DISCOVERING SOUTHERN AFRICA

OTHER BOOKS BY T V BULPIN

Lost Trails on the Low Veld
The Transvaal
Shaka's Country
To the Shores of Natal
The Hunter is Death
The Ivory Trail
Islands in a Forgotten Sea
Trail of the Copper King
The Golden Republic
The White Whirlwind
The Great Trek
Natal and the Zulu Country
To the Banks of the Zambezi
Low Veld Trails
Lost Trails of the Transvaal
East Africa and the Islands
Mountains of Africa
Tickey: The Story of a Clown
Southern Africa: Land of Beauty and Splendour
Scenic Wonders of Southern Africa
Illustrated Guide to Southern Africa
Majestic Southern Africa, Land of Beauty and Splendour

DISCOVERING SOUTHERN AFRICA

T V Bulpin

Published by Discovering Southern Africa Productions cc
Reg No CK 89-09448-23
P O Box 10, Muizenberg, 7950

Distributed by Tafelberg Publishers Ltd, P O Box 879, Cape Town, 8000

First Edition 1970 (Six impressions)
Second Edition 1980
Third Edition 1983
Fourth Edition 1986
Fifth Edition 1992
Sixth Edition 2001

© T V Bulpin 2001
ISBN 0-9583130-5-9

All rights reserved. No part of this book may be reproduced, stored in a retrieval system, or transmitted in any form or by any means, electronic, electrostatic, magnetic tape, mechanical, photocopying, recording or otherwise, without written permission from the publisher.

Discovering Southern Africa wishes to thank the many people who assisted in updating the information appearing in the text.

Text entry: Annie Sutherland and Celia Parker
Editorial consultant: Felicia Stoch
Population statistics (SA) consultant: Prof R Davies
Indexer: Melanie Cairncross
Production co-ordinator: Bert Cox
DTP: User Friendly, Cape Town
Imaging: Cape Imaging Bureau, Cape Town
Printed and bound by Interpak, Pietermaritzburg

FRONT COVER: Uruhap and Agrab, two hunters of the Kalahari (Photo T V Bulpin).
REAR COVER: Shumba, monarch of the Tshukudu Game Lodge in Mpumalanga (Photo Paul Changuion).

THOMAS VICTOR (T V) BULPIN
1918–1999

Author – Traveller – Adventurer – Photographer
Storyteller – Film-maker

This sixth edition of *Discovering Southern Africa* which you now hold in your hands is the final edition completely researched and written by T V Bulpin who, after a decade-long battle with skin cancer, regrettably passed away on 3 October 1999.

Tom was the name he preferred to be called, although he was widely known by the nickname T V. He was a highly intelligent man with a huge intellectual capacity; he was never shy to give his opinion on a subject, which was what made his writing so interesting. He was extremely strong willed and had the drive and passion to see a project through, no matter how long it took or what obstacles were in the way.

Tom had a great love for his country and the diversity of cultures. He believed in equality of all man but this was tempered by the fact that he had little time for fools or fanatics.

He was born on 31 March 1918 in Umkomaas, KwaZulu-Natal. His mother was Constance Florence Bulpin (née MacNab) of Aberdeen, Scotland. His father, Thomas Richard Bulpin, originally from Wales, was a journalist who came to South Africa on behalf of Reuters in anticipation of the Anglo-Boer War and, together with Edgar Wallace, became famous for extraordinary journalistic scoops during the war years.

Tom was expected to follow his father into journalism and he did start writing in his early teens, but at the age of 16 he entered the cinema business as a technician and cinematographer working on many productions dealing with Africa.

During World War 2 he enlisted with the S A Air Force, joined an anti-aircraft regiment and later became an aerial photographer serving in North Africa, Italy and Austria. On demobilization Tom went to Britain where he joined the Associated British Cinema Corporation and worked on the production of *Pathe News*, *Pathetone Weekly* and *Pathe Gazette*. He was then sent to cover Africa for their news and topical reels. By this time he had already started writing features for various magazines. Travelling all over Africa provided him with access to innumerable sources of information, which he was to put to good use in his books. The first one was *Lost Trails on the Lowveld* (1950) which, after four editions, was rewritten as *Lost Trails of the Transvaal* (six editions).

Tom then joined the publishing company Howard Timmins as a sales representative where he had an agreement that he would work for six months in a year; the other six months he concentrating on writing. During this period he wrote over 500 features for magazine and radio serials. Travelling through Southern Africa for months on end without touching home base, he continued to collect information, writing everything down in little notebooks which eventually amounted to several hundred, backed up with over 50 000 photographs.

This comprehensive research material was utilised to bring out a series of books on historical and biographical subjects such as *The Ivory Trail*, *The Hunter is Death* and *The Trail of the Copper King*, to name but a few. He also spent many months doing research on the islands of the Indian Ocean such as Mauritius and Madagascar which led to the book, *Islands in a Forgotten Sea*. This book is still widely recognised today as one of the most comprehensive histories of that region.

Tom hated editors changing or corrupting his words, or the English language, to suit themselves. This led him to start his own publishing company – he bought the company, *Books of Africa*, which he used to publish his own and works of other authors.

During this period he juggled the running of a business with travelling through Southern Africa collecting additional material for a series of booklets and for the first edition of *Discovering Southern Africa*. This edition, and subsequent ones, received world-wide acclaim and became known in the travel industry as the bible of travel (no disrespect intended) of Southern Africa.

Altogether Tom managed to produce over 2 000 booklets, pamphlets, newspaper and magazine features and travel videos and 29 books on travel, biographies and historical matters. Through these works we can quite comfortably give him the title of Doyen of Travel Writers.

Tom will be sorely missed by his family, friends and readers alike but he will be with us for many years to come through his printed works.

J A BULPIN

EXPLANATION

Discovering Southern Africa is intended to be a well-informed, loquacious and opinionated guide to the various territories comprising Southern Africa. The opinions expressed in the text are entirely those of the author. Each successive edition of the book has been revised and updated. The desire of the author was that this book be regarded as a dependable guide to the pleasures and excitement of travel, the wealth of fascinating discoveries to be explored, and the joy of life to be found in the sunshine of the great spaces of Southern Africa.

The spelling of place-names in Southern Africa is inconsistent. With names originating from so many different language groups and many of them containing odd sounds such as clicks, these inconsistencies are unavoidable. Only in recent times have efforts been made at least to impose uniformity of spelling, but a great deal of work has still to be done in this direction.

A major problem is that many place-names have originated from languages now antique and have been converted into the language forms of later successive occupants of the area. In the process of adaptation, such names have become badly distorted to the point of incomprehensible corruptions.

African grammar is composed of classes of words, each class identifiable by a particular prefix which usually simply means 'the', or presents the noun as singular or plural. Correctly, these prefixes would be spelt in lower-case letters, with the capital appearing at the beginning of the noun, thus *amaZulu* (the Zulu people), *baSotho* (the Sotho people), *maTebele* (the Tebele or Ndebele people), *uMzimkulu* (the Mzimkulu River), *iliGwa* (the Gwa or Vaal River), *uSutu* (the Sutu River).

For simplicity and in an effort to direct the reader of this book into correctly pronouncing African names and words, the prefixes have been omitted, unless by usage they have been incorporated into modern language forms.

The reader should remember that in African languages, particularly of the *Bantu* (correctly baNthu) group, the vowels are pronounced as follows: a as ah; e as eh; i as ee; o as o in or; and u as oo. African languages avoid putting two vowels together, as pronunciation would be difficult.

In providing an etymology for African place-names, the correct spelling is first given, followed by the interpretation. In subsequent use of the name, the spelling used on modern maps is used, and this very often means the dropping of the aspirate, thus *Mzimkhulu*, becomes *Mzimkulu*.

It is interesting to note that most tribal, generic, and ethnic names are names of convenience given to groups of people by foreigners. Thus, the Swazi people were so named by Zulus and European traders after the king Mswati; the *maTebele* were so named by the Sotho people and have accepted this name (meaning 'refugees' or 'runaways') in the form of Ndebele; the earliest known South Africans, the hunter-gatherer people, were named Bushmen or Bosjiesmens by Europeans who also named the early pastoral people of the Cape Hottentots. The pastoral people called the Bushmen *Sonkwa*. They had no generic name other than that they were *Khoikhowi* or *Khowekhowe* (people) or *Khowi* (an individual).

The name *baNthu* (meaning people) and *muNthu* (meaning 'an individual') was applied in the nineteenth century to the black people of Southern Africa as a term of convenience by Dr W H Bleek. Nowadays the name is only applied to the language group.

The Bushman language is unique in that it makes use of five different click sounds and several assorted supporting sounds exotic to foreigners. Spelling such a language is exceedingly difficult without the use of special characters which in themselves are incomprehensible and unpronounceable to foreign readers. The name *San* (pronounced Saan or Son with the 'o' as in 'on') imposed by Europeans on the Bushmen is meaningless to them. They never had the need for a generic name. There was no need for one as they were not aware of any other human beings on Earth. Each group knew itself only by its own name, generally that of their chief. The Sotho people called them *boRwa* (people of the South) and also *boQuo* (click people). The Nguni people (Xhosa–Zulu), who have no 'R' sound, changed Rwa to Tswa. The Kavanga people of Zimbabwe appear to have called them *Ndisnerepi* (wandering vagrants).

T V BULPIN

ABBREVIATIONS

$	Dollar (Namibia and Zimbabwe currency)
E	Emalangeni (Swazi currency)
L	Loti (Lesotho currency)
P	Pula (Botswana currency)
R	Rand (South African currency)
Mt	Metical (Mozambican currency)

The Metric System has been used.

An easy, quick conversion for measurements: 8 kilometres = 5 miles

Temperatures are given in Celsius (centigrade).
To convert Celsius to Fahrenheit, multiply by 9, divide by 5 and add 32.

A NOTE TO THE READER

The fifth edition of *Discovering Southern Africa* by T V Bulpin was published in 1992, two years before the 'New South Africa' came into being. Eight years lie between that edition and this one. As you will have read on a previous page, Tom Bulpin died late in 1999 while still working on this book. Given the timespan between the last two editions, the updating and rewriting of the text proved to be a major task. The physical rearrangement of South Africa's four provinces into nine areas required a concomitant rearrangement of the book's content. Although continuing to research and write during his illness, unfortunately, owing to failing health, Tom Bulpin was unable to complete the editing of the text before his death.

Much of the book relates the history of southern Africa and the specific places described. The names of countries, provinces and geographical areas used in the text are appropriate for the time of the incident being described – for instance, in the text describing events during the Anglo-Boer War, all references to provinces are given as they were at that time: the Cape, Natal, the Transvaal and the Orange Free State. The text relating to more recent history is not always so clear cut and the rule of thumb has been to use whichever wording makes the most sense in the context. Some things do not fit easily or neatly into the new geographical dispensation and have been left untouched.

The publishers have tried to ensure that the naming of geographical areas, towns and villages is correct and fits with the current situation. If in any doubt about directions given in the text, please consult an up-to-date road atlas.

In previous editions, population figures were provided for a number of the places mentioned in the book – giving readers an indication of the size of the place and a sense of what to expect. Since then, the demarcation of municipal boundaries has altered and is still in a state of flux. In 1996, South Africans participated in a full census and these figures, released by the government, were used to update the present text.[1] Up-to-date figures for individual Namibian towns were not available at the time of going to print and therefore remain unchanged from the last edition.

Discovering Southern Africa is essentially a travel book, even though it is loaded with historical information and anecdotes to entertain and intrigue. The author therefore included information about opening times, telephone numbers and contact details for many of the places described. As you, the reader, will appreciate, these are all things which can and do change. While every care has been taken to ensure that the information given is correct at the time of going to print, to avoid disappointment, please always contact the local tourist information office or phone the place you plan to visit beforehand to check opening times.

The publishers cannot be held responsible for any errors or omissions in the text.

We trust that you will enjoy your journey ...

---

[1] Statistics South Africa Census 96: Community Profile

CONTENTS

Prelude xiii

1	The Birth of the City of Cape Town	1
2	Adolescence of a City	21
3	Cape Town, Table Bay and Robben Island	33
4	The Cape Peninsula	52
5	The Southern Cape Peninsula	78
6	Sea and Sand. The Towns and Coast of the South-Western Cape	113
7	The Garden of the Western Cape	130
8	The Valley of the Eerste River	142
9	The Berg River Valley. The Valleys of the Huguenots and the Wagonmakers	176
10	The Valley of the Breede River	209
11	The Coast of Flowers	229
12	The Copper Way to Namaqualand	242
13	Cape Town to the Gariep (Orange) River	270
14	The Diamond Way	290
15	The Great Karoo, Bushmanland and Gordonia	315
16	Enchanted Waters, Magic Mountains. The Story of the Little Karoo	340
17	Cape Town to Mossel Bay	366
18	The Garden Route. Mossel Bay	386
19	The Eastern Cape. Port Elizabeth and the 1820 Settlers Country	410
20	The Eastern Cape. People, Places and Ghosts	436
21	East London. The Border Country and Ciskei	453
22	The Transkei and its Wild Coast	483
23	The South Coast of KwaZulu-Natal	504
24	Durban and the North Coast	524
25	The Land of the Zulus	544
26	The Wildlife and Game Reserves of the Zulu Country	565
27	Pietermaritzburg and the KwaZulu-Natal Midlands	572
28	The Drakensberg	600
29	The Golden Way from the Gariep to the Vaal	620
30	The Eastern Free State	644
31	The Northern Province. The Vaal to the Limpopo	665
32	The Witwatersrand	684
33	Johannesburg	708
34	Pretoria	741
35	Mpumalanga. The Highveld	753
36	Mpumalanga. The Edge of the Berg	770
37	The Lowveld, its People, Scenery and Wildlife	795
38	The Kruger National Park	811
39	The Northern and North-West Provinces of South Africa	829
40	Botswana	849
41	Lesotho	864
42	Mozambique. Maputo and the South	885
43	Mozambique. A Journey along a Coast of Coconuts and Coral	896
44	Namibia. The Northern Areas	905
45	Namibia. The Central Areas	924
46	Namibia. The Southern Areas	949
47	Swaziland	963
48	Zimbabwe. The Central Districts	992
49	Zimbabwe. The Ndebele Country	1008
50	Zimbabwe. The Eastern Districts	1021

Index 1039

*To the excitement of discovery,
the long views;
the other side of the horizon;
the surprise around the corner and the song of the wind.
To the fun of having a companion
and the pleasure of experiences that are shared.*

Prelude

WHY TRAVEL? WHY BE A TOURIST?

With a good book, compact disk, television, video or film, you can settle down snuggly and safely in your own home and save yourself money and trouble. But you still want to travel? The reason is easy to explain. The very essence of travel is excitement, the intellectual, personal and physical experience of venturing over the hills and far away, of seeing for yourself new places, meeting new people, making new friends, eating new foods, the fragrance of new flowers and plants, new sounds and melodies and the discovery for yourself of the natural and unnatural wonders of this wonderful planet Earth.

So you set out to travel in Southern Africa and find yourself confronted with what is the most diverse part of Earth. It can be truly described as a world in one country and a country for all seasons. To understand the reasons for this diversity open a map of Africa. You will see that the continent of Africa is the great divider between East and West. The sea on either side of it has vast differences in life-forms and climatic influences. On the East side lies the Indian Ocean with its warm tropical climate and Indo-Pacific species of marine life carried down the south-east coast of Africa in the Mozambique–Agulhas Current. The warm water evaporates easily as it flows, clouds are formed and favourable winds carry them over the coast to deposit rain on an eagerly receptive land made green and fertile by the gift of copious water.

The south-western coast of Africa provides a remarkable contrast. The South Atlantic Ocean on its eastern side contains in it the cold Benguela Current, a spin-off drift from the Antarctic. Its life-forms are very different from the warm-water species. The cold water resists evaporation. There is little save mist to reach a coast which is either a transitional desert in the south deteriorating northwards into the giant sand dunes of the Namib Desert. Follow a line of latitude across Southern Africa from this arid western side.

It is fascinating to see the land, the flora and fauna, gradually transformed the further eastwards you travel. First there is desert, then arid thornbush, then the grass-covered prairie country of the highveld, then the savanna country, the haunt of big game and of the immense variety and number of the wild animals of Africa, then the often snow-covered eastern edge of the high-lying central plateau, the Drakensberg range where most of the principal rivers of Southern Africa have their source. Eastwards the tumbling foothills fall away to a belt of tropical lagoons and swamps, then the dark-golden coloured sands where the waves of the Indian Ocean come tumbling joyfully on to the shores of Africa.

From this mix of climatic zones, eco-systems, and micro eco-systems comes the extraordinary diversity of life-forms in flora and fauna. To explore this vast area is to have the excitement of experiencing as you travel the immense changes of landscape and life, discovering for yourself at least some of the countless natural and unnatural wonders contained in this southern end of the mighty continent of Africa. In it you will see geological systems of incredible variety, you can stand on remnants of the earliest surface of Earth, see the petrified relics of the earliest known forms of life, visit the sites where the ancestors of man first stood upright in the ancient Garden of Eden, made tools, perceived the inevitability of death, wondered at the possibility of an afterlife, puzzled by myths over the riddle of the mysterious universe. In it you can step back for a while from the Plastic age to the Stone age, meet on a friendly basis with people from the most distant past and find their cultures worthwhile to treasure, their life-style with nature a lesson in harmony and consequent survival right from the time of counting on fingers and toes into the age of computers and the self-made conflicts and contradictions with which we frustrate and crucify ourselves today.

It is so easy to explore this magic world. It is said that long before humans appeared in Africa you could have walked from the Cape to Cairo along paths blazed by wild animals migrating seasonally north and south, east to west. With these ancient paths the wild animals found the easiest ways over the mountains, through the deserts and forests, avoiding problem areas where malaria-carrying mosquitoes lived, where tsetse flies killed off livestock. Man followed the wild animals. Roadmakers converted the ancient paths into the highways of today. They will take you comfortably in a normal vehicle to the most remote areas, the loveliest of places and lead you safely back providing you respect them by obeying speed and other traffic requirements and treat your fellow travellers with the courtesy you would have them give to you.

Road hogs suffer from a disease known as cancer of the rectum. They cannot bear to sit comfortably still in a motor vehicle. Their cancer hurts them. They must be up and about. They must drive faster, take chances, risk the lives of themselves, their passengers and pedestrians, all in order to save a few minutes of time with which they do not appear to do anything worthwhile. Avoid this style of mindless driving. Speed is the greatest killer on the roads of Southern Africa.

An elaborate railway network has been created over the face of Southern Africa. You can travel from Cape Town north to Dar-es-Salaam in Tanzania, from Maputo on the moist east coast to Walvis Bay on the arid west coast; you can have the mist of Victoria Falls moistening your face from the window of a luxury train crossing the Zambezi River on one of the most remarkable bridges in the world. You can cross mountain ranges, penetrate the savanna wonderland of big game in the comfort and security of what are tantamount to luxury hostels on wheels. You can drive your own vehicle, travel in coaches, large or small, walk, cycle or fly.

Nowadays if you have the time, an increasing number of travellers are even re-discovering the delights of sea transport rather than air in coming to Southern Africa. Travel time then becomes part of the whole tourist experience and not just a speedy convenience. The joy of seeing Table Mountain looming up over the horizon to welcome you is one of the most unforgettable experiences of any world traveller.

In Southern Africa there is waiting for you an accommodation infrastructure of hotels, guest houses, hostels, caravan parks and camping grounds to shelter you in comfort and cleanliness.

For health, if you require a particular course of medication, enquire before you leave from your regular supplier whether the medication is available outside your home country. If not, bring it with you. Medical insurance is a comfort. If you do fall sick or have a mishap while on tour it is a relief to know that you can be retrieved and returned all the way home to your own bed and doctor. This is not to say that medical services in Southern Africa are bad. You will never, in fact, fail to receive sympathetic treatment. Local doctors can be expected to be particularly well versed in local ailments. Take advice on such problems as malarial fever, sleeping sickness (from tsetse flies) and bilharzia (from infected rivers and water). Such problems are only experienced in tropical parts of the more northerly areas of Southern Africa.

From a safety point of view, Southern Africa does have a crime problem. This is closely associated with unemployment. In all countries, high unemployment figures inevitably result in a high crime rate. The biggest criminals in a country can be the fat cat money men and economists who devise spurious monetary policies supportive of their own interests, parasitic stock exchange gamblers, currency swindlers and speculators rather than productive working people. Crime becomes the only employment for people who consider themselves the innocent and uncomprehending victims of punitive fluctuations in such things as usurious interest rates arbitrarily imposed overnight to ruination of innumerable businesses small and large, and countless persons trying to own their own homes. Southern Africa has a nuisance problem with such financial disruption.

Do your financial transactions in your home country. Deal with the money world you know. Use the favourable rates of exchange between your country and Southern Africa to give yourself a bargain. Have as little as possible to do with financial institutions in Southern Africa. For the rest, follow the advice given to the author when he visited Madagascar to work on research for a book. He landed in Tamatave, the only passenger from a small island trading ship. It was a humid, stifling, sultry morning. Carrying his impedimenta he made his way to a small tin shanty customs and immigration shed about the size of a privy. Inside there was an officer in a pristine white uniform studying a girlie magazine and picking his nose with his thumb. He was startled to see me. I gave him my passport.

'How long do you want to stay in Madagascar?' he asked.
'Maybe twelve months.'
'Mmn. Doing what?'
'Getting material for a book. I'm a writer.'
'Mmn. Where do you want to go?
'All over.'
'Mmn. Do you have friends in Madagascar?'
'No.'
'Mmn. How will you travel?'
'Trains, buses, walk. I want to meet people. You can't in an aeroplane. You just see the back of the heads of the passengers in front of you. Smell stale recycled air.'
'Mmn. Can you speak Malagasy?'
'No.'

He suddenly looked very grave and re-perused my passport.

'Monsieur,' he said, 'You can't speak Malagasy. Your French, if you'll pardon me, is execrable. Not many people on this island can speak English.'

I became alarmed. Maybe the bureaucrat would refuse me entry.

'Do you think I'll have any trouble?' I asked. He saw my concern and gave me a pleasant smile.

'Monsieur, go anywhere you like in this great island of ours. But just don't do anything or go anywhere which your heart will tell you is wrong or bad. Nothing will happen to you on Madagascar, except pleasant things.'

He stamped my passport and handed it to me. Nothing bad happened to me on Madagascar. I went wherever I wanted to go. I made many friends. I had a great time.

Back in South Africa I wrote my book *Islands in a Forgotten Sea*. I still listen on the radio to Madagascar. Its music whispers to me from far away to return to friends and pleasant places. One day I will.

I wish to all visitors to Southern Africa equally happy memories of their stay, in my lovely country. Come back to us again; you have only seen a fragment of this land. The rest is waiting for you with open arms.

Chapter One
THE BIRTH OF THE CITY OF CAPE TOWN

Cape Town is a fortunate city. There are few other cities so splendidly displayed, so influenced by a benign setting of mountains which, by their presence, caused the foundation of Cape Town, directed its growth and provided it with so handsome a background.

The city and the mountains belong to one another. Cape Town without the mountains would not be quite so interesting. The mountains, Table Mountain, Devil's Peak, Lion's Head and Signal Hill, would still be superb without the city, but their offspring provides them with an animated contrast of capricious moods, an unfolding drama of events, an agreeable mix of sounds, aromas, scandals, all taking place beneath the overlooking piles of rock, like the gambolling of children around the feet of indulgent parents.

Look down upon Cape Town from the mountain heights, one of the great views of the world. The city in its metropolitan setting of 3 000 000 inhabitants is revealed in all its complexity of shape, detail and colour. It is spectacular by day, exquisite by night, especially beautiful in the early evening when a golden glow lingers from the sunset and, one by one, countless lights start to appear like stars descending from the milky way to dance and play in the city all night.

Sunset is a romantic time to view any city. Venality, for a little while, is at a lower level, the nighthawks are still to emerge, there is a small pause for rest and reflection. It is pleasant to think then of the past of the city, of the different stages of growth, of the cosmopolitan people who have contributed to its story and its culture. Africans, Asians, Europeans, all have played a part in the history of Cape Town, building it at the foot of the mountain they called its old grey father. All have laboured on the paths and roads which reach out from the city into the heart of the continent of Africa.

How did it all start? As mountains go, Table Mountain is no giant. It is only 1 086 m high but, standing next to the sea, every metre of its distinctive shape is visible. It is one of the most renowned shipping landfalls of Earth. It stands on the south-west end of Africa, its distinctive shape looming up as a gigantic beacon halfway on one of the principal trade-routes of mankind, the sea route around Africa linking east to west.

In making this mountain and positioning it so strategically, nature revealed a piquant sense of humour and sympathy to human needs. Not only was the mountain so positioned as to be seen from far out to sea, but its unique shape made it easily identifiable. To make it even more distinctive, nature provided it with a cloud table-cloth, adding to its fame as one of the natural wonders of the world.

The geological and climatological explanations for the creation of the mountain and its cloth are perfectly logical and understandable. In some ways, however, they are just too good to be true. First of all, about 350 million years ago, an accumulation of silt was eroded from the southern end of the land mass which was to become Africa. This silt, a mixture of sand, pebbles, shale and mud was deposited beneath a shallow sea on a base of granite and slate. Over millions of years the layer of silt thickened. Then came a great change. Either the sea receded or the mass of eroded material in some way was elevated above the level of the water. Exposed to the sun and rain, the silt dried, warping, cracking and eroding into deep valleys. Whole portions were completely carried away. Other segments remained isolated like irregularly shaped pieces of a broken jigsaw puzzle.

Table Mountain emerged from this jumble as one of the fragments of the original mass, looming upwards at first as a precipitous island in a primeval sea, gaunt, forbidding but eerily beautiful. In time the level of the sea receded still further, leaving Table Mountain and its companion mountains which form the Cape Peninsula separated from the mainland of Africa by what is known as the Cape Flats, a sandy remnant of the original bed of the sea. It was at this creative phase that nature must have looked at Table Mountain and, with some amusement, decided to provide it with a table-cloth. This spectacle was effected by ensuring that the angle and altitude of the mountain were correct, and that the prevailing south-east wind of summer collided with the mountain and was forced to rise abruptly to pass over the level summit.

The south-easter carries a heavy load of moisture picked up by the wind in its passage over the warm waters of the Mozambique–Agulhas Current which reaches the end of its flow in False Bay. Orographic condensation turns this moisture into cloud as the wind is forced to rise over the mountain top and suddenly cools. Tumbling over the northern edge of the tabletop, the wind falls immediately back to a lower and warmer level. The cloud disappears at this level and Table Mountain is left with its table-cloth. An amusing piece of folklore explains this remarkable phenomenon with an account of a never-ending smoking and gambling contest between the devil and a retired pirate known as Van Hunks. The details of this interesting contest make it undoubtedly the world's classic smoking story but they are best told elsewhere.

Who were the first human beings to see the majestic spectacle of Table Mountain and its cloud? Fossils and artefacts at least 15 000 years old have been found in caves in the Cape Peninsula. Until recently rock art on the walls of cave shelters on Table Mountain itself were reminders until they faded away, of the presence in former years of people of the Latter Stone Age.

Legends tell that Phoenician and Arab sailors, 2 000 and more years ago, were the first to reach the mountain from the sea. The Phoenicians, circumnavigating Africa for the first time from the West, are said to have landed at the foot of the mountain to rest, repair their ships, and replenish their food by planting and reaping crops of wheat. The Arab sailors, exploring the east coast of Africa, described Table Mountain as a magic place, with a magnetism which drew ships to doom. The eggs of the giant bird known as the roc were said to be found on its slopes and living there was a race of dwarfs known as the Wac-Wac.

The Phoenicians were looking for a way around the southern end of the African continent; the Arabs more particularly for an extension of their slave, ivory and gold trading enterprises on the east coast. To both the pioneer groups and the countless seafarers who followed them, Table Mountain became the eagerly looked-for beacon at the end of Africa. Fresh water could always be obtained there from the mountain streams. Meat could be bartered from the nomadic pastoral people of unknown name who grazed their herds in the area. The Wac-Wac on the other hand were simply hunters of game animals and gatherers of wild roots, fruits and sea foods. Neither they nor the pastoral people offered great trading possibilities. They were not sufficiently numerous or physically muscular to interest the rapacious slave traders who wreaked havoc on the east and west coasts of Africa. The early seafarers simply found the bay at the foot of the mountains to be a convenient resting place for repairs and the acquisition of food supplies in an atmosphere that was invigorating and free of any tropical diseases.

It was at this time that the island in the bay, known today as *Robben Island* (island of seals) started to play, for so small a place, a peculiarly important role in the story of Cape Town. This importance derived from three characteristics. Firstly the island, kidney-shaped, 3,5 km long, 2 km wide, 574 ha in extent and its highest point only 30 m above sea-level, has a strategic situation at the entrance to Table Bay. It lies 10 km from Mouille Point, the eastern side of the bay and 7 km from Bloubergstrand on the western side. Mounted on the island even old-fashioned cannon could command the entrance to the bay. Secondly, the island was protected by the sea from any predatory life-form on the African mainland. Thirdly, the geological structure of the island was economically interesting. It had a solid rock foundation of Malmesbury shale of good building quality, covered by windblown sand and the debris of ages of deposits of marine shells in various stages of decomposition, including deposits of limestone. Shrubs, grass and flowering plants, notably arum lilies and numerous species common on the south-western coast flourish on the island as well as exotic trees planted by man in modern times. As for wildlife, penguins and other sea birds nested on the place in prodigious numbers while seals lolled around completely tame and still to learn of man's rapacity.

It is not known who was the first European seafarer to see Table Mountain. The records of the discovery of the Cape of Good Hope by Bartholomeu Dias in 1488 are incomplete and make no mention of Table Mountain. The written story of Table Mountain and its bay started in 1503 when the Portuguese admiral, António de Saldanha, on his way to the East with a fleet of three ships, mislaid his position so badly that when he tried to double the Cape of Good Hope in the customary manner, far out to sea and then turn eastwards, he found himself approaching the mainland in St Helena Bay on the west coast. Lost and bewildered, with his little fleet scattered in foul weather, he sailed down the coast looking for the Cape of Good Hope. In this way he found himself quite inadvertently sailing into Table Bay and confronting the majestic mountain which was thenceforth known as Table Mountain.

Anchoring in the bay, Saldanha left his men on the shore to replenish water caskets while he and a party followed the fresh water stream to the foot of the mountain and then up the Platteklip Gorge which provides the only relatively easy climb to the summit. From the top Saldanha could see the whole of the Cape Peninsula as far as the Cape of Good Hope and this grand view of the classic peninsula shape cleared the confusion as to his whereabouts.

Back on the shore, Saldanha found his men trying to bargain for livestock with the resident pastoral people. The discord of two completely different languages made such bargaining extremely difficult. The haggling deteriorated into a squabble. The first recorded encounter of African and European on the site of the future city of Cape Town ended in bloodshed. António de Saldanha was slightly wounded himself. The Portuguese were driven back to their ship and they sailed off in disgruntled mood.

From thence on the bay was known to the Portuguese as the *Aquada de António de Saldanha* (watering place of António de Saldanha.) Seven years later, at the end of February 1510, Dom Francisco de Almeida, returning to Portugal after a bloody five year spell as the first Portuguese Viceroy of India, put into Table Bay with a fleet of three ships. The crew replenished drinking water from the mountain stream and a trade for livestock was started with a group of pastoralists who were living somewhere on the site of the present suburb of Woodstock. Everything seemed to be going well, with the Africans friendly, killing a sheep and inviting the Portuguese to a feast.

A fight developed for obscure reasons but said to have begun when the Portuguese attempted to take a man by force as a hostage or to meet their commander. The language barrier between the Portuguese and the Africans was impenetrable. The Portuguese were driven to the beach. Almeida decided that the prestige of Portugal demanded retaliation. On 1 March 1510, he landed on the beach with 150 men and marched to the African village. In a surprise attack the Portuguese seized a number of children and cattle. There were only about 80 African males in the village but they rallied to rescue their children and livestock. Sheltering behind bullocks trained for combat and to answer the whistled commands of their masters, they charged at the Portuguese, throwing stones and spears in a barrage. It was the turn of the Portuguese to be surprised. They retreated to the beach and were dismayed to find that the sailors who had conveyed them from the anchored ships had moved further eastwards, to the watering place which was more protected from an increasing wind.

There was a running fight as the Portuguese, many of them already wounded, retreated along the beach. Reinforcements reached the Africans, with 170 of their men harassing the heavily armed Portuguese. Almeida died with a spear through his throat. Seventy-five of his men including eleven officers died with him. The fact that 170 primitive African people could so overwhelm 150 well-armed European soldiers was considered to be one of the worst disasters in Portuguese history, especially as several of the casualties were members of illustrious families and Almeida was a nobleman of the high rank of Viceroy. Few Portuguese ships ventured into the bay at the foot of Table Mountain after this disaster.

Towards the end of the 16th century, seafarers of other nations started to sail around the Cape and they had no qualms in visiting the watering place of Saldanha. In 1591 the English admiral, George Raymond, with James Lancaster (later 'Sir') as captain of one of his three ships, sailed into the bay in search of fresh water and meat. The Englishmen landed on the beach, the first of their nation to do so. Then came, as they put it, *'certain savages, very black and brutish'*. Sheep and cattle were traded for the usual scrap metal, but then bartering degenerated into squabbling. The pastoralists would have no more of Admiral Raymond and his men and withdrew mistrusting the visitors and themselves misunderstood. A few days later, however, the Englishmen found a solitary man on the beach. They gave him a gift and indicated that they wanted cattle. Eight days later the man returned with a party of his fellows as well as a herd of cattle and a flock of sheep. The Englishmen traded as many animals as they wanted for two knives for an ox and one knife for a sheep. Raymond also sailed over to Robben Island. He found an unexpected bounty. There were so many sea birds, eggs and seals that the seafarers recorded that *'there can be no other island in all the world as full of fowl and seal as this. It is astounding'*. The Englishmen replenished their foodstore on fish, penguins and seals and then sailed on leaving behind on the island a number of sheep which were too thin and sickly to withstand a voyage.

The Dutch sailors made considerable use of Robben Island. In 1601 Joris van Spilbergen named it *Cornelia* after his mother. He had visited Dassen Island as he came down the west coast and named it *Elizabeth*. On that odd island he had been surprised, as all visitors have been, at the presence of the *dassies* (coneys) which have given the island its name. The origin of these little animals on an island so isolated from the mainland (where they are common) would have slightly puzzled Charles Darwin. Captain Van Spilbergen captured a number of them for food and released a few on his Cornelia Island as some exchange for the plump sheep which he found there, running wild after being left by some earlier voyager.

Captain Van Spilbergen seemed to have been a man partial to naming places after ladies but these attachments were not very long lasting. He was, however, responsible for the name of Table Bay which replaced the old Watering Place of Saldanha. The older name was moved northwards by the map makers to the present Saldanha Bay.

Leaving a few surplus livestock on Robben Island to fatten in safety and then be replaced in exchange with thinner animals by later voyagers became a courteous habit no matter whether the seafarers were friends or enemies. Another habit which started at this time on the island and the mainland watering place, was to inscribe stones with the name of a ship and the date of its visit. Underneath these stones letters were placed with requests that they be carried forward, east or west as required, by other ships. The courtesy was granted even in times of war. The so-called 'Post-Office Stones' became a custom of visitors to Table Bay and those letters which survive tell engrossing stories of sea fights, storms, wrecks, adventures, hopes, disappointments and the hardship of long voyages in appalling conditions, with bad water, worse food, dismal living conditions, and the ships haunted by the dreadful curse of scurvy, *'a disease which rots the flesh and makes the mouth like an open sore'*.

With the launching in 1600 of the English East India Company and in 1602 of the Dutch East India Company there was a considerable increase of shipping calling in Table Bay. Only the Portuguese continued to bypass the Cape, using as their refreshment place the islet of Mozambique, 3 000 km further north.

The Cape was extolled by nearly all the English and Dutch seafarers who called there. It was halfway on what could be a terrible journey. The climate was healthy, the water from the Fresh River (as it was called) tasted exquisitely pure and sweet. There was no malarial fever; and, as Thomas Aldworth, senior merchant for the English East India Company reported to his superiors, he arrived there *'with many of our people sick, they all regained their health and strength within twenty days'*. As for the local pastoralists, Aldworth found *'the natives of the country to be very courteous and tractable folk, and they did not give us the least annoyance during the time we were there'*.

Nobody knew what to call these indigenous African inhabitants. The clicks and odd sounds in their language made it extremely difficult for visitors to understand them or pronounce any word or name. The Dutch visitors overcame the difficulty by applying a nickname to the pastoralists, *Hottentot*, said by some to mean a stammerer, from the odd sounds in their speech and by others to have originated from a rhythmic word sounding like *huttentutton*, which the pastoralists are said to have repeated constantly while they danced. The smaller and less numerous hunter-gatherer people were eventually given by the Dutch the name of *Bosjesmans* (Bushmen) because they seemed to lurk in the cover of the shrubs. The pastoralists referred offhandedly to these people as *Sonkwa*. The origin and ancestral relationship of the hunter-gatherers and the pastoralists remains unknown. Their languages were similar but their lifestyles very different. They were both, however, essentially nomadic, wandering about in groups or small tribes, each group having its own name and not recognising any paramount power or generic name.

The seafarers had some peculiar ideas of winning friends and influencing the local inhabitants. They couldn't have had it much better. Scrap metal and junk trinkets bartered for fat slaughter animals, enough to provision one whole fleet, 39 fat oxen and 115 sheep, in exchange for *'a little brass which we cut from two or three old kettles'*. This was in 1612, but the old haggler's rule always prevailed *'Buy cheaper and sell dearer with bigger profit in the end'*. The English felt that things could be still better if they had a resident middleman who could ensure trade. To this purpose, in 1613, the chief of the local pastoralists, (whose name sounded like Cory) with another man, was lured on board a homeward-bound ship and kidnapped. The one man died on the voyage but Cory reached England where the plan was to teach him English and for the company to learn from him something of the possibilities of the Cape country for trade. Cory was even dressed in clothes of the current English fashion. He was accommodated in London in the home of Sir Thomas Smythe the founder of the English East India Company. He would lie on the ground crying and pleading *'Cory home go, Souldana go, home go'*, over and over.

Smythe eventually relented and sent Cory back to the Cape. As soon as he landed he bolted for home, tearing off his English clothing and reverted to traditional dress. The English were disgruntled. They complained that the bottom line bargaining price for livestock went up sharply after Cory's return. Scrap metal became scorned. Bright, brass kettles and other goods were demanded. Cory was blamed for educating his people and one cynical visitor wrote that it would have been better if Cory *'had been hanged in England or drowned homeward'*.

It was on the shores of Table Bay that, at this time, a development was taking place with consequences as to bedevil the whole turbulent story of Southern Africa. A plural society was being spawned from complete misunderstanding between persons of African and non-African origin. The division was not caused so much by colour, as by a barrier of separate cultures and languages, each with sounds extremely difficult for the other group to learn or pronounce. The two divisions in the Cape simply could not communicate or comprehend each other's life-style or ethos. They had to formulate assessments of each other by superficial observation during casual encounters.

To the Africans, the seafarers of whatever their origin, Asian or European, were, at first just curiosities and no threat because they did not stay long. As traders they were demanding rather than requesting. Even without the experience of Cory, it was inevitable that the rubbish they offered for livestock would soon become unacceptable. Their obvious disdain of the African's clothing, eating habits and hygiene was irritating. African clothing suited the climate and was the product of available dress materials. Their eating habits were to the taste of the Africans and, as for hygiene, the rancid fat they rubbed into their bodies might stink to the visitors but it drove away bugs. It was the visitors who looked sick near to death when they arrived, recovered in the healthy environment and then sailed away leaving behind such scourges as smallpox and venereal disease which caused heavy mortality to the indigenous people.

As for culture, the Africans had their music, traditions, legends and religion. The seafarers considered them to be barbarians with no schools or buildings better than huts, no signs of parliament, government, tax collections, churches or the evident signs of religion in the form of vestments, ceremonies, services, attendance registers and promises of rewards to come in another world. The Africans were bemused by this; they had not much belief in paradise to come and soon discovered the fact, particularly important for them, that none of the foreign religions had the least condemnation of slavery. The Ten Commandments and the golden rule of not doing to others that which you would not have them do to you were indeed preached but definitely not much practised. The vaunted superiority of Eastern and Western civilisations, to the Africans, amounted to nothing against the barbarous murders, wars, inhumanity and ruthless exploitation of the environment, which were so integral a part of the life-style of the newcomers.

Finally, there was the matter of land. The visitors saw no sign of fences, cultivation or private ownership. The African concept of collective ownership was completely contrary to the ideas of European and Asian people. Private property, to them, was sacrosanct, but here, beneath Table Mountain, there was no sign of any such thing. The whole land seemed to be wide open, up for the taking. Fences and trespassers-will-be-prosecuted signs, could come, followed by the whole complex rhythm of buying and selling, starting from free ground and working its value up by the sleight of hand of the land speculator, money lender and lawyer. To the seafarers this was called development. To the indigenous people it was incomprehensible. They were about to learn of the subtle nature of western civilisation very soon.

Notwithstanding disappointment in Cory as a source of information, the director of the English East India Company decided on establishing a permanent presence at the Cape. His method of effecting this presence was rather peculiar. From King James I he obtained a reprieve for seventeen condemned prisoners who were offered the choice of the gallows or the Cape. With some hesitation they accepted the Cape. They were joined voluntarily by three other convicts. On 5 June

1615, Cory and his people were somewhat disconcerted to see landed on the shores of Table Bay nine of these felons led by a celebrated highwayman and former yeoman of the Royal Guard known as Captain James Crosse. This little band was supposed to start a plantation, be grateful to their king for saving their lives, behave like Christians, and explore the country to see if they could discover anything which might be beneficial to England and to their honourable employers.

The means given to the men to allow them to effect this programme were so stingy as to horrify the crew and officers of the ship which had brought them. A few more comforts were provided but their resources were still miserable, a tent, some turnip seeds and spades, two knives, a short pike, a sword and a knapsack for each man, a store of bread, dried Newfoundland fish, a little wine and 'strong water' given to them as a final act of charity.

A shore party was sent to find Cory, trade with him for some livestock and promise him an English-style house if he would treat the settlers kindly. On the way to the meeting there was a brawl with the local inhabitants. One man was killed and several wounded. Cory, however, promised hospitality providing the settlers were armed with muskets and were prepared to fight for him against his enemies.

Captain Crosse and his companions felt themselves somewhat unwanted but a ship's whaleboat was given to them. This convenience allowed them to make their base in security on Robben Island. The idea was to stock the island with livestock bartered from the mainland pastoralists. Visiting ships could be provided with a dependable supply of fresh meat. The idea was interesting but it never had a real chance. Apart from bartering for livestock and filling water casks the islanders found additional interests on the mainland and Captain Crosse had his throat slit in a quarrel over women.

The whaleboat was wrecked on the island's rocky coast and the men were marooned. After eight months, a ship was seen on the horizon but seemed to have no intention of venturing into Table Bay. The islanders, by then were *'almost mad by reason of their several pressing wants and extremities'*. They had made a raft from the wreckage of the whaleboat. On this, four of the men attempted to paddle to the ship. They were overturned in a swell and drowned.

The next day the ship, homeward-bound to England, entered Table Bay. The surviving islanders begged to be taken away. Within a few hours of landing in England, the three were arrested for stealing a purse. They were hanged by special warrant of the Lord Chief Justice who, without further trial, simply revived their original condemnation which had been remitted because of their banishment.

In the following year, 1616, three more condemned men were sent to the Cape by the English East India Company. Finding nothing on the mainland or the island of the first 'settlement' these men, according to the chronicles of the voyage, *'presented themselves on their knees, with tears in their eyes, to the chief commander, Captain Joseph, most humbly beseeching him, that he might give orders that they might be hanged, which they much rather chose than to be there left on that cursed place'*.

Captain Joseph, it is said in one account, could not oblige the request. His orders were to convey the three men to Table Bay and that was all. He sailed off leaving them there but the captain of another English ship, arriving a few days later, took pity on them and carried them off to an unknown fate in the East. The island was left to its seals and penguins, although another account does say that Captain Joseph, in fact, hanged the men.

The English East India Company persisted in their interest in the Cape. In July 1620 six of their outward-bound ships arrived in Table Bay and found nine Dutch ships and one homeward-bound English vessel. Other ships arrived during the next couple of weeks. The bay must have taken on quite a festive appearance with everybody friendly and on the mend from the ailments of the voyage. The Dutchmen confided to the Englishmen that their company had the intention to occupy the Cape. This alarmed the English who saw their fresh water and food supplies falling under somebody else's control. The two senior English commanders, Commodore Andrew Shillinge and Captain Humphrey Fitzherbert, decided to forestall the Dutch. On 3 July 1620 they annexed the Cape to King James, hoisted the flag of St George and erected a cairn of stones on what they called *'King James his Mount'* (now Signal Hill).

Nothing resulted from this annexation. The English government and the East India Company were on friendly terms with the Dutch and quite happy to let them have the Cape if they wanted it. The English were overextended in their current colonisation of North America and the Dutch were prepared to promise them a continuance of supplies of fresh water and meat at the Cape. For the time being there was no change in the bartering, haggling, squabbling and occasional killing which passed for the beginning of civilisation and commerce in the Cape. Cory, who was generally blamed for the hard bargaining of the pastoral people, was one who came to a dismal end as a result of this trade. About 1625, some Dutch visitors finding him reluctant to part with cattle, killed him. This did not secure a lower price for cattle or friendlier relations with the pastoralists.

With Cory gone, the English visitors tried to find a replacement middleman between them and the pastoralists. About 1631 one of their ships bound for the East took aboard a beachcomber who they named Harry. He was given a round trip, taught some English on the journey, well-treated, and returned safely to Table Bay. Back with his own kind, he was appointed to the position of a sort of general factotum for visiting ships, keeping mail for ships which called, and supposed to become a middleman in the trade for livestock. Unfortunately Harry was not esteemed by the pastoral tribes. He and his people were lowly *strandlopers* (beachcombers) who lived largely on dead whales and the sea creatures washed up on shore. The superior pastoral people would have none of him.

To save Harry from being killed, the English removed him and a number of his clan to Robben Island where they could live safely, feeding on the seals, birds and marine creatures washed up dead or caught alive. On the island Harry could continue his career as postman and act as interpreter and negotiator in bargaining for livestock on the mainland. Some such an arrangement was very needful. In March 1632, just before Harry returned to the Cape, 23 of the crew of a Dutch ship had been killed when, it is said, they tried to seize cattle without payment to the owners.

Notwithstanding such disastrous occasions, the reputation of the Cape as a place of refreshment grew over the years. In 1647 this reputation received a considerable boost. On 25 March of that year the homeward-bound Dutch ship *Haarlem* had the misfortune of being blown by a south-east gale on to the beach at Blouberg on the northern end of Table Bay. Nobody was drowned but the ship stuck fast and it was carrying a valuable cargo. Most of the crew and passengers were taken aboard two other Dutch ships anchored in the bay, while 40 others were given passage to Europe aboard two English ships. The 60 men, who remained, led by a junior merchant, Leendert Janssen, stayed to salvage the cargo. They built a small fort on shore and, in the months they stayed there, worked, planted a vegetable garden, fished, hunted and rowed over to Robben Island to gather penguins, eggs and to club seals to secure train oil for lamps.

A few beachcombers were the only local inhabitants they at first encountered but after five months a group of pastoralists wandered into the area and were quite happy to trade cattle and sheep for what they considered to be fair exchange in items from the shipwreck. The shipwrecked men lived well and were even able to supply meat and vegetables to ships that called. In March 1648 a homeward-bound fleet of twelve Dutch ships arrived. The salvaged cargo, 60 healthy men and ample stocks of food were taken aboard and conveyed in good order to the Netherlands. The report compiled by Leendert Janssen and Nicolaas Proot, both members of the shipwrecked party, to the Dutch East India Company eulogised the Cape, its health, peaceful inhabitants, and possibilities of profit from seals, whales, fishing, and supplying food to passing ships. As a consequence of this report, the Company, on 20 March 1651, finally decided to establish a victualling station at the Cape. It was a momentous decision for Southern Africa.

Two ships, *Dromedaris* and *Reiger*, and a yacht *Goede Hoop* were commissioned to convey to the Cape a party of 70 men. The command was offered to Nicolaas Proot. When he declined the position, it was offered to a 33-year-old man, Johan (Jan) van Riebeeck, who had already seen service in the East with the Company as an under-surgeon and then as assistant clerk. After some trouble over private trading at Tonkin he had been recalled to Holland in 1648. He left the company, married Maria Quevellerius (also known as Maria de la Queillerie), made trading voyages to Greenland and the West Indies and then rejoined the Company with the rank of merchant at the pay of £4 11s 8d a month. He accepted the offer to lead the venture to the Cape where he was destined to rise to the rank of commander with a salary of £7 10s a month.

On his first return voyage from the East, Van Riebeeck had lived on shore at the Cape for three weeks while the cargo of the wrecked *Haarlem* was being loaded on the homeward-bound ships. He shared the opinion that the Cape was suitable for the establishment of a permanent refreshment station for the convenience of shipping. He was somewhat dubious, however, about the nature of the indigenous inhabitants of the Cape.

The instructions given to Van Riebeeck and the captains of the three ships were to proceed directly to Table Bay. The materials for a wooden building were included in the loading of the ships and, on arrival, this was to be erected close to the all-important watering place at the mouth of the Fresh River. A site for a fort had then to be selected and the stronghold built as quickly as possible. It was designed to accommodate about 80 men. Four small cannon of the type known as culverins were to be mounted on the fort's angles. Once secure in this fort, Van Riebeeck and his men had to take possession of a fertile extent of arable land suitable for vegetable and fruit cultivation. A professional gardener, Hendrik Boom, with his family were members of Van Riebeeck's party. Suitable pasture land for cattle had also to be obtained. The party was instructed not to injure any of the local inhabitants or their cattle but to endeavour to win friendship. The instruction did not indicate how this goodwill could be obtained and maintained if select sites for occupation, agriculture and grazing were also to be set up without negotiation or suggested payment. All nations except Portugal would be welcome to trade and even to occupy areas of the country for themselves beyond the Company's boundaries.

On Sunday, 24 December 1651, a fine easterly wind blew from the mainland of Europe. Like a flock of birds waiting to migrate, a whole fleet of Dutch merchant ships set sail for many far ports of trade. Amongst these vessels were the two ships and the yacht *Goede Hoop* conveying Van Riebeeck and his party to the Cape. The voyage was uneventful and, for those days, speedy. At the end of March 1652 the three vessels were approaching the turning point at the south-western end of the continent of Africa. Floating sea weeds, the vast flights of sea birds, the varieties of fish, the perfume of land, of the Cape mountains with their aromatic plants and flowers, all indicated that a great change was about to take place with the meeting of two great ocean currents and a blending of the cultures of East, West and Africa. The two Magellanic clouds, galaxies of stars, were eagerly watched for, poised in the heavens over the longed-for landmark of Table Mountain. At last, on 5 April 1652, about the fifth glass of the afternoon watch, the chief mate of the *Dromedaris* saw Table Mountain rise just above the horizon. There was jubilation among the company and a reward for the first person to see the renowned landmark, soon to be regarded as a gigantic welcoming sign to Van Riebeeck's Tavern of the Sea.

That night the little fleet approached the land to the south of the entrance to Table Bay. The wind dropped and they passed an easy night. The next morning was windless. While the ships idled, a boat was sent with the bookkeeper Adam Hulster and the mate of the *Dromedaris*, Arend van Leveren, to look cautiously into the bay and see whether there were any ships there. They returned to report that the bay was empty. On this good news, the *Dromedaris* and the *Goede Hoop* used an evening breeze to sail into the bay and anchor in the usual place off the mouth of the Fresh River. The *Reiger* joined them early the next morning, Sunday, 7 April 1652. It was a busy and exciting day for everyone.

Captain Coninck of the *Dromedaris* was the first to go ashore with six armed soldiers and a party of sailors. They landed just after dawn, caught delicious fish in a seine net, collected some herbs and found a box containing three letters left on 26 February by the Admiral of a homeward-bound fleet of eleven Dutch ships. The fleet had become scattered as far back as the last sighting of the shores of Asia. Only three ships had reached Table Bay and found it to be empty. Only one bullock and a sheep were bartered. Even fresh water was at low supply in the midst of a very dry season. Van Riebeeck was disappointed to learn that a number of horses for the use of his party had been on board one of the ships of the fleet, along with a collection of plants and fruit trees. The intention had been to leave these in the care of Harry if Van Riebeeck and his party had not already arrived in the Cape. These had presumably been carried on to the island of St Helena and would have to be fetched. Otherwise, all was well and peaceful in the Dutch trade with the East.

Later that afternoon, Van Riebeeck went ashore with a party to select the best site for the fort. The area of the future city of Cape Town had been well dehydrated by the summer season of the south-east wind. Wildlife as well as the pastoralists had abandoned the place until the winter rains came to refresh it. In a swamp close to the present Church Square, a few hippos garumphed at intruders. The only human inhabitants were Harry and his clan of beachcombers. With one of his companions he went with Van Riebeeck to the *Dromedaris*. Through him, Van Riebeeck learned that Harry's people, a very small clan, had a name which the Dutch wrote as *Goringhaikona*, the nearest they could get to recording the clicks and exotic sounds. Two larger clans of pastoralists habitually used the area for grazing when the rains came. They were the (Dutch spelling)

Goringhaikwa and the (Dutch spelling) *Gorachoukwa*. At least eight other pastoral clans had their grazing areas in what is now the province of the Western Cape. All these clans were nomadic, wandering about in search of the best grazing. They were generally peaceful, the country was large and there were not many of them. They could avoid one another. These were the people nicknamed Hottentots by the Dutch. They had no generic name for themselves.

Work started the next day, 8 April, on erecting the wooden house and store shed close to the mouth of the Fresh River. The site for the fort was selected where the fruit stalls stand today on what is known as the Grand Parade in the centre of modern Cape Town. One hundred men were selected from the three vessels to work on construction on shore and were housed in tents. Harry and his clan took up residence close to the camp and regarded themselves as of such importance, well-fed and treated, that when, at midday on 10 April, about ten of the Goringhaikwa clan approached the scene of construction, Harry and his followers jealously attacked them and it was the novel turn of Europeans in the Cape to restore order between rival African people.

On 24 April, Van Riebeeck and his family removed from the *Dromedaris* to the shore and occupied the wooden building. On the previous evening a hippopotamus had been killed in the swamp and on this animal the whole party feasted. They likened the flesh to veal and craved for more but hippos were difficult to kill with the muskets and balls of the period. For some time the principal items on the Cape menu were the fish which swarmed in huge shoals in Table Bay and were described by Van Riebeeck and his people as the most delicious they had ever tasted. These fish made a hard, cold, wet, miserable winter bearable. Everything else was in short supply. The few ships that came in to the bay were themselves in search of provisions. Some of them were in so sad a way that their plight emphasised the urgency of the successful establishment of a place of refreshment at the Cape. The *Walvisch* and *Olifant* which arrived on 7 May after four months sailing from Holland had between them lost 130 men. The remaining crew were on their last legs from scurvy.

The earth walled fort was at least nearing completion and the names of the four ships in the bay, *Dromedaris*, *Reiger*, *Walvisch* and *Olifant* were bestowed on the four bastions while the name of the yacht, *Goede Hoop*, was given to the whole fort. The 50 weakest individuals on the two recently arrived ships were brought ashore to recover, along with hard-tack provisions to support them for three months. The four ships then sailed and Van Riebeeck and his men were left with little for their comfort save the small yacht, the still unfinished fort, three more months of heavy winter weather, and short rations.

At least the rains transformed the vegetation and softened the soil. Hendrik Boom, the gardener, made haste to plant seeds and soon there were health-restoring vegetables and the scurvy was vanquished. Great herds of game animals also appeared in the area on what was apparently their seasonal migration. The sight of these wild animals made the longing for fresh meat almost an obsession but the hunters had little success with their simple weapons and lack of experience. In the whole winter season, only one young hartebeest was run down by dogs. For the rest, the wild animals outwitted marksmen, traps and pitfalls with agile impunity.

Whales in considerable numbers also appeared in the bay for winter was the season when they visited the South African coast to avoid the pack ice of the Antarctic. In the warmer waters they calved and relaxed, as though on holiday, blowing, grunting, breaching (leaping clear out of the water), lobtailing (slapping their flukes on the surface) and spy hopping (viewing the surroundings by standing vertically, with head and shoulders above the water). Van Riebeeck watched the antics of the whales with even more frustration than he observed the game animals on the land. He longed to distinguish himself by making quick profits for his employers but he had neither men nor means to establish a whale-oil factory.

What Van Riebeeck did do, was look to Robben Island for that little place always seemed to be productive of something interesting. The yacht was sent over to the island and came back with over 100 carcasses of sea birds and 3 000 penguin eggs, a very welcome addition to food supplies. Van Riebeeck decided that he must himself visit so prolific a provider. He found the island rather chaotic as a result of the last visit of the yacht. The penguin colony had been badly disturbed. Gulls had destroyed most of the remaining eggs of the colony. The seals which had once been so prolific were now little more than a lingering name to the island. The bemused penguins were still, however, sufficiently numerous as to allow the sailors to shepherd a whole flock of them down to the beach where they could be conveniently slaughtered and loaded on to the yacht.

Back on the mainland, Van Riebeeck decided it was time to examine the possibilities of the country behind Devil's Peak. This beautiful and fertile agricultural land delighted him. On his return to the fort he wrote a report on what he had seen and sent it by the next ship to the Governor-General and Council of the Dutch possessions in the East. He was of opinion that if a population of Chinese settlers could be introduced to farm this area (now known as Constantia) an unlimited supply of vegetables and other produce could be obtained for supply to shipping. Van Riebeeck was a great admirer of the industry of the Chinese. By their presence he considered that the whole area of the Cape would be transformed from wilderness to productive vegetable garden. The Dutch authorities, however, had no Chinese available at that time, convicts or others, to ship to the Cape. Nothing transpired from the scheme. Hendrik Boom, the gardener, was left with the assistance of a few labourers supplied from the garrison to slowly create the Company's vegetable garden close to the fort.

With Robben Island for the time being somewhat denuded as a source of food and profit, Van Riebeeck discussed the situation with Simon Peter Turvey, captain of the yacht *Goede Hoop*. Turvey told him how, as a mate aboard a ship in a Dutch fleet returning in 1651 from the East to Europe, he had met a French captain who had anchored his ship close to them at St Helena Island. The men of the sea had mixed socially for bouts of drinking and yawning. In his cups, the Frenchman had been boastful and voluble. He described in detail the success of his voyage, the richness of his cargo of seal pelts and the curious nature of the islands off the South African coast, especially Dassen from where he had just come. The stolid Dutchman listened and plied the Frenchman with liquor until his tale was told and he slid as gracefully beneath the table as only the French can do.

Van Riebeeck was fascinated at the story. Turvey was ordered to sail to Dassen Island and investigate. His instructions were *'Carefully examine into everything which may possibly bring any profit. This may secure you great honour as the first discoverer of further means of securing profit'*.

Profits were Van Riebeeck's bugbear and preoccupation in life. He had to provide them somehow in order to put the Cape establishment on a viable footing. So impressed was Turvey by his great opportunity that he was not the first man to venture out on duty already dreaming of the rewards before the task was done. Gold, ambergris, musk and ivory were all fortune-making items thought to be obtainable on the south-western coast.

Van Riebeeck waited anxiously for the return of the yacht. No ships visited the bay. Living conditions in the primitive fort were miserable. The feeling of isolation and insecurity made the men quarrelsome and insubordinate. Many would have deserted if there was any place where they could go. Discipline in the fort was severe, while outside there was a vast continent filled with unimaginable dangers. Lions seemed to be crowding around the fort, even attempting to assault the place.

'This night,' wrote Van Riebeeck *'it appeared as if the lions would take the fort by storm, that they might get at the sheep, they made a fearful noise, as if they would destroy all within but they could not climb the walls ...'*

While the yacht was away the annual migration took place of the Goringhaikwa people to the Cape with their flocks and herds. At the beginning of October their camp fires were first seen in the north. On the 9th of the month two of their men arrived at the fort. They were far stronger looking than the beachcombers of Harry. They were armed with spears and sticks, naked except for a well-prepared skin draped down over one of their arms as European gallants affected a mantle. Their arms and legs were decorated with ivory and copper ornaments. They were friendly, informed Van Riebeeck that their people would soon be coming to graze their livestock on the spring growth of fresh grass and herbs. Van Riebeeck was delighted. He showed them his stock of trade goods – copper, brass and other metals, tobacco and alcohol, gave them samples and entertained them hospitably before they returned to their people. Other small groups came and Van Riebeeck traded three cattle, four sheep, three elephant tusks and two young ostriches. The rest of the Gorinkhaikwa arrived a few days later and camped on the sites of the future suburbs of Rondebosch and Claremont. Everybody was friendly. Harry acted as interpreter, assisted by his niece, a bright child of about 11 years who was named Eva by the Europeans. She took up residence in the fort, was taught Dutch, Christianity, assorted European skills and industry and dressed like a young lady from Holland.

It was at this time that the yacht returned from its voyage of exploration. Captain Turvey was jubilant. He had, in fact, found the first substantial profit for his employers. Turvey had sailed directly to Dassen Island. Approaching what the Portuguese had originally named *Ilha Blanco* (white island) and Sir Edward Michaelhouse *Coney Island*, Turvey optimistically renamed it *Profyt Eiland* in the hope that it would be his source of wealth. Three hundred years later the renowned British naturalist Cherry Kearton described the island in his book *The Island of Penguins* as one of the natural wonders of the world. At that time there were over one million penguins as well as countless other sea birds nesting on the island. The donkey-like braying of the Jackass penguins could be heard as a strange booming sound from several kilometres away. The white colour of the island came from the birds' guano.

Turvey and his crew landed on the island but found only birds and dassies. They killed 20 of the dassies and considered their flesh to be delicious, They sailed on to the entrance of Saldanha Bay where they found another island, this one rocky, with a stony hillock as its centre. Living on the island were prodigious numbers of seals. The animals were swimming around in troops of thousands. The fish population of the sea could only be immense to support such a number of predatory seals and birds. It was an incredible sight. Turvey named the place *Vondeling* (foundling). Anchoring in the calm waters of Saldanha Bay, Turvey and his men loaded their craft with fish, eggs and venison from some antelope they killed with arrows. Two rather skinny sheep were also bartered from some pastoralists and these animals they decided to leave to fatten on one of the islands in the bay. In this way fate led them to their treasure. They landed the sheep on a little island which they named *Skaap* (sheep). Turvey and the mate explored the island without much hope of discovering any marvels. Suddenly, in a clearing they found a huge pile of neatly packed seal skins just waiting to be loaded. Around the skins were scattered tents and tools left by the hunters. The Netherlanders looked at each other incredulously. They had obviously stumbled on a French sealer's base. It seemed too good to be true. They scampered back to the beach and called all hands off the yacht to load up. With a lookout man watching in case the Frenchmen returned, they laboured all day and then sailed out of the bay in high spirits.

'Took some 2 773 skins,' Turvey gleefully noted in his log. *'The Frenchmen will swear when they return and find them gone.'*

Back at Vondeling Island, they explored the place hoping for another treasure trove of seal skins. They found the island covered with an asparagus of a bitter kind, reeds, thorny shrubs, tortoises and an occasional snake. Sailing off they again landed on Dassen Island, this time on a different side from their last visit. There they discovered another French sealers encampment, with huts made of whale ribs covered by seal pelts. A litter of cases, barrels, and implements was scattered around. There were no pelts waiting to be taken but they collected 12 000 eggs. And so proudly back to the Cape to be greeted by Van Riebeeck's congratulations and the order that they return to the islands as soon as possible to search for more of the Frenchmen's treasures.

The economic future of the Cape was now starting to reveal itself. The situation of the Cape Peninsula at the south-western end of Africa made it strategically and commercially important for the replenishment and repair of shipping. Notwithstanding the seasonal nature of rainfall and the shortage of water from perennial rivers, the soil was fertile, rich in humus and replenished by the chemicals of continually decomposing sandstone. Once agriculture could be established, with the fundamental essential of an industrious population, the Cape would easily fulfil its intended role as a tavern of the sea, supplying vegetables, fruit, and drinks to all who had the money to pay for them.

The two great ocean currents converging on the Cape of Good Hope carried with them a vast population of marine life, warm-water Indo-Pacific species with the Mozambique–Agulhas Current from the east, cold-water species especially huge shoals of pelagic fish, mainly pilchards and anchovies, carried up the west side by the plankton-rich Benguela Current. The sea on both sides of the Cape Peninsula was clearly destined to become the source of a huge industry in fishing, sealing and the collection of guano from the islands for sale as fertiliser.

All visitors to the Cape were captivated by the scenery and the lovely flora of one of the Earth's principal domains of wild flowers. It was a vast natural garden in a superb scenic setting. As the intended Tavern of the Sea expanded its facilities and reputation for hospitality so visitors would be attracted, if not to settle, then at least to see so remarkable a place. The first stirrings of a future tourist industry were taking place.

So far as food was concerned, the herds of game animals tantalised Van Riebeeck and even more frustrating were the flocks and herds of the pastoral people. On 20 October the Goringhaikwa finally arrived on their annual visit to the summer grazing grounds below Table Mountain. Their fat-tailed sheep and plump cattle were tempting creatures to see by people longing for fresh meat, not only for themselves but also to supply to visiting ships at the much desired profit for the Dutch East India Company.

The pastoral tribes were becoming known to Van Riebeeck and his people by the colloquial name of *Kaapmans* (Cape People), abbreviated at times to Capeys. Through the interpreters, Harry and his young niece, the Cape People repeatedly asked when the English were coming. They were reluctant to part with any large numbers of their livestock. The Netherlanders became aggrieved and thought that Harry had somehow prejudiced the Cape People against the Dutch because they had settled permanently on the traditional grazing grounds of the tribe. Van Riebeeck candidly recorded his thoughts in his diary.

'What would it matter if we took at once from them 6 000 or 8 000 cattle, there is opportunity enough for it, as we do not perceive that they are very strong in number, but indeed very timorous, coming often only two or three men driving 1 000 cattle under our guns.'

Without the sanction of his superiors in Holland Van Riebeeck could only fret at such easy profit denied him. Restraints by parent authority in Europe on the headstrong doings of colonial offspring were destined to become increasingly contentious as the years passed. His superiors, however, approved at least one urgent desire of Van Riebeeck. This was his demand for labour. Chinamen were not available and the Cape People were not much tempted to become labourers. They were not physically suited to become slaves and would find it too easy to run away. Imported slaves were regarded as the answer. The Cape settlement therefore became one more market for slave traders to dispose of their wares. The slaves came mainly from the nearest source of supply to the Cape, Angola, and they supplied the human material for the system of forced labour management which was considered to be normal in the world at that time.

A trade was opened with the Cape People. Flat copper bars and tobacco were bartered for cattle and brass wire and tobacco for sheep. By the end of January 1653 Van Riebeeck had acquired by this barter trade 230 head of cattle and 580 sheep. He still, however, felt aggrieved. In his writings he again observed that it would have been so easy to seize ten or twelve thousand head of cattle and to pack their owners off to India in chains to be sold as slaves. The only pity he felt to such action was the prohibition by his superiors.

The islands and the fisheries, meanwhile, were well exploited as providers of food and profit. Apart from its penguins, eggs, and seals, the shells and limestone on Robben Island were the beginning of the first manufactory in the Cape. Shells were collected and limestone quarried, with kilns to convert the raw material into lime-wash for painting buildings. Another interesting first for Robben Island was a *plakkaat* (edict) issued in 1653. This was the second proclamation concerning conservation. The first had regulated the felling of trees on Table Mountain. The second controlled the slaughter of seals, penguins and the collection of eggs on Robben Island. This measure of conservation was considered very necessary. After twelve months of 'harvesting' the island for foodstuffs its population of wildlife was in rather sad disarray.

Corporal Marcus van Robbeljaert was appointed to be commander of the island, with two French sealers and two Netherlanders under him to help with the herding of the cattle and sheep being sent there. Two small cannon were sent to the island and specific instructions to the commander *'to beware the sailors of the homeward fleets for, the good ones excepted, they are light-fingered and neither care for the devil or his dam'*. One of the two Netherlander herdsmen on the island set a good example of light fingering. He rifled the other's chest and had to be removed in chains back to the mainland.

Corporal Van Robbeljaert and his little community of islanders busied themselves in watching the livestock fatten, fishing and planting a garden where, as the Corporal reported with a touch of poetry, *'most things grew well, glory be to God, but the sweet potatoes we see nothing of'*. Another problem for the island was rabbits. Van Riebeeck had landed on the island eight rabbits, which he had brought with him from Holland. These had increased at such a rate that a greyhound to hunt them down had to be added to the population of the island.

While the islanders tried to solve the problems of their little world, Van Riebeeck was having an anxious time. On 18 January 1653, the galiot *Zwarte Vos* arrived with the news that war had broken out between the Netherlands and the Commonwealth of England under Oliver Cromwell. This was very bad news. The Netherlands was already at war with Portugal and Van Riebeeck in his fort had little defence against any attack by either of the hostile maritime powers. The fort was just about capable of keeping at bay the marauding lions and leopards, the available cannon were feeble and, to worsen matters, the local pastoral people were increasingly resentful of the Netherlander's occupation of the grazing lands. Even Harry and his beachcombers with young Eva sneaked away one day while the garrison was in church, stole 42 of the herd of 44 cattle then in the possession of the Company and murdered the young Netherland's herdsman.

Times looked bleak but ships continued to call for supplies. The vegetable garden was increasingly productive. If beef was in short supply, then penguins and their eggs from the islands provided good eating and the sheep on Robben Island fattened in security. A base for hunting seals was also established on Dassen Island. The French who at least remained in a state of mutually suspicious peace with the Netherlands, continued sealing from the islands in Saldanha Bay with one ship taking away a cargo of 48 000 skins.

The anniversary (6 April) of the arrival of Van Riebeeck and his party in the Cape was treated as a day of thanksgiving. At that date there was not much to give thanks for but four months later, with the spring flowers blossoming, there was a change for the better. On 15 August the yacht *Vlieland* arrived with the good news from the Netherlands that there was peace with the English. The oppressive sense of threat and isolation, which had gathered over the settlement, simply vanished away like the storm clouds of winter. International shipping returned to Table Bay, one of the ships bringing the first vine stocks all the way from the vineyards of the Rhine. The indefatigable gardener, Hendrik Boom, soon had them settled in the local soil along with a varied collection of fruit trees and the flourishing fields of vegetables. To the visiting ships, some with more than half of their crew dead or half dead from scurvy, Van Riebeeck's garden, orchard and vineyard at the Cape offered a new chance of life, a little cheer and the beginning of what became the famed cuisine of the Cape.

Cape Classic Cuisine, as it is called, is based on the essential foundation of fresh, tasty local produce, a good contribution from the vineyards and a subtlety of cookery which came from the blending of the skills of Europe, Africa and the East. The Dutch had acquired a liking in Indonesia for the exotic tastes of that country. These tastes were brought to the Cape to an increasing extent from 1654 onwards. It was in that year that four Indonesians were sentenced by the Dutch court of justice in Batavia to banishment, and hard labour for life. Their crime was resistance to Dutch seizure of their homeland. Three of the men were left on the island of Mauritius. The fourth was landed at the Cape. He was the first of many people to be banished from the East to spend their lives in Southern Africa. Most were from Indonesia, nearly, but not all were Muslims. For some reason they were indiscriminately known in the Cape as Malays. Their influence on cooking, architecture, building and industry became notable in the story of the Cape.

The uneasy relations with the Cape People continued. Resentment at the growth and obvious permanence of the European settlement was very obvious in the local inhabitants. They flaunted their herds and flocks within easy reach of Van Riebeeck's men but often declined to trade and continually and deliberately irritated the Dutch by asking when the Englishmen were coming. The soldiers wished to avenge the murder of the young herdsman, Van Riebeeck craved possession of slaughter animals for the ships. The whole situation could be resolved if only he could be permitted by his superiors to reduce to servitude what he described as an idle and useless people. To seize their herds of cattle and flocks of sheep would provide the settlement with its own pool of breeding stock, with quick profit possibilities of shipping the whole caboodle of the local population of Cape People as slaves to Batavia and the East. The project remained constantly on his mind.

In an effort to reach over the Cape People and find trading possibilities with less hostile tribes, the first party of exploration, seven soldiers under Jan Wintervogel, was sent out from the Cape in March 1655. In nineteen days the explorers only managed to travel a little beyond the site of the present town of Malmesbury. They encountered a few small groups of Bushmen, who had nothing to trade, and some pastoralists with herds of cattle but little enthusiasm to part with their livestock for the usual scrap metal.

Trading conditions at the fort made a sudden improvement on 23 June 1655 when Harry the prodigal reappeared accompanied by 50 strangers who brought 40 cattle for trade. Harry flatly denied having anything to do with the recent murder and theft of cattle. Van Riebeeck considered it wise to at least pretend to believe the man. Some trade for cattle and sheep was restored. Harry even volunteered to lead a party from the fort to the shores of False Bay in search of people prepared to trade their cattle. Particularly gratifying was the arrival of a large group of pastoralists under a chief named Gonnema, nicknamed the Black Captain because he used soot as a facial cosmetic instead of the red clay favoured by the Cape People. The newcomers built on the site of the future suburb of Rondebosch an encampment of two hundred huts, linked with a palisade and containing a huge *corral* (or *kraal* as such structures came to be known in Dutch) in which they secured their livestock at night. Van Riebeeck had the satisfaction of trading copper scrap for nearly 400 head of cattle and about the same quantity of sheep. The sheep were taken over to Robben Island for fattening in safety.

In the absence of Harry, two other local men did duty as interpreters, a beachcomber known as Klaus Das because he had learned Dutch working with the seal hunters on Dassen Island, and a Cape man nicknamed Doman because his demeanour seemed as grave and transparent as a *dominee* (parson). He was so highly regarded that Van Riebeeck in 1655 sent him on a round trip to Batavia to expand his knowledge of the Dutch and their language. He returned two years later not quite as angelic as he had seemed when he left the Cape, as will be seen later in this story.

A momentous change to the nature of the Cape settlement came in 1655. The directors in Holland revised their original concept of only having employees of the company stationed in what was intended as a simple trading station. The directors decided that company employees on completion of their service contracts in the Cape, if they did not wish to return to Europe or be posted to the East, could be settled as freemen on ground close to the fort and earn a living by producing food or by some other industry. With this decision, the Cape became a colony rather than just a service station on the East–West route. The directors of the Dutch East India Company unfortunately had much to learn about the peculiar nature of a colony. Their hope was to see the transplant into new soil of the same industrious peasantry that farmed smallholdings in Holland. They failed to appreciate that the contagious cancer of slavery persuaded a 'freeman' to take others into bondage, to become a squire, patron or slave master rather than a worker himself. Work was for slaves; the landowner automatically became a gentleperson in the local social scale, craving ever larger land holdings as the means to rise still higher in popular esteem, clamouring for more slave workers whose labour would reward the master with the profits to support an ever more demanding lifestyle.

The facilities offered to shipping were improved in 1656 with the opening of a hospital large enough to cope with sudden influxes of considerable numbers of patients. A strong wooden jetty was also completed and this was a great convenience to the loading of fresh water casks and general supplies. The first two inns were also opened, one by the wife of Sergeant van Harwarden, the other by Annetje de Boerin, wife of the gardener Hendrik Boom, an enterprising lady who already had secured the right to lease the company-owned herd of dairy cows and supply the community with fresh milk.

Four years after its establishment, the Cape settlement, transforming to a colony, presented a bustling scene. Practically every garden crop of that age was flourishing. Only potatoes and maize had still to be successfully introduced. The genius and industry of Hendrik Boom had created a garden so productive that it now even provided luxuries such as strawberries and blackberries and all things in such quantity that an export business to Batavia of high quality seeds had commenced. Oak and fir trees had been introduced; domestic livestock were flourishing, the wild animals were being driven away by professional hunters and the quality of their venison becoming appreciated as an alternative to the meat of domestic animals.

Wheat and barley at first proved difficult to cultivate, for their ripening time unfortunately coincided with the season of the desiccating southeasterly wind. Crops simply withered. Van Riebeeck then discovered that the south-easter was not nearly so venomous on the western side of Devil's Peak. An experimental crop was grown in the area known as *Ronde Doorn Bossien*, from a round grove of thorn trees which grew there. The results were excellent. *Rondebosch*, as the area came to be known, was developed as a wheat farm. A substantial building, known as the *Groote Schuur* (great barn), was erected to store the grain, as well as a redoubt to shelter a small guard of soldiers. The whole question of the security of the expanding settlement, especially now that families, under the freeman scheme, would be granted land beyond the protection of the fort, was causing concern. There was even a notion of digging a moat or canal from Table Bay to False Bay. This would act as a barrier between the indigenous tribes and the settlers. The projected separation of people was based rather on religion than anything else. Christians would live within the area on the western side of the 20 km long moat. Non-believers would live on the eastern side. The possessions of heathens could be seized without sin, and they could be enslaved. Professing Christians whatever their colour or ethnic origin, could not be kept in bondage or discriminated against in any way. Intermarriage was common.

The idea of the moat was conceived in 1656 by Ryklof van Goens, an admiral in the service of the Company. Van Riebeeck examined the idea but it was discarded as being too expensive. Alternative ideas were then considered including building a line of forts connected by a strong palisade or a thick hedge of wild almond trees running from the banks of the stream known as the *Liesbeek*, from a species of water plant, where it flows from the heights of the Bosbergen, along the summit ridge of the *Bosheuwel* (bush slopes), below the cluster of granite boulders known from their shape as the Hen and Chickens, and across the flatlands to the mouth of the Salt River. It took some time for this defensive scheme to mature.

The first two groups of freemen, five in the one group and four in the second, chose land for themselves on the outer side of the Liesbeek River. They were each gifted by the company with plots about 28 acres (or 13 morgen) in extent and were free of the burden of taxes for twelve years. The prospects looked good. More men decided to take their freedom in the Cape from company service and become property or business owners at no cost to themselves. Not all wanted to be farmers. Wouter Mostert had been a miller in the Netherlands. He set up a water-mill in the upper reaches of the Fresh River. Others became carpenters, tailors, wagonmakers, fishermen, hunters or innkeepers. A straggling little town started to grow in the afternoon shadow of Table Mountain.

Robben Island also gained in importance. There were 400 sheep, numerous pigs and 300 head of cattle grazing there in safety. Apart from caring for the livestock, the men stationed on the island were given a new duty in 1657. On the highest point of the island a pole, and later a platform, was erected on which pitch rings were set alight each night as a navigational beacon. The hill was named *Vuurberg* (fire mountain) and this was, in its simple way, the first lighthouse on the coast of Southern Africa. The modern lighthouse was built on Vuurberg in 1864. The hill was then renamed *Minto Hill* after Dr James Clephane Minto, surgeon-superintendent of the island in the 1860s.

Still another use for Robben Island was found by Van Riebeeck at this time. It was a very handy place to have right on the doorstep of the Cape settlement. All manner of problem human beings could be sent to it, like a maid sweeping dust under a carpet, and there accommodated well concealed from public view. Van Riebeeck was convinced at that time that Harry the interpreter was playing a treacherous game, pretending friendship but plotting with the Cape People to destroy the settlement before it entirely enveloped their traditional grazing fields. Meanwhile they were to demand ever higher values in trade for their livestock.

Van Riebeeck considered that Harry, as official interpreter, was becoming expendable. If Europeans found it almost impossible to learn the local language with its clicks and exotic sounds, some of the Cape People found it relatively far easier to learn Dutch in the form of a local version of it which started to develop as a convenient medium of communication. People such as the girl Eva and Doman could take over duties of interpretation and negotiation and it was here that Van Riebeeck had his brainwave. If Robben Island was difficult to reach for people who had no boats then it would obviously be just as difficult for boatless people to leave. The stone quarries and lime-making industries on the island provided ideal hard labour employment for prisoners.

Accordingly, in his diary for 10 July 1658, Van Riebeeck cynically noted: *'The ex-interpreter, or as the English call him, King Harry, was removed in a sheep boat out of his kingdom in this furthest corner of Africa to Robben Island with two of his companions'*. These three Cape men with some political prisoners exiled in chains from Batavia were the first to obtain what Van Riebeeck considered secure quarters where the massed arum lilies wave so freely in the wind on Robben Island. The irrepressible Harry, however, was destined to prove Van Riebeeck wrong by being the first prisoner to escape from Robben Island. He managed to hijack the same sheep boat, which had brought him to the island and in it made his way to freedom on the mainland. Very few other prisoners had the same audacity and good fortune in the years to follow.

Life in the infant Cape Town might have been on the rough side but it was certainly eventful and a place of interesting rumours. The legendary land of Monomotapa, the golden Ophir of

Solomon and Sheba, was reported to be within easy reach to the north. Friendly cattle-rich tribes were said to live just beyond the mountains. Parties set off in search of this wealth, one group south-eastwards to the foot of the mountains exploring an area whose few inhabitants described it so enthusiastically that the visitors jocularly named it the Hottentots Holland.

Later in October 1657 another party explored the valley of the river flowing northwards along the foot of a range of mountains which provided a barrier to further travel eastwards. A high cluster of granite domes seemed to stand sentry over this valley, guarding a sandstone world. Because they glittered in the sun after rain, like diamonds and pearls, the explorers named the highest peaks *Diamant* and *Paarl*. In February 1658 still another party of explorers managed to climb the mountain range close to the passage washed through it by the Little Berg River and from the summit look down on the long valley of the Breede River with still another range of mountains on the further side to block progress to the interior.

No quick wealth in gold or cattle rewarded these explorers. News of their travels, however, fascinated the stay-at-homes in the Cape settlement and provided relief from the continuous rumours of attack from the dispossessed original inhabitants. Eva, the young lady interpreter, was a great source of such assorted tales of riches and troubles to come. She treated listeners to elaborate accounts of the Nama people who she said had white skins, long hair, wore clothing and owned black slaves who tilled the soil, worked mines and built stone houses for their masters. The Nama, according to Eva, lived in style, had church services similar to those of the Dutch, decorated their women with elaborate jewellery, and flourished in comfort on the labours of the slaves. Such tales of gentlemanly living in Africa were beguiling to employees of the Dutch Company. These people of various nationalities had a background in Europe of hard living and poorly rewarded labour. It seemed to them that by being posted for duty to the south-westerly end of Africa, they had escaped from a humdrum existence into a new era of prosperity, of generous land grants, the award of monopolies in trading and professional occupation, of rights to own slaves, of the whole prospect ahead of them of a fat-cat society. The fact that the Dutch East India Company had intended to establish a productive community rather than a parasitic one did not bother them.

They were all transformed to land owners and moneygrubbers, wanting only lawyers, stock exchange manipulators, developers, promoters, usurers, speculators and swindlers to complete the social strata of the Cape. Even Van Riebeeck was in the real estate business. The Dutch East India Company, in 1657, granted him the land now covered by the suburb and sports fields of Green Point. When this area was found unsuitable for agriculture, Van Riebeeck received in 1658 a farm, 86,5 hectares in extent on the south-eastern side of the Liesbeek River. On this farm Van Riebeeck planted grapevines, naming the place *Wynberg* (wine mountain). The name was later transferred to adjoining high ground and Van Riebeeck's farm was renamed *Bosheuwel* (bushy slope).

The basic contradictions of a slave-based society became apparent when the first substantial number of slaves reached the Cape. On 28 March 1658, the *Amersfoort* brought 170 black Africans to the Cape. On the way from Holland, the *Amersfoort* had captured a Portuguese ship bound from Angola to Brazil with over 500 slaves. The ship was too decrepit to be a worthwhile prize. The Netherlanders relieved the slaver of 250 of the best of the Angolans and then allowed the Portuguese to continue their voyage to Brazil. Of the 250 slaves, 80 died before the *Amersfoort* reached the Cape and the remaining 170 were in a very miserable state. Two weeks later, the *Hasselt* arrived in Table Bay with 228 slaves. Before this influx there were only about 12 individuals in bondage in the Cape and these were from Indonesia and Madagascar.

Eighty-nine of the newcomers were sold off on credit to the local freemen. Prices ranged from £4 3s 4d to £8 6s 8d each, depending on physical condition, age and sex. The company put a number into its own bondage. A surplus of 172 was sent on to Batavia. In the Cape the slave owners reconditioned their new acquisitions by feeding them on seal meat, sea birds and eggs from the islands. The *Hasselt* had brought with the slaves seeds of their staple food, maize, but it would take at least a year before crops could be produced. A chain of events now began which baffled the slave owners. As soon as the slaves recovered their strength individuals took the first opportunity to run away. They knew vaguely that their homeland was north up the West Coast. They had no idea how far they would have to go or through what dangers of wild animals, hostile people, or the harshness of the desert country they would have to traverse. They simply wanted to go home. How many of them, if any, ever managed to reach their homes is unknown. It would make an epic story.

The owners were outraged at the behaviour of the slaves. Many of them were left to pay off the credit allowed them in buying the slaves, together with the cost of fattening. There was no little debate in the Cape about what to do. If the slaves were left in their emaciated condition, they couldn't run away, but they were unable to work. If they were reconditioned and ran away but were pursued, there was more expense. If they were caught, there was no profit in shooting, or imposing barbaric physical punishment, which would reduce their work capacity. Keeping slaves in chains also was a handicap on work. The females at least were expected to be more docile but even here there was a contradiction. The children they bore their owners were expected to be baptised and as Christians could not be added to the slave force. Legally, they had to be free and were not an asset.

There was also a feeling that the Cape People sympathised with the slaves and aided their escape. Ill feeling, attacks on farmers, theft of livestock and rumours of war bedevilled the Cape settlers. Even the young girl, Eva, left the settlement with some of her people, wishing Van Riebeeck goodbye with the ominous warning *'Mynheer Van Riebeeck, take good care. I shall not return for a long time, your land will now be full of war.'*

Van Riebeeck confronted problems at every turn. His term at the Cape was drawing to a close and his tribulations there did not leave him with much love for the place. He had done his duty there, according to the norms of the times. The settlement was firmly established but he was often criticised by his superiors in Holland, especially over deteriorating relations with the African people. The possibility of serious conflict was not a profitable prospect to the Dutch East India Company. The infant Tavern of the Sea had certainly achieved the purpose allocated to it by its parents in Holland, but as a teenager it was proving a little wayward, headstrong and unruly.

In 1659 there was a nasty setback when an unidentified disease attacked the domestic livestock at the Cape. About a quarter of the animals died. Robben Island, always considered so safe a grazing place, was badly affected. Of its flock of 520 sheep and 332 head of cattle, only 40 survived. Just when Van Riebeeck thought that he had achieved an ability to supply all demands for fresh meat from his own breeding animals he had to start almost from the beginning bartering livestock from the increasingly truculent tribes.

At least a little cheer that year came from the vineyards. Grapes were thriving magnificently in the Cape. On 2 February 1659 Van Riebeeck recorded in his diary his thanks to the Lord for the taste of the first wine produced in South Africa. He had made the wine himself. He was the only man in the Cape who knew how to make the delicate elixir. As he savoured the wine, Van Riebeeck could at least toast an excellent agricultural season, with bumper crops as some compensation for the problems with livestock. Fresh vegetables and fruit were sure remedies to the curse of scurvy. The produce of the Cape saved countless lives and no visiting ship, Dutch or friendly nation, was ever denied its full supply of health-restoring food. For vegetarians, at least, the Tavern of the Sea became a paradise.

When the Cape People returned in 1659 to their traditional grazing grounds, they found them sprinkled with neat farmhouses and tilled fields, all the largesse of the Dutch East India Company showing gratitude to its employees by generous gifts to them of other people's land. The Cape People were enraged. The Tavern of the Sea was now far too strong to be overrun by force. Doman, the angelic-looking interpreter, had returned to the Cape in 1658 from his visit to Batavia. At first he resumed his work in the fort. It was soon apparent that his round trip had taught him much about the European life-style. For a while he even wanted to change his name to Anthony as sounding more refined. The growing friction over land with his own people had its due effect on him. Abandoning his European clothes, he deserted the fort one night, became an adviser to the Cape People and leader of an aggressive band of cattle thieves. His advice to his people was to avoid any confrontation with superior European firearms but to harass them at night and in the rain when the old flint firelock guns were almost useless. He had observed that the principal motivation of white people was to make money and he felt that the best way to drive them away was simply to ruin them.

What Doman failed to realise was that the former Company employees now had their own stake in the Cape, liked the place, and it would take more effort to drive them away than the Cape People could muster. Van Riebeeck organised the freemen and the garrison into a militia and, by indefatigable action, rallied them to strengthen the farmhouses, keep their powder kegs dry, their weapons on the ready and to hold prayer meetings every Wednesday to ask God to withdraw his rage against them. Various reasons were given for this wrath of God, principally the goings-on in the taverns. Van Riebeeck and his superiors had no doubt, however, that the cause of the trouble with the Cape People was the direct result of the occupation of their land. They could no longer even get their livestock to the river to drink without trespassing on private property.

Meanwhile, the livestock disease continued its toll, but with the surviving animals becoming resistant. There was a rumour that Doman had told the Cape People to deliberately sell sick animals to the Dutch in order to infect their livestock as part of the policy of ruination. He also led raiding parties and was responsible for a surprise attack on a herdsman named Simon Janssen, killing him and driving away the cattle under his care.

A bounty of 137 shillings and 6 pence was put on the head of Doman, 55 shillings for each of the Cape People taken prisoner, and 27 shillings and 6 pence for each one killed. Vengeance and profit stimulated the militia. In one fire fight, three mounted militiamen led by the *fiscal*, Abraham Gabbema, encountered a party of five Cape men. Three were killed, one captured after being wounded, the other, also wounded, escaped. To the mortification of the militia, this man was Doman.

By the end of the year, however, conditions improved in the Cape. The garrison had been reinforced with 105 extra soldiers supplied by passing ships. More ponies had also been sent from Batavia, as well as several big, strong, vicious watchdogs. Doman's wounds had subdued the man and, in any case, the Cape People moved northwards in their usual seasonal migration. They would be back with their grievances in the following year but short of returning to them their ancient grazing grounds there was no answer to their problems. The Cape was now a colony. It would simply grow like the celebrated Topsy. Meanwhile, to provide security to the growing Cape Town, Van Riebeeck decided to deepen the fords across the Liesbeek River and the Black River, which it joined as a tributary. Watch houses would be built along the outer line of the settlement. These were named *Keert de Koe* (turn the cow), *Hout den Bul* (hold the bull) with *Kyck Uitt* (look out) at the mouth of the river. They were connected by a strong fence patrolled by a mounted force quartered in the watch houses. A thick hedge of bitter almond trees was planted along this barrier line.

Early in 1660 the Cape People wished to make their customary journey to the Cape, but they had lost their spirit to fight. Harry was now living with them after his escape from Robben Island. He and Doman sent a message to Van Riebeeck proposing a treaty of friendship and safe conduct to the fort. Van Riebeeck responded favourably and on 6 April a party of 43 of the leading men of the Cape People, including Harry, Doman and the chief of the tribe, Gogoswa, known as the Fat Captain to Van Riebeeck, arrived at the fort. It was an historic occasion, resulting, after considerable discussion, in the first peace treaty in Southern Africa between the indigenous people and Europeans.

The Cape People received little advantage from the treaty. There was peace. Nobody was to molest the other but the Europeans retained possession of the land they had occupied. The Cape People pleaded for the right to enter the area to gather bitter almonds and edible roots but even this was denied them. The bitter almonds were needed for the hedge. They could visit the fort along delineated roads. Europeans doing them wrong would be punished. The Cape People would endeavour to persuade the other tribes to trade with the fort. A feast of rice and bread, with a tub filled with mixed brandy and arrack, was then held in the courtyard of the fort.

A month later a similar treaty was negotiated with the Gorachoukwa people. They tried to raise the issue of the ownership of the land along the Liesbeek River but Van Riebeeck wouldn't budge. The Europeans would hold this area by the gun if necessary. There was nothing the tribes could do about that. The total number of individuals in the pastoral tribes living near the Cape was not more than about 15 000 and of the whole of their race in Southern Africa about 40 000 at most, fragmented and widely scattered. They had to accept the fact of occupation by a stronger power. They made their marks on the treaty and another party was staged in the courtyard of the fort. It went on with dancing, singing, feasting and drinking until one after the other the visitors fell to the ground and were carried outside to sleep. The party ended with only three or four men still on their feet out of the 100 who had attended, including Harry and Doman who had come to interpret.

Thus ended the first war between African and European people fought in the Cape. Van Riebeeck was delighted. The trade in livestock revived. In the general atmosphere of peace, four successive parties of explorers were sent northwards in search of the Nama people and the city of

Davagul or Vigita Magna where the legendary Monomatapa ruled in golden splendour. The Nama people were reached in their arid homeland. Some of them were induced to visit the Cape and peace, friendship and trade was established. Davagul, Vigita Magna and the Monomatapa remained in legends.

As for Jan van Riebeeck, he had done his best, worked hard and been a loyal servant to his employers. He dreamed of promotion to a position of importance in the East, working with what he called the more orderly people of Asia as a change from the primitive tribes of the Cape. He had been the midwife at the birth of the city of Cape Town but his directors in Holland had little appreciation of this. They often listened to carping accounts by visitors that the Cape was a dreary place, the anchorage exposed to violent gales, the meat tough, the little town a place of lodging and tap houses where strong liquor was sold by persons not having the fear of God before their eyes when they made their charges.

In 1660 the directors decided to transfer Jan van Riebeeck to India. His successor, however, Gerrit Harn, died on the way to the Cape from Holland. It took months before the authorities in Batavia heard of this misfortune and appointed one of their officials, Zacharias Wagenaar, to relieve Van Riebeeck at the Cape. In the months of waiting Van Riebeeck cleared up his effects. It is interesting to read that when he handed back to the company the farm of *Bosheuwel*, the improvements, for which he would be given credit, included 1 162 young orange, lemon and citron trees, five apple, two pear, nineteen plum, two olive, three walnut, forty-one other fruit trees and several thousand vines.

Zacharias Wagenaar finally arrived from Batavia on 2 April 1662 as commodore of two of the annual return fleet of nine ships, three of which were already safe in Table Bay but the other four were never heard of again. Such were the perils of sea travel at that time. Wagenaar took over the government of the Cape in a ceremony in the fort on 6 May 1662. Early on the morning of 8 May, Van Riebeeck and his family sailed for Batavia where he was appointed head of the Company's trading station at Malacca. In the three years he remained there as commander, his wife died. He then went to Batavia, married again and was employed by the Company as secretary of the Council of India. He died in 1677.

The city of Cape Town will always be associated with the memory of Van Riebeeck. On ground reclaimed from the sea at the foot of Adderley Street, the principal street of Cape Town, there stands a graceful bronze life-sized statue of Johan (Jan) van Riebeeck, created by the sculptor John Tweed and presented to Cape Town in 1899 by Cecil Rhodes. Next to Van Riebeeck stands a second statue, that of his wife Maria. Slightly larger than life-size, this statue was the work of Dirk Wolkberg. It was presented to Cape Town in 1952 by the Van Riebeeck Committee of Holland on the 300th anniversary of the landing of the couple on the shores of Table Bay. The statues stand at approximately the position where they would have reached the beach in what was known as *Roggebaai* (bay of skate fish), now buried beneath the reclaimed area of the Foreshore.

The fort built by Van Riebeeck has vanished entirely, replaced by the later castle. It stood on the site of the stalls on the southern side of the Grand Parade. The original vegetable garden, 18 ha in extent, cultivated by Hendrik Boom with the aid of 300 slaves, is now a botanical garden reduced in size to less than 6 ha. The rest of the former garden is occupied by the buildings of the Houses of Parliament, the town residence of the President of South Africa, the Anglican cathedral of St George the Martyr, the National Library of South Africa, the National Gallery, the South African Museum, the first synagogue in South Africa, built in 1862, and a cluster of buildings housing several departments of the University of Cape Town. An avenue of oak trees 1 km long, known as Government Avenue, traverses the site of the original garden and provides a pleasant walk.

In a curious way, however, the only still living link with Van Riebeeck is a remnant of the almond hedge he planted with the intention of separating the Cape settlement and civilisation, as Van Riebeeck knew it, from primitive Africa. Portions of the hedge still flourish and produce nuts, especially along the Bosheuwel ridge where the modern Klaassens Road follows it from the top of Rhodes Drive. For 300 years the tangled hedge has remained faithful to the task given it by Van Riebeeck. Like the fort, the almond hedge was never breached by hostile forces.

At the end of the Bosheuwel ridge, the old landmark of the Hen and Chickens rocks also remains although not in their original state. The larger granite boulder, resembling a fat hen, still sits on a saucer shaped nest with the ignominy of a surveyors beacon planted on her head to mark the north-east boundary of Van Riebeeck's original farm now known as Bishopscourt, the home of the Anglican Archbishop. The smaller boulders which made the chickens also remain, but gathered to form a rockery during the making of the Hen and Chickens Reservoir. Van Riebeeck must often have walked along this boundary to pick an almond and enjoy the view of the settlement he created at the Cape of Good Hope, the Tavern of the Sea, the future city of Cape Town.

There is no known authentic portrait in existence of Van Riebeeck or his wife. The two portraits thought to be of them and often reproduced on postage stamps, bank notes and in books, were, in 1984 proved in research by the portrait expert in Holland, Jonkheer F G L O van Kretschman, to be of Bartholomeus Vermuyder and Catharina Kettingh. The two were not even related to each other, let alone be Jan van Riebeeck and his wife. They were painted by Dirck Graey and are exhibited in the Amsterdam Rijks Museum. Just how they were palmed off on to South Africa as authentic portraits of the Van Riebeecks would make an interesting story.

Chapter Two
ADOLESCENCE OF A CITY

At the time he relieved Van Riebeeck as commander of the Cape, Zacharias Wagenaar was an elderly, well-experienced administrative servant of the Dutch East India Company, conservative by nature and in poor health as a consequence of his years of residence in the East. After the volatile Van Riebeeck, the new commander was not disposed to promote change or development.

He was happy to find the Cape peaceful, with deputations from the local tribes visiting the fort to wish him well and cement their friendship by enjoying free jollification. In return, the commander visited them, dispensing gifts of tobacco and strong drink, and confirming the barter trade for sheep and cattle. He also carefully enquired after the legendary city of Vigita Magna. The local tribes had never heard of the place. One of Wagenaar's few ventures, however, was to send out on 21 October 1662 still another expedition in search of this mystical city. Once again the explorers, thirteen volunteers led by Corporal Pieter Cruythof, with Pieter van Meerhof as assistant, travelled up the west coast as far as the arid homeland of the Nama people. The intention was to travel further but the Namas were at war with a neighbour. The explorers considered it advisable to return home. Early in the following year still another expedition was sent out to search for Vigita Magna. Drought and heat rather than any human hostility drove them back to the Cape. Commander Wagenaar then lost any further interest in investing money in searching for the fabulous city.

There were other matters to distract the settlers at the Cape. It was the age of great international rivalry about trade with the East. With no quick source of reliable news the Cape was at the mercy of rumours and gossip. The local people never knew whether a visiting ship was friend or foe. Some amusing contretemps occurred when a visiting ship sailed happily into the bay in need of fresh water and provisions, without knowing that the friendly Dutch of their previous visit were now their involuntary mortal enemies as a result of political squabbles in Europe.

In this uncertain atmosphere, the Company decided that Van Riebeeck's earth fort was in need of replacement by a more robust stronghold. Plans were drawn up in Holland for a proper stone castle. An engineer, Pieter Dombaer, was sent out to supervise the construction and Commissioner Isbrand Goske was instructed to select the site. Wagenaar was empowered to draw 300 soldiers from passing ships to work on the new stronghold while an assortment of convicts and slaves were to be sent to Robben Island to quarry stone and make lime from shells in kilns fired by wood from *Houtbaai* (wood bay). Commissioner Goske arrived from Holland on 18 August 1665. After eight days of inspections and discussions he selected a site 227 metres south-east of the old fort. Then began the largest constructional activity so far undertaken in the Cape settlement.

Saturday, 2 January 1666, was a gala day in the Cape. Practically every resident as well as the crews of visiting ships, soldiers and merchants, all dressed in their best, gathered to see four heavy pieces of stone work lowered into the foundation trench for the massive walls of the projected castle. Commander Wagenaar laid the first foundation stone, the resident clergyman, Johan van Archel, laid the second; the *secunde* (second in command), Abraham Gabbema, laid the third; the *fiscal* (law enforcement officer), Hendrik Lacus, laid the fourth. It was a great occasion with tables spread within the area marked by the foundation trenches, and heavily laden with beef, mutton, vegetables, fruit and eight heavy casks of Cape ale to toast the castle named Good Hope. A poem, specially composed for the occasion, was recited; there was music and jollification.

Commander Wagenaar was a sick man at that time. He had already asked the company to relieve him of his post. His successor, Cornelis van Quaelberg, reached the Cape from Holland on 25 August 1666 after a dreary voyage lasting eight months, much impeded by weather and the war between Holland and the England of King Charles II. At least the Cape was peaceful when he took over government. The local pastoral tribes had willy-nilly accepted the reality of their ineffectiveness against the expanding settlement. In any case, their ability to resist had waned. About a fifth of them had died by this time from some unidentified disease. Many of the survivors had moved away to the interior; others took servitude with the settlers or the company and started to merge with the population of slaves of various ethnic origins and especially with the progeny of slave women.

About three-fourths of the children from the slave mothers were from European fathers. White females remained in short supply in the Cape and there was in any case no colour bar. From this mix of humanity the future ethnic group of the so-called Cape Coloureds had their origin. The slave owners and their conservative allies considered the directive to be scandalous of the church authorities and the Company that all these children be baptised, brought up in the Christian faith, and, as Christians, be free persons even if their fathers disowned them. The slave mothers, if they became Christian, would also be released from bondage. This threat to the vested interests in slave ownership created a deep schism in the established Dutch Reformed Church. There were unpleasant scenes of protest, when slave women brought their half-breed children to be baptised. Cant and great argument split even families into contentious divisions.

From its beginning in the first church in the infant Cape Town, this squabble persisted through the whole story of Southern Africa. Eva, the young lady interpreter, was the first of the Cape people to become a Christian. She was baptised early in the regime of Commander Wagenaar. A short while later, on 2 June 1664, she married Pieter van Meerhof, the Danish mercenary soldier and amateur surgeon. There was a bridal feast in the residence of the commander and a wedding gift from the Company of £10. This was the first marriage in the Cape between a couple of African and European origin. Van Meerhof was promoted to the rank of surgeon at the pay of £3 a month and given the post of overseer of Robben Island where there was considerable activity in quarrying stone and making lime. The couple made their home on the island and it was there that Eva presented her husband with their first child, the first born on Robben Island, who was brought over to the mainland to be baptised.

Work on the new castle proceeded slowly. After 21 months of heavy labour, the 300 soldiers employed on construction had not even completed one of the five points of the building. Then, in May 1667, instructions were received from Holland to suspend further work and send the soldiers on to their original destination in Batavia. The threat of attack on the Cape by the English had so diminished with the destruction of their shipping by Admiral De Ruyter in the Thames that the expense of building the castle in the Cape was no longer a priority. Leaving the date 1667 on the stonework near the highest completed course of the castle wall, the soldiers were only too happy to sail off to the glamorous East.

Quarrying on Robben Island was also suspended. Van Meerhof was appointed head of an expedition to Madagascar where he and eight of his men were killed in a clash with the Malagasy at Antongil Bay. Eva was left a widow on Robben Island. She went to pieces, became an alcoholic, alternating between loose living on the mainland and disciplinary removals to Robben Island. She eventually died on 29 July 1674 and was buried within the church of the castle. A sad ending for an interesting person.

Commander Van Quaelberg also came to grief in the Cape. On 18 June 1668 he was summarily dismissed from his position and relieved by Jacob Borghorst, sent out from Holland for that purpose. The trouble was that Van Quaelberg had supplied a large visiting French fleet with provisions and repaired damage to one of their vessels at a time of uncertainty about the prospects of problems with France over trade rivalry in the East. Van Quaelberg left for Batavia where he was rehabilitated and rose to be Governor of Malacca and the distinguished admiral of a fleet which inflicted a serious defeat on the British off the coast of India.

Jacob Borghorst was an invalid when he landed and had no desire to remain in the Cape. His successor, Peter Hackius, was another sick man when he landed at the Cape on 18 March 1670. He was an experienced man, but his health had been ruined by long service to the Company in the East. At this stage in his life he was not much inclined to launch new ventures or to do much except keep out of trouble. The growing town was simply left to its own devices, its buildings increasingly taking on the so-called 'Cape-Dutch' appearance created by the number of Muslims banished from the East and employed as convict or slave builders, aided by the African slaves. They gave subtle variation to the architectural ideas of their European masters.

There was peace with England. The French, however, continued to cause some anxiety by sending fleets around the Cape, anchoring in Table Bay, requesting water and provisions and going into Saldanha Bay to reclaim the old islands of their seal hunters. In this setting Commander Pieter Hackius died on 30 November 1671 and was buried beneath the floor of the rough building used as a church within the area of the unfinished castle. Until a successor arrived, the Cape was governed by a committee of senior officials. To them, in February 1672, came instructions that the castle was to be completed to its original design as quickly as possible in order to confront what the Netherlands now considered the inevitability of a war with England and France who had combined in order to seize the rich trade with the East. Material and skilled workmen were to be sent out forthwith from Holland to complete the castle while quarrying of stone and the making of lime had to be recommenced immediately on Robben Island.

Since its founding ten years previously, 370 of the Company's ships, 26 French, 9 English and 2 Danish ships had been recorded as having visited Table Bay for supplies, having on board over 7 000 crew and passengers. All had drunk of the sweet waters of Table Mountain and replenished their stores from the produce of Van Riebeeck's Tavern of the Sea. It was time for the Company to regard their Cape settlement as reaching adolescence in its growth. In recognition of this fact the Cape was upgraded in its administration. Even before news of the death of Commander Hackius reached the Netherlands, his successor had been appointed. It was to be Isbrand Goske, the man who had selected the site of the castle. He was to have the rank of governor with a monthly salary of £25, a generous table allowance, formal quarters in the castle as soon as it was ready and a pleasure house in a garden setting at Rondebosch where he could relax and entertain visitors. It would be named *Rustenburg* (place of rest). Two senior officials were at the same time appointed to the posts of second in command and law enforcement.

Before the new Governor arrived to take office in the Cape a ship came in from Batavia. On it was Arnout van Overbeke, a justice of the high court at Batavia and admiral of the return fleet of 1672. He had been commissioned while the fleet was in Cape Town to investigate local affairs. Of immediate concern was to devise some legal basis for the creation by the Dutch East India Company of a colony in the Cape. The area had never been conquered. The settlement had grown unofficially without the previous inhabitants being able to do anything about it. The earliest known hunter-gatherer occupants of the area had been driven out by the pastoral people before Van Riebeeck's arrival. Both people were too weak to resist any invader and had no permanent vested interest in the Cape save hunting or grazing. Since Van Riebeeck's time, Gogoswa, the chief of the principal clan of pastoralists, had died. His son Osingkima, known to the Dutch as Prince Schacher, had succeeded him but the local pastoralists had largely disintegrated into small clans. Nevertheless, for want of a more paramount power, Commissioner Van Overbeke offered Prince Schacher £800 worth of assorted goods for the whole of the area from the Peninsula to Saldanha Bay. The pastoralists could graze their animals only where the Company or the freemen did not require the area. Peace was to prevail between the pastoralists and the settlers. The Company would protect Prince Schacher's followers if they were attacked.

Prince Schacher accepted the offer without demur. There was nothing else he could do. His people had already lost the area of the Cape Peninsula to the Company; this was simply recognition of fact. Other parts, such as the area of Saldanha Bay, were the grazing grounds of other pastoralists but they were not considered. Trade goods recorded as being only of the value of £2 16s 5d were actually given to Prince Schacher to consummate the 'sale'. The agreement was signed or marked by all concerned on 19 April 1672. A similar agreement was signed with the Chainoukwa for the Hottentots Holland area and the False Bay coast. Again the terms were £800 worth of goods for everything but only £6 16s 4d worth of assorted junk, liquor and tobacco were given to the representatives of the tribe. The legal gobbledegook of the two agreements, and the cynical complacency of the report to the directors in the Netherlands about the value of the goods actually handed to the two pastoral tribes emphasise the reality of the old proverb, 'a man is not a slave of his word', the basis of so many similar documents drawn up in pretentious legal language.

Governor Goske arrived at the Cape from Holland on 2 October 1672. News had already reached the Cape that war had commenced between the Netherlands and the combined forces of England, France and two ecclesiastical princes, the elector of Cologne and the Bishop of Munster. It was a formidable force for a small country such as the Netherlands to confront and the Dutch were also divided by feuds. They were, however, a hardy people and stubborn by nature. The

French grand army overran nearly half of the Netherlands but the Dutch settled their divisions, appointed William of Orange as their leader, held the English fleet at bay, breached the dykes and flooded the southern part of Holland to stop the French. Meanwhile they assembled a substantial fleet, not only to discomfort the English, but as a last resort to convey 200 000 people away from Europe to the Cape and off to the rich islands of the East. The castle being built at the Cape was now considered by the Dutch to be the frontier fortress of India. While they held it they could defy any attempt by their enemies to challenge their dominance in the East.

Governor Goske exerted every effort to complete the castle, meanwhile repairing the earth walls of the old fort. An outpost was also established in the newly acquired Hottentots Holland to which the people of Cape Town could retreat in the event of a successful onslaught on the town by the enemy. There were, at that time, about 600 Europeans resident or stationed in the Cape and times were exciting. An expedition was even organised to capture the British-held island of St Helena. This would handicap any ideas the British might have of attacking the Cape. Four ships then in Table Bay were fitted out and their crews augmented with men from the Cape garrison. On 10 January 1673 this pugnacious little force captured St Helena, a small British garrison being driven away. Four months later, the British recaptured the island but at least they were aware that an attack on the Cape would require a more considerable force than they had available in the area.

The castle at this time was sufficiently advanced in its construction to allow the garrison to move into it. The old earth fort was finally abandoned and demolished. Curiously, the urgency of building the castle declined at the same time as it was nearing completion. On 13 July 1674 a small dispatch vessel, gaily decorated with flags, arrived in the bay from the Netherlands bringing the tidings that the English had made peace with the Dutch. The French at that time lacked the naval power to be regarded as a threat, especially as they were now involved in war with other European powers. There was jubilation in the Tavern of the Sea, especially as the Dutch and English East India Companies, on 18 March 1674, joined in a special treaty of friendship to promote the honour and profit of each other.

Governor Goske had been sent to the Cape expressly to guide it through the troubled times of war. The presence of so senior a man was no longer necessary, so he requested permission to return to Europe. His successor, Johan Bax, promoted from his post as second officer on the island then known as Ceylon (Sri Lanka), relieved him on 14 March 1676 and the much honoured Isbrand Goske sailed for home. He left to the new Governor an exuberant little town, full of hope for the future and with only one problem, a 'war' which had been raging in desultory fashion for the previous four years between the neighbouring pastoral tribes. This affected the trade in livestock and made it difficult for hunters and explorers to travel safely outside the area which the company had purchased. The Cochokwa, under the chief Gonnema, were the principal tribe involved in a series of killings, raids and stock theft on several smaller tribes who increasingly looked to the Europeans for support. The 'war' petered out in the middle of 1677 when Gonnema found that he had lost too many of his own livestock. He sent messengers to Governor Bax asking for peace. A treaty ended the matter with the various pastoral chiefs finding Governor Bax to be a likeable and friendly man.

The castle by then needed only a moat and finishing touches for completion. As the Company was no longer interested in financing work on the structure, the Governor promulgated a regulation that required everyone, of any rank or sex, to contribute labour towards the digging of the moat. To set an example, the Governor, his wife and little son, all the company's officers, and the leading inhabitants of the town, gathered at the castle on 25 November 1677 and spent some time in excavation. Over the next months work steadily extended the moat but unhappily the Governor, although young and healthy, did not live to see its completion. A hard winter came early in 1678. He caught a cold and died on 29 June, leaving the second in command to control affairs until the Company appointed a successor.

The new man only reached the Cape from the Netherlands on 12 October 1679. He was rated only as a Commander, for peace made the Cape less important, but he was to prove one of the most energetic men ever to be head of affairs anywhere in Southern Africa. His name was Simon van der Stel. He was the eldest son of Adriaen van der Stel of Dordrecht. His mother was Maria Lievens, born in Batavia from a slave mother, Monyca da Costa, who came from the Coromandel coast of India and had married Heyndrich Lievens, Captain of the Citizenry of Batavia.

In 1639 Adriaen van der Stel was appointed to the command of the Island of Mauritius. Simon was born on 14 October 1639 on the ship *Cappel* taking the family to the father's new appointment. In 1645 the family returned to Batavia and in the following year Adriaen van der Stel was appointed Commander of the Dutch East India Company troops then engaged in the conquest of Ceylon (Sri Lanka). Shortly after his arrival in Ceylon, Van der Stel was captured in battle, decapitated and his head displayed on a spear to the Dutch troops and his family.

The Dutch East India Company had an obligation to the families of their employees. In 1659, Simon van der Stel was sent to the Netherlands to complete his education. When he finished his schooling he was employed by the Company and on 23 October 1663 married Johanna Jacoba Rix, daughter of a well-to-do Amsterdam family. Over the next thirteen years Van der Stel showed great competence in his work and then was rewarded with the offer of the post as Commander of the Cape. It was a big career opportunity at a far superior salary and he accepted with enthusiasm.

Mrs van der Stel declined to accompany her husband to the Cape. Her health was poorly and she remained in the comfort of Amsterdam until her death in October 1700. Van der Stel's four sons, Willem, Adriaan, Hendrik and Frans, and his daughter Catharina with his wife's younger sister, Cornelia, sailed with him, so he was well supported on the voyage. They were received when they landed on 12 October 1679 with such pomp as the Cape could mount to honour a new Commander, discharges of cannon and musketry, the cheers of onlookers who saw their new head of government as a short, dark-complexioned man, refined of manner, courteous, highly intelligent and very alert.

For the next twenty years Simon van der Stel was to control the colony until his retirement in 1699. He never left the Cape. The Castle was his home throughout this period of service, a dour pile built without any thought of beauty. It was a purely functional military edifice, its walls ten metres high and three metres wide built in the shape of a pentagon, each side 175 m long and leading to a bastion at each angle. The five bastions were named after the titles of the Prince of Orange who had led the Netherlands through the recent wars. *Leerdam* contained the kitchen and pay office; *Buren* contained the quarters for the officials of the company, including the Commander. There were chambers for the transaction of public business and storage space for foodstuffs and drinks. *Oranje* contained the arsenal and workshops; *Nassau* contained the powder magazine; *Catzenellenbogen* provided accommodation for the garrison. Below sea-level there were dungeons with graffiti carved and written on the walls and doors by inmates either awaiting transport to serve their sentences on Robben Island or for execution to Gallows Hill, the site of the modern traffic department.

There was little ornamentation to the castle. Above the entrance there was a pediment containing the arms of the six cities of the six chambers of the Dutch East India Company, with the monogram of the Company on either side. Over all was the lion of the Netherlands carved in stone. The archway to the entrance was surmounted by a bell tower. The quarters accommodating the Commander were spartan. It was only when Van der Stel was elevated in 1691 to the rank of Governor that the *Kat* was built across the interior grounds of the castle. This building contained more sumptuous quarters befitting a Governor and his staff, with reception rooms which today house the interesting William Fehr collection of paintings and memorabilia of former times in the Cape.

During the first days after his arrival, the Commander familiarised himself with the state of affairs of the Cape and inspected the town. Then, on 3 November, he rode out with an escort of soldiers to examine the countryside. The first night they camped at a place called *Kuilen* (pools) on the banks of a small stream which was tributary to the *Eerste* (first) River, the principal river draining one of the loveliest and most fertile parts of earth, a domain of wild flowers destined to become one of the principal wine and fruit farming lands of the Western Cape. It was then empty of people, free of any pollution and serenely beautiful. For five days Van der Stel explored this wild garden of infinite charm. Following the Eerste River up towards its source in the bosom of the mountains he reached a place which captivated him completely. The river divided there to form an island covered with trees. He camped on this island. It became known as *Van der Stel se Bosch*. (Van der Stel's Wood). There was no sign of other human beings. In his mind Van der Stel saw a picture of a thriving agricultural community, of rich crops and fat cattle grazing on the green pastures, drinking their fill of the amber coloured water of the streams.

Van der Stel returned to the castle and began to fulfil his dreams of a new Holland on the southern part of the vast continent of Africa. All that was good in the culture and industry of the Netherlands would be transplanted to grow on the soil of this fertile part of Earth. To Van der Stel this was no idle fancy. He was a small, dynamic bundle of energy and firm in the conviction that all things Dutch were the best. Before the year ended the first settler had occupied ground at Stellenbosch. Eight families followed the pioneer in May of the next year. All were tempted by the offer of as much free land as they could cultivate, selected by themselves, and only to be reclaimed by the Company if they ceased to cultivate it. The sole obligation to the Company was a tithe of the grain grown by the farmers. There was free use of all uncultivated land as grazing for cattle.

The growing Cape Town also received the beneficial attention of Van der Stel. The Company garden was replanned. It was divided into separate plots, with wind-breaking hedges. Vegetables were cultivated in some of the plots, fruit in others. There were nursery plots and experimental plantations of timber trees collected from all over the world. The wild flowers, herbs and trees of the Cape were also planted and studied to discover their special uses. In this carefully planned work, Van der Stel was ably supported by a renowned gardener, Hendrik Oldenland, trained as a medical doctor in Leiden who, apart from his practical duties, catalogued the various plants, with many interesting observations on their properties.

Van der Stel enlarged the garden on its southern side and on the north eventually built a large hospital and a lodge in which the Company slaves were housed. A pleasure lodge was also built on the site of the present statue of Queen Victoria. There Van der Stel entertained friends and visiting personages. Pathways and an avenue allowed people to walk through the garden. Before he retired, Van der Stel had the pleasure of being told by many visitors that nowhere else in the world was there a more varied display of trees and plants in so beautiful a setting.

Streets were laid out, wide and straight, while trees in great number were planted to provide shade, rest the eye, and beautify a town where the buildings were mainly a dazzling white from the use of the limewash which protected walls in place of unobtainable paints. Increasingly, the buildings carried in their design a touch of the East as well as of Africa and Europe. Prisoners and political exiles from Indonesia and India, many of them cultured and highly intelligent men, were being sent to the Cape. These personages, generally accompanied by a handful of followers and family members, at first felt themselves dreadfully detached from their familiar Eastern society. They received a little comfort when one of them, a man of great influence, Khardi Abdusalem, urged them to hold their faith without fear for they would one day live protected by a holy circle of *kramats* (saintly places) which would come into being at the tombs of holy men who would constantly intercede on their behalf with Allah. A line drawn connecting these *kramats* would form a magic ring. Within it the residents of Cape Town, not only Muslims, would live safe from fire, famine, plague, earthquake, tidal wave or attack by hostile forces.

In West Java, meanwhile, a grim drama was taking place. The ruler of Bantam, Sultan Ageng, was the last independent prince of any significance in Java. On 1 May 1680 he abdicated in favour of his son, Abdol Kahar, who reigned as Sultan Hadji because he had been on the pilgrimage to Mecca. There was, at that time, great rivalry between the Dutch and English East India companies for commercial privileges in the East. The young sultan favoured the Dutch, his father favoured the English. The old man decided to remove his son from power. He was supported by the English and Danish traders, some of his family and many of the Bantamese people led by Sheik Yussuf of Macassar, a man of powerful influence.

The young sultan soon found himself practically besieged in his castle. In this extremity he appealed to the Dutch for aid. His palace guard was already under the command of a Netherlands mercenary. The Dutch authorities in Batavia sent 300 Dutch soldiers to aid Sultan Hadji. They soon pushed the old sultan back into his own castle. This edifice, reportedly the most beautiful in Java, he was forced to abandon, blowing it up and taking refuge in the mountains. There he was captured by his son and severely tortured until the Dutch took pity and gave him sanctuary in Batavia.

The Dutch were now triumphant in Java. Sheik Yussuf maintained some resistance for a year but then he was forced to surrender. Revered as a saint and the last defender of the independence of the Bantamese people, the Dutch decided to banish him from the country for life. First they sent him to Sri Lanka but he was still considered to be a danger so, in 1694, he was shipped to the Cape, taking with him 2 wives, 12 children and 49 followers. His journey became a source of legend. It was told, for example, that on the voyage the ship ran out of drinking water, Sheik Yussuf dipped one foot into the sea and told the sailors to replenish their water casks. When the wondering men sampled the sea water they found it to be fresh.

Arriving at the Cape, Sheik Yussuf was taken to the then isolated farm of *Zandvliet*. There he remained until his death on 23 May 1699 at the age of 73. His heart was cut out and taken back by some of his people to his home in Indonesia. His body was buried on *Zandvliet*. The site was forgotten until, so the story goes, a herdboy on the farm lost some cattle. In fear of punishment from his master the boy lay down and wept. He fell asleep. As in a dream, there came to him a noble man in the clothes of a priest of the East. The man told the herdboy to look into a little valley behind a ridge. There he would find the missing cattle. The boy awoke. As promised he found the strays. As he drove them back over the ridge he found also a grave inscribed with the strange writing of Indonesia. He reported the find to his master. In such a manner was the burial place of Sheik Yussuf found, the first and most important of the *kramats* of the magic circle around Cape Town.

Sheik Yussuf's tomb is now an impressive memorial built in 1925 by Hadji Sullaiman Shah. The *kramat* is on a low hill with a grand view of mountains and farmlands. It is close to the banks of the Eerste River for the sound of running water is not only pleasant but is said to have magical curative powers. Visitors fill containers with water and leave them at the *kramat* overnight. The containers absorb some special gift of magic and the water is said to receive the qualities of healing.

Five other *kramats* complete the magic circle around Cape Town. Close to the road followed by countless people to the viewsite on the summit of Signal Hill, there is a pretty little domed building. In this *kramat* is buried Sayed Muhammad Hassan Gaibi Shah. On the slopes of Signal Hill, above the old quarry at the top of Strand Street, there is the third *Kramat* where lie the bodies of four holy men, the revered Khardi Abdusalem, Tuan Syed, Tuan Guru and Tuan Nurman. From this *kramat* the magic circle leads to *Oudekraal* where, from the scenic drive of Victoria Road, a concrete stairway leads up beneath the trees to a *kramat* where lies buried Nureel Mobeen who is said to have been banished to Robben Island. He escaped by swimming to the mainland supported on a plank. For the rest of his life he hid in the bush of *Oudekraal*. In his time he is said to have performed many miracles. Near his tomb, closer to the beach known as *Bakoven* (bake oven) from the shape of a granite boulder, another concrete stairway leads to a path which wanders up the banks of a stream to a number of graves, culminating in the tomb of Jaffer Java. These tombs, especially that of Nureel Mobeen, lie close to a stream, and the sound of running water.

The fifth *kramat* in the magic circle is on Robben Island. This is the tomb of Sayed Abdurahman Matura, Prince of Ternate, an island in the Molucca sea of Indonesia. He was banished to Robben Island in January 1744 and died there in 1755. The sixth *kramat* is in the Constantia valley. On the slopes of Islam Hill, close to the stream known as the *Spaanschemat* there is a cemetery overlooked by a small mosque with a minaret. Nearby, at the entrance gate to the farm *Klein Constantia*, again beside a running stream, there is the tomb of Abdumaah Shah.

To each of these *kramats* of the magic circle many Muslims travel on weekends, holidays and sacred days. They pray to the departed holy men for continued intercession with Allah and for the unbroken protection around Cape Town of the Magic Circle. The paths to these places are well trodden, not forgotten, the roads well used. To 'make the circle', visiting each one of the *kramats*, is much desired by all devout Cape Muslims.

In October 1684, the governing body of the Dutch East India Company, the Assembly of Seventeen, appointed one of its members, Hendrik Adriaan van Rheede, the Lord of Mydrecht, to head a commission charged with examining the affairs of the Cape and those of Ceylon and Hindustan. His lordship arrived in the Cape on 19 April 1685 and set about examining affairs. According to the colonial norms of the time the Cape was doing well. It was not only feeding itself and profiting handsomely from supplying ships but even starting to export food to the East. As far as its social system went, it was amazing how readily people from Europe adjusted their thinking to a slave-based colonial society. In their home countries slavery might be repugnant but by simply crossing an ocean they could walk ashore into a new world of buying, selling and ruthless exploitation of human beings. Such a society, in fact, perfectly revealed man's inhumanity to man with not the slightest awareness of any wrong to it.

The Lord of Mydrecht found nothing too objectionable to slavery in the Cape except for some legal and protocol problems in the ownership of slaves and in their emancipation. His lordship tried to improve things by making a law that imported slaves of both sexes, after 30 years of bondage, and slaves born in the Cape on reaching the age of 40, were entitled to freedom. As a contradiction to this glimmer of hope, emancipation was only as a favour on the part of the owner. There was a distinct reluctance by owners to free slaves until they were so old as to be useless. In order to save feeding them they were then emancipated. They were driven out to fend for themselves, usually by begging or as vagrants living in destitution in caves or crude shelters on the mountain slopes, where they were known as 'Bergies'.

His lordship did make it a law that slave children under the age of twelve were to be sent to school where they were to be taught the principles of Christianity, to read, write and conduct themselves respectfully to their superiors. Those over twelve years of age were to be allowed two afternoons a week for instruction in the Christian religion. They were to attend church services twice on Sundays. At the conclusion of the afternoon service, when the customary lengthy sermon ended, they were required to repeat the Heidelberg catechism. Some restrictions on punishment were also made. Excessive punishment drove slaves to desert and turn criminal. Fugitives who were captured were to be flogged and chained as a warning to others but such punishment could only be inflicted with the consent of the authorities. Punishment generally, to law breakers of any colour, remained severe. Robben Island was always accommodating. The slight rise at Green Point called Gallows Hill possessed a gibbet capable of hanging seven or more condemned persons at a time. Around it were the grim means for torture and execution by impalement or breaking at the wheel, sometimes from the feet up in order to prolong agony. There were ten wheels used for this limb-breaking.

So far as relations with the indigenous population were concerned, the original inhabitants had either dispersed or fragmented to insignificant numbers. The local Sonkwa (or Bushmen) were nearly extinct. The pastoral tribes living further from the Cape, such as the Hessekwa, the Inkwa and the Outenikwa who lived along the coast to the east, were friendly and prepared to trade significant amounts of their livestock for the usual junk. From the west coast, the Namakwa sent several representatives to meet the Commissioner. They came riding in to town seated on trained oxen. Some of these oxen also carried on their backs the simple skin huts which these nomads were accustomed to take with them as they wandered with their herds and flocks in search of pasturage. Even more interesting were the fine samples of copper ore which they showed the Dutch authorities. The Lord of Mydrecht was pleased that Van der Stel had already sent three abortive expeditions up the west coast to reach what were called the copper mountains. Prospectors were also busy fossicking through the mountains of the Cape Peninsula hoping to find such precious metals as gold and silver. One prospect shaft in the Steenberge had already yielded a strange ore which the people of Cape Town excitedly thought was silver. This was eventually identified in Holland as being manganese but the discovery at least stimulated what was the beginning of systematic prospecting in Southern Africa. Van der Stel was authorised to personally lead an expedition to the copper mountains of the Nama people.

The Lord of Mydrecht also approved of the foundation of Stellenbosch and the generous grants of free land there to stimulate such settlement. An officer known as a *landdrost* (magistrate) was appointed on 16 July 1685 to preside over a court established in Stellenbosch with jurisdiction over the whole country beyond the Cape Peninsula. The shortage of suitable settlers was well appreciated by the Lord of Mydrecht. In Holland every effort was already being made by the Company to stimulate emigration to the Cape, with particular attention to females. Of these desirable creatures there was a shortage in the Cape while in the Netherlands there was a surplus on account of so many men being away crewing ships or serving the Company as soldiers or merchants. Not many of the spinsters, however, were prepared to face a long voyage to the Cape and the uncertain prospects of marital bliss in so little known a part of Earth.

Before he left for India, on 16 July 1685, the Lord of Mydrecht showed the Dutch East India Company's high appreciation of Simon van der Stel for his constancy, dedication and loyalty, and their desire for him to remain in the Cape as long as possible. He was granted the superbly situated piece of ground beyond the last farm then occupied at Wynberg. The Commander selected this handsome estate himself, carefully taking into account the variety of soils, altitudes and microclimate, all factors of decisive influence in farming, and especially in viticulture. Title to the estate was granted on 13 July. The gratified Commander named it *Constantia*, presumably in honour of the young daughter of Commissioner Rijkloff van Goens who had that name, or simply that the name meant 'constancy'.

With the Lord of Mydrecht gone, Van der Stel launched himself into a considerable programme of work. Just over a month after the departure of the Lord of Mydrecht, Van der Stel left on an exploratory journey to the Nama country. It was a festive day, 25 August 1685, for Cape Town. There were fifteen wagons each drawn by eight oxen, eight carts and one coach to carry the Commander. Van der Stel had with him three personal slaves. In the party there were 56 Europeans, a Macassar prisoner of state named Dain Bengale with his personal slave, 46 drivers and a number of interpreters. There were 200 spare oxen, 113 horses and 8 mules. They all set out from the excited little town on what everyone hoped was a venture which would lead to the discovery of vast wealth, not only of copper, but of many precious metals and gemstones. The explorers after many adventures reached the Copper Mountains on 21 October and, guided by the Nama people, found copper ore of great richness and quantity. The Copper Mountains, however were about 500 kilometres from Cape Town. The two months it had taken to reach the area had seen the explorers forced to penetrate such rugged, arid country that there could be no way of carrying heavy ore all the way to Cape Town on the transport of the day.

On the way back to Cape Town, Van der Stel explored the West coast in hope of finding a harbour which could be used for the shipment of copper ore. Nothing of any use was found. On 26 January 1686 the Commander arrived back in the castle after an absence of five months and one day. The dream of a vast instant profit for the Company which had obsessed every commander of the Cape since Van Riebeeck, still proved elusive. The richness of the samples of copper ore tantalised everybody who saw them but it was to be 200 years before the copper mines of Namaqualand were to come into production.

To be back in the cool, green and well-watered Cape must have been a relief to all the members of the exploratory party. Van der Stel did not leave it again and the Cape flourished under his attention. He was always a great man for trees. The Cape was not well forested, except in the mountain gorges where trees found shelter from the winds and weather. These forests were fragile and already over-exploited for fuel and timber. From the experimental work in the Company's garden, the imported oaks seemed to do best in local conditions. Using his own farm of *Constantia*, the growing town of Stellenbosch, and farms run by the Company, Van der Stel cultivated oak trees. There were over 50 000 in the nurseries and 5 000 planted out by the spring of 1687. He offered young trees for nothing to whoever wished to plant them and eventually issued an edict that all farmers had to plant at least 100 trees on their farm and replace every tree that was cut down.

Stellenbosch, in the short time of its existence, was already showing signs of its future destiny as the prettiest town in Southern Africa. An annual fair was commenced in the town in 1686. Each year, from the 1st to the 14th of October, became a holiday season for the people of the Cape. They travelled to Stellenbosch to buy and sell without any restriction, to feast and drink the products of the country, to play games and compete in gun shooting at a target traditionally shaped like a parrot. The winner received a first prize of £5 and the title for the year of King of the Marksmen. There was also a pistol shooting competition for mounted riders who, at full gallop, shot at small targets. The last day of the fair was the birthday of Van der Stel. He was always present, along with many of the residents of Cape Town, the farming community, chiefs of the pastoral African clans, and passengers and crews of shipping in the harbour. There was great fun for all, with a final procession and a parade by the military who fired volleys in honour of the Commander while everyone wished him well.

A church, courthouse, residence for the magistrate and a mill were built in Stellenbosch in 1686. Van der Stel directed the design and construction of these public buildings and undertook considerable experimentation in agriculture. Crops such as rice, cassava, hops and olives were all tried without success. Vines were doing well but the wine was poor. The quality from the Stellenbosch farms was better than from anywhere else in the Cape but not up to the wines of Europe. On his farm of *Constantia*, in the Company's garden in Cape Town, at *Rustenburg* in Rondebosch and in the Eerste River valley at Stellenbosch, Van der Stel planted vines obtained from many countries, even from Iran (Persia) the reputed home of the grape. He experimented systematically with the harvest times, pressing and maturation in order to isolate the causes of inferior quality.

Van der Stel's hopes of expanding settlement of the Cape farming areas received support in September 1687 when some 50 individuals on the annual homeward fleet found the Cape so much to their liking that they petitioned the Commander for permission to remain as farmers. Unfortunately most of them were single, but 23 men, at least supposedly happily married, were formed into a party. At the end of the Stellenbosch fair, Van der Stel personally conducted them over the divide and into the lovely valley he named *Drakenstein* after the Lord of Mydrecht's estate in the Netherlands. In the following year the first batch of a stream of French Protestant Huguenot refugees fleeing from religious persecution in France arrived in the Cape. Van der Stel was delighted, although he would have preferred them to be Dutch. The Huguenots were, however, fine farming stock, experienced viticulturists and most of them were married. He settled them on glorious farmlands in what became known as *Franschhoek* (French glen), the upper valley of the Berg River.

The Cape prospered, notwithstanding the shortage of marriageable females, which continued to be a source of social problems. Each year saw more shipping anchoring in the bay. The demand for Cape foodstuffs seemed insatiable and the Commander continuously explored new possibilities of expanding the original settlement. In November 1687 he sailed around the Cape of Good Hope and into False Bay taking with him a party of surveyors and draughtsmen. Back in 1671 the *Isselsteijn*, a Dutch East Indiaman, had sheltered in the bay. The crew had reported so favourably that Van der Stel was keen to explore the area himself. The advantages of the bay were only too apparent. It offered shelter from the north-westerly gales which often created havoc to shipping anchored in Table Bay. The bight in which the *Isselsteijn* had anchored offered safe, sheltered anchorage, fresh water and excellent fishing. It had become known as *Isselsteijn Bay*, but was now renamed *Simon's Bay* after the Governor and recommended as a sanctuary from winter storms or wars in Europe which could affect Table Bay. The port and town which eventually grew at the harbour became *Simon's Town*.

The growth of the Cape Colony, generally, and the esteem in which Simon van der Stel was held by his directors in Holland, was marked on 1 June 1691 when dispatches reached the Cape that the Commander had been elevated to the dignity of a Governor. Van der Stel could look around him with considerable satisfaction. He had enemies but was generally well liked. Only the Huguenots had a grievance against him. He had refused their plan to be allowed to establish their own church. Appeals by them to the directors of the Dutch East India Company once again revealed the authorities in Holland to be more liberal than their local officials. They overruled Van der Stel and the French settlers were granted the complete religious freedom for which they had fled from France, and so many had died of persecution in their homeland.

For the next five years of his governance, Van der Stel busied himself on several improvements to Cape Town. The place had its problems. Garbage collection was left to the hyenas and other scavengers which came down each night from lairs on the mountain slopes and wandered at will through the dark streets. Heavy drinking and gambling in the taverns led to fights and murders. There was no police force. The shortage of females was the cause of violent brawls. Even slave women were in short supply.

Lions and leopards still frequented the countryside, occasionally venturing into the little town and dragging away the odd drunkard who had fallen asleep on the roadside. Gangs of runaway slaves provided a hardcore criminal element. They were a community of the lost. Their destitution and hopeless future gave them no alternative but to resort to robbery while the brutality of punishment when they were caught made them desperate. To die on the gallows was at least a quick way out but sentences of torture 'close to death', impalement, or to be broken on the rack or wheel was the more usual punishment with the mangled wretch dumped to die on Gallows Hill. The only possible mercy came from one of their comrades creeping into the town at night to put them out of their misery by strangulation. Pollution of drinking water was becoming a health hazard. Even the once pure Fresh River on which the shipping depended was carrying down to the sea unpalatable run off from dirty streets and the dirtier habits of human beings using it for washing their persons, clothes, utensils and as a form of waterborne sewage disposal for personal and industrial waste. The south-east wind of summer, known as the Cape Doctor, fortunately blew most of the stinks, miasmas and assorted bugs, insects and bacteria away and kept the town healthier than its population deserved.

An endless stream of thirsty and amorous sailors called at the Cape. Most of them were the crews of the Dutch East Indiamen, about 170 men on each ship. English ships, mainly used St Helena Island as a refreshment port and by-passed the Cape. Danish, French and an occasional Portuguese vessel also called. Amongst this motley company the majority were reasonably honest merchants, but others were pirates. Slave traders also frequented Table Bay, mainly taking human cargoes from East Africa, Mozambique and Madagascar to the West Indies, but always prepared to oblige local demand for what were advertised as sturdy, stout, Negroes, male or female. Auctions of slaves were periodically held on what became known as Church Square, a piece of waste land, once a marsh, which adjoined the grounds of the Dutch Reformed mother church of Southern Africa, the present *Groote Kerk* with its pleasant, leisurely sounding two-note clock chime marking the passing of the hours.

The auctions were held in the shade of a fir tree, known as the slave tree, reputedly planted by Van Riebeeck. Slaves were brought to this tree from the nearby slave lodge which later became the Supreme Court and then the South African Cultural Museum. They were exhibited on benches and auctioned. Slavery was only abolished in 1834. The dilapidated old tree was cut down on 9 November 1916 leaving only a stump on which was fixed a brass plate inscribed with the history of the tree. At the end of 1951 the stump and brass plate were removed and replaced by a granite plaque inscribed with the words *'On this spot stood the old slave tree'*. It is in the centre island of Spin Street opposite No 6.

Governor Van der Stel did nothing to ease the degradation of slavery. The dual morality of the time made the lot of those in bondage of little concern to the rest of the community. The development of Van der Stel's own estate of *Constantia* was based on slave labour and there was no available substitute. At least, however, he made Cape Town, for all of its people a far more agreeable place in which to live. In January 1693 he appointed Hendrik Oldenland, superintendent of the Company's Garden, to be the first town engineer of Cape Town. Considerable public works were commenced. The Heerengracht was improved; a new road entirely was made along the line of the canal known as the *Keisersgracht* which took water from the Fresh River to the castle moat. This new street was later named after C H Darling, the British Lieutenant-Governor of the Cape from 1852 to 1854. On the seaward side of this road, work began in 1697 on levelling the ground and this became the Grand Parade.

Most important of all was the building of the new hospital, larger, far better and more suitably located on a site between the upper end of the Heerengracht and Berg Street (now St George's Street). The hospital was designed to accommodate 500 patients, or 750 in an emergency. It was the last work by Van der Stel in his capacity as Governor. In 1696 he requested permission to resign his office and retire to his estate of *Constantia*. The directors gave him a final honour when they appointed his eldest son, Willem Adriaan, born in 1664, as his successor.

On 11 February Simon van der Stel left the castle and removed to his estate of *Constantia*. For the next thirteen years he lived there, farming, ranching cattle, planting thousands of oak trees and vines and producing fine wine. His reputation for hospitality, good food and wine attracted innumerable visitors to what was regarded as one of the most beautiful estates in the world. He obtained more grants of land, and grazing rights for his cattle until he controlled practically the entire Cape Peninsula outside the settled area of Cape Town. He ran a fishing and sealing industry at Saldanha Bay and was altogether a man for all seasons and activities. His one great disappointment came from his son, whose governance foundered in accusations of oppression and venality. He was recalled to Holland on 3 June 1707.

Simon van der Stel was left in the Cape without the companionship of any of his family. As death approached he became despondent. In his last will and testament, his scribe wrote: *'His excellency was overcome with the evil and weakness of human life, passing away like a shadow, knowing that nothing is more certain than death and, in contrast, nothing more uncertain than man's time and span upon this earth.'*

He bequeathed *Constantia* to his five children. None of them were interested in the estate, other than as a source of financial inheritance. Van der Stel wound up his affairs neatly. He freed several of his slaves who had been faithful to him for long, and to Francina Grutting, left a legacy of 3 000 guldens, half of his linen and a bed with all accessories. She had been brought up in *Constantia* since her birth and had already been long freed from slavery.

Simon van der Stel died at *Constantia* on 24 June 1712. After the estate was wound up it was divided into three sections in order to make it more saleable. Together with all livestock, 90 slaves, trees, vines, wagons and chattels it was sold at auction. A Swede, Captain Olof Bergh, a retired soldier and explorer of the Dutch East India Company, bought the section with the manor-house and lived there until his death in 1723. His wife, daughter of a slave woman, Angela of Bengal, then remained mistress of *Constantia* until it was sold ten years later to Carel Georg Wieser. A succession of owners followed. The estate went into decline until, after 66 years of indifferent management, it was sold on 15 December 1778 to Hendrik Cloete of Stellenbosch. A glorious revival then took place.

The other two sections were bought at the auction by Pieter de Meyer, an official of the Dutch East India Company. There was no longer a Van der Stel in the Cape, but the memory of Simon lingers over *Constantia* evermore.

There is no known completely authentic portrait of Van der Stel. A canvass showing a man thought to have been him, in a hunting party and considered nine-tenths authentic, was unfortunately destroyed in 1963 in a fire in the Napier collection in Ireland. Only a photograph of this painting remains. A second portrait, also of a huntsman, but of less authenticity, is in the *Rijksdienst Beeldende Kunst*, The Hague. This portrait however, is only considered one-tenth possible and nine-tenths of dubious authenticity. Photographic reproductions of these paintings may be seen in the Simon's Town Museum.

Chapter Three

CAPE TOWN, TABLE BAY AND ROBBEN ISLAND

As cities go, Cape Town, compared with those ancient places of Asia and Europe, is still a mere juvenile. In its relatively brief three and a half centuries, however, it has experienced interesting times and gathered memories of odd events and diverse people who have come to the Tavern of the Sea, dallied for perhaps just a little while or, beguiled by its beauty and atmosphere, remained for the rest of their lives.

Many of those who landed on the shores of Table Bay did so involuntarily. They were wrecked there. During the winter months when the prevailing wind was the north-western, Table Bay could become a death trap for shipping. There was simply no shelter from this wind. It is a wind, which can blow gale force for a merciless hour then deceptively lull, while it recovers breath for another big blow. Over 200 ships have been wrecked in Table Bay. The old Arab legend of a magnetic mountain at the southern end of Africa drawing ships to doom by some baleful force was perfectly valid if the insidiously lethal north-westerly was given the blame.

Some of the storms became legendary. April, May and June were the danger months in Table Bay. On 16 June 1722, seven Dutch and three English ships were wrecked. On 21 May 1737, eleven Dutch ships were at anchor in the bay preparing to resume their homeward voyage to the Netherlands. A storm had started during the previous night. By dawn the waves shouldering their way into Table Bay could only be described as lethal. One by one nine ships broke from their anchorage and were summarily driven on to the beach with a loss of 531 members of their crew. The cargo of the ships was strewn along the shore. A proclamation was hurriedly issued threatening summary execution of any person caught looting. Four men were caught and hanged on gallows erected amidst the wreckage as a grisly warning to pilferers.

A particularly famous wreck occurred during a storm on 1 June 1773. The Dutch East Indiaman *De Jonge Thomas* was soon in difficulties. She ran aground and began breaking up in the pounding of heavy surf. Employed as a dairyman for the Dutch East India Company and living in the farmhouse of *Klein Zoar* on the site of what became the suburb of Brooklyn was a man named Wolraad Woltemade. Born in about 1708 he had entered the service of the company, reached the rank of corporal in 1752 and in 1770 was in charge of the outpost of Muizenberg before becoming the Company dairyman. Hearing about the wreck, he rode to the beach and saw that the crew of the ship were almost helpless against the power of the sea. He rode his horse through the waves seven times. Each time he returned with two men holding on to the horse. On the eighth attempt Woltemade and his horse were themselves overwhelmed by a huge wave and drowned. Horse and man had saved 14 of the crew; 53 others managed to reach the shore on their own while 138 were drowned.

The Dutch East India Company named the first ship built for them after the tragedy *De Held Woltemade* (the hero Woltemade). His widow and sons living in Batavia were compensated. A statue of him was created in later years by the sculptor I Mitford-Barberton and erected in the grounds of the Old Mutual Insurance Society in the modern garden township of Pinelands which grew on the grazing fields of the dairy-farm he managed. A railway station was named after him on the old dairy farm grounds and this serves the mourners visiting Cape Town's principal burialground, the Woltemade Cemetery. The highest South African decoration for bravery was also named after him, the Woltemade medal.

The loss of life, ships and cargo from winter storms was the principal disadvantage of the Cape victualling station. With the means available at that time it was very difficult to do anything about this problem. Engineering on a massive scale was the answer but this would demand an expenditure of a considerable amount of money. After the disastrous storms of May 1737, it was decided that a breakwater (or mole) would have to be built at what became known as *Mouille Point* on the western side of Table Bay. To achieve this construction with as little expenditure as possible, all farmers bringing wagon-loads of produce for sale in Cape Town were required to use their empty vehicles to transport one load of stones to the construction site of the mole. By 1745, the mole had been extended 320 metres into the sea but then the work had to be suspended for a strange reason. A plague of locusts did such destruction to the farms of the Cape that the farmers had little produce. No more wagons came to carry stones and that was the sad ending of the mole of Mouille Point.

Nothing further was done towards providing artificial shelter in Table Bay although periodic north-westerly winds continued to create havoc. In 1831 six ships were wrecked and the British government who then ran the Cape were sufficiently disturbed as to appoint the first Harbour Board with the directive to plan protection works in Table Bay and to construct a stone pier into the sea from the bottom of Bree Street. This pier was completed but it proved to be almost useless. A second stone pier was then built from the foot of Adderley Street and a wooden pier near the site of the original stone jetty built by Van Riebeeck in 1656. None of these works provided any shelter for ships.

It was only in 1856 that Captain James Vetch, harbour surveyor to the British Admiralty, produced a plan for an enclosed harbour in Table Bay. The plan included an inner and an outer basin, protected by two breakwater piers. John Coode was appointed engineer-in-chief to give practical effect to the scheme which, as always in such a project, was modified to save money. The growth of the Cape Colony, the increased number of larger ships calling at Cape Town and the demand for facilities superior to loading and unloading into barges while precariously anchored in a windswept bay, provided considerable pressure towards the making of this harbour. The ultimate decider came in June 1857. A prodigious gale stormed into the bay. For three days a north-west wind blew at overwhelming force. Sixteen large ships and seven smaller boats were wrecked. The storm died, the sun shone, but five days later, on 14 June, the storm returned and wrecked two more big ships.

After a disaster of this magnitude construction of a proper harbour had to start, no matter the cost. It had an auspicious beginning. On 17 September 1860, Prince Alfred, the 16-year-old second son of Queen Victoria, at the start of a tour of the Cape Colony and Natal, pulled a silver trigger to tip the first truck load of stones into 1,8 metres of water to start the new breakwater. A bronze plaque on a stone pillar on East Pier road marked this construction which eventually resulted in the man-made harbour of Table Bay, a major engineering accomplishment by any world standard. The stone for the breakwater, known as the Western Breakwater, came from a huge quarry worked by hard-labour convicts just south of the construction site.

The Prince was a fitting man to launch so considerable a work. At the time of his visit to Cape Town he was a midshipman on the steam frigate *Euryalus* with ahead of him a distinguished lifelong career in the Royal Navy. His tour, the first royal tour of South Africa, was done mainly on horseback, from Cape Town along the coast to Durban, then over the Drakensberg to the Orange Free State where he was entertained to the greatest hunt known in history with the shooting on the farm *Bainsvlei* west of Bloemfontein of several thousand head of antelope in one afternoon of 'sport'. The prince shot 24 of the animals.

The strength of the construction of the all-important western breakwater was tested by many storms. In 1862, seventeen days of continuous gale so damaged the construction that there was talk of abandoning the whole concept as impractical. The engineers learned from experience, however, and persisted. During the night of 16 May 1865 a particularly vicious north-western started to blow. An enormous swell was pushed into the bay where three steamers and 25 sailing ships were at anchor. By dawn of 17 May 1865 they were all in trouble. Seventeen of the sailing ships and the mail steamer *Athens* were wrecked. Loss of life and cargo was severe. Some 60 000 tons of rock in the unfinished breakwater were shifted by the power of the sea. The breakwater, nevertheless, held firm and this was heartening. The storm actually served to spur on construction. A year later in the severe gales of 1866, no significant damage was done to the breakwater. For the first time shipping was protected in Table Bay and there was a collective great sigh of relief from all shipmasters trading to the Tavern of the Sea.

On 15 August 1867 Prince Alfred, then becoming known as the Duke of Edinburgh, visited the

Cape again, this time as the captain of the steam frigate *Galatea*. On 24 August he laid the foundation stone of what was named the Alfred Dock. He said that he was proud to have his name attached permanently to so great an undertaking. After that he left in the naval steamer *Petrol* on a visit to Knysna where he hunted elephants in the forest in company with the well-known Rex family, the Governor of the Cape Colony, Sir Philip Wodehouse, and a considerable party of staff and dignitaries.

Prince Alfred visited the Cape twice more while captain of the *Galatea*, in December 1868 and then again in 1870. By the time of his fourth visit the Alfred Basin and dock had been completed. The Prince officially opened it on 4 July 1870. At the same time he laid the foundation stone for a dry-dock 152 metres long × 17 metres wide × 8 metres in depth. On its completion in 1881 it was named after Sir Hercules Robinson, just appointed Governor of the Cape. The attractive clock and signalling tower at the entrance to the basin was built in 1883. The entrance is so narrow that it was from the beginning a problem to pilots and shipmates. It was known as the Cut. A small flat-bottomed double-ended ferryboat known as the Penny Ferry provided a service for pedestrians wishing to cross the Cut. The first ferryman, Abdul, spent his lifetime working the boat and was estimated at the time of his retirement to have covered a distance equal to twice around the world.

Prince Alfred did not again return to South Africa. He rose to the rank of admiral of the fleet, married the Grand Duchess Marie, daughter of Alexander II of Russia, and with her aid produced four daughters, Marie, who became Queen of Romania, Victoria, who married Grand Duke Cyril of Russia, Alexandra, who became Princess of Hohenlohe-Langenburg, and Beatrice who married Alfonso, the Infante of Spain.

Prince Alfred died in 1900. By that time Table Bay harbour had experienced vast changes. The discovery of diamonds and gold and the volatile expansion of trade and industry in the whole of Southern Africa imposed relentless pressure on the harbour and demanded ever-better facilities, security and expansion.

In 1890, 1 000 labourers and 600 convicts housed in what was called the Breakwater Prison commenced work on extending the breakwater to 1 430 metres in order to protect a water area of 27 hectares, creating what was named the Victoria Basin, with jetties and a new south pier. It took five years of work to complete this phase of development. Larger ships could then call at Table Bay and be berthed in safety but the outbreak of the Anglo-Boer war made the whole new facility inadequate within four years. Up to 50 ships were sometimes forced to anchor in the bay waiting their turn to discharge or load cargo, and were often double or treble berthed at wharf.

The end of the Anglo-Boer war provided some relief to the pressure on the harbour but by 1925 the situation was impossible with still larger ships demanding deeper water and larger berths. Work on a new basin on the south-eastern side of the Victoria Basin was commenced in 1926. There was, however, a limit to the size of the new basin. In 1913 the Cape Town municipality had constructed a recreation pier projecting from the foot of Adderley Street. For the time being, new harbour works were confined to the north-west side of this pier. The new basin was opened in 1932. It was 75 hectares in extent. It had a wide entrance to allow larger ships to berth in sheltered conditions but a serious problem was soon revealed.

On 25 January 1936, the largest ship so far to visit South African waters, the 43 000 ton *Empress of Britain*, arrived at dawn in Table Bay after a record-breaking run from Madeira. The big liner was carrying 387 wealthy passengers, including 30 millionaires on a cruise around the world and their arrival was considered to be of major publicity value in the development of a South African tourism industry.

The ship was docked at B berth without difficulty. Entertainment and tours around the Cape Peninsula and inland had been arranged for the passengers until the planned sailing time at noon on 28 January. A vicious south-easter, however, blew up and gleefully showed its power. The big ship was pressed so firmly against the quay that all the port's tugboats and all the port's men could not get the *Empress of Britain* out to sea again. At least, not until the south-easter died down. It took its own time.

The great liner left 30 hours late and this was a sad embarrassment to the Table Bay harbour. The battle between man and ship against the wind had been well reported around the world. A big audience of spectators watched every effort by the tugboats. It was rumoured that the problem wasn't just the wind. The liner was said to be stuck in the mud on the bottom and that it had been damaged by all the bumping. Fortunately it was in fact just the wind which reached peaks of 112 km an hour and caught the liner broadside on. At 6.37 pm on 29 January there was a little lull. The tugboats were waiting for the chance. They managed to get the ship out just in time. By 8 pm the wind was back at over 100 km an hour but the liner was far gone by then, heading around the Cape of Good Hope at full speed for Durban and India.

The wind had revealed that the new basin of the harbour was limited in its use. Shipmasters of the large ships expected to call at Table Bay would all think twice about visiting the place until a new harbour scheme was achieved, involving major engineering, construction and dredging. This work had already been started. With the threat of World War II looming, work was expedited and a massive exercise in construction, with a prodigious feat of dredging took place.

The new scheme involved major engineering construction and dredging work. The municipal pier had to be demolished together with most of the abortive new basin construction. Two new quay walls parallel to each other, 1 000 metres long and 670 metres apart, had to be built extending from the Woodstock beach towards the Victoria Basin; massive dredging of the area between the two walls yielded a spoil which had to be pumped by pipeline and deposited on the land (south) side of the project, completely burying the original shore and the historic landing place of Roggebaai. The spoil provided 140 hectares of landfill, known as the Foreshore, as a brand-new and very welcome addition to the available building space of the city area of Cape Town, already feeling somewhat compressed between sea and mountains.

It was a spectacular engineering concept. The quay walls were built departmentally by the South African Railways and Harbours and completed in 1940. The dredging contract was given to the Dutch firm of Hollandsche Aanneming Maatschappij, highly expert at projects such as this, possibly the most ambitious land reclamation scheme undertaken by any city.

The dredging operation started on 15 May 1935. Work was speeded up. By the outbreak of the war on 3 September 1939, 117 hectares of what was named the Duncan Dock after Sir Patrick Duncan, Governor-General of the Union of South Africa, was in use. The contract originally intended the whole new harbour to be completed by 8 July 1941 but the war delayed completion until 1 July 1945. The new harbour included a small craft harbour presided over by the Royal Cape Yacht Club, and the largest graving dock in the Southern Hemisphere, 360 metres long, 47,6 metres wide and 13,7 metres deep. It was named the Sturrock Dock after the Right Honourable F C Sturrock, Minister of Transport, and opened in September 1945. Bulk storage space for coal and liquid fuel was provided, as well as a 27 220 ton grain elevator and pre-cooling stores for 29 000 tons of fruit for what is the third-largest fruit export harbour in the world. There is also a floating dock capable of lifting 1 016 tons.

In 1966, a new bulk tanker berth on the north-eastern (seaward) mole of the Duncan Dock was opened. It is connected by three pipelines to the oil refinery at Milnerton.

Table Bay is the principal passenger and mail harbour of Southern Africa, and a haven for repairing, revictualling and refuelling passing ships. Its fishing industry is enormous, as nine-tenths of the fish eaten in South Africa is landed, processed and railed from Cape Town. From the harbour, South African trawlers work the Agulhas Bank; while fishing fleets from many foreign countries, far outnumbering the local ships, use Table Bay as a base, trans-shipping their catches on to refrigerated vessels for transport to their home countries, replenishing their own stores and fuel, and allowing their crews spells of shore leave.

Hake or stock fish is the principal export fish, and many thousands of rock lobsters are flown alive each season to supply the epicures of America and Europe. Kingklip, sole, snoek, silver-fish, hottentot, kabeljou and yellowtail are also the main local varieties; and there are many less numerous species. In the winter snoek season the fishing wharves are particularly busy, with the long, handsome, silver-coloured fish being landed by the hundreds of thousands, providing particularly delicious eating for those who care to go to the harbour personally and purchase the fish absolutely fresh. With abalone, oysters, mussels, crabs and prawns also landed in Cape Town, its seafoods are justly renowned. A seafood dinner and an evening trip on one of the launches which take visitors on excursions can be a very pleasant way of exploring the harbour. On a warm, windless, moonlit night in summer, such an outing can be memorable.

In 1969, the contracts were awarded for a new outer basin especially for the use of container ships. Heavy blasting of the rock of the seabed was needed to provide this new harbour with 22 deep-water berths. It was completed in 1975 and named after Ben Schoeman, the then Minister of Transport who opened it on 1 July 1977. The spoil from the dredging of this massive work provided the material for a new foreshore area of 180 hectares which buried the original coastline of Table Bay on the south-east side of the new harbour. This area, known as *Paarden Island* (island of horses), lay between the mouths of two rivers, the old Salt River (which still reaches the sea in very diminished form at the north-east corner of the Ben Schoeman Dock) and what is now the Salt River Canal which carries the water of the Black River and its Liesbeek tributary to the sea on the eastern end of Paarden Island. A canal connects the old Salt River to the Salt River Canal. Paarden Island remains at least something of an island completely overgrown not with lush vegetation but with a hodgepodge of factories. Back in the 1780s Arend van Kielligh, contractor of wagons and horses to the Dutch East India Company, grazed his livestock on Paarden Island, hence the name.

After all these large-scale harbour works, the historic Alfred Basin, still in use mainly for fishing vessels, with the waterfront facing into the Victoria Basin, was starting to look somewhat woebegone, its warehouses and other structures, architecturally interesting but showing their Victorian age. Their neglect put them in peril of demolition and there was some controversy as to what would replace them if they were sold off to the tender mercies of property speculators.

At this critical stage, however, the ministers of Transport and Environmental Affairs appointed a committee to investigate greater public use of the harbours controlled by the South African Transport Services. Arie Burggraaf, the assistant Chief Engineer of Portnet, was appointed chairman of what was called the Burggraaf Committee. The eventual recommendation of the committee was that the Victoria and Alfred working harbours be maintained as a colourful, animated, lively centre-piece for the revitalisation of the waterfront buildings for tourism, entertainment and related uses. The concept was largely the vision of Mike Myburgh, the Assistant General Manager of S A Harbours. It was brilliant.

In November 1988, Transnet established its first private company, Victoria & Alfred Waterfront (Pty) Ltd. Brian Kantor, Head of the School of Commerce of the University of Cape Town, was appointed Chairman with David Jack as Managing Director. Work started with a holistic approach rather than the often-conflicting piecemeal conceptions of private development. In the first five years of the ongoing project, the fading waterfront was transformed like a Cinderella. Prince Alfred and his revered mother would have been even more than delighted to have their names attached to such a glittering princess. Restaurants, cafés, cinemas, theatres, hotels, a waterfront brewery, innumerable speciality shops, the headquarters of the National Sea Rescue Institute, a mineral world with wonderful displays of gemstones and a scratch patch with finders keepers for all manner of lovely things, arts and crafts, a vast sea world aquarium, boat trips, the S A Maritime Museum, a giant Imax cinema, the endless movement of shipping, the old Breakwater Prison converted into the University of Cape Town's Graduate School of Business, seals basking on ledges as a lazy contrast to the coming, going, promenading, meandering and search by human beings for fun and food, day and night, in what has become one of the major tourism and recreational attractions of Southern Africa. The story of the man-made harbour of Table Bay has gone far from the very first attempt to provide a sanctuary for shipping.

The ferry boat for Robben Island has its base in the Victoria Basin. It is fitting at this stage in the story of the Tavern of the Sea to take the 13 km journey across Table Bay from the historic first harbour of Table Bay to the recent and smallest sanctuary, Murray's Bay, the neat modern little harbour of Robben Island. Murray's Bay was named after John Murray who, in 1806 was granted permission by the British authorities to commence whaling from the island. At the time the new British administration of the Cape was just starting to appreciate the varied charms and values of Robben Island. Its convenience as an isolation centre was obvious. In 1807 a Superintendent was appointed to the island and unwanted persons were thenceforth ferried over to be placed under his charge. These persons included young army officers who had got themselves into debt or some personal trouble. They were sent to the island to hunt rabbits and be kept out of mischief.

Most of the other arrivals were human wrecks of various sorts. Very little money was provided to maintain this growing island population of outcasts. Government authority had the happy notion that such people could simply be swept away, if not under the carpet, dumped on Robben Island with little prospect of ever returning, or of seeing their friends and relatives again. They were considered to be the living dead.

Robben Island at that time was a wretched place. The sick, mad and criminal were herded together in a number of shacks. They had nothing to do save look longingly at the distant Table Mountain and potter about the shore, gathering shellfish from the rocks and fishing. The island superintendent hit upon a scheme of setting one person to watch another. This provided the outcasts with occupation, creating such dissent and suspicion that there was little prospect of a rebellion or escape.

Persons banished to the island for political reasons formed a special group. They were generally individuals of some stature and intelligence. They found conditions on the island particularly intolerable with escape constantly on their minds. Several tried, some succeeded, but the sea was bitterly cold and the currents hazardous. Makhanda, the revered Xhosa mystic who led his followers on an abortive, bloody attack on Grahamstown on 22 April 1819, was one of the political prisoners of Robben Island. On the night of 9 August 1828 he led 30 other prisoners on a resolute attempt to escape. They overpowered their guards, seized the whaling boats on the beach of Murray's Bay and set out for the mainland.

Reaching the shore, the excited men, sensing freedom, plunged into the surf and made for the beach. Only Makhanda failed to reach the shore. He was drowned. The rest of the men scattered in several parties. Three of them were captured, others were shot, and some escaped. The three captured men, including a European man named John Smith, were hanged, their heads then fixed on stakes and mounted on Robben Island as a warning to others who had ideas of escape. John Murray was ordered to transfer his whaling industry to the mainland, as his boats were considered to be a temptation to would-be escapers. As for Makhanda, such was his mystic reputation that for over 50 years the Xhosa people refused to accept that he was dead. They called him by the title of Nxele and affirmed that he was still on Robben Island. One day he would return to lead them to victory against the whites. His personal mats, clothes and ornaments, were carefully kept for him. When, at last, all hope for his return was abandoned, a proverb found a lasting place with the Xhosa people, *Kukuza kuka Nxele* (the coming of Nxele), said to anybody who longed persistently for something which would never happen.

In 1843 a considerable change came to Robben Island. John Montagu, the newly appointed secretary to the Cape government, realised the urgent need for road construction in the colony. He proposed to the government that all the common convicts on Robben Island be brought back to the mainland and set to work building roads. The accommodation vacated by the convicts would be available for the housing of lepers, lunatics, beggars, paupers, chronically and terminally ill people, cripples and the blind. Political prisoners would remain on the island.

Montagu's proposal was accepted by the government. Quite a considerable exchange of island population took place. Among other things this exchange resulted in the closing down of the old leper colony in the valley *Hemel en Aarde* (heaven and earth) near modern Hermanus.

On the island the increase in population caused considerable activity in building. A substantial house was built for the superintendent, quarters for the military personnel who did tours of guard duty, a bakery, butchery, blacksmith's shop and other conveniences. A neat little Anglican church had been built in 1841 by Captain R J Wolfe, brother of General Wolfe of Quebec fame. A 200 metre long jetty was built in 1847 to convenience loading and unloading the ferryboats and a regular village started to grow as a centre for the island.

Conditions for the sick remained primitive. The lepers, particularly, lived in complete squalor. Their hospital was hopelessly overcrowded, with the kitchen acting after meals as a bathroom. Perhaps understandably, the lepers were described as a parcel of desperate characters, idle, insolent, insubordinate and, knowing the then incurable nature of their disease, reckless to a degree. Without adequate funds the succession of medical superintendents could do little and some of them were not particularly notable for their ability.

The island cemetery grew larger year by year. Dr John Birtwhistle was appointed surgeon superintendent of the island, to be succeeded by Dr James Clephane Minto, but there were continuing complaints and scandals of shocking conditions and maltreatment of patients, with the sick and poor treated as though they were criminals.

Eventually, in 1861, a government inquiry was ordered. There were 361 patients on the island at this time. Dr William Edmunds was appointed as medical superintendent, more money was provided, and conditions at last improved under a far more humane dispensation. Left to itself, Robben Island was an atmospheric little world of its own, not just a geographical outcast but with a curious piquancy of character, of stunningly beautiful dawns and sunsets and an interesting diversity of flora and fauna. Once man ceased trying to impose on the island a repressive, heartless and brutal social system, Robben Island responded happily to a little love and understanding.

The island was cleaned up. The 'capital' grew to a pretty village unofficially known as *Irishtown* because most of the nurses and officials stationed there came from Ireland. With such a community it could only be lively. There were dances and romances, picnics among the arum lilies or next to one of the great rock pools. Edmund's Pool was a favourite with its underwater forests of marine vegetation, anemones of exquisite colour and quaintly patterned little fish so tame that at the first sign of a picnic they rose to the surface in eager anticipation of a share of at least the crumbs of the good things of life. The main street of Irishtown, named after Dr John Birtwhistle, had a tramway with mule-drawn trolleys to transport people and goods. Schools were built as well as a library, recreation hall, fire station and general dealer. A second church, built from island stone and designed by the celebrated architect, Sir Herbert Baker, was built in 1895 by the lepers. It became their special church and was named the 'Church of the Good Shepherd'. The Church of the Province of South Africa provided the ministry.

On the summit of Vuurberg, the highest point of the island and the site of the first navigation beacon on the South African coast, a neat permanent lighthouse was built in 1864. The hill was renamed Minto Hill after the former medical superintendent. The lighthouse was at first lit with a paraffin lamp. In 1938, it was equipped with its own power plant and a 464 000 candlepower light, to keep its faithful watch over the entrance to Table Bay, with a red flash added to mark the position of the shipping hazard of Whale Rock.

The rocky north, south and western shores of Robben Island are well littered with the relics of at least 27 shipwrecks. One of them, the British ship *Rangatira*, has left its name on the bay where it was wrecked on 31 March 1916. The *Rangatira* was a ship of 5 758 tons owned by the Shaw Saville and Albion line. She was conveying a general cargo from London to New Zealand when, just before lunch, travelling dead slow through a dense fog on a calm sea, she ran on to the rocks on the north-west coast of Robben Island. All aboard and 2 000 tons of cargo were saved including crates of whisky, two brood mares, a 'fine Persian cat' and one cage with canaries. More of the cargo would have been saved but the salvage crew broached open cases of whisky. A drunken brawl took place on the wreck with several men injured. Others were arrested and given prison terms. Salvaging operations were impeded. The wreck broke up and the sunken hull still contains the balance of the cargo.

Another of the wrecks made Robben Island a genuine treasure island and gave it a sad little ghost story. In 1693 the Dutch East Indiaman, *Goude Buys*, outward bound from the Netherlands with a rich cargo of gold and other valuables for the trading stations in the East, came to grief on the west coast about 24 km north of St Helena Bay. Of the 190 individuals who had sailed from the Netherlands on this ship, there were fewer than a dozen who had not already died or were in process of dying from scurvy. Leaving the ship at anchor, seven men set off along the shore in search of assistance. Five of these died of hunger; one was found by the local Africans and safely taken to the Dutch East India Company post at Saldanha Bay; the other was eventually rescued after seven weeks of aimless wandering.

Quite a fleet of small ships was sent from Table Bay to rescue any survivors and save the cargo. The *Goude Buys*, meanwhile, drifted ashore and could not be salvaged by the available means. Only one person was found alive in the ship and he died soon after the rescuers arrived. The cargo, however, could be retrieved. The Cape yacht *Dageraad* was employed on that task. Heavily laden with goods, including a considerable value of specie, the yacht, in the misty early hours of 20 January 1694, ran ashore on the western side of Robben Island. The yacht was a total wreck. Sixteen of the crew drowned while all the salvaged cargo and treasure from the *Goude Buys* were scattered among the kelp and rocks of the island. Only fragments have ever been retrieved. The shipwrecked men were buried on the island. Among them was the skipper, and of him there is an island folktale. Over his grave is a ship's anchor. It is said that his ghost used to roam about the whole island, frightening everyone by its wailing. The anchor was put on the grave to hold down the restless spirit. It was thenceforth allowed to roam only as far away as the anchor cable length. The spirit guards the wreck, sitting on the rocks at night at the scene of the disaster, bewailing the mishap and hoping that the *Dageraad* with its precious cargo will somehow manage to sail again.

The fauna and flora of the island flourished during this period with some of the fauna, especially the exotics, more prolifically than was desired. The rabbit population and the introduced game birds such as the Chukar partridges and the peafowls became so numerous that hunters were welcome to visit the island and shoot as many as they pleased. Over 26 000 trees were planted on the island in the early 1890s by Dr S Impey. Unfortunately these trees were mainly exotic bluegums, rooikrans, cypress and monatocca. Their thirst for water on an island with an annual rainfall of only about 350 mm proved deleterious to the springs. Like the rabbits, their presence has to be controlled. Their benefit to Robben Island is dubious.

In 1913 the lunatics were removed from the island to mainland asylums and in 1931 the lepers were transferred to Pretoria. After all the years of their isolation on the island, it had been found that salt-sea air was actually deleterious to their condition. The wards they had occupied were destroyed by fire. Irishtown went into decline. From a peak population of 2 000 people in the 1920s, the place became something like a ghost town with empty houses and hospital wards. A green tangle of vegetation grew over the island's cemetery. For a time the lighthouse keepers and their families were about the only inhabitants of Robben Island. Then, with World War II looming, a new activity commenced. The South African Defence Force took over the island and prepared it as a fortress to guard the entrance to Table Bay. The harbour at Murray's Bay was built, as well as an airstrip, emplacements for three large cannon, and an anti-aircraft battery. No attack was made on Robben Island and throughout the war years it was a peaceful little world in a setting of global conflict.

At the end of the war came another era in the story of the island. The South African Navy established a base and training centre for seamen on what they called *SAS Robbeneiland*. During the war years and the period of Naval control a one-mile security zone was imposed around the island. The marine population flourished under this protection. Line fish, abalone and rock lobster increased to at least something like the numbers which must once have found a home in a typical West Coast kelp-bed eco-system.

In 1960 control of the island passed to the Department of Prisons. A new maximum-security jail was erected, built from the grey slate of the island. In 1962 the first political prisoners were sent to the island by a regime which was intent on reviving the historic use of the place as a dumping ground for individuals the politicians considered best out of sight and out of mind, at least by themselves. These prisoners included most of the then leadership of the African National Congress, headed by the revered Nelson Mandela. They remained on the island, doing hard labour in such occupations as rock quarrying, until the last of them were transferred to mainland jails on 15 May 1991. About 600 common-law criminals replaced them.

During this dismal reversion in the use of Robben Island there was at least one advantage. As a maximum-security jail the wildlife of the island and the surrounding sea was stringently protected from the usual depredations of fishermen, treasure seekers and assorted looters of nature. The fish population of the island coast flourished, the bird population of about 110 species increased spectacularly with even mainland birds such as cattle egrets and black-crowned night herons flying over to the island to breed in security. Penguins, which had been completely driven away from the island by mass slaughter, made a welcome return. In the 1970s the South African National Foundation for the Conservation of Coastal Birds (SANCCOB) found it convenient to release on the island penguins which they had cleaned of pollution from oil spills. At first the penguins simply used the island as a staging post on their return to their homes on islands such as Dassen. In 1983, however, after the release of 3 000 penguins, the birds realised that they would never again be slaughtered on Robben Island. In that year nine breeding pairs made their nests on the island. By 1990, 1 238 pairs nested there and the colony is now well established, with a population of about 4 000 on the eastern shores.

In 1996 the island was declared a national monument and museum by the South African Cabinet and the Department of Correctional Services (the old Department of Prisons) phased out its presence. Control passed to the Department of Arts, Culture, Science and Technology. In January 1997 the first parties of tourists visited the island on conducted tours, including the prison and the cell occupied for so long by Nelson Mandela. On 1 December 1999 Robben Island was declared a World Heritage Site by UNESCO. The island entered a new era in its history as a unique nature reserve with the jail preserved as a museum.

To visit the Robben Island Museum, catch the ferry from Jetty I in the Victoria & Alfred Waterfront. During the 30 minute trip to the island, a video is shown of the history of the island, setting the scene for the rest of the tour. The tour guides are former political prisoners who have first-hand knowledge of what it was like to be incarcerated on the island. After touring the maximum security jail, a bus tour takes visitors on a circular ride around the island – stopping at the house where Robert Sobukwe was held, the lime quarry where the political prisoners worked, the Leper Church and several other landmarks before stopping in the village. Departure of the ferries may be affected by bad weather and rough seas – to check the times phone (021) 409-5123.

To explore Cape Town it is fitting to start from the docks. The two main dock gates both face Table Mountain from slightly different angles and take the traveller on to what is known as the Foreshore. This is the 145 ha level area reclaimed from the sea during the vast dredging operations which were necessary for the construction of the Duncan Dock. The spoil from this dredging was pumped out on the landward side of the new harbour and completely buried the original shoreline.

When the dredging and pumping were over, Cape Town found itself separated from its harbour by a wide, open, windswept Foreshore, which (once the dust had settled) had great potential to provide the city, already compressed between mountain and sea, with a unique face-lift – a new approach and a new building area with exciting architectural possibilities. There is a legend originating from those days of wide, open spaces that currency notes of various denominations and countries were often blown from the persons of sailors returning to their ships after late-night revelries. After a really powerful summer south-easter, these notes could be found the next morning adorning the dock security fences which were then scavenged daily by vagrants in search of this treasure of the Foreshore.

The Foreshore of today yields few such items of value. A grid of roads and a hotchpotch of buildings have settled the dust and partially broken the wind. The original anchorage of Roggebaai is buried deep beneath the modern reclamation; traversed by the main thoroughfare known as the *Heerengracht* (gentleman's canal), the name given in former years to the canalised lower section of the Fresh River. The traffic junction of this thoroughfare outside the dock gates is the unmarked beginning of one of the most romantic highways in the world, the Cape-to-Cairo road, followed by countless travellers using many different forms of transport.

Further up the Heerengracht, there is a traffic circle around a fountain and ornamental pools where a happy and garrulous squawk of sea-birds habitually disport themselves. The site of the pools roughly marks the original shoreline. Growing in the vicinity are a few palm trees, displaced relics of a once-handsome row of palms standing along a vanished marine promenade.

Looking across the pools at the mountain is a the graceful bronze statue of Jan van Riebeeck, created by the sculptor John Tweed and presented to Cape Town in 1899 by Cecil Rhodes. The statue stands very near to the spot where this founder of Cape Town must have landed on 7 April 1652. Near to him is a second statue that of his wife Maria, presented to Cape Town in 1952 by the Van Riebeeck Committee of Holland. This statue is the work of the Dutch sculptor, Dirk Wolkberg. It is slightly larger than the statue of her spouse but the two make a benevolent pair, appearing to watch with parental interest the growth of the city they founded.

The statues and pools mark the end of the Foreshore. Among the various buildings standing on it is the Artscape complex, containing an opera house and theatre, both well equipped, with excellent acoustics and seating. Each year many performances of ballet, opera, music, drama and other theatrical entertainments take place at these two venues. Facing this entertainment complex is the Civic Centre, a massive municipal administrative building which acts as a good buffer for the south-easter, as well as housing numerous officials. Cape Town became a municipality in 1861 and a city in 1913.

Beyond the statues of Van Riebeeck and his wife is the main street of Cape Town, Adderley Street, named after C B Adderley, a member of the British House of Commons who, in 1850, gave considerable support to the people of the Cape Colony in their struggle to dissuade the British Government from turning the colony into a convict settlement. At the beginning of Adderley Street is an imposing bronze monument to those who fell in the two World Wars and the Korean War. It was sculpted by Vernon March, who modelled it on the famous Winged Victory (the Nike of Samothrace) in the Louvre. On the right-hand side of the street in front of the Medical Centre, just before the war memorial, there is a small bronze ship mounted on a pedestal erected in memory of Robert Falcon Scott, the explorer of the Antarctic. On the left-hand side of the street, opposite the monument, are the extensive buildings housing the Cape Town railway station, airways and coach terminus. An attractive and well-maintained garden sets this modern building to advantage, although its appearance is marred by a permanent flea market. This is the terminal station of the whole railway network of Southern Africa, Zimbabwe, Mozambique, Zambia, Namibia, and places as far away as Dar es Salaam in Tanzania and Benguela in Angola. The concourse of the main line section of the station displays the first locomotive to work from Cape Town after railway construction commenced in 1859.

Adderley Street, lined with commercial buildings, leads for nine blocks towards the mountain. It is the main shopping street of the central city area and is an animated scene during the week. New arrivals from overseas are immediately aware that there is a peculiar quality to the air in Southern Africa that seems to make everything a little brighter than it really is. Certainly Adderley Street on a clear morning has an attractive sparkle, with everybody on the run and fast-moving pedestrians and traffic showing an alarming tendency to ignore each other. Smartly dressed women drift at will through moving streams of vehicles, casually pushing prams laden with infants and shopping bags, quite undaunted by the proximity of noisy buses and cars and the hooting of exasperated drivers. Fashions in Southern Africa generally follow Europe and America, with a slight delay to cover shipping and handling. There is a similar mindless adherence to the same fads. The pedestrian traffic is, however, interestingly cosmopolitan, a many-hued throng presenting a well-dressed, amiable, perhaps overfed picture, with African ladies flaunting bright colours to particular advantage.

Shopping hours are mostly from 08h30 to 17h00 on weekdays. On Saturdays, while many shops close at 13h00, the larger fashion and department stores stay open later. Some open on Sunday mornings in the run up to Christmas and during the long summer holidays. After commercial hours the city area tends to become deserted as Capetonians abandon the city for homes and entertainment in the suburbs. Cafés with open doors become hard to find. However, for the young late-night reveller, there is a wide choice of clubs, discos and live music. Much of the basic household shopping is also done in the suburbs and, as with most cities, the centre of Cape Town has become increasingly a place for the offices of financial institutions, lawyers and accountants. Street children, known as 'strollers,' the homeless and beggars regard the city area as their own.

The buildings of Adderley Street are attractive, without any particularly noteworthy examples of modern architecture. The railway station is connected to the opposite side of Adderley Street by an underground shopping mall. Between the General Post Office and the railway station there is an extensive so-called Golden Acre development, a massive construction housing shops, restaurants, cinemas and offices on the site of Cape Town's first railway station. The clock in the old station used to be a great meeting-place. The clock in the new building has been re-erected in the same position. The site of the building was also that of an early reservoir built in 1663, the walls of which were salvaged, carefully removed and preserved in the precincts of the new building. At this reservoir, old-time seafarers filled their water casks and bartered for food. Most of the post office stones in the museum were found in excavations between this point and Darling Street. The Grand Parade Centre, just beyond the Golden Acre, was the site of Cape Town's first post office. The later post office, on the corner of Darling and Parliament streets, displays one of the post office stones in its entrance foyer.

At the Strand Street entrance to the Golden Acre, facing the escalator leading up to the modern station, there is a plaque on the wall showing the position of the original shoreline of 1693. In the floor, across the entrance to the Golden Acre there is a black coloured inlay marking the approximate position of the tidal zone of the sea. Opposite, on the wall of the railway station there is another plague, this one in memory of António de Saldanha who, in 1503, landed near this point. From here he ascended Table Mountain to ascertain his position.

Just up Adderley Street from the Golden Acre, there is a roofed alley known as Trafalgar Place. This is the centre for Cape Town's flower sellers where loquacious ladies and men of varied temperament offer wonderful flowers for sale, and combine any transaction with a colourful commentary on life in general.

The Grand Parade Centre building and the post office were built on what was originally part of the military parade-ground in front of the castle. The remaining portion of the Grand Parade north of the post office has remained open and is mostly used as a parking area, with occasionally some military event or public meeting taking place. Religious and political groups also hold meetings there. On Wednesday and Saturday mornings there is an open-air market displaying plants, books and second-hand bric-à-brac for sale. A line of fast-food stalls stands on the south side. By day and night the Grand Parade is colourful and lively.

The first earthwork fort was built on the site now occupied by the stalls. Nothing of it remains. The Castle of Good Hope which replaced it, was built on the northern end of the parade between 1666 and 1679. In it there is an interesting military museum containing uniforms and medals as well as other items relating to the Cape's military history. The defensive cross wall known as the *Kat*, built in 1691 across the interior grounds of the Castle, once contained the official quarters of the Governor and his staff. The ornamental balcony in front of the Kat was the scene of important proclamations and the swearing in of new governors. Today the Kat houses a fine collection of paintings, furniture and ceramics of the Cape, known as the William Fehr Collection. It is open to the public daily from 09h30 to 16h00. The Castle itself is open to the public from 09h00 to 16h00; in December and January from 09h00 to 16h30. Guided tours take place at 11h00, 12h00 and 14h00 daily (not on Sundays). Changing of the guard takes place at 12h00 daily, with full ceremonial on Fridays. The ceremony of the keys takes place at 10h10 daily. Closed on Good Friday, Easter Sunday, Christmas and New Year's Day.

Originally, around the walls of this Castle of Good Hope, there was a moat filled with water from a canal known as the *Keizersgracht*, connected to the Fresh River. The route of this canal is now followed by *Darling Street*, named after C H Darling, Lieutenant-Governor of the Cape from 1852 to 1854. Across this street, overlooking the Grand Parade, is the City Hall, a massive sandstone building in the Italian style, completed in 1905. The clock tower contains, apart from an excellent clock, the first and largest carillon (44 bells) in South Africa. The hall was the home for several years of the Cape Town Symphony Orchestra, a body of professional musicians giving concerts of a first-class standard often under the baton of international guest conductors. The orchestra now has based at the Nico Theatre Centre and carries on the tradition of good music. It also goes out into the community and plays at venues throughout the Greater Cape Town area. Further along Darling Street, beyond the walls of the Castle, stands the Good Hope Centre, an impressive exhibition hall designed by Dr Antonio Nervi of Rome and completed in 1977. The main hall seats 8 000 people and has the world's largest free-spanning cross-vault concrete roof.

Above the intersection with Darling Street, Adderley Street continues towards the mountain. On the left-hand side stands one of its most notable buildings, the *Groote Kerk* (great church). This, the mother church of the Dutch Reformed Church is Southern Africa, is also the oldest surviving church, completed in 1704 and enlarged twice since. It contains a magnificent pulpit carved by Anton Anreith. The original bell tower contains a clock with a pleasantly distinctive two-tone chime. The organ is superb.

Beyond the Groote Kerk, on the same side of Adderley Street, stands the old Slave Lodge, originally the quarters for slaves employed in the great vegetable garden founded by Van Riebeeck and maintained by the Dutch East India Company to provide fresh food for ships. In later years, when slavery came to an end, the lodge became the building housing the Supreme Court. Previously known as the South African Cultural History Museum, the Slave Lodge contains an interesting collection of furniture and articles from Cape Town's past. The customs and art of the Islamic people in the Cape are well presented. The museum is open Tuesdays to Saturdays from 09h30 to 16h30, closed on Sundays, Mondays, Christmas and Good Friday.

This museum is now one of fifteen museums and sites forming part of Iziko Museums of Cape Town – an organisation formed to rationalise and streamline those of Cape Town's museums which are funded by national government. Iziko, a Xhosa word meaning 'hearth', is also understood as 'the centre of cultural activity'.

Adderley Street ends with the cultural museum. A sharp right-hand turn takes traffic into the beginning of Wale Street (*Waale* or Walloon Street, where two individuals of that nationality used to live). A hospital maintained by the Dutch East India Company once stood on the corner opposite the cultural museum. Up Wale Street, on the left-hand side, stands the substantial concrete pile of the Western Cape Province Administration buildings. The archway underneath the buildings leads to Keerom Street where, among other buildings, stands the modern Supreme Court. Past the Provincial Administration buildings, Wale Street climbs the lower slopes of Signal Hill to reach what is known as the *Bo-Kaap* (high Cape) or Malay Quarter, an interesting area largely inhabited by Muslims, Many of the neat little cottages here have recently been restored; there are several pretty mosques; and the call to prayer can be heard at all proper hours. The various annual festivals, such as the Feast of the Orange Leaves held on the birthday of the prophet (the date varies in the non-Muslim calender) and Ramadan (in the ninth lunar month from new moon to new moon) are all devoutly observed. Weddings, funerals and *Tamat* (when a Muslim boy completes his study of the Koran) are all practised in the Malay Quarter. One of the restored houses, 71 Wale Street, has been converted into the Bo-Kaap Museum. Many interesting items are exhibited here of Muslim cultural life in the Cape. It is open Mondays to Saturdays from 09h30 to 16h30. Closed Sundays and Eid holidays.

A very diverse population of human beings made their homes in what become simply known, without formal naming, as Cape Town. Retired soldiers, sailors, time-expired employees of the Dutch East India Company, mercenaries, adventurers and wanderers of many different nationalities made their homes there. A fair sprinkling of retired pirates who, having made fortunes from their nefarious trade, 'turned honest' (as the saying went) and settled within the blue afternoon shadow of Table Mountain.

There were slaves – brown, black and yellow – from Indonesia, Mozambique, Madagascar, and West and East Africa. To communicate with one another, a new language of convenience was created, basically the official Dutch from the Netherlands, but modified by words and pronunciations derived from many other sources. It was a language increasingly spoken first by slaves, farmers and labourers, and then, willy-nilly, by the officials, clergy, traders and aristocrats – the language eventually recognised as *Afrikaans*.

The architecture of Cape Town was also influenced by the cosmopolitan population as well as by the available local building materials. The result was a pleasingly relaxed, unique, indigenous style which blended perfectly with the environment.

The culture of Cape Town developed as an interesting blend consequent on its geographical position at the bottom end of the tumultuous continent of Africa and half-way between East and West. Black, brown and white – all provided subtle touches to the music, foods, aromas and culture of the Cape. Many of the people of Cape Town are the descendants of various political personages and their followers from the East, especially Indonesia. Cape Town was once a place of banishment for such people who had resisted the seizure of their homelands by the great European commercial enterprises of the day, the East India companies, whose charters gave them powers of life and death over many peoples.

The irrepressible cheerfulness, diversity and joy of living of the people of Cape Town is amusingly displayed in the Cape Minstrels' Carnival held annually on 1 and 2 January. On these days there is great celebration. The origin of the carnival is uncertain. Some say that it started as an annual reminder of the ending of slavery in the Cape. To others it is simply a colourful way of starting the new year.

For several months before the end of the year, groups of individuals form what are known as minstrel troupes. Each troupe has its own costume, colours, songs and musicians. On the days of the carnival, the troupes pour through the streets of Cape Town and converge on the stadium at Green Point, where they compete with one another in singing, music and appearance.

The troupes move through the streets at a traditional half-run, half-walk known as the 'Cape Walk'. Many thousands of individuals participate, and each troupe can include men, women and children. Just watch these troupes go by, look at the faces of the individuals; and you will see the descendants of the human diversity who made a home in the shadow of Table Mountain.

The hospitality of Cape Town was integral with its reputation as the Tavern of the Sea. The descendants of the slaves as well as the freemen and the time-expired soldiers, sailors and officials who chose to remain in the area at the end of their contracts with the Dutch East India Company, created between them a notable industry in the provision of food and good cheer for the passing ship. *'He's riding home back to front on his horse'*, says one metaphor about a farmer returning from a night in a tavern; while this witty description of a sailor rolling back to the landing-place observes: *'His hold's full and some's on deck too!'*

Farmers, butchers, bakers, vintners and fishermen all worked to contribute to the bill of good fare offered by this Tavern of the Sea. To supply the fresh vegetables and fruits so essential for the repair of the ravages of scurvy and malnutrition of long periods at sea, the Company created the great vegetable garden, watered by the same mountain stream which provided drinking-water for the ships and the residents of Cape Town.

The original Company's Garden founded in 1652 by Van Riebeeck, with Hendrik Boom as the first gardener, covered 18 ha of ground. It was tilled by a work-force of over 300 slaves. The Company's Garden is now a botanical garden covering less than 6 ha of the original area, and planted with flowers, trees and shrubs collected from many parts of the world. In this pleasant garden there are delightful walks, an open-air tea-room, aviaries, lily ponds and statues of public figures. One of the statues is of the famous Cecil Rhodes pointing north, and is inscribed with the words: *'Your hinterland is there'*. On 27 December 1889, while walking up and down beneath the oak trees of Government Avenue which bisects the Garden, Rhodes talked Frank Johnson into organising the Pioneer Column, which occupied what is today Zimbabwe. The bronze statue was sculpted by Henry Pegram and unveiled in 1910.

The bell tower next to the aviary was built in the style of the Cape-Dutch slave bell towers. Dating from 1855, the bell signals closing time each evening. Between the statue of Cecil Rhodes and the lower end of the Garden there is an oak tree which has the remains of a pump embedded in its trunk about 3 m above the ground. The pump (dated 1842) is connected by pipe to a well 2,7 m deep and originally supplied fresh water. Near the well is a statue of the Governor, Sir George Grey. Sculpted in marble by Calder Marshall and unveiled in 1864, it was the first statue erected in South Africa.

The oldest tree in the Garden is a saffron pear (*Pyrus communis*), believed to date from Van Riebeeck's time. The original trunk is dead. The present four arms arose as suckers around the parent. Aloes flower in winter. Demonstrations of rose pruning are given at the end of each July. The various ponds are cleaned in September and surplus goldfish are sold to the public. These fish and a lantern made of white granite were presented to Cape Town in 1932 by Japan as a token of appreciation for kindness shown to Japanese immigrants when passing Cape Town on their way to South America. The sundial bears the date 1787, but its history is unknown.

The Garden is open daily from 07h00 until sunset. Closed Christmas and Good Friday.

The area of the old Company's Garden steadily diminished over the years as buildings were erected on much of it. Most important of the structures are the South African Houses of Parliament, originally built in 1885 and since much enlarged. Each January the National Assembly commences its sitting with some pomp and ceremony. A second session starts at the beginning of August.

Guided tours of Parliament take place throughout the year Mondays to Fridays from 09h00 to 12h00 on the hour. To book, phone (021) 403-2201 or fax (021) 403-3817. During sessions, ordinary sittings, for which it is possible to book in advance, may also be attended. Tickets are obtainable from Room V12 in the Old Wing via the Parliament Street gate. Visitors will need to present an identity document or their passports to gain entry.

In the basement of the Parliament building there is a magnificent library of Africana, the Mendelssohn Library The grounds and buildings of the Houses of Parliament are immaculately maintained, and there is a graceful statue of Queen Victoria among the trees on the lower side.

Immediately across Government Avenue from the terracotta brick Parliament buildings is the sandstone Anglican cathedral of St George the Martyr, designed by Sir Herbert Baker to replace an older cathedral on the same site.

Between the cathedral and the Garden is the building complex of the National Library of South Africa housing a massive collection of books dealing with Africa. Among them is the Grey Collection, donated to the library by Sir George Grey, a former governor of the Cape Colony. The collection is housed in the annexe and comprises about 5 000 volumes, including many medieval manuscripts, early printed books and first editions of famous works. There is a first folio Shakespeare (1623), easily the most valuable book, and a copy of the second folio (1632), as well as a 15th century copy of Dante's *Divine Comedy* and a 14th century copy of *Mandeville's Travels* (in Flemish). The library also contains the oldest book in South Africa, the four Gospels, a manuscript authentically dated about the year 900. In the foyer of the older section of the building there is a painting usually described as the landing of Van Riebeeck, but actually depicting Van Riebeeck's first meeting with the pastoral tribespeople. It was painted by Charles Bell who designed the famous Cape of Good Hope triangular stamps. Both the Mendelssohn Library in the Houses of Parliament and the National Library of South Africa are among the five copyright libraries of South Africa in which files of all periodicals and copies of all books published in the country are kept. The Library is open to the public on weekdays from 09h00 to 17h00.

Further up Government Avenue, on the same side as the Parliament buildings, stands *De Tuyn Huys* (the garden house), surrounded by beautifully kept formal gardens. Today this is the town residence of the State President of the Republic of South Africa. It was built in 1699 as a pleasure lodge in the Garden for the Governor, Willem Adriaan van der Stel, who used it to escape the confines of his more formal residence in the Castle. Later British governors resided there permanently, and many illustrious guests have graced its spacious rooms.

Government Avenue is itself a renowned feature of Cape Town. It is a fine 1 km long promenade though a shady tunnel of oak trees inhabited by a permanent population of doves, pigeons and American squirrels. Cecil Rhodes introduced these squirrels into the Cape. All live comfortably on handouts of bread and peanuts from the benevolent public. A discord of vagrant cats lives agreeably on the hand-fed doves, pigeons and an occasional unwary squirrel. A walk through the Avenue, feeding the animals or lolling on the numerous benches, are all pastimes which Capetonians and visitors have enjoyed for many years. As the Avenue terminates the direct route from the docks up Adderley Street, visiting seamen, immigrants and tourists seem to gravitate there naturally. As with Piccadilly Circus in London, an encounter with a familiar face is almost inevitable in the Avenue.

It is there, too, that the characters of the town, the eccentrics, deadbeats and dropouts, spend much of their time. Such individuals come and go in all cities and, in their deviation from convention, add a touch of spice to an otherwise staid, humdrum world. Cape Town has known some marvellous and attractively quaint characters among this community of bench sitters and Avenue promenaders. There was old 'Professor' Herbst with his long white beard and seafarer's attire, who sold love potions for a living; there was a woman who wore the same dress every day for years, it is said, to spite her husband who had once accused her of extravagance in buying clothes. Towards the end of her life the dress was an incredible garment made up of threads and patches. Then there was a mystery man, always-dressed in knickerbockers and carrying a paper-shopping carrier; there was also a rabbinical character that slept on benches and snored loudly. There was a man who lived well for years by coaxing plump doves and pigeons into a paper bag containing titbits. By catching and eating them curried, boiled, roasted or grilled, he even achieved some variety in his menu. Cape Town Charlie earned a living as a snake charmer and conjurer, performing each day to appreciative audiences in the Avenue.

In modern times there was Cas Lucas, a happy-go-lucky individual who claimed to have achieved his life's ambition by becoming Cape Town's top tramp. A frequently photographed pair were Iris Theodora Holmes and her son Anthony, who, for 48 years, fed the birds and squirrels in the Avenue each day. Around 1980, the reigning characters were a brother-and-sister team, Giesbert and Dagmar Westphal, known locally as the 'Sack People' on account of their strange attire made up of sacks. They spent their time strolling the streets deep in conversation or sitting on benches in the Avenue, tapping a collection plate with a gentle request to passers-by to give them 'something'. And always there is a new face, a new story among the familiar characters of the Avenue.

The upper portion of the present Garden is crossed by an open space containing ornamental ponds and a number of statues and monuments of persons and events, the most notable being a memorial to South African soldiers killed in the Battle of Delville Wood during the First World War. On the south-east side of this open space is the South African National Gallery, which exhibits a collection of European and South African art. There is a rather neglected garden of statues on the one side. The permanent European collection includes works representative of the main schools of English and Dutch paintings. Perhaps the best known is Gainsborough's Lavinia, and there are good specimens of the work of Raeburn, Reynolds, Romney and Morland. The Dutch pictures include works by Heremans, Vijtmens, Van der Kessel and other 17th and 18th century artists. There are paintings of the 17th and 19th century French schools, and works of such English painters of the early 20th century as Wilson Steer, Sickert, Rothenstein and John. The highlight of the permanent collection is the Sir Abe Bailey Collection of sporting pictures – one of the most distinguished of such collections in the world, including paintings and drawings by George Stubbs, Herring senior and junior, James Pollard and Munnings, among others. There is also a collection of leading South African artists. The Gallery is open Tuesdays to Sundays from 10h00 to 17h00. Closed on Mondays and Worker's Day.

On the opposite side of the open space stand the buildings of the South African Museum which has a notable collection of San rock art, the Lydenberg Heads, the only example of a quagga foal and 250 million-year-old Karoo mammal-like reptiles. The Whale Well with its skeleton of a blue whale is well worth a visit. The museum is open daily from 10h00 to 17h00. Closed on Good

Friday and Christmas. There is also a planetarium attached to the main building, with the same opening hours as the museum. The planetarium has shows daily including an evening show once a week. The museum and planetarium has a monthly programme of events – for up-to-date information of exhibitions and films, phone (021) 424-3330.

Just above the art gallery loom the twin towers of the Gardens Synagogue, built in 1905 alongside the original building which was the first synagogue in South Africa, erected in 1862. The picturesque old synagogue housing the Jewish Museum has now been linked by a walkway to a new specially designed museum building erected behind it. This expanded museum complex opened in November 2000. The Cape Town Holocaust Museum, the first and only Holocaust Centre in Africa, opened in 1999 next door to the Gardens Synagogue in the Albow Centre in Hatfield Street. It contains a permanent exhibition on the Holocaust including text and photo panels, archival documents and film footage, multimedia displays, artefacts, recreated environments and survivor testimonies. Both museums are open Sundays to Thursdays 10h00 to 17h00, Fridays 10h00 to 13h00 (the Holocaust Museum) and 10h00 to 14h00 (the Jewish Museum). Both museums are closed on Saturdays and Jewish holidays.

The handsome oak trees growing in front of the synagogue buildings have among them the remains of several planted in the time of Governor Simon van der Stel who introduced a large number of oaks to the Cape. Unfortunately, in the warm climate of South Africa, oak trees have a short life relative to their kind in Europe. The winters are not cold enough to send them into the deep sleep they need and they become subject to a fungal disease. English oaks are particularly susceptible to this disease. Turkish oaks (*Quercus cerris*) are now planted. Beneath the trees outside the synagogue is an area known as the Paddocks, once used as a paddock for horses kept in stables near Government House. Later a bandstand was erected there, but this was demolished in 1934.

Government Avenue continues past the museum and reaches on either side a pair of ornamental gateways guarded by pairs of stone lions. These gateways were once the entrance to a menagerie established by Governor Adriaan van der Stel. A beasts-of-prey park was situated on the right-hand side and a bird and antelope park on the left. The lions and lionesses guarding the gate were sculpted by Anton Anreith. The right-hand gateway now leads to a cluster of buildings housing several departments of the University of Cape Town, the Michaelis School of Fine Art, the Little Theatre and other cultural and educational institutions, one of which is constructed in neo-Egyptian style. It was built for the South African College (later the University of Cape Town) in 1839 as the first building erected in Cape Town for higher education. It was designed by Colonel G G Lewis of the Royal Engineers. Near to it is Bertram House, a Georgian brick building constructed in the 1830s as a town house for John Barker, an attorney. This museum depicts the British contribution to life at the Cape. The museum is open Tuesdays to Saturdays 09h30 to 16h30. Closed Good Friday and Christmas.

On the opposite side of the avenue from the museum are the grounds and building of Cape Town High School and the Gardens Commercial High School. Government Avenue ends where it is bisected by Orange Street. The imposing pillared entrance just across Orange Street leads to the Mount Nelson Hotel with its beautiful grounds, private property for the enjoyment of the hotel's guests. This is one of the oldest and best-known hotels in Southern Africa. The property was originally owned by the Honourable Sir Hamilton Ross who built a town house there which he called *Mount Nelson* when he settled in the Cape at the time of the first British occupation.

Besides the main artery of Adderley Street, the city area of Cape Town has many other interesting streets. Plein Street, named after *Stal Plein* (stable square), is a busy shopping street. At the top of Plein Street, at the square, there is an equestrian statue of General Louis Botha, the Roman Catholic Cathedral of St Mary, the tall building housing Ministers of State during the Parliamentary session and the Lodge de Goede Hoop, the first Masonic lodge in South Africa.

St George's, Burg and Long streets are also commercial streets. Burg Street bisects Greenmarket Square, which was the site of the original open-air vegetable market of Cape Town. It is now the scene of a flea market. On its one side stands the attractive Old Town House, built in 1761, originally the Burgher Watch House and later the civic centre and council house of Cape Town. It was replaced by the present city hall in 1905 and is now preserved as a national monument housing the Michaelis Collection of old Dutch and Flemish paintings. The pride of the collection, presented by Sir Max and Lady Michaelis, is a woman's portrait painted by Frans Hals in 1644. This painting is probably the most valuable in Southern Africa. The Old Town House is open Mondays to Saturdays from 10h00 to 17h00. Closed Sundays, Good Friday, Christmas and New Year's Day.

Unfortunately modern buildings have replaced most of the older structures in Cape Town. The few that remain are hemmed in by aggressive new developments. In Strand Street, after it bisects Burg Street, stands a handsome Lutheran church, built surreptitiously in 1774 by Martin Melck, a wealthy Lutheran merchant who erected it ostensibly as a store-room in the days when no religion was tolerated in the Cape other than the Dutch Reformed. The sexton's house adjoining this Lutheran church was built in 1787 and is now occupied by the Netherlands Consulate. On the south side of the church is the Martin Melck House, a fine specimen of an 18th century Cape-Dutch house, actually built after Melck's death in 1781, but named in his honour. It is now a business centre.

On the opposite side of Strand Street stands another graceful old house, built in 1702 and named the Koopmans-de Wet House after the family who acquired it at the beginning of the 19th century. It is now a historical monument and museum, containing an interesting collection of period furniture, antiques and prints. It is open to the public Tuesdays to Saturdays 09h30 to 16h30. Closed Sundays, Mondays, Good Friday and Christmas Day. At 40 Long Street stands the restored church and headquarters of the South African Missionary Institution. Built in 1799, this building, with its fine acoustics, played an important role in the history of Christianity in South Africa. It is open Mondays to Fridays from 09h00 to 16h00. Closed Saturdays, Sundays and public holidays. The building is a national monument and museum containing many interesting items related to mission work.

Between the top of Government Avenue and the slopes of Table Mountain lie the oldest residential suburbs of Cape Town. *Gardens* is a popular place for boarding-houses and rooms for business people. *Vredehoek* (peaceful corner) and *Kloof* (cleft) are also populated by working and business people of the city; *Oranjezicht* (orange view), originally a farm, was so named because the farmhouse had a view of the *Oranje* bastion of the Castle of the Cape of Good Hope; *Tamboerskloof* (drummer's ravine) is further west, against the slopes of Lion's Head; Devil's Peak, University Estate and what used to be a picturesquely decrepit slum area, District Six, all lie on the slopes of Devil's Peak. District Six, now demolished, once enjoyed an atmosphere of great vitality and gaiety, despite its conditions of anguished poverty. *'This is fairyland'* was the claim of graffiti carelessly scrawled on a dingy wall.

The eastern boundaries of the farm on which the suburb of Oranjezicht now stands were along the banks of the Fresh River. Although this river has been forced underground in the lower reaches of its flow through the modern city, the stream in its upper reaches remains on the surface; and, in the winter rainy season when there is a flow of water, it is pleasant to walk along its shady banks and find lingering there something of the atmosphere of Cape Town long ago.

To reach the beginning of this still-unspoilt upper valley of the Fresh River, go up what was once the outlying street of Cape Town, *Buitenkant* (outer side) Street. The street passes the lovely old Rococo house *Rust en Vreugd* (rest and peace), now a national monument and gallery for fine water-colours collected by William Fehr. Among these paintings are a number by the famous wildlife artist, Edmund Caldwell. The collection is open Mondays to Saturdays 08h30 to 16h30. Closed on Sundays, Mondays, Good Friday, Christmas and New Year's Day.

Beyond *Rust en Vreugd*, the street continues up the hill in the direction of Table Mountain. Passing the Gardens Shopping Centre, one reaches the imposing building and grounds of Highlands House, the Jewish Old Age Home. It is here that the Fresh River is free from its conduit and flows merrily down the lower mountain slopes through a beautiful, tree-filled valley, nowadays called the Van Riebeeck Park, attractively laid out with picnic spots and shady glades. Many lovely, perfectly maintained homes such as *Rheezicht* nestle among the trees on both sides of the valley. In former years a cobbled pathway known as the 'slave walk' made its way up this portion of the valley to wash houses where the clothes of Cape Town were laundered.

About 90 m above the ruins of these wash houses stand a pair of cottages which once comprised a water-mill. In former times at least five such mills ground corn from the power of the passing river, but nothing is left of them today. The growth of the town demanded a less haphazard water supply than filling pails from the passing stream. The water mills were a luxury that the river could no longer support. In 1868 the municipality bought them all out and they were closed down. A weir was built across the river at the point where it was joined by one of its principal tributaries from the mountain, the Silver Stream. From there the water was filtered and piped to the population of Cape Town.

Above this weir, on a steep slope of the tongue of land between the river and its tributary stream, stood a house whose ruins, more than half buried in shrubbery, still overlook the valley through a tangle of oak and fir trees. The view stretches as far as the distant waters of Table Bay. There are many legends about this house, which was called *De Grendel van de Platteklip Kloof* (the bolt of the flat stone cleft) because it blocked access to the upper reaches of the valley. Its isolated situation, the shadows of the trees and the tumbling rush of a waterfall beside it, certainly make it an ideal home for ghosts. Here, legend has it, lived Antjie Somers, the favourite bogeyman (or woman) of the Cape Coloured people. Antjie Somers is a mystical character who appears in many rhymes and tales, especially those told by mothers to frighten naughty children. In this area too, according to folklore, stood *Verlatenbosch* (abandoned bush), where the leprous son of a former governor lived in solitude. He had apparently been infected by playing a flute he had picked up, once owned by a leper and deliberately placed by an enemy of the governor where his son could find it. The sound of the flute is said still to haunt the area.

Just above the ruins of the abode of Antjie Somers, the Fresh River comes racing down over a series of flat rock surfaces. These give the name of *Platteklip* (flat stone) to the higher reaches and the great diagonal gorge which cleaves the front of Table Mountain, providing the easiest (but dullest) scramble up to the summit where the busy little river has its source.

Climbers have found over 350 separate routes, ranging from easy to very difficult, to the summit of Table Mountain. This great pile of sandstone, a mountain playground in the backyard of a city, is also a National Monument, National Park and recreational area belonging to all, with wild flowers in astonishing profusion, sizes and colours, ranging from the giant protea to the fragile disa, to be seen somewhere on the mountain throughout the year.

The level but rough and rocky summit has many points of interest. It is 3 km long, east to west, with its highest point, the 1 086 m Maclear's Beacon (Sir Thomas Maclear was a one-time Astronomer Royal), on the eastern end.

The western end of the narrow table plateau supports the distinctive concrete 'pimple' of the upper cable station, where the engines are housed which safely lift over 500 000 people to the summit each year.

The cableway was opened in October 1929. It had taken two years to build. Notwithstanding many hazards, nobody had been killed in the construction and no serious accident ever marred the working of this cableway. It was the brain-child of a Norwegian engineer, T Strömsoe. At the beginning of October 1997, after extensive reconstruction and updating made essential by the vast increase in tourism, a new cableway replaced the old. The upper and lower cable stations were rebuilt to accept larger, circular shaped cable cars, weighing 13 tons each and holding 65 passengers. They are similar to the cable cars used on Mount Tittis in Switzerland. These cars and increased speed allow 890 passengers an hour instead of the old 250 to reach the summit.

There are two carrying (or track) cables, 1 220 m long and 46,5 mm thick. They have a braking strain of 168 tons and are minutely inspected once each month. The two cabins counterbalance each other. One goes up as the other goes down, taking about 6 minutes to do the journey. The breaking strain of the hauling rope is over 36 tons. The driving engine is powered by electricity from Cape Town. If the power supply failed, the cabin would remain stationary until an auxiliary power supply is switched on.

The experience of going up the Table Mountain cableway is unique. There is tremendous drama in the great rock mass of the mountain. The cable cars revolve slowly as they travel and the view expands with every metre the car climbs, revealing the whole of Cape Town, with Table Bay and a long view northwards to the mountain ranges on the far horizon.

Climbing the mountain by foot and hand should not be attempted without expert advice, as several people are killed on it each year. The Mountain Club of South Africa, at 97 Hatfield Street, Gardens, phone (021) 465-3412, is happy to advise prospective climbers. This club also publishes an excellent guide and map for walkers and climbers, with all climbs rated. The Table Mountain aerial cableway works daily (weather permitting) from 08h00 to 18h00 in winter and from 08h00 to 22h00 in summer. It is always best to check with the cableway office as to whether they are running or not as often the wind can come up at short notice. It is also possible to pre-book tickets. Phone (021) 424-8181.

The narrow tabletop falls away sharply into the back table, a walker's rugged paradise, with gorges, wild flowers, pine forests, and a set of reservoirs supplying water to Cape Town. This back table eventually ends precipitately in the south in Orange Kloof. Its eastern precipices, beautifully wooded, overlook the southern suburbs of Cape Town. The twelve sun-drenched and bare buttresses of its western precipices, known as the Twelve Apostles, dominate the Atlantic Ocean suburbs such as Camps Bay

The actual western edge of the table, with the upper cable station and restaurant on its top, falls away almost alarmingly to the saddle of land known as Kloof Nek. This saddle links Table Mountain to one of its satellites, the 669 m high Lion's Head. This striking sugarloaf-shaped peak is connected by a long body to a rump known as Signal Hill, which overlooks the docks. Signal Hill has on it the ceremonial cannons of Lion's Battery which, by firing a shot at noon, each day cause the pigeons of Cape Town to take fright and the human populace to check their time. Lion's Head was once known as the Sugarloaf. The reason for the change of name is apparently either its shape, or the shooting there of the last Cape lion. For many years a look-out man was stationed on its summit to warn Cape Town with a small signal cannon and flags of the approach and identity of ships. A well trodden pathway spirals to the summit through sparkling groves of silver trees and lovely spring displays of watsonias, its final stretch up steep rocks facilitated by chains.

The climb is not unduly demanding and the 360-degree panorama is, if anything, aesthetically superior to the higher but more directional view from the top of Table Mountain. The road which climbs the lower slopes of Lion's Head runs past the domed *kramat* (tomb) of Mohammed Gasan Gaibbie Shah and leads to the summit of Signal Hill. There is a picnic site near the tomb, on top of the saddle of land linking Lion's Head to Signal Hill. A pair of old signal cannons are mounted on a look-out just above the tomb. Countless sightseers have travelled this road to view the scene at night, when the whole city lies glittering like a fairyland necklace elegantly suspended around the smoothly curved neck of Table Bay. Midnight on the last day of the year is a memorable time to be on this wonderful vantage-point. The glow of lights, firing of rockets, distant sounds of revelry, hooting of ships, whistling trains, the sound of bells, all rising from the city and echoing and reflecting from the watching face of Table Mountain, provide an almost dreamlike prelude to the coming year. Table Mountain is floodlit.

From the Signal Hill observation point it is pleasant to drive back to Kloof Nek and then along Tafelberg Road which starts at Kloof Nek and, with constantly changing views, lovely by day and night, follows the 350 m contour below the cliffs of Table Mountain, past the lower cable station to the slopes of the 1 001 m high Devil's Peak, which stands guard on the flank of Table Mountain opposite to Lion's Head.

Devil's Peak was originally known as the Wind Mountain. The reason for its two names is not only interesting but also explains several local weather peculiarities. An oft-told local legend introduces us to a retired pirate named Van Hunks. This rugged character, it appears, was accustomed to spend his days sitting beneath a clump of trees at what is known as Breakfast Rock on the summit of the saddle of land connecting Devil's Peak to Table Mountain. There he passed his time smoking a potent mixture of rum-soaked tobacco and viewing the shipping in the bay, speculating on the wealth of their cargoes. One day the Devil visited Van Hunks and the two began a smoking contest. This contest continues throughout the summer months. (In winter Van Hunks has rheumatism and cannot climb the mountain.) Proof of the competition is the marvellous, billowing, smoke-like cloud which in the summer season seems to begin at the clump of trees at Breakfast Rock, grows, expands and then rolls over the summit of Table Mountain to produce the phenomenon of the table-cloth. Penny Miller's delightful book for children, *The Story of Rory*, and her *Myths and Legends of Southern Africa*, provide us with an amusing account of Van Hunks, the table-cloth, and the last lion of Lions Head.

The scientific explanation for the table-cloth is equally fascinating. From it we learn something of Cape Town's famous south-east wind. This wind is as much a part of the Cape as Table Mountain. It has had a definite influence on the development of the city. It is the prevailing wind during the summer, appearing towards the end of October and petering out in February, leaving just before the most idyllic months at the Cape, March and April. In May the north-west wind appears, far less venomous in its impact, but the bringer of cool weather and up to 1 524 mm of rain during winter, turning the Cape into a green garden.

The famous south-easter, the 'Cape Doctor', which blows away insects, miasmas, smogs and pollution from the atmosphere of the Cape, is in fact not originally a south-east wind at all. It is born in the high-pressure areas (the anti-cyclones) which in the southern summer, girdle the Earth between latitudes of 35°S and 40°S. Cape Town's latitude is only 34°S; but the whirling masses of air rotating in an anti-clockwise direction, on account of the rotation of the Earth, throw out tongues of air which reach the southern end of Africa travelling from the south or south-west. The long line of mountains which lies just inland from the southern coast of Africa forces this air to pile up and move along it with compressed vigour. At Cape Hangklip the air suddenly finds itself released from this imprisonment. It sweeps around Cape Hangklip with what is known as 'corner effect' and, like a wild beast run amok, goes swirling across the waters of False Bay, picking up a high moisture content. It then collides head-on with the mountains of the Cape Peninsula. A number of things now take place.

The mountains force the wind to rise sharply, and what is known as 'orographic condensation' occurs. The moisture in the wind is suddenly condensed to a thick white cloud as soon as it reaches the cooler altitude of the mountain tops. The summit of Table Mountain, ideally placed and the highest point of the range, catches the bulk of this cloud which, with its thickness determined by the strength and height of the wind, rolls over the mountain as the famous table-cloth, draping itself over the edge like a tumbling waterfall which abruptly disappears in an almost straight line where the mist dissolves in the warmer air of a lower altitude.

Lower reaches of the wind, meanwhile, have rushed along the eastern precipices of the mountain chain. Devil's Peak, the wind mountain, acts as a corner-stone; and here the stream of air whips around in another corner effect. It pours down into the city area of Cape Town, the Table Valley of the Fresh River; and here, at last coming from a truly south-easterly direction and compressed between rows of buildings, it can play havoc, reaching speeds of 130 km per hour (hurricane force) on occasions, and from time to time breaking records with a speed of 150 km per hour and more. Unlike the north-western of winter which blows in spurts, the south-easter can maintain its force for days, but as a rule it slackens in the early hours, allowing people some relaxation in the mornings, and reappears about noon.

Chapter Four
THE CAPE PENINSULA

For the tourist, the exploration of the Cape Peninsula is one of the most famous travel experiences in the world. With the city of Cape Town and Table Mountain, the Peninsula is strikingly varied, combining scenery that is both dramatic and charming with a piquant atmosphere. From the time of its first discovery, the serenely beautiful Cape Peninsula, with its interesting ocean currents, its marine fauna and its unique scents and flavours, was accepted as a merging place of East, West and the great dividing continent of Africa. For the indigenous wildlife and people of Africa this was the cul-de-sac of their migration routes from north to south. Exotic people from East and West joined them in a veritable maelstrom of human history, cultures, activities, emotions and aspirations, colouring the majestic ambience of this most renowned and strategic Cape.

The geological origin of the Cape Peninsula is dramatic. Underlying the Peninsula there is a basement of granite. In several parts of the Peninsula this granite is revealed; for example, at the very tip of the Peninsula known as Cape Point. Here the granite is exposed to a relentless force. Surging in upon the Cape of Good Hope comes the full weight of the enormous rollers created in the welter and disturbance of the meeting of two great ocean currents, the Benguela and the Mozambique–Agulhas, at the end of the vast land mass of Africa. The coast of the whole Peninsula takes a heavy pounding, especially on the western side. Steep cliffs, detached rocks and oddly shaped pinnacles have been eroded by the restless water. In the granite. Beneath Cape Point itself there are caves, one of which is 51 m deep with a mouth 12 m in diameter, and approachable only from the sea.

On top of the granite basement, the higher levels of the Peninsula consist of sedimentary sandstone and quartzite laid down beneath the sea in comparatively recent geological times (about 300 million years ago). In a series of great convulsions this sedimentary mass was eventually elevated above the sea to form part of what geologists know as the Cape Super group. With its three related series of sedimentary deposits laid down under water in different conditions at different times this group provides the spectacular valley and mountain scenery of the Cape coastal area.

The sandstone is a coarse rock composed of large grains of sand stained red and brown with iron. At times this iron content cements the sand grains together to form ferricrete. Manganese is also present in dark layers; or, at places such as Bordjiesrif, it gives the rocks a generally darker hue. At various parts of the Peninsula attempts have been made to mine manganese, but it is too erratic to be profitably worked.

To the eye the surface of the southern end of the Peninsula consists of a line of hills on the eastern side, the highest points being Paulsberg (367 m), Judas Peak (328 m) and Vasco da Gama (268 m). On the western side of these hills lies a gently undulating plateau averaging 61 m above the sea and topped with a thin layer of very acidic soil containing little organic matter but chemically replenished by constant disintegration of the sandstone. Nature makes this unpromising looking soil a paradise for the ancient macchia-type vegetation known as Cape schlerophyll or, in Afrikaans, as *fynbos* (small-leaved bush), with no fewer than 1 800 species of plants lustily competing on the Cape Peninsula for existence in conditions which would be regarded by any gardener as hopeless.

To further complicate all forms of life on the Cape Peninsula, there are obvious signs of several former variations in the sea-level. Old sea cliffs, marine terraces, wave-polished boulders, shell deposits inland – all record variations in the sea-level which were so substantial that the Peninsula was often fragmented into two islands when the sea flooded across the glen of Fish Hoek and inundated the Cape Flats. Primitive man might easily have been marooned on these islands. The signs of their middens and artefacts certainly indicate that they were present in the area at a remote period. It is difficult even to guess the precise nature of the weather and other natural conditions prevailing at the time. It is unlikely, however, that the southern portion of the Peninsula was ever an area particularly salubrious to early man. The tip of the Peninsula probes southwards as far as the 34,22 degree of south latitude. This is getting close to the Roaring Forties with their interminable gales, and the Cape of Good Hope is noted for its winds.

In the dry summer months (November to March) the south-east wind is persistent, averaging 17 km to 40 km per hour, but having periodic tantrums which reach 120 km per hour and more. This is a peculiarly relentless and unavoidable wind. It influences the direction of the growth of trees (which all grow away from it) and exasperates man into defensive concepts of architecture and outdoor activity. It also, however, provides the Peninsula as a whole with a significant service. The south-east wind, is known as the 'Cape Doctor'. It disperses smog and stench, clears visibility, and makes life so difficult for insects that such pests as flies, mosquitoes and gnats are not a health problem to man on the Peninsula. They simply get blown away.

In winter (May to August) a north-west wind replaces the south-easter. This wind, however, is far less persistent. It does blow periodic gales of great violence and brings rain to the southern Peninsula (averaging 355 mm at Cape Point), but it lacks the venom of the south-easter. The carrier of rain is the bringer of life; and the north-wester alternates its 'blows' with days of sunny calm when the Peninsula, green, clean and fresh from its shower, is at its best.

The average temperature of the southern Peninsula is 20,3°C in summer and 15,5°C in winter. The long narrow Peninsula is three-quarters surrounded by sea. As such, it is very much influenced by oceanic conditions which, to complicate matters further, vary from the one side of the Peninsula to the other. In summer there is usually a difference of at least 6°C between sea temperatures on the eastern and western sides. In winter the difference is slight, but still noticeable at around 0,5°C, with the eastern side always the warmer of the two. This temperature variation influences the species of marine life as well as recreational and commercial fishing.

The drive around the Cape Peninsula, starting and ending at the statues of Jan van Riebeeck and his wife, where Adderley Street merges with the Heerengracht, is 143 km long. It requires at least one full day from the life of any traveller but no day could be better spent. A more agreeable medley of scenes, atmospheres, experiences, aromas, colours, interesting people, stories, myths and legends, it would be difficult to find anywhere else on the good planet Earth. Let's be off, then, on a journey of discovery from Van Riebeeck's Tavern of the Sea, to the Cape of Good Hope and then back with our thoughts full of a day never to be forgotten.

One block from Van Riebeeck's statue, down the Heerengracht towards the docks, there is a turn right into Hertzog Boulevard. Passing, on the right, the imposing Civic Centre and left, the Nico Theatre Centre, the road climbs the interchange which carries on it the beginning of National Road N2, the coastal highway which connects Cape Town to Durban and the far north coast of Natal and the Zulu country. Below this elevated dual carriageway (known here as the Eastern Boulevard), the docks and central city area of Cape Town provide a handsome sight. Table Mountain and its companions, Devil's Peak on the left, Lion's Head and Signal Hill to the right, dominate the scene. Immediately to the right (south) of the road is the area once known as District Six. This was a shabby but strangely picturesque home for the homeless, the destitute and the poor until the whole community was summarily driven out of what they sometimes called 'fairyland'. District Six was levelled to the ground in the name of apartheid. Its population was dispersed to distant areas, where it would be out of sight and out of mind to an uncaring political regime, just like the old days of Robben Island. The area is now to be rebuilt and the renaissance of District Six will be fascinating to see.

After 3 km there is a turn-off to the first of the southern suburbs of Cape Town ...

WOODSTOCK

The heavily built-up suburb of Woodstock was once a residential area known as *Papendorp* after a well-to-do inhabitant of those parts named Pieter van Papendorp. In 1881 when the place was granted a Village Management Board, the name Papendorp sounded slightly odd. The majority of its inhabitants who were all satisfied customers of the local pub, *The Woodstock*, arranged a change of name in honour of their favourite place of recreation. Whether the social downfall of the neighbourhood dated from this change of name is unknown, but nonetheless Woodstock became thenceforth substantially less select and far more congested.

In former years a toll-gate stood on the main road, and the property of the headquarters of Cape Town Tramways (Cape Town's transport company) became known as Tollgate.

Beyond the turn-off to Woodstock, the Eastern Boulevard continues its gentle climb up the slopes of Devil's Peak. On both sides of the road lie the suburbs of Devil's Peak, University Estate and the former District Six. Passing the Holiday Inn on the right, the Eastern Boulevard continues under a major traffic flyover and then, after 4 km from the start of our journey, at what is known as Hospital Bend, joins De Waal Drive which has come around the slopes of Devil's Peak from the upper portion of the city.

At this junction the route has reached its highest level on the slopes of Devil's Peak. From this point onwards there is generally a distinct reduction in temperature (especially in summer). The road leaves the built-up area below. On the left there is a fine view over the Cape Flats towards the mountain ranges on the near horizon. On the right, the beautifully wooded slopes of Devil's Peak rise upwards to the mountain's impressive jagged summit. Standing beside the road there is a small pillar erected as a memorial to those who died during the First World War.

De Waal Drive, which has now been joined, is named after Sir Frederic de Waal, first administrator of the Cape Province, who conceived the original route. It is cut into the slopes of Devil's Peak in finely graded curves. Its verges and grade separations are planted with indigenous flowering plants which provide many visitors with their first sight of the wonderful flora of Southern Africa.

The combined roads now take on the name of Rhodes Drive. The drive sweeps down the slopes of Hospital Bend. On the left is the vast complex of Groote Schuur Hospital, the buildings of the Medical School and, in perhaps unfortunate if convenient proximity, a cemetery. This coincidental grouping of interrelated human activities and inactivities should provide motorists with food for thought, but it seems to have little noticeable effect on the local brand of demon drivers. Hospital Bend is a favourite place for accidents. Speed freaks or those suffering beyond endurance the type of cancer mentioned in the prelude in this book are, perhaps, tempted into driving excesses by the convenient locations of the above-mentioned facilities!

Groote Schuur Hospital was founded in 1932 and became world famous when Professor Chris Barnard performed the first heart transplant operation there on 3 December 1967. The theatre he used for this renowned operation is now an historical monument.

Below the hospital and cemetery lies Main Road, a principal (and very congested) commercial thoroughfare, and the suburbs of Salt River and Woodstock.

Back at Hospital Bend, below the hospital, to the north and east the unbeautiful city jumble of concrete and bricks gropes upwards as though trying to engulf the unspoilt mountain heights. The story of the preservation of this lovely area is interesting. The mountain slopes were part of the farm *Welgelegen* (well situated) owned by the Van Reenen family. On this property Sybrandt Mostert in 1796 had erected a windmill known as Mostert's Mill and this is maintained today in good working order as a national monument. In 1891, Cecil Rhodes, Prime Minister of the Cape Colony, then only 38 years of age but master of the Kimberley diamond mines and one of the most powerful financiers in the world, bought the estate and commenced a programme of acquiring control of the mountain slopes all the way to Constantia Nek. On his death in 1902 this whole area was bequeathed to the people of South Africa. The brooding spirit of a remarkable man is an indefinable presence guarding this legacy from any spoilation.

Beyond Hospital Bend, 5 km from the start of our journey, the N2 coastal road branches off as Settlers Way and commences its long journey up the coast to Natal and the land of the Zulus. At this interchange De Waal Drive undergoes a change of name. As Rhodes Drive, it swings southwards, passing Mostert's Mill standing on the left-hand side of the road with its four arms held up to embrace the sun and the wind. The mill is open to the public daily from 09h00 to 15h00. Close to it a gracefully designed footbridge takes walkers over Rhodes Drive to a path leading beneath the stone pines, favourite trees of Cecil Rhodes who introduced them to the Cape from their home in Italy.

The path leads through the shade of the trees and up the slopes of the mountain. In a paddock to the left may be seen the walled cemetery of the original owners of the farm. Antelope of a number of species graze on the well-grassed mountain slopes. With easy gradients the path winds upwards. Eventually it reaches the memorial to Cecil Rhodes on a site particularly beloved by the man. From it is revealed the whole of the Cape Flats from Table Bay on the left to False Bay on the right, from the built-up suburbs below us to the mountain ranges on the northern horizon.

The Rhodes memorial was built by public subscription and unveiled on 5 July 1912. It is an impressive work. It was designed by Francis Masey and Sir Herbert Baker, mainly using granite, the favourite stone of Rhodes. The centre-piece is the first cast of the famous bronze statue by G F Watts: *Physical Energy*, the original of which stands in Hyde Park, London. The statue faces north, where Rhodes dreamed and schemed of so many things. It was presented to South Africa by the sculptor in regard and admiration for Cecil Rhodes. It is set on a granite base at the foot of a granite stairway guarded by bronze lions sculpted by J M Swan. At the top of the stairway, in what resembles a Doric temple, there is a bust of Rhodes, also sculpted by J M Swan and inscribed with the words:

> *'Living he was the land and dead*
> *His soul shall be her soul.'*

Silver trees, proteas and other species from the Cape floral kingdom flourish around the memorial. Stone pines provide shade to the parking area where a branch road from Rhodes Drive comes up to the memorial. A tea-room behind the memorial provides refreshment while paths lead upwards to join the contour path which wanders through the trees high on the slopes of Devil's Peak. The remains of three blockhouses still stand on these slopes where they were erected by the British during the time of their first occupation of the Cape (1795–1803). This was the period of the French Revolution. The British occupied the Cape in order to control its strategic situation and prevent the spread of French revolutionary ideas which were anathema to the conservative English ruling class. The forts or blockhouses were small but sturdily built. A number of the cumbersome cannon of the period were dragged with considerable effort to positions of vantage from which it was hoped any invading Frenchmen, along with their ideas of liberty and equality, could be blown away. No onslaught by the French ever occurred. The blockhouses are reachable by footpaths from the Rhodes Memorial or by road from the end of the scenic Tafelberg Road running along the lower slopes of Table Mountain, past the lower cable station. The smaller Queen's Blockhouse is a little below the end of the road. The King's Blockhouse is about one kilometre along the continuation of the road open to walkers to the east, while the Prince of Wales Blockhouse is close to De Waal Drive on a vantage-point overlooking the Groote Schuur Hospital. There is a path to it leading through a gateway and onwards for about one kilometre of easy walking.

The Queen's and the Prince of Wales blockhouses are in ruins. The King's Blockhouse, the principal of the fortifications, eventually became a convict station. About 40 hard-labour convicts and six warders were accommodated in the building and employed on a programme of afforestation of the treeless lower slopes of Devil's Peak. Frank Jarman, the first forester in charge of the project from 1893 to 1902 built a house and workshop just below the blockhouse, sharing the drinking water provided by a spring above the blockhouse.

The situation, high on the shoulder of the mountain, provided a prodigious view embracing the whole of the Cape Flats from Table Bay to False Bay. Devil's Peak, however, had not been originally known as the Wind Mountain for nothing. The situation of the blockhouse was such that it was exposed to the full blast of both of the prevailing winds of the Cape, the south-easter of summer and the north-wester of winter. Both winds hurtle around Devil's Peak, and the corner effect at the turn around the eastern shoulder of the mountains works them up to gale force. Indigenous trees, except in the protection of the gullies, had never found these slopes to their liking. The beautiful silver trees flourished, for they thrive in conditions of wind which blows away the parasites inflicting them in more protected areas and distributes their seeds.

For nine years forester Jarman worked diligently in planting exotic, fast-growing softwood trees on the mountain slopes. Then he was transferred to the Elgin area in 1902 and killed there in an accident. The trees he had planted on Devil's Peak grew lustily and his colleagues, remembering the sterling qualities of Frank Jarman, placed a memorial stone in the walls of his house, with the words *'He found these barren stony slopes treeless. He left them covered with trees'*. The memorial remains, a sad little fragment of a ruined wall, and a lost human endeavour.

The whole forestry station has vanished into these few half-buried walls. The trees are gone. A plantation of such inflammable timber in such a situation was ill conceived. The soldiers, the convicts and the foresters are just a memory. The sombre blockhouse remains as an historic monument, waiting for the Frenchmen who never came. The silver trees, displaced for a while by the plantation, have returned, triumphantly waving their lovely leaves in the wind, like swords defending the domain of wild flowers which cover the mountain slopes all around them.

From the seats below the Rhodes memorial, a site where Rhodes himself was reputedly fond of sitting, there is a panoramic view over the suburbs built on the eastern side of Rhodes Drive and De Waal Drive. To the north-east lies the suburb of Observatory.

OBSERVATORY

In 1821 the British Admiralty established in Cape Town a Southern Hemisphere branch of the Royal Observatory. The site selected (on the banks of the Liesbeek River) was then pleasantly rural and free from the glare of modern electric lighting. The purpose of the observatory was to set time and longitude. Many important research tasks were also given to this observatory and many distinguished scientists worked in it. Its principal instruments were the 1 m Elizabeth reflecting telescope and the 0,6 m Victoria refracting telescope. Apart from its observations, the observatory was given the task of setting standard time for Southern Africa; and, by remote electrical control, it fired the noon gun on Signal Hill.

In modern times the steady encroachment of urban areas, atmospheric pollution and floodlighting on nearby roads such as the Black River Parkway made work in the observatory increasingly difficult. In 1972 a new central observatory, the South African Astronomical Observatory, was created. A site was selected near Sutherland in the Karoo, where the skies are unpolluted and unaffected by clouds for at least 50 per cent of each year. The main instruments from the Cape Town, Johannesburg and Pretoria observatories were moved to this site. Cape Town remains the administrative centre. The astronomical staff spend about one week in every six at Sutherland. The rest of the time they spend in Cape Town analysing their data and preparing new programmes. Much routine and technical service activity, as well as the measurement of stellar distances, continues in the old Royal Observatory.

Visitors are welcome each month on the second Saturday evening at 20h00, weather permitting. Admission is free. There is a guided tour. Phone (021) 447-0025.

The buildings to the right of the observatory house the principal mental hospital of the Western Cape, *Valkenberg*, once the private home of Cornelis Valk. The manor-house was built in 1770 and is a fine example of the Cape-Dutch style. The football grounds of Hartleyvale are also nearby. South of Observatory lies the suburb of *Mowbray* which, like Woodstock, grew up around a roadside tavern.

MOWBRAY

In 1723 Johannes Beck, who had a tavern at Rondebosch, decided to build another wayside hostelry nearer Cape Town. In the following year, on the night of 20 July, while the tavern was being built, three slaves, in vengeance for some grievance, murdered a farm foreman named Behr and his wife on a farm close to the tavern. It is said that a baby of the murdered couple survived when its slave nurse hid the infant in the kitchen oven. The slaves were captured, condemned and executed in the usual barbarous manner. They were first broken on the wheel, then beheaded with their heads exhibited on stakes at the scene of the crime. The name *Drie Koppen* (three heads) was attached to the new tavern, with a sign-board displaying the heads. The name was passed on to the village which grew around the tavern. On 17 June 1850, however, the name of the village was changed to *Mowbray*, the name of a local estate owned by a man from Melton Mowbray in

England. The three heads were still depicted on the coat of arms of the municipality which was established in 1890. Three cups, presumably in memory of rollicking times in the tavern, were also included in this rather odd coat of arms.

ROSEBANK

South of Mowbray and immediately east of the Rhodes Memorial is the suburb of Rosebank, named after the estate on which it grew. Back in 1657 a group of free burghers (men released from servitude to the Dutch East India Company) settled on land granted to them on the site of the future Rosebank and named the area *Hollandse Thuijn* (garden of Holland). Always notable for its flowers, Rosebank is much used as a dormitory area for students of the University of Cape Town. In Cecil Road is situated the Irma Stern Museum devoted to the work of that artist. The museum is open Tuesdays to Saturdays from 10h00 to 17h00. Closed Sundays and Mondays, Christmas and 26 December, New Year's Day and Good Friday.

RONDEBOSCH

Originally named *Ronde Doorn Bosjen* (round thorn bushes), after a long-vanished landmark of a circle of thorn trees,the suburb is now covered with attractive residences, schools such as the Diocesan College (Bishops), Rondebosch Boys (high and primary), Westerford (high), Rustenburg Girls Junior and High, in whose grounds stand the original summer residence of the Dutch governors, hence the name Place of Rest. The original building was destroyed by fire and only fragments remain. Also in Rondebosch is the Silwood Kitchen, the renowned *cordon bleu* culinary school founded by the late Mrs Lesley Faull, author, *cordon bleu* chef, and great personality of South African cooking. Rondebosch Common is a large open space much used as a camping ground by the Dutch and British military during the long-drawn out Napoleonic Wars. It is now protected as an open space by proclamation as an historic monument. It is the home for several species of wild flowers. Overlooking it on the eastern side is the Red Cross War Memorial Children's Hospital. In the centre of Rondebosch stands a cast-iron fountain built about 1884 as a drinking trough for horses. It became the support for the first electrically generated street light in Cape Town with power provided from a privately owned generating plant at Westbrooke.

UNIVERSITY OF CAPE TOWN

Rhodes Drive continues from Mostert's Mill, immediately reaching a turn-off down Woolsack Road, past the residences, administrative buildings and faculties of Music and Ballet of the University of Cape Town, and then joins the Main Road through the suburbs of Rosebank and Rondebosch. The attractive complex of the Baxter Theatre stands at this junction.

The main cluster of buildings of the University of Cape Town lies on the right-hand side of Rhodes Drive, 6 km from the city centre where our journey began. The situation of the university is magnificent, with the serrated summit of Devil's Peak and the rugged cliffs of the back of Table Mountain forming a spectacular backdrop. A statue of Rhodes, great benefactor of the place, sits on the steps in front of the university, looking in pensive mood at the playing fields and beyond.

The University of Cape Town is the oldest in Southern Africa. It had its origin in 1829 as a private enterprise named the South African College, housed in the city area proper, with buildings including what later became the archives in Queen Victoria Street. The private college became a public venture in 1837 and then, as a university, was transferred to its present situation in 1925, when the foundation stone of the first building was laid by the Prince of Wales. The imposing site is on Rhodes's great gift of his Groote Schuur estate. Over 15 000 students study each year in the various faculties of this university.

Rhodes Drive passes below the creeper-covered walls of the university. On the left stands the one-time summer-house of the British governors, known as *The Belvedere*. Beyond it the dual carriageway curves around the end of the university campus and passes, on the left, the gateway leading to the lovely homestead of *Groote Schuur* (the great barn). This was originally built by Jan van Riebeeck as a grain store. It was converted by later English owners into a residence called *The Grange*, and then purchased by Rhodes as the nucleus of his great estate along the slopes of the back of Table Mountain and Devil's Peak. A disastrous fire practically destroyed the house in 1896. It was then remodelled for Rhodes in the Cape-Dutch style by the famous architect, Sir Herbert Baker. From the fire-blackened ruins rose the stately Groote Schuur manor-house of today. It is full of treasures, for Rhodes was a great collector of antiques and curiosities. The garden outside became famous for its hydrangeas, passion flowers and plumbago (Rhodes's favourite flower), all planted in great banked masses which he felt were appropriate to the prodigious scale of the African continent. A pleasant tradition was that each Christmas the hydrangeas were cut, and literally by the truckload – taken to decorate the wards of Groote Schuur and other hospitals.

Rhodes bequeathed his wonderful home as the official residence of the Prime Minister of the Cape (later South Africa). A second house on the estate, *The Woolsack*, was originally built by Rhodes as a summer home for his friend, Rudyard Kipling, and later became the official residence of the Deputy Prime Minister. It is now part of the university. Across the way from *Groote Schuur* is *Westbrooke*, originally bought in the early 1800s by Judge William Westbrooke Burton and today the country residence of the State President of the Republic of South Africa. The name was changed in 1995 to *Genadendal* (valley of grace).

NEWLANDS

Just beyond the entrance to *Groote Schuur*, 7,5 km from the start of its journey, the road reaches the Princess Anne traffic interchange. From here there is a branch leading right to the Rhodes Memorial and to the University of Cape Town. To the east (left) there is a turn leading down to Rondebosch and to Newlands Drive which leads beneath a fine avenue of oak trees, past the South African College Schools and through the north-western side of the suburb of Newlands.

It does not take a very discerning eye to appreciate that the lands on the eastern side of Devil's Peak and the back of Table Mountain are fertile, well watered and sheltered from the desiccating south-easter. With the highest average rainfall on the Cape Peninsula of over 1 500 mm a year, the mountain slopes are well forested, green, cool and a considerable contrast to the Table Valley where the Tavern of the Sea was founded. The area became known as *Nieuwland* (Newlands). At first it was a logging area and farm on the banks of the upper reaches of the Liesbeek River. Then, in 1700, the Governor, Willem Adriaan van der Stel discovered the charms of the area and built a country house there.

Newlands became one of the choicest residential suburbs of Cape Town. The houses built in the shallow river valley include many delightful homes in garden settings. Van der Stel's original house was used as a summer retreat by several of his successors. British governors also used it but it had a somewhat chequered career. Lord Charles Somerset added a second storey to it. It became a little top heavy and blew down in a storm on 12 August 1819. The house was then rebuilt on its present site, became partly ruined, passed into private hands of speculators who haphazardly sold off plots on its 64 morgen of ground. The remaining 29 morgen and the house were sold in September 1859 to Dr Jonas Michiel Hiddingh, a physician, politician and businessman.

From the Princess Anne traffic interchange Rhodes Drive changes its name to Union Avenue and provides a fine drive with the forest-covered mountain slopes dominating it on the right-hand side. The verges and grade separation of the road are lineal gardens of indigenous flowers while the attractive houses of Newlands drowse their days away in the shade of trees on the left. There is a turn-off to a picnic and barbecue site just after the interchange. At intervals along the length of the forest fronting the road there are parking places at the start of paths which wander to many parts of this lovely domain of trees. As a reminder of the pervading influence of Cecil Rhodes, bird-lovers will be interested to see and hear a small colony of the chaffinch, a common British bird introduced by him and nesting in the trees. Their song was a favourite of Rhodes.

In 1706, a part of this forest was granted to Willem ten Damme, who succeeded his father as chief surgeon to the Dutch East India Company in the Cape. He named his possession *Paradijs*. He built a cottage as a farmhouse, close to a perennial mountain stream flowing down into a deep valley known as *De Hel* (the abyss). It was to this 'paradise' amidst the trees that there came, for a little while, one of the most romantic couples in the story of Southern Africa. In 1797, when the British occupied the Cape for the first time, as a temporary security measure during the Napoleonic Wars, they sent out as governor an Irish gentleman, George Earl Macartney, recently raised to the peerage as reward for many years of diligent service to the British as an ambassador and governor. His wife declined to accompany him to the Cape but amongst the staff he brought with him from England was Andrew Barnard, appointed to the position of Colonial Secretary. He brought with him his wife Anne, daughter of the Earl of Balcarres. She took over the duties of the first lady of the British administration, charged with the organising of social functions and the making of friends with the *Kapenaars* (Cape people). With her husband she was allotted the Castle Residency for accommodation. This she furnished with tasteful informality. In the Council Room of the castle she held drawing-room receptions, dinners and dances with a lively band of six black fiddlers.

Lady Anne's personal history was interesting. Born in 1750, she was an artist of repute and author of the famous ballad *Auld Robin Grey*. She became involved in an unfortunate and lengthy love affair with Henry Dundas (later Viscount Melville, Secretary for War and the Colonies). His political ambitions required that he form an alliance with another powerful family. Lady Anne became something of an embarrassment. She was intelligent, attractive and artistic but at 43 years of age she was still dreaming of an impossible marriage to her lover. There must have been a great deal of hard talking behind the scenes. The upshot was that Lady Anne was married off to Andrew Barnard, a man thirteen years her junior with little hope of professional advancement without influential friends. What he got was Lady Anne and the appointment to Lord Macartney's staff as Colonial Secretary, a plum job for so young a man. So off he sailed with his talented wife, many horizons away from Henry Dundas, to Cape Town.

The Barnards enjoyed a good living in the Cape. Barnard proved efficient in his position and Lady Anne was a brilliant success as first lady of the administration. The Cape benefited from their presence. Lady Anne endeared herself not only to contemporary local society but also, through a sequence of letters she wrote to Henry Dundas, recording an amusing, perceptive and most readable picture of living in Cape Town.

As a rural escape from their official duties, Lady Anne and her husband were allocated the cottage in the woodlands of *Paradijs* estate. They found the cottage *'too old and crazy to be safe any longer'* (as Lady Anne described it). Barnard therefore set to work and built a 'wee cottage' on an 8-ha plot on the banks of the Liesbeek River. This estate the Barnards named *'The Vineyard'*. They moved there in 1800 and spent their spare time from duties in creating a dream garden, digging out the palmiet reeds and planting fruit trees and vegetables. The pity was that time was short. Lord Macartney retired on 20 November 1798. He suffered badly from gout and he did not like the hot Cape summers any better than the wet winters in the castle. He returned to England and died there in 1806 at the age of 69. He was succeeded as acting-governor by Major-General Francis Dundas until 10 December 1799 when Sir George Younge, an elderly baronet, took office as Governor. He only lasted until 20 April 1801 when he was dismissed on grounds of incompetence and accusations of corruption. Major-General Dundas once again became acting-governor and retained that position until the British handed the Cape back to the Dutch on 20 February 1803.

Lady Anne returned to Britain at the beginning of 1802. Her husband remained in his position until the Dutch took over and then joined his wife. Lady Anne, in the few years she had resided in the Cape, found herself a unique place in the history of the country. Three years later, in 1806 when the British reoccupied the Cape, Barnard was reappointed to his former position. He sailed to the Cape alone, while Lady Anne remained in Britain to settle affairs, pack and follow. Unfortunately Barnard died in October 1807 on a farm while on a journey in the interior of the country. Lady Anne was left a widow in Britain. She died in 1825 without ever again setting foot in the Cape.

The Vineyard at first was abandoned to dilapidation. Then the Governor, Lord Charles Somerset, restored the place as his country retreat. Later it passed into private hands. Fruit, grapes, flowers and vegetables, with pumpkins described as *'big as a barrel of beef'* were grown there. Then it became a hotel. The house was enlarged and new buildings constructed but in some indefinable way the amiable, hospitable and romantic personalities of the Barnards remain attached to it. The proud owner of *The Vineyard* today, Francois Petousis, a veritable prince of hoteliers, has carefully maintained its atmosphere and preserved within the body of the modern hotel something of the elegance and charm of bygone days. The garden is superb, the river still flows along the boundary, while the hospitality of the place is a legacy from Lady Anne.

The pleasant climate, fertility and plentiful fresh water from rainfall, mountain streams and springs not only attracted residents, but provided Newlands with a commercial property of considerable value. The possibilities of reticulating the pure water for domestic use and for the production of aerated drinks and beer were obvious. Jonas Hiddingh of Newlands House established the Cannon Brewery after buying the plant of the small pioneer Martienessen's Brewery. Jacob Letterstedt, a Swedish merchant who settled in the Cape in 1822, also entered the brewery business. He married the widow Dreyer and acquired her mill built in 1818. In 1840 Letterstedt built a new mill with a huge cast-iron water wheel. This was named the Josephine Mill after Crown Princess Josephine of Sweden. Things went well for him until a problem started to develop in the late 1840s. The British Government, in May 1841 proposed that Europeans condemned to long terms of imprisonment in India, particularly soldiers, be sent to Robben Island and, after serving their sentence, be liberated in Cape Town.

There was a public outcry in Cape Town. The scheme was abandoned but during the next year, in March 1842, a fresh proposal was made to ship out from Britain 50 boy convicts to be apprenticed in the Cape. Again public outcry aborted the scheme. The British government, however, seemed obsessed with the idea of clearing out their crowded jails of surplus individuals. Earl Grey, then Secretary of State for Colonies, made periodic suggestions but always withdrew when the local people reacted.

The controversy seemed to be dying down when, in March 1849, news reached Cape Town that, without further consideration of local feelings, a ship, the *Neptune*, had sailed from Britain with a load of convicts from Pentonville prison. The ship was sailing to Bermuda to pick up and convey to the Cape a number of Irish convicts who had been transported to the Caribbean to serve sentences for trifling offences during the potato famine in Ireland. They were certainly not hardened criminals but the Cape people still wanted none of them.

There was a considerable public disturbance. An anti-Convict association led by John Ebden was formed, supported by John Fairbairn, editor of the *Commercial Advertiser*. A pledge was adopted declaring that the undersigned inhabitants of the Cape of Good Hope would not employ or knowingly admit, provide work for, assist, associate with or support convicted felons. Petitions to the Queen, parliament and the people of England were drawn up. The country people supported the town people in a united opposition to the Cape as a convict settlement.

Nevertheless, at 22h00 on 19 September 1849 the good ship *Neptune* anchored in Simon's Bay with 282 convicts on board guarded by two officers and 47 rank-and-file soldiers. At daybreak the next morning the fire-alarm gong in the town house of Cape Town, and the bells of churches of all denominations tolled to warn the population of the arrival of the ship. Mass public meetings were held in Greenmarket Square and on the Grand Parade. The Governor, Sir Harry Smith, was informed that any person, company or government department in any way supplying the *Neptune* would be boycotted.

Weeks passed with the unfortunate ship lying at anchor and nobody allowed to land. On 10 October the names were published in the press of twelve men who were denounced as supplying provisions and aid for the ship. Among these names was that of Jacob Letterstedt. He found his businesses boycotted. With others denounced as supportive of government policy he was personally assaulted, abused, threatened, his effigy burned and his business premises damaged. The whole dismal affair dragged on until a dispatch from Earl Grey reached Cape Town on 13 February 1850 instructing the Governor to send the *Neptune* to Van Diemen's Land. There the convicts would receive pardon and be liberated. There was jubilation in the Cape. The ship was provisioned, a small sum of money collected to be given to the convicts and the *Neptune* sailed on 21 February 1850 after five dreary months at anchor.

Cape Town relaxed. The principal street, the Heerengracht, was renamed in gratitude after C Adderley, a member of the House of Commons who had ably championed the cause of the Cape in Britain. Those individuals who had supported the government, especially the twelve men who had been denounced in the press and suffered losses by boycott, damage or physical violence attempted to get some compensation. One of them, Captain Robert Stanford, was knighted for his services in breaking the boycott of supplies and received £5 000, but the rest received nothing. Jacob Letterstedt was particularly aggrieved at the ingratitude of the authorities. He felt that he had supported a government which did not support him. He decided to quit the Cape as soon as it was possible and move to France. This took some time.

Letterstedt's Josephine Mill and his brewery in Newlands were eventually sold to Ole Anders Ohlsson, a Swede who had emigrated to the Cape in 1860. He also bought the brewery and canteen interests of Jonas Hiddingh, created Ohlsson's Cape Breweries and built this up to become the then largest manufacturing enterprise in South Africa. In 1900 Ohlsson erected a large new brewery on the site of the old Mariendahl brewery he had bought from Hiddingh. He had already obtained rights to several of the perennial streams and springs in Newlands. He floated the Cape Town and Districts Waterworks Co Ltd and supplied potable water to the southern suburbs as well as using the water as the basis of his beer and softdrinks. In 1898 this company became a public utility run by the municipalities of Claremont, Rondebosch and Mowbray. Ohlsson entered politics, became a member of the legislative assembly for the Cape, was a great conservationist, protector of the last elephants of the Knysna forest and of Addo. He died in 1912 on his Newlands estate of *Montebello*, now the property of the South African College Schools.

Newlands is still a supplier of water to the southern suburbs of Cape Town. The forestry station and municipal waterworks lie among the trees on the mountain side of Union Avenue. The demands for water, however, have so far exceeded the capacity of local springs that the two reservoirs are now supplied by three pipelines, 51,5 km long leading from the Steenbras reservoir in the Hottentots Holland Mountains. Those suburbs fortunate to receive their water reticulated from the Newlands reservoir receive a most palatable supply. The springs near the brewery (now owned by South African Breweries) are still used. One of them, the Albion Springs, was for long the basis of the softdrinks bottled there by Schweppes until they moved elsewhere.

The Josephine Mill was restored. A fully operational milling museum was incorporated into the building and this is open to the public. It is open Mondays to Fridays 10h00 to 13h00;14h00 to 16h00 with conducted tours at 10h15, 11h30 and 14h15. The commodious building is also used for concerts. The museum of the South African Rugby Board is housed at the Sports Science Institute opposite the mill. It is open from 09h30 to 16h00 on weekdays and on Saturdays when a rugby match is taking place. The entrance to the Newlands rugby ground, home of the Western Province Rugby Union, is close to the mill, with the playing fields of the Western Province Cricket Club and the Kelvin Grove Sports Club on the eastern side of the suburban railway line. Ohlssons Brewery stands across the road from the Josephine Mill.

Union Avenue continues its pleasant way between forest and suburb and then, with a turn eastwards, reaches a crossroads 9,5 km from the start of our journey. To the left Newlands Avenue leads through an avenue of oak trees. Ahead, Union Avenue changes its name for a short distance to Paradise Drive. It bridges over the Liesbeek River and then divides into Protea Road which leads eastwards as a boundary between Newlands and the suburb of Claremont. The other branch, known as Edinburgh Drive, twists southwards, climbs Wynberg hill past Bishopscourt on the right and then down the southern slopes, with the suburb of Wynberg on the left: Constantia lies on the right while ahead is a distant view of False Bay and the end of the Cape Peninsula.

CLAREMONT

Claremont, which has an important commercial centre, is still sometimes referred to as the 'village' and its rugby team is known as the Villagers. It is today more like an infant city, with a major shopping centre and one of the most beautiful public parks in Southern Africa, the Arderne Gardens. The garden was originally part of the estate known as *The Hill*, in the halcyon days when Claremont was still a village in the centre of a quiet rural area. In 1840 an English immigrant, Ralph Arderne, acquired this estate. He was a lover of trees, and on the site he planted one of the finest tree collections in Southern Africa. From all over the world he acquired about 325 species of trees, including magnificent Norfolk Island pines, Indian rubber trees, Atlas Mountain cedars, North American swamp cypresses and many others. All flourished in Ralph Arderne's garden. The

Black River has its source in this garden. The spring was converted by Arderne into a delightful Japanese garden with bridges, ferns and water-fowl. Azaleas, rhododendrons and roses grow to perfection in the park and always provide a colourful show.

In 1927, hard economic times and the unfortunate death of Arderne's son and heir, Henry, forced the family to dispose of the fine estate. Of it 4,5 ha were acquired by the municipality and, saved from the mercies of property developers, converted into the public gardens of today.

Harfield Road, leading off from the park, was named after *Harfield Cottage*, famous in the annals of missionary work in Africa as the transit quarters of the staff of the London Missionary Society. In this cottage stayed eminent men such as Robert Moffat and Dr David Livingstone. Sir John Herschel, the famous astronomer, lived at *Feldhausen* in Claremont from 1934 and carried out research there. An obelisk marks the site of his telescope.

At the important intersection of Union Avenue with Newlands Avenue and Paradise Road (9,5 km from the city), turn sharp right off the double carriageway and follow the continuation of Rhodes Drive up the avenue along the bottom of the slopes of the back of Table Mountain. The road is a scenic delight and leads through what is without doubt one of the most attractive residential areas to be found anywhere in the world – the green and fertile expanse of the lands of Van Riebeeck's old farm of *Boschheuwel* (bushy hill), now known more generally as *Bishopscourt*, after the official residence there of the Anglican archbishop of Cape Town.

Boschheuwel was laid out in the sheltered valley of the upper Liesbeek River. The south-eastern rise took the name of *Wynberg* from Van Riebeeck's farm vineyard. The valley is now covered with lovely homes. A drive through the estate is a thoroughly enjoyable diversion from the main route of Rhodes Drive. A very pleasant little road to explore is Boshof Avenue, the first turn-off to the right down Paradise Road. This road passes through the gates of the old Boshof Estate. Shaded by a fine avenue of oaks, it continues past many a handsome home including, on the right, the original *Boshof* homestead with the date 1776 on its gable. Further on is the beautiful and secluded *Fernwood* (now simply the pavilion of the Parliamentary sports club). In its commodious grounds is contained what is surely one of the most delightful cricket fields to be found anywhere in the world where the game is played.

After 2 km, just beyond the point where Rose Street, the continuation of Boshof Avenue, joins Rhodes Drive, the drive passes the entrance to Kirstenbosch, one of the most famous botanical gardens in the world.

KIRSTENBOSCH

Kirstenbosch was named apparently after Johan Frederick Kirsten, an official of the Dutch East India Company. The area of the garden was at first a woodcutters' post. Kirsten was a German who was the Dutch East India Company official resident in Simon's Town and the owner of considerable property in Constantia.

In 1811 the area of the future garden became the property of Henry Alexander, the Colonial Secretary in the British administration. He was quite an individualist. He built a homestead with windowless bedrooms, as he considered such rooms would only be used at night. This interesting establishment was unfortunately burned down and later replaced by a tea-room. This was also burned down and eventually replaced by the modern tea-room. Another interesting construction in 1811 was the exquisite sunken bath in one of the springs of the Liesbeek River. It was built by Colonel Christopher Bird, in the shape of a bird. It became known as Lady Anne Barnard's Bath in memory of that notable lady. Some visitor started the custom of throwing a coin into the bath and making a silent wish to Lady Anne. The men who service this bath of crystal-clear spring-water appreciate the custom.

Colonel Bird was the assistant secretary to Henry Alexander. On the death of Henry Alexander in 1895, Cecil Rhodes bought the whole of Kirstenbosch and presented it to the people of South Africa with the intention that it become the site of a botanical garden. In 1911 Professor Harold Pearson confirmed its suitability and in 1913 it was proclaimed as the Kirstenbosch National Botanical Gardens. Professor Pearson became its first director. The garden encompassed an area of 497 hectares, including the entire overlooking slopes and back summit of Table Mountain right up to the highest point, Maclear's Beacon at 1 066 metres. In this virgin area Professor Pearson set to work to make a home for the collection, preservation and study of the indigenous flora of Southern Africa. The success of his efforts is gloriously self-evident. Over 4 000 of the 18 000 species of the flora of Southern Africa are happily gathered there with an all-year-round display of flowers amidst a magnificent collection of shrubs, plants and trees. Professor Pearson died in 1916. His grave in the garden has a fitting epitaph:

'All ye who seek his monument look around.'

Pearson's successor was Professor R H Compton who, from 1919 to 1953, carefully guided the garden until it became one of the principal botanical gardens of the world. The headquarters and shop of the Botanical Society of South Africa are in the gardens. Nature-study instruction is given to parties of school children and the Compton Herbarium provides an ultimate authority in the identification and classification of the flora of Southern Africa.

From Kirstenbosch, Rhodes Avenue climbs the southern slopes of the Liesbeek Valley, providing changing views of the fashionable residential area of Bishopscourt. Reaching the top of the slope, it swings sharply right over the Boschheuwel at the junction with Klaassens Road which leads eastwards through the trees to the suburb of Wynberg. A portion of Van Riebeeck's hedge of wild almonds still flourishes on the left-hand side of the road. Where the hedge passes over the highest point of the Boschheuwel there stands a trigonometrical beacon and close to it the well-known granite landmark known as the Hen and Chickens. The 'hen', still sitting on her nest, has a survey beacon on her head marking the south-eastern corner of the Bishopscourt estate. Klaassens Road is the boundary between Bishopscourt on the north of the ridge and, on the south side, the estate of *Klaasensbosch*. In 1693, Hendrik ten Damme, chief surgeon to the Dutch East India Company, was granted 65 morgen of this forested land. He built a farmhouse and country retreat where he entertained and relaxed. His son Willem, who succeeded him as chief surgeon, was the man who built the cottage of *Paradijs* in the Newlands forest. He inherited *Klaasensbosch* in 1707 and during his lifetime it became a place known for its hospitality and sylvan setting. There his youngest daughter, Helena, was courted by Hendrik Swellengrebel who rose to become the first locally born man elevated to the rank of Governor. The town of Swellendam combines the names of this amiable couple. A succession of owners followed. Wine and timber were produced on the estate. Willem Ferdinand Versfeld who bought it in 1809 for 46 000 gulden, expanded the property to nearly 300 morgen. Vineyards steadily replaced forest and *Klaasensbosch* wine became well known.

The trouble with the estate was that it suffered from what was known as the 'Constantia Blight'. It was lovely but it didn't pay. When Versfeld died his estate was insolvent. Friends backed the son Jan Willem in a takeover in 1829. He died in 1871 and left a widow to face another invasion of debt collectors and sheriffs. Two of her sons pooled their resources and credit in order to buy the estate but fate was relentless, even if it took its own time.

In September 1906 Arnold Wilhelm Spilhaus bought the estate. The thatched farmhouse looked romantic but it was not for him. He had it demolished and in its place built a massive home in the style of his ancestors who had emigrated to the Cape from *Tiefenort* (the low-lying place) in Germany. The new building was named *Hohenort* (high place). It was large enough to be a hotel, and that is what it eventually became while the surrounding vineyards disappeared, as had the forest, and were replaced by housing.

Rhodes Avenue winds off along the north-western boundary of *Klaasensbosch* through an avenue of chestnut trees, planted by Rhodes because he liked their nuts. The chestnuts give way to a lovely tunnel formed by oak trees. This area was acquired by Cecil Rhodes in order to preserve its beauty and to build a scenic drive around the mountain slopes above the estate *Bel Ombre* all the way to Constantia Nek. The forest above the road is named *Cecilia* after Rhodes. As with the rest of the area it was a gift to South Africa from Rhodes. Through it wind several paths and tracks leading to such beauty spots as the Cecilia Waterfall, and up to the reservoirs on the back of Table Mountain.

In 1728 Jan Zacharius Beck and his brother Jan Christoffel were granted 60 morgen of virgin land which was named *Goedgeloof* (good trust) on the south side of *Klaasensbosch*. The estate passed through a succession of owners, including, in 1870, an English doctor, James Hutchinson, who gave the area its French name of *Bel Ombre* (beautiful shadows). He built a Victorian-style home next to the earlier farmhouse. Two years later he sold the property, by then enlarged to nearly 3 000 morgen, to Johannes Rathfelder, owner of the well-known Rathfelder's Inn by the wayside at Diep River. He and his son Otto made good wine on the estate but the pressures to fragment and sell the land for a select housing estate eventually proved too great. Today all that is left of the wine farm are the two houses still standing side by side.

Rhodes Avenue continues its way and 5 kilometres from its beginning reaches the end of its journey at the traffic circle on the summit of the divide over Constantia Nek. The avenue merges there with the road from Constantia to Hout Bay. Beneath the trees on the right, opposite the Constantia Nek restaurant, there is a parking area used by climbers and walkers exploring the Cecilia Forest and up to the back summit of Table Mountain. The road to Hout Bay descends through an avenue of oaks while on the eastern side the road makes a curving descent to the green and pleasant area of Constantia. It is this road which we will follow.

Half a kilometre down the eastern side from the summit of Constantia Nek, the main road passes on its left side a bus stop at a small parking place. From here there is a fine walk down the tree-covered valley known as *De Hel* (the abyss). This circular walk, down one side of the valley, across the stream at its bottom and back on the far side has rewarded countless walkers with the moderately strenuous pleasure of exploring an unspoilt example of a Cape ravine forest surviving from the past.

From the parking place at *De Hel*, the main road continues its curving descent through the tall trees. The road is now descending the south-east slopes of the mountain ridge of the Cape Peninsula and passing through the estate of *Witteboomen* (silver trees). This area in past years was one of the principal homes for these beautiful trees, *Leucadendron argenteum*, unique to the Cape Peninsula. A whole forest of these grew on the slopes. The spectacle of their silver-down coloured leaves glittering in the sunshine and the wind made several people think that perhaps real silver in the ground was the cause of this extraordinary colour.

Even the great Simon van der Stel searched for this lode of silver. He employed professional miners from Holland to prospect the area. In the ravine of *Witteboomen* they sank a shaft over 30 metres deep. Nothing of value was found, but the rivulet which flows through the property is still known as the Silvermyn Stream.

The first owner of the area was Lambert Symonsz in 1697. Simon van der Stel, however, obsessed with the search for silver, bought him out only a few days after the bemused man had secured what he thought would be a delightful place in which to live. Until Van der Stel's death, the area remained part of *Groot Constantia*. Then it was sold and the inevitable chain of owners, bankruptcies and forced sales followed. The record of these sales is interesting. At a sale in 1833 the slaves were the first to be sold. The most valuable, Abraham, a blacksmith, fetched 2 000 rix-dollars. Neptune, a Mozambican slave had absconded but was sold in absentia, with the buyer gambling on his apprehension. Ontang, from Batavia, asked if he could buy his own freedom. This was allowed. Nobody else bid for him as he was aged, so he bought himself for four stuyvers (about two cents).

The Van Helsdingen family owned the estate for over 100 years, which was an unusual span of family ownership. Perhaps the reason was their fertility. Jan Guillaum fathered 18 children, and with such a brood it was perhaps difficult to find any other place to go which had sufficient accommodation. In 1875 Willem Adriaan van der Byl bought the estate. His descendants may still be found there growing grapes and fruit. The original farmhouse has long since disappeared. The present manor-house is Georgian with some traces lingering from the earlier building.

The main road we are following leaves the area of *Witteboomen* and for the next kilometre continues south-eastwards forming the boundary line between the estates of *Silverhurst* on the left and *High Constantia* on the right.

High Constantia has an imposing manor-house of a design rather surprising to see in an area so essentially associated with Cape-Dutch architecture. The building looks as though it belongs to an illustration to a novel of Scotland by Sir Walter Scott. Its occupants are just as unusual in this setting of vineyards and cellars, for *High Constantia* is the home in the Cape for the religious order of the Schoenstatt Sisters of Mercy, founded in Germany in 1914 by Father Joseph Kentenich. This lay movement was dedicated to Mary, the Mother of Christ. Members are active in professions, working as doctors, social workers, teachers and nurses. The movement has retreats, and retirement and holiday homes for its members in several parts of the world. The buildings at *High Constantia* were not constructed by the religious movement. Originally there was just a simple thatched house built on a farm named *De Witte Boomen* (the silver trees) lying on the hill slopes immediately north of *Groot Constantia*. Who built this house and started the farm is unknown but in 1806 it was unoccupied. The British government then transferred it to William Duckitt as a reward for services in improving agriculture in the Cape Colony.

Duckitt was a professional agriculturist whose influence on the Cape was considerable. He was not over-impressed by Constantia's farming possibilities. Wine, to him, was a luxury while bread was the staff of life. The wheatlands north of the Cape Peninsula drew him away. In 1813 he bought a farm near Darling and moved there selling his estate in Constantia to Jacob van Reenen. Three of his children remained in the Constantia area, married to the then owners of *Groot Constantia*, *Klaasenbosch* and *Tokai*.

Jacob sold the largest portion of *De Witte Boomen* to his brother Sebastiaan in 1821 and to this portion was given the name *Sebastiaan's Hooge Constantia*, later simplified to the *Hooge* or *High Constantia* of today.

The Van Reenens aspired to rival *Groot Constantia* in the production of high-quality wines. To this purpose they planted their vineyards with Muscat de Frontinac and Pontac grapes. From these grapes they produced good wine but this did not save them from the blight of Constantia, bankruptcy. *High Constantia* passed through the hands of a succession of owners. In 1902 it was sold to Robertson Fuller Bertram who had made a fortune on the Witwatersrand gold-fields as a stockbroker, speculative land owner and developer. The suburb of Bertrams in Johannesburg is named after him. Abe Bailey (later 'Sir'), was his partner.

Bertram planned to retire at *High Constantia* and he intended to do it in style. First of all he set out to rebuild the farmhouse but it fell to pieces. The only thing was to pull it down. The new manor-house was planned on sumptuous lines. Money was no object. There was granite from Scotland, English oak, with a grand staircase carved in England and dominating an entrance hall fit for the reception of a king.

The Bertrams entertained celebrities and aristocrats. The Prince of Wales once danced all night there. Musicians, actors and actresses enjoyed the Constantia hospitality. Because the guests were such a thirsty lot, Bertram is said to have decided to start making his own wine. In association with a professional wine-maker, Walter Stokes, he founded Bertrams Wines, producing a variety of alcoholic drinks, including liqueurs such as the traditional Van der Hum.

Where did all the fine wines and glamorous guests go, and all the fortune made on the Witwatersrand? Bertram went bankrupt. It was a classic case of the dread Constantia Blight. He died a very sad man in 1942. His wife and son died shortly afterwards. *High Constantia* fell under the auctioneer's hammer but the imposing mansion was difficult to sell. The farmlands were separated from the house and sold in sections. Somebody tried to turn the house into a hotel but the building wasn't too suitable for the purpose. The usual quick succession of owners followed. Then, in 1957 it was sold to the Schoenstadt Sisters of Mary who remain there today.

The estate of *Silverhurst*, opposite *High Constantia* on the main road, was at first named *Frankengift* when the 27 morgen area was purchased in 1716 by Johannes Franke from the estate of Simon van der Stel. Franke was a German shoemaker who had done reasonably well for himself in Cape Town. With his wife Catharina he settled down on his Constantia property, raised 11 children there and, by all accounts, was well satisfied with life.

The Constantia Blight only set in when the last of Franke's three children who had inherited the estate died. The almost inevitable succession of owners followed the auction of the property. In 1812 alone, the property changed hands three times in three weeks. With the disappearance of the Frankes from the estate, the name was changed to *New Constantia*. The farmhouse built by Franke was also changed in particular detail while the name of *Silverhurst* was given to the estate (because of the silver trees growing there,) by a Scott, William Gilmour and his wife, who acquired the estate in modern times.

Flowers and bulbs are grown at *Silverhurst* today but memories of the wine-making past, especially of its port, linger on. The slave bell dated 1815 stands quiet but remindful of the labours of the past. Across the main road from the entrance to *Silverhurst*, 3 km from the divide where Rhodes Avenue ended, there is a small cluster of shops, including the well-known *Old Cape Farm Stall*. From here a short approach road leads to the manor-house of the estate of *Groot Constantia* created by the renowned governor Simon van der Stel. In Chapter Two of this book the story has been told of the beginning of this estate and of its fragmentation when Van der Stel died in 1712. In 1778 Hendrik Cloete of *Nooitgedacht* farm in Stellenbosch bought the portion of the estate on which stood the manor-house and gave it to his son, also named Hendrik. The Cloete family who have been so intimately a part of the history of Constantia, came to the Cape with Jan van Riebeeck. Jacob Cloeten was a mercenary soldier from Cologne in Germany. In the Cape they became known by the name of Cloete. They were amongst the first of the free burghers settled on the banks of the Liesbeek River at Ecklenburg in present Rondebosch. From there they moved to the Stellenbosch area, obtaining the farm of *Nooitgedacht*.

The new owner of Constantia found the place half in ruin. He set to work with a will on restoration. A handsome new cellar was built, said to have been designed by the French architect, Louis Thibault. The sculptor, Anton Anreith, a friend of Cloete, gave him as a gift the famous pediment. The manor-house was almost completely rebuilt, converted from a double-storeyed building to its Cape-Dutch style elegance of today. The vineyard had been as much neglected as the house. Cloete planted 10 000 new vines and launched a programme of searching for the ideal cultivar for the area. A relative of Cloete, Johannes Colyn, had married a widow who owned *de Hoop op Constantia* (the hope of Constantia), a fragment of the original estate. Colyn had already commenced a systematic testing of each of the soil types and climatic micro-areas on this property. He and Cloete shared results and the same ambition to establish the Constantia area as a world leader in wine. They succeeded brilliantly, producing on their sections of the original estate two of the most celebrated of all wines – the legendary red and white Constantia wines.

The two men left no details of the making of these wines. Laboratory tests of the contents of a few surviving bottles found in the cellars of such collectors as the Duke of Northumberland reveal that it was a natural, unfortified wine. It had an alcoholic content of 13,42 per cent in the red, 15,01 per cent in the white and a sugar content in both of about 128 grams per litre. The flavour was that of a luscious raisin-like liqueur, with a subtle aroma. The two wines were a drink for the gods as well as for ordinary mortals. They were carried all over the world, and eulogised in the writings of many celebrated authors. Charles Dickens wrote in *The Mystery of Edwin Drood* of *'the support embodied in a glass of Constantia and a home made biscuit'*. Jane Austin in *Sense and Sensibility* advised her heroine Elinor Dashwood to try a glass of Constantia for it had *'healing powers on a disappointed heart'*. Alexander Dumas and Henry Longfellow and many others wrote fondly of these wines. Baudelaire, in his poem – *Les Fleurs du Mal* wrote *'Even more than Constantia, than opium, than Nuits I prefer the elixir of your mouth'*. They were sipped with appreciation by the captains and the kings. Princess Alice of Athlone liked to reminisce that her grandmother, Queen Victoria, drank a man-sized glass of Constantia wine every evening after dinner. Frederick the Great, Bismarck, the Kings of Holland, France and Britain drank the wine and beguiled their guests at state banquets with its taste and fragrance. Napoleon, in his exile on St Helena Island, found solace in drinking a bottle a day. On his deathbed the last thing he asked for was a glass of Constantia.

Strangely enough, the production of this and other wines was made possible in the Cape by the presence over the vineyards of a remarkable bird. Each year in November the steppe buzzards of Russia escape the approaching Siberian winter by migrating across Africa to the Cape. Until the end of March these raptors keep guard over the Cape vineyards, gliding, wheeling and coursing incessantly, killing or driving away the fruit-eating birds such as the starlings which are capable of destroying an entire harvest. The buzzards do not eat grapes themselves. By the time they return to Siberia, the grapes have been safely harvested and the wine is maturing in the cellars.

What happened to the two Constantia wines, the most celebrated wines ever made in Southern Africa? Henry Cloete, fourth generation of the Cloetes to own *Groot Constantia*, was not much interested in a farming life. He liked France and spent most of his time there. He returned to *Groot Constantia* in 1885 to find the estate in ruins with the vineyards destroyed by the fungal disease *oidium* and the root parasite *phylloxera*. He sold the farm at a public auction. It was bought by the Cape government and converted to a training and experimental farm under the direction of a German viticulturist, Baron Carl von Babow who knew nothing of the two celebrated old wines.

The South African government took over the estate in the early 1960s. In 1976 the estate was transferred to the Groot Constantia Control Board who, although still government owned ran it as a viable commercial wine producer.

In 1993 ownership of the Estate was again transferred, this time from the government to the Groot Constantia Trust, an article 21 company. The main objective of the company is to take the Groot Constantia Estate into trust, to fund it and commercially run it in all facets in order to promote and preserve it as a cultural historical monument, as an educational asset and as a wine producing estate. Today, a range of fourteen estate wines are produced and sold on the estate from 10h00 to 17h00 daily, except Good Friday, Christmas Day and New Year's Day. Tours of the cellar are conducted on the hour between 10h00 and 16h00. The historic farmyard, which includes the famous manor-house, Jonkershuis complex and beautiful Cloete cellar is open for visitors. Some leisurely walks under oak lined avenues may be enjoyed with a lovely ornamented bath a short walk from the manor-house. Furthermore the Estate offers two restaurants where the estate wines may be enjoyed as a pleasant accompaniment to good food, including traditional Cape cuisine. Vineyards have been established to produce the famed Constantia wines of yesteryear.

From the entrance to *Groot Constantia*, the main road continues through the residential area, past the Constantia Village shopping centre and, after 3 km, reaches the Alphen interchange with the Simon van der Stel freeway. Below the interchange the road continues to reach the suburbs of Wynberg and Plumstead; a turn right would take the traveller southwards to the end of the Peninsula. A left turn leads back to Cape Town. Just before this interchange there is a turn left of the Alphen road which leads past the Alphen Hotel and then into the residential area of Alphen and on to Hohenort and Constantia Heights. This area was originally the *Alphen* farm lying on the south side of the wine mountains of Wynberg. The farm, named after a village in the Netherlands, was granted to Theunis van Schalkwyk in 1714. The manor-house was built on it in 1753 by Abraham Leever, known as the Monsieur from Amsterdam, who bought the estate in 1748. The house is in the Cape-Dutch style but unusual in that it was double-storeyed, the upper floor supported on massive walls, insulating it from the extremes of heat and cold. Tall windows and high-beamed ceilings ensure ventilation from the winds of the Cape. The front and rear parts of the house are divided by a superb screen of yellowwood and stinkwood. The teak front door has a baroque carving and is painted to simulate marble. The house faces a large oak-shaded square with, on its sides, two cellars in Cape-Dutch style, a Victorian double-storey block known as the Dower House, and the Jonkershuis, probably the first building on the farm. It now houses the atmospheric *Boer 'n Brit* pub.

In 1801 *Alphen* was bought by Thomas Frederick Dreyer, a great friend of Lord Charles Somerset, Governor of the Cape. Lord Charles and Mr Dreyer were lovers of horses and hunting. *Alphen* became the base for the Constantia Hunt, complete with all its social trimmings of balls, dinners and entertainments. The Governor was a frequent visitor to *Alphen* and with him came that remarkable and enigmatic individual, Dr James Miranda Stuart Barry, whose portrait, a copy of the only one known, graces the sitting room of *Alphen* today.

Dr Barry was born around 1790 of unknown parentage. He was brought up by two individuals he always referred to as his uncle and aunt, the Royal Academician James Barry and his sister Mrs Mary Anne Bulkerley. James Barry died in 1806, a distinguished artist. Two of his patrons, General Francisco de Miranda, and David Stuart Erskine, the Earl of Buchan, took an interest in the youth and in 1809 Mrs Bulkerley took him to Edinburgh where he entered the university and studied medicine, graduating as a doctor in 1812. His thesis was dedicated to his two patrons. After them he derived two of his three first names, the first and his surname, coming from his 'uncle'.

In October 1812, young Dr Barry entered the United Hospitals (Guys and St Thomas's) in London and there qualified as a regimental surgeon. In this capacity he served in Plymouth and London and then was posted to Cape Town, arriving there on 1 August 1816 at the beginning of a remarkable career. Lord Charles Somerset was the Governor of the Cape at that time and Barry had a letter of introduction to him from the Earl of Buchan. Barry, apart from his regimental duties, was appointed physician to the Governor's family.

In appearance Dr Barry was small in stature, red haired with a rather high-pitched voice, prominent eyes, no hair on face and hands, and a notably effeminate disposition, manner, appearance and gait. There were rumours that Dr Barry was really a female but, of whatever sex, there was no doubting the competence of the individual as a surgeon. In 1819 Barry was ordered to Mauritius to deal with an epidemic of cholera. Back in the Cape in 1822 Barry was appointed colonial medical inspector. On 25 July 1826 he made medical history when he delivered the wife of T C Munnik of a son by the first successful Caesarean operation in Southern Africa. The grateful parents named their son James Barry Munnik. Years later these three names were given as Christian names to a godson of James Barry Munnik. This infant, James Barry Munnik Hertzog, became prime minister of South Africa.

Dr Barry could be brusque and even offensive in his speech. He made enemies of powerful officials by his insistence on more humane treatment of convicts, lepers and the outcasts on Robben Island and the old leper colony at *Hemel-en-Aarde*. He stopped unqualified persons from acting as doctors and clashed several times with the fiscal over the appalling conditions in the Cape Town jail. In June 1824 placards were posted overnight in the streets alleging an unnatural relationship between Dr Barry and the Governor. Notwithstanding the offer of a reward of 5 000 rixdollars nobody was apprehended for the scurrilous attack.

Dr Barry regarded *Alphen* as something of a home from home and he showed considerable interest in one of the winsome daughters of Mr Dreyer, who had fourteen children. Josias Cloete was also attracted by the young lady and the two fought a formal duel over her on the back steps of the manor-house. Neither of the contestants was injured. They shook hands and became the firmest of friends. What Miss Dreyer thought of the proceedings it would be interesting to know. Miss Dreyer eventually married Johan Gerhard Cloete of *Buitenverwachting*. Josias Cloete was an officer in the British army. He was promoted to the military command of Barbados in the Caribbean and married Anna Lewis, the daughter of the governor.

Dr Barry continued his career in the Cape. The feud with the authorities became more bitter. In 1824 he found a man named Elliot in the jail, lying filthy and verminous, without bed, pillows, blankets or any comfort, and with a broken leg. When the jailer was asked if there were any other prisoners with broken bones, he replied *'Only one'*. He showed Barry a convict from Robben Island, Jan Kiser, who had one leg fractured and the other surrounded by a heavy chain. The climax came when Dr Barry ordered a mentally deranged man to be treated in hospital and not simply thrown into the asylum. Barry stated that the man's state might be *'the result of bad treatment he had received in the jail'*. This criticism really upset the apple cart of the fiscal.

Barry was summoned to give evidence on 15 September 1825. He refused to take the oath or to answer questions. He was ordered to be imprisoned for one month for contempt of court. The Governor then intervened and overruled the sentence. Barry remained stubbornly persistent in his criticism of conditions. On 12 January 1826 he resigned all his official appointments. Public esteem for him was high but the administrative officials hated him. To settle what was becoming an awkward situation, he was promoted to staff surgeon and in 1828 transferred to Mauritius.

Promotions and transfers followed in steady succession, the West Indies, St Helena, Malta, deputy inspector of hospitals stationed at Corfu, and in 1858 to one of the highest medical ranks in the British Army, inspector-general stationed in Canada. There his health broke down. He was used to living in warmer climates. Bronchitis and influenza forced him to retire in 1859. He returned to London and died on 15 July 1865. Rumours about the sex of Dr Barry had intrigued so many people that the military authorities ordered an examination of the corpse. The person who laid out the body stated that Barry was a woman and, moreover, had given birth. To finally settle the mystery, the army surgeons reported to the register-general of Somerset House that Dr Barry was *'neither male nor female, but rather an imperfectly developed man'*. There was no evidence to support the story that as a woman she had given birth. Dr Barry, she or he, died still an enigma.

The Cloetes were a fruitful family. Jacob's great-grandson Hendrik had nine sons one of whom, also named Hendrik, was given Van der Stel's old farm by his father. Another son was Dirk, who remained farming on *Nooitgedacht*. His grandson, also named Dirk, was the Cloete who acquired *Alphen* in 1850. It is said that Dirk married a wealthy woman from Holland. She did not much like the country life at Stellenbosch. One day she returned from a visit to Cape Town to see relatives at *Groot Constantia*. She firmly informed her husband that she had bought a house near *Groot Constantia* and intended moving there. When he went to see the place, it was found that it was not only the magnificent *Alphen* manor-house but about half of the Constantia valley and most of the southern slopes of Wynberg.

The house was already well furnished but to it the Cloetes took many of their own treasures, including a magnificent 17th century kist which had contained the family effects from Europe when they sailed with Van Riebeeck. The new owners settled in and Dirk commenced a programme of planting vines. One of his sons, Louis, was sent to France to study wine-making. On his return he built the great cellar, renovated the manor-house, and started making wine.

The oldest son, Henry, inherited the estate but he was an advocate in Johannesburg and he left the running of *Alphen* to his younger brother, Louis. In the difficult political period leading to the Anglo-Boer war, Henry was pro-British. He served as British agent in Pretoria when the British diplomatic mission was withdrawn. When the war was imminent, Henry returned to stay in *Alphen* until peace came. With him came his wife Christina Deliana, daughter of Nicholaas van Warmelo who had brought the Nederduitse Hervormde Kerk to South Africa from Holland. She was very pro-Boer in the conflict and, unknown to her husband, set up a spy network based on *Alphen*. It was an excellent base, a great resort of high-ranking British officers such as Lord Kitchener and Lord Roberts. She found eavesdropping on their after-dinner conversations particularly informative. This information she placed in a hollow oak on the farm, where it was collected by undercover couriers and conveyed to Pretoria concealed in cases with false bottoms and hand-made dolls with hollow porcelain heads.

Apart from her espionage work, Mrs Cloete performed her wifely duties. She had four daughters and then at last came the longed-for son. Henry threw a great dinner to celebrate the birth of his heir. At the height of proceedings the nurse rushed in asking for a little brandy for the baby. There were roars of laughter from the guests and comments about a young chip off the old block. The next morning, however, the baby was dead.

Henry bequeathed *Alphen* to the eldest grandson produced by any of his daughters, on condition that the heir took the name of Cloete. Nicolette, wife of Hugh Bainsfather, produced this heir, christened Peter. An outstanding young man who played both rugby and cricket for Western Province, he was engaged to General Smut's adopted daughter, Kay. He became ADC to General Dan Pienaar in the Second World War. Flying back from Cairo, he and the general were killed when their aircraft crashed into Lake Victoria. His younger brother Sandy then inherited *Alphen* and changed his surname to Cloete. He was only 23 years old when he inherited *Alphen*. Confronted by heavy death duties, he was forced to sell off the bulk of the estate, leaving, by 1961 only the manor-house and 11 surrounding acres. With farming no longer viable, he and his second wife, Elsabe Turkstra, whose family then owned the Vineyard Hotel, decided to turn *Alphen* into a hotel. When he died in 1982 his eldest child, Nicolette, married to Dudley Hopkins, inherited one of the finest and most elegant hotels in Southern Africa.

THE CONSTANTIA WINE ROUTE

Groot Constantia, with its manor-house, cellars and vineyards, is the classic wine estate of the Cape. It is hospitable and proud to display its treasures to visitors. It is a provider of good food and fresh grapes, especially of the muscatel varieties, picked and sold from February to June. Wine of course is available throughout the year, in several varieties and vintages, its cellars open for inspection and the sale of their contents direct to the public. If no other of the great wine estates in the Cape are visited, *Groot Constantia* must not be missed. It is a unique part of the history of the people of South Africa.

Several other parts of the fragmented original *Groot Constantia* estate of Simon van der Stel are also open to visitors. A tour through the Constantia Wine Route, as it is known, is very rewarding, full of beguiling scenes and interest. Start this journey from the entrance to the *Groot Constantia* estate on the main Constantia–Hout Bay road. A kilometre down this road, just before it reaches the Constantia Village Centre, turn right at a traffic light into an oak-shaded street known as Ladies Mile and Ladies Mile Extension. Follow this road for one kilometre until it reaches another traffic light where it crosses the road named after the *Spaanschemat* (Spanish rushes) River.

The Ladies Mile road leads over the Simon van der Stel freeway and then continues for two kilometres until it ends by joining the lower main road. The Ladies Mile passes through a completely built-up area. In 1714 this was one of the three divisions of *Groot Constantia* sold at auction. The buyer, Pieter de Meyer, was simply the first of the real-estate speculators to pounce and feed on the recumbent estate of Simon van der Stel. Within days of his purchase, he resold

620 morgen of his purchase to Jan Brommert who then owned *Alphen*. Brommert sold *Alphen* to raise the money to pay for what was named *Bergvliet* (mountain stream) and started to develop it as a large farm. Unfortunately he died a short while later and *Bergvliet* passed into the hands of several successive owners.

Peter de Meyer had sold the second division of *Groot Constantia* which he had purchased to J J Kotze. This division was originally part of Van der Stel's estate known as *Klein* or *Petit Constantia*. The deed of sale included several provisions such as right of way over the *Bergvliet* estate, which were destined to provide considerable profit to legal luminaries. Kotze died soon after purchasing his land from Peter de Meyer. His widow Elsabe then married Johannes Colyn, grandson of Evert and Anne of Guinea, two well-known freed slaves who had made their home in Cape Town.

Johannes Colyn started to make wine on *Klein Constantia*, and it was good wine. His wife died and he was married again, this time to Johanna Appel whose mother was a member of the influential Cloete family.

In 1776 Johannes Nicolaas Colyn, tenth son of the family, acquired the farm. It was known as *de Hoop van Constantia* (the hope of Constantia). In order to settle estates, it was customary for all properties and assets to be sold at auction so that each member of the family could receive their proper share. If one of them wanted the whole estate he had to bid for it. To secure the property the bidder generally had to borrow money and carry with him a partnership of money-lenders and the instability of fluctuating interest rates and sleeping partners whose rapacity for profit was notorious. In this way Johannes Nicolaas junior secured the estate and, with his wife Anna Marie Auret, settled into producing wine and children. Their first son, Lambertus Johannes, was baptised five months after the wedding. This was not considered unduly hasty at the time. Lady Anne Barnard tells us that *'brides generally lay in with fine boys two months after marriage'*. When she remarked to a Dutch friend that this was perhaps a little early, the reply, with a twinkle, was *'not at all madam, the babies come exactly at the proper time but perhaps the marriages take place a little late'*. With some of the families, the wife was almost continuously pregnant for the first fifteen to twenty years of marriage. The parents found it impossible to remember the names of all their offspring and could only raise them with the aid of slave nursemaids.

In 1778, two years after Johannes Colyn took over *de Hoop van Constantia*, Hendrik Cloete acquired *Groot Constantia*. The two men appreciated their relationship. They became friends and colleagues in the making of wines, with remarkable results already told.

The eldest son of Nicolaas, Lambertus, succeeded his father in possession of *de Hoop van Constantia*. His wife was Leonora who eventually inherited from him considerable wealth. One of her sons lived on *Nova Constantia*; for another she built a house called *Sweet Valley* and this started the 'battle' of Constantia with the then owner of *Bergvliet*, Hendrik Oostwald Eksteen.

The Eksteen family had acquired the *Bergvliet* farm in 1769. Petrus Michiel Eksteen bought the property from the estate of the late Nicolaas Schott. Eksteen was a well-to-do man of German descent, married to Sophia Cloete, sister of the famed Hendrik Cloete of *Constantia*. Eksteen built the fine manor-house of *Bergvliet* as an addition to the existing buildings. With his wife he lived there in some style while he developed the farm to a considerable industry. It was a well-watered estate. Near the manor-house there was a pretty little lake known as *De Oog* (the eye), fed by a perennial spring, The *bergvliet* (mountain stream) which gave the name of *Bergvliet* to the estate, the Spaanschemat River, flowed in the shallow valley just below (west) of the manor-house. The construction of the modern Simon van der Stel freeway has displaced the river more to the west.

Petrus died in 1783. His son Hendrik Oostwald Eksteen bought the farm for 90 000 guldens. His brothers and sisters received their share of the inheritance while he and his wife Elizabeth Scholtz moved into the manor-house. Everything looked fine for the future of the couple and the estate.

When the British occupied the Cape in 1795, they found *Bergvliet* to be in a very prosperous condition. The owner, however, was a supporter of current French revolutionary ideals. This made him very suspect by the conservative British who regarded ideas of liberty, equality and fraternity as akin to the pox. Thus, when Mr Eksteen sent out invitations to his daughter's wedding at *Bergvliet* and addressed them to Citizen so-and-so, Lord Macartney sent a party of rough-and-ready dragoons to arrive on the scene at the height of festivities, shoulder their way into the food and devour it with the manners of a pride of lions. The practice of 'quartering' dragoons on to persons of known sympathies to revolutionary ideals became common. Feeding and accommodating such rowdy men subdued many farmhouses in the Cape, with young women sent far away for safety.

A climax came in the story of *Bergvliet* when the wealthy widow, Leanora Colyn of *de Hoop op Constantia*, built a house as a present for one of her sons on a portion of the original *Bergvliet* which she had purchased. She called it *Sweet Valley*. This farm lay on the south side of *Bergvliet* and was reached by a rough farm road crossing part of Bergvliet. When the Colyn family had bought *de Hoop op Constantia*, the original deed of sale dividing the property from *Bergvliet* gave the owners of *de Hoop op Constantia* rights in perpetuity to the use of this and other roads.

Hendrik Oostwald Eksteen didn't like the widow Colyn and she didn't care a fig for him. They disagreed in politics and practically everything else. She deliberately made full and flamboyant use of her right of way on the road across *Bergvliet*, galloping backwards and forwards each day to see her son, and sending wagons and carts to convey building materials for the new house and bring back thatching material for her own home. Eksteen seethed with rage. One day he put his slaves to work digging a deep ditch directly across the road. Leonora Colyn promptly appealed to the court and judgement was against Eksteen.

Thus began the so-called 'battle of Constantia'. It was a lawyer's delight, two wealthy people determined to fight each other to the bitter end no matter the cost. Advocates were briefed. The judge tried to persuade an out-of-court settlement but the contestants were adamant. Advocate Olaf Bergh, for Eksteen, pleaded that the deed of sale gave the widow rights to use the paths and roads of *Bergvliet* but not to go across it. Advocate Johannes Truter, for Leonora Colyn, responded that Eksteen, in personal pique, was simply trying to deny a right which had been enjoyed without argument for a hundred years.

Eksteen won the case. The widow appealed to the King in Council, the first time this had been done by a resident of the Cape. In 1827 His Majesty ruled in favour of Leonora Colyn. 'Ladies Mile', the road which runs through *Bergvliet*, was thenceforth named after this celebrated and costly squabble. It proved to be the ruination of Eksteen. Costs were awarded against him. They were murderous and he went insolvent. A nephew, Johannes Paulus Eksteen, bought the estate. In 1841 he sold off a substantial portion of the ground, now known as *Firgrove* and then in 1863, the rest of the farm to Willem Hertzog.

So far as Leonora, the redoubtable lady of the Ladies Mile was concerned, she died in 1839. Her son, Johannes Nicolaas, inherited *de Hoop op Constantia* while Lambertus Johannes got *Nova Constantia*. Johannes Nicolaas ran into hard times and went insolvent in 1857. *De Hoop op Constantia* was sold to John Robert Thompson. Eight other owners followed one another in possession of the estate. It was a time of the phylloxera disease and the vineyards were dead.

In 1881 Daniel Gerhardus Malan bought *de Hoop op Constantia* but was killed shortly afterwards when his wagon overturned. His widow Deborah Suzanna ran the farm with the aid of her eldest son Johannes who eventually inherited it. When he died the farm was, in 1942, sold to Solomon and Fanny Hirshfield. The manor-house became a museum and showplace of the Constantia area but its maintenance was costly. In 1961 a forced sale took place. The manor-house fell into near-ruin and the property was in danger of collapsing into the hands of developers.

Fortunately the Board of Management of *Groot Constantia* intervened. They bought the manor-house and the remaining thirteen hectares of ground and this was returned to *Groot Constantia*. The rest of *de Hoop op Constantia* estate is lost under housing development. But at least a little was saved.

To discover the fate of the other portions of the original *Constantia* estate, let us go back to the crossroads where Ladies Mile extension crosses the Spaanschemat River road. From this point, instead of continuing straight, turn right down this road. After another kilometre the road diverges left slightly, while the Klein Constantia road branches off diagonally on the right. For an all-too-short 3 km this road leads through trees and past gardens of flowers. The estate known as *de Hoop op Constantia* lies on the right with a glimpse of its lovely manor-house peeping through the trees. Passing a turn-off to the left leading to the estate of *Buitenverwachting*, the road enters the grounds of *Klein Constantia*.

By the side of a stream at the entrance to this estate there stands a neatly domed *kramat*, the tomb of the venerated Sheik Abdurachmau Matebe Shah. With two other political prisoners of high rank he was banished in 1668 to the Cape during the Dutch conquest of Indonesia. The three men were brought to the Cape in chains on the ship *Polsbroek*. One was sent to Robben Island, the other two spent the rest of their lives in Constantia, meditating and introducing to Islam the slaves working on the farms. Sheik Abdurachmau died in about 1681 on the site of his tomb while his companion Sheik Mahmoud was buried on Islam Hill a few kilometres away on the Spaanschemat River road.

Klein Constantia was part of Simon van der Stel's original estate of *Groot Constantia*. When Hendrik Cloete acquired the estate in 1772 and set out to revive its sagging agricultural industry, he soon discovered that some of the best wine-producing grapes flourished on this portion of *Constantia* and on the adjoining portion of *de Hoop op Constantia*. Both areas came under considerable cultivation of the grape varieties, Pontac and Muscat de Frontinac, used in the production of the famous red and white Constantia wines. There was no manor-house on *Klein Constantia* then, but on a particularly pleasant site, Cloete planted a grove of oak trees close to a mountain stream which was directed to feed a dam. A secluded guest-house was built in this pleasant area and named *Marlbrook*, the popular name of the renowned British general, the Duke of Marlborough whose powerful support put on the throne of England, William of Orange, defender of the Protestant faith. Both men were much admired by Hendrik Cloete. The death of Hendrik Cloete brought a decline in the fortune of *Groot Constantia* from the golden years of the production of the famed Constantia wines. His widow, Anna Catharina, had the task of controlling what seemed like a Cloete tribe of children and grandchildren. Fortunately she was a tough matriarch who seemed to revel in incessant family feuds. One of her sons, Johan Gerhard, in 1819, bought the 195 ha portion of the old estate known as *Klein Constantia*. He built the manor-house but failed to achieve notable success in farming. He sold the estate in 1840 to Abraham Brunt, and the game commenced of speculators buying and selling. One other Cloete, Dirk Gysbert, bought it in 1870 but went bankrupt three years later.

A succession of owners followed, most leaving *Klein Constantia* in a slightly worse state than when they acquired it. Some tried their best, but for so beautiful a place there seemed to be a blight. The Van der Byl family had it from 1890 to 1909. During this period the pioneer fruit nurseryman, Harry Pickstone, rented *Marlbrook* and planted there experimental orchards of fruit and beds of strawberries. In 1913, however, *Klein Constantia* was acquired by a couple who at least gave it some renown in the social life of the Cape. The couple were Mr and Mrs Abraham Lochner de Villiers. He had been a milliner in Paarl and was nicknamed *'La Mode'* from the name of his shop. He saved enough money from his business to take a holiday in Europe. Before departing he jocularly told his friends that he intended marrying a millionairess. He did. Clara Hussey, whose money came from the Pittsburgh steel mills, was the lady.

Back in the Cape the millinery shop was soon sold. Clara purchased *Klein Constantia* and with her husband set out to convert the somewhat run-down manor-house into a romantic scene of parties, balls, banquets, fun and games and all manner of social occasions. Some farming was also undertaken but not much.

Clara made spacious additions to the manor-house, including a chapel, a ballroom with a gallery for an orchestra and a swimming-pool renowned for what the servants discreetly described as 'moonlight frolics'. Clara often had 600 guests at her all-night parties, sometimes inviting all passengers and officers of passing cruise-liners to join in a grand jollification. A ghostly whisper of giggling and the popping of champagne corks is still said to be heard from the swimming-pool on some warm summer nights. The couple had no children. Lochner died in 1930 aged 61. Clara was four years older than him but she lived to the ripe age of 90 before dying in 1955. Jan de Villiers, nephew of Lochner, inherited the estate but he had insufficient finance to run the place. In 1963 he sold it to Ian Austin.

In 1980 Douglas Jooste, after the merger of his family-owned company, Sedgwick Tayler, with Stellenbosch Farmers' Winery, bought *Klein Constantia*. He set out to revive its capability of producing fine wines. One of his dreams was to recreate at least one of the two legendary Constantia wines of the days of Hendrik Cloete. Supported by the advice of Professor Chris Orffes, the authority on wine varieties, the viticulturist Ernst le Roux, the master wine-maker Ross Gower, and his own enthusiastic son Lowell, he commenced a ten-year period of experimentation.

All that was certain was that some unspecified areas of the estate had produced the grapes needed in producing the two Constantia wines, Muscat de Frontinac for the white and Pontac for the red wine. Both these cultivars had fallen out of favour in Cape viticulture but some relics of the original vines were found still growing where Van der Stel or Cloete had planted them. These were cloned and a vineyard planted of Muscat de Frontinac. The steppe buzzards then obliged by doing their job as guardians. The ripening grapes were selectively pruned by almost 50% and the remaining berries were left to a slow ripening until they had the appearance almost of shrivelled raisins with a taste like honey gathered by bees from the wild flowers and aromatic shrubs of the Cape. The first harvest was picked and crushed in 1986 and the young wine put into wood for a leisurely period of reflection and maturation. To the winemakers this was the most difficult part of the operation, as Ross Gower said, *'waiting for it, just waiting for it'*.

In 1989 the first bottle was opened and they tasted it. Was it exactly the same as the famed Constantia white wine of the past days? It is impossible to know. Taste it yourself. *Vin de Constance*, as it is named, has a luscious sweetness, a lingering fragrance of the Cape mountains, a taste which could only come from a combination of the soils, winds and lush vegetation of the floral kingdom of the Cape. The great experiment has now started with a vineyard planted with Pontac grapes. The objective is a red *Vin de Constance*.

The neighbouring estate to *Klein Constantia* is *Buitenverwachting*. It is reached by a turn-off from the Klein Constantia road a little less than one kilometre before it enters the *Klein Constantia* estate. From this turn-off it is one kilometre to the manor-house, cellars and restaurant.

The estate of *Buitenverwachting* (beyond expectations) with its *werf* (farmyard) in a magnificent garden setting has had, for so lovely a place, a curious history of disappointment. Originally the area was part of the estate of *Bergvliet*, itself a portion of *Groot Constantia*. In 1793 Hendrik Oostwaald Eksteen, owner of *Bergvliet*, sold 200 morgen of the estate to Cornelis Brink who sold most of it to his brother Arend in 1794.

Arend Brink gave his estate its name in 1796 and built the manor-house. He planted vines and had high hopes of fortune but beauty is sometimes treacherous. A cheque-book farmer can only last as long as his bank balance. In 1797 Brink sold the farm to Ryk Arnoldus Mauritius Cloete, a brother of Hendrik Cloete of *Groot Constantia*. Ryk was a lot different from Hendrik. His farming industry seemed to consist principally of borrowing money and speculating in slaves. He bought, sold, long-term leased and short-term hired human beings. He lived too well on the proceeds. Ryk Cloete went bankrupt. He moved to the family refuge of *Marlbrook* and left the mess to a liquidator to handle. The whole property and all its chattels was auctioned off and sold to another Cloete (Pieter Lourens). Of the roster of slaves it is interesting to see that their value ranged around 350 rixdollars for a skilled worker. The lowest was six rixdollars for a three-year-old boy who was bought by a free maid, Betjie by name, who bid from the crowd and, it is hoped, had the sympathy of the assembly who failed to run up the price, realising that the woman only had six rixdollars to her name and wanted to possess what was apparently her son.

Over the following years seventeen successive owners attempted to farm the estate with little success and several bankruptcies. One of the owners, Pieter Lourens Cloete, went so far as to change the name of the estate to *Plumstead* in the hope that this would bring better luck. It didn't, not to him.

In 1981, Richard Müller bought the estate and began a comprehensive programme of realising at last its potential as a producer of fine wine. In the midst of a considerable investment in capital and creativity, the new owner, however, found himself in an awkward position. It was the time of the so-called 'Cold War'. Richard Müller was accused of complicity in supplying the Soviet Union with high-tech computers. He found it expedient to leave South Africa and make his home in East Europe, continuing his projects on *Buitenverwachting* through a management trust. The work continued with complex three-directional ploughing. The clay and the top soils were mixed to a depth of one metre. This ensured that moisture be maintained in the soil and provided the depth necessary for root development. It was the intention that natural rainfall would be the sole source of moisture. Organic farming techniques were introduced with no artificial fertilisers, herbicides or pesticides.

In May 1989, Richard Müller's wife, Sieglinde, took over the estate from the trust and ambitious development continued under her direct management. Today the modern state-of-the-art cellar produces a range of fine wines. Visitors are welcome. There are tours, tastings and direct sale of wine to visitors during normal business hours. A considerable dairy industry also takes place on the estate and there is a restaurant of high repute. It is interesting to see that a small block of hanepoot table grapes, about 100 years old, has been left in the midst of the modern cultivars and still rewards the owner for continued life by yielding great bunches of delicious grapes.

Half a kilometre before the turn to *Buitenverwachting* on the Klein Constantia road, there is a turn to *Nova Constantia*. This was part of the estate of *Bergvliet*, sold in 1793 to Cornelis Brink, who promptly sold most of it, 172 morgen, to his brother Arend who used it to form the estate of *Buitenverwachting*. The remaining 28 morgen were sold to Hendrik Christian Carinus. He died and his widow sold the area to Lambertus Johannes Colyn, owner of the neighbouring *de Hoop op Constantia*. He built the manor-house, a charming example of the Cape-Dutch style and gave it the name of *Nova Constantia* (New Constantia). The manor-house is still there, handsomely restored by the Tupperware Company who bought it in 1972 to serve as their administration head office in Southern Africa. The rest of the estate has been fragmented into residential areas and is buried beneath houses and ornamental gardens.

The road continues through *Nova Constantia* and after one kilometre joins the Spaanschemat River road. To the west of this road the rest of the original *Bergvliet* farm has succumbed to the relentless urban sprawl and, like *Nova Constantia*, is buried beneath houses and tarmac roads. Only the farm names survive as memories of days gone by, *Fir Grove, Belle Constantia, Dreyersdal* (once owned by the Dreyers of Alphen), *Meadowridge*, and *Bergvliet*.

The road through the *Nova Constantia* estate reaches the Spaanschemat River road with, on its right-hand side, a cricket oval complete with a Victorian pavilion. This surprising sight in so intense an agricultural setting is the delight of David McCay, a Johannesburg banker with a passion for cricket, wine, and Constantia. In 1988 he purchased what is known as *Constantia Uitsig* (Constantia outlook), a 60 ha portion of the original *Nova Constantia* which he also bought. There was a neglected vineyard, a broken-down old cellar and a forlorn atmosphere; a little lost dog of a place, waiting to be put down by some real-estate speculator. The assets were a panoramic view and a rambling Victorian farmhouse on *Constantia Uitsig*, in a lovely garden shaded by trees.

The new owner, supported by an enthusiastic staff, set to work to reinvigorate the estate. A comprehensive planting of new vines transformed the vineyards. *Constantia Uitsig* may be the smallest wine farm in Constantia but the resolve was to make it one of the best. From the past years, only the wonderful old hanepoot dessert grapes were left untouched and each season they are still sold from a stall beside the Spaanschemat road close to the entrance of the estate half a kilometre from the turn to *Nova Constantia*. The farmhouse has been converted into a restaurant featuring traditional Cape cuisine with vegetables, herbs, salads and artichokes grown on the estate. The restaurant is rated as one of the ten best of the popular restaurants of South Africa. Twelve luxurious guest cottages have also been built in the setting of the shady garden. They accommodate guests from all over the world who relax in a peaceful setting far indeed from the sometimes unseemly scramble for wealth of the business world.

Beyond the entrance to *Constantia Uitsig*, the Spaanschemat River road continues southwards. After one kilometre it enters the area of the estate named *Tokai*, after the hills in Hungary where the decorative, subtly flavoured Tokai grapes had their original home and still produce a famous wine. In 1792 a German mercenary soldier, Johan Andreas Rauch, bought the land of *Tokai* but sold it in the same year to another German soldier, Andreas Georg Teubes, who in 1796 built the manor-house, designed for him by that indefatigable architect Louis Thibault. The house was a picture but within twelve months Herr Teubes put it up for auction, along with 70 000 growing vines, wagons, bullocks, wine caskets empty and full, good slaves and furniture of different kinds.

Johan Caspar Loos, a deacon to the German Lutheran community, became the next owner and he kept it until 1814. Then it was bought by Petrus Michiel Eksteen, son of the litigious Hendrik Oostwald Eksteen of *Bergvliet*. Wild times came to *Tokai*. Eksteen was a high roller, a rake and a profligate seemingly determined to ruin himself and his family. He wined, dined and lived on borrowed money and time. His wife was a Cloete, his sister the mistress of *Alphen*. In the beginning his credit was good. The parties he threw in the manor-house were famous. At one of them, on a New Year's eve a celebrated ghost story of the Cape had its origin.

A vainglorious young man, said by some to have been one of the numerous Eksteens, accepted a bet on a boast he had made that he could ride his horse up the steps, into the dining-room, around the table and then down the steps again. Egged on by his friends the young man called for his horse to be saddled, rode up the steps into the dining-room, around the table, had a drink of brandy from the saddle, poured a good tot into the horse's mouth and then, to loud applause and cheers, galloped off out of the room, across the stoep and took off over the high flight of curving steps. Horse and rider were killed. The ghosts of the two are said to come galloping out of the surrounding trees each New Year's eve and repeat the performance although this can not be much fun for them.

Petrus Michiel Eksteen eventually ran out of borrowed money and time. On 6 January 1849 a bill of exchange signed by Eksteen was presented to his bank for payment. Eksteen was bankrupt. A flood of promissory notes were presented for payment. Eksteen took to bed and died before *Tokai* was auctioned on 23 November 1849. Sebastiaan Valentyn Eksteen bought the estate for 77 200 guldens and it remained in the family until 1883 when the Cape government bought it.

The *Tokai* estate was given to the Forestry Department. Joseph Sturr Lister, the man regarded as the pioneer of forestry in Southern Africa, moved into the manor-house with his wife Georgina. He commenced the creation of the foundation forestry nursery for the government policy of reafforestation in the Cape and later throughout South Africa. Lister was appointed as the first Superintendent of Woods and Forests. His salary was £10 a month for himself and £5 for his horse. Both were also given free accommodation in the *Tokai* manor-house and stables.

Lister had learned the art and science of forestry in India where he had gone after completing schooling in Cape Town. At *Tokai*, Lister created an arboretum of trees collected from many parts of the world and cultivated to find which were most suited to South Africa where timber trees, especially quick-growing soft-woods, were in short supply. Pine and eucalyptus trees were planted in great quantity up the slopes of *Prinseskasteel* (Constantiaberg) while in the lower areas, American vine cuttings, resistant to *phylloxera*, were cultivated and supplied to the Cape wine estates to revive the vineyards destroyed by the disease.

It was all a considerable work, but a labour of love to Joseph Lister. His dedication to the lovely world of trees and plants was, perhaps, a little inspired by the knowledge that Robert Brown, the Scottish botanical scientist so famous in later years, while on the way with Captain Flinders to explore Australasia in the ship *Investigator*, arrived in Simon's Bay on 16 October 1802. Brown and his party wanted exercise and the chance to see something of the Cape. They set out to walk to Cape Town. Caught by a rainstorm and lost, they arrived at *Tokai*. The owner, then, was Johan Loos. He was away on business in Cape Town but a pleasant young lady received them graciously, fed them and then persuaded them to stay the night, bedded snug on feather mattresses while the rain pelted down all night on the thatched roof. The next morning they walked on, climbed Table Mountain and then, with a load of botanical specimens, walked back to *Tokai*. With the rain still pelting down they reached the manor-house at nine o'clock that night. When they woke in the morning they were surprised to learn that the surgeon and landscape painter from their ship had also stumbled into *Tokai*, soaked to the skin and very late in the night. They had been accommodated in the room next door. After a hearty breakfast with their host, they all went their way.

Forester Lister, after only three years' happy stay in *Tokai*, was transferred to King William's Town and eventually rose to be in charge of the forestry department of the whole Cape province. The plantation he created at *Tokai* flourished and today is the setting of a school of forestry. The Tokai Forest reserve provides pleasant walking, riding and picnicking for the public. It is open daily from dawn to dusk. Until recently, part of the old estate was the home for the Porter Reformatory with its two schools for boys and girls. The principal of the reformatory had his home in the manor-house which is preserved as a national monument.

The Spaanschemat River road, changing its name to Orpen Road, leads through the Tokai Plantation for two kilometres and then crosses the Tokai main road. The right-hand turn leads to the manor-house and with, on the way, a three kilometre long turn down Zwaanswyk Road to Allandale with its holiday cottages. The left-hand turn leads to the commercial centre of Tokai and the lower main road. Across this junction the Orpen road changes its name to Steenberg Road. It continues southwards with the great estate of *Steenberg* (stone mountain) on the right and the sombre Pollsmoor Prison on the left. The prison was built on the site of a former Grand Prix motor-racing track created just before the Second World War on the farm owned in the 1870s by Hendrik van der Poll and his wife Johanna Kirsten, after whose family Kirstenbosch is named. After 2 km the Steenberg road passes the entrance to the Steenberg estate, with the manor-house and original farm building still standing in superb condition.

Steenberg originally had the name *Swaaneweide* (feeding place of swans). Its first owner was an extraordinary young woman named Catharina Ustings who arrived in the Cape in 1662, a 22-year-old widow from Lübeck on the Baltic coast of Germany. What her short history had been it would be interesting to know. She survived the appalling conditions of a sea voyage from Europe to the Cape, landed just ten years after Jan van Riebeeck's founding of the Tavern of the Sea, and considered it wise to get herself safely married as soon as possible. A young, single woman could experience rather rough handling in those times and parts. Her choice of husband was Hans Ras. He was a former soldier who had become a free burgher settled in the valley of the Liesbeek River on property he had acquired from Jacob Cloete.

The marriage started with an uproarious wedding day. On the way home from the church the two wagons conveying guests and the married couple were raced against each other by highly intoxicated drivers. There was a collision. The incensed bridegroom received a knife between his ribs while he was involved in a brawl with the drivers. His wife pulled the knife out of her husband and managed to get him home but there was little joy in the marriage night.

Hans Ras survived the knifewound and had time to father several children before he was killed by a lion. Catharina married again but the new husband was murdered by one of the tribesmen. Catharina tried again but husband number three was trampled to death by an elephant. Catharina was persistent. A woman on her own faced many hazards in those days. She selected Matthys Michelse as number four. By that time she had also reputedly become the part-time mistress of Simon van der Stel. She persuaded the Governor to grant her the farm she named *Swaaneweide*. Van der Stel was pleased to oblige. Catherina and her husband in 1682 built their first house on this farm. By the time Simon van der Stel retired to his estate of *Groot Constantia*, Catherina was well established and a personality of some renown in the Cape. When the commissioner, Baron van Rheede tot Drakenstein, rode on inspection through the lowlands below the Steenberge, he and his party lunched with her, finding the food excellent but having some views about the lady. *'She rides bare-back like an Indian,'* the baron wrote, *'and her children resemble Brazilian cannibals.'*

In 1695 Catharina sold the farm to Frederick Russouw and moved to the valley of the Berg River. Russouw's wife, Christina Diemer, was a woman in the same resolute mould as Catharina. While her husband farmed, she provided a continuity of effective management which saw the farm develop to a considerable agricultural industry, especially after 1741 when the horrific wrecks in Table Bay induced the Dutch East India Company to make Simon's Bay a winter refuge for shipping. She became the principal supplier of provisions for ships anchoring off Simon's Town. She acquired the grant of additional land from Baron von Imhof, Governor-General of the Netherlands East Indies, including what she named *Imhoff's Gift*, the site of the modern village of Kommetjie. She and a gentleman friend, Carol Georg Wieser, a wealthy farmer, built two seaside cottages at what was destined to become a popular resort next to the natural tidal pool, the *kommetjie* (little basin) which gave the place its name. Her house was named *Slangkop* (snake peak) and his, next door, was Poespaskraal (higgledy-piggledy corral).

Christina also acquired land above Simon's Bay, built a house there named *Goede Gift*, farmed vegetables for the ships and grazed cattle to the very end of the Cape Peninsula. When she died in 1765, her son Nicolaas took over the estate and, with his wife Anna Marie, directed affairs for the next 36 years. For some reason, when the farm was transferred to him, it was named *Swaanswyk*. The farm continued to prosper and the manor-house was provided with a handsome new gable in the *holbol* style.

At the time of the death of Nicolaas Russouw in 1802 times were changing. The long years of the Napoleonic War were having an effect on the economy of the world. Daniel Russouw, who secured the property from his mother, was resourceful, however, and for the next 40 years he managed the estate with great ability. In his old age, however, he found conditions increasingly difficult. The problem which all fathers of large families have to eventually face, how to divide the inheritance among the children, also became demanding of solution especially as none of the rather fractious brood was keen on an agricultural life.

In 1842 Daniel solved his problems by selling the estate to two of his sons-in-law, Johannes Adriaan Louw and Fredrik Anthon Olthoff. From the proceeds his heirs each received 646 rixdollars and that was the end of the matter. Johannes Louw took on the management of the estate. His descendants continued in ownership of what became known as Steenberg until May 1990. The estate was then sold to the JCI (Johannesburg Consolidated Investment Company, Limited.) Under this ownership a vast transformation has come to *Steenberg*. The lower-lying portion, with soil of less agricultural potential, has been converted into an 18-hole golf-course directly fronted by 210 residential erven as homes for golf-lovers. The design of the central clubhouse is harmonious with the historic architecture of the estate. The houses of the golf estate are intended and to be compatible with the historic background in a concept of a park-like setting of relaxation and play for the wealthy on a superb golf-course. The sombre pile of the overlooking Pollsmoor Prison might provide cause for some reflection on the part of the players.

A state-of-the-art wine cellar is surrounded by new vineyards with cultivars selected to suit the chemical nature of the soils, micro-climate and altitude of the slopes of the Steenberge. The original historic buildings are maintained, with a restaurant housed in one of them.

The wine estates, of Constantia all lie with their backs resting against the narrow spinal range of sandstone mountains which run southwards from Table Mountain down the Peninsula to its tip at Cape Point, where the Cape of Good Hope provides the south-western end to the continent of Africa. A number of springs have their source on these mountains. Of some of these there is a curious legend concerning the final decline of the pastoral tribes who had once grazed their herds and flocks in the area of the Cape Peninsula and the Hottentots Holland.

After the 'purchase' by the Dutch East India Company in 1672 of the Cape Peninsula, the Hottentots Holland and most of the interior as far as what were called the Mountains of Africa, the once dominant tribes who had themselves supplanted the earlier inhabitants, and now been themselves swindled out of the area, fell to petty squabbling and dissipating their remaining wealth in live-stock by bartering for trinkets, scrap metal, alcohol and tobacco.

The Chainoukwa had been persuaded into selling their homeland of the Hottentots Holland to the Dutch East India Company for £6 16s 4d worth of junk. The tribe had then fragmented under two contentious leaders, Prince Dorha (the original paramount chief known as Klaas to the Dutch) and a rival chieftain known as Koopman. Dorha was married to the daughter of Goukou, the ruler of the powerful and wealthy tribe of the Hessekwa who lived in the area of the river known as the *Riviersonderend* (river without end). Goukou supported his son-in-law and, at first, so did the Dutch until there was a quarrel over cattle trading. A punitive force of 100 soldiers and 100 burghers was sent from Cape Town to settle the matter. Koopman gleefully joined in the attack on his rival. Dorha and two of his leading men were arrested. All their cattle were seized and shared between the attackers. Booty included the wife of Dorha, known as the *prinses*.

Dorha and his two companions were sent to Robben Island on 8 August 1683. Appeals on their behalf were made by several of the Dutch colonists who were friendly with Dorha, and by his father-in-law. The authorities in Cape Town relented. Dorha and his companions were allowed to return to the mainland and settle near the site of modern Muizenberg. He begged for the return of his wife but the *prinses* said she preferred to remain with Koopman. The two chiefs became mortal enemies. They both wanted the *prinses* and to get her were prepared to ruin themselves and their people. In the midst of this bloodshed, the *prinses* changed her mind and ran away to rejoin her husband. Koopman pursued her. He claimed to have killed her but legend says that she feigned death and escaped to hide in the great cave known from its shape as the Elephant's Eye below the summit of the 928 m high *Prinseskasteel* (castle of the princess), nowadays less romantically known as the Constantiaberg, which vaguely resembles the profile of an elephant's head.

In the cave the princes remained, hoping that the fighting would come to an end. Instead, in June 1701, Dorha was killed. Koopman was ruined and the Chainoukwa tribe dispersed. In her cave the *prinses* is said to have wept bitterly at the death of her husband and the dissipation not only of the tribe but of her entire race. She committed suicide and legend says that the springs on the mountain are forever reinforced with the magical sadness of her tears. They flow to the sea replenishing on the way lakes which fill the hollows in the flat land below the mountains, *Prinsesvlei* (princess marsh), *Klein Prinsesvlei* (little princess marsh), *Zandvlei* (sandy marsh), *Rondevlei* (round marsh) and *Zeekoevlei* (hippopotamus marsh). These lakes today provide recreational facilities to the people of the Cape Peninsula. Perhaps the tears still shed today by the sad *prinses* are as much for the degeneration of her lakes through pollution as for the dissipation of her people.

Chapter Five
THE SOUTHERN CAPE PENINSULA

The main dual carriageway road known as De Waal Drive, after passing the turn-off to Claremont, takes on the name of Edinburgh Drive. It leads through the fine residential area of Upper Claremont (here with a truly clear view of the back of Table Mountain and Devil's Peak) and passes on the right the fashionable area of Bishopscourt. At this stage the road climbs the slopes of what Van Riebeeck named the *Wynberg* (wine mountain). As it tops the rise of this hill, there is a fine view over the Cape Flats and towards False Bay, with a first glimpse in the distance of the tip of the Cape Peninsula which is the principal objective of this pleasant journey.

On the summit of the hill, 12 km from the city centre, there is a turn-off left past the stone pines, oaks and silver trees of Wynberg Park. By turning left here and again after passing the second traffic-light, the traveller enters the suburb of ...

WYNBERG

Wynberg, with its substantial and very congested commercial centre, is the site of a large military camp and hospital, established by the British when they occupied the Cape. In modern times many of the old cottages have been restored in what is locally known as 'Chelsea' style. In these delightful cottages a community of artists, craftspeople and would-be artists have made their homes and studios. The park and the open-air theatre of *Maynardville* are also in the Chelsea area.

James Maynard, after whom the park is named, was a timber merchant and member of the Cape Legislative Assembly. He acquired the estate in 1844. His grandson (through his daughter), William Maynard Farmer, inherited the estate in 1874. Having accumulated wealth in the exciting days of the diamond rushes, he lived in style and employed a gardener trained at Kew, London, who created a colourful ornamental garden of oleanders, hydrangeas, fountains and lawns. In 1949 the property was offered to the Cape Town municipality. It became a park and an open-air theatre which, in an idyllic setting, is the venue for an annual summer production of a Shakespeare play. The original homestead has been demolished, but several ghosts of its grand days reputedly linger on. These include a cast-off, unwed daughter with babe in arms and rapidly receding horse's hooves, said to be either the culprit fleeing or the father in pursuit.

Also in Wynberg, in magnificent grounds, is *Hawthornden*, the home of the late mining magnate Sir J B Robinson and his son-in-law, Count Labia. In 1976 this residence was donated to the Cape Provincial Council to be maintained as a cultural museum. It was built in 1880 and contains many fine late Victorian paintings and statuary. The Robinson and Labia family mausoleum is in the grounds. In the garages are two superb vintage cars.

KENILWORTH

Kenilworth is the suburb between Wynberg and Claremont. It grew as a residential area around the original homestead of *Stellenberg* farm. It was in this area that the Dutch governors had the kennels of their hunting hounds. The name Kenilworth was first applied to the estate and then to the railway station. The Kenilworth Racecourse, scene of the principal horse-race in the Cape, the Metropolitan Handicap, is in the lower part of the suburb adjoining the military base of Youngsfield.

From the turn-off to Wynberg and Kenilworth, 12 km from the city centre, the main double carriageway of the Simon van der Stel freeway continues down the southern slopes of Wynberg Hill. It crosses Wynberg Park by means of a bridge. With a splendid view of the farming and residential area of Constantia, the road descends until at a point 14 km from the city centre, it reaches a turn-off leading to the suburbs of Wynberg, Plumstead, Constantia and over Constantia Nek to Hout Bay.

The double carriageway continues southwards across an undulating, green and pleasant landscape. There are turn-offs to suburbs such as Diep River (via Kendal Road), Bergvliet and Meadowridge (via Ladies Mile Road). At 20 km from the city, a turn-off leads for 1 km to the suburb of Retreat on the left and on the right to the forest area of Tokai.

RETREAT, TOKAI AND THE OU KAAPSE WEG

The suburb of Retreat was always closely connected with the British Army which established there two camps, *Pollsmoor* and *Westlake*, both used as marshalling and resting-places for troops in transit to Asia or Europe, especially during the First and Second World Wars. With the interminable movement of manpower during these war years, countless numbers of men found themselves quartered in Retreat, and it remains an address remembered by many.

From the turn-off to Retreat and Tokai (21,5 km from the city), the Simon van der Stel freeway continues for 1,5 km and then reaches an intersection. To the left the turn-off leads to Steenberg, Lakeside and Muizenberg. To the right is the scenic *Ou Kaapse Weg* (old Cape way), which is a superb drive.

Passing the Westlake Golf Course and the Silvermine Maritime Headquarters of the S A Navy on the left, securely constructed in the depths of the mountain, the Ou Kaapse Weg commences a steady climb up the *Steenberg* (stony mountain). At a point 4 km from the intersection the road reaches a viewsite on the summit, with a turn-off leading to a parking area and, further on, to a toll-gate providing admittance during the day to picnic sites, pine forests and an old reservoir which once supplied drinking water to the residential area below the mountains. The whole area is known as the Silvermine Nature Reserve now part of the Cape Peninsula National Park and is rich in indigenous flora. Even the verges of the road are gardens of wild flowers, brilliant with colour, especially in spring. Paths take walkers on several routes to such interesting places as the great cave of the Elephant's Eye with its memories of the sad princess. Pause awhile at the viewsite and look down at the tidal wave of housing relentlessly pressing the fertile farmlands of Constantia back against the stony mountains. You can almost see, and certainly sense, the dynamics of this movement with ever increasing humanity involuntarily trampling to oblivion the good earth which feeds them.

There are many pleasant picnic places in the area of the nature reserve and the walks are delightful, notably the circular walk up the forest road which leads from the reservoir to the summit of the mountain and then down to the other side of the reservoir. Near the highest point of the road, a short walk away, the stone beacon on top of Noordhoek Peak (756 m above sea-level) may be seen. From this beacon there is a spectacular view of Hout Bay and the sea.

One kilometre further along the Ou Kaapse Weg, beyond the turn-off to the summit viewsite and toll-gate, there is another turn-off, this one being on the left-hand side of the road. A gate, open during daylight hours, allows access to another popular picnic area close to a waterfall which, in wet winter months, is an attractive spectacle. From this site there are walks to the Kalk Bay and Muizenberg mountains with their caves, wild flowers and glorious views over False Bay and in the direction of Noordhoek.

Beyond the waterfall turn-off, the Ou Kaapse Weg begins a curving descent with the Silvermine River flowing down the valley on the left-hand side. After 2,5 km the road passes on the right-hand side one of the original pits sunk in 1687 by prospectors searching for silver in the area. This was the first mining activity in Southern Africa undertaken by Europeans. No silver was found, only traces of manganese in quite unpayable quantities. The name *Silvermine* clings to the area, a reminder of a long-past disappointment.

One kilometre beyond the shaft the road reaches a crossroads. The right-hand turn leads past the Silvermine Retirement Village and then on to Noordhoek. The left-hand turn (gravel) leads by a rough route to Clovelly. The Ou Kaapse Weg continues southwards. After a further 3 km it reaches the Sun Valley residential area, where it passes the Sun Valley shopping centre, joins the main road running along the western side of the Peninsula from Cape Town to Cape Point, and a branch road leading to Fish Hoek. The Ou Kaapse Weg continues southwards, climbs out of the valley past the Serina kaolin mine, discreetly hidden behind trees, rises with easy gradients over a ridge of rocky hills and then, after a total of seventeen kilometres of travel from its start, descends to the False Bay coast and joins the main coastal road at Glencairn.

At the turn-off to Steenberg, Lakeside and the Ou Kaapse Weg, the main double carriageway of the Simon van der Stel freeway comes to an end, its eventual route still uncertain – either a tunnel through the mountains or to continue a further half kilometre to join Boyes Drive, cut into the mountains overlooking False Bay. *Boyes Drive* takes its name from George Boyes, a magistrate of Simon's Town whose enthusiasm for the road largely stimulated its construction in the 1920s. It is cut high into the slopes of the Muizenberg and Kalk Bay mountains. On the left-hand side there are superlative views over False Bay . On the right-hand side there are several pathways leading climbers into the same lovely area of wild flowers, caves and extensive views which is reached from the waterfall turn-off on the Ou Kaapse Weg, described earlier. Below lies the seaside suburb of Muizenberg which can be reached by taking the turn-off left from the present end-point of the Simon van der Stel freeway.

Muizenberg is 26 km from the city centre of Cape Town.

FALSE BAY

The coastal road is narrow and congested, especially on holidays and sunny weekends when half of the population of Cape Town seems to be travelling along it to reach their chosen recreational areas on the False Bay coast. With Muizenberg as the main centre, this coast is the principal recreational area for the people of the Cape Peninsula along with many others, vacationers and tourists from all parts of Southern Africa and overseas.

Muizenberg is justly ranked as one of the world's most famous seaside resorts. The glory of the place is its beach. It is the finest and most spacious on the coast of Southern Africa and one of the safest and liveliest bathing beaches to be found on planet Earth.

Muizenberg lies on the north-western end of False Bay, a 30 km by 30 km inlet of the sea held between the mountainous arms of the Cape Peninsula reaching south to the Cape of Good Hope, and the range of the Hottentots Holland reaching south to the Cape known as Hangklip from its overhanging shape. The name of False Bay originated from an unfortunate confusion experienced by several early navigators. They turned northwards after doubling either of the Capes. Instead of a clear passage up the west or east coasts of Africa, they found themselves forced into the predicament of the complicated sailing manoeuvre known as 'tacking' to get their ships out again in the teeth of contrary winds.

During the summer months, when the prevailing wind is the powerful south-easter, the warm Mozambique–Agulhas Current from the Indian Ocean flows down as far as the Cape of Good Hope. False Bay lies at the end of its journey down the east coast. The bay fills with sparkling blue water, about 22°C in temperature and well populated with Indo-Pacific species of fish. These are the conditions of summer-holiday time with False Bay at its best from November to April. The splendid beach on its northern side stretches east to west for 35 unbroken kilometres. Rudyard Kipling who knew and loved the Muizenberg beach was a regular summer visitor. With his friend, Cecil Rhodes, he swam in the azure water, strolled bare-foot along the beach and in 1895 wrote in his poem *The Flowers* the oft-quoted line *'White as the sands of Muizenberg, spun before the gale'*.

The bracing, unpolluted winds which sweep into False Bay, can be a pest in a really big blow, but the reputation of the summer south-easter as being the 'Cape Doctor' is based on a very real phenomenon. Insects and miasmas are blown away. Cecil Rhodes, whose lungs were weakened by years of tuberculosis, bought in 1899 a seaside cottage beside the coastal road on the south-western side of Muizenberg. In the last three years of his life he spent as much time as he could in this unpretentious little place, and the fresh air he loved to breath in long, deep breaths seemed to be his last links to sustaining life.

Muizenberg is cradled between sea and high mountains. Its magnificent beach stretches off eastwards for 35 km to the mountain range of the Hottentots Holland. From the traffic circle at Sunrise Beach in Muizenberg, Baden-Powell Drive follows the shoreline, providing an attractive panorama of glistening beaches, restless surf and serene mountain ranges on both sides of the great bay. There are kilometres of safe and enjoyable bathing, surfing and fishing stretches, such as those at *Strandfontein* (beach fountain), 6,8 km from Muizenberg; *Mnandi* (pleasant place); and *Swartklip* (black rock), 18 km from Muizenberg. From Swartklip the road veers inland to join Settlers Way (24,5 km from Muizenberg). Strandfontein has been developed as a recreational area for residential areas such as *Mitchell's Plain* (named, and misspelt, after Charles Michell, Surveyor-General and Civil Engineer of the Cape Colony). There is a large tidal pool, caravan park, some bungalows and wind-protected picnic grounds, as well as the Strandfontein Snake, Crocodile and Reptile Park. At Mnandi there is a large pool with slides and boat rides. At Swartklip there is a resort known as *Monwabisi* (the one which makes others happy) with the largest tidal pool in the Southern Hemisphere, picnic spots, camping and caravanning, shops and all facilities. It has been developed particularly as a resort for the residential area named *Khayelitsha* (home which is new).

Close to the shores of False Bay lie several lakes. These are fed by streams which have sources mainly in the mountains of Constantia and Tokai. Among these streams are the *Spaanschemat* (Spanish rushes), *Keysers* (after Johannes Keyser who was drowned there) and the *Diep* (deep). These streams meander seawards across built-up areas which were once fertile farmlands producing, among other things, some of the most delectable table grapes of South Africa.

On reaching the level ground of the Cape Flats, these streams half lose themselves in the sandy former sea bed in depressions which trap their flow. The streams become shallow lakelets such as *Zandvlei* (sandy marsh), beloved by canoeists, owners of small yachts, windsurfers and numerous birds. This expanse of water is fed by the Spaanschemat, Keysers and other streams. On its northern, western and eastern verges, the *Marina da Gama*, named in memory of the Portuguese navigator, Vasco da Gama, was constructed. This is an extensive luxury housing project with waterside sites opening on to a series of artificial canals leading from Zandvlei. It is an imaginative residential concept, first conceived in 1969 by David Jack of the Cape Town City Council Planning Department, and built on what was originally a garbage dump and wasteland. The land was systematically acquired over several years. This involved more than 1 000 separate land transactions by the project's principal motivator, John Bridgeman. It was opened in 1974.

The Diep River supplies water from the two connected lakelets known as Little Princess Vlei and Big Princess Vlei, farmed for the size of the carp living in their waters, and for their reflecting qualities on calm days. Two other lakelets fed by water from the mountains and other sources that is trapped by the sands are *Zeekoeivlei* (hippopotamus marsh), the largest of them all and a favourite haunt of yachtsmen, and *Rondevlei* (round marsh), a famous bird sanctuary established on 1 January 1952 as the first ornithological field station in South Africa. In this 105 ha sanctuary some 200 bird species make their home, or are occasional visitors. These birds include flamingo and pelicans. They are systematically studied in relation to one another, to food and to climatic conditions. Midsummer sees the vlei with its densest population. There are observation towers and a hide open to the public, and an interesting museum. Hippos were reintroduced to Rondevlei in 1981 in order to control the growth of vegetation.

Close to Rondevlei lie the extensive artificial lakes of the Strandfontein sewage disposal area. In these nutrient-rich lakes live an array of water birds rivalling any of the world's famous bird sanctuaries. Flamingos – both the greater and lesser species – pelicans, avocets, stilts, innumerable ducks and other birds visit the area seasonally or live there permanently.

Rondevlei is open to the public all year round, except for Christmas Day, from 08h00 to 17h00. During December, January and February, on Saturdays and Sundays the opening times are 07h00 to 19h00. An entrance fee is payable at the gate.

Apart from its vast recreational assets of safe swimming with no significant backwash, angling, boating and surfing. False Bay as the terminal of the Mozambique–Agulhas Current, is of great significance to marine biologists. There is a constant seasonal change in the nature of all its marine life. From April to June, for example, the rare and remarkable Argonauts drift into the Bay. These strange little creatures have no powers of self-locomotion. They are drifters at the mercy of wind, current and tide. A north-westerly wind followed by a south-easter washes them on to the shores of False Bay. Their exquisite, fragile shells, are easily damaged, especially those of the larger, more mature animals. If they are washed up in daylight the sea-birds swoop on them, destroying the shells in order to feed on the animal inside. A large, undamaged Argonaut shell is a valuable collector's piece. To secure such a prize, Argonaut hunters search the beach with torches at night at the time of an incoming tide. The shells are sold to collectors and shops all over the world.

There are good and bad years for Argonauts. Very little is known about their life cycle, the part of the Mozambique–Agulhas Current where they breed and the time it takes to make their shells. What is known about them is largely the result of studies done by Jeanette Power, a naturalist working in Messina, Sicily who managed in the 1830s to keep some alive in her aquarium; and the studies of Heinrich Muller reported in 1853. Their combined work on what is correctly known as *Argonauta Argo* cleared up some but not all of the ancient mysteries about this shell and its occupant.

The Argonaut is found in all oceans and the Mediterranean Sea. The naturalists of the Roman Empire were baffled at the finding of shells but with no sign of the maker of the shell. There was not even an indication that the maker of the shell had been attached to it by the usual muscle which connects mollusca to their shells. The small octopus-like creature with its eight tentacles, often found in the shell, was thought to be a parasite who had occupied a deserted shell. Studies by the two researchers already mentioned revealed that the female miniature octopus-like animal was indeed the creator of the shells. Two of the tentacles of the animal have an ingenious modification converting them into extendable specialised tools for the making and repairing of shells.

When hatched, the male and female Argonauts are naked and defenceless. If the female survives for the first critical ten days she starts to make her shell, just large enough to provide a refuge and, when she produces eggs, a secure container. The male is only about one-twentieth the size of the female and plays no part in proceedings other than a little romance. Whether the female eventually eats him is uncertain but he is certainly considered to be both expendable and consumable.

The name *Argonauta argo* was given to these wandering shells after the Greek hero Jason and his men, known as the Argonauts of the ship *Argo*, which in ancient legend sailed uncharted seas in search of the Golden Fleece. The shells are sometimes mistakenly known as *Paper Nautilus*, confused with the *Nautilus pompilius*, a different animal found only in the Pacific Ocean. It has 50 or more tentacles and is attached permanently to a far heavier shell. To walk on the False Bay beach at night with a torch and to see an Argonaut washed up unbroken at your feet provides a great thrill and yields a collector's treasure.

The winter months in False Bay bring a profound change. The north-west wind replaces the summer south-easter. The warm Mozambique-Agulhas Current is pushed back with all its varied life-forms. The cold Benguela Current, a spin-off of the Antarctic Drift, flows into the bay. The water temperature drops to around 15°C. Cold-water species of marine life displace the warm-water species. Swimmers need to be of a hardier breed but surfers, protected in their wetsuits, find wave conditions to be far more exciting. The waves are larger, although the shallow water of the False Bay littoral acts as a brake. It slows them down, making the coast particularly safe for swimmers as well as novice surfers who describe the area as being their nursery. The only current in False Bay is a leisurely clockwise movement along the coast. Sharks, including the Great White, although present in the bay (as they are in all oceans) prefer deep water and, in any case, feed on the copious supply of seals who have their home on Seal Island in the middle of the bay.

False Bay and the Cape Peninsula together provide Earth with a scenic, ecological and recreational treasure which demands the care of an authority with power to enforce compliance with its disciplines. False Bay should be removed from the abuses of irresponsible individuals and local authorities. There is no problem made by human beings which cannot be solved by them, if they want to. The only real problem is their disinclination to do anything until it is sometimes too late. Humanity's democratic right does not include the right to do anything harmful to the life or to the environment. Naughty children, and adult human beings, need at times to have their bottoms smacked. False Bay needs the discipline and loving care of the status of a marine national park. The unspoilt remaining areas of the Cape Peninsula, with its incredible incomparable floral kingdom, need equally resolute defence against piecemeal exploitation.

Muizenberg grew as the principal recreational area for the Cape Peninsula from the natural assets of a superb beach, Zandvlei, with its parklike verges, and the overlooking Steenberg with its caves, walking paths and wild flowers. The resort originated as a military stronghold intended to defend the narrow passage where the coastal road leads between the sea and the slopes of the mountain. The *Oudepost* (old post) building erected there in 1743 still survives. The village of Muizenberg took its name from the commander of this post, Wynand Muys, and the place was at first known as *Muysenburg* (Muys's stronghold). In the course of the years this name was corrupted to the Muizenberg of today. Wynand Muys died in 1759 with the rank of captain and was buried in the mother church in Adderley Street. The military post remained, keeping guard by the side of the rough track and regarded as the outer defence south of Cape Town.

Imagine the place as it was in those days. To the south there stretched a rocky coast overlooked by towering cliffs. Only wild creatures such as baboons lived there and these were so numerous that the soldiers, we are told, dared not go out unless they were in parties of five or six. The post building looked eastwards over False Bay with the beach stretching off, at that period a place only of birds, the basking seals and the endless murmur of the surf.

Northwards, the post was linked to Cape Town by a sandy track, only 25 km long but, by its roughness, involving quite a difficult journey for the soldiers and their carts. Close to this road, just after it left the military post, lay the shallow lake of Zandvlei, a place of pelicans, flamingoes, coots, wild ducks and wonderful reflections of dawns, sunsets and the distant shapes of Devil's Peak and Table Mountain. Wax-berries, milkwood trees and reeds grew around the lake while great shoals of baby fish found their way in from the sea up the estuary. The nutrient-rich waters of the lake acted as a nursery where the young fish could grow in safety until such time as instinct drew them to swim out once more to the open sea.

In the year 1795 a curious drama developed around the little outpost of Muysenburg. In Europe, the French Revolution was causing a vast disturbance to the social establishments of the world. The concepts of liberty, fraternity, equality and a better share for the common man in the good things of life were perceived as threats to the conservative rulers of many countries. For colonies, such as the Cape and Mauritius, these revolutionary ideas penetrated like waves sweeping on to a beach from a distant storm. The people of the Cape were already in some political agitation. The rule of the Dutch East India Company was in disrepute. There were many complaints of corruption, malpractice and favouritism. News reaching the Cape of the fall of the ruling house of France brought a real ferment to the population. Their administrators were all appointees of the Dutch East India Company, and supporters of the aristocratic order. The common people found the slogans of revolution to be catching, provided they were applied only to themselves. In the strange dual morality of a slave-owning society, the masters had no desire for the spread to their servants of any notions of the liberty they desired for themselves.

In this confusion the British sent an expedition to occupy the Cape. The French had invaded Holland and the ruler, the Prince of Orange, had fled to Britain for sanctuary. A republican government had been established in Holland. In the great struggling for supremacy in the Indian Ocean, it was essential that the British prevent the French from seizing the Cape. The understanding with the Prince of Orange was that the British would hold the Cape until the French were defeated and then return it to the House of Orange on the restoration of a conservative government in Holland.

A great argument commenced in the Cape. The administration favoured a take-over by the British. The common people preferred the French, if they were, indeed, to be taken over at all. They would, however, prefer to be left alone to talk of liberty and equality but keep the notions well away from the slaves.

In this peculiar play of politics the hitherto tranquil outpost of Muysenburg found itself suddenly called upon to fulfil a major role. On 11 June 1795 a British fleet sailed into False Bay and came to anchor before Simon's Town. A messenger galloped to Cape Town with news of this arrival and there was general consternation. The signal guns were fired one after the other, from one outpost to the next, to warn the countrymen of invasion and to summon them to the defence of Cape Town.

The military state of the Cape was hopelessly weak. Most of the regular garrison consisted of mercenaries and the British could deal with these simply by offering more pay. In any case, there was only a handful of men at Muysenburg and fewer than 100 stationed at Simon's Town. Reinforcements of 200 infantry and 100 gunners were hastily sent to confront the British. Their commander, Lt-Colonel C M W de Lille, however was for the British and, with the mercenaries, was hardly likely to make anything of a stand.

The reinforcements were trudging along the road to Muysenburg when a messenger rode past them carrying letters to the authorities in Cape Town from the two British commanders, Admiral Sir George Elphinstone and Major-General James Craig. The letters were friendly. They invited the head of the administration in the Cape, Commissioner Abraham Sluyskens, and the military commander, Colonel Robert Gordon, (a Dutchman of Scottish descent), to visit the British admiral who would receive them with honour and give them important information as well as a letter from the refugee Prince of Orange.

It was not politic for Sluyskens or Gordon to visit the British commander. Major-General Craig was invited to send an officer to Cape Town with the news and information. Meanwhile, the British were welcome to obtain provisions at Simon's Town. A great bustle of human movement developed, with countrymen rallying to Cape Town and troops being marched along the track to Muysenburg. Most of the men already sent under Lt-Colonel De Lille to Simon's Town were hurriedly ordered to fall back on Muysenburg and strengthen its armament in case of hostilities.

There were nothing much at Muysenburg just a simple building to house a handful of soldiers, a signal station and two mortars. The British messengers who rode past the place were not much impressed. In any case they did not really expect hostility. On 14 June, as a result of the invitation from the governing council at Cape Town, Lt-Colonel Mackenzie, Captain Hardy and Mr Ross, the secretary to General Craig who could speak Dutch, rode along the track to Cape Town and presented a letter from the Prince of Orange ordering the local authorities to admit the British as a friendly power, simply there to protect the Cape against invasion by the French.

There was some hard lying in Cape Town. The British told the local authorities that the French had occupied the whole of the Netherlands, the Prince of Orange had been forced to flee to Britain, and the French were treating the Dutch with severity. It was carefully concealed that the Dutch people had welcomed the French, that a national democratic government had been formed and the old order of the States-General headed by the Prince of Orange had been abolished.

The officials of the council of policy of the Cape were placed in a real quandary. To a man they supported the Prince of Orange but their allegiance was sworn to Holland and they had no instructions from its government or certain indication of events in Europe. They tried to play for time. They thanked the British for their offer of support against French attack, repeated their own offer of provisions, but meanwhile requested that only unarmed men be sent on shore and that General Craig come to Cape Town for discussions. The British party rode back to Simon's Town. Along the track to Muysenburg, cannon, supplies and reinforcements were being sent from Cape Town. The countrymen were also arriving in Cape Town. On 15 June, 200 horsemen from Stellenbosch were sent to Muysenburg where they joined the mercenaries and other soldiers, sleeping out in the winter weather, with the comfort of plenty of good food and wine, but no shelter, very conflicting thoughts and a confusion of news and rumours.

On 18 June General Craig, three senior officers and his secretary, rode to Cape Town, viewing on the way the reinforcement of Muysenburg and studying the landscape in detail. They partook of the good fare of Muysenburg and in Cape Town were courteously received. On 19 June the Council of Policy met with the general and heard his story of events and intentions. The British, he now emphasised, were only there to protect the colony. They would hand it back to Holland as soon as peace came. They would make no changes. The pay of the soldiers would come from the British. The mercenaries heard a beguiling whisper that the British actually thought them to be underpaid. There could be increases. There was some disappointment when the Council of Policy rejected the British proposals.

General Craig returned to Simon's Town, once again viewing the military preparations of Muysenburg when he stopped there for some wine with the garrison officers. The matter of the pay of the mercenaries and the rejection of the British proposals was discussed. Craig had sensed in Cape Town that there was dissent on many matters and he was a man who made the most of opportunities. He left Muysenburg garrison under far greater strain that on his arrival while he rode gaily on to Simon's Town.

Back on the flagship, Craig, Elphinstone and their advisers drafted in Dutch and German an address to the people of the Cape. This address was printed and then distributed on shore. It presented a lurid description of the French Revolution, the guillotine, horrors, emancipation of slaves, collapse of commerce, hardships and sufferings. In contrast there was the proffered hand of British friendship with definitely better pay for soldiers. This address mightily disturbed the Council of

Policy. It was becoming obvious that there was lurking at the Simon's Town end of the track from Cape Town a real subverter.

The council sent a message to the British requesting them to desist from any further messages, epistles or correspondence. The British replied with another carefully worded effusion of good intentions, horror stories and their own paternalism. The council replied by denying the supply of any further provisions. More men were sent to Muysenburg, horsemen from the country, Hottentot *pandours* (armed guards), the rest of the men from Simon's Town, leaving only one man there to spike the guns if the British landed. Cape Town was in a ferment. The senior officials were petrified by the horror stories of the guillotine and the ending of privileges. The mercenaries were highly restive; only the country people, rallying to the defence of Cape Town, wanted to fight. The officials had to affect a pretence of resolution, and have the mortification of being cheered in public for their supposed determination to oppose the British.

At Muysenburg the drama became unbearable. The mercenaries started to desert. Twenty-three of them slipped away to join the British. Two were caught, summarily tried and shot out of hand as traitors. The artillery men remained loyal but they and the countrymen were having a hard time. Although it was a mild winter, it was trying sleeping in the open, never knowing when the British would attack, wondering what was really happening behind their backs in Cape Town where the administration had never been trusted, wondering what was happening to their families in remote frontier farms, wishing the whole business would be resolved as quickly as possible.

In this confusion there arrived at Simon's Town two small American ships, one of them sent from Amsterdam to convey to the authorities at the Cape and Batavia news of events in Holland. The British seized the mailbags but by some means a newspaper was smuggled ashore and eagerly read in Muysenburg and then in Cape Town. From this, for the first time, the people of the Cape learned that Holland had become a republic, the rule of the autocratic Prince of Orange was no more, and the French were friends and the British were enemies.

The authorities of the Cape, like it or not, now had their policy made up for them. They had to deny the British any control of the colony. Their allegiance was to their country, not to a deposed ruler no matter how much they personally supported him. Half-hearted or not they had to prepare for war. On 29 June, therefore they ordered all possible combatant troops to be concentrated at Muysenburg. Simon's Town was abandoned entirely, the provisions there destroyed, the guns spiked and the ammunition thrown into the sea.

For the next few days there was a curious lull before the storm. The Council of Policy had to contend with something of a pocket revolution taking place in Swellendam and continued suspicion from most of the population. They ordered that nothing be done to provoke the British. They hoped that a fleet would arrive from Holland, or shortage of provisions would drive away the British. Three Dutch ships did arrive in False Bay but these came like lambs to the slaughter. Before they realised what was afoot they were captured by the British. Their advent actually stimulated the British into action in case a large Dutch fleet was approaching. They decided to capture Muysenburg and from the position force the Cape Town authorities to resume negotiations.

The big day was 7 August 1795. At the time there were 800 men garrisoning Muysenburg. Of these 200 were mercenaries of the so-called National Battalion and the British had reason to believe that they, like dogs, would not bite a hand offering them a bigger bone. Their commander, Lt-Colonel de Lille, was a loyal supporter of the Prince of Orange. There were also 150 Hottentot pandours who had not much enthusiasm to die. The artillery men and burgher cavalry from the country districts were more resolute.

To confuse the defenders, the British, for some time, caused certain of their ships to cruise around False Bay, as though preparing for departure. Under this diversion, the British landed 1 600 men at Simon's Town. Led by Major-General Craig this force of assorted sailors and soldiers set out along the track, mainly rocky, at times deep sand, which led to Muysenburg. Four large ships were sent to Muysenburg to bombard the fort, while a number of smaller craft made their way along the coast to protect the advancing land force and pepper any defenders with shot.

The outpost picket at Kalk Bay retired before the attackers. The ships then reached Muysenburg and fired a broadside. As expected, the mercenaries and their commander immediately abandoned the place and fled for safety into the reeds of Zandvlei. There was a prodigious squawking and whirring of birds. Flamingoes, pelicans, coots, terns, cormorants, kingfishers and what not all rose into the air.

The artillery men at Muysenburg had two twenty-four-pounder guns and with these they opened fire on the British ships, killing two men and wounding four on the *America*, and wounding one man on the *Stately*. The British gunners were firing high, trying to hit the trenches dug into the mountain slopes above the actual strongpoint of Muysenburg. The Dutch gunners had to contend with loose sand under their cannons. They had to reposition them each time they were fired. Two other British ships the *Echo* and *Rattlesnake*, arrived and made a foursome of the attackers. They kept up the cannonading until the British land party approached along the track to Cape Town. The burgher cavalry and the pandours had already made their departure.

With cheers the British occupied what they called Muizenberg and pursued the retreating garrison. As soon as they were out of range of the ships' guns, the Dutch forces did make a stand. From the north side of Zandvlei a party of artillery men under Captain Kemper opened fire on the British and it was the turn of the attackers to go into retreat. Casualties were slight: one British officer, one burgher, two artillery men and one pandour. The mercenaries were in full retreat and had fallen back as far as Lochner's farm at Diep River. Burgher cavalry reinforcements, however, were coming from Cape Town and slept that night by the side of the track.

Overnight De Lille and some of his men made their way back to the north shores of Zandvlei. The marsh was then larger and the track skirted its reed-covered shores. The British soon observed the presence there of an opposing force and set out to attack them, wading through water up to their waists and firing from cover in the reeds.

Suddenly a party of burghers and pandours appeared from behind some sand dunes on the British flank. The British withdrew, thinking they were in a trap. They retreated back to the cover provided by their own ship's guns. The two cannons, abandoned by the Dutch at Muysenburg but now repaired, were dragged on to firm ground and aimed northwards along the track to Cape Town. A considerable amount of firing took place. The mercenaries had not attempted any action. They now simply fled. They formed a new camp at Wynberg. Their behaviour was so craven that the disgusted burgher officers accused De Lille of treason. He was arrested and sent to Cape Town where he was brought before the authorities but found not guilty. For his own protection, however, he was kept in custody. The public were certain that he had assured the British that he would assist and not hinder them and were all for lynching him.

The British made themselves as comfortable as possible in Muizenberg. The transport *Arniston* arrived at Simon's Town bringing reinforcements from the garrison of St Helena Island. The Dutch authorities were informed of this reinforcement by letter and advised that many more men and armaments were on the way. The same terms as before of surrender were offered, but this time with the threat that further delay would lead to far more savage action.

The authorities in Cape Town rejected the letter. On 18 August the British were informed that resistance would continue. For the next few days the two sides scouted and skirmished without much effect. The Dutch were in difficulties. Their force was dwindling and there was little prospect of aid save through some miracle of a fleet from Holland. The mercenaries were quite disaffected; many of the burghers were slipping away home, worried about the safety of their families; the pandours were restive. On 1 September, the burghers and some pandours at least tried an attack on British outposts on the slopes of the Steenberg near Muysenburg There was some brisk firing but nothing was achieved. The attack had no support from artillery. The British by then had lost 5 men killed and 43 wounded. On the day of this attack the pandours mutinied. They had had enough. They marched with their arms to the castle and refused to fight any longer. They complained of insolent, incompetent officers, the ill-use of their families by Europeans while they were away from home, bad pay, insufficient rations, especially of brandy, and failure to receive a promised bonus for good behaviour.

Commissioner Sluyskens did what he could to pacify them with promises of better treatment to come but they returned to their quarters sullen, suspicious and with no intention of doing any more fighting. Hurried attempts to recruit more men in the country met with no success.

A plan was formulated for a night attack on Muizenberg but before this, on 4 September, a fleet of fourteen British ships arrived at Simon's Town bringing 3 000 fresh troops, with artillery and engineers. This was really the end of the matter. On 9 September the British issued another address inviting the inhabitants of the Cape to surrender and save loss of life. The Dutch authorities repeated their intention to fight on.

On 14 September an English force of nearly 5 000 men set out from Muizenberg along the way to Cape Town. The remaining Dutch force attempted to oppose them but there was little they could do. They harassed the oncoming British, killing one sailor and wounding seventeen soldiers. The Dutch, however, were not only outnumbered but they were betrayed from within. With De Lille still in custody, his successor, Major Van Baalen, proved even more reluctant to do battle. From his camp at Wynberg, he marshalled his force in such a way that it was quite ineffective. The artillery was so placed that the guns were useless. In any case, as soon as the British came along the track, the gallant major and his men simply bolted. The Wynberg camp was abandoned with everything in it. The disgusted countrymen felt themselves completely betrayed. They scattered and rode for home, leaving the mess to the authorities responsible and the place-name of Retreat, as a reminder of their disconcertment. The British camped for the night at Newlands and there, at midnight, consented to a Dutch request for a suspension of hostilities in order to arrange terms.

The next morning, 15 September 1795, General Craig travelled to Rustenburg, the country seat of the Dutch governors. The articles of peace were discussed and agreed to without much argument, except for one item. Five deserters from the British force had fled to the Dutch and Commissioner Sluyskens asked that they be pardoned. Craig declined but he was in a delicate position. Deserters from the Dutch side had joined his forces. After some thought he simply promised that, while he could not pardon deserters, he would ignore them as though they simply didn't exist. The next day, 16 September, the articles of capitulation were signed and the British took over the Cape. Lt-Colonel De Lille was rewarded by appointment as barrack-master in Cape Town. Other friendly officials received posts in the new administration. Commissioner Sluyskens returned to Holland. Colonel Gordon committed suicide in the garden of his Cape Town home on 5 October. It was said that he could not bear the jibe that the only time he had drawn his sword during the recent events had been when he led his men out of the castle and commanded them to lay down their arms in ceremonial surrender to the British troops paraded outside.

There was perhaps an understandable tendency to celebrate amongst the British forces. The Cape Town taverns did a roaring trade. Along the track from Muizenberg most of the farmhouses were looted, wine drunk, livestock stolen and some damage done. Even the grand manor-house of *Groot Constantia*, home of the renowned wine master, Hendrik Cloete, was visited by a stray party of roistering sailors who destroyed furniture, broke open several barrels of good wine and drank until they were incapable of any further activity. It is said that to make amends to the hospitable Mr Cloete, they, sometime later, presented him with a collection of cannonballs fired during the battle of Muizenberg. These cannonballs may still be seen at *Groot Constantia* ornamenting the pillars of the lower vineyard.

MUIZENBERG

The track from Cape Town to Simon's Town was a long one for thirsty men. The few wayside farmhouses were not places of refreshment and inns could only be established with profit when there was a steady demand by increased traffic along a better road. Such a state of affairs came about after the second British occupation of the Cape in 1806. Simon's Town in 1814 then became a base of the Royal Navy, and although the road from Cape Town still remained unmade it carried such a stream of travellers that wayside inns became viable.

One of the most celebrated of these inns was Merckel's Halfway House hotel established by George Merckel at Diep River. After Merckel's death in 1839 his widow Hester married a renowned character of the Cape, Johan Georg Rathfelder, a big burly man who had been born in Stuttgart in 1811, emigrated to the Cape in 1835 and, through his marriage, became the host of what was renamed as Rathfelder's Halfway House. Dressed in black leather, shell jacket ornamented with chains, jack boots and helmet, riding a big bay horse, he maintained at the hotel the hounds of the Cape Hunt and he, riding hard, was almost the prototype in Southern Africa of the Hell's Angels. Known as the 'King of the Landlords', he kept an excellent table and good order in the establishment, with a clientele of Anglo-Indians on recuperative leave, enthusiasts of the hunt, passing sailors and many distinguished guests including Prince Alfred of England in 1860. Rathfelder died in the hotel in 1873 and the building eventually became part of the former Eaton Convalescent Home.

Further along the road an equally famous wayside inn was established in Muizenberg in 1825 by two immigrants from Britain, the brothers Henry and Simon Peck. Farmer Peck's Inn, as it was called, was a rambling, thatched, white-walled building which stood on the site of the present tallest building in Muizenberg, *Cinnabar*. A sign on the front showed the gentle shepherd of Salisbury Plain, a benevolent- looking rustic with a lamb under his arm. Above the sign was another board displaying an atrocious poem, an effusion said to have been concocted by two midshipmen who, unable to pay their bill after a night in the place, presented the hosts with the poem and painted the inn sign instead of paying cash. The words were as follows:

> 'Life's but a journey,
> Let us live well on the road
> Says the Gentle Shepherd,
> The Gentle Shepherd of Salisbury Plain
> Multum in parvo! pro bono publico!
> Entertainment for man and beast, all of a row,
> Lekker Kost as much as you please,
> Excellent beds without any fleas,
> Nos patriam Fuguamis Now we are here,
> Vivamus, let us live by selling beer.
> On dorme a boire et a manger ici
> Come on and try it, whoever you may be'

In the pub there was another sign.

> This is a home for all those who haven't a home
> of their own, and a refuge for all who have one'.

The Pecks were reputed to be smugglers and purveyors of strong drink which had not known the seal of blessing of the revenue collector. They were occasionally in trouble with the law but around their inn the seaside resort of Muizenberg had its start. Simon died in 1850 and Henry in 1857. Rathfelder from the Halfway House then bought the inn and it was run by his daughter, an enormously fat woman whose contented appearance was considered a considerable advertisement for the place. She was married to Hendrik Hugo and, when he died, to Hendrik Auret. Apart from eating, she spent much of her time dozing in a double-sized rocking chair in a corner of the bar. A Kimberley syndicate bought the hotel in 1895 and renamed it the Grand. This place eventually vanished into history underneath the high modern building. The original inn sign is in the Africana Museum, Johannesburg. The name Peck's Valley lingers on in a valley above Muizenberg.

The old post building fortunately still remains in Muizenberg, with the overgrown defensive works on the mountain slopes above it. Zandvlei, where the battle of Muizenberg was fought, is now a recreational area, somewhat changed in shape, depth and nature by successive attempts by man to improve it. Birds and fish still flourish and the beautiful beach of Muizenberg stretches off unspoilt, free and spacious, for 35 km to the distant mountains on the east side of False Bay.

The village which grew up around the inn started with a few fishermen's cottages, gradually attracted holiday makers and became the rather atmospheric place of today, worth exploring strolling through the narrow streets of what is known as the 'ghetto', and then, in Beach Road along 'Millionaires Row', the imposing line of mansions that were mostly built in Edwardian times as holiday homes for the wealthy of Johannesburg. A magnificent feature of Beach Road are four adjoining houses designed by the celebrated architect, Herbert Baker. These houses *Crawford Lea, Rokeby, Sandhills* and *Swanbourne*, became the possession of Joan St Leger Lindbergh, great granddaughter of Frederick St Leger, founder of the *Cape Times* newspaper and daughter of A V Lindbergh, a Rand financier and creator, amongst other enterprises, of the Central News Agency. His daughter was a poet and philanthropist. She consolidated the four Baker designed houses and *Swanbourne* was opened on 28 August 1996 as the Joan St Leger Lindbergh Arts Foundation. In this handsome setting there are art exhibitions, lectures, readings and musical occasions. It is a fine cultural asset for all the people of South Africa. There is a tea-room, reference library and conference facilities. Open Mondays-Fridays 09h30–16h30. Phone (021) 788-2795.

Muizenberg has a pavilion, swimming pools, miniature golf, children's playgrounds, a promenade, water slides and a pond for small motor boats. Between Muizenberg and St James there is a very pleasant walkway, built from funds contributed by the Cape Town Municipality and various private persons, notably Mr Mendel Kaplan. The main road is narrow and congested with the walkway a pleasant alternative. Both walkway and road are 1,5 km long from Muizenberg to St James.

Trek fishermen still bring in hauls of harders (mullet), yellowtail, and other table fish. The beach stretches far away, inviting a swim, a paddle in the tidal zone, a night-time chance of finding an Argonaut, or a strange sea-bean, once thought to grow beneath the sea. These beans have supposed magic properties which make them much sought by African diviners for use in the procedure known as 'bone-throwing' used in attempts to predict the future or provide answers to human problems. The beans are now known to originate in the giant pods of the creeper *Entada pursaetha* which grows on trees overhanging rivers in tropical East Africa. Falling into the water, the beans, protected by a hard case, are carried down to the sea. They float off southwards in the Mozambique Current to its terminus at the Cape of Good Hope, 3 000 km or more away. A remarkable journey for a very peculiar bean.

From Muizenberg the main coastal road continues its way south-westwards, passing the railway station built in 1913 to serve the suburban line opened in 1882. Several interesting and contrasting buildings line the right hand side of the road and provide what is known as the Historical Mile of Muizenberg. First after the railway station, is the simple little building of *De Post Huys* (the post house) which sheltered Wynand Muys and his garrison. It has been restored in modern times and is preserved as an historic monument. When the British occupied the Cape, the old building became the quarters of the Commanding Officer of the Muizenberg garrison, with three batteries, a powder magazine close to the sea, and a barracks on the site of the later Muizenberg park.

Just beyond De Post Huys stand two buildings. The first housed the original post office of Muizenberg erected on the site of the old toll house where all passing traffic had to stop and pay their dues for the use of the road. Next to this building stands the Carnegie Library, built in 1911 from a grant made by Andrew Carnegie, the great Scottish philanthropist who made a vast fortune in America, then returned to Scotland and, in accordance with his belief that *'a man who dies possessed of wealth which he was free to distribute, dies disgraced'*, disbursed over £70 000 000 to the benefit of his fellow man, He died in 1919, aged 84.

The Carnegie library building in Muizenberg later became the police station while the post office became the magistrate's court. The two buildings fell out of use but on 21 June 1990 they were opened as the S A Police Museum, the first police museum in the Western Cape. The various aspects of police life are depicted in displays of antique furniture and memorabilia of police duties in the field. In the office, there are photographs of old police stations, chief magistrates, police officials and police detachments; historical snippets reflecting the development of the Cape police force prior to Union; and displays of uniforms and kits, arms and equipment. There are authentic reconstructions of police single quarters, a police inspector's office of about 1948, a charge office, a periodical court-room, and police cells, complete with one prisoner trying to escape and another trying to set the building alight! The full gamut of the world of crime is well represented in the displays portraying notorious crimes of the past and of weapons used by criminals. Behind the former library building, set in a terraced garden, there is an imposing statue of the first *fiscal* (law enforcement officer) in 1660, specially sculpted for the museum by Brigadier Buks van Staden. Visiting hours are Mondays to Fridays 08h00 to 15h30, Saturdays 09h00 to 13h00 and Sundays 14h00 to 17h00. Closed on public holidays and long weekends.

Next along the coastal road stands the elegant building named *The Fort*, built between 1929 and 1930 as the home of Count Natale Labia, who came to South Africa in 1916 as Italian Consul in Johannesburg and later his country's first minister plenipotentiary in South Africa. Count Labia married Ida, second daughter of the mining magnate, Sir J B Robinson. Their Muizenberg home was designed by the Cape Town architect, F M Glennie, as the official residence of the Italian legation. It was created on a grand scale. *The Fort* became a renowned social and diplomatic centre with receptions, parties and the visits of innumerable celebrated people in the world of diplomacy and the arts. Count Labia died in 1936. The title of Prince was conferred upon him posthumously in recognition of distinguished service to his country. His wife, Princess Ida, died in 1961. The house was leased as an embassy to the Canadian Government and then to the Argentinian Government. In 1983 it was presented by Prince Labia's son, Count Labia, with its treasures of art and design, to the people of South Africa. Now known as the Natale Labia Museum, the building, a national monument, was adapted for use as a museum and gallery in 1988. With its lecture rooms, gallery, restaurant and garden, it is an exquisite asset to the cultural life of the Cape. It is open Tuesdays to Sundays from 10h00 to 17h00. Closed Mondays and Worker's Day.

Continuing down the historic mile of the coastal road, there are several interesting houses such as *Canty Bay, Graceland, Knights* and *Rust en Vrede*, the mansion built in 1903 by the mining magnate Sir Abe Bailey. Graceland was the home of John Garlick, merchant prince and philanthropist. It is a superbly furnished and most elegant home in a garden which extends behind the house up the slopes of the mountains almost to the level of Boyes Drive. Paths take walkers through what is a sanctuary of wild flowers and beautiful trees. Perhaps the most interesting of all the buildings of the historical mile is the small, almost insignificant, thatched *Barkley Cottage*, bought in 1899 by Cecil Rhodes as a seaside retreat with a small bedroom and a living-room where great deals were planned. It was there that Rhodes spent as much of his remaining life as he could. He died there on 26 March 1902. His close friends and associates were gathered to see him for the last time. From his deathbed he concluded the planning and paper-work of the creation of the Rhodes Fruit Farms, destined to transform the entire fruit-growing and exporting industry of South Africa. He was only 49 years of age. It is said that his last words were *'So much to do, so little done'*. His doctors could only despair. There was so much the matter with this man that it was only his indomitable will that had kept him alive. From birth he had suffered from a congenital *Atrial Sertal* defect (hole in the heart). His lungs were shattered from tuberculosis and a drastic surgical procedure to arrest this wasting disease which had travelled the length of his spinal column, left him, at the age of 17, a eunuch. He panted rather than breathed. The south-easter with its rush of pure, fresh air, actually seemed to sustain him in the last months of his life. A hole was knocked through the wall of his house to allow the wind to sweep in to his sick bed. Physically he was a wreck but he had achieved so much and left so much to Southern Africa and the world that his memory will linger as long as man remains on earth.

Rhodes Cottage is open to the public Tuesdays to Sundays 10h00 to 13h00 and 14h00 to 17h00. Closed on Christmas. It is maintained with its original furniture and many interesting personal possessions and photographs concerned with the eventful life of a remarkable man.

ST JAMES

On 5 October 1858 the foundation stone of a small church was laid to provide a place of worship for the Catholic community living along the coast between Muizenberg and Kalk Bay. A number of Filipino fishermen, survivors of a shipwreck, had settled at Kalk Bay. They were Catholics and the nearest church to them was at Simon's Town. They supported the building of the new church. It was named in honour of the apostle and fisherman, St James, who was also the patron saint of Spain. Spanish was the language of the Filipino fishermen. A priest rode by horse from Wynberg each week to the church in order to say mass.

On 1 June 1874, Father John Duignam, an Irish priest who could speak Spanish was sent to serve the community. He was supposed to relieve only for six months but remained for 50 years. With his arrival, the St James Mission School was established close to the church, with Father Duignam and Francis Hilario as teachers to the children of the fisherfolk of Kalk Bay.

More people settled along the coast. The Cape Government railway decided in 1900 that a station was needed to replace a simple whistle stop alongside the church. They needed the site of the church for this station. John Duignam only assented on condition that the station be named St James. The indefatigable Duignam, supported by the Filipinos and other inhabitants of the coast, then set about building the handsome sandstone church of today. A larger school was also needed and this was also built of sandstone with the aid of Italian stone masons. The new convent school, named *Star of the Sea*, was opened at the beginning of 1908 with a staff of Dominican sisters transferred from the convent of Springfield. Father Duignam retired on 1 December 1925 and after a life of dedicated work, died in Bonnievale on 7 January 1931.

St James has a beach and tidal swimming pool sheltered from the south-east wind. An attractive residential area has been built on the overlooking mountain slopes with grand views of False

Bay. A walkway built close to the sea links St James to Muizenberg 1,5 km away. Beyond St James the coastal road continues for a further 1,5 km and then, at the entrance to Kalk Bay harbour, joins the road coming down the slopes from Boyes Drive.

KALK BAY, ITS HARBOUR, FISH, MOUNTAINS AND CAVES

Kalk Bay (lime bay) takes its name from former years when kilns were burned there in order to produce lime from shells for painting buildings. Quite a number of the white-walled homes of the Cape owed their smart appearance to the lime from Kalk Bay. The village had its beginning as a simple outspan place along the rough coastal track. In 1806 Abraham Kloppers, who had started trek fishing in Muizenberg, acquired some ground there, built a home and started to catch and dry fish as rations for slaves. A number of Filipino sailors who had been shipwrecked, also settled at Kalk Bay. In the days before refrigeration, the making of *bokkems* (kippers), the drying and salting of snoek and other suitable fish was the only means of preserving fish. A fisherman needed ample shore space on which to build the racks used for exposing the gutted fish to the warmth of the sun. The harbour is always a busy scene; but around June and July, the peak of the snoek season in False Bay, it is especially bustling. Catches of 40 000 snoek landed in one day in this compact little harbour are not uncommon. Fresh fish is sold in the harbour. There are two small tidal pools.

The mountain massif dominating the Muizenberg to Kalk Bay stretch of the False Bay coast is a superb recreational area for the energetic walker, cave explorer and nature lover. It is like a gigantic rock garden, ingeniously devised by Nature to shelter a vast variety of flowering plants, displaying their lovely blooms against a background of views across False Bay. There are paths to most places of interest in these mountains. Perhaps the most intriguing places to explore are the many remarkable caves, about which there is a story.

In 1924 a schoolmaster by the name of Johannes B Meyer spent a holiday at Kalk Bay. On learning that there were caves in the mountains, he occupied some of his time following the paths meandering up to the heights. His experiences entranced him so much that his holiday became a period of joyful discovery. The paths which made their way upwards, some steep and direct, others gradual and diagonal, rewarded him with memorable views. At his feet were gaily coloured wild flowers – heaths, proteas, everlastings, watsonias, scarlet-coloured flames and countless other lovely shrubs.

The caves added a touch of drama and adventure to this natural beauty. Several caves were already well known in the 1920s. Muizenberg Cave, with its enchanting moss-grown entrance, its low caverns and deep mysterious well, had not yet been totally disfigured by morons with their idiotic name painting; but the process had started, with a first date as early as 1873.

Clovelly Cave with its labyrinth of passages and chambers was sufficiently well known to be considered haunted by the local Coloured folk. Apparently a half-demented old mountain hermit had once made his home there and had amused himself by stealthily approaching visitors on the mountains and scaring them out of their wits with his sudden chuckle close behind them. Eventually he was found dead in his cave. The sinister echo of his chuckle is reputed to linger on in the cave, and it is said that a cold hand touches any interloper's shoulder the moment his light goes out.

The amazing Boomslang Cave, penetrating right through a ridge for 146 m, was discovered in 1911 by Arderne and Sampson. It was here that Meyer met a fellow explorer. It was an amusing chance meeting. Meyer started his cave journey from the low northern entrance, wriggling in on his stomach. At the same time, J C W Moore started from the southern side where the entrance is high and overlooks the Fish Hoek glen. The two men met in one of the chambers in the middle reaches of the cave and, with a candle burning on a ledge of rock, they enjoyed a chat about the mountains and the wonders of the caverns. Moore was a Kalk Bay man who knew the area well, and his knowledge stimulated Meyer to learn more about this fascinating place.

As a result of his explorations during his holiday, Meyer was privileged to discover two new caves which he named Central Grotto and Johles Cave, the latter a combination of his own name and that of a companion, Leslie van Blerk. He never forgot the pleasure of these pioneer explorations. In 1935 Meyer retired. He was a sick man, but he returned to Kalk Bay and made his home there, determined to devote what time he had left to a study of the mountains and to the discovery of more caves. During the following months he wandered over the heights and the more he explored, the more caves he found. The exercise and fresh air gave him a new lease of life.

A small band of friends gathered around Meyer, for he was a most amiable companion on the mountains. Knowledgeable, communicative, humorous, he knew many good yarns and was a fine hand at brewing coffee or grilling a chop. Through their activities, Meyer and his friends became known as the Moles. Meyer was recognised as First Mole. A certificate was awarded to his companions who had explored at least the dozen principal caves of the 95 assorted grottoes, caverns, pits and other exciting places mostly discovered and named by Meyer on the Kalk Bay mountains.

Alvin Meyer, Phillip Hitchcock, Anne Hefere, Leslie van Blerk, Horatio Nelson, Basil Harris, Arthur Patten and J W Hurlingh were some of the Moles. The pleasure they had in their various outings is reflected in the names they and the First Mole attached to their discoveries: Rest-a-Bit, Light and Gloom, Six Moles Cave, Moss and Diamonds, Drip-Drop, Sunbeam Cave, Noonday Rest, Mirth Parlour and many more. Some of these names have vanished from modern maps but most remain, many painted on to the rock walls of the caves by Meyer and the Moles. Countless later visitors have enjoyed pleasant days of adventurous exercise and relaxation in rediscovering these interesting places.

The heights of this sandstone mass consists of a number of parallel ridges. The ceaseless dripping and washing of water during the wet months of winter has eroded the rocks into curious shapes (such as the remarkable head overlooking Devil's Pit which resembles that of a latter-day South African prime minister) and modelled numerous caverns.

Of the caverns, the most extensive so far found is Ronan's Well. This cave was known before Meyer's time, but for many years it was thought to be only 68 m long. Then a modern cave explorer (or speleologist), Michael McAdam, followed a draught of air coming through a narrow crack and, with some difficult scrambling and a tight 2,5 m long squeeze, opened the way into an involved series of underground chambers, halls and crevices stretching for 365 m into the depth of what is known as Ridge Peak and thence out through two other caves, Aladdin and Robin Hood. Ronan's Well is not a cave for a beginner to explore, even the entrance is tricky – a rather sinister – looking grotto with a dark hole 5,5 m up its inner wall, which takes the explorer into the heart of the mountain.

Boomslang Cave, the second most extensive cave so far found is a safe, exciting 146 m passage through the ridge known as Cave Peak. There are several impressive chambers, a 9 m crawl on the northern end, and an impressive southern exit high over Fish Hoek. It was at the pool on the floor of this exit that the original discoverers disturbed a boomslang quenching its thirst – hence the name.

The third largest cave in these mountains was found by Meyer in 1941. The exploration of this cave must have given its discoverer many a thrill, as the first entrance found was a narrow 9,5 m deep pit, the descent of which required a rope ladder.

At the bottom end of this pit the cave stretches out in a succession of passages and chambers for 132 m. At the south-eastern end an easier entrance was subsequently found; a chimney 3,6 m deep connected through a low cavern and a narrow passageway with Annie's Hall, the first of the large caverns. Meyer, who named several of his cave discoveries after figures in Greek mythology, named this whole remarkable cave sequence Oread Hall, after the Oreads, the nymphs of caverns and mountains in Greek legend. The 13,7 m deep Devils Pit was another cave first explored by Meyer by means of a rope ladder. Now it is usually entered from a hole in the ravine below it which leads through Creepy Corridor and Herripilation Chamber for 36,5 m and then into the pit.

Among the numerous parties which Meyer conducted through the caves was one consisting of twenty lady teachers. Getting them through the section of Boomslang Cave where explorers are forced to crawl must have taken some coaxing, but generally he seems to have enjoyed having ladies accompany him on explorations. Several of his cave discoveries carry names such as Pollie's Cave, Beatrice Cave, Nellie's Pool and Dolly's Doorway.

The last cave found by Meyer and his Moles was a small cavern rather wistfully named Me Too. The First Mole sickened after that. In 1951 his health broke down completely. He recovered partially, made two more climbs and then died of lung cancer on 9 September 1952. He was 78 years old and the mountains had given him the gift of nineteen healthy years during which his diary records 1 700 climbs into the Kalk Bay mountains. Memories of him will linger over the mountains.

In later days Jose Burman and S MacPherson found a cave on the Red Afrikaner Ridge (named on account of the watsonias there) and fittingly named it Meyer's Memorial.

From Kalk Bay the coastal road continues past the entrance to the harbour and curves around the slopes of the mountains. After 1,5 km a fine view of Fish Hoek and its glen is revealed, with (on the northern side) the small residential suburb of ...

CLOVELLY

Few railway stations have ever displayed signs such as those of Clovelly station, prohibiting angling from the platform! At Clovelly the sea washes against the station. If the railway administration was not so firmly set against it, this little station could provide good fishing for travellers! Clovelly station was originally known as *Trappies* (little steps) because the original road descended as though down a staircase to the Fish Hoek glen.

The area of Clovelly was once a farm named *Klein Tuin* (little garden) owned by the De Kock family. An Englishwoman, a guest of the De Kocks, is said to have been responsible for the name of Clovelly because she fancied the place resembling the charming little fishing village in her native Devon. At Clovelly the Silvermine stream reaches the sea. A road to the right leads up the banks of this stream through the wind-sheltered residential area to the Clovelly Country Club and then, as a country lane, eventually joins the Ou Kaapse Weg and carries on to Noordhoek.

Across the Silvermine stream the road enters the area of Fish Hoek, with its centre 1,5 km from Clovelly.

FISH HOEK

Fish Hoek, part of the South Peninsula municipality, is almost unique in Southern Africa. It is a striking example of non-town-planning and it is also 'dry'! The original grant of the farm *Vischhoek* (fish glen) was made by the Governor, Lord Charles Somerset, to Andries Bruins in 1818. There were conditions to this grant. The farm lay directly on the road to the naval station of Simon's Town and some very thirsty sailors on shore leave. The prudent Lord Somerset therefore stipulated that no public wine house be kept on the farm. This condition was perpetuated in the township created in 1919. The municipality grew as one of the few teetotaller towns in thirsty Southern Africa. You could drink in Fish Hoek from your own supplies but, with bottle stores and bars absent, the town boasted a minimal crime rate. Nowadays there are still no bottle stores but restaurants and sports clubs are licensed. It grew as a residential area connected by railway to Cape Town. Despite its congested and unbeautiful layout, a dismal absence of trees, and its principal commercial street also part of the main coastal road carrying heavy traffic to the southern end of the Cape Peninsula, it is a relaxed, self-contained little town with a safe bathing beach.

The glen in which Fish Hoek lies cuts right across the Cape Peninsula. In comparatively recent geological times (Cretaceous 65–125 million years ago) the sea washed through the glen, leaving the southern portion of the Peninsula an island. The present floor of the glen is the sandy former sea bed. In a great rock shelter overlooking the northern side of this glen, prehistoric people once lived and dined on marine molluscs, fish and tidal life which teemed in the shallow waters below them. The rock shelter became known as the *Schildersgat* (painter's cave) from the rock art left on its walls by the early inhabitants. It is now more generally known as Peers Cave after Victor Peers and his son Bertram. In 1926 they commenced a painstaking exploration of the place which resulted in the excavation of the skull of Fish Hoek Man, a representative of the people who inhabited this part of Southern Africa 15 000 years ago.

Peers Cave may be reached by following the road from Fish Hoek through the glen to the western side of the Peninsula. At 3,5 km from the centre of Fish Hoek, there is a sign indicating the turn-off to the Fish Hoek sports ground and to Peers Cave. From the end of this road there is a path through a forest of Port Jackson trees, then over glistening white sand dunes and up the slopes of the ridge to Peers Cave and to another remarkable cave, Tunnel Cave (reached by the same path), in which interesting discoveries of artefacts have been made. The path ends at a beacon just above Peers Cave. From this vantage-point a fine view of the glen may be enjoyed.

The beach at Fish Hoek is gently sloping and provides safe swimming. An easy stroll may be taken through the rocks at the water's edge along the pleasant *Jager Walk*, named after a former mayor of the town, Herman Jager, who first proposed it in 1931. Trek fishing is carried out from the beach. In the restaurant on the beach there is an interesting memento of this industry started by Filipino fishermen who settled in the area in the 19th century. The first boat they used, the *Bonita*, was overturned in a False Bay storm. The crew were drowned. The prow of the boat now rests as the centre-piece of the seafood restaurant. It is a mute memorial to a sad tragedy in a modern setting of a fine sea-food dining place.

The False Bay Fire Museum displays antique and modern fire-fighting equipment. It is open by appointment only. Phone (021) 782-1327. Kaolin is mined in the glen near Sun Valley.

A cluster of 80 cottages and an excellent municipal caravan park provide accommodation just above the tidal zone of the beach.

GLENCAIRN

From Fish Hoek the main road passes the Sunnycove railway station and continues along the coast around the slopes of the 303 m high Else Peak to enter the valley of the *Elserivier* (river of *els* or alder trees). A branch road leads up this valley past many residences, the Rotary, MOTHs and Gordons camps, as well as the buildings of the *Welcome* farm, originally granted in the early 19th century to the well-known Brand family whose sons have played so distinguished a part in the administration of South Africa (Johannes Brand was President of the Orange Free State from 1864 to 1889). The wetland on the floor of the valley is of great interest to bird watchers. It provides protected nesting for many species of birds. The road continues up to Da Gama Park, a housing estate built for members of the South African Navy and named after the Portuguese navigator, Vasco da Gama. Another road leads over the dunes and down into the Fish Hoek glen where it links with the coastal road and the Ou Kaapse Weg.

The inlet at the mouth of the stream, marked on maps as *Elsebaai* (alder tree bay), has a small beach and a tidal swimming-pool. The residential area is known as *Glencairn*, so named, it is said, by a Scot who came from the original Glen Cairn. He was in the habit of wandering about this little valley playing his bagpipes. Glencairn is administered as part of Simon's Town, which is reached by the main coastal road 6 km from Fish Hoek (36,6 km from Cape Town).

When the south-east wind is not blowing, Glencairn beach can be very pleasant. In 1939 it was reported that a large number of people on this beach saw the spectral *Flying Dutchman*.

In the breakers between Glencairn and Simon's Town the tops of engine cylinders can be seen, all that remains of the SS *Clan Stuart*, a naval collier which was blown ashore there on 20 November 1914. The ship had been at anchor with her engines off when a south-easter carried her gently ashore. The crew ended the day playing billiards and drinking beer in the Glencairn Hotel. The ship settled in the sand and refused to budge.

One kilometre beyond Glencairn there is the Dido Valley Road turn-off right at a traffic-light. It leads to the naval residential area of Da Gama Park. A short way along this road is Topstones.

Topstones, more familiar to Capetonians and visitors as The Scratch Patch, the world's largest gemstone-tumbling factory, had an interesting beginning. In 1967 Bruce Baines finished his training as a lawyer in Cape Town, but decided not to enter practice. His interest lay in gemstones and the creation of beautiful things. He went to London and established a gemstone manufacturing and distributing business.

Then fate took a hand in the game. Bruce secured a contract to provide Mobil Europe with 40 million gemstones for use in a free-gift promotional scheme in garages. To produce these stones, Bruce, his brother and two other partners, had to set up a factory. The contract called for the gemstones known as tiger's eye to be a substantial part of the 40 million stones. Tiger's eye is of South African origin (Griqualand West) and a law forbade the export in unfinished form. There had to be a tumbling plant in South Africa and Simon's Town was the choice.

Such was the beginning of Topstones. Since its creation countless thousands of beautiful gemstones have been tumbled, polished and mounted in the factory. Outside there is a treasure-hunter's delight, a scratch-patch where fossickers have a real chance of finding all manners of lovely things amongst thousands of fragments of gemstones. Visits to the factory and shop may be made

Mondays to Fridays 08h30 to 16h45. Saturdays, Sundays and Public Holidays 09h00 to 16h30. The Scratch Patch also has a branch in the Waterfront.

One kilometre beyond the turn-off to Topstones and Da Gama Park there is a turn-off right which climbs Red Hill and leads to the west coast of the Peninsula. The views from this road are spectacular. The main coastal road, after another kilometre, reaches ...

SIMON'S TOWN

Simon's Town is spectacularly situated beneath a 678 m high ridge of mountains. The bay of Simon's Town was originally known as *Isselsteijn Bay* from a Dutch East Indiaman of that name which, in 1671, sheltered there from contrary winds. The crew of this ship found the bay so much to their liking that their reports eventually stimulated an exploration of the bay in 1687 by the Governor, Simon van der Stel. He recommended its development as an alternative winter sanctuary to Table Bay, which was exposed to north-westerly storms. The bay was renamed Simon's Bay in his honour. A wooden pier, barracks and two small forts were built there in 1743. In 1814 the British converted Simon's Town into a naval base for the South Atlantic Squadron. Additional workshops were erected, among them a mast house and sail loft that became the St George's Church, used by the Navy as a place of worship on Sundays when sail-making activities were not carried out. At the turn of this century substantial workshops and a dry dock were constructed. It is from this time that Simon's Town acquired something of the special naval atmosphere of a small English seafaring town, with narrow twisting streets. The handsome Admiralty House, at first a lodging house, was taken over by the British Admiralty as the home of the Commander-in-Chief of the South Atlantic Squadron. The Old Burying Ground records on its tombstones a colourful story of sea fights, cuttings-out and escapades of the period.

On 2 April 1957 the South African Navy took over Simon's Town naval base. The coming and going of naval ships and the activity of small craft in the fishing and pleasure boat harbour create a real seafaring atmosphere. Simon's Town is the home port for over 200 ocean-going yachts and power boats, many used by their private owners to pursue big game-fish (tunny and marlin) during the summer season off the Cape of Good Hope. The False Bay Yacht Club which incorporates the South African Marlin and Tuna Club has its quarters close to the harbour. The South African record bluefin tunny stands at 361 kg and was caught by Brian Cohen in December 1968.

Simon's Town is the terminus of the suburban railway from Cape Town. The train journey along the coast between Muizenberg and Simon's Town is a delight. It is worthwhile strolling down the main street of Simon's Town with its Historic Mile of period buildings and national monuments. The Simon's Town Museum is in the original Residency, built in 1777 for the use of the Governor on his periodic visits to the town. The museum contains a varied collection of interesting relics from Simon's Town's past. A section of the exhibits deals with the celebrated dog 'Just Nuisance' who was a great friend of sailors during the Second World War. There are many amusing stories about this naval dog and his love of sailors. He died in Simon's Town on 1 April 1944 at the age of only seven and is buried above the town. There is a memorial to him created by Jean Doyle, a bronze statue, on a rock on Jubilee Square in the centre of the town where he often stood and aided in collecting money for charity. The museum is open Mondays to Fridays from 09h00 to 16h00 and on Saturdays from 10h00 to 16h00. Sundays and public holidays from 11h00 to 16h00. The original police cells, including a 'black hole' (punishment cell) are in the basement. Next to the Simon's Town museum is the South African Naval Museum containing many interesting exhibits related to naval history and equipment. Ship models, a hands-on operations room and bridge of a submarine and a minesweeper. The museum is open daily 10h00 to 16h00 except Christmas Day, New Year's Day and Good Friday.

The Anglican St Francis Church, completed in 1837, although not in its present form, and claimed to be the oldest Anglican Church in the Peninsula, is situated next to the Simon's Town Museum.

Another interesting building is the Martello Tower built in 1796 by the British who, after seizing the Cape, wished to prevent possible attempts by Napoleon to occupy it. The tower was a copy of a French fortification which had caused the British no little grief when, in 1794, they set out to capture the bay of Florenzo in Corsica as a base for their ships blockading the port of Toulon. The British had never encountered such a fortification. It was deceptively simple, just a circular tower of stone garrisoned by two grenadiers, twenty seamen and armed with two cannon. Two British warships found themselves totally repelled by this fortification which stood on Cape Mortello and denied entrance to the bay. Six of the attackers died, 56 were wounded and the two ships severely damaged before the disgruntled British withdrew from the resolute little fort. It took a land attack launched the next morning to subdue the tower, and then only by smoking the defenders out by setting fire to damp wood piled around the sides.

That such a simple fortification could prove so difficult to subdue impressed the British command. They made a model of it, corrupted its name to Martello, built the one in Simon's Town as their first fortification there and eventually built 103 around the coast of England, and one more in South Africa at Fort Beaufort. The Simon's Town tower has a diameter of 12,57 m. It is 7,85 m high and has walls 1,83 m thick made of local sandstone. Inside, a ground floor and a first floor provided space for quarters for the occupants and firing positions through embrasures which covered all approaches. On the flat roof there was a base for a cannon.

This tower guarded the main powder magazine of the British fleet in Simon's Bay. With the nearby original Dutch battery known as *Boetselaar* it was the most southerly defensive work in the Cape. From the protective walls of Van Riebeeck's first fort, through his almond hedge and the magic circle, to the post of Muizenberg and then to the Martello Tower at Simon's Town, the old track had steadily found its way. South of the tower, the track deteriorated into a path leading down to the actual Cape of Good Hope. The only other structures of any note in Simon's Town were a store, magazine and barrack built by the Dutch in 1745, a small timber wharf, a second small battery known as *Zoutman*, and a scattered handful of houses. Simon's Town, for a while, was the end of the road and the southern end of civilisation, such as it was, on the Cape Peninsula.

The Martello Tower stands on naval property but may be visited by arrangement with the Simon's Town museum. To find the Martello Tower, drive through the town past the second gate into the dockyard, and follow the sandstone dockyard wall to its end. Then, still by the wall, turn sharply left into a narrow road called Martello Road leading to the sports ground. Turn left again with the wall towards the car-park. A stone wall with a gate surrounds the tower, which houses the museum. On the slopes overlooking Simon's Town stand several historic old gun batteries, including the Scala Battery with three guns of 9,2 inch (23,2 cm) calibre, capable of firing a projectile for nearly 40 km. Even older is the Zoutman Battery with a 9 inch (22,8 cm) muzzle-loading gun built in 1890. Numerous ruins of old fortifications remain, including all the ingredients for an interesting naval museum.

In past years, the *Stempastorie,* the house where the Rev M L de Villiers composed the music for the national anthem of the Union of South Africa, was open to the public. However, with the change of government in 1994 and the introduction of a new nathional anthem for South Africa, it was decided to close this museum. There is a privately run toy museum and warriors shop open at normal trading hours.

At the time of the Napoleonic wars a sad, half-forgotten drama took place in Simon's Bay. If the Dutch had their problems of disaffection amongst their troops and citizens at the time of the battle of Muizenberg, then so had the British in their navy. The wars with the French were long drawn out, the press gangs in Britain brutal and conditions on naval ships often dismal, with sickness, bad food and an officer caste who occasionally overlooked the fact that their subordinates were human beings. Such conditions had driven many desperate men to mutiny in past years. Obnoxious officers had been thrown overboard and honest men turned into pirates when they could no longer go home without being hanged for their actions.

British sailors taken prisoner during the wars learned that conditions in the French navy were far superior to those in the Royal Navy. Ratings and officers got on much better, the slogans of liberty, fraternity and equality were more than catchwords. On 7 October 1797 the crews of nine British warships anchored in Simon's Bay rose in mutiny, hauling up at the end of each ship's jibboom a jacket and sending rounds of cheers from one ship to the other until the sound echoed back from the cliffs overlooking the bay.

Commissioned officers and warrant officers were put ashore and the admiral in command, Admiral Pringle, was detained on board his flagship the *Tremendous*. Delegates were elected by the mutineers to state their case and a manifesto was drawn up listing grievances which included ill-treatment, oppression, extortion, bad food and corruption. In the manifesto the mutineers stated that they would permit no ill usage of any one, pillaging, bad behaviour, riot or thefts. They were loyal to their country and would return to duty at the first sign of the presence of an enemy.

News of the mutiny was carried post-haste by a horseman galloping along the track through Muizenberg to Cape Town. There was outrage amongst the British officials. The Governor was Lord Macartney, a conservative man in the social establishment of Britain and intolerant of any notion that the lower classes had rights of complaint. Troops were immediately dispatched to occupy Simon's Town and force the mutineers to surrender.

Admiral Pringle seemed more sympathetic although for a British admiral to be confined on his own ship by his own crew was unpardonable. The recent mutiny at Spithead had been brutally suppressed, but here was the same thing happening in Simon's Bay. The British ruling class considered French revolutionary ideals to be a virus more infectious than smallpox. Pringle was discreet, perhaps uneasily aware that some grievances were justified, and a little sympathy might be a better way of ending the mutiny than severe suppression. He discussed matters with the mutineers, promised to do what he could to redress their grievances, bring to trial any officer accused of ill-treatment and give amnesty to all mutineers if they submitted once again to naval discipline.

The mutineers accepted the offer. After five days of revolt the mutiny ended. But twelve days later, on 24 October, three more British warships arrived and their crews went into mutiny as soon as the anchors dropped in Simon's Bay. Again the mutineers were promised redress of grievances and they submitted to discipline. On 6 November, Captain George Stephens of the *Tremendous* was tried by court martial, charged by Philip James and other members of the crew with oppressive conduct and neglect of his duty to his subordinates. He had been dumped ashore in Simon's Town by the mutineers at the start of the trouble and was in high temper at his humiliation. His fellow officers in the court supported him. The sailors then insulted the court, it was suspended and the mutiny broke out again.

The trouble spread to Table Bay. Admiral Pringle was no longer in confinement. With Lord Macartney he arranged for the big guns of the Amsterdam battery in Cape Town to be aimed on the ships and the mutineers were summarily ordered to return to duty and surrender their leaders within two hours or be fired upon. The mutineers on the three ships concerned surrendered and 22 of their leaders were confined in the castle.

Another warship, the *Crescent*, then arrived in Table Bay on 16 October and anchored off Robben Island. There her crew mutinied and obnoxious officers were summarily offloaded on the island. A delegation was sent to Cape Town to present complaints to the admiral but he promptly arrested all the delegates. A warship was ordered to bring the *Crescent* up to anchorage in the range of the shore battery and one hour was given to the mutineers to surrender their leaders. Six men were given up and the mutiny ended.

Captain Stephens was honourably acquitted by the court martial. No other officer was brought to trial but the leaders of the mutiny had to face the music. On 21 November Philip James and Daniel Chapman were sentenced to death and duly hanged on the yardarm two days later. Two other leaders, Richard Foot and James Reese, were sentenced to death and executed on 24 November. Three other leaders received severe sentences, and the rest were given mercy.

No attempt was made to alleviate conditions in the various ships, whose crews mainly consisted of men forced into service by the naval press gangs. Lord Macartney simply noted that from the minutest investigation of the mutiny he could not discover the *'shadow of a grievance to be pleaded in its alleviation'*. Four men swinging on the yardarm didn't much disturb his lordship's sleep. Why they were prepared to die for what he considered to be such trivial grievances was quite beyond him.

Simon's Town is now part of the South Peninsula municipality, a part of the Cape Metropolitan area.

The main coastal road leaves Simon's Town (and the last petrol point for 55 km) and continues to the end of the Peninsula along a stretch of coast that is best described as one long ocean playground. Here are delectable little bathing places such as Seaforth and Boulders, which are sheltered from the winds of summer. *Seaforth* was named by an early settler, Captain Harington, whose wife was a niece of the Earl of Seaforth. A pathway links Seaforth to Boulders. It is pleasant to see a protected colony of penguins living among the granite rocks of Boulders and mixing on sociable terms with human beings. Other delightful bathing places in this area are Windmill Beach, Water's Edge Beach, Fisherman's Beach, Foxy Beach and Froggy Pond.

MILLER'S POINT

The climax of this stretch of coast comes 8 km from Simon's Town, at Miller's Point. In 1828 this beautiful locality was acquired by Edmund Miller who built a seaside cottage there called *Elsemere*. Until 1850 his family had the whole place to themselves and he conducted whaling operations in False Bay, mainly during the winter months when female right whales and humpback or fin whales habitually come into False Bay to calve. Then the estate passed into other hands. Today Miller's Point is a fine public coastal resort. In this superb setting, the then Cape Divisional Council imaginatively created a caravan park, with vehicles deployed on terraces that enjoy a view of sea and distant mountains which no luxury hotel could surpass.

Playgrounds, boat-launching facilities, a restaurant, a large tidal swimming-pool, green lawns, innumerable picnic spots and a profusion of wild flowers are among the attractions of this recreational area. For the canoeist and underwater swimmer there is a glorious garden beneath the ocean, with anemones and sea urchins of brilliant hues set in waving forests of seaweed where shoals of lively fish wander like butterflies in a magical world.

SMITSWINKEL BAY

From Miller's Point the road continues south along the coast for a further 5 km, passing many picnic and viewsites until, gaining steadily in height, it climbs diagonally along the cliffs 91 m above the bay known as *Smitswinkel* (the blacksmith's shop), a name suggested by a pair of rocks in the sea, one shaped like an anvil, the other like a bellows. Smitswinkel Bay is a favourite fishing spot, with a cluster of informal shacks built on the water's edge where their owners enjoy a happy privacy. Troops of baboons frequent this portion of the road. Human visitors are warned that it is an offence to feed wild animals. Baboons are amusing to watch but they can become nasty if they are tempted to climb onto cars by handouts of food.

The road now swings away from the coast and after 8 km reaches a junction with a turn-off to the left, taking the traveller for the final 13 km southwards to the end of the road at Cape Point. These final 13 km lead through the Cape of Good Hope Nature Reserve.

THE CAPE OF GOOD HOPE NATURE RESERVE

A visit to the Cape of Good Hope Nature Reserve at the tip of the Cape Peninsula is a most fascinating outing. The area has excellent roads and is easily accessible at all seasons of the year. The summer months (November to March) are inclined to be windy. The winter months (May to August) are pleasant, as the rainfall is hardly sufficient to disturb visitors for more that a few days each year. Spring (September and October) when the countryside is colourfully strewn with wild flowers is particularly lovely.

Walking trails lead to many pleasant and secluded places. At Buffel's Bay and Bordjiesrif there are enclosed tidal swimming-pools and at Buffel's Bay a launching ramp for boats. There are several picnic spots in the reserve and a field museum dealing with the area. Most tourists to South Africa visit the Cape of Good Hope Nature Reserve. The end of the road at Cape Point in fact, is one of the most famous coach terminuses in the world. With its sister cape, Cape Horn, at the end of South America, the Cape of Good Hope is one of the most celebrated of all capes.

At this stage it is perhaps necessary to clarify a persistent controversy about the waters washing the two sides of the Peninsula. Are these waters those of the Indian Ocean or those of the Atlantic Ocean? In actual fact the sea knows no oceans. Man, for the sake of geographical convenience, has applied a variety of names to portions of the sea, but the straight lines he draws between them are just as imaginary as the thread stretched across the lens of a telescope by sailors and shown as the equator to gullible passengers when they first cross the famous 'line'.

The sea knows only the differences of temperature and currents in its various parts, and these are the decisive influences affecting all forms of marine life. When the first sailors came down the west coast searching for an end to Africa and a sea route to the east, they discovered that the peninsula of the Cape of Good Hope was the most south-westerly point. It was not the most southerly point – this is Cape Agulhas, 170 km eastwards – but it was to them the most important, for on doubling it, they not only commenced the great swing eastwards, but changes in water temperature and marine life confirmed for them that they were entering a new world. No such significant changes were discernible on either side of Cape Agulhas at any season of the year. It was the Cape of Good Hope, which marked the blending of the cultures and life forms of East and West. It is here that two powerful currents of this part of the sea – the warm Mozambique–Agulhas Current coming down the east coast and the cold Antarctic Drift which forms the Benguela Current running up the west coast of Africa – have their collision course. The warm waters of the east finally lose themselves, but by their pressure ensure that the cold waters sweep on up the west coast and do not penetrate eastwards.

Few fish or other forms of marine life can tolerate a temperature change of 5°C or more in water. To the warm-water Indo-Pacific species living on the east side of Africa, and the cold-water species living on the south-west side, the difference between the two currents provides a barrier as impenetrable as a garden wall.

Modern geographers have drawn a straight line south from Cape Agulhas and marked this as the division of the Atlantic and Indian oceans. But this is purely a man-made convenience. The actual point of impact of the prevailing currents could never be a straight line. As with the cultures of East and West, so the sea currents with their different temperatures experience an erratic and varying blending. The cold Antarctic Drift surges up from the south and collides with the south-western coast from the Cape of Good Hope north-westwards. In summer the pressure of the warm Mozambique Current holds it roughly in that position and it sweeps northwards as the Benguela Current. In winter the Mozambique Current is weaker, and the meeting-place is slightly further east.

However, the Cape of Good Hope is always the beacon. It is one of the great landmarks of the world, proclaiming that this is where the two halves of the world, East and West, merge; where two ways of life have their frontiers and blend with the culture of the great dividing continent of Africa. It is here that two major ocean currents, each with an enormous influence on all forms of life, climate and scenery in their proximity, have a rendezvous and, simultaneously, a parting of the ways.

Luis de Camões, the poet genius of Portugal, tells of the legendary origin of the Cape Peninsula in the majestic verse of his *Lusiads*. The monstrous *Adamastor* (the untamed) was one of the 100 giants who rebelled against the gods of ancient Greece and attempted to take Mount Olympus by storm. Defeated by Hercules and Vulcan at the head of all the gods, the giants were condemned to eternal punishment. They were banished to the far places of the Earth and buried there beneath volcanoes and mountains.

Adamastor, the personification of the barbarism of ancient Africa, was condemned to a special transmutation. It is his body *'turned to rocks all rough and strange'* which forms the peninsula of the Cape of Good Hope. His spirit forever haunts this tomb. With Table Mountain as his workshop for storms and thunderbolts, he roams the surrounding seas in the form of howling gales and dark storm-clouds, raving dire vengeance on the sailors who disturb his seclusion. The pioneer Portuguese explorers were the sailors who first dared this rage of Adamastor. The vengeance which he cursed upon them still persists, as may be seen in the strange tale of the *Flying Dutchman*.

Apart from leaving a few middens – kitchen refuse of marine shells, game animal skeletons, etc – prehistoric human beings played no significant part in the story of the Cape Peninsula. Their ancient garbage dumps may still be seen at places such as Batsata Cove, Cape Maclear, Bonteberg and Rooikrans, where there was some natural shelter from the winds and drinking-water was available from springs.

Early human beings in these areas collected shellfish and lobsters, caught various fish species, foraged for bulbs, roots and edible vegetation, and hunted and trapped game in close competition with other resident predators, such as the now-extinct Cape lion and the lynx. There were probably not many game animals. The winds of the Cape Peninsula made life unpleasant for the larger animals and the absence in the soil of such essentials to their welfare as copper traces made the grazing unpalatable. Migrating animals which wandered about at will could visit the area seasonally but leave when they tired of the winds and grazing. Such migrants could have included Cape buffalo, elephant, black rhino and various antelope. Baboons were always present. They are today a source of amusement to all visitors and of interest to scientists in that they scavenge the beaches in search of sea foods in similar manner to prehistoric humans.

Bird life was varied, with about 150 species resident at different seasons of the year. A variety of sea-birds was always the principal feature. Jackass penguins landed on the beaches, while albatrosses, giant petrels, gannets, black-backed gulls, Hartlaub's gulls and cormorants were all common around the coast. Of the land birds, the malachite and orange-breasted sunbird were the most striking.

In the surrounding sea, Cape sea-lions, whales, porpoises, sharks, tunny, yellowtail and snoek were in abundance. On land, tortoises have always been common. The Cape of Good Hope Nature Reserve is, in fact, one of their great breeding grounds. A few Cape cobras, boomslangs, mole snakes, puff-adders and other snakes also made their homes in the southern Peninsula.

The modern history of the Cape of Good Hope began in a howling gale, which blew in the last three weeks of January 1488. Concealed in this gale, according to Luis de Camões was the sullen fury of the giant Adamastor and the termination of the age of legends. Down the west coast, probing, searching and enquiring, came the Portuguese explorer, Bartholomeu Dias. In a cramped cockle-shell of a ship, with his crew sick and frightened, he persisted in sailing southwards, hoping to find an end to the continent of Africa.

On 6 January 1488, off the south-west coast, they saw the lovely Cederberg range and named it *'Mountains of the Three Magi Kings'*. Then a storm enveloped them. The tiny ship was blown far from land, with Dias pitting his own resolution against the full force of nature. At last the storm abated. The sailors looked for land and found to the east nothing save the swirling sea. They swung northwards. In the storm they had unknowingly doubled the end of Africa. Only on 3 February 1488 did they reach land at what is known as Mossel Bay. The unseen cape around which they had found their way they named the *Cabo Tormentoso* (Cape of Storms).

Dias sailed on, with his crew in a mutinous and sulky mood. Beyond Algoa Bay, off the mouth of the Chalumna River, Dias was forced to turn back, leaving a stone pillar erected on a lonely headland known as the 'Rock of the Fountains'. But at least the weather was fine. Keeping close to the coast, they discovered Cape Agulhas, naming it 'Cape St Brendan', as it was on the feast day of St Brendan, 16 May 1488, that they passed it. A few days later they passed Cape Hangklip, looked into the spacious and lovely 'Gulf Within the Mountains' (False Bay); and then, in fair and gentle weather at last, the Portuguese historian Barros wrote, *'they beheld that great and remarkable Cape hidden for so many centuries, which when discovered revealed not itself alone, but another world of lands'*.

To this cape the Portuguese king eventually gave the name of *Cape of Good Hope*, abandoning the first name of the Cape of Storms. The name was applied to the whole cape, not simply to one point upon it. Dias spent a month anchored somewhere off its shores, resting his crew, writing his reports and perfecting a map of his voyage. Then, leaving another stone cross (no trace has ever been found of it), he sailed for home to report his finding to his king.

In the renaming of the Cape of Good Hope, Dias conveniently forgot his earlier 'Cape of Storms', but it – and the vengeance of Adamastor – did not forget him. In 1500 Dias once again set out to double the Cape of Good Hope. Again he encountered a terrible storm and this time his ship and a companion vessel was overwhelmed. They both lie somewhere in the deep waters off the Cape. Legend has it that in this disaster Adamastor had his revenge; and so the tale arose of a phantom sea captain and his ship, condemned forever to attempt the doubling of the Cape of Good Hope, but always frustrated by violent storms. The nationality of the unfortunate individual has varied with the telling through the years. Wagner, in his opera *The Flying Dutchman*, gave particular renown to the Dutch version, with Captain Van der Decken as the central character whose fate was redeemed by the constancy of a woman. But fundamentally the tale is rooted in the curse of Adamastor's fury and his vengeance on Bartholomeu Dias. This feud continues forever. It is in fact astonishing how many sailors navigating these waters have made serious reports about a sighting of the phantom ship. It is the world's most famous ghost story.

Since the time of its discovery, the Cape of Good Hope has remained a point of great interest to all voyagers. East and westbound travellers alike regard it as the half-way mark on their voyages. To double it in a storm is an achievement comparable to doubling Cape Horn. To sail around it in fair weather is a delightful experience. From the tiny 100 ton *Golden Hind*, Sir Francis Drake in the course of his round-the-world journey (1577 to 1580) saw it. In his log it is described as *'the fairest cape and the most stately thing we saw in the whole circumference of the globe'*. Few disagree with this enthusiasm.

In the early years the southern part of the Cape Peninsula was a windswept wilderness of wild flowers. A few fishermen and runaways from justice occasionally made their way down to the tip of the Cape, but there were no roads and no settlement in the area until the first quarter of the 19th century, when the British took control of the Cape and Simon's Town was developed as a naval base.

Farms were then allocated in the area. On 1 July 1816 John Osmond was granted the farm *Buffelsfontein* (buffalo fountain) also knows as *Uiterstehoek* (furthermost glen) which included the tip of the Peninsula. A condition of the grant was that the Naval Department retained the right to erect a lighthouse on any part of the farm which might be judged best for such a purpose. Access to this lighthouse was also to be permanently available.

Nothing was done about a lighthouse for some years, although the need for a beacon became increasingly urgent as the volume of shipping around the Cape increased. In 1823 the coastline was properly surveyed by Royal Navy chartists such as Captain Owen, and names were given to the various rocks, including Bellows (the dangerous outlying rock always covered in foam), Anvil, Whittle (in False Bay) and Dias Reef. Captain Owen, incidentally, also reported sighting the *Flying Dutchman*.

The first lighthouse, a prefabricated iron tower painted white with a red top, was erected in 1859 on Da Gama peak, the summit of Cape Point, 249 m above sea-level. This lighthouse, made by the Victoria Foundry Company in England, was 9 m high with a 2 000 candlepower flashing light. The first lighthouse keepers, J Coe and his assistant, H Franks, soon found that their light was too high. When the mists swept in, the light was often well above the clouds and quite invisible to any shipping. This was a dangerous situation but for some time nothing was done to rectify matters.

Apart from the lighthouse keepers, a few farmers established themselves on land in the southern Peninsula, but little is remembered of them. With bad roads, thin soil and incessant wind, they were forced to live on a subsistence economy. Horses, however, flourished in the area. The farmers managed to grow some barley and wheat. Milk and vegetables were produced for the shipping at Simon's Town. A few homesteads were built of local sandstone cemented with lime made from shells in the kilns at Buffel's Bay and Bordjiesrif. In these buildings the farmers passed their days. Remnants of the homesteads may still be seen, but memories of the personalities who lived in them and the events which took place have long since been blown away with the winds.

Occasionally a shipwreck occurred somewhere around the coast or there were sightings of the *Flying Dutchman*. One of the most famous of these was logged in 1881 by King George V when he was a midshipman on HMS *Bacchante*. The lighthouse keepers also reported sightings of odd vessels, with all sails set even in the worst weather, persistently trying to double the Cape. Even the coming of steamships did not end these rumours of sea ghosts.

On the night of 18 April 1911 a major disaster occurred when the 5 557 ton Portuguese liner, *Lusitania*, struck Bellows Rock. The lighthouse of Cape Point was completely obscured by the mist. The ship was a total loss, although fortunately only 4 out of the 774 people aboard were drowned. This disaster tragically emphasised the urgency of a change to the lighthouse. It was recorded that in some years the light was obscured by mist for as much as 900 hours. This was an intolerable situation.

A new site was selected lower down on the tip of Cape Point, only 87 m above the sea and overlooking the strange column of rock known as Dias Rock which stands guard there as though watching eternally for a return of the vanished ship of Bartholomeu Dias. On 25 April 1914 the foundation was laid for the new lighthouse. In this construction a 500 000 candlepower paraffin lamp was installed. In 1936 this lamp was converted to electricity, with a giant reflector and lens providing 19 000 000 candlepower, making the lighthouse the most powerful in the world. This light was later reduced to 10 000 000 candlepower provided by a 1,5 kw lamp.

The light at Cape Point can justly be described as one of the greatest shipping beacons in the world. Countless sailors have been guided by its tremendous beam. The giant tankers which make their way around the Cape, rusty freighters, trim ocean liners, pugnacious warships, sneaky submarines on the prowl – all regard it as a massive landmark. During the Second World War German submarines lurked by day beneath the waters and by night lay on the restless surface just beyond the beam of light, waiting patiently for prey. Several of these nocturnal prowlers reported sightings of the *Flying Dutchman*. Just before the war, in early 1939, crowds of holiday makers on False Bay beaches reported a weird-looking battered old sailing-ship making its way towards Muizenberg and then vanishing in a cloud of mist. This intriguing legend persists into modern times. It is a colourful part of the character and romantic atmosphere of the Cape of Good Hope, the commanding presence of which dominates one of the great strategic trade routes of the world.

The idea of preserving the southern portion of the Cape Peninsula as a nature reserve originated in 1928, when the whole area was threatened with development into seaside resorts, complete with *'Trespassers will be Prosecuted'* signs and forlorn, dilapidated shacks deserted for months at a time by owners who used them only during holiday periods.

Fortunately several public-spirited and influential Capetonians became interested in the area. Brian Mansergh, a Cape Town architect, had known the area since his youth and had often discussed its conservation with local farmers. In November 1928 he wrote to the Minister of Lands, pleading for the establishment of a nature reserve. His plea was rejected on the grounds of cost. Mansergh continued to promote the idea of a reserve, supported by a number of friends who gathered for a weekly informal lunch during which they discussed affairs in general. News of the formation of a syndicate to develop townships in the southern Peninsula particularly disturbed them. A patient spell of propaganda and systematic agitation followed. Dr Stacy Skaife, Dr Leonard Gill, Anthony Leyds and Henry Hope concerned themselves with arousing public interest. The key property in the area was *Smith's Farm*, owned by Norman Smith and his family. This was actually the farm *Buffelsfontein* or *Uiterstehoek*, originally granted to John Osmond, extending across the end of the Peninsula. The Smith family was approached. They approved the idea of conservation and agreed to sell to the conservationists rather than to the land speculators.

The Cape Town City Council was then approached, but the area was well outside their boundaries and individual councillors were not enthusiastic. One of the councillors, A Z Berman, summed up resistance to the idea by stating flatly that he would be against spending council money on an area where *'there was not enough vegetation to keep a scorpion alive'*. Another councillor, W F Fish, described it as *'wasteland, waterless and treeless'*.

The enthusiasts were not dismayed. They started to make plans for raising the money to buy *Smith's Farm*, fence it in, and make it pay for its maintenance as a nature reserve by erecting a tollgate on the road leading across it to the lighthouse and resorts such as Buffel's Bay and the famous fishing ledges at Rooikrans, places already much frequented by visitors.

At this stage Will and Percy Hare, owners of the farm *Bloubergvlei*, which was also in the area, offered their property to the projected nature reserve. This was provided that it would be maintained as a wilderness and that they would be allowed to live undisturbed in their seaside cottage at Brightwater; also that no road was ever to be built across what had been their land.

The whole concept of a nature reserve gained in stature. The Simon's Town municipality supported the idea. Its mayor, L C Gay, was particularly enthusiastic. The local morning newspaper, the *Cape Times*, gave it considerable editorial support. One memorable leader (23 November 1938) was amusingly specific: *'It seems almost treasonable to this stately peninsula of ours to think that its extreme end, now the only unspoilt part of our heritage, should fall into the hands of men who will cause it to pimple into a bungaloid acne'*.

The City Council, however, remained hostile to the establishment of a nature reserve, although a poll of the people of Cape Town revealed overwhelming support. Charles Duminy, chairman of the Divisional Council of the Cape, and Jerwyn Owen, its secretary, had fortunately also been interested in the project for some time. They put it to their council and the idea was at last officially accepted. On 11 April 1939, a special meeting of the council approved the purchase of

Smith's Farm. The Cape of Good Hope Nature Reserve came into being, with the specific object of preserving for all time the 'fairest Cape' in the state in which it must have been seen by Bartholomeu Dias and Sir Francis Drake. Norman Smith was appointed first warden with £250 a year as salary and free occupation of his farmhouse.

The Divisional Council spent £16 000 in purchasing *Smith's Farm* with its homestead and three privately owned bungalows. Crown land was added by the State. In 1941 the farms *Olifansbos*, *Theefontein* and *Krommerivier* were bought from the estate of D C de Villiers, as well as the Minicki family farm, *Klaasjagers*. Other land was acquired to consolidate the area. The last property to be purchased (in 1965) was a portion of *Wildschutsbrand*, owned by Mrs Jacoba Malherbe. This farm had been the first to be granted in the southern Peninsula and originally it had been the home of the first *field-cornet* (district officer) appointed over the area. The homesteads of all these farms have vanished, including, unfortunately, the one known locally as *Die Spookhuis* (the haunted house), a building with quite a number of tales about its unorthodox residents.

With this acquisition, the Cape of Good Hope Nature Reserve attained its present dimension of 7 750 ha, obtained by the Divisional Council of the Cape at a total cost of £63 500. Completely protected and carefully maintained, this nature reserve is a scenic and botanical delight. Game animals of the type which once roamed freely over the Southern Cape (eland, bontebok, hartebeest and mountain zebra) have been re-introduced. These, together with descendants of the indigenous population of grey rhebok, grysbok, steenbok, baboons, marine life, over 1 200 species of birds, dassies, tortoises (especially the Cape angulated tortoise) and other small wild creatures, live their natural lives in a setting which is peaceful, beautiful and quite unique.

The original homestead of Smith's Farm was converted into a restaurant and gift shop to cater for an increasing stream of visitors. In 1994 the number of annual visitors reached 443 500.

To cope with such numbers, a lease agreement was negotiated in 1995 with Concor Holdings (Pty) Limited for the self-financed construction and management of a modern complex of buildings and also the construction of a funicular railway to convey visitors from the road terminus to the viewsite on the summit of Cape Point. At the end of this lease, the ownership of this complex, including a restaurant, destination gift shop, information centre and funicular railway, reverts back to the Cape Metropolitan Council. The funicular track is 585 metres long and ascends 230 metres. The two coaches each have a capacity of 40 passengers and take three minutes to complete the journey. They replace a bus known as the Flying Dutchman which originally provided a service for those disinclined to do the walk. Utmost care was taken to preserve the environment during construction and many restrictions were placed on the developer with regards to the positioning of the funicular track, thus resulting in one of the most unique layouts accommodating varying gradients and curves.

In 1998 the number of visitors exceeded 750 000. It was apparent that a visit to the Cape of Good Hope was becoming an essential part of any tour of South Africa by international visitors.

A good walkway was made by the Western Cape Regional Council to the summit of Cape Point, with viewsites, and resting places. The original buildings, including the first lighthouse were restored. Since 1978 the South African Council for Scientific and Industrial Research (CSIR) have maintained on the summit an atmospheric trace gas research station with a laboratory, facilities and a 30 m high aluminium mask to provide experimental platforms and stratified air intakes.

This facility is managed jointly by the CSIR and the IFU (Frauhofer Institute for Atmospheric Environmental Research) in Germany. It is part of the World Meteorological Organisation Global Atmosphere Watch Network. There are nineteen other similar facilities maintained at strategic situations in the world. They keep a close, continuous watch on trace gases in the atmosphere, meteorological conditions and solar radiation.

Altogether the Cape of Good Hope Nature Reserve, with its fauna, flora, spectacular scenery, atmosphere and ongoing activity, is a very worthwhile place to visit and a credit to the staff who maintain it.

The gates to the reserve are open every day of the year at the following times:
07h00 to 17h00 in winter (April–September)
07h00 to 18h00 in summer (October–March)

From the turn-off leading into the Cape of Good Hope Nature Reserve, the main road commences its journey back to Cape Town up the west coast of the Peninsula. Carvings, crafts and curios are sold by wayside vendors. There are pleasant picnic sites beneath the trees on either side of the road and an ostrich show farm. At 8,5 km towards Cape Town, close to the junction with the road coming from Simon's Town over Red Hill, the Divisional Council has converted *Perdekloof* (horse ravine) farm into a recreational area with shady trees and green grass, ideal for a picnic. It is open from 06h00 to 20h00.

A further 3 km takes the road past ...

SCARBOROUGH

Scarborough consists of a cluster of cottages close to the oddly shaped roadside landmark known as Camel Rock. There is a pretty beach. When the wind is not blowing, the picnic and camping sites are pleasant. For 7,5 km beyond Scarborough the country is wild and bush-covered, with sandy bays such as *Witsand* (white sands) and many picnic sites and camping grounds in sheltered places along the way. After 5 km there is a crossroads with a turn-off left which leads to the recreational area of *Soetwater* (sweet water). A right turn provides a short cut through the housing estate of Ocean View to Fish Hoek. The main road now climbs the face of a cliff and reveals a large stretch of coast with tidal pools, the *Soetwater* park and a recreational area dominated by the graceful steel tower of *Slangkop* (snake peak) lighthouse.

The road now descends into the pleasant little resort known as ...

KOMMETJIE

Kommetjie (the little basin) takes its name from a natural inlet in the rocks which has been developed into a large tidal pool. This area is a favourite place for surf riders, as is Long Beach, especially in the summer months when the south-easter is blowing. The view north towards Chapman's Peak and Hout Bay is particularly impressive from here. Swimming in the tidal pool is safe; the water is relatively warm but troubled by pollution.

Originally this area was a farm granted in 1743 to Christina Diemer by the commissioner, Gustaf Willem van Imhoff. The farm was named *Slangkop*, but became more widely known as *Imhoff's Gift*. An adjoining farm, granted at the same time to C C Wieser, was *Poespaskraal* (higgledy-piggledy corral), the name of which, one suspects, has an interesting origin!

In those days this area was accessible only by a rough track and farms were used by their owners as grazing grounds for cattle. Farmhouses were built of local stone, painted with lime obtained by burning shells, and thatched with reeds from the lakelets near Noordhoek. These lakelets were also used to produce salt. Unfortunately, the homestead of *Imhoff's Gift* was destroyed by fire and only partly restored. One interesting building dating from that time was a shooting box erected for the Governor, Lord Charles Somerset, which later became *Honeysuckle Cottage*, eventually replaced with the modern house *Palm Villa*.

Holiday makers discovered the charms of the area, especially fishing and swimming. A few shacks were put up to provide more substantial shelter than the milkwood trees. Then the inevitable developer arrived, determined that if the public showed signs of liking the area, they could be induced to buy plots. A company, Kommetjie Estate Ltd, was formed in 1902 by a Cape Town builder and contractor, Anton Benning. The company laid out the resort named Kommetjie. A gravel road was built to Fish Hoek, its verges planted with the diverse-coloured flowering gums which make the route so beautiful in spring.

The resort was laid out by the surveyor, K N Teubes. A few of the cottages built in those days still survive. Even a railway was planned, but after 85 years the first train has still to arrive. Visitors come by car through the avenue of flowering gums, with the modern tarmac road following substantially the same route as the original track from Fish Hoek. It is a pleasant and pretty drive and along it has travelled a varied and interesting cavalcade of people.

Apart from fishing, surfing and swimming, attractions in the early days included shipwrecks. Back in May 1900, the *Kakapo*, was steered directly on to Long Beach. The ship was brand-new and on its maiden delivery from British builders to New Zealand owners. It was named after the rare species of flightless owl parrot of New Zealand. The reason why the wreck occurred is a little obscure. The weather was fine. The navigator said that a sad error had been made: the Sentinel at Hout Bay had been mistaken for the Cape of Good Hope. But even if there had been no confusion, a similar sharp turn around the Cape of Good Hope would hardly have taken the ship to New Zealand. Knowing what goes on when crews of ships stop for refreshment in Table Bay, it is a wonder more of them don't end up on Long Beach!

The crew of the *Kakapo* experienced little hardship as a result of the wreck. The ship went straight on to thick sand; the crew jumped over the side and walked away. The ship couldn't do the same, however, and was left to settle high and dry on that magnificent beach where surfers ride the high waves today. The ship was cut down and stripped of its valuables and plates. The ribs, keel and boiler remain to form a picturesque scene, used in modern times as a set in several motion picture films, including *Ryan's Daughter*.

A wreck that attracted very large crowds to the salvage auctions held on the beach was the *Clan Monroe* which struck the rocks just south of the basin on 2 July 1905. Fortunately the crew were all saved except for one man, a Lascar named Ormel Corsette, who was drowned while being taken ashore in a breeches buoy. He is buried on a sand dune near the Slangkop lighthouse. The ship carried a lethal amount of dynamite and cyanide destined for the mines, but there were other valuables aboard and these were auctioned on the beach.

The Slangkop lighthouse was built in 1914. It is the twin of the lighthouse on Dassen Island, a graceful steel tower in the classic lighthouse shape. The two towers were made in Britain and shipped out to South Africa in pieces. The Slangkop lighthouse was originally fitted with a lamp of 16 750 000 candlepower, making it the second most powerful on the coast of Africa after Cape Point.

A radio transmitter for communication with ships was also erected near the site of the lighthouse. The overlooking cliffs of *Slangkop*, however, contain irregular seams of manganese which interfered with the radio waves. The transmitter was moved in 1937 to a site near Imhoff Park and at a later stage to Klipheuwel on the Cape Flats. The sole reminder of this transmitter is Wireless Road, the name of the road leading to the caravan park.

During the Second World War a radar station was built on top of the Slangkop ridge and a track made to reach the site. The track to the concrete 'pillbox' buildings may still be followed. As with the walk along the beach to the wreck of the *Kakapo*, the walk up to Slangkop ridge provides a pleasant outing. The wild flowers on the ridge are varied and very beautiful, especially in spring.

The route from the village up the ridge leads past St Joseph's Church in Rubbi Road. This charming little church was erected in 1948 as a memorial to Joseph Rubbi, an Italian builder who lived, worked and died in Kommetjie. The church is notable for its marble and mosaics. Behind it stands a building used as a retreat by Catholic nuns and priests.

North of Kommetjie the road leads through an avenue of flowering gums. After 1 km a road turns off to the left and leads down to the Imhoff Park caravan park and to the beach at *Klein Slangkoppunt* (little snake peak point), from where there is a good walk up the beach of Chapman's Bay to the wreck of the *Kakapo*, more than half buried in the sand.

Seven kilometres from Kommetjie the main road reaches the Sun Valley residential area with a junction with the road which crosses the waist of the Peninsula to Fish Hoek. The coastal road bears left from this junction. After 1 km the road reaches a junction with the Ou Kaapse Weg (already described). Continuing left through the residential area, the main coastal road arrives in ...

NOORDHOEK

Noordhoek (north glen) is a rural settlement with an attractive little shopping centre shaded by oak trees, and situated just below Chapman's Peak. From the main road a side road turns off through the trees, passes the Chapman's Peak tea-room and leads down to the beach. When the south-easter blows, there are superb surfing waves at *De Hoek* (the corner), where the beach ends on the steep slopes of Chapman's Peak. There is some fine walking along the great beach which skirts Chapman's Bay all the way up to Kommetjie. The name 'Chapman', applied to the bay and the dominant peak on the north side, originated on 29 July 1607 when the *Consort*, under Captain David Middleton, anchored off this coast. The master's mate, John Chapman, was sent in a boat to see if there was any anchorage. His name was thenceforth attached to the peak and the bay. The estate and home of the late Sir Drummond Chaplin lies on the slopes east of the road. Kaolin is mined in the area.

In a lovely grove of milkwood and other shady trees there is a secluded cluster of mountain site cottages constructed in what is known as Monkey Valley. Each cottage is different, each with its own character. Each has a superb view of Chapman's Bay with its 8 km long glistening beach. It is a private nature reserve with one of the finest of all forests of the protected milkwood tree permanently defended from the woodcutter's axe. A multitude of birds and a variety of small mammals find sanctuary in it.

The original owner of this 4-ha paradise was an immigrant from the Netherlands named Jan Hesterman. Tradition has it that one day he saw a troop of baboons gambolling up the ravine. Unaware of the difference between baboon and monkey (there are no monkeys in the Western Cape), he called his farm Monkey Valley. In 1988 Monkey Valley was sold by his two sons to Jude Sole. She was enthralled with the beauty of it all, the murmur of the surf and the song of the birds, and was determined that this beautiful place should not be defaced by any injudicious property development. In this way was born the concept of an exclusive resort for a limited number of people sharing the pleasure of living in so sylvan a setting, each having the power to veto further development. Delightfully romantic log tree-houses and thatched brick cottages, all with spectacular views, were built in the forest overlooking the sea. Two private paths lead down to the unspoilt beach. Monkey Valley borders the world-famous Chapman's Peak scenic drive, a link to the pleasures of the Cape Peninsula.

CHAPMAN'S PEAK

For the next 11 km from Noordhoek the main road follows one of the world's most spectacular marine drives cut into the cliffs around the 650 m high Chapman's Peak. This famous scenic road was the brainchild of Sir Frederic de Waal, the same energetic first Administrator of the Cape Province after whom De Waal Drive was named. Stimulated by his enthusiasm, the road was built between 1915 and 1922 and still remains an engineering feat of the first magnitude. On the grave of the engineer responsible, Robert Glenday, in the Woltemade Cemetery, a stone quarried from Chapman's Peak was erected by his colleagues as a fitting memorial to a magnificent piece of work. From this road, with its numerous look-out points and (on the far side) picnic places, there are incomparable views back over the great beach of Chapman's Bay and north across the handsome sweep of Hout Bay to the 331 m high Sentinel which looms over the busy fishing harbour. The road itself, for most of its journey around Chapman's Peak, has been cut into the junction line of the Cape granite and the sedimentary Table Mountain sandstone laid down on top of the granite and brilliantly coloured in layers of red, orange and yellow silt. Dark lines of manganese may also be noticed. Many picnic sites have been created at the roadside in the descent to Hout Bay.

At the end of this great drive the road descends with a grand sweep into the residential and fishing village of ...

HOUT BAY

Soon after his arrival in the Cape in 1652, Jan van Riebeeck sent a party to explore the bay behind Table Mountain. The explorers found it to be a beautiful bay scenically, but dangerously exposed for shipping. In the valley there were mountain cypress trees *(Widdringtonia noeliflora)*, and from their presence the bay was named *Houtbaai* (wood bay).

Over the years the trees were cut down to supply timber for ships. In 1681 a lease was given over the area. A sawmill was built and a wagon track made to the bay over Constantia Nek. A community of woodcutters settled at Hout Bay but for some years it remained a remote and wild area with the last two elephants there only shot in 1689. A few fishermen started to work from the bay, however, and the area became regarded as an interesting possible expansion of the settlement at Cape Town.

During the American War of Independence, the French troops who garrisoned the Cape built a battery on the western end of Hout Bay harbour to defend the place from any possible British invasion. A second battery was built on the eastern side of the bay in 1799. Two years later the British troops occupied the Cape and built a blockhouse above the eastern battery. In 1804 the Batavian administration also contributed to these varied military constructions by building a battery. The ruins of these various structures still stand.

No invading force ever did threaten Hout Bay, but at least during the Napoleonic wars a French corsair captain, Malo le Nouvel, was driven into the bay by a great storm. He and his ship were taken prisoner by the British garrison.

A particularly beautiful architectural survival from this period is the homestead of *Kronendal* farm, built in 1800 and now a national monument. It houses a restaurant. The fishing industry of Hout Bay really started in about 1867 when a German immigrant, Jacob Trautman, settled at the bay and began catching and salting snoek to export to far away places such as Mauritius. The presence in the area of vast numbers of rock lobsters was also noticed. In 1903 the hulk of a British barge, R. Morrow, wrecked at Mouille Point, was bought, towed to Hout Bay and beached. It had been converted into a canning factory before being towed to Hout Bay. It continued as a factory until 1914 when an explosion in its refrigeration killed seven people. The remnants of the hulk remained in Hout Bay until after the Second World War when they were removed to make way for the substantial fishing harbour of today with two large factories on the shore.

A museum in the village displays interesting exhibits on the history of Hout Bay, including such early activities as manganese mining, conducted from the 1880s until 1909. The ore was sent down a chute to a jetty, part of which is still standing. The museum is open Tuesdays to Saturdays from 10h00 to 12h30 and from 14h00 to 16h30. Guided walks to places of natural or historical importance are organised by the museum. Phone (021) 790-3270.

The bronze leopard mounted on the rocks overlooking the bay is the work of the late sculptor, Ivan Mitford-Barberton, who lived in Hout Bay. There are daily launch trips around the bay and to the seals living on Duiker Island. There are sunset cruises to Cape Town and other sea trips on the pleasure launches and sailing craft.

There are some fine walks around Hout Bay. From the harbour area it is interesting to walk over the saddle of land connecting the Sentinel to the mainland. Duiker Island with its resident population of seals may be viewed from this walk. From the harbour a disused road climbs steeply to the old radar station built during the Second World War on top of the 653 m high Karbonkelberg. The views are stunning. For the really hardy there is a rough and surprisingly long walk along the coast to Llandudno. With its crevices and hard going, this is a day-long outing, even though it looks short on the map. It is dangerous and should not be undertaken without a guide.

Hout Bay is renowned as the rock lobster capital of the world. During the oppressive apartheid years of sanctions, Hout Bay was jocularly proclaimed as a republic independent of the rest of South Africa, with its own benign president, an authentic-looking passport, border posts, and a viable economy based on seafoods and the tourists attracted by the excellent eating and the scenic beauty of the area.

Harbours, whatever their size, are fascinating places to visit. There is always something happening. Fishing and pleasure boats glide over waters so rich in reflections that they seem to be in a magical world of their own. Fishermen mingle with visitors strolling along the quays. Seals laze in the waters. Gossiping, squabbling sea-birds fly just out of reach, always watchful for the handout of a fragment of food.

The Hout Bay harbourfront emporium of Mariner's Wharf was South Africa's first. Its world-famous fish market is built around the hull of the *Kingfisher*, an original 1940s trawler from the Cape Coast fleet. At the market the delicious local delicacy called snoek and other fish are smoked daily the old-fashioned way, live lobsters crawl around in the seawater tanks, and an incredible range of seafoods is available for the kitchen. Behind the *Kingfisher* is where to find Ye Olde Wine and Liqueur Shoppe, which is famous in its own right for having pioneered weekend trading. Conveniently open all week long for the needs of locals and tourists alike, it stocks the best from

South Africa's top wine estates. The Wharf's own special souvenir wine in a fish-shaped bottle is also sold here, a unique memento of a visit to Hout Bay.

Then there is the excellent Wharfside Grill Restaurant with its private dining cabins displaying fascinating relics from ocean liners such as the *Queen Mary*, ships of the Union Castle Line and the Navy. The Grill is regarded as one of Africa's top seafood restaurants. Expect to get a glimpse of the rich and famous here – the celebrity list is endless from the likes of German Chancellor Helmut Kohl and Archbishop Desmond Tutu, royalty and VIPs, sportspersons and filmstars.

There are also bars such as the Crayclub Bar, serving the grogs so beloved to seafarers from the days of yore. The Boatshed Tapas is also a particularly memorable restaurant of seashanty singing and casual seafood, right on the water's edge.

At the Pearl Factory customers are welcome to select their own oysters, which are then opened in front of them, each guaranteed to contain a pearl. The Mariner's Chest, Shell, Shipwreck and Artifact Coves are where thousands of shells, ephemera and relics of shipwrecks gathered from the world's oceans are on sale; along with handmade sea-art, marine antiques, scrimshaw, nautical books, paintings, brassware and fishing memorabilia. An incredible selection for anybody interested in the sea or maritime history.

Fish and chips are, inevitably, a special of the area. Alfresco meals on the quayside at the Seafood Bistro, or on the upstairs decks of the Wharfside Grill, offer great views of the surrounding bay and a beckoning harbour. Seabirds are always in attendance, approving companions to a pleasant way of satisfying appetites aroused by the ambience and scenic settings.

Stanley Dorman is the man who created Mariner's Wharf. Coming from a family which settled in Hout Bay in the 1890s he was prominent in, and an integral part of the Hout Bay fishing industry for over 30 years, prior to embarking upon his creation of South Africa's first harbourfront emporium. This emporium, Mariner's Wharf, the first section of which opened in 1984, was destined to become one of the Cape's top tourist attractions. Yet there were humble beginnings. Way back in the 1970s he and his wife Pam started by selling smoked snoek over weekends from a makeshift kiosk outside their small factory. From a paltry turnover of R18 on the first day, they have built a maritime empire.

Stanley Dorman's enthusiasm for all things related to the sea permeates the whole enterprise. In the nearby village he is busy with the creation of a craft village, aptly named Fisherman's World. Here he is re-erecting and rehabilitating its old fishermen's cottages, and even character buildings such as the original post office and the old gaol. The objective is to also incorporate into Fisherman's World a themed section devoted to the fisherfolk he admires. Their works, crafts, and special skills, such as net-making and shipwrighting, will encompass the lifestyle and tools of trade of a traditional coastal community. Look out for the half boat on the rocks alongside the Main Road – preserved as a landmark for prosperity, in similar style to what Stanley has done in elevating old fishing boats into the roofline at Mariner's Wharf. This is his personal tribute to the fishing families whose home has been Hout Bay for over one hundred years. Their forefathers loved the quaint harbour as a sanctuary, long before the advent of today's suburban sprawl, when the village was still a distant outpost in Cape Town's countryside.

A lovely grove of historical milkwood trees has likewise been thoughtfully preserved behind the Mainstream Shopping Centre (another Stanley Dorman development). This sensitively designed shopping centre is unique. Instead of one big mall, it has been built as an open cluster of 21st century buildings with unique passageway-into-time windows, reflecting how the shops (fifty in all) would have looked a century ago, the implements they used, and the products they sold. In its shady sylvan setting, which could be straight from the fairyland tale of a midsummer night's dream, there are seasonal outdoor entertainment and happenings.

Hout Bay's Mariner's Wharf and Fisherman's World are well worth a visit. Leave yourself plenty of time to take in the special ambience and attractions of what nature, history and the enthusiasm and foresight of a still very active local son of the valley has created, virtually single-handed.

Immediately out of Hout Bay village the marine drive reaches a junction with the road which comes down through the shady avenues of oaks from Constantia Nek. The main road veers left, bridges the course of the Hout Bay River, makes its way through an avenue of plane trees and then reaches a junction where a short road branches off left and leads to the fishing harbour. On the right-hand side up Valley road is the World of Birds wildlife sanctuary, the largest bird park in Africa.

THE WORLD OF BIRDS

The World of Birds is the creation of Walter Mangold. Always dedicated to wild life, he acquired land in Hout Bay and commenced breeding birds. In 1974 he had the misfortune of going into liquidation. He lost his land but kept his beloved birds. He leased fresh land close to his original breeding site. With no transport except a wheelbarrow, he moved his remaining possessions, birds and cages, to the new site. It took a full year of labour to get the venture going, struggling to feed the birds, pay innumerable bills. Then dogs broke in to the cages one night killing or maiming three quarters of the birds. This was about the final blow. The kindness of neighbours, Mr and Mrs Mitchell, alone gave him the strength to continue with his dream. They erected a security fence for him and in its protection he worked day by day in building cages and creating the present World of Birds.

The setting is lush. Squirrel monkeys play with visitors, delightful families of meerkats pose for photos like slightly disapproving Victorians. The birds are elegant and friendly, like the black swans in pensive mood, or the secretary birds talking about money and management matters to Walter Mangold in the green forest which provides the wild life with a natural home. The aviaries are so large that visitors can walk freely through them, mingling with the birds and mammals in a landscaped garden setting. Over 3 500 birds of 450 different species, South African and exotic, can be seen there along with a community of amusing little mammals. Many of the birds are free to come and go as they please. Open every day of the year from 09h00 to 17h00. Photographers are welcome. Phone (021) 790-2730.

The main road veers sharp right as it leaves the Hout Bay valley and climbs the slopes of the 436 m high mountain known from pronounced similarities in shape to Lion's Head overlooking Cape Town, as Little Lion's Head. To the right there are fine views of the valley of the Hout Bay River, while silver trees and many indigenous flowering shrubs ornament the estates on either side of the road.

At its highest point the road passes over the saddle of land connecting Little Lion's Head to the Twelve Apostles (the back of Table Mountain), and an entirely new vista of sea and mountain opens up. Immediately below lies the attractive little beach and residential area of Llandudno, with a road branching off left to provide access. The main marine drive is known as Victoria Road, for it was completed by Thomas Bain just before Queen Victoria's golden jubilee in 1887. It was a superb engineering feat by a master road builder and was his last great work. The road descends the face of the cliffs diagonally, with the sea on its left and the twelve great buttresses of the back of Table Mountain glowering on its right. From Llandudno there is a short walk south to Sandy Bay, a secluded area much liked by sunbathers in various stages of dress or undress. The wreck of a tanker, the *Romelia*, lies on the rocks where it came to grief in 1977 while being towed to a scrapyard in the Far East. The tow-rope snapped and the single towing-tug lost control.

Three kilometres from the Llandudno turn-off the road sweeps around a bend and reveals, especially on a sunny day, one of the finest views of the Cape. Across a sparkling stretch of sea, Lion's Head can be seen in its most handsome aspect, with the houses of Camps Bay and Bakoven in pleasingly multi-coloured disarray beneath it. The whole stretch of the Twelve Apostles (originally called the Gable Mountains; but given their present name by the British Governor, Sir Rufane Donkin) provides a panorama on the right, while on the left the sea rolls in through a mass of granite boulders, with many little coves and inlets frequented by holiday-makers and fishermen. One of these places, *Hottentotshuisie* (Hottentot's shack), developed over the years into the home of a curious community of permanent cave dwellers. Remnants of the wreck of the coaster *Bluff* lie on the rocks where it ran aground in 1965. Remnants of the tanker *Antipolis* also lie on the rocks here after being wrecked in 1977 while being towed with the *Romelia* to ship-breakers in the Far East.

Three kilometres along this interesting stretch of coast, the road leads past a path and stairway to the Bellsfontein *kramat* of the Muslim holy man, Nureel Mobeek. It is said that about 13 000 Muslim slaves were buried in the protection of this sacred place, part of the original *Oudekraal* farm of the Van Bredas. The farmhouse is now the site of a five star hotel. The road enters the municipal area of Cape Town at what is known as *Bakoven* (the bake oven) from the shape of a large hollow rock on the coast. This area is now a place of bungalows built down to the water's edge. Through it the Victoria Road leads directly into the suburb of ...

CAMPS BAY

Camps Bay was named after Frederick von Kamptz, an invalid sailor who, in 1778 landed in the Cape, married the widow of the owner of the original farm at Camps Bay, *Ravensteyn*, and made his home in the farmhouse which stood on the site of the former Rotunda Hotel. Nowadays, the hotel named *The Bay*, occupies this site. Camps Bay today is a well-to-do suburb built on the slopes of the Twelve Apostles and overlooking a spacious beach, much used by sunbathers and picnickers. There is a large tidal pool and surfers find sport in a cove (Glen Beach) on the north side of Camps Bay; but swimming, generally, is marred by very cold water and a frequent back-wash.

From Camps Bay two roads lead up the slopes of the mountain, join at Kloof Nek and finally enter the city area. One of these roads, Geneva Drive, branches right from Victoria Road just after it passes the pavilion. The other road, Kloof Road, branches right as Victoria Road leaves Camps Bay. This is a pleasant route around the slopes of Lion's Head past the Round House restaurant (an old shooting-box of the British governors); Stan's Halt Youth Hostel, built in the original stables of the shooting-box; and The Glen picnic area, with fine views of Camps Bay through the trees. There is a popular theatre, the Theatre on the Bay, in Camps Bay.

CLIFTON

On the coastal side, Camps Bay ends in a small headland preserved as a scenic and botanical reserve. Beyond this lies Clifton with its famous beaches (First, Second, Third and Fourth), all ideal for sunbathing and displays of feminine pulchritude, the coldness of the Atlantic Ocean providing bikini beauties with an excellent excuse not to swim. Informal (but expensive) little cottages (some not so little) are built on the cliffs overlooking the beach and are today very fashionable places in which to live. Several of these cottages were originally built as emergency housing after the First World War!

At Clifton, Lion's Head is much closer to the sea; and many of the houses along Victoria Road are built on stilts and piles. Roof-top parking is common. The name *Clifton* (place on a cliff) is a popular one. There are six Cliftons in the USA There is one in Canada and one on the cliffs overlooking the Avon River at Bristol in England. Before Bain made his Victoria Road, only a rough path provided a precarious way around the cliffs of what was then known as *Skoenmakersgat* (shoemaker's cave) from a hermit who lived there and earned a living of sorts as a shoemaker.

BANTRY BAY

From Clifton, Victoria Road is cut into the cliffs, winds tortuously around a mountain spur and passes through the heavily built-up area of Bantry Bay. Here, groups of apartment buildings cluster at the edge of a turbulent little bay. *Bantry Bay* was the site of a terraced botanical garden established in 1806 by Dr F S Liesching. The terraces have long since been overwhelmed by houses and flats and the first name, Botany Bay, has been forgotten. The first building there was Bantry House, constructed in the 1920s. It and the bay were named after Bantry Bay and the port of Bantry on the rugged south-western coast of Ireland.

At the end of Bantry Bay, Victoria road enters the suburb of ...

SEA POINT

The suburb of Sea Point is overcrowded and unplanned with narrow, densely built-up streets. Its principal advantage is a handsome ocean front and some overwhelmingly beautiful sunsets. At the earliest opportunity a traveller should turn left out of Main Road into Beach Road, a far more relaxing route which follows the coast. An almost continuous cliff of expensive but nondescript apartment buildings line the landward side of the road. Sea Point is Cape Town's most popular residential area. Some startlingly high rentals are paid for apartments whose principal asset seems to be what is free anyway – an elevated view of the very lovely sunsets.

Sea Point beachfront is laid out as a promenade with lawns, gardens and tidal swimming-pools, including Graaff's Pool where men may swim in the nude. This pool was named after Sir Jacobus Graaff who once had his mansion opposite, where a great block of flats stands today. The pool was originally a quarry from which stone was blasted to provide ballast for the suburban railway which once connected the city area with Sea Point. A concrete causeway carried a trolley from the quarry to the railway line. Along the beachfront there are children's playgrounds, amenities, and a large swimming-bath at the Sea Point Pavilion. A variety of hotels and restaurants flourish in the area. The ocean promenade is a favourite walk for people and their dogs taking the air on summer evenings. There are public conveniences for man and dog. The shoreline is rocky, making swimming difficult in places other than the tidal swimming-pools provided.

The first building in Sea Point was a country club named the *Heeren Huis* (gentlemen's house). It was erected in 1766. It stood on the southern end of Sea Point, just before Bantry Bay. In front of the site of this long-vanished building there is an exposure of rocks of such great interest to geologists that it is marked by a plaque carrying the following inscription:

'The rocks between this plaque and the sea reveal an impressive contact zone of dark slate with pale intrusive granite. This interesting example of contact between sedimentary and an igneous rock was first recorded by Clarke Abel in 1818. Since its discovery it has had an inspiring influence on the historical development of geology. Notable amongst those who have described it is Charles Darwin, who visited it in 1836.'

Between Sea Point and the slopes of Lion's Head lies the suburb of *Fresnaye* named, as are most of its streets, after places in France. Fresnay (as it is correctly spelt) is a town in Sarthe.

THREE ANCHOR BAY

The suburb of Sea Point ends on its north-eastern side at a small inlet known as *Three Anchor Bay* after three anchors originally used during the Napoleonic war years to hold a defensive chain across the inlet. It is now used as a base for pleasure craft and the operations of private fishermen. The sea is cold along this coast. •

GREEN POINT, MOUILLE POINT AND GRANGER BAY

From Three Anchor Bay the coast veers northwards for half a kilometre. Then it reaches Green Point, where a lighthouse was built in 1824. From this point the coast turns eastwards for a kilometre until it reaches Mouille Point where it swings south-eastwards at the beginning of the shoreline of Table Bay. It was at this point that the Dutch East India Company, between 1743 and 1746, attempted to build a *moeltjie* (mole or breakwater) to provide shelter for shipping in Table Bay. It was a forlorn effort. There was little money for a project which would have required massive engineering work to allow it to withstand the power of the sea. The French version of the name,

Mouille, was applied to the area in 1781. French troops assisting in the defence of the Cape built a battery at the point.

Altogether this is a hazardous coast for shipping, misty, gale-swept and the scene of so many wrecks that a lighthouse was built in 1842 on Mouille Point to supplement the light on nearby Green Point and guide shipping entering Table Bay at night. Even with two lighthouses however, there were still wrecks. The Mouille Point lighthouse was eventually demolished in 1908. The Green Point lighthouse, often erroneously called the Mouille Point lighthouse, was increased in power to 850 000 candlepower and, supplied with a deep-voiced foghorn, continues its duty of warning shipping of the dangers of the coast.

On the south-east side of Mouille Point there is a small bay named Granger Bay. This was once a base for whaling. Then, in 1854, Captain Robert Granger, made his home there in a cottage named *Sea Beach* and started a fishing industry. He was a merchant and shipping agent. On a squally evening in February 1857 he saw a small schooner, the *Miner*, capsize as it was leaving Table Bay bound for Hondeklip Bay. Captain Granger launched a dinghy and rowed out alone to the distressed ship. He rescued five people clinging to the side of the ship. The remainder were rescued by another boat. As a tribute to his gallantry, the inhabitants of Cape Town presented Captain Granger with a copper moderator lamp in the shape of the Green Point lighthouse, with, at its foot, his cottage and himself rowing his little boat. This tribute was later presented to the Cape Town municipality by Captain Granger's son.

Granger Bay in 1964 became the site of the S A Merchant Navy academy, moved there from Gordon's Bay. A spectacular building development has converted the bay into a marina with luxurious apartments.

The coastal strip known as Mouille Point is simply what used to be called *De Waterplaats* (the waterfront) of Green Point, the suburb which adjoins the city centre of Cape Town. The Green Point common is a large public commonage, immediately south of the Mouille Point coast. It was first a grazing area for cattle of the Dutch East India Company. The British, in the 1850s, created a horse-racing track there and the grandstand was the first building.

Today it is the site of several sports fields, such as the Metropolitan golf course, the Green Point stadium, tennis courts and athletic track. The City Hospital and the New Somerset Hospital have been built there. The Cape Medical Museum is at the New Somerset Hospital while at Fort Wynyard, named after Lt-General Robert Wynyard, there is the South African Museum of Coast and Anti-aircraft Artillery.

Beyond Green Point the main road enters the city area of Cape Town and the circular drive around the Cape Peninsula comes to an end 143 km from where it began at the statue of Jan van Riebeeck.

Chapter Six
SEA AND SAND

The Towns and Coast of the South-Western Cape

The south-western Cape is altogether a very remarkable part of the continent of Africa. It was not so long ago (geologically speaking) that Table Mountain loomed up as a precipitous outlying island in a shallow sea which reached as far as the slopes of the sandstone ranges known in former years as the 'Mountains of Africa'. When the sea receded, or the coastal land was elevated in Cretaceous times, 60 million years ago, it left behind its former sand bed. This dried and, through the combined efforts of man and nature, became covered with trees, shrubs and grass. It is known today as the Cape Flats in the south, and as the Sandveld lying up the south-west coast.

The Sandveld extends northwards up the coast as far as the mouth of the Olifants River. It is arid but nevertheless a great area for wild flowers and succulents. North of the Olifants River the Sandveld becomes a transitional desert, eventually merging with the Namib Desert of Namibia. The Sandveld was always regarded as a sort of backyard of the Cape. Compared to the fertile valleys of the *Boland* (upland) it lacked the prosperous glamour of the fruit and wine estates and the architectural beauty of the Cape-Dutch villages and towns. In years of reasonable rainfall it produced wheat. However, for most of its inhabitants, life was hard. They were always short of water; roads were poor; and there was very little money save from a small fishing industry on the coast, hampered by distance from markets.

THE LOBSTER ROUTE

The transformation of the drab little West Coast Cinderella into a real princess came largely through the construction of the magnificent west coast highway popularly known as the *Kreef* (lobster) Route.

The Cape rock lobster (*Jasus Ialandii*) is abundant along the west coast. The rock lobster, known as *kreef* in Afrikaans, is a very different crustacean from the crayfish of the Northern Hemisphere. Both animals, however, have flesh of delectable flavour, with the rock lobster considered by many to be the ultimate in seafoods. It is in great demand all over the world, particularly in France and Japan.

The catching of lobsters is controlled by a quota system which restricts commercial companies to specific tonnages determined by Government so that the lobster population is not left defenceless against the rapacity of commerce and totally destroyed. Private catches are limited to four lobsters a day for the catcher's own use. There is a minimum size limit of 89 mm in carapace length. This restriction particularly protects the female lobster which takes about ten years to reach the minimum size. Between the sizes of 65 mm and 89 mm she lays from 40 000 to 150 000 eggs each year. Because males grow at about twice the speed of the females, they comprise about 90 per cent of the commercial catch.

The season for catching starts on 15 November and lasts until 15 April. Eggs hatch in about October, with millions of tiny larvae drifting with the currents for an initial period of nine months. They moult and grow; and then, as transparent miniature lobsters, make their way inshore and find homes amongst the rocks and kelp. These miniature lobsters grow steadily, moulting their shells each year so that their growth can be accommodated in a larger covering.

By law, 25 per cent of the total catch of lobsters is retained in South Africa for local sale. The rest are exported. Cooked in a variety of ways, these lobsters are eaten in restaurants and on private tables. The Lobster Route is renowned for its seafood restaurants, with delicacies on the menu caught in the sea within sight of diners. Prices vary considerably. A good-sized lobster has a mass of about 500 g with the commercial quota being sold in wholesale quantities. Privately caught lobsters are sold at whatever price the catchers can get for them. There is a vast amount of illegal poaching.

Long before the road made it accessible there was never any uncertainty about the richness and nature of the endowment of this Cinderella coast. Some 60 million years ago something happened to our planet Earth which is as yet unexplained. From the regions of ice in the Antarctic, a cold current was spun off and flowed northwards towards the southern end of Africa. In the water of this current there was contained something of the very soul of the white continent of Antarctica, not only its cold but also a share in its natural riches of chemicals and minerals, carried down by glacial action from the land surface and then, together with the ice, dissolved into the sea.

The current, therefore, was richly endowed. Flowing northwards, it underwent a broadside collision with the warm Mozambique–Agulhas Current sweeping down the east side of Africa. The warm current was weakening at the end of a long run, but its sheer mass remained enough to deflect the cold current sufficiently westwards to prevent it affecting the east coast in any way whatever. Instead, as something like a cold river, 10°C in temperature, it was directed to flow up the west coast. The effect on this part of Africa was traumatic. The cold water hugged the coast with a caress of death, killing off the original marine life. Known as the Benguela Current, it was only about 150 km in width but this was sufficient to isolate the south-west coast from the far warmer Atlantic Ocean. Rainfall along the coast dwindled; all life-forms were affected; and a transitionary desert developed in the south, with a full desert (the Namib) in the north.

The original marine life-forms either died from cold or fled the area for warmer climes. In their place, however, came cold-water species, fewer varieties, but vast quantities of pelagic (surface living) fish such as pilchards and anchovies. These little fish flourished exceedingly on the rich stores of food in the cold current. Flowing up from Antarctica, the current (moving at a speed of about 3 km an hour) carries with it twenty times the amount of nitrogen found in the Mozambique–Agulhas Current on the east coast. On this nitrogen feed a prodigious population of plankton drifting with the current. One drop of water from this current contains about 30 million life-forms, and this is probably the most densely populated 'real estate' on Earth. Like rich pasturage in a lineal meadow of the sea, the plankton in their turn support vast shoals of pelagic fish, as well as crustaceans and shellfish known as filter feeders because they exist by sucking in plankton-rich water, feeding on the plankton and then expelling clean water. There developed a huge population of seabirds and seals living on these filter feeders and the pelagic fish. Then came human beings.

Prehistoric people scavenged the coast, living off the shellfish, fattening on the occasional gift from the sea of a stranded whale or other creature. The first Portuguese explorers observed the vast colonies of seals and birds along the coast and correctly associated their presence with the availability of sea foods. Sealers, mainly French, were the first commercial interests to exploit the animal life along the south-west coast. The Dutch followed, then the Americans. Seals and whales were the first attraction. Then the prodigious deposits of *guano* (bird's dung) covering the rocky islets caused the extraordinary episode of the Guano Rush, with thousands of ships (over 300 at one time anchored around one of the Saldanha islets) all busy loading smelly cargoes of one of the richest fertilisers known to man. The brawls, 'wars' and scandals of this guano rush provide a very peculiar story.

Lastly came massive commercial exploitation of the shoals of pilchards and anchovies, and the rock lobsters. Canneries were created at Saldanha Bay and St Helena Bay. Factory ships and swarms of trawlers appeared on the scene from hungry nations of East and West. There was a regular mania for ever larger catches. Science was enlisted to bolster the pure chance and instinct of ordinary fishing. Echo sounders, suction dredgers, complex netting, large trawlers; on all sides the talk was of 'bigger throughput' in the factories, bigger profits, more fish in the sea than had ever been taken out. A vast parasitic industry developed, with collapse so inevitable that only human greed was blinded to it. Marine life simply could not sustain such an onslaught.

All forms of marine life along the West Coast went into drastic decline. Frustrated fishermen blamed everything except themselves. The birds and seals were eating all the fish; kill the birds and seals. The unlimited shoals must still be there, hiding to escape capture. Scientists must devise more efficient ways of finding the fish; government must drive away the foreign fleets; the last shoals of fish must be left for South African fishermen to have the sole rights of extermination.

The Lobster Route has its start at the beginning of the Cape-to-Cairo road at the entrance to Table Bay harbour (foot of the Heerengracht). Follow this road, known here as Table Bay Boulevard. After 2 km, turn left on the road marked Paarden Island and Milnerton. The road leads north up the shores of Table Bay. After 3 km the road reaches an intersection; a left turn leading to the Ben Schoeman Container Dock, and a right turn into the light industrial area known as *Paarden Eiland* (island of horses), from its original use as a grazing ground for those animals. On the left-hand side there is an impressive view over Table Bay; the shipping and the mighty pile of Table Mountain are seen to great advantage. Unfortunately the beach is grubby – as it usually the case on the verges of a busy harbour – but the waves are much used by surf riders.

After 8 km the road crosses the river known as the *Liesbeek* (reedy stream) and reaches the lagoon at the mouth of the Salt River (sometimes known as the Dieprivier). In former years this river formed something of a delta. One of its channels reached the sea at the present mouth of the Liesbeek River, and the segment of land enclosed in this delta was Paarden Eiland. Modern reclamation of the land has changed the landscape, and the river now finds its way to the sea through a narrow lagoon much beloved by birds, canoeists and aquaplaners.

MILNERTON

On the right, meanwhile, the industrialisation of Paarden Eiland and Metro has given way to the residential area of *Milnerton*, named in 1902 after Sir Alfred Milner (the British High Commissioner in South Africa). It became a municipality in 1955. This is a pleasant, if slightly airy, part of the Cape. The west coast road leads up the eastern shore of the Salt River lagoon, with a handsome avenue of palm trees shading green lawns. Two bridges, one an historic old wooden bridge, cross the lagoon to reach what is known as Woodbridge Island. This 'island' (really an isthmus) was the property of the De Villiers Graaff family and their home, *Huis Zonnekus*, built in 1929, remains amidst a congested assembly of modern homes. From this area a lighthouse keeps watch over shipping and there is a popular golf-course, said to be the only true links in South Africa. The beauty of cultivated gardens prepares the traveller for the spectacular wild flower area just ahead.

After 11 km the road crosses a bridge over the seasonally flowing Salt River and sweeps close to the beach, passing on the right the old waterbird paradise and conservation area of *Rietvlei* (reedy swamp), once planned as a fishing harbour. In spring this portion of the drive is graced by a blaze of wild flowers. Cape daisies (*Dimorphotheca pluvialis*), golden gousblom (*Arctotis acaulis*) and many others carpet the sandy ground. But at any time of the year the drive is memorable, especially after the first 16 km where, at a crossroads, the road reaches the site of the oft-painted, endlessly photographed, classic view of Table Mountain and its companions, Devil's Peak and Lion's Head, which can be seen 10 km away across the restless waters of Table Bay. A walk along this lovely, spacious beach with its world-famous view is an experience to remember and, although the Atlantic Ocean hereabouts is on the cold side for bathing (15°C in summer), it is a most popular area for fishermen, picnickers, sunbathers, and all who love life in the sunshine.

At the crossroads there is a right turn leading to Table View residential area, and left for 2 km along the shore to ...

BLOUBERGSTRAND

The seaside village of *Bloubergstrand* (blue mountain beach) is named after the 331 m high hill which rises nearby. Seen from the sea, this hill has a tendency to take on a particularly blue appearance. The village itself was once an informal little place of weekend and seaside cottages; many of the older houses having partly been built with timber that had washed up on the beach. Nowadays it has become a fashionable place of residence with many expensive homes. The views of Table Mountain are superb. Surf riders are fond of the great rollers which sweep in from the Atlantic Ocean. Big Bay is a favourite resort for them. Shells are numerous and, in spite of the cold water, there are hardy people who even enjoy swimming. *Robben* (seal) *Island*, with its lighthouse and numerous buildings, lies due west across the Atlantic Ocean. The whole atmosphere of Bloubergstrand is that of the sea with its kaleidoscopic colour and capricious moods.

From Bloubergstrand there is a road running next to the sand dunes of the coast, with many stopping places favoured by fishermen and picnickers, many glimpses of wild flowers, and intermittent views over a sparkling beach to the now-receding bulk of Table Mountain. The Blouberg looms on the right with, on its summit, the ruins of a war-time radar and observation post.

THE BATTLE OF BLOUBERG

The first British occupation of the Cape after the battle of Muizenberg in 1795 was a holding measure. The French had invaded Holland. The Prince of Orange, the ruler of Holland, an ally of the British, had fled to England. There was fear that the French would take over the Cape and use it as a base to attack British trade around the end of Africa to the East. When peace came on 27 March 1802, the Cape was restored to the Dutch. Lieutenant-General Jan Willem Janssens was sent from Holland as Governor on the authority of the Batavian administration. He arrived in Cape Town on 23 December 1802.

Peace did not last long. On 12 May 1803 war was resumed between Britain and France. There was very little the people of the Cape could do about the resumed conflict. They had no naval resources and the garrison was feeble, short of all things of war and, mostly consisting of mercenaries, not very enthusiastic of involvement if either of the two contending powers decided to occupy the Cape. Holland could do nothing to aid them. Governor Janssens did his best to prepare the Cape for any attack, always hoping that the war would be played out in Europe, but to most of the local authorities there was a feeling of inevitable doom.

The day of truth came on the morning of 4 January 1806. A British fleet of 61 ships arrived from the north and were reported by the signallers on Signal Hill. The fleet anchored between Robben Island and Blouberg Strand. It must have made an impressive appearance. On board there were 6 654 troops under Major-General David Baird who had orders to occupy the Cape.

The British plan was to land the next day at *Losperds* (stray horse) Bay at Melkbosstrand. Overnight, however, a north-east gale blew up and landing was impractical. Not knowing how long the gale would last the general decided to make the landing at Saldanha Bay, protected from the winds but giving the troops a long march over sandy country before they could reach Cape Town.

A portion of the invading force was sent up to Saldanha Bay that night in order to occupy the place. The balance were to have left the next morning but when the sun came up on 6 January the wind dropped and the original plan of landing was possible although the sea was still rough. There was no resistance from the Dutch but 36 men of the 93rd Regiment were drowned when their landing craft was overturned by the surf. Military action started when a company of Burgher militia on reconnaissance killed one British soldier and wounded four others.

In Cape Town there was, meanwhile, a considerable bustle of military preparation although there was not too much that the authorities really could do. The signal cannons firing from hill to hill had alerted all the settled areas of the Western Cape to the British landing. As many men as could (or would) respond to the alarm, were riding into Cape Town and General Janssens mustered a little army of just over 2 000 men. It was a very mixed force. Most of the men were mercenaries, mainly Germans of the Waldeck 5th battalion, but with a mix of recruits from all parts of Europe. They were supported by 138 dragoons and 60 artillerymen from the Netherlands, 240 French marines from two ship anchored in Table Bay, 54 Javanese artillerymen, 181 Cape foot soldiers and 104 Mozambique slaves in the artillery train of 16 field guns.

At dawn on 8 January 1806, the advancing British invaders, about 4 500 strong, found themselves confronted by General Janssens men, drawn up about 4 km south-east of the Blouberg. The opposing artillery opened fire. The first few balls to land near the mercenaries put them into retreat. They considered resistance to be hopeless and they had no desire to fight simply for honour. The rest of Janssens army made at least a token resistance but faced with obvious British preparations for a bayonet charge by the Highland brigade, they fell back in general retreat. This was the end of the battle of Blouberg. The British lost 1 officer and 14 other ranks killed, 9 officers and 180 other ranks wounded and 8 men missing. When the Dutch force called a meeting that afternoon they found 337 of their men to be missing but whether dead, wounded or deserters could not be determined.

At 16h00 on the afternoon of 10 February 1806, articles of capitulation were signed in a cottage on the outskirts of Cape Town in the area then known as Papendorp (now Woodstock). The British then occupied Cape Town without further resistance. Terms of capitulation were generous. The inhabitants of the Cape were left in peace to their normal lifestyle. Only the regular troops which had garrisoned. Cape Town, and the French from the two ships in the bay, were taken prisoners of war and sent as such to Britain. There was no intention by the British of the Cape ever being returned to the rule of Holland or the Dutch East India Company.

MELKBOSSTRAND

Eleven kilometres from Bloubergstrand the coastal road reaches another seaside resort, *Melkbosstrand* (beach of milkwood trees). This is an informal little place particularly favoured by farmers who each summer holiday season, on 26 December, stage a day of *boeresport* (farmer's sports), when burly, sunbronzed rustic characters may be seen at tug-of-war and a variety of other antics. It is a picnicking place for Capetonians. The beach, rich in Atlantic Ocean shells, is a favourite haunt for walkers, but should definitely be avoided when the south-east wind is blowing during the summer months. From the village a tarmac road leads for 2 km to the Ou Skip Caravan Park. A further 2 km along the road lies the Koeberg nuclear power-station of ESKOM. Visitors are welcome at the Visitors Centre Mondays to Fridays 08h00 to 16h30, and on the second and last Sundays of each month from 14h00 to 16h30. Closed Saturdays and public holidays. Phone (021) 550-4668.

From the turn-off to Bloubergstrand, 16 km from Cape Town, the main Cape Town–Saldanha Bay road continues more inland on a straighter, less interesting course. Passing close to Bloubergstrand, at 27 km there is a crossroads, with a left turn to Melkbosstrand and a right turn leading for 10 km to the Cape Town–Namaqualand main road.

At 32,5 km there is a turn-off to the Koeberg nuclear power-station, and at 37,5 km a turn-off to the residential and industrial township of Atlantis, built in the first half of the 1970s.

At 41,5 km there is a crossroads, with a left turn leading for 3,5 km to the lovely beach known as *Silwerstroomstrand* (Silver Stream beach), developed as a camping and recreational resort, and a turn right leading for 11 km to the mission station of Mamre.

MAMRE

This mission was established in March 1808 as a result of an invitation extended to the Moravians by the then Governor, Lord Caledon. He invited them to create in the area a work similar to their highly successful activity at Genadendal near Caledon. Known as *Groenkloof* (green ravine), the area he offered had long been regarded as something of a sanctuary for the remnants of a few pastoral tribes who had once grazed their herds at the Cape. In 1701 a barracks had been built there for a garrison of ten men and a sergeant whose duty was to defend the area against stock thieves. This barracks fell into disuse and the Moravians found the old building half forgotten amidst a clump of oak trees. They named the place *Mamre* (amid the oaks), for it was there that Joseph had lived in the Holy Land. On the site they erected a church, a school and a water-mill, and laid out the present picturesque settlement of white-walled, black thatched cottages. With fertile and well-watered fields available for cultivation, Mamre in due course attracted a population of over 2 000 resident Coloured people. Today it remains the home of many families whose offspring work in Cape Town and return on weekends. With advancing years they eventually settle permanently at Mamre. The place is a favourite resort for artists and photographers. The cottages, garden, parsonage and church (this last with a primly plain interior) retain their original charm and it is pleasant to walk through the lanes and streets. The water-mill has been beautifully restored by the Rembrandt Company and is open to the public on weekdays from 09h00 to 17h00, and on Sundays from 14h00 to 17h00. Easter, particularly, is a time of reunion for the people of Mamre. They gather from far and wide to attend a succession of services in the church and to sing and listen to the music of their brass band. In 1789 in this Groenkloof area, the first four merino ewes and two rams were put to breed by their importer, Colonel Robert Gordon, thus beginning the wool industry in Southern Africa.

From Mamre a road leads for 17 km to Darling. The main Cape Town–Saldanha road continues north beyond the turn-off to Mamre for a further 29 km of rather dull scrub country and is then intersected (70,5 km from Cape Town) by a tarmac road linking Darling (15 km right) to the coastal resort of Yzerfontein (8 km left).

DARLING

Darling, with its population of 5 013, was laid out in 1853 and named in honour of the then Lieutenant-Governor, Charles Henry Darling. It became a municipality in 1955 and is the centre for prosperous farming activities. It is particularly noted for its dairy produce, grapes, peas, wool, export lupins and chincherinchees. Its spring flowers are renowned and an annual flower show is held in the third week of September. The Tinie Versfeld Wild Flower Reserve lies 12,5 km from the town on the tarmac road to Yzerfontein. Spring sees a spectacular display of wild flowers in this reserve and also at Waylands, Oudepost and Contreberg. A network of footpaths provides the visitor with some pleasant, easy walking. Seven kilometres north on the gravel road at Platteklip siding there is a memorial to Field-Cornet C P Hilderbrand of the Maritz Commando. He was killed there on 12 November 1901 when the Boers raided deep into the Cape Colony during the Anglo-Boer War. This was the most southerly scene of fighting during the war.

The Darling Museum presents the history of the local butter-making industry. There is also an art gallery featuring the work of local artists. The Duckitt Orchid Nurseries have a show each September. There is a basket factory in the town.

From Darling the traveller has a choice of three routes. One road leads eastwards for 32 km to Malmesbury, where it joins the main Cape Town–Namaqualand road, thus providing a circular drive back to Cape Town (total 175 km). Halfway along this road there is the well-known Mamreweg wine cellar, notable for its wines of the region. The second road from Darling leads north-eastwards for 24 km across flat, wheat-producing country and then joins the main road connecting Malmesbury with Saldanha. The third road from Darling leads westwards past the Tinie Versfeld Wild Flower Reserve and across the main Cape Town–Saldanha road for 23 km until it reaches the coast at the resort of *Yzerfontein* (iron fountain).

YZERFONTEIN

This is an exposed bay, windy in summer and always washed by the cold water of the Benguela Current. However, it has a fine beach and great rollers beloved by surfers. Nearby are the ruins of an ill-fated fish-canning factory (built just after the Second World War) with a 150 m long jetty which now provides a lee for surf riders and a vantage-point for fishermen. Dassen Island lies 10 km to the south-west. In the bay is the rocky islet known as *Meeurots* (gull rock), the nesting place for a large colony of sea-birds. For many years a derelict thatched cottage, a forlorn reminder of an old mystery, stood on the shore. In about 1910 two men, Matthys Schreuder and Johannes Genade, were murdered by an unknown assailant while they were fishing on a rock. For a long time afterwards their cottage was regarded as being haunted.

From Darling the R315 road leads through sheep and dairy-farming country which is filled with wild flowers in spring. Wild creatures can sometimes still be seen – steenbok, grysbok, hares, bat-eared foxes, ostriches and numerous birds. Puff-adders and mole snakes are common. After 15 km this road intersects with the R27, the main tarmac Cape Town–Saldanha road. If one crosses the R27, a further 8 km brings one to the village of Yzerfontein, now built up with weekend and vacation cottages of a very pleasant kind. Kilns used to burn shells for lime-making can be seen by the roadside. Some interesting hiking trails start at Yzerfontein. What is known as Sixteen Mile Beach is a lovely stretch of coastal scenery.

At the intersection of the R27 and the R315, if one turns and continues in the direction of Saldanha, a further 10 km along the West Coast road brings one to the turn-off to the West Coast National Park. A small fee is payable on entering the Park. Some 7 km from the turn-off the road divides. The right-hand road of this division provides a drive up the east shores of the lagoon, with many fine views and passing several old farmhouses. After 14,5 km this road reaches the village of Langebaan. To the left of the division, the road continues up the isthmus to Donkergat, passing on the way pleasant little settlements, such as Schryvershoek, Churchhaven (after 9 km) and Stofbergsfontein (at 11 km), originally created by fishermen. In 1666 a garrison of twelve men was sent from the Cape to occupy this area because the French were making a claim to Saldanha Bay and the lagoon, and were sealing on the islands. In those days, ships watered at a spring on the isthmus beneath what is today known as Postberg. For some years the Dutch and the French occupied the area alternately, but the Dutch were eventually left in possession. Ensign Izaak Schryver was once in command of the outpost. One of the small settlements established by fishermen bears his name.

The road leads above a beautiful beach, with cliffs providing a lee from the south-easters of summer. The bay is a favourite anchorage for yachts and houseboats. At a point 4 km from Stofbergsfontein, the road enters the Postberg private nature reserve. The original Dutch garrison was established at the freshwater spring near the shore. The property, known as *Oude Post*, was bought by a syndicate in 1949 and became a private nature reserve open to the public in August and September each year for the wild-flower season. Through this estate the road continues for 5 km and then ends at a locked gate at the entrance to a prohibited military area.

Beyond this gate the road reaches the site of the long-disused Donkergat Whaling Station, opened there in 1909 and closed in 1967. Many thousands of whales were captured from this station, humpbacks, right, blue, fin, sei, sperm and Bryde's, first described from Donkergat and named after the Norwegian who pioneered the station of *Donkergat* (dark hole). This area is now used for naval training and is closed to the public.

One kilometre further the road ends at Salamander Bay, where the ruins of several former fishing, whaling, and other concerns which came to grief there, still remain. The wrecks of several whale catchers and other derelict vessels lie in the bay. There is also a rather pathetic little sailors' cemetery, with tombstones dating back as far as the last century. There is an added touch of melancholy about this isolated cemetery; the tombstones record the deaths of very young sailors who had to be buried far away from their homes in Norway and other parts of Europe. The Salamander whaling station was opened in 1911 and closed after twenty years of slaughter. The Navy now uses the area for training purposes.

The name of the bay comes from the Dutch ship *Salamander*, which once sheltered there with its crew stricken with scurvy. From this northern point of the isthmus there is a panoramic view across the entrance to Saldanha Bay, with the modern harbour development on the opposite shore, the five bird islands, and Langebaan village on the eastern shore. Saldanha Bay is one of the great natural harbours of the world. It is a magnificent spread of sheltered water. On a still day or a calm evening it has a tranquillity and quietness which is dreamlike; the diminutive waves seem to sigh as they come to rest on the beach; the lights of Saldanha and Langebaan trail glittering pathways across the water. The only sounds are the distant murmur of the surf, the calling of the birds, and perhaps the 'putt-putt-putt' of some fishing boat.

THE WEST COAST NATIONAL PARK

South Africa – notwithstanding its historic background of vast open spaces and an unsurpassed richness in wildlife – has over the years been largely smothered by the private property of landowners who had little thought of conservation. There seemed to be so many wild animals, such a prodigious quantity and variety of vegetation and mineral wealth, that man could kill or exploit at will and, as the fishermen like to say, there would always be more for the taking. Unfortunately this was simply not true.

At the rate that uncontrolled destruction was taking place, South Africa was heading towards the total devastation of its marvellous heritage of wildlife and unspoilt landscape. It was Nature, rather than man, who intervened and, by making certain areas of the country seemingly unprofitable for exploitation, preserved them as wilderness areas. So it was with the area of the West Coast National Park. Saldanha Bay together with its appendage of *Langebaan* (long channel) is a wildlife area so unique that its destruction by man would have been a tragedy. Fortunately real estate 'developers' were kept at bay by a shortage of drinking-water in the area, and up to modern times the area remained inviolate from the establishment of seaside resorts or industries.

On 30 August 1985 the West Coast National Park was proclaimed over the 5 600 ha of the lagoon and its marshlands; 55 ha of the precincts, four islets – Jutten (47 ha), Malgas (19 ha), Marcus (11 ha) and Skaap (41 ha); and two sections of what is known as Sixteen Mile Beach (100 ha). As a result of subsequent negotiation with private landowners and Geelbek Annex (109 ha) the farms, *Bottelary, Geelbek, Abrahamskraal, Schrijvershoek, Flamingo Farms*, and the sand-dune area of *De Hoek* were added to the conservation area. The private nature reserve of *Oude Post* also joined the conservation area as the first contractual national park in South Africa. This area of wild flowers had been acquired by a syndicate in 1949, proclaimed a nature reserve in 1960, and became part of the West Coast National Park in August 1987.

The conservation of this area of lagoon wetlands, coast and islets is of enormous importance to wildlife. In this area live, either permanently or seasonally, 50 per cent of the world's population of swift terns, 25 per cent of the world's population of Cape gannets, 15 per cent of the world's population of crowned cormorants, and 12 per cent of the world's population of African black oyster-catchers. The tragically declining population of jackass penguins also find a sanctuary on the islets.

From September to April of each year there is an almost unbelievable influx of migrating wading birds such as curlew sandpipers. These little birds with other waders, sanderlings and knots etc., breed each year during the short Arctic summer on the Taimyr Peninsula in Siberia, where the Russians have preserved for them their ancient feeding and nesting grounds.

During the Arctic summer of continuous daylight there are enormous numbers of insects on which the birds feed. They nest, raise their chickens, and in August set out on a 15 000 km flight which terminates for most of them in the area of the West Coast National Park.

Flying at about 75 km an hour, the birds take about six weeks to do the journey, including wayside refuelling stops to feed. How the tiny mechanism of their body allows them to fly such a distance and find their way from the far north to the south, is a miracle of Nature. They remain in the south until April and then return to the Arctic. How many die on the journey is unknown, but each summer at least 55 000 of the little birds make a welcome return to the Langebaan Lagoon. There they potter around, feeding on crustaceans, molluscs and other denizens of the shore and wetlands.

Curiously enough, the numbers of migrating wading birds fluctuate over three-year cycles with the population of lemmings in the Arctic. Each third year sees a tremendous boom in the lemming population of the Taimyr Peninsula. The Arctic foxes feed on the lemmings and do not disturb the nesting birds. Many chickens are hatched and mature so fast that they are ready to join their parents in the flight south. The population explosion of the lemmings, meanwhile, is being dramatically reduced by the Arctic foxes. When the birds return for the next nesting season, the lemmings have been almost wiped out. The hungry foxes turn on the birds and feed on their eggs and chickens. This reduces the number of birds which fly south at the change of seasons. In the third year of the cycle, the lemmings start to increase again. The Arctic foxes also have large litters but the birds are left to nest, and their numbers increase. The young birds only nest when they are two years old. Until they reach that age, they remain at Langebaan, for the winter climate there is better than the summer climate of the Taimyr Peninsula. They never nest at Langebaan. When the urge comes to raise a family, they join the next migration north and build nests in a part of the world completely different from the sheltered waters of Langebaan.

Some 250 species of birds frequent Langebaan. There are huge flocks of Cape weavers, pied and wattled starlings, European bee-eaters, turnstones (which also migrate seasonally from Russia), swift terns, and fully a quarter of all the bird species found in South Africa.

The *Geelbek* farm was acquired on 30 June 1986 by the S A Nature Foundation who incorporated it into the West Coast National Park. Gold Fields of South Africa Limited financed the restoration of the superb old Cape-Dutch homestead and farm buildings, now used as an environmental centre.

The lower portion of the lagoon is a wilderness area with no human activity allowed. The middle portion is a limited recreational area and the upper portion is a multi-purpose recreational area. A tarmac road runs around the verges of the lagoon and traverses the Postberg area, with side roads open during the spring flower season. The ruins of the original military post (Oupos or Oudepost) may be seen on the shores of *Kraalbaai* (corral bay).

From the intersection with the Darling–Yzerfontein road, the main Cape Town–Saldanha road (70,5 km from Cape Town) continues northwards across the scrub-covered country. After 10 km there is a turn-off to the Langebaan Lagoon and the West Coast National Park. There is a tarmac road leading to the southern part of the lagoon and the isthmus separating it from the sea. The main road continues its way northwards. At 108,5 km from Cape Town it is intersected by a tarmac road linking Langebaan (11 km left) to the Malmesbury–Saldanha road (6 km right).

LANGEBAAN

Langebaan, founded in 1922, has a pleasant beach and is a characteristic lagoon-side holiday resort, with a collection of cottages, fishing boats, an anchorage for yachts, an air force crash-boat station, shops and municipal caravan parks. The population is 2 735. The town lies at the head of the lagoon where it joins Saldanha Bay proper. The connection is half blocked by Skaap and Meeu islands. Yachting, fishing and aquaplaning are favourite pastimes at Langebaan. Swimming is good but the water is cold. Wild flowers provide a colourful display in spring.

In 1997, the geologist Dave Roberts found fossilised footprints left by a woman 117 000 years ago in the sand dunes at Langebaan. These footprints are amongst the oldest so far found left by an anatomically modern human being.

In June 1998 the fossils were removed in a complex operation to the South African Museum in Cape Town. The move was made to save the footprints from the effects of vandalism and erosion. After the making of casts, the originals will be returned for safe keeping in the West Coast National Park.

Where the Cape Town–Saldanha road joins the Langebaan intersection, a right turn leads for 6 km to the Malmesbury–Saldanha road at the air force station and flying school of Langebaan Road. From this point a right turn (southwards) leads for 24 km to ...

HOPEFIELD

Hopefield, originally called *Zouterivier* (salt river), was established on the farm *Langkuil* in 1844. It was renamed in 1853 after two surveyors, Messrs Hope and Field, who laid out the town on a proper plan when it was anticipated that a trunk road would be built linking Cape Town with Saldanha Bay. The railway from Cape Town opened to the town in February 1903. It became a municipality on 2 April 1914. Hopefield has a population of 4 427 and is a farming and railway centre, with a cluster of stores, garages and houses built in the valley of the generally dry *Soutrivier* (salt river). It is the principal centre of what is known as the *Voorbaai* (before the bay), the area immediately east of Saldanha Bay.

Despite the unspectacular nature of this little town, it is perhaps as widely known among international scientists as is Johannesburg. The reason for this is that, in May 1951, Dr Ronald Singer, palaeontologist of the South African Museum, visited the farm *Elandsfontein* in the Hopefield district. Seven years previously Dr J G Smit of Wynberg had found a few fossils there while on a hunting trip and had reported this to Dr Singer.

As soon as Dr Singer reached the eroded sand-dune area of *Elandsfontein*, he realised the tremendous significance of the place. It is, in fact, one of the world's most important sites for the prehistorian. Originally a small lake in arid surroundings, it attracted to its shores a considerable variety of ancient life. Consistent work there has so far rewarded archaeologists with 6 000 important fossil bones and 3 000 man-made stone implements. The fossils include bone fragments of an extinct Neanderthal-type human, Saldanha Man. Remains have also been found of two extinct giraffe species, extinct buffaloes, lions, baboons, sabre-toothed tigers, zebrine horses, wild pigs, giant leopards, elephants, cave hyenas and skeletons of numerous modern game animals – rhinos, hippos and antelope.

The fossils date from a period ranging from 150 000 to 75 000 years ago. The stone implements found fall into three major groups. The first and most primitive group is a hand-axe industry known as the Cape Coastal Fauresmith; the second group belongs to the Middle Stone Age (Still Bay Culture); and the third group belongs to the Late Stone Age (Bushmen and Hottentots). Several other minor fossil sites have also been discovered in the area.

There are a number of historical farms in the Hopefield area. *Langrietvlei* on the Berg River was allocated to a free burgher in 1715. Today *Langrietvlei* is well known for its Guernsey and Hereford studs and natural fynbos honey. A replica of a *hartbeeshuisie* (wattle-and-daub cottage) can be seen at one of the entrances to the town. These cottages were commonly built by early cattle farmers in the Sandveld: walls were made by tying layers of reed between saplings and covering with a layer of clay.

A variety of hiking trails with prolific bird life are found at *Kersboschdam,* Phone (022) 723-0403 and *Langrietvlei* Phone (022) 783-0856.

From Hopefield the tarmac road continues northwards through flat sand country which, apart from August and September when it bursts into a colourful display of wild flowers, remains dull for most of the year. After 64 km the road joins the main Cape Town–Namaqualand road 4,5 km north of Malmesbury.

From the Langebaan intersection the main tarmac road continues north past the Langebaan phosphate quarries, a deposit thought to be fossilised guano lying on top of a former island. After 6 km there is a turn-off to Saldanha and the iron-ore loading jetty and terminus of the mineral line from Sishen in the Northern Cape. After a further 5 km there is a turn-off leading for 16 km to the most important town and administrative centre of what is known as the *Agterbaai* (the rear bay), the area north of Saldanha Bay. The main road continues for 20 km to Velddrif.

VREDENBURG–SALDANHA

Vredenburg (the town of peace) had a beginning somewhat less peaceful than its name. The strongest spring of fresh water in the area bubbles to the surface here on the boundary line separating the two farms *Heuningklip* and *Witteklip*. The original owners of these two farms, W Baard and C Loubser respectively, quarrelled so much over water rights that the spring was first known as *Twisfontein* (fountain of strife) and later as *Prosesfontein* (lawsuit fountain). In 1875, when it was decided to create a centre for the area, the site of this contentious spring was selected; a church was built there; and the name was changed to Vredenburg. Today it is the seat of a magistracy and the communications centre for the area. Numerous shops and garages line the principal street. In 1975 Vredenburg and Saldanha were united as Vredenburg–Saldanha. The combined area of 67 208 ha makes it the largest municipality (spacewise) in South Africa.

From Vredenburg the main tarmac road swings south-westwards, sweeps down past the great granite boulders of *Witteklip* (white stone) farm, and off through wheat fields for 12 km to ...

SALDANHA

The port of Saldanha is now part of the Vredenburg–Saldanha municipality, with a combined population of 22 563. Saldanha originally consisted of only a few shacks, erected by impoverished fishermen who earned a living by catching mullet and mackerel, drying them to make what are known as *bokkems* (kippers), and selling them to the local farmers as rations for labourers. Early in the 1900s, the partnership of Holland & Hinchliffe shipped up from Cape Town the machinery from a small factory which French interests had set up in Table Bay for the canning of rock lobsters. This venture had gone bankrupt. The new owners set the machinery going on the shores of Saldanha Bay and with a 'fleet' consisting of two ancient fishing boats, commenced an industry.

This North Bay Cannery Company (as it was called) was the start of the present fishing and processing industry in Saldanha Bay. The settlement, originally known as *Hoetjies Bay* from the word *houtee* (seal), began to grow steadily. The shortage of fresh water, which had handicapped Saldanha Bay since its discovery, was alleviated by a filtration plant which was built on the Berg River during the Second World War. From here water was piped to the area, allowing Saldanha Bay to be utilised as a naval base, a sanctuary for damaged ships, and a laying-up anchorage.

After the war, the naval facilities were converted into a training depot which eventually developed into the modern naval gymnasium. Three fish-processing and canning factories also began operating at Saldanha Bay after the war: the Saldanha Bay Canning Co (Pty) Ltd; Southern Sea Fishing Enterprises (Pty) Ltd; and the Spanish Pescanova Fishing Co. Gelatine-rich seaweed is harvested in the bay. The islands yields guano and eggs; and shoals of mullet are netted from the beach, especially at night.

In 1970 the government decided to develop Saldanha as the export harbour for iron, manganese and other ores mined in the Northern Cape. A direct railway was built to carry this ore from Sishen to Saldanha. The line was opened in 1976. Vast harbour operations were undertaken which developed Saldanha Bay into a major port for the use of large bulk carriers.

A very interesting, and quite unexpected, result of harbour developments in Saldanha Bay has been the establishment of aquaculture. One of the civil engineers who worked on harbour construction was Philip Steyn. Born in Pretoria, he grew up in Oudtshoorn and then went to the University of Stellenbosch to study civil engineering. After ten years of working for a Johannesburg firm, he was sent to Saldanha. While employed on harbour development, he met a friend, Vosloo Pienaar, who was working for the Department of Fisheries on a project of cultivating oysters in the Langebaan Lagoon. This project was yielding positive results, but the creation of the West Coast National Park terminated all commercial activity in the area.

Vosloo Pienaar moved to the Knysna Lagoon, but his work with oysters had aroused the interest of Philip Steyn. He was aware of the demand for such delicacies as mussels, clams and oysters.

In countries such as New Zealand there was a considerable sea-farming industry in the cultivation of green-lipped mussels. In France cultivation of shellfish had started 600 years ago. South Africa had the disadvantage of a coast with few lagoons or estuaries suited to sea farming. In Saldanha Bay, however, Philip Steyn perceived an almost ideal opportunity.

As a result of harbour works which included the building of an enclosing stone wall, a portion of the bay had been converted into a 28 ha tidal dam. Philip Steyn negotiated with the government for its use as a sea farm. After some initial mixture of suspicion, bewilderment and amusement, the authorities gave him the desired permission. In 1982 Philip Steyn started to farm in the sea, registered as the West Coast Maricult (Pty) Ltd, trading as Seafarm. In 1984 the first harvest was marketed. It was of superb quality.

The Mediterranean blue mussel (*Mytilus galloprovincialis*), considered to be more tasty than the South African black mussel (*Choromytilus meridionalis*), became the principal product of sea farm aquaculture. These mussels migrated to South Africa of their own accord by 'stowing away' on the hulls and anchor chains of ships. They found Saldanha Bay to be an excellent home. Its water is rich in plankton. Marine animals, such as mussels, which feed by filtering water and extracting the plankton, fatten very rapidly. The Langebaan Lagoon is said to support the densest population on Earth of microscopic animals and marine plants. Their concentrated presence gives the water a distinct green colour. By feeding on these minute organisms, the filter fish keep the water clear. They fatten rapidly. Unfortunately over-eating by the filter-feeders causes them to defecate far more frequently than normally. In the still waters of Saldanha Bay this faecal matter accumulates on the bed of the shallow bay and provides a difficult problem of disposal to the sea farmer.

The South African indigenous clam, *Macra glabrata*, is also harvested in sea farming. Like the mussels, they take up to six months to mature from seed, constantly enlarging their shells to accommodate their increase in body size. Indulgences in their appetite has also had an unfortunate consequence.

The Japanese oyster, *Crassostrea gigas*, also does very well in Saldanha Bay. The seed is obtained from Guernsey Island and Chile. They take nine months to reach marketing size. The shellfish spawn in summer and lose weight. Winter sees them plump. They also are hearty eaters.

Four other sea farms commenced production apart from Philip Steyn's pioneer venture: three in Saldanha Bay (Atlas, Sea Harvest and Lusitania) and one in St Helena Bay. Fish, such as sole, are a farming possibility of the future. The delectable rock lobster needs very special conditions of water; and its fastidiousness, and the fact that its principal diet is the black mussel, makes it a more difficult animal to farm.

SALDANHA BAY

The name *Saldanha Bay* comes from the Portuguese admiral, António de Saldanha, although, he never actually visited the place. In 1503, as commodore of a Portuguese fleet, he anchored below Table Mountain. For nearly 100 years thereafter the name Saldanha Bay (meaning, in its Portuguese form of *Agoada de Saldanha*, watering-place of Saldanha) was applied to what is now called Table Bay. It was the Dutch who changed the name. In 1601 they gave Table Bay its modern name and transferred the name of Saldanha to its present situation.

All the early visitors to Saldanha Bay were immediately impressed by the abundance of marine life in the area. Sea-birds and seals frequented the islands in immense numbers, and their plumpness was visual proof of the presence of huge shoals of fish on which they fed. Early in the 17th century the French started sealing operations in the bay, regarding the area as their possession.

Very shortly after Jan van Riebeeck settled at the Cape, he dispatched a yacht, the *Goede Hoop*, on an exploration up the coast. The crew of this vessel paid particular attention to the various islands, for rumours of the great profits made by the French fur sealers had penetrated to the Dutch. Immediately south of the entrance to Saldanha Bay the Dutch sailors found an island occupied by such a large number of seals that the animals sported in the sea in huge shoals like porpoises. It was an incredible spectacle, and the Dutch named the island *Vondeling* (foundling). When they landed there, they found it covered with bitter-asparagus, reeds and thorny shrubs. Tortoises were numerous and an occasional snake startled them.

In the bay they found five other islets which they named *Jutten* (Joyce's); *Malgas* (meaning 'mad geese', the name given to the beautiful sea-birds known as gannets); *Meeu* (gull); *Marcus* (after Corporal Marcus Robbeljaert, Commander of Robben Island); and *Schaapen* (nowadays known as *Skaap* Island, sheep island), because they left two sheep there as food for future ship-wrecked sailors in distress. Rabbits were later left on this island to replace the sheep, and their descendants still flourish. Gannets, penguins, cormorants and seals occupied all the islands of Saldanha Bay. On Skaap Island the Dutch found a pile of 2 733 sealskins neatly stacked by French sealers to await shipment. Thanking the Lord for such a gift and keeping a watchful eye over their shoulders, the Dutch loaded the skins on to their yacht and gleefully sailed off to Cape Town.

For some time after that there was a comedy of rivalries between the French and Dutch over the possession of Saldanha Bay and its islets. The French erected beacons of possession; the Dutch engraved the initials of their company (VOC) on to projecting rocks on the same islands; the French sealers promptly defaced them. The Dutch, however, had to win; they were occupying the Cape and were nearest to Saldanha Bay. In 1666 they established a small garrison at the principal fountain of drinking-water on the western shore of the Langebaan Lagoon. After a few changes of ownership over the next five years, with the French periodically chasing out the Dutch and the latter returning as soon as the French were gone, the area of Saldanha Bay eventually came under the control of the Dutch East India Company.

Drinking-water was always the great problem of Saldanha Bay. With so magnificent and sheltered a harbour, a perennial supply of fresh water would certainly have made it the site of Cape Town. Instead, for so many years, it served only as an occasional anchorage for ships, as a resort of sealers, and as a lair for pirates. In 1693 one of these adventurers, Captain George Dew of the *Amy*, had the misfortune to be caught there by a Dutch warship while his vessel lay careened on the beach. He and his crew were taken to Europe to stand trial.

The Dutch were also occasionally surprised in Saldanha Bay. On 21 July 1781 the *Middelburg* and five other Dutch ships were caught in the bay by an English squadron. The *Middelburg* was put to fire and sunk by her own crew, but her five consorts were captured. Many other ships have been sunk or scuttled in the bay and the bottom is littered with relics of these vessels. One of the most famous was the *Meerestyn* wrecked on 3 April 1707 off Jutten Island. Twenty years after this disaster, John Lethbridge, using a wooden barrel as a diving apparatus, salvaged a valuable booty of silver bars and ducatoons from this wreck. Odd coins and fragments of china can still be found in the sand and pools.

Perhaps the most extraordinary event in the early history of Saldanha Bay was the guano rush. In the mid 1830s Europe discovered the value of guano as a fertiliser. The greatest deposits known – those off the Peruvian coast – were all in the hands of monopolies. There were searches for other sources of supply, and attention was directed to the various islands off the coast of Namibia and the Cape. At first Ichaboe Island, off the south-western coast of Namibia, was the scene of a great rush, but then the deposits on the islands of Saldanha Bay were discovered. It is recorded that in August 1844 there were over 300 ships in Saldanha Bay loading guano from the islands. Several of the islands (particularly Malgas) were found to be covered with guano to a depth of 10 m. A flagstaff was planted in the centre of Malgas Island. From the staff, lines were marked partitioning the island like slices of a huge cake. Each slice was apportioned to a different vessel.

For some time Malgas Island presented the aspect of a fair, with tents, scaffolding and a boisterous crowd of men. Grog vendors and young ladies from the Cape hurried there to get their share of profits. Tent houses of business were erected, each sporting some flag with fanciful names such as 'Wapping', 'Sheerness' or 'London Docks'. Brawls and riots became commonplace, and a warship had to be sent up from Cape Town to restore order. A tax of £1 per ton was levied on all guano removed, and the government collected over £200 000 from this source. With guano selling in Europe at £6 per ton, the profits were enormous. These little islands rank as true treasure islands of the world. Preserved by the ammonium content of the guano were countless carcasses of birds and, on Malgas Island, the body of a French sealer named l'Ecluse. This mummy was shipped to Europe and for years was a famous exhibit in side-shows.

The southern end of Saldanha Bay consists of the lagoon known as *Langebaan* (the long channel), 16 km by 4,5 km in extent, and seldom more than about 6 m in depth. The lagoon is fed by water from the bay. It is cold at the northern end, but is progressively warmed by the sun until, at the shallow southern end, the water is generally 10°C warmer than the sea.

Flamingos, as well as many other waders and sea-birds, frequent the lagoon. Beneath the surface lies a deposit of oyster shells so enormous that it is rivalled in all the world only by the deposit in Chesapeake Bay in the United States. The origin of this deposit is a mystery. The shells (of a species *Cabria*) lie in huge flat beds, 3 m to 7 m thick and intersected by the tidal flow. In an area of about 6 square kilometres the deposit amounts to about 30 million tons.

The oysters probably died as a result of one of the following three causes. In the successive elevations and submergences to which this part of the coast was subject during Cretaceous times (60 million years ago), the lagoon seems to have been the estuary of the Berg River for a while. Silt discharged by this river could have caused the death of the oysters. Alternatively the oyster beds may have been elevated above the sea and the molluscs may have been killed by exposure to the air; but most probably the change in the prevailing temperature of the sea with the advent of the Benguela Current could have brought about their end. Whatever the case, the beds were left for man to discover in modern times and an industry for the making of lime and poultry food developed. Oysters have not been able to re-establish themselves in the lagoon naturally.

Saldanha became the terminus of the coast road and a branch railway from Cape Town. From Vredenburg, however, a road leads northwards on a journey through a countryside of wheat fields and oddly shaped outcrops of granite boulders. After 16 km this road reaches the sea at the pleasant little fishing village of ...

PATERNOSTER

The source of the name *Paternoster* (our father) remains unknown. One explanation is that the name refers to prayers said by Portuguese seamen when shipwrecked. This part of the coast was mapped in the 1790s by Captain Francis Renier Duminy, with the Dutch East India Company ship *De Meermin*. Perhaps he said a prayer at Paternoster and then named it, although more likely it takes its name from the fishing tackle known as the paternoster. Duminy Point, however, bears his name.

Today it is a place of white-walled cottages, with a fine beach washed by a cold sea. There is considerable activity in the catching and processing of rock lobsters, with a factory run by Paternoster Fisheries. This part of the coast is rich in lobsters, perlemoen and other seafoods. The rock lobster fishing season is from 15 November until 15 April.

From Paternoster a track runs south for 3 km along a rugged coastline to the lighthouse at *Cape Columbine* (named after the wreck there in 1829 of the barque *Columbine*). This 9 million candle-power lighthouse and radio beacon is a major navigational point for ships approaching the coast of Southern Africa from Europe and America. The lighthouse stands in the Columbine Nature Reserve which is noted for its spring flowers. The track continues for some kilometres along the coast and is used by line fishermen finding their way to the numerous promontories and bays. One kilometre beyond the lighthouse this track passes the rocky little bay named *Titties* or *Titus Bay*, from a fisherman who had the misfortune of being drowned there. There are many fine camping sites along this coast, but there are no facilities besides toilets. Wild flowers, fresh air and a rugged seascape make up the beauty of this part of the world.

North-west of Paternoster a gravel road runs for 16 km to *Stompneusbaai* (bay of stumpnose fish) on the shores of ...

ST HELENA BAY

This great bay received its name, *St Helena*, from the Portuguese navigator, Vasco da Gama. He discovered the bay on the day of that saint (7 November 1497) while on his pioneer voyage from Europe to the East. There is a memorial to this event consisting of three marble pedestals erected close to the main road at Stompneusbaai. On the beach somewhere here or near the mouth of the

Berg River (which the Portuguese called the River of St James), the Portuguese explorers careened (scraped the hulls of marine growths) their four ships and relaxed for a week after their four-month ocean voyage. It was there, too, that a foolish brawl developed between one of the sailors and a group of Africans – the first recorded clash on the shores of Southern Africa between Europeans and the indigenous people. Nobody was killed.

St Helena Bay is one of the world's principal fishing centres. The cold Benguela Current surges upwards along this part of the coast and brings to the surface large concentrations of nutrient salts. Huge shoals of anchovies and (before they were depleted by over-fishing) pilchards fed in the area on the plankton which flourish on the nutrient salts. The number of fish-processing factories which were built along the southern shore of the bay was such that the visitor might well have been pardoned for thinking that the area was an industrial suburb of a city.

Twelve busy fish-processing factories were established along the 21 km curve of the shore from Stompneusbaai to the mouth of the Berg River. In the heyday of pilchards, the scene was quite extraordinary during the catching season (1 January to 31 July). Wheat fields reach down almost to the water's edge, and only a tarmac road running along the coast provides a boundary line between agriculture and fishing. The factories stood between the road and the sea, with their jetty 'feet' in the water to receive the catches of one fishing boat after another.

From Stompneusbaai a tarmac road leads along the southern shores of St Helena Bay for 17 km and then joins the tarmac road from Vredenburg, right turn, 10 km; to Velddrif, left turn, 12 km.

After the turn-off to Vredenburg–Saldanha, the main west coast road continues across the sandveld. After 6 km there is a turn to St Helena Bay and a further 11 km brings the road to a turn-off which leads past the pumping station on the Berg River to Hopefield. The turn-off to Saldanha and St Helena Bay is half a kilometre beyond this. The west coast road then bridges over the Berg River and, 140 km from its start, reaches ...

VELDRIF–LAAIPLEK

As the road crosses the Berg River, it enters the river mouth harbour town of Velddrif–Laaiplek, a major fishing centre with a population of 1 389.

Velddrif, as its name indicates, was originally a fording place across the river for the road traversing the sandveld from Cape Town to the north. A pont was provided in 1899 to carry travellers and vehicles over the river. A bridge was only built in 1950. Inevitably, a store, blacksmith's shop and hotel came into being to serve travellers at the river crossing. *Laaiplek* (loading place), lower down at the mouth of the Berg River, was formerly a shipping point for the wheat grown in the area. In 1871 an enterprising Cape Town merchant, Johann Carel Stephan, son of a Norwegian seafarer, patched up the hulk of a sailing-ship, the *Nerie*, wrecked in Table Bay, and sailed it up to Laaiplek. There it was permanently anchored, and for years it served as a home, store and place of business for Stephan, who became known as the so-called *Koring Koning* (corn king) of St Helena Bay. As the general factotum of the area, he bought wheat in bulk, stored it in the holds of his anchored hulk, shipped produce to Cape Town, brought in assorted goods, and managed an export trade in salted snoek to the island of Mauritius and to Natal – where this fish was in favour as standard rations for workers on the sugar estates.

For nearly 30 years the tall, gaunt-faced Johann Stephan was the trading baron of the coast. His influence and that of his family will never quite vanish from the great bays of Saldanha and St Helena. The Stephans built stores, started fisheries and attracted to their employ a whole community of Italian and Portuguese fishermen – the Colombos, Carosinis, Sienis, Seras, Carnessas, Violas, Pharos, Dipoalas, Donighis, Tallies, Nimbs, Fioraventes, and many others whose descendants still fish and work in the area. The waters of the Benguela Current are the source of their prosperity.

Beginning in desperate poverty, the area has risen to some affluence. The first factory of the Berg River mouth was opened in 1944; and two years later Velddrif became a local authority, with municipal status attained in September 1960.

A new and deeper artificial harbour entrance was built in 1966 to bypass the silting river mouth. The future of this area seems assured for as long as there are fish in this most productive pocket of the Atlantic Ocean. The Cerebos Company recovers salt from polders on the left bank of the

Berg River. In the early 1980s the Owen Wiggens Trust created a resort and marina on the banks of the Berg River known as Port Owen, this is a marina for yachtsmen, fishermen and vacationers staying in waterfront cabanas and private homes.

Velddrif is known for its wonderful birdlife. The diversity of wading species is greater within the estuary area than anywhere else in South Africa. Bird watching and recreational tourism is overtaking fishing as the most important economic industry of the town.

From Velddrif there is a road leading eastwards for 65 km to Piketberg on the main Cape Town–Namaqualand road. A second road follows the left bank of the Berg River, past the old water filtration and pumping plant (24 km), and then returns to Hopefield (total 40 km).

The road to the north continues up the coast. After half a kilometre there is a turn-off leading for one kilometre to the Pelican Park caravan park one of three caravan parks in the area. Ten kilometres further on, the road reaches the seaside and residential area of *Dwarskersbos* (across the candle bush), created on the farm of that name owned by the Smit family. It is notable for the number of *Euclea polyandra* and *kersbos* (candle bush) growing there. Eleven kilometres from Dwarskersbos, the road passes the entrance to the 390 ha Rocher Pan Nature Reserve. During the winter rainy season, when this shallow lakelet fills with water, it becomes a great resort of aquatic and other birds, with at least 90 species already identified as frequenting the area. The Rocher family owned the area which now comprises the nature reserve.

Two kilometres beyond the entrance to the Rocher Pan Nature Reserve, the road crosses the Saldanha–Sishen railway line and, after another 7 km, there is a crossroads with the road leading from Piketberg to Elands Bay. The country is typical Sandveld – shrub-covered, level and containing many hollows which fill with water during the rainy season but are dry for the rest of the year.

The road climbs over a ridge and then descends into a more fertile valley which contains an impressive stretch of water, 10 km by 3 km, known as *Verlorevlei* (lost marsh), an all-year-round resort of countless aquatic birds such as pelicans, ducks, geese, coots and other species. Fish such as carp, kurpers and springers live in the water.

At 44,5 km from Rocher Pan the road, after following the shore of Verlorevlei for 2 km, reaches a junction at a bridge. On the left-hand side of the vlei a road continues for 3 km and then ends at the jetty and processing plant of the Elands Bay lobster-fishing industry at *Cape Desejado* (cape welcome), also known as Baboon Point. The Saldanha–Sishen mineral line tunnels through the sandstone pile of mountain at Baboon Point, and a path leads from the end of the road to the Elands Bay Cave which contains interesting rock paintings. The cave is being excavated and studied by the Department of Archaeology of the University of Cape Town. It was inhabited by man 15 000 years ago.

Back at the bridge, the main road crosses Verlorevlei. After 2 km the road reaches a turn to the village and beach of Elands Bay. This is a celebrated resort for surfers during the summer season of south-east winds, when powerful waves shoulder their way into the bay and break on a fine sandy beach. The small village has a few shops, a hotel and caravan park right on the beach.

Back at the turn-off to Elands Bay, the main coastal road continues northwards. After 17,5 km there is a junction with the Lamberts Bay–Leipoldtville Road. The road to Lambert's Bay leads westwards past the salt-pans at Krompoort and then turns northwards close to the coast. At 46 km from Elands Bay the road reaches the terminus of the Lobster Route at the fishing harbour and holiday resort of ...

LAMBERT'S BAY

Sir Robert Lambert, commander of the naval station at the Cape from 1820 to 1821, was responsible for the marine survey of the south-western coast of the Cape Colony. The bay which carries his name is notable for a small island which is the home of a large colony of sea-birds and provides a protective lee for a harbour very suited to fishing boats and small trading vessels.

The shores of the bay were then part of a farm named *Otterdam* owned by Gerrit Erasmus Smit. In 1887 the enterprising trader, Joseph Carl Stephan of Laaiplek, bought the site of the future town and used the natural harbour for bringing in trade goods and exporting wheat and other local products. The Marine Hotel was built by the Stephans at the harbour. Inland, east of Lambert's Bay,

James William van Putten, born in England of a Dutch father and French mother, established another hotel and trading station at what became known as *Van Puttensvlei*. This place was actually the first administrative centre and police post of the area.

Lambert's Bay, during the Anglo-Boer War, was the scene of the only known naval engagement between Boer and Briton. When General Jan Smuts raided the south-western Cape, he found anchored in the bay a small Royal Navy gunboat. The Boers opened fire from the shelter of the sand dunes. The Navy responded with a few shells. There was, fortunately, only one casualty – a marine by the name of Corporal Smallwood. Another small British warship, the HMS *Sybille*, was wrecked in the bay in a gale on 16 January 1901 after having landed a naval brigade. The site of the wreck was 8 km south of the harbour at Steenbokfontein, where the powerful gale had driven the ship during the night. One seaman by the name of Jones was crushed by a big wave against a cannon and killed. He and Corporal Smallwood are buried in the Dutch Reformed church cemetery in Lambert's Bay. Salvaged items from the ship are in the Sandvlei Museum in Lambert's Bay.

After the war, the Stephan brothers sold a portion of their land at the bay to the Cape Government for use as an outspan. The rest of the farm was sold to the government in 1909. A few people started to settle there. A school opened in 1915 and in 1918 Axel Landstrom and Co built the first rock lobster factory and founded the Lambert's Bay Canning Co. This development attracted many more people to find work and build homes. In 1929 Lambert's Bay became a local authority and in 1969 it became a municipality.

Two other fish-canning companies were established in Lambert's Bay but both were eventually absorbed by the Lambert's Bay Canning Co. The company nowadays has a production quota of 34 000 tons of fish (mainly anchovies yielding 10 000 tons of fishmeal) and 530 tons of rock lobsters. Pilchards, which used to be the principal edible fish for canning, have largely vanished from the south-west coast. The high profits from the export of rock lobsters have compensated for the collapse of the pilchard industry.

During May and June there are considerable catches of snoek. The anchovy population seems to be holding its own in spite of massive fishing. They appear, in fact, actually to have increased their number as their competitors, the pilchards, decreased. It is on these little fish, swimming in shoals of millions, that the predatory game fish, the birds which produce guano, and the fish factories all survive.

As the northern terminus of the Lobster Route, Lambert's Bay has several very good seafood restaurants. The rock lobsters come live and kicking straight from the holding tanks in the factory. The *Muisbosskerm* (mouse bush shield) on the beach 5 km south of the town is a unique 'boma'-style restaurant. Other open air restaurants notable for interesting seafoods are Bosduisklip and Plaaskombuis.

Apart from the excellent seafoods, the visitor to Lambert's Bay finds interesting photographic and visual opportunities in the busy little harbour. The colonies of gannets, penguins and cormorants on Bird Island are easy to see by means of a causeway, September to February being the best period to see the birds. The island yields about 280 tons of guano each year. About 5 000 pairs of cape gannets breed on the island, laying their eggs in September and October. Four species of cormorants also breed there in a long season from September to April. About 50 pairs of African (jackass) penguins live permanently on the island and breed throughout the year.

The Sandveld, after reasonable winter rains, is a glorious area for wild flowers. August and September are the best months, while aloes flower from May to August.

The Sandveld Museum is an interesting place to visit. It is open Mondays to Fridays 09h00 to 12h00, 14h00 to 16h00; Saturdays 10h00 to 11h00. The museum houses a remarkable collection of domestic and industrial items connected to the lifestyle of the people of the Sandveld. Life for them and their domestic animals, was hard. Note the horsemill, originally from the farm *Kleinfontein*. The horse that worked it was blindfolded and supported by a 'stagger stick' to prevent staggering and dizziness as it walked around and endlessly around in a dreadful, tedious chore which must have seemed incomprehensibly endless to the animal. There is a four by four desert route, 18 km long. Up to the time of writing no one has completed this route without getting stuck but if you want to test the capability of your vehicle then by all means try it. Contact Ron Saly (027) 432-1715.

Chapter Seven

THE GARDEN OF THE WESTERN CAPE

A river is a child of the mountains and the clouds. The winds act as matchmakers to the parents, carrying in the clouds. The mountains hold the clouds in their arms. The clouds rest on the mountains. From this pleasant union comes the water – pure, cool and sparkling. It bubbles out of the mountains from springs flowing to streams, then to rivulets, merging to form the rivers which by their energy create the valleys, gives them fertility and because it is itself a living thing, attracts to them innumerable other forms of life.

Amongst the scenic wonders of Earth, the folded sandstone mountains and valleys of the Western and Southern Cape provide a superbly rugged but curiously elegant landscape. Geologists refer to the area as the Cape Supergroup of sandstones laid down by the action of water between 500 and 250 million years ago.

The sedimentary deposits were laid down in three main groups. The oldest is known as the Table Mountain Group. This deposit was laid down during a period of an ice age in the Southern Hemisphere. There are few traces of any life-form of this time, but numerous scratches left by glacial action.

Above the Table Mountain Group a second deposit known as the Bokkeveld Group was laid down. The climate of the Southern Hemisphere had changed by then, and this assortment of mudstones, shales and sandstones is rich in fossils of a variety of shallow-water creatures which flourished in conditions warmer than those of the earlier ice age. The third series of sediments to be laid down is known as the Witteberg Group, and this is rich in the fossils of fish and marine plants.

The three groups were lifted above the level of the sea.. They dried, warping and twisting, and were then attacked by the rain. The soft rock was easily eroded and sculpted into all manner of odd shapes. Rocks were left balancing on precarious supports. The grotesque shapes of antique creatures seemed to be petrified into stones, all strange and eerie. Deep valleys were washed by the rivers and streams, and in them life flourished – a rich vegetation to supply food for mammals, birds, insects and reptiles.

Then man found the valleys attractive – prehistoric people of a variety of origins, and then exotic immigrants. All were influenced in their life-style by the sandstone setting. A culture and industry evolved, architectural styles, agricultural techniques – all were affected by the chemistry and nature of the rocks and the environment. It is fascinating to follow the rivers from their source through this lovely jumble of scenery and see how life has evolved along their banks, how the rivers have affected man and how man has affected the rivers.

Fruit, fruit juices, wine and flowers in great variety and considerable quantities are produced in these spacious valleys. Patient experimental work by nurserymen such as the pioneer, Harry Pickstone, and the modern government research stations, have succeeded in bringing into South Africa fruit varieties from all over the world. These are tested in local conditions. New varieties are also bred locally, and the most suitable are established commercially as *cultivars* (cultivated varieties) in the valleys of the Western Cape. It is interesting to know something of the origin of these beautiful and tasty immigrants from foreign parts.

In the royal family of fruit the apple is king. Its lineage is ancient. It has played a part in the human story since the days of Adam and Eve. No fruit other than the grape, the queen of fruits, has featured more in history and legend. The apple, whose natural home is on the southern slopes of the Caucasian Mountains, has been planted all over the world. Today there are 450 million apple trees bearing fruit. America has become the great home of the apple. Over 7 000 varieties are listed there, for the apple does not grow true to seed and varieties are common.

Three main varieties of apple are grown in the Western Cape. They are *Granny Smith, Golden Delicious* and *Starking*.

Although no longer of commercial interest, the earliest-bearing cultivar, harvested in February, is the *Ohinimuri*, a New Zealand selected mutation of *Dunn's Seedling*, a chance seedling found in the 19th century by a Mr Dunn of South Australia. The Ohinimuri (misspelt in South Africa as Ohenimuri) takes its Maori name from the Ohinimuri Country on the Thames River in the North Island of New Zealand. It is an apple with the advantage of early ripening, but the local disadvantage of a tendency to crack.

In March, *Golden Delicious, Starking* and *White Winter Pearmain* come into bearing. The last of these is one of the oldest commercially cultivated apples, originating in the Parma area of Italy (hence the name). This apple with its piquant flavour, was a standard feature in the orchards of medieval monasteries. It found its way to Britain, and the Pilgrim Fathers carried it with them to America where it is regarded as one of the classic varieties. It was introduced to South Africa by that great nurseryman Harry Pickstone. In modern times it has lost some of its popularity with consumers.

The Golden Delicious cultivar is one of the world's great commercial apple varieties and South Africa's second most important apple. It originated in about 1890 as a chance seedling on the farm of Anderson Mullins of West Virginia in the United States. The great American nursery of Stark Bros introduced it commercially in 1916. It was brought to South Africa in 1934 by six members of the Elgin Fruit Growers Co-operative (the Moltenos, Col Cunningham, H Blackburn, Miss K Murray, G Thomas and J Green) who shared the cost of importation. Each received four trees with which to commence cultivation. Miss Murray sent the first consignment of 400 single-layer trays of fruit from the trees to London where they were enthusiastically received. It is a magnificent apple, highly popular with producers and consumers. A bud mutation known as *Starkspur Golden Delicious* was discovered in America in 1959 by Philip Jenkins in Yakima, Washington. It was commercially introduced in 1961 by the Stark Bros Nursery and brought to South Africa in 1963 by the Department of Agricultural Technical Services.

The *Starking* cultivar is one of the most beautiful and tasty of all apples. It originated from the famous Hawkeye apple discovered in 1872 by Jesse Hiatt in Iowa, America. The parent was introduced commercially in 1895 by the Stark Bros. and by them given the name of Delicious, for the specimens sent to them by Hiatt for exhibition had arrived minus the original name. Only in the following year, when Hiatt sent more specimens for exhibition, did the Stark Bros, learn the original name given by Hiatt. This magnificent apple quickly became the most popular cultivar in America, providing one-fifth of the total apple production. In 1921 an all-red bud mutation of Delicious was found in Munroeville, New Jersey, by Lewis Mood. It was commercially introduced in 1924 by the Stark Bros, and named the *Starking Delicious*. Well over 100 million trees of this beautiful apple have been propagated since then and, notwithstanding tendency to mealiness in cold storage, it is deservedly one of the world's most popular varieties. A bud mutation known as *Starkrimson Delicious* was found in 1953 by a Mr Bisbee of Hood River, Oregon. This was introduced commercially in 1956 by the Stark Bros and brought to South Africa in 1963 by the Herold Nurseries of Magaliesberg. It has a brilliant crimson colour and a delicious flavour. It is the fourth most important cultivar in South Africa.

The *Granny Smith* apple originated in 1867 as a seed planted by Mrs Maria Ann Smith, wife of the mayor of Parramatta in New South Wales, Australia. It seems to have been introduced to South Africa in 1919 by Professor O S H Reinecke. Notable for its tangy flavour, handsome size, rich green appearance and excellent keeping qualities, it is in firm demand in the world fruit market. It is the most important apple in South Africa.

May sees the end of the apple harvesting in the Western Cape with the ripening of the *York Imperial*. This apple originated in the early 19th century on a farm near York in Pennsylvania. A farmer named Johnson was attracted to the tree by the attention given to it by small boys who visited it in early spring to eat the apples which had passed the winter covered by leaves on the ground. The excellent condition in which the fruit survived the winter months impressed the farmer. Jessop, a local nurseryman, propagated the variety before 1830 under the name of *Johnson's Fine Winter*. In about 1850 Charles Downing pronounced it to be the 'imperial of keepers' and suggested the name of York Imperial. It is a pretty little apple with a most distinctive flavour and excellent keeping qualities but with the disadvantage of small irregular size. In a world which prefers large things, the York Imperial has unfortunately lost much of its saleability, although its late ripening is still of some value to growers. It was introduced to South Africa in about 1906 by Pickstone.

Other varieties grown in the Western Cape, although not on any considerable commercial scale, are *Jonathan, McIntosh, Rokewood, Rome Beauty, Winter Banana* and *Wemmershoek*, a locally bred variety.

There is an endless search for better varieties and for varieties with ripening times which would extend the harvesting period both earlier and later. Over 130 varieties of Starking alone have been bred, with one of them, *Topred*, having become popular for cultivation on account of its brilliant colour.

The commercial apple grower has to be keenly aware of the preferences and demands of consumers. Lately there has been a tendency towards apples deviating from the traditional red, yellow or green colours. The tasty red-on-yellow *Gala* and its mutation *Royal Gala* (originally known as *Ten Hove Gala* and even more brilliantly red than Gala) have become very popular and are planted increasingly in the Cape.

Changing consumer preference has also led to a renewed interest in the famous old English apple, *Cox's Orange Pippin*, which was bred in 1830 by Mr M R Cox of Buckinghamshire.

It is impossible to visualise the apples of the future. Perhaps they will be the same varieties of today. Perhaps by careful breeding or the chance discovery of mutations, they will change in appearance, improve in flavour, extend in harvesting times, be superior in keeping qualities and approach the farmer's dream of perfection which may still be within his grasp in the apple which Eve gave to man and which he has never tired of eating.

The major apple-producing areas of the Cape are Grabouw, Elgin, the Long Kloof and the Koue and Warmbokkeveld near Ceres. About 4,5 million tons are exported each year and similar volumes are also sold on the domestic market.

If the apple is the king of fruits and the grape the queen, then the peach is undoubtedly the princess. Delicately coloured and exquisitely flavoured, it originated from China. From there it was brought to Persia and then to Europe where it took its name from the old French *pesche*, derived from the Latin *persicum* (Persian apple). Jan van Riebeeck introduced the first peaches to South Africa. He imported trees of the common yellow peach from St Helena, where they had been planted by the Portuguese. Harry Pickstone established the basic commercial varieties. Today the varieties most widely grown for the export market are the luscious *Rhodes* and *Culemborg*. They are both white-fleshed peaches ripening early in the season and were bred in South Africa. *Orion, Peregrine, San Pedro* and *De Wet* are also grown for the export markets. A mutation of the common yellow peach, the Kakamas peach is the most important of all fruit in the South African canning industry. Its story is told in Chapter Fifteen in the section on Kakamas.

In the Western Cape the peach areas are situated around Elgin, Ceres, Piketberg and the upper Berg River valley. Some 300 tons of peaches are exported each year. The vast majority of peaches are, however, not exported fresh but are delivered to canneries or sold on the domestic market. These are the yellow cling types, such as the *Kakamas* peach.

The Cape peach export industry received a new lease of life when a series of yellow-flesh nectarine varieties was imported during the seventies. The nectarine is in fact a smooth-skinned mutation of the peach, so called for the nectar-like flavour of its firm flesh. The imported varieties proved to be successful and about 550 tons of nectarines are now exported annually. The major varieties are *Sunlite, Flavortop, Armking* and *Fantasia*.

The apricot was introduced to Europe by the Arabs. It takes its name from the Latin *praecox* (early ripe). The old French variety known as the *Royal* is a popular commercial type grown in the Western Cape. The local variety *Peeka* (named after the initials of Mr P K le Roux, former Minister of Agricultural Technical Services), is also popular. The main apricot-growing areas are situated around Barrydale, Ladismith, Ceres, Montagu and Piketberg. At present the major export variety is *Imperial*. It is a locally bred variety originally named after Piet Cillie, one of the pioneers of the industry. Other local varieties gaining in importance are *Soldonne* and *Supergold*. In total, some 700 tons of apricots are exported annually.

The plum comes from the East, and its commercial establishment in the Western world was largely due to the work of the famous Luther Burbank of Santa Rosa in the United States. In the Western Cape the most popular type is *Santa Rosa* Locally bred varieties have in the meantime become increasingly important. The first local plum to be released to the industry in 1973 was *Songold*. It has since become the major variety in the Western Cape, followed by two other local varieties, *Harry Pickstone* and *Ruby Nel*. The latter was named after Reuben Nel, an erstwhile director of the Fruit and Fruit Technology Research Institute in Stellenbosch. *Harry Pickstone* obtained its name from the famous nurseryman of the Cape early this century, who was also closely involved with Cecil John Rhodes and his fruit farms in the Groot Drakenstein area.

The largest plum-producing areas of the Western Cape are the upper Berg River valley, Elgin, Villiersdorp, Stellenbosch, Wolseley and Ceres. Over 10 000 tons of plums are exported each season.

The pear is indigenous to Europe. It grows wild in England. The most popular varieties grown in the Western Cape are Packham's *Triumph*, an Australian pear introduced into South Africa in 1904, and Williams's *Bon Chretien* (good Christian), first propagated in England in the 1760s by a nurseryman named Williams working on stock bred by a schoolmaster named Wheeler. In America this pear was introduced by Enoch Bartlett in 1799, and what became known as the *Bartlett* pear is the most widely grown in the world today. Other popular pears grown in the Western Cape include the *Beurre Bosch* (butter pear) from Belgium, the *Beurre Hardy*, and the *Forelle*. In the Western Cape about 67 000 tons of pears are exported each season. The principal areas of production are Ceres and Elgin.

Minor fruits grown in the Western Cape include the greengage, a plum mutation introduced from France into Britain in the early 1800s by Sir Thomas Gage; the loquat or rush orange; the South American guava; the kiwifruit; and berries such as the loganberry, the piquantly flavoured cross between a blackberry and a raspberry which was the result of the work of Judge Logan in California in 1881, the youngberry, the blue berry, gooseberry and the tayberry recently introduced from Scotland.

The orchards of the Western Cape are beautiful and productive, and together with the vineyards and the wild flowers give the region its greatest renown. The grape, the queen of fruits, delectable to the palate and heady to the senses, has brought both joy and tragedy to human beings ever since they first sampled its flesh and drank its fermented juice. The vines, attractive to the eye and sensitive to the moods of Nature, undergo seasonal colour changes which provide the Western Cape with a striking spectacle. The Barlinka vine leaves in the Hex River valley are particularly spectacular in autumn when they change from green to brilliant scarlet. In this beautiful setting, when the mountains are sprinkled with early snow, the grape – royalty against a majestic backdrop- sumptuously, regally and graciously holds her last court of the season, and then retires gracefully to sleep until the warmth of spring, like the kiss of a young prince, revives her to begin the cycle of life and productivity once again.

Some 350 million vines grow in the Western Cape, producing 54 000 tons of dessert fruit for export each season. Approximately 310 million of these vines grow in an area 104 154 ha in extent, and from them over 5 million litres (909 998 leaguers) of wine is produced. South Africa is the fourteenth largest wine producer in the world. France is the largest with a production of 60 million litres followed by Italy, Algeria, Spain, Portugal, Rumania, the Argentine, Yugoslavia, Russia, Greece, Germany, Hungary, the United States of America and South Africa.

The English name grape is rather a curious misnomer. It is really a confusion of the French name for the fruit. The French call the grape a *raisin*; a bunch of grapes is *une grappe de raisins*. In English, the French name *raisin* is only applied to the dried fruit and the word *grappe* (bunch), anglicised to *grape*, is applied to the fresh fruit. It is anomalies such as this that cause the French to shrug their shoulders at the English!

Traditionally, the natural home of the cultured grape is said to be northern Persia. The ideal climate for vines is a long, warm summer and autumn, with little rain from the time the grapes start to ripen. Rain during this critical ripening period promotes the development of disease, cracking of the skin and watery fruit. Heavy rain is only necessary during the winter when the vines are dormant. The colder it is during the rainy season, the safer and more sound asleep the vines will be.

The quality of the grape is largely dependent on these climatic conditions as well as on deep, cool soil, not very rich, but well drained. In northern Persia all these conditions prevail. Man has taken the grape to similar areas in many distant parts of the world. Wine was made in Egypt as far back as 6 000 years ago. Since then the demand for the grape and its juice has always been so great that suitable growing areas have continually been sought all over the world.

The father of South African viticulture was Jan van Riebeeck. He brought the first vines to the Cape, and on 2 February 1659 he recorded in his diary his thanks to the Lord for the taste of the first wine produced in South Africa.

There is no way of knowing what varieties of grape Van Riebeeck introduced. The only hint he gives is when he states that the 'Spanish' grapes were not yet ripe. From this, it can be assumed that the first vines grown in the Cape originated from Spain. The first vines, wherever they came from, were almost certainly all varieties that were selected for wine-making rather than eating.

The still ubiquitous *Green Grape* probably produced the white wines, and *Hermitage* probably produced the red wines. Almost certain to have been among these pioneer varieties was the grape called by the Spaniards *Moscatel Gordo Blanco* (the fat white Muscadel), by the French *Muscat d'Alexandrie*, and known to South Africans by its shape as *Haanekloot* (rooster's testicle) or *Hanepoot*. This variety produces not only Muscadel wines but also Muscadel raisins. It is, in addition, a magnificent dessert grape with a sweet and piquantly musky flavour. Professor Perold, in 1926, wrote an account of the origin of the Red Hanepoot from the White original. *'From a reliable source I was informed that a Mr Cloete, fully one hundred years ago, one day in Constantia noticed a shoot with red grapes on a Muscat of Alexandria vine, marked this shoot, and afterwards propagated it. When it reached the fruiting stage, it bore only red bunches and thus the Red Hanepoot was born, evidently as a vegetative sport, bud variation'.*

Such was the auspicious birth of arguably the most delicious and subtly flavoured of all dessert grapes. Its skin, like that of the white hanepoot is unfortunately too thin to make the grape suitable for refrigeration and export. There are several other varieties of the hanepoot, such as the piquant Muscat de Frontinac, used in the making of the celebrated white wine of Constantia, and the Le Roux Hanepoot, with a rounder, whiter berry than its fellows. It is a vigorous bearer of rather short bunches, with the berries naturally loose and not requiring pre-thinning for export. It was named by Professor Perold after Mr P M le Roux of *Vredenburg* farm near Paarl. He was the first to grow what was a bud variation of the ordinary white hanepoot.

For 250 years after Van Riebeeck's time the Hanepoot grape remained the standard dessert grape. When the export market developed at the end of the 1880s the search for new varieties began. The Hanepoot always remained the favourite local eating grape, but its skin is far too delicate to allow it to travel well. In spite of every care taken in packing, entire shipments were often useless by the time they reached overseas markets.

Varieties of dessert grapes with tougher skins and good keeping qualities had to be found. Today the stars of many of the prosperous vineyards are the export varieties of grapes. It is interesting to know something of the work of the men who found or bred these varieties.

The most important of all export grape varieties grown in the Western Cape is the *Barlinka* which provides one half of the total grape export crop. This handsome black grape was found by Professor A I Perold of Stellenbosch University. In 1909 he observed it growing on the farm of Leon Roseau, near the village of Novi, 80 km west of Algiers. Roseau had obtained the grape from the natives of Algeria, and the cuttings sent by Perold to South Africa produced the Barlinka vines of today.

The origin of the name is unknown. The grape was apparently not a commercial success in its home in Algeria. In the Cape, Professor Perold planted cuttings in various areas, but the results were indifferent except in the Hex River valley where, by pure chance, the vines found their ideal climate, quality of soil and water supply from irrigation, with freedom from rain throughout their late ripening period.

On 2 April 1925, Professor Perold's wife took a box of Barlinka grapes with her on a ship sailing to Hamburg. During the first five days of her voyage the grapes were kept in her cabin. Then the box was placed in the cold store. On 8 May the box was opened in Hamburg and the grapes were found to be in perfect condition. This proved the export possibilities of the Barlinka even in simple preservation.

Nowhere else in the world are Barlinka grapes grown with such commercial success as in South Africa. Their brilliant success in the Cape stimulated others to try them, but the results were disappointing. These luscious, large, strongly skinned grapes are now truly a South African cultivar which have rewarded their new home with an unparalleled story of successful immigration.

The second most popular export grape is the *Waltham Cross*, which supplies about one-sixth of the total crop. This large yellow grape was bred in England by William Paul, a grower in the area of Waltham Cross. He developed it from the Turkish variety known as *Razaki Sari*. In 1871 he received a first-class certificate for the grape from the Royal Horticultural Society. Waltham Cross was introduced into South Africa at the beginning of the 20th century.

As with other fruit varieties, consumer preference for grapes are also changing. The very sweet, seedless varieties have become tremendously popular during the past few years. *Sultanina*, a variety widely grown for drying purposes, is now also marketed fresh. Exports of *Sultana*, also sold as Thompson Seedless, have increased to such an extent that it is now the third most important variety.

Alphonse Lavallée is another popular variety. This grape, of the same stock as the *Ribier*, was named after the well-known French viticulturist and author of the standard *Histoire Statistique de la Vigne et des Grands Vins de la Côte d'Or*, published in 1885. In 1925 Major E G Munro of the Covent Garden firm of George Munro Limited strongly recommended the *Alphonse Lavallée* to one of his South African suppliers, J R Frater of Paarl. The grape, which ripens early, was being imported to Britain from the Argentine and was fetching excellent prices. Mr Frater's son, Gerard, wrote to a Buenos Aires nurseryman and arranged for him to place some vine cuttings in the care of the steward of a Japanese boat leaving for Cape Town. From the steward's pantry, the cuttings were handed to the Fraters and the *Alphonse Lavallée* was introduced into South Africa. It was released to the industry in 1928.

The *Alphonse Lavallée* is a luscious grape but it has the unfortunate defect of cracking its skin if it rains near harvest time. This causes great losses in export. To solve this problem, Mr P K Siebrits of the farm *Keerweder* in Franschhoek, with his partner, Mr Coetzee, in 1956, started an experiment in crossing *Barlinka* with *Alphonse Lavallée*. The hybrid bunches were carefully tended and their seeds planted. Only 2 100 of these seeds germinated and one of the seedlings outgrew the others.

In 1959 this young vine produced its first berries. Bunches were sent overseas as an export test and the Fruit and Food Technology Research Institute in Stellenbosch made a careful evaluation. As a result patent rights were taken out by the breeders and what was named *Salba* was placed on the export list as a new cultivar. The name was derived from the 'S' of Siebrits, the 'al' of *Alphonse Lavallée* and the 'ba' of *Barlinka*. The black grape ripened later than the *Alphonse Lavallée* and just before the *Barlinka*. It did not crack in rain and the skin was strong enough to survive the handling of the export industry. The *Salba* mother vine is preserved by the Fruit and Food Technology Research Institute in Stellenbosch.

Grape farmers and researchers are always on the look-out for new varieties ripening at different times and complying with the demands for interesting flavours. During the 1980s the South African range of cultivars was extended with the introduction of several locally bred varieties which are well adapted to climatic conditions. Of these the white *Dauphine* and the *Bien Donné* are the most important. The black *La Rochelle* also shows promise, although production is still small. Muscat-flavoured grape varieties have also become very popular.

The principal stars of the dessert grape industry in the Western Cape all ripen during a lengthy season extending from December to June, and yield table grapes of superlative quality and flavour. Several varieties of dessert grapes of lesser importance are also cultivated in South Africa. These include *Almeria*, a late ripening grape from Almeria in Spain, a mutation of it bred in California and named *Calmeria*, and the giant black *Gros Colmar* introduced from the Caucasus to France and England more than 100 years ago.

The *Prune de Cazouls*, imported in 1910 by Professor Perold from Montpellier in France, was popular for awhile but now not much cultivated. The *Queen of the Vineyard*, an early ripening hybrid between the *Queen Elizabeth* and *Pearl of Csaba* was imported from Austria in 1936. The *Raisin Blanc*, imported by Perold in 1910 from Montpellier in France, and the *Red Emperor* were also once popular but are now seldom marketed. The handsome, large *Red Globe* grape is becoming established for its sweet flavour.

Search continues for ideal grapes suited to different areas and for earlier or later ripening time. Some of these are found by pure chance. An example of this is the variety known as *Golden Hill*.

In 1940 Douglas Hill of *Sandhills* in the Hex River valley, visited John Heatlie of *Orange Grove* farm. While wandering about the farm, Hill noticed a strange looking vine whose fruit was ripening at an unusual time. Hill asked for details. Heatlie told him that on the veranda of the *Orange Grove* homestead, there had once been a tin of geraniums. Among the flowers a vine had appeared which had seeded there by chance. The Heatlies watched with some amusement as the little vine struggled for life. When the geraniums were discarded the vine narrowly escaped destruction. Somebody, however, took compassion and transplanted it. When Hill saw it, it was bearing its first fruit and not at the usual time. The fruit itself was not particularly impressive, but its ripening time was certainly interesting. Douglas Hill took cuttings of the vine and on his own farm he grafted these cuttings on to old *Hanepoot* stock. The result was the tasty handsome *Golden Hill* grape, with its valuable ripening time which is between that of established varieties.

About 1,2 million tons of grapes are exported each year to many foreign countries. The profits together with profits from mass sales on the local market, as well as the proceeds from the wine industry, provide the finance for the beautiful homesteads, the high land values and the congenial way of life of farmers in the mountain valleys of the Western Cape. The Hex River valley is the major production area for dessert grapes of Southern Africa (75 per cent). The Paarl area also produces substantial amounts, while the lower Berg River valley is also gaining in importance, because it is an early-ripening area.

The export of deciduous fruit was controlled for many years by Unifruco Ltd, which was originally established as the Deciduous Fruit Board in Cape Town in 1939. Fruit is shipped by this body through the Cape Town harbour to more than 30 countries all over the world. The industry earns more than R1 000 million in foreign currency each year, making it the most important export earner in the country after metals, minerals, precious and semi-precious stones. The production and export of wines and spirits are controlled by the Co-operative Wine Growers' Association of South Africa (the KWV – the Koöperatiewe Wijnbouwers Veneniging van Zuid-Afrika) founded in 1918, with headquarters and cellars – gigantic cathedrals of wine – at Paarl.

THE WINES OF THE CAPE

Since Van Riebeeck's time, the viticulture or wine industry of the Western Cape has developed considerably. Vines, visually beautiful, having a romantic history and, fascinating in their subtlety and variety, are influenced by local conditions in the different natural areas of the mountain valleys where they grow. These areas differ from one another subtly, but decisively. Each is influenced by various climatic and topographical factors such as the blend of winds from moist coast and arid interior; temperature; and the chemistry of the soils (sandstones, shales and granites).

Van Riebeeck first planted small experimental vineyards in the Company's Garden near the Castle. He then planted over 1 000 vines on *Wynberg* (wine mountain), and gradually vines were planted further and further away. A variety of cultivars were planted. On *Constantia* estate in the Cape Peninsula, first Simon van der Stel and then Hendrik Cloete, and his relative, Johannes Colyn who farmed on *de Hoop op Constantia*, produced the earliest truly superior South African wines; these were the famous Constantia wines – one a highly regarded red and the other a little less popular white. They were sweet wines, apparently made from the late harvest grapes or what the Germans call *Trockenbeerenauslesen* (selected overripe grapes). They were skilfully blended by master winemakers who used mainly *Muscat de Frontignan* grapes for the white wine and the strange *Pontac* grapes with their blood red juice for the red wine. They were classed as natural wines, not fortified with brandy, and aged in wood for a few years. The red had an alcoholic content of 13,42 per cent and the white 15,01 per cent, with a sugar content of 128 grams per litre.

As pioneers moved into the interior, they settled in one river valley after the other. Each farm had its vineyard alongside its orchards, meadows and wheat fields. The first river valley to be settled and cultivated was that of the *Eerste* (first) River. Then the *Berg* (mountain) River valley, the *Breë* or *Breede* (broad) River valley and the *Olifants* (elephants) River valley where each in turn settled and cultivated. Each river had tributaries flowing through valleys of their own and each valley had a distinct character. The valleys were the mothers and the human cultivators were the fathers of a family of crops. To their family, the parents bequeathed something of the chemistry of the soil; something of the essence of the winds and rain; some of the effects of altitude and orientation; and a great deal which was owing to the farmers' skill and empathy with the soil.

There is no crop more sensitive to its inheritance than the grape, and wine is its essence and its offspring. In the making of wine, many delicate factors are involved: subtleties of environment, cultivation and, ultimately, the skill and fine instinct of the winemaker – the artist who blends and refines the juices of the grape to a liquid of delicate perfection, and then carefully nurses this infant in the womb-like security of his cellar.

Man introduced most of the standard wine grapes of Europe and the Middle East to the river valleys of the Western Cape. He learned by experience which varieties adapted best to the new setting. About 100 different varieties are cultivated in the Cape. The white grape varieties which adapted best are the *Chenin Blanc* (also known in South Africa as the *Steen* or *Stein*); the *Palomino* (French White); the *Green Grape* (*Sémillon*), which produces in France the fine, sweet white wines of Sauternes and Graves; the *Clairette Blanche*; the *Colombar*; *Muscat d'Alexandrie* (known in South Africa as the *Hanepoot*); *Ugni Blanc* (or *Saint Emilion*); and the *Cape Riesling*, which is similar to the French variety, *Cruchen Blanc*. The principal German variety *Weisser Riesling* (or *Rhine Riesling*), is increasingly being planted. This is the producer of the Moselles, the Spatlesen, Auslesen and Trockenbeerenauslesen wines. Other white varieties becoming increasingly popular are the *Sauvignon Blanc*, *Chardonnay* and *Merlot*.

The red grape varieties which adapted best include the *Cinsaut*, formerly known as the *Hermitage* from the hill overlooking the town of Tain-l'Hermitage, where a famous hermit, Gaspard de Sterinburg, a knight who wearied of the Crusades, settled to grow grapes and to meditate. This is the most widely grown red grape. Other red varieties include the *Pinot Noir*; the very successful local hybrid of *Hermitage* and *Pinot Noir* called *Pinotage*, developed in 1928 by Professor A I Perold; *Tinta Barocca* (the Portuguese 'tinted grape of the gorge'); *Shiraz*, the Persian grape taken to Europe from the town of Shiraz in Iran; the famous French *Cabernet Sauvignon*, a shy bearer, but the producer of superlative wine; and the Red *Muscadel* or *Muscat Red* (*Red Hanepoot*), which grows to such perfection in the Robertson area and the Little Karoo. This is a marvellous table grape and the producer of such excellent sweet wines as *Moscato* and *Marsala*. The white muscadel was the great grape of Arabia, and of the Saracens.

Distinctly separate areas of cultivation in the river valleys of the Cape emerged with the years, each area having its own characteristics. On 16 June 1972, official recognition was accorded these areas of origin. They were the Boberg (the upper valley of the Berg River), Overberg, Constantia, Durbanville, Little Karoo, Swartland, Olifants River, Paarl, Piketberg, Robertson, Stellenbosch, Swellendam, Tulbagh and Worcester. The Breede River valley was similarly demarcated on 27 December 1974. An additional area known as the Coastal Region was officially recognised on 17 February 1978.

Thirty-two wards, inclusive of the previous Durbanville and Constantia districts, were also demarcated for the production of wines of origin. Seventy-six individual estates were demarcated for the production of estate wines. Of these, 32 estates are in the Stellenbosch area.

In the beginning the production and marketing of wines in South Africa was controlled by private enterprise. During this time some fine wines were produced, but by the First World War there was hopeless over-production and uneconomic returns from chaotic marketing. To save the industry from ruin, the *Koöperatiewe Wijnbouwers Vereniging van Zuid-Afrika Beperk* (KWV) was established in 1918 under the chairmanship of C W H Kohler, a great champion and organising genius of the industry.

The purpose of the co-operative was to stabilise the industry by, among other means, production control, setting minimum producer prices, promoting the consumption of wine, providing the industry with a recognised corporate voice for negotiation, and improving standards of production. Marketing within South Africa was left to private enterprise in order to ensure that fair prices were returned to producers. The organisation was also to ensure absorption of surplus production and to use the surplus of high-quality wines and spirits to expand overseas markets, particularly in Britain and Canada, and even in the continent of Europe. As a result of thorough marketing, the Scandinavian countries (notably Finland) and even France, the great home of wines, developed an appreciation of the subtleties of South African wines.

The wine grapes are harvested in the Cape from January to March. This is a time of great activity in the vineyards. The scene is little changed from the time when man first began to cultivate the vine in the lost years of antiquity. A machine to harvest grapes has only recently been introduced, and on most farms each bunch is still picked by hand, placed in containers and conveyed in bulk to the presses.

The estates of origin have their own presses. The other producers (supplying about 80 per cent of the total crop) send their fruit to one or other of the 75 co-operative wine cellars scattered throughout the wine areas. Impatient queues of trucks and trailers form outside these cellars, waiting their turn to be weighed with their loads. The weight of the grapes is written up to the credit of the supplier, as is also the nature of the grapes, their variety, quality and sugar content. Some wines, such as the late-harvest ones, demand special delayed harvesting in order to ensure high sugar content and piquancy of flavour.

The grapes are unloaded into containers and wine-making begins. This is an entirely natural process. Man expedites and improves, but no part of it is synthetic. A grape crushed underfoot would automatically produce wine, provided the juice was not lost through evaporation, or saturation into the ground. Man is there to provide the ideal conditions. Like a parent discreetly promoting a good match for a favoured child, he expedites and influences events in order to achieve a desired end.

The grapes are fed into a mill which extracts and discards the stems and crushes the berries to produce a mixture of husks (skins) and juice, known as must. The juice of all grapes (except the *pontac*) would produce a white wine; it is the skins or husks which affect the colour and it is the bloom on the skins which contains the yeast – the living unicellular organisms of microscopic size which mingle with the juice, feed on the sugar, and by a process of fermentation, convert it into alcohol, carbon dioxide and other by-products. Yeasts, however, have different strains which produce different effects. It is at this stage, therefore, that man intervenes in the natural process and directs it along predetermined lines by cultivating special yeasts. The skill of the winemaker now comes into full play, and this is the science of oenology.

If a white wine is being produced, the husks are usually separated from the juice very soon after pressing. In the making of certain wines, the husks are left long enough to influence the acidity and piquancy of the wine. Once separated, the husks are re-pressed and the juice extracted is used in general wine-making, or it can be added to the main body of juice in carefully measured quantities in order to influence its flavour. Then, after being left to ferment slightly, the husks are pressed for the third time. The juice from this final pressing is distilled into spirits. The dry husks are used for compost.

The must, freed from the husks and all pips and flesh (which have been filtered out in various ways), is poured into stainless steel tanks for fermentation. Sometimes fermentation is done in small oak barrels. To ensure that fermentation occurs in the desired way, quantities of specially cultured grape yeasts are added. Fermentation then proceeds, generating considerable heat. As this heat can be detrimental to the wine, the must is cooled by refrigeration, and a temperature of 15°C to 18°C is maintained. The carbon dioxide escapes into the air and the sugar in the must is steadily converted into alcohol. If not controlled and influenced, fermentation would eventually cause the disappearance of all the sugar; the resultant wine would be very dry (or sugarless) to the taste. However, fermentation can be artificially arrested by subjecting the wine to low temperatures or high pressure. The yeasts become paralysed and are prevented from further action, and the wines have some sweetness, the amount of which depends on the stage when fermentation was arrested.

Some delicate, light table wines are known in Germany as Moselles if they are very light and as Hocks if they are slightly stronger in flavour. In France these wines are the Chablis and the Graves.

If all the carbon dioxide is allowed to escape, the wine will be a still one; if some of the gas is left, then the wine will be a Perlé. Sparkling wines such as the French champagnes are made from carefully selected natural wines. They are then subjected to a second fermentation, either in their bottles or in sealed containers. Carbon dioxide is retained in the wine and this constitutes the sparkle and fizz. Depending on the amount of sugar, sparkling wines can be *brut* (exceptionally dry); *extra-sec* (extra dry); *demi-sec* (medium dry); or *doux* (sweet).

Another method of retaining sugar in the wine is by fortification. At a carefully chosen moment in fermentation, pure wine spirit is added to the must. This spirit paralyses the action of the yeast and fermentation is arrested, leaving the desired amount of sugar in the wine. The fortified wines are full, with a stronger alcoholic content than the light natural wines; this is because of the artificial addition of pure spirits. The alcohol content of the fortified wines ranges from 17 per cent to 20 per cent; the natural wines have an alcohol content of 11 per cent to 14 per cent.

The sweetest wines are the Jerepigos: this is because the fortifying wine spirit is added to the must before any natural fermentation has taken place. This means that all the natural sugar remains in the wine; and the alcohol content, though pure in itself, is artificially added by the winemaker. Sherries, Ports and Muscadels are all fortified wines.

For the production of red wines, the husks are left with the musk; yeast is added and fermentation takes place either in open vats or tanks, or in closed steel tanks. The husks rise to the surface and form a head which is so solid that it can support the weight of a man. Under the direction of the winemaker, this head is periodically broken up and pushed down into the must. From this mixture comes the colour, flavour and tannin of red wines. The husks are eventually removed from the must at the discretion of the winemaker. Fermentation is allowed to proceed until the sugar content has been reduced to about 4 per cent. The wine is then pumped into wooden vats. The separated husks are pressed and all residual juice is extracted, some is returned to the fermenting must. In the wooden vats, fermentation continues until all the sugar content has vanished and the wine is completely dry. Small quantities of gases such as oxygen slowly percolate through the wood into the maturing wine. As these intruding gases gently work on the tannin and mineral salts which the wine has absorbed from its husks, the wine steadily mellows. Time is the only aid in the process of maturation. Man, always impatient, has tried methods of forcing wine to age quickly, but wine is curiously alive in its foibles – it clings to its raw, astringent and crude youth. It settles down only in its own good time and begins to mellow; but traditionally needs to enjoy at least three undisturbed years in the oak casks, and a reflective five-year period in bottles lying in a cool, dark, quiet cellar. Some of the fortified wines, such as ports, only reach their best after 100 years of maturation; sherries need 20 years of tranquillity in order to attain the really rich, nutty flavour and piquant aftertaste which they inherit from grapes such as the Palomino (or White French), from which they are made, and from the all-important *flor*.

Fortified sherry style wines, ranging from very dry to very sweet, start off as white wines. They undergo a second, very special fermentation in which the peculiar wine yeast called *flor* is used. This yeast was originally thought to be found only in the Jerez de la Frontera region in Southern Spain, hence the English name 'sherry'. Its discovery in the bloom of a locally grown grape made the production of this type of wine possible in the Cape. All the principal varieties are produced: *Fino* (dry); *Amontillado* (slightly sweet); *Oloroso* (sweet); and *Old Brown* (very sweet and full – almost a banquet of grape syrup and raisins).

Port style wines – Ruby, Tawny and small quantities of the aristocrat Vintage style port – are produced from grape varieties such as *Tinta Barocca, Hermitage, Souzâo* and *Tinta Roriz*. They are fortified during fermentation when the sugar content is 12 per cent, receiving an alcohol content of up to 20 per cent. They demand a combination of loving care and delicate skill from the winemaker. The English name originated from Oporto the city in Portugal from where this wine is shipped.

Rosé wines, which are among the lightest of all wines, can be made in various ways. Red and white wines can be mixed, but the best rosé wines are produced from grape varieties with red to light-black skins. The skins are left in the must just long enough for the fermenting juice to absorb from them colour, flavour and aromatic substance.

Brandy takes its English name from the Dutch *brandewijn* (burnt wine), meaning distilled wine. South Africa is the fifth largest brandy-producing country in the world, producing 36 million litres each year compared to Spain with 171 million litres, Germany with 117 million litres, the USA with 48,6 million litres, and Italy with 41,4 million litres. The production of brandy is financially the most important agricultural industry in the Western Cape.

The principal grape cultivars for the production of brandy are *Chenin Blanc*, *Cinsaut* (*Hermitage*), *Palomino* (*White French*), *Colombar* and *St Emilion* (*Ugni Blanc*). The grapes are pressed at 21°C sugar content. The husks are immediately removed.

So far as is known, the first brandy to be distilled in the Cape was in 1672 when a ship's cook from a Dutch East Indiaman anchored in Table Bay produced what must have been a pretty raw alcohol because it was drunk without significant maturation. For over 100 years Cape brandy was poorly rated; dismissed as 'Cape Smoke' or 'Dop brandy', fiery stuff, fit only for sailors or slaves. The gentry simply would not dream of drinking it. Then the British occupied the Cape; and the governors, such as Sir John Cradock and Lord Charles Somerset, set out to improve the quality of the local drink. Incentives were offered for quality; memoranda and treatises were published; and the advent of more people – settlers, and visitors – created an increasing customer demand for a better brandy.

In 1825 Francis Collison formed the Cape Wine Trade Committee to investigate all aspects of the production of good quality wine and, from it, superior quality brandy. Without good grapes to produce good wine, there can never be good brandy – the three are essential links in a subtle chain of cultivation, fermentation, distillation and maturation.

Collison established the first substantial high-quality wine and brandy business in the Cape. In 1842 Jan van Ryn, a 36-year-old Dutch immigrant, started the Van Ryn Wine and Spirit Company. The Cape Wine and Brandy Company also came into being; likewise E K Green; and in 1856 the Paarl Wine and Brandy Co was formed by a group of Paarl farmers and businessmen. Still later, in 1892, Johannes Henoch Marais settled on the family farm of *Coetzenberg* near Stellenbosch, after a profitable spell on the Kimberley diamond-fields. At Vlottenburg 'Jannie' Marais created the Lion Distillery in a building designed in the French chateau style and constructed from the round boulders in the bed of the Eerste River. When Marais died in 1915, this distillery, renowned for the quality of its product, became the Van Ryn Brandy Cellar when it was acquired by the Van Ryns. After the Anglo-Boer War, René Santhagens, a distiller, trained in France, moved from the Transvaal to Stellenbosch and started distilling brandy to the cognac method and maturing for at least three years in imported casks of French oak. His discipline in the selection of wine for distillation in copper pot stills and maturation became the ingredients, in 1909, of the first legislation aimed at the improvement of the quality of brandy in the Cape to the highest international standard.

To lovers of brandy there is one other very subtle, very essential magic in the production of the drink. In the cool, quiet darkness of the maturation cellars, there is a slow, delicate interplay of brandy, wood, air and something else. This something else is the ultimate mystery of maturation when, it is said, the angels work, turning the brandy into something golden, mellow and smooth. For their work, the angels take their share. From every cask of 300 litre capacity, for every year of maturation, a predictable nine litres of brandy vanish; that is, a disappearance of 36 bottles of brandy for every three years of maturation. This is said to be the angels' share in exchange for their work. They are very welcome, bless them.

Herbal brandies and wines of several types are also produced with a wide variety of flavours, aromas and effects. Vermouth demands approximately 30 different herbs and plants in its production. Liqueurs also require considerable subtlety in their blending. Van der Hum, a peculiarly South African liqueur with a tangerine flavour, was first blended in the early days at the Cape. The story is that, when the Dutch captured the island of Curacao from Spain, they found there a very pleasant liqueur made from oranges. When they settled in the Cape, they experimented to make a local version and used tangerines and mandarins in their tests. They liked the new flavour so much that they gave it a nickname of its own, *Van der Hum* meaning 'Mr What's His Name'. The drink seems to embody something of the essence of past years when pirates and East Indiamen anchored side by side in Table Bay. One can almost imagine, as one sips this liqueur, the glowering faces of rival captains as they gossiped over liqueurs of downed rum or savoured the sweet rich wines of Constantia, acquired at the inns of the Old Tavern of the Sea.

THE LABELLING, CERTIFICATION AND CLASSIFICATION OF WINE

Most wine-producing countries apply strict controls to the standards of wine and the claims made on the labels by producers. The South African Government applied a stringent discipline to winemakers. On 1 September 1973 the South African Wine of Origin Legislation became law. From then on, seals of certification were issued to wines attaining standards prescribed by the Government Wine and Spirit Board. This board consisted of a chairman and six members, all experts – two appointed from the liquor trade, two from the Government Research Institute at Nietvoorbij, and two from the KWV (Co-operative Wine Farmers' Union). Every Wednesday morning the board met at the laboratory of the Government Research Institute at Nietvoorbij near Stellenbosch. Each member retired to a cubicle and the wines to be tested were passed to them one at a time. Each member had three switches in his cubicle: green (approved), amber (passed with reservations) and red (denied). He could not see or hear his fellow members and his decision about the wine was transmitted electrically from the switches.

The seal of certification which the wine carried if it was approved by the board guaranteed the correctness of the information contained on the main descriptive label of the bottle. The seal was affixed to the top of the neck of each bottle. If the word estate appeared on the seal, then 100 per cent of wine in the bottle had to originate from the estate mentioned on the label. If the word in a blue band was on the seal, then 100 per cent of the wine in the bottle had to come from the specific geographical area claimed on the label.

If the word *vintage* appeared in a red band on the seal, then the vintage claimed on the label was correct, with at least 75 per cent of the wine from the vintage.

If the word *cultivar* appeared in a green band on the seal, the 75 per cent of the wine in the bottle had to originate from the type of grape described on the label. An identification number was also given to each wine and was printed on the seal.

Until 1990 certain wines also carried the designation *Superior* on a gold-backed seal. To achieve this high honour, the wine had to be of superlative quality, a real aristocrat of its kind, and was subject to the most stringent tests of the board.

Chapter Eight

THE VALLEY OF THE EERSTE RIVER

It is a delightful experience in travel to explore the wine and fruit producing valleys of the Western Cape Province. The principal valleys are those of the Berg, Breede (Breë) and Eerste rivers with their various tributaries. Each is beautiful, full of charming scenes and rich in fragments of history, with interesting towns, villages and farmlands, containing finely preserved examples of one of the most serene forms of domestic architecture to be found anywhere on Earth – the Cape-Dutch style.

The valley of the *Eerste* River, as its name (First River) indicates, was the first of the inland valleys to be settled and it deserves to be the first to be explored by any traveller. Scenically it is superb. Stellenbosch, which lies near the head of the valley, is without doubt the prettiest of all the small towns of Southern Africa; while the wines, wild flowers and fruits of the valley are among the finest in the world.

STELLENBOSCH

Stellenbosch, with its population of 58 909, has a situation, atmosphere, architecture and general appearance which all contribute to a unique charm. Essentially an academic and farming centre, it is largely free of the relentless pressures of industry and excessive population growth. Here, man has a chance to live in a more relaxed atmosphere, to take stock of the good things around him, conserve and beautify, and learn that it is more pleasant by far to live in the shade of a tree rather than that of a lamp-post. If developers, town planners, civil engineers and traffic authorities claim that old building, trees and open spaces are contrary to modern planning, then it is best that these gentlemen be transferred or removed to the Sahara Desert and for the good things to be left where they are.

Stellenbosch had its start in 1679. On 3 November of that year Simon van der Stel, the newly appointed Commander and future governor of the Cape for the Dutch East India Company, set out with an escort of soldiers on a journey to explore the countryside immediately eastwards of Cape Town. The first night out was spent camped on the banks of a stream they named *Kuils* River (river of pools). It was a tributary of the Eerste River, the principal river draining one of the most delectable parts of the world which they had ever seen. It was scenically lovely, only too obviously fertile, a domain of flowering plants, with a mild climate and an atmosphere exhilarating and healthy. There was no sign of human habitation. It was untouched, unpolluted and serenely delightful to mind and eye. The river had been first reported and named in 1655 by Corporal Willem Mulder, sent by Jan van Riebeeck to explore the area.

For five days Van der Stel and his party explored the wild garden. Following the Eerste River with its amber-coloured water up towards its source in the bosom of the mountains, they reached, on the afternoon of 6 November, a place which captivated Van der Stel completely. It was there that the river for a part of its course divided into two branches. Between the branches an island had been formed. Van der Stel and his party camped beneath shady trees on the island. It was named *Van der Stel se Bosch* (Van der Stel's Wood). After a happy stay there, they returned to Cape Town on 8 November, with the mind of the Commander full of dreams of a thriving community of farmers, of beautiful crops and herds of fat cattle grazing on the green pastures in the valley of the Eerste River, the source of life to the area, supplying drinking, irrigation and washing water, and power to drive a mill.

It must have been a delightful experience for Van der Stel and his men to explore the shallow valley. The river ran pure, unpolluted and cool, with the rich amber colour of streams flowing through the disintegrated sandstone and fynbos peat country of the Western Cape. The river was alive with fish, especially redfin minnows, frogs and other aquatic creatures. Birds sang and nested in the trees; antelope came to the water to drink.

Before the end of that year the first settler had made a home in the area. In May of the following year, 1680, eight more families followed the pioneer from Cape Town. All were tempted to make the move by offers of as much free land as they could cultivate, selected by themselves and only to be reclaimed by the Company if they ceased to cultivate it. A tithe of grain grown had to be given to the Company. The settlers had free use of all uncultivated land as grazing for cattle. The only restriction on the settlers was a total prohibition of the cultivation of tobacco.

By the summer of 1681 the settlement at what was known as Stellenbosch was flourishing. A crop of excellent wheat was reaped, so bountiful that it supplied the people of Cape Town with the making of several months of bread, a welcome relief from the usual rations of biscuits and rice. More families were tempted to move to so fertile an area. Quarrelling over selection of land demanded the personal attention of Simon van der Stel. In 1682 he rode up to Stellenbosch, settled disputes by limiting the size of individual estates, arranged for the area to be properly surveyed and for title deeds to be drawn up for each farm. To settle further disputes, a *heemraad* (county court) was created with four elected members from the local inhabitants. They were empowered to deal with trivial disputes with two members resigning each year and replaced by election.

There were about 30 families settled at Stellenbosch by the end of 1683. It was not entirely a place of milk and honey for them. The flourishing wheatlands soon attracted a resident insect population. For several seasons the insects enjoyed a banquet at the expense of the farmers. Then they settled down to a sensible share-and-share-alike basis and harvests improved.

The first school was built at the end of 1683, a *landdrost* (magistrate) was appointed with the incumbent given authority over the whole inland area, some 25 000 square kilometres of country at that time unexplored by Europeans and occupied by unknown people. Two years later, in 1686, a church was established and in that year a pleasant annual country fair had its beginning in Stellenbosch to celebrate the birthday on 14 October 1639 of its founder, Simon van der Stel. Van der Stel maintained a special interest in the town. He thenceforth made a habit of always being present at the festivities. He presided over a jollification of sporting occasions and feasting. After the wet winter months, October saw the wild flowers in bloom, the fruit orchards in blossom and the new leaves of the deciduous trees green and fresh, all reviving like the hopes of man after a cold season of dormancy, an offering of thanks by the plants that they had been spared destruction by winter weather and man and left once again to experience the joy of spring. Games, competitions, dancing, romancing and feasting attracted people in wagonloads all the way from Cape Town. Chiefs of pastoral tribes, passengers and crews of ships in Table Bay, country and townspeople, all joined in the fun. Marksmen competed by shooting at targets such as one made in the shape of a *papegaai* (parrot), the name given to the high hill, the *Papegaaiberg* (Parrot Mountain) overlooking the town. On its slopes the competition took place. The winner received a prize of about £5 and the title, for the year of King of the Marksmen. There was also a pistol-shooting competition for mounted riders who at full gallop shot at small targets. The last day of the fair was the birthday of the Governor. There was a final procession and a parade by the military, with volleys fired in honour of Van der Stel while everybody wished him well with rousing cheers.

During his annual visits Van der Stel commented on local affairs, criticised anything he considered distasteful, encouraged what he approved and adjudicated squabbles. He was always a great man for trees, especially oaks. He ordered that oaks be planted along the sides of each street, watered by furrows fed from the river, with water rights to all gardens. The presence of the river with its ample water was a great benefaction to the growth of a town. The trees were a legacy from Van der Stel of incalculable value, not only beautiful, but shading the streets, purifying the air, deadening the sounds of ever-increasing traffic, providing leaves for compost, timber for all manner of uses from firewood to furniture.

The approval or disapproval of Van der Stel in all matters concerning the growth of his town of Stellenbosch became a pervasive influence. The birthday of the founder is still celebrated each year on the Friday and Saturday nearest to 14 October. It is a genuine jollification centred mainly on the open space, *Die Braak* (the fallow land), in the centre of the town where the old Powder Magazine still stands, but spilling out an overflow of stalls, fun, hucksters, buskers and cheerfulness down almost every street.

The islet on which Van der Stel camped has long since disappeared beneath the streets and houses of Stellenbosch. The site was apparently where Noordwal-Wes Street turns into Pastorie Street. The Eerste River still flows near the site of the vanished islet and off down its shallow valley, its amber-coloured water shaded beneath a long, green arch of overhanging trees. This part of the Eerste River has so tangible an atmosphere of romance that it has always been one of the favourite walks for lovers. To explore the Stellenbosch of today, it is fitting to start here from the banks of the river. The exploration should be done on foot. Any form of wheeled transport should be parked beneath the riverside trees at some convenient spot along Noordwal-Wes Street or The Avenue. Where these two streets merge, Pastorie Street has its start and leads for one block before it ends at the eastern beginning of what was at first known as the Wagon Road to the Cape. This became *Dorp* (town) Street, the best-preserved old-time street in all Southern Africa.

Dorp Street is a street of architectural delights. Shaded by oak trees, with a furrow of running water on either side, the street is lined on both sides with many beautifully restored buildings, residential and commercial. On the corner of Pastorie Street, at the turn into Dorp Street, stands the imposing Theological Seminary, built upon the walls of the original *Drostdy* (Magistracy). For 100 years the power of the Stellenbosch magistrate was supreme over a vast area of frontiersmen, nomadic tribes, restless adventurers, hunters and explorers. The records of this old frontier magistracy have quite a few tales to tell of curious events and interesting people.

Drostdy Street branches off from Dorp Street to the right (northwards) just beyond the Theological College. In our Stellenbosch stroll, let us turn into this street. We shall rejoin Dorp Street later. Drostdy Street is not long but architecturally it is quite superb. First of all is the building known as Utopia, the offices of the Dutch Reformed Mother Church which stands next to it, dominating the street with a tall tower and a presence extending over the whole town.

The first church of Stellenbosch was a simple building which stood on the site of the present d'Ouwe Werf Hotel. It and several adjoining buildings built about 1680 were burned down in December 1710. The thatched roofs of these buildings were picturesque and excellent insulation from the weather, but they were vulnerable to fire. Sparks carried by the wind could spread a blaze from one roof to another at disastrous speed. A new site for a church was granted in 1717. When funds became available, a simple cruciform church was built there and inaugurated in about 1723. This compact little church served the community into the 19th century. A conservatory was added in 1807 and a classical gable in 1814. The growth of Stellenbosch then required a more commodious building and in 1862 the present neo-Gothic steeple church, designed by Carl Otto Hagen, was built on the site. This is the imposing church of today with a fine pulpit, also designed by Carl Hagen, and built by craftsmen brought from Holland with the special timber. There is a superb organ, a set of six bells and nine windows created by Leo Theron using coloured glass imported from France. The pieces are set in concrete.

The ruins of the original church were left until 1802. Then the site was sold and Wium's Hotel was built on top of the ruins. Aunt Betjie Wium, who ran the place for several years, gave it renown for the quality of her country-style food. In 1973 Gerhard Lubbe bought the old hotel and started a programme of restoration. The foundations of the church were carefully preserved. They can be seen in the basement beneath the present kitchen of the coffee garden in the shady setting.

The original hotel, now known as *d'Ouwe Werf* (the old yard), has been restored but its atmosphere remains of old-time hospitality and amiable living. Each room in the hotel has been given its own individuality and exquisitely furnished with antique pieces. When you enter the hotel, look at your reflection in the full-length mirror on the right-hand side. It is a magnificent ripple-free example of silvered glass. Think, as you see yourself exactly as you are, of all the fair ladies and gallant gentlemen of the past years who appraised themselves in this all-revealing mirror and then went on to meet friends, to be accommodated in elegant bedrooms, with huge antique double beds, heavenly made for dreams and the fulfilment of romance. Before you snuggle down to sleep, think for a little while of all the activities and inactivities, which have taken place in these selfsame beds. Remember such delights are never too late to experience. Insomnia is impossible in such elegant comfort.

Church Street, in which d'Ouwe Werf stands, has its start immediately in front of the Mother

Church. It is a short street, embowered by tall oak trees with fine views of the church steeple framed by the green leaves. As you stroll down this street, there are several interesting buildings and scenes. On the corner on the right-hand side, where Ryneveld Street crosses Church Street, stands Schreuder House, built in about 1709. It is an atmospheric place and, as part of the Stellenbosch Village Museum, is well preserved with its early Cape furniture and household objects. Sebastian Schreuder (or Schroder), who built the house, was a German. He was the messenger of the court and secretary of the public mill.

The Stellenbosch Village Museum at present covers some 5 000 square metres of the central part of Stellenbosch. The buildings occupying this area provide a stroll back in time into a lifestyle very different from that of today. The main entrance to the museum is situated at 18 Ryneveld Street. Just beyond this entrance, set in the wall of the next building along the street, is an original Queen Victoria period post-box. It is still in use and cleared each day. If you post a letter there, remember that times have changed since the old box was put into service. The days of penny postage and quick overnight delivery have been replaced by a system some 60 times the cost and which takes at least five times longer to reach Cape Town.

The Stellenbosch Village Museum is open Monday to Saturday (including public holidays) 09h30 to 17h00. Sundays and religious holidays 14h00 to 17h00. It is closed on Good Friday and Christmas Day. Apart from Schreuder House, it includes Bletterman House, built by Hendrik Lodewyk Bletterman in about 1789. He was the last of the frontier magistrates of Stellenbosch to be appointed by the Dutch East India Company. The furnishings are far more sumptuous than those in Schreuder House where the court messenger lived.

The third building of this unique museum is Grosvenor House in Drostdy Street next to the mother church. Christian Ludolph Neethling, founder of a family distinguished in South Africa in the legal and agricultural community, built this residence in its early form in 1782. Successive owners modified and enlarged the building, its present state being achieved in about 1803. The Collins family, who were amongst the later owners, named it Grosvenor House. In 1985 it was restored to its early 19th century state of a two-storeyed, flat-roofed town house, furnished in the life-style of well-to-do occupants. The former slave quarters are on the left-hand side of the building with many other interesting things to see.

The fourth house in the museum complex was the house of Olof Marthinus Bergh and his family who lived there in the late 1870s. The house had a thatched roof and gable but was altered to its present form in the 19th century. It is furnished with items from this period.

The house stands at the corner of Drostdy and Kerk Streets. A part of the back of the house displays how old edifices are archaeologically researched. Two more houses will eventually be added to the group, completing 7 000 square metres of very special restoration and conservation of a whole block of preserved buildings.

The people of Stellenbosch ate well and their cooking became renowned. It is based on locally grown vegetables of high standard, fruit and grapes for table and wine, fat sheep and cattle. It has always been a good life in Stellenbosch and as you stroll through the town centre you run a tempting gauntlet of restaurants and cafes. There are over 50 of them in a small area, offering practically everything a hungry person could desire; pancake houses, coffee houses, pavement restaurants, pub lunches, students' hangouts and romantic places for that special night out.

There are art galleries and thematic museums. Many of the specialised shops are little museums of their own, displaying private collections as well as things for sale: gemstones, copperware, hand-crafted jewellery, guns, clocks and chocolates. There are bookshops as befits a university town, while flower-sellers provide islands of brilliant colour in the midst of the pavement flow of humanity.

Drostdy Street ends just past Grosvenor House. Turn left (west) down Van Riebeeck Street which leads into Plein Street. Across Ryneveld Street, the street passes on the right the town hall. Built in 1941, this building has some interesting features, including a handsome staircase.

Outside the hall, presiding over the animated street scene, there is a charming life-size bronze of a cat done by the artist Nerine Desmond.

This is the town cat, modelled after a real-life cat who lived in one of the cafes. The cat has considerable presence. It sits on its pedestal, its tail wrapped elegantly over its paws, complacent but alert as it watches over its territory. Somebody started a fable about this cat. At certain seasons in the year, if you stoop down and look across its ears, you will see the moon rising over the mountains known as the Jonkershoek Twins. Stroke the cat's head and you will hear it purr. Make a wish and it will come true.

On the wall beyond the entrance to the library there is a frieze by the sculptor Ivan Mitford-Barberton. The frieze depicts the coming to the Cape of the French Huguenot settlers in 1688. On the left-hand side is a sternly repressive-looking monk threatening some sad-looking Protestants. As the eye moves to the right-hand side, note the changes of expression as the Huguenots are welcomed to the Cape by a benevolent-looking Governor.

Plein Street ends in a traffic circle in the middle of Bird Street. Beyond the circle lies *Die Braak*, the village-green of Stellenbosch, the scene of the annual birthday festivities. It was originally also used as a military parade-ground with the VOC-*Kruithuis* (Dutch East India Company powder-magazine or arsenal) still standing on the far side where Market Street reaches *Die Braak*. The tubby-looking little building is now maintained as a military museum. It is open Mondays to Fridays 09h00 to 14h00. Closed week-ends, public holidays and from 1 June to 31 August.

On the south side of *Die Braak* stands the mission church erected in 1823 and added to in 1840. It became the Rhenish Missionary Church and in 1862 the Rhenish School, the oldest boarding-school for girls in South Africa, was opened on its left (west) side in what was originally a private dwelling house. This was subsequently enlarged until it reached its present size in 1890. Later it became a hostel only. For the first time in South Africa, domestic science was taught there. It is now the P J Olivier Art Centre.

The Anglican Church, St Mary's-on-the-Braak, stands on the northern side of *Die Braak*, faced on the corner of Bloem and Market streets with a cluster of restored buildings now used as offices. Immediately down the left side of Market Street, in what was apparently the original smithy of the Rhenish Museum, there are the offices and information centre of the Stellenbosch Publicity Association. Books, brochures, maps, etc may be obtained there as well as locally made crafts, gemstones and other items in a gift and curio shop. Behind the information office stands the original Rhenish parsonage in a walled garden and lawn traversed by the mill stream. This building now houses a delightful toy and miniature museum created by the Stellenbosch Village Museum. It is open Mondays to Saturdays 09h30 to 17h00, Sundays 14h00 to 17h00. It's full of fun; don't miss it. Market Street continues on its way, reaches a junction with Herte Street and then bends southwards to reach, as does Herte Street, the well-preserved Dorp Street. Turning right (west) down Dorp Street, there are several interesting buildings. On the south side of the road, just across the *Aan die Wagen Weg* (along the wagon road) the original road leading to Somerset West, there is the beautifully restored *Libertas Parva*, built by Lambertus Fick, with its gable dating from 1783. It now houses the Rembrandt van Rijn Art Gallery while an outbuilding contains the Stellenryck Wine Museum. Both these buildings are open to the public Mondays to Fridays from 09h00 to 12h45 and 14h00 to 17h00, Saturdays from 10h00 to 13h00 and 14h00 to 17h00.

The two museums are maintained by the Distillers Corporation whose headquarters are in the building behind them. They house some stunningly beautiful exhibits. Superb sculptures by Anton van Wouw and an interesting collection of modern art and historic paintings are the treasures in the gallery. The fine art in the gallery is rivalled in the wine museum by the industrial art of the designers of the stills and utensils of the winemakers. Apart from wine itself, the containers, casks and bottles have provided their makers, who had an eye for the natural beauty of enduring wood and polished metals, with opportunities in design. The cabinets are filled with VOC-engraved glasses, decanters and silverware. Their elegant shapes are lovely to see. There are bottles of the famed Constantia wine, honey sweet, deliciously aromatic, the toast of Europe in the 18th and 19th centuries. In harvest time, a glass of freshly pressed grape juice or 'must' is offered to visitors and there is always a Stellenryck wine to taste.

Outside the wine museum stands a gigantic old grape press, a massive affair which must have required in its making the cutting down of a substantial tree and used the labours of several men to create it. It is today a well-known landmark. As you look at it, imagine the tree that provided the wood. Where did it grow; in which quiet forest did it mature from a tiny seed; who were the men who felled it; for how many hours did they work dressing the wood; what labour did the draught animals have in dragging the wood to the workmen, and then the finished press to the vineyards where the grapes were ripening in the sun?

Turning back up Dorp Street in our Stellenbosch stroll, we pass a long row of cottages built between 1817 and 1859 in the Cape-Dutch style and then converted into the Victorian style. Dorp

Street continues past Gi-Gi's Bistro and De Kelders Restaurant and then the garden and manor-house of *Vredelust* (desire for peace). Past the branch of Market Street, on the left-hand side, stands the landmark of the well-known *Oom Samie se Winkel*. The first owner of this building was Pieter Gerhard Wium who, in 1791, was granted the land together with a concession to trade in meat. In 1876 the property was subdivided. Johannes Christoffel Heyneke bought, for the princely sum of £225, the portion containing the present shop.

In May 1904, Samuel Johannes Volsteedt bought the shop for £1 000 and commenced business as a general dealer. He had been born on 27 May 1879 in the Faure district. Of farming stock, he suffered all his life from a weak back which made him unfit for an agricultural life. So he became a trader, and this was the beginning of S J Volsteedt, General Dealer, in a shop which became affectionately known as *Oom Samie se Winkel* (Uncle Samuel's shop).

Oom Samie traded in virtually everything. His shop breathed a symphony of aromas from lamp oil and roll tobacco to lavender. Surrounded by friends and pets, he presided over this establishment for 40 years. His gentle, caring nature made him a well-loved member of the community. On his death in 1944, his Coloured and Black customers formed a choir to sing at his funeral. On his grave was inscribed the simple epitaph: *'He was a good man'*.

Although Oom Samie is no longer in his shop to welcome us, the lady who now runs the place, Annatjie Melck, devotedly maintains it as yesterday's shop still in business today, buying, selling, trading or acquiring for you everything from chewing tobacco and musical spittoons through a whole range of most everything collectable and eatable: sweets, biltong, dried fruit and fish, good foods, spices, leather, home-made delicacies and the dry goods of yesterday and today. Part of the shop is a Victorian-style wine shop and a fully licensed restaurant where you tuck into a light meal and goodies in a setting of flowers, tame ducks and other friendly domestic animals, including a well-known cat named Warlock. The wine shop dispatches gift-packed local wines to addresses all over the world in quantities from six bottles to a full container load. There are rare vintages and a consultancy service for collectors. The shop is open every day of the week, including public holidays from 08h00 to 17h30. Phone (021) 887-0797 for the shop. (021) 887-2612 for the wine shop. Fax (021) 883-8621.

Up Dorp Street from Oom Samie se Winkel stands De Akker country pub on the corner of Herte Street. Above this street there is a long row of beautiful old houses, numbers 102 to 122. All were converted into double-storeyed residences in Victorian times but they still retain their original Cape-Dutch character. Opposite them is what was once the parsonage of the Reverend Meent Borcherds who in 1798 built and named his lovely home *La Gratitude* and modelled in its gable an 'all-seeing-eye'. How many passers-by have felt a trifle uneasy as they met its unflinching stare? Later it became the home of the Winshaw family whose head, William Winshaw, founded the Stellenbosch Farmers' Winery. The name of the house became the name of one of his most popular white wines.

Shaded by the oak trees at the higher end of Dorp Street, there are several specialist shops including, at no 145, the Gemstone Paradise with a superb private collection of the gemstones of South Africa as well as many lovely cut, faceted and polished stones. These beautiful stones, gathered from all over Southern Africa by Michael and Petra Schmidt, seem to harmonise in a subtle way with the colours and forms of Stellenbosch. Antique shops, jewellery manufacturers, a gunsmith and clockmaker, The Blue Orange farm shop and coffee house, the Jan Cats Seafood Restaurant, the Stellenbosch Hotel, the Dorp Street Gallery and De Soete Inval Pancake House are some places to visit on this part of the tour.

At 161 Dorp Street stands the interesting and atmospheric building of the Eendracht Village Hotel. The site of this double-storey building and the parking area behind it is on what was originally part of the island on which Simon van der Stel camped during his first exploration of the valley of the Eerste River. The island has long vanished but the river still flows merrily seawards past the east side of the parking ground.

The first building on the site was a simple little two-roomed thatched cottage erected by a French lady, Sarah Couchet, widow of Guillaume du Toit. She built her cottage after the disastrous Stellenbosch fire of 1710. She died in 1714 and a succession of owners added additional rooms and modification to the cottage in order to accommodate larger broods of children and relatives.

Archaeological research on the site of this old cottage has retrieved many interesting relics of the various owners. Chinese porcelain, kitchen utensils, fragments of linen, early smoking pipe bowls, and metal fragments from an early iron, copper and silversmiths workyard. A particularly interesting occupant of the cottage was the artist Jan Adam Hartman who lived there during the period 1790–1801. He practically rebuilt the place in a square shape with several additional rooms.

From 1890 to 1960 the building was substantially rebuilt to become a double storey students boarding house. This had to make way for the A P Venter Hall and Park. Then the Lutz Trust reconstructed the building using the original architectural style. It became the Eendracht Guest House and now the Eendracht Village Hotel. The atmosphere of the place is very tangible. Many people have lived in the house, there is a feeling of hospitality and welcome, reminders of the past years, of travellers, events, good eating and friendship. The building epitomises Stellenbosch since its very beginning with Governor Van der Stel encamped on the island site in what was first named Van der Stel se Bosch. Phone (021) 883-8843. Fax (021) 883-8842. Email lutzkor@iafrica.com.

Stellenbosch has understandably always been attractive to artists. Galleries sell their works. The University of Stellenbosch exhibits work of many South African artists in a gallery housed in the former Evangelical Lutheran Church at the intersection of Bird and Dorp Streets. The collection includes an endowment of 150 paintings by Maggie Laubser.

If you look up Bird Street as you cross it, you will see a pleasant touch to the architecture of the Checkers Centre. The canopy over the pavement has been so made as to allow an oak tree to grow through it.

The University of Stellenbosch had its origin in the early 1860s. Two professors of the Theological Seminary in the town, John Murray and Nicolaas Hofmeyr, with the local minister, Reverend J H Neethling, persuaded the residents of the town to support the establishment of the Stellenbosch Gymnasium which opened in 1866. From this Gymnasium grew an Arts Department which, in 1881, became the Stellenbosch College, renamed the Victoria College in 1887, the jubilee year of Queen Victoria's reign.

With the creation of the Union of South Africa in 1910, there was talk of the establishment in Cape Town of a single national university, but this was strongly opposed. In a memorandum submitted to the government in 1915, Dr D F Malan and a committee emphasised the importance of Stellenbosch as a cultural and educational centre for the Afrikaner. Their plea was reinforced in the same year when Johannes Henoch (Oom Jannie) Marais, owner of the farm *Coetzenberg* died. Amongst other bequests he left £100 000 towards higher education in Stellenbosch, and this was a substantial sum in those days.

The Government yielded to persuasion and in April 1918 the Victoria College became the University of Stellenbosch which (with its current enrolment of over 14 000 students) today dominates the town, not only physically with its impressive complex of buildings, including a superb underground library, but also culturally and socially with its atmosphere of learning, varsity life and sport. The central square of the University of Stellenbosch is named after Johannes Marais, the great benefactor of the university. His statue stands in the centre of the square. The square covers what is one of the largest underground libraries in the world, the J S Gericke Biblioteek, named after a former Vice-Chancellor of the university. The square is jocularly known to students as the Red Square of Stellenbosch. The amphitheatre on the right hand side is used by students for lunch-hour gatherings and concerts. The library has a floor area of 18 000 square metres and contains over 600 000 books, periodicals, microfilms, manuscripts and government publications.

The University of Stellenbosch has made a major contribution to culture, politics, science, agriculture and sport in Southern Africa. It has often been described as the nursery of South African rugby. Its sporting colours, a deep maroon, give countless individuals the pride of being known by the nickname of *Maties* (tomatoes). To sit in some pleasant little cafe, each with its own atmosphere and devotees, enjoying a pub lunch and watching the passing show, is to savour something of the atmosphere of a Continental university town. This could almost be a part of the Netherlands, with its neatness, scrupulous cleanliness and a particular polish to all the windows.

Johannes Marais also bequeathed £10 000 for the establishment of a public park. In 1919 the Jan Marais Nature Reserve was opened on 25 ha of ground near the centre of the town. In 1962 the park was declared to be a wild flower sanctuary conserving the richly varied flora which flourished on the site of Stellenbosch when Simon van der Stel first visited the area. The reserve is open daily from 07h30 to sunset.

The University of Stellenbosch also has a fine botanical garden in Neethling Street known as *Hortus Botanicus*. It is notable for its collection of ferns, orchids, bonsai trees and succulents, including such varieties as a *Welwitschia* from the Namib Desert. The garden is open weekdays from 09h00 to 16h30 and Saturdays 09h00 to 11h00. A visit to these gardens and to the University campus is very rewarding.

STELLENBOSCH FARMERS' WINERY

The largest of the 'big three' of the wine and spirit producers in Southern Africa is the Stellenbosch Farmers' Winery Ltd, whose extensive cellars are situated 1 km from Stellenbosch on the road to Cape Town down the west side of the shallow valley of the Eerste River. This company was the brainchild of an American doctor, William Charles Winshaw.

Born in Kentucky in 1871, he ran away from home at the age of twelve. With an old hobo, he canoed down the Tennessee River. In 1893 he was a Texas Ranger fighting in the Jacqui War on the Mexican border. He was a friend of Buffalo Bill and had numerous adventures until he decided to become a medical doctor. He qualified in New Orleans and practised in New Mexico. Then he met Lieutenant McGuiness who was buying horses for the British army in the Anglo-Boer War. Winshaw took on the job of caring for 4 500 horses shipped to Cape Town in 1900 on the *Laringa*.

The horses were delivered to the British army remount camp at Koelenhof near Stellenbosch. Winshaw joined the British army and served until the end of the war. He then settled in South Africa, practising medicine until he decided to turn farmer. From a Cape Town dentist he rented near Stellenbosch the farm *Patrysvallei* (partridge valley), later known as *Brown Hills* and started making wine in the kitchen with little more equipment than the stove and a few buckets.

From the beginning Winshaw managed to produce good wine. In 1909 he founded the Stellenbosch Grape Juice Works but it was a difficult time in which to establish a wine industry. There was over-production and little demand. In 1921 he went insolvent but his faith in wine remained unshaken. Two years later he joined G J Krige in a new venture based on Krige's farm. This fine farm, named *Libertas* (liberty), had first been granted by Simon van der Stel in 1689 to Jan van Oudenlingenland, who named the farm and then transferred it in 1690 to Hans Grimp. On Grimp's death, his widow married a well-known character in the history of the Cape, Adam Tas. It was purely coincidental that his name was part of the farm name, but the cellar of the farm, built in 1706, is named after him. Several of the modern company's wines, such as the ever-popular 'Tassies' or Tassenberg, Tasheimer and Oom Tas, are reminders of a stalwart defender of civil liberties.

In 1869 Gideon Krige had purchased the northern section of *Libertas* and founded a business as a distiller and wine and spirit merchant. In 1925 William Winshaw rehabilitated his estate, bought the farm and business from Krige, and founded the Stellenbosch Farmers' Winery Ltd. Winshaw remained as managing director of this company until 1962 when, aged 92, he retired. All his life he insisted on high standards of production and the healthiness of natural wine. He died at the fine age of 96, and his enthusiasm for the qualities of good wine had obviously served him well. His two sons, Jack and William, had worked with him in the creation of the company. William succeeded him in 1950, becoming chairman of the Stellenbosch Farmers' Wine Trust Limited which incorporated the original Stellenbosch Farmers' Winery and the wine firm of V H Matterson and Sons Ltd.

In 1960 the company merged with the South African Breweries Ltd by means of a share exchange. The Winshaw family continued management and the company expanded, in 1966 absorbing the Paarl firm of Monis Wineries and being renamed The Stellenbosch Wine Trust Limited. The magnificent *Nederburg* estate at Paarl, owned by Monis, was brought into the group at the same time. In 1970 Sedgwick Tayler was also acquired. In 1979 Stellenbosch Farmers' Winery became part of Cape Wine and Distillers Ltd but in 1988 was once again a quoted company on the Johannesburg Stock Exchange, and its spectacular growth continued without pause.

The company today markets nearly two-thirds of all wines sold in Southern Africa, employing over 3 500 people, and has an annual turnover in excess of R2 000 million. Amongst the wines produced in these modern cellars are the prestigious Zonnebloem range, sparkling wines such as Grand *Mousseux* (Mousseux means bubbling) and 5th Avenue Cold Duck, the Lanzerac range, Chateau Libertas, La Gratitude, Graca, Perlino Perle, the Autumn Harvest and Kellerprinz ranges, Capenheimer, Virginia, Roma White and surprises such as Pêche Royale, a delicious sparkling wine made from peaches. Last but not least was *Lieberstein* (love stein), the light semi-sweet stein wine introduced in 1959 and within five years becoming the largest-selling branded natural wine in the world, and largely responsible for popularising table wine in South Africa. Latest developments include huge successes with Hunters, Crown and Savannah, a variety of ciders and fruit juices, including Monis grape juice, Super Juice and Polar Ice.

Opposite the cellars on the farm *Oude Libertas*, the company has an impressive reception and training complex in the Oude Libertas Centre. Completed in 1977, the Oude Libertas Centre comprises conference and training facilities, a wine and entertainment centre and the Oude Libertas Amphitheatre, a focal point of the arts in the Western Cape. From December until March, a season of music, dance and theatre is presented under the stars providing a unique experience. Patrons are also invited to bring picnic hampers and the whole family along to the popular Sunday twilight concerts and enjoy supper on the lawns surrounding the amphitheatre. Brochures on the Oude Libertas Amphitheatre's annual summer season are available at Computicket, who handle bookings for all the performances, from mid-November. The atmosphere is as romantic as the setting.

The Oude Libertas restaurant is a delightful setting for a relaxed luncheon or an elegant dinner. Superb intercontinental food is served with a wide selection of wines, including a magnificent array of mature red wines. Happy visitors from around the world rate this restaurant as one of the best in the Cape.

Mon Repos (my repose), a charming farmhouse of *Oude Libertas*, is also home to the Cape Wine Academy, which has been involved in wine education for just over a decade. The courses offered by the CWA range from ones on a preliminary level to a four-year diploma course and courses on food and wine. Wine tours are conducted by trained guides Mondays to Thursdays at 10h00 and 14h30. Fridays 10h00. They start with a video presentation at the Oude Libertas Centre, followed by an extensive tour through SFW's renowned cellars, and are concluded by a wine-tasting. From September to May one can also taste wines on Saturdays between 09h30 and 14h00. It is advisable to book beforehand for tours by telephoning (021) 808-7569.

The Cape Town firm of architects – Mallows, Louw, Hoffe and Orme – designed this very attractive complex of buildings. They stand in the setting of huge old oak trees, with a vineyard in front of them.

DISTILLERS CORPORATION

The second of the 'big three' of the wine and spirits business in Southern Africa is the Distillers Corporation (SA) Ltd. Its origin was in March 1943 when Anton Rupert, a 26-year-old lecturer in Industrial Chemistry at the University of Pretoria, and a slightly older partner, an attorney named Dirk Hertzog, formed a partnership. The partners had little money but considerable courage. They created what they named the *Tegniese en Industriële Beleggings (Edms) Beperk* – Technical and Industrial Investments (Pty) Ltd – with a subscribed capital of £10. They could not afford an office but shared premises with the artist, Kobus Esterhuyzen. They had no money to pay salaries. Mrs Rupert became unpaid clerk, typist, telephonist, messenger and secretary.

From this humble beginning, in the midst of World War II, there were spectacular developments. The two partners were astute and they had a genius in acquisition, organising, and negotiations. They acquired shares in companies and became trustees of Union Distillers SA (Pty) Ltd. By March 1945 they were sufficiently established to allow them, as trustees of Union Distillers, to purchase the property, machinery and resources of the Farm Products Protection Association Ltd in Stellenbosch, which was in the process of liquidation. This purchase gave them possession of the 7 ha site of their present extensive and magnificent cellars in Stellenbosch. It was from this development that, on 11 June 1945, they created Distillers Corporation (SA) Ltd with a capital of £1 300 000.

The war was now over and South Africa could anticipate a great surge in opportunity. Anton Rupert, as managing director of Distillers Corporation, set out to gather a talented staff. Mr G H Schroeder became technical manager and Dr A Baumgartner became chief chemist and wine technologist. They created a laboratory for research into wine and spirits and commenced a programme directed towards the creation of products of the highest standard.

Without a long-term programme of growing vines themselves, the shortest way of achieving their aim was to draw into the young corporation a number of independent wine estates. These estates would retain their private ownership and name, but would be happy to allow Distillers Corporation to market their products. In this way Anton Rupert steadily added to his *'family of partners'* nineteen prestigious estates: *Allesverloren, Alto, Bonfoi, De Wetshof, Goede Hoop, Hazendal, Jacobsdal, Koopmanskloof, La Motte, Le Bonheur, L'Ormarins, Meerlust, Meerendal, Middelvlei, Mont Blois, Rietvallei, Theuniskraal, Uitkyk* and *Zandvliet*.

A major objective for Distillers Corporation was to produce brandy and spirits. By 1947 the Corporation had successfully introduced to the market such products as Rembrandt and Richelieu brandies, the La Residence range of sparkling wines, port, sherry, vermouth, various sweet wines and the Oude Meester range of 23 liqueurs. All these products were created in the difficult post-war period of shortages of equipment and bottles. A complex marketing organisation was created to sell and distribute the products. There were problems of supply of adequate quantities of rebate brandy and frustration from the somewhat antiquated South African liquor laws.

In 1951 Distillers Corporation introduced to South Africa the so-called 'cold fermentation' method of wine production which had been developed in California. It was a process suited to countries with warm climates and had been devised by Wilhelm Geiss of the Seitz-Werke in Germany, a great manufacturer of wine-making machinery. On their recommendation, four high-pressure tanks needed for the process were imported from Germany. After initial problems in the first year the process was successfully established. In it, the grape juice is fermented under very high pressure with temperature controlled under optimal conditions to produce wines of varying sweetness and predictable standards of quality. The first wine produced by this technique to be marketed was *Kupferberger Auslesen* – delicate and slightly sweet. It is still a great favourite. Related to it, Distillers produced by the same technique, but somewhat drier and lighter, what was called *Grunberger Stein*. The latter wines were marketed in the type of bottle known as a *Bocksbeutel* used by the Franconians in Germany.

Over the years there were inevitable product changes. Some wines, spirits and liqueurs vanished; others took their place; a few old favourites remained. The year 1960 saw a clash of interest between South African Breweries and Distillers Corporation. In May of that year South African Breweries acquired control of Stellenbosch Farmers' Winery and thus made a spectacular entrance to the wine business. Distillers Corporation resisted this development by legal action, fearful that South African Breweries, which controlled many major liquor outlets, would discriminate against Distillers' products in favour of those of the Stellenbosch winery.

Legal action failed to halt South African Breweries, but Anton Rupert was a tough man to beat. He countered the Breweries' move into wine by entering the beer business. The advertising industry and the public both had a good time from the ensuing 'beer war'. In the midst of this conflict, vodka was introduced to South Africa, with Distillers marketing Sputnik Vodka, named in honour of the launching of the first Russian satellite. French cognac was also introduced by Distillers, blended with local brandy to create the high-class Richelieu Brandy.

In 1964 the Drostdy Co-operative Cellars at Tulbagh were acquired by Distillers. This gave them control of the largest sherry maturation cellar in South Africa. The Witzenberg range of wines produced in the Tulbagh area was also acquired. In the same momentous year it was decided to build, on the slopes of the Papegaaiberg in Stellenbosch, a huge underground cellar on similar lines to the famous cave cellars in France and Germany where top quality wines were produced under ideal conditions.

The *Bergkelder* (mountain cellar) was opened on 7 November 1968. It is especially notable for its magnificent vats, carved in 1968 by the artist, Karl Wilhelm. Brought out from Germany to do the work, he completed all the vats in less than a year and then decided to settle in the Cape where his talents are a considerable asset and his work may be seen in many forms.

A stroll through the underground cellars is an unforgettable experience. Each barrel is a masterly example of the woodcarver's art. There is tangible magic to the place, with its shadows, silence and the presence of thousands of bottles of fine wine symmetrically packed into every vault and maturing slowly into the perfection which only time can give them.

The Bergkelder, with its meticulous control of temperature, humidity, light and noise levels, is primarily used for the maturation of its own wines. It is also used as a vinoteque where high quality wines acquired by private collectors are further matured in ideal conditions, increasing their value year after year.

There are conducted tours of the Bergkelder, Mondays to Saturdays at 10h00, 10h30 and 15h00. Tours for overseas visitors with special requirements in language can be arranged. The shop is open during normal business hours. Visitors can taste and buy Bergkelder wines. The Bergkelder is not open on public holidays. Phone (021) 888-3016.

In 1965 Anton Rupert merged his rapidly expanding liquor interests into one company named The Oude Meester Cellar, Distillers and Breweries Corporation Ltd, with a capital of R20 million. In the same year, in association with Whitbread of London and Heineken of the Netherlands, Rembrandt announced the building of a modern brewery in Wadeville (Germiston). Ivanoff vodka was introduced to the market, as well as Beefeater gin, distilled in South Africa.

In 1968, the year of the opening of the Bergkelder, Anton Rupert purchased the famous red wine estate *Alto*. The winemaker of the estate, P du Toit, was offered a share and was left to manage the place. The Fleur du Cap range of high quality wines were introduced with the opening of the Bergkelder.

In 1969 South African Distillers & Wines Ltd was acquired, and this gave Oude Meester control also of E K Green & Co, Van Ryn Wine and Spirit Co, Castle Wine and Brandy Co, and Henry Collison Ltd.

In 1970 the corporation launched Paarl Perle wine, and this sparkling light wine became the largest-selling wine in South Africa.

In 1971 the Stellenryck Wine Museum was opened in the original wine cellar of the Fick and later the Krige families in Dorp Street. An art gallery was created in the original homestead.

By 1972 the total assets of the group had reached R82 million, and the following year saw a bold and massive venture into the brewing business. In South Africa, beer is far and away the most popular alcoholic drink. Sorghum beer, the traditional drink of Africa, has 35 per cent of the total market for alcoholic beverages, with ordinary beer having 28 per cent. Wine (natural and fortified) has 21 per cent of the market. In an effort to obtain a share of the lucrative beer market, Anton Rupert and his colleagues created The Beer and Malt Investment Ltd Intercontinental Breweries to produce beer. South African brewing rights were obtained for the well-known German beers of Becks and Kronenbrau.

At the end of 1979 the 'beer war' ended. The South African Breweries Ltd, purchased Intercontinental Breweries from the Rembrandt Group and were left in sole control of the beer market. The two groups pooled their wine and spirit interests into a company named Cape Wine and Distillers Ltd. In this company Rembrandt, KWV and South African Breweries each had 30 per cent of the equity, with the balance of 10 per cent going to the public. Rembrandt and KWV pooled their interests into a joint company known as Rembrandt/KWV Investments. Oude Meester and Stellenbosch Farmers' Winery continued to operate as separate competitive companies. The name, Oude Meester, now only exists as the name of a brandy product. The company name is Distillers Corporation.

GILBEY DISTILLERS AND VINTNERS

The third of the 'big three' wine and spirit producers of Southern African, is Gilbey Distillers and Vintners (Pty) Ltd. It is part of the largest drink company in the world, International Distillers and Vintners of London. They have their South African headquarters in Stellentia Avenue below the slopes of the Papegaaiberg. This concern had its origin in Britain where the brothers Walter and Alfred Gilbey founded a company in 1857 and commenced importing Cape wines. For two years they did well. Then, in 1859 a treaty of amity and commerce was signed by Britain and France. This put French wines at a great price advantage. Thenceforth they paid the same customs dues as Cape wines and their product only had to cross the Channel to reach the British market.

Sale of Cape wines in Britain dwindled to insignificant quantities. The firm of Gilbey for many years was less interested in importing anything from South Africa than exporting to it a number of foreign products. Included in these was gin (made from the berries known as *Geneva* or *Juniper*). Gin was popularly known in South Africa as Holland's Squareface Gin because the drink originated in the Netherlands and came in a four-sided bottle.

An interesting sequence of events led to the establishment of Gilbeys in Stellenbosch. The beginning was based on the thirst of the gold-miners of the Witwatersrand. The prospectors and diggers provided a demand for strong drink which always remained far beyond the supply. A few grog shops were at first the only sources of alcohol. Their stock was somewhat limited, mainly to home-made brandy distilled from yellow peaches, corn or various wild berries. The result was pretty strong. When George Harrison found the gold in the main reef of the Witwatersrand, the only place to celebrate was in Koos Malan's grog shop, and the drink was said to have an effect similar to falling under a two-stamp mining battery.

More sophisticated drinks had to be brought into the Transvaal by ox-wagon. The romantic old transport industry from Lourenzo Marques (now Maputo) to Lydenburg was largely concerned with bringing in loads of liquor. Examining the contents of the rubbish middens at the side of the trading stations and staging posts along the old wagon trail reveals that there was heavy traffic in Holland's Squareface gin. The descriptive term 'Dutch Courage' derived from a story that soldiers were given tots of the drink to fortify them before going to do battle.

One of the men engaged in the transport industry was a Hungarian, Alois Nellmapius. Nellmapius acquired a fine farm, known as *Hatherley*, 16 km east of Pretoria. In October 1881 he negotiated a concession from the Transvaal government giving him the sole right to refine sugar and distil alcoholic liquor from corn and other sources. The concession was named *De Eerste Fabrieken* (the first manufactory). It was historic for the Transvaal and considered to be the beginning of industry in the South African Republic.

Nellmapius died in July 1893. The financier, Sammy Marks, took control of the Eerste Fabrieken distillery. In 1897, in an attempt to improve the product, he placed in various European papers an advertisement for an experienced distiller. This advertisement was seen by a 33-year-old man, René von Eibergen Santhagens. He had been born in Batavia (now Jakarta), the capital of Java. His father was Dutch, his mother French. The name, Santhagens, was pronounced in French with a silent 's' at the end, a slight matter which caused confusion in South Africa.

The opportunity was just what he needed. He was working as a distiller in the district of Cognac in France. His employer, the Marquis de Pellerin de la Touche, had a very vivacious daughter named Laure Emilie Louise Jeanne. She and René fell in love but she was only 18 years of age. He father insisted that René had to make more money somewhere and his daughter wait until she was more mature before he would permit the marriage. He offered to give René a glowing recommendation to speed him on his way, hoping, it would seem that this would be the last of him. René applied for the appointment at Eerste Fabrieken. Sammy Marks gave him the job and instructed him to acquire the latest distillery equipment. Amongst the equipment René included a small copper pot still. With considerable excitement on his part, and tears from Laure Emilie, he sailed for Lourenzo Marques and then travelled to Pretoria on the recently constructed eastern railway line.

René was a great success. He made whisky from grain and gin from juniper berries. There was no time for maturation but the liquor was what the mining community liked – strong. Within twelve months, Laure Emilie alternatively sulked and nagged her father into submission. He sailed with her to Cape Town and she became Mrs Santhagens in St Mary's Cathedral. They made a happy couple. Before René took his bride off to Pretoria, they explored the wine country of the Western Cape, including Stellenbosch. The possibilities of the Cape impressed René, but he had to return to Pretoria with his bride and concentrate on satisfying the gold-miners' thirst for raw spirits.

The outbreak of the Anglo-Boer War brought an end to the production of liquor at De Eerste Fabrieken. The distillery concentrated on producing pure alcohol for medical antiseptic use. At the end of the war, the new British administration cancelled the concession and the Santhagens returned to Europe. Both of them, however, had grown to like South Africa, and in 1903 René decided to commence distilling brandy in Stellenbosch. From the liquidators of the Eerste Fabrieken, René bought stills and other equipment, and this was the basis of the enterprise in the Cape.

In the Eerste River valley, René joined W A Krige of *Vredelust* estate near Vlottenburg. Then the brothers, J and C Marais, established the Golden Lion Distillers at Vlottenburg as a co-operative venture of local farmers. René became joint manager of the enterprise. The production of brandy, liqueurs, wines and fruit syrups was commenced.

René's genius as a distiller became well known. John X Merriman, Prime Minister of the Cape Colony, gave him the management of *Schoongezicht* and the project of producing a high-class brandy, Sir Lionel Phillips, the Rand mining magnate, became interested. With funds available, René bought in 1909, the farm of *De Oude Molen*, beneath the Papegaaiberg at the entrance to Stellenbosch. This farm, originally called *De Oudemool*, had been granted on 2 October 1701 to Jannetjie van Heijningen. The manor-house was built in 1710. There René created his celebrated distillery and maintained the manor-house as a beautiful home presided over by Madame Santhagens. In this home the couple, without a family but always devoted to each other, collected art and antiques. They loved dogs and horses; and René, who had served in the French army, collected swords and military weapons. René Santhagens died on 15 November 1937, leaving many bequests to his staff and charities. Madame Santhagens lived on in *De Oude Molen* manor-house until her death in July 1961 aged 81. It is said that she and her husband, both good-looking and always elegant in dress and manner, may still occasionally be seen driving through the grounds in a trap drawn by a superb white horse.

The various interests of René and his associates were bought in 1962 by Gilbeys, and in 1970 the wholly acquired shares were incorporated into Gilbeys Distillers and Vintners (Pty) Ltd. The manor-house of *De Oude Molen* and the water-mill which gave the place its name are perfectly preserved.

In 1972 the company acquired Bertrams Wines, a company with an established reputation in the wine trade. R F Bertram had in the late 1920s purchased the *High Constantia* estate adjoining the famous *Groot Constantia* in the Cape Peninsula. He built a cellar and produced fine wine from grapes grown on both estates. In 1939 Bertram's company was bought by G N Maskell, who expanded the concern and then sold it in 1959 to Simeon Blumberg. He moved the entire company to the Devon Valley, near Stellenbosch. In 1972 he sold the company to Gilbeys who, by this acquisition, became the number three wine and spirits producers and distributors of Southern Africa.

The Devon Valley complex consisted of a distillery and maturation cellar eventually producing a considerable variety of spirits and liqueurs such as Smirnoff Vodka, Gilbeys London Dry Gin, Bertrams Brandy, sherry and port, Malibu, Cinzano, Vermouth and Spumante; several different cream drinks such as Cape Velvet, rum, and coffee liqueurs; and the grand old favourite, Van der Hum. In 1995 the creation of these and many other drinks was transferred to the Oude Molen complex behind the Stellenbosch railway station. Groups are most welcome to visit the brandy museum. The Devon Valley facility was closed by Gilbeys but in 1996 the estate and cellars was bought by the Distillers Corporation for the purpose of producing their sparkling wines.

THE WINE ROUTE

The source of the wine used by the big three in production is, of course, mainly from the farmlands surrounding Stellenbosch. This is one of the most productive farmlands on Earth. The basic nutrient richness of the soils, decomposed sandstone, shales and granite, and the subtle variations in climate, often providing a single estate with micro-climates and eco-systems on different slopes of a single hill, was originally responsible for the vast variety of flowering plants. Now it is the secret for the cultivation of many different varieties of grapes and fruit, each variety requiring specialised conditions of growth. The whole area is scenically splendid. Exploring it is the delight of countless visitors.

In April 1971 a wine route was opened, the creation of three well-known farmers, Neil Joubert, then owner of *Spier*, Frans Malan of *Simonsig*, and Spatz Sperling of *Delheim*. The wine route could also be called a food route, a flower route, a brandy route or a fruit route. The purpose is to allow visitors to discover the area for themselves, following good, well signposted roads, taking their own time, choosing when and where to go, when to shop, what to buy and what to eat without any persuasion from salesmen or hucksters.

The members of the Wine Route offer conducted tours of their cellars and tastings of their wines. Several of them also provide attractive light lunches in delightfully atmospheric and lovely garden settings. Some also have fine restaurants featuring such delights as traditional Cape cookery. Over 260 wines are produced in the Stellenbosch area. Visiting the estates provides a pleasant way of discovering these wines, obtaining them direct from the cellars and meeting the people who create them.

Maps of the Stellenbosch Wine Route are available – the Information Office of the Stellenbosch Publicity Association and the Wine Route will gladly offer you advice and assistance. Their address is 36 Market Street, Stellenbosch, 7600. Phone (021) 883-3584 or 883-9633 (Publicity) and (021) 886-4310 (Wine Route). Fax (021) 883-8017.

THE OLD CAPE WAGON ROAD (R310)

Let us start our discovery of the Stellenbosch Wine Route by following the original road which connected Stellenbosch to Cape Town. This road, the historic Dorp Street when it leads into Stellenbosch on the western side of the town, is known today as R310 from its junction with the Adam Tas road. From this junction the old Cape Road turns southwards to carry the traveller over the hills and farmlands to Cape Town. It is an interesting journey with many pleasant diversions.

Passing on the left, the administrative office of Gilbeys, the road rises over the railway line and the bustling, if rather humbly named *Plankenbrug* (Plank Bridge) River, one of the principal tributaries of the Eerste River. Just over the Adam Tas bridge (as it is named) on the right-hand (north) side of the road, there is a small monument marking the site of a borrow pit (an excavation where gravel was extracted or 'borrowed' for the making of the road). In this excavation in 1899, Louis Péringuey, a French entomologist and archaeologist who became Director of the South African Museum in Cape Town, discovered stone implements proving the great antiquity of human beings in Southern Africa. The implements are of the type known as the Stellenbosch Culture.

Past the monument to the Stellenbosch Culture, the R310 road swings more southerly and passes on the left the cellars of the Stellenbosch Farmers' Winery with, on the right, a view over the vineyards to the charming old residence of *Mon Repos* and the handsome cluster of buildings of the Oude Libertas Centre. The roses flowering at the end of each row of vines are not simply decorative. Traditionally wine and roses go together, with rose-bushes providing, like the canaries to coal-miners, an early warning of the threat of some harmful condition.

Half a kilometre from the monument a road turns off right which leads to the Oude Libertas Centre, thence to a crossroads with a right turn leading beneath the trees to the Oude Molen Centre of Gilbeys. Ahead through the suburb of *Onder Papegaaiberg* (under the parrot mountain), the road terminates at the farmyard and cellar of the wine estate of *Middelvlei* (middle marsh), the home of J H Momberg and his family, producer of subtly flavoured wines (notably a pinotage). All are worth sampling. The estate is open to the public for tastings and purchases during normal business hours. Picnic lunches can be booked December to March. Phone (021) 883-2565. The rose garden is notable. Exotic pet goats and ancient tortoises wander at will while cows graze on the lush pasturage next to a dam with a calm surface full of reflections. There are fine walks through the trees to the summit of the Papegaaiberg from the highest portions of the streets on the right-hand (east) side of the suburb of Onder Papegaaiberg. From the summit the views of Stellenbosch and its mountains are superb.

Half a kilometre further along the R310 road from the turn-off to *Middelvlei*, there is another turn on the right-hand side which leads up the Devon Valley to the sparkling wine cellars of Distillers.

Four kilometres up the Devon Valley road there is a turn-off left leading to two wine estates. One of these is *Clos Malverne* (small Malvern), named after the hill in Britain known as Great Malvern. This is claimed to be the smallest vineyard on the Wine Route but the 9 ha under cultivation by the proprietor, Seymour Pritchard, allows his winemaker, Guy Webber, to produce high-quality wines which are sold during normal business hours. The Auret and Devonet blends of Cabernet Sauvignon and Merlot are especially worth tasting.

Close to *Clos Malverne* is the estate of *Louisvale*, owned by Hans Froehling and Leon Stemmet, with Marinus Bredell as winemaker. The estate is a portion of the old farm of *Nooitgedacht* which a previous owner divided into two sections named *Marydale* and *Louisvale* after two of his children. The present owners acquired the property in 1988. They are men with three principal loves in their lives. Chardonnay wine, the performing arts (especially ballet) and dogs. They produce on their estate an impeccable Chardonnay and its lighter version, Chavant. They breed the perky miniature Schnauzer dogs and also show an extraordinary Great Dane known as the Harlequin. The estate is open to visitors during normal business hours.

At 4,5 km from the start of the Devon Valley road there is a turn-off leading to *Protea Heights*, the private wild flower farm founded by Frank and Ivy Batchelor. This farm, which is not open to the public except by special arrangement, was the pioneer of wild flower cultivation in the Cape.

In 1920 Frank Batchelor, then a 21-year-old bookkeeper purchased on very easy terms from two uncles a 46 ha piece of their farm *Craighall*. This section of the farm he named *The Firs*, and there he made a living growing strawberries and gladioli. The venture was a success but at the same time he became aware of an unfortunate sequence of events. The Devon Valley had always been a paradise for wild flowers. The rare *Gladiolus blandus* (painted ladies) had the valley as their natural home, while proteas, ericas and pincushions provided such dazzling displays that the spectacle was almost fatal to themselves. Vandals descended on the flowers with a frightening determination to destroy them utterly by means of shovels and hand-picking. The spread of cultivation in the valley and the building of roads threatened the flowers with complete destruction. The dismal sight of all this change gave Frank Batchelor the idea of conserving the last of the valley's wild flowers by propagating them in a sanctuary of his own where visitors could see, but not harm them. With this object, in 1944 he bought 24 ha of the farm *Nooitgedacht*, and on this he laid out what became *Protea Heights*, a vast garden designed to look as the Western Cape could have looked if all its scattered flower varieties had ever grown together in one place. On this farm of flowers Frank Batchelor and his wife pioneered the development of South Africa's commercial protea industry. The theory was that if wild flowers were cultivated, their preservation would be assured. In 1948 the Batchelors harvested their first crop of proteas and these had a sensational reception at the Transvaal Horticultural Society's Spring Show. It was generally agreed that if proteas could be cultivated on a large scale, they would have a tremendous impact on the floral trade all over the world.

In 1953 *Protea Heights* was first open to the public, and from then on it became one of the major botanical attractions of the Cape each spring. An enormous number of proteas of many varieties flourish in the sanctuary. The *Leucospermum* species (pincushions) grow there to perfection while many of the wonderful *Serruria* genera have made the place their home. Amongst them is *Serruria florida*, the delicate blushing bride flowers whose original home was in so restricted a part of the Franschhoek Mountains that only careful cultivation in gardens such as *Protea Heights* has saved them from extinction. Even with this cultivation, the seed of the blushing bride reached a marketable value of over R1 000 for 1 kg and it remains a rare treasure. On *Protea Heights* it not only grows in profusion but, in 1947, with *Serruria aemula*, produced a red-tinted hybrid which Mrs Batchelor named the Maid of Honour.

The Batchelors were particularly interested in selective breeding, hybridisation and vegetative propagation of superior clones. Their achievements in this field were such that in 1971 the South African Wild Flower Growers' Association honoured the pioneers by establishing the annual Batchelor Prize for the best hybrid protea produced for the cut-flower industry.

Frank Batchelor willed *Protea Heights* to the South African Nature Foundation. On his death in 1977 his work in experimentation was continued, supported by the research and facilities of the Department of Horticulture of the University of Stellenbosch. *'Plant, and not just pluck'* was the dream of Frank Batchelor, with cultivation ensuring conservation. *Protea Heights* is a superb example of sustainable utilisation where conservation is not simply preservation but a harmony of man and nature, proving the profitability of wild flowers and thus ensuring their preservation.

Just beyond the turn-off to Protea Heights, the tarmac road leading up the valley reaches the turn-off to the Devon Valley Hotel, beautifully situated with a hillside garden looking out on a handsome view of mountains and valley. The wine list of this three-star hotel is fascinating to read and quite a piece of literature. All the wines of the Devon Valley are there including those made from the hotel's own vineyards as well as intriguing rarities, classics and exquisite drinks from far away cellars with poetic names.

The menu is Cape regional cuisine, based on the freshest home-grown vegetables, piquant farm cheeses, fruit from the hotel's own orchards.

After lunch or dinner savour one of the 50 different malt whiskeys, taste the liqueurs, enjoy a fine cigar. The setting is ideal for romance and friendship. The atmosphere is the result of countless happy hours filled with the pleasures of life in this most delectable valley.

Be sure to say hello to the 30 hotel cats, some of whom will always be found sprawled in the sunshine in front of the hotel. There are cats in every shape and size, ginger cats, Persian cats, Siamese cats, Turkish Angoras and even nondescript tabbies. They have one thing in common. They are all epicure fat cats, true gourmet. They know where the good things come from. They live high from the subtle aroma and luscious scraps of the hotel kitchen, only the very best for them. David Nathan-Maister is the man who runs this delightful hotel. He is justly proud of it.

P O Box 68, Stellenbosch, 7599. Phone (021) 882-2012. Fax (021) 882-2610.

Five hundred metres beyond the turn-off to the Devon Valley Hotel takes the road to the house of J C le Roux. In 1997 Distillers Corporation acquired this beautiful estate from Gilbeys. The buildings on the estate were transformed into facilities for the making of sparkling wines in the J C le Roux range and also a Cap Classique sparkling wine named in honour of the Hungarian viticulturist, Desiderius Pongracz.

The magnificent state-of-the-art cellars are capable of producing six million bottles of sparkling wine a year with ample room for expansion. Visitors are welcome for tastings and sales during normal business hours. There are guided tours with the whole process of making sparkling wine revealed from an overhead ramp which visitors can follow on their own with information boards to explain what they are seeing. Disabled people have full access to this ramp. For information or tour bookings, phone (021) 882-2590.

The whole estate has been superbly developed. The cellars stand in a veritable sea of vines covering the upper end of the Devon Valley. Looking over the valley from the summit of the high hill on the western side is the Devon Hill Cellar built there by a Swiss concern to produce wine for several Devon Valley vineyards. The view from the cellar is quite breathtaking.

The private road across the estate continues through a grove of olive trees. At the end of this grove, the road climbs up the hill slope, revealing a fine panorama of vineyards and mountains. A gate blocks further usage of the main Devon Valley road. Beyond this gate the road, now private, continues until, over the summit, 9 km from the start of the journey, the road joins the tarmac Bottelary road from Stellenbosch.

Just beyond the Devon Valley turn-off, R310 road to Cape Town and its airport passes on the left, 2 km from Stellenbosch, the buildings of the Plant Protection Research Institute. Just beyond, there is a turn on the right-hand side leading to the wine estate of *Verdun*, owned by J F and Kosie Roux. A charming homestead stands in a notable garden. A cellar produces a range of red and white wines which are sold to visitors during normal trading hours, but not on Sundays and some public holidays. Phone (021) 886-5884.

At 3 km from Stellenbosch the R310 road veers more southwards and from it at this point, M12, known as the *Polkadraai* (polka turn) road, leads westwards with the sweeping bends which give it the name of the popular old dance. The R310 continues its way down the shallow valley of the Eerste River. On the left-hand side lies the estate of *Vredenheim* (peaceful home), graced with a fine old manor-house and well-watered pastures for a variety of livestock. Elzabé Bezuidenhout, the winemaker, is a very busy lady creating a range of wines which are sold during normal business hours. Tours, luncheons and even accommodation are available by arrangement. There is a function room for hire and a garden setting, very suitable for weddings or parties. Cape kitchen products and gifts are obtainable in the tasting-room.

The road continues its pleasant way and reaches, 5 km from Stellenbosch, the small railway centre of Vlottenburg. Opposite the station, on the right hand side of the road, stand the cellars of the Vlottenburg co-operative where 12 000 tons of grapes from its members are pressed each year and 10 million litres of wine and grape juice are produced. Included in the range of wines are two rarities, a light-red Gamay Noir and a sweet red Muscat de Hambourg. Kowie du Toit is the winemaker and his products are sold during normal business hours.

The farm *Vlottenburg* was granted in 1687 to two French Huguenots, Pierre Rochefort and Gerrit Hanseret. In 1709 it was sold to Antonie Vlotman. It was from him that the name Vlottenburg originated. In 1772 Paul Roux bought the farm and it remains the possession of his descendants.

A second co-operative wine cellar, the Eersterivier, is reached by a road branching off to the right just before R310 rises over the railway line. With Manie Rossouw as its winemaker, this cellar is a notable producer of a considerable range of wines, including an award-winning Sauvignon

Blanc, and such delights as a Hanseret Claret, a Port-type, an excellent Pinotage, Jerepigo and sparkling wine.

Across the railway a road branches off to the left and after a short drive reaches an interesting architectural landmark of the Stellenbosch Wine Route, the Van Ryn Brandy Cellar. This attractive and unusual building to find in South Africa was built in 1904 by a gentleman named Boon. It was designed like a French chateau. The thick walls are made of large rounded river stones. The building is a bluish-grey in colour, with white borders around windows, doors and the pillars of the fence. Altogether it makes and imposing and distinctive novelty in the setting of the white-walled farmhouses of the Cape.

The building was erected to be the home of what was at first known as the Lion Distillery. The founder was Johannes Henoch Marais, who had made a fortune on the Kimberley diamond fields. Returning to the family farm of *Coetzenberg*, at Stellenbosch, he was responsible for several worthy projects and generous endowments, notably towards the founding of the university where his statue stands today in the Central Square.

On the diamond fields Johannes Marais had observed the thirst of the diggers in that dusty atmosphere, and the poor quality of the liquor being sold to them. In the Cape he also observed the depression in the wine industry. He benefited diamond diggers and farmers alike by founding his distillery.

Inside the building were installed cognac stills and a French two-column spirit still. A co-operative organisation was formed with the farmers who provided the grape juice for distillation. Excellent brandy was produced and the distillery flourished, bringing prosperity to the farmers and, no doubt, considerable jollity to the diamond diggers.

On the death of Johannes Marais in 1915, the distillery became part of the Van Ryn Wine and Brandy Company. It is a fascinating place to visit with the giant copper pot stills, the great barrels of brandy secluded for maturation in the dark cellars where, according to legend, the angels take their sip in the form of a predictable loss of liquid from every barrel.

Tours of the cellar take place Mondays to Fridays at 10h00, 11h30 and 15h00, Saturdays 10h00 and 11h30. The cellar is closed on Sundays and Good Friday, Christmas and New Year's Day. Brandy courses and advanced brandy courses are held periodically. There are evenings of music, lectures on brandy and hints for the kitchen. Phone (021) 881-3875.

One of the most beautiful of all the wine estates of the Eerste River valley is *Spier*. The manor-house and original farmyard building stand in a superb garden on the banks of the river, just left of the road shortly after it passes the turn to the brandy cellar. Handsome trees shade pleasant walks and there are many interesting architectural features including the slave bell, notable for its form.

Spier was originally granted on 17 September 1692 to Arnout Tamboer Jansz, a German mercenary soldier who had seen service with the Dutch East India Company. The Eerste River traversed the property in its southerly flow to the sea in False Bay. Jansz built a simple cottage on the east side of the river and commenced a successful farming industry in the production of wine, wheat and livestock. The first wagon road from Stellenbosch to Cape Town was on the west side of the river, with a railway line later built close to the road. Communications were therefore easy, the river was generous with its water, and the soil was sandy and deep, very suitable for the cultivation of such crops as grapes, strawberries, vegetables and fruit.

It is not known by what name Jansz called his farm but by the time he died in 1706 it was flourishing. His son inherited the place but, in 1712, sold it to Hanz Hendrik Harttingh who also came from Germany. He named the estate after his home town, a port on the Rhine, built where a tributary joined the great river. This tributary was named *Speyer* (from its reeds) but also known through the centuries in different spelling and languages, such as Speier, Spier and Speiere.

Several other owners succeeded one another as masters of *Spier*. In 1965 Neil Joubert acquired the estate. The farmyard by then was graced with its manor-house, *Jonkershuis*, cellars, including the oldest (dated 1767) wine cellar in South Africa, stables and other structures. Together they formed a classic cluster of Cape-Dutch style buildings sheltered on the west bank of the river in a rambling old-world garden shaded by some superb trees. Neil converted the slave lodge into a well-liked restaurant with a second restaurant in the original *Jonkershuis* (bachelor's quarters). Both restaurants had champagne breakfasts on Saturdays and featured the *Spier* wines, a tasty Edelsteen, Bukettraube, Special Late Harvest, a Port wine and a sweet natural wine.

On the death of Neil Joubert, Spier was sold in 1993 to Dick Enthoven whose family business is the Hollard Insurance Company. With the support of his wife, Angie, and the company, Dick set out to restore completely the whole historic complex of farmyard buildings and make of the now 600 ha estate and a resort for all, with picnics, wine tasting, conferencing and a celebration of the Cape's art, music, wines and fine foods. There are three restaurants: the Jonkershuis serves a Dutch East Indian buffet with superb desserts. The Cafe Spier features a Mediterranean menu and the Taphuis provides the meats and seafoods traditional to Southern Africa.

In the summer season, symphony concerts, opera and other musical entertainment are staged in a superb 1 100-seater amphitheatre. Exhibitions, conventions and a great variety of 'happenings' are presented all through the year. A comprehensive collection of the wines of Southern Africa (especially of the Stellenbosch wine route) are stored and sold in a spacious cellar. There is a gift shop, full of novelties, a veritable prince of farm stalls selling vegetables and fruit grown on the Estate, delicatessens, farm baked bread, jams, preserves, cold meats and all sorts of drinks to take home or carry out for picnics on the lawn, next to a delightful lake where ducks live in a happy paradise. *Spier* has become a sanctuary for birds, flowers and the rich heritage of nature in the valley of the Eerste River.

The perfectly restored manor-house is rich in its art, antiquities and furniture of the times of the Dutch East India Company. There is an Equestrian Centre housing horses and ponies which can be hired for horse-and-cart or pony rides, and a Children's Play Centre where toddlers can enjoy themselves under the watchful eye of a nanny. A brand new state-of-the-art cellar is now producing wine of superlative standard from the vineyards of the estate and there are plans for a hotel and golf-course on the south-eastern side of the Eerste River, which Dick Enthoven is clearing to once again become a home for trout and other lifeforms of pollution-free water.

Beyond *Spier* the main road continues down the river valley passing, at Lynedoch station, a hotel, farm stall and holiday cottages. The Annandale road branches off from this point crossing the Eerste River and continuing eastwards for 5 km through vineyards, passing the *Limberlost* farm of M Zetler, where strawberries and other fresh produce are sold in season, and then joins the main Stellenbosch–Somerset West road.

The main road R310 continues past the turn-off and down the fertile and pleasant valley. On the eastern side of the road lies the co-operative wine cellar of *Welmoed*. This cellar produces a large range of wines each year from over 10 000 metric tons of grapes originating from many farms as far afield as Stellenbosch and Constantia. Red, white, sweet and dry wines are all produced, and some excellent sparkling wines and grape juices. Wine is sold during normal business hours. Lunch is served at the cellar throughout the year, and this or a picnic beside the lake provides a pleasant opportunity to sample the wines. The winemaker is Nicky Versveld. *Welmoed* (good courage) was the name of a farm granted on 6 October 1690 to Henning Huising.

Beyond the cellars the road passes the magnificent farm of *Meerlust* (sea longing), owned by the Myburgh family. A tantalising glimpse of the homestead roof may just be seen nestling in its sheltered situation close to the river. The homestead is dated 1776 and is said to be haunted by the wistful ghost of a young woman, occasionally seen arranging cut flowers in the early mornings or standing at an upstairs window looking longingly at the sea, faintly visible in the distance.

The pigeon loft and manor-house of *Meerlust* are national monuments. *Meerlust* was granted on 13 June 1693 to the same Henning Huising who owned *Welmoed*. The two farms together made quite an estate. The dam on the farm attracts a considerable number and variety of waterbirds at all seasons. In the centre of the dam there is a windpump. It is said that, when the dam was made, this pump was started to provide the water to supply the artificial lake. Mr Myburgh went away on holiday and forgot to turn off the windpump. Like the famous broom of the sorcerer's apprentice, the pump simply went on and on pumping. It filled the lake and half drowned itself. Its controls are deep under water and nobody has so far been able to stop it from pumping. But why should they? It enjoys pumping. Visits to the farm may be made by appointment only. Phone (024) 843-3587. *Meerlust* specialises in red wines. Rubicon (a blend of Cabernet Sauvignon, Merlot and Cabernet Franc) is of superlative quality. The Merlot and Pinot Noir are also excellent.

Beyond *Meerlust* the R310 road bridges over the railway and R102 road leading to Somerset West. The Stellenbosch Wine Route does not continue further southwards. A turn right northwestwards up the R102 road would take the traveller for 12 km to join the Polkadraai road and a return to Stellenbosch.

THE POLKADRAAI ROAD (M12)

Just after this road has its start, branching off from R310 at 3 km from Stellenbosch, the traveller sees on the right-hand side of the road a tall single-jet fountain and a line of flagpoles. This is the impressive entrance to the estate of *Neethlingshof* (Neethlings garden) with the road into it leading through a magnificent avenue of stone pines (*Pinus pinea*). This avenue has become the emblem of the estate, featured on the labels of its wines. Planted at the time of World War I, the trees are said to be descendants of trees introduced by Cecil Rhodes to South Africa from Italy. In their Mediterranean home these trees form many noble avenues, beautifully described in music by Ottorino Resphighi in his symphonic poem *The Pines of Rome*. The *Neethlingshof* stone pines are the admiration of visitors and a delight to birds, squirrels and children who eat what are called the *dennepitte* (pine seeds) of the *dennebol* (pine-cone).

The avenue of *Neethlingshof*, with oak trees on the upper end, is 1 km long and then terminates at the manor-house (now a restaurant), cellars, and administrative buildings of the estate. Originally known as *De Wolwedans* (the dance of the wolves), this 273 ha estate was first cultivated in 1692 by a German, Barend Lubbe. In 1788 Charl Marais acquired the estate. He built the manor-house in 1814 in traditional Cape-Dutch style 'H' formation. After his death, his widow continued farming with the aid of her sons, Petrus (the elder) and Cornelius. Her daughter, Anna, in 1822, married Johannes Henoch Neethling, the owner of *Coetzenberg* farm at Stellenbosch, originally granted in 1693 to Dirk Coetzee.

In 1844 Neethling exchanged *Coetzenberg* farm with Petrus Marais for *De Wolwedans* and the name was changed to *Neethlingshof*. The head of the Neethling family in the Cape at that time was the father of Johannes, also named Johannes Henoch Neethling. He was a distinguished judge and the first born and trained South African advocate-at-law with a doctorate degree. After the death of Johannes Neethling in 1870, the estate passed to his daughter Jeanne, who had married Jakobus Louw. It remained in the possession of the Louw family until 1963 when Jannie Momberg purchased it.

In 1985 Jannie Momberg sold *Neethlingshof* to a German banker, Hans Joachim Schreiber, who resided in Singapore. He had visited South Africa on banking business, liked the Cape and had already purchased two estates there, the *Alphen* wine farm on the slopes of the mountain known as the *Helderberg* (clear mountain), bought in 1981 and renamed *Stellenzicht* because of its views of Stellenbosch, and in 1984 the *Klein Welmoed* vegetable farm in the valley of the Eerste River. The farms all experienced a spectacular transformation. The two wine estates had been only partly developed by their former owners. They both had a markedly different variety of microclimates, soils and altitudes. They presented an unparalleled opportunity for development into major producers of premium wine and the new owner had the vision, finance and courage which the estate needed.

The immediate task was to plan, and to find the right men to effect the transformation of two agricultural Cinderellas into princesses of the wine industry. A considerable industry began in replanting the vineyards with cultivars carefully selected for each of the micro-ecological areas with its own climate, soils, exposure to wind and altitude. The cellars were extensively rebuilt and equipped with state-of-the-art technology. Altogether, it was a superb application of applied science, human empathy with the possibilities of each area, testing and careful planning. Today *Neethlingshof* grows twelve different grape varieties, 55% white and 45% red on 165 of the estate's 273 ha.

While this was going on in the vineyards, the manor-house of *Neethlingshof* was converted into a restaurant. Five separate rooms in the manor-house now each have their special atmosphere. The main dining-room is known as the B C Square. It has a magnificent tapestry dated from 1750. Next to the Lord Neethling is the Palm Terrace where informal meals are served.

All of the wines of *Neethlingshof* and *Stellenzicht* are sold at *Neethlingshof*. The pride of the cellar is the *Neethlingshof* Weisser Riesling Noble Late Harvest, a champion in its class for eight consecutive years. One block of vines on *Neethlingshof* is used to produce this delectable wine. It is the most treasured part of the whole vast estate. In 1997 this wine won the international trophy of the German Wine Institute for the finest botrytis wine in the world. In the Veritas 1998 bottled wine competition, with 1 242 entries, *Neethlingshof* won 18 awards from 18 entries. *Stellenzicht* won a double gold for its Merlot/Cabernet Franc 1995. Four golds, 4 silvers and 1 bronze were also won. Syrah is the special pride of *Stellenzicht*. It is produced from Shiraz grapes. There is one very special block of these vines on *Stellenzicht* which yields grapes of the superlative quality essential for the making of this wine.

In 1996 Hans-Joachim Schreiber added more farms to his family of wine producers. *Hillandale* was planted with vines to supplement the *Stellenzicht* cellar and *Olives* was planted with vines to supplement *Neethlingshof*.

Wine-tasting and cellar tours are available at *Neethlingshof*. From the beginning of November until the end of April each year there are comprehensive tours of the estate on a tractor-drawn trailer. This tour includes a cellar tour and a private wine-tasting in an open-air venue named *iLanga* (the sun) and a barbecue lunch. The views are magnificent. For bookings phone (021) 883-8988.

Wines are sold from the *Neethlingshof* cellar weekdays from 09h00 to 19h00 (09h00 to 17h00 in winter); Saturdays and Sundays 10h00 to 18h00 (10h00 to 16h00 in winter). The superb frieze on the walls of the tasting room was created by The Painted House.

Schalk van der Westhuizen is the winemaker of *Neethlingshof*.

Less than one kilometre further along the Polkadraai M12 road from the entrance to *Neethlingshof*, there is a turn-off right at the shop and post office of Vlottenburg. This provides a most agreeable entrance and diverting drive into the vine-covered foothills of the *Bottelaryberg*, a ridge of hills lying east to west, fertile, beautiful, richly coloured and with the convivial name (mountain of bottling), suggestive of a pantry or buttery where many good things are produced to eat and drink. A little over half a kilometre from the start of this road it passes the entrance to the wine estate and cellar of *Overgaauw* owned by Braam van Velden, a third-generation descendant of Elizabeth Overgaauw who gave the place her name. With a fine modern cellar supplied with grapes from 130 ha of well-tended vineyard, the estate produces a range of wines, including some worthwhile novelties such as, in the whites the only Sylvaner in South Africa, a fine Cabernet Sauvignon, a blended Tria Corda in the reds, and a vintage port. Sales from the cellar are during normal business hours. Closed on Sunday.

For another all-too-short 2 km this rural road leads along the foothills past farms such as *Bonfoi* (good faith). Wild flowers bloom in a linear garden on either side of the road and the journey is altogether pleasant. Then there is a parting of the ways. Ahead stands the manor-house and cellar of the estate known as *Uiterwyk* (outer ward). Danie de Waal is the owner of this estate. His homestead was built in 1791. Through nine generations of ownership by the De Waals, the estate has known no change save in the techniques of the cellar and the cultivation of grapes which have kept apace with the times. Interesting wines to discover here include the only Muller-Thurgau produced in South Africa and Kromhout. There is a range of Chardonnays, Sauvignon Blanc, Merlot, Pinotage and the classic Cabernet Sauvignon. Wines are sold from the cellar during normal business hours. Closed on Sundays. Phone (021) 881-3711.

At the parting of the road, just less than one kilometre from *Uiterwyk*, the left-hand branch continues its rural way for 2,5 km and then reaches the unusual-looking cellar of the Jordan Winery. A pretty lake lies in front of this cellar and visitors are greeted by a flock of inquisitive geese who scrutinise all arrivals for approval, after considerable comment.

The Jordan Winery came into being in 1982 when Ted and Sheelagh Jordan purchased the 134 ha property with its handsome spread of hillside vineyards. It was an old farm but the new owners commenced a careful plan of replanting with modern virus-free high-quality vines. By the time the vines were ready to bear, a new generation of Jordans, Gary and Kathy, had taken over and, in the state-of-the-art gravity-flow cellar, commenced the creation of red and white wines of superlative quality. Sauvignon Blanc, Chardonnay and Rhine Riesling are the whites, with an interesting blend called Chameleon. The reds are Cabernet Sauvignon and Merlot, again with a blend called Chameleon. There are tastings and cellar sales of wine during normal business hours. Closed on Sundays.

Back on the Polkadraai M12 main road 6 km from the turn-off at Vlottenburg to the three wineries just described, the road passes the Polkadraai Farm Stall at the Vlaeberg road turn-off. This farm stall, run by the Zetler family, is noted for its early summer strawberries, which the customers can pick themselves if they so desire. At 3.5 km beyond the stall there is a turn-off on the right-hand side of the road leading for a half a kilometre to the manor-house, cellar and The Guinea Fowl Restaurant of the estate of *Saxenburg*, one of the most prestigious wine producers of the Stellenbosch Wine Route.

Saxenburg had its start in 1693 when Simon van der Stel granted the land to a free burgher, Jochem Sax. He built the manor-house in 1701 and gave the estate his name. Four years later the farm became the property of the brothers Olof and Albertus Bergh, two Swedish mercenary soldiers and explorers, retired from service with the Dutch East India Company. Olof Bergh, who retired as a captain, bought *Groot Constantia* when it was auctioned after the death of Simon van der Stel in 1712. He lived on that historic estate until his death in 1723.

A succession of owners followed in possession of *Saxenburg*. In 1989 it was eventually bought by a Swiss businessman, Adrian Buhrer, who, with his wife Birgit, commenced an ambitious programme of rehabilitating the estate and developing it into a showpiece of the Stellenbosch Wine Route. Nico van der Merwe as winemaker and the Buhrers' good taste and business acumen, the result is quite a story of success. It is immaculately managed, very beautiful to see and the home of a lively population of the guinea fowls who provide *Saxenburg* with the emblem for its Guinea Fowl range of estate wines while another *Saxenburg* range, *Les Deux Mers* (the two oceans), consists of blended wines. An elegant tasting-room provides an opportunity to sample and purchase these wines during normal business hours. (Sundays in season). The Guinea Fowl Restaurant is open for lunch daily, closed on Tuesdays, and open for dinner Wednesdays to Saturdays. Phone (021) 906 5232 to book.

The last wine estate to be reached from the Polkadraai road, *Zevenwacht*, has a turn-off just beyond the entrance to *Saxenburg*. This is an estate road 4 km long, gravel but in good condition. The turn-off to the road is only 1,5 km before the Polkadraai road ends by joining the Kuils River–Somerset West road. The town of Kuilsrivier, 1,5 km from the junction, has the benefit to caravanners of an 86 site three-star caravan park as a base for exploring the Stellenbosch Wine Route. The town has a population of 36 000. Its convenient presence is a reminder of Simon van der Stel camping in the vicinity on the banks of the Kuils River during his pioneer exploration of the area. There is a line of shops in the town on either side of the main road and, 3 km from the Polkadraai road, another turn-off right leading for 3 km to *Zevenwacht*. So you have a choice.

Zevenwacht consists of several things. First of all, *Zevenwacht* is really two estates. One is *Langverwacht* (long awaited), first granted on 8 July 1721 to Jean de Normandie le Roux. The second is *Zevenfontein* (seven fountains), granted in 1793 to Daniel Bosman. The farms had an indifferent record until 1979 when Gilbert Colyn, a Cape Town architect, acquired them with an interest in wine production.

The two farms of *Zevenfontein* and *Langverwacht* were combined. Their names were blended to make *Zevenwacht*, an estate of 353 ha. With much energy, Gilbert Colyn set out to invigorate a farming area of great potential in hill slopes, valleys, altitudes, soils and climates. The Sleeping Princess needed a lot of awakening but the ultimate results were dazzling.

A vast replanting of wine-grape cultivars took place and a modern cellar was built in front of the manor-house of *Zevenfontein*. A restaurant was opened in the manor-house and named Zevenwacht Pride. Fun places for children, barbecue sites for outdoor feasting, a retirement village, accommodation for groups of up to 30 people in the Look-Out on the summit of the Ribbokrant, trips through the vineyards in a tractor-drawn surrey, walks, horse-riding, and the pleasure of exploring a wild flower, fynbos and wildlife sanctuary conserving a substantial part of the area in its original state: all these are part of *Zevenwacht*. To manage development, a public company was organised with 2 000 shareholders now enjoying a proprietary interest in unique wineland development. Harold Johnson is the major shareholder and became the managing director of the estate in 1992. Zevenwacht Wine Cellars have been opened in Johannesburg and Durban with the products of the estate available for tasting and purchase.

THE BOTTELARY ROAD

The Bottelary road M23 runs east to west along the north side of the Bottelaryberg. From Zevenwacht estate and the town of Kuilsrivier on the western end of the fertile range of hills, let us find our way back to Stellenbosch along this route and complete a fine circular drive around the whole of the Bottelary range of hills.

One kilometre up the road leading from Kuilsrivier town to *Zevenwacht* estate, there is an intersection with the Amandel road. Turn left along this road. After 3 km the road leads into the Bottelary road just west of the Kuilsrivier golf-course. From there onward the road leads straight through fertile agricultural lands with the foothills of the Bottelaryberg on the right-hand side.

After 2,5 km the road reaches a turn-off left at the entrance to the estate known as *Hazendal*, after a man with the curious name of Christoffel Hazenwinkel to whom it was granted on 26 September 1704 by the Governor, Willem Adriaan, son of the illustrious Simon van der Stel. The manor-house was built in 1790 and is now a national monument and museum. A modern wine cellar complements the original building and allows for underground bottle fermentation. The whole farmyard is interesting with the original slave quarters, corrals, stables, workshops and other outbuildings still well preserved.

Hazendal was the possession of the Bosman family from 1830 and at least one of their wines, a Special Late Harvest, Hazendal Freudenlese, became especially notable. In 1994 the estate was bought by Mark Voloshin from Russia. The new owner commenced a considerable programme of restoration of the estate to its historic importance, with a restaurant serving Cape Classic Cuisine and a replanting of vines to provide a new cellar with the makings of a range of superior wines, including a Cap Classique bottle-fermented sparkling wine. Alongside the cellar is the small Marvol Museum with exhibits of Fabergé artefacts and an art gallery featuring Russian artists. Videos and films showcasing Russian arts and culture are shown regularly

Three kilometres beyond *Hazendal* along M23 lies the estate of *Koopmanskloof* (merchant's ravine) where, apart from wine and brandy distilled in copper stills and aged in Limousin barrels, Manzanilla and Calamata olives are grown and prepared for market on the estate. Stevie Smit, owner of the estate, makes Port-type wines in the traditional Portuguese way.

Four kilometres further along the road stands the cellar of the Bottelary winery, a co-operative with 40 producing farmers as members. The range of wines may be tasted and bought during normal business hours. A pleasant feature of harvest time each year is the opportunity given to visitors to join in the picking and pressing of grapes. Apart from the wines, the white and red grape juice is delicious. The original Bottelary (place of bottling) farm was granted on 18 October 1701 to J Rotterdam and M Liffering.

Continuing eastwards for another 2,5 km, the road reaches a turn-off right leading to the handsomely situated estate named *Het Hartenberg* (the heart of the mountain) by its first owners. This estate originated in 1692 when two bachelors, Coenraad Boom and Christoffel L'Estreux (or Esterhuizen), arrived in the Cape. They were granted permission to farm 60 morgen of land in the hills. They named the estate, cleared the land, planted 2 000 vines as well as wheat, and ran sheep and oxen. In 1704 L'Estreux became sole proprietor with a grant from the Governor, Willem Adriaan van der Stel. The conditions were that he farmed properly, replaced all trees that he used for wood, and gave one-tenth of his annual grain crop to the Dutch East India Company.

A succession of other owners followed L'Estreux. The homestead was built in 1849, and in the later years the name was changed to *Montagne*, but for various reasons the estate never fulfilled anything like its true potential. Lying in its setting in the high hills of the Bottelaryberg, the estate contains in its 172 ha a variety of soils, mainly decomposed granite and Malmesbury shale, and a range of altitudes and associated micro-climates which provide a winemaker with subtle challenges. In the hands of a succession of owners the estate often seemed on the verge of achieving its destiny as a premier producer of superior wines but was always handicapped by some problem.

In 1948 *Hartenberg* was bought by Dr Maurice Finlayson and his wife. Their sons, Walter and Peter, were winemakers. They realised the possibilities of the estate and in the 1960s planted new cultivars and modernised the cellar, but something was still lacking. Then in 1986 the estate was purchased by Windham Limited of Bermuda, run by Ken Mackenzie and his daughters, Fiona and Tanya. The original name of the estate was restored and *Hartenberg* was completely relieved of the last restraints on the fulfilment of its destiny.

Ken Mackenzie is a very remarkable man. Born in Pearston in the Eastern Cape in 1922, he had no more distinguished a scholastic background than failing matric after three years at the prestigious Michaelhouse. In later years he was destined to become a great benefactor of the school, and Mackenzie House is named after him.

Then Ken was caught up in World War II as a fighter pilot in the South African air force. With the war over, he was employed by an Australian, Noel Hunt, who was setting up a branch of his textile machinery supply company in South Africa. This was the launch into the commercial world of a young man who started his own business in the late 1950s with his wife Megan, one typewriter and the incalculable assets of courage, common sense and enterprise. Together they founded the multi-million rand enterprise of Kaymac.

Hartenberg is open to visitors in normal business hours with tastings and sales of wine from Monday to Saturday. The garden around the cellar is superb and a vintner's lunch is served outside during summer months and in the tasting-room during winter. The amiable catering manager, Sonette Rabie, has a genius for these luncheons. The estate wines include, apart from all the old favourites, a piquantly flavoured Special Late Harvest named *L'Estreux* after the pioneer owner, and *Zinfandel*, a light-bodied red. Neither should be missed. A rarity is *Pontac*, a curiously flavoured dark red wine derived from the only grape with juices red as its skin. It was the source of the famed red Constantia wine of former years.

The underground cellar is especially notable. It is romantic in its atmosphere and ornamented with superb stained glass by Karel Hans Wilhelm.

The Bottelary road M23 continues eastwards from the entrance to *Hartenberg*. After 1 km it passes the Devonvale golf-course at the turn which eventually leads, on a private road, to the Devon Valley. Another kilometre brings the road to a crossroads with R304. A turn left would pass the *Klawervlei* (clover marsh) wine estate, the quaintly named Antique Tractor where Murray and Kelly Tonathy preside over a charming guest-house, and then leaves the Stellenbosch Wine Route after 4 km, continuing to the Paarl Wine Route and reaching the N1 road after another 2,5 km.

A turn to the right at the crossroads would take the traveller into Stellenbosch after 6,5 km of travelling along the eastern slopes of the Papegaaiberg, passing several wine and fruit farms and pleasant places of accommodation. Directly across the crossroads, the road to the east takes on the name of the *Kromme Rhee* (crooked streamlet) road, crosses the railway line at the small rural centre of *Koelenhof* (garden of refreshment), built on the farm originally granted on 21 November 1694 to Simon de Groot but now owned by Attie Joubert. Half a kilometre further on, the road reaches the entrance to the wine and fruit-producing estate of *Simonsig*.

This productive estate had its beginning in 1953 when Frans Malan acquired the farm *De Hoop* from his father-in-law. He started to produce wine there. Production expanded. In 1964 he bought *Simonsig* and combined the two farms into one estate with the overall name of *Simonsig* (from the view of the Simonsberg). From the beginning Frans Malan practised innovation in cultivation and production and when he retired in 1982 he handed to his sons, Pieter, Francois and Johan, a legacy of agricultural skills.

A third farm, *Morgenster* (morning star), was added to the estate. Today *Simonsig* comprises 270 ha planted with nearly one million vines of about eighteen different varieties, and extensive orchards of peaches, plums and pears. The quality of production is high and visitors are welcome to see and taste for themselves. The wines of the estate can be purchased throughout the year during normal business hours. There are guided cellar tours at 10h00 and 15h00 on weekdays and 10h00 on Saturdays. Interesting to see is the making of sparkling wine using the Cape Classique method. This sparkling wine, known as Kaapse Vonkel, was the first to be made in South Africa. Most of the classic wine favourites are also produced on the estate. There is a pleasant playground to divert children while their elders are more seriously occupied in the tasting-room and cellar.

From the entrance to *Simonsig*, the Kromme Rhee road continues eastwards through a gentle rural landscape. It was here that the British army, during the Anglo-Boer War, maintained a large remount camp. Horses and pack animals shipped in from overseas were rested in quarantine and prepared for dispatch by train to the war theatres. The road passes the entrance to the government-owned experimental farm, *Kromme Rhee*, granted on 13 April 1698 to Hans-Pieter van Melchien. The road ends by joining the R44 Stellenbosch–Klapmuts road 3 km from the crossroads at Koelenhof station. A short drive but very enjoyable especially in the flower and blossom season.

THE KLAPMUTS ROAD (R44)

Another interesting drive from Stellenbosch is along the tarmac road leading north for 13,5 km to Klapmuts and the main N1 road which leads from Cape Town to Paarl and the north. This road, R44, has its start from the northern end of Adam Tas Road. It makes its way through some of the best Cape scenery, passing many neat farmlands overlooked by the 1 390 m high Simonsberg which provides this part of the world with a great landmark. Named after Simon van der Stel, Simonsberg was said to be his favourite mountain. It caught the last rays of the setting sun and has a shape which makes it the classic mountain of the Western Cape.

Just after the start of the road there is a turn-off to Franschhoek over Helshoogte. After 1 km the road passes on the right the entrance to the Nietvoorbij Research Institute for Viticulture and Oenology. This is the principal centre for study and research on the cultivation of the grape and the production of wine in South Africa. The national wine museum is housed in the institute. The name *Nietvoorbij* (don't pass by) comes from the hospitable original farm name.

Fine estates and farms lie on either side of the road as it curves and steadily rises on its way to the top of the dividing ridge between the Eerste River system and the valley of the Berg River. Fresh fruit in season is sold from the roadside while 4 km from Stellenbosch, on the right, is the estate of *Morgenhof* (morning garden), with an impressive group of buildings, carefully restored, standing in the valley below the road.

The story of this farm goes back 300 years, but its modern rejuvenation only came in 1993. It was acquired then by the French Huchon-Cointreau family of Cognac whose history in winemaking goes back to the beginning of the 13th century in France. Their immense experience and reputation has been transferred to this estate. An extensive programme of replanning and modernisation of cellar facilities has ensured a quality of wine production with a subtle blend of the Cape and France.

Wines can be tasted and bought during normal business hours (Saturdays and Sundays included). There are summer lunches under the oaks or in the old horse stable while in winter lunch is served in the tasting-room with an open fire-place for a good warm. The Ruby Port, Cabernet Sauvignon and a Noble Late Harvest are amongst the wines to try. There is a high-tech cellar which may be viewed from an observation platform, and a museum cellar where you can make your own wine during the harvest season. There is also an aromatic garden of herbs. Picnic basket lunches are available from October to April.

Back on the Klapmuts road, 1,5 km beyond the entrance to *Morgenhof*, there is a turn left to the estate of *L'Avenir*, (the future). This 70 ha estate was formerly a part of the *Kromme Rhee* farm with the grape harvest sold to *Nederburg*. In 1991 it was bought by Marc Wiehe, who came from Mauritius. He gave the farm its name and within a short period of intensive planning and construction transformed it into a wine producer in its own right, with a modern cellar. The first wines were released in 1994; Vin d'Estelle, a fruity off-dry white, and a red blend of Merlot and Cabernet Sauvignon called L'Ami Simon. A lot of water has gone under the bridge in a short time and, today, L'Avenir's Pinotage, Chardonnay, Cabernet, Chenin and Sauvignon are rated amongst the best of Stellenbosch wines.

A guest-house with eight luxurious rooms and a swimming-pool in a garden setting was also created. Guests have free rein to wander through the vineyards and relax in a lovely environment. Phone (021) 889-5001. Fax (021) 889-5258. Web page: http:www// adept/co.za/lavenir.

Back on the Klapmuts road, 2 km from the turn to *L'Avenir*, there is a turn right known as the *Knorhoek* (growling glen) road leading into the foothills of the Simonsberg and the outlying hill known as *Kanonkop* (cannon summit), once used as a signal point. Along this road lies the estate of *Muratie* (ruins). The present, deeply shaded homestead was built on the ruins of an earlier building. In 1925 the artist Georg Paul Canitz, bought the estate and produced there some famous red wine as well as many lovely paintings. He was a pioneer in planting the Pinot Noir cultivar in South Africa. On his death in 1959, his daughter, Annemarie, took over management of the estate. In 1988 *Muratie* was bought by Ronald Melck, the then Managing Director of Stellenbosch Farmers' Winery. The estate produces an excellent port-type wine and a muscat-type wine known as Amber, as well as high-quality red wines, including the ever-popular Pinot Noir. Wine is sold during normal business hours. Cellar tours are arranged by appointment only.

Just beyond *Muratie* lies *De Drie Sprongh* (the three forks), the wine farm and cellar of

Delheim Wines (Pty) Ltd. In 1938, Hans Hoheisen, a successful builder and keen conservationist, bought the 177 ha farm of *De Drie Sprongh* from Charles Nelson, a grandnephew of Lord Horatio Nelson of Trafalgar. The farm had originally been granted on 28 February 1699 to Lourens Campher. Higher up the valley an official of the Dutch East India Company was stationed in a small house with a signal cannon on a vantage-point. The duty of the official was to fire the cannon as a signal to local farmers that ships had arrived in Table Bay and were desirous of purchasing fresh provisions.

Hans Hoheisen had no farming experience, but in 1951 his wife's nephew, Michael 'Spatz' Sperling, arrived from Poland where his family had farmed for over 150 years. The two men joined forces and commenced a programme of planting on 45 ha a variety of grape cultivars and of creating a first-class cellar. The cellar was named *Delheim* after Deli, Mr Hoheisen's wife, and heim meaning 'home'.

The cellar is a prolific producer of fine wines. Notable are a Grand Reserve red, a well-known dry sparkling wine Pinot Noir Rosé Brut, a Noble Late Harvest Edelspatz, and a Late Harvest wine with the cheeky name and amusing label of *Spatzendreck* (sparrow's droppings), given to it as a joke by a friend when this wine was introduced. Spatz is a colloquial German name for the sparrow (or 'Sperling'), and this little bird appears on the label of several of Delheim's wines.

The Vintner's Platter Garden Restaurant is open Mondays to Saturdays 12h00 to 14h30 all year round. It is also open on Sundays for lunch from October to April. There are cellar tours Mondays to Fridays all year round at 14h30. From October to April, Mondays to Fridays, there is also a tour of the vineyards at 10h30. All year round at 10h30 on Saturdays there is a conducted cellar tour. Wine is sold during normal trading hours throughout the year. This fine estate has given such pleasure to so many visitors that it must be one of the best-known farms in the world. 'Spatz' and his wife Vera are two of the great characters of the Cape wine industry. Phone (021) 882-2033.

Back again on the main road to Klapmuts, very shortly after the turn-off just followed, there is the turn-off left to the Kromme Rhee road which leads to *Simonsig* wine estate and the rural centre of Koelenhof.

Eight and a half kilometre from Stellenbosch on the Klapmuts road another turn-off stretches left to Muldersvlei and the Stellenbosch University Agricultural College of Elsenburg built on the *Elsenburgh* farm granted on 23 September 1698 to Samuel Elsevier. The road then climbs through a lovely vale passing such well-known wine estates as *Kanonkop* (cannon peak), *Uitkyk* (outlook) and *Warwick*. *Warwick* was so named by Colonel William Gordon, commander of the Warwickshire Regiment during the Anglo-Boer War. He saw this delectable valley, fell in love with it, and purchased a subdivision of the original farm. He named his property *Warwick* after his regiment. In 1964 Stanley Ratcliffe bought it and today it produces red wine of excellent reputation.

The story of *Uitkyk* started in 1783 when Martin Melck bought the land and gave it to his son-in-law John David Beyers, who was married to Martin's 20-year-old daughter, Anna Katarina. The house is thought to have been designed by Louis-Michel Thibault, the renowned architect of the Cape-Dutch style. Everything about *Uitkyk* homestead is elegant, with the focal point of the facade a magnificent front door carved by Anton Anreith. The Beyers family lived on *Uitkyk* until 1920 when it was bought by George von Carlowitz, a Prussian immigrant who was the first to really recognise the potential of the varying micro-climates, rainfall and elevations of *Uitkyk* vineyards.

The 600-ha estate now has about 180 ha under vineyards. With as much as a 250 mm difference in rainfall, there are at least a dozen meso-climates on parts of *Uitkyk*. Therefore the estate offers ideal conditions for a variety of grape cultivars.

The first phase of the restoration of the homestead has been completed. The most recent development was the discovery of neo-Classical murals in the hallway of the house, underneath eight layers of paint. The work of uncovering these murals is slow and complex. The estate is open to the public. Visitors are welcome to taste and buy the estate wines and view the murals during normal weekday business hours, as well as on Saturday mornings.

Beyond *Uitkyk*, 11 km from Stellenbosch the road reaches the summit of the saddle of land connecting the Simonsberg massif to the outlying 522 m high point known from its shape as *Klapmutskop*. A *klapmuts* was a type of cap with earflaps worn by Dutch sailors in former years. The road starts to descend over this saddle into the valley of the Berg River and after half a kilometre passes the entrance to the estate of *Lievland*.

Lievland was originally part of the farm *Natte Vallei*, granted in 1715 to an ex-soldier and woodcutter named Juriaan Hanekom. The De Villiers family bought this property in 1770. Daniël Muller bought a second section of *Natte Vallei* in 1820. He named his farm *Beyerskloof*, and on it he built a cellar in 1823 and a manor-house in 1828.

After a succession of other owners, Baron Karl von Stiernhelm, a resident of Latvia who planned to escape the threatening pre-war atmosphere in Europe and move to the Cape, bought the estate in 1933. He died before the move, however; but the widowed Baroness Hendrika von Stiernhelm and her four children moved to the estate, which she renamed *Lievland* after the family home in Latvia.

The Baroness knew nothing about viticulture and she was almost broke. She was, however, a woman of courage. She studied viticulture under the famous Professor A I Perold, struggling meanwhile to raise her family and maintain the estate. At last, after four hard years, she produced her own wines with labels, Santa Monica and Beyerskloof.

In 1973 *Lievland* became the property of the Benadé family. New cultivars were planted, a new cellar was built, and the first wines with the *Lievland* label were marketed at the end of 1982. Paul Benadé owns the estate today with Abé Beukes as his winemaker. There is a fine underground maturation cellar and 65 ha of land under vines. The estate is open to the public and wine is sold from the cellar during normal business hours. *Lievland* red and white wines have been selected nineteen times by the Wine of the Month Club, four times by the Oaks Wine Club, and three times by the International Vineyards Wine Club.

Beyond the entrance to *Lievland*, the road descends, curving through lovely farming country and eventually joins the N1 road at the hamlet of Klapmuts, 13,5 km from Stellenbosch.

THE HELSHOOGTE ROAD

From Stellenbosch there is another tarmac road leading into the Berg River valley – this one over the pass known as *Helshoogte* (heights of the abyss). The drive along this road is one of the great scenic routes of the Cape, and part of what is known as the Four Passes circular drive from Cape Town to Stellenbosch over the Helshoogte Pass to the Berg River valley, then over the Franschhoek Pass to the upper Riviersonderend valley, then over the Viljoen Pass to Elgin, and finally back to Cape Town down Sir Lowry's Pass.

The road over Helshoogte starts from a branch off the Klapmuts road just after the road leaves Stellenbosch. It climbs steadily from its beginning. After 1,5 km there is a branch left which leads for 4 km up what is known as *Ida's Valley*, named, it is said, after a mistress of Simon van der Stel. Divided into two portions, this lovely farm was originally granted on 2 September 1692 to Francois Viljon (Portion A) and on 6 September 1692 to Gerhard Cloete (Portion B) The road is a short but pleasant drive up a valley filled with fruit-producing farms. The road ends at *Rustenburg* farm. On this estate, 5 km from Stellenbosch, is the well-known health resort, the High Rustenberg Hydro, founded in 1971 by the late Boris Chaitow and Co Saporetti. It is modelled on Champneys, founded in England by Stanley Lief, cousin of Boris Chaitow.

Half a kilometre up the Helshoogte road from the turn to *Ida's Valley*, there is a turn leading into the centre of Stellenbosch.

The summit of Helshoogte Pass is reached 7 km from Stellenbosch. It is a fine drive up a beautiful and well-made pass. All the way along this road there are spectacular views of Simonsberg and the valley of the Eerste River. From the summit there is a view of the magnificent pile of the Groot Drakenstein Mountains on the right. Simonsberg on the left, and, directly ahead across the valley, the flat summit of the Wemmershoek Table Mountain. At the top of the pass a branch road leads right to the wine farm and cellar originally created by John Platter and named *Delaire* (eyrie). It is now owned by Ruth and Storm Quinan and is notable for its dry red and white wines and a cheerful sparkling wine, all sold Mondays to Saturdays 10h00 to 17h00. There are light lunches. Good fare for picnics may be ordered in advance, or you can take your own hampers.

Another branch road at the top of Helshoogte Pass leads left to the farm with the Greek name of *Thelema* (good hope). This farm was bought in 1983 by David McLean. His family trust set out to rehabilitate the 157 ha of high-lying mountain-slope farmland, replacing fruit trees with high quality vines, mainly the classical varieties, Chardonnay and Cabernet. David's son-in-law, Gyles Webb, became the winemaker. He produced the first wine of *Thelema*, a Chardonnay, in 1988.

A beautiful area: orchards and vineyards cover the slopes and in winter snow often crowns the high summits. After pausing to admire the scenery and sip the wines of *Delaire* and *Thelema*, the traveller begins the descent into fertile valley of the Berg River. It was from here in 1687 that Simon van der Stel, at the head of a party of settlers, looked out with delight at the view. It is an area of flowers and flower farms, such as *Calenick* farm of Colin and Pamela Michell, famous for their cultivation of proteas. The Michell family originated from Calenick in Cornwall in 1860. Sir Lewis Michell was head of the Standard Bank and involved with Rhodes in the purchase of the Rhodes Fruit Farms. In the process he found an old fruit farm which he bought for himself and named *Calenick* after the family home in Cornwall. High mountains dominate the scene and memories linger of the days when wild animals roamed through what was named *Die Bange Hoek* (the fearful glen).

HILLCREST BERRY ORCHARDS

On the cool southern slopes of the Simonsberg lie the terraces of *Hillcrest Berry Orchards*. Raymond O'Grady and his wife Betty bought this farm in 1986. It was rather undeveloped but they appreciated its possibilities. Raymond had worked for ten years as Human Resources Manager for Anglo-American Farms. Betty was teaching French at the University of the Western Cape. They were both interested in the cultivation of berries.

There was much to be learned and the only way to obtain information was to go overseas. Berry farming in South Africa was in its infancy compared to the scale and standards of countries in Europe. To England, Scotland and Italy Raymond had to go, and then back to South Africa to apply his new knowledge to the cultivation of berries on *Hillcrest Berry Orchards*. For six patient years he tested the suitability of different altitudes of the slopes of the Simonsberg for different berries. There were problems, but each year he learned more of the fastidious berries, their affinity to soil, temperature, winds, water and altitude.

Hillcrest Berry Orchards is today a model berry farm. On the terraces grow several varieties of raspberries, youngberries, boysenberries, three varieties of English blackberries and the luscious Scottish tayberry (a cross between a Scottish raspberry and the American blackberry). New varieties of blueberries, blackcurrants, English gooseberries and wild strawberries are currently being trialed. Every year something new, something exciting.

Fifteen different jams are made on the farm, from pure, choice grade berries with absolutely no preservatives or colourants and as little sugar as possible. There are dessert toppings (or coulis), relishes, sauces including game sauce and vinegars, fresh berry drinks and many other delicious things. There is a shop and an open-air tea garden on one of the viewsite terraces where all these good things, and many more, may be tasted. No tour buses are admitted (parking not available). Booking for groups for the Tea Garden is essential.

P O Box 2091, Dennesig, 7601. Phone (021) 885-1629. Fax (021) 885-1624.

THE JONKERSHOEK ROAD

From Stellenbosch there is a road leading up the valley of the Eerste River to Jonkershoek, where the Eerste River has its beginning in a most lovely womb of mountains. The drive is not long but leads all the way through superlative scenery which is beautiful at all seasons, especially autumn, when the green leaves of the vines and trees turn the most delicate shades of red, yellow and brown.

The Eerste River has its source high on the mountain divide which separates the watersheds of the Riviersonderend which flows to the east, and a stream of amber-coloured water tumbling down on the south-western side and flowing off through the deep glen known as *Jonkershoek*, from Jan de Jonker, who was granted land there on 15 October 1692. This is a glorious scenic area of wild flowers and mountains, dominated on the western side by the 1 495 m high Jonkershoek Twins, with their double peak providing a stiff challenge to mountaineers and a dramatic subject for photographers and artists.

A path, part of the Hottentots Holland Wilderness Trail, leads down the valley from the divide.

This trail provides a strenuous two-day hike between the Highlands Forestry Station near Elgin, up the valley where the Riviersonderend has its source in an area renowned for its aromatic herbs such as the *buchu*, then over the divide into the Jonkershoek valley. From there the path winds down the valley, with many fine views and turn-offs to such spectacular features as what is known as the Second Waterfall, a sheer fall into a deep gorge, choked with ferns and varied vegetation, with a succession of sparkling pools, rapids and cascades. The turn-off into this gorge is complicated. The path has to find a way around giant boulders and hug the sides of sheer cliffs. Some simple climbing is necessary. Perseverance is well rewarded. At the head of the gorge the path reaches an amphitheatre where the Second Waterfall plummets down in a superb 100 m leap. When the author first visited this fall, there was a deep pool at its foot into which he dived and swam. However, on a second visit one year later, he found that a landslide had entombed the pool, filling it with boulders. The waterfall, however, is still beautiful; and fine contra-light photographs can be taken of it from the slopes above the landslide to the left. The morning is the best time for lighting.

Below the turn-off to the Second Waterfall, the main path continues down the valley for 4 km, passes the Jonkershoek Kleinplaas Dam, which now covers the site of what was known as the First Waterfall, and then reaches the bridge at the upper U-turn of the gravel road which leads from the gate at the entrance to the Jonkershoek Nature Reserve, 6 km lower down the valley. It is a fine 12 km long drive. The road leads up one side of the river and then goes down the opposite bank. The reserve is open throughout the year although the management reserves the right to close it when conditions are hazardous. No fires are permitted. Permits are issued at the gate between 07h30 and 17h00. Entrance fees are charged and there is an additional fee for hiking in the reserve.

Below the gate, the road and river pass through the grounds of the Nature Conservation Department whose buildings house some interesting exhibits accessible to visitors. The Assegaaibosch Nature Reserve is situated on the left bank of the river, and includes a garden of wild flowers, lawns and a picnic ground. It is open on weekdays from 08h00 to 16h15. The Nature Conservation Department also maintains here the well-known Jonkershoek fish hatchery. This hatchery is sacred to all lovers of freshwater fishing. In 1893 the Cape Government first rented from private owners this part of Jonkershoek. A professional pisciculturist, Ernest Latour, was employed there in the construction of pools for breeding trout. From that time, Jonkershoek became the principal fish hatchery in Africa and one of the best known in the world. From this mother hatchery, many of the streams and rivers of South Africa, Zimbabwe and East Africa received their populations of trout. Vast numbers of fish are still bred there and distributed to many waters, including the Eerste River itself which flows through the grounds of the hatchery. Its tributary streams provide the water for the breeding tanks and dams. As a reward for the service, the Eerste River became one of the best trout streams in Southern Africa, with excellent fishing during spring and autumn. Indigenous fish are also bred in the hatchery. There is an aquarium open to the public on weekdays from 08h00 to 16h15, and the hatcheries may be visited by permission of the officials.

The Okkie Jooste camping site of the Department of Education is across the road from the Nature Conservation offices.

The river and the road leave the grounds of the Nature Conservation Department and make their way down the valley in the shade of many handsome trees. Just below the entrance to the grounds of the reserve there is a turn-off to a splendid picnic ground extending for nearly 1 km beneath the trees growing on the right bank of the Eerste River. This picnic ground is maintained by the Stellenbosch municipality. In autumn, when the leaves are falling and the vegetation is as richly coloured as the amber water of the river, the scene is unforgettable.

The entrance to this picnic ground is 7,5 km from Stellenbosch. Less than 1 km lower down the valley, the road passes the homestead of *Nektar* (nectar). This serene building was, in its original form, designed by the famous architect, Louis Thibault, and built in 1780. The present gable was added in 1815. It is a delightful example of Cape-Dutch architecture. As with most of these old homesteads, the permanent fixtures include a ghost, this one said to be that of Louis Thibault, the architect who, liking the place as he had originally designed it, does not much fancy the later gable, and conservatively resists all other changes by irately knocking on the walls when any renovations or rebuilding is commenced.

Nektar was subdivided into two separate properties in the early 1940s. The portion containing the homestead and 5 ha was bought in 1941 by the late Major-General Kenneth van der Spuy, grand old man of the South African air force. The Major-General and his wife, Una, a well-known author of gardening books, then started the Old Nectar Nursery, renowned for its roses. The homestead and garden have been declared a national monument, and this is the only private garden to have been honoured in this way.

In 1970 the Peck family acquired the larger (255 ha) portion of the farm, known as *Glenconnor*. They planted high-quality grape cultivars on the cool northern slopes of the valley. In 1983 a cellar was established and a range of wines and a port were made on the estate under the Oude Nektar label. In 1989 the estate was acquired by Hans Peter Schröder. Born in Windhoek, Hans-Peter was educated in Stellenbosch. He went to sea and became a master mariner. Then he went to university in Japan and lived in that country for 23 years, becoming an international businessman before returning to South Africa with a charming wife and buying the estate in the idyllic Jonkershoek valley. He created an ornamental lake in the grounds as a sanctuary for birds, including swans. The cellars were upgraded and the vineyard replanted. In 1993 Hans-Peter purchased shares in Neil Ellis Wines (Pty) Ltd and leased the production facilities on the estate to Neil Ellis who commenced the creation there of a range of wines under his own brand name. The Oude Nektar wines have been phased out and are now collector's items. The estate is open for wine sales and tastings during normal business hours on weekdays throughout the year. From 1 September to 30 April the estate is open on Saturdays as well as from 11h00 to 16h00. Light lunches are available from 15 December to 31 January. Booking is essential.

The road continues down the valley, revealing many views of farmlands and mountains. High up on the mountain slopes on the right-hand side may be seen the fairy-like castle built by the magnate, Toni Hermle. It is named *Konstanz*, after his home in Germany on Lake Konstanz. Autumn colours are particularly lovely in this part of the valley. After 3 km more of travelling down this pleasant road, there is a turn-off to the Lanzerac Hotel and to the banks of the Eerste River where, across a causeway, in a fine stand of trees, the University of Stellenbosch has a sport and recreation area.

THE LANZERAC MANOR AND WINERY

The five-star Lanzerac Manor hotel is one of the best-known, best-loved of all hotels in Southern Africa. In fact, in 1976 the Lanzerac appeared in a prestigious Thomas Cook publication as one of the top 300 hotels in the world. It was described as *'by far the prettiest in South Africa'*. The story of how it started as the manor-house of a farm, attained its first eminence as a hotel and continued in its destiny to become the homely, comfortable but serenely elegant place of today, is both fascinating and beguiling .

Back on 28 February 1692 the Governor, Simon van der Stel granted to Isaac Schrijver, a soldier and prospector in the service of the Dutch East India Company, an estate named *Schoongezicht* (beautiful outlook) at the lower end of the Jonkershoek valley. The sergeant died on the estate on 15 October 1692.

Over the years the farm passed into the hands of several other owners who each contributed some building to the farmyard. The cellar was built by Coenraad Fick in 1815 and the main homestead also by him in 1830. In 1914 the farm was bought by Mrs Elizabeth Katherina English, an enterprising lady who cultivated grapes on the estate, with no less than 21 imported varietals planted. From them she bottled the first wine with the Lanzerac label. Mrs English made extensive modifications and additions to the buildings, including enlarging the manor-house by elongation. She had, however, a problem with the name *Schoongezicht*. The original estate had long since been fragmented into sections each having the use of the name. She decided that she needed a proprietary name for the wine and called her portion of the estate *Lanzerac* after a place, it is said, of which she had romantic memories.

Mrs English died in 1929. A bank controlled the estate for six years and then sold it to Johannes Tribbelhorn who made good wine in a fine cellar. In 1941 Angus Buchanan bought the estate. His wines, especially reds, won prizes but there was not much financial return. He sold *Lanzerac* in 1958 to the Rawdon family, Marie and her two sons, David and Graham. They were hoteliers but not winemakers. With fine perception they converted the estate buildings to a hotel. The vineyard was left to go back to nature. Stellenbosch Farmers Winery took over the *Lanzerac* name and continued producing its most popular wine, a delicious Rosé sold in a distinctive dew-drop shaped bottle. The grapes for it were no longer grown on the namesake estate.

The Rawdons were experienced hoteliers with an inborn hospitality and a genius in creativity. They knew that atmosphere was as important as comfort, service and impeccable food. They had limited finance, but they spent a year in renovating, converting farmyard buildings into rooms, each with its own character, furnished with antique pieces acquired by persistently foraging through dealers and spreading word that anybody needful of a little hard cash could find a ready buyer for the odd heirloom they had inherited from the past. The Rawdons planned and did the building work themselves, with the aid of a handful of specialist tradesmen.

In August 1959 *Lanzerac* opened its doors. Customers ventured in, curious to see what the Rawdons had done, ready to criticise, but instead a love story started between hotel and its guests. Nancy V Richards has recorded some memories and legends.

> *'There are many things that make the Lanzerac of the 'sixties and 'seventies memorable apart from its beautiful settings amongst oaks and mountains. There was the treacle-brown bar that welcomed thirsty souls like bees to a honey-pot, the inimitable translucent pink wine, four-poster beds, a supper and a cellar club, lingering cheese lunches and slabs of moist brown bread rich as a fruit-cake. Every bit as colourful were the guests who came to stay. Of course they had their share of 'sixties' celebrities – Ted and Ethel Kennedy, Ian Smith, Uri Geller, Jean Shrimpton, Cecily Courtneidge, Dame Edith Evans, Princess Alice, Laurens van der Post – but it was the regulars from abroad, affectionately known as the Swallows (because they came with the seasons), who carved the memories.*
>
> *'Top on the list of regulars is Lady Iris Southby, ex Mrs Robertson, after whom a corner of the bar is named and who is still welcomed there after 30 years. There was Tommy Whitson, the elegant English dame who came out annually on the Ellerman and Bucknall shipping line. In a flowing white gown with a scarf over her head she would walk the grounds at dusk each day. At her request her ashes have since been scattered under the willows at Lanzerac. There was her arch-rival, Bon Walton, who impressed the rest by bringing her Daimler out with her on the ship and, even at the age of 80, speeding from the docks through the driveway to Lanzerac in time for the first gin and tonic. There was the well-known comedienne Joyce Grenfell who came regularly with her husband and alarmed the staff on frequent occasions by removing her glass eye and placing it in a tumbler as she lay by the pool. Another local visitor was her brother-in-law Harry who had two wooden legs that were removed at night and tucked under the bed complete with socks and shoes. One morning, David Rawdon recalls, the chambermaid requested to know if she should bring another tea-cup 'for the master under the bed'. The stories are rife – and riveting. Molly Reinhardt summed up the Lanzerac mood in 1964 by writing: "It isn't a hotel, it's a way of life". They leave you to your own devices and if you haven't got any devices, it's not for you'.*
>
> *'But amidst all the glorious past of Lanzerac, it should never be forgotten that this jewel of the winelands, lay in the lap of Stellenbosch; Matie country. And in Lanzerac the students of this university town had a second Alma Mater. For them David Rawdon created a special bar to house their energy and exuberant drinking habits that nightly woke the neighbours. In that structure you will find the students today – but this time as white-aproned waiters serving at the humming country table of the amusingly named Vinkel en Koljander (six of one and half a dozen of the other). The famous rosé wine they serve is still in that same distinctive skittle-shaped bottle but now produced by Stellenbosch Farmers' Winery. Not since the days of Angus Buchanan in the 1940s have the grapes for Lanzerac Rosé*

> been grown on the estate – but wait a while, the new vines are in and by 1997 present owner Christo Wiese and his winemaker, Wynand Hamman, plan to have them pressed.
>
> 'The food at Lanzerac today is both classy and comfortable, like an updated version of its menus in the past. But turn the tables a few years and there in the kitchen you would have found David – his hands chocolate coated, guiding his disciples. You could not have missed Cookie – Coloured, broad-beamed and tough, stirring a mighty bobotie and kneading submission into mountains of dough. Laurens van der Post celebrated her virtue in his book African Cooking with a grinning photo. Cookie's laatlammetjie (late lamb), Sally, keeps tradition alive as an artist of the kitchen.'

There was a grey time in the story of Lanzerac. After David Rawdon sold in 1988 Lanzerac looked set to join the brassy big-time set with talk of timeshare and multi-million renovation. But luckily for lovers of the real Lanzerac legend it was not to be. In 1990 Christo Wiese, advocate, retail magnate, banker, businessman, wine-lover and ex-Matie, saved her in the nick of time *'because I wanted a wine farm'* he says simply. Christo Wiese has invested sufficient to restore Lanzerac to the fine, simple style to which she is accustomed. There are new Swallows – and new Amazons – but the oak trees provide the same shade and the kitchen still the same comfort.

The first renovations and extensions were completed in November 1992, with 40 rooms all en-suite, individually furnished and each having direct access to the gardens. A handsome compliment to the Mediterranean charm was achieved in the renovations. Two restaurants, the casual Lanzerac Terrace and the more elegant *Governors Hall*, offer country lunches and cream teas, hot soups, casseroles, salads with fresh ingredients, sandwiches and many other delights.

Realising the importance of not only faithfully preserving the historic architecture of the Lanzerac, but also maintaining a healthy respect for the ever changing and challenging hotel industry, Christo Wiese yet again decided upon a fresh new approach in 1996. By enhancing the existing features of the hotel and indulging in exciting ideas in a new venture of refurbishment, and management, envisioning a triumphant return to memories inherited from South African history at the Lanzerac. The time was emerging to pay homage to bygone ears and patrons of the country and to the diverse essences of her people. A noble transformation to celebrate a legacy of gleaming old yellowwood and creaking leather, beaten copper, majestic marble floors and rich oil paintings has been accomplished. Christo Wiese has carefully guarded the momentum, which the Lanzerac takes pleasure in honouring: *'Custodians of our heritage – Protectors of the future'*.

The hotel is situated 3 km from Stellenbosch at the entrance to the Jonkershoek valley. The vineyard around it provides a delightful setting, with its leaves changing colour with the seasons. Warm summers, snow on the peaks in winter, spring with its flowers, and autumn, perhaps the loveliest season of all.

As far as wine is concerned, the *Lanzerac* estate has been completely rejuvenated. By amicable agreement with Stellenbosch Farmers' Winery the *Lanzerac* trademark is shared. The vineyard has been replanted with all-new, virus-free clones, originating mainly from France. Under the control of winemaker Wynand Hamman, 300 tonnes of grapes are already being pressed each year, with the intention of doubling the amount by the year 2000. Three wines, a Chardonnay, Cabernet Sauvignon and a Merlot, are already being marketed from these estate grown grapes. They are marketed by the Stellenbosch Farmers Winery in imported French bottles featuring the distinctive new *Lanzerac* label. The famous old Rosé will still be produced by Stellenbosch Farmers Winery, in its traditional bottle, along with a Pinotage also made by the Stellenbosch Farmers Winery, but marketed in the new *Lanzerac* French-made bottle.

Phone (021) 886-5641 and 887-1275. Fax (021) 887-6998.

THE SOMERSET WEST ROAD (R44)

The road to Somerset West leads southwards from the western end of Dorp Street where the massive old grape press stands as a landmark in the grounds of Libertas Parva with its wine museum, art gallery and the administrative buildings of the Distillers Corporation. The road bridges over the

Eerste River, passes the turn to the Cape-Dutch manor-house of *Doornbosch*, (thorn bush) now housing a restaurant, and a turn on the right-hand side to the estate of *Libertas* with its magnificent manor-house dated 1771 and *Fleurbaix* (or Fleurbaai) granted on 28 July 1695 to Pieter Leveber.

After 2,5 km there is a turn on the left-hand side up Paradys Kloof road, leading eastwards into an agricultural area of immense fertility. Along the way the road passes the farm of Heiveld Herbs and the estates of *Stellenrust* and *Stellenzicht* (formerly the *Alphen* estate but bought in 1981 by Hans-Joachim Schreiber, owner of *Neethlingshof*, and renamed). The road passes the *Keerweder* (cul-de-sac) estate and ends, after 7 km, at the *Mont Fleur* conference centre built on the slopes of the Helderberg. This is an interesting drive but the road deteriorates in condition towards the end of its route.

Back on the Somerset West road, past the Stellenbosch golf-course in its woodland setting on the right, after 1 km, there is a turn-off on the right-hand side leading to the airfield and the modern industrial development of Technopark, a multi-million-rand complex for technical experimentation. At 4 km from Stellenbosch there is a turn left to Webers Valley, a rural residential area of small holdings. Just beyond this turn there is the entrance on the left-hand side leading to the estate of *Blaauwklippen* (blue stones).

This fine estate was granted by Simon van der Stel on 9 October 1690 to Gerrit Visser. The manor-house was built in 1789 by Dirk Wouter Hoffman and around it a varied cluster of farm buildings were created in succeeding years. These buildings today house a tasting-room, an interesting, well-displayed museum of domestic items, stables, a Country Shop selling home-made jams, konfyts and some outstandingly good Weinwurst salamis, chutneys and farm-made relishes, gifts and books.

A range of wines made by Jacques Kruger from grapes grown on the estate, are sold during normal business hours (not on Sundays). In the summer season, October to April, there is a Coachman's Lunch, served in the shade of the oaks. Horse-drawn carriage rides are available through the farmlands. The Medallion mushroom-growing cellars are also on the estate.

From the turn-off to *Blaauwklippen* the Somerset West road continues southwards, passing, after 1,5 km, the Mountain Breeze farm stall and caravan park situated in a plantation of pine trees. One kilometre beyond the farm stall, the Stellenrust road branches left through the pine trees and leads for 4 km to join the Paradys Kloof road, passing on the way the large vegetable farm of *Bonterivier* and vineyards of the *Stellenzicht* wine estate.

Another kilometre along the Somerset West road past this turn-off there is a crossing of the Annandale road. A right turn leads across the strawberry fields of the *Limberlost* farm of the Zetlers, then past a left turn to the *Welmoed* vegetable farm of Neethlingshof estate and then across the Eerste River to join the R310 Stellenbosch–Faure road.

A turn left on the Annandale road leads, after 2 km, past the entrance to the red wine estate of *Alto* with its cluster of Edwardian farmhouse, modern cellars and friendly tasting-room. Visitors are welcome to purchase some superlative wine during the usual business hours. Hempies du Toit, of Springbok rugby fame, presides over this renowned estate with its lovely views.

RUST EN VREDE

Another kilometre past the *Blyhoek* (Joyful Glen) farm the road reaches a division. Half a kilometre straight ahead lies the *Rust en Vrede* (Rest and Peace) estate of Jannie Engelbrecht, a Springbok of rugby fame who represented South Africa in 74 international matches. A graduate of the University of Stellenbosch with a BSc Agriculture and Honours in Economics, he purchased *Rust en Vrede* estate in 1978.

Originally a sheep farm named *Bonterivier*, it was granted by Simon van der Stel in 1694 to a gentleman with the interesting name of Willem van de Wêreld (William of the World). In 1780 vines were planted on the farm. It was subsequently divided into smaller parts, each given its own name, *Blyhoek* and *Rust en Vrede* being two of them.

Wine was made on *Rust en Vrede* until 1923. The cellar then became derelict until Jannie Engelbrecht bought the farm and set out with tremendous enthusiasm to transform it into the jewel it is today. He and his cheerful wife Ellen rehabilitated the historic manor-house built between

1780 and 1790 (but restored in 1825 after a fire), the original *Jonkershuis* (young gentleman's house) where the eldest son and heir always took up residence, the small winery and the coach house. All historic buildings erected in a line.

Jannie Engelbrecht produced his first wine in 1979. Red wines were his particular interest. The soils and climate of the estate suit them to perfection. On 40 ha he planted such classic cultivars as *Cabernet Sauvignon, Shiraz, Merlot* and *Tinta Barocca*. Maturation 225 litre barrels of Nevers oak were imported from Bordeaux, France. In 1984 Jannie and the architect Gawie Fagan designed and built a superb underground cellar with bottle maturation in ideal conditions of temperature and quiet rest. In 1987 Kevin Arnold, a South African champion winemaker and red wine specialist, was appointed the estate winemaker. Until he left to make his own wines in July 1997 he and Jannie produced many distinguished wines. The pride of the estate is known as the *Rust en Vrede* estate wine. It is a subtle blend of the Cabernet Sauvignon, Shiraz and Merlot vines, each contributing grapes of superlative quality, and the first of its kind produced in South Africa.

In 1993 *Rust en Vrede* has a very special honour. On the occasion when Nelson Mandela and F W de Klerk received the Noble Prize for Peace, a blind tasting held to select the wine for the banquet in Oslo chose *Rust en Vrede* Merlot 1989 as the wine to be served.

Jannie Engelbrecht is now retired. His son Jean has succeeded him in management, with Louis Strydom as winemaker and Neil Büchner as marketeer.

The estate welcomes visitors. The cellar is open during normal business hours, for inspection. Wine can be tasted and bought in a spectacular variety of bottles. The Merlot, Shiraz, Cabernet Sauvignon and, of course, the *Rust en Vrede* estate wine, are each in a premium class of their own.

At the division of the road, half a kilometre before *Rust en Vrede*, there is a turn right leading for 1 km to a subdivided part of the original farm. This part is named *Dombeya* (first to bloom) after a tree *Rotundifolia* sp. On this farm, Susanna Orr in 1985 started a weaving industry with a shop and tea-room. She trained the wives of farm labourers and today has a skilled force of weavers, spinners and dyers. They created a superb range of jerseys.

Back on the main road to Somerset West, just on the Annandale crossroads, stands the Mooiberge farm produce stall run by one of the best-known vegetable and strawberry farmers in the Cape, Sam Zetler, aided by his sons. Their industry produces amongst other things, strawberries and sweetcorn exported by air to many foreign markets. During the strawberry season (mid-August to mid-January) the industrious Zetlers export over 200 metric tons of strawberries of the Tiobelle, Tioga, Selecta and Parfaite varieties. To protect the extensive strawberry fields the Zetlers each year create a veritable army of scarecrows, including some amusing characters riding on bicycles and carts.

Two kilometres beyond the farm stall of the Zetlers, the road reaches the last of the wine estates in this area of the Stellenbosch Wine Route. This estate, backed by the Helderberg ridge, is *Eikendal* (dale of oaks) created by the Swiss company, A G Für Plantangen controlled by the Saager family. They built a spacious cellar in a setting of trees, lakes, picnic grounds and a show vineyard. With Josef Krammer from Austria as the winemaker, Cabernet Sauvignon, Merlot, a Special Late Harvest and Chardonnay are features in a list of thirteen wines, including two sparkling wines.

Wines are sold in business hours including Saturdays and Sundays. Sunday lunches are served 12h00 to 14h00 mid November to mid April. From May to September there is a hearty soup with bockwurst and home-baked bread. On Friday evenings (June to September) a Swiss fondue is served in a spacious dining-room with live entertainment. Swiss choirs sing and bands play; there are seasonal festivals; oysters and sparkling wine are served on Sundays. It is a fun place and a pleasure to visit at all seasons. Phone (021) 855-1422.

One kilometre beyond *Eikendal* there is a turn right which leads for 6 km to the end of the Stellenbosch Wine Route at Firgrove. On the way the road passes the beautiful estate of *Vredenburg* (peaceful place), granted on 24 January 1691 to Hendrik Elberts, and the cellars of the Helderberg Co-operative Winemakers, the oldest of the co-operative winemakers, especially known for port-style wine, jerepigo, sparkling wine and a range of 21 wines as well as red and white grape juice. Light lunches are served and the cellars are open every day except Sundays.

Just before the Helderberg cellars, there is a turn-off to *Raithby*, the Methodist mission station founded in 1842 as a sanctuary for freed slaves. It was named after Raithby Hall in Lincolnshire, home of Mrs Brackenbury who donated land for the mission.

The mission church, close to the restaurant, is a subtle reminder of the past, of all the hard work, patience and labour of so many people, first in bondage, then in service, which has gone into the making of all the lovely farms, buildings and meticulously tilled fields. Think a little of them, and toast their memory, as you wine and dine on the bountiful products of this delectable countryside.

Chapter Nine
THE BERG RIVER VALLEY

The Valleys of the Huguenots and the Wagonmakers

In the year 1687 the renowned Governor of the Cape, Simon van der Stel, decided it was time to establish a settlement in the valley where the Berg River has its headwaters in the superb cluster of mountains north of Stellenbosch. For this purpose, 23 men who fancied themselves as pioneers were gathered in Stellenbosch. At daybreak on 16 October, accompanied on horseback by Van der Stel and his attendants, the party made its way up the slopes of *Helshoogte* (heights of the abyss) probably following much the same route as the present road does to the summit. And it was at the summit that they paused and looked down, as modern travellers do, at a scene which has stopped for a little while the hearts of countless people in the course of their journey over this same road.

It was early one lovely spring morning that Van der Stel and his men first saw this valley. It must have seemed like a dream; richly covered in vegetation, with proteas, ericas, everlastings and the delicate blushing brides waving a welcome in the wind. Waterfalls tumbled down from the surrounding heights. The *Berg* (mountain) River, its waters stained by the soil of the Cape to the colour of amber wine, still free of any pollution by man, meandered along the floor of the valley, ornamenting it with many deep pools and calm reflections.

Flowing down to the Berg River from the Helshoogte summit was a tributary, the *Dwars* (traversing). It was along the banks of this tributary and the Berg River that the fortunate 23 pioneers secured their farms. Each farm was about 50 ha in extent, fronted by the river. To these farms the settlers brought their families and began the task of building homes, planting trees and laying out lands.

To this area, never before tilled by the hand of man, Van der Stel applied the name of *Drakenstein* (dragon rock), after the estate in Holland of the Lords of Mydrecht.

During the following year (1688) the 23 pioneers of the valley were joined by a band of 176 French Huguenot refugees who had fled from religious persecution in their own country. To the lovely Drakenstein Valley these newcomers added a subtle French atmosphere, and their skills in wine-making soon gave the area a particular renown.

Some of the most romantically beautiful farmhouses in the world were built in this valley: *Bien Donné* (well bestowed), *Le Rhône, Boschendal*, originally *Bossendaal* (bush and dale), *Languedoc, La Motte, De Goede Hoop* (the good hope), *Bellingham, La Terra de Luc* (Land of Luke), *L'Ormarins, Bethlehem, Champagne, L'Ecrevin* (Arie L'Ecrevin, the first owner) or *Lekkerwijn* (nice wine), *Delta, Werda, Zondernaam* (without name), *Weltevreden* (well satisfied), *La Paris, L'Arc D'Orleans, La Provence, La Bri, Bourgogne, La Dauphine*, and many other serene pieces of pastoral architecture. In these homesteads lived the forebears of some of the most numerous families in Southern Africa today: the Lombards, Fouchés, De Villiers, Du Plessis, Jouberts, Rossouws, Rouxs, Malans and others whose present numbers are proof of the virility of their ancestors.

At the time of the first settlement of the Drakenstein Valley, the area around the head of the Helshoogte Pass was a rugged mountain wilderness, dangerous for its wild animals as well as its heights. It was originally known as *De Bange Hoek* (the fearful glen), but its old terrors have long since vanished. The name remains in the corrupted form of Banghoek. The modern road twists down through scenery which is peaceful and lovely at any time of the year, but especially beautiful in spring and autumn.

One and a half kilometres below the summit of the pass there is a turn-off right (opposite the Helshoogte Garage) which leads for just over a kilometre to the fine old farmhouse of *Zeven Rivieren* (seven rivers). Immediately before reaching the farmhouse, the tarmac divides into two gravel roads. The branch to the left leads through the trees for 3 km before ending at *Wentworth* farm. The branch to the right leads for 4,5 km up the valley of the Banghoek River to farms such as *Rainbow* (the highest farm) and *Pear Tree* (the furthest farm up the valley). This is a mixed farming area. In spring the spectacle of the fruit trees (mainly plum, pear and peach) in blossom is superb. The flower farms such as *Calenick* seem to be on fire with the crimson colour of the proteas which they cultivate in thousands. In autumn the late grape varieties – Barlinka and Prune de Cazoul – turn the slopes scarlet with the colour of their leaves while the Almeria vines (especially on *Wentworth*) are golden. Against the blue background of the Groot Drakenstein Mountains to the right and the Simonsberg to the left, these colours are sensational.

The main road descending into the Drakenstein Valley leads for 4 km beyond the Banghoek turn-off and passes the turn-off to the superb *Hillside Berry Orchards* of Raymond and Betty O'Grady. The wayside Samburgh Inn stands lower down the road near what was originally the mission of *Pniel* (the face of God), established in 1843. This is now a substantial free-holding community. Most of the residents work in the fruit industry in the vicinity. Next to the mission church on the left-hand side of the road, is a short tarmac drive leading to the beautiful homestead of *De Goede Hoop* and its finely preserved cluster of Cape-Dutch style buildings, outhouses and bell.

The various farms such as *Bethlehem, Le Rhône, Languedoc* and *Boschendal*, are now part of Anglo American Farms Ltd. At 17 km from Stellenbosch, the road crosses the railway line at Groot Drakenstein station and joins the main road running the length of the valley. At the intersection stand the central fruit-packing sheds of the historic organisation, Rhodes Fruit Farms, now part of Anglo American Farms (Am Farms).

THE DRAKENSTEIN VALLEY

The Drakenstein Valley was the birthplace of the deciduous fruit export industry in Southern Africa. From the time of the first settlement in the Cape, fruit was produced and eaten with relish, but the only way in which such products could be exported was in dried form (principally raisins) or bottled as wine and brandy.

Refrigeration was not yet even a dream in the minds of inventors. Only one method of preserving grapes was devised. Some farmer (perhaps an individual excessively fond of that delicately flavoured muscadel, the hanepoot) discovered that this grape could be preserved for several months if bunches with long stems full of sap were cut. The tips of the stems were sealed with pitch or beeswax and the bunches were hung in the cool attics beneath the thatched roofs of the farmhouse. In such conditions the grapes would preserve their deliciously sweet and subtly musky flavour.

This ingenious dodge was actually the basis of the export fruit industry of Southern Africa. In the year 1886, at the time when the volume of fruit grown in the Cape so far exceeded the local demand that it was hardly worth the trouble of picking, somebody, writing under the *nom de plume* of 'Old Salt', suggested in a letter to the *Cape Times* that the original idea of preserving grapes could surely be used to achieve their export. The letter produced rapid results. Two months later, in April 1886, the *Cape Times* reported that a Dr Smuts had successfully transported to London several boxes of grapes with the stems of the bunches sealed with beeswax. The flavour of the grapes was superb. With prices in London reaching 15s per pound compared to the 1d per pound (roughly R1.50 compared to 1c) on the Cape Town market, this successful experiment was like a glimpse of heaven to the fruit growers of Southern Africa.

There was a great stirring in the farmhouses of the Cape. Many experiments were conducted, and two years later the Reverend Mr Legg made the first attempt to export a consignment of peaches in the cramped cold store of the *Grantully Castle*. The attempt was a failure, but the idea was fascinating to shipowners as well as to farmers. What a profitable new high-tariff cargo could be found for their ships if peaches, pears, plums, apricots, apples and citrus, as well as grapes could be made to survive the lengthy voyages of the day.

Brilliant confirmation of the whole idea came on 2 February 1892. Percy Molteno, manager of the Castle Steamship Company, and second son of Sir John Molteno, first premier of the Cape Colony, contrived by means of the cold store of the *Drummond Castle* to land in Britain the first

Cape peaches to be successfully exported. Fourteen trays of beautiful peaches survived the long journey to perfection. The peaches received such an ovation on the Covent Garden market, selling for 2s 3d each, that they might have been prima donnas in the nearby opera, with the applause being the merry tinkle of the cash registers echoing all the way back to the farming valleys of the Cape.

There were many heartbreaks to come. The cold stores on ships were hopelessly small and quite unsuitable for preserving fruit. Everything had yet to be learned about the delicate art of selective picking, pre-cooling and handling. Worst of all, the available fruit varieties were not very suitable for the highly competitive export trade. Fastidious palates overseas had their special preferences. Few of the local varieties produced in carefree fashion in the Cape quite measured up to international standards.

In the midst of these tentative ventures into the export markets, disaster struck the grape farmers. A bacterial disease known as *phylloxera* reached the Cape. This bacteria had first attacked the vineyards of the United States in 1854, then spread to France in 1863 and, notwithstanding stringent controls, appeared in the Cape vineyards in 1886. The grape farmers were ruined. There was just no answer to the disease apart from the total replacement of all vines by phylloxera-immune American stocks.

Fate, however, produced a man for the occasion. In 1885 a 20-year-old Englishman, Harry Ernest Victor Pickstone, born on 4 July 1865 in Manchester, came to South Africa for military service in what was known as the Bechuanaland Expedition. He liked what he saw of the country – its space, sunshine and opportunity – and decided to make the place his home. However, on his return to England at the end of his military service, he was attracted to Canada to join the Royal Canadian Mounted Police. The cold did not suit him and after eighteen months he returned to England. Then he went off to the California gold-rush. On finding no gold, he worked instead as a nurseryman in a climate and landscape which irresistibly reminded him of his first love, South Africa.

In 1892, therefore, Pickstone returned to the Cape as a man of destiny. He only had 30 shillings in his pocket when he landed in Cape Town on 15 March, but he had an all-important introductory letter to C D Rudd, partner of Cecil Rhodes. The letter had been given to him by John X Merriman, whom he had met in London.

Rudd was impressed by the young man, and it so happened that there had been some consideration by Rhodes about the prospects of a fruit industry in the Cape. Rudd introduced Pickstone to Rhodes. To that renowned individual the young man expounded a particular dream which was close to his heart. It was a dream of planting in the waiting soil of Southern Africa the finest fruit varieties gathered from all over the world. With these varieties he would experiment to find those most suited to local conditions. He would search for and systematically breed new cultivars perfectly adapted to this land. While the engineers solved the problems of pre-cooling, cold storage and transport, he would find the ideal fruit.

Rhodes asked Pickstone what he needed to commence the venture. Pickstone explained that he wanted to start a nursery and he had to have some means of earning a living. Rhodes was sympathetic. He advanced money to Pickstone to enable him and a partner to buy the farm *Nooitgedacht*, near Stellenbosch and plant on it an experimental selection of 50 000 fruit trees imported from overseas. Pickstone was also appointed, on an occasional basis, to serve as an extension officer, lecturing and demonstrating fruit cultivation. In his lectures he was forthright in his opinions about the over-use of water with fruit trees and vines by excess of irrigation, the need for biological control of insects, the use of mulch to save water, proper pruning, and compost as fertiliser to rejuvenate the soil.

The *Nooitgedacht* nursery was unfortunately rather short-lived. Pickstone and his partner disagreed. Pickstone left. In Cape Town he saw Rhodes and explained the difficulty. He still intended to start a nursery, and Dan Retief of Wellington had offered him the use of land for nothing. He needed £300 to get started. Rhodes and Rudd gave him £150 each. With this finance Pickstone started nurseries in Wellington, Hex River and Constantia.

The amount of work done by Pickstone can only be described as prodigious. He attended to nearly everything himself, including the production of an annual catalogue which, apart from listing available varieties, was packed with practical information on cultivation. His energy and dedication were boundless.

His brother, Horace, joined him. With the support of Rhodes they settled in the Drakenstein Valley and began there the famous nursery which has mothered so many of the commercial orchards of export fruit of Southern Africa. He acquired three farms, *Delta, Lekkerwijn* and *Meerlust*, on the level alluvial floor of the Berg River valley, with the Dwars River flowing through the estate and the Berg River providing a northern boundary. Here he commenced his great experimental industry. By 1896 Pickstone's trees were flourishing and Rhodes entered the fruit business with spectacular enthusiasm.

While the two men were walking through the drying yards of the Pioneer Fruit Driers factory in Wellington one day, Rhodes suddenly asked, *'Pickstone, you always stated that you had the greatest confidence in the fruit industry; now tell me, have you the same confidence today?'*

Pickstone didn't hesitate to reply, *'Much more, Sir, I am today dead certain'*.

Rhodes smiled, and said: *'I want to see you at Groote Schuur at an early date'*.

Pickstone went to Cape Town soon afterwards and saw Rhodes. Rhodes was beset with the problems of the Jameson Raid, the resultant ruination of his political career, and impending trial in Britain, but the dream of a massive fruit industry still had a place in his schemes. He staggered the young nurseryman by coming immediately to the point.

'Pickstone, I believe the farm I helped to buy for you is in the Groot Drakenstein valley, somewhere near the centre, isn't it?' Pickstone agreed, and Rhodes then said, *'I want to buy the Groot Drakenstein valley: how much will it cost?'*

Pickstone replied: *'It's a tall order, Sir. The valley is 15 miles long by two to three miles wide, and contains the small hamlet of Franschhoek, some good farms, and any amount of waste veld. In round figures it will cost £250 000'*.

Rhodes thereupon said *'Go and buy it'*. He left for England to stand trial without giving any further definite instructions. However, the original plan was slightly altered. Instead of the entire Groot Drakenstein valley, 29 farms in total were bought in the Franschhoek, Wellington and Tulbagh districts.

As recalled by Pickstone, *'In 1897 Mr Rhodes entrusted me with the purchase and management of the Rhodes Fruit Farms. These farms cost, approximately, £250 000, and were intended to stimulate export trade, more especially in dried fruit'*.

A trust company, the Rhodes Fruit Farms, was established, with Pickstone appointed as managing director and expert adviser for a period of five years.

Nearly every unit of the group of farms was graced with an original Cape-Dutch style homestead. Around these farmhouses stretch today the great orchards of apple, apricot, nectarine, peach, pear and plum trees whose luscious fruit is carried each summer season to many far countries by refrigerated train and ship. In their perfection this fruit will always be a reminder of the painstaking work of Harry Pickstone and the faith of Cecil Rhodes.

The formation of Rhodes Fruit Farms as a company was only achieved on 25 March 1902, with the formalities concluded by Rhodes's partners in the project. Leander Starr Jameson, Sir Charles Metcalfe and E R Syfret, gathered around the sick-bed of Rhodes in his Muizenberg cottage. It was the last project of Rhodes to reach fulfilment, for he died the following day.

Rhodes's holding company, De Beers, managed the farms, commissioned the first canning factory in time for the 1905–6 season, and in 1911 made the first profit from the enterprise. During the depression years of the late 1920s, several of the farms were sold. Amongst these was *Bien Donné*, which was acquired by the Government as a research farm. In 1936 Sir Abe Bailey bought Rhodes Fruit Farms but he died in 1941. The company was then acquired by a syndicate of four men, E J Crean, A B M McDonald, S J Richards and G H Starck. In 1969, however, a majority shareholding in the company was acquired by the Anglo American Corporation in association with De Beers and Rand Selection Corporation Ltd. Once again the farms were under the control of the financial interests directly descended from Rhodes.

Initially Rhodes Fruit Farms consisted of a 3 000 ha block of nineteen farms involved in the production of fresh and canned fruit, with all the wine production falling under the Boschendal label. Recently the fresh fruit division was sectioned off under a managment lease agreement and now trades as Imibala. The foods division has been sold to the Ferreira Group. From November to March harvesting is in full swing with about 1 400 people employed in picking, packing and processing. An interesting feature of the estate is the housing of the workers. A village of 110 cottages was designed by the celebrated architect, Sir Herbert Baker, and built on the farm named

Languedoc, with a modern extension added, known as New Languedoc. This village is worth seeing. Compared with the usual dreadful sub-economic housing estates, it is a delight.

Sir Herbert Baker also designed additions to Harry Pickstone's home, *Lekkerwijn*, which became the residence of his granddaughter, Wendy Pickstone. Harry Pickstone died on 1 November 1939. In the 47 years he had worked in South Africa, the genius and industry of this remarkable individual had been a joyful contribution to the well-being of man and the greening of planet Earth. In 1991, Wendy Pickstone sold the nursery to Mrs Lin Mehmel and her partner Mr H B Ambrosia. A great rejuvenation of the famous old nursery then started, putting back into its soil no damaging artificial fertilisers or pesticides but by symbiosis precisely what had been originally depleted by its years of use and export in literally millions of tins containing seedling fruit trees to the commercial orchards of Southern Africa.

The historic homesteads of *De Goede Hoop, Weltevreden, Boschendal, La Rhône* and *Bethlehem*, are all immaculately maintained and each seems to be lovelier than the other. *Boschendal* has been completely restored together with all the outbuildings, including a most fascinating poultry house (a real place for aristocratic birds). *Boschendal* was originally granted in 1685 to the Huguenot, Jean le Long, by Governor Simon van der Stel, it was at first named Bossendaal. In 1715 the property was purchased by Abraham de Villiers who, with his brothers Jacob and Pierre, arrived in the Cape on 6 May 1689 aboard the *Zion*. The *Boschendal* manor-house, notable for its graceful gable and its friezes adorned with acorn patterns, was built in 1812 by Paul de Villiers. *Boschendal* remained in the possession of the De Villiers family until 1879. It was later bought by Rhodes. Like most of these old Cape homesteads, it has its ghost. The *Boschendal* ghost is a wire-haired terrier puppy who joyfully scampers in through the doorway (open or shut) at the front of the house and out through the back in complete silence, except for the patter of its feet on the floor. Several people have often reported seeing it, generally just after midnight.

Boschendal and its outbuildings now contain a superb restaurant housed in the original cellar. A shop known as the *Waenhuis winkel* (wagon house shop) sells the wines and produce of the estate. The neighbouring homestead of *Le Rhône* has in its outbuildings the cellar for Boschendal wines and a *taphuis* where wines can be tasted and bought by the public. The Boschendal restaurant is open daily for lunch. It is closed at night. There is an open-air café. Picnic lunches are served beneath the trees every day during the summer season. Booking essential (1 November to end April). Phone (021) 870-4272 or 870-4274.

The upper (eastern) reaches of the Drakenstein Valley are graced with many interesting and beautiful farms. From the intersection where the road from Stellenbosch joins it immediately opposite the road leading to Pickstone's Nursery, the main road up the valley leads through a fine avenue of trees. On either side there are vineyards and orchards while the towering, red-coloured sandstone cliffs of the Groot Drakenstein Mountains dominate the valley from the western side.

After 1,5 km the road crosses the Dwars River tributary of the Berg. The entrances to several handsome farms lead off from the road. One of the most interesting, 3 km beyond the bridge, is the wine estate of *Bellingham*, first granted by Simon van der Stel on 21 October 1694 to a Netherlander, Gerrit van Vuren who was married to a Huguenot girl. The farm was named *Bellegam* on the deed of transfer. In French *bellegamme* means 'beautiful sounds' or 'tones'. *Gamme* is pronounced as 'gam'. Possibly the name was mispelt on the title deeds but its origin remains obscure. To compound the confusion, Gerrit van Vuren died shortly after acquiring the farm. On 14 July 1700 the estate was sold by public auction to Pierre Joubert and the name was written as *Bellinchamp*.

On 10 February 1742 Jean du Buisson bought the estate at an auction after the death of Pierre Joubert and the name of the farm then, surprisingly, was written as *Bellingham*. How and why the change took place remains unknown. There is a Bellingham in England and two Bellinghams in the United States of America. The one in Washington State grew as a port on the magnificent natural harbour named Bellingham Bay by Captain George Vancouver when he explored this part of the Pacific coast in 1792. Sir William Bellingham was a commissioner of the Royal Navy who had supported Captain Vancouver in his venture. The other Bellingham is in Eastern Massachusetts and was named after Richard Bellingham, Governor of the State. The Bellingham family in England and Ireland have played an influential part in the history of Great Britain and there is a Castle Bellingham. On 12 May 1812 Frances Bellingham assassinated Spencer Percival, the Prime

Minister of England. Whether there is a connection between the names in South Africa, England and the USA it would be interesting to know.

On 27 April 1759 the farm was bought by Jacob de Villiers from the widow of Jean du Buisson. His descendants were responsible for several developments. The H-shaped homestead was built with the date 1797 on its gable. The first wine cellar was built in 1800 and a water-mill was also constructed at this time.

On 25 September 1807, the farm was sold to Jacobus Roux who sold the estate on 30 March 1810 to Johannes van Niekerk who started subdividing the land and selling off portions. A succession of owners acquired the portion of the estate which retained the name of *Bellingham*. The beauty and fertility of the estate was only too apparent. It was ideal for the production of fruit and wine but, until Cecil Rhodes and the Pickstones could find practical answers to the problems of exporting fruit, it was hardly worth picking a crop. So far as wine was concerned, since the romantic days of Simon van der Stel and Hendrik Cloete at Constantia, the cultivation of grapes and the making of wine in the Cape had declined to the level of depression. Vineyards had been destroyed by the *phylloxera* disease and the general mood of despondency was reflected in dilapidated homesteads and weed-infested farmlands.

The renaissance of the Cape wine industry started just before and during the Second World War. So far as *Bellingham* was concerned, its man of destiny was Captain J Bernard Podlashuk. He had been a successful merchant in Germiston before the Second World War. He volunteered for the South African Air Force when the war broke out. In 1942 ill health caused him to be boarded out of the Air Force and he was advised to move to the coast. With his wife, Fredagh, he looked for a place in which to live and commence some worthwhile activity. 'Pod' (as he was known) and Fredagh were shown Bellingham. The homestead had been deserted for nearly twenty years; there was no electricity; the water supply was blocked; the farmlands were neglected; and the atmosphere was despondent. But Pod and Fredagh immediately fell in love with it. On 11 August 1943 they purchased the estate. Like a little lost dog, *Bellingham* responded to their offer of love and understanding.

While Fredagh rehabilitated the homestead and garden, Pod set out to restore the vineyards, cellars and outbuildings. By careful, intelligent development, personal taste and enthusiasm, shrewd promotion and a vast investment of energy, he created a range of wines which, in the peculiar way of wines, reflected something of his own subtle personality. The winemaker is the father of a wine and the good Earth is its mother. The taste, aroma and character of the liquid offspring derives from the nature of its parents – the chemistry of the mother soil, the intellectual intuition of the father.

Pod and Fredagh liked their wine dry and subtle in its flavour. The soils of *Bellingham* provided grapes with a piquancy of flavour which they needed to blend to their taste.

In 1951 they released Bellingham Rosé; and this, the driest Rosé produced in South Africa, gave the estate its first international recognition. In 1953 they released their Bellingham Grand Crû. South Africans were considered to prefer sweet wines of the Steen variety. To tempt them to try a wine as dry as the Premier Grand Crû demanded courageous and innovative marketing.

Pod tackled the problem by giving Bellingham wines a special elegantly fastidious appeal. He proclaimed them to be different, something sometimes a little difficult to find and buy, something for people with the taste and class to appreciate as very special without worrying about the price. The result of this presentation was brilliant. Wine writers and tasters noticed the quality of the Bellingham Premier Grand Crû. Controversy developed over the merit of the wine. This was all excellent publicity. The reward came in 1958 when the wine was selected as the first Cape table wine to be featured in a wine-tasting held in South Africa House in London.

Today there are over 60 brands bearing the name of Premier Grand Crû. The pioneer Bellingham Premier Grand Crû remains securely at the peak of this delectable mountain of exceedingly dry white wines, blended from Riesling grapes, containing no fermentable sugar and with an alcohol content of 11 per cent.

In 1957 Bellingham Shiraz was released as a tribute to Fredagh, and this was the first Shiraz to be introduced to the South African market.

Shortly afterwards Pod released what is the most famous of his Bellingham wines. This wine, Bellingham Johannisberger, was named and, in an affidavit on the original bottles, acknowledged to the foreman of *Bellingham*, Dirk Schwenke, who had managed to obtain cuttings from the original vines brought to the Cape by his grandfather from Schloss Johannisberg on the Rhine. The beautiful and distinctive bottle for this wine was designed by Fredagh Podlashuk. Its design duplicates the shape of the mountain overlooking the estate. Bellingham Johannisberger became one of the most popular wines ever produced in South Africa. It is just a little sweet, with a gentle aroma.

In 1972 the estate of *Bellingham* was bought by Union Wines and there have been vast developments in irrigation, planting, cellar accommodation, and the creation of a reception centre for tastings, lectures, presentations and banquets.

Pod and Fredagh remained owners of the homestead. This gloriously atmospheric building in a 2 ha garden setting was proclaimed a national monument. It was bequeathed through the Podlashuk Charity Foundation to the people of South Africa.

It is intended that the homestead become a cultural history museum. It is brimful of treasures collected over the years by the indefatigable Fredagh. In a huge garage is a wonderful collection of exotic motor cars used by the Podlashuks over the years and then 'pensioned off' as faithful old friends, never threatened with the scrap-heap. Captain Podlashuk died in July 1993.

The garden, created by Fredagh with the original help of thirteen Italian prisoners of war, is an old-world delight with nearly 1 000 varieties of roses apart from many other flowering plants, creepers and trees. There is a fine swimming-pool fed by pure mountain water, and several interesting sculptures, notably Aurora, the goddess of dawn; Aquarius, pouring water through an urn into the pool; and a delightful cat, created by the artist Nerine Desmond. The bronze of this sculpture is outside the town hall in Stellenbosch. The concrete replica in the garden of *Bellingham* sits on the steps of the wine cellar watching the homestead with such a complacent attitude that you can almost hear it purr.

Higher and closer to the mountains than *Bellingham* lies another superb estate *L'Ormarins*, first granted to the Huguenot, Jean Roi, and named after a village in the south of France. The present homestead was built in 1811 and is a joy to see in a setting of an old-world garden and pond.

In 1969 Anton Rupert bought the estate and his son Anthonij took it over in 1978. The property is immaculately maintained and an interesting range of wines is produced there under the L'Ormarins label. Especially notable is the Blanc Fumé and a Noble Late Harvest.

The cellar is modern. The original cellar has been restored, and in it is a magnificent set of wine vats, each carved with the name of a French Huguenot family. The carving was done in Bordeaux by the artist J. Mathlev and the vats were shipped to South Africa from France in 1983.

L'Ormarins is open for visits during normal business hours. Wine may be tasted and bought on the estate. The entrance gate is 1 km from that of Bellingham.

A little over 1 km beyond the entrance to *Bellingham* there is a turn-off leading to the Waterval caravan and camping site laid out beneath wattle trees growing on the banks of the Berg River, where there is river swimming and fishing.

The main road crosses the Berg River just beyond the caravan park and less than 1 km further on reaches the entrance to a spacious and beautiful picnic ground which is sublet by Safcol. This resort, laid out under the shade of trees on the banks of a stretch of the Berg River, is open from 10h00 to sunset on weekends and public holidays, and daily during school holiday periods. No overnight camping is allowed.

Half a kilometre beyond this picnic ground, the main road reaches a junction with a tarmac road coming from Paarl past the Wemmershoek Dam. This road is described later in the text.

The main road continues up the valley, and 2 km beyond the Wemmershoek junction passes the estate, store and butchery of La Motte.

The *La Motte* estate, named after a village near Toulon in France, was originally granted to Hans Hattingh, a German married to a Huguenot girl. In 1709 it was acquired by a Huguenot named Pierre Joubert, ancestral father of the South African Jouberts. The homestead was built much later in 1815. In 1970 Anton Rupert bought the estate and restored the historic buildings, erected a modern wine cellar and replanted the vineyards with the finest cultivars, especially reds. In 1985 Dr Rupert's son-in-law, Paul Neethling, and his wife Hanneli took control of the estate.

Wines may be tasted and bought during normal business hours.

Another kilometre takes the road past the buildings of the La Motte Forestry Station, the centre for an extensive afforestation of the upper area of the Berg River in what is known as the *Assegaaibosch Kloof* (assegai bush ravine).

There is a 13 km drive up the right bank of the river through this beautiful cleft in the mountains. Permits to enter Safcol forestry areas may be obtained from the Franschhoek Tourist Office. The Berg River has its birth high up where the Groot Drakenstein Mountains meet the Jonkershoek range in country so wild and broken that few men have ever drunk from the cold spring at the river's source. The vigorous young river leaps down in a spectacular fall. During the rainy season dozens of tributary streams all race to join the river in its course through this lovely valley.

The river swells rapidly in size. Overlooked by the gaunt cliffs of the Franschhoek Mountains, with trees crowding its banks, the river tumbles off, leap-frogging a long chain of pools which lie like a necklace of amber beads, each linked on the thread made by the flurry of white-water cascades. Ferns, orchids and wild flowers all find sanctuary here, while trout lurk in the pools.

From the turn-off to this forestry area, the main road continues its own way up the valley of a tributary of the Berg River, past the farm *La Provence*, first granted in 1694 to the Huguenot, Pierre Joubert. The homestead has been restored and the farm is now owned by Count Augusta. It is only open to the public by appointment. Its wines are made by the Franschhoek Vineyards Co-operative. Beyond the farm lies the hamlet of Groendal, formerly La Roux Dorp, and then, 15 km from the point where the Stellenbosch road joins it at Groot Drakenstein railway station, the road reaches the town of Franschhoek.

FRANSCHHOEK

Named after the Huguenot settlers who pioneered this valley, *Franschhoek* (French corner) is today a town with a population of 6 546. It became a municipality in 1881. After the beauty of Stellenbosch and the drive up the Drakenstein Valley, Franschhoek was something of an anticlimax with its main street largely denuded of trees. A tree-planting programme, however, is now under way. There are shops, a garage, some excellent restaurants, an imposing church and a public park. The town is being transformed into a beautiful resort as well as the commercial centre of the valley of the Huguenots.

At the far end of the road, through the town stands the impressive Huguenot Memorial Museum. The monument was erected to mark the 250th year (1938) of the Huguenots' arrival in the valley. The central figure is a woman standing with a Bible in her right hand and a broken chain in her left hand symbolising freedom from religious oppression. This is the work of the sculptor, Coert Steynberg. The three arches behind her represent the Trinity, and the globe at her feet leaves her poised in the regions of the spirit. Above the arches shines the sun of righteousness tipped by the Cross. The reflection pool below expresses tranquillity experienced after great strife. Against the handsome background of the mountains the monument is effective and beautiful. The adjoining museum was opened in 1967. The building housing it is an exact reconstruction of *Saasveld*, the Cape Town residence built in 1791 by Baron van Rheede van Oudtshoorn. When property development in Cape Town made the destruction of this house inevitable, it was demolished and as much of the material as possible was bodily removed to its present site. The museum contains items concerned with the history of the Huguenots.

The Huguenot Memorial and Museum stand in a very lovely garden, especially notable for roses which bloom during the summer months. The museum is open Mondays to Saturdays from 09h00 to 17h00. Sundays 14h00 to 17h00. Closed on Good Friday and Christmas. An extension to the museum is housed in an elegant example of modern architecture situated across the road from the original building. The memorial, museum and gardens were declared a conservation area in 1990.

The Franschhoek Vineyards Co-operative Ltd has its cellars in Franschhoek. Wine is sold to the public during normal business hours. Cellar tours are permitted by prior appointment. A full range of local wines is available for tasting and sale in the co-operative's wine centre.

Immediately before the Huguenot Memorial the main road divides. The right turn leads for 3 km to several farms such as *Stony Brook* and *Boekenhoutskloof* in the southern cul-de-sac of the valley. The tarmac road ends at the imposing Swiss-style building of the Mountain Manor hotel with its beautiful setting, fine garden, restaurant and the original cellar, *Die Binnehof*. A 5 km road branches from the tarmac road past estates such as *Champagne* (well known for its honey) and ends at *Robertsvlei* farm which is situated in a handsome bowl in the mountains.

The main road turns left at the Huguenot Memorial and begins climbing the Franschhoek Pass. This fine pass is justifiably famous for the beauty of its views as well as for the skill involved in its construction. It was originally a trail known as the *Olifantspad* (elephant's path). Like many of the mountain passes of Southern Africa, it was used from time immemorial by migrating herds of game. The game animals unerringly found the line of least resistance across the mountains and man simply followed their tracks. In 1819 one of the settlers of the Drakenstein Valley by the name of Cats received a government contract to blaze a better route than the old game trail and provide a usable track for wagons. Four years later the Catspad (as it was called) was improved by a military party under Major Holloway. This remained the route until the 1930s when a new road with an easier gradient was built. In 1965 work was completed on relocating the pass and today it provides a magnificent 6 km drive from the Huguenot Memorial to the summit, 520 m above the level of Franschhoek.

On the summit of the pass there is a track leading left for a short distance to an old forestry cottage. From there a path climbs northwards into the mountains and provides walkers and mountaineers with access to the Wemmershoek range of mountains. Wild flowers are very numerous here in spring.

The Franschhoek Pass descends for 7,5 twisting kilometres on its eastern side, bridges the Du Toit's River at the foot of the pass, and then enters the basin in the mountains in which the *Riviersonderend* (river without end) has its headwaters. This basin in the mountains lacks the fertility of the Drakenstein Valley and by comparison appears arid although it is improved by the presence of the Theewaterskloof Dam. The road skirts the north-eastern fringes of the man-made lake (impounding 480 million cubic metres of water), passes the picnic grounds at the old toll and, 10 km from the bottom of the pass, reaches a junction. A left turn leads to Villiersdorp and a right turn crosses the Riviersonderend, divides again, with a left-hand branch wandering off towards Caledon, and a right-hand branch crossing the floor of the bowl past many pleasant sheep-runs and fruit orchards, and eventually leading to Elgin and back to Cape Town down Sir Lowry's Pass.

Back in the Franschhoek valley it is interesting to explore the road which leads down the northern side of the valley to Paarl. From its branch 8 km from Franschhoek, this tarmac road first passes a State sawmill and then, after 1 km, the entrance to the recreational resort named *De Hollandsche Molen* (the Dutch mill), frequented by Capetonians during summer as a refuge from the south-easter. This resort is extensive with a large river-fed swimming pool. The place was founded just before the Second World War when a Dutch master builder, A W Diepering, discovered the site and built a tea-room there in the form of a windmill. The sails of this structure were blown away, but the odd building remains and provides an unusual sight.

Less than 1 km beyond De Hollandsche Molen, there is a turn-off leading to the Wemmershoek Dam, one of the principal suppliers of pure mountain water to Cape Town and parts of the Western Cape Province. The dam was opened in January 1958 and is notable for a 518 m long earth wall made watertight with a thick clay core. The man-made lake, 52 m deep in places, covers 308 ha. Across the water fine views may be seen of the various peaks of the Wemmershoek Mountains, particularly impressive in winter when covered in snow.

A permit is required to visit Wemmershoek Dam, valid only on the day for which it is issued. It is obtainable in Cape Town from the Administration Services of the Water and Waste Directorate which is situated on the 7th floor of 38 Wale Street. There are picnic sites below the wall of the dam and trout fishing is allowed in the river.

From the turn to Wemmershoek Dam the road continues through well-wooded and fertile farming country. Passing the lovely homesteads of *L'Arc D'Orleans* and *La Paris*, and the unlovely Drakenstein (Victor Verster) Prison, the road (7,5 km from its start) reaches the turn-off to Safariland, a game park and holiday resort, open daily 08h00 to 17h30. After a further 4 km, the road passes what used to be the original Paarl municipal caravan park and holiday resort of Wateruintjiesvlei, now privately run and named Boschenmeer. Just beyond this, on the opposite side of the road, lies the almond orchard and nut farm established by Nic Taylor. There is a farm stall selling a range of tree nuts such as almonds, Brazil, cashew, hazel, macadamia, pecan and walnuts. It is open daily 09h00 to 18h00. Beyond the entrance to the farm, 12,5 km from its start, the road passes under the N1 Cape Town–Johannesburg road and enters the municipal area of Paarl.

The main road down the Drakenstein Valley which the road from Stellenbosch joined at Groot Drakenstein station, 15 km from Franschhoek, leads down the southern side of the valley. The floor of the valley is covered with pine plantations, vineyards and orchards, while the pleasant scene is dominated from the south by the great bulk of Simonsberg.

Less than 1 km along the road there is a gravel turn-off leading to one of the most beautiful of all the homesteads of the Cape.

BIEN DONNÉ

The estate of *Bien Donné* (well beloved) was originally granted in 1691 to the Huguenot, Pierre Lombard, who had arrived in the Cape with his wife in 1688. He was described as being a sick man but an excellent farmer. A second farm, adjacent to the first, was granted to him in 1699. In 1762 *Bien Donné* was bought by Jean de Villiers of *Boschendal*. His son Dawid settled on the farm with his wife Johanna, produced sixteen children and, in 1800, built the manor-house and farmyard buildings.

Other owners followed for the large families usual in those days could not possibly remain together on a single property. Only by sale could each individual obtain a share of inheritance. After the disastrous *phylloxera* epidemic in the 1890s ruined most of the wine farmers of the Western Cape, Pickstone bought the estate for Cecil Rhodes.

In 1936 *Bien Donné* was bought by the South African Government and it became a fruit research farm. The Agricultural Research Council own the property today and manage it through the Infruitec/Nietvoorbij Fruit and Wine Institute in Stellenbosch. The manor-house and farmyard buildings have been restored as proclaimed historical monuments. They are under the administration of the Directorate of Cultural Affairs, Western Cape.

The manor-house is open to visitors. Research, breeding, evaluation and processing of new fruit varieties continues in the orchards. Manor-house and orchard tours are organised. There is a magnificent herb garden where exotic and indigenous herbs are grown, including the South African honeybush tea, a healthy, natural drink with a rice aroma, freedom from caffeine and good for allergies and the skin. There are tastings of fruit juices, new fruit varieties, herb products and regional cooking using herbs.

There is a restaurant in a pleasant setting, conference facilities and the manor-house is used as a setting for art exhibitions, music, lectures and workshops. Banquets featuring regional foods and drinks are regularly held in the manor-house. It would be impossible for any visitor to leave *Bien Donné* without any enthusiasm and appreciation of the benefits and flavours of fruit, nuts and herbs used in cooking or eaten fresh. There is a farm shop.

After 2 km of travel the main tarmac road reaches the hamlet of Simondium, named after Pierre Simond, the minister and head of the original Huguenot community. The place comprises a huddle of shops, post office, garage, church, hotel and two schools.

From Simondium there is another tarmac road turning off to *Bien Donné* 3 km away. Less than 1 km after leaving Simondium, there is a turn-off left, leading to the wine farm of *Le Plessis Marlé*, originally granted to the Huguenot, Charles Marais, and named after a village near Paris. The name has been corrupted to *Plaisir de Merle*. The carefully maintained homestead is dated 1764. This farm is now the possession of the Stellenbosch Farmers' Winery and is their largest vineyard. It supplies grapes for many of their wines such as the prestigious range of Nederburg. Beyond the turn-off to this farm, there is another turn-off, this one leading for 8,5 km to join the Klapmuts–Stellenbosch road. At 3 km along this road there stands the lovely farmhouse of Babylonstoren (tower of Babylon), the possession of the Louw family for several generations. Just beyond this farmhouse, there is a turn-off to the wine estate of *Backsberg*, one of the finest vineyards in the Cape.

The farm *Klein Babylonstoren* (little tower of Babylon) was named after the hillock which dominates it. In 1916 Charles Back, an immigrant from Lithuania, acquired this estate. He was joined by his son Sydney in 1938, by John Martin in 1955 as manager, and by Sydney's son Michael in 1971. The estate was developed skillfully until its 160 ha of vines (55 percent red varieties) became one of the most notable producers of fine quality wine in the Cape. Drip irrigation, with each vine receiving 9 litres of water twice a week, is used on the farm. Incessant care and labour have produced superb vineyards.

A modern cellar, including a beautifully designed cave cellar, allows the production of an outstanding range of wines whose quality reflects something of the pleasant atmosphere of the estate. There is an interesting little museum containing wine-making implements and a very amusing series of cartoons featuring 'Bull'. Visitors are welcome. Guided tours are conducted through the cellar, with the process of wine-making illustrated throughout the year by means of closed-circuit television.

A modern innovation has been the making of Backsberg Estate Brandy matured in Limousin oak barrels for three years, with the first release in 1994.

Wine is sold on the estate Mondays to Fridays from 08h30 to 17h00 and on Saturdays and non-religious public holidays from 08h30 to 13h00. With over 40 000 people visiting the estate each year, and many sending orders through the post, almost the entire production of *Backsberg* is sold direct to the public.

The road from Simondium which leads past the entrance to *Backsberg* joins the Klapmuts–Stellenbosch road after a further 5 km. The hamlet of Klapmuts and the junction with the main Cape Town–Johannesburg road lie less than a kilometre to the right. To the left is the beautiful 12 km drive to Stellenbosch.

Back on the main road which runs down the Drakenstein Valley, at 1 km beyond the turn-off to Klapmuts, the road passes first the Simondium (formerly Drakenstein) Co-operative Winery and then a series of vineyards, fruit orchards and nurseries. In spring this area is particularly beautiful. The Babylonstoren road leads to the crocodile farm of *Le Bonheur* (good fortune) which is open daily 09h00 to 17h00. At 9 km from Groot Drakenstein station the road passes the turn-off to the Berg River Resort and then leads under the railway line to the north and joins the old main road which enters Paarl. A turn left along the old road leads, after 1 km, past the Simonsvlei Co-operative Winery. Visitors are welcome and there are wine sales during normal business hours. Farm stalls, such as Strawberry King, sell strawberries of superb quality from September to December.

PAARL

The municipality of *Paarl* (pearl) with its population of 105 763, lies on the banks of the Berg River at the foot of a cluster of giant granite domes which surge 654 m into the sky and provide a remarkable contrasting landmark in a countryside dominated by folded ranges of reddish-coloured sandstone.

It was in October 1657 that Abraham Gabbema, a pioneer explorer from the settlement at the Cape, became the first European to reach the valley of the Berg River. The cluster of granite domes, moistened by rain, glistened so much in the sunlight that he named them the *paarl* (pearl) and *diamandt* (diamond) mountains, while the valley in which the town was destined to grow became known as the *Paarl-vallei* (pearl valley).

In 1687 the first farms were granted to settlers in the area. *Laborie, Goede Hoop, La Concorde* and *Picardie* were settled by French Huguenots in the following year. *Laborie*, on the slopes of the Paarl mountains, is now owned by the KWV who run it as a model wine estate. The restored homestead is used to entertain guests of the wine farmers' co-operative, and its period furniture is magnificent. There is a winehouse in an adjoining building and a guest-house. With many of the original farmlands which formerly surrounded Paarl converted into housing estates (productive of children rather than food and drink), it is commendable that an estate such as *Laborie*, with its homestead and farmyard facing directly on to the main street of the town, should be preserved as a living reminder of the past.

The town of Paarl had no formal beginning. It simply grew up haphazardly on either side of what was at first known as *De Kaapsche Wagenpad* (the Cape wagon road). In 1720 a church was built and this is often considered to have been the start of the town, although the first settlers were in the area in 1687 and there was a water-mill in operation by 1699. Several beautiful buildings were erected in the town. One of the best of these to survive is the *Oude Pastorie* (old parsonage), built in 1787. In 1937 the Oude Pastorie was bought by the municipality. In commemoration of the 250th anniversary of the arrival of the Huguenots, it was restored and converted into a cultural museum containing a fine collection of antique furniture, Cape silver, glass, copper and brassware. An interesting curiosity is a lace-making machine. Visitors should note the lock, handle and bolt on the door at the back of the main room. The museum is open Mondays to Fridays 10h00 to 17h00.

Another interesting old building is the homestead of *Vergenoegd* (contented) situated at 188 Main Street. This building is now used as a home for the aged. The original yellowwood and stinkwood doors and windows and the well in the backyard are features of this place.

Also facing Main Street is the Dutch Reformed *Strooidakkerk* (thatched roof church), consecrated on 28 April 1805 and still in use. The church stands in a spacious, shady churchyard amid flower-beds, smooth lawns and cypress trees. The interior, cruciform in shape, is severe in the Calvinist manner, but impressive. It contains a fine pulpit, galleries, and a sounding-board which must have amplified the words of many sermons. The place is deliciously cool during summers which are notable in Paarl for some very hot days. The architect, George Conrad Küchler, designed the church. Its gables are superb. The rather sun-baked little graveyard contains gabled vaults and some interesting tombstones.

The church is kept locked but visits may be made by request at the church office. There is often somebody working in the grounds or building who will open the door.

A walk through Paarl will reveal several other examples of architecture which survive from different periods. Zeederberg Square contains a variety of restored buildings which are worth seeing. Zeederberg House, dating from 1848, is a two-storeyed brick-built home with tall shuttered windows. The *Toringkerk* (tower church) in Main Street is another fine building. Of the various buildings erected in modern times, La Concorde – the administrative offices of the KWV and headquarters of the South African wine industry – is elegantly beautiful, with a fine entrance graced by some magnificent vines, the leaves of which turn blood-red in autumn. It was completed in 1958. The Gymnasium Primary School, opposite the museum, is notable for its fine Egyptian elements.

One very extraordinary construction in Paarl unfortunately no longer remains. A miller named Blake had a water-mill with a wheel so enormous that it resembled something from the famous Vienna amusement park. Harry Lime might well have taken a turn in it! The building, minus the wheel, is still in use as a municipal store.

Paarl became a municipality on 9 October 1840. The original wagon road became the long main road and a programme was commenced of planting oaks. The town is considered to be the third oldest in South Africa. The railway reached the place in 1859. It developed into a substantial and prosperous town, a farming centre, and the home of some specialised industries, notably the working of granite into building stone and tombstones, and the building of wagons and Cape carts. Paarl wagons were renowned and they played a major part in the exploration and development of the whole of Southern Africa. The middle reaches of the Berg River valley were often known as the *Val du Charron* (valley of wagons) or the *Wagenmakers Valleij* (wagonmakers' valley), and Paarl inherited this reputation when it grew as a centre for the industry. The prosperous wagonmakers erected some lavish homes for themselves reminiscent of the feather palaces of Oudtshoorn.

Culturally, Paarl played a major part in the establishment of the Afrikaans language. A man from the Netherlands, Arnoldus Pannevis, who taught classical languages at the Paarl Gymnasium, became increasingly aware in the 1870s that, while Dutch was the established language, the vast majority of people could hardly comprehend it. Over the years the common people had lost touch with High Dutch to such an extent that they had created not simply a dialect but a new language, Afrikaans. Pannevis discussed the matter with several of his colleagues and on 14 August 1875, at a meeting in the homestead of Gideon Malherbe (a farmer who was married to the daughter of Dr G W A van der Lingen, the principal of the Gymnasium), the *Genootskap van Regte Afrikaners* (Institute of True Afrikaners) was formed with the purpose of establishing Afrikaans as a written and accepted language.

With his colleagues, Pannevis worked on the grammar and vocabulary of the language. On 15 January 1876 they launched the first Afrikaans newspaper, *Die Afrikaanse Patriot*, printed on a simple little press in Malherbe's house. This press was from then on responsible for the production of many books in Afrikaans. It was in Paarl, in January 1896, that the first congress on the language was held and the ultimately successful campaign commenced to establish Afrikaans as an official language of South Africa.

The residence of Gideon Malherbe is now an Afrikaans language museum. It has been perfectly restored, the seven rooms of the upper floor displaying the history of the language while the five rooms on the ground floor are maintained as they were when the Malherbes were in residence from 1860 to 1921. It is a fascinating collection which should be seen by every visitor to Paarl. The Afrikaanse Taal Museum is open Mondays to Fridays 09h00 to 17h00. Phone (021) 872-3441.

On a commanding viewsite high on the slopes of the Paarl Mountains an impressive monument to the Afrikaans language has been erected and is visible for a considerable distance. It is reached by a tarmac road 5 km long, leading from Main Street just after it passes under the main Cape Town–Johannesburg road at the southern entrance to Paarl.

THE TAAL MONUMENT

The *Taal Monument* (language monument) was designed by Jan van Wijk. It is built of concrete and stands in a handsome setting of granite boulders and indigenous trees. The monument has several distinct features. Three linked columns symbolise the contribution of the enlightened West; three round shapes represent the magic, mystery and tradition of Africa; a low wall depicts the cultural contribution of the Indonesian people to Afrikaans; a rising wall merges into a covered corridor, symbolising a bridge, the way Afrikaans forms a link between Europe and Africa. The corridor leads to a 57 m high pillar which soars upwards from a spring of clear water at its base. This pillar is hollow, and light from the top pours down, illuminating the water at its base. A second pillar, parallel and close to the language pillar, symbolises the political growth of the Republic of South Africa. The monument was inaugurated on 10 October 1975. It is open daily from 08h00 to 17h00. Phone (021) 863-2800.

Today Paarl consists of an amiable mixture of assorted homes of many different architectural styles; vineyards, old oaks and young jacaranda trees – all gathered along the pivot of an 11 km long main street which stretches beneath the shade of trees to the northern boundary of the town.

One kilometre from the start of this main street at the turn-off from the main road to Cape Town there is a turn left marked Jan Phillips Drive. Jan Phillips was one of the most successful wagon-makers of Paarl. When the project of this fine scenic drive was first mooted, he contributed £5 000 of the £9 000 used for the construction. The gravel road, opened in 1928, with its 10 km of shady driving and spectacular views of the Berg River valley, is in its way an admirable memorial to the wagons and carts which, built at Paarl, left the tracks of their wheels on countless thousands of kilometres of the pioneer trails of Southern Africa.

Six kilometres along this road lies the picnic ground and entrance to the mountain reserve and wild-flower garden situated in the sheltered valley of the *Meulwater* (mill water), the stream which once provided power for the water-mill. The garden, dedicated to Lil de Villiers who founded the Paarl Town Beautifying Society in 1931, is one of the finest wild-flower reserves in the Cape. Spectacularly positioned on the mountain slopes, its collection of pincushions and proteas is particularly impressive (especially *Leucospermum reflexum*). In the late spring the masses of red, orange and yellow flowers provide the colour photographer with superlative opportunities.

Just beyond the entrance to the garden the road forks. The right-hand fork is the continuation of the Jan Phillips Drive, leading for a further 4 km along the mountain slopes and yielding magnificent views over the vineyards before it descends to join the tarmac road from Paarl to Malmesbury.

The left-hand fork (after the wild-flower reserve) climbs past the picnic ground known as Pienaarskamp, and then reaches a fork. The left-hand side leads onwards around the top of the garden and past what is still known as Breakfast Rocks where, in the energetic old days, walkers on what was then only a path, paused to refresh themselves. The habit has for so long been abandoned that the site is now simply and rather unromantically marked by a sign warning visitors not to light fires or pollute the water.

Past Breakfast Rocks the road continues climbing. After a total of 3 km the road reaches a sharp turn at a clump of pine trees. From this point a footpath leads to the top of the granite dome known today as Paarl Rock. There is no means of knowing precisely to what point Gabbema applied his names of Diamandt and Paarl. Some speculate that the names apply to the mass of rock known today as *Gladdeklip* (slippery stones) which lies to the left of Paarl Rock (as seen from Paarl), which certainly has a pronounced glitter in wet weather. Others are of the opinion that the names apply to high twin domes, nowadays known as Britannia and Gordon's rocks.

Paarl Rock, although substantially lower than the twins behind it, nevertheless dominates the town of Paarl. On the top is a beacon and an old ship's cannon which originally stood on Kanonkop and was used to inform farmers of the *Agter-Paarl* (behind Paarl) that shipping had arrived in Table Bay and required fresh provisions. The summit of Paarl Rock is littered with an extraordinary assembly of giant boulders. To the left of the beacon stands a strange vaulted and hollowed boulder, reputedly once used by a runaway murderer as his hiding-place. The smoke from his cooking fire eventually betrayed his retreat. He was arrested and hanged, but his curious hideaway is still haunted by his presence, for the wisp of smoke which betrayed him is said to be occasionally seen rising into the clear air at dawn. Passing beneath this boulder, the footpath finds its way to a truly colossal rock, easily visible from all around. The base of this rock is riddled with caves, niches and hollows in which one half expects to find standing a few petrified sentries. The acoustics of the main caves are remarkable – a whisper at the narrow end is amplified and penetrates the full length of the cave. The atmosphere of Paarl Rock is very reminiscent of the Matopo Hills in Zimbabwe.

From the parking area at Paarl Rock the road makes a sharp turn to the right and for a final half-kilometre climbs to its terminus at the foot of the two giant granite domes, Britannia (left) and Gordon's (right). A footpath leads to the top of Britannia with chains to provide help on the steeper portions. The view from the summit is impressive and the climb is easy and worthwhile. A very clear echo resounds from the face of Gordon's Rock (which is more difficult to climb). Just beyond the parking area the footpath to Britannia Rock passes the great leaning rock shelter with its natural rock table (about which there is a legend that poltergeists have been observed playing cards there). At this point a less-used path branches right and takes the climber up a steep slope, eventually leading to the summit of Gordon's Rock through a narrow cleft with a chimney rather awkward for stout people. A fine view of Britannia Rock, however, rewards the climber. The origin of the names Gordon and Britannia (or Bretagne) is obscure. It is said that a young man named Gordon slipped and was killed on the one rock.

From the top of these two granite domes the nature of the surrounding highlands of the Paarl Mountains may be seen. Gravel roads provide access to most parts of this highland. It is a catchment area for the Paarl municipal water supply. Wild flowers and small game are numerous in the area. A few pairs of black eagles still occur. There are several popular picnic grounds such as Tredoux Camp, Christmas Camp, *Renosterkop* (named after a tree stump shaped like a rhino), *Oulapklip* (where the Oukraal Club of athletic types who walked or ran up the mountains had their meeting-place), and Waboomkop, the highest point in the Paarl Mountains, from the summit of which may be seen a vast panoramic view. The reservoirs, Nantes and Bethel, built in the valleys leading down to the farms of those names, are stocked with black bass and trout.

Paarl is the headquarters of the KWV (Koöperatiewe Wijnbouwers Vereniging van Zuid-Afrika Beperkt), founded in 1918 as the umbrella organisation of the wine producers of South Africa. Its administrative office, La Concorde, is a notably attractive modern building in the Cape-Dutch style. The frieze over the main entrance, the gateway, gardens, interior, and the vines growing on trellises, all contribute to a sensitive piece of design. Also in Paarl is the main cellar complex of the organisation, heavy with the aroma of millions of litres of wine and spirits. From here some 70 per cent of South Africa's wine and spirit exports are handled.

The KWV has a permanent exhibition devoted to the wine industry. Lectures and wine-tastings are presented, and there are conducted tours every day of the week. For information on time and to book, phone (021)807-3007/8. On *Laborie* a restaurant and taphouse have been built on traditional lines. A cellar is stocked with the wines of the Berg River valley. These may be purchased during normal business hours. A festival of the Vine takes place each March when local winemakers introduce their product to the public.

Paarl is the starting-point each July for the KWV canoe marathon down the Berg River for over 230 km to its mouth at Port Owen. The race lasts four days and attracts many hundreds of entrants.

THE PAARL ARBORETUM

Paarl is fortunate in possessing a superb collection of trees gathered from all over the world. The trees grow in an arboretum covering a 2,8 km length of the east bank of the Berg River and occupying 31 ha with a fascinating and beautiful parkland, green and shady, with paths for walkers and joggers but no disturbance from vehicles.

The arboretum had its origin in 1957 when Mr A E Short, the town treasurer, recommended its establishment to the Paarl town council. The ground was a Crown grant made in 1910 and ideal for a riverside park, garden or recreational area. The town council accepted the idea of an arboretum. A great collection of trees started Municipalities all over Southern Africa were informed of the project, and 61 of them donated trees and shrubs and participated in a tree-planting ceremony to mark the establishment of the arboretum in October 1957 during the tercentenary celebration of the discovery of the Berg River valley. Professor H B Rycroft, then the Director of the National Botanic Gardens of South Africa, officially inaugurated the Paarl Arboretum.

For the next 30 years there was intensive work in planting and layout. Mr A M J Scheltens, who was in charge from 1959 to 1971, was largely responsible for developing the park into its present state, dividing it into six sections, each containing trees and shrubs originating from different continents, 48 species from South America, 185 species from Asia, 93 species from North America, and 113 species from Australasia. Today a total of about 4 000 trees of over 700 species grow in the arboretum. In shelters between each continental division there are detailed plans showing tree positions. Most of the trees also have identification plaques. The Paarl Arboretum is open 24 hours.

On the road to Suid Agter-Paarl lie three wine estates which are open to the public. *Fairview* is 2,8 km from Paarl, the road to it branching off from the old main road linking Paarl to Klapmuts, just beyond the turn-off to Franschhoek. *Fairview* estate, 2,3 km along this road, was bought in 1973 by C L Back, father of Sydney Back of Backsberg. On the death of Mr Back, *Fairview* was taken over by his son Cyril who was joined by his son Charles.

The estate produces a range of wines of excellent quality and is also renowned for its cheeses, made from the milk of Jersey cows and a herd of goats whose lively antics, including a spiral climb up a goat tower, are a source of amusement to visitors. Cheese and wine tastings and sales are held daily during normal business hours and cellar tours are arranged on request.

One kilometre beyond *Fairview* lies the estate of *De Leeuwen Jagt* (the lion hunt) with its original homestead and cellars handsomely restored.

Another kilometre take the road past the entrance to the estate of *Landskroon*, owned by the De Villiers family since 1874. Their red wines are notable and there is an excellent port-type wine. A large herd of thoroughbred Jersey cows, the Fairseat Jersey cattle stud, produce the ingredients for excellent cheese. Wine and cheese can be tasted and are sold to the public during normal business hours. From mid-November to the end of April there is a Vintner's Platter lunch from Mondays to Fridays between 11h30 and 14h30.

Brandy of superlative quality is produced in Paarl. It was on a rainy day in 1856 that the De Villiers brothers founded Paarlsche Wijn & Brandewijn Maatschappy Beperkt. They named the company after their town, which, in those days, was little more than a street with vineyards, and a solid day's horseback ride to Cape Town.

The De Villiers family was well respected in the infant town and entertained elegantly. The story goes that their home – opposite the small family cellar in Main Street so that they could keep a watchful eye on proceedings – was linked to the maturation cellar by underground bamboo pipes. A mere turn of the tap kept glasses filled and guests happy.

The De Villiers' ambition to create a brandy which pleased the most fastidious palates was realised, and their golden liquid soon glowed in the crystal glasses of the Cape aristocracy.

The arrival, in 1863, of the *Alabama* at the Cape provided the opportunity for the international debut of what was known as Paarl Rock Brandy. Raphael Semmes, captain of the famed Confederate raider, was so taken with the brandy that he stocked his officers' saloon with it and shared it proudly at every port of call. The result was requests to purchase from as far away as England and Europe.

Onze Jan Hofmeyr, leading political figure and man of culture, shared his enjoyment of Paarl Rock with Cecil John Rhodes who persuaded Hofmeyr to sell him 240 £1 shares in the company.

In the north, where gold and diamond fever ran high, the wealthy Randlords were far too sophisticated to drink the 'Cape Smoke' so popular amongst the diggers. They served Paarl Rock in their palatial homes and exclusive clubs.

Over 130 years have passed, but Paarl Rock is still made as it was in the days of the De Villiers brothers when one, or both, supervised every step. The original secret recipe – handed down from generation to generation – was stipulated in the company's *Akte van Overeenkomst*.

This brandy can never be plentiful. Only selected wines are used. Double distillation in traditional pot stills ensures purity and lightness. Maturation is only in vats made from French oaks over 100 years old. The young distilled wine and wood stay wedded for many years, whereafter the brandy is blended according to the De Villiers' original recipe. Over the years Paarl Rock has been rewarded with more than 200 medals at international brandy shows.

In 1949 it became necessary to move the cellar from the hustle and bustle of Main Street to a quieter corner in Dal Josafat. Visitors can view the distillation process in the quiet maturation cellars of Paarl Rock Brandy Cellar, and taste Paarl Rock in the De Villiers Dining-Room furnished with antiques from the De Villiers home and memorabilia of Paarl Rock history.

Cellar tours take place from Mondays to Thursdays at 11h00 and 15h00 and at 11h00 on Fridays. Phone (022) 862-6159.

From Paarl there are two main tarmac roads running down the valley of the Berg River to Wellington. Main Street North, on the western side of the Berg River, branches off from the top of Lady Grey Street and provides a pleasant drive through the northern residential area of Paarl. After 3 km the road passes the turn-off to the Jan Phillips mountain road. A further half-kilometre takes the road to a branch. A right turn leads to Malmesbury and turn-offs to Wellington. Continuing ahead, the road leads behind the granite mountains to Agter-Paarl, and then for 5 km past several fine vineyards, farms and estates such as Rhebokskloof, with its restaurant in a restored Cape-Dutch building and 450 ha of vineyards. At 8,8 km the road crosses the Klapmuts–Wellington road. A right turn leads for 8 km over the Paarl–Malmesbury road, across the Berg River bridge and into Wellington. Continuing down the western side of the river, the Malmesbury road also leads to a turn to another Berg River bridge into Wellington after 5,5 km (a total of 14 km from Paarl).

The second road to Wellington, travelling down the eastern side of the valley, leads from the bridge over the river at Huguenot station at the bottom end of Lady Grey Street. This road proceeds through the industrial area of *Dal Josafat* (dale of Joseph) and reaches Wellington after 10 km of travel. Two kilometres along this road from Paarl is a turn-off leading to the wine farm of Nederburg.

NEDERBURG

The most prestigious wine producer in Southern Africa, *Nederburg*, had its origin in 1792. Sebastiaan Cornelis Nederburgh, Chief Advocate of the Dutch East India Company, was in that year engaged in the investigation of various complaints, irregularities, abuses and problems in the administration of the Cape. In the course of his inquiry, the Chief Advocate was aided by Philip Wolvaart, to whom was subsequently granted a farm which he named after Mr Nederburgh. Nowadays the name is spelled without the 'h'.

The homestead of *Nederburg* was built in 1800. Farming commenced on the estate, but a succession of owners failed to raise the place to a position of any considerable eminence. The right man to appreciate the potential of the farm only came in 1937. In that year, a brewer from Bremen in Germany, Johann Georg Graue, acquired *Nederburg*. He was a dedicated, intuitive and eager winemaker and the possibilities of *Nederburg* excited him. Lying on the eastern side of the Berg River valley, the lands of the estate covered part of the foothills of the Klein Drakenstein Mountains. There was considerable variation in altitude, soils (sandstone, shale, granite) and directional slopes. The Berg River valley is a notably hot area in summer, but the directional variations of the *Nederburg* estate influence amounts of sunshine and exposure to the seasonal southeast wind. This wind – warm, unpolluted, healthy and locally rain-free – could vitally influence vine diseases and fungi.

Johann Graue began a detailed study of the farm in all its different parts. He replanted *Nederburg* with the finest vine varieties, especially cabernet sauvignon and riesling. The latest German innovations of control and cellar technique were also introduced, including cold fermentation. Aided by his wife Ilse and his only son Arnold, Johann Graue made spectacular progress. By 1953 *Nederburg* had won 8 gold medals, 158 first prizes and 104 trophies for excellent wines.

Unfortunately a disaster occurred. On 12 September 1953 at Youngsfield aerodrome in Cape Town, a military training plane accidentally landed on top of a light plane taxiing along the runaway. The pilot of the light plane was Arnold Graue, then 28 years of age. He was killed, and the effect on *Nederburg* was traumatic. For some time Johann Graue thought of letting the whole place go, for it was inextricably tied up with memories of his son.

At the time of the accident, the great wine farm was looking its best. It was the beginning of spring. Father and son had recently added to it a new farm high in the foothills. This acquisition they had named *Hochheim* after the area in the Rhinelands where the famous Hocks of German wines were produced. The two men had planned many innovative experiments on this high vineyard. Johann Graue could not simply abandon everything.

In 1955, two years after the accident, Werner Thielscher, one of Johann Graue's associates, went to Germany on business. In Weinsberg he found a young man named Günter Brözel working as a cellar and research assistant in the State Research and Training Institute for the wine industry. Born on 3 April 1934 Günter Brözel came from a family of winemakers and coopers. He was an articulate and sensitive individual, greatly dedicated to his career as winemaker. Brözel accepted the offer of a position as assistant to Horst Saalwaechter, who was the winemaker of *Nederburg*.

Brözel reached *Nederburg* on 6 February 1956 and found the farm on the threshold of a great change. Johann Graue had decided to withdraw gradually from the actual management, but to do so in such a way that *Nederburg* would live, progress and not be harmed by the change. In July 1956 he sold 50 per cent of the shares to the firm of Monis, producers of high-grade sherry type and sweet dessert wines in the Italian style, such as Marsala and Moscato. Roberto Moni, the founder of this firm, had immigrated to South Africa from Italy in 1905 and had created in Paarl a substantial business of high reputation.

The winemaker of Monis, Dr E N Costa, was regarded as a man of considerable skill. He took over the direction of *Nederburg*, with Günter Brözel becoming his principal technician. When Johann Graue died on 12 April 1959, he was comforted by the knowledge that his beloved *Nederburg* was in excellent hands. By the end of 1978 *Nederburg* had produced 22 wines which had been awarded the ultimate certification of Superior. In 1985 Günter Brözel gained the distinction of Winemaker of the Year at the prestigious International Wine and Spirit Competition held in Britain. He twice won the Diners Club 'Winemaker of the Year' award. *Nederburg*'s reputation became world wide, backed by more than 900 international awards. By the end of 1988 *Nederburg* had produced far and away a greater volume of wines which were awarded the certification of Superior than any other estate in South Africa.

The production of a late harvest wine, the first in South Africa to receive Superior certification, led the winemakers of *Nederburg* to achieve their ultimate goal – the creation of an *Edelkeur* (noble choice), the pride of the estate and the first of its kind to be produced in South Africa.

For such a wine to be produced, the South African wine law itself had to be changed. This law excluded the production in South Africa of wines similar to the Sauternés of France, the Trockenbeerenauslesen of Germany and the Tokai essences of Hungary. The winemakers of *Nederburg* sensed, however, that conditions in the Cape were near ideal for the production of this type of royal wine, and they longed to be allowed the opportunity to do so by law.

The technique of creating this type of wine had been pioneered by the Benedictine Abbey of Fulda in Germany. Carefully selected, specially cultivated noble grapes are used. Even before the first budding in spring the vines are carefully watched. Pruning, amount of rain, amount of sunshine, soil chemistry, humidity – all are regularly checked and studied. If conditions are considered suitable, the grapes are left to ripen to perfection in the sun.

At this critical stage a fungus, *Botrytis cinerea*, plays a vital part. This little spore lurks in the soil and on the leaves of the vines, hungry for sugar and filled with overwhelming desire to consummate a union with the good things contained in the berries. Within the ripening time, Nature must intervene with a very light drizzle providing 100 per cent humidity for at least 24 hours. A film of water forms over the sun-ripened grape just before it turns into a raisin. In this water film, the spore develops two fins. Aided by these fins, it swims over the surface of the grape and, as the skin is softened by the water and loses its resistance, the spore finds a weak spot and enters the berry, roots itself and starts to feed on the sugar.

As it feeds, the fungus extracts water at a faster rate than it does the sugar. The sugar content within the grape therefore rises in proportion to the volume of water. The grape shrinks, shrivels and becomes a raisin. The wind, now welcome, must blow away the exuded moisture until the sugar concentration is as near to the winemaker's ideal of a luscious 50 per cent as possible. Throughout this process, the winemaker – a voyeur with a magnifying glass – is testing and watching the love affair of berry and spore, picking a couple of berries here and there, putting them into a breeding disk under simulated conditions to see what will happen to the 'lovers' in the vineyard under possible climatic changes.

If the mists are insufficient, the soil must be saturated to provide moisture by evaporation. Weather conditions are decisive; the exact day of harvest must be selected just before the berries are in any danger of turning sour. Picking can only be done by hand, for it is selective. Normally a wine grape yield is 8 to 12 tons per hectare. From the royal grapes, 2 to 4 tons at most are produced. Even the harvesting is done under government scrutiny and discipline. With the harvest in, the winemaker turns midwife, the wine being the infant. Starting in 1962, two vintages were obtained but could not be sold. In 1969 the wine law was changed to allow marketing of a royal wine. More knowledgeable production commenced. Edelkeur could only be marketed if it was certified as Superior. An inferior vintage of an Edelkeur could only be used as an enrichment for other wines. Analysis of the 1984 vintage, which could be regarded as fairly typical, revealed a content of 12,26 per cent alcohol and 162,2 grams of sugar per litre. The wine had a rich golden colour and a sweet velvety smoothness on the palate.

Two other wines of *Nederburg* are especially notable. Eminence is made from the White Muscadel grape known as Muscat de Frontignan in France. The grapes are picked at a raisin-like stage and yield an aromatic wine, sweet and with magnificent Muscadel characteristics.

Nederburg Chardonnay 1984 was rated among the world's finest in a challenge by the international wine magazine, *Decanter*, to determine the best-tasting wines of this variety from ten countries. The tasting panel compiled a short list of 85 wines from the vineyards of France, Italy, Spain,

Portugal, Bulgaria, Canada, the United States, Australia, New Zealand and South Africa, dividing these into vintage groups with no other indication of provenance. Of the eleven wines selected from the Cape, an impressive six made it through to the finals (compared to four out of ten for France and nine out of twenty for the United States). When judging was over, *Nederburg*'s 1984 Chardonnay won second place in the tasting. The panel described the wine as a *'rich, full Chardonnay, high extract, good balance ... lovely bottle development'*. For the record, first place in the top ten was taken by Robert Mondavi Reserve Napa Valley Chardonnay 1985 of California.

Wine experts regard Chardonnay as the greatest white grape variety in the world. It yields a wine delicately dry with subtle wood maturation flavours. The variety originated in the Middle East. It was taken to France and became the classic ingredient in three of that country's premier wines – Chablis, White Burgundy and Champagne.

Nederburg is the scene of the annual South African wine auction, the principal event of the local wine industry. The auction was introduced in 1975. It takes place in April each year. The great estates of the Cape offer their finest wines for sampling by international buyers. Amid a lovely scene of sunshine, coloured tents, brightly dressed women, and serious wine authorities, quality is assessed and bids are made. The public may watch but only the trade may bid. Aided by the balmy weather (usual for this time of the year), generous sample tastings and vivacious company, the animated scene (becoming, perhaps, a little jollier towards the end) proceeds under the serene and benevolent gaze of the gracious old homestead. In 1979 a permanent hall, restaurant and other buildings, collectively known as the Johann Graue Centre, were built at *Nederburg* for use in these auctions and for exhibitions and functions.

In 1989, after 33 years of service at *Nederburg*, Günter Brözel retired. He was succeeded by Niewald Marais.

Just beyond the turn to *Nederburg* on the Wellington road, the Bo Dal Josafat road leads to the north and reaches the farm and homestead of *Schoongezicht*, now a restaurant and the centre for a considerable activity in the farming of *waterblommetjies* (*Aponogeton distachyos*), the small water flower which provides a delicacy for diners. They are known to the people of the Cape as *vleikos* (marsh food). The restaurant features these waterblommetjies on its menu, and each year at the beginning of October the place is the scene of a Waterblommetjie Festival where there is a great deal of good eating, drinking, jollification, and prizes for the person who can harvest the most flowers within ten minutes.

The restaurant is open daily (except Tuesdays) for lunch and tea; dinner Wednesdays to Saturdays.

DAL JOSAFAT

The area of Dal Josafat is the home of many industries, such as the cellars of Paarl Rock Brandy, jam manufacture, canning, packaging and other activities. Eastwards, towards the mountain slopes lies a lovely rural area of vineyards, olive groves and orchards, especially of guavas. A good way to see this area is to take the turn to Klein Drakenstein from the main road at Paarl East. This road leads for 8,5 km through the shopping centre of Klein Drakenstein and into the farming area. At 5,5 km there is a turn to the manor-house of *Mountain Shadows* was built in 1823 as the homestead on the farm *Deckersvlei* (thatcher's marsh). Today it is a perfectly restored and delightful place of accommodation, only 60 km from Cape Town and 7 km from the town of Paarl.

Apart from being a place of accommodation with a superlative cuisine and a renowned cellar of Cape wines, *Mountain Shadows* is also a centre for the discovery of the scenery of the Western Cape, and the excitingly varied sporting experiences of fishing for trout and bass in mountain streams, rock and deep-sea fishing within easy reach. Game and water birds are numerous, such as guinea-fowl, francolin, sandgrouse, Egyptian and spurwing geese, duck and teal.

Two kilometres before this turn-off there is a turn marked Dal Josafat. This leads past several farms and Cape-Dutch homesteads such as *Roggeland* (6,5 km), *Schoongezicht*, and the Dal Josafat Art Foundation.

The manor-house of *Roggeland* (ryelands) was built in 1778 as the homestead of the farm named *Dal Josafat*. For five generations the farm remained in the possession of the Du Toit family. It was Andries Bernhardus du Toit who built the present manor-house. A noteworthy interior feature of the house is its original four-leaved diamond-panelled *porte visite*, dating from 1821 and made from yellowwood and stinkwood. It separates the entrance hall from the dining-room. On the exterior of the manor-house is a curved staircase, used by goats to climb to their attic sleeping quarters.

The Hugo family eventually bought the farm. The homestead, now known as the Roggeland Country House, is owned today by Mildie Malan with Topsi Venter as the hostess. The two ladies pride themselves on the beauty, comfort and hospitality which they invite their guests to enjoy.

After 8 km this road joins the main Paarl–Wellington road 6 km from Wellington.

WELLINGTON

The traveller arrives in Wellington expecting to find something exciting and characteristic of the Western Cape. If he is willing to look beyond the rather dreary approach through the main street, which happens to be the unfortunate characteristic of most Boland towns, he will certainly find it.

The town was founded in 1840 after the church was completed as the centre for a farming community living in what was known as *Wagenmakersvallei* (wagonmakers' valley). The origin of this name is not certain, as there certainly was no wagon industry when the valley was named. Most probably, one of the first settlers was a wagonmaker by trade, and people spoke of *'the valley where the wagonmaker lives'*, or in Dutch *'De Wagenmaker s'n Vallei'*. A committee elected by local inhabitants, with Dr John Addey, a medical practitioner, as chairman, bought the farm *Champagne*, built the church and laid out the town. On completion, the Governor, Sir George Napier, was asked to give his name to the new town but replied that permission had been granted to a town near Klipdrift to be called Napier. He added, with thought *'Call it Wellington. It is a disgrace that in this colony no town bears that name'*. On 26 March 1840 the name of *Wellington* (after the renowned Duke of Wellington) was gazetted.

The original manor-house of *Champagne* farm has not survived. The house known today as *Twistniet*, at 31 Burg Street, was thought to be its manor-house, but research has revealed the fact that the original buildings were on the large grounds belonging to the Dutch Reformed Church in Church Street, where the manse of this church is built today. Unfortunately, the original buildings have been broken down. *Twistniet*, a national monument, is still worth visiting, although badly hemmed in by modern buildings. Built in 1811, it is a good example of the Cape-Dutch style.

The growth of Wellington (its population now stands at 45 224) was substantial after the opening of Bain's Kloof Pass in 1853, and the opening on 4 November 1863 of the Cape Town–Wellington railway, the first step of the long railway journey into the interior.

The scholastic importance of Wellington began with its farm schools, the two best-known being Mr M J Stucki's School in the Bovlei, and Mr C P Hoogenhout's in the Groenberg. They opened their doors in 1861 and 1864 respectively, and produced prominent figures in various fields, such as Paul Roos, Professor Gawie Cillié in education, and A F Markötter in sport.

The importance of Wellington as an educational centre became established when Dr Andrew Murray, a renowned minister of the Dutch Reformed Church, while on holiday in Kalk Bay on the Cape Peninsula, was given two volumes (*The Life and Labours of Mary Lyon* and *The History of the Mount Holyoke Seminary*) describing the founding in America of the Mount Holyoke College, a famous centre of church-inspired education. The account so impressed Murray that he resolved to establish a similar institution in Wellington where devout young women could be trained as teachers for evangelical and mission work.

Murray wrote to the principal of the Mount Holyoke College and asked if a teacher could be spared to come to South Africa. The appeal reached Miss Abbie Ferguson and, with Miss Anna Bliss, she sailed for the Cape in September 1873. On 19 January 1874, the Huguenot Seminary was opened in Wellington with 40 students. This was the small plant from which grew three large separate institutions: the Huguenot Girls' High School, the Huguenot College, later in 1916 becoming the Huguenot University College, and the Boland Teachers' College. The Huguenot University College closed in 1950, owing to the close proximity of larger universities, and its premises were taken over by the Huguenot College of the Dutch Reformed Church which concentrates on the training of social and mission workers and on Bible Study.

Dr Andrew Murray is suitably remembered in Wellington by a seated statue erected outside the church, and the preservation of his home, *Clairvaux*, situated near the town hall. Surrounding this house are the buildings belonging to the Huguenot College, of which the Samuel Hall, approached over a shady green lawn, is one of Wellington's most impressive buildings. The town is still the home of the Boland Teachers' College, and high and primary schools.

Industrially, Wellington is the centre of the South African dried fruit industry, where the Dried Fruit Board and the South African Dried Fruit Co-operative Ltd have their head offices. The industrial drying of fruit in South Africa had its start in the Valley of the Huguenots and the Wagonmakers' Valley. Men such as the renowned nurseryman H E V Pickstone of Groot Drakenstein, Piet 'California' Cillie of the farm *Vruchtbaar in die Bovlei*, and Senator Dan Retief of *Welvanpas*, also in the Bovlei, played major roles in establishing the dried fruit industry of South Africa.

In 1893 Petrus Cillie spent eight months studying the drying of fruit in California. On his return he was so filled with enthusiasm at what he had seen that he joined Pickstone in promoting the dream of a great fruit industry in South Africa. He organised the Pioneer Dried Fruit Company on his farm in the Bovlei, and this was the real beginning of the industry. The Wellington Fruit Growers (Pty) Limited was another of his creations. In March 1908, as a result of a meeting of farmers in the Hotel Masonic in Wellington, the South African Dried Fruit Company was formed with H E V Pickstone as its first chairman, a position he held for 30 years. In 1962, the company became the South African Dried Fruit Co-operative (SAD) which, from its headquarters in Wellington, with the Dried Fruit Board (founded in 1938), remains in control of an industry relatively small by world standards, but second to none in quality.

The fourth largest of the liquor distributors in Southern Africa, Union Wine Corporation, also has its headquarters in Wellington, while there are three co-operative wineries in the district: Bovlei, Wamakersvallei, and Wellington Wine Farmers' Co-operative. Wine is sold to the public from these co-operatives, and visitors are welcome during the harvest season. Two of these co-operatives have built facilities where not only their product may be tasted, but also the panoramic views over the mountains and vineyards can be appreciated.

Most of the vine cutting nurseries of the Cape are found in Wellington. There is also a large berry farming industry producing strawberries, raspberries, youngberries and gooseberries. Jams and berry vinegar are sold. Wild flowers are prolific throughout the year.

There are many fine private gardens in the town. Victoria Park is notable for its roses. The Coronation Arch commemorates the coronation of King Edward VII in 1902. Also carried on in the town is an industry unique to the area – piano-making.

In the vicinity of the town are situated several superb examples of Cape-Dutch architecture. *Versailles*, on Main Street, is a classic example of the H-shaped structure common to these houses. The great-grandfather of the present owner, Pieter Malan, donated land as a site for the Wellington railway station on condition that all passenger trains should stop there.

A cluster of these lovely old houses may be seen in the Bovlei area between Wellington and the foot of the dominant Groenberg massif. *Groenfontein, Lelienfontein* and *Welvanpas* are three of these homesteads. *Welvanpas* was granted in 1704 to Pierre Mooij whose 15-year-old daughter married Francois Retief in 1719. This couple were the grandparents of the Voortrekker leader, Pieter Retief, who was born in the Wellington district in 1780 and grew up on *Welvanpas*. *Hexenberg, Onverwacht, De Fortuin* and *Leeuwen Vallei* are other fine old houses.

Jacaranda trees flourish in the Wellington area and flower in November.

For an overview of the history of Wellington and its valley, a visit to the Wellington Museum is a must. Being a local history museum, everything on display, including the archaeological displays of Early, Middle and Late Stone Age implements and rock art, was collected locally. The section devoted to the history of Education includes the Huguenot archives which tell the story of the Seminary and College through documents and, visually, through photographs and furniture. Of special interest is a display of Egyptian antiquities presented to the Huguenot University College by Professor Leonard Woolley after his 1930–31 expedition to Tell El Amarna and Ur. This collection is considered to be one of the best in South Africa.

The scenic pride and joy of the Wellington district is the magnificent Limietberg range of mountains and the spectacular Bain's Kloof Pass which carries the road over its heights to Ceres and the Breede River valley. This mountain pass provides one of the most glorious scenic drives in Southern Africa.

BAIN'S KLOOF PASS

South Africans often do not realise how fortunate they are to live in a country which is not only beautiful, with an exciting atmosphere of unspoilt wilderness which is also accessible. The lovely mountain country above Wellington is a superb example of a scenic playground – all brought within the convenient reach of motorists, cyclists and walkers by means of an excellent road.

History tells us that Bain's Kloof Pass was first explored in 1846 by Andrew Geddes Bain, best known of all South African road engineers. At the time this busy engineer was working on the construction of Michell's Pass which was to lead a new road through the mountain barrier from the Breede River valley to Ceres. From his construction camp at the southern entrance to this pass, Bain faced the Elandskloof and Slanghoek ranges which provided so formidable a barrier between the valley of the Breede and the Berg rivers. He was intrigued by what appeared to be a natural gap in the obstacle which hindered easy transport to Cape Town. At that time the only roads from Cape Town to the interior went through Tulbagh Kloof (where the main railway line passes today) and the tortuous way over the Franschhoek Pass.

At the first opportunity Bain explored the apparent cleft through the mountains. Starting from the Wellington side, he set out before dawn one morning, climbed to the summit of the opening and spent a day scrambling along the boulder-strewn course of the Witte River whose erosive action has made this spectacular pass. By evening Bain had proved to his own satisfaction the practicability of the pass. After traversing the full length of the future road route, he arrived back safely at his construction camp at the entrance to Michell's Pass. The report he gave to his superiors reflected the excitement and pleasure at the discovery of a mountain passage at once so useful and beautiful.

As soon as Michell's Pass was completed, Bain set to work on the new pass. It was eventually opened in September 1853 with a cheerful ceremony. From then on the 18 km long pass became the established route through the mountains to the interior.

Many of the place-names originally given to remarkable portions of the pass survive as reminders of the pleasant, leisurely days of travel 100 years ago when surveyors could afford to leave a deliberate twist in a road or a tree or an overhanging rock, simply because their removal would scar the beauty of the scene. The names, Montagu Rocks, Bell Rocks, Pilkington Bridge and Dacres Pulpit, are still attached to features along the pass. Dacres Pulpit was the name applied to the rock overhanging the road with an unmistakable resemblance to the sounding-board of a pulpit. The Reverend Mr Dacres delivered a sermon there at the opening of the pass.

Such was the early history of Bain's Kloof Pass. Now take a journey along this most interesting scenic way. From Wellington the road to Ceres leaves the northern end of the jacaranda-lined Church Street and climbs steadily up the slopes of the Limietberg. The constant change of views is spectacular, and the pass has a singular air of the pioneer days when wagons laboured up the gradients and every metre gained seemed an achievement for the early travellers. Oak trees, gnarled and battered by the weather and mountain fires, line the route, inducing the wish that modern road engineers would plant more trees.

The Bovlei cellars stand next to the historic road from Wellington as it starts to climb up Bain's

Kloof Paass. The handsome modern buildings contain fermentation cellars, a modern grape press and processing facilities, a tasting, sales and reception room. Currently 73 wine-producing members of the Bovlei Co-operative supply the cellars with about 10 000 tons of grapes each season, and the range of varieties is considerable.

The grapes come mainly from three areas: Agter-Groenberg, Bovlei and Leeuwrivier. There are cool mountain slopes in the Bovlei and Leeuwrivier areas where white wine varietals such as Bukettraube, Sauvignon Blanc, Weisser Riesling and Riesling grow in slightly gravelly and sandy soils. On the northern slopes of the Agter-Groenberg and parts of the Bovlei and Leeuwrivier areas the soils are warmer and ideal for the cultivation of Cabernet Sauvignon, Pinotage, Cinsaut and Shiraz grapes. Full sweet wines originate from grapes with a high sugar content growing on the weather-protected slopes of the Bovlei and Leeuwrivier areas.

The Bovlei cellars on Bain's Kloof Road are open during normal business hours.

After 13 km of climbing, the road reaches the summit of the Pass. A tremendous view to the left (the west) may be seen. On the right a gravel track leads into the valley of the upper *Witte* (white) River. A chain prevents vehicles from using this track. Permission to use the track (and a key to the lock) must be obtained from the forester at the Hawequas Nature Conservation Station further down the main pass.

The track is worth exploring. The Witte River, whose erosive activity has produced this great natural pass through the mountains, is so named because its waters are comparatively free of the dark amber colour common to most of the peat-stained mountain streams of the Cape. It is one of the principal upper tributaries of the Breede River. Anyone who has followed the Witte to its source will agree that the valley through which it flows is one of the most beautiful in this world of mountains. In late winter and in spring, Paradise Valley (as it is called) is a blaze of flowers. A succession of pools provide fine swimming and interesting fishing for brown trout. The mountains which hem in the valley provide endless attractions for climbers.

There are interesting stories about this valley. On the left-hand side of the road stands a concrete memorial with these words engraved upon it: *'Ter Gedagtenis Aan die Durf en Heldemoed van L van Dyk; F van Dyk; C Krynauw; Lettie de Jager. Witrivier Kamp.23 Mei, 1895'*.

This memorial refers to a most poignant tragedy which occurred in the last century. A party of thirteen girls from the Huguenot Seminary in Wellington set out to climb the 1 689 m high Sneeukop on 22 May 1895. They were caught in heavy rain and made the classic climbing mistake of dividing the party into two sections; with the stronger going on, and the weaker lagging behind.

The first party got back to the seminary at 20h50 but the others failed to arrive. A search-party, with the aid of lanterns, set out to find them. The searchers, reached the stream and found that it had suddenly come down in flood, marooning the second party on the opposite bank. More rescuers with ropes were obtained from Wellington. At dawn one of them, C Krynauw, swam across the river with a rope; and food and drink were taken across. Then four of the rescuers set out to ferry Miss De Jager across the stream. The current and the icy water of early winter proved too much for them. They managed to lift the girl on to a projecting rock but the normally happy little stream seemed to be intent on claiming human victims that day. As the people on the bank stood watching in horror, the flood rose sharply. Three of the men and the girl were carried away and drowned, with nobody able to do the slightest thing to help them. The rest of the party were eventually rescued by being carried over in a basket manoeuvred along a rope like a miniature cableway.

The relic of a much more recent disaster could be seen until recently on the saddle of land over which the track passes at the entrance to Paradise Valley. At this wonderful viewsite stood the melancholy ruin of the great Hugo mansion which was burned down on 22 February 1949 when a bush fire, fanned by a strong gale, swept across the mountains and set the place alight. The house had been built by the late P J Hugo, the Wellington jam manufacturer, on ground originally known as *Oosterberg*, but renamed by him *Paradise Estate* when he acquired it in 1939. He died before he could achieve his ambition of retiring to the place. His estate sold it together with a large tract of surrounding ground to the Paarl Municipality for use in a projected water scheme. At the time of the fire only a caretaker was in residence.

In the process of creating his dream home, Mr Hugo exploited one really curious modification made to the topography. In 1856 Gawie Retief, a farmer from *Welvanpas*, with the help of Bain, blasted out a deep furrow diverting water from the Witte River through the divide and then releasing it to flow down the mountains on the Wellington side where it could be used for irrigation by a group of farmers who contributed £1 200 for expenses in a complex piece of construction. By means of this furrow a portion of the normal flow of the river was redirected from one side of the watershed to the other. The regular course of the river is a tributary of the Breede leading to the Indian Ocean on the east coast. But the furrow carries its flow to join the Kromme River, itself a tributary of the Berg River which flows to the Atlantic Ocean on the west coast. Amongst other changes caused by this diversion was the escape of eels from the Breede River system and their population of the Berg River. So far as Mr Hugo was concerned, he used the artificial flow of water to feed a magnificent swimming-bath in the grounds of his mansion.

The ruins of the house were reputedly haunted. In 1979 a nasty murder took place when an escaped convict found camped there a young couple and their dog. They were innocently hiking through the mountains, but were most brutally killed.

The succession of swimming and fishing pools on the upper reaches of the Witte River are all worth visiting. Mountaineers who care to follow the river to its very end will be delighted to find some fine cascades, each with magnificent fern-girt pools lying at their feet. The ultimate springs of the stream occur on the slopes of the great Slanghoek Peak, from whose summit may be seen a fabulous view overlooking the Breede River valley into the heart of the Hex River Mountains. In winter it is almost like viewing the snow-covered Himalayas.

At the foot of Bain's Kloof Pass at Antonies Vlei there is a popular recreational resort.

On the summit of Bain's Kloof Pass, just beyond the gravel turn-off up Paradise Valley, the main road enters a pleasant thicket of wattle trees with an attractive picnic ground. A cluster of private holiday cottages have also been erected here. Various paths descend to swimming-pools in the Witte River. A hotel, the Hotel in the Mountains, once stood at the summit of the pass but was burned down in 1976.

From the end of the path on the Ceres side of the old hotel site across the river, another path climbs up the banks and then veers downstream. This is the start of a fine walk. The path climbs steadily up a mountain slope rich in wild flowers and for 6 km finds a way into the Baviaanskloof. This is a handsome valley hemmed in by high peaks. A perennial stream – full of swimming-pools – courses down its floor. Near the head of the valley a path branches to the left and leads down to a picnic ground where a waterfall tumbles into a deep swimming-pool. The main path continues to the head of the valley where cliffs close in and the stream falls a sheer 25 m, rushing off through a series of rapids, pools and a jumble of mighty boulders. Care is needed in climbing through this gorge, but the scenery and the deep pools are magnificent. The walk to the head of the valley and back takes three hours. It is a delight at any season of the year. Permission must be obtained from the Forester at Bainsberg Forest Station.

Beyond the picnic grounds the main road begins its tortuous descent down the precipitous valley of the Witte River. This is one of the most celebrated road passes in Africa where strange rock formations and numerous wild flowers abound. Incessantly twisting, the pass descends, providing a succession of memorable views.

After 8 km of descent the road reaches *Wolvenkloof* (ravine of hyenas) where, on the site of the original toll-house, there is the popular Tweede Tol camping site, a series of deep swimming-pools, and a short turn-off left leading to the Bainsberg Forestry Station. From this forestry station there is a magnificent 13 km long circular path which leads the walker past waterfalls, wild flowers, indigenous forest, and high up to the summit of the Limietberg before returning to its starting-point via another route. The best time to do this walk is on a winter's morning when the Hex River Mountains, covered in snow, provide spectacular photogenic views. In February, however, disas may be seen, especially growing on the rock faces around one high waterfall, while wild flowers bloom at all times of the year. The walk is best done in an anti-clockwise direction. It is essential to obtain permission from the forester.

Beyond *Wolvenkloof* the main road tends to level off and keeps to the alluvial floor of the river valley. It passes Sebastiaan Kloof, where a locked gate provides access to a mountain club hut. After 8 km the main road reaches the Darling Bridge across the Breede River, a favourite camping area. One kilometre beyond the river there is a turn-off right leading eastwards to Worcester.

From Wellington the main road northwards crosses the railway line and passes several industrial sites. The Wellington Wine Farmers' Co-operative has its cellars opposite the railway station. It is open to the public during normal business hours on weekdays. The wines may be tasted and bought.

The road leads out of the industrial area. After 3 km it reaches a small fort built by the British during the Anglo-Boer War. This fort was the most southerly of a series erected to guard all major railway bridges. Smaller block-houses, each garrisoned by about seven men of the South African Constabulary, were built at intervals of 3 000 m from one another along the main lines of rail.

Beyond the fort the country changes, vineyards giving way to wheat fields and sheep-runs. After 23,5 km the road reaches the rural centre of *Hermon*, named after the Biblical place-name meaning 'exalted'.

From Hermon a road branches north-westwards and leads across wheat fields for 10 km to the village of Riebeek-Kasteel, lying in the centre of large vineyards on the slopes of an isolated 946 m high mountain formerly known as Van Riebeecks-Kasteel but now called Kasteelberg.

Six kilometres beyond Riebeek-Kasteel, the road reaches another village on the slopes of the mountain. This is Riebeek West, a rural centre notable for its vineyards and the fact that two of South Africa's prime ministers were born in the district: General J C Smuts on the farm *Bovenplaas* (above the flats), the high-lying portion of the old farm *Ongegund* and Dr D F Malan on *Allesverloren*.

Allesverloren was originally granted in 1704 by Governor William Adriaan van der Stel as a grazing area to Gerrit Cloete who farmed in Ida's Valley at Stellenbosch. The origin of the rather lugubrious name of *Allesverloren* (all is lost) is uncertain. There is a tradition that the owner, returning to his farm from Stellenbosch, found that the place had been raided, the livestock stolen, and the house set on fire. From this event, said to have taken place in 1705, the name probably originated. The walls of the original house eventually received a new roof but not in the Cape-Dutch style. The building with its many rooms (six bedrooms), is notable for superb ceilings and floors. In 1870, Daniel Francois Malan acquired what was then a 700 ha wheat farm. His eldest son, also named Daniel Francois, became a minister of the Dutch Reformed Church, entered politics, and became Prime Minister of South Africa when his National Party defeated the United Party of General Smuts in the 1948 general election. The Malan family still own the farm and produce there some fine wines including a notable port type wine. The farm lies on the mountain slopes next to the main road just before it enters Riebeek West. Wine is not sold on the farm.

Jan Christiaan Smuts was born on *Bovenplaats* on 24 May 1870. He was the second of six children and lived on the farm until he was eight, the family then moving 20 km away to the farm

Klipfontein. The homestead of *Bovenplaats* and adjoining buildings were intact in 1946 when Pretoria Portland Cement Company Ltd bought the farm for its lime deposits. However, work in quarrying caused parts of the house to fall into disrepair and be threatened with total demolition. Instead of this, the company chairman, Mr George Bulterman, decided on conservation. The task of restoration was given to the architect Gawie Fagan who, with his wife Gwen, researched the property in its original form. The restored building is as Field Marshal Smuts would have remembered it as the place of his youth. The original schoolroom in an outbuilding has also been preserved as well as the poultry house with its masonry roosts, a coachhouse, flat-roofed dairy and stable where Jan Smuts, at the age of five, nearly met his death when he fell through the loft between the startled mules.

The furnishings are authentic pieces of the period and there is an interesting collection of photographs in a museum housed in the outbuildings. The atmosphere of the place lingers long in the memory of all visitors. The restoration and preservation of the place is a credit to the Pretoria Portland Cement Company Ltd. The turn-off to the quarry and farm is off the main road to Moorreesburg as it leaves Riebeek West.

BARTHOLOMEUS KLIP

East of Hermon just off the main tarmac road, overlooked by the Elandsberge range, lies *Bartholomeus Klip*. It was named in memory of the massacre in Paris of over 2 000 Huguenot Protestants by order of the Catholic French court on St Bartholomew's night, 24 August 1573. Several thousand Huguenots, left France as exiles and settled in America, Britain, Germany and the Cape where they founded many families and had considerable influence in the agricultural and political history of South Africa.

Today Bartholomeus Klip is a superb country lodge in a shady setting of aged oaks and lush gardens. It is surrounded by a 4 000 hectare private nature reserve and part of *Elandsberge* farms, one of the largest wheat and sheep producers in the Western Cape. Guests have the pleasure of delightful walks or rides to see sheep dogs working the flocks of merino sheep and to see the wheat being sown and reaped.

There are guided trails in the nature reserve and evening game drives. There are herds of zebra, eland, wildebeest, springbok, bontebok and numerous smaller creatures such as the quaint little geometric tortoises who have this area as their natural home. An interesting attraction for guests to view is the attempt by careful breeding to recreate the quagga, which in former times inhabited the game plains of the Highveld in countless thousands before being blasted away by uncontrolled hunting.

Bird life is rich, including the blue crane and fish eagles calling from the lake. Vegetation includes such rarities as the spectacular dagger-leafed proteas.

The homestead of Bartholomeus Klip is a sumptuously renovated Victorian farmhouse with furnishings, decorations, fabrics and high beamed ceilings all combining to produce an atmosphere of past elegance in a modern setting of comfort. It is run by Nic and Nicole Dupper. The cuisine is regional Cape farm style served in generous portions.

There was an older farmhouse, long since vanished. Of this there is a story. In 1714 it was occupied by a Dutch settler, Franz Joosten van der Lubstadt who had a young wife, Maria Mouton. It was not a happy marriage. On 4 January the couple quarrelled. Maria fled screaming from the home, pursued by her husband. A Bengali slave named Titus ran to her rescue, tackled Van der Lubstadt, brought the man to the ground and held him down. A second slave, Fortuijn, an Angolan, ran to the scene. He was armed with an implement used to scrape mud off plough shares. He killed Van der Lubstadt. A horseman was then heard approaching. He was a neighbour looking for a runaway slave. Maria and her two slave allies hid the body of her husband behind a cattle corral until the man left, then pushed it into a porcupine burrow. She reported her husband missing.

Months passed. Then a neighbour visited the farm and found Maria drunk and in the arms of Titus the slave. The visitor reported what he had seen. Maria and the three slaves were arrested and taken to Cape Town for trial. Under torture Maria revealed the details of the killing of her husband.

Maria was condemned to be bound to a pole on Gallow's Hill, half strangled, scorched, allowed to recover and then strangled a second time until she was dead. The slave Fortuijn had his right hand chopped off and was then broken on the wheel from the feet upwards. Titus was impaled on a stake until, after 48 hours of misery, he died. The heads and right hands of the slaves were exhibited on a pole on the roadside to Bartholomeus Klip as a grim warning.

The main road from Hermon crosses the railway line and continues northwards across wheat fields for 10 km and then passes the dam of *Voëlvlei* (bird marsh), one of the major water supplies for the Western Cape.

Voëlvlei was originally a natural lake but had a small catchment area allowing it to collect little more than 1 m in depth of water. During the Second World War the military authorities were compelled to find a solution to the problem of supplying water to the harbour of Saldanha. A water scheme was hurriedly devised, feeding to the area water pumped from the Berg River. After the war this supply was extended to such places as Vredenburg and Velddrif, but the erratic seasonal flow of the Berg River proved a great problem.

To solve this difficulty a storage dam was built at Voëlvlei in 1952. The dam is 8 km long and 1,5 km wide, impounding 172 169 megalitres of water behind a rock-and-earth fill embankment, 17,73 m high. Water is fed into this dam from weirs in the Little Berg River where it flows through the Nuwekloof from Tulbagh, and from the Leeuw River and the group of streams known as the Twenty-Four Rivers. From these sources 82 500 megalitres of water a year is fed into Voëlvlei and stored there. During the dry summer months when the flow of the Berg River becomes sluggish, water is fed into it from Voëlvlei and supplies are maintained to users as far away as Cape Town in the south and Velddrif in the north. The dam is also used by yachtsmen for recreation and is stocked with bass. Permits to enter the area may be obtained at the gate. No camping is allowed.

Opposite the Voëlvlei Dam wall a branch road leads westwards for 13 km to Riebeek-Kasteel. This road crosses the Berg River by means of a concrete causeway (submerged in flood time) at *Sonkwasdrif* (fording place of the Bushmen), one of the few place-names in South Africa which is reminiscent of a long-vanished people. The causeway marks the end of the first day in the annual Berg River Canoe Marathon.

Eight kilometres north of Voëlvlei the main road reaches a junction. Straight ahead the road leads to the Nuwekloof and the upper valley of the Little Berg River. A left turn leads for 2 km to the village of *Gouda* which, built on a farm named after Gouda in Holland, had its own start as a railway station at first called Porterville Road. About the village still lingers a true corn-country atmosphere although the grand old days have passed when 300 ox-wagons a day could be seen bringing wheat to the railway station and the hotels were crowded with thirsty men.

The country around Gouda shelters such celebrated estates as *Lorelei* and *La Bonne Esperanza*; and their products of wheat, wine and wool are of high quality. Five kilometres from Gouda there is a left turn to Riebeek-West (22 km), while 8,5 km further on is a right turn (east) leading for 3 km to the mission station of *Saron* (named after the Biblical name meaning 'on the plains'), established by the Dutch Reformed Church. The mission – a great place for the making of velskoen – lies under the 1 499 m high Saronsberg which dominates this part of the country.

Five kilometres north of the Saron turn-off, the main tarmac road reaches the first of a series of bridges spanning what are known as the Twenty-Four Rivers, a succession of stony-bedded mountain torrents rushing down to feed the Berg River. Eighteen kilometres further on the road passes through a fine avenue of gum trees and, 30 km from Gouda, reaches the town of ...

PORTERVILLE

Founded in 1863 when F J Owen, an 1820 Settler, divided a portion of his *Pomona* farm into erven, *Porterville* was named after William Porter, the Attorney-General of those days. As the centre for a prosperous industry in sheep, cattle, fruit and wheat, Porterville grew into a pleasant little town. It attained municipal status on 24 September 1881 and became a magistracy in 1908. Outside the magistrate's court, next to the flagstaff, stands an old naval gun originally found on the farm *Dammetjies* where it had been mounted by the Dutch East India Company as one of their signal guns.

The *Olifantsrivierberge* (elephant's river mountains), which overlook Porterville from the east, are renowned for their wild flowers, rock formations and Bushman paintings. A spectacular drive climbs to the top of the mountain range. Continuing north from Porterville past a turn-off left leading westwards to Piketberg (23 km away), the main road travels towards Citrusdal (46 km away). Four kilometres out of Porterville there is a gravel turn-off right (east) marked Cardouw. The *Kardouw* (narrow pass) was an old route used by the pre-historic tribes to cross the mountain range. It is now disused, but after 9 km of travel on this road – which runs along the foot of the mountains – there is another turn to the right which takes the road 7 km up the spectacular *Dasklip* (coney rock) Pass to the summit of the range.

Dasklip Pass is swept by surging windstreams reputed to be superior to any other in the world. An international hang-gliding competition is held there annually from December to January.

Several farmers have settled along the top of the range, and a rough road finds a way over the plateau summit through a high world of striking rock formations, wild flowers and forests of waboom. The scenery is spectacular and in winter the high peaks of the Groot Winterhoekberge (2 076 m) are well covered in snow.

On the highest point of the pass there is a turn to the private Beaverlac Nature Reserve. After a further 4 km there is a fork, with the left-hand road leading to farms such as *Rockhaven* and *Phoenix Rock*. The right-hand turn continues for 2 km to the Groote Winterhoek Forestry Station. Permits to continue are now required, and the rough road (after a further 6 km) ends at a fork leading to two locked gates beyond which only walking is allowed. The views, grotesque rock formations and flowers are memorable.

There are several dozen caves in this mountain area decorated with galleries of Bushman paintings. There is a well-ornamented cave on the farm *Driebos*. The farm *Eselfontein*, on the top of Dasklip Pass, has some unusual abstract paintings which may be seen about 8 km along the road on a large rock standing on the marshy flats known as the Zuurvlakte. Further along the road towards the old *Winterhoek* farm, in a deep canyon known as *Die Hel*, (the abyss) there is a large cave close to a 9 m high waterfall. This was an important Bushman centre, for it was a source of ochre-white, off-white and pink pigments, with a lower cave yielding red. The walls of the caves are adorned with scenes of hunters and elephants.

Among the several other Bushman cave galleries in the area there is one on the farm *Noodbron*, 2 km south-east of the summit of Dasklip Pass, which contains a picture of a sailing ship with flags flying. The winds must have been rather contrary, for the flags are all flying in different directions. This unique example of rock art is in sad decay.

At Gouda, where the road to Porterville branches off, the right-hand road continues in company with the main railway line, passing a mass of rock known as Bushman's Rock, and twisting easily into the ravine through the mountains washed by the Little Berg River, the principal tributary of the Berg.

TULBAGH PASS OR NUWEKLOOF

In the entire length of what the pioneers at the Cape called the mountain range of Africa, the passage forced by the Little Berg River is the only easy and level way through the mountains into the interior. In March 1658, when Jan van Riebeeck sent out a party under Sergeant Jan van Harwarden on a journey of exploration, they found this natural pass. The surveyor Pieter Potter partly explored it, and then continued north along the ridge known as the *Roodezandberg* (red sand mountain). From the summit of what is known as the *Oude Kloof* (old cleft) he was the first European to look down into the inner valley of the mountains which, in 1699, Willem Adriaan van der Stel named the *Land of Waveren* in honour of an illustrious Amsterdam family with which he was connected.

For many years the Oudekloof of the Roodezandberg was the accepted way through the mountains. Then the more natural pass up the valley of the Little Berg River (Tulbagh Kloof) gradually came into use, with the road swinging in past Bushman's Rock, crossing and re-crossing the bed of the river, and then emerging into the Land of Waveren. In about 1850 a proper road was constructed up this ravine and it became known as the *Nuwekloof* (new cleft) to distinguish it from the old mountain passage. The modern tarmac road keeps to the side of the river opposite the old road and, 8 km from the Gouda turn-off, it enters the Land of Waveren at the railway station of *Tulbaghweg* (Tulbagh road). The view of the fertile valley is impressive with the high peaks of the Winterhoekberge lying to the north and the range of the *Witsenberge* (named by Van der Stel after Nicolaas Witsen, a director of the Dutch East India Company) providing a seemingly impassable wall to the east.

The Little Berg River has its watershed in a basin in the mountains with the Winterhoek valley forming the northern cul-de-sac, dominated by peaks such as the Kleinberg (1 551 m), Klein Winterhoek (1 957 m) and the Groot Winterhoek (2 076 m). In the centre of this basin, 4 km from the way out of the Nuwekloof, stands the town of ...

TULBAGH

When the first settlers came to the basin of the Little Berg River on 31 July 1700, Tulbagh, with its present population of 5 07 9, had its beginning. At first these pioneers were only interested in establishing farms but a centre for their area had to be created, with a church being built and a village laid out in 1743. In 1804 a magistrate was appointed for the district named in honour of Ryk Tulbagh, one of the best governors of the Cape.

The *Drostdy* (magistracy) was built on the farm *Rietvlei*, 4 km north of the church, and is a fine, if slightly severe example of Cape-Dutch architecture. It was designed by the famous Louis Thibault and is open to the public Mondays to Saturdays from 10h00 to 12h50, 14h00 to 16h30; Sundays 14h30 to 16h50. It is closed on religious holidays. The candle-lit cellar is well stocked, especially with sherry-type wine. It is a fine place to sample this pleasant drink in an atmosphere of cool shadows and rich aromas. The *Oude Drostdy* (old magistrate) is the emblem of Drostdy-Hof wines which are produced in the cellars a kilometre away. The *Oude Drostdy* is maintained by the Distillers Corporation as a museum.

The original church of Tulbagh is also now a museum housing an interesting collection of furniture and antique items such as a large patent penny-in-the-slot symphonium, a sort of deep-toned musical-cum-juke-box which played (and still plays) a large selection of the hit tunes of Victorian times. The museum is open week days from 09h00 to 17h00 except religious holidays. Saturdays 09h00 to 16h00 in summer; 10h00 to 16h00 in winter. Sundays 11h00 to 16h00. There are three annexes of the museum further up Church Street. The buildings and collections are worth seeing. Danie Theron, the renowned Boer scout, was born in a house in Church Street, now named after him.

Chris and Eleze Kemp maintain in Tulbagh a non-profit haven for injured owls. The sanctuary and its occupants welcome visitors daily except Sundays 14h00–16h00.

A severe earthquake devastated Tulbagh on 29 September 1969, killing nine people and causing considerable damage to property. A second minor quake occurred on 14 April 1970. After the disaster, however, some magnificent restoration work was begun. The main commercial street remains a rather drab stretch of sun-baked shops, but is beautified by flowers cultivated in a garden running the full length of the street. Church Street, however, is a delight with its long line of carefully restored buildings and pretty gardens which perfectly emphasise the pleasure of living if man blends with his environment without wantonly destroying it for the sake of venality.

One of the restored buildings was originally a winehouse, set in a spacious garden, and named *Paddagang* (frog's way) because frogs habitually hopped down the lane leading to the stream where they gathered during the mating season. Paddagang had its beginning in 1821 as a licensed winehouse (or taphouse). Jollifications and high jinks caused some alarm to the more sedate section of the residents of the town. Sunday happenings had to be slightly subdued, particularly during church times. Over the years, however, Paddagang remained a place of good cheer where fiddlers played and people danced. There was food and wine in abundance. The hospitable building still seems to retain its character, a memory of those past days and nights of merriment.

During the earthquake of 1969, the building was severely damaged but skillfully restored. The KWV Co-operative Wine Growers Association had, by that time, conceived the idea of opening a winehouse in each of the regions of the Western Cape notable for the individuality of their wines and food. For the Tulbagh region they acquired Paddagang. It was opened as a restaurant in 1974. Mary Malan was in charge of catering and trained as chef a most talented little lady named Netta Kock who presided over the kitchen for the next 22 years. Mary Malan's husband, Oom Piet Malan, was the host and entertainer. This amiable threesome established the reputation of Paddagang for piquantly flavoured Cape country meals. The garden, meanwhile, was rejuvenated and a vineyard of high-quality cultivars was planted.

In 1986 the Malans retired. It was a time of change for Paddagang, with the KWV deciding to relinquish control in favour of private ownership. They sold the buildings to the Tulbagh Wine Association and Michel Olivier ran it until April 1989 when the Paddagang Vigneron leased it. Elaine Rousseau took over management. In August 1989 she was joined by Tienkie Muller, and the two ladies formed a management team of considerable sensitivity to the beauty of Paddagang and its garden.

With Netta Kock remaining as the chef, they created a menu dedicated to Cape country cookery based on the produce of the Tulbagh area and traditional local ways of preparation. On the menu, apart from soups and starters, there are such main course items as Cape Babotie, Waterblommetjie Bredie, and Chicken Tulbagh style. Portions of the three combine to fill a delectable Cape platter. There is also always a dish of the day, and in the season this is often venison. There is a trout platter and a Vigneron's Platter, while the desserts feature such delicacies as traditional baked Malay Malva Pudding, Cape Gooseberry Pie and Cape Brandy Tart. A variety of breads are baked on the premises and there is a home-made sinful chocolate cake which needs to be tasted. Netta Kock died late in 1997. Her influence on Cape country cooking will long remain. Ronel Vermaak now manages Paddagang and maintains the excellence of its cuisine and hospitable atmosphere.

From the vineyards, the Tulbagh co-operative produce for the restaurant a range of Padda wines, ten at present, each with a distinctive padda label of a jolly-looking frog, and names such as Platanna, Paddarotti, Paddamanel, Paddapoot, Paddasang and Brulpadda. The wines were selected by a group of local wine farmers and other interested people who form the Paddagang Vignerons BK. The Krone and the Theron families are largely represented on this association. The wines make a collector's set, with the amusing labels created by Janice Ashby.

Paddagang is open for lunch every day as well as wine-tasting and sales till 16h00.

No visitor to Tulbagh should fail to explore the upper valley of the Little Berg River, which is a beautiful area at all seasons. Two main farm roads lead from Tulbagh up the valley. The one road passes the modern Dutch Reformed church, leads for 4 km to the original drostdy building, now the museum and sherry maturation cellar of the Drostdy Wine Cellars of the Distillers Corporation. Visitors are welcome and there are conducted tours at 11h00 and 15h00 each day except Sundays. Next to the Drostdy Wine Cellars stands the Tulbagh Co-operative Wine Cellars, producer of the well-known Witsenberg range of wines as well as a varied selection of other wines of high quality. Visitors are welcome; wine is sold during normal trading hours. The co-operative was founded in 1906. Today it has 123 members who deliver to it 14 000 tons of grapes each year.

The road passes the two cellars and leads off into one of the major wine-producing areas of the Western Cape. At 6,5 km from Tulbagh there is a turn-off to the vineyard of *Theuniskraal*, home since 1930 of the Jordaan family and producer of some excellent estate wines, especially the dry whites for which this upper valley of the Little Berg River is notable. *Theuniskraal* was one of the first estates in South Africa to make a delicate dry white wine. The farm is in an area of stony soil overlooked by protective mountains. The vineyards are sheltered from excessive heat and are ideal for white wines of very subtle flavour, especially from the Riesling cultivar. Wine is not sold from the estate.

Beyond the turn to *Theuniskraal*, the tarmac road continues across lovely farming country for a further 6,5 km before ending in the grounds of *Remhoogte*, the farm of Mr J Theron, a great producer of prunes, pears and apples. This is one of the finest estates in the Winterhoek valley of the Little Berg River. Its homestead is modern but the whitewashed stone-walled corrals, the flowers and the trees – especially beautiful during autumn – give it considerable charm.

The second farm road from Tulbagh branches of to the left from the road to the drostdy at the Dutch Reformed Church, passes the parsonage and after 2,5 km reaches a turn-off to the wine estate of *Montpellier*, granted in 1714 to Jean Joubert who named it after his home town in Southern France. It is now owned by the Theron family. From this estate come the Vlottenheimer range of wines and many other good products of the Winterhoek Valley. Wines are sold during normal business hours.

Four kilometres beyond this turn-off the road reaches the immaculate estate of *Twee Jonge Gezellen* (two young companions), where the well-known Mr N C Krone and his son Nicky produce a celebrated range of estate wines of origin. In the days when the Dutch East India Company first allocated farms in the Land of Waveren, this estate was granted (so the story goes) to two young bachelors – great friends – who named it *Twee Jongegezellen* (two young bachelors). Years later, when the Theron family acquired the estate, they subtly changed the name to the present form of *Twee Jonge Gezellen* (two young companions) because they were sensitive to local jokes insinuating that the Therons were descendants of bachelors. The Krones are related to the Therons on the female side. The family is notable for its dedication to quality, innovation and high skill in the complex creation of white wines of subtle delicacy in flavour and bouquet. The estate, with its homestead, flowering creepers and trees in a setting of vineyards and mountains, is a classic example of the Cape-Dutch style of domestic architecture, of which there is nothing more serene to be seen anywhere in the world. Labour relations on *Twee Jonge Gezellen* have been a model for some years in the Western Cape.

There is something magical in the atmosphere of the Land of Waveren. It is intangible, indefinable and elusive, but nevertheless perceptibly as real as a symphony composed of many things: sounds, perfumes, the presence of high mountains, streams rushing down to a fertile valley of serenity, fertility and the bounty of nature when human beings chose to live in harmony with an exquisite environment.

The estate of *Twee Jonge Gezellen* is an example of such harmony of human beings and nature. Since their acquisition of this estate, the Krone family have enjoyed a very special empathy with the place. Cultivation blends with the natural flora and fauna. The atmosphere is amiable. There is a pleasant mix of sophisticated skill and contented labour without which no industry can possibly succeed no matter how vast its finance.

A subtle example of the interplay of technology, labour, and the creativity of the Krone family is depicted in the introduction of the sparkling wine known as Krone Borealis. The renowned microbiologist, Professor Hugo Schanderl, head of Geisenheim, the great wine institute in Germany, gave the Krones the basic idea of creating a biologically stable sparkling wine with no preservatives or any unnatural additions which would influence the flavour. In 1969 the Krones started experimentation. The classic French method of champagne production devised in the 17th century by the renowned blind Benedictine monk, Dom Pierre Pérignon, was accepted as the basis of the experiment on *Twee Jonge Gezellen*.

The vineyards of *Twee Jonge Gezellen* are spread across a variety of slopes with consequent variations in the nature of the soil and micro-climates. The first task was to decide on the grape varieties which could best provide the essential juice and which flourished to the required state of perfection in the setting of the estate. Chardonnay, Pinot Noir and Pinot Blanc were eventually selected. In carefully studied areas of *Twee Jonge Gezellen*, and subject to stringent disciplines of cultivation, these varieties are nursed and pampered with selective pruning, thinning of leaves and precise control of fertilisation and moisture. When they are three-quarters ripe, the bunches are harvested at night, by hand. Night harvesting is essential. It is then that the grapes are cool and their juice piquant with the flavour of the soil and perhaps containing just a little of the sparkle of the stars.

The whole bunches are placed in old-fashioned basket presses. Only the first half of the juice is used; the rest goes to distillation. The juice is fermented with a multi-culture of yeast. It is left in the yeast until its taste is judged to have reached the standard set by the winemaker. The juice is then inoculated with malalactic bacteria which break down the harsh acidity, making the wine soft, harmonious and simultaneously introducing antibodies. It is these antibodies which make the wine biologically stable.

The wine is cold stabilised by being taken below freezing-point. It is then bottled with a particular strain of yeast which can ferment under pressure. As an effect of this fermentation, during the first three months the wine is loaded with negative ions, and this is regarded by French sparkling winemakers as an aphrodisiac.

For three and a half years the bottles are left to mature in peace in the first underground sparkling wine cellar in Africa. They are disturbed only by occasional shaking. During this period the process of autolysis takes place. The wine becomes very reductive. The yeast cells release certain enzymes which break down the cell walls, releasing amino acids, which are what our body cells need for upliftment and rejuvenation.

At the end of this period the bottles are placed in specially designed racks which tilt them down towards the neck. In a process known as *remuage* (riddling), they are regularly hand-turned to the right and left over a period of about a month. At the end of this period, all the sediment has found its way down into the neck of the bottle. The bottle is then taken to a freezing bowl (minus 35°C) and the top of the neck is frozen. The cap on the bottle is then removed. A small block of ice falls out with the sediment in a process known as *degorgement* (disgorgement). The bottle is then topped up with a teaspoon of special liquor consisting of wine and syrup.

Then the cork, cap and seal are put on and at last, *voila*, you have it!

But how did this delectable sparkling wine get its name of *Krone Borealis*? Nicky's son, also Nicky, suggested it. Bacchus, the god of wine, fell in love with Ariadne. She was a maiden disillusioned with men. Bacchus had told her that he was a god, but this she had heard before. She told him to prove it. He took off his crown and threw it to the heavens. There it formed the glittering constellation, *Corona Borealis* (crown of the north). The family name of Krone means crown. With the grapes being harvested at night beneath the light of the stars, the name is a final touch to the strange magic which goes into the making of a remarkable wine.

The road we have followed continues past this glorious farm for a further 5 km and then ends at the *Roodezandskloof* farm of Mr J Lombard, where prunes, peaches and grapes cover many hectares of the foothills of the Winterhoek Mountains. In spring, when the orchards are in blossom, in autumn when the leaves turn golden to red and the blue mountains are touched with snow, this area is unforgettable – a joy to the eye, a delight to any visitor, and an inspiration to any artist, writer or composer.

Tulbagh has an annual agricultural show which for years has been regarded as one of the very best of its kind and a credit to the community. Horses and a display of wild flowers are particular features of this show. As a convenience for visitors and exhibitors, a caravan park was created on the banks of the *Klip* (stone) River which flows through the valley next to the showgrounds. Rondalia, the motoring and tourist organisation, contributed substantially towards the initial costs of the park, and this was the beginning of what is today one of the best self-catering resorts in Southern Africa.

A succession of events influenced the development of the park. When Tulbagh municipality built a dam to provide water for the town and a modern sewerage disposal plant, the Klip River park was greatly benefited. Ample water for irrigation allowed it to be beautified with lawns, gardens and trees. It became an all-year-round resort, not just a convenience for one week in the year during the springtime agricultural show. Tourists discovered that it was a pleasantly relaxed and comfortable base for the exploration of the Tulbagh area, the celebrated Land of Waveren, with its wild flowers, scenery and charming architecture.

In 1974 seven cottages were built in the park and in 1988 a group of chalets was built on the right bank of the river. A lake was also created in the river when the valley was excavated to provide a rich topsoil for the sports field in a new residential township. Ducks and a variety of fish – bass, carp, bluegill, yellowfish and trout – were introduced for the pleasure of anglers.

The park became increasingly popular with visitors. A progressive town council served by an energetic town clerk, Matthew de Villiers Muller (known as Div), conceived a programme which, without in any way destroying the amiable atmosphere of the park, made it a centre for a new hall, cinema, indoor sports and theatre. A swimming-bath, tennis-courts and bowling-green are all adjoining amenities.

The park was increased in size to accommodate 250 caravans, each site on grass and close to modern facilities which are maintained to a high standard of excellence by a resident caretaker and his wife.

The success of this small town in creating so considerable a recreational asset for the use of visitors is a model for local authorities with the pride of their environment and the desire to facilitate the discovery of its beauty by offering reasonably priced accommodation of high standard. There is the added convenience of nearby shops, restaurants featuring Tulbagh country cookery, and the cellars of several famous wine producers open for visits, tastings and purchases. This is the grand life!

Chapter Ten

THE VALLEY OF THE BREEDE RIVER

The river known as the *Breede* or *Breë* (broad) has its birth in a cluster of streams tumbling down into a basin held in the palm of the half-open hand of the Western Cape mountains. It is a basin so fertile that it is often likened to the open end of the horn of Ceres, the goddess of agriculture. Nature has graced this basin with bountiful supplies of water, wild flowers, a crisp sunny climate and fertile soil. Man has seized the opportunity to fill it to overflowing with fruit, wheat, dairy products and wool, and has topped it with congenial living-places in a beautiful environment.

The basin is known as the *Warmbokkeveld* (warm buck veld) to distinguish it from the higher land to the north called the *Kouebokkeveld* (cold buck veld). The mountain ranges enclosing the basis consist of the Hex River Mountains to the east and south, the Witsenberg to the west, and the Skurweberg, Gydoberg and Waboomberg to the north. These massive piles of sedimentary material collect and store pure water from winter rains and snows. This water seeps into the basin below in the form of innumerable springs. The springs feed streams, which in turn fill dams that irrigate the farmlands and then unite to form two main rivulets, the *Dwars* (traversing) and the Titus. After flowing down many cascades, rapids and waterfalls, broadening into pools and resting in tranquil, tree-shaded stretches where trout play among the dapples of sunshine, the two rivulets eventually unite to form the river known as the Breede. With its new-found strength, the young river shoulders its way through the south-western rim of the basin, tumbles down a waterfall into a boiling pool known as the 'Coffee Pot', then finds a tortuous way through the mountains into the great valley which carries the river south-eastwards to the sea.

The basin where the Breede River has its headwaters was used by a number of prehistoric people as a hunting-ground from early times. Nomadic pastoral groups also found their way into the basin, clashing with the earlier hunter-gatherer people. In the middle of the eighteenth century a handful of European pastoralists found their way into the area. The mountains, however, held the basin in an iron grip. The sole link with the outside world was an atrocious track which followed the river through the mountains and was passable only by pack animals. Wagons had to be pulled to pieces, carried bodily through the pass, and then reassembled – not a profitable way of conveying produce to a market.

In 1765 the situation improved. Jean Mostert, whose farm *Wolvenkloof* (hyena ravine) was situated where the river found its way out of the mountains, built a road at his own expense, crisscrossing the bed of the river into the basin through what became known as *Mostertshoek* (Mostert's glen). The name of this enterprising farmer is commemorated by the 2 031 m high twin peak which looms above the eastern side of the pass and is the beginning of the Hex River range. The oak trees planted by Mostert still shade the *Wolvenkloof* farmhouse, but the road he made has long since been re-claimed by Nature.

By the 1840s a permanent road into the basin became essential in order to provide a gateway to the Karoo in the north. Work started in October 1846. Andrew Geddes Bain was the engineer in charge. He built the pass with the aid of 240 convicts. Opened on 1 December 1848, the pass was named in honour of the Surveyor-General of the Cape, Colonel Charles Michell. The Governor, Sir Harry Smith, performed the opening ceremony, during which at least half the local population rode through the pass in procession.

The route of the modern road, concreted in 1946, is substantially the same as that of the pass built by Bain. The original toll-house is maintained as a monument in the middle of the 8 km long route. The scenery of the pass is a majestic high peak, strange rock shapes and, winding their way down the slopes to join the young river, bustling mountain torrents. One of these tributary streams is the *Witels* (white alder), renowned among climbers and trout fishermen for its complex upper course which comprises 14 'swims' at points where the containing ravine is so narrow that explorers can only proceed by swimming, pushing their impedimenta ahead on inflatable mattresses. There are camp, picnic and viewsites at various points along the pass.

CERES

Ceres was named after the Roman goddess of agriculture. It has a population of 22 677. Its location is admirable. Apart from the Dwars River, several streams such as the Koekedouw flow from the overlooking mountains to the town. There is little danger of any shortage of water to inhibit growth, irrigation, the generation of power, and recreation in the form of swimming and angling. In order for the town to be beautiful, all that was needed was sensible gardening and an appreciation of the potential of such a well-endowed situation. In both these respects Ceres was very fortunate in its residents.

In 1864 Ceres became a municipality under the chairmanship of its magistrate, J A Munnik. Planting trees to shade the streets was a municipal priority. For this purpose Mr Munnik obtained a number of young oaks from Stellenbosch and Paarl. Eucalyptus trees, introduced into the Cape from Australia in 1827 by Sir Lowry Cole, the Governor, had already been planted. What was reputedly the largest specimen of its kind in South Africa grew on the banks of the Dwars River watching the traffic cross the Breda bridge. The trunk of this tree was 10 m in circumference and the crown 45 m off the ground. This old tree is, alas, no more.

Pin oaks and poplars were also planted and forests of pine trees (*dennebosse*) grew on the outskirts. Constantine William Carson served Ceres as chairman of its municipal management committee for nearly 30 years. A great gardener, he supervised the planting of many trees and flowers, laid out walks and paths and created recreational parks which are the green heritage of the town today. The autumn spectacle of poplar trees losing their leaves along the banks of the Dwars River is a superb reward for all the work of planting and conservation.

On 18 May 1912 the branch railway from Wolseley to Ceres through Michell's Pass was opened. Three special trains carried sightseers on a scenic journey. In 1929 the line was extended to the terminus at Prince Alfred's Hamlet. Today this railway route with its tunnels, cuttings and gradients is still a traveller's delight.

Ceres is now a prosperous town and a great resort for holiday-makers as well as a busy agricultural centre. It is warm in summer while in winter the snows on the mountains provide a fine spectacle and some opportunities for winter sports. The numerous pools and rapids of the Dwars, Titus and Koekedouw rivers offer trout fishing in settings of great beauty.

At the western entrance to the town, where the road comes in through a strange assembly of rocks, 33 ha of unspoilt mountain slope has been reserved as the Ceres Nature Reserve. Pathways lead to viewsites and rock shelters with galleries of prehistoric paintings. Wild flowers and wild creatures, dassies, baboons and birds, abound. Admission is free and the reserve is open daily.

In the town there is the *Togryersmuseum* (transport riders museum) with displays of the vehicles and many relics of the days when Ceres was a major point on the pioneer road to the interior. Countless fortune-seekers passed through it on their way to the diamond and gold-fields of the north. The museum is open Mondays to Fridays 08h30 to 13h00 and 14h00 to 17h00. Saturdays 09h00 to 12h00.

The residential areas of Ceres are notable for gardens. Throughout the year there are colourful displays of flowering plants and trees. Autumn has a special beauty. Along the banks of the Dwars River there is a delightful park of poplar, oak and other trees whose leaves change colour with the seasons from the green of summer through every shade of gold until, with the nostalgic, beautiful melancholy of early winter, they all are scattered by the winds. The pedestrian bridge over the river here is known as Lovers' Bridge, and from it there is a romantic view of the river and its trees.

In a large forest of pine trees the municipality has created an excellent resort known as the Pine Forest Resort. There is a swimming pool, a recreation centre, café, squash courts and a mini-golf course. Visitors can enjoy boating on a lovely reflection pool and take walks into the overlooking mountains. There is a second resort, known as the Island Holiday Resort, with a swimming-pool, playground and café. There are excellent walking trails, such as the Toll House trail and the Van Stadensrust trail.

On the banks of the Dwars River, in a garden setting, stands the New Belmont hotel with a restaurant, dining-room, swimming-pool, squash and tennis courts, sauna, jacuzzi and conference facilities, as well as an aviary and zoo. Originating in 1890 as the Belmont Sanatorium supervised by Dr Gustav Zahn from England, it was much resorted to by persons recuperating from pulmonary and nervous diseases. The present buildings were built in 1970 after an earthquake severely damaged the original sanatorium.

From Ceres there is a pleasant 10 km long drive along a tarmac road to the railway terminus and fruit-growing centre of Prince Alfred Hamlet. During the fruit season (January to mid-June) the journey is particularly delightful, while spring sees the orchards-apples, pears, peaches, plums and nectarines – in all the beauty of blossom time. During the season guided tours to the orchards and packing-sheds are conducted. Phone the Ceres Publicity Association (023) 316-1287.

PRINCE ALFRED'S HAMLET AND GYDO PASS

Prince Alfred's Hamlet was established on 8 December 1874. Laid out on the farm *Wagenboomsrivier*, owned by J G Goosen, it is a centre for the surrounding farms and a resting-place at the foot of the Gydo Pass which carries the road up to the Kouebokkeveld. When the branch railway was built in 1929 through Michell's Pass from Wolseley, Prince Alfred's Hamlet became the terminus and this gave it importance as the place of dispatch for fruit and other agricultural products. The Hamlet Hotel has a pleasant ladies' bar named after John Taylor. In the days of the thirsty transport riders, he opened the first hotel in the village, the long-vanished Commercial Hotel.

The Gydo Pass is named after the euphorbia plants which grow on the slopes of the *Skurweberge* (rough mountains). The pass begins 3 km out of Prince Alfred Hamlet and takes 7 km of climbing to reach the summit. Views of the basin of the Warmbokkeveld and the surrounding mountains are spectacular. In winter the pass is occasionally closed for short periods when snow falls on the mountains. Flowering plants are numerous, especially varieties of erica. In autumn *Protea repens* blooms in spectacular numbers. From the summit of this pass the road leads on to Citrusdal and the Cedarberg. The very interesting resort of Kagga Kamma with its resident Bushmen community, is reached along this road.

Another interesting drive from Ceres leads north-eastwards from the town. This modern tarmac road was originally part of the Great North Road – the Cape-to-Cairo road – followed by the pioneer explorers, hunters, traders, missionaries, prospectors and fortune-seekers who made their eager way along it to the interior of Africa. The museum in Ceres is thematically dedicated to the colourful and vital doings of the transport riders who passed this way before the modern N1 was constructed up the Hex River valley to the north.

The road leads past many fine farms. There is a turn-off after 11 km leading to *Lakenvlei* (lake of the marsh), a popular place for trout fishing during the season. This stretch of water, with its reflections of the overlooking mountains, lies behind a dam wall in the Sandrifskloof River. The river finds a spectacular route penetrating the Hex River Mountains. Its water, regulated and fed from the Lakenvlei lake, provides additional water for the irrigation of the Hex River valley.

One kilometre beyond the turn-off to Lakenvlei the road to the north reaches the foot of the

Theronsberg Pass. For the next 12 km the road climbs to the summit at the 1 091 m level. In winter this can be quite a journey, for the pass is occasionally blocked by snow. At all seasons the views are expansive, revealing the whole Warmbokkeveld basin in its setting of folded mountains.

The Theron family from *Leeuwfontein* (fountain of lions) have a thatched and gabled homestead dated 1770. Through this landscape of mountains and farmlands the road continues its winding way. Passing through Hottentots Kloof, it reaches, 30 km from Ceres, a turn-off to Citrusdal and this provides the opportunity for an interesting circular return route to Ceres. This branch road joins the road which has climbed Gydo Pass.

The old transport road we are following continues past this turn-off. At 35 km from Ceres the road passes the *Nuwerus* (new rest) farm homestead. There is a resting-place with water. After another 2 km there is a turn-off leading eastwards to join N1 at Touws River. Beyond this, our road leads directly towards the ridge of mountains which serves as the barrier between the arid area of the Great Karoo to the north and the far better watered area to the south. The transition is very apparent. Karoo Poort is a gateway through a garden wall. On either side of the wall the vegetation is very different. The gateway is actually the pass formed by the Doring River. At the southwestern entrance to the pass there is a shady resting-place near a farmhouse. As the road penetrates the pass, the familiar fynbos vegetation of the Western Cape dwindles. By the time the road leaves the pass, the succulents of the Karoo have taken over. Ahead lies the prodigious interior of Southern Africa; behind is the sandstone elegance of the Cape, with its own special way of life.

From the western end of Michell's Pass, the Breede River and the road follow a wide bend into the valley which leads south-eastwards to the Indian Ocean. The upper end of this seemingly uninterrupted valley is separated by a divide and forms part of the watershed of the Little Berg River which drains through the mountains at Nuwekloof Pass and then joins the Berg River which flows to the Atlantic Ocean on the west coast. The divide occurs in the middle of the town of Wolseley which lies 7 km from the entrance to Michell's Pass.

WOLSELEY

Wolseley was named after the renowned British general, Sir Garnet Wolseley. It was founded on 3 October 1893 and developed as a rail centre for the surrounding agricultural area, producing wine, fruit and such unusual things as *waterblommetjies* (water-lily flowers) which are a special delicacy in traditional Cape cooking. Its present population is 5 885. Fruit packing and dispatch are the principal occupations. Local produce is sold from a roadside shop in the grounds of the Wolseley Fruit Packers. The watershed between the Breede River, flowing to the East Coast, and the Berg River, flowing to the West Coast, is in the centre of the town.

Wolseley is 4,5 km north of the Breede River. The tarmac road crosses the river over a bridge guarded by two well-preserved blockhouses built by the British during the Anglo-Boer War. Both blockhouses have periodically served as residences, and they have a homely appearance in their serene rural setting of orchards and vineyards. One and a half kilometres away from the blockhouses and the bridge, the road joins the route descending the east bank of the river from Michell's Pass. From there it leads across the vineyards past the station and wine cellars at Romans River to the west of the valley where the Witte River flows out of the mountains to join the Breede. Here the road reaches a fork, one branch following the course of the Witte and crossing the mountains by means of Bain's Kloof Pass.

There is a co-operative wine cellar at Lateganskop. This is closed to the public but nearby is the *Bergsig* estate. From its 420 ha of vineyards comes a variety of grapes, crushed and fermented in the cellars to make some fine wines, including an excellent port type wines, a cabernet sauvignon and some delicious grape juice. Wines are sold from the cellars during normal business hours. There are co-operative wine cellars at Waboomsrivier and Botha. Both cellars sell wines to the public during normal business hours.

The tarmac road down the valley of the Breede continues south-eastwards. To the north the Hex

River Mountains are a grand sight. A complex mass of high peaks to the south and west seems to enclose the valley entirely. Orchards, vineyards, cellars and homesteads cover the level floor of the valley. The soil is a sandy alluvial deposit eroded by streams from the folded mountains of the Cape System and distributed over the floor of the valley, which needs only irrigation for the cultivation of fruit and grapes. Rainfall occurs in winter. About 720 mm falls in the western end of the long valley, decreasing to a skimpy 210 mm in the east. Little rain falls in summer and during this season, irrigation becomes the backbone of farming. Efficient utilisation of available water supplies makes this middle part of the Breede River valley the largest grape-producing area – mainly for wine and brandy – in the Cape. There are 55 co-operative cellars in the valley and several private cellars on estates. Of these cellars, two are sparkling wine cellars and two are brandy cellars.

The main road continues south-eastwards down the valley in close company with the railway line. At a point 38 km from Wolseley this road joins N1, the Cape-to-Cairo road, but leaves it again after a short union and 5 km further on, reaches the principal town of the Breede River valley ...

WORCESTER

Named after the Marquis of Worcester, the eldest brother of Lord Charles Somerset, Governor of the Cape at the time the town was founded in 1820. Before then, Tulbagh was the administrative centre for the frontier areas of the Western Cape. The development of agriculture and the importance of communications to the Hex River valley and the eastern valley of the Breede necessitated the establishment of a new sub-magistracy. At the end of 1818 two farms, *Roodedraai* (red corner) and *Langerug* (long ridge), were bought from the Du Toit brothers. On these farms the new town was laid out. On 28 February 1820 the first building plots were sold. Today Worcester has a population of 76 893.

The centre of the new town was a sumptuous, elegant *drostdy* (magistracy) built to the order of Lord Charles Somerset in such a way that it could serve as a shooting-box and residence when the governor was on official visits to the inland areas. Captain Charles Trappes was the first *landdrost* (magistrate) of Worcester. He supervised the construction of the residence in 1825, ensuring that it would be a building of lasting value. Now part of the Drostdy Technical High School, it is a historical monument and is regarded as the finest Regency Cape building in South Africa. Captain Trappes died on 5 September 1828 – his grave lies in the grounds of the drostdy.

Several other buildings from early Worcester still survive and one, *Kleinplasie* (little farm) the homestead of the farm *Roodedraai* (red bend) was built in 1800. This pleasingly austere-looking farmhouse was restored in 1977 and is now an office. One of the original outbuildings serves as a wine cellar which offers for sale an extensive range of the wines produced by various co-operative cellars and estates in the Breede River valley. The collector, connoisseur and bargain-hunter will find this wine shop a convenient and pleasant introduction to many novelties of vintage which would be difficult to find without visiting out-of-the-way cellars. Part of the original farmland of *Roodedraai* is now the showground of the Worcester Agricultural Society, which holds its annual show in February, the Winelands Festival in May, and the Young Wine Show in September.

It is also the site of the *Kleinplasie* Living Open-Air Museum, a fascinating display of period buildings, water-mill, and traditional farmyard, complete with farm animals. Many traditional industries are carried out in this museum: candle-making, bread-baking from flour ground by the watermill, witblits-making, and other activities of the old-time farmyard. There is a shop, tea-room and restaurant attached to the museum. The hours are Monday to Saturday 09h00 to 16h30. Sundays 10h30 to 16h30. Closed Easter Friday and Christmas. In the grounds of *Kleinplasie* there is also a cluster of pleasant little country houses which are rented to visitors.

The *Kleinplasie* Reptile World displays a collection of snakes, crocodiles, tortoises and other interesting life forms. There is a mini-animal park and picnic area. It is open Mondays to Saturdays 09h00–16h00. Sundays from 10h00 to 16h00.

The KWV brandy cellar in Worcester is the largest in the world. There are 120 copper pot stills in this giant distillery and the aroma of brandy is rich in the air. There are guided tours daily except Sundays and religious holidays. Phone (023) 342-0255 for times and choice of language.

The oldest surviving residence in Worcester stands at 3 Trappes Street. The original gaol was later converted into a residence. Church Street contains several fine buildings, most of them dating from 1840 to 1855. One of these buildings, now called Beck House, on the corner of Church and Baring Streets, facing Church Square, has been restored and is now part of the Worcester Museum. The building was erected in 1841 by D F Languérenne. He sold it in 1854 to Thomas Heatlie who in turn sold it in the same year to Cornelius Beck. In the garden behind the museum is a bathing-house fed by a stream. Beyond it, facing Church Street, a delightful cottage houses the Tourism Bureau. Next to Beck House, facing Baring Street, is Stofberg House now an exhibition gallery. A collection of works of four well-known Worcester artists, the sculptor Bill Davis, Hugo Naudé, Paul du Toit and Jean Welz, is housed in the Hugo Naudé Art Gallery in 113 Russell Street. It is open weekdays 08h30 to 16h30. Saturdays 09h00 to 12h00. Next to it is the Jean Welz Gallery, home of the Worcester Region of the S A Association of Arts, where exhibitions are held throughout the year. From 1919 Beck House was the home of a mayor of Worcester, Attorney J E J Krige. It is now maintained in its original state, a Victorian town house, complete with stable and coach-house containing a smart Cape cart and ensemble. The Worcester museum is open Mondays to Fridays 08h00 to 16h30. Also in Stofberg House there is a documentary and photographic exhibition of Worcester. It is open at the same hours as the museums.

The Dutch Reformed church, a fine example of the Gothic style, dominates Church Square. Completed in 1832, it had as its first minister the Reverend Henry Sutherland from Scotland, a renowned churchman of the period. The original spire was squat. In 1899 it was replaced by a tin spire. This was blown down twice and then, in 1927 was replaced by the present graceful spire. The pulpit was the work of a local craftsman, Wouter de Vos. The square in front of the church contains a garden of remembrance, designed by the artist Hugo Naudé, with several monuments and memorials.

In Church Street, next to the Tourism Bureau, stands the Congregational church, built in 1948 in classic Cape-Dutch style. In a beautiful garden setting, it is very photogenic, and contains furnishings of outstanding craftsmanship.

Worcester became a municipality in 1842. The advent of the railway in 1877 and the building of good roads to Cape Town and on into the interior made the town a place of consequence. The main street, High Street, became lined with places of business. Unfortunately in modern times this street has been robbed of the trees that once shaded it. Little remains to remind one of past years except for furrows on both sides of the street which are still filled with running water from streams.

The mountains overlooking the town provide a spectacular setting and are the recreational area of an active local branch of the Mountain Club of South Africa. Climbers such as Izak Meiring and Dr Auden have left their names on high peaks which they were the first to climb. Several great gorges in the mountains, especially Jan du Toit's Kloof in the Hex River range, are famous for their scenic beauty.

An attractive feature of Worcester is the Karoo Garden, originally established in 1921 at Whitehill, near Matjiesfontein in the Karoo. This situation proved inaccessible to the public, and the National Botanic Gardens requested a site from the Worcester municipality. Land was granted which encompassed the foothills of the Brandwag Mountain, where conditions of soil and climate were ideally 'Karoo'. A well-known local farmer, Charles Heatlie, donated additional land and the garden was brought to a total area of 154 ha, of which 10 ha is under semi-irrigation.

In July 1946 the original plants were transferred from Whitehill to Worcester. Under the skilful control of Jacques Thudichum, the first director of the new garden, the Karoo National Botanic Garden was opened in September 1948. The garden specialises in plant species from the arid areas of Southern Africa. Its collection of succulents is considerable. Stapelias bloom from January to mid-March: June is a good month for aloes; August, September and October see dazzling displays of many flowering plants. Stone plants, euphorbias, cycads, stem succulents, desert grapes, spekboom and brilliantly flowering mesembryanthemums are all plentiful. The garden is open daily until 16h30. There are interesting walking paths in and from the garden.

Near the garden there is a magnificent golf-course. Gliding is a popular pastime with good thermals rising from the floor of the valley. Soaring conditions make Worcester an all-year round gliding venue.

Notable in Worcester are the schools for the blind and the deaf founded by the Dutch Reformed Church in 1881. A braille printing press produces a weekly magazine as well as books in several languages. There are also homes and workshops for the blind, and a special department in the school for deaf-blind children. The Pioneer School for the Blind, the Institute for the Deaf and the Nuwe Hoop Centre for the Hearing-Impaired, equip students with the necessary skills for them to play an independent and self-fulfilling role in the community.

STETTYNSKLOOF AND BRANDVLEI

Worcester and much of the highly productive area of the middle Breede River valley depends for irrigation water on a dam and lake erected over a marsh known as *Brandvlei* (burning marsh) on account of the six hot springs which reach the surface there. With a temperature of 64°C and a flow of 1 814 400 litres per day these are the second hottest thermal springs in South Africa (after Aliwal North). The hot springs have no notable medical value. They were proclaimed in 1841 as public resorts and the farmer who then owned the land built a few simple amenities there. The water has to be considerably cooled before people can bathe in it. Reports state that two children, a horse, ox, ostrich and many dogs have died by falling into the scalding water. The water now loses itself in the lake of the dam, the springs being in the prohibited area of the Brandvlei Correctional Services Prison.

The lake is used for yachting, water skiing and power boating and supplies irrigation water through canals to the middle reaches of the valley of the Breede River. The lake in turn is fed by two streams; the *Smalblaar*, named after the smalblaar trees which grow in the area and produce a blossom which imparts a bitter taste to wild honey; and the more important of the two streams, the *Goudini*, which takes its African name *Kgo dani* (bitter honey) from this taste. In recent times the latter stream has been prosaically renamed the *Holsloot* (cavity ditch). Its source lies at the head of *Stettynskloof* (named after Stettin in Germany), a narrow rugged gorge where, in 1952, the Worcester municipality built a dam which supplies the town's drinking-water. The remaining flow of the Holsloot reaches the Greater Brandvlei Dam. The entire course of the stream is notable for its swimming-pools and trout.

A second dam, the Kwaggaskloof Dam, was built in 1983 and was at first linked to the Brandvlei Dam by a canal. The embankment of the original dam was also raised. The two dams, now completely joined, are known as the Greater Brandvlei Dam. The Papenkuils pumping station pumps water into the dam from the Breede River. The lake has a storage capacity of 460 million cubic metres.

From Worcester a tarmac road leads south-westwards for 3,5 km to the Breede River. Immediately across the river there is a fork. The left turn leads to the Greater Brandvlei Dam. The right (west) turn leads for 11 km to the town of Rawsonville. From the latter road there are two turn-offs at 7 km and 10 km; both are marked Louwshoek and climb for 22 km up Stettynskloof to the dam.

RAWSONVILLE

Founded in 1858 as a centre for the area known as Goudini after the stream, this town was named after William Rawson, one of the members of the first legislative council of the Cape Colony.

In former years Rawsonville was the centre for a considerable raisin-making industry. Today it still produces vast quantities of grapes but these are mainly dessert species and species used for the making of wine in several local co-operative cellars. There is a fine church and some of the streets are lined with jacarandas.

In the vicinity of Rawsonville there are several co-operative wine cellars and private estates which sell wines to the public during normal business hours. These cellars are Aufwaerts (dry white wines only); Du Toit's Kloof (try their port-type wine and grape juice); Goudini (a tasty variety of cultivars); *Lebenstraum* estate, owned by P P Deetleefs; Louwshoek-Voorsorg (a good range with an excellent hanepoot superior); Merwida (a good range including grape juice); and Nuwehoop (a good range including grape juice).

THE ATKV GOUDINIA SPA

Six kilometres north-west of Rawsonville, across the N1 main road from Cape Town to the north, there is a resort built at a hot spring known as the ATKV Goudini Spa. The spring is situated at the south-eastern base of a range of sandstone hills. The water surfaces at 40°C and is very pure, containing per litre only 32,8 mg silica, 13 mg magnesium carbonate, 11 mg sodium chloride and 8,8 mg potassium chloride. There is slight radioactivity. The ATKV (Afrikaanse Taal & Kultuur Vereniging) created a resort at the springs, which offers two enclosed swimming-baths, an open pool, a restaurant and shop, rondavels, flats and a caravan park.

There is a beautiful drive from Goudini through the *Slanghoek* (snake glen) to join the main Wolseley–Worcester road at Waboomsrivier. In the vicinity of Goudini there are several wine cellars which are open to the public during normal business hours. These are Badsberg Co-operative (dessert wines and grape juice). Groot Eiland Co-operative (try their port-type wine and grape juice), the *Opstal* estate, the Slanghoek Co-operative, and the private cellars of Lee & Jones.

From the road to Rawsonville, just outside Worcester there is a turn-off leading to Villiersdorp and Cape Town over the Franschhoek Pass. At 18 km there is a turn-off to the Kwaggaskloof portion of the Greater Brandvlei Dam. The tarmac road continues through a pleasant rural landscape, with the high mass of the Stettynsberg range looming on the western side. At 35 km from Worcester the road passes the Stettyn Co-operative Wine Cellars and at 49 km there is a turn-off into the mountains leading for 5 km to the estate of *High Noon*. The road then enters the municipal area of ...

VILLIERSDORP

This town was named after Pieter de Villiers, a local farmer who established the place in 1843. As with the Du Toits in the Worcester area, so the De Villiers family in the Villiersdorp district have played a major part in the development of the area. Sir David de Villiers Graaff provided the money and ground for the construction of a school in 1901, which, in 1907, became the well-known De Villiers Graaff High School. The town has a population of 4 825.

Villiersdorp is pleasantly shaded with oaks. There is a wild flower garden where 60 varieties of proteas grow, including those that are claimed to be the largest in the world, the giant king proteas, with pink and cream coloured flowers more than 0,3 m in diameter. Watsonias and ericas also flourish in great profusion. The mountain rose, *Cedro montana*, is indigenous to this area. The garden is 36 ha in extent with winding paths, suspension bridges over the river and five thatched summer houses for picnickers. The garden forms part of a 573 ha nature reserve. There is a herbarium and reference library. An annual wild flower show is held in the last weekend of September and a rose show in October.

The Dagbreek Museum and Restaurant is worth a visit. The 'Fruit Route' has its start there with visits to fruit farms. Phone (028) 840-2126 for further details. There are various mountain hiking trails in the Villiersdorp area and it is a charming and picturesque little town.

From Villiersdorp the road continues for 9 km, then reaches a junction; the left turn leading through the rural centre of Vyeboom to Elgin, and the right turn leading to the Franschhoek Pass and the Berg River valley (see Chapter Nine). The lake of the Theewaterskloof Dam covers part of the basin in the hills beside the road, and stores water from one of the principal tributaries of the Breede, the Riviersonderend, feeding it out for irrigation. The dam is used for sailing, fishing, windsurfing and other water sports. The name *Theewater* comes from the water having a colour resemblance to tea.

HEX RIVER VALLEY

From Worcester, the great N1 trunk road to the north leads north-eastwards for 3 km. It then makes a turn due north directly towards the passage between the Hex River range and the Langeberge which have their western start at this valley between the high sandstone mountains. At 8 km from Worcester stands the De Wet Co-operative Wine Cellar which sells its products to the public during normal business hours.

The road crosses the Hex River, traverses the well-cultivated table grape farmlands of *Glen Heatlie* and passes their farm stall. The road then enters the narrow cleft through which the Hex River has worked so tortuous a way that the original wagon route was forced to ford the river nine times. From this the *Hex* received its name, (properly *Ekse* meaning criss-cross).

The river passage of the Hex provides a spectacular entrance to one of the most productive of all the valleys in the sandstone mountains of the Cape. Bushman paintings on the walls of the rock shelters in the valley reveal that it was formerly an area of many wild animals. Giraffe and various species of antelope, lion, leopard, and even rhinoceros, found a congenial home in the valley. On migrations backwards and forwards these animals blazed the first path through the cleft of the Hex River, and this trail was later followed by Bushman hunters.

It is not known who the earliest European was to follow this ancient trail, but on 21 December 1709 Roelof Jantz van Hoeting was the first person to receive a licence to graze his livestock in the area described as *'under the mountains of Red Sand above the Rock of Lions'*. This was a momentous date for the valley – the beginning of its modern agricultural history and the advent of European settlement in an area which, until then, had belonged to the Bushmen and the wild animals which they hunted for their food.

Other cattle-keepers followed Van Hoating to the valley. Official names of farms began to feature in the records. On 8 December 1723, for instance, *Vendutie Kraal* (sale corral) was granted to Jacob van der Merwe, and the name of the farm hints at an established industry in cattle breeding and auction. In view of the value of land in the valley today, it is interesting to note that Mr van der Merwe paid 24 rixdollars for his grant and agreed to deliver one-tenth of his grain crop each year to the *landdrost* (magistrate) of Stellenbosch. The latter part of the deal he could quite easily evade by not growing any grain at all.

By the end of the 18th century six farms had been granted, covering all the best reaches of the valley. *Kanetvlei* (named after the type of reeds in the marsh there) was in the hands of the Stofberg family; *Roodesand* (red sand) was owned by the Jourdans and noted for the quality of its Madeira-type wines; *Vendutie Kraal* belonged to the Van der Merwes; *Modderdrif* (muddy ford) was owned by the Conradies; *De Doorns* (the thorns) was the home of the De Vos family, whose hospitable home was already recognised as the natural community centre of the valley; and *Buffelskraal* (buffalo corral), a farm at the upper end of the valley, was owned by another branch of the same De Vos family.

Each farm had a handsome Cape-Dutch style farmhouse. It was in one of these, *Buffelskraal*, that the tradition was born of the ghost (the *hex* or witch) who is supposed to haunt the Hex River Mountains. It is said that in the year 1768, just after the house had been built, one of its occupants was a beautiful girl named Eliza Meiring. She was so popular with the young bloods that she set any would-be suitor the initial task of bringing her a disa from the inaccessible precipices of the 2 249 m Matroosberg, the highest peak of the range. The very difficulty of the task was intended to deter unwanted suitors.

Unknown to Eliza, however, the one man she really favoured set out to surprise her by securing a disa. In the attempt he fell and was killed. The shock deranged the fair Eliza, and she had to be locked in an upper room of the house. One night she contrived to force a window open but in trying to reach the ground she slipped and was killed. It is said to be her spirit, lamenting the death of her lover, which wanders along the windswept peaks at night. The date 1768 and the initials

'E M' were carved into the window-sill, but later removed by renovators. This graffiti was thought to commemorate the tragedy. Now, when the moonlight glitters on the first sprinkling of winter snows, someone living on the valley floor is sure to remark: *'The witch is on the mountains tonight'*.

From Worcester, people like to point out the profile of Eliza the witch on the skyline of the Langeberge over the cleft of the Hex River. This legend provides a local version of the Swiss *edelweis* story and overlooks the fact that the original name of the river had nothing to do with any '*hex*' (witch).

Eliza may have suffered a tragic end, but most of her fellows in the valley at the time were a carefree lot with few worries save the effects on their figures of hearty eating, good wine and a pleasant life in the sunshine and crisp Karoo air.

Today, from the original farms of the Hex River valley, there are nearly 150 subdivisions. The value of any single subdivision is so greatly in excess of the original combined value of the first six farms that the comparison is ludicrous. In contrast to the quiet economic conditions of the cattle-grazing past, an economic revolution has come to the valley in recent times.

The change began in 1875 when the Hex River railway pass was surveyed by Wells Hood and built to carry the main railway from Cape Town to the north and the diamond-fields of Kimberley. Before the construction of the railway, most of the traffic to the north had followed the early road route through Ceres and Sutherland, but now the Hex River valley became accepted as the principal route to the interior. The early wagon trail over the criss-cross river was gradually improved until it became the Great North Road we know today, and the valley at last gained the advantage of first-class communications.

Seven years after the opening of this great railway pass – certainly the most famous in Southern Africa – the first tentative export of table grapes was made to Britain. In 1886 the grapes (red and white Hanepoot) were privately dispatched to Dr Smuts in London. Carefully packed in cork and charcoal dust, their stems sealed in beeswax and without any refrigeration, they arrived in excellent condition. This was the auspicious beginning of the great export grape trade of today. The Hex River valley is the principal South African centre and producer of dessert grapes of international quality and renown.

The railway to the north brought an increase in the demand for table fruit for the inland market. The Hex River valley farmers found that they had a slight advantage in the competition for new markets on the diamond and gold-fields. The railway station and locomotive depot built on De Doorns farm was, by rail, 200 km nearer the northern markets than Cape Town. Freight costs were therefore cheaper and the fruit was subjected to some 20 hours less of buffeting and heat from constant stoppages at sidings and crossing-points – common in goods railage in those days.

From this period the Hex River valley farmers started to become seriously interested in table grapes. They soon made a significant discovery. The Hex River valley had an ideal climate for vines, with a long, warm summer and autumn, with little rain from the time the grapes started to ripen. Not only do grapes grow superbly there, free of most diseases and blemishes, but the lengthy, dry autumn allows the fruit to remain on the vines until the very end of the season when market prices are excellent.

In the developing local market the Hanepoot remained the grape variety in greatest demand, but its weakness of a skin too soft to allow it to travel well was serious. Despite care and ingenuity in packing, the first 20 years of the table grape industry were seriously handicapped by this weakness of the Hanepoot – entire shipments were often useless by the time the grapes reached the markets. The answer was to find or breed other varieties of grape with tougher skins, which made them keep better.

The most popular of the varieties subsequently grown is the Barlinka introduced from Algeria in 1909. This large luscious black grape grows to perfection in the Hex River valley, and today the area produces the bulk of South Africa's export grape harvest.

Water is the only limiting factor in the development of the valley. Originally boreholes were the principal source of supply, going down about 150 m to the underground supplies in the Table Mountain sandstone. Rainfall in the valley is slight, and the main original source of borehole water was rain and snow on the overlooking mountains. Mineralisation of the water supply from salts in the Bokkeveld rocks and by pollution from fertilisers and pesticides affected this supply of water. In modern times two dams have been built on the Sand River: one at Lakenvlei on the Ceres side of the Hex River range. This feeds a second dam in the heart of the mountains. From here a tunnel 14,7 km long feeds water into the valley and then to the farms through a complex of pipes. Each farm is entitled to 1 500 cubic metres of water per hectare from November to June.

Late autumn and early winter (around the month of June) see the Hex River valley aflame with one of the world's greatest botanical spectacles. It is then that the leaves of the Barlinka vines and those of red varieties of grapes turn an almost unbelievable shade of scarlet. Green varieties of grapes have leaves which turn yellow.

The principal centre in the valley of the Hex River, 150 km by road from Cape Town is ...

DE DOORNS

Built on the farm *De Doorns* (the thorns), this town started as a railway station in 1875. It is now the principal commercial, administrative and educational centre for the Hex River valley.

The De Doorns Co-operative Wine Cellar sells its wines to the public during normal business hours.

Beyond the turn-off to the town, N1 continues its way up the valley. There are fine views of the Hex River Mountains, dominated by the highest peak, the 2 249 m high dome-shaped summit of *Matroosberg*, named after Klaas Matroos, a shepherd who once lived on its slopes. After 4,5 km the road passes the Bonny Brand fruit stall and soon starts to climb out of the valley along a serpentine pass up the edge of the escarpment to the 965 m level of the central plateau of South Africa. The spectacular old railway pass climbs the escarpment to the east of the road while the new pass, opened in 1989, carries the railway upwards through four long tunnels, a total of 16,3 km underground of the 30 km of track.

THE MIDDLE REACHES OF THE BREEDE RIVER

From Worcester south-east to Bonnievale, the Breede River valley, as befits its name, is broad, somewhat arid so far as natural rainfall is concerned, but beautifully fertile under irrigation. It is here that the Breede River is almost completely harnessed by man. Its water effects an almost magical transformation of a valley surface composed mainly of rather unprepossessing Malmesbury shales. By the touch of water the suitability of these shales for the cultivation of fruit and grapes has proved a gift to man. He has prospered on the water. The river, in exchange for its bounty, has not been so well rewarded.

During the winter months, when the rains and snow on the mountain tops cause the springs and tributary streams of the Breede to flow, the river is replenished and its waters are purified. The fruit trees and vines are asleep and little water is used by man. The holding reservoir of the Greater Brandvlei Dam fills up. With the arrival of spring the farms awaken. The whole valley is astir, flowers, blossoms, new leaves and new farming plans – all based on irrigation.

At this time the natural flow of the river dwindles. There is little rain; the sun blazes down from cloudless skies; the springs dry up; the merry little streamlets cease to flow. It is then that the water impounded in the Greater Brandvlei Dam is released to irrigate the thirsty farmlands. Up to 640 000 cubic metres of water a day is required by the farmers of the valley. The Breede River itself provides the main channel. Into that river the irrigation engineers release from the Greater Brandvlei Dam 560 000 cubic metres of water. Four weirs in the river divert this water into subsidiary concrete-lined canals. The first of these is Le Chasseur canal, 1 km downstream from the Greater Brandvlei Dam. Then, 44 km further on, is the weir feeding the Robertson canal. A further 20 km downstream lies the Angora canal and 6 km lower down is the weir feeding the Sanddrift canal.

The 560 000 cubic metres of water released from the Greater Brandvlei Dam is supplemented by the water of various minor streams along the way and by return flow. This return flow of water provides the balance between the 560 000 cubic metres released from the Greater Brandvlei Dam and the 640 000 cubic metres required by the farmers. It also, unfortunately, is responsible for the progressive mineralisation of the river from an initial 51 mg per litre to 401 mg per litre. Pesticides, artificial fertilisers and other pollutants are carried back into the river by the run-off water. This results in severe salinisation of the lower reaches of the river.

At the Sanddrift weir, the lowest in the river, all the remaining flow is canalled, apart from 30 000 cubic metres which by seepage escapes from bondage. At this point the salinisation has reached 401 mg per litre. At Drew, 23 km further downstream from Sanddrift, the flow of the river has been restored by 50 000 cubic metres of return flow and reaches 80 000 cubic metres a day. The pollution level at this point reaches the disastrous figure of 1 160 mg per litre. About 260 tons of salt is carried down by the river each day with about 48 per cent of it pure table salt. Such water is no longer suitable for irrigation except under very special conditions and subject to expensive purification procedures.

If all the water fed to each farm was used in irrigation without any return flow, there would be no problem from pollution. Each farm would retain its own pollutants and have the responsibility of neutralising their effects without rather scurvily rewarding the river for its bounty by washing into it such an unappetising mix of chemicals. As it is, the lower reaches of the river, while imposing to the eye, carry water which would need to be eaten with a knife and fork rather than drunk, if anybody was so ill-advised as to crave a taste of it!

The beauty and prosperity of the farms of the middle reaches of the Breede are, however, a delight to behold. From Worcester the main tarmac road down the valley leads south-eastwards in close company with the railway line. The Langeberge range dominates the valley on its northern side. Fine farms cover the approaches to the range. An interesting circular drive from Worcester is possible by taking one of the two tarmac roads which branch off at Overhex and Nuy (named from the willow trees growing on the banks of the stream). The road leads through this area to join N1 at De Wet and then back to Worcester. There are co-operative wine cellars at Overhex, 7 km from Worcester; at *Nuy*, 22 km from Worcester; and at De Wet, 8 km from Worcester. All sell wines and welcome visits. The port-type wine of Nuy is worth sampling. Another interesting road branches south from Overhex and leads to the co-operative wine cellars at Aan de Doorns and then across the Breede to the wholesale bulk cellars at Rondebosch. The road then meanders through the farmlands on the south side of the river, eventually rejoining the main Robertson road at Rooiberg.

The main road, meanwhile, has continued its direct path down the valley, passing the quarry and works of the Cape Lime Company 31 km from Worcester and then, after a further 2,5 km, reaches the co-operative wine cellars at ...

ROOIBERG

The *Rooiberg* (red mountain) Co-operative Winery was established in 1964 and today is the possession of 36 members whose vineyards lie north and south of the main road to Robertson in areas such as Vinkrivier, Goree, Riverside and Eilandia. The reputation and achievements of this cellar and its cellar-master, J C (Dassie) Smith, are exceptional.

In an area noted for its sweet Muscadel wines, the Rooiberg Co-operative always had as its objective the production of the dry wines which, at least in former years, were in greatest demand. The results were spectacular. In 1971 the cellar won the S A White Wine Championship. In 1978, 1982, 1983, 1984 and 1986 Rooiberg was the South African Champion Co-operative Cellar. In 1984 Rooiberg had a real vintage year, winning two championship trophies, four class winner trophies and twenty gold medals (eight for dry white wines, six for semi-sweet white wines, one for dry red wine and five for sweet dessert wines).

In 1986 Rooiberg won one championship trophy, four class winner trophies and eleven gold medals. The cellar and its cellar-master were awarded the General Smuts Trophy as overall South African Champion Winemaker in 1982 and 1984. Twenty-eight Rooiberg wines were awarded the distinction of the Superior classification by the Wine and Spirits Board.

From grapes grown in the relatively cool climate of the Vink River valley the cellar produces dry wines such as Riesling, an oak-matured Riesling, a Steen, a slightly sweet Colombar, a Chenin

Blanc, a semi-sweet Late Vintage and a Special Late Vintage. There is a White and a Red Hanepoot wine from the same valley. Try them as a liqueur, or when fishing or lazing beside a tranquil stretch of the river!

From the red soils of the Eilandia district come dry red wines, a Pinotage and a Cinsaut. There is also a Selected Dry Red and a Cabernet Sauvignon.

From the Goree area comes a delectable dry white wine, Clairette Blanche. From Riverside comes a smooth Ugni Blanc; also a Selected Dry White, a Premier Grand Crû, two Rosés (dry and semi-sweet) and an elegant Blanc de Noir. Pure grape juice is also produced in the cellar.

Several private estates also produce wine in the area. Notable is Graham Beck's farm with the Biblical name of *Madeba* (running water).

The main tarmac road past the Rooiberg Co-operative Winery continues its way south-eastwards. To the south on the slopes of the Sandberg ridge may be seen extraordinary wind-blown dunes of red sands carried high and naturally graded with the coarser grains on the lower slopes and the finer grains near the summit. Climbing a ridge, the road makes a grand approach, 46 km from Worcester, to the town of ...

ROBERTSON

This handsomely situated town, notable for its fine jacaranda trees, good wine and lovely rose gardens, was founded in 1852 and named in honour of Dr W Robertson, pastor of the Swellendam congregation at that time. A portion of the farm *Over Het Roode Zand* (beyond the red sands) was purchased from its owner, J van Zyl. In 1853 the first sale of plots was held in what was planned as a new church centre, eventually growing into a town built around an impressive Dutch Reformed church.

Traders, schools and government offices followed the church to the area and it grew slowly as a centre for the local agricultural community. Wagons and coaches were built there; furniture and cabinets, copperware and even clocks were made. The De Jong Type Press was established in 1875, and a substantial trading company was founded by the Barry family. In 1873 the town became the headquarters of the Cape Midland Railway Company which remained an independent concern until its absorption into the South African Railways in 1925.

With plentiful water from the Langeberge, farming flourished. Grapes, vegetables, almonds, olives and coriander are produced. The production of wine, brandy and the breeding of thoroughbred racehorses are major activities.

There is an interesting museum housed in Druid's Lodge in Paul Kruger Street. Built in 1863, it contains many relics of the past years. It is open Mondays to Saturdays 09h00 to 12h00. Closed on public holidays.

On the banks of the Breede River the municipality has created a resort known as Silverstrand. Here there are facilities for boating, a fine open-air swimming-bath, rondavel, chalet and flat accommodation and a caravan park. There is a restaurant and a golf-course.

The KWV created a taphouse, *Branewynsdraai* (brandy bend), situated in a pleasant garden notable for its superb old peppercorn trees. A cellar was created to stock a representative collection of the wines of this portion of the Breede River valley. The taphouse, situated in an elegant old Cape Dutch building, is now run as a restaurant under private management.

There are three co-operative wineries in the town: Clairvaux, founded in 1964; Roodezandt founded in 1953 with 52 members contributing 23 000 tons of grapes each year, and the Robertson Co-operative Winery.

The Robertson Co-operative Winery was founded in 1941 and is the oldest co-operative cellar in the Breede River valley. There are 40 members of the co-operative. With their farms in areas of subtle divergence in climate, the range of wines produced is impressive. Ten horizontal hydraulic presses crush 18 000 tons of grapes each year and produce juice of high quality. Rotor tanks and cold fermentation cellars are of modern design.

The cellar is proud of its Colombar wine, a crisp dry table wine of high quality. There are two special 'limited edition' wines – Baron Du Pon, each bottle numbered and packed in a wooden box, and a very special Bukettraube in 250 ml bottles only. The cellar also produces a white Muscat-flavoured grape juice of high quality. Wine is sold at the cellar during normal business hours. Visitors are welcome to enter a pleasant tasting-room and to join tours through the cellars.

From Robertson there are several very attractive drives and hiking trails. For the lover of scenery, fruit, wine and cheese, an exploration of these routes is recommended. The two-day, 38 km long Dassieshoek hiking trail starts from the Silverstrand resort and is highly recommended. There is an overnight hut. The 15 km long Boerbok trail finds its way through lovely farming and scenic country. There is an overnight hut. An 11 km long road leads into the foothills of the Langeberge as far as De Hoop, passing estates such as *Mont Blois*, (well known for its white Muscadel wine) and culminating in a shady cul-de-sac where mountaineers can begin their climb up slopes adorned with many lovely wild flowers. Another road into the foothills leads to the municipal nature reserve of Dassieshoek where climbers start a 23 km long path up Donkerkloof to the summit of the range. The reserve is open daily from dawn to dusk. The Boerbok trail is 15 km long and the Arangies Kop trail is 21 km long. Bookings and enquiries phone (023) 626-3112.

South of Robertson a tarmac road enters a fine avenue of giant eucalyptus trees, crosses the Breede River and then forks. The right-hand road leads for 22 km through the farming areas of La Chasseur and Agterkliphoogte, passing a succession of wine, fruit and other estates in an alluvial valley watered by a tributary of the Breede named the Poesjenels. The left turn at the fork also passes many fine farms. After 15 km it reaches the entrance to the *Vrolijkheid* (merriment) Nature Reserve created by Cape Nature Conservation. The reserve has two fine walking trails. The Rooikat trail is 19 km and fairly strenuous through the Elandsberg mountains. The Heron trail is an easy 3 km and includes an interesting bird hide with 175 species to see. Wildlife includes klipspringer, grysbok, grey rhebuck and springbok. Caracals (rooikat) occur but are seldom seen. Spring flowers are spectacular. Enquiries, The Manager, Vrolijkheid Nature Reserve, Private Bag X614, Robertson 6705. Phone (02353) 621.

At 17 km from Robertson the road reaches the charming little town of ...

McGREGOR

The Reverend Andrew McGregor, one of the Scottish ministers who served the Dutch Reformed Church, gave his name to this place. It was founded in 1861 in a situation and environment strangely reminiscent of a village in Scotland. The architecture, however, is pure Cape-Dutch and the inhabitants have taken pride in carefully maintaining a delightful assembly of buildings. The church stands in the centre of a garden of flowers. The houses are so immaculately whitewashed and topped with black thatched roofs that they almost appear to have gathered in their best Sunday-go-to-meeting clothes to listen to an open-air service by the estimable Dr McGregor! The housing estate created originally for the Coloured community was carefully laid out with neat little cottages in Cape-Dutch style, far more attractive than the dreary rows of buildings which pass for modern housing estates in many other towns. McGregor is an agricultural centre. A co-operative wine cellar was established in 1948 and is now well-known for its white and Muscadel wines. Wine is sold at the cellars during normal business hours.

In the days of wagons, McGregor was a great provider of whipstocks, the bamboo sticks to which the long thongs were attached to allow wagon men to discipline the spans of oxen. The Krans Nature Reserve, part of the commonage of McGregor, conserves flora, fauna and traces of prehistoric man. Paths provide pleasant walks.

There is an interesting continuation of the road directly through the town and then for 16,5 km up the slopes of the Riversonderend Mountains to the head of Boesmanskloof, a renowned area for wild flowers. The road reaches a sudden and disconsolate end at a precipice known as *Die Galg* (the gallows). Originally it was planned to continue right through *Boesmanskloof* (Bushman's cleft) to Greyton and then to Caledon on the southern side of the mountains. A sad story of financial muddle and incompetence aborted the project.

From the end of the road the Boesmanskloof hiking trail has its start and leads through handsome mountain scenery for 14 km to Greyton on the southern side of the Riviersonderend Mountains. This is a first class, fairly strenuous walk. There are no overnight facilities on the walk. A permit is essential. These may be obtained from the Manager of the Vrolijkheid Nature Reserve, Robertson. Phone (023) 625-1621.

From McGregor another road leads for 32 km to the foot of the pass which climbs from Bonnievale through the Riviersonderend Mountains to the little town of Stormsvlei.

The main tarmac road from Robertson down the valley of the Breede River proceeds eastwards from the town. There is a turn-off south to Bonnievale just outside the town. The main road continues over a level valley floor. At 7 km there is a turn-off north towards the mountains and this leads to the Sheilam cactus gardens, sometimes known a Little Mexico. This is a remarkable place to visit. It is actually a nursery for exotic cactus plants. About 3 000 of some of the weirdest and loveliest plants imaginable may be seen growing and flowering here. Mrs Winnie Schwegman developed the place and she exported her plants to many parts of the world. Visitors are welcome during normal business hours.

Shortly after the turn-off to the Sheilam cactus gardens, there is a turn-off south leading to Klaas Voogds station and then on to join the Robertson–Bonnievale road. Klaas Voogd was trampled to death by an elephant on the slopes of the Langeberge while he was tracking a band of Bushmen accused of raiding cattle. His name was applied to the Klaas Voogds River which waters several farms, including the estate of *Rietvlei* (valley of reeds) where the Burger family for five generations have been producing a red Muscadel wine. John Burger is the cellar-master today, and he faithfully follows the recipe of his ancestors, handed down to him by an ancient Coloured winemaker who knew, to perfection, how to make this fiery raisin-flavoured drink.

Further down the Klaas Voogds road lies the estate of *Burgershof* named after Jacobus Burger who started farming there in 1840. Hennie Reyneke, a descendant of Jacobus Burger on the female side, now runs the estate and producers dessert wines of high quality.

At 18 km from Robertson lies the town of ...

ASHTON

Ashton was originally known as Roodewal. When the Cape Midland Railway Company constructed the line from Worcester to Swellendam, the official sent to take charge of the station being built there is said to have had difficulty in pronouncing the name of Roodewal. He solved his difficulty by renaming the station after *Ashton*, his hometown in England. For several years from the opening of the line in 1887, Ashton was little more than a loading-point for goods carried through Kogmanskloof to and from the Little Karoo. Then, in 1940, the Langeberg Koöperasie Beperk established what became a substantial canning factory. Ashton grew into a small town around this factory and eventually achieved municipal status on 1 January 1956. Ashton has a population of about 8 360 people.

The Ashton Co-operative Wine Cellar, founded in 1962, handles about 22 000 tons of the wine grapes of the area from 86 members. Most of the product is sold in bulk but a small percentage is bottled and sold from the cellar during normal business hours.

Just south of the town, on the banks of the Kogmans River, lies the estate of *Zandvliet* (sand stream) renowned for the production of Shiraz wine. Paul de Wet is the winemaker, while his brother Dan runs the *Zandvliet* stud, one of the group of thoroughbred racehorse breeders of the BAR Valley (Bonnievale, Ashton, Robertson) Breeders who have produced some of the finest horses in South Africa.

Computer-controlled drip irrigation, a high limestone content to the soil, and the most modern cellar techniques all contribute to the production of fine wines. Sunny summer days, cool nights and frosty winters suit both vines and horses. Many a winner on the race-track has been bred on this estate, and its success toasted with Zandvliet Shiraz.

Further down the Kogmans River lies the *Excelsior* estate, once part of *Zandvliet* and now run by the brothers J S and F M de Wet. Their wines are sold in bulk to such buyers as Stellenbosch Farmers' Winery. The *Excelsior* stud is one of the BAR Valley Breeders with an impressive record of finely bred racehorses.

Beyond Ashton, the main road continues eastwards. After 1 km there is a division. Straight ahead, the road leads through Kogmanskloof and into the Little Karoo. A right turn leads south-eastwards down the Breede River valley, past two turn-offs to Bonnievale, and then 48 km from Ashton, after a very pleasant journey up and down over the foothills of the Langeberge, the road reaches the town of Swellendam (described in Chapter Seventeen).

BON COURAGE

Midway in its journey to the sea, the Breede River flows past the pleasant town of Robertson and then on into the rising sun through a landscape of vineyards, fruit fields and homesteads. Where the Klaas Voogds River joins the Breede, 9 km from Robertson on the Bonnievale road, lies the old farm of *Goedemoed* (good courage), with a serene Cape-Dutch homestead built in 1818. From the beginning of the 19th century this farm produced excellent wine from a variety of cultivars. Its soil was varied: rich alluvial river soil, shaly high ground, reddish-coloured sedimentary soils – each area receptive to particular cultivars; each area demanding a technical appreciation of its possibilities, an empathy and profound understanding on the part of the cultivating farmer.

In the 1920s *Goedemoed* was acquired by the Dutch Reformed Church who closed the cellars, rooted out the vines and used the estate as a training school for farm managers, planting there lucerne and fruit and breeding pigs. The venture did not prosper. In 1927 the property, already subdivided, was put up for auction. The highest bidder for the largest division was Willie Bruwer, a farmer from the De Hoop area in the foothills of the Langeberge just north of Robertson.

Willie replanted the whole estate with steen and muscadel grapes, vinifying and fortifying the juice and selling the product in bulk to the KWV. Then, when Dr Niehaus discovered *flor* yeast in the Western Cape, Willie Bruwer joined the resultant rush to the production of sherry.

The youngest son of Willie was André. Born and bred on a wine estate, he majored in wine making at Elsenburg Agricultural College and in 1965 settled on the *Goedemoed* farm. Some confusion in the use of the name *Goedemoed* became inevitable, for there were five other divisions, each under a separate owner. He decided to translate the Afrikaans name into the French *Bon Courage*, and this was the name which eventually appeared on the labels of his wines.

André made a deep study of the soils of his estate. In the cool, shaly high ground he planted cultivars such as Kerner, Chardonnay, Gewürztraminer, and Sauvignon Blanc. In the sedimentary soils he planted riesling; in the alluvial river soils he planted Muscadel and Colombar.

The whole estate was orchestrated into a thoughtfully managed wine-production operation. André Bruwer accepted the basic maxim that wine is produced in the soil; therefore harmonise the correct cultivar to the correct soil. In 1972 he introduced drip irrigation, providing for greater control of water supply and allowing the utilisation of the stony ground hitherto beyond the reach of cultivation.

In 1974 he modernised the cellar. In 1980 he purchased a neighbouring farm and extended his ownership to a total of 160 ha. In 1983 he started marketing a small selection of his wines himself, selling the bulk to Stellenbosch Farmers' Winery. In 1983 he received from the Wine and Spirit Board his first Superior classification for a Kerner special late harvest. In 1984 he received the Superior classification for Red Muscadel Jerepigo. In 1985 he received the Superior classification for a late-harvest wine made from Rhine Riesling grapes.

In 1986 André started night harvesting, accepting the fact that the quality of the grape, especially the subtle flavouring in the skin, is better if the grape is cool. Flavour is volatile and heat carries it away like a ghost fleeing before the dawn. The cooler the grape, and the sooner it is crushed after picking, the more subtle the flavouring of the wine; the cleaner and crisper with all its delicate elusive aromas and flavours.

André Bruwer has won numerous awards, trophies and prizes, and was judged S A Estate Winemaker of the Year for 1984, 1985 and 1986, after which these awards were abolished.

MON DON

Mon Don is another subdivision of the original old farm of *Goedemoed*. In 1901 Nicolaas Jonker purchased this fertile fragment of what was a huge and largely unworked property. He commenced farming wine grapes for bulk sale but prices were so low that in some years farmers simply emptied their vats into the drains, for there was no demand.

In 1944 Nicolaas Jonker died and his daughter Hannatjie inherited the estate. She was married to George Marais, chief librarian of the Carnegie Library in Stellenbosch, and for about 20 years the estate was left to the management of a foreman. There was little on it save a wine cellar without a roof and a rather unpromising-looking vineyard.

Times changed. Wine increased in value. Hannatjie's son Pierre studied at Stellenbosch University and in 1962 graduated in viticulture and wine-making. He settled on the farm and started planting high quality grape cultivars and producing wine with modern irrigation technology introduced to permit the cultivation of 80 ha of good land.

In 1972 Hannatjie sold the farm to her son on such generous terms that he decided to rename the place *Mon Don* (my gift). On his estate Pierre at first produced sweet wines from Chenin Blanc grapes and a sweet sherry type for the KWV. When the fickle market for this type of wine deteriorated, he replanted portions of the estate with dry wine varieties of grapes and extended his range with the addition of Harslevulü, Sauvignon Blanc, Gewürztraminer, Ugni Blanc, and others.

The *Mon Don* estate shares the characteristics of the middle reaches of the Breede River valley. The soil contains a high calcium content from outcrops of lime. Winter weather is cold enough to put the vines into a restful sleep. There is a high light intensity in summer, with hot afternoons but cool evenings and mornings. The prevailing south-east wind of summer makes itself felt at about 15h00 each day, bringing in moisture from the Indian Ocean. When the temperature drops by early evening, mists form. Harvesting on *Mon Don* is done early in the mornings at the coldest possible temperature. Grapes picked in hot weather are crushed and fermented separately.

Wines sold under the estate label include a slightly dry and a semi-sweet Colombar, a semi-sweet Chenin Blanc and a late harvest made from Steen grapes, with a pleasant honey-sweet flavour and bouquet. Wine is sold from the cellar during normal business hours, and visitors are welcome to visit the estate which lies 10 km from Robertson on the Bonnievale road.

VAN LOVEREN

In 1692 Guillaume van Zyl arrived in the Cape with a young bride, Christina van Loveren. The bride brought her trousseau packed in a superb Philippine mahogany kist. The fair Christina never saw the farm now named after her. In the 1690s the valley of the Breede was still an area of wild animals with only a few early human beings – hunters and pastoralists – wandering through the valley.

In the 19th century farms were created in the valley with one of them named *Goudmyn* (gold-mine). This farm prospered during the ostrich feather craze. When the boom collapsed, it went into something of a recession and was divided amongst the nine offspring of the Potgieter family.

In 1937 Nicolaas Retief purchased one of these divisions for his son Hennie. The division, 28 ha in extent, lay at the confluence of the Kogmanskloof tributary with the Breede and was simply known as *Goudmyn F*. This was a dull address, and Hennie's wife Jean suggested that they call their farm after her ancestor, who happened to be the young bride, Christina van Loveren. Her treasured Philippine kist had been inherited by Mrs Retief, and this lovely old bridal treasure-chest may still be seen in the homestead of the *Van Loveren* estate.

As on most of the wine farms of the Breede River valley, Hennie Retief at first concentrated on producing the sweet wines made from Muscadel grapes which flourish in the area as though it was their natural home. Then, in 1972, cold fermentation facilities were installed on *Van Loveren*. New cultivars were planted such as Colombar and Steen. In 1980 the Retiefs planted Sauvignon Blanc, Rhine Riesling, Harslevulü and Fernando Pires, two cultivars introduced to South Africa by the Retiefs.

Hennie Retief died in 1982 leaving two sons, Nico and Wynand. By that time the farm had been substantially increased in size with the acquisition of three neighbouring farms, *Schoemanshoek, Jacobsdal*, and a portion of *Goedemoed*. The cellar was also modernised with cement and fibreglass tanks with a total capacity of 1 000 tons and a capability for further enlargement to accept the 1 800 tons which is the pressing quota of the estate.

The great flood of 1981 put a large part of the estate under water for a while but left a legacy of rich new soil washed down from the Little Karoo and Kogmanskloof. The two brothers manage the estate in partnership. Nico is the viticulturist, with 60 ha of vines, 30 ha of fruit orchards and 5 ha of vegetables. Wynand is the cellar-master.

The brothers concentrate on white wine and are proud of a fresh, flowery piquancy. The light dry Harslevulü and the delicate Fernando Pires are their especial pride. They also produce a Rhine Riesling, a Sauvignon Blanc, a Chardonnay, a Gewürztraminer, and two Blanc de Noirs (dry from shiraz grapes and off-dry from muscat de frontignan). To complete the range there is a Colombar, a Blanc de Blanc, a special late harvest and a premier crû.

The floral bouquet of all these *Van Loveren* wines is a perfect complement to the glorious garden cultivated by Mrs Jean Retief around the original homestead. This garden is worth travelling many kilometres to see. It is like an oasis of colour in the midst of the pleasant green sea of vines. Flowering plants and trees originating from many countries have found a little paradise here. Roses and hydrangeas reach complete perfection. To relax in this cool garden on a warm summer day and sample some of the wines is to appreciate the strange alchemy of the soil, the perfume of the earth and the bouquet of a garden of flowers.

THE ROAD TO BONNIEVALE

The road from Robertson to Bonnievale takes the traveller on a joyous journey of discovery past many grand estates along the north bank of the Breede River. Three of the stud-farms of the BAR Valley Breeders lie along the road within a few kilometres of Robertson. First, 4,5 km along the road, lies *Riverton*, run by George and Duncan Barry. Another 4,2 km takes the road past *Saratoga*, owned by Fred and Harry Doms. Less than 1 km beyond this stud is the entrance of *Normandy* where Dr Tommy Foulkes, the veterinary surgeon and his wife combined scientific knowledge with artistry in the creation of a renowned stud for thoroughbred racehorses.

The *Klipdrift* wine farm of the Bruwer family lies along the river banks 3 km from Robertson while 1 km beyond it is *Die Vlakte*, the property of the Marais family. *Bon Courage, Mon Don* and

Van Loveren are next along the road. Their story has already been told. Close to *Van Loveren*, 16 km from Robertson lies the *De Wetshof* wine estate of Danie de Wet, one of the most distinguished of all the wine producers of the Breede River valley.

DE WETSHOF

De Wetshof has always been a great innovator. Danie de Wet skilfully assessed that the lime-rich soil was similar to the soils of Burgundy in France. Cool morning mists and the south-east wind of the afternoons also affected the ripening of grapes. In such a setting Danie broke from the established patterns of growing Muscadel grapes in the area. In 1973 he produced a Rhine Riesling, followed by a Sauvignon Blanc and a Chardonnay. They were the first of their kind to be produced in South Africa and were of such quality as completely to deserve the classification of Superior.

To crown his achievements, Danie was the first wine farmer in the Robertson region to produce a noble late harvest, the *De Wetshof Edeloes*, an exquisite dessert wine made in years of high humidity when *Botrytis cinerea* turns the grapes into little more than withered looking skin containing an elixir for the gods. The four great wines of *De Wetshof* are distributed internationally by the Distillers Corporation. Unfortunately they are not for sale at the cellar.

Beyond De Wetshof, the road continues its amiable way past the estate of Wolwedrift and Goedverwacht and then past the cellars and vineyards of the Weltevrede estate.

WELTEVREDE

Weltevrede (well satisfied) had its start as recently as 1912 when Klaas Jonker bought 290 ha of semi-Karoo scrub country. He invested muscle, patience and a great deal of skill in studying and cultivating his new farm. He started to produce good wine at a bad time of depression. It was pretty thankless pouring his wine into the gutter because there was no demand in the years of depression, but he lived on hope and persisted.

In 1969 Lourens Jonker inherited the estate. He acquired a neighbouring farm named *Muscadel*. The two farms were consolidated under the name of *Weltevrede* in 1974. The first wine bottled on the estate, a Colombar, was released two years later. From then on it was steady progress. In 1979 a fine reception hall was built. In 1981 the neighbouring farm *Riversedge* was incorporated into *Weltevrede*; and with 150 ha to cultivate, Lourens Jonker found himself in the position of producing twelve different wines of high quality. An underground cellar and a vinotique were built in 1984, and today visitors to the estate may taste and purchase, during normal business hours, a very interesting range of wines.

Weltevrede lies on the verge of the rural centre of ...

BONNIEVALE

At one time serving as a half-way railway crossing-point between Robertson and Swellendam, the station was simply named 'Vale'. In 1917 the name was converted to Bonnievale. In 1922 it became a village and in 1953 a town which today has a population of 3 625 and is renowned for its cheese and wine.

The founder of Bonnievale was Christopher Forest Rigg who, after a not-too-successful search for gold in the Barberton rush, saw the possibilities of irrigation in this part of the Breede River valley. He acquired all the land on which Bonnievale now stands. He laid out a canal system with a tunnel to carry water to Bonnievale. The irrigated farmlands were divided and sold to various individuals. Of his three children, two died in infancy. The third was Myrtle Rigg, the idol of her parents. She died in 1912. As a memorial to her, her bereaved parents built a charming little church. It is in Gothic style, with a door imported from Zanzibar, tiles from Italy, a solid lead roof, and stone from Bonnievale. On the death of the Riggs, the Myrtle Rigg church fell into disuse. It was restored in 1977 by the municipality and is now a museum.

Water flows in canals from the Breede River irrigation system to the fertile alluvial soil of the valley. The area is renowned for its production of Muscadel wines and sherry type wines. Cognac-type grapes yield fine brandy, and there are three co-operative cellars in the town and its vicinity. They are the Bonnievale Co-operative Wine Cellar where wines and grape juice are sold during normal business hours; the private cellars of the Van Zyl brothers on the main street; and the Nordale Co-operative Winery which sells its wines at the cellar.

Peaches and apricots are also grown in large quantities while gouda and cheddar cheese are produced under the 'Bonnita' label by the local cheese co-operative, Die Boesmansrivierse Koöperatiewe Kaasfabriek Bpk (one of the largest in South Africa). These cheeses are outstanding in a country which is not really renowned for producing cheeses much better than 'mousetrap' quality. There are daily tours through the factory. The yellow clingstone peaches of Bonnievale are also of superlative flavour.

A cheese shop on the eastern side of the town, where the road turns off to Stormsvlei, sells the local cheese during normal business hours. Seven kilometres east of the town, on the road to Swellendam, lies the Merwespont Co-operative Winery, founded in 1956. Its wines and grape juice are sold from the cellars.

The Mooivallei hiking trail is a 12 km walk in beautiful scenery. The trail is 8 km in the veld and 4 km on tarred road. The trail starts on the farm of Mr Phillip Jordaan, *Hooggelegen*, and it also ends there. No entrance fee is payable, and the trail is open to everyone.

The Kobus Steyn Nature Garden shows that even Bonnievale can have a piece of Namaqualand during spring. It is situated in Buite Crescent and is open to everyone.

From Bonnievale a tarmac road crosses the Breede River (where there is a camping ground and ramps for launching boats), passes the cheese co-operative and then leads for 20 km over the Riviersonderend Mountains to Stormsvlei. Another road 3 km long connects the town to the main road from Robertson to Swellendam.

The story of Swellendam and the lower reaches of the Breede River is told in Chapter Seventeen.

Chapter Eleven
THE COAST OF FLOWERS

The rugged coastline of False Bay around Cape Hangklip, past Hermanus, Danger Point and off to Cape Agulhas and Arniston, is one of the most beautiful in the world. Its waters, rich in fish, attract thousands of sea-birds. Its rocky promontories and cliffs are full of vantage points for anglers. Reefs, islets and capes are enriched by memories of shipwrecks and disasters. There are sandy beaches for swimming and sheltered bays where the waves seem far too lazy even to break. There are caves and pleasant camping grounds. Handsome mountains crowd close to the shore and above all there are wild flowers, dazzling in quantity, variety and brilliance of colour.

The road which follows the coast of flowers begins at Muizenberg where the beach of silver-coloured sand, which forms the northern cul-de-sac of False Bay, reaches its western end in the afternoon shadow of the mountains of the Cape Peninsula. From the traffic circle where Prince George's Drive reaches Sunrise Beach, the marine route, known as Baden-Powell Drive, leads eastwards close to the shore. This road provides access to an uninterrupted 30 km of beach where swimmers, anglers, surfers and sunbathers find recreation on a sandy coast gently sloping beneath a sea, warm in summer, cool in winter, safe and always beautiful.

At 3 km the road passes an enclosed area much loved by bird-watchers. Invisible from the road, behind low sand dunes, lies a series of artificial lakes, home to a vast and diverse population of aquatic birds – pelicans, flamingos, terns, cormorants and many others. They find life pleasant in nutrient rich water which is near the end of the cycle of the Cape Town sewage disposal system. To visit this bird sanctuary a day permit must be obtained from the Cape Town municipal offices.

Beyond these man-made lakes the road bridges a stream draining the largest of the natural lakes of the Cape Flats, *Zeekoevlei* (hippopotamus marsh). Once the home of hippos Zeekoevlei is now a venue for yachtsmen, aquaplaners and picnickers. Access to Zeekoevlei and to the artificial lakes is along a road which joins the coastal road at Strandfontein, 8 km from Muizenberg.

Strandfontein (beach fountain) was developed by the Cape Town municipality as a coastal resort adjacent to the residential township of *Mitchell's Plain*, named (and slightly misspelt) after Colonel Charles Michell, Surveyor-General of the Cape in the 1840s. The township was created in 1974. For several kilometres the coastal road forms the divide between residential and recreational areas including the beach named *Mnandi* (the pleasant place), a popular seaside resort.

The coastal road continues eastwards, revealing splendid views over False Bay and across to the Hottentots Holland Mountains. Seal Island lies 6 km from the coastline, its rocky shore crowded with seals and birds. Gulls nest in crevices and ledges of the cliffs overlooking the sea which, 16 km from Muizenberg, are protected as their special sanctuary, named *Wolfgat* (hyena cave).

Two kilometres beyond the gull sanctuary, the coastal road passes a turn-off leading inland (left) to the main N2 coastal road and (right) to the swimming and angling area of *Swartklip* (black rock). Just beyond Swartklip there is a seaside resort known as *Monwabisi* (the one which makes others happy). Designed to provide a recreational area for the residents of the nearby township of *Khayelitsha* (home which is new), *Monwabisi*, developed by the former Regional Services Council, has a large tidal pool, picnic grounds, shops, pavilion, chalets and caravan park.

MACASSAR BEACH AND SHEIK YUSSUF'S TOMB

Sheik Yussuf of Macassar was a prince of Bantam in Indonesia and a revered Muslim religious leader who was exiled to the Cape by the Dutch in 1694. Accompanied by 49 followers, 2 wives and 12 children, he was obliged to reside at an outpost on the farm *Zandvliet* (sand stream). When he died on 23 May 1699 at the age of 73, his heart was cut out and returned to Indonesia. His body was buried on a hilltop on *Zandvliet*. Since that time his gravesite has been regarded as a holy place by all Muslims. The *kramat* (sacred place) was built over the grave in 1925 by Hadji Sullaiman Shah Mohommed. It is an impressive memorial. The perfumed and beflagged tomb shelters within a domed chamber and is visited by many pilgrims who cover the tomb with thanks-offerings of brilliantly coloured silken quilts which are periodically removed by the guardian.

Old cannon guard the kramat and overlook a grand panorama stretching from Table Mountain to the end of the Hottentots Holland Mountains. Sheik Yussuf's kramat is the most important of six holy tombs, all built over the graves of Muslim religious leaders. All attract pilgrims. It is said that a line joins together all these kramats, making a holy circle which encloses Cape Town and brings peace and blessings to all those who reside there.

Sheik Yussuf's kramat is close to the beach of Macassar where a seaside resort has been developed. The beach is spacious and there is a large picnic area with numerous barbecue fireplaces.

Macassar Beach ends at the estuary of the Eersterivier. East of this, the coast is part of the well-wooded grounds of African Explosives and Chemical Industries, whose Capex fertiliser and explosives factory buildings stand among the trees. Entry to these grounds is prohibited. Where the company ground ends, the shoreline continues at what is known as Milk Bay. On this broad and gently shelving beach, one of the safest bathing beaches in Africa, stands the resort of Strand. To reach Strand, the N2 dual carriageway must be followed for 10 km from the point where the road from Muizenberg joined it. A traffic interchange then provides a turn-off to Somerset West (left) and back to the coast for 4 km to ...

STRAND

This holiday resort stretches for 3 km along the beach of *Milk Bay*. Originally intended as a seaside suburb for Somerset West, the place soon outgrew its parent and became a municipality of its own on 15 June 1896. Its original name was Somerset Strand, later abbreviated to the simpler form of Strand. Today the town has a population of 55 720 and is a popular holiday resort offering swimming, surfing, boating and the pleasure of a fine sandy beach of considerable size.

From Strand the road continues for 5 km parallel to what is known as the Harmony Coast and then reaches the resort of ...

GORDON'S BAY

An attractive seaside resort lying immediately below the Hottentots Holland Mountains, the town's namesake was Captain Robert James Gordon, an officer of the Dutch East India Company, who explored the area in 1778. Gordon's Bay became a municipality on 1 February 1961.

Though swimming is somewhat complicated by a rocky shore and large numbers of rather prickly sea urchins, Gordon's Bay is well protected from the wind and in summer its waters are warm. In winter, too, the climate can be delightful. False Bay is often calmer than an inland lake. At this time fishing boats and yachts in the harbour sleep easily on tranquil water so clear that, until you see the shoals of fish moving lazily beneath them, the boats seem to be touching bottom.

Adjacent to the harbour at Gordon's Bay are the buildings of the Naval College for cadet officers. The letters 'G B' and an anchor laid out in white stones on the mountain slopes above Gordon's Bay refer to the original name of this training school, when it was known as the General Botha Training College for merchant navy officers.

At Gordon's Bay the mountains crowd close to the sea and the famous marine drive cuts into their slopes. Two kilometres out of Gordon's Bay a turn-off left provides a spectacular route to the summit of the range where the imposing buildings of the Steenbras filtration plant stand. This plant supplies water to the Cape Peninsula and the towns of the Cape Flats. The 4 km long road up to the filtration plant reveals some magnificent views. At the plant there is a gate, and a permit to continue the journey is essential. Permits are obtainable from the municipal offices of Cape Town, Strand and Gordon's Bay. From the gate the road crosses the summit of the Hottentots Holland Mountains and then descends into the valley of the Steenbras River, now completely flooded by the waters of the Steenbras Dam.

Steenbras Dam, which has a surface of 380 ha, is one of the scenic showpieces of the Western Cape. Built in 1921 and later enlarged by raising the wall to a height of 22,1 m, it supplies Cape Town with drinking-water fed through three pipelines, 52 km in length, which end at the Newlands reservoir in Cape Town. The dam has also been developed as a major recreational area. Pines, covering 1 214 ha of land, have been planted around the reservoir, and a garden of wild flowers (especially of the protea family) has been laid out. There is also a picnic site beneath the pines. When the dam overflows during the winter rainy season (around August), the spillway makes a spectacular picture. A short way down the course of the river there is a fine natural waterfall.

From the Steenbras Dam the road continues for 5 km, then joins the main Cape Town–Port Elizabeth road on the east side of Sir Lowry's Pass.

Back to the marine drive which, as it continues along the mountain slopes from Gordon's Bay, overlooks a stretch of precipitous and rocky coast, one of the finest fishing areas in Southern Arica. Innumerable great catches of the teeming fish life of False Bay have been made here. But the coast has also claimed a toll of human lives, for it is an excessively dangerous area. Many an unwary or over-zealous fisherman has slipped on the cliffs or been caught on an exposed rock by a sudden wave.

At 3 km from Gordon's Bay the road reaches the mouth of the *Steenbras River* (named after the steenbras fish species). Beyond the river is Clarence Drive and, 8 km from Gordon's Bay, a roadside memorial dated 1 January 1950 tells us that it was G J V (Jack) Clarence *'whose vision, faith and determination helped to bring the road into being'*. Clarence was one of the directors of the Cape Hangklip Beach Estate Company which planned ambitious real estate projects.

At this point the drive enters its most spectacular stretch. It climbs around the cliffs and then, 3 km beyond the Clarence memorial, drops down to the beautiful (but dangerous) beach of *Koeëlbaai* (cannon ball bay). The beach is backed by the dominant pile of the 1 268 m high *Koeëlberg* (cannon ball mountain), so named, presumably, from the round boulders on the shore which look like old-time cannon balls. The scenery is superb but the sea is treacherous and unsafe for swimming. At the southern end of the bay is the *Blousteenberg* (blue stone or manganese mountain), where a small mine was once worked. The ruins of the jetty used to ship out the manganese may still be seen. There is a caravan and camping ground run by the Cape Town municipality and a deep cave in the cliffs at the northern end of the bay.

Nineteen kilometres from Gordon's Bay the road reaches the mouth of the *Rooiels* River, named after the red alder trees growing there. On the east side of the river a cluster of seaside cottages look down on a pretty beach marred for swimming by a tricky backwash. Across the river the road swings inland and climbs steeply, entering the area of the original Cape Hangklip Beach Estate Company. This region is renowned for its wild flowers. For their sake it is perhaps fortunate that the original grandiose township schemes for this area have produced only a scattering of fishermen's and weekend cottages. The everlastings, the watsonias and, above all, the proteas, have always flourished best in this environment of sweeping mountains and interminable wind.

Five kilometres from the Rooiels River is a right turn which leads to *Pringle Bay* (Rear-Admiral Thomas Pringle was in command of the Cape Station in 1796) and to the 452,6 m high landmark of *Hangklip* (hanging rock), the leaning mountain from which Cape Hangklip – the eastern end of False Bay – takes its name. An automatic lighthouse, a few cottages and a hotel are at the cape.

The gravel road continues for another 5 km and then rejoins the original main tarmac road which leads on to Betty's Bay.

The main road meanwhile has continued beyond the turn-off to Pringle Bay and the hotel at Hangklip. Wild flowers and several lakelets (stocked with black bass) make the drive both interesting and attractive. At 32 km from Gordon's Bay the road reaches a turn-off right which leads to the ruins of the old whaling station at *Stony Point*. Founded in 1907 by a Captain Cook, it was called the Southern Cross Whaling Station. In those days it was a lonely place served by no roads. Only the comings and goings of the four little whale catcher ships stationed there provided any link with the outside world.

Over the years other companies took over the running of the station; first the Shepstone Whaling Company under Captain Berntsen, and then in 1916 Irvin and Johnson, who ran the place until it closed down in 1928. Its rough-and-ready staff of whalermen wandered away to adventures in other parts. The buildings were left to rust. The hulk of one of the whalers, the *Balena*, still lies next to the remains of the jetty. West of Stony Point, in Silver Sands Bay, the swimming is good and there is fishing all along the coast, which is strewn with many interesting shells.

In November 1987 a group of Jackass penguins came ashore at Stony Point, found it to their liking, and made nests. Other penguins joined them but a leopard discovered the colony and in one night killed more than half of them. Cape Nature Conservation came to the aid of the surviving birds. The leopard was trapped, radio collared and released in the Koeberg Nature Reserve. A protective fence was erected around the penguin colony and the birds recovered their confidence in the area. The colony is now flourishing.

The leopard was later shot when it left the sanctuary of the Koeberg Reserve. A local resident killed it when he claimed that the animal had threatened him.

After the Stony Point turn-off the main road continues, passing a turn-off to Betty's Bay beach and picnic area and, after 1,5 km, the Betty's Bay shopping centre. It then enters the village of ...

BETTY'S BAY

This lovely area of mountains, sea and coast, is named after Betty Youlden, the daughter of the managing director of the first company to attempt development of the Cape Hangklip area, once a retreat for runaway slaves, who sought sanctuary there from the oppression of their owners. Tales are still told of pursuit and desperate defiance in the caves and hidden valleys of these mountains, when much human blood was shed in the course of an unhappy chapter of man's inhumanity to man.

In later years the area became a ranch owned by John Walsh of Caledon, who ran livestock there and organised a small fishing enterprise at Holbaai, sending fish across to the Kalk Bay market. He also exported everlasting flowers to Germany and Russia where they have traditionally been in demand for the making of wreaths. A reminder of those past days is the place named *Dawidskraal* (Dawid's corral) where, for many years a shepherd lived in the shelter of the milk-bush trees.

On the death of Walsh the property passed first into the hands of Youlden and then, in 1938, after the stock-exchange crash of Black Friday, into the possession of the Cape Hangklip Beach Estate Company controlled by Jack Clarence and Harold Porter. Their plans for massive development proved abortive. Betty's Bay grew into a rather haphazard collection of weekend and holiday cottages. There is one beautiful asset, apart from the scenic setting. The Harold Porter Botanic Reserve, was bequeathed by Porter in February 1958 to the National Botanic Gardens of South Africa. This reserve is now the permanent home for the magnificent wild flowers of the area and is famous for its red disas. Pleasant paths have been made which lead visitors through the reserve up the slopes of the mountains and as far as the waterfall in Disa Kloof where indigenous trees, identified by tags, provide a shady walk. There is fine swimming in the stream.

Forty-six kilometres from Gordon's Bay the road leaves the Cape Hangklip area proper and passes through *Elephant Rock Estate*, a protea farm named after an unusually shaped rock high up on the mountain, near the waterfall on the left-hand side of the road. Three kilometres further on, the road crosses the *Palmiet* (bulrush) River just above the lagoon at its mouth.

KLEINMOND

Three kilometres beyond the *Palmiet* River bridge (51 km from Gordon's Bay) the road reaches this holiday resort which, as the name *Kleinmond* implies, is built at the 'small mouth' to the sea of a river. The Kleinmond–Hangklip area has a permanent population of 3 882. Kleinmond itself is a great centre in summer for caravanners and campers, especially from inland farming areas. The lagoon is the venue for the 'Anything that Floats' competition which takes place in January each year. There is a fishing harbour. The long beach of Sandown Bay, spacious but steeply sloping, is rather dangerous for swimming but well liked by fishermen. A superb mountain backdrop is enhanced in springtime by magnificently blooming proteas. The Kleinmond Coastal and Mountain Reserve offers many fine walks.

From Kleinmond the tarmac road continues through a countryside full of flowers and strange rock shapes. Directly ahead looms the 1 168 m high Babylon's Tower on whose precipitous peak grow many rare flowers. June is a good month for proteas along this road; October to November is the time for everlastings, watsonias and chincherinchees. At 11 km a turn-off left leads for 5,5 km to the Highlands Forestry Station, a fine drive up a rough road with steep gradients. From the forestry station the road continues to Grabouw. Immense concentrations of wild flowers carpet the area.

Back at the main road, after 5 km a junction with the Bot River–Hermanus road is reached. A left turn leads for 3 km to a junction with the N2 Cape Town to Port Elizabeth road; a right turn goes south down the left-hand side of the Bot River lagoon, through wheat, onion and potato fields. At 13 km there is a turn-off to the Lake Marina township and at 14 km a turn-off to the Sonesta Holiday Resort. At 16 km the road reaches ...

HAWSTON

C R Haw was a one-time civil commissioner of the Caledon district. The resort named after him is now a popular holiday village especially used by the Coloured community. A road leads for 3 km to a beach at Harry's Bay and to a rocky inlet now developed into what is known as the 'New Harbour' with a slipway for fishing boats.

The Sonesta Holiday Resort at Hawston is one of the finest in the country, managed and administered by the Cape Nature Conservation Department. Attractively situated it has its own swimming and paddling pool, children's playground and various indoor and outdoor sporting facilities, including a beach and a lagoon for angling, surfing and yachting. Other amenities are a restaurant, snack-bar, shop etc.

Three kilometres beyond Hawston the road reaches the seaside resort and village of ...

ONRUS

The first Europeans to visit this area named it *Onrus* (restless) because of the everlasting droning of the sea. The coast here is rockbound with heavy surf. There is a small beach and a lagoon at the mouth of the Onrus River and a natural swimming-pool among the rocks. Well wooded, green and with the fresh clear air of this part of the coast, Onrus is a particular haunt of campers and caravanners who enjoy the fishing and relaxation.

Behind Onrus the mountains crowd close to the sea; only a green and pleasant terrace separates them from the surf. For 7 km beyond Onrus the tarmac road leads through wooded, attractive, country with pretty homesteads, diverse scenery and innumerable flowers. Then the trees suddenly divide, disclosing a vista of the immaculate and prosperous resort of Hermanus, its coast lined with cottages, seaside mansions, hotels and various retreats for tired millionaires, jaded business men and many ordinary people who appreciate one of the world's finest seaside areas for relaxation. Crisp air, rugged coast and mountains richly ornamented with wild flowers, waterfalls, ravines and grottoes create a restful and attractive atmosphere.

HERMANUS

Hermanus has had a curiously romantic history. Back in the 1830s a certain Hermanus Pieters wandered through the Caledon district. A man of some slight education, he earned his living by selling his services to the farmers as a shepherd-cum-teacher. He never remained in one place for long, but drifted from one farm to another.

One dry summer he passed through the valley of *Hemel-en-Aarde* (heaven and earth) which lies behind the mountains overlooking Hermanus. A leper station had been established in this secluded valley in 1814. From that time until the end of 1845 when the patients were transferred to Robben Island, it was a retreat of the abandoned. Hermanus Pieters heard from the lepers that there was a path known as the *Olifantspad* (elephant's path) which climbed over the mountains to the coast. It was used by an occasional individual who wanted to fish. Curiosity led Hermanus Pieters along this path. He reached the summit of the range and looked down in admiration at the beautiful landscape beneath him. It was intensely green, streaked with rivulets tumbling down to the sea. There was no sign of human habitation.

Following the path down to the shore, Hermanus Pieters found a congenial campsite at a spring almost in reach of the spray of the great rollers which pounded on the rocky coast. To a restless child of nature, this unspoilt wilderness was a terrestrial heaven. Each summer it became Hermanus's habit to camp at the place which later became known as *Hermanus Pietersfontein* (the spring of Hermanus Pieters). There he tended his flocks and herds, fished and wandered as free as the winds among the wild flowers and the heaths. The fountain of Hermanus Pieters is marked by a plaque next to the present Marine Drive.

In due course other people discovered the potential of Hermanus Pieter's fountain. Among them were some pioneers of fishing at Hawston: a German, Michael Henn, with his wife Henrietta, five sons, five daughters and inevitably (for the young Henn girls were reputedly comely), five young men to marry the girls. They were Thomas Montgomery, a ship's carpenter who turned up at Hawston and was gathered into the flock; James Warrington from Cape Town who was also added to the brood; John (Scotty) Paterson, formerly of the Royal Navy, who found his way to this little Henn house; Thomas Leff, a wandering Pole, who joined the clutch; and Harry Plumridge, a deserter from the Royal Navy who cheerfully found a roost for himself with the youngest of the Henn girls.

In addition to fishing at Harry's Bay, the Henns burned shells to make lime. There were huge, ancient deposits of shells strewn along the various beaches and in numerous kitchen middens left by prehistoric man. While making their way to one of these shell deposits at *Skulphoek* (shell corner), the Henns explored the area of Hermanus Pieters' fountain. Liking what they saw, they decided to move there. Packing their belongings into ox-wagons and into their boat the *Nellie* (originally the gig used by Dr Culhave, ship's doctor of the ill-fated *Birkenhead,* to reach Harry's Bay after the shipwreck) they made their way to the present site of Hermanus where Michael Henn built the first house. His sons and sons-in-law followed his persuasive clucking. Other people were attracted to the area and a hamlet grew. The first church, St Peter's, and a school opened in 1868.

In June 1891 the place became a village with its own management board. In the same year Walter MacFarlane built the first hotel, the Victoria (now the Astoria). It would have been fitting if the ghost of Hermanus Pieters could have been the first guest.

Fishing developed along with the holiday trade. The old *Nellie* and all the first fishing boats worked from the unique natural harbour, a rocky cove with a precarious entrance. It was a most unreliable shelter from what Kipling called 'the dread Agulhas roll'. Damage to the fishing vessels and a number of wrecks occurred before public agitation brought about the construction of a better harbour. The old harbour is now a museum with an interesting exhibit on whales and whaling. It is open Mondays to Saturdays 09h00 to 13h00, 14h00 to 17h00; closed on religious holidays and Sundays.

There is a delightful photographic museum housed in one of the original fisherman's cottages, now restored. Several of the photographs provide visual proof of fishermen's tales of gigantic catches in the past.

In September 1904, by which time its name had been abbreviated (the postal authorities had quietly dropped the 'Pietersfontein' in 1902) Hermanus was made a municipality. The place became renowned for its fishing, especially the kabeljou run from November to March. Prominent people such as Sir William Hoy, then general manager of South African Railways, were attracted to Hermanus. It became a fashionable resort for both the wealthy and the wise. Today the town boasts a population of 15 125. Sir William Hoy and his wife are buried on a hillock known as Hoy's Koppie, in the centre of Hermanus. A path leads to the summit from where there is a good view.

Some exciting catches have been made at Hermanus. On 28 April 1922 after five and a half hours of battle, W R Selkirk landed the greatest catch ever made with rod and line up to that date anywhere in the world: a 4 m long shark weighing 986 kg. Another record catch was a 50 kg kabeljou caught by the Hon W P Schreiner. Many other large fish have been landed.

The publicity of these catches lured anglers to Hermanus. Today it is a flourishing holiday resort. Yachting and aquaplaning take place in the great lagoon. A spectacular 6 km long scenic road (Rotary Drive) curves up the mountain slopes to a viewsite on the summit. Fernkloof Nature Reserve, opened in January 1960, is a 1 446 ha sanctuary for flowers, birds and game, with carefully graded footpaths which take even the elderly to many beautiful sites where wild flowers grow in their natural element. A fine golf-course, bowling-greens and other sporting facilities, as well as two superb bathing beaches (Voëlklip and Grotto), are additional attractions. A 12 km long footpath runs along the cliffs from the new harbour to the mouth of the lagoon. This track reaches all fishing points and is a fine walk embellished by many wild flowers and entrancing views. The track provides excellent vantage-points for people watching whales, such as the southern right whales, which frequent this coast from July to November to calve and mate. Hermanus even has a 'whale crier' who blows a horn made of sea bamboo to tell people that whales are in view. The whales, in their turn, seem to appreciate an audience and provide spectacular entertainment. They are totally protected on the South African coast.

A magnetic survey station is located in Hermanus; visitors are allowed on Wednesdays by appointment.

Wines (notably dry) from the Hamilton Russel vineyards in the Hemel-en-Aarde valley may be sampled and bought from a tasting and sales room in the town.

Hermanus is regarded as the principal centre of the *perlemoen* industry. The *perlemoen* takes its South African name as a corruption of the Dutch *perlemoer*, meaning mother-of-pearl, from the beautiful pearl-lined interior of its shell. It is known internationally as the Abalone, Venus's Ear or Olly Crock. It is one of several species of the *Haliotis* genus and is the largest of the South African shellfish.

In 1952 Brian McFarlane discovered that there was a market for the flesh of this shellfish. From a simple beginning in his kitchen, within four years he had built a factory in Hermanus, the Walker Bay Canning Factory, employing a number of people – part time and professional – as perlemoen divers. Two other factories were also opened in Hermanus for the canning of perlemoen. The product of these factories is distributed throughout the world. The annual 'Festival of the Sea', held in April, provides an excellent opportunity for the tasting of this delicacy. The demand for abalone has become such that perlemoen farming has developed into a substantial industry in the cultivation of the shellfish in artificial conditions.

From Hermanus the tarmac road runs for 18 km along the verge of the spacious lagoon of the *Kleinrivier* (little river). This is a particularly fine drive – the mountains crowd close to the road and in the winter months sparkling necklaces of waterfalls adorn the slopes, whispering through the air like a sigh.

STANFORD

Twenty-four kilometres from Hermanus is a small farming and road centre named after Captain Robert Stanford who owned the *Klein River* farm on which it was laid out in 1856. Stanford became a village in 1892 and a municipality on 22 December 1919. It has a population of 2 295.

From Stanford there is a 17 km drive to the 834 ha Salmondsdam Nature Reserve, created in 1962 by the Divisional Council of Caledon. The reserve is named in memory of Captain Robert Salmond, Commander of the ill-fated *Birkenhead*. The reserve is the home for most species of the game animals indigenous to these parts, a vast variety of flowering plants, and 124 species of birds. Spring is the best time to visit this reserve but there are always flowers in bloom. A mountain drive takes visitors to a high viewpoint. There are three hiking trails (Ravine, Waterfall and Mountain), each taking one day or less.

Beyond Stanford the main tarmac coastal road continues south across unspoilt bush-covered country frequented by small antelope. It is a fine area for flowering plants. After 17 km the road approaches the coast once more and a short gravel turn-off leads to ...

DE KELDERS

Consisting of a handful of cottages and a hotel, this place takes its name, which means 'the cellars,' from a curious underground cavern. There is a superb view over the great sweep of Walker Bay where whales flirt and laze and white sand dunes rise in strange contrast to the blue mountains of the coastal range. The natural cavern has a cool stream flowing through it A swim underground in the crystal-clear water is an interesting experience. Lady Anne Barnard visited the place in 1798 and left an amusing description of her journey to what was then called the *Drupkelder* (stalactite cave) – a lair of hyenas, full of bones, stalactites, stalagmites and other dripstone formations. There is a small charge to enter the cave. A glassed-in display depicting a Bushman family sheltered in the cave adds interest.

Three kilometres from De Kelders the tarmac road reaches the fishing harbour of ...

GANSBAAI

Built around the largest fishing harbour along this part of the coast, the village of *Gansbaai* (goose bay) is nondescript but the harbour with its fish-canning factory is photogenic. From the breakwater the views of Walker Bay and the coastal mountains are sweeping. Walker of *Walker Bay* was a master in the Royal Navy who must have been well pleased to have so handsome a stretch of coast named after him. A huge swell often shoulders its way into the bay bringing tremendous waves.

DANGER POINT

From Gansbaai the road continues in a south-westerly direction for 2 km and then reaches a turn-off leading for 8 km to the lighthouse at Danger Point. This is a worthwhile journey for Danger Point, menacing and rocky, is very atmospheric. The Birkenhead rock of sorrowful memory lies less than a kilometre off the point.

The wreck of the *Birkenhead* is one of the most celebrated of all maritime disasters. The *Birkenhead* was a steam transport conveying reinforcements from Simon's Bay to serve in the Eighth Frontier War. The ship struck the submerged rock off Danger Point at 02h00 on 26 February 1852. It practically tore open at the bottom and many soldiers were drowned as they lay asleep in their hammocks. The rest rushed on deck and were drawn up in good order. Two boats were launched which took the seven women and thirteen children on board, along with as many men as the vessels could hold. The gig was also launched with nine men. Within twenty minutes of striking the rock the *Birkenhead* went down, leaving part of the hull with the main mast precariously balanced on the rock.

The gig reached the coast near Hawston. The two other lifeboats met a coasting schooner which rescued them and then proceeded to the scene of the disaster. About 50 men were found clinging to the remnants of the ship. They were taken aboard the coaster and, carrying a total of 116 survivors, the little boat made its way to Simon's Town with news of the wreck. Sixty-eight men and eight horses survived a final buffeting by the surf and rocks, and managed to reach the shore. Nine officers, 359 men of other rank and 87 of the crew were drowned.

Set in the base of the Danger Point lighthouse is a plague commemorating the wreck of the *Birkenhead*. The lighthouse, with a 4 750 000 candlepower light, makes a fine picture as it stands guard over this point of dramatic memories. The gravel road ends at the lighthouse gate but a fishermen's track winds around the fence to the actual point, where there is a blow-hole linked to the sea by an underground chasm. At times of very high tide the great powerhouse rollers which pound upon Danger Point roar their way up this chasm and force a jet of water through the blow-hole. Fishermen have reported that the jet has been seen to reach a height of more than 10 m.

Four kilometres beyond the turn to Danger Point, another turn leads for 2 km to the small coastal resort of Franskraal. The coastal road continues through scrub and flower country. Two kilometres on there is a short turn-off leading to the coast at the mouth of the *Uilenkraal* (owl's corral) River. There is a fine beach and lagoon at this point and the area is popular for camping and caravanning, offering excellent bathing and fishing. To the south-east of this resort are the guano and seal islands of *Dyer* (Samson Dyer was an American negro who once worked guano on this island) and *Geyser* where fur seals have their rookery.

Beyond the Uilenkraal turn-off the tarmac road continues through undulating, bushy country. After 13 km the road reaches a crossroads. To the left there is a turn leading to the diminutive settlement of *Baardskeerdersbos* (beard shaver's bush), oddly named from the baardskeerde, a class of hunting spider, the *Solfugidae* (fugitives from the sun). There is a popular belief that this non-venomous little creature cuts the hair of sleeping people or other animals. The turn to *Baardskeerdesbos* also leads to the mission station of Elim and to Bredasdorp, all in fine wild flower country. A right turn at this crossroads leads to ...

PEARLY BEACH

The road taking travellers to this beach passes through magnificent wild-flower country. In early summer yellow, white and pink everlastings, as well as numerous pincushions, are in flower. The summit of a rise along the way gives a fine view of the coast, with a line of very elegant sand dunes looking steeply towards the blue of the sea. Swimming, fishing and hiking are pleasant pastimes for holiday-makers at Pearly Beach.

The tarmac main road continues from the Pearly Beach turn-off through hilly wild-flower country. After 14 km there is a turn-off leading to the resort of *Buffelsjagbaai* (buffalo hunt bay) where the Overberg Regional Services Council created a fine seaside resort. Five kilometres beyond the turn to Buffelsjagbaai, the tarmac main road ends at a T-junction. A turn right leads for 1 km to the house of the supervisor of the two fine coastal resorts known as *De Dam*, created by the Overberg Regional Council and built along a level terrace confronting a superb beach. A left turn at the T-junction leads inland through a lovely rural countryside of gentle undulations. Wild flowers and birds are numerous, with blue cranes an especial delight. There are fine farms with sheep, cattle and wheat. There are turn-offs to such rural centres as Viljoenshof and, after 23 km, a junction with a road leading for 9 km to the Moravian mission station of ...

ELIM

This is one of the most attractive and picturesque of the surviving old-time South African mission stations. It shelters in a well-watered hollow in an undulating plain noted for its spring everlastings.

On 12 May 1824 Bishop Hallbeck of the Moravian Church acquired the 2 570 ha farm *Vogelfontein* (bird fountain) from Johannes Schonken. On Ascension Thursday, 12 May 1825, the name was changed to *Elim* (palm trees), and a mission was established around the original farmhouse built in 1796 by a Huguenot named Louis du Toit. Neat little cottages were built to house the Coloured community, mainly freed slaves. A substantial church (severely plain as with all Moravian churches) became the pivot of the settlement.

An interesting later addition to this church was its clock. Just before the First World War the Reverend Mr Will, the then incumbent of Elim, went to Germany on furlough. He heard about a clock built in 1764 in Zittau, Saxony, by a renowned watchmaker named Prasse. This clock had been installed in the church at Herrenhut and for 140 years had kept time for the congregation. In 1905 the clock had been pensioned off and was lying unused. The Reverend Will secured the clock and shipped it to Elim where, in 1914, it started work again. With a slow, deliberate pendulum swing and a deep resolute tick, it still keeps excellent time.

One of the last of the working water-mills of the Cape is in Elim. Built in 1828 to replace an earlier mill, it had a Australian jarrah wheel. Its machinery was made entirely out of wood but in 1881 the mill was re-equipped with 5 442 kg of iron machinery. Thereafter only the waterwheel was of wood. A standby diesel engine was introduced in 1900 to supplement the wheel, and the mill ground local wheat until October 1972, when the great wheel ceased to turn because of the increasing popularity of commercial bread. In its heyday the mill had a curiously graceful air of old-fashioned elegance. Its heavy, slow-turning grindstones produced whole wheat flour of superb aroma and taste. The whirr of its racks, the rumbling of the grindstone and the merry splashing of water created an atmosphere of honest work and pride in its production.

The mill was declared a national monument in 1974. The buildings, for a long time dilapidated, were restored by the Rembrandt company. In the meantime, the old wheel had fallen into disrepair. Under the aegis of the Reverend Jacobus Wynand and Mr Paul Swart, a wheel restoration project was launched. The Caledon carpenter, Henry Olivier, together with two assistants made a new wheel of Burmese teak but using the original enormous old axle. The 100 old cogs of the crown wheel inside the mill were replaced with new ironwood cogs from Knysna, and the half-ton millstones were sharpened.

The restored mill was formally opened on 21 April 1990. Wholewheat flour ground at the mill is now sold. The whole of Elim needs to be restored to its former state. Only a few years back it was the scene of considerable activity involving production of sausages, salami, cigars, and the export of everlastings to wreathmakers in Germany. There was a small boarding-house and a lovely old-world garden. Fruit trees lined the streets, and there was a charming elegance to the whole mission.

From the junction with the road from De Dam, 9 km from Elim, the gravel road continues eastwards for 3 km to *Voëlvlei* (bird marsh) where there is a junction. The left-hand turn leads for 19 km to Bredasdorp; the right-hand turn leads through flat farmland sprinkled with numerous lakelets, marshes and dried-out beds of former lakelets. Aquatic birds are numerous and flamingos breed there. The road skirts the verges of the large *Zoetendalvlei* – a marsh and farm named after the wreck of the *Zoetendal* in 1673, and renowned as one of the principal breeding grounds of the first woolled sheep in South Africa. Twenty-three kilometres from the Voëlvlei junction, this road joins the tarmac road connecting Bredasdorp (left turn, 19 km) to Cape Agulhas.

Turning right, this tarmac road leads for 4 km to a cluster of fishermen's cottages which often feature in the paintings of South African artists. The unusual name of this little place – *Hotagterklip* (on the left side behind the stone) comes from the days of the first wagon track, when a stone outcrop imposed a sharp detour on all travellers. Most of the old cottages were allowed to fall into ruin, with the fishermen housed in the usual drab modern abodes. The original cottages have now been expertly restored.

STRUISBAAI

Two kilometres beyond Hotagterklip the tarmac road reaches the village and holiday resort of *Struisbaai* (straw bay) named, it is said, after fishermen's cottages built there in the past of straw. Another version of the name is that it used to be *Vogelstruis* (ostrich) Bay. Whatever the origin of its name, this handsome bay has a fine beach for swimming, fishing and shell collecting.

The tarmac road continues along the coast beyond Struisbaai for 8 km and then ends at the village, holiday resort and lighthouse at the most southerly point of Africa ...

CAPE AGULHAS

Cape Agulhas was first named Cape St Brendan because on the day of that saint – 16 May – Bartholomeu Dias passed by on his homeward voyage in 1488. The name *Agulhas* was originally applied to Struisbaai (*Golfo das Agulhas* – gulf of the needles) but later applied to the cape as well. According to De Castro in his *Roteiro*, the etymology of the name is interesting. It was at this cape that a remarkable change in magnetic forces occurred: *'It is an axiom with the pilots'*, wrote De Castro *'that here there is no variation in the needles of their compasses, which bear directly upon the true poles of the earth. Hence they call it the Cape of Needles'*.

To the men of the sailing-ships who lived close to the sea, the Cape of Good Hope was indisputably the meeting-place of the Indian Ocean Mozambique–Agulhas Current and Atlantic Ocean Benguela Current while Agulhas, with its tremendous rollers and rocky bottoms, was a place of magnetic change. To the eye, Cape Agulhas is not a dramatic point. A range of hills forms a wall separating the sea from the flat inland. A 12 million candlepower lighthouse and radio beacon stand permanent watch over the end of Africa. The land peters out into a flat and rocky projection which, at a depth of 60 fathoms, continues under the sea as the Agulhas Banks for 250 km before falling steeply into the 1800 fathom depths of the southern ocean.

The first lighthouse, dating from 1848, is the second oldest in South Africa. It has been restored. Open on Mondays 13h00–17h00; Tuesdays to Saturdays 09h30–16h45, Sundays 11h00–15h00.

The holiday resort of Agulhas consists of a few stores and the usual cluster of cottages thrown up in modern times. Fishing is good and tidal swimming-pools have been made along the rocky shore.

The tarmac road ends at Cape Agulhas. Retracing the road past Struisbaai to Bredasdorp, the spacious farm, *Zoetendals Vallei*, belonging to the Van Bredas is passed. Seven and a half kilometres beyond that point there is a gravel turn-off right to Arniston. This road leads across a fine stretch of level farming country (wheat and stock). At the immaculate *Prinskraal* farm belonging to Patrick Swart (7 km) there is a crossroads connecting the small coastal resort of De Mond to Bredasdorp. The principal road continues east for 7 km and then joins the tarmac connecting Bredasdorp to Arniston. A right turn leads down this road for 7,5 km, curving around an impressive line of giant sand dunes and then reaches the sea at the attractive little fishing harbour and resort of ...

ARNISTON OR WAENHUISKRANS

This fishing village takes its name from the disastrous wreck in the bay of the transport ship, *Arniston*. On the afternoon of 30 May 1815, homeward bound from Ceylon, the *Arniston* ran ashore under the influence of wind and a powerful current. It is difficult to understand exactly what happened after this mishap, for no boat appears to have been launched. Night came and some time before midnight the ship went to pieces. A carpenter and five sailors reached the shore alive but 372 other people were drowned, including 14 women, 25 children and Lord and Lady Molesworth.

About 2 km south of the village there is an enormous cavern eroded into the cliffs. It is known from its size as *Waenhuiskrans* (wagon-house cliff). The entire coastline in this region is notable for its bizarre marine erosion: arches, caverns and all manner of odd shapes are modelled into the long line of rocky cliffs. Near Arniston there is a magnificent natural archway. The great cavern of Waenhuiskrans is accessible only at low tide. If the Waenhuiskrans cavern could be entered from the land, it could certainly contain about six wagons complete with their spans of oxen. It is curious that interesting shells and seaweeds are often found on the floor of this cavern as well as the beans of *Entada pursaetha*, the so-called 'sea bean'. This creeper grows on the banks of rivers in the tropics and produces an enormous bean pod about 1 m long. The seed beans fall into the rivers and are distributed by the sea to many distant shores. Those found in the great cavern have travelled down with the Mozambique–Agulhas Current from the shores of East Africa. These tough, brown, much-travelled beans may also be found along the beach, together with a multitude of beautiful shells. Up the coast at *Ryspunt* (rice point) parts of the wreck of the *Clan McGregor* may still be seen although it ran aground as far back as 1902. Swimming, surfing and fishing are all good at Arniston. The fishing village itself has been attractively restored and is a treat for artists and photographers. The Kassiesbaai Craft Centre is in the fishing village. On the outskirts of the village Armscor created a rocket-testing range with an elaborate cluster of buildings and an observation tower.

Arniston is at the end of the 25 km long tarmac road from Bredasdorp. The road runs straight across exceptionally level but very attractive farming country. Handsome and historic estates such as *Nacht Wacht* (night watch) provide interest to the journey.

BREDASDORP

With a population of 10 603, this town is the administrative centre for the southern end of Africa. It originated in 1837 when the farm *Langefontein* was sold to the Dutch Reformed Church and laid out as a town. On 16 May 1838 the first erven were sold and the place was named in honour of Michiel van Breda, a leading member of the local community and church. Bredasdorp became a municipality in 1917. Wheat, wool and wild flowers are the principal products of the district. The town is clean and pleasant, situated on the slopes of a 368 m high hill called the *Preekstoel* (pulpit), on the ridges of which grow a profusion of giant proteas. There is a first-class small museum, the *Shipwreck Museum*, with a fascinating hall devoted to the theme of shipwrecks. Another room houses a collection of ancient vehicles and furniture. The museum is open Monday to Fridays from 09h00 to 16h45, Saturdays from 09h00 to 13h00; 14h00 to 16h45 and Sundays from 11h00 to 12h30.

There is also the *Agricultural Museum* which is open Monday to Fridays 07h30 to 13h00 and 14h00 to 17h00, and Saturdays from 08h00 to 12h00.

The Bredasdorp Wool Route, which is open from April to October, takes visitors on organised day tours of local farms. Bookings can be made via the publicity office, phone (028) 424-2584.

The Heuningberg Nature Reserve with its beautiful wild flowers and views extending to the Indian Ocean, offers a 16 km long (or shorter) trail along easy gradients. There is also a wildflower garden containing, among others, the Bredasdorp lily.

Bredasdorp is the venue for the 'Foot of Africa Marathon' which starts and ends in the town. It takes place in mid-October each year.

Seventeen kilometres from Bredasdorp the tarmac road reaches the small town of ...

NAPIER

Founded on 12 April 1838 when the first erven were sold, the place was named after the then Governor, Sir George Napier. It is today the centre of a prosperous wheat and wool farming area. The town has a population of 2 554 and possesses a substantial Dutch Reformed church and a street lined with stores and places of business. Considerable quantities of strawberries are grown in the district in the early summer.

From Napier the tarmac road winds through a sun-soaked, mellow and gently undulating land of wheat and sheep, sprinkled with many fine farms such as *Fairfield*, owned by the Van der Byl family. After 56 km of pleasant travelling the road reaches Caledon and joins the N2 road to Cape Town 114 km away.

Chapter Twelve

THE COPPER WAY TO NAMAQUALAND

The Copper Way, N7, which traverses the entire length of Namaqualand, might well be described as the way of citrus, gemstones and flowers. It begins at a traffic interchange on the Cape-to-Cairo road (N1), 11 km from the entrance to Table Bay harbour.

From the traffic interchange the double carriageway leads northwards, passing the housing estates of Bothasig and Bosmansdam, and impressive-looking but odorous chemical and refining plants with clusters of huge storage tanks.

There are turn-offs east to Milnerton (3,5 km from the start of the road), after 7 km to Durbanville lying in the hills behind the *Tygerberg* (leopard mountain) and, after 14,8 km, west to Melkbos and Atlantis. After crossing the Diep River the road points almost straight north-east through a pleasant, gently undulating rural landscape of wheat fields, with extended views to the east of the lovely mountain ranges of Groot Drakenstein in the Wellington area. Then, after a final 5 km of minor twists and 51 km from its start, the road reaches the town of ...

MALMESBURY

Malmesbury is the principal centre of the wheat-producing area named by Jan van Riebeeck *Het Zwarte Land*, the *Swartland* (black country) from the renosterbos which turns black during the dry and hot summer months. At the site of the town in the shallow valley of the Diep River, there is a tepid (32°C) sulphur chloride spring similar in its rich mineral content to the famous medicinal bath of Aachen in Europe. By 1805 this spring was already in use by a Dr Hassner. It had a reputation of curing sufferers of rheumatism. As early as 1744, a few people had settled around this spring and permission had been granted for them to establish a church and school at the site. At first simply known as Swartland's Kerk, this was the beginning of the present town. The name of *Malmesbury* was given to it in 1829 when the British Governor, Sir Lowry Cole, visited the site and renamed the place in honour of his father-in-law, the Earl of Malmesbury. The town became a municipality in 1896 and today has a population of 20 714. A congenial if rather awkwardly laid-out town, it is the centre for the production of wheat, oats and milk, with huge storage silos, flour mills and the largest grain distributor in Southern Africa. The Malmesbury district is in fact the largest wheat-producing district in South Africa. The biggest dry-land (that is, non-irrigated) wine farm in the Southern Hemisphere (*Rooidraai*) is situated in the Malmesbury district. Swartland Cellars with its full-bodied red wines and sweet Hanepoot is 4 km from Malmesbury. Malmesbury is also the start of the Swartland Wine Route.

There is a pleasant swimming-bath but the medicinal spring (nearby the swimming-bath in the centre of the town) has not been developed in modern times. This is a pity, for its potential is considerable. The first spa was destroyed in a fire.

In former years there was a Jewish population in Malmesbury substantial enough to support a synagogue. The attractive building now houses the Malmesbury museum with interesting relics, photographs and memories of people who played an important and enterprising part in the development of the town.

From Malmesbury the Copper Way, N7, continues north over rolling wheat fields with spacious views of the mountain ranges in the east. After 5 km there is a turn-off north-west to Hopefield and Saldanha. A further 16 km takes the road past the Langgewens Experimental Farm where wheat research takes place. At 11 km further on (32 km from Malmesbury) the road reaches a turn-off leading for 3 km to the rural and rail centre of ...

MOORREESBURG

A wheat, oats and wool centre which likes to claim that its district holds the densest population of sheep in the world. Moorreesburg is situated in the heart of the Swartland wheat belt. Founded as a church centre on the farm *Hooikraal* by the Dutch Reformed Church in 1898, the town was named after the Reverend H A Moorrees. It received municipal status in 1890. Today there are 8 280 people living there. Wheat is the principal product, and storage silos and mills predominate. The railway, built in 1902, carries from the district a substantial amount of the total wheat production of Southern Africa. Moorreesburg can accurately be described as an inhabited island in a sea of wheat.

There is an interesting wheat industry museum open on Mondays to Thursdays 08h00 to 17h00 and Fridays from 08h00 to 16h00. It is one of the only three such museums in the world.

The Copper Way (N7) continues its easy route north from Moorreesburg across fields of wheat. After 22,5 km the road bridges across the Berg River, climbs over a foothill spur of the Postberg and passes (after 5 km) the factory of the Cape Portland Cement Company at De Hoek. The limestone quarry of this factory is the third largest man-made excavation in Southern Africa and the biggest opencast limestone mine in Africa. It is the only quarry where limestone is being won at depth instead of from hills or surface workings. Just beyond the cement factory is a turn-off west leading to Velddrif (63 km), while 3 km from the factory (30,5 km from Moorreesburg) the road reaches the town of ...

PIKETBERG

This town lies at the foot of the sandstone cliffs of the Piketberg range which tower above the wheatlands to the maximum height of the 1 459 m Zebrakop.

In former years the impressive mass of the Piketberg served as a stronghold for the Bushmen. Many well-preserved galleries of their paintings, mainly monochromes in red, are still to be seen in the rock shelters on farms such as *Bushman's Hollow, Langeberg, Bangkop* and *Staweklip*, up on the heights. Around the base of the mountains the Kogikwa pastoral tribe roamed with their herds. Their leader, Gonnema, featured prominently in the records of the founding of the settlement at the Cape. It was during the various brawls between Gonnema's followers and the European settlers that the name of the *Piketberg* (outpost mountain) was first used. A small military post was established there to check the cattle-rustling activities of the Kogikwa.

European settlers began to establish themselves on farms around the Piketberg in the first quarter of the 18th century. The great herds of game which once frequented the area were steadily destroyed (in 1868 there were still twelve zebra grazing on Zebrakop) and the original inhabitants were driven into the wilderness of the north.

On 31 December 1835 the Government granted to the district the farm *Grootfontein* and there, on the mountain slopes, a church was built. Beneath it, like a congregation gradually attracted to listen to a discourse, the buildings of the town grew. With the coming of the railway in 1902, Piketberg became the centre of a prosperous agricultural area, producing wheat, fruit, maize and a variety of other crops. The town now has 6 915 inhabitants.

The Piketberg Museum exhibits many interesting items, many donated by the inhabitants of the town. Note the peculiar funeral hearse and bearer. The museum is open weekdays 09h00 to 14h00.

Of particular interest to visitors is the agricultural activity atop the Piketberg massif. It is said that the first European inhabitants of this mountain land were two sailors – one Dutch, the other English – who had deserted their ships and found sanctuary in these remote heights. Then, in about 1868, Mr J Versveld bought the farm *Langeberg* on top of the mountains for £300 and started to grow tobacco. Conveying crops to market from the isolated farm in the clouds was at first a problem. In 1889 however, Mr Versveld built the spectacular *Versveld Pass*, made famous by three loops designed to allow the passage of ox-wagons.

Versveld Pass opened the mountain summit to others – people who had formerly thought Versveld mad to have settled there. A prosperous community eventually made their homes on the heights, finding the area ideal for the growing of crops such as apples, pears, peaches and export proteas. Frank Versveld planted the first deciduous fruit orchard there in 1907. Buchu was also produced after the forester of Algeria (in the Cedar mountains), George Bath, started the industry, promoting a boom in the sale of leaves in 1918.

A fine new road built up the pass in 1943 rewards the traveller with a delightful exploration of a surprisingly beautiful rural area. The road reaches the summit 10 km from Piketberg, continues as a tarmac surface for a further 10 km and then ends after 3 km of gravel at a cul-de-sac 22,5 km from its start. From the summit there are wide views of fine avenues of trees, orchards, wild flowers and pleasant farms. There are Bushmen paintings in several rock shelters. On the farm *Dezehoek*, at the foot of the pass, there is a water-mill.

In the town there is a large co-operative fruit and potato-packing organisation, Piketko Ltd. Escorted sight-seeing tours can be arranged. Phone (022) 913-1166.

North-west of Piketberg, in a deep, fertile valley, lies the Moravian mission station established in 1888 on the farm *Goedverwacht* (well expected). It is now administered by a local committee. Its church, the Evangelical Fraternity Church in South Africa, was built by the community, using stones from the Piketberg massif. The road to the mission branches off from the tarmac Piketberg–Velddrif road, 14 km from Piketberg, and leads for 10 km into the valley.

The 2 500 people living at Goedverwacht have gardens producing a variety of fruit and vegetables. There is a disused water-mill and the street is lined with some magnificent old trees. Phone (022) 912-4207.

Voëlvlei (bird marsh) near the town is a shadowy and singularly silent wood of wild olive trees. There are picnic spots with toilet and barbecue facilities. For permission to enter, phone Dries Rossouw at (022) 913-2057, or Casper Rossouw at (022) 913-2056.

On the road to Elands Bay, 8 km north of Piketberg, is the export grape-producing farm of *Stenebrug*. From mid-January to mid-March table grapes of superb quality can be purchased from a stall on the farm. After another 20 km along the road to Elands Bay, there stands the wine cellar of *Winkelshoek* where a variety of wines and two types of brandy are produced. They may be purchased during normal business hours.

At 32 km from Piketberg is the small rail centre of *Eendekuil* (pool of the ducks), renowned for the quality of cheese produced in the local Sebraskop Co-operative factory. Cheese in South Africa tends to be erratic in quality but the Eendekuil cheese is very well worth sampling.

The Copper Way leads north-westwards from Piketberg across the pool-studded, level floor of a broad valley between the Piketberg and the Olifants River range. Completely covered in fields of wheat, oats and lupins, this valley is a fine spectacle in winter when it is delightfully green, or in spring when the wheat turns golden. Mountain ranges hem in the valley from all sides.

After 32 km the road reaches the foot of the Olifants River range and starts to climb what is known as the *Piekeniers Kloof Pass* (pass of the pikemen). The name comes from the conflict with Gonnema and his followers in 1675. After carrying out a raid, Gonnema and his people escaped into the mountains and were pursued by a party of European soldiers, including pikemen. The ravine originally climbed by the road was given the name which commemorates the disappointed pikemen who made the journey in vain.

This old pass served as the early gateway between the settled areas of the Western Cape and the wilder lands of the Nama tribe. It marked, too, a dramatic change in the landscape. Many early explorers travelled this way in search of mythical cities in the wilderness and the famed copper mountains of the north. On 7 December 1660, guided by Bushmen, Jan Dankaert crossed the mountains – the first European to do so. In February of the following year a second party of explorers made their way up this pass. One of the leaders, Pieter van Meerhoff, left his name on the rounded, 962 m high mountain overlooking the pass, *Van Meerhoff's Castle*. Simon van der Stel also made his way up the original pass on his classic journey to discover the source of the copper traded by the Nama people. With all the wagons and escorting soldiers, it must have made quite a cavalcade.

On 17 November 1858 a new pass was opened, built by the renowned Thomas Bain and named after Sir George Grey, the Governor. This pass began at the foot of Van Meerhoff's Castle at a small hostelry known as 'The Rest', built in the shade of tall gum-trees. Its route up the mountain slopes can still be seen below the line of the present pass built in the late 1950s. The latter was once more named the Piekeniers Kloof Pass – although the original pass of that name is really up the gorge which reaches the present road only at the summit.

After 6 km of climbing, the road reaches the summit of the pass at a fine viewsite, 519 m above sea-level. On the summit there are citrus groves. Oranges and orange-blossom honey are sold by the wayside during the winter season.

The road descends for 5 km on the eastern side of the mountain into the handsome valley of the Olifants River. Backed by a superb mass of mountain ranges, neat groves of citrus trees grow to perfection on the warm alluvial valley floor. In 1660, on the slopes of the mountains east of the river, the first European explorers under Jan Dankaert saw a vast herd of 200 to 300 elephants and named it the *Olifants* River (elephants river).

As the road reaches the floor of this fertile valley, 43,5 km from Piketberg, there is a turn-off east which crosses the Olifants River to the town of ...

CITRUSDAL

Aptly named 'the dale of citrus', *Citrusdal* has the orange as king. Beautiful citrus groves cover the landscape and a vast pack house marshals and dispatches the golden fruit to many customers all over the world. The town was founded by the Dutch Reformed Church in 1916 and became a municipality on 1 March 1957. Its population is 3 990. The superlative situation in which the town lies makes it a fine centre from which to explore the surrounding world of mountains, valleys, farmlands and wild flowers. During the citrus-packing season (May to October) a great bustle overtakes the town. A visit to the pack house, opened in 1946, is worthwhile. It packs over 60 000 tons of citrus each year. Wine is also produced in the area under the *Goue Vallei* (Golden Valley) label and may be purchased in the town.

The lovely old farmhouse of *Karnmelksvlei*, 19 km from Citrusdal, was built in 1767 and is worth seeing. Some interesting Bushman paintings may be seen near Citrusdal on the farm *Vlaksrug*, and up the Olifants valley where a series of paintings depict European men and women in costumes worn 250 years ago. There are also wagons and scenes of European hunters pursuing a lion.

A museum and traditional *Boerehuisie* in the town exhibit items on the history of the valley. An art gallery, *Die Kunshuis*, exhibits the work of local artists.

Several interesting and spectacular roads lead from Citrusdal into most diverse scenery. Two roads lead up the valley on either side of the Olifants River and take the traveller through kilometres of orange groves and fertile farmland until they culminate in cul-de-sacs. The road up the left bank of the river after 16 km of interesting travelling reaches the hot springs known simply as The Baths. These springs, 43°C in temperature, are claimed to be radioactive. They lie in a beautifully wooded ravine which enters the main valley. Amenities include open-air swimming-baths, jacuzzis and several private baths, a shop and varied accommodation, all in a relaxed old-world setting. There is a hiking and bird-watcher's trail.

The story of The Baths is interesting. In 1739 Jan Cruywagen reported to the Council of Policy on Bushman raids. Amongst his recommendations he suggested that a military post be set up in the Olifants River valley *'on the farm with the warm baths'*. Daniel van den Henghel, the controversial Acting Governor of the Cape and the only official ever to be chosen by drawing lots out of a hat, then decided that the Dutch East India Company should erect *'a handsome stone building'* and thatched bathing huts for visitors to the area. Today the Homestead, much modified, still stands on the original 18th century site. Van den Henghel's idea was an excellent one, but The Baths were many kilometres away from Cape Town, and it was difficult for the Company to maintain the property in good order. So it was that on 15 May 1778 a letter went out from the Castle of Good Hope, authorising Schalk Willem Burger, who owned *Karnmelksvlei*, a farm nearby, to move to The Baths with his family. He was to supply visitors who came to *'take the waters'* with poultry and produce and not only keep the Company House in good condition, *'maar ook dit behoorlyk te repareeren'* (to repair it properly).

In 1855, when the British had been in power at the Cape for 60 years, they decided to sell The Baths on behalf of Queen Victoria. The first private owner was John Lawrence Sharp, who paid £350 for The Baths and 81 morgen (69,3 ha) of ground. Several owners followed – Johannes Jacobus Wiese, the London merchant Richard Grisold, Aletta Burger with her eleven children and Johannes Petrus Kirsten. Kirsten paid £2 000 for the property, but sadly neglected it. A Commission of Enquiry, set up in 1895, found that the roofs were leaking, the floors were full of holes and pigs were scavenging amongst the cooking pots! A doctor, called in to give evidence, still maintained that despite these conditions, *'there is no doubt that the Oliphants* (sic) *River Baths, deserve the good repute for healing purposes which they have acquired'*.

So persuasive was he that the commissioners themselves formed a syndicate and bought The Baths, planning a railway line from Porterville and many other improvements. The Anglo-Boer War intervened, however, and in 1903 James McGregor bought the property at an auction on the Grand Parade in Cape Town. It then passed down to his children, grandchildren and great-grandchildren, who own The Baths today.

James McGregor was a very remarkable man. When he first rode over the mountains, a short stocky Scot in a crumpled hat and velskoene with his goods piled on a wagon, no one thought him anything much better than a vagrant. He was given a room in a backyard to store his things. He was *'die uitlander'* (the foreigner) nothing more. But James McGregor was shrewd – and hardworking. As a very young man he had been to Australia, digging roads and panning for gold. When he saw the valley – rich and fertile and almost untouched – he realised that he had come to stay. In 1869 he bought his first land, and then married the beautiful Lenie van Wyk, whose family had farmed there for generations. They made him promise, with his marriage vows, that he would never take her to his foreign land over the sea. When this was signed and sealed, he was accepted as one of them. He, they and the valley would never look back.

By 1900 James McGregor owned 50 000 morgen (42 800 ha) of the finest land and was popularly known as the King of the Olifants River valley. Three years later he bought The Baths, building good roads, an elegant balconied guest-house and several fine stone bath-houses, which are still there today. McGregor had three sons and seven daughters. When a young Norwegian engineer named Trygve Morch-Olsen arrived to build a bridge over the Olifants River, he married Lizzie McGregor. His energy almost matched that of his father-in-law and, twelve years after old James died in 1914, he added a gabled *dwarsgebou* (affectionately known as *Paddastraat*), a large swimming-pool, the boarding-house and bungalows.

Today James McGregor's great-grandchildren are still improving The Baths. It is to their credit that they have brought The Baths into the 20th century without disturbing the timeless peace and beauty of the area.

Eastwards from Citrusdal the Buffelshoek Pass finds a spectacular route over the mountains. For the first 7 km the road is tarmac, then it becomes a good gravel surface leading through entrancing scenery, passing many amazing rock shapes and (8 km from Citrusdal) a pretty 24 m high waterfall with a natural swimming-pool at its base. At 28 km a turn-off leads for 6 km to *Sandfontein* farm, a popular base for mountaineers visiting natural wonders such as the Sandfontein Arch. The main road penetrates a narrow ravine (at 32 km) and then emerges on to what is known as the *Kouebokkeveld* (cold buck veld). This is a fine, rugged mountain plateau studded with many beautiful farms which are dominated by a set of wild-looking mountains such as the Skurweberg in the west, the slopes of which, scarred by strange rock shapes, resemble an ancient battlefield where men once fought with such bestiality that the gods were offended and punished the warriors by petrifying them into weird rock formations.

At 55 km the road has a tarmac surface. A further 14 km takes the road through the hamlet of *Op de Berg* (on the mountain). From here, there is a turn-off leading through very rugged country to the Cedar mountains and to Wuppertal. At 93 km there is a tarmac turn-off west into the fruit-farming valley of the *Achterwitsenberg* (behind the Witsenberg). This is a very beautiful drive which ends in a cul-de-sac. The tarmac road first leads for 5 km through the pass; then there is a gravel turn-off signposted 'Witsenberg Vlakte'. This turn-off stretches for 26,5 km past many fruit farms and comes to an end at the great pool known as *Visgat* (fish hole), where the Olifants River tumbles into the head of its upper gorge. For the adventurous there is an exciting journey – swimming or riding on lilos – through this gorge with a one-and-a-half-hour walk back. The scenery is superb.

The main Citrusdal road (after the turn-off to the Achterwitsenberg) descends via the spectacular *Gydo* (euphorbia) Pass into the Ceres valley, reaching Prince Alfred Hamlet at 101 km from Citrusdal and Ceres at 110 km. This route provides a fine circular drive – Cape Town–Citrusdal–Ceres–Cape Town – and is highly recommended, especially in September or October when the orchards are in blossom.

THE CITRUS INDUSTRY

If the Caucasian apple is the king of fruits and the Persian grape the queen, then their royal relative from Asia is a true Chinese mandarin – the citrus, resplendent with luxuriant deep-green leaves and fruit so rich in colour that it sometimes seems to be made of solid gold.

How the citrus family left its home in the tropical rain forests of southern China and the Malay archipelago and found its way around the world into pleasant sanctuaries such as the Olifants River valley, is an historical romance featuring the Arabs and the Portuguese in principal roles as carriers and cultivators of the golden fruit of the sun.

In the beginning the Arabs carried the sour orange, the lime and the lemon from their Asian home and planted them throughout the Middle East, along the north coast of Africa, into Spain, and down the east coast of Africa as far as modern Zimbabwe, where the first European settlers were surprised to find lemon trees of the common Indian *Jamburi* variety growing along the banks of the Mazowe River.

The Crusaders, in turn, among other good things adopted from the Arab culture, introduced the apricot, sour orange, lime and lemon to the more northerly parts of Europe. The sweet orange only followed later, some time in the 15th century. Precisely how it was introduced is an interesting speculation. When Vasco da Gama doubled the Cape of Good Hope in 1498 and made his way up the east coast of Africa, the Arab ruler of Mombasa received him with a boatload of the produce of the place, including 'citrons, lemons and large sweet oranges'. Some writers think that Da Gama took the sweet orange back home with him, and certainly the Portuguese claim the honour of growing the first sweet oranges in Europe. They say that the first sweet orange tree of the western world grew in Lisbon, in the garden of the Count St Laurent; and that this tree, if not actually brought by Vasco da Gama, was certainly introduced at about the time of his return from his visit to the East. However the sweet orange came to grow in Europe, it became known as the *Portugal orange* and was popularly believed to have originated from the voyage of Vasco da Gama.

There is no doubt at all, however, about precisely when and how the sweet orange was introduced in Southern Africa. On 11 June 1654, the yacht *Tulp* brought the first trees to Cape Town from the island of St Helena where they had been planted by the Portuguese for the enjoyment of sick sailors. In Cape Town the trees were planted in the Company's Garden. On 26 July 1661 the first fruits were plucked by Jan van Riebeeck and pronounced *'very good'*.

Other sweet orange trees (the familiar old seedling type) were also imported from India. At the time the St Helena trees bore their first fruit, Van Riebeeck had 1 162 young citrus trees growing in his garden – the first South African orchard, containing an interesting assortment of seedling oranges, lemons and the *Citrus maxima*, known as *bombolmoes* in Tamil, *pampelmoes* in Dutch, and known to the British as the *pummelo* or *Shaddock*, after Captain Shaddock who introduced it to the West Indies where its bud mutation, the grapefruit, first developed.

From Van Riebeeck's pioneer citrus orchard, trees became dispersed over the expanding settlement of the Cape. In the latter half of the 18th century when the Olifants River valley was first portioned out to settlers, the citrus family reached *Hexrivier* when this farm was granted to C J Mouton. The Moutons later married into the Visser family. Today the owners of this fine estate are proud to show visitors one of the original seedling orange trees planted in the valley by the first Mouton. The old tree still bears a palatable and juicy fruit after more than 200 years of changing seasons! It is now an historical monument.

The famous *Washington Navel* is the real backbone of orange production. This delectable fruit originated in the early 19th century at Bahia, Brazil, where it was possibly a mutation of the earlier *Selecta* orange introduced by the Portuguese. In 1869 the Reverend F I Schneider, the first Presbyterian missionary in Bahia, sent a eulogistic report about the orange to the United States Commissioner of Agriculture. In reply the missionary was asked to send a few trees to Washington for testing, which he did the following year, 1870. This proved to be a momentous date in the history of orange growing.

In Washington the Department of Agriculture propagated the trees. In 1873 the first budded specimens were sent to various parts of the United States to see how they would grow. Two of the trees were sent to Mrs L C Tibbets, in California, who planted them in her yard. There they flourished, and from these two trees arose the entire naval orange industry, not only of the United States but also of most of the world. One of the parent trees is still alive. Its seedless offspring, all grown from cuttings, must run into many millions. Think of that next time you cut a juicy navel orange!

The Washington Navel was introduced to South Africa in 1903 by that indefatigable nurseryman, Harry Pickstone, who also introduced to this country the second great commercial variety, the *Valencia Late*. This orange came into being at almost the same time as the Washington Navel. In 1876 an assorted, unlabelled package of orange trees was shipped by the famous British nurseryman, Thomas Rivers, to the Californian grower, A Chapman.

Chapman cultivated the trees but only one proved of any value. This single tree, however, was worth a fortune, for its fruit, although it bore seeds, ripened later in the season than the Washington Navel.

Chapman named the orange the *Rivers' Late*. A Spanish grower, however, identified it as a variety grown in Spain under the name of *Naranja Tarde de Valencia*. Chapman accordingly changed the name of his tree to the *Valencia Late*. Under this name it was introduced to massive commercial growing. Chapman's single tree, probably a chance find of Thomas Rivers somewhere in southern France, became the parent of a prodigious number of offspring.

As in America, the two varieties of orange described above contribute the great bulk of the 761 130 tons of citrus fruit grown in South Africa each year. Both varieties do exceptionally well in South Africa. On the intensely competitive world markets the fruit is highly regarded.

Of the main orange-growing areas of South Africa (Mpumulanga, Northern and North-West provinces, Eastern Cape, and Western Cape, mainly the Olifants River valley), the Olifants River valley is the smallest producer (about 100 000 tons a year) but its product is of supreme standard – for a good reason. The valley of the Olifants lies in a winter rainfall area of very low humidity. The hot summer and crisp frostless winter make it a particularly congenial home for the citrus family. Soil chemistry and climate combine naturally to produce a fruit with thickish skin but a 'rag' or tissue finer than, for instance, the Lowveld orange, produced in an area of summer rainfall and high humidity. Palatability of the fruit depends on a delicate balance between acidity and solids, or sugar. This balance must be fine or the end result will be either too tart or too insipid. It is generally considered that the Olifants River valley is almost ideal in flavour and tissue.

All industries have their problems. With citrus production, most of the basic difficulties – pests and parasites – have yielded to science. One practical problem that remains is the propagation of a really satisfactory mid-season orange. At present there is an awkward gap of about three weeks between the last Washington Navel and the first Valencia Late. This delay seriously embarrasses the entire industry, particularly the pack houses. They have to employ numerous staff for the season and during those weeks they remain idle in their homes and hostels.

There have been many attempts to breed a satisfactory mid-season orange. The famous Dr R Nortjie of Clanwilliam found a bud mutation on an old seedling orange tree which had come into some favour among local growers in the Olifants River valley. This mid-season tree is, paradoxically, a seedless seedling. Known as the *Clanor* (a combination of the names of Clanwilliam and Nortjie), it has not yet been grown in sufficient quantity to have discernible commercial impact. Constant research continues in order to find an ideal mid-season orange variety as well as early and late-season fruit.

CITRUSDAL TO CLANWILLIAM

The Copper Way N7 continues from the turn-off to Citrusdal northwards down the left bank of the Olifants River. This is a beautiful drive down a magnificent river valley, noted for its wild flowers and fine mountain scenery. At 27 km there is a turn-off east to the Algeria Forestry Station and, 22,5 km further on, the road reaches the great dam in the Olifants River. This dam, completed in 1935 to a capacity of 67 million cubic metres in its lake, was expanded in 1968 by raising the height of the wall. It supplies water to the town of Clanwilliam and to the Bulshoek barrage, which feeds the water to 12 140 ha of irrigated farmland. The lake is popular for recreation. Across its surface are spacious views of the Cederberg mountain range and other peaks. The Olifants River is excellent for canoeing with challenging rapids, especially from below the dam wall to the road bridge and then down to the junction with the Jan Dissels stream. Reeds, narrow channels and various obstacles combine with strong currents to make this an exciting river for the adventurous. Anglers find seven varieties of fish in the river and dam. The yellow fish (*Barbus capensis*) can reach more than 11 kg in mass.

One and a half kilometres beyond the dam (51,5 km from Citrusdal) there is a crossroads leading to Lambert's Bay (west) and east to the pleasant little town of ...

CLANWILLIAM

This town lies in the well-watered valley of the Jan Dissels stream where most things grow well, subtropical as well as deciduous fruit trees and many vivid flowers, notably red-hot pokers.

In the early years Clanwilliam was known as Jan Dissels Vlei. In 1814 the name was changed by the Governor, Sir John Cradock, in honour of his father-in-law, the Earl of Clanwilliam. At the time of the arrival of the 1820 Settlers, five Irish parties were sent to settle in this area, but they did not find the valley of the Jan Dissels stream to their liking. Most of them went off to the Eastern Cape. A handful, however, remained. One of them, Captain W Synnot, became Deputy Landdrost of the district. A descendant of one of these settler families, Charles Fryer, became the first mayor of the town when it acquired municipal status on 12 July 1900.

Several interesting buildings survive from the early years and are worth seeing, such as the gaol (built in 1808), the original landdrost court, and a typical Irish settler home.

An art gallery, *Die Kunshuis,* exhibits the work of local artists. It is open daily during normal business hours.

Clanwilliam today has a population of 4 816. It is a prosperous agricultural centre serving a district which produces citrus, rooibos tea and vegetables. A convenient tourist centre, it is much frequented during the spring by visitors admiring the profusion of wild flowers which cover the countryside.

The *rooibos* (red bush) tea plant (*Aspalathus linearis Linearis*) grows wild on the mountains. A Russian Jew, Benjamin Ginsberg, and a South African, Doctor P le Fras Nortier, a bosom friend of Dr C Louis Leipoldt the writer, were the fathers of the industry. This tea is now cultivated, dried and packed in Clanwilliam and widely exported. About 6 000 tons are produced each year. Guided tours of the rooibos tea factory take place Mondays to Thursdays from 10h00 to 16h00 every two hours and on Fridays at 10h00, 12h00 and 14h-00.

Velskoen (felt shoes of untanned skin) are made in the town at Strassbergers.

A wild-flower garden, recreational area and caravan park are situated on the shores of the Clanwilliam lake at Ramskop. There is an annual spring show of wild flowers.

THE CLANWILLIAM DISTRICT

Several interesting branch roads from Clanwilliam penetrate the surrounding countryside, the Cederberg and its companion mountain ranges. One road crosses the Pakhuisberge (pack house mountains) to Calvinia (153 km). From this route tourists can turn off to view the wild flowers in the Bidouw valley, to visit the picturesque Rhenish mission station of Wuppertal and to Bushmans Kloof.

The road heads east from Clanwilliam and climbs the *Pakhuis* (pack house) Pass, passing an extraordinary collection of rock shapes. After 14,5 km the grave of the renowned writer and individualist, Dr C Louis Leipoldt (28 December 1880 to 12 April 1947), is reached. This grave, in a Bushman rock shelter complete with a gallery of faded paintings, is worth visiting. The rock containing the shelter is made up of a pile of sandstone boulders, a veritable Bushman's castle. To the left of the grave a path passes through a cave to a perennial stream which flows through a rugged valley choked with giant rocks and guarded by *dassies* (coneys).

A parking and picnicking area is next to the grave and a great deal of fine walking and scrambling about can be done in the vicinity. The site was a favourite haunt of Louis Leipoldt. Such was the amiable nature of the man that visitors may be sure that he shares in the pleasure of their outing and is present, a silent and happy ghost, at their camp-fires.

Five kilometres beyond the grave, after passing the Kliphuis camping ground, the road reaches the summit of the pass and commences a winding descent to the plains of the Karoo, sweeping in from the east like a primeval sage-green coloured ocean breaking on the rock cliffs of the high mountains. Below the pass there is a cluster of buildings known as *Pakhuis* (pack house). Then, 13 km from the summit, the road crosses a causeway over the rather bucolically-named *Brandewynrivier* (brandy river) with the *Travellers Rest* farm on its east bank offering accommodation. Two kilometres further on there is a turn-off on the right hand side signposted Bushmans Kloof. The main road continues on its way to Calvinia, with a turn-off 3 km further on to the Bidouw valley and Wuppertal.

BUSHMANS KLOOF

Bushmans Kloof is a special place, where it is easy to step from this modern age and return to the stone age. To the hunter-gatherer people of the past years it must have been a paradise, felicific and delightful. Two perennial streams tumble down, pure and sparkling, from the overlooking mountains. Each stream finds its way with many a cascade and waterfall down narrow ravines. In the cliffs there are caves and snug rock shelters. At least 126 of them were decorated with paintings by the /Xam (Cape Bushmen) who lived, generation after generation for countless years in a setting where the rushing sound of water makes a symphony throughout the days and nights.

To the woman folk some of these shelters made ideal homes. Water was within reach and wild olive trees gave shade and protection. There were no endless chores of fetching and carrying water and firewood for wearisome distances. Rich vegetation covered the downland plains on either side of the ravines. Bulbs, berries, fruits, nuts, flowers and greens were there for the picking.

To the men it was a hunters dreamland. Fat antelope, especially eland and springbok which were their favourite food, were lured from the dry Karoo to the mountain slopes by the rich grazing and water. Flowers galore and the colours and shapes of the sandstone rocks ornamented the whole wild garden and made it a place of delight to the minds of all who have ever seen it. The nectar of the flowers provided the indigenous bees with the makings of sweet dark honey, a food source that was prized by the /Xam and yielded them an alcoholic drink.

For how long the hunter-gatherer people lived in this wilderness it is impossible to know. So far as they were concerned, for generations they were the only people in the entire world. They knew nothing of history, discoveries, conquests, barbarous killings or the need for senseless slaughter. They did not even have cause to name themselves as a people, tribe or nation. Through myths and stories they explained their presence to their children and the riddle of the mysterious universe.

The downfall of this ancient culture came with the advent of pastoralist people and European settlers. Powerful colonialists either killed or drove the indigenous residents away. Their culture vanished. Nothing remains of all of those past years save the enigmatic paintings on the rock walls of the caves and shelters. Their supplanters kept little record of the early people of the Western Cape, their names or their stories. The proliferation of game animals that abounded in the Cape were indiscriminately and unsustainably killed for either sport or the pot.

Bushmans Kloof Wilderness Reserve is a National Heritage Site. It borders South Africa's largest proclaimed wilderness area originally named in A G Krihaan: *The Sederberge*. Nestled between the Cape's floristic kingdom and the Great Karoo the area's brief winter rainfall, together with hot dry summers, make this environment more ideally suited to indigenous wildlife rather than agriculture.

Capetonian businessman Bill McAdam purchased the land in 1991. In 1992 his son Mark made his home on the property. Both are lovers of African wilderness. Together they carefully planned a programme of restoring and rehabilitating the area to its former glory, turning a vision into a reality. It was a major exercise in sustainable conservation, eliminating the early agricultural practices and reintroducing breeding herds of indigenous game animals. Eland, gemsbok, red hartebeest, black wildebeest, springbok and the endangered bontebok and cape mountain zebra now once more roam in the area. Another aspect of Bushmans Kloof's conservation efforts includes the monitoring and protection of rarer endemic floral species and the introduction of the Clanwilliam yellowfish to its river systems.

Viability to this 're-birth' vision is achieved and maintained by the creation of a luxury game lodge. Harmonious in its setting and with accommodation for twenty guests, it offers a unique wilderness experience and ensures complete exclusivity. There are professionally conducted late afternoon and evening game drives, guided rock art walks, self-discovery hiking and mountain bike trails, ideal wildlife photographic opportunities, bird watching and swimming in crystal clear mountain rock pools. Set on rolling lawns, the lodge also has a well-stocked library, sauna, swimming pool, billiard room, lounge, fully licensed bar and conference facilities. The sound of silence is only interrupted by the gentle songs of the sunbirds and the nearby mountain streams, invigorating both the body and the soul.

BIDOUW VALLEY

At 3 km beyond the turn-off to Bushmans Kloof on the R364 road to Calvinia, there is a turn-off to the Bidouw valley and the mission station of Wuppertal. After 14,5 km along this road, there is a turn-off leading eastwards down the valley of the stream known as the Bidouw from the plants of that name (*Chrysanthemoides monilifera*) which grow there. The valley is renowned for its spring flowers, at their best in August and September. After 29 km (rather rough, with numerous gates), the road reaches a ford over the Doring River at Uitspanskraal – deep when the river is in spate. After it crosses the river, the road deteriorates into a rough but passable track which finds a rather solitary way across a harsh stretch of arid Karoo country, watched over from the western horizon by the summits of the Cederberg Mountains. After 51,5 km of travelling from the river crossing, the road reaches the main gravel road from Calvinia (56 km) to Ceres (209 km).

WUPPERTAL

Beyond the turn-off to the Bidouw valley the road continues its sharp descent for a further 18 km and then reaches Wuppertal (69 km from Clanwilliam), a most attractive little oasis in a very rugged wilderness. The western slopes of the Cederberg Mountains are arid, but from the mountains flow beautiful streams. Nature's kiss of life to the area. Among these streams is the *Tra-Tra* (bushy). Where it tumbles from the high mountains it washes a deep valley, narrow and hemmed in by harsh peaks. The valley floor, however, is fertile and green, producing all manner of vegetables and fruits, excellent corn and tobacco. Rooibos tea flourishes on the slopes, figs, quinces, peaches, pomegranates and blackberries all thrive.

The mission station of Wuppertal had its origins in 1829 when Johan Gottlieb Leipoldt, grandfather of Dr C Louis Leipoldt, the poet-physician, arrived in the Cape from Germany with three missionaries, Theobald von Wurmb, G A Zahn and P D Luckhoff. On 1 January 1830 Leipoldt and van Wurmb bought the farm *Rietmond*, 2 563 ha in extent. There they established the first Rhenish missionary farm in South Africa and named it *Wuppertal* after the valley at the Wupper River in the Rhineland where the Rhenish Mission Institute was situated in Barmen.

From its start the mission was concerned with the temporal as well as the spiritual welfare of the people resident in the area. In 1834 another farm of 20 000 ha was bought to be used for grazing. In 1838 a number of newly freed slaves from adjoining farms settled on the mission. They were trained by the missionaries as shoemakers, tanners, millers, bricklayers, joiners and thatchers. They learned to build homes and even the church, which was consecrated in 1834.

The people prospered for nearly one hundred years. Then a decline commenced in the 1960s. Young people left to seek employment in the outside world. The handcraft industries of Wuppertal went into depression. On 17 October 1965, the Reverend H K Diehl of the Rhenish mission, handed Wuppertal over to Bishop P W Schaberg of the Moravian Church whose resident minister, assisted by a council of inhabitants, runs the place today.

The village consists of a store, three terraces of neat photogenic little cottages – each with garden and plot – and a meandering street with water flowing in furrows as well as coursing down a natural bed in the valley floor. In the village, excellent *velskoen* (felt shoes) are still made; tobacco is dried and worked into rolls; rooibos tea is sorted and packed, dried fruit, beans and goats are produced. In short, a great deal of productive activity takes place, which is surprising to any traveller descending the steep pass into the isolated valley. At Christmas time there is a festival of carol singing at the mission and the mountains echo to the voices of the people of Wuppertal.

The village is dominated by the *Vaalheuningberge* (tawny honey mountains) to the south and the *Krakadouw* (woman's pass) range to the west. The original 'woman's pass', an old pathway, penetrates the mountains from Wuppertal to Clanwilliam and is a spectacular but strenuous walk. From Wuppertal a gravel road leads south through rugged and sandy country and eventually, at Matjiesrivier, joins the road from Algeria to Ceres. This road requires a four-wheel drive vehicle.

CLANWILLIAM TO LAMBERT'S BAY

A tarmac road leads westwards from Clanwilliam to the coast. After 29 km the road reaches a railway station, built in 1910 as a centre for the handling of goods consigned to Clanwilliam and Lambert's Bay. The name *Graafwater* (excavation for water), a rather lowly name but comprehensible in an area so arid, came from the farm there owned by Erasmus van Zyl. In 1920 a township was laid out and Graafwater became a church and commercial centre. Thirty-two kilometres north of Graafwater, on the Vredendal road, there is an interesting old cave (now an historic monument) known as the *Heerenlogement* (gentleman's lodging) where the initials and names written and engraved on the walls by about 170 early travellers reveal that the place was used as a shelter in the 18th century.

Olaf Bergh, the first explorer of Namaqualand, sheltered in the cave in November 1682. There is a dependable freshwater spring at the approach to the cave and this was a considerable convenience to travellers. Bergh named the place *Dassen Berghs Fontein* from the number of *dassies* (coneys) living there. His name is the earliest engraved on the rock face. Among many other interesting visitors who left their mark was the Governor, Simon van der Stel, in the course of his journey to find the copper mountain of the Nama people in 1685.

A cast-iron pot in the cave, 1,23 m by 1 m by 0,6 m in extent, was used there by unknown persons. There are galvanised-iron forts on the farms *Heerenlogement, Klipfontein* and *Graafwaterplaas*. On *Klipfontein* farm the owner, Mr J V de Jongh, has a private museum and there is a stone marked with the names of Olaf Bergh and other travellers. Before visiting these places, it is wise to enquire at Graafwater about access to these properties.

The gravel road continues from Graafwater westwards for 30,5 km, traversing some interesting wild-flower country and then, 59,5 km from Clanwilliam, enters the fishing harbour of Lambert's Bay (described in Chapter Six).

THE ROCK WILDERNESS OF THE CEDERBERG (CEDAR MOUNTAINS)

This mighty rock wilderness of sandstone is a superb recreational area. Walkers, climbers, lovers of nature, photographers and artists find themselves in a realm of inexhaustible scenic beauty: novel rock shapes, rich flora, clear atmosphere and challenges to adventure through strange caverns and ravines, and climbs to the summits of many high peaks.

Access to the mountains is easy. From the Copper Way (N7) there is a gravel turn-off 27 km from Citrusdal on the way to Clanwilliam. This turn-off crosses the Olifants River by means of a low-level concrete causeway. For 16 km it finds a rugged route with steep gradients through the *Kriedouw* (difficult passage) over the Nieuwoudt Pass. From the summit of this pass there is an impressive view of the mountains. The valley of the *Rondegat* (round hole) River lies below the pass. To the left is the 1 745 m high Krakadouw Mountain, while in front towers the 1 513 m high Middelberg Ridge.

In the valley below is the forestry station of Algeria, founded in 1904 by George Bath, the first forester of the area. The gnarled old cedar trees (*Widdringtonia cedarbergensis*) growing on the mountains and the general appearance of the area reminded Bath of the Atlas Mountains of North Africa. For this reason he named the new station *Algeria*. Bath blazed the paths which penetrate the range, built the first mountain hut at Middelberg, and gave such names as Crystal Pools to the lovely swimming-pools in the heart of the range where he decided to build a second hut. He also established the plantation of cedar trees which preserves this variety of cypress.

Today the range is a proclaimed wilderness area. Paths meander through the mountains, taking the walker to all manner of remarkable places. There are caves, waterfalls, stupendous viewsites and astonishing formations such as the Wolfberg Arch and the Maltese Cross, a rock pillar standing 9 m high, like an ancient totem pole in an eerie setting of rock shapes reminiscent of the petrified forms of worshippers of some forgotten god of ancient times. These bizarre rock shapes are a feature of the range, masquerading as myriad different things – faces, animals, bridges, archways. The fiery colours of the sandstone formations, the heady clarity of the air, the brilliance of the stars at night and the magnificence of the wild flowers make the atmosphere unique.

In the trees around the Algeria Forestry Station, a fine camping ground is enhanced by the river which forms a natural swimming-pool. This is the base camp for many excursions into the range. The main path leads up through the plantation of cedar trees, past a beautiful cascade to the first hut at Middelberg. From the Middelberg hut, paths take visitors for days of walking and climbing to places such as Crystal Pools, Sneeukop (1 931 m), the strange Wolfberg Arch and Cracks, as well as to many other interesting places. The pride of the mountains is the lovely snow protea (*Protea cryophila*) which grows only above the snowline and is pure white; it blooms around March. A close second to this flower is the blood-red Cedarberg pincushion. Rooibos tea is also common in the foothills. The strange elephant's foot plant (*Diascorea elephantipes*), from which cortisone was originally obtained, is also common. The round-leafed buchu (*Agathosma betulina*) with its pleasant aroma flourishes on the mountains.

Permits for hiking are available from the forestry office.

From Algeria roads lead up and down the valley of the Rondegat River. Downriver the road passes through fine scenery for 30,5 km to Clanwilliam, up river the road begins a spectacular climb over the *Uitkyk* (look-out) Pass, past farms and forestry centres such as *Driehoek* (14,5 km); *Eikeboom* (16 km); *Rypvlei* and *Paardekloof* (19 km); *Dwarsrivier* and *Sanddrif* (27 km); and *Kromrivier* (35 km).

Dwarsrivier, Sanddrif and *Kromrivier* (crooked river) are farms belonging to members of the Nieuwoudt family who have lived in the mountains for many years. The first Nieuwoudt (Gerrit) got himself into a rather awkward situation when he killed Coenraad Fiet, the first magistrate of Clanwilliam, in a duel. Sentenced to life imprisonment, he was reprieved. On his release he retired deep into the mountains to what was then (and still is) a very isolated farming area. Today there are three Nieuwoudt families (those of Polly, Rensie and Jan) in the mountain area. All are renowned individualists. *Nieuwoudt Pass* is named in honour of Swart Andries and Ernse Nieuwoudt who contributed money for its construction.

At *Sanddrif*, Polly Nieuwoudt maintains a camping ground next to the Sand River. This is the starting-point of many walks and climbs to places such as the Wolfberg Arch and Cracks.

At *Kromrivier*, Rensie Nieuwoudt maintains bungalows and a caravan park for the use of mountaineers. There is a shop supplying fresh milk, home-baked bread and fresh fruit in season. This farm makes an excellent base for walks to the Maltese Cross, the 2 027 m high Sneeuberg and many other spectacular parts of the range. A map of the hiking trails and the Wolfberg Cracks is available. There is also horse-riding on mountain trails.

Beyond the turn-off to *Kromrivier*, the main road from Algeria continues. After 4 km a track to the right leads through a gate to a massive rock (at 1,5 km) on which there are Bushman paintings of elephants and men. The track ends 1,5 km further on at a marvellous honeycomb of caves and weird rock formations known as the *Stadsaal* (town hall). There is an entrance fee, payable at Matjiesrivier or at the entrance gate.

Three kilometres beyond the turn-off to the Stadsaal, the main road from Algeria joins a rough road at *Matjiesrivier* coming south from Wuppertal. The Wuppertal section should only be attempted by a four-wheel-drive vehicle but the gravel continuation southwards is reasonably surfaced and provides a spectacular route to Ceres, 110 km away. On the way this road crosses the Kouebokkeveld, bridges over the Grootrivier (19 km from *Matjiesrivier*) joins the tarmac Ceres–Citrusdal road (53 km from Grootrivier) and then continues for a further 38 km down the Gydo pass to Ceres. This is a true scenic switchback drive. The gravel road is in fair condition but demands cautious driving. There are many extraordinary rock formations to be seen, especially in the Zuurvlakte area.

From the hamlet of *Op de Berg* (up the mountain) a road leads eastwards past the strange rock formation known as the *Katbakkies* (cat faces) through handsome scenery for 4 km to reach *Kagga Kamma* (plentiful water) a huge wilderness estate whose owners, Willem de Waal, his son Pieter and Pieter Laubser, his cousin, have invited back to the mountains descendants of its original Bushmen population who were driven away to the arid areas of the Kalahari and now have the opportunity of a return to the lands of their ancestors.

CLANWILLIAM TO NAMAQUALAND

After Clanwilliam the main tarmac road, the Copper Way (N7), continues north down the left bank of the Olifants River. The country becomes more arid, but there are kilometres of irrigated farmland along the banks of the river and many fine views. The canal carrying irrigation water keeps close company with the road. At Kransbrug there is a huge siphon which diverts water from the western to the eastern channels of the river as part of the Olifants River irrigation scheme. At 47 km from Clanwilliam the road bridges the Olifants River; and 6 km further on there is a tarmac turn-off west to the railway centre of *Klawer* (3 km), named from the wild clover growing there, and to Vredendal (27 km). The Klawer Wine Co-operative is 3 km outside the town. Diagonally opposite the cellar there is a gallery of Bushman paintings in a rock shelter.

Twenty-one kilometres further on from Klawer (74 km from Clanwilliam), the Copper Way N7 reaches the sunbaked little town of ...

VANRHYNSDORP

At the entrance of Namaqualand, this town is named after Petrus Benjamin van Rhyn, first member for Namaqualand in the old Cape Legislative Council, and a leading public figure in the district.

First explored by Europeans in 1662 (Pieter Crythoff), then in 1682 (Olaf Bergh), and in 1685 (Simon van der Stel), the area around Vanrhynsdorp was first settled in the 1740s. The farm on which Vanrhynsdorp stands, *Troe-Troe,* received its unusual name from a Nama war-cry *Toru-Toro*, meaning 'return, return'. Lying on the verge of Namaqualand to the north of the *Matsikamma* (mountains that yield water), the farm was a good site for a town. In 1850 a Namaqualand congregation was established, and on 8 September 1866, at a meeting of male church members, Petrus van Rhyn offered to provide a church building for ten years on condition that each member paid one shilling a year towards maintenance.

The church was the beginning of Vanrhynsdorp. A township was eventually laid out in 1887 and this became a village management board in 1904 and a municipality in 1913. The town is a rural centre with a population of 4 028. It lies at a crossroads leading to several interesting parts of the north-western Cape. There is a museum housed in the original gaol. It is open Mondays to Fridays from 08h00 to 13h00 and from 14h00 to 16h30.

There is a remarkable *Kokerboom Succulent Nursery*, reputedly the largest succulent nursery in the world, which should be visited by all lovers of plants. Phone (02727) 9-1062.

THE WILD FLOWERS OF NAMAQUALAND

There is an intriguing mystery about Namaqualand. It is one of the great floral kingdoms of the world, but why do the flowers grow there in the first place? The area is quite unpredictable in its moods and seasons; hot, drought-stricken, plagued by searing winds, rocky, with sandy soil, and so seemingly barren as to make a human gardener recoil in horror. It is mystifying why the flowering plants don't simply pull up their roots, pack their seeds in their little portmanteaus, and head for places where the air is cool, the soil rich and deep, the streams brimming with pure sweet water, and the rain falls often in lovely big drops.

The search for an answer to this puzzle is an interesting exercise in the appreciation that any form of life must harmonise with Nature in order to flourish. Man sometimes considers himself an exception. He thinks that he can contend with Nature and therefore pays a bitter price. These flowers of Namaqualand harmonise with a harsh environment and flourish.

To understand the mystery of the flowers, it is important to realise that Namaqualand was not always an arid area. Nature changes continuously; nothing is permanent except the driving force of Creation and the basic building blocks of the universe, matter and energy. All indications show that Namaqualand, in comparatively recent geological times, was well watered. Along the whole south-western coast of Africa rivers flowed to the sea, rain fell and the vegetation was luxuriant and varied.

The soils of Namaqualand have several geological origins. Prodigious dome and whaleback shapes of granite hills dominate the central and northern parts of the area. Sediments of the much more recent Nama and Cape deposits cover other parts of the surface. Windblown sand eroded from granites and sediments alike is mixed in different proportions and covers other parts of the area. Such a variety of soils, irrespective of climatic conditions, would offer widely different opportunities for life in an irregular patchwork quilt of micro-habitats. Some of these ecological habitats blend; others are so sharply divided that they could well be the arbitrary political boundaries of adjoining countries inhabited by life-forms entirely foreign to one another.

This basic geological infrastructure of Namaqualand always influenced a diverse vegetation, with climate being the ultimate controlling force. In the history of Namaqualand weather there lies an enigma. About 50 million years ago, for some inexplicable reason, the currents of the southern ocean underwent a drastic change. A flow of cold water from the Antarctic was directed northwards. This current is a spin-off from the wild weather of the icy southern sea. In its water is contained the essence of icebergs and the breath of the South Pole.

The current reaches the south-western end of Africa at the Cape of Good Hope. Pressure from the warm south-flowing Agulhas–Mozambique Current deflects the cold current up the western side of Africa. Like a cold river about 150 km wide, the Benguela Current (as it is known) flows up the coast. Its arrival had a shattering effect on a comfortably established climatic area. The cold water resists evaporation. From being a well-watered region, the south-western coast of Africa deteriorated and became arid. A major desert – the Namib – developed in the north and a transitionary semi-desert – Namaqualand – in the south.

The early vegetation experienced a crisis. Most of the vegetation died, but a few survivors clung to the summits of the highest peaks where enough water condensed from mist or clouds to provide these isolated plants with the essentials of their former way of life. But on the low-lying plains where most of the plants died, the rivers were fossilised. The winds turned the sun-drenched surface of the land into an area of dust and sand. The gravels originally carried to the mouths of rivers were dispersed up the coast by the powerful current to form pebble beaches filled with the shells of marine molluscs such as oysters, killed by the cold water. Mixed in the gravel with these fossil oyster shells were diamonds.

Amongst the surviving plants were succulents and members of the daisy family (*Iradaceae*) both tenacious, wily and courageous families of plants capable of adapting to their transformed habitat. They even discovered advantages in the arid conditions. The extinction of many other plant species made life less competitive as far as living space was concerned. The soils with their varied origins not only retained their fertility but, during dry years when little could grow, were rested and replenished with chemicals released by rocks disintegrating from the action of sun and wind.

The plants made several adaptations in order to flourish in the area. They produced seeds which could hibernate through several years of drought, simply lying dormant where chance had deposited them. As soon as they sensed that weather conditions were favourable, they became complete opportunists, growing at such speed that Namaqualand people say they can hear the stirring of life after a good fall of rain. A rustle of spring occurs all over Namaqualand. Debussy's *Springtime Rounds* perfectly depicts the joy, the stretching, the growing of all these little plants.

They have to grow and mature quickly in case the favourable weather deteriorates. As an additional safeguard, a proportion of the seeds will not germinate, remaining dormant for one or several years more. In their growth, the plants keep low to the ground and do not waste time or substance by producing long stems. They flower and confront the last problem of their existence in Namaqualand – the shortage of pollinators. In the arid years most of the pollinators die. When a good year comes, there is vast competition among the plants for the services of a few survivors. The plants court the pollinators, not only with brilliantly coloured flowers, but also with several cunning devices.

Apart from colours, the flowers have patterns and mock images with which to tempt the pollinators. Insects are susceptible to ultra-violet; therefore some of the flowers contain patterns in ultra-violet (invisible to the human eye) which are very attractive to an insect. Other flowers have mock images of lady beetles, bugs or wasps in exactly the right position for an amorous pollinator to settle and, while exploring the charms of the image, inadvertently pollinate the flower.

It is impossible to predict a good flower season in Namaqualand. The transformation from drabness to almost unbelievable beauty is dependent on such capricious climatic conditions that the whole area can change almost as quickly as Cinderella putting on her gown and appearing at the ball. The visitor to Namaqualand can either see its floral dress in truly dazzling display, or be so disappointed as not to believe that so magical a transformation can ever take place.

About 4 000 species of plants grow in Namaqualand, their distribution influenced by local conditions. Average annual rainfall varies in certain areas as well as the nature of the soils. The best-watered part of the floral area is along the valley of the Olifants River. In the upper reaches of this valley the rainfall stimulates a merging of the flowers of Namaqualand with the fynbos of the Western Cape. Ericas, proteas, pincushions and many other flowers compete with the mesembryanthemums and daisies. Along the valley, citrus estates cover much of the original wild garden, but patches of it may still be seen in remaining uncultivated areas and on the slopes of mountain ranges such as the Cederberg.

The region of the Olifants River is always worth exploring, even in a dry season. It is here that *Aspalanthus linearis* (rooibos tea) grows wild as well as being cultivated. Oranges, especially navels, ripen during the season of the flowers, with wayside stalls offering them to travellers.

Eendekuil sweetmilk and cheddar cheese should be sampled – they are amongst the best in South Africa – and there are some interesting wines to be tasted in the cellars at Citrusdal, Klawer and Vredendal. Fishing (seven edible species in the river), canoeing, swimming, a flask of wine, a slice of cheese and sunset reflecting on the Olifants River, provide a pleasant ending to a day spent viewing the flowers. There is an attractive caravan park at Algeria, while the Cedarberg Hotel in Citrusdal is known for its table.

Clanwilliam lies in the middle reaches of the valley of the Olifants. Experiencing lower rainfall than Citrusdal, the fynbos type of vegetation has dwindled. There are more succulents and dry area plants whose growth is notably closer to the ground. In the Ramskop Wild Flower Garden of Clanwilliam, which contains a good representative collection of Namaqualand plants, they attain their best growth living under natural but protected conditions where rainfall is artificially supplemented in times of drought. The lake in the Olifants River provides a background (not too characteristic of the arid areas) to the garden. When the weather is hot, a swim there is a pleasant way of relaxing. The water's-edge caravan park provides an amiable stopover and there is a very good hotel in the town.

From Clanwilliam a tarmac road leads west across what is known as the Sandveld to the fishing harbour of Lambert's Bay. This Sandveld is a 50 km wide strip of transitionary desert, the southern extension of the Namib Desert, which reaches its end at Lambert's Bay where rainfall averages about 130 mm a year. North of Lambert's Bay the rainfall dwindles to an average of 50 mm at Port Nolloth. North of that little port, rainfall can best be described as a drop and a promise. To live in this sandveld, the vegetation has to be tough. But it is still beautiful. Mesembryanthemums *(vygies)* provide almost translucent shades of shimmering colour. Skilpadbos *(Zygophyllum species)* have a strange affection for the sandy wastes, while many interesting succulents manage to flower even in a dry season. Sea mists are common in the area, and these provide at least some moisture to supplement the skimpy rain.

East of Clanwilliam a gravel road climbs the mountains and passes the grave of Dr C Louis Leipoldt. Situated here is a pleasant picnic spot, and the rock formations are spectacular. On the eastern side of the mountains a road branches off southwards and leads to Bushmans Kloof, the famous Bidouw valley and to the mission station of Wuppertal.

The Bidouw valley is a very special place for all lovers of flowers. It is fortunate that the farmers living there are also flower lovers and are tolerant of the sightseers who drive into their valley each spring. For 29 km the valley is a linear garden. With a rainfall of up to 400 mm each year and a perennially flowing river, the valley supports a rich vegetation. Mass floral displays carpet the valley floor and slopes with patches of brilliant colour. There are several graceful homesteads built in the Cape-Dutch style. Their owners are to be congratulated for lovingly maintaining these serene old buildings, and allowing the flowers to bloom and seed before ploughs or livestock are released to disturb the valley by cultivation or grazing.

North of Clanwilliam lies the Knersvlakte, with Vanrhynsdorp, Klawer and Vredendal as the principal centres. The rainfall is not more than 200 mm a year, but in this area the plants grow in countless millions if there is the slightest encouragement from the weather. The land surface is sedimentary, part of the Nama Group laid down about 500 million years ago. Dominating a landscape of a gently rolling pebble-covered plain of reddish soil is the landmark of the Matsikamma mountains, composed of Table Mountain Sandstone dated at 350 million years. The name *Knersvlakte* (jarring plain) comes from the noise made by the rocks on the wheels of wagons.

Vanrhynsdorp is a convenient centre from which to explore this area. Gravel roads lead to such places as the valley of the *Kobee* (flow away) River and to the summit of the mountain massif known as *Gifberg* (poison mountain), where remnants of the ancient vegetation of the area may be seen. Chincherinchee plants, which are poisonous to livestock, flourish on this mountain. On the plains lies the domain of the Asteraceae family, the daisies of many different colours and forms; of particular note being the beetle daisies which, with their beetle patterns, ingeniously lure live insects to join the feast of nectar. Also present are the richly coloured botterbloms, the *Arctotis* species of white, golden and deep-red; *Dimorphotheca sinuata*, the Namaqualand daisy found in many gardens, but here blooming free and happy in the midst of a lonely wilderness.

The Knersvlakte stretches up past the railhead of Bitterfontein. Then the road traverses what is considered by many to be the true heart of Namaqualand, the area of granite. Giant dome and whaleback shapes of rock give the area a drama and an atmosphere dating back 360 million years when these prodigious masses of igneous rock surged up through the primeval surface of Earth.

With a rainfall of around 150 mm a year, the granite area is rich in copper and other minerals. It is here that the kokerboom grows and many members of the *Liliaceae* family. In the valleys, flowers of nearly every Namaqualand species flourish, especially in wheat fields left to rest for a season. Springbok is the best centre for exploring the granite area, with roads leading off in all directions to many interesting places. There is a well-kept caravan park with rooms on the outskirts of the town and two hotels in the town itself. However, facilities can become a little congested at the peak of a good flower season.

North of the granite area lies the *Richtersveld* where the rainfall is usually less than 50 mm a year. A permit to visit this rugged area is essential and may be obtained from the Department of Nature Conservation in Springbok. The traveller also needs to have the confidence to drive a motor vehicle into so harsh a world. The rewards of a visit, however, are exciting, with dramatic scenery, many marvellous succulents and astonishing patches of flowering plants joyfully making the most of an annual rainfall which could fall in less than an afternoon in some more favoured part of Earth.

Explore each of these distinct parts of Namaqualand if in search of flowers, each part is different and contains many worthwhile features unique to itself.

From Vanrhynsdorp a tarmac road stretches west to areas irrigated by the Olifants River. This road penetrates spectacular wild-flower country and after 24 km reaches the town of ...

VREDENDAL

With a population of 11 744, *Vredendal* (the dale of peace) is the principal centre of the Olifants River irrigation scheme. The origin of the name is uncertain. It is said that in 1668 a group of stock traders clashed with a band of cattle-rustlers who had stolen cattle at *Bakleiplaas*. After a running fight, with three of the rustlers killed, the cattle were recovered and peace restored at the site of modern Vredendal.

In 1732 the first farm in the area was granted to Pieter van Zyl. Stock farming was the principal activity in the area, but where the Olifants River flooded its banks during the winter rains a little agriculture was practised. The possibilities of irrigation were evident – fertile, low-lying soil, arid, but on the banks of a perennial river, with copious water simply flowing to the sea.

Sir Thomas Smartt, Minister of Agriculture, inspected the area, and on 16 February 1911 an irrigation district was proclaimed. From the water, the first vineyards were planted, with Senator Dan Retief the pioneer wine farmer. The first wine cellar was built on his farm *Bakleiplaas*, now called *Boomvlei*.

There are now over 800 farmers involved in irrigation from the Olifants River. The principal product is wine, with the large co-operative wine cellars of Vredendal and Spruitdrift. Raisins, lucerne and vegetables, especially tomatoes, potatoes and squashes, are also produced. The railway link to Cape Town, opened in 1927, provides a direct route to a major market.

Iron ore is mined at Garieb Mine on the road to Vanrhynsdorp. Dolomite is crushed and marble processed at Cape Lime. Both mines can be visited.

The town was laid out in 1933 and became a municipality in 1963. It is surrounded by kilometres of vineyards, vegetable fields and fruit orchards.

The tarmac road continues from Vredendal down the irrigated valley. After 21 km the road reaches a gravel turn-off leading for 32 km to the coast at Strandfontein, a holiday resort frequented by the farmers of Namaqualand. The main tarmac road crosses the Olifants River, passes the small centre of Lutzville, founded in 1923 by Johan Lutz, and (30,5 km from Vredendal) reaches

Koekenaap (river where meat was cut), composed of a cluster of shops and garages loitering around a railway station. Here the tarmac road ends, but the road continues with a good gravel surface, passing through wild country for 51,5 km until it joins the Copper Way (N7) at the hamlet of Nuwerus, from where the traveller can complete a circular drive back to Vanrhynsdorp.

VANRHYNSDORP TO THE NORTH

From Van Rhynsdorp the main tarmac N7 road continues north through fine wild-flower and succulent country. Arid and searingly hot for much of the year, it is a typical piece of Namaqualand scenery – an immense, gently undulating plain covered in low scrub and rocks, with the escarpment of the central plain lying like a long ridge of mountains on the horizon to the east. The water is brackish and the stream beds are saline. Gypsum is mined in the area. At 22 km there is a turn-off to the strangely named *Douse the Glim*. Despite the size of the sign, this is simply a farm. The name, it is said, was given by a tired surveyor who, in his tent one weary night, irately told his assistant to *'douse the glim'* (put out the light) and go to sleep.

After 66 km the tarmac road enters more rugged country and skirts the rural hamlet of *Nuwerus* (new rest), perched on a hill slope known as *Erdevarkgat* (antbear hole). The road bypasses it and continues over low, rocky hills for a further 14,5 km to the railhead of Bitterfontein. Here in a shallow valley the 465 km long railway from Cape Town comes to a sudden and disconsolate end at a pile of coal and a drab cluster of corrugated iron sheds and railwaymen's houses. The line to the place was opened in 1927, but north of this point Namaqualand was left to the mercies of road transport. Only heavy transport vehicles are encountered from now on, engaged in an endless shuttle service between the railhead and points far and wide.

The tarmac road bypasses Bitterfontein and continues north for 63 km through increasingly rugged country until it reaches the village of ...

GARIES

This little town is simply one long street consisting of a church, houses and shops built along the banks of the stream named by the Nama *Th'aries* (Garies) because of the couch-grass growing there. The population is 1 460. In 1983–84 Garies was the centre for the so-called 'rotten milk culture'. An organisation known as Kubus Nurseries was started in the town by Adriaan Nieuwoudt to produce a milk culture said to be the secret of Cleopatra's beauty. The eventual product, a range of cosmetics, was to be known as Cleosec. Vast numbers of people invested millions of rands in obtaining milk cultures from the nursery. These cultures were bred as a sort of smelly cottage industry in homes all over South Africa. The dried cultures were returned for purchase by the nursery. Rival nurseries started in other parts of South Africa and the industry developed into a get-rich-quick mania. Vast amounts of money poured into Garies. Nursery promoters were enriched and talked of the whole world cultivating the kubus culture and all women anointing themselves with Cleosec. In 1984 the strange business collapsed with numbers of people ruined and left with little save the knowledge that Cleopatra's beauty secret (if she had one) was something idiotic like bathing in asses milk. Participants in the scheme were considered to be the asses. At the time of its collapse, Kubus Nurseries had debts in excess of R39,5 million.

From Garies a farm road leads westwards to a cluster of boulders at a site called *Letter Klip* (lettering stone) where the names of several early travellers are engraved, as well as a coat-of-arms engraved by British soldiers garrisoning a small Anglo-Boer War fort built there.

The valley of Garies is hemmed in by a rocky and wild-looking assembly of mountains. The road climbs steeply out of the valley up heavy cuttings and makes its way north through rugged country. After 5 km a gravel turn-off west leads to Hondeklip Bay (85 km) and 35 km further on another turn-off leads to the same fishing and seaside resort.

HONDEKLIP BAY

This little coastal resort and fishing harbour once had a lobster-processing factory. In former years *Hondeklip Bay* was used as a port for the shipment of copper. The name comes from a rock shaped like a seated dog. The head, unfortunately, was struck off by lightning. There are camping grounds and the place is a holiday resort for local farmers. Limited self-catering accommodation is available. On the way to Hondeklip Bay the road descends the escarpment by means of a pass named *Messelspad* (from the dressed stone embankment). Below the escarpment lies the village with the sad name of *Soebatsfontein* (fountain of pleading), where a goat herd named Hendrik Stievert, in 1798, is said to have pleaded with Bushmen for rights to use water from the spring.

Five kilometres north of the turn-off to Hondeklip Bay (45 km from Garies) the Copper Way N7 passes the hamlet of ...

KAMIESKROON

Kamieskroon is hemmed in by huge granite masses of mountains known as the *Kamiesberg* from the Nama name *Th'amies*, aptly meaning 'a jumble'. The *Kroon* (crown) of Kamieskroon, about 1,5 km from the village, is a prominent height with a huge cleft rock on the summit.

Seven kilometres west of Kamieskroon, the *Skilpad* (tortoise) Wild Flower Reserve was established in 1988 by the World Wide Fund for Nature. In 1999 it became the nucleus of the Namaqualand National Park with a generous endowment of land from Leslie Hill, a naturelover and collector of succulents. It is open during the flower season. Apart from the flowers and tortoises, several small mammals may be seen. Enquire at Kamieskroon Hotel. Phone (027) 672-1614.

Kamieskroon is, in fact, the descendant of an earlier town. Six kilometres to the north, the Copper Way (N7) twists through heavy granite country dominated by great domes and whalebacks of deep-seated rocks and then descends into the narrow valley of the Wilgenhoutskloof. Here are the ruins of an abandoned settlement, founded in 1864 by the Dutch Reformed Church as the site of the first church in Namaqualand. Known as *Bowesdorp* after the district surgeon, Dr Henry Bowe, the town could not develop in the narrow ravine. In 1924 the church, school, police station, post office and shops were all transferred to the present site of Kamieskroon. The ruins of the earlier place provide a melancholy, ghostly touch in the ancient granite landscape.

From Kamieskroon there is a turn-off east to the early *Leliefontein Mission*, founded in 1816 by the Reverend Barnabas Shaw and named after the *Lanticeschia aethiopica* lilies which flourish in the area. Close to the mission site, in this arid setting, is an old Nama settlement with the lovely, liquid Nama name of *Ouss* (fountain). At Nourivier, near Leliefontein there are fine examples of the traditional huts of the Nama people. This is great mountain bike trail country.

The N7 road continues northwards through massive granite country, the route taking many twists, climbs and descents. This is Namaqualand at its most rugged – a difficult land in which to live, populated by some weather-beaten characters working hard for their livelihood.

The first *kokerbooms* (quiver trees) – *Aloe dichotoma* – appear on the granite slopes. The kokerboom, an aloe species, is extremely slow-growing and lives for more than 100 years. The Bushmen made pincushion-type quivers for their arrows from the fibrous core. At 45 km from Kamieskroon the road passes the small rural centre of Mesklip and 21 km further on (66 km from Kamieskroon) the Copper Way (N7) reaches the curiously Wild-West town of ...

SPRINGBOK

The area of this town was once a favourite haunt of springbok and these entrancing little antelope gave the place its original name *Springbokfontein* (springbok fountain). The story of Springbok is essentially the story of copper mining in Namaqualand (described further on). Suffice to say here that the town was laid out in 1862 by the copper-mining concern of Messrs Phillips and King, which had purchased the land (a farm named *Melkboschkuil*) from its owners, the Cloete family, in 1850.

The first sale of plots took place on 28 October 1862. The town is situated in a narrow valley between high granite domes of the *Klein Koperberge* (small copper mountains). An odd little hillock stands in the middle of the valley as though on sentry duty. The town developed around this hillock but suffered a grievous setback in the late 1870s when rich copper was found at Okiep, causing nearly every inhabitant to move off to the scene of this new discovery.

The fountain of Springbok continued, however, to supply good drinking-water. As other copper deposits were located in the vicinity the town was established as a communications, administrative, educational and commercial centre for the miners. On 27 June 1922 it received a village management board, and on 26 June 1933 it acquired municipal status. Today, with a population of 10 708, it is one of the most important points on the N7 road between Cape Town and Namibia. It is a centre for tourists visiting the many wild flower regions and other interesting areas of Namaqualand and the Northern Cape. The place retains much of the atmosphere of the early days of the copper boom. There is a museum housed in what was originally the first Dutch Reformed Church, later the Synagogue and then, when the Jewish Community dwindled with the ending of the copper boom, the property of the municipality.

Just beyond the airport about 15 km south-east of Springbok is the Goegap Nature Reserve, including the Hester Malan wild flower garden on ground presented in 1965 by the Okiep Copper Company. This interesting sanctuary preserves the flora and fauna of the area, including gemsbok and other antelope. It is open daily. There are hiking, horseriding and 4 × 4 trails.

THE COPPER MINES OF NAMAQUALAND

Copper mining in Namaqualand dates back to a period long before the advent of the European in South Africa. The Nama tribe worked the metal, producing tools, weapons and ornaments, and used these items to barter with neighbouring tribes.

In December 1681 a party of these early miners visited the settlement at the Cape and presented to the Governor, Simon van der Stel, such excellent samples of copper that he immediately sent the metal off to Holland for inspection by the Directors of the Dutch East India Company. The result was an instruction that the source of the ore be found. The first major prospecting expeditions ever organised in South Africa were sent off, one after the other, to locate the so-called copper mountains of Namaqualand.

Each expedition managed to penetrate further north than the one before it. Eventually, in August 1685, Van der Stel himself led a major expedition on the copper trail, equipped with 15 wagons, a boat for crossing rivers, 2 small cannon to impress local tribes, 56 Europeans and a camp following of tribesmen and slaves. The assembly must have made a picturesque and colourful cavalcade as it moved through the lovely mountainous countryside of what is now the granary of South Africa.

It had been an excellent winter in the Cape. Good rains had fallen and the exploring party travelled for kilometres across a multi-coloured mosaic of flowers. Few ventures into unknown country could have been as delightful and fascinating. To top it all, the expedition was successful. On 21 October, Simon van der Stel reached the fabled *Koperberg* (what is known today as Copper Mountain West); and the three shallow prospect shafts sunk by his men yielded quantities of ore of impressive richness.

Two hundred years were to pass, however, before this discovery was worked by Europeans. Its remote location precluded earlier attempts at mining the ore, for the cost of primitive transport and the limited value of copper in the old days made it unprofitable to develop such far-off mines.

The 19th century saw world industrialisation and a steady rise in the value of copper. In 1836

Sir James Alexander became the father of Namaqualand copper mining. He re-examined Van der Stel's old prospect shafts and other outcrops in the Richtersveld at places such as Numees and Kodas. He then formed a company in London to promote a mining venture.

The difficulties of opening up mines in so remote and rugged a territory were formidable. Men had to be found who were prepared to work in complete isolation from the outside world, their only form of communication a laborious ox-wagon transport system which carried the ore to the Gariep River. From there it was floated in barges down to *Alexander Bay* (named after Sir James Alexander) and then shipped to Swansea in Wales, where it was milled, smelted and refined.

Despite the problems associated with mining, other companies became interested in Namaqualand copper. The 1850s, in fact, brought a rush to the area. Mushroom companies and syndicates were established even in some of the smallest towns of the Cape Colony. Men poured into the copper area, brain-washed with fallacies that copper lay thick and pure on the ground like overripe apples in an orchard.

The 'copper rush' collapsed as soon as the newcomers found that both hard work and substantial capital were needed in order to extract copper from its mother reef. Two companies remained; the Concordia Company; and a partnership of two Welshmen, Messrs Phillips and King. The latter sold out to the Cape Copper Mining Company in 1880. The two companies were both energetic, successful and fortunate in that the ore they were working was astonishingly rich, producing upwards of 31,5 per cent copper from the parent load. In the 1870s the Okiep Mine ranked as the richest copper mine in the world and by 1904 had produced over one million tons of ore.

The mines constructed their own narrow-gauge (2 ft or 0,76 m gauge) railway between Port Nolloth and Okiep. This private railway was opened on 1 January 1876 and served as the principal outlet to the sea for 68 years. Only in 1942 were running operations abandoned in favour of road transport. The last engine in use, the *Clara,* is preserved in Nababeep. The railway was 146 km long and must rank as one of the most remarkable ever operated. Motivation was at first provided by 60 mules. These hardy animals were hitched, three to a passenger coach and six to each coupled pair of freight trucks. Passengers travelled free.

This strange assembly started off at 6 a.m. from Port Nolloth. For 76 km to Anenous the line traversed completely barren country. Relays of mules were stationed at staging posts but providing them with water and fodder was a considerable problem.

The mules took seven hours to cross this thirsty land. Beyond Anenous the line climbed the Klipfontein range. This took four hours. At the top of the climb there stood the Klipfontein hotel. The train stopped there for the night. It left the next morning at 8 am and reached the terminus at Okiep at about 5 p.m.

Travelling up from the coast, most of the freight trucks were empty. Going down they were heavily laden with copper. For nearly 88 km they freewheeled with little need of traction. The 60 mules simply ambled along while the drivers attended to the brakes. Steam locomotives were introduced for the first 35 km in 1886. In 1893 they continued to the terminus at Okiep. In times of drought, however, the mules took over because they used far less water than the steam engines.

In 1937 the two working companies merged to become the Okiep Copper Company which operates the mines today. A major economic factor in the life of Namaqualand, the mines have an annual output of some two million tons of ore from two principal mines – Spektakel and Carolusberg – and several smaller workings.

A visit to the modern mines is a fascinating experience. The first impression the visitor receives is of the high degree of mechanisation. However, the old-time miners, especially those from Cornwall, were magnificent craftsmen who devised a technique of mining which is still in use today; the difference is that the tools of the modern miners have become infinitely more efficient and powerful. In the old days, too, ore had to bear a tremendous concentration of metal in order to become profitably mined. Nowadays, mechanisation and modern flotation and smelting processes have reduced working costs to such an extent that ore which the early miners discarded as unprofitably lean can be quite payably worked.

The milling and concentrating of the copper ore makes a particularly interesting spectacle. The company has three mills, each capable of handling more than 2 000 tons of ore every day. In these mills the ore is ground fine and converted into a pulp which flows into flotation machines. Here the copper separates from the waste matter by attaching itself to bubbles formed in the machines from the addition of detergents. These bubbles are collected and pumped to a thickener where the heavy copper settles and, after passing through a filter, emerges from the process as a damp concentrate.

The concentrate is dried and then taken to the smelting plant where it is exposed to carefully controlled heat in a reverberatory furnace with a working temperature rising to 1 600°C; this reduces the concentrate to a molten matte containing about 50 per cent copper. The process of smelting is a fireworks display, especially at night. The waste material (slag) provides a particularly awesome spectacle. After being trammed away by an electric locomotive, it is poured down the side of a waste dump in a vivid burst of colour like a waterfall of fire.

The matte is carried off in huge steel ladles to what is known as a converter. By means of compressed air which is blown through the molten matte, the converter oxidises unwanted sulphur to a gas and removes iron by turning it into a silicate which is skimmed off. What remains is molten copper, 99 per cent pure. This is carried off, also in ladles, and poured into moulds fitted on to a huge wheel, 6,7 m in diameter. Each mould contains 159 kg of blister copper, and by the time the wheel has turned full circle the copper has cooled into bars. These bars are the finished product of the mine. A fleet of heavy transport vehicles takes them down to the railhead at Bitterfontein, from where they are entrained to Cape Town to be included among South Africa's varied exports. The blister copper is refined overseas.

Visitors to Namaqualand are struck by the effects of the copper-mining industry on the arid countryside. Well-kept houses, recreation centres, tarmac roads and other signs of civilisation flourish in an environment which, without copper, would be solitary and bare. Just as rain can touch this barren land with magical fingers and turn it into an amazing garden of wild flowers, so copper has given the wastelands wealth which has lasted through 150 years of intensive mining activity. From geological signs and discoveries, mining will continue to be a major factor in the economy of Namaqualand for many years to come.

The prospecting shafts from the original Van der Stel expedition and the smelter smoke-stack of the original Springbokfontein mine are preserved as national monuments. Many interesting relics of early mining are to be seen at Okiep. The abandoned stations, embankments and culverts of the old narrow-gauge railway run alongside the Copper Way, between Springbok and Steinkopf, and then close to the road to Port Nolloth.

SPRINGBOK TO VIOOLSDRIF

Beyond Springbok, the main N7 road passes the old smelter stack of the original Springbokfontein mine, crosses high granite hills and, after 6 km, reaches a turn-off west leading for 13 km to the substantial copper-mining town of *Nababeep* (the water behind the little hill). This town is managed by the Okiep Copper Company. There is an interesting museum devoted to the story of copper mining in Namaqualand. Outside the museum stands one of the narrow-gauge trains, a fusspot of a little locomotive named *Clara*, and a few coaches. The museum is open Mondays to Fridays at 10h00 to 13h00 and 14h00 to 17h00; Saturdays from 10h00 to 13h00.

The main N7 road continues north. After 1,5 km (8 km from Springbok) it passes the outskirts of the copper-mining centre at the fountain known as *Okiep* (originally O okiep), from the Nama *U-gieb* (the great brack). Here the old smelter stack, built in 1880, still stands – a reminder of the early boom years of copper mining. In a stone building near the hotel there is also a remarkable Beam pump built in Cornwall in 1882. The mine at Okiep is still very active and a mining community live in the town today.

At Okiep a gravel road branches north-westwards and leads via the drift at Goodhouse to Namibia. The main tarmac N7 road continues northwards through huge granite outcrops. Many kokerbooms grow on the slopes. Relics of early mining activity may be seen. The embankments of the abandoned narrow-gauge railway keep company with the road through the hills.

The landscape levels off into an arid plain notable for its spring displays of wild flowers. At 48 km from Springbok the road reaches the mission station of *Steinkopf*, originally founded for the Nama people by the Rhenish Mission Society but now run by the Dutch Reformed Church. Named after the Reverend Mr Steinkopf, the mission is an interesting place. In it still stand the curious round *matjie-and-sack* (reed and sack) houses built by the Nama people in a world where shelter from the sun is of greater importance than protection from an insignificant rainfall. From Steinkopf a tarmac road R382 branches west to Port Nolloth (see further on).

Close to Steinkopf at Kinderlê is the communal grave of 32 Nama children murdered, it is said, in the 19th century by Bushmen, while their parents were in church at the mission.

Still in a northerly direction, the N7 road crosses arid plains dotted with rocky hillocks. After 13 km a turn-off right takes travellers 39 km to the date plantation at Henkries. The plantation can be visited by permission of the Management Board in Steinkopf. Straight ahead looms a mass of mountains, and 51 km from Steinkopf the road commences a gradual descent among huge piles of boulders gathered together as though swept from the plains by giant charladies. At the bottom of this 14 km descent, 114 km from Springbok, the road reaches the Gariep (Orange) at the fording place known as *Vioolsdrif* from a shepherd, Viool, who once lived there. A modern bridge across the river takes the road on into Namibia. At the bridge the Gariep River is dominated by a spectacularly coloured line of high cliffs and the area is rich in the beautiful decorative Vioolsdrif stone. Relentless summer heat blankets the valley, but irrigation from the river allows successful production of tropical fruit, dates, citrus, lucerne, vegetables, corn and other crops. A cluster of farmhouses, a police post and a garage are situated at the bridge. This sun-baked but dramatic frontier post of South Africa is also the terminal point of the N7 Copper Way. The customs and immigration posts are open at all times.

THE RICHTERSVELD NATIONAL PARK

The Richtersveld was named after the Reverend W Richter of the Rhenish mission seminary at Barmen in Germany. It consists of the north-western end of Namaqualand, a harsh and arid wilderness with a rainfall varying from 5 mm to 200 mm a year and a temperature range from 0°C to 52°C. A few perennial springs somehow or other manage to reach the surface at the foot of as gaunt a jumble of rocky mountains as could be seen in a nightmare of the nether world. Altogether, not too salubrious an area in which to live. Nevertheless, highly specialised life-forms have made a home there. Vegetation is confined to desert living succulents, several of them rare species, including *Aloe dichotoma* (the giant aloe) and *Pachipodium Namaquamun* (the elephant's trunk or *halfmens*, half human).

The Gariep (formerly Orange) River which forms the border with Namibia, provides a sharp contrast to the arid areas north and south of its banks. Trees and aquatic birds flourish in its valley. Spiders, scorpions and insects are fairly numerous. Tortoises, lizards and snakes find a living somehow. Of the mammals, Hartmann's mountain zebra, grey rhebok, kudu, duiker, steenbok, klipspringer, coneys, leopard, aardwolf, baboons, vervet monkeys, jackals, bat-eared foxes, otters, water mongoose and ground squirrels, have adapted themselves to some harmony with the wilderness. About 2 000 human beings, mainly Nama people, herd goats and a few sheep, cattle and donkeys in the area. For them the Richterveld has always been a communal home, with the few springs regarded as treasured assets.

Life has never been easy for any of the inhabitants of this wilderness. A few base minerals have been found and some, such as quartzite at Lekkersing, are worked. The demand by collectors for the rare succulents of the Richtersveld has prompted the establishment of a communally owned nursery. Tourism also brings in some revenue, with four-wheel-drive vehicles and mountain bikes penetrating into the most difficult country. Canoeing down the Gariep River has also become increasingly popular. The grandeur and immense power of the landscape is an attraction for visitors.

There are many natural wonders to see. Near Anniesfontein, 5 km from the Gariep River, is the *Wondergat*, a large cave regarded in some awe by the Nama who say that it is the sanctuary of the god, Heitsi Eibid. He hides his treasures there and will kill any interloper. Over the whole wilderness there is the feeling of the brooding presence of some primeval power. The hot winds which swirl over the rugged mountains sometimes carry a strange moaning sound which is said to be the singing of some restless spirit who haunts the rugged area.

There are a few small community centres such as *Sendelingsdrift* (missionaries ford) on the Gariep River, Khubus, and the strangely named *Riemvasmaak* (tie with leather thongs). Of this place it is said that some years ago a policeman arrested a Bushman, tied a leather thong around his neck and led him for 50 km through the wilderness to the police post.

In 1973 the Richtersveld was the scene for another but far larger forced removal. The Government summarily dispersed the entire resident population. The whole area was taken over by the South African army as a training ground for mechanised warfare. There was intense resentment by the people of the Richtersveld. Harsh it might be but it was still home to them.

Political times changed in South Africa. On 16 August 1991 a national park was proclaimed consisting of 162 445 hectares of the Richtersveld lying within the final great bend taken by the Gariep River. The park was created with the full co-operation of the returned people of the Richtersveld. The National Parks Board hired the land from them, paying an agreed annual rental into the Richtersveld Gemeenskap Trust. The succulent nursery would also be run by the National Parks Board and its profits paid into the Trust which is managed by trustees elected by the Richtersveld community. The park is controlled by a committee of four representatives of the National Parks Board and five elected representatives of the community.

This park will conserve a unique area, a true mountain desert region, one of the world's great homes of succulents and life-forms which have adapted successfully to seemingly impossible conditions.

From Steinkopf (48 km from Springbok) a tarmac road R382, leading to what is known as the Diamond Coast branches westwards from the Copper Way (N7) and stretches to the edge of the Namaqualand plain. After 10 km the road passes the abandoned railway station of Klipfontein where a couple of kokerbooms grow on the old platform, as though waiting hopefully for a train.

The road now descends through successive terraces, each more arid than the one before. At 18 km from Steinkopf the road reaches the bottom of the pass known as *Anenous* (side of the mountain). There is a turn-off south to *Spektakel* (spectacle) at 59,5 km from Steinkopf; 13 km further on the road passes the works of the Diamant-Quartzite Industries and the Namaqualand Quartzite Company, which produce an attractive building stone. At 79 km from Steinkopf there is a turn-off south to *Kleinzee* (the 'small sea' or lagoon at the mouth of the Buffels River) 45 km away where Consolidated Diamond Mines have a mine in a prohibited area. Just before the gate of the mine at *Grootmis* (great mist), a road stretches for 96,5 km to Springbok, climbing the interesting Spektakel Pass – a fascinating drive on a gravel road. Fourteen and a half kilometres beyond the turn-off to Kleinzee, on the main route 93 km from Steinkopf, the road reaches the coast at ...

PORT NOLLOTH

The cluster of houses of Port Nolloth confronts a diminutive harbour protectively enclosed in the arms of a reef of rock. A pretty stretch of beach and calm water within the reef are visually inviting to the holiday-maker. The Benguela Current sweeping up the coast, however, is bitterly cold and the little port is plagued by contradictory weather conditions. The cold sea (16°C maximum) resists evaporation, with the result that the coastal terrace on which Port Nolloth lies is an unprepossessing semi-desert – level, sandy and scrub-covered – with a rainfall of 45 mm a year, mainly from great clammy banks of mist which blanket the place intermittently between February and June and precipitate about 2 mm of moisture in 24 hours. From October to March, the southerly winds tend to blow at gale force. February can be oven hot; July ranges from cool to cold; the latter month, however, together with August and September, is the best time to visit the Diamond Coast.

Port Nolloth is an odd, isolated little desert port, but despite its weather problems it has a distinctive atmosphere. A hardy character, memories of past things, tough men and women and forgotten adventures make the Diamond Coast unique.

Port Nolloth goes back to the time of the copper boom, long before diamonds were found. Originally known as *Robbebaai* (bay of seals), it was surveyed in 1854 by Captain M S Nolloth and proved to be the most practical harbour on the Namaqualand coast for the shipment of copper ore. In March 1855 the proposed harbour was named after its surveyor by the Governor, Sir George Grey, and Port Nolloth was established.

At first, copper ore was laboriously conveyed to the place by wagon. The draught animals suffered badly on the tortuous old road. In 1876, however, the narrow-gauge railway was opened to the copper mines. After a preliminary spell of animal-drawn trains, a task force of steam locomotives, real puffing billies, worked their way backwards and forwards along the line, taking trucks of ore to the port. A town was laid out at the port, destined to be dominated for years by enterprises such as the Cape Copper Company, the South African Copper Company and the Okiep Copper Company.

Nobody was very satisfied with Port Nolloth. The opening in the reef allowed only small vessels of the coastal type to enter the harbour, while the cost of imported coal made the narrow-gauge railway an expensive enterprise. When the railway was opened from Cape Town to Bitterfontein and the development of heavy trucks made road transport practical, the narrow-gauge railway fell into disuse and was eventually rooted up, leaving a chain of 'ghost' stations and remnants of culverts and cuttings. Left in operation was an 8 km stretch from Port Nolloth to some freshwater springs from which the Okiep Copper Company railed water to the town at 1d per 18 *l*. Only in 1949 did the town secure its own water supply from boreholes.

After being abandoned by the copper companies, Port Nolloth went into decline. Then commercial fishing developed in the area. Three rock lobster canning factories – John Ovenstone Ltd, Hicksons Canning Co and Port Nolloth Visserye – were established. In 1930 Port Nolloth acquired a village management board and on 1 July 1945 it obtained municipal status. Today 4 839 people live in the town. What really got the place going, however, was the spectacular discovery of diamonds. Port Nolloth is also the only holiday resort on an otherwise prohibited-entry diamond-mining coast. *McDougall's Bay* (named after a pioneer trader, miner and fisherman, Donald McDougall, who settled there in the early years) has a picturesque cluster of shacks on ground leased from the municipality.

THE DIAMOND COAST

It is difficult for man to comprehend the mood of Nature in the creation of the Diamond Coast. Harsh and grim? Cynical and ruthless? The icy seas, oven-baked land, freezing nights, barrenness and solitude, the thirst – even the few springs callously salty to torment what life there is – would certainly suggest a savage fury. And yet, when all was done and Nature had relieved a harsh mood, the power of Creation looked down on the deformed landscape and compassion came. In a way which no man has ever convincingly explained, diamonds appeared in the marine terraces along the beach, making this Cinderella land one of the richest places on Earth.

Why man took so long to find these diamonds is yet another mystery. Rumours of their existence circulated for many years, but the great discovery only occurred on 15 August 1925. Captain Jack Carstens, son of William Carstens, a storekeeper in Port Nolloth, was home on leave from service in the Indian army. He took to prospecting, abandoned his military career and with his cousin, Percy Hughes, pegged claims 10 km south of Port Nolloth. There Carstens found the first diamonds at Oubeep and the news, quickly reported by Carstens senior, the local correspondent for Reuters, attracted a rush of prospectors.

A partnership consisting of Kennedy, Misdall and J P White went up to Alexander Bay but had no luck. On his way back Kennedy stopped at what was known as The Cliffs, where he had noticed red soil and traces of gravel when on his way north. Within a few days Kennedy found fourteen small diamonds. This, the second discovery, stimulated tremendous local excitement and a little later a storekeeper from Steinkopf named Rabinowitz found 334 diamonds at Buchuberg north of The Cliffs.

In the midst of the excitement, another Steinkopf storekeeper, Mick Caplan, went to Alexander Bay with a small party of workmen. They pegged twenty claims and found some magnificent diamonds.

Now prospectors, option hunters and diamond buyers flocked to the Diamond Coast. Namaqualand seethed with excitement and rumours. Company promoters and mining experts such as the famed Hans Merensky hastened to the area. One of the most discerning of all geologists, Merensky, soon noted that diamonds were invariably found in association with beds of gravel interspersed with fossilised shells of *Ostrea prismatica*, a warm-water oyster, probably killed off when the cold Benguela Current made its appearance along the coast. He looked for a place which had concentrations of these shells and took options on claims pegged at Alexander Bay by Caplan's party, a syndicate of attorneys and merchants, led by I Gordon. All Merensky's instincts told him that this was the richest area. He set out to secure control of the entire so-called 'oyster line' around the shores of the bay. For a total of £17 000 Merensky gained control of what became one of the world's richest natural treasure chests. Under a single flat stone the prospector found 487 diamonds. Within a month 2 762 diamonds totalling 4 308,9 carats had been found in Alexander Bay.

Hans Merensky hastened to Cape Town and saw the Prime Minister, warning him that the sensational finds would certainly incite a stampede of fortune-seekers to the Diamond Coast and that, in the harsh conditions, most of the hopefuls would simply die of thirst or hunger. There could be no repetition of the wild rush to Lichtenburg. Most of the diamondiferous coastline was in any event already in the hands of big companies.

The Government took rapid action. On 22 February 1927 all further prospecting for diamonds along the Namaqualand coast was prohibited. This measure, drastic but essential, brought the entire coast under tight control. As it was, when the co-called Hans Merensky Association halted operations in accordance with the Government ban, they had, in one month's work, already found 6 890 diamonds weighing 12 549 carats and valued at £153 000. Further unlimited exploitation of these fields could only bring about a collapse in the market value of diamonds. At this point the Diamond Syndicate, guided by Ernest Oppenheimer, intervened, undertaking to buy the entire output of the Namaqualand fields and to place the stones on the world market in an orderly fashion to maintain prices. Oppenheimer also bought his way into Merensky's Association. By July 1927 he had obtained £500 000 worth of shares and had become the dominant personality on the Diamond Coast.

The problem of operating the coastal alluvial fields was comprehensively solved by the Government. The coast became a state diggings, with the exception of discoverers rights on distinct geological deposits, of which there were six altogether. Of these the 'Oyster Line' and the 'River Gravel' areas went to Merensky; the 'Pebbly Limestone Line' at The Cliffs to Kennedy; the 'Buchuberg' area to Rabinowitz; and the 'Operculum Beds' to the Gelgorcap Syndicate. After some legal wrangling, the sixth deposit, the 'Extension of the Oyster Line' also went to Merensky and his Association. By wheeling and dealing Merensky and Oppenheimer then bought up the other discoverers' rights and made themselves sole controllers of Alexander Bay, obliged, however, to sell their production to the Government.

On 1 May 1928 work was resumed along the Diamond Coast in areas controlled by the Merensky Association and on the State diggings, controlled by the Government. The strictest security precautions were enforced on the fields. Barbed wire and guards kept unauthorised persons out, but the very severity of the restrictions became a challenge to many ingenious individuals who, over the years, used every possible scheme to smuggle diamonds through the security screen.

Public resentment, especially from the people of Namaqualand, of Government preclusion of their hopes for fortune, and of the exclusive monopoly of the Merensky Association, was considerable and understandable. It seemed that the newly discovered riches of the area, like the oil of the Middle East, would be looted for the benefit of only a few individuals, companies and non-resident shareholders. Namaqualand would be left to its poverty in the incongruous setting of one of the most richly endowed parts of Earth. Successful diamond smugglers were applauded as poor Robin Hoods robbing the rich.

Port Nolloth was bursting at the seams with an influx of would-be diggers, many from as far away as Lichtenburg. All were disgruntled and existing in appalling conditions of squalor. Among them moved the IDBs (illicit diamond buyers) and all manner of adventurers waiting for the main chance. Among this community it was not considered a crime to rob the State or Merensky's diggings and simply a misfortune, rather than a disgrace, to be caught. The atmosphere became electric with open talk that the restricted areas should be rushed by force.

In December 1928 an abortive effort was made to rush Buchuberg. This was restrained only by vigorous police action. When the men involved were taken back to Port Nolloth in handcuffs, an angry crowd demanded, and secured, their release. This was the beginning of what became known as the Namaqualand Rebellion.

The crowd threatened to storm Merensky's monopoly at Alexander Bay unless the Government made some land available for public working. More policemen were rushed in by the authorities. Money was voted for the relief of would-be diggers, whose condition was becoming deplorable. Port Nolloth was reminiscent of a dead-end town of lost souls. Starvation and frustration were etched on nearly every face.

A stormy meeting was held by the diggers and an ultimatum was sent to the Government. Unless some ground was made available as a public diggings by 28 December, the diggers would storm Alexander Bay. The Government replied by sending in still more policemen; voting funds for the relief of poverty among the would-be diggers and offering employment on roadworks and the railways in various parts of South Africa.

The offer was shouted down at a meeting. A fresh ultimatum was sent; Alexander Bay would be stormed on 7 January 1929 unless public diggings were proclaimed. The atmosphere at Port Nolloth became even more pugnacious. Scores of policemen arrived. Diggers were increasingly truculent. Bars and tea-rooms were crowded with men holding meetings while police patrols marched up and down the two sandy streets of the town.

Diggers were also squabbling among themselves. Considerable friction existed between the local men and those who had rushed to Namaqualand, mainly from the Lichtenburg diamondfields. Both groups tended to work separately and this weakened their cause. The general plan was to hold a mass meeting on 7 January and then drive out in trucks to Alexander Bay, where they would establish themselves around the outer fence and lay siege to the place for three days to allow for further negotiations. After that if there was no satisfaction there would be serious trouble.

At Alexander Bay, police mounted machine-guns and preparations were made to resist attack. Truckloads of police reinforcements arrived. January 6 passed with a great bustle of opposing sides preparing for the climax. The squabble between the Namaqualanders and the Lichtenburgers (as they were known) mounted. Only the leadership of the renowned Manie Maritz of Anglo-Boer War fame and the 1914 Rebellion kept the two sides to a single purpose.

Dawn of 7 January found Port Nolloth seething with excitement and frustration. Committees of Namaqualanders and Lichtenburgers met to organise proceedings, but simply squabbled for five weary hours while 2 000 impatient would-be rebels clamoured for leadership. At 15h00 a mass meeting was called. Two thousand men gathered for the occasion. Manie Maritz counselled caution. The rebellion fizzled out. A deputation was appointed to interview the Minister of Mines on 25 January.

For the next 48 hours a howling south-west wind swept over the Diamond Coast and even the most militant man lay low for shelter. The broken spirit of the rebellion was scattered by the winds. When calm returned, only poverty and despondency remained. Manie Maritz was appointed by the Government as a welfare officer for the area and poor relief was given to the would-be diggers. But no diamond areas on the coast would ever be available for public working – they were to be a prohibited zone for all time. Profits of the big companies were inviolate.

Diamonds found along the Namaqualand coast are gemstones of particularly fine quality, recovered along the line of an ancient beach (hence the association with fossil oysters) and by marine dredging from deposits beneath the sea north of Oranjemund. Alexander Bay (84 km north of Port Nolloth) and *Kleinzee* (small sea) the lagoon of the mouth of the Buffels River, where diamonds were first found by a building contractor named Alberts, 56 km south of Port Nolloth are the two principal areas of coastal recovery. There are substantial deposits on the coast which are kept in reserve. Outside the area of the original discoverers' claims, the Diamond Coast of Namaqualand is operated as a state diggings. Casual visitors to the fenced areas, unless they are vouched for by persons employed on the fields and issued with a permit, are unwelcome. Of the total of 9,1 million carats of diamonds produced in South Africa in 1989, the State-owned Alluvial Diggings

(Alexkor) yielded 140 000 carats, more than 90 per cent of gem quality. The output is restricted and co-ordinated so as not to depress the market value of diamonds.

Alexkor Ltd allows tours on Thursdays, starting at 08h00. Bookings are essential at least 24 hours in advance – Phone (027) 831-1330. There is a museum open weekdays 07h30 to 12h30. The hill east of the Alexander Bay gate is famous for the number and variety of lichens, over 26 species. Flamingoes and other aquatic birds frequent the estuary of the Gariep River.

Chapter Thirteen

CAPE TOWN TO THE GARIEP (ORANGE) RIVER

The N1 road, the Cape-to Cairo road, is the great north–south trunk route of Africa. It begins, unmarked by sign or monument, at the foot of the Heerengracht, just in front of the entrance to the Cape Town docks. This is the road that leads from Cape Town through Bloemfontein to Johannesburg and Zimbabwe, then northwards across the Zambezi River, through the seemingly interminable brachystegia forests of Zambia, the nyika wilderness of Tanzania, the savanna game plains of East Africa, and down the Nile to Egypt and the Mediterranean.

This has always been a road of adventure, hope and romance. From the time of the first settlement of the Cape, Jan van Riebeeck and his pioneers looked wistfully at the mountains of the north and east wondering what lay beyond – what riches, strange people and natural marvels. As the road was blazed stage by stage into the interior, it became a pathway for explorers, hunters, missionaries, traders, prospectors and farmers. Fortune-seekers poured by the thousands up the trail to reach the gold and diamond areas. Tented wagons, bicycles with sails, stylish and outlandish carts, rickety old motor vehicles, footsloggers and hitch-hikers, record-breakers, freaks, runaways from law, and escapers from society – all have helped to beat this great road into the ground. Stories rich enough to fill a thousand books have originated along this road and built up to a climax of human comedy or drama whose ending is often lost in mystery.

From its start at the foot of the Heerengracht the road keeps below the concrete Eastern Boulevard. It follows the fence of the Cape Town docks for 1,5 km, keeping to the verge of Table Bay. The bulk of Table Mountain is on the right – the great beacon heralding the south-western end of Africa – and also the beginning of the route into the interior.

After 1,5 km, where there is a branch left to Milnerton, the shores of Table Bay swing northwestwards. The road says goodbye to the sea until, after over 7 000 km, it will reach the shores of the Mediterranean. It continues north-eastwards. Passing at 7 km the clover-leaf Koeberg road interchange which takes traffic off to Muizenberg and Milnerton, it continues along the verges of the Ysterplaat air station, where fledgling helicopter pilots train in their odd insect-like machines.

On the right is the housing estate of Kensington; on the left in the near distance are the refineries and the chemical works of Caltex and Fisons. After 14 km, at a traffic interchange, the N7 road to Namaqualand and Namibia turns off. Modern housing estates crowd close to the verges.

For 7 km the road climbs around the slopes of the Tygerberg providing the traveller with spectacular views of the great housing developments of the Cape Flats and the city of Cape Town – a particularly magnificent spectacle at the end of each day when the lights are coming on and Table Mountain is silhouetted in the fiery glow of sunset.

At 19 km from Cape Town the road reaches the turn-off to Parow and at 24 km the turn-off to Bellville. Housing developments abound. Each dwelling seems so close to its neighbour that the borrowing of foodstuffs and utility items may be made by means of outstretched arms through windows. The entire area is, in fact, a congested light home industrial site, specialising in the production of babies and with little of beauty save the view of Table Mountain.

In the beginning this area was the sandy bed of a shallow sea separating the mountainous Cape Peninsula from the high ground of the interior. The sea receded and left mankind with what seemed an insurmountable problem. The former sea bed, known as the Cape Flats, had been left as a sandy, windblown wilderness, poorly drained, with little vegetation and soil lacking in the essential mulch and compost of vegetative matter which gives fertility.

Even roads across the flats were a problem. Sand blew over them as quickly as they were made. Wagons could sink up to their axles in areas which were nearly quick sands. So what could be done with such a wasteland? The solution was found in 1845 by John Montagu, Secretary to the Cape Government. He imported a variety of exceptionally hardy, sand-loving shrubs from Australia, including the wattle, Port Jackson and hakea. These were planted on the Cape Flats along with Hottentot figs. Within an astonishingly short time these shrubs completely overwhelmed the sand. In an area where even grass had never before taken root, the exotic vegetation simply smothered the loose sand in greenery. By binding the sand, the vegetation made the Cape Flats habitable to man. The basic fertility of the sand was revealed once it became firm. With the addition of humus from the exotic shrubs and manure, the sand supported vegetable and flower gardens. Suburbs and townships developed on ground reclaimed by the alien vegetation which, despite its tendency to run riot and become a pest in modern times, has performed an invaluable function.

The Cape Flats provided the built-up Cape Peninsula with generous space for expansion into a level and open area. All cities would regard with delight such a perfect answer to their problems of congestion and expansion. The northern suburbs and most of the satellite towns of Cape Town have been built in this area. Some of these satellite towns are growing at a pace which makes them substantial centres in themselves. It is a pity that, given the available level space, some of these developments do not result in something better than the characterless, ad hoc hotch potches of congested nondescript buildings which abound and pass as smart and modern. Private enterprise has little interest in devising a pleasant, warm environment. Gardens, boulevards and attractive buildings are not as profitable as concrete boxes hemmed in against one another in narrow streets. Public authorities and town planning are usually so ineffectual as to be non-existent. It seems that such authorities confine their activities to discreetly turning their backs on the venality of private developers. Architecture is often judged simply by height, the tallest building being the most admired. For the tourist, therefore, these satellite towns of Cape Town on the Cape Flats are dull and sometimes down right hideous.

The northern suburbs and satellite towns are linked to Cape Town by an electrified railway (the main line to the north) and by turn-offs from N1, or a badly congested highway known as Voortrekker Road. To reach this road from the centre of the city drive, (as for the trip around the Cape Peninsula) up Strand Street from its intersection with Adderley Street. Passing the walls of the Castle, the road continues under the traffic interchange where the Peninsula road turns off. Its name becoming first Newmarket and then Albert Road, the route leads through a congestion of warehouses, dingy shops and run-down residences until, 3,5 km from the start, it reaches a busy traffic circle in the centre of the suburb known as Salt River. A left turn at this circle leads into Voortrekker Road which rises over the railway tracks at Salt River station, continues through a densely built-up area and then, 5 km from the centre of Cape Town, enters the suburb of *Maitland*, named after Sir Peregrine Maitland, Governor of the Cape in the 1840s.

Light industrial and commercial establishments line the road until, on the left, the open space of the Wingfield military aerodrome is reached and, on the right, the seemingly endless wall marking the confines of Cape Town's principal cemetery. It is known as *Woltemade* after Wolraad Woltemade who, in 1773 heroically lost his life while rescuing men from a shipwreck at the mouth of the Salt River.

GOODWOOD

Eleven kilometres along the way the traveller enters the area of Goodwood. It has a population of 314 197, a volatile housing development and a busy cluster of industries. The place was originally a horse-racing track (hence the name, after the English racecourse), but this sporty beginning has long since been forgotten. Today its growth is such that it has suburbs of its own, notably *Vasco* (named after Vasco da Gama, the first Portuguese navigator to reach the East), and *Elsies River* (after Elsie van Suurwaarde, who farmed on the banks of the river in the 1690s).

PAROW

The houses of Goodwood merge with the buildings of the next town, *Parow*, named after Johann Parow, a German sea captain who settled in the area after his ship, the *Kehrwieder*, had been wrecked in Table Bay in 1865. Parow is another busy industrial and commercial area. It has a handsome civic centre, with a carillon of twelve bronze bells which ring daily at 08h00, 12h00 and 16h30. There are extensive housing estates such as *Tiervlei* (leopard swamp), and a huge hospital, the Tygerberg Hospital, which also serves as a teaching hospital for the medical and dental faculties of the University of Stellenbosch. Eighteen kilometres from Cape Town, Parow merges with the buildings of the city of Bellville.

BELLVILLE

Bellville had a rather humble but honest beginning as an outspan place at the 12-milestone point on the road from Cape Town to the interior. The original milestone still stands at the corner of Voortrekker and Durban roads. The original outspan place is now the *Hardekraaltjie* caravan park, so named (hard little corral) because it was situated on firm ground after the haul from Cape Town over the sandy Cape Flats.

When Durbanville was founded in 1836, it was at first named D'Urban in honour of the Governor Sir Benjamin D'Urban. What has now become the major railway centre and goods depot of Bellville started as a siding simply known as D'Urban Road, for it was the nearest station to the town now known as Durbanville.

The name Bellville was given to the place on 18 November 1861 in honour of Charles Bell, Surveyor-General of the Cape and the designer of the famous triangular postage stamps. The town at first grew slowly, only becoming a municipality in 1940, but after that it developed rapidly. It became a city on 7 September 1979. Today it has a population of 264 735 .

Bellville has many substantial buildings and a magnificent civic centre and theatre. The occasionally flowing Elsies River finds a way through the congested city centre and a pleasant park has been created in its valley.

Overlooking the city is the 415 m high *Tygerberg* (leopard mountain) which, in former years, had on its summit a signal cannon. When ships entered Table Bay, this cannon was fired to inform farmers that there was a potential market for fresh produce. Other cannons were placed on vantage-points in the interior. Their gunners, hearing the Bellville signal cannon, would then fire their cannons to relay the message to surrounding farmers.

The summit of Tygerberg is now a nature reserve, 60 ha in extent. It conserves many indigenous plants and a number of small animals. The view of the Cape Flats is spectacular. There are hiking trails. The reserve is reached from a parking area and gate at the end of Totius Street in the fashionable hillside suburb of *Welgemoed* (cheerful), the amiable name of the old farm there whose manor-house, built in 1704, still stands, but is not open to the public. The reserve is open Mondays to Fridays 08h00 to 16h30. Saturdays, Sundays and public holidays 09h00 to 18h00. Phone (021) 913-5695.

DURBANVILLE

Durbanville was originally known by the rather naïve name of *Pampoenkraal* (pumpkin corral). In 1836 it was renamed *D'Urban* after the Governor, Sir Benjamin D'Urban. The name eventually became D'urbanville in order to avoid confusion with D'Urban in Natal. Both places eventually dropped the apostrophe for the sake of simplicity. The nearest railway station was 6 km away and was named D'urban Road, later becoming the Bellville of today.

Durbanville remains a rural town and an attractive residential area for people working in the congested industrial and business areas of Cape Town and the northern suburbs. Its situation is pleasant. It is a centre for good riding country, with panoramic views of the mountains. Horse-races and gymkhanas are periodically held there by the Cape Town Turf Club.

Durbanville became a municipality in 1901. Today it is a town with a modern shopping area, many fine homes, and a few interesting buildings surviving from earlier times. In High Street there is one of the only two surviving windmills in the Cape. Visits are allowed by appointment. Phone (021) 919-4507.

The Dutch Reformed Church in Weyer Avenue was built in 1826 in the classic Cape-Dutch style, complete with ring-wall, cemetery and cypress trees. In Durban Road there is the private *Eversdal* residence built in 1680 and containing many interesting household items from the period of its construction. King's Court in Church Street dates to about 1890. Built in the Victorian style, it has fine cast-iron trellis work and handsome stairs.

Near Durbanville there are beautiful farms, such as *Altydgedacht* (always in the mind), a wine estate dating from 1698. The estate is open for wine sales Mondays to Fridays 09h00 to 17h00 and Saturdays 09h00 to 13h00. The *Bloemendal* (dale of flowers) wine estate is also close to Durbanville and is open for wine sales Mondays to Fridays 09h00 to 17h00 and Saturdays 09h00 to 13h00.

In the town there is an interesting clay museum housed in *Rust-en-Vrede* (rest and peace), the original magistracy built in 1850, now a cultural centre. The museum is open Mondays to Fridays 09h30 to 16h30, Saturdays and Sundays 14h00 to 16h30.

The Durbanville Nature Garden is along Race Course Road. It is a garden of indigenous plants, open daily 08h00 to 16h30.

From Bellville the N1 road divides at a point 21 km from Cape Town. The N1 road swings north-eastwards towards Paarl; the branch passes through Stikland and on to the municipality of Kuilsrivier, 25 km from Cape Town.

KUILSRIVIER

Kuilsrivier (river of pools), with its population of 248 387, was founded in the 17th century as a cattle corral of the Dutch East India Company. Governor Simon van der Stel had camped on its banks at the start of his pioneer exploration of the valley of the Eersterivier in 1679 and ever since then it has been recognised as a staging post on the early road to Stellenbosch. It is marked by a milestone recording fifteen miles from Cape Town. The old milestone is in the entrance hall of the municipal building. From this time on, Kuilsrivier has been a traditional resting-place; and its attractive, shady caravan park is a legacy from the days of the outspan. Today it is a busy little industrial town and the centre of the pioneer school for the care and education of epileptic children. It is an excellent caravan base for visits to the modern Stellenbosch wine route (See Chapter Eight).

The N1 road, from the turn-off to Kuilsrivier, continues its way northwards heading towards Paarl and the mountain ranges. The 1 390 m high bulk of Simonsberg – among the handsomest of Cape mountains – dominates the scene on the right.

Flyover bridges cross the road at junctions to Kraaifontein at 32 km from Cape Town and to Stellenbosch at 40 km. From this turn-off the Tygerberg Zoo is reached. It is open daily from 09h30 to 17h30. Just off the road, 48 km from Cape Town at the little centre of *Klapmuts* (so named from the overlooking hill, the shape of which resembles the Dutch sailor's hat of that name), there is a cluster of garages, wayside cafés and a hotel. Roads to Agter Paarl and Franschhoek (see Chapter Nine) lead off left and right while, 56 km from Cape Town, a major turn-off left takes the traveller into the town of Paarl (see Chapter Nine).

The road now burrows under the main railway line, bridges across the Berg River and, 60 km from Cape Town, after shedding turn-offs to Wellington and Franschhoek, reaches the toll-gate at the beginning of one of the finest scenic mountain passes in Southern Africa ...

DU TOIT'S KLOOF PASS

A French Huguenot by the name of Francois du Toit gave his name to this fine mountain pass. He secured from the Governor, Simon van der Stel, the farm *De Kleyne Bos*, lying at the foot of the Klein Drakenstein Mountains, just below the saddle allowing access to the gorge on the east side of the range which carries the road today.

The need for a road through this gorge was apparent from an early period for it would provide a direct link between the valleys of the Berg and Breede rivers. In 1824 the first attempt at building a pass was made by Detlef Schönfeldt, a former lieutenant in the 45th Würtemburg Hussars. Using £1 527 raised by himself and the public, he made a rough track of little use other than to walkers; wagons crossed it at their peril. Schönfeldt had such faith in the future of the pass, however, that he purchased most of the gorge and planned to finance road construction by means of tolls. He died with his project unfulfilled, but several others became interested in the pass. In 1846 it was surveyed by Colonel Michell and the road inspector, Andrew Geddes Bain. Their estimated cost of £340 000 made construction prohibitive. For nearly 100 years nothing further was done to the pass other than the construction in the 1920s of a private track up the Drakenstein slopes and over the saddle into the gorge, where a Paarl farmer, J le Roux, had a buchu-producing farm.

Finally, in 1935, with the establishment of the National Roads Board, the project of this pass was re-examined. One of the great roadmakers of South Africa, P A de Villiers, was then an engineer of the board and he surveyed the route. His report, made in 1940, estimated construction costs of £260 000. Building commenced in 1943 with 500 Italian prisoners of war as labourers. The 40 km long pass climbed to 820 m above sea-level and traversed a 223 m long tunnel through Kleigat. It was opened on 26 March 1949. The final cost of construction was £750 000.

The summit of this pass is reached 77 km from Cape Town. Here many travellers pause awhile for their last look (or a first if they are coming down from the north) at Table Mountain in the distance across the valley of the Berg River. The towns of Paarl and Wellington lie directly below. This is a superb view and viewpoint. The mountain slopes are rich in wild flowers. From the summit of the pass a footpath and also a private road on the left (north) side leads to a telecommunications tower and to the beautiful *Krom* (crooked) River with its swimming-pools and Mountain Club hut, the base for many fine climbs and walks up the surrounding high peaks.

In the 5 km from the head of the pass down to the tunnel, the traveller is treated to spectacular views of the great bulk of the 1 655 m high Du Toit's Kloof peak. In winter when the peaks are covered in snow, many beautiful waterfalls grace the left (north) side of the pass. Wild flowers are sold at a farm just before the tunnel entrance.

Beyond the tunnel – a favourite rendezvous for baboons – the road bridges the Elandspad River, up whose valley there are fine walks and famous trout-fishing pools. The Mountain Club of South Africa has a hut at the top of this valley. The entire area of the pass offers wonderful recreation for climbers, hikers and fishermen.

In March 1988 an alternative route through the Klein Drakenstein Mountains was opened. A tunnel, known as the Huguenot Tunnel, 3 913 m long, was opened. This tunnel burrows underneath the Klein Drakenstein Mountains and emerges on the east side to rejoin the original road at the crossing of the Elandspad River. P A de Villiers, the man responsible for the 1949 pass, was again involved in the basic planning of the new pass. He had by then retired from Government service, but assisted the South African firm of Van Niekerk, Kleyn and Edwards and the Swiss firm of Electrowatt Engineering Services in feasibility study and design. The tunnel shortens the journey by 11 km. The road continue down the valley of the *Molenaars* (miller's) River, a favourite water for trout fishing. The total cost of construction, including a viaduct on the western approach over the Hugo's River, the largest curved structure in South Africa (536 m long and 16 m wide), was R198 278 900, the most expensive 10 km of road built in Southern Africa up to that time.

At the 74 km point from Cape Town (via the tunnel) or 85 km via the old pass, the road passes a hotel, garage and wayside fruit stall. For 9 km beyond the hotel the road descends through the valley of the Molenaars River, overlooked on both sides by towering cliffs and peaks. At 83 km from Cape Town the road crosses this mountain river and emerges from Du Toit's Kloof Pass into the broad, alluvial and stony valley of the Breede River. Ahead (north and north-east) lies the handsome sandstone range of the Hex River Mountains with the Mostert's Hoek Twins on the left and the *Brandwag* (sentry) Mountain (1 809 m) straight ahead.

The valley of the Breede River (see Chapter Ten) is one of the principal grape and deciduous fruit farming valleys of the Western Cape. The road passes through neat vineyards where some of the sweetest grapes in Southern Africa (notably hanepoot) are grown. During the season, January to April, grapes and other fruits, nuts and jams are sold at several farm stalls by the wayside. After 8 km of vineyards a crossroad leads right to the small village of Rawsonville and left to the Goudini Spa holiday resort (see Chapter Ten).

On the far side of the valley of the Breede River, 24 km from the exit of Du Toit's Kloof Pass and 107 km from Cape Town, a turn-off left goes to Wolseley and, shortly ahead, a turn-off right enters the principal centre of the valley, the town of Worcester (see Chapter Ten).

The N1 highway to the north passes at 113 km from Cape Town a crossroad, the right turn leading into Worcester and the left turn to the beautiful Karoo Botanical Gardens. Three kilometres further on stand the wine cellars at De Wet. The road crosses the Hex River and enters the lower end of the famous Hex River Mountain Pass, where the Hex River finds a narrow passage between the Kwadouw and the Hex River Mountain ranges. The passage was so tortuous that the pioneer wagon track was forced to ford the river nine times and from this the river was first named the *Ekse* (criss-cross). The name later became corrupted to *Hexe* and then to Hex.

Just before the road crosses the railway there is a fruit kiosk on *Glen Heatlie* farm, which is noted for its grapes.

The story of the Hex River valley is told in Chapter Ten. The great north road (N1) traverses the full length of this valley and it is a spectacular journey with snow-covered mountains in winter, superb greenery of cultivated vineyards in spring and summer, and one of the world's most exciting botanical spectacles in autumn (about June) when the leaves of the barlinka grape vines turn blood red in colour.

At 139 km from Cape Town, N1 passes the turn-off to De Doorns, the principal centre of the valley. Keeping close company with the main railway to the north, the road approaches the head of the valley. The highest mountain of the Hex River range, the 2 249 m high *Matroosberg* (named after Klaas Matroos, a shepherd who once lived there), dominates the whole valley.

There are fruit stalls and irrigation dams on either side of the road. One great vineyard succeeds the other. At the head of the valley the road commences a serpentine climb up the escarpment edge of the central South African plateau and reaches the summit 965 m above sea-level at a point 162 km from Cape Town. At this point it is nice to pause awhile and look back down the valley. The whole of the journey along a finely engineered road has provided travellers with an unforgettable experience in the sheer joy and excitement of a beautiful landscape of mountains, valleys and farmlands.

On the summit of the climb the traveller now has his back to the sandstone world of the Western Cape. Ahead lies an entire new world in the form of the high-lying Karoo Sequence of sediments which cover the great bulk of the interior of South Africa, arid in the south, well watered in the north.

THE HEX RIVER VALLEY RAILWAY PASS

The road pass provides a dramatic transition from the low-lying Western Cape to the high central plains, but it is the railway pass which is even more sensational. It is, in fact, the most famous railway pass in Africa. The original pass was built between 1874 and 1876 at a cost of £500 000. The location engineer, Wells Hood, who surveyed the route of the line, did a magnificent job given the limitations of technical resources in those early days of railroad construction.

From the road coming up the valley, the route of this original pass can be seen clearly. From De Doorns, 477 m above sea-level, the railway, in 25 km, climbed to Matroosberg station at 959 m above sea-level. The ruling gradient of the pass was 1-in-40 uncompensated at curves. If put together, all the curves in the pass would take a train through sixteen complete circuits. There was one tunnel 180 m long. For passengers, the pass was a great scenic thrill but for the trains it was a serious handicap and bottle-neck on the route to the north. The ruling gradient on the line from Cape Town was 1-in-66. To climb the pass, all trains had to be double-banked; that is, at least one other locomotive had to be attached to the train (usually pushing from the rear) from De Doorns up the pass. Speed was slowed and loads were restricted.

Nevertheless, the original Hex River Pass carried all traffic between Cape Town and the north for 113 years. In all that time it had a fine record for safety. All manner of specialised railwaymen played a part in keeping the pass in operation; gangers, patrolmen, men who recharged the nine automatic greasers which lubricated the flanges of the wheels of passing trains at intervals along the pass, men who greased the sides of the rails at curves to ease friction, signalmen, wheel tappers, drivers and many others.

Only one serious accident ever occurred on the pass. On 10 September 1914, at 18h00, a troop train conveying 500 men of the Kaffrarian Rifles was derailed on the way down the pass. The coaches rolled over the side at a point marked by a monument, midway between the stations of Tunnel and Matroosberg. By a miracle only 10 men were killed and 40 injured.

During the Second World War it was realised that the old pass would have to be replaced. In 1943 money was granted to ease the grades to 1-in-40 compensated and the curves improved from the original minimum radius of 100 m to an easier 200 m. This made things a little easier for the trains but was still not good enough for modern transport needs.

In November 1945 the railway engineer, W H Evans, suggested an entirely new location for the line which would provide a grade of 1-in-66 compensated and a minimum curve radius of 800 m. Four tunnels would have to be made; two of 0,8 km each, one of 2,4 km and one of 13,5 km. There would be a saving of 8 km in distance, the elimination of 5 200 degrees of curvature and 110 m of false rise in level. All this would add up to the ending of the bottle-neck. Train running time could be reduced by 23 minutes going up the pass and 36 minutes down to Cape Town. Heavier loads could be carried and there would be a considerable decrease in running costs.

The scheme was approved, construction equipment ordered, and work started on the tunnels in 1948. In April 1950 the whole project was halted in view of current economic constraints. By that time 1 170 m of tunnel had been excavated. Instead of proceeding with the new pass, the old pass was electrified and continued to carry the increasingly long and heavier trains.

Between 1974 and 1976 the lower section of the line between De Doorns and Orchard stations was improved, including the first tunnel. Then, at last, in 1979, the decision was made to proceed with the entire new pass, this time elaborated with a crossing loop in the main tunnel. This would improve the carrying capacity of the pass each day to 42 trains instead of 31 trains along the single-line track.

The whole project was a considerable exercise in engineering. The contract for the main Tunnel No 4 (13,5 km long) was awarded to Comiat in 1980. The contracts for Tunnel No 2 (1,1 km) and Tunnel No 3 (1,2 km) were awarded to Cementation in 1985. On the west side, the main tunnel enters directly into a nearly vertical mountain face. On the east side the tunnel emerges into a 600 m long, 16 m deep cutting. The crossing point is in the middle of the tunnel. The grade is 1-in-66 except in the crossing loop section where it is 1-in-200. The pass is electrified throughout. The total cost was R130,52 million. It was opened on 27 November 1989.

From the summit of the Hex River road pass (162 km from Cape Town) the N1 road passes a turn right to Montagu and a turn left to Ceres. Over rolling and increasingly arid country the road continues until (183 km from Cape Town) it reaches the town of ...

TOUWS RIVER

On 7 November 1877 a station named Montagu Road was opened on the newly built railway from Cape Town. On 1 January 1893 its name was changed to *Touws River* (river of the pass). Touws River is a major staging post on the way to the north – a junction for the now abandoned branch line to Ladismith – and was a great coaling depot, until the line was electrified on 14 May 1954. An open-air steam museum preserves a magnificent Class 23 locomotive.

There is a 2 700 ha nature reserve conserving wild flowers, birds and mammals, including the rare black variety of springbok. Bushman paintings may be seen in Pienaarskloof. In 1990 warm underground mineral springs were discovered but have still to be developed.

Sheep, wheat, lucerne and barley are produced in the district. Touws River became a municipality on 1 January 1962 and is now inhabited by 6 323 people.

The N1 road leads from Touws River in an easterly direction, passing through a complex of semi-arid hills and valleys of tillite and shale. It is a curious landscape and, as the road passes *Tweedside* (32 km from Touws River), with its wrought-iron gates and rows of gum-trees, the military graveyard 11 km further on, and (239 km from Cape Town) the turn-off right to Matjiesfontein, one can sense an unusual story about the area ...

MATJIESFONTEIN

Matjiesfontein (the fountain of mat-rushes) is the 'capital' of this area. It is worth turning off the main road at least for an inspection. The story began when a Scot, James Douglas Logan, destined to be known as the 'Laird of Matjiesfontein' was on his way to Australia in 1877 at the age of 20. Instead of continuing on his journey, he left the ship at Simon's Town on the Cape Peninsula. In somewhat straitened circumstances, Logan became a porter on Cape Town railway station. From this position he literally worked his way up the line to become District Superintendent of the Touws River–Prince Albert Road section of the railway.

He took a liking to the wild landscape of that part of the world. It suited his health and he felt he could make his fortune there. He resigned from the railway and opened a hotel in Touws River where his name is still retained by the Loganda Hotel. Matjiesfontein, however, was the place which appealed to him most. Little was there other than a few rough buildings and the surrounding wilderness, but he saw hidden virtues. He paid £400 for a 2 998 ha farm which he named *Tweedside* and built a homestead, bought handsome wrought-iron gates, and planted thousands of hardy eucalyptus trees. Gradually he bought up neighbouring properties until he owned 51 390 ha of ground. Logan sank innumerable boreholes, planted huge orchards of fruit trees, built a handsome shooting lodge and made *Tweedside* one of the model farms of Southern Africa. At the same time he developed Matjiesfontein. He imported real London lamp-posts and built a large windmill to crush wheat and used its power to generate electricity – his house was the first private residence in South Africa with electric lighting. He also pioneered waterborne sewerage and piped water to Matjiesfontein from a 50 000 litre a day spring on his farm. He made money by selling the water to the railway. A steam train consumed 250 000 litres of water on the journey across the arid Karoo from Touws River to De Aar, and any dependable supply on the wayside was invaluable. The thirst of the locomotives was only curbed in modern times, first by condenser tenders which reconverted steam into water, and later by electrification.

Logan suffered from a weak chest. His liking for his adopted home was connected with the beneficial effects of its dry, crisp air on his health. He set out to develop Matjiesfontein as an international health resort. His success was astonishing. He built a substantial hotel, complete with fountains playing in the bright sunlight. Lady Sprigg, wife of the Cape Prime Minister, opened the place by turning on the fountains and thereafter it became a resort of the élite. Aristocrats came by sea all the way from Europe to enjoy the life-giving air of Matjiesfontein. Lord Randolph Churchill, the Duke of Hamilton, the Sultan of Zanzibar, Cecil Rhodes and many other notables visited the place.

A keen sportsman, Logan twice brought out Lord Hawke's cricket team which actually played in Matjiesfontein. When the health of George Lohmann, the great English cricketer, broke down, Logan prolonged his life for many years by employing him in the warm sunshine and keen air of Matjiesfontein. Lohmann died in Matjiesfontein on 1 December 1901 and was buried in the cemetery at Monument, beneath a tombstone which records him as one of the cricketing greats of all times.

On Matjiesfontein railway station Logan maintained a magnificent dining-room for the refreshment of railway passengers (there were no dining-cars in those days). He also opened a mineral water factory at Matjiesfontein, managed a chain of restaurants on other railway stations and entered the Cape Parliament as Progressive member of the Legislative Assembly for Worcester. His home remained at the elegant *Tweedside Lodge* built at Matjiesfontein. Among his other activities, he was an expert amateur magician.

With the outbreak of the Anglo-Boer War, Matjiesfontein became the headquarters of the Cape Command and many of the crack British regiments of the day came there, among them the Coldstream Guards and the 17th Lancers. Other visitors were men such as Douglas Haig and Edgar Wallace, both of whom later became famous.

The Matjiesfontein hotel was used as a military hospital and its turret became a look-out post. The hotel still stands in its original state and London lamp-posts still light the main street. Logan died in Matjiesfontein on 30 July 1920. His son, James, continued to run his father's interests. A keen botanist, he made a study of the rich flora in the area between Matjiesfontein and Sutherland. The mounted collection of game animals' heads in the hotel was also acquired by young Logan, who lived in *Tweedside Lodge*, planting succulents in the garden and becoming almost as well known in his way as his father. He died at Matjiesfontein in 1960. His sister had married Colonel Buist and they continued to reside at *Tweedside Lodge*. Their son, Major John Buist, eventually succeeded to the management of the extensive family interests in the area. In 1969 Major Buist sold the village of Matjiesfontein, together with the Lord Milner hotel, to David Rawdon.

The new owner was a highly accomplished hotelier. He set out to restore Matjiesfontien to its former Victorian glory. The village was opened in mid-1970, a unique resort offering a museum, a fine hotel with a superlative menu, a traditional *losieshuis* (boarding house), and swimming, riding, shooting and relaxation in the pure air of the Karoo. *Tweedside Lodge*, with its twelve rooms and thirteen cellars, is a wonderfully atmospheric museum piece, depicting a remarkable family life-style. The village is an entertaining, worthwhile and tasteful restoration. It would be apt if the railways would restore the original dining-room in the station building, where the staff, with commendable enthusiasm, started a railway museum on their own.

Fittingly, Matjiesfontein is reported to be one of the most richly haunted areas in Southern Africa. The ghosts of the hotel are all jovial; they can afford to be, since they do not have to pay the hotel bills. The click of billiards and cues is heard when there is nobody in the billiards room; glasses clink and laughter and whispered conversation linger in empty rooms. A great number of people from all walks of life passed through the place; convalescents wounded during the Anglo-Boer War, chest sufferers, unusual visitors from overseas, soldiers and sailors. Such was the hospitality of Matjiesfontein that many felt welcome to return – albeit discreetly after they died.

The Logan family entertained living visitors so frequently that they were always tolerant of unseen residents. The family has a delightful story of one invisible resident who caused no trouble except that he (or she) could not open doors and would rattle doorknobs until a member of the family obliged by opening the door. Although the ghost appeared to be well mannered, it was also rather touchy ...

On one occasion, after Jennifer Buist's marriage, she was busy packing presents when there was a great rattling at the door. For a while she was too engrossed in her packing to oblige the ghost. The rattling mounted to an impatient crescendo. Rather crossly, she flung open the door, saying 'Oh come on in if you must, but don't make such a damn noise about it'. A puff of cold air rushed past her, rattled its way irritably through the window – and was never heard of or felt again!

Jean du Plooy, the housekeeper, related another story of touchy ghosts in Matjiesfontein. She was alone in the hotel while it was being refitted. The night after the workmen had finished laying new wall-to-wall carpets, Jean was awakened by a ringing at the door. She clambered out of bed and went downstairs, expecting to have to turn away some would-be guests. She opened the door and was confronted by five rather peculiar travellers – all she could see of them was their upper bodies! In her astonishment, she blurted out the thought most in her mind: 'For God's sake, don't make a mess of the new carpets!' The ghosts stared at her blankly, looked down at their invisible feet, and vanished ...

James Douglas Logan, the founder of Matjiesfontein, is buried in a little graveyard at Monument, next to the Cape-to-Cairo road, 10 km before it reaches the turn-off to the hotel and railway station. Born in Reston in Scotland on 26 November 1857, he died at Matjiesfontein on 30 July 1920. His wife, Emma, died on 29 March 1938 and is buried close to him, as is their son, James, who was born in 1880 and died in 1960. He was known during his lifetime as 'Daddy Jim'.

Also in this atmospheric cemetery is the grave of George Alfred Lohmann, the great cricketer, born on 2 June 1865 and who died on 1 December 1901. There is the grave with a monument to Major-General Andrew Wauchope, born in Scotland on 5 July 1846 and killed in action at the Battle of Magersfontein on 11 December 1899. Several other graves lie in the cemetery, some nameless, others recording names of soldiers and visitors who died at Matjiesfontein. There is also a celebrated ghost, a British soldier in the uniform worn during the Anglo-Boer War. His arm is in a sling and he has a bloodied bandage around his head. It has been reported that he is often seen standing beside the N1 road at the turn-off to the cemetery. Motorists stop, thinking that there has been an accident and that he needs help, or a lift, but he vanishes instantly. It is uncanny how often he has been clearly described by people of widely different origin who know nothing of Matjiesfontein and its band of ghosts.

The N1 road continues for 28 km and then (267 km from Cape Town) enters the town of ...

LAINGSBURG

This town stands on part of a 10 278 ha farm known as *Vischkuil-aan-de-Buffelsrivier* (fish pool of the Buffalo River). The farm was bought for £800 by Stephanus Greeft, who planned to develop a township there. By 1879, however, this project had fared so poorly that only a single residence existed in the place. Then the railway came and a cluster of corrugated iron shacks was erected there around a siding named Buffelsrivier. The name conflicted with that of the Buffalo River at East London, so was changed first to *Nassau*, and then to *Laingsburg* in honour of John Laing, the Commissioner of Crown Lands in the Cape. The town was properly laid out in 1881 and became a municipality in 1904. Today 3 656 people live there.

Laingsburg lies more or less on the junction point of the winter rainfall (west) and summer rainfall (east) areas. Its own rainfall is negligible – about 50 mm a year. Despite this, goats and sheep flourish, and wheat, lucerne and fruit are grown along the Buffels River. Between 1953 and 1956 an irrigation dam with a wall 28 m high was built in the river at Floriskraal, 24 km south of Laingsburg, and supplies water for considerable farming activity.

A typical little town of the Great Karoo, Laingsburg had a unique Victorian atmosphere easy to sense if one took a stroll down its side streets at sunset. The architecture was quaint and some of the houses were embellished with involved wrought-iron work. Windpumps drew water from the depths of the seemingly dry river course and gardens were spectacular. Quinces, figs, pomegranates, grapes, and many colourful creepers and flowering shrubs flourished in the soil and climate. There were odd little corner shops and *losieshuisen* (lodging-houses), the latter invariably draped with some character lolling on the veranda regarding strangers with an open stare, while his old woman peeped out through a window.

The skies are generally aflame at dusk; there are no more spectacular sunsets to be seen in the world. Strangely shaped hills loom close by; long trains incessantly come and go; car headlights move over the deep spaces of the Karoo and drivers stop in Laingsburg for fuel and refreshment.

The little town – an oasis in the wilderness – always seemed to be part of a bygone world where, at sunset, travellers could step back 50 years by simply wandering off the main street. However, tragedy struck in 1981 when the Buffels River came down in flood and swept most of Laingsburg away. The town is being rehabilitated, but unfortunately the modern buildings hardly compare to the glorious old homes washed away by the flood.

From Laingsburg the N1 road climbs over the hills. At 14 km east of the town the road bridges over the Geelbeks River. A well-preserved example of an Anglo-Boer War blockhouse stands guard on the right bank of the river. Twenty-seven kilometres further on, the road passes Koup station, where the Regional Services Council created a caravan, camping and resting-place with water, shade and toilets. Across the railway line, 4,5 km on, the road enters as 'howling' a stretch of wilderness as any would-be recluse could desire. If 10 mm of rain a year falls on this area the few inhabitants consider themselves well served. To the eye the scene has an eerie fascination, especially in the long shadows and colours of sunset. The mountain wall of the Swartberge acts as a great barrier in the south, preventing rain-clouds from penetrating to this parched rock-strewn wilderness which seems to undulate gently, like the petrified surface of an ancient lunar sea.

THE KAROO

The African name *Karoo* (a thirstland) describes perfectly this area of minimal rainfall, scanty soil, coarse surface rubble, and numerous outcrops of rock concealed by little vegetation other than clumps of the hardy renosterbos.

This landscape is part of what is known to geologists as the Karoo Sequence which occupies fully one-half of the entire area of Southern Africa. It consists of an enormous, high-lying, shallow basin, arid in the south, but where it forms the highveld of the well-watered Free State, North-West and Northern provinces, it is covered with grass. The Karoo Sequence is a sedimentary series of shales and sandstones laid down on a base of glacial tillite and, in parts, with a roof of basaltic lava. The Karoo and its extraordinary landscape is described in Chapter Fifteen. To many travellers the landscape is boring and seemingly interminable, especially during the hot hours of the day. However, many interesting scenes and surprising places are hidden away in odd corners.

Provided some rain has fallen, spring (September to October) sees even the most arid areas of the Karoo transformed into a garden with a multitude of flowers carpeting the ground and the smell of pollen heavy on the warm air. Particularly striking are the glowing, iridescent mesembryanthemums (*vygies*) with their masses of mauve, magenta, pink and white flowers.

Eighty six kilometres from Laingsburg, the N1 road reaches the railway station of Prince Albert Road, with a cluster of buildings, hotel and garage. From here a tarmac road branches off east for 42 km to the town of ...

PRINCE ALBERT

This picturesque little Karoo municipality has a population of 4 837. It lies at the entrance to the spectacular Swartberg Pass. It was founded in 1842 as a church centre on the farm *Kweekvallei,* and on 31 July 1845 named *Prince Albert* in honour of the British Prince Consort. Watered by perennial mountain streams, it is famous for its fruit, especially peaches in January and grapes in March. One of the last working water-mills in Southern Africa may be seen grinding corn in the town.

In the hotel there are four extraordinary paintings of unknown origin. Two of the paintings, oils in sumptuous gilt frames, depict a romantic woodland scene with a lady, elegant in Victorian dress, standing next to a pool. All is peaceful in the one painting. But in the companion painting she is looking down into the pool and the surface is stained with blood. The legend is that the lady did her husband in. His body lies in the pool. It is said that the blood stain varies on different days and so does the expression on her face.

The other two oil paintings are coldly bleak pictures of a snowy landscape with broken trees. They are said to depict scenes of Delville Wood. There are figures in the paintings. They are said to change their position on different days. Some disappear. Others reappear.

They are known as the haunted paintings.

Beyond Price Albert Road N1 continues its journey north-eastwards across the Great Karoo. After 25 km, water and shade can be found at the national road camp at Palmiet siding. At 48 km the road reaches the small railway centre of ...

LEEU-GAMKA

An unlovely modern name combines the Afrikaans and the African word for 'lion'. Once called Fraserburg Road, this little place consists of a cluster of commercial buildings standing at the junction of the road to the isolated town of Fraserburg, 115 km away.

Past Leeu-Gamka the road (N1) continues across the Great Karoo. The Nuweveld Mountain massif dominates the northern horizon. After 77 km, the road passes a turn-off right to Oudtshoorn, and then (left) a turn-off to the Karoo National Park. The road (N1) then bridges over the railway and (479 km from Cape Town) reaches the principal town in this part of the Great Karoo ...

BEAUFORT WEST

Travellers like to style this town the 'oasis in the Karoo'. Although local rainfall only averages 200 mm a year, this figure is far higher than the rainfall in much of the surrounding country. In addition, the situation of Beaufort West – below the southern heights of the Nuweveld range – provides it with a dependable supply of fresh mountain water. The town is built on the banks of the *Gamka* (lion) River which, although usually dry, occasionally floods its banks. In 1877 it completely overflowed the town.

In the second half of the 18th century, farmers first started to penetrate the Karoo, settling in what was known as the *Nuweveld* (new veld) and the *Koup* (or *Gouph*), a African name which means 'a level plain'. Scarcity of surface water confined the human population to areas with springs, and the relatively well-watered site of the present town was once the haunt of nomadic African people. Bushmen paintings of horses, ostriches and game animal can be seen in rock shelters at places such as Grootplaat on the town commonage. With the advent of Europeans, the site of Beaufort West became a farm, *Hooivlakte in de Carro* (hay flats in the Karoo). Its owner, Abraham de Klerk, the local *field-cornet* (district commandant), nurtured a farm which became known for the quality of its stock and produce, sheep, cattle, horses, corn, barley and fruit – and for its hospitality.

More settlers arrived in the area, especially after the ill-fated Slagtersnek Rebellion, when a number of the men implicated were banished to the Karoo. On 27 November 1818 the district was proclaimed. The farms *Hooivlakte in de Carro* and the adjacent *Boesjemansberg*, destined to be the site of a proposed town, were bought for £1 025. The new district and town were named *Beaufort* as the Governor of the Cape, Charles Somerset, was the son of the Duke of Beaufort. The *West* was added later in order to distinguish the place from Fort Beaufort and Port Beaufort in other parts of the Cape.

The town was laid out in 1820 and the first erven were sold in March of the following year. The Government offices were the pivot of the growing town. The first landdrost, J Baird, made furrows which still channel water along the sides of the streets. He also planted pear trees which still shade the streets today, a pleasing feature of the town.

In 1836 Beaufort West became a municipality, the first in the Cape under a new ordinance permitting the formation of elective municipal councils. The town hall was the first in the Karoo. It was designed by James Bisset in 1864 and opened in 1866. It is now a national monument.

Great changes took place in the area. Arthur Kinnear introduced the first merino wool sheep. The drought of 1849 precipitated the disappearance of the huge herds of plains game, killing off countless thousands of animals which once grazed in the area. A description of this event, recorded by Sir John Fraser, son of Reverend Colin Fraser, the Beaufort West pastor, is worth quoting:

'One day a travelling smous (pedlar) came to Beaufort West and brought the tidings that thousands of trekbokken (migrating antelope) were coming from the north, devouring everything before them. About a week after the smous had left Beaufort West, we were awakened one morning by a sound as of a strong wind before a thunderstorm, following by the trampling of thousands of all kinds of game – wildebeest, blesboks, springboks, quaggas, elands, antelope of all kinds – which filled the streets and gardens and, as far as one could see, covered the whole country, grazing off everything eatable before them, drinking up the waters in the furrows, fountains and dams wherever they could get at them; and, as the poor creatures were all in a more or less impoverished condition, the people killed them in numbers in their gardens. It took about three days before the whole of the trekbokken had passed, and it left our country as if a fire had raged over it. It was indeed a wonderful sight.'

The passing of game animals marked in a tragic way the end of old times in that part of the Karoo. Huge flocks of merino sheep replaced the game and Beaufort West developed as a commercial centre. The first bank in the town was floated in 1854 by John Charles Molteno (later first Prime Minister of the Cape). A newspaper, *The Courier*, was founded in 1869. The railway from Cape Town reached Beaufort West in 1880 and it became a major locomotive depot and marshalling yard on the way to the north. A great dam with a retaining wall 63 m high was built in 1955 in the Gamka River high up in the Nuweveld Mountains and provides copious water. Beaufort West is now a bustling centre with a population of 28 607. It offers the traveller along the Cape-to-Cairo road a variety of accommodation, garages, restaurants and other amenities. There is a modern airport. The Dutch Reformed church with its 46 m high tower is a notable landmark. A museum in the town is open Mondays to Fridays from 08h30 to 12h45; 13h45 to 16h45; Saturdays 09h00 to 12h00. A section of the museum is dedicated to the life and work of the renowned heart surgeon, Professor Christiaan Barnard, who was born in the town in 1922.

THE KAROO NATIONAL PARK

Notwithstanding the modern aridity of the area, the Karoo has had an extraordinary geological history. Between 250 and 125 million years ago it was a vast swamp supporting a forest inhabited by a considerable variety of creatures now mostly extinct. This was the age of the *dinosaurs* (terrible lizards) and the dried-out sediments of the Karoo provided a graveyard for one of the world's richest deposits of fossilised skeletons. The terrible lizards were succeeded by prodigious herds of plains game, especially such animals as springbok, *gnus* (black wildebeest), red hartebeest, kwagga, blesbok and eland. They flourished best when the Karoo was in a transitionary stage, with a little more surface water than it has today. Their numbers were depleted by increasingly frequent dry spells and the blood-lust of hunters who, like fishermen, deluded that numbers were inexhaustible, simply killed for sport or for meat and leather. The vast free-range grazing areas required by the herds of antelope also became restricted as more white settlers entered the Karoo and were allocated huge sheep-runs by the Government. These runs were fenced in with barbed wire and the sheep artificially watered from windpumps. The wild animals, precisely at the time when they needed still larger grazing areas to compensate for the dwindling vegetation, found themselves increasingly restricted and destined for extinction. Nobody at that time had the slightest comprehension that the wild creatures were one of South Africa's most valuable assets. They were simply regarded as vermin and ruthlessly, mindlessly wasted.

It was only in the middle of this century that some people became aware of the total irresponsibility of an uncaring Government and private enterprise in their treatment of the environment. At first dismissed as a crowd of cranks, these people started to agitate that something be done before it was too late. The wilderness areas of South Africa were dwindling at such a rate that they were already far below the minimum extent of ten per cent of the total land area of any country which should be conserved as watersheds, nature sanctuaries and areas of recreation.

In Beaufort West a number of people, notably William Quinton, a farmer and bird lover, started a movement to secure the establishment of a conservation area. The municipality proved receptive to the idea. The National Parks Board and the South African Nature Foundation were supportive. The Beaufort West municipality donated 7 209 ha of the town's commonage as the nucleus for a national park.

Funds were raised by the Nature Foundation and private bodies. On 7 September 1979 the Karoo National Park was proclaimed. It consisted of the area donated by the Beaufort West municipality and two farms *Stolshoek* and *Buttersvlei*. It now covers a total of 32 792 ha, with the ultimate dream (as money becomes available) of expanding the conservation area to over 100 000 ha.

The purpose of this national park is essentially to conserve the flora and fauna of the Karoo. The conservation area covers a diversity of altitudes from the low-lying Karoo plains to mountain slopes and the high-lying plateau summits. Some 61 species of mammals, 184 species of birds (including 20 breeding pairs of black eagles), many species of reptiles (including 5 different species of tortoises, 37 different lizards and geckos), a diverse collection of insects, and a very fascinating flora, all live in this area. There are opportunities for the discovery of new species.

In December 1988 a rest camp was opened in the park. The camp is connected to N1 by a tarmac road. It has an information centre, swimming-pool, air-conditioned chalets, caravan park, restaurant, curio shop, and conference facilities. Sixty kilometres of roads are being constructed. There is a three-day self-guided hiking trail, the Springbok Trail, with two overnight huts, and a mountain-view rest camp (with simple accommodation) on top of the Nuweveld Mountains. There are several short walks such as the Pointer Trail, and the 400 m Fossil Trail, where fossils can be seen in *situ*. This 400 m trail is suitable for wheelchairs. It reveals the Karoo environment as it was 240 million years ago.

Altogether, this is a very fascinating national park and a delightful place to visit on the way between Cape Town and the north. It is open throughout the year but the hiking trail is closed during the hot period from 1 November to the end of February. The entrance gate on the N1 road is open 05h00 to 22h00. The reception desk is manned from 07h30 to 20h00.

The N1 road continues from Beaufort West in a north-easterly direction, crossing a level plain at the foot of the Nuweveld Mountains. After 40 km the road climbs a spur of the mountains and then reaches a turn-off northwards to the railway station (50 km from Beaufort West) of ...

NELSPOORT

As far back as the 1850s, David Livingstone wrote about the beneficial qualities of the South African climate for all patients suffering from pulmonary complaints. In 1889 Dr E Symes Thompson of the Royal Colonial Institute of London said of the Karoo: *'We find the region characterised by excessive dryness of air and soil, where, at a level of less than 1 000 m above the sea, remarkable purity and coolness of air are secured with an almost complete absence of floating matter; great intensity of light and solar influence; great stillness in winter, a large amount of ozone, and a degree of rarefaction of proved value in cases of phthisis'.*

Many chest sufferers began visiting South Africa. Consumption, or as it is now called, tuberculosis, was a common complaint in the damp, smoggy climate of Europe, but the illness was rife even in sunny South Africa, where living conditions in slums such as District Six in Cape Town were the breeding ground of fearsome diseases.

In 1891 Dr Alfred Anderson became Medical Officer of Health for Cape Town. He was immediately confronted with the disgraceful conditions in slum areas where people were dying of many different diseases, largely deprived of care and medication. The Government and the affluent section of the population simply pretended that the situation did not exit. To make matters worse, during the Anglo-Boer War, plague broke out and much of the slum areas had to be destroyed, with the result that there was increasing congestion in remaining areas.

Tuberculosis became so rampant that Dr Anderson established the Society for the Prevention of Consumption, but he received little Government money or support. Then, in 1911, John Garlick, founder of the merchant house which bore his name and a public-spirited individual, joined Anderson's society. Garlick was appalled at the inroads made by tuberculosis, particularly on the coloured people. He had also recently read Thomas Mann's novel, *The Magic Mountain*, which told of a sanatorium in the Alps where victims of the disease were nursed back to normal life.

In 1918 John Garlick offered Dr Anderson a donation of £25 000 to be used to set up an institution for consumptives. It was estimated that this establishment would require £75 000, and Garlick's generous offer influenced the Cape parliament and the public to give additional support. The total sum collected was £108 000.

A search was made for a suitable site for a sanatorium. The attention of the committee was drawn to a farm near Nelspoort, *Salt River*. The Salt River flowed through a valley in the Nuweveld Mountains and there was ample water for drinking and irrigation, with well-nigh perfect climatic conditions for a sanatorium.

The farm was bought and Dr Peter Allan, a Scottish doctor with experience in pulmonary complaints, was appointed as director. By the end of 1920 the sanatorium had been planned. Several Cape municipalities contributed additional funds and on 24 July the Prince of Wales conducted the official opening of the Nelspoort Farm Sanatorium for Tuberculosis. The first patient had already been admitted on 5 May of the previous year.

The sanatorium was steadily enlarged over the years and additional facilities were provided, such as an X-ray theatre, and new techniques introduced such as pneumo-thorax lung collapsing. In 1947 the British royal family visited the hospital, which then had 460 patients. In 1969 psychiatric patients were admitted and for a while Nelspoort treated both tuberculous and mental cases. Today, however, Nelspoort is entirely devoted to mental patients. Tuberculosis is now more of a socio-economic problem, still breeding in poverty and malnutrition, but treatable by curative drugs in the patient's own home.

Passing the turn-off to the sanatorium, the N1 road continues through the hills for 17 km and is then joined by the loop road leading through Nelspoort. After 19 km (75 km from Beaufort West) the road reaches a major junction at a well-known landmark – the three dolerite-capped hillocks known as the Three Sisters. To the left, the Diamond Way (N12) branches off northwards to Kimberley and the Northern Cape (see Chapter Fourteen). The right turn of the road crosses the railway line and swings in a north-easterly direction around the slopes of the Three Sisters. Twisting and turning around the hillocks of the Karoo, the road makes its way across a landscape which, though essentially arid, can be green and pleasant in a summer of good rains. At each watercourse or fountain stands a cluster of homestead and farm buildings surrounded by willow trees, busy windpumps and sheep corrals. Many are fine modern Karoo farms such as *Skietkuil*, belonging to P van der Merwe and well watered by Gabriel's stream.

At 42 km from Three Sisters, N1 reaches a crossroads with the tarmac R63 coming from Victoria West to the north-west (left) and leading south-east for 43 km to ...

MURRAYSBURG

Murraysburg is a particularly picturesque little town of the Karoo. As always in an arid area, its secret is a reasonably generous supply of water. The *Buffels* (buffalo) River which winds rather unhurriedly across the Karoo and several deep boreholes supply the town which has shady tree-lined streets to keep the place cool, relieve glare and rest the eyes with some green in an otherwise arid landscape.

Murraysburg was founded in 1856 when the Dutch Reformed Church acquired from a Mr Burger his farm *Eenzaamheid*. A town was laid out as a church centre and named in honour of the Reverend Andrew Murray, pastor of Graaff-Reinet, and 'burg' from the first part of the name of Mr Burger.

Wool and water combined to give the town prosperity. On 26 July 1883 it became a municipality, and today has a population of 4 335.

The R63 road from Murraysburg to Graaff-Reinet (98 km to the east) provides an interesting drive across a Karoo landscape ornamented with clumps of trees, following the course of the Buffels River for the first 36 km and passing through the *Oubergpas* near Graaff-Reinet.

At 104 km from Three Sisters the N1 road reaches the typical Karoo town of ...

RICHMOND

This town was founded on 11 October 1843 when the presbytery of Graaff-Reinet formed a new congregation for that region of the Karoo. A portion of the farm *Driefontein* was bought, and erven were sold there on 19 April 1845 during the course of a gathering for *nagmaal* (communion). The town was named after the Duke of Richmond, the father of Lady Sarah Maitland, the wife of the then Governor of the Cape, Sir Peregrine Maitland.

Driefontein farm was well-watered and a great game haunt. The three fountains from which the farm took its name still bubble to life in the Wilgersloot. The banks of the Ongers River, which flows through the town, once provided cover for numerous lions. In this setting Richmond grew slowly, its history marked by lengthy droughts and occasional violent floods. During the Anglo-Boer War it was twice attacked by the Boers and eight little forts were erected by the British on the surrounding hills. Today Richmond is a clean and pleasant Karoo town. Gardens abound with flowers and the streets are shady beneath eucalyptus trees.

From Richmond the N1 road continues north-eastwards across the Karoo plains. Three kilometres from the town at the branch right to Middelburg, there is a shady resting-place with water. At 62 km from Richmond the road reaches the town of ...

HANOVER

Like Richmond, this town was formerly a part of the Graaff-Reinet district and was known simply as *Bo-Zeekoerivier* (upper hippopotamus river). As the farming population of the area grew, a community centre became necessary and in 1854 the 8 656 ha farm *Petrusvallei*, belonging to Gert Gous, was bought for 33 333 rixdollars. The vendor requested that the proposed town be named *Hanover*, as his ancestors had come from that town in Germany.

The site of the town lay at the source of a powerful spring (204 570 litres per day) at the foot of a cluster of hillocks. Thus, well-watered and the centre for a famous merino sheep area (the world record price at the time was paid for a locally bred merino ram), the town grew steadily. Today it has a population of 3 668. Hanover's first magistrate, C R Beere, took up office in October 1876. He laid the streets out around a handsome Dutch Reformed church. He had trees planted and built a footpath to the summit of *Trappieskoppie* (hillock of little steps), from which point there is a commanding view of the town and countryside. A stone pyramid was erected on top of this hillock in memory of Mr Beere and his good works. He died in Hanover on 9 November 1881. Hanover's first minister, the Reverend Thomas Francois Burgers, became the second president of the South African Republic in the Transvaal.

The N1 road continues from Hanover north-eastwards across the Karoo plains which become perceptibly better covered with vegetation as rainfall increases to an average of about 250 mm a year.

At 3 km from Hanover there is a tarmac turn-off to Philipstown and the Vanderkloof Dam (see further on). At 22 km from the town the road crosses the railway line from De Aar to Noupoort; 51 km further on it joins the N9 road coming from George and Port Elizabeth, and then reaches the town of ...

COLESBERG

An important junction on the road to the north, Colesberg is fittingly beaconed by one of the most conspicuous landmarks along the entire length of the southern section of the Cape-to-Cairo road. This is the 1 707 m high, remarkably symmetrical hillock known as *Cole's Kop,* which is discernable from all directions for a deceptively long distance.

Pioneer travellers in the area knew this landmark by several names. *Toringberg* (towering mountain) because it was conspicuous from far away: *Toornberg* (mountain of wrath) and *Tooverberg* (enchanted mountain) because as travellers approached, it seemed to recede further into the distance. At its foot was a marsh which provided water for a host of game animals. In 1814 a mission station was established there by Erasmus Smit in the hope of bringing peace to what was a very unruly frontier area of the Cape Colony. A second mission station, *Hepzibah*, was established a few kilometres away and the two stations soon attracted 1 700 Bushmen, causing great alarm among frontier settlers who felt their security was threatened. In 1818 the Cape Government intervened, putting an end to the mission work.

In 1822 the farmers petitioned for a town to be established in the area and this was granted by Lord Charles Somerset, the Governor. A 15 417 ha extent of ground in the area was presented by the Government to the community, to be administered on their behalf by the local church council. In November 1830 the first erven were sold. The town was named after Sir Lowry Cole, the Cape Governor at the time.

As a frontier town, Colesberg flourished on trade with the interior. Gun-powder and alcohol passed through the place in such quantities that in 1837 a magistrate, Fleetwood Rawstone, was stationed there to impose order in the town. On 19 June 1840 Colesberg was made a municipality. In the face of all the disturbances of frontier life it became the centre of a considerable stock-breeding area for horses, sheep and cattle, which flourish in the crisp air.

Nowadays Colesberg is inhabited by 12 738 people. Though the town is slightly off the main road, it is worth turning aside and driving through the streets which have a distinct atmosphere of a century ago. A rather higgledy-piggledy but attractive jumble of Victorian buildings is built around a cluster of hillocks. The churches in the town are worth inspecting. The fine Dutch Reformed church with its white walls dominates the main street. Christ Church, the Anglican church, contains many notable objects. Its first rector, Dr C Orpen, was a considerable scholar who presented his library, which included many rare books, to form a nucleus for the town's library. His wife was a titled lady. Through the good offices of her family connections, the church was beautifully decorated with a stained-glass east window, a carved oak lectern, an oak pulpit and many other handsome items.

In the museum the original window-pane can be seen with, scratched into it, the letters 'DP', made by the first diamond found in South Africa. John O'Reilly brought this mysterious looking glass-like stone into the town early in 1867. It had been found on the farm *De Kalk* in the Hopetown area (see Chapter Fourteen). In Draper and Plewman's store, he showed the stone to Lorenzo Boyes, the Acting Civil Commissioner of Colesberg. Boyes tested the stone by scratching the initials of the store, DP into a window pane. He then looked at the two letters and declared to the anxious O'Reilly: *'I believe it to be a diamond'*.

There are several Anglo-Boer War battle sites around Colesberg. Many soldiers from both sides are buried in the military cemetery at the north-east end of town. At first the town was held by the Boers. When the British took over they camped in the surrounding hills and dragged two 15 pounders (field guns) up to the top of Coleskop to defend the town. Many of the hills in the district are named after the regiments who held them, e.g. Gibraltar and New Zealand Hill. Skietberg, situated just behind the hospital, is the height where the Boers mounted guns and fired on the British in Coleskop. There is a monument on Suffolk Hill, just outside the town, dedicated to the men of the Suffolk Regiment who died on 6 January 1900 and another, on the farm *Yardley*, dedicated to the men of the Worcestershire Regiment who died on 12 February 1900.

Beyond Colesberg the N1 road continues through the northern limit of the Great Karoo. After 30 km the road reaches the Gariep (Orange) River at Bothasdrif, now spanned by the handsome Serfontein Bridge. Across the river the road enters the Free State. At this point it is interesting to know something about the most important river in South Africa ...

THE GARIEP (ORANGE) RIVER AND ITS DAMS

The source of this great river is more than 3 000 m above sea-level on the mountain plateau of Lesotho just behind the Drakensberg peak known as *Mnweni* (the place of the fingers), or The Rockeries. Its course, 2 250 km long, ends in the Atlantic Ocean at the diamond-mining centres of Alexander Bay and Oranjemund. Named the Orange River on 17 August 1779 in honour of Prince William V of Orange by Captain (later Colonel) Robert Jacob Gordon, who explored its lower reaches, the river was known to the Bushmen as the *Nu Gariep* (great river).

The Gariep (as it is known today), carries 23 per cent of the total water run-off of South Africa to the sea. At flood periods, 11 330 cubic metres of water per second flow down the river. The two principal tributaries of the Gariep – the Vaal and the Caledon – together supply half of the total discharge of the river. The Vaal River has already been thoroughly harnessed by man, but the Gariep and the Caledon are only now starting to play a major role in modern development, irrigating 29 400 ha of dry Karoo land, supplying 455 million litres of potable water per day, and generating 177 000 kW of continuous power from 20 hydro-electric sites.

Heavy rains in the highlands of Lesotho – at least 2 000 mm per year – as well as heavy snowfalls, feed the river prodigious volumes of water. In summer the flow reaches its peak; in winter the river is often reduced to little more than a series of deep pools linked by a trickle of water.

At all times the water of the Gariep is free of the blight of bilharzia. The water freshets of melted snow effectively destroy the snails which carry bilharzia in tropical rivers. Even mosquitoes are no great problem along its course. The abundant fish eat the larvae, and the type of mosquito that breeds there is not a malaria carrier.

Along its middle and lower reaches, the Gariep flows through the most arid country in South Africa. At its mouth the rainfall does not exceed 50 mm a year. The river is the bringer of life to the northern area of the Karoo, Bushmanland and the north-western Cape. As with the Nile, there is a startling contrast between the green islets and banks of the river and the surrounding arid landscape. The shallow river valley has many areas suitable for irrigation. The water and silt carried by the Gariep nourish a variety of crops.

Many people dreamed of taming the great river and using its water for irrigation or the generation of power. The middle Gariep, from Buchuberg to the Augrabies Falls, first attracted serious attention. Private individuals started to pump water from the river to irrigate flat alluvial land on the banks. In 1872 a survey was made of this area but there was no finance for any ambitious schemes. In 1883, however, a 32 km long canal was dug at Upington to provide water for irrigation. This was the beginning of harnessing the Gariep for the service of man.

In 1912 Dr A D Lewis, Director of the Department of Irrigation, rode and walked down the Gariep from near Upington all the way to the sea. His detailed report is the classic study on the river. Harnessing the Gariep became his special dream. In 1928 he first proposed what was then the startling idea of transferring water from the Gariep at a point near Bethulie and leading it through a tunnel 82,8 km long under the divide and then allowing it to flow into the Teebus stream which would carry the water to the Brak River and through it to the Great Fish River valley (a prime area for irrigation) and thence by another tunnel to the Sundays River valley.

The whole concept was staggering in its implications. It would transfer water from the Gariep (flowing westwards to the Atlantic Ocean) to rivers flowing eastwards to the Indian Ocean and stimulate the creation of at least 2 000 new irrigated farms in agricultural areas of great potential value.

The idea was too immense for immediate acceptance, but there was no doubt that eventually something would have to be done. South Africa is essentially a thirsty country. About 65 per cent of it receives less than 500 mm of rain a year. Crops can be grown only if this rainfall is supplemented by irrigation. To complicate the problem, only 9 per cent of the total rainfall reaches the rivers. The balance is evaporated in the dry climate or escapes by penetrating to underground formations. The Gariep River carries 14 per cent of the total run-off in South Africa. Most of this water is evaporated in the long middle and lower reaches of the river, where it flows through desert-like conditions. What remains is poured into the sea.

For sixteen years the dream of A D Lewis remained on paper. Only in 1944 were field surveys and drilling begun. In 1948 a technical report was presented to the Government. It proposed the construction of a gigantic diversionary dam in the Gariep River and a tunnel to carry the water to the Great Fish River valley. A second dam and possibly a third one would be built lower down the river to stop and regulate the flow to irrigated areas as far down as Augrabies.

In 1971 the Hendrik Verwoerd Dam was completed after three years of work and named after the then Prime Minister. This is now the Gariep Dam. It consists of a dam wall 914 m long and 88 m high with a storage capacity of 5 673,8 million cubic metres and covering 360 square kilometres. The dam overflowed for the first time during February 1972.

The tunnel was completed in 1975 and, 82,8 km long and 5,35 m in diameter, it is the second largest water-supply tunnel in the world. Through it, about 25 per cent of the water of the Gariep River is diverted from the *Oviston* (Oranje-Vistonnel) intake tower. At maximum flow it transfers 57 cubic metres of water per second to the Teebus stream and thence to the Grassridge Dam and on to the Great Fish River.

The second dam, originally named in honour of P K le Roux, a former Minister of Water Affairs, but now named the Vanderkloof Dam, was constructed 130 km below the Gariep Dam. This dam has a wall 765 m long and 107 m high, making it the highest dam wall in South Africa. It stores 3 236 million cubic metres of water and feeds the canals of the Vanderkloof irrigation system, with 174 000 ha of land suitable for development under irrigation. The main canal, on the right (north) bank of the river, is the largest in South Africa. It is 14 km long with a capacity of 57 cubic metres of water per second. It feeds the Ramah branch canal which is 81,1 km long. The Vanderkloof canal system is extended into the Gariep River canal, 112 km long, which feeds water into the Riet River settlement near Jacobsdal where 4 540 ha of land is under irrigation and a further 7 400 ha is planned.

In 1966 and 1967 a serious drought emphasised the need to transfer water from the Great Fish River to the Sundays River for use on the citrus farms. To do this, a canal and tunnel scheme carrying 22 cubic metres of water per second was constructed. This system starts with a weir at Elandsdrift near Slagtersnek. From there, an aqueduct 108 km long finds a complex route through the Bosberg range. The 13,1 km long Cookhouse tunnel, completed in 1978, takes the water through the Bosberg. The water is released into the Little Fish River near Somerset East. After 40 km of free flow down the river, the water reaches the De Mistkraal weir. From there it is diverted into the Skoenmakers canal which carries the water to the Sundays River valley, providing water for up to 30 000 ha.

To see the Gariep Dam, take the N1 road out of Colesberg for 39 km to Norvalspont, the site of a pont ferry over the Gariep River established by a Scotsman in 1848 in the days before a bridge was built across the river. The name of the hotel there, the Glasgow Pont hotel, is a reminder of the name of the actual pont which carried thousands of travellers across the river in the early days. Three kilometres away, across the river, is the Gariep Dam Resort.

A road R58 leads from Norvalspont for 4 km to a fine viewsite overlooking the Gariep Dam. During the summer floods, when the river overflows the wall, the scene is awesome. From the viewsite the tarmac road continues along the southern shore of the lake, providing anglers and boat enthusiasts with access to the water. At 36,8 km from the viewsite the road reaches the town of ...

VENTERSTAD

Named after Johannes Venter who owned the farm on which the town was laid out in 1875, this is an agricultural centre and a resort catering for visitors to the Gariep Dam. It became a municipality in 1895 and has a population of 4 142.

The R58 road continues for 34 km from Venterstad and then reaches a junction. The south branch leads to Burgersdorp and Aliwal North. A left turn north takes the road for 15 km to the town of Bethulie. On the way to Bethulie the road bridges across the eastern end of the Gariep Dam. The main railway line from East London to the north also crosses the dam on the same bridge. At 1 152 m, this is the longest rail bridge in South Africa.

THE VANDERKLOOF (P K LE ROUX) DAM

To visit the Vanderkloof Dam, take the tarmac road R389 which branches off from the N1 road 3 km north of Hanover. After leading for 73 km across flat Karoo landscape, this branch road makes a sudden descent into a valley. Here, in a relatively fertile setting, surrounded by an assembly of strangely shaped hillocks, lies the small, odd-looking town of ...

PHILIPSTOWN

Founded in 1863 as a church centre, the town remains much as it was when it was first built. Some interesting buildings exemplify the style of architecture popular at that period, among them the original sandstone church and the parsonage which is still in use. The town was named after Sir Philip Wodehouse, Governor of the Cape. Merino sheep farming is the principal local occupation.

The R48 road leads north from Philipstown through interesting scenery sprinkled with flat-topped and rhino-horn-shaped hillocks. After 45 km the road reaches the town of ...

PETRUSVILLE

Like Philipstown, this little centre lies in a fertile valley surrounded by a cluster of high hills. Named after Petrus van der Walt, owner of the farm *Renosterfontein* on which the town was laid out, *Petrusville* is an agricultural centre.

From Petrusville the R48 road continues north for 7,8 km and then joins the Hopetown–Luckhoff road, crossing the Gariep River 7 km further on at Vanderkloof, the original construction camp, just below the high wall of the Vanderkloof Dam. The name *Vanderkloof* is an odd mixture of the name of Petrus J van der Walt (see Petrusville) and *Kloof* (ravine). The view of the dam and river is impressive. The road continues into the Free State to the town of Luckhoff, 34 km away.

Chapter Fourteen
THE DIAMOND WAY

The Diamond Way to the north (N12) begins its journey at a famous landmark in the Karoo – the triple hillocks known as the Three Sisters. At this point the Diamond Way branches due north from the Great North Road (N1) which has come up from the Cape and which swings in a north-easterly direction in its long journey across the Karoo to the maize and gold-fields of the Free State and then far away through the heart of Africa. Meanwhile the Diamond Way leads through Kimberley and across most of the great diamond-fields of Southern Africa. Both roads link up again in Johannesburg.

From Three Sisters the tarmac road of the Diamond Way twists north-westwards through a rocky pile of arid hills, following the course of the *Soutrivier* (salt river), the banks of which are shaded by green acacia trees. Farms such as *Brakfontein* (9 km) and *Jasfontein* (41 km) make effective use of the stream's erratic flow and, in the heart of the thirstland of the Karoo, reveal what can be achieved by the magic touch of water.

At intervals along the highway a considerate roads department has planted peppercorn and other drought-resistant trees to provide shady resting-places. In addition, there is a pump supplying drinking-water at a point 46 km from the start of the road. A further 14 km from this pump (60 km from the start of the road) brings the road to the town of ...

VICTORIA WEST

Despite the arid appearance of the countryside, Victoria West is the centre of a wealthy farming activity in the production of wool. The town seems smaller than it is when viewed from the Diamond Way which traverses it at right angles to the long main Church Street, lined with shops, garages and public buildings. The street burrows into the western hills along a watercourse.

The town originated in 1843 when the Dutch Reformed Church purchased for 23 000 rixdollars portions of the farms, *Zeekoegat* and *Kapoksfontein,* for the purpose of building a church and creating a centre for a then isolated but developing region. At the request of the churchwardens, the Governor of the Cape, on 25 September 1844, approved the name of Victoria West, in honour of the Queen. A church was built and consecrated in 1850, erven were laid out and sold, and the town began its life beneath the clear blue skies of the Karoo.

On 24 December 1855 the division of Victoria West was created by Government proclamation, the specific situation in the west of the colony being emphasised in order to distinguish the place from the division of Victoria East established near Queenstown in the Eastern Cape. A municipal council was proclaimed for the town on 28 January 1859.

The discovery of diamonds at Hopetown in 1886 contributed to a surge of progress in Victoria West. The town lay on the main route to the north. The flood of fortune-seekers making their way to Hopetown and then to Kimberley, used Victoria West as a staging post.

Diamonds lured the railway from Cape Town as far as Kimberley, but for obscure reasons the line bypassed Victoria West by 12 km. The town, therefore, had to be satisfied with a station at first named Victoria West Road, later renamed *Hutchinson,* in honour of the Governor, Sir Walter Hely-Hutchinson. In 1904 a branch line was built from Hutchinson to Victoria West and from there to Calvinia.

Years of floods (such as in 1871 when 62 people were drowned after a cloudburst sent a wall of water down the usually dry watercourse) and years of extreme aridity (in 1922, only 26 mm of rain fell in twelve months) – as with all Karoo towns – kept the local pendulum of prosperity swinging between ruin and riches. Through it all, however, Victoria West developed, producing a surprising number of people who made a name for themselves in the outside world. With a population of 8 413, it is today a typical example of a Karoo town flourishing in the sunshine.

An interesting museum, notable for its Stone Age exhibits and some remarkable fossil fish, is housed in the library buildings. It is open on weekdays from 07h45 to 13h00 and from 14h00 to 16h45. Closed weekends and public holidays.

From Victoria West the Diamond Way (N12) continues northwards across the railway line and over a rugged stretch of arid Karoo. The roads department has established resting-places shaded by clumps of trees, and boreholes to supply drinking-water at points 12 km, 48 km and 49 km from Victoria West. At 55 km the road crosses the Ongers River at a place overlooked by the stool-shaped hill known as Leebskop. The surface of the Karoo in this area is covered with piles of dark-coloured dolerite fragments, as though Nature had gathered them into neat heaps in an effort to tidy up relics of ancient hills. The road leads for 32 km over an arid, flat plain, with hills watching rather aloofly from the horizon. In the midst of this plain, 102 km from Victoria West, the Diamond Way reaches ...

BRITSTOWN

This communications centre lies half-way between Cape Town and Johannesburg on the Diamond Way, and is a junction point for the tarmac road which leads to Upington.

Britstown was named after Hans Brits, a man who had accompanied Dr David Livingstone on a venture into the interior and then settled on the farm *Gemsbokfontein*. In 1877 an association of local men, headed by T P Theron, purchased a portion of this farm on which they founded a community centre and built a church, giving the place to the churchwardens to manage. The town became a municipality in January 1889 and today has a population of 4 278. There is a museum housed in an old church next to the municipal offices.

In a region having a total average rainfall of only 250 mm a year, Britstown is a centre for sheep farming. Situated 19 km from the town is an irrigated area watered by a dam in the Ongers (or Brak) River. This irrigation scheme was originally started in 1895 as the private venture of what was known as the Smartt Syndicate. This concern built two dams, planted lucerne and wheat, and grazed sheep, karakuls and Clydesdale horses. Unfortunately the syndicate was liquidated in October 1954 and the assets of its considerable enterprise dispersed. The massive flooding of the Ongers River in March 1961 destroyed the Smartt Irrigation Board Dam, but it was reconstructed by the Government in 1964 and today irrigates fertile agricultural land where crops flourish on sunshine and ample water.

From Britstown the Diamond Way crosses the railway line linking De Aar to Namibia and continues northwards. After 1 km a tarmac turn-off (N10) leads east for 48 km to ...

DE AAR

This railway centre, the name of which means 'the vein', is the second most important railway junction (after Germiston) in Southern Africa. When the railway was built from Cape Town to Kimberley, the administration purchased from J G Vermeulen a large portion of his farm *De Aar* and established there in 1881 a marshalling yard and junction. Hot in summer, bleakly cold in winter, De Aar had an evil reputation among railwaymen and passengers alike for being a deadly dull place in which to live, and was notorious for such inordinate delays that Parliamentary pressure eventually had to be invoked to induce the trains to leave more quickly! It was originally planned to name the place *Brounger Junction* after William Brounger, the colonial railway engineer and head of the railway department, but this name did not survive. The farm name *De Aar* refers to underground water supplies, said to occur in a vein. At first comprising simply a couple of gangers' cottages and a ramshackle wood-and-iron hotel, De Aar has now grown into a substantial, well-planned modern town with parks, gardens and amenities. It became a municipality in 1904. Its present population is 27 647. The lives of the people living there will always be influenced by the endless coming and going of trains.

Back on the Diamond Way, 2 km beyond the turn-off to De Aar, there is a tarmac turn-off (N10) stretching to Prieska and from there to Upington and Namibia. The Diamond Way proceeds across arid, harsh country, littered with dark-coloured fragments of dolerite rock. After 56 km the road reaches a resting-place with shady trees and drinking-water. The journey continues a further 17 km across an open scrub-covered plain and past a low ridge of rocky hillocks to reach (73 km from Britstown) the small town of ...

STRYDENBURG

Lying on the verge of a large pan filled during the rainy years with shallow, salty water, *Strydenburg* (the town of strife) received its rather lugubrious name on account of incessant squabbling over – of all things – the choice of its name. The place was laid out by the Dutch Reformed Church in 1892 on the farm *Rooipan*, originally owned by the brothers N and B Badenhorst. Experiencing a slow, sunbronzed growth, it became a municipality in 1914 and is today, with a population of 1 982, a neat little farming centre of the Karoo, dominated by a handsome Dutch Reformed church built of local stone.

The Diamond Way (N12) leads north-westwards from Strydenburg over an open, level plain covered in Karoo scrub. Several shady resting-places have been made by the roads department, notably at 16 km and 46 km from Strydenburg. After 59 km the road reaches the sunbaked little town of romantic memories ...

HOPETOWN

With a population of 7 905, Hopetown is situated on an arid slope leading down to the Gariep River. In 1850 Sir Harry Smith, the Governor, extended the northern frontier of the Cape Colony as far as the Orange (Gariep) River, and the few individuals in the Hopetown area – wandering Griqua and renegade Europeans – were allowed to claim ownership of land. Nineteen farms were granted to those who claimed early residence, and a steady influx of new settlers occurred once the area was no longer a no man's land.

The need for a community centre was soon obvious and the choice for a site fell on a farm named *Duvenaarsfontein* after a nomadic cattle herder who had in former years occasionally watered his stock there.

On 18 February 1854 the community was established by the Dutch Reformed Church and a town laid out, with a church – a rough, frontier-type building – being made out of mud and manure. The origin of the name *Hopetown* is odd. It is said locally that the widow of the first owner of the farm (Michiel van Niekerk) wore a necklace to which was attached a small anchor. One of her servants admired this anchor and was very impressed when told that it represented hope. The servant made an ingenious imitation from tin, which was nailed above the entrance to the farmhouse. When the house was demolished, the symbol of hope was preserved and eventually fixed above the door of another house by a local farmer's wife, Mrs Curry. The little token was considered to be the good-luck emblem of Hopetown which became a municipality in September 1858.

For the first few years the town flourished on sheep farming. Then, in the momentous year 1866, Schalk van Niekerk, son of the first owner of *Duvenaarsfontein*, visited a neighbour, Daniel Jacobs of the farm *De Kalk*. He noticed a 15-year-old boy, Erasmus Jacobs, playing with a glittering stone. Van Niekerk was no prospector but he was so taken with the stone that Mrs Jacobs induced her son to give it to him. Van Niekerk, in turn, gave the stone to John O'Reilly, a travelling trader. He took it to Colesberg and showed it to the magistrate, Lorenzo Boyes, who tested it by scratching into a window-pane the two letters 'DP', an interesting memento which may still be seen in the museum at Colesberg. The stone was then sent to Grahamstown to a local medical man of some general scientific reputation, Dr W A Atherstone. He proved it to be a 21,25 carat diamond (1 carat equals 200 milligrams). It was bought for £500 by the Governor of the Cape, Sir Philip Wodehouse.

Nobody knew the origin of the diamond. It was thought to be an isolated specimen, perhaps carried into the area in the crop of a wild ostrich. But in 1868, on the farm *Zandfontein*, a Griqua diviner, known as Booi, picked up a magnificent white diamond weighing 83,5 carats. He took it to Hopetown where Schalk van Niekerk acquired the stone in exchange for a wagon, a span of 10 oxen, 500 sheep and a horse. In due course Van Niekerk sold the stone for £11 000 to Lilienfeld Brothers in Hopetown. It was eventually bought by the Earl of Dudley for £30 000. This stone was named the Star of South Africa. Its discovery marked the beginning of what may be called the diamond epoch in the story of Southern Africa.

Suddenly, Hopetown was living up to its name. Fortune-seekers poured in from all over the world. Business boomed and, when the great rushes to the Kimberley area took place, Hopetown became the main source of supply, with local farmers making a fortune as transport riders.

The railway proved the evil genius in this prosperity. As with Victoria West, the line passed Hopetown 15 km to the east, leaving the town with the sole consolation of a siding known as Orange River. Hopetown sank into the doldrums.

In 1897 a disgruntled local inhabitant conjured some life back into the place by claiming a rich new find of diamonds on *Rooidam* farm. Within three weeks, 10 000 diggers rushed to the place, and Hopetown boomed once again. It was then discovered that *Rooidam* was a fraud. Loads of diamondiferous soil disguised as bags of maize and forage had been brought to the farm from Kimberley. Well 'salted' with diamonds, this formed the bait for a sucker-rush. Diggers abandoned Hopetown in disgust and the place fell into disrepute.

Alluvial diamonds were later found on several farms along the banks of the Gariep River near the town. *Brakfontein* (or *Higgshope*) proved the richest. Between 1923 and 1953 diamonds worth £1 360 666 were recovered from these fields (a total of 131 070,25 carats). Although most of the diggers rushed to Lichtenburg in 1927 as the Hopetown fields became exhausted, an occasional stone is still found in the area. No one can say for certain that another great discovery may not again bring boom times to Hopetown.

A road leads east from Hopetown, crosses the railway line at Oranjerivier station and thence for 49 km to the private township at Orania, a former construction camp of builders of the Vanderkloof Dam on the Gariep River. The place became a retreat for die-hard supporters of Dr Verwoerdian-style apartheid, with his widow, Betsie Verwoerd as its principal resident.

From Hopetown the Diamond Way (N12) continues north-eastwards and, after 3 km, crosses the Gariep River. A turn-off 2 km further on leads to Salt Lake (35 km), a prolific supplier of high grade salt, and to Douglas (73 km). The main tarmac road proceeds across the Karoo plains and after 20 km reaches a turn-off east to the mainline station of Witput. At 35 km from Hopetown the road crosses the branch railway line from Belmont to Douglas, and 15 km further on there is a wayside resting-place with shade and drinking-water.

The Karoo now gives way to less arid thorn country and rocky hillocks. Old battlefields of the Anglo-Boer War lie along either side of the road. At 56 km a memorial situated on a hillock west of the road pays tribute to British soldiers killed at Enslin and Graspan in November 1899.

In their advance to relieve Kimberley, the British under Lord Methuen used Oranjerivier station as base, fighting their way up the line of rail. The Boers first opposed them from the koppies at Belmont station and then successively at such railway centres as Enslin and Modder River. At the Battle of Magersfontein the Boers, under General Jacobus de la Rey, introduced trench warfare for the first time. These trenches may still be seen together with graves and several memorials.

The Diamond Way continues north-eastwards along the route of the British advance, keeping in close company with the main railway line. A resting-place with shade and drinking-water is reached 57 km from Hopetown. A further 7 km brings the road to a turn-off east to Jacobsdal (24 km), just before the small railway centre of Heuningneskloof. At 73 km the road passes the Riet River Agricultural Research Station where the surroundings (the site of the Battle of Modder River) become pleasantly green, irrigated by water from the Riet River. The road crosses the river at the village of the same name, 83 km from Hopetown, and a further kilometre takes the road past Modder River station.

The road now leads northwards through low hillocks rising from a plain covered in grass and acacia trees. After 115 km of travel from Hopetown, a long avenue of peppercorn trees provides shade and marks the approach to ...

KIMBERLEY

The story of the diamond city of Kimberley has made it one of the best known cities in the world. To its name is attached a considerable glamour and romance. With diamonds as the emblem of affection and Kimberley the source of the glittering stones set in many of the world's great pieces of jewellery and engagement rings, it is understandable that this sunbronzed city has a place in the hearts of the world's lovers. Certainly, Kimberley has an aura as if Eros, in association with Venus and Cupid, is employed there in the design of dreams.

The saga of Kimberley and its diamonds originated during a phase of volcanic activity which occurred about 60 million years ago towards the end of the Cretaceous period. Groups of volcanic pipes (or throats) were blown up through Earth's crust from deep down. Through these pipes flowed a soft, waxy, blueish volcanic rock known as kimberlite. On the surface this kimberlite weathered to so-called 'yellow ground'. Being soft, it easily eroded along with any volcanic cones which might have piled up above the pipes. Below the surface the kimberlite in the pipes formed what is called 'blue ground', while at greater depths it became what is known as 'hardebank'.

In some inexplicable way, diamonds were accumulated by the kimberlite on its way up from the depths. A diamond is composed of carbon which has been subjected to tremendous pressure. Kimberlite itself contains no carbon, but simply acts as host to the diamonds which must have been formed deep down and then been carried by the material surging up the volcanic pipes. Not all the pipes contain diamonds, but of 150 found so far, 26 of them do, to degrees varying from 29 carats per 720 000 kg of kimberlite at the Premier Mine near Pretoria, 19 carats at Kimberley, and lesser quantities elsewhere.

Many other kimberlite pipes were entirely eroded away and their diamond content dispersed along the beds of rivers (as at Hopetown and Barkly West), or among the gravels of abandoned watercourses where subsequent discovery by man caused the great rushes to places such as Bloemhof and Lichtenburg in the Transvaal.

While the first diamond rush was taking place at Hopetown, a second and far greater discovery was made in 1870 in the gravels of the Vaal River at Barkly West. At the height of the rush to these river diggings, diamonds were found in the mud brick walls of the farmhouse of *Bultfontein*, (hilly fountain) owned by Cornelis du Plooy. The house was rapidly dismantled. The site is now the colossal hole in the ground of Bultfontein Mine.

In December 1870 diamonds were found by the children of Adriaan van Wyk, playing next to Du Toit's Pan on their father's farm *Dorstfontein* (dry fountain). A whole army of diggers stampeded to the place. Against such a flood of humanity a landowner could do nothing save make money from claim fees and watch his farmlands literally disappear in an appalling cloud of red dust and dumps of rubble abandoned by the diggers.

In May 1871 a new discovery was made on the farm *Vooruitzicht* (outlook), owned by the brothers Diederick and Nicolaas Johannes de Beer. Then, on Sunday night 18 July 1871, a servant named Damon, employed by Fleetwood Rawstone, one of a party of men from Colesberg who were digging at Du Toit's Pan, appeared at his master's tent with three diamonds he had found on a hillock nearby. This marked the discovery of Colesberg Koppie, and started what was called the New Rush, the greatest of all the diamond rushes. It attracted to South Africa some of the most flamboyant characters in the world and produced a staggering fortune in precious stones. By the mass activity of the diggers, it resulted in the sinking of the Big Hole of Kimberley Mine, the largest man-made hole in the world.

The Big Hole has a surface area of 17 ha and a perimeter of 1,6 km. Over 22,5 million tons of ground was removed from it, yielding 14 504 carats of diamonds (the equivalent of 2 722 kilograms) before operations ceased on 14 August 1914. As an opencast working, it is 215 m deep. Shafts extended it to the 1 100 m level before the pipe started to pinch out. Water seepage steadily filled up the hole until it was 133,6 m from the surface. Pumping has lowered the level of the water and the excavated pipe is now revealed.

Kimberley (named after the Secretary of State for Colonies, the Earl of Kimberley) grew up as the centre of the new rush. A twin town, *Beaconsfield* (named after Benjamin Disraeli, the Earl of Beaconsfield), developed as the centre for the Bultfontein, Wesselton and Du Toit's Pan mines. The two towns were eventually amalgamated in 1912 to become a city.

These early diamond towns were at first great tent camps which were slowly replaced by tin shanties and permanent buildings. Life was uproarious, with rumours, rows, bad smells from non-existent sanitary arrangements, dust, heat, shortages of water, and a plethora of insects, vermin, loafers, thieves and swindlers. Political squabbles over the ownership of the diamond areas raged between Britain, the Orange Free State, the Griqua and the Tlapin tribes, emphasising the general insecurity of life.

The British, in the grand imperial manner in vogue at the time, took control of the areas which the Keate Award had declared the possession of the Griqua, whose chief promptly ceded to the British the territory known as Griqualand West. By that time there were 50 000 people living in Kimberley. Such individuals as Cecil Rhodes and Barney Barnato were amongst the throng beginning to elbow their way from scratch to fortune.

The first rushes to diamond pipes such as Colesberg Koppie saw the entire exposure pegged out into claims. Seven hundred claims were marked off on Colesberg Koppie, many overlapping the pipe on to completely valueless ground. An area slightly less than 3 ha actually proved the most profitable. At first, each claim was separately worked and there was no indication that the pipe would extend to any depth. As the claims were worked deeper, chaos resulted when separate workings became difficult and dangerous. Amalgamation of claims became the only solution, and it was through this fortuitous circumstance that the organising genius of men such as Rhodes and Barnato grasped the opportunity which led to fortune.

The spectacle of these vast opencast mines, looking like overturned antheaps, must have been staggering. Thirty thousand men worked at one time in the Big Hole; and the sounds of pounding, digging, shouting, grinding of winches, and all the hubbub of mining gave to Kimberley a strange husky sort of voice which could be heard day and night for some kilometres across the veld, as though the town was muttering to itself.

Suddenly confronted with this flood of gems from South Africa, the world price of diamonds (which until then had been extremely rare gemstones) fell very considerably. At the same time, however, diamonds were now within the reach of the general public. With such a glamorous background of rarity and mystic beauty they became fashionable throughout the world and the accepted emblem of romance. Demand increased after the first decline and Kimberley flourished considerably, with successful diggers washing in soda-water, booking all-day rides on visiting merry-go-rounds, lighting cigars with £5 notes, as well as all the other nonsense which accompanies an excess of money in such a madcap society.

Kimberley underwent a metamorphosis, with money providing the cocoon out of which a dusty caterpillar, transformed into a butterfly, emerged complete with social graces, libraries, fine buildings, theatres, gardens and civic airs. Old Nicolaas de Beer, owner of the land on which the town was growing, took one last look at it, sold out for 6 000 guineas and moved to quieter parts in the Transvaal. The family name, in the form of De Beers, remained as a collective term for the entire mining activity as it was slowly amalgamated by Rhodes into the mighty concern of today, De Beers Consolidated Mines Ltd.

Kimberley became a municipality in 1877. By 1882 a tramway connected the place to Beaconsfield and the streets were illuminated by the first electric lights in Southern Africa. Cecil Rhodes had begun his political career by becoming the diggers' representative for Barkly West in the Cape Legislative Assembly. In 1890 he became Prime Minister of the Cape Colony. It was on Kimberley Market Square on 16 July 1886 that F W Alexander, an itinerant produce dealer, publicly crushed samples of reef which he had acquired on the newly discovered Witwatersrand. This started a rush of financiers from Kimberley to secure holdings in the world's richest gold-fields. It was also in Kimberley in 1887 that Rhodes and his cronies planned the famous concession with Lobengula and the subsequent occupation of what was at first named Rhodesia, but now Zimbabwe. The simple little office and boardroom in which Rhodes conceived many of his great coups still stands in its original state in Warren Street. It is now a museum.

In 1888 the great amalgamation took place between Rhodes's De Beers Mine and Barney Barnato's Kimberley Central Mining Company. Barnato received a cheque for £5 338 650 for the Big Hole. Rhodes was acknowledged as the veritable king of diamonds, the controller of the great bulk of the world's production and the recipient of a personal daily income far beyond the earning capacity of the average man's lifetime. By means of this unparalleled income he financed his dealings on the Witwatersrand, in Zimbabwe and elsewhere. The great hole in Kimberley provided him with an inexhaustible flow of money which, like the hair on Samson's head, was the source of his power.

Kimberley spread out around the mines. In 1889 the Kenilworth Model Village was established by the De Beers company to house employees. At that time plans were already under way to convert the opencast working into underground operations. The headgear of the Kimberley Mine was erected in 1892 and all activity at the Big Hole was thenceforth conducted through shafts and adits.

The year 1892 also saw the Kimberley and World Exhibition, the first of its kind to be held outside London. At that time the diamond city was the gayest and most vivacious place in Southern Africa. Even learning and religion were flourishing in the town. A School of Mines was opened in 1896. Strangely enough, in 1903 it was transferred to Johannesburg where it became the University of the Witwatersrand. Among the religious groups which thrived in Kimberley were the Seventh Day Adventists. In 1885 Pieter Wessels, founder of the denomination, on reading his Bible, decided that the Fourth Commandment explicitly ordained the seventh day (Saturday) as the Sabbath. Arousing considerable argument over the matter in his church, he was excommunicated. He promptly started the Seventh Day Adventists in a small corrugated-iron church, situated on the corner of Blacking Street and Dyer Place in Kimberley. It was amply financed by the sum of £451 438, paid in 1891 by the De Beers company in exchange for the Wesselton Mine, a Wessels family property.

The outbreak of the Anglo-Boer War in October 1899 saw Kimberley besieged by the Boers for 154 days from 14 October 1899 until 15 February 1900. Rhodes was in Kimberley for the entire siege. His quarters at the Sanatorium Hotel provided a favourite target for the Boer artillerists. To escape the shelling some 3 000 women and children were accommodated in underground workings at the De Beers and Kimberley mines. A famous gun named 'Long Cecil', firing a 12 kg shell, was designed and built in the De Beers workshops and used to shell the Boers. The designer, an American engineer, George Labram, was himself killed when a Boer 'Long Tom' secured a direct hit on the Grand Hotel while he was dressing for an appointment with Rhodes.

With the war over, Kimberley resumed its diamond mining. The Honoured Dead Memorial, designed by Sir Herbert Baker on a plan selected by Rhodes, was built in memory of the people of Kimberley who were killed in the siege. Similar in conception to the Nereid Monument of Xanthos, it was built of granite procured from the Matobo Hills of Zimbabwe. Rudyard Kipling wrote the inscriptions, and the original 'Long Cecil' stands guard on a stylobate of the memorial. The death of Cecil Rhodes in Muizenberg on 26 March 1902 saw an end to the king of diamonds.

As is the nature of life, however, his crown prince was already on the way, for in November of that year a young man named Ernest Oppenheimer arrived in Kimberley as a representative of Anton Dunkelsbuhler, a European diamond-merchant concern. When Beaconsfield and Kimberley combined to become a city in 1912, Ernest Oppenheimer became its first mayor and was by then already on his way to securing massive power in the world of finance.

In 1912 Kimberley became the home of the first flying school in Southern Africa, known as the Aviation Syndicate School of Flying. An aerodrome, about 3,5 km from the present airport, was used. A wonderful box-kite affair of a flying machine, a Compton-Paterson biplane, was used by an instructor named Paterson. This machine formed the training foundation of the future South African Air Force. The hangar has been reconstructed and there is a replica of the original flying machine. The monument is open Mondays to Saturdays 09h00 to 17h00. Sundays 14h00 to 17h00. Public holidays 10h00 to 17h00.

The 1930s saw the collapse of the diamond industry during the world depression. Kimberley experienced a very bleak time, but its situation as the commercial, administrative and communications centre of the Northern Cape guaranteed it some importance even without the glitter of diamonds.

Today, with a population of 197 256 Kimberley is an educational centre and the seat of the Anglican Bishop of Griqualand West. With the restoration of diamonds to their former value, it remains essentially the diamond city. It is the headquarters of De Beers Consolidated Mines, where the gemstones of Southern Africa are sorted and dispatched. It is certainly the only city in the world where – unlike the unfortunate Irishman digging for gold in a London street – men may still be seen profitably searching for and finding diamonds on the sites of demolished buildings and excavated pavements and roads. The 'blue ground', the kimberlite, was scattered in these constructions during the first hectic days of the rush, before men quite realised the value of its contents.

For the visitor, Kimberley offers an atmosphere redolent of old excitements. There is, of course, the Big Hole. From an observation platform the visitor can visualise the place, and particularly the crater pipe itself, seething with a lava of human activity. A completely reconstructed street, lined with original buildings of old-time Kimberley, forms a wonderful museum on the edge of the Big Hole. Here may be seen a bar, church, and Barney Barnato's Boxing Academy; tramcars, luxury private Pullman railway coaches used by the millionaires; complex machinery for the recovery of diamonds; bicycles with sails for wind power; the original headgear which lowered many women and children to safety during the siege; and a replica of the original De Beers homestead. The Big Hole and the Kimberley Mine Museum are open daily from 08h00 to 18h00; closed on Christmas and on Good Friday. A unique tram service connects the Kimberley Mine Museum with the City Hall in Market Square. The City Hall, built in 1899 in the Roman-Corinthian style, is itself a national monument. The tram route from it goes past several historical buildings and places of interest. The tram runs between 09h00 and 16h15 on a regular schedule of five round trips each day, Mondays to Fridays; and seven round trips on Saturdays, Sundays and school holidays.

In contrast are the modern workings with their recovery processes, the glittering finished products from uncut diamonds and the ultra-intelligent police dogs which guard the diamond areas. De Beers conduct guided underground tours of their Bultfontein diamond mine. The tours start each weekday at 08h00 and take about two and a half hours to complete. Visitors to the mine have to don real mine worker gear such as safety shoes, hard hat, overall with light reflecting strips, battery and head lamp, as well as a survival pack. These tours must be pre-booked at (053) 842-1321. The minimum age for these tours is 16 years of age. The Bultfontein mine is one of the oldest and deepest diamond producing diamond mines in the world. Surface tours of the Bultfontein diamond mine are done every weekday at 09h00 and 11h00. The minimum age for these tours is 8 years.

Digging for diamonds was thirsty work and Kimberley had a very considerable number of bars and 'watering holes'. Some of them still remain in business. The Halfway House Inn and the Kimberlite Hotel both have drive-in bars where customers on horses are still welcome. The Star of the West is on the tram-route to the Big Hole. Public transport stops here long enough for passengers to have a quick one.

There are several interesting museums and galleries to visit in Kimberley. The Alexander McGregor Memorial Museum at 10 Chapel Street was created as a memorial to a former mayor of the city. It is open Mondays to Fridays 09h00 to 17h00; Saturdays 09h00 to 13h00; Sundays

14h00 to 17h00. It houses a science centre, geological specimens from all over the world and a selection of old-fashioned dresses and uniforms. The McGregor Museum in the Sanatorium in Atlas Street has a display on the Anglo-Boer War, exhibits on the evolution of prehistoric humans and more recent history, particularly of the Northern Cape; there is also a Hall of Religions. Built by Cecil Rhodes in 1897 as an hotel and health resort, after the siege of Kimberley it was refurbished and renamed Hotel Belgrave. In the 1930s it became a convent school. Finally in 1971, it became the McGregor Museum's headquarters. It is open Mondays to Saturdays 09h00 to 17h00; Sundays 14h00 to 17h00; public holidays 10h00 to 17h00. Closed Good Friday and Christmas.

Also part of the McGregor Museum is the bungalow built for C D Rudd, now maintained as a fine example of the architecture and furnishings of what might be styled a diamond palace, comparable to the 'feather' palaces of the Little Karoo and the 'sugar' palaces of Natal. Visits to Rudd House and also Dunluce (the residence of John Orr of departmental store fame before he donated it to the McGregor Museum) can be arranged at the McGregor Museum. These houses are two of Kimberley's most famous houses and are good examples of the opulent life-styles of years gone by. The Belgravia Historical Walk leads visitors to thirty-three of Kimberley's most historical sights. A guided ghost trail tells the story of so-called ghost sightings in Kimberley, amongst them a lone bagpiper still playing his bags at the Magersfontein battlefield, a riderless horse running at Carter's Ridge and a uniformed British soldier walking up and down at the Kimberley Golf Club.

The William Humphreys Art Gallery was founded in 1952 when William Humphreys, the Member of Parliament for Kimberley for 25 years, donated his collection of paintings to the city. Housed in the Civic Centre, this collection has been considerably expanded to include works by many South African artists, European and Cape furniture, and other items. The gallery is open Mondays to Saturdays from 10h00 to 13h00 and 14h00 to 17h00; on Sundays and public holidays from 14h00 to 17h00. Closed Good Friday and Christmas.

The Duggan-Cronin Gallery in Egerton Road, has the same opening hours as the McGregor Museum (closed on Saturdays between 13h00 and 14h00). It exhibits a staggering collection of over 8 000 photographs taken by A M Duggan-Cronin who immigrated to South Africa from Ireland in 1897. Working for the De Beers company as a manager in their labour department, he indulged in the hobby of taking these unique photographs of African tribespeople before they adopted European dress. Such pictures can never be retaken and, in addition to being of historical value, they are superb photographic works of art. There is space in the building for the exhibition of only a small portion of the total collection.

On the southern outskirts of Kimberley, a portion of the battlefield of Magersfontein (428 ha) has been proclaimed a national monument. It was here, on 11 December 1899, that the Boers, 8 200 strong and commanded by General P A Cronje, were attacked by 12 500 British soldiers commanded by Lieutenant-General Lord P S Methuen. The British were attempting to relieve the siege of Kimberley but their advance was so decidedly brought to a halt at Magersfontein that it was two months before they recovered and finally relieved Kimberley. The Boers had created strong defensive positions in a single line of trenches and behind several low stone walls. The British attacked without realising the strength of the Boer positions. Altogether 239 of the British were killed and 663 wounded, mainly men of the Highland Brigade. The Boer losses were 87 killed and 149 wounded. A field museum, viewing-post, tea-room and some picnic sites are situated at the battlefield.

The Kimberley Africana Library in Dutoitspan Road is worth visiting. It houses one of the best collections of Africana in South Africa and is greatly used for research. It is open on weekdays from 08h00 to 12h45 and 13h30 to 16h30.

Among the many memorials in Kimberley is a superb equestrian statue of Cecil Rhodes sculpted by Homo Thorneycroft. The horse was actually modelled from Rhodes's personal animal which he often rode in Kimberley. Spread across Rhodes's knees is a map of South Africa. He is dressed in the clothes he wore at the great indaba with the Ndebele in the Matobo Hills.

In the gardens of the Civic Centre stand a fountain and statue sculpted by Herman Wald in the form of a diamond sieve held aloft by five life-sized diggers. A bust of Sir Ernest Oppenheimer, first mayor of Kimberley City and diamond financier supreme, is also in the garden.

Railway enthusiasts can see several interesting steam locomotives at the marshalling yards in Austin road, Beaconsfield. Permits must be obtained at the Paul Sauer Building, Kimberley station. There is a Railway Museum at the Kimberley station. This museum also displays a map of the rail lines used during the Anglo-Boer War amongst other interesting railway displays.

For recreation the people of Kimberley frequent two pleasure resorts: Riverton and Langleg, 26 km away on the Vaal River, where pastimes include boating, fishing and swimming. There are bungalows and sites for caravans, camping and picnicking.

The Kimberley satellite township named after the baTlhaping chief, Galeshewe, was established in 1871. The route to it starts at the city hall. The road leads past the house and grave of Sol Plaatje, founder member of the African National Congress and its first general secretary. He was an outstanding writer, author of the first novel in English written by a black South African. His home is a national monument. Galeshewe has many interesting buildings, old and new. Robert Sobukwe, founder of the Pan African Congress lived there. A lively and animated township to visit.

GRIQUALAND WEST AND THE NORTHERN CAPE

Kimberley is the gateway through which travellers along the Diamond Way from Cape Town to Johannesburg may turn aside from the beaten track and enter the great spaces of sunshine and bush-covered plains of Griqualand West and the Northern Cape, where spectacular developments are taking place against the background of a history involving hunters, prospectors, missionaries and wanderers of the wilderness.

Take the tarmac road (R31) leading west from Kimberley across the bush-covered plains to the great bend of the Vaal River. After 22 km there is a turn-off to *Nooitgedacht,* where glacial pavements and rock engravings may be seen. The engravings are of uncertain age and origin but probably done by Bushmen. At this point the river is a fine stretch of water which the main road crosses by means of a handsome solid-looking bridge of dolomite stonework. The original toll-house still stands guard. Downriver from the bridge there is a great pool which, according to African legends, is the haunt of a giant serpent. A swimming-pool and camping and recreational area have been created on the right bank of the river where the road makes its crossing.

The traveller is now in really romantic diamond country. Immediately across the bridge, on the eastern side of the road, looms Canteen Koppie, now a nature reserve preserving the site of the great rush to what was known as Klipdrift. There are signs everywhere of considerable disturbance to the landscape: mounds of gravel, pits, holes, excavations. old implements, rusty machinery abandoned at the site of rich finds long exhausted – all still remain, while the broad river flows silently by, retaining the secret of when and how the diamonds came to be mixed up in its gravel and from where they originated.

The area around Canteen Koppie almost resembles an illustrated geology textbook. The striated rocks at *Nooitgedacht* (16 km away) indicate that about 220 million years ago the area was under ice. After the ice melted, prehistoric man moved in. Canteen Koppie is rich with their artefacts. Iron Age people arrived, followed by Koranna tribespeople and in 1849 by missionaries of the Berlin Missionary Society who founded a station on the left bank of the Vaal and named it *Pniel* (the face of God). The most momentous occasion of all was in January 1870 with the arrival of a party of prospectors from Natal, led by Captain Loftus Rolleston. They discovered diamonds in the gravel of the river, an event which put an end to the tranquil labours of the missionaries. It was as though an earthquake had suddenly rocked the place.

Diggers rushed to Pniel and across the Vaal River to Klipdrift where a noisy, uproarious camp established itself, notorious for gun-running, strong liquor and illicit traffic in stolen diamonds. The site of this camp, just beyond Canteen Koppie (35 km from Kimberley) is now the town of ...

BARKLY WEST

With a population of 11 922, Barkly West, to say the least, experienced a very lively beginning. The diamond diggers had no sooner pitched their tents on the site of the town – the old fording place known as Klipdrift – than a number of individuals appeared on the scene claiming ownership of the ground and the right to levy taxes. First to arrive was the Koranna chief, Jan Bloem. The diggers, led by Roderick Barker, armed themselves, formed a laager on the site of the English church and offered to fight for their independence. Bloem fled. He was followed by Chief Jantjie of the Tlapin tribe and then by the Griqua people, both of whom were driven away in confusion.

The Orange Free State claimed the south side of the river and a magistrate was established at Pniel. The Transvaal claimed the north side. In June 1870 President M W Pretorius arrived to effect control. The diggers, however, would have none of him. Led by Roderick Barker, they threatened to pull down the Transvaal flag if it was hoisted over them. Pretorius tried again three days later and introduced Hugh Owen to the diggers as their magistrate. In a yelling mob the diggers surrounded the Presidential party, tore up the flag, dumped Owen in a boat and sent him off to the south bank of the river, threatening to tar and feather him if he tried to return. Pretorius retreated to the mission station of Hebron (now Windsorton), from where he tried to negotiate with the diggers, who simply ignored him. Forming a mutual protection society, they elected Stafford Parker as President of the so-called Klipdrift Republic and declared independence.

President Parker, with his white top hat and massive set of whiskers, was one of South Africa's classic characters. His speech, in accepting office, was simple: *'If you have any confidence in me, support me loyally, and for Heaven's sake don't allow any tipsy fool to say pitch him in the river'*.

President Parker ruled with rough justice in the form of common-sense trials and punishments such as tarring and feathering, being hauled through the river, pegging out a man on the ground, or simply running him out of camp.

In December 1870 John Campbell arrived in a top hat crowned with an ostrich feather. He had been sent by the government of the Cape Colony, which also laid claim to the diamond area. The whole unseemly squabble about ownership was eventually taken to arbitration and the Keate Award gave the area to the Griqua people. Complete chaos resulted on the diamond-fields, with supporters of rival claimants threatening one another. The British eventually persuaded the Griquas to cede the area to them and, at the close of the singularly stormy year of 1870, Sir Henry Barkly, the Governor of the Cape, visited the diggings to establish order, administration, and a High Court for Griqualand. As a result of this visit, the camp at Klipdrift received the name of *Barkly West* and commenced a more sober career. The majority of diggers abandoned the place when the great diamond pipes were discovered at Kimberley, but diamond recovery from the gravel beds of the Vaal River has continued (and is likely to proceed for many years to come) along the 160 km stretch of the river above its confluence with the Harts.

Barkly West became a municipality on 3 January 1913. It is an atmospheric little town, especially on a Saturday morning when a row of offices is opened. Diamond buyers meet the local diggers and intense negotiation takes place over the sale of stones found during the week. There is an interesting museum containing minerals and prehistoric artefacts found along the Vaal, as well as early photographs of the diggings. The museum is open Mondays to Fridays from 08h00 to 16h00.

The course of the Vaal River is a particularly interesting sight, characterised by breakwaters where diggers still labour during the dry season (June to November) and scars of enormous mining activity. The river has many pools, rapids, waterfalls and features with odd names such as *Gong-Gong* (a Bushman ideophone from the sound of water falling over the rocks). There is *Beaumont's Folly* – the great pool below the Kimberley Bridge where George Beaumont transported piecemeal and at great expense a substantial dredger which he erected, launched and floated in 1898 in the hope of recovering diamonds from the bottom, only to be defeated by the rocks. *Bosman's Fortune* is where A Bosman, in the same pool that had ruined Beaumont, erected breakwaters and from the river bottom recovered a small fortune in diamonds. There are many other places of forgotten hopes and stories rich enough to fill several books. St Mary's Anglican church in Barkly West, built in 1871 as the first church building on the diamond-fields, is brimming with memories of the diggers. The gravels of the Vaal River are a rich source of gemstones and decorative pebbles, providing a rewarding pastime for the collector who fossicks there. Cecil Rhodes's house later became the residence of the manager of a local bank.

From Barkly West the tarmac road (R31) continues north-westwards, keeping a few kilometres north of the course of the Vaal River. The length of the river is lined with the signs of mining, and frequent turn-offs lead to places such as Waldeck's Plant (16 km), Longlands (19 km), and

Delportshoop (25 km). All these places have odd little community centres, some of them almost ghost towns, with a hotel, a few stores and government offices.

On the left (south and east) bank of the Vaal lies Sydney-on-Vaal, now a farm but once a settlement of 30 000 people, with a church, hotel, hospital, and a unique library established by the renowned bibliophile, Sidney Mendelssohn. The diamond boom town of *Droogeveld* (dry veld) had a population of about 20 000 inhabitants. There is nothing left of it save ruins and piles of washed gravel.

THE VAALBOS NATIONAL PARK

In April 1986 the Vaalbos National Park was established on 23 000 ha of land, most of it a former cattle ranch managed from Sydney-on-Vaal. This national park conserves an interesting botanical area where the thorn savanna blends with the grasslands of the highveld. It is being restocked with a variety of game, including black and white rhino, Cape buffalo, giraffe, Burchell's zebra, kudu, blue wildebeest, red tsessebe, eland, gemsbok, hartebees, springbok duiker, steenbok and warthog.

Bird life is varied and includes the martial and fish eagle, the lappetfaced whitebacked and cape vulture, crimson breasted and the rare yellow form of shrike, secretary bird, pale chanting goshawk and kori bustard. Good roads have been made by the hard work of local people using gravel from old diamond diggers' heaps. There are two picnic sites but no overnight facilities. Bungalows may be hired at Sydney-on-the-Vaal. The park is open from half-an-hour before dawn to half-an-hour after sunset.

Delportshoop lies close to the confluence of the Vaal and Harts rivers. At this point the Vaal swings off to the south-west. The tarmac road continues westwards. At 31 km from Barkly West the R31 road reaches a crossroads where a turn-off leads south to Schmidtsdrif, and north to various diamond-mines along the course of the Harts River, including Bellsbank, where diamonds are found in strange volcanic fissures. Jasper, agate and tiger's-eye are common to the area. Eight kilometres beyond the crossroads lies the huge opencast working of Ulco (Union Lime Company), beyond which the road climbs the escarpment of what is known as the *Ghaap, or* Kaap from the old African name *Ghab* (plateau). The scenery is of an immense featureless, open, bush-covered dolomite plain where *Acacia giraffe* trees flourish, as well as a singularly rich number of many hundreds of varieties of grass for which the Northern Cape is noted.

The carboniferous landscape is of great interest to the discerning geologist, for it represents the resurrected pre-Karoo surface stripped of its sedimentary cover but little changed by later erosion. To the west along the ranges of the Langeberge and Korannaberge it merges with the Kalahari and is buried beneath the sands. Sink holes, underground rivers and surprisingly powerful springs (all characteristic of dolomite) are a feature of this great plain.

At 65 km from Barkly West the R31 tarmac road reaches the railway centre of *Koopmansfontein* (merchant's fountain). The R31 continues westwards for 52 km then reaches a turn north leading for 10 km to Danielskuil and thence for 58 km to the historic centre of ...

KURUMAN

An attractive, clean and modern town, Kuruman was once so remote that it took eight days of hard travelling by ox-wagon to reach it from Kimberley. The town lies at the foot of a range of low hills and is characterised by a remarkable feature, the famous 'eye', the source of the Kuruman River.

At a place known to the Africans as *Gasegonyana* (the small calabash), 20 million litres of crystal-clear water gush out from the dolomite every day at a rate of flow which slackens only slightly during the worst droughts. The town draws its water supply directly from this spring, an incalculably valuable asset for any community centre in the wilderness of Africa.

The residue of water tumbles into a fine pool occupied by a parcel of fat, grossly over-fed bream and barbel fish. Lilies rest on the surface of the water. Tall shady trees cluster around, beneath which are picnic sites, a tea-room and caravan park with comfortable chalets. Water is led from the pool through two canals to irrigate a 6 km length of the valley which, as a result, is green and fertile. The valley is known from its shape as *Seodin,* meaning an elbow in the river.

The name *Kuruman* apparently derives from a Bushman chief, Kurumane who once lived there and was killed by the Tlapin people on the hill overlooking the town. The first known Europeans to reach the place came in an expedition from Cape Town in 1801. Led by P J Truter, a member of the Council of Justice, and Dr W Somerville, Assistant Commissioner of Graaff-Reinet, the party was joined on the Gariep River by the missionaries Johan Kok and William Edwards. The expedition reached the 'eye' of the Kuruman River and Edwards established a mission there for the Tlapin tribe. Johan Kok joined him. Edwards, however, was recalled by the London Missionary Society after a year and Kok was murdered by two of his servants in 1808. In 1816 Robert Hamilton arrived, followed in 1821 by Robert Moffat. The two missionaries bought land from Mothibe, Chief of the Tlapin tribe, and set to work to establish the mission and an irrigated garden. This became the best-known mission station in Africa, a famous frontier outpost and the base for so many historic journeys of exploration by such people as David Livingstone that the Kuruman 'eye' was described as a fountain of Christianity in Africa.

Today the cluster of original buildings erected by the London Missionary Society still stands, surrounded by a riverine forest and a garden. Giant syringa trees (almost the trademark of missionaries in Southern Africa), huge pear trees, old figs and pomegranates all flourish. The almond tree under which Livingstone proposed to Mary Moffat in 1845 is dead, but its trunk still stands and the wind whispers gently through the leaves of the tree shading it.

The original church built in 1838 is beautifully preserved and still in use as a mission church with clean mud floors, great wooden beams holding up a thatched roof, and wonderful acoustics. Moffat's homestead is restored and is in spic-and-span condition. The original wagon-house, Hamilton's house and outbuildings are nearby. The cemetery is half overgrown and filled with the melancholy graves of the children of missionaries who found life on the frontier too much for them. They rest in the shade of a giant kameeldoring tree. About the whole station lingers an atmosphere and a character of calm confidence and tranquillity. All is still, as though the place is set in a dream world. The mission is now run by the United Congregational Church of Southern Africa, successor to The London Missionary Society which is no longer in existence. In 1981 the Kuruman Moffat Mission Trust was formed to mobilise support for the restoration of the mission buildings. A considerable amount of work was done under direction of the Reverend Alan Butler. It was at this mission that Robert Moffat reduced the Tswana language to writing, printing there the first Tswana Bible. The small cast-iron press which printed this first Bible in Africa has recently been returned to the mission and is back in use for printing in the old school-room. Education continues to be a prime task of the mission today. The conference facilities are in constant use by church and community organisations as they work together for the upliftment of the region. A library to house the considerable collection of books and records was due for completion in 1999.

The town of Kuruman was laid out in 1887 by Captain Levenson and in 1916 it became a municipality. The number of inhabitants now totals 9 327. It is the centre of a substantial district particularly important for the production of cattle, asbestos, manganese, lime and iron. The Kuruman Hills were mined for Cape blue asbestos for many years since 1912. At first exploited by primitive opencast workings, the industry developed through the enterprise of such men as O'Conner and Weimgartner. Large-scale companies such as Dominion Blue Asbestos and Cape Blue Asbestos, which were created to exploit deposits of high grade Cape blue asbestos. High grade manganese ore at Black Rock and high-grade haematite found in 1940 at *Sesheng* allowed for the development of enormous mining industries, with Kuruman as the central town. In modern times asbestos has fallen out of favour and mining for it is no longer a major industry.

Kuruman is situated at a major crossroads in the communications network of the Northern Cape. East of the town a fine, straight tarmac road (N14) leads for 139 km to Vryburg, over a seemingly boundless plain of grass patched by shrub and low thorn trees. There are few landmarks of special note other than occasional small rural centres such as Lykso (72 km from Kuruman) which serves as a half-way point on the journey. North-west of Kuruman a tarmac road (R31) extends for 60 km to the manganese-mining centre of Hotazel. Another tarmac road (N14) leads from Kuruman for 65 km to the iron mine at Kathu.

MANGANESE AND IRON

Between the Koranna and Langeberge ranges on the west and the Asbestos and Kuruman ranges on the east, lies a level plain. Although not notable for its scenery, this plain is covered with a parkland of trees including many magnificent *Acacia giraffe* trees, otherwise known as *kameeldoring* in Afrikaans or *mukala* in Tswana. In a forest on the farm *Kathu,* where water is plentiful, these trees reach perfection.

It would appear that in former geological times this area was part of the bed of a shallow sea. From the surrounding mountains prodigious amounts of manganese and iron were leached into this bed and its shores. The deposits lie on, and immediately below the surface, and are probably the largest in the world.

Black and red rocks are clearly visible on the surface and were evident to the earliest human beings to reach the area. Prehistoric people used red ochre (associated with iron ore) as a cosmetic. White flaky iron oxide crystals known as specularite (or *blinkklip,* shiny stone), was worked into the hair, and was particularly sought after. Some outcrops of it, such as the hillocks called *Logagena* or *Gatkoppies*, were riddled with excavations. The specularite was traded to distant tribes. Manganese was also mined, ground to a powder and used as a cosmetic and as a remedy for stomach complaints.

The first European travellers to explore the area all noticed these mineral deposits. Apart from the iron and manganese there was crocidolite or blue asbestos and the hardened forms of asbestos known as tiger's-eye (golden), hawk's-eye (blue) and cat's-eye (green). Jasper (including a handsome brown and black striped variety) and prodigious amounts of limestone also occur.

Hinrich Lichtenstein, William Burchell, the Somerville-Truter expedition of 1801 and the missionary Robert Moffat, all gave accounts of these treasures.

In 1872 the geologist George Stow was sent by the British Government to report on the area. He examined the Asbestos Mountains and found them to be composed of a series of fine jaspers of a yellowish-brown colour. Iron ores, haematite, galena and magnetite were common. Asbestos and tiger's-eye were the first minerals to be mined in the area by Europeans, being relatively easy to work and reasonably portable in an area without proper roads or railways. Miners, both black and white, fossicked through the hills, working surface outcrops and sharing the proceeds with the landowners.

In 1906 the geologist, Dr A W Rogers, surveyed the area. In his report he recorded asbestos, iron and the manganese outcrop of the hillock named Black Rock, a prominent landmark at the centre of a vast deposit of manganese. Unfortunately, the area was inaccessible, the nearest railway being 350 km away.

In 1915–17 a full-scale land survey of the area was undertaken by Dirk Roos and Hendrik Wessels. They were responsible for surveying and naming many of the farms: *Wessels* (named by Roos after his colleague) *Mamathwane* (bats), and the celebrated *Hotazel*. This farm on the Gamagara River was surveyed by Roos assisted by J W Waldeck. The day was blazing hot and in the camp that evening Roos practically collapsed. '*What a day, what a place! Hot as hell!* he exclaimed. '*That's it*', said Waldeck '*the perfect name*!' So they called the farm *Hotazel* without realising that the ground beneath them was almost solid manganese.

In 1918 Plaatjie, assistant to the prospector Casper Venter, found a diamond in a suricate's (meerkat's) burrow at Postmasburg. Venter prospected this area thoroughly and found a kimberlite pipe with a surface extent of 1,4 ha and ranked nineteenth in the world listing of diamond pipes. Venter sold his rights for £80 000 to the West End Diamond Mining Company formed to work the pipe.

Many diggers and prospectors were attracted to the area by the discovery. Among them was Captain Thomas Shone who arrived in 1922 from the Western Transvaal. He became one of the most active prospectors in the area and developed an interest in manganese. In 1925 with Reg

Saner and John Dale-Lace, he formed Union Manganese Mines and Minerals Ltd, secured options over several farms where manganese was present and tried to find a market. The area's remoteness remained the principal problem.

In Pretoria meanwhile, a Dutch engineer, Cornelis Frederik Delfos, had in 1920 founded the South African Iron and Steel Corporation Ltd (Iscor) and was struggling to raise the capital to create a steel industry. Private enterprise would not back the idea but in 1924 the newly elected Pact Government in South Africa (National and Labour parties) announced their support in anticipation of a vast increase in the demand for iron and manganese ore, the essential ingredients of steel, Dr A L Hall, the geologist, was sent to the Northern Cape to report on the deposits. He returned again in February 1926 with Dr A W Rogers who had twenty years earlier reported on Black Rock. Their report showed conclusively that iron and manganese were present in quantity.

This report encouraged other people to prospect and take options on farms. A J Bester and Niels Langkilde formed South African Manganese Ltd in 1927 and secured options on several farms such as *Kapstewel* where their prospectors, S Griffiths and W J Marais, found manganese, with a richness of 55,4 per cent. Overseas demand was for manganese with a value of at least 50 per cent. Representatives of several overseas manganese buyers from America and Europe visited the area. One of them, Norman Pickett, eventually leased the mining rights of Union Manganese and formed the Manganese Corporation which opened the Mancorp Mine on *Beeshoek* farm. His company also persuaded the Government to build a railway to Postmasburg, guaranteeing to ship 200 000 tons of ore in the first year and at least 350 000 tons a year after that for nine years. If the company failed to meet its target, it would be penalised by £100 000.

In November 1930 the railway reached Postmasburg and the company found itself in difficulties. It was not producing enough manganese of the quality demanded by its buyers, and had to buy manganese at high prices from other producers. Several hectic board meetings followed. Captain Shone left and joined S A Manganese which was also in difficulties, but not burdened by guarantees to the railway. Shone found markets for the manganese and the company also sold iron to a Natal steelmaker. To facilitate its workings the railway was extended to *Lohatla*.

Next to the *Lohatla* farm was *Gloucester* where Gloucester Manganese, run by Guido Sacco, was mining manganese. In 1935 this company was absorbed by the Anglo-Transvaal Consolidated Investment Co which also took over on a royalty basis the mines of the struggling Manganese Corporation. The combined organisation was named Associated Manganese Mines of South Africa Ltd. (Ammosal for short, or Assmang on the stock exchange).

With Guido Sacco as managing director, this new company became very active. The *Beeshoek* mine was closed and its plant moved to *Gloucester*. A second mine was also started on *Bishop*, but a new problem arose when about 600 black miners died of relapsing fever caused by a tick-like insect brought down by migrant labourers from Malawi. In the primitive barrack-type accommodation at the mines, the insects had flourished, as did hookworm. The overseas demand for manganese also suddenly flattened. Germany had been stockpiling in anticipation of war and had plentiful supplies. Life was not easy on the manganese fields and the mines seemed to move from crisis to crisis. The war was imminent, however, and armaments needed steel made from iron and manganese. Things had to improve.

In 1937 the Government sent three geologists to the area to examine it in detail for strategic minerals. F C Truter was allocated the Postmasburg area, D J L Visser the Langeberge, and Leslie Boardman the manganese and haematite deposits. Boardman was particularly impressed with the iron ore on such farms as *Bruce, King* and *Sishen* (*sesheng*, the new place). As a result of his report the South African Iron and Steel Corporation (Iscor) took options on *Sishen*. The town is now known as *Dingleton*.

The war started in 1939. In 1940 Boardman was sent back to the Northern Cape to investigate manganese, especially at Black Rock, and to assess its potential in case the Allies needed more of the metal for armaments. Boardman was an authority on manganese and had examined deposits all over South Africa: from Du Toit's Kloof in the Cape, Caledon, Swellendam, the Cederberg, and the Western Transvaal – nothing, however, remotely equalled what he found in the Northern Cape.

At Black Rock, Boardman found that Associated Manganese Mines of SA had already taken options on three farms. Boardman described the field with enthusiasm and the company decided to commission the famous geophysicist, Oscar Weiss, to undertake a full exploration. Weiss had specialised teams working in many parts of the world and he called in one of them. Using a gravimeter, this team reported positively on the Black Rock field. Associated Manganese took up their options and decided to start mining immediately.

Leslie Boardman returned to the area, this time in the employ of a private company, African Metals Corporation (Amcor), which had been floated by H J van der Bijl, a great figure in the South African steel industry. Amcor had formed an association with S A Manganese and they were running a joint company, Manganese Iron Mining Ltd, mining iron at *Lohatla* and Kapstewel.

Using a magnetometer, Boardman conducted a careful geophysical search of the area near Black Rock. The instrument detected a great deposit of manganese below the sands on the farm *Wessels*. More deposits were found on the farms *Smartt, Rissik, Goold* and *Mamathwane*. What the instrument had detected was the greatest manganese deposit in the world.

S A Manganese bought *Smartt*. Boardman continued prospecting. Farmers were always coming to him with reports of manganese. A diviner from Lichtenburg, a Mr van Rensburg, was employed by the farms to find water and he reported seeing black rocks beneath the surface on farms such as *Langdon* and *Hotazel*. Almost unwillingly Boardman was induced to visit these farms. He was staggered at what he found on *Hotazel*. The magnetometer overshot its own scale! Only an ore body of unimaginable size could have had such an effect.

Boardman immediately secured options on the farm. Mining eventually started there in 1958, with the village of Hotazel being built to house the workers, and the railway extended to the place from Sishen in 1960. Mining at *Mamathwane* started soon afterwards. In 1975 S A Manganese and Amcor merged to form Samancor (South African Manganese Amcor Ltd).

Iron mining had started at Sishen in 1953. In 1973 a second mine was established particularly to feed an export market along a railway line built for 350 km to the harbour of Saldanha Bay. To house the additional workers a new town was created in the parkland on the farm *Kathu*. This town, named Kathu, became a municipality in 1980. It is the largest of the mining towns. It has a fine nature reserve, the Khai-Appel Nature Reserve, and the streets are shaded with superb *Acacia giraffe* trees which are carefully protected.

In company with the railway, a road (R385) continues from Sishen for 64 km past *Lohatla* (place of the vaalbos (*Tarconanthus camphoratus*), and after another 57 km reaches the workings of the Manganese Corporation at Beeshoek. The road then enters the town of ...

POSTMASBURG

This atmospheric town is built in a hollow, originally with a marsh as the town centre. It is surrounded by a prodigious dolomitic plain covered in grass, low shrubs and stunted thorn trees. The marsh is now the man-made Makou Dam in a pleasant park and garden setting, with a municipal caravan park and recreational facilities.

Postmasburg was founded when the local farming community decided that a centre was needed for a church and trade. They selected as a site the area known to the Africans as *Tsantsibane* and *Sibilung*, and to Europeans as *Blinkklip* – each name deriving from the glittering stones found there on the surface. The town was proclaimed on 6 June 1892 and named after Professor D Postma, one of the founders of the Reformed Church (Doppers). A village management board was created at the same time. In this state the little town remained until prospectors found rich deposits of minerals and precious stones.

First there were diamonds, originally found in 1918 by Casper Venter and his assistant Plaatjie. The West End Diamond Mining Company worked the discovery successfully until 1935. The 45 m deep opencast working was then flooded with water from the dolomite. Diamonds are still produced in the vicinity of the town.

The discovery of manganese followed. As the centre for this mining activity, Postmasburg became a municipality in 1936 and since then has grown rapidly, with a present population of 17 392. It has a substantial railway marshalling yard, with the line electrified to Kimberley and doubled for most of the way. Sheep, goats and cattle are farmed.

From Postmasburg a main road (R385) leads eastwards, climbing through a low ridge of hills and after 50 km reaching a turn-off, 10 km long, to the village of ...

DANIELSKUIL

This little place with a population of 9 842 received its name, meaning Daniel's pool, from a sinkhole in the dolomite known as Daniel's Den and used by the Griqua as a depository for prisoners. Asbestos, diamonds, marble and lime in the area are the source of the village's prosperity.

Danielskuil lies at the foot of a ridge of hills where several asbestos mines of various sizes are located. In modern times, however, this mineral has become unpopular for health reasons and is not of much worth. On a hillock overlooking the village there is a small fort built by the British during the Anglo-Boer War. Twenty-two kilometres south of the village, across what is known as the Great Pan (a dried-out lakelet), lies the railway station of Silverstreams. Eight kilometres west of this place is Lime Acres, the huge quarry of the Northern Lime Company, working a deposit of limestone found in the 1950s by the geologist, Digby Roberts.

Seven kilometres beyond the quarry, on the summit of a low ridge, is the Finsch Diamond Mine on the farm named *Brits*. This great diamond pipe was first prospected by Henry Samuel Richter. In 1930 he found signs of a kimberlite pipe when he outlined changes in the vegetation. He sank two prospecting shafts, but the mining commissioner warned him that the farm was owned by the Government and no prospecting for precious stones was allowed there.

Richter, however, was certain there were hidden riches on the farm. To evade the prohibition, he found two partners, Stephanus van Niekerk and Joe Cawood, who secured a permit to prospect for asbestos on *Brits*. Using the permit as a blind, Richter started prospecting for diamonds of which he found excellent examples. He was wild with excitement and talked too much. The news leaked out and the three partners had a violent quarrel in the hotel at Danielskuil. Richter was charged with illegal prospecting and fined, while the partners were ordered off the farm. Richter wandered up to the Kalahari and died in the valley of the Nossob.

Nothing further happened on *Brits* until 1956. Then, a diamond digger from Lichtenburg, Danie de Bruin, who had found diamonds at Bellsbank in some of Richter's old prospect shafts, heard of the find on *Brits*. He secured a licence to prospect for base minerals, sending a digger, Jan Krieg, to prospect the farm. Nothing encouraging was found and De Bruin allowed his licence to lapse.

In his café in Postmasburg, Thorny Fincham had heard of the search. He secured prospecting rights, pegging three large base mineral claims on *Brits*. He made no attempt to work them, but in 1959 granted a twelve-month option on them to Willie Schwabel who moved to the farm with his son Ernst. For twelve months the Schwabels worked on the farm until their option lapsed. Willie Schwabel joined Fincham as a partner in Finsch Base Minerals, the name combining their two surnames. Another digger, Brahm Papendorf, was offered 10 per cent of the company if he could use his influence to persuade the Department of Mines to allow precious stone prospecting on the farm. This was suitably arranged, and Finsch Base Minerals was replaced by Finsch Diamonds, in which Fincham held 55 per cent, Schwabel 35 per cent and Papendorf 10 per cent.

The partners were all stony broke after the long wait and pulling of strings. The little café in Postmasburg had had to carry a lot of expenses, but then came the day of reckoning. Borrowing a rotary pan and watched by Government and police officials, the partners washed their first gravel. Two diamonds appeared in the first sieveful; there were three more in the next sieveful. Within two hours they had recovered 26 diamonds.

Naturally, De Beers took note of such a find. In 1962 they started tests and eventually bought the partners out for R4,5 million. The mine was opened in 1964. Its workers are housed in the village of Lime Acres.

From the turn-off to Danielskuil the main road (R31) continues east over a level, featureless grassy plain covered with dense shrub and low trees. After 51 km the road reaches Koopmansfontein, situated at the junction of the road to Kuruman, and from there continues east to Kimberley.

From Postmasburg a gravel road (R386) leads south over an enormous open plain. To the west lies the long ridge of the Langeberge. Low shrub and thornbush blanket the plain until the road reaches and crosses the low range of the Asbestos Mountains and, 52 km from Postmasburg, reaches ...

GRIQUATOWN

Situated in a fold of the Asbestos Mountains amid trees and sunshine, Griquatown is small and quite nondescript but undoubtedly has a character which stems from a curious past.

When Europeans first settled in Cape Town they encountered a small pastoral tribe, the Xurikwa, living in the area of Piketberg. Apart from several bad habits and a considerable amount of mixed blood, these people received from Europeans so many corruptions of their name that the term Griqua (or Grikwa) by which they eventually became known is, in effect, a simplification.

Under the leadership of a freed slave, *Adam Kok* (Adam, the cook), who had reputably been in charge of the kitchen of a Cape governor, these people wandered away from their original homeland. After numerous adventures, they settled in the area of what was at first known as *Karrikamma* or *Klaarwater* (clear water), now Griquatown. There, in 1804, the London Missionary Society established a station for the benefit of these people. This became the centre for a very polyglot crowd of Griqua, one faction led by Adam Kok I, the second by Andries Waterboer. There were also Tswana tribal fragments and half-breeds known by the proud tribal name of Bastards.

It was on 7 August 1913 that the name of Griquatown was finally adopted. The settlement had the distinction of being the first town to be founded north of the Gariep River. It was here also, in 1812, that the wife of the missionary, Cornelius Kramer, had the misfortune of becoming the first white woman known to die north of the Gariep River. In 1821 Mary Moffat, later the wife of David Livingstone, was born in Griquatown. The old mission house, built in about 1826 is now the Mary Moffat Museum. It houses collections devoted to the story of missionary work in the area, especially that of Robert Moffat who worked there, as well as Griqua relics and general household objects. The museum is open Mondays to Fridays 08h00 to 13h00; 14h00 to 17h00.

In 1819 Adam Kok II (son of Adam I) moved to Campbell then to Philippolis and finally, in 1862, right across the Drakensberg to Griqualand East.

During this period (the 1820s) the remaining Griquas, under the chief Andries Waterboer and leaders of smaller factions, ruled over the substantial portion of country still known as Griqualand West. Griquatown became a place of some importance – a base for hunters and traders venturing into the interior and a sanctuary for many renegades and desperadoes. The discovery of diamonds at Barkly West in 1870 terminated the dominion of the Griqua when the British, to quote President J H Brand of the Orange Free State, *'jumped the country'* and incorporated it into the volatile British Empire.

The second and last chief of the Griquas was Niklaas Waterboer. The second chief (Niklaas Waterboer) had a son who was called Andries but was never a chief. It is stated that two Griquas (Niklaas and Andries) both died in Griquatown in 1896, (these were sons of former chiefs). Chief Niklaas Waterboer lived in a house on the plot later known as *Geeljarts*. On this plot there are some large syringa trees under which it is stated that the chief had two murderers hanged. These two men were brothers named Mablala. They were accused of the murder of their own father.

In Griquatown may still be seen the original *Raadsaal* (council chamber) of the Griqua and next to it the execution tree where they hanged cattle thieves and murderers. The grave of the chief Andries Waterboer is guarded by two cannon, old Niklaas and old Grietjie, presented to the Griqua by Queen Victoria, and named by them after their chief and his wife. There are several other interesting mementoes of the days when this little town was the capital of an independent state with its own flag and coinage.

The area, especially at Niekerkshoop, is famous for tiger's-eye. The stone is polished in Griquatown. The population of Griquatown is 5 288. About twenty groups of Griqua still live in South Africa today.

From Griquatown the R64 tarmac road leads east over a featureless plain covered with dense, low scrub. Amongst the principal inhabitants of this wilderness are numerous kudu, a large antelope notoriously devoid of traffic sense. Several signs warn motorists to beware of colliding with the creatures.

After 46 km the road reaches the faded village of Campbell, lying in a shallow valley on the shrub-covered plain at the edge of the Ghaap Plateau. Named after the Reverend John Campbell, this little place is situated at the head of a well-watered gorge known to the Griqua as *Knovel Vallei* (valley of wild garlic), which provides an easy route up the escarpment of the Ghaap Plateau. The Griqua settlement was founded there in 1811, with the first mission church built in 1831 by the Reverend John Bartlett of the London Missionary Society. Bartlett's church has been restored and stands in a pleasant setting behind the Livingstone bottle store.

From Campbell the R64 tarmac road leads for a further 39 km to Schmidtsdrift and Kimberley (108 km). A branch road (R385) follows the gorge, revealing some handsome views over the low-lying country and, after 31 km, crossing the Vaal River to reach the town of ...

DOUGLAS

With its inhabitants numbering 9 872 Douglas was founded in 1848 as a mission established by the Reverend Isaac Hughes on the farm *Backhouse*, close to the ford of Kokounop across the Vaal River used by early travellers making their way to the north. This strategic ford had been the site of bitter contention between the Bushmen and Griquas, whereafter it was known to the Bushmen as *Go Koo Lume* (where we had a hard time).

In 1867 a group of Europeans from Griquatown signed an agreement with the Griqua chief, Nicholas Waterboer, giving them the right to establish a town at the ford. The place was named after Lieutenant-General Sir Percy Douglas. It flourished as an agricultural centre with land irrigated by water from the Vaal. Attaining municipal status in 1905, its prosperity attracted a branch railway from Belmont in 1923. Lucerne, wheat, potatoes, cotton, vegetable seeds and an occasional diamond are the products of Douglas.

Twelve kilometres from Douglas, the Vaal River joins the Gariep at the irrigation area of Bucklands. At Driekops Island in the Riet River, east of Douglas, may be seen hundreds of stylised engravings carved in the rock by prehistoric people. The site is reached via a turn-off on the main Douglas–Kimberley road marked Plooysburg with, after 8 km, a turn-off through a gate leading through two more gates to a parking area at the site. The engravings are inundated when the river is in flood.

From Douglas the R385 road continues south past Salt Lake to join the Diamond Way (73 km). Another road (R357) leads north-eastwards across gently rolling country, densely bushed and populated with numerous game animals such as springbok and kudu. To the east the Vaal River flows in great, lazy loops and coils. After 45 km the road joins the tarmac road from Campbell (32 km). The combined roads continue eastwards for 6 km to cross the Vaal River at Schmidtsdrif. From there the tarmac road leads due east for 71 km to Kimberley over a level bush-covered plain.

Situated 30 km along this road at Doornlaagte, is a prehistoric site, a Stone Age water-hole unearthed by the roadmakers. Half-way between Schmidtsdrif and Kimberley, the tarmac road passes a curious isolated hillock which has been used as a gravel quarry. This hillock, known as Bakenkop (beacon summit), marks the centre of South Africa at its widest point, for it stands half-way between the east coast at St Lucia and the west coast at Oranjemund.

The game farm of De Beers Consolidated Mines lies next to the road at Rooikoppies near Schmidtsdrif. Further on is a private zoo on the farm *Teneriffe*, created by C P Mathewson.

SCHMIDT'S DRIFT

Of all the odd characters who enlivened Griqualand West's early days there was none stranger perhaps than Willem Schmidt, hot-headed and great-hearted; trader, farmer and founder of Schmidt's Drift.

Capricious fate brought him Schmidt's Drift through the race he hated most – the English. Schmidt was a Dutch trader who, for his services as guide to Sir Charles Warren's expedition with the object of annexing Griqualand West in 1871, was rewarded with the gift of a farm, *Bobbejaan's Kloof*, and a strip of ground on the Vaal River.

The site was a happy choice for though his store and farm paid well, the income was small compared to that which accrued to him as Kimberley grew, and the traffic, halted on the banks of the Vaal, became heavier each day. All day long the massive flat iron pontoon which he constructed, plied a busy trade. At 7/6d a wagon his wealth grew.

But the river, which had brought him prosperity, returned to take his entire fortune in one mad rush. In 1894 Willem Schmidt, watching the floods rise to an unheard of height, saw his property washed down the river. Though he had been warned of impending floods he had always replied: *'The Lord provided and He may take away'*. Perhaps that was why he remained optimistic and, further inland, rebuilt the hotel and store which still stand today. The local Africans regarded Schmidt as a king. His neighbours knew him as a generous man, a quiet man but with a quick temper and an unforgiving memory.

He once built a church for his neighbours but he soon fell out with the parson. In a rage he turned the church into a store. Schmidt's temper was roused in odd ways. The sight of a dog while he was engaged in his favourite pastime of feeding wild birds, would rouse him to an almost ungovernable degree. Many innocent passers-by were astonished to see a gun wildly waved in front of them. He died, a bachelor, in 1899. His grave is near the beacon marking the flood. His pontoon is now a water tank behind the present hotel.

THE DIAMOND WAY TO THE NORTH

From Kimberley the Diamond Way (N12) makes its way northwards over a level plain covered with grass and low bush. Sixteen kilometres from the city there is a turn-off west to the pleasure resort of Riverton, managed by the municipality of Kimberley. At 41 km the road reaches the small railway centre of Windsorton Road from where a tarmac turn-off stretches eastwards for 12 km to the odd little diamond-miners' village of ...

WINDSORTON

Built on the banks of the Vaal River, this atmospheric place was originally the mission station of Hebron. Diamonds were discovered in the gravels of the river and a crowd of diggers rushed to the place, establishing themselves in an uproarious camp. The missionaries went into retreat and the diggers' camp was named *Windsor* after P F Windsor, a merchant who owned the land on which it developed.

Diamonds are still found in the area but the prodigious upheaval of the past is now a memory the scars of which are still clearly visible on the landscape. A drink in the local pub can be rewarding for yarns as well as refreshment.

From the Windsorton turn-off the Diamond Way (N12) continues across level shrub country. After 26 km (67 km from Kimberley) the road reaches the Vaal River and, on its south bank ...

WARRENTON

This town originated in 1880 when a syndicate of eighteen men bought the western portion of the farm *Grasbult*, on the left bank of the Vaal, with the intention of irrigating the fertile land there and producing vegetables for the Kimberley diggers. In those days and in such an area, fresh vegetables were almost as valuable as diamonds and as a result the enterprise of the syndicate proved highly profitable.

A town was laid out on the south bank of the river and named after Sir Charles Warren, leader of the Warren Expedition to the Tswana country and surveyor of the local frontier line with the Transvaal and Orange Free State. In 1888 diamonds were discovered on the town lands and a rush to the place ensued. Mining continued until 1926 when the last diggers wandered away. The town was then left to develop into an agricultural and railway centre with such enterprises as a cheese factory providing employment for its population, which has since reached a total of 18 411.

Warrenton became a municipality in 1948 and is today a pleasant little rural centre producing maize, ground-nuts, cheese and china clay.

At Warrenton the Diamond Way undergoes a major division: the main road, (N12), veers north-eastwards (see Chapter Thirty-Nine) and enters the North-West Province, while a tarmac road, known as the Road to Africa, (R49) crosses the Vaal and continues north. After 16 km the R49 road reaches ...

THE VAAL-HARTS VALLEY IRRIGATION AREA

In 1873 it was discovered that the Vaal River, in the approach to its confluence with the Harts, was 140 m higher than the latter river, with a high ridge separating the two valleys. However, the time was inopportune for any development and the first settler in the valley of the Harts, the well-known Francis 'Matabele' Thompson, only made his home in the area on *Cornforth Hill* in 1874. Troubles with the neighbouring tribes in 1878 delayed still further any development until 1881 when Cecil Rhodes sent surveyors into the area to devise an irrigation scheme.

Nothing came of Rhodes's plan nor of several subsequent schemes. In 1933, however, the Government, spurred on by depression, reinvestigated the project. The Vaal-Harts Valley Irrigation Scheme, the largest in the Southern Hemisphere and, at that time, the second largest in the world, came to fruition. The Vaal-Harts Storage Dam was built in the Vaal River at a site above Fourteen Streams. From this dam a grand canal was dug to lead the water from the Vaal for 120 km into and up the valley of the Harts, thereby irrigating 1 200 smallholdings of varying size from 25 ha to 40 ha. From this water the valley of the Harts, originally a wilderness of vaalbos and kameeldoring trees, was transformed into a huge garden of lucerne, ground-nuts, maize, watermelons and other produce. Any residual water from the canal finds its way back to the Vaal through the Harts River.

At 21 km from Warrenton the tarmac road to Africa, R49 reaches a turn east leading for 1 km to the pleasant town of ...

JAN KEMPDORP

This centre was originally known as Andalusia in honour of the Spanish Andalucian donkeys imported to work on the irrigation project. The town became the headquarters of the officials concerned with the irrigation scheme. During the Second World War, an internment camp was built at Jan Kempdorp where 2 000 Nazi sympathisers were interned, mainly from South-West Africa (Namibia). A second camp was built at Ganspan, 10 km from Jan Kempdorp. This camp held 180 South African internees. Nine of them escaped through a tunnel which may be seen in the remnants of the camp. A vast depot was also constructed at the town in order to store ammunition well out of reach of possible coastal invasion. In January 1954 Andalusia became a town and was named *Jan Kempdorp* in honour of the Minister of Agriculture. A rural centre shaded by fine trees, it attained the status of a municipality on 1 April 1967. The population is 14 533.

From the turn to Jan Kempdorp the R49 road continues north, keeping close company with the railway and leading in a straight line through rich irrigated fields. After 18 km there is a turn-off east leading for 3 km to the rural centre of ...

HARTSWATER

Laid out in 1948 as a town for the northern section of the Vaal-Harts irrigated area, Hartswater has grown up to the sound of gurgling water in irrigation canals and is surrounded by trees and wide expanses of fertile fields. It became a municipality on 1 April 1960 and has a population of 4 782.

From Hartswater the tarmac road (R49) continues north across the irrigated fields. The drive up the length of this irrigation scheme is akin to crossing a vast garden 40 km long and occupying 400 000 ha. Sixteen kilometres north of Hartswater the scheme ends and the traveller feels a slight shock at the sudden transition back to the wilderness of shrub and aridity. Seven kilometres beyond this point (24 km from Hartswater) the R49 road to Africa reaches the small rail centre of ...

TAUNG

From *Taung* (the place of the lion), a branch railway leads west to the Buxton quarries of the Northern Lime Co. It was in this quarry that one of the most celebrated of all fossils was found. In 1924 Professor Raymond Dart of the University of the Witwatersrand offered £5 to the student who brought him the best fossil. From the quarry at Taung, one of his students, Josephine Salmons, brought a baboon skull. The skull was interesting and Dart was told that the quarry was rich in fossils. Mr M de Bruyn who worked in the quarry agreed to collect any fossils revealed in blasting and send them to Professor Dart. In a box of these fragments Dart found the cast of the inside of a skull of a five-year-old boy whose features were half ape, half man. His front teeth were flat and the canines of an ape were missing. From the position of the hole where the spinal cord joins the brain, it was apparent that the boy had walked upright instead of on all fours like an ape. The molar teeth, however, were big like those of an ape and the brain size was far smaller than that of a human being.

The discovery created a sensation. The creature was named *Australopithecus africanus* (southern ape of Africa) and hailed as the long-sought missing link between ape and man.

West of Taung is the largest cheese factory in Southern Africa, *Reivilo*, an odd name derived from the spelling in reverse of the name of the Reverend Mr Olivier who presented the land for the centre. Visitors to the factory are welcome. The Taung Travertyn works, mining gemstones, is situated in Taung itself. Marble is worked in a factory producing a variety of subtly hued and elegantly designed tiles, baths, pillars and other creations.

The tarmac road (R49) north of Taung leads across a vast flat savanna – parklike in places, with green grass and areas of handsome trees. At 9 km a turn-off leads to Amalia. The road continues past the railway junction point of Pudimoe (*Pudumong*, place of the wildebeest) at 12 km from

Taung, leaving an area of tribal African occupation and reaching a vast grassy plain – magnificent ranching country. Here, 60 km from Taung, sheltering in a slight hollow in the plain, lies the town of ...

VRYBURG

Inhabited by 33 999 people, *Vryburg* (the town of liberty) had a real swashbuckling origin. A long spell of disturbance between the Tlapin tribe of Chief Mankwarane and the Koranna, led by David Massouw, resulted in the employment by these rivals of European mercenaries. David Massouw offered each recruit a farm as well as a share in all loot. Commanded by Sarel Cilliers, a force of over 400 Europeans was raised to support David Massouw, while Mankwarane also presided over a pocket army.

A desultory little war followed, with four of Massouw's followers being killed – two mercenaries and two of his own men. On 26 July 1882 peace was arranged and 416 farms were given to mercenaries. The occupants of these farms decided to organise their own state. In August 1833 they formed the Stellaland Republic with Gerrit Jakobus van Niekerk elected as the first president. The name of Stellaland is said to have arisen after a comet appeared while fighting was in progress. A party of mercenaries, sitting around their camp-fire in the veld, were discussing the proposed republic and its name, for which various suggestions were made. One of the men, lying on his blanket gazing at the wondrous spectacle of the sky, proposed that the republic be named *Sterland* (star land), as he considered that in no other part of the world could the stars be seen so vividly. The name was accepted but changed to the more euphonious *Stellaland*.

As a capital for the republic, the town of Vryburg was laid out on a site known to the Africans as *Huhudi* (running stream). A postal service was organised, a flag designed and the republic launched as a proper, if diminutive, state. Its life, however, was short. A second pocket republic, Goshen, had been established further north and disturbances there induced President Paul Kruger of the Transvaal to annex the area. The British intervened and sent an expeditionary force under Sir Charles Warren to 'remove filibusters from (British) Bechuanaland and restore order in the country'. Warren and his men occupied the area without resistance in 1885, and from then on it became part of what was called British Bechuanaland. The Stellaland flag was sent to Queen Victoria and hung in Windsor Castle until 1934 when King George V returned it to Vryburg where it is now displayed in the museum housed in the handsome town hall.

The Stellaland flag is worth seeing. In the centre, on a dark-green background, is a shield surmounted by a star. On the shield is a white hand holding a *korhaan* (bustard). Representative of Mankwarane are two fish (totems of the Tlapin tribe) pierced by a sword. A scale depicts justice and there is another star. Stellaland postage stamps are rarities. The museum is open daily from 07h00 to 17h00.

British Bechuanaland became part of the Cape Colony in 1895, and today the land of stars is a prosperous ranching area, with Vryburg a great sales yard and railage centre for livestock. Beef, butter, milk-powder, buttermilk and other products are the exports of Vryburg. The days when the town was a frontier resort for renegades, freebooters and outlaws such as Scotty Smith are gone forever, although some of the atmosphere of those halcyon days still survives.

On Fridays from 08h00 onwards a cattle auction is held at which about 4 000 head are sold. Heavy trucks bring in the slaughter stock and the ranchers and stockmen provide a very colourful gathering. A meat-canning concern has its factory in Vryburg and 10 km away at *Armoedsvlakte* (poverty plain) is situated a veterinary research and bull-testing station.

Ruins of the old gaol – a home from home for many interesting characters – may still be seen. Outside the modern civic centre plays a pretty little fountain, next to which stands a bronze of President Gerrit van Niekerk, looking very paternal with his king-sized bushy beard, and viewing with interest the rapidly changing scene around him. Six kilometres out of Vryburg, on the road to Tosca, lies the fine Swartfontein Recreational Resort, where there are facilities such as a swimming-pool, café, caravan and camping sites and cottages. Next to it is a nature reserve named after Leon Taljaard, a councillor of the town. A large variety of game animals find a home in this resort which is open Mondays to Thursdays from 14h00–18h30, and on Fridays, Saturdays and public holidays from 08h00–18h00.

From Vryburg the main tarmac road (R49) continues north across a seemingly boundless plain of grass and acacia trees. After 20 km the road passes the Boereplaas Holiday Resort, and 46 km from Vryburg reaches the small trading centre of Stella, laid out in the form of a star next to a salt-pan known to the Africans as Schwaing (place of salt).

At 85 km from Vryburg lies the trading centre of Setlagoli, from where there is a turn-off to *Madibogo* (the fording places) railway station. This is a flat world of red soil, maize, ground-nuts and cattle. Acacia trees are the principal natural feature.

At 114 km from Vryburg the road reaches the trading centre of Maritsane. Beyond Maritsane (a total of 156 km from Vryburg) the R49 road reaches ...

MAFIKENG

The town of *Mafikeng* (place of boulders) was originally known to Europeans as Mafeking. The birth of Mafikeng was similar to that of Vryburg. In 1881 the Rolong tribe was divided into two factions, both of which recruited European mercenaries with the usual promises of farms. The consequences of this was the establishment of a pocket republic named Goshen. A 'capital' was created at Rooigrond (18 km from Mafikeng) and A Delaney was elected as president.

Goshen never amounted to much and its inhabitants squabbled aimlessly. Paul Kruger attempted to annex the republic to the Transvaal but the British Government intervened in 1885 and sent Sir Charles Warren in command of an expeditionary force to occupy the whole of what became known as British Bechuanaland. In the course of the expedition Sir Charles laid out the town of Mafikeng on the banks of the *Molopo* (river). A British administrator, Sir Sydney Shippard, was appointed and the roughneck semi-military Bechuanaland Border Police was raised to control the area. Mafikeng was the administrative centre and it grew into a rough-and-ready frontier town inhabited by tough troopers and a rugged crowd of farmers, traders, hunters and adventurers.

In 1895 British Bechuanaland was annexed to the Cape. Life in Mafikeng, the remotest town in the Colony, started to settle down, with the Jameson Raid that same year drawing off many of the former Bechuanaland Border Police. On 10 September 1896 Mafikeng became a municipality. On 14 October 1899, a few days after the outbreak of the Anglo-Boer War, a Republican force under General J P Snyman besieged the town. Colonel Robert Baden-Powell and a garrison of 800 men held the town for 271 days until 17 May 1900, when it was relieved by a combined force of Rhodesians from the north and Imperial troops from the south. The siege of Mafikeng had so captivated the imagination of the British public that, when news of the relief arrived, celebrations in the streets of London reached such unparalleled heights of emotion that a new word thenceforth appeared in English dictionaries: *Maffick* (exult riotously). It was during the siege, when Baden-Powell organised the boys of the town into a non-combatant corps to keep them out of mischief and assist in the conduct of the town, that the idea was born for the future Boy Scout movement.

There are many relics in Mafikeng of the siege days. The fort on Cannon Koppie has been restored as an historical monument. The Anglican church, designed by Sir Herbert Baker, was built of Rhodesian granite in memory of those who died in the siege. Old cannon and other bric-à-brac of battle are preserved in various parts of the town. There is a fine museum in the old town hall, housing exhibits mainly concerned with the siege. The museum is open Mondays to Fridays from 08h00 to 16h00; on Saturdays from 10h00 to 13h00. History tours to historical sites are conducted by arrangement with the museum.

Subsequent to the war, Mafikeng continued to develop slowly. Excitement erupted in 1924 when alluvial diamonds were found 5 km from the town. Some 500 diggers rushed to the area but it proved only moderately rich and eventually petered out. Prosperity in Mafikeng today is based on cattle, dairy products, maize, cement and its importance as a railway junction and marshalling yard close to the border with Botswana. Until February 1965, Mafikeng was the seat of the British administration of the then Bechuanaland Protectorate. Their buildings were situated on what was known as the Imperial Reserve, an area adjoining the town, which had been preserved for the exclusive use of the British Government.

With the creation in 1977 of the so-called Tswana homeland of *Bophuthatswana* (that which binds the Tswana), a capital was established on the outskirts of Mafikeng and named *Mmâbatho* (mother of the people). Situated here, apart from residences, is an administrative and council building, a large stadium, a university (Unibo), and a hotel containing the usual gambling casino, nightclub, theatre presentations and varied entertainments. Bophuthatswana, under the apartheid policy of the then South African government, became an independent Bantustan in 1977. It was fragmented into several sections with a total area of 4 187 813 ha inhabited by nearly two million people. The head of state was Lucas Mangope, who survived several attempts at removing him from power and a constant agitation for a reincorporation of the Bantustan into South Africa. In 1980 Mafikeng was incorporated into Bophuthatswana. With the change of government in South Africa in 1994 and the ending of apartheid, Bophuthatswana became part of the North West Province of South Africa.

Cooke's Lake provides a pleasant recreational area for the people of Mafikeng as well as visitors. There are fishing opportunities, picnicking and a caravan park. Thirty kilometres from Mafikeng a great sink-hole has occurred in the dolomite. Over 60 m deep and 70 m by 50 m wide, it is filled with crystal-clear water.

In the Lutlamorong village created by the writer and mystic, Credo Mutwa, visitors are welcome to see something of the ancient lifestyle of the Tswana people. There is a lion park at Manyame game lodge and a crocodile breeding station.

From Mafikeng the tarmac R49 road to the north continues, passing Mmabatho at 5 km and at 25 km reaching the border customs and immigration post of Botswana at Ramatlabama. The post is open from 07h00 to 20h00.

Chapter Fifteen
THE GREAT KAROO, BUSHMANLAND AND GORDONIA

Vast, moody, lonely, melancholy, autumnal in its moods and stillness. Remote, elusive, harsh in the midday sun, but transformed by the approach of night into a place of gorgeous sunsets, with cool shadows rising out of valleys and hollows, slowly enveloping the land in a dark blanket of sleep while the heavens sparkle with so brilliant a display of stars that the Karoo seems to be washed with a soft dew of their falling light.

There are several ways of seeing the Karoo. The tarmac Cape-to-Cairo road (N1) which crosses part of the area is described in Chapter Thirteen. For most travellers along this great north–south highway of Africa, the Karoo simply represents a hot and dreary non-scenic intrusion between the fertile Western Cape and the grasslands of the highveld. To the discerning, especially those who make the journey in the early morning or late afternoon, the Karoo is far more appealing, for at that time of day the landscape is modelled into interesting shapes by oblique light and its crystal-clear air is cool and invigorating.

This chapter is for those who have sensed the intrinsic nature of the Karoo and who wish to know it more intimately by leaving the beaten track and journeying to Bushmanland, Gordonia and the verge of the Kalahari where the springbok play.

In the language of the early African people, the name *Karoo* indicated a thirstland – very dry but not actually a true desert. Geologists apply the name to a sequence of sediments laid down over two-thirds of the interior of Southern Africa; dry only in the south, covered in grass in the better-watered highveld of the Free State, the North-West and Northern Provinces, and blanketed with trees further north in countries such as Zimbabwe and Zambia.

The sediments were laid down by water between 250 and 150 million years ago in a series of different deposits of immense thickness, in places over 7 000 m. The origin of this material, however, is a mystery. Some ancient surface comprising mountain ranges, volcanoes, hills and valleys must have been eroded completely, the debris dispersed in solution and then redeposited as though Nature, dissatisfied with some early creative work, had erased it and started again with something new.

Buried in these layers of silt are the fossils of many animals and plants which existed in the swamplands, lakes and seas during the period of the formation of the Karoo. The water subsequently dried up and vanished like a mirage in the geological history of Earth, leaving behind the high-lying surface of the central plateau of Southern Africa.

Apart from its content of fossils and coal, the layers of sediment contain a particularly notable intrusion. Some disturbance in the molten depths of Earth caused igneous matter to travel upwards through the soft layers of shale and mudstone. Forcing its way through horizontal and vertical lines of weakness in these sediments, the igneous matter cooled to form hard dolerite rock which, when it reached the surface vertically, was exposed in the form of strange walls of stone known as dykes, stretching aimlessly across the country as though constructed for unknown reasons by some vanished people. In places where the dolerite spread out horizontally, it solidified in layers of hard rock known as sills, which resist erosion long after the softer sediments around them have disintegrated. In the same way as a roof, the sill protects what is below it, with the result that fragments of higher levels of land remain like pieces of an ancient jigsaw puzzle, the surface of which was once the face of the land but whose segments are now scattered over the floor, irregular in size but uniform in height. These are the distinctive 'koppies' of South Africa – table-tops, pouf-tops, or rhino horns, oddly shaped hillocks each characterised by a hard dolerite top of different size and shape.

The sediments of the Karoo are virgin and rich, but to awaken fertility water is needed, a precious bringer of life in a region where it sometimes does not rain for years. When rain does fall, the surface, only thinly protected by vegetation, is more often damaged than aided by sudden run-offs of water from short-lived but violent storms. In addition, every watercourse is impeded by man with dams and weirs. The flow of streams is in any case erratic but, even without being impounded by man, the water seldom gets anywhere. It flows into hollows, lingers for a while in shallow lakelets and then disappears, leaving behind dried-out *pans*, ghost lakes with hard, smooth, level floors caked with mineral salts.

In 1854 in America, Daniel Hallady invented the windpump, the perfection of which in 1883 by Stuart Perry, made the Karoo inhabitable by significant numbers of people. Over 200 000 of these pumps work in South Africa today, drawing up water through boreholes and pouring it into small reservoirs and drinking troughs. The plaintive creaking and groaning of these hard-working devices provides the Karoo with one of its most characteristic sounds. There are few parts of this wilderness where a windpump may not be seen, either nearby or on the furthest horizon.

Before the windpump was introduced, the Karoo was the home only for life-forms which could tolerate drought conditions, such as springbok, gemsbok, the suricate (*meerkat*) and the tortoise. Water obtained from the windpumps made possible the introduction of sheep, over 35 million of which now flourish in Southern Africa, mainly in the Karoo.

The most prolific variety of sheep in this area is the woolled merino which originated in Spain. The black-headed Persian mutton sheep is also common, as is the *dorper* (a mixture of the Dorset Horn and the Persian), and the karakul, which is bred for its handsome skin. Sheep provide the Karoo with its principal industry, the production of wool and mutton.

The scarcity of surface water, understandably, made the Karoo unattractive to early man. A few prehistoric groups wandered into the area but generally departed at the earliest opportunity. Europeans entered the Karoo from the south, but before the introduction of the windpump their settlement was confined to the few oases where water was available although it was brackish, unpalatable, smelly, and undependable.

The traditional southern entrance from the Western Cape to the Karoo was from Ceres through Karoo Poort. The first track to penetrate far into the interior of Southern Africa made its way through this natural passage. It was the route followed by early explorers, hunters, missionaries and most of the extraordinary human cavalcade which, lured by the discovery of diamonds and gold, poured into Southern Africa. The highway later fell into disuse and was almost forgotten when the modern road and railway were opened through the valley of the Hex River. The old road was subsequently revived and today it carries traffic to several towns such as Sutherland and Fraserburg. For the connoisseur of travel, it provides the means for a nostalgic journey off the beaten track to places seldom visited, along a route crowded with memories of adventures and characters and where many scenes and aspects of life peculiar to the Great Karoo are revealed.

From Ceres the R46 tarmac road stretches north-eastwards across the floor of the fertile fruit-producing area of the Warmbokkeveld. Fine farms line both sides of the road and turn-offs lead to such places as Onder-Swaarmoed (at 3 km) and Lakenvlei (at 11 km). After 12 km the road reaches the foot of the Theronsberg Pass and for the next 12 km climbs steadily to the 1 091 m high summit. The views from this pass are superb, especially in winter when the mountains encircling the basin of the Warmbokkeveld are often covered with snow. The pass is frequently closed owing to snowfalls, while the Hex River Mountains to the south provide at least a little opportunity for winter sports.

The Theron family, after whom the pass is named, settled on *Leeuwfontein* (lion fountain) farm during the 18th century, and their thatched and gabled homestead is dated 1770.

The tarmac road continues, rising and falling through a world of panoramic views and castellated mountains. The road descends the Theronsberg Pass and winds through Hottentots Kloof, passing a turn-off to Citrusdal and the Kouebokkeveld 30 km from Ceres. The journey is interesting and prepares the traveller for entrance to the Great Karoo.

The road continues past a resting-place with water in the midst of the kloof. The *Nuwerus* farm buildings stand beside the road 35 km from Ceres. At 2 km beyond this homestead the tarmac road veers eastwards to join N1 at Touws River. The road to the Great Karoo now becomes gravel surfaced. Ahead can be seen Karoo Poort, the cleft in the mountains which forms the gateway between the fertile, well-watered Western Cape and the arid Great Karoo.

Karoo Poort is actually the passage made through the mountains by the *Doring* (thorn) River. For 4 km the road keeps close company with the river as it twists through the mountains. The floor of the pass is level and the journey demands no climbing or descent. Near the farmhouse at the south-western entrance to the pass a shady resting-place is reached, beyond which a considerable change in vegetation and scenery occurs. The erica, protea, renosterbos and characteristic flora of the Western Cape dwindle and disappear. Dark-green karee trees *(Rhus lancea)* and the lighter-green wild willows (*Salix capensis*) line the banks of the river, the bed of which is thick with reeds. As the road reaches the north-eastern side of the pass, the vegetation transforms completely, with drought-resistant succulents, mesembryanthemums, ganna, milkbush, brakbos and other shrubs taking over. A hardy acacia tree puts in an occasional appearance.

The sedimentary cliffs of the *Witteberge* (white mountains) on either side of the pass have been curved and warped by the stresses of their original deposition and drying process. The gravel road leaves the pass beneath these natural arches. The traveller sees before him the vast panorama of the Bokkeveld Karoo – a level, open, shallow valley through which the Doring River swings northwards and then westwards eventually to become a tributary of the Olifants just south of Klawer.

The road divides beyond the end of Karoo Poort, 45 km from Ceres. One branch, R355, leads northwards up the valley of the Doring to Calvinia, 213 km away. The other branch, R356, veers north-east across the broad valley towards the mountain heights at its eastern end. The wheels of many wagons, the feet of many eager travellers seeking fortunes in diamonds and gold, blazed this route into the heart of the Great Karoo.

For a while the gravel road keeps within a few kilometres of the east bank of the Doring River. Irrigation from this river and its tributaries brings life to orchards, fields and vineyards on estates such as *Inverdoorn*. Over the entire valley broods a strange, sombre pile of dark-coloured Dwka Shales, known as the *Perdeberg* (horse mountain), a remnant of a former higher level of the valley. A melancholy atmosphere surrounds it as though it remembers past years, but is now forlorn, the last of its kind awaiting an inevitable end through erosion.

The road passes the foot of this 620 m high landmark, twice crossing the Doring River and continuing across a semi-desert landscape painted with colour – delicate blues for the sky, olive-green for vegetation, splashes of vivid shades in the spring when the succulents bloom and convert the wilderness into a garden.

Ahead lies another landmark, an overhanging peak known as *Klein-Hangklip* (small hanging rock) (744 m high) which forms part of the mountains on the eastern side of the valley of the Doring. In former years many travellers outspanned and rested beneath Klein-Hangklip, for the place marked the end of the journey across the hot and arid Bokkeveld Karoo.

Beyond this landmark the gravel road starts to ascend the heights, reaching the summit 65 km from the exit of Karoo Poort. Behind, the traveller has a last view of the mountains of the Western Cape, the Hex River range, the Cederberge and the Witteberge. The road continues, descending and climbing the grain of mountains and tributary river valleys of the Doring. It is a bone-dry, hot and rugged world, but nevertheless provides an interesting scenic and travel experience.

At 106 km from Karoo Poort the gravel road joins the tarmac road R354 coming in from Matjiesfontein (71 km away) on the N1. Another kilometre takes the tarmac road across the *Bobbejaanskrans* (baboon's cliff) River, beyond which lies the entrance to the pass known as *Verlaten Kloof* (lonely or abandoned ravine). This great cleft in the face of the mountains carries the road steadily upwards. There are several pleasant resting-places along the way, with shade and water provided by windpumps. The summit, 1 571 m high, is reached after 21 km, and the road then begins to cross the cold and often snowbound plateau of the *Roggeveld* (rocky prairie).

Five kilometres from the top of the pass the road passes a pleasant resting-place with toilets and water. After a further 10 km (188 km from Ceres and 143 km from Karoo Poort), the tarmac road reaches the isolated little town of ...

SUTHERLAND

Founded in 1857 and named after the Reverend Henry Sutherland, the town was created on the farm *De List* as a centre for the wool producing district of the Roggeveld, which has the bleak reputation of consistently being one of the coldest areas in Southern Africa. Parts of Mpumalanga do at times experience lower temperatures than Sutherland but, with an average minimum temperature of 6,1°C and periodic heavy falls of snow, the town (lying 1 456 m above sea-level) and its surroundings can be rather chilly.

Despite a shortage of water, Sutherland is an amiable place characterised by a few interesting buildings surviving from the Victorian period. The town became a municipality in 1884. It has a population of 2 023.

Beyond Sutherland the gravel road continues over the Roggeveld, reaching after 13 km a turn-off to the entrance of the South African Astronomical Observatory, the buildings of which, awkwardly positioned, look down aloofly from the cold summit of a 1 750 m high ridge. The observatory was created in 1972 when the main instruments from the observatories in Cape Town, Johannesburg and Pretoria were moved to this site (away from the glare and pollution of cities) where the sky is brilliantly clear and largely unaffected by clouds. The principal instrument is the 1,9 m reflecting telescope, formerly housed in the Radcliffe Observatory in Pretoria. There is also a 1 m reflecting telescope, formerly mounted in Cape Town; a 0,75 m reflecting telescope; and a 0,5 m reflecting telescope. The buildings of the observatory on top of the ridge are visible from many kilometres away. Visitors are only allowed during daylight hours and visits must be booked at least a day in advance. Phone (023) 571-1182.

Beyond the turn to the observatory the gravel road continues over an arid, undulating Karoo landscape where sheep flourish on the scanty vegetation and windpumps provide the source of life. After 100 km the road reaches the town of ...

FRASERBURG

Fraserburg was named in 1851 after two people, the Reverend Colin Fraser, the Scottish Dutch Reformed minister of Beaufort West who had pioneered the establishment of a new congregation in the western Nuweveld, and Gerrit Jacobus Meyburgh who had exerted himself for the establishment of the town.

This centre of wool production, with a population of 2 637, is situated high on the cold plateau of the *Nuweveld* (new prairie). Fraserburg is worth exploring, for in the side streets may be found several well-preserved Victorian buildings, with elaborate wrought-iron decorations, verandas, doors, windows and interior furnishings of great interest to antique dealers.

One particularly extraordinary building is known as the *Peperbus* (pepper box), a six-sided building erected in 1861 and designed as an office by the Reverend Carl Bamberger. The reason for its eccentric design is unknown. Over the years it served as an office for the municipal market master, the magistrate and for the church. A small powder-magazine used by British forces during the Anglo-Boer War stands on the hills overlooking the town.

During the winter months there is considerable hunting activity in the district, especially for springbok and various other plains' game.

From Fraserburg the gravel road continues across the Karoo with its sheep-runs, isolated homesteads and long clear views. After 95 km the road enters ...

LOXTON

In 1899 the Dutch Reformed Church bought from A E Loxton, the farm *Phezantfontein* (fountain of pheasants) on which was founded a village to serve the sheep-farming community. In 1905 Loxton became a municipality and today has a population of 837. Although it is a sleepy, hot little place, numerous trees have been planted and the town shelters in a hollow in the valley of the upper Sak River, away from the searing winds of the Karoo. There is normally a scarcity of water but occasionally the situation alters – in March 1961 a violent storm caused such flooding that the dam above the town burst and three-quarters of the buildings in Loxton were destroyed or damaged.

From Loxton, roads diverge to several parts of the Karoo. At the town, the old road from Ceres joins the R63 tarmac route (84 km long) leading eastwards to Victoria West where it joins the modern Diamond Way N12 proceeding to Kimberley and the north. Along this road, 47 km from Loxton, lies the holiday resort of Melton Wold.

A gravel road, R381, leads south from Loxton for 111 km across an interesting stretch of Karoo, descending (as a tarmac road) the spectacular Molteno Pass to Beaufort West. Extraordinary rock formations, deep ravines, the Karoo National Park (see Chapter Thirteen), and some fine farms may all be seen along this road.

North-west of Loxton a tarmac continuation of the R63 road from Victoria West leads for 62 km, passing a resting-place with water (44 km from Loxton) and reaching ...

CARNARVON

The town of Carnarvon, with its population of 7 389, lies in the central Karoo in a setting of flat-topped hills. The town originated as a Rhenish mission station where, in about the year 1850, 110 African refugees from various tribal disturbances in the north were settled. In 1860 a village named Harmsfontein was established. In 1874 the name was changed to *Carnarvon* in honour of the British Colonial Secretary, Lord Henry Carnarvon. In 1882 the village became a municipality. Trees have been planted to provide shade and water is obtained from boreholes. The town is a busy farming centre, served by the branch railway from Hutchinson to Calvinia.

The Appie van Heerden Nature Reserve conserves an interesting local flora and a number of wild animals indigenous to the area.

There is a museum exhibiting about 700 different items related to the region. Several old houses survive. At the museum there is a fine example of a corbelled dwelling – a giant, stone, beehive shaped building unique to this part of the Karoo and similar to those built in the Mediterranean by megalithic people. These buildings are pleasantly cool in summer but perfectly snug during the harsh winters. They were built by the early stock farmers, who were the first to settle permanently in the Karoo.

From Carnarvon the R63 tarmac road leads westwards, keeping company with the railway line. After 35 km a turn-off leads to an interesting national monument, the homestead of the farm *Stuurmansfontein*, an example of the corbelled style of architecture. The method of construction of the homestead on this farm in the 1850s incorporates stone and timber, and effectively promotes coolness. After a further 95 km (130 km from Carnarvon) the road reaches ...

WILLISTON

In a setting of arid hills, the town of Williston originated as a Rhenish mission station founded in 1845 on the banks of the Sak River and named *Amandelboom*, after a wild almond tree under which the first missionaries, J H Lutz and F W Reinecke, pitched their tent. About 600 people of diverse origin were living in the area at the time. The purpose of the mission was to impose some order on a rather shiftless community. Sheep farmers were attracted to the area in the 1860s and a village developed around the mission. It was named *Williston* in 1919 in honour of Colonel Hampden Willis, Colonial Secretary of the Cape Colony in the 1880s. The town became a municipality in 1881 and today has a population of 3 069.

From Williston the R63 tarmac road continues west across the Sak River, passing a resting-place with shade and water 2 km from the town and continuing across a more fertile and better-watered part of the Great Karoo than has been traversed so far. The Sak River and its tributaries (when they contain water) flow sluggishly over a plain where they are easily intercepted and diverted by means of weirs, dams, polders and other constructions. By this means farmlands are irrigated and crops such as lucerne and wheat are cultivated. The shallow valley of the Sak River is famous for the *saaidam* system of irrigated farming which takes place in the river bed. Grain is sown in the shallow river bed as soon as the seasonal flow ends. Enough water remains in the soil to allow the crops to ripen without the necessity of rain or further irrigation. The name of the river, *Sak* (sinking), refers to the way the water disappears into the sandy bed for long stretches of its course.

At 90 km from Williston a tarmac turn-off R27 stretches north to Brandvlei and Upington, while the R63 tarmac road continues west and, 111 km from Williston, reaches ...

CALVINIA

Founded in 1845 and named after John Calvin the religious leader, *Calvinia* is a pleasant if isolated little town lying at the foot of the Hantamsberg. Sheep are bred in the area on a very considerable scale and, after Harrismith, in the Free State, this is the second largest wool-producing district in Southern Africa.

Calvinia (with a population of 8 358) is the terminus of the branch railway from Hutchinson which reached the town on 13 August 1917. One of the steam locomotives which worked this line, a Class 24, built in 1949 by the North British Locomotive Company, is now preserved in the garden of the local museum. Housed in the old synagogue building, the museum was opened in 1968 and contains an interesting and well-displayed collection of items of local history. There are photographs and mounted specimens of unusual sheep, period furniture, and a delightful example of a confidence trick – a four-legged ostrich chick skilfully contrived by a local itinerant carpenter who charged people one penny to peep at his odd little pet. The museum is open weekdays from 08h00 to 13h00 and from 14h00 to 17h00; on Saturdays from 08h00 to 12h00; and Sundays from 15h00 to 17h00 by appointment only.

A rockery in the centre of the town contains a good collection of aloes. Four kilometres out of the town, at the foot of the mountains, lies the Akkerendam Nature Reserve, 2 568 ha in extent and conserving the flora and fauna of the area. There are two hiking trails and several picnic places in the reserve which is open daily from sunrise to sunset. One of the trails, known as the Kareeboom Route, has been specially created for use by elderly people. It is two kilometres long. The second trail, the Sterboom Route leads to the plateau summit of the Hantam Mountains, at least seven hours of good walking. There is also an 'Historical walk about Town' route which reveals several interesting buildings.

Drought is the curse of the district, with water often scarce and inclined to smell. In compensation Nature delights the area with some of the most blazing sunsets and dawns imaginable. The dolerite-topped Hantamsberg also provides a fine sight. The name *Hantam* comes from the edible roots of the *Pelargonium bifolium* plants, known as heyntame, which grow there.

Each year the Hantam Meat Festival is staged at the height of the wild flower season in August. There is folk dancing, athletic and equestrian marathons are staged as part of the festival and the quality of the local mutton is proved in several traditional cooking procedures.

From Calvinia the tarmac road R27 continues westwards. After 2 km there is a gravel turn-off leading south through Bloukranspas for 215 km to Karoo Poort and from there for 45 km to Ceres. The main tarmac road proceeds west for a further 30,5 km, reaching an interesting wayside memorial commemorating the last battle of the Anglo-Boer War, which was fought at this place. The memorial contains an actual rifle used in the conflict.

The tarmac road follows the fertile valley of the *Oorlogskloof* (ravine of war), reaching at 35 km from Calvinia a turn-off leading for 117 km to Clanwilliam through Botterkloof and over Pakhuis Pass. Beyond the turn-off, the tarmac road continues over a high, open plateau fairly well watered and grassy, with low shrubs. At 69 km from Calvinia the road enters ...

NIEUWOUDTVILLE

Named after H C Nieuwoudt who owned the land on which the Dutch Reformed Church, in 1897, created a centre for the district, the town is a place of sandstone houses, dominated by a picturesque church built of dressed sandstone in neogothic style. Windpumps provide water and many trees have been planted to shade the town.

On the farms around Nieuwoudtville there are interesting examples of stone buildings. There is an original horse mill at *Kookfontein*. The homesteads on *Ouplaas, Groenrivier, Sewefontein, Papkuilsfontein* and on *Lokenburg*, the first farm in the district sold with title deeds, are all interesting to see. There are *Kapsteilhuise* (A-framed houses) still being lived in on the road south to Clanwilliam. These houses were thatched with what was known as *Sonkwas* grass, from its use by Bushmen *(Sonkwa)*.

The spring display of wild flowers around Nieuwoudtville is extremely beautiful if there have been reasonable winter rains. The Nieuwoudtville Wild Flower Reserve, established in 1974, conserves on 115 ha a variety of over 300 species of indigenous flora, including the red cat's tail *(Bulbanella* sp.*)*, which is unique to the district.

The *Oorlogskloof* (ravine of war) is 5 570 ha in extent and conserves magnificent fynbos country. There are several hiking trails, day hikes and two four-day routes with camping facilities. The name comes from a battle there between settlers and the followers of Jantjie Klipheuwel, a Bushman captain. Bushman paintings are numerous in the area. Some of the best preserved glacial tracks in South Africa may be seen 6 km south of Nieuwoudtville on the road to Oorlogskloof.

The pretty 100 m high Nieuwoudtville Falls in the Doring River provides a fine spectacle, especially after rains. There is a picnic and camping ground at the Falls. The caravan park is pleasantly laid out in a setting of wild flowers.

Sheep and wheat farming are the principal agricultural activities. Rooibos tea is cultivated and harvested between December and March. There is a processing plant in the town which may be visited. The population is 1 255.

From Nieuwoudtville there is a tarmac road R357 leading north-eastwards for 63 km to the town of ...

LOERIESFONTEIN

Said to be named after the birds known as *loeries* or *louries (Turacus corythaix)* which frequented the area in past years, Loeriesfontein is a wool and salt producing centre of some importance. It became a municipality in 1958 and is notable for its displays of spring flowers. It is at this time of the year, in September, that Loeriesfontein stages its annual agricultural show, which features American saddle-horses, with breeders exhibiting from all over South Africa.

There is a working horse-mill at Rheboksfontein, 25 km from the town, and salt-pans at places such as Dwaggas.

The main tarmac road R27 to the west continues from Nieuwoudtville for 8 km across fields of wheat, heather and proteas. Reaching the edge of the escarpment, the road commences a 6 km long descent of the Vanrhyn's Pass. On the way down, the road passes a picnic site with water and a tremendous view west over the coastal terrace of Namaqualand. At the bottom of the pass the tarmac road proceeds over this terrace, famous for its wild flowers in spring. At 52 km from Nieuwoudtville the road reaches Vanrhynsdorp (see Chapter Twelve).

At a point 21,5 km before the tarmac road from Victoria West and Loxton reaches Calvinia, a tarmac road R27 branches northwards and leads for 126 km up the valley of the Salt River to ...

BRANDVLEI

The rather bleak little town of *Brandvlei* (burned marsh) became a municipality on 1 October 1962. The Sak River normally reaches its end at the large dried-out marsh near the town. The last trickle of water not ambushed on its journey by weirs, dams and irrigation polders is finally evaporated by the heat. However, this despairing surrender to the Karoo does not always occur without a final show of spirit. In 1961, for example, a flash flood inundated the town to such an extent that it was cut in two. Afterwards, Brandvlei took some time to join itself together again. A scorching sun in summer and icy winds in winter pose certain problems for the townspeople with regard to personal comfort.

From Brandvlei, roads branch to places such as Loeriesfontein (121 km) and Vanwyksvlei (149 km). *Verneuk* (deception) Pan may be reached from Brandvlei but the route is complicated and involves the opening of several gates. The surface area of the pan is hard, dried out, completely flat, and notable for its mirages. On 14 April 1928, Sir Malcolm Campbell, in his Bluebird car, made an unsuccessful attempt at breaking the world landspeed record on the pan.

From Brandvlei the R27 tarmac road to the north follows the long since dried-out *Grootvloer* (great floor), the bed of the Sak River when it flows to join the Hartbees. Sheep, jackals and bat-eared foxes (whose poor traffic sense sees many of them lying dead on the road) flourish happily in a flat area devoid of any features, save occasional piles of dolerite rock fragments, remnants of hills which have vanished. After 136 km there is a turn-off east to Verneuk Pan (115 km). A further 2,5 km sees the road pass through a ridge of dolerite covered with kokerbooms. This is a nature reserve maintained by the Kenhardt municipality. Ten kilometres further on, 148 km from Brandvlei, the tarmac road reaches ...

KENHARDT

In the wild frontier days of the Cape Colony, this area was a lair for rustlers and outlaws. On 2 September 1868 the Government promulgated a Border Protection Act calculated to bring a degree of law and order to the unruly frontiersmen. A magistrate, Maximillan Jackson, together with 50 policemen, was ordered to establish an outpost on the site of Kenhardt. The police party had to fight its way to the place, driving the rustlers away and arriving on 27 December 1868 to find two ramshackle shacks on the banks of the Hartbees River and the name Kenhardt, of unknown origin, lingering over this old resort of renegades, outlaws and adventurers. The policemen made a camp under a giant kameeldoring tree.

The town developed around the tree and became a municipality in 1909. Today 4 012 people live there. Karakul and dorper sheep provide the district with a quieter but more prosperous living than the banditry of former years.

From Kenhardt, roads radiate in various directions. The main R27 tarmac road to the north continues for 70 km, reaching the south bank of the Gariep (formerly known as the Orange) River at Neilersdrift, crossing the river by means of a bridge to reach Keimoes (3 km away), where it joins the main Upington–Kakamas road (40 km from Upington).

A particularly interesting gravel road follows the course of the Hartbees River (on the banks of which Kenhardt stands), leading for 90 km to Kakamas and passing on the way great dunes of red sand and many wonderful kameeldoring trees with their boughs weighed down by nests of social weaver birds. Scattered about are strange granite domes and piles of rock. In the spring vast areas of wild flowers bloom, an astonishing sight in a landscape basically so harsh and wild. Gemstones are numerous. *Tourmalines,* so-named from the Singalese *toumali* (mixed colour) gemstones, are found in a considerable variety of colours, including the exquisite watermelon tourmaline, red on the inside, green on the outside. There are shades of pink, known as rubellik, and blue, known as indicolite. Crystals are also found that gradually change colour from one end to the other.

UPINGTON

The island-strewn section of the Gariep River between Upington and the Augrabies Falls is particularly rich in memories. For many years the densely wooded islands served as strongholds for river pirates, bandits, rustlers, renegades and desperadoes. The renowned Captain Afrikaner had his hide-out close to the site of modern Upington. His lieutenant was a Polish forger named Stephanus who had escaped from Cape Town gaol while awaiting execution.

Stuurman was another famous river bandit who headed a crowd of vagabonds. The activities of these adventurers of the Gariep eventually provoked a substantial punitive expedition whereby they were rooted out and driven away into the northern wilderness.

One of the great centres for all these people of the river was the ford known as *Olijvenhoutsdrift* (ford of the olive wood trees). In 1870 a chieftain, Klaas Lucas, who lived at the ford, appealed for the establishment of a mission station in order to settle the area. The Reverend Christiaan Schröder was sent up from Cape Town. From Klaas Pofadder, who claimed ownership of the area, he secured permission to establish a mission. The foundations of the Olijvenhoutsdrift Mission, as it was called, was laid in 1873. By 1875 the mission was complete and in 1883 Schröder built a parsonage next to it. These buildings still stand today and are maintained as a museum preserving the natural and cultural history of the lower Gariep River and the southern Kalahari. The museum is open weekdays from 09h00 to 12h30 and 14h00 to 17h00; Saturdays from 09h00 to 12h00. In the grounds of the museum there is a monument to the donkeys used in former years to motivate the irrigation system used by farmers to raise water from the river. At the offices of the S A Police in Schröder Street there is a memorial dedicated to the camels used by the police to patrol the southern Kalahari.

In 1884, when the river pirates were finally driven away, a town was founded at Olijvenhoutsdrift and named after Sir Thomas Upington, Prime Minister of the Cape Colony from 1884 to 1886. This became the administrative centre for *Gordonia*, the area north of the Gariep named in honour of Sir Gordon Sprigg, Prime Minister of the Cape four times between 1878 and 1892.

Upington grew rapidly. It is the centre of a region characterised by a variety of activities and considerable natural wealth. Pioneer settlers such as Johan (Japie) Lutz and the Reverend Christiaan Schröder dug the first irrigation canal in 1890. A pontoon ferry service was started at Olijvenhoutsdrift and the town became a busy commercial centre most pleasantly situated on a river which was ideal for boating, fishing and recreation, and never likely to run dry.

The second-longest railway bridge in Southern Africa (1 067 m) was built over the river to carry the railway from De Aar on its way to Namibia. A branch line was built down the north bank of the Gariep as far as Kakamas. Lucerne, sultanas, raisins, peaches, apricots, cotton, wheat, maize, peas, wine, karakul pelts, cattle, wool, mutton and dates are produced in the area. Salt is obtained from several pans while scheelite (or tungsten), copper and pegmatites are mined. Wood from the wild olive trees is worked into furniture and decorations.

The celebrated Scotty Smith (George St Leger Gordon Lennox), reputedly the Robin Hood of South Africa, a highwayman, horse thief, rustler and adventurer, settled and married in Upington after he had quietened down. He died of influenza on 26 October 1919 and is buried in the local cemetery. The museum exhibits items associated with this enigmatic character.

A fine collection of mineral specimens from the district is exhibited in the museum. Spitskop, 13 km north-west of the town, is maintained as a 2 700 ha nature reserve, open daily from 08h00 to 17h00. Thirty-seven kilometres of roads lead through the reserve, and there is a telescope at the look-out on top of the hillock. Olijvenhout Island has been beautifully developed as a park with sports fields, a tourist resort with a caravan park, varied accommodation, a swimming-pool, restaurant, numerous flowers and trees, and an avenue of date palms 1 041 m long. It is known as the Eiland Holiday Resort.

A bright, clean and cheerful place, Upington can be excessively hot in summer, although evenings are invariably cool. The town possesses an international airport and a population of 54 724. It is an industrial development point.

The mud-rich water of the Gariep, like that of the Nile, brings life to the arid world on both sides of the river and to a complex of islands. Originally mudbanks formed by the river, these islands were permanently established by a dense growth of vegetation and are now intensely farmed and connected to the banks by means of bridges. Situated on Olijvenhout Island is an agricultural research station with most of the various crops cultivated along the river adjoining each other.

Sultana and hanepoot grapes are grown along the river in about 10 000 ha of vineyards. From the grapes wine is made in Upington by the Orange River Wine Cellars Co-operative which commenced production in 1968. Visitors are welcome to tour the cellar anytime before 19h00 during weekdays. Cellars at Groblershoop, Grootdrink, Keimoes, Kakamas and Upington all contribute to a total of 70 000 tons of grapes which are crushed and the juice supplied to the central wine-making co-operative, the largest in Southern Africa. Visitors are welcome at the Upington co-operative on Tuesdays at 09h00 and 15h00. Wine is sold direct to the public during normal business hours.

Sultanas, seedless and muscadel raisins are dried on a vast scale and exported to many parts of the world. The cement-floored open-air drying yards may be seen on nearly every farm. The S A Dried Fruit Co-operative is situated south of the river at Upington and is claimed to be the most modern in the world, with 150 tons of sultanas and raisins packed each day. The product is of superb quality and is absolutely hygienic. Visitors are welcome at the factory Mondays to Thursdays at 09h30 and 14h30 and on Fridays at 9h30. Dried fruit can be bought at the factory during normal trading hours.

Dates grow to perfection along the Gariep but have hitherto not been extensively cultivated on account of the low price of imported dates from the Middle East. This is now changing. The local date is of magnificent size and flavour. The hygienic conditions under which it is handled make it an infinitely superior product. Cultivation is being expanded as a result of difficulties involved with the rising costs of supply from the Middle East.

Dates are not easy to produce, although the palms grow without trouble in perfect local conditions. They flourish on intense heat and plenty of water from irrigation. Humidity (and especially rain) during the ripening season has a deleterious effect on the fruit, but fortunately this is not much of a problem locally. The difficulty lies in pollination. There are male and female palms. In their oasis homes the palms grow close together and the wind carries the pollen. Under cultivation the palms are too far apart. A vast amount of hard work is required, with pollen being collected from the male flowers and either sprayed over the female flowers, or the bunch of male flowers cut off and suspended next to the female bunch for the pollen to be spread by wind and insects. The pollen can be stored in a deep-freeze and used when required. Portions of the male flower are also inserted into female buds for maximum pollination. It is a tedious job to do in the heat, and uneconomical if the palm trees grow too tall. Bunches of ripening dates must also be protectively wrapped as a defence against birds and rain or dew.

Research is being done on the best method of date cultivation for the Gariep River area and other suitable parts of Southern Africa. There are many different species of dates, such as the Deglet Noor, Medjool, Thoory and Zahidi, each with its own flavour and character. The dates ripen in March; and fresh fruit bought in the area is delicious.

Cotton is another crop very largely produced along the Gariep River. A ginnery in Upington is open to visitors when it is in production towards the end of summer. Lucerne, wheat, maize, peas, lentils, citrus and numerous other products are also grown in the fertile mud of the Gariep.

From Upington, roads follow both banks of the Gariep. On the south bank (the left-hand side) a tarmac road leads to the rural centre of Louisvale (15 km from Upington) and then reaches a turn to the bridge linking Kanoneiland to the banks of the river (26,5 km from Upington).

KANONEILAND

Kanoneiland, the largest island in the Gariep, is intensely cultivated. A tarmac road leads across the bridge from the south bank. After 3 km this road reaches the small commercial and administrative centre of *Kanoneiland*. The name of the island originated from the period of the war against the river pirates. In 1879 a force of 80 policemen under Captain Dyason was sent from Kenhardt to deal with troublesome elements on the Gariep River. The river people followed their normal tactic of hiding in the dense foliage on the islands. *Kanoneiland* is said to have been bombarded with a small cannon for several days, and so received its name. The river people eluded capture, however, and other punitive police and military forces had to be sent to the area until, in April and July 1879, final attacks led by Commandants McTaggert and Alexander Maclean of the Cape Mounted Rifles finally cleared the river of unruly elements.

European settlers subsequently found the valley of the Gariep River to be fertile and commenced farming there, although the area was almost overpoweringly hot. Settled in 1928, Kanoneiland really consisted of a number of islets separated by narrow channels of the river. A 2 533 ha extent of rich land was available for cultivation, with unlimited water for irrigation.

The first islanders secured the aid of Johan Lutz from Olijvenhoutsdrift and dug the first irrigation canal. Crops were planted and harvests were rich. A prosperous community developed on the island, and in 1939 a board of local management was created. A church was built in 1951.

Periodic floods have inundated the island but, being itself an offspring of the river, it is resilient and the retreating waters have always left behind a rich layer of silt.

The tarmac road crosses Kanoneiland and bridges over the Gariep to the north bank. There, 4,5 km from the turn-off to the island on the south bank, the road joins the main N14 tarmac road from Upington down the north bank of the river. From here it is 26 km to Upington.

From the turn-off to Kanoneiland, the road down the south bank of the Gariep converts to gravel and continues to Kakamas. The road N14 along the north bank is completely tarmac and beyond the turn-off to Kanoneiland it continues for 14 km reaching at 40 km from Upington ...

KEIMOES

Klaas Lucas, one of the leaders of the river people, established a village named *Keimoes* (mouse nest) on account of the colonies of mice found living on the site in twig nests. The modern town, with a population of 7 123 and a municipality since 1949, is a farming centre of considerable importance. A restored waterwheel stands next to the main street. Overlooking the town is *Tierberg* (leopard mountain), the highest point in the area. It is preserved as a nature reserve. A road leads for 4 km from the town centre to a look-out on top of the hill, from where a tremendous view of the irrigation areas of the Gariep is revealed. Flowering aloes are spectacular during winter, and spring sees many species of succulents in full flower.

From Keimoes the tarmac road continues down the north bank of the Gariep River, passing a range of hills composed of basement complex rocks and granite pegmatites (the Kheis System) aged well over 2 000 million years. The green, irrigated fields of the river valley appear very youthful compared to these weather-beaten ancients. Many gemstones are found in this area, notably rose quartz, amethyst, amazonite, garnet, beryl, tourmaline, river stones, agate, onyx, jasper, and blue, green and brown tiger's-eye.

There are turn-offs north to Lutzputs 2 km from Keimoes, and again at 38 km just before the tarmac road crosses the Gariep. At 40,5 km from Keimoes, the road reaches ...

KAKAMAS

The early pastoral Koranna tribe gave *Kakamas* its name, but the meaning is controversial. It was apparently applied to the fording place now known as Bassonsdrif, where they watered their cattle. It is said that a buffalo cow set up residence in the reeds at this ford and occasionally charged the herdsmen. From this came the name, although another explanation is that it simply means 'poor pasturage'. In 1895 a movement began in Cape Town for the settlement of the poor on the land. The Reverend Christiaan Schröder remembered his abandoned mission station on the banks of the Gariep, and his impression that the area was ideal for irrigation and intensive farming. At a conference in Worcester on 5 March 1895 he recommended the valley of the Gariep River as a suitable site for the projected settlement. Under the auspices of the Dutch Reformed Church, and with the Reverend Schröder in charge, this settlement was established in 1898.

The first irrigation canal at Kakamas was opened on 4 July 1898. By 1900 there were 95 settlers in the area each receiving £12 in capital from the church and being left on their own to clear bush, level dunes, lead irrigation water, dig tunnels through obstructions and turn the river valley into a giant garden. The indefatigable Johan Lutz played a considerable part in the creation of canals and tunnels.

The general intention was to farm fruit, with peaches growing very well. Then in 1928, the Reverend H P van der Merwe sent up a few thousand sultana vines from Robertson. These took to local conditions with such enthusiasm that the sultana became the staple crop for the Gariep River valley farmers. Today the area is the principal producer of sultanas in Southern Africa. The cement-floored sultana and raisin drying yards, and the overshot waterwheels, perfected by Piet Burger from an ancient design of the Egyptians and used in lifting irrigation water from the canals, became a characteristic sight of the Kakamas area. Fourteen of these Egyptian-type waterwheels are still in use. Also of Egyptian influence is what is known as the Transformer Building in the town. From this building hydro-electric power was supplied to the people of Kakamas. It is being developed as a museum.

As far as peaches are concerned, it is interesting to know that this area produced the mutation known as the *Kakamas peach*, the standard canning peach of South Africa. The first peach grown in South Africa by Jan van Riebeeck was known as the *St Helena* variety, for he imported the tree from St Helena Island where the Portuguese had planted them. A variety known as the *Apricot peach*, from the colour of its flesh, and a white-fleshed variety, the *Parvie,* flourished later.

The St Helena peach took to South African conditions so well (especially on the highveld) that today it grows wild in many areas, such as Lesotho. It is popularly known as the Yellow peach. See Chapter Thirty, in the Zastron section. The Kakamas peach is a mutation of this common yellow peach. Prior to its discovery, no satisfactory canning peach had been grown in South Africa. A great deal of experimental work was carried out to find or breed such a variety. Professor Reinecke of the Elsenburg Agricultural College in Stellenbosch, in particular, busied himself in experimenting with peach varieties collected from many parts of the world.

One of Reinecke's students, A D Collins, became a teacher of agriculture at Kakamas where he furthered the professor's interest in peach varieties. In 1933 he forwarded to Reinecke a batch of seedlings from the Kakamas area, one of which showed immediate promise. Collins forwarded propagation material from the parent tree during the same year. This was the beginning of the Kakamas peach, with its characteristics of vigorous growth, prolific cropping, large fruit of good yellow colour, perfect shape for canning, finely textured flesh, delectable flavour, and retention of its firm shape throughout the canning process. The South African canning industry developed around this peach, with 75 per cent of all canning peaches deriving from offspring of the one original tree found by chance. The first trees, sold to the public by nurserymen in 1938, came into bearing in 1943. In their first year of bearing they increased the total volume of South African canning two and a half fold.

Superb dates, sultanas and seedless raisins are grown under irrigation.

Orange River Wine Cellars (Co-operative) Ltd have a branch cellar in Kakamas. Local wines may be tasted and purchased during normal business hours.

The South African Dried Fruit Co-operative has a receiving depot in Kakamas. Their products are sold at the depot during normal business hours.

What had begun as a settlement of economically distressed people, flourished on irrigation and grew into a prosperous community. In 1926 a branch railway was opened to Kakamas from Upington. In 1954 the town received a village management board and on 1 December it became a municipality. The number of inhabitants has now reached 7 021.

From Kakamas the N14 tarmac road continues down the south bank of the river reaching a division after 10 km. The right-hand branch continues as R359 along the river to the Augrabies Falls and the left-hand road leads to Pofadder and Springbok.

The turn to Augrabies (tarmac) passes the rural centres of Marchand (14 km from Kakamas) and Augrabies (24 km). The Augrabies Falls hotel is reached a further 9 km along the road and the Falls themselves 39 km from Kakamas.

AUGRABIES FALLS NATIONAL PARK

Derived from the African *oukurubes* (the noise-making place), the name *Augrabies* describes the gigantic gorge into which the Gariep River roars headlong with a rising cloud of spray which can, during a flood season, be heard and seen from a considerable distance.

Geologists consider the gorge to be the finest example in the world of weathering of granite by water action. Over the passage of time the Gariep has cut a knife-edge wound through this prodigious barrier of rock. In a series of preliminary cascades and falls, the river drops about 100 m, shouldering its way through a narrow gap to hurtle down yet another 100 m in a combined cascade and final sheer fall of 56 m. At the bottom lies a deep pool reputedly haunted by a mighty water serpent, In addition, a fortune in diamonds is thought to have been washed down the river over the ages, and to lie trapped in this great hole. Certainly, the hole and the gorge provide a home for many giant mud barbel *(Clarias gariepinus)*, a fish reaching a length of 2 m.

For 18 km the river boils and rushes through the granite gorge, dropping over 300 m in a series of rapids and minor falls. The average depth of the gorge is 240 m. The main gorge is joined by several tributary gorges, the entire formation presenting a scene of savage primeval power and force in a setting of utter wilderness. Strange noises, echoes and the ceaseless, daring flight of swifts, which especially seem to like the gorge, add to the atmosphere.

The flow of water over Augrabies varies very considerably. In the midst of a dry winter the flow can dwindle down to a mere stream. At the peak of a wet summer in the main watershed of the river (Lesotho and the highveld), the spectacle can be stupendous. The river overwhelms the entire upper portion of the gorge, with nineteen great waterfalls hurling into it and creating an infernal combination of spray, water and menacing sound.

Augrabies is justifiably regarded as one of the six great waterfalls of the world occurring in a first-class river. Each waterfall has its own special character. The wonderful spectacle of Victoria Falls, the queen of them all, has a feminine beauty and the intensely green surroundings soften the nature of the fall. Augrabies is essentially masculine – ruthless and brutal in a harsh and fearsomely arid landscape. During peak floods about 400 million litres of water race over Augrabies every minute. The peak flow of Victoria Falls is about 750 million litres of water a minute, but Augrabies is concentrated into the head of its narrow gorge, while Victoria Falls is spread out over the whole 2 000 m length of the long trough into which the Zambezi tumbles.

In former times the area of the Augrabies Falls was the resort of early African people who fed on fish and the several edible roots, wild fruits, beans and the berries of the wild raisin trees (*Rhus viminalis* and *Zizphus mucronata)* which flourish there. Klaas Pofadder was the last of the leaders of these people to rule in the area, with his base on the island named after him. The first European to see the Falls was a Swedish mercenary soldier, Hendrik Wikar, who had deserted his post in Cape Town in 1775 as a result of debt and wandered north to the Gariep River, reaching Augrabies in October 1778.

In 1967 the Augrabies Falls National Park, centred on Klaas Island, was opened, conserving as a wilderness area 5 403 ha of the south bank of the river. The waterfall and gorge are now accessible throughout the year, whereas formerly it was impossible to reach the vicinity of the waterfall during flood times, for the river spread above and around the gorge, completely overwhelming all approaches. Bridges and causeways have now been built, as well as a series of protected outlooks on the very edge of the gorge which allow the visitor to view in safety the waterfall in full flood – one of the world's great spectacles.

Five people are known to have been carried over the Falls. Only one survived. Hugo Truter, a 20-year-old national serviceman stationed at Upington, visited Augrabies with some friends on Saturday 10 October 1981. They crossed the suspension bridge over the gorge above the Falls and were scrambling through the rocks next to the river when Truter slipped and fell. He bounced on some rocks, felt a searing pain in his back and half lost consciousness. The current carried him over the waterfall. At the bottom of the gorge he regained consciousness.

Horrified, his friends ran to the National Parks Board office to seek help. With the officers they looked down into the gorge and saw Truter clinging to a rock. Ropes were obtained and, with great courage, one of his friends, Johannes Lombard, was lowered down to the river. He swam to his friend, comforted him and assisted him to the side of the gorge. The two were hauled to a ledge half-way up the side. Two members of the Cape Town Fire Brigade, who were on holiday at the Falls, were lowered to join them. They gave Truter a sedative. An overhang of rock made it impossible to lift the injured man higher. The police were summoned from Upington and a helicopter requested from Pretoria.

Eventually at 20h00, Truter was lifted by the helicopter and flown to the military hospital in Pretoria. He sustained no permanent injury. The waterfall had apparently thrown him forward, away from the suction of the pool at its foot. On a previous occasion, police divers had tried to recover a body from the pool. They went down 50 m into the pool before giving up, as the water was icy cold and pitch dark.

The National Parks Board has its office, restaurant and shop on Klaas Island, with a museum displaying the rocks, gemstones, fauna and flora of the area. The walls of this complex of buildings contain a great variety of decorative and semi-precious stones, all found locally. Over 100 species of aloes are grown in the garden next to the central building. Trees such as the karee, wild olive, Cape willow, kokerboom, and species of acacia flourish in the area, including the beautiful *Schotia brachypetala* with its flame-red flowers, as well as numerous succulents.

The population of wild animals is increasing under protection. Monkeys, baboons, klipspringers, steenboks, springboks, various wildcats and other creatures may be seen. Bird life is varied and numerous. Lizards are plentiful, especially the Cape red-tailed flat lizard (*Platysauros capensis*) which has a particular liking for granite country in most of Southern Africa.

A road 12 km long leads to the western portion of the park at Fountain. From this road branches lead to various outlooks over the gorge and other places of interest. A complete exploration of these roads and a return journey to the park headquarters comprise a total of 42 km. A three-day hiking trail known as the Klipspringer Trail may be followed, with overnight accommodation provided by two huts.

The north bank of the Gariep, from where the best views of the waterfall may be had, consists of a wilderness area 4 012 ha in extent, to be maintained in this state, with hiking trails. Gemsbok and red hartebeest have been introduced. A 20 m long suspension bridge across the river above the waterfall provides access to this area. A visit to this first-class national park is highly recommended. Summer is the best season, with maximum flow of the river, even though the weather can be stiflingly hot.

From the turn-off to Augrabies, 8 km west of Kakamas, the N14 tarmac road continues to the west over the arid plains of Bushmanland. In spring, wild flowers flourish in great profusion while red sand dunes and curious piles of dolerite and pegmatite fragments provide variety to an otherwise flat landscape. The road passes small rural centres such as Bladgrond (70 km from Kakamas) and at 84 km a turn-off north for 51 km to *Onseepkans* named from the orange-thorn trees *Parkinsonia africana* growing there. It is a settlement on the banks of the Gariep which was laid out in 1916 for the cultivation under irrigation of citrus, lucerne, beans and other crops. With a summer temperature of about 50°C, this is a very sunbaked little place, but the fields are beautifully green.

The N14 tarmac road continues for a further 46 km and, 130 km from Kakamas, reaches ...

POFADDER

The chieftain, Klaas Pofadder, once had his principal centre at the springs on the site of the present town. In 1875 the Reverend Christiaan Schröder established a mission there and named the place in honour of the chief. Pofadder himself came to grief after raiding livestock from farmers in the Springbok area. He was pursued and shot at the springs which have since borne his name.

In 1918 a town first named Theronsville was laid out at these springs. The old name of *Pofadder* (puff-adder), however, persisted and eventually became generally accepted and has given the little town the distinction of an unusual place-name. In 1937 the first village management board was elected.

With a rainfall seldom exceeding 50 mm a year, Pofadder is a centre for karakul and other sheep, but periodic droughts in an already arid environment cause grievous damage. In 1959 the entire livestock population had to be transported by the Army to better grazing until rains came to revive a remarkably resilient vegetation.

In this arid setting, Pofadder is an atmospheric and attractive little town. Of interest to ornithologists is the presence on the farm *Banke* of a population of red larks (*Certhilauda burra*). How they came to be there and nowhere else, is a puzzle.

From Pofadder a road, R358, leads for 49 km to the agricultural settlement of Onseepkans on the Gariep River. This is an interesting drive and the rock formations, granite, schists and pegmatites are very remarkable, especially across the Gariep River on the road to Warmbad.

The main N14 tarmac road from Pofadder continues for 24 km and then reaches a turn-off leading to Pella, Swartkoppies, Little Pella and Goodhouse. The mission station and oasis of Pella is reached after a drive of 3 km along this road and then 9 km down a turn-off.

PELLA

Originally founded in 1814 by the London Missionary Society as a sanctuary for people driven out of the Warmbad area of Namibia by various disturbances, the mission was named after the ancient town east of the Jordan river which became a refuge for persecuted Christians.

In 1872 drought induced the London Missionary Society to abandon Pella, but it was reopened in 1878 and developed by the Roman Catholics into the present substantial settlement. Their pioneer missionary, Father J M Simon, who became the first Vicar Apostolic of the Gariep River, and his associate, Father Leo Wolf, were responsible for most of the hard work involved in establishing the station. It took them seven years to build the church. They had no experience of building and for reference only had a general encyclopedia. Today they are buried in the church they built themselves, later consecrated as a cathedral.

The situation of Pella is striking. It is particularly strange to arrive there in the evening. The date palms, the sharply serrated mountains, the dry desert air, the pervading incense-like perfume of the wild flowers (in July and August) and the aromatic shrubs used for fuel by the residents, all combine to conjure up an image of Arabia. There is no other place in Southern Africa quite like this.

Life in Pella is not easy. During the summer months temperatures hover around 60°C and sometimes it does not rain for years. Goats, karakul sheep and dates are produced in the area. The dates, which ripen in March, are in considerable demand, for their flavour is delicious. On the farm *Klein Pella* along the road to Goodhouse, 14 km beyond the turn-off to Pella, dates are produced on a large scale. The owner, Rudolf Niemoller, introduced drip irrigation to cultivate dates of the *Medjool* variety from Morocco, and produces fruit of superb quality and delicate flavour from palm trees obtained from California.

In the 1930s a shepherd found a strange-looking rock lying on the sandy plain west of Pella. He took Bishop Simon to see it. Thinking it was a meteorite, Bishop Simon tried to penetrate it with a metal drill, but it caused hardly a scratch. They left the rock lying on the sand.

During the Second World War, geologists of the Geological Survey searching through the area for strategic minerals, were shown the so-called meteorite. It turned out to be no meteorite, but a unique mixture of corundum and sillimanite, the refractory mineral used in the making of bricks required to withstand the tremendous heat in the furnaces of steel and glass-making industries. *Sillimanite,* named after the American chemist, Benjamin Silliman, was well known, but the mixture with corundum made the composite one of the hardest rocks of all.

The geologists told a local base metal prospector, Peter Weidner from Goodhouse, about the stone and the fact that there were five hillocks of it, the *Swartkoppies* (black hills) of Pella. Nobody knew whether the rock had any value. Weidner took a chance and pegged the hillock. Working incessantly he sent samples all over the world. When he started getting orders, he devised a mining and crushing technique for super hard rock. The five hillocks have now completely vanished, having been dispatched piecemeal to furnaces in Japan, America and Europe. In place of the hillocks is a deep quarry. The works of the mining company, Pella Refractory Ores, stand 4 km beyond the turn-off to Pella on the Goodhouse road.

The corundum-sillimanite mine and the zinc-lead mine at Aggeneys provide employment for the men of the area. Water is pumped from the Gariep, thereby developing the residential areas at the mines into oases in the wilderness. A road known as *Charlie's Pass*, after Charlie Weidner, son of Peter, links Pella to the Gariep and provides easy access through the mountains to the river, with a picnic and swimming place next to the pump station. Another road leads directly to the mines.

The area around Pella is a treasure-house of gemstones; green-blue malachite-stained rocks, red oxides of iron, jaspers, smoky and rose quartz, silvery micaschists and enough other lovely treasures to build a veritable fairy city in this hot but sweet-smelling wilderness.

From the turn-off to Pella and Goodhouse the main tarmac N14 road continues westwards across the desolate plains of Bushmanland.

At 60 km from Pofadder, the road reaches *Aggeneys* (place of water) where considerable mining developments concerning lead, silver, zinc and copper are taking place at Black Mountain Mine, close to what was for a long time simply a cluster of farmhouses, post office and store standing in the desert.

From Aggeneys the N14 road continues south-westwards, passing through a ridge of rocky hills and then crossing an immense plain covered in low scrub and broken by a few isolated and lonely-looking hills scattered around the horizon. Sheep and karakul farmers find a living in this wilderness, but drought is a curse and drinking-water very precious. After 104 km (164 km from Pofadder) the road reaches Springbok and the main N7 highway of Namaqualand. The Namaqua 4 × 4 route starts in Pella. It leads for 642 km to the mouth of the Gariep River at Alexander Bay. This route provides a unique travel experience. Information may be obtained from the Tourism Office, Springbok. Phone (027) 712-1543.

GORDONIA

Gordonia is the area north of the Gariep River which borders on the Kalahari. Hot and flat, it is nevertheless full of interesting features – great sand dunes, salt-pans, farms, wayside trading posts, elegant kameeldoring trees, nests of the social weaver bird and, in the north, the Kalahari Gemsbok National Park.

From Upington, the principal centre of Gordonia, roads radiate to all parts of the region. Thanks to the quality of modern road construction, it is now possible to explore the area without the shattering experience of corrugations and pot-holes which made Gordonia notorious to motorists only a few years ago.

From Upington, the main tarmac road N10 to Namibia leads to the north-west over a vast plain. After 6,5 km a turn-off north to the Spitskop Nature Reserve is reached. After 15 km, there is a turn north to a cluster of salt-pans such as Grootwitpan and Norokel where salt is gathered from the dried-out floor. This road, R360, continues northwards for 153 km until it joins R31 at a crossroads 66 km from the frontier of Namibia at Rietfontein or, by turning north up R31, reaches after 84 km, Twee Rivieren at the entrance to the Kalahari Gemsbok National Park.

The N10 road, from the turn-off of R360, continues westwards. At 61 km from Upington there is a crossroads. The main N10 road continues west for a further 71 km, reaching the border of Namibia at Nakop. To the south a road branches off for 11 km to the railway station of Lutzputs, from where there are roads to Keimoes (45 km) and to Kakamas (52 km). *Lutzputs* (Lütz's wells) is named after that pioneer of irrigation, Johan Lütz. To the north a road leads to the Kalahari Gemsbok National Park. Although gravel, this road is now maintained in reasonable condition after years of being famous for being the worst corrugated road in Africa.

At 23 km from the crossroads this road is joined by a road 58 km long which joins the R360 road from Upington to the North. The gravel road meanwhile, from its turn-off from the N10 near Lutzputs, continues northwards, ascending to a higher plateau and passing farms such as *Swartmodder* (32 km) and *Bokhara* (47 km).

A further 17 km brings the road to a turn-off to Namibia, and 5 km beyond this point (69 km from the crossroads on the main tarmac road) stands a solitary tree in a landscape devoid of trees. Considerate road engineers have placed seats and a table beneath its shady boughs. People travelling with a dog should draw their pet's attention to this tree, as there is no further convenience for some distance.

The road proceeds over the seemingly boundless plains, reaching after 5 km the Albion Pan. Thirty-five kilometres beyond the tree (104 km from the crossroads) the road passes the small centre known as *Noenieput* from a noenie tree which grew there at an old drinking well dug by the Bushmen. A school with a hostel provides for the education of children from many isolated farms.

Beyond Noenieput the road passes a substantial pan at Abiquasputs. A turn-off leads to the Dutch Reformed Church mission of Rietfontein (127 km from the crossroads). The road to the Kalahari Gemsbok National Park swings to the north-east. At 157 km the road passes Koopan-Suid, with its store and petrol pump. A further 24 km brings the road to the turn-off to ...

LOCH MAREE

This salt-pan lies 5 km west of the main road. The track leading to it is poor, and permission must be obtained from the landowner whose farmhouse stands at the turn-off. The pan is an extraordinary sight and a geological marvel. It is 24 km in circumference and covered with a layer of salt 1 m thick, the equivalent of 9 million tons, with concentrated brine below the surface. The salt is particularly pure. The shimmering white surface of the pan is surrounded by red sand dunes. With deep-blue skies and, around February, masses of yellow-coloured botterbloms, the spectacle is unforgettable. When it rains, water collects in the pan but there is seldom enough to cover more than a section of the dry floor. The shallow water is blown about by the prevailing winds, sometimes covering one portion of the pan and then, within a few hours, blown over another portion by a change of wind. The pan is occasionally worked for salt, but the bad road leading to it has impeded development.

From the turn-off to Loch Maree the main road continues for a further 9 km, reaching a turn-off to the Rietfontein mission station (68 km away) and Namibia. The main road continues north-eastwards. After a further 13 km (204 km from the crossroads) the road passes the turn-off to Lentlands (or Leitlands) Pan, an old retreat for Scotty Smith, the celebrated horse thief and rustler. The name of a nearby farm, *Scotty's Fort*, provides yet another reminder of the escapades of this irrepressible character. He made this area his home in the 1890s, remaining there for several years. The book *Scotty Smith* by F C Metrowich gives a detailed account of his life.

The countryside is now amply covered with trees, many of them acacias laden with the cumbersome community nests of the social weaver birds (*Philetairus socius*). These little birds select a suitable tree and join forces in building a roof of twigs somewhere in the branches where there is shade and security. Under this roof individual pairs build their nests in a dense 'condominium' which can remain in use for generations of birds. A few predatory snakes also take up residence, living on the eggs and chickens.

At 207 km from the crossroads, the road reaches a small garage at a junction with the R360 road from Upington and the R31 road leading from Kuruman in the east to the Namibia frontier in the West near Rietfontein. After 23 km this R31 road turns east to Askham and Vanzylsrus, and the main road continues north. There is a pleasant little motel at this point with a swimming-pool.

After a further 3 km there is a turn to Molopo and Grenspan. The road now reaches the border of Botswana. From there on the road follows the dry bed of the Nossob River in the middle of which is situated the border between South Africa and Botswana. After 61 km the road reaches the entrance to the Kalahari Gemsbok National Park 273 km from Upington.

KALAHARI GEMSBOK NATIONAL PARK

This is a unique park and one of the most fascinating wilderness areas in the world. Although the park is bisected by the Botswana–South Africa border, there is no boundary fence and the wild animals have complete freedom of movement in a well-balanced ecological area. The Botswana side of the park, known as the Gemsbok National Park (1 087 000 ha in extent) is a complete wilderness unserviced by roads or public access. The area consists of aeolian sand covered in shrubs and a few acacia trees. Little surface-water is present. However, when it rains during summer (usually in the form of thunderstorms), water collects in shallow pans. The wild animals which frequent the area, together with a few wandering groups of Bushmen, have adapted themselves to these arid conditions and regard the area as a happy home well free of interference from the outside world, other than the activities of an occasional poacher.

The western border of the Botswana section of the reserve runs down the centre of the *Nossob* (black water) River. The floor of this shallow river valley is firm and well covered with trees and grass and has ample water below the surface. A considerable concentration of wild animals live in the valley, particularly springbok, gemsbok, hartebeest and wildebeest. Predators such as lion and cheetah prey on the game while numerous scavengers such as brown and spotted hyenas and jackals keep the area clear of any carcasses.

The border line, happily, is marked simply by a line of small concrete beacons, allowing the wild animals complete freedom of movement. The South African side of the park consists of 970 000 ha of country stretching westwards to the frontier of Namibia. Through this area occasionally flows another river, the *Auob* (bitter tasting), in a grassy, tree-covered valley narrower than that of the Nossob. The floor of this river valley is firm, with water occurring beneath the surface and an occasional surface flow during a very wet season. Between the two rivers (which join at the southern end of the park) lies an area of dunes and scrub-covered sand scattered with several pans and watering-places.

The park was originally a pure wilderness area resorted to by nomadic tribes, hunters and renegades such as the celebrated Scotty Smith. One of his hideaways, *Scotty's Fort*, lay to the south of the area where he hunted, concealed stolen livestock and, rather oddly, exported the skeletons of Bushmen to museums. The excellent condition of many of these skeletons aroused suspicion about his manner of obtaining them. In 1912 his permit for this trade was summarily withdrawn. His favourite part of the area was at Seven Pans, but what he did there is a mystery.

Scotty Smith guided into the area various parties searching for the so-called 'lost city' of the Kalahari (a hoax perpetuated by an American showman). Scientists such as the celebrated Dr W H Bleek and his daughter Dorothea, with Maria Wilman, Director of the McGregor Museum, who were studying the Bushmen, also used his services. In 1913 he took into the area the underground water expert, Major C A Anderson, whose task it was to select sites for boreholes. They went up the Auob River and then crossed the dunes to the valley of the Nossob.

The two river valleys had been surveyed into farms for European settlement. Major Anderson's report, however, was so unfavourable that the project was changed to the establishment of a number of smallholdings for Coloured goatherds and shepherds. These people built small houses from fragments of calcrete and eked out a precarious existence, mainly by hunting game and making biltong.

The depletion of wildlife in the area became apparent to several people supportive of conservation, notably a well-known farmer and community leader, Willie Rossouw of *Loubos*, and Piet de Villiers, the Inspector of Lands at Upington, known as the 'King of the Kalahari'. They induced Piet Grobler, Minister of Lands, to join them on a hunting expedition to the area. Instead of hunting, however, they revealed to him that the wildlife was on the verge of being exterminated.

Piet Grobler was a conservationist. He was appalled at the wanton killing which he saw. At one of their camp-fires he decided to proclaim a game reserve in the area and this was done on 3 July 1931. The various farmers in the area were resettled in the valley of the Kuruman River and Johannes le Riche was appointed as the first ranger, with one assistant, a constable named Gert.

Thus began the extraordinary association of the Le Riche family with what became the Kalahari Gemsbok National Park. The family was of French Huguenot descent. After wandering about the interior of South Africa, they had settled as traders and farmers at the mission station of Rietfontein south-west of the new national park. Le Riche and his assistant took over an abandoned *hartbeeshuisie* (hard reed house) left at Gemsbokplein by one of the departed farmers, and this became their headquarters. They had two horses and a small cart. There was a severe drought; no windpumps (the original farmers had removed them); hardly any water, and nearly every human being in the area seemed to be a poacher.

It was an epic effort for the two men to patrol the park. The distance from the Nossob River to *Wêreldend* (world end) formerly known as Union End, and back was 650 km, including a 250 km stretch without water. However, in 1934 it rained. The two rivers came down in flood. With the water came mosquitoes. Almost everybody contracted malarial fever and both Johannes le Riche and his assistant died. Joseph le Riche, younger brother of Johannes, was appointed ranger with another constable, Gert Mouton. Their first task was to clear mud from all boreholes and wells clogged up by the recent floods. Mosquitoes by the million still infested the area and both men contracted malaria. In addition, long grass grew as a result of the rain, followed by a year of heat and dryness. The grass died and a series of devastating fires swept through the area.

Drought, floods, fires and poachers all seemed to conspire towards the destruction of the park. But its assets were unique. It was a remarkable conservation area possessing a resilient population of wild animals and a completely dedicated staff. To aid Le Riche, Piet Moller was appointed ranger and stationed at Mata-Mata. In 1938 the 1 087 000 ha piece of Botswana adjoining the park was proclaimed a national park and this was placed under South Africa for administration and policing. Le Riche and his staff had the sudden addition of more than double the original area to supervise.

By this time all permanent human residents in the combined areas had been relocated. Nomadic Bushmen groups remained, having been given every possible inducement to stay and continue their traditional way of life. Their subsistence hunting had little effect on the wild animals in the park. They became trackers and allies of the conservationists in the war against poachers.

Tourists were already coming to the park. To accommodate them, bungalows were built in 1940 where the Nossob and the Auob rivers met at *Twee Rivieren* (two rivers). A new house for the warden was also built of corrugated iron, oven-hot during the day and refrigerator-cold at night. Le Riche found it better to sleep outside. All available money was spent on boreholes. In one year they bored thirteen holes of between 55 m to 113 m in depth. Four were dry, five were full of brine, two only yielded 700 l of potable water an hour. The other two were more useful. The deepest they ever bored was 372 m and this hole yielded good water. The more water they provided, the more wild animals were attracted into the area to places where they could be protected from poachers.

Fortunately, poaching was considerably affected by the Second World War. Guns, ammunition, motor vehicles and petrol were all in short supply from 1939 to 1945. During this period the wild animals increased their numbers to a spectacular extent, with the population controlled only by water supply. Troops of eland 1 000 strong could be seen, while springbok, red hartebeest and gemsbok flourished in great herds. The poachers eyed them longingly and waited for the war to end. Peace for mankind would mean death to wildlife.

At the end of the war the onslaught began. The conservationists were almost overwhelmed. In one major counter-action they arrested 22 poachers in the first week of June 1948. The rangers often found 100 or more carcasses, with the best parts cut off to make biltong and the rest left to rot. A particularly galling fact was that several of the most active poachers proved to be relatives of the Le Riche family! They considered it a challenge to make fools of the rangers.

The wretched business of making biltong seemed to be an obsession with many of the farmers south, west and north-west of the park. They would find out when the rangers had returned from a patrol and then launch a raid into the park, using four-wheel-drive vehicles and trucks. Many wild chases resulted when the rangers tried to intercept them. Sometimes the rangers were lucky; many times they were frustrated. The poachers used decoys and all manner of strategies. After one arduous chase the rangers topped a dune and found in the hollow below them a pick-up truck stalled across the track, blocking the way. In the back sat a half-tipsy young man strumming a guitar and drinking wine. He told them that he was on his own and had come there to practise his instrument in solitude. Was there a law against it? By the time the rangers had dealt with him, the rest of his party had disappeared over the horizon, with a few stragglers left here and there to delay the pursuers.

A fence was built between the park and Namibia. Before it was sealed, there was a big drive of game from Namibia into the park. Animals left outside would have to take their chance against hunters. About 2 000 gemsbok were, however, driven into the sanctuary as well as considerable numbers of other species.

The park was becoming increasingly popular with the public. More facilities had to be provided, which meant that more water had to be found. Additional huts, rooms and caravan parks were built at Twee Rivieren and Mata-Mata. A camp was established in the Nossob valley in 1966 and a road opened across the dunes to link the two rivers.

By this time the two sons of Johannes le Riche, Christoffel (who had been born in the park in 1936) and Elias, had joined the staff as rangers (Christoffel in 1958 at Mata-Mata and Elias in 1963 at Nossob). When Joseph retired on 31 July 1970 after 36 years as warden, Christoffel succeeded him. Christoffel's position as ranger at Mata-Mata was taken by Isak Meyer. More roads were made to allow the rangers quicker access to all parts of the park and aeroplanes were used to locate poachers. Scientific research also commenced and in 1971 M G L Mills became the first resident scientist. Before he was transferred to the Kruger National Park in 1983, he had obtained a doctorate for his thesis on the brown hyena.

In 1980 Christoffel le Riche died. He was succeeded by his brother Elias, with Dawie de Villiers assuming the post of ranger at Nossob. Under the continuous care of the Le Riche family the park has become what it is today – one of the finest in the world. It is under constant improvement in the facilities it offers to visitors and in the conservation of its population of wild animals. A tour through the park is a unique experience.

From Twee Rivieren a road follows the valley of the Nossob for 3,5 km to its junction with the Auob. There the road divides, one branch leading north-westwards up the valley of the Auob for 112 km to the camp, shop and ranger post of *Mata-Mata* (the very nice place). This camp lies on the frontier of Namibia.

The drive up the Auob is delightful, not only for the wildlife, but also for trees and clouds (in summer). The trees, such as the kameeldorings, are superbly graceful and ideally suited to a desert world of glaring, relentless sunshine, generously providing dense, cool shade pervaded by a pleasant aroma issuing from their bark, leaves and blossoms. The wood provides excellent fuel for cooking fires, adding a piquant flavour to meat, tea, bread, flapjacks and coffee. The clouds of the summer thunderstorms tower like gigantic dream mountains in the sky.

A second road leads up the valley of the Nossob, adjoining and occasionally crossing the Botswana border. From the junction with the road up the Auob, this route extends for 102 km, reaching a turn-off known as the Dune Road which traverses the sand country between the Nossob and the Auob. The 52 km journey provides travellers with the sensation of being on a ship negotiating a grassy sea of sand. Few features may be seen save occasional windpumps. Pans and trees are sparse. Gemsbok, hartebeest, steenbok and ostriches are particularly fond of the area. At the end of its run this road reaches the Auob valley, joining the road at a point almost midway between Mata-Mata Camp and the junction of the Auob and Nossob valleys.

From the turn-off to the Dune Road the road up the Nossob valley continues for 53 km and then reaches Nossob camp where there is a ranger post, shop and accommodation. From here the road continues for 134 km up the valley to World End, formerly the extreme northern tip of the park where the road reaches a dead end. There is a resting-place but no accommodation.

The Nossob valley is not as green as the Auob but wild animals are plentiful, especially hartebeest and gemsbok. Springbok occur in very large numbers all over the park, and their sprightly movements and *pronking* (prancing) provide amusement for visitors. Wildebeest, eland and kudu are well represented. The presence of predators is unpredictable but they are always somewhere in the area. About 170 species of birds have been recorded in the park.

Late summer is the best time to visit the park, as winter is too dry. The summers are hot but the evenings are cool and afternoon thunderstorms continually refresh the area. Cloud formations and sunsets are spectacular. Vegetation is at its best in summer and the wild animals concentrate in the river valleys to enjoy the grass and water.

The camps are informal, and the staff courteous. There is little evidence of bureaucratic authority, and the natural ecological balance of the park allows for a management fortunately devoid of culling operations and curio and by-product manufacture from the carcasses of its wild animal inhabitants.

The park is open daily from dawn to dusk, with the hours varying slightly between summer and winter. There is a restaurant at Twee Rivieren and shops with basic supplies at all these camps.

On the road south (61 km from Twee Rivieren), there is a junction with the R31 road branching east. This road, maintained in good condition, leads along the usually bone-dry valley of the

Kuruman River, past rural centres such as Witdraai (where the old camel patrol of the police had their headquarters), Askham, Cramond, Ontmoeting and Vanzylsrus (159 km) where there is a cluster of stores, houses and a hotel in a hot sandy setting.

From Vanzylsrus the road veers south-eastwards and, after 108 km across a bush-covered, featureless plain, reaches the manganese-mining centre and railway terminus of Hotazel. From there the R31 road leads for 61 km to Kuruman where it joins N14, the route followed by travellers from the North-West Province visiting the Kalahari Gemsbok National Park.

From Hotazel a road R380 leads southwards alongside the railway for 59 km to *Dibeng* (place of the well) and from there on for 30 km to Sishen (*Sesheng*, the new place) with its huge iron mine. From Sishen, also known as Dingleton, roads lead to Kuruman (66 km), Kimberley (263 km) and to Upington (207 km). This last road N14 provides an interesting return journey to Upington for travellers interested in completing a grand tour from that riverside town to the Kalahari Gemsbok National Park and back through the rugged Kalahari sand country. Along the road 37 km west of Sishen is the small but enterprising town of ...

OLIFANTSHOEK

Founded in 1897, *Olifantshoek* is said to have taken its name from the tusk of an elephant which was used as payment for the ground on which the town stands. With a population of 7 742, the town is a ranching centre supplied with water from a nearby dam. Mining for iron is carried out in the vicinity. The town lies in a parkland in a valley on the eastern side of the Langeberge.

From Upington the main tarmac road to the south, N10, bridges over the Gariep and then follows the left bank of the river, passing scenes of agricultural activity. After 114 km the road reaches ...

GROBLERSHOOP AND THE TURN-OFF TO THE BUCHUBERG DAM

Groblershoop was originally known as *Sternham* after a man named Stern who, in the 1920s, farmed in the area and built a small pump station to supply water from the Gariep River. This enterprise was unfortunately destroyed in the 1925 floods. Even before this, in the 1890s, an individual named Litchfield had a small hydro-electric generator and pump on the Gariep. He was aware of the irrigation possibilities of the river valley. Since 1872 people had been farming along the course of the river and laboriously raising water for irrigation. In 1895 Litchfield submitted proposals to the government for an irrigation scheme, but nothing came of it.

In 1904 W B Gordon, an engineer in the service of the Cape Government, visited the area. On 6 August he submitted a report to the Secretary of Public Works in Cape Town, recommending the Litchfield proposal of irrigation. Nothing came of this.

In February 1911, Alfred Lewis, Sectional Engineer of the Irrigation Department in Cape Town, visited the area in the course of a detailed study of the lower reaches of the Gariep. One of the finest water engineers South Africa has ever produced, he became Director of Irrigation from 1921 to 1941. In his classic study he followed the Gariep River, travelling along its banks by cart and horse, but mainly on foot. His awareness of the potential of the river was profound. His achievement in carrying out this study, accomplished under the most trying physical conditions of extreme heat and rugged terrain, has been unsurpassed by any scientific investigator in South Africa.

Lewis recommended the construction of a dam at *Buchuberg* (or *Boegoeberg)*, named after the buchu plant (*Barosma betulina*) growing on the hill slopes, and an irrigation canal 130 km long to feed water to 4 000 morgen of irrigable land.

Lack of money inhibited the project, but during the great economic depression the Carnegie Commission (1929–32) recommended that unemployed persons be provided with work on public projects. Their pay would be low, but better something than nothing. Instead of the degradation of a dole, they would be creating something of permanent value and be stimulated by work and achievement.

The Department of Irrigation was instructed to commence work on several irrigation projects which would provide immediate employment and a long-term prospect of settling people on irrigable land as a means of rehabilitation from financial destitution. The various projects were financed by grants from the Department of Labour. Amongst the projects launched was the scheme of Lewis to construct a dam at Buchuberg and the irrigation canal.

Work started at Buchuberg on 23 May 1929. The project was to create a barrage rather than a dam. A concrete wall 622 m long and 10 m high was built across the river bed at Zeekoebaardsdrif. Sixty-eight sluice-gates raised by a travelling crane were included in the construction to allow floodwaters to sweep through and relieve the dam of silt. The wall would divert water into the canal and a storage lake to supply irrigation as far down the river as the Augrabies Falls.

With no towns in the vicinity, a construction camp of tents and shanty houses was created on the site, and this had stores, a school and a clinic. Labourers received 7s 6d in day in wages and conditions were rough. *'Buchuberg was built without beer or bread'* was a popular description, but there was a fine atmosphere to the whole project. In compensation for hardship, the labourers had the hope of securing an irrigated patch of land when construction ended. The dam became their particular thing. They wrote poems about it, sang songs and danced at night to the tune of catchy little melodies about the high price they were paying to bring the waters of the Gariep to farmlands, factories and homes. *'Buchuberg Dam is a Wonderful Dam'* is still occasionally played as a catchy little foxtrot of those times.

Engineers at the site, such as Adolf Aslaksen, Sven Eklund, Gordon Allen, and Mr Kokot, controlled the work of 250 labourers, nearly all of whom were married with sunbronzed families who cheerfully made the most of very difficult conditions.

The dam was completed in 1933 and in 1934 the first water was directed into the 121 km long canal, supplying 6 600 ha of farmland divided into 5 ha plots, each with a small stone house. It was a festive occasion, with speeches, prayers, a barbecue, and everybody present requested to gather a stone and deposit it on a single pile which would provide material for a monument to the workers on the project. Nothing came of this. In 1938 however, when the Voortrekker Centenary ox-wagon trek was held to synchronise with the laying of the foundation-stone of the Voortrekker Monument in Pretoria, it was decided that the building of the Buchuberg Dam monument would go ahead with the original stones. This served to commemorate the construction of the dam as well as the *Ossewa Trek*.

Lucerne, cotton, potatoes, sultanas and fruit of many kinds are now produced along the banks of the Gariep by over 700 farmers.

Groblershoop, named after the Minister of Agriculture, Piet Grobler, was founded in 1936 on the site of the original Sternham as a centre for the Gariep River irrigation area south-east of Upington. It has grown rapidly to become a busy and modern little town. One kilometre out of the town, on the main N10 road, there is a tarmac turn-off eastwards which leads for 34 km to the Buchuberg Dam. The dam has been developed into a considerable recreational centre, with swimming, boating and fishing for carp, barbel and yellow-fish of large size. There is a very commodious caravan park.

One kilometre before the N10 road from Upington reaches Groblershoop, a tarmac turn-off R64 leads eastward across the Gariep for 135 km to Griquatown and from there to Kimberley. At 10,5 km along this road a gravel turn-off north to Witsand is reached. This road serves many farms, amongst them, after 66 km, the farm *Doornaar*, owned by Mr P M Maritz who maintains the Witsand Holiday Resort there with bungalows and a camping ground for people wishing to visit ...

THE ROARING SANDS

Consisting of a white dune 'island' which contrasts with a surrounding sea of red Kalahari sand, the roaring sands or *witsand* (white sands) extend in the form of a tongue about 9 km long and 2 km wide. Whereas the dry surrounding sands are coloured by the presence of iron oxide, the white dunes are peculiar for the amount of water contained in them.

The origin of these isolated white dunes is obscure. It is probable that they originally consisted of normal wind-blown Kalahari red sand which accumulated over a supply of water. The water, reaching the surface under pressure, removed the iron oxide and with it the red colour. This chance freedom from a coating of foreign matter, combined with the dry atmosphere and the smoothness and uniform size of the individual sand grains as a result of ceaseless wear from wind movement, provides suitable conditions for the roaring effect.

The smooth surface of the sand grains allows for considerable contact if the sand is disturbed. Friction results and sets up vibrations which produce the strange sound. The roaring issues from completely dry sand lying on the surface. If it rains, the sand is dampened and the sound vanishes until dry weather returns. Extreme cold also seems to mute the sands. It is therefore useless visiting the area in a wet season. The locals relate very conflicting stories about the sand. Some say that it will only roar during the months which contain an 'R' in their names. The truth is that the sands know no calendar – they roar when they are dry and conditions are suitable. The driest months are in winter from May to October. The summer months are very hot, with frequent thunderstorms which subdue the roaring for several days.

The southerly face of the dunes is the best place to hear the roaring, which is distinct when the sands are violently agitated and subsides to a hum when the sands are poured or gently moved. A person sliding down the dune can be heard 100 m away. Even the act of moving a finger backwards and forwards through the sand produces a roar which will occur day or night. A strong dry wind blowing in the dunes at night produces an eerie rumbling.

The dunes are also notable for the occurrence of fulgurites caused by flashes of lightning which strike and fuse the sand. The fulgurites consist of thread-like or tube-like strings of fused sand, glazed and mirrored in parts and up to 2 m long. Short, fragmented fulgurites are numerous and the local people collect and sell them as souvenirs to visitors. The white sands are very photogenic, especially towards sunset.

The road to the white sands is in reasonable condition when dry but should be negotiated in daylight. There are several signposted turns which can easily be missed at night.

From Groblershoop, the main N10 road continues south, leaving the fertile valley of the Gariep and crossing arid country. After 15 km there is a turn to Buchuberg Dam, and after another 5 km a turn to the railway station of *Putsonderwater* (well without water), rather sadly named in an area so arid. At 56 km from Groblershoop the road reaches a crossroads. To the east 3 km away, lies the railway station of *Draghoender* (dragoon) where soldiers of that regiment were reputedly stationed during the Anglo-Boer War. To the west of the crossroads lies ...

MARYDALE

Established in 1902 by the Dutch Reformed Church, *Marydale* was named after the wife of G P Snyman who owned the farm *Kalkput* on which the town was laid out. The population is now 1 704. Sheep and cattle are farmed in the area and considerable mining activity, mainly for asbestos, was carried out in the vicinity. The Koegas Asbestos mine, 24 km to the east, was the largest producer of blue asbestos in the world. The mine centre at Westerberg was of substantial size and a real oasis in the wilderness famous for its gardens producing oranges, other fruit and vegetables. The decline in demand for asbestos has badly affected the district and left it with a legacy of the ill-health of many people exposed to the asbestos fibres.

From Marydale the N10 road continues in a south-easterly direction through arid but asbestos-rich country where mining activity was once extensive. After 73 km the road passes through the Doringberg range of hills and reaches ...

PRIESKA

Lying on the south bank of the Gariep River, the town takes its name from an ancient fording place known to the Koranna people as *Prieskab* (place of the lost goat). Many early European travellers used this ford on their way to the north and it became a well-known staging post. A trading station and mission were established there and the town developed around these places. The population now numbers 11 527.

Prieska is the centre for sheep farming while irrigated farmlands in the valley of the Gariep produce lucerne, vegetables, maize and fruit. Considerable mining activity is carried out. The Prieska Copper Mine, situated at Copperton (64 km from Prieska), produces copper and zinc. Salt-pans yield salt, and Prieska is the principal centre for the mining of tiger's-eye gemstones.

Overlooking Prieska is *Die Koppie* (the hill) on whose summit stands a small fort built by the British during the Anglo-Boer War. Garrisoning the fort must have been akin to being stationed in an oven. The hill is a nature reserve where a good collection of aloes and other flowering plants flourish. Another fine collection of aloes grows in the garden named after Ria Huysamen, a local lady who collected them. They bloom in July and August. Four kilometres from the town centre is a riverside resort known as *Die Bos* (the wood). The Gariep River here is fine for swimming, with many trees whose deep shade is a precious asset in an area extremely hot in summer.

There are two hiking trails in the Doringberg range, the T'Keikamspoort and the Oranjezicht trails. Both reward the hiker with spectacular scenery and unusual flora.

In the municipal offices is a collection of gemstones and mineral specimens from the district. The disastrous collapse of asbestos mining, and the deleterious affects of its fibres on the health of miners and their families, is a sad legacy.

From Prieska the N10 road continues south-eastwards over arid country. After 129 km the road joins the main road, N12, the Diamond Way, linking Cape Town to Kimberley. The junction point is 3 km north of Britstown. For this road see Chapter Fourteen.

Chapter Sixteen

ENCHANTED WATERS, MAGIC MOUNTAINS

The Story of the Little Karoo

In the year 1689 a party of travellers from the Cape set out on a venture into the interior. The chief Hykon of the Inkwa tribe, living somewhere in the eastern Karoo, had sent messages to the commander of the Cape settlement inviting the opening of trade. Ensign Izaak Schryver, at the head of a party of soldiers and guides, was sent on the long walk along the coast and then across the mountains into the unknown to find the chief.

An ancient pathway made by migrating elephants and other wild creatures provided a way over the barrier of mountains between the coast and the interior. Up this path, through Attakwas Kloof the travellers made their way. They reached the summit (west of the modern Robinson Pass) on 27 January 1689 and looked out like eagles from its heights. Below them, to the north, they saw a very remarkable part of the world – so remarkable in fact for its geology, scenery, flora and fauna that there is nothing quite like it to be found anywhere else on this whole beautiful planet Earth.

The travellers descended to the floor of a basin contained between two great walls of mountains, the *Swartberge* (black mountains) on the northern side and the *Langeberge* (long mountains) on the south. The floor of the basin was a veritable garden of flowering plants especially of numerous species of succulents. So pervasive was one genus, the *Sceletium* (known as the *Ganna*) with 22 members, that the travellers named the place *Cannaland;* and this for long remained the name of what is now called the Little Karoo.

Let us wander through this Cannaland and discover its natural wonders.

The Little Karoo seems so arid but it is one of the most amazing examples on Earth of a landscape entirely fashioned by water. In it may be seen an almost unbelievable sequence of creative 'happenings', where Nature used water and sediments in particularly brilliant fashion to form a part of Earth of subtle beauty and with a highly potent, very localised influence on the life-forms making a home there.

In the beginning there was only water. An ancient sea washed over the area. This sea was rich in nutrients. On the surface floated colonies of the blue-green algae known as stromatolites. A multitude of tiny creatures lived in the sea. Their shells and skeletons fell to the bed of the sea and formed a belt of limestone 140 km long and about 1 000 m thick. The period of deposition was between 600 and 800 million years ago. The deposit of limestone is known to geologists as the Kango (or Cango) Group. Where it remains on the surface, it weathers to form a blue-grey coloured rock known as *Olifantklip* (elephant stone) because of its resemblance to the hide of an elephant.

Vast quantities of other sediments were deposited by the sea over and around the belt of limestone. Washed down by the rivers from the continental mass of Africa, these sediments were deposited in the series of layers known collectively to geologists as the Cape Supergroup. The layers were deposited in three main sequences. When the sea receded (or the land rose), they dried, warping and folding in the process, providing Earth with the glorious mountain-and-valley sandstone world of the Western Cape. The Little Karoo is part of this surface, a level sedimentary basin set between two parallel ranges of mountains; the Swartberge in the north-west and the Langeberge–Outeniqua range in the south-east. Complex in their shapes, vivid in their colouring with reds and oranges derived from iron-oxides, these mountains are supreme examples of the use of sediments and water in the creation of a landscape of serene beauty.

By 250 million years ago this phase of creation was complete. Like a human artist who experiences different phases of work, Nature then turned the modelling tools and paintbrushes of water to something entirely different. The sea flooded in once again; the basin of the Little Karoo was submerged. Wave action eroded into the mountain slopes and deposited a spoil of soil and pebbles to create a conglomerate, particularly richly coloured red, which accumulated as foothills to the parent ranges when the sea once again receded and they were left exposed. Soft in structure, these so-called Enon Conglomerates have bizarre shapes and are easily eroded by wind and water.

With the surface of the Little Karoo once again dry, Nature used the rain-water and the run-off of mountain streams to create a real subterranean treasure-chest. For the past millions of years the limestone belt had been left undisturbed by anything other than the occasional tectonic stirrings of earth. About twenty million years ago one of these earth movements brought the limestone into the weathering zone close to the surface. Acidic rain-water soaked its way from the surface into cracks caused by earth movements of the limestone. Chambers were formed as the acidic water dissolved the limestone.

About one million years ago there seems to have been a general uplift in the Little Karoo. The water in the chambers seeped away, leaving empty spaces. Perhaps this was what Nature had intended, for these dark chambers became subterranean art galleries. It is nice to think of the power of Creation finding relaxation there, decorating the chambers with all manner of lovely *Speleothems* (cave things) such as stalactites, stalagmites, helictites and flowstones. All these were fashioned by the rain-water soaking down, picking up carbon dioxide from the humus in the soil above the caves, forming bicarbonate by dissolving the limestone and then depositing this on the ceilings, walls and floors of the chambers to form all the magical 'exhibits' in the underground 'art galleries'.

But where is the pleasure to an artist if his works cannot be exhibited to others? To arrange this, a stream known as the *Donkergat* (dark hole) was influenced to flow from the mountains at right angles directly across the underground chain of caverns. The stream eroded a valley, and this cut across the limestone belt. An entrance to the caves was revealed. In time, bats and prehistoric man found the entrance and made their homes there.

THE DREAMLAND OF THE GANNA

Why Gannaland? The *Sceletium* genus of plants which gave this area its original name of Gannaland or *Kannaland* is numerous. But in themselves the members of the genus are rather nondescript. Compared to the almost luminous beauty of the flowers of the countless mesembryanthemums which grow there and the aloes which seem to set the mountain slopes on fire with their reds and oranges, the flowers of the ganna are small and colourless; and yet the plants had enough presence to dominate the area. The reason, however, is not too hard to find.

If the leaves of the ganna, particularly those of the *Sceletium anatomicum* species of the Aizoaceae family of succulents, are dried and then chewed by any animal, hallucinations and intoxication are induced. Wild animals discovered this, especially the eland and the ostrich. Man also found the plants to be the key to fancies and dreams. For the prehistoric people who first made their homes in the basin between the ranges where so many of these desirable plants grow, the area became something of an Elysium. It was a dreamland where, to escape reality, all they had to do was harvest enough leaves to dry and store in a skin pouch and then chew whenever so inclined. The leaves were considered to be so potent that they were even said to be used in revival of the dead and, oddly enough, as an abortive. The leaves contain mesembrine, a relative of cocaine. They are known popularly as *kougoed* (chew things). They are considered similar, in some of their effects, to the *ginseng* of the East, which is said to be rejuvenating, stimulating and aphrodisiacal – altogether a rather remarkable little plant! It is even a source of soap, and this was one of the earliest exports from the Little Karoo.

Botanists, understandably, have a fascinating time in the Little Karoo. The area is a home for succulents, a part of Earth which particularly suits these specialised little plants. More species grow there than anywhere else. For botanists a new discovery is always possible on any outing. In this botanical kingdom there are humble little plants growing by choice in the rockiest soil. They mimic the rocks and pebbles so perfectly in shape and colour that they are hard to find although there are so many of them. The *Crassulaceae* and the *Anacampseros* include many of these odd plants which have adapted themselves ingeniously to an environment of baking sunshine and unpredictable rainfall. In this setting they shelter among the rocks which reflect away much of the heat, allow rain-water to penetrate the earth but shade the ground while the plants collect the water and store it in fleshy leaves – many of them with a double protection of a waxy surface, resistant to any evaporation.

The *Geraniaceae* family are the parents of the geraniums cultivated in the gardens of the world. This family has some real prodigals amongst its offspring. Included in these is the so-called Bushman's Candle (*Sarcocaulon patersonii*), with a stem which secretes so inflammable a resinous concentration that they burn even when green. They were, in fact, used by many people prehistoric and modern to light dark caves and give brilliance to many a camp-fire.

The *Liliaceae* family include not only the lovely lilies, but also the aloes, gasterias and the haworthias. The haworthias, named after Adrian Haworth, the leading English authority on succulent plants, who lived from 1768 to 1833, include some extraordinary botanical characters. A notable species is *Haworthia truncata* or *perdetande* (horse's teeth), much sought after by collectors for its strange appearance and for its medicinal value. Only the tips of the leaves of this plant appear above the surface and are so arranged that they have the appearance of a set of horse's teeth.

The aloes of the *Liliaceae* family, especially *Aloe ferox*, provide the brilliant floral displays of the winter months. To see them flowering in the setting of the deep clefts and valleys of the sandstone mountains is one of the finest of all botanical spectacles.

The *Compositeae* family of succulents include the daisies which carpet whole areas of the Little Karoo with massed flowers in the spring.

The *Asclepiadaceae* family include stapelias, the carrion flowers and star-fish flowers which attract their insect pollinators, not with a sweet aroma, but with the foul stench of putrefaction. Their shapes and colours are almost reptilian but their odour attracts to them numerous insects.

The *Euphorbiceae* family include the milkbush plants and the nabooms. The *Portulacace* family include the spekboom or elephant's food, while the *Aizoaceae* or *Ficoidceae* include the ice-plants and the vygies (called the *mesembryanthemums* – midday flowers – because they stay in bed late and go to sleep early, revealing the full beauty of their evanescent, glowing colours only around noon). Then it is that they open fully; literally millions of flowers on countless plants in a variety of colours which seem to include almost everything except black! Spring in the Little Karoo, with a good mesembryanthemum season, is dazzling. The ganna shrubs are part of this family, but without the brilliant flowers. The Ganna (*Salsola aphylla*) is a shrub which flourishes in the dry watercourses and provides food for ostriches and livestock.

Who the first people were to see this kingdom of succulents, how and when they came, is unknown. It would seem that by the Late Stone Age the Little Karoo was the home of a number of family groups of the hunter-gatherer people called Bushmen by Europeans, for they had no known collective name for themselves.

These interesting people were never numerous. Family groups or small clans attached themselves to selected hunting and food-gathering areas and made their homes in the caves and rock shelters. They were not warlike, there were never enough of them for that. Each group kept a distance from the others. Hunters would clash if they intruded into the preserves of another family.

Perhaps 1 000 of these people at most lived in the Little Karoo at the time the first Europeans arrived and written history commenced. Before that there is not even legend. The names of their clans, families and leaders are unknown. They were people of dreamland, almost like the fairy folk of Europe or the mythological creatures and gods of ancient Greece. If it were not for their artefacts left on the floors of their caves, and especially the galleries of pictures painted on the rock faces, their existence would be almost unknown. When more powerful and numerous people arrived, the Bushmen vanished. They were not regarded by their supplanters as being much more than wild creatures. Their ancient hunting-grounds were simply considered to be vacant land with no proprietary rights for Bushmen. As vacant land it was settled by farmers and granted by the Government in reward for any services. The Bushmen residents, if they tried to resist, were exterminated and nobody recorded any history of their kind. There was extreme difficulty in communication. The Bushman language was unique. It was a 'click' language, very exotic and complex for other people to learn to speak or devise a written means of record. There are five different click sounds in this language, associated with 25 supporting sounds, all exotic to other people.

The galleries of rock paintings left by the Bushmen are their principal memorial. From these paintings we receive a glimpse of their life-style, an indication of the days of old when the Little Karoo was the home of eland, buffalo, elephant, rhino, ostrich and countless antelope. There are pictures of the people, their ceremonies and dances, and of mythological creatures such as water people and odd bird-like figures. There are not many of these galleries. Rock shelters with walls suitable for painting were scarce. But even on the few suitable walls there is no evidence of rival artists erasing somebody else's work in order to make room for their own. There were not many artists, and amateur work was not encouraged. The pictures were probably painted by professionals, mendicant artists and entertainers who visited the various Bushman groups, giving them news of friends and relatives who had wandered off to join other families or clans. Tales of hunting, ghosts, myths and legends would be told and would be worth many a good meal for such a travelling artist. An individual who knew the secrets of making the colours and how to paint upon the rocks illustrations of the stories told would be a doubly welcome visitor.

It is pleasant to imagine the audience sitting entranced, listening and watching with deep appreciation. It is considered that the Bushmen were a harmless little people, or at least as near to that happy state as it is possible for humans to be. They lived close to nature and in a degree of peace. The country was large, they could move away to avoid competing with others. This they eventually did completely in order to avoid competing with more powerful newcomers. But when you visit some of their rock shelters, the atmosphere is so tangible that you feel that, like the fairies, they are perhaps still there but just living on another plane. Perhaps Nature took compassion on them in their time of crisis. A cloak of invisibility was simply, completely and effectively placed over them. They still wander free on their old hunting-ground, the dreamland of the ganna.

A LEGEND OF THE WATERMAIDENS

The so-called 'mermaid' frieze from the overhanging cliff shelter in Ezeljagd's Poort is one of the most renowned and intriguing examples of rock art in South Africa. The paintings were first reported in 1837 by J E Alexander in his book, *A Narrative of Exploration among the Colonies of Western African and of a Campaign in Kaffir-Land*. Years later, in 1875, a farmer named D Ballot from *Molensrivier* copied the drawings. From an old Bushman known as Afrikaander he secured this interesting legend about the mythological creatures who reputedly lived beneath the water.

> *'I know many stories of Waterwomen which my mother has told me and I will tell baas* (master) *one of them'.*
>
> *'There was once a girl who all the people said was so good-looking. One day the girl went out to walk along the river, and came to a large water-hole over which a krantz* (cliff) *was hanging'.* Here old Afrikaander stopped short, and advised me never to go near a water-hole over which a krantz is hanging, for, says he, *'Met zoo een gat is dit nooit helder nie, baas'* (with such a hole is it never clear, master), and then continues his story.
>
> *'Well, baas, I told you that she stopped at the hole to look at some flowers which were very attractive, and which were drifting near her, till at last one of them came so near that she stooped over the water to pluck it. but she had hardly touched the flower when she was caught by the hand and dragged into the water.*
>
> *'Now, as the girl did not come home, her mother went to look for her, and traced her tracks to the hole wherein she had been dragged, and when she saw that the tracks did not go any further, she knew at once that the Water women had caught her child, for she was a clever woman. She therefore ran in the veld and there gathered some shrubs which she knew the Water women were very fond of. When she had enough of these shrubs, she ran home, dried them hastily by the fire, and ground them into a fine powder. Then she ran back to the hole, and threw the dust over the water. When she had done this, she went and stood a little way off and waited. She had not waited long when she saw her child coming out of the water and walking towards her. She was unhurt, but the Water women had loved her so much that they had licked her cheeks quite white and this remained so ever afterwards.*

> 'She told her mother that the people who live under the water had such fine houses, and that they live in great abundance. As I have said, the girl's mother was a very clever woman, and she had instructed her child from her youth how she should behave, and what to eat if she should fall into the hands of the Water women. If they ask you: "What will you eat, fish or meat?" you must say, "I eat neither; give me bread to eat". If you ask for fish or meat, it will be certain death to you; as the Water women are half fish, half flesh, they would think that you would want to eat them'.

This legend was sent by Mr Ballot to Dr W Bleek in Cape Town, the renowned authority on Bushmen. He never published the legend, but fortunately it was kept by his secretary, Miss L Lloyd. Nearly 100 years later it was found by Mr J Leeuwenburg of the South African Museum in a folder of her letters in the library of the University of Cape Town.

A VERY REMARKABLE BIRD

The ostrich was once numerous throughout the continent of Africa. There are about twelve forms of the bird, each with its own characteristics and occupying particular areas where they have adapted themselves to harmonise with the local climate and environmental conditions. In the basin of the Little Karoo, the ostrich found its ideal habitat. It was here that the species *Struthio camelus* made its home. In a dry climate, extremely healthy to them, with plenty of water in streams, a rich food supply of herbs, succulents (including the ganna, for which they had a great liking) and other delicacies such as the sandstone pebbles which they liked to swallow as an essential aid to their digestive system, they developed as handsome, athletic birds with magnificent feathers, especially those of the male. A cross between the resident ostrich and North African variants produced *Struthio camelus* var, domesticus Swart, which has been selectively bred to create the so-called Oudtshoorn or South African ostrich of today. A notable infusion of exotic blood reached the local ostriches from the Sahara north of Timbuktoo. A few specimens of this variety of ostrich were sent from Morocco to a breeder named Rabie in Mossel Bay. These birds had feathers known as the Evans type, after Oscar Evans of *Melrose* farm in the Bedford district of the Eastern Cape. He was a great authority and champion of the ostrich industry. He had travelled to the Sahara Desert to find ostriches with superior characteristics which could be bred into the local birds. The Evans-type feather was small and white with notably stronger flues than the larger feathers of the local birds. In 1911 the South African Government sent a party of four men to the Timbuktoo area to obtain specimens of the local ostriches. The four men were R W Thornton, principal of the Grootfontein Agricultural College; J M P Bowker, an ostrich farmer in the Middelburg district; F C Smith, a staff member of the Agricultural College at Middelburg, and H Oldershaw, an ex-British sergeant-major who knew the Timbuktoo area, its people and languages.

These four men had to overcome daunting difficulties of climate, bad water, sickness, a precarious political situation with incessant skirmishing between Arabs and the French Foreign Legion, and the presence of a rival American party also searching for this particular type of feather. With the exertion of considerable effort, the South African party, employing Arab hunters, managed to obtain 200 ostriches and succeeded in getting 150 of these birds to Kano in Nigeria. From there they were taken by train to Lagos and shipped safely to Cape Town.

The cross-breeding experiment was conducted under the supervision of Frank Smith at Grootfontein Agricultural College. An ostrich hybrid was evolved with a superb feather. Unfortunately the First World War broke out at this stage. The collapse of the feather market frustrated the search for the perfect feather, but the breed had been achieved. Long after the four men had died, the revival of demand for feathers of quality saw their expedition to the Sahara finally justified.

In the Little Karoo the male ostrich grows to a height of about 2,2 m and a mass of 90–120 kg. The females are smaller and have drabber plumage, but every part of both male and female birds is valuable to man, not just their feathers. Their meat is tasty and extremely healthy, high in protein and low in fat content. Apart from tender fillet, the deboned cuts yield an extraordinary range of cold meats – mince, sausages and casseroles, smoked brawn, ostrich ham, meat loaf, garlic polony, french polony, hamburger patties, liver pàtè, neck, curried tripe and, strangely enough, a stomach which looks and tastes like the finest ox tongue. Their skins make excellent leather; they have been used as pack animals or even trained to pull carts; while their bones and offal are steam digested and milled to yield a protein-rich fodder supply. Bones are sent to bone meal factories.

The ostrich adapted itself admirably to the habitat of the Little Karoo. It is a bird designed to cope with semi-desert life. It can survive without water for long periods, but under flood conditions it is sufficiently versatile to be able to swim. Two-toed feet and muscular legs enable the birds to reach speeds of about 80 km an hour, with a stride of 3 m, making them formidable sights as they race to safety across some open space such as a dried-out pan. Their speed, however, is of short duration, about 3 km. They drop from exhaustion and, perhaps realising their limitations, generally expect to escape aggressive attention by hiding. The chicks scatter, melting into the grass or feigning death, while the parents lower their heads to the ground in order to reveal as little of themselves as possible.

Normally they are docile creatures, but romance can go to their heads. During the mating season the scales of legs and beak of the male birds turns a bright pink. With their long naked legs, the birds look as though they are dressed in circus tights! They become aggressive and their kick can be dangerous. The male bird makes his presence known by means of a booming call which is commonly confused with the distant roar of a lion. He displays his beautiful feathers to the hen in an elegant mating dance, bending his knees, falling to his haunches and swaying from side to side. The hen lays her first egg approximately fourteen days after mating, and thereafter one every second day until she has a clutch of 12 to 15 eggs in her nest, a hollow scraped by the birds in the ground. This simple nest is often shared with other hens. Males and females take turns in sitting on the eggs, the dark-coloured males at night and the grey-coloured females during the day, but this is not a rigidly followed duty sequence. The incubation period is 42 days and the chickens take 2 years to mature, with their prime-feather period falling in the years between 3 and 12. The male has a plumage of 240 g of wing feathers (much used in high fashion) and 1 kg of body feathers (used in dusters). The life span of an ostrich is 40–50 years on average but some birds have been known to live well over 60 years. Predators catch many ostriches on their nests. The black-backed jackal developed a special technique for raiding nests by rolling one egg to the edge of the rim, kicking it smartly backwards against its fellows, and then dining well out of the resulting omelette! Each egg weighs just over 1 kg and provides excellent eating, especially when scrambled and sprinkled with ostrich biltong. An egg takes 1½ hours to boil.

Ostrich feathers were used as a decorative item of dress by the early African tribes and exported from Southern Africa from the days of the first traders and hunters. They were always valued as decorations and curios, as well as having a functional use in the making of dusters. The feathers, when brushed, are charged with static electricity, and dust is attracted and adheres to them.

The ancient Egyptians had a high regard for ostriches. They domesticated them and used the feathers as a symbol of justice because the stalks ran exactly in the centre of the flue. In the Little Karoo a local story relates that in 1865 there was a severe drought. Only the ostriches seemed indifferent to the period of thirst, while most other creatures died or fled the place. The European settlers who had always hunted the birds were forced to exist largely on the spoils obtained from the ostriches. They found the meat to their liking and the handsome feathers of the male birds provided a saleable item. The idea of domesticating the birds occurred, but wire fences with which to contain them had yet to be devised. Lucerne (an alfalfa grass developed in Lucerne, Switzerland) had to be introduced to the Little Karoo as a staple food and much conservative opposition to the domestication of the bird had to be overcome. Hunters claimed that tame birds would not breed, and that their feathers were inferior and not as curly or lasting as those of wild birds. Dealers were suspicious and offered lower prices for feathers obtained from domesticated birds.

Yet the idea of domestication spread. The birds were easy to domesticate. Pet ostriches were to be seen on many farms. Eggs were easy to hatch and the chickens grew up perfectly amenable to human control. They could tolerate arid conditions with greater resilience than many other forms of life.

They were accident prone (even breaking their own legs in an excess of high spirits when habitually performing a gyrating dance of welcome to the rising sun or in a dance of joy at the approach of rain). They were nearly free of disease and parasites in their natural home. The notion that domesticated birds did not breed, or that their feathers were inferior, soon proved to be unfounded.

A farmer in the Graaff-Reinet district, Von Maltitz by name, is said to have been the first to domesticate the birds on a large scale. Another farmer, Arthur Douglas of Grahamstown, brought the idea to complete practicability. He also perfected the incubator, investing time and money in improving a primitive device he had imported in 1868 and developing exact control of temperature, correct humidity and automatic turning of eggs. The Eastern Cape farmers played a particularly important part in the development of the ostrich-feather industry into South Africa's first great earner of export profits. The subsequent introduction of the wire fence and lucerne to the Little Karoo made large-scale domestication possible in that area in perfect weather conditions. The incubator was the device which allowed farmers to control hatching and, by systematic removal of eggs, to induce the hens to lay more eggs. This allowed the rapid increase of stock.

When fashion adopted the feather in the period known as *Art Nouveau* (new art), there was a tremendous boom in the Little Karoo. Land values shot up to £600 a hectare and breeding pairs of birds fetched £1 000. By 1880 the ostrich industry was a markedly profitable feature of the South African economy. In fact, a feather-brained mania took place in the Little Karoo. Palatial homesteads and manor-houses known as feather palaces were erected, and around them great flocks of ostriches enjoyed a pampered existence in the lucerne fields. The cocks were clipped every nine months, each yielding about 0,9 kg of feathers. With prime plumes fetching £250 a kilogram, the profits were enormous.

During the year 1880 no less than 74 000 kg of feathers were exported, valued at £900 000. In 1904 the output passed 210 000 kg, valued at over £1 million from 385 370 birds. In 1913 the figures were 464 581 kg of feathers exported, worth over £3 million. There were 750 000 ostriches in the Little Karoo at that time. The boom reached its zenith between 1910 and 1912. Ostrich feathers held a distinguished place in the export economy of South Africa, second only to gold, diamonds and wool. In many other parts of the world – the Argentine, Australia, Algeria, America, even Europe – attempts were made to farm ostriches, but the Little Karoo remained the paradise of the big birds, the only area where, with a minimum of upkeep of feeding them their preferred diet of lucerne, such succulents as ganna, and marble sized stones, they attained complete perfection.

Then came the First World War. Shipping was not available for such frivolous cargoes as feathers. *Art Nouveau* in all its forms – fashion, architecture, art – suddenly became ostentatious. Austerity became the order of the war years, with women in uniform or overalls. The feather trade collapsed and at the end of the war it did not revive. The feather-brained era was succeeded by the scatter-brained age of the 'flapper' and the Little Karoo experienced a complete depression.

The ostrich population dwindled, but later years have brought a profitable recovery and there are now approximately 200 000 birds in the Little Karoo producing 120 000 kg of feathers a year on the 350 farms which maintain them. Today the industry is firmly established under the organised, one-channel marketing system of the Klein Karoo Landboukoöperasie Bpk, founded in 1945. This organisation was responsible in 1947 for the first feather auctions and in 1964 for the first ostrich abattoir, capable of processing 40 000 birds a month. The ostrich certainly pays well for its keep, not only in the profitable harvest of feathers every nine months (usually coinciding with the bird's moulting pattern) but also after processing. Tender high-grade ostrich meat makes very good eating. The thigh meat is made into biltong. One ostrich egg alone is the equivalent of 24 fowl's eggs. Boom time may have passed, but a thriving industry has replaced it; duster feathers and high quality plumes, for instance, formerly sold at about R13 and R36 per kilogram respectively, now fetch prices of R80 and R800 per kilogram – an over 300 per cent rise during the last ten years. Likewise ostrich skins, formerly R10, now cost R1 500. All in all, a mature 15-month-old bird is worth about R1 200. Breeding pairs selected according to quality of feathers fetch up to R4 000.

One of the great tourist attractions of the Little Karoo is a visit to the ostrich show farms. Daily from 08h00 to 16h30 at *Cango* and *Safari* and from 08h00 to 17h00 at *Highgate*, these farms conduct tours during which the visitor is shown details of one of the world's most unique industries.

Safari farm is graced with an authentic 'feather palace' homestead, built during the boom days. The Edwardian homestead of *Highgate* also attracts attention, while the reception building of the Cango farm is the early factory of the Schoeman Tobacco Company. There are shops in which various products are displayed, including ostrich leather items, shoes, bags and the beautiful jackets and coats of the two distinctive types – characteristically pocked body skins and the smooth, glazed leg skins – and ostrich biltong. Eighty-five per cent of the leather processed at the Oudtshoorn tannery, however, is destined for export to the Far East, USA, West Germany, Italy,

France, Spain and England. The making of the much-prized ostrich leather jackets and coats has recently begun in Oudtshoorn by a talented couturière, Nerina Aling. Meat is exported to Europe and America and distributed all over Southern Africa. This remarkable bird is the basis for a considerable industry employing a wide range of people from farmers to processors, manufacturers, couturiers, artists, curio and gift manufacturers.

OUDTSHOORN

The largest town, principal centre and 'capital' of the land of the ostriches. Oudtshoorn is situated on the banks of the Grobbelaars River tributary of the Olifants River and lies in a strategic central position in the basin between the mountains. The site of the town was originally the farm *Hartenbeesrivier*. When the settler population in the Little Karoo increased, making it desirable that a community centre be established, the farm owner, C P Rademeyer, donated 4 ha of ground and a church to provide the nucleus for a town. The church was completed in April 1839.

In 1847 a surveyor, John Ford, divided the farm into 500 erven and the first sale of plots was held on 15 November of that year. The place was named *Oudtshoorn* after the family name of the Baroness Gesina E J van Reede van Oudtshoorn, the wife of the Civil Commissioner of George, E Bergh, who was the superior administrative officer for the area which included the Little Karoo. Oudtshoorn became a magistracy in 1855 and a municipality on 1 September 1863. There are at present 53 589 people living in the town.

As the principal centre of the Little Karoo, Oudtshoorn grew steadily. The Olifants River and its tributary, the Grobbelaars, provided water for fine gardens and the surrounding green fields of lucerne on which the ostriches fed. Oudtshoorn became the 'feather capital' of the world, with great flocks of ostriches still providing a spectacle to be seen nowhere else in the world.

The demand for feathers was associated with the introduction of *Art Nouveau* (new art) in Europe, America and Japan. After the heavy formality of the art forms of the early 19th century, there was towards the end of the century a joyous attempt at emancipation in all forms of creative work. This had a very special influence on the life-style of people living in the sandstone world of the Little Karoo.

Art Nouveau was inspired by nature. Fashion designers, carvers, painters, architects: all were swept along by the exciting new style. The straight lines of the past were eschewed. The forms of nature took over, with the complex shapes of trees, flowers and feathers used in all forms of art. Wood-carvers, jewellers, wrought-iron workers, interior decorators, stained-glass artists, clock makers: all were stimulated to create new works.

In the Little Karoo an interesting development of *Art Nouveau* appeared in a relationship of feathers and sandstone. Money poured into the area from the sale of feathers. Despite attempts in other countries, there was nowhere else on Earth where the ostrich flourished nearly as well or produced comparable feathers. The profits of the feather industry stimulated many activities in the Little Karoo, and one of these was architecture.

The local sandstone with its exquisite colours suited designs in the *Art Nouveau* style. It was easy to work and readily available. Twelve architects established themselves in the Little Karoo and developed a singular style, particularly in the design of so-called feather palaces, the mansions put up in towns and as manor-houses on the farms of the 'feather barons', the new rich captains of the feather industry.

The prince of the sandstone architects was Charles Bullock who immigrated to the Cape from England in the early 1890s. Employed by the Public Works Department, he was posted to Oudtshoorn. He found the area at the crest of its feather boom with a tremendous demand for building. Everybody who was making money seemed to want to spend their new wealth on an imposing residence in the new style. Bullock resigned from the Public Works Department and set up practice designing public buildings and private residences, using local sandstone combined with imported stained glass, wrought iron, teak panelling and staircases, decorative ceilings made of papier mâché, and as many 'follies', ornaments and elaborate decorations as the finances and tastes of his client allowed.

Amongst Bullock's creations was the celebrated Olivier Towers. Built in 1903, this was a double-storey manor-house on the grand 'feather palace' scale and was considered to be the most beautiful of its kind. Dressed yellow-brown sandstone was used throughout . The cast-iron brackets and balcony railings were imported from the famed collection of the Saracen decorative foundry of Walter MacFarlane at Glasgow. There was an octagonal tower above octagonal rooms and a second tower like a witch's hat over the main entrance. There were twenty rooms decorated in full *Art Nouveau* style with the hall and grand dining-room panelled in imported teak.

This building unfortunately no longer exists, but its memory is preserved as the emblem on the labels of the products of the local co-operative winemakers. Several other buildings designed by Bullock have survived, however. One of these is Gottland House, erected in 1903 for a local attorney, M C Lind. This highly decorated building also has the almost obligatory octagonal tower covering an octagonal room. There are also elaborate wrought-iron railings, papier mâchè ceilings with pressed designs, and stained glass carrying patterns of the French lily and vines.

Another local attorney, J Foster, flush with the profits of the boom, commissioned Bullock to create a double-storey mansion named by its owner *Rus in Urbe*, but popularly known as Foster's Folly. This mansion was built of sandstone in its lower levels, burned bricks on its upper storey, and the inner walls of mesh-plastered panels. It had teak panelling, a teak staircase, false gables, encoustic tiling, papier mâchè ceilings, stained glass with the French lily motif, twenty commodious rooms and a cellar large enough to store a vast collection of wines and spirits.

Mr Foster was a member of the Cape Legislative Assembly and a real high roller. Rumour had it that he maintained a wife and a mistress, both living in style in separate parts of the mansion. Entertainment was lavish. When the feather boom collapsed in 1914, Foster went bankrupt. Rumour had it that he hid from his creditors in the cellar, reported himself as dead and, in disguise attended his own funeral, the coffin filled with sandstone fragments. He was never seen again in the Little Karoo. The Standard Bank took over the property and sold it to the educational authorities. The mansion was used as a teacher's training college until 1924, then as a hostel for girls and offices for the C J Langenhoven Commercial School. It became vacant in 1972 and fell into disrepair. It has been restored.

Another notable building in Oudtshoorn designed by Bullock is the former Boys' High School, now the C P Nel Museum. This handsome sandstone building has a clock tower 27,5 m high and was saved by public subscription from the danger of demolition. It was built in 1907 with a handsome green dome.

C P Nel was a local businessman who in 1953 bequeathed to the town his lifelong collection of historical objects. This collection forms the nucleus of the present museum which has the ostrich as its principal theme. There is a series of exhibits displaying the evolution of this remarkable bird, including stuffed models of the birds, maps of their natural habitat and displays of fashion during the feather boom period. One amusing little exhibit is the old glass chemist's bottle of ostrich-aphrodisiac pills, results guaranteed! Ostrich breeders insist that mealies are just as effective for Struthian sex appeal! Apart from ostriches, the museum houses replicas of period shops with their stocks, a collection of vehicles, carts and automobiles, and many other interesting exhibits, altogether making this one of the finest of all small town museums of Southern Africa. The museum is open on Mondays to Saturdays 09h00 to 17h00; Sundays from 14h00 to 17h00.

One of Bullock's most exquisite designs was on commission from J H J le Roux, a cattle breeder from *Baakenskraal,* to build a town house of sandstone in full *Art Nouveau* style. This house is now part of the C P Nel Museum in Oudtshoorn and its preservation is assured. Its stained-glass door-sides and windows, its wrought-iron work and period furniture are outstanding examples of the work of the day. Its wallpapers and carpeting are sumptuous.

Fireplaces fascinated Bullock. In 1907 he created for R Sladowski an *Art Nouveau* town house containing four superb elaborately decorated fireplaces. The barge-board at the front gable of the house is decorated with dragon-design carpenter's lace.

Another architect contemporary with Bullock was a man from Holland with the almost improbable name of Johannes Egbertus Vixseboxse. He had immigrated from Holland in 1888 and gone to work in the Transvaal where he was employed in the Public Works Department and later as government architect of the Orange Free State. He returned to Holland during the Anglo-Boer War. In 1903 he joined Charles Bullock's office in Oudtshoorn and worked with him on several important buildings such as the Boys High School. In 1910 Bullock died of pneumonia. Vixseboxse, with a partner, Wontink, who had once been his assistant in the Orange Free State, became Bullock's successor in the remaining years of the feather boom.

Like Bullock, Vixseboxse found sandstone very much to his liking and he designed a number of outstanding buildings. The most remarkable of these was commissioned from him in 1911 by Edwin Edmeades, who was then mayor of Oudtshoorn and the owner of a substantial business in wagon-making.

The contractor, A Rogers, an expert stonemason, built the Edmeades mansion from the design of Vixseboxse. There are twenty rooms with four superb fireplaces, each decorated with delft tiles carrying merchant-ship and windmill designs. The ceilings are of pine; the panelling of teak. The French lily is the dominant decoration. The mansion was built on a commanding site and is today a national monument used as a hostel for the Teachers' Training College. Several other of Vixseboxse's creations still survive in Oudtshoorn although others, such as the Gaiety Theatre in High Street, have vanished. Vixseboxse died in Johannesburg on 18 January 1943 aged 80.

High Street, the commercial centre of Oudtshoorn at that time, was said to have had only one business open on Jewish holidays. The feather boom had attracted over 300 Jewish families to the area. They dominated the feather trade. Most of them originated from Lithuania where pogroms in Tsarist times forced many people to emigrate. The Little Karoo Jews mainly came from two parts of Lithuania: a very conservative group from Chelm, and a liberal group from Shavli. The two groups could never agree. There were two *shuls*, no co-operation and an opinion that there were two separate paths to heaven.

Rich men lived in style in feather palaces; poor men tramped the country roads carrying on their backs sacks to hold the feathers they bought from the farmers. One of these traders, Max Rose, immigrated to the Little Karoo in 1890. Within ten years he became the so called 'Ostrich King' of South Africa, controlling a vast trade in feathers. He possessed a magnificent farm of his own where he kept 10 000 birds and produced feathers of superlative quality.

Many of the farms had on them homesteads as elaborate as the mansions in Oudtshoorn. Bullock designed several of these homesteads, while most of the practising architects of Oudtshoorn were kept busy applying *Art Nouveau* to the countryside. Other homesteads were designed in neo-Cape style but still using sandstone as building material. One of the finest examples of this style of building may be seen on *Welgeluk* (successful), the huge ostrich farm nowadays visited by thousands of tourists and widely known as the *Safari* Ostrich Show Farm.

Welgeluk had originally been owned by Pieter Olivier. At the height of the feather boom he commissioned the local architects, Bridgeman and Freeman, to create a homestead and this they did with style. The house has seven bedrooms and is especially notable for its stained glass and the usual 'follies' of gables and towers. The Lipschitz family who own the farm today, acquired the estate during the depression of 1932.

The history of the Lipschitz family in the Little Karoo is indicative of the rise and fall of life and business in a boom-to-bust economy. In 1904 Nathan Lipschitz arrived in Cape Town from Europe. He was 15 years of age. In Cape Town he found employment with a local watchmaker. After a year he was offered a better position with a jeweller in Oudtshoorn.

One morning the 16-year-old apprentice went to work and found the business locked. The owner had fled the place to evade his creditors. There were dozens of watches and clocks waiting for repair. Nathan opened his own business forthwith and worked night and day to create N Lipschitz Jewellers and Watchmakers. In his spare time he rode by horse many times for 85 km to the town of Ladismith where he courted Rachel Danilar. When he was 27 years of age, he married her. They remained together for 66 years.

In his jewellery shop, Nathan started buying and selling ostrich feathers. He decided to start farming himself and in 1917 hired *Rooiheuwel* in the foothills of the Kammanassie Mountains. After three years he gave up the farm and bought a house and land in Oudtshoorn. Then, in 1932, during the depression, he and a partner, Bramwell Butler who had won over £135 000 in the Calcutta Sweepstake, bought the farm *Welgeluk* from Pieter Olivier. It was a magnificent estate with 177 ha under irrigation and 1 498 ha of prairie country ideal for ostriches. It was also graced with its seven-bedroomed feather palace.

In the first year, the farm proved far more profitable than the jewellery business. Lipschitz bought out Butler and appointed a manager, Theunis Muller, to run the farm. An adjoining farm was bought and added to the estate, making a total of 359 ha under irrigation and 1 540 ha of open veld. It became an enormous business. In 1945 Harry, one of Nathan's sons, was demobilised from the South African Air Force and, with his brother Hilton, became a full-time farmer on the estate.

Another family then joined in the development of the estate. Back in 1856 Abraham Velenski had come from England and bought unseen a farm in the Prince Albert district of the Karoo. The arid Karoo was quite a change from the countryside of Britain.

To reach his property he bought an ox-wagon and trekked to the place. It took some years to recover from the shock of what he found but then the family grew to like the rugged, sun-drenched landscape. In about 1868 they bought the farm *Zeekoegat* (hippopotamus hole) adjoining *Welgeluk* and moved into the Little Karoo. One daughter married M S Lipschitz (no relation to Nathan Lipschitz). Her husband built the handsome ten-bedroomed Montagu House in Oudtshoorn. There the union produced ten children. The family acquired 34 farms in the Little Karoo. One daughter, Sophelia, married Jack Fisch whose father had been brought out from Europe by E K Green as a distiller. He later became a farmer in the Calitzdorp district.

When the feather boom collapsed at the outbreak of the First World War many farmers of the Little Karoo left the area. Others converted their farms to the growing of such crops as tobacco, lucerne and fodder, wine grapes and fruit. *Art Nouveau* was regarded as ostentatious and replaced by austerity. Jack Fisch was one of those who remained. Starting from the depths of the depression years, when feathers seemed to be valueless, he found markets in the manufacturing of feather dusters. He developed this enterprise into a thriving industry as well as managing his own farm.

Feathers slowly revived in value with re-acceptance into high fashion and for decorative uses. Ostriches were also found to yield skins for leather goods; their meat came into favour; and today every part of the bird has a commercial value. Ostrich meat, strangely enough, first found favour in Switzerland where it was marketed as South African turkey. Now restaurants in many parts of the world offer delicacies such as ostrich steak, ostrich neck (like oxtail), a variety of cold cuts of excellent flavour and, of course, the huge eggs, making delicious omelettes or scrambles.

One of Jack's five children, Derek, started exporting feathers and in 1956 established and formed his own company Derek Fisch (Pty) Ltd. He built this company into an international concern. He made 40 journeys to various parts of the world developing markets. He started an ostrich leather tannery in France which he eventually sold to French interests in 1972. In 1980 he sold Derek Fisch (Pty) Ltd to the Klein Karoo Co-operative and it now exports the bulk of the feathers and leather produced by the entire ostrich industry.

Derek Fisch then concentrated on farming. He made his home on the estate of *Onverwacht* (unexpected) with its grand old ostrich 'palace' farm house, where his manager Stephen Muller lives, while he has built an unpretentious house for himself on the southern boundary of Oudtshoorn.

In 1956 Derek and his great friend Harry Lipschitz combined and created the *Safari* Ostrich Show Farm with 3 000 ostriches on Harry's farm and over 8 000 on Derek's property, Karoo Valley Farms. Harry's wife Ida, a Swellendam lass of considerable resolution, concerned herself with the management of the tourist side of *Safari* Ostrich Show Farm together with Harry and Derek who also attended to their respective farming operations. Ostriches are selectively bred and feathers of high quality are produced along with the by-products of this most amazing bird. Harry's son, Stan, now carries on the farming of ostriches and Hereford cattle.

The *Safari* Ostrich Show Farm is visited by many thousands of tourists each year. They are welcomed in a central reception area containing a restaurant, tea-room, curio shop, conveniences and cool areas in a lovely garden setting where visitors can sit and relax. Every hour multilingual guides take parties of visitors on a tour of the estate. They are shown the breeding area, with gigantic incubating sections which hold 1 500 eggs, pens with breeding birds, birds on their nests, ostrich chicks, feeding pens, ostriches of various ages, their magnificent plumage, the manner of their handling and the way they are plucked.

Visitors are given an opportunity to ride an ostrich and the tour ends with a race by experienced jockeys. After that, tea, cold drinks or a pleasant lunch on ostrich steak (like tender beef), ostrich egg omelette sprinkled with biltong, ostrich stroganoff, or even ostrich neck (like oxtail), all washed down with local wine or grape juice. Memories of *Safari* farm are made like this and carried to many parts of the world!

Apart from feather barons and architects, Oudtshoorn has been the home of several accomplished people. One of the most revered was Cornelis Jacob Langenhoven who, as an attorney, settled in the town in 1899. Apart from his legal work, he was a prolific writer and a great champion of the Afrikaans language. His writings are notable for their homely humour and sympathy for his fellow men. He held sway in the old coffee house in High Street, strolling there from his office, soberly dressed with a fine walking-stick and a flower in his buttonhole. He was always ready to treat his café admirers, as the French literary figures love to do, with a series of witticisms directed at all and sundry, but especially at the English and their ways. On his death in 1932, Langenhoven's home *Arbeidsgenot,* was presented by his widow to the South African nation. It is open to the public and is perfectly preserved as an atmospheric example of the home life-style of a professional man during the period. It is filled with his personal belongings, including many odd little carvings of Herrie, the droll elephant who features in his book *Sonde met die Bure*. The carvings were sent as presents to Langenhoven by numerous admirers of Herrie.

In 1918 Langenhoven wrote *Die Stem van Suid-Afrika* which became the national anthem of South Africa. His enthusiasm for his native tongue largely contributed to Afrikaans being placed on the statute book in 1925 as one of the two official languages of South Africa.

Arbeidsgenot may be visited Mondays to Saturdays between 09h00 and 17h00. Closed Sundays and religious holidays.

The *Kango Koöperatiewe Tabak en Wynmaatskappy* in Oudtshoorn produces an interesting range of wines under the Rijckshof label. Fresh grape juice is also sold. The Klein Karoo Landboukoöperasie Bpk has its headquarters, ostrich tannery, abattoirs and factory in Oudtshoorn. It is the central marketing organisation for ostrich products.

THE ROAD TO THE NORTH AND THE CANGO CAVES

From Oudtshoorn a fine tarmac road leads northwards for 26 km, following the valley of the Grobbelaars River through the foothills of the Swartberge until it reaches the famous Cango Caves and a branch road turning eastwards to the Swartberg Pass, De Hoek and Kruisrivier. The scenery is beautiful, reminiscent of the Apennines of Italy.

Five kilometres from the centre of Oudtshoorn the road passes the Cango Crocodile and Cheetah Ranch, a rather novel enterprise to find in ostrich country. About 300 crocodiles as well as numerous other wild creatures, including lions and cheetahs, are maintained in this ranch and tours are conducted daily every half hour from 08h00 to 16h15. Cheetahs are bred very successfully in this delightfully planned zoological garden created by Andrew Eriksen and his wife Glenn.

At 14,5 km from the centre of Oudtshoorn, the road passes the attractive building erected in 1909 as the headquarters of the Schoeman's Tobacco Co. This building is now the reception office, curio shop and tea-room of the Cango Ostrich Show Farm run by Daniel Lategan.

Half a kilometre beyond the Cango Ostrich Show Farm, opposite a hill covered in aloes flowering in June, there is a turn-off leading to the Cango Angoré Rabbit Farm, started in June 1990 by Johan Kock and his wife Denise, with Arona Weidemann as their partner. The buildings were once part of the Spies Tobacco Factory on the farm *Roodewald*. German angora rabbits are bred on the farm and their wool is used to produce handmade jerseys and other items of clothing.

One kilometre beyond the Cango Angoré Rabbit Farm, the road (16 km from the centre of Oudtshoorn) enters Schoeman's Kloof and makes a lovely winding way through this handsome ravine. After 6,5 km there is a branch leading eastwards to the superbly situated Oudtshoorn municipal Cango Mountain Resort, with its caravan park and chalets at the foot of the Koos Raubenheimer Dam. From this resort a gravel road continues eastwards through the foothills of the Swartberge, past the turn-off to the 61 m high Rust-en-Vreugde waterfall and eventually joins the tarmac road from Oudtshoorn through Meirings Poort to the Great Karoo.

Five kilometres beyond the turn-off to the Cango Mountain Resort, the main road reaches a division. One branch leads westwards, branching to provide a fine drive through Kruisrivier to Calitzdorp, or climbing the Swartberge by means of the spectacular Swartberg Pass; the other division continues north and terminates at the entrance to the Cango Caves, 30 km from Oudtshoorn.

THE CANGO CAVES

The foothills on the southern side of the Swartberge range contain a deposit of limestone which, wherever it occurs in the world, is an indication that systems of caves decorated with elaborate formations of dripstone may be present. Explorers of this area have not been disappointed. So far, more than 30 caves containing dripstone formations have been found in the area and there are probably many more whose entrances, perhaps because they have become blocked by land slides or matted vegetation, have yet to be discovered.

The cave system popularly known as the Cango Caves is one of the great tourist features of Southern Africa. Many thousands of people visit these caves each month and find every facility available; restaurant, curio shops, crèches and a pet-room. Few visitors to this subterranean wonderland ever leave the place disappointed.

Bushmen were the first to discover the caves in what they knew as the Kango (water or wet mountains). The entrance of the caves was used as a dwelling by these prehistoric people. They decorated the walls with paintings of the various game animals which they found in the area. These early people would have had very limited knowledge of the caves for, without portable light, it would have been impossible for them to have penetrated far into the depths.

In 1756 the government awarded the first land grant in the area to Phillip du Pre, whose farm was called *Cango-Matjiesrivier*. It was the first time that the name Cango was used officially. Later, in 1760, Hermanus Steyn of Swellendam named another farm grant *Combuys aan de Cango* (kitchen of the Cango). The homestead of this beautiful farm may be seen in the valley on the right-hand side of the road as it approaches the turn-off to the caves. The entrance to the caves is located on this farm.

The year 1780 brought a very dry season, during which farmers had to travel long distances in search of grazing. The presence of water in the Swartberge came to their notice, and thus it chanced that Jacobus van Zyl, of the farm *Doornrivier* on the south-east side of the valley, obtained grazing rights on *Combuys* farm. Van Zyl was a road builder as well as a farmer. In 1779 he had been appointed to supervise road construction in the Little Karoo.

The discovery of the Cango caves took place quite accidentally. It is said that a group of Van Zyl's cattle strayed and his slave, Klaas, went in search of them. While journeying through the Combuys farm, he noticed the cave opening. On his return, he told the tale to Barend Oppel, a Dutch seaman and teacher, who was then a boarder with Van Zyl, and tutor to his children. Oppel was an adventurer at heart, and regarded this discovery as an ideal opportunity to escape the daily routine. He set off for the cave mouth with Klaas and, in his turn, told Van Zyl of his findings. On 11 July 1780, the farmer accompanied them to the caves. They entered the caves with torches and descended to the floor of the first great chamber by means of leather harnesses. In this fashion the chamber known as Van Zyl's Hall was discovered. It is pleasant to imagine the pioneer's awe as they stood looking up at the tall formations such as Cleopatra's Needle, 9 m high and at least 150 000 years old. The small group of pioneer explorers scratched their names into a rock face nearby the entrance, Barend Oppel's name remaining legible until recent times.

It is not known how much further Van Zyl and his party continued their exploration. Over the years visitors penetrated deeper into the sequence of chambers, each one being given a fanciful name until, 762 m from the entrance, a dead end appeared to have been reached. Cave experts were certain that the sequence continued, for a draught of fresh air was felt, but dripstone formations and rockfalls had blocked the passage.

In 1820 Lord Charles Somerset became the first British Governor to visit the caves. Later, in 1822, the writer and traveller, George Thompson, visited the caves. In his book *Travels and Adventures in Southern Africa*, he provided the first illustrated description of the caves. This book was published in London in 1827. Thompson was accompanied on his visit by Commandant R P Botha, a veteran of the Border wars and District Officer of the Cango at that time. He farmed locally on *Nooitgedacht*, which had been granted to him by the Dutch East India Company for his services during the wars. The second hall of the Cango Caves, Botha's Hall, is named after him.

In the absence of official control during this early period, considerable damage was effected to the caves. Souvenir hunters eagerly made off with glittering speleothem trophies and daubed their names over the Bushmen paintings at the entrance. Even after the Government had appointed the first *veldkornet* (district officer) to the area, no responsibility was taken for the caves.

By 1820, however, concern for the maintenance of the caves at last began to take root. On 27 July of the following year, the Governor, Sir Rufane Donkin, issued a table of regulations – the first active attempt to protect the caves. Vandalism and the work of insatiate souvenir hunters had now become painfully apparent. Speleothem formations had even been attacked with axes, for no law provided restraint for such wanton destruction. The District Officer took responsibility for the caves and was further given the task of introducing visitors to the caves and levying entrance fees. A fine of 50 rixdollars was imposed on anyone found damaging the formations. The money from this was to be employed in the improvement of education in the district.

Later in 1858, when Oudtshoorn became a Divisional Council area, administration of the caves fell to members of the council. Their task was to make the caves accessible to the public and to curtail vandalism. Under their management, roads to the caves were constructed and repaired, iron railings were introduced to the caves for the safety of visitors, and a large iron gate was erected in the entrance, allowing tighter control over vandalism. In 1891 Mr H van der Veen, the owner of *Combuys aan de Cango,* was appointed supervisor of the caves. In the same year, he employed the first full-time cave guide. This was the celebrated Johnnie van Wassenaar, who conducted innumerable parties through the caves until his retirement in 1934. During his 43 years of service, he opened many of the side chambers in the caves and once spent 29 hours underground exploring new areas. This was a record until 1976, when a party of four spent 50 hours exploring Cango Four.

It must have been a memorable experience to visit the caves during those early years. The road to the area was a makeshift affair and groups of travellers, complete with camping equipment, bumped and jostled their way in wagons on this arduous pilgrimage to see *'one of the most romantic and wonderful sights to be found in the colony'* (Oudtshoorn Courant 1880). Each visitor paid two shillings to enter and view the caverns by candle-light. Provision was also made for guano collectors – upon payment of ten shillings, the visitor was entitled to take away a 230 lb bag of guano, provided that he was willing to get down on his own hands and knees to collect it.

In 1896 the first proper geological survey was made of the caves. The geologist, George S Corstorphine, assisted by H M Luttman-Johnson, examined the caves and drew up a report and sketch plan. By that time the caves had been explored as far as the Devil's Workshop. In January 1897 a new chamber was seen through a crevice in the side of the Bridal Chamber. An adventurous boy, the son of Mr T E Anderson, the magistrate of Prince Albert, squeezed through the crevice and was the first to enter the chamber, but he could not explore very far. Johnnie van Wassenaar and Luttman-Johnson enlarged the crevice and were then able to explore two interesting side chambers, the first of which was named Wassenaar's Room, and the second, Luttman's Room.

Further exploration by Johnnie van Wassenaar revealed a cluster of eighteen new chambers, many of them decorated with speleothems of great beauty. It was a time for discoveries as, in the same month, J Walter and a Mr Oldfield discovered twelve more side chambers, making a grand total of thirty new chambers found in seven days. One of the new chambers was named the 'Monkey Rope' on account of a speleothem with the appearance of a rope being climbed by a troop of monkeys. Another of the new chambers was named 'The Mushroom' after the huge toadstool-shaped formation found in it.

News of these discoveries attracted further exploration. On 3 February 1897 a party of five visitors, G Innes, F Meyer, A Murray, C Mitchell and B Bergh, found seven more chambers, one of which was named the *'Courant Chamber'* after a representative of the local newspaper, the *Oudtshoorn Courant*, present in the party. Yet another chamber was found when George Innes broke through from the Treasure Chamber to what was then called *'Innes Chamber'*.

As the years passed, the ever-growing stream of visitors and the interest of influential people contributed to the advancement of the caves. On 24 June 1921 the management of the caves was taken over by the Oudtshoorn municipality. More attention was paid to facilities within and around the caves. Candle-light and paraffin lamps, for instance, had hitherto provided a rather inadequate lighting. Magnesium flares were used in photography, and black deposits resulting from this method can still be seen on some of the formations in Van Zyl's Hall. A visit from the Prince of Wales in 1925 prompted the purchase of the first small generator, and electric light pierced the subterranean darkness. This rather unreliable machine, which never completely replaced the candles, became progressively more laboured as tour groups penetrated deeper into the caves and more lights were switched on. The well-trained ears of the cave personnel could easily determine which part of the caves a party had reached by listening to the frenzied drone of the generator!

In 1930 a sum of $600 was donated and a small wooden building was erected at the entrance to serve as a tea-room. In 1967 a new building complex was constructed at the entrance, and this now houses a restaurant, curio shop, crèche, toilets, showers and personnel accommodation. Parking facilities were also created and a tarmac road to the caves from Oudtshoorn was perfected. Well lit by electricity and manned by a staff of professional guides, the Cango Caves are visited by over 170 000 people each year. No serious mishaps have occurred since the caves were opened to tourists.

The first sequence of caves is known as Cango One. The floor of this section has a rise and fall of only 15 m and is thus ideal even for the elderly tourist. There are innumerable beautiful dripstone formations to be seen in the main chambers and antechambers which branch off in different directions. The largest chamber is Grand Hall, stretching 107 m across. The highest dripstone formation is a column 12,6 m high which is found in Botha's Hall.

The mystery surrounding the continuation of the Cango caves was only solved in modern times. In 1956 the Speleological Association did a survey of the caves and noted that, when atmospheric pressure dropped outside, there was a flow of air out of the caves. When the barometric pressure mounted outside, there was a reverse flow of air into the caves. This verified the fact that there was an extensive continuation of the cave sequence. Two of the professional guides working in the caves, James Craig-Smith and Luther Terblanche, assisted by Daart Ruiters, devoted their spare time to exploration. In the last chamber of the recognised sequence, the Devil's Workshop, they tracked the source of a draught to a small crevice. For months they painstakingly worked on expanding this crevice. At last, in August 1972, they broke through into a fairyland, a 270 m extension of the sequence never before seen by man and of overwhelming beauty in its formations.

This extension of the caves was named Cango Two or the 'Wonder Cave'. The Speleological Association experts were then called in to explore the discovery thoroughly. At the end of the sequence they found a perennial stream flowing back towards the entrance and disappearing into a course about 20 m below the level of the caves. Several attempts were made to explore this stream, but rock obstructions and the level of the water provided a barrier.

In 1975 a pump was brought to the stream and this reduced the water level sufficiently to allow teams of workers to clear obstructions. After a great deal of work, on 2 August 1975, a party which included Hans Oosthuizen, Luther Terblanche, Michael Schultz, Floris Koper and others, managed to penetrate up the bed of the stream and enter what is known as Cango Three, a sequence of chambers 1 600 m long, with an extension known as Cango Four. The new cave sequences are closed to the public. They involve strenuous agility and Cango One is quite enough for most people. The pure crystalline beauty of the dripstone formations in the new cave sequences is thus preserved, since human beings carry destruction into caves. Their body warmth heats the air in the caves; limited supplies of oxygen are replaced by carbon dioxide; and artificial light stimulates the growth of algae. Cigarette smoke is a curse, depositing a patina of nicotine over the pure white lime. Humans must relieve themselves and the disposal problem in deep caves, without causing bacterial complications, is insurmountable. Another curious local problem is that people incessantly eat biltong in the caves. Ostrich biltong is tasty, and practically every visitor to the Little Karoo buys a few packets. Fragments of this and other foodstuffs thrown on to the cave floor in so humid and sheltered an atmosphere leads to serious invasions of bacteria and cockroaches. It is probably just as well that the inner sequences of the chambers are so secluded.

The entire cave sequence originated as a fault or crack in the rock up to 91 m in width. Nature sealed up this fault with calcite. Water soaked in and, after slowly eroding the huge chambers, drained away. Rain-water dripping down through the roof picked up carbon dioxide from plant roots and humus in the upper soil. Passing through the calcite, the carbon-rich water carried with it calcium carbonate which is only soluble in carbon dioxide.

Dripping through the ceiling of the caves, the water encountered air far less rich in carbon dioxide. With the balancing action of nature, carbon dioxide was then transferred from water to air. The calcium carbonate, unable to be transferred with the carbon dioxide, solidified – a minute amount from each drop of water – and over hundreds of thousands of years decorated the cave sequence with dripstone formations of astonishing beauty and variety of shape.

In this way, Nature laboured in the dark for countless years and finally gave man the privilege of seeing a work which is still in full progress, changing, growing and being perfected. Cango One is the introduction; the new sequences are for scientists and students to study and to guard against spoliation of any kind. The Caves are open daily all year round except on Christmas. Three tours are offered: the 2-Chamber and Full Tour (from 09h30 to 15h30 every hour on the half hour) and the 6-Chamber Tour (from 09h00 to 16h00 every hour on the hour). Phone (044) 272-7410.

TWO ROADS TO THE SOUTH

From Oudtshoorn two roads lead southwards and cross the Outeniqua range in order to reach the sea. The one road crosses the undulating floor of the Little Karoo basin and after 35 km reaches the foot of the Outeniqua range where it joins what used to be called the Road of South Africa which leads to the Long Kloof and also to Uniondale and Graaff-Reinet. The road is described in the section 'The Road to the East'.

The other road south from Oudtshoorn leads past the two famous ostrich show farms of *Safari* (5 km) and *Highgate* (7 km) and then, after climbing the Robertson Pass over the Outeniqua range, reaches the coast at Mossel Bay 83 km away. The story of *Safari* has already been told. Both *Safari* and *Highgate* ostrich show farms have been visited by so many tourists that they must be two of the best-known farms in the world.

The story of *Highgate* started in 1850 when William Hooper emigrated to South Africa from the village of Highgate, north of London. He was the son of Alexander Hooper, a high official in the Bank of England whose signature appeared on issues of bank notes in 1805, giving the usual guarantee of payment in gold on demand. William Hooper settled with his family at Blanco near George and it was there, in 1861, that a son named William was born. He grew up to become a worker in the Cape postal service. He was employed in the rural post office at Le Roux near Oudtshoorn. The pay was low, so he took on a job managing a stock farm which stretched from the present-day Oudtshoorn airport east and southwards to the foothills of the Outeniqua Mountains.

The domestication of ostriches had just started and William bred birds to sell the chicks. In 1887 the Standard Bank subdivided the farm and William obtained the portion south of the Olifants River, the present *Highgate*. William and his wife, Hester, made their home there in a small cottage which still stands next to the feather-plucking pens. There they lived hard but happily, struggling to pay for the farm and, in 1891, starting a family with the birth of their first child, named Alex.

The feather boom came, gave them prosperity, and then slumped. The Hoopers survived on general farming. William died in 1917 and Alex inherited the property, keeping a few ostriches but concentrating on growing lucerne and producing honey. In 1920 he married Idchen Arenhold, daughter of an Eastern Cape doctor. Their first son, born the following year, was named Will. It was at this time that they named their farm *Highgate* after the family home in England.

In 1937 Alex was approached by local hoteliers and the Oudtshoorn municipality to allow visits to his farm by conducted parties of tourists, especially from overseas, who came to see the Cango Caves and expressed a desire to visit an ostrich farm. The following year *Highgate* was opened as a show farm with 100 visitors in the first 12 months.

In 1940 Alex Hooper died. His son Will was only 18 years of age when he inherited *Highgate* and he had serious problems to face with the outbreak of the Second World War. The farm was closed to the public and only in 1947 was it reopened at the request of the South African Railways. There were 800 visitors that year. The subsequent development of *Highgate* into a great tourist resort was carefully managed by Will and his wife, Beryl. Today Will's son, Alex, manages the family business, farming ostriches, producing magnificent feathers, running a considerable curio industry.

Many thousands of people visit *Highgate* farm each month. The reception area is shaded by a grove of magnificent peppercorn trees planted in 1902. In their shade visitors refresh themselves and are serenaded by an excellent farm choir composed of members of the staff. There is a restaurant in the original farmhouse featuring meals of ostrich eggs and meat, as well as other delicacies and the local wine of the Little Karoo. There is a delightful area for barbecues, a cactus garden and a wonderful collection of succulents growing in a wild garden behind the homestead. There is a shop filled with interesting novelties of the ostrich industry, incubator rooms, and a museum with a collection of such odd things as the articles found in the stomachs of ostriches.

Multilingual guides escort visitors on tours of the farm, with many interesting scenes of the feather industry. An exciting ostrich race, a real 'feather derby,' is the climax of all visits. *Highgate* is open daily from 07h30 to 17h00.

THE SWARTBERGE

The range known as the *Swartberge* (black mountains) provides a 200 km long barrier between the Little and Great Karoo. It is one of the most beautiful and spectacular mountain massifs in Southern Africa. To the Bushmen the range was known as the *Kango* (water or wet mountains) from the number of streams which had their source on its slopes. The highest point of the range is the Seven Weeks Poort Mountain, 2 326 m above sea-level. The range, notwithstanding its name of Swartberge, is composed of red-coloured sedimentary sandstone, warped and twisted into many extraordinary shapes, and coloured still further by the presence of yellow lichens growing on the precipice faces. Visually this magnificent range is in many parts overwhelmingly beautiful. It glows with a rich warmth of colour, reminiscent of an active volcano which is in the process of cooling. In fact, the only way to picture some of the great gorges and river passages – notably Seven Weeks Poort – is to draw a poker across the embers of a dying fire; the passage left by the poker, glowing red and orange on either side in all manner of surprising shapes and beautiful tones, would not be more colourful than Seven Weeks Poort or the precipices of Meirings Poort.

The Swartberge have had a curiously romantic history. A typical event concerning these mountains dates from the period of the Anglo-Boer War. A band of Boer guerrillas raiding into the Little Karoo found themselves hotly pursued by British soldiers. They determined to cross the Swartberge and escape to the vast spaces of the Great Karoo where they hoped to rejoin the main body of their commando, led by General Jan Smuts.

Since the passes through the mountains were all closely guarded by the British, the raiders decided to lead their horses directly over the range. They set out to climb the great heights, the horses struggling up the cliff faces and the men sustained by the thought of reaching the summit ridge and then being able to look north into the safety of the Great Karoo.

Darkness came before they had reached the summit. Clouds enveloped the heights by the time the men finally arrived at the top. Too cold to sleep and with everything too damp to enable them to light a fire, they sat shivering until dawn. They then started to grope their way down the northern face of the mountains which was shrouded in dense mist. It was not until nearly 16h00 that they descended out of the clouds. They expected to find themselves looking down on the Great Karoo, but instead they were astounded to find beneath them a long, narrow canyon, hemmed in by precipices. On the floor of this ravine 305 m below, they could see a few primitive-looking mud houses scattered about amongst the aloes and the bush.

Thinking that some African people must have found a retreat in the eerie place, the Boers left their horses in a ravine. In a body they went down to investigate, reaching the bottom just after sunset. As they approached the nearest house, a shaggy giant of a white man, heavily bearded and dressed in goatskins like Robinson Crusoe, appeared and spoke to them in a strange, long-drawn out, outlandish type of Dutch. He introduced himself as Cordier, who lived in the house with his wife and a brood of half-wild children. He knew all about the visitors, for one of his sons had been up in the mountains that morning. Hearing the sound of men and horses, he had stalked the party in the mist, observed their numbers and then slipped down to report to his father. Cordier was the head of a small community living in the ravine. He offered the visitors a rough but kindly hospitality, feeding them goat's milk and wild honey. He had vaguely heard of the Anglo-Boer War, but none of the contestants, either British or Boer, had ever penetrated this valley of isolation in the Swartberge. For two nights the visitors remained as guests of this 'Swiss Family Robinson'. Then their host and some of his sons guided them along secret paths across the rugged mountains, until at last they looked down on the northern plains, and so made their escape across the barrier of the Swartberge. This account of how the secret valley was discovered appears in the book *Commando* by Deneys Reitz.

The history of this hill-billy community was strange. According to them, a party of *trekboers* (nomadic farmers) had been wandering along the northern slopes of the Swartberge at the beginning of the 19th century. Smelling water and sweet grazing in the hidden valley, a number of domestic animals owned by the migrant farmers stampeded during the night. The animals found their way down the gorge forced through the Swartberge by the Gamka River which flows north to south directly across the concealed valley from the Great to the Little Karoo. Following the tracks of their missing livestock, the trekboers discovered the valley. They were delighted with the perennial water and farming possibilities of its alluvial soil. It was uninhabited, although the presence of numerous paintings in caves, as well as wooden peg ladders reaching up the precipice faces to wild hives, were proof of the original presence of Bushmen.

The nomadic farmers ended their wandering forthwith and settled in what became known as Gamkas Kloof or *Die Hel* (the abyss). Eventually, sixteen small farms were occupied in the valley. The owners, shut in by the mountains and increasingly uninterested in the outside world, became self-dependent, living entirely on the produce of their farms, making their own clothes and indulging in their one luxury – a potent alcoholic beverage made from wild honey.

In 1921 the Dutch Reformed Church established a school in the valley, and the inhabitants developed a cash crop of Hanepoot grapes which they dried into raisins and conveyed by pack donkeys out of the valley to sell to the outside world, principally through the co-operative in Calitzdorp. On the proceeds they purchased clothing, sugar, coffee and a few other luxuries. In 1962 a hair-raising road which twists, rises and falls was made into the valley, thereby allowing the advent of representatives of burial societies, insurance agents, sellers of encyclopedias and politicians at election time into this once-lost valley. All of the families left the valley in recent years. It is planned that the area will become a national park.

For the tourist there are some magnificent drives through the Swartberge. One and a half kilometres before the main road from Oudtshoorn terminates at the Cango Caves, there is a turn-off to the west, signposted Prince Albert. This road leads along the southern slopes of the Swartberge through 27 km of ruggedly attractive country where the towering mountains may be viewed from many angles. After 27 km the road reaches a turn-off which leads to Kruisrivier (29 km); to a branch road to Oudtshoorn (43 km); and eventually to Calitzdorp, (58 km from the original turn-off). This road provides a fascinating circular drive, Oudtshoorn–Calitzdorp–Oudtshoorn, taking the traveller through magnificent foothill scenery and past many beautiful and curious rock formations and caves.

Meanwhile the main Prince Albert road, after the turn-off to Kruisrivier and Calitzdorp immediately starts to climb the Swartberge by means of the Swartberg Pass, without a doubt one of the most sensational passes in Africa. The road ascends steadily for 7 km, climbing magnificent mountain slopes covered in watsonias and proteas. Eventually, 1 568 m above sea-level (over 1 220 m above the level of the Little Karoo), the road crosses a saddle on the summit ridge of the range. If the southern side of the pass has been scenically exciting, then the northern side can only be classed as sensational.

The road immediately commences a most involved descent. Just below the summit ridge, in a stand of pine trees, lie the ruins of the old building originally erected to shelter convict labourers employed on the construction of the pass between 1881 and 1888 by Thomas Bain, son of the famous Andrew Geddes Bain, builder of Bain's Kloof Pass. This ruined building is reputedly haunted by the ghost of an unfortunate traveller caught in one of the snowstorms which often block the pass in winter. Just beyond the ruins of the old building, 1,5 km from the summit of the pass, the road crosses a perennial stream of crystal-clear water around which may be seen many lovely watsonias in spring.

Directly beyond the stream is a forestry station, while 1,5 km further on, a turn-off provides a rough, wild and woolly switchback-railway-type drive to Gamkas Kloof (57 km to the west). This road to the secluded valley is not to be carelessly followed but, for those prepared to drive with caution, it yields many remarkable views with a final descent into the valley that is breathtaking.

The Swartberg Pass continues to descend for 10 km with zigzags, serpentines, twists and stiff gradients carrying it down the face of a flame-coloured precipice. The road then winds out of the mountains through a canyon full of echoes, the rock strata of which are warped, arched, and daubed with splashes of vivid colour as though Nature, putting on overalls and preparing to turn painter, had tested brushes and colour effects against the rocks.

Ten kilometres from the northern entrance of the Swartberg Pass the road enters the little town of Prince Albert and then goes on to join the main N1 Cape-to-Cairo road. Prince Albert is a convenient and interesting turning-point and base for anybody exploring the Swartberge. Local architecture is attractive; fruit is superb during the summer season; and there is an atmospheric, snug hotel (see Chapter Thirteen). From Prince Albert, there is a road eastwards leading back to the Little Karoo through the Swartberge by means of another spectacular pass, Meiring's Poort, and this provides a fine round trip from Oudtshoorn.

This east road from Prince Albert branches off from the Swartberg Pass road 3 km south of the town, following a settled valley, passing several handsome farms and revealing many impressive views of the mountain range. At 47 km from Prince Albert the road joins the tarmac highway stretching south from Beaufort West. After a further 5,5 km the combined roads reach the rural centre of *Klaarstroom* (clear stream), lying in a fertile setting of lucerne fields. After 3,2 km of travel through this cultivated area, the road reaches the entrance to ...

MEIRINGS POORT

Meirings Poort is named after Petrus Johannes Meiring who owned the farm *De Rust* (the rest) situated at the southern (Little Karoo) entrance to the pass. In 1854 when the roadmaker, Andrew Geddes Bain, was trying to find a route for a road to link the Great and Little Karoo, Petrus Meiring drew his attention to the ravine penetrating the range from his farm. Bain rode through the pass and considered it to be ideal. The entire ravine had been worn through the range by escaping floodwaters which resulted from occasional downpours in the Great Karoo. The draining stream, simply known as the *Grootstroom* (great stream), had eroded for itself a reasonably level floor littered with giant boulders and overlooked by colossal precipices. Any road made through the ravine would have to cross and re-cross the stream 26 times, but the route was perfectly practical and exactly the type of pass which Bain loved; grand and majestic to behold, with brilliantly coloured sedimentary sandstone precipices, and the whole place full of odd rock shapes and echoes.

After some delay in the raising of funds, work was started on the pass in August 1856. Labour was recruited from farms on either side of the pass and, under the supervision of Thomas Bain, son of Andrew Bain, construction proceeded quickly. On 3 March 1858 Meirings Poort was opened to traffic and was considered to be such an asset to the farmers of the Great Karoo, who could now send their produce through the mountains to be shipped from Mossel Bay, that a party of 300 horsemen and 50 carts carrying ladies made an opening tour through the pass. The Civil Commissioner of Oudtshoorn, Lieutenant-Colonel A B Armstrong, opened the pass. He broke a bottle of Bass's Best Ale on a rock and named the pass after Piet Meiring, who held open house for the whole party on his farm, where feasting and dancing continued until dawn chased away the night as well as all the merry horsemen and their ladies.

Meirings Poort remains one of the most romantically lovely of all South African road passes. It is 12,9 km long from its northern to its southern entrance and is full of beautiful scenes and interesting features. Three kilometres from the northern entrance there is a pathway branching off from the road and leading to a waterfall. A further 3 km takes the road past a tablet commemorating the famous Senator C J Langenhoven and his well-beloved literary character, Herrie the elephant. The modern tarmac road has overwhelmed several of the charming corners of the pass (well remembered by seasoned travellers of the route), but the scenic splendour remains and there are many pleasant picnic sites and resting-places where the motorist can pause awhile and admire the towering cliffs with their fantastic patterns of warped and twisted rocks, numerous flowering plants and rugged piles of boulders.

It is through this splendid natural gateway that the road makes the transition from the Great to the Little Karoo. The beauty of the pass prepares the traveller for a general transformation in the landscape. Behind is the aridity of the Great Karoo with its isolated sheep farms, scarcity of water and absence of cultivation. Ahead the traveller is immediately confronted by the intensely cultivated and picturesque ostrich country of the Little Karoo. Three kilometres beyond the southern entrance to Meirings Poort lies the hamlet of De Rust.

From De Rust a road, part tarmac, part gravel, branches eastwards, leading for 73 km to the hot springs at *Toorwaterpoort* (pass of the enchanted water). This is an interesting drive and the springs are worth visiting. The water is beneficial and the setting is restful. The water, 1 200 000 *l* a day, reaches the surface at a temperature of 45°C. In former times, subterranean gases such as methane rose to the surface with the water. Escaping through various fissures, these gases used to catch fire and burn intermittently as will-o'-the-wisps. Later excavations to lead the water to the bath-house largely ended this occurrence.

There is a legend that the medicinal value of the spring was first discovered by a wandering group of Bushmen. One of their party was incapacitated and left at the spring to die. The waters, however, proved healing. The invalid rejoined the group and the spring became known as the 'enchanted water'. The railway from the Little to the Great Karoo penetrates the Swartberge through Toorwaterpoort.

The main tarmac road from De Rust continues for 34 km following the valley of the Olifants River to Oudtshoorn. On the way it passes beautiful, strangely shaped, red hills composed of Enon Conglomerates. There are ostrich farms and fertile fields, with homesteads dating from the years of the feather frenzy. The *Mons Ruber* (red mountain) wine estate lies opposite Le Roux station, while the *Doornkraal* (thorn corral) wine estate of Gerrit le Roux, famous for its superb manor-house, has a winehouse beside the road near Oudtshoorn where you may taste the products of this estate.

THE ROAD TO THE EAST

At the foot of the Outeniqua Pass, 35 km from Oudtshoorn, the main R62 road to the east branches off and leads along the northern side of the Outeniqua range. It is a fine drive down a shallow valley which seems to become increasingly fertile with every kilometre travelled. To the north lies the mountain range known as the *Kammanassie* (place of perennial water), while innumerable streams flow down from the slopes of the Outeniqua. Here, in rock shelters and caves, the Bushmen people once lived. Galleries of their art, painted on the rocks, may still be seen, including fascinating pictures of what seem to be mermaids.

After 72 km the road reaches a division. The right-hand branch (R62) continues down what is known as the Long Kloof, the second largest fruit-producing area in South Africa (after the Western Cape). The left-hand branch (R57) veers north-eastwards. It climbs over a rocky ridge and then, after 12,5 km, reaches the town of ...

UNIONDALE

Uniondale had a rather odd beginning. In 1856 the owners of each of the two portions of the farm *Rietvallei* laid out two rural townships named Hopedale and Lyon. The townships adjoined one another but the owners disagreed until the Dutch Reformed Church settled the rivalry in 1865 by building a church in the centre of the area and marking the union of the townships by naming the place *Uniondale*.

For some years Uniondale was a very quiet backwater hindered by lack of communications. It acquired municipal status on 12 February 1884. The ostrich-feather boom gave it an injection of prosperity, for feathers not only fetched high prices but could be relatively easily transported through the Swartberge range to what was then the nearest railway station, Prince Albert Road in the Great Karoo.

Wagon and cart building, the manufacture of furniture and the rearing of cattle, horses, sheep and Cape goats also flourished in and around the little town. With a rainfall of 250 mm a year and the surrounding hills looking very arid, the dale of Uniondale fortunately is still well watered by a perennial stream. A water-mill with a fine big wheel is a reminder of a local industry of former times. This mill was built in 1852 by James Stewart and remained in service for 100 years. It was restored in 1977 and is now a national monument. A second national monument is a small fort built by the British during the Anglo-Boer War. It is situated on a high vantage-point reached by a gravel road. The present population of Uniondale is 3 425.

The 9 km drive from Uniondale through Uniondale Poort to Avontuur is magnificent. The road runs through a beautiful ravine overflowing with vivid colours and extraordinary sandstone rock formations. Resembling a miniature Seven Weeks Poort. Uniondale Poort is resplendent with flowering aloes, yellow lichens and other plants. There are galleries of Bushman paintings.

The road from Uniondale to the junction of the road down the Long Kloof has been the scene of several curious reportings of a ghostly female hitch-hiker, who secures a lift, preferring (it seems) motor cyclists, and then vanishes in a manner most disconcerting to the driver!

Beyond Uniondale the R57 road rises steeply for 4,5 km. At the summit of the rise there is a left turn to Oudtshoorn (132 km away), while ahead, along the edge of the dry, arid north-eastern corner of the Little Karoo, lies the Swartberge range. The Swartberge have lost much of their height by the time they reach their eastern extremity here, but the range still presents a formidable barrier to the road seeking a way of escape from the Little Karoo. The road leads north-eastwards towards the mountains. Forty kilometres from Uniondale there is a turn-off to Oudtshoorn and to the hot springs at Toorwaterpoort. Immediately beyond this point the road enters what is known as *Gwarriepoort*, a dry shallow valley full of flowering aloes and the *Euclea undulata* (gwarri) trees which give the pass its name. The pass provides a natural passage around the eastern end of the Swartberge, out of the Little Karoo and on to the higher plateau of the Great Karoo. After 17 km of steady climbing, the road emerges from the pass, enters the Great Karoo and, 63 km from Uniondale, reaches the town of Willowmore (see Chapter Twenty).

THE ROAD TO THE WEST

From Oudtshoorn a fine tarmac road (R62) leads westwards for 39 km to the town of Calitzdorp. This is an interesting drive passing places such as the *Greylands* ostrich farm (13 km from Oudtshoorn), with its fine nature reserve and feather-palace homestead. The tourist keen to explore the basin between the mountains will find it interesting to turn off this main road (10 km from Oudtshoorn) on to the old road which accompanies the branch railway line leading to Calitzdorp. Along this route lie many large ostrich farms where there is always activity in the handling of birds with their nests and chickens, and the growing, reaping and dispatch of crops. At 38 km from Oudtshoorn along this concrete-surfaced road, a gravel turn-off leads to the hot-water springs of the Calitzdorp mineral baths, and 16 km further on lies the town of ...

CALITZDORP

This sunny and colourful little town is situated against the western end of the basin through which the Olifants River flows before joining the Gamka. In former times the area was richly populated with game, especially buffalo, and many of the local farms retain the memory of these animals in their names. *Buffelsvlei*, the farm on which the town of Calitzdorp stands, was one of these resorts of buffalo. It was granted in September 1821 to J J and M C Calitz. In those days this area was remote with no proper roads. Ox-wagons took five weeks to journey to Cape Town and back. Hunting and ranching were the local activities, with cattle being driven to market along rough trails across the mountains.

By 1845 the local farmers had prospered sufficiently to make them think of a community centre. In that year, *Buffelsvlei* was selected as a church farm, with services held under a large orange tree. In 1857 a proper church was erected and around this building the town slowly grew. On 22 April 1913 Calitzdorp became a municipality. When the branch railway from Oudtshoorn reached the town on 24 November 1924, its development into a prosperous agricultural centre became inevitable. Today it has a population of 3 657.

The Calitzdorp Co-operative Cellars, situated on a handsome viewsite on the old Oudtshoorn road, sell wine and grape juice. Dried and fresh fruit of renowned quality is also sold there and in roadside shops. There are two wine estates on the outskirts of the town *Boplaas* (upper farm) and *Die Krans* (the cliff) owned by Carel (Boets) Nel. Their Muscadel-type wines are worth tasting. Their port-type wines are of such a standard that Calitzdorp is known as the 'port' capital of South Africa. Wine is sold on both estates and at the co-operative during normal business hours.

Boplaas is well-known for its brandy, distilled in an old Santhagens pot still. The estate was the first to make brandy under the new legislation and has exported brandy since 1880. Colombard grapes are used exclusively to make this brandy.

Seventeen kilometres from the town lies the Calitzdorp Spa. A mineral-rich hot spring, with a temperature of 50°C at its source, reaches the surface on the banks of the Olifants River just before it flows into a ridge of high hills and, at the bottom of the gorge joins the Gamka to form the Gourits River. A resort has been developed around the springs with swimming-pools (35°C), private baths, saunas, a restaurant, caravan park and several chalets and huts. The chalets are built on a high viewsite with a grand panorama of the plain stretching to the Swartberge range.

From Calitzdorp a highly attractive road (gravel) leads eastwards for 53 km to Vanwyksdorp. This road climbs the *Roodeberg* (red mountain) Pass. On the summit, 24 km from Calitzdorp, there is a pleasant picnic spot and an old 'luck heap' where travellers deposited stones in order to bring them good fortune and a safe journey. Such luck heaps are common in Zululand and Natal where they are known as *Vivane*.

The original main road from Calitzdorp to the west found a way through Caledon Kloof. This road is now disused but provides a superb trail for hikers. The tarmac road (R62) from Calitzdorp proceeds north-westwards and, after 8 km, crosses the Gamka River, flowing beneath towering cliffs. Three kilometres further the spectacularly located *Huisrivier* (house river) Pass begins and carries the road 665 m above sea-level. Some splendid scenery may be viewed.

Twenty-seven kilometres from Calitzdorp, a gravel turn-off leads northwards through the Swartberge to the Great Karoo by means of what must surely be one of the loveliest and most remarkable mountain passes in the world, the famous ...

SEVEN WEEKS POORT

The origin of the name *Seven Weeks Poort* is elusive. It is said that it was originally named *Zerwickspoort* after the Reverend Louis Zerwick, a missionary at the Zoar mission station which stands close to the turn-off to Seven Weeks Poort. This mission was established in 1816, long before the road was made, and was then a real oasis in the wilderness. *'Like the garden of the Lord, as thou comest into Zoar'* (Gen.14:2–8). Petrus Joubert, grandfather of the famous General Piet Joubert of the Transvaal, founded the station for the South African Missionary Society. After seventeen years the Berlin Missionary Society took over, building a church and a school next to Zoar at *Amalienstein* (named after Amalie von Stein, a great benefactress of missions), and growing superb fruit which, in dried form, won first prize at the Crystal Palace Exhibition in London in 1851. During the First World War, the Dutch Reformed Church took over the station. Amalienstein flourished on water from the stream which flowed out of Seven Weeks Poort; and it was during this period, it is said, that the name originated.

Another explanation of the name is that wagons smuggling Cape brandy to the interior avoided the revenue officers by travelling to the Cape through this pass, with the return journey from Beaufort West to Cape Town taking seven weeks. Still other stories claim that commandos flushing out rustlers took seven weeks to clear the pass, while it is also said that the name comes from the everlasting flowers (known as Seven Weeks) which flourish there or from the East that it took seven weeks for the first road to be surveyed through the pass.

Even if the name is puzzling, there is not the slightest doubt about the supreme beauty of the pass. Prometheus himself must have passed this way through the Swartberge and split the range asunder with a breath of fire. Glowing coals of red, orange and yellow seem to form the towering cliffs, while their summits, topped with dark-green growth, are like blackened, charred embers. What prehistoric man must have thought as he first found his way through this fantastic pass would be interesting to know. He must have found it a terrifying experience.

The ruins of the toll-house still stand, and attached to the place is a story that the ghost of the toll-keeper may still occasionally be seen, especially on stormy nights. He appears in the road, swinging his lamp. When any vehicle stops he disappears with a chuckle.

The gravel turn-off from the main tarmac road leads through the pass for 21 km. On the northern side it joins a gravel road coming from the Great Karoo and Laingsburg. This road continues eastwards through *Bosluiskloof* (cleft of ticks) to the Gamka Dam. Seven Weeks Poort is dominated by the 2 328 m high Seven Weeks Poort Mountain, the highest peak of the Swartberge range.

There are picnic sites along the pass, while 13 km from the entrance is the little farm, *Aristata*, situated in very handsome surroundings. There is a superb swimming-pool on this farm and beautifully clean mountain water. Once there was an inn there. The farm is named after the rare *Protea aristata* which grows in the pass and blooms at Christmas time.

The main tarmac road from Calitzdorp, after passing the turn-off to Seven Weeks Poort (27 km from Calitzdorp), crosses the Zoar River 3 km further on. There is a turn-off to the mission of Zoar and, 9 km from Seven Weeks Poort, a turn-off to Hoeko. This tarmac turn-off leads up a fertile valley into the foothills of the Swartberge. After 2 km the road passes the birthplace of the writer, C J Langenhoven, and then continues along the foothills. The tarmac ends after 7 km, but a good gravel road eventually proceeds as far as Ladismith and provides an interesting drive. Beyond the turn-off to Hoeko the main tarmac road from Calitzdorp continues for 16 km. At 48 km from Calitzdorp, the road reaches the town of ...

LADISMITH

Handsomely set against the mountains, Ladismith is overlooked to the north by some of the finest peaks of the Swartberge, two of which are particularly notable. Directly above the town soars the 2 126 m high *Toringberg* (towering mountain), so named because of its steep cliffs and its sharp peak (as seen from the east).

Immediately to the west of the Toringberg stands one of the most famous mountains in Southern Africa, the *Toorkop* (enchanted peak) 2 197 m high and an extraordinary landmark from whichever angle it is viewed. A folk tale relates that a witch, while trying to cross the range one night was thwarted near the summit. In her rage she split with her wand the great rock dome before her. Today it remains divided into the eastern and western pinnacles, so oddly situated in relation to each other that the mountain takes on a different appearance in varying lights and from each point of the compass. The northern aspect, observed from the Cape-to-Cairo road between Beaufort West and Laingsburg, is particularly strange; the peak looks like a recumbent face which has a bulbous nose, protruding chin and a cigarette stump between the lips.

Climbing the two halves of the dome of the enchanted mountain is an outstanding feat. The east side rates as an E-climb. The west side is even more difficult. It is about 2 m higher than the east side and rates as an F-climb with some nasty moments of exposure, which makes climbers think that the mountain is not too friendly towards them. There is an absence of comforting hand grips. The final 122 m of the west side is a severe and exposed test for any climber. The west side was first climbed in 1885 by a 19-year-old local farmer from the north side of the Swartberge, Gustaf Nefdt, while the rest of his party remained at the base of the dome. To prove his success he left one of his socks under some rocks on the summit. Fourteen days later he repeated the climb and lowered a rope to help up two friends. He retrieved his sock. The next ascent was not accomplished until 1907 when the celebrated climber G F Travers-Jackson was successful. The mountain remains one of the major climbs in Southern Africa.

The area to the south of this odd mountain was first settled by Europeans in the middle of the 18th century. As in other parts of the Little Karoo, strong men wandered across the southern mountains, hunting, grazing cattle and hoping to escape the grasping hand of the tax-gatherer. Cogmans Kloof was the entrance to the Little Karoo which most of these pioneers used. Riding hard on their heels on his horse Bob, came the indefatigable Pastor Robertson, visiting the scattered pioneers, holding services in wagon houses and under trees.

Ladismith started in this way as a permanent place for worship. In 1851 a portion of the farm *Elands Vallei* was bought for £1 000 from Balthazar Kloppers. In 1852 this was laid out by

William Hopley into 138 erven and named in honour of Lady Juana Smith, wife of the Governor, Sir Harry Smith. The spelling was *Ladismith* to differentiate it from Ladysmith in Natal. At first administered by the Dutch Reformed Church, the town received local government in 1862 and became a municipality in 1903. The ostrich feather craze converted Ladismith into a boom town, with 50 000 birds feeding on the lucerne fields around the town. The farmers paid fortunes for breeding pairs, while their wives enjoyed the profits by going on mad spending sprees.

The feather crash in 1914 brought the district to bankruptcy. Economic relief and rehabilitation only came in 1925 when the branch railway was opened connecting Ladismith to the main line at Touws River. This link provided an outlet to markets. Nowadays the district produces excellent fresh and dried fruit, wine, lucerne and dairy products, including some notably good cheese, especially Gouda and Cheddar, which is sold in the local co-operative cheese factory and widely distributed under the brand name of Towerkop. The local home-made milk tarts are delicious. In 1981 a tremendous flood severely damaged the railway line. It has been replaced by road transport.

Ostriches also still flourish but the bitter memory of the crash keeps men sober when they think of those remarkable birds. Ladismith is now a level-headed and pleasant little town of 4 733 inhabitants. Beautiful mountain scenery and fertile farmlands are its proudest assets. A first-class nature reserve is being created by the municipality on 6 000 ha of high, hill country south of the town. There is a rich flora and an interesting population of fauna.

High on the slopes of the overlooking Elandsberg a little light may be seen continuously shining, although not too visible in daylight. This light originated on 31 May 1963 when a 37-year-old man, Stanley de Wit, a Ladismith welder and a great walker, was wandering along the slopes. It was a hot day, and he was delighted to find a stream of cool, clear water. He decided to mark the site for the benefit of others. He erected there a bicycle dynamo, driven by a small water-wheel, to supply power for a 6-volt bulb. This little electrical installation was later changed to a 12-volt motor-car alternator feeding a 12-volt bulb. To service the light, he climbed to the site 268 times up to April 1992, when the author of this book first met him. The light only failed on two occasions when drought conditions caused the water flow to dwindle.

From Ladismith the tarmac R62 road leads south-westwards for 79 km across a rugged and interesting semi-arid landscape. Rivers such as the *Groot* (great) and the *Touws* (pass) meander through this sandstone wilderness on their way to join the Gourits. In spring, mesembryanthemums (*vygies*) provide fantastic patches of concentrated colour. At 53 km from Ladismith a gravel turn-off stretches for 3,5 km to the hot springs of Warmwaterberg. These springs, surfacing on the farm *Uitvlugt,* have a temperature at source of 40°C. They are rich in iron and slightly radioactive. A small resort has been created there where sufferers from skin diseases and rheumatism find relief and relaxation. It is a pleasantly old-world place.

From the turn-off to Warmwaterberg the tarmac road gradually approaches the southern range of mountains (which in this part of the Little Karoo is called the Langeberge) and directly against these heights, 79 km from Ladismith, reaches the little agricultural centre of ...

BARRYDALE

Barrydale lies at the northern entrance to the Tradouw Pass which leads through the Langeberge to Swellendam. The Barry merchant family of Swellendam laid out this township in 1882 as a church and trading centre on a portion of the farm *Tradouw Hoek*. In 1921 Barrydale became a municipality and today it is the quiet centre of a productive fruit-farming area, renowned for the quality and sweetness of its crops, and the vivid colour of the mesembryanthemums growing on the mountain slopes.

From Barrydale the tarmac road continues westwards along the foothills of the Langeberge. Immediately beyond the town there is a tarmac turn-off leading through the Tradouw Pass to Zuurbraak and the R2 coastal road. The road to the west continues across a rugged countryside, the valleys filled to the brim with fertility. Grapes, apples, quinces and other deciduous fruits flourish there, as well as sheep and cattle. The road proceeds over the Op de Tradouw Pass (27 km from Barrydale) and past the turn-off to the Poortjies Kloof Dam (35 km from Barrydale). At 63 km from Barrydale the road reaches the mineral baths and town of ...

MONTAGU

Lying at the historic entrance to the Little Karoo – the scenically splendid Cogmans Kloof – Montagu grew as a staging post for travellers coming through the kloof. An added attraction was the presence of a hot, radioactive spring (19 mach units) which, bubbling up at a temperature of 43°C has been a boon to many visitors. There is another radioactive hot spring at Baden, 13 km from Montagu. In 1981 a tremendous flood caused havoc to the main mineral spa area, washing away the caravan park and causing the original Baths Hotel to close down. The area around the mineral springs has since been restored to include a new hotel and over 100 holiday chalets.

Montagu was founded in January 1851 when the first erven were sold in the town which had been laid out on the farm *Uitvlugt* (originally occupied in 1841 by P Swanepoel). The town was named after the energetic and popular Colonial Secretary, Sir John Montagu who, during his ten years of office at the Cape (1843 to 1853), was the originator of the first great road-building programme in Southern Africa. Montagu became a municipality in 1895 and a magistracy two years later. It now has a population of 8 521.

The town is the centre for wine and fruit producing activities. There are four wine cellars in the area. Wines are sold during normal business hours. The rugged area north of Montagu, known from the *Fockea edulis* plants growing there as the *Koo*, is famous for its export-quality apples, pears, apricots and peaches. A tarmac road leads for 78 km through this region in a winding, climbing route over Burger Pass and the Roodehoogte to join the N1 Cape-to-Cairo road at the summit of the Hex River Pass. At 29 km along this road Mr D P Burger of the farm *Protea* has developed a unique tourist attraction through conveying passengers by tractor and canopied trailer on a three-hour trip to a viewsite on top of the Langeberge, overlooking the town of Robertson on the southern side.

Montagu is graced with several Cape-Dutch and Georgian style buildings, 23 of which have been declared national monuments. There is a museum open weekdays from 09h00 to 13h00 and 14h00 to 17h00. Saturdays and Sundays from 10h30 to 12h30. It is housed in a former mission church built in 1907.

The Montagu Country Inn, built in 1875, still has its hospitable doors open for travellers and visitors to the Little Karoo. Recently renovated to three-star standard its reputation for country excellence of food and comfort persists into modern times.

Fine scenery and wild flowers (particularly mesembryanthemums) have made Montagu a popular resort, especially during winter when the climate is mild and swimming in the hot springs and exploring the mountains provide pleasant occupations.

There are several excellent walks up the various valleys and two hiking trails, Blou Punt (15,6 km) and Cogmans Kloof (12 km), served by well-appointed stone overnight cabins. There is also a nature garden boasting a large selection of indigenous flowers and a short walking trail to the top of Bessiekop. 'Lovers' Walk' between Montagu and the hot springs leads through a magnificent ravine. It is a pleasant, easy stroll, especially at sunset when the birds are tucking themselves into bed with a last twitter as some hen nags her mate for coming in a trifle late. Baboons and dassies call from their retreats on the face of the cliffs, while klipspringers, black eagles and large mountain tortoises are often encountered. The rocks are rich with colours of red, purple and orange. The warm water from the springs meanders down the floor of the ravine, gradually cooling as it goes. Trees shade the pathway and the twists and curves tempt the walker on to explore further, with new scenes and experiences around each corner. Tea and cakes are served to visitors by local ladies between the end of June and the end of October.

COGMANS KLOOF

From Montagu the main tarmac R62 road linking the Little Karoo to the valley of the Breede River continues for 6 km and then joins the main Worcester–Swellendam road, R60. During these 6 km the traveller is rewarded with a wonderful concentration of scenery. *Cogmans Kloof* takes its name from an African pastoral tribe which once lived there. The road was built by the famous engineer, Thomas Bain, and opened on 28 February 1877.

In the middle of the pass is Keurkloof, a ravine which supplies drinking-water to the town of Ashton. A track wanders up this gorge for 6 km while, at the entrance beneath wattle trees, there is a fine shady camping ground with barbecue sites and toilets.

There is a short but picturesque tunnel, 15 m long, running under a rocky ridge known as *Kalkoenkrans* (turkey crag). Perched on the ridge above the tunnel is a small fort built by the British during the Anglo-Boer War. It served as a guard point blocking the way to the Western Cape from the Little Karoo. The fort was garrisoned by a company of Gordon Highlanders who had their camp on the site of the original road construction camp below Kalkoenkrans. Lt Col Sidney of the Royal Field Artillery selected the site of the fort and it was known after him. He was the Commandant of Montagu under martial law. The view from this fort is superb, the overlooking mountains being notable for their extraordinary folded sandstone formations, their vivid colours, the lichen growing on the rocks, and the aloes flowering during winter.

Chapter Seventeen

CAPE TOWN TO MOSSEL BAY

From Cape Town the main coastal road to the east (N2) leading all the scenic way along the seaboard to the Eastern Cape, Kwazulu-Natal and Mpumulanga, is one of the oldest and most romantic highways in Southern Africa. Herds of game animals wandering along the coast, prehistoric hunter-gatherers, the early pastoralists with their herds of sheep and cattle, migrating tribes moving down from the north into the cul-de-sac of the south; all combined to blaze this ancient route. When Europeans arrived in the Cape and explored the coastal area, they followed old trails, converting footpaths into wagon trails and wagon trails into the highways of today.

The N2 highway along the east coast of Southern Africa is known, when it leaves Cape Town, as Settlers Way. It starts on Rhodes Drive just beyond Groote Schuur Hospital, 5 km from the centre of Cape Town. It leads out on to the Cape Flats, past numerous traffic interchanges to suburbs, housing estates and satellite townships such as *Pinelands* (the first garden city to be established in South Africa, laid out in 1919 on a section of the *Uitvlugt* forest reserve. A municipality in its own right from May 1948); *Athlone* (the Earl of Athlone was Governor-general of the Union of South Africa from 1924–1930); *Langa* (the sun): *Nyanga* (the moon); *Gugulethu* (our hope); *Manenberg* (named after Henricus Maanenberg, a Netherlands missionary); *Epping* (home of the municipal market); *Bonteheuwel* (dappled slopes); and, after 16 km, Cape Town International Airport.

The road, a finely engineered dual carriageway, leaves the built-up confines of Cape Town, with Table Mountain receding into the blue directly behind it. With the influx of people from country areas in search of work, squatter camps have spread further and further out along the N2. However, within what were previously known as the 'black' townships, a vibrant cultural life has developed, especially in the arts and music, and a number of companies now offer township tours.

At 28 km from Cape Town the road passes the military training depot of the South African Cape Corps, the nuclear accelerator facility of the Council for Scientific and Industrial Research and then, at 31 km from Cape Town, an intersection with turn-offs to Stellenbosch and to the False Bay coast at Swartklip and thence for 21 km to Muizenberg. From this point the highway veers eastwards, passing a turn-off to the housing estates at Macassar, to Firgrove and to the Methodist mission of *Raithby*. Beyond this turn-off the concrete road passes the extensive grounds occupied by the explosives and fertiliser factories of African Explosives and Chemical Industries. At 46 km from Cape Town, the road reaches a traffic interchange, with branches leading south to Strand and the Coast of Flowers (see Chapter Eleven) and, for 2 km, to the town of ...

SOMERSET WEST

Lying in a superb mountain environment, the commercial centre of Somerset West – one long street – is not particularly distinguished by architectural beauty. However, the residential area is exceedingly pleasant. Fine gardens and many beautiful homes are owned by retired as well as business people who find the attractions of the area ample compensation for spending a significant proportion of their lives commuting to Cape Town by train or road. The population is 29 782.

The best part of Somerset West may be seen by following the road to the Helderberg Nature Reserve which turns off from the main road at the top of the commercial area. This road leads for 5 km through the residential area of the town, passing the entrance to the famous Cape Dutch homestead of *Vergelegen* and ending at the gateway to the magnificent estate of *Loursford* with its manor-house of recent but handsome style and construction.

The Helderberg Nature Reserve is reached by a turn-off to the left, 3 km from the start of this branch road. The reserve is situated on the south-eastern slopes of the 1 138 m high Helderberg, and its 245 ha area extends well up to the rock faces of this impressive mountain. The reserve, proclaimed on 23 September 1960, is intended as a permanent sanctuary for the indigenous flora and fauna of the Hottentots Holland area. In 1988 it received the Sasol award for the best bird sanctuary in a nature reserve. Skilfully developed, with pleasant paths, it is one of the show-pieces of the Western Cape. The reserve is open daily from 07h15 to 18h00. Picnic places are situated in a grove of oaks. Light lunches and teas can be enjoyed at the kiosk.

From the Helderberg Nature Reserve a path leads up to the highest point on the mountain, the Helderberg Dome. This is a strenuous but very worthwhile walk. Even before one reaches the actual summit, the views from the lower reaches of the path magnificently reveal the whole area of the Hottentots Holland. Permission to climb the Helderberg from within the nature reserve must be obtained from the ranger in charge.

The *Helderberg* (clear mountain) is so named because it is seldom obscured by cloud or mist. It constitutes the northern arm of the great amphitheatre of the Hottentots Holland range and, as with all mountains which project as a spur, the view from the summit is panoramic, revealing in breathtaking detail a countryside not only handsome, but filled with romantic human associations.

In 1657 the first Europeans – three cattle traders from Cape Town – made their way into this area and found living there about 500 members of the small Chainoukwa clan. The prosperity of these people and their proud claim that they were living in the choicest part of the entire world, in addition to the visual beauty of the area, induced the Europeans to improvise the rather quaint name of the *Hottentots Holland.*

Fifteen years later the Chainoukwa parted with their cherished homeland. For an assortment of trade goods and scraps, they sold the area to two representatives of the Dutch East India Company, and the wild flowers and streams of their 'Holland' knew their people no more. The new owners only established a cattle post and outstation, but the desirable qualities of this fair countryside were too self-evident not to arouse the cupidity of every visitor to the Hottentots Holland. Among these visitors was the Governor, Willem Adriaan van der Stel, son of the revered Simon van der Stel. The story of how he lost his heart and reason to the fair charms of this area provides a lugubrious chapter in the records of the Cape.

It was contrary to the rules of the Dutch East India Company for its officials to own ground, but there were ways of evading such regulations. The choicest farmlands in the Hottentots Holland were soon in the possession of the Van der Stel family. *Parelvallei* (pearl valley) was granted to the Governor's brother, Frans, on 11 March 1699, while the superb stretch of country which Willem van der Stel named *Vergelegen* (far away) was granted to the Governor himself by a visiting dignitary on 1 February 1700.

Vergelegen became an obsession with Van der Stel. He enlarged his holdings by the expedient of granting adjoining land to subordinate officials and then immediately buying it back. Along the valley of the stream known as the *Lourens* after an individual unfortunate enough to have been drowned in it, Van der Stel developed one of the most famous South African farms. A magnificent homestead formed the centre for a whole cluster of industries: workshop, water-mill, tannery, winery, granary, groves of fruit trees, corn lands, and a vineyard of over half a million vines.

Since the Governor was so preoccupied with the delights of agriculture, it was inevitable that his subordinates would follow suit. In South Africa the most unexpected people frequently have a tendency to turn farmer at the slightest opportunity, often with unfortunate results to their farms – but that is by the way. In Willem van der Stel's time, senior civil servants were more engrossed in agriculture than in affairs of State. It is reputed that even the Company-appointed clergyman of the Cape showed an inclination to postpone Sundays if chickens were hatching on his farm. As for the Governor, he was more often on *Vergelegen* than at his post in the Castle.

Inevitably, of course, trouble ensued. Reports started to trickle through to the Company in Holland; officials were said to be using their position to secure markets for their own produce; the Company's slaves and materials were being used on private farms, plus a whole series of detailed complaints and accusations.

Looking down on the tranquil fields of *Vergelegen* today, it is difficult to imagine the storm that raged over the question of the farm's possession. Van der Stel was not the kind of man to take accusations with a smile. Not only was his position as governor at stake but also his ownership of these fertile lands. He tried to use force to silence his critics. The famous Adam Tas, leader of the agitation against the Governor, was imprisoned while others were summarily arrested and deported to Holland and Java.

The end was unavoidable. Van der Stel had simply allowed the charms of *Vergelegen* to run to his head. With his senior officials he was recalled to Holland in April 1707, while his brother Frans was ordered to take himself off to some territory outside the Company's possessions. *Vergelegen* was repossessed by the Company. The dwelling-house, considered too ostentatious for any farmer, was ordered to be demolished. The 526 ha of ground was divided into four separate farms and sold by auction – the section on which the condemned homestead stood, alone retaining the name *Vergelegen.*

The end of the dreams of Van der Stel lingers as a melancholy memory in the fair land of the Hottentots Holland. Down the years many other settlers came to the area and many beautiful farms were granted. None of them, however, has quite the atmosphere of Van der Stel's old farm with its intangible mood of lost hopes and forgotten jealousies.

Upon viewing the interlinking farmlands today, it is easy to imagine the dazzling white homesteads and pleasant to think of the bustle and industry which resulted when their first owners took possession of the virgin land. Examples of these farms are *Laaste Gift,* so named because it was the last grant of Governor Louis van Assenburgh before his death in 1711; *Lourensford,* one of the divisions of *Vergelegen,* which is named after the ford leading over the Lourens River to the original water-mill; *Rome,* with its seven hills which suggested the name; *Morgenster* (morning star) with its superb farmhouse; *Land-en-Zee-Zicht* (land and sea view), whose unique view inspired the name; *Brinksburg, Erinvale, Republiek* and *Weltevreden.* All these and many others provided snug livelihoods for the people – the Munniks, Malans, Morkels, Moolmans, Hendriks, Brinks and Theunissens – who made up the community of this pleasant land during the course of the last century.

It was this community which eventually founded the village of Somerset West in a way typical of many South African centres. In 1817 the farmers of the district decided to establish a church of their own to avoid the inconvenience of having to travel to Stellenbosch. They combined to buy land which they called the Pastorie Estate and applied for permission to establish a township. By 1820 the church was ready, with building plots and wide roads radiating from it in a carefully laid-out plan calculated to place the church at the centre of the future town. On 13 February 1820 Lord Charles Somerset had the pleasure of granting permission for this centre to bear his name. The church is now an historical monument.

The mountains which overlook this interesting area are serenely beautiful. Attached to the Helderberg in a succession of summits are Guardian Peak (*Haelkop* or hail peak); *Pic sans Nom;* (peak without name); New Year Peak; The Triplets; Sneeukop (at 1 590 m the highest point); Landdroskop; Klein Vallei; Valleiberg; Langkloofberg; Moordenaarskop; and the curious Sugar Loaf. After this, the range loses height to the level of Sir Lowry's Pass. Attached to each of these mountains is a tale. The modern climber finds traces of many half-overgrown paths wandering through the valleys and along the ridges, blazed there not only by the migrating herds of game, but by the first men – renegades, some of them, flower pickers in more recent times – or those odd souls one occasionally encounters who lead a hermit's life in the solitude of the heights.

Robbers and bandits also blazed these trails. The sinister name of *Moordenaarskop* (murderer's summit) serves as a reminder of a tragedy which occurred around the end of the 18th century. It was then, it is said, that travellers crossing the mountains were frequently pillaged by robber gangs hiding in the mountain valleys. To end the misdeeds of these gangs, the government called upon a commando of Stellenbosch and Swellendam burghers. Led by four field-cornets, the commando hunted for the robbers and found them at bay in an inaccessible ravine. Thereupon a young burgher, Barend Saayman by name, together with another, volunteered to be lowered by ropes to the place where the robbers were hiding. His offer was accepted but the result was tragic. Barend Saayman was killed by the fugitives while his companion barely escaped with his life. Only later were the robbers captured or shot.

Upon learning what had happened, the Directors of the Dutch East India Company ordered the Governor of the Cape to grant to the widow and children of the man who had sacrificed his life, a farm which had to be named *Barend Saayman's Eredood* (Barend Saayman's honourable death). To each of the four field-cornets a suitably inscribed silver jug was presented. The farm awarded to Barend Saayman's widow, situated in the Riversdale district (its name now prosaically changed to *Surrey*), subsequently passed into hands other than those of the descendants of Barend Saayman. In recent times a gentleman in Stellenbosch, Mr Beyers, had in his possession one of the silver jugs.

Somerset West has a busy, modern commercial centre. As it leaves the shopping area the main street crosses the Lourens River, with the original stone bridge preserved at the side of the modern structure. The road continues past many fine estates eventually to reach the village of Sir Lowry's Pass and the foot of the road pass over the Hottentots Holland Mountains.

SIR LOWRY'S PASS

Migrating herds of game blazed the first way over the Hottentots Holland Mountains, the range which provided so formidable a barrier between the areas of the Western and the Southern Cape. Prehistoric hunter-gatherer and pastoral people followed the trail of the animals and gave the pass its original name of *Gantouw* (pass of the elands).

The old pass followed a stiff route directly up the mountain wall with no twists or zigzags to ease the gradient. European pioneers used the same track and it became a most laborious wagon route. At a point 4,3 km from the start of the modern pass the tarmac road crosses the route of the old trail. There is still a little-used gate where the trail crosses the railway line above the modern road. This wagon trail goes directly up a small ravine, today followed by the Eskom power lines, and then over the summit. It is a worthwhile scramble to follow this old trail.

The scars of the wagon wheels worn deep into the rocks may be clearly seen. It is easy to imagine the shouting, cajoling, cursing, whip-crashing, grunting, rumbling and groaning as the vehicles made their tedious way up the pass. On the summit, amid a natural garden of wild flowers, stands the ruin of a small fort with two cannon lying at ease beside it. These weapons were mounted there in 1734 and used as signal guns summoning farmers in the *Overberg* (referring to the area east of the mountains) to Cape Town in times of trouble, or inviting them to bring provisions for sale when shipping arrived in port.

As settlement increased east of the mountains, so transport pressure on this old route became a problem. A great clamour arose for the making of a new and properly graded pass. No money, however, was allocated in those days for public roads.

Lieutenant-General Sir Galbraith Lowry Cole, an Irishman who had served under the Duke of Wellington in the Peninsula War, was Governor of the Cape at the time. He took a chance and authorised construction. His superiors in London promptly accused him of wantonly using official funds. The Governor almost ended by paying the bill himself. Public support forced the Secretary of State eventually to sanction construction. There was rejoicing in the Cape at what was in fact an epoch-making decision.

Planning began on the new pass, the first substantial road making in Southern Africa done by the State. The Surveyor-General in the Cape, Major C C Michell, advised against simply trying to patch up the original pass. He advocated a new route with easier gradients. The cost would be about £7 000, but the road would be usable for all vehicles. Work commenced on 14 January 1829. The new pass was opened on 6 July 1830 by Mr D J van Ryneveld, the Civil Commissioner of Stellenbosch. Accompanied by Major Michell and other officials, he drove up the pass in a cart drawn by only two horses. Two royal salutes were fired from small cannon, one at the top and the other at the bottom of the pass named in honour of the Governor. After that, four heavily laden ox-wagons descended without brake blocks.

The new pass (substantially followed by the modern tarmac highway) reached the summit in a setting of oddly shaped rocks. From the summit there is a superb panoramic view of the Cape Peninsula, False Bay, the Hottentots Holland and Cape Flats. As one travels up the old pass, this grand view fades away like a vignette as the rocky sides of the ravine narrow and close. The new pass has the contrary effect of opening up the view as the road reaches the summit and few travellers can resist pausing to admire the scene. At sunset it is enchanting.

The summit is 452,6 m above the level of the great curve of False Bay and it is reached 6 km from the bottom of the pass (57 km from Cape Town). Immediately over the summit there is an entrance gate to the Steenbras reservoir (see Chapter Eleven). The first 23 km long stage of the

Hottentots Holland Hiking Trail also starts at the summit. This is a magnificent walk through possibly the finest wild flower area on Earth, eventually ending in the Jonkershoek valley above Stellenbosch.

Beyond the summit of the pass lies a new world. When the loquacious Lady Anne Barnard travelled over the pass in 1798, she described the view ahead as being that of *'the new Canaan opened to my eye, hillock upon hillock, mountain behind mountain, as far as the eye could reach'*. The area actually consists of a high-lying bowl drained by the river known as the *Palmiet* after the palm rushes which grow there. Set in a ring of mountains, the height and situation of the area combine to give it a special quality. The air is fresh and a crispness in winter is ideal for keeping fruit trees healthily dormant for months of rest. A coolness in summer and dew from the sea breezes, combined with 1 200 mm of winter rainfall a year absorbed by well-drained soil, make the area a heaven for flowers, trees and the agricultural industry of man.

From the summit of Sir Lowry's Pass, the N2 descends easily into the basin of the Palmiet with scenes on all sides of afforestation, water conservation and intense activity in the growing of fruit, particularly apples, pears, peaches and plums. After 8 km a tarmac turn-off leads for 3 km to the town of ...

GRABOUW

This town is the commercial centre for what is the largest single export fruit producing area in Southern Africa (36 per cent of the export total). The town was created on the farm *Grietjiesgat*, acquired on 22 November 1856 by Wilhelm Langschmidt, who named the place after Grabouw, the village of his birth in Germany. The farm was situated at the ford across the Palmiet River where a store had already been opened in 1832 by William Venables. Langschmidt took over the store. This was the beginning of a town which the new owner apparently resolved to populate himself, for he was the father of 23 children, including 3 sets of twins. The population has since risen to 15 993.

Grabouw is today a rather unbeautiful town in a lovely setting of green trees, farms and mountains. Instead of allowing the place to remain a pleasant habitation, a forest town, the civic planners have been misguided by traffic authorities into thinking that motor vehicles are more important than people and trees. All roadside trees have been cut down. Grabouw is a town of streets, pavements, shops and garages. It became a municipality in 1956. Perhaps one day the streets will be planted with apple trees and an annual apple festival held at blossom or harvest time.

Rather to the mortification of Grabouw, the district of which it is the centre is better known by the name of Elgin. The reason for this is that in 1902, when the railway known as the Caledon Extension was built over Sir Lowry's Pass, it passed about 1,5 km from Grabouw to a station named Elgin situated on the farm *Glen Elgin* of the Molteno brothers. This station was intended as the dispatch point for the produce of the district, eventually becoming internationally known as the place in South Africa *'where the apples come from'*. The name *Elgin* (with the 'g' pronounced as in 'get') originated in Scotland. The original place seems to have had nostalgic memories for several expatriates, for the name has been copied in Canada and Australia, and occurs seven times in the United States.

THE APPLES OF ELGIN

When the railway line linking Cape Town to Elgin and thence to Caledon was opened, the principal products loaded on to the trains were wheat, oats and everlasting flowers which were exported in considerable quantities, mainly to Germany where they were used in the making of wreaths. Fruit was grown in the area but not on any substantial scale.

One of the farmers of the Palmiet River basin was a remarkable individual, Dr Antonie Viljoen of *Oak Valley*. A medical man born in Caledon in 1858, he had studied medicine at Edinburgh University, practised in the Transvaal, returned to the Cape, and in 1899 purchased the portion of *Palmietrivier* farm which he named *Oak Valley*. He returned to the Transvaal to serve in the Boer forces during the Anglo-Boer War. He was captured by the British and was returned to his farm in the Cape on parole, after agreeing to pay the salaries of the two men who guarded him – a unique way of being prisoner-of-war!

Dr Viljoen planted oaks on his farm and experimented with various crops, but found nothing really remunerative. In 1902 he was elected to the Cape Legislative Council and when, in 1905, he told the Cape Minister of Agriculture, John X Merriman, about the agricultural problems of the district, Merriman advised him to try apples. This was the beginning of a vast industry.

Dr Viljoen purchased 24 assorted apple trees from Harry Pickstone, the great nurseryman. These trees were planted close to the homestead on *Oak Valley*. A patient wait for them to produce a crop followed. In 1912 the first apples were ready and, on an auspicious day, Dr Viljoen invited friends and neighbours to sample the fruit. It was excellent.

Dr Viljoen resolved to embark on the large-scale production of apples. He was aided in this industry when, in 1913, the elder of his two daughters, Hannah, married George, son of James Rawbone, a well-known forestry officer of the Cape Government. George Rawbone became a real son to his father-in-law and joined him as a partner in the apple-growing venture. From then on the family name was Rawbone-Viljoen.

The First World War delayed the apple project. Dr Viljoen was knighted in 1916 but unfortunately died in 1918 before he could see his plans to fruition. However, he did at least see vast orchards of young trees growing on his estate and on the properties of his neighbours. On his estate he also left 20 000 oak trees, a condition of his will being that they remain undisturbed. These lovely trees are as much his memorial as the apple industry. His second daughter, incidentally, he christened Oaklene.

The local farming community had everything to learn about apples correct varieties, cultivation, picking, packing and dispatch. When Miss Kathleen Murray, a neighbour of Dr Viljoen, picked her first apple crop she sent 25 boxes to the Johannesburg market. The agent returned to her a cheque for £1 a box. At the same time he complained that the apples had reached the customers in such a state that it was hardly possible to find one good bite between the bruises.

In 1923 a number of the local farmers created the Elgin Co-operative Fruitgrowers Ltd. A library of technical books on apple cultivation was founded and a start was made to the systematic study of the problems and possibilities of apple production.

In 1931 three of the leading farmers organised the Elgin Fruit Company as a joint venture in packing and marketing. Depression, followed by the Second World War, impeded progress in the industry. The end of the war, however, saw a tremendous surge of technical development in every aspect of the growing, refrigeration and marketing of fruit in general and apples in particular.

The Palmiet River lent itself to water storage and irrigation. With the introduction of sprinkler irrigation the area was transformed. Instead of 100 trees to 0,4 ha 470 trees could be planted, with a consequent five-fold increase in production. Improved fertilisers and the method of sod culture (where a covering of natural grass is left between trees in order to enrich the soil with humus, retain water and impede erosion) were used. Then, in 1959, Edmond Lombardi introduced the Italian Palmette System of cultivation on his farm *Applethwaite*. This idea, perfected in Italy from an ancient practice, involved the planting of fruit trees close together and training them to form continuous walls, each tree linked to its fellow for mutual support by grafting, with the main branches tied down into a horizontal position. This technique brought apple trees into bearing after four years instead of eight. It was further developed to suit local conditions. Today it is a mixture of the Duret Spindle Bush, the New Zealand Hawke Bay Multiple Leader Method and the original Palmette System. The Eikenhof Dam was built as a co-operative venture by some 100 of the farmers and the water provides the life-blood of the area.

Apple production became an industry and Elgin today produces 70 per cent of the apples grown in South Africa. The big farms installed computers to solve intricate problems of production and marketing. On *Applethwaite* farm the genius of its owner resulted in the creation and introduction to the market in 1966 of the pure apple-juice beverage known as 'Appletiser'. In creating this drink in association with Professor H R Luthi of the Department of Agriculture at the Swiss

Federal Institute of Technology, Edmond Lombardi solved the apple producers' problem of what to do with lower grades of fruit and gave to the world a drink free of additives or preservatives.

Picking, packing and handling techniques were transformed in a manner far removed from the traditional ways. *Glen Elgin* and *Applethwaite* farms established their own packing houses. The smaller producers banded together in 1948 to form, with the Elgin Fruit Company, the Elgin Fruit Packers' Co-operative. A second co-operative packing station, Kromrivier Apple Co-operative Ltd, was formed in 1972. A third co-operative, the Valley Co-op, was formed in 1982 by nineteen farmers. The combined output of apples and fruit juices from all these enterprises today amounts to a significant factor in the economy of South Africa.

The main varieties of apples grown in the area of the Palmiet River are the Ohinimuri, ripening in February; the White Winter Pearmain and the Golden Delicious, both ripening in March; Granny Smith, Starking, Starking Delicious, Starkrimson Delicious. Top Red, Oregon, Spur, and Red Chief in March/April. The last apple to be picked, during the month of May when the season ends, is the York Imperial, Pears, plums, nectarines and citrus are also produced.

The Elgin Apple Museum, housed in an old cottage on the banks of the Palmiet River, contains interesting examples of early machinery as well as historic photographs of the area. It is open Mondays to Fridays 09h00 to 17h00. Weekends by prior arrangement. Phone (021) 859-2042.

There are kiosks which sell the apples and other fruits of the district. One is run by the Elgin Fruit Packers' Co-operative (Elpaco) at the entrance to their huge pack house; another is Peregrine, at the eastern turn-off to Grabouw from (N2); a third is situated at the Kromrivier Apple Co-operative (Kromco) and a fourth at the turn-off to Houhoek. Visits to fruit farms and packing stations can be arranged. Phone (021) 859-9030 for details. Elgin–Grabouw is on the Four Passes Fruit Route linking Elgin to Vyeboom, Villiersdorp, Franschhoek and Stellenbosch. The four passes are Sir Lowry's, Viljoen's, Franschhoek and Helshoogte.

From the turn-off to Grabouw, the N2 continues eastwards, crosses the Palmiet River and after 2,5 km reaches a crossroads with a left turn to Grabouw, Elgin and Villiersdorp. A right turn leads through the apple orchards to the forestry station of Highlands. The Peregrine farm stall stands at the crossroads and offers fruit, juices and other good things to eat and drink. At this point the N2 is 68 km from Cape Town.

The N2 continues past a succession of orchards, especially lovely in spring when the trees are in blossom. After 5 km the road passes the Kromrivier Apple Co-operative and farm stall selling the fruit of the area to passing travellers. Just beyond this pack house is a tarmac turn-off, the Valley Road, which leads to the lovely farming area in the valley of the Krom River. A further 2 km takes the road past the entrance to the Lebanon forestry station and ahead, on the slope of a hill, a large white 'K' forms a landmark for the farm *Korteshoven*. At 5,5 km further on (81 km from Cape Town) there is a turn-off leading to ...

HOUHOEK

Houhoek (ravine glen) lies in a narrow fertile valley known as *Poespas* (higgledy-piggledy). Down this valley, where the Jakkals River flows, the old road and the railway originally found a complex twisting route out of the mountains (the railway still follows this route). The railway station of Houhoek stands at the top of the actual ravine which gives it its name, and the surrounding countryside is dominated by a fine cluster of high peaks. Wild flowers and trees cover the slopes and floor of the valley.

In former years the transport wagons out spanned at this pleasant spot for a rest and refreshment. An inn was built there which became a regular staging post. Lady Anne Barnard stayed there in 1798, eating boiled chicken *'fit for an emperor'*. Lady Duff Gordon was another visitor who, in 1861 recommended the place, for she found it *'all clean and no louses'*. The present buildings were erected in 1834 and extended in 1861, while the gigantic eucalyptus tree which stands at the door, as though hopeful of a free drink, was reputedly planted in 1875.

There are many stories about this inn. After the railway was built, the inn supplied meals to passengers. It is said that the innkeeper made handsome profits by serving the soup course so hot that diners were unable to consume it in time to eat the rest of the meal before the train moved on.

The pub is notable for its collection of old school ties, cut or forcibly removed from wearers during past forgotten celebrations. There is also a collection of about 200 foreign bank notes, mostly signed by owners who nailed them to the wall of the bar for safekeeping against future need or thirst. The habit is said to have been started by a young lord who left a ten shilling note glued to the ceiling of the bar so that on his return from abroad (broke as usual) he could once again enjoy the delights of the cellar.

A story is told about the eucalyptus tree. Its alcoholic tendencies are said to make it flourish on the aroma of good liquor which floats out from the bar. Its leaves rustle appreciatively when any good jokes are told inside, but it drops twigs on hearing stale stories. A teller of real chestnuts is said to have been killed by a falling bough. Since then his ghost reputedly haunts the inn, tugging at people's sleeves in the hope of inducing them to listen to his tales. Another ghost is said to be that of a man who died of indigestion or over-indulgence; the inn is haunted by his hiccups.

Beyond the turn-off to Houhoek, the modern N2, instead of following the old route down Higgledy-Piggledy Pass, takes the mountain crossing in its stride. It rises purposefully to the 341 m high summit and, with a glance at the view over the wheat fields of the Overberg, commences a sweeping descent. The summit ridge is a good place for wild flowers, especially pink everlastings. At the bottom of the pass (5 km from Houhoek) in a mass of protea bushes, there is a turn-off to Hermanus and to the small town of ...

BOT RIVER

This little town takes its name of *bot* (butter) from the days when the pastoral tribes resident there supplied butter to traders from Cape Town. A large number of proteas and their hybrids are cultivated in the area today and exported to florists all over the world.

From the turn-off to Bot River and Hermanus, the N2 continues on a switchback journey over hill and dale through wheat fields which are green in winter, gold in spring and drab in summer. The landscape has a spaciousness and variety which add interest to the journey. At 21,5 km from Bot River a turn-off leads to Greyton and Genadendal (see further on) while a further 2,5 km brings the road to the entrance (24 km from Bot River) to the town of ...

CALEDON

In itself a rather drab, sun-baked little town of 8 994 people, Caledon has the saving grace of lying in a handsome environment overlooked by the 2 607 m high Swartberg and confronted by the 2 687 m high Tower of Babel mountain to the south. The town also possesses two remarkable assets, one of which, in fact, stimulated the founding of Caledon.

On the slopes overlooking the town, seven springs of chalybeate (iron-rich) water originally bubbled to the surface, one of which, curiously enough was cold and the other six thermal. The water, in contact with rocks heated by pressure deep under the ground, is warmed to a steady temperature of 49,5°C, with 909 000 *l* reaching the surface each day.

As with the 73 other known hot springs of Southern Africa, these thermal springs of Caledon are not related to volcanic activity. The principal feature of the water, besides its warmth, is that it is free of any organic matter and has a large amount of iron in solution along with a variety of other less important chemicals. Compared with the waters of the famous spas of Europe and America, the waters of Caledon rate very highly. At the 1893 Chicago World Fair, in fact, they secured first prize against all comers.

The early African people discovered the springs long before Europeans came to the Cape and it was these early people who contributed the place-names of the area. They called the springs *Disporekamma* (hot water), while the river into which the water flows was called the *Hakwa* (zebra) River. This is the river on the banks of which Caledon stands today.

Whether the early people made any use of the springs for medicinal purposes is not known, but Europeans have always had an irresistible urge to jump into such natural baths on sight. From the time that Europeans settled in the Cape, the Caledon springs became increasingly famous. Actual development started in 1710 when Ferdinand Appel secured a grant of the area on condition that he build there a house of accommodation for invalids and visitors.

Just how effective such medicinal baths are in curing human ailments has always been a matter of some debate. Taking the waters is a fetish with many, and certainly does no harm. One rather suspects that these medicinal baths were more effective in former years when people normally washed less and in water which was often not very pure. Relaxing in a nice hot bath of absolutely clean water would do anybody a power of good if their normal ablutions only consisted of using perfume to counter body odour!

At all events, the hot springs at Caledon became popular and were developed as the years passed, with a variety of shelters and accommodation erected there for the convenience of visitors. The town of Caledon grew almost as an adjunct of these baths, being founded in 1813 and named *Caledon* in honour of the late Governor, the Earl of Caledon.

At the beginning of the 20th century the spa reached a notable height in its development, with a company named The Golden Baths Ltd erecting quite a remarkable hotel and sanatorium with accommodation for 200 guests, public rooms, recreational facilities and gardens of a most spacious and impressive nature. Old photographs of the place reveal it as being quite the equal of similar establishments anywhere in the world in those days of elaborate Victorian decorations and uncomfortable-looking furniture.

All this glory, alas, was destined to go up in smoke. In the early hours of 5 June 1946 the hotel was burned down, with a total loss of some £200 000. What set the blaze going is a mystery. The staff and the 29 guests just managed to get safely out of the place before the flames soared up to the heavens like a Guy Fawkes night bonfire. It was a miserable night for a fire, with a howling north-wester blowing and just enough drizzle to wet the unhappy, if fortunate survivors. There was no fire brigade in Caledon and at dawn a melancholy ruin was all that remained of what had once been a glittering social centre.

The place was never rebuilt. It remained a ruin until 1961 when the Caledon municipality obtained possession of the site. Their development of the place was somewhat low budget. Only on 1 September 1990 was a new resort hotel, The *Overberger*, opened at the springs. The warm mineral water is now drawn out mechanically and led through the Victorian mineral bath which is part of the site of the resort and hotel. The bath is open to casual visitors as well as hotel guests. For information regarding opening hours phone (028) 214-1271.

The second great asset of Caledon is its world-renowned wild flower garden and reserve. This garden was founded in 1927 as a result of the zealous work of a group of nature enthusiasts, J Dunsdon, F Guthrie, L Langschmidt, B Newmark and J B Taylor. Part of a 214 ha nature reserve covering the slopes of the Swartberg, it was laid out in 1933 by an itinerant landscape gardener named Cecil Young, and then developed to its present standard by its curator, C de W Meiring.

The garden, covering 56 ha, is notable for its wonderful variety of indigenous flowers, superb examples of one of the richest flora in the world. Added attractions are the pleasantly casual layout of paths and bridges, the pretty little valley, and the odd natural feature of the so-called 'Window Rock' with its view of the surroundings. The garden is open daily from 07h30 to 17h00.

There is a fine cultural museum in the town, portraying a Victorian household. Barley, onions, wheat and wool are produced in the district. Southern Associated Maltsters have in the town the largest malt-producing plant in the Southern Hemisphere. A wild flower show is held at Caledon every September and a Beer and Bread festival in March.

From Caledon a road branches south-eastwards to Bredasdorp (see Chapter Eleven). Caledon is also a convenient centre for a visit to Greyton and to the romantically situated mission station of Genadendal, 27 km north of Caledon up the road which branches off from the N2, 2,5 km before it reaches the town. This is a pleasant drive over undulating wheat fields, especially lovely in November when the colours are golden and harvesting is in progress.

GENADENDAL

The mission station of *Genadendal* (the valley of grace) was founded by the Moravian Missionary Society in 1793 in what was called *Baviaanskloof* (ravine of the baboons) where, in 1737, an earlier worker of the Society, Georg Schmidt, had attempted to establish a station for the conversion of the resident pastoral tribe to Christianity. This effort had failed, ending after five years in a squabble over the unordained missionary's right to administer baptism to his converts.

The new venture, however, flourished. In 1806 it received its present name and became a model of its kind, with a thriving population converted to the Christian and Western way of life. The village with its streets of neat black-thatched, white-walled cottages, the church and manse, the water-mill and the magnificent groves of oak trees – all survive to this day and preserve with them the flavour of life in the Cape 150 years ago. There is an interesting museum.

The Genadendal Hiking Trail has its start at the Moravian mission church. It provides a circular route, 25,3 km in length with overnight facilities at 14,3 km. It is a tough but magnificent walk, with permits and reservations necessary – contact the Manager, Cape Nature Conservation, Vrolijkheid Nature Reserve, Private Bag X614, Robertson, 6705. Phone (023) 625-1621.

From Genadendal the gravel road continues eastwards for 4,5 km to the small, beautifully situated village of ...

GREYTON

A relaxed and pleasant little place, Greyton was founded by Herbert Vigne who, in 1846, bought the farm *Weltevreden*. He laid out a town in 1854, which he named after the then Governor of the Cape, Sir George Grey. It became a municipality in 1910, and today is a popular weekend and hideaway resort. It lies in the afternoon shadow of some of the finest peaks of the Riviersonderend range. Into one of the mountain ridges, the *Wa en Osse* (wagon and oxen), a particularly beautiful gorge known as *Noupoort* (narrow pass) finds a way close to the summit of the 1 465 m high Kanonberg. This provides a fine walk, while a walk through the Boesmanskloof is also spectacular, with a vast variety of flowering plants to be seen.

The Boesmanskloof trail covers a distance of 15,8 km. It links the villages of Greyton and McGregor (formerly known as Lady Grey), which are situated respectively to the south and the north of the Riviersonderend range. At one time the trail was the only direct link between the two villages, and the story goes that rugby teams from the two little towns had to cross the mountain at weekends in order to engage in a friendly match.

The trail starts to the north-east of Greyton, at the end of the Boesmanskloof, and leads to the top of the mountain as far as *Die Galg* (the gallows), where it joins an historic pass which was built just before the Second World War. The labourers who worked on the construction of the pass were vagrants who had been rounded up by the authorities in the Cape Town area and held under prison conditions. They were employed as manual labour by the Cape Provincial Administration at a minimal weekly wage. Construction methods were primitive. They involved the use of pick-axes, shovels and donkeys. In 1941, when the road had been completed as far as Die Galg (about 15 km from McGregor), work was stopped as a result of the embezzlement of funds.

At a leisurely pace, the walk may be completed in five or six hours. Drinking water is plentiful, and there are many pools for bathing especially at Oaks Falls. During the winter months nine spectacular waterfalls, which drop into the river from a great height, are clearly visible from the footpath. A large variety of proteas, ericas and disas grow along the trail. Wildlife occurs in abundance, and fresh leopard tracks and droppings are frequently observed. The river contains a variety of fish, and a rare species of frog occurs in the moist areas.

There are no huts along the trail. Camping-out at night is prohibited. However, private accommodation at either end of the trail is available.

Clearly marked notice boards indicate the start and finish of the trail. Particulars and permits may be obtained from the Manager, Cape Nature Conservation, Vrolijkheid Nature Reserve, Private Bag X614, Robertson, 6705. Phone (023) 625-1621. Hikers may be required to show their permits at any time, and are therefore advised to keep them available.

On the road to Krige, 1,5 km from Greyton, a pleasant camping ground with simple facilities is situated in the wood on the banks of the Riviersonderend. There is canoeing and swimming. The camp is run by the local authority. From Greyton the gravel road continues eastwards along the slopes of the Riviersonderend range where many fine views of mountain and rural landscape may be seen. On the farm *Nethercourt* may be viewed the little cave know as *Het Ziekenhuis* (the hospital) in which ailing travellers were sheltered in former years. After 33 km the road joins the N2 which has come from Caledon (48 km away) over the wheat fields, and now enters ...

RIVIERSONDEREND

Lying astride the N2, 168 km from Cape Town, *Riviersonderend* (river without end) is a municipality with a population of 2 635 It was established in 1925 as a centre for the farming community in the fertile valley of this river with the romantic name. In itself it possesses little of tourist interest, but its setting, dominated to the north by the Riviersonderend range of mountains, makes it a convenient centre for exploring the area. Indigenous forests survive in the mountain ravines.

From Riviersonderend, the N2 continues eastwards over wheat fields where superb photographic possibilities may be found, especially when the wheat is golden ripe and being reaped. There are turn-offs to Protem after 5 km, to Napier after 10 km and, at 20 km, a turn-off to the village of ...

STORMSVLEI

A small rural centre on the banks of the Riviersonderend, *Stormsvlei* (marsh of storms) has a holiday resort with river swimming and camping grounds in the shade of trees. A tarmac road crosses the river and leads through the Riviersonderend Mountains for 19 km to Bonnievale in the valley of the Breede River.

East of Stormsvlei, the N2 continues through more rugged country as the Riviersonderend Mountains peter out into hillocks covered with the red flowering *Aloe ferox*. Ahead lies the great mountain wall of the Langeberge, with the Breede River flowing down from the north-west. After 24 km there is a turn-off to Bredasdorp and 7 km further on, the road reaches the bridge across the Breede River. The town of Swellendam lies 5 km beyond the river bridge (36 km from Stormsvlei).

SWELLENDAM

In a well-watered valley beneath the most spectacular peaks of the Langeberge range lies this attractive town of 11 394 people. It is said that from the shadow of some of these peaks – the Clock

Peaks, individually known (from east to west) from the hours as ten, eleven, twelve, one – it is possible to estimate the time of day.

Swellendam has experienced an eventful past. The area was once famous for its game animals. Lion, rhino, hippo, elephant and ostrich abounded, as well as antelope in great numbers and variety including eland, zebra, hartebeest, the bontebok and the now-extinct quagga and bluebuck. The concentration of game and the congenial nature of the countryside attracted the Hessekwa tribe, who erected their principal kraals in areas such as Bonteboskloof, where the graves of their last leaders, Klaas and Markus Sababa, may still be seen.

With the advent of Europeans, many fine farms were established along the slopes of the mountains where perennial streams provided ample water, and along the banks of the Breede River. Among them were *Grootvadersbosch*, home of Captain Benjamin Moodie, descendant of the wild lairds of Melsetter and a great coloniser whose grandson led the Moodie trek into Zimbabwe; *Rhenosterfontein*, the fine farm of the Van Reenens; *Bruintjiesrivier; The Glen; Rietvlei (Oude Post);* the superb *Klipperivier*, now a guest-house but once the home of the famous F W Reitz, politician and man of progress whose son Francis William became President of the Orange Free State; *Somerset Gift,* and *Rotterdam*, home of the renowned *landdrost* (magistrate), Anthonie Faure. All these and several other farms still have their original homesteads, many of which are characterised by interesting architectural features. Cattle, horses, sheep and wheat were farmed in the area, In order to provide an administrative centre, the Dutch East India Company authorities decided in 1743 to establish civil authority over this remote frontier portion of what was then the unwieldy district of Stellenbosch.

Johannes Rhenius was appointed as the first magistrate. Together with his councillors he selected for his seat a particularly charming locality in the valley of the Cornlands River, which tumbled down from the clock peaks of the Langeberge range. A *drostdy* (magistracy) was built in this pleasant situation. In the same year that it was completed – 1747 – the new district was named *Swellendam*, in honour of Governor Hendrik Swellengrebel and his wife, Helena ten Damme.

The original drostdy was substantially renovated in later years. Beautifully preserved as a national monument, it is today one of the architectural gems of Southern Africa. It houses a museum containing an interesting collection of period furniture and household bric-á-brac dating back over the years since the place was built. The Drostdy Museum is open weekdays from 09h00 to 16h45 Saturdays, Sundays and public holidays from 10h00 to 15h45. It is closed on 25–26 December, Good Friday and 1 January. There is an extension of the museum in *Mayville,* the Victorian period home of the Steyn family. The museum shop is housed in the old goal. The cells are open for visitors.

Swellendam has been the scene of lively and varied human activity. For a short while it was even one of the capitals of the world! On 17 June 1795 the citizens of the town, enraged by the misrule of the Dutch East India Company, gathered at the drostdy, dismissed the landdrost and declared an independent republic with a local resident, Hermanus Steyn, as president. The pocket republic lasted only six months (17 June to 4 November 1795). The first British occupation of the Cape provided a new regime and the little republic quietly expired.

In 1798 Swellendam consisted of twenty houses scattered along the river valley. It was not until 1802 that the place acquired even a church. For years it was simply the eastern frontier village on what was known as the *Kaapse Wapad* (the Cape wagon road) or *De Groote Wagen Weg* (the great wagon way), the pioneer road to the east blazed by cattle traders, hunters and explorers. The drostdy was regarded by these people as something of an inn and many celebrated travellers found hospitality there in the course of their travels.

As the years of the first half of the 19th century passed, Swellendam steadily developed into the prosperous administrative and commercial capital of what was known as the *Overberg* (over the mountain) area. The wool industry of Southern Africa was first established commercially in the Overberg, with Swellendam as the centre. Wool farming provided the stimulus for the town's development; and its long main street, running up the right bank of the Cornlands River, became lined with a varied collection of buildings, including the warehouse and trading headquarters of the merchant prince of the Overberg. Joseph Barry, and his home, known as the *Auld House*. It is worth walking along the main street – preferably towards evening when it is cool, for few trees have been left to fend off the daytime heat and glare. Odd gables, gateways, relics and fragments of many interesting old buildings survive as well as several lovely old thatched residences. It is easy to visualise this street in the 1850s, when traders, farmers, travellers and wagon builders lent to the place a bustle and importance.

In 1864 the Great Western Agricultural Exhibition was held in Swellendam. This was the peak year of the old order. A newspaper, *The Overberg Courant*, had appeared in 1859 and there were amenities such as a race-track, library and literary society. The Barrys had organised a shipping service. A coaster connected the mouth of the Breede River to Cape Town. The district anticipated a brilliant future. Unfortunately, 1865 proved a disastrous year for Swellendam. On 17 May a spark from a baker's oven started a fire that practically razed the town. The flames, carried by a powerful wind from one thatched roof to the next, destroyed 40 of the fine old houses. Even more destructive to the prosperity of the town was a persistent drought. Little money remained in the district and many of the ventures of the Barrys (Barry and Nephews) fell on evil times. Joseph Barry died in the same year. After 45 years of prominence in the Overberg, the Barry concerns went bankrupt in 1866, leaving a huge void in the commerce of the Overberg.

Many memories of the 'golden years' when the town was a hub of commence still linger in Swellendam. The jingle, *As jy lekker wil lewe koop by Barry Newe* (if you want to live nicely purchase at Barry Nephews), is still occasionally sung by children playing in the long main street. Today Swellendam remains a picturesque town, an important rail and road centre and an interesting stopover for those journeying along the modern N2 highway which has replaced the old wagon road to the Cape.

Opposite the Drostdy Museum is a craft centre containing a blacksmith shop, shoemaker, charcoal burner, coppersmith, cooper, and a working water-mill where stone-ground flour may be bought.

The 11 300 ha Marloth Nature Reserve lies in the foothills of the Langeberge, 5 km from the centre of the town up André Whyte Street. Climbs and walks into the mountains are popular. There are several short walks and a 76 km long circular hiking trail with five overnight huts. The route can be shortened to 54 km or 48 km. Permits are necessary, and bookings must be made through the Manager, Marloth Nature Reserve, P O Box 28, Swellendam, 6740. Phone (028) 514-1410.

THE BONTEBOK NATIONAL PARK

Six kilometres from Swellendam, just off the main road east of the town, is the entrance to a 2 786 ha national park preserving a handsome expanse of the country in something of its original state when man first discovered it. Dominated by the tall peaks of the Langeberge and fronting on some fine stretches of the Breede River, this national park provides a sanctuary for species of game animals that once roamed this part of Southern Africa. Chief among these animals is the bontebok, a species of antelope peculiar to the sandy flat fynbos country of the southern end of Africa and, until a handful of local farmers granted them protection, almost on the point of extinction. In 1931 the National Parks Board established a sanctuary for bontebok near Bredasdorp, but the area provided poor grazing and the animals failed to flourish.

In 1960 the Bontebok National Park at Swellendam was established and the animals in the old Bredasdorp sanctuary were translocated to a new and ideal home where, according to old records, they were originally present in great numbers. Grey rhebuck, steenbok, grysbok, and duiker were already in the area. In addition to bontebok, the National Parks Board reintroduced red hartebeest and Cape mountain zebra. In the healthy environment these animals have all thrived. The park today is an attractive and interesting place, with beautiful aloes flowering in winter and many trees, including *Acacia karroo*, wild olive, milkwood, yellowwood and candlewood. Over 470 plant species have been identified in the park, 190 species of birds and 35 mammalian species. Gravel roads lead motorists to all parts of the park.

A visit to the Bontebok National Park – so conveniently situated to Swellendam and the N2 – is thoroughly recommended. A pleasant picnic site and caravan park are situated among a grove of acacia trees on the banks of the Breede River. Fishing and swimming are permitted in the river. There is an office and curio shop at the park entrance. The park is open from 1 October to 30 April, 08h00 to 19h00; 1 May to 30 September, 08h00 to 18h00.

The Breede River forms the southern boundary of the Bontebok National Park. Beyond the park the river flows across an undulating coastal terrace, meandering around the hills and descending gentle towards the sea. This is wheat country, dotted with flowering aloes in winter and great flocks of sheep grazing in the meadowlands.

From the Buffeljags River, 10 km along the main N2 road east of Swellendam, a gravel road winds its way southwards parallel to the Breede and serves various farms lining the river banks. After 29 km this road reaches the quaint little former river port named *Malgas* from the gannet sea-birds. From here a pont, the last of its kind working in South Africa, conveys traffic across the river. From the west bank a road stretches for 60 km to Bredasdorp. The pont operates from 06h00 to 18h00 daily. This is a picturesque and enjoyable means of crossing the river which, at this point, is sufficiently broad and deep to have allowed the penetration of coasters in former years from the mouth, 40 km away. On the western bank of the river there are some interesting buildings, including a church. They were built by the firm of Barry and Nephews.

The shipping service, alas, no longer works. In the 1850s when the merchant house of Barry and Nephews dominated trade in the Overberg area, it was found that three full weeks were needed for wagons to transport goods to Cape Town. The Breede River was obviously perfectly navigable in its lower reaches, and the enterprising firm acquired a fleet of small sailing vessels and built a store at Malgas.

The Breede River mouth is in St Sebastian Bay, with Cape Infanta on its south side. The bay offers little protection from the prevailing south-easterly winds which can be violent. The river mouth is wide but blocked by the sandbanks usual in rivers. Sailing vessels had a tricky time entering what was called Port Beaufort. Once across the bar into the river, navigation was more simple, but if the wind was in a treacherous mood a sailing vessel could suddenly find itself becalmed at an awkward point and end up on the beach.

To overcome this problem, the Barrys had a special steamer built on the Clyde. Named the *Kadie*, this perky little 150-ton coaster arrived at the mouth of the river on her maiden voyage on 26 September 1859. She steamed across the bar without difficulty and from the banks of Port Beaufort picked up practically everybody of importance in the district. With flags flying and all on board very merry on good wine and brandy from the Breede River valley, the ship steamed upriver to Malgas and there unloaded cargo and those passengers who could find their way home. It was a very happy occasion on the Breede River.

For the next six years the *Kadie* carried to Cape Town cargoes of butter, bitter aloes, wool, sheep and grain valued at many thousands of pounds, and brought back trade goods to stock the Barry stores. The *Kadie* crossed the bar on 240 voyages. Then, on 17 November 1865, she struck the rocks on the west bank of the river and was totally wrecked. The ship's bell and some salvaged furniture are in the Barry home in Swellendam, the *Auld House*.

Other coasters continued the trade to Port Beaufort. The last was a famous little ship named the *Chubb*, 172 tons with a draught a little over a metre. Built originally as a waterboat for Simon's Town, she was bought in 1933 by Dart and Howes for £100. The new owners removed the water tanks and put the ship on the Breede River run, carrying fuels, oils and other cargoes for the farmers and traders. The railways soon complained that the trade was 'unfair' competition, and the *Chubb* was transferred to the run to Port Nolloth. She ended up on the shore at Paternoster.

Nowadays only pleasure craft and fishermen sail across the bar of the Breede River. From Malgas a road leads for 20 km down to Witsand at the mouth of the river, where there is a holiday resort, launching ramps, a fine beach and a small harbour for fishing and sporting boats. Many fine fish, including giant grunter and cob, are caught in the river mouth and bay. Boating on the river is superb but always dangerous at the mouth as a result of unpredictable winds. Oysters flourish in the warm waters, and there is an old jingle that *'in St Sebastian's Bay you can find pearls'*. The hint of their presence at the mouth of the Breede provides a fitting culmination to a river which, along its entire course, brings man so much pleasure and prosperity.

From Swellendam, the N2 proceeds over undulating wheat country. At 8 km from the entrance to the Bontebok Park the road descends into the fertile valley of the river known after some old adventure as the *Buffeljags* (buffalo hunt). In this pleasant setting there is a tea-room, garage and small trading centre near the railway station. A road branches off at this point to reach the sea at the mouth of the Breede River.

Beyond the Buffeljags River the road climbs out of the shallow valley with fine views of the Langeberge range to be seen north of the road. After 1,5 km, there is a turn-off to Barrydale and the Little Karoo through the pass known as ...

THE TRADOUW PASS

The branch road to the Tradouw Pass leads north-eastwards close to the Langeberge range. At 6 km a cairn stands marking the site of *Oupos* (old post), a small military stronghold established there in 1734 by the Dutch East India Company as a defence against Hottentot and Bushman groups who were marauding and resisting settlement by Europeans in the area. Three kilometres further on, in a well-watered valley lying at the foot of the mountain range, the road reaches the station of the London Missionary Society, founded in 1809 at *Suurbraak* (sour marsh). Today it consists of a 1 km long cluster of cottages on either side of the road with an attractive village green around which the more important buildings stand.

Beyond Suurbraak, the road passes the fine *Lismore* farm of the Barry Trust and then, 6 km from the mission, reaches the turn-off north to the *Tradouw* (women's pass) which follows a most beautiful route for 17 km to Barrydale on the northern side of the mountains. This pass, originally blazed by the Bushmen and named by the Hottentots, is notable for its waterfalls in winter and wild flowers in spring. Bushmen found the caves in its cliffs to their liking, and there are several galleries of rock paintings. Twelve kilometres from the start of the pass there is a magnificent swimming-pool in the river, reached by a branch track. The pass was opened to traffic in 1873, having been built by Thomas Bain to provide a trade route between the Little Karoo and Port Beaufort at the mouth of the Breede River. It has been substantially rebuilt in modern times.

From the turn-off to the Tradouw Pass the road from Swellendam leads for 25 km past the historic farm of the Moodie family, *Grootvadersbosch* (grandfather's bush), with its forest of stinkwood and California redwoods, and then arrives at the town of Heidelberg.

From the turn-off to Tradouw Pass and Barrydale, the main coastal road, N2, finds an undulating route over wheat-covered hills. There is a turn-off to Port Beaufort 37,5 km beyond the Barrydale turn-off. After another 3 km (50 km from Swellendam) the road reaches the town of ...

HEIDELBERG

With its population of 6 415, Heidelberg lies in an attractive setting on the banks of the *Duivenhoks* (dovecote) River. In 1689 the explorer, Izaak Schryver, first camped at this pleasant place and found so many doves there that he gave the river its rather unusual name.

Settlers found their way to the valley. As early as 1725 Andries Gous received a grant there of the farm *Doornboom* (thorn tree). For some years the area was considered to be a part of the Riversdale district. Then, on 14 September 1855, the Riversdale church council bought for £5 000 a portion of the farm *Doornboom*. The purpose was to lay out a town which they named *Heidelberg* after that ancient city in Germany, the source of the Heidelberg Catechism and, like the new Heidelberg, built on the banks of a river.

A church and school became the twin centres of the new town. The first erven were sold on 21 November 1855. In 1862 the place inaugurated its first town management board under the chairmanship of Joseph Barry (son of Thomas Barry, one of the two well-known Barry nephews). Wool, tobacco, corn, dairy products, cattle and ostrich feathers were the products which put the community on its feet. The opening of the railway in 1903 provided the essential link with the outside world.

From Heidelberg the main coastal road (N2) continues eastwards for 29 km and then reaches ...

RIVERSDALE

This town was at first part of the Swellendam district. Church services were periodically held in a room set aside for the purpose on the farm *Zeekoegat* (hippopotamus hole) owned by Hillegert Mulder, a man renowned for his hospitality towards travellers on the road to the east. The farmhouse still stands and is known as the *Ou Pastorie*.

Watered by the Vet River, many other fine farms flourished in this area, a well-known one being *Barend Saayman's Eredood* (subsequently known as *Sussex*) mentioned at the beginning of the chapter. The residents of these farms decided that a community centre was desirable in an area as prosperous as theirs. Money was contributed and on 21 July 1838 the farm *Doornkraal* (thorn corral) was purchased from Hermanus Steyn. On 16 August the first erven were sold in a town named after Harry Rivers, the Civil Commissioner of the Swellendam district. Rivers, a civil servant who had found himself in hot water for autocratic behaviour in his former post in Grahamstown, had mellowed after transfer to Swellendam. He became popular, and eventually ended his career as Treasurer-General of the Cape Colony.

Today Riversdale is an amiable and clean little farming centre. It has 9 759 inhabitants and is resorted to by travellers as a staging post on the road to the east. For some reason the town has always been the home of 'characters' and there are many tales to be heard in the pubs about individuals such as Henry Meurant, a magistrate renowned for his sage decisions and the man who, in 1861 in Cradock, published the first work written in Afrikaans. A typical local story of a Riversdale character concerns one Dik Koos Saayman, a fat and happy old farmer. Dik Koos – a total illiterate who kept his farm accounts accurately in his head – had the habit every week of visiting the town in his cart and conducting his business. At the end of the day he drove to the pub, leaving his cart in the care of a little boy. After having one for the road, he would collect a couple of bottles of brandy already wrapped up and waiting for him.

The local *dominee* (parson) at this time was something of a holy terror who strongly disapproved of Dik Koos. One evening he lay in wait. When Dik Koos went in for his drink, the parson walked up to the boy, told him to run along, and stood holding the horses himself. The whole town was agog at the news of his attempt to shame Dik Koos. Dik Koos finished his drink, collected his bottles, paid his money and walked outside, watched by many. Without blinking an eye he went to his cart, paused, then fumbled heavily in his pocket for a moment. Producing sixpence, he gave it to the astounded parson and with a *'Thank you I usually only give a tickey but as it's the parson this evening, I'll give sixpence'*, he drove away.

The Riversdale district is also well known for the rather pungent and curiously antiseptic aroma produced by species of agathosma which flourish in these parts. The area is also good for wild flowers and aloes. In the Van Riebeeck Garden of the Jurisch Park there is a magnificent collection of local aloes which bloom in May and June, while mesembryanthemums are equally spectacular in spring. The late Mr Werner Frehse, acting town engineer from 1950 to 1972, was responsible for this garden, the planting of trees in the streets and the creation of the Werner Frehse Nature Reserve. His work created a floral spectacle which brought many travellers to a halt on the N2 as they admired it. Unfortunately, after his death in 1972, the garden was allowed to decline.

Mounted in Riversdale there is a Class 7 locomotive of the type used when the railway was opened in the town in 1903. There is an interesting museum in the town.

For those travellers with the time and inclination to appreciate lovely and interesting things, there are two fascinating drives from Riversdale. To the south-west a gravel road leads down to the coast through what is almost a forgotten rural world where may be seen one of the most primitive types of architecture ever devised by man. This road stretches for 41 km to the mouth of the Duivenhoks River. Projecting into the blue of St Sebastian Bay is what is known as *Puntjie* (the little point), on which stands an extraordinary cluster of seaside buildings architecturally known as *kapsteilhuisies* (truss-style houses). This odd place started as a holiday resort for the local farmers. Shortage of modern building material stimulated somebody to erect a kapsteilhuis as his ancestors had once done; then others followed the style. Each building consists of a thatched roof built at ground level with no side walls at all and a floor space of about 6 m by 5 m. A window in one end and a recessed door in the other completes the primitive but extremely snug structure. Such buildings were used in Europe in ancient times.

Similar or more elaborate kapsteilhuisies may be seen in other parts of South Africa, but nowhere quite as numerous or as lovely as these. On the way to Puntjie, where the road passes through the rural settlements of Brakfontein and *Vermaaklikheid* (jollification), elaborations of kapsteilhuisies may be seen with low, whitewashed side walls elevating the roofs above ground level. The atmosphere of this part of the world is rather reminiscent of Ireland – poor but pretty.

Puntjie was privately owned for many years by Mrs Molly Lazarus (née Davids) who bought it in 1960 from a previous owner, the gentleman-politician, Major Piet van der Byl. Major Piet – the stories have it – allowed local farmers to build kapsteilhuisies at Puntjie for a nominal ground rental of 4 shillings, and perhaps they showed their pleasure by voting for him. It is a fact that, in a strong Nationalist area, the locals voted United Party for years and at the same time had their seaside fun. Only kapsteilhuisies may be erected at Puntjie so that its charm will be preserved.

The second drive from Riversdale leads northwards to the Langeberge. After 10 km the tarmac road crosses a bridge over the lovely upper reaches of the *Kafferkuils* (named from a species of rush) River which flows through delightfully verdant country with the high peaks of the Langeberge looking down serenely. Across the river lies the Garcia forest station, also the start of Garcia's Pass which takes the road through to the Little Karoo.

In 1868 Maurice Garcia, Civil Commissioner of Riversdale, with the assistance of a few convicts, constructed a bridle-path through the mountains following the deep gorge of the Kafferkuils River. This pass (10 km long) provided a short link through fine scenery between Riversdale and Ladismith in the Little Karoo. Between 1874 and 1877 Thomas Bain constructed a proper road through the pass. This route provides travellers with a most spectacular gateway into the Little Karoo. It replaces the older, now-disused Plattekloof Pass which followed the Duiverhoks Rver through the mountains.

Garcia's Pass is particularly renowned for its wild flowers. A ruggedly beautiful circular tour may be made by taking the Van Wyksdorp turn-off 4,5 km from the end of the pass (25 km from Riversdale). This road leads eastwards along the northern slopes of the Langeberge. High mountains, deep ravines, red-orange coloured sandstone cliffs, innumerable waterfalls in the rainy season and farmhouses against a background of serrated peaks, together form a dramatic landscape.

At 72 km from Riversdale the road crosses the Gourits River flowing in a deep gorge. Nine kilometres further on the road passes an old toll-house at the entrance to Bergkloof, the beginning of what is known as *Cloetespas* after the family owning ground on the southern end of the mountain passage. Cloetespas is a picturesque and little-known mountain pass, still guarded by the ruins of blockhouses built to watch over it during the Anglo-Boer War. After 23 km of twisting and turning, the road reaches *Herbertsdale*, a former mission station founded by the Reverend Mr James Herbert. Down the fertile valley of the Langtou River the road continues through masses of winter-flowering aloes and eventually rejoins the main coastal road, N2, at Cooper siding after a 130 km drive from Riversdale. By means of the coastal road it is 59 km from Cooper siding to Riversdale.

From Riversdale the N2 coastal road continues eastwards for 12 km and then reaches a tarmac turn-off south to Stilbaai. This road leads over slightly rolling country for 25 km to the mouth of the Kafferkuils River where lies the fishing harbour and resort of ...

STILBAAI

Divided into an east (resort) side and west (harbour) side on the banks at the mouth of the Kafferkuils River, *Stilbaai* (still bay) is an almost classic example of the South African countryman's ideal of a holiday resort. There is a fine swimming beach, excellent boating on the river, and varied estuary and coastal fishing. Between June and October Southern Right whales come into the bay to mate and bear their young. These attractions, together with an equable climate, soon lured man to the area for his living as well as recreation. Prehistoric people made their homes on this coast, artefacts of the Middle and Later Stone Age are numerous, and it was on this coast that Dr C Heese found the evidence of what is known as the Still Bay Culture. Bone implements dating back 40 000 years have been found by Dr C Henshilwood. There is an interesting collection of these artefacts in the office of the local tourism bureau in the *Palinggat* homestead.

Interesting features of the coast dating from the period of early inhabitants about 2 000 years ago are the numerous fish traps known as *vywers* (ponds) which are still in use. These are dams made of boulders built up to form low barricades between the high and low water marks. At high tide the fish enter these dams to feed among the rocks. When the tide recedes, the fish are left behind and often thousands of mullet are caught in a single trap. The traps are still maintained in their former condition and the bottoms are cleared of debris in order to make it easier to catch the fish.

When Europeans first entered the area, they found several unusual natural wonders, caves, strange rock formations such as the *preekstoel* (pulpit) 3 km east of Stilbaai, and an extraordinary number of eels populating the streams. These eels – a local delicacy with a record weight of 7 kg – frequent all the streams and many are incredibly tame. On *Platbos* farm, for instance, where the De Jager family live in the original 1814 homestead, there are springs full of these eels which eat from the hands of visitors! The *palinggat* (eel hole) is a study centre of the peculiar habits of eels. They are fed at 11h00 each day except Sundays and religious holidays.

Shells and drift seeds (such as the *Entada pursaetha* and *Entada scandens*), washed down from the tropics to this coast by the Mozambique–Agulhas Current, are often found in considerable numbers. It was here that Dr John Muir of Riversdale collected many of the shell specimens which are part of the Muir Collection in the South African Museum in Cape Town. His detailed study of the strange, wandering drift seeds is also the definitive work on the subject and is published as *Botanical Survey No 16* by the Government Printer. It is interesting to know that some Stilbaai oldtimers such as J Dekenah (a man rich in local lore) induced these seeds to grow. Although they produced creepers with bean-like leaves, the plants did not flourish in the temperate climate and never developed the huge 0,9 m long seed pods characteristic of their kind in the tropics.

Until the great smallpox epidemic of 1713 wiped out most of the indigenous tribes, there was friction along this coast between settlers and the earlier people. There is a local story that relates that the last of the earlier people – a tall, light-coloured individual who had resisted the settlers and set himself up as a rustler – was eventually cornered and killed on a rock offshore where he had swum for safety. His retreat had been the rock shelter at *Jongensgat* (the cave of the young man) and his death took place at Grootjongensfontein.

Such bitter memories of the old times seem alien to this pleasant coast. Today man lives there in harmony. At *Melkhoutfontein* (fountain of milkwood trees) there is a pleasant village of fisherfolk, with a little churchyard in which may be seen the graves – decorated with shells – of fishermen drowned in the cruel sea; for their calling, even in the waters of the still bay, is a matter of skill, risk and interminable battle with the elements.

Stilbaai itself was surveyed into plots in 1894. Early buyers such as Frans van Wyk secured choice properties for £7 10s each. No road was made to the resort and visitors travelled by wagon to a point on the river from where boats ferried them and their belongings down to the coast. Riversdale inhabitants went there for Christmas while the farmers of the Little Karoo travelled down during March after the grape harvest was in, with their wagons always loaded with barrels of wine, brandy and *witblits* (white lighting). Their holiday camps were jolly affairs, with the old folk gossiping and the young people dancing all night, every night, beneath the stars on a specially cleared piece of ground which was literally danced into a smooth, rock-hard surface by the time the season was over.

With the advent of motor vehicles, a road was built. A pontoon was opened across the river in

1930 and worked (until it was replaced by a bridge in 1955) by a celebrated character named Eepie, who never seemed to forget anybody no matter how long they had been away. Wooden bungalows were erected on plots in the higgledy-piggledy fashion common to old resorts with no disciplinary local authority. Many of these bungalows were built on stilts above the level of spring tides and all had freshwater wells dug into the sand underneath them. Most of these bungalows were built by the Dekenah brothers, who habitually knocked up a house in ten days and nights flat. To the fury of neighbours they often worked all night by the light of the moon. Even though a good many of the bungalows look as they have been built in the pitch dark, Stilbaai has always been a singularly happy and totally informal place. Concerts and church services were held in the *planksaal* (plank hall), with everybody – including the parson – barefoot and relaxed. Sports, pastimes, romances, picnics and friendships all flourished in the sunshine against the murmur of the waves on the beach.

Stilbaai became a municipality in 1965 and that same year the road was tarred. With a permanent population of 3 221 it remains a place of many happy ghosts and beautiful wild flowers.

The main coastal road (N2) continues eastwards from the Stilbaai turn-off for 24,5 km over level wheat country and then reaches the town of ...

ALBERTINIA

This town was named after the Reverend J R Albertyn of Riversdale, who planned the establishment of a separate church community east of Riversdale. For various reasons the project was delayed. He had long left the district before the town had its birth on the old farm *Grootfontein*. It was proclaimed a town on 18 November 1904.

With its population of 3 465 Albertinia has had a quiet history. Like every other town, however, it has a feature special to itself. In 1925 W R van As started mining yellow and red ochre from deposits first noticed by Sir John Barrow in 1797. This industry today is the principal source of ochre in South Africa. It is exported all over the world as a natural earth colour used in the manufacture of paints and for imparting colour to cement and linoleum.

Kaolin is also found in the area, while another unusual local industry – largely practised by the Coloured people – is connected with the masses of red flowering *Aloe ferox* which flourish between Albertinia and Mossel Bay. During winter the leaves are collected and drained of their bitter-tasting sap. This sap is concentrated by boiling and is exported from the area which is one of the world's two principal sources (the other being the West Indies) of an important ingredient in many medicines.

At 8 km east of Albertinia, the N2 reaches a gravel turn-off leading to the coast 27 km away at the mouth of the Gourits River. The N2 road actually crosses the deep gorge of this river 8 km further on. Most travellers pause here to view the spectacular twin rail and road bridges 270 m long and 75 m above the river. Bungee jumpers make use of these facilities.

The Gourits River, draining the arid areas of the Little and Great Karoos, is essentially a fluctuating river with long spells of slight flow followed by short but most violent floods. The *Gourits* is named after the Gourikwa tribe who once lived along its banks. At its mouth (at the end of the 27 km long turn-off mentioned earlier) there is a good beach with the usual nondescript collection of bungalows, most of them forlornly locked up for eleven months of the year. A track down the coast leads to several vantage-points for fishermen, including the rocky stretch known as The Fisheries, where Mr Gulliman started an industry mining deposits of amorphous silica. Deposits of this silicrete provide the principal material for the furnace bricks used in the South African iron and steel foundries.

Beyond the high bridges over the Gourits River, where a picnic area is situated at a good viewsite, the main coastal road (N2) continues eastwards for 5 km and then reaches a turn-off leading to the coast. This road follows the broad alluvial valley of the lower Gourits where masses of aloes grow. At 12,5 km there is a turn-off (R325) to the mouth of the Gourits River 38 km away, and, 2 km further on, a turn-off for 34 km to Kanon, the first of three coastal resorts ...

FRANSMANSHOEK, KANON AND VLEESBAAI

These resorts owe their names to the visits (of varying fortune) made by three ships. On 11 September 1763 the French warship *La Fortune* was wrecked during a heavy gale near the mouth of the Gourits at a place known as *Fonteintjies,* after a small freshwater fountain situated close to the beach. The rocky point projecting into the sea there is known as *Fransmanshoek* (Frenchman's corner) and is covered in vivid ochre-coloured lichen, making a striking picture with the waves breaking on its jagged rocks. A sandy area nearby is said to be the burial site for many of the drowned sailors. Several cannon from the wreck were washed up on the beach. The Reverend M Johnson of Riversdale, who had a bungalow near the mouth of the Gourits, dragged three of them away and mounted them in front of his home. These cannon gave the name of *Kanon* to the huddle of seaside bungalows which stands there today, forming the sort of fishermen's holiday resort which always looks windy even when it isn't.

Vleesbaai, which is reached by a turn-off 3 km beyond the turn-off to Kanon, consists of a fine (if exposed) bay with a sandy beach and a throng of holiday bungalows trying to stop themselves from sliding down the slope on which they have been built. The bay received its name on 8 July 1601 when two Dutch ships commanded by Paulus van Caerdon sailed along this coast searching for signs of one of the pastoral tribes who could sell them fresh meat. The local tribes were well known for their cattle trading. Because of this the Portuguese had already contributed one name, *Cape Vacca* (cape of the cows). One of the two Dutch ships, the *Hop van Holland*, put into what the crew named *Visbaai* after the fish they caught there. The second ship, the *Vereenigde Lande*, found the pastoralists and their herds in what the Dutch named *Vleesbaai* after the meat they bartered there. Through some latter-day confusion, the modern resort known as Vleesbaai has been built on the shores of Visbaai.

This stretch of the Southern Cape coast is a renowned fishing area and many spectacular catches have been made. Whales frequent the coast, coming into the bays to calve. There are large kitchen middens of sea shells, artefacts, clay pots and other bric-à-brac left there by the beachcombers and fishermen of prehistoric times. Scenically the coast is dramatic; a succession of bays and cliffs, with the Langeberge range on the northern horizon.

From the turn-off to Kanon and the other resorts the main coastal road (N2) continues for 14 km then passes a second turn-off leading to the three resorts. A further 4 km takes the road to a turn-off proceeding inland to Herbertsdale and 12 km further on, 35 km from the Gourits River bridge, the N2 coastal road reaches a turn-off to the port and holiday resort of Mossel Bay.

Chapter Eighteen
THE GARDEN ROUTE

Mossel Bay

Mossel Bay, the sixth harbour of South Africa and a major holiday resort, has a population of 43 639 with a very considerable addition in numbers during vacation periods. The town is attractively (if slightly) awkwardly) situated on cliffs and a narrow terrace between them and the sea. Cape St Blaize dominates the town with an 80 m high cliff, on the summit of which stands a lighthouse winking seductively at passing ships with a 20 000 candlepower lamp. The harbour lies below this cliff with space for fishing vessels, coasters and other small craft. Heavier vessels lie out in the roadstead and are serviced by lighters.

On 3 February 1488 the Portuguese explorer, Bartholomeu Dias, after doubling the Cape of Good Hope in a vicious storm, became the first European navigator to sail into Mossel Bay. Dias named the bay the *Angra dos Vaqueiros* (bay of the cowherds) after the African pastoralists and their herds who could be seen wandering along the shore. What the pastoralists in turn thought of the miracle before them – a sailing-ship appearing on the hitherto empty waters of the bay – is unfortunately unrecorded. Dias did try to communicate with them but a volley of stones rewarded his efforts and he sailed off on his voyage of discovery.

On 20 November 1497 Vasco da Gama reached the bay. His charts are marked with the name *Aguade de Sâo Bras* (watering-place of Saint Bras), for it was on the feast day of this saint that Bartholomeu Dias had originally visited the place. The corrupted version of this name is still retained in Cape St Blaize.

Da Gama established friendly trading relations with the African herdsmen. Thenceforth many Portuguese ships called to obtain fresh water and meat and to leave messages for other seafarers expected to pass that way. These letters and messages were often left hanging protectively in such things as old sea boots tied to the branches of a milkwood tree growing close to the fountain of fresh water which the sailors used to fill their casks. Messages were also left carved into rocks; and a cast of one of these may be seen in the local museum.

The old 'post office tree' and the little fountain, both now declared national monuments, may still be seen close to the beach. A letter-box in the shape of a navigator's boot has been erected there. Any letters posted in it receive a special post office franking. Close to the post office tree, one of the Portuguese visitors, John da Nova, in 1501 erected a small shrine. This was the first place of Christian worship in South Africa. An old pensioned-off steam locomotive, rusting away rather sadly, stands near the site.

On 4 August 1595 Cornelis de Houtman of Holland visited the bay. He named it *Mossel* (mussel) Bay from the pile of shells of that mollusc which he found on the floor of the huge open cavern (known today as Bats Cave) just below the modern lighthouse. Mussels and oysters were collected in the tidal zone along the shore by the Dutch sailors. These shellfish are still gathered each spring tide in Mossel Bay and marketed throughout Southern Africa. There is an oyster hatchery in the old aquarium building at the Point.

Over the years many ships called at Mossel Bay in search of refreshment or shelter from storms. With its rocky little island covered by seals, the bay became well-known and was marked on the early maps of the African coast as a sheltered and convenient anchorage. In 1734 the Governor of the Cape, Jan de la Fontaine, visited the bay by sea and erected there a stone beacon of possession, with the arms of the Dutch Republic and the monogram of the Dutch East India Company.

It was not until 1787, however, that the first permanent settlement was made on the site of the present town. In that year a granary was built there. In July of the following year the first shipment was made of wheat grown in the surrounding countryside. From that date Mossel Bay started to develop as a port for the Southern Cape and the Little Karoo. At first a ward of George, it became a separate magistracy on 18 March 1848. The name given to it was *Aliwal* (after the place in India where the Governor, Sir Harry Smith, had won a notable victory), but the older name of Mossel Bay proved more popular and lasting.

In the boom years of ostrich farming, some 800 000 kg of feathers were exported annually through the port. A breakwater and jetties to allow small craft to dock were built in 1912. The railway line reached Mossel Bay from Cape Town in 1905 and, although ostrich feathers no longer provide a rich export cargo, ochre, wool and fruit products still attract ships to the bay. The first submarine pipeline built on the coast of Southern Africa also allows oil tankers of considerable size to discharge into a cluster of storage tanks built in the industrial area known as the *Voorbaai* (fore bay). A vast modern development, known as Mossgas, is concerned with the refining of natural gas produced by boreholes in the seabed. There is a Mossgas information bureau close to the beach where Bartholomeu Dias landed. An exhibition there depicts the search for oil in South Africa. The Oribi Oil Field, the first to be productive off the coast of South Africa, came on stream on 12 May 1997. Situated 140 km south of Mossel Bay, it produces 5 000 barrels of oil a day, about one fifty of the total requirement of South Africa. The crude oil is refined in Cape Town.

With its equable climate, moderate rainfall of 375 mm a year, attractive scenery, beautiful beaches, natural swimming-pool in the rocks below the lighthouse, caves (such as the Tunnel Cave) and Seal Island with its 2 000 seals, Mossel Bay has always had a strong appeal to holidaymakers. Fishing and water sports are good and there are trips to Seal Island. Although Mossel Bay has developed slowly and never been fashionable in the sense of smart hotels and sophisticated entertainments, the farming community of the Southern Cape and the two Karoos have a great affection for the place. In the summer holiday season – especially around Christmas – they gather there in enormous camps. Some of the beaches, especially the ones known as *Die Bakke* (water trough) and Hartenbos, are particularly popular. The caravan parks are especially good.

There are several interesting museums in the town. They form the Bartholomeu Dias Museum complex. A replica of the original granary has been built on the foundations of the old building. This is used as an information centre for the museum complex. The original municipal and community centre built in 1858 is now the Local History Museum, with more exhibits in the original municipal office building erected in 1879. The building erected in 1901 as a grain mill is now the Maritime Museum and houses a replica of one of Bartholomeu Dias's ships, a caravel built in Portugal and sailed to South Africa as a gift from the people of Portugal at the time of the 500 year anniversary of Dias's voyage.

The original post office tree and the fountain of fresh water used by early visitors to replenish their water casks, are part of the museum complex. There is also the fine Shell Museum housed in an extension of the mill building. A cluster of Muslim graves is situated in the area.

Apart from the municipal area of Mossel Bay itself, the whole stretch of the coastline of the bay is an area of recreation and holiday resorts. The N2 coastal road is known, from Mossel Bay onwards to the Storms River bridge, as the Garden Route. It makes a grand sweep along the verges of the bay and rewards the traveller with lovely views of blue water, inviting beaches, the islet and its seals, and the majestic Outeniqua range of mountains watching serenely from the near horizon.

For the first 5 km from Mossel Bay the Garden Route is hemmed in closely between the cliffs and the shore. Past *Voorbaai* (before the bay), with its railway marshalling yard and industrial area, the coastal belt widens slightly and 6 km from Mossel Bay the road reaches the resort of ...

HARTENBOS

Named after the river on the banks of which grow the rushes of that name, *Hartenbos* is a resort particularly popular with farmers. The influx to the place of recreation-seeking humanity during the holiday season is almost unbelievable. Individuals employed in such enterprises as tea-rooms are left with a stunned expression for some weeks after the rush is over. Some 80 000 holiday-makers flock to the limited area in December and January. Most of them are farmers who habitually lead an isolated life, but enjoy a brief spell of gregarious existence, tolerating overcrowding for the sake of meeting old friends, exchanging news, lazing on a fine beach, reopening sporting rivalries, being harangued by cultural and religious leaders, watching folk-dancing in an open-air amphitheatre, and allowing opportunity for the young folk to meet one another. The ATKV (Afrikaanse Taal en Kultuurvereniging) has the management of most of the area.

There is a Voortrekker museum at Hartenbos containing interesting exhibits from the pioneer days, including some fine dioramas. It is open Mondays to Fridays from 09h00 to 16h30. Saturdays 10h00 to 12h30.

The Garden Route bridges the Hartenbos River 3,5 km from Hartenbos. From here there is a branch tarmac road swinging northwards and leading over the mountains for 80 km to Oudtshoorn by means of the spectacular *Robinson Pass*. Built by the famous Thomas Bain and opened in June 1869, this pass was named after M R Robinson, the Commissioner of Roads. The pass carries the branch road 838 m above sea-level from Mossel Bay and rewards the traveller with wonderful views. At Ruiterbos on the southern slopes of the pass is the Eight Bells Mountain Inn.

Four kilometres beyond the Hartenbos River the Garden Route crosses the Little *Brak* (brack) River and passes through another popular holiday resort with numerous shacks and bungalows and a pretty little beach at the mouth of the river which gives the area its name.

Ten kilometres beyond Little Brak River the Garden Route reaches the Great Brak River with its holiday resort, lagoon and beach. About this area there is an interesting tale ...

GREAT BRAK RIVER

Apart from being a picturesque resort with a cluster of bungalows built on a low island in the lagoon of the Great Brak River, this area will always be associated with the name of one man.

When the first bridge was built across the river, its construction had to be financed by means of a toll. The keeping of the toll was put out for tender in 1859. The successful tenderer was Charles Searle who had emigrated to South Africa the previous year and, with his family, was staying near George with his brother.

Searle settled next to the bridge on the farm known as *Voorbrug,* operated the toll, built a store, and gradually acquired 1 713 ha of choice land. In 1875 he started a water-mill and two years later a wool washer. In 1884 he sold the growing business to his sons and two years later a beginning was made with a boot and shoe factory, employing only two men. The following year a tannery was opened and soon a village, whose inhabitants were nearly all dependents of the Searle enterprise, grew up at Great Brak River. Searle's Limited became one of the best-known shoe and boot manufacturers in Southern Africa. The present population of Great Brak River is 7 351.

The original Great Brak village is at the north end of the estuary. It has a pleasant village character, with well kept, attractive and interesting old buildings. It has gardens, trees, vegetable plots, horses and farm animals.

On the north-eastern edge of the village Watsons Shoe Factory was founded by the Searle family in 1886, where many of the local inhabitants were employed. A retail Watson's shoe shop was opened in the centre of the village next to the factory.

There is a hiking trail along the river to the top of the wall of Wolwedans Dam. At the start one passes the attractive new municipal buildings on the river's edge, Pine Creek holiday chalet and caravan resort and the Boat Builder. Along the river which runs in a deep gorge of indigenous trees is the hydro-electric plant which supplied electricity to Great Brak River from 1924 to 1973. It is now linked into Eskom and can still give its small contribution.

Around the lagoon and its surrounding beaches are numerous bed and breakfast establishments and two caravan and camping resorts. On the sea front from the mouth of the river, a sandy beach stretches 10 km to the wreck at Glentana in the east and 20 km to Mossel Bay yacht club in the west. There are excellent hiking trails.

Near the mouth at the southern end of the estuary is the Island which is connected to the eastern shore of the estuary by a single lane bridge. On the dunes to the east of the mouth lies Hersham and to the west lies Southern Cross, with many holiday homes of timber frame structure which characterises the area. Whales and their calves are frequently seen between May and September.

From the Great Brak River village there is a gravel road (the original road) leading to George. From this road there is a most beautiful drive leading to the forestry station of Jonkersberg and the Ernest Robertson Dam which supplies water to Mossel Bay. A permit to visit the dam is necessary and is obtainable from the Mossel Bay municipality. It is worth the trouble. The road was constructed in the 1840s by Henry Fancourt White and it provides a magnificent scenic drive.

In 1745 the Great Brak River was determined to be the eastern boundary of the Cape Colony. East of the river was the wilderness of Africa.

From the Great Brak River bridge the Garden Route climbs above the coastal strip. With a lingering view behind of Mossel Bay and Cape St Blaize and an exciting glimpse up the coast of beaches, bays and cliffs, the road twists inland. For the loss of the seascape the traveller is compensated by handsome panoramic views of the whole length of the Outeniqua range.

The traveller is now in a different world – a higher terrace about 250 m above the sea. The change in scene is so remarkable that few can disagree with the description given of it in the 1780s by the French traveller, Le Vaillant: *'We had to climb a very difficult and very steep mountain. The scenery which now appears richly rewarded all our trouble. The land bears the name Outenikwa, which in the Hottentot tongue means "a man laden with honey". The flowers grow there in millions, the mixture of pleasant scents which arises from them, their colour, their variety, the pure and fresh air which one breathes there, all these make one stop and think Nature has made an enchanted abode of this beautiful place'.*

The Garden Route leads across this amiable landscape, crossing such torrents as the Gwayang and the *Maalgat* (whirlpool) rivers. Several branch roads tempt the traveller to turn off and explore the surrounding countryside. Eight kilometres from Great Brak River a road branches off south (right) down to the coastal resort of Glentana. This is a fine 7 km long drive descending steeply to the coast and yielding impressive views of Mossel Bay. There is a pleasant beach at Glentana, the usual collection of bungalows and, about 1 km up the coast, the wreck (visible at low tide) of a 120 m long floating dock which came to grief there in a howling gale while being towed to Durban in October 1902. The crew escaped but the brand-new dock was a total loss.

Seventeen kilometres from Great Brak River there is another turn-off south (right), leading for 7,5 km along a tarmac road to the pretty little bay known as ...

HEROLD'S BAY

Named after the Reverend Tobias Herold of George, *Herold's Bay* is set in the steep cliffs with a collection of bungalows looking down on a safe swimming-beach. Paths lead along the coast to such fishermen's vantage-points as Voëlklip and Skotsebank, and it is altogether a pleasant and intimate little resort.

From the turn-off to Herold's Bay the Garden Route continues its pleasant way past the George airport and then, 27,5 km from Great Brak River, reaches a turn-off to the town of ...

GEORGE

George, with its population of 93 814, is one of the great junctions on the N2 Garden Route, for it not only lies next to this wonderful coastal trunk road, but is the terminal for the important N12 road leading over the Outeniqua Pass to the Little Karoo and Beaufort West with, branching off it, the N9 road leading to the Long Kloof and north across the Great Karoo.

In a setting of great natural beauty, 226 m above sea-level on the plateau terrace between the Outeniqua range and the sea, George has always been admired by visitors. It can hardly help being beautiful, even though many of its lovely trees have vanished beneath the axe of a modern age which shows little inclination to replace them.

The town of George had its birth shortly after the second British occupation of the Cape. The earlier Dutch administration had already felt the need to establish an administrative centre further east than Swellendam in order to provide more effective control over this part of the Cape. The new British Governor, the Earl of Caledon, was in agreement with this need. He sent Lieutenant Collins to investigate the matter. As a result, on 12 October 1809, the Governor recommended to the Colonial Secretary that a new magistracy be established in the area of Outeniqualand.

The new district was proclaimed on 23 April 1811, and Adrianus van Kervel was appointed as the first landdrost. To Van Kervel fell the interesting task of laying out the new town known as *George Town* after the reigning King of England, George III. The first erven were presented free to six woodcutters whose labours would provide materials for the construction of the town.

York, Meade and Courtenay streets were the first to be laid out. The landdrost decreed their width to be 91 m. Trees had to be planted on both pavements *'not only for ornament but for defending passengers from the scorching rays of an almost vertical sun'*.

With plentiful supplies of amber-coloured water, good soil, and an amiable climate, gardens flourished in the town. It became a place of flowers, with the beautiful Outeniqua Mountains providing a background to a middle distance of green forest and a foreground of every flower colour imaginable.

In 1837 George Town became a municipality. The 'town' part of the name fell out of use and it became more simply known as George. The growth of the town was leisurely. It was an administrative outpost, a staging post for travellers proceeding east, and a centre for the timber-cutting industry in the surrounding forests. Mine props, railway sleepers, hardwood for furniture and softwood for boxes, all came from the George area. The industry was at first parasitic, trees simply being cut down. In 1896, however, a nursery was established at Witfontein for the purpose of re-afforestation. From then on, considerable planting of trees began around George, mainly exotic softwoods such as pines.

The railway line from Cape Town reached George on 25 September 1907 and was carried on over the mountains to Oudtshoorn by means of seven tunnels, involved cuttings and steep gradients. The picturesque branch line through the coastal lake country to Knysna was opened in 1928.

Dairy farming, the growing of hops for beer-making (first started by a man named Stietz in 1829) and vegetables are the principal agricultural products of the George district.

Close to George the London Missionary Society in 1813 established a station named *Pacaltsdorp* after the Reverend Charles Pacalt, the German missionary who founded it.

At Saasveld, 8 km east of George, is South Africa's training centre for foresters. It was established in 1932 and is housed in a handsome building with furnishings and woodwork made of a large variety of indigenous timber.

George is famous for its wild flowers. The scarlet lily or George lily (*Cyrthanthus purpureus*) is unique to the area, while proteas, ericas, watsonias and the *Gladioli splendor* cover the mountain slopes with carpets of colour.

The George Museum, which owes its creation to a public-spirited resident, Mr C O Sayers, is housed in the old drostdy where its large collections are well displayed. One of its most interesting exhibits is a collection of old phonographs, many still in working order.

OUTENIQUA PASS

An all-tarmac road (N12) from George climbs over the Outeniqua range, giving access to routes on the northern side into the Little Karoo, the R9 into the Great Karoo, and R62 through the Long Kloof to link up with the N2 road near Humansdorp. It is a magnificent alternative to the coastal road.

From its start in the town of George, the road confronts the massive mountain barrier of the Outeniqua. For 3,5 km the road leads westwards below the face of the range, searching for a gap through which to pass. Deciding that the only course to choose is the bold one of climbing directly over the barrier, the road sweeps northwards, passing the Witfontein forestry station, the gravel turn-off signposted Montagu Pass, and a turn-off to the village of *Blanco* (white), originally the construction camp of Henry Fancourt White (after whom it is named). He was the engineer who built the Montagu Pass. The road then ascends by means of the Outeniqua Pass one of the most majestic road passes on the continent of Africa. Six kilometres up this pass there is a viewsite with a parking bay and a toposcope built on a vantage-point and identifying various interesting parts of the countryside. This is a fitting place to pause awhile and learn something of the Outeniqua range and its remarkable road and rail passes.

The *Outeniqua* Mountains were named after the tribe who formerly lived there. This pleasant name actually means 'the people laden with honey'. They used to remove rich stores of honey from the hives of the swarms of bees flourishing on the nectar of the wild flowers growing on the mountain slopes.

The range, rising to 1 579 m on George Peak, serves as the barrier between the coastal terrace and the unique world of the Little Karoo, the basin which acts as an intermediate step to the central South African plateau. The problem of crossing the barrier of the Outeniqua has provided travellers and road builders with no little exertion.

The first Europeans to cross this range consisted of a party led by Izaak Schryver. Hykon, then chief of the Inkwa tribe living near the modern town of Aberdeen, had sent messengers to Cape Town in 1687 offering to trade. The result of this was Schryver's expedition. In January 1689 he led his men over the mountains, following an ancient elephant path through what was known as Attakwa's Kloof after the tribe of that name who once lived at its foot on the seaward side.

Attakwa's Kloof remained for years the regular pass over the Outeniqua. It lay just to the west of the modern Robinson Pass in the area of the Ruiterbos forestry station. It has now reverted to an overgrown and forgotten track.

A second pass over the Outeniqua lay east of George. This climbed the slopes of the 1 113 m high *Duiwelsberg* (devil's mountain) and descended the northern slopes of the Outeniqua into the Long Kloof. This old pass, known as the Duiwelskop Pass, with its splendid scenery, like Attakwa's Kloof, is no longer used but provides a fascinating walk for those energetic enough to follow its route from the modern forestry settlement of Bergplaas.

The third pass over the Outeniqua was built in 1812 after the establishment of George. This pass, known as *Cradock* Pass in honour of the Governor, Sir John Cradock, was built by the first magistrate of George, Adrianus van Kervel. It was an appalling 8 km long climb. From the viewsite at the toposcope on the Outeniqua Pass it is easy to see the route that the Cradock Kloof Pass follows. Its course is clearly marked by whitewashed cairns erected during the time of the Voortrekker Centenary in 1938. The pass climbs steeply up a shoulder of the mountain, crosses the railway line in a clump of trees and then rises in a fierce gradient to the summit. This was a dreadful pass. From the time it was built travellers' complaints about it were incessant. It was described as fit only for baboons.

The fourth pass over the Outeniqua range was the *Montagu Pass*, opened in 1847 as a replacement for Cradock Pass. This pass is still in use and may also be seen from the toposcope on the Outeniqua Pass. Its gravel surface seems to curve like a yellow-brown cobra up the valley immediately east of the viewsite. The pass was named after John Montagu, Colonial Secretary of the Cape in the 1840s, whose enthusiasm for good roads resulted in the first ambitious programme of road construction in Southern Africa. The old toll-house still stands at the foot of this pass. The ruins of a blacksmith's shop may be seen half-way up the pass where it was built to repair vehicles damaged in the difficult mountain passage. The original toll fees for users of Montagu Pass were 3d a wheel, 1d for each animal drawing a vehicle, and 2d for any other animal. The pass was built by Henry Fancourt White, an experienced road engineer recruited from Australia. After the building of the pass, Henry Fancourt White remained in the area as a road inspector. In 1849 he built a beautiful home in *Blanco* (white), the village named after him. The house was named *Fancourt*. Later financial depression ruined him. He lost his property and died poor. His son Montagu White, however, made money on the Witwatersrand and bought *Fancourt*. He restored it to full glory with a magnificent garden. In this setting Montagu White staged a party in 1916. He and his guests feasted on mushrooms and all died of poisoning. Dr Krynauw, a retired neurologist, purchased the property in 1939 and he made it one of the showplaces of the Garden Route.

The railway pass is also known as the Montagu Pass. It provides train travellers with a journey never to be forgotten. It was opened on 6 August 1913 after three years of difficult construction. From George to the summit at Topping the pass is 24 km long. It passes through eight tunnels and climbs 516 m at a ruling gradient of 1-in-36 compensated. From Topping it descends 146 m over 10 km to reach the basin of the Little Karoo.

The modern Outeniqua Pass which carries the tarmac road over the mountains was located by P A de Villiers, the National Road Board's location engineer who will always rank as one of the great road builders of South Africa. Its whole conception and execution – bold and majestic – ensures its status as one of the world's grandest road passes and makes it a pleasure to see.

The summit (799 m above sea-level) is reached 14 km from George, 10 km from the foot of the pass. The altitude of George is 226 m above sea-level. From the summit of the Outeniqua Pass the road descends into a fertile valley so full of fruit farms that it resembles the bounteous harvest basket of Ceres. Having descended, 10,5 km from the summit (24,5 km from George), the road reaches the northern foot of the pass. At this point the N9 road turns off eastwards and leads through the northern foothills of the Outeniqua Mountains down the long fertile valley between this range and the mountains known as the *Kammanassie* from the original *T'Kami 'Nasi* (the place of perennial water). The scenery is impressive, the tarmac road excellent. The valley becomes increasingly fertile as the road travels further eastwards. Fruit stalls sell the seasonal produce of the valley, including the aromatic honey bush tea grown in the mountains, sold from the stall at the junction of the Uniondale–Long Kloof roads.

Seven and a half kilometres from the turn-off from the N12 road to Oudtshoorn, the original gravel road turns off to George over Montagu Pass. At 72 km from the N12 turn-off the N9 road reaches an important division. The N12 veers north-eastwards to Uniondale (see Chapter Sixteen). The branch R62 leads eastwards for 12 km to Avontuur and thence down the great fruit producing valley of the Long Kloof. Avontuur is a rural centre and terminus of the narrow-gauge railway running down the Long Kloof and popularly known as the Apple Express (see Chapter Twenty).

THE SEVEN PASSES ROAD

The prodigious difficulties encountered by road engineers in the building of the N2 coastal trunk road between Cape Town and Durban are perfectly illustrated by the complex stretch of country between George and Knysna. Here, between the mountains and the sea, there is a narrow belt of country averaging 24 km in width. It consists of a plateau terrace at the foot of the mountains, falling sharply to a narrow coastal belt of lakes and lagoons. The terrace is deeply bisected by the gorges and ravines of successive streams and rivers and, to add to these formidable barriers, the well-watered landscape with a rainfall of up to 2 540 mm a year on the mountains – is densely wooded with luxuriant primeval high forests, tangles of shrubbery and such masses of wild flowers, erica's and creepers as to justify fully its description as the garden of South Africa.

To appreciate fully the difficulties of the road engineers and the way they surmounted them, take (before following the great highway of today) the earlier alternative route known as the Seven Passes Road, which was the first link between George and Knysna. This gravel road is maintained in excellent condition. It feeds several important forestry stations as well as providing tourists with a fascinating and leisurely scenic drive.

The Seven Passes road branches off from the modern Garden Route (N2) 3 km outside George. It immediately leads into difficult road-makers' country with a 3 km long descent into the valley of the Swart (black) River. In former times this descent was a nightmare. The first wagon track simply slithered almost straight into the valley. With their wheels *remmed* (braked with blocks), the wagons wore the road into a channel more than 2 m deep and so narrow that a man could not pass between the banks and the sides of the vehicle. Down this chute the wagons went with a loud cracking of whips by the drivers to warn any travellers not to start coming up in the other direction. A first-class disaster would occur if two wagons encountered each other on the pass.

This hazardous pass and the rest of the pioneer road to the east became so notorious that eventually, in 1861, a select committee was set up to investigate the matter. As a result work at last began in 1867, on the first properly made road between George and Knysna. The famous Thomas Bain had the task of locating and constructing the new road. The Seven Passes Road followed today is substantially his work. He must have had a fascinating and energetic time sorting out the difficulties of the route, and a great deal of satisfaction in seeing it completed.

Across the Swart River there is a shady picnic site. The road then rises for 3 km through the forest to the level of the plateau where, against a magnificent background of the Outeniqua Mountains, stand the gates of Saasveld, the college for the Department of Forestry. There, in a delightful environment, the young foresters of South Africa receive their training. *Saasveld* takes its name from the ancient castle in Holland, the original seat of the ancestors of the Van Reede van Oudtshoorn family. Baroness Gesina E J van Reede van Oudtshoorn became the wife of E Bergh, Civil Commissioner of George, and owned a portion of the ground on which Saasveld now stands.

This ridge was originally occupied by a farm with the rather lowly name of *Pampoenkraal* (pumpkin corral), the property of Barend Stander, a man fortunately renowned for his hospitality. He was often called upon to extend this courtesy because, 1,5 km east of his farm, the road descends to the crossing of the *Kaaimans* (leguaan's) River. The leguaan is a species of monitor lizard growing to over one metre in length. The road now makes an easy descent but, before the engineering of Thomas Bain, it required the labours of 32 oxen to effect a wagon crossing of the murderous gradients. The river torrent often ran so wild that travellers were delayed for days on end. The notorious *Kaaimansgat* (leguaan's hole) near which the old road found its fording place was reputedly a mermaid's pool haunted by water spirits.

No sooner is the road across the Kaaimans River than it has to cross the Silver River in a pretty pass. Then it climbs 1,5 km to a crossroads at a little rural post office and store known as Ginnesville, 14 km from George. From here a road known as White's Road branches down to the coast at Wilderness.

Beautiful farms, such as *Woodifield* and *Pieter-Koen* (Jan Pieter Koen, grandson of a famous director of the Dutch East India Company, settled here in the 1750s), may be seen on either side of the road. *Barbierskraal* (barber's corral) is another old name in this area where a foreman labouring to improve the original track swore that he would not shave until the task was achieved. It is on record that he grew an uncommonly long beard.

Six kilometres east of Ginnesville the road traverses another thickly wooded river valley, this time the valley of the river nowadays known as the *Touw,* said to be a corruption of the original African name, *Krakede Kau* (maiden's ford). A picturesque river pass today, it was a fearsome toil for the oxen before Bain relocated the road. Right on its eastern summit a tarmac road branches off to Wilderness while the gravel road veers left and continues across another of the plateau segments of this terraced country.

Six kilometres further on (26 km from George) the road reaches the turn-off to the forest stations of Woodville, Bergplaas and Kleinplaat. If you have the time, it is worth turning aside here. For 16 km the road burrows through the forest right up close to the mountains where the forestry settlements of Bergplaas and Kleinplaat lie. From here the energetic can follow the original road, now quite disused, which gave up the struggle with the river crossings and made its way over the mountains via the pass known as *Duiwelskop* (devil's peak) and descended on the northern side of the range into the Long Kloof. This was the route all the early travellers took, including Sir Harry Smith on his 950 km six-day ride to reach Grahamstown when news spread to Cape Town that the Xhosa had invaded the Eastern Cape.

One and a half kilometres before Woodville there is a turn-off north leading to an enormous yellowwood tree, 600 years old, 31 m high with a girth of 9 m.

Bain pushed his own new road due east over all obstacles. Across the valley of the Diep or Swart River, he found a way past Lancewood (34 km from George) across to Hoogekraal valley, over the plateau where the Karatara forestry station and the rehabilitation settlement of the Department of Health Services and Welfare are situated. The name *Karatara* is said to come from an African name meaning the hill of horses. Down and up the sides of the shady valley of the Karatara River the road goes past the forestry centres of Barrington (where Henry Barrington had his farm) and Farleigh. Then, winding, climbing and falling through forests, plantations, wild flowers and fields of erica, with cottages peeping from the wayside, their chimneys smoking contentedly, the road (42 km from George) comes to the deep and beautifully wooded valley of the *Homtini* (the place of the difficult passage).

Bain completed the Homtini Pass in 1882. It is a classic piece of old-time road-making, with dramatic views and the indefinable elegance of its curves. The river itself is a gorgeous torrent of amber water, tumbling down from the deep forests of the mountain slopes to the north.

All travellers along this road should turn aside at some stage in their journey and drive into the primeval high forest. An excellent opportunity occurs 1,5 km beyond the east summit of the Homtini Pass. Here, just where the tarmac starts, there is a road branching off to the *Goudveld* (gold-field) forestry station. The intriguing name is itself an invitation. Take this side road.

The entrance to the forestry station lies 1,5 km from the start of the turn-off. Drive in through the arch and secure a permit from the forester (during normal working hours only). Continue past the forestry offices across the grid and into the forest. A most entrancing drive runs along a good gravel track which tunnels through the tall indigenous trees. After 3 km there is a junction. Take the Jubilee track to the left. A thick carpet of ferns covers the verges of the road and the trees meet overhead. Another 3 km further on, a sign directs the traveller to the left for 1,5 km down a track to a picnic site on the banks of an exquisite little stream known as Forest creek. Here gold was prospected in former times, and a faint 'tail' of yellow dust can still be found in a pan today if you try your luck.

The track continues across the creek for 1,5 km to Natbos, where there is a picnic site in the shade of a gigantic 400-year-old yellowwood tree, and then ends at another picnic site at Droërug.

Back on the main track, continue out of the indigenous forest through a plantation. After 3 km the road reaches the forestry settlement of Millwood. Here in the late 1880s there was a bustling town of prospectors and gold-diggers. One thousand men rushed into this sylvan area in 1886 when alluvial gold was found in several of the streams by an inspector of roads, C F Osborne. On 6 August 1886 John Courtney found reef gold in the overlooking hills and excitement reached a fine pitch. By the end of 1887 the town of Millwood had 7 hotels, 25 shops, 3 banks, 7 butchers, 4 bakers, a police station, post office, 3 newspapers and 40 mining syndicates. About 400 people lived in the town, while 600 prospectors searched for gold in the forest. Machinery was brought in; adits, shafts and trenches were dug. The sound of dynamite explosions rumbled incessantly through the trees. Now nothing remains. One has to search and scramble to find the foundations of the houses, the rusty machinery, the caved-in excavations. The gold was there, but only enough to tantalise. The prospectors went broke. The ericas, the trees, the wild flowers and mountains reclaimed their own. All that is left today is the ghost of a vanished town. In the cemetery there are over 100 graves.

The Oudtshoorn Mine was the most promising venture on the Millwood field. When it proved a failure, the spirit went out of the rush. Millwood was so named after an overshot sawmill waterwheel originally run there by a Mr Franzen.

Back on the main Seven Passes Road (now tarmac), pass the forestry centre of Rheenendal. For 6 km continue over a fertile plateau with many fine views of the mountains and the long belt of forest. Then the road reaches a turn-off. The tarmac road sweeps on to Keytersnek and Knysna, 13 km away. The Seven Passes Road proper reverts to a gravel surface and turns sharply left. For 3 km it descends steeply down the *Phantom Pass* (so named after the phantom moths common there), rewarding the traveller with charming views of the delightfully green and completely rural valley of the Knysna River lying below. From the bottom of the pass the road runs for a further 5 km along the banks of the river and then joins the modern N2 coastal road just before it bridges across the upper end of the Knysna Lagoon (82 km from George by the Seven Passes Road).

By modern standards this old road is quite inadequate, except for sightseeing. When the modern road came to be built, P A de Villiers – the location engineer – abandoned the plateau terrace entirely. He boldly took the road from George straight down to the sea, blasting and cutting a spectacular route through country totally impassible to the old-time engineers. In the process of this construction a classic example was presented of the changes which can be brought to an area by a new road. The whole coastal stretch from George to Knysna was completely transformed by this road. From a remote wilderness of bush and lake it developed within a few years of the coming of the road into a lotus land of pleasure and recreation, with a considerable industry in hotels, motels and caravan parks.

From George the N2 coastal road (the Garden Route) descends steadily to the coast. Passing after 3 km the turn-off to the Seven Passes Road and, 5 km further on, the turn to Victoria Bay, the road crosses the Swart River and sweeps downwards, revealing some of the finest road making in Southern Africa. The view here has given delight to countless travellers. In all the world there can be few more serenely beautiful scenes of river and coast. Here the dark amber-black waters of the Kaaimans and the Swart Rivers merge and, with a great tidal ebb and flow, make their way down a deep valley to the sea.

VICTORIA BAY

Victoria Bay, 3 km from the turn-off by a tarred road, is worth seeing. It consists of a small bathing beach set in a tiny bay from which there is clearly no exit by land at either end. A row of seaside houses, a small concrete pier, a tea-room and caravan park make up the amenities. In the 1840s there was a project to turn this little bay into a landing harbour. There are several places of accommodation in the vicinity, mostly higher up at the main road. It is considered to be one of the best surfing areas of Southern Africa. During the winter months some very big waves work this part of the coast.

All land masses with shores exposed to deep water have surf but the waves are not always entirely suitable for the sport of surfing. Southern Africa possesses several beaches where conditions are ideal or almost ideal for surfing. Surfers regard as perfect a wave which breaks sufficiently early and far from the shore to give them a long run and provide the chance of trying out manoeuvres and skills. A big wave breaking too near the shore is spectacular to see but useless for surfing. The waves must be powerful, with all the muscle and weight of a heavy swell, having a wall at least 3 m to 5 m high and the ability summarily to 'wipe out' or 'dump' a surfer, thereby making the ride high and wild, taxing his stamina, skill and experience. The surfer does not compete with the wave; he wishes to harmonise with its movement, stealing some of its power to carry him along. He cannot fight such a wave; he can only ride it to the point of tolerance. If its power exceeds his capacity, he will be 'wiped out', his board broken, and he will possibly have the nasty experience of being unceremoniously dumped on the rocks or beach.

The isolated volcanic islands of Hawaii (the home of surfing) rise abruptly from the tremendous depths of the Pacific Ocean. They are exposed to waves originating from a variety of disturbances. Huge seismic waves originate from earthquakes; so-called *tsunami* waves are caused by earth movement on the bed of the sea, while the complex play of wind on water over the huge expanse of the Pacific Ocean produces waves of prodigious power.

Waves emanating from such disturbances can travel for immense distances without losing much energy. As they finally approach a land mass, they come under the influence of the shallowing sea bed. Wildly undisciplined in the outer ocean, the waves travel at speeds varying from 25 km to 32 km an hour. As the water shallows, they are braked from below by the rising sea bed. The crest eventually falls forward over its own base, the power of the wave is broken and it expires on the beach.

The principal surfing beaches of Southern Africa are at Elands Bay on the south-west coast of the Western Cape Province, where the south-east winds of summer produce a heavy swell; Chapman's Bay on the Cape Peninsula, where the summer south-easter produces some giant waves at Long Beach and De Hoek; Muizenberg and Kalk Bay, where the north-westerly wind of winter produces small but lively waves; Victoria Bay; the celebrated St Francis Bay, and Nahoon at East London, where a very consistent reef wave of great power breaks.

Just beyond the Kaaimans River bridge (a handsome curved concrete structure), a somewhat inconspicuous gravel turn-off on the right leads down to a place ideal for riverside picnics, and providing access to a handful of houses on the opposite bank. The Kaaimans River is a pleasure for canoeists, and the waterfall up the course of the Swart River can only be seen from such a craft.

The N2 road follows the east bank of the river, rising steadily as it nears the sea. The branch railway from George to Knysna crosses the mouth of the river by means of a bridge, after making its own spectacular descent to the coast through tunnels and cuttings. Countless photographers must have paused at this point in the hope of seeing a train crossing the bridge. The Outeniqua Choo-Tjoe (as it is called) runs between George and Knysna twice daily except on Sundays and certain public holidays. To check operating times and make reservations, phone (044) 382-1361.

This branch railway, built in 1928, has a 30,4 km route which the puffers take about two and a half hours to complete. It is a highly diverting journey and a most enjoyable alternative way of seeing the lake country.

The coastal road now swings sharply around a shoulder of the cliff. Ahead and below stretches one of the loveliest views imaginable of seascape and forest-covered downland. The road descends to sea-level and 13 km from George reaches ...

WILDERNESS

Wilderness had its start on 16 January 1877 when George Bennet purchased for £500 what was known as Lot 497 (H), originally surveyed in 1850 by M J Adams. Bennet decided that his purchase should have a name and called it what it was: a wilderness of dense forest and bush falling from the interior right down to the edge of the lagoon of the Touw River.

The area having no road access of any kind, Bennet constructed a rough track down from the Seven Passes Road and built a homestead on the site of the modern luxury hotel. There he lived until his death, the property passing into the hands of his widow's second husband in 1886. In May 1905 the property was acquired by The Wilderness Estate Company (Montagu White and Associates) who divided it into plots, built a new road (White's Road) to provide access and converted the farmhouse into a boarding-house run by Hannie and Alida van Niekerk.

The venture did not prosper. In 1921 the estate was auctioned. A new company, The Wilderness (1921) Ltd, took over, with one of the directors, Owen Grant, later acquiring sole ownership. With some genius he converted the farmhouse-cum-boarding-house into the beginning of the renowned Wilderness hotel. Plots were sold and the modern resort came into being. With its beautiful (but dangerous) beach, spacious lagoon, superb boating river and magnificent scenery, Wilderness is today one of the finest of all South African resorts.

There is a small nature reserve, entered from the road at the right-hand side of the Wilderness hotel, in which a footpath leads up one side of a thickly wooded valley and back to the starting-point, with three sign posted alternatives, each a little longer than the preceding one. This is the haunt of many of the area's birds and is a recommended excursion.

From Wilderness the N2 road continues in a fine drive which runs along the narrow strip between the sea and the chain of lakes; the Langvlei, Rondevlei, Swartvlei and Groenvlei. Oddly enough, each of these beautiful little lakes has the reputation of being haunted. Groenvlei, with its greenish waters is reputedly a particular haunt of water spirits who can be heard singing as they float on the surface in the light of the moon. Bushman paintings in several caves in the Outeniqua mountains and Little Karoo, strangely enough, depict women with fish tails, so the legends date from a long time ago. Ghostly carts with horses are also said to have been seen galloping across the waters of this still and peaceful little lake. All these lakes have resorts on their banks. Any ghosts present certainly do not interfere with the pleasures of boating, yachting, swimming and fishing.

The main lake is Rondevlei which forms part of a nature conservation research station, the buildings of which stand on the eastern shore. All the lakes are saline to varying degrees. Rondevlei is fifteen parts per thousand saline in content. Swartvlei is the deepest of the lakes, averaging around 6 m. The water of all the lakes is rich in food and fish flourish – especially the smaller species which have found a sanctuary for themselves where there are no predatory fish and only a few otters with the numerous birds which feed in the calm waters.

Swartvlei is best for fishing with steenbras, grunter and harder in its waters. Groenvlei is good for bass. About 160 species of birds frequent the lakes. They explore the surrounding coastal terrace for food by day and return to the trees around the lakes at night. A rich symphony of calls and songs provides an accompaniment to the kaleidoscopic changes of dawn and sunset. The chorister robins of the area seem to act as the prima donnas.

Eilandsvlei, Langvlei and Rondevlei are connected to the sea by a natural channel known as The Serpentine which joins the rivers at Ebb and Flow to feed the lagoon at Wilderness. Canoeing through The Serpentine or up the Touw and Ebb and Flow is a delightful experience, for the river valleys are natural wildlife sanctuaries, with glorious trees and such singing of birds that the verdant valleys resemble the entrance to paradise.

Thirteen and a half kilometres from Wilderness, the Garden Route (N2) reaches the turn-off to the nature conservation office at Rondevlei and to several holiday resorts on the shores of the lakes.

From this turn-off to Rondevlei, the coastal road continues eastwards for 1 km and then bridges across Swartvlei. A further 2 km of pleasant driving along the coastal terrace brings the road (16,5 km from Wilderness) to the village of ...

SEDGEFIELD

Sedgefield has a happy inactivity as its most considerable industry. It is an ideal place in which to relax. It is the centre for several holiday resorts situated on the lakes and sea coast. The coast is reached by a tarmac turn-off from the N2 Garden Route as it passes through the village. The turn-off follows the verge of Swartvlei and leads to a pleasant assembly of seaside houses overlooking a sandy beach. Just before crossing the bridge to the coastal resort, there is a gravel turn-off signposted Swartvlei. This passes the caravan park and camping ground and then climbs the dunes to end at a sort of belvedere overlooking a wide bay with its right arm ending in a barren crag named Gerickespunt, accessible only on foot at low tide. Notwithstanding this inconvenience, the point is a fishing harbour, with several boats generally resting on the beach. In an easterly direction, the beach extends smooth and level past the estuary of Swartvlei all the way to Buffels Bay.

Four kilometres east of Sedgefield the main N2 coastal road reaches the fresh water lake known as *Groenvlei* (green marsh) or Lake Pleasant. This beautiful lake is in a delightful setting and its charms were well appreciated by a discerning flock of swans which used to live there permanently, breeding in the beds of reeds and providing a pretty spectacle as they cruised over the calm waters. They are no longer in residence but perhaps will some day return. Black bass and bluegill fish abound in the lake. For the bird-watcher there are many interesting scenes and studies in this area. A canoe allows for exploration of the lake, with opportunities for photographing the nests of birds which live in the reeds. Sunset on the lake is often very lovely.

Beyond Lake Pleasant the coastal road continues for 2 km, then passes a turn-off to Karatara (see the Seven Passes Road). A further 9 km of driving through a natural garden brings the road to the Goukamma River. A tarmac turn-off leads for 6 km to the resort of Buffels Bay and the ...

GOUKAMMA NATURE RESERVE

This reserve was created by the Cape Provincial Administration to protect a characteristic area of the coastal dunes and the bird sanctuary of the *Goukamma* (river of Hottentot figs). It contains some of the highest vegetated dunes in South Africa and includes Groenvlei Lake which has no in-flowing river nor any link with the sea.

The reserve offers a number of hiking trails for which one can obtain a permit on arrival. There are also a few self-catering units for visitors wishing to stay for a few days – bookings should be made in advance. Angling and boat licences for Groenvlei are obtainable at the reserve's office. To book accommodation, contact the Manager of the Goukamma Nature and Marine Reserve at P O Box 331, Knysna, 6570. Phone and fax (044) 383-0042 or (044) 343-1855.

Once in possession of a permit, a member of the public has access to several attractive nature trails. The adventurous visitor may continue through the whole reserve, to emerge at Groenvlei at the Lake Pleasant hotel.

The entire area is a good place to see waterbirds. The commoner ones and those most likely to be seen by the casual walker are the Egyptian goose, yellowbill duck, blacksmith plover, both the Cape and water dikkops, crowned plover and black-backed gull. There are three species of kingfisher (the pied, giant and brown hooded). The black Cape raven is a common sight. In the bush there are many greater double-collared sunbirds, red-winged starlings and Cape canaries. More than 200 species of birds have been recorded.

Beyond the turn-off to the nature reserve the tarmac road continues for 3,5 km to the small resort of Buffels Bay (Buffalo Bay) where there is a large beach café and caravan park.

Beyond the turn-off to the Goukamma Nature Reserve and Buffalo Bay, the main coastal road (N2) continues for a further 6 km, climbs a rise and then makes a grand descent to the great lagoon of Knysna. At the bridge the Seven Passes road comes in to join the N2 road. At this point there is a branch road turning off to Brenton and the pretty little church of Belvidere. This road is worth taking. The church lies 2 km from the turn-off and is surrounded by trees, the Belvidere homestead and a few creeper-covered cottages.

Belvidere church might well be regarded as a lesson in Norman (12th) century architecture to anyone who has not seen it in its native Europe. It has many of the features of the Norman style: interlaced arcading, a massive entrance arch in two orders, a round-headed chancel arch, rounded apse, and capitals based on Norman originals. The stained-glass windows are interesting, especially those in the apse, which came from the bombed ruins of Coventry Cathedral in Britain.

Belvidere was acquired in 1833 from George Rex by Lieutenant Thomas Duthie, a Scottish army officer in the Cape Town garrison. He married Rex's daughter Caroline. Belvidere House was their homestead and they built the church in the 1850s. It was consecrated on 5 October 1855. The oak trees growing around the church and homestead grew from acorns presented to the lieutenant by George Rex.

One and a half kilometres before the church, the main branch road turns sharply to the right and climbs steeply through plantations of pine and gum trees. Wild flowers and erica are in profusion, while the views are spectacular of the great lagoon of Knysna on the one side and Buffalo Bay on the other. Many varieties of erica bloom around April. After 7 km the road reaches the resort of Brenton-on Sea. *Brenton*, originally part of the famous *Melkhoutkraal* estate, was named after Sir Jahleel Brenton, the British admiral who opened Knysna harbour.

From the bridge across the upper end of the Knysna Lagoon, the Garden Route makes a handsome 6 km long drive down the northern shores to the town and holiday resort of ...

KNYSNA

Knysna is one of those places to which most people who see it say they would like to retire. Its 32 057 inhabitants live in the mildest of climates, with 762 mm of rain considerably falling mainly at night and distributed over the four seasons in order to keep the area perennially green. Its situation between the great inland forests and the shores of the tranquil lagoon, the wonderful sunsets reflecting over the waters, the Outeniqua Mountains watching from the horizon, the spectacular gateway to the sea through The Heads, are all additional attractions.

The Knysna lagoon is a rich field of study for the scientist. Its bottom varies from a deep mouth to the sea, through deep to shallow channels and mud banks further inland. Over 200 different species of fish flourish in it, including a rare species of sea-horse *Hippocampus capensis* unique to the estuaries of the Garden route.

At the lagoon end of Long Street, just past Thesen's factory, are the premises of the Knysna Oyster Company. Knysna lagoon is one of the few places on the South African coast whose water is (so far) sufficiently unpolluted to allow for such an undertaking. An area of 13 ha of the lagoon is reserved for the cultivation of oysters. Finger-nail sized baby oysters, known as spats, are imported from overseas hatcheries. For two years they are fattened and grown in plastic mesh bags attached to timber racks in the intertidal zone. Then they are harvested, cleaned and purged in fresh sea water and about 300 tons of them placed on the market each year. The Thesen's Island tavern of the oyster company offers visitors the chance to taste and buy oysters in any amount.

For anglers the Knysna estuary is one of the world's great sporting areas. The variety and number of fish, the pleasant climate, varied conditions and beauty of seascape, all combine to provide an exciting experience. There is an ample supply of bait.

The concreted road leading from Knysna around the east shores of the lagoon to The Heads, yields many handsome views. Near the end of this road a tarmac turn-off climbs to the top of the Eastern Head and terminates at Coney Glen. The views from this road (especially towards sunset) are superb. Wonderful as these views are, however, the aspect of the shore at the foot of the steep concrete road presents one of the most magnificent seascapes in South Africa. A more splendid confusion of red rocks and blue ocean can scarcely be imagined.

A puzzling thing about Knysna is the meaning of its name. It apparently originated as the African name of the river flowing into the lagoon. The original form of the name is uncertain, but it is said to have been *Zthuys Xna* (place of wood). There are several other forms of the name.

The first settlers of the Knysna area were all attracted to the place by its beauty although, once they were there, they were inclined to think that perhaps they had been lured to ruin by a siren. Almost impossible lines of communication made the area seem more difficult to get out of than into. Only a South African bullock wagon, made of the hard timber of the Knysna forests, could have survived the first dreadful track that was blazed to connect Knysna to George.

The first settlers – Van Huysteen, Van Rooyen, Jerling, Read, Meeding, Weyer, Barnard, Vosloo. Terblans and others of the days of the Dutch rule – all selected superb farms for themselves. Of these farms the finest was without doubt *Melkhoutkraal* (milkwood corral), first granted in 1770 to Stephanus Terblans. It was his farm which included the whole basin containing the Knysna lagoon.

On the death of Terblans the farm was sold by his widow in 1796 to her second husband, Johan van Lindenbaum. He resold the property to a trader, Richard Holiday, who died in 1802. Two years later the ownership of *Melkhoutkraal* was taken over by a man who will always be identified with Knysna as the real founder of the town, George Rex.

So much romance has been attached to the person of George Rex that it is interesting to learn a little about this extraordinary character whose enigmatic and forceful personality has become part of the folklore of Southern Africa. He arrived in the Cape in 1797, at the time of the first British occupation. A man of distinguished bearing, he was well educated, accomplished, intelligent, obviously well connected, but extremely taciturn.

In Cape Town, George Rex was appointed Marshal of the Vice-Admiralty Court, Notary Public to the Governor, and Advocate to the Crown. He met Johanna, the young widow of a well-to-do ships captain and merchant and settled down with her and her children.

When the British occupation ended, he remained in the Cape. In 1804, at the age of 39, he purchased the farm *Melkhoutkraal.* To reach this farm George Rex made a coach journey on a grand scale. His lady and four children rode with him in a coach bearing a coat of arms and drawn by six fine horses. Riding alongside the coach was a retinue of friends and retainers. To the awed locals the journey resembled a royal procession – even the name of the man, George Rex, conjured up images of royalty travelling incognito.

Stories spread that George Rex was the son of George III of England and the fair Quakeress, Hannah Lightfoot. Modern research does not confirm this belief and there is no record of George Rex ever having made such a claim. But his life-style and grand manner convinced the residents of the Cape, and especially those of Knysna, that the man in their midst was indeed of royal descent. His company was sought by many distinguished visitors.

At Knysna, Rex found a fellow Briton, James Callander, a retired shipwright already in residence in a home he had built near The Heads. Rex rebuilt the farmhouse of *Melkhoutkraal*, as the place had been burned down during a Xhosa raid along the coast. Rex turned it into a magnificent home known as 'the old place'. When his common-law wife Johanna died, Rex took as his second common-law wife her daughter from her original marriage. With the amiable aid of this pretty young woman, his family increased to a total of six sons and seven daughters. Edward, the eldest son, was deaf and never married. John the second son, was his father's right-hand man and considered by those who met him to be an individual of *'princely manners and conspicuous ability'.*

The daughters, mainly educated in Cape Town, were comely, made good marriages and attracted to Knysna sundry gallants such as Lieutenant Thomas Duthie who married Caroline Rex and made his home at *Belvidere* on the west side of the lagoon; Captain John Fisher Sewell, who married Maria Rex; and Mr Atkinson of Arnagh, who married Sarah Rex.

Melkhoutkraal blossomed into one of the show estates of the Cape. Gardens, water-mill, blacksmith shop, orchards, vineyards, oak trees, all flourished under the care of George Rex. The farm was expanded to cover an area of 10 125 ha, including the whole lagoon area and The Heads. On this estate Rex engaged in a variety of enterprises. He kept ostriches; his daughters spun silk from the silkworms fed on groves of mulberry trees; Rex men hunted elephants in the forests, sealed at Plettenberg Bay, cut timber, and influenced the government to develop Knysna into a port.

Knysna as a harbour seemed to be the answer to the problem of transport. It was surveyed by James Callander. The scheme was considered practical and on 11 February 1817 the naval transport brig, the *Emu,* made an attempt to enter the lagoon. Unfortunately the vessel struck a sunken rock as it entered The Heads and was damaged so badly that it became necessary to run her ashore within the entrance. Nobody was drowned. A second naval vessel, the *Podargus*, was hastily sent up from the Cape in May 1817 to rescue the stranded crew and retrieve the stores of the *Emu.* Captain Wallis of the *Podargus* accomplished his mission, sailing in and out of the lagoon, and reported so favourably on the harbour and the vast forests that the Admiralty decided to commence shipbuilding there. Rex promptly presented them with 16 ha of lagoonside land. This site, named *Melville* (after Viscount Melville, the First Sea Lord at the time of the British occupation of the Cape, and the man loved so wistfully by Lady Anne Barnard), became the scene of a great deal of labour as the hull of a large brig slowly took shape from local timber.

Unfortunately a fire seriously damaged the hull on its stocks and the project was abandoned. The site of the George Rex slipway, situated by the side of the lagoon, is marked by a pillar and is most easily visited by river. The nearest land access would be from the point where the Seven Passes road takes a sharp left-hand bend by a side road to the right, barred by a gate and 'private' notices. Doubtless the farmer would allow any serious enquirer to cross his land.

The wood from which the ship had been constructed was salvaged and part of it now forms the handsome triangular table in the council chamber of the Knysna Regional Services Council, the offices of which are in Market Street. The wide stinkwood planks have acquired a beautiful lustre through continual polishing. The table may be viewed by permission. Ask on the first floor at the enquiries counter.

Knysna, notwithstanding the set-back in shipbuilding, was established as a port. Up to the time of his death on 3 April 1839, Rex had the satisfaction of seeing 162 ships call at Knysna, with only four wrecked in the course of their visits. In 1831 Rex even launched his own 127-ton vessel, the *Knysna*. In this ship, built at Westford on the Knysna River, just below Phantom Pass, John Rex explored the coast, becoming the first to sail into the Buffalo River at East London. Fifty years after she was launched, the stout little *Knysna* was still in service carrying coal along the coast of England.

George Rex's grave may be seen close to the site of his original homestead on *Melkhoutkraal*. The turn-off from the N2 Garden Route is marked. It can also be reached by taking Assegaaiweg, about 600 m from The Heads road, but on the left-hand side. Opposite this road at two large shady trees a gravel road turns right. Take it and then turn almost immediately left to cross a deep stream, beyond which is a stone-walled enclosure sighed over by two tall pine trees. Rex's son, George junior, and his wife Jessie, are also buried there. The younger Rex family lived at *Hunter's Home*, adjoining *Melkhoutkraal*. Their house has vanished but the beautiful wood known as Ashmead, once part of their estate, survives as a holiday camp.

On the death of George Rex, his estate was fragmented amongst his thirteen children. No descendants of the male line of the Rex family remain in Knysna. One of the best known of George Rex's descendants was the late circus clown Stompie, really Wentworth Fitzwilliam Edward Dupreez, sometimes known as King Stompie from the romantic stories of his ancestor's origin. He was partner to the celebrated clown Tickey.

In 1825 the Governor, Lord Charles Somerset, decided to found a village at Knysna. Fortunately, for once he did not also name the place after himself or any of his relatives. George Rex granted 121 ha for the proposed town, while the old Admiralty dockyard of Melville was added to it in 1844.

The beauty of the situation and, perhaps, the social standing of the Rex family, made it fashionable to settle in Knysna. The Honourable Henry Barrington, younger son of Viscount Barrington, came in the 1840s and founded an estate at Portland on land bought (like Belvidere) from the Rex family. Colonel John Sutherland also came soon after the death of George Rex. When Rex's heirs fragmented the *Melkhoutkraal* estate, he purchased the old homestead. The Rex family moved to Rexford, known to them as 'the new place' closer to The Heads; and thereafter they gradually faded from the local scene. The Sutherland family laid out the township of Newhaven, now part of Knysna town, and the process of fragmenting the old Rex lands was well under way. They were divided into erven, plots, smallholdings and otherwise 'improved' (to use the jargon of estate agents).

Apart from the Rex family, another family particularly associated with Knysna is that of the Thesens. This family of twelve sailed from Norway in 1869 intending to settle in New Zealand. A storm off Cape Agulhas blew their schooner *Albatross* back to Cape Town. While there, one of the sons, Hans, sailed to Knysna on contract and reported so enthusiastically about the place that the family settled there, purchased an island in the lagoon, and on it commenced boat building and furniture manufacturing. In 1974 the business was acquired by a Johannesburg finance house, bringing to an end the long association of the family and the firm.

In its heyday Knysna as a port exported wool, timber and railway sleepers. An average year such as 1886 saw 89 vessels trading with the place. The Thesens, with their Knysna Steamship Service, had two coasters, the 635-ton *Ingerid* and the 23-ton *Agnar*, permanently on the service; and trade was flourishing.

The village became a magistracy on 29 April 1858 and a municipality in 1881, combining the areas of Melville, Eastford and Newhaven under the name of Knysna. The first railway was planned as a narrow gauge half-metre-wide line by the South Western Railway Company, which hoped to connect with the Port Elizabeth–Avontuur line. The present standard gauge was opened on 17 October 1928. The railway killed local shipping. The harbour was deproclaimed in December 1954 and a picturesque activity ended with the last pilot, Reuben Benn, fourth generation of Benns to hold that post, transferred to Port Elizabeth. The railway connects Knysna to the main line at George. With a steam puffer known as the Outeniqua Choo-tjoe it provides a delightful journey of two and a half hours through lovely scenery.

There is a museum in Knysna which, although still young, contains a wealth of material concerning the history of the town, with hundreds of old photographs of absorbing interest. A collection of George Rex items has been started. As the years pass, this will become a museum of truly national rank. It is housed in Millwood House, originally built in the mining village of Millwood.

It was later dismantled and transported to Knysna when the gold-fields were abandoned. It is a national monument.

Today Knysna is a favourite holiday resort, residential area and scene of considerable activity in the making of furniture and boats. Speculation in property and improving the natural beauty of the area by means of townships, suburbs, golf-courses, supermarkets and so on, are standard preoccupations of the population.

Across the lagoon is a glaring example of local insensitivity to the natural beauties of the site. The Heads have been ruined for all time through the haphazard building of houses over the heights of the left-hand side. This acquiescence by the authorities to the claims of profit-making has irreparably spoilt one of South Africa's most famous views by covering a noble bastion with a scattering of nondescript houses that could just as easily have been built anywhere else.

Leisure Island is another example of local development. Originally a sandy island known as Steenbok Island, it was purchased from the Duthie family in 1929 by George Cearn, a wealthy visitor to Knysna. Considered to be a crank by the locals, he built a causeway to the island, spent £500 000 and ten years in draining and laying out his treasure island, and then another ten years in selling, at substantial prices, building plots with fabulous views and a romantic atmosphere.

There are many pleasant things to do in Knysna, walking trails in the forest, viewsites, delicious sea foods, delicacies and local drinks. Knysna is well known for its honey produced in the forest, the special flavours coming from the variety of wild flowers. In 1983 Lex Mitchell started a brewery in Knysna using mainly locally grown ingredients such as hops and malt. His products have become national beverages of piquant flavour. Double-thick cream produced on *Gansvlei* farm is another local delicacy. Ham, smoked from yellowwood shavings on John Dormeyl's farm, and cheese produced in the Italian manner on *Golden Pond* farm by Ann and Frank Lamberti, provide very special delicacies.

THE KNYSNA FOREST COUNTRY

Southern Africa is notable more for its wide open spaces and savanna country than for great forests of timber trees. Such forests require, for one thing, at least 750 mm of rain a year and only limited humid areas in the country attain or exceed this annual figure. In South Africa there are 255 150 ha of indigenous forest, mainly controlled by the State, and 972 000 ha of exotic forests of plantations owned by the State and private enterprise. Altogether, therefore, only one per cent of South Africa is covered in trees, compared to 25 per cent of the United States.

Of all the indigenous forests in South Africa, the coastal forest stretching from George to near Humansdorp is the largest, covering some 40 500 ha, with a further 68 860 ha planted with exotics (pines, eucalyptus and wattle). Known as the Midland Conservancy, this forest area is 177 km long and 16 km broad, lying along the coastal terrace between the sea and the inland mountains. The indigenous areas are covered with a luxuriant mixture of tall and ancient trees, wonderful ferns, creepers and wild flowers. Animal life, as in most high forests, is limited to a few varieties of forest-dwelling antelope, numerous birds and, until recently, a lingering remnant of the herds of elephant which once frequented the area.

From the time Europeans discovered this forestry area it was ruthlessly exploited. The finest hardwood trees, 600 years old and more, were cut down to provide railway sleepers and timber for ships. It was not only mature trees which were cut, but wagon tracks were blazed to reach them, crushing literally hundreds of young trees in the course of dragging out logs and sawn timber.

An entire community of professional woodcutters derived their livelihood from the Knysna forests. Like fishermen who incessantly take and never replenish, they all firmly believed that the forest was inexhaustible. They cut at will. Government control came very late. In 1874 Captain Christopher Harison was appointed conservator, but he had limited control over the tree cutters.

In 1886 a French forester, Comte de Vasselot de Regne, was appointed by the Cape Government to investigate the state of the forests. He was appalled to find that fully three-quarters of the indigenous forest had been seriously damaged by wanton cutting. He prohibited further indiscriminate cutting and divided the forest into sections. The felling was thenceforth permitted only in specific sections of the forest, while other sections rested. Those portions of the forest which had been completely destroyed, as well as other suitable areas, were reafforested with exotics.

Notwithstanding these measures, the demand for timber continued to bring destruction to the forest. In 1913 the Forestry Department introduced fresh control measures by marking trees for destruction and these were allocated to registered woodcutters by means of the drawing of lots. The woodcutters had to pay a nominal charge for the trees and were then free to sell the timber for what they could get. It was an absurd arrangement. The woodcutters on the whole were not a particularly intelligent crowd and, left to the hazards of chance on the one hand and the hard bargaining of timber merchants on the other, their situation became increasingly miserable.

The number of woodcutters dwindled. In 1932 there were 500 of them registered. In 1939 this number had decreased to 258. Their average annual income was little more than £20 per man. The government then realised the absurdity of a situation where some of the most beautiful and majestic trees in Africa were being destroyed with no significant gain to the State. The ultimate prospect was a community of poor whites, no matter how picturesque their way of life. There was no profit to anybody save a crowd of timber dealers and speculators.

In March 1939 the Woodcutters' Annuities Bill passed its final stage in Parliament. The 258 remaining woodcutters were banned from further private work in the forests and compensated with a pension of £25 a year. Settlements were established for them and employment found in public works and in the Forestry Department. Considerable public agitation and resentment arose over this abolition of the ancient Knysna profession of woodcutting. It was, however, obvious to all except romantics that the primeval forests were simply being destroyed by a group of men whose hard work was completely misplaced in a mass destruction which rewarded them if they were lucky, with a pittance.

From 1939 onwards, trees for cutting were carefully selected by the Forestry Department and auctioned as they stood to the dealers. The ancient forests of Knysna are now solely under the control of the State. It would be a tragic day indeed if any caprice of politics once again allowed wanton destruction of one of the most beautiful and tranquil areas on Earth.

From Knysna there are several very fine drives through the forest country, while walkers will find that the loveliest scenes are reserved for them alone as a reward for their exertions. The Terblans Walk (6,5 km long) is a pleasant circular route starting and ending at the Groot Draai picnic spot. The Kranshoek Walk is 9,4 km long, with short variations. It starts at the Kranshoek picnic site.

A short but exceptionally interesting drive from Knysna starts with the gravel turn-off leading up the left bank of the Salt River, just as the N2 road enters the built-up area of Knysna. This Salt River road makes its way up the river valley and then climbs north into the overlooking hills, revealing many handsome views. At the summit there is a junction. The left-hand branch continues north over rugged country to an open plateau on which stands the Gouna forest station, from where there is a magnificent forest drive to Diepwalle on the Avontuur road. The right-hand branch swings eastwards and after 3 km of varied views reaches the Concordia forest reserve. At this point there is a branch to the right leading down the slopes to Grey Street in Knysna. The views are memorable.

The longest route through the Knysna forest country is the road to Avontuur across the Outeniqua range by means of Prince Alfred's Pass. This road starts as a tarmac turn-off from the main N2 coastal road 7 km east of Knysna on the way to Plettenberg Bay. After 1,5 km there is a gravel turn-off west leading to the Concordia forest station and linking up with the Salt River road already described. The main tarmac road leads on northwards through pine and eucalyptus plantations. After a further 3 km the tarmac ends and the gravel road enters the indigenous forest. Fourteen kilometres from the start of that road it reaches the Ysterhoutrug picnic site, considerately laid out by the Forestry Department. One and a half kilometres beyond this site there is a turn-off to the west leading for 183 m to what is known as King Edward VII Tree, one of the big trees of the forest. This one is a yellowwood, 625 years old and 39 m high from the ground to the start of its branches. The tree received its name in 1924, when Professor J F V Phillips entertained at a picnic luncheon in its shade, the visiting members of the British Empire Parliamentary Association.

The traveller is now in the main forest of Knysna, the old feeding-ground of the elephants. One and a half kilometres beyond the turn-off to King Edwards Tree there is a turn-off east to the Diepwalle forestry station.

ELEPHANTS WALK

The forestry station of *Diepwalle* (deep walls) is in the heart of the main Knysna forest. The road from Knysna to Avontuur over Prince Alfred's Pass takes the traveller past this forestry station, and it is from there that hikers commence what is known as the Elephant Walk, a circular trail of 18,2 km leading through some of the most beautifully luxuriant high forest imaginable. The walk takes about six and a half hours, with two shorter alternatives. The path is well marked, many of the trees are numbered, and there are eight giant yellowwoods to be seen on the way, together with a host of interesting smaller trees, plants and wildlife. Each spring the elephants of the Knysna forest used to migrate through the area, changing from their winter feeding grounds in the Harkerville forest to those in the Gouna forest for the summer season. In autumn they moved back again. In 1876 a census of the Knysna elephants revealed that there were nearly 500 living in the forest. Thirty years later there were only 30 elephants left. In 1920 there were only twelve elephants. In 1962 only ten were counted. There were only four survivors, including one calf in the 1990s. These dwindled to one last elephant and it is very silent on the old Elephant walk. Poachers, sporting and ivory hunters have done with the elephants. A permit for humans to do the Elephant Walk must be obtained from the forestry station at Diepwalle.

A second and even more spectacular hiking trail, known as the Outeniqua Hiking Trail, starts from Diepwalle leads for 150 km along the full length of the Outeniqua range, linking Diepwalle to the Witfontein forestry station near George. There are seven huts along the way. The trail can be divided into sections and joined or left at various points. It is an outstanding wilderness trail and a delight for all lovers of nature.

One and a half kilometres beyond the turn-off to Diepwalle there is a turn-off to the Kransbos forest station. A further 6 km (26 km from the start of the road) leads to the beautiful *Dal van Varing* (dale of ferns) where there are picnic sites and a fine walk leads through an enchanting forest world of giant ferns. On the left-hand side of the road, a short distance away from the Dale of Ferns, a signposted branch will take the visitor to the top of Spitskop (933 m), a fine viewpoint.

One and a half kilometres beyond the Dale of Ferns, the road reaches the Buffelnek forestry station perched on a hilltop looking out on majestic views of the inland mountains. The road now makes a steady 5 km long descent until it reaches the valley of the Kruis River, leading to Plettenberg Bay 39 km away. Seven kilometres along this turn-off there is the famous viewsite of Perdekop. The continuation of the road makes a pleasant return route to Knysna via Plettenberg Bay.

The main road to Avontuur continues for 6 km, then reaches a picnic site in a river valley. A further 11 km of travel leads to the tiny rural centre of De Vlugt where there is a store and a causeway across the clear waters of the Keurbooms River. The road is now 50 km from its beginning and at the start of the spectacular Prince Alfred's Pass. For 13 km the gravel road makes a convoluted ascent up this pass before reaching the summit, 1 046 m above sea-level. The descent on the northern side of the mountains is much easier. It is only 5 km long before the road reaches Avontuur and joins the tarmac R62 road leading down the Long Kloof. Avontuur, 872 m above sea-level, is the terminus of the narrow-gauge railway up the Long Kloof from Port Elizabeth. The beautiful mountain pass road is now 68 km from its start at the turn-off on the Garden Route (N2), 7 km east of Knysna.

PRINCE ALFRED'S PASS

This fine pass, still in much the same well-maintained condition as when it was originally built, is one of the most spectacular mountain crossings in Southern Africa. Andrew Geddes Bain located the route in 1856 and his son, Thomas, had the actual task of constructing it, using for labour a force of about 270 convicts who were housed in a building erected for them at De Vlugt. Construction work was exceedingly heavy. A complex passageway had to be blasted up what was known as Reeds Poort, with bridges crossing the Fuchs River, which at this spot tumbles down through a canyon in a series of lovely cascades and rapids. The road had to continue, skirting the slopes of a valley known as Fuchs Kraal, climbing over a saddle (known as Voor die Poort) at the head of this valley, and then twisting and steadily rising to the place where the mountains touch the clouds.

The pass was completed in May 1867. It was named after Prince Alfred, the Duke of Edinburgh, who, in company with the Rex family, had hunted elephant in the Knysna forests in 1864. It is a fine example of the work of Andrew Geddes Bain and his son Thomas, two of the greatest road builders who ever worked in Southern Africa. It is a pass full of charm, of majestic views, of lovely forest vistas, and (in the latter part) of gentle rural scenes. There is no way of traversing this pass quickly. By modern standards it is narrow and twisting, but aesthetically, throughout its length, it is a complete scenic delight.

From Knysna the N2 Garden Route leads eastwards. Three and a half kilometres from the town centre there is a concrete turn-off to The Heads. The main tarmac road climbs steadily out of the basin containing the Knysna lagoon. After 5 km there is a crossroads. A tarmac turn-off to the north leads to Prince Alfred's Pass and Avontuur (already described). A gravel turn-off south leads for 5,5 km to the beach at the mouth of the *Noetzie* (black) River, a pretty little place hemmed in by seaside houses, five of which, through a whim of their owners, are designed like castles. Back in 1913 when the first plots were sold in the area, a Rhodesian (Zimbabwean) named H S Henderson bought several plots as an investment. In 1932 he designed and built a house for himself on one of them and it happened to resemble a castle. Other owners followed precedent. The result is an attractive little place of most unusual appearance.

The coastal road continues eastwards through the eucalyptus and pine plantations of the Kruisfontein forest station. Ten kilometres from Knysna a gravel track branches off south into the plantation, leading to the Brackenhill Falls, a series of cascades in the Noetzie River, 1,5 km away. Six kilometres beyond this turn-off, 16 km from Knysna, the coastal road enters the indigenous forest known as the Garden of Eden. Here there is a picnic site and a very beautiful walk through a portion of the forest where the Forestry Department has identified many of the trees.

One and a half kilometres beyond the Garden of Eden, 18 km from Knysna, there is a gravel turn-off to the Harkerville forest reserve. A permit from the forester will allow the traveller to drive for 11 km through the reserve, ending at a clearing with a path leading for 91 m to a viewsite over the rocky coast. There is a fine, but demanding, Harkerville coast hiking trail, with a circular route taking in forest and coastal scenery. Overnight huts provide accommodation. The trail starts and ends at the Harkerville forest station and passes through the 1 828 ha Sinclair Nature Reserve. Phone (044) 382-5466 for bookings.

The Garden Route is now traversing a beautifully forested landscape, but one which also possesses some unhappy memories. It was in this area in October 1802 that a Xhosa raiding army swept through the forest. At *Moordlaagte* (the dale of murder) the warriors surprised five wagons carrying to safety families of the local farmers. The women and children were seized as hostages and four men were killed. One of them, Wolfaardt by name, was brutally ill-used and his body tied to a tree in a copse known as Wilke's Kraaibos. *Benekraal* (corral of bones) is another place-name marking the site where the raiders slaughtered a large number of cattle. Retribution came on the elevation known as Kaffir Kop; where a commando attacked the raiders, rescued the captive women and children and killed most of the Xhosas.

At Harkerville, 20 km from Knysna, there is a turn-off to the south leading to the Kranshoek forest station (7 km away). Six kilometres further on there is a turn-off on the left leading to Wittedrif (8 km away) and then over Prince Alfred's Pass to Avontuur (79 km away). Five kilometres further along the coastal road there is another turn-off, this one leading to Robberg (10 km away) and to Beacon Island (3 km away). One kilometre beyond this junction there is the main tarmac turn-off to the south leading for 1 km to the amiable coastal resort of Plettenberg Bay, 32 km from Knysna. The road leads first to the business centre, the street of which is lined with an assortment of commercial buildings. The village lies well above the sea, and from it roads stretch down to the shore. Views from the village are panoramic, embracing a vast sweep of ocean, shore, coastal terrace and mountain range. The variety of scenery is exciting to every taste.

PLETTENBERG BAY

With a permanent population of 10 758 Plettenberg Bay has a vast influx of visitors during the Christmas holiday season. Fortunately, its three spacious beaches and the grassy slopes of the hills overlooking them, have ample room to contain the holiday-makers.

Plettenberg Bay, sheltered by the great natural breakwater of Cape Seal (Robberg), offered sailors a degree of protection from storms. The early Portuguese explorers named the bay *Formosa* (beautiful), for its situation, backed by the handsome Outeniqua and Tsitsikamma ranges, was very satisfying to the eye. The present name resulted from a visit to the bay of the Governor, Joachim van Plettenberg who, after a rough journey from Cape Town, reached the place on 6 November 1778 and erected there a stone pillar as a mark of possession by the Dutch East India Company. Van Plettenberg's pillar still stands on the site of its original placement.

Ten years later the government erected a shed at the bay and attempted to establish the place as a port for the forest area. The ship *Meermin* loaded the first cargo of timber there in August 1788. The harbour never flourished, for the bay was a tricky roadstead. The warehouse fell into ruin and the relics remain today as a memento of wasted effort.

In the 1820s a member of the Rex family of Knysna built a farmhouse and inn. This pioneer hostelry still survives as the Formosa inn, with portions of the original buildings incorporated in the lounge and pub. Forest Hall, built in 1863 by William Newdigate, a younger son of a British aristocrat, remains in the possession of his descendants and is an elegant guest-house.

Attached to the shore of Plettenberg Bay is a rocky islet known as Beacon Island after a navigational beacon erected there in 1772 as an aid to the checking of chronometers. In 1912 this islet became the site of a Norwegian-run whaling industry. A collection of corrugated iron buildings grew up on the islet. When the Norwegians abandoned the place in 1920, the buildings were converted into a rather rough-and-ready boarding-house. In 1940 the Beacon Island hotel was erected on the unique site, with the islet tied to the mainland by a tarmac road. A new hotel was built on the islet in 1972. The beacon of Beacon Island, several times renewed, still stands on the islet, with the slip way of the whaling station and one of the blubber pots.

Safe swimming, excellent fishing, a most equable climate and a beautiful situation, are the assets of Plettenberg Bay. It is today very much a rich man's darling of a holiday resort, with many elaborate seaside 'cottages' occupied for the holiday season.

A tarmac road 10 km long leads from the town (a municipality since 24 October 1960) south down the coast to Cape Seal and the prominent red sandstone peninsula known as the *Robberg* (seal mountain). This famous fisherman's resort is a nature reserve 243 ha in extent. Scenically spectacular, with pathways providing many interesting walks, the peninsula has a rich intertidal life, a considerable variety of birds and a remarkably varied environment. There is a huge cave (once the home of prehistoric beachcombers) and there are many dramatic viewsites showing towering cliffs and white waves breaking on rocks. The Greek ship *Athena* was run aground in the north lee of Robberg in 1967 and still lies there just below the spectacularly situated Robberg caravan resort. Remnants of the wreck in 1630 of the Portuguese ship, *São Goncales,* may be seen in the municipal offices.

From Plettenberg Bay the main N2 coastal road continues north-eastwards. After 8 km the road bridges over the *Bitou* (a species of shrub) River and 1,5 km further on crosses the handsome river known as the *Keurbooms,* after the trees of that species (*Sophors capensis*) which grow on its banks. This is a superb boating river and the Regional Services Council maintains a fine holiday resort on the west bank.

The Keurbooms and the Bitou unite at their mouths to form a broad lagoon. Just across the river there is a 5 km turn-off to the south-east, leading to the holiday resort, popular with fishermen, of ...

KEURBOOMSTRAND

This small resort lies at the end of a tarred by-road where the hills slope steeply down to a sandy shore broken by many outcrops of rock. Once a collection of ramshackle huts, Keurboomstrand has become respectable in recent times, although many of the houses remain tightly bolted for most of the year.

From the road's end through Arch Rock caravan park, a narrow path (signposted) leads through luxuriant coastal bush to *Matjiesfontein* (mat rush fountain) cave (20 minutes' walk). Where the path forks towards its end, take the left-hand path. The cave is really a characteristic overhanging shelter, occupied for many thousands of years in the Late Stone Age. In 1928 and the 1950s it yielded to excavators valuable information about the people who lived there. Much of what the archaeologists found may be seen in the National Museum in Bloemfontein. All that the visitor now sees is a narrow path between the rock face and a pile of sea shells. What he may not realise is that the pile is a gigantic midden, slowly accumulated over countless generations by a shellfish-eating people who, not unlike those of our own day, carelessly chucked their rubbish over the edge. When one thinks about it and studies the size of their dump, it can be a sobering thought!

The Keurbooms River is usually considered the boundary between the two forest worlds overlooked by the Outeniqua and the *Tsitsikamma* (clear water) mountain ranges. From the bridges across the Keurbooms River, the N2 Garden Route climbs steeply and diagonally up the face of the cliffs until it reaches the level of the coastal terrace, twisting, rising and falling through attractive wild flower and forest country. For the road-makers this Tsitsikamma country has provided considerable difficulties. It is split by the deep ravines of several rivers and covered in dense primeval forest. For many years, in fact, this stretch of country was considered to be impassable.

Only in 1868 did Thomas Bain (the road-maker) and Captain Harison (the forester) arduously cut a path through the forest and discover that a practicable route could be found for a road linking Plettenberg Bay to Humansdorp. Work on this road stated in 1879, with the indefatigable Bain in charge. Convict labour provided muscle for the work, while the engineering skill and aesthetic taste of Bain located and controlled a complex route including three superb crossings of the great chasms of the Groot, Bloukrans and Storms rivers. The completed road was opened to Humansdorp in 1885. The route located by Bain was substantially followed by the original N2. It is a beautiful drive, a genuine garden route and a lasting reminder of the genius of Thomas Bain.

Modern traffic demands, however, made the original route increasingly impractical. It remained as a scenic delight for leisurely tourists but a problem for heavy transport or for people in a hurry. At a point 15 km from Plettenberg Bay the original N2 divides. A new toll section of the N2 continues due eastwards. The original road, now known as R102, swings southwards towards the sea. Let us follow this old road before we follow the new route.

Eleven kilometres from the Keurbooms River the road passes the Keurbooms River forest station. After 10 km of varied plantation, forest and open country, where watsonias are spectacular in spring, the road commences the steep descent into the gorge of the *Groot* (great) River. For 3 km the road descends steep slopes covered in forest and ferns. After losing 223 m in altitude, the road reaches the floor of the gorge near the lagoon and mouth of the Groot River, in what is known as Nature's Valley. Here, on a small alluvial plain more than half buried beneath the forest, stands a cluster of seaside cottages. There are picnic sites on a pretty little beach and on both sides of the bridge across the Groot River. This is a cool and beautiful place for a roadside luncheon. At the first of these picnic sites a signposted path leads through the forest to Kalander Kloof, a fine walk with the air filled with the calling of the sombre bulbul birds.

The Groot River marks the western boundary of the Tsitsikamma Coastal National Park (described later). On the banks of the river there is a delightful campsite named after the French forester, Comte M de Vasselot. From the bridge over the river, 34 km from Plettenberg Bay, the road begins to climb out of the gorge. After 3 km of twists, rises and handsome views, the road regains the altitude of the coastal terrace and continues eastwards through dense plantations. At 3 km from the top of the pass, the road leads through the Platbos indigenous forest. On the roadside in the Platbos forest there are several picnic sites and a gravel turn-off leading to Covie.

Six kilometres from the top of the Groot River pass the road passes the Bloukrans forestry station and then commences the descent of the Bloukrans Pass. As in the Groot River Pass, the road has to lose 183 m in altitude in 3 km of winding down the sides of the river gorge and then bridging across the Bloukrans River. This is a particularly charming pass and the 5 km the road takes to climb the height on the left bank of the river provides travellers with many lovely views.

The top of the Bloukrans Pass is 50 km from Plettenberg Bay. The road now leads over the coastal terrace through plantations of exotic trees. After 3 km the road passes the Coldstream sawmill. A further 3 km takes the road through the Lottering plantation and, 5 km east of this settlement, 64 km from Plettenberg Bay, there is a turn-off to the south leading for 11 km through plantations and forest and then descending the coastal cliffs to the narrow and spectacularly rocky stretch at the mouth of the Storms River. The traveller is now in the ...

TSITSIKAMMA FOREST AND COASTAL NATIONAL PARK

The coastal national park consists of a narrow strip of coast about 76 km long, lying between the mouth of the Groot River in the west and (in the east) the mouth of another river also known as the Groot. Between these two namesake rivers the cliffs press close to the sea, making a bold rocky coastline, wild, unspoilt and beautiful to the eye. Through these high cliffs the Storms River has washed a narrow cleft through which its amber waters flow to the sea.

Boating, swimming, skin-diving, walking, and (strangely enough, in a national park) angling are the pastimes in this pleasant wilderness.

At the end of the road are beach cottages (some remarkably ugly for such a spot), the restaurant and office, to which intending visitors must go immediately to make or confirm their bookings. The restaurant stands on the site of another of the many strandloper middens of the coast and a show-case there contains specimens of the objects found when the restaurant was constructed.

From here a rough path leads eastwards towards the mouth of the Storms River, passing a small field museum a short distance from the start. The river is spanned by a suspension bridge but walkers are reminded that this path eventually comes to a dead end. Here is a cave once used by prehistoric beachcombers, with an interesting museum showing some of the things they used and bones of the animals and fish on which they fed. From a small jetty, canoes go up the Storms River for 3 km through primeval forest scenery of great beauty and interest.

In the opposite direction from the restaurant, a coastal path known as the Otter Trail, follows the length of the entire national park to Nature's Valley and provides a strenuous five-day walk. Shelter is provided in bungalows at four points, but all food and bedding must be carried.

A first-rate book, *Tsitsikamma Shore* by R M Tietz and Dr G A Robinson, is on sale in the shop. Packed with information and illustrated with colour photographs, it is compulsory reading for anyone staying more than a few hours who wishes to learn more about the fascinating life of the shore.

From the turn-off to the Storms River mouth the N2 road continues eastwards. After 5 km there is a gravel turn-off to the south leading for 366 m to Storms River village (a small centre serving the Tsitsikamma forest area), and then continuing down the original pass made by Bain across the Storms River, rejoining the modern road at Pineview. This is a very beautiful drive 16 km long and well worth doing. The Bluelilliesbush forest station lies east of the river crossing.

The modern N2 road, after passing the turn-off to Storms River village, traverses the Tsitsikamma forest reserve and, 1 km beyond the turn-off to the Storms River village, there is the entrance (on the northern side of the road) to what is known as De Plaat, the magnificent forest section of the Tsitsikamma Forest and Coastal National Park. At a turning place for vehicles there are a few show-cases with wood sections and drawings of plants. A path to the right leads to a yellowwood tree of a majesty and nobility that transcends anything that the human race has so far produced. There are several others in the vicinity of impressive size and the forest is usually loud with the unfamiliar calls of the birds of the canopy, audible rather than visible.

Three kilometres east of this forest turn-off the road reaches the gorge of the Storms River and the spectacular Paul Sauer bridge which carries the road across the deep gash washed by the river through the sandstone. The bridge is 191 m long in a single span 130 m above the river. It was designed by Ricardo Morandi of Rome and built like two giant drawbridges made of concrete. A platform was first constructed on either side of the gorge. The two halves of the bridge, in vertical form, were then erected on hinges. On completion the two halves were lowered, meeting perfectly in the centre. It was opened to traffic in 1956 after two and a half years' construction work. It replaced the entire original Storms River Pass. Purely functional but cleanly beautiful in appearance, it is one of the very few bridges of its kind in the world.

There is a restaurant overlooking the Storms River bridge. There is also a picnic ground on the south side of the road just before it reaches the bridge and a small caravan park.

The Storms River marks the end of the Garden Route. The road, after crossing the river, leads on into the Eastern Cape.

THE TSITSIKAMMA TOLL-ROAD

To overcome the problem of the circuitous old road, three new bridges were constructed between 1980 and 1984 as part of a toll road which branches off from the original road at a point 15 km from Plettenberg Bay and rejoins it at a point 48 km from Plettenberg Bay. The length of the toll-road section of N2 is 27 km. It shortens the old scenic route by 9 km and, by eliminating all passes, allows much higher traffic speeds with considerable saving in fuel, especially for heavy transport vehicles.

The three all-concrete bridges consist of, firstly, the Bobbejaans River bridge, with a deck 286 m long and 170 m above the river bed. The single arch supporting the bridge is 165 m long. This bridge cost R6 million. It was designed by Watermeyer, Legge, Piesold Uhlmann (in conjunction with Freeman Fox and Partners).

The second bridge, over the Groot River, has a deck 301 m long supported by an arch 189 m long. It is 172 m above the river bed. It cost R8 million and was designed by Jeffares and Green (in association with G Maunsell and Partners).

The third bridge, over the Bloukrans River, has a deck 451 m long supported by an arch 272 m long and 216 m above the river bed. It cost R11 million and was designed by Liebenberg and Stander. It is the largest concrete bridge in Africa and the fourth largest of its kind in the world.

All three bridges were built by Murray and Roberts Civils (Cape) (Pty) Ltd and Concor Construction (Pty) Ltd. The arches were constructed in stages by means of the suspended cantilever system using temporary suspension and tie-back cables. Six-metre segments were constructed on travelling formwork carriages which cantilevered out from the previously constructed segments.

To re-establish the indigenous vegetation disturbed by the construction work, 100 000 plants and trees were replanted at a cost of about R1 million.

The bridges and the toll-road were opened on 8 June 1984 after three years of work. With the three massive bridges in a 15 km length of road, the whole construction is a superb piece of engineering.

Chapter Nineteen
THE EASTERN CAPE

Port Elizabeth and the 1820 Settlers Country

After crossing the Storms River, the N2 road continues along the coastal terrace, with the Tsitsikamma Mountains looking down serenely from the north and the Indian Ocean a few kilometres to the south. Between ocean and mountain there lies a natural garden of trees and flowering plants. Through this lovely wilderness the road finds a pleasant entry into the Eastern Cape.

The Blueliliesbush forest reserve is situated 4 km from the bridge and the Witelbos forest reserve is 14,5 km further on, dominated by the handsome 1 251 m high *Witelskop* (peak of the white alders), the great landmark of the eastern end of the Tsitsikamma range.

Thirty-two kilometres from the Storms River bridge, the road passes the eastern end of the Tsitsikamma where there is a turn-off leading over a saddle in the mountains to join the tarmac road running up the Long Kloof 6 km away (see further on). This turn-off, known as the *Kareedouw* (pass of the karee trees), provides a handsome drive with many lovely wild flowers along the roadside.

Forty kilometres from the Storms River the road passes the mission station of *Clarkson*, established in 1839 by the Moravian Mission and named after Thomas Clarkson, the co-worker of Sir William Wilberforce, the great campaigner for the abolition of slavery. The mission was created for the benefit of the Fingo and other tribal people who found refuge there from various disturbances.

Clarkson is overlooked by the last substantial peaks of the Kareedouw Mountains, a short range which is a continuation of the Tsitsikamma, running from the Kareedouw Pass eastwards. Eight kilometres further east the road passes close to a prominent 359 m high peak and the range then peters out, literally passing under the road and continuing only as a ridge which eventually sinks beneath the sea at Cape St Francis.

Beyond the ridge the road traverses the open mouth of the famous fruit-producing valley of the Long Kloof and, 68 km from the Storms River, reaches the junction of the main tarmac road into the Long Kloof (see further on). As the mountains have dwindled, so rainfall (no longer precipitated by the heights) has diminished and the country is drier and more spacious, becoming undulating scrub-covered terrace. After a further 18 km of travelling (86 km from Storms River) the road reaches the town of ...

HUMANSDORP

This town is an agricultural and railway centre on the narrow-gauge line from Port Elizabeth to Avontuur in the Long Kloof. The area of Humansdorp, dominated by the Kouga Mountains, was originally known as the Parish of Alexander, after the Reverend Alexander Smith, the Dutch Reformed minister of Uitenhage who periodically visited the community and held services in a building on the farm *Geelhoutboom*, 11 km from the present town. In the 1840s the local community began agitating for a church and district centre. The administration was not keen on the idea, but in 1849 Matthys Human offered a gift of 606 ha of the farm *Rheeboksfontein* for a township and commonage. The government accepted it and in 1853 a town named after Matthys Human was laid out with 300 erven, half being sold to endow a church.

The Humansdorp district produces forage, oats and sheep, but it was always a difficult area for agriculture, with extremes of drought, flood and grass fires. Numerous stories have resulted from the colossal fire which swept the whole coastal terrace in 1869. Entire spans of oxen were caught in yoke and roasted alive. Many people died and homesteads were destroyed. The fire broke out on 9 February 1869 when the thermometer registered 59°C in the sun, and a fierce north-westerly wind was blowing. The Civil Commissioner of Humansdorp, Mr J J le Sueur, has left an interesting account of this disaster:

> *'A very wet season about the middle of 1868 had been succeeded by drought and great heat which prevailed for some months before the fire occurred. The heat had prepared for instant ignition the grass, shrubs, and brushwood, then unusually plentiful in consequence of the heavy rains that had preceded the dry weather. Veld burning (that barbarous system or "want of system" of agriculture) had been going on for some time, and on a calm night, bright dots and streaks and reflections in the sky marked the localities where it was being practised. The heat was most intense on 9 February, a scorching hot wind from the north, blowing like a sirocco, withered and dried up all that came within its influence. Everything, therefore, combined to make ready for combustion the plentiful grass and bushes so that where there fell cinders or sparks (from the fires kindled to burn the veld), which a strong gale of wind bore along to an almost incredible distance, a new centre of flame instantly burst into destructive activity, and then in turn gave origin to many others.*
>
> *'The loss of life in this district amounted to twenty. Of these, four were Europeans and the rest Natives. Of the Europeans three consisted of a mother with an infant in her arms and a child by her side, who fled before the fiery blast until they were overpowered, and then sank victims to the flames'.*

This fire covered the coastal area from near Port Elizabeth to the vicinity of George. Many of the wonderful forest areas it destroyed have never recovered and are today little more than open expanses of scrub.

Humansdorp became a municipality in 1906 and its population is now 10 877. It is a busy centre for the area of St Francis Bay. Humansdorp Park, originally laid out on the plan of the crosses of a Union Jack, with an ornamental fountain in the centre, shelters several rare and interesting trees and also contains the municipal caravan park. There is a nature reserve at the Seekoei River pool and the pleasant 4 km Boskloof trail which rewards walkers with the sight and sound of many birds. Humansdorp lies in an area noted for its fynbos (erica), and many flowering plants and shrubs. A fynbos festival is held in the town each year. The aroma of the wild flowers is sweet in the spring air. The bees produce honey with a delicious flavour.

From Humansdorp a gravel road leads southwards over the rolling coastal plains which are notable for brilliant displays of erica in May and many other flowering plants through the year. After 16 km there is a turn-off leading for 10 km to Oyster Bay, a coastal resort especially favoured by fishermen. After a further 13 km the road reaches the seaside resort of Sea Vista, and a further 10 km (36 km from Humansdorp) brings the road to its end at the Cape St Francis lighthouse.

ST FRANCIS BAY

This handsome and spacious bay is one of the great recreational areas in Southern Africa. It was named in 1575 after the saint by the Portuguese navigator, Manuel Perestrello, who described the landfall well, naming the area *serras* (mountains), for it was there, in his own words, that *'all the mountain ranges, which are continuously tacked on to one another from the Cape of Good Hope along the coast, give out here and come to an end'*. The 2 750 000 candlepower lighthouse built in 1876 actually stands on Seal Point at the western end of Seal Bay, which has Cape St Francis for its eastern end. This lighthouse is a massive cylindrical tower 28 m high, with the original keeper's quarters at its base.

In his description of the bay, Perestrello does not say whether he actually landed there. But if he did walk upon that wonderful beach of shimmering sands, it is certain that he would have stopped immediately to collect a shell, for in all the world there are few beaches more richly supplied with these beautiful jewels of the sea.

Scenically the environment of Cape St Francis is a rather flat, fynbos covered plain, the air saturated with the pungent, almost antiseptic, odour of the *agothosma* species of plants which flourish there. The cape itself is not dramatic, simply a flat sandy promontory petering out into the sea. But the bay on the south-western side, sheltered between the arms of Cape St Francis and Seal Point, is handsome with a spacious beach and excellent swimming and surfing. The white tower of the lighthouse dominates the bay with, unfortunately, the usual nondescript collection of seaside houses and cottages boarded up forlornly for most of the year.

For many years Cape St Francis was very difficult to reach, its only access being a sandy track. Seaside resort developers gradually discovered the possibilities of the area. Its real fame began in 1961 when Bruce Brown produced his surfing film *Endless Summer*. He visited the area and found the 'perfect' wave washing along the eastern side of Cape St Francis. These waves, called Bruce's Beauties, after their discoverer, work with a north-westerly wind coupled to a ground swell at low tide. This combination occurs mainly in the winter months (May to September) and provides a ride of at least half a kilometre. The waves are immensely powerful, relentless surges of water sweeping in from the outer ocean with a crashing, rumbling rush. Riding them is a wild experience in which the surfer is called upon to use every skill and reflex he possesses as he is carried forward at such speed that there is little time to think.

Smaller waves known as Bruce's are fairly common. They require a westerly wind, a low tide and a light swell. These waves also work on the east side of Cape St Francis. Generally, superb waves occur on the west side (Seal Bay), especially with the westerly winds in winter. They do not reach the size of Bruce's Beauties, but are always exciting and very lovely to watch, with their long white plumes trailing behind them as though each wave is a line of knights in armour, charging down upon a trembling shore, pennants and banners flying.

Apart from surfing, the swimming is good and the fishing exciting on this western side of St Francis Bay. Sea Vista, situated on this part of the coastline, is a holiday-house area of the more superior kind with some very attractive homes, white-walled and black-thatched but, as usual, boarded up for most of the year.

The Sea Vista resort looks out over a spacious beach across the surfing waters of what is known as *Krombaai,* from the *Krom* (crooked) River which reaches the sea there. The lower reaches of this river have been developed into a marina and the banks are lined with the holiday houses of boating enthusiasts. The Krom River, apart from its boating, is notable for the wild flowers growing along its banks. Aloes flower in winter and ericas and arum lilies bloom to perfection. Countless birds make their homes in the area. The Churchill Dam, which supplies Port Elizabeth with much of its water, lies across the middle reaches of the Krom River.

From Humansdorp the old coastal road continues eastwards for just over 6,5 km and then reaches a turn-off leading to the resort known as Paradise Beach 11 km away. Paradise Beach lies on the right bank of the lagoon formed by the Seekoei and the Swart rivers. This is a famous bird sanctuary, resorted to by at least 57 varieties of aquatic birds, including flamingos and swans. It is said that when the ship *Cape Recife* was wrecked on Cape St Francis on 20 February 1929, two swans were released from a crate on the deck by a member of the crew. They flew ashore and settled on the Krom River. As a result of their breeding the number of swans has increased enormously. At times 150 of these lovely birds may be seen together in such sanctuaries as the one at Paradise Beach.

There is good swimming and fishing at Paradise Beach and a considerable seaside resort housing development.

Back on the old coastal road, 5 km east of the turn-off to Paradise Beach, there is a turn-off to *Aston Bay* (named after Aston Manor in N W Birmingham, England), a resort developed on the left bank of the same lagoon of swans as Paradise Beach (which is on the right bank). Fishing, swimming and the birds are the attractions.

On the N2 coastal road, 10 km east of the turn-off to Humansdorp, there is a turn-off leading for 4 km to the coastal resort of ...

JEFFREYS BAY

Jeffreys Bay had its beginning as a trading store built in 1849 on the shores of St Francis Bay. In those days, before the opening of the narrow-gauge railway from Port Elizabeth to Humansdorp and on to Avontuur (the Apple Express), the beach in front of the store was used for landing and offloading cargo from coasters. It was named *Jeffreys Bay* after the senior of the two partners in the venture, Messrs J A Jeffrey and Glendinning.

The coasters vanished after the railway was opened but the beach of Jeffreys Bay was soon discovered by holiday-makers. The swimming is excellent and this part of St Francis Bay is especially rich in shells. Numerous people living in the area spend much time collecting shells for sale to visitors or for making into ornaments and novelties. Known as *skelpie* (shell) hunters, the collectors have provided apt common names for several of the shell varieties found on their familiar beaches: violets, tops, rose-buds, angel wings, dollies, butterflies, jam tarts, plates and tear-drops. The book, *Marine Shells of Southern Africa* by D H Kenelly, describes these shells in detail. In Jeffreys Bay the Charlotte Kritzinger Shell Museum houses a wonderful exhibition of shells originally collected by the late Miss C Kritzinger.

In modern times surfers have discovered the great rollers of St Francis Bay, and Super Tubes Point at Jeffreys Bay is one of the finest surfing areas in the world. Almost as good are the waves at Kitchen Windows, Magnatubes, Tubes and The Point. Winter is the best season, with westerly winds bringing in the big rollers. The surfing community include visitors from as far afield as Australia and provide Jeffreys Bay with its most picturesque inhabitants. To watch them riding the wild waves is a spectacle not easily forgotten.

Jeffreys Bay became a municipality on 3 January 1968. It is growing rapidly as the usual real-estate developers cover the landscape with seaside homes. Numerous rooms, chalets, flats, cottages, etc are available for renting by visitors. There is a 28,7 ha nature reserve in *Noorskloof*, named after the indigenous *noorsboom* (*Euphorbia triangularus*). The population is 11 366.

From the turn-off to Jeffreys Bay 10 km from Humansdorp, the main coastal N2 road continues eastwards, descending into the shallow valley of the river known from the species of fish as the *Kabeljous*. After traversing a stretch of open sandveld country, covered with flowers in a good rainy season, the road (15,5 km from Humansdorp) reaches the bridge over the Gamtoos River.

The *Gamtoos* takes its name from a pastoral tribe which once lived in these parts. It is a river of major importance in the economy of South Africa, for its broad alluvial valley has lent itself to irrigation. At the mouth of the river there is a fishermen's resort with a camping site. A hotel is situated just upstream from the bridge at the site of the original ferry service across the river. A tarmac road runs along the left bank of the river for 7 km and then joins the tarmac road leading from Loerie to the picturesque little railway junction of Gamtoos. This is an interesting drive (see the section on Baviaanskloof) in Chapter Twenty.

The N2 road continues eastwards from the Gamtoos River, climbing steadily to a higher coastal terrace. After 11 km the road reaches a tarmac turn-off leading to Hankey and Baviaanskloof.

Beyond this turn-off the N2 road continues for 4,5 km to a turn-off to the rural centres of Thornhill and Sunnyside and, after a further 3 km, reaches the spectacular bridge over the ...

VAN STADENS GORGE

The *Van Stadens* River is named after Marthinus van Staden, a pioneer farmer in those parts. With its precipitous sides the gorge was a major road obstacle for years. The first proper road across it was completed in 1867, but floods repeatedly destroyed the river crossing however often it was remade. Traversing the gorge was always hazardous. Eventually a better road and bridge were constructed in the early 1880s, but the descent on both sides of the river remained dangerously steep.

Finally, on 12 October 1971, after four years of construction and the expenditure of R1 275 000, the spectacular modern bridge was opened. It eliminates completely all descents and ascents and spans the deep gorge so smoothly that many travellers speed over it without even realising that they have just crossed one of the greatest bridges in the world.

The four-lane bridge is the fourth longest concrete arch bridge in Southern Africa and the ninth longest in the world. Its main span is 198 m long (or twice the length of a rugby field). There are also several approach spans. The bridge deck rises 125 m above the bottom of the gorge. The overall length is 366 m and the overall width is 25 m. It was built by the Italian engineering firm of Impresa Ing A & P di Penta.

The earlier road may still be followed to the bottom of the gorge where there is a picnic site. It is a beautifully forested gorge and there are pleasant walks up and down the banks of the river.

The eastern side of the gorge has been preserved as the Van Stadens Gorge Wild Flower Reserve and Bird Sanctuary, which conserves 373 ha of fine wild flower and forest country. There are many attractive walks in this reserve and a pleasant picnic ground. The reserve is open daily from sunrise to sunset. The book, *Wild Flowers of the Eastern Cape* by A Batten and H Bokelman, is the standard guide to the flora which is amazingly varied.

The turn-off to the Van Stadens Gorge Wild Flower Reserve (and down to the bottom of the gorge) is 1 km east of the bridge. At this point there is also a turn-off leading to Uitenhage 22,5 km away. The N2 road continues eastwards across a level, well-wooded plain. There are several turn-offs to such places as Van Stadens River mouth, Sea View and Kragga Kamma. After 42 km the road reaches the city of ...

PORT ELIZABETH

With a population of 775 254 Port Elizabeth is the third port and fifth largest city in South Africa. Originally founded on a narrow coastal shelf compressed between the sea and a steep rise to a high plateau, it was most awkwardly situated. The city has escaped its early constriction by spreading up the rise and then projecting its new suburbs in all directions over the high plateau. Here, gardens and mankind flourish in a more spacious environment generously endowed with water, sunshine and good soil. All things grow well, and places such as Walmer enjoy the shade of many magnificent trees planted there in previous years by considerate people.

Originally, a pastoral tribe grazed livestock in the area and watered them in the stream they named *Kragga Kamma* (stony water), now changed to Bakens, at the mouth of which there was a small lagoon and the best landing beach on the shores of Algoa Bay. The first Europeans to visit the bay were the early Portuguese navigators who named it the *Bahia de Lagoa* (bay of the lagoon). Bartholomeu Dias, on his pioneer voyage of discovery in 1488, sailed along the east coast as far as a headland now known as *Kwaaihoek* (angry corner) 14,5 km west of Cape Padrone, the sandy *Pontas do Padrão* (point of the pedestal) which marks the eastern end of Algoa Bay. On Kwaaihoek, called by the Portuguese the Penedo das Fontes (rock of the fountains), Dias erected a pillar in honour of St Gregory, hence the modern corrupted name of Cape Padrone. Another Portuguese name lingers over the western cape of Algoa Bay, *Cape Recife* (cape of the reef). A replica of the pillar in honour of St Gregory, hewn from the same quarry in Portugal, stands in the mayor of Port Elizabeth's garden.

The Portuguese made no use of the *Bahia de Lagoa* (Algoa Bay), since it offered scant shelter and the few African residents on the shore had little to trade. Not until January 1690 was any interest shown by Europeans in taking possession of the area. A galiot from the Cape, the *Noord*, visited the bay for the purpose of securing possession, but the skipper, viewing the bay lashed by a howling gale, considered it worthless and sailed away again.

In 1752 Ensign August Beutler visited the shores of Algoa Bay during an overland journey from the Cape. He camped on the shore of the bay and erected at the mouth of the *Bakens* (beacon) River a beacon of possession bearing the arms of the Dutch East India Company. Nothing further was done, for the exposure of the bay to the south-east gales of summer made it a death-trap for shipping. A harbour to serve the Eastern Cape, however, became increasingly essential and, for want of anything better, Algoa Bay slowly came into use as a landing-place for men and goods.

In August 1799 the authorities of the first British occupation of the Cape built a stone redoubt 24 metres square overlooking the mouth of the Bakens River and dominating the landing-place of Algoa Bay. It was named *Fort Frederick* after the Duke of York. A garrison was stationed there. This was the beginning of the present city which, with the landing of the 1820 Settlers, was visited by the Acting Governor, Sir Rufane Shawe Donkin, on 6 June and named by him *Port Elizabeth* in memory of his beloved wife who, at the age of 28, had died of fever in India two years earlier. The old fort was the first stone building to be erected in the Eastern Cape and is well preserved on a handsome viewsite overlooking the harbour. Sir Rufane built a stone pyramid to the memory of his wife on the hill above the landing-place of Algoa Bay. The monument, with its touching inscription, stands in the Donkin Reserve, with the old 15 000 candlepower lighthouse beside it watching the shipping in the busy harbour of today.

Port Elizabeth became a seat of magistracy in February 1825. Notwithstanding many dreadful shipwrecks in the bay when entire fleets were sometimes blown on to the beach by sudden gales, Port Elizabeth developed as a major port with a secure artificial harbour eventually built in 1928. The worst shipping disaster occurred on 31 August 1902 when 19 out of 28 ships in the anchorage were wrecked.

Industry flourished in the growing town, with Frederick Korsten founding the first manufactory (a tannery and smithy) in 1811. Today the city is one of the principal centres in Southern Africa for the automobile industry, while over 700 factories are engaged in the production of a great variety of commodities.

As a holiday resort, Port Elizabeth has much to offer in the way of fun and enjoyment of life in the sunshine. Summer sea temperatures are pleasantly warm (21°C to 25°C) without becoming sticky, and the beaches of Algoa Bay offer splendid swimming. Humewood, Hobie and King's Beach (where the British royal family swam during their 1947 visit) have been imaginatively developed with changing rooms, tea-rooms, a miniature railway, promenades, tidal baths and children's paddling pools. A particularly pleasant adjunct to this ocean front is Happy Valley, once the boggy course of a stream but now most skillfully converted by the municipal gardeners to resemble a playground of fairies from *A Midsummer Night's Dream*, with reflecting pools, lights, masses of flowers and the greenest of lawns.

The famous Port Elizabeth snake park, museum and oceanarium complex on the Humewood beachfront is now known as Bayworld. The museum has many beautifully displayed exhibits of natural history (especially marine life), settler history, early transport vehicles and sailing-ships. Of considerable literary interest are some of the original illustrations and text pages from *Jock of the Bushveld* by Percy Fitzpatrick, the classic work of South Africa's gold-rush and hunting days. *Jock of the Bushveld*, with over 100 editions to its credit, has never been out of print since its publication in 1907 and has given pleasure to countless people. Its author, James Percy Fitzpatrick, died in his home *Amanzi*, overlooking the Sundays River valley, on 24 January 1931.

The snake park next to the museum is one of the best known of its kind in the world and the display of assorted reptiles is fascinating.

The oceanarium contains a varied, animated and colourful collection of fish and marine life. Stars of this assembly, occupying a large central tank, are a number of delightful dolphins whose antics are a joy to see. The bottle-nosed dolphins were all caught in Algoa Bay or bred in the aquarium. The first two stars of the dolphin show were the females Haig (caught off King's Beach on 16 October 1962) and Lady Dimple (caught in November 1963).

The Bayworld complex is open daily from 09h00 to 16h30, except for Christmas Day. The Oceanarium's public programme consists of seal and dolphin presentations and penguin talks which take place daily at 11h00 and 15h00.

Another considerable asset to Port Elizabeth is the Settlers' Park Nature Reserve, a 54 ha wild flower reserve situated on the banks of the Bakens River. Proclaimed a reserve in 1938, this interesting piece of riverine scenery preserves part of the landscape, flora and fauna of the area in its original state. Indigenous flora (water-lilies on the pools of the river; trees such as yellowwood, milkwood and keurboom in the deep gorges; coral aloes on the cliff faces; the orange-scarlet *Aloe pluridens* flowering in June and July; the Namaqualand daisies and other spring flowers) as well as a variety of fauna (springbok, blue wildebeest and waterfowl) animate an attractive scene.

Yachting and boating on the lower reaches of the *Swartkops* (black hills) River at Redhouse and the North End Lake, and a great variety of organised sports on excellent playing-fields, all contribute to the enjoyment of life in Port Elizabeth.

Port Elizabeth is the home of the dual-medium (English and Afrikaans) University of Port Elizabeth, which began its first academic year on 1 March 1965. Several fine schools, such as Grey High School, are also established in the city. The King George VI Art Gallery, opened in June 1956, is accumulating an interesting collection of works of art and frequently exhibits loan collections. Admission to the art gallery is free. It is open Mondays to Fridays 09h00 to 17h00 (closed Tuesday mornings); Saturdays, Sundays and public holidays 14h00 to 17h00. There is an interesting historical museum in the restored parsonage of the Reverend Francis McCleland. He was the Colonial chaplain and lived there until his death in 1853. Now known as No 7 Castle Hill Museum, the parsonage is open Tuesdays to Fridays from 10h00 to 13h00 and 14h00 to 17h00 Saturdays from 10h00 to 13h00 and on Mondays from 14h00 to 17h00.

A campanile 52 m tall stands on the harbour-landing as a memorial to the 1820 Settlers. Built in 1923, it has a 204-step spiral staircase leading to the top. It is open Tuesdays to Saturdays 09h00 to 12h30 and 13h00 to 17h00. Sundays from 14h00 to 17h00. Closed on Mondays. A carillon of 21 bells rings changes from the campanile every day at 08h32 and 18h02. Another notable memorial in Port Elizabeth is the Horse Memorial standing at the junction of Cape and Russel roads. The work of Joseph Whitehead, it was erected by public subscription in recognition of innumerable horses which perished during the Anglo-Boer War.

Port Elizabeth is a sunny, friendly sort of place and a favourite holiday resort for many people.

PORT ELIZABETH DISTRICT

There are several roads from Port Elizabeth leading to beautiful places. The Marine Drive from the city around Cape Recife and along the western coast is one of the most interesting.

From the city hall, drive south along North Union Street, leading first into Humewood Road, then Beach Road, and eventually becoming Marine Drive. On the way the harbour is passed on the east side and then the terminus and depot of the narrow-gauge (61 cm) railway, the so-called Apple Express, which connects Port Elizabeth with Avontuur in the fruit-growing valley of the Long Kloof and also with Patensie in the Gamtoos valley.

The road develops into a fine double carriageway running along the ocean front with a long line of hotels, apartments and residences situated on the landward side, all with fine views over the playgrounds of King's Beach, Humewood and the blue haze of Algoa Bay.

Three kilometres from the city hall the road passes the oceanarium, museum, snake park and the hill named after Alfred Brooks, mayor in 1928, the summit overlooking the bay and, on the south side, Happy Valley.

The road leads onwards past sunny beaches, green lawns and the entrance to Sea Acres holiday resort and caravan park. Six kilometres from the city hall there is the bus terminus of Summerstrand, and from here the road becomes the Marine Drive proper. Past the Humewood golf-links the road cuts across the base of Cape Recife with its black-and-white banded lighthouse with a 4 067 000 candlepower lamp. The cape is covered in dense thickets of Port Jackson willows planted there in 1873 to settle drift sands. Fourteen kilometres from the city hall the road reaches the south-western shores of the cape and leads along a rocky coast liked by fishermen for its vantage-points and the variety of catches to be made there. Numerous camping sites lie sheltered among the trees. Permits to camp may be obtained at the Regional Services Council resort known as The Willows, which the road reaches 18 km from the city hall.

The Willows is a first class and justly popular resort with a tidal swimming-pool, restaurant, some fine walks along the rocky shore, interesting fishing and a grassy, clean camping and caravan area. There are other resorts at Beachview, Willowglen, Maitland and Willowgrove.

Beyond The Willows, Marine Drive continues along a rocky fishermen's and walkers' coastline, with numerous parking areas, benches and barbecue sites. Six kilometres from The Willows the road reaches *Skoenmakerskop* (shoemaker's peak), a small coastal residential area with a line of houses watching the sea and a tea-room for refreshment.

From Skoenmakerskop the road turns inland through thickets of Port Jackson, willows and tall gum trees. After 3 km there is a turn-off westwards leading for 8 km past many pleasant little country estates and ending at the fine sandy beach of Sardinia Bay. There is a walking trail (the Sacramento Trail) linking Skoenmakerskop and Sardinia Bay. It is highly recommended.

The main tarmac road continues northwards inland for 4 km beyond this turn-off and then, 30,4 km from the city hall, joins the Port Elizabeth–Sea View Drive. A turn right (east) into this road would lead directly back to Port Elizabeth (6 km), passing on the way the residential municipality of ...

WALMER

Notable for its fine flowering and evergreen trees, the present site of Walmer was originally the farm *Welbedacht* belonging to Anthony Muller. This forested area was laid out as a town in 1853 and named after the seat of the Duke of Wellington in Kent. Walmer has been a municipality since 22 April 1899.

If the left turn (west) is taken at the intersection of the Port Elizabeth–Sea View Drive, the road continues over a green, rolling and bushy countryside, past such residential areas as Charlo, Greenshields Park and Mount Pleasant, eventually reaching the coast again at Sea View, 24 km from the junction (30,5 km from Port Elizabeth via Walmer, or 27 km by an alternative inland road branching off at Sea View).

SEA VIEW

A coastal resort popular with anglers, Sea View is the start of a particularly handsome stretch of the coastal drive leading to many fine beaches and fishermen's vantage-points. The road rises and falls along the slopes of the coastal hills, providing the traveller with panoramic views of sea, beach and stretches of rocky coast. Picnic and camping sites are numerous.

Six kilometres from Sea View the road reaches the Maitland River mouth, where a fine beach is dominated by enormous sand dunes. The road swings sharply inland at this point passing an attractive grassy camping site (Regional Services Council) towered over by a gigantic sand dune. Three kilometres from Maitland River mouth the road reaches a left turn (west) to Van Stadens River mouth, a pleasant 19 km long drive ending at the mouth of the river with a magnificent beach lying below a cluster of huge sand dunes. At the mouth of the river (a lagoon for most of the year) the Regional Services Council has created another fine recreational area with bungalows, caravan and camping sites, and a restaurant. Boating, swimming, walking, fishing and sliding down the steep sides of the dunes are the pastimes here. From Van Stadens River mouth there is a road running inland for 16 km back to the Port Elizabeth city hall.

ADDO AND THE ELEPHANTS

A most interesting and varied circular drive from Port Elizabeth leads to the Addo Elephant National Park, the Sundays River valley, and back to Port Elizabeth through the town of Uitenhage.

From the city hall of Port Elizabeth the route leads up the long Main Street of the city, then branches right along the old Grahamstown road through the industrial areas, and (now known as R335) continues slightly inland to the small centre of *Swartkops* (black hills) on the river of that name, one of the greatest yachting waters of Southern Africa. Swartkops is situated 13 km from the city hall on the original Grahamstown road, and 6,5 km further on across the river there is a tarmac turn-off left (north-west) leading to Addo and the Sundays River valley.

This road leads through level scrub country for 34 km (53 km from Port Elizabeth) and then reaches the small railway centre of Addo, originally called by the Africans, *Kradouw* (river passage) from the fording place there across the Sundays River. Addo (the European corruption of the name) is the junction of the branch railway up the Sundays River valley from the main Port Elizabeth–Johannesburg line. One and a half kilometres north of Addo there is a tarmac turn-off leading north-westwards up the Sundays River valley.

The R335 road continues northwards and, with the railway, marks the western boundary of the Addo Elephant National Park. Passing *Lendlovu* (place of the elephant), the road continues until, after 9,5 km, it reaches the railway station of *Coerney* (the small bush). Here the tarmac ends. A turn-off crosses the railway and enters the Addo Elephant National Park. The R335 road continues northwards, reaches a turn-off eastwards to Paterson, and then starts to climb into the foothills of the *Zuurberge* (sour mountains). On the slopes of the mountains there is the Zuurberg inn. The gravel road continues, serving many farms, until it eventually reaches Somerset East.

ADDO ELEPHANT NATIONAL PARK

The 9 712 ha Addo Elephant National Park is an area of singular interest to botanists, zoologists and lovers of big game. An extraordinary assembly of tough, drought-resistant plants, shrubs and stunted trees combine to produce the famous, and in the old days notorious, Addo Bush, blanketing the slopes and heights of a cluster of foothills of the Zuurberg range. Spekboom (which elephants find particularly palatable), boerboom (with its lichen and long strands of moss), gwarri, acacia species, aloes, creepers, mesembryanthemums, and a great variety of other hardy evergreen plants find conditions to their liking in this rugged wilderness and combine to produce a thicket which requires the full power of modern bulldozers and tools to penetrate it. In former years it was quite impenetrable.

The Addo Bush (of which the elephant park is a part) covers a total of about 26 000 ha. As the Eastern Cape became settled, game animals – elephant, buffalo and antelope – retreated into this bush, tramping erratic pathways through the thicket and developing so evil a temper against mankind that hunters who persisted in harrying them in their last retreat, did so at considerable risk. Even donkeys fleeing from hard work found sanctuary in the Addo bush and reverted to a state of wildness and cunning.

A crisis in relations between settlers and the wild animals of the Addo Bush took place when the adjoining Sundays River valley was being developed under irrigation as a great citrus and farming area. There was an increasing demand that all wild animals, especially elephants, be exterminated from the area. A professional hunter, Major P J Pretorius, was accordingly employed in 1919 by the Provincial Administration for the purpose of eradicating the elephants from the Addo.

Pretorius spent 12 months in what he described as: *'a hunter's hell, here it was a hundred square miles or so of all you would think bad in Central Africa, lifted up by some Titan and plonked down in the Cape Province'*.

In a systematic hunt in these difficult conditions and with numerous narrow escapes, Pretorius shot 120 elephants in the Addo Bush. Only fifteen elephants were known to survive, but it was at this stage that the vast publicity given to Pretorius's hunting adventures produced a reaction from the public sympathetic to the unfortunate animals fighting so resolutely for life in an erstwhile sanctuary which had now been turned into a slaughterhouse.

The hunt was called off and the surviving elephants – some wounded, all completely terrified of man – were left alone in a retreat in what was known as the Harvey Bush, where they fed on spekboom, prickly pears and the spoil of occasional nocturnal raids on adjoining farmlands. There was much uncertainty about their future, and farmers once again started to vociferate their complaints about damage to crops.

On 3 July 1931, however, a far-sighted Minister of Lands, P G W Grobler, proclaimed the Addo Elephant National Park. Ranger Harold Trollope was sent there from the Kruger National Park with instructions to concentrate all elephants in the area proclaimed a national park and to find a means of containing them there. This was no easy task.

Trollope reached the Addo area in August 1931. Supported by Mr R A Hockley, a member of the National Parks Board, and the Harvey brothers (local farmers who were sympathetic to the elephants and had left them undisturbed in the bush on their property), he studied the new national park and its problems. His decisions were practical and sensible. Firstly, the park had to be prepared to receive its population of elephants, with water supplies assured. Secondly, the elephants would have to be driven into the area by making the greatest possible noise behind them and lighting fires. Once in the confines of the new park they would have to be retained there by log fires kept alight at 457 intervals all night, every night, until they became used to their permanent home or until a better way was found of containing them.

The big elephant drive took place in the first week of October 1931 and was a success. By 8 October, twelve elephants were in the park, with only a few stragglers remaining outside – a cow and a small calf which had been left behind in the stampede, and a lone bull. The drive had been quite an epic of hard work in most difficult and dangerous conditions. The cow and calf followed the herd into the park, but the lone bull, an outcast and full of old bullet wounds, charged Trollope and his men and had to be shot, making him the only casualty of the operation.

The next few years in the history of Addo Park saw a prolonged struggle to contain the elephants in their area. It proved an impossible task despite the most painstaking efforts of Ranger Trollope and his successor Graham Armstrong who took over in 1944. Under protection the number of elephants increased to 25. From their point of view, they made most intelligent use of the Addo sanctuary, raiding the neighbouring farms and retreating back to the park when the farmers' tempers made outside conditions hazardous.

Stories became commonplace of the raids, of narrow escapes by people, and of brushes with trains and railwaymen at sidings such as Lendlovu, where guards switching points for a crossing in the dark hours occasionally mistook an elephant for a pile of maize sacks. Coerney railway station was also the scene of periodic visitations by the elephants, with trains being held up and operating staff fleeing for safety. Two elephants were killed in collisions with trains.

Once again the clamour mounted for the elephants to be destroyed totally. They were said to be purely a destructive nuisance and, in the dense bush, not even visible to tourists. Hundreds of letters of complaint and claims for compensation for damaged fences and crops reached the National Parks Board, while in 1949 a petition was sent to Parliament by the farmers asking for a definite end to the matter.

The elephants, however, cantankerous as they were, also had their supporters. Wildlife enthusiasts did their best to defend them. An Addo Park Advisory Committee was formed under the chairmanship of the mayor of Port Elizabeth; individuals such as James and Eileen Orpen donated boreholes to provide the elephants with dependable water supplies; and the Citrus Co-operative dumped low-grade oranges into the park as supplementary food.

Then, in 1951, the real turning-point came in the history of the park. Mr L D Summerley, local manager of the Waygood-Otis Lift Company, offered to donate old lift cables for the building of an elephant-proof fence to enclose the park. Old tramlines from Port Elizabeth and Johannesburg were also presented for use as posts. In this way the famous Armstrong Fence evolved.

The idea of some form of fence around the park had always been considered. In 1934 Ranger Trollope had suggested that an electrified fence be used and 16 km of this was actually completed in 1940 before the work was abandoned. The elephants, at first frightened by the electric shock, had discovered that the standards could be pushed down with impunity and the fence no longer presented a barrier to them.

The Armstrong Fence, however, made of steel wire lift ropes, proved to be the answer. With prodigious exertion, Ranger Armstrong built the fence. A post office hole-digging machine made the post holes; 64 km of lift cable and the old tramlines provided the material. In September 1954 the fence was completed, and by this means the elephants were most successfully contained.

Today the Addo Elephant National Park is so magnificent an asset to the Eastern Cape that it is difficult to imagine the place as ever having been endangered. The elephants (232 at 1997 count), secure in their fenced reserve, have recovered confidence and are more easily seen. Buffalo, black rhino and numerous antelope such as kudu, bush buck, eland, red hartebeest and Burchell's zebra also flourish, along with a most fascinating diversity of flora. Water supplies have been further assured by incorporating into the park what is known as Caesar's Dam, an old elephant wallow scooped out into a dam by an ostrich shepherd named Caesar. The present dam was built by the Cape Sundays River Settlement Company.

The park is open throughout the year from 07h00 to 19h00. There is a restaurant, curio shop, and a small caravan park.

THE SUNDAYS RIVER VALLEY

One and a half kilometres north of the village of Addo (53 km from Port Elizabeth) on the way to the Addo Elephant National Park, there is a tarmac turn-off leading in a north-westerly direction up the fertile valley of the Sundays River.

The Sundays River has its source in the Sneeuberg range in the Great Karoo. Dependent on the periodic Karoo thunderstorms, the river flows erratically in its upper reaches, but its original African name, *Kukakamma* (grassy water), emphasises that, relative to the drought-prone landscape across which it flows, the river verges have always been attractive to man. The origin of the European name of the river is obscure, but possibly it is derived from a family, the Sontags, who originally settled on its upper reaches.

European settlers first appeared in the valley between 1818 and 1820. Farms were granted but life was fraught with hazards such as wild animals, especially elephants which regarded the valley as being their own. The whole area was also dangerously near the strongholds of the African tribes then pressing down from the north.

The first settlers, nevertheless, pioneered irrigation from the river, leading water over the rich alluvial soil which covered the 48 km length of the valley and experimenting with a variety of crops. One of these farms, owned by Jacobus Scheepers, had the great asset in an arid area of a dependable spring of pure water. The farm was purchased on 3 April 1818 by the Moravian Mission and converted into the mission station of *Enon*, named from the biblical *Aenon* (a spring). The brilliantly red conglomerate sandstones in the area originated the name of the Enon Conglomerates, a distinct geological system.

The year 1819 saw fighting with the Xhosa people. The entire valley was plundered by raiding bands, with 31 people killed. Everything had to be rebuilt. A particularly attractive little church was opened at Enon in 1821. With its solid walls and cool white interior, this church survives as a reminder of the frontier passions and hardships of the past.

Successive raids into the valley during the various frontier upheavals seriously disrupted farming. Despite this, the natural fertility of the valley made it inevitable that prosperity would follow as soon as tranquillity came to the frontier areas. Meanwhile, men lived with one hand on a plough and the other hand on a gun. The name Commando Kraal, applied to the area around the village of Addo, comes from the rallying point on the site of the area's present primary school which the local men used as a stronghold commanding the historic fording place across the Sundays River. A feeling still lingers about the place, with its relics of old-time inn, wagon works and forges, of the days of alarms and the constant coming and going of early travellers.

The late 1870s saw significant changes coming to the Sundays River valley. In 1878 the Trappist monks established a mission named *Dunbrody* after the ancient abbey in the county of Wexford. This mission was unsuccessful, largely on account of drought, but in 1882 the Jesuit order took it over and they still run the place. Particularly momentous was the arrival of James Somers Kirkwood, a well-known auctioneer from Port Elizabeth who travelled up the valley in 1877 to attend a sale. He climbed to The Lookout at Hillside, where the spectacle of the alluvial valley floor covered in luxuriant vegetation fired his imagination. He visualised a tremendous development in irrigation, including barge transport on the river with a port at its mouth.

After settling at Hillside and proving his irrigation theories in practice, Kirkwood started to buy farms in the valley. By 1883 he owned 21 of them, He then formed the Sundays River Land and Irrigation Company Limited, and shares were offered to the public for a major enterprise in irrigation. The flotation proved a total failure and most bitter disappointment to Kirkwood and his colleagues. The public were just not interested. In a time of depression there was no capital for such a long-term project, no matter how worthy. The desired quick returns from ostrich farming were at the time far more interesting to those with money.

Kirkwood's dreams simply collapsed. He was declared insolvent in 1887 and died two years later. It is fitting that the memory of this worthy man will always remain in the valley he loved so much. The principal modern centre and terminus for the branch railway up the valley, the town of *Kirkwood*, bears his name. It was founded in 1913.

Kirkwood's assets were taken over by the Guardian Assurance and Trust Company. A manager, a renowned character named Arthur Goldhawk, was appointed to manage the estate. Farming continued on an individual basis. Then, in 1893, a syndicate of valley farmers and Port Elizabeth businessmen bought the Sundays River Estate. They formed the Strathsomers Estate Company (so named after one of Kirkwood's first names and the Scottish word *strath*, meaning a broad valley) and commenced a substantial farming activity in lucerne and ostriches.

The first large-scale irrigation work in the valley (and indeed in South Africa) was the Korhaans drift weir, completed at the end of 1913. This weir irrigated 4 856 ha of land which the company offered for sale at £20 per hectare in order to attract settlers.

A comprehensive new Irrigation Act introduced in 1912 by Colonel H Mentz, Minister of Lands, really exposed to the discerning the full potential of the Sundays River valley. A consolidated effort was needed, and the stimulant for this came largely from the lower end of the valley where, in 1906, the Addo Land and Irrigation Company had been formed with one of its directors, J W Babcock, planting the first large-scale citrus orchards on his farm *Carlton*. A second company operating in this lower area was the Cleveland Estate Syndicate, formed in 1912 with a highly ambitious project of irrigating vast stretches of land towards the mouth of the river.

The man destined to weld into a whole the various enterprises in the lower part of the valley was Sir Percy Fitzpatrick, the mining financier and politician always remembered best by the public as the author of *Jock of the Bushveld.* On a visit to the valley in 1913 he saw the fine orchards on Babcock's farm and immediately appreciated the potential of the area. He purchased a block of farms near Addo and formed the Sundays River Settlements Limited, with the intention of attracting an influx of new settlers to the valley.

In 1914 Sir Percy's company absorbed the Cleveland Syndicate with its assets of irrigation development. With great vigour he set out to raise capital and to prepare ground for an influx of settlers expected at the end of the war, but he experienced many setbacks. The war years saw the collapse of the ostrich feather industry, while the Eastern Cape was in the grip of a ruinous drought. Substantial water storage during good years would have to be effected to tide the valley over such periods of crisis. A prodigious flood in 1916 gave the government the embarrassment of having to grant drought and flood aid to the same valley farmers. The Sundays River would definitely have to be disciplined. The result, after discussion, planning, argument and inevitable court litigation, was Lake Mentz completed in 1922.

While the government built Lake Mentz, the land-owning companies continued their programmes of development. The years of waiting for the waters of Lake Mentz ruined several of them and caused considerable recrimination that the companies had stimulated sales of land by over-sanguine propaganda. The usual glowing real-estate brochures had been published and many British settlers had purchased land simply by selecting smallholdings from a map. On arrival in South Africa they had found their property still under bush, with no prospect of any financial return for several years and, to make the situation worse, a drought so serious that drinking-water had to be brought in by the railway. Life in the sunshine, so rosily advertised in the brochures, became a matter of sweat and dust.

Sir Percy Fitzpatrick and his company were the most severely criticised. It was his enthusiasm which had attracted most of the immigrants who now felt aggrieved at their hardships. A great argument also developed in the valley towards the end of 1921 when, with Lake Mentz nearly completed, it began to appear that there would be a shortfall in the long-awaited water supply. Irrigation plans would have to be curtailed. Management squabbles and a major lawsuit over the dismissal of its managing director, General John Byron, added to the difficulties of the Cape Sundays River Settlements Company. In 1923 it went into voluntary liquidation. The unfortunate Sir Percy, like Kirkwood, must have regarded the valley as a beloved mistress turned traitor. The assets of the company were taken over by the government.

In spite of squabbles and disappointments, the shattering of over-rosy dreams, and the heartbreak of facing the reality of water limitations even with Lake Mentz, the valley progressed. Lucerne provided a cash crop; citrus groves were being planted and, in 1924 the Sundays River Citrus Co-operative Company was formed to control marketing. At its start it had 60 members owning 60 000 trees.

March 1928 saw Lake Mentz overflowing for the first time. The railway from Addo to Kirkwood had been opened in January 1927 and now, with water, transport and organised marketing, the valley changed from a duckling into a swan. Sir Percy Fitzpatrick at least had the satisfaction of seeing many of his predictions become a reality before he died in 1931. He was buried beside his wife on the top of Outlook Hill which dominates the valley.

Droughts, floods, the siltation of Lake Mentz and many other problems have plagued the valley, but in 1936 220 000 cases of oranges were exported under the Outspan trademark introduced that year for South African citrus. In 1947, after the setback of the war years, 1 million cases were exported. In 1989 the Eastern Cape produced 172 365 tons of the total South African citrus crop of 761 130 tons. The Sundays River valley is the principal producer in the Eastern Cape. Lake Mentz is now known as Lake Darlington. It holds 187 million cubic metres of water.

A drive up the Sundays River valley leads the traveller through a superbly fertile and most charming world. From the tarmac turn-off north of Addo, the road leads north-westwards. After 3 km it reaches the packing station of the Sundays River Citrus Co-operative at Hermitage. On all sides stretch the citrus groves, particularly beautiful in October when the trees are in blossom and the air is sweet with perfume. The fruit is picked in early winter.

Five kilometres from Hermitage lies Sunland, where there is a turn-off leading to the fine viewsite known as The Lockout. One and a half kilometres further on, the tarmac road crosses the Sundays River and for the next 18 km continues through beautifully tilled citrus groves and farmlands with the dark-green trees as neat and disciplined as any army on parade. The road then crosses the Sundays River for the second time and after a further 3 km (32 km from Addo) reaches the principal centre of the valley, the town of ...

KIRKWOOD

Named after the unfortunate James Kirkwood whose story has already been told, Kirkwood was founded in 1913 as a centre for the valley. It became a municipality in March 1950 and today has a population of 9 866. It is the terminus of the branch railway from Addo and the site of a pack house of the Sundays River Citrus Co-operative. The town is particularly notable for the beautiful roses which grow there.

Eighteen kilometres beyond Kirkwood the tarmac road joins the main tarmac road linking Uitenhage to Jansenville. Immediately ahead, dominating the landscape, looms the 1 799 m high bulk of the Cockscomb Mountain, the highest peak of the Groot Winterhoek range. The road has found its way through a valley any visitor will long remember. In summer (the best time to see it) it can be oven hot, but the late afternoons are cool and reminiscent of a man who has worked hard all day in the heat, but now relaxes with a sundowner.

The road now traverses a level alluvial and arid valley covered in low scrub, aloes, cacti and euphorbias. Botanically this area is the home of the elegantly angular crane flower (*Strelitzia reginae*) which blooms from January to May. Ostriches, angora goats and sheep are the principal products of the area. The tarmac road, turning left (south-east), leads over the foothills of the Groot Winterhoek range, past (after 27 km) a turn-off stretching eastwards to Steytlerville, and at 32 km a turn to Addo. After 37 km there is a turn to the Springs recreation resort and then, 6,5 km further on (43, 5 km from the junction with this tarmac road), reaches the town of ...

UITENHAGE

With a population of 174 442, Uitenhage is a clean, modern and bustling industrial town notable for its fine trees and pretty gardens. The town had its start when Jacob Abraham Uitenhage de Mist, Commissary General sent by the Batavian Government in 1802 to take over the Cape from the British, toured the Colony, inspecting even its remoter frontier regions.

De Mist found four families settled in the valley of the Swartkops River. These people had made their way to the area in 1790 when a party of hunters roamed into the valley, found it to their liking and petitioned for permission to settle there. De Mist considered their choice of homes so handsome that he decided to establish a town there as a seat of a frontier *drostdy* or magistracy. (The word *drostdy* actually comes from *drossardschaap*, meaning a bailiwick).

De Mist selected the farm of Gert Scheepers as the site of the town, for it was well watered by a cluster of powerful perennial springs. In November 1804 the government purchased this farm for £400, with the widow of Scheepers retaining until death the right of residence in the farmhouse. She lived in the loop-holed, two-roomed, mud walled house on the site of the later locomotive works until the fine old age of 90, spending some of her time with her son-in-law, the well-known Van Staden of *Winterhoek* (winter glen).

Uitenhage was given its name in honour of Jacob Abraham Uitenhage de Mist on 25 April 1804 by the first landdrost, Captain Ludwig Alberti, formerly commander of Fort Frederick at Algoa Bay. Notwithstanding numerous alarms of Xhosa raids, the town grew fairly rapidly as a centre for the frontier area. The residency of the landdrost remains as a fine piece of construction from this period. A municipality was created on 11 June 1877. Apart from being a centre for mixed farming, Uitenhage began its industrial life as a centre for wool washing. In the 1870s eleven wool washeries were in operation on the Swartkops River, depending on ample supplies of soft water. This was the beginning of a substantial textile industry.

At one time Uitenhage was world renowned for being the home of a working baboon. The signalman at Uitenhage railway station, James Wide, had lost both legs in an accident. He trained a large baboon to work the points and to harness a collie dog to a trolley on the line and see that his master was conveyed to and from his cottage. The baboon's method of working the signals was a famous spectacle. He pulled the levers, looked around to ensure that the correct signals had been moved and then watched the approaching train, catching the various offerings thrown to him by the passengers. For nine years he carried out his work without a mistake until his death in 1890.

The principal modern industries in Uitenhage are concerned with transport. The railways repair rolling-stock and manufacture spares in eighteen workshops. Goodyear Tyre and Rubber Manufacturers, Volkswagen and several component manufacturers have their plants close to the town. Visitors can book for conducted tours of the factories – for information about the tours phone Goodyear (041) 994-6911 and Volkswagen phone (041) 994-4111.

The municipality maintains a fine recreational area at The Springs, 12 km north of the town on the tarmac road to Jansenville. At this resort there are two swimming-pools, a picnic area, flood-lit tennis-courts, a caravan park, chalets and rondavels. Uitenhage draws part of its water supply from this source and visitors are shown the springs, known as 'The Eyes' by arrangement with the manager of the resort. Nature trails lead into the beautiful hill country of the 25 000 ha Groendal Wilderness Area.

The Cuyler Manor Cultural Museum with a unique water-mill is situated 5 km from the town on the Port Elizabeth road. Originally built as a homestead for the landdrost of Uitenhage, General Jacob Glen Cuyler, this complex now houses a mohair demonstration farm and a herb garden. Once a year there is an unusual festival in honour of the prickly pear, reviving its uses as well as arts and crafts of former years. The Drostdy Africana Museum in the town traces local history. In an adjacent hall Volkswagen have a car museum. The railway station, built in 1875, has been converted into a railway museum, a delight for visitors who can roam through an authentic station of the Victorian period, complete with all the furnishings, equipment and with carriages and a Class 7A locomotive on the permanent way. These museums are open Mondays to Fridays from 10h00 to 13h00 and 14h00 to 16h30. Closed on Christmas.

In the town there are a number of interesting historic buildings. The court-house, with its fine Victorian clock tower, built in 1898, is worth seeing.

Gardens in the town are notably beautiful. The municipal botanical garden in Magennis Park has a fine collection of plants and trees, with a nearby Olympic-sized swimming-pool. Cannon Hill Park has a look-out tower with a 360 degree view of Uitenhage. The tower was built to commemorate the coronation of King George VI. The decorative main gate commemorates the coronation of Queen Elizabeth II. The cannon of Cannon Hill came from the shipwreck of the *Amsterdam*. There is also a collection of the succulents which are indigenous to the area.

Strelitzia Park is the home of three species of strelitzia (crane flowers) indigenous to the area. At Willow Dam there are picnic areas. Art-in-the-Park is held on the first Sunday of each month, and there is a glorious little steam train pulled by Little Bess, used originally in the construction of Lake Darlington in the Sundays River. It is one of only two such locomotives in the World.

A tarmac road leads south-eastwards over the aloe-covered foothills of the Groot Winterhoek, Elands and Van Staden ranges of mountains. After 14 km of travel along this tarmac road there is a crossroads, with a left turn to Port Elizabeth (34 km) and a right turn up the Elands River valley, a fine drive leading to the Gamtoos valley. A further 8 km (22,5 km from Uitenhage) sees the road join the main coastal N2 road linking Port Elizabeth to Cape Town.

The direct road from Uitenhage to Port Elizabeth leads eastwards past the Cultural Museum (5,5 km) and at 10 km reaches a turn-off to the town of ...

DESPATCH

The rather odd name of *Despatch* seems to have stemmed from the days when the town was originally a railway centre used largely for the dispatching of bricks which were produced locally. It became a municipality in 1945. With its population of 17 714, it is now a residential area for people working in Uitenhage and Port Elizabeth.

Beyond the turn to Despatch the tarmac road continues past outlying residential areas of Port Elizabeth such as Redhouse, Perseverance and (21 km from Uitenhage) a turn to Bethelsdorp. This place was founded in 1803 by Dr J T van der Kemp of the London Missionary Society as a settlement area for remnants of the original African tribes. The community developed around a huge salt-pan 3 km by 1,5 km in extent. Each holder of a residential plot in the settlement was entitled to a *baan* or polder in the salt-pan. In this polder the owner could evaporate brine and secure the salt. Nowadays a company leases the whole area, pays a rental each year and works all the polders as one unit. In summer the salt-pan resembles a frozen lake with piles of snow like salt gathered ready for packing.

Beyond the turn to Bethelsdorp the road continues for 13,5 km and then reaches Port Elizabeth.

THE ROAD TO JANSENVILLE AND STEYTLERVILLE

At the junction where the road up the Sundays River valley meets the road from Uitenhage, the left turn described earlier leads for 43,5 km to Uitenhage. The right turn proceeds north-westwards along the tarmac R75 road through a rugged landscape covered in dense bush and a multitude of flowering aloes. This is good country for kudu, and roadside signs warn the traveller that these noble antelope are notoriously lacking in traffic sense, particularly at night.

After 46 km the road reaches the railway station and small trading centre of *Wolwefontein* (fountain of hyenas).

At Wolwefontein the R75 road divides. One road R329 continues north-westwards over more open arid country, with hills on either side, and where flocks of sheep and goats graze. After 27 km the road passes the railway station of *Baroe* (the place of the baroe plants (*Cyphia volubilis*), with a turn-off north leading for 34 km to the railway junction of *Klipplaat* (stony flats).

The R329 road continues from Baroe and after 6 km leads through Waaipoort, a pretty pass through a vividly coloured ridge of high, rocky hills. A further 16 km takes the road through a second pass, *Noorspoort* (pass of *Euphorbia triangularus* trees), and then (25 km from Baroe) reaches the town of ...

STEYTLERVILLE

This little town of 3 790 inhabitants on the banks of the Grootrivier was established in 1875 by the Dutch Reformed Church and named after the Reverend Abraham Isaac Steytler who used to hold services in the district. The situation is a warm, arid plain between the Baviaanskloof range and the Grootrivierhoogte, a high ridge of hills where rainfall is inclined to be erratic. The Dutch Reformed church is the most notable building, while in the George Hayward Hall there is an interesting little local history museum which is opened on request.

From Steytlerville the tarmac road R329 continues westwards up the floor of the wide valley. After 85 km the road reaches the town of Willowmore. See Chapter Twenty.

The tarmac road R75 which turned north from Wolwefontein continues for 53 km to the town of ...

JANSENVILLE

Founded in 1854 and named (with a slight misspelling) after Lieutenant-General Jan Willem Janssens, Governor of the Cape Colony in 1803, the town is situated on the banks of the Sundays River. The population is 4 644. It is a centre for sheep and goats. The quality of wool from locally bred Cape angora goats is renowned and it is a major centre for the breeding of these animals.

From Jansenville the tarmac road R75 continues north through Soutpansnek and after 83 km reaches the small town of *Adendorp*, named after John Adendorff who, owning a woolwashery on the site. He saved himself from bankruptcy in 1855 by laying out a town on his property which was well watered from the Sundays River. Eight kilometres further the road joins N9, the main road from George, and then enters Graaff-Reinet.

PORT ELIZABETH TO GRAHAMSTOWN AND THE SETTLER COUNTRY

From Port Elizabeth, N2 leads northwards out of the city by means of a magnificent double carriageway, complete with a spectacular series of traffic interchanges and flyover bridges. Hugging the shores of Algoa Bay, the road reveals to travellers many fine views over sparkling beaches and the spacious reaches of the great bay. Offshore to the north may be seen the two rocky islets of *Jahleel* and *Brenton* (named after Admiral Sir Jahleel Brenton), while further out to see lies the islet of *St Croix* (the islet of the Cross), so named because it was once thought that the pioneer explorer, Bartholomeu Dias, had erected a cross there in 1488 to mark the furthest point of his voyage of exploration. The actual remnants of this cross, dedicated to St Gregory, were later found 14 km west of Cape Padrone (originally known as the *Pontas do Padrão*, point of the pedestal). A replica stands there today on the headland now known as *Kwaaihoek* (angry corner) as named by the Dutch, but which the Portuguese had called the *Penedo das Fontes* (rock of the fountains) and the British, *False Islet*.

At 7,5 km from the centre of the city the road crosses the mouth of the Swartkops River by means of the Settlers bridge. This is a great river for yachtsmen. The left bank is lined with a free-and-easy-looking collection of water's-edge bungalows and unconventional houses.

Beyond the river the road continues north-eastwards, leading over level country covered in low, stunted scrub. The coast veers off in a more easterly direction, with the road gradually finding its way inland.

At 12 km from the city there is a turn-off north-westwards to Addo and the Sundays River valley. A further 4,5 km (16,5 km from Port Elizabeth) brings the road to the mouth of the river known as the *Coega* (place of acacia trees), where the Salnova Salt Company recovers salt from a pattern of geometrically shaped evaporation polders built in the shallow water of the lagoon.

A further 14 km (30,5 km from Port Elizabeth) brings the road to the Sundays River, with a holiday resort known as *Pearson Park* situated on its banks. This lower reach of the Sundays River offers fine boating. A track leads to the beach at the mouth where there is a massive barrier of sand dunes.

From the valley of the Sundays River the road climbs over low scrub-covered hills. At 45,5 km from Port Elizabeth there is a traffic interchange where the N10 tarmac road branches off on the start of its journey inland to join N1, the Cape-to-Cairo road, at Colesberg and to carry traffic on to the great north–south trunk road of Africa (see Chapter Thirteen).

Settlers Way, N2, continues north-eastwards. One kilometre from the interchange there is a turn-off stretching eastwards (R72) to Alexandria and Port Alfred. The road now traverses an area of low undulating hills with pineapple, dairy and sheep farms worked in difficult conditions of unreliable rainfall. Spineless varieties of prickly pears are cultivated to provide stock feed in times of drought.

The road curves downwards into the shallow valley of the Bushman's River, where it crosses the river 78 km from Port Elizabeth. The road then climbs steadily out of the valley over undulating hills covered in scrub and numerous aloes which flower in May and June. This is the country where descendants of the 1820 Settlers occupy most of the farms. The area is enriched by memories of these settlers such as the Slaters and the Gushes and the contentions they experienced in the form of a difficult erratic climate, periodic and seemingly interminable droughts, raids and wars with the frontier tribespeople, and all the uncertainty of existence in a primeval land.

Frequent turn-offs from the main road lead to 1820 Settler villages such as Seven Fountains, Salem and Sidbury. For those who are able to explore these byways at leisure, there are many interesting scenes of rural landscapes and frontier-type farmhouses of the period. Salem, particularly, is worth visiting. The turn-off leading southwards to this village (situated 16 km from the main road) is 101 km from Port Elizabeth.

Salem (peace) was founded in 1820 by Hezekiah Sephton and his party of 344 settlers. Several of the houses they built are still standing: compact, double-storeyed (for economy of roofing material), and stoutly built. The church with its thick, strong walls served as a fortress in times of danger.

In the records of this church there is an account of the last time it was used as a stronghold. The people of Salem retreated to the church when a band of Xhosa warriors raided the area. There was a great bustle of calling on the Lord, cleaning of guns and drying of powder. In the midst of this excitement there walked a man of peace, Richard Gush. Wearying of all the talk of approaching bloodshed, he took off his coat and went out unarmed to the warrior chieftain.

The Xhosas received him in silent surprise. Gush fell to lecturing them severely on the impropriety of their conduct. Abashed, the chief excused the behaviour of his people. *'We are hungry'*, he said, *'that is why we attack you'*. Gush eyed the settlers' livestock in the hands of the raiders, but decided to take the chief at his word. Returning to the church, Gush collected 6 kg of bread, 4 kg of tobacco and 12 pocket-knives. These he carried back as a gift to the warriors. As the records have it, he once more *'expostulated with them on their great wickedness. The parties shook hands and the Caffres went away and were seen no more in the vicinity of Salem!'*

The original fortress-church of Salem is now a school for the descendants of the Xhosa warriors. It is an atmospheric building filled with contrasting memories of old alarms, of happy little weddings, of baptisms and long sermons, of simple rustic schoolteachers, and pupils such as Theophilus Shepstone who became famous in Natal, and Mary Moffat who grew up to marry Dr David Livingstone. The village green outside the church (especially on a summer afternoon with a game of cricket in progress) could have been transported with the Settlers all the way from England.

At 4,5 km north-east of the turn-off to Salem, Settlers Way (N2) reaches a turn-off to Alicedale (30 km) and Highlands (16 km). Another kilometre takes the road across the upper reaches of the river known as the *Kariga* (place of steenbok). Patches of typically stunted Eastern Cape bush alternate with cultivated lands. A further 6 km (113 km from Port Elizabeth) brings N2 (Settlers Way) to a turn-off leading south to Kenton-on-Sea (48 km) and to Alexandria (48 km). N2 now reaches the picturesque Howison's Poort where a reservoir is situated immediately downstream in one of the tributaries of the Kariga River. There is a pleasant picnic site at the foot of Howison's Poort. The reservoir has been stocked with trout and black bass and it is used for boating. The first road up the valley was built in the 1830s by Alexander Howison, working on a public subscription from the inhabitants of Grahamstown who wanted a dependable link with Port Elizabeth. The modern road, following the same route, climbs steadily up the fertile valley of the stream. It is a pleasant drive, with the Stone Crescent hotel built to provide refreshment half-way up the valley. After 6 km the road reaches the top of the valley and descends for 6 km down a well-wooded hill slope past the caravan park and turn-off to the mountain drive, and (120 km from Port Elizabeth) enters the miniature city of ...

GRAHAMSTOWN

The original capital of the Eastern Cape Province, *Grahamstown*, was founded in 1812 by Colonel John Graham. The intention was to establish a military outpost on the troubled frontier in order to effect pacification after the Fourth Frontier War. A line of blockhouses was built to guard from the heights the prodigious valley of the Fish River which formed the frontier line – the line of collision – between European settlers expanding from the south and African tribal groups migrating from the north.

The choice of the site of Grahamstown was admirable. It was made by Colonel Graham while he was resting in the shade of an acacia tree which grew on a position today marked by a memorial on an island in High Street opposite Fishers building. The river known to the Xhosas as the *Qoyi* (rushing) has its headwaters nearby in a number of streams bubbling to life on the slopes of the overlooking heights. In the valley below, close to the tree under which Graham rested, they unite to form the river whose name was corrupted by Europeans into the familiar *Kowie* of today.

A straggling little town grew up around the military camp. In its early years it was reputed to be a slovenly place, simply an army camp-following of traders and canteen keepers leading a precarious life at the whim of the soldiers and very much dependent on the ability of the military to defend it from the onslaught of primitive tribes. The site of the town was actually the abandoned farm of *Rietfontein*, with the original farmhouse of Lucas Meyer restored from its burnt-out, looted condition and converted into the officers' mess of the garrison.

Grahamstown became the administrative capital of the district named *Albany* (after the city of Albany in America where the father of the first magistrate, Colonel Jacob Cuyler, had once been mayor). An interesting and most varied population was attracted to the town. The famed (and ill-fated) Voortrekker leader, Piet Retief, was one of the leading businessmen in the place, owning amongst numerous other ventures, a windmill for the grinding of wheat.

In April 1819 Grahamstown was attacked by 10 000 warriors led by the renowned diviner, Makhanda. Only a most resolute defence saved the town from total destruction.

The following year saw the advent of the 1820 Settlers to the Eastern Cape. Grahamstown became their particular centre. A great bustle came to the place with 174 registered ivory traders dealing in tusks and many more engaged in the traffic of skins. In those days great herds of game animals wandered through the frontier areas. Regular fairs were held and at least 50 000 skins and many tons of ivory passed through Grahamstown each year.

By 1830 the town had grown considerably, with an imposing High Street and many fine buildings, including the *drostdy* (official residence) completed in 1826, which subsequently became part of Rhodes University. The erection of this building by Piet Retief had been commenced in July 1822 but during the four years it took to complete, several other contractors had a hand in the work. The house was demolished in 1935 to make way for the modern administrative centre of Rhodes University and only the arched gateway remains.

The present St George's Cathedral also had its beginning in this period, firstly as a rather ill-constructed church completed in 1828 as the first Anglican church in Southern Africa and, secondly, after Grahamstown became a bishopric in 1853, converted piecemeal (as funds became available) into the imposing structure of today with its numerous memorials, tablets, regimental colours and other items.

In the 1830s Grahamstown ranked as the second-largest town in Southern Africa. It had a horticultural society; a weekly newspaper, *The Grahamstown Journal* (first issued in December 1831); a substantial commercial hall where social occasions could be held (today the Eastern Districts Court of Justice); a municipality promulgated in April 1837; and the Albany Library, founded in 1842. All this progress was made in the teeth of periodic alarms, frontier disturbances and wars with the tribes who were still trying to migrate southwards.

Frontiersmen, ivory traders, farmers, hunters and soldiers thronged the streets of the town. With them mingled an increasing number of men of culture and learning: Robert Godlonton and L H Meurant, journalists and authors of note; Thomas Pringle the poet; John Centlivres Chase; the famous road builder, Andrew Geddes Bain; and Dr William Atherstone whose versatile genius saw him perform the first successful operation in the Cape using an anaesthetic. He was also the originator of the Botanic Gardens, a scientific and literary society, and the identifier of the first diamond found in Southern Africa in 1867.

The first school in Grahamstown was opened in 1849 and the building is still in use as the Good Shepherd School. The second, opened in January 1850, was the Assumption Convent School for girls. In August 1855, St Andrew's College was founded by Bishop John Armstrong. This was the first of the prestigious public schools of Grahamstown, the purpose of which was to provide the type of church-controlled training in Christian citizenship that was the pride of the illustrious English public schools.

The second prestigious school to be established in Grahamstown was Graeme College (1873). In the following year Bishop Nathaniel Merriman established the Diocesan School for girls as a sister school for St. Andrews. In 1876 the first Catholic Bishop of the Eastern Cape, the Right Reverend Bishop Rickards, founded St Aidan's College (now closed) under the management of the Society of Jesus (Jesuits). In 1894 the Methodist Church founded Kingswood College. In 1896 the government rebuilt a small private school founded in 1892 by Miss Bertha Mingay and converted it into the Victoria Girls' High School. In 1894 the Grahamstown Training College was founded by the Anglican Sisterhood of the Community of the Resurrection. In its day it was responsible for the training of many female student teachers. The principal educational institution in Grahamstown is Rhodes University, founded in 1904. The main building of the university was designed in 1911 by Sir Herbert Baker. At first a university college, Rhodes attained full university status in 1951.

Among the other schools in Grahamstown are St Paul's Theological College, the P J Oliver High School, and a School of Art and a School of Music, both attached to Rhodes University. The buildings in which these schools and colleges are housed are notably handsome and the grounds in which they stand are spacious and exceedingly beautiful. The Students' Union of Rhodes University used to occupy a particularly interesting old building known as *Selwyn's Castle*, a castellated house built in 1835 as a home for Major C J Selwyn.

Grahamstown is truly a city of schools. The original commercial importance as a frontier town largely vanished in modern times with the building of railways. Grahamstown was left well off the main routes from the coastal ports to the interior. With little significant industry except ceramics and electric lamps to motivate its way of life, it has, instead of the overall of the workman, accepted the cap and gown of the student as its characteristic dress. Social and commercial life are very much influenced by the school and university calendar and activities are very relaxed during vacation periods. The population is 62 637.

Apart from its public library, Grahamstown is the home of the South African Library for the Blind. It also possesses several first class museums. The Albany Museum incorporates the Observatory Museum (open weekdays 09h30 to 13h00 and 14h00 to 17h00; Saturdays 9h30 to 13h00; closed on Sundays), Fort Selwyn (open on request only), the Provost Prison (open on request only) and the Natural Sciences and History Museums (open weekdays 09h00 to 13h00 and 14h00 to 17h00; 14h00 to17h00 Saturdays and Sundays). The History Museum contains many interesting relics of the 1820 Settlers and some fine paintings by Thomas Baines. The Observatory Museum in Bathurst Street contains period furniture, a clock and the only *camera obscura* in South Africa, a very remarkable optical device which projects a panoramic view of Grahamstown on to a round screen in a darkened room. The history of the diamond industry is depicted, including the identification by Dr W G Atherstone in Grahamstown of the first diamond found in South Africa. The building was purchased and restored in 1980–82 by De Beers Consolidated Mines Ltd in order to commemorate the beginning of the diamond industry in South Africa.

The National English Literary Museum is open to the public on weekdays. The Rhodes University Museum is another interesting museum containing items relating to the university. The former training college museum in Anglo African Street contains an original steam-driven Wharfedale printing machine twin of the one used to produce the *Eastern Star* which commenced publication in 1871 in Grahamstown and eventually moved to Johannesburg where it became *The Star*.

Among the architectural relics of past days is the Provost building with its round tower and loop-holed walls built in 1836 as a military prison. Another interesting building is *Fort Selwyn*, a redoubt on Gun Fire Hill, built in 1836 and named after Major Selwyn who was the commanding officer of the Royal Engineers in the Eastern Cape. It still contains a battery of guns. Around Artificer's Square there are groups of restored cottages and others in New and McDonald streets.

The oldest post box in South Africa is still in use at the corner of Worcester and Somerset streets. Mail posted in it is franked with a special post mark.

Behind Fort Selwyn stands the imposing 1820 Settlers National Monument. This building was the result of a campaign started by Thomas Bowker to revive pride in the heritage of the English-speaking people of South Africa. In 1960 the South African Parliament voted R100 000 towards the cost of the monument. Mr Bowker died in 1964 but his enthusiasm lingered on to carry the project forward with numerous supporters and contributors. The result was the construction of a complex of two conference halls, one seating 500 people and the other 200 people; a theatre with a seating capacity of 914; a restaurant; a shop; and a magnificent commemorative interior containing an eternally bubbling fountain rising from a millstone, depicting man's dependence on bread and the skill and labour which produce it.

The abstract sculpture of the interior, created out of indigenous yellowwood, is a three-dimensional integration with the concrete wall and represents the merging of the cultures of Britain and South Africa. The rectangles and diagonals symbolise the Union Jack with the Cross of Christ dominating the whole. The yellowwood radiates towards the lantern roof which is opened to the sky in good weather.

The theme of the monument is taken from *St. John 10:10*, *'That all might have life and have it more abundantly'*. The design was by Richard Wade and Kevin Atkinson. The building was opened on 13 July 1974.

Outside the complex there is a bronze of a settler family by Ivan Mitford-Barberton. The building stands in a floral reserve where the flora of the Eastern Cape is cultivated. There is a nature reserve on the slopes of Gun Fire Hill. The view from the monument presents a superb panorama over Grahamstown in its setting of hills and valleys.

The J L B Smith Institute of Ichthyology was originally a research department of Rhodes University forever associated with one of its great professors, after whom it is named. It is now independent of the university as a National Museum Institute with ongoing research on the marine and freshwater fish of Southern Africa. It is open to the public Mondays to Fridays 08h30–13h00 and 14h00–17h00.

The Botanic Gardens were founded in the 1850s, the second oldest in South Africa and containing a variety of interesting trees and cycads. There is a small military cemetery in the gardens and, by repute, a ghost. The beautiful Lady Juana Smith, wife of the Governor, Sir Harry Smith, is said to have liked the gardens so much that she lingers there as an occasional intangible and inexplicable whiff of Spanish perfume in the evening air. Another reserve, the Thomas Bain Reserve, has been established in Howison's Poort, with a variety of game animals originally indigenous to the area and reintroduced.

A particularly fine feature of the Grahamstown environment is the Mountain Drive which turns off from N2 at the caravan park. This road leads for 17 km through handsome stands of trees and there are many panoramic views. The drive passes such interesting places as the first reservoir of Grahamstown, built in 1860 and named after Sir George Grey, Governor of the Cape. The road climbs to the summit of the ridge, Dassie Krans, where the view provides a fitting climax to any visit to this amiable, atmospheric and serene little city, sometimes known as the City of the Saints on account of the 40 churches situated there.

It is a delightfully diverting little city to explore with several trails and walks.

From Grahamstown, Settlers Way (N2) stretches eastwards, climbing out of the valley of the Qoyi River up the slopes of the hill named after Makhanda, the leader of the Xhosa attack on Grahamstown in 1819, and along the summit of a high ridge. At 4,5 km from Grahamstown a tarmac turn-off leads northwards to Fort Beaufort, while a further 12 km brings the road to one of the most impressive and romantic viewsites in Southern Africa.

The end of the ridge is marked by a pair of radio and telecommunications towers erected on the 847 m high Governor's Kop. From the summit may be seen a superb view across the valley of the Great Fish River, the old frontier of Kaffraria, the meeting-place of two great migratory waves of humanity – black from the north, white from the south – and the scene of innumerable clashes, brawls, fights, wars, heroics and outrages. The line of watch-towers built by the British Army to guard this troubled frontier still looks out from the heights. The scene stirs the imagination and is beautiful at all seasons, with the range known as the *Amatole* (place of weaned calves), across the valley, often topped with snow in winter.

The road steadily descends into the valley. Wayside stalls offer pineapples, oranges and iced fresh fruit juices for sale. At 23 km from the summit (39 km from Grahamstown) the road passes *Fraser's Camp*, named after Colonel G S Fraser who led several commandos during the frontier wars. At this place a stall offers ice-cold pineapple juice and a variety of snacks. Accommodation is available.

For a further 12 km the road continues its tortuous descent, enhanced by many interesting views. At 49 km from Grahamstown the road reaches the bridge across the Great Fish River, the old frontier line of so much disturbances. The river for long marked the end of the Eastern Cape Province. For the continuation of the N2 road, see Chapter Twenty-One.

GRAHAMSTOWN TO PORT ALFRED AND PORT ELIZABETH

The route R67 from Grahamstown through Port Alfred and thereafter as R72 west along the coastal road to Port Elizabeth, provides the traveller with an interesting and scenically most varied journey. The exit from Grahamstown is especially spectacular. The tarmac road rises out of the city, climbing a hill slope covered in plantations of fir and gum trees. Reaching the summit line, the road follows the top of a high ridge with fine views on either side of the downlands of the coastal terrace and many well-cultivated farms of citrus and pineapple.

After 15 km the tarmac road starts to descend. At 20 km from Grahamstown the road reaches the Bloukrans Pass, a 5 km long traverse across a valley, the slopes of which are thickly grown with flowering aloes and bush. It was here, on 22 April 1911, that there occurred the so-called Bloukrans Bridge Disaster. A mixed train was derailed while crossing the high railway bridge and 28 people were killed when their coaches tumbled into the gorge.

Beyond the pass the tarmac road continues south-eastwards across an undulating grass-covered plain patched with light acacia bush and huge pineapple fields. At 38 km from Grahamstown there is a turn eastwards leading to Trappes Valley, and 3 km further on (41 km from Grahamstown) the road reaches the little town of ...

BATHURST

One of the most picturesque municipalities in South Africa, *Bathurst* has a population of 4 410. It was named after Earl Henry Bathurst who was the British Colonial Secretary at the time of the 1820 Settlers. The town was originally planned as the principal centre of the settlers area. In May 1820 Captain Charles Trappes of the Seaforth Highlanders was appointed its first magistrate. The tent he pitched as a combined residence and office was intended as the beginning of a town. The seat of magistracy, however, was transferred to Grahamstown. Bathurst was left as a quiet little rural centre. In this rustic state it still remains with its buildings dominated by some magnificent trees, notably flowering kaffirbooms which grow in the streets and many gigantic wild figs, one near the hotel with a spread of 120 m. The atmosphere of Bathurst is enriched by memories of early settler alarms, achievements and disappointments.

The Anglican and Wesleyan churches are both national monuments and each contains a Settler Bible. In their stormy day, both acted as retreats and strong points for the settlers during times of attack by Xhosa warriors. Christmas Day 1834 saw Bathurst abandoned entirely as a result of one of these attacks, with the district overrun by raiders for several days.

Bathurst is generally considered to be the pineapple capital of Southern Africa. Pineapples originated from Brazil and the Caribbean. Christopher Columbus found them on the island of Guadeloupe and took them to Europe. The Dutch introduced them to the Cape from Java, but they were little cultivated. In about 1860 they were planted in Natal, probably from crowns originating from Sri Lanka. In 1865 a Bathurst farmer, Charles Purdon, went into the shop of a Grahamstown barber, Lindsay Green, for a haircut. In his shop the barber had some pineapples from Natal. Purdon secured about 40 of the crowns and planted them on his farm *Thorndon*. They grew to perfection. Everything suited pineapples in that area. The novelty of the fruit rewarded growers with high prices and pineapples became the rage. Cultivation spread from Bathurst to the southern sector of Albany district and up the coastal belt to East London. South Africa now ranks as the eighth largest producer in the world after Hawaii, Brazil, Malaysia, Taiwan, Mexico, the Philippines and Thailand.

The water-drawn wool mill built in Bathurst in 1821 by Samuel Bradshaw is a national monument. It was used to make coarse cloth and was the home of the wool industry of South Africa. Corn milling was also done there. It is open daily except Thursdays. The Bathurst Agricultural Museum exhibits over 1 200 historical items, some unique. It is open daily (except Wednesday) 09h00 to 13h00 and 14h00 to 16h00.

Summerhill farm, on the outskirts of Bathurst is open to the public. On it stands what is claimed as the largest pineapple in South Africa, a 16 m high structure devoted to the story of pineapples.

The farm buildings have all been maintained in their original state, the cultivation of pineapples and chicory can be seen, there is a Xhosa village, walking trails and motorised tours, a mini-farm with baby animals, restaurant, pub and children's playground.

From Bathurst a gravel road leads westwards to the Horseshoe Bend Nature Reserve, 6 km from the town. Near the entrance to the reserve there is a viewsite overlooking the horseshoe bend in the Qoyi River, a classic and much-photographed example of a river meander. The road descends steeply, ending at a fine picnic site on the banks of the Qoyi River, 9 km from Bathurst. This is a very worthwhile drive. Several species of antelope and numerous birds find sanctuary there. Among the flowering plants is *Strelitzia reginae* (the crane flower) which flourishes to perfection.

From Bathurst there is a turn-off leading eastwards for 2 km to Bailies Beacon where, on a fine vantage-point, there is a toposcope identifying the various interesting points in the surrounding countryside, including the different places where parties of the 1820 Settlers were allocated land.

The main tarmac R67 road continues southwards across a richly grassed coastal plain where there are sheep and cattle farms. After 15 km the road makes a scenic entrance to the town and port of ...

PORT ALFRED

The town is one of the most attractively informal and picturesque of all the holiday resorts of Southern Africa. It is situated where the Kowie or *Qoyi* (rushing) River reaches the sea, with a spacious beach at its mouth. It is a fine river flowing through a well-wooded valley with innumerable twists.

When the 1820 Settlers came to the Eastern Cape, they viewed the mouth of the Kowie with interest. At that time the estuary consisted of a swampy mixture of islets, canals and reeds confined east and west by the low hills known as the East and West banks. The area was entirely unpopulated and a great resort for birds and fish.

Several individuals conceived the idea of a port at the mouth of the river. In 1821 the government, at their suggestion, sent a small brig, the *Locust*, to sound the entrance to the river, and this was the first vessel ever known to sail the waters of the Kowie. The bar across the entrance to the river varied from 1 m to over 2 m in depth, with reasonably deep water further inland. A rich fishing ground lay in the roadstead east of the river mouth close to the *Fountain Rocks*, so named on account of the swell which at high tide spouted up there in a jet of water.

As a result of this investigation, Mr J Dyason was appointed pilot and harbour-master of the Kowie, a flagstaff was erected on the East Bank and a boat's crew appointed. This was the beginning of Port Kowie. A special light-draught schooner, the *Elizabeth*, was built to serve the port; and on 9 November 1821 this little vessel successfully entered the river. Unfortunately, on her next voyage from Port Elizabeth the schooner was totally wrecked on Cape Recife.

Other coasters soon replaced the wreck, for there was a genuine need for a port to serve the Settler country. But, like all shallow river mouths, the Kowie was a death-trap for sailing vessels. A sudden drop in wind or an unexpected rush of tidal water could defeat the genius of any sailing master and land his vessel unceremoniously on the beach.

For the next ten years the government struggled to develop Port Kowie into a harbour. The town which grew up on the banks of the river was at first called *Port Frances* in honour of the wife of Colonel Henry Somerset, son of the Governor, but in 1860 the name was finally changed to Port Alfred in honour of Prince Alfred who was on a visit to South Africa at the time.

The efforts to develop a harbour failed. In 1831 the office of harbour-master was abolished and the port was left to a few fishermen and the enterprise of private individuals. Among these was William Cock who in 1836 settled there, building on the West Bank what became known as *Cock's Castle*. His daughter, Mary, has left her name on *Mary's Cove*. For years these private individuals laboured, trying a series of schemes to open the river mouth. Cock was the motivating force for most of these efforts and it was he who changed the flow of the river to a new channel below the West Bank.

A vast amount of energy and money was expended on the Kowie by Cock and other people. Ships came and went, but the number that were wrecked was considerable and professional ship-masters detested the place because of its dangers and uncertainties. The only saving grace was that Port Elizabeth, the nearest harbour, was also a great hazard to shipping.

In 1857 the government once again launched a scheme to develop the port. Piers were built, a steam tug was stationed there in 1863 and a dredger employed in deepening the channel. A company, the Kowie Harbour Improvement Company, had the running of the port. This was the golden age of the harbour, with ships such as the 340 ton *Icon* trading there. Larger ships anchored in the roadstead and were serviced by lighters. In this way the mailships of the Union Steamship Navigation Company paid regular visits from 1875 onwards, with 101 ships landing 12 750 tons of cargo in Port Alfred in 1876.

The year 1881 saw a great activity, with a railway being built from Port Alfred to Grahamstown. The constructional materials and rolling-stock were all shipped to the harbour. Included with this material was the steelwork for the 61 m high bridge over the Blaauwkranz where the railway disaster took place in 1911. The railway was built by a private company, the Kowie Railway Company, which went into liquidation in 1886 and was taken over by another concern. It is interesting to know that two of the locomotives used on this railway are still preserved, one on a pedestal in the Cape Town railway station and the other in the Port Elizabeth Museum.

Port Alfred harbour fell into disuse in the 1890s. There has been periodic talk of reopening it, but today the river is confined to yachts, power boats and canoes used in a paradise of fine scenery. The climate is pleasant and there is excellent swimming, surfing, fishing, scuba diving and recreation. The beaches of Port Alfred are renowned for their variety of shells.

The river is navigable by small boats for 24 km. The Kowie Canoe Trail up the river, which includes a tramping trail through the indigenous forest, is very popular. There are launch trips and boats and canoes to hire for the exploration of the river. Bird life is extensive and there is a bird sanctuary in the central business area of the town. The Royal Alfred Marina and small-boat harbour has been constructed near the river mouth. It is interesting to note that the walls of the Marina, created in 1988, are packed with hand-laid stones to match the work of the settlers in the 1840s on the banks of the re-routed river.

The population of the town is 17 627. There is a museum which has as its main theme the Qoyi River. It is open from 09h00 to 12h30 every day except Sundays. The Royal Port Alfred Golf Club is one of the finest in Southern Africa and is renowned for its spectacular sea views.

The Kowie Nature Reserve is situated 8 km north of Port Alfred. It conserves 200 ha along the river banks, with cycads, flowering plants and fine scenery. There are hiking trails.

The coastal R72 road from East London (150 km) leads through Port Alfred on its way to Alexandria and to a junction with N2 at 50 km from Port Elizabeth. This tarmac road provides access to several coastal resorts.

North-eastwards up the coast, the road (after 4 km) reaches the Rufane River, with a pleasant beach at its mouth. A further 7,5 km takes the road to the Rietrivier, where a short gravel turn-off leads to the lagoon mouth. A 20-minute walk up the beach (eastwards) leads to the group of rocks known as the Three Sisters. Another 4 km up the R72 road takes the traveller to the twin rivers known as Kleinemonde west and east. Both rivers have fine lagoons at their mouths and small resorts consisting of private bungalows and shacks.

Another 4,5 km takes the road past a turn-off to the Great Fish Point lighthouse built in a prohibited area down a 5 km long gravel road. A permit to visit the lighthouse can be obtained from the publicity office in Port Alfred, phone (046) 624-1235.

Another 4,5 km beyond this turn-off there are the ruins of Fort D'Acre, built during the days of frontier disturbance as one of the British military strongholds guarding the line of the Great Fish River. The river is 1 km beyond the fort. Just before the bridge there is a turn-off leading to the mouth of the river where there is a holiday resort overlooking a fine, sandy beach. The distance to the river from Port Alfred is 25,5 km. Across the Great Fish River the coastal road continues up a delectable coast for 152,5 km to East London (see Chapter Twenty-One).

South-west of Port Alfred, the coastal road R72 provides a drive through pleasant downland country with grassy hill slopes rolling towards the sea. An interesting feature is the number of dewponds, each with a collection of wild ducks and geese. Patches of trees and fine herds of cattle ornament the landscape.

At 13 km there is a gravel turn-off to the small hamlet of Southwell (19 km) while at 23 km from Port Alfred the road crosses the Kariga River, a spacious and most attractive expanse of water with an informal huddle of cottages on its banks. The *Kasuka* River nearby takes its name from the number of leopards which used to inhabit the area. It has a fine lagoon. A further 0,5 km brings the road to a turn-off leading to the seaside resort of Kenton-on-Sea which lies on the east side of the broad mouth of the Bushman's River, known to the Xhosa as the *Qhora* (the place where tobacco pipes are made). Superb boating on the river, a spacious beach, handsome sand dunes and interesting rock formations all contribute towards a pleasant recreational area. Besides a hotel, there are cottages available for rent.

Five kilometres from the Bushman's River there is a tarmac turn-off to Boknes and Cannon Rocks. The main road continues for 20 km past pineapple and chicory fields and fine dairy country to the town of Alexandria. The turn-off to Boknes and Cannon Rocks provides an alternative route to the same town. Along this turn-off, after 1,5 km, a gate on the eastern side takes the traveller on to a track (1,5 km long with three gates) ending at a path which stretches over bush-covered dunes and across a miniature 'Sahara Desert'. Beyond this 1 km wide stretch of windswept sand, there looms the curious island-like, isolated rock known as the 'rock of the fountains', where Bartholomeu Dias reached his furthest point of exploration and erected his stone cross to St Gregory. It is a moderately stiff walk to the rock (apparently once an islet), but is worth the effort.

The original cross was shattered into some 5 000 pieces and the site forgotten. In 1935 Professor Eric Axelson found the fragments. They were painstakingly reassembled into the original cross which now stands in the Library of the University of the Witwatersrand. A replica of the cross was erected in 1940 on the rock of the fountains at *Kwaaihoek* (angry corner). On 12 March 1988, exactly 500 years after Dias planted his cross, a cross made in Portugal from the same material as the original, and brought to South Africa on a replica of Dias's ship, was erected there.

At 4,5 km beyond the turn-off to the Dias Cross memorial, there is a crossroads. A left turn (tarmac) leads for 1,5 km to the beach and lagoon of the small holiday resort of *Boknes* (father's river), where there is a camping ground. A right turn (gravel) leads to a turn-off after 6 km to the fishing resort and sandy beach of Cannon Rocks. Two old cannon and an anchor are mounted at the beach.

Beyond the turn-off to Cannon Rocks the gravel road continues along the coast past the Rustfontein store and Cape Padrone. After 13 km the road reaches a turn-off to Midfor. The coastal scenery is spectacular with a sandy mass of high dunes and a view seawards of Bird, Seal and Stag islands.

The R72 road now veers inland and leads through the beautiful Alexandria state forest. This is an indigenous high forest with many superb trees, well populated with vervet monkeys, bushbuck and wild pigs. There is a picnic site at Langebos 4 km from the Midfor turn-off, while a further 1,5 km takes the road past the Alexandria forest station. There is a 2-day circular hiking trail as well as a forest walk.

For a further 8 km the road leads across open pasturage country patched with forest. Then, 30 km from the turn-off to Cannon Rocks, the road, after a most enjoyable journey reaches the town of ...

ALEXANDRIA

Named after the Reverend Alexander Smith who ministered to the population in the district, *Alexandria* was established in 1840. Today, it is the centre of a considerable industry in the growing of chicory and pineapples. The chicory-drying factory is claimed to be the largest in the world. Visitors are welcome. The summer months November to April see full production. The town is the railhead of a branch line from Port Elizabeth. A few of the original houses still survive, including the gaol, now used as a residence in Drews Lane.

From Alexandria the tarmac R72 road continues westwards across a pleasant agricultural countryside of chicory, pineapple, wheat and mixed livestock farms. Passing through a small bushy valley (Soutkloof), the road (20 km from Alexandria) climbs into a pile of hills. At 30 km from Alexandria the tarmac road reaches the summit of an attractive pass and descends easily through the shallow Thorn Kloof, with wheat and maize lands set among low, rolling hills. At 49 km from Alexandria the road joins the N2 Port Elizabeth–Grahamstown road at a point 54 km from Port Elizabeth. The circular drive from Port Elizabeth to Grahamstown, Port Alfred, Alexandria and back to Port Elizabeth, provides a diverting and varied tour of a total of 338 km through the best parts of the 1820 Settler country.

Chapter Twenty
THE EASTERN CAPE

People, Places and Ghosts

The tarmac road from Port Elizabeth to the north (N10), for the first 45,5 km of its journey, is part of N2 (Settlers Way) leading to Grahamstown and on to KwaZulu-Natal and Mpumulanga. A major traffic interchange marks the parting of the ways. The road to the north has its own start by leading over a slightly undulating plain. After 21,5 km it reaches the small twin rural and rail centres of Paterson (named after John Paterson, a member of the Cape Legislative Assembly and proponent of a separate province in the Eastern Cape, who established the village in 1879) and Sandflats where there is a gravel turn-off leading for 27 km to the Addo Elephant National Park. The main road N10 crosses the railway line and is immediately confronted by a steady climb up the densely bushed slopes of the range known as the *Zuurberge* (sour mountains) from the taste of the grazing. After 19 km of interesting journey up the *Olifantskop* (elephant's peak) Pass, the road reaches the summit of the range, 720 m high, where there is a comprehensive view over a countryside covered in the blue-green bush typical of the Eastern Cape. This is classic *zuur* (sour) grazing country with dense patches of stunted-looking but extremely hardy bush.

While the road has climbed over the Zuurberge, the railway to the north has found a circuitous route through the mountains by joining the valley of the Bushmans River which has taken a good few millions of years in times of better rains to erode a passage for itself. From the foot of the Olifantskop Pass there is a turn-off leading for 18 km to the Bushmans River valley and the agricultural centre and railway junction of ...

ALICEDALE

When the railway was constructed, the engineer in charge named the station after his wife, Mrs Alice Slessor, whose maiden name had been Dale. Alicedale became the junction for the branch line to Grahamstown and today is a busy little town of 3 383 residents, with a pleasant recreational area on the banks of the lake at the dam built on the Nuwejaars River.

The main road to the north, N10, meanwhile, has descended to the northern side of the Olifantskop Pass. The inland side of the range is far more arid than the coastal belt. The road descends into this drought-ridden wilderness, crosses, 12 km from the summit, the erratically flowing upper reaches of the Bushmans River, then (36,5 km from Paterson) passes through the small rural centre of Middleton. The traveller is now in the valley of the Great Fish River and for many kilometres the effects of irrigation can be seen as the road leads northwards.

At 14 km from Middleton the road passes a memorial to ...

THE SLAGTERSNEK REBELLION

The roadside memorial to the Slagtersnek Rebellion was unveiled on 9 March 1916. It was erected on the site of the gallows used in executing five of the men involved in a most unfortunate affair in the year 1815. It was a particularly stormy period in the seldom-peaceful history of Southern

Africa. Frontier disturbances, raids and wars were frequent; and many of the individuals living in the frontier areas were not only as rugged as the mountains, but inclined to be trigger itchy.

Frederik Bezuidenhout, a farmer of the banks of the Baviaans River, had a series of disagreements with a shepherd named Booi. The shepherd complained to the authorities at Cradock and Graaff-Reinet, and Bezuidenhout was repeatedly summoned to court. Each time he responded by writing an apologetic letter and suggesting that the matter be settled by the local *field-cornet* (district officer) visiting him on the farm.

For reasons unknown the field-cornet did not do this. Eventually a small force of *pandours* (Coloured soldiers) under white officers was sent to arrest Bezuidenhout. Bezuidenhout declined to be arrested. With two companions he withdrew into a cave and defended himself. He was eventually shot dead by one of the pandours.

At Bezuidenhout's funeral one of his brothers, Johannes, swore that he would avenge the death. A farmer named Hendrik Prinsloo of *Bruintjieshoek* became involved in the affair. He invited Johannes to join him in a movement to drive the British out of the country on the grounds that they favoured blacks and enacted legislation affecting the land ownership of the Boers.

Bezuidenhout and Prinsloo proceeded to organise an uprising on the eastern border. About 60 farmers joined and the Xhosas were asked for support. By November 1815 the insurrection was being actively planned, with Johannes Bezuidenhout as the leader.

The authorities sent an armed force to arrest the insurgents. On 13 November Hendrik Prinsloo was arrested and taken to Van Aardtspos, a military post and the site of the memorial. About 60 armed Boers thereupon rode to the post and demanded the release of Prinsloo. When the commanding officer refused, the Boers made a vow to see the rebellion through faithfully. They then dispersed, as they were expecting support from the Xhosas.

On 18 November, the military commander of the border, Jacob Cuyler, landdrost of Uitenhage, came upon a group of rebels at Slagtersnek. After some negotiation, most of the men dispersed and another twenty surrendered. They were escorted to Van Aardtspos. Over the next few days several other men surrendered. Others took to the mountains, including Bezuidenhout.

On 24 November a force of about 120 Boers and pandours under Commandant W Nel and Major G Fraser were heading for the Tarka River when they heard that Bezuidenhout and his party were riding towards the Winterberg. The troops pursued them and captured two men, Abraham Bothma and Andries Meyer, who stated that the rest of the party had reversed their tracks and were heading for the Tarka River. The troops gave chase.

On 29 November in a ravine between the farms *Oxford* and *Spring Valley* the troops ambushed Bezuidenhout, Stephanus Bothma and Cornelis Faber with their families. The Fabers and the Bothmas surrendered but the Bezuidenhouts refused. Bezuidenhout, with his wife and young son, fought it out until all were wounded, Bezuidenhout dying of his wounds. He was buried a few kilometres away on the farm *Rocklyn*.

The rebels were tried in Uitenhage. Some were acquitted, others imprisoned or banished, six were sentenced to death. Of these, one was reprieved by the Governor. The others were Hendrik Prinsloo, Stephanus and Abraham Bothma, Cornelis Faber and Theunis de Klerk. On 9 March 1816 they were hanged from a single gallows at Van Aardtspos, at the spot where they had made their original vow four months earlier. A large number of people were ordered to attend the execution as a warning. The hanging was badly done. The rope broke while four of the men were still alive. There was a highly emotional scene as they and many of the spectators pleaded for clemency.

Cuyler, who was in charge, stated that he did not have the power to grant clemency, and the men were hanged separately. The rebellion was not a popular movement amongst the farmers, particularly in regard to the idea of enlisting support from the Xhosas. The execution, however, created considerable ill feeling.

At 2,5 km beyond the Slagtersnek memorial the N10 road passes the small rural centre of Golden Valley. After 7 km the road reaches the railway and road junction of *Cookhouse*, a village notable for little other than its oven-like heat in summer. Its name comes from a small stone kitchen erected there by troops garrisoning the area during the years of the frontier wars.

From Cookhouse there is a turn-off leading westwards for 24 km to the town of ...

SOMERSET EAST

Lying firmly against the bushy 823 m high cliffs of the Bosberg range, Somerset East is a pleasantly relaxed town with a long main street unfortunately somewhat devoid of trees. The mountain background, however, is impressive with patches of forest and numerous waterfalls (sixteen of them visible from the town). The Bosberg Nature Reserve, proclaimed in 1967, covers 2 050 ha of the southern slopes of the range. There are good walks, including a 15 km circular hiking trail with an overnight hut on the summit of the Bosberg. The views are exciting, especially over the Bestershoek valley. The 33 km scenic Auret Drive leads to the summit of the range from where many lovely views may be had.

The district is famous for its merino sheep, boerbok and angora goat stud-farms. Somerset East, in fact, originated as a farm (known as *Somerset Farm*) which was founded there in 1815 by the Governor, Lord Charles Somerset. This farm was developed to supply meal and oat hay to the frontier garrisons and also to experiment with crops such as tobacco. Although, the farm served a useful purpose, its production was ended in 1825 and a village (named *Somerset* after the Governor) was laid out on its grounds. The 'East' was added to the name later to distinguish the town from Somerset West near Cape Town. On 13 April 1825 the first erven were sold. In February 1837 it became a municipality, and today has a population of 16 390.

The original Georgian-style farmhouse was built in 1818 for the superintendent of *Somerset Farm*. Subsequently it became the *drostdy* (seat of magistracy), then the Methodist manse and then the Dutch Reformed parsonage. It is now the Somerset East Museum exhibiting many interesting items and pictures of the early days of this frontier area. It is open weekdays 08h00 to 13h00 and 14h00 to 17h00, or by appointment. There is a tea-room in the building. In another building which used to be an officers' mess there is a collection of the paintings of the artist Walter Battiss. He spent his childhood in Somerset East and lived in this building. The exhibition is open weekdays during the same hours as the main museum. Thirteen buildings in the town have been proclaimed national monuments.

Somerset East is notable for its flowers, both cultivated and wild. Roses flourish to perfection, producing some wonderful displays in summer. Rose-petal jam is a product of the area and can be purchased with other delights in the museum tea-room. Bestershoek is a recreational area for picnics. It has a pleasantly situated caravan park. The co-educational dual-medium Gill College High School is well known.

From Somerset East the tarmac road, R63, continues westwards for 51 km to the town of ...

PEARSTON

Pearston is the centre for a rich pastoral and agricultural district. Irrigation water is available from fountains of the Vogel River. Fruit and vegetables are cultivated.

The town had its start on 21 September 1859 when the Dutch Reformed Church bought part of the farm *Rustenburg* from Casper Lötter and had it surveyed into irrigation and residential plots. The town was named after the Reverend John Pears of Somerset East, who ministered to the local congregation. A village management board took over the place in 1861 and a municipality was created on 8 June 1911.

Pearston is a sunny little town with the detached, relaxed atmosphere peculiar to most places which have no rail or major road connection to the outside world. It is served by road transport to Somerset East, Cradock (87 km) and Graaff-Reinet (72 km).

From Cookhouse, meanwhile, the tarmac N10 road continues northwards up the valley of the Great Fish River, closely hemmed in by high cliffs covered in thornbush. The alluvial valley floor, wherever suitable, is intensely irrigated and very productive. Several turn-offs mark the way. At 13 km there is a tarmac turn-off to East London, another one to the same place after 6 km. At 24 km from Cookhouse a turn-off stretches westwards to that place of lugubrious memories, Slagtersnek. *Slagtersnek* (butchers' col or saddle) was so named after the killing there on 28 December 1811 of the landdrost of Graaff-Reinet, Anders Stockenström, and thirteen others by a Xhosa armed force.

After 80 km of travel up the valley from Cookhouse the main tarmac road, N10, reaches the pleasant, busy town of ...

CRADOCK

A major road and rail centre on the route to the north from Port Elizabeth, Cradock is a pleasant, spacious and clean country town. It was built on the banks of the Great Fish River and dominated by a handsome Dutch Reformed church erected in 1868 as a replica of St Martin-in-the-Fields in London.

The story of Southern Africa consists of a series of leapfrogs: government drew boundaries; pioneers leaped over them; government was forced to redraw boundaries. Cradock had its beginning in such a manner. Families such as the Van Heerdens, Lombards and Van Rensburgs settled in this area when it was well beyond the recognised frontier.

After the 1812 Frontier War the soldier-governor of the Cape, Sir John Cradock, decided to strengthen the frontier by creating the two sub-districts of Uitenhage and Graaff-Reinet. On 10 June 1812 Andries Stockenström (son of the ill-fated Anders Stockenström of Slagtersnek) became deputy magistrate at Van Stadens dam in the valley of the Great Fish River. He soon changed his seat to the farm *Buffelskloof* owned by Pieter van Heerden, which lay in a particularly pleasant and strategic position close to a spring of sulphur water.

Sir John Cradock visited the place and approved it as the site for a town. The farm was bought for 3 500 rixdollars. The homestead was converted into a gaol and official buildings were erected. From Stockenström came a suggestion that the place be named Cradock. On 21 January 1814 this name was officially approved. From then the town grew, becoming a municipality in 1873 and developing a considerable charm and character over the years. The town has 29 168 inhabitants.

With rich soil irrigated from three government irrigation dams (Grassridge, Lake Arthur and Kommandodrif), Cradock is the centre for considerable farming activity in lucerne, fruit, dairy and poultry products. Lake Arthur is a favourite recreational place for boating of all kinds.

There is a good viewsite overlooking the town from Oukop, a hillock next to the N10 road just as it leaves Cradock for the north. At the Karoo Sulphur Springs the municipality has developed a resort with swimming and facilities for picnicking and caravanning. The Van Riebeeck Karoo Garden with its succulents, shrubs and wild pomegranates is worth visiting.

MOUNTAIN ZEBRA NATIONAL PARK

Situated 24 km from Cradock, this is one of the most scenically beautiful and interesting of all the national parks in Southern Africa. It may be reached by following the main N10 road running northwards from Cradock. After 3 km there is a tarmac turn R61 leading north-westwards to Graaff-Reinet. At 5 km along this tarmac road there is a gravel turn-off south into the foothills of the Bankberg range. Eleven kilometres of travel brings the road to the entrance of the park where the ranger's house and office lie tucked away in a valley 3 km further on.

The park was started in 1937 when the National Parks Board bought the farm *Babylonstoren* to use as a sanctuary for one of the rarest animals, the Cape mountain zebra (*Equus zebra zebra*). The smallest of the zebras, the mountain zebra stands a mere 1,2 m high. Beautifully striped with a distinct dewlap beneath its throat, it is a lively, sure-footed creature which once inhabited many of the mountain ranges of the Cape, especially the Outeniqua. European hunters largely shot them out, but in the 1997 count there were 241 mountain zebra in the park while a further 400 are known to exist elsewhere. These are the only survivors of a breed once numerous.

The Mountain Zebra National Park covers an area of 6 633 ha on the slopes of the Bankberg. Apart from zebra, there are mountain reedbuck, grey rhebok, klipspringer, steenbok, duikers, kudu, eland, black wildebeest, red hartebeest, springbok and 150 species of birds, including ostriches.

Vegetation is particularly interesting and typically Karoo, with many fine karee, acacia, wild olive, white stinkwood and kiepersol trees, and a great variety of flowering plants, shrubs and aloes growing there. Mesembryanthemums make a handsome display. After good rains in April the entire landscape is covered with flowers such as the purple-mauve *Moraea polystacha* (blue tulip).

Roads lead from the ranger's house to several parts of the park, and those climbing to the heights of the range (especially to Kranskop) reveal magnificent panoramas of a landscape covered with oddly shaped hillocks. Walking is permitted in the park along the many paths. Horses may be hired by the hour. This is classic commando country where armies could manoeuvre like fleets on the surface of a seemingly boundless ocean. With the herds of antelope grazing on the heights, the wild flowers and the Bushman paintings on the rocks, the scene is superb and a living museum-piece of the romantic days of old. The park is open daily from 07h00 to 19h00 (1 October to 30 April) and from 07h00 to 18h00 (1 May to 30 September).

Facilities in the modern rest camp include caravan and camping sites, bungalows and a restaurant. There is a museum in the original homestead of *Doornhoek*. The Mountain Zebra Trail provides a three-day walk.

From Cradock the N10 road crosses the Great Fish River by means of the Gilfillian bridge. It then climbs steeply northwards out of the river valley, taking a last look at the little town resting on its banks. At 3 km north of Cradock there is a tarmac turn-off R61 stretching north-westwards to the Mountain Zebra National Park (17 km) and to Graaff-Reinet (140 km).

The road continues northwards over the great plains of the Karoo. Scattered over the high-lying landscape is an assembly of rocky hillocks (the genuine, unique breed of South African koppie). Among their assorted shapes may be seen table tops, pointed and round tops, rhino horn and pouf-seat tops. In this truly South African setting it is easy to understand the hardiness and independence of the pioneers. The landscape is on a prodigious scale, seemingly infinite, always with more distant hills peeping over an endless horizon. Such a scene is an insidious temptation to trek on, to escape from authority and the irksome taxman, and to lose oneself in the blue.

After 35 km the road crosses the upper reaches of the Great Fish River. Twenty-four kilometres further on there is a turn-off stretching eastwards to Hofmeyr (50 km) and then, 97 km from Cradock, the road merges with the tarmac N9 road coming from George and Graaff-Reinet. Together the combined roads lead past the town of ...

MIDDELBURG

Founded in 1852 as the middle point (hence the name) between the older towns of Cradock, Colesberg, Richmond and Hofmeyr, *Middelburg* lies on the banks of the Little Brak River in the great basin which forms the watershed of that river. The town attained municipal status in 1913 and is the centre for a substantial farming activity mainly with sheep. The Grootfontein College of Agriculture is situated 3 km from the town.

From Middelburg the tarmac N10 road to the north stretches on past the Grootfontein College of Agriculture and, in company with the railway, begins climbing up the Carlton Hills, reaching the summit 1 804 m above sea-level, 10 km from Middelburg. Three kilometres further on, the road passes through the *Noupoort* (narrow pass), with the railway running below it in a tunnel. The road then descends to the level of another high plain on which, 39 km from Middelburg, lies the railway junction and marshalling yard of ...

NOUPOORT

When the railway being constructed from Port Elizabeth cut its way through the 'narrow pass' and reached the site of the town in 1884, *Noupoort* had its beginning. The town was actually laid out on the farm *Hartebeeshoek*, but because the narrow pass was the principal feature of the area, the name of Noupoort came into use. As a coaling depot, junction (to De Aar), staging post and marshalling yard, Noupoort became one of the most important railway centres in South Africa. Its existence is dominated entirely by the continual passage of trains. The population is 6 795.

From Noupoort the tarmac N9 road continues northwards across a high, open and windswept plain, bitterly cold in winter. Rocky hillocks are scattered around in some general disorder. At 16 km north of Noupoort the traveller sees for the first time one of the best known of all these hillocks and one of the principal landmarks of Southern Africa, the famous Colesberg Koppie. A further 34 km of travel brings the road to the slopes of this distinctive beacon on the way northwards. At this point, 50 km from Noupoort, the Cape-to-Cairo (N1) road coming from the south joins the road from Port Elizabeth, and together the roads lead to the crossing of the Gariep River and the long journey northwards.

N9 ROAD SOUTH TO GRAAFF-REINET AND GEORGE

In the original planning of the National Road network of South Africa, this road (now known as N9) was identified as N1 and called the Road of South Africa. There was considerable controversy about this at the time. In recent years the identification N1 has been given to the Cape-to-Cairo road and the identification N9 given to the old road which merges into the modern N1 at Colesberg.

Let us follow the N9 southwards from Middelburg, where N10 from Port Elizabeth joined it.

Keeping close company with the railway line, the road makes its way down the eastern verges of the Renosterberg. It is a rugged stretch of country with, on all sides, some pretty wild-looking mountains of the *Sneeuberge* (snow mountain) range. The road crosses the range by means of the pass known as *Lootsberg* after Hendrik Loots who was killed there when his cart overturned and crashed down a steep slope. The summit of the pass is 1 785 m above sea-level and it is often closed because of snow. The summit is 52 km from Middelburg.

Below the pass, there is a tarmac turn-off eastwards which leads over the *Wapadsberg* (wagon road mountain) Pass for 88 km to Cradock. This road passes the turn-off to the Mountain Zebra National Park 8 km from Cradock.

The main N9 road continues south-westwards from the foot of the Lootsberg over the floor of a high-lying bowl in the mountains. At 57 km from Middelburg, N9 reaches the railway station of *Bethesdaweg* (Bethesda Road) where there is a turn-off leading for 27 km to ...

NIEU BETHESDA

The attractive and interesting little town of Nieu Bethesda lies in the southern foothills of the Sneeuberge and is dominated by the highest peak of the range, the 2 502 m high *Kompasberg* (compass mountain), so named in 1778 when Governor Joachim van Plettenberg and Colonel Jacob Gordon examined the area and considered that from the summit of this mountain they could encompass a panoramic view of the whole countryside.

In the arid setting of the Karoo, the site of the future town was generously watered by perennial streams flowing down from the mountains. On the inspiration of Andrew Murray, the renowned parson of Graaff-Reinet, the Dutch Reformed Church founded a village there in 1875. On giving the place the biblical name of *Bethesda* (place of flowing waters) from *John 5: 2–4*, he used the words in Dutch *'Laten sy dese plaats nu Bethesda noemen'* (Let us now name this place Bethesda). In later years a mistake in translation turned the *'nu* (now) into *nieu* (new) and this incorrect form is still used.

The village flourished as an agricultural centre endowed with such copious supplies of perennial water that every plot and garden was entitled to a twice-weekly irrigation flow by deflecting the streams running down the sides of the streets. Pear and other trees were planted in the streets, and by 1886 the town had grown sufficiently to become a municipality.

Today it is a delightful little place to visit. Its population is 953. The atmosphere is amiable and it is a pleasure to walk through the streets and find a place so unspoilt by any modern development. There are interesting houses, a water-wheel mill erected by B J Pienaar, and a handsome Dutch Reformed church built of local stone with gas chandeliers and carved wooden pews. Nieu Bethesda is noted for its historic architectural integrity.

There are walks, climbs and what are called Sneeuberg Farm Trails organised by a group of local farmers. Horses are available for trail riding, and accommodation is provided on some of the farms. It is great back-packing country. Significant fossil discoveries have been made in the district.

An extraordinary feature of Nieu Bethesda is the so-called 'Owl House'. This was the home of Helen Martins who was born in the town on 22 December 1898, the youngest of six children. She went to school in Nieu Bethesda and then moved to Graaff-Reinet where, trained as a teacher, she taught for several years. She married Johannes Pienaar, but the marriage was a failure. Helen continued teaching in Graaff-Reinet with spells of travel, including a time in Muizenberg where she worked as a waitress. In the 1940s, the ill health of her parents eventually made her return home to nurse them until their death.

She married again, to a retired furniture restorer named Niemand. Divorce followed after three months. She was then 54. For the next 17 years she lived alone, employing a very talented assistant named Koos Malgas and, at different times, two other men, Piet van der Merwe and Jonas Adams, to help her in the creation of an astonishing gallery of cement sculptures in what was called the Camel Yard.

She remained in the family house, becoming increasingly reclusive and interested in Oriental mysticism as well as other religions and their symbolism, devoting the rest of her life to a very special form of art. She incessantly read Omar Khayyam and William Blake and developed a special empathy with light and its reflections. She made ground glass with the aid of a mealie grinder in an outhouse. She ground the glass to meticulously graded sizes and colours. The glass was embedded in brightly coloured bands of paint to form an almost infinite variety of patterns and shapes giving every room a distinct theme. With this ground glass she covered the walls of her house. She had no electric light, but at night candles and paraffin lamps were lit at carefully selected sites and there were a myriad of reflections from the ground glass.

Her only known income was from the State old-age pension. She seemed to live on tea, bread and an occasional hot meal sent in by her neighbours. Most of her money went to pay Koos Malgas and the other assistants, and to buy the materials, mainly cement and chicken wire used in her art. She never sold any of her art or sought human company. She did have friends within the village but on the whole they frowned upon her work.

Her eyes started to fail as a result of age and her working with ground glass. She became increasingly frail but refused to move to an old age home. When she realised that she could go on no longer, at the age of 78, in 1976, she committed suicide by the agonising method of drinking caustic soda.

Her faithful assistant, Koos Malgas, became a menial in Worcester with little chance of continuing his talented artistry. Then in 1991, a group of enthusiasts known as The Friends of the Owl House, found Koos Malgas and persuaded him to return to Nieu Bethesda, help restore the Owl

House and continue artistic work. The Owl House Foundation was formed in 1996 and is committed to the long-term preservation of the Owl House and the care of Helen Martins' remarkable work, The Nieu Bethesda local council, art lovers, local residents, The Friends of the Owl House and PPC Cement (Pty) Ltd are members of this Group. PPC Cement (Pty) Ltd is justly proud to be associated with the work of Helen Martins. They are the principal patron of the Owl House. There are about 400 cement statues in the Owl House including over 90 owls. She kept four live owls as pets.

Helen Martins left no explanation of her work, which occupied her for over 25 years. It is a fascinating, thought provoking and remarkable place to visit, recognised as a significant example of the phenomenon of Outsider Art. A play, a book and a film have been produced on the reclusive life of Helen Martins. Her house is now preserved by the municipality as a museum. Her strange creations – owls, camels, human figures and various other creatures of fantasy – are preserved in the Camel Yard at the back of the house. Perhaps it is all best interpreted simply by the words worked by Helen in bent wire lettering on the fence of the house: *This is my world.*

From the turn-off at Bethesdaweg railway station, the N9 road continues south-westwards, traversing a high-lying bowl in the mountains – fine sheep and angora goat country – cold in winter, hot in summer. After 15 km the road leaves this area by means of the Naudesberg Pass and descends to the level of a lower plateau. After 11 km there is another turn-off leading for 23 km to Nieu Bethesda. Gradually descending through rugged hill country, the road crosses the Sundays River just above the point where it flows into the Vanryneveld Pass Dam and then, at the outskirts of Graaff-Reinet, passes the memorial to the famed leader of the Great Trek, Andries Pretorius. The sculpture by Coert Steynberg faces Pretorius Kloof, where Andries Pretorius had his farm *Letskraal*. After 1,5 km (106 km from Middelburg) the N9 main road enters the town of ...

GRAAFF-REINET

One of the historic towns of the Cape Colony, Graaff-Reinet still retains some of the atmosphere and presence of the days when it was a frontier town and its streets were peopled by a colourful crowd of wanderers, hunters, explorers and pioneers. The district gave birth to a hardy, independent and rugged assembly of human beings, some of whom were to become great Voortrekker leaders, such as Andries Pretorius and Sarel Cilliers.

The town had its beginning on 19 July 1786 when the Governor of the Cape, Jacob van de Graaff, in an effort to settle a troubled frontier, proclaimed the establishment of a new district embracing the sprawling, sunburned area which extended from the Gamtoos River to the Great Fish River, and from the sea to the Seekoei River. A new town was planned to administer this district, and the site chosen was in a most spectacular concentration of scenery near the source of the Sundays River. At this place the river burrows into a complex cluster of flat-topped mountains which form part of the Sneeuberge massif. In the course of finding a way through this range, the river formed a huge horseshoe-bend and deposited a rich layer of alluvial silt which, with the perennial flow of water, the crisp, sunny climate and 250 mm of rain a year, combines to make the area particularly fertile. Overlooking the site is a guardian peak, *Spandau Kop*, named by a Prussian settler, Werner, after the fortress in Spandau near Berlin.

The site of the town (originally the farm of Dirk Coetzee) was well chosen by Herman Woeke, the first landdrost appointed to the new district. The name of *Graaff-Reinet* was given to the town in honour of the governor and his lady, Cornelia Rijnet. It was at first spelt *Graaff-Rijnet*. A *drostdy* (residency) was built in 1786 on a site adjacent to the modern Seamans Garage but was replaced in 1804 by a more imposing official residence, the restored building now serving as the Drostdy hotel. In its early years Graaff-Reinet was a rough-and-ready little town in which most of the early buildings met their end by simply collapsing as a result of their primitive construction.

After the first drostdy came a church and school and, eleven years after its founding, the town could boast one street lined with clay buildings. Progress was slow, however, impeded by frontier uncertainties and political disturbances. In 1795 the local inhabitants assembled in the town, whereupon they expelled the resident landdrost, Honoratus Maynier, and declared a republic with Adriaan van Jaarsveld as president. The establishment of British rule in the Cape brought the little republic to its end in February 1796. The Great Trek (1834 to 1838) lured away many of the best local farmers. Economic conditions remained in a state of depression for many years, with inadequate communications isolating the district from any worthwhile market for its produce.

The passage of years did not, however, prevent Graaff-Reinet from developing its special character. Some most interesting buildings were erected. Reinet House, built in about 1805 as the parsonage of the first minister of the local Dutch Reformed church, is a supreme example of Cape-Dutch architecture. In the garden may be seen growing the famous old grape-vine, one of the largest in the world. Planted in 1870 by the Reverend Charles Murray, the son of the Reverend Andrew Murray, this vine is of the Black Acorn variety, the stem of which attained a circumference of 3,1 m in 1983 when fungus-infested wood was removed, leaving a number of separately growing stems. At present the vine covers 125 square metres and still bears excellent grapes. Reinet House is now a museum containing many interesting period pieces. Included among the exhibits are two gloriously Heath-Robinson-type inventions, a hand-held machine for pipping raisins, and a machine for peeling peaches. In the yard of the museum is a working water-wheel and mill. Reinet House is open throughout the year. Mondays to Fridays from 08h00 to 12h30 and 14h00 to 17h00; Saturdays from 09h00 to 15h00; Sunday and public holidays 09h00 to 12h00.

A tragedy occurred on 1 April 1980 when the building was partially destroyed by fire. However, the museum has been rebuilt.

Parsonage Street leading from the museum to what was originally the drostdy (now a hotel), is lined with some fascinating examples of South African architecture, many well restored. The Old Residence at Number 1 Parsonage Street which houses a firearm collection is open Mondays to Fridays 08h00 to 12h30 and 14h00 to 17h00. Also in Parsonage Street is the restored church building of the London Missionary Society which now houses the John Rupert Little Theatre.

A powder-magazine built in 1833 still keeps a rather sinister watch over the town from an overlooking hill. The present Dutch Reformed church, surely the most graceful in Southern Africa, was built in 1886 and designed by the architect J Bisset on similar lines to Salisbury Cathedral in England. The town hall, constructed in Renaissance style, was opened on 1 May 1911. The charming little Dutch Reformed mission church, consecrated in 1821, now the Hester Rupert Museum, is another unique asset preserved and restored for the town by the Rembrandt group of companies and named after the mother of Dr Anton Rupert, the guiding spirit of the company who was born in Graaff-Reinet. The Hester Rupert Art Museum exhibits an admirable and provocative collection of the work of many leading South African artists, which is constantly being expanded. The museum is open on weekdays from 10h00 to 12h00 and from 15h00 to 17h00.

The main building of the Drostdy hotel has been restored to its original charm, while behind it is the superb *Stretch's Court* named after Captain Charles Stretch, Government Surveyor of Graaff-Reinet, who bought the area in 1855 and subdivided it. Cottages were built there mainly for labourers. These later fell into disrepair, but in 1966 the Historic Homes of South Africa acquired the properties and perfectly restored the entire court. The cottages now form part of the hotel. As the result of the conservation programme of the Save Reinet Foundation, numerous buildings have been restored and proclaimed national monuments, of which the town now has 220.

On the banks of the Sundays River a beautiful little park has been laid out and named after Herbert Urquhart, a popular mayor of the town. This park is particularly pretty at night when the trees are illuminated by lights and the atmosphere is almost tropical. It contains a caravan park, camping sites, rondavels and holiday chalets.

Graaff-Reinet (with a population of 34 238) is the centre for many sheep, cattle, horse and dairy farms. Wool and mohair are the principal products. Lord Charles Somerset sponsored the introduction of merino sheep to the district, and the headquarters of the Merino Stud Breeders' Association of South Africa is situated in Graaff-Reinet. The mohair industry was also started in Graaff-Reinet. The first public auction of imported stud angora goats to be held in South Africa took place in the town in 1857. The present strain, the world-famous Cape angora, is a result of a century of cross-breeding.

The town is also an important educational centre. The cultural history of Graaff-Reinet is described in detail in the book *Graaff-Reinet* by Dr C G Henning.

An unusual monument in Graaff-Reinet is a plaque on a large boulder in College Road. It honours the Jewish pedlar, known as a *Smous*, who contributed so much to the development of South Africa.

THE VALLEY OF DESOLATION

From Graaff-Reinet an interesting 14 km drive leads to the summit of the overlooking mountain massif west of the town, ending at what is known as the Valley of Desolation.

The tarmac R63 road leaves Graaff-Reinet on its way to Murraysburg. Passing the Urquhart Park (1,5 km from the town), the road skirts the verge of the Vanryneveld Pass Dam in the Sundays River. The dam, covering 1 000 ha, has a wall 353 m long and 32 m high. The Karoo Nature Reserve of the Department of Nature and Environmental Conservation adjoins the dam. The reserve occupies 14 500 ha and virtually surrounds Graaff-Reinet, except for a corridor to the south of the town. The Valley of Desolation falls within the reserve, as does the Vanryneveld Pass dam where there is prolific bird life to delight bird-watchers. Hiking trails, ranging from a few hours' walk to a two-day excursion, have been laid out in the reserve. There is also a game viewing area, open 06h00 to 18h00 over weekends and during holiday seasons, 8 km from the town on the Murraysburg road. The entrance rondavel, manned by nature conservation officials, is adjacent to the road. No charge is levied to drive on the circular gravel road through the well-stocked area. A game hide has been built and a picnic site is provided. It is essential to book for the hiking trails at least one month in advance. Phone (049) 892-3453.

The road continues past the memorial to Gideon Scheepers, designed by E Hough. Commandant Scheepers was executed near there during the Anglo-Boer War. Six kilometres from Graaff-Reinet a gravel turn-off leads to *Winterhoek* farm. At 1,5 km along this turn-off west, a tarred branch road to the left takes the traveller in a steady, steep climb of 8 km up to the summit (1 500 m above sea-level) of the mountain massif. The views of the surrounding country and Graaff-Reinet make the diversion well worthwhile.

The road terminates at a parking site, from where a footpath leads to the various viewsites along the edge of the Valley of Desolation. The valley is actually a cleft in the rock-strewn plateau summit of the massif and is an example of bizarre natural erosion. Littered with rocks and boulders, and with the crumbling edges of the precipice worn into all manner of jagged shapes, the valley falls sharply away from the plateau summit, yielding fine views over the plain of the Great Karoo.

Leaving Graaff-Reinet through Munnikspoort, the N9 road continues south-westwards over an arid plain. After 47 km the road crosses the river known as the *Kamdebo* (green place) from the colour of some of its pools and their surroundings. Then, 58 km from Graaff-Reinet, the road reaches the town of ...

ABERDEEN

Aberdeen, with a population of 6 453, is one of the towns of the Karoo which retain an agreeable old-world charm. Situated on the high plains of the Kamdebo and backed by the Sneeuberge Mountains, it was created on the farm *Brakkefontein* by the Dutch Reformed Church as a community centre in 1855. A year later it was named after the birthplace in Scotland of the Reverend Andrew Murray, then the Dutch Reformed minister of Graaff-Reinet, a man whose powerful personality had considerable influence over this part of the world.

The Dutch Reformed church provides the town with a handsome centre, its 51,5 m high steeple being visible from a considerable distance. It is claimed to be the highest steeple in South Africa. Curiously enough, the tower is 45,7 cm off-centre, a sort of leaning steeple of Aberdeen.

There are several interesting buildings, including the magistrates court and the post office. There are fine gardens and in spring there is generally a spectacular display of wild flowers of several species. There is a nature reserve at Fonteinbos on the banks of the Kraai River, with walks, picnic sites and an interesting population of wild animals. The white stinkwood *(Celtis africana)* is indigenous to the Kamdebo mountains. The area is a good source of fossils of the age of the dinosaurs, and the tracks of the 'terrible lizards' may be seen in the sedimentary rocks.

The quality of locally produced wool is superb.

From Aberdeen the N9 road continues south-westwards over the high plains of the Karoo. After 84 km the road reaches a jumble of hills and bridges over the Groot River at the Beervlei dam where there is a picnic site but, unfortunately, seldom much water in the dam.

After a further 12 km there is a turn-off to Beaufort West and another 17 km sees the turn-off to Steytlerville and Port Elizabeth. Three kilometres from the turn-off, the road completes its steady descent from the high plain and, 116 km from Aberdeen, reaches the town of ...

WILLOWMORE

This is a curiously old-world Karoo town with several interesting buildings dating from the Victorian and Edwardian periods. It is the administrative centre of a large district lying on the border of the summer and winter rainfall areas. It would be pleasant to imagine that it enjoys the best of both worlds, but the weather never seems to have made up its mind about the district, resulting in an interesting effect on the vegetation. Drought-resistant plants such as *Obesa euphorbia* and *Horrida euphorbia* grow in the area and find conditions congenial, if only because most normal plants have long since given up in despair and left space for others.

The town had its beginning in 1864 when J P Aughanbough purchased from William Moore a portion of the farm *The Willows*. A tennis-court was built on part of the ground which became a centre for local sporting activities. This thereafter led to the establishment of trade. The name Willow-Moore was first applied to the place and later simplified to *Willowmore*. Ten years after the tennis-court had been built a church and a magistracy were established. After a further ten years, on 28 February 1884, Willowmore became a municipality. The railway connecting Cape Town to Port Elizabeth reached the town in 1900.

Today Willowmore (population 6 899) is the centre for a considerable farming industry which produces ostriches, sheep, goats, lucerne, and (in the fertile Baviaanskloof) citrus and tobacco.

BAVIAANSKLOOF

From Willowmore a gravel road leads eastwards through the Baviaanskloof wilderness area, 175 000 ha in extent, to join the coastal N2 road and reach Port Elizabeth. For the traveller exploring Southern Africa, this road (rough in places, with steep gradients and incessant curves) provides an exciting drive through 171 km of rugged, brilliantly coloured sandstone mountains, hills of red Enon Conglomerate, and ravines.

At a junction 30,5 km from Willowmore, the road is joined by a gravel road coming from Uniondale 50 km away. The combined roads now leave the Karoo area and enter the great *Baviaanskloof* (ravine of baboons). For 43,5 km the road runs through a narrow cleft in the mountains filled with plants such as geraniums and arum lilies and many lovely acacia trees.

Seventy-four kilometres from Willowmore the road reaches the principal centre of the Baviaanskloof, a cluster of stores with a police post, named *Studtis* after a German who once traded there. Fine wild fig trees shade the area and a branch road leads for 24 km into the Baviaanskloof Forest Reserve where, in places such as Doringkloof in the Kouga mountains, the rare and unique Baviaanskloof cedar trees (*Widdringtonia schwarzii*) may be seen growing.

The road continues beneath red cliffs with many strange rock formations. After travelling 25 km the road reaches a small farming centre known as Colesplaas, where there is a store and petrol supply. Beyond this place the road climbs a high ridge, and for 8 km the journey is graced with magnificent scenes of rocks, ravines, a richly varied flora and majestic views. At the far side of the pass after a steep descent, the road winds through a valley shaded by fine peppercorn, acacia, and wild fig trees. Thirty-two kilometres from Colesplaas, the road reaches a gate at what was originally an agricultural settlement, now taken over by the Forestry Department. From this gate the road commences a steep ascent and reaches the summit after 10 km of climbing. The views are superb; the mountain slopes are richly covered with proteas, ericas and other flowering plants.

On the summit is a solitary farm, *Berg Plaatz*, and the road passes the signpost demarcating the boundary between the Willowmore and Humansdorp districts. The road traverses a high plateau where the traveller can admire the wheat fields, proteas, pincushions and panoramic views of the towering mountains. The road then descends steeply down a narrow pass occasionally edged by hair-raising precipices.

Forty-five and a half kilometres from Colesplaas the road reaches the bottom of the pass in a valley quite choked up with vegetation. A beautiful clear stream, the *Witrivier* (white river) flows down this valley and the road crosses it by means of twelve successive causeways. It is a delightful drive with several fine shady places in which to rest and picnic. The valley suddenly opens into a basin in the hills containing the Cambria forestry station and the Goedehoop Nedersetting, a church settlement. Flowering aloes, orange groves, cacti, succulents, geraniums, and acacia trees with their sweet-smelling blossoms, grow on the alluvial floor. There are several fine farms.

Fifty-six kilometres from Colesplaas the road reaches a turn-off at a small store. This turn-off leads to *Armmansvriend* (poor man's friend) and to a memorial to Tjaart Johannes van der Walt who was killed on 8 August 1802 about 8 km away on a site marked by a small white commemorative stone in the centre of a field in the farming area of the Cambria agricultural settlement. His death occurred during one of the wars of the period. His remains were exhumed and removed to the present site where a memorial hall has been erected to serve the local community. A plinth stands over his grave.

From the turn-off to this memorial site the road twists through a most magnificent cleft in the mountains. The colours and folded formations of the sandstone cliffs reflect in the river pools and the journey is extremely winding and varied for 13 km. The road then emerges from what is known as the Groot River Pass and enters the alluvial valley of the Gamtoos River with its beautiful irrigated farmlands. After 2 km the road reaches the small centre of Heroncliff 71 km from Colesplaas. From here the road, now tarmac, continues down the Gamtoos valley for 24,5 km to the village of Patensie.

Any traveller venturing through Baviaanskloof, the 171 km stretch from Heroncliff to Willowmore, will have lasting memories of the journey. In summer the air is sweet with the smell of acacia blossoms. Plumbagos are in flower, as well as agapanthus, red-hot pokers, oleanders, and some proteas, although their season is really winter. Wild fig trees, pelargoniums and a mass of greenery grow in vividly red soil.

Birds chatter and call. The air is warm. Crystal-clear streams tumble down, the slopes in cascades and waterfalls. Rivers such as the Kouga work their way through complicated scenery. Odd farms linger in isolated places, with men, some of them hill billy types, dressed in blue overalls and women bare-footed, gazing at passing traffic in curiosity. A visitor is usually suspected of being a revenue, forestry or water department official come to expropriate their land.

Guinea-fowl call; baboons bark; an occasional fat puff-adder slithers across the road, sluggish and sinuous. Tortoises large and small abound: this is their primeval sort of country. Echoes sound in the hills – a distant shot – fish glide silently in the pools and there is stillness and solitude.

The wind whispers and tells of old adventures. The streams gossip interminably as they bustle along. *Mtunzini* (the place of shadows) the Fingo people called this area. It is an ideal place for ghosts and one can understand their reluctance to leave it.

THE GAMTOOS VALLEY

When the road through Baviaanskloof emerges from the Groot River Pass, the traveller is confronted with an altogether different scene. The mountains still crowd in on either side, but the valley is densely settled, highly developed, and has an atmosphere far removed in years of progress from the wilderness of Baviaanskloof.

The Gamtoos valley lends itself splendidly to irrigation. It has water supplies which at times have proved more than ample when heavy rains bring the rivers down in flood. Five and a half kilometres from Heroncliff, on the main tarmac road to Patensie, there is a turn-off leading to the Kouga Dam 8 km away in a deep gorge of the Kouga River. This fine dam contains 130 million cubic metres of water and was completed in 1967, having a wall 365 m long and 94 m high. It feeds irrigation water to many farms in the valley. Its scenic setting is pleasant and there is a picnic ground situated below the dam wall.

Beyond the turn-off to the dam the main tarmac road continues down the valley, with irrigated farmlands on either side and many lovely gardens of flowers cultivated around the homesteads. Aloes flowering in May and June turn the hillsides red. Twenty and a half kilometres from Heroncliff there is a gravel turn-off to the north, leading to the valley of the Eland River and from there to Port Elizabeth. The main tarmac road, 24,5 km from Heroncliff, reaches the town of ...

PATENSIE

This is a busy little agricultural centre and the terminus for a branch of the narrow-gauge railway from Port Elizabeth. The name of *Patensie* is said to have originated from an early African place-name indicating a resting spot for cattle. Citrus, tobacco and vegetables for the Port Elizabeth market are the principal products.

From Patensie the tarmac road leads down the valley through a landscape covered in flowering aloes. The narrow-gauge railway accompanies the road closely. After 14,5 km the road reaches the town of ...

HANKEY

With a present-day population of 9 263, *Hankey* had its beginning in 1822 when the London Missionary Society purchased ground on both sides of the Gamtoos River. To this area they transferred some of the surplus population from their overcrowded mission station at Bethelsdorp. The Reverend J G Messer was appointed first missionary and the station was named in honour of William Hankey, the treasurer of the society in London.

The irrigation possibilities of the flat alluvial valley floor were only too apparent. William Philip, a son of Dr Philip, one of the leading missionaries of the society, cut a tunnel to divert water from the river to the fields. The young man was sadly rewarded for his enterprise – he drowned with John Philip Fairbairn on 1 July 1845 in the Gamtoos during a flood. Sudden floods have always been a menace in such a wide, flat valley. The years 1847, 1905, 1916 and 1932 all saw prodigious floods which did great damage and caused considerable loss of life. Emma Hughes and Alice Hullock, 17 and 13 years old respectively, drowned in the Klein River on 27 February 1875.

In 1876 the London Missionary Society sold their property. Hankey was proclaimed a public village in 1881 and a municipality in 1905. This first municipality was abolished in 1951 but on 1 March 1963, Hankey was once again given village management board status. Today it is in the centre of irrigated farmlands producing citrus, tobacco, fruit and vegetables.

Camping is allowed in the pleasant park known as Yellowwoods, situated 1 km from the town on the road to Klein River.

From Hankey the main tarmac road climbs a ridge with a turn-off 1 km away leading to a fine viewsite looking out over the whole valley. After a further 17 km the road reaches the railway centre of ...

LOERIE

Named after the bird *Turacus corythaix*, Loerie is simply a railway station with a few shops and houses. However, several things contribute to give it an importance beyond its size, for it is the site of one of the main water storage dams of the Port Elizabeth municipality.

The station is one of the busiest on the narrow-gauge railway from Port Elizabeth. The limestone quarries of the Eastern Province Cement Company are connected to the station by an aerial ropeway 9 km long. There are two separate parallel ropeways. One, a bi-cableway built in 1932, consists of two steel ropes, a stationary track rope and a haulage rope. The second ropeway, built in 1954, is a mono-cableway and consists of one endless rope which carries as well as hauls.

The speeds and carrying capacities of the two ropeways are very similar. They run simultaneously or individually and take an hour to carry a bucket container from the quarry to Loerie where the narrow-gauge railway takes over the load, hauling about 120 trucks of limestone a day to the junction of Chelsea, from where the cement company has its own narrow-gauge railway to take the trucks to their factory in Port Elizabeth.

The ropeway is completely straight. It climbs for about a third of its route and then descends to Loerie. The descending weight of the evenly spaced buckets helps to raise the ascending buckets and consequently makes the ropeway very economical to operate. The driving engines are at the Limebank quarry which was first worked in 1932 when the ropeway was opened.

From Loerie a tarmac road branches off and leads to Gamtoos 9 km away where the narrow-gauge railway has a junction. A branch goes up the valley to Patensie while the main line continues to Humansdorp and the Long Kloof. The situation of Loerie is handsome and there is a pleasant picnic area just outside Loerie on the road to Patensie. For railway enthusiasts, there is the opportunity to take a trip on the Apple Express, operated by the Apple Express Steam Train Society, Private Bag 13130, Humewood, Port Elizabeth, 6013 or phone/fax (041) 507-2333 for a timetable of excursions departing from Port Elizabeth.

From Loerie the tarmac road climbs steeply out of the valley of the Gamtoos, winding through hills covered in aloes, cacti and dark-green bush. After 7 km of climbing, the road reaches the summit where there is a viewsite and resting-place offering a grand view of the valley and the ranges of the Elandsberg and the Groot Winterhoek. The scene is dominated by the 1 759 m high peak known to Europeans as the Cockscomb but named by the African the *T'Numkwa* (mountain of the clouds). To some the outlook is so vast that it is known as the Valley of a Thousand and One Hills.

The tarmac road continues for a further 3 km and then, 10 km from Loerie, joins the main coastal N2 road at a point 35 km from Port Elizabeth.

Back at Willowmore, the N9 road continues south-westwards over an arid plateau encircled by mountains. Passing through Buyspoort, it then reaches the point of a considerable change in scene. For 17 km the road makes a steady, easy descent through what is known as *Gwarriespoort* from the gwarri (*Euclea undulata*), a shrub much browsed upon by game and domestic animals and notable for its sweetish, slightly astringent berries and the flavour of honey made by bees from its blossoms.

The pass is dry but full of flowering aloes and succulents. It takes the road down from the level of the Great Karoo into the basin of the Little Karoo. The scenic change is dramatic. The pass provides a natural passage around the eastern end of the Swartberge range, and the Little Karoo makes an inviting picture of high mountains and a jumble of hills.

At 26 km from Willowmore there is a turn-off to Oudtshoorn and the hot springs of Toorwaterpoort. There are other turn-offs to Oudtshoorn further along the road. At 63 km from Willowmore the N9 road reaches the town of Uniondale, already described in the chapter on the Little Karoo. From Uniondale, N9 continues for 13 km and then is joined by R62 coming from ...

THE LONG KLOOF

After the western side of the Cape Province, the Long Kloof is the second-largest deciduous fruit producing area in Southern Africa. Its fertility is very evident to the eye, for practically the entire length of the valley is one huge export fruit orchard, backed by handsome mountains and watered by perennial streams.

The fine tarmac road, R62, running down the Long Kloof passes through a succession of rural fruit-growing and dispatch centres such as Avontuur, Haarlam, Misgund, Louterwater, Joubertina, Assegaaibos, and so on – each a cluster of houses and commercial buildings scattered around a railway station, church and school. Spring in the Long Kloof (September and October) is a period of blossoms and wild flowers. During the summer, wayside stalls sell the fruit of the valley to passing travellers.

Towering mountains crowd in on the valley from north and south, now advancing, now receding, leaving some new vale filled with farms and homesteads. The tarmac road and the narrow-gauge railway run down the centre of the valley, criss-crossing each other like two strings holding together a necklace made of farms, towns, villages and packing stations.

In former times the valley was the home of Bushmen. Their paintings may still be seen on the walls of many of the rock shelters. African pastoralists who supplanted the Bushmen hunters have contributed many of the place-names which are still in use in the valley. *Gwarina* or *Querina* (the ravine of the eland); *Kouga* (place of the hippopotamus); *Traka* (place of the women); *Humtata* (plain where the Hottentot figs grow). These and many other names survive as reminders of a vanished people whose disappearance was largely due to the pressure of European settlement.

Izaak Schryver's expedition of 1689 was the first European venture into the area. Hunters, botanists and explorers followed after him. The first European settlers appeared in 1740. These people, always the despair of the authorities in Cape Town, were of the breed of pioneers who, on their own initiative and quite contrary to the wishes of government, constantly expanded the frontiers in an attempt to keep one step ahead of the tax-gatherer. He, however, inevitably followed after them.

By 1773 about eight homesteads had been built in the Long Kloof. Men such as R Kamfer (*at Kamfer*); M Zondagh, on the farm *Avontuur* (adventure); John Kritzinger on *Onzer;* Tjaart van der Walt on *Warmbad* (warm bath); and Jan de Buys on *De Ezeljacht* (the donkey hunt) were some of the pioneers of the area. Jan de Buys was the father of one of the most notorious and toughest of all South African frontiersmen, Coenraad de Buys. He was born on the farm *Wagenboomrivier* (wagon tree river) but had his own farm *De Opkomst* (the rising) near Kareedouw. His wild lifestyle and his practice of polygamy on a large scale sent him wandering off as an outlaw into the northern wilderness where, at Mara on the southern slopes of the Zoutpansberge in the Northern Transvaal, he founded a tribe of his own descendants, the Buys people.

During the early frontier wars, the Long Kloof was invaded by marauding Xhosa warriors. Many memories survive of wild fights, escapades and adventures. In those days the valley was remote and tediously difficult to reach by wagon or horse. Even now there are minor valleys such as the Hoeree valley (attached to the main Long Kloof) which are as difficult to enter as the famous Valley of Hel in the Swartberge.

Avontuur is a small village at the head of the narrow-gauge railway running down the valley to Port Elizabeth. This line is of considerable interest to the railway enthusiast. The train service, popularly known as the Apple Express, is busy during the fruit-picking season when thousands of trucks of fruit are conveyed to the harbour at Port Elizabeth for shipment. Passengers are not particularly catered for on the Apple Express – a bus service provides a faster alternative – but enthusiasts can always find a seat in second and third class accommodation in the caboose. During holiday periods a special passenger train runs from Port Elizabeth to Loerie.

From Avontuur there is a magnificent drive over Prince Alfred's Pass to Knysna. Avontuur is situated in the Long Kloof 12 km from the point where the road to Uniondale and the Great Karoo branches off. Just 0,5 km from the turn-off to the village on the main road, there is another turn-off leading for 9 km to Uniondale. This road runs through a beautiful ravine filled with rich colours and extraordinary formations of the local sandstone. Resembling a miniature Seven Weeks Poort, Uniondale Poort is resplendent with flowering aloes, flaming red and orange cliffs, yellow lichens, and caves containing galleries of Bushman paintings.

Twenty-three kilometres down the Long Kloof from Avontuur there is a turn-off to the farming area of the *Bo-Kouga* (higher Kouga). The village of *Misgund* (envied) lies 8,5 km further on, and the village of *Louterwater* (clear water) a further 6 km down the valley. Fruit orchards which line both sides of the road provide a magnificent spectacle in spring when the trees are in blossom.

Seventeen kilometres from Louterwater there is a turn-off to the farming area of the *Onder-Kouga* (lower Kouga), and after another kilometre (65,5 km from Avontuur) the road reaches the principal town of the Long Kloof ...

JOUBERTINA

Named after the Reverend W A Joubert, pastor of Uniondale from 1879 to 1892, *Joubertina* was founded in 1907 when the Dutch Reformed Church acquired from Daniel Kritzinger sufficient land to create a church centre. It became a municipality in July 1971 and has a population of 4 453. With its position in a handsome setting of mountains, it is a busy farming centre and station for the Apple Express. The original landowner, Mr Kritzinger, was a teetotaller and he stipulated as a condition of the transfer of his land that no liquor would ever be sold from the town. Joubertina still has a prohibition on the sale of liquor. A descendant of Mr Kritzinger, however, sold a portion of his inherited farm on the outskirts of the town, and on this the Kloof hotel was built. It has a liquor licence.

Keeping company with the narrow-gauge railway, the road continues down the valley for a further 43 km and then reaches the village of ...

KAREEDOUW

Kareedouw (pass of karee trees) is a timber and farming centre. From it a tarmac road branches off to cross the mountains and join the coastal N2 road, traversing the pass which has given the village its name. Wild flowers on the mountain slopes are prolific. Three kilometres from the village, down the Long Kloof, is the narrow-gauge railway centre of Assegaaibos. Here a gravel road branches off on a spectacular route to Zuuranys, the lower Kouga valley and the strange area of the Moordenaars River.

GHOSTS AND THE MOORDENAARS RIVER

The gravel road from Assegaaibos railway station climbs steeply for 7 km to the summit of the *Zuuranys* (sour anys shrubs) and then descends into a broad farming valley where (9 km from Assegaaibos) it joins a gravel road which has come 18,5 km from Essenbos in the Long Kloof. From this junction the road leads past several farms and then makes a sudden steep descent into the ravine of the *Kouga* (hippopotamus) River. The causeway across this river is 17 km from Assegaaibos and is situated in a spectacular setting of cliffs. A fine series of pools lie upstream and downstream. The whole area, however, is private property and the very tempting camping grounds can only be used with the permission of the farmers.

The road climbs steeply out of the ravine and after 2 km reaches a turn-off leading to farms such as *Joubertkraal* and *Sewefontein*. This left-hand turn-off rewards the venturesome traveller with splendid scenery. The right-hand road continues for a further 2 km and then passes through the farmyard of *Brandekraal*. For the next 5 km there is some rugged travelling to be done and the road yet again descends steeply, this time into the ravine of the *Moordenaars* (murderers) River. The floor of the ravine lies 24,5 km from Assegaaibos. At the bottom of the pass there is a sharp turn downstream just before the road crosses the river and climbs the further slopes to reach farms on the northern side of the valley.

The road downstream is rough and leads through a wild and eerie landscape, terminating after 4 km on the farm *Boskloof,* owned by Mr J H ('Bang Jan') Ferreira. Half-way to this farm lies the abandoned farm of *Jammerfontein* (fountain of sorrow) which is reputedly the most haunted place in South Africa. The story behind the reputation has been related in detail in books such as *Myths and Legends of Southern Africa* by Penny Miller.

The farm was originally the possession of Jan Prinsloo, a man renowned for his breeding of horses and notorious for the harsh manner in which he treated his servants. Eventually a number of his servants decided to kill him after he had flogged two of their women to death. Prinsloo heard of this plan and tried to escape on one of his horses. He was chased back into his horse corral and, among the terrified animals, was skinned alive, and parts of his body were eaten.

This event took place on the stormy night of 15 January at the beginning of the 19th century. Since then the farm has had several owners, all of whom have abandoned the place. Unpleasant manifestations are said to take place on the same night each year, invariably accompanied by a thunderstorm and always in the presence of horses.

The original farmhouse of Jan Prinsloo is a total ruin overgrown with dense bush. It lies close to the Moordenaars River 1 km from the start of the road. A second farmhouse was built 0,5 km further down the road by an owner hoping to avoid any unpleasant occurrences. This farmhouse is also in ruins. A further 0,5 km down the road among the trees are some graves, said to be those of British soldiers killed in the area during the Anglo-Boer War. *Boskloof* farm is 1,5 km further on.

Jammerfontein farm lies in a setting of high, red-coloured sandstone mountains. In former times this area was the lair of renegades and men who preferred the solitude of the wilderness and wanted nothing to do with government, law, religion or any other restraints of society. By all accounts, Jan Prinsloo was a brooding, erratic, violent character who found his way into this forbidding and remote gorge and there defied the efforts of the tax-gatherer, police and parson to reach him. He built the homestead himself, dug a water furrow to irrigate his lands, and built stables and a corral to house the horses he bred – the only living things for which he had any affection.

Perhaps it was inevitable that something violent would take place in so wild and remote a setting with such a strangely sinister atmosphere. To visit the place is an experience. In January the air is hot and thunderstorms charge the atmosphere with electricity as the dark shadows of the clouds drift over the mountains. For those who wait through the night for something to happen, the day dawns with the visitor realising long afterwards that perhaps something did occur. What was thought to be natural at the time – a particular sound or the noise of horses fighting in the thicket – cannot now be reasonably explained because there are no horses there.

Giant tortoises move ponderously through the undergrowth. Snakes threaten death with their hiss. There is a tangible silence in the night. Even the stream seems muted. Some birds do sing and horses, wild or tame, conceal themselves from man in the thickets. There is no need for signs which say 'Keep out' or 'No Trespassing', for many things conspire to make the place hostile.

From the turn-off at Assegaaibos to Zuuranys and Jan Prinsloo's ill-starred kloof, the R62 road down the Long Kloof continues for 18 km and then joins the main coastal N2 road at a point 18 km from Humansdorp. The coastal road then proceeds to Port Elizabeth and Algoa Bay.

Chapter Twenty-One
EAST LONDON

The Border Country and Ciskei

Across the Great Fish River, the N2 highway enters the *Ciskei,* meaning on this side (south) of the Kei River. The road climbs the steep euphorbia-covered eastern side of the valley of the Great Fish River. After 4,5 km, at the top of the rise, the road emerges on to an open grassy plain. After 3 km there is a turn-off leading to the mouth of the Great Fish River, while a further 6 km takes the road to a turn-off leading through Ebb and Flow (41 km), Kidd's Beach (72 km) and on to East London.

From the turn-off to the Great Fish River mouth, N2 continues eastwards for 8 km and then (73 km from Grahamstown) reaches the small town, lying in a bowl in a cluster of hills covered with stunted acacia trees of ...

PEDDIE

Beginning its existence as an earth-stockaded fort shaped like an eight-pointed star which was built in 1835 to protect the Fingo (*amaMfengu*) tribe who took refuge there from troubles in the Transkei, *Peddie* was named after Colonel John Peddie of the 72nd Highlanders. On 28 May 1846 the European and Fingo residents of the district were besieged in this fort by 9 000 Xhosa warriors. A relief force eventually reached them from military posts situated at the Great Fish River.

Fort Peddie became a magistracy in 1848 and the town developed around the old fort and government buildings. The earth fort has long since vanished, but the line of watch-towers built in 1841 to protect communications with Grahamstown may still be seen at the original sites: Fort Peddie, Piet Appel, Fraser's Camp and Fort Selwyn (Grahamstown). A few relics of the old military buildings (hospitals, church and quarters) from the troubled period of the successive frontier wars still stand in the town.

Peddie became a municipality in 1905 and is an agricultural and trading centre.

From Peddie the tarmac N2 road continues northwards across undulating country lightly covered in acacia trees. At 6 km from Peddie a gravel turn-off stretches to the coastal resort of Hamburg (46 km). At 15 km from Peddie the road descends into the *Keiskamma* (shining water) River valley. Thick acacia and euphorbia bush cover the slopes of the valley. On the right bank of the river stands the old Line Drift hotel. The road crosses the river here (18 km from Peddie) and then climbs the left-hand side of the valley to a semi-arid plain thinly covered in grass and acacia trees.

After proceeding 31 km from the Keiskamma River, there is a tarmac turn-off which leads to Alice (59 km) and Keiskammahoek (41 km). One kilometre further on (50 km from Peddie) the road crosses the Buffalo River and enters the town of ...

KING WILLIAM'S TOWN

Originally established by the London Missionary Society in 1826, King William's Town has had a somewhat chequered career. In 1835 the Xhosas destroyed the mission, driving the missionaries away. In due course the Xhosas in their turn were chased away by Sir Benjamin D'Urban, the formidable governor of the Cape who, on 24 May 1835, in the hope of bringing peace to the troubled area, proclaimed a new district which was named Queen Adelaide Province. Here a new town was to be created at the site of the old Buffalo River mission station. The town was named after the reigning British monarch, William IV.

Plans for the first King William's Town proved abortive because the British Government was reluctant to expand territorial ownership over the area. The mission continued, however, and the name of King William's Town remained attached to this part of the valley of the Buffalo River. A few traders were attracted to the place and a local industry developed in the spinning of coarse silk from silkworm cocoons gathered from the acacia trees. Gum arabic was also prepared.

In 1846 King William's Town and the mission were destroyed by the Xhosas. At the end of the war Sir Harry Smith, governor of the Cape, revived the idea of a town. The old site became the administrative centre of the newly proclaimed province of British Kaffraria. As a military centre the town soon outgrew the ruins of the old site. It became the principal base for operations in the subsequent frontier wars. It was a very cheerful, bustling type of frontier town abounding with the rumours, ceremony, and comings and goings of a garrison stronghold. Many bizarre and exciting scenes must have taken place in the town: redcoats drilling; prisoners in chains, transport riders bringing in the impedimenta of war; hordes of human skeletons fleeing in 1856 from the mystical cattle killings which ruined the Xhosa people.

In approximately the year 1857, the German Legion, a mercenary force serving in the British army was disbanded and 2 500 men settled in the area. The empty countryside became populated with stolid farmers. After Prince Alfred's visit in 1861, King William's Town became a royal borough; and later, after the annexation of British Kaffraria to the Cape and the final pacification of the frontier areas in 1878, King William's Town became a prosperous centre of trade for the tribal areas. The town remained a garrison station for imperial regiments until 1914. It's easy to imagine the place at the time when social life was dominated by the doings, scandals and gossip of the officers' mess. Legacies of those days include a town hall which contains an excellent little theatre for concerts and stage shows, and the Kaffrarian Museum, housed in a graceful building. This museum, founded in 1884 by the King William's Town Naturalists' Society, contains among its treasurers one of the world's finest and most complete collections of African mammals. This unique assembly of 25 000 specimens was largely the work of the late Captain Guy Shortridge, a former curator of the museum, an author, and a world authority on his subject. The layman will find this collection staggering. It contains a variety of rarities including a black lechwe from Zimbabwe (only one other is known); web-footed hares from Calvinia; silver moles from Namaqualand; a 5,5 m high giraffe from the Kaokoveld (the world-record specimen); and, dear to the hearts of all animal lovers, that most famous of all hippos, Huberta. After ambling a full 800 km down the coast of South Africa she endeared herself as the country's national pet. She eventually came to an unhappy end when she was shot in the Keiskamma River in 1930. The Amathole Museum (formerly known as the Kaffrarian Museum) is open weekdays from 09h00 to 13h00 and 13h45 to 16h30; Saturdays from 10h00 to 12h30.

The South African Missionary Museum was established in 1973 in the old mission church in Berkeley Square. The museum depicts the life and work of missionaries in South Africa and is open Mondays to Fridays from 09h00 to 13h00 and 13h45 to 16h45.

The public library, founded in 1861, contains a fine collection of books on Africa. There is a botanical garden where five conservatories are laid out in a most pleasant environment on the left bank of the Buffalo River, opposite the caravan park.

The well-known Dale College for boys was founded in 1861 as the Diocesan Grammar School but renamed in 1877 after Sir Langham Dale, the Superintendent of Education. It is an important part of life of King William's Town, along with the Kaffrarian High School for girls (founded in 1875), the school of the Convent of the Sacred Heart, and the De Vos Malan School for Afrikaans-speaking children (founded in 1933). There is also a technical institute which offers commercial courses after normal working hours, with facilities for apprenticeship and post-apprentice training.

There are several handsome churches in King William's Town, such as the Holy Trinity church, built by the military in 1856; the Roman Catholic church; and the Presbyterian church. The town also has several national monuments. Notable amongst these are the British Kaffrarian Savings Bank (the town's own banking establishment, founded in 1860), Grey Hospital, the town hall, the South African Missionary Museum, and the Daines Wing of the Amatole Museum.

Industrial King William's Town is the centre for tanning, footwear, soaps, candles, clothing, sweets, cartons, light engineering, grain milling and toy soldiers. The tanning of hides and skins commenced in King William's Town more than a hundred years ago. The King Tanning Company's factory is today the largest of its kind in the country. It produces leather for local and foreign trade. On the outskirts of the town lies *Zwelitsha* (new era), the site of the huge mill of the Good Hope Textile Corporation and its housing estate for workers. The population of King William's Town together with Zwelitsha is 105 111.

King William's Town is the junction for several major roads: the R346 to the north; the important link (R63) through Fort Beaufort to Cookhouse and the N10 to the north; a short link (R63) through Komga, rejoining the main coastal road (63 km) north of East London; and the continuation of the main coastal N2 road to East London. All these roads reveal many interesting scenes.

KING WILLIAM'S TOWN TO COOKHOUSE

This important all-tarmac road (R63) links the main coastal N2 road and the N10 road from Port Elizabeth to the north. It also allows the traveller access to the beautiful mountain country of the Amatole range, the Hogsback and the Katberg.

The R63 road branches off from the coastal N2 road just before this route crosses the Buffalo River from Grahamstown into King William's Town. From this point (1 km from King William's Town) the tarmac road climbs out of the valley of the Buffalo River and continues over an undulating plateau covered in stunted acacia trees. To the north loom the forest-covered slopes of the *Pirie* (named after the Reverend A Pirie of the Glasgow Missionary Society) and the Amatole Mountains. The huts, land and herds may be seen of the *Ngqika* (Gaika) section of the Xhosa people who inhabit this part of what is known as the Ciskei.

At 19,5 km from King William's Town there is a turn-off to the industrial township of Dimbaza. Two kilometres further a turn-off leads to the village of Keiskammahoek, 19 km away. The road travels a further 3 km over the saddle of land known as Debe Nek where the *Debe* stream has its source. The name *Debe* comes from the curious natural depressions on the surface of the Debe Flats, resembling the tribal incisions which people such as the Bhaca cut into their faces. The forest-covered mountain slopes crowd in from the north. Passing the railway station, store and hotel of Debe Nek, the road continues westwards, traversing an arid plain whose thin grass contrasts with the green of the indigenous forests on the overlooking mountain slopes. A curiosity of this area between the upper Buffalo and Keiskamma rivers is the presence of giant earthworms (*Microchaetus*) growing to over 3 m in length. The burrowings of these creatures create mounds and hollows about 3 m by 2 m in extent over a large area known as *Kommetjievlakte* (plain of little saucers). The Xhosas, for the same reason, apply the name of *amaLinde* (the hollows) to another area. The excavations of the giant worms are beneficial and they are harmless. The large number of worms is one of the reasons for the East London coast being considered a fisherman's paradise.

After a further 12 km (39 km from King William's Town) there is another turn-off to Keiskammahoek (94 km) and Fort Cox. Yet another kilometre takes the road across the Keiskamma and into the village of Middeldrift, which lies in the shallow valley of the river.

For a further 19 km the tarmac road continues westwards over an open rolling plain (notable for its flowering aloes in winter) and then, 57 km from King William's Town, enters the picturesque town of ...

ALICE

Named after Princess Alice, daughter of Queen Victoria, *Alice* is pleasantly laid out around a central park. It became the magisterial and administrative centre of the district of Victoria East, and later the first capital of Ciskei when that area was made into a so-called Bantustan.

Alice had its start as a mission station founded in November 1824 and named *Lovedale* after Dr John Love of the Glasgow Missionary Society. After being abandoned during the Frontier War, this station was re-established in 1836 on its present site on the west bank of the Tyumi River. It was there in 1841 that a school was opened. Although the mission had again to be abandoned during the 1846 war, with the buildings converted by the military into a fort, the importance of the place as an educational centre began to increase.

The military later built a fort for themselves on the east bank of the Tyumi River, named *Fort Hare* (after Major-General John Hare, the acting lieutenant-governor of the Eastern Cape). From 1847 the missionaries returned to Lovedale, developing schools and a hospital. In the same year the town of Alice was founded and named.

Alice is the centre for the University of Fort Hare, founded in 1916 as a university college, and now developed to accommodate over 3 400 students. Also situated in the town are the Lovedale High School and the Lovedale Hospital which provides training for student nurses and midwives. The Federal Theological Seminary of Southern Africa, consisting of four colleges representing the Anglican, Congregational, Methodist and Presbyterian denominations, stands in a fine parkland and trains 100 theological students annually. The Lovedale Mission of the Church of Scotland operates the Lovedale Press which has a considerable output of educational books, as well as the Lovedale Farm which supports a superb herd of dairy cows.

Citrus, beef, milk, wool, mohair and tobacco are the agricultural products of the district.

THE ALICE COUNTRYSIDE

Alice and the district of Victoria East provided the setting for many battles during the frontier wars. The scenery becomes dramatic nearer the mountains in the north or down the colossal valley of the Great Fish River, where relics of the old military forts make an exploration of the area an interesting experience.

The road to the south descends into the Great Fish River valley through Victoria Post and Breakfast Vlei. The river is crossed at Committee's Drift (57 km from Alice). A steady climb of 2 km brings the road to a junction with the tarmac road stretching from Fort Beaufort (64 km) to Grahamstown (15 km). An interesting circular drive through Fort Beaufort back to Alice is provided.

The road to the north branches off from the main tarmac road just as it enters Alice from King William's Town. Passing the University of Fort Hare, the gravel road makes its way up the valley of the Tyumi River, enhanced with aloes (flowering in June) and fine citrus estates. In previous years the valley was the stronghold of the Xhosa chief, Ngqika; and the road passes the sites of the British settlements of Woburn, Juanasberg and Auckland which were destroyed on Christmas day during the Frontier War of 1850.

After 16 km a turn-off leads for 20 km to the pretty little village of Seymour. This is a beautiful drive which passes the shores of the Kat River dam on the way. The road to the north continues past this turn-off and after 5 km (21 km from Alice) starts to climb the *Amatole* (place of weaned calves) mountains by means of a spectacular pass. At 31 km from Alice the road reaches the summit and enters the popular resort area known as ...

THE HOGSBACK

The Xhosas call the Hogsback area *Qabimbola* (red clay on the face). The Xhosas obtained from numerous clay pits in the area the type of clay they traditionally used to cover their faces. The valley of the Tyumi River was a stronghold of the tribe, and the mountain known to Europeans as Gaika's Kop is said to have been the particular centre of the great Xhosa leader, Ngqika.

The first Europeans in the area were soldiers stationed at Fort Mitchell, built on the slopes of the height known as Tor Doone where a watch was kept on the stronghold of the Xhosa chief. The outline of Fort Mitchell is still visible as well as traces of the first road built from Fort Hare to this outpost. The graves of several soldiers killed during the frontier wars lie next to this old military trail at places such as Komkulu. Colonel Mitchell built the fort, and the road pass was also named after him.

After the frontier wars ended, European farmers settled on the high plateau overlooked by the three mountains whose summit ridges give rise to the name of *Hogsback*. The gorgeous indigenous forest growing along the escarpment of the Amatole range became a forestry area. A hotel, the Hogsback Hydro, was built to convenience travellers. Farmers such as Colonel Bowker, owner of the farm *Arminel*, and Mr Summerton, a professional gardener who introduced apples, hazelnuts and berry fruits to the area, were among the first to build homes in the vicinity of the village of Hogsback.

There are several beautiful forest walks at Hogsback, with drives for vehicles, viewsites, big trees and a waterfall known as the Kettlespout which, when the wind is strong, is actually blown upwards for about 10 m, curling back to fall behind the ridge of the escarpment. There is interesting trout fishing in the area and superb wild flowers abound.

During the years 1933 to 1977, Professor Robert Houghton and his wife Betty created the beautiful garden of Little Timbers on 20 acres of fertile ground. It became one of the show gardens of South Africa with a collection of plants from all over the world. Rhododendrons and camellias are an exquisite feature of the garden, with azaleas and roses.

In 1988 Professor H B Rycroft, retired director of the National Botanic Gardens at Kirstenbosch, with his wife Jean, bought the garden and continued its loving care.

From Hogsback village the main road continues over high grassland set among hills and mountains. Well-watered and richly grassed, this is excellent cattle country. With turn-offs after 11 km to Happy Valley and after 18 km to Whittlesea, the road (47 km from Hogsback) reaches Cathcart.

A beautiful and most interesting road also leads back to the main King William's Town–Alice road. This route is known as the Wolf Ridge road. It descends the western slopes of the Amatole escarpment through the forest reserve where there are fine views of the Amatole range and the basin of the Wolf River. The gravel road descends on the right bank of the Wolf River past numerous tribal villages until it joins the Middeldrift–Fort Cox–Keiskammahoek road after a total of 28 km. Middeldrift, on the main King William's Town–Alice road, is 17 km away along the right-hand turn-off. Turning left to Keiskammahoek 7 km away, the traveller is taken through the notorious Boma Pass where 700 men of the British Army were ambushed by Xhosa warriors on 24 December 1850. Twenty-three of the soldiers were killed before the rest fought their way through to Keiskammahoek. This was the bloody beginning of the Eighth Frontier War. On the following day, Christmas day, the Xhosas attacked the settlements of Woburn, Juanasberg and Auckland in the Tyumi valley and totally destroyed them, killing 84 European settlers during the course of a hectic series of fights.

From Keiskammahoek an interesting scenic road passes the Devil's Staircase on its way to Stutterheim, or branches south to Pirie and the Alice–King William's Town road.

ALICE TO FORT BEAUFORT

From Alice the tarmac R63 road continues westwards across the foothills of the northern escarpment. It is semi-arid cattle country covered in acacia bush. After 21 km the road reaches ...

FORT BEAUFORT

This town was started during the interminable disturbances of the successive frontier wars. The *Kat* (wild cat) River, on the banks of which the town stands, flows through a warm, fertile valley which is ideal for citrus. This valley was the scene of many contentions. It was too fruitful to escape the competitive and envious attentions of man. For some years after the Fifth Frontier War of 1819, government forces, having driven the Xhosas across the Keiskamma River, attempted to maintain the whole area between the Great Fish and the Keiskamma rivers as a neutral buffer zone. Forts were built to preserve the peace. In this way *Fort Beaufort* was founded in 1822 as a military stronghold named after the ducal title of the father of Lord Charles Somerset, the governor of the Cape.

The position of the fort was extremely strong, being built on a level tongue of land between the Kat and Brak rivers, the steep banks of which enclosed the place almost like a moat. This natural strength served Fort Beaufort well, for it was often used as a place of safety during the disturbances of the time. On 7 January 1851 it withstood a full-scale assault from a Xhosa army.

Fort Beaufort was surveyed as a town in 1837. A strategic military highway known as the Queen's Road was constructed from Grahamstown across the valley of the Great Fish River, through Fort Beaufort and onwards to the mountain strongholds of the Xhosas, ending at the foot of the Katberg. The road was built by that indefatigable road-maker, Andrew Geddes Bain, using military labour. Completed in 1842, it was named in honour of Queen Victoria who was crowned in the year the building of this road commenced. It was the first major South African highway to be properly constructed. Its route is still followed by the modern tarmac road to Grahamstown, and the original fine stone bridges still span the Kat and Great Fish rivers.

Fort Beaufort became a municipality in September 1883. Today it is a pleasant and modern town, the centre for considerable farming activity, especially citrus, with the Kat River packing sheds dispatching many thousands of cases of oranges every June to October.

The original fort, a Martello Tower, built in 1857 on the same design as those used for the national defence of England, may still be seen. It is similar to the fort at Simon's Town on the Cape Peninsula and a whole chain of forts built to guard the coast of Britain, all copies of the original fort built by the French at Cape Mortello on the island of Corsica. A permit and key to visit the fort must be obtained from the town clerk. There is an interesting historical museum which contains many relics from the years of frontier incident and uproar. The museum is housed in the original military mess house built about 1830. It is open Mondays to Fridays from 08h30 to 13h00 and from 14h00 to 17h00; Saturdays from 08h30 to 12h45. Closed on Sundays and public holidays.

Ten kilometres from Fort Beaufort, on a most picturesque site, stands the Methodist Healdtown Institute named after James Heald, treasurer of the Wesleyan Methodist Missionary Society. The Institute was established in 1855. African students receive technical education. There are several interesting buildings in Fort Beaufort dating from the time of the founding of the town. It is worth exploring the side streets.

THE FORT BEAUFORT COUNTRYSIDE

From Fort Beaufort there are several interesting drives. To the south the original Queen's Road provides an all-tarmac route directly across the valley of the Great Fish River to Grahamstown. At 9 km from Fort Beaufort this road passes a turn-off to a sulphur spring, frequented by many local people. Climbing and winding, the tarmac road reveals grand views of the valley of the Great Fish River and eventually bridges the river at Fort Brown (49 km from Fort Beaufort).

This fort is now a police post. Its tower still watches over the vast valley, its flowering aloes, cattle and sheep farms, thick stunted bush and sunbronzed farmhouses. Fort Brown was built in 1813 and was first known as Hermanus's Kraal. During the 1834 war it was held against several attacks. After the war it was strengthened with a tower containing a powder-magazine, a swivel gun and an underground tunnel which led to a water supply. From then it was named after Lieutenant Robert Brown of the 75th Regiment and was completed in 1838. During the 1846 and 1851 wars it survived several attacks and finally, in 1873, it became a police post. The Andries Vosloo Kudu Reserve extends down the valley of the Great Fish River from near Fort Brown to Double Drift. It provides a sanctuary for several species of antelope.

Six kilometres from Fort Brown the road descends to the lowest level of the valley by means of the *Ecca* Pass named in corrupted form from the *iKhakha* (bitter tasting) river. There is a steep climb up the southern cliffs of the valley through thick bush where many euphorbias and aloes grown. This pass has given its name to exposure there of the geological deposit known as the Ecca Group. Superb views of a prodigious and most atmospheric valley are revealed. At 64 km from Fort Beaufort a turn-off leads to Peddie (69 km) via Committee's Drift. The Ecca Nature Reserve, 134 ha in extent, preserves many features of historical, geographical and environmental value. The bush begins to thin out with the rise in altitude. Prickly pears and aloes cover the slopes. At 69 km from Fort Beaufort the road reaches the summit of the climb, a grassy undulating plateau covered in wattle, fir and eucalyptus trees. At 73 km from Fort Beaufort the road joins N2 and leads to Grahamstown 6 km away.

From Fort Beaufort a magnificent tarmac road follows the valley of the Kat River through an amiable rural landscape of citrus groves and fine irrigated farms such as Millbank and Olive Cliff. Today the area is peaceful, but during the frontier wars this valley was the scene of violent fighting. A branch railway line, known as the Kat Valley Express, leads up this valley from Fort Beaufort to Seymour and provides an interesting journey for train enthusiasts.

There are small wayside villages such as Lower Blinkwater (13 km) and Tidbury's Toll (22 km), with a turn-off to the east at Lorraine (23 km) which provides a pleasant drive along a tree-lined road past Bonkazana to Alice. At 53,3 km a turn-off leads to the village of Balfour and thence to several interesting places such as Maasdorp, Post Retief, Jurieshoek, McKommenshoek and other rural hamlets snuggling in the valleys below the towering Katberg. A road also ascends the Katberg Pass from Balfour.

Post Retief is a national monument. It was built as a military stronghold in 1836 on the farm of Piet Retief, the Voortrekker leader. There are several other fortified farms in the district such as *Sipton Manor, Rietfontein, Hammonds* and *Stoneyfield.*

Beyond the turn-off to Balfour the main tarmac road continues up the valley of the Kat River, passing close to the shores of the irrigation dam. There is a turn-off to a recreational area 39 km from Fort Beaufort and after a further 3,5 km a turn-off to the village of ...

SEYMOUR

Seymour is a rural village and the terminus of the branch railway from Fort Beaufort. It originated in 1833 as a military stronghold called Elands Post. It was subsequently named after Colonel Charles Seymour, Private Secretary to Sir George Cathcart, governor of the Cape. It is an atmospheric little place, although a trifle decayed through the closing down of various enterprises. It is handsomely situated. The Kat River Dam, built in 1969, provides a fine recreational area. The hotel building was originally the officer's mess, built in 1852.

Beyond the turn-off to Seymour (from where a road skirts the verges of the dam to join the Alice–Hogsback road), the main tarmac road proceeds directly towards the face of the overlooking mountains and steadily climbs the magnificent Nico Malan Pass. At 61,5 km from Fort Beaufort the road reaches the summit 1 438 m above sea-level, after climbing 650 m from the level of Seymour in the valley below. The journey is delightful, revealing fine scenery on the way.

From the summit of the pass the road crosses a high grassland watered by many clear streams where trout play in the rapids and pools. At 24,5 km from the summit there is a turn-off to Hogsback and Cathcart. The tarmac road continues on its easy sweeping way past the Waterdown Dam and, 38,5 km from the summit of the pass, reaches the village of *Whittlesea*, a small rural centre for a prosperous sheep and cattle area. It is named after Whittlesea in England, birthplace of the governor, Sir Harry Smith. A road branches off beyond the village to the Katberg Pass.

Beyond Whittlesea the R67 tarmac road proceeds for 34,5 km and, 132 km from the start at Fort Beaufort, reaches Queenstown.

WHITTLESEA DOWN THE KATBERG PASS

A road (mainly gravel) from Whittlesea provides a spectacular scenic journey down the Katberg Pass to the valley of the Kat River. For the first 25 km this road winds sinuously over high grassland. It then climbs the northern slopes of the Winterberg range by means of what is known as Devil's Bellows Nek, reaching the summit after 14 km. Passing a turn-off 2,5 km further on which leads through Doringkloof to Post Retief and Adelaide, the road starts to descend the Katberg Pass.

The road winds and zigzags through a deep indigenous forest where trees, ferns and flowering plants cascade down the cliff faces like a green waterfall. The Katberg forestry station lies 12 km from the summit. From this place there are drives and walks into the Branderskop area and the Katberg forest area, where picnic spots are situated and lovely scenery may be viewed. Another kilometre brings the road to a turn-off leading to the Katberg hotel (51,5 km from Whittlesea).

A further 5,5 km of descent brings the road to a turn-off to the village of Balfour. Six kilometres further on (63 km from Whittlesea), the road joins the main tarmac R351 road which leads up the valley of the Kat River from Fort Beaufort. The drive is unforgettable and has splendid photographic possibilities. It should be done in good weather.

From Fort Beaufort the tarmac R63 road continues westwards along the foothills of the mountains. After 15 km there is a turn-off which descends into the valley of the Great Fish River to Gardiner's Drift and Riebeeck East. A further 21 km (35 km from Fort Beaufort) brings the road into the town of ...

ADELAIDE

Named after Queen Adelaide, wife of William IV of England, *Adelaide* had its start as a military post established on the banks of the Koonap River in 1834. It was at first known as *Post Retief*, after Piet Retief, the ill-fated Voortrekker leader who farmed nearby on *Mooimeisiesfontein* (pretty girl's fountain). Adelaide today has a population of 11 857. It became a municipality in October 1896. The centre for a lush farming area, it is a pleasant little town with a central square faced by an array of shops and business premises. The Our Heritage Museum, with an interesting collection of glassware, may be visited. It is housed in the original parsonage of the Dutch Reformed church built in 1859.

From Adelaide the tarmac R63 road continues westwards through the foothills of the *Baviaansrivier* (river of baboons) range, with the great Winterberg range lying to the north. At 2 km from the town a turn-off leads to Tarkastad (98 km). After a further 13 km (24 km from Adelaide) the R63 tarmac road reaches the town of ...

BEDFORD

Lying at the foot of the *Kaga* (reedy) mountains, Bedford was laid out in 1854 on the farm *Maaström*, belonging to Sir A J Stockenström. The town was named after the Duke of Bedford and is today the centre for considerable industry in the rearing of cattle and sheep, with several studfarms situated in the area. The population is 8 444.

From Bedford the R63 tarmac road proceeds in a westerly direction beneath the heights of the Kaga mountains. After 10 km there is a turn-off to the north which leads to the farming settlement of Glen Lynden in the beautiful Baviaans River valley. It was here that the 1820 Settler poet, Thomas Pringle, had his home, called *Emigrants Cabin*, now a national monument. Beyond the turn-off to Glen Lynden, a further 11 km brings the road to a junction with the main tarmac N10 road travelling from Port Elizabeth to the north at a point 19 km north of the railway junction of Cookhouse.

KING WILLIAM'S TOWN TO THE NORTH

King William's Town is the starting place for the tarmac R346 road to the north which, after leaving the town, steadily climbs through foothill country covered in dense medium-high acacia trees. Ahead lies the high mountain ridge which marks the end of the coastal shelf and the steady rise of the country towards the central plateau of Southern Africa. During winter the high peaks of the Amatole, covered in snow, look down aloofly from the north-west on a landscape of brown grass and acacia trees.

At 11 km the tarmac road crosses the Izeleni stream and, 1 km further on, a turn-off west leads to the Pirie Trout Hatcheries and the Rooikrans and Maden dams, all lying in handsome mountain and forest country. The trout hatcheries at Pirie are open to the public daily (except on Sundays) from September to April. The road now traverses a densely inhabited tribal area, climbing steeply up a well-bushed ridge decorated with aloes which flower in June. It is a picturesque drive with interesting views of the downland country.

At 27 km from King William's Town the road reaches the summit of the ridge. Here, in a clump of wattle trees, a turn-off to the west provides a magnificent scenic drive to the Evelyn valley, Mount Kemp, and to a memorial built over the grave of the great Xhosa chief, Sandili, situated behind the Mount Kemp Store (11,5 km). The road continues northwards across a grassy, open plateau covered in cattle, maize fields and wattle plantations. The peaks of the Amatole are well revealed to the west. At 35 km from King William's Town a turn-off to the west leads to the Kubose and Kologha forests and to the forest sanctuary. Sandili's grave may also be reached along this road (21 km). He was buried there on 9 June 1878 after being mortally wounded in a skirmish on 29 May during the Ninth Frontier War. He was chief of the Ngqika section of the Xhosa tribe. Two British soldiers killed in the same war were buried, one on each side of him, reputedly as guards to ensure that his turbulent spirit would roam no more. Three kilometres further on (40 km from King William's Town), the road enters the town of Stutterheim and joins the N6 road from East London to the North.

KING WILLIAM'S TOWN TO KOMGA

From King William's Town the tarmac R63 road leads directly towards the Transkei through the Ciskei and Komga, thereby saving 52 km compared with the main N2 road which goes to East London before continuing to the Transkei. This road leads over open grassland. Immediately outside King William's Town the road passes through *Bisho* (buffalo), the Xhosa name for the Buffalo River. This was created as the capital of Ciskei when it was made an independent state. Its administrative buildings, stadium, hotel, casino, international airport and other costly structures were gifted by the South African taxpayers and assorted investors to the independent state. The structures looked at the time like a load of expensive furniture fallen off a furniture removal truck in a political accident and with nobody to claim it.

THE CISKEI

The Ciskei, with an area of 793 827 ha and a population of 821 500, became an independent bantustan on 4 December 1981 under the leadership of Lennox Sebe. There was considerable ill feeling and resistance to the establishment of this state. Eventually on 4 March 1990, a bloodless coup ousted Lennox Sebe and Brigadier Oupa Gqozo became the new head of state, to the accompaniment of considerable jubilation and some looting. Brigadier Gqozo announced that he would discuss reincorporation of the Ciskei with South Africa and the development of a democratic community to replace oppression. The area is now part of the Eastern Cape Province with Bisho as the capital.

Twenty-five kilometres from King William's Town the road crosses the main railway line to the north at Kei Road station and, 64 km from King William's Town, reaches the town of ...

KOMGA

The name of *Komga* is a European corruption of the African *Gama* (red clay). The town is an agricultural and railway centre. On the road between it and Kei Road there is an interesting little memorial marking the spot where Major H G Moore on 24 December 1877 won the first Victoria Cross to be awarded in South Africa. This occurred at the beginning of the Ninth Frontier War.

Six kilometres beyond Komga (74 km from King William's Town) the road rejoins the main coastal N2 road and descends into the valley of the Kei River (see Chapter Twenty-Two).

KING WILLIAM'S TOWN TO EAST LONDON

From King William's Town the N2 road climbs out of the acacia-covered valley of the Buffalo River. Passing a turn-off to the industrial centre of *Zwelitsha* (new era), the road reaches the level of a grassy, acacia-dotted plain where, 20 km from King William's Town, stands the village of ...

BERLIN

Founded in 1857 by men of the disbanded German Legion who settled in the area. Berlin was for years simply a small rural village. In recent years it has changed into an industrial centre, a part of the general development of the border area. It is now part of the East London municipality.

Beyond Berlin the main road gradually descends to the coast, passing *Mdantsane* (named after a Xhosa chief). A vast housing area created for African industrial workers and then, 60 km from King William's Town, reaches ...

EAST LONDON

The city of East London is the only river port of any significance in South Africa. Developed at the mouth of the Buffalo River, the harbour has a working depth of 12 m at low water. Its six quays on the east bank and seven wharfs and quays on the west bank can accommodate substantial ocean going ships. Among other facilities is the Princess Elizabeth Graving Dock.

The harbour possibilities at the mouth of the river originally named by the nomadic pastoral tribes *Ingaad! ab* (river of buffaloes), and by the Xhosas *Bisho* (also meaning buffalo), were apparent to the first European explorers, but the need for development there only arose in 1835. After the Sixth Frontier War when British control was extended to the area between the Keiskamma and the Kei rivers, Colonel Harry Smith, then chief of staff to the governor, rode to the river mouth to examine its potential as a port where supplies could be landed. As a result of the visit, the brig *Knysna*, owned by the famous George Rex, was sent to the Buffalo River to trade, arriving on 19 November 1836. A Union Jack was nailed to a tree on Signal Hill overlooking the left bank of the river, and a mixed cargo was landed by means of the ship's boats.

The success of this experiment was marked by giving the river mouth the name of Port Rex. For a decade nothing more was done to the harbour, since the British Government had relinquished control over the area. Then, in 1847, the Seventh Frontier War broke out and the mouth of the Buffalo River immediately became of major importance. Fort Glamorgan was built to defend the place and, on 28 April 1847, the barque *Frederick Huth* arrived to unload military stores. After this the harbour was used regularly. A village grew up and on 28 December 1847 was officially (if rather stupidly) named East London. The following month the area was annexed to the Cape Colony. From 1851 organised parties of settlers – many of them German mercenary soldiers from the disbanded German Legion – made their homes on both banks of the river. Since most of these ex-legionnaires were bachelors, the *Lady Kennaway* was sent out from Britain in 1857 with a cargo of 157 Irish lassies. These beauties arrived in East London on 20 November, probably the most welcome cargo ever landed in the Buffalo River harbour!

In 1856 work commenced on the first training walls at the mouth of the river. From then on the harbour was steadily developed into its present state. The completion of the C W Malan Turning Basin in 1937 allowed substantial ships to enter the river, and it was no longer necessary for passengers to be offloaded in wicker baskets into lighters from ships anchored at sea. A considerable contribution to marine engineering came in 1961 when the harbour engineer of East London, Eric Merrifield, devised the unique concrete interlinking block known from its shape as the *dolos* (a witch-doctor's name for the knuckle-bone used in divination). This is now in use all over the world in breakwater construction. The strange shape of the *dolosse* ensures that they become permanently entangled once in the sea, and provide breakwaters of enormous strength.

East London has a population of 500 158. It is the centre for numerous industries and for extensive trade with the Transkei. A vast number of pineapples are grown in the area and canned in the huge Langeberg factory. There is an agricultural research station in East London. The area rates as one of the ten principal pineapple producers in the world. As a holiday resort it has tremendous potential, being richly endowed with a congenial climate and a string of superlative beaches and river mouths where boating, fishing, swimming and recreational delights are available for those who like to enjoy themselves in the sunshine and fresh air.

The commercial centre of East London, built along the principal thoroughfare of Oxford Street, is not particularly notable but the suburbs are attractive. The coastline is superb, combining most of the best features of the Cape and Natal beaches; the clear water of the Cape and the warm sea temperatures of Natal; the spacious sandy beaches of the Cape and the shady evergreen shoreline trees of Natal; the absence of excessive summer heat and the humidity experienced in Natal; and the safe swimming conditions of the Cape where there are few sharks or dangerous back or side washes. All these characteristics unite to create a most enjoyable playground for man.

Among the principal suburbs and places of interest in East London are *Panmure* (named after Lord Panmure, Secretary of War at the time when members of the German Legion settled); *Vincent* (after Amelius Vincent, a leading figure on the Cambridge Village Management Board in the 1870s); *Quanza Terrace* (after the wreck of the *Quanza* in 1872); and *Cambridge* (after the Duke of Cambridge, British Commander-in-Chief when the German Legion was disbanded).

The three main beaches are *Orient* (named after the Russian ship *Orient,* wrecked there on 29 July 1907), Eastern beach and Nahoon beach, situated at the mouth of the Nahoon *(Nxaruni,* the name of a chief who lived there) River. These are only a few among the delectable necklace of bays, lagoons, inlets, promontories and beaches strung along the length and breadth of coast where the Indian Ocean meets the shores of Africa north and south of the mouth of the Buffalo River.

East London possesses one of the best museums in Southern Africa. Among its fine natural history exhibits is the first coelacanth to be discovered in modern times. This strange fish, long thought to be extinct, was caught in 1938 near East London. The museum also exhibits the only dodo egg in the world, as well as a magnificent collection of marine shells and a finely presented series of exhibits depicting man through the ages. The museum is open weekdays from 09h30 to 17h00; Saturdays from 09h30 to 12h00; Sundays and public holidays from 11h00 to 16h00.

There is a zoo containing about 1 200 animals in Queen's Park. It is open daily from 09h00 to 17h00. In its 30 ha grow many handsome trees and plants, including the rare *Umtiza listerana* and many lovely strelitzias and flame lilies. On the beachfront is an aquarium open daily from 09h00 to 17h00. Feeding-times are at 10h30 and 15h00. Seal shows take place at 11h30 and 15h30.

The Ann Bryant Art Gallery is open on weekdays from 09h00 to 17h00; Saturdays from 09h30 to 12h00. Gately House, situated at the bottom of Caxton Street, is another interesting place to visit. This was the home of John Gately, the first mayor of East London in 1875. In 1966 the house with its Victorian furnishings was bequeathed to the municipality and is preserved as a national monument. It is a delightful example of a well-to-do life-style during the last century. It is open Tuesdays to Thursdays from 10h00 to 13h00 and 14h00 to 17h00; Fridays from 10h00 to 13h00; Saturdays and Sundays 15h00 to 17h00; closed on Mondays.

There are several buildings in the city which are historically interesting; the railway station, built in 1877; the Drill hall, built in 1906; St Peter's church, constructed in 1857; and the city hall, situated in Oxford street, where stands the equestrian memorial to the men of the Colonial Division who fell during the Anglo-Boer War.

Surfing is spectacular at Nahoon beach, a favourite area where a reef wave of considerable power occurs sufficiently reliably to allow competitions on an international level to take place.

Caravanners have a particular affection for East London. It was here that the municipality created the first large-scale modern caravan park in Southern Africa. It gave pleasure to many thousands of visitors.

THE EAST LONDON COASTLINE AND THE CAPE WILD COAST

Exploring the coastline of East London and what is known as the Cape Wild Coast, the traveller is rewarded by the discovery of many pleasant and amiable resorts where rivers become calm lagoons before reaching the sea and waves play lazily on the beach.

As already mentioned, many of these resorts combine some of the best features of the Natal and Cape beaches. Fishing is interesting and richly varied as are shells, which combine species from the tropical seas of the north with those from the temperate waters of the south.

The roads following the coast north and south from East London pass through a green and attractive countryside where picnic and camping sites can be found. African tribal life is in many parts picturesque, and it is interesting to know that it was here that the Xhosa people migrating down the north encountered and mingled with the pastoral tribes who first inhabited the area. The pioneers have now vanished from the region, but many traces of their original presence are retained in the culture and dress of the local tribes people. The language of the local Xhosa tribes people (especially with its strange-sounding clicks) has been influenced, as have most of the place-names (particularly river names), which have been hopelessly corrupted from their original form into Xhosa, English or Afrikaans forms.

THE COASTAL RESORTS SOUTH-WEST OF EAST LONDON TO PORT ALFRED

The tarmac road travelling down the coast south-west of East London leaves the city at the seaward end of Oxford Street. It descends into the valley of the Buffalo River, passing Queen's Park and its zoo set among trees and gardens. The road then crosses the river by means of the handsome five-span bridge built in 1978 immediately upstream from the curious old double-decker steel bridge which the road originally shared with the railway. The view of the river from the bridge is impressive. Downstream may be seen the bustle of the harbour, upstream, where the river flows down from the interior, magnificent opportunities for boating are provided.

Immediately beyond the bridge a turn-off descends the west bank to the mouth of the river and continues from there as a marine drive along the coast, rejoining the main road after 15 km.

The main road proceeds from the bridge in a south-easterly direction, passing the East London Airport at 9 km and rewarding travellers with a delightful journey along a level, green, lightly bushed coastal terrace. At 12 km the road is joined by the marine drive and at 17 km there is a crossroads with a turn-off to the west leading to Mount Coke (the mission station named after Dr Coke, founder of the Methodist Missionary Society) and east to the coast and the mouth of the Igoda River where there are camping sites and holiday cottages.

Another kilometre takes the road across the *Igoda* (shallow valley) River. The name accurately describes the course the river follows through hills well covered with a considerable variety of bush, euphorbia species and trees. The area is pleasantly parklike. At 24 km the road descends into another attractively wooded, shallow valley through which flows the river known as the *Gxulu* (agitated).

At 6,5 km from the Gxulu River (30,5 km from East London) the road reaches a turn-off which leads for 3 km to the coastal resort of ...

KIDD'S BEACH

Named after Charles Kidd, a mayor of King William's Town in the 1860s, *Kidd's Beach* originated as a coastal resort particularly popular with the people of King William's Town. Today it is an amiable (if untidy) huddle of seaside cottages which look out on to a rocky shoreline. There is a tidal pool for swimming and a sandy beach at the mouth of the river.

From the turn-off to Kidd's Beach the tarmac road continues south-westwards along the parklike coastal terrace. After 1,5 km (33 km from East London) a turn-off west leads to Mount Coke and King William's Town. The coastal road swings left, passes substantial fields of pineapples and then descends into the well-wooded valley of the river known as the *Ncera*, after the species of grass used for thatching which grows there. At 1,5 km beyond this river (39 km from East London) a turn-off stretches for 4,5 km to Christmas Rock, and for 9 km to ...

KAYSER'S BEACH

Named after John Kayser who owned the land during the 1880s, *Kayser's Beach* is a popular resort for fishermen.

Beyond the turn-off to Kayser's Beach the winding tarmac coastal road continues, passing fields of pineapples and swinging more inland across a gentle succession of green, lightly bushed hills. At 49 km from East London the road descends steeply to the river known to Europeans as the *Chalumna* and to the Xhosas as the Tyalomnga.

Three kilometres beyond the river crossing there is a turn-off leading southwards for 9 km to the mouth of the Chalumna. The main tarmac road continues through a tribal area lightly bushed with low acacia species and covered with green grass, sisal plantations and maize fields. After 11 km (67 km from East London) the road descends into the ruggedly handsome, thickly bushed valley of the river which still bears the pleasant original name of *Keiskamma*. The scenery of rolling hills and an interesting collection of succulents and euphorbias growing along the river banks is dramatic.

Eight kilometres beyond the river (80 km from East London) an important junction is reached. One branch veers westwards and makes its way inland for 25 km over gentle hills covered in thick bush. The Crossroads Supply Store is passed on the way, after which the tarmac road reaches Peddie and joins the main N2 Cape Town–Durban road.

The left-hand branch at the junction continues for 4,5 km and then reaches a turn-off to the east which descends to the alluvial floor of the valley of the Keiskamma and then follows the bank of the river for 16 km before reaching its mouth, at which lies the holiday resort of ...

HAMBURG

Hamburg is an informal little fishermen's resort with a spacious beach, excellent swimming and boating on the river. A huddle of cottages and stores stands on the bush-covered hill slopes which overlook the estuary of the river. It was founded in 1857 by members of the disbanded German Legion and named after Hamburg in Germany.

Beyond the turn-off to Hamburg the main tarmac road proceeds, passing a turn-off to the Wesleyan mission station of Wesley and then approaching the coast. This is a delightful coast which is as yet unspoilt by so-called developers or other 'vepers' (venal persons) who assault nature by looting it for their own profit. The road crosses a succession of rivers – the Gqutywa, Bira, Mgwalana and Mtati – each with a pretty lagoon at its mouth. The Mpekweni River, 25 km from the turn-off to Hamburg, has a camping ground on its left bank.

The Old Woman's River is 10 km further on where a turn-off north leads to Peddie. A further 2,5 km brings the tarmac road to the bridge across the Great Fish River. From this point the road has been described in Chapter Nineteen.

THE COASTAL RESORTS NORTH-EAST OF EAST LONDON

The coastline from East London to the mouth of the Great Kei River, shelters a succession of popular holiday resorts all with fine beaches, lagoons and river mouths, rocky vantage-points for fishermen and patches of coastal forest where campers and picnickers can find shady retreats.

Immediately north-east of East London proper lies the mouth of the river known to Europeans as the *Nahoon*, a corruption of the Xhosa *Nxaruni* (said to have been a chief who once resided there). The Nahoon area is nowadays a suburb of East London lying 3 km from the centre of the city. The river provides a fine stretch of boating water and there is a spacious beach pleasantly situated at the mouth where swimming is safe and there is exciting surfing.

The second coastal resort north-east of East London is Bonza Bay, reached by a turn-off from the main road to the Transkei, 9 km from the city centre. This is a 4,5 km turn-off to the sea at the mouth of the river known to Europeans as the *Quenera* – a name which has, through the years, undergone a succession of involved corruptions from the original African *!Kani lab* (river of elands). At the mouth of the river lies Bonza Bay, an attractive little bay which has a pleasant beach and good sea and lagoon swimming and boating. The township area is known as *Beacon Bay*, combining the names of the original farm *Beaconhurst*, and *Bonza Bay (*the name of which is said to have been given to it by an admiring Australian). The Quenera and Nahoon rivers border the area and provide kilometres of interesting possibilities for boating, canoeing, aquaplaning, swimming and fishing.

The third coastal resort north of East London lies 12 km from the city along the N2 Transkei road and is reached by a 7,5 km turn-off to the coast.

GONUBIE

The pleasant little seaside town of Gonubie lies at the mouth of the river known to the Xhosas as *Qunube* after the wild bramble berries which grow along its banks. Apart from giving the town its name, this river (and the lagoon and beach at its mouth) provides a delectable recreational facility for visitors to this sunny and relaxed part of the world. To enhance these natural assets, the local municipality has, with commendable energy, created several amenities such as a tidal paddling pool for children and, in a shady setting along the banks of the river, one of the loveliest caravan parks in Southern Africa.

The coast north-east of Gonubie supports a necklace of pretty little bays, river mouths and recreational resorts casually strung out along the shoreline and reached by a tarmac loop road which branches off from the main N2 road at a point north of the turn-off to Gonubie (17 km from East London). This loop road, leading to the East Coast resorts area, provides a very pleasant 23 km long drive which traverses a green and gentle rural landscape.

Crossing the old East London–Transkei road, the loop road travels eastwards for 3 km before reaching a turn-off 7,5 km to the coast at the mouth of the *Kwelera* (river of aloes) where a cluster of seaside shacks and cottages look out over a rocky fishermen's shoreline. A lagoon and beach are situated at the river mouth. From this branch road to Kwelera Mouth there is a turn-off stretching for 3 km to Sunrise-on-Sea.

From the turn-off to Kwelera Mouth the main tarmac loop road continues across fields of pineapples. After 4,5 km a turn-of leads eastwards for 3 km to the splendid beach at the mouth of the Bulugha River, where swimming is safe and the fishing is interesting. This area (known as Fisherman's Cove) is a fine holiday resort throughout the year.

From the turn-off to the Bulugha River mouth the tarmac loop road continues past the turn-off to Cintsa Mouth West (4,5 km) and, at 7,5 km, a turn-off 6 km long leading to the mouth of the Kefani River and thereafter for 7,5 km to Cintsa Mouth East. At both these river mouths there are fine beaches, lagoons, good swimming and fishing, holiday camps and caravan parks. At Cintsa Mouth East there is also a Regional Services Council parking and camping ground. The *Kefani* (or Cefane) River is said to take its name from a man who once resided there. The *Cintsa* is said to be named after the 'crumbling' of its banks by floodwaters.

The village of Cintsa is a pretty resort and place of retirement. It has grown on the banks of the Cintsa lagoon in an area of rolling hills and sub-tropical dune forest. Bird life is varied, with 197 species so far identified. The shoreline is a 17 km long part of the Strandloper Trail. The wreck of the *Atalaia* which sank in 1647 lies between Cintsa and Cefani. It was located in 1980 and some of its cannons are now in East London Museum.

From the turn-off to the mouths of the Kefani and Cintsa rivers, the tarmac loop road proceeds. After 1,5 km a turn-off stretches for 12 km through pretty scenery and tribal country past the Tainton school, joining the N2 Transkei road at a point 40 km from East London. The tarmac loop road meanwhile continues for 4,5 km and then rejoins the Transkei road at a point 32 km from East London.

At a point on the N2 Transkei road 41 km from East London, there is yet another turn-off which leads to the coast at Haga-Haga. This road travels eastwards over gentle hills with euphorbia-covered slopes, and well cultivated farmlands. After 12 km a crossroads is reached at St Anthony's Store. The road leads for a further 12 km in an easterly direction straight to the coast, past pineapple and maize farms and numerous tribal settlements nestling in lightly bushed country. Once at the coast the road descends suddenly and steeply to a line of cottages, stores and places of accommodation built along a rocky coastline at a resort with the odd-sounding name of ...

HAGA-HAGA

A small coastal village, *Haga-Haga* looks out at the sea from the foot of a pair of hills. It is said to take its name from the ceaseless murmur and movement of the waves upon the shore. It is the centre of an interesting stretch of coast where a spacious beach at the river mouth provides lively fishing and a good area for collecting sea shells. There are several beautiful walks.

From the junction at St Anthony's store a road marked Kei Mouth turns to the north. For 9 km this road crosses gently rolling country lightly bushed and very green. Occasional trees, fine farms (pineapples and sheep) and tribal settlements may be seen. This road then joins the R349 road connecting with the N2 road which travels to Morgan Bay and Kei Mouth.

This R349 road to Morgan Bay and Kei Mouth branches off from the N2 road at a point 57 km north-east of East London and leads eastwards over gently rolling hills for 29 km before reaching the turn-off south to Haga-Haga, described above. From this junction the road continues for a further 15 km and then reaches a turn-off 8 km to the delightful little resort of ...

MORGAN BAY

Morgan Bay takes its name from A F Morgan, master of the Royal Navy ship *Barracouta* which was used in the survey of the coast of south-east Africa conducted in 1822 by Captain W F Owen. The master's name was applied to Cape Morgan (on which today stands an automatic lighthouse) and the little bay sheltered in its southern lee.

The holiday resort lies on the right bank of the *Ntshala* (or *Nchara*) River, so called from the crabs found there. The river forms a pretty lagoon which is the centrepiece for a singularly romantic and quite charming stretch of coastline. South-west of the village with its atmospheric hotel and water's-edge caravan park, the coastline develops into a handsome line of cliffs over the top of which leads a track to one of the most beautiful and unspoilt areas in Southern Africa. This area is known as Double Mouth and consists of the lagoon formed by two small rivers: the *Quko* (or *Khukho*), meaning something spread out, and the *Gondwane* (river of wild figs). The traveller is confronted with an almost-dreamlike scene of calm water, green hills, and an exquisite coastline of rocks alternating with dark-yellow coloured beaches. Fine shells litter these stretches of sand, and amongst the natural gems of the sea may be found cornelian beads and fragments of Ming china washed up on the shore from the forgotten wrecks of early sailing vessels.

North-east of the village a pleasant 5 km long walk leads to Kei Mouth over the ridge of Cape Morgan, past a drowsy indigenous forest where bushbuck and duiker lurk. In this forest may be seen the unbeautiful workings of the Cape Morgan Titanium Mine. In 1954 an asbestos miner, Trevor Miller, on holiday in Morgan Bay, noticed a black deposit on the beach. Samples showed this deposit to be rich in ilmenite, rutile and zircon. He followed the traces, pegged claims and exported the first 150 tons in 1958.

Once again on the R349 road at the turn-off to Morgan Bay the road continues eastwards to the coast, passes pineapple fields and over hills for 9 km to the village and holiday resort of ...

KEI MOUTH

This little place takes its name from the *Kei* (great) River which flows sedately through a jumble of low hills, depositing upon the beach a peace offering to the ocean of flotsam, jetsam, and tree trunks carried from the inner parts of South Africa.

The village consists of an informal collection of cottages, stores and places of accommodation built on the slopes of a pile of hills which tumble down to the sea. There is a spacious beach and good rocky vantage-points for fishermen. Sea shells can be collected, and a walk of 1 km through a coastal forest (a haunt of blue duikers) takes the visitor to the mouth of the river. The climate is cool and the sea-water warm. With the addition of plenty of sunshine but no humidity, all these factors contribute to make an attractive holiday resort. There is also a ferry to take passengers and motor vehicles across the Kei River.

Beyond the Kei River, of course, lies the Transkei. Kei Mouth is the last of the holiday resorts on the East London and Border coastline.

EAST LONDON TO THE NORTH

The road N6 to the north from East London, finds an easy, well graded route from the city, rising steadily through the coastal hills, passing farmlands and patches of bush country. Keeping close company with the main railway line to the north, the N6 road passes villages such as Macleantown and Kei Road and then, after 87 km, reaches the town of ...

STUTTERHEIM

Lying on the southern slopes of the Kologha Mountains which form an eastern spur of the Amatole range, Stutterheim is pleasantly situated with forest-covered mountain slopes providing many recreational possibilities such as good walks (e.g. the two-day Kologha hiking trail), fishing, boating, swimming in the rivers, and numerous picnic spots and scenic features such as waterfalls and viewsites. Ferns and wild flowers are numerous. Four well-marked paths lead from the Kologha picnic site near Eagles Ridge to several interesting places. Gubu Dam is well known for trout.

The first Europeans to settle in this well-watered area were missionaries of the Berlin Missionary Society who, under Pastor Jacob Ludwig Dohne, established the Bethal mission station in 1837. Twenty years later men of the disbanded British German Legion were settled in the area then known as Dohne's Post where a small fort had been built on the site of the present caravan park. In the same year the town was founded and named after the commander of the German Legion, Major-General Baron Richard von Stutterheim. Several interesting ruins from this period may still be seen in the town.

On 20 May 1879 Stutterheim became a municipality and at present 24 819 people live there. Today it is the centre for a considerable timber industry, with sawmills producing transmission poles, mosaic floor blocks and building materials. The town is also the centre of the Eastern Cape Grassveld Region. The Dohne Agricultural Research Institute conducts extensive experiments (especially with sheep and cattle) on its research farm 8 km north of the town. The Dohne merino sheep breed was created in the research station and has become an established mutton and wool producer in sour-grass conditions. Merino sheep, Jersey cows and Bonsmara beef animals are bred in the district. Citrus fruits and timber are produced.

From Stutterheim the N6 road continues northwards climbing the steep slopes at the eastern end of the Kologha range. Alongside the road the main railway line also proceeds in an involved serpentine climb up the same ridge. After 5 km the tarmac road passes the small rail centre of Dohne, with its turn-off to the east which leads to Komga, 48 km away. A further 5 km of steady climbing through plantations of pine and wattle trees takes the road past Fort Cunynghame. The old fort was built during the Ninth Frontier War (1878) and named after General Cunynghame. Eight kilometres further on, the road reaches the top of the ridge and continues its journey over rugged, grassy, stony country patched with wattle-tree plantations. After 9 km the road crosses the Thomas River and then proceeds over an undulating plateau for a further 21 km until (48 km from Stutterheim) it reaches the town of ...

CATHCART

In the early 1850s Cathcart was originally a military post built on the overlooking Windvoëlberg. In 1876 the first erven were sold to create a town named after Lieutenant-General the Honourable George Cathcart, governor of the Cape from 1852 to 1854. In 1881 the town became a municipality. It is a quiet rural centre surrounded by extensive sheep farms.

From Cathcart the N6 road carries on climbing over a rugged countryside with the main railway line tunnelling and twisting in close company. After 19 km both the road and the railway reach a fine viewsite which has an extensive outlook across the valley of the Swart Kei River into a great bowl dominated to the north by the high, stool-shaped mountains of the Stormberge range and its numerous spurs and outliers. This is a majestic scene peculiar to South Africa – rocky, arid, enormous, romantic in atmosphere and strangely comforting in its harshness.

The road and railway descend into this bowl and continue northwards across its floor through stunted acacia bush past numerous sheep farms. Stony hillocks (many flat-topped) look down on a rugged landscape.

At 40 km from Cathcart there is a turn-off east to Engcobo (130 km). After a further 17 km the road (57 km from Cathcart) reaches the town of ...

QUEENSTOWN

The principal town of the Cape Midlands, Queenstown is also the commercial, administrative and educational centre of a prosperous farming area. It is a communications, road and railway centre and staging post of considerable importance.

Queenstown, named after Queen Victoria, was founded in 1853 on the banks of the Komani River by the governor, Sir George Cathcart. It is said that some years earlier an official on government business had passed that way. He reported to his superiors that he had found a site for a town in the area, so ideal that it was fit to be named after Queen Victoria herself. The town was intended to be one of a chain of border posts and had a most unusual layout. In accordance with the instructions of the governor that the town be a stronghold for the defence of the frontier area, the surveyor, Thomas Holden Bowker, designed the town around a hexagonal open piece of ground from where cannon or rifle fire could be directed down the six thoroughfares which radiated from it. This hexagonal town centre is now a handsome garden with a pleasant fountain as its dominant feature.

Lying on the banks of the Komani River, with a refreshing climate and plentiful water obtained from the surrounding heights, Queenstown grew rapidly. In 1876 it became a municipality and is today one of the most important towns in Southern Africa.

Queenstown possesses an impressively modern commercial centre; and its cultural, sporting and recreational assets are numerous. The Frontier Museum and Art Gallery contain many exhibits worth seeing, including an old steam-engine and a replica of a cottage of the early frontier days. At the beginning of June each year the Queenstown Art Society holds an exhibition of paintings and sculptures by artists from many parts of Southern Africa. There is a well-stocked library and the collection of shell work of Miss R Lock, exhibited in a gallery in 1 Lamont Street, has a unique charm. The Queenstown Collectors Museum, founded in 1988 by Mr Rex Abbott, has on show a considerable variety of interesting exhibits. At Louis Motors, opened in 1990, there is a collection of unique motor vehicles.

Queenstown is pleasantly situated. From the overlooking heights many handsome views are provided. The slopes of the Madeira Mountain were proclaimed as the Lawrence de Lange Nature Reserve in May 1964. A 7 km long gravel road leads through this reserve to the summit of the mountain from where a sweeping panoramic view may be seen. Blesbok, springbok, zebra, other game animals, and ostriches roam the reserve and the flora is varied and interesting. In winter (July to August) the *Aloe ferox* is in full bloom, while in spring and early summer (October to November) the numerous species of acacia trees are covered in yellow and red flowers. The tambookie thorn (*Erythrina acanthocarpa*) is especially notable at this time. Cycads may also be seen and fine specimens may be found 6 km south of the town at Fincham's Nek. The reserve is open daily 08h00 to 17h00 all year round, except in wet weather. The Longhill Nature Reserve is adjacent to the Lawrence de Lange Nature Reserve and is open at the same time.

Five kilometres from Queenstown, on the road to Lady Frere, lies the Bongolo Dam, the town's main source of water. In a fine setting of hills, the dam has been developed as a recreational area where there are picnic sites. The Queenstown Power Boat and Yacht Club is based at the lake and has a summer weekend tea-room in its clubhouse. The lake is stocked with black bass and bluegill fish. Another substantial dam is the Waterdown Dam, 50 km from Queenstown on the road to Fort

Beaufort. With an earth wall 55 m high and 260 m long, this dam supplies water for irrigation and is well stocked with trout. Bushman paintings in the area are amongst the finest known.

Queenstown is notable for its gardens, with roses flourishing in great numbers. The Walter Everitt sunken gardens have been developed where the road enters Queenstown from the south. The garden has a succession of ponds frequented by swans and aquatic birds, and a great variety of ornamental shrubs, trees and flowers. A caravan park has been laid out here next to a drive-in tea-room.

Queenstown is altogether a pleasant and modern country town with an amiable and relaxed atmosphere. At present the population is 54 387.

Queenstown is the junction for a branch railway and a road (R61) leading west for 61 km to ...

TARKASTAD

The name *Tarkastad* has an obscure origin. Most likely it derives from the African *traka* (women) and the Afrikaans *stad* (place or city). The name, however, is a confusion of the corruptions of the early language and then the addition of the stad. It could also derive from a Xhosa name meaning a place of birds. Whatever the origin of its name, Tarkastad was established as a church centre by the Dutch Reformed Church in 1862 and became a municipality in 1864. The present population of the town is 4 954.

It is a pleasant little town. Notwithstanding its remoteness at the end of a branch line and well off the beaten track, it is neat, clean and well looked after. Wool and various agricultural crops are produced in the district.

Tarkastad is also a centre for trophy hunting of East Cape and Karoo species of game animals. Professional hunters use the town as a base; and there is quite a considerable industry in game breeding, capture, sale, equipment of hunting parties and preparation of trophies.

There are some notable scenic landmarks in the district, including the oft-photographed pair of flat-topped hillocks known as Martha and Mary.

From Queenstown the N6 tarmac road climbs northwards through the mountains, with Hangklip dominating the landscape from the east. Angora goats and aloes flourish in its rugged setting. Lay-bys created by a considerate roads department allow travellers to rest awhile and view the surroundings. Numerous flat-topped mountains crowd the horizon. The landscape is wild and the air has the clarity of the verges of the Great Karoo.

At 49 km from Queenstown there are turn-offs west to Sterkstroom (12 km) and Dordrecht (48 km), described further on in this chapter. The road continues northwards and after a further 5 km crosses the branch railway line from Sterkstroom to Maclear. Ahead looms the high continuous ridge of the *Stormberge* (storm mountains) running east to west. At 57 km from Queenstown, the road starts to climb the range by means of the *Penhoek* (sharp-pointed glen) Pass. For 7 km the road climbs steadily up the grassy, rock-strewn slopes. The summit of the pass is 1 844 m high (65 km from Queenstown), from where the road traverses a grassy and windswept mountain plateau with no tree or bush to be seen. Cattle and sheep farms cover the heights. At 7 km from the summit there are turn-offs east to Dordrecht (34 km) and west to Molteno (35 km).

The road continues through rugged rock and hill country where fine farms abound. After a further 33 km (106 km from Queenstown) the road reaches the town of ...

JAMESTOWN

A rural centre for a substantial farming activity in sheep and grain, Jamestown shelters in a hollow on the northern slopes of the Stormberge. It is the terminus of the branch railway from Molteno and has always been a staging post on the route to the north, the early transport men having used it as a place of rest and repair after or before crossing the Stormberge.

The farm on which the town stands, *Plessies Kraal*, was owned by Johannes Jacobus Wagenaar, known to his English-speaking friends as 'James'. With a syndicate of his friends he laid out a village on a portion of his farm. The first 405 lots were auctioned on 22 December 1874. Eight years later what had become known as *Jamestown*, after the farm owner, received its first village management board and on 4 December 1943 eventually became a municipality. Its growth has not been very spectacular, but Jamestown has no pretensions of being anything other than a friendly little rural centre, the terminus of the branch railway which was built to the town in 1930. The population is 3 582.

From Jamestown the N6 road continues northwards through rugged, rocky sheep country where the cliff faces of numerous high hills provide ideal nesting ledges for a large population of vultures. After 6 km there is a turn-off leading eastwards to Lady Grey (58 km). After a further 6 km the road finally emerges from the Stormberge range and makes its way on to a superb agricultural plateau where wheat, barley, dairy cows and sheep are farmed. On the far eastern horizon looms the great pile of the *Witteberge* (white mountains), covered in snow in winter, and the complex mountain massifs which build up to the Drakensberg.

At 24 km from Jamestown the tarmac road passes the Vineyard Cheese Factory. For a further 16 km the road traverses fertile farming country dominated to the west by the bulk of Stormberg Peak. At 40 km from Jamestown the road travels through a spur of hills dominated by the Plaatkop. A further 5 km takes the road across the branch railway linking Aliwal North to Barkly East. There is a turn-off to the east 6 km further on, leading to the hot springs at Aliwal North. Fifty-six kilometres from Jamestown the road enters the town of ...

ALIWAL NORTH

With a population of 22 502, Aliwal North was founded as a centre for the territory north of the Stormberge which had been newly annexed by that volatile governor, Sir Harry Smith. On 19 September 1848 Sir Harry had visited the site and at a meeting of local settlers was requested to establish a town. On 12 May 1849, John Centlivres Chase, newly appointed magistrate for the area, laid the foundation-stone for an administrative building and held an auction sale of erven in the town named after Sir Harry Smith's victory in 1846 over the Sikhs at Aliwal in India.

The site of the new town was at the strategic ford across the Gariep River known as Flotfontein, where a frontiersman, Pieter Jacobus de Wet, had settled on a farm named *Buffelsvlei* in 1828. On this farm two powerful thermal springs at a temperature of 94°C reach the surface. The larger, 2 182 000 *l*, and the smaller spring, 1 227 000 *l* a day, are both highly mineralised, principally with sodium chloride, calcium chloride, calcium carbonate and aluminium sulphate. They have so high a content of methane, nitrogen and carbon dioxide that a funnel placed over the eyes of the spring could trap enough gas to maintain a cooking fire in the first restaurant built there. These springs originate at a depth of about 1 280 m where the water is heated. Through artesian pressure the water rises to the surface so rapidly that much of the heat is carried upwards as well. From early times the springs were highly regarded for their properties in curing rheumatism, arthritis, lumbago, neuralgia, etc. People became accustomed to visiting them to enjoy their qualities.

Aliwal North grew as a frontier town of the Cape, a transport centre and health resort. A pontoon was floated in 1872 to convey travellers across the Gariep River. Just below the pont, D C Greathead erected a giant water-mill which was driven by the river, while pleasant homes were built on vantage-points along the banks.

In 1882 Aliwal North became a municipality and in 1885 became the railhead of the line from East London, competing for the trade of the booming diamond-fields of the north. Hotels and warehouses were built and many colourful gardens were cultivated. The streets were shaded by handsome trees and a park was developed and named after the romantic and beautiful Lady Juana Smith, wife of the governor.

The continuation of the railway across the Gariep along a relocated route destroyed the significance of Aliwal North as a railhead on the main line, but the town remained an important staging post and branch railway junction, the centre of rich farming activity, endowed with boundless water from the Gariep River and the hot springs.

The hot springs have been lavishly developed. In a setting of green lawns, a warm Olympic-sized swimming-pool holding 2 273 000 l of water (27,7°C) has been constructed. There is a second outdoor pool built over the eye of a hot spring containing water of a temperature of 31,1°C. Built directly in the eye of the main spring is a completely enclosed 'wonder' pool where the water is 34,4°C. Since the water is heavily impregnated with natural gases, the effect is like bathing in warm champagne.

There are two warm children's pools (27,7°C), an exercise centre, sauna, jacuzzi, playgrounds, picnic areas, caravan and camping parks and numerous other worthwhile amenities which today attract over 150 000 visitors each year. The hot springs resort is open from 06h00 to 22h00 (October to March); from 07h00 to 18h00 (April to May); from 08h00 to 17h00 (June to August); and from 07h00 to 18h00 (September).

The Aliwal Spa is continuously being upgraded. New facilities include chalets, a putt-putt course, braai lapa, upgraded caravan park and various water features.

The town council is also busy with the construction of a new resort, the Islands Spa. The main recreation facilities consist of a lake area approximately 17 ha in extent on which canoeing, windsurfing, rowing and fishing are allowed.

There are also interesting museums in the town. The old library building was erected in 1876 and used as a library until 1987 when it was put into use as a museum. Gogga Brown, famous palaeontologist and entomologist, was the librarian from 1860 until after the Anglo-Boer War. Currently the museum houses an interesting soap collection, a photo history and items used at the springs, an old pharmacy, kitchen utensils and articles, a palaeontological collection, clothes of yester-year and various other exhibits depicting the history of Aliwal North.

The old Dutch Reformed church was built in 1864 by the parishioners themselves to save money. In 1925 the church building was sold to the municipality for £2 000, after which it was used until November 1987 as a market-hall, cinema and storehouse. The town council then decided to restore and use the building as an extension of the museum complexes.

The Buffelspruit Nature Reserve, situated on the banks of the Kraai River, was proclaimed on 27 January 1978 as a local reserve. The aim of the reserve is to maintain breeding populations of indigenous species and to encourage public recreation and environmental education. Only wild animals that were indigenous in the area have been re-introduced. Animals most frequently seen on the indicated routes are springbok, blesbok, black wildebeest, ostrich, eland, zebra, red hartebeest, gemsbok, reedbuck and steenbok.

Beyond Aliwal North the N6 road crosses the Gariep River by means of the General Hertzog Bridge and enters the province of the Free State (see Chapter Twenty-Nine).

Aliwal North is the gateway to some of the most spectacular scenery in Southern Africa, the rugged mountain world of the north-eastern Cape. This was an old domain of the Bushmen, the type of country which they loved, full of caves and rock shelters with plenty of water, and herds of the game animal which they particularly liked to hunt – the eland. Experiencing this area at all seasons is an exciting discovery of a very special part of planet Earth.

From Aliwal North, a tarmac road (R58) leads eastwards for 48 km directly towards the *Witteberge* which, in winter when they are often covered in snow, fully justify their name of the 'white mountains'. At the foot of these mountains, hidden in a cul-de-sac valley, lies the picturesque town of ...

LADY GREY

With a population of 4 913, Lady Grey is completely dominated by the high range of the Witteberge. The town originated in 1858 when the Dutch Reformed community purchased the farm *Waaihoek* from the Botha brothers and laid it out as a church centre. The first church was built, and a town was established, named after the wife of the Cape governor, Sir George Grey.

Lady Grey, a trading and administrative centre for a rugged mountain area, is beautifully situated. Its valley is well wooded and a journey up to the reservoir is very worthwhile. The reservoir is the centre for a nature reserve and was built in 1925. A steep road climbs out of the valley over Joubert's Pass, crossing a high ridge until it eventually joins the R58 road to Barkly East near a railway station with the rather damp name of Drizzly. The drive is rough but worthwhile, and the snow-covered mountains are very lovely in winter.

The R58 road and the railway both follow difficult routes between Lady Grey and Barkly East. The railway route is particularly involved, comprising eight successive reversing sections where the train zigzags its way up and down steep slopes.

From Lady Grey, the R58 road skirts the southern slopes of the Witteberge range, yielding many tremendous views, especially at 9 km from Lady Grey station where the road climbs steadily towards the fourth reversing station on the railway, and 15 km further on, where the road crosses a high ridge.

The gravel road continues eastwards along the southern slopes of the Witteberge which are grassy and ideal for sheep. At 53 km from Lady Grey station, the road passes the station of New England, a centre for many handsome farms. Five kilometres further on is a turn-off north-eastwards to Lundeans Nek. A further 4 km takes the road across the willow-lined Kraai River, swiftly flowing through a precipitous gorge which provides several zigzags and other engineering problems for the railway to surmount.

Climbing out of this gorge, the road reveals fine views of the whole length of the Witteberge range – fairyland when covered in snow. At 73 km from Lady Grey station there is a turn-off to Dordrecht and, 3 km further on, the road enters the town of ...

BARKLY EAST

Lying 1 820 m above sea-level, Barkly East has the chilly distinction of experiencing some of the coldest weather in Southern Africa, with an average of 93 nights a year when the temperature drops below freezing-point. Snow is usual in winter. Notwithstanding the coldness of winter, the district has always been desirable to man. Bushmen hunted the game animals grazing on the rich pasturage in the area and found shelter in sandstone caves. Europeans settlers wandered in during the first half of the 19th century. To provide a religious, educational and trading centre for this community, Sir Henry Barkly, the governor of the Cape, proclaimed the establishment of a town in December 1874 which received his name in the form of *Barkly East*. A portion of the farm *Rockypark* was purchased as the site for the town and on it the Dutch Reformed community built a church. Captain Nesbitt, a survivor of the wreck of the *Birkenhead*, established a water-mill in the Langkloofspruit, having apparently resolved to move as far away from the sea as possible. By 1881 the town had reached the status of a municipality. The population is now 7 295. In 1886 a newspaper, the lively little *Barkly East Reporter* was published. The town became a busy centre of considerable agricultural activity in the production of wool, maize, wheat and potatoes. Eventually, by means of a 1-in-36 gradient and eight reversing stations, the railway managed to reach the town in December 1930.

Today 600 000 sheep and many thousands of other livestock graze in the surrounding mountains, often in areas so remote that a farmer has to be a pretty agile mountaineer in order to visit his pasturage. The cold winters kill livestock parasites; sheep and cattle flourish. Rustlers also prosper, however, and this jumble of mountains still sees a never-ending war between farmers and the men who cut their fences at night and spirit away a loot of prime cattle and sheep into secret valleys and hideaways in Lesotho and elsewhere.

Apart from its scenic setting, Barkly East is a centre for trout fishing. The municipal dam is well stocked, and the Langkloofspruit which flows through the town lands has yielded many rainbow trout of up to 5 kg in mass. Yellow-fish in the Kraai River weigh up to 2,3 kg and provide good sport and excellent eating.

The district is considered to be the best partridge-hunting field in the world and it certainly surpasses anything of its kind in Southern Africa. Bird life is generally plentiful and the grass-covered mountain slopes are the home for many rooiribbok and vaalribbok.

It is a fine centre for horse riding, with several bridle-paths which are a delight to follow.

From Barkly East a particularly beautiful drive leads up the valley of the Langkloof and over Barkly Pass to Elliot. Leaving Barkly East lying in the midst of a great bowl in the mountains, the R58 road winds southwards, commencing a long, steady climb up the river valley, overlooked on both sides by high sandstone buttresses containing many caves and weirdly shaped rock formations. There are superb galleries of Bushman paintings. On the farm *Denorbin* there is a panel of polychrome paintings, 32 m in length, in one rock shelter. Magnificent sheep and cattle farms are scattered along the floor of the valley.

At 43 km from Barkly East, there is a turn-off east to Rhodes through the Tembu Pass. At this point the R58 road reaches the summit of Barkly Pass, built in 1885. Spectacularly beautiful, it reveals many majestic views of crumbling sandstone cliffs. The view from the summit, especially to the west along the great wall of the Drakensberg, is magnificent, with a superb 'castle of the giants' (Vanzylsberg) dominating the road. The Tafelberg lies further west, and the range ends 35 km away at the towering sandstone cliffs of *Xalanga* (vulture).

From this point the road starts to descend and after 9 km reaches the foot of the mountains. After a further 9 km of travel across undulating country at the foot of the massive wall of the Drakensberg, the road reaches the town of Elliot, 63 km from Barkly East. It is a memorable drive.

ELLIOT

The town of Elliot is handsomely situated in a grassy, spacious valley at the foot of the Drakensberg, curtain-like buttresses of orange-coloured sandstone provide a majestic backing to the green lowlands. Named after Sir Henry Elliot, a former chief magistrate of the Transkeian territories from 1891 to 1902, it became a municipality in 1911. Its situation and brisk climate have made it a very pleasant place in which to live.

The area around Elliot is renowned for its mushrooms. The Xhosa people, in fact, know the town as *eCowa* (mushroom). The mushroom appears on the coat-of-arms of Elliot.

The rock formations of the sandstone heights have been modelled by erosion into extraordinary shapes. Notable are 'The Pillars' and 'Giant's Castle', a circle of huge sandstone rocks like the ruined stronghold of a primeval race. There are hiking trails such as eCowa Trail (three to four days) and the Baster Footpath which leads for 30 km to Maclear and reveals stunning scenery.

There are several very beautiful drives to places such as *Waterkloof* farm (8 km), from where there are fine views of the rock teeth formations of the Drakensberg. The Gillie Cullem waterfall (18 km) is one of the most spectacular waterfalls in South Africa. It is in a lovely setting of indigenous forest and sandstone cliffs. A footpath leads up a ruggedly beautiful ravine to the top of the waterfall.

The Otto du Plessis Pass (40 km) provides a spectacular link from Elliot to Barkly East through the Tsomo valley. The Barkly Pass has already been described. On the summit of the pass, 18 km from Elliot, there is a turn-off 2 km long to Kransies, from where there is a vast panoramic view with, on a clear day, even a glimpse of the sea 80 km away. The Satansnek Pass (20 km) on the road to Engcobo has memorable views.

The Thompson Dam (3 km) lies in a nature sanctuary, with many birds and game animals, angling, boating, barbecue and picnic facilities and a caravan park. Views from it of the Drakensberg are spectacular. Bushmen paintings are numerous in many caves.

Elliot is a farming and railway centre with a population of 11 491.

Elliot lies astride the tarmac R56 road which leads from Kokstad all the way along the eastern slopes of the southern Drakensberg and through the jumble of mountains which marks the southern end of the range. The road eventually comes to its own end at Middelburg in the Karoo. It is one of the great scenic roads of South Africa.

From Elliot, let us travel north-eastwards up this road and find a way back to Barkly East so spectacular that few travellers will ever forget it.

The road leads through superb farming country with the high wall of the Drakensberg looming down from the west. After 20 km there is a turn west to Noah's Ark, and from here may be seen the curious-looking mountain with a hole bored through its centre, which gave the district its original name of *Gatberg* (cave mountain). The mountain is known to the Africans as *uNtunjenkala* (the crab's opening). It provides a remarkable landmark to a delectable countryside.

For another 30 km the road leads past many fine farms and richly grassed dairy country, with stands of wattle trees and such a variety of views of the mountains that the journey is continually interesting. At 50 km from Elliot the road reaches the village of ...

UGIE

The curiously named village of Ugie lies on the south bank of the Nxu River. It was founded in 1863 by the missionary William Murray. The river flowing through green fields with herds of cattle grazing on the slopes of the Drakensberg foothills so reminded the missionary of the Ugie River in his Aberdeenshire Scottish homeland that he gave the name to his new home in South Africa. It is a charming little place with the willow-lined river twisting down from the great orange-coloured sandstone cliffs of the mountains. The view of the village from the road coming in from the south (Transkei) is especially appealing. Rock paintings in the area show pictures of ox-wagons and redcoat soldiers. They are amongst the last paintings to have been done by the Bushmen.

After another 19 km of travel, the R56 road reaches the town of ...

MACLEAR

Named after Sir Thomas Maclear, the celebrated and popular Astronomer Royal at the Cape from 1834 to 1879, the town was established in 1875 as the magisterial centre for the district originally known as *Gatberg* from the weirdly shaped mountain in the south.

Maclear lies in the valley of the Mooi River, an attractive stream (as the name implies) full of trout and with shady tree-lined banks. Caves in the overlooking mountains contain galleries of polychrome Bushman paintings exemplifying the later and most sophisticated techniques used by these artists. The Tsitsa Waterfall, 26 m high, is beautiful.

The little town experienced many troubles in the course of its early years. During the rebellion of 1880, Maclear was besieged for over a month and the pioneer magistrate, J R Thomson, supported by loyal Mfengu tribesmen, had a bad time. It was at this stage that Hamilton-Hope, the magistrate of Qumbu, with three Europeans, attempted to reach Maclear. They were killed on the road.

At the end of the insurrection in 1881, the Maclear district received its present name, becoming an area of European settlement. From then on, Maclear became a prosperous farming area, notable for its cheese and dairy products, cattle, maize, wheat and potatoes. The railway from Sterkstroom was opened in 1902. The present population of Maclear numbers 8 030.

The R56 road continues northwards to Kokstad and Mount Fletcher (see Chapter Twenty-Seven and Chapter Twenty-Eight respectively).

NAUDES NEK TO STERKSPRUIT

From Maclear a scenic road, R396, branches westwards on a most spectacular journey. This is the road we will follow. For the traveller exploring the southern Drakensberg this is an exciting experience in both driving and scenic beauty.

From Maclear the gravel road leads up the beautiful green valley of the *Pot* (pot-hole) River, a clear, fast-flowing stream whose banks are shaded by many graceful trees. Handsome farms shelter below towering cliffs of sandstone. After 24 km the road crosses the Pot River and commences a steady climb up the slopes of the Drakensberg. Scenery is on a large scale and many examples of soil erosion are interesting. At 73 km from Maclear the road reaches the 2 920 m high summit of Naudes Nek Pass. This is the highest road pass in South Africa open to general traffic. For 19 km the road makes a steep and involved descent, Snows in winter are often heavy. Red-hot pokers flower in March, staining the slopes with colour. Immediately to the north-west looms the 3 300 m bulk of *Makhollo* (great mother), known to Europeans as Ben Macdhui, one of the principal peaks of this part of the Drakensberg. It is the highest mountain in the Eastern Cape.

At the foot of the pass is a picnic site and a memorial to Stefanus Naude and his brother Gabriel who first blazed this route over the Drakensberg. The road was located by the engineer George Mandy and constructed, finance allowing, between 1890 and 1911. It was intended as a military road linking Maclear with Lundeans Nek and was built to facilitate the pursuit of rustlers and the movement of troops around the southern border of Lesotho.

Beyond the memorial the road finds a way down the valley of the Bell River, passing a succession of farms. After 12 km (105 km from Maclear), the road reaching the village of ...

RHODES

The village of *Rhodes,* established in 1893 as a church centre on the farm *Tintern,* was named after the famous Cecil Rhodes, who sent the village a gift of stone-pine trees which, today, provide the place with so handsome a feature. The village comprises a couple of dozen earth-walled shacks and corrugated iron cottages, most of them used only occasionally by the mountain farmers when they come to the village to attend *Nagmaal* (Communion) or to escape from the winter snows.

In its day, Rhodes experienced hectic times. Race-meetings were held regularly, with bookies travelling from Durban and wagonloads of liquor being dragged over the mountains from East London. The polished horns of Wydeman, doyen of the oxen who drew the liquor wagons, were mounted in the bar of the Horseshoe hotel when he died, and toasts were proposed in his honour.

Dice, billiards and some celebrated fights provided nightly entertainment at the hotel. Visiting wool buyers such as Maurice Rosenberg presided over big card games. Bill Hocking, the host, and Joey van der Walt, the barman, saw piles of coins changing hands. So many cowboy types habitually rode their horses directly into the hotel that a Bushman, Thys Volstruis, was employed on a piecework basis to sweep up the droppings. Costs were debited to the rider's bill! When business was slack, the Bushman, keen to make a fast buck, would anxiously slap the horse's hindquarters. His plaintive plea *'Kom, toe jong'* (come, please fellow) is still remembered.

From March to September there is generally snow on the high Drakensberge, and skiing is a popular sport in the area. The population is 395.

From Rhodes the road continues amid fine scenery down the valley of the Bell River. Red-orange coloured sandstone cliffs and high, black basalt peaks crowd the side of the fertile valley. After 8 km there is a turn-off to Maartenshoek where a giant cavern contains a gallery of Bushman paintings. At 17 km there is a turn-off to Bokspruit. After a further 12 km the road reaches Moshesh's Ford, where memories of the splashing hooves of rustler bands and the passing of raiding warriors linger beneath the willow trees.

Moshesh's Ford lies at a crossroads. Continuing eastwards, R396 leads for 34 km to Barkly East. A left turn (south) leads for 50 km through rugged country to the top of Barkly Pass. A right turn leads north as the R393 road into a scenic wonderland. The road crosses the river and climbs the steep northern slopes of the valley, an area littered with great blocks of sandstone, a lovely place in which to rob a stage-coach. There are turn-offs to Barkly East and Funnystone. The road seems to ascend to the skies and the atmosphere is wildly beautiful. Past the trading station of War Trail and a lonely police post, the road (30 km from Moshesh's Ford) reaches the summit of what is known as *Lundeans Nek* from a Swede who owned a trading station there in the 1880s.

From Lundeans Nek on the summit of the Witteberge is revealed a tremendous view over the mountains of the southern part of Lesotho. The summit is a place of winds, snow and airy solitude. The police post at the summit (now rebuilt in a more protected situation 1 km lower down the south slope) was the base for a ceaseless war against rustlers. In the records are many accounts of raids, pursuits and captures among the valleys and heights of this mountainous world.

In former years a police outpost stood even higher in the Witteberge on the mountain named Snowdon. For fourteen years a celebrated individual, Constable Erasmus, was stationed there. His only connection with the outside world was a bridle-path to Lundeans Nek. When winter came, the bleak weather forced him to retreat to the main police station but in spring he returned to the heights. While he was at the police outpost, rustlers lay low or followed more distant trails, for his administration of justice was swift, rough and ready.

The road descends the steep northern slopes of the Witteberge and after 8 km passes the Upper Telle trading station. Three kilometres below this station is a turn-off leading up the valley of the Telle River to what is known as *Dangers Hoek*, after Richard Dangers who owned a trading station there. The road comes to a dead end after 12 km. The valley is spectacularly beautiful, burrowing into the private underwear of the great basalt Drakensberg range, revealing the frilly, delicately coloured cave sandstone undergarments. The road ends at the village of Nomlengana, dominated by the great heights of Nduzikontaba and Makhollo.

Beyond the turn-off to Dangers Hoek, the main road continues down the rocky slopes of the Witteberge, following the valley of the Telle River, the boundary of Lesotho. After 17 km there is a turn-off of 15 km leading to the border post of Telle Bridge. The post is open 08h00 to 16h00. The main road swings westwards into the valley of the Famine River. Climbing through this valley and overlooked by brilliantly coloured sandstone cliffs, the road makes its way over a ridge, passing the hospital of Mlojinini, built on a picturesque site. Sixty-four kilometres from Lundeans Nek, the road reaches the dusty village of Sterkspruit, built on the left-hand side of the rocky valley of the *Sterkspruit* (strong stream).

The road described, from Maclear to Sterkspruit, can be classed as one of the most spectacular scenic routes in Southern Africa. Gravel throughout, it has tremendous gradients. There is no pleasure in doing the journey in wet weather, but in fair weather, and when the mountains are covered in snow (not thawing), it is a dramatic experience.

From Sterkspruit a road leads for 49 km to the town of Zastron in the Free State (see Chapter Thirty).

STERKSPRUIT–BARKLY EAST–ELLIOT

The road from Sterkspruit to Barkly East is almost as spectacular as the road from Maclear, just described. From Sterkspruit this road swings westwards, climbs out of the valley and continues across a rugged, rocky and densely settled tribal area. Prickly pears grow amongst the rocks and everywhere erosion and abuse of the soil by poor farming techniques are apparent. After 25 km the road passes through the small rural centre of *Herschel*, named after Sir John Herschel, astronomer at the Cape from 1834 to 1838.

The road climbs and twists over the ridge which forms the western end of the Witteberge range. At 11 km from Herschel a turn-off leads westwards to Aliwal North. A further 4 km takes the road past Lady Grey station. In a cul-de-sac in the Witteberge range, 3 km away, lies the picturesque situated town of Lady Grey, where we join the R58 road already described from Aliwal North.

ELLIOT TO THE WEST ALONG R56

Leaving Elliot, the tarmac R56 road crosses the railway line and continues south-westwards, steadily climbing a spacious, grassy slope – treeless, save for clumps of wattles – and providing handsome views of the Drakensberg. After 7 km there is a division. One road continues south-westwards and after another 23 km reaches the Transkeian town of Cala. The R56 road turns westwards at the division and continues its way, keeping close beneath the sandstone cliffs of the southern Drakensberge, an area known here as *Xalanga* from the number of vultures which roost on the heights. After 66 km of travel from Elliot, the road reaches the town of ...

INDWE

The Ndwe River, on whose banks the town lies, takes its name from the blue cranes which frequent this pleasant valley. The town had its origin in the discovery of coal in the area. The Cape government badly needed coal for use by the steam locomotives on its expanding railway network. Coal deposits in the Ndwe valley and elsewhere in the Stormberg Mountains, which lie at the end of the Drakensberg, were unfortunately of low grade, productive of more ash than heat, but they did offer a cheaper source of power than the import of high-grade coal from Europe.

The Indwe Railway Collieries and Land Company was formed to mine the deposits at the Ndwe River and to build a railway line to convey the coal to awaiting consumers. For this purpose a branch railway was built from a junction at Sterkstroom on the main line from East London to the north. The railway was planned eventually to continue to Natal. It was opened as far as Maclear in 1903 but was never continued.

Mining started in 1895 and about 6 000 tons of coal a month was supplied to the Cape railways. To house the mineworkers, a town was laid out in 1896 by the surveyor, E G Hall and named *Indwe* after the river and its blue cranes. The mining of high-grade coal in Natal and the Transvaal, unfortunately, proved the death of the local coal industry. In 1917 what was known as the Indwe Company went into liquidation. Mining on a small scale was continued for some time in order to supply the town with fuel. Even as late as 1946, the mine was still producing about 100 tons of coal a month. From its local coal resources the town of Indwe was the fourth town in South Africa to have a domestic power supply.

Indwe in its mining days had three successive newspapers and was a very lively little place with a cultural society and club. It is today an agricultural centre notable for wool, beef, maize and wheat. The present population is 6 936.

From Indwe the R56 road continues westwards across farming country overlooked by fine outlying sandstone cliffs at the end of the Drakensberg. As the great range dwindles into hills, so the rainfall lessens and the country becomes increasingly arid. At 23 km from Indwe, the road climbs a ridge, traversing a high plateau covered with sheep and cattle farms. Passing turn-offs north to Mackay's Kop and Barkly East, the road reaches the town of ...

DORDRECHT

Dordrecht lies in a shallow valley on the banks of a lake formed by a dam in the Holspruit. Tall sandstone cliffs overlook the town whose long main street is dominated by the tower of the Dutch

Reformed church. The town had its origin on 19 July 1856 when the Dutch Reformed Church acquired from L J Buys his farm *Boschrand*.

A town was laid out as a church, administrative and trading centre for an agricultural district covered with sheep and cattle farms. The town was named after the ancient city in Holland. It became a municipality in 1867. Seams of low-grade coal were found near the town and mining was conducted by people such as H Lichtenstein and J D van Niekerk.

When the railway from Sterkstroom to Maclear was built, a squabble developed between the Indwe company (mainly the De Beers company from Kimberley) and mining interests in Dordrecht. The Indwe company were financing the building of the line and they bypassed Dordrecht by 5 km to avoid carrying coal from the place at a cheaper rate than the coal of Indwe. Dordrecht was literally left out in the cold (and in winter it is very cold). Only in 1931, as a result of much persuasion and political string-pulling, was the line relocated to take in Dordrecht.

Pleasantly sunny in summer, Dordrecht has in its vicinity many caves containing fine galleries of Bushman art. The lowest temperature ever recorded in South Africa (–16,8°C) was at Buffelsfontein near Dordrecht on 11 August 1991.

The population of the town is 8 765.

The R56 tarmac road continues westwards along the length of the Stormberge range. After 5 km a gravel turn-off follows the railway through the mountains for 52 km to join the N6 road from East London to the north. At 14 km beyond this road junction lies the railway junction of ...

STERKSTROOM

The name *Sterkstroom* (strong stream) comes from the Hex River which flows past the town. It was founded in 1875 by the Dutch Reformed Church and became a municipality in 1898. At one time coal was mined in the town grounds but, like all coal found in the Stormberge area, it was of low grade and is no longer worked.

The town is the junction for the branch line from Maclear. Sterkstroom has a nature reserve with a caravan park and picnic facilities.

From Dordrecht, meanwhile, the R56 road has led westwards along the Stormberge for 36 km and then reached the N6 road from East London to Aliwal North which has already been described. The circular route we have followed provides any traveller with an unforgettable experience in the discovery of the scenic drama of South Africa.

If we continue westwards along R56, across N6 for another 32 km, we will reach the town of ...

MOLTENO

Molteno lies 1 580 m up on the slopes of the Stormberge. The town was founded in 1874 by George Vice on his farm *Onverwacht* and named after the then prime minister of the Cape Colony, John Charles Molteno (later Sir). Most of the streets were named after cabinet ministers. There was initially great promise to the town with the discovery of coal in the Stormberge. The town site had good water from the Stormbergspruit and a solid agricultural base in merino wool production, cattle, wheat and forage.

The poor-grade coal proved unprofitable, especially after Union in 1910 when higher-grade coal from the Transvaal was introduced to the Cape. However, the town progressed because of its agriculture and importance on the main railway line to the north. It is the junction for the branch line to Jamestown.

It is a notably friendly place with a population of 9 780 shaded by many handsome trees whose planting has beautified the town. The Kaffrarian Steam Mills and Simba Quix have factories in the area. Bricks and tiles of high quality are produced at Cyphergat. The 'ghost town' of Cyphergat was originally the mining village for the Cyphergat Coal Company. Excellent clay was a by-product of the coal mining activity, and the chimney of the brickworks, built by Alexander Lawrie, still stands with his initials 'A L' on it.

There are fine Bushman rock paintings in several caves. Fossils are numerous and the area is rich in succulents. Three extinct volcanoes on the eastern side of the district yield semi-precious stones. Scenery is spectacular, especially at Wonderhoek and the Boesmanshoek Pass on the road to Sterkspruit. There is a fine view of the town from Van Straaten's Drive.

The heir of George Vice, the founder, presented to the town a handsome sandstone building and this houses a public library, a museum of cultural history and a gallery of South African art.

The town was the home of Johannes Meintjes, a very creative and productive artist and writer. For several years he acted as curator of the Molteno Museum and librarian of the George Vice Library. He wrote 36 published books and created more than 1 200 oil paintings as well as numerous other works in pencil, ink crayons, charcoal and distemper.

He died on 7 July 1980, aged 57 years, on the family farm of *Grootzeekoegat* (great hippopotamus hole). His library and many of his works of art were presented to the Molteno High School by his widow, Mrs Ronell Meintjes, and these are exhibited in the chronological order of creation. The original homestead of *Grootzeekoegat* is a grand old place with walls 90 cm wide and woodwork of yellowwood. It is near the site of one of the abandoned coal-mines, Cape Colleries, 20 km from the town.

The district is well populated by game animals and wild fowl. There is controlled hunting on several farms.

There is a dam used for recreation. On the banks of its lake there is a wildlife sanctuary and a caravan park which includes an old railway carriage with four compartments available for hire.

From Molteno the R56 tarmac road leads north-westwards through the rugged Stormberge landscape. Snow, hail and thunderstorms are an often very spectacular occurrence in the area. It was here, at the Stormberg railway junction, that there took place, on 10 December 1899, one of the heaviest battles of the Anglo-Boer War. The British suffered a sharp defeat and lost over 700 men.

Close to the Stormberge railway junction, 19 km from Molteno, a road branches off leading for 58 km to the town of Hofmeyr. Another 9 km brings R56 to a junction with a road leading northwards for 38 km to the town of ...

BURGERSDORP

At first known as Klipdrift, *Burgersdorp* (citizen's town) was founded on 27 December 1847 when the farm *Klipfontein* of Gert Buytendach was purchased as a church centre for a wool and livestock farming area. The town is handsomely situated. It rests on the banks of the Stormbergspruit and is overlooked to the east and south by the jumble of hills which mark the beginning of the Stormberge range.

In 1861 a theological seminary was founded in the town by the Dutch Reformed Church. This was later moved to Potchefstroom as the start of the university there.

The town played a notable part in securing the place of the Afrikaans language in South Africa. A memorial to this struggle was erected on Burger Square in 1892.

A British blockhouse known as the Sentinel, built in 1901, still keeps watch over the town and is one of the several national monuments. Included amongst these is the old gaol. It was here that Piet Klopper was executed for taking up arms against the British. He was the first Colonial to be so punished.

There is a museum in the original parsonage. The population of Burgersdorp is 12 176.

From the turn-off to Burgersdorp, 37 km from Molteno, the R56 road steadily turns westwards, leaving the mountains behind and traversing the arid plains of the Karoo. After 34 km the road reaches the town of ...

STEYNSBURG

The town was founded as a church settlement in 1872 and was named after Douw Steyn of *Bulhoek* farm, the grandfather of President Paul Kruger. The original farmhouse, where Paul Kruger was born, has been renovated and preserved as a national monument. Steynsburg became a municipality in 1892 and is a great merino wool centre with several stud-farms in the vicinity. The population is 5 939.

Ten kilometres beyond Steynsburg on the R56 road stand two classic-shaped South African flat-topped koppies, known as *Teebus* and *Koffiebus* (tea caddy and coffee caddy). It is here that the 82,8 km long tunnel from the Gariep Dam has its outlet and pours water into the Teebus River which carries it southwards to irrigate the Fish and Sundays river valleys.

Close to the outlet there is a turn-off south leading for 37 km to the town of ...

HOFMEYR

Hofmeyr is a centre for the production of wool and salt recovered from the beds of several shallow lakes. It was founded on 25 February 1874, first with the name Maraisburg. To avoid confusion with Maraisburg on the Witwatersrand, the town was renamed in 1913 in honour of Jan Hendrik (Onze Jan) Hofmeyr, a renowned political champion of farmers and a stalwart supporter of the establishment and development of the Afrikaans language. The old name of Maraisburg is still applied to the district and the magistracy. It is connected by a branch railway to Schoombee, a village 43 km west of Steynsburg. Named after a local farmer, *Schoombee* is a centre for wool, salt and stud-farms.

At 41 km from the Schoombee junction, the road and railway from Steynsburg reach the railway junction of *Rosmead* named after Lord Rosmead (Sir Hercules Robinson), a former governor of the Cape. Nine kilometres further west brings the R56 road to its end in the town of Middelburg (see Chapter Twenty).

Chapter Twenty-Two
THE TRANSKEI AND ITS WILD COAST

From East London the N2 road to the Transkei and KwaZulu-Natal proceeds in a north-easterly direction. This great highway extends across the undulating and perennially green expanse of the coastal terrace, where deep valleys have been eroded by a multitude of streams and rivers during the course of their journey to the sea. Banana and pineapple farms, clumps of acacia bush bedecked with gold-coloured, sweet-smelling flowers in spring, and numerous tall evergreen trees cover the attractive parklike landscape.

There is a turn-off to Gonubie after 10,5 km and at 16,5 km the turn-off to the East Coast resorts loop road. This loop road returns to rejoin the main road 30,5 km from East London. At 40 km there is the turn-off to Haga-Haga and at 56 km the turn-off to Morgan Bay and Kei Mouth.

The N2 road swings inland and at 60,5 km is joined by the direct road from King William's Town through Komga. After 2,5 km the N2 begins to descend into the valley of the river known to the early pastoral people as the *Kei* (great) and to the Xhosas as the *Nciba*. This river truly deserves its name, not only for the vastness of its valley, but for the fact that it has long been a divider in the affairs of man, providing a natural frontier between tribes and a memorable landmark for all travellers.

The road descends the southern side of the valley through a hot wilderness of euphorbias, aloes and acacia bush. The railway line follows a more circuitous descent, with the Great Kei cuttings being famous among railway enthusiasts. The road completes its route after 7,5 km but the train takes 24 km to descend the 330 m to the bridge across the river.

The valley is spectacular in all seasons. During winter the aloes are in flower; in spring the blossoms of the acacia trees perfume the warm air with a sweet fragrance. Dominating the valley on the southern side are the cliffs of the 576 m high *Moordenaarskop* (murderers peak) where, in September 1847 during the War of the Axe, five British officers were surprised and killed. To the Africans the height is known as *Sihota* (place of seclusion).

The Kei River, 70,5 km from East London, marks the border of ...

THE TRANSKEI

The Transkei consists of 4 287 000 ha of agricultural and pastoral land extending along the coast from the Kei River to the border with KwaZulu-Natal on the Mtamvuna River. The area consists of three distinct tribal territories divided into 26 magisterial districts, all of which now form part of the Eastern Cape.

The first tribal territory consists of the Transkei proper, the area between the Kei and Mbashe (Bashee) rivers. The second tribal territory is known as Tembuland and lies between the Mbashe and Mtata rivers. The third territory is Pondoland, lying from the Mtata River to the border of KwaZulu-Natal.

These territories cover the 480 km from north to south, while east to west they extend about 160 km from the coast inland. As a whole, these areas are graced with extremely beautiful scenery such as the magnificently rugged Wild Coast and a grassy midland – emerald green in summer, drab brown in winter – traversed by several fine rivers flowing through deep valleys. The entire landscape is given an extraordinarily picturesque appearance by the distribution, as well as sheer number, of rondavel-type homes in which the resident population live.

Inhabiting the Transkei are about 3 168 000 people who belong to the various tribal groups.

They are pastoralists and agriculturalists by occupation, their land supporting 1 386 000 head of cattle, 2 226 000 sheep, 1 400 000 goats, 101 000 horses and 415 000 pigs. Fully 70 per cent of the land is for common grazing; 24 per cent is arable; 3 per cent is planted with forest; and 3 per cent is residential. Apart from wool and mohair, the area each year produces substantial crops of maize and corn which, together with milk, form the staple diet of the people. About 1 000 tons of tea are produced each year on two estates at Magwa and Majola in Pondoland and fibre is produced from *Phormium tenax* plants. Forestry is being extended, with 73 505 ha of indigenous forest and 60 000 ha of plantations being cultivated.

Tradition says that the first inhabitants of the Transkei were hunter-gatherers and nomadic pastoralists. In about the year 1600, a section of the Hlubi tribe of Natal wandered southwards, hunting and seeking new lands in which to settle. The Hlubi people were part of the great migratory wave of humanity which was steadily moving down the coastal belt of south-east Africa. All speaking a similar language (the Zulu–Xhosa of today), this group claimed a common origin in a place called eMbo in the far north. One section of these migrants, under a leader named Nguni, developed into the great tribe of the Zulu. Another migratory wave, under a leader named Dlamini, entered the area of Natal.

The Hlubi section of these people sent still further south an advance party which rebelled against its parent group and (it is said) killed their leader. Led by a woman known as Xhosa, they encountered the pastoralists, found sanctuary with them and blended to form the tribe which they apparently named after the woman who was its first leader. The language of the newcomers was retained by the combined group but was much influenced by the 'click' sounds of the pastoralists and hunter-gatherers. The use of these clicks was apparently regarded as fashionable and became widespread. It is notable that the migrants who remained in the north employed fewer words containing such clicks. The Zulu language, for example, has the same variety of clicks as Xhosa but a much smaller number of words which contain them.

Other related people followed behind the Xhosa vanguard. The pressure pushed the pioneers forward as far as the Great Fish River where they encountered Europeans advancing from the south in a similar but counter migratory movement.

The inevitable clash resulted in the nine successive frontier wars (or Kaffir Wars, as they were originally called) and the ultimate annexation of the Transkeian territories by the Cape Government in 1879. The territories were then divided into magisterial districts for the imposition of law and order, but the tribal chiefs always had a considerable measure of local authority. District councils were established in the 1880s. In 1895 these councils combined to form two general councils, one meeting in Butterworth in the south and the other in Pondoland. These two councils, which exercised local control over tribal life, were amalgamated in 1931 to form the United General Council of the Transkeian Territories, popularly known as the *Bunga* (meeting and discussion). In May 1963 this became the Legislative Assembly of Transkei when the territories received their independence as a bantustan. Paramount Chief K D Matanzima became Prime Minister of the new government. Political and economic conditions in Transkei were unsatisfactory to many people. There were accusations of corruption and nepotism. In August 1987 Matanzima resigned. He was replaced by Stella Sigcau. After 88 days, on 31 December 1987, General Bantu Holomisa took power in a coup. He announced his intention of ridding the government of corruption and calling for a referendum on reincorporation into South Africa. The Transkei is now once again a part of the Republic of South Africa.

Beyond the bridge over the Kei River the N2 tarmac road commences a steady and scenically spectacular climb out of the valley. The road ascends for 16 km before reaching the 765 m high level of the grassy, rolling midland plateau. The road continues for a further 18 km across this spacious world of summer thunder-clouds, grassy slopes, cattle herds and white rondavels scattered over the landscape like grains of starch dropped on an emerald-green carpet.

At 34 km from the Kei River bridge the road reaches the valley of the *Gcuwa* (overgrown) River on the acacia-covered slopes of which lies the town of ...

BUTTERWORTH

Known to the Africans as *Gcuwa*, from the river, Butterworth is the oldest town in the Transkei. It was originally a Wesleyan mission station built in 1827 on the banks of the Gcuwa River near the seat of Hintsa, chief of the Gcaleka section of the Xhosa tribe. The first missionary, the Reverend W S Shrewsbury, named the station after Joseph Butterworth, the treasurer of the Wesleyan Missionary Society. Although it was burned down three times during the frontier wars, the mission was always rebuilt. In December 1877 a magistrate was stationed there. Upon the establishment of law and order, a collection of traders and commercial people created by their joint activity a town which became a municipality in 1904.

Butterworth has developed as a substantial industrial centre. In the vicinity of the town are two handsome waterfalls; the Bawa Falls in the Qolora River with a drop of nearly 100 m, and the cascades on the Gcuwa River, tumbling down 90 m. The population of the town and surrounding district is 96 219.

GCALEKALAND

From Butterworth several drives traverse the charming countryside inhabited by the section of the Xhosa tribe known as the Gcaleka after a chief who ruled over them around 1750. These drives lead by devious scenic ways down to the coast, here truly 'wild' and quite magnificently beautiful. The most important of these side roads stretches south-east from Butterworth. After 31 km of winding, the road reaches the village of ...

CENTANE (KENTANI)

Centane takes its name from a nearby hill named kwaCentane after a local headman who once had his home there. It is a picturesque and typical Transkeian village – one street of shops, a post office and magistracy; horsemen riding in to attend to business, and womenfolk in their tribal costume wandering into and out of shops. The regal gait of these women results from their practice, handed down from generation to generation, of balancing loads on their heads.

Centane, notwithstanding its diminutive size (a population of 622), features largely in the history of South Africa. The area around it was the scene of many clashes between elements of the Xhosa tribe and British forces. The village was established as a military post where, on the misty morning of 7 February 1878, the last battle of the Ninth (and final) Frontier War took place.

Captain R Upcher was in command of the post at the time, having under him 436 European and 560 Fingo soldiers. A combined 5 000 strong army of Xhosa warriors from the Gcaleka and the Ngqika (Gaika) sections of the tribe attacked the government force which was entrenched in a rough quadrangular earthern fort built near Moldenhauer's Hill store. The Xhosas had been well motivated by Xito, a renowned magician who had so thoroughly assured them that they were invulnerable to bullets that they attacked *en masse*. The two great chiefs, Sarhili and Sandili, were present to witness the promised total defeat of the government troops. Instead, a sad débâcle followed.

The advancing warriors were simply mown down by heavy fire. With their faith shattered, they broke and fled, pursued by cavalry. Three hundred of them were killed while the government force lost only two men. Sandili and his Ngqika fled south of the Kei River while Sarhili and his Gcaleka became refugees, hiding in the forests and endless hills of their homeland. The chief eventually surrendered and spent the rest of his life in retirement near Elliotdale. His followers were resettled in the Willowvale district while their former homeland, largely depopulated, was united with Fingoland and Idutywa to become the nucleus of the present Transkei. Centane grew into an administrative and communications centre, with a village management board proclaimed on 12 June 1932.

From Centane, roads lead down to several coastal resorts whose scenic beauty and angling, swimming and recreational possibilities make them superb holiday resorts. The most southerly resorts are reached by a gravel road which turns off just before the road from Butterworth enters the village.

The road descends steadily for 6 km through a handsome jumble of bush-covered hills where the tilled fields and rondavel huts of the Xhosa tribespeople occupy all suitable ground. The road then reaches a turn-off stretching for 20 km to the mouth of the Kobonqaba River, where a cluster of seaside shacks stand watching the site of the wreck of the *Jacaranda* (see further on). The main road continues its winding descent. At 20 km it passes the Kei Mouth forestry station, with a turn-off just ahead leading down to the left bank of the Kei.

The main road now traverses a green coastal terrace where clumps of palm and indigenous forest grow. At 26 km it reaches the coastline at the pleasant resort of ...

QOLORA MOUTH

The *Qolora* (steep place) River is named after the gorge through which it reaches the sea. This stretch of coastline is very typical of the Wild Coast. The river emerges from its gorge and, as though weary after its tortuous journey through the hills, rests in a pretty lagoon until at last it finds its way to the sea. A spacious beach extends between the lagoon and the sea. A series of rocky promontories provide fishermen with ideal vantage-points. Green grass, sundu palms, wild banana palms and a variety of indigenous trees crowd together on the verges of the sand. The general effect created is pleasing and relaxing to the eye and mind.

Holiday-makers come here to fish, swim and play golf on a scenic course. There are walks or rides to several interesting places such as The Boiling Pot, a rough inlet from the sea; The Gates, where the river flows through a narrow crevice; and The Blow Hole, where high tide forces a spurt of water high into the air. A 7 km walk south-eastwards down the beach leads to the mouth of the Kei River, while a similar walk in the opposite direction ends at Khobongaba Point and the site of the wreck of the *Jacaranda*.

The *Jacaranda* was a 2 000 ton Greek coaster. On the windy night of 18 September 1971, while riding high with empty holds, her engines are said to have failed. The little vessel ended up so securely wedged in a narrow crevice in the rocks that it looked as though she had been snugly berthed. Captain Kokkios Paulos phoned his owners in Greece by means of the ship's radio, informing them of his predicament. Nothing much could be done about the situation at that distance, but the conversation between them would have made interesting listening. The captain, his wife and fourteen crew members then abandoned ship by means of a rope-ladder strung from the prow to the rocks, leaving the good ship *Jacaranda* to her fate. There she remained with no intention of ever leaving.

Another interesting walk or drive over a rough track can be followed inland for 4 km to that pool of poignant memories where the young medium Nongqawuse (sometimes known to Europeans as Nongqause) claimed to have held communion with the ancestral spirits. The pool lies in the river known as the *Gxara* (the precipice) after the deep gorge through which it flows. At this pool Nongqawuse used to sit and look into its waters where she claimed to see the faces of ancestral spirits. Their voices came to her promising that they would help the Xhosas drive the Europeans away provided that, as a sign of faith, the tribespeople would destroy all their cattle and crops.

A great commotion arose amongst the Xhosas at news of this revelation. Men travelled from far to speak with the medium and her diviner uncle, Mhlakaza. Crowds gathered to gaze into the pool where many claimed to see the faces of their own ancestors and hear them demanding total faith as the price of support from the supernatural world. Some witnesses told in bated breath of how they had seen whole armies of ghost warriors waiting to emerge, eager for war and jeering at the timidity of the Xhosas.

There commenced a dreadful fever of cattle killing and crop destruction. The great majority of the Gcaleka section of the Xhosas implicitly obeyed the dream voices heard by Nongqawuse. Fortunately, the Ngqika section of the tribe exercised their reason and remained aloof.

For those who believed, the climax was destined for 18 February 1857. The sun would rise blood-red and the land would be filled with fat cattle, new crops and vast armies of reincarnated spirits ready to restore the Xhosas to their past glory and greatness.

It was truly a terrible dawn for many thousands of deluded people. The sun climbed out of the Indian Ocean as usual and the Gcaleka saw before them ruination and the prospect of starvation. They had nothing left. It is estimated that 25 000 people died of hunger. The remainder only survived through the compassion of neighbouring tribes and Europeans who fed them. The discredited medium fled for safety but was arrested by police near King William's Town. She died in obscurity and was buried on *Glenshaw* farm near Boknes on the coast close to Alexandria. The pool of spirits in the Gxara, with its troubled surface and wild surroundings, remains as a memorial to folly. In winter, flowering aloes provide a particularly handsome setting, although the area is always beautiful. The river meanders through the hills until it comes to rest in the lagoon at its mouth before finally rushing through the barrier of sand to the waiting sea.

EXPLORING THE WILD COAST

The best way to explore the Wild Coast is to follow the gravel road which twists, rises and falls parallel to the coast from Centane to Port St Johns and Lusikisiki. From this road, branches lead off to the various coastal resorts. The scenery is entrancing throughout the journey. For the photographer and artist there are innumerable views and scenes which are charming and often overwhelming. The road crosses the homelands of the principal section of the Xhosa, Tembu and other tribes. Displayed to the traveller, in splendid variety, is one of the most unique landscapes on Earth. There are green hills, deep valleys and gorges; grassy pastures ornamented by clumps of indigenous forest and palm trees; herds of grazing cattle, goats and sheep; neat rondavel dwellings with doorways invariably facing east and roofs decorated with odd charms against lightning; friendly little pigs which act as mobile garbage disposal units; beautifully poised and statuesque women in their tribal dress; the absence of fences or any other sign or private property (land ownership is communal). These are merely a few of the ingredients comprising the atmospheric, elegant and curiously old-world land originally known to Europeans as Kaffraria.

In the same way as the other administrative and trading centres in the Transkei, Centane lies on top of a ridge with its avenue of trees providing a landmark which is visible from many kilometres away. The road from it follows a north-easterly direction and commences a winding descent into the valley of the river, the name of which *(Khobonqaba)* is said to indicate a deserted precipice. After 8 km the road crosses this river and 1,5 km further on reaches the first of the turn-offs leading to coastal resorts. This turn-off stretches for 24 km over pleasant downland country. It ends at a fine lagoon formed at the mouths of two rivers, the *Nxaxo* and the *Nqwasi*, both said to be named after former tribal headmen.

The lagoon provides a fine stretch of water for boating and aquaplaning while the islets and swamps further up the two rivers are good nesting places for crested cranes. These beautiful birds are numerous along the Wild Coast. Very fortunately for themselves, they are regarded as taboo by the tribespeople. It is believed that if one of these birds is killed, death will come to the killer's family.

A fine beach lies between the lagoon and the sea. Swimming is safe; there are oysters in season and fish all through the year. Birds, monkeys and shells are numerous while the local tribespeople are expert bead workers.

At the turn-off to Nxaxo Mouth the main road from Centane continues its undulating way north-eastwards. After 8 km (17 km from Centane) there is a junction with a road branching westwards which eventually leads to the main inland road, the N2, traversing the Transkei. The road being followed veers eastwards and proceeds along what is known as the Cats Pass, the summit of a narrow ridge from where tremendous views, especially northwards into the valley of the river known as the *Qora* (place of clay), may be seen.

At the end of the Cats Pass there is a junction. One road descends the river valley while the other continues eastwards, passing the cluster of buildings of the Dutch Reformed Church mission hospital at *Tafalofeffe* (the plain of help), 24 km from Centane.

A further 15 km takes the road to the forestry station of *Manubi*. This forest, comprising 1 361 ha of indigenous trees and shrubs, provides a very fine drive for those who turn aside and, with permission from the forester, explore some of the tracks. The forest has always been a retreat for game animals. Its name is said to have been derived from a local chief, Manyobi, who hunted in the area.

The road continues its descent. After travelling a further 7 km from the forestry station, it eventually terminates 46,5 km from Centane at the coastal resort of ...

MAZEPPA BAY

Without doubt one of the most beautiful coastal areas in Southern Africa, this bay was named after a coastal trading ship, the *Mazeppa,* which (captained by a man named Allen) used the place in the 1930s in order to land goods.

Swimming and fishing are excellent here. A little island connected to the mainland by a suspension footbridge provides vantage-points for fishermen as well as some handsome views up and down the rugged coastline. Between the island and the *Clan Lindsay* rocks, where the ship of that name was wrecked in 1898, there is a sheltered beach fringed by sundu palms. Known as First Beach, this is a splendid swimming area while further south lies the spacious Second Beach, with Shelly Beach still further south, but both within pleasant walking distance.

The attraction of shells, numerous middens left behind by prehistoric beachcombers *(strandlopers)*, fine walks, kite fishing, and the clear air of the Wild Coast, make Mazeppa Bay an outstanding holiday resort.

The main road from Centane continues past the turn-off to Mazeppa Bay and immediately descends to the bottom of the Qora Valley. This is a magnificent scenic drive. The river is crossed after 6 km and the road then makes an involved climb up the northern slopes. After 11 km a branch leads westwards to Butterworth. A further 10 km brings the road to a junction with the main gravel road running from Willowvale (west) to Qora Mouth (east). This junction is 51 km from Centane.

QORA MOUTH

From the junction point of the Centane road, 33 km of very pleasant driving is provided to the mouth of the Qora River. The landscape is typical of the Transkeian downland countryside; rich grass, deep gorges, patches of indigenous forest, the innumerable huts of the Gcaleka, and the buildings of several wayside trading stations. It is worth stopping at some of these trading stations where the bustle of a group of tribespeople doing their shopping provides an animated scene and the costumes are fascinating. Some of the stores such as the one at *Ncizele* (the grassy place) sell beadwork, carvings and curios – prices are not exactly cheap but there are many interesting items to examine.

At the mouth of the Qora River lies a fine beach and an oyster bed. The swimming and fishing possibilities are excellent. It was at this place on 14 November 1887 at about 23h45 that the 1 390 ton fully rigged iron ship *Idomene,* bound for London from Rangoon and carrying a full cargo of rice, ran straight into the rocks. The ship was totally wrecked. The captain and twelve of the crew were drowned while eleven men safely reached the beach.

From a botanical point of view it is interesting to note that the Qora River marks the northern limit of the sundu palms. Beyond the river, palm trees are absent for some distance before the lala palm appears, becoming the characteristic plant of the coast.

Resuming the journey from the junction point where the road turns off to Qora Mouth, the main gravel road continues westwards for 1 km and then enters the village of ...

WILLOWVALE (GATYANA)

With a population of 1 371, Willowvale received its name from a number of willow trees which originally grew in the valley, behind the old residency. The local tribespeople know the place as *Gatyana* after a former headman who had his home there. The Paramount Chief of the Gcaleka section of the Xhosa tribe has his seat (great place) at Nqadu close to Willowvale.

The tribal history of the Willowvale district is particularly interesting. Hunter-gatherer and pastoral people originally inhabited the area, but towards the end of the 17th century they were displaced by the Xhosas who absorbed many characteristics of the pastoral people, including the use of 'clicks' in speech and the amputation of the top joint of the little finger.

In about the year 1750 the Xhosas split into two great sections. The senior section remained in the Willowvale area and became known as the *Gcaleka* after their chief. The second section moved south of the Kei River and were known as the *Rarabe*, also after their own chief.

The first half of the 19th century saw great troubles in the land of the Xhosa. Disturbances in far-off Zululand sent waves of refugees southwards in search of new homes. The Xhosas were themselves restless and inclined to push southwards where they clashed with European settlers, the result of which were the successive frontier wars. Eventually the British invaded the land of the Gcaleka in 1837. William Fynn was established as a political agent at the then Xhosa capital of Holela in the Centane district. A long series of brawls took place, inducing the British to apply ever firmer control over the Xhosa people.

In 1856 the disaster concerning the medium Nongqawuse and the cattle killing occurred. Further disturbances caused the British to drive the Gcaleka northwards across the Mbashe River and to leave their old homeland almost denuded of population. In 1864 their chief, Sarhili was allowed to return to the area with some of his followers. A British officer was stationed with him as consul and 40 000 Fingo (Mfengu) tribespeople were also settled in the area.

Fighting inevitably broke out between the Xhosas and the Fingos. This was the start of the Ninth (and last) Frontier War in 1877. After several minor clashes, the Xhosas were defeated at the Battle of Centane and the bulk of the Gcaleka were once again driven north of the Mbashe River. In 1878 a police camp was erected on the site of Willowvale and on 2 January 1879 a magistrate, Mr F N Streatfield, was appointed. He surveyed the district and was the actual founder of Willowvale, which acquired a village management board on 17 July 1933. Since the Gcaleka were allowed to return to their old homeland, the district has been at peace.

Europeans first arrived in the Willowvale area in about 1839 when the Wesleyan Missionary Society founded a station named *Beecham Wood* after the Reverend John Beecham, the general secretary of the society. This station was abandoned in 1858 when the population was depleted as a result of the cattle-killing episode of Nongqawuse. Nothing remains of the station today except the place name.

The Malan Mission was founded in 1876 by Major C H Malan, officer commanding the 75th Regiment. He intended it to be an interdenominational mission but it was later taken over by the United Free Church of Scotland. *Fort Malan*, built in 1877, was named after the mission. *Fort Bowker*, built in 1860, was named after Colonel J H Bowker. Apart from these places, Europeans made no attempt to settle in the area and the whole Willowvale district remained a tribal reserve.

Beyond Willowvale the gravel road continues north-eastwards parallel to the Wild Coast, following a meandering, up-and-down route through superb scenery. Initially the road descends to the bottom of the pretty valley of the river known as the *Nqabara* (place of the steep descent). On its banks, under the Mbongo hill, lies the grave of the great chief Hintsa, who was shot in the valley in 1835 when he tried to escape from a British force. A road leads down to the mouth of the Nqabara River and the Dwesa forestry station and nature reserve, the first large reserve to be established in the Transkei. It comprises a fine stretch of indigenous forest where various species of game animals have been introduced, such as blesbuck, buffalo, hartebeest, as well as wart-hog. Bushbuck and blue and grey duikers were already present when the area was fenced. The camp is situated in an evergreen forest within easy walking distance of the sea. The walking is excellent and the camp provides accommodation in log cabins as well as sites for caravans and tents.

The Nqabara River is crossed at a point 28 km from Willowvale. A further 12 km of travelling brings the road to the Mpozolo trading station on the verge of the prodigious valley of the Mbashe River. This is one of the great viewsites of Southern Africa. The Mbashe (also known to Europeans as the Bashee) finds so tortuous a way through the seemingly interminable hills that a portion of its middle course bears the amusing name of Colley Wobbles. Few travellers at this point in their journey fail to pause and admire an outlook that is airy and most serenely beautiful. The name *Colley Wobbles* originated in 1859. Lieutenant George Pomeroy Colley, a Transkeian Special Magistrate, surveyed the area and, upon looking down at the extraordinary meander in the river, remarked to his staff: '*How that river wobbles!*'

'Yes Sir', said one of his staff. '*In fact, it Colley Wobbles!*'

Lieutenant Colley eventually attained the rank of General Sir George Colley and was killed in the Battle of Majuba.

At 45 km from Willowvale the road bridges the Mbashe River and starts to ascend the northern slopes in a stiff climb. On the summit, 54 km from Willowvale, the road joins the main gravel road stretching from Elliotdale (Xhora) and the main inland road to the mouth of the Mbashe River. The drive down to the coast, 35 km from this junction, crosses fine hill country yielding handsome views of the great river valley and dense coastal forest. Where the road ends, the Mbashe relaxes after its journey in a lazy lagoon bordered by another good beach and a series of rock outcrops which oblige fishermen with vantage-points. This assembly is watched over by a 225 000 candle-power lighthouse which stands on a tall steel trestle like a lonely being from another world looking for its fellows who are lost somewhere in space.

The coastal road from the mouth of the Mbashe (35 km long) rejoins the original route from Willowvale which now continues inland. After 4 km a turn-off leads to the mouth of the Qora River and a further 1,2 km brings the road to a turn-off to Mpame and Mqanduli. The road now descends to the floor of the beautiful valley of the Qora River where many fine views may be seen before the ascent to the other side.

At 12,5 km from the junction of the Willowvale road, there is a pleasant camping spot next to the Qora River at the bridge. The surroundings are completely wild and well wooded.

A further 6,4 km brings the road to a turn-off to Mpame. Continuing left (west), after 13 km, the road reaches the Lutubeni Mission and a junction with the main gravel road leading from Mqanduli and the interior to the coast. It is 30,8 km from the Willowvale junction to this point.

Once the main gravel road is joined (turning right or eastwards), the traveller is conveyed towards the coast through green and pleasant hill country. After 7 km there is a turn-off to the Wilo forestry station and a further 11,6 km brings the road to the trading station of Ncwanguba, standing in a tall cluster of eucalyptus trees. At this point there is a junction with a turn-off to the right (south-east) stretching over the hills for 19 km to one of the most remarkable coastal scenes in Africa.

THE HOLE IN THE WALL

This natural feature consists of a huge detached cliff rising up from the sea in the form of a precipitous island at the mouth of a small river known as the Mpako. Through the centre of the cliff the pounding waves have worn a substantial tunnel.

The Hole in the Wall is known to the local Africans as *esiKhaleni* (the place of the sound). The great rollers shoulder their way through the cavern with a rumbling, sullen roar which in stormy weather can be heard for a considerable distance. The cavern is regarded with suspicion among the Bomvana tribespeople who inhabit this part of the coast. They are great eaters of shellfish. Many a food gatherer, tempted to explore the cavern at low water, has been caught by an unexpected roller and chafed to death on the barnacles.

A local tale tells of a rough and over-intrepid trooper of the old Cape Mounted Rifles who, for a wager of a bottle of whisky, attempted to swim through the cavern. He vanished inside and was never seen again. Numerous people have attempted to climb the 'wall' containing the hole. It is possible, but is no easy exercise. A Bomvana tribesman who watched a party of experienced European mountaineers reach the summit, tried his hand the next day. He climbed to the top but, when he had to get down again, he lost his nerve and sat plaintively hollering for help for the next three days until news of his plight reached a camping party whose members, fortunately for him, could climb.

The name of the Hole in the Wall was applied to it in 1823 by Captain Vidal of the *Barracouta*, one of the ships on an expedition (under Captain W F W Owen RN) sent out by the British Admiralty to survey the coast from the mouth of the Keiskamma River to Lourenzo Marques (Maputo). Vidal reported to Owen that *'twice they approached the beautiful but harbourless Kaffir Coast, the first time, within half a mile, at a most interesting spot, where two ponderous black rocks arose from the water's edge, upwards of eighty feet above its surface, exhibiting through one of them a phenomenon of a natural archway, called by us the Hole in the Wall'*.

The coast on either side of the Hole in the Wall is precipitous and notorious for the number of ships wrecked there. Divers constantly find odd fragments of many unfortunate vessels, while beads and coins are often discovered in the pools. Among the tribes living along the coast are descendants of people shipwrecked, whose ancestors, of European and Asian descent, mingled with the African population who gave them shelter. One small tribe resident in the vicinity is known as the *abeLungu* (European people) who claim that they originate from these shipwreck survivors.

There is accommodation available at the Hotel in the Wall, and a cluster of privately owned seaside shacks.

At the Ncwanguba trading station, where the road branches off to the Hole in the Wall, the main gravel road continues to the coast and after 16,5 km reaches the resort known as ...

COFFEE BAY

The origin of the name Coffee Bay is obscure. A local story tells of a ship which was wrecked in 1863, depositing its entire cargo of coffee beans on the beach. Some of the beans are said to have taken root. For several years coffee shrubs tried to grow but eventually gave up the struggle and died, unable to flourish so far from their natural home.

Three small rivers, the *Nenga* (river of the whale), *Bomvu* (red), and *Maphuzi* (place of pumpkins), reach the sea in the area of Coffee Bay. The local tribespeople usually refer to the place as *Tshontini*, the name applied to a dense wood there. Today Coffee Bay is one of the most popular holiday resorts on the Wild Coast. An informal little village is fronted by a superb beach, snugly contained in a setting of green hills. Swimming, fishing, walking, riding, and having a thoroughly enjoyable and lazy time, are the major occupations. There is a spectacularly situated golf-course.

After 3,5 km of travelling on the road from Coffee Bay to the interior, just before the trading station of C R Ilott, there is a turn-off north which will take the more venturesome traveller on to the scenic route running parallel to the Wild Coast. This road (rough for the first few kilometres) descends into the valley of the river known as the Umtata or *Mthatha* (the taker) because of its destructive and dangerous floods. At 3 km from the turn-off the road reaches a low-level causeway which is impassable when the river is in flood.

Beyond the causeway the road improves and climbs steeply out of the valley. At the summit (5 km from the causeway) a turn-off leads westwards to the Cancibe hospital. A further 1,5 km brings the road to a junction with the gravel road which stretches to the mouth of the Umtata River from Ngqelini and the interior. This junction is 10 km from the turn-off on the Coffee Bay road. A turn-off eastwards down this road reaches the coast at the mouth of the Umtata River after 7 km where there is a spacious beach, fishing and a cluster of seaside shacks.

Seven kilometres after leaving Umtata Mouth the gravel road passes the junction of the road leading from Coffee Bay. The gravel road continues westwards and soon begins to descend into the well-wooded and beautiful valley of the river known as the Mdumbi. This is one of the most verdant valleys in the Transkei. At 4 km from the junction of the Coffee Bay road, the bridge over the river is reached where the climb back to the summit begins. At the top the road reaches a junction.

The main road continues ahead to Ngqeleni and the interior. The scenic route, signposted 'Presley's Bay' and 'Old Bunting', swings off to the right (northwards), providing a fine drive through rugged hill and forest country. After 4,8 km there is a turn-off eastwards to Presley's Bay and Lwandile. A further 2 km brings the road to a turn-off leading to the coast at the mouth of the Mtakatye River. The road crosses the Mtakatye River in the midst of a fine valley. After a further 5 km the road finds the main gravel road (which is in good condition) stretching from Libode and the interior down to the coast of Hluleka. At the coastal terminus of this road lies the Hluleka nature reserve which comprises some delightful beaches, a rich flora and excellent walking. There is a very beautiful indigenous forest.

Turning westwards (to the left), the road ascends smoothly for a further 22 km (46 km from the junction of the Coffee Bay–Umtata Mouth road) until it reaches the site of the long-abandoned mission station of *Buntingville*, founded in 1830 by the Wesleyans and named after the Reverend Dr Jabez Bunting. The mission was moved to New Bunting in 1864 and the original site is now known as Old Bunting.

At this point there is a turn-off to the right (eastwards) leading to Tombo and the coast, which passes through some fine scenery. After 6 km of travel along this road, there is a division. The left fork of the road veers northwards past the turn-off to the pretty Mpande Beach. After 26 km the road reaches the Dutch Reformed Church Mission hospital of *Tsilemele* (the place where help is given), built on a slope in the green valley of the Singangwana River. After a further 16 km the road joins the main gravel Umtata–Port St Johns road. This junction is 42 km from Old Bunting and 88 km from the junction of the Coffee Bay and Umtata Mouth roads.

Turning eastwards down this road, a turn-off is reached after 7 km which follows a very beautiful route for 11 km down the left bank of the river known as the *Mngazi* (place of blood) after tribal battles which took place in its valley in former times. At the mouth of this river lies a spacious lagoon and a fine beach with a rugged coastline stretching south to the great cliff face known to Europeans as the Brazen Head and to Africans as *Ndluzulu* after the thundering sound of the surf. Bird life is especially rich, with about 130 recorded species. The entire valley of this river is a supreme example of a perfect landscape of hills, river, forest and seascape. A project for the development of a harbour for the Transkei was mooted at the mouth of the Mngazana River.

From the turn-off to the mouth of the Mngazi River, the main Umtata–Port St Johns road continues eastwards through superb scenery for 12 km. Reaching the banks of the great river known as the *Mzimvubu* (home of the hippos) the road comes to a major junction. The left branch veers sharply to the north and crosses the Mzimvubu River by means of the Pondoland bridge. The right branch (now tarmac) continues straight down the right bank of the river, past wayside kiosks selling fruit, curios, basketwork and carvings. After 3 km the road reaches that delightful little place at the mouth of the river ...

PORT ST JOHNS

Known to the Africans as *Mzimvubu*, Port St Johns, with its population of 1 958 has one of the most beautiful and scenically spectacular situations imaginable. The Mzimvubu River reaches the sea after cutting its way through a high ridge. This passage, known as The Gates of St Johns, is dominated by two great cliffs of sandstone. On the right (western) bank stands the 378 m Mount Thesiger; on the left (eastern) bank looms Mount Sullivan. Both are thickly covered in indigenous forest and provide the giant 'posts' for the gateway which heralds the river's approach from the interior to the sea.

Port St Johns takes its name from the saint, but the reason for this is obscure. The name does not appear on any of the early Portuguese maps although in 1552 one of their galleons, the *Saint John*, was wrecked 89 km north of Port St Johns at the mouth of the Mtamvuna River. The popular theory is that the site of the disaster was in later years mistakenly thought to have been the mouth of the Mzimvubu and the name applied accordingly. Another theory is that the buttress of Mount Sullivan (on the left bank) resembles a full-length figure of a man, robed and hooded in the same way as the apostles are depicted in biblical paintings. This likeness may be viewed from the right bank on the site of the original harbour works of Port St Johns.

The Portuguese named the Mzimvubu river after *Saint Christovão*. The first English name of the place was *Rosebud Bay*. In October 1846 the schooner *Rosebud* became the first vessel known to attempt a passage across the sand-bar at the mouth of the river and to open the harbour to trade. Other ships followed. In spite of many of them being wrecked, the river mouth became the accepted port of call for coasters conveying goods for trade with the Pondo and other local tribes.

Notwithstanding the considerable difficulties of transporting goods inland from the mouth of the river, an increasing number of ships visited the harbour. The name of Port St Johns became established. The British Government decided that it was essential to exert control over the area, especially in view of the possibilities of foreign powers landing there and the place being used by gun-runners. In July 1878 an agreement, by means of which the harbour of Port St Johns was ceded to the British, was made with the chief Nqwiliso, who ruled over the independent Pondo tribe living on the western side of the Mzimvubu River. In August 1878 General Thesiger (later Lord Chelmsford) and Commodore Sullivan arrived at Port St Johns in the *Active*. On 31 August they hoisted the British flag at what was known as White's Landing Place downstream from the lower ford across the river known as Davis Drift. *Fort Harrison*, a stronghold named after the captain commanding the garrison, was built on the right bank close to the ford and was held by troops until 1882 whereafter the garrison was stationed at the mouth of the river. The site of the fort is about 6 km above the Pondoland bridge.

The area along the river banks was at first administered as an enclave known as the St Johns River Territory, with a resident magistrate and harbour-master. On 15 September 1884 the territory was annexed to the Cape Colony. The population at the time comprised 110 officers and men of the garrison, 92 European officials and traders with their families, and 106 African servants. A wooden wharf was built on the right bank of the river where a succession of small craft landed cargoes such as whisky, beads, blankets and trade goods, and carried away maize, ivory, hides and other products of the Pondo.

In the warm, drowsy atmosphere of Port St Johns the garrison and traders led lives of extreme isolation. Drinking and gambling were the principal pastimes. Some renowned dice games were held beneath a drooping wild fig tree growing nearby the wharf. During one of these games a visiting Norwegian ship's captain was obliged to wager parts of his vessel. The bell of his ship, the *Clan Gordon*, is still in use outside the town hall.

The days of the river trade are over. The last coaster, the *Border*, called at the harbour in December 1944; and today the bar across the mouth allows only very light craft to enter the river. The garrison has also long since vanished, but the atmosphere from the picturesque early days remain. There are very few visitors to Port St Johns who are not receptive to the relaxed, easy-going feeling inherited by the little town from its past.

Port St Johns became a municipality in 1935. The first councillors had the management of an almost dreamlike little place inhabited by a picturesque crowd of individualists, beachcombers and escapees from society. Memories of many of these individuals form part of the amiable story of the town. There was a ragamuffin known as Captain Kettle with his dog Billy Bones. Together these two roamed the countryside, making a dashing entrance into the town on the odd occasion. On one such occasion when Port St Johns was *en fête* to receive the Prime Minister, Captain Kettle made his appearance and, dressed in his usual rags, strolled down the centre of the main street bowing to the crowd, while his mongrel dog trotted proudly at his heels.

The famous wandering hippo, Huberta, arrived in the village in March 1930 and for six months took up residence in the river. Notwithstanding its name of *Mzimvubu* (home of the hippos), none of her kind had been seen in the river for years. She grazed on the gardens in the village, over-turned a few boats, caused several upsets and quite a few laughs and then wandered off southwards to her untimely death.

Relics of old shipwrecks, such as cannon retrieved from the celebrated wreck of the *Grosvenor*, salvaged silver coins and sea-washed beads, may be seen in the town. Gardens and vegetation are luxuriant, and handsome beaches stretch on either side of Cape Hermes, on which promontory there stands a 5 000 candlepower lighthouse and a radio beacon.

There are many magnificent walks through the forests, over the hills and along the coastline. Pathways meander to most of the places. Viewsites and picnic spots are scattered along the way. Many of these trails were blazed and also described by one of Port St Johns' characters of former years, the author C R Prance, who wrote an interesting little booklet *Rambling Routes for Hikers*, giving details of the paths. Fishing, swimming, walking, bird and butterfly watching, boating and sleeping in the sun, are the activities and inactivities of Port St Johns.

Third Beach is part of the Silaka nature reserve. It has fine swimming and fishing spots such as Bird Rock and the Sugar Loaf. A hiking trail begins here and leads down the coast to Coffee Bay. This is a superb walking experience. The full hike last five days. There are four overnight huts with bunks and furnishings which include large missionary cooking pots.

On the left-hand side of the Mzimvubu River a road leads down from the Pondoland bridge to Agate Terrace and on to Poenskop where there is a beautiful beach and many fishing spots in a magnificent stretch of coastal scenery. There is a tea-room at Agate Terrace and a caravan park.

From Port St Johns the main road (3 km upriver) crosses the Mzimvubu by means of the Pondoland bridge which, in May 1953, replaced the picturesque but unhurried Camerondale pontoon. On the left bank of the river the road enters Eastern Pondoland and begins a steep, winding and most beautiful climb out of the valley of the Mzimvubu, where many fine views of the towering Gates of St Johns may be seen.

At the Gemvale trading station, 11 km from the bridge, stands a small roadside memorial to the indefatigable Bishop Bransby Key who was fatally injured there in an accident. At this point a turn-off leads for 10 km to the coast at Seaview and the mouth of the Mntafufu River where there is a cluster of cottages. Gold was once found here and efforts were made by two successive companies to extract the metal. The last company, floated in 1932 by Eli Tom Ball, a famous Pondolander who ran the store at Gemvale, proved that, although gold was present, it occurred in unpayable traces.

Beyond Gemvale the main road twists and climbs for 13 km in a picturesque journey through the hills of Eastern Pondoland. It then reaches a turn-off to the coast which ends at Manteku and Bucele. After a further 1,5 km the road arrives at the summit of its climb where it traverses a lovely green rural plateau sprinkled with the white-walled rondavel huts of the tribespeople and patched with dense indigenous forest in the valleys.

A further 16 km (42 km from the Mzimvubu bridge) brings the road to the village and magisterial centre of ...

LUSIKISIKI

This pleasant name is derived from the sound of the reeds which rustle in a nearby marsh. Proclaimed a village in 1932, Lusikisiki is now a bustling trading and road transport centre.

A long central street provides an animated spectacle of tribespeople in their national costume doing their shopping or gossiping in the shade of the stores' verandas. The men (often riding into the village on horseback) attend to their business at the offices of the government or at the various labour recruiting offices particularly those of the Witwatersrand mines which are invariably identified by the sign *Kwa Teba* (place of Mr Taberer). The late Mr Henry Taberer was a pioneer of labour recruiting in the territory and his name is immortalised by the organisation which took over his personal activity.

Thirteen kilometres north of the village lies the seat of the Paramount Chief of East Pondoland. This centre, named *Ohwakeni* (the elevated place), is also a scene of considerable activity.

THE LUSIKISIKI DISTRICT

One and a half kilometres south of Lusikisiki on the main road to Port St Johns, a gravel road branches off eastwards. This road leads through fascinating and varied scenery to one of the wildest stretches of the famous Wild Coast, where features such as the site of the *Grosvenor* wreck and the superb Magwa Falls can be seen. Fishing on this coast is among the finest in Southern Africa.

Six kilometres along this road a turn-off stretches southwards for 27 km to the coastal resort of *Mbotyi* and to the *Magwa* (wonderful) Falls. Following this turn-off for 8 km, a second turn-off is reached which leads to the waterfalls. This road traverses grassy downland country where large plantations of tea are grown. After 3 km there is another turn-off which leads through these plantations. The traveller is advised always to bear right at any division not signposted, as there are several branch roads through the plantation. After 5 km (22,5 km from Lusikisiki) the road ends at the dramatic Magwa Falls where the river leaps a sheer 142 m into a narrow gorge below.

The Mbotyi road, meanwhile, continues to the coast past the three-step cascade known as Fraser Falls, through a fine primeval forest and terminates on the Wild Coast at the delightful little fishermen's and campers' resort of Mbotyi (31 km from Lusikisiki).

The main gravel road continues eastwards from the point where the Mbotyi–Magwa road turns off (6 km from Lusikisiki). After 1,5 km a track branches off north-eastwards to the Mateku Mission station and the 142 m high Mateku Falls where a stream tumbles headlong into the densely forested valley of the Msikaba River. The Mateku Falls are worth seeing only after rain. The track is poor but a good view is yielded from the Msikaba road.

The main gravel road continues for a further 36 km and ends at South Sand Bluff at the mouth of the Msikaba River, where an automatic 2 000 candlepower lighthouse stands. On the left bank of the Msikaba River lie the grounds of the Mkambati leper hospital established in 1922 as a sanatorium for those suffering from what is today a curable disease. The area is also worked as an immense cattle ranch. A pathway extends along the coast to groves of carefully protected palm trees belonging to the species *Jubaeopsis caffra* (known to the Pondo as Mkambati), and to several magnificent scenic attractions such as the Waterfall Bluff where a river plunges straight into the sea over a high cliff. The entire coastal area between the Msikaba and Mtentu rivers is being developed as the Mkambati Nature Reserve, the largest nature reserve in the Transkei with accommodation provided in log cabins and with hiking trails leading to many lovely places, including Waterfall Bluff.

On its way to the Msikaba River, the main road sends tracks down the coast to several coastal points such as the mouth of the Mkweni River and Kilroe Beach. One of these places is known as Port Grosvenor where, in 1885, an abortive attempt was made to develop a harbour for West Pondoland. The attempt proved disastrous. The East Pondoland chief, Mqikela, gave two identical monopoly concessions to two rival traders, a Captain Turner and a man named Rethman, neither of whom would allow the other to function. Only one ship, the *Sir Evelyn Wood*, called there with a cargo for Captain Turner, whereupon Rethman disputed landing rights so effectively that it was forced to sail away.

THE WRECK OF THE GROSVENOR

The name of *Port Grosvenor* was taken from one of the most celebrated of all shipwrecks. A few kilometres down the coast from Port Grosvenor (the turn-off is 26 km from the turn-off to the Manteku Mission) lies a rocky little bay known as Lwambasi. On 4 August 1782, the English ship *Grosvenor*, sailing in from India on a dark night, literally collided head on with Africa. The consequence was dismal for the ship. Although only 14 of the 150 people on board were drowned, the survivors experienced severe hardships on land. Having no strong character to bind them together, they split up into groups, each one making its own way in search of shelter and distant Cape Town.

After four months, six sailors managed to reach a frontier farm near the site of modern Port Elizabeth. The news they brought of the disaster prompted the government to send a relief expedition. The party found twelve more survivors, but the fate of the rest remains undiscovered. For years rumours persisted that some of them, including several women, were living with the tribespeople.

In 1790 an expedition set out from the Cape to investigate these rumours. On a tributary of the Mngazi River the expedition found a mixed community comprising about 400 descendants of people of various non-African origins who had been shipwrecked along the coast. Among them were three old white women, apparently English, whose origin was obscure. The expedition arrived at the site of the wreck of the *Grosvenor* but saw nothing of the ship and no survivors.

Over the years other travellers journeying along the coast visited the site of the wreck, finding several ship's cannon, ballast and other fragments. Included among these relics, however, were reported to be gold and silver coins. The result of these reports was an increasingly eager search for a fortune in bullion (£1 314 710) which was reputed to have been listed on the bill of lading. Rumours persisted that even the fabulous peacock throne of Persia (looted at about this time) was part of the ship's cargo.

A succession of syndicates and companies went bankrupt in their search for the treasure of the *Grosvenor*. Nowadays, on visiting the site of the old disaster, one is likely to find more interest in viewing the wreckage left behind by the various companies than in expecting to see something of the ship itself. The amount of debris is impressive as is the variety and ingenuity of the techniques which have been employed to salvage the ship.

The first *Grosvenor* treasure recovery syndicate known was formed in 1883 when a group of spiritualist-hypnotists, guided by a ghost, made an idiotic effort at searching for buried treasure!

Several individuals followed in the hunt, including a local trader, Alexander Lindsay who, in 1896, systematically blasted away rubble and sifted sand to recover a substantial number of coins. Lindsay showed his findings to others and in 1905 he formed the Grosvenor Recovery Syndicate. A steam-driven crane was dragged to the site where it scraped the sea bottom with a heavy chain. Many coins and fragments of the wreck were dragged to the surface by this means, but the company's finance was exhausted without any worthwhile return.

In 1907 Lindsay organised a second venture, the Grosvenor Treasure Recovery Company. With £10 000 as capital he planned to use a suction dredger and divers to reach the wreck. The dangerous situation of the wreck (close inshore in a rocky little bay, combined with rough seas and the lack of shelter of the Wild Coast) totally defeated the venture which ended in disaster after a diver was drowned when his air hose was severed by a sharp rock.

In 1921 Martin Webster, a Johannesburg mining engineer, floated the Grosvenor Bullion Syndicate Ltd with a capital of £35 000. He had a plan of tunnelling under the sea bed, solidifying the sand with liquid cement and boring directly into the hull of the wreck. This involved a substantial mining operation. A diver was employed to examine the sea bottom and he claimed to have located a mound in the floor of the bay large enough to be the wreck buried under the sand. By November 1922 the tunnel had bored 122 m through sandstone, which was easy to work but allowed a dangerous amount of seepage from the sea. At one stage a black mamba took up occupation in the tunnel and refused to budge. This delayed work by several days until the reptile could be located and ejected. Then money ran out, work became desultory, and in 1925 the tunnel collapsed. A new tunnel was started; and in 1927 a wealthy individual, Theodore Pitcairn, bought out the venture. He allocated £27 000 to continuance of work but, when the funds were exhausted in 1929, the venture was abandoned.

In 1938 the Grosvenor Salvage Co Ltd was formed by Gerhardus van Delden. His project was to build a horseshoe-shaped breakwater, 396 m in length, around the site of the wreck. The water inside would then be pumped out and the treasure recovered on dry land. £35 000 was needed as capital and work started in January 1939. Rock was blasted from a quarry and carried by a tramway to the two arms of the breakwater which groped out to embrace the bay. The trouble was that the bay had no intention of being embraced. As fast as the breakwater arms were extended, storms simply lashed them to smithereens. By the end of the year the whole venture had collapsed in chaos, to the recriminations of shareholders and disgruntled employees out of a job.

Next to appear on the scene was F W Duckham whose project was to use a Michigan mobile grab crane to fish up the wreck piecemeal in a steel bucket. The Second World War delayed this venture but in 1946 the Grosvenor Salvage Co (Duckham) Ltd was floated, a road was built and the crane ordered. When it arrived in South Africa, there was insufficient money to pay for it and the venture collapsed.

Duckham then organised the Duckham Marine Salvage Co (Pty) Ltd. Another crane was ordered but again there was no money to pay for it on its arrival. Investors were now becoming very chary of risking money in the recovery of the *Grosvenor* treasure. A few private enthusiasts were left to carry on the search. The idea of the grab crane was abandoned (unfortunately, perhaps, for the little steam crane used by Lindsay in his pioneer effort had at least produced some results). Instead, water jets, worked at high pressure from a raft, were used in an effort to remove the overburden of sand. Frogmen were employed and the Grosvenor Treasure Co (Pty) Ltd was floated in 1951 to work on the project.

It appeared that three major fragments of the wreck lay beneath water less than 10 m deep, but were also buried under about 2 m of sand as well as rubble from the ill-fated breakwaters of Van Delden. A professional diver was employed to work from a small ship, the *Steenbok*. Several cannon and other bric-a-brac were located on the bed of the bay (which is actually a gully). Explosives were used in an attempt to reveal more of the wreck but work was made difficult and dangerous by heavy weather, treacherous currents, turbid water and sharp rocks. In June 1952 the venture was abandoned.

The only items so far recovered from the *Grosvenor* have been cannons (one placed at the old Fort, Durban; two in the Umtata Museum; one in the park at Port St Johns; and one in the grounds of the Royal hotel, Lusikisiki) and the various gold and silver coins recovered by individual searchers. Sidney Turner, the trader, found enough of these in 1880 to make a bracelet for his daughter, to melt down for a silver cup, and to be able to sell about 3 000 coins to a bank. Alexander Lindsay's steam crane also collected several hundred coins. The remaining cargo still lies at the bottom of the dangerous little gully on the Wild Coast. How much is there and how best to reach it, no man knows.

LUSIKISIKI TO NATAL AND KOKSTAD

The main gravel road leads north-westwards out of Lusikisiki and over the seemingly endless hills of Pondoland. After 1,5 km a turn-off stretches eastwards to Ohwakeni (11 km) and the important mission station of Holy Cross (40 km) founded in 1911 by an Anglican missionary, Robert Callaway, and famous for its hospital and the handsome church built in 1925.

Providing a contrast, the extraordinary residence of the late herbalist, Kgotso Sethuntsa, is passed by the main gravel road 3 km beyond the turn-off to the mission. Painted entirely a pale blue colour, this mansion is known as *Mount Nelson* and reflects the scale on which the famous Pondo healer practised.

The main gravel road continues for a further 27 km over the grassy hills. Thirty-three kilometres from Lusikisiki there is a turn-off on to an interesting 49 km long scenic drive to the small village of *Tabankulu* (the great mountain). On the way may be seen a spectacular example of a river meander, a great horseshoe bend in the course of the Mzimhlava River. Tabankulu originated in 1894 when two traders, Blenkinsop and Meth, opened a store there. Other traders joined them and in 1909 a village was laid out. Beyond Tabankulu the road joins the main N2 road.

The gravel road continues for 11 km beyond the turn-off to Tabankulu along a high ridge sprinkled with myriad huts on either side. After 46 km of travel from Lusikisiki, the road reaches the trading centre and village of ...

FLAGSTAFF

This little place had its origin in 1875 when two traders, Z G Bowls and G Owen, secured rights to the area from the Paramount Chief of Eastern Pondoland. They erected a store and did a roaring business, but found it difficult to keep customers away when they closed on Sundays or holidays. Accordingly the traders erected a flagstaff next to their store on which a white flag was flown on the days when the store was closed. This not only kept customers away, but gave the future village its European name. Today it is a busy trading and road transport centre surrounded by substantial plantations of black wattle trees which grow on the village commonage. Flagstaff is known to the Africans as *Siphageni*.

At 1,5 km out of Flagstaff, a turn-off leads eastwards to Holy Cross Mission and the Mkambati leper hospital (71 km away). Five kilometres beyond the wattle plantation in a handsome avenue of tall eucalyptus trees, there is a turn-off to *Emfundisweni* (place of learning), the training school for young men destined for the high office of administration.

The main gravel road continues through fine, rolling, high hills with deep, wooded ravines. Incessantly rising and falling through this lovely country – one of the most romantically beautiful expanses in Africa – the road (31 km from Flagstaff) reaches an important junction close to the trading station of *Magusheni* (place of sheep), where a large flock of these animals is once said to have perished after being caught in a storm.

From this junction a tarmac road turns north-westwards and leads for 49 km over high hill country, joining the main N2 road at the foot of Brooks Hill. The second branch turns eastwards.

After passing a turn-off (at 19 km) to Harding and Durban the road makes its way over a beautiful green pastoral landscape covered in innumerable rondavel huts, maize fields and herds of cattle. A further 8 km sees a turn-off to Mtentu and Holy Cross Mission, while another kilometre down a hill slope takes the road into the magisterial village (27 km from the junction at Magusheni) known as *Bizana* (the little pot), after the stream of that name which meanders nearby.

From this trading centre the tarmac road continues eastwards over a high undulating plateau covered in green grass, huts, maize and cattle. To the north there are views across the great valley of the Mtamvuna River which marks the boundary of the Transkei and KwaZulu-Natal. At 16 km from Bizana there is a turn-off which descends steeply into the valley of the Mtamvuna, the views are spectacular. This road crosses the river after 27 km and, after climbing out of the valley, traverses some superb hill country and eventually (41 km from Bizana) joins the N2 road at Izingolweni, from where the surface is tarmac to Durban. This route provides a very beautiful alternative to continuing from Bizana directly to the coast. The latter road descends steadily across green hills. The blue sea emerges from the distant haze, and 37 km from the turn-off to Izingolweni (53 km from Bizana) the road crosses the Mtamvuna River by means of the handsome C H Mitchell Bridge, entering KwaZulu-Natal 3 km south of Port Edward.

Just before this bridge is the entrance to the Wild Coast Sun hotel and casino. There is an interesting exposure on the beach here of what is known as the Mzamba fossil beds, best seen at low tide. The cliffs are full of limestone caves and are encrusted with fossils dated about 60 million years ago. There are about 120 different shell species as well as bones of various creatures, sharks' teeth and huge fossilised tree trunks.

BUTTERWORTH TO IDUTYWA

From Butterworth the N2 road of Transkei continues north-eastwards over the undulating grassy plateau covered by the rondavel homes of the tribal people, all conservatively the same, with their doorways invariably facing east towards the rising sun. On many of the thatched roofs may be seen small patches of soil supporting a species of plant used as a charm against lightning.

The costumes of the people are particularly striking, especially those of the women. Braided skirts and orange-ochred shoulder cloths are the convention. Although rigid conservatism demands that everybody dress exactly the same, the cumulative effect is extraordinarily charming. The women smoke long-stemmed pipes and wear many metal armlets and turban head-cloths. Custom dictates that all items of costume and every colour, bead or decoration have a particular meaning.

Periodically the traveller may see boys dressed in the weird costume of the *Khwetha,* the circumcision lodge of puberty. With their faces and bodies daubed with white clay and strange reed dancing skirts wound around their waists, they provide a touch of ancient magic to a unique landscape.

At 33 km from Butterworth the road crosses a stream with the singular-sounding name of *Ngxakaxa* (the ditherer) and, after travelling north-eastwards for a further 2 kms, reaches the town on the acacia-covered slopes of the Mputi River called ...

IDUTYWA

The name *Idutywa* (place of disorder) originated from a tribal disturbance which occurred in that area during an invasion by raiders from Natal.

The town was laid out in 1884 near the site of a military and police post established in 1858 by Colonel Gawler at what was known as the Idutywa Reserve. It is today a magisterial, railway and trading centre with a population of 9 632. It became a municipality in 1913, with its first mayor, W E Warner, holding office for 20 years.

From Idutywa a branch leads south-eastwards for 32 km to the magisterial centre of Willowvale. This little village, with its cluster of stores and hotel, is the point of departure for the popular fishermen's resort at the mouth of the Qora River.

IDUTYWA TO VIEDGESVILLE

The main Transkei road (N2) continues north-eastwards steadily climbing out of the acacia-covered valley of Idutywa. At 16 km there is a turn-off west stretching to the pretty little town of *Engcobo* (place of long grass) founded in 1875 by the resident commissioner, Walter Stanford (later Sir), as the administrative centre for the Tembu tribe. A further 8 km of travelling along the main Transkei road over the grassy plateau takes the road to the brink of the acacia and aloe-covered valley of the Mbashe (Bashee) River. The tarmac road winds down for 4 km to the valley floor where the river makes a sultry way towards the sea.

At 28 km from Idutywa the road crosses the river and steadily rises out of the valley for 13 km, passing through the Mtentu cuttings. Returning to the level of the plain, the road continues across this world of rondavels, ox-drawn sledges, horsemen and statuesque women in their elegant orange-ochre costumes. After 5 km there is a 31 km turn-off south-east to Elliotdale, known to the Africans as *Xhora*. After a further 17 km (64 km from Idutywa), the road reaches the trading post, railway and road centre of *Viedgesville,* named after a German trader who established his headquarters there.

VIEDGESVILLE TO THE WILD COAST

From Viedgesville a road branches eastwards to some of the most popular resorts on the Wild Coast. At 13 km from Viedgesville this road reaches the small magisterial centre of *Mqanduli* (the dresser of grindstones), where a man once lived who was famous for this skill. The centre comprises a cluster of stores, administrative buildings, garages and a hotel.

At 23 km from Mqanduli lies another small magisterial village, originally named *Elliotdale* after Sir Henry Elliot, Chief Magistrate of the Transkeian territories from 1891 to 1902, but now known as Xhora. It is the administrative centre for the Bomvana tribal area. The village was founded in 1878 and is situated in handsome, rugged hill country. The Bomvana people who live in these parts are a picturesque and amiable crowd, notable tobacco growers and smokers, and inclined to be conservatively primitive. Their tribal name derives from a chief, Bomvu, who ruled over them in about the year 1600. A younger son of this ruler created a tribe of his own and it became known as the *Bomvana* (little Bomvu tribe). The tribe is closely related to the Pondo living further south.

Beyond Elliotdale a good road leads for 40 km through delightful scenery to the mouth of the Mbashe River where there is a great resort of fishermen at what is known as The Haven. The scenic setting for this sport is superb, with fine beaches and forest-clad hills rolling down to the sea. A couple of kilometres from Elliotdale along the road to the Mbashe mouth, it is worth turning aside to view the famous Colley Wobbles, the series of involved curves in the Mbashe River, one of the world's most remarkable examples of a river meander.

Just outside Mqanduli on the road to Elliotdale, a turn-off proceeds eastwards for 67 km through delectable downland scenery to several interesting spots on the Wild Coast. One of the best known of these is the Hole in the Wall.

VIEDGESVILLE TO UMTATA

From Viedgesville the N2 road continues north-eastwards over the undulating coastal plain where the hill slopes are scattered with rondavel huts seemingly as numerous as the stars in the Milky Way. Also prominent are cattle herds and herdboys, sheep and their shepherds, and groups of women who balance their water containers so skilfully on their heads that, even if the container happens to be an unglamorous paraffin tin, they still contrive to look graceful and dignified, a feat unmatched by any other race on Earth.

At 17 km from Viedgesville the tarmac road commences an easy descent down the southern slopes of the valley of the Mtata River, approaching (3 km ahead) the city of ...

UMTATA

The capital of the former Transkei, Umtata is a pleasant hill-slope town, the terminus of the railway from the south and a road junction and communications centre of considerable importance. Together with the surrounding districts, it has a population of 239 750.

The nearby Mtata River is said to have received its name from the *thathe* or sneezewood trees

(*Pteroxylon utile*) which flourish along its banks. It supplies the town with a generous amount of water and contains several beauty spots, including a pretty cascade a couple of kilometres downstream. As it is a notably treacherous river when it floods, another theory suggests that the name is derived from the word *thatha* (the taker), owing to the damage and the fatalities through drowning caused by the flooding river.

From early times the Mtata was regarded as the boundary between the lands of the Tembu and the Pondo tribes. The *Tembu,* who take their name from a chief who ruled over them in about the middle of the 16th century, were among the earliest people to settle in the Transkeian area. Their origin is obscure, but they are generally considered to be part of the Lala offshoot of the great Karanga tribe of Zimbabwe.

Incessant border brawls with the Pondo north of the Mtata River gave the chiefs of both tribes the idea of creating a buffer strip between them. To this end, both the Tembu and Pondo tribes granted farms along the river to Europeans in the 1860s. In 1875 Tembuland was ceded to Great Britain and divided into four magisterial districts. A site about 8 km west of the present town was selected as the seat of one of these magistracies, with Major J F Boyes pitching his tent there in 1876.

In 1877 Bishop Henry Callaway arrived as the first bishop of the new Anglican diocese of St Johns, which serviced the Transkeian territories. He acquired one of the Mtata River farms where he erected his headquarters, including a church, school and hospital, the forerunner of the present substantial Sir Henry Elliot hospital.

The town of Umtata was laid out in 1879 and grew rapidly. In 1882 the first village management board was elected and on 10 November of the same year the town became a municipality. It became a city in June 1981. There is a handsome building in Umtata which seated the *Bunga* (Parliament) and an impressive town hall built in 1907 stands overlooking a superb garden. Other features are a substantial Anglican cathedral, numerous official buildings, and many pleasant homes in the residential areas. The University of Transkei (Unitra) was founded in 1976 as a branch of the University of Fort Hare but became an autonomous university on 26 October 1986. It is situated on the southern side of the town and has 4 000 students.

A 460 ha nature reserve was proclaimed in 1983 at Luchaba, 5 km from Umtata. There are picnic and boating facilities. A second nature reserve, Nduli, 100 ha in extent, lies 3 km from Umtata on the N2 road to the south.

PONDOLAND

North of the Mtata River lies the land of the Pondo, an area of immense scenic variety: precipitous river valleys, the greenest of downland country, lovely patches of indigenous forest, and as rugged a piece of coastline as any fisherman could desire.

Two closely related tribes inhabit this area, the Pondo and the Pondomise. Both had a common origin and were involved in the great migration of people down the east coast from a legendary home in the far north known as eMbo. Tradition has it that Mpondo and Mpondomise were brothers who divided the original tribe in about the year 1500. They formed part of the vanguard of the main migration and their language belongs to the modern Zulu–Xhosa group.

The people of Pondoland dress in a manner similar to their Xhosa and Tembu neighbours, but incorporate a different colour scheme. Pale blue is the dominant colour instead of red-orange. White – originally the colour of mourning – was once worn after the death of a revered chief for so protracted a period that this colour became permanently established. Subsequently, the habit of using blue in washing was adopted from the Europeans, and this new shade of clothing became popular as opposed to the less practical white. Nowadays all gala dress is a pretty shade of pale blue, while red-orange is still worn by young boys and girls.

Residences are of the same rondavel type as those built by the Xhosa. The doorways also face east towards the rising sun.

The principal road through Pondoland branches off eastwards at Umtata and leads through some of the most spectacular and fascinating scenery in Africa. Crossing the Mtata River (1,5 km from the town), the road proceeds eastwards over hills densely settled by tribal people. At 6 km from Umtata a turn-off to the south-east leads to the village and magistracy with the bleak name of *Ngqeleni* (the cold place). From this point the road continues down to the Wild Coast fishing and camping resorts such as the mouth of the Mtata River. Fishing along this coast is good, and the mouths of the several small rivers which reach the sea there provide suitable vantage-points and pleasant camping sites.

The main road continues past the turn-off to Ngqeleni and (26 km from Umtata) reaches the magisterial village named after the Pondo chief, *Libode*. From there on the road finds an involved way through spectacular scenery. Steadily losing altitude, the road descends into the valley of the river bearing the sombre name of *Mngazi* (place of blood) where vicious tribal fights of former years took place.

Dominating this great valley (51 km from Umtata) is a gigantic pile of rock, a veritable fortress known as *Mlengana* (the hanging one). Its huge cliffs seem to lean out over the valley and the atmosphere is one of brooding savagery. This is one of the most memorable of all landmarks. There are many legends to the place, Europeans like to call it Execution Rock and fancy that some early chief had his victims dragged to the summit, from where they were thrown to their death. However, on the northern side of the river there is a precipice (also known as Mlengana) which was actually used as a place of execution. The great rock itself can be climbed on its eastern side. Among the legends surrounding it is one in which a circumcision lodge of tribal youths attended their mystic training in seclusion on the summit. A fire swept across the grassy top and all of them perished, either by being burned to death or in their attempt to jump to safety.

The road curves around the great rock, yielding panoramic views of the valley. The best time to do this journey is in the cooler hours of the late afternoon when the cliff faces are emphasised by the deep shadows of oblique light. The atmosphere of this rugged area is then both wild and romantic and the colours are varied and deep.

At 81 km from Umtata at the Tombo trading station, a turn-off leads for 16 km to the mouths of the Mngazi and other rivers where fishermen find sport and holiday-makers relax in fine camping grounds. For a further 12 km the main road climbs and twists, with handsome indigenous forest covering the slopes. Running along the right bank of the great river known as the Mzimvubu, the road (95 km from Umtata) reaches a junction. The left branch crosses the river, while straight ahead the road continues along the river bank for 3 km and then (97 km from Umtata) reaches the picturesquely situated town of Port St Johns.

UMTATA TO KOKSTAD

The tarmac N2 road leaves Umtata on the banks of the Mtata River in a great bowl in the hills and climbs over slopes green in summer but sleepily brown in winter. Sheep, cattle, maize and the rondavel huts of the Pondomise tribespeople may be seen on all sides. After 35 km a turn-off west is reached, leading for 4,5 km to the village of *Tsolo* (sharply pointed), so named after a pointed mountain which provides a landmark 23 km away. The village was originally established in 1879 under this mountain. The first European inhabitants were besieged in the stone prison building for eight days during the Pondomise uprising in 1880. Close to the modern village is the Mbuto School of Agriculture, established in 1903.

The main road continues past the turn-off to Tsolo. After 11 km it descends into the densely inhabited valley of the fine, often-flooded river known as the *Tsitsa* (the one that spouts out). A magnificent 125 m high waterfall occurs in this river downstream from the bridge. It is reached from the road which branches off down the left bank to the *Shawbury* Mission (15 km) founded by the Wesleyans in 1839 and named after the mission benefactor, William Shaw. The waterfall is especially worth seeing during flood time. A guide should be obtained from the mission station, if only to control numerous urchins who volunteer their services and can be a nuisance. The track continues for a rough 2 km and then there is a walk of another kilometre to a handsome viewsite. Afternoon light is best for photography.

From the bridge across the Tsitsa, the main road climbs out of the valley over undulating grassy slopes. Traversing a densely populated area, the road (57 km from Mutate) descends a slope after 10 km and passes through the small village of *Qumbu* (place of budding or bursting), with its avenue of jacarandas.

Continuing over rolling green hills, the N2 road proceeds from Qumbu for 11 km and then descends into the badly eroded valley of the river known as the *Tina* (said to be so named because of the otters there). With its complex meanders, this river provides some interesting scenery as the road climbs its left bank. At 27 km from the river (39 km from Qumbu) the road descends steeply and passes through the village of *Mount Frere* with its one long street of commercial buildings situated on the hill slope. Founded in 1876 as a magisterial centre for the Bhaca tribe, the village was named after Sir Bartle Frere, the Governor of the Cape and High Commissioner. The Africans know it as kwaBhaca (the place of the Bhaca).

The N2 road continues through the village and descends steadily over 10 km of attractive countryside into the valley of the Mzimvubu River, which reaches the sea at Port St Johns. There is a pleasant picnic site at the bridge across the river.

The N2 road climbs out of the valley over 11 km of rugged country, then leads along a high ridge from where fine views to the north may be seen of deep valleys, mountains and a regular milky way of the white-painted rondavels of the Bhaca tribespeople.

The impressive Insiswa Mountains, with their periodically worked copper deposits and patches of forest, dominate the road to the north. Many streams tumble down the slopes in waterfalls and cascades during the summer rainy seasons. Passing (at 33 km from Mount Frere) the turn-off to Tabankulu and the Insiswa forest reserve (1,5 km further on), the road descends to the crossing of the river known as the *Mzimhlava* (home of the *Mhlava,* the mealie grub parasite of maize) at the foot of the mountain range. At 6 km beyond the river (41 km from Mount Frere), the road passes *Mount Ayliff,* a cluster of houses, trees and stores sheltering at the foot of a high ridge. The place was named after William Ayliff, Secretary for Native Affairs in the Cape Government, who visited the area in 1878 and accepted the local Xesibe tribe as subjects of the Cape. The diminutive village grew as the administrative centre for this tribe and is known to the Africans as *maXesibeni.*

Beyond Mount Ayliff the N2 road continues up the valley of the Mmvalwini stream, densely populated by the Xesibe tribespeople, with high hills towering on either side of the road. At 19 km from Mount Ayliff there is a turn-off to Bizana (39 km) and Port Edward (119 km).

The N2 road now commences a steady climb up the slopes of Nolangeni, the 2 013 m high mountain which dominates the area. After 6 km of climbing, the road reaches a point 1 610 m high at *Brooks Nek* where L M Brooks once had a trading station. From this point the road starts to descend, passing after 6 km the turn-off to Pietermaritzburg and the south coast of Natal, and then, after a further 3 km (35 km from Mount Ayliff), entering the town of Kokstad (see Chapter Twenty-Seven).

Chapter Twenty-Three
THE SOUTH COAST OF KWAZULU-NATAL

The great coastal highway of Southern Africa, the N2 from Cape Town, descends the northern side of Brooks Nek over the often snow-covered heights of Nolangeni Mountain and reaches a turn-off leading for 4 km to the town of Kokstad (see Chapter Twenty-Seven). Beyond this turn-off the N2 tarmac road leads north-eastwards across an undulating grassland dominated to the north by the bulk of Mount Currie.

After 21 km the road reaches the mountains known as *Ingeli* on account of their fragmented, precipitous nature. Amid slopes and ravines blanketed with fine patches of indigenous trees, the road passes through the Langerwacht and Ingeli forests, which lie along the summit ridge of the Ingeli range. At 29,5 km the road reaches the Ingeli forest lodge and a turn-off to the government forestry settlement of ...

WEZA

This centre, the name of which means a fording place, is one of the largest forestry plantations in KwaZulu-Natal. The plantation was started in 1923 as a labour settlement, mainly for people who had been involved in the Rand riots of the previous year.

Additional people were settled there during the period of the depression of the 1930s. With the return of better economic times, the majority of these settlers rehabilitated themselves and wandered off to more rewarding fields of employment. The original corrugated iron buildings erected to house the first settlers remained and, during the Second World War, Weza became a prisoner-of-war camp for Italians captured in North Africa.

A timber sawmill had been built in 1939. When the main plantations began to reach maturity this small mill was replaced in 1953 by what was then the largest mill in South Africa. The Weza State Forests were proclaimed a nature reserve in 1994. There are delightful hiking trails. The forest is well populated with about 360 species of birds, including the Cape parrot. There are tree dassies, baboons, vervet and samango monkeys, nyala and other antelope.

At 8 km beyond the turn-off to Weza (37,5 km from the Kokstad turn-off) the N2 road reaches a major division. One branch leads on to Umzimkulu and Pietermaritzburg (see Chapter Twenty-Seven) while the second branch swings south-eastwards through superb forest country and, descending gently, passes a second turn-off to Weza (after 13 km) and, at 52,5 km from the Kokstad turn-off, reaches ...

HARDING

This town was established in 1813 as a magisterial and police post on the rather unruly frontier between KwaZulu-Natal and Griqualand East. Named after Walter Harding, the Natal Supreme Court Judge, it became the administrative centre of the district of Alfred, replacing the earlier centre of Murchison. The area is inhabited by a number of tribes of diverse origin such as the Mawu and the Jali who derive from the Pondo; the Cele, Nhlangwini and Nyuswa who are of Zulu origin; and one mixed tribe, the Nkumbini, founded by the British ivory trader Frank Fynn and still ruled by one of his descendants.

For a lengthy period the border area was a no man's land of gun-runners, smugglers and a retreat for a number of shady characters. In this setting Harding grew into an atmospheric little town, becoming a municipality in 1911. At first very remote, Harding was eventually connected to the outside world by means of a modern road and subsequently a narrow-gauge railway from Port Shepstone, opened in 1917 for the purpose of transporting to market the considerable timber resources of the district.

The nature of the countryside around Harding is aptly demonstrated by the narrow-gauge railway. The road from Harding to Port Shepstone is 77 km long. To complete the same journey, the narrow-gauge railway follows a circuitous 122 km long route which winds, climbs and descends, giving the little puffers a very hard time. What with stops, starts, hesitations, reversals, shuntings, heaving and squealing of brakes, the procedure resembles the love life of a nervous spinster.

The trains originally took nine hours to make the journey, speeded up today to seven hours by use of diesel locomotives instead of the picturesque old puffers. Railway enthusiasts find a travel experience such as this fascinating, if only to discover what happens to the train during its lengthy trip. An outing at night, particularly, seems like a venture into darkness. The original puffers were completely masculine: a bundle of pipes exuding hot air amid various grunts, steams, pants, gasps, blow-offs, swear-words when one of the crew put his hand on a hot pipe, and peculiar smells, all of which comprise the body odour of a living, mechanical creature working very hard for its living of coal, water and a spot of grease. The puffers moaned and complained incessantly, sizzling at other engines when they encountered them at crossing points. They rattled merrily downhill, groaned at the gradients and zipped along the straights, squealing around curves like small boys pretending to go quickly. In the darkness the headlights illuminated only two fragile-looking rails which stretched ahead into a void so inky that it seemed as though the puffer had taken a wrong turning and abandoned the world around the previous bend. The line, known as the Alfred County Railway, is now run by a private company.

From Harding the N2 road continues, descending towards the coast through a seemingly interminable jumble of hills. At 35 km there is a turn-off to Gundrift and after a further 5 km a turn-off to the farming area of the Oribi Flats. Passing the trading centre of *Izingolweni* (place of wild cats), founded in 1870 as a half-way point and police post between Harding and Port Shepstone, the road continues its winding descent. There is a turn-off to Port Edward 1 km beyond Izingolweni (39 km from Harding) and at 53 km the road passes the trading centre of Paddock. The railway station there is a National Monument. The resident caterers will gladly open the museum house to visitors. At 4,5 km beyond this little place there is a loop road turn-off to the Oribi Gorge Nature Reserve, with the second leg of the loop to the gorge being reached after a further 4,5 km. Beyond this point the road descends rapidly for 12 km past many smallholdings and shacks before reaching Port Shepstone, 77 km from Harding.

THE ORIBI GORGE NATURE RESERVE

The loop road to this reserve provides a magnificent scenic spectacle. From the turn-off on the Harding road 12 km from Port Shepstone, the tarmac road leads through a densely settled tribal area. Hugging the edge of the escarpment, the road reveals fine views of the valleys of the *Mzimkulu* (great home of all rivers) and its tributary, the *Mzimkulwana* (little Mzimkulu).

At 16 km from Port Shepstone the road commences a steep descent into the valley of the Mzimkulwana River which forms the lower end of the Oribi gorge. Scenically splendid, the slopes of this ravine are covered in dense indigenous forest, home of about 250 species of birds.

At the end of the descent, 21 km from Port Shepstone, the road crosses the river near the ruins of the buildings formerly occupied by the Umzimkulu Lime Company, now removed to another quarry site. The road climbs steeply to the heights dominating the left (north) side of the river. The summit is a plateau known as the Oribi Flats, consisting of a tongue of high land between the deep valleys of the converging Mzimkulu and Mzimkulwana rivers. On the edges of this tongue of land are a series of wonderful sites from which to view the two valleys.

Once on the summit (24 km from Port Shepstone), the road reaches a turn-off to the Oribi Gorge hotel, in the grounds of which lie most of the viewsites for the Oribi Gorge. The hotel stands 1,5 km from the turn-off. For an entrance fee visitors are allowed to follow a private road leading to off-photographed scenes such as Baboon's Castle, Lehr Falls, Horseshoe Bend and The Heads, all of which are worth seeing. The *Fairacres* estate on which the hotel stands, is a green and pleasant natural parkland where there are many fine trees, wild flowers, and exotics such as flamboyants, bougainvillaeas and the 'yesterday, today and tomorrow' flowers which are at their best in spring. There are many picnic spots.

Beyond the turn-off to the hotel, the tarmac road continues westwards over the grassy Oribi Flats with fields of sugar cane and plantations of trees stretching on both sides. After 3,5 km there is an unmarked turn-off to the right leading for 0,5 km to one of the most impressive views in Southern Africa. The track is rough but at its end lies the Hanging Rock, projecting over the edge of the precipice of the Mzimkulu River. The gorge is immense and the great river provides a fine spectacle as it rushes through the rocky rapids far below.

From the turn-off to the Hanging Rock the road continues westwards over the Oribi Flats. After 3 km there is a junction. Straight ahead the road continues over the Oribi Flats to rejoin the main Harding road at Izingolweni (29 km). Turning left (south), the scenic road commences a descent through an exquisite indigenous forest into the gorge of the Mzimkulwana River where the road enters the Oribi Gorge Nature Reserve. At a point 37 km from Port Shepstone the road crosses the river and then starts to climb the southern side of the gorge. After 3 km of climbing, the road passes the entrance to the tourist camp and rangers' quarters all built on a handsome viewsite.

The Oribi Gorge Nature Reserve, 1 837 ha in extent, was proclaimed in 1950 and, to the delight of botanists, ornithologists and walkers, conserves a large portion of the great gorge of the Mzimkulwana River. Towering sandstone cliffs – red-orange in colour – dominate a gorge choked with a tangle of trees, flowering plants and ferns. Baboons and leopards find a home on the faces of the precipices. Duikers, bushbuck, oribi, monkeys and a variety of wild cats roam through the forest while many beautiful birds nest in the branches of the trees. There is a picnic site with barbecue facilities for day visitors. Six trails of varying length take walkers to many interesting places in the reserve.

Immediately beyond the entrance to the camp, 40 km from Port Shepstone via the scenic drive, the road joins the main N2 road at a point 24 km from Port Shepstone. The entire 64 km provides a superb circular drive.

PORT SHEPSTONE

The terminus of the south coast railway from Durban and the narrow-gauge railway to Harding, Port Shepstone is also the principal administrative, judicial, commercial, industrial, educational and transport centre on this portion of the KwaZulu-Natal coast.

The town has experienced a romantic history. The presence of marble at what is known as Marble Delta, on the north bank of the broad Mziimkulu River a few kilometres from its mouth, attracted attention in the 1860s and a sprinkling of settlers made their homes in the area. Among them were several men of enterprise; such as the Aiken family and William Bazley, an engineer whose endeavours opened the river mouth for shipping. He made it practical for the first coaster to enter the river on 8 May 1880 and to anchor at what had been named *Port Shepstone* in honour of the secretary of native affairs in Natal, Sir Theophilus Shepstone.

From then on, a regular shipping service linked Port Shepstone to Durban. Sugar, lime and marble blocks were shipped out and a great variety of goods were brought in for local trade. Harbour facilities were built and a town was laid out in 1882. In that year a party of 246 Norwegian immigrants landed at the place, which has since then benefited from a substantial community of these hard-working people. A charming little church on the outskirts of Port Shepstone continues to serve as a centre for those of Norwegian descent. The population of Port Shepstone is cosmopolitan. There are members of at least twenty African tribes, descendants of English and German settlers as well as Norwegian, Indians of Hindu and Muslim persuasion, and several other groups.

With the opening of the railway from Durban in 1901, the harbour fell into disuse, but the importance of the town as a distributing centre continued and it became a municipality in 1934. The population has now reached 16 268. The river remains one of the handsomest rivers in Southern Africa although, sadly, it has silted up in modern times. A 27 000 candlepower lighthouse keeps watch over the entrance and serves as a beacon to passing ships. The harbour is being revamped into a marina with space for at least 200 yachts and pleasure craft with walk-on moorings directly from the golf-course. A waterfront and fishing harbour is also planned. The attractions of Port Shepstone as a holiday resort, apart from the river, are a beautifully situated 18-hole golf-course, varied coastal and river-mouth fishing, a tidal swimming-pool, a sandy beach, and superb scenery inland. Industrially, substantial amounts of sugar are produced through the mill of the Umzimkulu Sugar Company. Timber and lime are also produced in the area. Subtropical fruits, such as litchis, bananas, pawpaws and avocado pears are grown, as well as coffee. For railway enthusiasts, and all those who enjoy an unusual outing, there are regular pleasure trips on the narrow-gauge railway run by the Port Shepstone and Alfred Country Railway Ltd. The pleasure train is known as the Banana Express. There are two-and-a-half-hour trips to Izotsha station and six-hour round trips on Wednesdays as far as Paddock and Oribi Gorge, with a two-hour barbecue stop at Paddock. There are specials, such as a Christmas Eve champagne breakfast run, a New Year's Eve barn-dance run and special steam safaris for tour groups to Harding and other interesting stations on the line.

Each year during the summer season there is a tube race down the Umzimkulu River. The race is limited to 1 000 entrants. It starts from the Umzimkulu Limeworks Kube quarries and ends near the river mouth. Using motor-car inner tubes, people from all over South Africa participate.

THE SUGAR COAST

The coast of KwaZulu-Natal with its warmth, friendly atmosphere, luxuriance of vegetation; fertility in all things, especially subtropical fruit and flowers; beaches and lagoons just made for fun lovers on vacation, is a sweet coast altogether. Not surprisingly it is also a major sugar producing area of Southern Africa with its downlands covered in a green sea of sugar cane, sprinkled like a coral sea with islets. Each islet consists of a mill or refinery surrounded by the homes of the workers.

The wild species of perennial grass of the genus *saccharium,* popularly known as sugar cane, grows in several tropical countries but the cultivated species seems to have originated in New Guinea. The sweetness of its juice made it a desirable cultivar in every country which had a suitably warm climate with a rainfall of at least 1 000 mm a year. Sugar cane grows from cuttings. It matures in 8 to 24 months, depending on climate. Replacement growth known as ratoons automatically appears after the old growth is cut. This self-rejuvenation continues for several years before a cane field needs to be replanted with new cuttings.

Harvesting is done generally by hand. The cane is then transported to a mill which crushes it. The sucrose rich juice is purified by the addition of lime and heating to boiling point. Impurities settle as mud which makes a good fertiliser. The clear juice is decanted and evaporated first into a rich, sweet-smelling syrup and then into sugar crystals. The crystals are separated by centrifuging leaving behind a thick brown liquid known as molasses, which provides a feed for livestock and can be used as a source of alcohol and a variety of chemicals. Nothing is wasted. The residue of the cane, after being crushed is known as *bagasse.* It provides fuel for the sugar mills, makes excellent paper or board and has several other chemical applications.

Altogether sugar cane is a sweet gift from nature to all living things even with the most rudimentary of taste buds. In former years it was a rarity, expensive and much sought after. The ancient Greeks and Romans had no sugar. They used honey as a sweetener. Arab traders introduced the cane from New Guinea to other parts of the world. The juice became a most desirable sweetmeat notable as a quick replenisher of energy and also sought for medicinal purpose.

Systematic cultivation started in India about the first century. The Arabs carried the cane, to which they gave the name of *sukkar*, to Egypt, Sicily and Spain. The British Isles and the more temperate parts of Europe where the cane would not grow, only received it as a sweet, expensive novelty and medicine, during the time of the Crusades in the 12th and 13th centuries.

The trade in sugar and spices by overland routes from the East, made Venice wealthy and other European nations envious. They set out to open trade routes for themselves. Christopher Columbus sailed westwards in search of such a route. Bartholomeu Dias and Vasco da Gama sailed eastwards, discovered the Cape of Good Hope and opened the trade route between the spice and sugar islands of the East and the continent of Europe.

Africa had wild canes which people chewed as a sweetmeat but the sugar content was too low to be commercial. It was only in 1847 that a cultivated cane species was brought to Natal from Mauritius and proved to be a commercially viable crop by Edmund Morewood on his north coast farm of *Compensation*. In 1851 he produced the first sugar from a crude little homemade sugar mill (see Chapter Twenty-Four). From this beginning has grown the multi-billion rand high-tech industry of today, with all its legacy of trials, tribulations, technical triumphs, rivalries, takeovers and wheelering-dealering.

Morewood's proof of the practicability of sugar cultivation had almost the same effect on Natal as the discovery of gold and diamonds had on the inland areas. A whole new vision of prosperity was revealed. The 1850s became an era of immigration with groups and parties of unemployed persons in Europe sponsored and financially aided to make a new start of life in Natal which they dreamed would prove to be a land of hope and fortune. Many of the newcomers received something of a shock when they arrived and viewed the land allocated to them. John Bazley and his family, after a tedious voyage from Britain and a seemingly interminable ox-wagon trek down the south coast from Durban, looked from a hilltop at the rugged landscape of their farm in the valley of the Fafa River. Bazley consoled his party with a simple *Nil Desperandum* (never despair). He gave the farm this name and by hard work became one of the pioneer sugar farmers of the south coast.

In 1850 the brothers Thomas and Lewis Reynolds emigrated from England's west country to Natal. They had no money but eventually found work on the north coast at *Oaklands* estate on the south bank of the Umhlali River, close to Morewood's pioneer sugar farm. On *Oaklands* they planted cane and built an ox-powered mill in 1852 to produce sugar. In 1860 Lewis made a momentous move to the *Canonby* estate where he worked, gained knowledge of sugar and saved enough money to allow him in 1873 to buy the 3 000 hectares *Umzinto* estate on the south coast for £5 000.

Lewis intended to float the Alexandra Central Mill Co Natal Limited but he died in 1875. His brother Thomas took over the estate, with two sons, Frank and Charles to support him. The *Umzinto* estate had been founded in 1857 by a Cape Town company that had been granted the land and built a sugar mill there driven by a 16-horsepower steam engine, described by John Robinson, editor of the *Natal Mercury* as *'a work of magnitude and solidity that seemed decidedly out of place in such a wild bushland region'*.

The company started to crush cane in 1861 but when John Robinson the journalist re-visited the place in 1871 all he could write about was to describe it as *'a monument of desolation and failure, with weeds covering the hills that are vocal with rustling cane leaves, and growing unchecked up to the very door'*. Robinson was, however, not too pessimistic. *'If this estate should fall into the right hands'*, he wrote, *'it can hardly fail to become one of the most prosperous enterprises in Natal'*.

The Reynolds family provided the right hands, notwithstanding problems. The Anglo-Zulu War of 1878–9 was a setback, but it at least sent the price of sugar skyrocketing to £45 a ton. With the war over, the Reynolds optimistically set up a second mill *Esperanza* (hope) four kilometres from the mill at Umzinto. Their first crushing in 1884 came at a time of the collapse of sugar prices. This was dismaying but the Reynolds persisted. Thomas Reynolds died in 1885 but his two sons, Frank and Charles remained steadfast. In 1889 they took over the *Equeefa* sugar estate. A week later the Equeefa mill boiler burst, killing five people and wrecking the mill. The attendant had weighed down the safety valve in order to secure more power.

The remnants of the *Equeefa* mill were hastily added to the old Esperanza mill to help it take on the load of crushing cane from the two estates. More capital was then needed to build a new mill and for expansion. For this the brothers turned to their uncle, James Reynolds, a wealthy Liverpool merchant. With his backing and chairmanship, Reynolds Brothers Ltd was launched in April 1891 with a share capital of £100 000. The sugar industry on the south coast of Natal was now entering the realm of high finance and it was at this stage that a 33-year-old man, Charles George Smith, was appointed as the new company's agent in Durban. He was destined to become one of the dominant personalities in the sugar industry of Southern Africa.

Charles Smith had been born in London in 1858. When he was three he came to Durban with his immigrant family. Life in Natal proved difficult for the family and they returned to Britain where they found themselves in hard times. The eldest son, Herbert, developed tuberculosis and the mother, Emma, decided in 1873 to send him and Charles back to Durban. She, and a third son, Arthur, born in England, followed the next year.

Charles Smith then aged 15, worked his passage back to Durban on the small barque *Priscilla*. It was a rough journey. In Durban Charles found work with a firm of general merchants, Black & Baxter. This company had just established the *Equeefa* Estates Plantation near Umzinto and Charles Smith was sent down the south coast to work in their store. From the beginning of his career, therefore, Charles Smith was concerned with the cultivation of sugar cane, as well as general and livestock trading. He learned very quickly.

He returned to Durban to work for W B Lyle, mainly on the sugar side of their business. There he met another young man, Richard Addison, one of the family of Dr H W Addison who had migrated to Natal in 1848 from his hometown of Addington in Kent. For two years he practised medicine in Pietermaritzburg. Then he bought an abandoned farm on the Mvoti River, named it *Addington* and settled down to raise crops and a substantial family of fourteen children.

Apart from children, sugar cane soon proved the most prolific crop on the farm. In 1862 Dr Addison crushed his first crop on a 12-horsepower steam driven mill. With this achievement, Dr Addison left the estate to be run by his 22-year-old eldest son with the unusual first name of Friend. The reason for this name was that Addison liked to at least always have one friend in his family. He moved to Durban to become district surgeon and superintendent of the government hospital on the bayside. This hospital was moved in 1878 to the back beach and was named *Addington Hospital* after Dr Addison's home town.

Friend Addison developed the farm, became a colonel in the Natal Mounted Rifles, bought the farm *Gledhow Mount* on the opposite side of the Mvoti River, and persuaded his brother Walter to manage it while he went off to the wars. By the turn of the century, *Gledhow* had grown to 4 000 hectares under cane. The mill on *Addington* had been moved to Gledhow and substantially enlarged. The two brothers controlled the planting and milling operation through a private company registered in 1911 as Addison Brothers Ltd. *Gledhow* was ideally situated to be the nucleus of a major sugar industry. It needed to add to its assets dynamic human control. The Addisons gave it that until 1919 when Friend decided to retire. In the 1914–18 war Walter's two sons were killed. They had been trained to take over the estate but with their death the Addison brothers decided to sell the company. It was bought by a syndicate of C G Smith, Frank Reynolds, William Pearce and the three Cookes brothers. They renamed the company the Gledhow Sugar Estates and under them it continued its growth, not only growing its own cane to feed its destiny as a gigantic mill, but also taking in the sweet harvests of many independent growers, including seventeen farms leased to ex-servicemen on favourable terms providing their cane was given to the *Gledhow* mill for processing.

Of the new owners, the story of C G Smith and Frank Reynolds has already been told. William Pearce, the third of the quartet, had been born in the Old Fort in Durban in 1855, the son of a British soldier who took his discharge in Natal from the 45th Regiment and opened a roadside inn on the *iLovu* (Illovo) River on the south coast. His father died, the widow was left with the new inn to run, no money and six small children to raise. She married again and battled. William Pearce was apprenticed to a wagon builder, working from dawn to sunset each day for five shillings a day wages.

He finished his apprenticeship when he was nineteen and went off with two friends to the Pilgrim's Rest gold rush. They opened a smithy there, made enough to buy a claim, made a little more money but not enough to make them stay, sold the claim and returned to Natal, where they read the news that the purchasers of their claim had found rich gold, £13 000 in six weeks and were anticipating a fortune.

William started transporting to the gold-fields with two old wagons. He worked the business up until he had twelve new wagons with spans of oxen. He received contracts to cart sugar from the south coast mills to the railhead at Isipingo, got married and in 1889 started growing arrowroot and then sugar cane on the flatlands of the lower iLovu River. By 1906 this enterprise had grown to the extent that it demanded a modern mill. To finance this William Pearce approached C G Smith in Durban. The result was the floating of Illovo Sugar Estates Ltd in 1906. C G Smith was chairman, William Pearce managing director and Frank Reynolds of Reynolds Brothers Ltd and Edward Saunders of Tongaat as directors. Saunders later sold his shares to George and Fred Crookes and the individuals who eventually bought and developed the giant mill at *Gledhow* were now together.

The Crookes family originated from Yorkshire. Samuel Crookes immigrated to Natal in 1860 at the age of 21. He was apprenticed to a wagonmaker in Durban for five years. Then he moved down the south coast to the Mpambanyoni River where he set up a wagon-making and repair business for himself. The south coast railway was still to be built and there was heavy transport demand by the developing sugar industry. Samuel married the daughter, Fanny, of Joseph Landers, one of the sugar producers in the valley of the Mpambanyoni. This lady presented him with three sons, George, Fred and John, all born with sugar on their minds and destined to become major players in the sweet industry of cane growing and milling.

Samuel bought the cane farm *Ellingham* west of Umkomaas and moved there with his family. The farm prospered. In 1880 Samuel bought the farm *Maryland* in the Mpambanyoni valley, added to it another farm in the valley, *Restalridge,* combined the milling machinery of his three farms on to *Maryland* and found himself on the way to becoming a sugar magnate. The next step was to buy the *Renishaw* estate and mill, centralise all milling operations there, steadily increase capacity and by the time the south coast railway was opened to Renishaw in 1898 Samuel Crookes had a substantial company. His three sons joined him in the business under the name of Samuel Crookes and Sons from 1903 until 1913 and then as the registered company, Crookes Brothers Ltd.

The south coast sugar producers became known for technical innovation and for the construction of private narrow-gauge railway systems conveying cane from outlying plantations to mills which became increasingly centralised and demanding of larger supplies of cane for crushing. At first driven by spans of oxen, the railway system elaborated until the Reynolds Brothers decided to use steam power. In 1900 they ordered from the Avondale works in Bristol the first of a fleet of 20-inch gauge locomotives. This perky little pioneer puffer did its work so well for so many years that it now stands in proud retirement outside the Durban sugar terminal. Other locomotives from the fleet, when they were retired, were shipped over to the United States where one of them still draws a tourist scenic train in Colorado. The Knebworth West Park and Winter Green Railway in England became home to Sezela's No 4 locomotive which had hauled cane from 1916 to 1975.

Sezela's rail system built on a 24 inch gauge connected the mill to John Bazley's old estate of *Nil Desperandum* 22 km away. Illovo's system had 113 km of rail while Crookes Brothers had 60 km for their *Shaka's Kraal* Estate. *Gledhow* and *Pongola* also had their miniature railways. *Pongola* had a fleet of 13 diesel locomotives and nearly 2 000 cane trucks. It was only in 1984 that heavy road transport replaced the willing little trains. They are now collectors' pieces with many amusing memories of odd mishaps, runaway trains pursued by frantic drivers who had got off in order to relieve themselves and neglected to put the brakes on, unexplained midnight excursions, ghost trains and tough women taking over combined driving and stoking duties when their menfolk were sleeping off various jollifications and wages could have been lost.

Through tunnels and cuttings, across often flooding rivers, with bridges and causeways deep under water, even across what was for years the longest suspension bridge in South Africa (137 m over the Mzimkulu River) nothing stopped the sugar producers. The bridge was washed away in floods in 1931 and 1933, rebuilt in England and shipped out for emergency erection in just 24 days, survived more floods until 1959 and then was carried away bodily by the triumphant river only to be rebuilt again. Through drought and flood the producers made sugar and money and the aroma of their industry lies gently over the green hills of the Natal coast.

Like the ostrich farmers of the Little Karoo with their feather palaces, the cane farmers rewarded themselves by building sugar palaces. The manor home on *Beneva,* built by E W Hawksworth;

the beautiful homestead named *Eden,* built by William and Elizabeth Pearce on a hilltop overlooking Illovo; the superb *Lynton Hall* at *Umdoni Park,* built by Frank and Charles Reynolds in a setting of trees and conserved flora and fauna. Frank Reynolds was a great admirer and friend of Louis Botha, general and first prime minister of the Union of South Africa. At Umdoni Park he built a mansion and named it in honour of General Louis Botha for his use as a holiday home. On the general's death Frank Reynolds placed the ownership of the house into a trust with use of the place for the successive Prime Ministers of South Africa. The park is open to the public.

Frank Reynolds was knighted in 1916 for his service to Natal and South Africa. His great colleague, C G Smith, was knighted in 1923 in recognition of his services to South Africa in parliament, industry and the humanities. His lifelong devotion to the sugar industry provided the magnetism and cement to bind together what could have been a fractious brood of separate companies. His firm, C G Smith and Company were selling agents, financiers and providers of secretarial services, especially for the south coast planters and millers. Over the years he continuously persuaded them to the benefits of amalgamation.

In 1906 he was instrumental in creating the Natal Sugar Association with recognition and statue that sugar was an international commodity and producers should have a mutual bond and forum for discussions and collective negotiation. In 1919 the Natal Sugar Association became the South African Sugar Association and in 1936 this became the quasi-statutory controlling body of the industry with C G Smith as its chairman.

Sir Charles George Smith died in Durban on 24 April 1941. His dream of an amalgamation of the south coast sugar interests associated with him only came to fruition in 1975 when a complex operation brought together into C G Smith Limited the four great sugar mills of Gledhow, Pongola, Sezela and Umzimkulu, with the warehousing operations and S A Sugar Distributors. Two years later, the Illovo, Doornkop and Noodsberg mills brought the tally to seven, when C G Smith Sugar bought them from Tate & Lyle. Then in 1980, Barlow Rand took 54% controlling interest in C G Smith & Company and C G Smith became a subsidiary of C G Smith Foods Ltd.

By that time C G Smith Sugar had become the largest sugar-producing company in Southern Africa with its agricultural estates producing 1 200 000 tons of cane a year and its seven mills with a capacity to produce 800 000 tons of sugar a year.

In the early 1990s, the unbundling of Barlow Rand saw C G Smith Sugar listing on the Johannesburg Stock Exchange in 1992 and then, in 1994, now as a subsidiary of C G Smith Foods Limited, changing its name to Illovo Sugar Limited. By this time, the company had added the Umfolozi Mill to its sugar producing stable and its capacity had increased to one million tons of sugar a year.

In May 1997, Illovo Sugar made a gigantic step forward with the R1,62 billion purchase of the British company Lonrho Sugar with its three mills, four estates and two hotels in Mauritius, two mills and estates in Malawi, one mill and estates in Swaziland and the Glendale mill in South Africa which has now been closed down. From the 1997 production of one million tons of sugar, the group's sugar-making capacity has jumped considerably to 1,5 million tons in 1998 with further significant expansion prospects down the line. Added to this are the group's downstream production lines of furfural products, diacetyl, ethyl alcohol, lactulose and dextran, each with material shares of their respective local and world markets. South Africa on its sugar coast has an industrial giant, one of the biggest in the world, with prospects far beyond the dreams of its pioneers.

THE LOWER SOUTH COAST OF KWAZULU-NATAL

The Mzimkulu River, reaching the sea at Port Shepstone, marks the division between the South Coast and the Lower South Coast of KwaZulu-Natal. From this point a subtle change occurs, the climate south of the river is more temperate, the humidity far less in summer, there is less coastal forest; and green grassy plains predominate, patched with the lala palms characteristic of this part of the coast. A succession of sandy bays, rocky promontories and river lagoons provide the setting where a great deal of enjoyment may be had from living and holidaying in the sunshine.

From Port Shepstone the R61 road branches off from the N2 and leads south-westwards down the coast past a succession of resorts and crosses a number of rivers, the first of which is reached

1,5 km from Port Shepstone. This is the *Mbango* (disputed) River, a boundary line of past squabbles between rival tribes. At 5 km from Port Shepstone the road crosses the *Boboyi* River, named after a type of grass growing on its banks. After another 1,5 km the road reaches the *Izotsha* River, where the Zotsha clan once lived. The perky little narrow-gauge railway from Port Shepstone to Harding has so far kept the road company, but at a point known as Shelly Beach it turns inland, crosses the road and vanishes into the hills.

The R61 road continues close to the coast from Shelly Beach over a green terrace of grass and lala palms. At 11 km from Port Shepstone the road crosses the *Mhlangeni* (place of reeds) River, and enters the municipal area of the resort of ...

UVONGO

This resort takes its name from the river known as *iVungu,* itself named on account of the onomatopoeic sound of the wind and the waterfall murmuring through the gorge. The river reaches the sea after tumbling 23 m over a pretty waterfall into a lagoon. The pool at the foot of the waterfall is 27 m deep, making this the deepest estuary in Natal. A compact little beach is situated on the seaward side. Features such as *Strelizia* (wild bananas) and trees clinging to the overlooking precipice face combine to form a delectable holiday resort.

The municipal area consists of three coastal resorts: St Michaels-on-Sea on the right bank of the Mhlangeni River; Uvongo Beach 3 km further south, the commercial centre and resort at the mouth of the Vungu River; and *Manaba* Beach, 1,5 km further south, aptly named after a Zulu word indicating a place of ease and relaxation. The three resorts combined in October 1954 to form a holiday town which possesses a considerable variety of attractions such as boating and swimming in the rivers; bathing beaches at St Michaels-on-Sea and Uvongo Beach protected from sharks; three tidal swimming-pools; and interesting fishing at Uvongo Beach and the Point at St Michaels-on-Sea. The scenic setting is a green coastal terrace covered in lala palm parkland. *Uvongo* Beach, originally the farm of the great fisherman, T G Lilliecrona, was fortunate in being thoughtfully laid out by an owner who was also a professional surveyor. Consequently it is one of the prettiest of the Natal coastal resorts. The Thure Lilliecrona Park on the banks of the Vungu River commemorates this owner. A nature trail follows the banks of the river above the falls. The Uvongo bird park, open daily from 09h00 to 17h00, exhibits a considerable collection of birds.

Beyond Uvongo (19 km from Port Shepstone), the tarmac main road immediately crosses into the municipal area of ...

MARGATE

The popularity of Margate as a holiday resort among inland and Zimbabwean visitors is so immense that it has occasionally been described as the seaside suburb of Johannesburg. It is a bright and cheerful place, particularly favoured by young people who like plenty of organised entertainment.

Margate is built around a fine sandy beach where there is a pretty swimming-pool for children and shark-protected sea swimming, as well as a tidal swimming-pool, a fishing pier and numerous other vantage-points for anglers, pleasant walks up and down the coast, and a small lagoon for canoeing at the mouth of the river known as *iNkhongweni* (the place of entreatment). This name stems from an old legend that the tribal people living there were so mean that travellers had to entreat them for hospitality. Things have changed in Margate since those churlish times!

Margate was originally a coastal farm owned by Hugh Balance. In 1919 he began to develop the farm as a resort. After a slow start the place received international publicity in 1922 when a so-called sea monster was washed up on the beach. The controversy surrounding the nature of this creature created considerable attention, which resulted in the charms of Margate being publicised at the same time. In 1948 Margate became a municipality and today 7 059 people live there. In April 1973 a modern airport (the second largest in Natal) was opened 4 km from the town. This is the scene for the annual Margate air show and the Experimental Aircraft Association conference.

From Margate the main tarmac road continues south, following a scenic marine route. After 5 km (24 km from Port Shepstone) it reaches the holiday town of ...

RAMSGATE

This resort was originally a coastal farm situated at the mouth of the river known as the *Bilanhlola* (marvellous boiler) because some of its pools appear to bubble and boil as if by magic.

In 1922 a wandering painter and violin-maker named Paul Buck discovered the beauty of the area and settled on the right bank of what he called 'Blue Lagoon'. The romantic home of the amiable Paul Buck was soon unearthed by journalists and writers whose accounts of his carefree way of life and the delightful setting of his self-built home attracted the attention of many others. A holiday resort grew up around the lagoon. Despite its rather stodgy name of Ramsgate, it remains a colourful and sunny little place on the coast of lala palms.

The art gallery attached to the tea-house of the Blue Lagoon is worth a visit. The batik work is superb and the food in the tea-room, which includes Chinese specialities, is good. There is boating on the lagoon and river, and protected sea bathing; fishermen's vantage-points such as Little Billy and Blue Bay are numerous. Together with a fine sandy beach, these are the assets of a resort town whose sole industry is the enjoyment of living.

From Ramsgate the main R61 coastal tarmac road continues southwards, crossing the Little Bilanhlola River, closely following the shoreline for 3 km and then sweeping more inland. After 5 km the road crosses the river with the name (of which there are various corruptions) of *Mbizana* (the place of little pots), so called on account of the small pot-holes in its rocky bed. At 1,5 km beyond the river there is a turn-off to the resort of ...

SOUTHBROOM

Established by Alfred Eyles on the farm which he named after his family home in Wiltshire, *Southbroom* has a pleasant beach with a shark-protected bathing area, several fishing vantage-points and two sheltered lagoons at the mouths of the Mbizana and Mkobi rivers. There is also a spacious area for aquaplaning, two tidal pools, an 18-hole golf-course and the River Bend crocodile farm. The crocodile farm is open Mondays to Fridays 08h30 to 16h30; Saturdays 08h30 to 13h00; and Sundays 09h00 to 16h30. Feeding-time is 15h00 on Sundays only.

Beyond the turn-off to Southbroom the R61 road proceeds southwards over an undulating mass of hills, well covered in trees and lala palms. After 2 km (34 km from Port Shepstone) there is a turn-off to the resort of ...

MARINA BEACH

This is one of the most spacious beaches in Natal. There is shark-protected bathing, a tidal swimming pool and a lagoon in the mouth of the river known as the *Mhlangamkulu* (place of big reeds). This lagoon is part of the private resort known as San Lameer. From the mouth of the lagoon southwards to the mouth of the Mpenjati River, lies the Trafalgar Marine Reserve administered by the Natal Parks Board. This reserve, 1 500 ha in extent, protects an offshore fossilised forest and the Yengele forest, a fine remnant of a coastal dune forest with a 'Black Lake', named after its peat-stained water.

The R61 continues beyond the turn-off to Marina Beach over rolling coastal hills covered in sugar cane, banana plantations, pawpaws, lala palms and patches of bush. During the next 20 km the road passes a number of turn-offs to coastal resorts. At 1,5 km there is a turn-off to the private leisure resort of San Lameer; at 3 km a turn-off to Trafalgar; and at 5,5 km to Palm Beach, lying just south of the river known as the *Mpenjati* from the reedy species of grass growing on its banks.

The coastal resorts of Munster and Portobello lie 10 km from Marina Beach, with Glenmore and Ivy Beach immediately to the south. *Munster* was named by an Irish surveyor after his home town and lies in a particularly verdant setting with safe bathing and interesting fishing possibilities. The Von Baumbachs and the Stoppels, two German missionary families, were the earliest European settlers in the area.

On 24 January 1933 Glenmore Beach was the scene of the wreck of the 150-ton fishing trawler, *Nightingale*. The vessel was totally lost but the crew were all saved. The anchor, rudder and propeller are displayed on the lawn in front of the Kinderstrand building at Glenmore.

A more celebrated wreck was that of the *Ivy* under Captain C Orr which occurred at Ivy Beach on 22 March 1878. The ship was a barque of 319 tons, carrying a full cargo (including 200 cases of gin, 650 cases of wine and spirits, 200 cases of ale and stout, and 200 cases of sundries) from London to Durban. The ship became securely wedged on a tongue of rock about 60 m from land and was left high and dry at low tide. The lower South Coast of Natal, in those days, was not very populated, but every individual (and there were some wild ones) in the area rushed to the scene. A lengthy party commenced which still rates as the most hectic ever held on the coast, with several individuals developing delirium tremens. The anchor of the *Ivy* may be seen at the holiday resort run by the Suid-Afrikaanse Onderwys Unie (the T O Strand) which fronts on to Ivy Beach.

After the turn-offs to these various coastal resorts the R61 road continues across a green parkland. At 21 km from Marina Beach there is a turn-off to ...

PORT EDWARD

This attractive town (with a population of 2 028) had its start in 1925 when T K Pringle acquired the area and named it *Banner's Rest*, for it was there that he intended to 'strike the banner' and retire. He laid out a township on the coast and named it *Port Edward* in honour of the then Prince of Wales.

It became a village in 1947 with the formation of a health committee. The village became famous for a postal service consisting of an African named Welsh pushing a wheelbarrow. Estimated to have pushed this 'vehicle' over 1 000 km a year, this individual met the railway bus each day on the main road, collected the mail and trundled it back to the village for delivery while the bus went on to Bizana. Welsh often slept in his barrow if the bus was delayed.

Port Edward has a pleasant beach overlooked by what is known to Europeans as Tragedy Hill and to the tribespeople as *isaNdlundlu* (that which is shaped like a hut). The 'tragedy' occurred in

1831 when a Zulu raiding band cornered a refugee party of Langeni tribespeople and some of the followers of Frank Fynn, on this hill. They were all killed and, up until recent times, it is said, their bones still covered the hill. On marine maps this hill is a landmark known as North Sands Head. Fragments of pottery and many interesting beads (including rare cornelian beads of great age) – the relics of shipwrecks – have been found on the beach.

Good swimming is provided from the beach and the area is protected by shark nets.

The road to Port Edward turns off at a crossroads, with the right-hand (west) turn-off leading to the Banner's Rest store and then inland for 35 km to Izingolweni, or branching off for 3 km down the banks of the Mtamvuna River, the border with the Eastern Cape. The road ends at the site of the original pont which for years was the only means of crossing the river. It provided a most picturesque scene on the coastal road to the Cape. The site is now a very pleasant caravan park.

The ferry service started in 1935 when the storekeeper of Banner's Rest launched a boat in order to attract customers from the areas south of the river. The name *Mtamvuna* (the reaper of mouthfuls) was given to this river on account of the damage done to crops by its floodwaters. It is a beautiful river flowing through fine scenery and its water is to a large extent still unpolluted and unsilted. Many legends have been attached to it. Its pools are said to be inhabited by water spirits, mermen and mermaids. Evil people are said to be swept out to sea if they do not confess their sins before attempting to cross the river.

In 1943 a proper vehicular ferry service was commenced about 11 km above the mouth of the river. This position was found to be unsuitable and the ferry was moved to its final position at the site of the present caravan park where it worked until May 1959 when it was swept out to sea during a violent flood. A new pont was introduced and this continued in service until 1967 when the handsome *C H Mitchell Bridge* was opened nearer to the mouth of the river.

At the peak of its activity the pont carried an average of 4 720 vehicles and 60 000 passengers across the river each month. Many travellers still remember with pleasure when their journey was broken by the picturesque pont being hauled across the river on a thick rope pulled by a crew of singing men. The pont was sold, cut into sections and removed to the Kyle Dam in Zimbabwe where it was reassembled and used for various purposes, including an appearance in a film.

In 1971 the Umtamvuna Nature Reserve was established on 3 137 ha of riverine forest upstream from the site of the old pont. Several antelope species and about 80 bird species live in this rich botanical area, with fine displays of spring wild flowers. Cape vultures nest in overlooking cliffs.

Beyond the crossroads leading to Port Edward and the pont site, the main road continues down the coast, passing through an extraordinary deposit of deep-red coloured sands. This 'red desert' is unique. According to legend, it was created by cattle that Shaka concentrated there during his celebrated raid against the Pondo tribe. The penned cattle decimated the vegetation, and wind erosion then exposed the sandstone bedrock which erodes into the extraordinary red sand. These sands are particularly beautiful at sunset.

After 3,5 km (55 km from Port Shepstone), the road reaches the end of KwaZulu-Natal on the banks of the Mtamvuna River. Crossing the C H Mitchell Bridge, the road continues into the Eastern Cape, reaching the Mzamba village market of crafts and the entrance to the Wild Coast Sun resort (see Chapter Twenty-Two) and then turning inland to reach Bizana 56 km from Port Edward and eventually, after 119 km joining the main Cape Town–Transkei–Natal road (N2).

PORT SHEPSTONE TO DURBAN

From Port Shepstone the N2 road crosses the Mzimkulu River by means of a bridge spanning the mouth. Now badly silted, the river still ranks as the largest to reach the sea on the South Coast of

Natal and fully justifies its name which means 'the great home of all rivers'. It marks the boundary between the Lower South Coast of Natal (the so-called Hibiscus Coast from the prolific growth there of the exotic flowering hibiscus trees), and the South Coast, known as the Strelitzia Coast on account of the number of wild banana plants of that family which grow there.

Two kilometres after crossing the bridge the N2 reaches a turn-off to the coastal resort of ...

UMTENTWENI

A relaxed little resort town, *Umtentweni* received its name from the river which in turn is named after the spiky mtentweni grass which grows on its banks.

As its assets this town has the handsome river, a lagoon and a pretty, sandy beach with fishermen's vantage-points such as Shaka's Rock, Splash Rock and Shad Alley. For swimmers there is a tidal pool and a bathing area protected from sharks. A balmy climate and an agreeable environment complete the list of attractions for retired people as well as those in search of a peaceful and easygoing holiday.

North of Umtentweni the N2 road twists through green hills, descending and climbing a succession of valleys of rivers such as the *Mhlangamkulu* (the river of big reeds); the Dombe (a species of sweet wild cane growing there); the *Kotswana* (little dried-up one); and the *Njambili* (the two dogs). This river received its name, the tribespeople say, because it consists of two streams flowing side by side like two dogs coursing after an antelope. Where the streams meet at the mouth, the dogs have pounced on the antelope (represented by the sea). In between these rivers are turn-offs to four small coastal resorts which combine to form the municipality of ...

BENDIGO

Four seaside resorts were created on the original coastal farm of *Bendigo*. They are Sea Park, Southport, Anerley and Sunwich Port. In 1967 these resorts amalgamated and adopted the original farm name for the new municipality. Each resort retains its individuality and has special features such as bays, beaches, tidal pools, shark-protected swimming, fishing and recreational facilities.

Three kilometres north of the Njambili River the N2 reaches a turn-off to the coastal resort of ...

UMZUMBE

It is said that in former years a band of cannibals and renegades created a stronghold for themselves on the banks of the river known as the *Mzumbe* (the bad kraal).

In 1828 when Shaka himself led the Zulu army on a great raid down the coast, the local Hlongwa tribe suffered severe loss of life and massive destruction of their villages and farmlands. One very interesting relic survives in the area from this great Zulu raid. Following a path which stretched towards the coast, the Zulu army climbed a ridge overlooking the valley of the Malukaka, a tributary of the Mzumbe. On this high ridge Shaka followed the custom of propitiating the spirits by picking up a pebble in the toes of his left foot, placing it in his right hand, spitting on it and depositing it by the side of the path. His followers observed this procedure and, one by one as they passed the site, every member of the Zulu army duplicated Shaka's action. A large mound of pebbles accumulated next to the path.

A pile of pebbles such as this is known as *isivivane* (a luck heap). They are regarded with reverence by Africans, particularly this one, on account of its association with the memory of the great Shaka. It is a classic specimen of its kind, impressively situated on a strategic height in the midst of a rolling sea of hills. The pathway besides which it stands seems to be as old as the hills themselves. The feet of countless travellers have tramped it deep into the ground. Surrounded by the superb panorama of scenery, the pile of pebbles stands next to the pathway which climbs, descends and twists incessantly through this prodigious landscape, conjuring up a picture that is completely African. The luck heap lies 10 km from Umzumbe up District Road D453. A guide should be obtained from Govender's store, beyond which the road is rough for 3 km, degenerating into a track and involving a final walk of 0,5 km along the path.

The coastal resort of Umzumbe is a pleasant place half lost in trees and palms. Fishing from the rocks is good.

Beyond the Mzumbe River the N2 South Coast road traverses a 3 km expanse of bush, crosses the *Mzimayi* (place of cattle) River and, 21 km from Port Shepstone, reaches the coastal resort of ...

HIBBERDENE

Named after C Maxwell-Hibberd, a former Postmaster-General of Natal who was the first to retire to this pleasant place, *Hibberdene* possesses a tree-fringed beach and fishing vantage-points such as the flat rocks known as Reefs End. It is a good place in which to have a thoroughly lazy time.

From Hibberdene the N2 road continues northwards. After 4,5 km the road bridges across the river known as the *Mhlungwa* (the division), for it was here that Shaka, on his great raid down the coast, is said to have divided his army into two sections to form a great pincer attack against the Pondo.

At 10,5 km from Hibberdene (32 km from Port Shepstone) the road reaches the resort of ...

MTWALUME

The river which gives the area its name is itself named after the *mtwalume* trees growing on its banks. The bark of these trees is used as a specific medicine against dysentery, and the name means 'what it carries must stand upright', an odd reference, presumably, to the effect it has on loose stomachs! The beach is pretty and there is a tidal pool and a shark-protected swimming area.

The N2 road crosses the Mtwalume River, the valley of which is thickly bushed, and after 4,5 km reaches a turn-off to the resort of ...

IFAFA BEACH

The river known as *iFafa* (the sparkling one) reaches the sea through a lagoon at Ifafa Beach. Swimming is good, there is a plentiful supply of karanteen bait for fishermen, and the area has a reputation for shad, rock fish, salmon and sharks. The lagoon and lower reaches of the river offer fine boating and canoeing possibilities. It is a favourite area for paragliding, offering magnificent sea views.

After crossing the Fafa River the main coastal road continues through a hilly landscape covered in sugar cane. After 8 km (44 km from Port Shepstone) the road reaches a turn-off to the sugar-producing centre of ...

BAZLEY BEACH

Bazley Beach, named after the sugar pioneer John Bazley, is a quaint, isolated little seaside village with no shopping amenities. It has a stretch of unpolluted, sandy beach on a coastline popular with windsurfers and jet-ski riders. There is a fine caravan park.

Fourteen kilometres further up the coast, the road reaches ...

SEZELA

Legend has it that the Sezela River was named after a notorious crocodile responsible for the deaths of many people. This reptile was known as *Sezela* (the one who smells out), for it persistently hunted its prey like a dog, or a diviner 'smelling out' victims. Shaka, when he led his army down the coast, was told about the monster and he decided to procure its skin. A great hunt was organised and the crocodile was found and killed. Its name still lingers on the river, which was originally known as the *Malangeni* after the tribe living on its banks.

In 1914 Reynolds Brothers Ltd, one of the largest sugar-producing concerns of Southern Africa, erected a mill at Sezela. The mill is fed with cane brought in on an extensive narrow-gauge railway system, and the company produces there over 120 000 tons of sugar each year.

The Reynolds brothers, Frank and Charles, were sons of Thomas Reynolds who, with his brother Lewis, acquired vast landholdings on the Natal South Coast. Before that, they had developed a considerable sugar industry on the North Coast on *Oakland's* estate near Shaka's Kraal where, among other things, they produced rum known as Umhlali Water.

Their first sugar mill, named Esperanza, was built in 1882 at Umzinto on the South Coast. This mill was served by a narrow-gauge railway system whose route included one tunnel of over 230 m in length through solid rock and a suspension bridge over the Mzinto River spanning 80 m at a height of 10 m. The old Esperanza mill was replaced in 1899 by the new Esperanza mill which was eventually removed in 1952 to the Phongolo River to crush the cane grown on the irrigation settlement. The mill at Sezela now handles most of the cane grown by the company on the South Coast. The mill is situated on the Sezela River lagoon which, having suffered the effects of agricultural and industrial activity in the past, has been restored to its natural indigenous beauty and is now a recognised environmental jewel on the south coast, attracting local fishermen, tourists and conservationists alike.

Beyond the Sezela River the N2 coastal road continues northwards over a fine rolling mass of hills well covered in sugar cane and patches of indigenous forest. This area was originally owned by the Pennington family whose name remains over the coastal resort of ...

PENNINGTON

The original Pennington was killed by a leopard in the bush on his estate. His two sons continued to farm in the area and to run a transport business. The estate was a superb piece of natural parkland, well-watered with two rivers flowing through it, the *Nkhomba* and the *Nkhombana*, both named after the palm trees, *Jubaeopsis caffra* which flourish there.

The Penningtons sold part of their estate to the sugar producer, Sir Frank Reynolds, who built his home there on what he named *Umdoni Park* after the *mdoni* or water myrtle trees growing there. On this beautifully wooded estate Sir Frank built a seaside mansion for General Louis

Botha, the first Prime Minister of the Union of South Africa, whom he admired. This lovely home, *Botha House*, eventually became a holiday residence for the prime ministers of South Africa. A public holiday area has developed close to the beach, and Umdoni Park has been left in trust by the Reynolds estate for the enjoyment of the public.

Pennington lies 1,5 km south of the river known to the Africans from its destructive floods as the *uMezi weZinto* (doer of things). On the north bank of this river, 51 km from Port Shepstone lies the railway junction and resort of ...

KELSO

The original farm, owned by S J Abrams, was named *Kelso* after a place on the Tweed River in Scotland. There is a small lagoon and a pleasant beach.

The main coastal road leads north from Kelso through a green parkland of trees, palms and grass. It crosses the river known as the *Mzimayi* (place of cattle) and after 5 km reaches ...

PARK RYNIE

In 1857 the land on which Park Rynie has been developed was acquired by the firm of Norsworthy & Co. A partner in this firm was a Mr Hoffman whose wife, Catherine Renetta, was nicknamed 'Rynie'. Consequently *Park Rynie* is named after her. During the First World War a whaling station was created at Park Rynie by a company known as Park Rynie Whales Ltd. A breakwater known as Rocky Bar Pier and a landing ramp were built.

From Park Rynie a turn-off from the N2 road leads for 7, 5 km to the town of ...

UMZINTO

The centre for one of the principal sugar-producing areas of Natal, Umzinto developed as the busy railway terminus of a branch of the main South Coast line, and also for the narrow-gauge line inland through Highflats to Ixopo and Umzimkulu. The road from Umzinto to Highflats (59,5 km) leads through superb hill scenery, passing on its way the small trading centre of Braemar.

Umzinto is named after the river *uMezi weZinto* (the doer of things) from the damage it does when in flood. It was in the Umzinto area that the first public sugar company in Natal commenced production in 1858, using as labour the first Asians to be imported for the purpose, a group of men from Java. By 1865 Umzinto had grown to be the magisterial and principal centre for the Alexandra District of Natal. It remains a major industrial town on the South Coast of Natal. It is a busy little town with one long main street notable for shops selling silks, spices, from the East and gold jewellery.

The 2 189 ha Vernon Crookes Nature Reserve named after the sugar magnate was established near Umzinto on 4 January 1973. There are picnic sites, walks and drives in fine hill country. There are five overnight self-service, fully equipped, thatched rondavels, and a 20-bed tree house and small laboratory suitable for study groups. Numerous antelope species live in the reserve. Bird life is prolific. It is open from 07h00 to 18h00 daily. Phone (032) 342-222 for information.

From the turn-off to Umzinto the N2 road continues through a green parkland for 4,5 km and then 52 km from Port Shepstone, reaches a turn-off to the town and resort of ...

SCOTTBURGH

This resort was named after John Scott, governor of Natal when the place was originally surveyed in 1860 as the first township in Natal south of Durban. Before the railway was built, an attempt was made to use the bay at the mouth of the Mpambinyoni River for the export of sugar. Several coasters traded there but the bay offered scant shelter from rough seas. A number of fishing vessels also used the place as a base at the beginning of the 20th century. The nearby Aliwal shoal provided rich fishing grounds and the industry flourished for several years.

Scottburgh became a municipality in 1964 and the population now numbers 5 828. Today it is a popular seaside resort with a fine beach fringed by lawns and trees. Attractions include shark-protected bathing, a tidal pool, a miniature railway and an 18-hole golf-course.

In 1985 Reynolds Brothers opened Croc World, a large-scale crocodile-breeding farm with exhibition and lecture facilities, a shop, restaurant and other amenities. It is open daily from 09h00 to 17h00. There is a trail through the coastal forest, with trees identified, and a bird-watching hide. Feeding-times for the crocodiles, alligators and snakes are 11h00 and 15h00 daily. There is a large walk-through eagle camp and authentic Zulu dancing.

From Scottburgh the N2 descends into the valley of the river which the Africans rather ingeniously named the *Mphambinyoni* (confuser of the birds), for its course meanders to such an extent that (it is said) even the birds fail to find their own nesting places. Across the river the road finds a way through dense coastal forest where so many palms of the strelitzia family grow that this part of the coast truly deserved its old name of the Strelitzia Coast.

Crossing the river known as the *Hlongwa* (after the resident tribe), the road after 6 km reaches the resort of ...

CLANSTHAL

The site on which *Clansthal* developed was originally a farm named by its German owner after a place in Hanover, Germany. On the hill overlooking the resort stands the 240 000 candlepower lighthouse of Green Point which beams its warning light over the offshore shipping hazard of the Aliwal Shoal.

The Aliwal Shoal is a 1,5 km long, 1 km wide ridge of rock lying in the sea 4 km off the coast. It is so near the surface that in rough weather the ocean swells break on it in a line of white foam. The shoal was first reported in 1849 by the captain of the barque *Aliwal* which narrowly avoided colliding with it. The first ship known to be wrecked on the shoal was the *Nebo,* a 2 600 ton steamer on her maiden voyage in 1884. The crew were all saved but the ship was totally lost as well as 4 500 tons of railway material destined for Natal. Several other ships, such as the *H C Richards* in 1893 and the *Amy Lykes* in 1970, have come to grief on this shoal. The *Amy Lykes* was on a record-breaking run to Durban when she hit the shoal at 11h00 on a calm morning. Over 3 000 tons of cargo had to be dumped before she could be pulled off by two tugs. On 11 August 1994, the Norwegian tanker *Produce* struck the shoal at 14h30. Ski-boat fishermen and a SAAF Puma helicopter from the Durban-based 19 Squadron rescued her crews of 34, including four women.

The shoal provides the south coast of Natal with its finest deep-sea fishing ground. Diving on the shoal and the wrecks around it attracts scuba divers from all over the world. It is, in fact, regarded as one of the top diving sites in the world. The shoal has the additional attraction of being home to the ragged toothed sharks. *'Come dive with the Raggies on Aliwal'* is a catch phase for scuba divers who find these sharks to be amiable and amusing. Ragged toothed sharks of the family *Odontaspididae* grow to lengths of up to 3 m. They have nasty looking teeth but designed for grasping rather than cutting purposes. The result is that the shark has to swallow its prey whole and this excludes from its menu anything as large as a human being. The shark is therefore amiable rather than dangerous to humans and, in fact, they happily swim amongst divers but can become excited over scraps from skin-divers' speared fish.

A curious thing about these sharks is the appetite of babies during the 9–12 months gestation period. After the yolk supply in their own eggs is consumed they happily feed on the rest of the eggs in their mother's uterus, then on smaller brothers and sisters, eggs and, finally, in a grand banquet on yolk capsules stored away by the mother and back packed with a couple of dozen unfertilised ova.

From Clansthal the N2 coastal road follows a scenic route through a forest of palms, casuarina trees and indigenous bush interspersed with fields of sugar cane. The road crosses the Hlongwana River and veers slightly inland to pass through the residential area of Widenham, returning to the coast to reach, 74 km from Port Shepstone, the river and resort of ...

UMKOMAAS

The European name of *Umkomaas* is a corruption of the African name for the river, the *Mkhomazi* (place of cow whales). The shallow waters of the river mouth have always provided a favourite place where cow whales can comfortably give birth to their calves. Shaka, the Zulu chief, is said to have witnessed the spectacle and then named the river.

The town of Umkomaas, with its population of approximately 8 000, originated with an attempt in 1861 to develop a harbour in the mouth of the river. Several coasters called there to load sugar but the river entrance was made hazardous by a sand-bar and difficult currents. As a result, the shipping venture failed. The opening of the South Coast railway in 1897 finally solved the transport difficulties of the planters.

Umkomaas was established as a town in 1902 and is today the centre for the factory of the South African Industrial Cellulose Corporation (SAICCOR) known as Sappi Saiccor which produces chemical cellulose pulp for conversion offshore into products such as viscose, rayon and cellophane. There is a fine 18-hole golf-course. The beach is rather restricted and the sea generally muddied in summer by the floodwaters of the river. However, there is an enclosed tidal pool for swimming, boating on the river and angling for fish such as salmon, garrick, grunter and shad.

The N2 road bridges across the mouth of the Mkhomazi River and continues northwards, passing a wayside market place where fruit and handicrafts may be bought. This is the area where the Luthuli tribe lives. They are a particularly talented people in arts, crafts, and trading. About 450 of them have stalls displaying and selling a multitude of local handicrafts and curios. Litchis sold in January are notably sweet. Bananas of several different varieties are sold. This market is worth seeing on any day of the week. Known as the Umnini market, it is next to a large modern garage, restaurant and convenience built in 1989 by the KwaZulu Finance Investment Corporation in association with Shell South Africa.

After 6,5 km the road crosses the river known as the *Mngababa* (place of jealousy) on account of an old tribal feud.

The coast on either side of the Mngababa River is rich in titanium, and a considerable industry developed here in the years after the Second World War. Recovery of titanium unfortunately caused the sea to become badly polluted, and the industry was ended. The N2 road passes through the area of titanium-rich sands, crosses the Msimbazi River and enters the area known as ...

KINGSBURGH

This borough received its name from Dick King who passed along the coast on 26 May 1842 at the start of his great ride to Grahamstown to secure reinforcements for the British garrison besieged in Durban.

Kingsburgh consists of several separate coastal resorts each with its own individuality. The combined urban area became a borough on 1 August 1952. The most southerly of the resorts is Karridene, 9 km from Umkomaas. The man after whom the resort is named, W Karri-Davis, was a Rand mining magnate who built a recuperative home there for people suffering from miners' phthisis. It has a pleasant beach; there is boating on the river and a fine golf-course.

Adjoining Karridene is the resort of *Illovo Beach* situated on the south of the river named after the *Cordia caffra* (iLovu) trees growing there. The N2 road bridges the broad river and reaches a turn-off leading inland for 87 km to Pietermaritzburg. On the coast opposite this turn-off lies the resort of *Winklespruit*, the name of which, with a slight misspelling, is derived from the Afrikaans *winkel* (trading store). On 10 May 1875 the schooner, *Tonga,* carrying a mixed cargo of groceries, was wrecked there. The salvors erected on the beach a small store from which the salvaged good were sold. Another version of the name is that it derives from periwinkles found there.

Further up the coast lies the residential area and resort of *Warner Beach*, founded in 1910 as a settlement for pensioners and named after the government surveyor T A Warner. Over the years this settlement developed, as has the whole of the Kingsburgh area, into a commuter residential area for people working in Durban. It has a fine beach with fishing and shark-protected swimming.

Warner Beach ends on the south banks of the Little Amanzimtoti River. On the north side stands the residential area and resort known as Doonside, originally a railway station named *Middleton* after Frank Middleton, Natal government surveyor, who was assisted by T A Warner of Warner Beach. To end confusion with Middleton in the Cape, the postal authorities changed the name to *Doonside* from a nearby house called *Lorna Doone* after the heroine of R D Blackmore's famous novel. Doonside is the most northerly of the resorts included in Kingsburgh.

Kingsburgh has collectively 8 km of sandy beaches. Shark nets protect four of the beaches. There are two tidal swimming pools.

The south bank of another river named by Shaka forms the northern limit of Kingsburgh. It is said that in the year 1828, when he was returning to Zululand with his army after raiding the tribes of the south, he camped on the banks of this river. Shaka's attendant filled a calabash of water for Shaka to drink. Upon drinking it, Shaka murmured with pleasure '*Kanti amanza mtoti*' (So, the water is sweet). As always, his followers acclaimed his every saying. From this event arose the name of both river and the modern town on its north bank ...

AMANZIMTOTI

Acquiring municipal status on 1 January 1962, Amanzimtoti combines the residential assets of a beautifully wooded coastal ridge within easy commuter reach of Durban, 27 km away; the industrial area of the Isipingo flats; and the Inyoni Rocks beach. This seaside resort consists of a long stretch of coast with a sandy beach, several rocky vantage-points for fishermen, swimming pools and shark-protected sea swimming areas. There is boating on the river, an interesting 4,5 ha bird sanctuary on Umdoni road, and a nature reserve, Ilanda Wilds (20 ha in extent), with walks along nature trails where 126 species of indigenous trees and shrubs flourish.

From the business centre of Amanzimtoti the N2 road continues northwards, passing through the residential and industrial area of Umbogintwini and then descending to cross the river called *emBokodweni* (place of round stones) after which the industrial area is named.

Durban is now only 19 km away and its buildings are clearly visible over a flat expanse of ground once covered in sugar cane but now being developed as the industrial area of Prospecton. The river flowing through this area, the *Isipingo*, derives its name from the siphingo shrubs *(Sentia indica)* which grow on its banks. In 1969 this river was diverted into the Mbokodweni to prevent flooding of Prospecton. The Mlazi River which also fed this lagoon was canalised out to sea in 1952 during the construction of the originally named Louis Botha Airport, now the Durban Airport. The result has been the total degradation of the once pretty Isipingo lagoon.

ISIPINGO

Isipingo is a residential township and holiday resort with a pleasant beach. The industrial and commercial areas are centred at what is known as Isipingo Rail.

The celebrated Dick King owned a farm on the site of Isipingo Rail. His homestead is now the headquarters of the local traffic department. If this had been the case in Dick King's day, he might possibly have been caught for speeding.

The N2 road continues from Isipingo directly across the coastal plain, past the airport, across the river known on account of its colour as the *Mlazi* (river like whey), past intensive housing development in areas such as *KwaNdosi* (place of the Ndosi clan), through the industrial area of *Mobeni* (place of sugar cane) and the congested business area of Clairmont, and then into Durban, 118 km from Port Shepstone.

Chapter Twenty-Four

DURBAN AND THE NORTH COAST

The metropolitan area comprising Durban, Pinetown, Inanda and Umlazi is home to close on 2 million people. Not only is the city of Durban (population 866 120) one of the loveliest and cleanest great harbours of the world, it is also an industrial centre of considerable importance and a major holiday resort which enjoys a non-stop, all-year-round season.

In the beginning it would appear that the present harbour of Durban consisted of a great lagoon which was fed by streams such as the Mhlatuzana and the Mbilo. About 100 million years ago the entire coastline subsided beneath the sea. The land eventually rose again, but to a lower level than before its submergence. The former lagoon had now become a bay almost landlocked by two elevated spits of sand formed from the silt brought down by the rivers. Sand spits such as these are a common feature of the Natal coast, where the powerful inshore current carries the silt north of the river mouths. The two sand spits of Durban comprise: in the north, what is known as the Point, composed of silt brought down to the former lagoon by its rivers; and in the south, what is known as the Bluff, probably composed of silt washed down by the river known as isiPhingo.

It is interesting to imagine this drowned lagoon at the time of the advent of man. It must have been a spacious and grand expanse of water with nothing to break its solitude save the play of the wind, the sea-birds flying incessantly over the surface, and the splashing and grunting of hippos lazing in the shallows. Around the verges of the bay where the city of Durban stands today, grew a forest, dense and secret; a place where the silence was broken only by the isolated sounds – plaintive or menacing – of wild animals.

A few African people, consisting initially of the Lala tribe and later mainly of the Luthuli clan, refugees from tribal disturbance in the north, found sanctuary in the forest around what they called *Thekwini* (the lagoon), and in the almost impenetrable bush of the high ridge of the Bluff, known to them as *siBubulungu* (the long, bulky thing). In constant fear of raids from their neighbours, these people eked out a living by planting crops in burned-out patches of bush, hunting game, and catching fish in the bay, using complex traps consisting of long fences made of reeds and poles which encircled the shallows.

The first Europeans to visit the area were mostly survivors of shipwrecks who tramped up and down the coast in search of rescue. One of these individuals was Rodrigo Tristão, who, surviving the wreck in 1552 of the Portuguese galleon *Saint John*, became the first European known to make his home in the area. He settled among the local Africans and found a living by hunting and fishing. Little did he realise that the simple hut in which he lived was standing on the site of a future city and that the tranquil bay would one day be lined with wharves and sheds.

Over the years, other odd characters found their way to the shores of the bay. It is noted in old shipping chronicles that even a penitent pirate who turned honest, sequestered himself from his former companions in that lonely place. A few traders occasionally visited the area, but there was little of commercial value since the resident Africans were poverty stricken and possessed neither ivory nor slaves for export. To this stretch of coast the Portuguese navigator, Vasco da Gama, had applied the name *Natal* (nativity) because he had first seen it on Christmas Day 1497. The entrance to the bay became known as the *Rio de Natal* (river of the nativity).

Fate took a hand in shaping the future of the Rio de Natal. In the north, 250 km away, the Zulu nation was formed at the beginning of the 19th century. Their wealth provided a market for trade. In 1823 merchants from the Cape chartered a brig named *Salisbury* commanded by Lt James King and sent it up to the coast of Natal in hope of finding a suitable harbour to use as a base for trade with the Zulus.

With Lt King sailed a friend of his, Lt George Farewell and J A Thomson, one of the merchants who had chartered the ship. In November 1823 the *Salisbury* eventually anchored in front of the entrance to the Rio de Natal. The explorers were interested in the place, but hesitated, thinking that the entrance would prove too shallow for a ship to pass. Fate once again took a hand in the game. A squall blew up. The ship was anchored dangerously close to the shore. If the anchor dragged the consequences would be disastrous. The explorers found their minds made up for them. With a few rolls and an alarming bump, they sailed straight across the bar. To their delight they found themselves safely on the waters of the great harbour, completely protected from the weather.

This was the real beginning of Durban. The explorers were jubilant at what they had found. They returned to the Cape to organise a trading venture, hopeful of government support in the establishment of a settlement. The government proved hesitant, but private means and men were found. In May 1824 the 25 ton *Julia*, under the command of a young man, Henry Francis Fynn, was sent to the area with a party on board who were to commence the settlement. It was these men who cut the first clearing in the bush *'opposite the present church of St Paul's in Durban, where the railway station stands'*, and built there a house, 4 metres square, made of wattle and daub.

Thus Durban was created by a population of 26 hard-living traders and ivory hunters. Life for these men was solitary and precarious. The Zulus tolerated the settlement as being convenient for trade, but kept a sharp watch on the activities of the settlers by means of a garrison established in a stronghold suggestively named *uKangel' amankengane* (watch the vagabonds). From the name of this has been derived the modern corruption of *Congella*, now a suburb of Durban.

The name of Durban was itself bestowed on 23 June 1835 when the traders and the missionary Reverend Allen Gardiner held a meeting for laying out of a town. They named the place after the Governor of the Cape, Sir Benjamin D'Urban, the apostrophe being later conveniently forgotten.

The advent of the Voortrekkers in 1838 and the dismal events surrounding the killing of Piet Retief and many of his followers, left the settlers of Durban in a state of alarm. They joined forces with the Voortrekkers. Durban became a part of the short-lived Natal Republic. In May 1842 Durban reverted to British control with the arrival of a garrison under Captain Thomas Smith. The soldiers made their stronghold in what is now known as the Old Fort. In this defensive work they withstood a siege by the Voortrekkers of 34 days (relieved on 26 June 1842). It was during this siege that Dick King made his celebrated 950 km ride in ten days to carry news to Grahamstown of the predicament of the garrison.

DICK KING AND HIS RIDE

Richard (Dick) Philip King was born in England in 1813 and was nine years old when his family came to South Africa in a group of 1820 Settlers. He grew up in the hard environment that was the frontier and consequently became resolute, tough and taciturn, prepared to try his hand at anything. He first arrived in Natal in 1828 as the servant of two explorers, Dr Alexander Cowie and Benjamin Green. King liked what he saw of Port Natal and remained there while the two explorers went on to Mozambique where they eventually died of fever.

Dick King worked for several of the ivory traders and accompanied Captain Allen Gardiner, the missionary, on his exploration of the inland areas and the Drakensberg in 1835. He was in Durban when the news of the killing of Piet Retief and his men at *uMgungundlovu* reached the ivory traders. Dick King set out immediately to warn the Voortrekker encampments below the Drakensberg, reaching them a day after the Zulu army had wiped out their advance camps. He remained with the trekkers, defending the rear camps, and then returned to Durban when the Zulus withdrew.

Together with Robert Biggar, several other ivory traders and their African followers, Dick King fought the Zulus and narrowly escaped when most of this little army was wiped out at Ndondakusuka. A few surviving traders and Dick King hid on Salisbury island. He remained in Durban when the Voortrekkers arrived and the area became part of the Natal Republic.

When the British arrived and the Voortrekkers besieged them in what is known as the Old Fort, Dick King was on board the trading vessel *Mazeppa,* which was anchored in the bay. The British garrison was in a hopeless position: short of food and ammunition, and completely isolated. Their only hope was relief from the Cape.

On the night of 25 May 1842 one of the senior traders, George C Cato, went aboard the *Mazeppa* and woke Dick King. The commander of the garrison, Captain Thomas Smith, had sent a message asking King to ride to Grahamstown and warn the authorities there of the danger in Port Natal. King asked no questions. He dressed hurriedly, went ashore, woke his 16-year-old servant Ndongeni and selected two good horses, a saddle and stirrups. At midnight a boat ferried them across the bay, with the horses swimming behind. They landed on Salisbury island and there Ndongeni decided to ride with his master, although he had no saddle. They whispered a farewell to the boatmen and set out across the shallow mangrove swamps, following a secret path to avoid Voortrekker picket posts.

On the far side of the bay dwelt a friendly chief named Mnini, who agreed to obliterate their trail. Then began a journey of nearly 1 000 km. There were reputedly 122 rivers and streams to ford and no road or continuous path to follow. There were wild animals and unknown dangers to face as well as the prospect of descending and climbing one deep valley after another.

For Ndongeni the journey became unbearable. Without saddle or stirrups he still managed about half the distance and was then forced to stop. Dick King, on his horse Somerset, reached Grahamstown after ten days, despite a delay owing to sickness. Reinforcements were hastily shipped from Port Elizabeth to relieve the siege in Port Natal. The first of these arrived in the bay on 24 June, followed shortly afterwards by others. On 26 June the siege was broken.

Dick King and Ndongeni were rewarded for their ride. Ndongeni settled on a grant of land he was given on the northern bank of the Mzimkulu River, where his grave lies today. Dick King also received a grant of land at Isipingo, south of Durban. He opened a butcher's shop in Kings Street, Durban and later, in 1859, moved to Isipingo where he ran a sugar mill. He died in Isipingo in 1871. His house became the headquarters of the Isipingo Traffic Department.

The impressive equestrian monument to Dick King was erected on the Durban embankment in 1915. It was designed by Wallace Paton and sculpted by H H Grellier. The monument was financed by public subscription organised by Miss Ethel Campbell, who knew Ndongeni and wrote a book about the great ride.

Near this statue, in the Guild Hall arcade, is the African Art Centre, which displays and sells a tremendous collection of African arts and crafts. Profits are used to promote the traditional artistic heritage of the African people.

When Natal was proclaimed a British colony and annexed to the Cape on 31 May 1844, Durban commenced its growth as a port and gateway to the interior of Southern Africa. Settlers came from Europe; explorers, hunters and prospectors passed through the place with their eager eyes fixed on distant horizons, merchants established stores and warehouses. For several years ivory and skins were the principal exports.

An early problem concerned the depth of the bar (the shallow entrance to the harbour). The bar was formed by the debris and soil eroded from the interior by the rivers and deposited along the coast, forming sand barriers across the entrances of all river mouths or inlets. Deepening this bar, which in 1855 had a low-water depth of little over 3 m, was an exceedingly difficult task. Years of hard work by the primitive dredgers of the period eventually improved the position by removing 10 million tons of spoil from the entrance and increasing the depth to 6 m by 1898. Today it is over 15 m deep at low water. The harbour is by far the principal cargo port of Southern Africa, with 18 million tons of cargo handled each year compared to the 6 million tons handled in Cape Town, South Africa's second-largest port. Among the facilities of Durban harbour are the Prince Edward Graving Dock, 352 m long, a floating dock 106,7 m long, a grain elevator storing 42 000 tons; specialised ore-loading facilities, coaling and oil-fueling facilities, bulk oil storage, and the bulk sugar export terminal with three massive storage silos with a combined capacity of 520 000 tons. Public tours of the sugar terminal can be booked. Phone (031) 301-0331.

The city of Durban originated as a scattering of wattle-and-daub shacks, half hidden in the dense coastal forest. As it grew, streets were hacked through the trees, with West Street (named after the Natal governor, Martin West) becoming the principal thoroughfare and *Smith* Street as the second most important street, named after Captain Thomas Smith, commander of the British garrison during the siege. Other important streets are: *Aliwal*, named after the victory in India of the Governor of the Cape, Sir Harry Smith; *Gardiner*, named after Captain Allen Gardiner, the pioneer missionary of Natal; *Field*, named after William Field, first magistrate; *Grey,* named after Earl Grey, Secretary of State for Colonies; *Russell*, named after Lord John Russell, the British Premier; and the *Snell* Parade, named after Edward Snell, a well-known merchant. To lend a touch of sanctity to the proceedings, *George* and *Andrew* streets were named after the saints. The rest of the city and its suburbs steadily expanded around this commercial nucleus. The residential areas, with their freely growing gardens, handsome flowering trees, brilliant sunshine, tropical warmth, and long views over the blue of the Indian Ocean, are amongst the fairest on Earth.

The famed Botanic Gardens had their beginning in 1848 when the Natal Agricultural and Horticultural Society was formed and acquired the ground for a garden. The Gardens are open 07h30 to 16h45 daily.

The Durban Philharmonic Society, organised in 1853, brought music to the town with a 12-piece band which was the ancestor of the later Durban Symphony orchestra.

Horse-racing started in 1852. The July Handicap (one of the richest horse-races in Africa), is run in Durban, which today remains a major venue for this sport. The Greyville racecourse is the scene of spectacular social gatherings.

Rickshaws, as a picturesque form of transport, were introduced to the town in 1893 by Sir Marshall Campbell, a sugar magnate. He imported the idea from Japan and trained stalwart Zulus to pull the rickshaws by himself demonstrating the techniques of drawing them. The rickshaws he imported were single-seaters but these were adapted locally into two-seaters. Notwithstanding the hostility of modern traffic authorities (who considered them a hindrance on the streets) the rickshaws long remained a feature of the Durban scene, enjoyed by visitors, and the pride of the lavishly costumed Zulus who drew them. The costumes were fantastic and the presence of these curious vehicles became a unique aspect of Durban life, much regretted when they were eventually banned from traffic congested streets. The oddly decorated vehicles and gaudily outfitted drawers still provide a colourful sight along the beachfront. These man-drawn vehicles were invented by an American missionary, the Reverend Jonathan Goble, who went to Japan in 1853 with Commander Perry. As his wife was an invalid, the missionary needed some form of transport for her. The idea of a rickshaw became fashionable in Japan, especially with high-class Geishas, while tourists also thought the vehicles novel and amusing.

Durban became a municipality in 1854 and a city in 1935. In many ways it is unique. Although it is the busiest port on the continent of Africa, it is spruce, clean and well ordered. Within easy reach of the great inland mining and industrial complexes of the interior, it is almost a seaside suburb and playground for their residents. Throughout the year there is an influx of fun and holiday-seeking vacationers. The climate is hot from January to March, and warm to temperate throughout the rest of the year. The beaches are highly developed as recreational areas, having amusement parks, games, rides, gardens, entertainment and varied facilities for fishing, surfing and swimming. Although bathing is complicated by shelving slopes and a notorious back and side wash, the water has a temperature range of 21°C to 25°C and swimmers are protected by effective shark netting and all-year-round life-savers.

The City Hall, a close replica of the city hall in Belfast, Northern Ireland, was opened in 1910. Apart from municipal offices, the building houses on its second floor an art gallery exhibiting a substantial collection of paintings, statuary, ceramics and other art.

The Natural History museum (housed on the first floor of the City Hall) displays a notable collection of mammals and birds, including the most complete dodo (the long-vanished bird king of the old pigeon empire in Mauritius) to be seen anywhere in the world. Attached to the main museum, but housed in the old Court House behind the City Hall, is the Local History museum exhibiting many interesting items concerned with past years in Durban. Included is a reconstruction of the wattle-and-daub cottage of Henry Francis Fynn, one of the pioneers of Durban; an old sugar mill which still works; Miss Fann's Fancy Repository, and reconstruction of shops from the past. The art gallery, museums and library, all housed in the City Hall, are open Mondays to Saturdays 08h30 to 16h00; Sundays 11h00 to 16h00; closed Christmas and Good Friday.

Another interesting museum is the Natal settlers' Old House Museum, featuring a replica of an original Durban house in a garden setting, built in 1849 by John Goodricke. The story of Natal is revealed here in a collection of pictures, maps, guns and other items of interest. The Old House

Museum is open Mondays to Saturdays 08h30 to 17h00; Sundays and public holidays 11h00 to 17h00.

The Old Fort in which the British garrison withstood the siege, is perfectly preserved and in it seems to linger the atmosphere of the pioneer days of Port Natal. The Warriors' Gate, shrine and headquarters of the Memorable Order of Tin Hats (MOTHs) is situated adjacent to the Old Fort where numerous military relics and trophies are contained in the MOTH Museum of Militaria. There are conducted tours of the Old Fort, and the MOTH museum is open Tuesdays to Fridays and Sundays from 11h00 to 15h00; Saturdays from 10h00 to 12h00.

On the ocean front may be found the famous Fitzsimons Snake Park where a remarkable collection of reptiles is exhibited and anti-venom serum sold. The snake park is open daily from 09h00 to 17h00.

Durban's Sea World (comprising aquarium and dolphinarium), at the foot of the West Street pedestrian mall, exhibits in huge tanks many of the fish fauna of the Indian Ocean, including sharks. Research is done in the Oceanographic Research Institute on game fish, reef fish and bait organisms. Sea World is open daily from 09h00 to 21h00. The fish are fed at 11h00 and 15h30.

Some of the attractions of Durban's beachfront include: miniature golf-courses and putting games; a model yacht pond; children's paddling pools; motor boating and other delights; numerous novelty rides and amusement park entertainment and a lovers' rendezvous at the Blue Lagoon (the mouth of the Mngeni River); the Umgeni River Bird Park exhibiting about 2 000 birds 1 km up the river from Blue Lagoon; a mini-town with its own drive-in cinema and replicas of buildings in 1-in-24 scale; a sunken garden and a large ice-skating rink close to the beach. Of considerable interest to visitors is the Indian market at the top of Victoria Street just off the top end of Smith Street. African and Eastern curios, as well as many different varieties of curry, may be obtained here, blended to order from volcanic-eruption strength, through mother-in-laws tongue strength to newly wed mild.

Most of the Indian population of Durban follows the Hindu religion. The Sri Vaithianatha Easvarar Alayam temple in Umgeni road is the oldest and largest in South Africa. The Muslim section of the population make use of a mosque – the largest in Southern Africa – at the corner of Grey and Queen streets. Both of these groups stage annual festivals in Durban. The Hindu firewalking rituals, held at Easter, and the Kavady festivals in February and July, when penitents pierce various parts of their bodies with daggers, fish-hooks and needles, are bizarre but fascinating spectacles.

The beautiful gardens of Durban have already been mentioned. Apart from the Botanic Gardens with its renowned orchid house exhibiting over 3 000 plants, and a garden for the blind, there is Albert Park with its trim-track facilities; the Amphitheatre gardens behind North Beach, which have an open-air auditorium and sunken gardens; Mitchell Park and its superb lawns, trees, monkeys, aviaries and penguin pool. Medwood Gardens in West Street, opposite the City Hall, provide a pleasant little retreat in the city centre, with a graceful illuminated fountain; the Robert Jameson Park has a magnificent rose garden; and there is a Japanese water garden on the north side of the Mngeni River.

Private gardens, especially in the residential areas of the Berea, are lovely. The views of the city and harbour from this elevation are worth seeing. Also in the Berea area, in the beautiful old family home known as *Muckleneuk* of the late Sir Marshall (Mashu) Campbell, the sugar magnate, is the Campbell Collection. This consists of the Mashu Museum of Ethnology, the William Campbell Furniture Museum, and the Killie Campbell Africana Library and Museum, bequeathed to the University of Natal by William Campbell, son of Sir Marshall Campbell. Visits to these museums can be arranged by appointment only. Phone (031) 207-3432. Apart from one of the world's most important collections of Africana, visitors may see the unique series of paintings by Barbara Tyrrell, depicting the costumes worn by the tribal peoples of Southern Africa. On this assembly of several hundred exquisitely detailed paintings was based Barbara Tyrrell's classic book *Tribal Peoples of Southern Africa*. Included in the Africana are many unpublished manuscripts. The material for several important books has been researched from the wealth of information contained in this elegant home of *Muckleneuk.*

The late Miss Killie Campbell, eldest daughter of Sir Marshall, was also a renowned gardener. In the grounds of the house, her professional gardener, William Poulton, who had been trained at the famed Kew Gardens in Britain, bred several new varieties of bougainvillaea, including one named after Killie Campbell. Several other variations are named after other members of her family. Killie Campbell died in September 1965. The house and its collection was presented to the people of Durban as a museum housing the unique collection of Africana assembled by Killie. It is now maintained as a study centre by the University of Natal.

Burman Drive, a short, very attractive route from Durban (Umgeni Road) to North Ridge Road, winds for 3 km through forest country where birds and monkeys abound. Another drive leads along the Esplanade and Maydon Road around the head of the bay. Branching east into Edwin Swales VC Drive, off the main South Coast road, the route climbs the Bluff where fine views are revealed of the panorama of shipping in the great harbour, the fair city of Durban, and the blue waters of the Indian Ocean sweeping in towards a golden shore.

In 1974 a 27 ha area was established as the Bluff Nature Reserve. This area lies east of Wentworth Hospital and has been developed with wilderness trails.

ANGLING FISH AND SHARKS

The angling calendar of the Natal coast is varied and exciting. The commonest fish is barracuda, taken from the shore or by line during two seasons: December to April and June to August. Bream and musselcrackers are caught from October to January; salmon from May to September; shad from April to January; skate from September to March; and sharks principally between November and March.

The main event in the angler's calendar takes place during the first half of June, when enormous shoals of sardines appear with such regularity that opinionated anglers lay bets and endeavour to prophesy the exact day when the first shoals will be sighted. The sardines perform this annual migration along the coast from the Cape to as far north as Durban. Their proximity to the shore depends on winds and other local influences. Sometimes they keep well out to sea and frustrate the shore anglers. In other years the little fish are driven into the waves and thousands of them are washed up on the beaches.

Throughout their migration, the sardine shoals are accompanied by predators such as game fish, sharks and masses of birds, especially gannets. A prodigious number of the fish (really pilchards) are eaten, but their breeding rate is so high – each female lays about 100 000 eggs – that an enormous casualty rate is essential to prevent the sea from being swamped with fish. Anglers follow the shoals to catch the predators, while the little fish are sought by everybody interested in tasty eating. Near Durban (where water temperatures are presumably becoming too warm) the shoals turn tail. Keeping further out to sea, they return in the flow of the Mozambique–Agulhas Current to the southern end of Africa to complete their breeding life-cycle.

Sharks and the larger fish which eat the sardines practically feed themselves to death. Sharks are ruthless characters, little more than stomachs with fins. There are many of them in the warm waters of the African east coast. The visitors to the coast should bear their presence in mind and know something about their habits and the precautions which have been adopted against them.

Eighty of the 400 known species of sharks and their close relations, dogfishes, inhabit the sea around Southern Africa. The reason for this concentration is that the fish, seals, penguins and other creatures to which sharks are partial, are in plentiful supply. Although human beings are more of a novelty on the shark's menu, they nevertheless provide very acceptable provender for eight species of sharks. If, through accident or carelessness, human beings appear within easy reach in water conditions suitable to sharks, they will be attacked.

Little is known about the habits of sharks but, for some reason, records show that very few attacks take place in water below 20°C, while in water above 25°C attacks are common. Most of the eight species of sharks which are dangerous to mankind are concentrated in the warm Mozambique Current. Off the Natal coast conditions throughout the year make them extremely dangerous. The sharks are at the height of their activity during summer owing to the high water temperature and the fact that flooding rivers discharge so much silt into the sea on the Natal coast that the water becomes turbid, the result of which is a 3 km wide brown ribbon running the length of the coast. It is in this strip that death lurks.

Natal beaches tend to shelve steeply into deep water, a condition which attracts sharks, while further down the Mozambique–Agulhas Current, off the Cape coast, the beaches shelve more gradually. The shallow water deters the sharks from venturing in too close, the water temperature dwindles below the danger level, and the rivers do not pollute the sea with mud to anywhere near the same extent as off the coast of Natal. Sharks are still present – they are found in all oceans – but they cause little trouble unless provoked. In False Bay, where the Mozambique–Agulhas Current ends, many great white sharks (the most fearsome of all) live on the rich concentration of fish and seals, but seldom attack people swimming and surfing off the gently sloping beaches. Occasionally there is a clash between sharks and fishing boats. Sharks apparently resent competition, and in the deeper waters of Macassar beach in False Bay they have been known to rub tentatively against the sides of boats, an ominous action they employ to 'taste' a potential victim. They generally disregard the boats once the tasting proves them to be unpalatable, and swim off. One gigantic individual, known locally as 'the submarine', is a great white shark of such formidable proportions that it would be perfectly capable of staving in the sides of a fishing vessel. It is renowned for its exploratory rubbing against the sides of boats but it has never attacked. Giant great white sharks have been caught in False Bay and exhibited in America and Europe.

Many vicious attacks have been made on human beings along the Natal coast. To prevent this from occurring and to study the sharks, the Provincial Council maintains the Natal Shark Measures Board which has its headquarters in Umhlanga Rocks.

Under the control of the board, bathing beaches at various resorts are protected by large nets suspended in the water but not necessarily forming continuous barriers. In order to survive, sharks have to keep moving constantly. They are highly nervous of either a reef or net standing between them and the open sea. They might be trapped at low tide or prevented from making a quick getaway. Every year off Durban, about 400 sharks are caught in nets and die as a result. Their struggles in turn serve to drive other sharks away.

Where the use of nets is impractical owing to powerful currents at certain resorts along the coast, continuous metal fences are erected around bathing areas. Persistent fishing and hunting for sharks also depletes the shark population. Several species have commercial value; their flesh, livers and fins are exported to the East where they are regarded as delicacies.

One of the most notorious sharks, the great white, is also known as the white death, blue pointer, or simply as the man-eater shark. The film *Blue Water, White Death*, depicts these and other species of sharks in all their power and ruthlessness. Many of the remarkable underwater sequences in the film were taken in the deep sea off Durban. Great whites grow to about 12 m in length and are capable of swallowing a human being whole. Even larger individuals are sometimes sighted, such as 'the submarine' in False Bay, reputed to be at least 15 m long. Teeth 127 mm in length have been found. It is estimated that the fish from which they came must have been about 30 m long. One shark of 5 m, caught off the South African coast, contained in its stomach the foot of a man, half a goat, two pumpkins, a wicker-covered scent bottle, two large fish, another shark and various other oddments.

Also a very dangerous shark is the Zambezi river shark. Similar in nature to the great white, it is an aggressive, mobile, ever-hungry stomach that swims. It favours shallow, muddy water and frequents estuaries, lagoons and even ventures up rivers for some distance. A formidably audacious creature, it reaches a length of 3 m.

The blue shark, attaining a length of 6 m, is a deep-water shark. It seldom approaches near enough to shore to be a nuisance to man.

The mako shark is also a deep-water shark. Speedy, dangerous and up to 5 m in length, it generally keeps out to sea, but does not hesitate to charge boats which disturb its hunting. It leaps clear of the water, sometimes landing in boats, creating havoc and huge splashes.

Hammerhead sharks have weirdly shaped double-hammer heads with eyes on the extremities. They grow to more than 7 m. They are aggressive but for some reason are not as dangerous in South African waters as in some tropical parts of the world. They provide anglers with great sport on the Wild Coast, where kite fishermen catch them in deep water at places such as Mazeppa Bay.

Whale sharks, a whopping 15 m in length, usually do not attack unless provoked.

Long-fin and bulldog sharks are also killers but fortunately avoid shallow water close to the coast.

The grey shark grows to 3 m but remains out to sea. It provides good eating and is considered a fine sporting fish by fishermen. The dusky or ridgeback grey shark is the commonest species found off the Natal coast.

The tiger shark reaches a length of 5 m and is a great menace along the coast, endlessly scavenging close to the shore. A 5 m specimen taken at Durban had in its stomach the head and forequarters of a crocodile, the hind leg of a sheep, three seagulls, two intact 1 kg cans of green peas and a cigarette tin.

THE OLD NORTH COAST ROAD

Along this road (essentially the Sugar Way), the traveller journeys as though on a ship, across an undulating sea of green sugar cane where occasional inhabited islands, consisting of towns and mills, emerge from the plantations. An interesting circular drive leads from Durban up this Sugar Way to Stanger, and back via the main N2 road (Shaka's Way) which, coming down from KwaZulu joins the old North Coast route at this point and then sweeps on southwards to Durban, hugging the coastline.

From Durban, the old North Coast road leads out of the city past the beautiful fairways and trees of the Windsor Park golf-course. At 4,5 km it crosses the river known as the *Mngeni* (place of acacia trees). On the left bank of the river, the road meanders through the handsome northern suburbs of Durban, with their sunny-looking houses, gardens and trees.

At 10 km from Durban the road passes through the Indian residential area of *Avoca* (named from the poem by Thomas Moore in which he writes of the 'sweet vale of Avoca') and at 11 km reaches a junction. Straight ahead (north-westwards) a road continues through the residential area of *Duff's Road* (named after Thomas Duff, a sugar cane farmer in the area during the 1870s) past the great African township of *kwaMashu* (the place of Mashu, the Zulu name given to Sir Marshall Campbell, the sugar magnate and introducer of the rickshaw to Durban). From here, a fine scenic drive stretches up into the green hills, reaching the magisterial centre of *Inanda* (the pleasant place) 24 km from Durban. The tarmac road ends at this point, but two gravel branches (especially the left branch) lead to some beautiful viewsites overlooking the great Valley of a Thousand Hills, through which flows the Mngeni River. This is a superlative piece of hill country, with several special features of interest.

In 1904 the famed Ohlange Institute was founded by Doctor John Dube in the Nanda Hills. Dube, a pastor of the American Board of Missions, had visited America and been much influenced by the work of Booker T Washington.

When he returned to Natal, Dube resigned his mission post and founded his institute. It was unique for that time in that it was African-controlled, although its teachers were paid by the government. It is a school which educates pupils up to matriculation standard, and has academic, commerce, trades and agricultural sections. Holding 700 pupils and a staff of thirty, the building and all the plant were erected and are maintained by Africans. Dube himself was a brilliant man, who not only founded the institute and the Natal Native Congress but also started the newspaper *Ilanga Lase Natal*, and was the first African to be awarded the degree of Doctor of Philosophy by the University of South Africa. He died in 1946.

Another interesting establishment in the area was the *Phoenix Settlement*. In 1893 the earnest young lawyer, Mahatma Karamchand Gandhi, was sent to South Africa from India to participate in a Transvaal lawsuit. On the train inland from Durban he was ordered out of the first-class section on the grounds of his colour. He spent a cold night on Pietermaritzburg railway station cogitating on the meaning of racial prejudice. This experience was the great turning point of a momentous life.

After settling the lawsuit out of court, Gandhi decided to make his home in Natal and aid his fellow Indians who were to be debarred from the vote in Natal's first responsible government. For the next twenty-one years Gandhi was a powerful figure in the world of the South African Indian. His experience influenced much of his future career and the formulation of the famous doctrine of *satyagraha* (passive resistance).

Trains seemed to play a particular part in the life of Gandhi. Reading Ruskin's *Unto the Last* on a train one day, he determined to mould his life in accordance with its teachings. He established the Phoenix Settlement in the Nanda district. It was a farm settlement where all workers drew the same wage and produced in spare time the influential newspaper *Indian Opinion*. When Gandhi returned to India in 1914 he left a trust to manage the settlement.

Two years after Gandhi's departure, the renowned African prophet and faith healer, Isaiah Shembe, founded his village of *ekuPhakameni* (place of spiritual uplift). Shembe had been born in the Drakensberg about 1869. At an early age he began to have visions. He claimed divine guidance, became a faith healer and preached throughout most of South Africa. Eventually, he settled in Durban in 1911 and formed his Nazarite church.

Shembe then bought thirty-eight acres of land in the Nanda district and founded ekuPhakameni. He died on 2nd May 1935, leaving his son, Johannes Galilee Shembe, to carry on control of an all-African religious movement, notable for its spectacular ceremonies and four big festivals each year, in January, April, July and September. Shembe's grave at ekuPhakameni has become a shrine for the movement, one of the most active of all African churches.

EDMUND MOREWOOD AND THE SUGAR INDUSTRY

Edmund Morewood was a travelling man from Britain who arrived in Durban during the time of its control by the Voortrekkers as part of the Republic of Natal. In Durban he was appointed harbour-master and superintendent of customs. He retained this position until the second British occupation.

Morewood then became manager of an experimental cotton plantation on the Mdloti River. On the North Coast he met several former sugar planters from the island of Mauritius. Hard hit by the temporary collapse of sugar prices in 1847, they had migrated to Natal and, like Morewood, were trying to find crops suitable for cultivation in their new homeland.

Among these immigrants from Mauritius there was frequent speculation about sugar prospects in Natal. An indigenous variety of cane, known as *iMpha*, flourished and was eaten with relish by the Africans but its sugar content was so low as to be uncommercial. Nevertheless, speculation continued. In September 1847 the Durban firm of Messrs Milner Brothers, which maintained a trade with Mauritius, made a trial importation of a cargo of seeds and shoots of various Mauritian and Réunion island crops. Included in the cargo were 40 000 tops of an inferior variety of sugar cane, known as *Mauritius Red Cane*.

This mixed cargo was sold by auction and a number of people experimentally planted the cane. The Milner brothers disseminated such information about the cultivation of the cane as they had been able to glean on the islands, and all Natal watched the experiment with interest. '*What a change would come over the spirit of affairs here*', wrote the *Natal Witness* wistfully on 22 October 1847, '*if, instead of the useless iMpha – sweet cane – a like quantity of the genuine plant were raised and manufactured*'.

The following year, one of the best known of the North Coast's early settlers, Ephraim Frederick Rathbone, arrived from Mauritius. He was interested to see the luxuriant growth of the patches of cane imported the previous year, and was very full of the matter when he journeyed up to the Mdloti River to become an overseer on the Cotton Company's estate, under Edmund Morewood.

Rathbone made Morewood interested in sugar. From a small patch of the imported cane, growing on the farm of Mr Pell at the Mngeni River, he secured some tops to plant an experimental ha on the Cotton Company's ground in February 1849.

The Cotton Company, however, was not interested in sugar. The project would have languished but, late in 1849, Morewood left the company to take up a farm of his own named *Compensation*, between the Tongati and Mhlali rivers. He had received this farm from the government as 'compensation' (hence the name) for land he had owned in Durban which was required by the State. Morewood had become personally interested in sugar. In October of that year he removed the growing cane to his own farm and, with such funds as he possessed, he struggled to prove sugar as an economic crop for Natal from the Cotton Company's farm.

In 1850 Morewood built a crude sugar mill, the first in Natal. With this he managed to produce the first sugar from his first crop in 1851. This success set many hearts beating at a faster rate. *Compensation* farm became a focal point of interest. Innumerable visitors journeyed up the North Coast to the farm to view the beginning of Natal's sugar industry. Hospitality was a strain on Morewood, for he was a bachelor. He had little on his farm save an untidy house, a galvanised iron sugar manufactory and very well-tilled fields. Cane from Morewood's plantation was carried all along the coast of Natal. In addition, tremendous publicity was given to the North Coast as an ideal sugar-growing area. Many new settlers hastened to obtain farms.

The sugar industry went ahead at a great rate. One plantation after another was commenced. In July 1853 M Jeffels of the IsiPhingo River area imported the first proper sugar mill and plant. By 1855 sugar was being produced on a commercial scale, with a third mill at Springfield, that of the Natal Sugar Company of J B and H Milner, adding its output to that of the first two establishments.

The industry had no easy beginning. Transport was non-existent and roads along the coast were atrocious. Occasional floods also did great damage. In April 1856 most of the young cane plantations were half washed away and the mills, all established near the banks of rivers, suffered grievous damage. In the four days' downpour, from the 12th of that month, 686 mm of rain fell. The Mngeni River came down 6 m high, and for a few days Durban was part of its mouth.

'The Springfield Plantation, three miles from Durban, was under water', wrote Bishop John William Colenso. *'The current rushed through the mill with a depth of nine feet and an impetuosity which enabled it to carry the heavy pans of the boiling battery clean out of the masonry. During the height of the flood, a large elephant was swept past the mill, struggling with the stream and sounding a furious alarm with its trumpet'*.

To many, the problem of plantation labour seemed to be the greatest stumbling block in the establishment of sugar. There was an immediate clamour that some measure should be introduced to import cheap and plentiful labour.

To a number of those in the sugar industry, this clamour of labour scarcity was unreasonable. *'During many years' residence here in Natal'*, wrote Morewood to the *Natal Mercury* on 18 January 1853, *'I have never experienced such a want, and could name many persons who are in the same position. The plain fact is that those who treat the natives properly can at all times secure the number of servants they require, and the cry of "want of labour" is almost exclusively raised by persons who either cannot afford to employ servants or expect unreasonable returns for small pay and cheap food'*.

The craze for cheap labour, however, had already warped the outlook of Natal planters too much for them to approach such a problem with foresight. They pointed out that they were establishing the industry in the face of the fact that sugar could be dumped in Natal by foreign growers at a price uneconomic to local farmers. Therefore, cheap labour and tariff protection was imperative. Those who considered that any industry established on such a basis could turn out more bitterness than sweetness for the country were soon shouted down.

One petition after another was sent to the Governor, praying for aid in the labour problem. The government duly investigated the question of overseas recruitment. In the end, on 16 November 1860, the barque, *Truro*, arrived in Durban with the first load of 341 Indian labourers, mainly Hindus, recruited from the Madras Presidency.

It was the start of a new epoch in Natal. Nineteen other immigrant ships followed, bringing 6 000 Indian labourers. The planters were delighted. The Indians were under contract at 10 shillings a month for the first year. This was increased each year, until the labourer received a maximum of 14 shillings a month in the fifth year. Labourers could be arrested by the police if they were found more than a mile from their place of employment. Females received five shillings a month with annual increases of 6d a month. Rations and quarters were provided by the employers. At the end of five years' service the labourer was free of his contract and could do as he pleased. Naturally his pleasure was not to continue working for 14 shillings a month. The free tickets which the planters were obliged to offer back to wretched conditions in India were also not much in demand. As early as 1856, Baboo Naidoo, an interpreter and high-caste man, had opened the first Indian store in Natal. It was in Field Street, Durban and sold Asiatic condiments and delicacies.

Morewood's enterprise had certainly popularised the Natal North Coast. As for himself, he recovered nothing from his labours. Short of capital from the start, he spent what little he had in establishing sugar cane as a practical crop. Then he went bankrupt before he could enjoy any legitimate reward. He left Natal and removed to England, then to Germany, and then to Brazil, where he died. The Morewood Memorial Garden is a national monument dedicated to his memory. It has been erected on the site of Morewood's primitive little factory. The foundations of the factory buildings have been conserved and the pond is on the site of the original mill pond from which Morewood drew water for the factory. Nothing is left of Morewood's mill but there is a replica of one of the early mills built in later times. From Morewood's pioneer work has developed a major industry with fifteen large mills producing about two million tons of sugar a year from cane grown on 418 000 ha of land.

The North Coast is the largest of the five sugar-producing areas of South Africa with 112 385 ha covered in cane and three mills, Darnall, Gledhow and Maidstone. Zululand is a close second with 108 665 ha under cane and four mills, Amatikulu, Entumeni, Felixton and Umfolozi. The Midlands of Natal is the third region with 78 192 ha under cane and three mills Eston, Union Co-op and Noodsberg. The South Coast is fourth with 69 322 ha under cane and two mills, Sezela and Umzimkulu. Mpumulanga (Northern Irrigation Region) is fifth with 49 972 ha and three mills, Komatipoort, Malelane and Pongolo.

Today the North Coast is one of the most important economic areas in Natal. Since Morewood's pioneering days the sugar industry has developed into an immense activity. From the 1860s, when there were twenty-seven small sugar mills turning out about 2 000 tons a year, the industry on the North Coast has three giant mills at Darnall, Gledhow and Maidstone combining to produce some 600 000 tons of sugar a year, nearly half of the total output of South Africa.

Administratively, the area has developed along with its population. Inanda became a separate administrative post back in 1851 when L E Mesham was sent there, and in 1854 was promoted from Assistant to the first full Resident Magistrate. Several other new magistracies have been established since then. In 1894, the Norwegian mission station of *Maphumulo* (the place of rest) became an administrative seat. W R Gordon, last of the border agents, transferred there as first magistrate from the old, so-called, *Insurance Office*, first established by Captain Walmsley.

In January 1890 F E Foxon had been sent to *eMbumbulu* (the place of the round knoll), to open a Native Administrative office. In 1894 this office was removed to the high *Ndwedwe* (narrow tableland), lying between the coastal plains and the beautiful valley of the upper Mdloti River. There it remains today, looking at what is without doubt one of the most superb views to be seen in South Africa.

The old North Coast road continues northwards from the point where the Inanda road branches off (12 km from Durban). Five kilometres from the junction, the road passes the town 18 km from Durban, known as ...

MOUNT EDGECOMBE

Named in honour of the Earl of Mount Edgecumb in Cornwall, with its name slightly misspelt in Natal, *Mount Edgecombe* was once a sugar community and the creation of the Campbell pioneer family, with a garden setting of hibiscus in many shades, cannas, bougainvillaeas and fine trees. A picturesque Hindu temple graces the exit of the town on its northern side. The Mount Edgecombe Sugar Mill was closed down in 1994 and it is envisaged that the whole area will become a distinctive, middle-sized town on Durban's northern periphery, catering for a variety of residential employment and recreational needs of lower, middle and higher income groups.

THE CAMPBELL FAMILY

Mount Edgecombe will always be associated with memories of the Campbell family and their company, The Natal Estates Ltd. The Campbells were of Scots descent and in the 1840s had their home in Glasgow where William John Campbell, at the age of 14, became a railway man and family breadwinner.

Times were not easy in Scotland but he was a hard worker. By the time he was 29 he had become manager of the line between Glasgow and Paisley. In 1850 William decided to emigrate to Natal under the Byrne Emigration Scheme. With his wife Mary and three small children he landed in Durban on 28 June 1850 and was allotted 70 acres of land at Richmond. The quality of land there dissatisfied him. He wanted to grow sugar cane. He exchanged his land at Richmond for land on the Mdloti River and named his new farm *Muckleneuk,* which in Scottish means 'big bend'. The big bend in the Mdloti which he could see from his farm reminded him of a similar view from his home in Glasgow above the River Cart.

Campbell's first cane was crushed in his own steam mill in 1861. From this beginning started what was to become one of the largest miller-cum-planter cane growing estates in Southern Africa with its own sugar mill and refinery. Campbell's two sons, William and Marshall, grew up with sugar in their minds, hearts and blood. Both joined their father in sugar production as soon as they finished school. Marshall Campbell, known to the Zulus as *Mashu,* soon proved a natural leader. With a partner, David Don, he acquired the sugar mill at Mount Edgecombe and in 1895 established the company named Natal Estates Ltd. Most of the sugar estates surrounding Mount Edgecombe were steadily acquired by this Company.

Marshall became a member of the Natal Legislative Council. He represented the coast district in the Upper House of the Natal Parliament and became a Senator for Natal on formation of the Union of South Africa in 1910. He was knighted shortly before his death in 1917 and left many pleasant memories of himself. Not least of these was his introduction of rickshaws to Durban and the naming after him of the vast township of *KwaMashu* (the place of Marshall).

Sir Marshall was succeeded by his son William Alfred Campbell, generally known as 'Wac'. Born in 1880 on the Cornubia Sugar Estate near Mount Edgecombe, he became Managing Director of the Natal Estates Ltd when he was 32 and retained that position until his death in 1962 at the age of 82. 'Wac' was responsible for many innovations in the sugar industry. The Natal Estates Ltd was developed into a massive sugar producing enterprise, the first in Natal to use large scale irrigation with water lifted from the Mngeni River, and fed into an extensive network of canals and storage dams. He introduced electricity to the sugar factories, good housing, and created recreational facilities for his staff and visitors, including the magnificent Mount Edgecombe golf-course, one of the finest in Southern Africa. The course was opened with 9 holes on 24 April 1926 and then extended to 18 holes in 1935.

'Wac' was a hunter and owner of the *Malamala* game farm in the Sabi-Sand private game reserve next to the Kruger National Park. This, and adjoining land, became the winter hunting resort of the Campbell family. The story of how this farm was later developed into the renowned game viewing luxury resort of today is told in Chapter Thirty-Seven.

Over the last 30 years, pressures for urban development have built up around Mount Edgecombe and have created the need for the move away from a company-run 'sugar' village into a viable modern town. The 'new' Mount Edgecombe Estate initially managed by a local authority in the form of a town board, is soon to become part of the Durban Metro. A Natal Victorian architectural theme has been introduced to harmonise with the design of a new clubhouse (no longer wood and asbestos) and this together with extensive landscaping, gives Mount Edgecombe Estate its own character. A second 18-hole golf-course and housing estate replacing some of the original The Natal Estates Limited sugar cane fields has been created.

Five kilometres further on, the road passes through the village of Ottawa, and a further 3 km (27 km from Durban) brings the traveller into the atmospheric village of ...

VERULAM

Lying on the slopes of the valley of the river known as the *Mdloti* after the wild tobacco plants found on its banks. Verulam was established in 1850 with the influx of British immigrants to Natal. A party of these people, led by Thomas Champeon, under the patronage of the Earl of Verulam, made their home around the future village which later became the magisterial seat for the county of Victoria. Today, Verulam is a modern town where intriguing glimpses may still be seen of the elegant homesteads, gardens and cemeteries dating back to the genteel but antique days of 'sugar barons'. The original settlers' Methodist Church still stands in Church Street. The Shri Gopalall

Hindu Temple was opened by Mahatma Gandhi in 1913. The Hazelmere Public Resort nature reserve, 304 ha in extent, provides a pleasant recreational area. There is swimming, watersports, nature walks, and campsites.

Crossing the Mdloti River (28 km from Durban), with a turn-off north-west to Canelands (1 km) and Ndwedwe (32 km), the old North Coast road continues northwards across the cane fields and, 34 km from Durban, reaches the town of ...

TONGAAT

A 6,2 km long main street, shaded by jacaranda and poinciana trees, leads past an interesting mix of new and old commercial buildings. The name *Tongaat* comes from the Thongathi River, so named from the *Strychnos makenil* trees growing along its banks.

The population of the town is now mainly Indian. Two of their temples are notable: the Juggernathi Puri (a national monument) and the Vishmarorp. There is a market renowned for its subtropical fruits, including very delicious litchis in December. The first railway building has been preserved and is now used as a library. The Amanzimnyama Park gardens provide a pleasant stroll and the river has fine reaches with many views and offers a glimpse of wildlife.

Tongaat was proclaimed a township on 21 June 1945. North of the village, the old North Coast road bridges the river (41 km from Durban), passing the handsome, white-coloured office (with its pretty fountains) originally built for Messrs Moreland Molasses (now Voermol). Just beyond this complex stands the equally imposing entrance to the Tongaat-Hulett Sugar Estate mills and office. A beautifully laid out golf-course in a setting of palms and other trees, surrounded by a green sea of sugar cane, makes this one of the most pleasant parts of the North Coast.

This area is the historic home of the sugar industry of Natal. Past the wayside Fairbreeze hotel, the road (48 km from Durban) reaches *Compensation*, the farm on which the pioneer, Edmund Morewood, produced the first commercial sugar in Natal in 1851. There is an interesting memorial to this endeavour. From *Compensation* a gravel road branches westwards for 1 km where a turn-off south leads for another kilometre to the site of Morewood's first sugar mill.

THE SAUNDERS FAMILY

The town of Tongaat will always be associated with the name of the Saunders family whose founder in Natal was James Renault Saunders, one of the leading personalities of the sugar industry in South Africa. He was born in Port Louis, Mauritius, on 3 January 1818. He was the son of James Ferguson Saunders who had reached Mauritius in 1810 in the service of Major-General Abercrombie, sent by the British to capture what was then known as the *Isle de France* (Mauritius), described by Captain Keating, one of the British naval officers, as *'a vile nest of buccaneers against our Oriental commerce'*. The famed corsairs of the Isle de France had, in fact, caused much grief to British trade with the East.

With the capture of Mauritius and the ending of the Napoleonic wars, James Ferguson Saunders settled on the island. He became a merchant in partnership with a Dane named Johan Wiehe. In 1823 the Saunders family returned to Britain where the father established a sugar importing business, Saunders and Company, and stood for parliament. His son was educated in Britain at Charterhouse.

The year 1830 saw economic problems. Saunders and Company in Britain and Wiehe et Saunders in Mauritius both came to grief. James Renault Saunders finished his education in a difficult period. In 1837 he returned to Mauritius and found employment managing a sugar estate named *La Laura* after his mother. It was a time of great disturbances in the sugar industry of Mauritius. The British had finally abolished slavery as from 1 February 1835. Slave owners received compensation for their emancipated slaves, and the British allowed Mauritian sugar to be imported into Britain on the same terms as the product of the West Indies. This gave the planters a simultaneous fresh capitalisation and a vast new market for their product. The trouble was labour. The freed slaves almost to a man refused to accept employment in the sugar industry which had for them more bitter memories than sweet. They wanted freedom from bondage and the chance to remake at least something of shattered lives. The answer was the recruitment of cheap labour from India.

James Renault Saunders returned to England in 1850 and on a visit to Germany met Katherine Wheelwright, studying painting and languages. He married her in 1851. In 1854, with his wife and baby daughter he immigrated to Natal to manage affairs for a property syndicate named The Natal Company of which he was a partner. Among the assets of the company was Edward Chiappini's Tongaati Sugar Estate. By 1860, the year in which it was dissolved, the syndicate had acquired 100 000 acres of land in Natal. Included in this was the farm *Buffelskloof.* On this farm, 144 one acre erven were laid out by the surveyor George Adam. This was at first called the village of Victoria but then became the township of Tongaat. On the adjoining farm of *Klipfontein*, the owner, Jan Meyer, had been killed by a leopard in 1857. The farm had been acquired by The Natal Company and the homestead, with the name of Tongaat House, became the residence of the Saunders family. Saunders became a great leader of the residents of Victoria County north of the Mngeni River. He worked for several years to persuade the government to build a bridge across the Mngeni River. This first bridge, known as Queen's Bridge, was eventually opened on 22 September 1864. There was great delight among the community south and north of the river that at last they had a road link more reliable than a fording place often unusable through floods.

Unfortunately the Queen's Bridge only lasted three years. The Mngeni then rose seven metres in a flood and washed away the entire structure. The military immediately constructed an emergency temporary pontoon bridge, to be paid for by tolls. The bridge remained intact for many years and was very profitable from the tolls.

Saunders also achieved the construction of a bridge over the Thongathi River, the formation of an efficient police force, a greater autonomy for Natal, and the introduction of Indian indentured labour on the sugar plantations. On his death in July 1892 he was succeeded by his youngest son, Edward, then 31 years of age.

Edward Saunders continued his father's objectives of expansion and development. In 1895 he formed a partnership with a Scots financier, William Mirrlees, and founded The Tongaat Sugar Company Ltd. In the same year the Natal Central Sugar Company at Mount Edgecombe, founded by Marshall Campbell, later The Natal Estates Ltd, showed its confidence by lending Tongaat £61 000 to build and equip a larger mill and other related expansion. The partnership between Mirrlees and Edward was dissolved in 1898 and in 1899 Edward floated the new Tongaat Sugar Company Ltd, with its head office in Liverpool, while further expansion took place in 1904 to cope with increasing quantities of cane.

In 1918 Edward was responsible for moving the Company's head office from Liverpool to Tongaat. A second sugar mill was built at Maidstone and for a period of five years both mills ran concurrently. In 1928 the first mill at Tongaat closed down and the area of Maidstone became the centre point around which the company's head office, employees' homes, and recreational facilities were built. The mill continued to produce sugar down to the present time.

Edward Saunders died on 10 September 1939. His eldest son, James, who served in the Coldstream Guards during the first World War, was killed in France on 4 November 1918, just one week before the War ended. Thus the mantle of succession fell on Edward's younger son Edward Douglas, known as Douglas, who was born at Tongaat on 13 August 1901. He had been appointed assistant general manager in August 1927, and joined the board of Tongaat two months later. He took over control of Tongaat as Managing Director in 1939 and was appointed Chairman in 1941.

Douglas was a man of many parts, who placed his indelible stamp upon this area called Tongaat, upon The Tongaat Sugar Company and on everything for which Tongaat stood. Like his father and grandfather before him, he was a hard-headed businessman. He had a brilliant brain, knew what he wanted and worked tirelessly towards the aims he set himself. He did a great deal to enhance the statue of Tongaat as a sugar entity. His acquisition of the Prospecton Mill at Isipingo, and thereafter the Central Factory mill at Canelands, changed the entire economic structure of the company. He stood by his word and expected others to stand by theirs. He set a great example and in doing so laid the foundation for the philosophy followed by The Tongaat-Hulett Group today.

The developments for which his name will go down in history relate to the change of the Tongaat social scene. Tongaat in the 1930s, and prior thereto, was known as a most unhealthy location. Malaria epidemics and slum areas were but two difficulties which had to be overcome. Douglas therefore determined that he would convert Tongaat into a township where people of all races, colours and creeds could gain a feeling of belonging; could gain an improvement in their standard of living and a feeling of pride in themselves and in their community. He was determined to eliminate filth and introduce beauty in its place.

He gathered around him two associates, each of them progressive and intelligent men, R G T Watson, known affectionately as 'Watty' and Dr Paul Labushchagne. This trio set about the formidable task of transforming the slum of Tongaat which had built up over the years. Gwelo Goodman, the well-known South African artist, was a personal friend of Douglas and provided him with invaluable advice with regard to the kind of architecture which should be used. Goodman suggested that Cape Dutch architecture should be used in the transformation of Tongaat. Goodman died in 1939 but his architectural influence can be seen today in many buildings in Tongaat and the nearby township of Hambanati, such as the Market, Post Office, Health Centre as well as many employees' cottages.

Douglas resigned his executive position as Chairman in 1963 and finally retired in 1969. He was succeeded by his son, Christopher, who continued to expand the activities of the Company by diversifying into the 'food, clothing, shelter' theme from the commencement of his chairmanship.

From the turn-off to the Morewood Memorial Garden, the old North Coast road continues northwards over the fields of cane. After 4 km (55 km from Durban) the road passes the small rail centre of Umhlali, dominated by the white building of the Victoria County Farmers' Association overlooking from a hilltop the surrounding ocean of sugar cane.

Another kilometre takes the road across the river known as the *Mhlali*, after the monkey-orange *(Strychnos spinosa)* trees growing on its banks. On the left bank of the river once stood the Shaka's Kraal sugar mill, demolished in 1961, with a ramshackle township attached to it. Each spring a few jacaranda trees nearby shed their blossoms like purple tears at the sight of such dilapidation.

Passing a turn-off to Glendale (28 km), the old North Coast road continues northwards through a tribal area covered with grass and lala palms. At 63 km from Durban, the road passes the *Groutville* Mission station, established in 1844 by the Reverend Aldin Grout of the American Board of Missions. Close to the mission station there is a high rock mass on which Shaka used to sit, watching the training manoeuvres of the men stationed in the garrison villages around Dukuza.

Three kilometres beyond Groutville, the old North Coast road twists down into the valley of the river known as the *Mvoti* after a man who once resided on its banks. Immediately ahead, clustered on a hilltop which emerges island-like from the ocean of sugar cane, may be seen the town of Stanger. Passing the mill and workers' houses of the Melville Sugar Estates, the old North Coast road (72 km from Durban) enters the busy centre of ...

STANGER

Laid out as a town in 1873 and named after William Stanger, the Surveyor-General of Natal, *Stanger* was built on the site of Shaka's last great capital, *kwaDukuza* (the place of he who was lost). About 2 000 of the traditional beehive-shaped Zulu huts were built in Dukuza. The royal hut was built near the site of the former police station in the centre of modern Stanger. An old *mkuhla* tree (Natal mahogany), known as Shaka's Indaba Tree, still grows in front of the municipal offices.

In its shade the king used to conduct meetings. It was here, towards sunset on 22 September 1828, that the great Zulu king was assassinated by two of his half-brothers, Mhlangana and Dingane. In the centre of what is now largely an Indian commercial town, a memorial stands in a small garden, marking the site where the great leader of the Zulu nation was buried. Each year, on 22 September, the Zulus have a public holiday, Shaka Day, and there is a gathering at the monument to honour the king.

Stanger became a borough in 1949 and has a population of 36 273. It is the commercial, magisterial and railway centre for one of the most important sugar-producing districts. The Natal North Coast museum of regional history is situated in Stanger. It is open Mondays 12h00 to 16h30; Tuesdays 08h00 to 10h30; Wednesdays and Fridays 12h00 to 16h00; and Thursdays 08h00 to 13h00. South African Pulp and Paper Industries (Sappi) have a large paper mill at Stanger. It converts what is known as *bagasse* (the pulp of sugar cane left after the extraction of the juice) into high quality coated and other paper. Tours of the mill are conducted – Sappi required 24 hours notice. Phone Thabile on (032) 437-2109.

Blythedale Beach, 8 km from Stanger, is something of a seaside suburb for the town.

From Stanger a branch road leads 10 km north-west to the sugar centre of Kearsney, always associated with memories of the pioneering Hulett family.

From Stanger the old North Coast road continues northwards for 6 km past the small centre of New Guelderland, and then joins the main N2 road, Shaka's Way, which links Durban with Zululand. Named (but misspelt) after Gelderland in Holland, this was the site for the settlement of 80 immigrants from the Netherlands. T Colenbrander brought them out and erected a big house and a sugar mill on land watered by the river known as the *Nonoti* from the *Mnono* trees (*Strychnos henningsii*) which grow there. The settlement did not flourish and was abandoned.

SHAKA'S WAY

What was the second main road from Durban to Zululand leads north from Durban along Stanger Street. Along this route Shaka and his army tramped the first paths. The great tarmac highway of today follows these old trails blazed by warriors, hunters and ivory traders.

Five kilometres from the centre of Durban, the road crosses the Mngeni River at what is perhaps ironically known as the Blue Lagoon, a muddy expanse of water in an untidy setting of concrete blocks. On the north bank of the river, 76 ha has been preserved since 1977 as the Beachwood Mangrove nature reserve. This area is used as a nature conservation educational centre. Across the river the road continues through the well-to-do suburbs of Durban North, where the roadside is beautified by flowering plants, especially a great variety of cannas which provide a gorgeous spectacle in November.

At 9,5 km from Durban the road passes Virginia airport, used by light aircraft. The farm on which the airport stands was originally owned by a Mauritian sugar planter, Melidor Cheron, who named it after his daughter Virginia, a singer once known as the 'Nightingale of Natal'. She and her Irish husband, Ancrum McCausland, in 1920 built the first hotel, the Victoria, 6 km further up the coast near the mouth of the *uMhlanga* (the place of reeds) River. This was the start of ...

UMHLANGA ROCKS

The site of this fashionable resort was originally part of the sugar estate of Sir Marshall Campbell, The Natal Estates Ltd, which had its headquarters at Mount Edgecombe. A track was made from

Mount Edgecombe to Umhlanga Rocks, and the area became popular with local farmers who leased small plots on the ocean front where they built vacation cottages. William Alfred Campbell, son of Sir Marshall, built his family home *Nganalana* there in 1925. In the coastal forest of Hawaan (an Indian name) he staged annual hunts. This lovely coastal forest, 26 ha in extent, has been preserved since 1980 as the Umhlanga Lagoon Nature Reserve, part of the green belt of Umhlanga. It is notable for its trees including the rare *Cava coa aurea.* There is an interesting Stone Age shell midden at the mouth of the lagoon, unfortunately partly destroyed in 1981 when the lagoon mouth changed position.

In 1931 Umhlanga Rocks became a village under its own health committee. Additional cottages, places of accommodation and stores were built. The first hotel, the Victoria, was rebuilt and named the Umhlanga Rocks hotel. The first beach cottage, The Oyster Box, became The Oyster Box hotel of today. The cottage had been built in 1869 and for years was used as a navigational point by passing shipmasters who found its corrugated iron roof easy to spot amid the green setting of coastal forest. The automatic lighthouse was built in 1953.

In December 1957 the entire Natal coast suffered a severe setback as a holiday area when several shark attacks on bathers took place. Sharks, of course, were always present in the Indian Ocean but had never been a major problem. With the tremendous increase in holiday-makers along the coast and the pollution of the sea by the spoil of rivers, drainage, industry and sewage systems, sharks seemed suddenly to have become aware that human beings were tasty.

As a solution to the predicament, Umhlanga Rocks erected shark nets in 1962. Two years later the Natal Sharks Board was established to study and deal with the problem of sharks. The headquarters of the board was built on a hill overlooking Umhlanga Rocks. From here the field staff service 425 nets which protect 46 recreational beaches along the 400 km stretch of coast from Port Edward in the south to Zinkwazi in the north. There is also a base station at Uvongo on the South Coast. Visitors are welcome at the Umhlanga headquarters and may see presentations on Tuesdays, Wednesdays and Thursdays at 09h00 and 14h00. There is a lecture on sharks, a film and a conducted tour of the laboratories.

In 1970 Umhlanga Rocks became a borough, and two years later it amalgamated with the adjoining residential township of La Lucia to become the Borough of Umhlanga.

Crossing the Mhlanga River, the coastal road continues north and after 7,5 km joins the main N2 highway which has come up all the way from Cape Town. Three kilometres north along this road there is a turn-off to La Mercy beach and the resort at the mouth of the *Mdloti* River known as ...

UMDLOTI

The Mdloti River received its name from a species of wild tobacco plant growing on its banks. A spacious lagoon, a pleasant shark-protected beach with an enclosed tidal pool, comprise the resort which is situated amongst trees and lawns.

In 1885 a Catholic missionary, the Reverend Louis Mathieu, founded *Oakford* on a farm on the Mdloti River bought from a Mr Oaks. On 2 April 1889, with the aid of eight Dominican sisters, he started a school which became one of the best known educational establishments in Natal.

The N2 road, Shaka's Way, continues up the coast where many pleasant glimpses of the sea and beach are provided. Casuarina trees growing along the shoreline are an indication of the many Mauritians who have settled on the North Coast, producing sugar and remembering their island home by introducing to Natal their favourite tree (originating from Madagascar, where it is known as the *filaos* tree).

After 8 km of pleasant travel from the Mdloti River, the road reaches a turn-off to ...

TONGAAT BEACH

The *Thongathi* River takes its name from a species of tree which grows on its banks. The resort is a relaxed, informal little place with bungalows shaded by whispering casuarina trees. Westbrook Beach is pleasant, shark protected, and there is good fishing.

Beyond Tongaat Beach the road continues north for 2 km, crosses the Thongathi River and then veers slightly inland, leaving the sea out of sight behind bush-covered coastal dunes. After 7 km a turn-off is reached, leading to the coast at Compensation Beach, Ballito Bay and, 2 km further on, a turn-off to the resort of Shaka's Rock.

BALLITO, SHAKA'S ROCK AND THOMPSON'S BAY

Ballito was established in 1953. The developer, Dr Rubinstein, for unknown reasons gave the place the Italian name of a brand of stockings called *Ballito* (little ball). It has grown into a very popular resort with good swimming, fishing and a variety of accommodation.

Shaka's Rock is said to have been a seaside resort favoured by Shaka during the last years of his life when his capital was established on the site of modern Stanger. The high rock mass forms a natural cliff where, it is said, Zulu warriors suspected of lack of courage were required to prove themselves by jumping into the sea. Enemies of Shaka are also said to have been thrown over it. Together with the adjoining resort of Ballito Bay, Shaka's Rock today forms a fine recreational stretch of coast with shark-protected swimming, a large tidal pool and a pleasant coastal pathway.

Thompson's Bay is just north of Ballito up Compensation Beach Road and Dolphin Crescent. There is a tidal pool and a pleasant beach on the south side of the bay. There is a rock with a naturally formed hole in which, legend has it, Shaka liked to play when he visited the seaside in holiday mood.

At a point 2,5 km beyond the turn-off to Shaka's Rock and Ballito, there is a turn-off to the coastal resort of ...

SALT ROCK

Salt Rock is a likeable little resort, popular with fishermen and those people who prefer a quiet holiday beside the sea. The rock in front of the hotel is said to have been a source of salt to the Zulu people. There is a popular country club, the venue for many bowls tournaments.

North of the turn-off to Salt Rock (46 km from Durban), the road continues for 6 km reaching a turn-off to Tinley Manor Beach, which lies on the coast just north of the Mhlali estuary. Sugar cane covers the coastal terrace and there are turn-offs to small coastal resorts such as Blythedale Beach and Zinkwazi Beach where there is a lagoon and protected beach. At 73 km from Durban, the N2 road, Shaka's Way, is joined by the old North Coast road, the Sugar Way. The combined roads continue through vast plantations of cane, passing the Huletts sugar mill and employees' village at Darnall, crossing the river known as the *Zinkwazi* after the white-headed fish eagles and then, 85 km from Durban, reaching a gravel turn-off which stretches for 11 km to the mouth of the Thukela River.

THE HULETT FAMILY

James Liege Hulett, was born in Sheffield on 17 May 1838, the son of James Hulett, a schoolmaster. In 1857, just turning 19 years of age and with only £5 in his pocket, he landed in Durban and went up to Pietermaritzburg to work as a chemist's assistant. In the following year his father, mother and three sisters joined him in Natal. He leased a 160 acre farm in the area surveyed as settler lots by John Moreland (Mount Moreland), built a house and commenced general farming. The terms of purchase were to pay £1 per acre after a certain number of years.

He struggled for some years, made a little money by managing for a company a cotton farm named *Driefontein* where he married Mary Balcomb in 1860 and traded in Zululand. Hulett saved enough to lease 600 acres in the valley of the Nonoti River 8 km north-west of Stanger. The farm was named *Kearsney* after the hamlet near Dover in England. There he planted vegetables, cotton, indigo and coffee but without much success. Then, in March 1877 the government imported tea plants from Assam. These experimental plants proved the making of James Liege Hulett. By 1892 he had founded a tea industry in Natal, formed J L Hulett and Sons Ltd and expanded into sugar cane cultivation and refining. He became the biggest tea producer in Natal. He built on Kearsney a beautiful manor-house, together with a chapel which, replaced in 1906 by a more substantial building, is today a national monument.

In 1883 James Hulett was elected to the Legislative Council as member for Victoria County. His four sons, Albert (the eldest), William, James and Edward, were all farming around Kearsney. They merged their interests with those of their father. The headquarters were at Kearsney and from this centre the company spread its control over agricultural enterprises particularly tea grown at Kearsney and the Kirkley Vale and Bulwer tea estates and then sugar in 1903.

With the granting in 1893 of responsible government to Natal, James Liege Hulett became secretary for native affairs. His services to the colony of Natal resulted in a knighthood bestowed upon him in 1902. In the following year, on the fall of the Pine Ministry he was invited to form a new government for the colony. He declined the honour as his business responsibilities were becoming formidable. Just before his knighthood his company purchased 3 000 acres at Wagon Drift, Umhlali and established in 1903 at Tinley Manor a state-of-the-art sugar mill for that age which produced 2 000 tons of sugar in its first year.

Other sugar mills followed; Darnall in 1905, Amatikulu in 1907 and, shortly afterwards, Felixton, both in Zululand. On 2 January 1901 Hulett also opened his own private railway from Stanger to Kearsney to bring supplies to his factories and carry away their produce. In 1910 the decision was made to build in Durban a central refinery, known as Huletts Refinery to process raw sugar from all the company mills, and from other mills as well. In that year, Sir J L Hulett became a senator in the newly established Union of South Africa. It was also time for him to retire from business. He built a manor-house in Durban and left Kearsney. His son Albert succeeded him as managing director of the company. He also lived in Durban.

Sir James Hulett died on 5 June 1928 after an eventful life of 90 years. His son Albert succeeded him in the chairmanship of the company. He died in 1948 and was succeeded as chairman of the company by his son Guy.

During the period of Guy Hulett's chairmanship, the company continued to expand. During the early 1950s the Darnall mill was completely rebuilt, at Felixton the Ngoye Paper Mill was established where surplus bagasse was converted into fluting and line paper. A second paper mill was established towards the end of the 1950s at Piet Retief.

In 1953 the interests of Zululand Sugar Millers and Planters (Pty) Ltd, established by George Armstrong and his son Athol in Empangeni, was acquired. The Triangle Sugar Company in Zimbabwe, was also acquired. With 295 000 acres of land it is one of the finest irrigated sugar estates in the world, capable of producing 300 000 tons of sugar a year. It was created by Murray McDougall, a man of extraordinary energy. Shortly afterwards Sir J L Hulett & Sons Ltd, in partnership with the Colonial Development Corporation, established a sugar estate at Mhlume in Swaziland.

In October 1962, one month after the death of William Campbell, Guy Hulett was one of the major role players in a proposed take-over bid of The Natal Estates Ltd. This resulted in a short but very bitter stock exchange battle which, at the beginning of November of that year, seemed to end in victory for Sir J L Hulett and Sons Ltd. The victory turned into sudden defeat when a consortium of companies headed by C G Smith & Co, and The Tongaat Sugar Company Ltd, took over Sir J L Hulett & Sons. Although the company name of Hulett was retained, various family members resigned. Ross Armstrong was appointed Chairman of Huletts in Guy Hulett's place.

The Armstrong family is another well-known 'sugar' family, whose mill, acquired by the four Armstrong brothers in 1892, and called Central Factory, was based at Verulam. Ross, was the son of Robert Armstrong, one of the original founders of the Central Factory. In 1946 Central Factory was taken over by The Tongaat Sugar Company Limited. One of the four Armstrong brothers, George, together with his son, Athol, also established The Zululand Sugar Millers & Planters in 1911, which, as previously mentioned, was subsequently acquired by Sir J L Hulett & Sons in 1953. Ross Armstrong remained Chairman of Huletts Sugar Corporation Limited as it then became known, until 1964, at which time Chris Saunders became Chairman of both the Huletts and Tongaat organisations.

Various acquisitions, expansions, sales and diversifications followed the take-over, resulting in The Natal Estates Limited becoming part of the sugar division of Huletts. Changes of name took place: in 1970 Huletts Sugar Corporation Limited became Huletts Corporation Limited, and The Tongaat Sugar Company Limited became The Tongaat Group Limited. The various divisions of both organisations carried on and improved the 'food, clothing and shelter' theme.

The Tongaat Group Limited acquired a greater investment in the Hulett Corporation Limited and on 1 April 1982 these companies were merged into one company, The Tongaat-Hulett Group Limited. Chris Saunders, great grandson of the original James Renault Saunders, became Chairman of the new Group which, closely linked to the Anglo-American Corporation, continues its role today as one of the principal industrial groups of Southern Africa.

The gravel turn-off to the mouth of the Thukela River takes the traveller to several interesting places. One kilometre from the start of the turn-off stands Fort Pearson, looking out from a hilltop over the Thukela River and far north into Zululand. This fort was built by the British army in 1878 when they were preparing to invade Zululand. The fort dominates what was known as the lower Thukela drift. A great military camp was pitched beneath it, close to the river were the British army prepared their attack.

Little more than 1 km beyond the fort, the road passes the so-called 'Ultimatum Tree'. Under this wild fig tree, which grows on the banks of the river, the Zulu headmen sent to meet the British commander on 11 December 1878 were given the ultimatum to take back to their king Cetshwayo. The demanding terms of this ultimatum resulted in the Anglo-Zulu War.

The gravel road continues down the right bank of the Thukela River. Leaving the canelands behind, it penetrates an attractive belt of coastal forest and then ends at the shallow bay at the mouth of the river. Some attractive camping sites are situated under the trees, but this is a wild and unspoilt piece of coast where the waves tumble ashore like invaders on a solitary beach. In 1967, 104 ha of this coastal area was established as the Harold Johnson Nature Reserve. There are walking trails, and the coastal vegetation and wildlife are interesting. Butterflies and birds are prolific.

Beyond the gravel turn-off to the mouth of the river, the N2 road continues northwards for 4,5 km and then (89,5 km from Durban) reaches the traditional boundary between Natal and Zululand, the great river known to the Zulus as the *Thukela* (startling) on account of its size, the power of its floods, and the colossal valley which it has eroded in its middle reaches. Across the river lies *kwaZulu* (the place of Zulu).

Chapter Twenty-Five
THE LAND OF THE ZULUS

The main N2 coastal road, Shaka's Way, which links Durban to what used to be called Zululand but is now known as *KwaZulu* (the place of Zulu), crosses the traditional frontier, the Thukela River, by means of the John Ross Bridge. John Ross was a 15-year-old boy who, in 1827, under the instructions of his master, walked from the ivory trading settlement of Durban all the way to the Portuguese fort at Lourenzo Marques (Maputo) to obtain urgently needed medicines. The courtesy of the Zulus saw him safely through his journey. He duly returned to his sick comrades with medicines and assorted comforts.

The road is at this stage 88 km from Durban and, once across the river, climbs out of the valley of the Thukela. After 1 km there are turn-offs – west to the Mandini mill of S A Pulp and Paper Industries Ltd, and east to a recreational area on the northern side of the mouth of the Thukela River, where a cluster of vacation cottages and a caravan park have been built. *Mandini* (place of *Euphorbia tiruculli* trees) was selected in 1945 as the site for the construction of a large papermill. Known as the Tugela Mill, this industry employs a considerable number of people who are housed in a village known as Mandini, managed by a health committee.

Seven kilometres north-east of Mandini is the industrial centre of *Isithebe* (the name of a small traditional grass mat), created in 1971 by the Bantu Investment Corporation. About 90 industries have been established there.

Beyond these turn-offs, the main coastal road continues northwards over an undulating terrace covered in sugar cane. At 16 km from the Thukela River the road bridges across the river known as the *Matigulu* (a pre-Zulu Lala name) meaning water that scrapes away. The Huletts sugar mill stands on its banks. At the mouth of this river there is a research station where the feasibility of cultivating prawns under artificial conditions is studied. The Amatikulu Nature Reserve has been created on the coast between the mouths of the Thukela and Amatikulu rivers. The Zangozolo tented camp is built on wooden platforms with a panoramic view. Vegetation and wildlife is varied. Beyond the turn-off to the nature reserve, the N2 continues its way north-eastwards. A further 5 km across the cane fields takes the road past the railway junction of ...

GINGINDLOVU

After Cetshwayo defeated his brother Mbulazi in a struggle for succession to the Zulu throne, he triumphantly established a new residence for himself which he named *Gingindlovu* (the swallower of the elephant). It is now a village and railway junction from where a branch line leads to Eshowe. In April 1879 a British force, on its way to relieve Eshowe (besieged by the Zulus), defeated a Zulu army at a site marked by a monument 3 km from Gingindlovu. The battle of 'Gin gin I love you', as the British soldiers called it, opened the way for an advance on Eshowe.

Half a kilometre north of Gingindlovu, a tarmac turn-off stretches for 21 km to Eshowe (see further on). The N2 coastal road continues through the green sea of sugar cane and, 19 km from Gingindlovu, reaches a turn-off leading for 2 km to the village of Mtunzini.

MTUNZINI AND THE UMLALAZI NATURE RESERVE

The pleasant name of *Mtunzini* (place in the shade) applies to an attractive resort in a green, park-like setting on a ridge with a view of the Indian Ocean. This was a favourite holiday place for John Dunn, the European chief of a section of the Zulu people living along the coast between the Thukela and the Mhlatuze rivers. By the time he died in 1895 at the age of 61, Dunn had married 49 wives. His offspring numbered 117 and these, together with numerous followers and dependants, formed a small group of their own to add yet another patch to the complex ethnic 'quilt' of South Africa.

The Umlalazi Nature Reserve, established in 1948, received its name from the *Mlalazi* (place of whetstones) River. The reserve lies 1,5 km east of Mtunzini and covers 1 028 ha of coastal dune country and swampland inhabited by numerous bushbuck, reedbuck, blue and grey duiker and many birds. The river is amply populated with fish and a few crocodiles. The vegetation is interesting; mangroves grow on the islets and around the lagoon. There is a mangrove trail for walkers at low tide. There are other trails, picnic sites and a pleasant tea-room where rooms may be hired.

The area is notable for a grove of giant raphia palms, growing to heights of 25 m and carrying the largest leaves of any plant. They are conserved in the Raphia Palm Monument, reached along a winding boardwalk. The rare palm-nut vulture lives only in the vicinity of raphia palms, feeding on the palm nuts.

Beyond the turn-off to Mtunzini, the N2 coastal road, after 3 km crosses the Mlalazi River and passes a turn-off leading to the Umlalazi River resort. Close by, 4 km from the river, there is the wayside Forest Inn motel and caravan park. The N2 road then enters the area of the Port Durnford state forest. Port Durnford simply consists of an exposed roadstead which was occasionally used by the British for landing supplies during the Anglo-Zulu War. A 6 000 candlepower lighthouse watches over the place today. The name comes from Midshipman Durnford, who served with Captain William Owen in the survey of the coast in 1822.

The N2 coastal road proceeds in a northerly direction, with glimpses of the Ngoya forest, a superb piece of indigenous forest covering the inland slopes. After 9 km, the road reaches the entrance to the University of Zululand, opened in 1960 and at present attended by 5 077 students. A further 3 km sees the road crossing the river known on account of its floods as the *Mhlatuze* (forceful). Two kilometres further on, there is a turn-off to the sugar-producing centre of *Felixton*, named after its pioneer planter Felix Piccione. The sugar mill there is the largest in South Africa. After a further 6 km of travel through the cane fields, the road, 31 km from Mtunzini, reaches the busy town and sugar centre of ...

EMPANGENI

In 1851 a mission was established by the Norwegians nearby a stream on whose banks grew a number of *mpange* trees (*Treema guineensis*). It is from these trees that the name of *Empangeni* is derived. The mission was later moved to Eshowe, but the original site was still regarded as a pleasant situation and in 1899 a magistracy was established there. The opening of the Zululand railway in 1903 made Empangeni a major staging post and later the junction of the branch line to Nkwalini and the sugar estates in the productive valley of the Mhlatuze River.

By 1906 Empangeni had become a village. In 1913 George Armstrong built a sugar mill there, now run by Zululand Sugar Millers and Planters Ltd. As a result, the place progressed into a town which achieved full municipal status in 1960. Today Empangeni is a busy and pleasant town shaded by some handsome trees. It is inhabited by 26 420 people.

From Empangeni, the main coastal road continues northwards, past the mill of Zululand Sugar Millers and Planters Ltd, and through cane fields and timber plantations. After 14 km the road crosses the Enseleni River, where there is a turn-off to the ...

ENSELENI NATURE RESERVE

Established in 1948 at a bend in the river known as the *Enseleni* (place of the badger), this 293 ha reserve incorporates a picnic ground and nature trail. Amongst the wildlife are zebra and antelope species such as nyala, impala and blue wildebeest; while a very rich plant life comprises mangroves, papyrus, and some grand old wild fig trees lining the banks of the river.

One kilometre beyond the Enseleni River, a turn-off 15 km long leads across a level, grassy plain to ...

RICHARDS BAY

Admiral Sir Frederick William Richards, after whom this great natural harbour is named, was commander of naval units during the Anglo-Zulu War. The port lies at the mouth of the landlocked bay of the Mhlatuze River, 180 km north-east of Durban and 92 square kilometres in extent. In its original state this bay provided a home for a vast population of aquatic birds, attracted to the area by a rich supply of fish. Crocodiles and sharks also frequented the waters eating each other as well as the fish. Hippos were numerous; and the celebrated wandering hippo, Huberta, is thought to have started her strange travels from this lagoon in 1928. She eventually walked as far down the coast as the Keiskamma River, south of King William's Town, where she was killed by hunters. Huberta is now the star exhibit in the Amatole Museum in King William's Town.

Hunters and fishermen frequented the bay and it was there that John Dunn shot a giant crocodile just over 7 m long (a South African record). The potential of the bay as a harbour was apparent to all the early visitors. In 1826 two ivory traders, King and Isaacs, planned to develop the area but without any result. In 1897 a detailed survey of the bay was carried out, the results of which proved its suitability as a harbour. The area of the sheltered expanse of water was twice that of Durban; the mouth was open to the sea and, although only 3 m deep, could be dredged to allow the passage of very large vessels. A second survey in 1902 again confirmed the harbour possibilities of the bay.

In 1935 1 200 ha of the bay was proclaimed a game reserve while the adjacent land on its northern side was, in 1945, declared the Richards Bay Park. The town of Richards Bay was laid out alongside this park on the elevated northern shore of the lagoon, overlooking a fine stretch of water. Established as a health committee in 1954 and a municipality in 1981, the town has a population of 62 852.

From being a quiet little holiday resort, Richards Bay has developed into a major port, connected by railway to the coal and other mines of the interior and accepting, for loading, bulk carriers of very deep draught. The new harbour was opened on 1 April 1976. In developing Richards Bay as a deep-water harbour, an attempt was made to preserve at least a part of the lagoon by building a berm across it. This barricade isolated the harbour from the sanctuary area to the south. A separate mouth to the sea was cut through the dunes to serve this area.

The Richards Bay coal terminal is the largest in the world. Several major industries have also been established at Richards Bay. Alusaf (Pty) Ltd has there the only aluminium reduction plant in South Africa. It produces 170 000 tons of aluminium each year. Indian Ocean Fertilizer (Pty) Ltd also has a major industry at Richards Bay producing phosphoric acid fertiliser.

Richards Bay Minerals mine heavy sands north and south of Richards Bay, recovering a variety of rare earths, titania, rutile and low-manganese iron. Central Timber Co-operative has a wood-chipping plant, and the Mondi Paper Company has a large pulp and linerboard mill at the port. It uses more than 6 000 tons of timber a day.

The N2 coastal road continues northwards from the turn-off to Richards Bay through vast plantations of gum trees and sugar cane. Magnificent casuarina trees grow at railway centres such as *Nseleni*. After 13,5 km the road passes the state forests at *kwaMbonambi* (place of the Mbonambi tribe) and a sawmill at Penicuik siding 3 km further north. A turn-off to the east leads to Eteza and for 40 km to the coast at Mapelane where the Natal Parks Board maintain a camping ground and furnished log cabins. The highest forest-covered dunes in the world occur at Mapelane. The artificial mouth of the Mfolozi River has been cut to the sea at this point. The name comes from *maPhelane* (place of strychnos berries), an edible berry.

Kilometres of gum plantations stretch off to the north. Twelve kilometres from kwaMbonambi, the road crosses the river known as the *Msunduze* (the pusher) on account of its destructive power during floods. A further 5,5 km takes the road past Mfolozi village, the Safari motel and to the bridge across one of the most important rivers in Zululand, the *Mfolozi* (zigzag) River. This river is notorious for its violent floods. The Zulus have a proverb about it '*The Black Mfolozi chooses its ferrymen for victims*' (a man dies at his trade). Many people have learned the truth of this proverb.

The Mfolozi is also famous for the big-game area, the Umfolozi Game Reserve, contained between the two upper divisions known as the White and Black Mfolozi rivers. There is a turn-off 5 km north of the bridge over the Mfolozi to the village of Mtubatuba and to the resort of St Lucia.

MTUBATUBA

In 1903 the North Coast railway line from Durban was opened to the coal-mine at a place known as *Somkhele,* after the local chief. A siding on the line, just north of the Mfolozi River, was named *Mtubatuba,* after Somkhele's son and heir, *Mthubuthubu* (he who was pummelled out) a reference to the manner of his birth. This siding was close to the swampland of reeds, papyrus and mud formed by the Mfolozi River where it reaches the flat coastal belt and, like all Zululand rivers, found its flow impeded by the absence of any further significant fall in altitude. The river dithered about, trying to find a way to the sea across the sand flats. Percolating through the swamps, the river shed its load of silt – a rich alluvial deposit which attracted the attention of sugar cane planters.

In 1911 the south side of the river was made available for settlement and, two years later, the north side was also offered to planters. The swamplands had kept out Zulu settlers. Europeans were given the chance of cheap virgin land, provided they could find a solution to the problems of malarial fever, bilharzia and floods.

To serve the area, a concession contract for a sugar mill was granted to D W Maxwell, and the St Lucia Sugar Company was floated in London. This company was stricken with troubles from its inception. All the machinery for its mill was aboard the *SS Centurion,* the first ship to be sunk by a submarine in the First World War.

When the mill was eventually opened in 1916, the quality of cane grown along the Mfolozi was found to be inferior in purity and sucrose content. Involved arguments among the planters concerning prices followed this discovery. In the midst of these troubles, in 1918, the Mfolozi came down in one of its periodic violent floods. The alluvial flats were completely devastated. Giant wild fig trees which had defied the river for over a hundred years were carried away as flotsam. Houses floated away down river and the village which had grown around the mill was entirely ruined. The store, bank, hotel and houses vanished. Only the bank strong-room remained, resting in mud and leaning over like a miniature Tower of Pisa.

The mill had been on the verge of bankruptcy before this disaster. After a struggle to raise fresh finance, it was put up for auction in December 1923. The only bid was by a co-operative society formed by the planters and led by George Heaton Nicholls. The bid of £30 000 was accepted and the Umfolozi Co-operative Sugar Company was formed. A Land Bank loan was secured to finance rehabilitation of the mill. In June 1924 crushing was resumed. In March of the following year, the Mfolozi River came down in flood once again and half the new mill was destroyed.

This second disaster taught the sugar producers a lesson. They salvaged what they could from the wreckage and rebuilt the factory, on a higher, safer site named River View. The first crushing in the new mill started on 23 July 1927. Large-scale drainage of the swamplands also commenced by means of concrete canals.

The railway siding of Mtubatuba developed as a trading and administrative centre for this sugar and timber producing area. A branch court of the Hlabisa magistracy was established there in 1932. In 1946 the full court of Hlabisa was transferred to Mtubatuba and it was established as the administrative centre for the district. In 1950 the first health committee was appointed and Mtubatuba became a village. Today it is a busy trading and communications centre.

The Lake Eteza nature reserve, covering 350 ha, was created in 1976. In this area there is a shallow lakelet where waterfowl breed in a papyrus swamp.

From Mtubatuba, a tarmac road stretches eastwards for 24 km through plantations and portions of the evergreen coastal forest named by the Zulus, *Dukuduku* (a place of groping in the dark, trying to find a way) because its denseness and wild animals made it a fearful place. Thirteen kilometres from Mtubatuba there is a roadside picnic site in the midst of this lovely forest. Two kilometres further on, there is a turn to Monzi and, after a further 9,5 km through forest and plantations, the road reaches the bridge across the estuary of Lake St Lucia. On the opposite bank lies the village and resort of ...

ST LUCIA

During the Cretaceous period, about 100 million years ago, the flat coastal area of Zululand, Maputoland and Mozambique lay beneath the sea. The Indian Ocean washed against the slopes of the Lubombo Mountains and laid down a rich deposit of coral and shells for man to unearth whenever he excavates the former sea bed.

This ancient sea bed eventually became the coastal plain of today when the waters, for some unknown reason, receded. Rivers which had originally reached the sea along the line formed by the Lubombo range, were now confronted by a barrier of sand about 100 km wide. This coastal terrace proved a complex obstacle to the rivers, whose flow was impeded by the flat nature of the plain and by chance depressions which trapped the water, forming shallow lakelets. A final ridge of high sand dunes piled up by wind action along the shore held the rivers back, creating lagoons, lakes and swamps.

Lake St Lucia, known to the Zulus as *eCwebeni lase Entlengeni* (lagoon of rafts), originated when a number of rivers, notably the Mfolozi, Mkhuze, Mzinene, Nyalazi and Hluhluwe, combined their water to form a vast estuary system, roughly in the shape of the letter 'H'. The left limb of the 'H' consists of what is known as False Bay, 25 km long, 3 km wide and less than 1 m deep. The crossbar of the 'H' is the so-called Hell's Gates, a windswept, treacherous stretch of water lying between the cliffs. The southern 'gate' is formed by what was known as Goose Point, but now known as the Ndlozi peninsula, frequently used in former years as a base camp for hippo hunters. On the west shore opposite the north 'gate', Jack Lister built a resort at Lister's Point.

The right-hand limb of the 'H' is Lake St Lucia proper, a vast and beautifully wild stretch of water – 40 km long, 10 km wide, with an average depth of less than 1 m. Three reed-covered islands lie on its surface. The largest is Bird Island. The other two are *Lane Island* (named after William Lane of the Natal Parks Board who used to fish there) and *Fanie's Island* (named after a Zulu headman who lived on the opposite mainland). Another local chief was Makhakhathana, at whose village on the north bank David Brodie established a trading post. The shallow crossing to the east shore is named after him.

Fanie's Island separates the lake from its southern reach which empties into the estuary channel. A shallow finger of the lake beset with mudbanks, this channel gropes towards the sea where it used to unite with the mouth of the Mfolozi River. Catalina Bay was used as a base for Catalinia flying boats during the Second World War.

The whole lake system has always been fed as much by the sea as by the various rivers flowing into it. Immense evaporation of water in the hot climate and erratic flow from rivers, the water of which is increasingly used for agricultural purposes, cause the lake to become seasonally more and more saline, with False Bay having a salinity which at times rises to more than three times that of sea water (110 parts per thousand). The Mfolozi River, originally the principal supplier of fresh water to the lake, was deflected by canals and irrigation projects and no longer supplied any fresh water to the lake. This proved so disastrous that a 250 km link canal was constructed to divert water from the Mfolozi back into the lake, but has since been closed off.

Large shoals of fish – kob, grunter, mullet, mud bream and others – have always frequented the lakes, and the grunter run in October is still a major sporting event for fishermen. At the estuary the fish are prey to numerous big game-fish and sharks, while crocodiles haunt the entire lake, particularly at the mouths of the tributary rivers. About 700 hippos are the principal species of a resident population of mammals. Over 350 species of birds, including several species of aquatic birds, find rich feeding in the area, with flamingos (greater and lesser), pelicans, fish eagles, ducks, geese, goliath herons, kingfishers and cormorants being particularly prolific and providing many wonderful spectacles.

The name *St Lucia* was first given in June 1554 to the mouth of the Thukela River by survivors of the wrecked Portuguese ship, the *Saint Benedict*. The same party named the St Lucia estuary, the *Rio de la Medaos do Ouro* (river of the sands of gold). In 1575 one of the survivors, Manual Perestrelo, was sent to map the coast. He moved the name of St Lucia from the Thukela River to the St Lucia Estuary, and the name Rio de Medaos do Ouro to what is now called Kosi Bay.

During the 19th century there was considerable hunting activity around the lake, for it was a great resort of game animals, especially elephant. Hippos were shot in vast numbers. Antelope were shot for their skins and meat. The first nyala to be recorded were found there in 1849 by George Angas and named after him, *Tragolaphus angasi*. The rich fish resources of the area were also noted and there were plans to establish a port.

On 27 April 1897, the 36 826 ha covered by the waters of Lake St Lucia were proclaimed a game reserve. The land surrounding the lake, 1 km wide and comprising a total of 12 545 ha, was proclaimed the St Lucia Park in 1939, while an area of 2 247 ha at False Bay was also proclaimed a park in 1944. In these reserves live reedbuck, bushbuck, nyala, impala, grey and red duiker, suni, steenbok and bushpigs. The whole expanse has an exceedingly varied and interesting vegetation consisting of grasslands, patches of forest, mangroves and ferns. For walkers there are wilderness trails which follow the verges of the lake.

These outings are conducted between April and October by professional rangers and usually last three or four days. Launch trips on the lake are also organised by the Natal Parks Board. In 1977, 12 873 ha was established as the Eastern Shores Nature Reserve. There are wilderness trails and coastal camping sites.

The best time to visit the area is in winter, when it is cooler. Apart from the hotel at the estuary the Natal Parks Board maintains five open-air camping areas and three hutted camps.

From the bridge where the road from Mtubatuba crosses the estuary, there is a division of routes. To the left, the tarmac road leads north. After 2 km this road reaches the Crocodile Centre run by the Natal Parks Board. The centre is open to visitors and provides a very interesting and instructive series of exhibits. From this centre, young crocodiles are supplied to various commercial farms where they are raised for their skins. They are also judiciously placed in rivers where their extinction by hunters has affected the ecological balance of fish life.

From the Crocodile Centre one road continues north, passes the airstrip and, after 35 km, reaches the caravan park and fishing area at Cape Vidal. The other road swings east, passes the entrance to the Iphiva camping ground and, on reaching the coast, turns west to the mouth of the lake. The beautiful grounds of the Sugarloaf caravan and camping ground, run by the Natal Parks Board, are reached by passing through the village and the National Parks Board main reception office.

St Lucia is a relaxed and friendly fishermen's resort. There is a swimming-pool in the Sugarloaf camp, crocodiles and sharks make estuary or sea swimming dangerous. Fishing and relaxation, bird-watching, hiking and boating on the estuary and lake are the main pastimes. The northern part of the lake is used by the military as a testing ground for missiles and rockets and is therefore a prohibited area.

CAPE VIDAL AND THE WRECK OF THE DOROTHEA

On the night of 31 January 1898 a decrepit old barque named the *Dorothea* was abandoned by the crew about 8 km east of the coast above the estuary of Lake St Lucia. There was no loss of life. The barque had simply leaked itself into a sinking condition. The scratch crew, under a skipper named H Marthisson, launched two boats on a calm sea and were picked up by passing steamers. The barque was on its way from Lourenzo Marques (now Maputo) to Durban, supposedly to be patched up after having been bought as a hulk by a Doctor Kelly who headed a syndicate of Johannesburg businessmen. The ship had been mouldering on the beach at Lourenzo Marques for over a year before the syndicate bought it, expressing the intentions of repairing the ship in Durban and then using it for fishing. They changed the name to *Dorothea* in place of the earlier *Ernestein*, re-registered it under the American flag and employed a Captain Vibert to patch it up. Eventually the *Dorothea* limped out on its last voyage which ended with the ship washed on to Cape Vidal.

Cape Vidal is simply a ledge of rock protruding into the sea 40 km up the coast from the estuary of Lake St Lucia. A road now leads from the village of St Lucia to a holiday resort built at Cape Vidal but in those days there was no easy approach. The name of *Vidal* had been bestowed on the Cape in 1823 by Captain W Owen, commander of the two Royal Navy survey ships, *Leven* and *Barracouta*, then engaged on a survey of the eastern coast of Natal. Lt Alexander Vidal was one of Owen's officers.

Nothing more would have been heard of the *Dorothea* or its graveyard on Cape Vidal but an interesting rumour spread amongst seafarers. It was said that illicit gold buying and theft on a fantastic scale was proceeding on the Witwatersrand gold mines. The *Dorothea* had been bought by the syndicate as a means of smuggling their loot out of the country. Some 120 000 ounces of gold were reported to have been concealed among the ballast in the ship's holds. This rumour soon produced results. Three months after the wreck, the Natal Government sent the salvage ship *Alfred Noble* to investigate the wreck. The *Dorothea* was located with its masts still above water. Bad weather prevented any attempt at salvage.

Then, very furtively, in June 1899, the syndicate of original owners and some leading shipping men of Durban financed a small steam fishing boat, the *Nidaros,* with an experienced crew, professional diver and a surfboat to sail up to Cape Vidal. The wreck was still easy to locate. The diver went down and to his intense excitement found some pigots of yellow metal lying among the timbers. He was hauled to the surface and the pigots examined. They were found to be copper.

The salvors made a second try. They anchored their surfboat above the wreck and were preparing to lower the diver when a heavy sea capsized the boat. Four men drowned, including the diver and the commander of the salvage party, Captain Wakeford. The salvage attempt was abandoned.

On the 25th of the next month (July 1899) the *Hansa*, a tug commanded by Captain Vibert, who had repaired the *Dorothea* in Lourenzo Marques, sailed to Cape Vidal while an overland party travelled up the coast to establish a shore base at the wreck site, the *Hansa* lowered her surfboat but it was promptly capsized and lost. The tug returned to Durban for another boat but, back at Cape Vidal, the salvors found the weather too bad. Salvage efforts were abandoned until later in the year when the sea could be expected to be calmer.

At this stage in proceedings the Anglo-Boer War broke out. Despite the hostilities, in December 1899, a 29 ton vessel, the *Countess of Carnarvon*, was chartered by a syndicate headed by a Mr Hall. Under Captain J P Nansson, and with several professional divers on board, the little ship made its way to Cape Vidal and the salvors began work. At the end of their activities they returned to Durban, reporting that only some 'curios' had been recovered.

At least a dozen individuals and small groups of speculators made plans to search for more 'curios'. The next substantial salvage attempt started on 22 July 1901. Captain George Vibert once again appeared, this time in command of a pocket-sized steamer named the *Fenella*. Apart from the salvors, the government this time insisted on a policeman being present on board to scrutinise any findings. The sea was rough, the policeman seasick, no salvage work was possible nor reported.

A few private groups then ventured to Cape Vidal but there was little they could do. The wreck, by then, had been covered by sand. It was too close to a dangerous shore to be reached from the sea unless the water was very calm. The powerful surf made reaching it from shore a very tricky operation.

In 1903, however, the Honourable Thomas Hassall decided to make an attempt. He chartered the tug *Ulundi* and, with government support and an expert diver, sailed up to Cape Vidal in December 1903. Nothing resulted, or was reported.

The next large attempt was by a 247 ton coaster named the *Penguin* owned by C Smith and Co of Durban, commanded by J Jorgenson and with a well-outfitted party of salvors on board led by a Scandinavian salvage expert named C E Frees. They set off on 13 August 1904 from Durban hopefully enough but off the mouth of the Mhlathuze River ran into a very heavy sea. The hatches of the ship were staved in and the ship had to be abandoned. Eleven men were drowned, the ship went down with all equipment and the survivors had a grim forty-hour battle in open boats without food or water until the storm abated and they reached the beach.

The promoters of the ill-fated venture were not deterred. At the end of October 1904 they sent a second ship, the *Good Hope* up to Cape Vidal, a sizeable land party went up as well. On the beach two large marquees, and several bell tents were erected. Two divers worked from surfboats. A substantial company, the Dorothea Treasure Trove Syndicate, was launched in the Transvaal, with Sir Edward Murray as chairman and a prospectus describing the gold in the wreck as consisting of 120 000 ounces packed in twelve boxes and three leather bags, all placed at the foot of the foremast and covered in six inches of cement. Nothing was reported as having been found of this gold by the syndicate.

Several more individuals, syndicates and groups followed this attempt. One of the largest was in 1906 when the S A Salvage Co, a £25 000 concern, financed Captain Gardiner and his ship, the *Alfred Noble* on another venture after the treasure. Nothing resulted. Then, in 1908, the Dorothea Barque Treasure Syndicate Ltd was organised by one of the keenest of all the salvage men, S E Hall. Around November 1908, a crack diver, S Abrahamson, spent six weeks on the salvage attempt at Cape Vidal. He was reported as having found only wood and anchor chains half buried in the sand.

This was the last large scale attempt at finding the *Dorothea's* gold. A few small parties persisted but nothing resulted. It was rumoured that, in fact, the gold had been found by an earlier salvage party but never reported for fear that as it was originally stolen, the Government could seize the lot. There is no answer to the mystery.

The *Dorothea* still lies beneath the green-blue water at Cape Vidal. There is nothing to be seen of the ship save wreckage left by the various salvage groups, rusting chains, poles and other debris. The ships anchor and chain, recovered by one of the parties, was left there as well. There is nothing else at Cape Vidal save broken human hopes and solitude.

MTUBATUBA TO THE GAME RESERVES

Three kilometres north of the turn-off to Mtubatuba and Lake St Lucia, the main coastal N2 road reaches a second turn-off of considerable importance to tourists. This is the road leading northwestwards to the game reserves of Hluhluwe and Umfolozi, and thence to Nongoma, Melmoth and Eshowe. The very heart of Zululand is penetrated by this route which passes the sites of several historic Zulu centres and battlefields, and reveals some of the most majestic scenery of a romantic country.

After 21 km this turn-off reaches yet another turn-off (15 km) which leads northwards through an open area of tribal settlement to the entrance gate (and thence for 17 km to the camp) of the ...

HLUHLUWE GAME RESERVE

Without doubt one of the best known and most popular game reserves in the world. Hluhluwe is 23 067 ha in extent. The reserve covers a superb piece of Zululand hill country, cut by the deep valley of the Hluhluwe River which has given the place its name. The river, in turn, received its

Zulu name from the thorny monkey rope (*Dalbergia armata*) which grow on its banks. Hluhluwe was proclaimed a game reserve in 1895 and its varied landscape, ranging from densely forested lowlands to open hill summits, provides a sanctuary for a considerable diversity of flora and fauna. Rhino, both black (about 100) and white (about 500) are easily seen. There are also buffalo, nyala, kudu, waterbuck, impala, giraffe, zebra, blue wildebeest, bushbuck, steenbok, reedbuck, red and grey duikers, wart-hog, bushpig, leopards, cheetahs, monkeys and baboons, hyenas, an occasional lion, crocodiles, and vast numbers of birds.

There is a fine observation hide overlooking a water-hole. This hide, known as Munywaneni, is at its best during the dry winter months when the wild animals make use of its perennial source of water.

Hluhluwe has an atmosphere entirely its own and remains imprinted in the memories of innumerable tourists on account of the variety of sights, experience, impressions, and the most satisfying tranquillity experienced there. The reserve is open throughout the year and is traversed by 80 km of all-weather roads. The history of the reserve is told in the next chapter.

From the turn-off to the Hluhluwe Game Reserve, the main gravel Mtubatuba–Nongoma road continues north-westwards for 7 km over low hills covered in acacia bush and fairly densely inhabited by tribal people.

At 27 km from Mtubatuba, the road reaches a turn-off south leading to the ...

UMFOLOZI GAME RESERVE

A 47 743 ha expanse of wilderness, Umfolozi is one of the most important game sanctuaries in the world. At the time of its proclamation in 1895 the last significant numbers of white (square-lipped) rhino in Africa lived in this lovely wilderness. This species, once on the verge of extinction, has been carefully safeguarded at Umfolozi and today flourishes to such an extent that each year a surplus population is immobilised by tranquillising darts and shipped off to zoos and other game reserves. Over 500 surplus white rhinos have been removed in this way, leaving a balance maintained at about 900 white rhinos, the number estimated as being safe for the carrying capacity of the reserve. There are also about 300 black rhinos in Umfolozi.

Umfolozi is an undulating, bush-covered wilderness area contained between the two great branches of the *Mfolozi* (zigzag) River, the *Mfolozi emnyama* (black Mfolozi) and the *Mfolozi emhlophe* (white Mfolozi). Hills overlook the reserve from the north and the atmosphere is particularly romantic. As with Hluhluwe, Umfolozi may truly be said to preserve not only the wildlife of Zululand, but also something of the indefinable charm and tradition surrounding one of the most storied and fascinating parts of Africa.

There are about 300 species of birds and, apart from rhino, the reserve also carries a substantial population of bushbuck, zebra, blue wildebeest, waterbuck, duiker, steenbok, reedbuck, klipspringer, kudu and nyala. There are numerous buffalo, giraffe, baboons, hyenas, cheetahs, leopards and a very remarkable group of lions whose story provides one of the most incredible episodes of conservation in Africa.

Lions in Zululand had long been shot out. In 1958, motivated by some totally unknown factor, a male lion found his way from Mozambique across 300 km of inhabited country and established himself in Umfolozi. Throughout his travels he had been tracked, hunted and pursued by the usual trigger-itchy goon squad but had given them all the slip. In his book *Bushlife of a Game Warden,* Nick Steele described very well the feelings of the rangers and conservationists regarding the adventures and perils of this lion, and their delight when he safely reached the reserve. The arrival of this lone animal was itself remarkable, but even more curious was the fact that, after a few years of celibate existence, he was joined by several females. The result of this is a healthy and happy lion population in Umfolozi, who occasionally visit Hluhluwe to feed on the plump antelope there.

The Umfolozi Game Reserve is open throughout the year. About half the area has been set aside as a wilderness through which parties of up to six people are escorted on three-day walking tours.

Sixty-seven kilometres of all-weather roads take the traveller around the reserve. A hide overlooking a water-hole provides a fine observation place. The history of Umfolozi is told in the next chapter.

From the turn-off to the Umfolozi Game Reserve, the main Mtubatuba–Nongoma road continues north-westwards, climbing steadily through taller and denser bush. Numerous game animals including rhino, may be seen, for the road is now traversing what is known as the Corridor, a belt of wilderness, 21 598 ha in extent, which provides a natural link between the Hluhluwe and Umfolozi game reserves. This section was added to the Umfolozi and Hluhluwe reserves in August 1989. The combined area makes a total of 92 408 ha conserved for wildlife. The road continues for 23 km beyond the turn-off to Umfolozi, climbing through lovely hill country and yielding many pleasant views of a green and almost classic expanse of Zululand scenery. With a final panoramic view over game areas, the road tops the escarpment and leads across a grassy, undulating plateau to enter, after 4 km (53 km from Mtubatuba), the magisterial seat and small village of *Hlabisa,* named after the Zulu clan of that name.

The gravel road proceeds across grassy hills, densely settled with tribal people whose cattle and maize lands are spread out on either side. The road finds a way through a narrow valley, well wooded with trees and wild banana palms. Climbing steadily, the road reaches another plateau and open grassveld, with low hill slopes. At 87 km from Mtubatuba there is a turn-off north to Mkuze (47 km). The road climbs a ridge of hills on the summit of which, 99,5 km from Mtubatuba, stands the village and administrative centre of ...

NONGOMA

KwaNongoma (the place of the diviner) comprises one street lined with stores, houses and administrative buildings which overlook a vast stretch of surrounding country. Founded in 1887, the village was built on a high ridge which was selected as a good strategic situation in what was then a very troubled part of Zululand. In fact, Nongoma was destroyed in June 1888 by supporters of the chief Dinuzulu and was only reoccupied two months later by government forces.

MTUBATUBA TO THE NORTH

From the turn-off to Nongoma, 3 km north of Mtubatuba, the main coastal road continues north-eastwards through plantations of eucalyptus, pine trees and sugar cane. At 17 km from Mtubatuba, at Nyalazi railway siding, a turn-off east leads for 12 km to Charter's Creek on Lake St Lucia (see earlier).

After 3 km the road crosses the Nyalazi River and after a further 8 km crosses the Hluhluwe River. Occasional patches of light bush and lala palms appear amongst the sugar cane and eucalyptus trees. At 49 km from Mtubatuba, the road reaches the small railway centre of Hluhluwe, from where turn-offs lead to False Bay (17 km east) and to the Hluhluwe Game Reserve (17 km west to the entrance, plus 12 km to the rest camp).

The N2 tarmac road continues north-westwards across gently rolling country covered in huge plantations of sisal. Elegantly shaped fever trees grow along the watercourses. Nine kilometres from the village of Hluhluwe, the road passes the small railway centre of *Ngweni* (place of the leopard), situated in the midst of the sisal estates. Beyond this, the road continues. In the distance on the eastern side, emerges the southern beginning of the *Lubombo* (the ridge), a continuous mountain wall of dark basalt rock which stretches far to the north.

At 12 km from Hluhluwe there is a turn-off known as the lower Mkuze road. The road leads north-eastwards for 75 km to the small forestry centre of Mbazwana where it joins the road leading from the magisterial centre of Ubombo to the Sodwana Bay National Park and Lake Sibaya (see further on). It is an interesting drive through the fringes of the Mkuze Game Reserve.

At 33 km from Hluhluwe, the N2 road crosses the Msunduze River on whose banks lie the plantations of the Msunduze Sisal Estates where piles of white sisal may be seen at the drying sheds. The road continues across fields of sisal alternating with patches of savanna covered in grass and acacia trees of various species. Fever trees growing in the watercourses are especially handsome with their deep-green leaves and greenish-white bark.

At 47 km from Hluhluwe, the N2 tarmac road reaches a turn-off leading eastwards for 8 km to the entrance of the ...

MKUZE GAME RESERVE

The approach to the Mkuze Game Reserve is picturesque. The road finds a natural passage through the Lubombo Mountains, forested with many tall trees and clustered with tribal huts. At the entrance to the reserve is a caravan park, with the office and Mantuma hutted camp 9 km further on. The reserve, quite apart from its game population, is a botanist's delight, consisting of 36 000 ha of natural parkland. The variety and elegance of the trees must be seen to be appreciated.

Mkuze contains a dense population of impala, blue wildebeest, nyala, kudu, bushbuck, reedbuck, red duiker, steenbok and black and white rhino. Bird life is extremely diverse and their songs very lovely. Excellent roads (100 km) and a comfortable hutted camp at Mantuma make this a delightful piece of wilderness.

The reserve is named after the Mkhuze River which forms its northern and eastern boundary. The river received its name from the aromatic trees (*Heteropyxis natalensis*) which grow along the banks. It is also notable for other handsome trees such as giant wild figs. The river is one of the principal feeders of Lake St Lucia and its mouth has always been a notorious lurking-place for crocodiles. Most of the river water, however, is nowadays used for irrigation and the flow is therefore erratic.

Mkuze (a misspelling of Mkhuze) was proclaimed a game reserve in 1912. An additional area, the Nxwala state lands, was added to the reserve in February 1982. The history of the reserve is told in the next chapter.

There are three well-designed hides at Bube, Msinga and Malibali pans, where considerable numbers of wild animals drink, especially in the drier winter months.

There are one-day walks and three-day wilderness trails through the reserve, which is open throughout the year. Summer months, however, are very hot and walks are best done during the cool months, April to October.

From the turn-off to the Mkuze Game Reserve, the N2 road continues north-westwards below the bush-covered slopes of the Lubombo. After 9 km the road reaches the rural and rail centre of Mkuze, baking in a warm summer sun near where the Mkhuze River passes through the Lubombo. Overlooking the area is the 520 m high peak which Europeans call Ghost Mountain. Known more prosaically to the Zulus as *iTshaneni* (the place of the small stone), this mountain is considered taboo. A secret cave somewhere near the summit is used as a burial site for the chiefs of the Gaza clan (the ruling family of the Shangane tribe of Mozambique). Tales are told of strange lights and weird sounds which issue from this mountain, and the superstitious will not approach its slopes.

At the foot of this enchanted mountain in the valley of the Mkhuze, lies the battlefield where, on 5 June 1884, the bold Zibebu and his Mandlakazi section of the Zulu people were defeated by the Suthu section of Dinuzulu, supported by 115 European mercenaries. Until recently, the battlefield was still littered with bones from this fight.

From Mkuze, the road continues north-westwards, crossing the Mkhuze River. Three kilometres from the village is a turn-off which leads eastwards for 12 km in a steep and spectacular climb to the magisterial village of Ubombo on the plateau summit of the Lubombo ridge. This is a most interesting drive and the variety of flora is especially fascinating. The display of flowering aloes in late summer is superb.

Ubombo is the administrative centre for a part of the forest-covered coastal belt known nowadays as Maputaland. Beyond the village to the east, a road descends steeply into this wilderness of trees, reaching the coast, 89 km away at the ...

SODWANA BAY NATIONAL PARK

This park comprises a narrow strip of forest-covered sand dunes 413 ha in extent. Proclaimed in 1950, it has a camping ground which is particularly popular with fishermen, especially during the winter holiday season. In summer it is extremely hot and humid. A few antelope such as suni, duiker, steenbok and reedbuck, as well as bushpig, frequent the area along with a wealth of bird life. The name is derived from an isolated streamlet known to the tribespeople as *Sodwana* (little one on its own). Precautions must be taken against malarial fever. There is a shop which sells foodstuffs and petrol.

From the forestry centre of Mbazwana, 15 km before the road reaches Sodwana Bay, there is a turn-off to the north which leads for 16 km to the Baya camp of the Department of Nature Conservation on the shores of Lake Sibaya, the largest fresh water lake in Southern Africa.

From the turn-off to Ubombo, the N2 tarmac road continues north-westwards for a further 7,5 km before reaching a turn-off to the east. This turn-off leads for 23 km, climbing a well-located route 600 m up the Lubombo to Jozini, the site of the Pongolapoort Dam. *Jozini* (named after a tribal headman) overlooks the wall of what is the fifth largest dam in South Africa. The village was created to house the construction workers on this project, which was completed in 1969. The dam impounds 2 446 million cubic metres of water supplied by the river named by the Zulus the *Phongolo* (like a trough) because, being long and deep, it has few crossing places. The dam irrigates a vast area for the cultivation of sugar, rice, coffee, fibre crops and subtropical fruits.

MAPUTALAND (FORMERLY TONGALAND), NDUMO AND KOSI BAY

The sweltering hot, feverous, bilharzia-ridden but otherwise happy wilderness of Maputaland, seems always to be under threat to be considerably altered from its present primeval state. For some reason its totally undeveloped condition has always been an irritant to certain people. Many schemes for the development of this flat, sandy, forest-covered area have been promoted. Few bother to think that Maputaland might conceivably be best left in its present state – a giant wilderness where game animals could perhaps be ranched for the world venison market, edible fish farmed in the shallow lakelets; wild fruits propagated to provide mankind with new flavours; and where a magnificent winter recreational area might be developed, including controlled safari hunting as well as game-viewing resorts.

A visit to Maputaland, as it is now, is a unique experience for the botanist, the bird and game enthusiast, and for the person who simply wants to relieve his mind of the tensions of city life by returning to nature.

Maputaland occupies an area of 7 000 square kilometres. In Cretaceous times (100 to 60 million years ago) this flat, sandy tract of country was the sea bed. Waves washed against the cliffs of the Lubombo. The sea receded, leaving a stretch of sand covered with shells. Shallow depressions, gathering fresh water spilled into them by rivers such as the Phongolo and Mkhuze meandering their way to the sea, formed the numerous shallow lakelets which are such a feature of Maputaland today.

A fine example of these lakes is *iSibayi* (an enclosure with no visible outlet). No rivers feed this natural reservoir of fresh water, crystal clear and held in a setting of sparkling white sand. Seventy-seven square kilometres in extent, with an average depth of 13 m, it is separated from the sea only by a coastal sand dune. It is nearly 20 m above the level of the sea. Fed by powerful springs rising through the sands of the bottom, it maintains its level in spite of immense evaporation. It is a home for hippos, crocodiles, fish and vast numbers of birds, including the vulturine fish eagles. Flying over it is an experience, the hippos, crocs and fish can all be seen clearly visible wandering about on their underwater ways.

A prodigious number of trees flourish in Maputaland, among them some of the most majestic wild fig trees in Africa. Several acacia species, including the elegant fever trees, also grow to perfection. The trees form a belt about 40 km wide stretching from the Lubombo eastwards. They peter out into a strip of lala palms which give way to open grassy coastal flats, followed by a thin line of coastal forest and a wall of tall sand dunes, resembling a dyke built by nature to keep the sea from flooding the lowlands. These topographical features terminate in a stretch of glistening beach where rocky fishermen's promontories jut out into the languid blue of the Indian Ocean.

This wilderness was always a great resort for game animals. Over 200 species of birds are to be found here. Fish, crocodiles and hippos teem in the lakelets and rivers.

Several tribal fragments also inhabit the area, the largest of these being the Tembe tribe, who are (according to tradition) related to the Karanga people of Zimbabwe. A portion of the Tembe tribe live in Mozambique where the capital city of *Maputo* is named, in corrupted form, after their chief Mabudu. The name of *Tonga* was indiscriminately applied to all the people in this part of the world by the Zulus. Its origin is obscure. For many years the area was known as Tongaland. Its rather odd history is told in *Natal and the Zulu Country*. The name Mabudu was applied to the lower reaches of the Phongolo and Usutu rivers after their junction, the Portuguese knowing the river as the Maputo and the English as the Maputa. From this spelling variation has come the name of Maputaland, after what is the largest river in the country. The Portuguese name for Maputaland was *Terra dos Fumos* (land of smokes) from the bush fires resulting from the incessant cut and burn technique of shifting cultivation.

Jozini acts as a gateway to Maputaland. From the village, one road leads south along the Lubombo to the magistracy of Ubombo and to Sodwana Bay. Another road proceeds north, crosses the Phongolo at the foot of the dam wall and, after 3 km, reaches a junction. Both branches from this junction stretch north to Ndumo Game Reserve, but one road keeps to the high country, while the other makes its way through the trees of the lowlands. The latter road is the shorter, but enquiries should always be made in Jozini as to which road is the more suitable. Their condition varies from fair to execrable.

The lowland road travels eastwards down the left bank of the Phongolo to the old fording place and store at Otobotii (*oThobothini,* referring to the willowy thobothi trees which grow there), 6 km from Jozini. From here it swings northwards, finding a picturesque way through the trees for 41 km before rejoining the upland road.

The upland road, meanwhile, makes it way northwards high up on the slopes of the Lubombo, yielding interesting views over the low country. After 48 km the road reaches a junction from where a turn left leads for 8 km to the magisterial and trading village of *Ingwavuma* (named after the river, itself named after the species of tree, *Pseudocassine transvaalensis).* From this isolated little centre with its tremendous views, an old road (not always open except for walkers), descends for 23 km down the Cecil Mack Pass to Swaziland where it joins the main Golela–Manzini road. A turn right at the junction before Ingwavuma takes the road down the eastern slopes of the Lubombo through a dense forest to join the lowland road after 24 km (72 km from Jozini).

The united roads continue northwards through the forest, where many interesting succulents (including the carrion flower) grow by the wayside. After 19 km the road crosses the Ngwavuma River, with tall fever trees on its banks. One kilometre further on, the road passes the Ndumo trading station and after a further kilometre (72 km from Jozini via the lowland road) reaches the entrance (with the camp 6 km away) of the ...

NDUMO GAME RESERVE

This reserve, 10 117 ha in extent, was named after Ndumo, a Tembe chieftain who once lived on the slopes of the overlooking hill. Proclaimed in 1924, it conserves one of the most gorgeous arboreal and riverine landscapes on Earth. Trees form a primeval forest through which the roads literally tunnel. Game animals roam this forest: shy nyala (about 2 000 of them), impala, suni, bushbuck, duiker, bushpig, black and white rhino. The density of the forest makes it difficult for the game to be seen. The trees, however, are the stars of the reserve. Of the estimated 200 different species growing there, there are no examples more beautiful to be seen anywhere else. The riverine forests of fever trees and wild figs are superlatively lovely. The powerful, majestic uSutu River, which forms the northern boundary of the reserve (and the frontier between South Africa and Mozambique), is made even lovelier by the handsome trees growing on its banks.

Some 390 species of birds may be seen in the reserve, while the series of shallow lakelets, fed by floodwater overflow from the Phongolo and uSutu rivers, contain an astonishingly rich population of fish, crocodiles (feeding on the fish), and about 400 hippos living well on the luxuriant grazing around the verges. With fish eagles sending their eerie cry over the calm waters, hippos 'gallumphing', fish splashing, spur-wing geese honking and hissing, and the crocodiles moving with such sinister silence and stealth that scarcely a ripple reaches the surface, these lakelets almost belong to a dream world.

There is a crocodile-breeding station at Ndumo. Eggs are hatched and the young protected for the first three years of life. They are then released in waters where their kind has been depleted by hunters, the result of whose activities has seriously affected the balance of fish life.

Ndumo is open throughout the year, but November to March is excessively hot and humid. From April the weather becomes cooler and vast numbers of birds flock to the area. During the coolest months, May, June and July, bird life is at its most prolific. But at all seasons, even in sweltering heat, Ndumo is worth visiting.

There are a number of rest huts and campsite accommodation. Book through the KwaZulu-Natal Nature Conservation Service, P O Box 13069, Cascades, Pietermaritzburg, 3202.

For those adventurers who wish to see still more of the Maputaland wilderness and who possess a strong, reliable vehicle, a sandy track stretches eastwards from the road to Ndumo at the point where the road from Ingwavuma joins the lowland road from Jozini (31 km from Ingwavuma). This track tunnels through the forest for a further 23 km and then crosses the Phongolo at the fording place, *Makhane's Drift*, named after a chieftain who once lived there.

The track then continues through the forest, passes the southern tip of the Tembe Elephant Park and across the belt of lala palms whose fermented sap provides the local tribespeople with the unique facility of being able to freely acquire unlimited quantities of intoxicating liquor. The result is that many alcoholic mothers give birth to inebriated babies, who, when they eventually die of old age, are still in the presumably happy state, never having known sobriety, and all for nothing.

TEMBE ELEPHANT PARK

The Tembe Elephant Park, named after the Tembe tribe, is 30 000 ha in extent with its northern boundary on the frontier of Mozambique. The entrance gate is 72 km from Jozini. There is a tourism office and a small tented camp which can accommodate eight people. Only one party of day visitors is also allowed at a time into the park apart from guests in the park.

Only 4 × 4 vehicles are allowed into the Park. Trail guides accompany each party. The tourism route includes a hide overlooking a pan in the Muzi swamp. It is a sandy area covered in dense woodland and thickets of assorted tropical and subtropical forms. Apart from elephants, wildlife includes white rhino, giraffe, water buck, kudu, impala, nyala, reedbuck, wildebeest, duiker and suni. Bird life is prolific.

Malarial fever is endemic and the Park is very hot and humid in the summer months.

At 57 km from Makhane's Drift the track reaches the remote trading post of *Maputa*. From this little centre the track proceeds north-eastwards over an open landscape of grassy flats and sandy hillocks. Branch tracks lead eastwards to the chain of lakes known to Europeans as Kosi. These magnificent lakes – *Hlangwe* (reedy place), 8 km long, 5 km wide and 50 m deep; *oKhunwine* (the place of firewood); *uKhalwe* (the distant one); and their estuary *enKovukeni* (ebb and flow) – received their collective European name in 1822 as a result of a mistake made by the pioneer marine surveyor, Captain Owen, who marked them on his chart as being the mouth of the 'omKosi' (Mkhuze) River. The lakes contain numerous fish which are caught in complex reed traps constructed by the local tribespeople.

THE KOSI BAY NATURE RESERVE

The Kosi Bay nature reserve of 20 ha was proclaimed in 1950 on the shores of Lake Hlangwe. The ranger in charge has the additional task of patrolling the beach where the leatherback and loggerhead turtles nest in one of the few sanctuaries provided for these interesting creatures.

There are camping sites but sandy access roads inhibit caravans. There are three furnished lodges. Book through the KwaZulu-Natal Nature Conservation Service, P O Box 13069, Cascades, Pietermaritzburg, 3202.

There are walking trails with guides. Fishing is good. Crocodiles and bilharzia prevent swimming. Malarial fever is endemic. A four-day hiking trail provides a wonderful circular walk around the lakes.

The track from Maputa, meanwhile, continues north-eastwards for 24 km past the Kosi Bay store, crossing the frontier line between South Africa and Mozambique. Eight kilometres beyond the Kosi Bay store, a turn-off to the coast leads through an exquisite parkland, ending at a lazy little bay with a high, sandy headland jutting protectively into the sea to form Ponta Do Ouro. Originally the Portuguese called the mouth of the Kosi lakes the *Rio de la Medãos do Ouro* (river of the sands of gold), of which name Ponta do Ouro is the sole remnant. A small lighthouse watches over the point, a lonely little outpost marking the frontier between South Africa and Mozambique and the most easterly point of South Africa. Good fishing, and the beautiful phosphorescent sands at night, make this an interesting place for the adventurous to visit.

The entire 100 km long coast between the Mozambique frontier and Sodwana Bay is now protected as the Kosi Bay Coastal Forest Reserve and Maputoland Marine Reserve. Mabibi coastal camp has been created by the Department of Nature Conservation as a centre for the southern part of this coastal park. It is 148 km from the N2 turn-off leading through Jozini to Sodwana.

From the turn-off to Jozini and Maputaland, 10,5 km from Mkuze, the N2 tarmac road leads north-westwards across a bush and aloe-covered plain dominated to the east by the massive wall of the Lubombo. At 19,5 km from Mkuze the road crosses the railway line at Candover station, passes a turn-off to Magudu (40 km) with its taboo forest used as a burial place for the chiefs of the Ndwandwe tribe. The name comes from a chief of the Ndwandwe tribe who lived on the overlooking mountain. The forest is reputably haunted by packs of invisible hounds and ghostly hunters who drive intruders away.

From the turn-off of R69 to Magudu, the N2 continues over a rolling plain, covered with acacias and sisal estates.

At 30 km from Mkuze, the N2 road climbs a ridge. In a finely located route it descends into the valley of the Phongolo River where fields of sugar cane are irrigated. At 33,5 km from Mkuze, the road crosses the Phongolo and leads westwards up the valley of this important river. After 3 km there is a turn-off north-eastwards to the border of Swaziland at *Golela* (a gathering place of wild animals), the traditional hunting ground of the Nyawo chiefs. From the turn-off to Swaziland, the left-hand branch of the road continues westwards to the town of Pongola (Phongolo) and then westwards to enter the province of Mpumulanga. The great N2 coastal highway of South Africa then continues north-westwards and ends at Ermelo where it joins N11 on its way north, over the highveld of Mpumulanga.

ESHOWE AND THE ZULU COUNTRY

One kilometre north of Gingindlovu, on the N2 coastal road of Zululand, a tarmac turn-off stretches westwards to Eshowe and from there to several interesting places in the heart of the Zulu country. One kilometre after this turn-off commences, a monument is passed, marking the site of the battle of Gingindlovu, fought in April 1879 when a British force on its way to relieve Eshowe from a Zulu siege, defeated a Zulu attack. Beyond this battle site the road climbs 500 m up the sugar cane covered hill slopes, from where the lovely countryside may be viewed. After 21 km the road reaches the summit, entering the municipal area of ...

ESHOWE

The town of Eshowe is built on the site of a gorgeous hilltop forest known on account of its silence and dark recesses as the *Dlinza* (a grave-like place of meditation). Since 1952, 203 ha of this forest have been protected as a nature reserve, with the town surrounding it. Within its confines live bushbuck, blue and red duiker, wild pigs, vervet monkeys and numerous birds. Fine drives and walks yield many delightful scenes of tall trees, fern-grown glades, streams and waterfalls. In a central glade, known as the Bishop's Seat, church services are occasionally held; and every three years a nativity play specially written in 1953 by Selwyn Moberley is performed in this natural amphitheatre.

Eshowe overlooks a fine view from its hilltop and the altitude contributes to a refreshing climate. The sounds of the cool breezes of Eshowe sighing through the trees are, in fact, said to have given the place its attractive name. This may be so, although the Zulus say the name is derived from the xysmalobium shrubs growing there, which they call *ishowe* or *ishongwe*.

Eshowe originated in 1860 when Cetshwayo built his *eSighwagini* (abode of robbers) kraal in the area and granted the Norwegian missionary, Ommund Oftebro, permission to establish what became known as the *kwaMondi* mission, from the Zulu version of Oftebro's first name. It was here, after the disaster of iSandlwana, that a British force was besieged by the Zulus for ten weeks until 3 April 1879, after the battle of Gingindlovu.

After the Anglo-Zulu War, Eshowe became the administrative centre for the British resident commissioner, Melmoth Osborn. To support him, a force of Zulus, the Reserve Territorial Carbineers, popularly known as the *Nongqayo* (restrainers), was created. A *beau geste* type fort, built for them at Eshowe, is now a picturesque museum housing an interesting collection of Zululand relics. It is open weekdays from 07h30 to 16h00 and weekends from 09h00 to 16h00.

In 1887 Eshowe became the capital of the whole of Zululand and in 1892 the first sale of erven established its future as a town. Tall trees and colourful gardens, a magnificent swimming-pool in the forest, Rutledge Park with its lake full of waterfowl, and Ocean View Game Park, just off the road to Gingindlovu, all contribute towards making Eshowe one of the most pleasant small towns in Southern Africa. The population is 24 921.

From Eshowe a very interesting scenic route to Empangeni may be followed. This road branches off from the Eshowe–Melmoth tarmac road 8 km from Eshowe, and runs along the verge of the tremendous valley of the Mhlatuze River, once one of the great game areas of Zululand but now extensively planted with sugar cane. Impressive views, the numerous Zulu huts and tribal villages, the acacia trees and euphorbias – all make the journey picturesque.

At 27 km from Eshowe, a monument on the left (north) side of the road marks the site of Shaka's great capital of *kwaBulawayo* (place of the man who was killed) which was situated on the summit of a rounded hill, now overgrown with thick grass and a few euphorbia and other trees. It is fascinating to imagine the day in 1824 when Henry Fynn, the ivory trader, was the first European to visit the place from the new settlement at Port Natal (Durban). There the rugged adventurer found an African city of several thousand huts. He was ceremoniously welcomed by the great Zulu king in the presence of 12 000 warriors in full war dress, while 10 000 girls in exquisite bead costumes danced in his honour. It must have been a spectacle of splendour unsurpassed on the whole continent of Africa.

One kilometre beyond the site of kwaBulawayo, a memorial draws attention to a kei-apple tree growing at the roadside, known as Coward's Bush, where Shaka reputedly tested by means of some ordeal those of his men accused of cowardice.

The gravel road descends to cross the *Mhlatuze* (forceful) River and, 45 km from Eshowe, joins the tarmac Nkwalini–Empangeni road 12 km from the latter town.

ESHOWE TO ULUNDI AND NONGOMA

This road R66 takes the traveller through fine scenery to several of the most interesting historical sites of Zululand. From Eshowe the tarmac road leads for 6 km, passes a turn-off to the site of kwaBulawayo (see above), and then makes a grand descent into the valley of the Mhlatuze River. This huge valley, overlooked by a jumble of high hills, was once a haunt of big game and a favourite hunting-ground of the Zulu kings. This is a supreme piece of Zulu country, with the huts of the tribespeople perched on the hill slopes and the river twisting lazily down the valley like a sinuous python.

The road bridges across the Mhlatuze River 17 km from Eshowe, passing the trading centre and railhead of *Nkwalini* (place of the red-legged pheasant) 3 km further on, with a tarmac turn-off leading down the valley to Empangeni. The road then starts to ascend the steep northern side of the valley, a magnificent drive which reveals many exciting views. After 6 km the road reaches the summit and continues through the high hills until, 48,4 km from Eshowe, it reaches the village of ...

MELMOTH

When the British government annexed Zululand in 1887, several magistracies were established, one of which was named *Melmoth* after Melmoth Osborn, the resident commissioner and chief magistrate of the country. The high hill country surrounding the village was ideal for the growing of trees, particularly wattle. In 1926 a factory was established in Melmoth to process the bark of the wattle tree for the production of tanning extract. The village is now a trading centre for a considerable industry in the growing of trees to obtain timber, wattle extract and paper-making material.

From Melmoth the R66 tarmac road climbs steadily through fields of sugar cane and plantations of trees. After 4,5 km a turn-off R68, known as the Battlefields route, leads to Babanango and Dundee. At 14 km further on along the R66 there is a turn-off to Katazo (*Ntabe Khathazo,* the hill of khathazo plants) and from there to Nkandla. The road is now on the summit of the escarpment, in what is known as the mist belt. The plantations of trees are particularly dense and green as a result of the water which condenses from the winds as they rise from the coast and top the summit ridge of the hills.

On the summit the road passes a monument marking the *Mthonjaneni* (place of the little fountain) which gives this ridge its name. From this spring the Zulu kings drew their drinking-water which was reserved for their personal use. A grand view reveals to the west the valley of the Mkhumbane, the traditional birthplace of the Zulu nation and the residence of all their early kings.

The road descends the western slopes of the Mtonjaneni ridge and at 24 km from Melmoth reaches a turn-off R34 leading westwards to Vryheid. Five kilometres along this turn-off there is a turn-off signposted Dingane's Kraal, an important historical site 4,5 km away in the valley of the Mkhumbane.

DINGANE'S KRAAL

About 300 years ago, according to tradition, the man named *Zulu* (heaven) who founded the Zulu nation, found his way into the warm, bush-covered valley of the stream known as the *Mkhumbane* (stream of the hollow). He settled in the valley with a handful of dependants and eventually died there. His grave is marked with a euphorbia tree planted at what is known as *kwaNkosinkhulu* (place of the great chief).

When Shaka became the king of the Zulus, he built a capital on the right bank of the Mhodi tributary of the Mkhumbane. This capital he named *kwaBulawayo* (place of the man who was killed) in memory of the persecutions of his youth. When he expanded his territorial control over what is now Zululand, he moved this capital south to a site overlooking the Mhlatuze valley (see earlier).

In 1828 Shaka was assassinated by two of his half-brothers, Mhlangana and Dingane. Dingane became king and built a new capital in the valley of the Mkhumbane. This capital he named *uMgungundlovu* (the secret plot of the elephant), a name which referred to the intrigue surrounding the assassination of Shaka.

It is worth visiting the site of uMgungundlovu, where the hard floors of many of the huts and other interesting relics may be seen. In its heyday, uMgungundlovu was an enormous hut city and the centre for endless ceremonial activities, military parades, dances and affairs of state of the Zulu nation. The scenic setting of the valley is impressive. To the north looms the principal landmark of this part of the world, the flat-topped 1 448 m high *Nhlazatshe* (green stone) Mountain. Immediately west of this mass of rock stands the stool-shaped mountain known as *isiHlalo sikaManyosi* (the seat of Manyosi).

Manyosi was a famous fat man and favourite of Dingane. Dingane found it amusing to display his gluttony to visitors by letting Manyosi eat, at one sitting, his fill of an entire goat and then look for more. Manyosi's pampered life ended when he said something out of place and Dingane had him starved to death. The stool-shaped mountain is his memorial.

It was at uMgungundlovu on 5 February 1838 that Dingane massacred Piet Retief and 70 of his men. The scene of the murder was the Zulu place of execution, known as *kwaMatiwane* after a chief named Matiwane who had been killed there. A memorial marks the site. This massacre resulted in war between the Zulus and the Voortrekkers. After the Battle of Blood River a Voortrekker force advanced on Dingane's capital, reaching uMgungundlovu on 20 December 1838. They found the entire place with its 2 000 huts abandoned and set on fire by the Zulus.

A large mission of the Dutch Reformed Church was later built on the ridge overlooking the site of uMgungundlovu. The mission occupies the position where the Reverend Francis Owen established his camp in 1837 and endeavoured to persuade Dingane to allow the establishment of a permanent mission. From this height, the pioneer missionary watched with horror as the Zulus killed Retief and his men, and then marshalled their army for a great raid against the camps of the Voortrekkers situated below the Drakensberg. A tangible atmosphere still lingers about the scene where these events took place. The valley remains in its original state, covered with a parkland of flowering aloes, euphorbias and flat-topped acacia trees.

From the turn-off to Vryheid and Dingane's Kraal, the R66 road continues for 11 km and then bridges over the White Mfolozi River, flowing through an acacia-covered bowl in the hills. In the centre of this bowl, 4 km beyond the bridge, the road reaches a turn-off leading to the memorial on the site of the battle of Ulundi.

ULUNDI

In 1873, when Cetshwayo became king of the Zulus, he founded a new capital which he named *uluNdi* or *oNdi* (the heights) and which Europeans know as Ulundi. On 4 July 1879 the British army under Lord Chelmsford advanced on the capital and the last battle of the Anglo-Zulu War took place there. About 17 000 Zulus made a rather dispirited advance on the British who, 5 000 strong, were drawn up in square formation about 2 km from the capital. The Zulus lost about 1 500 men in the attack, while British fatalities amounted to 12 – the spear was simply no match for the rifle. The battlefield is still sprinkled with numerous bullets and other bric-à-brac of war. Visitors to the site (marked by a memorial building), are usually received by urchins who offer for sale various items presumably recovered by them from the scene of battle. Ulundi was burned down by the British. By this act the independence of the Zulu nation was ended.

The modern administrative centre of Ulundi has been built 3 km from the memorial.

OPATHE GAME RESERVE

The *Opathe* (place of ambush) Game Reserve consists of 9 000 hectares of a conservation area notable for its extraordinary biodiversity within the flora and fauna kingdom. The reserve extends from the southern banks of the White Mfolozi River over three rugged river valleys, that of the Opathe, nKongolwane and Kwibi rivers. Within its conservancy there are highveld grasslands, mist belt, valley bushveld, sand thornveld, lowveld, shadowy areas of thambothi woodland, cliff hanging vegetation like green waterfalls tumbling down over precipices, springs, wetlands, granite cliffs and sparkling gneiss formations of rock. Hills and valleys provide superlative scenery.

A four-wheel drive vehicle is essential to visit the Opathe Game Reserve. A trail for these vehicles has been created by the Department of Nature Conservation assisted by the Delta Isuzu Corporation. This track, known as the *mKhosini* (place of kings) Trail winds and climbs through awesome scenery.

There is limited accommodation in the fully furnished and serviced original farmhouse of *Mars*. All provisions must be brought with visitors. The nearest shops are at Ulundi one-and-a-quarter hours drive away. The reserve is in process of being restocked with the fauna indigenous to the area. Bird life, is prolific, with several raptor, grassland and wetland species.

The R66 road continues northwards, climbs the hill slopes overlooking the Ulundi basin and, after 10 km, reaches the small centre of *Mahlabathini* (place of white sands), founded in 1869 as a seat of magistracy. From this rather dilapidated place, a commanding situation being its principal asset, the road descends into the bush-covered valley of the *Bekamuzi* (behold a kraal) River, 13,5 km from Mahlabatini. This valley was once a hunting area renowned for its elephants, but wildlife has long since been replaced by man. The road climbs another bush-covered ridge and, after 9,5 km, descends to cross the Black Mfolozi River. Rising, falling, twisting and turning, the road continues for a further 23,5 km. After a long climb, it reaches Nongoma (see earlier) and a choice of roads stretching to the coast or inland.

ESHOWE TO NKANDLA, ISANDLWANA AND RORKE'S DRIFT

From Eshowe a spectacular scenic drive follows the edge of the valley of the Thukela River to Nkandla and thence to Kranskop, Babanango, Nqutu, iSandlwana and Dundee. The first part of the road to Nkandla is mainly gravel and should be avoided in wet weather. Careful driving in dry weather rewards the traveller with superb scenery.

The road leads westwards from Eshowe through extensive plantations of sugar cane. After 13 km there is a turn-off to the Entumeni nature reserve, a 564 ha area of evergreen mist belt indigenous forest. It was proclaimed a reserve in 1970. The name is derived from the wild bitter-apple trees growing in the vicinity. Dabulamanzi, a renowned officer of the Zulu army during the Anglo-Zulu war, had his stronghold there. The British garrison of Eshowe attacked it on 1 March 1879 but without notable success.

At 22 km from Eshowe a turn-off stretches for 4 km to the sugar mill and village of Entumeni. The road continues for a further 24 km through the cane plantations and then reaches the first of a number of superb viewsites looking out over the huge valley of the Thukela River to the distant landmark of Kranskop on the KwaZulu-Natal side of the river.

For the next 31 km the road follows the edge of the prodigious valley which justifiably gives the river its Zulu name of *Thukela* (startling). Patches of indigenous forest cover the hills which are also clustered with numerous tribal huts.

The name *Nkandla* (place of exhaustion) is applied to the rugged forest-clad edge of the Thukela valley. This wildly beautiful piece of country was the scene of the Bambatha revolt in 1906. A number of tribesmen, led by the petty chief Bambatha, made an armed protest against the imposition of taxes. The Mhome gorge in the heart of the Nkandla forest where Cetshwayo is buried was their stronghold. Some bitter fighting took place in the area before the revolt was suppressed and Bambatha killed.

The village of Nkandla, 77 km from Eshowe, was established as a seat of magistracy in 1887. It is a straggling, attractive little place, shaded by wattle and eucalyptus trees.

Two kilometres outside Nkandla a road branches off for 32 km to join the R68 road from Dundee and Nqutu. The combined roads make a spectacular descent into the valley of the Thukela, crossing the river after 18 km at Jameson's Drift. The road then climbs the cliffs on the KwaZulu-Natal side of the valley, reaching Kranskop after a further 34 km of scenic splendour.

From the junction outside Nkandla, the west road continues for 2,5 km, reaching a turn-off to Melmoth 48 km away. A further 13 km takes the road to a turn-off of 3,5 km which joins the tarmac Melmoth–Babanango road at a point 12 km from the small rural centre known as *Babanango* (father, there it is). The name is derived from a high hill which serves as a landmark for the area and is a convenient place from which to explore the grassy middleveld and the battlefields of iSandlwana and Rorke's Drift.

From Babanango the R68 tarmac road leads westwards over the grassy hills. There are turn-offs after 16 km to Nkandla; after 18 km to Vryheid (75 km); after 30,5 km to Kranskop (100 km); and 40,5 km from Babanango a turn-off leading for 9,5 km to the site of the battle of ...

ISANDLWANA

The scene of this renowned battle of the Anglo-Zulu War is the plain at the foot of the isolated, sinister-looking hillock which the Zulus called *iSandlwana* (something like a small house). This is the name given to the second stomach of a cow, the shape of which the hill is considered to resemble.

On 20 January 1879 the British army, about to commence an invasion of Zululand, set up camp at the foot of iSandlwana on a site which consisted of open, high ground and which seemingly dominated the surrounding country. Deep dongas, however, invisible from ground level, lay scattered at the approach to the site, providing magnificent cover for any attacker with the wit to exploit them.

On 22 January, while the British commander Lord Chelmsford was out on reconnaissance, a Zulu army of about 17 000 men led by Ntshingwayo overwhelmed the camp and killed 864 British soldiers and 470 of their African allies. The Zulus suffered about 1 000 casualties.

The battlefield is clearly marked with whitewashed boulders which indicate the position of the various units engaged in the action. A small field museum is situated on a hill overlooking the battlefield, where maps and a relief model of the scene on the day of the battle are displayed. There is also a collection of shields from the different Zulu regiments and uniforms and badges of the British units.

To reach Rorke's Drift, where a small British garrison was attacked immediately after the battle of iSandlwana, the main tarmac road must be rejoined and then followed through the trading centre of Nqutu (23 km). From here the main road to Dundee must be taken across the Buffalo River to a turn-off 19 km from Nqutu (32 km from Dundee), which leads for 18 km to the Swedish mission station of ...

RORKE'S DRIFT

James Rorke farmed and traded on the site of the mission until his death on 24 October 1875. In 1878 the Swedish Missionary Society acquired the property and founded the *Oscarberg Mission,* named after the Swedish king. The mission, under the Evangelical Lutheran Church of Southern Africa, is still very active.

At the outbreak of the Anglo-Zulu War, the main British force was marshalled near the mission. On 11 January 1879 it invaded Zululand by crossing the Buffalo River at the drift named after James Rorke. It was this force which made its camp at iSandlwana and suffered such grievous defeat. A small garrison under Lieutenant G Bromhead, with Lieutenant J R M Chard of the Royal Engineers in overall command, had remained at the mission station. When news of the disaster at iSandlwana reached them at 15h15, the 139 men at the mission hurriedly braced themselves for a Zulu attack.

Two Zulu regiments commanded by Dabulamanzi were sent to pursue refugees from iSandlwana. At 16h30 they approached the mission. They had received no orders to attack the place, but were heady with the victory of iSandlwana. About 600 Zulus charged the sandstone building of the mission but were driven back, trying a second time without success. The main body then lined up on the overlooking hill and peppered the buildings with bullets, meanwhile launching a series of onslaughts during which the parsonage, which was being used as a hospital, was set on fire. The attack went on until about 04h00 of the next day, 23 January. Dabulamanzi then realised that he was badly exceeding his orders in conducting an attack on entrenched soldiers. He had so far lost about 400 men while 15 British soldiers had been killed and most of the others wounded.

The remnants of the two Zulu regiments withdrew, leaving the members of the little garrison to bandage wounds and put out the fires. These men ultimately received high praise for stubborn courage and heroism shown in the face of heavy odds.

Chapter Twenty-Six
THE WILDLIFE AND GAME RESERVES OF THE ZULU COUNTRY

The story of man and wild animal in Zululand is not very edifying. It is sad but true that the most beautiful and peaceful areas of Earth have been, and remain, those which man, for various reasons, has not been able to disturb or (in his own description) improve. According to geologists, the planet Earth is nearly 500 thousand million years old. It took Nature that considerable period of time to create the surface of Earth as we know it today, and not even the most powerful telescope has revealed anything in outer space more beautiful or amiable to life.

Man, nevertheless, in his short span of existence has always held the opinion that he can manage things much better. The Zululand game reserves provide fine continuing studies not only of wild animals but of man – also an animal – firm in his conviction that his wisdom is superior to that of Nature, that he has the power and the right to play God, to dispense death even if he has not the ability to create life.

The scene of the sad little drama is set in the bush, the hills and the valleys of Zululand, where the great African savanna sweeps down from the north. The savanna is still home to the most numerous and diverse population of wild animals to be found anywhere on Earth. This vast parkland extends from the borders of Ethiopia south for 4 000 km, until it finally peters out in the Addo bush near Port Elizabeth. Before the invention of the gun, this savanna was the great haunt of big game and nowhere was this more so than in the south-east coastal area between the Phongola and Thukela rivers.

The prehistoric hunter-gatherer people preyed upon these wild animals for food, but lethally their bows and arrows were limited and they killed for the pot, not simply for sport. The Iron Age tribes, with their spears and traps, made a greater impact on the wildlife, but not to any decisive extent. It took the gun and the commercialisation of killing by professional ivory, horn, hide and biltong hunters really to launch the onslaught on the domain of wild animals.

When Shaka became king of the Zulus and commenced the creation of a warrior nation, he saw their country at its most glorious. Travellers of those times describe the Zulu country as teeming with wildlife. With Shaka assassinated and his half-brother, Dingane, driven out by the Voortrekkers and their ally Mpande, the domain of the wild in the Zulu country was thrown open for the first time to European hunters and traders. Mpande had been placed in his position of power by the white man, hence the white man could do no wrong.

A time of killing commenced. Each winter season parties of hunters travelled up from Durban. The summer months of fever gave the wild animals some respite when the hunters retreated to the safety of a healthier climate, but the onslaught of the killers was severe. From 1840 until 1870 the slaughter continued until the only remaining populations of wild animals of any significance were in the areas in which the presence of tsetse fly made conditions unpleasant for hunters.

Tsetse fly were the carriers of the livestock disease called by the Zulus *uNakane* (the pest). Nobody at that time knew that the tsetse fly carried this disease. The Zulus thought that it was caused by a species of grass or by cattle grazing on grass infected by the saliva of wild animals. Europeans, who called the disease nagana, had several theories, including a suspicion that the tsetse fly was responsible. The disease affected all domestic animals, even dogs. Man was not fatally infected in Zululand, but the loss of cattle, horses, draught oxen, and even the hardy donkey, effectively dissuaded hunters and settlers from entering fly-infested areas. The tsetse fly was thus the pioneer conservationist, as wild animals were immune to the disease carried by the fly. Their continued existence in the Zulu country became dependent on the presence of the tsetse fly.

The situation whereby a fly could hold man at bay became increasingly frustrating to hunters and would-be settlers. Nobody had the temerity to suggest that the tsetse could be ignored and selected wild animals species ranched for their venison, hides and horns. The mere idea of selectively breeding such species as eland for their unique meat-to-bone ratio and for the richness of their milk was scorned.

Pressure mounted on the Colonial Government of Natal to do something about nagana. The correct man for the job arrived in 1894 in the person of Surgeon-Major David Bruce, posted to the British garrison in Pietermaritzburg. He was a medical man of considerable reputation. Assigned to the garrison in Malta, he had discovered the cause of Malta Fever, which annually killed many people. He found that the disease was carried in goat's milk. The governor of the island at the time was Sir Walter Hely-Hutchinson. When Bruce was posted to Pietermaritzburg he found that Sir Walter had just been appointed Governor of Natal.

The two men discussed the nagana problem and Bruce agreed to being sent to Zululand to study the disease. With his wife he travelled by wagon to the remote administrative post of Ubombo, where he was accommodated in a simple wattle-and-daub hut, the veranda of which served as a laboratory.

Within two months Bruce found that nagana was caused by the *Trypanosoma* parasite which lived in the blood of various wild animals, but did not give them the disease. Tsetse fly fed on the blood of these infected animals and carried the parasite to domestic livestock. At this stage in his research, Bruce was recalled to his regiment. Back in Pietermaritzburg he wrote his classic preliminary report, *The Tsetse Fly Disease of Nagana Zululand*.

In 1896 Bruce and his wife were sent back to Ubombo where he continued his research for two years. He sent an infected dog to London and the parasites in its blood were described in 1899 as a new tsetse species, *Trypanosoma brucei*, named after Bruce. This parasite was assumed to be the cause of nagana, but it was later discovered that it only caused a mild infection in cattle.

Bruce continued his research on the life-cycle of the tsetse, discovering amongst other things its odd mode of reproduction whereby the female gives birth to a single, full-grown larva.

While Bruce worked on his research, there were major political developments. In 1897 Zululand was annexed to Natal. There was an immediate stirring among land-hungry Europeans. A wild stampede for farms would have occurred, but the British Government imposed a five-year delay before any land would be made available for settlement.

In 1895 hunting had been prohibited in five areas of Zululand where game animals still survived – the same areas where tsetse fly occurred. At this time, C D Guise sent a letter to the Zululand Administration, informing it that the white rhino was on the verge of extinction. Unless it was protected, it would soon wind up only as a museum exhibit. He suggested that the remaining white rhinos be totally protected. Sir Walter Hely-Hutchinson was sympathetic. In 1897 he proclaimed as game reserves four of the five areas where hunting had been prohibited, namely Hluhluwe, Umfolozi, Umdhletshe and St Lucia.

Between 1895 and 1896 the livestock disease known as rinderpest swept the length of Africa like a forest fire. About 750 000 head of cattle died in South Africa, including 80 per cent of the cattle in Zululand. In the Eastern Transvaal the disease at least had a beneficial effect. In a way as yet unknown it killed the tsetse fly, but unfortunately this process was not duplicated in Zululand.

Bruce completed his two years of research at Ubombo and returned to the army. In 1898 he published his *Further Report on the Tsetse Fly Disease of Nagana in Zululand* and this secured him a Fellowship of the Royal Society. He was only 44 years of age and recognised as a master of experimental medicine.

In 1902 the five-year moratorium on land settlement in Zululand expired. A clamour for farmland ensued. A railway was opened in 1903 as far as a coal-mine at Somkele near Mtubatuba, and this made most of the coastal area accessible, with the terminus only a few kilometres from the borders of the Hluhluwe and Umfolozi game reserves.

A Delimitation Commission had the task of dividing Zululand into areas for new settlement and for the original population. The four game reserves were left intact; and a fifth one, known as Hlabisa, was created, but was abolished in 1907. A flood of eager settlers arrived to take up cheap, virgin land. The four existing reserves were soon surrounded by farms. To protect the reserves the first game conservator was appointed to Zululand in 1911, in the person of Frederick Vaughan Kirby, author and hunter. He was stationed in Nongoma and patrolled the four reserves by mule wagon.

Kirby had to confront a very difficult situation. There was mounting agitation that the game reserves be deproclaimed, all wild animals slaughtered, and the land made available for settlement. The wild animals were considered vermin; killing them would deprive the tsetse fly of food; the fly would die and nagana would vanish from Zululand. Nobody entertained the idea of prevention or cure. After the departure of Bruce, only a few amateur naturalists continued research in Zululand.

Glossina pallidipes was the species of tsetse fly which Bruce had studied. Then, in March 1915, J M Robertson captured a tsetse fly in the court-house at Ubombo, where he was a clerk. The magistrate, R A L Brandon, sent the fly to the Durban Museum. The curator, E C Chubb, mistakenly considered it to be a new species, which he named *Glossina brandoni* after the magistrate. It was later found to be a specimen of *Glossina austeni*, which had already been found in Central Africa.

Chubb asked Brandon to catch more specimens of tsetse fly and on 25 April 1915, in the valley of the Mkhuze River, the magistrate caught several *G. pallidipes* and one new species which was named *Glossina brevipalpis*. These three species – *G. austeni*, *G. brevipalpis* and *G. pallidipes* – comprised the tsetse population of Zululand. What was to be done about them and the disease they carried was the cause of great controversy.

Poor Vaughan Kirby found his game reserves under bitter attack. His only ally seemed to be Dr E Warren, director of the Natal Museum in Pietermaritzburg. Of all the scientists, Warren was one of the very few who defended the wild animals. Concurring with Professor E A Minchin of Britain, he was adamant that *'the extermination of wild animals would not remove the trouble. The tsetse fly would simply transfer their feeding to other creatures, birds, domestic animals, reptiles, man. Nagana or sleeping sickness would remain endemic'*.

Along with the rest – farmers and transport riders – even the esteemed David Bruce was explicit in his opinion.

'Wild animals should not be allowed to live in fly country,' he said. *'Not only should all game laws restricting their destruction in fly country be removed, but active measures should be taken for their early and complete blotting out'*.

Warren and Kirby did what they could.

'We must endeavour to stop this wild outburst of bloodlust,' Warren wrote to Kirby. *'Some voice on the side of the wild animals should be raised.'*

Time after time Warren made his point.

'The great essential is to eliminate the fly, not the game. It is a fallacy to think killing the game will kill the fly. The experiment of slaughtering game is doomed to almost certain failure'.

The problem was how to eliminate the fly or the disease. For this there was no answer. The killers partly had their way; all game outside the reserves was to be shot. In August 1917 the first concentrated hunting commenced in the Ubombo district. The whole area was cleared of wild animals, with over 25 000 wildebeest alone being destroyed. Hunters flocked to the scene from all over South Africa. It was a degrading spectacle and the commencement of a sorry chapter in the history of the country.

Vaughan Kirby watched the shambles with disgust and horror.

'What has been gained by this slaughter?' he wrote to the Provincial Secretary. *'I do not hesitate to affirm that you can only find one reply thereto, and that is "nothing, absolutely nothing". Briefly stated, then, the position is this, that the game has gone but the fly remains. Believe me, no member of the public is ever going to admit that the measures taken have been futile, though every one of them knows it, so it remains with the administration to review the situation and to admit failure, and to put a stop to this worse-than-cruel-slaughter'*.

His protests were ignored. In February 1919 the Ngwavuma district was thrown open to hunters in a new proclamation and there was a regular stampede to the area by what seemed to be every trigger-happy idiot in South Africa. The killers were arrogant, bombastic and triumphant. The one official in all Zululand who was on the side of wildlife was in despair.

'That damnable proclamation,' Vaughan Kirby wrote to Dr Warren. *'It is an absolutely broken-spirited man that now addresses you'*.

The sheer scale of the slaughter, however, attracted the attention of other people, and not all of them were killers. The chief of veterinary research in South Africa, E Montgomery, met the Natal Provincial Secretary and told him flatly that the destruction of game was unlikely to lead to any beneficial result. The Transvaal Game Protection Association also made strong representations.

The Natal Administration became confused. Notwithstanding all the slaughter, nagana was still present in Zululand and in 1920 there occurred a serious crisis.

In 1919 a settlement area comprising 72 farms had been opened for returned soldiers. The farms covered a jumble of low, bush-covered hills west of the Umfolozi Game Reserve, drained by a watercourse known to the Zulus as *Ntambanana* (little vein) which follows a tortuous route on its way to join the Mhlatuze River.

For the first year this new settlement flourished. The settlers commenced ranching and, with good rains and excellent grazing, their livestock fattened. More farms were allotted and the settlers were optimistic. Then the tsetse fly discovered the plump livestock, the rains failed and the settlers faced ruination. They could not make rain, but they could blame the Umfolozi Game Reserve for harbouring the tsetse flies. A great agitation to abolish the game reserve and to shoot everything in it followed.

A conference was held in Pietermaritzburg in August 1920. The settlers attended, certain that the answer to their nagana problem lay in the deproclamation of the game reserve. They had to be reminded that most of them had been warned of the presence of nagana. The Zulus had never settled in the area because of the disease. All game animals had been destroyed in the farmlands by means of a major game drive in 1919. The drought had induced wild animals to leave the reserve and enter the farmlands in search of water. The continuous shooting of wild animals resembled the search for gold at the end of a rainbow. Every animal – wild and domestic – including birds and reptiles, would have to be destroyed if the tsetse were to be starved to death.

The troubled officials simply did not know what to do. The veterinarians knew little more about the disease than what Surgeon-Major (later Sir) David Bruce had discovered. The suggestion that the settlers should never have inhabited the area before the problem was solved, produced howls of rage. It was decided that shooting the animals might placate the settlers. Umfolozi was deproclaimed, but there was a stay of execution when Vaughan Kirby and Dr Warren reminded the government that Umfolozi was the home of the last white rhinos. Even in those days there would have been a public outcry if these animals were shot. Before this drastic step was taken, it was imperative that the whole problem of tsetse and nagana should be studied.

A veterinary service officer, Dr H H Curson, was stationed in the Ntambanana settlement area while R H T P Harris, a plant inspector of the Department of Agriculture, was sent to the Umfolozi Game Reserve to study the bionomics of the tsetse fly. Harris had no training in entomology; he was simply sent to the Cedara College of Agriculture for a one-month crash course and then packed off to Zululand with very little equipment other than a donkey wagon. In April 1921 he made his way to the Ntambanana area where, with six assistants, he scoured the bush in search of tsetse fly. There were none to be found. At the end of May he moved his establishment to the Umfolozi Game Reserve.

In September 1921 Harris made a permanent base on the ridge known as *Conjeni* (the prominent place) overlooking the right bank of the White Mfolozi River. It was a good choice for a base. In his corrugated iron house and laboratory, Harris was connected to civilisation by a rough track he had cut through the bush to Empangeni. Between his base and the Ntambanana settlement a shooting zone was set up as a buffer by the farmers. There was a fording place across the river where an ancient pathway from the coast made its way inland to Hlabisa.

This pathway wound through the bush of the Umfolozi Game Reserve, which lay in the triangle of land contained within the converging Black and White Mfolozi rivers. It was a beautiful and tranquil area to the eye, with no visible hint of the problem presented to Harris for solution.

The area was largely uninhabited by humans. A few Zulus had once managed to find refuge from tribal wars on the hill they called *Mpilo* (the healthy place) because it was high enough to be free of fever. Where the path climbed to the top of the hill known as *Dengezeni* (place of broken pots) there were signs of early human activity in the form of debris from some tribal battle. Beyond these slight traces, the area was completely wild; indeed, so solitary and full of ancient mysteries that it was considered a fearsome place by many tribespeople. Where the pathway crossed the summit of the Dengezeni hill, a luck heap had been created on which each passing traveller deposited a stone and prayed to his ancestral spirits for safe conduct on the journey.

At this place, then, Harris settled himself down to study the tsetse. Driving an ox or a donkey ahead of them as bait, Harris and his assistants tramped through the bush, forming an opinion as to the distribution of the flies and catching specimens for laboratory study.

In his hot little laboratory, Harris kept specimens in battery jars with mosquito netting over the top. Each morning the specimens were all fed from a herd of goats kept for that purpose. A Zulu, whose firm conviction it was that Harris was mad, had the task of holding the goats down and placing the jars face downwards against bare patches shaved on the animals' sides.

In these conditions Harris learned much of the life of the fly. He found that it was an oddly primitive insect, possessing little sense of smell and guided to its prey by crude sight only. Large mass attracted the insects, but they were quite unable to distinguish what was alive or dead without close personal inspection. Dummies or motor cars drew them as quickly as a live animal.

He found that the eyes of the tsetse seemed to be irritated by glare and that they clung to the shade of the bush and always attacked the shady part of an animal. At night they roosted on bushes and tree trunks and only flew if disturbed. In moonlight or lamplight they would attack, but they were certainly much less liable to bite at night than during the day.

When the donkey Harris used as bait to catch the tsetse fly died of nagana in January 1923, he found that a dummy donkey was even more effective than a live animal, provided it was bigger. When he tried out a young zebra as bait, he found to his surprise that the flies still preferred to attack the dummy. This gave him the first idea of devising a trap of some kind. An inverted packing-case with a hessian skirt around the bottom and gauze-covered windows trapped 82 tsetse flies in a few hours. At the same time Harris tried devising a tsetse poison which could be applied to animals by means of a dip, but this was found to be impractical. Experiments at bush clearing also showed that the fly could cross a buffer zone of 450 m with ease.

Harris's experiments at least provided a stay in the execution of the wild animals. While he laboured, the controversy continued over his head. Dr Warren enlisted the support of several scientists, and such conservationists as Lt-Col James Stevenson-Hamilton, warden of the Kruger National Park, and the writer-artist, Harry Stratford Caldecott. Against their pleas for conservation were such influential persons as General J C G Kemp, Minister of Agriculture, and Dr Claude Fuller chief of the Division of Entomology. Both were on the side of the killers. As an added complication, Fuller detested Harris.

Harris's five-year contract ended in October 1926 and he was withdrawn from Zululand. Things seemed to be quiet and the farmers were claiming that their mass game slaughtering had proved effective. On the strength of this, new settlement areas were opened at Hluhluwe and Mkhuze. Within two years, however, the whole picture changed. Once again nagana swept Zululand. Once again the settlers were clamouring for action. They insisted that the cure they had formerly tried with some apparent success should be tried again. This time every wild animal throughout the whole length of Zululand should be slaughtered and the game reserves completely abolished. General Kemp supported them.

At the height of the crisis, Fuller resigned to take up an appointment in Mozambique, where he was killed in a road accident. In South Africa the problem of nagana was transferred from the entomology to the veterinary department.

Harris was hastily sent back to Zululand in January 1929. He was opposed to the wholesale extermination of animals. He advocated, as a man groping in the dark, that all wild animals outside of the reserves should be exterminated. Those in the reserves should be reduced to such a low figure that some practical step towards controlling their fly parasites could be undertaken.

Towards this end, an organised slaughter campaign was commenced in 1929, with 70 paid hunters constantly on the job killing everything except rhino (which were protected). From June 1929 to November 1930, 26 162 wild animals were shot by these hunters and nearly all survivors driven into the three reserves.

Vaughan Kirby had retired at the end of July 1928 and so was spared the sorry spectacle of the slaughter. His successor, Roden Symons, was not so fortunate. A wiry, rugged character, Symons had relieved Kirby on several occasions in the past and for some years had been warden of the peaceful Giant's Castle Game Reserve. When he was sent up to Zululand to replace Kirby permanently, he stepped right into trouble. It had been decided to place the game warden under Harris, who, although an able and extremely intelligent man, had one great failing – a complete inability to get on with his fellow men.

Symons only lasted a year with the abrasive Harris and the game slaughtering. To replace him there came to Zululand one of the best known of all its latter-day people, Captain Harold Potter, a tall lean young man whom the Zulus promptly named *Mthwazi* (monkey rope).

Potter had one month with Harris at Umfolozi. Then, to his relief, he was ordered to establish himself in the Hluhluwe Game Reserve. So it was in August 1929, in that most beautiful of places, that 'Monkey Rope' Potter pitched his tent beneath a wild fig tree, on the top of a dominant and healthy 769 m high ridge known as *Luhlaza* (the green one), on account of its verdant grass.

In this place Potter lived a serene life, surrounded by the wild animals he loved so much. It was a remote and solitary station where no visitors called. Only an old footpath wandered through the hills, climbing the ridge where forgotten travellers had superstitiously left behind a luck heap on the saddle before descending into the rhino-inhabited bush.

One old African with the poetic name of *Ndwangu* (dishcloth) and his family were the only inhabitants of the place. The rhino and buffalo came tripping over the tent guide-ropes at night. By 1930 Potter had a snug little wattle-and-daub house in which to shelter his wife and family while four game guards and one ranger, another well-known Zululander named Edward Lightning, helped him in the war against poachers. Under Potter the Hluhluwe Game Reserve was developed. The animals, once wild and wary from much shooting, soon became extraordinarily tame, with buffalo almost as safe as cattle for the visitors who started coming in 1932. White rhino were enticed over from Umfolozi by means of a trail of corn and treacle; while impala and nyala, which had been completely exterminated, were reintroduced in 1935 from Mkuze. Other exotic animals – eland, giraffe and ostrich – were also introduced experimentally and roads were made.

Early in 1934 the first huts were opened for visitors' accommodation in what was known as Hilltop Camp. Many thousands of tourists started to pass through the place each year. Few failed to be thrilled and to tell a story of some encounter with a rhino. One animal character, a black rhino bull named Waltzing Matilda by Australian visitors during the war, became probably the world's best-known and most photographed wild animal.

Matilda, in some ways, typified Hluhluwe. He was a battle-scarred individual, minus one horn from a fight, and of extremely regular habits. In his home on the *Manzamnyama* (black waters) stream, he was particularly accessible. Everybody could depend on seeing him and nearly everybody got a thrill when he pretended to charge. He died, lamented by all, of old age, rheumatism and rainy weather, in August 1951. All over the world he lived on in countless tourist stories of narrow escapes, although few appreciated that he was not really more bad-tempered than other rhino. It was just that opportunities for scaring people came his way more often and he enjoyed them. He was a great advertising asset for Hluhluwe and conservation in general.

The other reserves were not as fortunate as Hluhluwe. At Umfolozi intensive shooting of game took place. Harris had also concentrated on his original idea of a trap to catch tsetse. In April 1930, aided by W Foster and S Deakin, he produced and patented the well-known Harris trap. By January of the following year 32 of the traps had caught 19 147 flies. By April, 90 traps had caught 176 563 flies and, by September 1931, 983 traps were in use with a catch of 2 088 508 flies. The total catch for 1931 was 7 299 992.

From then on, fewer and fewer flies were seen and caught. In 1938 a total of 29 000 traps caught only 428 flies and it was jubilantly thought that the end of the tsetse was in sight. Harris retired with much honour in 1940 and the farmers were all thriving.

Then the tsetse came again. For the first time it became clear that the slaughtering of game and the extensive trapping had hardly affected the fly at all. The tsetse were subject to cycles controlled by their own parasites, mainly a wasp which laid its eggs inside tsetse pupae. The tsetse increased in numbers and so did their parasites. The parasites killed the tsetse and then died themselves from lack of food. The tsetse increased again. Thus, in the rhythm of Nature, the tsetse had come and gone in almost regular 10-year cycles, and nothing man had done up until then had greatly affected it.

At the end of 1940 nagana was present again in Zululand and reached a peak in 1942. The farmers were once more in uproar and clamouring that all game in the reserves should be shot. The government replied by appointing Dr E B Kluge in 1942 to take charge of tsetse operations. Trapping was continued, although it was obviously no solution. Between 1942 and 1946, some 60 000 head of livestock died of nagana in Zululand. There was no appreciable effect on the tsetse. In their new base, known as Nagana, established in 1944 on the northern bank of the Black Mfolozi, the scientists could only battle on.

Then at last the solution arrived. In 1945 experiments were commenced to spray DDT (*dichloro-diphenyl-trichloro-ethane*) by means of aircraft over tsetse-infested areas. The Mkuze

Game Reserve was selected for the first trial and the results were startling. After three applications of DDT the fly density dropped to approximately 8 per cent. The forest-living *G. austeni* still persisted, but its capacity to infect cattle with the fatal nagana was so slight as to be negligible. The fly which carried the disease to cattle was *G. pallidipes*, but fortunately it could not survive the DDT.

In April 1947 the aircraft spraying campaign was extended to Umfolozi and Hluhluwe. Since 1948 not a single tsetse of the malignant *G. pallidipes* variety has been caught in the Mkuze Game Reserve, which once teemed with them. A similar record of progress was reported at Umfolozi and Hluhluwe. The introduction of the DDT-arsenic dip for cattle seemed to seal the fate of the tsetse forever. From May 1953 onwards, not one single tsetse fly of the fatal type could be found in Zululand. Aerial spraying ended on 30 January 1954, after an eight-year battle which had cost £2 million.

In the empty bush of many parts of Zululand the bones of over 143 000 wild animals lay mouldering in mute remembrance of man's blundering in the dark, with nothing to guide him and his only motivation blind panic and ignorance.

Over the years, under careful protection, the game reserves of Umfolozi and Mkuze were reinhabited by wild animals wandering into them from such places as Hluhluwe where they had not been hunted, or from the wilderness of Maputoland. Umfolozi and Mkuze were opened to tourists, and the discovery of their beauty and natural wonders by visitors soon made the game reserves of Zululand world renowned.

However, none of these game reserves have been, or are today, safe sanctuaries for wildlife. Their future has always been precarious, at the mercy of political change or economic pressure. Would-be settlers, black and white, eye the virgin lands with deep desire. Settlers in adjacent areas mutter incessantly about the effects of wild animals wandering out of the reserves. Damming of water for irrigation purposes reduces the flow of the rivers passing through the reserves. Increasing scientific control in place of the more patriarchal old-time game warden has meant more slaughter in the name of population control. Biltong, hides and curios are manufactured in the reserves. Adjoining farmlands become hunting areas, but at least provide insulation between the inner wilderness and the outside world. Management becomes the accepted thing, with computers to check and calculate the permissible breeding levels, to discipline changes of vegetation, population distribution and way of life in the old free-and-easy wilderness. Nature has been pushed just a little into the corner. The story of man and wild animals in Zululand continues as a serial, with a climax still to come.

Chapter Twenty-Seven

PIETERMARITZBURG AND THE KWAZULU-NATAL MIDLANDS

Pietermaritzburg is situated in parklike surroundings; a city of flowers and bright colours. The hollow (originally known on account of its warmth as 'sleepy hollow') in which the city developed and is now very wide awake, is the valley of the *Msunduze* (the pusher) River named for its habit of 'pushing' masses of driftwood down its course during flood time. With good rainfall (1 000 mm a year), deep soil and a climate conducive to the growth of vegetation, the site of the city became one of the main stops on the pioneer wagon road from Port Natal (Durban) to the interior.

The Voortrekkers, who appreciated fertile and pleasant situations for their towns, chose the site for the capital of their Republic of Natal. After the defeat of the Zulus in the battle of Blood River, they laid out a town on the banks of the Msunduze in the traditional Dutch manner; wide streets with water furrows for irrigation of gardens on either side, and plots so large that they seemed more like small farms.

The town was founded in 1838 and named in honour of the two leaders of the Voortrekkers in Natal, Pieter Retief and Gerrit Maritz. The former was killed by the Zulus and the latter died of natural causes just prior to the establishment of Pietermaritzburg. Statues of the two men stand in the garden outside the Voortrekker museum, which displays an interesting collection of relics of the period. The thatched double-storey home of Commandant Andries Pretorius, who led the Voortrekkers to their victory at Blood River, is part of the museum complex. The museum is open Mondays to Fridays from 09h00 to 16h00; Saturdays from 09h00 to13h00. Closed Sundays and religious holidays.

In the halcyon days after it was first established, Pietermaritzburg must have been a delightful little capital of a rural republic of extreme simplicity: white-walled, black-thatched cottages built in Cape-Dutch style, each surrounded by an irrigated garden of fruit trees, vegetables and flowers; the streets filled with an unhurried traffic of wagons, horsemen and pedestrians; Zulu men and women in traditional dress; rugged-looking hunters, traders and visiting farmers conducting business; missionaries and explorers coming and going to and from the far interior of Africa.

Simple government buildings were erected, including a small hall in which, on the first Monday of January, April, July and October, assembled the august members of the *Volksraad* (people's council), the ruling body of the Republic of Natal.

One of the early buildings which has survived is a double-storey residence built in 1846 by Petrus Pretorius at 333 Boom Street. This interesting thatched house still retains its original yellowwood ceilings and tiled floor. It now contains a small museum.

The collapse of the Natal Republic in 1843 brought British administration and a garrison to Pietermaritzburg. A military stronghold, Fort Napier, was built on an elevation overlooking the town. In December 1845 the first British Governor, Martin West, was established in the town, which from then on became the capital of the British colony of Natal.

Fort Napier is well preserved and contains artillery pieces and other interesting military relics. St George's garrison church was built in 1897 and also contains relics of the British military units.

The market square of Pietermaritzburg was a meeting-place for traders and hunters, as well as local businessmen. Transport vehicles outspanned there, resting, repairing or offering for sale a great variety of tusks, skins, horns, agricultural produce and goods imported from foreign countries. Shops, hotels and small industries were founded. The first newspaper of Natal, *The Natal Witness*, made its appearance on 27 February 1846. Its editor, David Buchanan, used the local gaol as his editorial office while he was imprisoned there for contempt of court. The address *'Pietermaritzburg gaol'* appears on several issues of the paper.

In 1848 Pietermaritzburg received a village management committee and in 1854 it became a full municipality. The Legislative Council of Natal sat in Pietermaritzburg and in 1893, when Natal received responsible government, the town became the seat of Parliament with two Houses, a Legislative Council and a Legislative Assembly. The Assembly building was later used by the Natal Provincial Council. The Legislative Council building contains the offices of the KwaZulu-Natal Provincial Administration. Both buildings may be visited by appointment.

The imposing city hall, said to be the largest all-brick construction in the southern hemisphere, was completed in 1900 on the site of the original Volksraad hall of the Natal Republic. The hall contains some fine stained-glass windows and a clock tower 47 m high with a Westminster chiming clock and a carillon of twelve bells. Another notable building is the Old Supreme Court opposite the City Hall. Completed in 1871, it was converted in 1990 into the Tatham Art Gallery. The exhibits include a number of French and English paintings, china, glassware and an elaborately gilded ormolu clock. This fine piece with moving figures was built in London in the last century, reputedly for an Indian rajah. The gallery is open Tuesdays to Fridays from 10h00 to 18h00; weekends 10h00 to 16h00. Closed on Mondays.

The Natal Museum, founded in 1905, is one of the five national museums of South Africa. A large collection of African animals is displayed and there is a notable exhibition of marine molluscs, fish, geological specimens and a first-class ethnological gallery. The Hall of Natal History contains a reconstructed street from Victorian Pietermaritzburg. The museum is open Mondays to Saturdays 09h00 to 16h30; Sundays 14h00 to 17h00. Closed Good Friday and Chrismas.

Another interesting museum is Macrorie House, maintained by the Simon van der Stel Foundation. The house, built about 1862, was the residence from 1869 to 1891 of William Macrorie, Bishop of Pietermaritzburg, who arrived at a time of great dissent in the Anglican church. The renowned Bishop John William Colenso challenged various dogmas and established the Church of England in Natal, with its own cathedral of St Peters, completed in 1872. Bishop Macrorie became head of the Episcopal Church of the Province of South Africa, with St Saviour's as his cathedral. Bishop Colenso is buried in front of the altar of his church (St Peters). In Macrorie House are displayed many items from Victorian times. It is open Tuesdays to Fridays from 09h00 to 13h00, and on Sundays from 11h00 to 16h00.

The old Government House is another reminder of the past. Originally the official home of Lieutenant-Governor Benjamin Pine in the 1860s, it is now the Natal College of Further Education.

In the Tatham Gallery gardens several monuments reflect the city's history. On the corner opposite the City Hall is the striking monument commemorating the men who gave their lives in the Anglo-Zulu War of 1879. Cloete's cannon in front of the monument was cast in Scotland in 1812 and brought to Natal in 1842 by Colonel Josias Cloete. When the Supreme Court building was used as a post office, the cannon used to be fired to let the townspeople know that the mail had arrived from Durban. Continue into the gardens and you will see on your right the War Memorial Arch dedicated to those who fell in the service of their country in two world wars. The arch is flanked by two German field guns captured by the South African forces in German South West Africa in 1915. About turn, and you will be facing the South African War Memorial, erected by the people of Natal in honour of the colonists who died for their sovereign and country during the Anglo-Boer War 1899–1902.

Part of the city's charm lies in the central network of quaint, narrow, pedestrian lanes between Church and Longmarket streets. This area became the financial centre of the young capital and housed four different stock exchanges between 1888 and 1931. Visitors will be attracted by the many small shops, the Edwardian Harwin's arcade (1904) and Theatre Lane, site of the old Scott's Theatre which was very popular before the turn of the century.

The Garden of Remembrance in Leinster Road is a picturesque reminder of the servicemen who gave their lives in two world wars. It contains the famous Weeping Cross of Delville Wood, said to ooze sap on the anniversary each July of the First World War battle in which many South Africans died.

Also evident is the later contribution of the city's Indian population, descendants of indentured labour brought to Natal in the 1860s to work in the sugar cane fields. They added a distinct Eastern blend – Hindu temples, Muslim mosques, colourful saris and spice shops. The main Hindu temple in Pietermaritzburg is the Sri Siva Soobramoniar and Marriamen temple in lower Longmarket Street. Established in 1898, the temple is the focal point of the Firewalking Festival held annually on Good Friday. Here, in the temple grounds, about 50 devotees end a 10-day fast by walking barefoot across pits of glowing coals. The temple is open to visitors on Mondays to Saturdays from 07h00 to 18h00; Sundays from 08h00 to 18h00.

Gardens, trees and parks are the city's chief glory. *Alexandra Park*, 65,5 ha in extent, was founded in 1863 and named after Queen Alexandra of England. This park comprises the Jan Smuts stadium, the cricket oval, a cycle-track, swimming-bath, the superb rock gardens created during the great depression, by unemployed men, and the Mayor's garden with its roses and avenue of palms. In May each year, an open-air art festival, 'Art in the Park', is held in the shade of an avenue of plane trees along the banks of the Msunduze River. The Diamond Jubilee Pavilion and bandstand are interesting reminders in the park of Victorian elegance.

Next to Alexandra Park is Kershaw Park with its public tennis-courts. *Wylie Park,* 8 ha in extent, was presented to the city by Mrs G H Wylie, together with a legacy to finance its development, particularly as a garden for indigenous plants and the lovely azaleas which are the floral emblem of Pietermaritzburg. The park was opened in 1958.

The Botanic Gardens (44,5 ha) were founded in 1870 by the Botanic Society of Natal and in 1969 were taken over by the National Botanic Gardens of South Africa. This garden contains a superb collection of trees gathered from many parts of the world, some of them the largest of their kind growing in South Africa. There is an avenue of plane trees, spectacularly beautiful when their leaves change colour. Plants indigenous to Natal are cultivated in a special section of the garden.

The Queen Elizabeth Park was established in 1960, 8 km from the city centre on the main road to the north. This 93 ha park contains the headquarters of the KwaZulu-Natal Parks. Game and Fish Preservation Board, as well as indigenous trees, shrubs and flowering plants, birds (including blue and crested cranes) and antelope of different species. There are walks and picnic sites.

The Doreen Clark Nature Reserve, 5 ha in extent, was established in 1969. It conserves a beautiful evergreen forest with a picnic area and a pathway.

The bird sanctuary, situated next to the main road to the north, is a popular roosting place in the evenings for hundreds of egrets. A number of beauty spots on the outskirts of the city provide pleasant drives and recreational areas for residents and visitors.

Eight kilometres from the city centre on the old Howick road is the viewsite known as World's View, 1 083 m above sea level. Traces of the original wagon road to the interior may still be seen climbing the escarpment at this point. A map set into the paving stones identifies landmarks of interest. There are picnic sites under the trees and several green-belt trails. The old Howick road continues for 4 km to the village of Hilton and then joins the main N3 road a kilometre further on.

Henley Dam, 22 km from the city on the Bulwer road, is another recreational area worth visiting. The Natal Canoe Club uses the lake. Pleasant picnic spots are provided. The area is open daily from dawn to dusk. Permits for parties of over six people must be obtained from the city engineer.

Pietermaritzburg has a population of 573 844 and is a considerable centre for industry. It retains its administrative and judicial importance and is the home of many fine schools and also of the University of Natal. The Pietermaritzburg and Durban campuses of the University of Natal together have 11 540 students. The former principal thoroughfare, Church Street, was converted in 1990 into one of the most attractive shopping malls in South Africa, featuring fountains and a bandstand. It is a delight for visitors, with a variety of shops and attractive buildings, including one of the most atmospheric and best-known bookshops in Southern Africa, the strangely named partnership of Shuter and Shooter. Exploring Pietermaritzburg yields many interesting scenes of streets, alleys and historic buildings.

There are several fine walking trails in the hills and valleys around Pietermaritzburg. Maps and details of these trails, along with brochures, souvenirs and videos of the city, can be obtained at the Publicity Association's information bureau at the corner of Longmarket Street and Commercial Road. Phone (033) 345-1348.

PIETERMARITZBURG TO DURBAN

There are several ways of travelling to Durban from Pietermaritzburg. One of the more strenuous routes is by canoe. In January of each year a race begins in the centre of Pietermaritzburg on the Msunduze River, as far as its confluence with the Mngeni and from there to the sea at Durban.

Another testing route (by road) is the Comrades Marathon, held at the end of May or early in June each year. Reputedly one of the world's most demanding athletic events, this race was started in 1921 by Victor Clapham, an ex-soldier member of the Comrades of the Great War, hence the name of *Comrades Marathon*. The course is over 90 km long, and alternates each year with either an uphill or downhill route. The first race was won by 39 year old Arthur Newton. At 72 years of age this remarkable athlete was still running competitively and had by then covered over 160 000 km.

The race is now organised each year by the Comrades Marathon Association and is a gruelling test of endurance, ranging in altitude from 30 m at the Durban post to 610 m in Pietermaritzburg. In the first race, 34 men took part; now over 15 000 men and women of different races and nationalities compete. All hope at least to complete the course within eleven hours in order to secure a medal proving that they are Comrades of the Road. A silver medal is awarded to those who finish within 7 hours 30 minutes. The record for the downhill race was set in 1978 by Alan Robb at 5 hours 29 minutes and 14 seconds. The uphill record, set by Bruce Fordyce in 1981, is 5 hours 37 minutes and 29 seconds. Bruce Fordyce won the race nine times.

For the more conventional road user, the superbly located dual carriageway from Pietermaritzburg to Durban provides a delightful drive through kaleidoscopic views. From Pietermaritzburg the road leads south-eastwards past the borough caravan park and commences a winding, steady descent through the green hills of Natal. The outlying suburbs of the city are reached via turn-offs. Near the turn-off to Mkondeni stands a little church built by Italian prisoners of war during the Second World War. About 5 000 Italians, detained in a camp at this spot, transported on foot stone from a quarry 2 km away in order to build the church. Consecrated on 19 March 1944, it is the only remaining feature of the camp. The stone lion in front of the building, sculpted by the Italians, once stood in the middle of the camp.

The road, 11 km from Pietermaritzburg, passes the residential area of *Ashburton,* originally the farm of William Ellis who, having made money in the Australian gold-rush, settled in Natal and named the property after his home town in Dorset.

Four kilometres beyond Ashburton, a turn-off leads for 8 km to the Natal Lion and Game Park and the Zoological Gardens. It is open from 09h00 to 16h00 daily and contains a variety of wild animals in addition to lions. This was the first lion park to be established in Southern Africa by Dick Chipperfield of Chipperfield Circus fame. It is scenically handsome on the verge of the Valley of a Thousand Hills. It is a centre for the training of animals for motion picture productions. The Boswell family of circus fame run the place and it is the base for Brian Boswell's circus.

Three kilometres beyond the turn-off to the lion park, a tarmac turn-off (18 km from Pietermaritzburg) provides a direct route to the south coast resorts of Natal. A further 5 km takes the traveller past the village of *Camperdown* founded on the farm named after the British naval victory over the Dutch in 1797. The area will always be remembered as the home of John Vanderplank and for the beginning of the wattle industry in Natal.

Vanderplank was a well-to-do Englishman of Dutch ancestry. He acquired land in Tasmania and returned to England to prepare for permanent emigration, marry his fiancée, Louisa Whitechurch, buy his own ship and in it sail off to establish a new home. The ship was obtained and named *Louisa* after his intended bride. The young lady then declined to leave her native land. Vanderplank had to sail without her. Arriving in Port Natal, he was commissioned by the Volksraad of the Natal Republic to sail to Lourenzo Marques and rescue the survivors of the ill-fated Louis Trichardt trek.

Back in Port Natal, John Vanderplank found the country so much to his liking that he decided to settle. He acquired farmlands such as *Camperdown.* In the 1840s he obtained from his eldest brother, Charles, in Australia, the seeds of the black wattle, which he planted at *Camperdown* in order to form hedges as they did in their natural home. He also stimulated the growing of sugar cane in Natal, became a member of the Legislative Council and, among numerous benevolent works, established on his *Camperdown* farm several distressed, nearly destitute members of the Byrne settler party. He gave them smallholdings free of any charge for the first year, then charged one shilling a year for subsequent years. The estate was eventually broken up and sold in the mid-1920s. Several of the original settlers then acquired their own properties.

So far as the wattles were concerned, to Vanderplank's surprise, the seeds developed into trees instead of shrubs. The local soil and climate had obviously affected their growth. It was not until 1887, however, that the value of wattle bark as a source of tannic acid became known. By that time, seeds from Vanderplank's pioneer trees had been carried to many parts of Southern Africa and mass cultivation was commenced.

Four kilometres beyond Camperdown (27 km from Pietermaritzburg) the road reaches the railway junction of *Cato Ridge*, originally the estate of G C Cato, one of the pioneers of Durban. Cato Ridge has developed as a railway centre and is a parting place of both rail and road, the original routes to Durban providing a scenic journey along the edge of the Valley of a Thousand Hills while the new routes swing off more to the west.

THE VALLEY OF A THOUSAND HILLS

The Valley of a Thousand Hills is the deeply eroded and most majestic valley of the river known as the *Mngeni* (the place of acacia trees). The course of the river is not very long, but from its source in the well-watered hills near the height known as Spioenkop in the Natal midlands, and fed by numerous tributaries, the Mngeni has been a vigorous influence on the landscape and economy of Natal. It feeds the Midmar Dam; provides the spectacle of the Howick and Albert falls and, in its final 65 km journey to the sea, finds an involved way through the beautiful Valley of a Thousand Hills. At the head of the valley looms a dominant, flat-topped height, monarch of all the 'thousand hills'. To the Africans this mass of sandstone is known as *emKhambathini* (place of giraffe acacia trees). Europeans know it as the Natal 'Table Mountain'. A climb to the top (960 m) is very rewarding. The plateau summit should be a nature reserve, for it is the home of many magnificent wild flowers and the views are breathtaking. The mountain is best climbed from the Pietermaritzburg side by taking the road past Bishopstowe.

At the foot of emKhambathini the Mngeni River flows into the lake formed by the Nagle Dam, one of Durban's principal sources of water. The dam, named after William Nagle, chairman of the works committee of the Durban city council when it was built in 1950, is reached by a tarmac turn-off from the old Pietermaritzburg–Durban road, 3 km from Cato Ridge. This superb 16 km drive descends to the floor of the valley, where the Debe tribe have their homeland. These people, whose residences and farmlands may be seen on every suitable site in the valley, were formerly much harried by Zulu raids and also by gangs of cannibals who once haunted the area like evil figures in a nightmare. The mountain tops, especially emKhambathini, provided sanctuaries for the tribespeople who stubbornly clung to the valley. Today they may be seen often wearing traditional dress and are renowned for their beerdrinks, weddings, dances and faction fights (mainly over women and cattle-rustling).

The road ends at the dam where there is a tea-room and picnic area situated in a handsome parkland of trees. Many lovely flowers flourish in the valley, such as the ink flower, *Cynium adoensis*, with its snow-white petals which turn ink-black when crushed; the orange-coloured snake lily, *(Haemanthus natalensis)* which blooms in spring from buds resembling the heads of snakes; arum lilies *(Richardia africana)* abounding in marshy places; red-hot pokers *(Kniphofia* sp.*)* and magenta-coloured watsonias, blooming in February; exotic Mexican sunflowers which have run wild; coral-coloured fire lilies *(Cyanthus* sp.*)* which spring up in winter, especially in areas where grass has been burned; *Aloe ferox* and other flowering aloes ornamenting the rock faces.

From the turn-off to the Nagle Dam, the old Pietermaritzburg–Durban road continues along the southern verge of the Valley of a Thousand Hills. Many panoramic views are revealed, especially along the top and around the cliffs of what the Africans know as the Ntshangwe (sharp ridge). Bird life is worth watching, with kestrels and white-necked rovers soaring past the cliff faces and ground hornbills foraging along the slopes.

The road passes the Inchanga Park Mobile Home Estate 5,5 km from Cato Ridge, and the small centre of Inchanga (a European misspelling of Ntshangwe) 3 km further on. At 12,5 km there is a viewsite which generally seems to be infested with people persistently offering bazaar curios for sale. This area is known as *Drummond*, apparently in honour of Sir F C Drummond, an immigration commissioner during the 1870s. The road passes the railway station of the same name, 14 km from Cato Ridge, and the two hotels in the area, Rob Roy and the Thousand Hills hotel, both of which have grand outlooks over the valley.

A further 6 km takes the road to *Botha's Hill*, a small trading centre named after Cornelis Botha, who had a wayside inn there known as Botha's Halfway House. This was in the 1850s when the place was a staging post on the road from Durban to the interior. From Botha's Hill a gravel road descends very steeply into the Valley of a Thousand Hills and eventually joins the road to Nagle Dam at the bottom of the valley.

For 6,5 km the road continues from Botha's Hill along the verges of the valley, then reaches the residential area of Hillcrest and, 27,5 km from Cato Ridge, rejoins the main Pietermaritzburg–Durban road. The old scenic road cannot be driven at speed; it is essentially for those who have the time to sightsee and is thoroughly worth taking. On a clear day the views into the great valley are breathtaking. Strangely enough, it is not known who first conceived the name of the Valley of a Thousand Hills. Before the First World War, it was simply known as the Umgeni valley.

From Cato Ridge the main freeway linking Pietermaritzburg to Durban sweeps eastwards, losing altitude steadily but rising and falling over lovely downland country. There are turn-offs to places such as *Shongweni* (place of Xysmalobium shrubs) and Assagay (47 km from Pietermaritzburg). The Durban municipal Shongweni Dam is situated near the road. At 22 km from Cato Ridge (49 km from Pietermaritzburg) the road reaches the residential area of Hillcrest and is rejoined by the old road which follows the verge of the Valley of a Thousand Hills.

The road descends from Hillcrest through a green parkland where trees and flowers flourish. There are many delightful residential areas on the cool heights where man finds relief from the humidity and summer heat of the Durban coast. The first of these garden towns is reached 56 km from Pietermaritzburg.

KLOOF

In 1851 William Swann Field, the first collector of customs for Natal and first magistrate of Durban, was rewarded for his services by the British Government who granted him a farm named *Richmond* (after the Duke of Richmond) on the hill slopes high above Durban. The following year, William Field brought his brother John from the Cape and settled him on the farm, eventually transferring ownership of the 2 268 ha estate to him in 1867. John Field became a well-known man in the area. *Field's Hill* is named after him while his son-in-law, William Gillitt, acquired a neighbouring farm which he named *Emberton* after the family home in England. Another piece of this farm was named *Hill Crest*, both portions being the sites of modern residential townships. *Richmond* farm remained in the possession of the Field family until 1901 when, on the death of John Field's widow, it was subdivided into residential areas. The attractiveness of the area at once made it popular, with several well-known business men from Durban building homes in what was at first known as *Krantzkloof* (precipice cleft), later abbreviated to Kloof.

Kloof became a municipality in 1961. The name is derived from a deep 10 km long cleft through the hills. The stream known as *eMolweni* (the place of high cliffs) flows into this cleft over a fine waterfall. The Krantzkloof Nature Reserve was established in 1950 over a 500 ha area and is 5 km from the centre of Kloof along a tarmac road. There is a picnic site immediately above the waterfall. The forested cleft is a sanctuary for bushbuck, bushpigs, blue, red and grey duiker and numerous birds.

From Kloof the main road descends the steep Field's Hill and it is from this point that travellers first see Durban in the distance, half lost in the blue haze of the Indian Ocean. At the bottom of the hill, 60 km from Pietermaritzburg, the road reaches ...

PINETOWN

In 1849 the Wayside hotel was built as a staging post on the coach road from Durban to Pietermaritzburg. The following year a town was surveyed around this hotel and named after the governor, Sir Benjamin Pine. The situation was pleasant – a parklike setting of flowering trees.

The place must also have been very atmospheric. In those days lions and elephants roamed about, and travellers along the road simply did not know what to expect round any corner. Pinetown became a municipality in 1948 and now has a population of 383 055. It is a popular residential area for people working in Durban. The altitude of 343 m is sufficient to elevate it above the heat and humidity of the coast. Numerous industries have also been established in the area.

From Pinetown a road branches southwards for 5 km to the Marianhill monastery, founded in 1882 by the Roman Catholic order of Trappists. Another road branches off to *Sarnia*, an industrial and residential area named by its first owner, Captain Drake, after his birthplace in England. From here a road leads to Durban through ...

QUEENSBURGH

In 1924 the townships of Malvern, Escombe, Northdene, Moseley and Cavendish were united under one local authority which became a municipality in 1954 with the name of Queensburgh. Queensburgh is a residential area on the outskirts of Durban. The North Park Nature Reserve, 52 ha in extent, was established in 1968 in the municipal area and preserves a stretch of coastal lowland forest rich in bird life. There are paths and a picnic site.

Near Queensburgh is the Kenneth Stainbank Nature Reserve, a 214 ha area established in 1963 on a piece of land granted by Mr Kenneth Stainbank. A Zulu military outpost, *Ndaba nKhulu* (the great discussion), once stood in this area which later became part of a farm named *Bellair*, granted to Robert Dunn in 1847. The Stainbank family acquired it in 1857. A delightful wilderness area on the outskirts of a big city, it provides nature trails and picnic spots. Bushbuck, grey, blue and red duiker, impala, zebra and nyala inhabit the reserve, as do many birds and small mammals.

The main Pietermaritzburg–Durban road continues eastwards from Pinetown. After 1,5 km it enters the municipal area of ...

NEW GERMANY

In 1847 two enterprising men, H Jaraal and P Jung, bought 6 272 ha of virgin ground on the outskirts of Durban where they planned to grow cotton. Naming the estate *Westville* after Martin

West, the governor of Natal, they set out to attract settlers, A group of 183 Germans immigrated to the place in 1848, making their homes on small farms, each 85 ha in extent.

Cotton proved unsuccessful but the settlers cultivated vegetables and New Germany (as the area became known) flourished. Today it is an industrial and residential area.

The main road continues through a parkland of flowering trees: scarlet-flowered kaffirbooms *(Erythrina* sp.*)* blooming in July and August, the blood-red kaffir honeysuckle *(Tecomaria capensis)*, flowering in April, cassia species producing golden blossoms in May and June, wild bananas *(Strelitzia* sp.*)* with their orange and purple 'bird of paradise' flowers and, in autumn, the orange flowers of the 'lion's tail' *(Leonutis leonuris)*. Many other indigenous plants flourish on these green slopes, while man has introduced shades of bougainvillaea and so many other ornamental trees, shrubs and creepers that no season is without some plant in full bloom.

The road steadily descends *Cowie's Hill*, named after William Cowie who came to Natal with the Voortrekkers. Close to the road on the hill slopes lies the Paradise Valley Nature Reserve (28 ha) established in 1963, with walks and picnic sites on the banks of the river known as the *Mbilo* (bubbling). At the foot of the hill, 64 km from Pietermaritzburg, lies ...

WESTVILLE

The town of Westville is a strictly non-industrial area on the outskirts of Durban, sufficiently elevated (about 300 m) to enjoy a cool climate and a fine view. It has grown on the old farm named after Martin West, the first Governor of Natal. The 162 ha campus of the Durban-Westville university is situated in the municipal area. It was opened in 1972 and has 6 500 students. The town had its beginning, pleasantly enough, as a tree which shaded the site of the first *outspan* (staging post) on the main road from Durban to Pietermaritzburg. In 1848 a London merchant named Jonas Bergtheil chartered a sailing ship, the *Beta*, to convey to Natal a party of 35 German farmers and their families. They settled in the area of Westville to grow cotton on a farm named *Wandsbeck* owned by Jonas Bergtheil. When cotton proved impractical through lack of machinery, the farm was divided and sold by auction. It remained a farming area until the 1920s, with one store and a small school. Only in 1932 did it receive a health board and in 1956 borough status.

The Bergtheil House museum exhibits items related to the founding and growth of the town. There are three nature reserves. The Palmiet Reserve of 70 ha and the Roosfontein Nature Reserve have superb walks, with 140 species of trees and 145 species of birds.

Beyond Westville, the main road continues eastwards to Durban. Crossing the north–south N2 coastal highway, the road passes through the suburb of Mayville, climbs over a rise where in former years there was a toll-gate and, on the summit of what is known as Berea, enters Durban, terminating in the centre of the city 80 km from Pietermaritzburg.

PIETERMARITZBURG TO KOKSTAD

The main tarmac road to the south, R56, from Pietermaritzburg climbs through the suburbs and out of the valley of the Msunduze River. The road leaves the built-up areas through an avenue of palm trees lined with pleasant homes and lovely gardens. After 16 km the road passes through the trading centre of Thornville where a turn-off leads eastwards to join the main Pietermaritzburg–Durban road.

Beyond Thornville the road proceeds across a succession of green valleys and hills, superlative dairy, poultry and general farming country. The first creamery in Natal was, in fact, established in this area at Nelsrus in 1899. Sugar cane, wattle, pine and gum trees flourish in the region which forms part of the mist belt of high rainfall lying along the edge of the middleveld escarpment of KwaZulu-Natal. In October and November the wattle trees are in blossom and the air is rich with their perfume. Farm stalls sell citrus fruits in November and a delicious, tangy blackberry jam is made from local wild brambles.

Thirty-six kilometres from Pietermaritzburg the road reaches ...

RICHMOND

During the influx of British settlers in 1850 several towns and villages were founded in the midlands of Natal. The first settlers in the area of modern Richmond, mainly farm labourers, were all from Beaulieu, the seat of the Duke of Buccleuch in England. The settlers established a centre they at first named *Beaulieu-on-the-Illovo*. The difficult pronunciation of the rather involved name, especially for Africans, caused the settlers to change the name to *Richmond* after another estate of the Duke of Buccleuch. Today the population is 3 049.

Lying on the banks of the Lovu River, Richmond lacks any spectacular features as a town and is cursed with a main street lined with tin-shanty stores. However, it is at least notable for the beauty of its gardens. The Bhaca tribespeople who live in the area are also renowned for their costumes and beadwork. On Tuesdays, in particular, Bhaca brides have a habit of coming into the town in order to register their marriages and are always superbly dressed for the occasion.

The luxuriance of the surrounding countryside is delightful. Branch roads leading to rural centres such as Eastwolds take the traveller through fine scenery. The road to Eastwolds descends into the valley of the Mkomazi River, crossing the river below the huge red-coloured sandstone cliffs known as *Hela Hela* (standing in a line). It is in this area that tea is grown by the Sapekoe Tea Estate. Across the river, half-way up the southern slopes, there is a resting-place with a fine view. Slightly higher, where the road crosses a small stream, a pathway leads to the summit of Hela Hela where a tremendous viewsite overlooks a world of hills and river valleys. Below the cliffs in the river valley lies the 498 ha Soada Forest Nature Reserve, established in 1967 to preserve a lovely expanse of indigenous forest.

Byrne village, 14 km north-west of Richmond, was another area of settlement under the Byrne Immigration Scheme. It was unsuccessful as a settlement, but today is a charming little retirement and weekend retreat. The Richmond, Byrne and District museum is in Richmond. From Richmond the tarmac road R56 to the south crosses undulating farmlands and plantations of sugar cane. After 6 km there is a turn-off stretching to Mid-Illovo and just beyond this point the road starts a descent into the spectacularly beautiful valley of the Mkomazi River. For 9 km the road finds a way down the slopes of the valley, revealing many impressive views of the landscape and homes of the Bhaca tribespeople. The floor of the valley is warm, and a picnic site is situated on the far side of the Josephine bridge across the river. Orchards of citrus fruit flourish in the valley.

The road climbs the southern side of the valley and, in so far as is possible, the views are even better than those from the northern heights. After 3 km a turn-off leads eastwards for 33 km to Highflats. The main road tops the heights of the river valley and continues for a further 24 km before reaching, 48 km from Richmond, a turn-off to ...

IXOPO

The village of *Ixopo* is situated in the gentle rural valley of the stream from which it receives its odd-sounding name (correctly spelt *eXobo*), an onomatopoeic word representing the sound of a person squelching through a bog. Established in 1878, it is an amiable little rural centre in a green setting of trees and luxuriant grazing. A narrow-gauge railway carries the agricultural produce of the area down to the coast at Umzinto.

The pleasant drive to the south along R56 continues over grassy hilltops covered in wattle trees and patches of indigenous bush. The narrow-gauge railway closely follows the road and, although trains are not very numerous, it provides a picturesque touch to a charming landscape.

After 1,5 km of travel from Ixopo there is a turn-off to Highflats (24 km) and from there to Umzinto on the coast, providing a beautiful drive through a veritable sea of hills. Eighteen kilometres from Ixopo the road reaches the *Mzimkulu* (great home of rivers), the border between KwaZulu-Natal and the Cape. Across the river stands a huddle of stores, a hotel and the terminus of the narrow-gauge railway, together comprising the hamlet known as Umzimkulu.

The R56 road proceeds through a densely settled area, especially in the valley of the Bisi River where a vast assembly of huts may be seen. At 39 km from Umzimkulu the road joins the main Cape Town to Durban coastal road (N2) and continues for 40 km to Kokstad.

KOKSTAD

The town of Kokstad (with a population of 21 036) had its beginning in 1862. In that year the Griquas – an assorted group of 2 000 people – migrated from Philippolis in the Free State across the Drakensberg to what was originally a no man's land but which from then on was called Griqualand East. The Griqua leader was Adam Kok III. After an adventurous journey driving 20 000 head of livestock over very difficult country, he and his followers formed a *laager* (fortified camp), on the slopes of the mountain which they named after Sir Walter Currie (commandant of the Frontier Armed and Mounted Police) whose support had allowed them to settle in these new lands.

On a spur on the southern slopes of Mount Currie the Griquas erected a substantial building protected by sod defensive walls. Around this stronghold each Griqua family erected a hut. In 1860 the Reverend William Dower of the London Missionary Society visited the Griquas. He was asked to remain and establish a mission. He agreed on condition that the Griquas came down from Mount Currie to a site chosen for a town. This was arranged and in the middle of 1872 a cavalcade of Griquas descended to the site of the future town which received the name of Kokstad. A 'palace' was built for Adam Kok near the site of the present post office. The town was laid out in a handsome situation. Surrounded by high hills and mountains, it lies on the banks of the bustling upper reaches of the *Mzimhlava* (home of the mealie grub) River.

Kok allocated a 1 214 ha farm to every male Griqua over the age of 18. It was good farming country, but winter was bitterly cold, with regular snowfalls on the mountains. The Nguni tribes had for this reason avoided the area. The Griquas, inclined to be improvident and indolent, began to sell their farms to Europeans and to live merrily on the proceeds. Soon uproar developed and in 1874 Griqualand East was annexed to the Cape Colony, the district of Mount Currie defined, and Kokstad converted from the seat of a rough-and-ready Griqua republic, into a magisterial centre. Adam Kok was pensioned off and eventually died when he was thrown from his cart in an accident. Kokstad grew as the centre for East Griqualand. It became a garrison stronghold during the Basuto War (1880–81), with a detachment of Cape Mounted Rifles stationed there. Oak trees were planted to shade the streets. The first hotel, the Royal, was opened by an American negro who also started, in 1881, the newspaper, the *Kokstad Advertiser*. On 5 April 1892 Kokstad became a municipality. It has developed into an important agricultural centre and railhead from which is dispatched a considerable proportion of the cheese and other dairy products of South Africa. Horse breeding, stock raising and general agriculture flourish in a notably crisp, healthy climate.

Many magnificent farms surround the town. Trout in the streams, finely bred horses for polo, and numerous sporting facilities make Kokstad a social centre of some importance. The town is graced with a rather elegant little civic hall, with a bandstand and a memorial to the men of the Cape Mounted Rifles who played an important part in quelling the frontier disturbances of former years.

The Mount Currie Nature Reserve lies 5 km from the town, off the Swartberg road. There are walks and climbs, and a fishing dam is stocked with rainbow trout, large-mouth bass and bluegill. There are picnic, caravan and camping sites. A national monument in the nature reserve marks the site of the laager erected by the Griqua people when they arrived in the area on 12 May 1863. The reserve is open from dawn to dusk.

PIETERMARITZBURG TO UNDERBERG

The tarmac R617 road leaves Pietermaritzburg, passing the Fort Napier Hospital and the residential area of Edenvale with its hospital. Twelve kilometres from the city, at what is known as Plessislaer, the road starts to climb out of the densely populated valley of the Msunduze River. A turn-off leads to the Henley Dam at 15 km. With fine views of the river valley, the road continues climbing steadily. At 40 km from the city, the road reaches the head of the valley where flowering aloes on the heights provide a magnificent display.

The road traverses high, rolling hill country, covered with plantations and rich, grassy farmlands. At 44 km from Pietermaritzburg the road passes the Boston rural centre. Six kilometres further on, a turn-off to the north-west leads to Impendle (10 km). The road climbs Lundy's Hill, reaching the verge of the spectacular valley of the Mkomazi River. An involved descent commences to the alluvial floor, a densely inhabited tribal area. At 65 km from Pietermaritzburg the road crosses the Mkomazi River and climbs the slopes of the right bank, revealing many panoramic views of the great valley, where both its beauty and severe erosion resulting from abuse of the soil by bad farming practices may be seen.

After 10 km of curves and gradients, the road reaches the level of the midland plateau, traversing an area of plantations and tribal settlement. At 82 km from Pietermaritzburg the road enters the village of *Bulwer,* named after the Governor, Sir Henry Bulwer. Founded in 1889 as the seat of the Ipolela division, it is a quiet little trading and administrative centre.

From Bulwer the R617 road continues over plantation-covered hills. This rural landscape is extremely pleasant and, 11 km from Bulwer, there is a particularly superb panoramic view of hills, mountains and grassy slopes. The road proceeds across farming country, with the Drakensberg ahead and the isolated peak known as Garden Castle looming in the foreground of the range. At 37 km from Bulwer the road curves around the 1 905 m high *Hlogoma* (place of echoes), making an impressive descent into the beautifully situated village and railhead of Underberg (see Chapter Twenty-Eight).

PIETERMARITZBURG TO KRANSKOP

The R33 road to the north-east climbs out of the valley in which Pietermaritzburg shelters and for 9 km curves up the slopes, revealing fine views of the city and its well-wooded surroundings. Once on the summit of the rise, the road continues over a plateau covered in acacia trees. At 13,5 km from Pietermaritzburg there is a turn-off to *Wartburg*, a village named after the castle in Germany where Martin Luther translated the Bible into German. At 3 km further on, the road starts to descend into the valley of the Mngeni River. At 17 km from Pietermaritzburg a turn-off leads for 3 km to the oft-photographed ...

ALBERT FALLS

The Mngeni tumbles over the Albert Falls in an attractive setting of trees and plants. Unfortunately recent floods have washed away most of the large trees, and the Falls, only 7 m high, are rather overpowered by the railway bridge just upstream and the dam wall above that. The path from the parking area provides a pleasant walk. There are picnic sites and fishing. Immediately above the waterfall a lake has been created in lovely surroundings. On its shores, the Natal Provincial Council established in 1975 the Albert Falls Public Resort, where boating and fishing are favourite pastimes. The 816 ha area around the 2 274 ha lake contains a nature reserve, proclaimed in 1975. Swimming in the lake is not advisable, as there is a slight risk of bilharzia infection. The lake holds 290 million cubic metres of water. Prince Albert was the consort of Queen Victoria.

A little over 1 km from the turn-off to the Albert Falls, the R33 tarmac road bridges across the Mngeni River, climbing the northern slopes of the valley. Passing another turn-off to the Albert Falls, the road (after 15 km) reaches the village of ...

NEW HANOVER

Pleasantly situated in the timber country of the mist belt, *New Hanover* consists of a simple cluster of stores, post office and police buildings, a railway station and hotel. It was named after Hanover in Germany by German settlers.

From New Hanover the R33 road climbs steeply out of the valley up *Garbutt's Hill,* named after a man who had an inn to succour those stuck on what was once a very muddy and steep road. The summit is reached 7,5 km from New Hanover and yields a grand view of hills and green valleys.

The road traverses an undulating plateau covered in plantations of wattle, gum and pine trees, sugar cane and sisal. At 52 km from Pietermaritzburg there is a turn-off of 15 km to the village of *Dalton*, named after North Dalton in Yorkshire. For a further 16 km the main tarmac road crosses a landscape of maize, wattle and dairy farms and reaches a turn-off of half a kilometre leading to the birthplace of the famed General Louis Botha, now a historical monument. Five kilometres further on (73 km from Pietermaritzburg), the road enters ...

GREYTOWN

In 1850 a town was surveyed on the banks of the Mvoti River and named after Earl Grey, the British colonial secretary. Since its founding, the town has experienced a lively history. Close to the frontier of Zululand, it was subject to periodic alarms of invasions and occasionally resembled an armed camp.

Claims concerning the discovery of gold, silver and coal in the vicinity also caused local excitement. The introduction, around 1890, of the cultivation of wattle for the tannic acid in its bark actually gave the area its principal industry. Today the whole countryside surrounding Greytown is covered in trees. Timber is the economic king of what is known as the Umvoti district.

Greytown became a municipality in July 1915 and today has a population of 11 530. Situated in the mist belt of Natal, it has a congenial climate and a green and refreshing environment.

There is an interesting museum housed in an attractive old residency building which was built in 1886 as a home for the magistrate.

In 1975 the Umvoti Vlei Nature Reserve was established. It comprises 267 ha and lies 11 km south of the town. It is a major sanctuary for wildfowl. Lake Merthley is a recreational resort for water sports and fishing. Sugar, maize, cattle, wattle, timber, avocado pears, carrots and kiwifruit are the products of the Umvoti area. Greytown, with its kiwifruit co-operative, is known as the Kiwi capital of KwaZulu-Natal. One of the largest hybrid seed companies has its headquarters in the town. Vast numbers of shoes are produced in the town and vicinity.

Greytown is an important junction for several roads. The R74 tarmac road leads north-eastwards through plantations of trees and across fertile farmlands. After 21 km there is a turn-off to the Natal Tanning Extract factory, and to *Hermannsburg*, the headquarters in Natal of the Hanoverian Missionary Society, founded there in 1854 and named after Hermannsburg in Germany.

At 33 km from Greytown, the road reaches an important junction. A turn right (east) continues for 69 km to Stanger and the north coast of Natal, an interesting drive through a spectacular jumble of hills and deep valleys. Tea estates, timber and banana plantations line the way and there are tremendous views of the valleys of the Mvoti and Thukela rivers.

At the turn of R74 to the coast, a branch road continues northwards and after 1,5 km enters the village of ...

KRANSKOP

Founded in 1894, *Kranskop* (precipice peak) received its name from one of the great scenic landmarks of Natal, the 1 230 m high peak which stands 12 km away like a sentry keeping eternal watch over the prodigious valley of the Thukela River. Known to the Zulus as *iTshe lika Ntunjambili* (the rock with two openings), this mass of sandstone has several legends attached to it. A cavern may be seen near the summit and it is said that there is a second entrance to the mountain, which opens magically. Maidens weary of carrying water from the river below the cliffs nearby need only say *iTshe lika Ntunjambili* (let me come into your house) and the secret doorway will roll open. The sound of revelry lures them in to what at first seems to be a wonderland but always ends as a prison. No maiden ever returns, and the sound of sobbing is said to be heard when the nights are quiet, lingering about the precipice face like a sigh.

The village of Kranskop is the terminus of the railway from Pietermaritzburg and is a centre for timber plantations.

From the village a road descends into the valley of the Thukela River, providing travellers with one of the most spectacular journeys in Africa. From Kranskop village the road leads for 4 km through plantations of trees, then reaches the edge of the gigantic valley of the Thukela River. An involved descent begins down the side of this great gash in the landscape. At 23 km from Kranskop there is a viewsite from where is revealed an almost overwhelming panorama of the valley, the river below doing a great U-turn, with the lovely hills of Zululand to the north.

At this viewsite stands a simple memorial to H B Jameson, Natal's Engineer Superintendent of Roads who pioneered the construction of this road, fittingly known as the Jameson Road. From the memorial the road continues its descent down slopes overgrown with a rich variety of trees, shrubs, euphorbias and flowering plants. The valley is densely inhabited by a number of Zulu-speaking clans whose thatched huts provide a completely African touch to the landscape. After 12 km (35 km from Kranskop) the road reaches the river and crosses into KwaZulu by means of the Jameson bridge. The northern side of the valley is as spectacular as the southern side. For 19 km the road climbs a difficult and steep way until it finally reaches the summit where it joins the road to Nkandla.

From Greytown the R74 tarmac road leads north-west to Muden and Weenen. Muden is the most easterly site for Bushman paintings. Another tarmac road leads north to Keate's Drift, Thukela Ferry, Pomeroy, Helpmekaar and Dundee. In this area the tribespeople still live in the traditional way, the stores deal in beads, salempore cloth, etc. Aloes are superb in winter. Game and hunting ranches such as Bambata's Kraal are found in this rugged area. Montelle Safari lodge lies between Greytown and Muden. Muden, on the banks of the Mooi River, is a centre for citrus estates and the production of orange wine. Established by the missionary Heinrich Rottche, *Muden* was named after his home in Germany.

PIETERMARITZBURG TO THE NORTH

From Pietermaritzburg the main N3 road to the north makes a handsome exit from the city, rising steadily through suburban areas where the homes are notable for their flowers and trees. At 6 km from the city lies the KwaZulu-Natal Parks, Game and Fish Preservation Board headquarters in the Queen Elizabeth Park – a pleasant setting of trees, picnic spots and drives. There are panoramic views of the city and the surrounding hills. At 11 km from Pietermaritzburg the road reaches the summit of the climb and passes through the residential area of ...

HILTON

In 1857 Joseph Henderson bought a farm named *Ongegund*, situated on the cool green heights above Pietermaritzburg. He renamed his farm after Hilton Park in Staffordshire where his wife had enjoyed walking as a girl. In 1860 Gould Lucas, magistrate of Ladysmith, purchased a portion of this farm, intending to retire there. In 1868 a friend of his, Reverend W V Newnham, organised a school in Ladysmith but the venture did not prosper and in 1872 was transferred to the original farmhouse on *Hilton*. From this small beginning the Hilton College of today has developed as one of the most prestigious schools in South Africa. The area of Hilton is beautified by trees and gardens. The railway station now houses the Umgeni Steam Museum run by the Preservation Group of the Railway Society of Southern Africa. The society maintains a number of coaches and a handsomely restored Class 15 AR 4-8-2 steam locomotive. This train uses a portion of the original track from Pietermaritzburg opened on 1 May 1884. There is a curio shop selling railway items.

From Hilton the finely graded N3 double-carriageway to the north continues through the midlands of KwaZulu-Natal. To the left of the road, 2,5 km from Hilton, lie the immaculate farmlands of the Cedara Agricultural College. There are turn-offs to Bulwer and Merrivale 3 km further on. After another 4 km (30,5 km from Pietermaritzburg),there is a turn-off to ...

HOWICK

The town of Howick lies in one of the most amiable and beguilingly beautiful parts of Southern Africa. The midlands of KwaZulu-Natal, just 1 048 m above sea-level, are a green, well-watered, fertile and temperate area midway between the coast and the Drakensberg range.

During the middle of the 19th century, the British Government granted a number of farms in the midlands. Amongst these were *Oatlands, Woodlands* and *Stocklands*, granted on 2 April 1849 to Reverend James Archbell, a Wesleyan missionary. The Mngeni River flowed across Archbell's lands, and the main road to the interior (at that time simply a rough wagon track) forded the river just above the 93 m high waterfall known to the Africans as *kwaNogqaza* (place of the tall one).

It was a dangerous ford, especially in times of flood, but the situation was a natural staging post on the journey to the interior. Transport animals could be rested, watered and grazed, and travellers found the area very agreeable.

On 23 November 1850 the government put up for sale the first erven in what was named *Howick* after the Northumberland home of Earl Grey, the then British colonial secretary. A former ship's purser named Lodge erected a small inn close to the river and was paid by the government to maintain a punt for the ferrying of travellers across the river. He became an unhappy first resident of the future town. On 16 January 1851 the river was in flood. A traveller arrived and insisted on crossing. Lodge rowed the man across the river safely while his two horses were given to a servant and Lodge's own twelve-year-old son to ride across the river. The servant crossed safely but the horse young Lodge was riding lost its footing and the current rolled it over. The boy was carried over the waterfall. His body was recovered from the deep pool at the foot of the waterfall. He was buried next to the pool, with a cairn to mark the site.

Over the years, as traffic on the road to the interior increased, there were periodic disasters at the fording place. In 1872 the Government built a wooden bridge to replace the ford. Known from its shape as the Bow-String bridge, this structure was itself carried over the waterfall in a flood. Fording the Mngeni River at Howick remained a danger, with several more fatal accidents there until 1903 when a substantial new bridge was opened.

The new bridge made the ford safe for travellers but it did not stop fatalities. Two weeks after the opening of the bridge an Indian woman washing clothes in the river was carried over the waterfall. Her body struck a ledge on the rock face behind the fall about 30 m down, bounced and then became lodged on another ledge about 50 m from the top. Several schemes were advocated for the removal of the body. Dynamite and a round of artillery fire were amongst the suggestions. Then a soldier, Gunner Mapleson of the 78th Battery, at that time in camp in Howick, volunteered to do the job. He had been a steeplejack in civilian life. He suggested that a derrick be erected on top of the waterfall. From this he would be lowered on a plank seat protected from the water by a roof. The derrick was built. After a couple of tests using a sack of rocks as ballast, Mapleson made the hazardous descent. He reached the body, attached a rope to it and then was hauled to safety. The body was brought up immediately afterwards.

The first known suicide at the waterfall took place in 1906 when James Kerr threw himself over the top. This started a dismal series of suicides. In 1940 a schoolboy attempted to dive over the fall. Watched by friends who had egged him on, he kept perfect balance for over half-way, then spun over, crashed into the side of the waterfall and was killed. Divers were called in to recover the body from the pool below the waterfall. Sharp rocks obstructed them and giant eels twisted through the gloom 10 m beneath the surface. The divers found the floor of the pool littered with odd things – relics of wagons; huge wheels rolled over the falls by some apprentices protesting against bad treatment in a local blacksmith shop; one complete wagon which had been deliberately rolled over the waterfall during the making of a 1919 film entitled *The Voice of the Waters*. The divers did not find the body of the schoolboy, but it floated to the water surface on 29 November, five days after the tragedy.

One murder has been known to have been committed at the waterfall. This was in October 1952 when a gang of drug-runners and burglars threw one of their members over the fall. Two members of the gang were eventually sentenced to death for the crime. The list of tragedies is continuous.

Many thousands of tourists view the waterfall each year. It is certainly the most often photographed waterfall in South Africa. There is a restful caravan park and tea-room on the site of the original outspan place and the beauty of the waterfall is renowned.

The town of Howick has grown into a busy centre of some 14 841 inhabitants, many of them employed in the factory of the S A Rubber Manufacturing Co, which uses a portion of the flow of the river for the generation of electric power. There is a cultural museum in the town. It is open Tuesdays to Fridays 09h00 to 12h00 and 14h00 to 15h30; Saturdays 10h00 to 13h00 and Sundays 10h00 to 15h00.

There is fine walking and riding country around Howick. The tarmac road which leads from Howick to Rietvlei on the Craigieburn Dam is not only a lovely drive in itself but provides access to four other waterfalls. One and a half kilometres out of Howick the road passes the entrance of the Umgeni Valley Project of the Natal branch of the Wildlife Society of Southern Africa. This excellent project had its origin in 1974 when the society, for almost a quarter of a million rand, purchased a game ranch, part of the old *Stocklands* farm, on the banks of the tributary of the Mngeni known as the *Gobongo* (hollow thing). The farm was converted into one of the world's most successful environmental education projects. Over 100 000 people, mainly children, have visited and stayed in the area since its opening. There are camps, experienced educators, walks, and programmes aimed at the development in the individual of an ecological conscience by a close encounter with nature, unspoilt and utterly lovely. There is also an interesting Howick Tour trail which takes walkers to several historic buildings.

It is in this gentle wilderness that the Gobongo tributary forms two of the waterfalls. The upper is the Cascade Fall, 25 m in height. It is a very beautiful flurry of white water with a fine swimming-pool at its foot. It has, however, also claimed at least one human life. Around 1944 a young local man, John Taute, started to climb down Cascade. He slipped, struck a ledge, got swept down, and was so badly injured that he never recovered. He died in 1948.

Further down the Gobongo there is the exquisite Shelter Fall, 37 m in height and occurring at the head of a secluded ravine with a delightful path leading to its foot. In April 1897 a 17-year-old schoolgirl, Mary Fynn, tried to climb the rock face next to the waterfall. She fell and disappeared in the pool at the bottom. A young Port Shepstone man, Alfred Kinsey, dived in to save her. Both were drowned. Their bodies lie side by side in the Howick English churchyard.

Ten kilometres further along the road to Rietvlei, there is a turn-off leading to the other two waterfalls. This turn-off leads through the private property of South African Pulp and Paper Industries (Sappi) and is closed to the public from 1 June to 31 October each year when there is a fire hazard to the timber plantations. The gravel road leads for 3 km to a gate where an entrance fee is charged. Another 3 km of driving leads to a viewsite of the superb Karkloof Fall, 105 m in height and the tallest of the five Howick waterfalls.

The Karkloof Fall occurs in the tributary of the Mngeni known as the *Mlambomunye* (single stream) to the Africans. The name of *Karkloof* (ravine of the cart) is said to have been given to the area on account of the abandonment there in about 1845 of the wreck of a heavily laden cart which overturned and for several years remained as a landmark by the roadside.

In September 1938 three young men attempted to climb the rock face to the right of the waterfall. They were near the top when one of them, Dean Griffiths, put his hand on a loose rock and fell. He was killed instantly.

There is a fine picnic ground at the waterfall and a second one above the fall at the fifth and smallest of the five Howick waterfalls. This fall is the Woodhouse Fall, about 10 m high but a very lovely rush of water. It is named after a farmer, William Woodhouse, who, in the 1880s, was fording the river just above the fall. His horse tripped and threw him. The horse scrambled out but its rider was carried over the fall. His body was subsequently found in the pool at its foot. The two waterfalls occur on the original farm *Shafton Grange*, first granted to James Methley and later the home of his grandson, the well-known conservationist Roden Symons, once the game conservator of the Giant's Castle Game Reserve and later of the Zululand game reserves. The property is now the possession of Sappi who maintain the picnic ground as a public resort.

An interesting inhabitant of this area in the early 1870s was John Goodman Household. Roaming about the hills of this beautiful midland, he watched the birds gliding over the valleys, the eagles, swallows, swifts and rock pigeons soaring on the updrafts. He envied them the excitement of flight. Household shot a vulture and carefully measured its wingspan in proportion to its weight. With this figure as a guide he designed a glider to carry himself. Made of bamboo, a few steel tubes, oiled silk and paper, this glider was completed in about 1871. The pilot's seat was suspended, like a swing, by a rope from the wings. Unfortunately the glider declined to fly.

Household built a second glider. When it was completed, he and his brother Archer, assisted by some of their farm workers, carried the contrivance one moonlit night to a suitable launching site on the edge of a ravine. Secrecy was desirable for fear of the ridicule of neighbours.

After much effort, the glider was launched with the intrepid Goodman Household seated in the swing seat. It soared away into the evening shadows, climbing to nearly 100 m, crossing the valley and then attempting a landing on the far side. Unfortunately the glider crashed into a tree-top. Household was catapulted into a pool of water and broke his leg. The glider was wrecked. While the pioneer aviator was confined to bed, the crumpled little flying contrivance was dumped in a loft. Household's parents were unsympathetic to further adventures. He was never allowed to try flying again. The historic glider was eventually thrown away and forgotten. This was the earliest attempt by man to fly in Southern Africa.

In 1980 the Karkloof Nature Reserve was established by the Natal Parks Board on 223 ha, including a fine yellowwood forest.

MIDMAR DAM

Just upriver from Howick, the Mngeni River has been contained to form a lake known as *Midmar* from a castle in Scotland. The lake holds 178 million cubic metres of water. In 1968 the Natal Parks Board created the Midmar Public Resort Nature Reserve, encompassing 1 822 ha of the lake and 2 844 ha of its verges. Fishing for carp or bass, yachting, swimming and various sports on water and land are popular pastimes. Riding and hiking trails may be followed and launch trips are organised. There is a restaurant and water's-edge camping ground, while chalets and cabins provide accommodation. The game park is a home for white rhino, eland, impala, blesbok, springbok, wildebeest, reedbuck and red hartebeest. Waterfowl flock to the area in large numbers. It is altogether a first-class, splendidly managed development which harmonises with its surroundings.

From the turn-off to Midmar and Howick, the main N3 tarmac double carriageway continues, winding and climbing through the grassy hills of Natal. This is a delightful journey along a finely located road. Turn-offs lead to villages such as Dargle, Tweedie, Lion's River, Curry's Post, Balgowan and Nottingham Road, all of which are worth exploring. Without exaggeration, this may be described as one of the loveliest pieces of downland country in Africa. The valleys are filled with the murmur of streams, cascades and waterfalls. Fat herds of dairy cows grazing, horses, patches of indigenous forest and many handsome farms contribute to a delightful landscape. At *Balgowan*, named after a village in Scotland, stands the famous Michaelhouse school. Nearby, on the *Tetworth* farm of John Parker, the first trout were introduced to Natal in 1882.

After 42 km of travel from Howick, the N3 road sweeps down over the hills to the valley of the willow-lined Mooi River on the banks of which stands the town of ...

MOOI RIVER

Named after the river *Mpofana* (little eland) which flows through this green and fertile valley, *Mooi River* (beautiful river) originated in 1921 on the farm of *Mooirivier* owned by J N Boshoff, the man who became the much-esteemed President of the Orange Free State. The town became a municipality in 1969 and at present has 8 051 inhabitants.

Stock-breeding is a major activity in the area. The stock sales held on the first Wednesday of each month provide an animated spectacle. The National Co-operative Dairies, Midlands Hides and Skins and Mooi River Textiles all carry out substantial industries in the town.

Trout fishing in the rivers of the district is good, while the Giant's Castle Game Reserve is reached 58 km west of the town. The Mooi River Waterfall is about 24 km from the town on the Middle Rest road. It is 80 m high and 50 m wide. In flood times it is very spectacular.

In 1978 the Craigieburn Public Resort Nature Reserve was established on 330 ha of land on the road to Greytown. There are picnic sites, fishing and boating facilities. Several farms in the Mooi River valley offer the chance of farm holidays with accommodation in huts and chalets. There are walking trails, four-wheel-drive trails, canoeing, fishing, shooting eleven rapids in the river on inner tubes, and wandering at will close to nature. For more information, phone Country Kitchen at (033) 263-2918.

Beyond Mooi River the N3 road to the north passes a turn-off (after 25 km) to the rural centre of Willowgrange. At 31 km from Mooi River the road reaches a turn-off to ...

ESTCOURT

In pioneer days, when the road to the north was simply a rough wagon track, Clem Heeley erected an inn and trading store at the fording place over the Bushmans River where C Florey acted as ferryman. Problems with Bushman cattle raiders in 1849 prompted the Government to send a military force to the area. A fort was erected on the hill dominating the fording place. This fort was rebuilt in 1874. It is still standing and is reputedly haunted by numerous ghosts who, for various reasons, have become attached to the place. The fort was designed as a substantial stronghold, with water tanks in the basement, a drawbridge, moat and (reputedly) two secret tunnels. It was built by Lt-Col A W Durnford after whom it is named. It is now a museum open daily from 09h00 to 12h00 and 13h00 to 16h00. A number of traditional Zulu huts have been built in the grounds and some fine aloes flower in winter.

A village was established under the protection of the garrison. By 1863 it was decided that a name be given to the place. *Estcourt* was the name selected by the inhabitants, in honour of Thomas Estcourt, an English parliamentarian who had sponsored the immigration of settlers to the area. Estcourt became a municipality in 1914; its present population is 12 085.

Lying at the edge of the thorn country of the KwaZulu-Natal midlands, Estcourt is the centre for a considerable industry in livestock. The Estcourt co-operative bacon factory produces great quantities of sausages, ham and other foodstuffs. Nestlé have a large factory there, while other products include hard and soft board, nylon goods, plastics, animal feeds and textiles.

The Bushmans River provides trout-fishing opportunities, while 4 km upstream from the town lies the Wagendrift Dam, greatly used for fishing and water sports. In 1973 the Natal Parks Board converted 758 ha of the lake and surrounding area into a public resort and nature reserve, with campsites and picnic places. The waters of the lake cover the site of Veglaager where the Voortrekkers withstood an attack by the Zulus on 10 August 1838.

At the head of the lake is the 264 ha Moor Park Nature Reserve, established in 1967 as a sanctuary in the acacia thorn country for blesbok, zebra, wildebeest, impala, kudu and other game animals. There is a picnic site for visitors and a trail.

At the time of the Voortrekkers, Gerrit Maritz had his wagons in laager in the centre of the meander of the Bushmans River overlooked by the site of Fort Durnford. A Zulu army attacked this camp on 17 February 1838 but was driven off.

Estcourt is connected to the historic Voortrekker centre of Weenen by means of a road and, until 1983, a narrow-gauge railway which was a delight to enthusiasts from many parts of the world.

WEENEN

The railway to Weenen was 0,5 m gauge and 46,5 km long. It was opened in 1907 and closed in 1983. It was a perfect specimen of its kind. The train depot was at Weenen from where, each weekday, the train left at 08h15, reaching Estcourt at noon. The return journey commenced at 13h15, ending in Weenen at about 16h20. On Saturdays the train left Weenen at 07h15. Two locomotives (Hanomag Garretts) worked the line, relieving each other every three weeks. Built in Germany in 1928, these locomotives could haul 185 tons on 52 axles on a ruling gradient of 1-in-33. The line passed through savanna country amply populated by pythons. Since these snakes are protected, they had right of way, and the train would stop to allow them to cross the line.

Weenen is an interesting place to visit in its own right. Situated 35 km by road from Estcourt in acacia thornbush country, it was founded in 1838. The name means 'weeping', a reminder of the massacres inflicted on the Voortrekker camps in the area after the assassination of Piet Retief and his men by the Zulus. The Bushmans River provides water for irrigation. Crops produced are vegetables, lucerne, citrus and ground-nuts. The town is also a trading centre for the Cunu and Thembu tribes who live in the vicinity.

Weenen became a municipality in 1910. A small museum, housed in a building erected in 1838 by Andries Pretorius, is open by arrangement. The Weenen Nature Reserve, 4 908 ha in extent, was established in 1975 in the thorn country outside the town. Picnic and caravan sites have been laid out, and the reserve carries an interesting population of wildlife indigenous to the Natal Midlands.

From the turn-off to Estcourt, the N3 tarmac road continues north-westwards over grassy hill country, patched with herds of cattle and numerous acacia trees. At 18 km there is a turn-off to Winterton and the Drakensberg. Shortly after this turn-off the old main road diverges from N3 and leads north-westwards, passing a wayside plaque marking the site where a British armoured train was wrecked by the Boers on 15 November 1899. During this event, Winston Churchill was taken prisoner. Those killed are buried in a cemetery nearby.

A further 1,5 km brings the road to a turn-off leading for 8 km to a monument marking the site of the Blaauwkranz massacre on 16 February 1838. The Zulu army, fresh from the killing of Piet Retief and his men at uMgungundlovu, surprised a number of Voortrekker camps. During a wild night they killed 41 men, 56 women, 185 children and 250 African retainers. About 500 Zulus died in the fighting.

Battlefields and military graves may be seen on either side of the main road as it continues for a further 14,5 km from the Blaauwkranz turn-off. Sixteen kilometres from the turn-off from Estcourt, the old road reaches the town of ...

COLENSO

Colenso is another of the wayside towns on the road to the north which originated as a collection of business establishments and hotel at the fording place of a river. The river in this case was the Thukela, the largest in Natal. The Zulus still refer to Colenso as *eSkipeni* (the place of the boat). Bishop John William Colenso, after whom the town is named, was a renowned religious leader in those days. Founded in 1855, Colenso became a municipality in 1958. It has a population of 3 936.

The British army made attempts to relieve the siege of Ladysmith, using Colenso as a base. One of the major battles of the Anglo-Boer War was fought on 15 December 1899 when the British tried to drive the Boers off the heights north of the town, but instead were themselves driven down to the south bank of the river, with 165 men being killed and 1 002 wounded.

The Thukela River provides the water for a large Eskom generating station and is also used for boating and fishing. The Thukela Drift Nature Reserve, 98 ha in extent, was created in 1973. There is a fine view from it of the Colenso battlefields.

From Colenso, the old main road bridges across the Thukela River and climbs easily up the same Colenso Heights which gave the British army so much trouble. Once on the summit of the ridge, the road continues through a tribal area of grass and acacia trees. This is cattle country, with views of the Drakensberg to the west. At 23 km from Colenso the road reaches the town of ...

LADYSMITH

The *Klip* (stony) River, on whose banks the town lies, is (to say the least) very erratic – sometimes hardly moving, at other times washing away half the town. This is good cattle country. The ranchers who first settled in the region were a rugged crowd who, in 1847, proclaimed the independent Klip River Republic, with Andries Spies as commandant. This pocket republic only survived for a few months before British authority over the area was declared.

The British planned a town as an administrative centre for the Klip River District, proclaiming it on 20 June 1850. It was named *Ladysmith*, in honour of the wife of the Governor, Sir Harry Smith, and provided a suitable partner for the town of Harrismith, just across the border, founded at the same time by the Orange Free State Republic.

Ladysmith became world famous during the Anglo-Boer War when it was besieged by the Boers from 2 November 1899 until 28 February 1900. Several of the most celebrated battles of the war were fought around the town, the sites of which are easy to reach: Wagon Hill and Caesar's Camp are within walking distance while Lombard's Kop and Umbulwana Hill are located after a short drive. A museum, housed in the municipal buildings in the town, displays many interesting relics of the siege days.

Ladysmith became a municipality in 1899 and today has a population of 89 293. It is an important road and railway junction where the main routes from Durban to the interior diverge to what was formerly the Orange Free State and Transvaal. Ranching and horse breeding are considerable activities, as is the cultivation of corn, soya beans, oats, fruit and vegetables. The climate is warm to hot. With ample water from the river and the Windsor Dam (8 km away) gardens flourish. There are facilities for water sports. Aloes thrive in great numbers on the surrounding hills and a visit to the various battlefields is recommended.

The N3 main road, meanwhile, has continued its way north-west from the point where the old road diverged 18 km from Estcourt. At this point a turn-off leads to Winterton and the Drakensberg resorts. The road continues as the Thukela toll-road. After 53 km there is a turn-off to the ...

SPIOENKOP PUBLIC RESORT AND NATURE RESERVE

This resort and nature reserve (4 400 ha in extent) were created in 1975 at the dam in the Thukela River, 40 km west of Ladysmith. Also included are two game parks. There are facilities for water sports, swimming and walking along a game trail.

Beyond the turn-off and traffic interchange to *Spioenkop* (spy peak) and Ladysmith, the N3 continues north-westwards as a toll-road. Passing, after 12 km, the Tugela Oasis garage, restaurant and rest-room complex, the road reaches the toll-gate 4 km further on. There is a turn-off to Ladysmith just beyond the toll-gate. The N3 road now confronts the escarpment of central South Africa and, 7 km further on, the start of the climb up ...

VAN REENEN PASS

Built in 1856 and named after Frans van Reenen who farmed at its foot and pointed out to the road surveyors the feasibility of the route, this finely located and sweeping pass is one of the major road and railway passes of Southern Africa. The modern road substantially follows the route of the first road. In the 15 km from the bottom of the pass to the summit at Windy Corner, the road climbs 580 m.

The railway pass follows an involved route,. employing bridges, tunnels and great curves along the contours, it climbs 681 m in the course of its 61 km journey from Ladysmith to the summit.

As with most other South African passes, this pass was originally blazed by migrating herds of game animals – notably zebra, hartebeest, blesbok and wildebeest – which moved seasonally between winter grazing in the warm midlands of Natal, and summer grazing on the highveld where, after sleeping through the frosty winters, the grass rejuvenates each spring with sweet-tasting young growth.

The hooves of countless animals unerringly found the line of least resistance up the escarpment.

Man followed – first the nomadic hunters who lived on the game animals, and then (especially after the Zulu disturbances at the beginning of the 19th century) as migrating or refugee groups in search of safety and new homes. European adventurers, hunters, renegades and deserters from the British army garrison on the coast were next in the procession of travellers. Then came the Voortrekkers in search of a promised land.

From the top of Van Reenen Pass, the modern N3 road enters the Free State (see Chapter Thirty).

What used to be the original N3 main road from Ladysmith to the Transvaal has now become the N11 to Mpumalanga. Leading north-eastwards out of Ladysmith, the road passes the railway marshalling yard of *Danskraal* (dance corral) where tribespeople danced in welcome to Voortrekker allies against the Zulus. The road proceeds over open, grassy undulating country. The Platberg Colliery stands next to the road 23 km from Ladysmith. The road crosses the barrier of the range known to Africans as *uNdi* (the heights). Europeans know it as the *Biggarsberg* after Alexander Biggar, one of the pioneers of Port Natal, who had a slight accident in his cart there when accompanying the Voortrekkers on their way to the Battle of Blood River.

In the midst of the Biggarsberg, 49 km from Ladysmith, is a motel pleasantly situated in an area known as *Fort Mistake*. This name refers to the ruin of a small fort, named Fort Selby, built on a high summit overlooking the area. The fort consists of two structures built of stone, without mortar or foundation. One of the structures is conical in shape and the only one of its kind in South Africa. The buildings were never roofed and, since there was no supply of water nearby, the military value would have been very doubtful. They were built as part of a chain of signalling stations during the Anglo-Transvaal War in 1880. The name of Fort Mistake came from a cartographer misplacing Mount Mkupe and Fort One Tree Hill.

The little fort makes every passer-by aware of its presence. Perched on the heights of the Biggarsberg, it looks out into the great power heart of South Africa – the area of coal and electricity – and seems to brood over memories as it watches the changes of today. Its awkward situation and strange construction have always been something of a mystery, to passing travellers.

Beyond the motel the N11 tarmac road continues for 6 km and then, at the Sunset Rest hotel, reaches an important junction. The N11 road continues north to Newcastle while a turn-off east, R68, leads for 26 km to Dundee and the coalfields of KwaZulu-Natal.

DUNDEE

The presence of coal in Natal was observed by many early travellers. The Voortrekkers, during their battles with the Zulus, found coal in the beds of streams such as the *Steenkoolspruit* (coal stream). In 1839 the British garrison commander in Durban, Captain Jervis, sent samples of coal to the Governor of the Cape.

In their kitchens farmers burned coal obtained from surface outcrops on their lands. It was one of them, Peter Smith of *Talana* farm, who started sending wagonloads of coal to be marketed in Pietermaritzburg. This enterprise, in 1862, actually started the coal industry. In 1880 the first proper geological survey was made of the Natal coalfields, by which it was proved that workable deposits were found on the farms *Dundee* and *Coalfields*.

By that time, Peter Smith had already marketed over 7 000 tons of coal. With Dugald MacPhail and Charles Wilson as partners, he developed mining substantially, forming the Dundee Coal and Estate Company. In 1882 he laid out a town on the farm *Dundee* to create a centre for the coalfields. In 1902 this township became a municipality and today has 24 920 inhabitants.

Dundee has a unique museum situated on the Talana battlefield. A section of the museum, which is housed in the original farm building of Peter Smith, the founder of the town, depicts the military history of the area, the agricultural history of the Biggarsberg, and his original home and workshop which have been restored. A replica of an old mine building houses the Chamber of Mines Coal museum, the Consol Glass museum, the Corobrik Heritage display and a reproduction of a street scene in Dundee in 1912. A miner's cottage has been relocated to the museum and depicts the life-style of a coal-miner in the 1920s. The Talana museum covers 8 ha of ground and includes an historic rose garden, the Smith family cemetery, as well as the military cemetery. Marked trails lead from the museum premises to the cairn marking the position where Gen Sir William Penn Symons, Commander-in-Chief of the British forces in Natal during the Battle of Talana, was mortally wounded, and up Talana Hill to the British military forts and gun emplacements. The name *Talana* (little shelf) comes from a flat-topped hill which overlooks the area.

In the town itself, a number of lovely old homes and buildings have been preserved and many have been declared national monuments. The Indumeni–Isandlwana MOTH Shellhole has a museum containing a collection of military medals and weapons. The Consol Glass factory allows visits and is a remarkable place to see. Coal-mines are not the most beautiful examples of man's impact on the environment, but in this part of the world they at least occur in a green, pleasant and healthy area. There are estimated to be reserves of 2 700 million tons of high-quality coal in northern Natal, lying close to the surface.

Dundee is the principle centre for the exploration of the battlefields of KwaZulu-Natal. It is a source of information and guidance for visits to several fascinating, if melancholy, scenes of tragedy, heroism and the bloody drama of military history.

Tarmac roads lead from Dundee to nearby coal-mining and farming centres such as Glencoe, Wasbank and Dannhauser, all of which are on the main railway line from Durban to Mpumalanga.

GLENCOE

Glencoe lies in the centre of the coal-mining industry of Natal. From its start as a railway village – the junction of the main line to the north and the line to Vryheid and the Eastern Transvaal (now Mpumulanga) – it became a borough in 1934 and today has a population of 11 231. Named after the mountain valley of sad history in Scotland, Glencoe is a centre for cattle and stock breeding. Its high-lying situation in the Biggarsberg range gives it a fresh, invigorating climate.

The Donald McHardy Dam provides a recreational area.

Ten kilometres south of Glencoe, in the valley of the *Wasbank* (washing ledge) River, lies the village of Wasbank. Close to it are the substantial buildings of the Maria Ratschitiz mission, established there in 1886. The mission was funded by the village of Ratschitiz in Czechoslovakia as a memorial to a small girl, Maria, who had been drowned. The church has some fine painted murals, stained-glass windows and wood carvings of saints.

The mission was founded by the Trappists, an austere branch of the Roman Catholic Cistercian order of monks. This order, whose rule committed its members to a vow of silence, had been founded at La Trappe in Normandy in 1664. The Marianhill monastery near Durban is their principal centre in South Africa. Apart from their religious practices and teaching, they are agriculturalists. Around their Maria Ratschitiz monastery and mission, they worked a farm 8 000 acres in extent, producing a variety of crops including grapes from which they made wine.

Many members of their order were Germans and the two world wars made life extremely difficult for them. The farm demanded a larger labour force than they could muster. The use of local African labour was complicated by the order's vow to silence and their acts of penance when they had to carry heavy loads of stone from the Wasbank River to the mission.

They worked on however until the Second World War. Then the OMI Catholic Order took over but this could not provide sufficient staff to run what had grown into a very substantial agricultural industry. The Franciscans then took over. Their members, however were mainly British and not much inclined to agricultural distractions from their religious lifestyle. They abandoned the mission and it was taken over by a private company called the Church Agricultural Projects with a board of directors made up of bishops representing the Anglican, Catholic and Lutheran churches combining into an ecumenical venture.

North of Hattingspruit lies the coal-mining centre of ...

DANNHAUSER

Lying on the main railway line half-way between Durban and Johannesburg, Dannhauser had its beginning in 1872 on the farm *Palmietfontein* owned by Renier Dannhauser. With a population of 4 152 it is a busy farming ad coal-mining centre.

Beyond Dundee the tarmac road R33 leads north-eastwards. After 6 km there is a turn-off (R68) past the Dundee Agricultural Research Station leading to Nqutu and the battlefields of Rorke's Drift (46 km) and iSandlwana (see Chapter Twenty-Five). The R33 tarmac road proceeds, reaching 27 km from Dundee a turn-off leading for 20 km to the battlefield of ...

BLOOD RIVER

The site of this clash is marked by a laager of 64 full-sized wagons cast in bronze and erected around a pile of rocks placed in the centre of the site by survivors of the battle. A strangely deceptive position for a decisive conflict, it is situated in the midst of a wide, grassy, treeless plain which is today peacefully covered with farmhouses and grazing cattle. A few isolated hills look down aloofly on the scene.

The Blood River (known to the Zulus as the *Ncome* or 'praiseworthy' river from its plentiful water and green banks) meanders tranquilly across the plain. Deeply eroded dongas, causing unexpected hindrances, hold the secret of the military character of the area.

It was here on 15 December 1838, that Andries Pretorius and 464 men, riding towards Dingane's capital uMgungundlovu to wreak vengeance for the killing of Piet Retief and his followers, found a campsite which either Providence or the perspicacity of their leader selected for its invulnerability. A sharply edged donga, 4 m deep and invisible from the level of the plain, leads down to a junction with the Blood River. The camp was situated on the tongue of land where the donga joined the river, thus being securely protected on three sides. With their wagons drawn up in a tight defensive laager, the men inside were secure from all save cannon fire.

Only foolhardiness could have caused the Zulus to attack such a camp. At dawn on 16 December 1838, a force of about 10 000 Zulus, commanded by Ndlela, made the sad mistake. Charl Celliers who was present, described the battle.

'They came down on the camp with great courage and, if I am not mistaken, endeavoured four times to take it by storm. Each time they were driven back. We could both hear and see their commander, who wished to repeat the attack, but the men refused to do so'.

About 3 000 Zulus died in the course of that clamorous morning. By the time they had been driven off, the donga was choked with corpses and the river so stained with blood that it will for ever more be known as *Blood River*. Only four Europeans had been wounded. The details of this battle and the events surrounding it may be found in *Natal and the Zulu Country*.

From the turn-off to Blood River, the R33 tarmac road continues north-eastwards over open, grassy country. After 41 km the road passes the Stilwater hotel. A further 6 km (74 km from Dundee) brings the road to the town of ...

VRYHEID

After the Anglo-Zulu War of 1879 the British fragmented Zululand into thirteen petty states. In this way they hoped to control the area by reducing the Zulu people to minor tribal elements. Considerable rivalry and fighting resulted between the thirteen appointed chieftains. Cetshwayo, the Zulu king, son of Mpande the brother of Dingane, was given only a small portion of his original state. On his death in 1884 his heir, Dinuzulu, became involved in heavy rivalry with Zibebu, chief of the Mandlakazi section of the Zulus.

In order to obtain support, Dinuzulu offered rewards of land to any mercenaries who would fight for him. In 1884 a group of Europeans formed the Committee of Dinuzulu's Volunteers. After several clashes they and Dinuzulu's men defeated Zibebu in the Battle of Ghost Mountain. Details of this complicated chapter in South Africa history are recorded in *Natal and the Zulu Country*. The mercenaries then expected their payment. Dinuzulu found himself confronted with demands from 800 applicants who claimed, rather dubiously, to have supported him. Zululand was not big enough to allocate to all these land-hungry individuals farms of the size which they wanted.

After some unpleasantness and intervention by Britain, the mercenaries had to be content with a grant of land in the northern part of the country. On 5 August 1884 this area was declared the 'New Republic', with the town of *Vryheid* (liberty) founded as its capital. This independent state only survived until 1887, when it was absorbed into the South African Republic (of the then Transvaal). After the Anglo-Boer War, Vryheid became part of Natal.

The town became a municipality in 1912. At present the population is 30 767. It is a centre for coal-mining and ranching and is particularly important for communications. Vryheid's importance as a communications centre has stimulated what has been called the Energy–Domoina Route linking the Mpumulanga coal, electric power and Sasol chemical plant areas with the harbour at Richards Bay and the coastal resorts of Natal. This route was, oddly enough, followed by the tropical cyclone Domoina on 31 January 1984 when up to 900 mm of rain fell on an area which was in the grip of a ruinous drought. The transition in one day was shattering.

Vryheid is also a major centre on the Northern Natal Battlefields Route, with, close to it, several battlefields of the Anglo-Zulu War and Anglo-Boer War periods.

Several interesting buildings remain in the town as a link with the days when it was the capital of an independent state, with its own flag, coat of arms and laws. The seat of the *Volksraad* (people's council) was built in 1884 with a large front room which served as the *Raadsaal* (council chamber). A fort and gaol were built behind this building. The Lucas Meyer house, built for the widow of the president of the state, is a nice example of Cape-Dutch revival style, with art nouveau decorations. It is now a museum. The Dutch Reformed church, built by Scottish stonemasons, is a handsomely imposing building.

The *Knabbelhuisie* is a remarkable example of co-operative home industries. Everything handmade in the Vryheid area can be seen and purchased there.

On Lancaster Hill, overlooking the town, the Vryheid Nature Reserve was created and leased to the Natal Parks Board in 1985. It is 720 ha in extent and has been stocked with numerous wild animals. There is a picnic site and a bird-watching hide. There are several pleasant hiking trails around Vryheid. The Klipfontein Public Resort Nature Reserve, 4 562 ha in extent, is 6 km south of Vryheid and has recreational facilities for fishing, boating, picnicking and camping.

From Vryheid a road leads southwards for 96 km to Babanango. At 48 km along this road stands the Mhlungwane trading store, from where a turn-off leads to the monument erected on the site where Louis Napoleon, the Prince Imperial of France, was killed on 1 June 1879 during the Anglo-Zulu War.

The R33 tarmac road continues northwards from Vryheid, climbing gently through grassy country, with the *Skurweberg* (rough mountain) lying to the west and the Zungwini Mountain to the east. At 12 km the road passes the site of the Battle of Nkambule where, on 29 March 1879, a Zulu army of 17 000 men attacked a British fort held by 2 000 men. The Zulus were driven off, losing about 2 000 men, an event which marked the turning-point of the Anglo-Zulu War.

The R33 road continues through pleasant, hilly country scarred by numerous coal-mines and forested by dense plantations of trees. At 50 km from Vryheid the road reaches ...

PAULPIETERSBURG

Situated beneath a high ridge and dominated by the bulky mass of rock known as *Dumbe* from the edible tubers of that name which grow there, *Paulpietersburg* was named after President Paul Kruger and Commandant-General Pieter Joubert of the South African Republic. The town became a municipality in 1958 and now has a population of 7 146. It is a centre for coal-mining, timber cultivation and for the hot springs of the Natal Spa which, 16 km away, have been considerably developed into a pleasant resort offering swimming, recreation and accommodation. The Phongolo Bush Nature Reserve, 858 ha in extent, was created in 1972 to conserve an evergreen forest in the vicinity of Paulpietersburg. It may be visited by arrangement with the officer in charge. Phone (0381) 2492.

From Paulpietersburg, the R33 tarmac road continues northwards for 56 km to Piet Retief (see Chapter Thirty-Five).

From Vryheid a tarmac road R601 (joining R69) leads eastwards for 67 km to *Louwsberg,* named after David Louw, a pioneer in the area, and proclaimed a town in 1920. North of the town is the entrance to the ...

ITALA GAME RESERVE

Established in 1972, this excellent wildlife area, 29 653 ha in extent, covers a beautifully rugged area of the valley of the Phongolo River. It is well populated with wildlife. There are game-viewing trails and a superbly situated camp named *Ntshondwe* (pointed) after a prominent peak overlooking the reserve. There is a swimming-pool, restaurant, shop and other facilities. The name comes from the Zulu *iThala* (the shelf).

From the turn-off of the R68 road leading to Dundee, the N11 tarmac road from Pietermaritzburg to the north continues across grassy country. Herds of dairy cows, maize fields and several coal-mines provide evidence of the richness of the area. To the west are fine views of the highveld escarpment while the Chelmsford Dam in the middle distance enhances the scene. The Chelmsford Public Resort covering 6 014 ha was created at this lake in 1975. There are facilities for boating, fishing and swimming as well as a game park and sites for camping, caravanning and picnicking.

The road crosses the Ingagane River, passing the Ballengeich and Kilbarchon collieries, the Ingagane power-station (the largest in Natal) and a turn-off to the Normandien Pass, an interesting but precipitous route into the Free State – not to be attempted in wet weather. At 41 m from the R68/Dundee turn-off, the road reaches ...

NEWCASTLE

Founded in 1864 and named after the British colonial secretary, the Duke of Newcastle, the town is today a major centre for the production of steel. The Iron and Steel Corporation has substantial works there, and the glare of blast furnaces at night is a characteristic sight.

Coal and water are in plentiful supply and form the basis of a varied local industry. A major portion of South Africa's pig-iron requirements originate from Newcastle as well as high carbon ferro-manganese, red oxide and calcium carbide. The factory of the Durban Falkirk Iron Company manufactures Defy stoves, enamel baths and other items. Textiles, rubber goods and cement are also produced in the town.

Newcastle is inhabited by 225 723 people. There is good fishing in the rivers and there are beauty spots such as the waterfall in the Ncandu River 16 km from the town on the road to Muller's Pass. There are hiking trails at Moorfield, Holkrans and Bergwaters, with fine scenery and overnight huts. Newcastle is an excellent base on the Northern Natal Battlefields Route.

From Newcastle a fine tarmac road (R34) leads to the town of Memel in the Free State. After 16 km this road passes a turn-off to the Schuinshoogte battlefield, where, on 18 February 1881, a British force of 311 men clashed with a Transvaal patrol. In the skirmish 65 of the British and eight of the Transvaal patrol were killed. Also on this road, 3 km away, stands *Fort Amiel*, named after Colonel Amiel who built it during the Anglo-Zulu War. The escarpment is climbed by means of *Botha's Pass*, a finely graded ascent up grassy hill slopes yielding pleasant views. Numerous sheep, cattle, storks, and sakabula birds live on these slopes. The pass was named after a farmer, Rudolf Botha, who lived at the foot of the pass. At 47 km from Newcastle across the Free State border, the road reaches the town of ...

MEMEL

Situated in a bowl in the hills, the site of Memel has always been renowned for the richness of its grass. In 1890 it was reported by a traveller that the basin was so overgrown that his wagon was invisible from 15 m away. The first farm, *Allenvale,* was acquired by a Mr Green. The opening of the road pass from Newcastle attracted to the site of the town a blacksmith, a toll-keeper and a trader. During the Anglo-Boer War the British built a line of forts along the top of the escarpment from Botha's Pass to Klip River. The town, laid out in 1911, became a municipality in 1913. The 1914 Rebellion was largely planned on *Allenvale* farm by General Christiaan de Wet, the then owner. The name *Memel* (surrounded by water) is of Prussian origin.

From Memel the R34 tarmac road continues north-westwards to Vrede, 56 km away. An interesting return drive from Memel to Newcastle is possible via a gravel road (64 km long) down *Muller's Pass*, named after Joel Muller who lived on *Eikenhof* farm at the foot of the pass. Below Muller's Pass a gravel branch road leads southwards, serving farms on the lower slopes of the escarpment. This is a pleasant route to take. Several passes lead from it up the escarpment into the Free State.

Under no circumstances should these roads be attempted in wet weather. The author, who had-covered over a million kilometres of African roads of all kinds, once found himself in a pickle in pouring rain near the summit of Normandien Pass, and had to slide his vehicle down part of the way in reverse. The language, regrettably, was as hard as the weather.

The road running along the face of the escarpment eventually joins the main Ladysmith–Newcastle road at a point 41 km from Ladysmith, or 58 km from Newcastle at a turn-off to the pass named after Thomas Collings who farmed at its foot.

From Newcastle a tarmac road leads eastwards for 37 km to the town of ...

UTRECHT

In 1854, six stock farmers secured permission from the Zulus to graze cattle in the area. They promptly declared the creation of an independent republic named after Utrecht in Holland. In 1860 this cattlemen's republic joined the South African Republic (Transvaal). After the Anglo-Boer War, Utrecht became part of Natal. With a population of 2 957, it is a centre for agriculture, beef production and coal-mining. It lies beneath the *Balele* Mountains named after the Hlubi chief *Langalibalele* (the sun is hot). It is an interesting little rural town with some fine examples of Victorian–Edwardian architecture. There is a museum in the old parsonage.

The main N11 tarmac road from Newcastle to the north proceeds from the town. Immediately outside Newcastle, there is a turn-off to Memel and at 6,5 km a turn-off to Utrecht and the Iscor steelworks. The road begins climbing steadily up the slopes of the escarpment.

At 35 km the road reaches the foot of the pass of Laing's Nek with the Inkwelo motel and a turn-off to O'Neill's Cottage. Majuba Mountain dominates a scene enriched by memories of the Anglo-Transvaal War.

MAJUBA AND LAING'S NEK

Laing's Nek Pass, 1 676 m high, was named after Henry Laing who farmed on the Natal side of the escarpment. At the outbreak of the Anglo-Transvaal War, the Transvaal forces occupied the summit of the pass, a very strong natural position. On 28 January 1881 the British tried to force a way up the pass. From their excellent shelter the Transvaal men held them at bay and then drove them back, with 82 of the British soldiers killed and 112 wounded. Only 14 Transvaal men were killed and 29 wounded. It was a sobering setback for the British. In an effort to outflank the defence of Laing's Nek they were then lured into a sad folly.

The flat-topped height of *Majuba* (the place of rock pigeons) is 2 146 m high and overlooks Laing's Nek. On the moonless night of 26 February 1881 a British force of 554 men, led by General Sir George Colley, quietly climbed to the summit of the mountain. The intention was to entrench themselves on the top during the night and by dawn to have the Transvaal force blocking Laing's Nek Pass at a considerable disadvantage.

When it grew light on 27 February, the 3 500 Transvaal men holding Laing's Nek discovered the British presence on Majuba. Expertly using every scrap of natural cover, they worked their way up the slopes. The British soon found themselves in sad trouble. The Transvaal men were magnificent shots and completely outnumbered the British. Any soldier revealing himself on the skyline of the mountain was immediately shot. The fight became a rout and ended at 18h00, when Nature mercifully intervened, bringing mist, rain and darkness. By then the summit of Majuba was littered with the dead bodies of 92 British soldiers, and a further 134 wounded. Among the dead was General Colley. The Transvaal force had lost only one man dead and five wounded.

As a result of this and other setbacks, the British were prepared to negotiate. Under the mediation of the kindly President J H Brand of the Orange Free State, a British representative met Paul Kruger and other Transvaal representatives in the homestead of the *Mount Prospect* farm owned by John O'Neill. A treaty of peace was signed on 23 March 1881, thus terminating the Anglo-Transvaal War. O'Neill's Cottage is now a national monument.

The summit of Majuba is best reached from the northern side. At 6 km from the turn-off to O'Neill's Cottage, the main road reaches the summit of Laing's Nek Pass and a further 2,5 km takes the road to a turn-off to Kwaggasnek and Majuba. The turn-off leads for 4 km to a gate bearing a sign marked Majuba. Through this gate the track leads for 0,75 km to a parking place very agreeably situated in the shade of an old wattle plantation. Here visitors may leave their cars and walk up a path to the summit. Some scrambling is required in steep places, but the path is otherwise quite practical. The views are superb and there are many lovely wild flowers. On the summit stands a stone memorial cairn, erected on 7 October 1935 by veterans of the battle and by public subscription. Graves may be seen as well as a memorial marking the place where General Colley fell. A trigonometrical beacon has been placed on the highest point. There is a windswept airiness about the place, with waving grass and the clouds very near overhead. A sudden thunderstorm in summer will send visitors down the slopes with a strong impression that the battle is still being fought.

From the turn-off to Majuba the N11 tarmac road continues for 5 km and then, 46,5 km from Newcastle, reaches ...

CHARLESTOWN

When the railway from Durban to the Transvaal was opened on 7 April 1891, it terminated at a customs and immigration point named Charlestown in honour of Sir Charles Mitchell, the Governor of Natal. Charlestown remained the terminus of the line until 1895 when it was eventually opened all the way to Johannesburg. Today, the town is a small trading centre.

At 3 km north of Charlestown the N11 road crosses the Coldstream which was originally the frontier between Natal and the Transvaal. A further 1,5 km (51,5 km from Newcastle) takes the road into the town of Volksrust (see Chapter Thirty-Five).

Chapter Twenty-Eight
THE DRAKENSBERG

The extraordinary scenic and botanical diversity of Southern Africa has, by the genius of Nature, been created over a prodigious period of time. A succession of distinct eco-systems range from pure aeolian desert (the Namib) on the west coast where the cold Benguela Current inhibits rainfall, through the arid sedimentary areas of the Karoo, to the semi-desert Kalahari thornveld, then the grass covered highveld, then the windblown and spectacularly beautiful Clarens Sandstone formation in the central part of the country, supporting a spectacular climax of an outpouring of a mass of basaltic lava which originated about 200 million years ago, forming the rainy 'roof' of South Africa. East of this basalt mass lies the fertile coastal terrace of high forest, wild flowers, the lovely Cape folded mountain ranges of sedimentary rock, the downlands of the East coast, the lagoons and sand dunes and finally the warm waters of the Mozambique Current of the Indian Ocean, providing plentiful rain.

The geological disturbance associated with the basalt eruption must have been truly colossal. The crust of the Earth split open, allowing a mass of molten matter to surge up from the depths and to spread out over the surface. This igneous matter congealed to form a 1 500 m thick layer of dark-coloured volcanic basalt. Exposed to wind and rain, the basalt was soft and porous, containing numerous pockets and bubbles of gas which formed cavities known as amygdales, filled with mineral matter such as agate and quartz crystals.

This 'roof' of basalt once covered a substantial part of Southern Africa. Being exposed to the weather, it was continually drenched with rain by clouds which swept in from the Indian Ocean. The crumbly basalt summit was eroded into deep ravines and the sides were washed away to form sheer cliffs. The whole island-like mass of rock eventually dwindled in size and today remains as the highland of Lesotho, the principal watershed and rainy 'roof' of Southern Africa.

On the eastern side, this island of basalt appears as a continuous wall of dark-coloured rock, known to the Nguni-speaking people of KwaZulu-Natal as *uKhahlamba* (the barrier) or simply as *uluNdi* (the heights). For the Sotho-speaking people living on the heights, the *Luteng* (highlands) of Lesotho, the edge of their world is an abrupt 1 500 m precipice which they call the *Dilomo tsa Natala* (cliffs of Natal). A party of European hunters in the last century heard the story of legendary dragons which had their lairs somewhere in the southern part of the basalt mass. Out of this legend came the name of *Drakensberg* (dragon mountain), first given to one height (Draken's Rock 2 727 m high), 50 km west of Matatiele. The name *draken* in the form of *Drakensberg* was later applied to the full length of the eastern wall of the basalt mass because, in the Clarens sandstone at its base, there are numerous tracks left by extinct dinosaurs.

From the east, the summit line of the basalt island is as level as the top of a badly decayed, crumbling wall. Few isolated sharp points emerge above the general level. The Drakensberg create an overpowering impression of tremendous rock faces, deeply eroded into crevices and gorges; crumbling buttresses and isolated ridges left behind by the retreat of the main wall. The ceaseless wear and tear of rain, ice, snow, wind; and the erosion of innumerable streams combined to produce a veritable master-work of erosion on a gigantic scale.

The summit maintains an average height of about 3 200 m above sea-level. The highest point, 3 482 m, is incongruously named with a double diminutive, *Thabana Ntlenyana* (small mountain that is a little nice). On its slopes the *Mkomazana* (small Mkomazi River) has its source.

The wall of basalt is 250 km long, stretching from the Sentinel in the north to the southern end at Xalanga in the Eastern Cape Province. Along this entire length, the basalt, from the 1 800 m level, rests on top of a layer of Clarens Sandstone vivid with colours – orange, yellow and red, largely originating from iron oxides – which contrast brilliantly with the dark basalt. Below this sandstone lies a succession of sediments known to geologists as the Red Beds, the Molteno Beds and the Beaufort Beds. Each rock system provides variation of scenery, form and colour, and each tends to erode into shapes peculiar to it. A cross-section of these different formations, as revealed in a deep gorge, is a fascinating visual display of the ceaseless power of creation at work with the tools of fire, water and wind; eroding, erupting, washing, blowing away and piling up.

The tremendous variation in altitude of the Drakensberg cliffs makes the area a home for diverse forms of life. The summit is an Alpine belt, where life is adapted to conditions of snow, hail, ice and vicious thunderstorms. Species of erica thrive in these harsh conditions as well as tough grasses and everlastings *(Helichrysum* sp.*)*. On the rocks grow algae, lichens and mosses. Apart from a few birds, animal life is scarce.

Below the 2 800 m level of the Alpine belt is the sub-Alpine belt extending down to 1 800 m. This is a zone of tussock grass and scrub, where ferns, cycads and trees shelter in the gullies. The lower and more protected the gullies, the denser the trees and the richer their variety. Below this belt, at the 1 200 m level, is the Montane belt where proteas such as the sugarbush *(Protea multibracteata)* flourish and also many grasses. In areas sheltered from the weather and protected by rock from grass fires, grow podocarpus forests of yellowwood and other timber trees. About 1 000 species of plants thrive in the three belts of altitude.

Most of the wild animals of the Drakensberg live in the Montane belt. The rich grazing and ample drinking-water attracted many antelope, such as gnus, blesbok, eland, red hartebeest, zebra, reedbuck, mountain reedbuck, grey rhebuck, grey duiker, klipspringer and oribi. Some became permanent residents; others migrated with the seasons.

Man was attracted to the Drakensberg from prehistoric times. The antelope provided food; the pure water of the streams was good to drink. The forests yielded firewood; and the sandstone was eroded into numerous overhangs, shelters and caves which provided accommodation for early residents such as the Bushmen. It was also a healthy environment with no endemic diseases such as malaria or bilharzia. In fact, it was in the Drakensberg that the Bushmen reached the heights of their stone age culture. Unfortunately, it was also in the Drakensberg that their kind was brutally wiped out when African and European immigrants seized their ancient hunting-grounds, regarding them as mere cattle-rustlers when they resisted encroachment.

There were never many Bushmen in Southern Africa. They lived in small groups, hunting in specific territories and claiming as their possession the caves in these areas, decorating many of them with galleries of paintings. About 2 100 caves and rock shelters, containing 150 000 paintings, have been found so far. The caves situated around the basalt 'island' contain the most splendid of these galleries. The sandstone surface lent itself to rock painting and a considerable range of natural colours was available, mainly derived from earth colours mixed with alluminoid binders made out of animal blood. The colours were applied with brushlike instruments in so expert a manner that mistakes or signs of accident are very rare. The artists must have learned their skills on less permanent surfaces and only applied themselves to rock faces when they were proficient.

Most of the paintings in the Drakensberg were completed between 800 and 200 years ago. They are fading rapidly, their deterioration inevitable because the rough rock surfaces are exposed to air, dripping water, damp and smoke from fires. Some of the colours, more fugitive than others, have already vanished.

Nothing is known of the artists and very little about the history of their people. The paintings give the impression that they lived well and enjoyed life. The men hunted and feuded; the women collected wild fruits and roots. At night they made merry, with feasts and festivals, mimes, rituals and dances. All these activities were depicted by the rock artists, whose paintings serve as the only record. Even the names of the clans and their leaders are only sketchily remembered by their supplanters, and then only in connection with conflict. They had no known generic name for their kind. The Sotho people called them collectively *boRwa* (people of the south) or *moRwa* for an individual. An ideophonic name was also applied to them, *boQhu* (people who click), from the whip-like sound of their click language, the, 'Q' representing a click sound. The Nguni people of the coast (Zulu, Xhosa), who have no 'R' in their language, converted the *Rwa* of the Sothos to *Thwa*, and called the Bushmen *abaThwa* (plural) or *umuThwa* (singular), applying a meaning that the name indicated a person or people of inferior type.

It was in the early 18th century that the Bushmen first confronted intruders to their hunting-grounds. Iron Age people migrating from the north entered Natal, and a section of these newcomers, the Zizi tribe, reached the Drakensberg. The Zizi were not a martial people but they were decidedly stronger and far greater in number than the Bushmen. They were pastoralists, attracted to the lower slopes of the Drakensberg where their livestock could graze. They steadily pushed the Bushmen back against the wall of rock, fighting with them, capturing their women and, at the same time, adopting some of their customs and peculiar manner of speech, notably the click sounds which were a novelty to the newcomers.

The Zizi largely eliminated the Bushmen of the Drakensberg, but soon experienced trouble themselves. Other migrating groups of Iron Age people started crowding them from the north-east. In the same way as the Bushmen, the Zizi found themselves pressed against the Drakensberg. They retreated up the passes and eventually found sanctuary in the deep gorges of Lesotho where the Bushmen had also found their last retreat.

Along the grassy foothills of the Drakensberg, the Zizi were replaced by the people known as the Ngwaneni. A period of chaos in the area ensued. A few Bushmen remnants clung to the most inaccessible areas and resorted to cattle raiding in order to compensate for the loss of their former hunting-grounds. Surviving groups of the Zizi hid in caves and were reduced to such destitution that they turned cannibal. Their hide-outs are still remembered as the scene of many horrible feasts.

Raiding Zulu bands periodically looted their way through the foothills of the Drakensberg. The Ngwaneni were driven off to seek sanctuary far in the south, only to return after the death of the Zulu king, Shaka. Under a chief named Zikhali, the remnants of the tribe once again built their beehive-shaped huts along the lower slopes of the Drakensberg. Here they still reside, especially in the area dominated by the mountain once known after their chief as *Zikhali's Horn*, but now called Cathedral Peak.

The first known Europeans to see the Drakensberg were, strangely enough, the survivors of a shipwreck. In 1593 the Portuguese ship, *Saint Albert,* was wrecked on the Wild Coast. The survivors, 125 Portuguese and 160 slaves, set out to walk to the old trading station of Lourenzo Marques (Maputo). They decided to march inland, hoping to find more food and to have less trouble fording rivers. It was May when they reported sighting on the horizon the snow-covered Drakensberg.

Hunters of the Cape reached the southern portion of the basalt mass during the first quarter of the 19th century. In October 1835 the missionary, Allen Gardiner, with two wagons driven by Dick King and Henry Ogle, arrived in the area near the modern town of Underberg. In his diary Gardiner described how he saw a rugged mountain which he named *Giant's Castle*, for he fancied that it resembled Edinburgh Castle. This mountain was renamed in 1865 by the surveyor Dr Peter Sutherland. He called it *Garden Castle* in honour of his second wife, Jane Garden Blaikie. The name Giant's Castle was then applied to another height of the basalt wall, the 3 314 m high mass of rock which provides a great landmark and corner-stone of the main basalt mass 50 km north of Garden Castle.

The Voortrekkers descended the escarpment from the central plains to the midlands of Natal by means of several passes north of the main wall of the Drakensberg. However, the mountain wall was clearly in view, and many of them hunted and selected farms for themselves in the foothills. These were men such as Adriaan Olivier, who settled on *Tugela Hoek* at the foot of the pass known as *Sungubala* (where you overcome a difficulty). This was one of the traditional routes up the escarpment to the central plains. The modern road is named Oliviershoek Pass.

Missionaries such as the Reverends C W Posselt, W G Gülden-Pfenning and C Zunckel commenced work at Emmaus, Emangweni and Hoffenthal, stations run by the Berlin Mission Society. Woodcutters also arrived, attracted by the forests of timber, to commence a destructive industry.

MONT-AUX-SOURCES

In 1836 two French Protestant missionaries, the Reverends T Arbousset and F Daumas, explored the summit of the basalt mass, travelling from the Caledon River valley in the west. They reached the edge of the Drakensberg cliffs at the plateau summit known to the Sothos as *Phofung* (place of the eland). The missionaries soon realised that they had found one of the natural wonders of

South Africa – the continental divide and the source of three important rivers. They therefore named the 3 282 m high summit *Mont-aux-Sources* (mountain of springs). On the slopes of the crest overlooking the high Mont-aux-Sources plateau, the Thukela, Elands (Namahadi) and western Kubedu rivers have their source. The Thukela flows eastwards, reaches the edge of the plateau and leaps into space, falling 614 m. The fall is not sheer, being broken, but the main fall is 183 m high. Near its source, the Thukela flows alongside the Namahadi River before tumbling over the edge of the cliffs. The Namahadi River veers away northwards, plunges over the edge of the basalt in a spectacular fall of its own. While the Thukela flows eastwards across Natal to reach the Indian Ocean, the Namahadi joins the Vaal, its waters eventually reaching the Atlantic Ocean on the west side of Africa. The continental divide is between the spring sources of the two rivers.

At the foot of the Mont-aux-Sources plateau, where the main mass of basalt forms a prodigious amphitheatre, a woodcutter named Dooley commenced work cutting trees on land named after him. Nearby, a farm named *Goodoo* was purchased in 1903 by Walter Coventry who, in a casual way, started to accommodate the occasional visitor who wanted to explore the Drakensberg. The spectacular beauty of the Mont-aux-Sources area became renowned. In 1906 the Natal Government Minister of Agriculture and Lands, W F Clayton, proclaimed as a national park the unoccupied area below the amphitheatre. The Natal Government Railways publicity department sent a photographic team to the area. As a result practically every guidebook to Natal and passenger coach on the railways was from then on decorated with photographs of the Drakensberg.

Lack of funds badly hindered any development. At one stage just prior to Union in 1910, the government actually decided to abandon the whole scheme. Fortunately, one of the members of the management committee of the park, Colonel J S Wylie, bought the area containing the park. After the formation of the Union of South Africa he sold it back to the government on condition that it be retained for all time as a recreational area and national park. The park was initially 3 330 ha in extent. More land was added, including the 762 ha Rugged Glen nature reserve. The park attained its present size of 8 094 ha, administered at first by an advisory committee, and then from 1942 by the Provincial Council of Natal. Since 1947, the park has been run by the Natal Parks, Game and Fish Preservation Board.

The first hostel accommodating visitors was opened when Mr and Mrs F C Williams leased *Goodoo* farm from its owner, Walter Coventry, and converted the original farmhouse into quarters for twelve visitors. Mr Coventry became lessee of the whole park in 1919 and was appointed park superintendent in 1924, earning a salary of £5 per month. He busied himself in building a road from the outside world to the hostel, as well as in blazing a series of bridle-paths to various interesting places in the park.

Climbers steadily began to explore the precipices. The 3 165 m high peak known as the Sentinel, which looms up as a jagged mass of isolated rock marking the northern end of the basalt wall of the Drakensberg, was first climbed on 17 October 1910 by W J Wybergh and N M McLeod. The Inner Tower was first scaled on 13 June 1913 by Father A D Kelly and J E Miller, the same two climbers conquering the 3 047 m high Eastern Buttress on 10 July 1914.

The mountaineer, Tom Casement, ran the climbers' hostel of Rydal Mount in the Orange Free State. Accompanied by his renowned Sotho guide, Mlatu, he brought parties into the Mont-aux-Sources area from as early as 1908.

In 1926, when Walter Conventry resigned as superintendent of what was called the Natal National Park, he was succeeded in turn by Otto and Walter Zunckel, of the early missionary family. The hostel in the park was enlarged and became an atmospheric place, filled with talk of climbing, hiking and adventure in this superb rock wilderness.

In 1910 a Drakensberg Club had been formed with Judge Broome as the first president. During the First World War this pioneer association became defunct, but on 15 April 1919 the Natal Mountain Club was established. In July 1920 the club held its first regular camp in the Mont-aux-Sources area. As a result, the national park received vast publicity from the photographs and glowing descriptions taken back home by those who had participated in the outing.

The first guidebook to the Drakensberg was published in 1927 by a member of the Natal Mountain Club which, during this period, built a stone hut on the summit of the Mont-aux-Sources Amphitheatre. This shelter gave many people the pleasure of spending at least one night on the heights, and of watching the dawn break over the lowlands of Natal.

Walter Coventry had built the bridle-path from the hostel to the summit of the Mont-aux-

Sources Amphitheatre – a distance of 22,5 m. With two chain ladders spanning the final rock face, this path has allowed several thousand people to experience the thrill of walking or riding to the summit of Mont-aux-Sources at all seasons of the year. Other paths stretching to most parts of the national park were made, including a superb 11 km long path leading up the Thukela River to its spectacular gorge near the foot of the waterfall. Without any climbing necessary, this is one of the finest walks in Southern Africa.

The popularity of the Mont-aux-Sources area increased very rapidly. The national park contained such a variety of scenes, climbs, walks, swimming and fishing facilities, flora, picnic spots and riding trails that few visitors failed to return home without pleasant memories. Otto Zunckel, the lessee of the hostel, ran his establishment in a relaxed manner, which made it a natural resort for outdoor lovers. Climbers came from all over the world. The Zulu guide, Charlie Sentinel, escorted so many people to the top of the Sentinel that overseas newspapers carried reports when he fell while climbing and suffered serious injuries. The Amphitheatre Wall was first climbed during this period. On 19 April 1935 Doyle Liebenberg, Amlee Metter, Mary Lear and Mark Frank found a route up the precipice.

The atmospheric old hostel, unfortunately, was burned down on 10 December 1941. The new, larger establishment was built in far more luxurious style. In March 1947, when the British royal family stayed there, the title of 'Royal' was added to the name of the Natal National Park. Carefully conserved by the Natal Parks Board, the Royal Natal National Park has become one of the tourist show-pieces of Southern Africa and a delightfully exciting place to visit.

There are 31 different walks in the area of the park. Climbing possibilities are innumerable, ranging from easy to extremely severe. The famous Devil's Tooth, an isolated spire of rock, was first climbed on 6 August 1950 by David Bell, Peter Campbell and Ted Scholes. It remains one of the most complex climbs in the Drakensberg where many exposed parts of the rock wall provide mountaineers with sensational challenges.

THE CAVERN

Apart from the hostel, accommodation in the Mont-Aux-Sources area was provided by private lodges such as the beautiful Cavern. The cornerstone in the dining-room of this well-beloved resort is a relic of its beginning in 1910 when a Mr Rogers bought the area as a farm from its first owner, Charles Putterill, who had acquired the land in 1907.

In the 1930s Walter Coventry, after resigning from his appointment as superintendent of the Natal National Park, found the call of the Drakensberg too powerful to resist. He bought and moved to the Cavern, ranching cattle there and running a small guest-house mainly for the accommodation of friends he had made during his years running the hostel in the National Park.

In 1941, Judge Thrash bought the Cavern from Mr Coventry. His intention was to develop a ranch, but the sour veld of the area made this uneconomical. William Carte, was employed by the Judge as farm manager. He had met and married Ruth Blyth at The Oaks, at Byrne, near Richmond. Bill, as he was known, was an enthusiastic farmer and Ruth, having completed a domestic science course in England, was keen to establish herself in the hospitality business.

In 1942, the young couple bought the Cavern from Judge Thrash. The guest-house could accommodate fifteen people in thatched rondavels with separate ablution blocks. Bill started a quarry where, using his own explosives, he blasted sandstone for building. The stone was transported to the main building site on a sleigh with oxen and later by Ford truck. Josias Gambu, who lived at Langkloof, was trained by Joe Ball senior to cut and dress stone, and the main building still has the charm of this stone craftsmanship.

The farm supplied fresh produce for the guest-house. Farm animals often confronted guests amongst the buildings. Life was not without problems – there was no refrigeration for eleven years and meat was stored in a water cooler, jelly set in bowls carefully placed at the edge of the stream. A pelton wheel, located in the Glen provided minimal electric power to light the farm house. Bill installed a small diesel-engined power generator, but only in 1976 was Eskom power available.

For many years the water runway down the mountain was the only water supply for the house. 'Rhodesian Boilers' (44 gallon oil drums suspended over an open fire) provided hot water to the rudimentary ablution blocks. Evening entertainment included games of wit and action, favourites being dumb charades and carpet bowls. The Saturday night dance was a highlight! A radiogram powered with an extension cable through the lounge window to a car battery was used for music.

Sadly, Bill became ill and died in 1954, leaving his wife and four young children: Ros, 12 years; David, 9 years; Peter, 7 years and Anthony 6 years. With the encouragement of her family and the help of many Cavernites and her strong faith, Ruth persevered. She successfully faced all the hardships of impossible roads, difficult communications, inexperience in building and untrained staff. She took daring chances and with the guidance of regular customers who had become her friends, she developed the guest-house into a successful holiday venue. The foundations she laid are evident in the beautiful resort today, and her influence is still respected.

In 1972 Ruth's sons, Peter and Anthony with their wives, Jean and Rhona, bought the Cavern and have carried on Ruth's successful recipe which makes the Cavern (in a phrase coined by guests in the 1950s) the resort of many happy returns!

The main access road to the Royal Natal National Park is through the town of Bergville, 46 km away. The approach road yields some grand views of the Drakensberg, with many of the best-known heights clearly visible.

BERGVILLE

In 1897 a cluster of trading stations and houses was built close to the banks of the Thukela River on the farm *Kleine Waterval,* owned by a retired sea captain named Wales. In 1903 this village received the name of Bergville. It progressed slowly as the natural trade, administrative and communications centre for the tribal area of the Ngwaneni, a European farming area, and the overlooking stretch of the Drakensberg. Bergville became a municipality in 1962 and is the terminus of a branch railway from Estcourt. During the Anglo-Boer War the British built a blockhouse near the town and this is now a museum and national monument. Scenery and climate are both superb and the municipality maintains a tourist resort. The population is 2 468.

South of the Royal Natal National Park there is a ruggedly beautiful stretch of the Drakensberg overlooking the tribal area of the Ngwaneni people. The foothill country is wild and not easily accessible. Valleys lead up to the basalt wall. Dominating the rocky landscape is a height considered by many to be the most beautiful of all Drakensberg peaks: *Mnweni* (place of fingers), so named from the spires of rock which provide a severe test for climbers. Sometimes known as The Rockeries, this peak is 3 116 m high. Behind it, the Gariep River has its source on the high moorlands of Lesotho. There is a magnificent cave next to a waterfall at the foot of Mnweni which is generally used by climbers for accommodation.

Immediately south of the Mnweni area a ridge of mountains projects eastwards from the main wall of the Drakensberg. This ridge is known as *abaMponjwana* (the place of little horns), on account of its sharply pointed assembly of peaks. On this ridge are grouped some of the best-known heights of the Drakensberg: the 3 004 m high Cathedral Peak; the 2 918 m high Bell; the 3 009 m high Outer Horn; the 3 017 m high Inner Horn; and an oddly shaped collection of lesser peaks known by names such as the Mitre and the Chessmen.

THE MPONJWANA RIDGE

The spectacular Mponjwana Ridge overlooks on its southern side one of the most beautiful gorges eroded into the basalt wall of the Drakensberg. Here the river known as the *Mlambonja* (river of the dog) draws its water from at least a hundred separate springs. Tumbling down in waterfalls and rapids and broadening into many deep pools where trout dodge from sunbeams to shadows, this river finds a tortuous way through the sandstone foothills, flowing off to join the Thukela as one of its most important tributaries.

The valley of the Mlambonja attracted human beings from at least as far back as Stone Age times. The valley was sheltered; there was plentiful water; and game animals were attracted to the area by the excellent grazing. The Bushmen pioneers lived well. In the valley of the Mlambonja there are about 150 rock shelters, formerly used by the Bushmen. These shelters contain some of their finest galleries of rock art.

The largest gallery is found in what is known as the Elands Cave in the sheltered and verdant valley of a tributary stream of the Mlambonja. This stream is called the *Mhlwazini* from the Bushmen's tea trees *(Catha edulis)* growing there. In the Elands Cave are painted 1 639 separate figures, including some of the most beautiful polychrome artwork done on rock faces in the world.

Close to the Elands Cave, the river known as the *Ndidima* (place of reverberations) flows down to join the Mhlwazini as a tributary. The Ndidima originates on the summit of the Drakensberg. Tumbling over the cliff face in a tremendous fall, the river flows through a deep, narrow valley half choked with gigantic boulders, while the other half is covered in one of the most dense and unspoilt indigenous forests to be found in the whole area of the Drakensberg.

Bushmen found the valley of the Ndidima particularly idyllic. Protected by its situation and depth from the worst of the Drakensberg weather, it had spacious rock shelters, permanent water, firewood in the forest, and fat antelope grazing on the grassy foothills. Even modern visitors are tempted to take up residence in so favourable a retreat.

There are seventeen main rock shelters in the Ndidima valley, which contain nearly 4 000 separate rock paintings, most of them polychrome and many attaining a high standard of art. Notable among these rock shelters is the one known as *Sebayeni* (the corral) from its use by later pastoralists as a shelter for livestock. In this shelter are 1 146 paintings and, although they have regrettably faded, they still reveal the art of the Bushmen at its most sophisticated level.

It would be interesting to know when the last Bushmen vanished from this area. In 1925 two European sheep farmers grazing their animals in the foothills, took shelter from a storm in the Elands Cave. On a ledge they found carefully hidden away a Bushman's complete hunting outfit: bow, leather case, bark quiver, 22 poisoned arrows, poison and iron knives. All the items were in such excellent condition that they looked as though they had hardly been there for six months. The bundle was carefully wrapped in fresh-looking skins and was concealed beneath some grass which appeared as though it was not more than four months old. The find was sent intact to the Natal Museum in Pietermaritzburg. Of the owner, there was no trace. Perhaps this was the only remaining Bushman in the Drakensberg, the last of his kind to view the high peaks and fading paintings left by forgotten artists on the rock walls of the caves.

During the period of this discovery in the Elands Cave, the foothills between Cathedral Peak and Champagne Castle were being used as seasonal grazing grounds. Each winter farmers from the Orange Free State sent flocks of sheep and herds of cattle to the area, grazing them on land leased or bought from the government. A farmer from Kransfontein in the Orange Free State, I J M (Ryk Isak) Buys, was the principal user of the area for grazing. In the watershed of the Mlambonja River he had by 1918 acquired eight farms: *Solar Cliffs, Brotherton, Gewaagd, Tryme, Inhoek, Schaapkraal, Hopeton* and *Leafmore*. These lands are no longer farms, but their names still feature on modern maps.

Tryme farm, said to have been named by its surveyor in honour of his horse, was sold by Buys to one of his foremen, Sybrand Vermeulen, who made his home there. Visitors to the mountains today are familiar with the name of the horse from the massive hill overlooking the Cathedral Peak hotel and from the little shop, the Tryme store, attached to the hotel.

Another of Buys's foremen, Willem Oosthuizen, bought *Leafmore* and *Hopeton* from him. *Solar Cliffs* was sold to Anton Lombard, *Brotherton* to Stoffel van Rooyen and *Gewaagd* to Jan Roux. In 1937 the farms *Inhoek* and *Schaapkraal* were sold to Philip van der Riet, then farming on *Olivia,* north of Mont-aux-Sources. Van der Riet bought these farms for the specific purpose of creating a mountain holiday resort. His son Albert, who had hunted, fished and climbed in the area, told his father of the immense possibilities. The two farms lay close to the Drakensberg in a superb setting dominated by Cathedral Peak and the Ridge of Little Horns. The Van der Riets wasted no time. They carefully selected the site for their hotel and started to build. The bad access road was improved and during Christmas 1939 the first guests arrived at the Cathedral Peak hotel. It is today one of the outstanding resort hotels of Southern Africa, its reputation created by the imaginative management of Albert and his son William. The hotel is a favourite conference centre and a great place for lovers, with a quaint stone art thatch chapel with huge glass windows looking at an awesome view. Many a romance has reached happy fulfilment there. The gardens are superb, with rainbow trout farmed in a series of ponds in the hotel grounds. An interesting modern development has been the acquisition by the hotel of a Squirrel 350 B2 helicopter which lifts passengers to the very top of the mountains to sip sparkling wine while they watch the sun set.

An interesting development in the Cathedral Peak area started in 1935 at the Empire Forest Conference. A problem was raised at this meeting, concerning farmers who complained that streams were running dry on account of exotic softwood trees being planted at their headwaters. It was decided to commence intensive research on this controversial matter. After much study the watershed of the Mlambonja River was selected as the site of what became the Cathedral Peak Forest Influences Research Station and Cathedral Peak Mountain Catchment Research Station.

In 1938 H M (Mike) de Villiers was appointed officer in charge of this research station. A start was made in erecting headquarters on what was originally the farm known as *Gewaagd* (risky or hazardous). The Second World War halted research plans. When Mike de Villiers returned to his post in 1945, he really began work. An entire complex of access roads and paths were made. The main access road had to climb steeply up a route which Mike de Villiers most skilfully located. This is fittingly named Mike's Pass, in his memory. The contract to blast the cuttings was given to G R Monzali, an Italian engineer who had built, amongst other things, the railway bridge over the Gourits River in the Cape. Unfortunately, Monzali broke his back in a truck accident just after he had started work on the cuttings. He persevered with the job, however, and the summit of what is known as the Little Berg was reach in May 1949. A drive up Mike's Pass is quite a scenic experience, during which the traveller cannot fail to admire the ingenuity of the road's location and construction. On completion of Mike's Pass, the top of the Little Berg could be reached and research commenced. The initial programme was to select ten catchment sites. Each of these streams was gauged. A central meteorological station was established with a network of rain gauges over each catchment. One catchment was subject to light intensive grazing while the rest were planted with trees. Research proceeded until 1972, with results proving that pines consumed far more water than natural grasslands. The farmers' original complaints were therefore justified.

This research having been carried out, a new programme of work was commenced. The Mountain Catchment Act had stipulated that the principal function of the Drakensberg was to provide optimum water and to allow environmental management and human recreation – the basic concept of wilderness areas. Afforestation was therefore terminated. No further farming or other development is allowed in the area. Pure water and human pleasure are the two products of the Drakensberg. The wilderness is to be maintained in its present state, with (strange as it may seem) fire being the principal tool of conservationists.

Totally protected grasslands create enormous fire hazards. Complete protection is therefore impractical, since fires – accidental or deliberate – are inevitable. Total preservation would in any case allow the encroachment of secondary, woody vegetation over the grassland. Different burning techniques are being studied, and this will influence future management of the whole Drakensberg catchment area.

The paths originally made by the Forestry Department (now Natal Parks Board) have opened up the entire area from Cathedral Peak to Champagne Castle. Permits to enter the catchment areas are readily available from the Parks Board offices. Nature lovers, walkers and climbers are welcome in wilderness areas especially during summer when the grass is green and the fire hazards are low. It must be remembered, however, that these are carefully controlled areas. An unplanned fire can cause immense damage and for years retard a complex programme of experimentation.

THE CATHEDRAL PEAK AREA

This portion of the Drakensberg is essentially the catchment area of the Mlambonja River. The main access route is by the tarmac road which branches westwards from the Bergville–Loskop road at a point 10 km from Bergville and 20 km from Loskop. The gravel road leads directly up the valley of the Mlambonja towards the Drakensberg. After 4 km the road passes the *Emmaus* mission with its large hospital and theological training school. Founded in 1847 by the Berlin Missionary Society, this mission was named after the place 16 km from Jerusalem known as *Emmaus* (hot springs). For the next 14 km the road leads through the homeland of the Ngwaneni people, with many handsome views of the mountain wall providing a background to the huts and fields of the tribal farmers. At 18 km from the junction, the road passes the turn-off to Mike's Pass and then, nearby, the turn-off to the Cathedral Peak Forestry Station. Opposite lies the turn-off to the caravan park and camping ground maintained by the Parks Board. A further 4 km brings the road to its terminus at the Cathedral Peak hotel, 22 km from the junction with the Bergville–Loskop road.

A closer approach to the main wall of the Drakensberg can only be achieved on foot, horseback or on a four-wheel-drive vehicle. A network of paths spreads from the Mike's Pass forestry road and from the hotel towards the mountains. The valley of the Mlambonja provides a particularly beautiful walk. In its upper reaches, the river is joined by tributaries such as the *Qalweni* (place of bamboos); the *Tseketseke* (place of red ants), and the *Xheni* (place of the bundle). In these deep valleys are innumerable waterfalls, swimming-pools, towering cliffs and forests of trees and ferns.

Another tributary of the Mlambonja, joining it just below the hotel, is the *Mhlonhlo*, which received its name from the 'elbow-shaped' precipice of sandstone projecting into the valley like a cape. The path finds a way up the Mhlonhlo to beauty spots such as the Doreen, Albert and Ribbon falls, and to a magnificent forest of ferns. These paths up the river valleys are pure delight for walkers, with crystal-clear water to drink, many delightful picnic spots and a constant change of scenery as the valleys twist and rise.

Yet another tributary of the Mlambonja which reaches that river below the hotel is the *Ndumeni* (place of thunder), named after the dome-like summit in the Drakensberg where the noise of summer storms always seems to reach a climax and where the river has its source. The path following the valley of this river provides the walker with a joyful experience of majestic scenery; a constantly changing panoramic view; a dreamlike indigenous forest; the Rainbow Gorge; and branch paths climbing steeply up to the bulky sandstone massif of Tryme.

A different path leads from the hotel up the Mhlonhlo valley. Branching north to climb the steep sandstone cliffs, the path passes the landmark known as Mushroom Rock and from there ascends to the top of the Little Berg, the intermediate stepping-stone between lowland and the actual escarpment. From this high, grassy plateau, the entire length of the Drakensberg from Cathedral Peak to Champagne Castle may be viewed. The path leads to a little tarn, a real enchanted pool where lovely reflections are captured on its surface. It is, however, a strangely elusive pool; one day it may contain water but the next day there is no sign of such a pool. Photographers and artists are left wondering whether they had, in fact, ever seen in it the glorious reflections of the mountain massif.

Beyond the tarn, the path continues until, as do most of the other paths, it joins the contour path which runs along the foot of the escarpment all the way from Cathedral Peak to Champagne Castle. This path provides enthusiastic walkers with a full two to three day walk if the whole journey is completed. Otherwise, part of the way may be done, which takes less time. Whichever length is chosen there are few walks in Southern Africa to equal it.

Above the contour path is climbing territory. The great heights loom like a battle phalanx of heavily armoured giants. They have their occasional weaknesses where steep passes lead to the summit, but most of them present a formidable challenge.

Cathedral Peak (3 304 m), at the end of the Mponjwana ridge, is actually one of the easier climbs with a choice of 'C' category routes. It was first climbed in July 1917 by D W Bassett-Smith and R G Kingdon. At that time it was already called Cathedral Peak, but the person who gave it that name remains unknown. Only by a long stretch of imagination can any similarity between the mountain and a cathedral be found, but the name was probably suggested by the adjoining presence of the extraordinary and unmistakably shaped peak known as the Bell.

The Bell (2 918 m) provides one of the most interesting climbs of the Drakensberg and was conquered for the first time on 17 January 1944 by Hans and Else Wongtschowski. The easiest ascent is in the 'E' category. It has attracted so many climbers in recent times – many of them sadly lacking in experience – that it is a wonder that more people have not been killed climbing it. Fatalities include Ian Dawson and Charles Barber, killed in September 1970.

Next to the Bell looms the Outer Horn (3 009 m). A 'D' climb, the Outer Horn was conquered in July 1934 by a party comprising some of the best-known climbers of the Drakensberg: Doyle P Liebenberg, T Wood, H G Botha-Reid, 'Doc' Ripley and F S Brown. Although easier to climb than the Bell, the Outer Horn is exposed, and on 13 October 1959 Miss Fielette van Rooyen was killed there.

Next to the Outer Horn is its twin, the Inner Horn (3 017 m). A 'C' climb, it was first climbed in 1925 by a group headed by H G Botha-Reid. On 13 July 1942 Auguste Hellemans, from what was then the Belgian Congo, was killed on this mountain. He is buried in the forest of wattle trees close to the hotel. Next to him lies Hans Marcus, who on 21 October 1947, was killed in a fall from Baboon Rock.

On the main face of the Drakensberg, south of the junction with the Mponjwana ridge, are several remarkable mountains. Projecting out on their own are two jagged-looking peaks, The Pyramid (2 914 m) and The Column (2 926 m). The Pyramid, an 'E' climb, was first ascended in 1936 by H F Howes-Howell, O B Godbold, Naomi Bokenham, H C Hoets, C Axelson and S Rose. On 29 December 1950, Michael Stephens was killed while climbing this mountain.

The Column, an 'F' climb, was first scaled on 9 December 1945 by one of the most legendary of all Drakensberg climbers, the New Zealander, George Thomson. Thomson, a builder by profession who deliberately sought contracts in the Drakensberg area so that he would have opportunities to climb, was responsible for many sensational first-climbs. Climbing alone and watched with bated breath from below, he managed to reach the summit of The Column using no mechanical aids whatsoever. On his way down he fell 15 m, badly gashing his leg, yet managed to reach the bottom safely.

Just south of The Column and The Pyramid, the summit line of the Drakensberg reaches one of its highest points by means of the 3 281 m Cleft Peak, so named from the deep vertical gash on its face. There is an easy 'A' category climb with a first recorded ascent in 1935 by Doyle P Liebenberg, 'Doc' Ripley and party. There are more difficult ways of reaching the top of Cleft Peak, but the 'A' path followed by many groups in modern times is a magnificent experience for walkers, yielding particularly sensational views.

Just to the south of Cleft Peak looms the 3 285 m dome of Ndumeni with, with just below the summit, the strange assembly of spires and buttresses known to the Africans as *Qolo la maSoja* (ridge of the soldiers) and to Europeans as The Organ Pipes. Easy paths lead to The Organ Pipes and, through a gap in The Organ Pipe wall, to the summit of Ndumeni.

Still further southwards rear the buttresses of the 3 065 m Windsor Castle; the 3 076 m Little Saddle; lesser heights such as the Sugarloaf and the Sphinx; and finally the 3 078 m Ndidima Dome where the magnificent waterfall of the Ndidima River leaps down from the summit plateau.

Next may be seen The Witch, The Vulture's Retreat and, in the foreground, the lower 2 596 m Eastman's Peak, a climb of 'C' category, first conquered in 1935 by H A Eastman and party. This peak marks the end of the Drakensberg area usually climbed or walked by people based in the Cathedral Peak hotel or the caravan park. Beyond this point lies the Cathkin Peak–Champagne Castle area.

THE CATHKIN PEAK–CHAMPAGNE CASTLE AREA

From the point 16 km from Bergville where the access road branches off to the Cathedral Peak area, the main road continues south-eastwards. Keeping parallel to the Drakensberg, the road crosses undulating foothill country, particularly beautiful around Easter when cosmos flowers are in bloom. After 8 km the road passes a short turn-off to the Kelvin Grove caravan park, pleasantly situated and from where fine views of the Drakensberg may be seen.

The main gravel road continues south-eastwards. After a further 5 km it reaches a crossroads. To the north a road branches off for 13 km to the agricultural centre of *Winterton*, founded in 1905 and named after H D Winter, Secretary for Agriculture. Ahead the road proceeds for 11 km to

Loskop; to the south the access road leads to the Cathkin Peak–Champagne Castle area. This road leads up the valley of the *Sterkspruit* (strong stream), taking the traveller through some beautiful foothill country.

The valley of the Sterkspruit, like the valley of the Mlambonja, was always attractive to human beings. For some reason, a very odd assortment of Europeans made their homes there at different times: hermits, woodcutters, nameless men who lived and died in solitude, cattle-rustlers such as Pat McCormick, remittance men, and also a more respectable breed of farmers who settled in the valley and worked hard to establish farms and build homesteads. It was to this valley in 1858 that David Gray, who ran a hotel at Weston, moved. He settled first on a farm named *The Nest* and then, in 1863 removed to an adjoining site which he named *Cathkin* after Cathkin Braes near Paisley, his home town in Scotland.

The imported name of Cathkin was rather unfortunately applied to one of the most handsome of all the Drakensberg peaks, the 3 194 m *Cathkin Peak*. This fine mountain, one of the cornerstones of the whole range, stands at the point where the basalt wall veers to the south. Cathkin Peak stands on its own, dominating the whole escarpment in so definite a manner that the Africans have called it *Mdedelele* (make way for him), the name applied to a bully.

David Gray and a surveyor of the Royal Engineers, Captain Grantham, were jointly responsible for naming another of the Drakensberg peaks, this time with a bit more originality. Grantham was busy on a survey of the Drakensberg when he and Gray decided to try and climb Cathkin Peak, a formidable prospect. After climbing two-thirds of the way, they felt that they had gone far enough. They settled down to rest and to drink a bottle of champagne they had carried with them, destined for enjoyment on the summit.

On removing the bottle from the haversack, they found it to be half empty. After some argument as to who had snatched a surreptitious drink (they had taken turns to carry the haversack), they resolved to blame the mountain. They renamed Cathkin Peak, *Champagne Castle*, and for years the mountain was inflicted with the unwieldy double name of Cathkin Peak or Champagne Castle. Only in comparatively recent times did the confusion end when map-makers transferred the later name to the hitherto unnamed 3 351 m summit on the main wall of the escarpment. The Champagne Castle of today is one of the highest points on the summit of the escarpment.

Another interesting settler in the Sterkspruit valley was Carter Robinson. In July 1910, when he was only 21 years old, he bought the farm *Benjamin*, which nestled in the afternoon shadow of Cathkin Peak. He erected the first building on the site of the present Monk's Cowl Forestry Station. He was a lover of trees and pleaded so strongly to the government for conservation that in April of 1922 the Cathkin Peak Forest Reserve was proclaimed, covering some 40 400 ha between the Njesuthi and Mlambonja rivers.

In January 1924 Carter Robinson was appointed honorary forester and the following year was placed on a salary basis at £5 per month. He resigned in 1934 and in the same year the government bought his farm *Benjamin*, developing it into the Monk's Cowl Forestry Station, with J van Heyningen appointed as the first full-time forester.

Apart from agriculture, recreation and forestry, the area beneath Cathkin Peak has seen diverse excitements such as claims of gold discoveries. The first occurred in November 1891 when J T Howe reported finding gold on a spur of Cathkin Peak. In February 1892 there was a rush to the Phutini valley where J M Sayman claimed a find. Nothing worthwhile resulted. In 1916 it was claimed that cinnabar had been discovered in the valley of the Nkosasana, where the earth is notably red in colour. There was a short-lived rush by fortune-seekers.

In the field of recreation, however, no disappointment has been experienced in the Cathkin Peak area. A string of recreational resorts has been built along the access road. Eight kilometres from the junction with the main Bergville–Loskop road stands the hotel known as The Nest, built in 1943 by David Gray, grandson of the original David Gray who had settled on the farm of that name. The hotel was later taken over by Ernie and Edelweiss Malherbe and became a great place for bowlers, walkers and riders. Bridle trails lead to the various beauty spots and Bushman caves. A further 3 km takes the road past the El Mirador hotel, built in 1940 by Captain H G Whelan on part of *Heartsease* farm. Just beyond the hotel is the MOTH sanctuary of Mount Memory, dedicated in 1948 as a place of reflection and a memorial to those killed in the two world wars.

One and a half kilometres further on, a turn-off leads to the Cathkin Peak hotel started in 1929 by Carter Robinson. After 3 km the road passes the turn-off to the Dragon Peaks Park and to the

Drakensberg Boys Choir school. The school was founded in 1954 when R W Tungay, a Durban journalist, bought the farm *Dragon Peaks*, and on 23 January 1967 his son John opened the school. Today it houses 120 boys whose touring choir-groups are known throughout Southern Africa and in many overseas countries. The school is now controlled by a board of directors and is a non-profit-making concern. The Tungay family run the Dragon Peaks Park, with Russel Tungay as manager. This is one of the major holiday resorts in the Drakensberg.

Five kilometres beyond the turn-off to the school and the caravan park, the road reaches a turn-off to the Monk's Cowl Forestry Station and the entrance to the grounds of the Champagne Castle hotel, founded in about 1930 by H Martens on the farm *Woestyn*. From the forestry station and the hotel, foot and bridle-paths lead into the mountains and to beauty spots such as the Sterkspruit Falls. This is magnificent walking country, and the assembly of great peaks provides a challenge to mountaineers. The camping and caravan park run by the Forestry Department provides close access to the mountains.

In 1973 the two forestry areas of Mdedelele and Mkhomazi were declared to be wildernesses, the first to be so declared on the African continent. Three years later the Drakensberg Policy Statement of the Natal Town and Planning Commission was published. This important policy statement protected the entire Inner Berg from unsympathetic development. Public recreation and tourist facilities could be developed in the foothills but not in anyway to unfavourably influence the environment.

From this beginning more wilderness areas were proclaimed. Between 1976 and 1986, 20 000 ha of privately owned land was also acquired and substantially the whole length of the Drakensberg from Mont-aux-Sources to the Cape border came under permanent protection.

Cathkin Peak is a stiff 'E' climb. After resisting many early attempts, it was first conquered by a party consisting of G T Amphlett, Tom Casement, W C West, Father A D Kelly and two guides, Tobias and Mlatu on 12 September 1912. A relentless mountain to climb, Cathkin Peak demands great stamina and perseverance. It is always dangerous; on 20 September 1955 Keith Bush was killed in a fall on this mountain. The Mountain Club hut in the Mhlwazini valley is named in his memory.

Champagne Castle is an easy 'B' category climb up Gray's Pass, first explored in 1860 by David Gray and Captain Grantham.

Immediately behind Cathkin Peak is the sinister-looking Monk's Cowl, 3 261 m high. This is an 'F' climb, first completed in May 1942 by H Wongtschowski, A S Hooper, E Rhute and J Botha. On 28 January 1938, Richard Barry had been killed trying to scale this mountain which demands great respect from all climbers.

Just to the north of Champagne Castle is the strangely shaped ridge known as the Dragon's Back, culminating in one of the oddest of all Drakensberg peaks, the 2 408 m high *Ntunja* (the eye). Also known as *Gatberg* (cave mountain), this mountain contains a great natural hole gouged out immediately beneath its summit. The mountain stares out over the countryside like a one-eyed giant. It was first climbed in 1888 by A H and F R Stocker, and the more difficult south peak, an 'F' climb, by the same two mountaineers on 19 August 1888.

From the turn-off to the Cathkin Peak area, the main Bergville–Estcourt road continues south-eastwards through a parklike area of tribal huts, cattle and trees. Crossing the Little Thukela River (7 km from the turn-off) the road leads past a turn-off to the Injesuti camp, formerly known as Solitaire but now part of the Giant's Castle Game Reserve. A gravel road which needs to be driven with care, especially in rain, leads for 31 km to the camp. The scenery is superb and there is excellent fishing for rainbow trout. Many walking trails lead through unspoilt wilderness.

From the turn-off to Injesuti camp, the main road continues south-eastwards. After 3 km it passes the railway station of *Loskop* (separate hillock), 34 km from Bergville. For a further 9 km the road continues through the tribal area. At 48 km from Bergville it reaches a junction. Ahead lies Estcourt 19 km away; to the right (south-west) lies Ntabamhlope (25 km) and Giant's Castle (57 km).

The south-western turn-off leads past the little rustic railway station of Draycott, with a turn-off to the agricultural research station of Die Hoek. The gravel road now climbs steeply up a sandstone height from whose slopes may be seen a panoramic view of the acacia-covered, badly eroded timber plantations. Wild cosmos flowering in late summer provides a magnificent display.

Passing many fine farms with richly grassed hills and valleys, the road skirts the western slopes of the massive flat-topped sandstone pile of the 1 983 m high *Ntabamhlope* (white mountain), which is a landmark in this area. At 25 km from the turn-off the road reaches a junction with a gravel road coming from Estcourt. At this junction point stands the White Mountain lodge.

The road continues past the resort in a southerly direction, rising and falling, with many lovely views of the Drakensberg to the west and Ntabamhlope, like a giant table, to the east.

The road proceeds through a tribal area and descends into the valley of the Bushmans River, a great trout stream which flows in a bustling rush of crystal water. There are massive displays of cosmos flowers on its banks in late summer. At 4 km from White Mountain lodge there is a turn-off leading for another 4 km to the Hillside camp of the Giant's Castle Game Reserve. At 11 km from White Mountain the road joins the main road leading directly from Mooi River (46 km) and following the valley of the Bushmans River for 9 km to the entrance of the Giant's Castle Game Reserve. Just before the entrance, Bill Barnes, a retired warden of the reserve, established a trout farm where some very delicious fish are sold at reasonable prices. From the gate it is a further 9 km to the main tourist camp of the ...

GIANT'S CASTLE GAME RESERVE

This reserve consists of 34 638 ha of beautiful, unspoilt country – a wilderness of grassy hills and deep river valleys lying at the foot of the great wall of the Drakensberg. The Drakensberg are at their most majestic where they overlook this game reserve. For a distance of 35 km the mountain wall maintains a height of around 3 000 m, with many prominent peaks rearing their heads to the clouds. North of the reserve may be seen the distinctive landmark of Cathkin Peak, beyond which the Drakensberg swing out of sight to the west. South of Cathkin Peak and its companion, Champagne Castle, the Drakensberg stretch in a southerly direction, where may be seen peaks such as the 2 986 m *kwaMfazo Gaya Mabele* (the old woman grinding corn), and the 3 212 m *Njesuthi* twins, at the source of that quaintly named river, the *Njesuthi* (well-fed dog). Following these is the unmistakably shaped Thumb; Bannerman (resembling the profile of Campbell Bannerman, seen very clearly from the warden's house at Giant's Castle); several other high peaks and, finally, the majestic 3 314 m mass of basalt known as Giant's Castle.

This is one of the great landmarks of the Drakensberg. Like Cathkin Peak, it acts as a cornerstone behind which the main wall swings to the south-west. The rock mass of Giant's Castle remains so prominently exposed that the Africans have their own name and legend for it: *iNtabayikonjwa* (the mountain at which one must not point). They say that the mountain resents being pointed at, creating bad weather as a result.

In former years, the rich grazing and perennial water in the area of the present game reserve attracted a substantial population of game animals. Eland, red hartebeest, gnu, blesbok, and a considerable variety of smaller antelope such as oribi, klipspringer, grey rhebuck, reedbuck and mountain reedbuck, especially, flourished in the area. Now under conservation, they may be observed in a superb setting.

Drawn by the antelope and the congenial environment, Bushmen hunters of the Late Stone Age made their homes in the sandstone caves of the Giant's Castle area, where some of their finest rock art may be seen in numerous galleries of polychrome paintings. There are more than 50 rock shelters in the area, containing about 5 000 paintings. Main Cave and Battle Cave are the two most important, containing 546 and 750 paintings respectively. A site museum at Main Cave displays an excavated hearth, models of Bushman figures and a collection of artefacts.

The area of Giant's Castle was proclaimed the Giant's Castle Game Reserve in 1903. A beautiful camp situated in a garden of wild flowers has been built to accommodate visitors. Mountain huts have also been erected at various points. Hikers and riders may use the paths; the streams are well stocked with rainbow trout. Climbers and walkers find endless fascination in what is one of the scenic show-pieces of Southern Africa. The Bushmans River Trail is an easy and quite delightful 3 km long walk, self guided by means of signs and leading from the camp to Main Cave and revealing many interesting scenes and views. Of special interest is the Lammergeyer hide where, every Saturday morning from May to September, meat and bones are put out on which the huge lammergeyer vultures feed. The path from Main Camp to the summit of Giant's Castle is 34 km long, yielding thirteen hours of unforgettable walking and easy climbing.

Of historic interest is the monument on the top of Bushmans Pass. On this site three men from Major A W Durnford's force were killed in 1873. They were in pursuit of Langalibalele and his Hlubi tribe, who were fleeing into Lesotho after refusing to surrender their guns to the government of Natal. There is a picnic ground for day visitors near Main Camp. At Hillside, 30 km from Main Camp, there is a caravan and camping ground which is also the base for pony trails lasting two or three days.

South-west of Giant's Castle, the great rock mass of the Drakensberg not only maintains its imposing height, but actually culminates in the 3 482 m *Thabana Ntlenyana* the highest point in Southern Africa. The river valleys and foothills below this stretch of the Drakensberg are particularly beautiful, and a drive through the area is a memorable scenic experience.

A gravel road leads southwards through this area, branching off from the main Estcourt–Giant's Castle road 28 km before it reaches the game reserve. After 13 km the road passes the holiday resort of Glengarry, situated on the banks of the Little Mooi River. Walking and trout fishing in a handsome setting are the pleasant pastimes here.

Eight kilometres beyond the turn-off to Glengarry there is a turn-off which leads for 4 km to the ...

KAMBERG NATURE RESERVE

Established in 1951, this 2 232 ha reserve is situated in the valley of the upper Mooi River. The valley is overlooked by a particularly beautiful ridge of Clarens Sandstone, while at the head of the valley looms the great massif of Giant's Castle. There is a trout hatchery in the reserve and the Mooi River is well stocked with brown and rainbow trout. A 12 km long stretch is available for fishing. There is a picnic ground for day visitors and a hiking trail which leads up the valley. The reserve is open from dawn to dusk.

From the turn-off to the Kamberg Nature Reserve, the main gravel road continues southwards. The *Kamberg* (crested mountain) provides a landmark to the immediate east. The hilly country is richly grassed and provides grazing for fat herds of dairy cows. After 11 km there is a turn eastwards leading for 28 km to Nottingham Road. The road winds, climbs and descends, passing the Inzinga waterfall. At 28 km there is a turn to Bulwer and Impendle.

After some involved climbing, the road at 32 km reaches the summit of Carter's Nek, 1 981 m high. From here, there is a tremendous view of the southern Drakensberg, dominated by the twin summits of Hodgson's Peak. The road descends and, at 45 km, reaches a turn-off leading for 14 km to the ...

LOTENI NATURE RESERVE

This reserve, created in 1953, is 3 984 ha in extent and is situated in the green valley of the upper *Lotheni* (ash-coloured stones) River. There are delightful walks and fishing for brown trout in a 16 km stretch of the river. The scenery is superb and there is an interesting population of birds and antelope, including eland, reedbuck, oribi, duiker and bushbuck. The reserve is open from dawn to dusk. The Loteni Settlers Museum is contained in the original homestead of the Root family.

VERGELEGEN NATURE RESERVE

This is another conservation show-piece created by the Natal Provincial Administration in the southern Drakensberg. The 1 159 ha reserve was established in 1967. It lies in very rugged country near the headwaters of the *Mkhomazi* (Umkomaas) River. There is excellent fishing for brown trout and fine walks. The reserve is open from dawn to dusk. There is a picnic site for day visitors. No caravanning or camping is allowed. The name *Vergelegen* means 'far situated'.

From the turn-off to the Vergelegen nature reserve the main gravel road continues its winding way southwards. After 4 km the road crosses the Mkhomazana River and a turn-off leading for 48 km to the village of Impendle. After a further 8 km the road reaches a turn-off westwards in a most spectacular route up the valley of the Mkhomazana River and, by bridle and 4 × 4 route, up the Sani Pass to Mokhotlong in Lesotho.

THE SANI PASS

The *Sani Pass,* named after the Sotho mountain chief Rafolatsani, known as Tsani who lived on top of the pass, is the principal route up the Drakensberg from Natal to Lesotho. It was opened in 1913 as a bridle-path by James Lamont, a trader in Lesotho. In 1949 David Alexander commenced a regular transport service using four-wheel-drive vehicles. The track was improved in 1958. When Alexander left the area, transport up the pass was taken over by the Mokhotlong Mountain Transport Company. The road leads from Himeville up the valley of the *Mkhomazana* (little Mkhomazi) River through scenery which becomes increasingly rugged with every kilometre. At the approaches there are farmlands and trout hatcheries. After 10 km the road reaches Giant's Cup Motors. This is the base for the Mokhotlong Mountain Transport Company, run by Mike Clark. From here, loads of goods are conveyed up the Sani Pass in four-wheel-drive vehicles. At 10h00 each day there is also a tourist service up the pass in a four-wheel-drive vehicle. The journey to the top of the pass (24 km) takes two and a half hours. At the top of the pass stands the highest hotel in Southern Africa. The Mountaineers chalet is a six-bedroomed lodge, licensed, with a kitchen in which guests must cook their own meals. From this comfortable abode in the skies, visitors visit *Thabana Ntlenyana,* at 3 482 m, the highest point in Southern Africa. The summit is 16 km from the Mountaineers chalet.

Giant's Cup Motors takes its name from the gap between the twin mountains (3 257 m high) which stand to the south of Sani Pass. The Reverend Allen Gardiner gave the mountains this name, but they were renamed Hodgson's Peak after a tragic occurrence in 1862 when a farmer, Thomas Hodgson, was killed there while pursuing a band of Bushmen cattle-rustlers. This mountain is 6,5 km from the Mountaineers chalet.

Just after Giant's Cup Motors, the road passes the Sani Pass hotel and then starts the climb up the Drakensberg escarpment. The route leads upwards through a jumble of giant sandstone boulders. The river rushes down the pass through a succession of pools, waterfalls and cascades. Vividly coloured cliffs of sandstone tower over a narrow gorge choked with a rich vegetation. Baboons and other animals flourish. Fishermen, walkers, climbers and nature lovers find a special paradise in this lovely valley.

At 25 km from the start of the turn-off the pass reaches the South African police border post, open from 08h00 to 16h00 daily. Passports are needed if the traveller intends proceeding beyond this border post. The rest of the pass is 7 km long, with Mokhotlong 48 km from the summit.

The main road beyond the turn-off to Sani Pass continues its scenic route through the foothills of the Drakensberg. Trees of considerable variety, many flowering, cover the countryside and line the road in a handsome avenue. These trees are mainly the result of the enthusiasm of a local farmer, the late Kenneth Smallie Lund, and his wife Mona. Kenneth Lund bought *Hazeldene* farm in 1937. He married Mona three years later. They were both tree lovers, but very few indigenous trees could stand the sharp temperature variation in the Drakensberg foothills and the powerful winds of winter.

The Lunds started to experiment with exotic trees. They created their own nursery, planting about 4 000 trees each year on their farm and selling or giving away the balance. They enthused the whole district, especially cultivating oak, maple, plane, poplar, elderberry, alder, birch, cypress, liquidambar, crab-apple, tulip trees, flowering cherries and many other varieties. On *Hazeldene* they created a 40 ha nature reserve around an artificial lake, carefully selecting the trees they planted there so that the colours reflecting in the water would be exquisite. It is in this nature reserve that the ashes of Kenneth Lund were scattered when he died in 1982. Autumn (April to May) is the finest time to see the trees in colour.

It is in the midst of this man-made wonderland that the road, 2 km from the turn-off to Sani Pass, reaches the town of ...

HIMEVILLE

Founded in 1893 by the Border Mounted Rifles sent to police the area, Himeville was named in 1902 after Sir Albert Henry Hime, Governor of Natal. It became a small magisterial and trading centre and a great base for trout fishermen. The nearby Himeville Nature Reserve, 105 ha in extent, comprises two lakes amply stocked with trout. Boats are available for hire and there is a comfortable little camp. The local hotel, run for three generations by the Aldous family, is a renowned fishermen's resort, with The Trout House serving superbly cooked fish. The fishing season is from 1 September to 31 May.

There is an interesting little museum in Himeville, created by Mrs Diana Nagy. It is in the old fort and prison, with exhibitions in the cells. It is open Wednesdays and Fridays to Sundays 10h00 to 12h00.

From Himeville, a tarmac road leads southwards for 5 km to ...

UNDERBERG

The railhead and trading centre of Underberg lies beneath the 1 905 m hill known as *Hlogoma* (place of echoes). The village is beautifully situated among hills and plains, with a fine view of the Drakensberg. There is excellent trout fishing in the district. Underberg had its origin at the end of the 19th century, when Michel and Benast opened a store to serve the pioneer community of settlers who had obtained farms there in 1886. It was expected that the site of the store would be the nucleus of a village but a Government Commission found the place overlooked by the hill, defenceless from any attack in those troubled frontier times, and also on privately owned land.

The site of Himeville was selected for the district centre, and in 1902 a magistrate was appointed. Rivalry developed between the two villages and the situation was compounded in 1917 when a branch railway was built to serve the area and, for some unknown reason, terminated at Underberg. Himeville was left in the cold. There were accusations of underhand persuasions with the railway engineers. For several years there was bitterness between the two villages. Then Kenneth Lund intervened with his trees. He gave trees to both villages and people started to mellow in their shade. Kenneth and Mona then offered to give an oak tree to each person in the two villages who would undertake to plant it in a line along the road connecting the two villages. The oaks were planted and they flourished. The villages were reconciled and old feuds were forgotten.

A very readable little local newspaper, the *Mountain Echo*, is published in Underberg.

Beyond Underberg, a tarmac road stretches westwards towards the Drakensberg. After 4 km there is a division of the road; the right-hand division continues for 32 km to the Drakensberg Garden hotel. Dominating this area is the remarkably shaped pile of sandstone which, in 1835, Captain Allen Gardiner named *Giant's Castle* on account of its close resemblance to the castle of Edinburgh. The original name was *maXholozholo* (many rocks). In later years the surveyor, Dr Peter Sutherland, renamed this mountain *Garden Castle*, after the maiden name of his second wife, Jane Garden Blaikie. The name of Giant's Castle was then applied to the mountain further north, on the main wall of the Drakensberg.

The road continues beyond the hotel for 4 km to the Garden Forestry Station, from where a path climbs the valley of the Mlambonja River, passing Pillar Cave eventually to reach the summit of the Drakensberg at Marshai pass. The upper valley is dominated by the sharp peak of the 2 997 m high Rhino Horn (*Ntaba Ngcobo)*, named after the Ngcobo clan who live there). The main wall of the Drakensberg averages about 3 100 m in height in this part of the basalt mass.

At the division of the road 4 km from Underberg, the left fork continues in a south-westerly direction, passing a turn-off to Swartberg 5 km from Underberg and, at 29 km, reaching a junction. The left turn-off at the junction leads for 5 km to the Bushmans Nek hotel, situated in the valley of the Ngwangwe River.

The road ends 3 km further up the valley at the Bushmans Nek police border post. Beyond this post (open from 08h00 to 16h00 daily), there is a bridle-path which ascends the Drakensberg to Jonathan's Gate on Bushmans Nek. A five-hour walk into Lesotho along this path takes hikers to Jonathan's lodge in the Sehlabathebe National Park, a place notable for its rock formations and scenic beauty. The Bushmans Nek Pass is dominated by the 3 028 m high Devil's Knuckles, known to the Sothos as *BoRwa Babararo (*three Bushmen). *Thabantseu* (the mountain of eagles) also overlooks the area.

The Bushmans Nek hotel is built on *Silverstreams* farm. One kilometre beyond the Bushmans Nek police post there is a hut at the start (or end) of the Drakensberg hiking trail – a five-day walk between the police post and Sani Pass. There are four huts providing overnight accommodation at staging posts along this trail. This is a fine walk which tempts many holiday-makers to linger over the journey, swimming or fishing in the mountain streams, taking photographs or simply revelling in a world of mountains and hills.

THE SOUTHERN DRAKENSBERG

The Drakensberg lying south of the old Cape–Natal border yield some spectacular scenery. The road following its length passes through an attractive landscape of hills and farmlands. However, there have as yet been few recreational developments in this area comparable to the northern Drakensberg resorts. But, for the motorist, the climber, the walker, the trout fisherman, the photographer, and the skier (for the southern Drakensberg experiences the heaviest falls of snow in South Africa), this stretch of massive rock precipices provides some exciting possibilities.

To explore this area, it is best to start from Underberg. Three kilometres back on the road to Bulwer a gravel turn-off R617 leads to Coleford, traversing some of the most beautiful farming country on Earth, especially so in late summer when the grass is velvety and masses of cosmos flower in patches of vivid colour.

Three kilometres from the turn-off the R617 road crosses the Mzimkulu River, a bustling, rushing flow of clear trout water. Twisting, rising and falling over endless grassy hills, the road continues southwards. At 20 km from Underberg there is a turn-off east to Bulwer and, 3 km further on, the road descends into the green, immaculate farming valley of the Ngwangwane River. In this fertile valley lies ...

THE COLEFORD NATURE RESERVE

Created in 1948 as a public resort for walkers, riders and trout fishermen, this reserve is 1 272 ha in extent. Immediately across the river (20 km from Underberg) lies the hutted camp of the Natal Parks Board. The reserve is good for rainbow trout. Bird life is interesting and gnus, blesbok and red hartebeest graze on the hill slopes. Eland are bred here. James Cole was the original owner of the land.

One kilometre beyond the camp a turn-off to the west stretches to Bushmans Nek (43 km). The R617 road now leaves the Coleford Nature Reserve and, after 3 km (32 km from Underberg), reaches the Ndwana River, cascading through a shallow valley carpeted with grass and cosmos flowering during Easter. The Ndwana River marks the border line of Griqualand East. The R617 road climbs the southern heights of the valley, revealing fine views of mountains and river. At the summit (46 km from Underberg) lies the small rural centre of *Swartberg* (black mountain), situated in a spacious, grassy bowl in the hills and flanked by a dark-coloured range in the south.

From Swartberg the R617 road leads westwards, traversing superb cattle country; a rich, grassy upland graced with many charming rural scenes. At 23 km from Swartberg the road crosses the Mzimvubu River, where a turn-off on its right bank leads to Cedarville. A further 23 km of rural travel brings the road to another turn-off (12 km) to Cedarville, a dairy-farming centre founded in 1912, sheltering at the foot of the Cedarberg on a richly grassed plain.

A further 12 km brings the R617 road to a junction with the R56 road coming in from Kokstad 52 km away to the east. After joining this road and turning west (right) a pleasant valley is reached, set against a background of the Drakensberg. In this valley, 5 km from the turn-off and 63 km from Kokstad, lies the town of ...

MATATIELE

The name *Matatiele* is apparently derived from the Sotho *Madi-i-Yila* (the ducks have flown), which is applied to the wild fowl which used to frequent the marshes in the area. However, it could well also refer to some of the rough customers and tough 'birds' – the pioneer inhabitants of this town on the frontiers of Lesotho, Natal and the Cape; an ideal area for the livestock rustlers of old.

The town originated with the arrival of Adam Kok and his Griquas in 1864. Near a broad, reed-grown lakelet frequented by innumerable aquatic birds, Adam Kok established a 'magistrate': a grimy chronically half-drunken character by the name of Peter O'Reilly. With a mud hut, serving as a court-house, built on top of a hillock known as Materies Kop, this representative of civilisation attempted to impose law and order on a turbulent countryside. It was said that any rustler wishing to run stock through the area need only send O'Reilly a bottle of whisky the day before and a bleary eye would be closed on proceedings. The isolated state in which the man lived was described by the missionary, William Dower, who, approaching the magisterial seat on a visit, received an urgent message from the incumbent: *'Hold hard. Send me some soap and in an hour I'll be presentable enough to see you'.*

The general turmoil in Griqualand East (as the area was called) induced the Cape Government to intervene in 1874. A respectable magistrate, G P Stafford, replaced the pioneer, but times remained unsettled. The outbreak of the Basuto Gun War in 1880 saw the area in so uproarious a state that the four Europeans stationed on Materies Kop were forced to slip away on 4 October of that year and to abandon the magisterial post. The place was overrun and eleven Hlubi tribesmen who were part of a force attempting to guard the government building were killed.

For twelve months the area remained chaotic, but the rule of law was eventually reasserted. Troublesome elements were driven away and the district was opened to European settlement. A new magistracy was built on the site of the present Matatiele town hall, with a detachment of the Cape Mounted Rifles to garrison the place.

Gun-running, smuggling and cattle-rustling continued in the area for years. Some rather picturesque individuals made their homes in the Matatiele of old. The local hotels – the Royal and the Masonic – were notorious places for brawls and gambling (especially the Royal, whose owner, Alec Payne, was a great card player). Many tales, both lurid and amusing, date from this period. A typical example concerns a memorable game which took place in the Royal hotel one night. A visiting commercial traveller cleaned out the local gamblers. At 05h00 everybody retired to sleep, with the game due to be resumed at 11h00 to allow losers a chance to recover their losses. The commercial traveller, however, sneaked out with his winnings, left enough to pay for his bill and fled for Natal.

When Alec Payne woke up and heard the news, he ordered a fleet horse to be saddled. Stuffing cards and money into the saddle-bags, he jumped on and rode in pursuit of the traveller. He returned triumphantly the next day, bringing with him the traveller's trousers, and all his money. The Royal hotel has been demolished but the façade has been preserved as part of a modern shopping centre.

Men such as Bill Wollenschlaiger habitually rode their horses right inside the hotels and into the bars, standing their horses as well as themselves to a drink. Charles Castle staked his farm *Compensation* in a game and lost it to Alec Payne. Payne left for Kokstad in the post cart the next day to transfer the farm to his name. Castle clambered into the cart with him. The two gambled all the way to Kokstad, with Castle winning not only his farm back, but half the hotel as well.

A regular character in the area was the trader James Cole. Known as 'King Cole', he arrived penniless in the area. On his death in 1943 he was reputedly a millionaire. Another successful early trader was J A E Taylor. Apparently he had family troubles. On his death he bequeathed a substantial sum towards the founding of hospitals in Matatiele and Mount Fletcher. There was a condition that nobody with the name of Taylor would ever be admitted to them alive or dead.

From the beginning of the 20th century, Matatiele started to reform. More women and policemen arrived and the hitherto predominantly masculine society was subdued. On 1 January 1904 Matatiele became a municipality. The arrival of the railway in April 1924 finally ended the town's isolation. Today it is a prosperous agricultural centre, the railhead of the line from Pietermaritzburg, and a great place for trade with the Sotho people who ride in across the Drakensberg. Horses (especially polo ponies) are bred here and the town is also a centre for the dairy industry in the fertile *Mabele* (kaffircorn) valley. The Wilfred Bauer Nature Reserve has been established on the road to Qacha's Nek.

From Matatiele a scenic drive (gravel) leads for 34 km to Qacha's Nek in Lesotho. The border posts are open daily from 08h45 to 16h00.

The R56 road to the south ascends from Matatiele over a ridge, yielding fine views of the Drakensberg. The road passes through a tribal area largely settled by Sotho people. After 8 km a turn-off stretches to *Ongeluksnek* (accident ridge), the pass over the Drakensberg used by the Griquas on their migration. The name of the pass refers to an unfortunate incident when one of the Griquas was killed there during an eland hunt. Immediately north of Ongeluksnek, dominating Pack Ox Nek, is the 2 727 m high *Draken's* (dragon's) Rock, said to have been the origin of the name *Drakensberg*. Footprints of dinosaurs may be seen in the Clarens Sandstone below the mountain.

The R56 road continues southwards, following the course of the Kenega River, which flows through a jumble of rocky hills. At 38 km from Matatiele, the road crosses the river at Kenega Drift, close to the site of some sulphur springs. Proceeding southwards through the eroded, arid, rocky tribal area, the road (after a further 24 km) crosses the Tina River. There is a pleasant picnic and camping site on the right bank of the Tina River where the road bridges across it. After a further 9 km (71 km from Matatiele) the road reaches the village and magisterial centre of Mount Fletcher, built on a ledge on the slopes of the 2 142 m high Castle Rocks, *Mount Fletcher* was named after the Reverend John Fletcher, one of the leading British Methodists. It was founded in 1882 as an administrative centre for the surrounding district largely inhabited by members of the Hlubi tribe. Although only a small one-horse type of place, Mount Fletcher is at least notable for the castle-shaped mass of rock towering above it.

From Mount Fletcher the road continues southwards over a stony ridge, revealing panoramic views of the Drakensberg and the rugged landscape of the tribal area. Descending into the valley of the Luzi River, the road crosses the river by means of a bridge 12 km from Mount Fletcher. A turn-off on the right bank leads westwards to Naudes Nek pass and Rhodes.

The R56 road continues southwards, climbing a rocky slope and passing over what is lugubriously known as *Moordenaars* (murderers) Nek. It was here that Hamilton Hope, the magistrate of Qumbu, and three other Europeans attempting to reach the besieged town of Maclear, were killed in 1880. Traversing a grassy, less stony and level plateau for 9 km, the road then descends into a wide valley littered with picturesque huts and dominated to the west by the Drakensberg. In the centre of this valley (44 km from Mount Fletcher) the road crosses the willow-lined Tsitsa River at Halcyon Drift, whereafter the countryside improves rapidly.

South of the river the road traverses the Maclear district, a farming area of red earth and fine alluvial river valleys watered by streams stocked with trout. The traveller is rewarded with many pleasant views of the Drakensberg range and its foothills, handsome and blue in the clear air. The road leads through the hills and, 64 km from Mount Fletcher, makes an impressive descent into the valley of the Mooi River, on whose pleasant banks lies the town of Maclear (see Chapter Twenty-One).

Chapter Twenty-Nine

THE GOLDEN WAY FROM THE GARIEP TO THE VAAL

From the point where it crosses the Gariep River from the Northern Cape into the Free State, the N1, the Cape-to-Cairo Road, becomes a golden way, traversing a gold-coloured land of maize, wheat and sunflowers. The surface of the land is the classic prairie country of South Africa, the veld with its grasslands stretching from one horizon to the other, while beneath it lies a treasure trove of gold, uranium and diamonds. The bridge over the Gariep River is 35,5 km from Colesberg. Upstream lies the great wall of the Gariep Dam. Just less than a kilometre further along the road, there is a turn-off to the recreational resort at the lake, and thence for 48 km to the picturesque little town of Bethulie on the upper shores of the man-made lake.

The Gariep Dam has been described at the end of Chapter Thirteen. Suffice to say here that it is an impressive engineering feat and, especially in summer flood time, an awesome sight when the river overflows its restraining wall. The holiday resort (built there by the former Orange Free State Provincial Administration) and the hotel both provide very agreeable accommodation.

From the Gariep Dam resort a road leads eastwards along the northern shores of the lake to the town of ...

BETHULIE

A mission station was founded by the London Missionary Society in 1829 for the benefit of the Bushmen. It was then known by the lugubrious name of *Moordenaarspoort* (murderers' pass) from a fight between Sotho and Griqua raiders. The London Missionary Society transferred it in 1833 to the French Missionary Society which gave it the name of *Bethulia* (chosen by God). The town, established in 1863, was at first named Heidelberg but in 1872 renamed *Bethulie* after the mission. The original mission buildings still stand, among them the oldest European-built house in the Free State, named after its builder, the Reverend Jean Pellissier, the first French missionary to be stationed there. The house is now the Pellissier House Museum, housing a collection of items devoted to local history.

The atmosphere of Bethulie is pleasantly old world. The nearby presence of the Gariep Dam has rejuvenated what was something of a forgotten place into a holiday resort with opportunities for boating and angling. There is a nature reserve and park in the centre of the town. Bethulie has a present population of 6 718.

Patrick Mynhardt, the actor, was born in the town and he has given the place a renown from his deliciously droll monologue called *The Boy from Bethulie,* which depicts with subtle humour the life of a small boy growing to manhood in so amiable a place.

The main railway line to East London from the north crosses the valley in which the town lies by means of a spectacular concrete viaduct. The road and railway from Bethulie southwards crosses the Gariep River by means of a combined road–rail bridge, 1 152 m long and 51,5 m high, the longest in South Africa.

Above the bridge, the Caledon River joins the Gariep. The *Tussen-die-Riviere* (between the rivers) game farm lies on the wedge of land 22 000 ha in extent between the two rivers some

10 km from Bethulie. This game area is open to the public, but is closed during the May-to-August hunting season. There are three walking trails, game-viewing roads, picnic sites, accommodation, a dense population of wild animals and interesting *Klipstapel* (stone mound) rock formations of eroded clusters of basalt rocks.

From the turn-off to Bethulie, 8 km from the point where the N1 crosses the Gariep River, the north–south trunk road of Africa continues its way northwards past rocky hillocks for 45 km and then reaches a crossroads. A turn right leads for 42 km to Bethulie. A turn left leads directly into the town of ...

SPRINGFONTEIN

An artesian fountain (known colloquially as 'a fountain which springs') gave the farm *Springfontein* its name. In 1904 a portion of it was laid out as a town. Lying on the main railway line from the Cape to the north, the place became an important junction for the line coming up from East London and also for a line to the diamond-mining centre of Koffiefontein. In 1912 Springfontein became a municipality. Sheep and maize are the products of the district.

For another 25 km the N1 continues northwards over the prairie country and then reaches a turn-off to the town of ...

TROMPSBURG

Trompsburg was named after Jan and Bastiaan Tromp, owners of the farm *Middelwater* on which the town was laid out in 1892 when the railway from the Cape to the north reached the place. It grew as a centre for a cattle and sheep producing district with 200 merino sheep farms carrying 200 000 sheep. Plentiful underground water and a brisk climate are assets to the town, which became a municipality in 1902. The population is 3 957.

At Trompsburg, the former route of the N1 from Colesberg rejoins the modern road. The earlier road, now known as R717, crosses the Gariep River at Bothasdrif 30 km from Colesberg. It continues for another 24 km through a jumble of rocky hillocks, passes the small rural settlement of Waterkloof and then, 4,5 km further on, reaches the town of ...

PHILIPPOLIS

Founded in 1823 when a mission school was established for the benefit of the resident African clans, Philippolis was named after the Reverend Dr John Philip, superintendent of the London Missionary Society's operations in South Africa.

In 1826 a section of the Griqua tribe, led by Adam Kok, settled there. A straggling village of shacks and huts grew up around the church while a few trading posts, the residence of Adam Kok, his council chamber, gaol (including gallows) and the homes of the missionaries gave the place some importance.

The Griquas eventually decided to move away. On 10 February 1862 the Orange Free State government bought the area for £400 from the Griquas, who then wandered off on what proved to be an epic trek through the mountains of Lesotho to Griqualand East. A magistrate, Jean Francis van Iddekinge, was appointed to Philippolis. It developed as a European type of village, although the narrow streets survive as a reminder of the original Griqua inhabitants. Today, Philippolis consists of one long main street and a few tortuous sideways. The population is 3 800.

Of interest is the Trans Gariep museum, having as its main theme the history of Adam Kok and the Griquas. It is open Mondays to Fridays 10h00 to 12h00. The distilling kettle, an exhibit of the museum, is used every year on 6 April when Philippolis stages its ever-popular Witblits Festival.

From Philippolis R717 swings north-eastwards. After 3 km there is a crossroads, with turns leading to Springfontein and Jagersfontein. At 23 km from Philippolis the road crosses the branch railway from Springfontein to Koffiefontein, and another 33 km brings the road to Trompsburg and its reunion with the N1.

From Trompsburg the N1 continues northwards and, keeping close company with the railway line, after 38 km across the Free State plains reaches the town of ...

EDENBURG

Edenburg was founded on 15 January 1862 when the farm *Rietfontein* was bought for 60 000 rixdollars as the site for a church centre. With plentiful water available and situated on the main north–south transport road, the town had an optimistic beginning when the first erven were sold on 24 February 1862. The name of Edenburg was given to it by the church elders. It became a municipality in 1890 and today has a population of 5 422.

Originally a great area for plains' game, it is now a prosperous cattle and sheep farming centre. The old Berlin Mission Society station of Bethany lies on the Riet River, 22 km away.

The N1 continues northwards across the plains. After 25 km the road passes *Tierpoort* (leopard pass) where the resort known as Tom's Place stands on the lake shores of the dam built in the Kaffir River.

After another 50 km the N1 reaches a series of turn-offs leading into the city of ...

BLOEMFONTEIN

With its population of 334 641, Bloemfontein is the capital of the province of the Free State. It is also the judicial capital of South Africa, the seat of the Court of Appeal. Centrally situated on the highveld plains at an altitude of 1 392 m above sea-level, it experiences a warm summer and a dry, cold winter. With an average rainfall of 500 mm, the countryside is intensely green in summer, gardens flourish and the soil is fertile. The city is attractively situated at the foot of a cluster of flat-topped hillocks with spacious views from the summits of heights such as Naval Hill.

Bloemfontein (the fountain of flowers) originated as an outspan at a spring where water could always be found, and game animals and wild flowers abounded. The site of this fountain, marked by a column and a mosaic of the city emblem, is now rather unromantically confined in a large concrete drainage canal. Behind it, in Victoria Park, there used to be a fine municipal caravan park where countless travellers rested and, in the old days, watered their draught animals at the fountain.

To the African tribes the fountain was known as *Mangaung* (place of cheetahs). In 1840 the first European known to settle there, Johannes Brits, built a simple homestead 300 metres from the fountain and started to farm. Six years later, in March 1846, the farmer was startled to see a group of horsemen and wagons approaching across the veld. In the van of this party rode an officer of the Cape Mounted Rifles, Major H D Warden, seconded to the responsibility of being official British Resident on the central plains of South Africa.

Major Henry Douglas Warden was something of a romantic figure. He was the son of an illegitimate offspring produced by one of the lusty Stuart princes and an Edinburgh beauty. Warden had, early in life, become a professional soldier. Now here he was, far from the elegance of Princes Street, Edinburgh, riding across the veld in search of a suitable site for his official residence and the building of a strong point for a small garrison.

Warden liked Bloemfontein. Its central situation and the dependable supply of water from the fountain made him choose the place as his official residence. After some hard bargaining with Johannes Brits, Warden bought the farm for £37 10s. Brits (who later complained about the sale price and received another £50) and his somewhat bemused family moved to a new farm in the vicinity of the present town of Harrismith. Warden and his men built a tiny fort of mud and stones which they named Fort Drury, of which nothing remains today. Only the ghost of the name lingers on a block of apartments erected on the site of the fort that watched over the original 'fountain of flowers'.

Warden had been sent to his post simply as official British Resident on the central plains. At first he had little power other than the influence of his personality on the sunbronzed farmers, hunters and traders who either settled or wandered over the face of the veld. To Warden's little fort, however, on 14 January 1848, came the Governor of the Cape, Sir Harry Smith. A meeting of plainsmen voted for the establishment of British rule over what was to be called the Orange River Sovereignty.

There was violent disagreement over this development. Many plainsmen had trekked away from the Cape to escape British rule and they had no intention of meekly allowing it to overtake them yet again. Six months after the meeting these hardy dissidents mustered their strength and received reinforcements from the Transvaal. Led by Commandant-General Andries Pretorius, they appeared before Fort Drury on 17 July 1848 and gave Warden summary notice to quit.

Warden was helpless. His supporters at the fountain of flowers consisted of a mere 45 African soldiers, 42 loyal civilian males and 200 of their dependants. After a short parley, Warden received three days to abandon his fort and within that time he led his men away. Back on the double came the doughty Sir Harry Smith. Pretorius rode south to meet him. On 29 August 1848 at Boomplaats, a tough, day-long skirmish occurred which resulted in the flight of Pretorius and the return of Warden to the 'fountain of flowers'.

For the next six years the Orange River Sovereignty prevailed. Bloemfontein grew as an administrative centre. With a garrison of 450 men, Warden built a new stronghold (Queen's Fort) on one of the dominant hillocks. This became the key British military base on the central plains of South Africa. Lion hunting was the principal diversion for the officers of this garrison. The surrounding plains at that time still teemed with such enormous numbers of game that the antics of the herds provided standard amusement for the residents of the village who watched from the shade of their verandas. The Anglican cathedral was built in 1850, and its elegant interior and windows are a reminder of those times.

The Orange River Sovereignty did not flourish. Many of its inhabitants remained resentful towards British control. The British Government in turn was not enthusiastic about this addition to its empire, calling it *'a valueless territory not worth retaining, always causing trouble, and moreover an endless expense to the Home Government'*.

To the consternation of the loyalists, Sir George Clerk arrived in Bloemfontein in February 1854 with the news that he had been sent to liquidate the Orange River Sovereignty. For a few days there was uproar in Bloemfontein, with celebrations on the one side and blank despair on the other. On 11 March 1854, the British flag was lowered over Queen's Fort and replaced with the flag of the new republic. Sir George rode out of the town at the head of the garrison. The republicans were left to elect for themselves a *Volksraad* (people's council) and, as first president, an amiable, intelligent trader by the name of Josias Hoffman. The old *Raadsaal* (council chamber), built in 1849 by Major Warden, is now preserved as a national monument and may be seen in St George's Street.

The village of Bloemfontein then found itself to be one of the world's capitals, albeit of a diminutive rural state whose total population numbered only 12 000 souls scattered over a vast plain with hardly any communications or assets and a threat of trouble from the Sotho people who lived in the east.

President Hoffman tried his best, drawing up a liberal constitution and, by personal friendship with Moshweshwe, leader of the Sothos, maintaining a precarious peace. But he had many enemies. After nine months he was ousted from office, accused of high treason for presenting to Moshweshwe a keg of gunpowder. He was replaced as president in 1855 by Jacobus Boshof, a magistrate from the Cape and Natal.

President Boshof found that it was required of him to be a combination of superman, lawyer, diplomat, administrator and soldier. Under the circumstances he managed extremely well. His pocket republic and its village capital were placed on a business footing. As a result of basic administrative order and the stirrings of prosperity in a fertile and healthy land, immigrants started to trickle into the place. Bloemfontein grew. In spite of troubles and petty wars with the Sothos and the people of the Transvaal, the old 'fountain of flowers' soon found itself at the centre of a respectable town.

President Boshof resigned in 1859 and was somewhat ineffectively replaced by M W Pretorius, the President of the South African Republic in the Transvaal. He attempted to be a dual president but soon went. On 5 November 1863 Johannes Brand – a lawyer from the Cape – was elected President of the Orange Free State. For the next 25 years under this wise and likable man the little rural republic entered its golden age of independence.

President Brand's daughter, Kitty, told the author that, when her father arrived with his family in Bloemfontein, the members of the Volksraad gathered to greet them – all soberly dressed in black, correctly mannered, grave of demeanour and densely bearded. Suddenly, in the midst of formalities, they all hurriedly left the room in some agitation. The Brands asked what was happening, half expecting to be told that some emergency had occurred. They were informed that no calamity, rumour or war ever disturbed the Volksraad members half as much as the fact that coming up the garden path was Mr Drinkwater, the local debt-collector!

Through wars with the Sotho people, quarrels with Britain over ownership of the diamondfields, and nagging economic problems Brand steered the republic along the stony road of independence. The simple little phrase he used when things looked bleak, *Alles sal reg kom, mits elkeen sy plig doen* (everything will come right, provided everybody does his duty), was sometimes the only hope of a gloomy Volksraad. The beautiful twin-spired Dutch Reformed mother church is a pleasant reminder of the days of President Brand. The President laid the cornerstone of this building in 1878.

There was a lengthy struggle to secure finance to build a railway and to persuade the more rural republicans that its advent would not drive the state to ruin. Eventually, in the midst of great public celebration, the railway to Bloemfontein from the Cape was opened on 7 May 1888. Unfortunately, President Brand had not lived to see the culmination of one of his special projects. He had died two months after finally persuading his Volksraad to approve its construction. His successor, Frederick Reitz, also a lawyer, found himself at the head of a republic which, through Brand's good work, was in a far healthier financial state than it had ever been in the past.

President Reitz could relax in a handsome presidency (built in 1884) and be saluted by the cannon and band of the smartly dressed State artillery – 100 men led by a finely whiskered German officer, Captain F W Albrecht. The population of Bloemfontein had by then reached 2 000. The original frontier character of the place had changed. More substantial buildings had been erected and the plains' game had been hunted almost to the point of extinction. In this massive slaughter a local farmer, Andrew Bain of *Bainsvlei*, had particularly excelled. Among his hunting achievements was the organisation in August 1860 of entertainment for the visiting 16-year-old second son of Queen Victoria, Alfred. Prodigious herds of antelope were stampeded through a narrow pass on Bain's farm, where numerous hunters were concentrated to ambush the animals. Five thousand game animals were slaughtered in one day during the course of this particular hunt.

President Reitz was an intelligent man in the same mould as Johannes Brand. He lived, however, in far more complex political times than his predecessor had. The graceful Raadsaal, built in 1893 and subsequently the seat of the provincial council, housed many acrimonious debates on issues such as unity with the South African Republic in the Transvaal. Reitz, like Brand, was against unity. When he resigned in 1896, the year of the Jameson Raid into the Transvaal, he was replaced by Marthinus Theunis Steyn, a farmer and lawyer, who was an ardent supporter of union. The Orange Free State was drawn into the quarrels which culminated in the Anglo-Boer War.

Bloemfontein was declared an open city. Five months after the war started, it became the unhappy duty of Dr B Kellner, who was then mayor, to surrender the capital to Lord Roberts, whose footsore but cheerful 'Tommies' marched in without opposition on 15 March 1900. The occupation marked the end of an epoch in the history of Bloemfontein. For the remainder of the war, the town was a major communications and remount centre for the British army.

With Lord Roberts had marched a naval brigade with a small battery of 4.7 guns. In the general search for suitable campsites, the sailors were allocated the flat top of what was formerly known as the mountain of Bloemfontein, from then on known as Naval Hill. Other units occupied this elevated site after the sailors had left. A remount camp for the Wiltshire Regiment was established below the slopes, where some of the troopers – inspired by the famous white horse of their home county – laid out a similar figure with the words *For Remounts* worked underneath in whitewashed boulders.

At the end of the war, Bloemfontein became the capital of the Orange River Colony and developed considerably as the centre of a communications complex and a rich agricultural area. With the Union of South Africa proclaimed in 1910, Bloemfontein became the judicial capital (the seat of the Supreme Court of Appeal) and an important educational centre with the establishment there of the University of the Orange Free State and many fine schools such as Grey College, founded in 1856 on a financial grant from Sir George Grey, Governor of the Cape Colony. Glen Agricultural College, opened in 1919, is situated just outside the modern city, and (among other achievements) is famous for its experiments in proving the fertility of the Kalahari aeolian sands, the basic research which started the great Vaal-Harts irrigation scheme.

With its central position and crisp climate, Bloemfontein is a suitable place for conventions and sports gatherings. Its sports facilities are excellent.

The clear highveld air has also made the city attractive to astronomers. The Boyden Observatory was built at Maselspoort in 1927 by the Harvard University of America. Today it is an international research station equipped with a fine 1,52 m reflecting telescope and two 0,41 m refracting telescopes. The observatory is now owned by the University of the Orange Free State. Visitors are allowed about the time of the first quarter. For further details phone (051) 441-7605.

On the summit of Naval Hill stands the original building of the Lamont-Hussey Observatory, built in 1928 for the purpose of observing binary stars, of which it discovered over 7 000. Its principal instrument was a 0,68 m refracting telescope. The observatory was originally under the control of the University of Michigan in America but astronomical work was completed there in 1972. The building now houses a unique theatre and cultural centre.

Today Naval Hill is a pocket-size game reserve known as the Franklin Game Reserve, established in 1928 and named after J S Franklin who was then mayor. Its 198 ha area is maintained in its original wild state and serves as a home for herds of springbok, eland, zebra and blesbok. The road which encircles the summit of the hill yields fine photographic views of the city, its suburbs and surroundings. Couples find it a pleasant place in the moonlight.

There are many interesting and unique things to see in Bloemfontein apart from the stars. There is a fine zoo and a magnificent rose garden in Kings Park; a first-class orchid house and a botanical garden. There is an annual rose festival with visitors taken on a tour of rose gardens. *Maselspoort* (oddly named 'measles pass') has river boating, swimming and holiday facilities. The National Museum with its outstanding anthropological exhibition is open Mondays to Saturdays 08h00 to 17h00; Sundays and public holidays 12h00 to 17h30. The Military Museum in Queens Fort, with its relics of the wars South Africa went through, is open during Tuesdays to Fridays 10h00 to 12h15 and 13h00 to 16h00. The Old Presidency, built in 1885 and designed by the well-known Lenox Canning in the Scottish-Baronial style, is open Tuesdays to Fridays 10h00 to 16h00;

Sundays 14h00 to 16h00. Freshford House, another worthwhile museum to visit, depicts the lifestyle of the Edwardian era, and is open Mondays to Fridays 10h00 to 13h00; weekends 14h00 to 17h00. Other museums include the first Raadsaal – the oldest existing building in Bloemfontein, built in 1849 by Major H D Warden – which is open weekdays 10h00 to 13h00; weekends 14h00 to 17h00, and the National Afrikaans Literature Museum, open weekdays 08h00 to 12h15 and Saturdays 09h00 to 12h00.

Many historic buildings and impressive memorials, such as the General J B M Hertzog statue with its 33 fountains, may be seen. The 34 m high obelisk of the National Women's War Memorial underneath which lie the ashes of the famed Emily Hobhouse who did so much to alleviate the plight of Boer women and children in the concentration camps during the Anglo-Boer War. The War Museum on the same grounds, with its relics of the Anglo-Boer War, is open weekdays 09h00 to 16h30; Saturdays 09h00 to 17h00; Sundays 14h00 to 17h00.

Bloemfontein became a city on 17 March 1945. It is a neat, bustling city, a pleasant stopover for those travelling north or south along the great N1 trunk road of South Africa.

BLOEMFONTEIN TO KIMBERLEY

From the central position of Bloemfontein, roads stretch to most parts of the Free State. West of the city, a tarmac road R64, crosses the level plains to Kimberley, passing numerous salt-pans, shallow depressions in the veld where rain-water collects during summer, washing in mineral salts from the surface of the plains and, over vast periods of time, concentrating deposits which are now recovered by various salt-producing companies.

It is interesting to see the vast number of smallholdings on the outskirts of Bloemfontein. Each one is owned by some individual who generally works in the city but devotes his spare time to the growing of vegetables or other cash crops to be sold at the local markets. Each smallholding usually has at least one windpump on a borehole, raising water which is used for irrigation.

After 69 km of travel, the road reaches the town of ...

DEALESVILLE

Laid out on the farm *Klipfontein*, owned by John Henry Deale, the town became a municipality in 1914. Dealesville is a centre for general farming (sheep and maize), for the recovery of salt, and for a number of thermal mineral springs frequented by sufferers of a variety of ailments. One of these springs reaches the surface on the town lands. Fifteen kilometres from the town lies the spring known as Baden-Baden, while 37 km away is the spring of *Florisbad* (named after Floris Venter who developed the mineral spring), famous for its fossil deposits. In 1932 Professor Thomas Dreyer discovered a skull there of Florisbad Man, which dates back more than 40 000 years.

The R64 road continues westwards past several salt-pans which lie on a prairie land so flat that there is little opportunity for rain-water to drain away. Flamingoes find this area very much to their liking. After 54 km the road reaches the town of ...

BOSHOF

Named after President Jacobus Nicolaas Boshof, the town was founded in 1855 on the farm *Van Wyksvlei* as an administrative centre for the western part of the Orange Free State. It became a municipality in 1872. Today 5 780 people live there. The Chris van Niekerk Museum is worth visiting. There are various themes, such as the life of Senator van Niekerk, and the history of Afrikaner folk-dances, which originated in Boshof. The museum is open Mondays to Wednesdays and Fridays 10h00 to 13h00 and 15h30 to 16h30; Thursdays 08h30 to 13h00 and 14h00 and 16h30. Of interest is a municipal nature reserve situated on the outskirts of the town. There are several hunting farms in the vicinity.

West of Boshof the R64 road crosses a more arid landscape dotted with a few acacia trees to break the monotony. After 45 km the road crosses the boundary with the Northern Cape and after 53 km reaches the city of Kimberley (see Chapter Fourteen).

BLOEMFONTEIN TO THE SOUTH

The N6 road which leads to East London has its start in Bloemfontein. Leading south out of the city, this road leads across fertile mixed-farming country, passes after 15 km the shooting range where National Bisley Championships take place. After 62 km the road reaches the town of ...

REDDERSBURG

On 20 August 1859 the farm *Vlakfontein* was purchased for £1 500 by the Dutch Reformed Church, which laid out a town and named it *Reddersburg* (town of the Saviour). It became a municipality in 1889 and today has a population of 4 103. It is an agricultural centre.

From Reddersburg the N6 road swings south-eastwards over the high, grassy prairie country. Low, bush-covered hillocks and numerous antheaps cover the surface. There are endless vistas of the type of highveld scene (especially attractive towards sunset) peculiar to South Africa. The roads department has considerately created several resting lay-bys (notably on the banks of a stream 16 km from Reddersburg). After 72 km the road passes through a ridge of hills by means of a natural passage known as Wilcocks Poort. A dense thicket of acacia trees covers the banks of a stream; Kinderman Park is situated there with picnic sites, golf-course and the Smithfield Dam. Just behind this attractive area, sheltering in the lee of a rocky ridge, lies the little town of ...

SMITHFIELD

Smithfield had its start in September 1848 when that hard-riding governor, Sir Harry Smith, laid the foundation-stone for a church planned as the centre for a town named in his honour. It was laid out on the farm *Waterval* belonging to C S Halse. The selected site of the town was soon found to be unsuitable through lack of water. In November of the following year, erven on a new site were sold on the well-watered farm named *Rietpoort*. Smithfield flourished in its new setting. It became a municipality in 1860. The church, built between 1860 and 1862 is worth seeing. Smithfield is a farming centre for the southern Free State and Lesotho border areas. The population is 4 411.

The Caledon River Museum is worth a visit. Exhibits include rooms devoted to General C R de Wet and President J P Hoffman, an 18th century kitchen and the old Traacha wool washery. The museum is open Mondays to Fridays 10h00 to 12h00, and 14h00 to 16h00.

There are good riding and walking trails around Smithfield. The Stokstert hiking trail, 22 km long, leads to many interesting places. There are two overnight huts and a brisk highveld atmosphere. Fauna and flora is varied and the trail reveals much of the huge Caledon River conservancy, created by conservation supporting landowners. It conserves 300 000 ha.

South-east of Smithfield, the N6 makes its way over grassy cattle and sheep country. After 15 km the road bridges over the handsome Caledon River and 24 km further on reaches ...

ROUXVILLE

Founded in 1863 as a church centre laid out on the farm *Zuurbult* owned by Petrus Weppenaar, Rouxville was named after the Reverend Pieter Roux who ministered to the district by riding there every three months from the older town of Smithfield. A rural town with a population of 5 442, Rouxville is the centre for prosperous farming in merino sheep and Afrikander cattle. Its situation is pleasant in a hollow overlooked by some handsome hills to the north-east.

The Witstinkhout adventure trail for hikers starts at Rouxville and provides a four or two-day walk with overnight facilities.

South of Rouxville, the N6 leads over the plains which build up to picturesque hill country, stony and lightly bushed. After 33 km the road reaches the Gariep River. The General Hertzog Bridge carries it over into the town of Aliwal North in the Eastern Cape (see Chapter Twenty-One).

BLOEMFONTEIN TO THE SOUTH-WEST

From Bloemfontein the road numbered R706 leads south-westwards for 113 km to ...

JAGERSFONTEIN

In 1870, J J de Klerk found a diamond on the farm *Jagersfontein,* originally owned by a Griqua named Jagers. A great rush of fortune-seekers took place. Diamonds were found in a volcanic pipe. Many beautiful stones of superb quality have since been recovered from this pipe, ranging from blue-whites to sapphires. In 1893 the Excelsior Stone (971 carats) was found, the largest diamond to be discovered until the Cullinan Diamond was found near Pretoria in 1905. At the start of the rush the government, on 29 August 1870, proclaimed the farm to be a public diggings. The original farmhouse was bought to serve as an administrative office. A large eucalyptus tree acted as a gaol, with prisoners tied to the trunk.

The diamond workings were subsequently consolidated to form one big mine run by the De Beers company. The excavation for this mine is comparable to the big hole in Kimberley, with steep sides and tremendous depth. The town, which became a municipality in 1904, has a population of 5 773. Pleasantly situated, it is an interesting example of a mining boom town of former years. The original mine-staff quarters have been converted into the Charlesville Old-Age Home.

From Jagersfontein, a road numbered R704 leads westwards across grassy plains where blue cranes, the bird emblem of South Africa, gather in groups. Many of these groups consist of three birds, but whether all are male or female, or an agreeable mixture, is known only to the birds. After 12,5 km the road reaches ...

FAURESMITH

Named after two individuals, the Reverend Philip Eduard Faure and the popular governor, Sir Harry Smith, *Fauresmith* was founded in 1842, making it the second-oldest town in the Free State.

Fauresmith is set among high ridges which have squeezed the growing town into a horseshoe shape. An extraordinary feature of the town is the railway line which runs up the centre of the main street. The spectacle of a steam locomotive happily puffing its way through traffic was almost unique. At Inhambane in Mozambique there is a similar line running along the main street. Berlington in the state of Iowa, in the USA, has the same feature. The local Fauresmith flyer (now drawn by a diesel) hits the main drag of Fauresmith at 06h00 and returns at 11h00 on weekdays. Train enthusiasts and nervous motorists should check these times beforehand in case of changes.

A retired puffer is permanently mounted in the middle of the main street in the centre of the town. As if it were one of the town's oldest inhabitants confined to a rocking-chair, this elderly locomotive now spends its time watching the traffic go by and wishing there was still enough steam left in its boiler to allow it at least a few more whistles at the girls. A fitting comparison to this retired puffer is the quaint little town hall which also stands on the main street. An example of genuine Victoriana, it definitely disapproves of both the puffer and modern goings-on.

In 1926 a veld reserve and laboratory were established on ground situated just outside the town. Dr M Henrici, a Swiss expert, was for 30 years in charge of a research project which involved studying the effects of weather and grazing on the vegetation of this part of the grass-covered veld.

It became a municipality in 1859 and now has a population of 3 593.

From Fauresmith the R704 road continues north-west through fine sheep and maize country, with poplar trees a superb golden colour in early winter. The Kalkfontein Dam lies immediately to the north of the road. It is a great place for yellowfish angling. After 53,5 km of pleasant travel, the road enters ...

KOFFIEFONTEIN

The habitual making of coffee by transport riders at the fountain is said to be the reason for the sociable name of *Koffiefontein.* The town recognises this pleasant tradition by means of an ornamental fountain (situated at its eastern entrance), designed to resemble a huge coffee-pot pouring out a drink.

In June 1870 one of the transport riders picked up a diamond near the fountain. This started a rush to the area. By 1882 Koffiefontein was a boom town with four mining companies working there. Several buildings in the town remain from this period, notably the Central hotel with its corner tower.

In 1892 Koffiefontein became a municipality and today has a population of 9 763. Diamonds obtained from a volcanic pipe are still being mined there by the De Beers company. The mine is in a security area but visitors are occasionally permitted to tour the workings if they apply to the manager. A game farm in the vicinity of the town, also owned by the mine, is open to visitors on Sundays.

During the Second World War Koffiefontein was a prisoner-of-war camp for about 2 000 Italians. A few memorials of their presence remain, including two wall paintings of Mussolini and the Italian king. These are protected to mark the former site of the camp. Eight hundred pro-Nazi South Africans were also interned there, including John Vorster, who (many years later) became Prime Minister and then State President of South Africa.

Bushman paintings may be seen in the area. A local factory produces cheese.

From Koffiefontein the traveller has several roads to choose from. To the west, a road (R705) leads for 43 km to the town of ...

JACOBSDAL

Named after Christoffel Johannes Jacobs, owner of the farm on which the town was laid out, *Jacobsdal* has a population of 4 750. It became a municipality in 1860 and is an attractive little place, its streets shaded by trees. Ample water is available from the Riet River on whose banks the town stands. An Anglo-Boer War blockhouse is situated on the outskirts of the town and numerous salt-pans may be seen in the vicinity. Wine is produced in the Landsicht cellar where it may be tasted.

Still another road, the R48, leads south-westerly from Koffiefontein over a grass-covered plain, good sheep and maize country. After 45 km this road reaches ...

LUCKHOFF

Established in 1892 and named after the Reverend H J Luckhoff, this town is a quiet centre of a sheep-farming and general agricultural district. It has a population of 2 611.

From Luckhoff the R48 road continues south-westwards for 38 km and then reaches the bridge crossing the Gariep River below the walls of the Vanderkloof Dam (see Chapter Thirteen).

From Bloemfontein a road, the R702, leads south-eastwards over fertile mixed-farming country. After 71 km this road reaches ...

DEWETSDORP

Named after the father of General C R de Wet, the town was laid out in 1880 on the farm *Kareefontein*. It became a municipality in 1890. The population is 7 772. There is a superb golf-course.

From Dewetsdorp the R702 road continues south-eastwards for 35 km and then reaches a crossroads at Jammersdrif on the Caledon River. There it joins the R26 which traverses the beautiful sandstone country of the Eastern Free State (see Chapter Thirty).

THE ROAD TO LESOTHO

From Bloemfontein the N8 road to Lesotho leads east out of the city and over the fertile farmlands which, with their smallholdings and windpumps, are so dear to the Free State urban worker who longs to get back on the land in all spare hours. After 5 km the road passes the turn-off to the Bloemfontein International Airport and the recreational resort of Maselspoort. Ahead lies open country for 38 km and then the road reaches the railway junction of Sannaspos, the scene on 31 March 1900 of a violent clash between Boer and British forces during the Anglo-Boer War.

The water supply for Bloemfontein came from a barrage in the Modder River at Sannaspos. General C R de Wet decided to attack the place and, by disrupting the water supply, seriously embarrass the British garrison in Bloemfontein. On the night of 30 March he marshalled 1 500 men for a surprise attack. Information received indicated that a British convoy on the way from Thaba Nchu to Bloemfontein was encamped for the night near Sannaspos and this would provide very acceptable booty for the Boer force. Brigadier-General R G Broadwood, a senior British officer, was also at Sannaspos with 1 700 men.

Just before dawn on 31 March the Boers launched their attack, catching the British fast asleep. There was chaos. At Koornspruit the British convoy was captured. At Sannaspos, Broadwood hastily marshalled his men and attempted a stand, but his defeat soon turned into ignominious flight to Bloemfontein. The British lost 428 prisoners, 6 missing, 117 wounded and 37 dead. Boer losses were 3 dead and 5 wounded. They captured 80 wagons and 7 cannons.

For more information, phone the War Museum in Bloemfontein at (051) 447-3447.

From Sannaspos, the N8 road continues eastwards and reaches the industrial development area of *Botshabelo* (place of refuge) established in 1979 as something of a sanctuary for about 350 000 individuals unsettled by the establishment of the fragmented bantustan known as Bophuthatswana. The inhabitants refer to the town as a monument of apartheid. A considerable number of industries have been founded there, drawing on the labour force living in Botshabelo and in the adjoining area (64 km from Bloemfontein) of ...

THABA NCHU

One of the best-known landmarks on the highveld is the 2 138 m high *Thaba Nchu (Thaba Ntsho, the black mountain)*. This was the stronghold of the Rolong tribe whose chief Moroko became an ally of the Voortrekkers in 1836 when they entered the Free State plains from the Cape. His people had been much harried in the tribal disturbances known as the *Difaqane* (or *Mfecane* in Zulu). With his people and two Wesleyan missionaries, the Reverends James Archbell and J Edwards, Moroko moved to Thaba Ntsho in 1833. For nine head of cattle and seventeen sheep and goats, he purchased the area from Moshweshwe, the Sotho chief and settled there. The town grew as a trading centre for an area of dense African population. In 1873 Thaba Nchu acquired municipal status and in 1966 was proclaimed a border industrial area. A portion of the town was included in the adjoining bantustan (now defunct) which had a population of about 150 000 people.

The Maria Moroka National Park on 3 400 ha of attractive country is contained in a natural amphitheatre overlooked by Thaba Ntsho 10 km south of the town. Maria Moroka was the mother of the reigning chief, Robert Moroka and served as regent before he reached maturity. There are walking and riding trails in the park and a good population of wild animals, including rhinos.

Two casino hotels provide entertainment and accommodation.

From Thaba Nchu, the N8 road continues eastwards through fertile agricultural lands. At 21 km there is a crossroads to the railway centre of *Tweespruit* (two streams), 3 km to the north, and to Hobhouse, 42 km to the south. For another 39 km the N8 road continues eastwards with the mountains of Lesotho on the near horizon. The road then joins the R26 north–south border road, with a turn-off to the Lesotho border post and Maseru 14 km to the north.

Another tarmac road (R48) linking Bloemfontein to Kimberley keeps close company westwards with the railway. After 80 km this road reaches the town of ...

PETRUSBURG

Petrusburg was named after Petrus Albertus Venter who provided money for the purchase of the farm *Diepfontein* on which the town was laid out in 1896 as a church and commercial centre for a prosperous agricultural area. There are numerous salt-pans in the surrounding countryside, their shallow water well used by flamingoes. The population is 6 053.

From Petrusburg the R48 road continues westwards and, at 120 km from Bloemfontein, reaches the village of *Perdeberg* (horse mountain), the scene of one of the major battles of the Anglo-Boer War.

THE BATTLE OF PAARDEBERG (PERDEBERG)

The war museum at Perdeberg station is open daily 08h00 to 17h00. Controlled by the War Museum in Bloemfontein, this museum records the events of a chaotic and bloody military episode of the Anglo-Boer War which took place between 17 and 27 February 1900. There are two viewpoints, one on *Oskoppies* (ox hillocks) which provides a panoramic view of the whole battlefield, and one on the banks of the Modder River where General Cronjé had his laager.

General P A Cronjé, retreating eastwards from the Battle of Magersfontein, was forced to a halt on 17 February 1900 in the region of Vendusiedrif by bombardment from a British force under Lieutenant-General J D P French, attacking from a northerly direction. While Commandant J F de Beer delayed the British advance, Cronjé and his 4 000 men dug themselves into fortified and well-camouflaged positions over a 3 km length on both banks of the Modder River. It was a strong defensive position but susceptible to bombardment.

The British field commanders wanted to use their artillery to force the Boers into surrender, for Cronjé and his men were surrounded. Unfortunately for the British soldiers, Lord Roberts, the commander-in-chief, was unwell and absent from the scene. Lord Kitchener, the acting commander-in-chief, was a great man for frontal attacks. He ordered such an onslaught although the approaches to the Boer positions were over open ground with no cover from the sharpshooters in the trenches.

Two British divisions attacked from the south and from the west. With support fire from artillery on Gun Hill and Signal Hill, Colonel O C Hannay was ordered to cross the Modder River at Vanderbergsdrif and attack the Boers from the east. Hannay realised that Kitchener's order of attack was futile and would lead to unnecessary and heavy loss of life, but he had his orders and Kitchener refused to listen to reason. Hannay knew that his men would face certain death. He sent most of them off on various duties and then attacked the Boers with 50 selected men led by himself.

Hannay and many of his 50 men were killed in the attack. A total of 1 200 British soldiers died in the senseless frontal attack, the greatest loss suffered by the British in a single day during the whole course of the war. The British were dismayed. In this state of confusion they were attacked at 17h00 on the afternoon of 18 February by two resolute Boer units led by General C R de Wet against the British position on Oskoppies, and by General P R Botha against the British positions on the ridges at Stinkfontein. Both positions were captured after very slight resistance.

The next day, 19 February, under commandants C C Froneman and F J Potgieter, 50 Boers broke through to Oskoppies where they joined Cronjé and plans were discussed for the relief of his force. All plans, however, proved abortive. On 19 February Lord Roberts returned to his command and set about clearing up the mess. He had 90 pieces of artillery and these commenced a continuous bombardment of the Boer position.

That night the British moved closer to the Boer position. Oskoppies was recaptured by the British and Cronjé was completely surrounded. The Boers ran out of artillery ammunition on 20 February, and were short of food and clean drinking water. The stench of decomposing bodies all around them demoralised even the tough Boer sharpshooters. They had no medical services and no hope of escaping the humiliation of surrender. They resisted stubbornly until the morning of 27 February. The British by then were less than 90 m from the Boer fortified position. Cronjé had no alternative but to surrender with his 4 000 men.

From Perdeberg, the R48 road continues westwards for 49 km and then reaches Kimberley.

BLOEMFONTEIN TO THE NORTH

From the centre of Bloemfontein it is 12 km north to the N1 which has bypassed the built-up areas. The N1 continues northwards for 6 km, then reaches a turn-off where the original N1, now called R30, branches off north-westwards to Brandfort and the gold-fields. The modern N1 continues straight north-eastwards across the central plains, past maize and sunflower lands, sheep and cattle pasturage and acacia thorn trees. The road crosses the Great and Little Vet rivers, and eventually, after 96 km, reaches the town of ...

WINBURG

This town has the distinction of being the oldest town in the Free State. Built around a central square and overlooked by low hills, Winburg has an atmosphere of the rural tranquillity of former times. Without possessing any notable architectural features, it is nevertheless a typical agricultural town of the central plains. Cattle, sheep, horses, wheat and maize flourish in a brisk highveld climate (1 441 m above sea-level) with a rainfall of 550 mm a year.

The town originated with the advent of the Voortrekkers. In 1835 Andries Hendrik Potgieter led a party of trekkers into the area and for 42 head of cattle purchased from the local African chief the rights to the vast stretch of country between the *Vet* (fertile) and the *Vaal* (tawny coloured) rivers. An administrative, church, educational and commercial centre for the area was essential and a search for a suitable site began. After some argument the farm *Waaifontein* was selected and the owner, Jacobus de Beer, named the place *Wenburg* (victory town) because he had defeated rival offers of alternative sites. The name was later spelt Winburg.

For several years the little town was the only administrative centre on the central plains. At first it was an outpost of the Natal Republic and from 1841 the seat of a landdrost who was appointed by the Volksraad in Pietermaritzburg. The British annexation of Natal left Winburg independent as the capital of the central plains. With the advent of the British to the central plains in 1846, Bloemfontein was founded as the centre of their administration. In 1848 Winburg became the seat of a British-appointed magistrate. Although Bloemfontein developed as the main centre of the Orange Free State and the capital of the republic which replaced British government, Winburg remained the administrative centre of its own district. The population has now reached 10 637.

There are two museums in Winburg: the Voortrekker Museum, and the house in which President M T Steyn was born. A monument to the Voortrekkers stands on the southern outskirts of the town.

From Winburg the N1 road to the north leads through extensive fields of maize and sunflowers. Six kilometres from the town the N5 road branches eastwards towards Harrismith and KwaZulu-Natal (see Chapter Thirty). At 32 km north of Winburg the N1 suddenly descends into the bush-covered Sand River valley. At this point an interesting diversion is made possible by taking the tarmac branch road leading eastwards for 9 km to the irrigation dam at ...

ALLEMANSKRAAL AND THE WILLEM PRETORIUS GAME RESERVE

In 1960, at *Allemanskraal* (public corral) on the Sand River, the Department of Lands completed the construction of an irrigation dam designed to supply water for the cultivation of produce for the nearby Free State gold-fields. The great dam, its lake and shores have been developed into a major recreational area, with yellowfish and carp in the lake providing interest for anglers. Boating, yachting, aquaplanning and swimming (in a beautifully situated swimming-bath built on a site overlooking the lake) are other activities to be enjoyed.

The bushy heights surrounding the lake were a favourite resort for prehistoric man. The summit of *Doringberg* (mountain of thorns) contains the ruins of an extensive settlement (about 7 000 huts) of early Iron Age people, presumed to be the long-vanished Leghoya tribe or the Taung tribe who built huts and cattle corrals out of stone. The huts were so tiny that only one person (they were normal-sized individuals) at a time could occupy them in any comfort, and then only if they slept sitting up.

This interesting area and much of the lake's surroundings have been converted into a 10 520 ha game reserve named in honour of Senator Willem Pretorius, a former member of the Orange Free State Executive Committee, whose enthusiasm for the project materially furthered its successful development.

A game reserve was urgently needed to provide a sanctuary for the fast-vanishing species of highveld game – springbok, black wildebeest, blesbok, red hartebeest, eland, zebra, impala and white rhino – which had once flourished there in prodigious numbers. An earlier attempt to establish a game reserve on the 10 278 ha farm *Somerville* near Bultfontein was unsuccessful as it was too remote from tourist routes and situated in drought-stricken country. It degenerated rather dismally into something of a private shooting area reserved for the favoured few.

The new reserve, however, was beautifully grassed, well watered and accessible to the public. Its wooded ravines and heights provided a most attractive scenic setting for the game animals. The more fortunate amongst the surviving game population of *Somerville* were translocated to the new area; buffalo and white rhino were reintroduced from Zululand. Today the Willem Pretorius Game Reserve is well established, an asset to the Free State, and a delight to all lovers of the wilderness and the rich wildlife of birds and game animals. It is thoroughly worth visiting. The accommodation provided, together with a restaurant and store, is excellent. On the summit of Beckersberg in the game reserve, a group of pre-historic stone corbelled huts and livestock corrals have been restored. There is a site museum.

From the turn-off to Allemanskraal the N1 continues northwards across the Sand River. On the northern bank of the river, on an elevation just off the road, stands a small monument marking the site of the signing of the Sand River Convention on 17 January 1852 by which the independence of the Transvaal was recognised by the British. Seventeen kilometres north of the Sand River (49 km from Winburg), the N1 reaches the town of ...

VENTERSBURG

The centre for an agricultural district producing maize, wheat and livestock, Ventersburg lies on the farm *Kromfontein*, which was originally owned by P A Venter, the chief field-cornet of the area and a great friend of the Sotho chief, Moshweshwe. Venter died in 1857 and his son, B G Venter, inherited the farm. He allowed his farmhouse to be used for church services when a community was created in the area in 1864. The town grew up around this farm church, with the first erven being sold in 1871. There are now 10 279 people living there.

Ventersburg is connected by a short road to the main railway line at a station formerly known as Ventersburg Road but, since 1927, called *Hennenman* after P F Hennenman, a local farmer.

The N1 road continues due north from Ventersburg across rich agricultural lands. One kilometre from the town it crosses the R70 tarmac road linking the gold-fields to Senekal, on the N5 main road to Natal, while 46 km from Ventersburg the N1 is rejoined by the division which left it just before Brandfort to travel as the R30 north over the gold-fields. Three kilometres beyond this junction lies the town of Kroonstad but, before this town is described, let us examine the branch of the N1 which has travelled up from Bloemfontein through Brandfort and the Free State gold-fields.

From the division of the two roads, 18 km north of Bloemfontein, the north-western branch, R30 leads through a forest of acacia trees with several shady resting-places at the roadside. After 5 km the road crosses the *Modder* (muddy) River, where there is a turn-off leading for 1,5 km to the Glen Agricultural College and to Maselspoort (16 km away). After a further 30 km of travel the road, now 53 km from Bloemfontein, reaches the outskirts of the town of Brandfort, with a turn-off bypassing the built-up area and leading on to the gold-fields.

BRANDFORT

An agricultural and communications centre, Brandfort was established on the farm *Keerom,* first occupied in about 1838 by Jacobus van Zijl. Van Zijl became an elder in the community of the Bloemfontein Dutch Reformed Church and in 1866 planned a church centre on his farm as a convenience for the local inhabitants. He named the place *Brandfort* (burnt fort) after a small fortification on *Keerom* farm which had been burned down during one of the frequent brawls with the Sotho tribespeople. The first erven were sold on 30 October 1866, houses were built, and in 1874 Brandfort was proclaimed a town. It has grown into a centre for wool, maize and general farming activity and has 11 620 inhabitants.

From Brandfort a road leads north-eastwards for 59 km to join the N1 at Winburg. The R30 road to the gold-fields bypasses the outskirts of Brandfort, curves past the hillock overlooking the town, and stretches northwards across a gently undulating plain covered in maize, sunflowers and (in winter) long, golden-coloured grass. Maize is the important product here, and the road enters the outskirts of both the Free State gold-fields and what is known as the Maize Triangle of South Africa, the principal agricultural pantry of the country. The first town to be reached, 42 km from Brandfort, is dominated by a huge silo holding 350 000 bags of maize. This is the town of ...

THEUNISSEN

Named after Colonel Helgard Theunissen, commandant of the local commando during the Anglo-Boer War, *Theunissen* was proclaimed a town in August 1907. The colonel was the founder of the town and also its first mayor. Amply watered from the *Erfenis* (heritage) irrigation dam, the town is the centre for a rich farming district. There is fishing, boating and swimming in the dam lake and a caravan and camping park on its banks. Many fine farms may be seen in the area.

Beyond Theunissen the R30 road continues northwards, passing the Star diamond-mine and then, after 24 km, reaching a major parting of the ways. To the north-west the R30 road leads to the gold-fields. To the north-east a road proceeds to the mining centre of Virginia, 16 km away.

THE GOLD-FIELDS OF THE FREE STATE

There is a bitter-sweet element about the discovery of most of the gold-fields in the world. The Free State gold-fields are no exception. To the eye these gold-fields consist of a plain so flat and featureless that the pioneers considered the one small hillock in the area remarkable enough to be named *Koppie Alleen* (lonely hillock). Particularly subject to droughts, the area was regarded as a wasteland, and the few farmers resident there made a precarious living.

During the great gold discoveries on the Witwatersrand, an occasional prospector wandered south into this area. It so happened that 13 km north of the modern town of Odendaalsrus, a trader named Gustav Furst owned a tin-shanty store on a farm named *Zoeteninval* (sweet surprise). Near this store there appeared a definite reef on the sandy surface of the veld. Furst pointed this out to one of the prospectors, Archibald Megson, and a syndicate was formed consisting of Furst, Megson, Alick Donaldson and George Haines.

The syndicate sank an adit into the reef and found traces of gold. Samples were taken to Johannesburg in 1894 but the mining houses there were not interested. The samples were unimpressive and the area was considered unlikely to possess any major gold deposits. As a last resort, the syndicate (after salting their samples to make them more spectacular) scraped up enough money to send two of their members, Donaldson and Haines, to London. The two men sailed from Cape Town on the *Drummond Castle* which struck a rock off Ushant at midnight on 16 June 1896. Donaldson and Haines were among the 250 people drowned in the disaster.

The remaining two partners gave up in despair. For 35 years the prospect shaft in the Zoeteninval reef lay abandoned. Gustav Furst vanished from the scene but Megson still wandered round the area, doing odd jobs and periodically trying to induce some visitor to take an interest in the reef. He was considered to be a local 'crank' but he nevertheless persisted.

In 1930 Megson happened to meet Allan Roberts, a Johannesburg mining engineer. Megson told him about the reef, whereupon Roberts inspected it and collected samples from the adit. Megson's faith was infectious and Roberts decided on a gamble. In Johannesburg he floated a £50 000 company called Wit Extensions Ltd. Megson received £400 for his remaining interests in the reef and the company secured options on the surrounding farms. This was the first worthwhile sum of money invested in the area.

A few hundred metres away from the original prospecting adit, the company sank a drill on the farm *Aandenk* (keepsake). The drill bored down 1 263 m and found nothing payable. At this stage, the company had exhausted its funds. The borehole was abandoned and the company withdrew, ceding its rights to the Transvaal Mining and Finance Co Ltd. The new company searched around for a while and then ceded its rights to the African German Investment Company, run by the well-known mining man, Hans Merensky. Merensky's reputation as a prospector was such that others became interested in the area simply because he was active there. A second company, Western Holdings, took options south of Odendaalsrus.

The geologist of Western Holdings, a Hungarian named Oscar Weiss, examined the area with brilliant perception. He noticed that all the geological evidence indicated that any extension on the Witwatersrand into the Free State was not likely to be part of the main Reef Series. Unfortunately, this series was not related to magnetic shales which could be detected at deep levels by the type of magnetometer used in the spectacular discovery of the Western Rand gold area. Weiss knew, however, that the Ventersdorp System of basic lavas lay immediately above the Witwatersrand System and was a fairly reliable indicator of the latter's presence. By means of a gravitational torsion balance he could delineate the areas of the Ventersdorp System, since its masses of thick lava produced local anomalies in gravitation which could be measured with his instrument. The thickness of the lava could also be reasonably gauged, and drilling could be directed to areas where the lava was at its thinnest and most fragile.

The gravitational torsion balance of Oscar Weiss proved to be the key which fitted the locked door, previously tapped upon so feebly by the first syndicate of prospectors. Using this delicate instrument, Weiss directed his clients to a spot where the lava was thin and the Witwatersrand System (if, indeed, it lay below) was reasonably accessible.

The place selected by Weiss was on the farm *St Helena*. It was there, in April 1938, that the diamond drill first broke through into the subterranean treasure-vault of the Free State. At a depth of 737 m, a reef was intersected which yielded, on assay, 11,8 dwt to the ton. This find shook the mining world. The reef (like the Zoeteninval reef) was a freak bearing no relationship to the Witwatersrand System, but its discovery and gold content were enough to spur on the search.

The Second World War hindered work, but the discovery on *St Helena* and the development there of a payable mine largely occupied the thoughts of all prospectors. At the end of the war the whole area bustled with prodigious activity. About 500 boreholes were sunk at a cost of well over £3 000 000. The result certainly justified the effort; 100 boreholes produced samples yielding gold in excess of what was then the payable minimum of 150 inch dwt; 15 boreholes produced values of over 500 inch dwt; 9 boreholes produced values over 1 000 inch dwt. The champion of them all was sunk on the farm *Geduld* (patience). On 16 April 1946, the entire mining world was thrown into a dither by the announcement that this drill, at a depth of 1 195 m, had intersected the Basal Reef and returned an assay amounting to the staggering figure of 23 037 inch dwt.

The Free State was proved to be the new El Dorado, with an estimated R10 000 million worth of gold waiting to be mined from a field roughly 50 km long by 20 km wide. Amid the general excitement, it is interesting to know that one of the prospecting companies remembered the borehole which had been sunk by Allan Roberts at *Aandenk*. They cleared out this borehole, resumed drilling and, after going down 135 m further, reached the gold-bearing Basal Reef.

The effect of all these discoveries on the area can best be appreciated by a visit to the modern towns which sprang up with extraordinary rapidity in order to house the mineworkers.

From the division of the road 24 km from Theunissen, the north-eastern branch continues for a further 10 km, then reaches the mining town of ...

VIRGINIA

Virginia grew up around the original railway station of that name and today has a population of 62 841. Virginia became a town in 1954 and within three years had become the second largest town on the gold-fields and the fourth largest in the Free State. With the development of the gold-fields, the Harmony Gold Mining Co, the Meriespruit OFS Gold Mine and the Virginia OFS Gold Mine were established in the vicinity.

The town lies in attractive surroundings on the south bank of the Sand River where the municipality has developed a recreational resort in Virginia Park, with a 9 km long boating stretch, swimming, fishing and a variety of holiday accommodation and sportsfields.

From Virginia a tarmac road continues to the north-east. After 16 km it reaches the town of ...

HENNENMAN

The town had its beginning as a railway station called Ventersburg Road, which served the town of Ventersburg 17 km to the east. The discovery of limestone in the area resulted in two cement factories, Anglo Alpha and Whites Portland, being constructed, and a town grew up around the railway station. On 25 May 1927 at a public meeting held at the railway station, it was decided to rename the place in honour of P F Hennenman, a local farmer of Dutch descent who had settled in 1860 on the farm *Swartpan* on which the town was being built.

The discovery of gold on 16 April 1946 on the farm *Geduld*, which lay to the west of Hennenman, stimulated the growth of the town considerably.

Welkom, the largest town of the gold-fields, lies 32 km east of the road division between Theunissen and Virginia. The road passes several pans much frequented by aquatic birds such as flamingos. The pans are fed by additional saline water pumped from the mines whose deep-level workings encounter great quantities of it.

WELKOM

This city was laid out in 1947 on the farm with the pleasant name of *Welkom* (welcome) by the Welkom Township Company. From the beginning it was planned as a garden city with a commercial centre built around a handsome central square. It became a municipality in 1961 and a city on its 21st birthday, 14 February 1969. The population has reached 203 285.

Understandably, it has no historic monuments, being entirely dominated by the headgear of the gold and uranium mines of the St Helena Gold Mining Co, the Welkom Gold Mining Co, Western Holdings, Free State Geduld Mines, President Brand Gold Mining Co, and President Steyn Gold Mining Co.

The oldest town on the gold-fields of the Orange Free State lies 5 km from Welkom ...

ODENDAALSRUS

When the Dutch Reformed Church established a village on the *Kalkkuil* farm belonging to Jesaja Odendaal, the name *Odendaalsrus* (Odendaal's rest) was given to the place. A few traders established themselves there but the village was short of water and extremely isolated. It was connected to the outside world only by a sandy track leading for 33 km to the railway whistle-stop which later became the town of Hennenman.

Memories still remain in Odendaalsrus of the original postal contractor, Weeber, who used to stagger into the village late at night, carrying mail-bags on his shoulders and using his horses as pack animals, having abandoned his cart which had stuck fast in the sand. One ramshackle little hotel run by Harry Woodburg provided an ever-open door (it was broken and couldn't be closed); water was sold from a well owned by I J van Vyver; there was a mill worked by MacMaster; four stores were owned by J Bridger, H Levy, J Cohen and a curmudgeon of an Irish bachelor, J Stewart, who periodically went on a spree and provided business for a solitary lawyer, Andries Hauptfleisch. Altogether, Odendaalsrus lived up to its name of 'rest'. It was a quiet but curiously cheerful little place, with Archibald Megson, the prospector, being one of two reigning characters. The other was Piet Nelson, who claimed by devious connections to be a descendant of Admiral Lord Nelson.

The secretary of the village management board, W Furst, received a salary of £2 a month. He couldn't live on such a sum and eked out a living by playing an old horned gramophone in the local pub. He received a slight increase in his salary in 1912 when Odendaalsrus became a municipality, but things still remained very quiet!

Thirty-four years later, when the golden bombshell burst with the sensational results of the borehole on *Geduld* farm only 4,5 km away, there were still only 40 dwellings in the place. Odendaalsrus is now a bustling mining town of 65 398 people. There is little to remind it of the past, save a memorial marking the site of the first abortive borehole sunk by Allan Roberts, and the original prospect adit on the Zoeteninval reef.

From Odendaalsrus a tarmac road runs north for 9 km and reaches the newest town of the goldfields ...

ALLANRIDGE

Named in honour of Allan Roberts, the man who sank the pioneer borehole at *Aandenk*, the town of Allanridge was founded in 1950 and designed by William Backhouse, who also planned Welkom. It became a municipality on 21 December 1956. With a population of 19 390 it is a fine example of a modern mining boom town. The place is hygienic, well ordered and a far cry indeed from the rip-roaring gold towns of former days.

Allanridge is the centre for the Lorraine Gold Mining Co. Huge fields of maize surround the town like an ocean. A large pan is situated on the outskirts of the town and is a favourite resort for flamingos.

From Allanridge, the R30 road to the north continues for a further 50 km through the maizelands and then reaches the agricultural centre of ...

BOTHAVILLE

Bothaville was laid out in 1891 on the farm *Gladdedrift* (slippery ford) owned by Theunis Louis Botha who planned to call it Bothania. It was proclaimed a town in 1893 under the name of Bothaville and became a municipality in 1914. The town is pleasantly situated on the banks of the Vals River where there are recreational facilities with swimming, boating and angling. The vast maizelands of the Maize Triangle stretch seemingly without end around the town.

From Bothaville the R30 road leads northwards over highly productive agricultural country with pasturage for sheep and cattle and fields of ground-nuts, maize, wheat and sunflower seeds. The road descends into the shallow valley of the Vaal River, crossing the river after 41 km. A further 6 km brings the road to the mining town of Orkney in the North-West Province. The R59 road leads north-eastwards for 48 km from Bothaville and then reaches the town of ...

VILJOENSKROON

The town of *Viljoenskroon* was laid out on 13 May 1921 on the farm *Mahemskuil* (pool of crested crane birds) and named after the owner of the ground, J J Viljoen, and his riding-horse, Kroon. It became a municipality in 1925, and is the centre for a considerable agricultural industry in the cultivation of maize, sunflowers, ground-nuts, potatoes and wheat. Stud cattle are bred in the area, and gold, uranium and coal are mined.

A nicely laid-out town, Viljoenskroon has a population of 24 076. On the farm *Sandfontein* near the town there is a museum devoted to tractors, with an interesting collection of early and later models. The museum is open daily 09h00 to 16h00.

From Odendaalsrus a tarmac road stretches eastwards for 61 km to join the N1 at the entrance to the town of ...

KROONSTAD

It is said that *Kroonstad* (city of Kroon) was named after a horse. This interesting animal appears to have been rather a loser. Owned by one of the Voortrekkers, 'Lang' Adriaan de la Rey, father of General Koos de la Rey, the horse reputedly came to grief in a pot-hole in a stream which flowed across the site of the town. The stream became known as *Kroonspruit* after the horse's misfortune. In August 1854, when Joseph Orpen, the landdrost of Winburg, selected the site of a new town on the banks of the *Vals* (treacherous) River, he simply applied to it the established place-name. The first erven were sold on 20 April 1855.

Lying on the main N1 route to the north, Kroonstad became a major staging post. The railway reached it on 20 February 1892. Over the years it became a strategic junction and marshalling yard on the north–south line and the line to Natal. Today Kroonstad is a bustling agricultural, educational and administrative centre, with a population of 86 925.

A number of monuments, historical buildings and memorials can be seen in Kroonstad. The Sarel Cilliers Museum on the first floor of the public library presents a theme exhibition of the history of Kroonstad. It is open Mondays to Fridays 10h00 to 17h30, and the second and fourth Saturday of the month, 09h00 to 12h00. Sarel Cilliers, one of the Voortrekker leaders, lived on the farm *Doornkloof*, 45 km east of Kroonstad on the old road to Lindley. The farm now belongs to the Voortrekker movement. The farm may be visited. The original homestead is preserved. There is a walking trail, various species of game animals and the graves of Cilliers and other pioneers. The farm is open Mondays to Fridays 08h00 to 17h00. A fine statue of Sarel Cilliers, by the sculptor Coert Steynberg, stands in front of the Dutch Reformed church in Cross Street. There are professionally managed hunting facilities in the district. A recreational resort, known as Kroonpark, has been developed along the banks of the Vals River.

From Kroonstad, the N1 continues northwards as the Kroonvaal toll-road over flat maize and sunflower farmlands. At 55 km from Kroonstad the road reaches the R720 turn-off leading to the town of ...

VREDEFORT

The area in which *Vredefort* lies is devoid of any great scenic beauty, but is extremely fertile. It was once the home of prodigious herds of game – blesbok, springbok and black wildebeest. Bushmen hunting-clans roamed the area, and their paintings may still be seen in numerous rock shelters, especially along the banks of the Vaal River. With the arrival of the Voortrekkers, and their defeat of the Ndebele at the Battle of Vegkop (19 km south-west of Heilbron) in 1836, the Vredefort area was settled by cattle farmers such as the Van Rensburgs, Schoemans and Bothas.

Hunting was the principal industry in the old Vredefort. At first the area was popularly called *Riemland* (thong land), after the quantity of skins and thongs produced there. The name *Vredefort* (peaceful fort) originated as a farm name during the period when there was dispute in the Transvaal over the question of the presidency. A Transvaal commando under Marthinus Wessel Pretorius invaded the Orange Free State. At *Laerplaas* on 19 May 1857 this commando was halted by men of the Orange Free State. After the usual wild threats had been made, good sense prevailed and everybody returned home without there being any casualties.

The area was left to develop in peace. More settlers arrived and a community centre became a necessity. A commission from the Kroonstad Dutch Reformed Church visited the area and selected as the site of the proposed town the farm *Vredefort* whose owner, Jacobus Scheepers, had named it in memory of the peaceful conclusion to the threatened war between the Transvaal and the Orange Free State. The town was laid out in 1876 and the first erven were sold on 20 April of that year. As a staging post on the north–south road, and the centre of a prosperous agricultural industry, Vredefort soon grew into a town. It received an added boost in 1886 when a discovery of gold was claimed by C J Bornman on the farm *Weltevreden*. Other claims of gold finds were made on the farm *Lindequesfontein*. For a few years the so-called Vredefort Gold-Fields attracted some attention, with one moderately sized mine, the Great Western, producing gold before the field fell into disuse.

The Vredefort area is well known to geologists on account of the so-called Vredefort Dome of granite which is exposed there. Maize, sunflowers, millet, corn, ground-nuts and cattle provide the riches of the Vredefort area today.

Lying 15 km across the farmlands north of Vredefort, is the town of ...

PARYS

The man who surveyed this town, Schilbach, was a German who had participated in the siege of Paris. He found that the site of the proposed town, lying on the banks of the Vaal River, reminded him of the French capital on the Seine, so he named it *Parys* (Paris).

Parys became a town in 1887 and today has a population of 43 431. Its attractive situation makes it one of the most popular of all the highveld holiday resorts. The broad Vaal River (about 1 km wide in places) is studded with tree-covered islands. Several of these, such as Woody and Long islands, have been developed as resorts by the town council. Boating, fishing and swimming provide relaxation on the river. The south side of the bank has been turned into a first-class resort for caravanners, campers and picnickers, with holiday bungalows available for hire. This is a very pleasant pleasant place for a stopover. The willow trees of the Vaal are curiously old world in their character. Fireflies dart like fairies through their graceful leaves at night. Fish rise to feed where the willow leaves touch the water and trap insects carried down by the stream.

A wonderful variety of birds nest and call in this green paradise of trees and water. At night it is pleasant to walk beneath the willows. Cross to one of the islands. All is quiet and it is nice to be alone for a little while. Listen to the silence – only the gentle gurgling of the water; the sound of frogs; the twittering of a bird comforting its chickens in some tiny nest; the sighing of the willows as the night breeze whispers stories of seeing a river nymph hiding in the shadows.

The town is a centre for the growing of tobacco as well as the production of maize, ground-nuts, sunflower seeds and corn. There is a museum in the town.

Parys, as we have seen, lies on the willow-shaded banks of the Vaal River. However, the road which has taken us to the town does not cross the river into the North-West Province at this point. It swings north-eastwards and takes the traveller across a landscape which is of interest to the discerning who know that the ridges of hills over which the road crosses, form part of what is known to geologists as the Vredefort Dome, an exposure of ancient granites emerging from the thick cover of the later-Karoo sediments. The form of the dome consists of a central cone of granite surrounded by concentric ridges of quartzites belonging to the Witwatersrand System. The exact nature and origin of this exposure is controversial.

At 17 km from Parys, the road reaches a junction with the N1 which has come up for 101 km from Kroonstad. A left turn on to the N1 will take the traveller for 16 km directly to a bridge over the Vaal into Gauteng (see Chapter Thirty-One). Continuing eastwards across the N1, the R59 road from Parys, after 19 km, reaches ...

SASOLBURG

As its name indicates, *Sasolburg* is the township established on 8 September 1954 to house the workers of Sasol South African Coal, Oil and Gas Corporation). With a population of 83 505,

Sasolburg is a modern town completely dominated by the chemical works which, night and day, reveal proof of enormous activity by belching out flames, fumes, smoke and an all-pervading, rather sickly sweet (and certainly king-sized) 'body odour' which can be smelt from a considerable distance.

The siting in 1954 of the Sasol plant in this part of the Free State was determined by the presence of vast deposits of low-grade coal (an estimated 600 million tons) and the proximity of the Vaal River in the immediate vicinity. From the river Sasol satisfies its thirst for 36 million litres of water a day. In exchange for its diet of water and low-grade coal, Sasol produces each year a considerable variety of chemicals for the national and international market. It is often referred to as the chemical hub of South Africa. A gas pipeline feeds gas to industrial users on the Witwatersrand, while a number of major chemical manufacturers of fertilisers, super phosphates, synthetic rubber, plastics, soft detergents, etc have their plants in the immediate vicinity of Sasol and draw on it for essential materials. Sasol exports considerable quantities of hard, high-melting point Fisher-Tropsch waxes and also kogasins – both essential materials in a great variety of manufactured products. A full list of the chemicals produced by Sasol makes bewildering reading. They include ammonia, solvents and phenolics.

The only inland refinery in South Africa, Natref, is situated in Sasolburg where the full range of fuels and diesel are produced from crude oil.

Sasolburg is a clean, pleasant town with a proper appreciation of the fact that trees with their shade, beauty, restfulness to the eyes, quietening effect on noise, and purifying influence on the air, are more important to an urban area than motor vehicles. Some 72 000 trees have been planted in the town. There is an attractive pedestrian mall; an excellent theatre; and a Highveld Garden, 6 ha in extent, where flora indigenous to the highveld may be seen. It is open daily from 10h00 to sunset. The Abrahamsrust Pleasure Resort on the Vaal River is maintained by the municipality as a recreational asset to the town. Two hiking trails, Leeuwspruit and Riemland Eco-route offer educational hiking to nature lovers.

Six kilometres north of Sasolburg, the road bridges over the *Vaal* (tawny-coloured) River, the borderline between the Free State and the original Transvaal (now divided into four separate provinces). This great river, the principal tributary of the Gariep, supplies over four million people with water and supports the most important industrial complex in Africa.

From Sasolburg you may either cross the Vaal River to Gauteng or take the R82 to Gauteng via Deneysville and the Vaal Dam to enter Gauteng on the N3 at Villiers.

THE VAAL RIVER

Known to the Bushmen as the *Gij 'Gariep* (tawny coloured river), and to the Zulus and Sothos as the *iliGwa* (erratic) River, the *Vaal* (tawny) has its source near Breyten in Mpumalanga. It has been thoroughly harnessed at many points along its course.

In 1923 the Rand Water Board built a barrage across the river, creating a reservoir some 65 km in length and 7 m deep, with a storage capacity of 62 million cubic metres. From this rather hideously named *Loch Vaal*, the Rand Water Board extracts 1 045 million litres of water a day and supplies an area of 12 000 square kilometres including the whole Witwatersrand, Pretoria, Gauteng and Sasolburg.

In 1936 the Vaal Dam was built upstream from Vereeniging. This dam stores 2 580 million cubic metres of water in a lake nearly 10 km wide in places and stretches back for 100 km. It has a circumference of 700 km and is up to 52 m deep. It controls the flow of the Vaal and feeds the barrage of the Rand Water Board. It also supplies users lower down the river, such as the Free State and Klerksdorp mining areas, which draw 218 million litres a day for use in the Klerksdorp mining area, and numerous riparian and other users all the way downriver.

Famous for its yellowfish, carp and barbel, the Vaal and its dams also provide great recreational possibilities. Angling, boating, swimming and aquaplaning – all are enjoyed on the waters of this majestic river which meanders its way across the sunny veld, its banks lined with handsome willow trees. The Vaal Dam Nature Reserve on the northern bank conserves typical highveld vegetation.

Two recreational and residential townships have been created on the Free State side of the Vaal Dam. The one resort is *Deneysville,* established in 1939 on the farms *Wilhelmina* and *Witpoort*, 24 km from Sasolburg. It was named after Colonel Deneys Reitz, who was Minister of Lands when the dam was built.

The second resort situated 38 km from Sasolburg on the banks of the Wilger River, is *Oranjeville*, established in 1919 and named in honour of the Netherlands Prince of Orange who was involved with the upliftment of South Africa. Both places are used for boating, fishing and general recreation. Deneysville is a particular resort for yachtsmen with four yacht clubs, boat builders, repair yards and chandlers. It faces a 300 square kilometre stretch of water free of bilharzia and malaria with excellent winds for sailing. Both resorts offer accommodation of a good standard and have a friendly atmosphere of happy relaxation in a healthy, pleasantly warm climate.

Chapter Thirty
THE EASTERN FREE STATE

The eastern part of the Free State is composed of one of the most beautiful, brilliantly coloured sandstone landscapes to be seen anywhere on Earth. Its features are: isolated flat-topped mountains, their precipice faces coloured red, orange, gold and yellow, strangely shaped or balancing rocks; meandering rivers whose banks are lined with willow trees; deep soil; richly rewarding to the producer of maize, fruit (notably cherries and yellow peaches), dairy products, wheat and vegetables. There are spectacular cloud formations and summer thunderstorms on a vast scale; a romantic history and an untapped literary treasure trove of legends, fairy-tales and traditions about long-vanished Bushmen, early Sotho tribes, cannibals and the first European settlers such as that droll character, Renier de Winnaar, whose tall tales are still told with many a chuckle in the homesteads of today.

Three kilometres north of Winburg on the N1, the north–south trunk road of Africa, the N5 road to the Eastern Free State and KwaZulu-Natal begins, branching off eastwards across the open, gently undulating highveld. At first there are few features of note. The landscape is sun-drenched, spacious and airy, green in summer, brown in winter. At 7 km there is a turn-off to Marquard and Clocolan; at 60 km there is a crossroads with a turn south to Marquard, and north to Ventersburg and Welkom. After a further 3 km (67 km from the start of the road) the hollow of the Klipspruit stream is reached, on whose banks stands the town of ...

SENEKAL

The centre for an important food-producing district, *Senekal* is a busy and modern rural town named in honour of Commandant Frederik Petrus Senekal, who was killed in the Second Basuto Gun War of 1865. The town was laid out in 1874 on the farm *De Put* (the well) owned by F Malan. It grew as a church, school and trading centre for the farming community. The population now numbers 19 351.

The Dutch Reformed church, built in 1896 and restored in 1960, is a handsome sandstone building with some fine stained-glass windows. The church is enclosed in a remarkable wall of petrified trees which was erected by the congregation under direction of the Reverend D P M Olivier in 1929. The fossils were found in the valley of the Sand River, east of Senekal. They belong to various species of the plant division Coniferophyta which flourished in the Southern Hemisphere 250 million years ago. The petrified trunks are particularly well preserved specimens of trees which once covered what was, in those distant years, the vast swamplands of central South Africa.

The N5 road climbs easily out of the shallow valley sheltering Senekal and continues eastwards. After 5 km there is a turn-off to Arlington and Lindley and 1,5 km further on brings the road to a turn-off to Rosendal and Ficksburg. The road is now making its way through rugged country dominated by isolated flat-topped hills. One of the largest of these is Biddulphs Berg. On this mountain and in the surrounding area may be seen the remains of numerous prehistoric corbelled houses. On 29 May 1900 a British army unit commanded by Lt Gen Rundle attacked a Boer force which had established a strong position on Biddulphs Berg. The battle was complicated by a veld fire. At first the smoke provided cover for the British. Then the wind changed directions and the fire swept over many of the wounded. Both sides withdrew, with the Boers victorious. In this setting it is interesting to see the homes of the local Sotho tribespeople, decorated by the womenfolk in gay colours and designs, providing many striking examples of folk architecture in the rural landscape.

At 34 km from Senekal, the road reaches a turn-off to the town of ...

PAUL ROUX

A rural centre lying among sandstone cliffs in the valley of the upper Sand River, the site of Paul Roux was once an early resting-place of the Voortrekkers and a staging post of the old post carts. The modern town is notable for its characteristic sandstone buildings. It was founded in 1911 on the farm *Wassou* as a centre for an area of mixed farming, including the growing of poplar trees for the making of safety matches. The name of the village comes from the Reverend Paul Hendrik Roux of the Dutch Reformed Church, a general during the Anglo-Boer War.

From the turn-off to Paul Roux the N5 road to the east continues its way, traversing a pleasant rural landscape of farmlands and isolated hillocks. After 39,5 km the road reaches the busy, progressive town of ...

BETHLEHEM

This is a major farming, communications, administrative and tourist centre and a very fertile and productive area in the Eastern Free State. It was founded in March 1860 on the farm *Pretoriuskloof*. Its site was well selected. The Jordaan River, flowing through *Pretoriuskloof*, provided a dependable supply of water and the climate was healthy. The town was proclaimed in 1884 and became a municipality in 1902.

A brisk climate and an attractive situation enabled Bethlehem to grow rapidly, especially after February 1905 when the railway reached it along the important route from Bloemfontein to Harrismith and on to Natal.

Today Bethlehem has a population of 56 464 and is the centre for the regional offices of several Government departments and commercial concerns operating in the Eastern Free State. There is an agricultural research station near the town. The town has always been an important church and educational centre – its name (and that of the Jordaan River) was given by F P Naude, a devoted churchman and one of the original owners of the site. In Hebrew, *Bethlehem* means a 'house of bread'. In the Holy Land, the Jordan River flows through some of the most fertile areas of the Middle East.

An interesting museum is housed in the old Nazareth Mission church which, built in 1906, was the second mission church in the Free State. The museum is open Mondays to Fridays from 10h00 to 17h00.

In addition to being a centre for tourism in the Free State, Bethlehem is a pleasant holiday resort in its own right. The Jordaan River has been dammed to form what is known as Loch Athlone, on whose shores a magnificent pleasure resort has been created, with a complex of bungalows, club buildings, slipways, a caravan park, swimming-pool, super-tube, water and other sport facilities, and a tea-room. The centre-piece, however, is a most unusual feature in an inland resort: a restaurant built in the form of the favourite old Union Castle mail steamer, the *Athlone Castle*. Painted in the same colours as the ship, the building used to house many items retrieved from the Athlone Castle when it was scrapped. Mr C M van Heerden, manager and creator of the pleasure resort, collected these items – steering-wheel, lamps, compass, etc – and designed the restaurant, which was opened on 6 December 1957. Boating, fishing and swimming in a heated swimming-pool are recreations in this resort. Pretoriuskloof, below the dam wall, is a nature reserve with a rich bird life. It is open from 08h00 to 17h00.

The Wolhuterskop Nature Reserve is 5 km from Bethlehem on the road to Fouriesburg. It is open from dawn to sunset and offers a walking and riding trail with an overnight hut. The trail starts at the Loch Athlone holiday resort. The walking trail is 13 km to the overnight hut and 5 km back to Loch Athlone. The riding trail is 10 km long and starts at the entrance to the nature reserve, where there are stables. The ride takes one and a half hours.

From Bethlehem the N5 road to the east continues through beautiful country. This part of the route makes a very pleasant drive. The landscape is fertile and varied, with rocky ridges and lovely farms in the valleys. In July wattle trees bloom and perfume the air, while masses of flowering cosmos adorn the roadsides over Easter. There are many fine views of the Maluti Mountains of Lesotho in the south – always beautiful, particularly when covered in winter snow.

At 7,5 km from Bethlehem a turn-off stretches to Clarens and the Golden Gate. At 35 km from Bethlehem, on the left side of the road near the horizon, there is a hill topped with radio masts. The western side is steep, while the eastern side has a gentle slope. This is *Groenkop* (green peak), site of the famous Christmas Night attack of General De Wet. The British were positioned on Groenkop to provide support for units constructing blockhouses. The British sentries were not too alert. De Wet and his men climbed up the western cliffs which were considered insurmountable. It was a chaotic and bloody Christmas night on the table topped summit of Groenkop.

At 45,5 km from Bethlehem, the road reaches the town of ...

KESTELL

Taking its name from the Reverend J D Kestell of the Dutch Reformed Church, this rural centre is inhabited by 4 418 people and is dominated by its rather unusual-looking church built in the Byzantine style, and designed by Gerard Moerdyk. The village was founded in 1905 on the farms *Mooifontein* and *Driekuil,* and has grown into a trade, church, school and administrative centre for the farming area.

The N5 road to the east continues from Kestell across the spacious, gently rolling highveld. All around are well-kept farmlands, sheep-runs, maize lands, wheat-fields, herds of blesbok and cattle. To the south there are views of the Maluti and Drakensberg ranges. At 19 km there is a turn-off to Witsieshoek, and another turn-off to the same place 19 km further on. At 45 km from Kestell, the N5 road reaches the important eastern Free State town of Harrismith where it joins the N3 road linking Johannesburg to Durban.

HARRISMITH

The centre for one of the eight principal wool-producing districts in Southern Africa, Harrismith has a population of 33 725. Lying 1 615 m above sea-level, the town has a fine, crisp climate and a handsome situation in a valley where the *Wilge* (willow tree) River flows beneath the slopes of a 9 km long, 2 377 m high, table-topped sandstone pile topped with the usual basalt layer, known as the *Platberg* (flat mountain). From its presence the Zulu name of the town is *Intabazwe* (place of the mountain).

Founded in 1849, *Harrismith* was named after the glamorous, hard-riding British Governor, Sir Harry Smith, whose beautiful Spanish wife is commemorated in the name of the neighbouring town of Ladysmith in Natal.

The first Harrismith was laid out by Robert Moffat (son of the famous missionary) on a site near Majoorsdrif on the Elands River, about 25 km from the present town. Erven were sold in May

1849. The site was found to be deficient in water, however, so the present situation of the town, on the farm of Jan Snyman, was selected. Jan's old homestead stood in a little valley, along which courses the clear water of the Halle stream. This stream has quenched the thirst of the town since it was relocated in January 1850.

Afrikaans and English settlers were attracted to the area, the latter mainly people who had been brought to Natal under the Byrne Scheme and had found the climate and prospects of Harrismith more congenial.

Harrismith became a municipality in 1874. During the diamond rush to Kimberley it boomed, becoming a busy staging post on the Natal transport route. At least 50 wagons toiled up the escarpment from Natal each day, and Harrismith became a customary place of rest and refreshment. Hotels, public buildings and stores sprang up. The discovery of gold on the Witwatersrand attracted still more transport vehicles, and in 1892 the railway from Natal to Harrismith was opened. Political problems, however, kept the railhead in Harrismith until 1905; then the link to Kroonstad through Bethlehem was opened.

A major base of the British army during the Anglo-Boer War, Harrismith has since then progressed steadily to become what it is today – a pleasant, spaciously laid-out town with several handsome churches and public buildings. A relic from the British Army occupation are regimented badges made of white painted stones on the surrounding hills. These are now preserved as national monuments.

The President Brand Park along the banks of the Wilge River boasts fine trees, a prolific bird life and a caravan park. The environment of the town offers enjoyable riding, walking and climbing. Angling is popular in the Wilge River.

The annual Harrismith mountain race, the Berg Marathon, run on the second Saturday of October, is one of the foremost cross-country athletic events in Southern Africa. The course comprises a stiff 609 m climb in 5 km up *One Man's Pass* (named from a solitary rock figure) to the top of the Platberg, then a run along the summit and down to the town by means of an old zigzag bridle-path used by pack animals of the British army during the Anglo-Boer War. The race had its origin when Major Belcher of the British army returned to Harrismith after being stationed there during the Anglo-Boer War. In exchanging reminiscences with the locals, he casually referred to the Platberg as 'that small hill of yours'. One of the locals immediately bet him that he could not reach the top in under 60 minutes. The major won the bet in style and then donated a floating trophy to the first person to reach the top in a race.

The slopes of the Platberg are forested, and among the trees are many fine oaks. A mountain drive branches off from the N3 road (which goes to Johannesburg) 2 km from Harrismith and leads for 6,5 km to the plantation gate. There are fine views, picnic spots and easy walking routes to the summit of this very majestic mountain. Permits to enter the municipal forests are available at the town hall or at the entrance to the forest.

Also worth seeing are the municipal waterworks 4 km from the town along the slopes of the Platberg. From there a blockhouse, built by the British garrison and now a national monument, is easily reached. Originally one of the eight National Botanic Gardens of South Africa, the area is now managed by the Harrismith municipality. Some 114 ha in extent, the Platberg Nature Reserve conserves the flora of a very interesting botanical region. It is open daily 07h00 to 19h00.

Next to the town hall is a remarkable fossilised tree, 27 m long and estimated to be 250 million years old. A small museum is housed in the town hall, which is a National Monument.

Harrismith is a considerable industrial centre and its factory shops are well known. On the outskirts of the town there is the industrial area of Industrigwa, with two residential areas, *Tshlame,* a family name of the Mopedi family, and *Khglanyoni* (crying birds), from the song of the birds in the surrounding grasslands. These developments are relics of the former bantustan of Qwaqwa. Harrismith has a particularly well-informed tourist office. Phone (058) 622-3525, P O Box 1001, Harrismith, 9880.

Continuing eastwards from Harrismith, the N3 road penetrates an impressive mass of sandstone mountains which tower like sentinels guarding the verges of the highveld plains. This makes a fine drive and an impressive gateway between the Free State and Natal. At 5 km from Harrismith the road passes Plover's Burrow country lodge, built in a 130 ha game farm at the foot of the Platberg. It makes a friendly base for exploring this corner of South Africa with its walking, riding, climbing, trout fishing and handsome scenery. After 20 km the road reaches the hamlet of *Swinburne.* Named after Sir John Swinburne, a pioneer gold prospector who landed in Durban in 1808, bringing with him the first steam engine to work in Southern Africa. There is a handsome old bridge in Swinburne, a National Monument built in 1884 and worth a short detour to see it.

Eleven kilometres beyond Swinburne the N3 road reaches the village of Van Reenen. At this point the road is on the 1 680 m high summit of the Van Reenen Pass. With the beginning of the descent it enters Natal. At Van Reenen, next to the Engen garage, there is the Llandaft Oratory, reputably the smallest church in the world. It seats eight people and was built to commemorate the heroism of Llandaft Matthew who was killed in 1923 in a mining disaster in the Burnside Colliery in Natal. At 2,5 km from Van Reenen, a turn-off down the old road leads to a viewsite known as Windy Corner. This is a worthwhile detour to follow, for there is a fine view of KwaZulu-Natal and the long line of the Drakensberg. The story of the Van Reenen Pass is told in Chapter Twenty-Seven.

THE ROAD FROM HARRISMITH TO HEIDELBERG

The N3 road leads northwards from Harrismith, curving around the western end of the massive landmark of the Platberg. After 3 km there is a turn-off to the mountain drive and, just beyond that, a turn-off leading for 48 km to the village with the picturesque name of *Verkykerskop* (far-lookers' hill). A *verkyker* is a binocular or telescope. The 2 153 m high Tafelkop is near the village.

The tarmac road continues north-westwards over a landscape which is beautifully verdant in summer. The streams are lined with willows and there are fine farmlands and maize fields. Handsome isolated sandstone hillocks, resembling feudal castles, tower over the countryside. The great pile of basalt mountains of Lesotho may be seen on the southern horizon.

After 50,3 km the road reaches a turn-off to the town of ...

WARDEN

This amiable place with its 6 078 inhabitants was named after Charles Warden, a well-liked magistrate of Harrismith. The tall grain silo and the towering church steeple denote the town's importance as an agricultural, church, and school centre. Warden was laid out in 1912 on the farm *Rietvlei.* It became a municipality in 1920. The sandstone church seats 1 700 people and is a National Monument. Its construction started in 1917 in a period of prosperity. During the depression of 1920–22 building was suspended. In 1923 in order to generate sufficient income to finish the building, the farmers arranged a massive sale of livestock. For this they donated 6 000 sheep and 1 500 cattle. An amount of £10 500 was collected and the church was completed. Its total cost was £40 000.

From Warden, the N3 road continues north-westwards. At Easter, the countryside is covered with huge patches of cosmos flowers – pink, plum and white – making a lovely sight as they wave in the wind. The mountains of Lesotho are gradually lost in the haze of the southern horizon. Gently undulating maize and sunflower fields stretch all around. Few prominent landmarks are seen. The colourful, tastefully decorated homes of the Sotho farm workers are worth noting.

At 45 km from Warden there is a turn-off to Memel and Vrede, and at 60 km a turn-off to Heilbron and Frankfort. At 75 km the road passes the small village of Cornelia which, in summer, is beautifully set amidst emerald-green pasturage and fat herds of cattle and sheep. *Cornelia* was founded in 1918 and named in honour of Cornelia Reitz, the second wife of F W Reitz, President of the Orange Free State from 1889 to 1895. On the banks of the Skoonspruit, 10 km north of the village, lies an important fossil site.

At 108,6 km from Warden, the road reaches the town of ...

VILLIERS

Situated in the great maize-producing triangle of the Free State, *Villiers* was founded in 1882 and was laid out on the two farms *Pearson Valley* and *Grootdraai*, owned by Lourens de Villiers after whom the town was named. It became a municipality in 1917. Villiers is situated on the left bank of the Vaal River where a pleasant recreational area with fine willow trees shading a good stretch of water has been created. Fishermen have a particular love for the place. There are warm and cool pools for swimming and the river water is free of bilharzia. Fishing is exciting and pleasant in a beguilingly beautiful setting of shady trees and, in February and March, masses of exquisite cosmos flowers.

From Villiers, a tarmac road branches westwards for 34,5 km to the ...

JIM FOUCHÉ HOLIDAY RESORT

Created by the former Provincial Council of the Orange Free State, this resort is situated on the shores of the lake of the Vaal Dam, near where the Wilge River joins the Vaal. The resort was named after J J Fouché, a former president of South Africa. It is a spacious and handsomely laid-out resort and appeals particularly to anglers who catch yellowfish, carp and barbel there.

Bird life is very rich in the area. Horse-riding is pleasant and boating superb.

From Villiers the N3 road continues northwards, crossing the Vaal River. Maize, sorghum and wheat fields cover the landscape, while sheep and cattle graze on rich pasturage. After 26 km there is a turn-off to Grootvlei power station. At 31 km a crossroads is reached with turn-offs to Vereeniging and Balfour. At 53,7 km from Villiers, the R23 road linking Ladysmith to Johannesburg joins the Harrismith road at a point 9 km south-east of Heidelberg (see Chapter Thirty-Five).

HARRISMITH TO KERKENBERG AND OLIVIERSHOEK

The R74 road leading from Harrismith to Bergville in KwaZulu-Natal by means of the Oliviershoek Pass provides the traveller with some dramatic changes of scenery. The road commences at a turn-off to the south from the N5 road, 1,5 km from Harrismith on the way to Bethlehem. After 8 km there is a turn-off of the R712 road to Qwaqwa and Golden Gate.

The R74 road crosses a pleasant agricultural landscape where colourful patches of cosmos flower during Easter, and the grassy countryside is dominated by several high, isolated flat-topped hills. These flat-topped hills or mountains have great character, Resembling islands in a sea, they tend to be individualistic and atmospheric, each having some legend or history attached to it. Early tribes used many of them as strongholds similar to the feudal castles of Europe, for the summits were easy to defend and generally accessible by only one or two routes. It was also possible to support (at least for short sieges) quite a number of people and their livestock on the summits.

At 32,5 km from Harrismith a turn-off leads for 3,5 km to Retiefklip, situated at the foot of a particularly stately example of these flat-topped massifs, the impressive 2 083 m high sandstone pile known as *Kerkenberg* (church mountain).

It was here, on 7 October 1837, that Piet Retief and his Voortrekkers (pioneers) arrived in 54 wagons and made camp. From the edge of the escarpment close to Kerkenberg, Retief first viewed Natal. Close to this viewsite, which he named *Blijde Vooruitzicht* (joyful prospect), an easy pass led downwards. Known today as *Oudeberg* (old mountain) or Step Pass, it was used by Retief and fourteen of his men when he set off on his first visit to Port Natal and to Dingane in Zululand.

From Port Natal (Durban), Retief sent two of his men back to the camp at Kerkenberg with samples of fruits from Natal and with the good news that the trekkers would be welcomed as fellow settlers by the ivory traders already resident there. There was jubilation at the Kerkenberg camp. The day after the arrival of this good news was a Sunday, and also the 57th birthday of Piet Retief. His 22-year-old daughter, Deborah, marked the occasion by painting her father's name on the side of a very strange rock formation at the foot of the Kerkenberg. This little memorial (carefully protected as a National Monument) may still be seen on what is known as *Retiefklip.* Each year, on 16 December (the Day of the Vow, now the Day of Reconciliation), a church service is held at Kerkenberg.

From Kerkenberg the Voortrekkers moved their camp to the edge of the escarpment. A steady stream of wagons joined them, each filled with jubilant people, excited at the prospect of seeing and settling in what they considered to be their promised land. At dawn on 14 November 1837, this surge of happy humanity started to descend the escarpment, using passes named De Beers, Bezuidenhouts and Middledale. For details of what befell them in KwaZulu-Natal, see Chapters Twenty-Four and Twenty-Five.

Beyond the turn-off to Retiefklip the R74 road continues southwards. The road crosses the canal bringing water pumped from the Thukela River in KwaZulu-Natal to feed the Sterkfontein Dam. At 44,2 km from Harrismith the road reaches the KwaZulu-Natal border at the summit of Oliviershoek Pass, 1 737 m above sea-level. Adriaan Olivier farmed in the glen at the foot of this pass when it was made in 1871. From the summit the road makes a curving descent and eventually reaches the town of Bergville, 80 km from Harrismith.

THE TUGELA (THUKELA)–VAAL SCHEME

The Thukela–Vaal water transfer scheme is a notable achievement in engineering ingenuity in attempts to solve a very complex problem: namely, the supply of water to the heavily industrialised, mining and densely populated areas of Gauteng, the North-West Province and the northern Free State. The Vaal River, which supplies this area, is already totally harnessed and cannot carry any additional load imposed by the increased demands of growth. The problem, therefore, was to supplement the water of the Vaal by transferring water in bulk from the flow of other rivers.

The Thukela River in KwaZulu-Natal, the second largest river in South Africa, offered a useful amount of water surplus to current demands in KwaZulu-Natal. The Thukela, however flows from its source on the summit of Mont-aux-Sources, falls over 850 m in five successive vertical drops down the cliff faces of the Drakensberg, and then flows eastwards for 322 km to the Indian Ocean. To draw a beneficial contribution of water from this river to the Vaal (which has its source on the eastern highveld and then flows westwards to join the Gariep River on its way to the Atlantic Ocean), would mean lifting the water up the highveld escarpment and feeding it into the Wilge River, which flows to join the Vaal River as one of its principal tributaries.

To achieve this water transfer from one watershed to the other involved a very sophisticated exercise in technological ingenuity. It was achieved in two phases: a transfer of 130 million cubic metres of water in the first phase, and another 217 million cubic metres in the second phase.

The first phase involved the Spioenkop Dam in the Thukela River, 10 km east of Bergville. This dam was completed in 1972 with a 55,5 m high wall and a 427,7 m long crest. The lake covers 1 540 ha and has a capacity of 282 million cubic metres of water. The purpose of this dam is to regulate the flow of the Thukela for downstream areas of KwaZulu-Natal.

Upstream, 37 km above the Spioenkop Dam, the Driel barrage was built to serve as the main obstruction point on the Thukela River. With three large gates to cope with floodwaters of 3 110 cubic metres per second, the barrage is equipped with five pumps which have a capacity to raise a total of 1 642 cubic metres of water per day and to feed the water (at a 90 m higher level) into a concrete-lined main canal which carries the water back westwards for 38 090 m and then discharges it into the forebay of the Jagersrust pump station. Three smaller weirs, Putterill, Clifford Chambers and Khombe, were built to direct floodwaters into the main canal and save pumping costs.

The water fed into the Jagersrust forebay is then pumped through a steel rising main tunnel and canal system up the escarpment and into the Sterkfontein Dam. This dam, in the valley of the *Nuwejaarspruit* (new year stream), was, in its first phase, built with an earthfill wall 69 m high and a crest 2 290 m long. The area covered by the lake was 5 073 ha, containing 1 203 million cubic metres of water. This phase was completed in 1977.

In the second phase, completed in 1985, the wall was raised to 933 m, with a crest of 310 m. The full capacity of the lake became 2 617 million cubic metres, covering 6 940 ha. In its final size, Sterkfontein Dam became the largest dam in South Africa in respect of volume content of the dam wall. It is the only dam in South Africa to qualify for inclusion in the *Icold Register of the World's Largest Dams*. From the Sterkfontein Dam the water is released into the Nuwejaarspruit and through it to the *Wilge* (willow) River, and thence to the Vaal.

The second phase of the scheme also involved the construction of the Woodstock Dam above the Driel barrage. This dam wall has a height of 49 m, a crest of 865 m and a capacity of 383 million cubic metres. It regulates flow in order to supply the pumps at the Driel barrage with a constant flow. Increased pumping capacity was provided at Driel and another pumping station, the Kilburn pump station, was built at the Jagerspruit forebay to pump water through a concrete canal into the Kilburn Dam built at the foot of the escarpment. This dam has a 51 m high earthfill wall, 825 m long in its crest and containing 36 million cubic metres of water. From this dam, water is transferred up the escarpment by four pump turbines driven by off-peak power from the national grid. This water is fed into the Driekloof Dam built in the upper reaches of the Sterkfontein Dam. It has a rockfill wall with a clay core 46,6 m high, 500 m long in the crest and containing 35 600 000 cubic metres of water. This dam overflows into the Sterkfontein Lake.

A classic pumped storage scheme takes place between the Driekloof Dam and the Kilburn Dam. Water is pumped up by surplus off-peak energy and, during high-value peak times, it is fed back through the same tunnels and thus drives four reversible turbo-generator sets, each 250 megawatts in generating mode.

To summarise a complex water transfer scheme, water from the Thukela flows into Woodstock Dam, then via the Thukela to the Driel barrage. From there it is lifted 90 m into the main canal. The water flows along this canal until it reaches the Kilburn low-lift pump station at Jagersrust. From there it is pumped to the Kilburn reservoir.

During low-peak electricity demand, water from the Kilburn Dam is pumped 450 m up the escarpment by Eskom's reversible hydro-electric plant to the Driekloof Dam. The Driekloof Dam overflows into the Sterkfontein Dam but always retains enough water so that, during Eskom's high-value peak time, there is enough to flow back and profitably generate power. The whole project was carefully conceived to harmonise with the environment. It is highly efficient.

WITSIESHOEK AND ITS MOUNTAIN RESORT

The river known to Europeans as the Elands and to the Sotho people as the *Namahadi* (place of plenty) has its source on the summit of Mont-aux-Sources, very close to the source of the Thukela. It tumbles down in a spectacular waterfall and then flows northwards through an extremely rugged glen, in itself magnificent and made doubly impressive because it is backed by the high Maluti range of Lesotho. Dominating the glen to the north is a magnificent specimen of a flat-topped sandstone mountain, named by the Bushmen *Kwakwa,* meaning 'whiter than white', either because of its winter snows, or because it is coloured by the droppings of vultures which, from time immemorial, have used it as a nesting area.

In approximately the year 1839, a group of Kgolokwe tribespeople, led by a chief named Whêtse, made their way to this glen where they found a precarious sanctuary during the Zulu disturbances. Made destitute by incessant raids, they turned rustlers themselves and set out to recoup their losses by stealing the cattle belonging to European farmers who settled in the Free State. This enterprise provoked a punitive reaction. In 1856 a commando was sent out against Whêtse's rustlers. The chief and his followers retreated to a great cave, still known as Whêtse's cave, near Monontsha. Besieged there, Whêtse made his escape through a tunnel, but his power was broken. Only his name in the corrupted form of *Witsie* remains in the area.

The government of the Orange Free State retained possession of *Witsieshoek* (Whêtse's glen) but in August 1867 allocated a portion of the area to the friendly chief, Paulus Mopeli, a brother of the famous Moshweshwe, chief of the ruling Kwena tribe of Lesotho. With 200 of his followers Chief Paulus made his home in the area. In 1874, at his request, the Dutch Reformed Church opened (on ground given to it by the Orange Free State) a mission station in Witsieshoek to serve the inhabitants. The Reverend G Maeder was the first missionary. From this mission originated the Elizabeth Ross Hospital (named after the wife of one of the missionaries) and a theological school.

In 1873 Chief Koos Mota of the Tlokwa tribe was also allocated a portion of Witsieshoek. It is the descendants of the Kwena and the Tlokwa people who live in the area today. On 19 June 1953 these people became the first tribe in South Africa to be granted tribal authority of their homeland, this being the first step towards the form of self-government known as a *Bantustan*. In 1969 the Witsieshoek area became the official homeland of the *baSotho ba Borwa* (Sotho people of the south) where territorial authority was exercised and an administrative centre known as *Phuthaditjhaba* (meeting-place of the nations) was established. To its inhabitants the Witsieshoek area is known as Qwaqwa after the flat-topped hill which dominates the region. The Qwaqwa area is 72 690 ha in extent and about 200 000 people are settled there. It was the smallest and poorest of the Bantustans, all now creations of the past.

Eight kilometres along the R712 road from Qwaqwa to Golden Gate there is a Basotho Cultural Village Museum which reveals the traditional lifestyle, architecture and art of the Sotho people. Tourists visit a chief in his *Khotla* (court), taste a sip of traditional beer, listen to music and watch dancing, visit the *Ngaka* (traditional healer) and visit the houses of the chief's wives, decorated with the vibrant colours known as *litema*. The village is open daily 09h00 to 16h00.

On 27 October 1972 a holiday resort was opened by the Bantu Development Corporation near the terminus of a spectacular road leading up the slopes of the Drakensberg to the Sentinel Peak and Mont-aux-Sources. This road provides one of the finest scenic experiences in Southern Africa.

Witsieshoek can be easily reached. Four kilometres from Kestell on the road to Golden Gate a well-maintained road branches off for 29 km to Phuthaditjhaba. Another road branches off from the main road to Oliviershoek 7 km from Harrismith. This tarmac road leads past the Sterkfontein Dam for 24 km to join the Kestell–QwaQwa road. From Phuthaditjhaba the road continues past Whêtse's cave to Monontsha and the Lesotho border. One kilometre before the centre of Phuthaditjhaba, a road branches eastwards to the mountain resort.

It is a drive enhanced by spectacular scenes. After 20 km the road reaches a toll-gate where a permit must be obtained before proceeding. The road continues climbing past some remarkable rock shelters, caves and overhangs. After a further 4 km there is a junction, the left turn leading for 1 km to the rest camp, the right turn continuing for 6,5 km to a terminus confronting the Sentinel. At this point, 30,5 km from the start in Witsieshoek, the road is 2 680 m above sea-level. From the road terminus, the original bridle-path carries on to the chains which provide access to the summit of Mont-aux-Sources. This is a superb four-hour walk which should not be missed by any lover of beautiful scenery, fresh air, high mountains, summer flowers and winter snows.

Accommodation at the resort (which is 2 100 m above sea-level) is comfortable. Winter snows are usual and violent summer thunderstorms are always spectacular. To experience one at this altitude is to be part of it, not beneath it. In fact, it is almost the same as being in a box of fireworks into which a lighted match is dropped. Everything literally seems to blow up in a strangely abrupt sequence of bangs, rumbles, flashes, patterings, downpours, hailings, floods, clatterings, rattles and, finally, a dead silence. One gets the feeling that the thunderheads (the *donderkoppen* of legend) are really alive – rough noisy fellows, barging around the sky, brawling, shouting, cursing, roaring and swearing like a gang of toughs on the rampage, who suddenly vanish down an alley when the police arrive. Sometimes they return just as suddenly after the police have left and have another go at tearing up the sky and flushing it down the drain. It can be quite an experience!

At the Witsieshoek mountain resort meals are served in the restaurant, which is fully licensed. No preparation of food is allowed in the bungalows. Horses, haversacks, etc, are available for hire. Phone (058) 713-6361.

THE MAIZE TRIANGLE

The northern and eastern parts of the Free State and the southern part of the North-West Province/Gauteng form what is known as the Maize Triangle, the pantry of South Africa where the bulk of the maize, wheat and sunflowers are grown.

Maize (corn or mealies) is so staple a food in Africa that it is perhaps surprising to learn that it is an exotic crop, introduced to Africa in comparatively recent times by the Portuguese and carried into the interior by hunters, missionaries and explorers. Maize is indigenous to America. The Portuguese explorers discovered the crop growing there and took it home with them to Europe. From there it was carried to Africa where the indigenous population found it easy to grow, prolific as a food crop, and superior in most ways to the millet which was their traditional staple food.

There was a 'maize revolution' in Africa. The African people gave it their own names, such as *mlungu* or *mbila*. The Dutch-speaking pioneers in South Africa called it the *mielie* as a corruption of the Portuguese word *milho* (grain).

It is interesting to travel through at least a part of the Maize Triangle and to eat there some 'corn-on-the-cob', maize-meal porridge, maize-rice, samp or tender young sweet corn cooked in several ways as an accompaniment to roast meals. Man and beast relish the corn; the sweet-tasting stalks provide silage feed for livestock; and the cobs can be converted into a fuel fully capable of running motor vehicles.

A rewarding way to discover at least a part of the Maize Triangle is to take the R26 road leading north from Bethlehem. For 52 km this tarmac road leads through what, in summer, is a veritable green sea of corn, and then reaches the town of ...

REITZ

Reitz was founded in 1889 on the farm *Stampkop* as a trading and staging post for transport riders. At first known as *Singer's Post* after the owner, the town developed as a natural centre for the corn country. After using the name of Amsterdam, in 1899 it was eventually named after President Francis William Reitz of the Orange Free State, who proclaimed it to be a town. It became a municipality in 1903.

A large grain elevator dominates the town and it is the headquarters of one of the largest co-operative agricultural societies in South Africa, the Free State Co-operative. Flowers and trees grow around it. Reitz is a well-kept agricultural town and has a population of 15 985.

At 31 km north of Reitz, the R26 road passes the landmark of two similar hillocks, with the railway centre of *Tweeling* (twin) named after them. Another 36 km to the north the road reaches the town of ...

FRANKFORT

Pleasantly situated on the banks of the Wilge River, Frankfort was laid out on the farm *Roodepoort* and named by Albert von Gordon after Frankfurt in Germany. Why the name was misspelt in South Africa is unknown.

The town is a typical inhabited 'island' in a sea of maize fields. Churches, schools, shops and administrative offices were built, and it became a popular retirement place for elderly farmers. The Wilge River is a particularly pretty river – excellent for boating, swimming and fishing, with long lengths agreeably shaded by the wild willow trees which gave it its name. The population is 12 400. National Co-operative Dairies have a large butter factory in the town and the Free State Co-operative has its premises there. The entrance to the Vaal Dam Nature Reserve is 15 km to the north-west.

West of Frankfort, 58 km across the cornlands, on the R34 road stands the town of ...

HEILBRON

Heilbron (the spring of salvation) takes its name from a strong spring in the vicinity, said to be reminiscent of a curative spring near the ancient town of Heilbron in Germany. It is the railway centre for a busy agricultural industry in the production of maize, millet, wheat, sunflowers and milk. The population is 24 245.

At the Uniefees Dam 2 km from the town, there is a recreation resort with swimming, fishing, boating, camping and caravanning facilities.

VEGKOP

Twenty kilometres south of Heilbron a tarmac road R725 leads to *Vegkop* (battle peak), the site of a renowned clash between the Voortrekkers and the Matabele (Ndebele) force of the chief Mzilikazi. Vegkop is actually a bush-covered ridge. On its summit there are the stone ruins of a substantial prehistoric settlement of African people who made their homes there in former years.

The site of the battle is marked by a memorial. There is a camping ground, a museum and buildings used in gatherings held in memory of the Voortrekkers.

The battle took place on 16 October 1836. A Ndebele raiding force of about 6 000 men came upon 50 Voortrekker wagons outspanned in defensive laager formation on the flats beneath the ridge. There were only 35 men in the laager under Sarel Cilliers. They withdrew into the shelter of the laager. The Ndebele, commanded by Mkhalipha, tried to take the laager in a wild rush, but learned the bitter lesson that spears were no match for guns. They managed to kill two of the defenders and wound fourteen, but they lost 400 of their own men. They hurled 1 137 spears into the laager, but failed to penetrate the defences.

The Ndebele withdrew, taking booty of 50 000 sheep, 5 000 cattle and 100 horses. The loss of their horses prevented the enraged Voortrekkers from pursuing the Ndebele. Vengeance came later, when the Voortrekkers combined under Hendrik Potgieter and raided the Ndebele stronghold at Mosega in the Transvaal.

South-west of Heilbron, the R34 road leads for 45 km to the town of ...

EDENVILLE

Edenville was established in 1912 on the farms *Erfdeel-Noord, Langland* and *Welgelegen*. It became a municipality in 1922 and is the centre for a rich agricultural area in the Maize Triangle. The population is 3 873.

South of Heilbron the R57 road leads through cornlands for 45 km to the town of ...

PETRUS STEYN

Situated in the heart of the corn country, Petrus Steyn was laid out in 1914 and was named after the owner of the farm on which it was founded. Today it has a population of 9 795. In a healthy and bracing climate, with never a shortage of corn to eat and milk to drink, Petrus Steyn is a busy railway centre.

From Petrus Steyn a tarmac road, the R707, leads south for 35 km to the town of ...

LINDLEY

Laid out in 1875 on the banks of the Vals River on the farm *Brandhoek* which had been donated to the Dutch Reformed Church, Lindley was named after the American Presbyterian missionary, Daniel Lindley, the first ordained minister to the Voortrekkers. The situation of the town is pleasant. It was proclaimed a town in 1878 and grew as a centre of prosperous farming. In February 1902 the town was razed to the ground by the British army, but after the war it was rebuilt and one of its residents, John Collister-Oats, led a campaign to plant many thousands of trees.

There is an attractive recreational resort on the Vals River, with a caravan park making it a popular recreational area in the Maize Triangle. There is a large powdered-milk factory in the town. The population is 9 577.

From Lindley the R76 road leads west for 36 km to the railway centre of Steynsrus, and thence for 48 km to Kroonstad. To the south-east the R76 road leads for 58 km to Bethlehem; and this concludes our discovery of the tranquil rural area of the Maize Triangle.

THE GOLDEN GATE

At a point 7,5 km before the main N5 road reaches Bethlehem from Harrismith, a tarmac turn-off R711 leads southwards in a drive through elegant sandstone country past fields of wheat and maize, and orchards of yellow peaches. Then, by means of the *Noupoort* (narrow passage), the road passes through the Rooiberg range and, at 28 km reaches the curiously old-world little town of ...

CLARENS

Laid out in 1912, *Clarens* was named after the place in Switzerland where President Paul Kruger died. It is a quaint little town, spread over a slope where some odd public buildings are looked down upon by a collection of high, very superior sandstone mountains. Three kilometres from the town lies a picnic and recreational area known as Leibbrandt Kloof. The town has a population of 2 536. The name of Clarens is attached to the geological formation known as *Clarens Sandstone*, notable for the brilliance of its colours, red to orange and golden yellow.

There are two hiking trails which reveal the colourful flora and handsome rock formations of Clarens Sandstone. Horse riding from four venues is popular, while fishermen catch bass and trout in local waters. It is a friendly, popular, clean town with several places in which to eat and stay. A memorial of convivial days and nights is Cinderella's castle, a structure built of 55 000 beer bottles (empty).

From Clarens, the tarmac road R711 swings up the valley of the Little Caledon River. This is one of the world's most beautiful examples of a sandstone valley, deeply eroded and modelled by the bustling river. The road leads beneath a series of towering cliffs, one of which is known as Gladstone's Nose, a prominent appendage situated in the middle of an unmistakable face. In this lovely area, 21 km from Clarens, lies the ...

GOLDEN GATE HIGHLANDS NATIONAL PARK

This unique park was established in 1963 to conserve 4 792 ha (subsequently increased to 11 500 ha) of Clarens Sandstone highlands, unsurpassed in their variety of rock shapes and colour. A great number of wild flowers – notably arum lilies, watsonias, fire lilies and red-hot pokers – flourish in the area. Bird life includes the magnificent lammergeyer, with a wing-span of nearly 3 m, the black eagle, jackal buzzard, blue crane, secretary bird, rock pigeon, guinea-fowl and numerous waterfowl. Game animals include eland, blesbok, springbok, black wildebeest and smaller mammals.

The whole area provides superlative riding, walking, and climbing opportunities, which yield innumerable interesting scenes. Great caverns and rock shelters are set in a landscape where the colours are spectacular. The rock shapes are surprising and there is an undeniable elegance conjured up by the old-world farmhouses and graceful trees (especially willows and poplars) which line the banks of the streams.

There is crisp mountain air to breathe, crystal-clear water to drink; the atmosphere is serene and quiet. Amid the many lovely scenes which charm the eye, the National Parks Board has developed a magnificent recreational area, complete with a variety of accommodation ranging from the luxury of the Brandwag Camp to delightful self-catering chalets, huts, rooms and a fine caravan park and campsite. There are restaurants, snack-bars and curio shops. Tours are conducted during school holidays and over weekends. There is a stable of riding-horses and a network of paths for walkers to follow, including the two-day circular Rhebok Hiking Trail 30 km long with overnight huts.

The road through the park is always open. One kilometre beyond the camp of *Glen Reenen* (named after the Van Reenen family, the original owners of the area, who are buried in the little cemetery near Gladstone's Nose) there is an entrance gate leading to the game park where a number of antelope live in their natural state. There are many fine picnic spots at Glen Reenen which are open from one hour before sunrise to half an hour after sunset.

Beyond the turn-off to the game park, the main through road traverses fine scenery for 37 km as far as Kestell, where it joins the R57 road to Harrismith.

THE ROAD ALONG THE LESOTHO BORDER

This road (R26) provides an all-tarmac drive through some of the finest scenery in Southern Africa. Starting in Bethlehem, it leads southwards past the Loch Athlone holiday resort and the Wolhuterskop Nature Reserve, across a fertile, green, agricultural landscape. After 50 km the road reaches the town of Fouriesburg. This first section of the road actually yields the dullest scenery, but the alternative route R711 through Clarens provides a scenic route which joins the road at Fouriesburg. This is the recommended scenic route which rewards the venturesome traveller with beautiful scenery during any season of the year.

From its beginning at Clarens where it turns off from the tarmac road to the Golden Gate, this road leads through the little town itself and, after 1 km, past the turn-off to Leibbrandt Kloof with its picnic spots (2 km away).

The tarmac road continues south-eastwards down the valley of the Little Caledon River, an undulating rural landscape adorned with willow and poplar-lined streams, sandstone cliffs, weird rock formations and neat farmlands. After 13 km, the road starts climbing the summit of a long ridge. On the summit, 14,5 km from Clarens, the traveller is treated to a view almost overwhelming in all directions, but particularly to the south and east into the massive mountain pile of Lesotho. Nearby, at Surrender Hill, 4 314 men under General Marthinus Prinsloo surrendered to the British during the Anglo-Boer War. They had been manoeuvred into the cul-de-sac of the Brandwag Basin and could not get out. There is a monument to the British dead, as well as interesting relics of the war.

At 19 km from Clarens there is a turn-off to Hendriksdrift and the Lesotho border. At 26 km from Clarens the road joins the main road leading from the Lesotho border post of Joel's Drift to Fouriesburg. At 36,5 km from Clarens the road reaches the town of ...

FOURIESBURG

This rural centre with its population of 7 814 was laid out as a township in 1892 on the farm *Grootfontein* owned by Rooi Stoffel Fourie, after whom the town was named. Although a somewhat nondescript little place, it is handsomely situated with the mountains of Lesotho only a few kilometres away, a picturesque assembly of sandstone flat-topped hillocks in the surrounding area, and the pretty picnic area of Meiringskloof (also a nature reserve) nearby. The town has considerable trade and traffic relations with Lesotho through the Caledonspoort border post 8,8 km away.

Places of historic interest in Fouriesburg include the house in which President M T Steyn lived, built in 1897 by D J Kriel, and situated on the corner of Reitz and Robertson streets. The Dutch Reformed church, built in 1894, stands on the site where Paul Kruger's commando made their camp when they supported the Free State against the Sothos. Fouriesburg also has a number of impressive sandstone buildings. The *Nagmaal* cottage on the corner of Martin and Theron streets was built in 1894. It is still occupied.

There are a variety of walks and trails in the hills and mountains surrounding Fouriesburg. The five-day Brandwater Hiking Trail, which starts and ends at Meiringskloof, is the longest trail in the Free State and also has the largest sandstone overhang in the Southern Hemisphere. Hikers use overhangs as overnight sites. Another trail, the Bushmans Caves Trail, leads for 30 km to Ficksburg with an overnight hut.

The Wyndford holiday farm near Fouriesburg, on the Butha Buthe road, also offers a variety of short walks. There are sporting facilities, a swimming-pool, and cottages for hire.

From Fouriesburg, the R26 border road continues south-westwards across well-cultivated farmlands dominated by high, flat-topped sandstone hills with vividly coloured cliff faces. At 32 km from Fouriesburg the road passes through a parklike valley, where fine orchards of peach trees are laid out, and the heights of the Witteberge look down from the west.

Continuing south-westwards across a landscape of grass and maize lands, beneath skies notable for their summer blueness and gigantic afternoon thundercloud formations, the road passes numerous flat-topped hillocks. Especially remarkable is the one 43 km from Fouriesburg at the Sekonyela railway siding. Three kilometres beyond this hill, the road is joined by the R70 road coming south from Rosendal. A further 3 km sees a turn-off north to Senekal (66 km). One and a half kilometres beyond this turn-off (46,5 km from Fouriesburg), the road enters the town of ...

FICKSBURG

Sheltered by the tree-covered heights of the 1 854 m high Mpharane Mountain to the west, with the Caledon River boundary with Lesotho immediately to the east, Ficksburg has a fine, crisp, highveld climate (the town is situated 1 629 m above sea-level), a good rainfall and an attractive environment. Consequently, the area has always provided a pleasant home for human beings.

Numerous paintings in caves and rock shelters indicate that the Bushmen found the area around Ficksburg to their liking. Various Sotho tribes settled in the area, where many memories still linger of raids and invasions, especially those which occurred during the troubled early years of the 19th century when the whole interior of Southern Africa underwent a period of war and ferment.

Europeans wandered into the area in the mid-1830s and made their homes along the fertile banks of the Caledon River. Life on the frontier, however, was precarious and subject to the endless depredations of expert rustlers and stock thieves. Among the pioneers was Commandant-General Johan Fick, after whom the future town was destined to be named. He became a renowned figure during the frontier wars with the Sothos. He and his wife are buried in front of the town hall, which was built in 1895.

The frontier area remained in a state of turmoil for over 30 years, and the history of this prolonged period reads with the excitement of romantic fiction. During those troubled years, Johan Fick rose to the rank of Commandant-General. On the founding of the town in June 1867, *Ficksburg* was the name given to it in his honour. The town of Wepener, further south, was founded simultaneously with the similar purpose of pacifying the newly conquered territory along the Lesotho border.

Ficksburg rapidly developed into a busy town, always having considerable trade relations with Lesotho. Today it remains an amiable and attractive place with 28 449 inhabitants. It is notable for its fine gardens, parks and recreational areas, such as the Meulspruit Dam. Grain, maize, fruit and livestock are the products of the district. The Bushmans Caves Hiking Trail, 30 km long, with an overnight hut, leads from Ficksburg to Fouriesburg. Another trail, the Banke Trail, leads for 42 km with overnight facilities.

Ficksburg is the principal cherry-producing centre in South Africa. Blossoms in springtime are exquisite. At the height of the season each year in November, a cherry festival is held in the town. The museum features the cherry industry and the life of Commandant-General Johan Fick. It is open on weekdays from 10h00 to 16h00.

Summer thunderstorms and violent hailstorms are a problem to farmers, and Ficksburg is the home of the Farmers' Hail Insurance Co-operative which provides compensatory protection for more than 10 000 members.

From Ficksburg the R26 road continues south-westwards close to the the Caledon River border of Lesotho. The countryside, neat and parklike in appearance, with tall gum, pine and willow trees, is well grassed and there are numerous fine farms. Handsome and curiously elegant sandstone hills dominate the scene. At 34 km from Ficksburg a turn-off leads for 3 km to the town of ...

CLOCOLAN

Lying in the centre of a rich agricultural area, where maize, potatoes, wheat and cattle are produced, Clocolan has a fine, crisp, well-watered climate. It is in a setting of green grass and is dominated to the north by the 1 820 m high *Hlohlowane* (ridge of the battle) Mountain.

The Kwena people under the chief Mohlomi made their homes in this area but were often raided by other tribes who envied them their prosperity. Memories of many fights linger about the area. Matiwane and his footloose Ngwaneni people raided the area; the Zulus came, and also the Ndebele. Endless disturbances drove away most of the early inhabitants.

Europeans arrived and a trader built a store beneath Hlohlowane Mountain, corrupting its name into the *Clocolan* of today. In 1906 the town was laid out in a hollow, close to the store on the two farms *Rienzi* and *Harold* (named by their surveyor after the Italian hero and the last Anglo-Saxon king of England). The town adopted the name of the store. Built around a central square, it has grown to its present modern state, with a population of 11 832. There is a large grain silo and industries include maize, corn, fruit and trade with Lesotho.

The Koranna Hiking Trail leads for 32 km from Clocolan to Excelsior with an overnight cave.

From Clocolan, the R26 road continues southwards across a landscape of grass, maize and low, flat-topped sandstone hillocks, many of which display on their slopes queer, balancing and oddly shaped rocks. The countryside is neat and immaculate, especially in summer when the grass is green and the sky is a rich blue filled with wonderful cloud 'castles'. After 32 km the road reaches (in a fine setting of hills and trees) the town of ...

LADYBRAND

With a population of 16 352, Ladybrand is sheltered in the rocky sandstone arms of the high ridge known as the *Platberg* (flat mountain). This area has long been an attraction to man. In the caves of the Ladybrand district may be seen many interesting and beautiful Bushman paintings. Especially notable are the caves at Rose Cottage (3 km from the town), Modderpoort (11 km from the town), and on the farm *Tandjiesberg* (22 km from the town). Unfortunately, most of these paintings have been badly disfigured by vandals who scrawled graffiti over them. Fossils and prehistoric artefacts are also found in the district. In 1934 the fossilised remains of *Diathrognatus* was found close to the Leliehoek pleasure resort. Scientists consider this prehistoric animal to be the link between mammals and reptiles. The fossil (the only one of its kind in the world) is now exhibited in the museum in Bloemfontein.

There was tribal chaos in the first half of the 19th century, as was the case in the whole Lesotho border area. Cannibalism in the mountains and raiding and renegade bands from Natal (mainly Zulu and Ndebele) combined to make life unpleasant in the region.

The first Europeans arrived on the Free State plains towards the end of this period, succeeded by a period of frontier disturbances and war between the Sotho people, the British and then the Orange Free State governments. Eleven kilometres north from Ladybrand is the flat-topped hill of Viervoet where, on 20 June 1851, a British-led force suffered defeat at the hands of the Sothos. The hill was the stronghold of the Taung people under the chief Molitsane. It was stormed by the British force. Sotho reinforcements counter-attacked, retook the stronghold and drove the British force off to Bloemfontein.

Battles and quarrels continued along the frontier until, in the 1860s, Europeans finally secured the area as far as the Caledon River. To pacify and hold this so-called 'Conquered Territory', towns such as Ficksburg, Wepener and Ladybrand were created.

Ladybrand was founded in 1867 and named after Lady Catharina Brand, mother of J H Brand, President of the Orange Free State. The site was originally known as *Mauershoek*, after an individual who once lived there. With plentiful supplies of water, the town rapidly grew into an important trade, administrative and agricultural centre, in a pleasant environment. Places such as Leliehoek have been developed into parks, and the sheltered situation of the town stimulates fine gardens and the growth of handsome trees. There are walks, such as the two-day Steve Visser Hiking Trail, and riding trails leading from Leliehoek to interesting places such as The Stables, a cleft in the rock where the Boers concealed their horses during the war with the Sothos in 1858.

Connected in 1905 by means of a branch line to Modderpoort on the main Bloemfontein–Bethlehem railway, Ladybrand is a trade centre on the Lesotho border. Maize, grain, cheese, dairy products and livestock are the agricultural industries.

At Modderpoort a unique cave church was created in 1869 by the Anglican Society of St Augustine, a small monastic group who used the cave as a chapel and also as living quarters for more than a year until they managed to build a house. In 1902 the Anglican Society of the Sacred Mission took over the area. Today they continue to work there, with Modderpoort serving as their headquarters. On the fourth Sunday of each August, a special service is held in the cave church.

From Ladybrand the R26 border road continues south-westwards, climbing up the ridge which overlooks the town. After 3,5 km, a tarmac turn-off leads for 18 km to Caledon Bridge, the main border post of Lesotho, with the capital of Maseru lying just across the Caledon River, which forms the frontier at this point. The customs and immigration office is open from 06h00 to 22h00.

The R26 tarmac road proceeds southwards from the turn-off to the Lesotho border post, reaching a fork after 12 km. The right-hand branch leads for 58 km to Thaba Nchu and thence for another 64 km to Bloemfontein.

From the turn to Thaba Nchu and Bloemfontein, the north–south road continues over green and pleasant border country. The mountains of Lesotho lie to the east and isolated hillocks loom like precipitous islands in an undulating sea of grass. Lying at the foot of one of these hillocks (which rather resembles a Stone Age mound), 54,5 km from Ladybrand, is the small town of ...

HOBHOUSE

This little place, with its population of 2 183, was named after Emily Hobhouse, who laboured during the Anglo-Boer War to alleviate conditions in the British concentration camps. It was founded in 1912 and is the centre for an agricultural area producing cheese, maize, wheat and livestock.

From Hobhouse, the R26 road continues south-westwards across fertile country bordering on the Caledon River. This is a spacious, well-grassed and open area where occasional sandstone hills look down serenely on the well-kept farmlands.

After 31 km the road crosses the Caledon River at Jammersdrif and, 36,3 km from Hobhouse, enters the town of ...

WEPENER

With a population of 8 828, Wepener was one of the towns established by the Orange Free State in the newly conquered territory along the Lesotho border. It was laid out in 1867 and named in honour of Lourens Wepener who was killed on 15 August 1865 while leading an attack on Thaba Bosiu in the war against the Sothos. It is an agricultural and trading centre, sheltered by a high ridge and pleasantly situated on the banks of the Jammersberg River. In the graveyard on the banks of this river there lie several British soldiers killed in battles with the Boers in 1900.

From Wepener the R26 border road continues southwards, crossing open grasslands, maize fields and luscious-looking pasturage with grazing herds of cattle. Flat-topped hills dominate an amiable rural landscape. One and a half kilometres from the town there is a turn-off to Bloemfontein (117 km), while a further 26 km takes the road past a turn-off to the south-east leading for 4,5 km to the town of Zastron. The main R26 road continues south-westwards for 30 km, ending its route at Rouxville.

ZASTRON

The town of Zastron has its scenic setting in what is almost a classic South African landscape. *Koppies* (hillocks) in the variety of flat-topped or pointed shapes so peculiar to South Africa, protrude from the long grass of the plains. On the horizon loom the blue mountains of Lesotho. The atmosphere is clear and unpolluted. From the top of the hills you seem to be able to look so far that what you see might well be a glimpse of the mountains of Fairyland.

The story of Zastron is inextricably linked with two brothers, Jan Hendrik and Petrus Renier de Winnaar. Both were farmers in the Cape. Jan was the younger brother who owned the farm *Lukaskop* near Aliwal North. Like most of the frontiersmen of the Cape Colony, he found the northern horizon to be an irresistible attraction. Vast herds of game wandered over the highveld prairie country. The pursuit of these animals lured men onwards, across the Gariep River into what was then known as the Trans Gariep. Jan Hendrik crossed the river and settled with his family on *Vlakfontein* in the Smithfield area. From there he hunted northwards and eastwards into the valley of the Caledon River. The fertility of that area would have delighted the heart of any farmer. The scenery was superb; the herds of antelope – springbok, gnus, blesbok and hartebeest – seemed countless in their numbers.

In 1838 Jan Hendrik moved his home to the foot of a sandstone mountain named *Aasvoëlberg* (vulture mountain), much used by those scavenging birds as a roosting-place. His brother Renier joined him. The area was a no-man's land at the time. Remnants of the original Bushman inhabitants still clung to their rock shelters and caves. Outlaws and rustlers such as Jan Letelle and Poshuli, had their strongholds in secret valleys.

For two years Jan Hendrik and Renier had a fairly precarious time in their new home. Then they were visited by the renowned Kwena chief, Moshweshwe, who was steadily gathering together fragments of the Sotho people and consolidating them under his protection to form a nation. Moshweshwe could hardly claim ownership of the area around Aasvoëlberg but he was a great man for giving away the possessions of others. He and the De Winnaars got on well with one another. Moshweshwe 'granted' the land they had occupied to them in exchange for a favour. Moshweshwe had a great liking for yellow peaches, fresh, dried, converted to jam or drinkable as yellow peach brandy. The De Winnaars shared his taste. Like the famed Johnny Appleseed in America who planted apple seeds wherever he went, the De Winnaar brothers carried sacks of yellow peach pips in their wagon and planted them at random. The hardy fruit-trees grow in most unlikely places and bare luscious fruit. Moshweshwe requested that they plant many yellow peach trees on their land and give him an annual tribute of fruit and its various products. The De Winnaars happily staked out what became jocularly known as the Yellow Peach Republic. This happy little 'yellow peach state' unfortunately did not survive long.

The Caledon River valley was in political ferment and the general insecurity forced the De Winnaars to leave the area. They returned, but in 1855 were once again driven away. Cattle-rustling, feuds, raids and killings made life precarious. There were innumerable vicious clashes between rival Sotho tribes, Bushmen, white frontiersmen, renegades, bandits and settlers. Sir George Grey, the British Governor of the Cape, attempted to act as mediator in an ominously deteriorating situation. A meeting was held at Smithfield and a treaty was drawn up calculated to regulate conditions in the frontier area.

There was a short lull in the uproar but rustling and raiding soon recommenced. Poshuli and his raiders, and the men of another petty Sotho chief named Lebenya, swept over the whole area of the southern Caledon River valley and westwards to beyond the Aasvoëlberg. All settlers were driven out and their belongings seized.

In 1858 war was declared by the Orange Free State against the Sotho people. The Free State force invaded the Caledon valley from the north and south but it was outmanoeuvred in a skirmishing series of fights fought by highly mobile opposing armies of mounted men. The Free State force reached the famed stronghold of Moshweshwe (Thaba Bosiu) but learned to their cost that it was impregnable. To their mortification, they were forced to retreat and negotiate a truce with Sotho forces who were raiding deep into Free State territory. News of the success of Moshweshwe disturbed every tribe in South Africa. The Sothos had proved that white men were not invincible. There were rumours of a general onslaught of black against white all over the country.

Sir George Grey rode up from the Cape. It was essential that he mediate a peace. His own garrison at the Cape was hopelessly weak, with most of the troops stationed there urgently ordered to proceed to India. A general war in South Africa could become a disaster. Sir George Grey visited Moshweshwe on his mountain and arranged for a meeting to be held on 14 September 1858 at the mission station of Beersheba. Nine commissioners were appointed to represent the Orange Free State at this meeting, and one of them was Jan Hendrik de Winnaar. Moshweshwe never arrived for the meeting. A blind boy spirit medium had informed him that in a dream he had been warned that evil would befall Moshweshwe if he attended such a meeting. No man of high rank was sent to represent Moshweshwe.

Sir George had to ride all the way back to see Moshweshwe at the French mission station of Morija. The chief was not much interested in a peace treaty. He felt that he had the better of the

Orange Free State. His conditions for peace practically amounted to the extinction of the Orange Free State. To oblige Sir George Grey, however, he did agree to send a bevy of senior representatives to a meeting in Aliwal North. There, on 29 September 1858 a treaty was signed defining such issues as boundaries, and providing means of punishing rustlers and other wrongdoers. In this new boundary dispensation, the area of Aasvoëlberg reverted entirely to the Sotho people. Jan Hendrik and Renier legally lost their farm land although they still spent much of their time there, defying the efforts of rustlers and raiders to eject or ruin them.

The whole frontier area simmered down like a pot going off the boil but left very close to the flames. Cattle-rustling and periodic raids continued. In 1865 war broke out again between the Orange Free State and the followers of Moshweshwe. This developed into a vicious and nasty affair with brutal killings and the superbly mounted and well-armed Sotho forces raiding deep into the Orange Free State. The Free Staters were outnumbered and outgunned. The flat-topped hills of the frontier area provided the Sothos with strongholds as impregnable as the feudal castles of Europe had been in the Middle Ages.

It was only after three years of frontier chaos that the British intervened. The Sotho country became a British protectorate with an imposition of order. A new frontier line was drawn up and peace came to what was surely one of the loveliest scenic areas ever turned into a battleground by the rapacity and rivalry of man.

In the general agreement, Jan Hendrik and Renier received at least some of their land back in 1869. Compared to the original grant from Moshweshwe, it was just a 3 530 ha farm, which Jan disgruntledly named *Verliesfontein* (the fountain of loss). Nevertheless, it was still a substantial property. The ground was so fertile and well-watered that Renier liked to tell people that crops such as pumpkins grew so fast that you could see the seeds germinate and the leaves develop. Once when he walked home to fetch his pipe, he said, the runners followed so rapidly that they reached the house before him, climbed on to the roof and deposited pumpkins there to ripen in the sun. As for the yellow-peach trees, the fruit fell upon the ground so thickly that the land seemed to be covered with gold after a magic hailstorm.

Jan Hendrik died on 3 June 1874 at the age of 77 years. By that time the need for a town in the area was urgent. The nearest centre for church, school and business was Rouxville, 30 km away. Renier had a story that an Englishman had presented him with a pair of binoculars so powerful that, sitting on top of Aasvoëlberg on a Sunday, he could see the good people of Rouxville being led into church by dignified old Dominee Albertyn. Renier could see so clearly that he could identify each person. And what was more, he could clearly hear them singing and the dominee holding forth in sermon although they were over 30 km away.

Even with such a magic convenience as these binoculars, the people of the Aasvoëlberg area had to have their own town. *Verliesfontein* was the choice for a site. There was considerable controversy about the choice. The local farmers considered that the fertility of the soil was too great to be wasted by being covered with streets and buildings. From their gardens, the townspeople would also be able to produce their own vegetables and fruit, leaving the farmers without a market for produce. Renier's portion of the farm, his home known as *Reniershof* (Renier's garden), was pointed out as an example of this wondrous productivity.

In 1876, however, *Verliesfontein* was laid out as a town named Zastron in honour of the maiden name of the wife of the Orange Free State President, J H Brand. It is said that whenever the President visited the area he commanded Renier to join him for dinner at the camp-fire, give an account of his adventures during the troubled years, and tell his wonderful stories and legends, to the delight of all his listeners. He was renowned for his inventions, including self propelled hot-air balloons with different models for politicians, swindlers and bible punchers. Duels with the *donderkoppen* (thunderheads) and outwitting the Devil gave humour to countless listeners.

Always with Renier was his inseparable companion, a wizened, seemingly ageless little Bushman, simply known as *Boesman.* Boesman sat at Renier's feet when the stories were being told. If he saw any doubt on the listener's face, he eagerly made a point with a convincing *'Dis reg, baas'* (it's correct, master).

A typical Renier story concerned the great hole through the summit of the Aasvoëlberg. It appears that Renier and Boesman were fishing in a stream below this mountain when the Devil, escorted by a troop of baboons and a number of vultures, arrived on the scene. Renier had a reputation for the making of brandy from yellow peaches. He even flavoured his tobacco with the fruit. When he and Boesman went fishing they poured a little of their brandy on to the water. The fish rose to the surface to drink, and danced . They even allowed themselves to be caught by hand, hoping for at least one last drink.

The Devil asked for a drink and a smoke. Renier obliged with a drink. It was strong stuff and he gave the Devil a generous portion. The Devil repeated his request for a smoke. Renier saw his chance. He had with him his trusty old *pangeweer*, a type of gun requiring liberal doses of gunpowder (and a strong nerve to fire it). He produced the gun.

The Devil looked at the weapon.

'What's that?' he asked.

'My new pipe,' said Renier, *'you get a wonderful smoke from it'.*

He loaded the gun with a mix of tobacco and gunpowder, and slipped in a few rocks and some nails. *'Here,'* he said, *'put it in your mouth and I'll light it. Draw hard to get it going.'*

The Devil did as instructed. Renier lit the fuse. There was a colossal explosion and a cloud of smoke. Baboons and vultures scattered. There was a startled exclamation from the Devil: *'Wraggies Renier, daardie twak is darem sterk!'* (Heck Renier, that tobacco is rather strong!). There was a second explosion. Through the smoke Renier saw the Devil's head hurtling off towards the summit of Aasvoëlberg. It hit the cliff with a crash, bored a hole through the sandstone and disappeared into the distance. The Devil's body sped off in search of its head and was not seen again in the Zastron area for some time.

On 6 December 1883, Renier went out riding on his beautiful *skimmelperd* (roan horse), with seemingly not a care in the world. He felt sick the next morning and died peacefully after three days in bed. He was then aged 102 years although there is a little mystery about the exact date of his birth. He explained his longevity on this confusion. Whenever the old man with the sickle came to investigate the matter as a possible fault in his bookkeeping, Renier hid under his bed. His legacy to South Africa is a host of droll, amusing stories.

As for the pleasant little town of Zastron, it became a municipality in 1881. As the principal distributing centre for this part of the Free State, a trading base for Lesotho, as well as a very productive agricultural centre, it has developed into a pretty town with a recreational area and caravan park in *Eeufeeskloof* (centenary cleft) where there are roads leading to viewsites high in the mountains, a dam and a network of paths. This is also the starting-place for the two-day circular Aasvoëlberg Hiking Trail.

THE BUSHMEN OF THE ZASTRON DISTRICT

The Zastron area was always favoured by Bushmen, the caves in the surrounding sandstone hillocks provided some of their most celebrated strongholds. Visiting these caves today is a fascinating and (if their history is known) at times poignant experience. On the farm *Lichtenstein*, for example, is the Cave of the Hippopotamus, so named because the hippo is the dominant figure in a gallery of rock paintings. Some of the last surviving Bushmen lived in this cave, the floor of which is still littered with the fragments of their pots. It is said that they were all treacherously murdered by a vicious half-breed freebooter named Danster, whose stronghold was nearby at Danster's Nek. Jealous of the Bushmen, he invited them to a carousel, got them drunk and then had their throats cut.

Close to *Lichtenstein* is another farm, *Glen Roza*, whose owner, hunting dassies in 1946, was caught by a sudden storm. Seeking shelter, he stumbled into what is now know in his honour as the Hoffman Cave. This cave contains one of the finest galleries of polychrome rock paintings to be discovered. Farmer Hoffman found a frieze 4,5 m long and 1,5 m wide, which, in a splash of vivid, almost unfaded colour, gracefully preserves the memory of a vanished people and the game animals they hunted. This is a veritable gallery of Bushman master-works, where eland, especially, are magnificently depicted. The cave is situated in a deep and broken ravine which leads to the Gariep River.

The fate of the inhabitants of the Hoffman Cave is not known. But in the 2 026 m high rock massif known as Genadeberg (19 km south-east of Zastron) there are a number of Bushman caves of which there are particularly poignant memories. It was here in the year 1830 that a punitive commando cornered a band of Bushmen accused of rustling cattle. The commando found the

Bushmen on the western side of the heights, living in rock shelters beneath a series of waterfalls.

A succession of fights and sieges followed. The Bushmen withdrew cave by cave towards the innermost valleys of the massif. Finally, they fled to the great cave of their chief in the eroded corner of the heights known as Poshuli's Hoek. This cave (big enough to house a thousand people) is made of a colossal arch of rock suspended across a scooped-out shelter in the sandstone. During the rainy season a fall of water thunders noisily across the entrance and a tangle of thorn trees and loose boulders makes the approach difficult.

The name of the Bushman chief was Korei. He was a wizened, one-eyed little man whose daring and skill as a bowman gave him a formidable reputation. One of the commando, 14-year-old Jacobus du Plessis, who could speak the Bushman language, made his way to the cave. Waving the Bushman sign of truce (a jackal's tail tied to the end of a stick), he nervously entered the rock fortress.

The Bushmen received him courteously. He was conducted to the inmost recesses of the cave where he found the wild little chieftain seated in the centre of a circle of his followers. It must have been a barbaric sight; the cave full of echoes, shouts and dark shadows in whose depths sat a savage circle of near-naked hunters with bows in hand, their heads bedecked with poisoned arrows filleted into thongs fastened around their foreheads.

In the centre of the circle, Du Plessis faced the chief and nervously stuttered out his message: futility of resistance; safe conduct if the chief surrendered, with Du Plessis himself to take the chief by the hand and walk beside him to the commandant's presence. The wrinkled little face peered at the boy from the shadows. *'Go. My eyes cannot bear the sight of you. Begone. Tell your commandant that our hearts are strong, and we will claim a price today before the score between us is settled!'*

Twice again Du Plessis returned to parley with the Bushmen. Each time the number of warriors who received him was less, but their resolution remained. Seven Europeans fell to the whizzing arrows until at last a storming-party, protected by shields formed by their duffel-coats, rushed the cave. The silence was final. No Bushman survived. Today the cave remains a place of memories, scarred by the marks of innumerable bullets.

The *Genadeberg* (mountain of grace) was named much later when a surveyor, M C Vos, scrambled up to erect a beacon and unsettled a rock which so narrowly missed the head of one of his assistants that it was considered an act of grace that the man escaped. The 2 209 m high peak immediately east of the town is *Vegkop* (battle summit), the stronghold of the chief Poshuli which, in 1849, was stormed by Lourens Wepener and his men in a bitter and bloody battle.

Chapter Thirty-One
THE NORTHERN PROVINCE

The Vaal to the Limpopo

The Vaal River, fully harnessed to the industries of man, is also a great recreational asset. Its water is naturally muddy but free of such hazards as crocodiles and bilharzia which make the more tropical rivers of Africa dangerous to man. Anglers and boatmen frequent the river. Its banks are lined with willow trees, waterside residences, pleasure resorts, hotels, caravan parks and picnic sites. Yellowfish and barbel of large size are caught. Canoes, power-boats and aquaplaners find great sport on the calm waters.

The N1 bridges over the Vaal a short distance downstream from the Vaal barrage which holds back the river to form Loch Vaal, the principal water supply take-off, for what is known as the Vaal Triangle or the PWV area, (Pretoria, Witwatersrand and Vereeniging). The N1 road, as a dual-carriage toll-road (the Kroonvaal toll-road) continues northwards for 60 km and then reaches the outskirts of Johannesburg. It detours around the city to avoid the centre, resuming its way northwards. Before joining it, let us explore the riverine area along the north bank of the Vaal River.

Shortly after crossing the Vaal the N1 reaches a turn-off east (R42) which leads for 16 km to ...

VANDERBIJLPARK

In 1920 Dr Hendrik Johannes van der Bijl, 33 years of age, was brought back to South Africa from America where he was an established scientist, and given the post of Technical Adviser to the South African Government, whose Prime Minister was then General J C Smuts. It was a momentous appointment. An industrial revolution was taking place in South Africa and Hendrik van der Bijl was the man selected to plan it on the basis of two gigantic state undertakings – *Escom* (Electricity Supply Commission), since renamed Eskom, and *Iscor* (Iron and Steel Corporation). It was to supply the water for this industrial revolution that the great Vaal Dam was constructed.

It was an exciting time for a scientist and engineer. Pretoria was the site of the first steelworks and Dr Van der Bijl was considering an extension in Vereeniging when the Second World War commenced. He became Director of War Supplies. The urgency of converting South Africa from an importer of essential finished products to a manufacturer was emphasised when the war steadily cut links with traditional overseas suppliers.

The Pretoria steelworks had reached the limits of growth. Dr Van der Bijl, as far back as 1922, had already stated an opinion: *'The future of the industrial development of the Transvaal must, of necessity, lie along the banks of the Vaal River'*. In 1941 the Director of Iscor decided on a new steelworks in the Vereeniging area. Dr Van der Bijl began the search for suitable ground with space for the creation of a massive industry. One morning Colonel K Rood, MP for Vereeniging, and a friend of Dr Van der Bijl, took him to a grassy expanse of open veld along the Vaal River, west of Vereeniging. It was a perfect site. On its 10 000 hectares, Dr Van der Bijl visualised the vast mill and a garden town to house the workers.

The advantages were numerous. Plentiful water, coal from nearby fields, high ground with prevailing winds to disperse and minimise dangers of pollution, natural slopes for drainage towards the river, and an existing infrastructure of communications and transport to the area.

While the erection of a new plate mill in Vereeniging progressed, the site for the new steelworks and town was acquired – an eventual total of 95 square kilometres, much of it the original possession of the Vereeniging Estates company, established by Samuel Marks. The planning of the mill and the town then commenced.

On 28 November 1944 the Vanderbijlpark Estate Company was registered as a non-profit-making company with its income and assets applied solely towards the objectives of the company and the constant improvement of the town for the benefit of its citizens. Land for the town was transferred to this company by Iscor at cost and it had the task of creating the town, with rights to resell land for residential, business or other purposes.

It was anticipated that the town would accommodate at least 200 000 citizens. The design was given to a young team of technicians and administrators, well briefed by Dr Van der Bijl.

'My experience,' he said, *'thus far in building a town has made me only too conscious of the tremendous complexity of the problem and the need for a substantial element of modesty, and I might say, even humility, in approaching a task so colossal and formidable as that in dealing with the lives of nearly a quarter of a million of one's fellow human beings. The mere fact that many others have associated themselves with me in this enterprise, makes me more conscious of the immensity of the responsibility. I visualised a town with people living in surroundings and under conditions which would be conducive to a healthy, happy and productive life. For this reason I was determined that ample provision should be made for parks, playing grounds, health clinics, hospitals and schools.'*

Dr Van der Bijl intended to live in the town himself. He was planning his home when he died on 2 December 1948 at the very height of his career. His town was established and became a municipality on 29 October 1952. Today it has a population of 483 361. It is a classic example of an industrial township of the 20th century, with over half a million trees planted and many delightful gardens and recreational areas. Loch Vaal on the Vaal River provides a spacious playground for the citizens of the town.

The Vaal Triangle Technikon has been established in the town, and also the Vaal Triangle campus of the Potchefstroom University for Christian Higher Education.

From Vanderbijlpark the R42 road leads eastwards for 10 km and then enters the town of ...

VEREENIGING

In 1878 the geologist and author, George Stow, discovered coal on the farm *Leeuwkuil* (lion pool), on which Vereeniging stands today. The so-called Vaal Valley Coalfields were rapidly exploited by a company floated by Isaac Lewis and Samuel Marks, which was given the imposing name of *De Zuid-Afrikaansche en Oranjevrijstaatsche Kolen- en Mineralen-Mijn Vereniging* (The South African and Orange Free State Coal and Mineral Mine Association).

At the same time, the railway line from the south was under construction and had reached what was known as Viljoen's Drift, directly opposite the site of the future town. The latter was already starting to grow as a centre for coal-miners and as a railhead, for there was a delay before the Transvaal Republican Government completed the link from the Vaal to the Witwatersrand. The first train completed this journey from the south through Vereeniging to the Rand on 15 September 1892.

The town at the bridge across the Vaal was named *Vereeniging* (association or union) because it was there that the Cape, Orange Free State and Transvaal joined hands by means of the railway.

Vereeniging was richly endowed for an industrial town. Record prices were paid at the sale of the first erven on 29 April 1892. Not only were coal and water in plentiful supply in the vicinity, but there was also glacial conglomerate to provide fire-clay, dolomite for calcium and lime, black reef to supply silica, and excellent quarry stone for building purposes. The railway provided transport and it was even proposed at one time that steel barges be used to carry coal down the Vaal to the point nearest Kimberley.

Vereeniging today has a population of 342 704, and is the centre of considerable industry. With an estimated reserve of 4 000 million tons of high-grade coal in the area, coal-mining is a major activity. Mines such as the Cornelia Colliery produce over 4 million tons each year. An entire battery of giant thermal power-stations – Highveld, Lethabo, Taaibos, Vaal and Vereeniging – cluster around the coal-mines and the landscape is festooned in every direction with high-tension grids carrying power to the Witwatersrand and to busy industries.

The town of Vereeniging is itself the venue for diverse industrial activities. Vereeniging Refractories, the Union Steel Corporation (which produced South Africa's first steel ingot in 1913), the McKinnon Chain Company, African Cables Ltd, Tubemakers of South Africa (Tosa), Massey-Ferguson, and the South African Farm Implement Manufacturers Ltd, are among the substantial industrial concerns which produce a wide variety of heavy and light industrial items in Vereeniging.

Situated on the Vaal midway between the Barrage and Vaal Dam, the town is also a popular resort. The river is broad and deep, lined with fine willow trees on its banks which offer many pleasant sites for campers and picnickers. Boating, swimming, aquaplaning and fishing are all pastimes to be enjoyed along the tranquil course of the great Vaal River. An interesting little museum can be visited in the town.

From Vereeniging the R42 road leads westwards for 46 km to Heidelberg, passing on the way the Suikerbosrand where the Transvaal Provincial Council created a fine nature reserve with a well-developed holiday resort at Kareekloof. The entrance is 32 km from Vereeniging up the turn-off to Daleside. There are fine hiking trails in the 13 500 ha nature reserve, with six overnight huts at strategic places, each with five beds.

The R26 road leads due north from Vereeniging. After 3 km the main road reaches a large traffic circle from which branch roads radiate to industrial areas such as Duncanville and Unitas Park, and to the old M27 main road to Johannesburg. The R26 road continues northwards. After 16 km it reaches a turn-off to ...

MEYERTON

Meyerton was proclaimed in November 1891. The town was named after Jan Meyer, then the Witwatersrand member of the Volksraad. The place is now a busy maize and industrial centre.

From Meyerton the R26 road continues northwards through a fertile area of smallholdings. After 10 km there is a turn-off to the rural centre of Daleside from where there is a road 11 km long to the Kareekloof Public Resort in the Suikerbosrand Nature Reserve. The R26 road continues for 27 km and then enters Johannesburg.

The old Vereeniging–Johannesburg road, meanwhile, makes its way northwards into the hills of the *Gatsrand* (ridge of caves). Smallholdings – vegetable, dairy and poultry farms – line the roadside, and the subtle change in atmosphere (a sort of 'body odour') makes one sense the approach to a big city. At 18 km from Vereeniging the road passes through the small centre of *De Deur* (the door), then climbs easily over the heights of the Gatsrand and descends into the valley of the *Klip* (stony) River, crossing the river at Jackson's Drift, 9,5 km from Vereeniging. The shallow valley is grassy and fertile. In former years it was a great area for transport men who brought loads of everything imaginable to the booming Witwatersrand. They grazed their draught animals in the valley. More than 1 000 wagons reached Johannesburg each week and the demand for grass and water was insatiable. At Jackson's Drift itself a man named Jackson opened a small store and hostelry. There is still a hotel and a resort there. Nearby, a miller named Wienand once had a water-mill with a great lumbering wheel. The water-mill has long since vanished. The area is now known as *Eikenhof* (garden of oaks). There are several resorts along the way.

Across the Klip River the main road confronts the long rise of the *Witwatersrand* (the ridge of white waters), the lid of one of the world's richest geological and mineral treasure chests. The main tarmac road makes its way up the heights of the Witwatersrand, following the course of a tributary stream of the Klip River and passing the Meredale Pleasure Resort.

Eight kilometres from the Klip River crossing (46,5 km from Vereeniging), the road reaches a junction with N13, on the outskirts of Johannesburg. The road is now on the heights of the Witwatersrand at *Baragwanath*, an area named after John Albert Baragwanath who, in the early days of Johannesburg, owned a small hostelry (the Concordia hotel), which stood at the junction of the roads. The family were of Cornish origin, their name meaning 'white bread'. Baragwanath's son, Orlando, was one of the great-hearted company of prospectors in Southern Africa. Together with Fred Lewis, he was the first to peg the Copper Belt of modern Zambia. The Chris Hani Baragwanath hospital is the largest and most modern in Africa.

From its entrance into Johannesburg at this point, until it leaves the built-up area of the city at its northern limit, the M27 road now becomes a spectacular 26 km long freeway which passes at some places over the roof of the city and at others cuts deep into the ground. There are many spectacular views of Johannesburg. The story of the Witwatersrand and the city of Johannesburg is told in separate chapters (see Chapters Thirty-Two and Thirty-Three).

The N1 road, after skirting the centre of Johannesburg, eventually links up on the northern side of the city with N3 from KwaZulu-Natal and M27 which has crossed the centre city from Vereeniging. The combined roads form the dual carriageway known as the Ben Schoeman Highway which leads northwards, gradually losing altitude as it crosses undulating, grassy country with pleasant views of the Magaliesberg range of mountains to the north-west. Several streams make their way across the road. Among them is the *Jukskei* (yokes-key or yoke-pin) along whose course the first tantalising traces of the gold of the Witwatersrand were found by Pieter Marais in 1853. The Ben Schoeman Highway, named after a former Minister of Transport, is beautifully located and built, but shamefully ill-used by some of the most irresponsible, idiotic and abusive drivers to be found anywhere on Earth. Youths use this highway as a missile track. For some reason the authorities originally allowed a speed limit of 130 km an hour on parts of the road. As a result there were 18,4 deaths for every 100 accidents – the worst record for any highway on the continent of Africa. Recent speed restrictions and other disciplines have improved matters.

Thirty kilometres from Johannesburg there is a turn-off to the small centre known as Halfway House, where a cluster of shops, garages and a hotel stand on the site of an old staging post of the original coach service. In summer the countryside here is extremely pleasant. The roadside farms produce fine crops of peaches, plums and other deciduous fruit. Along with eggs, honey, cream and home-made jams, these edibles are sold to passing travellers from stands and kiosks. The area is known as Midrand.

At 8,5 km north of the turn-off to Halfway House, there is a parting of the ways. The Ben Schoeman Highway continues for a further 20 km, culminating in a grand approach to Pretoria, 58 km from Johannesburg (the story of Pretoria is told in Chapter Thirty-Four), while the N1 road swings off to bypass Pretoria. After 6,5 km it reaches a turn-off to ...

CENTURION

In 1964 a municipality was created by merging the townships of Doornkloof, Irene and Lyttelton. The 20 000 ha area received the name of *Verwoerdburg* after the then Prime Minister of South Africa, Dr Hendrik Frensch Verwoerd, who was assassinated in 1966. Lyttelton was established in 1904 on a portion of the farm *Droogegrond* (dry ground) owned by a Mr Ball whose five daughters established a company to develop a township, proclaimed in 1908 and named after General Sir Neville Lyttelton, who had succeeded Lord Kitchener as Commander-in-chief of the British Army in South Africa at the end of the Anglo-Boer War. It became a popular residential area for people working in Pretoria who found its rural atmosphere relaxing. Two large country clubs, *Zwartkop* and *Irene*, were built there to provide recreation. The Waterkloof Air Force Station is in the immediate vicinity of Lyttelton. *Irene*, was named after Irene Violet Nellmapius, the daughter of a well-known figure in the days of the South African Republic, a Hungarian named Alois Nellmapius, who promoted various industrial and property developments, including a block of nine model farms. He developed these farms on a large portion of the 16 000 acre farm *Doornkloof* (thorn ravine) which he purchased from its original owners Daniel and Stephanus Erasmus.

In 1909 General (later Field-Marshal) Jan Christiaan Smuts purchased 4 000 acres of the farm. As a homestead on this portion of the farm, he bought the timber and iron officers mess of Lord Kitchener's old headquarters in Middelburg in the Transvaal. The building was carefully dismantled and removed to *Doornkloof*. It was re-erected and, with later additions giving it eleven bedrooms and several large living rooms, it became known as the 'Big House'.

Doornkloof remained the home of Field-Marshal Smuts until his death on 11 September 1950. His ashes, and those of his wife Isie, are scattered on the nearby Smuts Koppie. The house is now a museum containing the original furniture and many personal belongings of a politician and soldier of world stature. The museum is open weekdays from 09h30 to 16h30; weekends and public holidays 09h30 to 17h00. Closed 24 December, Christmas Day, Workers Day and Good Friday.

In December 1994 the town council of Verwoerdburg was dissolved and a new municipality was established. Suggestions for a new name were invited from the public and put to a vote. The majority chose *Centurion* after the cricket ground, built there in 1986 as an international venue and named Centurion Park in honour of all cricketers scoring centuries. It is a growing town with a man-made lake created by the municipality on the Hennops River. This attractive recreational area contains, among other features, a water organ with 600 nozzles and 280 coloured lights. There are fine sporting facilities.

Four kilometres beyond the turn-off to Centurion there is a turn-off to Kempton Park and Pretoria; 2 km further on a turn-off leads to the Pretoria suburb of Waterkloof; after 8,5 km the road reaches a traffic interchange with the eastern highway, N4 to Komatipoort and Mozambique. This crossing is 53 km from the centre of Johannesburg. The N1 road continues its sweeping way north. After 3 km a turn-off branches to the Pretoria suburb of Waverley and East Lynn; after 7 km to Wonderboom and Cullinan and at 18 km to Pyramid and Wallmannsthal.

To the north the road now traverses an interesting geological area. With a far mountain rim out of sight, fully 100 km away, this acacia-covered plain seems boundless. To the untrained eye it is an immense and completely flat plain, but to the discerning geologist this landscape is a lopolith on a colossal scale, known as the Bushveld Igneous Complex. Its formation was spectacular ...

THE BUSHVELD IGNEOUS COMPLEX

About 600 million years ago a considerable disturbance occurred beneath the surface of this part of the world. In between the sedimentary layers of the Transvaal System a molten mass of magmatic material intruded, consisting of a mixture of dark-coloured basic rocks (carrying platinum, chromite, nickel and iron), and later a reddish acid granite (which carries tin and tungsten).

As this material forced its way into the subterranean layers of the Transvaal System, it was fluid and soft. The centre of the overlying landscape subsided into this undermining fluid, rather like lead melting in a pot and subsiding when heated from below. A gigantic basin formed (a lopolith) whose rim consisted of remnants of the original high-lying Transvaal System, now in the form of an encircling chain of mountains known in its various parts as the Magaliesberg, Strydpoort, etc. This mountain rim dips inwards towards the basin, whose floor is extraordinarily flat. Below it the lopolith, shaped by the weight and pressure of the intrusive magma, takes the form of the bulging curve of a convex lens pointing down into the depths. This is the Bushveld Igneous Complex, famous for its succession of rock types and associated ore deposits. It also has a small, beautifully preserved crater known as *Tswaing*.

THE TSWAING CRATER MUSEUM

This most interesting geological 'happening' is in the form of a crater known as the Pretoria Salt Pan or, by the Tswana people, as *Tswaing* (the place of salt). The crater is 1,13 km wide, more or less circular and holds a calm saline lakelet about 3 metres in depth.

The rim is 60 metres higher than the surrounding plain and is thickly wooded with acacia and other trees. The crater was originally 200 metres deep but gradually filling with material eroded into it from the rim. The surface of the crater is 100 metres below the rim. Drilling into the crater reveals that its bottom is solid granite.

The sediment filling the crater at present is 90 metres deep, its liquid content enriched with dissolved salts of carbonic acid and sodium bicarbonate. This salt and soda content is constantly replenished by weathering of the crater rocks, mainly granite, and evaporation of the lake, which itself is maintained by rainfall.

The Moloko and Tswana speaking people who settled in the area produced salt by boiling, evaporating and filtering water from the crater lake. Boer farmers settled around the crater in the second half of the 19th century and they started to produce salt from the lake. Then the soda deposits were discovered, the only known natural soda deposits in South Africa to be exploited commercially.

Between 1912 and 1956 a company named South African Alkali Ltd produced salt and soda from the crater. In 1919 large quantities of valuable soda-salt liquid were found in the sedimentary matter below the crater floor. The company sank boreholes into the crater floor and installed electric pumps to extract the mineral rich liquid. The liquid was pumped from the crater floor up to a storage reservoir on the crater rim. It was then gravitated down to a factory below the crater where it was reduced to soda-ash and salt. The soda-ash was the really profitable product of the crater. It was used in the manufacture of glass, caustic, baking and washing soda, pulp, paper, soap, detergents and as a softener of acid water. The factory ceased production in 1956.

The origin of the crater has provided some controversy. It was originally considered to have been a volcanic blow hole. Later opinion, however, is that it was the consequence of a meteorite collision with the Earth about 220 000 years ago.

The meteorite was of the type known as a *chondrite*. About 92% of all meteorites are stone meteorites and 84% if these are chondrites because of the presence in them of *chondrules* composed of silicate materials that have melted and then re-solidified. Chondrite meteorites shatter on impact whilst iron meteorites (7%) and stony-iron meteorites (1%) are stronger.

Apart from the visual and geological interest of the crater, the 90 metres of sediment below the lake, undisturbed since it was deposited in a closed geological system, provide scientists with a rich source of fossilised pollen and algae reflecting climatic changes since the crater originated. It is a unique source of palaeoenvironmental and palaeoclimatic information.

In 1993–94 the National Cultural History Museum based in Pretoria bought the two farms on which the crater is situated. This site of 2 000 hectares in being developed as an Enviro-Museum, The Tswaing Crater Museum. It is a unique and fascinating place to visit. It is open daily 08h30 to 16h00.

At 38 km from Pretoria up the N1 road there is a turn-off to the burgeoning centre of *Hammanskraal*, where a road branches off west to the crater of Twaing. Hammanskraal was named after someone who built a corral there in the old days to protect cattle against lions. This area was always frequented by predators. Right up until the 1930s an occasional lion still hunted in the thornbush. There are numerous stories of desperate adventures with these resolute animals. A number of early travellers vanished without trace in the course of traversing what was known as the Springbok Flats. Today ground-nuts and maize replace much of the thornbush. A tall grain elevator at the railway junction of Pienaarsrivier (21 km further on) is one of the principal landmarks in the flat landscape.

The Springbok Flats are the home of a section of the interesting, artistically talented and colourfully dressed Ndebele tribe. Some 10 km west of Tswaing there is a traditional Ndebele village where visitors are welcome.

THE NDEBELE

About 1600 AD, when the Nguni people who subsequently became the Zulus had just migrated down the east coast into Natal, a small party detached itself from the main body and, under a chief named Musi, wandered into the Transvaal. They settled about the site of modern Pretoria. There Musi's son *Tshwane* (the little ape) came into his inheritance. When his time came, he died and bequeathed his name to posterity as the African name for the Apies River.

The original tribal name of these settlers is unknown. The Tswana-speaking people of the central plains dubbed them *maTebele*, indicating a 'refugee people' or 'people who hide'; and this name the newcomers happily incorporated into their own tongue in the form of *Ndebele*. It was the same name which was to be applied 200 years later to another group of people, refugees from the Zulu country, who became the grim warriors of Mzilikazi. In exchange the Nguni people named the Tswana people baSotho (or Basuto), and this is the name by which they became best known in the Transvaal and Free State.

These first Ndebele were a peaceful crowd of people. No great wars or excitement took place in their lives. Legend, with its easy explanations of forgotten events, simply tells us that when Tshwane died he left six ambitious sons who each refused to bow to a brother. The whole tribe, accordingly, was split up into six groups: each independent, but all acknowledging a common origin.

One group, under Manala, remained at the original tribal home and built a village at Wonderboompoort, just north of modern Pretoria. A second section under Ndzundza removed to the Olifants River. Their latter-day chiefs, with the family name of Mabogo (Mapoch), were destined to win some fame.

Of the rest of the brothers, Dhlomu is said to have gone back to Zululand, two others lost their identity in later years, while the sixth, Mathombeni, wandered up northwards and eventually settled in the bush along the southern slopes of the Strydpoort Mountains. There, in the course of years, his descendants quarrelled and split up: some settling near modern Potgietersrus, others remaining near the mountains where their latter-day chief Mamukebe obtained some renown and the honorific name of *Zebediyela* (the diplomat) on account of his prudent and peaceful reign at a period of much trouble between European and African.

Several other minor sections of the Ndebele people are distributed over the former Transvaal, including a small group known as the Black Ndebele, who live near Potgietersrus and came to the Transvaal separately.

These scattered groups of Ndebele people are nowadays surrounded entirely by the more numerous Tswana–Sotho people. With stubborn conservatism, however, the Ndebele have retained their own personality. They have few customs other than a simple ceremony known as *Luma*, performed each year in February, when their chief ritually samples the first fruits of the harvest. They are noted for the distinctive architecture of their villages. Their huts are elaborately decorated in many colours and with most intricate patterns. Their womenfolk, likewise, are remarkable for their elaborate costume, made up of heavy rings of beads worn around neck, waist and legs.

The Ndebele have been a peaceful and never numerous people. How they came to develop their unique culture of building residences so exquisitely decorated with wall paintings, and how they elaborated their bead costumes remains unknown. There is nothing like it to be seen anywhere else in the world.

The village in the *Klipgat* (stone cave) area west of the Tswaing crater is inhabited by the Ndzundza section of the Ndebele. Their chief Nyabela was banished to the Pretoria area from Sekhukhuneland by the Boer government after the Mapoch war of 1882–83. He died there in 1902. The village is known as *Mapoch's* from the family name of their chiefs. The village is a brilliantly photographic place to visit and the arts and crafts of the people are a delight to see.

At 93 km from Pretoria, the N1 road reaches a turn-off leading for 8 km to the town and resort of ...

WARMBATHS

Jan Grobler and Carl van Heerden were hunting in this area one winter when they noticed a cloud of vapour rising in the cold air. They rode to the spot and found a powerful hot spring (22 730 l an hour, at a temperature of 62°C) bubbling to the surface amid a morass of soggy vegetation. The spring was later found to have been a death-trap for numerous wild animals. When it was cut open, a vast accumulation of skeletons – including those of elephants – were recovered from the mud where they liked to wallow.

The Sotho tribespeople knew the area as *Belabela* (the boiling place). The two European discoverers of the hot spring settled in the vicinity of what first became known as *Het Bad* (the bath). Carl van Heerden established a farm around the hot spring, draining the swamp with a furrow and cleaning out the morass. People with ailments began to arrive to take the waters, camping, and digging their own baths in the mud, which they encircled with screening shelters of reeds and blankets.

The baths soon attained considerable renown and became as popular in the old Transvaal as did the Caledon baths in the Cape. In 1873 President Thomas Francois Burgers visited the place. He considered it so great a national asset that he persuaded his Volksraad to purchase the area of the baths which from then on came under State control. Little development, however, took place in the area for another ten years. Then it was surveyed by the government and the hot springs were proclaimed as public baths. They were enclosed and roofed. A township was laid out on an adjacent farm. The township site proved unpopular. Hotels and boarding-houses were built closer to the baths and eventually the present town of Warmbaths was laid out, receiving its first health committee in 1921. Today 28 189 people live in the town.

The hot baths have been magnificently developed. Over 750 000 people visit them each year, not only for health reasons but also for the pleasure (especially in winter) of swimming in the 32°C swimming-baths. Medicinally, the springs are rich in sodium chloride, calcium carbonate and other chemicals. They are also slightly radioactive. Anything immersed in the water is subjected to a degree of irradiation. Visitors are confident that the baths have a definite effect on them, especially after a course of the waters lasting from one to two weeks, when what is described as 'bath reaction' is very marked. Devotees believe that taking the waters is beneficial in cases of rheumatism and other arthritic ailments. The Warmbaths Hospital has a special institute for rheumatic research, developed by the Transvaal Provincial Administration in conjunction with the baths. Specialised treatments and expert advice are available with a variety of different baths, underwater massage, bubble-jet, saunas, vapour inhalation, electro-galvanic and other scientifically controlled and programmed treatments.

Wheat, ground-nuts, maize and citrus are the products of the district. Commerce in the town itself is principally orientated towards catering for visitors to the hot springs.

The Warmbaths resort is open from 07h00 to 17h00 daily.

Veering in a north-easterly direction from Warmbaths, the original N1 road finds a scenic way through the tree-covered foothills of the *Waterberg* (water mountain). Several shady resting-places are located along this stretch of the road. An arresting landmark 8 km from Warmbaths is the 1 308 m high Buyskop. A story is told of this height. A group of followers of the frontiersman and outlaw, Coenraad de Buys, were once attacked in the region and retreated to the hilltop, where they withstood a stubborn siege. Days passed, and their food and water supplies approached exhaustion. Suspecting, however, that the besiegers were also suffering privations in the summer heat, the leader of the De Buys party, in sheer bravado, scaled a vantage-point atop the cliffs. From there he taunted the besiegers by offering them his last skin bag of water. When the besiegers sent a man up the slopes to collect the bag, the leader insolently threw it at his head. This apparent proof of plentiful water supplies on the summit dispirited the besiegers so much that they withdrew, leaving the De Buys party to continue their journey in peace.

Immediately beyond Buyskop is a turn-off east to the Maroela Nature Resort, the railway station of *Eersbewoond* (first habitation) and the Loskop Dam. The road then continues through the foothills past the Klein Kariba Hotel and Holiday Resort (11,5 km from Warmbaths) and Floyd's Motel, 19,5 km from Warmbaths.

The old N1 road crosses the upper reaches of the *Nylstroom*, which the Voortrekkers mistook for the headwaters of the Nile (hence its name), and at 31 km from Warmbaths reaches the town on the banks of that river ...

NYLSTROOM

The principal centre of the fertile Waterberg area, this town was proclaimed on 15 February 1866 and laid out on the farm *Rietvallei*, purchased from Ernest Collins. It grew to be an agricultural centre and railway junction for the line to Vaalwater. It has a present population of 18 410. The headquarters of the large agricultural co-operative, the NTK, are in Nylstroom. The manufacture of peanut butter from the enormous local ground-nut crop is an important industry. Table grapes are also grown in the area.

There is a museum devoted to a former prime minister of South Africa, J G Strijdom, who was known as the 'Lion of the North'. The museum is open Mondays to Fridays 0800 to 16h00; Saturdays 10h00 to 16h00. Closed Sundays and Christian religious holidays.

The old N1 road continues from Nylstroom in a north-easterly direction along the foothills of the Waterberg. Fine trees provide shade along the undulating road, the scenery is pleasant, and there are many wayside resting-places. After 8 km the road passes the Stokkiesdraai Motel, with its mineral baths and recreational facilities.

The road twists around the foothills. To the east there is a good view of a famous landmark of the Springbok Flats, the 1 337 m *Kranskop* (cliff peak) which the Voortrekkers are reputed to have regarded as the remnant of a pyramid. Known to the local tribespeople as *Modimolle* (place of spirits), the mountain is thought by them to be a resort of ghosts and the taboo site of graves of ancient chiefs.

After 17 km from Nylstroom, the old road joins the new N1 which, as the Kranskop toll-road, has come 20 km directly from the turn-off to Warmbaths. The N1 continues for another 24 km and then reaches the town of ...

NABOOMSPRUIT

This pleasant little town, whose name means 'stream of the euphorbia tree', is red and green in colour. The rich, deep-red colour of the soil is perpetuated in the locally made building bricks, and the trees are vivid green. Fine jacarandas line the streets.

Naboomspruit has often been the butt of big-city newspaper jokes. For years it was considered the epitome of a Southern African *dorp*. In the 1920s it certainly was an odd little town, complete with a private, patent narrow-gauge railway, which ran for 34 km to Singlewood on the Springbok Flats. The railway, the creation of Major Frank Dutton, boasted a locomotive known as *Tshongololo* (the centipede) which could jack itself off the line, undergo a change of wheels, and take to the road to cope with an unscheduled service!

The Waterberg, behind the town, is a richly mineralised area. A discovery of tin made there in 1910 by a local prospector, Adolph Erasmus, led to the founding of the town. The discoveries, made on the farms *Doornhoek* and *Welgevonden*, attracted a rugged crowd of miners to the area. A collection of bars, stores and a gaol was erected to serve them at the nearest railway point. This centre grew until, in 1919, it became a village.

In 1925 Adolph Erasmus found platinum on the farm *Rietfontein* and the fresh influx of miners gave Naboomspruit the impetus to become a town in 1938.

In addition to mining, Naboomspruit is the centre for considerable farming activity. Maize, ground-nuts and citrus flourish in the area. The original narrow-gauge railway was later converted to standard-gauge and extended to reach the enormous citrus estate of *Zebediela*, 84 km away. Named after Mamukebe, an Ndebele chief, also known as *Zebediyela* (the diplomat or one who concedes), the estate is one of the largest citrus producers in the world, with more than 600 000 trees bearing over 60 000 tons (400 million oranges) each year. This colossal agricultural industry had its start in the 1890s when W H Gilfillan, surveyor-general of the South African Republic, observed that the area of the estate was substantially lower in altitude than a tributary of the Olifants River flowing southwards through the Strydpoort Mountains. By deflecting the flow of this stream, water could irrigate the fertile plain below the mountains.

The Anglo-Boer War prevented Gilfillan from developing his discovery. When the war ended, however, he bought two farms in the area, *Uitkyk* and *Schaapplaats*. He tried to finance his plans by farming ostriches but the outbreak of the First World War practically ruined him. The escalation in demand for fresh fruit, however, made it only too obvious that there would be a fortune in the large-scale cultivation of citrus in the area.

Gilfillan carried his idea to a financier, Isidore Schlesinger, who bought the farm and divided it into 1 200 plots, each two hectares in extent. These plots were skilfully advertised in brochures and periodicals. They were offered at £67 each, with purchasers entitled to live on them while the combined orchards would be cultivated, the fruit picked, packed and marketed as a profit-sharing co-operation.

The brochure was attractive. The whole concept proved tempting, especially to army officers demobilised with a small gratuity. Life in the sunshine, with clubs and sports seemed so much better than going back to office work in some city. The plots were sold, houses were built, but time passed in preparation of the orchards, building canals and starting the project. Only in 1926 was the first crop picked. By that time many of the settlers had gone bankrupt and their plots taken back by the company. There was considerable ill-feeling and accusation of a deliberate delay in bringing the project to the production stage in order to squeeze out the small owners.

Zebediela grew from this unfortunate beginning into what is today a prodigious industry in the production of Navel oranges (harvested August to September) and Valencia oranges harvested in November and December. The branch railway from Naboomspruit was built in 1928. From then on, each year larger numbers of oranges were dispatched to markets in many far parts of the world. Over 30 000 cases of oranges are dispatched each day during the season.

In 1974 the government bought the estate and it was then Government-managed by the Lebowa Development Corporation.

The Waterberg has many beauty spots, streams, gorges, valleys and hot springs. The larger hot springs have been developed by various private enterprises. The temperatures are about 39°C. The Nylsvley Nature Reserve conserves a 3 100 ha flood plain of the Nylstroom. It is 20 km south of Naboomspruit and was created by the Transvaal Provincial Administration.

From Naboomspruit, the N1 road continues north-eastwards along the foothills of the Waterberg. Trees shade many wayside resting-places and travelling is pleasant. At 22 km from Naboomspruit there is the Fiesta Park Motel, which also has a caravan park. Eighteen kilometres further on, the road reaches a picnic and resting-place at a site of poignant memories, *Moorddrift* (the ford of murder), where the road bridges across the Nylstroom. Moorddrif was the scene of a gory event which took place in September 1854. Two Voortrekker parties, totalling 33 people, were travelling in the area with Hermanus Potgieter when they were attacked at Moorddrif and slaughtered by local Tlou tribespeople. What started the massacre remains unknown but, once it began, the attackers made a particularly brutal job of things. Then, realising the inevitability of retribution, the 2 000 Tlou tribespeople concerned fled for safety into the depths of a prodigious cave known today as *Makapansgat*, after their chief Makapane. What befell them there is told further on in this chapter. Immediately across the Nylstroom, known to the tribespeople as the *Mohalakwena* (place of fierce crocodiles), the N1 road reaches a branch leading eastwards to Groblersdal (124 km), the Loskop Dam, Middelburg and down to KwaZulu-Natal. This all-tarmac route is much favoured by people travelling from Zimbabwe to the coast of KwaZulu-Natal, as it avoids the congestion of Pretoria and the Witwatersrand.

Eleven kilometres beyond this turn-off (51 km from Naboomspruit), the N1 road enters the town of ...

POTGIETERSRUS

Pieter Potgietersrus, to give this town its original name, was named in memory of Commandant-General Pieter Potgieter who was killed at Makapansgat while directing a punitive attack on the tribespeople responsible for the massacre at Moorddrif. His grave is beneath a pile of stones in the grounds of the municipal buildings. The town was founded on 25 September 1858. Today it is a busy and modern place, with a population of 10 028. Its residential streets are shaded by handsome trees and its gardens overflow with bougainvillaea, poinsettia, poinciana and jacarandas, all of which thrive in the warm and well-watered climate.

The town lies on the floor of a wooded pass which provides the national road and the branch road into the Northern Province bushveld with an easy natural route through the Waterberg. The centre for a considerable industry in tobacco production, Potgietersrus has huge sheds for sorting, grading and packing the leaves. Ground-nuts, sunflowers, castor oil plants, cotton, rice, citrus, maize, millet and wheat also flourish in the region, while the north-western bushveld is a major cattle-ranching area.

Thirty-seven kilometres from Potgietersrus is the Zaaiplaats tin mine and its refinery.

The Arend Dieperink Museum, named after its founder, is one of the finest small-town museums in Southern Africa and is well worth a visit. Its aloe garden contains more than 4 000 plants of 212 different species. They flower in about June and July. The museum is open Mondays to Fridays from 07h30 to 16h00. Closed weekends and public holidays.

In the caravan park there rests in honoured retirement a Class 19D Steam locomotive, pensioned off from arduous duties in 1980.

Immediately outside the town, off the road to Pietersburg, there is the nature reserve and game-breeding centre of the National Zoological Gardens of South Africa. It is open to the public from 07h30 to 16h00 weekdays; 08h00 to 18h00 weekends. There is an interesting mix of exotic and indigenous animals. There are picnic areas. Several hunting farms are situated in the district and are notable for their kudu and impala.

The Doorndraai Dam Nature Reserve is 45 km south-west of Potgietersrus. The reserve covers

7 229 ha with the dam 600 ha in extent. The reserve is home to a variety of bushveld trees and plants, with an interesting population of animals. Fishing and boating take place on the dam. The reserve is managed by the Northern Province Nature Conservation.

Beyond Potgietersrus, the N1 road makes its way up the long valley which provides a route through the mountains. At 3 km from the town there is a turn-off to the Percy Fyfe Nature Reserve which lies 27 km from Potgietersrus. The reserve is a breeding station for tsessebe, roan and sable antelope. It is open to the public. Pietersburg lies a further 38 km beyond it. This road provides an interesting drive through spectacular granite outcrops, but the surface is mainly gravel. Potties Pride holiday resort lies 12 km along this road from Potgietersrus.

Fourteen kilometres from Potgietersrus on the main tarmac N1 to Pietersburg there is a gravel turn-off for 11,5 km to the caves of ...

MAKAPANSGAT

These extraordinary limestone caverns lie on a private farm. The homestead is passed on the way to the caves. The gravel road terminates at a gate. Permission must have already been obtained from the Bernard Price Institute of the University of the Witwatersrand in order to proceed. Beyond this point a rough track leads for about 2 km to the entrance of the caves, which lie in a wild and beautiful ravine whose slopes are covered in aloes, euphorbias and forest trees. To the right the valley is bordered by a high cliff of red sandstone. This rugged and primeval setting was the scene of sanguinary events which were climactic in the history of the caves.

The caves themselves are colossal, and only when one enters them can their size be fully appreciated. The two main entrances, one below the other, slope into each other and huge chambers branch off from them into the depths. Stone barricades, ashes of long-dead fires and sinister memories are all that remain in the caves from the days of the siege.

Much excavated by archaeologists, the caves have yielded many important discoveries, dating as far back as the Upper Chelles Acheul period, well below the level of the Early Stone Age. Man continued to discover and make use of these strange caverns from those distant days. In exploring them today, it is fascinating to visualise the long succession of prehistoric people who made their homes there. After the Moorddrif massacre in 1854, the caverns became a stronghold for the Tlou tribe. With their leader (whose proper name was Makapane) these people retreated into the great caves, believing that the natural cave water and their stores of grain would see them through any siege.

A punitive commando, led by Commandant-General Piet Potgieter, made its way to the caves and a grotesque struggle followed. The tribespeople fired from the impenetrable dark in the depths of the caves at anybody who appeared in the bright light at the 600 m by 150 m entrance. This fire was formidable.

On 6 November 1854 Potgieter was himself shot dead by a sniper lurking in the shadows of the caves. The 29-year-old Paul Kruger (then a field-cornet) was nearby and he dragged Potgieter's body away.

For 30 days the commando besieged the caves. Then a party of Europeans, observing that the defence had become notably weaker, stormed the caves. They found them to be a place of death, permeated by an overwhelming stench of putrefaction. Some 1 500 tribespeople lay dead of starvation and thirst – only a handful had managed to slip away.

Once more the great caves were left to themselves. Now only rock-pigeons bill, coo and flutter through the shadows and the silence of Makapansgat. The disease known as *Histo plasmosis* is endemic in the caves. Unauthorised visits by casual sightseers are discouraged.

Much research continues in the caves, especially with the fossil pig species, *Potamochoeroides shawi*. These fossils are found associated with those of *Australopithecus*, the hominid first found in the Sterkfontein caves (see Chapter Thirty-Two) and considered to be the ancestor of mankind, the 'missing link' with the more primitive apes. Discoveries in East Africa at first indicated that the specimens *Australopithecus afarensis* found there were the oldest. More recent research in the Makapansgat caves by P Bender has indicated that *Australopithecus africanus*, the species found in the Sterkfontein caves, by association with the fossil pig, may be older than previously thought, at least as old, 3,5–4,3 million years, as the East African fossils and, therefore, at least contemporary or earlier as the origin of man.

From the gravel turn-off to Makapansgat, the N1 road continues its easy climb to the plateau summit above the pass. Twenty-two kilometres from Potgietersrus the road reaches the summit of the rise and finds itself 1 297 m above sea-level on an open, grassy plateau with the high ridge of the Strydpoort Mountains stretching off to the east.

Five kilometres further on (27 km from Potgietersrus), the road reaches a junction east. The sign 'Eersteling' is a reminder that the traveller is passing through an interesting mining field. It was at Eersteling that the first gold rush in the Transvaal occurred. In 1871 Edward Button, a pioneer prospector from Natal, claimed a find of payable gold. The discovery did not prove to be valuable but it attracted a flood of fortune-seekers to the Transvaal.

The old gold-field at Eersteling is worth visiting. It lies 4,5 km from the N1 road in a superb setting backed by a range of mountains. It is a small field around a central hillock. The surrounding area is scarred with old adits, rubble dumps, rusting machinery, stamp bases, and the famous chimney. This chimney, built of imported Aberdeen granite, transported all the way from Scotland by ship, train and ox-wagon, was the smoke-stack of the Eersteling Mine. Once the tallest building in the Transvaal, it is a fine example of industrial architecture. A legend spread at the time that the chimney represented the strength of the British empire and, if it could be pulled down, the empire would collapse. During the Transvaal War of 1880–81 several local inhabitants tried to destroy the chimney using spans of oxen in a futile effort to drag it down. It survived and still stands today, a curiously elegant ruin.

As befits an old field, tales are told of hauntings. It is said that at certain times on particular days and nights, sounds of digging may be heard, although there is never any sign of work done. The clamour of nocturnal jollification is also sometimes heard. The old diggers were a happy breed even in their poverty. Any one who enjoyed some luck would give a party. The sounds of merriment are said still to echo over the field, to the accompaniment of midnight sharings of bottles of Holland's Squareface Gin. Five kilometres beyond the turn-off to Eersteling, the R101 road passes the handsome grounds of the Ranch Hotel.

At 11 km beyond the Ranch Hotel the road passes a turn-off south-east to Zebediela (40 km). Thirteen kilometres further on (a total of 64 km from Potgietersrus), the N1 road enters the principal town and capital of the Northern Province ...

PIETERSBURG

Lying 1 312 m above sea-level in a slight hollow (known to the Africans as *Polokwane*, the protected place) amid an open, grass-covered plateau, Pietersburg originated on 11 November 1884 when the *Volksraad* (people's council) of the South African Republic approved the farm *Sterkloop* (strong stream) as the site of a new town. The farm was bought for £1 500 and on 31 July 1886 a magistracy was established. The town, named after Commandant-General Pieter Joubert, grew rapidly, for it was a natural centre for communications and agriculture in the Northern Transvaal.

A bright and modern miniature city, decorated with flowering trees and pretty fountains, Pietersburg has a population of 37 152 and enjoys a considerable amount of commercial bustle. It is a major staging post on the road to the north and along the scenic R71 road which leads east over Magoebaskloof to Tzaneen and the Kruger National Park. Along the road, at a site marked by a huge star of David painted on the slope of an overlooking mountain, 40 km east of Pietersburg, is *Zion City Moria*, the centre of the Zion Christian church, founded in 1910 by Edward Lekganyane. With a following today of an estimated seven million people, it is the largest independent church in Southern Africa. Its leader is Bishop Barnabas Lekganyane. The annual gathering at Easter attracts over three million followers of the church.

Garages, hotels and shops line the N1 as it passes through Pietersburg, offering travellers the goods, fuel, repairs and refreshments they need to continue their journey.

The town has a 3 200 ha nature reserve which shelters more than 1 000 head of game, many lovely trees and 195 species of birds. An interesting hiking trail, known as the Rhino Trail, winds for 20 km through the reserve.

At the northern entrance to Pietersburg the verges of the N1 road have been converted into a gallery of industrial sculptures similar in concept to Frogner Park in Oslo. Various artists have created some very unusual-looking work, using improbable material such as steel pipes, old railway sleepers and diverse pieces of scrap metal. The results are diverting. A collection of over 600 paintings is housed in the civic centre, including work by many of South Africa's leading artists.

There is a very interesting museum containing the work of the photographer Hugh Exton, who had his studio in Pietersburg. There are 22 000 of his glass negatives in the collection, and many photographs are of great historical value. The museum is in the civic plaza in the centre of the town. Another museum, devoted to the cultural history of the area, is housed in a fine example of late Victorian architecture. This building known as the Irish House, has a clock tower and wrought-iron decorations.

The original air force station west of Pietersburg has been converted into the Pietersburg Airport. Silica quartz is mined at Witkop on the outskirts of the town, and silica metal is produced in large quantities.

The University of the North at Turfloop is east of the town on the R71 road to Tzaneen. Its buildings are decorated with African motifs.

The N1 road continues northwards from Pietersburg, descending gently off the plateau and entering an area which becomes increasingly heavily bushed with stunted acacia trees. The road passes through a cluster of hillocks and, 40 km after leaving Pietersburg, the traveller sees ahead in the haze of the northern horizon, 72 km away, the long line of the Soutpansberg range.

Fifty-one kilometres from Pietersburg the road passes through an assembly of small granite domes, a foretaste for the north-bound traveller of the enormous granite domes the road must pass in Zimbabwe. These granite domes are disfigured by idiots daubing their initials on them. A gentleman from the public works has to be frequently employed there with a ladder and paint remover.

An important milestone is passed 61 km from Pietersburg; the Tropic of Capricorn, indicated by a sign at the point where it crosses the road. Immediately ahead a forest of magnificent euphorbia trees serves to emphasise the great changes in the vegetation as the road leads on into warmer and lower-lying regions.

Seventy-two kilometres from Pietersburg a tarmac turn-off stretches east to Soekmekaar (22 km) and Tzaneen (97 km). Five kilometres further on, the road crosses the railway nearby the small centre of *Bandelierskop*, said to be named after a *bandelier* (shoulder cartridge belt) mislaid there by a member of a Boer commando.

The 1 171 m high hillock of that name is immediately to the east of the road. Six kilometres beyond Bandelierskop lies the Lalapanzi Motel and 11 km further on (95 km from Pietersburg) is the Adams Apple Motel.

The N1 reaches the southern slopes of the Soutpansberg range 113 km from Pietersburg, and then enters the handsomely situated town of ...

LOUIS TRICHARDT

Set in an extremely beautiful situation, backed by the Soutpansberge range, this town has a warm climate, 940 mm of rain a year and rich soil all of which combine to produce a green and congenial environment, inhabited by 8 486 people.

In 1836, two advance parties of Voortrekkers reached the Soutpansberge. The first party, under Johannes van Rensburg, pushed on eastwards, hoping to reach a Portuguese trading port in Mozambique. They were massacred somewhere in the bush. The second party, under Louis Trichardt, camped nearby the site of the modern town. They planted crops and made exploratory journeys into what is now Zimbabwe and to the east in search of the Van Rensburg party. In a valley in the Soutpansberge, at Mara, Louis Trichardt and his followers discovered a community of offspring of the frontier adventurer Coenraad de Buys, who had made his home there in about 1820.

Trichardt and his followers left the Soutpansberge in September 1837 in an attempt to reach Lourenzo Marques (now Maputo). This venture cost most of them their lives. Later, other pioneers followed Trichardt's trail to the Soutpansberge. In 1847 a renowned leader, Hendrik Potgieter, explored the area and selected the site for a town which became known as *Zoutpansbergdorp* (salt-pan mountain town).

At that time, the area of the present Northern Province was teeming with game animals. Zoutpansbergdorp, the northernmost town of the old Transvaal, became a base for the ivory trade. An unruly crowd of hunters and traders made the place their home. After the death of Hendrik Potgieter in 1852, the town fell under the control of Stephanus Schoeman, who married the widow of Potgieter's son (who was killed at Makapansgat). The town was renamed Schoemansdal. Conditions there became chaotic. The incessant brawling and the quarrels between ivory hunters and local African tribes culminated on 15 July 1867, when the town was abandoned by the Europeans and totally destroyed by the Venda tribespeople. Today nothing remains of the place other than piles of rubble and a few fruit trees growing wild in the bush.

For some years the area remained under the control of the Venda people of the Soutpansberge. Few Europeans ventured into the area, and those who did, such as the famous safari trader, João Albasini, made their homes in private forts. At the end of 1898, after a petty war with the Venda, the South African Republic regained control of the area. The town of Louis Trichardt was proclaimed as an administrative centre for the Zoutpansberge on 15 February 1899. Today it serves as a centre for communication, administration, afforestation and large-scale vegetable farming.

Angling and boating can be enjoyed on the Albasini Dam, 20 km east of the town. Hunting opportunities in the district are numerous. There are several game farms and professional hunters. The Ben Lavin Nature Reserve lies just off the N1 road as it approaches Louis Trichardt from the south. It is the property of the Wildlife Protection Society of South Africa.

Fort Hendrina, one of three iron forts erected in the Transvaal, was originally built at Klipdam in 1888. It was moved to various sites and then presented to the town of Louis Trichardt in 1969.

Beyond Louis Trichardt, the N1 road begins to climb the Soutpansberge range. The road finds a way up the southern slopes of the range over a winding and attractive scenic pass. The summit is reached 10 km from Louis Trichardt and at this stage it is fitting to know something of ...

THE SOUTPANSBERGE (ORIGINALLY ZOUTPANSBERGE)

The range takes its name, which means 'salt-pan mountains', from a large salt pan lying at its western end. The pan has a powerful brine spring, and has been a source of salt for different people from prehistoric times.

The mountain range is slightly longer than 130 km and its highest point is the 1 753 m Lejume. Its composition is sedimentary – rather coarse, reddish-coloured sandstones, grits and conglomerates, part of the Waterberg Group laid down about 1 700 million years ago.

The summit of the range is a fertile, well-watered healthily cool plateau which has proved attractive to human beings since very early times. Bushmen made their homes there and, at about the beginning of the 18th century, a fragment of the Rozvi people of Zimbabwe wandered south and discovered the delights of this delectable range of mountains. They named it *Venda* (said to describe a pleasant area), ejected the Bushmen, and settled there themselves to become the Venda people of today.

The Venda still live on the pleasant plateau atop the mountains. Their huts, the picturesque costumes of their women and their traditional way of life may still be observed. At night their drums thud as young girls are put through the elaborate and prolonged rituals of puberty, including the famous *domba* (fertility) dance of the python.

In the Nzhelele valley are ruins of the Zimbabwe-style stone walls the Venda erected around their first settlement, Dzata. In the valley of the Mutale River lies the curiously sinister lake of Fundudzi, an old venue for tribal sacrifice, enveloped in superstition and reputedly the retreat of the python god of fertility. There are enchanted waterfalls such as *Phipidi* (named after a chieftainness) and haunted forests, the latter said to be so full of ghosts that few men dare to venture into them. Magnificent walks can be taken through this land of forests and plantations. There are interesting climbs to the summit of peaks such as Hangklip (1 718 m), where lies the taboo burial-ground of the early chiefs of the Venda tribe; the famous Maghato, the Lion of the North, and his son Mphephu. From the heights there are striking views of the flat bushland of the Northern Province.

There are fine hiking trails in the Soutpansberge. A worthwhile drive leads west from Louis Trichardt, past the site of Schoemansdal, now just a cemetery (15 km), as far as the western end of the range (73 km), where it joins the tarmac road from Pietersburg to the village of *Dendron*, so named from the Greek word for trees, which cover the surrounding country. From here it is possible to drive on a tarmac road for 71 km eastwards along the northern slopes of the range, past the salt pan and Waterpoort, to rejoin the N1 road 33 km north of Louis Trichardt.

On 13 September 1979, the Venda homeland became autonomous, with the status of a bantustan. A capital named *Thohoyandou* (head of an elephant) after a renowned early chief, was created but the whole political rigmarole proved abortive. The Venda homestead is now once again a part of South Africa.

As has already been described, after leaving Louis Trichardt (984 m above sea-level), the N1 road immediately commences its ascent of the southern slopes of the Soutpansberge through the wooded country of the Hangklip Forestry Reserve. Five kilometres from Louis Trichardt the road passes the park-like grounds of the Clouds End Hotel. Ten kilometres from Louis Trichardt the road passes the Mountain View Hotel, right at the top of the pass.

At the summit, 1 524 m above sea-level, a gravel turn-off west is marked 'Bluegumspoort 16 km'. This is a beautiful drive along the summit ridge of the western Soutpansberge, revealing a succession of charming rural scenes – only to be seen in Africa – an intermingling of farms and tribal huts. Here are fine trees including one remarkable avenue-like stretch of tall bluegums, serene indigenous forests, and arresting views across the lowveld. The gravel road ends at a farm gate.

After the turn-off to Bluegumspoort, the N1 road curves into the heart of the Soutpansberge, passing the grounds of the Punch Bowl Hotel (11 km from Louis Trichardt). The road then begins a circuitous and scenic descent into the central valley of the range. At 16 km from Louis Trichardt, the Ingwe Motel regards the view from a vantage-point on the slopes. From here, the road enters a final descent to the fertile valley floor, where citrus groves and farmlands flourish on the red soil. At 22 km from Louis Trichardt the N1 road reaches the famed scenic pass known as Wylie's Poort. The old gravel road through the pass is still to be seen following the stream through the range. The modern road burrows straight through the cliffs by means of two tunnels, opened on 18 November 1961. These two, the 274 m long northern tunnel and the 457 m long southern tunnel, were built after serious washaways destroyed the original pass in 1953.

WYLIE'S POORT AND TSHIPISE

Wylie's Poort was named after Lieutenant C H Wylie who located the original road to the north through it in 1904. To the Venda, the passage is known as *Manaledzi* (place of the stars). Before the deep gorge was blasted open to allow construction of the first road, its facing cliffs almost touched at the top. Baboons could jump across, and it was said that from its depths the stars could be seen shining in the middle of the day. The yellow-coloured lichen high on the dark sedimentary cliffs of Wylie's Poort gives a spectacular touch to an impressive and atmospheric mountain passage.

Immediately north of Wylie's Poort a gravel turn-off stretches east towards the Venda capital of Thohoyandou. At 29 km from Louis Trichardt another turn-off leads west to Waterpoort (27 km) and a little place with the odd name of Alldays (97 km). The Cape-to-Cairo road now makes its way through a charmingly sylvan passage which leads out of the Soutpansberge and, 31 km from Louis Trichardt, into the northern bushveld. Children stand by the roadside, selling seed pods of baobab trees, and the first baobab trees appear just after the road leaves Wylie's Poort.

The landscape is a gently undulating, densely bushed plain. Evergreen mopane trees replace thorny acacia as the most numerous species and the botanical world is dominated by the wonderful baobab trees, which are carefully protected here. The N1 road continues northwards through this parkland. At 39 km from Louis Trichardt there is a turn-off to the Njelele Dam (22 km). This dam, completed in 1948, has a storage capacity of 31 million cubic metres and irrigates 1 867 ha of farmland. Nineteen kilometres further on is the tarmac turn-off to the well-known Tshipise mineral baths (31 km). The name *Tshipise* is a Venda word meaning a hot spring. A popular resort, under the same administration as Warmbaths. Tshipise makes an agreeable stopover for travellers and holiday-makers. The spring, which yields 227 366 l a day at a temperature of 65°C, has been attractively developed in a fine natural parkland of acacia and baobab trees. Poincianas (flamboyants), jacarandas, frangipani and bougainvillaea flourish in the area. The resort is open daily and there are three pools as well as private baths for sufferers from rheumatism. Nearby, on the farm *Nonsiang*, there is a particularly huge baobab – 25,9 m tall and 19,2 m in circumference. It is estimated to be about 4 500 years old and contains about 181 840 l of water.

At Tshipise there are shops, a restaurant, butchery, post office and bank. There is an excellent caravan park and accommodation in chalets and bungalows.

From the turn-off to the Tshipise spring, 60 km from Louis Trichardt, the N1 road continues for a further 34 km through a fine parkland of mopane and baobab trees. Then, 90 km from Louis Trichardt, the road enters the old copper mining centre of ...

MESSINA

Messina takes its name in corrupted form from *Musina* (the spoiler), the word used by early African miners to describe copper, which they found intruding into the iron ore they were smelting. What is known to geologists as the Messina Fault occurs in the area. Hydrothermal action precipitated into this fault a variety of minerals and, from prehistoric times, the area of Messina has been the scene of mining activity. For many years it was the largest copper producer in South Africa. The Messina district also produces substantial amounts of iron ore and magnesite. There are large deposits of asbestos. Diamonds are found in several areas and mined at Venetia. Where the road to Tshipise crosses the Sand River, 10 km from the town, may be found one of the world's geological wonders. In the bed of the river on either side of the old causeway may be seen exposures of what is known as the Sand River Gneiss. Dated at 3 852 million years, this is the oldest datable rock so far found in Africa and amongst the oldest on Earth. This ancient granite has been intruded in more recent times by dolerite in the form of a curious pattern of dark coloured lines. The whole combined mass of rock weaves as though still in liquid motion, instead of having remained in its solid state almost since the birth of Earth.

The Venda call this usually dry river *Munyengedzi* (the river that always brings water). It is notable for the sudden violence of floods.

The Messina area is rich with the relics of prehistoric people. In the valley of the Limpopo River stand several flat-topped remnants of an ancient eroded plain. To early man, these isolated, steep-sided hillocks made natural strongholds. The paintings on the walls of caves, old barricades, fortifications and piles of rubble, provide archaeologists with a valuable field of study. One of these hillocks, *Mapungubwe* (place of jackals), was a stronghold of the long-vanished Leya tribe. It remains a taboo place of strange legends and superstitions. To archaeologists, it has proved to be a veritable mountain of treasure, having yielded beads, bangles, ornaments and plate – all of gold. Mapungubwe is 72 km west of Messina, near the junction of the Shashi and Limpopo rivers. It is an interesting drive through well-wooded ranching country. Near Mapungubwe is another notable hill, *Matshete*, and the hot springs at Evangelina.

By the time Europeans appeared on the scene, the area of modern Messina was covered with bric-à-brac from early mining activities. Adits, shafts and rubble dumps were numerous. The early miners, known as the Musina people, used their women as labourers, utilising iron tools fastened on to wooden handles, ladders made of thongs, and haulage systems consisting of baskets attached to leather thongs. They could work as far down as the water-level, after which they were forced to dig new shafts as they had no pumps or pipes with which to drain their mines.

The ore from the mines was broken by hammers, winnowed in baskets and then placed in furnaces fanned by bellows made of skins. The molten metal-iron or copper-was poured into moulds scooped out of the ground and generally shaped somewhat like cooking pots, each one with a cluster of small legs at the bottom. These strangely shaped ingots were standard trade items, accepted all over Southern Africa and hammered by smiths into a variety of tools and ornaments.

In the 1880s, a prospector in Zimbabwe, John Pasco Grenfell, met a renowned hermit known as Wild Lotrie, who told him of the group of disused mines at Messina. The Anglo-Boer War delayed exploration but in 1901 Grenfell visited the site, guided by Magushi, last known survivor of the Musina tribe. A quick inspection of the workings made Grenfell certain that he was on the surface of a great copper deposit long since abandoned by the early miners.

At the end of the Anglo-Boer War, Grenfell organised a company and sent a prospecting expedition led by Everard Digby to examine the Messina area thoroughly. Their findings staggered the expedition members. The farm *Bergenrode* on the Sand River was, as they described it in a report, *'a veritable mountain of copper ... there must be millions of tons of copper'*.

On 11 March 1904 Grenfell secured a 'discoverer's certificate' for the first claims pegged in the Messina area. In January 1905 the Messina (Transvaal) Development Company Ltd was established to mine the area. The road from Louis Trichardt through Wylie's Poort to Messina was opened in 1907. From then on the Messina area developed. At first the copper ore was carried south in ox-wagons but, when the railway reached Messina from the south on 4 May 1914, the improved transportation enabled production at the copper mines to be increased to a high level.

The village of Messina, the residential and trading centre for the workers, grew with the mines. In 1915 a health committee was formed and on 1 December 1968 Messina became a municipality. Today it has a population of 19 062. The town is notable for its beautiful poinciana (flamboyant) trees, which flower in spring. Just outside the town, on the road to Malala drift, a wonderful old hollow baobab tree grows. Known from the shape of one of its branches as the 'Elephant Trunk', it is preserved in a special little park named after Eric Mayer, a well-known painter of baobabs.

The railway station of Messina has won awards as the best-kept and most beautiful station in South Africa. On 15 January 1915 Frank Bretag, the first station-master of Messina, planted a baobab on the platform. This tree has been a keen train watcher ever since! Other baobabs and many lovely flowering trees grow in the station grounds. There is a collection of historic photographs and old vehicles, including a stage-coach.

The N1 road continues northwards from Messina through densely wooded mopane country. A gentle slope leads for 16 km to the banks of the Limpopo River. Here the Beit Bridge, opened in 1929, and the customs posts of South Africa and Zimbabwe mark the end of the South African section of the N1 (the Cape-to-Cairo road, the Great North Road of Africa), which has led all the way from Cape Town through 1 996 km of remarkably diverse scenery. The Limpopo River was named by the Ndebele *iliMphopho* (river of the waterfall). The Tswana know it as *Noka eya Udi* (river with steep banks). The Venda call it *Vhembe* (the gatherer) and the Mozambique tribes call it *Mete* (the swallower), the two last names referring to the river in flood.

The customs post is open from 06h00 to 20h00 daily. Beyond it, across the *'great grey-green, greasy Limpopo River'* where the curious elephant received its trunk (if Kipling is to be believed in his *Just So* story), there lies Zimbabwe and a long, long journey through the heart of Africa for those travellers with an urge to explore far places, to cross savanna and desert, to behold great rivers, mighty waterfalls, the snows of Kilimanjaro, vast herds of game, secret lakes full of flamingos – and at long last the shores of the Mediterranean.

THE VENDA COUNTRY

From Louis Trichardt a tarmac road leads eastwards along the southern slopes of the Soutpansberge. The vegetation is luxuriantly tropical, with farms producing tropical fruits, nuts, sisal, tea and coffee. Roadside stalls offer for sale varied products. At 42 km from Louis Trichardt the road enters the Venda tribal area. Another 17 km takes the road past the Dzindi Fisheries and Crocodile Farm. Nine kilometres further on (66 km from Louis Trichardt), the road reaches a turn-off leading for 2 km to *Thohoyandou* (head of an elephant), the Venda capital.

The Venda area (707 513 ha in extent) is worth seeing. Roads through it are being expanded and surfaced. Visitors are welcome and there are several beauty spots such as the Phiphidi Falls and Lake Fundudzi. The old copper furnaces at Tshimbubfe are particularly interesting.

Domba dances may be seen by arrangement with Mr Nemurunzini at 082 721-2910, Beth Mashawana at 072 174-5775 or Mashudu Dima at 082 401-9756. There is a museum at Thohoyandou with a full-size chief's residential hut, and a collection of drums and other Venda items. The museum adjoins the national stadium. Woodcraft, basketry, pottery and mats are produced by Venda craftspeople and sold at various wayside stalls.

The population of the Venda area is about 505 000. Their area secured its nominal independence from South Africa in 1979, but its history as a bantustan was dismal. Its first leader, President Patrick Mphephu, was accused of abuses of power. On his death there was a wave of murders connected with witchcraft rituals and the sale of human parts for magical use. Popular protests, riots and agitation pressurised President Frank Ravele to dismiss a cabinet minister accused of participating in witchcraft, and to promise reforms.

There was mounting agitation for the reincorporation of the Venda people into South Africa. The army, under a South African commanding officer, Brigadier P G Steenkamp, then intervened. President Ravele and his cabinet resigned, and the Venda Defence Force's chief of staff, Colonel Gabriel Ramushwana became sole ruler in mid-1989. Although his rule was relatively liberal, there was still a great deal of corruption, oppression, unhappiness and poverty. Even convicts in gaol showed their grievances in April 1990 when they staged a mass break-out from the prison in Thohoyandou, marched to the government offices, presented their complaints and then marched back to gaol. The Venda Bantustan ended in 1994 with reincorporation into South Africa.

From the turn to Thohoyandou the tarmac road continues eastwards. After 60 km the road crosses into Gazankulu, the former self-governing territory of the Shangane people. Another 2 km brings the road to the entrance of the Kruger National Park (134 km from Louis Trichardt). The Punda Maria camp is 7 km beyond the gate.

Chapter Thirty-Two
THE WITWATERSRAND

The *Witwatersrand* (ridge of white waters) is one of the geological wonders of the world and for long has been our planet's principal source of gold. To the eye it consists of a narrow rocky ridge about 80 km long, stretching east to west, with its centre point or hub, the city of Johannesburg, lying 1 748 m above sea-level. Bleak, dry, hazy and swept by frost-laden winds in winter (May to August), the Witwatersrand is green, warm, and pleasantly well washed during the summer months (November to March) by a rainfall of 813 mm which generally falls in the form of spectacular afternoon and evening thunderstorms.

Geologists find the mystery of the Witwatersrand and its treasure-chest of gold to be quite a puzzle. Many theories have attempted to explain the origin of the complicated exposure of rock known as the Witwatersrand Supergroup. This supergroup is sedimentary and is composed of rocks such as quartzite (hardened sandstone), shale and slate (hardened shale). The actual outcrop on the Witwatersrand is about 8 km wide and consists of a succession of upward-sloping layers or series of beds, known from north to south as the Hospital Hill Series, the Government Reef Series, and the Jeppestown Series, all grouped together to form the Lower Witwatersrand Beds. Two other layers, the Main-Bird Series and the Kimberley-Elsburg Series, are together classed as the Upper Witwatersrand Beds.

The nature of the lower beds is largely shale, while the upper beds consist mainly of quartzites impregnated with bands of conglomerate which are composed of quartz pebbles bound together in a fine matrix of siliceous cement containing iron pyrites. The conglomerate is similar in appearance to the favourite old Dutch sweetmeat of almonds in burnt sugar known as *banket*, and it is by this name that it is popularly known.

On the Witwatersrand itself there are three important bands containing this conglomerate: the Main Reef, the Main Reef Leader, and the South Reef. They occur close together and are collectively called the Main Reef Group of Conglomerates. On the Far West Rand, a less important member of this group, the Carbon Leader, is present. At Klerksdorp and in the Free State, the Vaal Reef and Basal Reef, both belonging to the Bird Reef Group, are the principal gold carriers. For the past 70 years these reef groups have together yielded the great bulk of the world's gold.

The origin of this remarkable rock system is cause for much controversy. That it was deposited by water action about 2 500 million years ago is certain, but whether by means of marine, river or even glacial action, remains a mystery. It seems most probable that the site was once an inland sea or lake. Rivers flowed into this ancient sea, depositing a rich spoil eroded from the higher-lying landscape of the Archaean surface of Earth. Included in this deposit, apart from pebbles, sand and silt, were green diamonds, gold and other minerals such as carbon, uranium, iron pyrites and chromite. The distinct layers at the bottom of the sea resulted from variations in the nature of the sediments carried in from time to time, the effects of currents, and the changing level of the inland sea.

Eventually this basin (a dream sea of gold) silted up and vanished. Its ancient bed was left to dry and solidify. During the course of time it was twisted, tilted, faulted, and subjected to extreme fluctuations of heat and cold. Lava intruded into it from subterranean depths. Its richly varied mineral content was partly dissolved and re-precipitated. The ghost of the old dream sea of gold was metamorphosed, and the only verification of its nature is that the gold is there and that water played some part in its establishment, all else is conjecture.

Few early writers of descriptive books on South Africa give much mention to the Witwatersrand. If they do, their description is usually an uncomplimentary reference to the bleakness of the place in winter. Of the summer months, curiously enough, very little was ever noted, although the Witwatersrand at this time has such a spacious and exhilarating freshness to its character, that those who know it best find the summer ample compensation for the drabness of winter.

Scenically the Witwatersrand is unexciting. With its altitude of nearly 1 800 m above sea-level it is a place of rocky, treeless hillocks, plain brown in winter, but green in summer, when the sky can be like a deep blue sea through which there sail and float a dreamy world of cloud ships, and castles, and snow-white fairy islands.

Long before the first Europeans came to the Transvaal, African people made their homes upon the Witwatersrand. In several places the ruins of their village may still be seen, crude stone walls of huts and livestock corrals, all abandoned and left in ruin when raiders and refugees such as the Ndebele (Matebele) invaded their country to escape Zulu disturbances in the south. On the hills in the Eagle's Nest area at Mondeor, Aasvogel Kop, and towards Mulder's Drift, these ruins are numerous. They are melancholy ghost-villages left behind by a vanished people. The defensive stone walls serve only as rockeries for aloes and various succulents. The grass that grows so thickly now in the passageways where countless people once walked, probably has its roots in ground fertilised like the scarlet flowers of the aloes by human blood spilt by such invaders as the savage Matebele who were not exactly gentle sightseers when they visited such scenes as this.

European farmers started to settle on the Witwatersrand around the middle of the nineteenth century with the arrival in the area of the Voortrekkers. Altogether some 75 families established farms along the ridge, running cattle, and planting maize, with a few yellow peach and peppercorn trees for fruit and shade. Of their early deeds and adventures hardly anything is known. They had a drab subsistence living in an isolated situation with no access to any market. If gold had never been found, even the names of these old settlers would scarcely be remembered. They made no history in themselves. Fate simply found them in their solitude. As though by magic, a city sprang up and today their family and farm names are immortalised in the names of suburbs where massive blocks of flats and a prodigious variety of residences now cover the area of their old farm lands.

On the farm *Doornfontein* (fountain of thorn trees) Frederick Bezuidenhout lived. Both his own name, in the form of Bezuidenhout's Valley, and the name of his farm, are part of the modern city of Johannesburg. The 5 000 acres which once yielded him a precarious living in agriculture yielded a fortune in property values alone. *Judith's Paarl*, was the name given to another section of the *Doornfontein* farm, laid out in 1896 as a suburb of Johannesburg. Judith Bezuidenhout, wife of the owner, described it as the *Paarl* (pearl) of the old estate, hence the name. So it was also with the *Turffontein* (fountain of clay), farm of J A Booysen; the *Langlaagte* (long dale) farm, divided up among several people, and many other properties whose owners lived in simple little mud and thatch farmhouses, and would have thought themselves well-to-do if they possessed £50.

There is no indication that any of the prehistoric inhabitants or the early farmers found any mineral deposits other than iron. Somehow, however, a rumour spread abroad that gold was present in the Witwatersrand. As early as 1806 John Barrow published a map of the Transvaal on which the high-lying ridge was indicated and marked as supposedly rich in gold.

The first discovery of gold in the vicinity of the Witwatersrand took place in 1853 when Pieter Marais, a man with experience of the Australian and Californian gold-fields, searched the verges of the ridge in the hope of finding alluvial gold. On 8 October he found a few tantalising specks of gold in a river which has its source on the summit of the Witwatersrand. He named the river the *Jukskei* because he also found in it an old wagon yokes-key. The gold specks had almost certainly been washed down from the heights, but Marais found no positive lead and abandoned the search.

The next discovery in the vicinity of the Witwatersrand was made in 1874 when an Australian, Henry Lewis, found gold on a farm named *Bloubank* (blue ridge) in the Magaliesberg, about 29 km north-west of Krugersdorp. Quite a rush to the scene of this discovery resulted, but little gold was ever recovered there and the excitement petered out.

Several other prospectors fossicked around the Witwatersrand at various times. In 1881, one of them, Stephanus Minnaar, found some gold on the farm *Kromdraai* (crooked bend) 17 km north of modern Krugersdorp. A miniature rush took place to this farm, when it was eventually declared a public diggings on 8 December 1885. Some gold was recovered, but the deposits were too erratic to be payable. A second find was made by J E Erasmus on the nearby farm *Tweefontein* (two fountains), and this discovery attracted to the vicinity of the Witwatersrand its first mill, erected by Sigmund Hammerschlag. This pioneer mill recovered something over £750 worth of gold before the yield petered out.

These early finds on the verge of the Witwatersrand brought little more than heartache to the men who tried to work them. They served, however, the important purpose of attracting to the scene the type of prospector who was hardly likely to abandon the trail once he had found the first faint traces of gold. Among these diehards was Frederick Struben, son of one of the best known of the early settlers of Pretoria.

In January 1884, Struben started to prospect the farm *Sterkfontein* (strong fountain) which adjoined *Kromdraai*. Gold traces had been found on this farm on several occasions in the past. Struben thought it so promising that he floated the *Sterkfontein Junction Mining Syndicate*. With his brother Harry he set out to find the origin of the gold traces and eventually discovered a gneiss vein on a farm named *Wilgespruit* (willow tree stream). The quartz was the richest so far found on the Witwatersrand. Struben named it the Confidence Reef. He displayed some spectacular samples to President Kruger, and could boast of assay values of over 900 ounces to the ton. The brothers erected a five-stamp mill in the Wilgespruit gorge (near modern Florida), but the results were depressing. In six months the Confidence Reef returned a miserable £261 12s 6d worth of gold. The Strubens were bitterly disappointed. They little realised that, in its curious way, destiny had used them for a special purpose and for this, in after years, they were amply compensated.

At the very height of the Strubens' excitement about the reef, two down-at-heel individuals arrived at their camp and asked for work. Struben needed a handyman to help in the camp. He looked over the two applicants and selected for the job, George Walker, a Lancashire man who had been roaming around South Africa for some ten years without much profit.

The second was a quiet individual who passes through the pages of history almost like a ghost whose passage has made an indelible impression, but whose substance is quite intangible. The name of this man was George Harrison. He seems to have come from the Australian gold-fields, but beyond that nothing is known of his origin, age, or appearance. When his more loquacious and forceful companion, perhaps inevitably, secured the position in Struben's camp, Harrison shouldered his kit in silence and went on to the *Langlaagte* (long dale) farm directly on top of the Witwatersrand, where he had heard that Johan Oosthuizen, son of one of the part-owners of the farm, wanted a man to build a house.

It was late in 1885 when Harrison tramped up the slope to the top of the Witwatersrand. We can imagine the man, sun-tanned and with his clothes shabby and weatherbeaten, tramping along, his feet swishing through the long grass, while his eyes contemplated the serenity of the scene around him, with the summer thunder-clouds high in the sky, and the long tailed sakabuli birds fluttering so heavily in the pursuit of their beloveds.

At *Langlaagte* Harrison introduced himself to Oosthuizen and secured the job of building the house. With the security of shelter and three meals a day, the man could then look around him with interest. There was not much to see.

Langlaagte was divided among four owners, Gerhardus Oosthuizen, Andries Breedt, Anna Oosthuizen and Petronella Oosthuizen, whose son had given Harrison the building job. The farm was in open country and remarkable principally for a small grog-shop run by a man named Koos Malan, who had some reputation for the potency of his peach brandy. There was also a small smithy run by a wandering English blacksmith named George Honeyball. Everybody was short of money. Honeyball complained sourly that, after numerous jobs done for F J Bezuidenhout of *Doornfontein* (thorn fountain) farm, the worthy owner of 5 000 acres couldn't pay his bill of 10s and instead offered a sheep in full settlement.

Harrison started work. In his off time he rambled around the farm, chipping rock and examining samples. When and how exactly it happened we do not know, but one day he found an outcrop of the Main Reef of the Witwatersrand on Gerhardus Oosthuizen's portion C of the Langlaagte farm. We can only imagine the initial puzzlement of the man. The Main Reef was the curious conglomerate of which he could have had no experience whatever. He must have crushed a sample dubiously, perhaps simply because he had nothing else to do. He washed the dirt in his old black pan, and then looked down in astonishment to see the first gold ever won directly from the great treasure house of the Witwatersrand.

The date was sometime in March, 1886. Towards the end of that month George Walker arrived, despondent that the fiasco of the Confidence Reef had put him out of work. We like to imagine

Walker's face when Harrison quietly showed his friend the golden samples from the Main Reef.

The two men tried to keep the find a secret while they continued prospecting. Koos Malan's grog-shop, however, soon loosened Walker's tongue. Rumour of the find started to spread. The two men decided that it was time to safeguard the discovery. In his simple little farmhouse, they broke the news to Gerhardus Oosthuizen. The farmer was thrilled at the prospect of a fortune. On 12 April 1886, he worked out and signed an agreement with the prospectors. This was the birth notice of the Witwatersrand and is worth quoting in full.

> *'Contract entered into between Mr Gerhardus Cornelis Oosthuizen on the one part and George Harrison, George Walker on the other part, for the prospecting of gold or precious metals on the quarter farm Langlaagte, the property of the first-named. Firstly. The first signatory agrees and binds himself according to the Gold Law to give to each of the signatories, one claim, reef or alluvial, wherever they may choose. Secondly, that when the other signatories have prospected the farm and found no payable gold or precious metals this contract shall be null and void. Thirdly, when they shall have found payable gold they shall be entitled to a stand and also water to work their gold or mineral with machinery or without machinery.'*

From the date of the signing of this agreement, the prospectors could work in the open. Rumours of the find were already attracting other prospectors to the scene like vultures descending on a kill. Even the blacksmith, Honeyball, was trying to trace the reef. He collected a variety of useless samples and carried them over to the Strubens to have them tested. There was no gold in his quartz, but the Strubens sent Godfrey Lys, who was working for them, over with Honeyball to inspect the farm.

No magician ever materialised a rabbit with greater speed than the whisper of gold produces prospectors. The solitude of *Langlaagte* was gone forever. Men were fossicking around all over the farm. Old Gerhardus Oosthuizen packed up and left the place for a more tranquil scene in the Bushveld. Most of his neighbours did likewise. The days of growing maize and herding cattle on *Langlaagte* were past. Now there was a frenzy in the air, with every man searching for an extension of the conglomerate reef.

Harrison and Walker worked at a great rate proving the discovery. When they were absolutely certain of it, Harrison secured a letter from Oosthuizen introducing him to President Kruger. With this letter he proceeded hotfoot to Pretoria in the last week of July, 1886. In the capital he signed a declaration affirming his confidence in the payability of his discovery, and asking that it be declared a public gold-field.

Two days later, on 26 July, a petition supporting his request was sent from the Witwatersrand, with the signatures of 73 men, including George Walker. In this petition the signatories stated that *'they have been informed and are convinced that gold in payable amount has been found on the portion of the farm Langlaagte. That they are assured of the fact both from personal experience and by the prospector of the said farm named Harrison who has prospected there with the consent of the owner. That they therefore humbly request the Government to take steps to have the said property thrown open as a public digging under the existing gold law'.*

The Government responded to this petition by sending a commission to examine this new field, and to report on the advisability of declaring the area a public gold-field. The two men appointed to the committee were Johann Rissik and Christian Johannes Joubert. By the simple chance of their appointment, the names of these two commissioners was destined to be immortalised in the name of Johannesburg.

The two commissioners could hardly have appreciated the honour that was to come to them when they first viewed the site of the future city. Winter had set in on the highveld, the night winds were sharp enough to chap the knuckles and lips, while the mornings saw the gold-fields white with frost.

Some of the men who made their way to the scene at the very start of the rush have left us remarkable impressions of the place as it was on the threshold of destiny. Willem Auret Pritchard, a young surveyor from the Cape, was one of these pioneers who hastened to the scene, driving along in his Cape Cart, anticipating good commissions in beaconing-off stands and claims. He arrived on the Rand on 22 August 1886. He found it completely desolate. There were no trees for shelter or firewood and no refuge anywhere from the cold dry wind. There was a shortage of everything. One *smous* (pedlar) had arrived, a man named Jackson from Jackson's Drift. All he had for sale was stale bread. He was the first trader of the Witwatersrand.

Another early arrival was Julius Jeppe, who rode over to the Rand from Pretoria as soon as he heard of the discovery of gold. His description deserves quoting in full.

> *'It was a cold, dark night'* he wrote, *'and between eight and nine o'clock I found myself on the crest of a ridge – now known as Hospital Hill – and looking over the wide expanse to the south for my brother, Carl Jeppe's, camp fire. In the wide flat veld at my feet I saw three camp fires at distances of about half-a-mile apart. I made for the most easterly of the three, and by sheer luck I found that it was Carl's. There I found my brother with Henry Nourse – the best sportsman and the finest athlete South Africa ever produced – and Jan Meyer, who was the field-cornet of the locality, as well as the representative of Bezuidenhout, the owner of the farm Doornfontein. The spot was called Meyer's Camp and it was east of what is now the Natal Spruit, where the Meyer and Charlton Mine stands at present. They were in a tent which was sufficiently large to hold Jan Meyer's kartel – his big Dutch bedstead of riempies* (leather thongs) *– on top of which he had his feather mattress. Henry Nourse was asleep on the floor. Carl Jeppe was sitting on the bed trying to persuade Jan Meyer to give him a water-right on Bezuidenhout's farm. It had been arranged previously between Carl Jeppe, the owners of the farm, and Jan Meyer, that they should peg off plots of ground next morning for prospecting purposes. Well, the water-right was under discussion when I arrived. There was a good deal of arguing, a certain amount of indulgence in "creature comforts" – you have all heard of square face gin – and a good deal more arguing. But eventually Jan Meyer's consent was won, my brother obtained his water-right. Early next morning the three of them – Carl Jeppe, Henry Nourse and Jan Meyer – went out with pegs, and a surveyor's chain and they marked out the ground subsequently known as the Henry Norse and the Spes Bona.'*

The claims they pegged on *Doornfontein* farm consisted of 30 in the name of Carl Jeppe, and 34 in the name of Henry Nourse. Both properties flourished and Jeppe's claims saw the erection in October 1887 of the first ten-stamp battery to be erected to work the main Reef Series. This battery stood on the left-hand side of modern Commissioner Street, just before Fordsburg Dip.

Of the other men mentioned in Jeppe's description, Henry Nourse was a renowned personality of the Transvaal, a typical restless adventurer of the golden years of South African prospecting. Born in the Cape in 1857, the descendant of a British naval officer, he had fought and roistered his way through innumerable escapades and actions on the diamond diggings and the alluvial goldfields. He had been agent to George Moodie in the hey-day of the Pioneer Reef in the Kaap Valley. With W K Dow and Ignatius Ferreira, he had started the coach service of Dow & Co, linking Pretoria with the uproarious mining camp of the *Duivel's Kantoor* (devil's office). Now here he was on the Rand, pegging 34 claims which were to be worth a fortune.

The two other camp fires seen by Jeppe on the site of Johannesburg were those of Sam Wemmer in the centre, and Ignatius Ferreira in the West. Wemmer's name became immortalised in the name of *Wemmer's Pan* in the southern suburbs of Johannesburg. Ignatius Ferreira's name is written so vigorously in the pages of the history of South Africa as to need little introduction. He was the descendant of a Portuguese who had been shipwrecked in the Cape. Since his youth he had been involved in nearly every frontier adventure and uproar in the troubled progress of the country. It has been truly said that no single generation, white or black, in Southern Africa, ever went through life without bloodshed and trouble. The weaklings panicked and fled the country to calmer parts. The strong remained and fought it out, knowing the prize to be worth the effort.

Ferreira was one of the toughest of the tough. He had first heard of the Rand discovery while searching for gold in the Limpopo River valley. Hastening to the scene, he made his camp on

Turffontein (fountain of clay) farm, five blocks south of modern Commissioner Street. The strength of his personality and his judicious camp site, made his wagon a nucleus for others. A digger's town grew up around him with such speed that we are told of a farmer who arrived on the scene with a wagon-load of produce for sale. He sold all his produce and then received such tempting offers for his oxen as slaughter animals, that he sold them. He left his wagon and walked home to fetch a span of donkeys to pull his vehicle away. When he returned he found his wagon so hemmed in with shacks that he had to dismantle it entirely in order to carry it away.

Apart from Jackson's stale bread, and Koos Malan's peach brandy (said by drinkers as having the same effect as falling under a two-stamp mining battery), somewhat better fare was soon obtainable on the Rand. Arthur Edgson, who ran a hotel and coach staging post at Muldersdrif, moved his establishment to Ferreira's camp. He called the place the Central Hotel. It consisted of a bar, dining-room, and three bedrooms. Around this relatively princely hotel, dozens of grog-shops and so-called boarding houses sprang up like weeds flourishing for a short time in dank soil. A good few of these places were of the type where the lodgers had their moneybelts bolted around their underpants with a padlock before they went to sleep.

Edgson's Hotel provided accommodation for the two Government commissioners when they reached the Rand early in August. They were met there by about 250 men whose names and personalities, good and bad, will always be part of South Africa's mining history; Cecil Rhodes, J B Robinson, Hans Sauer, B Geldenhuis, H Ellis, and many others, all individuals of the most contrasting types brought together by only one common feeling, their faith in the future of the Witwatersrand.

The commissioners were well wined and dined. They had no doubt about the meaning of the events around them. Men were pouring on to the Rand in hundreds every day and among them were representatives of many of the great financial houses of the world. This was no poor man's diggings. It had all the signs of developing into the greatest gold rush the world had ever known.

With this knowledge the commissioners returned to Pretoria. They advised their Government to throw the whole Witwatersrand open as a public gold-field, with official policy inclined to grant mining leases to properly financed companies. There was no alluvial gold. The conglomerate reef would demand a major mining effort to work it, with costly machinery and immense investment of capital.

The Government responded to the report as rapidly as possible. Carl von Brandis, one of the most popular men every to hold office in the Transvaal, was appointed as Mining Commissioner, with Jan Eloff as his assistant. They rode to the Rand immediately and set up their office in a tent. From the moment the canvas was up, the tent was jammed from dawn till dusk with vociferous diggers registering claims, making complaints and asking advice from the kindly man who was to become known to them as Mr Von Brandis, the father of Johannesburg.

At night when Von Brandis and Eloff closed the office, they simply turned it into their bedroom, Von Brandis sleeping on top of the table, and Eloff underneath. In after years Von Brandis wistfully remarked that he had often envied his junior the comfort of the relatively soft earth. He had occasionally thought of summarily ordering his junior to sleep on the iron-hard table top. Delicate issues of social prestige, however, persuaded Von Brandis to remain on top, rolling crossly from side to side while Eloff snored loudly and contentedly on the good earth underneath.

To Von Brandis fell the historic role, on Monday 20 September 1886, of reading to the excited diggers the proclamation throwing open as gold-fields the farms *Driefontein* and *Elandsfontein*. The following week *Doornfontein* and *Turffontein* were thrown open. *Randjeslaagte* and *Langlaagte* followed on 4 October, while seven days later came *Roodepoort, Klein Pardekraal* and *Vogelstruisfontein*.

In the midst of all the clamour and excitement, the original pioneers were almost bemused. Gerhardus Oosthuizen ceded all rights for 30 years to his portion of the *Langlaagte* farm to the Paarl Syndicate run by H J Schoeman and D F du Toit, who gave him a rental of £100 a month. With this to keep him comfortable for the rest of his life, Oosthuizen quit the scene of gold with no expressed desire ever to return.

George Walker ceded his claim on 2 September 1886, to J M J van Rensburg for £350. He eventually died virtually penniless, wasted with miner's phthisis and alcohol, living largely on a grant from the Chamber of Mines, and handouts given him by various persons who liked to hear some very romantic descriptions of his part in the discovery of the Rand.

As for George Harrison, who started it all, on 16 November 1886, he sold his Discoverer's Claim, No 19, to F W Marsden for £10. Then he vanished from the scene as quietly as he had come. One tradition says that he died of fever somewhere in the hills around Barberton. Another tradition says that he tramped through the Rand three years later, took a long look at the place and expressed the opinion that he was sorry he'd ever done it. Then he tramped off down the dusty road and was seen no more. The golden Witwatersrand and the metropolis of Johannesburg are his memorials.

The site of the discovery of the Main Reef is preserved as the George Harrison Park, 5 km west along the Main Reef Road from the centre of Johannesburg. Old mine workings may also be seen there, as well as an interesting ten-stamp battery of the type used to crush ore in the early days.

The reason for George Harrison's abrupt disappearance from the scene was probably due to his own disappointment at the nature, rather than the immediate value of his discovery. Gold is found in two main types of deposit: alluvial and lode or reef. The prospector, generally an individualist, always dreams of finding a rich alluvial deposit in a stream. With the minimum requirements of capital, the prospector could set up a simple recovery plant and extract gold with little investment other than hard work. There is no happier a man in the world than a prospector who discovers and recovers payable gold from such a 'small working' (as they are called).

The gold-bearing reefs of the Witwatersrand were lode deposits which required the investment of enormous amounts of capital. Individual prospectors could not cope with such discoveries, for they were immediately at the mercy of financiers. Of these gentlemen, it was said that the only time one of them ever seemed to have a glint of kindness in his eyes was when one of his eyes was made of glass and happened to reflect the light!

A simple prospector such as George Harrison fled the scene when the financiers moved in. If one such as he was lucky, he took something away with him; if unlucky he left in rags. Out of the finds these prospectors left behind them, the financiers created a colossal industry. A lode such as the Witwatersrand Main Reef might be difficult to work, involving complex chemical problems of how to release the gold from the rock. From a business point of view, however, while an alluvial deposit was patchy and unpredictable, a reef could be measured, tested, assayed and evaluated as a long-term industrial prospect worthy of vast investment and the employment of an enormous concentration of money, labour and technical expertise.

When the gold-bearing reef of the Witwatersrand was first discovered, it was exposed by open trenches which were dug along its length. The reef was narrow – only 1 m wide for most of its length – and dipped steeply below the surface at an angle of about 20 degrees. The trenches were made as deep as possible, but there were limits to such surface workings. The average proportion of gold in the Witwatersrand reef was 15 g per metric ton (8,75 pennyweights per short ton). For payability of maximum profit, a very minimum of non-gold-carrying ore would have to be extracted. With the reef being so narrow this meant that highly specialised mining techniques were called for. When it became evident that the reef would reach a very deep level, it was even more essential that as little non-productive waste matter as possible be mined, for every rock would have to be hoisted to the surface. The deeper the mine, the more costly the hoisting would be; the more non-productive matter fed into the mill, the more expensive the whole process of gold recovery would become.

In practice, a shaft is sunk to the lowest level planned for current working. On the Rand the deepest level reached so far is 3 428 m. From the shaft, drives are sent out at various levels to intersect the sloping reef. From these drives stopes are worked up the reef, with the excavated ore gravitating down to the drives where it is trammed by electric haulage to the hoisting shaft. The stopes are kept as narrow as possible, excavating the width of gold-bearing reef with just enough space on either side to allow the miners to work. Ventilation and refrigeration on a massive scale have to be provided to make conditions tolerable for human beings; since the deeper the mine, the greater the heat and humidity.

The ore hoisted to the surface is crushed in mills to a fine powder. Mercury is then introduced and this amalgamates with about 70 per cent of the gold. This amalgam is separated from the rest of the material and heated to vaporise the mercury. The gold remains. The mercury vapour is condensed for re-use. The balance of gold has a recalcitrant nature and its recovery demands a more complex chemical process. A solution of sodium or calcium cyanide is introduced which dissolves the gold, producing gold cyanide. Extremely fine zinc powder is then added which displaces the gold in the cyanide solution. The mixture is filtered and the gold is precipitated in the form of black powder. This powder is mixed with fluxes and subjected to heat. Most of the impurities separate to form waste slag. What remains is known as bullion or unrefined gold.

Bullion contains an average of 88 per cent gold, 10 per cent silver and 2 per cent base metals. Bullion is sent to a central refinery, the Rand Refinery in Germiston, for the elimination of all undesirable matter by means of the standard treatment, the Miller Chlorination Process, invented in Australia. This process introduces chlorine gas to the molten gold. Impurities form metallic chlorides with the gas and, being lighter than gold, rise to the surface where they are skimmed off. The remaining matter is known as monetary gold, 99,5 per cent pure gold, while 0,5 per cent is silver. This refined gold is cast into bars weighing about 12,5 kg each. On these bars the exact purity as determined by assay is stamped. A bar stamped 9960 would mean that it is 99,60 per cent pure gold, and is acceptable for monetary and most industrial purposes, as well as for the making of jewellery.

The space age and modern electronics demand gold of ultimate purity. To achieve this purity, refined gold is subjected to additional treatment such as electrolytic refining, during which an electric current is passed through the gold. This current deposits absolutely pure gold on to a cathode. Pure gold is used in electronics to plate vital contacts, and also in printed circuits where high conductive reliability and corrosion resistance are essential. Space apparatus, too, demand this gold. Thin layers are used to provide an outer casing for satellites, since the metal reflects 98 per cent of infra-red radiation and acts as a barrier against solar radiation of high intensity. Astronauts' visors are plated with pure gold to protect them from both ultra-violet and infra-red radiation.

Since gold was discovered in the Transvaal, more than 35 million kilograms (1 100 million ounces) have been recovered. Large mines such as the Vaal Reefs and the Harmony Mine mill more than 5 million metric tons of ore each year. The world's richest mine, West Driefontein, produces 74 000 kg (2,4 million ounces) of gold every year. Apart from gold, also recovered are uranium, silver, platinum and various base minerals of considerable value to industry. Over 500 000 men are employed in the gold-mining industry in the Transvaal (now fragmented into four separate provinces).

The deepest gold-mine in the world is the Western Deep Levels, the main shaft of which goes down 3 581,7 m. The second-deepest gold-mine is the East Rand Proprietary Mine, with a shaft of 3 428 m. To maintain a reasonable working temperature for the miners, the East Rand Proprietary Mine uses 36 284 tons of ice each day.

On the Witwatersrand, the temperature rises 12,2°C for every 61 m descended beneath the surface. The deep mines are working in temperatures of 46,1°C. Although ore is known to extend beyond the 15 244 m level, the technical difficulties of operating at such depths would be staggering and the costs of hauling ore to the surface immense.

By the middle of the 1890s the Witwatersrand was producing over 2 000 000 ounces of gold a year from nearly 200 separate mines. Employed on this production there were over 9 000 Europeans drawing an average wage of £502 a year, and 64 000 Africans whose individual remuneration in cash and food averaged £48 a year.

Out of every thousand employed, five men died and eleven were injured in accidents. In comparative figures this meant that in 1896 one human life was the price of every 11 858 tons of ore mined, or every £23 702 of gold won.

Most of the European miners were of British origin, with such a preponderance of Cornishmen that the Rand underground was, in language and atmosphere, almost a province of Cornwall. Even the engineers and executives adopted the Cornish dialect when they went down the mines. If they retained their normal accents, they were considered as 'putting on side', and were not much regarded by their 'Cousin Jack' employees. Miners worked long hours and suffered grievously from the dread mining disease of phthisis. In their spare time they had an obsession with racing whippets for prize money. Their own families often went short of nourishment to allow the purchase of expensive dog foods supposed to contain secret additives to give the little mutts extra zip in their acceleration.

The African miners came from nearly every tribe in Southern Africa with a good few coming from as far as Malawi and Tanzania. Most of them could speak only their tribal language and had a very simplistic idea of the world. There is quite a saga to be written about their experiences in reaching the mines, in making their way down lonely paths through the bush, in tramping for hundreds of miles to the Witwatersrand and there finding a part for themselves to play as individually minute but vital cogs in the whole complex machine of the mining industry.

In the beginning there was no systematic recruitment of mine workers. Men, African or European, were simply attracted to the Rand by its golden reputation. The cost of living in the place was high, but wages of both black and white workers left them a small margin above their respective standards of living to allow them to effect some saving. To both Africans and Europeans this margin of saving was the real inducement for their labour on the Rand. By far the greater number of them journeyed to the mines intending to make this saving as rapidly as possible and then return home with a minute portion of the wealth of the Rand for themselves. To attain this satisfying ambition the miners had to be prepared, not only for arduous and dangerous work, barrack-like living conditions but also to run the gauntlet of a host of rackets and pitfalls all ingeniously contrived by an unpleasant crowd of human parasites to relieve them of their wages.

It would be fascinating to have some individual record of the average African mine worker of those early years. The book, *The Ivory Trail*, recording the adventures of the famous S C Barnard, known as Bvekenya, one of the greatest *blackbirders* (or illicit recruiters of African labour), provides some account of the business of recruiting. It became profitable, as the demand for African labour increased, for Europeans to busy themselves in recruiting labourers for work on the mines. These recruits were transported to a particular employer. The recruiter received for his efforts a 'capitation' fee for each worker supplied to an employer in a whole and reasonably hearty state.

By the very nature of his employment the recruiter was generally an individual of rugged character. In the old days there was scant control over his activities and techniques. He tramped along the complex of paths which had been blazed through the bush as the first highways of Africa. At each village the recruiter talked to the men, describing in tempting detail the money, adventure and food to be found at the mines.

The best time to recruit was in the years of drought or other hardship. Famine always stimulated the men to leave home and seek work. It was accepted that as soon as a man enlisted the recruiter would clinch the contract by standing him a square meal on the spot. This was the equivalent of a military recruit in the old days receiving the 'King's shilling' from the recruiting sergeant. From that moment the recruit was on the payroll, and liable to serious trouble through breach of contract if he changed his mind or ran away. Another advantage of the meal was that it provided visible demonstration to others of the immediate advantages of recruitment. The greatest advertisement the recruiter could have was his ability to provide a really hearty meal, even in a time of famine. For this reason most of the early recruiters were renowned hunters with generous quantities of venison or elephant meat always ready for the pot.

The successful recruiter would gradually accumulate a sizable gang of Africans who would follow him along the path, enjoying the regular meals and egging on waverers to join them in their happy state. Some enlisted several times, others tried once, and then never again. The women never liked the men going away. It was conventional for the men to sneak off and for the women to show their love by struggling to detain them.

So far as the recruiter was concerned, his destination was a depot at some road or rail-head. Here he would hand over his gang to a labour agent who would pay him the capitation fee depending on the age and vigour of the recruits, generally about £7 for an adult and £4 for a youth. The recruiter would then withdraw to his gin stocks for some relaxation while the Africans were sent to the Rand by train, cart, or even on foot, in a large organised party.

To a man from the primitive bush, the experience on reaching the Rand must have been quite overwhelming. They would be shepherded out of some noisy railway station into a busy, sophisticated street. Generally led by an imposing Zulu boss boy they would make their way to some compound, their minds bedazzled and bemused by the remarkable sights and sounds around them, their eyes full of an almost numb animal-like terror at the nature of the white man's modern world.

In the compound they would be medically examined, deloused, fed, and outfitted with the workaday uniform of the mines; heavy boots, strong trousers and shirts, and mining helmets. This uniform they wore night and day for the duration of their contract. The helmets were considered particularly impressive and they loved to take them home as proof to their women of the nature of the miner's life and its dangers.

On the mines they would be allocated work, which, by the very nature of the primitive African and the fact that most of them only contracted to do 15 months work, could not demand any skill whatever. The average African mine worker, in fact, had a somewhat circumscribed idea, to say the least, of the part he played in the vast juggernaut of the mining industry. He was one of the countless thousands of other tiny cogs, all rotating strictly on their own confined axis in the body of a giant machine. Perhaps the worker spent his time at the bottom of a mine, operating a drill or shovelling rocks. Perhaps he worked on the surface in the mill, enveloped in such a flood of ear-splitting sound as to cut him off entirely throughout his working hours from the normal world of speech. Perhaps he was allocated some specialised task which kept him busy for his contract period on an occupation at once essential, but almost pathetically lowly in the vast industry along the Rand.

The reward of all this labour came to the workers when they set off home. Coming to the mines, the Africans had been ragged, poverty stricken, half-starved and known to all and sundry as *Momparas* or bumpkins. Returning home they were *Magayisas* or rich ones. They had spent very little of their wages during their working months. Returning home they loaded themselves up with treasures. They had new jerseys in stylish football colours, hats, scarves, and cumbersome, gaudily decorated tin or wooden trunks packed with blankets, cloth, and gewgaws for their women. A final touch of affluence would be the acquisition of a concertina or guitar on which to play with seemingly endless identical repetition, a single simple harmony to accompany the whole long journey home.

Bvekenya met one of these Magayisa once, a hundred miles from nowhere, struggling along the path home carrying a large grandfather clock. Bvekenya asked the man what he intended to do with this strange object. *'It will tell my wives when to feed me'*, the Magayisa replied.

From the early years of the Rand there was controversy over the part the unskilled African worker was destined to play in mining. There was general appreciation of the fact that European navvies and skilled miners would be far more productive than the primitive African. These same European workers were used in gold-mines in many countries such as Australia and America and, notwithstanding the higher cost of wages, these mines were profitably worked from ore of very mediocre grade. The inefficiency of cheap African labour was notorious but its availability and low superficial cost produced a pattern of labour relations which pervaded the entire economic life of Southern Africa. This pattern, in short, made it conventional in Southern Africa to accept low individual efficiency from the migrant labourer, but to find compensation in the fact that such labour was readily available at very low rates. The labourer was also below the bottom rung of the ladder of human progress, lacking even any awareness of the most rudimentary ideas of organised demands for improved conditions.

Once the mines accepted the migrant labourer as the basic muscle of the mining industry, the logical policy came to be better, more reputable recruitment than the efforts of the private recruiters, more efficient dispatch of the recruits to the mines, and good care in accommodation, feeding and hospitalisation, for a sick or dissatisfied worker was not only a direct loss through absenteeism, but he was also a bad advertisement to the mines when he returned home and broadcast any complaints to his tribespeople.

The difficulties the primitive African faced in finding his way to the mines were only too obvious. Not only did he have to wrench himself away from the familiar environment of home and chance himself upon the hazards of a strange and alien society, but from the start he ran the gauntlet of parasitic chiefs who expected the lion's share of his earnings, recruiters whose techniques were often as gentle as those of the old British naval press gangs, and endless red tape, bullying and officiousness by Government petty bureaucrats stationed in isolated administrative posts.

As a final harassment, the labourer, travelling on foot, was mulcted of so many fines, tributes and other impositions by police and farmers over whose lands he had to pass, that it was something of a miracle that labourers managed to reach the mines at all. Having once completed their contracts it was another even greater miracle how the workers ever managed to find their way home again with any portion of their wages still intact. As a last imposition, they were often held up and robbed by a collection of so-called 'highwaymen', white and black human rubbish who lurked in the bush and seized by force the treasures and wages of the returning labourers.

All the considerations mentioned above contributed to the idea of a properly organised, central labour organisation to handle the recruitment, transport, distribution to the various mines, and safe return home, of African labourers. It took some years, however, before all mines could agree to such a joint effort, or the time became opportune for its establishment in 1901 in the form of the

Witwatersrand Native Labour Association. In the meantime recruitment continued along haphazard lines with nothing more organised than the Government appointment, in 1893, of a Labour Commissioner to impose some safety checks on working conditions. From that time detailed statistics became available of mining operations, accidents, labour relations and employment figures.

The unskilled African mine workers provided the basic foundation of the entire human community on the Witwatersrand. Above them came the skilled European miners who provided the brains for the Africans' brawn. Those next in the social scale were considered to be the successful merchants, brokers, the minor speculators, and also, as is the nature of things in modern society, a scattering of undetected rogues and well-to-do swindlers. These had by then made medium fortunes in Johannesburg from the sharpness of their wits and found in local society a convenient firmament in which their talents could glitter with little chance of police action or being outshone by the brighter, more genuine luminaries found in older established communities elsewhere.

The aristocrats who lorded it over this whole community of miners and middle class were the big financiers, the so-called Randlords, who controlled the workings of the Rand gold-mines through their companies and share holdings.

Ten main financial houses dominated the Rand at this period. Of these the largest was the firm of *Wernher, Beit and Co* who operated on the Rand through a local organisation, Hermann Eckstein and Co, popularly known as *The Corner House*. The financial resources of this concern were formidable and its reputation in business considered to be absolutely impeccable. Julius Wernher and Alfred Beit, who controlled it, were protégés of the fabulous Paris diamond merchants, Jules Porges et Cie. They had been well trained by their master in the intricacies of finance and the complexities of employing and controlling large numbers of people. Their ventures on the Rand, since the very beginning when they had financed Robinson, included some of the best and largest properties on the Rand. They were technically advanced and in the happy position of possessing not only immense financial resources of their own, but the close and eager support of the most powerful financial houses in Europe, including the House of Rothschild.

In their operations Julius Wernher was the calculating brain working from London. Beit was the active and vivacious local director, while Hermann Eckstein was their methodical lieutenant. Their executives were a shrewdly selected set of men who all played a major part in the history of the Rand. Lionel Phillips, a Londoner who had been with Beit since the Kimberley days; a Frenchman, Georges Rouliot; James B Taylor, a Natal man; and James Percy Fitzpatrick, best remembered by the public perhaps for his beloved literary classic *Jock of the Bushveld.*

A close second in size and power to Wernher, Beit & Co was the *Consolidated Gold Fields of South Africa* founded by Cecil John Rhodes. Rhodes, at this period, was at the height of his power. His remarkable career could only have developed in such spectacular fashion in a young country as rich in opportunity as South Africa. He had emigrated from England in 1870, arriving in South Africa as a sickly youth of 17 years, with very little money and not much enthusiasm at the prospect of a farmer's life in Natal with his brother Herbert. He suffered from a hole in the heart defect and had been castrated in a drastic surgical procedure when he contracted syphilis as a university student.

The following year the two young men abandoned their farm and joined the Kimberley diamond rush. From this point in his life the story of Cecil Rhodes takes on something of the quality of a fairytale. What enchanting godmother he had, who touched him with a magic wand, we have no means of knowing. The sickly youth was quite transformed. Everything he handled seemed to turn to diamonds or gold. By the time he was 20 he had made sufficient money to allow him to enter Oriel College. For the next eight years this extraordinary person alternated between the academic tranquillity of Oxford and the fearsome no-holds-barred human scramble on the Kimberley diamond-fields. When George Harrison discovered the Witwatersrand main reef, Rhodes had already attained full academic honours along with fabulous wealth and power after eight years of contrasting, dutiful, study in England and unparalleled virtuosity and dominating leadership in financial organisation and control in Southern Africa.

On the Rand, after a hesitant start, when his technical advisors misguided him into the belief that the new discovery was just another Barberton, Rhodes had made up the leeway with his customary speed. By the mid-1890s Rhodes was the dominating figure on the Witwatersrand. Wernher and Beit might have had a larger organisation there, but they were quite overshadowed by the personality of Rhodes. Their two giant concerns were on amicable and co-operative terms.

Their combined financial resources reached staggering proportions. Rhodes would not have been human if he had not become heady with his own power. He felt himself to be the tool of destiny in Southern Africa. He knew that he had the means to shape its still new and pliable form. He overshadowed it, just as he dominated the world diamond trade; his Chartered Company had all Southern Rhodesia in its sole control; he had members of the British royal family on his boards of directors and he had attained such personal political power that he was Prime Minister of the Cape.

Rhodes' principal henchman was his partner, Charles Dunell Rudd, joint managing director of the Gold Fields company, and an old associate of his on the Kimberley diamond fields. He was nine years older than Rhodes and was responsible for the methodical management, while Rhodes controlled policy and enterprise. The two men held the 200 Founder's shares in the original Gold Fields of South Africa Ltd, and these carried three-fifteenths of the profits of the company. The two men received another two-fifteenths of the profits as remuneration while they held their managerial positions. As a personal income Rhodes at this time was receiving some £300 000 each year. When the original Gold Fields company was re-organised in August 1892, as the *Consolidated Gold Fields of South Africa Ltd,* Rhodes and Rudd received the right to 8 per cent of its profits. The first annual accounts of the new company, which had been re-organised mainly to embrace deep level properties, showed a profit of £207 455 and declared a dividend of 10 per cent. The founders' shares where transformed to the Company in 1895 in exchange for 100 000 R1 shares which were valued at the time at £12 a share.

The third of the great Rand mining concerns was the Johannesburg Consolidated Investment Co run by one of the most unusual personalities produced by either the Kimberley or Witwatersrand rushes. This individual was the nimble-witted, elusive Barney Barnato, whose real life story, if staged as a play, would be dismissed as quite unbelievable.

Barney Barnato started life in the East End of London. He was named Barnett Isaacs in those days, and had no known aspirations other than to follow the humble career of his father, a simple Jewish shopkeeper running a poky little store in Aldgate. Forced by lack of money to leave school at the age of 14, Barnett became a learner barman in the King of Prussia bar, owned by his brother-in-law, Joel Joel. Long hours of washing glasses in the bleary-eyed, loud-voiced atmosphere of a particularly sleazy type of bar, provided the impressionable Barnett with an interesting finishing school and a high cultural polish to his character. All the assorted expressions, questionable jokes, brash good fellowship, and low humour of a world peopled by drunkards left an impression on Barnett which he never lost. To a youth of 14, the ultimate sharpening of his character came when his respected superiors taught him the secrets of successful short-changing of fools and drunkards, and the unerring ability to assess just how much, and how ready, an individual was for plucking.

Passing out from his 'finishing school', Barnett went on the stage, working an act with his brother Henry and doing the rounds of the cheap music halls. At this period came the change of name. Isaacs seemed to lack glamour. Searching around for an alternate, Barnett remembered the stage manager calling him on stage with a slurred 'Barney too!' From this came the name Barnyto, then Barneto, and eventually the Barnato which was to make no little commotion and create no mean respect for itself in the mining circles of the world.

The theatrical partnership came to grief when diamonds were discovered in the Cape. First Henry, and then Barney made a hurried way to the scene. Barney actually arrived in Cape Town with little save his personal clothing and all his money invested in 40 boxes of rather venomous cheap cigars which the young man considered might be sold at high profit to the diamond diggers. He had to walk the 600 miles to Kimberley as he had no money to pay for transport.

Barney was in his element on the diamond fields. Kimberley was like a gigantic bar, crowded with gamblers, touts, wide-boys, tough guys, hard-cases, and swindlers. To a man trained in the bar-room technique of keeping one ear cocked to the cash-register and the other to the gossip and rumours, mixed up with the jokes and inanities of drunkards, Kimberley provided unparalleled opportunities. Within five years of his arrival Barney Barnato was one of the princes of the world of rough diamonds and at the beginning of a tremendous struggle with Cecil Rhodes for the right to wear the ultimate crown. Rhodes won, through a superior genius for deploying financial allies, but the terms of victory left Barnato not only a life governor of De Beer's Consolidated Mines, but also its largest single shareholder, and one of the wealthiest men in the world.

Barnato's principal henchmen were his nephews, Woolf, Solly and Jack, the sons of Joel Joel of the King of Prussia bar. These young gentlemen, at the time their successful uncle summoned them to Kimberley, had been reduced to earning spare money by investing their bar tips in a flock of homing pigeons. These birds they hawked around as children's pets. As the birds returned home to the bar in most dependable fashion by escaping as soon as anybody started to play with them, the partners could never run out of stock no matter how many pigeons they sold.

Other associates of Barnato who were destined to leave their names in mining history, were the engineers John Hays Hammond and Gardner Williams; Barnato's deputy on many company boards, William Rogers; Ernest Oppenheimer and Gustav Imroth, nephew of the remarkably named, Anton Duenkelsbuehler.

Barnato's entire organisation was noted for its liveliness and quick-thinking. When news reached Kimberley of the Witwatersrand, Barney and Solly Joel hastened there, riding in a resplendent private coach and four, appropriately gilded, and padded with red plush. There was a tale that Barney had bought the thing from a bankrupt Cinderella pantomine company. On the Rand, Barnato bought his way into a variety of properties, organised his *Johannesburg Consolidated Investment Company*, and amused himself in his spare time as the central figure in a society of visiting players, pugilists, punters, and promoters of profitable propositions. The letter 'P', for some reason, had great attraction to him in the profession of his male and female acquaintances.

After the big three companies on the Rand, there were several smaller concerns whose activities, however, were large enough to make them play a significant part in mining and financial history. The J B Robinson group was the largest of these companies. Its efforts were concentrated mainly, but not exclusively, on the West Rand, and its leader was the famous J B Robinson, whose opinionated nature and reputation for ruthless business methods, made him the most unpopular of all the big Rand financiers.

Sigismund Neumann, who controlled such properties as the West Rand Consolidated Mines, was another of the big ten Rand Company directors who had started financial life in Kimberley. George Albu, with his *General Mining and Finance Company* had also originated in Kimberley. On the Rand he ran the highly profitable Meyer & Charlton property, which, in 44 years of working life, returned £26 for every £1 share. Abe Bailey, a protégé of Rhodes, founded the *South African Townships Mining and Finance Corporation*, and was another of the financial stars. He was considered to be a great 'sport' and had quite a reputation with the gloves.

Adolf Goerz, who founded the *Union Corporation*, had originated as an investigator of the Deutsche Bank. He was one of many German Jews to emigrate to South Africa with the discovery of diamonds and gold. George Farrar, on the other hand, had originally come to South Africa from England in order to sell mining machinery. He went into big business, and organised the *Anglo-French Group*. With Carl Hanau he founded the *East Rand Proprietary Mines* in 1895, and was a most active man in both business and politics. His partner Hanau usually looked the complete part of the big time financier, with a most imposing presence, immaculate dress, and a fabulous astrakhan coat. Surmounting everything was a silk top-hat which he wore so frequently that it was popularly considered that he slept in it.

Sam Marks and Isaac Lewis, two Russian Jews, who ran the *African & European Investment Co*, also ranked with the top ten companies. Their interests, however, were largely concerned with landed properties and secondary industries. They seemed to have their hands on nearly every spare piece of land in the Transvaal. Some 300 separate farms, covering 3 000 000 acres of the Transvaal, were held by this concern. The two partners conducted their affairs mainly in Yiddish, although Marks learned Dutch so well that he became very friendly with President Kruger. An amusing story tells us of an encounter between the two on the Pretoria railway station. The departure of the train to Johannesburg was delayed but President Kruger was in high good humour. *'Tell you what, Sammy,'* he said. *'Let's you and I have a race up the platform. If you win, you become President: if I win, you turn Christian!'* Marks declined. History missed its most memorable race!

Marks was one of the few of the Rand financiers with whom Kruger ever chose to exchange a joke. For the rest of the financial giants, the old President had little time and fewer words. They moved in a world of which he knew little, and had the greatest mistrust. Their opinion of him was similar to that expressed in after years by Chief Justice Kotzé, who looked back on Kruger through somewhat bitter eyes, and described him as *'obstinate and impatient of contradiction, abrupt and at times uncouth in manner, egotistical and selfish, with an eye to his own advancement'*.

That the President was also shrewd, determined and courageous, was generally admitted. Barney Barnato, of all the big financiers, had the greatest sympathy for Kruger.

> 'The Transvaal Government', he said, 'is like no other government in the world. It is indeed, not a government at all, but an unlimited company of some 20 000 shareholders which has been formed to exploit a large territory, and after being unable for 30 years to pay any dividend or even to pay its clerks, suddenly struck it rich. There was neither capital nor skill in the company itself for development, and so it leased the ground to those who had both ... They had a hard time in the early years and Kruger thinks they are entitled to all they can get now. That is all right and quite in my line'.

Kruger's opinion of the financiers varied from heavy suspicion to outright hatred. Rhodes, as the dominant leader of the big men, and the most resolute promoter of British expansion in Africa, was a figure who loomed large in Kruger's mind from the very beginning.

> 'In spite of the high eulogiums passed upon him by his friends', wrote Kruger sourly in after years, 'he was one of the most unscrupulous characters that have every existed. The Jesuitical maxim that the end justifies the means formed his only political creed. This man was the curse of South Africa'.

We have no counter opinion of Kruger uttered by Rhodes. The two men were entirely dissimilar in background, circumstances, culture and ambition. Kruger personified a rural state: Rhodes thought in global terms. Kruger was sedate; Rhodes was explosive. Kruger was conservative to the point of reaction; Rhodes could only have shouldered his way to the top of the mining world by being mercurial in decision and an aggressive, ruthless promoter of new ideas and projects. The rigidly conservative suit of administrative clothing in which Kruger insisted on dressing the Transvaal could only appear both inadequate and slightly ludicrous to a man like Rhodes, just as Kruger was constantly resentful at the bursting of the seams in the suit by the staggering growth of the mining industry.

Visits to the gold-mines are possible only if you are able to go on 'stand by'. Due to production and safety constraints, the Chamber of Mines runs tours of gold-mines for specialist interest groups on request. Members of the public can join these groups if there is space. The tours include several hours underground and are therefore not advisable for anyone who suffers from claustrophobia. Children under 16 years of age are not allowed. Phone (011) 498-7100 for information.

The African loves to dance. He regards it as a recreation, an exercise, an opportunity for display – the supreme expression of his zest for life. A miner's work is arduous and dangerous, his society exclusively male. He lives in barrack-like compounds for the duration of his contract period (usually at least one year) and his women are far away back home. For him the journey to *eGoli* (the place of gold) is the greatest experience of his life, a completely new environment, life-style, type of labour and society.

Men from about 50 different tribes work on the Witwatersrand. To converse with one another, and the European mineworkers, they quickly learn a simple language common to all, known as *Fanakalo* (like this). Fanakalo consists of mainly a Zulu vocabulary interspersed with odd words from several other African languages while English and Afrikaans provide the technical terms.

In his leisure time, the African mineworker takes part in sport, watches films, attends self-improvement classes in subjects such as reading, writing and various handicrafts. There is singing, tribal music, African jazz and also dancing; in this manner he can revert to the skins and adornments of his own people, can look and feel his best when dancing in groups of his own kind, displaying to others his physical prowess and competitive spirit.

The dancers organise themselves into teams, each having a manager as well as a music and dance director. Costumes are designed and rehearsals are held in preparation for Sunday mornings – the big day for tribal dancing.

The music is powerful, the rhythms explicit and demanding. Variations are imposed on a basic rhythmic theme which is established at the beginning of the piece. Most of the melodies are pentatonic (consisting of five notes) but some of the tribes, particularly those from the Northern Province and Zimbabwe, use hexatonic (six-note) and even heptatonic (seven-note) scales. The principal dances are as follows.

The various tribes of the Nguni-speaking group – Zulu, Hlubi, Bhaca, Nhlangwini, Pondomise, Pondo, Zingili and Swazi – who live along the south-east coast, specialise in what is known as the *Ndlamu* dance, performed by young men in single or double lines who stamp their feet in different ways to diverse tempos. Each tribe has its own complex variation of this dance. Music is provided by clappers, bells and various kinds of drums. From all the groups, individuals spring forward at different times and perform a *giya* or war dance; jumping, brandishing sticks, throwing their bodies about and shouting vainglorious self-praise.

In the same Nguni-speaking group, the Xhosa perform an *amaKhwenkwe umleyo* (young men's shaking dance); with rapid backward and forward movement of the knees, the dancers make their chests and spines ripple, tinkling small bells strapped across their upper bodies.

The Bhaca tribe have an amusing dance of their own, known as the *isiCathulo* (boot dance). Of this dance, it is said that a missionary once forbade his community to perform their traditional dances, as he considered them to be pagan. They were taught a more 'genteel' Austrian folk-dance. It happened that some of the tribesmen working in the docks in Durban were issued with wellington boots. The 'new' dance, performed in these cumbersome boots, became popular and there was nothing the missionary could do, since the idea was originally his!

The Sotho–Tswana-speaking tribes have a completely different series of dances from the Nguni-speaking tribes. The Sothos perform a *Mohobelo* (striding dance), making a unique entrance to the dancing area by sliding, striding, slithering and hissing. They favour high kicks and stamping, leaping and twisting into the air. Another of their dances is the *Stapu* (walking dance), in which they move rhythmically backwards and forwards.

The Pedi tribe of Mpumalanga perform a *Kubina dithlaka* (pipe dance). Each dancer plays a pipe of a different tone. As they dance, they blow their pipes in succession, producing a series of unique melodies, like the chords on a concertina. Leg rattles and drums provide the rhythm.

The Tswana or Lete people from Botswana also have a *Kubina dithlaka* (pipe dance) which is similar to that of the Pedi tribesmen, but varies slightly in sound, melody and performance.

The Shangane–Tsonga people from Mozambique perform a modern dance known as the *Makwaya*. Providing a source of great amusement, the participants poke fun at the modern world and the ways of the white man, their bosses on the mines, the missionaries back home, the tax-collectors and Government officials.

The Tswa from Mozambique perform a complex *Nzumba* or *Ngalanga* (step dance), using small wooden xylophones for music.

The Tshopi tribe from Mozambique have the *Ngodo* (orchestral dance), and musically this is the most fascinating sound in Africa. Wooden xylophones are used and the standard of playing is excellent. An outstanding player is highly regarded and honoured by his people. Orchestral performances in the homelands are superb – a full *Ngodo* has up to sixteen movements.

The Ndawu tribe, also from Mozambique, perform a *Mutshongolo* (stumbling dance), which involves skilled acrobatics. The men burst into the dancing area; somersaulting, throwing themselves on to the ground and bouncing along on their hands and toes, clowning in many ingenious and amusing ways. Their drummers are masters of rhythm, and a good performance always brings the house down.

EXPLORING THE WITWATERSRAND

The Witwatersrand is not regarded by many people as a holiday resort. Any traveller condemned to negotiate the full 96 km length of the Rand from Springs to Randfontein during a rush-hour period (from 16h30 onwards on a Friday) would consider himself to be in purgatory.

The towns and cities are linked together by kilometres of similar-looking streets congested with seemingly demoniac drivers and heedless pedestrians. Look-alike shops – commercial clones – line the streets and there are few exceptional features.

This does not imply that the towns and cities are unpleasant. Towns such as these may be seen in most industrial and mining areas of the world, but at least the inhabitants of the Witwatersrand have the consolation of being able to breathe reasonably unpolluted air at least during the summer months. They can bask in generous sunshine and, leaving their high ridge, can escape to the vast, rolling kilometres of open veld where claustrophobia is unimaginable.

Winter is a bleak season – dry, hazy and swept by frost-laden winds. Grass-burning is common, polluting the atmosphere, blackening the landscape which, as a result, seems to be in mourning. Spring transforms the place into a beautiful Cinderella. Green, warm and washed by thunder-storms, she is sparkling, vivacious and stimulating. In autumn, she reluctantly sneaks back as late as possible before the stroke of midnight into the drab colours, smog, cold and toil of winter.

Activity along the Rand east and west of Harrison's discovery expanded rapidly as prospectors discovered the lie of the Main Reef and learned more of its peculiar nature. The West Rand was centred around the *Randfontein* farm bought by J B Robinson. It developed under the impetus given by the faith of its financier-owner. Robinson, after acting as purchasing member of Beit's syndicate, had detached himself from that body. He took with him as his share of the venture, the West Rand property, which the dominant members of the syndicate considered to be the least valu-able. All his life Robinson felt galled that the one property which carried his name, the *J B Robinson Mine*, produced a fortune in gold, but never yielded him a farthing for it was retained for working by the syndicate. The *Randfontein* property, however, which cost Robinson only £500 to buy, yielded him compensation enough to satisfy most men.

The East Rand developed in the same fashion, as the prospectors extended their knowledge of the position of the Main Reef. The first farm to be proclaimed there was *Klippoortje* (stony pas-sage) on 17 January 1887. From then, there was a succession of discoveries along the East Rand. These discoveries were not only of gold. In December 1887, a German prospector named Johann Gauf found a deposit of medium quality coal. The importance of the situation of this coal far out-weighed inferiority in quality. The fuel hungry Rand had to cart in its coal laboriously by ox-wagon all the way from the rich coal seams at Witbank. Gauf's discovery was a real boon.

Gold soon followed coal in mining on the East Rand. One of the best known of the pioneer ven-tures was developed on the farm *Elandsfontein* (fountain of elands) which, we are told, had been acquired by its owner, J G Meyer, in exchange for a bullock wagon. As a farm, the place had never yielded its owner enough to make him consider it was worth its price. At the height of the rush to the Rand, however, a trader John Jack from Lake Chrissie in the Eastern Transvaal, happened to cross *Elandsfontein*. He diverted himself by prospecting the farm, and found gold.

This was the start of the Simmer & Jack Mine, floated by John Jack and his trading partner, August Simmer. One of the characters of the boom days was the manager they employed, an Australian prospector named Charles Knox. In less fortunate days, Charlie Knox had been as tough as the best of them. He had prospected the farm in detail for his employers and lived on lit-tle better than the celebrated South African hard-tack diet of mealie pap and boerewors. Appointed mine manager in reward for his labours, Charles Knox blossomed out into a classic picture of a successful prospector, with silk top-hat, black frock coat, umbrella, and a sizable gladstone bag.

The Simmer & Jack Mine produced, as its offspring, the town of Germiston. This was laid out in May 1887 to house the mine workers. John Jack named it in memory of the farm near Glasgow on which he had been born.

The Simmer & Jack mine continued in operation until 1964, by which time it had produced 448 000 kg (15 802 469 ounces) of gold.

GERMISTON

Germiston became a municipality in 1903 and a city in 1950. It is today the largest railway junc-tion in Africa and a major industrial centre. It is the site of the world's largest gold refinery, the Rand Refinery, with an annual output of 73 per cent of the world total of gold produced outside Russia. There are over 2 000 factories in Germiston which has 164 249 inhabitants. Among its recreational facilities is Germiston Lake (a 57 ha expanse of water), the largest on the Witwaters-rand and a favourite place for boating, swimming and picnicking, with a 40 ha surrounding park.

At the western entrance to Germiston stands a remarkable illuminated fountain which resem-bles the working headgear of a gold-mine with skips travelling up and down. It is named after W A Boshoff, a local mining magnate. The various tailings dumps around Germiston include some of the largest and most colourful of their kind. Photographers and those interested in mining his-tory find the area rich in fascinating scenes and relics. On the old Balmoral Mine a huge tailings wheel, 16 m in diameter, still stands on its original supports.

The busiest civil airport in South Africa, the Rand airport, is close to the city. The 94 ha Rondebult Bird Sanctuary has a variety of 102 species of resident and migrant waterfowl. It was established in 1971 as a sanctuary, a joint venture of the Germiston City Council and the Transvaal Nature Conservation Division. There are observations hides. It is open daily 07h00 to 17h00. A number of highveld species of antelope and other animals also have their home there.

The greater Germiston area, with a Local Council, was formed on 26 October 1994. It includes Germiston, Bedfordview, Palm Ridge and Katlehong. The Katlehong Art and Cultural Centre in Germiston displays the artistry of the African People of Katlehong.

BOKSBURG

In September 1886 a prospector by the name of P J Kilian found gold on the farm *Leewport* owned by Carl Ziervogel. It was not a very prosperous agricultural area and Ziervogel had been trying to sell his property but had found no buyers. Kilian's discovery changed the picture. A second prospector, Adolf Vogel, also registered a claim for a discovery on an adjoining unallotted farm named *Vogelfontein*. On 10 March 1887 the two farms were proclaimed as public diggings.

Ziervogel opened the first gold-mine on the East Rand, the Ziervogel Gold Mining Company, with an American manager and a staff of young miners from Cornwall. Lack of capital crippled this pioneer mining venture. In 1894 the owners sold the property to the Johannesburg Consolidated Investment Company. Mining rights passed through various hands but over 100 years after its discovery gold is still being produced on *Leeuwpoort* by the ERPM (East Rand Proprietary Mine), which proved to be one of the most profitable of all the Witwatersrand mining ventures.

Other mines were also active in the area, and the need for a town convenient to them all became apparent. The Government surveyors abstracted land from *Leewpoort* and adjoining farms. In 1887 the first stands were offered in a town which was named *Boksburg* after Eduard Bok, the then Attorney-General of the South African Republic. Government offices, shops and two hotels, the Masonic and the Central, were hastily erected. The town started to grow. During the next year, 1888, coal was discovered right on the boundary of the town, and this gave Boksburg a considerable importance. Coal was urgently needed on the Witwatersrand and here was a worthwhile deposit in the heart of the gold-mining industry. The first coal-mine was Gauf's Mine, named after its manager, J L Gauf. The Good Hope Mine was started by T R Ziervogel, the Ferndale by the Reverend R E Davies; and there were several others.

High grade fire-clay was also found near Boksburg and the town grew rapidly. It was fortunate that the first mining commissioner appointed to the place was Montagu White. On reaching the town, this official was not much impressed with the place. He said afterwards that he considered it one of the 'most uninviting spots he had ever seen'. The country was then in the grip of a severe drought. The grass was dead, and the two things dearest to him – trees and water – were almost non-existent.

The Government had already received urgent pleas from the transport riders to provide water for their draught animals. A small dam had been built by the government at *Vogelfontein* to satisfy the thirst of the transport animals but it was hopelessly small and more mud than water. White was instructed to do something about the problem. He did this willingly. He used convicts to build a dam across the stream and visualised a lake on so magnificent a scale that President Paul Kruger was aghast when he saw the size of the project during a visit in 1889. *'White'*, he said, *'this will not be a dam. It will be an inland sea, what will happen if the wall breaks?'* The old President, however, was partial to Boksburg. He owned a farm nearby named *Geduld* (patience) which he later sold at good profit when gold was discovered on it.

The President forgave White, but there was a problem. In the drought there was no water to fill the dam. Half the local miners were wagering that the dam would never fill and the other half were prophesying a general inundation if it did. It remained depressingly empty for two years. It became known as White's Folly. Then, one summer night in 1891, there was a thunderstorm that sounded like the crack of doom. The rain came. In the morning the good (and bad) people of Brakpan awoke to find White's Folly overflowing with water. It has never been empty since then. In 1898 Boksburg held its first regatta on the lake and attracted 10 000 people.

By that time Montagu White had planted 40 000 trees around the lake in what is now know as Plantations. The problem of transporting the coal and fire-clay from the town had been eased by the surreptitious building in 1889 of what was called the Rand Tramway, a light railway from Johannesburg to Boksburg, and thence on to Springs. The line had to be built as a tramway supposed only to carry passengers. The established lobby of transport riders in the Pretoria Volksraad resisted ideas of a railway, as such a construction would undermine their business. The little railway came, with the rolling-stock brought up from the coast in pieces carried on ox-wagons.

The coal-mining, unfortunately, ended disastrously. An underground fire broke out in 1894 on the Holdfast Coal-Mine. It was inextinguishable. It spread to the other mines and the gases made it impossible to resume work. However, gold-mining continued.

A famous mine developed in these parts was *The Chimes*. This was the result of the discovery of gold in September 1887, on a farm named *Benoni*. The Chimes mine became a particular haven for Cornishmen on the Rand. The Cousin Jacks, with no SPCA to restrain them, were devotees of dog fighting, and some murderous affrays were organised there. Another local entertainment took place each payday. A long line of cabs would arrive from Boksburg, then the nearest town. As soon as the men knocked off, they would choose their cabs and for high stakes race one another to one of the Boksburg pubs, causing an appalling cloud of dust from an execrable road. There was a regular sweepstake to be won by the first cab to reach the pub.

A considerable variety of industries were established in Boksburg other than mining. Electric motors, transformers, nuts and bolts, bitumen, veneered and laminated board, concrete piping, detergents, domestic appliances and many other useful things are produced in the town today.

Boksburg has several interesting buildings including an impressive Civic Centre, the old Law Courts designed by Sytze Weirdo for the government in 1890, the St Michael and all Angels Anglican Church designed by Sir Herbert Baker, with magnificent mural paintings by John Henry Amshewitz and the old post office in market street, now the headquarters of the Boksburg Arts and Cultural Societies.

Boksburg became a municipality in 1903. Its population is 263 178.

From the centre of Boksburg it is 8 km to the centre of the town of ...

BENONI

It is said that the irregular shape of the farm on which the modern town stands, wedged between two older farms, gave its original surveyor so much trouble that he borrowed from the Bible the name Rachel had given Benjamin – *Benoni* (son of my sorrow). Gold was discovered on the farm in September 1887 and in due course the celebrated mine by the name of The Chimes commenced production there. For some reason this mine was a great centre for Cornishmen who comprised the total white work-force. The book *Lost Trails of the Transvaal* relates that the collection of shanties which served as the mine's housing estate was a favourite place for gambling and dogfights.

The town of Benoni only came into existence in March 1904 when the first sale of stands took place. The foundation and early development of the town was largely due to the work of Sir George Farrar, chairman of the mining syndicate which owned the ground. On his instructions thousands of trees were planted, the Homestead lake was stocked with rainbow trout, and the town laid out on spacious grounds. Today there are over 30 parks, with walks and nature trails, and five lakes with more than 40 km of shoreline. On 1 October 1907 it became a municipality and today 366 343 people live there.

Benoni is one of the most pleasant towns on the Rand. A 44,2 ha nature reserve, the Korsman Bird Sanctuary, has been established as a safe home for 160 species of birds and several species of mammals. There are first-class sporting facilities at Willowmore Park, Rynfield Children's Park, known as Bunny Park, provides a delightful children's playground with hundreds of rabbits, tame sheep and birds. Bullfrog Pan in Rynfield is a sanctuary for the African bullfrog *(Pyxicephalus adspersus)*. Sandpan and Leeupan are conserved wetlands used by a multitude of birds.

For those who believe getting there is half the fun, there is the Benoni Lakes Express – a vintage steam train from Johannesburg. The train stops at Northmead Station next to the Danie Taljaard Park, which is an ideal spot for picnicking and watersports.

A variety of industries are centred in the town, producing batteries, jute, asbestos products, light castings, valves, brake linings and wheel rims, railway trucks, hose-piping and teapots.

The commercial centre of Benoni contains an attractive pedestrian shopping mall and a considerable variety of shops. A monthly large-scale flea market is held in the centre of the town. Street entertainments, arts and crafts, exhibitions and a considerable amount of good eating provide an enjoyable local life-style. A drawcard is the Benoni Lane of Fame, where the footprints of well-known people are embedded in the concrete.

Outside Benoni, at a place with the Hebrew name of *Jatniel* (God gives), are the headquarters of the religious sect known as the Latter Rain Mission which had its origin in 1927 when nine women members of the Pentecostal movement developed the belief that, through a regimen of prayer and fasting, the Holy Spirit would descend upon them, giving such powers as healing, prophecy and the ability to speak in 'tongues'.

After nine months of prayer and fasting, one of the group, Mrs Mara Marta Fraser, claimed that God had spoken to her and directed the establishment of a church. It was named Latter Rain because of a belief that, after Jesus went to Heaven, there was an outpouring of rain of the Holy Spirit. According to the sect, the Second Coming of Christ is near and will be preceded by another outpouring of holy rain.

Female members of the sect wear a neat blue dress and in South Africa are popularly known as *Blourokkies* (blue dresses). Male members wear beige suits, white shirts and black ties. Shoes are removed before attendance at services and prayer is a way of life. The sect is known for its cleanliness and self sufficiency. At Jatniel members busy themselves in workshops, a printing press, gardens and other activities. The well-known blue dresses are made at Jatniel and members wearing them may be seen all over Southern Africa and overseas.

Eight kilometres from the centre of Benoni lies the next East Rand town of ...

BRAKPAN

With its population of 171 361, *Brakpan* was originally a farm named on account of a small lakelet of brackish water which was found in the vicinity. The area came into prominence when coal was discovered and the first railway in the Transvaal, the old 'Rand Tram', was built to carry coal from this and other East Rand coal-mines to Johannesburg.

The town of Brakpan had a slow beginning and only became a municipality in August 1919. Besides being a mining town, it has developed into a modern industrial centre. Recreational facilities include Hosking Park and Jan Smuts Park created on the shores of the VFP Dam.

The last East Rand town is reached 6 km from the centre of Brakpan.

SPRINGS

This town was established on the farm of *Springs* which was named on account of the number of fountains there. The importance of the area increased when coal was discovered in 1888. In 1890 the first railway in the Transvaal, the so-called 'Rand Tram', was built to carry coal from the East Rand coal-mines to Johannesburg. The line terminated on the *Springs* farm and six collieries commenced operations in the area.

The railway terminus formed the nucleus of a town whose first inhabitants were principally Welshmen employed as coal-miners. Inevitably, the Springs Male Voice Choir was established and became well known in the Transvaal. The coal-mines, however, underwent several unfortunate experiences. The ZASM Colliery, situated between the present railway station and the town hall, caught fire early in 1899 and had to be closed. On 21 March 1907 a major subsidence occurred in the Great Eastern Colliery, causing the houses of the mine captain and engineer to collapse into the excavation, with one of the mine captain's children being killed.

Coal-mining in the area was gradually abandoned. It was replaced by gold and industry. Springs became a municipality in November 1904 and has a population of 163 303. It is now a substantial industrial centre where factories produce paper (Sappi), cosmetics (Vanda), glass (Pilkington), foodstuffs (Irvin & Johnson) and many other items.

Recreational facilities include the Murray Park pleasure resort; Blesbokspruit, a bird sanctuary; President Park; the Pioneers Park with its novel layout; the Springs Indoor Sports Centre; and the spacious P A M Brink Stadium, home of the Falcons Rugby Union. In the library is a fine frieze painted by the wandering artist, Conrad Genal who, after deserting from the French Foreign Legion, walked all the way from North Africa to South Africa, earning a living by decorating the walls of hotels, churches and private buildings with delightful friezes, mostly of African scenes.

There is a spacious modern theatre and an art gallery associated with the library.

From Springs, the main road eastwards leaves the Witwatersrand, crossing typical highveld maize country. After 29 km the road passes through a rural centre with the French name of *Delmas* (the little farm) which, with a population of 4 192, is the rail and commercial centre for the surrounding farmers.

A further 42 km brings the road to the rural coal-mining centre of Ogies, built on the farm *Ogiesfontein* (fountain of the little eyes) belonging to Jan Visagie.

Another rail centre in this flat world of coal, maize, beans and potatoes is *Kendal*, named after the town in north-western England which lies at the gateway of the Lake District.

Twenty-seven kilometres beyond Ogies (98 km from Springs) the road joins the main N4 road from Pretoria to Mozambique at Witbank, the coal metropolis of Southern Africa.

THE WEST RAND TOWNS

From Johannesburg, the Main Reef Road to the west passes the old workings of the Crown Mines, in its day one of the richest gold-mines every worked, but now no longer in production. Part of it has been converted by the Chamber of Mines into the Gold Mine Museum with an old-time restaurant, smelter, underground workings and rides on steam trains. The museum is open daily 08h30 to 22h00.

The main Reef Road continues through a complex of mines, dumps and industries. At 6 km the road passes the George Harrison Memorial Park where the first payable gold was found on the Witwatersrand. At 13 km from Johannesburg there is a turn-off to Florida with its lake and recreational area.

At 19 km from Johannesburg the road reaches the town of ...

ROODEPOORT

Many of the pioneer miners of the Witwatersrand worked in this area where *Roodepoort* (the red pass) was first established as a mine camp. On the farm *Wilgespruit* just north of Roodepoort, Fred and Harry Struben worked their Confidence Reef. Others such as J G Bantjies, H G van der Hoven and G Lys worked on the farm *Florida* and A P Marais on *Maraisburg*. A town to serve these various mining enterprises was laid out on the farm *Roodepoort* and the first stands were sold in February 1887. With its 'family' of suburbs and associate townships such as Maraisburg, Florida, Discovery and *Ontdekkers* (discoverers) Park, Roodepoort now occupies a 140 square kilometre extent of the Witwatersrand. Apart from its mines it is a rapidly developing industrial area. It became a city on 1 October 1977 and the population now numbers 279 342. The area around Florida lake facilitates activities such as swimming, boating and picnicking. A monument commemorating the discovery of gold in the area stands on its shores. The bronzes were sculpted by Dale Lace. A museum in the town exhibits interesting relics of early mining and the pioneer days.

Each year an eisteddfod is held in Roodepoort and attracts entrants from many parts of the world.

From Roodepoort, the Main Reef Road continues westwards through *Witpoortjie* (the small white pass), a popular picnic resort. From the Witpoortjie railway station a path passes for 8 km down a precipitous ravine to a fine 76 m high waterfall and pleasure resort accessible only by road a long way round through Krugersdorp. Facing the Witpoortjie railway station is a wayside hotel which for many years has offered refreshment to passers-by.

In 1889 a famous gun-fight took place near this hotel. Two bank robbers, John McKeone and Joseph Terpend, had held up the Standard Bank in Krugersdorp, absconding with £4 500. A posse set off in pursuit of the thieves who were making good their escape. While passing Witpoortjie, one of the pursuing posse remembered that a well-known racehorse named Atlas was quartered in a stable behind the hotel. He flung himself on to the horse and raced after the robbers who, to their dismay, found themselves being overtaken by what seemed to be a whirlwind.

On passing the wagon of an impoverished woodcutter, they tried to lighten their load of £1 503 worth of gold nuggets by tossing their saddle-bags on to the wood piled on the wagon. They had the hope of retrieving the gold later. This strategy was to no avail. Nemesis in the form of the racehorse overtook them and a blazing gun-fight ensued. The two men surrendered and were imprisoned. It is said that, when the woodcutter unloaded his wagon and found the bags of gold, he gave thanks to the Lord for gifts received, retired to the bushveld and bought a farm. He and the gold were not seen again.

Passing through the Lewisham and the Luipaardsvlei Estate Mining area, the road (11 km from Roodepoort) reaches the town of ...

KRUGERSDORP

For a variety of reasons, Krugersdorp is the most atmospheric town on the Witwatersrand. During the period between 8 and 18 December 1880, a great gathering of Transvalers was held on the farm *Paardekraal* (horse corral) on which Krugersdorp was destined to be built. The stalwarts of the old Transvaal Republic had assembled to stage a massive protest against the annexation of their country by the British. A triumvirate was appointed – Paul Kruger, Piet Joubert and M W Pretorius – with full powers to act. The 6 000 men at the gathering all solemnly swore to stand united until independence was restored. As proof of their oath, each man placed a stone on a cairn. After the short but salutary Anglo-Transvaal War (1880–81), when independence had been won, it was resolved that once every five years on 16 December a celebration would be held at the cairn, combining the giving of thanks for independence and remembrance of the victory over the Zulus at Blood River. A permanent monument to mark the site was erected at *Paardekraal*, but unfortunately the original cairn of stones has vanished.

On 25 April 1887 the Republican Government resolved to purchase a portion of *Paardekraal* and on it was founded the town of *Krugersdorp*, named in honour of the President, Paul Kruger. This town became the administrative centre of the West Rand gold-fields. Its importance was soon established with substantial Government buildings. The original magistrate's court building, which had its foundation-stone laid by President Kruger on 18 September 1890, still stands. Hitching posts for horses are a convenience outside and the atmosphere is reminiscent of innumerable court cases of the past. The town hall, with its elegant clock tower, had its foundation-stone laid by the British Governor, the Earl of Selborne, on 10 May 1907. In its hall there have been held many functions, stormy political meetings and entertainments by travelling artists such as the famous old Steele-Payn Bell Ringers. A spacious new Centenary Hall was added in 1987 but it was carefully designed to blend with the original building.

There is a handsome 37 ha Coronation Park, first-class sports amenities and a bustling commercial centre. Enhanced by flourishing vegetation, Krugersdorp became one of the most pleasant towns on the Rand and its council has systematically set out to beautify the place with gardens and trees.

At Doringkop, 13 km south of Krugersdorp, the Jameson Raid came to a sudden end. The renowned Dr 'Jim' and his band-reduced to a forlorn collection of prisoners – were marched into Krugersdorp, which they regarded as something like their 'Krugerloo'. The five burghers who fell in the fight were buried in Krugersdorp, while the graves of Jameson's men lie alongside the railway line to Randfontein.

Krugersdorp stands a brisk 1 749 m above sea-level on the summit of the Witwatersrand. Its population has reached 208 284. It is situated near the western end of the ridge where there is, within walking distance of the town centre, some fine rugged scenery, with the heights falling away sharply to the bush-covered lowlands. Several attractive picnic, camping and swimming places are situated in the ravines along the edge of the escarpment. The Crocodile River has its headwaters here in a number of tributary streams which flow off the watershed of the Witwatersrand.

The road from Krugersdorp to Pretoria passes through some particularly dramatic scenery. Muldersdrift Hill has been the scene of many famous hill-climbing races for automobiles, cyclists and athletes. The sweeping panorama seen from the top of the hill is known as World's View. Below Muldersdrift Hill, on the road to Pretoria, is the South African Lion Park, a 354 ha privately run game reserve where visitors can drive along 16 km of trails, viewing a variety of game animals and, especially, lions. The lion park is open daily 08h30 to 17h00.

Immediately west of the town, 5 km away on the Rustenburg road, is the Krugersdorp Game Reserve which preserves the indigenous fauna and flora of the Witwatersrand prior to the discovery of gold. A fine example of conservation has been set by the Krugersdorp municipality. The reserve occupies 1 400 ha of grassy highveld, falling off to a lower level through bushy valleys. It supports a dense population of eland, zebra, springbok, blesbok, oryx and other antelope, as well as lion and white rhino which are contained in separate enclosures. About 165 species of birds may be seen there. Facilities for hunting are available during the season. An attractive camp with bungalows and a swimming-pool has been built in a sheltered valley. A tea-room offers refreshment, and a circular road, (16 km long) provides a very pleasant drive. The reserve is open daily from 08h30 to 18h00.

Apart from gold, a considerable variety of economic minerals are mined in the Krugersdorp district, including high-grade manganese, iron, asbestos, dyes, lime and dolomite. There are three uranium plants within the municipal area, one of which was the first recovery plant in Southern Africa, opened on 8 October 1952 on the first mine in the world (the West Rand Consolidated) to produce uranium as a by-product of gold.

From Krugersdorp, the Main Reef road veers sharply south-westwards past the vast mining properties of the West Rand Consolidated Mines (5 km) and the Randfontein Gold Mining Company at Robinson (11 km). At 14,5 km from Krugersdorp the road reaches the town of ...

RANDFONTEIN

The last of the West Rand towns, Randfontein was originally attached to Krugersdorp but became a municipality of its own in January 1929. *Randfontein* (fountain of the ridge) was originally a farm owned by Louis le Grange. During the first wild scramble for mining areas after the discovery of the Main Reef, J B Robinson, acting on little more than rumours of gold and his own instinct, secured options over the area.

Robinson's instinct proved wonderfully rewarding. In 1889 the Randfontein Estate Gold Mining Company was floated, then the largest mining enterprise on the Rand. It was destined to produce a fortune in gold. A town to serve the mine was proclaimed on *Randfontein* farm in May 1890. With its 133 030 inhabitants, it is today a major mining and industrial centre. There are two pleasant recreational areas at the Riebeeck and Robinson lakes.

From Krugersdorp two main roads continue westwards, taking the traveller through interesting scenery to Rustenburg and Mafikeng. One road leaves Krugersdorp from a suburb once known as *Blikkiesdorp* (shanty town) which has now become the respectable Dan Pienaarville. Immediately beyond this suburb, the main road reaches the edge of the Witwatersrand. Fine views to the north are revealed with the well-bushed escarpment falling away sharply to the low country.

The road begins to descend. The scenery is now ruggedly hilly and the vegetation changes rapidly. There are turn-offs at 10 km to Muldersdrift (13 km) and Pretoria (64 km). The road then reaches the 8 km long turn-off (12 km from Krugersdorp) leading to the world famous ...

STERKFONTEIN CAVES

One of the world's most important anthropological sites, these caves have their entrance in a low, rounded hillock of dolomite forming part of the Isaac Stegmann Nature Reserve.

The caves were discovered in 1896 on the farm *Sterkfontein* by an Italian limestone prospector, Guglielmo Martinaglia. The caves were rich in bat guano. Extracting the guano unfortunately led to considerable destruction of the spectacular dripstone formations in the cave, many of which were broken up and used for the making of lime. Countless wonderful fossil relics of ancient animal fossils must also have been destroyed.

The caves consist of six large chambers connected by passages. The largest chamber is the Hall of Elephants, 23 m high and 91 m long. The other chambers are: Milner Hall, Fairy Chamber, Bridal Arch, Lumbago Alley, Fossil Chamber and the Graveyard. At a depth of 40 m lies an underground lake which is completely still and has about it an atmosphere of such enchantment that local African people regard it with considerable awe. Its waters are reputed to have healing power and to be effective against blindness. Ceremonies are performed on the verges of the subterranean lake and water is carried away for the sick.

Prehistoric animals once inhabited the caves. Many interesting fossils and other relics have placed the caves among the world's major archaeological sites. Between 1936 and 1951 Dr Robert Broom of the Witwatersrand University carried out considerable excavations in the caves. Among his discoveries was the exceptionally well-preserved skull of what was first named *Plesianthropus transvaalensis*, now known as *Australopithecus africanus* (the southern ape of Africa), a species of early man who was thought to have lived about two million years ago. The skull, that of a female, was nicknamed 'Mrs Ples'. The discovery of this primitive creature was hailed as the finding of the 'missing link' between man and ape. Subsequent discoveries of similar fossils in East Africa indicated that these, *Australopithecus afavensis*, were older than the Sterkfontein fossils, and lived approximately 3,5 to 4,3 million years ago. Still more ongoing research in the Makapans Caves of the Northern Province (see Chapter Thirty-One) has, however, revealed *Australopithecus africanus* as being much older than originally thought, at least the same age as its East African rival in claiming the dubious honour of being the first of the human kind of ape.

In 1994 Ron Clarke of the Witwatersrand Medical School's Palaeoanthropology Research Unit, while checking the contents of a cardboard box of fossils found in the cave, found four bones of a hominid left foot. In 1997 Clarke found four more hominid foot bones in another box as the medical school. A fifth bone was also found which did not fit the others.

More similar bones were then found at Sterkfontein. Clarke named the discovery 'Little Foot'. The fossils had been found in what was known as Silberberg Grotto in the caves. Two excavation workers, Stephen Motsumi and Nkwana Molefe, began a close search of the grotto, a deep, dark cavern of considerable size with many fossils exposed on the walls and ceiling. One discovery followed the other. It became apparent that this little creature with human and ape features had experienced the mishap of falling 15 metres into the grotto and died face downwards on the floor. For 3,5 million years the skeleton remained embedded in rock and dripstone formations. It is the oldest hominid skeleton found anywhere and takes the study of human beings a big step back to the origin of their kind in the African garden of Eden.

The *Sterkfontein* farm was acquired in 1921 by Mr Stegmann whose heirs presented the site of the caves to the Witwatersrand University in 1958. The Robert Broom Museum at the caves exhibits many fossils found in the area. There is a restaurant and a picnic site. Guided tours are held at frequent intervals – Tuesdays to Saturdays from 08h30, last tour begins at 16h00; Sundays from 09h00, last tour begins at 16h00. A bust of Dr Broom examining the skull of 'Mrs Ples' stands at the entrance of the caves.

Chapter Thirty-Three
JOHANNESBURG

Johannesburg – at the centre of the Witwatersrand, the largest urban complex of Southern Africa with a population exceeding four and three quarter million – has 760 792 inhabitants. Together with *Soweto* (south-western townships) and the northern municipalities of Randburg and Sandton, the population is over 2 000 000. Known in Zulu as *eGoli* (the golden) it is the capital of the province of *Gauteng*, formed in 1994 when the original province of the Transvaal was split into four provinces. The name *Gauteng* comes from the Sotho, *Goudeng* (golden place) derived from the Afrikaans word *goud* (gold). Apart from its new administrative position, Johannesburg has, since its founding, been the principal financial, mining and industrial centre of Southern Africa.

The story of the discovery in March 1886 of gold on the Witwatersrand has been told in the previous chapter. The two commissioners, Johann Rissik and Christiaan Johannes Joubert, sent from Pretoria to inspect George Harrison's discovery and to assess its profitability, reported back their opinion that it was, in fact, of enormous long-term economic value. The farms along the line of reef were declared to be public diggings and F C Eloff, private secretary to the State President, Paul Kruger, was sent from Pretoria to find a central site suitable for a town.

Eloff rode over the area, gazing in wonder at the hotchpotch of humanity crowding into the new El Dorado. He found a vacant piece of ground, a Government owned farm named *Randjeslaagte* (dale of little ridges). It had never been sold, cultivated or considered of value. It was situated off the known line of reef, unwanted by prospectors or farmers, unlikely to be undermined by any working but quite suitable for building. The surveyors, Robert Ockerse and J E de Villiers, were instructed by the government to lay this farm out as a future town. They completed their work on 3 December 1886. The name Johannesburg was written for the first time on their plans of streets and stands. Who made the decision to name the town is unknown. With all the romance of prospecting and enormous human enterprise of mining behind the creation of the future city it was a pity that some less stodgy name could not have been given to it. The two commissioners, Rissik and Joubert, both had Johann or Johannes as first names. It is said that President Kruger, on hearing that the town had been named Johannesburg, asked why it had not been named after him. The reply was *'Your honour, your names are Stephanus Johannes Paulus. Indeed, we have named Johannesburg after you, Sir'.*

The *afval grond* (left-over piece of ground) of *Randjeslaagte* was a triangle of land sandwiched between three farms – *Braamfontein* (bramble bush fountain) to the west; *Doornfontein* (thorn fountain) to the east and *Turffontein* (peat fountain) to the south. As it belonged to the government, the state would make the profit out of the sale of stands and not the owners of the adjoining farms. The southern boundary became Commissioner Street; the western boundary Diagonal Street and the eastern boundary of the triangle, End Street. The apex is on top of the hill which became known as Hillbrow, where Clarendon Place meets the line extension of End Street. The Randjeslaagte Beacon is erected at this historical apex of the triangle.

On 8 December 1886, only five days after the completion of the survey, the first 986 stands were auctioned and realised the sum of £13 000. The first building to be erected was a corrugated-iron hut into which Carl von Brandis, the mining commissioner and his assistant Jan Eloff moved from their tent in order to collect revenues in greater comfort. A gaol was the second building. Civilisation had laid the foundation of the golden city.

Johannesburg at the end of 1886 presented the classic picture of a rough-and-tumble mining camp. To the eye there was neither order nor apparent design to the place. Wagons and shacks littered the landscape as though scattered by the dusty whirlwinds of the highveld. Open-cuts, trenches, and shallow prospecting-shafts provided a death trap for men, drunk or sober, homeward-bound from the canteens in the dark of night.

There was nothing made or organised in the future city. The first Diggers' Committee was elected on 8 November 1886. It was immediately confronted with the almost nightmare task of laying the foundations of law and order beneath the feet of a community of diverse origins, boisterous nature, and headstrong singleness of purpose to find wealth.

There were no made roads made leading to Johannesburg. The feet of the advancing multitude and the wheels of their wagons, simply followed the straightest line of least resistance to the golden Rand. The first sight of Johannesburg's hotchpotch of holes and shacks must have made an aesthete think of a garbage dump but, to the gold-seekers, it was their idea of heaven.

The town grew by the hour with each newcomer trying to improvise some shelter no matter how crude, while those who had this basic comfort were constantly trying to improve it. Some fruity descriptions of the comforts of home on the Rand have been left for us by the pioneers. Fisher Vane has described a typical miner's hut of the period.

> *'In one corner the beds were lying; they were not made – I don't think they ever were after the first time. Two stretchers with two sacks of straw on each, and a blanket apiece, with a coat or two thrown over them: these were the beds. They were on the bare ground, which was baked hard by the heat.*
>
> *'The earthen floor was littered with bits of bread, tea leaves, coffee grounds, odd scraps of meat, hard and dry, sundry potato peelings, scattered dottles of tobacco, and a few other miscellanies too numerous to mention. This pleasant assortment was the accumulation of a week.'*

Hotels and boarding houses were literally bursting at the seams trying to accommodate all possible customers. Some of them reached the ultimate in hospitality when they devised an elastic scale of charges to cover every grade of accommodation, from luxury of a bed in a room of your own, down to permission for the sum of 2 shillings to use the lee-side of the building for shelter from the wind.

Boarding houses consisting of tents or tin shacks were even more profitable than gold-mines in the first few years of Johannesburg. An attractive advertisement for one such enterprise has also been left us by Fisher Vane, who seems to have had an eye for such things. He put up in a digger's home-from-home consisting of two minute tin huts and a patched-up tent. Two thirds of this tent was occupied by a bed in which slept the host and his gossip.

> *'The remaining third of the tent was the boarding house. It contained a small table chiefly. A plank placed on two boxes squeezed between the table and the bed, along with two or three odd chairs, served to seat the adult members of the family and the boarders, to the number of eight or ten.*
>
> *'As we could not all sit down to table together, two or three had to squat outside while the others dined or supped, and the outsiders slipped in one at at time as the seats were vacated.'*

The social pivot of the Rand remained for some time Edgson's Central Hotel. The dining room of this place was the first public hall used for a variety of entertainments staged by itinerant performers. The first professional indoor entertainment ever given in Johannesburg consisted of Madame Ferreira's 'Opera Company', billed to hold the dining-room floor for the last few days of September 1886. This refined company, on closer inspection of the programme, consisted largely of '*Sleight of hand tricks, very cleverly performed by Signor Ferreira, songs by Signor Carlo, and fire-eating by Signor Marcellini*'.

The opera company had been preceded by only a few days, as the first public entertainment, when Fillis's circus had pitched a storm-battered and well patched-up tent, and given its first performance on 27 September 1886. The tent had just previously been blown down in Pretoria, and the slits in the sides revealed where the audience had been forced to cut themselves out.

It is fascinating to trace the making of a modern city, so close to us in time that we can record nearly all the first events in its history, even down to the first burglary. The Central Hotel had this experience on the night of 22 October 1886, when three thirsty diggers broke into the liquor storeroom. The first Chief of Police of Johannesburg, John McIntosh, tracked the villains down by following the scent of their breath.

The first church service of Johannesburg also took place in the dining room of the Central Hotel. Bishop Bousfield of Pretoria came over in November 1886, and gave communion to the first congregation. His journey to the Rand was uneventful when compared to the later visit of Bishop Merriman. That dignitary travelled up from the Cape by cart, experiencing all the difficulties of bad roads and worse accommodation. To get away from vermin-infested pubs, and the roistering of drunken men, he accepted hospitality one night from a wayside farmer. He enjoyed an excellent dinner, but was slightly shaken when the time came for bed. The host conducted him to the only bed in the only bedroom. It was a large four-poster with a feather mattress which seemed to be three feet deep. Into this antidote against insomnia the bishop, the host, and the host's plump wife all sank with conflicting emotions. After some hesitation the Bishop joined the other two in a trio of snores. When he awoke he found himself sharing the bed with the wife, the farmer having crept out before dawn to attend to his cows.

The first couple to be married in Johannesburg were J P Frost and A S Oosthuizen who took this bilingual plunge on 14 December 1886. The first death in a mining accident on the Rand occurred on 4 December 1886, when Charles Johnson was hit on the head by a falling stone as he was being hauled up a shaft in a bucket. The first free fight, large enough to be called a riot on the Rand, took place on Saturday night, 6 February 1887, when the entire Rand police force was put to flight after a tremendous brawl in a canteen in Ferreira's camp.

Life was never quiet in Johannesburg. A mining camp without its full quota of sudden death and public violence would be as unnatural as a melodrama without a villain. In the flood of humanity pouring into the place the driftwood of rogues, swindlers, and bully-boys had to be carried along with the main body of hard-working, kindly, and reasonably honest seekers after gold. By the very notoriety of their actions the more flamboyant sections of a community always appear to make more history. Their more humdrum, work-a-day contemporaries pass by nameless and almost unnoticed until one realises that the vast city of today was not built by swindlers and murderers, but by the individual toil of all its law-abiding people. They must have found the colourful doings of their noisier contemporaries to be so much handicap and nuisance.

To the Government of the South African Republic, the problems of coping with this international human influx were formidable. No matter what was done for the town, Johannesburg outgrew any administrative suit provided for it far faster than any growing boy ever burst the seams of his trousers. The postal department, in particular, had an experience which must have amounted to a postman's nightmare. The first post office of Johannesburg consisted of an empty soap box in the ubiquitous Central Hotel. This box was serviced by runner to and from Pretoria three times each week. On arrival the mail was simply dumped in the soap box and left to the grimy hands of the diggers to sort for themselves. With letters pouring into the soap box from all over the world, the chaos of mail days resembled the elegance of a collapsed rugby scrum.

A corrugated-iron shack was built as soon as possible to replace the soap box. The first postmaster, C A Dormehl, was appointed with a salary of £12 10s 0d a month and a staff of junior clerks. Mail was distributed by the clerks standing on the verandah and reading out addresses from the envelope. A telegraph connected the place to the outside world on 26 April 1887. Working in the shack, was considered by the clerks to be purgatory. It became, as a result of these conditions, the scene of the first labour disturbance on the Rand. On 8 December 1887, the clerks downed their pens and walked out in protest at a combination of intolerable conditions and delays in the payment of their salaries. They were all sacked on the spot.

The first school was started in November 1886, when 21 pupils were enrolled by a private teacher named Duff. From that simple start, education was a major problem to every parent in Johannesburg. There had never been enough qualified teachers in the Transvaal to cope with its original population. Now, within a period of one overwhelming year, there were almost as many people on the Rand as in the rest of the country. Any state would have found such a demand embarrassing. To complicate the issue further was the fact that very few of the newcomers spoke a word of Dutch, the language of the South African Republic. They were all *Uitlanders* (foreigners) with little real ambition ever to merge themselves permanently with the older inhabitants whose agricultural interests and culture were vastly different from their own ambitions and nature. The seeds of future contention were planted on the Rand as soon as the numbers of the newcomers not only exceeded the proportions of a national minority, but threatened to turn the tables on the original inhabitants, and make them the minority in their own country! It is impossible not to feel sympathy for the little Republic faced by such an awkward predicament.

The President of the Republic, Stephanus Johannes Paulus Kruger, was then 62 years of age and in his first term of office as head of the state. He paid his first visit to Johannesburg on 14 February 1887. He rode into the town through arches carrying the loyal greetings usual on such occasions but he was frankly suspicious of the place. He was an astute man who, lacking any great pretence to education, relied on his good sense and a sharp intuition to guide him through the complexities of diplomacy and state-craft.

Kruger had received news of the Witwatersrand gold rush with mixed feelings. The new field would certainly provide relief from current economic troubles brought on by the collapse of Barberton, but intuition must have warned him that the cost of this sudden prosperity could, in the long run, be high. Just how high he was only to realise long afterwards when, in his autobiography he wrote: '*It is quite certain that, had no gold been found in the Transvaal, there would have been no war. No matter how great the influx of Englishmen, no matter how varied and manifold their complaints, the British Government would not have lifted a finger in their defence, had it not been tempted by the wealth of the country*'.

With some intuitive forebodings, the President faced the diggers on his first visit. The Mining Commissioner standing on a rough platform in front of the Government offices read an address to him. The watching crowd of diggers made such a noise as they pushed and swayed in their efforts to secure a better view that the President summarily told them to shut up.

The President understood English well enough to know what people were saying, especially about himself, but he seldom chose to talk that language. He addressed the diggers in Dutch, making a curious speech, more threatening than diplomatic on such an introductory occasion, long before any serious political trouble had occurred on the Rand. The local newspaper reported him as saying:

> '*He had his secret agents in Barberton and on the Rand, and had found some who, perhaps, did not work, or whose ideas were not exactly as he wished at the Kaap Goldfields but his latest reports from there were to the effect that the population was as satisfied as it could be.*
>
> '*He wished to make his laws so that everybody could obey them and be contented with them; but he wished everyone of whatever nationality to understand that if there were any disturbances here, he would first call the diggers to catch the diggers who were disobedient (laughter) and if they failed he would then use the burghers.*'

After a night's rest, the President was in a better mood. He spent the following day listening to deputations from the diggers, who carried to him various requests, suggestions and complaints. In the evening the diggers stood him to a dinner at the Gaiety Hotel and everybody became a trifle more friendly. The President left the next morning, and must have carried away with him personal observations to provide material for much thought and reflection.

The new gold-field was on the verge of production, with a staggering effort in transporting by ox wagon every piece of machinery, building material, stone and commodity from the nearest railheads far beyond the borders of the Transvaal. Over one thousand wagons were reaching the Rand each week bringing in its requirements although there were no made roads and none so far planned. The cost of living was sky-high, with stores having so little difficulty in selling the most exorbitantly priced rubbish that many enterprises removed themselves bodily from their original homes in Natal or the Cape and set up business in the happy traders' over-charging grounds of the Rand. Everything they had, from creaky floor-boards to corrugated iron roofs, and all their counters and stock, was hauled up for hundreds of kilometres by long suffering oxen.

Newspapers were already being published. There were six on the streets by the end of 1887, the first being the *Diggers News* which had started on the 24 February. Like most newspapers catering for a digger population, they provided strong reading matter. Editors were indifferent to libel or defamation. Their columns were full of abuse, lurid language, and such sex as could be worked up from times when the reigning beauty habitually allowed herself to be auctioned each night while she displayed her charms standing on a billiard-table, dressed in corsets, and voluminous drawers edged with plenty of lace.

The religious communities were also busy organising themselves. In laying out the town, the government had reserved seven free stands for churches. The Anglicans, Catholics, Presbyterians, and Baptists were all soon busy with plans for buildings. There is a tradition that the Jewish community was the last to request the government for a free stand. Their representative returned crestfallen when Kruger offered only half a stand as they believed in only half the bible. Johannesburg incidentally, by that early time, was already nicknamed 'New Jerusalem' or 'Jewsenburg' from the number of immigrants of that persuasion.

The Salvation Army was active from the beginning of Johannesburg. We have the record of one disgruntled digger who suggested *'Let's peg off the Market Square, and then if the Salvation Army comes 'ere a'blowing of that 'ideous trumpet, we'll 'ave them up for jumping'.*

'Jumping' of claims was the major source of sensation in the town at that time. The Gold Law of the Republic stated that if any claim remained unworked for fourteen days, or if ownership lapsed through non-payment of fees or disobedience to the letter of the law, then the claim could be 'jumped' by anybody else pulling out the original owner's pegs and replacing them with his own.

It became profitable for the sharp gentlemen of the day to become professional claim jumpers. Any desirable claim was watched most carefully for the slightest technical breech of the law. A man going to pay his licence fee a minute after time would find that his claim had been jumped. If an owner fell sick, or some circumstance impeded his working of the claim, his pegs would vanish exactly on the expiration of the legal time limit.

The jumpers eventually allowed greed to cause their own downfall. On 16 July 1887, Johannesburg was outraged to hear that a gang of these opportunists led by W P Fraser, a leading light in the Diggers Committee, had jumped a large number of claims held by several public companies. The Diggers' Committee was pledged to fight the claim-jumping evil. To have one of its members involved in the scandal was just too much.

The largest gathering of people thus far held in the town, collected in Marshall's Square. When Fraser tried to explain his actions he was shouted down and pursued through the streets by the crowd singing *'We'll hang old Fraser on a sour apple tree'*. The alarmed man found refuge with some ladies he had invited to dinner at Heath's Hotel. Pressing invitations for him to step outside eventually produced his reluctant promise to resign from the Diggers' Committee.

The crowd realised that investors all over the world would soon lose faith in the Rand if claim-jumping continued. Accordingly they organised a proper Vigilance Committee, sent telegrams of reassurance to the principal stock exchanges of the world, and continued public agitation for some days, burning at the stake effigies of the jumpers, and making such a clamour that Fraser was eventually forced to withdraw his pegs publicly from the jumped claims.

The reign of the claim-jumpers on the Rand ended in the adoption by the Vigilance Committee of the resolution: *'That any person attempting to jump claims in future shall be drummed out of Johannesburg'.*

Thenceforth the sharp gentlemen had to find other occupations. They were probably not unemployed for long. A gold rush is too fertile a field for social parasites. Opportunities for making money were endless in early Johannesburg and nimble wits could always find some scheme for profit.

Gambling, of course, was a normal entertainment, although the American type of card-sharp never became a standard character in Johannesburg. Horse racing started on 30 December 1886. The first theatre, the Theatre Royal, opened its doors in June 1887, while Fillis's' circus erected a permanent corrugated iron arena for itself in the town with seating accommodation for 1 600 people. Prize fights were also staged regularly. Any men having grievances to settle could turn their quarrel into cash by settling the argument in public with bookmakers laying the odds and the press publishing blow-by-blow descriptions.

Recreational areas were allocated to the town from an early period. At the end of 1887 a vacant piece of land was laid out as a park, and named after Christiaan Joubert, the first chief of the newly created Mining Department. In the same year the Wanderers Club was started, and duly received the grant of a generous extent of ground to provide playing fields for Johannesburg. The ground lay at the foot of Hospital Hill where, 60 years later, it was completely overwhelmed by the railway station. It was originally named Kruger's Park after the President.

The creation by Montagu White of the artificial lake in Boksburg set a pleasant precedent on the Witwatersrand in dealing with the ever increasing volume of water being pumped out of the developing mines. If nature had forgotten to give beauty spots to the Witwatersrand, human beings could make them. A whole string of artificial lakes came into existence along the Rand. These sheets of water, many of substantial size, often reflected the vividly coloured rubble and tailings dumps which rose up like mountains next to every mine. Nature contributed an interesting share to the lakes when wildlife discovered them. Aquatic birds adopted the lakes as homes, fish flourished and even otters settled down happily to represent the world of mammals in what is one of the most remarkable examples of an artificial landscape to be seen anywhere on earth.

The prodigious human effort in developing the Rand, building a city, and changing the landscape in so surprising a fashion, was not only matched but was quite dependent on the efforts of the transport men who had the task of carting up the bag, baggage, and persons, of the rush. Johannesburg grew as rapidly as the transport service allowed it and the expansion of the service involved the acquisition of many thousands of transport animals.

In the very beginning the only regular postal service to the Rand was the thrice-weekly runner linking Pretoria to Edgecombe's Hotel. The runner was soon replaced. By its first birthday Johannesburg was linked to Pretoria, 50 km away, by three coaches a day run by Dow & Colquhon, who had the convenience along the route of a staging post and inn known as the Half-way House.

One coach a day also linked Johannesburg to Kimberley, 494 km away. This service was run by Heys & Co, who had 58 coaches and one thousand horses working on the road. A count of wagons on the same road in 1889 revealed that an average of two thousand five hundred wagons a month were making their slow way from Kimberley to Johannesburg. At the same time another two thousand five hundred wagons each month left the Natal railhead 457 km away at Ladysmith, and headed for the Transvaal. A third, but smaller, wagon stream came up from Bloemfontein 463 km away in the south. Added to this deluge of vehicles was a substantial in-pouring of coal wagons from the East Rand coal-fields, and a persistent stream from every direction of carts and wagons bringing in fresh produce from farms in the surrounding countryside. Feeding all the transport animals, especially in winter, was a problem which turned every transport man, if not grey, at least to very strong drink.

Some of the individual loads which were carried became famous. One boiler for the Wolhuter mine took the best part of a year to be dragged up to the Rand. On the last leg of its journey, the wagon carrying this bulky object became so bogged down in a swamp that at one time, in the height of a wet spell, only the load was left projecting above the mud. How this load was eventually retrieved when the rains ended, and was duly delivered to the Wolhuter mine, would make quite a saga. The question of its fate was the subject of a great deal of betting on the Rand with sightseers trooping out to view the predicament of the wagon and the efforts at its rescue being made by the transport men.

The construction of a railway link to the Rand became the most urgent need of the day. The fact that this need was so obvious did not, however, exactly stampede the contemporary politicians into any rapid decisions. History in Southern Africa has mostly been made by the little men, the prospectors, miners, hunters, traders and farmers who expanded frontiers quite unofficially. Politicians have seldom been in the van of progress. Rather they panted along well in the rear, lured on in pursuit of the pioneers solely by the bait of collecting taxes.

After a great deal of talk, and not a little obstructionism, especially by farming representatives in the Volksraad who had a financial interest in road transport, or the supply of feed to the draught animals, a concession was eventually granted to the Netherlands Railway Company to build what was called a tramway from Johannesburg to the East Rand. The name 'tramway' was given as a camouflage to this enterprise, in order to make it more palatable to the opponents of a railway.

The line was built in 1889, and was immediately remarkable for the fact that all of its permanent way and rolling stock of 42 trucks and 6 steam engines had to be carried up to the Rand by ox wagon. The line was opened on 17 March 1890. This was the first railway in the Transvaal. It ran 14 miles from Park Station in Johannesburg to Boksburg.

The price of coal in Johannesburg dropped from 26s a ton to 6s a ton. The transport men were so annoyed at the loss of their livelihood that one of them attempted to sabotage the line. On the night of 8 May 1890, the last train from Boksburg collided with a heavily loaded coal wagon outspanned on the line. The train was going too slowly to be seriously damaged. The overturned wagon had to be removed, a mound of coal shovelled away, and the wagon driver arrested.

Progress was not impeded again on the Rand tramway in any physical way. In the Volksraad, however, opposition to railways remained both strong and articulate. One crowd of rustics from the Bronkhorstspruit ward went so far as to submit a memorial on 28 July 1890, protesting that they had been bamboozled into their original acceptance of the Rand tramway, by being told that it was to be worked by animal power. Now they had found that steam was being used. The 'tramway' had been built, therefore, under false pretences. The memorialists prayed that no extensions be allowed to the line. They would rather have it suppressed.

We can smile at simplicity of this type, but human progress has invariably been achieved against the bitter will of many people and, in fact, must count itself fortunate if the great majority are not so much against advancement as to stamp it out entirely. The little Rand 'tramway' at least did manage, not only to survive, but to be extended, first in October 1890, to the area on the East Rand known as 'The Springs', where six new collieries started work, and then, on 10 February 1891, to Krugersdorp, on the West Rand. The modern electric trains which speed along this route today are very far removed in comfort and cleanliness from the grimy, ricketty little Puffing Billies which pioneered the way. It is a pity that one of the wheezy little engines hasn't been retained and mounted at the spot just outside Germiston where the first collision occurred with the obstreperous coal wagon. It would be an exceedingly quaint monument to the endless struggle between progress and conservatism in South Africa.

The initial prospector's rush to peg claims along the Rand was over by the end of 1886. The financiers by then were already busy with their complex manoeuvres. Among them were characters even more individualistic than the early prospector.

The first financier to reach the Rand was Joseph Benjamin Robinson, a 46-year-old man who had been born at Cradock in the Cape. He had joined in the Kimberley rush but lost all he owned. He was hard pressed for cash and distinctly at a loose end in the diamond world when news reached Kimberley of the discovery at the Rand.

At first the Kimberley diamond magnates were dubious of the field. Barberton was still a melancholy memory with most of them. They suspected the worst about the Rand. Then a travelling produce merchant named F W Alexander arrived in Kimberley from the Rand, bringing with him some samples of the main reef. On 16 July 1886, he publicly crushed and panned the samples before a gathering in Kimberley of some of its wealthiest men. There was a sensation when they saw the result.

A great bustle of preparation commenced all around for a quick start to the Witwatersrand. Robinson went to see Alfred Beit, the Kimberley representative of the great financial house of Jules Porges & Co., of Paris. Beit was interested in the idea. He knew Robinson well. The man was personally disliked and with something of a tricky reputation. There was no doubt, however, that, given support and the spur of big money, he was the man most likely to shoulder his way through a frenzied crowd in a gold rush.

Beit financed Robinson, relieving him of current embarrassments, and allowing him £25 000 in cash to back any property deals on the Rand. On 18 July, Robinson was on his way to the Rand. He arrived there so far ahead of any rivals that he had the pick of the field. He spent £31 500 on properties which were worth £18 000 000 within a few years.

Among his acquisitions were the outright purchase of Portion B of *Langlaagte* for £1 000 and a lease over Petronella Oosthuizen's Portion D for £150 a year rental. An option to purchase this property was also taken, and exercised two months later for £6 000. Robinson also bought himself into a syndicate formed by Jan Bantjes to work *Vogelstruisfontein* (the fountain of ostriches) farm, and obtained a half interest in the mining lease over *Turffontein*, including 50 claims pegged there for Jacob de Villiers by a prospector named Gerrit du Plessis. These claims eventually became one of the richest gold-mines in the world, the Robinson Mine. Acting on pure hunch, Robinson also bought seven unprospected farms covering 40 000 acres on the West Rand. He was certain that the gold reef ran in that direction. Time proved him correct.

Robinson's rivals in the financial world followed hard on his heels to the Rand. They found that while Robinson might have snapped up most of the obvious bargains, there were still many opportunities on the Rand for the venturesome financier. William Knight, who followed Robinson very quickly, acquired the *Driefontein* (three fountains) farm from the Strubens for £45 000, a pleasant bonus to the Strubens for their earlier disappointments. All other known discoveries of the Main Reef were soon taken up by financiers. Cecil Rhodes, after some initial uncertainty, spent £65 000 on securing a string of properties, including *Luipaardsvlei* (leopards marsh) which cost him £40 000 in cash and £20 000 in shares for the fortunate owner.

By the end of 1886 the financiers had completed their initial buying. Leaving the geologists and consulting engineers to detailed exploration of the Rand, the big men busied themselves in floating companies, and raising the cash for the coming activity. The excitement of the outside world at the golden prospects of the new field was demonstrated by the speed with which companies could be floated. Rhodes' *Gold Fields of South Africa Ltd* was floated in London on 9 February 1887. Its capital of £125 000 was over subscribed immediately. The success of this company was such that it yielded Cecil Rhodes over £300 000 a year in dividends. When he sold his founder's shares, he received £1 300 000.

Among the other pioneer companies was William Knight's *Witwatersrand Co,* floated on 8 January 1887, the first to be registered in the Transvaal. The *Jubilee Gold Mining Co,* floated in Pietermaritzburg in December 1886, was the first to get a mill working for the specific purpose of crushing the Main Reef. This was a small three-stamp battery which started its noisy life in Natal Spruit on 11 April 1887.

The Crown Reef was registered on 8 March 1887. Its property, the Crown Mines, was destined to become one of the most famous gold-mines in the history of mining. It started milling in January 1888, a date on which several other great ventures such as the *Robinson Gold Mining Co,* also dropped their first stamps.

In those days, life in Johannesburg was about as comfortable, private and quiet as trying to sleep in the midst of a major construction site. Holes were being dug on every side. Buildings were being erected or demolished. An appalling cloud of dust covered everything. Wagons rumbled in day and night bringing foodstuffs, mining tools, people and still more people.

In several unusual ways, however, Johannesburg quickly developed into a ready-made town. It was the age of corrugated iron. Traders moving to Johannesburg from other areas brought with them their stock and premises, the latter being dismantled and carried in pieces on wagons. In other South African towns spaces began to appear along the commercial streets; buildings simply accompanied their owners in the rush to the golden city.

Even newspapers such as *The Star* transplanted, removing staff, press and accommodation from other centres such as Grahamstown to commence publishing in Johannesburg. Grog-shops, canteens and bars sprang up like weeds.

Within twelve months Johannesburg was the second largest town in the Transvaal, rapidly overtaking Barberton, the largest, with Pretoria lagging well behind. By the end of 1889, 17 875 kg (630 499 ounces) of gold had been recovered from the Witwatersrand main reef. Businesses were booming; a hospital and a stock exchange had been founded; the Chamber of Mines was organised in April 1889 as the representative body for the mining industry; and workers were forming unions. The first strike, on 7 September 1889, was aimed at achieving a 48-hour week as well as pay increases. Citizens began agitating for a municipality and direct representation in the government of the South African Republic.

To supply a rapidly growing city such as Johannesburg with services would have taxed any government. In 1890 drinking-water was still supplied by a public company. The demand on the limited resources was so great that taps at times yielded little more than a trickle of liquid mud. The transportation of goods was chaotic. Vast numbers of draught animals consumed all the grazing. The environment of Johannesburg, littered with the skeletons of numerous unfortunate oxen and horses which had died of starvation or overwork, began to resemble a desert. The proposed railway from the Cape to Johannesburg met with considerable opposition. Transport riding had become a major industry. The men working this service thought that they would be ruined by the railway. They had no interest in the well-being of the public. They had a powerful anti-train lobby in the Transvaal Volksraad. Every effort was made to stop the construction of a railway line.

Despite opposition the railway from the Cape reached Johannesburg on 15 September 1892. There was great excitement when the first train arrived. The last stage-coach to carry mail departed the next day, after which the trains took over. For the first six years of its life, an entire town and a considerable mining industry had been built and maintained by the carrying power of wagons and coaches. Bricks, timber, water, food, clothing, cumbersome machinery – all were brought to the town by thousands of stoic oxen, mules and horses. The story of these draught animals and the transport men who ran the service provides a romantic chapter in the history of South Africa.

The opening of the railway heralded a new epoch in Johannesburg. The tempo of its growth accelerated as a result of the greater carrying capacity of the trains. Amid the glitter of opulence now appearing, black and white miners laboured in primitive conditions and lived in bleak, company-provided accommodation. The self-styled upper social strata – financiers, company promoters, businessmen, gamblers, swindlers, illicit gold buyers, thieves, usurers and prostitutes – lived in style and gave the town its ostentatious facade.

Gambling became increasingly a mania in Johannesburg. Pritchard Street was the main trading thoroughfare in those days, but the hub of the town was a portion of Simmonds Street in front of the Stock Exchange. This area, known as 'The Chains' (since all vehicles were kept out by means of chains), contained rows of offices which housed various brokers. The street was always filled with people of all nationalities. It was here that the cosmopolitan nature of Johannesburg could really be appreciated. In a number of diverse languages and accents, trade was conducted, deals were made, shares were sold, rumours, gossip and tips abounded. Horse-races, prize-fights, claim-jumping, swindles, chorus-girls, organised coups against rivals, or the great gambles of the previous night when £80 000 and more changed hands at cards – all were subjects for excited discussion, debate and dissension.

By the middle of the 1890s there were 200 separate mining companies working from head offices in Johannesburg. A Witwatersrand gold-mine was cynically described as consisting of a hole in the ground with a fool at the bottom, a liar on top, a swindler in the stock exchange, and a crook in the seat of the managing director. There were then 75 000 men working in the mines. Their excavations had resulted in colossal profits for the financiers and considerable grief for the women left widowed. For every 11 858 tons of ore mined (worth, at the time, £23 702 in recovered gold), one man had been killed. The number injured and totally disabled in accidents was appallingly high. Even more miserable was the number dying a slow death as a consequence of the progressive wasting disease of miners *phthisis*. This was a lethal disability common to rock drillers and other workers exposed to inhaling minute particles of inorganic matter with which the atmosphere underground was charged as a result of drilling and blasting. About one in six of drillers died from this silicosis. Those who survived the perils of the mines, fell prey to the social dangers of Johannesburg – strong drink, footpads, confidence tricksters, the high cost of living and incessant gambling. From the time a miner collected his pay, he was fair game to a host of parasites. On pay-days, lines of cabs waited at the mines to take the men to town, where the bars, girls and card-sharps were waiting expectantly.

Dominating Johannesburg at this time were the so-called 'Randlords' – the heads of the principal mining houses, men whose profits were astronomical. Chiefs among these mining financiers were Julius Wernher and Alfred Beit, who ran Wernher, Beit & Co, and many of the most profitable mines, including the fabulously rich Crown Mines and Rand Mines.

The second-largest company was the Consolidated Gold Fields of South Africa, run by Cecil John Rhodes and Charles Rudd. From this company Rhodes drew a personal income of £300 000 a year. Next in line was the Johannesburg Consolidated Investment Company, run by the flamboyant Barney Barnato. He revelled in the money-making scramble of Johannesburg. He built himself a huge mansion in the town, complete with imported English butlers, chambermaids and footmen. In this establishment he spent most of his spare time playing poker for high stakes with a crowd of big-time gamblers.

Sigismund Neumann, J B Robinson, George Albu, George Farrar, Carl Hanau, Sammy Marks and his cousin Isaac Lewis (who, conducting their business in Yiddish, acquired control of more than 300 farms in the Transvaal), and Abe Bailey (a large-scale speculator), were all men whose audacious achievements and ruthless coups were regarded by themselves as worthy of knighthood (received by several of them from King Edward VII) or even the Nobel Prize.

Early in the second half of the 1890s, the Randlords started conflicting with the Transvaal government. The financiers considered the government to be inept and to be standing in the way of still bigger profits. The clash resulted in the Jameson Raid, a futile effort on the part of Cecil Rhodes and his financial allies to dislodge the Transvaal government by means of a paramilitary invasion of armed men from what was then called Bechuanaland (Botswana), led by Dr Leander Jameson, Rhodes's principal assistant.

The working class of Johannesburg kept aloof from the squabble. They had nothing to gain from it. Better wages, shorter working hours and more humane treatment was what they wanted. They were not going to get this by fighting for the randlords. The Government rewarded them for their neutrality by granting Johannesburg municipal status. The first *burgemeester* (town master), Johannes de Villiers, was appointed in September 1897 to preside over an elected council.

The town continued to grow. A family of suburbs was steadily spawned from the original parent: Hillbrow, Mayfair, Rosebank, *Rosettenville* (laid out by Levin Rosettenstein and his son Albert) were all created at this period. Johannes de Villiers found himself in charge of a town with more than 100 000 inhabitants. Half these people were European – mainly British, and Russian Jews. European males outnumbered females by 24 to 1. As a result of this disparity there were 591 hotels and bars within the municipal limits, and almost the same number of brothels.

The first motor car was brought to Johannesburg in January 1897 by J P Hess. Within two years traffic was complicated by an assortment of animal-drawn and motorised vehicles. Streets and shops were electrically lit, entertainments were diverse – flashy music-halls, circuses, open-air prize-fights, lotteries, horse-racing at Turffontein, wax-works and a great variety of dingy dives.

Over the heads of this boisterous community the political storm continued. On 11 October 1899 the Anglo-Boer War broke out. Johannesburg became almost deserted as trainloads of refugees fled the place. The rumbling noise of ore being ground day and night was stilled as mill after mill closed down. For the people of Johannesburg the quiet seemed like the end of the world, so accustomed were they to this 'voice' of the town.

The Anglo-Boer War has been called the last of the gentlemen's wars, although it is not particularly clear what special business the social elite had in shooting one another in the first place. With many of this elite in Johannesburg society it was said that the nearest they actually got to being gentlemen was the evening suits they affected. So much, however, is true about the Anglo-Boer War, whilst the rest of the Transvaal was turned into ruin, the gold-mines were not only left unscathed, but often as carefully guarded by both sides from danger of loot or sabotage as any fine lady in a tale of knight errantry.

Johannesburg, stripped of three-quarters of its population, was placed under martial law from the outset of hostilities. The Government relieved the mines of whatever specie could be found, and made a small effort to continue work on some of the properties in order to secure finance for the war. Engineering works were also taken over and converted to the manufacture of armaments. The works of Thomas Begbie & Co were largely used for this war-time purpose until the whole enterprise was blown sky-high on 24 April, 1900. The explosion smacked so much of sabotage that the government expelled all remaining British subjects six days later. They also stiffened their own administration by replacing Commandant D E Schutte with Dr F E T Krause as Special Commandant or military governor of the Rand.

Dr Krause, in his book, *Critical Examination of Evidence Relating to the Discovery of the Main Reef* provides some distraction from his expressed theme by giving us a glimpse behind the scenes on the Rand during the war. '*As the fortunes of war began to turn against the Boers*', wrote Dr Krause, '*and because it was believed and accepted, that the Gold mining magnates were mainly responsible for the war, a strong movement backed by high officials, was started, which insisted upon the Gold Mines being destroyed and Johannesburg being laid in ashes. The burning of Moscow was the historic example justifying the carrying out of this policy. President Kruger and General Botha were strongly opposed to such a policy and I, as military governor, was commanded to and held personally responsible to counteract and to stop any attempt in that direction*'.

Investors in Europe were officially reassured that no harm would be deliberately done to the mines. As the Boer forces had no intention of making a defensive stand on the Rand, there was little danger that the mines would be even accidentally damaged by hostilities.

The British army, advancing from the south under Lord Roberts, crossed the Vaal at Parys and invaded the Republic on 24 May 1900. The Boers, under Louis Botha withdrew with little resistance until they reached the Klipriviersberg, just behind Baragwanath, the last ridge dominating the approach to the Rand. There they determined to make at least a token stand before the British could occupy the Rand. In Johannesburg a few republicans, understandably bitter at the course of events, made a last minute move to damage the mines.

> 'Only a few days before the surrender', wrote Dr Krause, 'I was fortunate enough to give the "coup de grace" to a last minute attempt of Judge Kock (he styled himself "General") and a contingent under his command, by personally arresting and disarming him, with the assistance of my Commandant of the Special Police, S H van Diggelen, and in dispersing his band. It was the discovery by Kock of some 120 000 ounces of gold still in one of the mines, and his protest that the gold had not been sent to Pretoria, that was the reason for calling at my office and so providentially falling into my hands. This gold was sent to Pretoria, then forwarded to the President at Machadodorp, and there some of it was minted into blank discs. It is possible, in fact probable, that, in the confusion, some of the boxes may have been stolen and buried somewhere in the lowveld, and so the story about the lost Kruger millions presumably has its origin from that possibility.'

The British Army, meanwhile, trundled its lethal impedimenta up to the line of the Klip River and occupied the crossing points such as Jackson's Drift and Van Wyk's Rust. After testing the Boer positions, Roberts resolved to shoulder his way through any opposition at Doornkop, the approach to the Reef town of Florida. The resultant Battle of Doornkop took place on the afternoon of 29 May. It was a warm enough affair while it lasted. The Gordon Highlanders had the task of clearing the way to the Rand. They did the job at a cost to themselves of 21 killed and 86 wounded.

On the same day the British right flank occupied Germiston. Johannesburg now lay defenceless before the British army. On 30 May Lord Roberts sent in a Grenadier guards' officer, Major Davies, with a demand for surrender. Dr Krause and Jan Meyer, the Volksraad representative, rode out to see Roberts and arrange for the British entry. The next day, 31 May 1900, Lord Roberts and Lord Kitchener led the British army into a golden city which looked about as cheerful as a lost dog, used to one owner and now claimed by somebody else. The Republican *Vierkleur* flag outside the courthouse was replaced by a silken Union Jack, especially worked for the occasion by Lady Roberts. The keys to the safe of the local authority were handed over and the new order came to Johannesburg.

The Boer army retired eastwards down the railway to Lourenzo Marques and prepared for a resolute phase of guerrilla warfare. President Kruger, tragic in defeat, sailed off to Holland as an exile for the rest of his life.

It was generally thought that the war was over. The 20 000 men remaining under arms in the Boer army, the so-called 'bittereinders' were not expected to delay the inevitable for much longer. The two Boer republics in the Orange Free State and Transvaal were considered to be prostrate, utterly defenceless before the might of the British Empire and the rapacity of international finance. They could be looted at will, their natural riches pillaged with the approval of a paternal British government, with no consideration whatever for the inhabitants black or white. The equity owned in the companies was the only interest to be considered and the owners were mainly British.

A joyful crowd of speculators, avaricious and greedy for profits, poured into Johannesburg. There was expectancy of an immediate boom, with the mines entering an area of unparalleled production and expansion. Capital flooded into the hastily re-opened stock exchange, property markets were buoyant, the share market lively. Anybody with the wit to launch some new project, could be sure of enthusiastic support.

The mines longed to resume production but the immediate problem was labour. The African mine workers had dodged white men's bullets and slipped away for home as soon as hostilities had started. There was little prospect of attracting them back to work so long as shooting continued with the '*bittereinders*'. Most white able-bodied men were in the opposing forces. Their release for mining work could only be expected with the complete cessation of hostilities. But here was a real problem. The Boer '*bittereinders*' refused to admit defeat. The British army floundered. Never before had it encountered guerrilla warfare of such resolution. It resorted to unconventional responses to unconventional resistance. Boer civilians were rounded up into concentration camps, hastily and not too well organised; hundreds of little blockhouses were built to guard rail and road bridges which were easy targets for sabotage. Instead of being freed to work on mines, men were deployed for dreary months of guard duties in these miniature forts. Casualties increased at an untenable rate. The initial *jingoism* (exaggerated mindless patriotism) of the British public which had seen them support the war in the beginning, started to be replaced by admiration for the courage of the Boers and a guilty feeling that they had been deceived in the nature of the conflict from the beginning. The whole war had been a fabricated sham with their manhood paying a price in blood for the benefit of a minority of speculators and swindlers. Returned soldiers to Britain carried home tales of atrocious working conditions on mines, bad pay, and dreadful accidents with casualties exceeding those suffered in the war.

The British liberal party in opposition was winning anti-war support. The ruling Unionist (conservative) party felt threatened in the next election. The money men were aggrieved at the hindrance to the expected quick profitability of investment in the Transvaal so long as shooting continued. The British military censorship made a desperate effort to suppress the daily litany of South African war woes published in newspapers which were increasingly clamouring for an end to the whole bloody business.

Amongst the throng of speculators who poured into Johannesburg in the search of bargains on the heels of the British army was a financier, Harry Freeman Cohen. He booked into Heaths Hotel, a hostelry much favoured by journalists. Of these individuals there was a plethora in Johannesburg, especially international war correspondents who were gathered there to cover the expected final stage of the war and the peace negotiations. The quick end to fighting, however, had just not happened. The British army instead was floundering in a nasty morass of guerrilla warfare. The *bittereinders*, refused to surrender and were prepared to fight it out against all odds.

Amongst the journalists in Heaths Hotel, Cohen met a 26-year-old man who had been born in London in 1875. He was the illegitimate son of Polly Richards, a small time actress in a repertory company run by a lady whose speciality was acting the part in tights of what a critic described as a very full figured Shakespearean Hamlet. On the birth certificate of her baby, Polly Richards found it prudent to write a fictitious father's name, Walter Wallace, with a profession given sardonically as 'comedian'. The little 'joke' was brought up by a Billingsgate fish-porter's wife who, as a foster mother, charged five shillings a week to rear him while the real mother went back to the stage. He hardly ever saw her again. The foster mother was fortunately, kindly, sober and honest. Her husband was a drunkard but she was a strict member of the temperance movement. She took the little boy to their meeting and he discovered that they kept small libraries. He educated himself largely in these temperance libraries. When he was 18 Edgar Wallace, for that was the boy's given name, enlisted in the British regular army and became a medical orderly. He started writing poetry in Aldershot barracks and continued his writing in 1896 when he was posted to the small army hospital in Simon's Town, the British Naval base on the Cape Peninsula. He became well-known as the 'soldier poet' with his work published in the *Cape Times* newspaper as well as various magazines in South Africa and Britain. As a rather bashful private he was even invited to dinner in the City Club, Cape Town, to meet Rudyard Kipling, who liked his poems but advised him '*For God's sake, don't take to literature as a profession. Literature is a splendid mistress but a bad wife*'.

Wallace noted the great man's advice in his diary but he had already made up his mind. He had also fallen in love with Ivy, the 18 year old daughter of the Wesleyan minister in Simon's Town, the Reverend William Caldecott. Marriage was out of the question on army pay. He borrowed £18 from the girl's mother and on 12 May 1899 bought with this amount his honourable discharge from the British army. He immediately set to work in Simon's Town, a one-man factory, determined to make money as a freelance writer. He didn't make too much but at least his reputation spread and he became friendly with a young Welsh journalist, Thomas Richard Bulpin who was attached to the Reuters News Agency Bureau in Cape Town waiting for the anticipated beginning of the Anglo-Boer War. After five months the Anglo-Boer War commenced on 11 October 1899. Bulpin recommended Wallace to Reuters. He was appointed by Reuters as their second correspondent with the western division of the British army. With his formal credentials, a salary of £25 a month and £100 expense money, the equivalent of six years pay in the army, Edgar Wallace considered that he was on the way to a literary career. After several months of covering British victories and defeats, he found himself eventually in Heaths Hotel, Johannesburg with Bulpin, talking to Harry Cohen.

Edgar Wallace had a problem with British military censorship. They didn't much like what he wrote. They were trying to suppress stories of British casualties and reverses, Boer resistance and the scorched earth response of the army to guerrilla warfare – burning farmhouses and herding civilians into concentration camps. The British public, after the first month's of being worked up into a state of mindless jingoism were having second thoughts. Patriotic fervour was being eroded by sober fact. Casualties were mounting and what exactly were the young men dying for? The opposition British Liberal party was exploiting the mounting anti-war sentiment and the ruling Unionist (conservative) party was becoming alarmed at their prospects in the next general election.

Cohen, Wallace and Bulpin did some hard talking. Cohen had an office in London managed by his brother Caesar Cohen. They were large scale speculators and investors in various stock markets with daily exchanges of lengthy telegraphic communications. Edgar Wallace had already devised a telegraphic code with the London *Daily Mail* which he was confident would give the British military censorship some difficulty in breaking. He needed for it, however, a seemingly innocent carrier. The Cohens provided the answer. The first long message sent through them provoked an enquiry from the censor. Wallace had anticipated this. The message was decoded for the censor and shown to be the authentic details of a complex stock exchange purchase. After that it was easy. The Cohens were trusted financial men. They were the perfect carriers and they loved what they were doing. They had valuable access to advance information which would affect share prices up or down. They needed no other reward which might betray them as covert couriers of uncensored reports.

In London things reached such a pitch that it was said that when the British government needed correct information about what was really happening in South Africa, they sent out for the latest issue of the *Daily Mail*. This newspaper carried Wallace's, Bulpin's and Reuters' dispatches in detail. Officially censored dispatches were published with full credit. The uncensored ones carried no mention of the source, although in the uncensored ones the style was revealing. Lord Kitchener, who took over command of the British army when Lord Roberts returned to Britain, particularly hated all war correspondents, especially Edgar Wallace and threatened hell fire and brimstone if anybody even mentioned his name. But there was nothing he could do. The code and method remained unbroken.

Edgar found time to marry his Ivy in Cape Town. He left her pregnant in a cottage in Mowbray while the guerrilla war dragged on to conclusion. It was not only the British public; Ivy in her small way; and the financiers who, for different reasons were praying for the ending of the war, but also the families of the Boer '*bittereinders*'. The British destroyed almost every farmhouse in the two former republics and 26 251 Boer women and children died in the concentration or 'refugee' camps into which they had been herded. Compared to the 3 990 Boer and 5 774 British soldiers killed in battle, the civilians as usual had suffered the most. Even if it meant the loss of independence and the looting of their country by the financiers, the survivors wanted an end to the blood and tears.

Peace negotiations started in Pretoria in the beginning of April 1902. Lord Kitchener had his official residence there in the Victorian architectural gem of Melrose House. Negotiations lasted there for six long drawn out weeks. There was the strictest security. Kitchener was determined that absolutely nothing would reach the press without official approval. The *Daily Mail*, however received a nightly resume of negotiations. The Cohens did handsomely on the rises and falls of share prices in response to good or bad reports on progress or stalemate in the negotiations.

Eventually every point of argument was settled, except one. This stickler was the question of independence. The British were adamant. The two Boer republics would be absorbed into the British Empire. The Boer negotiators bargained stubbornly for some concessions to their national pride but they got nowhere. It became a final decision of continued war or surrender. The '*bittereinders*' wanted to fight, the civilians wanted peace and the chance to live for another day. To resolve this obdurate problem the Boers arranged with the British for a 'Peace' camp to be held in Vereeniging. All the major Boer role players attended a gathering held in a big marquee, surrounded by barbed wire and armed guards. For fifteen days the Boers argued and this was one event with security Kitchener was confident no outsider could possibly break. The Melrose House breach could only have been through the comings and goings of caterers, soldiers and negotiators. The editor of the *Daily Mail* long afterwards confessed succinctly that the breach was rather costly but worth it.

The Vereeniging marquee was another matter. There were no comings and goings. Smaller tents around the central marquee provided accommodation for all concerned. There were no telephones or communications. Actually it was very simple for the indefatigable Edgar Wallace. The railway line from Johannesburg to Vereeniging passed close to the camp. All Wallace wanted to know was a twice-daily report on proceedings. To get this report he had an informer employed in the marquee. In the mornings and afternoons Wallace or one of his colleagues was a passenger on a passing train. The informer had a bad cold. He always happened to be outside the marquee as the train passed, blowing his nose on one of several different coloured handkerchiefs representing yes, still arguing, and no. For fifteen days Wallace and the *Daily Mail* (courtesy of the Cohens) kept the world and the stock exchanges on tenterhooks with carefully prepared hot and cold stories based on these simple three colours.

The stories were filled out with personal details of the Boer negotiators and what Wallace and Bulpin had been able to glean beforehand of their conflicting opinions. The detailed stories of argument in the marquee read so convincingly that the corps of war correspondents camped outside the barbed wire actually sent a deputation to Edgar Wallace protesting about the leakages and asking him to desist because he was embarrassing them. Bulpin who worked closely with him in creating the scoops for the *Daily Mail* and other papers subscribing to Reuters wire service, summed the business up with the comment '*An amazing fellow was Edgar. If the facts were slow coming in, he applied logic to possibilities, jumped ahead of the facts, and waited for them to catch up. Most times they did. In which case the story was already written and in the setting room of the newspaper. He would just signal them to rush into print. Nobody could beat him*'.

On 31 May 1902, the Vereeniging conference finally agreed to the British demand. Shortly before midnight a deputation left for Pretoria to carry their surrender to Kitchener and to sign what was named the Peace of Vereeniging. Wallace already had the story in London while they were still in transit. All staff of the *Daily Mail* editorial and printing, were locked into their London office for the night to prevent any chance of leakage. At dawn the *Daily Mail* was on the streets with the glad tidings of peace. Only on the next day was the official announcement made in the House of Commons. It left General Lord Kitchener mortified and apoplectic. All he could do in his rage was instruct the chief censor to write a letter on 1 July 1902 to Edgar Wallace. '*In consequence of you having evaded the rules of censorship subsequent to the warning you received, you will not in future be allowed to act as war correspondent and further, you will not be recommended for the medal*'.

Wallace sent the letter to the *Daily Mail*, who published it. In the meantime, as soon as he broke the story of peace, Edgar rushed off to Ivy in Cape Town. In the midst of negotiations on 23 May, she had given birth to a daughter. He also had news for her. Harry Cohen had found his connection with the press so exciting and profitable in its power to influence share prices that he had decided to own a paper himself. He had bought the suspended *Standard and Diggers News*. He had appointed Edgar Wallace as its editor on the then handsome salary of £2 000 per annum. The two men had decided to rename the paper the *Rand Daily Mail* in honour of the association with the London *Daily Mail*. Several of Edgar's associates from Reuters including Bulpin, would be joining him on the staff. For a man of 27, after so short an experience of professional journalism, it was a tremendous advancement.

The new paper came out in the autumn of 1902. Johannesburg was a rich field for journalism and Edgar Wallace was in his element. For the first time in his life he had plenty of money. He and Ivy settled down to some stylish living in Johannesburg. He revealed himself as a real high roller, entertaining, indulging his inherited fascination in the theatre, planning to start writing plays, and gambling. He and Bulpin wrote lively copy for his own newspaper and also continued to feed the London *Daily Mail* with features on such topics as the current Chinese cheap labour controversy; the slums of Johannesburg; the sartorially impeccable, autocratic Lord Milner, the British High-Commissioner, suggesting that South Africa would be pleased if that gentleman would be relieved of his office.

Within seven months, Edgar Wallace confronted a problem. Being an editor was very different from being a glamourous roving war correspondent. His writing style was selling the newspaper but making for himself some powerful enemies. Harry Cohen became uneasy. His motivation in buying the newspaper had been to use it to support his numerous and very considerable financial interests, and to influence the share market. He was the owner of the paper and, simply, its policy had to be decided by himself, not the editor. Cohen and Wallace started to quarrel. The climax came early in 1903. Cohen had guaranteed £250 000 towards a government loan of £30 000 000 for the development of various gold-mines. The anticipated profits of these mines was dependent on such factors as cheap labour, loose control of safety conditions and other aspects of management. Cohen anticipated a high return on his investments. He demanded unstinting support from his newspaper for his interests. He didn't receive it, so Wallace went, along with editorial integrity. Cohen sold the newspaper to Abe Bailey.

Edgar Wallace returned to London, taking his wife with him. Their infant daughter had died in Johannesburg of meningitis. The couple left in heavy debt from their high living and arrived in London with six shillings between them, but the asset of Edgar's reputation as a war correspondent. The London *Daily Mail* unhesitatingly gave him employment on its editorial staff. The salary of £15 a week didn't compare to his editor's remuneration in Johannesburg but he was on Fleet Street, only 28 years of age and the world was before him. He settled down and started to write. His first play, based on the life of Cecil Rhodes, was staged in Cape Town. It was a failure but he wrote more than a dozen others which became smash hits. His first book, *The Four Just Men*, was published in 1906 at his own risk to the printer because he couldn't find a publisher. With the book almost ready from the printer, Wallace realised that he couldn't pay for it. In his despair at the prospect of a debtors prison, a publisher by the name of George Newnes approached him. Newnes had been shown the printed sheets by the printer and quite liked the book. He offered to pay the printer's bill and gave Wallace £100 in cash for all rights to the book's royalties. Wallace had to agree. The book sold several million copies, was made into a film and radio and television series. Every publisher in the world was then at Wallace's door. He wrote 140 other books and became the largest selling author the world has ever known. His royalties were prodigious but he lived so extravagantly that he was always in debt – he kept a string of race horses and mistresses; his family never worked. He wrote many short stories and film scripts. The British Lion Film Corporation was created for the express purposes of transferring his scripts to the screen. When he was 56, Radio-Keith-Orpheum studios in Hollywood commissioned him to write a blockbusting script which they knew was within the capacity of his incredible imagination. He went to Hollywood, wrote the script, collected his money and was about to return to Britain when he died very suddenly, strangely enough, of drink. He had never drunk alcohol in his life. When he wrote he sustained himself on endless cigarettes and big pots of freshly made strong tea with so much sugar that the drink was almost solid syrup. He died of sugar diabetes. The film was *King Kong*.

On the Witwatersrand, meanwhile, a drama was being played out between the mine owners, their workers and the people of Southern Africa. The Transvaal, in those post-war years, was being ruled as a Crown Colony with Lord Milner as Governor, assisted by an Executive Council of officials, and a Legislative Council to which non-official members were appointed by the government. The new regime was giving tremendous change and direction to Transvaal affairs and, in a country as fundamentally rich as Southern Africa, even a moderately sensible, let alone a progressive government, could produce remarkable results.

Commissions had been established to examine most aspects of life in the Transvaal. As their findings were published and when they were acted upon, there were profound changes. The mining department was completely reorganised and the staff found for a comprehensive geological survey of the Transvaal. A forestry department was also established and the first plantations were made in the Transvaal in 1903 in order to meet the demand for pit props and general timber. A water commission also produced a report which was destined to have far reaching consequences. Acting on its findings the Rand Water Board was formed in 1903 with its members made up of representatives of Johannesburg, the Reef municipalities and the mines. It was delegated the responsibility of supplying water to the entire Rand and given full power to raise loans for the financing of any large project.

The assets of the former company were taken over and found to be capable of supplying only three million gallons a day, mainly from boreholes on the farm *Zuurbekom*, 28 km south-west of Johannesburg. The Water Board had to augment this supply as rapidly as possible from new boreholes on *Zuurbekom* and *Zwartkoppies*. Eventually, when these areas were completely exploited the Board searched for a new source of supply. Advised by its engineer, W Ingham, the Board, in 1913, decided on constructing a barrage across the Vaal River. This was completed in October 1922, and remains today the principal water source of the Witwatersrand.

Another post-war commission of particular interest to the mines was formed in November 1902. It was given the task of inquiring into the incidence of miners phthisis. Everybody was agreed that some supervisory system would have to be devised in order to improve and control working conditions. Miners phthisis was becoming increasingly worse as the mines reached deeper levels. Of 1 377 rock drill miners who continued work underground during the war years, 225 died of phthisis. In 1902 the new rock drill known as the 'water leyner' was introduced and this promised some relief from the trouble. Water was pumped through the shaft during drilling in order to drown the fatal dust. Curiously enough, the drillers, whose health had so much to gain from using this new device were so conservative in their working techniques that they resisted the change.

The commission confirmed that miners phthisis was 'a silicosis produced by the inhalation of minute particles of inorganic matter with which the mine atmosphere is charged'. The water-drill, better ventilation, and general cleanliness seemed to be the logical preventatives. There was some talk of a respirator, and the Chamber of Mines offered prizes for any new ideas. Half the battle against phthisis, however, was won with general awareness of the real cause of the trouble. Human ailments are most terrible when their origin is cloaked in mystery.

The work continued of getting the established mines back into production and here the basic problem remained one of labour. A large number of British soldiers took their discharge in South Africa and to secure local demobilisation they had to produce a guarantee of some employment. To secure this guarantee, most of them accepted labourers' work on the mines. This provided some relief for the labour scarcity, at least until the soldiers found something better for themselves to do. Any idea about increasing wages on the mines in order to influence demobilised soldiers into permanent employment was regarded as pure heresy. Mine owners had a thing about wages. With them it was a taboo subject. While the war was still raging, the Chamber of Mines had met in Cape Town and actually decided, in a full blossoming of their wisdom, to reduce African miners wages when the mines reopened from the established 47 shillings and one penny paid a month to 30 shillings a month.

The whole question of long-term labour policy on the mines was receiving considerable attention at this time. It was only too obvious that, without a reliable flow of labour, the anticipated mining growth would be seriously stunted. A great deal of argument took place over what was to be done. Just after the war a full-time recruiting organisation known as the Witwatersrand Native Labour Association was organised as a communal effort on the part of the mines to obtain a regular supply of labour without division of effort and costly competition among themselves.

All manner of schemes were proposed to produce the necessary workers. Madagascar was suggested as one source of labour. A group of owners favoured European unskilled labour, with men to be imported from places such as Hungary, Russia or Italy. The latter suggestion was discussed in detail in 1903 when a representative of the Italian Immigration Department visited the country.

The Witwatersrand Native Labour Association redoubled its efforts with recruiters sent as far afield as what was then Nyasaland (Malawi) in 1903. Working conditions were also improved with better food, a free evening ration of a quart of sorghum beer, introduced in 1902, and more comfortable quarters. The labour shortage continued, however, and a report published on 19 November 1903, by an investigating commission reported flatly that the mine's requirements of 129 000 workers a year in excess of their present supply could not possibly be met in Africa.

There was some furious quarrelling over this report. The contention that Africa with its millions of inhabitants could not fill more labour demands was considered to be absurd by many. The big guns in the mining industry, however, nearly all supported the principle of imported labour. Their inclination now lay in the direction of China. Their attention had been drawn to this recruiting ground by such people as P Leys, an ex-Consul General for North Borneo who, writing in *The 19th Century* magazine in February 1902, had recommended the Chinaman as the ideal worker. The Witwatersrand Native Labour Association confirmed that they could not possibly meet the labour demand directed at them from any source in Africa.

Supporters of Asiatic labour, by having in their ranks many of the most influential men in the mining industry, gradually swung official sanction to their solution of the problem. Early in 1903 the Chamber of Mines sent H Ross Skinner to the East to study details of the recruitment, feeding and accommodation of Chinese labourers. On 16 July 1903, the Chamber carried the whole idea another step forward. Carl Hanau introduced a resolution to the monthly meeting of the Chamber of Mines declaring it to be in favour of the importation of alien labour under legislative restrictions preventing the labourers from settling permanently in the country. The resolution was passed.

It became the official policy of the mines, notwithstanding the continued arguments of the minority, notably F H P Cresswell, General Manager of the Village Reef General Mining Company, who championed the cause of white mining labour.

The Native Labour Commission, which sat from 21 July to 6 October 1903, finalised the whole issue with the majority's report supporting alien labour. The minority report disagreed radically with the findings of the majority but this was over-ruled. At the end of December 1903 the Legislative Council, persuaded by mining members such as Sir George Farrar and Sir Percy Fitzpatrick, passed a motion calling for Chinese labour. The government published the necessary draft ordinance on 6 January 1904. A new order came with a vengeance to the Transvaal mines. Notwithstanding the uneasiness of the local population, the protests of the liberal opposition in Britain and the dismay of the champions of European labour, the steamer *Tweeddale* sailed from Hong Kong for Durban on 25 May 1904. It carried on its decks the first batch of 1 055 Chinese labourers destined for work on the mines.

The advent of the Chinamen had several effects which substantially influenced Johannesburg, South Africa and Britain itself. The inhabitants of the Transvaal were hostile to the introduction of so exotic a crowd of workers. Public meetings of protest were held in Johannesburg but invariably broken up by organised gangs of hooligans trucked in from the mines. The men were paid the equivalent of a day's shift work to stamp on the floor, break chairs, pick fights and chant. *'Who are we, who are we? 'We are the men who want the Chinee'*.

The new British administration was supportive of the mine owners, many of whom had been or were awaiting knighthood from the court of King Edward V11 for their services in bringing the wealth of the Transvaal into the control of Britain. The local police force quite happily arrested anybody at the meetings who resisted molestation by the hooligans.

The Johannesburg newspapers were all affected. Their staff well knew what was going on but any notions they had of editorial integrity were soon shattered. They were expected to be subservient to the newspaper owners. Most of the owners had interests in mining. There was no future for journalists deluding themselves with ideas of independence or moral high ground. If truth was considered harmful to the making of money it was suppressed and distorted. If journalists did not like it they were fired. The Dutch speaking inhabitants of Johannesburg referred contemptuously to the printed media by the old Dutch word *pappekak* (diarrhoea). English readers agreed and picked the term up in the anglicised form of poppycock journalism. Local newspapers lost credibility. They became regarded as mouthpieces of the Chamber of Mines and big business.

The editor of the Johannesburg evening newspaper, *The Star*, W F Moneypenny, on 3 December 1902, the day after the Chamber of Mines passed their resolution approving Chinese labour, published an editorial disagreeing with them and ending with the words *'The present editor of The Star withdraws'*. He left in disgust. Sir Alfred Milner, the British High Commissioner promptly put his private secretary, G G Robinson into the editor's chair and this guaranteed dutiful support for Chinese labour and any other actions by the mine owners and financiers.

The Chinamen were employed on the same rates of pay as the Africans, with contracts for three years work before being returned home. The government took the opportunity of the change, however, to enforce as standard practice, the recommendations of the medical experts involved in a recent inquiry on the mortality rate on the mines. The Chinese, incidentally, appeared to be a sturdier crowd than the Africans and it is worth repeating a newspaper description of the first batch to reach the Rand from the *Tweeddale* on 22 June 1904.

> **'Their baggage was simple',** noted The Star, *'and not of much greater proportions than that Kaffirs usually carry. They had their wicker-worked baskets, their little pillows, made of bamboo sticks, the simplest of contrivances, their sleeping mats, and their tin pannikins. They appeared in the best of good humour, joked amongst themselves, and were most obedient to the overseers. They were clad in blue overalls made of the material usually worn by stokers. Their cleanly appearance was striking after the long train journey. They averaged 5 ft 4 in in height but a few reached 5 ft 8 in They are muscular, intelligent in appearance and from appearances should be serviceable for the work for which they are intended. Their pigtails, over two feet in length were entwined on their heads for the most part.'*

The new Comet and Cason mines were the first two mines to be staffed by Chinamen. It was not intended that the Chinese be mixed with Africans. The first batch was led off to the compounds, and from the start the men were the centre of considerable attention. The mining experts waited impatiently to learn if the work output of the new labourers would justify all the hopes placed in them. The population of the Transvaal waited nervously to see whether their fears of Asiatic bogeymen would materialise. The politicians of both South Africa and Britain kept up a running commentary and a steady barrage of questions about the entire innovation.

Probably no other body of workmen in the history of industry have ever had their behaviour and productivity more keenly observed than this company of Chinamen, which, by September 1905, numbered 46 895. With 122 437 Africans and 18 510 Europeans as fellow workers, the Chinese were partly responsible that year for producing a gold output of 4 909 541 ounces, over one million ounces higher than anything ever before attained in the Transvaal.

As workmen the Chinese were industrious, but inclined to be reckless. Their casualty rate per thousand from accidents was 6,8% compared to 5,3% for Africans and 4% for Europeans. Off duty they were clean, sober, and reasonably healthy, apart from some beriberi brought with them from China. For entertainment they enjoyed amateur theatricals and gambling, which latter pastime brought no little grief to many of them, for they were hard losers, often choosing suicide as the only escape from their debts. In the first half of 1905 the Chinese earned £317 084. Of this £15 744 was remitted to China. The balance remained for pocket money and to settle gambling debts.

The European population of the Transvaal had expected the worst of the Chinamen. Nobody ever really understood the newcomers. They remained something in the nature of bogeymen whose occasional misdeeds received considerable attention. There was an inevitable flow of desertions. With the Africans, such deserters could simply lose themselves among their own people. A Chinese deserter, however, was an outlaw from the moment he slipped away from his compound. All hands were against him. Realising this, the Chinese deserter was invariably a desperate man.

Of the 46 895 Chinese in the Transvaal in September, 1905, 2 543 had been convicted by the police of a variety of offences, ranging through riotous behaviour, desertion, robbery or assault. Of this number, 1 735 men had deserted and 250 were still at large. Disease and accident had killed 629 men. A lively trade in opium had also commenced with over 3 500 lbs of the drug openly imported into the Transvaal by the usual batch of so-called 'reputable' merchants who justified the trade with the old standby that *'if they didn't do it, somebody else would'*.

From the public's reaction to the Chinamen it became obvious to the mine owners that the next general election in Great Britain would see much attention given to the matter, for the liberal opposition had always been hostile to the idea. It took little foresight, in fact, to predict that the bubble of cheap Chinese labour on the Rand was doomed to a sudden end.

The whole argument about the Chinamen was brought to a sudden climax on 4 December 1905, when the ruling British Unionist Party resigned after five years of office. The Liberal Party of Sir H Campbell-Bannerman formed the new government. Seventeen days later the new premier announced the suspension of Chinese recruitment until the British government could learn the opinion of the Transvaal people through a duly elected and truly representative local legislature. There was jubilation in the Transvaal at the news, and still more celebration on 19 February 1906, when the new British Parliament was ceremoniously opened. In his speech from the throne, the King stated that responsible government was to be given to the Transvaal.

The year 1906 may safely be described as pre-eminently the year of politics in the Transvaal. Everybody in the country seemed to be arguing, finding a political home in one or other of the new parties, and working up a temper about the various issues, particularly the Chinese question. One rather imagines that the Transvaal was a good place to be out of at this period. South Africans have always taken politics with a good measure of passion, noise and bitterness. The first election year in the Transvaal set a standard for legal injunctions, threats, fights, effigies burned at the stake, and a great display of extravagantly worded banners, mainly attacking or defending the Chinamen.

On 8 March 1906, the British Government announced the appointment of a Committee of Inquiry into Transvaal affairs, with the particular task of deciding on the basis of the new constitution. The gentlemen dispatched from Britain on this committee must have felt themselves dropped into a hornet's nest. South Africa has often been described as a graveyard of overseas political reputations. Its problems often seem transparent from a distance, but strangely opaque on closer inspection.

After the hearings of the Committee of Inquiry, the Transvaal was left for a short while to its political dog-fight. One wonders what the old guard would have thought of the noise and passion. Nearly all the leading actors in the Transvaal of the pre-Anglo-Boer War years had already taken their last bows on the golden stage and wandered away into the darkness beyond the stage door. Paul Kruger had died in exile in Switzerland on 14 July 1904. With all his stubbornness, reaction, and faults he will always be remembered as the old lion of the Transvaal. His great opponent, Cecil Rhodes, had preceded the president on 26 March 1902, leaving a fortune to be disbursed for worthwhile and progressive causes. Alfred Beit, the financial genius, also vanished from the scene in this period. He died in July 1906, and left £1 200 000 for development in Africa, £200 000 for the founding of the Witwatersrand University, as well as many other bequests.

On 31 July 1906, Winston Churchill introduced the new Transvaal constitution into the British parliament. A new political epoch was ushered into the country, and it is worth quoting from his introductory speech.

> *'The guiding principle in conferring Responsible Government on the Transvaal was to make no difference between Boer or Briton, but to extend to both the fullest privileges of British citizenship.*
>
> *'The government had adopted the voter's basis for the division of the constituencies and also the principle of manhood suffrage. Males over 21 years of age who had resided in the Transvaal for six months would be allowed to vote under the secrecy of the ballot.*
>
> *'The government had decided to have single-member districts and to adopt the old magisterial districts for electoral purposes.*
>
> *'The government's final decision was 34 members for the Rand, 6 for Pretoria, and 29 for the rest of the Transvaal.*
>
> *'Either Dutch or English could be spoken in the new Parliament.*
>
> *'Chinese labour would end, with all recruitment prohibited after November of that year'.*

There was no mention of the Black population. They simply did not exist although they were the majority. Women, of any colour, had no vote.

Polling day for the first Transvaal government was set for the 20 February 1907. The end of all the quarrelling came as a relief to the country. The result was a victory for the Dutch *Het Volk* or People's Union party led by Louis Botha and violently hostile to Chinese labour. They won 37 seats while the Progressive party, largely the mouthpiece of the mine owners, and pro-Chinese, won 21 seats. There were also 11 odd seats held by minor parties who would all vote with the Het Volk government, providing its policy was liberal. The Chinese issue had been the principal reason for the defeat of the Progressive party.

The new government of Louis Botha had to assume a load of troubles. There was a general depression in the Transvaal with unemployment and numerous petitions to government for aid and relief. In the midst of it all there occurred the first really major labour disturbance on the Rand mines. It started with a strike of 60 Europeans on the Knight's Deep on 1 May 1907. The complaint of the men was the reduction of footage by 10 shillings a fathom from £3 15s 0d to £3 5s 0d, and the introduction of a third African rock driller to the supervision of each European. The men claimed that the extra drill in a team would be an added hazard to health on account of the dust, and that it was impossible for one man to supervise three rock drills and at the same time observe all mine safety regulations. The Transvaal Miners' Association organised the strike.

On 22 May 1907, this Association proclaimed a general strike in an effort to stop any black-legging. Meetings became increasingly rowdy and bitter, while the government sent troops to the Rand to maintain order, and prevent the Chinese from fishing in troubled waters.

Fights and minor riots broke out all over the Rand. Fortunately General Louis Botha returned on 30 May to the Transvaal from a visit to Britain. He immediately interviewed a deputation from the miners and by his moderation saw that trouble was reduced to a minimum. It was not an easy problem for a man with a background of farming and military activity to solve. He agreed, however, to an arbitration board, which was what the men had been asking for over the last three years. The strike then petered out during the first week of June 1907. The government subsequently found itself unable to arbitrate on the recent dispute as it had no legislative powers. It decided, however to devise suitable legislation to deal with any future disputes. The workers lost this first major strike in South Africa. The lasting effect was the appearance of the Dutch speaking miner on the Rand, and the return to Britain of a steady stream of men of the old school who declined to accept any adjustment to their accepted standard of living. From this date on the accents of Cornwall were increasingly replaced underground by the gutturals of Dutch and the developing Afrikaans language.

The year 1907 ended with the general depression still in full swing all over the world. There was great political talk of union in South Africa as an antidote to all local economic ills. So far as the mines were concerned, they were all working at top pressure, with a new record of 6 450 740 ounces of gold produced in 1907. Mining activity not only provided the country with its major income, but was also beginning to produce a curious side-effect. On 7 February 1908 the first major earth tremor was felt in Johannesburg. Minor tremors had been occasionally felt before that, but they were too slight to attract much attention. From the February tremor onwards, however, these disturbances became regular phenomena along the Rand as the earth started to compensate by slips and re-adjustments for the astonishing excavations conducted beneath its surface.

When the politicians finally agreed on the draft Act of Union, uniting the two former Boer states, South African Republic and Orange Free State, and the two former British colonies – Cape of Good Hope and Natal, the Union of South Africa was born on 31 May 1910. It had, in fact, an auspicious beginning with a parallel return to prosperity all over the world. The South African mining industry looked forward to a tremendous future, with no great trouble clouding its horizon, with no worrisome technical problem beyond hope of comprehension. Even the involved labour position was quiet and free of disturbances.

The last Chinamen were repatriated to their homeland in February 1910, and that whole experiment ended. The Chinese even took home with them the ashes of their deceased comrades packed in tin tea boxes for burial in the soil of China.

The fear, ill-feeling and prejudice around the controversial figures of Chinese cheap labour had a long-lasting influence on the story of Southern Africa. To the Boers it was a particularly bitter humiliation.

The Boers were still trying to adapt themselves to their defeat in the war and the new order of British Colonial rule. The loss of their independence had been given a slight sugar coating in that at least the whole of South Africa, like Cinderella, would now be transformed from a drab kitchen drudge of the international financial world into a diamond and gold bedecked princess, with prosperity for all. Instead, the insatiable greed for profits of the so-called Randlords of the mining industry, their total lack of any social responsibility, the destructive unsustainability of their parasitic industry on the environment and their arrogant disregard of the local population, Black or White, emphasised Boer belief that the war had been launched by the British for the sole purpose of looting the country of its natural wealth for the benefit of an exotic crowd of financial gangsters and their overseas shareholders. The whole caboodle were gorging themselves at a veritable banquet of treasures, watched hungrily through the windows by the indigenous people denied even the left-over crumbs of low paid labour, their very culture and life-style threatened by the introduction of a completely alien people.

Discontent and feelings of injustice simmered. The looming First World War also complicated the whole unhealthy political situation. The Germans had shown sympathy to the Boer cause in the Anglo-Boer War. The rivalry for colonies between the two imperial powers of Britain and Germany stimulated the Germans to taunt the British by criticising their inept military record during the Anglo-Boer War and other minor colonial wars. They gave the Boers the impression that if Germany was victorious in the anticipated coming war with Britain, Boer support might be rewarded with restoration of independence rather than just a transference from one empire to the other of the riches of the old republic.

Boer desire for a German victory in turn stirred up the jingoism of the British. They suspected the worst from the signs of revival of the prostrate Boers. There were fights in bars and a great deal of unpleasantness, especially in the slum suburbs of Johannesburg where the working class lived in dreary circumstances.

British victory over Germany was a dreadful disappointment to the Boers. The British celebrated, the Boers were once again dispirited and humiliated. When Dr D F Malan, the Cape

Nationalist Party leader visited Johannesburg, his public meeting on 17 April 1918 was violently broken up by an English speaking crowd. Members of his audience were assaulted. The National Club building was attacked, its furniture dragged into the street, set alight, and the whole place vandalised.

Three men in their late teens, D H C du Plessis, H J Klopper and H W van der Merwe, were very disturbed by these events. The three met the next day and found seclusion in a walk to the summit of the rocky ridge overlooking the suburb of Kensington. Looking out over the panoramic view of Johannesburg, they decided to create an organisation devoted to the defence of their people, the Afrikaners, their culture and language, and to restore them to their just place in South African politics and economy. It was a momentous decision with consequences far beyond their conception.

On the evening of 5 June 1918, they convened a meeting in the home of D H C du Plessis, in the suburb of Malvern and founded what they named *Jong Suid-Afrika* (Young South Africa). The intention was to draw together young Afrikaners in a purely cultural, friendly society, to provide aid, support and advice to those in need.

For the first two years the society was open and benign but it failed to attract members. Times were too harsh for many people to have money and inclination for purely cultural matters. By 1920 there were only 37 members. Meetings were public, held in Dutch Reformed Church parsonages and halls, but the British still regarded them as suspicious relics of pro-German supporters. There was much discussion among the 37 members about the future of the society. It became obvious that something would have to be done otherwise the society would simply fade away.

On 21 September 1920, the 37 members reached a decision. *Jong Suid-Afrika* was transformed into the *Afrikaner Broederbond* (Afrikaner Brotherhood) with new rules of membership. It was still culturally inclined but the intention was to make of it a fellowship exclusively for Afrikaners. It would be a counter to the English-speaking clubs and such secret societies as the Free Masons who were dedicated to the preferment in all things of their own members. From thence on the Broederbond would work to benefit only fellow members by supportive actions and preference. On 26 August 1921, at a meeting in the old Carlton Hotel in Johannesburg, it was decided that the Broederbond would become a secret brotherhood. Membership would be by invitation only for Protestant Afrikaner males on the strictest language and social lines. Even marriage to a non-Afrikaner woman would preclude membership.

The Broederbond developed a credo defined in a circular sent to all members in 1939 by their then chairman, Professor J C van Rooy.

> *'The primary consideration is whether Afrikanerdom will reach its ultimate destiny of domination in South Africa. Brothers, the key to South African problems is not whether one party or another shall obtain the whiphand but whether the Afrikaner Broederbond shall govern South Africa.'*

By its 50th birthday in 1968, the Afrikaner Broederbond had experienced phenomenal success. They had increased from 37 founder members to 8 154 members in 560 cells scattered all over South Africa. The Broederbond was feeling very satisfied. Henning Klopper, one of the original 37 founder members, and the first chairman of the Broederbond, was one of the speakers at the 50th anniversary celebrations. Looking around at the assembled brothers he said proudly:

> *'Do you realise what a powerful force is assembled here tonight between these four walls? Show me a greater force on the whole continent of Africa. Show me a greater force anywhere else, even in your so-called civilised nations.*
>
> *'Looking at public life in South Africa we are glad that the Afrikaner Broederbond gives leadership in every facet and sphere and is indispensable there. Everywhere Broeders are manning the front lines.'*

The Broeders could certainly count many gains. They were volatile. Within another ten years their membership had reached 12 000 in 810 cells. Most influential Afrikaans speaking men were members. They could boast that since the National Party, their political wing, had come to power in

1948, every successive prime minister had been a Broederbonder along, with few exceptions every member of their cabinet. The civil service was dominated by them with appointment and promotion impossible without at least the approval, if not membership, of the Broederbond. The army and police force was completely under their thumb with Broederbonders as senior officers. Peripheral to these forces were covert operations such as BOSS (Bureau of State Security), CCB (Citizen Cooperation Bureau) and other dirty work and information gathering organisations, some of them very strange indeed. The South African Railways, harbours and airways were firmly under their control. The South African Broadcasting Corporation had Broederbonders in the top positions. They had made great progress in the printing and publishing industry. They published daily newspapers and periodicals distributed throughout South Africa. They had become the decision makers of South Africa

They had made equally powerful progress in commerce, industry, insurance and finance. Even the Reserve Bank, with its stranglehold powers over the economy of the country, was controlled by the Broederbond. Its governor was also on the State President's Advisory Council. The bank had full power to make or break the economy of the country with a spurious policy based on manipulation of interest rates, favours to Broederbond-controlled banks and enterprises and the ability to ruin overnight countless small businesses and individuals by strangling them with sudden hikes in bond and overdraft rates.

The Broederbond had become the stronghold of the super Afrikaners, the rich and powerful, sworn to support and prefer one another. They had manoeuvred their members into dominant positions in Southern Africa. They had infiltrated into culture, sport and education. The Afrikaans universities were dominated by Broeders. They devised an entire educational system known as Christian National Education. They were besotted with the dream of imposing the Afrikaans language as the sole official language for all the diverse peoples of Southern Africa. Non-Afrikaans-speaking white people in South Africa would be tolerated but only as inferiors. To deal with the vast majority of Black South Africans the ideology of *Apartheid* (separateness) was elaborated in great detail by the inner councils of the Broederbond. It was planned to keep the Black and White ethnic groups permanently segregated with the Whites securely on top and Broeders in supreme power for the next ten thousand years. They institutionalised nepotism, corruption and racialism to their advantage but not to that of their fellow human beings.

The trouble with the Broederbond was that in its impressive surge to power it left behind its own constituency of the Afrikaner working class. As the exclusive home of the rich and powerful it fell into the trap of considering that what was good for the rich minority was also good for the poor majority. It failed to realise that 12 000 Broeders could not hope to dominate the entire country. Its exclusiveness made it many enemies. Squabbles and rivalries within its ranks developed into factional feuds. Its cloak of secrecy became porous. It was impossible for there to be sufficient talent in their limited membership for enough efficient individuals to be provided to fill all positions of decision making of importance in the country. There were too many dud generals promoted by pure favouritism in police and army. The public lost all confidence in them. Corruption protected by secrecy became a way of life. Brutal suppression to protect privilege was the order of the day

Greed for power and money and disregard for the vast majority of South Africans turned the Broederbond into an anti-social political deformity stumbling about like Frankenstein's monster treading on other peoples toes with all manner of aggressive acts inimical to the interests of the majority. The Broederbond was also infected with Nazism. Hitler was their role model. Meetings were bedecked with banners proclaiming the Black danger, the Jewish menace, the Communist anti-Christ.

The Broederbond spawned crack-pot right wing groups such as Oswald Pirow's New Order, Wichardt's Grey Shirts and the *Ossewa Brandwag* (ox wagon sentries) who planted a few bombs and grew beards swearing never to shave until the Nazis won the war.

The Broederbond became increasingly self destructive. It became an isolated entity in its own country while Nazi sympathies during the Second World War brought it into international disrepute. The basic contradictions became only too apparent of a corrupt secret society foisting its own members and self interests on to society and still expecting them to be admired, respected and trusted. The Broederbond had to collapse. In doing so it left a hard core of fanatics, known as the new Bittereinders, to continue the lost cause of the racial supremacy of the few. This hard core provided the motivation in South Africa for what was known as the Third Force, a group which committed acts of murder, sabotage, brutality and terrorism to impede any fancied threat to their own supremacy.

The Broederbond found itself in an increasingly untenable position of its own making. The contradiction of the members of a small secret society trying to impose their will on the vast majority of the 40 million population of South Africa isolated them. The basic corruption and deceit of nepotism resultant from the foisting on by a minority to the majority of people in South Africa of leaders and decision makers whose loyalties were not for the country or its people but for their own secret little set became only too apparent. Few of these Broederbond appointees were competent to hold their jobs. The public lost all trust in them. Their Nazi sympathies made them repugnant to the outside world. They simply had to go. They went – pushed out rather than shot out. There was no bloody revolution.

The African National Congress which replaced them was not a social revolutionary party in the right or left wing sense. Their constituency empowered them to replace the apartheid regime without changing the social system. The bloodbath of a social revolution was therefore avoided. This relatively peaceful change did, however, have an unfortunate flip side to the coin. The new regime found the seats of administration left vacant for them, still temptingly warm with all the comfortable perquisites, high salaries, privileges, security and easy money corruption of their former occupants. The Broederbond was replaced by a Blackbond whose members had little comprehension of the cause of the severe problems of poverty, unemployment, associated crime and the despair of the mass of their own supporters who could not comprehend why, in a country of so much coal, iron, base and precious metals and stones, they were left in abject poverty with only the fortunate members of the elite, black simply replacing white, sitting at the same banquet table as the Randlords, while they starved. Such is the ongoing enigma of Southern Africa, its uncaring social establishment simply changing colour, with a hangover of a few Broederbond relics, untrustworthy, still lingering in positions of power on the excuse that, for the time being there is nobody able to replace them no matter how incompetent they are in the control of law, the economy and aspects of decision making.

Johannesburg became a city in 1928. By 1960 it had more than one million inhabitants. Today it is the centre of the most densely concentrated population in Southern Africa, all of whom live along the Witwatersrand in various municipalities which, with little vacant ground separating them, form one built-up area nearly 100 km long.

The city of Johannesburg developed from a gauche, untidy and quite unbeautiful mining camp. From the beginning it was purely mercenary, a regular painted lady with all the characteristics of her kind. Few of its citizens regarded it as being anything other than a convenience. It was knocked around, subjected to a great deal of ill-usage, exploitation and harsh treatment, and regarded by many people as a purely temporary affair, which grew against all expectations. This growth often astonished its inhabitants who, having made their fortunes, left Johannesburg with a smirk. On returning for a nostalgic visit in later years they found the place transformed like Cinderella.

In the space of the lifetime of a single human being, Johannesburg grew through every stage: bouncing babyhood; brawling youth; tarty girlhood; mindless teenager, flaming wanton; finally reaching a degree of maturity, preoccupied with money and having the self-consciousness of a respectably married one-time dancing girl, now primly hugging a fur coat around the bosom she once displayed with brazen abandon.

It is not possible to see much of the Johannesburg of old, since it has always been a place in the process of being pulled down and rebuilt. Local architecture always tended to be admired for little more than its height. In slum suburbs such as *Fordsburg* and *Jeppestown* (created by the estate company of Lewis Ford and Julius Jeppe) and *Vrededorp* (peaceful town) odd glimpses may be seen of the original mining camp – bleak, sleazy and sordid – where some rather battered-looking characters wander around the tougher areas. An extreme contrast is provided by the northern suburbs, residential areas as handsomely and beautifully developed as in any city on Earth. By means of these suburbs – Houghton, Killarney, Randburg, Rosebank, Sandton, Saxonwold and others –

man has turned a former treeless grassveld into a parkland of shady trees, lawns, gardens and pleasant homes.

The best way to begin an exploration of Johannesburg is by viewing the city from some high observation point. The highest natural point in the area of the city and of the whole Witwatersrand, is at Northcliff, the 1 808 m high *Aasvoëlkop* (peak of vultures). A fine panorama of the northern and north-western suburbs may be seen after an easy climb to the top of this peak. For the less energetic there are viewsites on the top of high buildings, yielding magnificent vistas of the city.

The highest building in Johannesburg is the J G Strijdom Tower, situated on Hospital Hill. This unbeautiful tower, resembling a large ramrod used by old-time artillery men, was completed in 1971. It was erected as a microwave transmitting centre for the South African Posts and Telecommunications Department. Its construction in the midst of a congested residential area was controversial. At times, local residents pelted rubbish at the monster growing in their midst. Telecommunications engineers, however, are a breed not notable for their aesthetic consideration. The site of the tower suited them and up it went, with no concession being made to appearance. The tallest building in Africa, the tower (named after a former Prime Minister of South Africa) is 269 m high. It was built with an observation room, revolving restaurant and souvenir shop near the top. The view of the city area as seen from the top is dramatic, especially at sunset. The tower is at present closed to the public for security reasons.

The suburb of Hillbrow in which the tower stands has some pretensions of being a cosmopolitan bohemian sort of place. It is certainly a hang-out of vagrants, layabouts, drug addicts and dropouts. Several of the shops in the area remain open until a late hour, or do not close at all, providing the nights with a little more liveliness than the funereal state of some other areas. Unfortunately, the few local residents trying to live up to the pseudo-Bohemian reputation of Hillbrow are as drab and boring as similar mindless people the world over. Scenically, there is a fine artificial waterfall on Pullinger Kop, on the approach to Hillbrow, but it works rather erratically.

The second highest building in Johannesburg is the tower erected in the suburb of Brixton for the South African Broadcasting Corporation. This tower is 235 m high and has a steel transmitting antenna on top, adding a further 52 m in height. Used for television and audio high-frequency radio transmissions, the tower was named in honour of Albert Hertzog, a former Minister of Posts and Telegraphs, but is today referred to simply as the Brixton Tower. This is a notably graceful construction, especially at night when skilful lighting causes it to resemble a giant red-hot poker. The view from the observation platform is superb and reveals the whole of the Witwatersrand, stretching from east to west, where so many lights twinkle at night that the area seems to be a continuation of the Milky Way. The scene is not only impressive but also instructive, It was formerly an essential item on the agenda of all visitors to the city, for it effectively dispelled the popular misconception that Johannesburg is built on top of underground mine workings. Unfortunately the tower is now closed to the public for security reasons.

From this tower it is easy to see that the gold-bearing reef approaches the surface in a narrow belt, plunging diagonally downwards to tremendous, as yet unplumbed depths. Mining operations are concentrated along this belt of reef, known as the Main Reef of the Witwatersrand. No mining takes place on either side of the reef, as all workings are vertical or lateral. Work in the central part of the reef has now ceased, for levels have been reached below which it is unprofitable to mine and to haul ore to the surface. The deepest mine in the central area adjoining Johannesburg was the Crown Mines, in its day one of the richest mines in the world. The workings of this mine reached a depth of over 3 000 m before operations were discontinued.

As seen from the Brixton tower, the mine workings – headgear, slag and tailing dumps, mills, dams storing water pumped from the mines as well as storm water – stretch in a long line, dividing the city into two halves, with the southern suburbs on the south side, and the city area, Hospital Hill and the northern suburbs to the north.

In both used and disused mine workings, constant movements of rock occur as the earth adjusts to the stresses and strains which result from the removal of vast quantities of material. These subterranean adjustments cause dreadful accidents in mining. However, their only surface physical effect on Johannesburg is to send tremors through the ground beneath the city. Buildings shudder but the vibrations are not strong enough to do significant damage. The periodic rumbles and shakes are part of life in Johannesburg. Visitors find them mildly alarming. The true 'Joburgers' or 'Joeys' (as the residents of Johannesburg or 'Joeys' are called) regard them with indifference.

Another instructive aspect of the towers is their play with lightning, especially during summer when electrical storms involve them in high drama. Both towers have been struck on countless occasions by the full force of lightning on the grand scale common to the South African highveld. The towers simply shrug off bolts of lightning which could illuminate a fair-sized town. The steel antennae on top of the towers are connected to the steel reinforcement of the concrete structures. This in turn is connected to copper strips buried in the earth. Nobody in either tower even realises that the structures have been hit.

The building most notable (at least for its bulk) in the city centre is the Carlton Centre. On the top (50th floor) of this building, an observation area is open to the public from 09h00 to 23h00 daily. There is a restaurant on the top and the view, especially of the built-up central city areas, is very impressive.

As seen from above, it is particularly obvious that the original surveyors of Johannesburg laid out the town in straight streets and square blocks – a completely functional plan without any adornment of boulevards, ornamental approaches or open squares.

The principal streets of the city are: *Commissioner,* named in honour of the Government commissioners involved in the proclamation of the gold-fields and the establishment of the city; *Eloff,* named after F C Eloff, private secretary to President Kruger when Johannesburg was laid out; *Harrison*, named after George Harrison who found the first payable gold of the Witwatersrand; *Jeppe*, named after Carl Jeppe, pioneer mine and property developer; *Joubert,* named after Christiaan Johannes Joubert, one of the first mining commissioners; *Loveday,* named after R K Loveday, first representative of the diggers in the Volksraad; *Pritchard*, named after W A Pritchard, who surveyed much of early Johannesburg; *Rissik*, named after Johann Rissik, one of the Government commissioners after whom the city itself is named, *Von Brandis*, named after Carl von Brandis, the first mining commissioner and *Hollard*, with its fountain of dolerite boulders and reflecting pools, named after Emil Hollard, lawyer and financier. The second and third stock exchanges used to be on this street, while in proximity are the head offices of many of the major mining houses. Close by, also, is the imposing Rand Club with its sumptuous interior modelled on Michelangelo's Farnese Palace in Rome. Around these edifices of big business, this modern central business district of Johannesburg is a classic example of urban decay, an incongruous comparison of enormous riches and sordid squalor, the end result of a get-rich and fly-by-night social system.

The buildings in the city centre are contrived mainly of concrete and glass and were simply designed to occupy the maximum space permissible. One of the few buildings linking Johannesburg with its past is the Rissik Street post office, designed by Sytze Wierda, head of the Public Works Department in the original South African Republic. The laying of the foundation-stone of this building in 1897 was a great occasion for the people of Johannesburg. The erection by the Government of so substantial a building was visual reassurance that authorities considered the town to be permanent, and that it would not become a dilapidated, abandoned place of ghosts, exhausted mines and long-departed dancing-girls. The post office had a ground floor and two upper floors, and was attractively designed and faced with red bricks. With two cupolas and a central bell tower, the building was the pride of Johannesburg.

After the Anglo-Boer War, the British added a top storey and a clock tower. In the process they removed the cupolas and the central bell tower. In exchange (to commemorate the coronation of King Edward V11 in 1902) they installed a clock which had been made in England by the same firm which had manufactured Big Ben, its chimes being identical. Ever since it was first set in motion, this clock has, with a few technical interruptions, told Johannesburg the time in a loud, clear, authoritative voice. The chime was taken from the fifth bar of Handel's aria from the *Messiah* 'I know that my Redeemer liveth'. The chime says in its four quarters,

> 'All through this hour,
> Lord be my guide,
> And by thy power,
> No foot shall slide'

The old building is now quite dwarfed by the towering modern glass and concrete skyscapers, but it retains a subtle charm, a mellowness of design and colour making it architecturally superior to the buildings around it. A new main post office of the usual concrete type was opened in Jeppe Street in 1935.

Immediately behind the Rissik Street post office, on a site once occupied by the Standard theatre, there is a garden in which a fountain plays, with eighteen bronze impala antelope jumping through the jets of water and a rainbow which is formed at various times of the day. The fountain was given to Johannesburg by Harry Oppenheimer, in memory of his father, Sir Ernest, the renowned mining magnate. The bronze impalas are the work of the sculptor Hermann Wald.

On the opposite side of the post office in Rissik Street, stands the Johannesburg city hall with its solid stone facings. It was designed in the Italian Renaissance style by a Cape Town firm of architects, Hawke & McKinley. Constructed between 1910 and 1915, it has now been refurbished at great expense to house the Legislative Assembly of the Gauteng Provincial Administration. Its interior has been decorated in warm African colours. An imposing assembly hall replaces the former Duncan hall. The new Metropolitan Centre and the Civic Theatre are on Hospital Hill.

One and a half kilometres west of the Legislative Assembly hall, off Bree Street, stands the Oriental Plaza, a lively and interesting modern shopping centre containing about 300 shops in an area of 9 ha. Opened in 1974, this shopping centre replaced the hotchpotch of shops under Indian management which lined Fourteenth Street, Pageview. Though picturesque, these shops were hopelessly cramped, unhygienic and dilapidated. The street was considerably congested. The new centre was a joint project in urban renewal of the State Department of Community Development and the Johannesburg City Council. The architecture is imaginative and it consolidates the separate businesses in one attractive, harmonious building complex. The oriental atmosphere is stimulating and, as in the original Fourteenth Street, there are many unusual novelties and bargains to be found.

A major feature of the central area is the railway station, the largest on the continent of Africa and very nearly the size of Grand Central in New York. The entrance to the original concourse building is at the northern end of Eloff Street. It was erected in the 1930s and was originally decorated with murals by the South African artist J H Pierneef. This concourse also contained the first locomotive to serve the Witwatersrand. The little 'puffing billy' was carted in pieces up to Johannesburg by ox-wagon in 1890.

Behind this building is the modern station, completed in 1966 and covering 22 ha with platforms and tracks. The main concourse is 168 m long, 43 m wide and 18 m high. It contains a variety of shops, restaurants and snack-bars. Escalators convey passengers down to the various platforms. Adjoining the station is the airways terminal and railways head-office building in a garden setting. A railway museum is housed in a part of the station building, and this contains many exhibits particularly fascinating to train enthusiasts.

The churches of the city area also add some architectural interest to the mass of concrete buildings. Among them is an impressive mosque, the Madressa Himayatil Islam. This building, standing at the corner of Market and Nugget Streets, has a minaret 30 m high, which is equipped with a powerful public address system in order to save the muezzin the fatigue from climbing for the five daily obligatory calls to prayer. The floor is electrically heated for the comfort of the devout at prayer. The mosque was founded in 1916 and has been enlarged in recent years.

The Roman Catholic Cathedral of Christ the King, built in 1960 in End Street, is of unusual design. A variety of materials were used to produce a finish of mellow brick, red granite and stained glass which floods the interior with crimson, viridian and golden light.

The Anglican St Mary's Cathedral was built in 1926 and designed by Sir Herbert Baker, an architect whose creative genius gave South Africa many of its finest buildings. The cathedral, with its imposing appearance, was constructed from hammer-dressed sandstone.

The Great Synagogue in Wolmarans Street was built in 1913 and designed with a magnificent dome by Theopile Scheerer in the style of Santa Sophia in Istanbul.

Overlooking the city area of Johannesburg from the north is the Hospital Hill ridge, densely covered with flats and other buildings. Part of this ridge is named after the Johannesburg general hospital, which was built on it. On the summit of the ridge stands the Johannesburg fort, a grim old stronghold built in the 1890s and designed by Colonel A H Schiel, a professional German soldier in the employ of the South African Republic. The purpose of the fort was to keep the boisterous digger community in order. A garrison of the State artillery was maintained there, together with armaments of cannon and machine-guns.

Happily, the fort was never used for military purposes. After the Anglo-Boer War it was converted into a prison. It is now a museum. Above its main entrance is the carved coat of arms of the former South African Republic (*Zuid-Afrikaansche Republic*), reputedly the work of the famous sculptor Anton van Wouw.

Close to the fort, built on the original parade-ground of the garrison, is the building of the Medical Research Institute designed by Sir Herbert Baker. To the west is the Metropolitan Centre, the vast administrative office-block of the City Council, and near it the Civic Theatre, the home of ballet, opera, drama and music. In front of the theatre is a fountain consisting of three bronze figures dancing, with water playing at their feet. The sculptor Ernest Ullman created the bronzes.

Still further to the west along the same ridge lie the two universities of Johannesburg. The oldest, the University of the Witwatersrand, strangely enough, originated in Kimberley in 1869 as a training institute for the mining industry. An offshoot of the institute was established in Johannesburg after the Anglo-Boer War. In 1906 it became the Transvaal University College, with a branch opened in Pretoria in 1907, which later became the University of Pretoria.

For some years the Johannesburg college only taught mining and technology but various other departments were gradually added. In 1922 it became the University of the Witwatersrand. The Johannesburg City Council had already presented a 32 ha site to the college at Milner Park. From the handful of buildings erected there in 1922 the present massive complex has arisen, housing over 15 000 students. Opposite the entrance to the university there is a delightful little fountain with two bronze antelopes drinking. The bronzes were sculpted by Ernest Ullman. The University of the Witwatersrand uses English as the medium of tuition. To its west, close to the Brixton tower and the audio-visual studios of the South African Broadcasting Corporation, lies the campus of the Rand Afrikaans University. Established in 1966, this Afrikaans-medium university is housed in a magnificent complex of modern buildings. It has an enrolment of 8 500 students.

Johannesburg is fortunate in that it possesses many open areas in the suburbs around the central city. There are approximately 600 parks and gardens within the city limits, providing over 4 000 ha of open space, recreational areas, picnic grounds and walks.

The best-known and oldest park in Johannesburg is *Joubert Park*, laid out in 1887 on 6,43 ha of vacant ground close to the city centre. Named after Christiaan Johannes Joubert, first chief of the Mining Department, this park is a green oasis set among asphalt streets and concrete buildings, where office workers eat their lunch under the trees and mothers, children and old people emerge from the shadows of their flats and enjoy the sunshine and fresh air. Situated in the park is a floral clock, giant open-air chess board, conservatory of tropical plants, restaurant and fountain. At Christmas, carols are sung and the park is illuminated. There is an art gallery and an open-air mart where any artist can exhibit his work and sell directly to the public.

The Johannesburg Art Gallery is housed in a building designed by Sir Edward Luytens as a fine example of British classical architecture. The gallery started as the private collection of Lady Phillips, wife of Sir Lionel Phillips, one of the mining magnates. Between 1904 and 1909 she collected from her wealthy friends a considerable amount of money for the purpose of creating an art gallery for Johannesburg. The first part of the building was opened in 1915 and another section in 1940. The gallery was finally completed in 1986. It is open Tuesdays to Sundays 10h00 to 17h00; closed on Christmas and Good Friday.

Bezuidenhout Park lies in the eastern suburbs, at Dewetshof, and is of considerable historical interest. It was originally the heart of the farm *Doornfontein* owned by F J Bezuidenhout when the rush to the Witwatersrand took place. The farm lay well away from the gold-bearing reef and, although it was prospected, no gold was found on it. The Bezuidenhouts, however, made a fortune by selling land for townships. Suburbs such as Bezuidenhout Valley, Doornfontein and Judith's Paarl were laid out on their property. The nucleus of the farm, with the homestead and the Bezuidenhout family graveyard, remained intact. Old Bezuidenhout died in 1900 and his son, Barend, in the 1920s. The Johannesburg City Council subsequently bought what remained of the farm. The deed of sale contained the condition that 40 ha, encompassing the homestead, garden, dam, cemetery and the original trees (mainly *Acacia karroo*), be preserved.

Bezuidenhout Park is therefore a unique combination of historical monument and recreational area, where such facilities as a miniature railway, children's playground and swimming-pool, tea-room, sports grounds, picnic spots, a caravan park and a walking area are provided in parkland.

In the suburb of Houghton Estate, a 17,45 ha expanse of ground covering part of the foothills of the Witwatersrand was presented to the city in 1937 by one of the major mining houses, the Johannesburg Consolidated Investment Company. This area was to become a permanent home for the spectacular collection of South African wild flowers exhibited at the 1936 Empire Exhibition which was held in Johannesburg. Since then the rocky hillocks have been converted into a garden of indigenous flora, dedicated to the memory of Field-Marshal J C Smuts, an enthusiastic naturalist as well as politician. The garden originally formed part of the grounds of *Hohenheim*, the home of Sir Percy Fitzpatrick, author of *Jock of the Bushveld* and also a director of the mining company which presented the property. The garden is known as The Wilds.

Another notable park donated to Johannesburg by a mining house is the Hermann Eckstein Park, situated between Saxonwold, Parkview and Parkwood and just over 100 ha in size. In 1903 Wernher Beit & Co offered the area to Johannesburg, asking that it be named after a late senior partner in the firm, who had started a private zoo on the estate before his death. These animals formed the nucleus for the Johannesburg Zoological Gardens which today cover 55 ha of the area and exhibits over 600 mammals, 1 300 birds and numerous reptiles. In another section of the park (45,32 ha in extent) is a lake, known as the Zoo Lake, very popular with boating enthusiasts, while other attractions include extensive picnic grounds, an illuminated fountain and a restaurant.

The western suburbs are provided with a 45 ha reserve, known as Melville Koppies. Left entirely in its natural state, with the original flora and remains of an Iron Age furnace, it is a national monument and a sanctuary for birds and other wildlife.

Brixton has the Kingston Frost Park – 3,39 ha devoted to the cultivation of numerous aloes collected from various parts of Southern Africa. Emmarentia, in the northern suburbs, named after Emmarentia Botha, wife of the owner of the farm, proclaimed a township on 22 April 1937, has the attraction of a fine 125 ha area, known as the Johannesburg Botanical Gardens. A garden of herbs flourish in one part and in another section more than 12 000 rose-trees are under cultivation. There is a refreshment kiosk which is open weekends and public holidays. There are guided tours every first Tuesday of each month at 09h00 (summer only).

Other parks include Rhodes Park in Kensington (24,9 ha) containing a small lake and a restaurant, and Pioneers' Park in La Rochelle, on the shores of Wemmer Pan (88,87 ha). In this park stands the James Hall Museum of Transport, housing a collection of old automobiles, trams, buses, steamrollers, tractors, and many other vehicles of former years. The museum is open Tuesdays to Sundays 09h00 to 17h00. A restaurant provides refreshments and there are picnic grounds for relaxation. Boat trips are offered on the lake. On the northern shores stands a miniature town known as Santarama. It is open daily from 10h00 to 17h00. Inspired by the famous Madurodam miniature city in Holland, Santarama has a scale of 1:25 and is run for charity by the South African National Tuberculosis Association. Included in this exhibition is a replica of the *Dromedaris*, the ship which brought Jan van Riebeeck to the Cape.

In the suburb of Doornfontein, 3 km east of the city hall, lies Ellis Park, named after a former mayor, J Dowell Ellis. It is the principal venue in the city for rugby, tennis and swimming. The headquarters of the Golden Lions Rugby Union are situated here and many great matches have taken place on its playing-fields. With a seating capacity of nearly 100 000 people, the Ellis Park Rugby Stadium is an international test-match venue for all visiting teams. The Central Gauteng Tennis Association also has its headquarters and 23 courts at Ellis Park. All major tennis tournaments in Johannesburg are played there and it is a standard venue on the international circuit. The largest swimming-bath in Johannesburg (built to full Olympic standards) is also to be found at Ellis Park and is the scene of international competitive swimming. Open-air boxing matches are also staged at Ellis Park. There is a superb stadium for athletics.

In 1888 a group of sportsmen banded together and formed a sports club called the Wanderers. They rented from the government a substantial piece of ground, which became known as Kruger's Park. The first railway station of Johannesburg was built nearby and named Park Station. An English cricket team, captained by Aubrey Smith (later a famous actor) was the first international side to visit Kruger's Park, where they played against the local team in January and February 1889. From that time onwards, the Wanderers grounds became internationally known as a centre of sport in Southern Africa and the venue where many great sporting events subsequently took place.

The Wanderers sports fields were taken over by the S A Railways to expand the station and the club moved to Kent Park in 1945. On the old site of the club, where Aubrey Smith had once led his white-flannelled men into combat, the gigantic modern railway station was built. The

Wanderers Club in Kent Park is today the setting for many important sporting events. It has the largest club building in South Africa.

Milner Park next to the University of the Witwatersrand, was the first home of the Rand Show (the largest of its kind in Africa), staged each Easter by the Witwatersrand Agricultural Society. Smaller agricultural, livestock and industrial shows were also held during the year on the 40,5 ha showground. A larger showground has now been created between the western border of Johannesburg and Soweto.

Other recreational areas, such as the 44 ha Gillooly's Farm in Bedfordview, are used for staging events such as dog shows as well as being used for picnicking, James Gillooly ran a dairy on this farm until the City Council bought it in August 1943 and opened it in 1944 as a picnic resort.

While possessing many parks, Johannesburg is also richly endowed with libraries, museums and galleries, several of which contain unique collections. One of the proudest possessions of the city is the Johannesburg Public Library and the group of specialised museums originally contained in the same building but now moved to the old produce market building and known as Museum Africa.

The library originated as a privately run subscription service housed in the boardroom of the City Chambers. By 1891 the infant library had grown to such an extent that a librarian was appointed and a series of moves to a succession of ever larger accommodation commenced. In 1905 the Reference Library was founded by the addition of the technical books owned by Major Seymour, an American mining engineer. The present home of the library on the western end of Market Square, facing the Legislative Assembly, is one of the handsomest buildings in Johannesburg. It was built in 1935 from a design by John Perry.

Museum Africa attempts to tell the story of life in Southern Africa from the Stone Age to the Computer Age. Johannesburg Transformation looks at some of the ways in which change has swept through the life of the city and its people. It also houses the museum of rock art, a geological museum and the Bensusan museum of photography, a remarkable display of early photographs and equipment presented by Dr and Mrs Bensusan.

The Bernard Price Museum of Palaeontology is the premier museum in South Africa wholly devoted to palaeontological research. It forms part of the University of the Witwatersrand, but is housed in a separate building off Showground Road in Brixton. The museum depicts the geological periods of the Earth and contains a vast collection of fossils, including a treasure trove of ancient bones recovered from the huge cave of Makapansgat. The deposits in this cave are so enormous and of such scientific value that teams of excavators will be kept busy for years to come. Detailed collections feature the bone, tooth and horn artefacts of early man-apes such as *Australopithecus*, whose discovery revealed that man was present very much earlier than was previously thought, and was hailed as the 'missing link' between man and ape.

The Bernard Price Institute of Geophysical Research is separate from the museum although named after the same man. Bernard Price was an electrical engineer and a considerable benefactor of the University of the Witwatersrand. The Institute of Geophysical Research is famous for its study of complex subjects such as thunderstorms.

Summer weather in Johannesburg is pleasantly mild – days are warm to hot, and nights are cool and refreshing. Most of the rainfall occurs in summer, usually in the form of spectacular afternoon thunderstorms which occur suddenly and are of short duration. In the early morning the sky is generally clear. At about 11h00, white cumulus clouds appear and build up steadily until they form gigantic cloud 'castles' resembling great dollops of whipped cream floating lazily through the warm air. At lunchtime, the clouds convert into an ominous black mass, and tremendous electrical charges (both positive and negative) separate within them. Drops of water turn to ice and fall as hailstones, sometimes as large as pigeon eggs, which cause immense destruction to crops, car windscreens, and insect and bird life. The contact in the clouds between hail and water seems to generate still greater electrical imbalances – flashes of 100 million volts are not uncommon in such huge clouds.

Lightning flashes as the clouds disgorge their electrical burden. Most of the lightning is hidden within the clouds, but about one in every six bolts strikes the Earth, releasing energy for a mere one thousandth of a second. Currents of approximately 100 000 amps are possible, but about 58 per cent of them are less than 30 000 amps. Electrical storms such as these provide an awesome spectacle. They should be viewed from a safe place. About 60 people are killed by lightning in

South Africa each year, generally struck in exposed situations. Modern buildings are protected against lightning. The two high telecommunications towers in Johannesburg are sometimes struck several times in the course of a single storm, but conductors take the discharge safely to earth without anyone in the buildings even being aware that anything untoward has taken place. Motor vehicles are unaffected, aircraft are occasionally struck but escape with minor damage. Electrical power lines and telecommunication networks suffer the greatest inconvenience.

A considerable amount of research on lightning has been carried out in South Africa. Dr (later Sir) Basil Schonland started studying the subject at Somerset East in the 1920s. When the Institute of Geophysical Research was founded in Johannesburg, Dr Schonland became the first director. Between 1933 and 1935 particularly, much information on lightning, as well as on radar and earth tremors, was accumulated by this institute. Working with an improved version of a camera invented in England by G V Boys, Dr Schonland and co-workers such as Dr E C Halliday and Professor D J Malan, all renowned authorities on lightning, managed to secure many high-speed photographs of lightning and to time the flashes to a few millionths of a second.

Other aids were developed, such as cathode-ray oscilloscopes and counters which could check the number of strikes on power lines and exposed points. It is an intensely interesting but very difficult and dangerous subject to study. Many problems remain unsolved, including weird phenomena such as ball lightning, often seen in Zimbabwe and occasionally in the northern provinces of South Africa. Since the Second World War, however, several protective systems against lightning have been devised and much more is now known about these spectacular disturbances.

Experimental work has been carried out extensively by the universities and by organisations such as the Electricity Supply Commission and the former South African Posts and Telecommunications Department, because of the effect of lightning on electrical transmission and communications service. The Council for Scientific and Industrial Research (CSIR) conducts research on lightning and the improvement of protective measures. When protection systems are contrived, instruments known as lightning-flash counters are used to establish the number of flashes which occur during a storm. Ground flashes are ones that cause damage to life and property; and the CSIR's National Electrical Engineering Research Institute has developed to a degree not possible before, a counter which differentiates between inter-cloud flashes and flashes to the ground.

The high-lying areas of the provinces north of the Vaal River, Lesotho, Zimbabwe, Zambia, Madagascar and parts of Australia experience some of the most violent electrical storms on Earth. As with Johannesburg, these are areas of summer rainfall which occurs in very localised thunderstorms. In the tropics of Africa, Malaysia and South America, thunderstorms take place on more than 100 days a year.

The Bernberg Fashion Museum, a section of Museum Africa, is contained in a suburban house on the corner of Jan Smuts Avenue and Duncombe Road in Forest Town. The house has been reconstructed to include a complete circuit covering two different displays; the first comprises costumes of various periods, worn by models standing in beautifully designed period interiors; the second involves collections of various accessories displayed in wall cases. A fascinating range of fashion-plates is exhibited on the walls. Also included are complete wedding groups, a reconstructed dress salon of the 1920s, an art gallery from 1910, a kitchen, various children's costumes and all the bric-à-brac of high fashion – underclothing, smoking-caps, buttons, gloves, shoes, shawls, purses, cigarette-holders and jewellery. The collection is superbly mounted and should not be missed, as there is no other museum like it in Southern Africa. It is open Tuesdays to Saturdays 09h00 to 13h00, 13h30 to 17h00.

The Museum of Man and Science is housed in a suburban residence at 111 Central Street, Houghton. It contains some splendid exhibitions of the history and way of life of the Bushmen and other peoples of Southern Africa. Artefacts, costumes and photographs are used in an exposition of primitive life-styles and the endless ingenuity of man in fashioning, out of minimal resources, his basic necessities.

The National Pharmacy Museum and Archives, maintained by the Pharmaceutical Society of South Africa, displays a collection of medicinal plants and antique laboratory equipment. The museum is accommodated in Pharmacy House, 52 Glenhove Road, Melrose.

The Planetarium is situated in the grounds of the University of the Witwatersrand. It was brought to Johannesburg at the time of the city's 70th birthday celebrations in 1955 and was later sold to the University by the Festival Committee. Since its opening to the public in 1960, this wonderful place of optical magic has introduced over one million spectators to the beauty and mystery of the Universe. The images of about 9 000 heavenly objects can be presented in any period from 2 000 years ago to 5 000 years ahead. There are shows on Fridays at 20h00, Saturdays at 15h00 and Sundays at 16h00.

The South African National Museum of Military History contains a lavish display of lethal equipment and the uniforms (equally lavish) of the military men of past years. The exhibition is mounted in the Hermann Eckstein Park, off Erlswold Way, Saxonwold. More people visit this museum than any other in Johannesburg. Tanks, armoured cars and military aircraft are displayed, including a Hawker Hurricane, a De Havilland Mosquito and a Spitfire, together with planes of the First World War. There are battle flags, medals, decorations, uniforms, insignia, war photographs, steel helmets, rifles, hand-guns, swords, daggers, knives and bayonets. Also included is a German one-man submarine. Many fine paintings of battle scenes and portraits adorn the walls. The museum is open daily from 09h00 to 16h00; closed on Christmas.

On a 10 ha site surrounding the No 14 shaft at Crown Mines, a mine museum and entertainment complex, known as Gold Reef City, has been created. This is a re-creation of old-time Johannesburg. There are replicas of a mine village, railway with a steam train, milling area, study facilities, opportunities for visitors to go underground, and also to see a gold pour. There is a large amusement park. Visitors can also see displays of tribal and gumboot dancing here. The City is open daily except Mondays 09h30 to 17h00. Closed on Christmas.

There are many interesting walking trails around and in Johannesburg. Booklets and maps may be obtained from the Public Relations Office, Civic Centre, Braamfontein.

Many of the suburbs and satellite townships around Johannesburg contain places of interest which are worth visiting. Some of the original suburbs have grown into towns in their own right, especially in the northern areas.

RANDBURG

Randburg is one of the young municipalities mothered by Johannesburg. It was created in 1959 when thirteen of the original northern suburbs combined to form one municipality, complete with a shopping centre, civic centre and light industrial area. Randburg has 37 parks and an art gallery (housed in the municipal building) exhibiting contemporary South African art.

The Randburg Waterfront has been a major redevelopment of the area and is now one of South Africa's top entertainment and shopping complexes. Built on the site of an old riversand quarry, a tributary of the Jukskei River was diverted during construction to form a lake. The complex, a mix of shops, restaurants, cinemas and fleamarket, was built around the lake. It is open all year round.

SANDTON

Another creation of Johannesburg, situated in its northern areas, is the municipality of Sandton which, with Randburg, has a combined population of 362 481. The name *Sandton* is a combination of the names of the original suburbs of Sandown and Bryanston which merged with northeastern Johannesburg in 1966 and formed a new town in a spacious parklike setting. There is a spectacular modern shopping centre, Sandton Square, which includes a re-creation of a medieval Italian square. Sandton has plenty of room for recreation and an African market in Atrium Centre where curios and handicrafts are made by very talented workers and artists.

In the Sandton area lies the original 1 000 ha farm named *Kyalami*, after the Zulu *kaya lami* (my home). This old farm is now the site of the Kyalami Country Club and the Kyalami motor-racing track, built in 1961. On 1 January 1968 this track became the venue for the annual Grand Prix of South Africa, one of the races included in the World Championship circuit.

The South African National Equestrian Centre has its home in Sandton, next to the Kyalami

Country Club. At 11h00 every Sunday displays of dressage in the unique riding disciplines of the Spanish Riding School in Vienna, are given. White Lippizaner stallions perform in the only riding school outside Vienna to display this precision training. A breed which originated from a mixture of Kladruber horses from Bohemia, small Italian horses, and Arabian horses, produced these magnificent stallions. They were a species bred at Lippiza stud-farm, founded in 1580 by the Austrian archduke, Charles. From the beginning this breed was trained in dressage in the celebrated Spanish Riding School founded in Vienna by the English Duke of Newcastle and Antonius de Pluvinal, riding-master to Louis XIII of France, who developed extraordinary training methods for the techniques riders call 'high school', 'carriage work', 'hunting' and 'hack'.

Several noblemen in the Austro-Hungarian Empire obtained some of these horses. At the time of the Second World War, Count Jankovich Besan had a number in his stables at Orgelak in Hungary. With the collapse of the Nazis, he fled. About twelve of the horses were removed from the war zone by the stud manager and accountant. These horses reached Bavaria where the count reclaimed them. In 1946 they were transferred to the estate of Lord Digby in England. In 1948 the count brought them to South Africa, where they were placed on a farm in the Mooi River district of Natal. In 1964 six of the horses were sold to National Chemical Products, a manufacturer of horse feed, who transferred them to Waterkloof in Natal and used them to establish a South African Lippizaner breed, the offspring of which perform at Kyalami.

The southern suburbs of Johannesburg are less glamorous than those in the north, but they contain some of the principal sporting venues, such as the horse-racing course at Turffontein, and the Rand Stadium in La Rochelle, scene of soccer and open-air boxing matches. South-west of the city limits lie the South Western Townships known as *Soweto*, the principal residential area of the African population since the earliest days of Johannesburg. It is now a substantial town with its own administration, sports fields, shopping centres and parks. The population is 904 166.

To the east of Johannesburg lie towns such as Bedfordview and Kempton Park (446 109 inhabitants). Kempton Park became a city in September 1992. It had its beginning in 1896 when Karl Frederick Wolff, who had been born in Kempton, the capital of Algau in South Germany, bought a portion of the farm *Zuurfontein* (sour fountain) and laid out a town. Today it is a residential and industrial centre adjoining the Johannesburg International Airport and the World Trade Centre. The Johannesburg International Airport, 20 km from the centre of the city, is South Africa's principal airport, opened in 1953 and enlarged over the years to cope with larger aircraft and ever-increasing numbers of passengers. The main runway is 4 411 m long and can accept all modern aircraft at maximum loads. The airport is the home base of South African Airways, the largest airline in Africa. The road from the airport to the centre of Johannesburg makes an impressive entrance to the city through Settlers Park and its three gold-lit fountains. Views are impressive of the skyline of the city.

Five kilometres to the west of Johannesburg lies the small George Harrison Memorial Park, which preserves the actual site of the first discovery by George Harrison of payable gold from the main reef of the Witwatersrand. Old mine workings may also be seen there, as well as an interesting ten-stamp battery of the type used to crush ore in the early days of gold-mining. The park is always open.

From the site of his memorial park, the spirit of the original prospector might well look out at the city, the mines and the factories which have developed all around the original exposure of reef. He would see a vast, sprawling, burgeoning, energetic city, where everybody always seems to be in a rush, preoccupied with getting to work to make money, getting home again, and then rushing off at night to spend some of their gains on entertainment.

At night Johannesburg is a glittering place to see from the air, or from a high point. Cinemas and theatres attract crowds while restaurants feature foods of many nationalities, particularly German, Greek, Italian and Portuguese, large communities of whom live in the city. Their characteristic music – from the oompah bands to the soulful singing of the *fado* – is part of the song of the city of gold, a sound it hums and murmurs to itself by day and night as it works and plays. It is the song of a bass drum-beat of industry; a baritone of men at work that is dangerous and hard;

a song of the falsetto of moneymen safe on the surface, counting profits, losses and loot; and of the lonely sighs of families who have lost somebody in the utter darkness and profound silence of the deep mines in the bowels of the Earth. Between 1903 and 1997, 55 877 miners had been killed in mine accidents, how many died of injuries or disease is not recorded. In the same period 47 229 tons of gold had been produced.

Chapter Thirty-Four
PRETORIA

With a total of 692 352 inhabitants, Pretoria lies 1 363 m above sea-level (382 m lower than Johannesburg). When the townships of Soshanguve, Ga-Rankuwa and Mabopane are included, the population of the area is over 1 million. The city enjoys a warm, well-watered climate very conducive to gardens (beautiful throughout the year) and the production of subtropical fruit. Summer is hot and moist, winter dry and cool. Spring, however, is the best time to visit Pretoria, for the colours of the flowers can then only be described as brilliant.

The city is attractively situated where the highveld falls away to the lowveld in a succession of parallel valleys separated by rocky ridges. In this sheltered setting Pretoria has spread out in a colourful complex of green gardens, shady streets, red roofs and reddish-coloured ridges of rock. There are some notably imposing and beautiful buildings in the central area, such as the Union Buildings, containing the principal government offices and standing in a magnificent formal garden; the City Hall in Paul Kruger Street, surrounded by superb jacarandas; several elegant old buildings surviving from the days of the South African Republic; many handsome modern commercial centres; and the almost overpoweringly dominant building of the University of South Africa, situated on the hills at the southern entrance to the city.

The desirability of the area as a place of residence was apparent to human beings from a very early period. About 500 000 years ago groups of Early Stone Age people made homes along the slopes and on the level summits of the Magaliesberg, especially near Wonderboompoort where they ambushed game animals migrating through the pass.

At Wonderboomnek these early people manufactured crude stone tools and weapons. They were succeeded by people of the Middle Stone age (100 000 to 30 000 years ago) and they by people of the Late Stone age (30 000 to 2 000 years ago). The area of the future city of Pretoria, therefore, was continuously occupied for some 500 000 years.

The first known Iron-age black people to settle in the area came about 1000 AD These were pastoralists, agriculturalists and smelters of iron. Next, about 1500 AD arrived sections of the Tswana–Sotho speaking people. Then, about 1600 AD there arrived sections of the Nguni people migrating down the east coast into modern Natal where they fragmented into tribes such as the Zulu. Some disturbance sent a small group of these people westwards where they made their homes on the future site of Pretoria, on the banks of the river which became known as the *Tshwane* (little ape) or in Afrikaans *Apies,* from one of their early chiefs.

This first settlement was established about 350 years ago. The people involved were dubbed *maTebele* (refugees) by the earlier Sotho-speaking groups living on the highveld. The descriptive name, in the Nguni language, became the tribal name of *Ndebele* by which these pioneers are still known. Their descendants may be seen in and around Pretoria. Ndebele residences are usually elaborately decorated with bizarre but beautiful patterns painted by the women, who also affect a complex, colourful (but rather unwieldy) ornamentation of heavy bead necklaces and anklets.

In about the year 1825 a second group of refugees from the Zulu country arrived in the valley site of the future Pretoria. These newcomers – also dubbed maTebele by the Sotho people – were a formidable crowd of renegades led by a renowned chief, Mzilikazi. They also built villages along the banks of the Apies River. It was there that the first known Europeans to reach the area (traders and missionaries) visited Mzilikazi.

In 1832 a Zulu army drove Mzilikazi westwards, out of the sheltered valley of the Apies. He and his followers eventually settled north of the Limpopo River in the area of modern Bulawayo in Zimbabwe. The site of Pretoria was abandoned, with only a few of the original Ndebele people remaining, scattered in hiding-places in the vicinity. In this state the Voortrekkers found the Apies Valley when they entered the Transvaal in 1837.

Several farms were established along the banks of the Apies. Farmers irrigated their fields from the river, finding profitable relaxation in hunting the herds of antelope which abounded in the area. The famed trek leader, Andries Pretorius, owned a fine farm, *Grootplaats* (great plateau), near the junction of the Apies and Crocodile rivers. Shortly after his death in 1853, it was suggested that a central capital be founded for the Transvaal and be named in honour of the dead leader. It would be the site of the *Volksraad* (people's council) of the South African Republic.

Pretorius's son, Marthinus Wessel, selected as a site for the new capital portions of the farm *Elandspoort* (elands pass) which he purchased for £825. On 11 August 1854 work was started on the erection of a church in the centre of the present Church Square. After initial uncertainty about the exact form of the name of the new town, the *Volksraad* on 16 December 1855, accepted the pleasant-sounding version, *Pretoria*, based on the distinguished family name of Andries Pretorius.

The town was laid out by a self-trained surveyor, Andries du Toit, and by 1860 incorporated large gardens and snug little houses. The first suburb, Arcadia, was already being developed by Stephanus Meintjes whose name has been commemorated by *Meintjeskop*, the hillock site of the Union Buildings. Traders had built the first stores and, overlooking the central square, a simple *Raadsaal* (council chamber), where the Volksraad held its meetings, was erected by the government.

The peaceful, rustic atmosphere of early Pretoria did not prevent the place from experiencing exciting events. In the early 1860s, when Marthinus Wessel Pretorius was the first President of the South African Republic, quite a small-scale civil war raged over Pretoria. Pretorius attempted to unite the Orange Free State with the Transvaal, but he had many political enemies. Bullets flew and the squabbles culminated in a minor battle fought on 5 January 1864 in the bush near Silkaatsnek, a passage through the Magaliesberg.

Pretorius resigned in 1870 and was replaced as President by the kindly and cultured Reverend Thomas Francois Burgers, who had to steer the little republic through troubled times of near bankruptcy, incessant disturbances with the African tribes, the excitement of the first discoveries of payable gold in the Eastern Transvaal, and the political crises culminating in the British annexation of the Transvaal on 12 April 1877.

By this time, Pretoria had grown into an imposing town, for Burgers had stimulated the building of schools and the creation of amenities such as public parks. The first park, Burgers Park, was established as a botanical garden in 1874. There are now 140 parks in the city.

The British established a garrison in Pretoria and attracted an influx of immigrants and money. New buildings were erected and the future generally looked secure. However, trouble was soon to come.

Between December 1880 and March 1881, Pretoria was besieged during the Anglo-Transvaal War of Independence and several skirmishes took place on the outskirts of the town. When the British withdrew, Paul Kruger was established in Pretoria as the President of the restored republic. For the next nineteen years his forceful personality dominated life in the developing town, as it did throughout the Transvaal.

Pretoria grew rapidly as the capital of what had now become a real golden republic after the dramatic discoveries of gold at Barberton (1884), the Witwatersrand (1886), and the subsequent massive influx of diggers and *uitlanders* (foreigners) attracted by the prospect of fortune.

The handsome new Raadsaal, built on the site of the original council hall, saw many tense and momentous debates. The Palace of Justice, which also overlooks the square, was used as a military hospital during the British occupation in 1900 and then became the headquarters of the Transvaal Provincial (now Regional) Division of the Supreme Court. The great trial of the Jameson raiders in 1896 was held in Pretoria, and the town experienced the mounting tensions which culminated on 11 October 1899 in the outbreak of the Anglo-Boer War. The raadsaal is an interesting place to visit, especially if one has some knowledge of the events and intrigues which centred around this building. The book *Lost Trails of the Transvaal* contains an account of these times.

Pretoria survived the war unscathed as an open city. Occupied by the British under Lord Roberts on 5 June 1900, it was there that the Peace of Vereeniging was finally signed late at night on 31 May 1902. Having achieved a new status as the capital of the British colony of the

Transvaal, Pretoria continued to grow. On creation of the Union of South Africa in 1910, it became the administrative capital of the new state. Cape Town became the legislative capital, the seat of parliament, in a cumbersome arrangement of dual capitals to placate rivalries between the Cape and the Transvaal. The handsome Union Buildings, designed by Sir Herbert Baker, were built at this time out of orange-red coloured sandstone. The total erection cost amounted to £1 180 000. The buildings were completed and occupied by the various Government departments at the end of 1913. The two wings – west and east – represent the two language groups, English and Afrikaans. The clock in the right-hand tower is known as 'Oom Paul'.

In front of the Union Buildings stands the Delville Wood War Memorial, built as a tribute to South African troops killed in the First World War. There is a fine equestrian statue of General Louis Botha, South Africa's first prime minister, and statues of two other late prime ministers, Mr J B M Hertzog and Field Marshal J C Smuts. There is also an impressive Police Memorial and the Pretoria War Memorial commemorating Pretorians who died in the two world wars and the Korean war.

The Union Buildings are surrounded by a spectacular garden. The garden is always open. In spring it is ablaze with colour and is a superb spectacle. Green lawns and brilliantly coloured flowers are dominated by the red-orange sandstone buildings, with a deep-blue sky above them. The amount of photographic film exposed by visitors must add significantly to the profits of the photographic industry.

An ever-growing community of civil servants expanded the population of Pretoria, while in 1928 the Union Government decided on the establishment there of the South African Iron and Steel Industrial Corporation (Iscor). This great venture into steel production commenced operation in 1934, and the glow of blast furnaces became a feature of the night sky of Pretoria. Many other industries were developed around the steel industry. Most steel production in South Africa is now done away from Pretoria.

Pretoria became a municipality in 1903 during the first British annexation and on 14 October 1931 was proclaimed a city. Today it covers an area of 632 square kilometres. The two principal streets are Church and Paul Kruger streets which cross each other at the original Church Square, still the centre of the city. The square is graced with a superb statue of Paul Kruger guarded by four burghers, sculpted by Anton van Wouw.

At the southern end of Paul Kruger Street stands the railway station, founded in 1910 and designed by Sir Herbert Baker. A fine old steam locomotive, ZASM No 238, is preserved in the station as a national monument.

Also in Paul Kruger Street is the City Hall designed by F G McIntosh and opened in 1931. The massive clock tower contains a carillon of 32 tubular bells made in Chicago and donated to the city by George Heys, the great coach operator. The grand organ in the hall was also made in Chicago. A tympanum by Coert Steynberg symbolises the growth of the city. There is a colonnade of fountains as well as murals and statues of Andries Pretorius and his son Marthinus Wessel, the founder of the city. Superb jacarandas grow in the garden.

On Republic Square in Church Street is the imposing State Theatre, opera house and theatre complex. Next to it an impressive fountain plays, erected in memory of Johannes Gerhardus Strijdom, prime minister from 1954 to 1958. The fountain comprises a sculpted group of charging horses and a giant bronze bust, the work of sculptor Coert Steynberg.

In spring (September–November) the whole city is transformed into a magnificent floral picture. It is at this time that the spectacle of flowering jacarandas may be seen – a feature that is world famous. An annual Jacaranda Carnival takes place in October.

About 66 000 of these trees grow in Pretoria, introduced by chance. A few trees had been grown in private gardens, notably a pair imported from South America and planted by Mr J D Celliers in 1888 at his home *Myrtle Lodge* in Sunnyside. Then James Clark, a local horticulturist, ordered some mixed seed from Australia. Included in the selection were seeds of *Jacaranda mimosifolia* from Brazil. The seeds developed into healthy seedlings and in 1906 Mr Clark presented some trees to the Pretoria municipality.

The trees were planted in Bosman Street and from these ancestors originate the beautiful avenues of today.

In 1962 Mr H Bruinslich, the Director of Parks, saw the white jacaranda in South America and introduced this variety to Pretoria, where it may be seen today growing in several streets.

East of the Union Buildings lies the residential area of Bryntirion where, in a magnificent garden setting the State President has his official residence. The State President's home was designed by Gerard Moerdijk and built in 1940. It was formerly known as *Libertas* but is now named in Zulu *Mahlambandlovu* or in Shangane *Mahlambandlopfu* (early hours of the morning).

The National Zoological Gardens of South Africa are situated on approximately 60 ha in the very heart of Pretoria. Since being established in 1899, the National Zoological Gardens have grown to such an extent that today this zoo enjoys world-wide recognition. It is the largest zoo in South Africa and the only one with national status. Approximately 140 mammal and 320 bird species are housed in beautiful parklike surroundings. A separate aquarium houses 300 fish species from both freshwater and marine environments and several amphibian and invertebrate species. Reptiles from all over the world are housed in the adjacent Reptile Park. An overhead cableway provides a spectacular view over the zoo and the surrounding city. A variety of souvenirs are on sale at the zoo shop and refreshments are available at the restaurant and at kiosks situated throughout the zoo.

The National Zoological Gardens, the Aquarium and the Reptile Park are open daily 08h00 to 17h30 in summerl and daily 08h00 to 17h00 in winter.

The Transvaal Museum in Paul Kruger Street is renowned for its exhibits of prehistory and natural history. Included is the Austin Roberts Bird Hall, a model on which to base all collections of birds. This exhibition is definitive and shows all examples of South African avifauna, arranged according to the Roberts Order. Dr Austin Roberts compiled the standard work *Roberts' Birds of South Africa* in which every bird, in addition to being arranged in natural order, was given a number. This number is the standard reference in all books on South African birds.

The lower part of this hall is devoted to bird life in general, showing by means of excellently mounted specimens, features such as the 27 orders of living birds, feeding methods, flight, nests and nesting, falconry, and the usefulness of predatory birds. There is also a collection of eggs.

A 'quiz' case contains a number of the commoner birds. Visitors may guess the name of a particular bird, then press a button which illuminates the correct bird.

Two other exhibits are notable: a dodo skeleton and an accurate reconstruction of the first known bird, the Archaeopteryx. There are two impressive displays on the evolution of life.

The museum is open Mondays to Saturdays 09h00 to 17h00; and Sundays 11h00 to 17h00. Closed on Christmas and Good Friday.

Also for bird lovers is the Austin Roberts Bird Sanctuary, established in 1955 by the City Council and situated in Boshoff Street off Queen Wilhelmina Avenue. More than 100 indigenous bird species, including black swans and ostriches, as well as a variety of mammals, such as blesbok, duiker, steenbok and springbok, are to be seen here in natural conditions. The hide is open on weekends and public holidays from 07h00 to 17h00. A small museum displays some of the birds frequenting the sanctuary.

Adjoining the Transvaal Museum is the Geological Survey Museum, of particular interest to those with some knowledge of geology and mineralogy. Beautifully housed and displayed in a new building, it is one of the most attractive museums in the country. The exhibits are splendid and the labelling equally so.

The collection commences with the basics of the solar system, the planets, Earth and its interior. Passing on to a study of geological processes at work, the collection shows the origins of different rocks, with a comprehensive section devoted to the chemical construction of minerals. Chemical analyses of a large number of these minerals are carefully indicated by means of coloured symbols.

Precious and semi-precious stones are included in a section where there is a case containing reproduction of the world's largest diamonds.

The room devoted to economic minerals is packed with information. The maps showing where they occur in the world, together with the production statistics, are interesting even to the non-geologist.

A large oval stone used as a simple crusher, is an interesting relic in the museum, dating back to the early days of gold-mining in South Africa when, in 1871, rumours of payable gold sent hundreds of prospectors rushing to Eersteling (near Pietersburg). All that remains on the site today is one of the crushing sheds and a solitary smoke-stack standing in the veld. For a further account of this event see Chapter Thirty-One.

A notable exhibit is an exquisite Italian mosaic table, inlaid with semi-precious stones. It is a masterpiece. This museum is open Mondays to Saturdays 09h00 to 17h00; and Sundays 11h00 to 17h00. Closed on Christmas and Good Friday.

The African Window, the National Cultural History Museum's showcase for culture and an exhibition centre, is located in the old Mint Building in Visagie Street (between Botswana and Schubart streets). It is set in beautiful grounds and has plenty of secure parking. The building and even the site have a history. Known as the Convent Redoubt (probably because of the neighbouring Loreto Convent, still present today as a school), the site in 1880 was a military camp during the Anglo-Transvaal War. Ten years later, the site was the location of a prison and the place of public execution. Once the Pretoria Central Prison was completed, in 1907, the old gaol was vacated. In 1923, the Royal Mint, built by J J Kirkness, was erected on the site. It is this building, though greatly modernised, which now houses the African Window.

The African Window houses a number of exhibitions and is filled with exciting historical and contemporary cultural objects. Culture and identity are not static, but are continually created and re-created. Creating Hananwa – The People of the Blue Mountain looks at how history has impacted on the identity of a particular group of South Africans, the Hananwa, living in Northern Province.

One exhibition is dedicated to Bushman rock art. It boasts twelve fine rock engravings, of exceptional quality. Using these artistic examples, access to power explores the vast spiritual world of these most interesting people.

The Rainbow Collection is a visible storage exhibition, the first of its kind in South Africa, although the concept has been used in a number of museums overseas. This exhibition, made up of approximately 1 500 objects ranging from stone tools to fine porcelain, to artworks to household appliances, many of which have never been displayed before, provides a window into the vast collection of the National Cultural History Museum.

Another exhibition, Reach for the Stars, explores the relationship that people have had with the heavens, throughout the world and throughout time.

What do museums do? Why even have museums? What is the history of this museum? The Museum World attempts to answer these questions.

Through the People's Choice Exhibition Project, different groups of people have the opportunity to research and curate exhibitions based on objects in the Museum's vast collection. Making Music, the first exhibition in this series, was curated by the Vuma Wethu Traditional Dancers. The second exhibition in the series, Go Dira Dijo, was curated by the Atteridgeville and Salsville Luncheon Club.

Three temporary exhibition spaces are filled with dynamic, changing temporary exhibitions, curated by the museum and by cultural groups and individuals from outside the museum, including curators from countries such as Mexico, Poland and Bangladesh.

The African Window accommodates conference facilities, a cafeteria, an internet café and a shop, and shows art, foreign and cultural films. It is open seven days a week from 09h00 to 17h00. Phone (012) 324-6082 with any enquiries.

Of great historical interest is Paul Kruger's house, 60 Church Street. A great deal may be learnt about the character of one of South Africa's most famous presidents by a visit to this house in which he lived from 1883 to 1900, before he went into exile in Switzerland. The impression is gained of a man who had little regard for elegance, even less for comfort, and none at all for pomp and show.

The surroundings are simple and modest, and even the official reception room holds little to impress those whom he met there. One exception to the general austerity of the house is the tasteful curtaining, handsomely draped in the fashion of the time.

The museum contains many relics of Paul Kruger – small things such as his pipes and personal belongings. One of the first telephones installed in Pretoria may be seen; also the *Vierkleur* (the ZAR flag) that flew for the last time in 1900 when he left the Eastern Transvaal for exile in Clarens in Switzerland, little realising that he was leaving his home for ever. There is the desk before which he must have spent many an anxious hour, and the chair (bearing the arms of the Transvaal Republic) in which he was often photographed. The official dinner service bears the same arms and two porcelain cups are ornamented with portraits of the President and his wife.

At the back of the house stands the President's State coach in which he was installed as

President for the fourth and last time in 1898, and his private railway coach. This railway coach should be compared with that exhibited at the Kimberley Mine Museum, for the contrast between Cecil Rhodes and the austere President is another pointer to character! This coach, built for the NZASM in the Netherlands, was originally two coaches which were joined together in South Africa on arrival. A painted board with the arms of the Republic is said to have been attached to the coach when the President travelled in it, and is thought to have been removed by British soldiers. It was subsequently found in London and returned to the museum.

In addition, the museum is a repository for documents and other material concerning the life of President Kruger. An illustrated brochure, giving detailed information about the exhibits, is available for sale. The house is open Mondays to Saturdays 08h30 to 16h00. Sundays 09h00 to 16h00.

Also of considerable historic interest is *Melrose House*, in Jacob Maré Street near Burgers Park. This magnificent example of a Victorian home was built in 1886 by George Heys who, born in 1852 in Durban, had settled in Pretoria during the first British annexation. He established a coach service which extended to many parts of the old Republic. His Pretoria home contains some superb period furniture, stained glass, porcelain, silver and works of art. On 31 May 1902 the Treaty of the Peace of Vereeniging was signed in this house, finally bringing to an end the tragedy of the Anglo-Boer War. Melrose House is open to the public Tuesdays to Sundays from 10h00 to 17h00. Closed on Mondays and religious holidays.

The Pioneer Open-Air Museum in Silverton preserves a restored house and farmyard of the pioneer period. It was built seven years before the founding of Pretoria. It is open daily from 08h30 to 16h00.

Another interesting house is Zwartkoppies Hall, the home of Sammy Marks. He was a renowned speculator and entrepreneur, and the house with its furnishings is a sumptuous example of a Victorian life-style in the setting of the Transvaal. It is now the Sammy Marks Museum and contains exquisite examples of Victorian silver, glass, porcelain and furniture. It is open Tuesdays to Fridays from 09h00 to 16h00; weekends 10h00 to 16h00

The Pretoria Art Museum in Arcadia Park is open Tuesdays and Thursdays to Saturdays 10h00 to 17h00; Wednesdays 10h00 to 20h00; Sundays 12h00 to 17h00. Closed on Mondays. Contained here are several hundred paintings by South African artists, as well as the Michaelis Collection. The Pierneef Museum in Vermeulen Street exhibits a representative collection of the paintings of this fine artist. It is open Mondays to Fridays 08h00 to 16h00.

The Van Wouw House in Brooklyn was the home of the sculptor Anton van Wouw, and exhibits much of his superb work. It is open Tuesdays to Fridays 10h00 to 16h00.

The Museum of Science and Technology in Skinner Street is open Mondays to Fridays from 08h00 to 16h00. Closed on Saturdays, Sundays and all public holidays. It is the only one of its kind in Africa where the exploration of space is depicted.

The South African Police Museum in Pretorius Street is open Mondays to Fridays from 08h30 to 15h30; Saturdays 8h30 to 12h30 and Sundays from 13h00 to 16h00. Closed on public holidays. The museum exhibits several relics – some of them gruesome – of past crimes including gambling, smuggling and narcotics.

There is a Post Office Museum in the old Bank of Africa building on Church Square. It is open Mondays to Fridays 07h30 to 16h00; closed on public holidays.

The Pretoria National Botanic Gardens (on the road to Witbank) are open daily from 06h00 to 18h00. The gardens, 77 ha in extent, contain 30 000 species of indigenous plants grouped according to the various climatic regions of South Africa.

Protea Park in Groenkloof is the home of a collection of proteas, aloes and Namaqualand flowering plants, while in Springbok Park in Pretorius Street grow numerous indigenous trees.

The beautiful Johann Rissik Scenic Drive, which is reached from the Fountains traffic exchange and along Nelson Mandela Avenue, provides fine views of Pretoria. On the summit ridge of the drive stands the perfectly maintained Fort Klapperkop Military Museum. As a sequel to the Jameson Raid the government of the South African Republic erected this fort and three others in 1897 in order to protect the capital. Formerly occupied by the military in 1898, it has now been lovingly restored in landscaped grounds and equipped with a series of dioramas and other exhibits to illustrate the military history of South Africa. The building is worth studying and would have been a difficult place to storm before aircraft rendered all such positions almost indefensible. The fortress itself, entered by means of a drawbridge and gate, is built around a small courtyard.

A second fort, Fort Skanskop, is also worth visiting. It was built near the present Voortrekker Monument and was erected at the same time as Fort Klapperkop. Fort Klapperkop is open daily from 08h00 to 17h00 (closed on Mondays). Closed on public holidays.

Pretoria has a proud tradition of academic and research excellence. It is home to the National Library of South Africa and there are in its area four universities. The University of Pretoria is the largest residential university in South Africa with nearly 50 000 students enrolled in 11 faculties and 141 departments. UNISA is a correspondence university with 128 000 students world wide. Medunsa is the medical university of South Africa. Vista University has a campus in Mamelodi. There are five technical colleges and the Pretoria Technikon which has 16 000 students.

There are twelve technological and research institutes, including the Council of Scientific and Industrial Research (CSIR), the Human Sciences Research Council (HSRC), the Medical Research Council (MRC), the South African Bureau of Standards (SABS), the Council of Geo-science, many institutes of the Agricultural Research Council (ARC), and a number of museums.

There are also many fine schools. The South African Mint and the Government Printer have their plants in the city. The laboratories of the South African Bureau of Standards maintain a nation-wide vigilance over the standards of manufacture throughout the country.

At 8 km on the N4 freeway to Witbank lies *Scientia*, headquarters of the South African Council for Scientific and Industrial Research (CSIR), home of fourteen different divisions for scientific and technological research, development and implementation. It employs a total of about 4 200 people and is by far the largest institution of this nature in Africa. Visits by appointment only.

Twelve kilometres north lies the famous Onderstepoort Veterinary Institute (OVI). This institute was founded in 1908 by a very dynamic young Swiss veterinarian, Dr Arnold Theiler, who was knighted for his outstanding work in finding solutions of great economic importance for several diseases of livestock. Onderstepoort was the first facility of its kind on the continent of Africa and is one of the best in the world. It has been responsible for finding vaccines for the control of veterinary illnesses such as distemper, blue tongue, horse sickness and botulism. It was at Onderstepoort that mineral deficiencies were proved to be the cause of livestock diseases, a discovery which prompted research on similar problems throughout the world.

The institute is situated on the farm *De Onderstepoort* (below the pass) and covers an area of 200 ha. The modern foot-and-mouth disease laboratory is housed on the adjacent farm *Kaalplaas* (bare farm) with an area of about 2 700 ha. Onderstepoort provides the only faculty of veterinary science in South Africa where students from many parts of Africa train as veterinary surgeons.

On the northern outskirts of the city is the *Wonderboom* (wonder tree) Nature Reserve, containing a huge wild fig tree and the remains of one of the forts built to defend Pretoria. The tree is about 1 000 years old and covers 0,5 ha. The reserve is open daily from 08h30 to 16h00.

Pretoria is an attractive, sunny, colourful city, with many areas of recreation and sport, such as the 85 000-seat rugby stadium named after Robert Loftus Versveld, a former administrator of the game. Another pleasant recreational area may be found at Fountains at the source of the Apies River, where there are gardens, picnicking grounds, a swimming-pool and caravan park. Shady trees, green lawns, flowers, swans, water birds and a delightful miniature railway with a real 'puffer' following an attractive route, are features of this resort. The Fountains valley was proclaimed the first nature reserve in Africa in 1895. The fountains springing from dolomite produce a flow of crystal-clear water which was the basic reason for human settlement in the area and the origin of the city of Pretoria.

MAMELODI

The principal residential area for the work force of Pretoria has the singular name of *Mamelodi* (the whistler). The name is said to have originated from the African name for President Paul Kruger and is sometimes applied to the whole of Pretoria. The President is said to have been fond of imitating the call of birds, although others say that he was asthmatic and whistled as he breathed.

The story of Mamelodi is an interesting microcosm of the story of South Africa itself. When Pretoria was founded in 1855 there were African people living in the area, especially along the course of the river known to them in its upper reaches as *Ntshabohloko* (the river of healing) and its further reaches as the *Tswane* after a Ndebele chief of that name. Europeans, translated the name of Tswane into the Afrikaans *Apies* (little ape) by which it is known today. Sotho and Tsonga people also lived along the river which had a perennial flow of drinkable water. Life was not easy, with tribal conflicts, raids and subsistence farming.

The coming of Europeans provided work opportunities for labourers on farms and public works and domestic employment for females. Pay was marginally above subsistence. Basic rations were generally included in the pay package. Workers were left to erect accommodation for themselves and such structures were generally ramshackle shelters of corrugated iron or scrap material for there was no permanence of occupation. Workers came and went, there was little security of tenure and a continuous change of population. People drifted in from the tribal areas, worked for a while and then often returned to their rural homes where their hearts really lay.

A tin shanty in some employer's backyard, with at best a pit toilet and, maybe, access to an outside tap of cold water was not conducive to hygiene or comfort. Employers could argue that this was actually an improvement on the traditional life-style of the black people who were therefore content to labour on low wages providing only that their bellies were also kept filled with *mieliepap* (maize porridge) and the occasional luxury of some tough meat which butchers supplied under the description of 'boys meat'.

There was no permanence in living on employers' property. If workers lost their jobs they would be summarily told to leave. An increasing number of people, by choice or necessity, started to make homes on vacant land at such places as the property of the Berlin Missionary Society. Providing they were church members they could live on the private property of the church but conditions were primitive, with no running water or sanitation, roads or lighting. Water and firewood had to be carried in on the heads of the women from some distance away.

Living conditions remained in this unsatisfactory and unhygienic state when the British took over after the Anglo-Boer War. The new Transvaal government, in 1905, did recognise the spontaneous development of two defined black 'locations'. These were known by them as Schoolplaats and Marabastad . Nothing much was done to these 'locations' save to define their boundaries. They were left to sprawl out within these boundaries as an improvised assembly of shacks, huts and ramshackle abodes which made them resemble giant scrap yards with no hygiene or amenities.

One other 'location' area, established in 1905 was named *Lady Selborne* after the wife of the British Governor, Lord Selborne, of the Transvaal and Orange Free State. It developed with a little more substance than the other areas and in 1923 was proclaimed to be a black residential area where the inhabitants could have proprietary rights instead of being regarded as squatters. This supposed security only lasted until 1958 when the black residents were summarily moved out to other 'locations' and Lady Selborne became a white residential area.

Mass chivvying and forced moving of ethnic groups occurred in the real boom days of apartheid under the dispensation of the then minister of native affairs, H F Verwoerd. In 1952 he announced that what had become 82 separate squatter camps and 11 locations around Pretoria would be consolidated into three black residential areas. Pretoria had become, by then, a centre for numerous industries. The influx of low paid unskilled labour, especially during the years of the Second World War, had got out of hand. With even scrap material for home building in short supply, 'location' residences became increasingly decrepit in their structure.

The three consolidated black residential areas planned to absorb this anarchic urban growth were: (A) *Atteridgeville* named after Mrs M P Atteridge, a Pretoria City Councillor who, in 1936, asked for its establishment to alleviate gross over-crowding in the squalid earlier black townships. It had its official start in 1940 and today has an estimated population in excess of 150 000 people. It is an industrial town in its own right with amenities, facilities, recreational areas, and its own Community Council. From Atteridgeville a considerable number of people moved to a later township with the contrived name of *Soshanguve* (So=Sotho; Sha=Shangane; Ngu=Nguni; Ve=Venda). The name was derived from the four main tribal elements settled there. It was established to house non-Tswana people. (B) *Klipfontein* (stony fountain) only now being developed. (C) *Vlakfontein* (shallow fountain). On this old farm the present town of *Mamelodi* has been developed. *Vlakfontein* (shallow fountain) was a farm lying on the lower approaches to the Magaliesberg range, on the eastern outskirts of the city of Pretoria. A few early people of unknown name or kind had lived in the area and traces of their stone walled settlements may still be seen on the overlooking heights. The *Moretele* (Pienaars River) flowed through the farm.

The original farm was divided into three parts and these passed into the hands of a succession of European owners. A number of Africans also made their homes there, especially after the founding in 1882 nearby of *De Eerste Fabrieken* (the first manufactory) in the old South African Republic. It was a distillery producing gin and alcohol for the thirsty gold-mining industry. The Anglo-Boer War saw the end of distilling but the factory continued as a bottle making operation using sand from the *Moretele* River *(*named from the plant *Urginea capitata*). Its bottles were sold to the newly formed South African Breweries and its employees were the first substantial force of industrial workers in the Transvaal. The bottle factory closed in about 1920.

The development of *Vlakfontein* started in 1945. In June 1953 it was proclaimed a township and in July 1962, at the request of the inhabitants the name was changed to Mamelodi. The population today is in excess of 250 000 people.

There are several interesting things to see and experience in Mamelodi. Traditional initiation rights for boys and girls take place in the overlooking mountains. There are herbalists and s*angomas* (diviners), a lively, informal business sector next to Denneboom station, a freedom square named after Solomon Mahlangu, a 20-year-old freedom fighter who was hanged when John Vorster was prime minister of South Africa, the Moretele Park where pop music festivals take place, the SOS village for twilight children, the barrack-like male hostels built during the apartheid era for migrant workers, an informal settlement of squatters named after Stanza Bopape, a political activist killed by the Civil Cooperation Bureau, the great specialists in dirty tricks for the apartheid government.

On the high ridge dominating Pretoria from the south stands the military centre of *Voortrekkerhoogte* (pioneer heights); the *Zwartkop* (black peak) air force station; the army and air force residential area of Valhalla; the head office building of the Iron and Steel Corporation, constructed out of stainless steel; the South African Air Force Memorial, commemorating members of the South African Air Force who sacrificed their lives in war and peace-time service; and ...

THE VOORTREKKER MONUMENT

This monument is the most imposing in South Africa. It originated in 1936 when the Sentrale Volks Monumente Komitee invited international architects to submit designs for the monument. The fundamental idea of the monument, whatever form it took, was that it should commemorate the fortitude, courage and intransigence of the Voortrekkers. At the same time the monument had to harmonise with Africa's vastness, solitude, mystery and the underlying drama of a savage and often brutal past.

Gerard Moerdijk, a South African architect specialising in churches and public buildings, produced the design which resulted in the Voortrekker Monument of today. His conception of the great structure was bold. Searching for a design homogeneous to Africa, he accepted the fact that, apart from the Cape-Dutch style, the European on this continent had still to produce something which had not been copied from Europe or America.

The Cape-Dutch style would have been gauche in the severe setting of the Transvaal highveld. Its relaxed tranquillity did not, in any case, reflect the stormy dynamism of the Voortrekker period. The Voortrekkers themselves had not built any great structures; wagons and simple *hartbeeshuisies* and *kapsteilhuisies* suited their needs. Since the Bible was their greatest cultural influence, had the Voortrekkers set out to build anything imposing, they would doubtless have followed precedent and erected an altar of thanksgiving. Accepting this postulate, Gerard Moerdijk set out to design an altar in African style, using pure African motifs for decoration and theme.

The ruins of stone enclosures built by the medieval Karanga people of Zimbabwe gave Moerdijk his solution to the problem of an architecture which was truly homogeneous to Southern Africa. The Karanga people had migrated south of the Zambezi River some time after the birth of Christ. Finding themselves in a world dominated by granite, they had harmonised their life-style with this type of rock, farming on its soil, mining the minerals associated with granite and using fragments of the rock to build enclosures around the residences of their chiefs. The architecture was unique: Without learning the technique of roofing or mortar, the builders devised a style which blended perfectly with the vastness of Africa.

Moerdijk went to the ruin known as Great Zimbabwe, near Masvingo. He studied it and adopted the same technique of piling small granite units one on top of the other to give the effect of massive scale. He, of course, used cement and, strangely enough, this one divergence from the original method was destined to cause complications in expansion and contraction.

The leading decorative motif of Great Zimbabwe – the chevron pattern on the *Imba Hura* (great enclosure) – was built into the facade of the monument. It represented water and associated fertility, the dominant influence in African life controlling so much human migration and activity. With its small stone unit construction and the chevron decorations, the facade of the monument is essentially African in its patterns and forms.

Grafted on to the four corners of this mighty altar are four busts depicting four leaders of the Great Trek: Piet Retief, Andries Pretorius, Hendrik Potgieter, and a symbolical, nameless leader. In the front stands a bronze by Anton van Wouw of a Voortrekker woman with two children huddled in her skirts.

Above the figure of the woman loom the heads of wildebeest, representing the dangers confronting civilisation. This symbolism was suggested by the episode during which Piet Retief was seated chatting amiably to the Zulu king, Dingane, and their conversation was disturbed by a thunderous singing and stamping outside the royal enclosure. *'What is that?'* asked Retief, *'My regiment of wildebeest dancing'*, answered Dingane with a smile. Over the main entrance is mounted the head of a solitary buffalo, the most dangerous and determined of all animals when wounded. Inside is a spacious crypt, designed with the idea that it might be used as a repository for the remains of great South Africans. In the centre of the crypt lies the sarcophagus, planned to contain relics of some of the pioneers. On it are the words *Ons vir jou, Suid-Afrika* (We for thee, South Africa). The surrounding shadows and quietness are tomb-like, but in the roof a circular well has been left which drenches the entire 30-metre-square hall with light.

The great hall is dominated by African patterns and designs. Light filtering into the lower portion is tinted with the peculiar brown-yellow of the African landscape, while the heights are the colour of the deep-blue sky.

Radiating across the floor from the centre wall are symbolic wave patterns representing the expanding influence of the pioneers, while all around on the wall where these waves break, is a bas-relief frieze made of Italian marble. It is 93 m long and 2,3 m high, reputedly the second largest in the world, the larger being the frieze at the altar of Zeus at Pergamum.

The frieze depicts in tableau form scenes and episodes from the Great Trek: Louis Trichardt with the kindly Portuguese Governor of Lourenzo Marques; the descent of the Drakensberg, Piet Retief and Dingane signing the ill-fated treaty, surrounded by their men. Well in evidence is the Zulu king's mobile human spittoon (a kneeling youth with outstretched cupped hands).

One by one the scenes are presented to the promenading visitor. Each depiction has been created with careful attention to authentic detail. Direct descendants of the Voortrekkers posed for the human figures. Original items of furniture and dress were carefully copied. When it became desirable to include a Voortrekker's dog, for lack of any positive guidance in the records, a special dog was deliberately bred and then modelled from life. Two casual references in Voortrekker records suggested a breed. In his diary Louis Trichardt noted: *'The bitch caught a rietbok this morning.'* This suggested a female greyhound, for reedbuck are very quick. In Voortrekker records of the Bloukrans Massacre, a passage relates: *'The people awoke to the barking of dogs'*. As the watchdog the Dobermann pinscher was selected. The pup produced by the greyhound–Dobermann pinscher match was featured in the frieze.

The frieze was modelled in clay in South Africa and translated in Italy into marble from the Apennines, the same as that used by Michelangelo.

Thirty metres above the floor of the great hall is the domed ceiling which forms the roof. Two hundred and sixty steps lead to the roof and from it may be obtained a sweeping view of the surrounding countryside. The domed roof adds a final touch of drama. The dome is a segment of a globe on which South Africa is marked in bas-relief. Marking the position of Blood River is an aperture, so situated that once a year at precisely 12h00 on 16 December (the date of the Battle of Blood River), a ray of sunlight shines directly through this opening, illuminating that portion of the frieze showing the Voortrekkers making their vow to God to build a church if He granted them a victory over the Zulus. At noon exactly, this ray of sunshine floods over the words *Ons vir jou, Suid-Afrika*.

Construction of the monument began late in 1937. Granite was quarried from an outcrop in the Northern Transvaal which had yielded material for the building of a prehistoric walled settlement. The monument cost £350 000 to erect and was opened on 16 December 1949. The monument is surrounded by a wall carved to represent a laager of 64 full-size wagons standing in a garden of indigenous flowers. Close by is a large amphitheatre where open-air religious services, meetings and exhibitions of folk-dancing are staged. A national gathering takes place there every year on 16 December.

Adjoining the tea-room is a museum which displays many interesting relics and contains a series of dioramas showing well-constructed interiors of Voortrekker homes. The three rooms, together comprising a Voortrekker cottage, exhibit many interesting objects of the time.

Among other exhibits are weapons, bullet moulds, African artefacts, leatherwork and clothing. One case contains 22 types of women's bonnets.

There are some photographs of considerable interest, including one of Louis Trichardt and another of his surviving children taken in Lourenzo Marques. Two trek wagons in good condition stand outside the museum.

A curiosity in the form of a lampshade made from a tin, with perforations allowing light to shine through, is paralleled in Morocco, where similar shades are still used and also sold to tourists in large quantities.

The series of ten tapestries, stitched by nine ladies of the Railways Culture Society to designs by Mr W H Coetzer, are notable. Depicted are scenes of Voortrekker history, a task which took eight years to complete, with 3 353 600 stitches and 130 different colours of wool being used.

The Voortrekker Monument, situated in a 54 ha nature reserve, is open daily 09h00 to 16h45.

HARTBEESPOORT DAM

Thirty-two kilometres west of Pretoria lies the irrigation dam of *Hartbeespoort* (pass of the *hartbees,* a species of antelope), completed in 1923 and overflowing for the first time in March 1925. With a wall 149,5 m long and 59,4 m high, the dam is fed by the waters of the Crocodile and Magalies rivers and covers 1 883 ha at a maximum depth of 45,1 m. Its capacity is 186 cubic metres. The dam supplies irrigation water through 544 km of canals to 15 976 ha of land on which tobacco, wheat, lucerne, fruit and flowers are produced.

Also a great recreational area, Hartbeespoort Dam is used by several boating and fishing clubs as well as by innumerable private people. On its shores lie residential areas such as the picturesque assembly of weekend cottages and hideaways known as *Kosmos* (so named by the founder of the township, Johan Schoeman, when one moonlit night he was rowing on the dam and the brilliance of the stars that reflected on the water reminded him of the universe), and the township of *Schoemansville* (founded in 1925 and named after General Hendrik Schoeman, father of the founder, Johan Schoeman). A tarmac road skirts the dam, passes through a tunnel 56,6 m long and crosses the dam wall, yielding many fine views. Kosmos, 9 km beyond the dam wall, is a particularly colourful little place enhanced by bougainvilleas, poinsettias, jacarandas, flamboyants (*Poinciana regia*), hibiscus and other flowering plants.

Numerous places of recreation such as tea-rooms, wayside kiosks, camping grounds, amusement parks, a hotel, snake park, menagerie, etc. have been created around the lake. Especially notable is the aerial ropeway run by the Hartbeespoort Dam Cableway Company. This ropeway, 1,2 km long and rising 400 m from the lower station to the highest point of the Magaliesberg range, provides a dramatic 6 minute ride, ending with a superb view from the summit. It is open daily from 08h00 to 18h00 and on Saturday nights until 22h00.

The Hartbeespoort Aquarium, said to be the largest freshwater aquarium in Africa, is another interesting feature of the area. Displayed here is a vast collection of exotic and indigenous fish, seals, crocodiles and marine birds. It is open daily from 08h30 to 17h00. Performing times for the seals are Saturdays 11h00 and 15h00; Sundays and public holidays 11h00, 13h00 and 15h00. Feeding times during the week are at 11h00 and 15h00.

Close to the Hartbeespoort Dam is the atomic research centre (the Atomic Energy Corporation of South Africa) built at *Pelindaba* (end of the discussion), the former home of the author Gustav Preller who gave the place that name when the waters impounded by the Hartbeespoort Dam enveloped his farmlands. Around July, flowering aloes are very beautiful in the vicinity, especially where the road to Johannesburg passes through the hills alongside the Hennops River. A picnic place is situated at the river.

THE RIETVLEI NATURE RESERVE

With 3 500 hectares under conservation this is one of the largest municipal nature reserves in South Africa. It is well stocked with wildlife.

Chapter Thirty-Five

MPUMULANGA

The Highveld

The grassy plains of the eastern highveld are deceptive. To the eye they are open areas – green in summer, drab brown in winter. Rural by nature, they provide farmlands where crops such as maize, sorghum and sunflowers are cultivated. They are also the adopted homeland of prodigious numbers of cosmos – white, pink and maroon flowers originating from Mexico, brought to Southern Africa as cultivated plants but long since escaped over garden walls and run riot on these wide plains.

This calm rustic simplicity is little more than skin deep. Immediately beneath the surface is hidden a gigantic powerhouse, a source of energy so vast that it will keep the heart of South Africa beating for perhaps a thousand years or more. How did this powerhouse originate?

Between 250 and 125 million years ago, Nature, using water as a creative tool, laid down a thick series of sediments known to geologists as the Karoo Sequence. In rainy, humid and swampy conditions on the surface a huge forest grew, providing a home for many strange primeval creatures. As the trees flourished, died and were replaced by others, their trunks, together with the carcasses of dinosaurs and other animals, were interred in a cemetery of mud.

As the mood of Nature changed, water was replaced by fire and wind in the creation of a new landscape. The cemetery dried up, grass covered its surface and, perhaps as a kind gesture before the Creative Spirit departed on other chores, flowers were sprinkled over the area in fond memory of trees long since gone and deep forests that have vanished. It is this burial-ground beneath the grass and flowers that contains an estimated 60 billion tons of coal, at least half of which is bituminous and lies within 300 m of the surface. It is this deposit – the eighth largest in the world – which provides South Africa with its energy heart; coal that can be burnt, converted into electric power, gas, liquid fuels, chemicals and raw materials for innumerable industrial processes.

Complementing these deposits of coal is water, of which there is ample on the eastern highveld. The west-flowing *Vaal* (tawny-coloured) River and the east flowing *Nkomati* (river of cows) and *Usutu* (dark brown) rivers originate on the watershed running north–south through the eastern highveld. A feature of the highveld plains is the number of shallow lakelets or pans – hollows in which water collects – which provide happy homes for a considerable population of water-fowl. After a good rainy season, the view from an aircraft reveals many hundreds of these lakelets scattered over the plains like spots of blue paint dropped by accident on a beautiful green table-cloth.

Endowed with energy and water, the area is understandably bustling with human activity in harnessing, conversion, packaging, exporting and marketing of its assets. Much of the once pure atmosphere is now polluted by industrial smoke and fumes. In winter this pollution is particularly bad, the worst in South Africa and amongst the worst in the world. As far as holiday-makers are concerned, the region would not exactly be regarded as a paradise. However, the area possesses a certain drama and impressiveness and there are recreational features worth exploring. Roads are excellent; and to journey past some of the huge thermal power stations, coal-mines and liquid fuel plants of Sasol II and III at Secunda, is an awesome experience.

The electric grid system of South Africa run by Eskom (Electricity Supply Commission) is based in this region. The grid system begins at the 1 600 000 kW generating plant built in 1962 at Camden, near Ermelo. Eighteen other large generating stations have been constructed to contribute energy to this grid which strides across the face of South Africa by means of 80 000 km of transmission line, feeding electric power at 400 000 volts from one end of the country to the other. The largest of these power stations in the eastern highveld are Kriel, generating 3 000 000 kW, and the new stations at Matla and Duvha, each with an output of 3 600 000 kW. Two more giants,

Ilanga and Tuluka, are to be built in the area, and each will have a capacity of 6 000 000 kW. They will be the largest thermal power-stations in the world.

The two Sasol plants, producing liquid fuel and diverse chemicals from coal, are far and away the largest of their kind in the world. At the time of construction they comprised the largest single engineering project in the world. These plants gulp one-third of the coal produced in South Africa. In order to feed Sasol II, the largest coal-mine in the world, Bosjesspruit Mine, is designed to yield up to 25 million tons of hard black coal a year. Mines in Germany produce 45 million tons each year, but of the type known as lignite, a soft brown coal with a high water content.

The two Sasol plants, together with the original Sasol I in the Free State, are designed to produce about 50 per cent of South Africa's oil requirements. Various coal-mines – some opencast, others underground – provide all domestic requirements and are calculated to export from Richards Bay 40 million tons of bituminous coal and 4 million tons of anthracite each year. In the opencast mines such as Rietspruit, Kleinlopje and Ermelo, massive machines remove overburden, gulping 80 tons of earth at a time. Huge mechanical shovels load the coal into 136 ton haulers which convey the coal to a crusher. It is then stockpiled, blended and loaded on to trains over 1 km long, destined for Richards Bay.

The first main road and rail communication to penetrate this natural powerhouse of South Africa was the route from Pretoria to the east. Originally created to connect the then South African Republic with the sea, this railway, known as the Eastern Line, unwittingly found its way across the surface of the powerhouse of South Africa, opening the area for discovery and development. The road which accompanies the railway to the east starts from the centre of Pretoria, in Church Square, where Anton van Wouw's fine statue of President Paul Kruger stands surveying the bustle and noise of the modern world.

The route leads for 6,5 km along Church Street through the densely built-up city. After 1,5 km Church Street crosses the Apies River by means of a bridge guarded by a set of stone lions presented to Paul Kruger by Barney Barnato, one of the Rand mining 'lords' of the last century. Another kilometre takes the street past the Union Buildings, looking down aloofly from the splendour of their garden setting. Shops and flats give way to suburban houses and gardens. Then, quite abruptly, Church Street reaches the open countryside and becomes the Eastern Highway, N4, a smoothly graded, gracefully curving dual carriageway which snakes across the rolling highveld.

Immediately outside the built-up area, 8 km from Church Square, the road crosses the main road to the north, the N1 road. Across this road a turn-off to the left stretches to the suburb of Silverton, originally laid out on 1 January 1890 on Mundt's farm as a recreational area for the citizens of Pretoria. Today it is a small town, but it still possesses some rural charm, with greenery interspersed amongst the concrete and some open space preserved as the Pretoria National Botanic Garden and Botanical Research Institute (open to the public daily from 08h00 to 17h30).

Passing the entrance to this garden, the road continues eastwards. The vast complex of buildings occupied by the Council for Scientific and Industrial Research (CSIR) stands on the right-hand side of the road. There are turn-offs to suburbs such as Val de Grace; Menlo Park; Willows; *Eerste Fabrieke* (first manufactory), the site of the first manufactory (a distillery) in the old Transvaal; Rayton; and Cullinan, the site of the Premier Diamond Mine discovered in 1902 by Thomas Cullinan. It was here, in 1905, that the largest of all diamonds was found; a 3 024,75 carat stone from which was cut the 530 carat Star of South Africa, the smaller Cullinan II, III and IV stones, and several brilliants, all of which are set in the British Crown Jewels. A 2-hour tour of the surface mining area takes place daily at 10h30. No children under 10 years of age are allowed on the tour. Phone (012) 734-0081 to book 24 hours in advance.

The road now follows the shallow valley of the Pienaars River, well wooded with acacia trees and sheltering fields of maize and lucerne. At 18,5 km from Church Square, the road crosses the Pienaars River, commencing a gentle climb through a low range of hills. There are turn-offs to place such as Avondzon; Cullinan; and Bapsfontein, a recreational resort renowned for its 'pop' music concerts. The Willem Prinsloo Agricultural Museum is on the old road to Bronkhorstspruit. It is open daily from 08h00 to 16h00.

Leaving the valley of the Pienaars River, the road continues eastwards over a spacious, sundrenched expanse of highveld, richly green in summer and, at Easter, brilliant with the colours of countless cosmos flowers. Clumps of eucalyptus, pine and wattle trees provide shade from the brightness and warmth. At 45 km there is a turn-off north which leads for 45 km to the Ndebele Traditional Village and museum. This project, known as *Vuko Tsoga* (wake up – arise), displays the unique architecture, wall finger painting and beadwork of the Ndebele people. At 7 km east from the turn to the Ndebele Village the N4 road reaches a turn-off to the town of ...

BRONKHORSTSPRUIT

Named after the Bronkhorst family, *Bronkhorstspruit* is a farming centre with a population of 19 972. Originally a station opened when the Eastern Line reached the site in 1894, it was laid out as a town in 1905. The town is famous chiefly for being near the site of the ignominious defeat suffered by the British 94th Regiment on 20 December 1880 at the commencement of the Anglo-Transvaal War.

The road proceeds eastwards, crossing the actual Bronkhorstspruit 56 km from Pretoria, and traversing the airy, spacious highveld plain. There are few landmarks save turn-offs to places such as Delmas and the town of Bronkhorstspruit (58 km); Wilgerivier and Nooitgedacht (70 km); Balmoral and Kendal (82 km); Verena and the Highveld Steel and Vanadium Corporation (92,5 km) usually disgorging a horrible pollutant into the highveld atmosphere. There are also turn-offs to Clewer and Verena (98 km); Lynville and Ferrobank (101 km); and 104 km from Pretoria a turn-off to Springs and to the town of ...

WITBANK

Named after a large outcrop of white sandstone, *Witbank* (white ridge) was formerly used by transport drivers as an outspan place for wagons.

The presence of coal in the area was perceived in the early years. It was visible on the surface and in the beds of streams. Sporadic attempts were made to exploit the deposits but wagon transport was too impractical. The building of the Eastern Line made mining possible and in 1896 Samuel Stanford started to work a mine at Zeraatsfontein. This was the beginning of the original Witbank Colliery Company. Today, the Witbank district is the largest coal producer in Africa, having 22 mines, a carbide plant and a cyanide factory. An estimated 75 000 million tons of coal lie close to the surface in this part of the highveld. In seams 2 m to 5 m thick, it is ideal for mechanical mining, thus securing the future of Witbank as a coal-producing centre for centuries to come.

Witbank was proclaimed a town in 1903. Becoming a municipality on 8 November 1914, it today has 167 186 inhabitants. It is a typical modern mining centre in an area with few pretensions to beauty, but in summer at least the atmosphere is well washed by thunderstorms and reasonably unpolluted for such an industrial centre. The climate is brisk and healthy. The Witbank Dam, completed in 1954 in the Olifants River, provides a recreational area with boating, fishing, and swimming facilities as well as a nature reserve.

The town has a splendid cultural centre with a town hall, civic theatre and banqueting hall of large size and the most modern design, a real credit to the town.

A particularly fascinating fragment of history linked with Witbank concerns Winston Churchill. On the night of 13 December 1899 this bedraggled-looking but quite irrepressible character appeared out of the dark and knocked at the door of the house owned by the manager of the Transvaal and Delagoa Bay Colliery. During the previous night, he had escaped from a prisoner-of-war camp in Pretoria and, concealed in an empty coal truck, travelled to Clewer siding near Witbank. Now he was in need of food and shelter. Fortunately for him, the occupant of the house was an Englishman, John Howard. Churchill was hidden, first in the underground stables of the mine and then behind some packing-cases in the mine office. Meanwhile, a hue and cry for him raged all over the Transvaal, with a reward of £27 being offered to bring him in 'dead or alive'.

Early on the morning of 19 December Churchill stowed away in a railway truck loaded with wool consigned to Lourenzo Marques (Maputo). It was a tedious journey. On the first night the train stopped at Waterval Boven; the next night it stopped at Komatipoort. At last, late in the afternoon of 21 December, the train reached Lourenzo Marques. After some argument with the British Consul, the grimy escapee was identified as Winston Churchill and a telegram was sent to the mine manager, Howard, with the terse news: *'Goods arrived safely'*.

As a token of his thanks, Churchill presented inscribed gold watches to the six men at Witbank who aided his escape. The mine shaft where he was hidden (now disused) was named the Churchill shaft. A plaque was erected to mark the event, but vandalism resulted in its removal to a safer place in the grounds of the local MOTH organisation.

The N4 road continues from Witbank for 30 km in an easterly direction across the highveld and then reaches a turn-off to the town of ...

MIDDELBURG

In 1859 the government of the South African Republic decided to found a town half-way between Pretoria and Lydenburg (hence the name of *Middelburg*). Nothing resulted from this plan, but in 1864 the Dutch Reformed Church bought the farm *Sterkfontein* (strong fountain) from L de Jager and in 1866 a town was laid out which the Church named Nazareth. A few houses and stores were built around the new church, but for years the settlement remained so lifeless that a popular jibe developed about nothing good ever coming out of Nazareth. This joke stung the residents (altogether only seven houses in the town), who petitioned that the name revert to the original Middelburg.

The town has since grown into a modern agricultural, industrial and communications centre with a population of 85 880. Situated near the coalfields, the town has plenty of water. Power is supplied by the giant Komati Power-Station and two others in the district. A ferrochrome mill produces stainless steel, and other industries have been established in the vicinity.

The Little Olifants River flows past the town, and the Kruger Dam (3 km from the town) is a well-developed recreational facility offering swimming, fishing, water sports, a restaurant, caravan park and other accommodation. The town is, in fact, a convenient staging post along the road to the east and also for north–south travellers who, on their way to and from the coast, bypass the traffic congestion of the Witwatersrand–Pretoria complex by turning off from the N1 and taking the all-tarmac N11 from Potgietersrus, south past the Loskop Dam to Middelburg and then on to Ermelo where they have the choice of following the N2 road on a magnificent coastal route all the way across KwaZulu-Natal, the Eastern and Western Cape to Cape Town. The N11 continues from Ermelo south to Volksrust and thence to Durban.

There are several interesting structures in the town which date from the days of the South African Republic. These include the railway station and Meyers Bridge (both built in 1890), and the Memorial Church which now serves as a museum. Fort Merensky lies 13 km from the town and is described in the next section.

There are two excellent hiking trails in the area: the Botshabelo Trail of four hours, and the Klein Aasvoëlkrans Trail of six hours.

LOSKOP DAM AND FORT MERENSKY

From Middelburg a fine tarmac road, N11, branches north from the N4 road to the east. It descends from the highveld through varied scenery to Loskop Dam (48 km) and from there to Groblersdal and Potgietersrus (198 km).

After 8 km of travel along this road there is a turn-off left (west) leading for 5 km to Fort Merensky. In 1865 the Berlin Mission Society bought a farm in the valley of the Olifants River, where the Reverend Alexander Merensky established a mission named *Botshabelo* (place of refuge). Out of local stone he built a flat-roofed residence, church and protective fort. Local tribesmen were employed as builders, and the construction of the little fort is an interesting example of combined African and European ideas. It is perfectly preserved as part of the Botshabelo Open Air Museum. The Museum is open to day visitors from 08h00 to 18h00 – the Ndebele craftswomen can be seen at work between 10h00 and 16h00. Three hiking trails start from the old mission which lies in the centre of a nature reserve.

From the turn-off to the fort, the N11 tarmac road continues northwards across the highveld plain, traversing an area densely settled by African people. The road then drops into a bushy, shallow valley and, 38 km from Middelburg, descends a spectacular pass flanked by cliffs. Beyond this pass the road reaches an alluvial valley covered in bush and dotted with farms. At 44 km in the valley lies the Kloof motel. At 48 km the road reaches the *Loskop* (separate hillock) Dam.

Completed in 1938, the 40 m high, 475 m long wall of the Loskop Dam stretches across the Olifants River, impounding 362 million cubic metres of water which irrigate 28 168 ha of land. The area around the dam was developed by the Transvaal Council for Public Resorts (Overvaal Resorts, then Aventura, now Mpumulanga Parks Board) as a recreational area offering boating, fishing, a swimming-bath, restaurant and varied accommodation. A 12 755 ha nature reserve surrounding the dam is well stocked with game animals such as white rhino, giraffe, blue wildebeest, zebra, sable, antelope, kudu, waterbuck, impala, nyala, bushbuck, blesbok, reedbuck, mountain reedbuck, klipspringer, grey duiker, oribi, steenbok, and bird life which is particularly rich. Bus tours are conducted into the reserve and there are nature trails leading from the camp. Water from the dam is used for irrigation on many farms in the lower reaches of the river valley.

There is a privately owned cheetah sanctuary where these endangered animals are bred.

From the Loskop Dam, the R35 road continues northwards for 32 km and then reaches the agricultural centre of ...

GROBLERSDAL

Groblersdal, in the past sometimes known as the Canaan of the Transvaal, was laid out on the farm *Klipbank* and proclaimed a town on 9 March 1938. It was named after the owner of the farm, W J Grobler, who played a large part in the creation of the Hereford and Loskop irrigation schemes. The town is the centre for these well-watered farmlands which extend for 121 km on either side of the Olifants River. Maize, sunflowers, rice, fruit, vegetables and tobacco are produced. It is the terminus of a branch railway from Pienaarsrivier.

From Groblersdal, the R35 road continues north for 21 km and then reaches ...

MARBLE HALL

Marble Hall was laid out in 1942 and proclaimed a town in 1945. It is an agricultural centre producing such crops as citrus, grain and grapes, as well as being a residence for workers in the marble lime mine. Fifteen different varieties of marble are mined here in what was originally known as *Marmerhol* (marble hole). The name was Anglicised, with a touch of poetry, to Marble Hall by, it is said, British soldiers in the Anglo-Boer War when they were shown the deposit. They confused the meaning of *hol* with *hall*. The 'hole' was a strange depression, muddy at the bottom and a death trap for many wild animals. Marble and lime were exposed on the sides.

It is said that, in 1913, Christoffel Visagie was hunting in the area with his family. He fell sick with malarial fever and looked as though he was going to die. His wife packed him into their wagon and set off for home in Pretoria. On the way they passed the marble hole. Mrs Visagie selected two fine blocks of white marble, loaded them into the wagon with her husband, and went on to Pretoria where she considered he could die in comfort and be decently buried. She had also recently lost one of her children.

In Pretoria there was a stonemason by the name of Thomas Taylor. To this gentleman, Mrs Visagie took her two blocks of marble and asked him how much he would charge to carve them into tombstones. The marble was of superb quality and he asked her where she had obtained it. She was a little secretive but, as it happened, only one tombstone had to be carved as her husband recovered. He visited Taylor to recover the unused block of stone and the two men became friendly. In due course, Visagie took Taylor to see the remarkable marble hole.

The two men then went into partnership to work the marble but there were no roads or railway. Transporting blocks of marble by ox-wagon was not practical and they were forced to abandon the project. In 1929 the Marble Lime Company was formed to work the deposit. A branch railway from Pienaarsrivier was constructed in 1936.

From the turn-off to Middelburg the N4 main road to the east continues a gentle climb out of the valley of the Little Olifants River. Traversing typical highveld country, the road passes plantations of wattle trees and numerous shallow pans (lakelets) which are a feature of this part of the highveld. The decorated huts of Ndebele people may also be seen, adding touches of bright colour to a landscape already painted by Nature with green grass and a deep-blue sky. From January to April the cosmos flowers provide a brilliant spectacle.

There are turn-offs to Hendrina (4 km); Arnot power station (26 km); Carolina (45 km and 65 km); and then at 65 km a turn-off left (north), leading for 3 km to the town of ...

BELFAST

With a population of 9 187, Belfast is the highest railway station (2 025 m above sea-level) on the Eastern Line. The farm *Tweefontein* (two fountains) was proclaimed a town on 30 June 1890 in anticipation of the opening of the railway four years later. The owner, Richard O'Neill, had come from a family living in Belfast, Northern Ireland, and so the new town was named after his ancestral abode. He was, for a long time, the principal figure in the community and opened the first store in the town.

The Belfast district is high lying, well watered, and has a crisp, healthy climate ideal for sheep and dairy farming. Numerous mist-belt plantations of wattle and gum trees flourish. The rivers provide good fishing, with trout and bass being found in several lakes and streams.

A branch railway meanders northwards from Belfast over the principal watershed of Mpumalanga. The railway serves rural centres such as Dullstroom 35 km away which, at 2 076 m above sea-level, is the highest railway station in Southern Africa. The name of *Dullstroom* does not refer to a lack of social life but is derived from Wolterus Dull, who directed an immigration scheme there in 1883.

The area around Dullstroom is a windswept grassland of numerous streams, merino sheep and wild flowers. Dominating the landscape is the 2 332 m high *Die Berg* (the mountain) of the Steenkampsberge range, the highest point between the Vaal and Limpopo rivers. A trout festival takes place in Dullstroom on the first Saturday of October each year. Fishing attracts many visitors to the area. There is excellent accommodation. The South African Bird of Prey Trust have established 9 km from Dullstroom on the Lydenburg road a breeding and educational facility for indigenous birds of prey. The facility is open to the public with flying displays, a restaurant, shops selling leatherwork, fine linen and period furniture and delicatessen.

The road to the east continues from the turn-off to Belfast, losing altitude as it traverses increasingly broken country. After 6 km the road passes a monument to the Battle of Berg-en-Dal, fought there on 27 August 1900. This was one of the most vicious small battles of the Anglo-Boer War.

The Boers, commanded by General Louis Botha, held exceptionally strong positions on the ridge at Berg-en-Dal. They were determined to delay any further British advance along the Eastern Line. The British mustered over 20 000 men in order to take the position by storm. At 11h00 the British artillery opened fire on the homestead buildings of *Berg-en-Dal* (mountain and dale) farm and the surrounding hillocks. The Johannesburg Police (some of Botha's best men) who were holding these positions experienced a barrage of fire. Nevertheless, the Johannesburg Police held their positions. When the British infantry tried to advance, they were received with a hail of bullets which killed 12 men and wounded 103. However, the British resolutely saw the attack through, and by evening the Boers were forced to abandon the position and retreat to Machadodorp.

Beyond the monument to this battle, the road makes its way for a further 16 km across the highveld before reaching a turn-off to the town of ...

MACHADODORP

This town was named in honour of Joachim Machado, the Portuguese surveyor and governor of Mozambique, who located the route of the railway from Lourenzo Marques (Maputo) to Pretoria. The town started as a railway station, built when the line was opened on 10 July 1894. There are now 4 502 people living there. Machadodorp is the junction of the line to KwaZulu-Natal through Breyten. At 1,5 km from the town there are radioactive thermal sulphur baths resorted to by sufferers from gout and rheumatism. The springs reach the surface at a temperature of 27°C and radioactivity is 12,3 mache units. Cattle, horses and sheep flourish on the surrounding farmlands. Trout fishing in the streams is good and the fish, fresh or smoked, may be purchased from wayside stalls. The climate is brisk and cool.

From the turn-off to Machadodorp, the main road continues eastwards through more rugged country. After 1,5 km there is a turn-off to Dullstroom and, 6 km further on, a division of the road. To the right the new national road, N4, leads to Waterval Boven and on to the lowveld down the valley of the Elands River (see Chapter Thirty-Six). To the left, the old road continues eastwards for a further 15 km, with the landscape gradually building up to a most dramatic change. Passing the Bambi motel and a turn-off to Lydenburg at 248 km from Pretoria, the road reaches the edge of the highveld and commences a steady descent down Schoemanskloof to reach the lowveld. The change in climate, scenery, vegetation and atmosphere is striking (see Chapter Thirty-Six).

The N4 road from Pretoria to the east traverses the northern side of the South African powerhouse, while other roads penetrate the heart of the area. The R29 tarmac road leading eastwards from Springs on the Witwatersrand leads directly to some of the largest centres and thence to the borders of Swaziland. From a sightseeing point of view the journey is not recommended in winter, for the area is unattractive – a hideosity of smog so foul that it stifles the breathing, chokes the throat and stings the eyes. Understandably, the grass is dead during this season, much of it burned black, and the atmosphere still further polluted by fires. It takes the summer rains to wash the man-made filth from the face of the land and the sky. The grass then turns emerald green and the clouds pile up like huge masses of snow-white whipped cream.

Beyond Springs the road stretches across a vast plain covered with maize, sunflowers and cosmos plants flowering by the million at Easter time. After 37 km the road passes the village of Devon, a cluster of buildings gathered in a hollow around a bulky grain silo. A further 12 km takes the road through Leandra, a small centre whose name incorporates the names of the neighbouring township of Leslie and *Evander* (after Evelyn Anderson, wife of the managing director of the Union Corporation Ltd which developed the far east gold-mines).

These townships provide commercial facilities for a cluster of mines, power-stations and the prodigious conglomeration of pipes, towers, smoke-stacks and chemical-mechanical processing bric-à-brac known as Sasol II and III built at Secunda. The headgear of the far eastern mining-area mines such as Winkelhaak, add to the complexity of an industrial scene. The giant power-stations of Matla and Kriel are worth visiting, especially Kriel with its curiously Aztec-shaped pyramid buildings, curved cooling towers, tall straight chimneys and mirror-surfaced lake, providing artists with extraordinary opportunities in composition. Incongruously interspersed among this futuristic array of structures are the cottages of Ndebele and Sotho farm labourers, most of which are decorated with elaborate colours and patterns by proud housewives.

Passing the rural centre of Trichardt 87 km from Springs, the main road continues past turn-offs to power-stations and mines until, 113 km from Springs, it reaches the town of ...

BETHAL

Potatoes, maize and sunflowers are the principal products of *Bethal*, named after the last and first parts of the first names of Elizabeth du Plooy and Alida Naudé respectively, two sisters who were wives of the owners of a portion of the farm *Blesbokspruit* on which the town was proclaimed in 1880. In 1921 Bethal became a municipality and has since grown into a substantial commercial, educational, communications and administrative centre with a population of 33 956. The Eastern Agricultural Co-operative and the National Potato Co-operative both have their headquarters in the town. There are twenty coal-mines and three gold-mines in the vicinity. A recreational area and caravan park have been established on the shores of the Bethal Dam. At the end of April each year, the town stages a National Potato Festival. There is a museum in the town and it is on the tourist route known as the Energy–Domoina Route leading to KwaZulu-Natal and the Lowveld.

From Bethal the main tarmac B29 road continues eastwards over the plains. After 31 km the road passes the hill known as *Tafelkop* (table top) on whose level summit there are the ruins of a prehistoric settlement of the Leghoya tribe. They built their curiously cramped little dwellings out of stone. They were annihilated by later invasions of more powerful tribes such as the Ndebele. Beyond Tafelkop the B29 road continues for another 24 km and then reaches the town of ...

ERMELO

In 1871 the Reverend F L Cachet founded a parish which he named *Ermelo* after a town in Holland where he had once lived. A town was laid out for the parish, and its situation soon made it the largest centre in the eastern highveld. The area is rich in coal and anthracite, worked by three large mines – Ermelo, Spitzkop and Usutu. The Camden Power-Station opened by Eskom in 1967 and fed with coal from the Usutu Mine, forms the beginning of the South African grid system.

Maize, potatoes, beans, lucerne, sunflowers, sorghum, wool, cattle, pigs and timber are the products of the district. The Nooitgedacht Research Station, 4 km from the town, conducts research on the agriculture of the eastern highveld. The station has been responsible for the breeding (from Basuto stock) of the Nooitgedacht indigenous pony.

The population of Ermelo is 50 530. The civic centre, completed in 1977, is one of the most impressive to be found in the smaller towns of South Africa. Housed in the centre is a spacious administrative office and two halls. The attractive garden surrounding it is enhanced by a magnificent fountain designed by a local resident, Mrs Heila Brink.

Several large dams in the vicinity of Ermelo, such as the Jericho and the Westoe, provide recreational areas with fishing and boating facilities. A nature reserve and municipal tourist resort is situated on the shores of the *Douglas Dam* (named after William Douglas, a former town engineer), 6 km from the town. At the dam named after Mr J W Pet, a former mayor of the town, there is a bird sanctuary.

Roads diverge from Ermelo to several towns in Mpumalanga, to Swaziland, and southwards to KwaZulu-Natal. To the north-east, a tarmac road leads for 8 km reaching a branch, with a left turn continuing for 22 km to Breyten and the north, and a right turn proceeding north-eastwards for 29 km to reach ...

LAKE CHRISSIE

The village of Chrissiesmeer has developed on the western side of Lake Chrissie, a natural lake 24 km in circumference and up to 3 m in depth. Numerous aquatic birds, including flamingos, congregate there. The lake lies in a hollow surrounded by grasslands and always attracted vast herds of plains' game which have, unfortunately, been destroyed. However, to meet the demand for venison, local farmers breed blesbok, substantial herds of which may be seen. *Lake Chrissie* was named after Christiana, the daughter of President M W Pretorius. Good views of the lake may be had from a gravel road leading to *Rooibank* (red ridge) via the northern shore of the lake.

From Lake Chrissie there are turn-offs to Breyten and Carolina. The R39 main tarmac road continues eastwards into the timber country of the eastern highveld mist belt. High precipitation along the edge of the highveld makes conditions ideal for the cultivation of trees, particularly wattle, fir and eucalyptus. At 27,5 km from Lake Chrissie (3,5 km beyond a turn-off to Carolina) the road passes the Jessievale sawmills, with a turn-off to Lothair after a further 25 km. There is a pleasant wayside resting-place 2 km beyond this turn-off.

The tarmac road continues east through plantations of trees. There are turn-offs to Amsterdam (33,5 km) and Badplaas (56,5 km). At 61 km from Lake Chrissie the road passes Lochiel with its store, garage and hotel. At 78,5 km from Lake Chrissie a turn-off provides a very steep and rough descent for 10 km to the Mhlondosi Valley, the site of the New Paarl Goldfield and the ghost mining-town of ...

STEYNSDORP

Today, little more than a store bearing the name of Steynsdorp remains. The mounds of several hundred buildings lie buried under bush and long grass as though in a graveyard, unmarked by memorial or tombstone. The story of this place and its rise and fall is strange.

In July 1885 two prospectors, Austin and Painter, worked their way through the valley. They found traces of gold down the entire course of the stream. Somewhere in its middle reaches they thought that they had discovered payable deposits. They pegged claims and a rush of prospectors ensued after the news leaked out. By April 1886, what was at first known as Painter's Camp was the centre for a considerable gathering of prospectors, all busy seeking a share in this new find.

Gold was certainly present in the area. A prospector's pan will today reveal traces of gold from many parts of the stream and the overlooking heights. Unfortunately, the gold occurred only in patches. Finding a payable deposit defied the most energetic prospectors. Traces simply tempted them to search on and on.

Painter's Camp was renamed in honour of Commandant J P Steyn who visited the diggings on 21 February 1887 and *Steynsdorp* was laid out as a town. It grew at a phenomenal rate, with about 3 000 diggers using it as a supply source and, drinking centre. Canteens, grog-shops, so-called hotels and other places of accommodation were more numerous than anything else. Upon viewing the mounds in the grass today, it is difficult to imagine Duprats Royal Hotel, Bremers Store, Fullertons Store, Sheriffs Store, the government offices, banks, or the office of the local newspaper, *The Observer*.

All that remains of the several hundred hopeful little mines and the thousands of claims are the half-healed scars of adits, shafts and cross-cuts. The reefs which proved so hard to find, and so deceptive to those who did discover them, but which were famous in their day – the Ingwenya, Bank of England, Mint, Southern Cross, Unity and Comstock – have been forgotten.

The stone walls of the gaol were the last of man's structures to withstand the wind and rain. The gaol was the scene of one of the few lynchings to occur in the course of events during South African gold rushes. One of the local constables, G Milhorat, and his wife Lizzie (formerly a well-known Barberton barmaid) were murdered by their servant, Jim Zulu, on the night of 19 January 1889. Jim Zulu was arrested and locked in gaol. The next night a crowd of diggers – some with their faces blackened, others masked – broke into the gaol, seized the murderer and hanged him from the slaughter poles of one of the local butchers.

The Steynsdorp rush was an excitable affair. The very uncertainty of the finds allowed speculators and swindlers to run rife. Salting was practised to a fine art. The pubs were places of rumours. Just how much genuine gold was mined remains uncertain. What is definite, though, is that through the years prospectors met with more disappointment in this valley than anything else.

The prospectors, miners, business men, gamblers, boozers and crooks, began to drift away. The town already lay in ruins at the outbreak of the Anglo-Boer War. It was then abandoned entirely to looters and the odd vagrant. Eventually, the bush and grass silently reclaimed the New Paarl Goldfield. Only memories and the ghosts of the excitable company of gold-mad men and women linger in that dark valley. Silence blankets the hills and valleys; the rumours, arguments, quarrels and shouts have been blown away by the winds into the vastness of eternity.

The gravel road continues down the valley of the Mhlondosi for 10 km and, 20 km from the turn-off on the main tarmac road near Lochiel, joins the gravel road leading from Badplaas to the old asbestos mine at *Diepgezet* (deeply sited). The valley is now a place of African settlement.

The main tarmac road, R39, proceeds from Lochiel past the turn-off to Steynsdorp. After a further 7 km (85,5 km from Lake Chrissie), it reaches the Oshoek police, customs and immigration post on the border of Swaziland (see Chapter Forty-Seven). The post is open from 07h00 to 22h00.

ERMELO TO MACHADODORP

Eight kilometres from Ermelo, the R36 tarmac road to the north-east (after the road to Lake Chrissie and Swaziland has veered off) continues for a further 22 km, reaching the town of ...

BREYTEN

Named after Nicolaas Breytenbach who owned part of the farm *Bothasrust* on which the town stands, *Breyten* lies on the watershed between the Vaal River system which flows westwards to the Atlantic Ocean and the Komati and Olifants rivers which flow eastwards to the Indian Ocean. The source of the Vaal River is a spring situated 2 km from the town from where it courses through a mass of cosmos flowers. For about one metre the infant river is unpolluted by man. After that it has problems. The spring is easily accessible along a road branching off from the main tarmac road to Carolina at the end of the railway yards where 'puffer' enthusiasts may observe a whole collection of retired steam locomotives gently rusting away in well-earned leisure.

Breyten was founded in 1906 when the railway line from Springs reached the site of the town. Sheep, maize and coal are the principal products of the district, supplemented by high rainfall which provides plentiful water and rich grazing. Klipstapel, the highest point on the watershed, is close to the town; and ruins of early stone settlements are scattered in the vicinity where the Leghoya tribe inhabited substantial villages, generally built for security on top of flat-topped hills. As a tribe they have disappeared and their settlements are in ruins.

From Breyten the main R36 tarmac road continues northwards over grassy sheep and maize country. After 2 km there is a turn-off to Lake Chrissie, and at 22 km the road reaches the town of ...

CAROLINA

In 1882 the farmers of the present Carolina district decided that it was time to found a town as a centre for their area. The wagon trail to the newly discovered gold-fields in the Kaap Valley passed through the area. The stream of traffic induced the need for a trading and staging post. Mr C J Coetzee offered a section of his farm *Steynsdraai* as a site, provided that the town was named after his wife, Carolina. Other land was added to this nucleus and on 22 June 1885 the town was proclaimed. Apart from being an important communications and trading centre with a population of 9 871, Carolina produces wool, timber, cattle and milk.

Carolina can be very cold in winter. The lowest temperature (−14.7°C) was recorded there on 23 July 1926. This was the record low temperature in South Africa until 11 August 1991 when −16,8°C was recorded in the Dordrecht district.

From Carolina the R36 tarmac road to the north continues for 48 km to Machadodorp, crossing on the way (at 23 km) the Komati (Nkhomati) River, with the original elegant stone bridge still standing next to the modern structure. Another tarmac road leads westwards from Carolina for 44 km to the town of ...

HENDRINA

Named after Hendrina Beukes, wife of the owner of the farm on which it was established, *Hendrina* became a village in 1923. It is a centre for maize production, coal-mining and two Eskom power-stations, Arnot and Hendrina. There is a museum of local history which includes among its exhibits a spinning-wheel brought to the country by Emily Hobhouse. The museum is open Mondays and Fridays, 10h00 to 13h00 and 15h00 to 17h30; on Tuesdays, Wednesdays and Thursdays 15h00 to 17h30; Saturdays 10h00 to 13h00. The population is 13 039.

From Carolina the R38 tarmac road stretches eastwards, passing through patches of tree plantations and making a winding, easy descent into the valley of the Komati River. After 50 km the road reaches the resort of ...

BADPLAAS

During the period 1860 to 1870, Jacob de Klerk traded with the Swazi people living in the valley of the Komati River. They showed him a natural feature in the area in the form of a thermal spring, reaching the surface at 53°C at a rate of 25 000 *l* an hour. The Swazis found the waters beneficial for a variety of complaints and De Klerk spread its fame amongst Europeans. From then on the spring was resorted to by people suffering from rheumatism. During the cool months from May to August a tent town was erected in the vicinity of the healing waters.

As the years passed, a few shacks were erected at the site, a tent boarding-house prospered for a while and then the Transvaal Government erected a few brick rondavels, followed by a hotel. The spring was led into a reservoir and the water piped to a series of baths. Thus the place was launched as an established health resort.

There is today on the site of the old *Badplaas* (bath farm) a considerable variety of accommodation, several shops, restaurants and other facilities. The medicinal water is fed into several private baths for use by invalids and into four magnificent recreational swimming-baths (two warm and two tepid). The Transvaal Board of Public Resorts (later Aventura now the Transitional Local Council of Badplaas) created the resort, now part of the Badplaas Centre. It is set in spacious surroundings with the great valley backed by the handsome range of high hills known to the Swazis as *Ndlumudlumu* (place of thunder).

From Badplaas the R38 tarmac road continues across the valley of the Komati River. After 1 km there is a turn-off to Lochiel and Diepgezet. The road passes Theron's Rest Camp and a turn-off to Machadodorp 8 km from Badplaas. A further 3 km takes the road across the Komati River. Immediately upstream stands the wall of the Kafferskraal Dam. The road climbs the northern slopes of the river valley where the country is grassy and open with many pleasant views. Near the top of the climb the road leads through the plantations of the Nelshoogte Forestry Station. The summit is 40 km from Badplaas, and from it may be seen the prodigious Kaap Valley – the Valley of Death of the prospectors – lying to the north amidst seemingly endless hills.

There is a viewsite and resting-place on the summit. The road makes a bold descent down a finely located pass, reaches the valley floor and, in a forest of gracefully canopied *Acacia siebeviana* trees, 63 km from Badplaas, joins the main Nelspruit–Barberton road 10 km from Barberton (see Chapter Thirty-Six).

BADPLAAS–MSAULI–BARBERTON

From Badplaas a dramatic scenic road leads to Barberton through the valley of the river known to the Swazis as the *Mtsoli* (unpredictable). This gravel road is very steep in places and sometimes rough, but quite usable in dry weather if carefully negotiated. It is 116 km to Barberton via this route for which a full day's journey should be allocated.

The drive commences with the turn-off to Lochiel, 1 km out of Badplaas on the direct tarmac road to Barberton. The gravel road leads down the valley of the Komati River. After 12 km a junction is reached from where the R541 turn-off leads southwards for 22 km to Lochiel to join the main Lake Chrissie–Swaziland road. The scenic road to Barberton marked Diepgezet continues down the valley. At 13 km there is a turn-off to Tjakastad and at 49 km a turn-off up the Mhlondosi valley to Steynsdorp which, after 20 km, joins the main Swaziland–Lake Chrissie road, R39.

The main gravel road leads on through a mountainous, bushy landscape. At 57 km the road crosses the Komati River and 2 km further on passes the opencast workings of the Msauli asbestos mine owned by African Crysotile Asbestos Ltd. The deposit was discovered in 1942 by two prospectors, Eyssel and Cronjé.

Beyond the mine, the road crosses the Msauli River, the corrupted name of which (Mtsoli) is applied to the mine. This fine torrent of water comes down in violent flood periodically, hence the name, meaning 'unpredictable'. The road climbs through impressive mountain country along the border of Swaziland, reaching the summit 13 km from the mine where it joins the Barberton–Havelock Mine road, R40, at a point 2 km from the border. The view from here is majestic.

Turning towards Barberton, the road follows the contours of the high country, a scenic wonderland with mountains stretching as far as the eye can see. Above the road the spectacular 20 km long aerial ropeway was constructed connecting the Havelock Mine to Barberton.

The road penetrates dense plantations of trees as it twists around the mountain contours. At 27 km from the junction with the Havelock road, the road reaches the verge of the Kaap Valley. For 12 km the road makes a steep descent which demands very careful driving. The road is an unforgettable experience with endless possibilities for the photographer along the whole 116 km long route from Badplaas. Barberton lies at the foot of the descent (see Chapter Thirty-Six).

From Ermelo a road, R65, leads eastwards for 79 km to the town of ...

AMSTERDAM

Originally known as Roburnia, the town was founded in 1866 by a Scot, Alexander McCorkindale, who organised the settlement of a number of his compatriots in this portion of the eastern highveld. McCorkindale divided the area into three, with Lake Chrissie as the centre for what he called Industria; Derby as the centre for Londina; and Roburnia as the capital of New Scotland.

Fifty Scottish settlers arrived and began farming sheep on estates such as *Lochiel, Waverley,* and *Bonny Brae.* Unfortunately, the rest of McCorkindale's schemes never matured, for he died of fever while planning the construction of a harbour in the bay of Lourenzo Marques. Roburnia was renamed Amsterdam in 1882 and is today a quiet little town with only McCorkindale Square to commemorate its founder.

From Amsterdam the road continues for 16 km to the customs and immigration post on the Swazi border at Nerston (see Chapter Forty-Seven). The border post is open from 08h00 to 16h00 daily.

ERMELO TO KWAZULU-NATAL

Beyond Ermelo the N2 main tarmac road leads south-eastwards over the grassy plain, passing after 13 km the Camden Power-Station whose thermal generating plant is fed coal on an endless conveyer belt from the Usutu Colliery at a rate of 5,5 million tons a year. The Camden Power-Station feeds 1 600 megawatts of electricity into the national grid, enough to supply two cities the size of Johannesburg. The power-station consumes 40 500 megalitres of water annually. It is the anchor of the national grid of South Africa. The road passes rural centres such as Sheepmoor, crosses the Vaal River 12 km from Camden, and the Ngwempisi River after a further 8 km. It continues through dense plantations of trees. Sawmills are situated at Iswepe and Panbult and the Ngoya Paper-Mill is passed at 96,5 km from Ermelo. At 104 km the N2 road reaches the town of ...

PIET RETIEF

In 1883 the surveyor G R von Wielligh laid out a town in the mist belt of the eastern highveld. It was named *Piet Retief* after the ill-fated leader of the Voortrekkers. Piet Retief has an annual rainfall of 1 000 mm and trees flourish in the area. The town is a centre for timber, paper and wattle bark production. Mica, kaolin and iron are also found in the district. Piet Retief became a municipality in 1932. Today its population is 27 518. The district includes the 100 square kilometre area of the 'Little Free State', surely one of the smallest independent states ever known. Between 1886 and 1891 this pocket state of 72 inhabitants was ruled by its own president. On 2 May 1891 the republic was incorporated into the district of Piet Retief as Ward 1.

Living in Piet Retief are a number of German families, descendants of settlers of the last century. Their brass bands are a feature of the social life of a town notable for its gardens and the jacarandas enhancing its streets. The Dutch Reformed church, built in 1921 and designed by Gerard Moerdijk (who designed the Voortrekker Monument), is a prominent feature of the town.

From Piet Retief the N2 road to KwaZulu-Natal continues southwards for 4,5 km through dense plantations of saligna trees. The road reaches a junction from where the tarmac road, R33, continues to the south, descending into the valley of the river known on account of its tortuous course as the *Mkondo* (zigzag) but, through a faulty translation, called by Europeans the *Assegai*. The road continues until, 18 km from Piet Retief, it passes through the rural timber centre of Moolman.

After a further 4,5 km of travel through plantation country, the R33 road steadily descends into the great shallow valley of the Phongolo River. At 31 km from Piet Retief a turn-off leads for 12 km to the Piet Retief Mineral Baths. The main tarmac road continues to descend, traversing open grassland where cattle are farmed. At 41 km from Piet Retief the road crosses the Phongolo River, the boundary between Mpumulanga and KwaZulu- Natal. For a further 15 km the road continues southwards over a grassy plain, covered with plantations of saligna and wattle trees. Fifty-six kilometres from Piet Retief the road reaches the town of Paulpietersburg (see Chapter Twenty-Seven).

Back at the junction 4,5 km from Piet Retief, the main tarmac N2 road swings south-eastwards, soon commencing an easy descent into the valley of the Mkondo River which it crosses 16 km from Piet Retief. At 38 km there is a turn-off north, leading for 23 km to the Swazi border post of Mahamba. The post is open from 07h00 to 22h00 daily. The road descends through bush-covered hills with fine canopied acacia trees and plantations of sisal growing by the wayside. At 66 km the road passes the mission hospital known as *Itshele Juba* (rock of the dove). At 96,5 km from Piet Retief, the road reaches the sugar-producing centre of ...

PONGOLA

The Pongola Government Water Scheme was started in 1932 with an extension being completed in 1956. There are 154 irrigated plots and a sugar mill is situated near the village. Subtropical fruits are grown in the area as well as sugar cane. Farm stalls sell produce to passing travellers.

The N2 road down the valley provides an interesting and varied drive, rising and falling over riverside hills, with fertile farmlands and forests of acacias and euphorbias lining the way. At 27 km there is a turn-off leading for 6 km to the Swazi border post at Golela. The post is open from 07h00 to 22h00 daily. After 3 km the road bridges across the Phongolo River and enters KwaZulu-Natal. The village of Mkuze lies 34,5 km further on (see Chapter Twenty-Five).

To complete a tour through the south-eastern part of the highveld, a tarmac road, R543, should be followed which leads westwards from Piet Retief past the village of Dirkiesdorp (51 km) and from there a further 43 km across the grassy plains to the town of ...

VOLKSRUST

In 1888 the South African Republic decided to create a town on the border with KwaZulu-Natal where the road from the coast reached the top of the escarpment at Laing's Nek Pass. Dorie de Jager, sister of Dirk Uys who fell at the Battle of Laing's Nek on 28 January 1881, suggested the name *Volksrust* (people's rest) for it was there that the Republican army had concentrated and rested during the battles of the Anglo-Transvaal War (1880–81).

Volksrust became a municipality in 1904 and has a population of 20 227. It is the communications centre of a district which produces maize, sunflowers, sheep, cattle and milk. The main railway and the R23 road linking Durban with Johannesburg passes through the town, hence there is a constant coming and going of trains and road traffic. The mountain of Majuba overlooking the town from the south, may be easily climbed (see Chapter Twenty-Seven). During the Anglo-Boer War there was a large concentration camp at Volksrust. A memorial records the names of the 772 people who died in the overcrowded conditions.

The town has some fine parks. The Mahawane Dam provides fishing and water sports facilities.

The N11 road from Durban to the north continues across the highveld plains which turn emerald green in summer. Elegant willow trees line the banks of the streams. High hills add variety to a rural landscape of maize and dairy farms. After 42 km this road passes through the town of Amersfoort and another 58 km brings it to Ermelo.

From Volksrust the R23 road, originally the main road from Natal to Johannesburg, leads north-westwards towards the landmark of *Perdekop* (horse peak) which looms 1 920 m high. It is situated 29 km up the road. In former years when horse sickness was endemic on the highveld, the area surrounding this miniature mountain was inexplicably free of the disease. The result was the village of Perdekop became a centre for the breeding of horses.

At 45 km from Perdekop the R23 road reaches the town of ...

STANDERTON

Pleasantly situated on the banks of the Vaal River, *Standerton* was founded in 1878 and named after Adriaan Hendrik Stander, the owner of the farm *Grootverlangen* (great desire) on which the town was created. The 1 641 m high Standerskop overlooks both the town and the site of the original fording place across the river.

In former years great herds of antelope frequented this area, attracted by the ample water and rich grazing. Nowadays the district produces wool, meat, and dairy products. During the Anglo-Transvaal War (1880–81) 350 British soldiers were besieged for four months in Standerton. The Republican force occupied Standerskop from where they peppered the town with bullets at the rate of about 800 pot shots a day aimed at anything in British uniform. A newspaper, *The Standerton News*, was published in the town throughout the siege.

A pleasant park is situated on the banks of the Vaal River. Adjacent to the town there are angling facilities, lawns, a swimming-bath, restaurant and barbecue sites. The Grootdraai Dam also has facilities for water sports, camping and caravans. There is a nature reserve, 128 ha in extent, at Standerskop. The original bridge over the Vaal River, Kruger Bridge, opened by President Kruger in 1891, still stands.

Leaving behind the landmark of Standerskop, the R23 road continues across maize and dairy country, delightful in summer but drab in winter when the grass is dead and generally burned to induce early grazing. After 56 km the road reaches ...

GREYLINGSTAD

The Dutch Reformed Church established *Greylingstad* in 1909 and named it after one of the pioneers of the district, Mr P J Greyling. Greylingstad is a maize, dairy and railway centre. During the Anglo-Boer War a fort was built on an overlooking hill by the Scottish Rifles, who also painted the initials of the regiment 'S R' on the rock.

Crossing a landscape of grassy plains, rocky hillocks, maize and sunflower fields, the R23 road after 24 km reaches ...

BALFOUR

Balfour was originally proclaimed a town in 1898 with the rather un-euphonious name of McHattiesburg after F S McHattie, owner of the farm *Vlakfontein* on which the town was planned. It was renamed *Balfour* in 1906 in honour of Arthur James Balfour, the British Prime Minister who made a speech on the local railway station and was highly regarded during those difficult years. The Springfield Collieries are situated a few kilometres away, while maize is the principal local product.

The R23 road continues across grassy, farming country with ridges of rocky hills protruding to the north and south. At 33 km the road joins the main N3 route from the Witwatersrand to KwaZulu-Natal through the Free State. A further 6 km brings the combined roads to ...

HEIDELBERG

The town of Heidelberg is situated at the foot of the 1 903 m high ridge of the *Suikerbosrand* which received its name from the number of sugar bushes (*Protea caffra*) which grow there, along with numerous other species of highveld flora.

The town was founded in 1862 when a German, H J Uekermann, established a trading station at the crossroads of the original wagon trails linking Pretoria, Potchefstroom, Durban and Bloemfontein. The trading station became an important communications centre and Uekerman purchased for £7 10s a portion of the farm *Langlaagte*, laying out a town which he named after his old university in the town of Heidelberg in Germany.

During the Anglo-Transvaal War (1880–81), Heidelberg was temporarily the seat of the triumvirate government of the South African Republic, bustling with the excitement of commandos and politicians coming and going. After the war, the discovery of gold on the Witwatersrand resulted in a flood of traffic along the roads and the town flourished, also becoming something of a pleasure resort with two hotels built beside the willow-lined banks of the Blesbok stream.

Today, Heidelberg retains its importance as a communication centre. The population numbers 83 011.

A pleasant recreational area may be found in Karee Kloof where visitors may swim, picnic and camp in a setting of trees, flowers and lawns. The farmhouse on *Diepkloof* in the Suikerbos Rand Nature Reserve, built by Jan Marais in 1850, has been restored as a museum and a visitors centre. There are attractive walks in the reserve which conserves 13 000 ha of highveld flora and fauna.

The original railway station, a fine period piece built of sandstone, was opened in 1895 when the railway line from Johannesburg to Natal was completed, with a final ceremony of linking the tracks at Heidelberg. In 1961 a new station was built. The old station fell into disuse but fortunately was not demolished. In 1969 it was partially restored by the Simon van der Stel Foundation with the intention of converting it into a cultural history museum.

In 1974 the Rembrandt Tobacco Corporation rented the building and grounds from the municipality. The corporation fully restored the station and moved three old goods sheds into a closer complex. A transport museum was established. The station is complete and at the platform stands a Type 16 C steam locomotive, built in 1919 by the North British Locomotive Co Ltd and retired in 1975. It weighs 136 tons and has a tractive effort of 13 154 kg. Behind the locomotive is a set of passenger-coaches and two dining-saloons, 'Illovo' and 'Liesbeek'. In the sheds is displayed a collection of veteran cycles, motor cycles and motor cars. The Heidelberg Transport Museum was opened in 1975. It should not be missed by any visitor to the area. The museum is open Tuesdays to Saturdays from 10h00 to 13h00 and 14h00 to 17h00; Sundays from 11h00 to 17h00; closed Mondays and religious holidays.

There are several other interesting buildings from the days of the Transvaal republic. The Dutch Reformed Church, built in 1890 is known as the *Klipkerk* (stone church), from its handsome sandstone construction.

The Town Hall, designed by Gerhard Moerdijk and built in 1939 from sandstone, has in front of it an obelisk containing the busts of the triumvirate, Paul Kruger, P Joubert and M W Pretorius, who headed the government of the Transvaal Republic, with Heidelberg as the capital from 1880–83.

From Heidelberg the N3 road sweeps over the highveld past maize, dairy and vegetable farms and many modern housing developments. After 35 km the road reaches ...

ALBERTON

After the Anglo-Boer War, a syndicate of developers bought the farm *Elandsfontein* from Johann Meyer who had trekked there in 1844 from Prince Albert in the Cape. A town was laid out and named after one of the members of the syndicate, General Hendrik Alberts.

Not too notable for scenic beauty, the town at least has the asset of being situated on the outskirts of the Witwatersrand where the air is cleaner away from the pollution of dusty mine dumps. It was for this reason that it became popular as a residential area. With a population of 220 000 it is now an industrial and dormitory town. The Newmarket horse-racing track is in the town area and is a popular venue for punters.

From Alberton the N3 dual carriageway sweeps onwards. Climbing the ridge of the Witwatersrand, the last open spaces left behind, the road passes the workings of the City Deep Mine whose shaft probes 3 245 m into the earth to the reefs of gold. At 11 km from Alberton the N3 road reaches Johannesburg.

Chapter Thirty-Six
MPUMULANGA

The Edge of the Berg

The transition from the eastern highveld to the lowveld is achieved within a few dramatic kilometres, involving a complete transformation of landscape. From the cool, open, grassy plains the escarpment falls away to a veritable ocean of greenery – trees and bush, the savanna country of Africa, the haunt of big game – surging in from the east, sweeping down from the north. Plants and soil have their own distinctive perfume. The atmosphere is laden with memories of the adventures of hunters and prospectors. Winds and weather are so warm and sultry that they seem to have been carried by the Indian Ocean all the way from the mysterious East.

The main N4 road and the Eastern Line railway linking Pretoria and the Witwatersrand to Mozambique run side by side, reaching the edge of the escarpment to make a dramatic descent down the pass of the Elands River, the historic gateway between the highveld and the lowveld. At the summit of the pass, 13 km from Machadodorp, the main road divides into a loop, with one division (R539) descending Schoemanskloof and the other (N4) passing the railway centre of ...

WATERVAL BOVEN

The building of the Eastern Line (as it was called) between Pretoria and Lourenzo Marques (now Maputo) constitutes a very lively chapter in the history of railroad construction. Building commenced from Lourenzo Marques in 1887 and in 1894 reached the site of Waterval Boven 304 km away and 1 971 m in altitude. It is said that, by that stage, as many men had died in the construction of the line as there were sleepers on the permanent way. Fever, heat, lions, alcohol, fights and accidents had resulted in the deaths of many workmen. On the station platform of Waterval Boven stands a poignant little memorial to all those forgotten workers. It consists simply of one of the countless boulders moved to make way for the line and a short section of the rack railway which enabled locomotives to haul the trains up the steep face of the escarpment. Once the line reached Waterval Boven, the remainder of the construction over the highveld to Pretoria was a relatively simple matter.

Waterval Boven (above the waterfall) received its name from the waterfall at the head of the valley of the Elands River. To reach this point on the highveld, the railway had to climb 208 m between the stations of *Waterval Onder* (below the waterfall) and Waterval Boven 14 km away. From Waterval Onder the railway and road ran steadily down to the sea at Lourenzo Marques (Maputo) 290 km away. Pretoria, the terminus of the Eastern Line, is 1 400 m above sea-level and 566 km from Maputo.

When the line reached Waterval Boven, a marshalling yard and railway depot was created there and in 1898 the place became a village.

From Waterval Boven the tarmac road makes its way to the edge of the escarpment and then descends through a tunnel. At 4 km there is a viewsite and a turn-off leading to the original railway tunnel – 213 m long – through which the rack railway made a 1-in-20 gradient climb. The rack railway was 4 km long and was worked by three special locomotives, each capable of hauling a 140-ton load. Puffing and grinding along at about 8 km an hour, these little locomotives pushed the trains up from the rear, while the normal locomotive pulled at the head of the train. In this way passengers had ample opportunity to view the beauty of the rushing waterfall tumbling down right next to the line. The modern railway pass, relocated to the other side of the valley, may be seen from the viewpoint. A walk through the old tunnel is interesting and the waterfall is always worth seeing, especially during the summer when the Elands River is in flood.

At the bottom of the pass, 8 km from Waterval Boven, the road and railway reaches Waterval Onder, a small railway centre drowsing in a warm, sylvan setting. It was here that President Paul Kruger and his Government enjoyed a brief sanctuary from 30 June to 28 August 1900 during the last stages of the Anglo-Boer War. The corrugated iron building used by President Kruger as a temporary State residence and office has been preserved. Known as Krugerhof, it stands in the grounds of the Wayside inn, built in 1879 as a staging post for coaches.

Trout, tropical fruits, nuts and other good things are offered for sale at wayside stalls. The journey down the valley is delightful as the N4 road traverses a parkland of trees and flowers where the busy Elands River flows through a succession of pools and rapids well stocked with trout.

At 10 km from Waterval Onder the road passes the Malaga Hotel and at 31,5 km reaches the small centre of *Ngodwane,* (place of little stumps) so named from the Godwane River. Here the South African Pulp and Paper Industries (Sappi) have a paper-mill, accompanied by the odours apparently unavoidable in this type of activity. At 3 km beyond the trading centre, a turn-off climbs the eastern heights of the valley, passes through the Berlyn forestry conservancy and, after 14,5 km, reaches the old gold-rush centre of Kaapsehoop, from where the road makes a scenic descent for 29 km to Nelspruit.

Beyond this turn-off to Kaapsehoop the main tarmac road continues down the valley of the Elands River, past the small centre of Elandshoek half buried beneath tall trees. Twenty kilometres from Ngodwane the road reaches Montrose Falls, rejoining the old main road (R539) which has descended the escarpment through ...

SCHOEMANSKLOOF

In 1848 P A Schoeman settled on *Mooiplaas* (pretty farm) in the valley named after him. The left loop of the N4 road to the east reaches the top of this valley at a point 248 km from Pretoria. The Bambi Protea Hotel stands on the summit of the descent to the lowveld.

The drive down Schoemanskloof is a memorable experience for, apart from being a natural gateway between the highveld and lowveld, it is extremely beautiful in its own right. With handsome trees, high cliffs, and fine farms where the road reaches the valley of the Crocodile River, the greenness and fertility of the area become more apparent metre by metre, as the road loses 800 m in altitude during the course of its journey.

Tobacco and maize fields, groves of citrus trees, lines of silver oaks, elegantly canopied acacia trees, flowering plants and trees splash the scene with colour. Farm stalls sell local produce. There are shady resting-places, spectacular views and a new scene around every bend, contributing towards an atmosphere of exhilaration and excitement.

After 47 km the road down Schoemanskloof rejoins the N4 road which has come from Waterval Boven down the valley of the Elands River. The reunited roads cross the Crocodile River just above the Montrose Falls, where the river tumbles 12 m into a deep pool.

From the Montrose Falls the road climbs over the shoulder of a high ridge. Descending the eastern side, the road reveals fine views of the valley of the *Ngwenya* (Crocodile) River and, after 5 km, reaches a tarmac turn-off leading for 8 km up the valley of the Houtbosloop to the Sudwala Caves, and from there to Sabie.

THE SUDWALA CAVES

One of the principal tourist attractions of Southern Africa, these caves are of special interest to geologists and speleologists. Beautifully situated, the entrance is hidden in a green forest which cloaks the precipitous side of the hill known as *Mankelekele* (crag on crag).

The caves are surrounded by a natural botanical garden. Aloes, blooming around August, are particularly prolific, with the yellow blooms of *Aloe recurrifolio* colouring the rocky slopes with gold. Wild pear trees blossom in white; while the scarlet-flowered *Erythrina caffra* and many other creepers, trees and plants provide colour throughout the year.

In this superb setting Mr P R Owen, the late owner of the area, and his two sons, Theo and Philip, created a unique dinosaur park where there are displayed life-sized replicas of these creatures of the past, modelled by Jan Theron van Zijl under the supervision of the palaeontologist, Dr André Keyser. A tour through the park takes the visitor back between 250 and 100 million years, providing an experience not to be forgotten.

Prehistoric man discovered the Sudwala Caves. At the beginning of the 19th century they were used as refuges by sections of the Swazi people. One of their kings, Sobhuza I, is said to have hidden in the caves to escape Zulu raiders. On Sobhuza's death, his heir Mswati was still a minor. An elder brother, Malambule, and one of Sobhuza's brothers, Somcuba, acted as joint regents. When Mswati came of age, both regents decamped with substantial portions of the royal cattle.

Somcuba built a *stat* (capital) for himself close to the caves at what is still known as *Statspruit* (capital stream). He used the place as a retreat whenever Mswati attempted to recover the stolen cattle. He even created a defensive alliance with the Lydenburg Republic. There is an old legend that the caves (whose end has not yet been reached) lead all the way under the mountains to the town of Lydenburg.

In approximately the year 1854, Somcuba was taken by surprise and killed by a Swazi punitive regiment. Those of his followers who were not wiped out continued to live in the area under one of Somcuba's headmen, Sudwala. The caves became his sanctuary and subsequently were named after him.

The area later became a farm, *Sudwala's Kraal*, and in the early years of the 20th century the caves were exploited for their deposits of bat guano. A few visitors explored the caves, but it was only when P R Owen acquired the farm that a road was built to the entrance. A resort was then developed to accommodate visitors on the floor of the valley of the *Houtbosloop* (woodbush stream). This stream has its origin in an amphitheatre of forest-covered mountains. It tumbles over the precipice in a high waterfall, notable for its rainbow during the summer rainy season, and then flows down to join the Crocodile River through one of the loveliest valleys in South Africa.

Serious exploration and mapping of the caves were largely the work of Harold Jackson, a master speleologist who devoted much of his leisure time to a systematic probing of the secrets of Sudwala. It was difficult work. The tourist sections of the caves comprise a small proportion of the full length which simply vanishes away into the dolomite mass. Local legend decrees the end to be many kilometres away.

A pleasant characteristic of these caves is a steady current of fresh air which provides some comfort to explorers. Unfortunately, falls of rock, underground streams and mud make exploration of its full length difficult. The rewards have been the discovery of many superb speleothems and entire chambers, magnificently decorated by Nature with all manner of dripstone and flowstone formations. In the 500 m length of the caves open to tourists may be seen dripstone formations such as the oft-photographed Screaming Monster, so dominant and powerful that those who first discovered the formation could be pardoned for regarding it with superstitious awe. It is highly likely that this formation was worshipped by prehistoric man.

The ceiling of these caves is particularly interesting, providing a perfect complement to the dinosaur park outside. On the ceilings, especially on the domed ceiling above the Screaming Monster, are fossilised colonies of blue-green algae known as *stromatolites*. These primitive algae were alive when the Earth's atmosphere consisted mainly of nitrogen and carbon dioxide. Floating on the surface of warm shallow water, these algae converted the carbon dioxide into oxygen by means of photosynthesis and were largely responsible for creating an atmosphere suitable for the higher forms of life we know today. Such stromatolites, one of the earliest identifiable forms of life in Southern Africa, flourished about 2 000 million years ago.

The largest cavern in the sequence of the Sudwala Caves has been named the P R Owen Hall, the high ceiling of which is decorated with stromatolite fossils. Having excellent acoustics, fresh air, a natural stage and seating on the tiered sides, this hall of the mountain kings is used for concerts by visiting choirs and orchestras.

The caves are open daily from 08h00 to 16h30 – the last tour starts at 16h00. On the first Saturday of every month, special tours are conducted lasting six hours and penetrating as far the Crystal Rooms, well beyond the normal tourist route. This tour is strenuous but very rewarding. It is necessary to book well in advance.

There is an à la carte restaurant and a swimming pool in the resort.

From the turn-off to the Sudwala Caves the N4 road continues down the fertile valley of the Crocodile River. Handsome scenery comprises granite domes dominating a rugged valley where every portion of arable land is planted with groves of citrus trees, litchis, mangoes and avocado pears. Pecan trees shed their ripe nuts in July and August, and roadside stalls offer them and many other tasty things for sale to passers-by.

Plants flower continuously throughout the year: aloes in June; bougainvillaea and poinciana (flamboyant) trees in spring and early summer.

After 5 km the road crosses the Crocodile River, passing a turn-off to the rural centre of Schagen and the Crocodile Country Inn.

At 3 km beyond the Crocodile River bridge there is a turn-off to *Alkmaar* railway station (named after the small town in Holland) which serves a rich agricultural area. Magnificent subtropical fruit estates adjoin one another, among the most beautiful of these being *Riverside*. This famous farm was created by Hugh Hall, a pioneer of the valley who settled there in 1890. He commenced a tremendous agricultural industry, producing so many tomatoes and mangoes that the railway authorities granted him a special siding called *Tomango* from the combination of the names of the two crops. When this title achieved fame as a trade name, the siding was renamed *Mataffin* in honour of Matafini, a Swazi chief who in 1887 had eloped from his native land with a girl intended as bride for the Swazi king. In the then uninhabited valley of the Crocodile River Matafini found a love-nest for himself until changing times and tax-collectors made life unbearable.

Beyond the Crocodile River bridge the road finds a way for 22 km through this pleasant garden of cultivated and indigenous plants and then reaches the principal centre of the valley ...

NELSPRUIT

Half buried beneath flowering jacaranda and poinciana trees, Nelspruit is one of the most attractive towns in Southern Africa. Situated in the middle of the valley of the Crocodile River, the town is well laid out in a parklike setting. Warm to hot in summer, the climate is pleasantly cool in winter. The town developed into the most important commercial, communications and administrative centre of the valley and has 25 532 inhabitants. Since 1994 it has been the capital of the province named *Mpumulanga* (the rising sun).

Nelspruit is named after the Nel brothers – Andries, Gert and Louis – who, in 1890 at an auction of farms in the valley, purchased the farm on which the town now stands. Two years later the Eastern Line was opened to the place and the town was born as a tin-shanty railway station, around which was eventually built a couple of stores, hotel and police station. Nelspruit was proclaimed a town in 1905.

The conquest of malaria in the 1930s freed the entire valley of the Crocodile River from the domination of the mosquito. Nelspruit became a municipality in 1940 and since then has grown steadily. One-third of South Africa's export oranges are produced in the district, while tobacco, nuts, litchis, mangoes, avocado pears, vegetables, cattle and timber are also produced on a large scale.

The Research Institute for Citrus and Subtropical Fruit has its headquarters outside Nelspruit, and the Lowveld Botanical Garden is situated in the town itself.

Nelspruit is a major tourist centre. Roads radiate from it to many of the most beautiful and interesting parts of the lowveld. Hotels and caravan parks in the town are convenient for stopovers and, in addition, several days can be profitably spent exploring the surrounding countryside.

A building in Nelspruit with an unusual story is the first town hall, built in 1951. It was designed by F H Moerdyk in the Spanish/Mediterranean style with a breezeway and fountain in the centre courtyard to provide a cool atmosphere in the heat of the lowveld. The interior wood panelling of the building was made of kiaat which was obtained from Villa Louise in Mozambique where it was grown commercially. It was cut and sawn to specifications of the designers. It was railed to a Nelspruit cabinetmaker who prepared the wood for the panelling as well as for the furniture to be used in the building.

The architect designed the building in the form of a square with a supper room on the northern side and the offices on the eastern side. The western section was taken up by the actual town hall and cloakrooms. In 1956 the southern side was demolished and further offices built. Below the supper room on the northern side of the building the municipal market was housed.

When the present market was built in town the fire brigade took over the premises. When the fire brigade moved, the traffic department took over the space, and later other departments.

The clock tower was designed in such a way that the public could have access to the tower from which they could view the town. However, someone maliciously damaged the mechanism of the clock which put an end to this privilege. It took some time for the local watchmaker to repair the clock. The clock struck on the hour and half-hour and was switched off in July 1988 when the building was sold to the present owners.

It is gratifying to note that the Mkhuhlu tree (*Trichilia emetica*) in front of the building has been retained. Next to this tree Nelspruit's first water supply in the form of a well, some 18 metres deep and yielding 2 700 litres of water per day, was dug in 1924. The well, however, was not used for very long. An irate town dweller dumped the contents of his sanitary bucket down the well after a fight with the village council. The well water was subsequently unfit for further human use.

To solve the water crisis, the town fathers finally decided to institute a water scheme. A reservoir was built in Mostert Street which was fed by water pumped from the Crocodile River – the start of Nelspruit's present-day water reticulation scheme. In the meantime the unused well was covered with a cement slab (in 1929) and was completely forgotten until its fortuitous rediscovery in 1990. The owners of the old town hall, by then converted into the present Hotel Promenade, realising the value of the find in front of their building, kindly erected over it a modern-day wishing well. The Nelspruit Lions Club was allocated the happy task of distributing to deserving welfare organisations a monthly turn to benefit from the well's takings.

From Nelspruit, the main road and railway to the east continue down the valley of the Crocodile River. Immediately outside the town the road passes through the immaculate citrus groves, orchards and fields of Crocodile Valley Estates (Pty) Ltd. At 6 km from Nelspruit the road passes the head office, packing station and wayside kiosk of this company. It is interesting to learn something of its history ...

CROCODILE VALLEY ESTATES

In 1925 Ivan Solomon, a young Pretoria lawyer, was engaged to liquidate a company formed to sell plots in the eastern Transvaal. This company had sold about 600 plots, mainly to soldiers returning from the First World War and to would-be immigrants from Britain. The intention had been to develop a community citrus estate with large-scale irrigation and a central pack house.

Unfortunately, the company went bankrupt although many plots had been sold, mainly in

Britain. Ivan Solomon visited the plots in the Crocodile valley and became convinced that the scheme, in fact, had considerable potential but simply needed more capital. He set out to persuade the plot holders to provide more money and not merely to liquidate the venture. He visited Britain and consulted the Plot Holders' Association, formed by owners to look after their interests. They declined to 'throw good money after bad', so Ivan Solomon returned to South Africa where he prompted a small group of people to support him. In this way the interests of the Plot Holders' Association were acquired. The remaining plot holders, scattered in many parts of the world, were all traced and persuaded to sell their interests.

During the depression years of the 1930s, Ivan Solomon struggled to establish the fortunes of the company. He ran his legal practice, served as mayor of Pretoria for a record term and, in addition, possessed the enthusiasm to turn farmer on a vast scale. In the face of pessimism and criticism, he struggled to finance the venture and to gather a staff whose zest kept them working even when there was no ready cash to pay their salaries. In the company's archives may be found an old school slate on one side of which is written 'cheques have arrived' and on the other side 'no cheques yet'.

Faith triumphed. In the citrus groves of the estate today, 100 000 trees bear fruit, yielding 5 per cent of the total South African export crop of oranges. From mid-April until early September the pack house is the scene of tremendous activity in the packing each day of about 250 tons of fruit consisting of 1,5 million oranges.

Ivan's son, Dennis, joined him in management in 1955. Dennis's son, Mark, was born on the estate and the African workers made him an honourary chief, *Nkosi Mabele Ingwe* (chief of the spots of the leopard).

The original 20 km long irrigation canal built by the old Plot Holders' Association still serves as the main artery of the irrigation system, using water from the Crocodile River. This water also drives the turbines which generate power for pumping and light. Irrigation is by sprinkler system and the estate is highly mechanised. A system of bulk handling designed by Dennis Solomon, who has a Master of Science degree in engineering, is used today by many other estates.

The estate is also the home of one of the finest pedigreed herd of Jersey cattle in Southern Africa, the Croc Valley Jerseys. Three of the bulls produced by this herd have received the highest award possible, that of Preferent Sire. The herd is established as one of the highest milk producers in South Africa. Beef cattle are farmed by the estate on a separate ranch, *Croc Ranch*, in the bushveld near Phalaborwa. On this ranch a new breed of cattle, known as Huguenots, are bred from Charolais and Zebu-type Africander parent stock. These animals combine the hardiness and easy calving characteristics of the Africanders with the large frame and beefiness of the European Charolais.

In 1956 the estate acquired a forestry area in the Pilgrim's Rest district – *Goedgeloof* plantations and sawmill – in order to manufacture wooden boxes for the pack house. Another acquisition has been the *Kloof* farm in Schoemanskloof. This estate, almost derelict when purchased in 1967, is now a large producer of wheat, avocado pears, soya beans and pecan nuts.

The main N4 road continues eastwards through a roadside garden of red *Bauhinia galpinii* (pride of the Kaap), yellow acacia and elegant palm trees. At 7,5 km from Nelspruit the road passes through a gateway of granite domes. On the eastern side of this ridge there is a resting-place and picnic spot in the shade of some wild fig trees. This pleasant place is unfortunately ill-used by certain individuals who will carry a full can of beer a thousand kilometres but decline to place the empty can in the nearest rubbish bin a mere metre away.

The road continues through beautifully wooded country down the valley of the Crocodile River. Oleander and frangipani trees line the verges of the road. At 13 km a turn-off leads to White River, providing tourists with an interesting alternative scenic route back to Nelspruit.

Three kilometres beyond the White River turn-off is a turn-off south to Uitkyk. This gravel road supplies the connoisseur of scenery with an exciting off-route drive with a choice of two ends. The road climbs steeply into the granite mountain complex. After 5,5 km there is a turn-off to Mara. By following this turn-off the traveller, after 23 km of scenic switchback journey, will rejoin the main N4 road near Boulders station. The other branch of the gravel road, after a great deal of winding and climbing, eventually joins the Claremont–Nelspruit road and, after 30 km, finds its way back to Nelspruit down Henshall Road.

The main N4 road, after the turn-off to Uitkyk, travels through the spectacular Crocodile River poort where the river forces its way through a narrow boulder-strewn pass in the ridge of granite mountains. Some of the heaviest work in the construction of the Eastern Line was undertaken in this passage. Earth and rock moving machinery was unknown in those days and all labour was performed by humans. The tough cosmopolitan crowd of navvies recruited for the work were housed in a construction camp known as Poort City, built at the east end of the passage. This was a notorious place for riotous living, rough customers, and a daily lottery run by the doctor, based on the highest temperature reached by any of the numerous malaria sufferers!

Another memory of those days is the name *Gould's Salvation Valley*, applied to a valley leading into the Crocodile River poort. This valley was reputed to be free of tsetse fly. During the Barberton gold-rush it was located by a transport man, Tom Gould, and used as a route for wagons carrying goods from the railway at Krokodilspoort station.

The main N4 road passes the turn to Salvation Valley 22 km from Nelspruit. After a further 15,5 km the road leaves Crocodile Poort, bridges over the Crocodile River and, 40 km from Nelspruit, reaches turn-offs leading to Barberton and to the railway junction of Kaapmuiden.

From Kaapmuiden the main road continues eastwards, past the Kudu Lodge caravan park and through a warm world of sugar cane, citrus and pawpaws. Intensive cultivation under irrigation may be observed. At 13 km there is a turn-off to Magnesite, Kaalrug and the Senekal mine. At 18 km the road reaches *Malelane* (place of small lala palms), set in an ocean of sugar cane and dominated by a sugar mill.

At 4,5 km beyond Malelane, the main road reaches turn-offs to Piggs Peak in Swaziland and to the Malelane gate of the Kruger National Park. Sugar cane now prevails over the landscape like a green flood of vegetation which has drowned the original bush.

At 18 km from Malelane there is another turn-off to Piggs Peak and, 1 km further on, the road passes the small centre of *Hectorspruit* which had its start in 1891 when the surveyor of the Eastern Line, Servaas de Kock, named the station after – of all things – his pet pointer dog!

A further 10 km takes the road past the railway centre named *Tenbosch* after the Dutch royal palace, *Het Huis ten Bosch*. Here a turn-off leads to the Crocodile River holiday township. The N4 road to the east passes a turn-off to the Strydom block of agricultural farms 25,5 km from Hectorspruit. After a further 2 km (64 km from Kaapmuiden) the road reaches a division where the left-hand turn leads for 3 km to the frontier town of ...

KOMATIPOORT

The Crocodile River reaches the end of its course when it flows as a tributary into the *Komati* (river of cows). The confluence occurs immediately west of the mountain ridge of the Lubombo which forms the frontier between South Africa and Mozambique. The combined rivers have forced a passage through the high ridge to reach the coastland of Mozambique.

Komatipoort (pass of the Komati) was founded when the railway known as the Eastern Line was built from Lourenzo Marques (now Maputo) to Pretoria. The railway constructors used the river pass to penetrate the Lubombo. It was convenient to have a railway centre close to the frontier on the western side of the mountains and so Komatipoort came into being. Its situation was hot and feverous. Malaria was endemic in the area and it was not until the 1930s that the mosquito-carried pest was brought under control.

Komatipoort had an uproarious beginning. The contract for the construction of the railway from Lourenzo Marques to the South African border was obtained by the Delagoa Bay and East Africa Railway Company floated in London at the beginning of 1887. There was no great difficulty in the construction of the line over flat, sandy country to what was considered by the contractor's company to be the border. Sir Thomas Tancred with 200 Europeans and 3 000 African workers completed this part of the construction on 14 December 1887. A great argument then began as to the exact position of the border. Three Swiss lawyers were given the task of settling the issue. They took twelve years to reach a decision. Meanwhile, however, the Portuguese government completed the line to Komatipoort, 93 km from Lourenzo Marques. This work included the building of the vital bridge across the Komati River. A Netherlands firm, Von Hattum & Co, had the contract to continue the line for the remaining 473 km to Pretoria. The line was completed on 2 November 1894. The story of its eventful construction is told in *Lost Trails of the Transvaal*.

Komatipoort was established as a railway marshalling yard, locomotive depot and customs post. From the beginning it had a reputation for being a resort of smugglers and some very rugged and shady human beings. The canteen-keepers were notorious. One so-called hotel, run by Spiro Salon, was raided by a police patrol. A man was found dying in the stable while a corpse was hidden underneath the bar counter.

The outbreak of the Anglo-Boer War in 1899 gave the Eastern Line and Komatipoort vital strategic importance as the only route to the outside world for the South African Republic. The British organised several raids on the line by saboteurs. The most successful was by Sergeant Ludwig Steinacker, a German serving in the British Army. He was an audacious gamecock of a little man who liked to boast that he was really a Prussian baron. In Natal, he was given a commission to raise a small force of rough riders and lead them through the bush to destroy the railway bridge across the Khomati River.

In May 1900, men were recruited in Durban for this task. They were fitted with the best arms, equipment and two horses for each man. Mules carried the explosives. In great secrecy Steinacker led his men north, climbing the Lubombo in Zululand and then continuing north along the plateau summit. On the way, Steinacker picked up recruits from the assorted renegades and refugees who had always used these remote heights as a hideaway. Ragged, short of food and mostly stony-broke, they were recruited into what was officially named Steinacker's Horse but called by the Boers, the Forty Thieves.

From the village of Chief Lomahasha, Steinacker sent a reconnaissance to spy on the Komati bridge from the summit of the range. The strength of the guard was soon assessed as beyond the strength of the Forty Thieves. Steinacker switched his tactics. On 17 June 1900 he managed to blow up a bridge near Malalane, wreck a freight train and halt all rail traffic for fourteen days. Leaving the Boers to clear up the mess, Steinacker led his men south into Swaziland. Their activities in that country caused some grief to the Boers (see Chapter Forty-Seven). Steinacker was rewarded with promotion to the rank of major and authorised to recruit a force of 400 men. When their activities provoked the Boers into major retaliation in Swaziland, Steinacker occupied Komatipoort. For the rest of the war he completely blocked the Boers transport link to Lourenzo Marques. For this activity Steinacker was promoted to the rank of Lt Colonel and, at the end of the war, rewarded with a DSO. He had hoped to be appointed warden of the Sabi Game Reserve (now Kruger National Park) or for Steinacker's Horse to be retained as a border guard but the force was disbanded and its men scattered back into the bush. For the end of Steinacker, see Chapter Thirty-Seven.

Komatipoort is still a place of memories of hectic times of the past and many strange characters. The summer heat remains, but its streets are well shaded by jacaranda and poinciana trees. Trains incessantly travel the Eastern Line while the Crocodile bridge entrance gate to the Kruger National Park lies 13 km to the north, ensuring a steady flow of tourists and visitors passing and stopping in the town.

From the turn-off to Komatipoort, the N4 road continues eastwards. Bridging across the Komati River, with a turn-off south to Swaziland after 1 km, the road passes the Doeane Motel and, at 4 km from the turn-off to Komatipoort, reaches the South African customs and immigration post on the Mozambique border.

NELSPRUIT TO BARBERTON

From Nelspruit the tarmac R40 road branches southwards from the N4 road to the east, just before it enters the town. This road climbs steadily past numerous fruit-growing smallholdings with wayside kiosks offering a variety of agricultural products for sale. At 14 km from Nelspruit the road tops the rise whereupon the traveller is confronted by one of the great views of Southern Africa, a most majestic panorama of the notorious Valley of Death of the old-time prospectors.

The great valley received its sinister name on account of the malarial fever once endemic there. Innumerable prospectors died during the search for gold in this valley of the river known to the Africans as the *Ngwenyana* (little crocodile), but to Europeans as the *Kaap* (cape) from various high cliffs which project into the valley like a cape projecting into a sea. The effect is particularly suggestive of this idea when the valley is shrouded in mist.

The verges of the valley are covered in vegetation, including flowering plants such as *Bauhinia galpinii* (pride of the Kaap), indigenous to the area and producing masses of blood-red coloured flowers in summer. On the floor of the valley grow many of the graceful paperbark thorn trees (*Acacia siebeviana*) with their canopied branches.

At 29 km from Nelspruit, a turn-off leads for 32 km to ...

KAAPSEHOOP

The old mining village and former boom town of *Kaapsehoop* (hope of the cape) is situated on top of the cliffs overlooking the valley from the west. Near the village is a cluster of more than a thousand sandstone rocks, many of them weathered into such strange shapes that they seem to have been sculpted by an artistic demon. A stream runs down the valley in the midst of this assembly of rocks, and in the upper portion lies one cluster of rock shapes which so resembles a group of petrified demons on convention that the area is known as the *Duiwelskantoor* (office of the Devil). Old fortifications made by early tribespeople may also be seen among the rocks.

Gold was discovered in the stream in 1882. A rush to the area ensued and Kaapsehoop was created as a centre for the prospectors. Traces of gold and asbestos were found, together with many signs of prehistoric mining, but no really payable deposits were located. Kaapsehoop, however, became the base for prospecting in the Kaap valley. It was there that one of the most persistent prospectors, 'French Bob' (Auguste Robert), discovered the Pioneer Reef on 2 June 1883. This was the greatest discovery of gold so far made in South Africa. It resulted in a rush to the Kaap valley and the eventual founding of Barberton.

Kaapsehoop was largely abandoned but in later years asbestos mining and afforestation commenced in the area. Old prospectors still search the streams, finding an occasional nugget or enough alluvial gold to tempt them into continuing long after all hope should have vanished. In 1976 the author met an irrepressible character named Ernest George Sparg, 74 years old and with 32 years of prospecting in the area behind him. He was sitting panning gold in a furrow, removing useless pebbles from the pan with his fingers and throwing them over his shoulder to add to an accumulation of several hundred thousand piled up in a long ridge behind him formed as he periodically changed his operating position. Future geologists might well be baffled as to how this ridge was formed.

Roads lead from Kaapsehoop down to Ngodwane in the Elands valley (14,5 km) and back to Nelspruit (29 km) along the verge of the cliff. The latter road is very spectacular and numerous interesting minerals such as asbestos, serpentine, stitchtite and others may be seen in cuttings and mining dumps.

From the turn-off to Kaapsehoop on the floor of the Kaap valley, the main tarmac R40 road continues for a further 8 km, reaching a turn-off to Badplaas. Just beyond this turn-off the road crosses the Queens River, named after Moyo, a Swazi queen who once ruled over a military centre established there. Passing through a fine forest of paperbark acacias, the road, at 45 km from Nelspruit, leads into the gold-mining town of romantic memories.

BARBERTON

In the midst of all the excitement surrounding the discovery by French Bob of the Pioneer Reef at what was known as Moodies, after George Moodie, a surveyor who owned the land, a party of prospectors comprising Graham Barber, his two cousins (Fred and Harry Barber), and two other men, Edward White and Holden Bowker, found their way into the narrow gorge just to the east of the modern town of Barberton. They noticed a white thread of quartz high up on a cliff. Graham Barber scrambled up and took some samples. With his companions he panned the samples in the Umvoti stream which ran through the gorge. The result sent a wave of excitement throughout the world and resulted in one of the greatest gold-rushes ever known.

On 24 June 1884, three days after Graham Barber had reported his find, the mining commissioner of the area, David Wilson, arrived to inspect the discovery. Already local prospectors were stirring. It was inevitable that a great rush would follow and that a town would come into being. The mining commissioner broke a bottle of Holland's Squareface Gin over a sample of Barber's Reef and named the site of the prospector's camp *Barberton*.

The speed with which the town grew was astonishing. Shacks and shanties sprang up like weeds, and in almost similar disarray. At first, town planning was influenced by the whereabouts of about 200 canteens, dozens of gin palaces, two stock exchanges and numerous bars. These were the social pivots of the boom town. Streets were directed towards them, around them, into them – but seldom past them without a pause. Nor was there a shortage of hitching posts outside them for use by horses and pack animals.

For the first few years Barberton's population was predominantly masculine with some very remarkable characters emerging among the thousands who used the town as their base. The few reigning beauties in the town (such as Cockney Liz, the Golden Dane and Trixy) did a roaring trade, with some of them being auctioned off in the evenings, using top-hatted gentlemen as auctioneers such as the famous Stafford Parker, one-time president of the 'diamond diggers republic'. Cockney Liz, the most celebrated of these ladies, arrived in Barberton in June 1887, leaving in September 1889 after having made her fortune. Where she came from and where she went, including details of her life, would make good reading.

Rumours and excitement were the order of the day. Many impudent frauds were perpetrated, but many real finds were made, among them the richest and most famous gold-mine in the world at the time. This was Bray's Golden Quarry on the Sheba Reef, found in May 1885 by Edwin Bray. In this mine, it was said, the gold was not embedded in rock but rather the rock was set in solid gold. It was the greatest producer in the world for some years. A separate town, known as Eureka City, grew up to serve this mine. When the gold was exhausted the town was abandoned; and its ruins today provide an interesting sight for visitors.

The riches of Bray's Golden Quarry, curiously, were among the factors contributing towards the ruin of Barberton. The world began to expect too much of the place. Fraudulent company promoters easily sold shares in useless properties simply by describing them as being close to the Golden Quarry. The entire Kaap valley was covered in claims and hopelessly over-capitalised. The vast numbers of loafers, layabouts and dead-beats attracted to the place were a curse, while the profits from the payable mines hardly equalled the amount of capital being poured into the valley by overseas investors.

The crash was inevitable. The Valley of Death lived up to its reputation, for dozens of companies collapsed and the hopes of innumerable overseas (particularly British) investors were ruined. Many a titled board chairman found himself dodging missiles in the form of worthless share certificates in Barberton properties. The name of the town was said to be indelibly printed in the memories of investors. By 1888 the great boom was over and investors were turning their attention to the newly discovered Witwatersrand.

Barberton and the Kaap Valley were left to settle down to a more humdrum, hard-working but quite prosperous life. The valley, richly if erratically mineralised with gold, nickel, chrome, titanium, copper, asbestos and gemstones such as jasper, onyx, budstone and verdite, will be a centre of mining for an indefinite period. Chert from a road cutting near Daylight Mine containing the earliest known traces of life – fossil bacteria and algae dated at 3 200 million years – was used by the American National Aeronautics and Space Administration to compare with moon rock samples. The rich soil of the valley floor and the warm climate allow for the production of crops such as cotton, tea, coffee, subtropical fruits, pecan nuts and sisal. Eucalyptus and fir trees flourish on the mountain slopes.

Barberton has a total of 24 870 inhabitants. It became the terminus for the 20,36 km long aerial ropeway which carried over the mountains to the railhead the entire output of the Havelock Swaziland Asbestos Mine.

From a tourist point of view, Barberton is not only an atmospheric and interesting place, with its poinciana and jacaranda trees, but it is also a convenient base from which several fine scenic drives diverge to places such as Kaapsehoop, the Havelock mine in Swaziland, the Agnes goldmine and Eureka City. Many mining sites, such as the Pioneer Reef at Moodies, either working or disused, are also linked by usable gravel roads leading through breathtaking scenery.

Barberton was for some years the home of Percy Fitzpatrick, the author of the classic tale of the low country, *Jock of the Bushveld*. In front of the town hall stands a bronze of the famous dog, Jock, modelled by Ivan Mitford-Barberton. The lounge of the Impala Hotel is adorned with a *Jock of the Bushveld frieze* painted by Conrad Genal. He was an itinerant artist born in Germany in 1875. He joined the French Foreign Legion, deserted when his unit was on its way through the Suez Canal for duty in Vietnam and then made his way from Cairo to South Africa, earning a living on his way by decorating the walls of many hotels, churches and other public places in his distinctive and talented style.

The flora of the Kaap valley is magnificent and includes the much-cultivated Barberton daisy (*Gerbera jamesoni*) named after R Jameson, a member of the Durban Botanic Garden who found the flower growing at Moodies when he visited it in 1885. He took the flower back to Durban. The nature reserve above Moodies is named after Miss Cythna Letty, the renowned botanical artist. Another interesting botanical area is the Barberton indigenous tree park where about 100 species of trees grow. The park is traversed by the Fortuna Mine Trail, a circular walking trail of 2 km which should not be missed. This trail passes through the 600 m long tunnel dug to convey gold-bearing ore to the old Fortuna Mine mill. A torch and good walking shoes are necessary, but the walk itself is easy. The 44 km Gold Nugget Hiking Trail, a fine three-day walk with two overnight huts at Agnes Top and Lone Tree's Hill, passes many interesting scenes. A third trail, the Pioneer Trail, is a walk with an overnight hut. Like the other trails it rewards the walker with exciting views and relics of early mining. For details of these walks, enquire at the publicity office.

There is an interesting museum in the town depicting the history, geology and archaeology of the area. It is housed in the library building. Attached to the museum is the restored *Belhaven,* once the residence of the Nisbet family. It is preserved as a fine example of the life-style of a well-to-do Barberton family of the last century.

There are several other interesting buildings surviving from Barberton's past. The Globe Tavern has been restored. It is now a private residence but the outside is worth seeing. It was built in 1887. Stopforth House, built by James Stopforth, a baker and general dealer who came to Barberton from Pilgrim's Rest in 1886, is a national monument. Fernlea House, built in the early 1890s by Thomas Lee, who ran a photographic and drapery business, has been restored by the Transvaal Provincial Administration. The Masonic Temple dates from 1884. Perhaps the most interesting of all is the surviving facade of the Transvaal Share and Claim Exchange, Trust and Agency Company Ltd. This was the first stock exchange in the Transvaal and some pretty hectic deals were made there. It was situated in a wood-and-iron building next to a pub called The Dives. The pub caught fire and the flames spread to the stock exchange. Both were burned down.

A second exchange, De Kaap Gold Exchange, closed when the Witwatersrand drew most of the speculators away from Barberton. The building was bought in 1899 by the property tycoon, Sammy Marks, who sold it in 1910 to the municipality. It was used for a while as a library and museum. It was later abandoned and became so dilapidated that it had to be demolished, leaving only the imposing arched facade, which has been preserved as a national monument.

Parked in sheltered retirement outside the caravan park is a well-preserved old steam locomotive. This puffer worked on the branch line from Kaapmuiden to Barberton for many years. With the coming of diesel engines, it was replaced and then disappeared. Its number was found on a photograph in the museum. The puffer was located in Port Elizabeth. It was brought back to Barberton under its own steam and made its final journey through the streets of the town on loose rails which took it to its place of retirement. With a last toot on the whistle, the fires were damped down and the puffer relaxed to rest after all its years of travel.

From Barberton a tarmac road (R38) runs down the valley of the Kaap River to Kaapmuiden on the eastern N4 road from Nelspruit to Komatipoort.

Three kilometres along this road is a gravel turn-off climbing up the steep heights to the Havelock Mine (39 km) in one of the most spectacular drives in Southern Africa. At the beginning of this turn-off a number of regimental badges made of stone and cement may be seen. These were built on the site of a training camp during the Second World War. The area is maintained as a garden of remembrance. At 8 km from Barberton a gravel turn-off leads to Fairview Mine (11 km) and to Eureka City, the ghost town of Brays Golden Quarry. One kilometre beyond this turn-off there stood what was known as Jock's Tree, a shady acacia tree whose canopy provided shelter for many camps of the celebrated dog Jock and his master, the author Percy Fitzpatrick. The tree has died and the memorial has been moved to a similar tree nearby.

Five kilometres further on (14 km from Barberton), the road reaches the small centre of Noordkaap, where the Bougainvillaea Hotel is the proud possessor of a superb acacia tree whose canopy is perfect. Inside the hotel the wandering artist, Conrad Genal, painted (in 1936) a lively series of monochrome friezes depicting a tribal hunt, a Zeederberg coaching episode, and other scenes of the African bush.

The R38 road continues northwards down the river valley. Turn-offs lead to the Consort Mine (3 km) and the Sheba Mine (8 km), the latter a very fine drive. At 39 km from Barberton the road passes Louw's Creek, an old mining area now concerned with the production of sugar cane and mangoes. A further 5 km of travel brings the road to *Revolver Creek,* named after the murder there of a prospector, James Mayne, in July 1887. When a search was made in the creek for his belongings, his revolver was found lying on a rock which he had chipped for gold. The rock did contain gold and the name of Revolver Creek was attached to the discovery. Ten kilometres further on (53 km from Barberton), the tarmac road joins the main eastern N4 road at Kaapmuiden. From here the traveller has the choice of turning west to Nelspruit (39 km) or east 68 km to the frontier of Mozambique at Komatipoort.

NELSPRUIT TO THE NORTH

The tarmac R40 road to the north-eastern lowveld leaves Nelspruit, crossing the Crocodile River after 1,5 km. Immediately a parting of the ways is reached. The right-hand fork R40 leads to White River and northwards across the lowveld; the left-hand fork (R37) travels north-westwards along the edge of the escarpment, eventually rejoining the lowveld road as R36 road far in the north at Tzaneen. A pleasant journey is provided by taking the left-hand fork northwards along the edge of the escarpment, returning along the lowveld road.

The road commences a long and steady climb out of the valley of the Crocodile River, through a lovely avenue of African flame trees flowering around January. Stretching over the hill slopes into the distance are sweetly scented orchards of oranges, mangoes, avocado pears, litchis, pawpaws, pecan nuts and other tropical fruits, creating a scene of warmth and fertility.

Turn-offs lead to places such as the *Houtbosloop* (wood bush stream) valley (33 km), the

Sudwala Caves (17 km away) and, 21 km further on, to White River. As the road gains altitude, the air cools and freshens. The road enters a zone of the most extensive plantations of pine and eucalyptus found anywhere on Earth. This area is not only of considerable beauty, but also retains many memories of some of the earliest Transvaal alluvial gold-fields.

It was here, on 6 February 1873, that one of the most renowned of the old-time prospectors, Tom McLachlan, found alluvial gold. A public diggings around the slopes of the dominating peak known as Spitskop was proclaimed by the government and a lively crowd of diggers rushed to the place in the hope of finding fortune.

Stories about the adventures of these diggers make fascinating reading. Some of them found fortunes, others were ruined by delusions. One of the diggers, John Swan, found gold but in an awkward situation where there was no water to allow for alluvial working. Carefully keeping the site of his discovery a secret, Swan started to dig a race (artificial watercourse) to lead water from a stream several kilometres away. Swan's Race, as it came to be known, was one of the diggers' marvels during the age of gold. Swan had begun digging his race in 1878 and for five years he laboured intermittently, financing operations with gold nuggets removed from his secret find. Then a company secured a concession over land which neatly blocked his contour line. The company made him an offer: if he would reveal the situation of his mine, they would form a company to work it and he would receive a royalty of 20 per cent. He refused, abandoned his race and went off to the Barberton area where he died of fever while prospecting in the Valley of Death. His mine has never been found, but portions of his race may still be traced, following the contours for several kilometres and then ending abruptly.

The main tarmac road continues to climb steadily, passing Hendriksdal station and revealing many views of tree-covered hills and distant valleys. At 54 km the road passes over a high saddle and reaches a junction. To the west the R37 road sets off to climb the Long Tom Pass over the Drakensberg to Lydenburg. To the right a branch road leads for 7 km to the town of Sabie.

LONG TOM PASS

The majestic Long Tom Pass, with its smooth tarmac surface and carefully planned gradients and curves, closely follows the route blazed by the pioneer wagon drivers transporting goods from Lourenzo Marques to Lydenburg. The section from Lydenburg over the Drakensberg was notorious for its gradients and hair-raising drops. The old route may still be seen twisting precariously up the western heights to what was known as Sabiesnek. Rising and falling across the four so-called Devil's Knuckles (a graveyard of many wagons), the road dropped down to Spitskop and from there crossed the lowveld in a dangerous journey through bush haunted by big game, mosquitoes and tsetse flies. The wagons took an average of ten days to reach the coast of Lourenzo Marques (Maputo) via this road.

The old transport road was blazed in 1871 by a commission appointed to that task by the people of Lydenburg. The discovery of gold brought heavy traffic to the route and it became one of the most romantic of roads, with a host of characters tramping along it in search of fortune.

The modern all-tarmac road provides panoramic views of the valley of the Sabie River. Densely planted with pine and eucalyptus trees, this green valley is dominated by the peaks of the 2 210 m *Mauchsberg* (named after Carl Mauch, the German geologist who predicted the discovery of gold in the Transvaal) and the 2 287 m *Mount Anderson* (named after the two land-surveyor brothers, H M and W A B Anderson).

At the junction with the road from Sabie, there is a pleasant picnic and camping ground with a spectacular view. From here the road climbs through the plantations of *Olifantsgeraamte* (elephant's skeleton) and *Renosterhoek* (rhinoceros glen). After 3 km the road passes the Olifants- geraamte Forest Station. The journey is altogether pleasant and diverting, enhanced by views and rich vegetation.

At 11 km from the junction the road passes a sign marking the last position held during the Anglo-Boer War by the Boer forces covering one of their famous Long Tom cannons after which the pass is named. A fine picnic site with a superb view is situated 400 m further on, where it is interesting to pause awhile and to imagine the Long Tom in action.

'Long Tom' was the nickname applied by the British soldiers to the Creusot artillery pieces used by the Boer forces. With a calibre of 15 cm and firing a 38 kg shell for 10 000 m, these ponderous guns were laboriously trundled by the Boers into situations both awkward and surprising to the British.

On 7 September 1900, General Redvers Buller and his Natal army captured Lydenburg after marching from the valley of the Crocodile River against slight resistance. The defending Boer forces withdrew to the heights of the Drakensberg up the road now known as Long Tom Pass. With them they dragged a Long Tom and some smaller artillery pieces. The British had no sooner made themselves comfortable for the night in Lydenburg than the Long Tom opened fire on them from the mountain top.

On 8 September the British advanced up the pass in order to dislodge the Boers. A series of clashes took place, with the Boer rearguard withdrawing to a succession of strong positions along the road. A cold mist eventually enveloped the mountain and fighting died away. The next morning (9 September) Buller resumed the attack. His men reached the summit of the pass from where, to the east, the stupendous view of the lowveld was revealed to them.

Below the summit the road fell away abruptly and the British could observe the Boer wagon convoy slowly retiring over the Devil's Knuckles, a particularly tortuous portion of the old road. The British sent their cavalry in pursuit as fast as the steep slopes would allow. They soon found themselves under heavy fire, with the deep voice of the Long Tom rumbling through the valley and its shells causing considerable damage to the attackers.

All day the action continued, with the Boers stubbornly keeping the British at bay. Night saw the British bringing up artillery to dislodge the Boers. At dawn on 10 September the British opened fire, with the Gordon Highlanders being given the task of clearing the road over the Devil's Knuckles. Battle raged for most of the day. Only at 16h00 did the Boers withdraw from the Devil's Knuckles, sending thirteen of their wagons tumbling down a precipice to prevent them from being captured by the British. The main Boer force had meanwhile escaped with the Long Tom, bag and baggage, to new and secret positions in the far-off hills.

The Devil's Knuckles lie 13 km up the pass from the junction with the Sabie–Nelspruit road. The position where the Long Tom was last in action is marked by a sign. If men had to die in battle, it was at least in a setting of overwhelming beauty.

Three kilometres further up the pass lies the Long Tom Forest Station and, after a further 5 km, the Blystaanhoogte Forest Station. The summit of the pass – 2 149 m above sea-level – is reached after a further 6,5 km from the junction with the Nelspruit road. The road is dotted with interesting things. Just beyond the Blystaanhoogte Forest Station is a sign marking the portion of the old road known as The Staircase. Nearby is preserved one of the Long Tom shell craters. There is a fine viewsite. Just before the summit there is a camping place at what is known as Whisky Spruit.

The summit acts as the division between the headwaters of the Sabie River (flowing east) and the Spekboom River (flowing west). In the 1920s the area of the division was the scene of a minor gold-rush to what was known as the Mount Anderson Gold Field. The signs of mining activity may still be seen in the form of rubble dumps, trenches, shafts and adits. Here, the Jackpot, Little Joker, Formosa, and several other small mines flourished for a short while.

West of the summit the road descends steadily through a rocky, undulating moorland, with flocks of sheep and troops of baboons wandering through the grass. After 19 km of easy descent, the road reaches the town of Lydenburg, 46,5 km from the junction with the Nelspruit–Sabie road.

Back at the foot of the Long Tom Pass, a turn off leads for 10,5 km through gum and pine plantations to the town of ...

SABIE

The beautifully situated little town of Sabie is named after the river originating on the divide at the summit of the Long Tom Pass. This river flows down through a handsome tree-grown valley to a waterfall where the town has been built. The name of the river – *Sabi* – derives from the Shangane word meaning 'fearful' and refers to the crocodiles and sudden floods which formerly made the river dangerous in its lower reaches.

Sabie was originally a farm named *Grootfontein* (great fountain) pioneered by D J Badenhorst and then sold to P de Villiers in 1864 for £7 10s. In 1880 H T Glynn bought it for £600. He and his son (also H T Glynn) farmed and became celebrated as big-game hunters.

The Glynns were renowned for their hospitality. Early in 1895 they were entertaining a party of friends at a picnic at the Klein Sabie Falls. The bottles remaining from lunch were placed on a ledge of rock and used as targets in a shooting match. The bullets chipped the rock and exposed what proved to be gold-bearing reef. The picnic was forgotten with the guests turning prospectors. Samples were crushed and panned. The results revealed good gold. The Glynns and their friends pegged a long stretch of what they named the Sandstone Reef. One of the picnickers, Captain J C Ingle, prospected the reef in detail to prove its extent and mining operations were commenced.

Thus the town of Sabie had its start. The Glynns-Lydenburg Gold Mining Company was floated to exploit the discovery. Mining operations were subject to immense technical difficulties. The rock was dolomite and subject to flooding, while chemically the ore was very refractory. Nevertheless, the miners persisted, and by the time the mine closed down in July 1950, 35 172 kg (1 240 646 oz) of gold had been extracted.

The town of Sabie grew up as the child of the mine, with the branch railway from Nelspruit reaching it in 1913. On 24 September 1915 it attained the status of a village with a health committee under the chairmanship of the popular Mr H T Glynn, known as the Squire of Sabie. On 1 January 1924, Sabie became a town. Today, with a population of 7 705, it is a bustling trading and communications centre, with a considerable industry in the production of timber.

The timber industry developed from the mines. The slopes of the mountains, acting as catchment areas for the Sabie River, had always been well covered with trees. With the opening of mines arose a demand for pit-props. A number of private woodcutters started work, causing enormous destruction to the natural forests, cutting down innumerable beautiful hardwood trees to make props or poles. The names of several of the old parasitic woodcutters still linger over the areas where they worked. Vosloo's Forest, Gabriel's Forest, Bokwa's Forest (named after the nickname of Jan Stolz, brother of Gabriel), Maritz's Forest and others. Several sawmills were started, most of them worked by water-power.

The demand for timber soon reached such a peak that the exhaustion of natural resources was inevitable. The first man to start planting trees was W Patrick of Elandsdrift Mine. Other mines followed his example. The first government plantations were established in the Transvaal in 1903 at places such as Lichtenburg, Machavie, Woodbush, Pan and Ermelo. In 1920 the Department of Forestry opened an office in Sabie. In 1922 the first white labour forestry settlement was started in Berlyn (Kaapsehoop) and several others followed. As a result of these settlements, millions of trees were planted. The area around Sabie today contains one of the largest man-made forests in the world. In Sabie there is a museum devoted to forestry, which depicts the different woods and the history of the industry.

Sixteen kilometres from Sabie, on the road to the east, lies the D R de Wet Tree Breeding Station, where experimental breeding and cross-pollination of trees takes place with a view to improving timber quality and yields.

Trees dominate the entire landscape. The main tarmac road to the north makes its way through green wooded country where ferns line every stream. Watsonias, proteas, red-hot pokers, nerinas, ericas and a rich profusion of other wild flowers flourish. The road leads along a narrow shelf of land with the Drakensberg towering to the west. To the east the dramatic cliff face of the escarpment falling sheer to the lowveld nearly 1 000 m below.

Driving or walking through these vast plantations is a delight. There are many lovely views, and waterfalls are spectacular, the Sabie Falls being within the confines of the town. The Bridal Veil Falls are 7,5 km from the town and the Lone Creek Falls 9 km. The Horseshoe Falls may be seen 3 km further along the same road which wanders through the trees up the left bank of the Sabie River and past the beautifully situated municipal caravan park. Trout fishing is good and hiking trails are exciting.

Several minor roads branch off east and west from Sabie to various forestry stations, down to the lowveld or to pleasant places such as the Mac-Mac pools (11 km from Sabie) where there are changing-rooms and picnic and barbecue sites next to some fine swimming-pools. In this pretty river alluvial gold was discovered in 1873 by Johannes Muller. An excited crowd of diggers pegged claims along its course. The odd name of Mac-Mac was given to the field by President Thomas Francois Burgers who encountered so many Scotsmen there when he visited the area. Most of the gold was recovered from the portion of the stream above the 100 m high twin waterfall which tumbles down into a spectacular ravine. A fine roadside view may be had of the Mac-Mac Falls (sometimes known as the Two Scotsmen), 13 km from Sabie along the tarmac road to the north.

After a further 3 km of travel along this road, a fine picnic site created by the Forestry Department is reached. A further 6,5 km (22,5 km from Sabie) brings the road to a junction. The east turn (right) leads for 5 km to the town of Graskop. The west turn (left) climbs up the mountains, crosses a saddle known to the prospectors as the 'divide', and then, amidst many beautiful views, descends into a lovely, misty valley, surely one of the most romantic in the world. Through this valley flows the Pilgrim's River, and 9,5 km from the junction of the road to Graskop (32 km from Sabie), the tarmac road enters that most delightful little mining centre of many memories ...

PILGRIM'S REST

With a present-day population numbering about 1 650 people, Pilgrim's Rest has thoroughly enjoyed a past which has been naughty, uproarious, gay, tragic, adventurous and, at times, outrageous. To connoisseurs of mining history the story of the Pilgrim's Rest rush is a classic. The little town – now merely a wistful ghost of itself – was declared a national monument in 1986. It is one of the most perfect examples to be seen anywhere in the world of a mining town born during the excitement of an alluvial gold-rush.

In 1873 a prospector known as 'Wheelbarrow' Alec Patterson (on account of his habit of pushing his belongings ahead of him in a wheelbarrow) found alluvial gold in the middle reaches of the stream running through the valley. He settled down to work his find. He was soon joined by a second prospector, William Trafford who, since it seemed to him that his weary pilgrimage in search of fortune was at last over, named the valley Pilgrim's Rest.

A rush took place to the valley as soon as news of the discovery spread. The middle reaches of the stream proved the richest and some very fine nuggets of alluvial gold were found there, especially during 1875. By the end of that year, Pilgrim's Rest comprised 21 stores, 18 canteens, 3 bakeries and a variety of other establishments.

Hostilities between the Transvaal government and the Pedi tribe (who lived west of Pilgrim's Rest) caused a setback in 1876. There was by this time a tendency for syndicates and companies to take over from the more happy-go-lucky diggers. The Anglo-Transvaal war of 1880–81 also affected the field. It was taken over in 1881 by a financier, David Benjamin, who offered the government a monthly payment of £1 000 in exchange for a concession.

Benjamin formed the Transvaal Gold Exploration and Land Company to exploit the field. For some years the company was poorly rewarded for its efforts. Then, in the 1890s a prospector, C Robinson, was employed to explore the area. He unearthed a complete mineral treasure chest. One of his discoveries, the Theta reef, alone yielded over 141 750 kg (5 million ounces) of gold in 50 years of continuous working.

In an environment healthier, more beautiful and romantic than any other gold-field in the world, Pilgrim's Rest was a persistent producer of gold right up to 1972 when mining ceased. Towards the end of its mining life the holding company diversified and developed into the largest forestry enterprise in Southern Africa. A detailed history of Pilgrim's Rest may be found in the book *Lost Trails of the Transvaal*.

There are several interesting museums in the town, such as the Miner's House museum, the Shop museum and the Alanglade House museum. Tours are conducted through the village and the original mine reduction works. There are demonstrations of digging and panning for gold. There is a 7 km long rambler's trail, bridle-path and trout fishing in the Blyde River. An excellent information office is open daily. The museums open daily from 09h00 to 13h00 and 13h30 to 16h15.

From Pilgrim's Rest, the road finds an amiable way down the left bank of the stream. Immediately outside the town, across a bridge over one of the tributaries of the stream, there is a division. The west branch (left) leads over the mountains to Lydenburg (58 km), climbing steeply through the Morgenzon Forestry Reserve. At 10 km this road reaches the summit where there is a plaque commemorating Jock of the Bushveld and the transport riders who used this route in former years. After a further 3 km there is a turn-off leading for 10 km to the Mount Sheba Hotel, set in a beautiful natural forest. From the turn-off to the hotel, the main road descends the western side of the Drakensberg and after 15 km joins the tarmac R36 Ohrigstad–Lydenburg road.

THE PANORAMA ROUTE

The northern branch (right) of the road outside Pilgrim's Rest continues down the left bank of the Pilgrim's stream, meandering through a green and delightful stretch of country, with tall hills crowding the valley and innumerable signs, relics and bric-à-brac of mining visible on the slopes.

Past the Vaalhoek mine the gravel road, 21 km from Pilgrim's Rest, reaches a turn-off west to Ohrigstad (30,5 km). The gravel road at present being followed bears east (right) and after 1,5 km reaches another turn-off. The right-hand branch continues east to Graskop (34 km) on the scenic Panorama Route. The left-hand branch continues past a little tea-room (the Manx Café) and then makes its way to the Blyde River Gorge.

The Panorama Route provides the traveller with a superb circular tarmac drive back to the junction where the road from Sabie divided east to Graskop, or west to Pilgrim's Rest. From the junction at Vaalhoek, the Panorama Route leads through an area settled by African people and rises steadily to cross over a divide after 5 km, entering the Goedgeloof plantation. The road winds through extensive plantations, passes at 13 km the London plantation and at 16 km the Blyde forest reserve.

At 19 km the road reaches the Waterval spruit, where there is a fine picnic site just downstream from the bridge, with a natural swimming-pool set among tree ferns and green grass. A further 5 km (24 km from the start) brings the road to a turn-off leading for 3 km to the Blyde forest station and state sawmill, and Berlyn Falls. This waterfall should not be missed. It has a sheer, 80 m fall. Excellent vantage-points reveal the entire drop and the deep pool at its foot. Afternoon light is the best for photography. Wild flowers are spectacular, especially watsonias in late summer.

Continuing from the turn-off to this waterfall, the main road (after 1 km) reaches a turn to some fine swimming-pools in the Blyde River. Little more than 500 m brings the road (25,5 km from the start) to a turn-off left leading for 8 km to what is known as God's Window, a cleft in the edge of the escarpment which provides a grand view down into the lowveld. From the parking site of God's Window, a path and motoring track lead along the verge of the escarpment to the Lowveld panorama and nature reserve, a lovely patch of indigenous forest with a stunning view. In this reserve flourish many flowering and aromatic plants. The air is delightfully cool and some of the subtle fragrances of the low country rise up to merge with the crisp winds of the highveld.

From the turn to God's Window, the main road continues to meander. After 1,5 km it crosses a river, reaching a turn-off to the right stretching for 1,5 km to the Lisbon Falls. This is a fine double waterfall set in superb scenery. There is a picnic site at the Falls. Afternoon light is the best for photography.

From the turn-off to the Lisbon Falls (27,5 km from the start of the road), the Panorama Route continues for 5 km and then reaches a turn-off left leading to the much-photographed Pinnacle and Driekop gorge. After a further 1,5 km, the road (34 km from its start) reaches the village of ...

GRASKOP

A pleasant little centre from which to explore the escarpment falling away to the east, *Graskop* (grassy peak) was originally the farm of Abel Erasmus, a renowned character during the 1850s who played a considerable role in the adventurous days of hunting, prospecting and the imposition of law and order over a turbulent area. The village is now a timber centre and the terminus of the branch railway from Nelspruit. It has a population of 1 293.

From Graskop, the circular drive is completed with an easy 5 km run to the junction with the Sabie–Pilgrim's Rest road. The circular drive stretching from this point through Pilgrim's Rest down to the junction at Vaalhoek and then returning via the Panorama Route through Graskop is 48 km long.

A very interesting and beautiful 37 km drive leads from Graskop down Kowyn Pass to the lowveld. From Graskop this tarmac road skirts the edge of the escarpment, revealing magnificent views of the low country. After 3 km the road passes the Panorama rest camp and a further 1,5 km brings it to the top of the pass known as *Kowyn* after the Sotho tribal chief who once lived there. Near the top of the pass is a picnic spot and a plaque marking the opening of the modern pass on 3 October 1959.

The road continues to descend the escarpment, passing through dense plantations of gum and pine trees, providing a fine drive. At the bottom of the pass, 14,5 km from Graskop, Rand Mining Timber have their depot. One more kilometre brings the road to a branch leading to Bushbuck Ridge. The road continues eastwards, rising and falling incessantly through plantations and a luxuriant, green, rural countryside settled by people of the Shangane tribe. There are many impressive views. At 37 km from Graskop the road joins the main tarmac R40 road leading from Tzaneen and Phalaborwa in the north down to White River and Nelspruit.

THE BLYDE RIVER GORGE

Back at Vaalhoek, where the Panorama route branched off, the left-hand road continues northwards along the edge of the escarpment. Passing the little Manx Café, post office and garage, the road proceeds for 7 km and crosses the *Blyde* (joyful) River just above its confluence with the *Treur* (sorrowful) River. Close to this crossing there is a turn-off leading to the remarkable potholes of Bourke's Luck, named after Thomas Bourke, one of the Director's of the Transvaal Gold Mining Estates which had concessions over the area.

The origin of the two river names is interesting. In 1840 the Voortrekker leader, Hendrik Potgieter, led a party on an exploratory journey to Lourenzo Marques. The womenfolk remained on the cool and healthy heights near Graskop, while most of the men rode down across the lowveld searching for a route to the coast. The time for their return came and passed. After the disasters which had befallen other trekkers on the route to the coast, the waiting party became despondent. They named the stream on whose banks they were camped, the *Treur* (sorrowful), and set out for home. Potgieter, however, after an adventurous journey returned safely, overtaking the women as they were fording the river from then on known as the *Blyde* (joyful) on account of the happy reunion.

Near the confluence of the two rivers there was in recent times a profitable little gold-mine known as Bourke's Luck, where a hydro-electric power-station supplied electricity to Pilgrim's Rest. The course of the rivers, especially at their junction, is notable for strange rock formations and pot-holes. A parking place and a series of foot-bridges allow visitors clear views of the gorge.

Below its confluence with the Treur, the Blyde River tumbles down into one of the most spectacular gorges in Africa. The two best viewsites are easily reached by means of tarmac turn-offs from the main road following the edge of the escarpment. Thick green grass covers the heights. The verges of the gorge are fringed with stamvrug shrubs *(Bequaertiodendron megalismontanum)*. In January these shrubs are covered with bright-red fruit, which is sold in baskets by children. The fruit has a distinctive flavour and is delicious to eat, either fresh or as jam.

Tremendous panoramas of the lowveld are revealed as the road leads onwards. The prodigious flat-topped bulk of Mariepskop may be seen in the middle distance. The Blyde River, 800 m below, forces a tortuous passage beneath towering red-coloured sandstone cliffs, painted with yellow lichen and modelled with shadows and a lovely haze of blue. Dominating the gorge are the triplet peaks known on account of their shape as the Three Rondawels.

The viewsite turns-off are 9,5 km, 16 km, and 19,5 km respectively from Vaalhoek. The last turn-off leads to the Blydepoort holiday resort originally created by the Transvaal Provincial Administration. This is a luxurious establishment, complete with restaurant, supermarket, sporting facilities, piped music, heated swimming baths, etc. Nature trails for walkers and riders lead to many interesting places. Paths meander into the gorge below where, in a magnificent setting of towering red-coloured sandstone cliffs, lies the Blyderivierspoort Dam with its 72 m high wall. All this development, and the roar of motors on roads and lake, contrasts sharply with the erstwhile remote and tranquil gorge. However, portions still remain where the sweet sound of silence may be heard by those with the energy to walk or ride away from the throng.

THE ECHO CAVES, OHRIGSTAD AND LYDENBURG

From the entrance to the Blydepoort holiday resort, the tarmac road winds onwards for 28 km up a fertile valley and then joins the R36 road coming from Lydenburg. Turning left (southwards) from the Blyde River gorge road junction, the R36 road leads through farmlands and after 1,5 km reaches a gravel turn-off to the right stretching for 3 km to the Echo Caves.

THE ECHO CAVES

The Echo Caves are situated in a hill spur at the head of the Molapong valley and occur in dolomite, a rock notable for water-worn caves and sink-holes. There are two entrances to the caves. The second one (popularly known as the Cannibal Cave) on the south-western side of the spur consists of a vertical shaft leading down to a complex sequence of passages which eventually join the series of caverns linked to the first entrance. These caverns contain some fine stalactites and stalagmites. The name of the caves derives from the echoes made when some of these formations are gently tapped. The caverns from the vertical shaft are home to a vast colony of bats. Hopefully their dark retreats will not be disturbed, for bats are invaluable and interesting little creatures, fully entitled to being conserved.

One section of the caves is 400 m long, the second section is 307 m, and the largest chamber is 100 m long and 49 m high.

The area of the Echo Caves was occupied by man during the Middle and Late Stone Ages (51 000 BC to 10 000 BC) and many interesting artefacts have been found. Bushman paintings may be seen in several rock shelters. The various caverns also served as sanctuaries for the local African tribes in times of war. In 1923 Mr J H Claasens bought the farm containing the cave area. The local Africans showed him the caves. Assisted by his son Johan he opened the Echo Caves to visitors. It was a difficult economic time and the Claasens had a struggle to finance development. Johan was studying to be a dentist. When he qualified and established a successful practice in Barberton, the young man invested most of his income in building a motel, shop and cafeteria at the caves. He persuaded the National Monuments Commission to declare the place a National Monument.

Visitors started to come. It was at this stage, while planning a dance hall in an old rock shelter, that Johan found interesting stone artefacts. Johan showed these to Dr J J Malan of the Bushbuckridge health centre. He was a qualified archaeologist as well as a medical doctor. He identified the artefacts as being particularly fine examples from the Middle Stone age. The result was the creation of the Museum of Man in the Bushman rock shelter next to the main approach road. A picturesque little art gallery exhibited the paintings and sculptures done by a local missionary, the Reverend Paul van Zyl. Mr Claasens died in July 1978 and is buried below the museum.

Recently the Caves were closed to the public owing to problems of access to private ground and inadequate facilities for visitors.

From the turn-off to the Echo Caves, the main tarmac road continues southwards down a rugged valley where many flowering aloes and euphorbia trees grow. Fruit, tobacco and vegetables are farmed in deep, red soil. At 21 km from the Blyde River junction there are turn-offs: at 18 km left to Kaspersnek and a tarmac road R355 right to Burgersfort and Sekhukuneland. A further 3 km brings the road to the village of Ohrigstad with its memories of past days and troubled times.

OHRIGSTAD

Ohrigstad was founded in 1845 by the Voortrekker leader, Andries Hendrik Potgieter, who had heard that the British claimed all land south of the 25th degree of south latitude. Accordingly, he abandoned the early Voortrekker settlement at Potchefstroom and moved north to the new town, which he named *Andries-Ohrigstad* in joint honour of himself and a Dutch merchant in Holland, George Ohrig, who had sent aid and encouragement to the trekkers.

The site of Ohrigstad was safely above the 25th degree of south latitude. Unfortunately it was soon found to be plagued by mosquitoes and excessively hot in summer. As a result of malaria being endemic in those days, Potgieter abandoned the town in 1848 and removed with his followers to the Zoutpansberge, where he established a new settlement. The remaining inhabitants of Ohrigstad stayed in the place for another year and then were also forced to move by the voracious mosquitoes. They established the town of Lydenburg, leaving Ohrigstad to the ghosts. Only in recent years, with the conquest of malaria, has the fertile valley of Ohrigstad been resettled. Ruins and graves of the original settlement may still be seen.

SEKHUKHUNELAND

The tarmac turn-off marked Burgersfort 3 km north of Ohrigstad provides a fascinating journey leading into a rugged, not often visited, part of Mpumalanga, previously known as *Sekhukhuneland*. This is the home of the Pedi people whose traditional rulers bore the family name of Sekhukhune. It is an extraordinary part of South Africa, a portion of what is known to geologists as the Bushveld Igneous Complex. Its landscape is almost lunar-like. Sharp mountains rise steeply from the floor of a vast plain lying like a wedge between the two rivers known to Europeans as the Olifants and the Steelpoort which flow down deep ravines, with many a twist and rapid as they shoulder their way through the mountains towards the distant sea. To the Pedi, the Olifants is known as the *Lepelle* and the Steelpoort is named the *Ndwase*. The *Steelpoort*, it is said, received its European name when a hunter named Scholtz shot an elephant where the river had a passage through the mountains. It was approaching night and the hunter left the dead elephant until the morning when he returned to cut out the tusks. He found that the tusks had been stolen (*steel* means steal) and gave the name to the river and the mountain passage.

There are signs of mining in every direction for it is a richly mineralised area. After 35 km there is a turn-off north leading for 46 km to the mine of Penge, for long the world's principal producer of the long-fibred variety of asbestos known as *amosite* from the initials of the company which mined it, Asbestos Mines of South Africa. Back in 1888 Johannes Rissik, was appointed to the difficult task of surveying the complex mountain country of Sekhukhuneland. On the south bank of the Olifants River, deep in the mountains, he surveyed several possible farms. Two of them he named incongruously *Penge* and *Streatham* after London suburbs. The South African namesakes baked in summer temperatures exceeding 40°C and lay in the wildest of mountain settings.

Prospectors rather than farmers followed the survey. Farmers had their doubts about the area but prospectors would go anywhere in search of gold or precious stones. What they found, however, was a variety of base minerals, including asbestos. With no means of transportation to any market the discoveries remained unexploited but not forgotten. In 1907 the geologists A L Hall and H B Wayne examined the area. The extent of the asbestos deposit startled them. As a consequence of their report mining started in 1910. It had to be on a vast scale to justify the expense of the building of a tarmac road and the creation of a small town to house the workers. With two associated mines at Weltevreden and Kromellenboog, the Penge mine attained an output of over 40 000 tons of amosite asbestos each year. The mine operating company was named *Egnep (Penge* spelt backwards).

Shortly after the turn-off to Penge mine, the R555 road reaches Burgersfort. Today this is a railway dispatch station for a variety of base minerals such as asbestos, chrome, iron ore, alusite and vanadium. Wheat, lucerne, tobacco and citrus are also produced in the area. The name of the place, however, is remindful of hectic events of the past.

The Pedi tribe who live in the area are of Tswana origin. They wandered into this mountainous land from the west and found living in it a minor group of Karanga people from Zimbabwe. These people were dispossessed and the remnants absorbed by the newcomers. Fearful that the Karanga ancestral spirits would resent the extinction of their descendants the newcomers prudently adopted the name of the earlier people the Bedzi. With no 'z' sound in their language, the nearest the Tswana could get to this name was to call themselves the Pedi.

Like their Sotho relatives, the Pedi discovered the defensive value of hills and mountains. They found one cluster of three strange hillocks to be excellent for this purpose. They were *Modimolle* (place of the spirits), *Mosego* (place of cutting) and *Tjate*, a most astonishing hillock. It consists of a gigantic pile of loose rocks dumped on the level floor of a bush-covered plain. The whole pile of rocks is honeycombed with caves, crevices and secret chambers. It was a superlatively strong retreat, difficult even for a modern army to subdue without resorting to gas or flame throwers.

Three successive mini-wars were fought by Pedi and the Government of the Transvaal. The story of these clashes are complex and best read in *Lost Trails of the Transvaal.* The fort at *Burgersfort* was built in 1876 during the first of these 'wars'. It was garrisoned by an odd little 'foreign legion' of recruits named the Lydenburg Volunteers, commanded by a German named Conrad Hans von Schlickmann. He claimed to have been a captain in the Franco-Prussian war and had received the Iron Cross. The fort was named in honour of President Burgers of the South African Republic. It was a bleak, sexagonal mud-walled enclosure, protected by a ditch, a parapet and a drawbridge. Only traces of this fort remain. Its only connection with the outside world was a footpath. It was dominated by the 1 416 m high triple summit of Morone Mountain, one of the strongholds of the Pedi.

The garrison of Burgersfort had a rough time. They suffered casualties in raids, counter-raids and ambushes. Von Schlickmann was killed on 17 November 1876 in a raid up Mahera's kloof. His successor was an Irish adventurer named Alfred Aylward who brought with him 70 recruits from the Kimberley diamond diggings. With the aid of these rough diamonds and a group of men brought in by one of the most preposterous characters ever known in South Africa, the so-called Gunn of Gunn and Lord of Farquhar, Aylward held the fort until the British took over the Transvaal and disbanded the volunteers in June 1877. The Pedi then looted and destroyed the fort. The last heard of Aylward was that he went to America, claimed to be a general and eloped with an heiress. The last heard of the Gunn of Gunn was that he was in jail.

The British had to continue the mini-war against the Pedi. Under the command of Sir Garnet Wolseley, a force of 2 000 Europeans and 8 000 Swazi warriors under Matafini was sent to the Pedi country. Before this force, the Pedi warriors withdrew into the stronghold of Tjate. On 25 November 1879 the British set out to dislodge them. For three days and nights there was almost a nightmare battle. Then the Pedi seemed to simply disappear. Only 300 women and children emerged from the caves of Tjate and surrendered. Sekhukhune was reported as having escaped. He was tracked to the top of the Lulu ridge of mountains and then to a cave in a secret valley cradled on the summit. For three days chief Sekhukhune kept the government forces at bay. Then he surrendered and was sent off with some of his councillors to prison in Pretoria. With his people he had fought a determined fight. Their casualties are unknown but the government forces lost 42 Europeans and 500 Swazi. Control of the Pedi tribe was divided between two chiefs of the royal house, Mampuru and Ramoroko, missionaries were given sites for the establishment of stations and prospectors started a search for mineral wealth.

There was one more mini-war in the Pedi country. When the British withdrew from the Transvaal in August 1881, the restored republic set out to gather taxes in order to finance itself. There was trouble with several of the African tribes who declined to pay. The Pedi at this time were very divided. Chief Sekhukhune had been released from captivity when the British left. Mampuru, one of the two men appointed by the British to replace him, resented the restoration of Sekhukhune and murdered him. Mampuru then fled for refuge to a friendly Ndebele chief named Nyabela who had a stronghold in a complex of caves in one of the precipices looking down on the Steelpoort River. It took no little effort on the part of the government force to subdue this and other strongholds. *Lost Trails of the Transvaal* has the details of this mini-war.

Mampuru was eventually surrendered by his ally and hanged in Pretoria. The Pedi tribe had not given him much support for they resented his killing of Sekhukhune. They live quietly, mainly in the open plain between the Steelpoort and Olifants rivers. The branch railway from Belfast on the Eastern Line terminates at Steelpoort, a centre for the mining of chrome and magnetite. Good roads provide access to most parts of the Pedi country. It is an interesting experience in travel to visit the sites of the various armed clashes of the three mini-wars. Cartridge cases and spent bullets may still be found amongst the rocks. The scenery is unforgettable and the various mineral exposures are fascinating. The tarmac R37 road from Lydenburg to Pietersburg traverses the country as well as the R555 we have been following.

From Ohrigstad, the R36 tarmac road continues southwards down an intensely cultivated valley. The landscape is fertile and pleasant, with the sandstone cliffs of the valley at times crowding in and then receding. Roadside kiosks offer for sale cold milk, vegetables and fruit. Tobacco, peaches, sunflowers, maize and other crops flourish on almost every part of the valley floor.

At 42 km from the Blyde River gorge turn-off, a turn-off leads over the mountains for 29 km to Pilgrim's Rest. The stage-coaches used this road during the gold-rush, and memories linger on of highwaymen and ambuscades. After a further 5 km the road climbs over *Verraaiersnek* (traitor's ridge) where a handsome view is revealed from the summit. The road descends the other side through a fertile alluvial valley.

At 60 km the road crosses the *Spekboom* (bacon tree) River, called the *Mombeza* by the Africans, in whose upper valley several small gold-mines were once worked. A further 11 km brings the road to a turn-off right leading to Burgersfort (56 km) and Pietersburg (209 km). Immediately ahead, 72,5 km from the turn to the Blyde River gorge, lies the town of ...

LYDENBURG

The lugubrious name of *Lydenburg* (town of suffering) was applied to the town when it was founded in 1849 by those disgruntled inhabitants of Ohrigstad who did not choose to move further north when Hendrik Potgieter abandoned the fever-stricken settlement. While Potgieter led his supporters far north to the Zoutpansberge to establish a new settlement, the dissident section was left to create their own new town. A church, magistrate's residence, school and gaol were erected, as well as a cluster of houses. In the years of political squabbling amongst the Voortrekkers, Lydenburg in 1857 even proclaimed itself a republic independent of the government in Potchefstroom. The quarrel was only patched up in 1859 when Lydenburg once again became part of the South African Republic.

From Lydenburg a trail was blazed to the sea at what was then named Lourenzo Marques (now Maputo). This transport road, spanning the Transvaal Drakensberg, descending the escarpment, and penetrating the savanna country of the lowveld and Mozambique, became the principal trade route for the Voortrekkers. Lydenburg was its inland terminal. Some very rugged individuals earned their living as transport riders. The full story of those years, with all the excitement of the discovery of the alluvial gold-fields of the Eastern Transvaal, makes fascinating reading.

When the British annexed the Transvaal in May 1877, they immediately found that they had inherited the makings of a war with the Pedi tribe of the chief Sekhukhune. A small garrison was established in Lydenburg during this period. When the Anglo-Transvaal War broke out in 1880, the 94th Regiment was stationed in Lydenburg under the command of Lieutenant-Colonel R P Anstruther. When he was ordered to march to Pretoria with the bulk of the regiment, they were ambushed near Bronkhorstspruit. There were 66 men killed, 90 wounded (of whom 21, including Anstruther, died later), and the rest were taken prisoner. Second-Lieutenant W H Long, a young man of 22, was left in Lydenburg in command of a detachment of 50 men. He constructed a small strongpoint which he named *Fort Marie* after his wife. The republicans had possession of the town but they made no serious attempt to take the fort. They occasionally peppered the place with rifle fire. There was a desultory artillery dual between two small republican cannons and a home-made British gun constructed from the barrel of an Abyssinian pump, so fashioned that it threw a 1 kg ball.

At the end of the war the British withdrew. The little fort fell into disuse. In 1889 stones from it were taken for the construction of a gunpowder room. The room still stands, with the names of some of the British soldiers inscribed by them on the stones. It is a proclaimed national monument.

Two other national monuments in Lydenburg are the first Dutch Reformed church (completed in 1852, with the first service held by the Reverend A Murray). A later church was completed in 1894. The tall pulpit of this second church was built of kiaat and is a replica of the one in the Mother Church in Stellenbosch. It also has a fine organ. The earlier Voortrekker church has ceilings of yellowwood. The original school building, completed in 1851, served the children of Lydenburg for many years. It was restored by the National Monuments Council in 1973 and proclaimed a national monument.

Lydenburg became a municipality in 1927 and has a present population of 21 600. It is today, notwithstanding its name, a cheerful little town. It is the centre for an agricultural community and for the hatching of fish, particularly trout. The Lydenburg Provincial Fisheries Institute was created by the Transvaal Provincial Administration in 1949, with the purpose of providing a variety of angling fish species, to control undesirable fish species, and to supply information to trout farmers.

On the banks of the Sterkspruit, 12 km from the town, is situated the De Kuilen Trout Hatchery, said to be the largest in the southern hemisphere. It can accommodate ten million trout eggs which are supplied to fish producers, as well as young fish for the restocking of rivers.

The rivers and dams in the Lydenburg district are well stocked with fish and most of them are in beautiful situations. The P T C du Plessis Dam in the Sterkspruit has a surface area of 9 323 ha and is a great place for trout angling. There are three spectacularly lovely waterfalls in the Dorps River, 16 km north-east of the town. Two of the falls are next to each other, tumbling over a cliff into a deep pool that feeds the third fall, a total drop of 244 m. The Lydenburg municipality has a hydro-electric generating station at this point. The municipality generates 40 per cent of its power requirements from the river.

The Dorps River is also an excellent trout fishery. The F C Braun park on its banks provides a delightful setting where anglers fish and their good wives barbecue trout. The bad ones stay at home and do other things. The Ohrigstad, Buffelskroon and Raubenheimer dams also are excellent for fishing.

The Spekboom River is another lovely river in a spectacular valley. This river has been, and is occasionally still worked for alluvial gold in what is known as the Finsbury Gold-Field. The Finsbury trout kloof is also in the vicinity. From the bridge over the Dwars River there may clearly be seen a remarkable geological occurrence in the form of chromotite bands in anortosite – spectacular to laymen and famous among geologists.

On the Ohrigstad road, 11 km from Lydenburg, Mr Heysteck has created a collection of life-sized statues of various wild animals and birds.

The museum in the town exhibits, amongst many other interesting things, three replicas of the seven terracotta so-called Lydenburg heads found in the Sterkspruit valley by Ludwig von Bezing. They are dated to the 5th century AD. Their purpose is unknown. Six of the heads have human faces and one is that of a wild animal. The originals of these heads are in the South African Museum in Cape Town.

The Gustav Klingbiel Nature Reserve, 2 200 ha in extent, on the road to Long Tom Pass, is the home for numerous wild creatures, including leopards, many birds and a varied flora. In it there are ruins of stone-walled villages and agricultural terraces dating from medieval times. A footpath leads to these ruins and there is a fine hiking trail with an overnight hut.

ABEL ERASMUS PASS

Beyond the turn-off to the Blyde River gorge, the tarmac R36 road continues northwards and immediately begins to climb the bush-covered slopes of the Drakensberg by means of the Abel Erasmus Pass. The ascent is 6,5 km long, during which fine views of the mountains are revealed. Once the summit is reached, the road commences a long and involved descent down the northern side into a grassy, bush-covered valley settled by African people. The route followed by the original road may still be seen and is marked by signs as the old coach road.

At 18 km from the Blyde River gorge turn-off, there is a track branching left and leading for 2,5 km to a viewsite known as the Devil's Pulpit. The road now enters a spectacular gorge dominated by high, red-coloured sandstone cliffs daubed with yellow lichen. There are picnic sites by the wayside, and a plaque commemorating the opening of the pass on 8 May 1959. It was named after Abel Erasmus, the well-known early inhabitant of the Graskop and Ohrigstad areas. The pass took three years to build. It rises 365 mm over the Drakensberg from Ohrigstad, and then descends 800 m to the lowveld.

At 21 km from the Blyde River gorge turn-off, the road reaches the tunnel named after a former prime minister of South Africa, Mr J G Strijdom. The tunnel, 133,5 m long, provides a dramatic gateway to the low country. The views are spectacular, especially of the Olifants River emerging from the mountain massif and flowing off across the savanna plains of the bushveld.

Beyond the tunnel the tarmac road continues its sweeping descent. At 24 km from the Blyde River gorge turn-off, the road reaches the bottom of the pass where, in a pleasant setting, lies the Manoutsa caravan park with its restaurant and inviting swimming pool.

Six kilometres further on is a turn left leading for 96,5 km to Tzaneen, while 3 km beyond this turn-off, on the banks of the Olifants River under the shade of some huge wild fig trees, lies the River Lodge Motel.

The tarmac road proceeds eastwards. After 13 km the Blyde Park shopping centre, close to the bridge over the Blyde River, is passed. Across the bridge, 2,5 km further on is a turn-off south leading for 27 km to the public resort of Swadini at the Blyderivierspoort Dam and also to places such as Kampersrus and Klaserie.

SYBRAND VAN NIEKERK RESORT (SWADINI)

This magnificent resort created by the Board for Public Resorts of the Transvaal Provincial Council (Aventura), was opened in September 1982 at *Swadini*, below the Blyderivierspoort Dam. Swadini was the name of a local chief who once had his village close by. The resort's facilities include a swimming-pool (which is heated in the winter months), boating, angling, walking, climbing and game and bird watching. There is a restaurant and shop.

A further 3 km beyond the turn-off to Swadini and Kampersrus takes the road past the Blyde trading store, with a turn right (south) to Bedford and Klaserie. The Rietspruit jam and canning factory stands beside the road 2,5 km further on. A further 9 km brings the road to the railway centre of Hoedspruit where it joins the main north–south R40 road of the lowveld (Tzaneen to Nelspruit).

ABEL ERASMUS PASS TO TZANEEN

At the foot of the Abel Erasmus pass, between the Manoutsa Caravan Park and the River Lodge Motel, the R36 tarmac road leading to Tzaneen branches northwards, crossing the Olifants River at a point overlooked by a handsome baobab tree. The bridge lies at a point 26 km from the summit of the Abel Erasmus Pass (101 km from Lydenburg and 100 km from Pilgrim's Rest). Here the Olifants River flows powerfully and many pools occur in which lurk crocodiles, hippos, barbel and yellowfish. Handsome trees line the river banks.

After crossing the bridge, the tarmac road leads northwards through a wild garden of trees, flowering shrubs and plants which blanket the gently rolling plains of the lowveld. Immediately to the west lies the long line of cliffs of the Drakensberg, a romantic sight, both visually beautiful and filled with memories of tribal wars and the bitter-sweet story of Louis Trichardt's trek.

As the main road proceeds northwards secondary roads branch off, several of them to extremely interesting parts of the lowveld. Nine and a half kilometres from the Olifants River bridge there is a turn-off east to Leydsdorp, a gold-rush centre of the 1890s. (See section in Chapter Thirty-Seven on the Murchison Range). The country around the Murchison Range is beautifully wooded.

The main tarmac road continues north through very attractive lowveld country. Nine and a half kilometres beyond the turn to Leydsdorp, the road passes the Shiluvane Mission of the Swiss Presbyterians, founded in 1886 in the territory of the Shangane chief, Xiluvana.

The road now crosses a fertile and densely settled portion of the lowveld, with tribal areas and European farms lying on either side of the road. From this lovely parkland, fine views of the mountains may be had to the west and east. Nine and a half kilometres from the Shiluvane Mission there is a turn-off west up the valley of the *Letsitele* (river of the wide crossing place) where fine subtropical fruit estates flourish on the water of the mountain streams. After 26 km of travel through thick bush country, a turn-off leads westwards for 6,5 km to the rural centre of Trichardtsdal, while 8 km further on (43,5 km from the Olifants River bridge) there is a crossroads where turn-offs lead east to Gravelotte and west to *Ofcolaco* (Officers' Colonial Land Company), formed co-operatively by a number of British army officers as a settlement scheme after the First World War.

The gravel road through Ofcolaco is worth taking for those who have the time and a rugged vehicle. The road passes through citrus groves and over fertile fields, heading for the Drakensberg. Climbing the escarpment by means of a spectacular pass, it reaches the plateau summit known as *The Downs* (from its resemblance to the Surrey Downs) where the family of the renowned prospector, Orlando Baragwanath, farmed potatoes amidst the clouds. The road then drops by means of the Jan Smuts Pass into the wild valley of the aptly named *Mohlapitse* (clear, deep water) stream, whose upper reaches are a paradise for walkers and climbers. Finally, the road stretches off to the west across the lunar-like scenery of the Bushveld Igneous Complex with its asbestos and chrome mines.

The main tarmac R36 road, meanwhile, continues northwards. Eight kilometres from the Ofcolaco turn-off (51,5 km from the Olifants River bridge) another turn-off leads for 18 km to Leydsdorp and the Murchison range.

Roadside kiosks offer fruit to passing travellers, especially during summer. The road finds an attractive way through well-wooded foothills until, 13 km from the Letsitele turn-off (83,5 km from the Olifants River bridge), it enters the attractive, modern town of Tzaneen.

Chapter Thirty-Seven
THE LOWVELD, ITS PEOPLE, SCENERY AND WILDLIFE

TZANEEN

Tzaneen lies in a hollow on the banks of the Letaba (*Lehlaba* or sandy) River, a bustling mountain torrent along whose length are situated some of the most productive farms in the northern lowveld. Tea, all kinds of subtropical fruits and vegetables such as avocados, mangoes, litchis, bananas, coffee, cotton and citrus nuts, flowers (especially carnations), winter vegetables, potatoes, and enormous quantities of timber are produced in the area. As the rail, commercial and administrative centre for so prosperous an activity, Tzaneen is the principal town of the northeastern lowveld. The population of the town is 6 138.

The origin of the name *Tzaneen* derives from a section of the boKgaga tribe who broke away from the parent group and settled in the area, calling themselves the *baTsaneng* (people of the small village). In 1905 Lord Milner established an experimental tobacco farm in the area of the present Merensky High School. As a result, Tzaneen cigars and Letaba cigarettes as they were called became well known.

The development of farming stimulated the extension in 1912 of the Selati railway line as far as the farm *Pusela*. It was there, around the sheds of the railway siding, that the town of Tzaneen was laid out, eventually receiving its first public body (a health committee) on 24 May 1924. The conquest of malarial fever, largely (as in Zululand) the result of a visit by the famed Professor Swellengrebel of the League of Nations, as well as the tireless work of Dr Siegfried Annecke, vanquished the old mosquito phantom of the lowveld. Today life is as pleasantly healthy there as in any other part of Southern Africa, providing proper precautions are taken. The Dr Siegfried Annecke Research Institute in Tzaneen is a stimulating place to visit. It is concerned in both malaria and bilharzia research and is open weekdays 09h00 to 16h00 (closed lunchtimes). Dr Annecke gave his life to the scientific war against malarial mosquitoes. Just when the battle seemed to have been won with 1966 the first year with no new cases of malarial fever reported, the health officials, notwithstanding Dr Annecke's warning, prematurely relaxed preventative measures. There was a disastrous revival of mosquitoes. Dr Annecke committed suicide in frustrated despair.

There is a museum in Tzaneen with a good ethnological section. It is open Mondays to Fridays 09h00 to 17h00 and Saturdays 09h00 to 13h00.

MAGOEBASKLOOF

The circular drive up Magoebaskloof returning to Tzaneen through George's Valley and the Letaba valley, or straight on to Pietersburg, is a scenic delight for any traveller. The magnificent road leads under the slopes of the 2 127 m *Wolkberg* (cloudy mountain), passing the lovely cascades of the upper Letaba, the waters of the Ebenezer Dam, the trout streams of the Haenertsburg district, and the forest-covered gorges of Magoebaskloof containing the handsome waterfall of Debegeni. The tour is a superlative botanic experience, for the valleys are veritable gardens of fruit, flowering plants and forest trees of great variety, and the escarpment edge is green, cool and delightful.

Travellers should take the R71 road up Magoebaskloof which branches off west 4 km from Tzaneen on the road to Duiwelskloof. Plantations of trees, tea and subtropical fruit cover the valley. The roadside is lined with 'pride of India' trees (flowering in December and January in shades of bright pink and mauve); bauhinia or 'pride of the Kaap', in pink and red; cassias and acacias in yellow. Eleven kilometres from the turn-off, the road passes the sawmill of De Hoek, where a gravel turn-off to the north is worth taking. The main road continues in a steep spiral. After 10 km it reaches the summit where the branch road will eventually rejoin it after 19,5 km of complex travelling.

The gravel branch road is steep and sometimes slightly rough. It passes through a vast primeval forest containing waterfalls, cascades, ferns, majestic trees, fine views and other delights. Five kilometres from the start an 800 m long branch leads down to the spectacular waterfall known as *Debegeni* (place of the big pot) on account of the deep pool shaped like a pot at the foot of the waterfall. The Ramadipa River, which feeds the waterfall, is a powerful flow of clear water. In former times the tribespeople believed that this waterfall was the home of several spirits. They left presents of food and beer beside the pool to be consumed overnight by supernatural diners.

Swimming and picnicking at the foot of the Debegeni Waterfall is allowed, but no camping. The rocks are very slippery and several people have been killed trying to climb the waterfall or attempting too much of the big slide.

It was in 1894 in this sylvan setting that a vicious petty war was fought between the Transvaal Government and the Tlou tribe of the chief Makgoba, whose name, corrupted to Magoeba, is applied to the valley today. Times were generally restless and there was resistance to paying taxes. Makgoba's followers (about 500 warriors) made so skilful a use of the deep forests of the gorge that the Government punitive force found it exceedingly difficult to dislodge them. Only in 1895 was Makgoba finally cornered in his forest retreat. A party of Swazi warriors fighting on the government side tracked him down. In single combat he was defeated and his head cut off. Today only his name lingers on in memory of a long-forgotten mini-war.

Beyond the turn-off to the Debegeni Waterfall, the gravel road follows a steep and very lovely route through mixed patches of dense indigenous forest and plantations. After 3 km the road passes De Hoek Forestry Station. A further 2 km brings the road to a camping ground with simple facilities, in a woodland setting.

At 11 km from the Debegeni Waterfall, the road reaches the summit and joins the main gravel road leading from the Tzaneen–Pietersburg road to Woodbush. A turn left along the road brings the traveller after 5 km to the main tarmac road at the top of the Magoebaskloof Pass 25,5 km from Tzaneen, thus ending a very fascinating drive. Just before joining the tarmac road, a forestry road passes a memorial to Alexander James O'Connor (1884–1957), a one-time director of forestry who was responsible for much of the afforestation of this area. He was the first forester of the Woodbush district.

The Woodbush forestry station is reached on turning right at the junction of the road coming up from the Debegeni Waterfall and De Hoek. This is another magnificent drive along the edge of the escarpment. A particularly fine view may be had from a site 600 m from the junction. At 6,5 km from the junction, the road reaches the Woodbush forestry station, always renowned for its trees. Heavy rainfall and deep, rich granite soil are ideal for trees such as yellowwoods, red stinkwoods, ironwoods, cabbage trees and many others, including the lovely *Ochna o'connorii* (redwood) named after the pioneer forestry officer in the district. The spring leaves of this tree are first a deep red, changing to green, while its masses of flowers are a brilliant yellow in late spring and its seeds are red. The resulting colour combinations are dazzling.

Beyond the Woodbush forestry station, the gravel road continues through beautiful avenues of oak trees, plantations and indigenous forest where moss drapes the trees. At 5 km from the forestry station the road reaches the wall of the D A P Naude Dam, built in 1958 to supply Pietersburg with water. There is a fine camping ground beneath the trees. The area is popular with anglers for the Broederstroom River is amply stocked with trout. Permits for camping must be obtained from the forestry office. Fishing permits must be obtained from *The Elms*, Haenertsburg.

After a further 2 km the gravel road leaves the area of the Woodbush forestry station. Continuing down the verdant valley of the Broederstroom, it passes beautiful farms such as *Greymists* and *Cloudlands*. At 13 km from the Woodbush forestry station it joins the Magoebaskloof–Haenertsburg gravel road which, after 9,5 km, joins the main tarmac Tzaneen–Pietersburg road. Many interesting side roads in this area lead through fine scenery. Although they meander considerably these roads all eventually take the traveller to some identifiable junction with a main road. Particularly lovely is the drive to *Houtbosdorp* (wood bush town), actually just a trading station, and thence to Duiwelskloof, a route described further on in this chapter.

GEORGE'S VALLEY AND THE LETABA VALLEY

This circular route (the first part being the main Tzaneen–Pietersburg road) provides one of the loveliest drives in Southern Africa. The 15 km section from Tzaneen to the turn-off to the De Hoek forestry area and the Debegeni Waterfall has already been described. Beyond this gravel turn-off, the main R71 road winds and climbs steadily for 10,5 km, before reaching the summit of Magoebaskloof. The scenery is superb, grand views being revealed of tree-covered mountain slopes and the lowveld stretching off to the east like a mysterious green sea.

The two great tea estates – *Grenshoek* and *Middelkop* – of *Sapekoe* (South African tea, from the Chinese word *pekoe* for tea) cover vast areas of the hill slopes with a dense green blanket constantly moistened by sprinkler irrigation. In 1963 tea cultivation was started in South Africa on these estates. Douglas Penhill, former managing director of the Kenya Tea Development Association, was persuaded to immigrate to South Africa. With the Industrial Development Corporation providing finance, and experts recruited from several tea-growing areas of the world, the venture proved successful. Tea of a quality considered excellent on the international market is now being produced to a significant extent. The estates are continually active: plucking from September to May, pruning in June and July, and tidying in August.

Half-way up the valley (22,5 km from Tzaneen) lies the Magoebaskloof Lodge and above it a fine viewsite. At 25,5 km from Tzaneen, the road reaches the summit and the gravel turn-off to the Woodbush area already described, including the circular route back to Tzaneen past the Debegeni Waterfall. The main tarmac R71 road continues towards Pietersburg, 69 km away. After a further 3 km the road passes the Magoebaskloof Hotel, at the head of the spacious valley.

Just beyond the hotel, there is a gravel turn-off which leads southwards through fine scenery for 9 km to the Ebenezer Dam and, at 12 km, joins the tarmac road running down George's Valley to Tzaneen. The tarmac road to Pietersburg passes this turn-off and the Stanford College, a private English high school.

A further 5 km brings the road to a junction just outside the old mining and forestry village of *Haenertsburg*, named after C F Haenert, whose discovery of gold was the start of a small rush in 1887 to what was called the Woodbush gold-field. Haenertsburg is a picturesque and amiable little place in a spectacular mountain setting. There is an unusual war memorial and Long Tom Monument commemorating everybody who lost their lives in the various South African wars. There are several hiking trails into an area of pure fresh mountain air, waterfalls, lakes, forests and wild flowers; birds and interesting little mammals abound. There is a hilltop cemetery fully worth a visit even if you don't intend to stay.

The R71 road proceeds westwards from Haenertsburg for 61 km to Pietersburg. A magnificent return route to Tzaneen is provided by taking the R528 tarmac turn-off branching southwards, an opportunity which should not be missed.

Passing the Ebenezer Dam, completed in 1958 and designed to stabilise the flow of the Letaba River, the tarmac road is joined by the gravel road which branched off from the top of Magoebaskloof. A series of lovely cascades in the Letaba River is passed and the road leads on down the valley known as George's Valley, 11 km from the turn-off. Overlooked by the towering Wolkberg, this valley received its name from George Deneys, a road ganger who lived there. He was an amiable soul who liked his work so much that he often included detours in his roads to allow travellers a better chance of viewing the scenery. Aloes and flowering shrubs were also planted to beautify the verges, and seats and picnic tables made of rock are scattered along the wayside for the relaxation of passers-by.

The road descends the escarpment through George's Valley in a sweeping pass, with massive mountains overlooking the Bergplaas plantation and the lush farmlands of the Letaba valley with their crops of subtropical fruit and nuts. The road terminates at Tzaneen, 50 km from the top of Magoebaskloof. It is altogether a magnificent 75,5 km circular route.

THE WOLKBERG CAVES

On *Mizpah* farm, on the lower slopes of the 2 128 m high *Wolkberg* (cloudy mountain) there is a remarkable sequence of caves. They were discovered in 1927 when Jan Meintjes, son of the owner of the farm, was out hunting. He shot and wounded a mountain reedbuck. With the hunter's dog in hot pursuit, the reedbuck ran for safety. Meintjies followed the trail of blood. He found that both animals had fallen down a 20 m shaft. There was a wild fig tree at the top of the shaft, with its roots growing down the side.

Meintjies descended the shaft with the aid of the roots. He found his dog and the reedbuck both dead from their fall. At the bottom of the shaft a tunnel led away into pitch darkness. Meintjies did not have a torch. He climbed out of the shaft and went home to tell his family of his discovery. With his elder brother, he returned to the shaft, taking ropes and torches. They hauled the two dead animals to the surface and then set out to explore the cave. They found themselves in a veritable underground fairyland, a sequence of passageways and chambers decorated with speleothems. The floor was covered with what looked like snow. Dripstone formations in spectacular variety gave each successive chamber the appearance of a subterranean art gallery.

An underground lake blocked easy access to the real depths of the caves. Exploration is still ongoing by the Cave Research Organisation and South African Underwater Diving Union. The farm was bought by the Transvaal Provincial Administration (now Northern Province). It is now protected from exploitation by miners extracting bat guano or destroying flowstone formations to make lime.

The caves are not open to the general public as the entrance is difficult. There are plans for future visits by conducted parties prepared to canoe over the calm waters of the underground lake and, in exchange for a strenuous effort of caving, see the full beauty of an underground world of enchantment.

From Tzaneen, the lowveld tarmac R36 road continues northwards past the great dam in the Letaba River and thence up a densely wooded valley, passing the turn-off to Magoebaskloof (4 km); the *Westfalia* estate of the late eminent geologist, Dr Hans Merensky, its romantic-looking man-made lake in a setting reminiscent of Tchaikovsky's *Swan Lake*; the turn-off to Politsi; the tree-breeding station of the Forestry Department at Zomerkumst; and the tea plantations of Sapekoe at Grenshoek. At 18 km from Tzaneen, the road reaches the picturesque little town of ...

DUIWELSKLOOF

The name *Duiwelskloof* (glen of the Devil) originally belonged to a farm. It is said to have been given on account of the sticky mud which impeded the passage of transport wagons in the old days. Rainfall is normally high in the area, but modern tarmac roads have defeated the mud and travellers may therefore admire without difficulty the forest-covered, intensely green hills which crowd the valley. Gardens are magnificent. Especially notable are bougainvillaea, poinsettia and frangipani in many colours; jacaranda trees which flower in October and November; potato trees, flowering in December and January; bauhinia creepers, cassias and acacias, flowering in January. Duiwelskloof is a rail centre for the timber and subtropical fruit-growing industry. It was proclaimed a village in 1920. The population of Duiwelskloof is 647.

DRIVES FROM DUIWELSKLOOF

The plantation and forest covered hills around Duiwelskloof are threaded with roads which take the venturesome traveller to many interesting places. A short but very beautiful drive leaves the village centre via Mabel Street, climbing the hill slopes west of Duiwelskloof. After 2,5 km, there is a branch left leading to a private estate. Continuing right, the road (at 5,5 km) enters the *Westfalia* estate of the late Dr Hans Merensky, always to be remembered for his work in the discovery of platinum and diamond deposits in South Africa. For 8 km the road winds through the trees of this fine estate, then crosses the railway line and joins the main Tzaneen–Duiwelskloof road at a point 5,5 km from Duiwelskloof. The round trip is 19 km long.

A very spectacular drive through the tree-covered hills begins opposite the old railway station of Duiwelskloof. Turn left up the road marked Modderspruit, which climbs the slopes of the 1 368 m Dickiesberg. After 2,5 km there is a fork; the right turn, marked Weltevreden, should be taken. After 3 km of climbing, the road tops the summit at a magnificent viewsite known as World's View. From this site may be seen a breathtaking panorama over the Letaba valley, with Tzaneen in the middle distance. In the background looms the great range of the Drakensberg dominated by peaks such as the Wolkberg and Kruger's Nose.

From the viewsite the road descends steadily through plantations of tall gum trees. At 9,5 km it passes through the indigenous forest known as the Donald Grant Nature Reserve, preserved by his family in memory of a local farmer who was killed during the Second World War. At 11 km the road joins the main tarmac road linking Tzaneen with the realm of Modjadji and her Lobedu tribe. A right turn leads for 14 km to join the main tarmac Tzaneen–Duiwelskloof road at a point 10,5 km from Duiwelskloof. The total distance for the round trip is 35,5 km.

If the traveller turns left at the junction with the Tzaneen–Modjadji road, he will enjoy an equally fine drive stretching 21 km from the junction and returning to Duiwelskloof, a total of 32 km. This road passes the turn-off leading to *Narina*, the home and private nature reserve of the late naturalist, artist, author and great character of the lowveld, Charles Thomas Astley Maberly. Named after the gorgeous *Narina trogon* birds who live there, this little sanctuary of nature was used by 'Mabs' (as he was known) as his own retreat where he studied and painted birds and game. Wild boars, monkeys and many other animals made the place their home and lived on such amiable terms with the beloved Mabs that it would have been easy to believe stories that he, like Dr Doolittle, could talk to them. He was brutally murdered in his home in 1972 by some vagrant, but his memory will continue to linger over an area he knew and loved so well.

THE REALM OF THE RAIN QUEEN

Duiwelskloof is the principal centre for the tribal area of the Lobedu people, the ruler of whom, with the dynastic title of *Modjadji*, is the famed Rain Queen whose mystic reputation and claim to eternal life provided Rider Haggard with the idea for his novel *She.*

The Lobedu (pronounced Lo-bair-du) tribe is an offshoot of the Karanga people of Zimbabwe, whose unique culture of building stone walls around their settlements has enriched the country with so many interesting ruins. During the 16th century a princess of this tribe fled south with a few followers, eventually finding a sanctuary in the valley of the Molototsi. The princess had carried with her full knowledge of the rain-making magic of her ruling family. She and her successors used this magic to considerable effect, instilling in tribes as far away as Swaziland a fear that if they offended the Lobedu queen, she would withhold the rain. The successive queens of the Lobedu tribe found it politic to remain invisible. Legend spread that *Modjadji* (the ruler of the day), as the Lobedu queens were titled, was immortal. Terror caused by the stories of magic powers of this strange being not only protected the tribe from being attacked, but brought them prosperity from the propitiatory gifts sent to the queen.

The inner secrets of Modjadji remain a mystery. The ritual of rain-making is highly complex, involving strange sacrifices and many magic ingredients – some gruesome, such as the skins of previous Modjadjis who, becoming too old to rule, were obliged to sip poison from a cup and were then secretly replaced by a young person. Modjadji is now far more accessible but is not likely to be seen on a casual visit.

From Duiwelskloof the main tarmac road leading northwards up the valley towards Muketsi and Munnik should be taken. After 5,5 km there is a turn-off right leading to Modjadji's capital. At 9,5 km there is a turn-off left to Leeudraai, and at 11 km another turn-off left stretching to gaKgapane, the offices of the baLobedu regional authority. It is essential to secure a permit from the administrative officer here. *Kgapane* was a chief of that area.

Beyond the turn-off the road continues for a further 2,5 km to a turn-off leading to the *Medingen* Mission, named after its benefactor in Germany, the Fraulein Von Meding. Shortly afterwards (14,5 km from Duiwelskloof) there is a junction. Straight ahead, the road stretches on towards Tzaneen in the drive already described, passing the old home of Charles Maberly and after 6,5 km the turn to Duiwelskloof via World's View.

Turn sharp left to reach Modjadji's capital. The road leads eastwards down the densely settled valley of the Molototsi – well wooded, warm and overlooked by high hills. After 10 km there is a turn right running for 4 km up to the slightly cooler heights where Modjadji's capital lies, 27,5 km from Duiwelskloof.

Modjadji's capital is a rather dusty and hot place, shaded by a few wild fig trees. It is necessary to pay a fee for sightseeing at the tribal office. The queen's courtyard is worth a glimpse but visits to the whole place are complicated by hordes of urchins who need to be very resolutely handled. One guide should be obtained from the tribal office and all visitors should take the short drive (3 km) to the summit of the ridge, where there are fine views and a remarkable forest of cycads may be seen. December to February sees many of these strange plants in seed and there are also scarlet bauhinia creepers, yellow and white acacias and other flowering plants. The hill ridge is possessed by a wild, primeval loveliness, like some lost island rising steeply above the surrounding ocean of bush. Ancient stone walls are being excavated.

A careful watch must be kept for urchins who damage motor vehicles by climbing on them or by pilfering from them. The cycads are protected plants and urchins offering to sell seedlings should be discouraged. There is a picnic ground with facilities for barbecue.

From Duiwelskloof the main tarmac R36 road continues northwards, passing the turn-off to Modjadji (5,5 km) and, after 16 km, the vegetable-farming centre of *Muketsi* (a fertile place where crops multiply). Just beyond Muketsi, the road divides. The left-hand division, R81, in a spectacular climb, ascends the escarpment to Munnik (21 km) and from there crosses the highveld plateau to join the N1 road to reach Pietersburg (58 km). The right-hand turn is the continuation of R36. It climbs the escarpment, reaches the railway junction of *Soekmekaar* (seek each other), said to have been given to it by two surveyors, Devenish and Rissik who, working in the area at a time of heavy mist, got lost and spent some days wandering about trying to find each other.

The R36 road continues from Soekmekaar, passes *Groot Spelonke* (the great cave) and then, after 45 km from Muketsi, joins the N1. From Muketsi a gravel turn-off left provides another spectacular route up to the highveld, past the trading centre of Houtbosdorp (36 km from the turn-off) and thence over the 2 000 m high summit ridge into the lovely Woodbush forestry area already described, and to places such as Magoebaskloof (53 km) where the main Tzaneen–Pietersburg road is joined.

TZANEEN TO NELSPRUIT

From Tzaneen the fine tarmac R71 road stretches south-eastwards through a veritable garden of subtropical fruitlands, with wayside stalls offering produce to passers-by. Rich, deep soil, rain, mountain streams and near-tropical warmth combine with industrious man to transform this entire area into a farmland of immense productivity. On the western side stretches the Drakensberg; to the east the mighty bushveld extends seemingly to the other side of the Earth. In August the citrus groves are laden with both fruit and sweet-smelling blossoms. Bougainvillaeas in many shades grow to perfection and the wild flowers of spring are profuse.

After 27,5 km the road crosses the Letaba River and 1 km beyond it a tarmac road R529 turn-off leads north-eastwards to *Eiland* and *Letaba* ranch. This turn-off passes vast citrus groves and a succession of homesteads notable for their gardens and flowering trees such as poincianas and silver oaks. After 35 km the road enters the ...

HANS MERENSKY NATURE RESERVE

In October 1950 the Transvaal Provincial Administration purchased the farm *Eiland* (island), named from the presence of an island in the Letaba River which flows through the property. In a small marsh on this farm, a thermal spring bubbles to the surface with an occasional surge of gas.

The flow of water – about 180 184 *l* an hour – remains at a constant temperature of 104°C. From early times it had been used by the local Africans as a source of salt and as a medicinal treatment for rheumatism.

Other farms were added to *Eiland* and the whole was proclaimed a nature reserve. The area around the spring was transferred to the Mineral Baths Board of Trustees (later Aventura), who transformed the area into a holiday resort, possessing a restaurant, garden and a variety of accommodation built in a parklike setting of indigenous trees. The thermal spring is fed into a large open-air swimming-bath surrounded by lawns.

The rest of the nature reserve – a parkland of mopane and combretum trees – was conserved as a sanctuary for game animals and a very rich bird life. Dr Hans Merensky, the prospector and mining magnate, provided a fully equipped borehole. The administration named the place in his honour, as he had played a large part in mining developments in nearby Phalaborwa. The reserve shelters a growing population of impala, zebra, blue wildebeest, sable, kudu, waterbuck, wart hog, duiker, steenbok, klipspringer, bushbuck, reedbuck, eland, giraffe, tsessebe and Sharpe's grysbok.

The tarmac road traverses the Hans Merensky Nature Reserve and, 3 km from the entrance, passes the impressive cluster of buildings of the *Eiland* mineral bath. A further 5 km takes the road out of the reserve on the eastern side. The road now has a well-maintained gravel surface. It continues past several subtropical fruit and cotton estates. There are turn-offs to Rubbervale (10 km), Gravelotte (19 km) and to Phalaborwa (32 km). At 37 km from the Hans Merensky Nature Reserve the road ends at the entrance to the ...

LETABA RANCH GAME RESERVE

The reserve was an expanse of wilderness which was converted by several previous owners into a private game reserve. Adjoining the Kruger National Park, it contains a lively wild animal population: 4 000 impala, 400 wildebeest, 300 zebra, 200 buffalo, 100 kudu, 50 sable and a mixed batch of giraffe, duiker, klipspringer, steenbok, waterbuck, wart hog, hippos, crocodiles, lions, leopards, cheetahs, hyenas, wild dogs and baboons. Previous owners developed the place as a resort with a hotel and eighteen camps, each having five to nine rondavels where visitors could look after themselves and view the game at will. The reserve later became part of the Venda homeland and was made available for hunting safaris. It is not open to the public.

From the turn-off to *Eiland* the main tarmac R71 road continues southwards past Rubbervale, the rail centre where a forgotten attempt was made to produce rubber from wild vines. Twenty-five kilometres from the turn-off (53,5 km from Tzaneen) the road reaches a crossroads at the small mining and commercial centre of ...

GRAVELOTTE

Fritz Reuter, a former dragoon in the Prussian army, named this place after the battle fought on 18 August 1870 in the Franco-German War, *Gravelotte* is a railway and trading centre for mining activity in the richly mineralised Murchison Range. Gold, cinnabar, mica, felspar, silica and emeralds are produced in the vicinity, while the Alpha shaft of the Consolidated Murchison mine – the largest and richest antimony mine in the world – is the deepest sunk by man in the recovery of a base metal.

Overlooking the little centre is the 874 m high Spitskop, the highest point in the Murchison Range. The entire area is rugged and bush-covered, profusely scarred by the continuous mining activity of the past as well as of the present. It is enriched by a human story abounding with lost hopes, weird characters, dead-beats, hard-ups and never-say-diers.

THE MURCHISON RANGE

From Gravelotte a gravel road leads westwards to Leydsdorp, the former centre of the Murchison Range. At 4 km along this road there is a short turn-off to an enormous baobab tree whose hollow trunk was once used as a bar by an enterprising liquor seller. This individual, catering for some very thirsty men in a very hot climate, found that the hollow trunk kept the bottles cool, and used it accordingly.

Leydsdorp is a further 7 km beyond the baobab tree. Nothing much is left of the once roaring mining camp. It has been said that the substantial cemetery is the liveliest part of the remaining town. This is rather unfair. The cemetery may be full – drink, the Devil and the mosquitoes conquered the prospectors of the Murchison Range – but at least some of the houses along the main street are still occupied. The canteens, hotels and stores have all closed down. The local newspaper, *The Leydsdorp Leader*, first published as a neat little eight-page tabloid on 24 October 1891, is now a rare collector's piece. Its pages, filled with the excitement of the gold-rush days, read like a piece of elaborate fiction. Could such things have happened in this quiet little place?

During the last century the Murchison Range, which rises abruptly from the bush-covered lowveld, was considered remote, sinister and cursed with malarial fever, relentless heat and wild animals. In 1870 Edward Button and James Sutherland prospected the area and found gold traces in several streams in the range they named after the famed geologist, Sir Roderick Murchison. The finds were not payable. The best was in what they named the Wildebeest Gully of Mount Eureka, but even this proved disappointing. They wandered off further eastwards to another range which they named after Dr Peter Sutherland, the geologist and surveyor general of Natal. They found more traces of gold there, but again nothing really payable. In 1888, however, new discoveries of gold attracted a considerable rush of prospectors to the Murchison Range. The entire area was pegged out into claims with dozens of little mines being started by a pretty wild crowd of men.

The Murchison Range soon proved a richly mineralised area although the deposits of gold and other precious minerals and stones (such as emeralds) were patchy and erratic, and were contained in refractory ore. Very few of the mines showed worthwhile profit. In London it was said that a new grade had been added to the list of liars: a liar, a damn liar, and a prospector of the Murchison Range.

The boom days of this part of the Murchison Range began in 1888 when about 600 prospectors, lured by rumours of gold, rushed to the area, pegging many hundreds of claims. Old maps still record the names of their hopeful claims: French Bob, Homeward Bound, Horseshoe, Dirty Dick, Great Bonanza and many more.

French Bob (Auguste Robert) was the leading prospector in this rush. Around his camp, pitched on the site of Leydsdorp, mushroomed a commercial and administrative centre comprising shacks, stores and bars. In 1890, this place received the name of the then State Secretary, Dr Willem Leyds. The Government laid out a town as the seat for a mining commissioner for what was called the *Selati Gold-Fields*, after Shalati, chieftainess of the Tebula tribe who lived in those parts.

The first rush soon petered out but others followed. Since then there has always been some mining (and quite a lot of salting) in the Murchison Range. Leydsdorp went into a long decline, with waves of men coming and going but always leaving behind a few hopefuls to keep at least a fragment of the town alive.

It was to serve this erratic mining area that the notorious Selati Railway Company was floated in Brussels on 2 February 1892. From its inception this company was a fraud. A pair of Continental company promoters secured a concession to build a railway from Komatipoort to a terminus in the Murchison Range, at a point somewhere on the stream known as the *Selati*, from the local tribal chieftainess of that name. The swindling, intrigue and double-crossing surrounding this so-called Selati railway contributed to a very involved story. Contractors are said even to have put additional curves into the line in order to make it longer. By the time construction started in 1893 there was almost nothing for the railway to serve. The line never penetrated the bush further than the Sabie River bridge in the present Kruger National Park. However, a vast amount of money was mulcted from investors in Europe and from the Government of the South African Republic. The promoters eventually landed in gaol but the money was never recovered. The line was only completed in 1922 to serve the farming and forestry industries around Tzaneen and to carry copper to the coast from Messina.

On the 33 km journey through the Murchison Range from near Gravelotte, the railway and the R526 road together find a way past emerald, mica and other mines. Claim beacons are scattered all over, and the treasures still hidden in the ground remain a challenge to prospectors. The road eventually links up with the R71 tarmac road, and the railway with a heavy mineral line from Phalaborwa. The Murchison Range area still shelters a fair number of wild animals. Kudu and giraffe are frequently seen from the road. A drive through the Range at night can be rewarding.

From Gravelotte the main tarmac R71 turns eastwards and, passing the mine workings of the Consolidated Murchison Ltd and the huge *Croc Ranch*, proceeds across a level, tree-covered plain. After 45 km there is a turn-off to the Kudu rest camp. A further 6 km takes the road to a junction with the tarmac R526 road coming up from Mica and the south. Ahead looms a line of oddly shaped hillocks. Immediately beyond them, 61 km from Gravelotte, lies the mining town of Phalaborwa, with the entrance gate to the Kruger National Park 4 km further on. This entrance gate is open throughout the year from dawn to dusk.

PHALABORWA

Phalaborwa is a town with a spectacular past. Geologists say that about 2 000 million years ago a gigantic volcanic eruption took place in the area. A volcanic pipe resulted, richly loaded with minerals and metals such as phosphate, copper, zirconium, vermiculite, iron, mica and gold. On the surface the mouth of the pipe is 10 square kilometres in extent. It was first discovered by a party of skilled metal workers from the Karanga tribe of Zimbabwe who wandered southwards through this area many generations ago. Finding themselves in a fever area, they retraced their steps to a wild parkland contained by rocky hillocks rising sharply from the plain, an area they found to be more salubrious. They named the region and themselves *Phalaborwa* (better than the south) and settled there, mining iron and copper at the base of the rocky outcrop known as the *Lule* (steep hillocks).

At the beginning of this century European miners rediscovered the prehistoric workings. Men such as William Valentine, Tucker, Cleveland and Scannell defied the curse of fever to work copper in the area. In 1938 the Transvaal Ore Company commenced mining vermiculite from the world's largest known deposit. In 1935 the Merensky Trust amalgamated Vermiculite (Pty) Ltd and the Phalaborwa Phosphate Co.

Phosphate production by the Phosphate Development Corporation Ltd (established in 1952) resulted in the birth of the town of Phalaborwa. It was laid out and in 1957 proclaimed a business, recreational and administrative centre for the area.

Forskor (the Phosphate Development Corporation), a multi-million rand concern, was financed by the Government through the Industrial Development Corporation. The purpose was to make South Africa self-sufficient as far as possible in the vital phosphate concentrate used in agricultural fertilisers and hitherto largely imported from Morocco. At Phalaborwa there are sufficient reserves of apatite to provide Southern Africa with phosphatic requirements for hundreds of years.

Close to the apatite deposit is a huge outcrop of copper ore. The Phalaborwa Mining Company Ltd, another multi-million rand project financed by a consortium of international companies, is delving into a deposit estimated at 300 million tons. In place of the once-solid Lule kop, a colossal opencast working 1,5 km long and 2,4 km wide is being excavated by bulldozers at a rate which, per day, fills 2 000 vehicles, each containing 40 tons. The intention is to mine 12 million tons of ore a year, producing 80 000 tons of copper, not only supplying South African requirements of blister and anode copper, but leaving two-thirds of the outcrop for export. Of this output, 45 per cent is exported to West Germany. Magnetite (iron ore) is also produced in the area and 8 million tons of concentrate are sent to Japan each year.

With a total of 10 713 inhabitants, the town of Phalaborwa was spaciously laid out on the farm *Laaste* in a natural parkland setting. It was proclaimed in July 1957. Watered by 457 mm of rain a year, and basking in a summer temperature of around 37,7°C, it is a garden town enhanced by flowering trees (flamboyants, jacarandas, frangipani), bright flowers and intensely green grass.

Five kilometres before the tarmac road enters Phalaborwa from Gravelotte, the tarmac R40 turn-off south leads through woodland so dense and level that it seems like a green ocean in the midst of which odd islets of rocky hillocks provide occasional landfalls. After 8 km the road passes the Andrew Motel. At 38 km the road reaches a junction with the R526 road coming directly from Gravelotte (33 km). Five kilometres from this junction (43 km from Phalaborwa) the tarmac road passes the small mining and rail centre of Mica, comprising a store, station and some storage sheds shimmering in the heat. Mica may be seen glittering in nearly every rock.

Four kilometres south of Mica, the road crosses the Olifants River – a fine, typically African river full of hippos, crocodiles and fish. The flat bushveld scenery is interrupted by a line of weirdly shaped hillocks. A further 2 km sees a turn-off to the Hippo Pools holiday resort.

The R40 road continues southwards, with the Drakensberg looming to the west over the sea of bush. Several private game reserves are maintained in the area and game animals such as giraffe are often seen. At 22 km from the Hippo Pool turn-off the road reaches the communications, road and rail centre of *Hoedspruit* (hat stream), consisting of a cluster of stores and a motel standing at a crossroads where a tarmac road branches off westwards to the Abel Erasmus Pass and to Lydenburg. (see Chapter Thirty-Six). The South African Airforce has a base here.

Seven kilometres south of Hoedspruit there is a tarmac turn-off east which leads to Ingwelala and the entrances to the nature reserves of Klaserie and Timbavati. Both these reserves consist of blocks of farms, each owned by private individuals or companies. No fences divide the farms. Individual owners maintain their own residences and rights. Wild animals roam at will. The owners collectively employ a staff of a warden and rangers to control the reserves.

Klaserie is the largest of the reserves but is not open to the public. It takes its name (in corrupted European form) from the river called Motlasedi.

Timbavati takes its name in corrupted form from a river correctly named the *Mbabati* (place of the bushbuck). There are 25 farms in this 75 000 ha private nature reserve. Three of these farms accept guests and offer accommodation in attractive, atmospheric lodges. Guests are taken by couriers on game-viewing drives in open vehicles and are given a close encounter of an exciting kind with the wilderness by day and night. There are bush camps, hiking trails and hides. Wildlife is prolific and includes the occasional sighting of a rare white lion. The Timbavati game lodges are named *Motswari* (to cherish); *Mbali* (blossom); *Ngala* (lion); and *Tandatula* (like the quiet).

The road leading to the wildlife areas is tarmac for the first 17,5 km until it crosses the Klaserie River. At 31 km there is a gravel turn to Acornhoek, with a turn-off to Ngala Lodge 7 km along this road. The main gravel road continues eastwards. At 36 km there is a turn-off to Tandatula Lodge; at 38 km the entrance to the Klaserie Reserve; at 40 km the entrance to the Ntsiri Nature Reserve; and at 44 km the entrance to Ingwelala. At 45 km there is an entrance to Motswari Game Lodge. The road ends on the boundary of the Kruger National Park, 50 km from its start on the main Hoedspruit road. There is no public entrance here to the Kruger National Park.

From the turn-off to the above-mentioned private nature reserves, the R40 road from Hoedspruit continues south. At 23 km from Hoedspruit there is a tarmac turn-off leading to the trading station of Casketts, the Thornybush Game Lodge, and the Cheetah Inn. Thornybush consists of a 4 000 ha expanse of wilderness and a comfortable lodge. The area is well populated with wild animals, especially cheetah. There are game drives day and night.

Beyond the turn-off to Casketts, the main tarmac road continues for another kilometre and then, 24 km from Hoedspruit, reaches the small rural centre of Klaserie where a tarmac road branches north-westwards to Kampersrus, Swadini and to the Abel Erasmus Pass.

Seven kilometres further south, the main tarmac road reaches a turn-off leading eastwards for 3 km to the rural centre of Acornhoek. From this centre there is a road (38 km long) leading to the Orpen Gate of the Kruger National Park, open daily from dawn to dusk. The road leads through game country and provides an interesting drive.

Acornhoek, which seems to have received its curious name as a result of a mispronunciation of the Afrikaans *eekhorinkie* (squirrel), is the centre for a large area settled by African people. From it a tarmac road leads south-eastwards for 10 km to a turn-off to the railway station of Rolle. From this turn-off the road, now gravel, continues for a further 33 km, reaching the entrance to ...

MANYELETI GAME RESERVE

This reserve was opened on 27 June 1967 for particular use by the African tourist and lover of wildlife. At 3 km from the entrance there is a fine camp from where a network of game-viewing roads explore an area of bush adjoining the Kruger National Park. The name *Manyeleti* (place of the stars) comes from a stream and marsh in which the reflections of the stars are notable. Originally the reserve consisted of five privately owned farms whose owners used them principally for shooting. In the 1960s these farms were bought by the then Department of Bantu Affairs for the purpose of converting this handsome piece of wilderness into a game reserve. Its popularity is such that over 30 000 people visit it each year.

The Manyeleti Game Reserve contains a population of about 7 000 impala, 1 000 wildebeest, 500 zebra, 375 giraffe, 140 waterbuck, 16 white rhino and a number of buffalo, sable, nyala, steenbok, reedbuck, bushbuck, duiker and elephant. Amongst the predators are usually about 100 lions, 25 cheetahs and numerous leopards, hyenas, jackals, and wild dogs. Bird life is rich and there are many fine trees, notably mahogany.

The reserve is open daily from sunrise to sunset between 1 March and 15 January.

A MEMORIAL TO STEINACKER AND HIS ADVENTURERS

The savanna parkland east of the R40 road between Hoedspruit at the Sabie River has to it the subtle allure which Field-Marshal Smuts described as the intangible, siren call of the bushveld, an undefinable attraction which has drawn many people to wander off down silent glades, hunting, prospecting, following trails which led to nowhere and have long since been lost. Scattered through this lovely wilderness there are nameless graves, small piles of stones at best. Each one could tell a tale but, alas, they lie there in silence, all memories forgotten. To tempt you to wander a little yourself, I will tell you just two stories about events and people who died amongst these trees. Both concern the colourful Lt Col Ludwig Steinacker. I learned the details when I was following the trail of his strange life story and it led me into the area.

From his main base at Komatipoort (see Chapter Thirty-Six), Steinacker had several piquet posts at strategic places where his men could block communication between Mozambique and the Boer guerrilla forces operating against the British. One of these posts was a small fort built on the farm *Orinoco*, 16 km north of Bushbuck ridge. It was named *Mpisana's* after a local Shangane petty chief. The fort was garrisoned by about 30 men under the command of Captain 'Farmer'

Francis. From this fort, the garrison raided farms below the escarpment, seizing cattle and becoming a thorn in the side of the Boers.

The Boers retaliated. General Ben Viljoen ordered two of his best commandants, Moll and Schoeman, with an ample body of men, to terminate the activities of the garrison. Early on the morning of 6 August 1901, the Boer force moved silently through the bush to the fort. The garrison was completely surprised. Their intelligence officer, Buchan Brown, had assured them that the nearest Boer force was many miles away.

Their sleep was shattered by the whistles of the Boer officers. The commando rushed the fort. They cleared the outlying trenches at a jump. There was a four-metre high wall surrounding the fort. The Boers emptied their guns over the top of the wall and followed behind the bullets. There was a tough fight and the fort was theirs. Farmer Francis was killed, two of his men wounded and twenty-four taken prisoner. Six Boers were killed and thirteen wounded. Fifty African cattle guards were captured and shot out of hand. No cattle were recovered by the Boers. There was galling evidence to them that 4 000 prime animals had been sent to Komatipoort a few days before the attack.

Farmer Francis was buried near the fort. His personal belongings were bundled up and sent to his sister in England. She put the unopened bundle in a closet and forgot about it. Some time later she was tidying up and found the bundle. She opened it. Amongst her brother's things was his service revolver. She examined it wonderingly and accidentally pulled the trigger. The revolver was still loaded with the last bullet left after the fight at Mpisanas. She was shot dead.

The capture of Mpisana's fort was the last serious action involving Steinacker's men before the end of the Anglo-Boer War. Steinacker was left at a loose end. His hopes of appointment as warden of the Kruger Game Reserve, or for his troop of rough riders to be appointed a permanent border guard under his command, were denied. He tried to obtain a permanent commission or at least be granted a pension but received nothing.

Eventually he used his gratuity to go farming on *London* farm near Bushbuck ridge. He tried tobacco and coffee but failed. He was ruined and the company who owned the farm kicked him off. For a while he lived with Griffiths, the native commissioner at Graskop. Then Jack Travers of the farm *Champagne* between Acornhoek and Bushbuck ridge offered Steinacker a job as a handyman working for food, accommodation and a little pocket money.

Steinacker lived on the farm with little prospect until the outbreak of the First World War. He then became truculent and off-hand about Germany's coming victory. Travers eventually gave him notice to quit. Steinacker ignored the notice. Travers sent to Bushbuck Ridge for the police. A sergeant was sent to remove Steinacker to an internment camp. Steinacker asked the policeman to wait while he packed. After a few minutes he stumbled out of his room frothing at the mouth. In the heat and dust he fell to the ground and died from a dose of strychnine. He had a revolver, a diary full of abuse and not even a sixpence on him.

He was buried in a shallow grave with a few stones piled over him to keep hyenas away. As for the rest of the 600 men of Steinacker's Horse, and countless wanderers, adventurers and fortune seekers who followed the siren voice of the lowveld, where do they all sleep tonight?

From the turn-off to Acornhoek, Orpen Gate and Manyeleti, the main tarmac road continues south through a green, fertile area densely settled by peasant farmers. There are fine views to the west of the Drakensberg, with patches of plantations in between areas of cultivation and natural parkland.

After 30 km the R40 tarmac road starts to climb the Bushbuck Ridge, reaching the trading and administrative centre of Bosbokrand on its summit (34 km from the Acornhoek turn-off). Magnificent views are revealed of the surrounding country from the heights. A turn-off leads for 35 km to Graskop.

The Bushbuck Ridge is a densely settled area occupied mainly by Shangane people. The tarmac R40 road continues over cultivated fields with yellow flowering acacias growing on the verges and many fine views to be had over the lowveld and of the Drakensberg escarpment. The F C Erasmus Forestry and Nature Reserve of the Department of Forestry lies on the eastern side of the ridge and there is an entrance 6 km from the summit. After 9 km of travelling from the summit, the tarmac road descends the southern side of Bushbuck Ridge, passing a turn-off to Graskop (35 km). Ten kilometres from the administrative centre on the summit, the road reaches a turn-off leading through the F C Erasmus Forestry and Nature Reserve and then eastwards across the lowveld for 30 km to the small trading centre of Newington and the entrance to the ...

SABI SAND GAME RESERVE

This private nature reserve is named after the two principal rivers which flow through it. The reserve consists of a block of nineteen farms occupying 62 308 ha on the western boundary of the Kruger National Park. The area was originally surveyed by W H Gilfillan who, although the farms were buried deep in the African wilderness, gave them incongruous names such as *Nantes, Toulon* and *Alicecot.*

The farms were acquired by various owners, some of whom (such as the Transvaal Consolidated Lands Co) started ranching, while others used their properties for shooting. In 1926 one of the farms, *Sparta*, was bought by two friends, Frank Unger and Charles Varty, both engineers and nature lovers. They built a camp on a fine site overlooking the Sand River, and each winter season went there to rest and relax.

In 1927 William Alfred Campbell of Natal Sugar Estates, bought the farms *Eyrefield,* portions of *Marthly,* and *Malamala* (sable antelope). A lodge was built on *Malamala* and this became the winter hunting resort of the Campbell family. The remaining farms in the area were acquired by various other owners.

In 1934 several of these owners collectively organised the Sabi Private Game Reserve and subscribed towards the cost of appointing a full-time ranger, Donald Kirkman, who was manager of the *Toulon* cattle ranch for its owner, the Transvaal Consolidated Lands Co. The company had decided to abandon ranching and their farm was purchased by Mrs M E Whitehead, who also owned *Flockfield* and *Charleston.*

At the end of the Second World War the various owners gradually arrived at the idea of creating what they named the Sabi Sand Wildtuin, with W Campbell as president and Stephen Roche (who had bought *Toulon* from Mrs Whitehead) as chairman. Another notable change of ownership occurred in 1962 when W Campbell died. His son Urban opened *Malamala* to visitors. Two years later he sold the farm to Loring Rattray who already owned two other farms in the area, *Exeter* and *Wallingford*. The Rattray family developed *Malamala* to its present status as a major game-viewing resort with an international reputation.

On 27 January 1965 the Sabi Sand Wildtuin was proclaimed a private nature reserve. Harry Kirkman, cousin of the first warden, was then warden of the area. Better roads were built and new game-viewing lodges were opened to the public; *Londolozi* (to protect) on the farm *Sparta*, owned by the Varty family, and Sabi Sabi with two lodges; Bush Lodge, on the farm *Loodswaai*, bought in 1979 by Hilton Loom and Pieter Milne: and River Lodge on the farm *Kingston*, leased from Mrs Irene Chalkley, widow of the original landowner.

The success of *Malamala* induced the Rattrays to open two additional resorts, Kirkman's Camp and Harry's Huts. These lodges and camps are comfortable, beautifully situated and very atmospheric. The garden setting of *Malamala* is as renowned as its wild animals. Londolozi is handsomely situated with a dining-room built half-way up a huge ebony tree. The two Sabi Sabi lodges, one on the Sabie River, the other known as the Bush Lodge, are superb in their situation, design and ambience of informal elegance in the midst of the wilderness of Africa.

The Sabi Sand area is well populated with wild animals in considerable variety. The flora is equally varied with many magnificent trees. Trails burrow through a wild garden; the bird-life is prolific; and at such hides as Wart-Hog Wallow and Puzamanzi in the Sabi Sabi area, about 130 species may be seen.

The Sabi Sand Game Reserve is separated by a veterinary fence where it adjoins areas of tribal settlement. The original Selati railway line, the construction of which provided so peculiar a chapter in the history of Southern Africa, led through the western side of the area. Its route may still be seen, with an occasional grave where construction workers were buried when they died of fever, booze, fights or were killed by wild animals. Newington, where there is an entrance gate to

Sabi Sand, was once a siding on the line renowned for its lions. Passengers waiting for trains generally spent their time perched in thorn trees. The attention of the authorities having been directed to this uncomfortable state of affairs; they obligingly provided ladders to facilitate tree climbing in an emergency. The Selati line has been relocated and Newington is no longer a station.

Apart from the gate at Newington, there are entrances to Sabi Sand from the airfield at Skukuza in the Kruger National Park (*Malamala* is 24 km from the airfield and *Londolozi* 30 km) and from the main tarmac road leading from Hazyview to the Paul Kruger Gate of the Kruger National Park. The turn-off to Sabi Sand is 37 km down this road and 20 km from the Paul Kruger Gate. The Sabie River lodge is 14 km along this road.

The Sabi Sand area shares with the lowveld its atmosphere of adventure and romance inherited from the days of the safari traders, hunters, prospectors, transport riders, renegades and explorers who blazed the first trails through the bush. The Sabi Sand Game Reserve is an extremely interesting example of private nature conservation. All fences within the reserve have been removed and wildlife is completely free to roam throughout the area. Imaginative management by the various owners has seen this wild garden become one of the tourist show-pieces of Southern Africa.

Easily accessible as Sabi Sand is from the outside world, visitors are transported into an entirely different environment from the cities, pressures and artificialities of the modern human lifestyle. From accommodation in almost dreamlike lodges, they are taken on game-viewing drives by experienced ranger-couriers. Sitting in open four-wheel-drive vehicles, they are taken along tracks which burrow through the bush. Birds, mammals, trees, aromas, atmosphere and experiences are of a nature which few of the visitors have ever known before. There are night rides, dawn and sunset excursions. The vehicles penetrate deep into the wilderness, and many visitors discover for the first time that nature is within touching distance. The rangers are trained to interest their guests in observing not only big game, but all manner of small things such as beetles, lizards, trees and grasses. They provide an informed interpretation of the basic drama of life in the wilds, and of the singular behaviour and habits of all living things.

The problems of conserving wilderness are part of the fascination of visiting such an area as Sabi Sand. Always under pressure from the amorphous, mindless spread of human population and development outside its boundaries, such wilderness areas have to be cared for and many peculiar and complex influences studied. With their habitat artificially prescribed, albeit in an area as large as this, game animals are no longer free to migrate with the seasons. Their continued, rather than seasonal presence affects vegetation. The human presence and its accompanying roads, tracks, petrol fumes and waste matter also affect the wilderness. Droughts and floods, the invasion of exotic plants, all need observation and, at times, subtle control. Knowledge of these problems and discussion of them in the relaxation of the lodges is an education to many visitors. They leave Sabi Sand with thoughts and moods far deeper than just the excitement of close encounters with nature in the raw.

From the turn-off to Newington and the Sabi Sand Game Reserve the main tarmac R40 road continues south over undulating foothill country. After 4 km the road passes the Jock Caravan Park. A further 8 km takes the road past the Meriti Huts and nursery, notable for spectacular bougainvillaeas and bauhinias, as well as many other flowering plants.

A further 4 km takes the road to a turn-off leading westwards to Graskop. Immediately beyond this turn-off, the road crosses the Sabie River to reach a turn-off west to the town of Sabie. Along this road, 1,5 km away, lies the Sabie River Sun Hotel and, further along the road the Hazyview Protea Inn and the Casa do Sol Hotel, each in a setting of trees and gardens.

One kilometre beyond the turn-off to Sabie, the main tarmac road reaches a turn-off stretching east via the Paul Kruger Gate for 54 km to Skukuza in the Kruger National Park. Less than 1 km beyond this point (35 km from Bushbuck Ridge) the road reaches the small commercial centre known as Hazyview.

A further 2 km south takes the R40 tarmac road to a turn-off leading to *Kiepersol* (cabbage tree) and 1 km beyond this lies the Safari Caravan Park. At 9 km from Hazyview there is a tarmac turn-off leading eastwards for 8 km to the Numbi gate entrance to the Kruger National Park. The gate is open daily from dawn to sunset throughout the year. The landscape is rolling, fertile and profusely settled by peasant farmers. At 1 km beyond the Numbi turn-off, the main road passes a roadside market-place known as *eDayizenza* (the place where things are made and sold). A variety of locally made curios and handicrafts are sold here.

Ahead looms one of the great landmarks of the eastern lowveld, the rocky height known as *Lugogodo* or *Legogote* (place of the klipspringer). The road passes to the west of this distinctively leaning mountain. It climbs steeply up an attractive pass. At the summit it reaches an area of plantations and farms, where the Winkler Hotel is situated in the midst of a spacious garden and lawn. Two kilometres beyond this hotel is a turn-off leading to the farming centre and railway terminus named *Plaston* after an old-time ganger, Dirk van den Plas.

Another kilometre sees a tarmac turn-off leading north-westwards and providing an alternative parallel route to the main road from Hazyview. A short turn-off branches from this road to the Pine Lake Sun Hotel. After a further 3 km (37 km from Hazyview) the main road reaches the town of ...

WHITE RIVER

The situation of the town of White River is a well-watered and intensely green plateau elevated slightly above the level of the surrounding lowveld. Flowering trees shade its streets while the area is irrigated and tilled into productive farmland where vegetables, timber and subtropical fruit flourish in great variety and profusion.

White River received its name from the stream which waters the area. Known to the tribespeople as *Manzemhlope* (white waters), this fertile area attracted European settlers in the 1890s when families such as the De Beers, Swarts, Stoltz's and Wolhuters made their homes there.

After the Anglo-Boer War the so-called White River Settlement was launched for the settlement of demobilised soldiers. A 26 km long canal was dug which led water to the farm *Witrivier*. A town was laid out and a school and government buildings were erected as a nucleus. Irrigated smallholdings were provided on easy terms, but the project was a failure. It was nearly impossible to farm economically on such small units in that area. Many of the settlers went bankrupt but others, planting crops such as tobacco, managed to pull through. The White River Farmers' Association was formed but had a chequered career. By 1911 the area was practically ruined and in 1914 the *Witrivier* farm was sold to a syndicate for £10 000 on easy terms. The syndicate, mainly comprising local men, brought new life to the place. Sixty thousand citrus trees were planted. The enterprise prospered, with a branch railway being built from Nelspruit in 1926. In 1928 the White River Estate was formed to manage the area. The Danie Joubert and the Longmere dams were built to irrigate the area. Today more than one million cases of citrus are exported each year, along with pine and gum wood, vegetables, subtropical fruit and flowers. More than 2 500 farmers living on smallholdings and farms within an 8 km radius of the town, make this the most densely populated farming area in Southern Africa.

The town received its first public body, a health committee, on 29 October 1932 and became a municipality on 1 January 1974. The population now numbers 5 943.

From White River the R40 tarmac road continues southwards, passing through a fertile landscape of fruit farms, beautiful trees and flowering plants. After 4 km there is a turn-off west to Sabie and a further 3 km sees a turn-off east to Plaston, Just beyond this turn-off is a roadside market-place (known as Kraal Kraft) which sells locally made curios and agricultural produce. A further 5 km (13 km from White River) takes the road past the former Drum Rock Hotel, now the head office of the Mpumulanga Department of Environmental Affairs and Tourism. The road descends into the citrus and subtropical fruit growing valley of the Crocodile River. At 18 km from White River there is a tarmac turn-off to Sabie. The R40 road then crosses the Crocodile and, at 21 km from White River, reaches the town of Nelspruit.

Chapter Thirty-Eight
THE KRUGER NATIONAL PARK

The Swiss are credited with the establishment in 1592 of the first known prohibited hunting area. The United States of America in 1872 proclaimed the first national park at Yellowstone. In South Africa the Hluhluwe and Mfolozi game reserves were declared in 1897, and on 26 March 1898 President Paul Kruger signed a proclamation for the founding of a government game park in the Eastern Transvaal, between the Crocodile and Sabie rivers. In this way, the reserve which was to become the Kruger National Park was born.

The area placed under protection was a small portion of the present national park but contained a variety of natural forms in three main vegetative areas; a grassy, rather sour thornless parkland in the west; a strip of bush willow parkland with sweet grazing in the centre; and on the eastern side a dry acacia savanna parkland with sweet grazing. These areas provided habitats of considerable difference for many forms of animal life. The palatability of grazing largely influenced the distribution of antelope and the associated presence of predators. The eastern part of the newly proclaimed government game park was therefore a resort for the greatest numbers of wild animals.

Adversely, the area had attracted the most intensive hunting by man. So drastically had the wild animal population been reduced that it had become apparent that, without protection, none of them would survive. As an area of human settlement the new game sanctuary was limited. Malaria fever was endemic; bilharzia present in the rivers. Tsetse fly had, until 1896, killed off any domestic livestock and it had yet to be proved that the pestilential fly had disappeared during the rinderpest epidemic of that year. Its absence was noted, but it could just as suddenly reappear.

The mosquito and the tsetse fly had, therefore, prevented the settlement of human beings in the area, allowing them to play the role of temporary predators only during the winter hunting season when fever was not so prevalent. A few African people, mostly refugee elements from neighbouring tribes, found an uneasy sanctuary in the bush, but fever and bilharzia debilitated them and the tsetse fly destroyed their livestock.

The area had at least been well explored. Pathways blazed by safari traders led directly from the coast inland across the lowveld of the Eastern Transvaal. In addition, the paths were tramped by ivory hunters and slave raiders. Voortrekkers such as Louis Trichardt, Johannes van Rensburg and Hendrik Potgieter also crossed the area, trying to open communications with the Portuguese coastal ports.

The advent of the Voortrekkers to the Transvaal stimulated increasing trading traffic along the paths. Traders such as the Italian, João Albasini (the famous *Juwawa*, as the Africans called him), sent so many parties of porters carrying goods along the paths that he created a depot and staging post near Pretoriuskop and planned to turn the entire lowveld into a new Portuguese colony named the Colonoa Da Santa Luiz.

The demand for trade goods in the Transvaal soon far exceeded the carrying capacity of porters. Albasini claimed that the path his porters followed was free of tsetse and this gave rise to the hope of a wagon route. The Voortrekker settlers in the Ohrigstad area blazed the route which became known as the 'Old Wagon Road'. Although found to be not entirely free of tsetse, it came into use as the first negotiable route with no insurmountable physical difficulties such as mountains or rivers to negotiate. The name *Pretoriuskop* dates from this period, either as a result of the death there of a hunter by that name or the visit in 1865 of President Marthinus Wessel Pretorius, who travelled down the road as far as that point (a landmark on the road) to inspect the route and to indulge in a little hunting.

The discovery of gold in the Eastern Transvaal at Spitskop in 1873 opened a romantic chapter in the story of South Africa. The transport of goods along the Old Wagon Road became a way of life for a singular breed of men known as transport riders – rough, tough, resourceful, and courageous. These men and their patient spans of oxen took the lumbering wagons into the most improbable and difficult places. They paid a price for their audacity, however, by leaving the wrecks of vehicles. their graves, and skeletons of countless oxen scattered along the Old Wagon Road.

In 1875 Alois Nellmapius, the Hungarian entrepreneur formed a transport company and experimented with exotic draught animals such as camels, mules and donkeys, hoping to find them resistant to tsetse fly, but they died as easily as the oxen. The only real solution to the problem of transport was provided by the building of the railway, the Eastern Line from the coast to Pretoria. It was opened on 1 January 1895. Thus the era of the transport riders ended and the Old Wagon Road was left to its ghosts, of whom, it is reputed, there are many.

After it was proclaimed a game park, the area saw no further hunting except for the activities of poachers. The police sergeant at Komatipoort was allocated the task of looking after the 4 000 square kilometre area, but there was no further development before the outbreak of the Anglo-Boer War in October 1899. Komatipoort became the base of a rather irregular British force of cavalry known as Steinacker's Horse, after its commanding officer, a German, Lieutenant-Colonel Ludwig Steinacker. This force indulged in a good bit of hunting for the pot, but their presence at least kept out the professional game slaughterers (known as 'biltong hunters') who have been responsible for the heaviest onslaughts on wild animals in Southern Africa.

At the end of the war, the new British administration accepted the idea of the game sanctuary and appointed a warden for what was called the Sabi Game Reserve. The person selected for the post was Major James Stevenson-Hamilton, a short, peppery man of considerable intelligence, resolution, and sympathy as far as wildlife was concerned. For his headquarters the new warden selected a point on the Sabie River where the railway known as the Selati Line, a branch from the main line at Komatipoort, reached the river. Originally known as Sabi Bridge or 'Reserve', the place soon adopted the name which the Africans gave to Stevenson-Hamilton – *siKhukhuza* (he who scrapes clean). The modified form of *Skukuza* is today the name of the principal camp and administrative centre of the park. The meaning of the name is said to have derived from Stevenson-Hamilton's reputation for 'cleaning out' all illegal residents, poachers, hunters, blackbirders (illegal labour recruiters) and the like, from the area of the game reserve.

The facilities of Skukuza were at first rather primitive. The railway had been constructed in 1893 as part of a fraud perpetrated largely on overseas investors. It had never been completed and consisted of a pair of light-weight rusty rails vanishing rather unevenly into the bush, a blockhouse at the railhead and a gangers' trolley. Nevertheless, the line provided a link with the outside world, and the trolley could carry in stores.

Stevenson-Hamilton appointed to his staff two rangers, both former members of Steinacker's Horse: Gaza Gray who was stationed at Lower Sabi, and Harry Wolhuter who was stationed at Mtimba, near Pretoriuskop. The three men had to look after the entire area, patrolling on horseback or on foot. To add to their responsibilities, they had also to supervise a block of ranches lying north of the Sabie River. These ranches were in private hands but were undeveloped, with no communications or occupants.

It was in August 1903 during the investigation of a report of poaching in the area of the ranches that Harry Wolhuter had his incredible encounter with a lion. Caught after sunset in desolate country, Wolhuter came upon a lion in search of dinner. The lion was probably more interested in the horse than the rider. The horse bolted and Wolhuter fell on top of the lion which then turned its attention to him. Seizing Wolhuter by the right shoulder, the lion dragged him for 55 m, purring with gruesome satisfaction at the thought of a meal and snarling viciously each time Wolhuter's spurs caught in a root or stone.

Wolhuter lay on his back, his face pressed into the lion's mane. The stench was foul and the thought of being eaten infuriated him. He suddenly remembered his small sheath knife attached to his belt. It had always been loose, however, and he was afraid that it might have fallen off. He groped for it cautiously, the lion growling as he moved. To Wolhuter's delight the knife was still there. He drew it out. Feeling for the lion's heart beating above him he stabbed upwards twice. With a great howl of agony the lion dropped him. Before it could bite again, Wolhuter stabbed it in the throat. Drenching the prostrate ranger with blood, the lion stumbled off to die.

In fearful pain Wolhuter staggered up and managed to climb a small tree. Using his belt, he strapped himself to the trunk in case he fainted. It was just as well he did. A second lion arrived to investigate the commotion. Rearing up against the fragile tree, it gave Wolhuter a lengthy, soul-chilling stare. At this critical stage one of Wolhuter's dogs, all of whom had bolted when the lion attacked, returned to find its master. It began to bark at the lion and so goaded it that the animal left the tree and tried to catch the dog.

After about an hour, some of Wolhuter's African game guards who had ridden ahead to prepare a camp, came to find out what was delaying him. They fired shots to drive the lion away and helped Wolhuter to camp where they dressed his wounds.

At daylight they found the first lion dead with two knife-wounds in the heart. The second lion had vanished. The skin of the lion and the knife are exhibited in the library at Skukuza. Also on display is a remarkable composite knife, presented to Wolhuter by T Williams of London, the manufacturer of the knife which had saved his life. The site of Wolhuter's adventure is marked by a memorial stone and the preserved stump of the long-dead tree.

In the same year as Wolhuter's misadventure, the area of the park was considerably enlarged. Between the rivers known as the *Letaba* (sandy) and the *Luvuvhu (mvuvu,* the *Combretum glomeruliflorum* trees growing on its banks) stretched a 5 000 square kilometre extent of wilderness – hot, inclined to be arid and dominated by mopane trees. The area was proclaimed the Shingwedzi Game Reserve and placed under the control of Stevenson-Hamilton. With his small staff, however, there was nothing much he could do with the new reserve. He travelled up to inspect the area which seemed to be almost devoid of any kind of animal life.

The *Shingwedzi* (ironstone) River, after which the area was named, was lined with tall trees and contained deep pools of water, even in times of drought. At a place called Malunzane on a tributary of the Tsende River, Stevenson-Hamilton found a hut deserted by a labour recruiter for the mines. He selected this lonely place for a ranger post and in 1904 stationed there a curious character by the name of Major A A Fraser. He became one of the legends of the lowveld. He was a man whose principal diet seemed to consist of pipe tobacco and whisky, his friends a very mixed pack of dogs, and his recreation the reading and rereading of a vast collection of back numbers of *Field* magazine. He was not much interested in anything else. The area under his authority was so huge that it was not really possible to control the poachers, blackbirders and renegades who frequented it, especially at the junction of the Limpopo and Pafuri rivers, known on account of their presence as Crooks' Corner.

The area then at least partially protected included most of the present Kruger National Park, but as it consisted of three parts – the Sabi Game Reserve, the Shingwedze Game Reserve, and the block of ranches between the Sabie and Letaba rivers – there was no guarantee of permanency to this protection. Also, Stevenson-Hamilton was disturbed at loose talk of the whole area being 'thrown open' for shooting. He countered with the idea that the area should rather be consolidated into one national park and 'thrown open' to the public as a magnificent spectacle of wildlife. He realised that as long as the area remained closed to the public they could hardly be expected to support its preservation, especially as their tax money was its only means of finance.

In 1912 the Selati railway was at last completed. Only one return train a week travelled the line, but the existence of the railway generally attracted more attention to the lowveld, with much talk of future development.

The first World War broke out in 1914 and Stevenson-Hamilton went off to rejoin the army. Major Fraser, with his pack of 25 dogs, took charge of the three areas for most of the time. He was not a great man for paperwork. A story relates how he once dumped a bag of coins on the desk of a surprised magistrate and told him that it was the tax gathered from staff in the reserve. The magistrate asked for copies of vouchers and receipts. Fraser simply snorted and walked out, asking over his shoulder whether the magistrate had no memory!

One very important event occurred during the war years. In 1916 a commission was appointed by the Government to inquire into the matter of game conservation. When Stevenson-Hamilton returned at the end of the war, with the rank of Lieutenant-Colonel, he was delighted to learn that this commission had recommended that the area under protection be converted into a great national park *'where the natural and prehistoric conditions of our country can be preserved for all time'*.

The end of the war unfortunately also saw a clamour for land for the resettlement of returned soldiers. African squatters were also pressing for more land; prospectors were fossicking around in search of coal, gold, copper and other minerals. All that was needed was a big discovery to send conservation ideals to their doom on a mining tailings dump. The principal landowner north of the Sabie River, the Transvaal Consolidated Land Company, was also very restive. In 1922 they commenced ranching on the farm *Toulon,* just across the Sabie River from Stevenson-Hamilton's headquarters. They provoked a test case (which they lost) by shooting a wildebeest on the grounds that it was destroying the plants or crops by eating grass.

In the midst of this renewed controversy, the South African Railways had a real brainwave. During the winter months of 1923 they introduced a novel tourist service, a 'round-in-nine' tour by train. This tour took holiday-makers through the best scenery of the Eastern Transvaal and included a merry night in Lourenzo Marques (now Maputo). At first the tourist train was scheduled to pass through the game reserve at night without stopping, an arrangement so stupid as to be unbelievable. It was soon changed, however. The train stopped at places such as Newington (then part of the reserve) where a ranger escorted the tourists on short walks into the bush. The public adored it. At last the hitherto forbidden areas of the wilderness were open to them, and a visit to the game reserve became the most exciting prospect for any holiday.

In August 1923 Colonel Deneys Reitz, the Minister of Lands, accompanied by members of the Transvaal Provincial Council, made an inspection tour of the reserve. He left it enthusing about the concept of a national park. The Wildlife Protection Society was also agitating for a national park and the South African Railways had started featuring the game reserve in its publicity. The biggest problem, in fact, was private ownership of the country between the Sabie and the Olifants rivers. Great controversy raged over these ranches.

As a compromise, a western boundary line was devised, leaving in the area of the future park 70 privately owned ranches which had to be expropriated. The remaining ranches, forming the big block between the Sabie and its tributary, the *Moyetlamogale* (river that is fierce when in flood), known to Europeans as the Sand River, were excluded and deproclaimed. This unfortunately included some of the best sable and roan country and most of the mountain reedbuck and red duiker country in the south-west. However, the park would at least remain a self-contained block and most of these deproclaimed ranches eventually formed part of the privately owned Sabi Sand Game Reserve (see Chapter Thirty-Seven).

Before the National Parks Bill could be considered by Parliament, there was a change of Government. Fortunately, the new government (Nationalist) was also sympathetic to the concept of conservation but a delay ensued while it settled down to office. The new Minister of Lands, Piet Grobler, a grandnephew of President Kruger, was particularly enthusiastic about the idea of a national park.

During the final period of waiting there were several events. Brown locusts were plaguing the entire country in 1925 and had to be resolutely battled. Farmers along the southern border complained vociferously about the activities of lions. To deal with this, a new post was established at *Malelane* (place of the small lala palms) and a new ranger, Harold Trollope, appointed to it. An experienced hunter, he tackled the lion problem to such effect that most of the predators in the southern area were totally destroyed. Trollope, who was somewhat over-daring, took his elderly father-in-law, Glen Leary, on a leopard hunt. The leopard surprised the inexperienced Leary in the long grass, wounded him fatally. He died later in hospital.

Many enthusiasts rallied to the support of the national park concept during the final period of anxiety when it was thought that perhaps something might yet cause it to be stillborn. Keen photographers such as Colonel F R Hoare and the American, Paul Selby, distributed excellent pioneer game pictures throughout the world. Charles Astley Maberly, the artist-naturalist, wrote letters to the press and to individuals, his exquisite drawings of mammals and birds winning considerable support. The publicity department of the Railways appointed Harry Stratford Caldecott, an artist, to promote the park as a tourism attraction. In creating posters, articles and pictures, he also (in close consultation with Stevenson-Hamilton) conceived the name Kruger National Park. It was the ultimate inspiration and an apt choice, serving as both a memorial to a remarkable man and a sentimental touch to win the support of many people. The name was first used in print on 14 December 1925, in a leading article in *Die Burger,* a Cape Town morning paper.

Enemies of conservation also tried to rally. Sheep farmers sent a deputation to their members of parliament condemning the idea. Would-be landowners tried to pull individual strings. Veterinarians, whose reputation in the history of conservation in Africa is particularly notorious, also raised their voices in support of slaughter, talking hysterically about a possible return of tsetse fly to the reserve or the uncontrollable spread from there of some dire livestock disease.

Considerable negotiation took place in the acquisition of the privately owned ranches north of the Sabie. Alternative land was exchanged outside the reserve; direct purchases were made; the government-owned mining ground between the Olifants and Letaba rivers was transferred. At last, on 31 May 1926, Mr Piet Grobler moved in Parliament the second reading of the National Parks Act. There were no dissidents.

Under the administration of a board of control comprising ten members – eight appointed by Government, one by the Transvaal Administration and one by the Wildlife Protection Society – the park was launched. It was Mr Grobler's intention that each province would eventually appoint a member, the Government four and the Wildlife Protection Society one. None were to receive payment save for expenses. Politics would not influence appointments or preferments.

Stevenson-Hamilton hurried to Pretoria to congratulate and be congratulated. Piet Grobler immediately insisted that there be no more shooting of lions. The park was to be a sanctuary for all living things except man (who would alone be controlled).

It was a year of great change and activity in the newly created national park. It was the desire of the Board of Trustees that roads should be made as quickly as possible and the park be opened to visitors forthwith. The economics of the park were that the State would pay for management and maintenance, but the public would pay for development. They could hardly be expected to do that unless they could visit the park and learn to regard it as something peculiarly theirs.

The first road was laid down from Sabie Bridge to the Olifants River, the second from Sabie Bridge to Pretoriuskop; and the third from Sabie Bridge to Crocodile Bridge. The first three tourist cars entered the park in 1927, using the entrance at Pretoriuskop. Among the passengers was a seven-year-old boy, Douglas Jackaman, who was so impressed by what he saw that he later became a camp manager in the park.

No accommodation was provided for visitors; they made their own camps in thorn-bush enclosures, the only facility the park could provide. Nobody knew how the estimated 100 000 wild animals living in the park would react to motor cars of the Tin Lizzie type, so visitors carried weapons for their protection. There was never any need to use them. From the beginning the wild animals seemed completely indifferent to motor cars and tourists, as long as they remained in their vehicles.

Some of the old hands in the game reserve were glad to retire before the expected flood of tourists came. Both new and experienced rangers found themselves heavily involved with rapidly increasing tourist traffic and, until rondavels could be built, had to accommodate many visitors in their own restricted little homes. Pulling motor vehicles out of the mud, repairing broken cars, advising and entertaining visitors – all demanded considerable time until separate tourist officers could be appointed as the flow of visitors increased to justify the expense. Proper camps were built and placed in the hands of private contractors who negotiated rights of catering and trading from the Board of Trustees. These contractors varied as much as the celebrated parson's egg.

Everything was casual. Tourists could come and go at any time, day or night. Speeding was no problem – the roads were too bad – but night driving soon had to be stopped, as many wild animals were being dazzled by headlights and killed as a result.

The opening of the park to visitors throughout the year also had to be summarily ended. The effects of rain on the primitive roads was chaotic. In March 1929 a large party of round-the-world American tourists arrived by luxury train at Crocodile Bridge. With the train serving as a base, groups set out in two big trucks to visit the park. A tremendous rain storm completely bogged them down and one truck overturned on crossing a stream. People in summer dress were drenched and had to perch in thorn trees to avoid lions. Hector Macdonald, the local ranger, and his staff eventually reached them with blankets and food. They spent the night crammed into two small picket huts at a place named after the old headman, Gomondwane. The tourists regarded it as a adventure; but trouble followed when several of them contracted malarial fever. The resultant publicity was bad. From the following year (1930) only the Pretoriuskop area, with its better roads and freedom from mosquitoes, was left open throughout the year. The rest of the park was closed from the end of October until the end of May. Fortunately the Pretoriuskop area experienced its best game concentration during the summer months when several species (notably zebra and wildebeest) moved into it from the east. A large permanent camp for tourists was created there, and in 1931 a full-time camp manager, Captain M Rowland-Jones, was appointed to its control.

The popularity of the park increased at a tremendous rate. More roads and accommodation were built. Every year the number of visitors reached a new record. In 1931 it was decided to open to the public the area north of the Letaba River. For this purpose, a low-level concrete bridge was constructed across the Letaba and a road built as far as the rangers' camp of Punda Maria, where it joined the original Ivory Trail, now a proper road leading to Pafuri and laid down by the Witwatersrand Native Labour Association. The road was opened in 1933 and a new ranger, H R Kirkman, a Natal farmer and former manager of the Sabi Ranch, was appointed to the staff so that three ranger posts could be maintained in the northern area. *Punda Maria* had originally been established by the colourful ranger Captain J J Coetser who, in Swahili, jocularly named the place *Punda Maria* (striped Maria) after his wife who liked striped dresses. The name was for some time corrupted to Punda Milia.

Apart from roads and tourist accommodation, the park was confronted with the problem of water supply. Tourists needed pure water. The existing surface water supplies in many parts of the park, notably the northern areas, were so insignificant and subject to erratic drought conditions that it would never be possible for wild animals to concentrate in any appreciable numbers. The establishment of artificial water-holes seemed to be the answer but for this finance was needed.

It was the subject of boreholes that first brought the public to the aid of the park. Mr J H Cloete of Clocolan bequeathed money for the erection of a windpump. Bertram Jeary, a wildlife enthusiast from Cape Town, launched a nationwide movement to raise money for boreholes. The park authorities were quite overwhelmed at the response. Towns subscribed money; individuals such as Mrs Armour Hall and Mrs Eileen Orpen each donated money for one borehole. Mrs Orpen and her surveyor husband (J H Orpen) surveyed the western boundary and cleared bush at their own expense. Mrs Orpen presented the park with land and considerable amounts of money for water boring and windpumps. Many other benefactors followed suit. By the end of 1933, two drills were at work and within the next two years twenty productive boreholes were sunk, with windpumps erected to raise the water to the surface. Most of the water was rather saline, unpleasant to human taste, but highly palatable to wild animals.

A new problem presented itself. Some game animals prefer muddy water to clean water in such things as troughs. The most successful boreholes were those that augmented existing supplies. Lions would drink anywhere, preferring clean water; antelopes and elephants liked their drinks dirty. Elephants and buffaloes also enjoyed a muddy wallow. Such was their habit and they wanted nothing else. To encourage them to accept clean water or to remain in arid areas dependent on artificial supplies when instinct warned them to migrate because of prevailing drought, would be a time-consuming if not impossible task.

In 1938 foot-and-mouth disease spread amongst domestic livestock throughout Mozambique and the Eastern Transvaal. Veterinarians immediately resorted to large-scale extermination of all infected cloven-hoofed animals, generally making themselves unpopular amongst the local inhabitants. A great deal of panic and confusion resulted. On the one hand, movements were being restricted (motor vehicles were even being made to drive through troughs of disinfectant to prevent the tyres from transmitting the disease) but, on the other hand, cattle were being gathered in vast herds for periodic dipping or inspection. To the lay public, the position was ludicrous.

To add to the local problem, the summer of 1938–39 was excessively wet. All the rivers were in flood and vast numbers of carcasses of cattle slaughtered by the veterinarians were washed out of mass graves into which they had been bulldozed. They were swept away downriver. The stench of carcasses simply left to rot in the veld was insufferable and there was a feeling of total disgust at the mishandling of a disease whose pathology still remained a mystery. Fortunately the antelope population was highly resistant to foot-and-mouth disease and no outbreak occurred in the park. However, all domestic cloven-hoofed animals in the park, whether infected or not, were destroyed. The loss of many head of cattle, including those which had recovered from the disease, was incomprehensible and, to the African population especially, unforgivable.

At the peak of this tragedy, the Second World War broke out in September 1939. No little panic resulted over the long, unguarded border with Mozambique. Tales spread of German spies slipping backwards and forwards across the park and of planned invasion by mythical forces. The Portuguese, however, exercised reasonable control over Mozambique. Apart from alarms and excursions on the South African side nothing occurred. In fact, the wild animals benefited from the war. Poaching with guns ceased almost entirely with ammunition being used elsewhere. Until petrol was rationed during the final years of the war, more tourists – particularly soldiers on leave – visited the park than ever before, carrying its fame to many far countries. During the last three years of hostilities, only the Pretoriuskop section of the park remained open to tourists at any time during the year It seemed like old times in the rest of the park. The rangers were left in solitude and a car on the roads was considered an event.

At this time a few hermits and outcasts found their way into the wilderness, for such a place has always been the resort of the lost and lonely. In the early 1940s one particular wild man made his home along the banks of the Olifants River. For about five years he roamed around what was then a very remote stretch of country. The man was usually naked and had a number of lairs secreted in the bush. He made particular use of antbear (*aardvark*) holes which he enlarged and improved into reasonably snug retreats. He had apparently originated from the Acornhoek area where some domestic upheaval had deranged him. He lived reasonably well on roots, fruit and venison. The park tolerated his presence, if only because he seemed harmless, happy and (since the war had depleted the staff) very difficult to catch. He was an expert at hiding. If discovered, he bolted with the speed of a tsessebe, leaping over bushes as if pursued by a lion and apparently impervious to such things as thorns or fatigue.

Unfortunately he developed a habit of raiding rangers' picket posts and pilfering such items as knives, pots and clothing. A patrol of five African rangers were so irritated by one of his raids that they tracked him down to a hollowed-out antheap. At 02h00 they stormed the place. The wild man was asleep behind a fire, into which the rangers threw a blazing stick so that they would have more light. The wild man shot up and, charging through the cordon of rangers, vanished into the night.

Ranger Leonard Ledeboer then sent an anti-poaching patrol down the right bank of the Olifants River. They surprised the wild man drinking at a pool. He bolted, but this time was out of luck. He tripped over a rock; injuring his leg so badly that his flight was reduced to a hobble. The rangers pounced on him. He lay on the ground, trussed up, his eyes filled with the terror of a captured wild beast. The rangers followed the trail back to his lair which consisted of a cave filled with the spoils of many hunts and raids on picket posts. He was taken away to be tried for killing game and ended his days in a lunatic asylum.

Another outbreak of foot-and-mouth disease occurred in the Eastern Transvaal in 1944. On the double, the veterinarians again arrived with their rifles, but this time they encountered resistance. Farmers saw them off their property. At meetings with veterinarians, fat cows and calves which had completely recovered from the disease were produced. There was no further killing. A cordon system was introduced to isolate infected areas and the disease died out by itself without the slightest contamination of the park.

The end of the war in 1946 saw great changes of staff. Most momentous and sad of all was the departure of the revered warden Lieutenant-Colonel J Stevenson-Hamilton. He had been born on 2 October 1867. At the end of the war he was 79 years of age. Forty four years of his life had been spent in the park which was as much a part of him as he was of it. He had established a unique record of dedication and total service to a high ideal. To choose a replacement for such a man was singularly difficult. Once the successor had been selected, the task which confronted him would be awesome.

The choice was Colonel J A B Sandenbergh of the South African Air Force, an administrative officer of high reputation with a background of farming, hunting, and life in the Eastern Transvaal. Stevenson-Hamilton approved of him, and on 30 April 1946 the heartsore warden left his beloved 'Cinderella' (as he liked to call it) for retirement in White River, where so many others from the park have spent their last years. His book, *South African Eden*, will always remain the classic record of the early years of the park.

The park was reopened to the public in 1946 under new control. In his valediction, Stevenson-Hamilton warned that whoever controlled the future should keep a sharp watch on glib ideas such as development, improvement and scientific research; these could simply be a camouflage for exploitation. Nor should the park ever be converted into a glorified zoo and botanical garden dotted with scientific experimental stations, hotels, shops and public recreation grounds. Such developments would initiate the liquidation of all wildlife.

Reflecting on his years in the park, Stevenson-Hamilton had even regretted the period of predator control. For a while this had been carried out with the good intention of rapidly replenishing the antelope population by protecting them from predation. To him, everything had its place in nature, which could quite happily function without the management of man. If things were left alone, the balance would be restored. Man's interference only deformed nature, the tides of which would still inexorably take their course. A national park was essentially a place where man could stand aside and watch the creative force of nature at work. He could study and compare its changes to those made by himself in the outside world. The comparison, whether good or bad, would always be instructive.

Sandenbergh did not completely agree with Stevenson-Hamilton. He reintroduced predator control but banned controlled burning which has always been a subject of great controversy. To an airman flying the length of Africa, the characteristic scene below him is not (as some would have it) the glint of sunshine on empty bottles and tin cans but one of columns of smoke rising to the heavens from the incessant fires of the shifting cultivation of peasant farmers, or the wanton destruction caused by accidental conflagration. In a continent where rainfall is generally confined to a few months a year, the rest of the year sees the land so dry that any spark is enough to start a fire. A particularly wet season produces long grass which cannot be disposed of by the insufficient animal population. It dies in the dry season and becomes a menace. Safety precautions are taken in the form of the fire-breaks burned into mountain sides and bush by foresters and rangers, leaving hideous geometric patterns. Deliberate burning is also practised in order to remove dead grass, stimulate new growth and prevent vegetative changes. But fire is as ruthless a tool as the rifle of the hunter. Mistakes are unremediable and the gross pollution of the atmosphere by smoke is offensive to all the senses. A great deal of research has still to be done on this subject and one of the park's deficiencies was a lack of systematic information on which management could rely for the creation of policies.

A vast amount of study was waiting to be done. On the practical side, the park was also completely unfenced; tourist accommodation was very patchy; trading arrangements with the various private concessionaires left much to be desired; and the fact that 38 376 tourists visited the park in the first season of its reopening was a warning that there would soon be a human flood to control, shelter, supply and feed. The visit to the park in 1947 of the British royal family, and their accommodation at Skukuza in specially built luxury cottages, gave the place tremendous post-war publicity. Every dignitary, touring sports team, and nearly every visitor to South Africa, wanted to see the park. As the park was obviously destined rapidly to become one of the great tourist attractions of the world, its management would require delicacy and skill.

Water supplies continued to cause serious problems. Sandenbergh launched another 'water-for-game' fund which brought in money for a further 46 boreholes. Biological research was also commenced with the appointment in 1951 of a biologist and senior research officer.

Major changes in the entire administrative structure of the park were also imminent. The relatively easy, romantic years were over. In February 1952 a Pretoria firm of accountants headed by Professor P W Hoek, was appointed by the Board of Control to investigate the administration and to make recommendations for more efficient and economical handling. The so-called Hoek Report was submitted in August 1952 and, with a considerable portion of its contents being highly confidential, was for some years the subject of controversy. One of its recommendations was that the Board be reduced in size to six specialist members appointed by the Minister of Lands, and that this board – consisting of a naturalist, biologist, accountant, tourism expert, nominee of the Wildlife Protection Society, and a practising civil engineer – should elect a chairman who would be the Director of National Parks. Directly responsible to him and his board would be a head of biological services, a controller, and a head of tourism and development.

The Board, however, decided to appoint a full-time park director, to whom the departmental heads would be subordinate. This post was advertised in January 1953. Out of 80 applicants from all over the world, Mr Rocco Knobel was appointed to the post on 1 April 1953. The son of a missionary in Botswana, he had a background of administrative work in such positions as assistant director of the Johannesburg Municipal Welfare Department and as chief professional officer of the *Armesorgraad van die Witwatersrand* (Council for the Care of the Poor of the Witwatersrand). The warden of the park was from then on left purely in charge of conservation, while control of tourists became the responsibility of a tourist manager in the person of H C van der Veen who had formerly been the principal officer in that department.

Colonel Sandenbergh resigned at the end of 1953 and the then senior ranger, Louis Steyn, was appointed to succeed him. The following year experienced good rains after a long dry spell and was spent in a considerable exercise in management and organisation. Experiments were started in the various vegetational areas, with a vast network of 3 800 km of fire-break roads commenced and eventually completed to divide the park into 400 different blocks. The entire park – its administration, vegetation and wildlife – was to be brought under close control. Improvement work was also expedited on all camps and roads, with the entrance gate at Orpen (named after the wife and husband benefactors of the park) completed to replace the old gate on the farm *Rabelais*, named by the surveyor after the French satirical author.

Veld management by means of burning was a subject of continuous argument. In 1955 a three-year rotational burning programme was introduced, with a two-year rotational programme in the long-grass area of Pretoriuskop. It was again a season of good rains. The park was looking superb and with the seasons remaining favourable for the next four years, it was in fact a good time to study the effects of burning during times of plenty.

The whole park – vegetation, birds, insects and mammals – seemed to be blossoming. Tourist traffic in 1955 brought in over 100 000 visitors (101 058) for the first time. All facilities were under pressure, particularly the privately run trading stations and restaurants, which on 1 December were taken over by the Board. From then on they became integral parts of national park management, a factor which was to the advantage of tourists and the park. All the camps were growing at such a rate that some of them (notably Skukuza) were becoming vast, sprawling complexes of rondavels. Pretoriuskop received a swimming-pool in the following year, while the houses for staff at the administrative centre of Skukuza were becoming so numerous that the place began to look increasingly like a village.

Several new research programmes were launched. Considerable activity also commenced in the eradication of exotic plants. To cope with the proposed extensive developments in roads (over 2 000 km by 1972) and camps, a Department of Works was also established in 1958 under the direction of a qualified civil engineer. A major task involved the complete fencing off of the park boundaries. This work commenced in 1959. The southern boundary along the Crocodile River was completed first. In 1960 the western and northern boundaries were fenced, and then the eastern frontier with Mozambique. Later, heavy cable, as it became available, was added in order to make the fences even elephant proof.

The purpose of the fences in impeding the movement of game animals was to curb the spread of diseases, facilitate boundary patrolling and inhibit the movement of poachers. The fences were breached in many places by wandering animals but they gradually became more used to being confined. Many of them, however, notably zebra, wildebeest, and elephant, showed a marked inclination towards east–west seasonal migrations. The years of good rain were providing excellent foodstuffs which lured across the frontier from Mozambique many elephants which were under pressure there from hunters and peasant farmers steadily burning off the bush to extend their lands. The first aerial census of elephants was conducted in 1959 and revealed the number in the park as being 986. As with most of the mammals (especially the browsing species), the elephants increased their numbers rapidly during the good years.

After considerable debate, carnivora control was terminated in December 1958. A new policy was introduced whereby control would only be imposed on a temporary and local basis where carnivora were endangering some declining prey population. Such a situation could periodically occur as it did, for example, in 1960 when there was an outbreak of anthrax, a disease to which kudu and roan antelope were particularly susceptible. The roan suffered severely in this outbreak with so many dying that their continued presence in the park was threatened. A state veterinary surgeon was appointed to the park in 1960 to study diseases of wild animals and to devise measures of control which, it was hoped, would be an improvement on the usual large-scale slaughtering which passed for veterinary treatment.

By then Stevenson-Hamilton, aged 90, had died of a stroke on 10 December 1957. His ashes, and those of his wife Hilda were eventually scattered in the park on 10 April 1979 at an outcrop of granite south of Skukuza know as *Shirimantanga* (early gardener) after a man who formerly lived there.

The warden, Louis Steyn, retired on 20 April 1961. His departure marked the end of the tradition where the patriarchal figure of the dedicated warden-conservationist was the head of the national park. He was replaced by the chief biologist, A M Brynard, who assumed the title of Nature Conservator, with the research and ranger sections united under one control into a single

Nature Conservation Department. Dr U de V Pienaar was promoted to Chief Biologist while Henry Wolhuter became Senior Ranger.

The new management was immediately confronted with two very dry years after the period of plenty. The erratic weather pattern of Africa has always been a major problem to all forms of life. To any management where dependability of supply is essential to stability and future planning, this unpredictable pattern is disconcerting. The original African population sought to counter capricious weather with the magic of rain-making whereby a good weaver of spells could at least make a fortune if nothing else. The few tribal groups which formerly inhabited the area of the park all practised rain-making. Close to the Punda Maria camp for visitors there is a well-forested and most handsome hill known as *Gumbandevu*, after a headman who once lived there. His daughter Khama practised rain-making. To her came supplicants bringing presents of snuff, hoes and livestock. At the foot of the mountain a goat would be sacrificed in such a way that its prolonged death cries would summon the spirits. Taking some of the animal's bones as well as the magic ingredients, Khama would then climb the hill. In a secret bower she would weave the spells until clouds appeared and rain fell. Whether this occurred in the homeland of her clients is unknown, but certainly the area around the hill was always green and the summit covered in a fine stand of ironwood trees. The hill is taboo. It is said that the sound of ghostly drums and singing may sometimes still be heard in the quietest hours of the night.

Modern management did not possess the magic resources of Khama, so an emergency drilling programme had to be launched, with the park acquiring its own boring machine. A long period of creating artificial watering holes ensued. The tourist camps were also very thirsty places. With ever-increasing tourist traffic there would obviously soon be many more people visiting the park each year than there were game animals. The existing camps were expanding. New camps, such as Olifants (opened in 1960), perched on a high cliff over the Olifants River, were being developed and several others planned. Additional roads were being constructed. Dust caused by the traffic resulted in a decision to tarmac the surface of all arterial roads. Picnic spots were provided, such as the one on the Lower Sabie road under the great Mkuhlu tree in 1959, and at Hlangulene and Manzene in 1963. With better roads, more of the park was opened throughout the year; Skukuza from 1962; Lower Sabie, Crocodile Bridge and as far north as the picnic spot at *Tshokwane* (named after a Shangane who had once lived there) in 1963; and the whole area as far as the Letaba River in 1964. Also that year, the number of visitors reached 216 680, exceeding the 200 000 a year mark for the first time, with 56 686 motor vehicles using the roads.

The wildlife population, too, was increasing. A programme commenced whereby species which had been shot out in former years were reintroduced. On 13 October 1961 the first batch of four square-lipped (white) rhinos were translocated from Zululand. As a result of the success of this operation, over 300 of these animals were introduced by 1972.

A less happy event in 1964 was the shooting of 104 hippos in the Letaba River which had become very dry and its remaining pools overcrowded. These were the first herbivorous animals to be destroyed in the park for reasons of over-population. The entire subject of the wild animal population – its increases and decreases – was a matter of considerable interest and study. In August 1964 the first aerial census of elephant and buffalo was conducted by means of a chartered helicopter. A total of 2 374 elephant and 10 514 buffalo were counted. A veterinary laboratory and an office block were opened in Skukuza. Several additional veterinary and research officers were appointed, with comprehensive programmes of study involving the participation of visiting students and scientists whose papers, on completion, could be expected to throw considerable light on many aspects of ecology and wild animal behaviour.

The rains returned in 1965, but the year was more notable for the Board's convening in Pretoria of a conference on the theme of the overprotection of nature, a rather surprising subject for a conservation body. The conference, held on 30 November, adopted a resolution advising the Board to cull those herbivorous animals whose population levels were thought to be increasing beyond natural controls. In the park such species were considered to be elephant, buffalo, zebra, wildebeest, impala and hippo. Culling quotas were determined in 1966. It was the intention that the results of the operation would be checked each year by aerial census, while the effects on vegetation would be observed through transect points. Meat and animal products would be disposed of to best advantage. For this purpose a plant known as a by-products depot was constructed at Skukuza. Biltong, bone-meal, canned and cooked meat, skin, ivory and trophies were to be produced.

With the aid of immobilisation of drugs, the animals could be destroyed from helicopters in the most modern, humane manner. The capture, translocation and sale of live animals was also commenced. A game-capture official was stationed at Tshokwane, with holding pens erected to corral the animals before they were redistributed to other less populated areas of the park, or translocated to outside places. The ingenious plastic-and-net corral method of capture devised by Jan Oelofse of the Natal Parks Board was introduced. This allowed entire herds to be caught with a minimum chance of injury. The year 1968 saw the whole operation fully launched, with the sale of products amounting to R37 000, mainly the proceeds of the shooting of 1 242 impala, 237 wildebeest, 390 buffalo, 355 elephant and the killing or capture for sale of 276 zebra.

The public was slightly puzzled at the news of these developments. They were not visually aware of any over-population of wild animals and would be likely to regard the establishment of a meat industry as aesthetically offensive in the setting of a game reserve. The reason for such a necessity, and the fact that veterinary restrictions made it impossible to build the factory outside the park, would have to be explained. As it was, the popularity of the park with tourists grew each year. In 1968 306 346 people visited the park (exceeding 300 000 a year for the first time). Facilities were also expanding and improving at an equal rate. Electric power from Eskom was fed into the park to light the camps while strenuous efforts were made to solve the water problem. Each year more boreholes were drilled. The mining magnate, Charles Engelhard, donated R120 000 for the construction of a dam in the Letaba River, and work was started in 1971 on a pipeline from the Olifants River to Satara camp, with thirteen branch pipes along its length leading to drinking-water sites for wild animals.

The park was enlarged in 1968, with the addition of the wild and hitherto remote area between the Limpopo and Luvuvhu rivers (the so-called *Pafuri* Game Reserve, named after Mphaphuli, a Venda chief). The few people living there were resettled in land excised from the park between Shangoni and Punda Maria gate, while the rugged area of the old Crooks' Corner became the site of a new ranger post. Although the population of game animals there was very slight, it would certainly improve under protection. Also, this area was historically and scenically one of the most interesting places in the park.

Further changes in management occurred on 13 March 1970 when Nature Conservator A M Brynard was promoted to the Pretoria head office to replace R J Labuschagne, who had resigned as Deputy Director of National Parks. Chief Biologist Dr U de V Pienaar was promoted to the position of Nature Conservator, with P van Wyk appointed as Chief Research Officer and Don Lowe as Senior Ranger. Further reorganisation in May 1974 resulted in Rocco Knobel becoming Chief Director of National Parks, with A M Brynard as his deputy. In 1979 Rocco Knobel retired and A M Brynard became Chief Director.

The year 1970 was the driest ever known in the park. Most rivers, except the Sabie, stopped flowing. Animal mortality throughout the park was dreadful, with hundreds of dead hippos befouling what little water remained in the rivers. Fortunately, the year ended with rains so heavy that the African cycle of drought to flood see-sawed to full circle. Chocolate-brown water gushed down the dry river courses, causing the rivers to reach very high flood levels. The new Engelhard Dam spilled over for the first time on 9 January 1971.

The extent of some of the downpours may be gauged from the fact that in one night Punda Maria received 219 mm. The ghost of old Khama on her mountain must have been working overtime! The park soon looked its best. Vegetation revives so rapidly after rain that its stirring and growth is almost audible. Unfortunately for the game animals, not only was culling in full swing but anthrax broke out in the northern areas in September and October 1971. The already small population of roan antelope was nearly wiped out while kudu were also very badly affected. Animals such as impala, wildebeest, buffalo, elephant, and zebra were already being systematically culled, but to supplement the wild animal population a programme commenced whereby cheetahs were imported from South West Africa in order to increase the then small numbers. On 17 May 1971 the first two black rhinos were reintroduced to the park after their kind had become extinct in the 1930s. A further eighteen black rhinos were sent up from Natal and twelve from the Zambezi valley of Zimbabwe in 1972. Resettlement schemes were also under way in the park for such rare antelope as eland, tsessebe, oribi and roan. A prophylactic protection against anthrax was developed in 1971 and the remaining roan population was immunised by dart syringes fired from a helicopter. The future of this species in the park now seems to be more secure.

Boreholes (362 in the park by the end of 1979), as well as 316 windpumps, were steadily stabilising drinking-water supplies. Plans were made for many more watering-places. The tarring of main roads was also progressing well. At the end of the 1 April 1996 to 31 March 1997 period, there was thirteen tourist camps in the park, each of which contained varying numbers of huts and rondavels: Skukuza, 200; Pretoriuskop, 148; Satara, 110; Olifants, 103; Lower Sabie, 102; Shingwedzi, 95; Letaba, 93; Berg-en-Dal, 100; Punda Maria, 26; Crocodile Bridge, 20; Orpen, 12; Balule, 4; and Nwandedzi, 1. There were also small, private camps which could be hired for parties of one to fifteen persons. Restaurants in all the main camps had reached a very high standard, with a trading turnover of R22 496 049. The shops had a turnover of R57 920 078. Total income from trade and tourism in the 1996/7 year was R200 966 788 with 906 999 visitors.

The estimated population of larger wild animals reveals the figures of impala as being 120 000; buffalo 20 000; zebra 23 000; wildebeest 14 000; elephant 8 300; kudu 9 500; giraffe 3 800; waterbuck 3 000; hippo 3 000; lion 1 500; sable antelope 800; reedbuck 1 000; leopard 900; tsessebe 1 200; eland 300; wild dog 150; nyala 1 300; roan antelope 120; cheetah 200; white rhino 1 700; black rhino 250.

The Kruger National Park of today, 1 948 528 ha in extent, differs considerably from the vision cherished by Stevenson-Hamilton, but this was largely inevitable. Relentless pressure from the public has resulted in the development of a tourist resort and vacation area in the setting of a park. Tourist facilities are of a high standard, with accommodation ranging from camping grounds to luxury chalets. Restaurants and shops are well run and stocked with a great variety of goods. Tarmac roads make the whole park accessible in all seasons. Enormous problems have had to be tackled in the supply of potable water and the disposal of waste material of all sorts.

With far more humans visiting the park in the course of a year than there are wild animal inhabitants, it is difficult for the average tourist, who undoubtedly experiences a great deal of pleasure there, to assess the park according to its original intent, that it be a sanctuary of the wild, where mammals, birds, insects, reptiles and plant life would be left undisturbed to pursue their own destiny in complete contrast to the developments and onslaught of man on nature outside. This is not the case today, however. The park is, in fact, intensely managed, with controls imposed on most things including vegetation.

Over-management has at times had unfortunate effects, including in some years a drastic reduction in the population of such animals as blue wildebeest and zebra. The by-products depot in Skukuza represents a substantial profit-making vested interest which needs to be regularly supplied with raw materials. Such raw materials can only be carcasses.

The question of culling is delicate and controversial. If it has to be carried out, the decisions should be made known to the public, with reasons accessible to all. For it is the public who own the Kruger National Park, not the officials, the Board or any single pooh-bah, private club, party or society. The public are entitled to ask questions, to argue, and to secure valid proof that the park, in fact, cannot carry more wildlife than it does and that man with his rifle, box of matches and poison is, in fact, better qualified to manage the wilderness than nature itself.

The northern part of the park has been badly disfigured by the construction of pylons carrying high-tension cables from the Cahora Bassa hydro-electric station in Mozambique. No sooner was this gigantic undertaking in power transfer from the Zambezi River to South Africa ready to provide electricity than politics cut off its nose to spite South Africa's face. The Renamo rebel movement sponsored in Mozambique by the South African apartheid Government sabotaged the line and for years nothing was transmitted. Electrical engineers and post office telecommunications technicians are notorious for ruining the landscape by insensitive planning, callously justified solely by mechanical convenience and so-called 'national need'. An even worse threat to this part of the park is the fact that prospectors from the Iron and Steel Corporation (Iscor) have found deposits of coking coal in the northern area. Railways, slag heaps, mining townships, complete with amenities such as drive-ins, supermarkets, and assorted hideosities, lurk menacingly on the drawing boards for this piece of wilderness. Very sharp watch has to be kept on the 'lunatechs' and 'idiotechs' (lunatic and idiot technicians) – the organisational men, chartered accountants and graduate masters of business administration – lest they destroy with glib persuasion the entire concept of a national park, carve it into a money-making area, and fulfil Stevenson-Hamilton's most pessimistic vision. Perhaps one or two elderly lions would be left, chained to stakes near the roads, trained to snarl at tourists occasionally in exchange for being pelted with an empty beer can.

A visit to the Kruger National Park, notwithstanding the problems of the place, is an extraordinary experience. With the bulk of the park open throughout the year, it is possible for the tourist to see the wonderful changes of vegetation from season to season; the migratory birds that come and go; the periods of love and courtship between animals, with innumerable duets and duels in the sun. During the spring and early summer when the birds are nesting, baby elephants stumble around on rubbery legs; zebra foals are so dainty as to be unreal; little giraffes stretch their necks even further to take a snack; impala fawns gambol about their graceful parents.

Wilderness trails are available for visitors who wish to get close to nature. A maximum of eight people at a time are escorted by rangers. Nights are spent in simple camps and the walking is delightful. The age limit is between 12 and 60 years. Bookings must be made well ahead, as the trails are very popular.

An unforgettable travel experience is provided by journeying one way through the full length of the Kruger National Park and returning along one of the two scenic drives of the lowveld, the R36 or R40. There are several variants of this route, depending on where the tourist enters the park. Numbi Gate, in the south-west of the park, is a good entrance to start the 'grand tour'. About twenty per cent of all visitors to the park pass through this gate. It is 8 km from the R538 road and 35 km from White River.

The Pretoriuskop camp is situated 9 km from Numbi gate. The road from the gate passes through the ridge of rocky hillocks which, in previous years, represented welcome landmarks to the transport riders bringing wagons through the tsetse areas of the lowlands. Shabeni is the imposing height to the north of the road. To the south looms the rather insignificant hillock of Pretoriuskop. By the roadside may be seen the restored grave of the hunter, said to have been the original Pretorius, who had the misfortune of dying there.

In summer this area is normally luxuriantly grassed and the tall forest trees beautifully green. In this area game animals are far more numerous in summer than winter, but throughout the year there is always something interesting to be seen in the bush. The reintroduced rhino population is largely concentrated here while sable antelope may often be seen. Trees are particularly impressive. In spring the forest is adorned with the blossoms of species such as the wild pear tree which produces masses of white flowers. Acacias scent the air with the sweet perfume of their yellow or white blossoms. The camp of Pretoriuskop is notable in spring for its spectacular red-flowering trees of the *Erythrina* species.

The camp itself, the third largest in the park, has excellent facilities and is pleasant, relaxed and informal. A swimming-pool provides a very welcome asset during the warm summer months. The Pretoriuskop area has always been extremely popular with tourists, with several drives – short and long – radiating from it. A perceptible atmosphere of the pioneer days lingers about the place.

The main tarmac road, known as Nhape road (from Nhapi hill), leads eastwards from Pretoriuskop to Skukuza, 47 km away. The gravel Hippo Pools road and the parallel Doispane road provide an alternative 61 km drive to Skukuza, revealing many pleasant views of the Sabie River, its hippos and riverside forests. The Doispane road is said to have received its name from a game guard nicknamed 'Dustpan', who was once stationed in those parts. Near the junction of the Doispane and Hippo pools roads, a short turn-off leads westwards to the reconstructed site of the inland depot of *Juwawa*, named after João Albasini, the safari trader of the 1830s.

The most interesting of the roads radiating from Pretoriuskop is the original transport trail which leads south-eastwards and is known as the *Voortrekker* (pioneer's) road. It is marked with stone beacons in memory of Jock, the hero of the most famous dog story ever written, *Jock of the Bushveld* by Percy Fitzpatrick. It passes on the way many well-known landmarks of the transport days, including (at 14 km) Ship Mountain, a rocky hillock which resembles the battered hull of a ship which had the misfortune (during the Stone Age perhaps?) of turning turtle. Most of the game animals of the park may be seen along this road. Especially numerous are giraffe, klipspringer and sable antelope

After 40 km the old transport road (now well surfaced with gravel) joins the road from Skukuza to Malelane. Turning southwards along this road, the tourist reaches after 19 km the entrance gate known as *Malelane,* from the small lala palms which flourish in those parts. This is the third most frequented entrance to the park, with over 18 per cent of the total traffic. The area is notable for its bougainvillaeas and spring flowers. The Crocodile River, the southern boundary of the park, flows nearby. There is an interesting 23 km drive up the left bank of the river to the western boundary of the park, an area to which wild dogs seem partial. The attractive tourist camp of *Bergen-Dal* (mountain and dale) lies north-west of Malelane.

Retracing the route for 11 km to Crocodile Bridge, the traveller reaches a turn-off which leads eastwards. Buffalo, impala, elephant and kudu are generally seen along this road and the trees, such as fine canopied acacias, are handsome. The ground is carpeted with the sweet grazing beloved by most herbivorous animals. Towards the end of the drive there is a turn-off stretching for 3 km to a viewsite overlooking the Crocodile River. Hippos laze in a pool and very faded Bushman paintings may be seen in a rock shelter covered with flowering aloes in June.

Crocodile Bridge is a small but very pleasant camp situated on the banks of the river known to the Swazi as the *Ngwenya* (crocodile). The railway bridge of the now disused Selati line, which runs through the park, crosses the river at this point and there is also a low-level bridge for motor vehicles. It is an entrance gate to the park, through which about 5 per cent of visitors pass. Facilities include a small store, some neat bungalows and a pleasant caravan park. The area has always been a great resort of buffalo, while the sweet grass on the flats beneath the Lubombo range attracts herds of zebra and wildebeest. Kudu, waterbuck and impala are also very fond of the area.

From Crocodile Bridge the main tarmac road leads northwards through an interesting landscape of flat savanna, with many fine trees and well populated with game. At 13 km the road reaches a gravel turn-off known as the Randspruit road which provides an alternative way to Skukuza. At the turn-off point a stand of old bluegum trees marks the site of a former trading station run by an Italian by the name of Sardelli. Just beyond the turn-off, at the stream named after the petty chief Gomondwane, the tarmac road passes a small memorial to the Dutch exploration party which in 1725, before being driven back, reached this point after journeying from the fort at the bay of Lourenzo Marques.

After 22 km (35 km from Crocodile Bridge) the tarmac road enters the camp of Lower Sabie. This is one of the larger camps in the park, where there is a fine restaurant and store and the facilities are excellent. Many of the bungalows and huts overlook the Sabie River and, since the camp is situated in some of the best game country in the park (lion being especially numerous), it is particularly popular with visitors from overseas. Without being picturesque, the camp is a pleasant and convenient centre from which to explore several very interesting drives.

From Lower Sabie the main tarmac road continues up the right bank of the Sabie River in one of the most rewarding drives in the entire park. The riverine trees are imposing and the luxuriant sweet grazing and perennial water attract considerable numbers of wild animals, making the area popular with many tourists. Impala are particularly partial to this area where warmth, food and water are available. Since they, in their turn, constitute 19,85 per cent of food for lions (with zebra 15,95 per cent; wildebeest 23,72 per cent; and buffalo 9,27 per cent as an alternative choice of menu!), it follows that the area is well populated with predators of all species. Bushbuck, waterbuck and kudu are also very partial to the thickets on the banks of the Sabie, while hippos and crocodiles are common in the river itself.

At 43 km from the Lower Sabie camp, the tarmac road reaches Skukuza, the administrative centre and largest camp in the park. Built in a pleasant situation on the banks of the Sabie River, Skukuza has had the misfortune of 'just growing' (like the famous Topsy) into a gangling unplanned array of tourist accommodation, a restaurant, shop, post office, open-air cinema, museum and the Stevenson-Hamilton Memorial Library, built in 1960 by the Wildlife Protection Society. Staff are accommodated in 125 houses; there is a school, clinic, club, staff golf-course and other sports facilities. Skukuza is actually a growing village, which certain field staff have suggested, with sardonic humour, should be deproclaimed, excised from the park, fenced off, given municipal status and its colony of officials required to pay normal tourist admission fees to see the wild animals.

Skukuza was in previous years renowned for its hyenas. Vast colonies lived around the camp feeding on garbage and tourist hand-outs, sleeping and breeding in such places as stormwater drains. At night they sounded like a craze of lunatics at their annual picnic benefit, for which type of jollification Skukuza was certainly a world winner. The hyenas roamed around the camp freely, contributing to visitors' memories of night sounds and sights. Unfortunately the inevitable happened. In 1966 two tourists in Olifants rest camp were severely bitten by hyenas, and this necessitated the erection of game-proof fences around all the camps. The hyena population of Skukuza was banned, purged and packed off to the graveyard. The nights are now respectable and silent, which is a pity. Every tourist longs at night to hear the voice of Africa – the roar of a lion, the sound of drums, or the lunatic cackle of a hyena. Hyenas make a great variety of sounds, but the unforgettable giggle (really a sound of excitement and rage) is something to hear. Any management with imagination would leave a garbage pile within earshot of each tourist camp!

A tarmac road 12 km long connects Skukuza to the Paul Kruger gate, opened on 21 March 1973, and now the busiest entrance and exit for officials and tourists, with about 25 per cent of the total traffic.

The main arterial tarmac road leaves Skukuza, crosses the Sabie River and leads north-eastwards into the central portion of the park, an area of sweet grazing where the highest density of game animals live. Impala, giraffe, kudu, wildebeest and zebra frequent this area throughout the year. After 11 km a tarmac turn-off south links up with the lower Sabie road, and the Salitje gravel road leading eastwards into fine game country.

At 19 km the main tarmac road reaches a gravel turn-off north which traverses excellent game country, passing the picnic sites of Hlangulene (28 km), Mzanzene (57 km), and (at 68 km) joining the road linking Orpen gate to Satara. Just beyond this gravel turn-off there are tablets set into a large granite boulder commemorating the proclamation in 1898 of the original Sabi Game Reserve, and then the Kruger National Park in 1926. The memorial was unveiled in September 1933 by Mrs Stevenson-Hamilton.

Fourteen kilometres beyond this memorial (33 km from Skukuza) the tarmac road reaches the picnic spot and tea-room of Tshokwane, famous for its perky population of those comic characters of the bird community, the hornbills, and the lovely blue-coloured glossy starlings. The Shangane name for these cheeky little birds is *Makwezi* and it compares them to the colour of a shooting star. *Tshokwane* was the name of a Shangane headman living there in former years. As far as wild animals are concerned, this is one of the most lively areas in the entire park. It is here that game-capturing operations and corrals are centred. Interesting drives along gravel roads branch out in several directions; south to join the Salitje road; west on the Hutomi road; and east to the finely situated Eileen Orpen Dam built in 1969, where there is a look-out allowing visitors the chance of watching the wild animals coming to drink.

Beyond the dam, the gravel road continues north for 19 km and then joins the Louis Trichardt road. On the way it is worthwhile taking a short turn-off east which climbs to the summit of the flat-topped hill known as Nwamuriwa, from where there is a tremendous view over the vast savanna plains of the park, with Tshokwane clearly visible in the middle distance. Beyond this turn-off, the road passes the Lindanda Memorial, erected on the site of Harry Wolhuter's celebrated adventure with the lions.

The main tarmac road, meanwhile, continues its interesting journey northwards. After 15 km it reaches a memorial to the Voortrekker, Louis Trichardt, erected at the spot where his pioneer trail crosses the modern road. This old trail has been developed into a good gravel road for tourists. To the west it winds for 19 km through a parkland of big game, frequented by giraffe, impala, wildebeest and zebra. It then joins the road leads through Hlangulene picnic site to the Orpen–Satara road. To the east, the Louis Trichardt road leads for 13 km to join the Lindanda road from Tshokwane.

Keeping close to the frontier line with Mozambique, the gravel road swings northwards and continues for a further 24 km to reach a pleasant picnic site situated on a cliff overlooking a waterhole in the Nwanedzi River. From there the road continues across a grassy savanna (where steenbok are particularly common) until, after a further 47 km, it reaches a junction. Continuing north for 13 km, the road terminates at the picnic place enhanced by an impressive view of the gorge carved out by the Olifants River as it penetrates the Lubombo range. Back at the junction, the turn westwards also leads for 13 km and then reaches a causeway across the Olifants River at hippo pools and the bungalows of the small Balule rest camp. Across the river, the traveller has the choice of swinging west to join the main tarmac road of the park or turning north-eastwards and driving for 10 km through good game country before reaching the spectacularly situated Olifants camp.

The main tarmac road meanwhile, beyond the crossing with the Louis Trichardt road, continues northwards across a vast, grassy, level parkland. Elephant, giraffe, waterbuck, zebra, wildebeest, impala, buffalo and lion are often seen. At 35 km from the Louis Trichardt road (50 km from Tshokwane), the road reaches the large modern camp of Satara, with little claim to atmosphere or beauty, but possessing a fine restaurant and shop. However, it does lie in the centre of some of the best game-viewing country in the park, and as such it is a comfortable base. The presence of lion and hyena often enliven the nights. The name *Satara* was given to a farm originally surveyed there. The surveyor had an Indian servant who suggested the name, meaning in Hindi the '17th' farm to be surveyed.

From Satara a tarmac road leads westwards to the Orpen gate through a lovely parkland of bush-willow and acacia trees, where a great variety of game may be seen. After 6 km the road reaches a turn-off to the picnic site on the river known as the *Mbabati* (or *Timbavati*) on account of the numerous bushbuck living in the splendid riverine forest. The Timbavati River is essentially a series of pools linked together by a surface flow brought on only during the rainy season. Nevertheless, the pools are permanent and provide water to one of the largest concentrations of game in the park. From the picnic spot a gravel road continues southwards for 37 km along the right bank of the river and then rejoins the Satara–Orpen road. Both of these riverside drives are very worthwhile.

The road from Satara to Orpen, after the turn-off to Timbavati at 6 km, leads westwards for a further 11 km, reaching the road which turns up the right bank of the river, and then carries on southwards eventually to enter Skukuza. The Orpen–Satara road continues from this crossroads for a further 26 km to reach the entrance gate of Orpen, 43 km from Satara. The drive is splendid throughout, revealing views of elephant, zebra, wildebeest, giraffe, lion and wild dog.

Orpen is a very pleasant little rest camp with a small shop. Nearby on the banks of the Timbavati River a separate caravan park called Maroela was established, a very attractive little place where caravanners can be close to nature in the form of lion, leopard, elephant and other game which frequently wander around this part of the world.

From Satara camp, the main tarmac road continues northwards across the grassy plain populated with herds of impala, wildebeest, zebra, and many giraffe, waterbuck and kudu. Crossing the Olifants River by means of the high-level bridge opened in 1972, the road skirts the left bank of the river for a few kilometres and then, 46 km from Satara, reaches the tarmac turn-off to the camp of Olifants, 11 km away.

Olifants, perched on top of a high cliff overlooking the *Olifants* (elephants) River, is the most spectacularly situated camp in the park. Opened on 3 June 1960, it is modern in its design and has a fine restaurant, shop and observation point which looks out on as superb and wild a piece of Africa as the heart could desire. Game watching could not be easier. From a comfortable seat, or the window of a bungalow, an eagle's-eye view may be had of many kilometres of river, lined with handsome trees and the resort of elephant and many different antelope. Sunsets and dawns are glorious.

From the Olifants camp an interesting drive may be followed for 48 km along a gravel road up the right bank of the *Letaba* (sandy) River to Letaba camp, with the Engelhard Dam spread out in a spacious sheet of water where the wall holds back the river. Elephant, bushbuck, buffalo and waterbuck frequent the verges of the river.

The main tarmac road, after the turn-off to Olifants camp, continues north for 19 km (65 km from Satara), reaching what is considered by many to be the prettiest camp in the Kruger National Park. Letaba camp is shaded by beautiful trees on the high right bank of the Letaba River. A fine restaurant and store provide amenities, while the bungalows are informally arranged around a central garden brimming with flowers and interesting plants. Monkeys play incessantly in the trees; elephants feed in the reeds and wander around outside the camp; leopards have always been common; and hippos and crocodiles find a home in the river. Bird life is especially rich. The atmosphere is redolent of Africa, of big game, interesting characters and old adventures.

Several worthwhile drives radiate from Letaba. A gravel road leads westwards for 50 km and a tarmac road south-westwards for 48 km, both of them ending at Phalaborwa gate, opened in 1961 to replace the old Malopene gate and nowadays the fourth most frequented entrance to the park, with over 16 per cent of all visitors passing through it. The border area there is watched over by a ranger stationed at *Mahlangeni* (the place of reeds). The tarmac road passes the spectacular Masorini hill, about 10 km from the Phalaborwa gate, where an interesting Iron Age village of the Phalaborwa tribe has been reconstructed. There is an information centre and a picnic site.

The main tarmac road continues northwards from Letaba. Crossing the river, it enters a more arid area dominated by mopane trees, a favourite haunt of elephant, eland, roan and tsessebe. After

45 km the road reaches the picnic and resting-place named *Mooiplaas* (nice farm) where there is a fine look-out over a permanent water-hole in the Tsende River. From here the traveller has a choice of two roads leading northwards and ending at Shingwedzi camp. The journey via the main road is 61 km past the ranger post of *Mooiplaas*. The more easterly road is 69 km long and closely follows the frontier of Mozambique. Game animals are not numerous in this arid, hot area of vast mopane woodlands where baobab trees dominate the landscape.

Shingwedzi (iron stone) camp is a pleasantly informal place notable for its trees, brilliantly flowering impala lilies (*Adenium multiflorum*), and very varied bird life. There is a good restaurant and store, and the place is tinged with an atmosphere of the wilderness. Leopards stalk baboons through the tall trees; monkeys and the loveliest of birds move through the branches. Elephant, impala, waterbuck, buffalo, kudu, zebra and wildebeest wander along the banks of the Shingwedzi River. A fine 56 km drive leads to the Tshange look-out point where an immense view may be had over the great mopane parkland stretching westwards to the ranger post named after the chief, Shangoni.

To the east of the camp a magnificent river drive follows the southern fringe of the large Kanniedood Dam. A great variety of game may be seen around this picturesque dam, including nyala antelope.

The Shingwedzi area straddles the Tropic of Capricorn. North of the Olifants River the soil rests on a limestone base as opposed to the granite of the south. The grazing is good, but lack of dependable surface water has inhibited any dense population of wild animals. The climate is warm to hot. The tourist finds himself in a world which differs from the other parts of the park.

The main road continues north-westwards across a level plain of grass and mopane trees. After 32 km the road reaches the picnic and resting-place of Babalala, built around a large wild fig tree. A further 16 km (48 km from Shingwedzi) takes the road to a parting of the ways. Continuing northwards, the right-hand branch of the road leads for 35 km to the Luvuvhu River, so-named from the mvuvu trees growing on its banks. The left-hand road swings north-westwards and, after 21 km, reaches the camp of Punda Maria, with the Punda Maria gate 8 km to the west.

Punda Maria is picturesquely (if rather awkwardly) situated on the steep slopes of a hill. Although one of the older camps, it is comfortable, informal and pleasant, and has a small restaurant and shop.

The story has already been told of Khama, the rain-maker, who practised on the nearby hill of Gumbandevu. About 48 km north of the camp, overlooking the Luvuvhu River, lies another hill with a notable history. On this hill a group of early people, the Lembethu, built a stronghold and stone-walled settlement. Their local chief, whose dynastic title was Makahane, was the last of his line to rule on the hill and had a reputation for insanity and cruelty. Many atrocities were committed on this hilltop, with people being thrown over the cliffs. Today, the stone ruins seem to abound with ghosts (especially at night).

Makahane's cruelty was eventually his undoing. The Paramount Chief received so many complaints that he sent his son (Makahane's brother) to kill the madman. In a dance of welcome to his brother, Makahane was stabbed to death. He lies buried in front of his throne, a seat built into one of the stone walls. The hilltop was afterwards abandoned and the old settlement now forms an interesting ruin for visitors walking the Nyalaland Trail.

A second ruin, named *Thulamela* (place of giving birth), is close to Makahane's stronghold. It was also built on a plateau overlooking the Luvuvhu River. It was carefully excavated and reconstructed between 1993 and 1996 into something close to its original state. It was the seat of a ruler and home to about 2 000 people. Many interesting relics have been found there, including gold jewellery. The history of this centre with its stone walls is unknown. From the skeletons found there the place appears to have been abandoned about 1550 after an occupation lasting about 300 years. The reason for the abandonment of this substantial stronghold is not known. The skeletons found there are all of people who had died a natural death. There is no known tradition of the name of the people who built the place or any details of their life-style and history.

The whole area north of Punda Maria is a densely forested and most rugged extent of sandveld. The Luvuvhu River is a handsome stream, typically African – sulky, erratic and enigmatic. Some large crocodiles (uncommonly fat) live in its pools, hippos are numerous; and elephant and buffalo like the area. Baobab, syringa, ironwood, mahogany, ebony and sycamore fig trees cover a landscape of deep valleys and red-coloured mountains. In the heart of this lovely wilderness, little trodden by man, is a touch of humour. Surrounded by huge nyala trees lies a warm spring, the name of which is *Shalungwa Siyafa* (we are dying). It refers to one of the famous old-timers of the park – the well-digger, dam-maker, ranger and hard case, Bill Lamont – who, because he persisted in working through the heat of the day, was given this name by his workers as they claimed they were all dying.

Punda Maria, as previously mentioned, was built as a ranger post to block the famous Ivory Trail. Following this romantic old trail of poachers and blackbirders, the tourist makes an interesting journey to the northern end of the park. The road leads north-westwards for the first 17 km past the slopes of Gumbandevu and then joins the direct road coming up from Shingwedzi. Near the junction is a short loop road passing the water-hole known to the Africans as *Shikuwa* (the fig tree) but to Europeans as *Kloppersfontein,* after Hans Kloppers, a hunter who often camped there.

The road now swings northwards and leads through an undulating wilderness of mopane and baobab trees. A famous landmark on the way is Baobab Hill, on top of which a solitary baobab stands sentinel. On its western side could be found drinking-water; on its eastern side there was a camping site often used by the great poacher *Bvekenya* (S C Barnard), whose story is told in the book *The Ivory Trail*. The road continues until, 42 km from Punda Maria, it reaches the deep riverine forests on the banks of the Luvuvhu. From here a side road turns west up the river for 3 km to a hippo pool, revealing a fine view of the river and a glimpse of the Valley of Giants, where a community of baobab trees flourish like the living relics of a lost world.

Turning east, the main road continues down the southern bank of the Luvuvhu past the turn-off leading to the old ford across the river (now a modern high-level bridge) and for a further 13 km through the riverside forest of fever trees and sycamore figs. Elephants, the lovely nyala, bushbuck, impala, zebra, hippos, crocodiles and pythons flourish in this tropical setting. A fine picnic and resting-place is situated beside the river and there is a turn-off along which the actual junction of the Luvuvhu with the Limpopo River may be viewed. The point of land projecting between the two converging rivers was originally the notorious Crooks' Corner. The whole area, once so celebrated for its tough characters and their adventures, is now part of the park. Plaques mark the sites of graves and interesting places connected to events and the characters of Crooks' Corner. A memorial to Bvekenya was unveiled on 19 September 1986.

The road being followed passes through a magnificent forest of fever trees and then ends at the police border post of Pafuri, where the genial Harold Mockford for many years managed the depot of the Witwatersrand Native Labour Association (Wenela). From this oasis in the wilderness, a sandy road enters Mozambique. Another road returns in a westerly direction and after 11 km joins the main road already followed from Punda Maria. In this most pleasant place, then, our journey regrettably ends, leaving a longing to return once again to see the cheeky glossy starlings; to breathe in the air, touched perhaps with the earthy aroma of newly cut potatoes from the fruits of the Phyllanthus shrubs; to meeting interesting people; to feel close to nature for just a little while before civilisation envelops you once more in its depressing rush.

The Kruger National Park is open throughout the year. Travel in the park is limited to daylight hours and the rules are very simple: stay in your car, keep to the road and observe speed restrictions (40 km on gravel; 50 km on tarmac).

Chapter Thirty-Nine

THE NORTHERN AND NORTH-WEST PROVINCES OF SOUTH AFRICA

Several roads traverse the seemingly endless plains of the Northern and North-West provinces of the former Transvaal, providing travellers with the chance to explore a portion of South Africa which contains a surprising number of scenic wonders both natural and unnatural.

From Krugersdorp on the edge of the Witwatersrand, 32 km from Johannesburg, the R24 tarmac road leads westwards past many smallholdings and nurseries. After 5,5 km a turn-off to the Krugersdorp Game Reserve is reached. This reserve is a very worthwhile exercise in conservation and, with its chalets, caravan park and swimming-pool, a most pleasant base for persons discovering this part of the Witwatersrand (see Chapter Thirty-Two).

The road loses altitude as it continues westwards, passing (11,5 km from Krugersdorp) the rural area of Tarlton with its dog-racing track, ostrich show-farm and asparagus-growing industry. At 21,5 km the road passes the Orient Hills where fresh trout are sold from wayside stalls. There is a trout hatchery at Maloney's Eye, where fresh and smoked trout are sold weekdays. At 29 km the road reaches the village of ...

MAGALIESBURG

Magali (or Mohale) was chief on the Po tribe who lived in the area of the village on the southern side of the handsome mountain ridge known after him as the *Magaliesberg*. Tobacco and citrus are produced here. The warm climate and scenic beauty have resulted in the establishment of several holiday resorts much frequented by people seeking an escape from the cold winters of the Witwatersrand. A branch railway connects *Magaliesburg* (Magalies Town) to Pretoria. Along this line runs what is known as the Potato Express, a mixed train which, at times, is still drawn by a puffer, making a day-long journey which provides train lovers with a pleasant outing.

THE MAGALIESBERG

Consisting of a flat-topped ridge of quartzite and red-coloured sediments of the Transvaal System, laid down about 2,500 million years ago, the Magaliesberg looms up like a wall of rock 120 km long, its highest point 1 852 m above sea-level. The slopes and summit are richly wooded and numerous streams have their source on the ridge. In former years this area was renowned for big game, including elephant. The first European hunters and traders who visited the range called it the Cashan Mountains after Khashane, chief of the Taung tribe who lived there.

The ledges on the precipice faces of the range have always provided good roosts for vultures. About 250 breeding pairs of the species, *Gyps coprotheres,* have their nests there. Thermal air currents rising from the heated rocks of the mountain facilitate the lazy, spiralling flight of vultures which may usually be seen here circling the sky. An amusing spectacle occurs when gliders are flown in the area. The vultures seem to regard them as bigger birds in their pecking order. They fly along with the gliders, turning and manoeuvring in perfect unison.

From the village of Magaliesburg, the R24 road branches off from the main Johannesburg–Mafikeng road, R509. Leading into the foothills of the Magaliesberg, R24 eventually reaches Rustenburg. On the way this road provides access to the various holiday resorts in the area. There are interesting hiking trails.

From Magaliesburg the R24 road follows a green and most pleasant valley. By the shady wayside are situated nurseries and resorts such as the Wicker Tea Garden and Lovers Rock Pleasure Resort; Boys Town, run by the Roman Catholic Church; and Camp Caplan of the United Progressive Jewish Congregation.

After 7,5 km a turn-off leads to the hamlet of Hekpoort and from there to Pretoria, or by means of a turn-off right through the actual *Hekpoort* (passage of the gateway) back to Krugersdorp. This is a fine natural pass by means of which the road climbs the Witwatersrand, passing the turn-off to the Sterkfontein Caves and then continuing to Krugersdorp. The distance is a total of 44 km from the Magaliesburg–Rustenburg road which meanwhile proceeds westwards along the length of the Magaliesberg, passing many farms where citrus, subtropical fruit, flowers and vegetables are produced. After 8 km from the turn-off to Hekpoort, the road reaches the hamlet of Doornkloof, from where a gravel road leads northwards to climb the Magaliesberg by means of Breedtsnek. This drive is very worthwhile, revealing grand views and interesting scenery.

After 13 km of climbing up this well-maintained road, a turn-off stretches for 4,5 km to the Utopia Holiday Resort overlooking the dam of Buffelspoort, a fine area for swimming and general sporting activities. Opposite the turn-off to this resort, there is another turn-off leading for 3,5 km to the Sparkling Waters hotel, beyond which the road continues for 13 km, passing *Parrots Paradise* where John Brown Rough founded his exotic parrot-breeding farm in 1969. After descending a handsome pass down the cliffs of the Magaliesberg, the road joins the main tarmac R24 road to Rustenburg.

From Doornkloof, where the road turns off to the top of the Magaliesberg, the main tarmac R24 road continues westwards along the mountain wall. Peach orchards, maize fields and shady indigenous trees line the route. From here the Magaliesberg is revealed at its best. In Retief's Kloof, a favourite resort for nature lovers and mountaineers, sequences have been shot for feature films on themes such as the Voortrekkers descending the Drakensberg. The streams are clear and there are fine waterfalls and deep pools. Adding to the spectacle is the Olifantsnek Dam, built in 1928 where the Hex River finds a way through the mountain wall by means of a narrow pass. The concrete wall of the dam – 24 m high and 134 m long – impounds enough water to irrigate 2 428 ha of farmland where citrus, tobacco and other crops are cultivated on the northern side of the range.

The road skirts the verges of the lake, revealing fine views of the mountains across the water. Elephants found their way through this pass in former years. The modern road, following their old trail, emerges without difficulty on the northern side on to the vast plains of the bushveld. Just below the pass, 33 km from Doornkloof, the road passes the citrus farm of *Boschfontein*, once the home of George Rex, grandson of the founder of Knysna, who settled there to hunt and farm. The modern resort of Hunter's Rest now stands amongst the citrus groves.

From Hunter's Rest the tarmac road continues westwards through a veritable garden of indigenous trees, orchards, tobacco fields and citrus groves. Wayside stalls offer a variety of fruits, honey, nuts and other produce for sale. After 1,5 km the road passes a turn-off which joins the Rustenburg–Pretoria road and at 4,5 km a turn-off leading to Kroondal. The road proceeds and, at 8 km, passes the Cynthiana hotel on the outskirts of the town of Rustenburg, 14 km from Hunter's Rest.

RUSTENBURG

The town of Rustenburg lies in a real garden setting of luxuriant vegetation and warmth backed by the superb Magaliesberg Range, whose forest-covered slopes and ravines give rise to hiking trails and many pleasant recreational possibilities. Jacaranda and poinciana trees enhance the streets with their shade and flowers. Gardens are notable for hibiscus, frangipani, poinsettias and bougainvillaeas of many different colours.

The town was founded in April 1851 when a church was established there. The town was laid out in September of the same year. The Reverend D E Faure named the place *Rustenburg* (town of rest) after Rustenburg in the Cape.

For some years the town was a frontier post, a resort of hunters, explorers and prospectors who used it as their base for ventures into the far interior, the Kalahari, and the world of trees and granite hills north of the Limpopo River. Men such as Henry Hartley the hunter, and Karl Mauch the geologist, equipped their expeditions from the trading stores of Rustenburg. Paul Kruger grew up in the area on the farm *Buffelsfontein* (buffalo fountain), owned by his father, Casper Kruger. In 1863, at the age of 16, Paul Kruger acquired a farm of his own called *Boekenhoutfontein* (fountain of beech wood trees). This farm north-west of Rustenburg now contains a museum, the earliest surviving pioneer cottage (built in 1841) and the Kruger homestead built in the 1870s. In front of the civic centre in Rustenburg stands a fine bronze of President Kruger, the work of the French sculptor, Jean Jacques Achard.

Rustenburg was the scene of several important events in the history of the South African Republic. It was there, on 16 March 1852, that a momentous meeting ended the almost fatal rivalry of the two Voortrekker leaders, Andries Hendrik Potgieter and Andries Pretorius. A period of peace in the stormy story of the Transvaal was ushered in by the acceptance of the Sand River Convention with the British. The reunion between the two rivals took place in the grounds of the Hervormde Kerk. The corner-stone of the original church on this square has been preserved.

In Kerk Street stands a marble replica of the stump of the original syringa tree under which the Reformed *(Hervormde)* Church was founded in 1859 as a separate body from the Dutch Reformed Church.

During the Anglo-Transvaal War of 1881, a British garrison was besieged in the town but survived without any major attack or casualty. Several small British forts were built on the overlooking hills during the Anglo-Boer War.

Rustenburg became a municipality in April 1918 and today has a population of 98 919. It is the centre of a magnificent farming area, home to the Magaliesberg Co-operative Tobacco Growers' Association, the Rustenburg Co-operative Packhouse Company Ltd where Outspan oranges are packed, the United Tobacco Company with its factory and the Tobacco Research Institute.

Rustenburg is also the centre for a considerable mining industry. The two largest platinum mines in the world are situated on the outskirts of the town. The workings of Rustenburg Platinum Mines Ltd comprise the world's largest underground mining operation. The source of platinum is the Merensky Reef, discovered in 1924 in the Lydenburg district by A F Lombard. It was traced and proved into the Rustenburg locality and other areas of the Transvaal by the geologist, Hans Merensky.

The town is situated on the verge of the remarkable geological feature known as the Bushveld Igneous Complex, notable for its high mineralisation. Asbestos, chrome, granite, lead, marble, slate and tin are mined in the district.

South-west of the town lies the Rustenburg Nature Reserve, an area of 2 898 ha proclaimed a nature reserve in 1967. It is situated on the summit and northern slopes of the Magaliesberg. The vegetation on the summit, 400 m above the level of the plain, is extremely varied and the views are superb. The Waterkloof River also has its source here and flows through a natural garden. Trees such as syringa, boekenhout and several acacia species are numerous. A two-day hiking trail in the reserve may be followed and there is a place at which to stop overnight. There are 230 species of birds and an interesting population of mammals, including the elusive brown hyena, leopards and aard wolves (maned jackals). There is a two-hour circular walking route.

Overlooking the town is the small Kwaggapan Reserve with its stone look-out tower from where Rustenburg and its surroundings may be viewed. The Paul Budenstein Park contains duck ponds and thatched shelters for picnics.

The Nederduitsch-Gereformeerde Kerk, built in 1850, is a national monument. During the Anglo-Boer War it was transformed into a hospital by the British. Six of the British soldiers who died here were recipients of the Victoria Cross. The graves of five of them lie in the small military cemetery next to the rebuilt Anglican Church. This pretty little church, built in 1811, is also a national monument. It was rebuilt on its present site in Van Staden Street in 1907 when township development threatened its original position.

There is a museum in the town hall. It exhibits local history and archaeology. It is open Mondays to Fridays 08h00 to 16h00; Saturdays and public holidays 09h00 to 13h00. Closed Christmas, Good Friday and New Year's Day.

Rustenburg Kloof in the Magaliesberg has been developed by the municipality into a fine recreational area with swimming, picnic sites, bungalows, caravan and camping sites. There are three swimming-pools, two of them with solar heated water. There are also several privately run resorts in the amiable setting of red-coloured mountains. From the Ananda hotel there are two hiking trails which lead into the Magaliesberg.

RUSTENBURG TO THE EAST

From Rustenburg the R27 tarmac road to Pretoria stretches eastwards along the northern side of the Magaliesberg, in which verdant area several resorts are situated. The Omaramba Holiday Resort lies 4,5 km from Rustenburg, the Bergheim Holiday Resort 12 km, and nearby it the Wigwam hotel, set in superb grounds and built in a very novel manner. The Buffelspoort Holiday Resort is situated at Marikana, 30 km from Rustenburg; and 2 km further on is the Mountain Sanctuary Park. From the Buffelspoort Resort a gravel turn-off leads to the Buffelspoort Dam where the fishing is good, and there are facilities for water sports as well as picnic and camping grounds on the lake verges. This gravel road joins the road previously described which climbs the southern side of the Magaliesberg from Doornkloof.

After a pleasant 58 km drive east the road reaches a turn-off leading 13 km eastwards to the town of ...

BRITS

When the Pretoria–Rustenburg railway line was constructed, a station was created amongst a cluster of granite hills on the farm *Roodekopje* and named after its owner, Gert Brits. The site of Gert Brits's farm was warm, subtropical and fertile. The building of the Hartbeespoort Dam provided a vast amount of water for irrigation and Brits became a centre for the production of tobacco, wheat, vegetables, flowers and fruit including table grapes.

Brits became a municipality in 1944 and has a present population of 26 438. In 1963 it was proclaimed a border industrial area and the town now has a number of factories, including the production of optical fibre, tools, engine components, tyres and gas (Afrox). High-quality granite is quarried by two concerns and cut and exported for extensive building projects. The Magaliesberg Grain Co-operative has its head office and huge silos in Brits.

Near De Wildt, east of Brits, there is the Margaret Roberts Herbal Centre where this renowned authority has a large herbal garden with a variety of herbal products. It is open on Wednesdays 08h30 to 16h00. There are demonstrations and lectures.

The De Wildt Cheetah Research Centre is also nearby. It was here that cheetahs were born in captivity for the first time. It is open on Tuesdays, Thursdays and weekends, with tours at 08h30 and 13h30 – booking is essential. Phone (012) 504-1921 or (012) 504-1554.

Forty-eight kilometres from Brits lies the city of Pretoria.

RUSTENBURG TO PILANESBERG

From Rustenburg, the main R27 tarmac road to Swartruggens leaves the town, travelling north-westwards for 6 km and then reaching a tarmac turn-off, R565, to Derdepoort and the Pilanesberg.

This turn-off passes through the Tswana residential area of Phokeng, largely inhabited by workers of the Bafokeng platinum mine. At 17 km the road reaches a turn-off to Paul Kruger's old homestead of *Boekenhoutfontein*, now a national monument and museum, open Tuesdays to Sundays and public holidays from 10h00 to 17h00. Beyond this turn-off the road continues through a part of the former Bantustan of *Bophuthatswana* (that which binds the Tswana), the homeland of several of the 59 different Tswana tribes of South Africa.

At 38 km a tarmac turn-off stretches for 9 km to the interesting geographical occurrence and recreational area of the ...

PILANESBERG

Phalane was a Tswana chief whose followers settled in the area of the subconical volcanic mass of rock (1 682 m high) subsequently named by Europeans the *Pilanesberg*. The Pilanesberg is one of the largest and most interesting examples in the world of alkaline rock. It is 27 km in diameter, almost circular in shape, and looks like a bushy cluster of six rings of high hills composed of volcanic rock and syenites.

In the centre of this rock wilderness there has been created the vast resort known as Sun City. Practically every known facility for entertainment, gambling, sport and recreation may be found in this resort. A wildlife sanctuary has also been established in the setting of the surrounding hills. With its game-viewing trails, water-holes and tented camp, it provides a remarkable contrast between primeval nature and the sophisticated glitter of the hotels; very plush places indeed, with all the atmosphere of staying in a large-scale cash register where the chink of coins in slot-machines and the rustle and perfume of banknotes may be heard and smelt at all hours. Several restaurants provide an interesting range of foods; there are superb swimming-pools, an exciting water slide, a spectacular garden at the Lost City hotel, an 18-hole golf-course, a lake for water sports, and many other sporting facilities such as pin bowls, a vast stadium for sporting events or pop concerts; and a magnificent theatre where some superb shows are presented.

The R27 tarmac road from Rustenburg to Swartruggens, after the turn-off to Derdepoort and the Pilanesberg, continues through well-wooded country, gently climbing the slopes of the eastern end of the Magaliesberg. At 8 km there is a turn-off leading to the Ananda Holiday Resort and back to Rustenburg, passing the turn-off to Rustenburg Kloof.

Citrus groves line both sides of the road, bearing their golden fruit around the month of June. Roadside stalls offer fruit and other products for sale. The famous Magaliesberg vultures circle overhead, and the colours of earth, sky and vegetation are vivid. The road descends the northern side of the Magaliesberg on to a great plain, densely covered in low bush. At 21,5 km a turn-off leads to Vlaklaagte and the farm *Shylock* on which stands the ruins of one of the substantial towns of stone huts and passageways built by Tswana people in former years.

Across the Koster River, 32 km from Rustenburg, the road passes the Oom Paul School. The road continues westwards until, 58 km from Rustenburg, it reaches the town of Swartruggens, where it joins the R509 tarmac road from the Witwatersrand through Magaliesburg to Mafikeng.

MAGALIESBURG TO MAFIKENG

From Magaliesburg the R509 tarmac road which we left in order to reach Rustenburg, proceeds westwards across plains covered in maize fields. Small railway and commercial centres line the route each with tall maize silos as their principal landmarks. From Derby, 53 km from Magaliesburg, a road leads to some interesting caves 27 km away, on the road to Ventersdorp.

At 69 km from Magaliesburg, the road reaches the town of ...

KOSTER

When the railway was opened to Mafikeng in 1910, Koster was established as a siding consisting of one tin shanty. The siding lay on the farm *Kleinfontein*, owned by Bastiaan Hendricus Koster, who named the place after himself. It became a village in 1913 and a municipality in 1930 and is now an agricultural, slate and diamond-mining centre. Near here, on 11 November 1970, 167 diggers raced to stake their claims in one of the last diamond rushes to take place in South Africa.

The Koster Dam provides recreational opportunities.

From Koster the tarmac road continues eastwards for 34 km and, at the town of Swartruggens, joins the R27 road previously described which leads from Rustenburg.

SWARTRUGGENS

Also known as Rodeon, *Swartruggens* (the black ridge) is a rural and railway centre situated at the foot of a low, bush-covered ridge. The town originated in 1907 when the railway line was built from Krugersdorp to Mafikeng and Swartruggens station was built on the farm *Brakfontein*. A scattering of stores, a church and school grew up near the station. A township was eventually proclaimed there and given the name of Rodeon. The population is 4 575.

From Swartruggens the R27 road continues westwards over acacia-covered hills into the fertile valley of the Groot Marico River where many beautiful lucerne, orange, tobacco and cattle farms flourish in the warm climate and fertile soil. At 29 km from Swartruggens the road passes through the small rural centre of Groot Marico, laid out on the farm *Wonderfontein*, owned by Francois Joubert, and granted its first health committee in 1927. The Marico River, after which the place is named, contributes to the agricultural prosperity of the town and is crossed 1,5 km west of the town. The name of the river is a corrupted form of the Tswana name, *Maligwa* (the erratic river).

Thirty-three kilometres from Groot Marico the tarmac road reaches the Klein Marico Poort Dam, built across a passage through a ridge of hills. There are facilities for waterskiing and angling. Three kilometres beyond the dam, the road passes the grave of Diederik Coetzee, and 3 km further on (39 km from Groot Marico) reaches the town named after his brother-in-law ...

ZEERUST

In its early days, *Zeerust* (Coetzee's rest) had the reputation of being wild and woolly. It is still easy to imagine a rugged crowd of hunters and prospectors bound for the far interior, heading down its one main street and enjoying a final fling in the hostelries. Today it is a pleasant enough rural town in a green and fertile setting of trees and long grass, backed by a high ridge of hills.

The town originated in 1864 when an itinerant builder named Walter Seymore was engaged to erect a church and fortification on the farm *Hazenjacht,* owned by Casper Coetzee. Coetzee died before the church was completed but his brother-in-law, Diederick Coetzee, continued the work, laid out a town and named it in memory of old Casper who was buried there. The first erven were sold on 20 March 1867. Zeerust became a municipality on 18 March 1936 and today the population numbers 8 944.

The town is a centre for cattle ranching, sheep, corn, wheat, tobacco, fruit and vegetables. There is mining in the district for chrome, fluorspar, lead and andalusite.

A museum housed in the civic centre is devoted to local history and is open from 09h00 to 12h00 and 13h00 to17h00 weekdays.

City dwellers wishing to escape the rigours of city life for a while will find the Marico bushveld in the Northern Province an area of great charm and tranquillity. Various farms and game ranches in the area offer visitors an opportunity to explore this area at leisure.

The Marico bushveld is the world of the champion story-teller, Oom Schalk Lourens, the literary character immortalised in the books of Herman Charles Bosman. It is a region known for its potent *mampoer* (home-distilled brandy) produced by successive generations of locals from peaches, apricots, and in fact any fruit except grapes. But, above all, the Marico is typical bushveld terrain, with a great variety of indigenous plants and trees, an abundance of birds and game species and a scenic charm which will surprise those who expect only fields of sunflowers and maize.

Accommodation on the farms varies from rustic hunting lodges to charming cottages. All are situated in lovely surroundings and offer a refuge in which the nature lover especially will revel. Anglers and water-sport enthusiasts will enjoy the many dams in the area. At the Marico Bushveld Dam, also known as Riekerts Dam, camping and ablution facilities are available. Boating and waterskiing are popular pastimes. The adjacent Marico Bushveld Nature Reserve contains more than 60 species of indigenous plants and a great many birds. The Kromellenboog Dam caters for day visitors only, and also boasts a rich bird life and good angling opportunities.

Hikers will delight in the many opportunities afforded them in this region and enjoy the diversity of landscapes ranging from open grasslands to densely vegetated kloofs. Areas such as the Enselsberg and the Groot Marico River valley are particularly scenic.

From Zeerust a tarmac road, R49, leads north to the rural centre of Nietverdiend (60 km) and from there for 40 km to the border with Botswana at Kopfontein. The Botswana post is named Tlokweng, from where it is 20 km to Gaborone.

From Zeerust, the R49 road to Mafikeng swings south-westwards, passing through the fertile valley of the *Mosega* (the divider) River. After 14 km the road reaches the railway siding of *Sendelingspos* (missionary's post) in the midst of the shallow valley. This fine agricultural area has been amply fertilised by the blood of mankind. In former years it was the home of the Hurutshe tribe who (in the custom of the Tswana-speaking people) erected two substantial towns, known as *Tshwenyane* (place of the little baboon) and *Kaditshwene* (place of baboons). These towns consisted of thousands of mud huts, the inhabitants of which prospered on agriculture, mining and working iron, as well as trading. Good fortune, unfortunately, has always attracted envy. The *Ndebele* (maTebele), then living near the site of modern Pretoria, started to raid them.

In May 1831, in the midst of an ominously developing situation, two French missionaries, Prosper Lemue and Samuel Rolland, arrived in the area and secured permission from the Hurutshe chief to establish a mission close to the site of the present railway siding of Sendelingspos. In February 1832 the missionaries effected their settlement, building a house and laying out an irrigated garden. Within a few months, however, the Ndebele invaded the area. The missionaries fled to Kuruman for safety and the Hurutshe tribe was practically destroyed. Having overthrown them, the Ndebele themselves settled in the fertile valley of the Mosega.

A second party of missionaries, this time American, arrived. With the permission of Mzilikazi, chief of the Ndebele, they rebuilt the former French station at Sendelingspos and settled there in 1836 to commence work among the followers of Mzilikazi living in the valley with their cattle.

Both the Zulus and the Voortrekkers then appeared on the scene. The Ndebele fought the advancing Voortrekkers south of the Vaal River in 1836. They were raided by the Zulus in July of that year; and in November, in the Nine Days' Battle with the Boers, were soundly defeated and driven north on a refugee trail which eventually took them to the highlands north of the Limpopo. In the face of this upheaval, the missionaries fled. All that remains of their venture is the simple railside monument marking the site of their pioneer settlement.

Beyond Sendelingspos the road gradually leads out of the valley into more open, level and lightly bushed country. The hills recede into the east. At 13 km from Sendelingspos (29 km from Zeerust) there is a turn-off north to Ottoshoop and south to Lichtenburg. *Ottoshoop,* named after Cornelius Otto, a former magistrate of Zeerust, is now little more than a railway station. Around 1895 it was the scene of a gold-rush after Michael Kelly made a discovery in the vicinity. A proper town was laid out, but unfortunately the rush proved abortive. Near Ottoshoop there is a sink-hole in the dolomite, filled with clear water of unknown depth. It is known as *Bobbejaangat* (baboon hole). The tarmac road now traverses a fine open grassland and parkland, where handsome karee and acacia trees flourish. At 43 km from Zeerust there is a turn-off south to the huge cement factory at Slurry (1,5 km). A further 6 km brings the road to the original border of the Cape Province, with the town of Mafikeng 14,5 km further west (64 km from Zeerust).

The factory of the Pretoria Portland Cement Company at Slurry was established in 1916 on the farm *Rietvallei* where a huge limestone deposit reaches the surface. It was called Slurry on account of the name applied to the raw materials used in cement manufacture when the wet process is used. Managed by a famous character in the cement business, an American, Ezekiel Davidson, this factory was skilfully developed into one of the biggest and most efficient in the world. At present consumption, the limestone deposit there is estimated to be sufficient for the next hundred years.

The R505 road branching to Lichtenburg from the railway station of Ottoshoop, 14 km before Slurry, leads southwards over a high grassland seemingly so boundless and smooth that the traveller is distinctly aware of the gentle curvature of the Earth. After 1,5 km a turn-off stretches to the source of what is known as the *Molopo* (meaning river), with another road to the same remarkable spring turning off at 21 km from Ottoshoop. A well-developed holiday resort has been created at this gigantic spring, where swimming and boating may be enjoyed in superbly clear water.

South of the turn-off to the source of the Molopo, the road enters the diamond-mining area where patches of the landscape resemble the site of a large-scale war. The human industry and energy expended in the massive disruption of this landscape was almost beyond description. Local place-names such as Elandsputte, Bakerville and Grasfontein are legendary in the history of diamonds. There is a turn-off to Bakerville at 30 km; at 50,5 km the road reaches the diamond centre of ...

LICHTENBURG

Lichtenburg commenced its development in conventional fashion, then experienced some of the most hectic events in the entire history of Southern Africa.

In 1859 Hendrik Greef settled on the farms *Elandsfontein* and the copiously watered *Doornfontein*. On 25 July 1873 a town was proclaimed on portions of these farms. President Thomas Francois Burgers named the place *Lichtenburg* (the town of light) in the hope that it would give rise to progress on the western plains. It was some time, however, before the light could be lit, for the place was remote. Progress was slow, and the village only attained the status of a health committee in 1902 and a municipality in 1904.

Maize farming became the principal occupation in a district which remained half asleep until the year 1926 when there came a change, shattering in its suddenness. On 13 March of that year Jacobus Voorendyk (son of the postmaster of Lichtenburg), together with a labourer named Jan, was digging holes for fence poles on his farm *Elandsputte* (eland's wells). As they dug the last hole of a series, Jan suddenly exclaimed *'Master, here is a diamond!'* Jacobus looked at the 0,75 carat chip in disbelief. He washed it in a bucket of water, realising that it could be glass for all he knew about diamonds.

He saddled a horse and rode with the chip to see his father in Lichtenburg. The two men took the stone to Mr Bosman, the science master of the Lichtenburg High School. *'It looks like a piece of bottle to me,'* he said dubiously.

'Try it in acid,' said Voorendyk. The little chip was placed in a bottle of acid and left on a shelf. That weekend the men almost tiptoed back to see it. There it lay, sparkling in the bottle of acid. There was no doubt about it: this was the first diamond found at Lichtenburg.

The story of the rush that followed is beyond the scope of short description. Nowhere in the world has there been a wilder or more frenzied scramble for fortune. Within twelve months there were over 100 000 people on the diggings. In many of the great claim-pegging races organised by the authorities, over 30 000 men – some hired athletes, others even on crutches – raced one another over the veld in an avalanche of diamond-crazed humanity. Each man hoped to peg a claim on a fancied position of newly proclaimed mining area.

On *Elandsputte* farm, the scene of the first discovery, there were 32 000 diggers. With Voorendyk taking 15 per cent on all diamond finds, 50 per cent on claim fees, and selling water at 6d for a 50 l barrel, he made £4 000 in the first month and £48 000 in three months. He eventually made a fortune. His farm resembled a fairground, with butchers, bakers, tea-rooms and boarding-houses springing up like weeds. Pagel's Circus arrived, as did merry-go-rounds and a prayer of four Dutch Reformed Church parsons who were intent on supervising the morals of the diggers. Schools were started, social workers appeared, doctors and midwives. Shrouding the entire scene was a permanent cloud of dust so appalling that it was like a London fog. Motorists had to switch on their headlights in the daytime. At night the dust settled on the cool faces of sleepers. It was said that when a true Lichtenburg digger breathed, a cloud of dust moved in and out of his mouth!

Many magnificent diamonds were found. The rush which had started at *Elandsputte* swept like a tornado over the veld, following the run of diamonds apparently buried in the gravels of an antique river course. Bakerville, Grasfontein, Carliesonia, Skelmkoppie and many other places became areas of digging. It is worth taking the road to Zeerust just to see these fields, mainly clustered 15 km north of Lichtenburg. The road leads for kilometres across a landscape which has been uprooted on a large scale. An atomic bomb could not have caused more prodigious a disturbance. The great rush has long since ended, petering out in about 1935, by which time over 7 million carats of diamonds had been found. A few minor discoveries were subsequently made in isolated pot-holes and pockets. Even today, a few hopefuls still root around amid the rubble hoping to find that which so many others have sought in the selfsame place, but have perhaps overlooked.

A total of 29 690 people now live in Lichtenburg, which has settled down to become a sober, prosperous and attractive town. A commercial centre has been built around a magnificent square, the lawns and fountains of which are shaded by a most elegant collection of karee trees. An equestrian statue of General Jacobus (Koos) de la Rey, the renowned leader in the Anglo-Boer War, stands on the square. Maize, sheep and cement contribute to the town a prosperity which, although not as meteoric as the diamond-fields, is far more lasting. The local Co-operative Agricultural Society handles about one-fifth of the total maize production of South Africa. There is a fine library in the town and a museum devoted to the history of the diamond-fields and the life of General De la Rey. The museum in the civic centre is open Tuesdays to Fridays from 10h00 to 12h30 and from 13h15 to 17h00; Saturdays from 09h00 to 13h00. There is a large game reserve and breeding farm on the outskirts of the town.

From Lichtenburg the tarmac R52 road leads south-westwards over a vast, level plain covered in maize and sunflower fields interspersed with plantations of gum trees. Here the mealie and sunflower are king and queen of the Earth. The small rural centres passed along the way are all made prominent by tall grain silos standing next to their railway stations.

The road, 40 km from Lichtenburg, reaches Biesiesvlei where it joins the N14 main road linking the N1 north of Johannesburg to Namibia. After a further 19 km the N14 enters the village of *Sannieshof*, named after Sannie Voorendyk, wife of the Lichtenburg postmaster of diamond discovery fame. The post office, the start of the village, was opened in 1920. Residential stands were sold there in 1928 and a village came into being, originally named *Roosville* after Tielman Roos, Member of Parliament for Lichtenburg. The fair Sannie defeated the politician, however, and in 1952 the place was renamed after her and the post office.

Twenty-one kilometres from Sannieshof (80 km from Lichtenburg) the N14 road reaches a short turn-off of 1,5 km leading to ...

BARBERSPAN

A natural freshwater lake 25 square kilometres in extent, Barberspan is known to the Africans as *Leghadighadi* (the deep water-hole) and is fed by flood spill from the Harts River (known to the Africans as *Kollong*, the place of flowing water). It is a proclaimed bird and fish reserve, frequented by immense numbers of birds such as flamingos. Shaped like a basin with a hard, flat bottom, the depth of water can be as much as 8 m, depending on the rains. Although the water is brackish, it is well liked by cattle which flourish there. Carp, yellowfish, mudfish, and the barber (barbel) which give the lake its name, thrive in the waters, the record carp having weighed 24,5 kg. Freedom from bilharzia and mosquitoes makes this a pleasure resort where swimming, boating, aquaplaning and fishing are favourite pastimes. No shooting is allowed. It is a great place for organised fishing competitions which attract a considerable crowd of enthusiasts. A fishing licence for Barberspan may be obtained from any local magistrate.

From Barberspan the N14 road continues south-westwards. After 5 km the road passes the Barberspan station, dominated by the usual tall grain silo. After a further 14 km (100 km from Lichtenburg), the road reaches the town of ...

DELAREYVILLE

This town is situated in a slight hollow in the centre of which is a lakelet (or pan). These pans occur frequently on this flat landscape since there is no run-off of rain-water, which then tends to collect in the slightest depression. Most of these pans are saline and salt is recovered from them. The two principal pans near Delareyville produce about 70 000 sacks of salt a year.

Delareyville was founded in 1914 when the first erven were sold and the town named after the famous General Jacobus Hercules (Herculaas Koos) de la Rey of the Anglo-Boer War. A statue of General de la Rey stands in front of the municipal offices. The battlefield where he won his great victory over Lord Methuen on 7 March 1902, during the Anglo-Boer War, is 20 km north-east of the town.

Maize is the principal agricultural product.

From Delareyville the R506 tarmac road branches south from the N14 and, in company with the railway line, continues across the flat maize and sunflower lands. After 5 km a turn-off east to Ottosdal is reached and a further 19 km takes the road past the rural centre and grain silo of Migdol. For a further 19 km the maize lands stretch without a break, then begin to peter out into stonier soil covered in grass, where flocks of sheep and herds of cattle graze. Low hills appear, and the road, 30,5 km from Migdol, passes the substantial Wentzel Dam in the Harts River, where fine camping, caravan and picnic sites are shaded by numerous trees. Three kilometres further on, sheltered by a ridge of bush-covered hills, lies the town of ...

SCHWEIZER-RENEKE

The town lies on the banks of the Harts River at the foot of the hillock known as Mamusa, used as a stronghold in former years by the Koranna chief, David Massouw. In the year 1885 the cattle-rustling activities of these people provoked a small-scale war with the South African Republic. The hill stronghold was captured, with ten Europeans killed, and the Koranna driven away. The stone fortifications of David Massouw may still be seen on top of the hill. The summit yields an excellent view of the town, laid out in 1886 and named after two of the Europeans killed in the punitive attack, Captain C A Schweizer and Field-Cornet C N Reneke. In a fertile valley shaded by handsome acacia trees, the town has flourished on the production of maize, sunflowers, groundnuts, cattle and sheep. The population is 26 313. There are some excellent Bushman paintings 5 km from the town.

From Schweizer-Reneke the R506 tarmac road leads south-westwards across a level, open parkland of acacia and karee trees where substantial maize and mixed farms flourish on rich, dark-red coloured soil. One and a half kilometres from the town there is a turn-off south to Bloemhof (56 km), while 90 km from Schweizer-Reneke the road reaches the town of Christiana and joins the Diamond Way, N12, from the Cape to Johannesburg. Alternatively, from Schweizer-Reneke the tarmac R504 road may be taken, leading for 29 km to the small rural centre of *Amalia*. Named after Mrs Amalia Faustmann, a well-known church personality in Schweizer-Reneke, this little farming centre was founded as a church community on 23 April 1927. From there a good road continues westwards for 42 km until, at the railway centre of Pudimoe it reaches a junction with the main R49 tarmac road linking Kimberley to Mafikeng.

The main N12 tarmac road from the Cape to the Witwatersrand, sometimes known as the Diamond Way, branches off from the Kimberley–Mafikeng road at Warrenton on the Vaal River (see Chapter Fourteen). During the low-water winter season alluvial diggers may generally be seen here searching for diamonds in the gravels left by the receding water. The road leads under the main railway line, passing the station of Fourteen Streams and (4 km from the bridge) a turn-off south to the diversionary weir in the Vaal River which supplies water to the Vaal-Harts irrigation scheme. This weir was completed in 1935 and diverts water from the Vaal to the valley of the Harts River in the Cape where 1 200 smallholdings produce rich crops from irrigated lands. At the weir, the impounded Vaal provides fine boating and fishing opportunities. There is a camping ground with simple facilities and a small shop.

At 2,5 km from the turn-off to the weir, the road reaches the Northern Cape border. The landscape consists of a vast plain covered in grass and a scattering of acacia trees. It is inclined to be bleak in the dry, cold winter months but green and pleasant in summer. In the midst of this plain, lying in the shade of trees growing on the right bank on the Vaal River, 42 km north-east from Warrenton, on the N12, is the town of ...

CHRISTIANA

A town where the houses stand on plots so large that they could be miniature farms, Christiana is essentially a rural centre. Towering maize storage silos are the principal landmark.

The town was the offspring of the diamond mania during the late 1860s. In *Lost Trails of the Transvaal* it is related that during the unseemly and bitter arguments concerning possession of the diamondiferous reaches of the Vaal River, President Marthinus Wessel Pretorius of the Transvaal laid claim to the area. In order to emphasise ownership of this portion of the Transvaal, a town was hurriedly laid out on the banks of the Vaal and the first erven sold on 25 November 1870. To this place was applied the name of *Christiana* in honour of the daughter of President Pretorius.

In 1872 diamonds were found in the river gravel at Christiana. The subsequent rush to the area stimulated the growth of a digger's town, inhabited by some notably rough and tough characters. A few diggers still work the Christiana field and occasionally a good diamond is found. The town, however, is nowadays mainly the home of a far more sober-minded crowd of people whose excitement is derived from the pleasures of good fishing and boating on the river, a sulphur bath 6 km out of town, camping and caravan sites beneath the riverine willows, numerous islands on the river and some interesting prehistoric engravings on the rocks. The population has reached 15 017.

From Christiana, the main N12 tarmac road continues north-eastwards over flat, lightly bushed country. The diamond diggings lie to the left of the road. After 6 km there is a turn-off to the sulphur baths, well developed by the Transvaal Provincial Council for Public Resorts (Overvaal, now Aventura). The sulphur springs are tepid (36,7°C) but highly mineralised. The holiday resort (known as the Rob Ferreira Mineral Baths after the chairman of the Mineral Baths Board of Trustees) comprises warmed private baths; a fine open-air swimming-bath (filled with filtered water from the adjacent Vaal River); a restaurant, numerous recreational facilities; and an interesting Diggers' Museum. A game reserve adjoins the resort.

Beyond the resort the N12 road passes the scene of another of the old diamond rushes where countless pits and gravel dumps provide the sole reminder of the feverish activity which once took place there.

Twenty-four kilometres from Christiana the road passes a large salt-pan, one of the peculiar depressions which form the principal feature of this otherwise level country.

At 47 km from Christiana the road reaches the town of ...

BLOEMHOF

This town, the name of which means 'garden of flowers', is a maize centre dominated by tall storage silos. Dairy products, salt and malt are also produced there.

The town had its origin in March 1866 when James Barkly laid out a town on his farm and named it after a garden of flowers cultivated there by his daughter. In those days a pontoon known as the North Star provided a ferry service across the Vaal River adjoining the town. The great storage dam of Oppermansdrift has now been built on the site of the old river crossing. The town is inhabited by 14 752 people.

The dam, generally known as the Bloemhof Dam, has a wall 4,5 km long and has a capacity of 1 273 million cubic metres. The lake provides excellent opportunities for water sports, swimming, angling and cruising. There is a caravan park on the shores. Another riverside recreational and camping area is at Die Hoek. There is, 17 km from the town, the S A Lombard Nature Reserve, where highveld game animals are bred for the restocking of farms.

From Bloemhof the N12 Diamond Way continues across the flat, grassy plain notable for its brown-red coloured soil, maize lands, sheep-runs and scattered acacia bush. After 9 km the road passes the scene of another of the chaotic old diamond rushes. Here the landscape is reminiscent of a world war battlefield scarred by innumerable holes, trenches, cuts and stacked with piles of rubble. This rush took place along the course of the Bamboesspruit and its tributaries. An occasional digger still searches through this narrow, 64 km long jumble, hoping to find by modern means what the old-timers overlooked in their frenzy. Five kilometres further on there is a turn-off east leading to the railway junction and village of Makwassie. At 64,5 km from Bloemhof the road reaches the town of ...

WOLMARANSSTAD

The town of Wolmaransstad lies in the shallow valley of the *Makwassi* stream, so named on account of the number of aromatic wild spearmint bushes *Groton gratissimus*, growing along its banks. In 1876 a trader, Thomas Leask, opened a store on this site. On 16 February 1891 a town was established there by proclamation and named after J M A Wolmarans, a member of the Executive Council of the South African Republic.

The town was planned as a centre for the farming community, with maize being the principal local product. The population numbers 21 664.

MAKWASSIE

The railway junction and village of Makwassie lies 14 km south of Wolmaransstad. It was the site of a mission station established in 1822 by two Wesleyan missionaries, Thomas Hodgson and Samuel Broadbent. This was the first mission station in the Transvaal. It was there, on 21 July 1823, that the first European baby was born in the Transvaal, a son to Mrs Broadbent.

The mission was abandoned in 1824 because of incessant disturbances amongst the tribes and the ill health of the Reverend Broadbent. In 1905 the railway from the Cape to Johannesburg was built, with a station named after the *Makwassie* (spearmint bushes) stream which watered the area. Two years later a village was laid out next to the station. The place grew as a junction for a branch line to Wolmaransstad and places north.

Maize and ground-nuts are cultivated on a large scale in the area. There are large silos for the storage and loading of maize, grain, sorghum and (the first of its kind in the world) for ground nuts. There is a large ground-nut factory in the village built by the South-Western Transvaal Agricultural Co-operative Ltd.

The branch railway connects Makwassie on the main Cape–Johannesburg line to Wolmaransstad and, 45 km north of Wolmaransstad on the R505 road, to the town of ...

OTTOSDAL

Laid out in 1913 as a church centre on the well-watered farm *Korannafontein* owned by G P Otto, the town was proclaimed in 1918. It is a farming centre for maize, sunflowers and ground-nuts.

Eight kilometres north of Ottosdal the extraordinary slate known as wonderstone is quarried. This is a fine-grained stone which can be carved, turned on a lathe or worked into flexible strips or sheets as thin as 2 mm. It is capable of withstanding enormous heat and is used for insulating spacecraft. It is exported to many countries.

There is a Garden of Remembrance in the town, containing the bodies of British soldiers killed in the Anglo-Boer War.

The branch railway and R505 road continues northwards from Ottosdal through vast fields of maize and sunflowers. After 48 km there is a crossroads with the N14. The R505 road continues north for 37 km and then reaches Lichtenburg. The N14 road leads eastwards from the crossroads and, after 20 km, reaches the railway junction and town of ...

COLIGNY

In the last session of the Transvaal parliament before the Union of South Africa was formed in 1910, the late General Jacobus de la Rey, Member of Parliament for Lichtenburg, secured approval for the construction of a railway line from Welverdiend, on the main Cape–Johannesburg line, to Lichtenburg, and from a junction to Delareyville and Schweizer-Reneke. The line was opened on 11 May 1911 and the junction was on the farm *Rietvlei*. As that was the name of another station in the Transvaal, the junction was renamed Treurfontein. To complicate the matter, the Dutch Reformed Church congregation was known as Welgemoed.

When the village became a municipality in 1923, it was named after Gaspard de Coligny, the French admiral and Huguenot leader who had died in the Massacre of St Bartholomew in 1572. Several descendants of Huguenots live in the vicinity of the junction, farming maize and sunflowers on a large scale. The congregation and the railway junction also changed their name in honour of the Huguenot leader.

Apart from its agricultural activity, Coligny has substantial railway repair workshops and is an educational centre for the district. There is some diamond-mining activity in the area.

The 1914 'Armed Protest' took place on the *Rietvlei* farm during the First World War.

From Coligny, the N14 road leads eastwards alongside the railway line for 53 km and reaches ...

VENTERSDORP

In 1866 a church centre was established on the farm *Roodepoort* (red pass) owned by Johannes Venter. The place was eventually proclaimed a town on 17 February 1888 and named after the owner of the farm. The town lies in the valley of the *Schoonspruit* (clear stream) which is contained in the Rietspruit Dam. An irrigation canal stretches from this dam to Klerksdorp and supplies copious water for agriculture.

Ventersdorp is therefore a well-watered and pleasant place in a very fertile setting. Maize is the principal agricultural industry. It is quite a sight from June to August to see the long queues of farm vehicles delivering their crops to the giant silos for storage and dispatch.

There is a museum with an interesting collection of rifles used in the Anglo-Boer War. The cemetery in the centre of the town contains graves of British and Boer soldiers killed in the Anglo-Boer War. Included amongst them is what is known as 'The Grave with Eternal Flowers'. It is there that an Irish soldier named Shaw lies buried. He protested against the destruction of farms and sided with the Boers. He was arrested, court martialled and executed by a British firing-squad.

There are diamond diggings at Swartplaat and Swartrand still being worked. Two water-mills in the Schoonspruit date from the previous century.

From Ventersdorp, the N14 road leads eastwards across the maize fields of the old Transvaal for 83 km to Krugersdorp. The R30 road leads southwards for 72 km to Klerksdorp.

From Wolmaransstad the N12 tarmac road continues over gently undulating grassy plains covered with maize fields and patches of thorn bush. At 37 km from Wolmaransstad there occurs an especially dense thicket of these thorn trees (*Harpagophytum procumbens*), known as the *Leeuwdoorns* (lion thorns), a great stronghold for predators in the days when the plains were alive with herds of game. The village of Leeuwdoringstad lies to the south.

LEEUWDORINGSTAD

This amiable village was laid out next to the railway station built in 1908 and named *Leeuwdoorns* from the surrounding thicket of thorn trees. The village lies on the farm *Rietkuil* formerly owned by A Strachen. It was proclaimed in December 1920 and received a village council in October 1958.

The village is the centre for a considerable agricultural industry in maize, sunflowers and ground-nuts. It is the headquarters of the South-Western Transvaal Co-operative Agricultural Society. There is a game reserve at Klipspruit on the Vaal River. The river provides recreational opportunities along a frontage of 20 km.

Being closely attached to the railway has not always been to the advantage of Leeuwdoringstad. On 17 July 1932, a freight train of 32 trucks loaded with 1 200 tons of dynamite exploded there. Wreckage was strewn as far away as 10 km from the accident and the sound of the explosion is said to have been heard several hundred kilometres away. Incredibly enough, only five people and a herd of cattle grazing in a nearby field were killed, but nearly every house in the village was damaged. There is a museum in the village, containing photographs and information about this disaster and the district in general.

After 51,5 km from Wolmaransstad, the N12 road reaches a turn-off north to the Dominion Reefs mining area, the first sign of gold-mining activity in what has so far been entirely a diamond region.

After a further 21 km a turn-off leads to Hartbeesfontein while 6 km further on (81 km from Wolmaransstad), the road reaches the substantial mining town of ...

KLERKSDORP

Klerksdorp originated with the arrival in the Transvaal of the first Voortrekkers. Early in 1838 an intrepid character, C M du Plooy, settled on the banks of the *Schoonspruit* (clear stream) and set himself up as master of a 16 187 ha farm named *Elandsheuvel* (eland's slopes). Other trekkers joined him. In exchange for the construction of a dam and water furrow, they received rights to half of the huge farm. There they settled, and the collection of rough dwellings which they erected subsequently received the name of *Klerksdorp*, from Barend le Clerq, the patriarch of the early settlement.

For some years Klerksdorp remained a quiet rural village, its principal buildings consisting of a church and a store run by James Taylor and Thomas Leask, which contained under one roof practically every possible commercial activity.

In 1885 traces of gold were found on the farm *Ysterspruit* (iron stream) by a farmer named Van Vuuren. Then, in August 1886, A P Roos found gold on the town commonage. A tremendous boom started, with what was named the Schoonspruit Gold-Field being regarded as a new Barberton. Over 4 000 diggers drew lots for rights to mine the town lands in July 1888, and the shacks they erected caused the town to sprawl in an untidy and unlovely manner, as if it was composed of corrugated iron and dust.

By the beginning of 1889 there were 200 commercial buildings, including 69 canteens and one stock exchange. At the end of the year the boom suddenly collapsed. There was no doubt about the presence of gold in the area but, compared to the spectacular finds on the Witwatersrand, the discoveries all consisted of low-grade ore. Most of the companies floated to exploit the Klerksdorp reefs were too over-capitalised ever to show a profit on such grades. Many went bankrupt. Those that remained drastically reduced their capital. Their continuing activities, combined with agriculture (principally maize production), brought the area to its present state of prosperity.

Gold and uranium are largely mined in the area today. The Central Western Co-operative Company – the largest grain co-operative in the southern hemisphere and the second largest in the world – has its headquarters in the town. Numerous mills, silos and elevators demonstrate that Klerksdorp is one of the leading grain towns of the world. Sussex cattle are bred in the area. The town is a bustling, modern place with an impressive commercial and civic centre. The population is 239 070.

Visits to mines can be arranged – for information phone the tourism office on (086) 111-1888.

The Faan Meintjes Nature Reserve lies 15 km from the town. It is a home for 30 species of game and 150 species of birds. There are attractive drives, a choice of three hiking trails, and facilities for lectures, accommodation and recreation.

The John Neser Dam, a few kilometres from the town, provides opportunities for water sports.

The Klerksdorp Museum is housed in a sandstone building erected in 1891 as a prison and used as such until 1973. The museum depicts scenes from prison life, geology, archaeology and social history. It is open weekdays 10h00 to 13h00 and 14h00 to 16h30; Saturdays 09h30 to 12h00 and 14h00 to 17h00. Next to the museum is the old warden's house with its Victorian exhibitions.

The beautiful station building, which was officially opened in 1897 by President Paul Kruger, was declared Klerksdorp's first national monument in 1983. Also of interest is Hendrik Potgieter Road, the oldest street in what was previously the Transvaal. The old cemetery houses the graves of British soldiers and the 968 children who died in Klerksdorp's concentration camp. A monument in memory of the women and children was also erected in this cemetery.

Annual festivals include a one-day street festival in October and the annual agricultural show in April.

An interesting excursion is the 12 km long Oudorp Hiking Trail, which winds through the oldest parts of Klerksdorp.

Thirteen kilometres south of Klerksdorp lies the mining centre of ...

ORKNEY

Simon Fraser, a pioneer of gold-mining in the Western Transvaal, came from the Orkney Islands of Scotland. The adit of the mine he worked on the farm *Witkoppies* (white hills) near the site of Orkney may still be seen. The ore was trundled to the surface by wheelbarrow! The adit is still in use as a ventilation shaft for the Orkney Mine.

The town was proclaimed on 20 March 1940. It was named after the Orkney Mine and became a municipality in March 1962. Today it has a population of 12 369. It is the centre for the Vaal Reefs Exploration and Mining Co Ltd. The town lies on the banks of the Vaal River and the town council has created the Orkney-Vaal Holiday Resort with angling, swimming, water sports, and numerous facilities for entertainment, refreshment, relaxation and sport.

The town is attractive, well-planned and possesses fine gardens and many trees as well as a modern commercial centre.

Thirty kilometres north-west of Klerksdorp lies the agricultural centre of ...

HARTBEESFONTEIN

It is said that in 1837, when Hendrik Potgieter led an attack against Mzilikazi and his Ndebele people, a number of his followers were left in a laager for two weeks. One of the men went hunting. He wounded a *hartbees* (a member of the *Alcelaphus* species of antelope), pursued it and discovered a spring of crystal-clear water on a hillock. He liked the area and subsequently obtained it as a farm which he named *Hartbeesfontein*. He later exchanged the farm for two oxen. The new owner, a Mr Grobler, built a house on the site of the present police station.

The farm had several owners, was sub-divided and, without any planning, became a relaxed residential centre with a church and a few stores. Maize, sunflowers, and ground-nuts are produced. Avocado pears, citrus and subtropical fruits also flourish in a warm, well-watered and fertile area.

Thorn and other trees grow in great profusion and it is altogether a very pleasant little place.

From Klerksdorp the main road, N12, now a double carriageway, continues north-eastwards over open, grassy plains covered with maize fields, plantations of gum trees, and cattle farms. After 10 km from the road passes the mining township of ...

STILFONTEIN

In 1888, Charles Scott, who had immigrated with his family from Strathmore county in Scotland, working on his farm *Strathvaal*, found the outcrop of a gold reef which he named Strathmore Reef. The reef contained good gold, but was very broken and vanished beneath an overburden of dolomite and basalt. After the death of Charles Scott, his son Jack continued to search for the reef. In 1895 he obtained an option over the farm *Stilfontein* (quiet fountain). Two years later a borehole on it intersected the lost reef and assayed 101 inch dwt of gold. Three more boreholes confirmed the presence of the reef. In 1949 the Stilfontein Gold Mining Co was registered, with Jack Scott as its chairman. Two shafts named Charles and Margaret were sunk and production commenced in 1952. Other mines were also created to work the reef. With uranium added to the gold output, the Stilfontein area developed rapidly.

A town was laid out in 1949 and serves four important mines – Stilfontein, Hartebeesfontein, Buffelsfontein and Zandpan. It has grown rapidly into a modern and vigorous mining town which is worth visiting. The parks are handsome and a shopping centre has been built around a garden and fountain. An attractive building houses the town council which administers the place. Generally the town is neat, well laid out, (without any traffic-lights), modern and functional.

From Stilfontein the N12 double carriageway continues north-eastwards, passing after 3 km the Hartebeesfontein Gold Mining Company's complex of dumps, shafts and works.

The country becomes increasingly wooded, with indigenous acacias and plantations of exotic gum trees flourishing. Past the turn-off south to Orkney (24 km from Klerksdorp) the road proceeds over this landscape of bush and low hills. At 46,5 km from Klerksdorp the road reaches the attractive town of ...

POTCHEFSTROOM

Founded by the Voortrekkers as their first town north of the Vaal River, Potchefstroom was once the capital of the original South African Republic. It was in November 1837, after the defeat of the Ndebele in the famous Nine Days' Battle, that Andries Hendrik Potgieter, leading his men back to their wagons in the south, forded the river they named the *Mooi* (beautiful) on account of its green and pleasant banks. Potgieter decided then that a town should be established at the site of the crossing, and a weeping willow tree was planted to mark the spot.

At the end of 1838 the town was laid out on a site about 11 km upstream from modern Potchefstroom. The wet season of 1840 revealed that the reason for the site being so vividly green was that it was actually a marsh. A new town was hurriedly laid out downstream, this time on a better-chosen site. It was planned on a spacious scale with broad, straight streets running in the direction of the compass points. Each street was lined with water furrows. There were erven of 1,2 ha each and three vast squares for a church, market and outspan. The town received the name of *Potchefstroom* (stream of chief Potgieter). The original site is only recorded by history as being the *Oudedorp* (old town).

Potchefstroom experienced a stormy political period during its time as capital of the Republic. Even after 1860 when Pretoria became the state capital, Potchefstroom still remained a place of political and cultural importance. During the curious Boer Civil War of 1862–64, Potchefstroom changed hands several times after siege and counter-siege, during which the vicious sound of rifle fire often echoed down the streets.

It was in Potchefstroom that the first glimmer was seen of the future gold wealth of Southern

Africa. On 20 March 1867 the first agricultural show in the Transvaal was held in Potchefstroom. Among the displays was a collection of 100 mixed mineral specimens recently gathered in the country by the German geologist, Karl Mauch. Mauch received a prize of £5 for his collection. The variety of his samples impressed on many people the possibilities of the as-yet-untouched mineral resources of the country.

In November of the same year Mauch returned to Potchefstroom from a prospecting journey to the north, accompanied by the famous hunter, Henry Hartley. To the Potchefstroom newspaper, *The Transvaal Argus*, fell the excitement of publishing the first news of Mauch's claim to have found a gold-field of enormous wealth on the Tati River in Botswana. This story, reprinted all over the world, started the first rush to Southern Africa, attracting a stream of adventurers to Potchefstroom where they completed their outfits and prepared for ventures into the interior in search of gold and game.

The Anglo-Transvaal War of 1880–81 saw a British garrison of 203 soldiers, 48 civilian men, women and children, and 61 African servants besieged in the Potchefstroom fort, where the soldiers remained securely bottled up for the duration of the disturbance. All these alarms and excursions from the past have left with Potchefstroom an atmosphere and a character peculiarly its own.

The town, the first municipality of the Transvaal, lies in one of the most fertile and well-watered areas of Southern Africa. The springs of the Mooi River are powerful, and Potchefstroom is one of the few remaining places in Southern Africa to retain the amiable luxury of having irrigation water gurgling down furrows on either side of the streets for use by gardeners.

With a cold, dry, frosty highveld winter and a warm summer with a good rainfall of 609 mm, the valley of the Mooi River is a healthy and productive place in which to live. Irrigation is largely practised and fruit, vegetables and maize are produced. Grain silos dominate the town, while more day-old chicks are hatched and marketed here than from anywhere else in the country. Culturally, Potchefstroom retains considerable importance, for it is a university town. The campus of the Potchefstroom University for Christian Higher Education is spacious and beautiful. The enrolment is over 9 000 students. Both Afrikaans and English medium schools are numerous. Potchefstroom is also the headquarters of the General Support Base North West (GSB North West) of the South African National Defence Force (previously the Western Transvaal Command), with its substantial military camp and one of the world's most famous artillery ranges.

Industries such as organ-building and sausage-making are carried out locally. The largest malt factory in the world and the principal chalk and crayon factory in Southern Africa are situated outside the town. The malt factory markets 50 per cent of all sorghum in South Africa and 85 per cent of the packed product.

One of the treasures of Potchefstroom is the restored residence of President Marthinus Wessel Pretorius which, combined with the stable, coach-house and smithy under the oak trees, creates an interesting museum depicting the culture of the last century. The main museum depicts the Great Trek and the story of the South African Republic. The only wagon surviving from the Battle of Blood River is exhibited here. The Totius House Museum preserves the memory of Jacob Daniel du Toit, well known under the *nom de plume* of Totius. He was a poet, translator of the Bible and advocate of the Afrikaans language. Many heirlooms and other items are displayed in this example of a town dwelling of former years. The Totius Garden of Remembrance on the banks of the *Wasgoedspruit* (laundry stream) contains the Totius statue and monument. The Goetz/Fleischack Museum reflects the opulent Victorian life-style of two prominent families of German descent.

Other interesting replicas and buildings include the old fort, powder-magazine, the Selbourne Hall on the site of the original Potchefstroom Agricultural College, the *Hervormde* (reformed) Church, the magistracy and post office, the Gunners' Memorial, the Centenary Monument sculpted by Coert Steynberg, and the Garden of Remembrance with the concentration camp monument.

Tom Street is a superb avenue 6,84 km in length and lined by 710 oak trees. The town is notable for many other lovely trees, with over 15 000 planted to shade the streets. There is also a handsome conservatoire of music, a theological seminary, a fine library, the Agricultural College and Research Institute, and a splendid museum of local history and art. There are numerous churches and schools in the town and an extensive recreational facility for swimming, boating and angling at a pleasure resort on the banks of the Mooi River Dam. The population is 102 118.

Beyond Potchefstroom the main N12 road crosses the Mooi River and leaves the town in an easterly direction, winding and climbing through low hills. Plantations of gum trees alternate with maize fields and clumps of acacia bush. This pleasant rural landscape, scattered with many fine farms, is particularly green in summer.

Roads branch off at 10 km to Vereeniging and at 40 km to the town of *Fochville*, laid out during the First World War and named after Marshal Ferdinand Foch, Commander-in-Chief of the Allied Forces in France. Beyond the turn-off to this town, the road climbs over a long ridge of acacia-covered hills. High on these hills, 47 km from Potchefstroom, may be seen to the south the monument to Danie Theron, a renowned figure in the Anglo-Boer War and the scourge of the British army. He was eventually killed while scouting British positions from the top of this hill. The site of his death is marked by a tall monument which appears rather odd from a distance but is worth closer inspection. The metal sculpture on top of the plinth symbolises the flame of liberty. A path leads to the summit of the hill, where some interesting ruins remain of the defensive stone walls built by prehistoric African tribes. Similar walls can be found on the summits of many hills in the Northern and North-West Provinces. The settlements they protected were nearly all abandoned when the Ndebele destroyed the tribal structure of the area.

The signs of considerable mining activity are now visible, for the road is traversing what is, in fact, one of the world's richest gold-mining areas. At 50 km from Potchefstroom where the N12 road reaches an important crossroads, with branches leading to Fochville (south) and Carletonville (north), it is interesting to learn something of the story of this wealthy mining area.

THE FAR WEST WITWATERSRAND MINING AREA

The Mooi River (on the banks of which stands the town of Potchefstroom) has its birthplace in a series of powerful springs which gush out of dolomite formations. One of its principal tributaries, the Mooirivierloop, flows down a long, shallow, grassy valley stretching up to the high ridge of the Witwatersrand. Among the springs of this tributary is the famous *Wonderfontein* (wonderful fountain), which rises out of the dolomite near the railway station of Bank, flowing from a great cave as a perennial stream of the clearest water imaginable.

The splendid water of the valley captivated the attention of the Voortrekkers. As early as 1842 they started to settle there on farms such as *Buffelsdoorn* (buffalo thorn) owned by the Harmse family; Wonderfontein owned by the Oberholzers; and *Welverdiend* (well deserved), whose pleasant name is said to have derived from its first owner, F G Wolmarans. Searching for new grazing and weary after a long ride, he off-saddled there and rested in the shade of a bush. He fell asleep so peacefully that when he awoke he was gratified to think that he had enjoyed such a well deserved rest.

Notwithstanding its copious water, the dolomite soil of the area was not rich agriculturally. As early as 1895, however, the area was prospected and there was a general feeling amongst geologists that the main reef of the Witwatersrand extended under the dolomites to the west. In the period 1898 to 1899, D J Pullinger sank a series of boreholes in the area and one of these, on *Gemsbokfontein*, struck gold.

The Anglo-Boer War retarded development but, when peace came, the Western Rand Estates Ltd was formed to work the area. The main reef was found on farms such as *Libanon* and *Venterspost*. In 1910 the first shaft, known as the Pullinger Shaft, was sunk on *Gemsbokfontein*, but water flooded in from the dolomite when it was only 29,5 m deep. Several other equally abortive efforts were made, but there was no technical answer at that time to the flooding problem and work petered out. It is ironic that nowadays the Pullinger Shaft is used to supply domestic water to the Venterspost mine on whose property it lies.

Several years passed, during which time the cementation process was perfected as a means of overcoming underground water problems. Modern geophysicists also entered the picture. Dr Rudolf Krahmann, a German geophysicist, studied the area with the aid of a magnometer, a delicate instrument which allowed him to trace the magnetic shales known to occur in relation with the main reef group. The results were so remarkable that the New Consolidated Gold Fields Company became interested. Options were taken up on the whole valley. In 1932, Western Witwatersrand Areas Ltd was formed for the specialised task of proving and developing the area.

Immense activity ensued in the vicinity of *Wonderfontein*. In the space of a few short years the barren valley was transformed by tarmac roads, townships and enormous new working gold-mines. Of these, the one on the aptly named farm *Blyvooruitzicht* (joyful prospect), registered on 10 June 1937, and the nearby West Driefontein mine are two of the richest gold-mines in the world. In 1965 their yield in pennyweights of gold per ton of ore was 12,5 dwt and 16,4 dwt, respectively, compared to an average of 7,5 dwt for the industry.

The fact that these mines produce at all is a miracle of applied science, for the technical difficulties of working through dolomite are immense. When the first Blyvooruitzicht shaft was sunk in 1938, water burst from a fissure at a depth of 430 m, flooding the shaft at the rate of 1 818 000 *l* an hour.

Some 917 cubic metres of broken brick and 14 438 packets of cement were tipped into the shaft to form an underground concrete plug through which work was continued. The shaft was completed in June 1941, reaching a depth of 1 536 m. Milling operations started in February 1942 and, by December 1950, 741 360 kg (2 615 028 oz) of gold had been produced. The principal town in this remarkable mining area known as Westonaria is ...

CARLETONVILLE

Named after Guy Carleton Jones, the resident director of the New Consolidated Gold Fields Ltd, *Carletonville* (with its present population of 15 657) was proclaimed in 1948 and on 1 July 1959 became a municipality. In its area are included the townships of Carletonville and extensions. Oberholzer and extensions, Welverdiend, Blyvooruitzicht, Bank, Blybank, West Wits and Water's Edge.

From the Fochville–Carletonville crossroads (50 km from Potchefstroom) the N12 road continues north-eastwards passing the wayside Kraalkop Hotel (53 km) and then climbing over a ridge of hills to descend into the Wonderfontein mining valley. At 63 km the road passes the Kloof Gold Mining Company; at 66 km there is a turn-off north to Carletonville; and a further 1,5 km brings the road to a turn-off to the mining areas and townships of Libanon, Westonaria and Venterspos.

Ahead to the north and east, the long ridge of the Witwatersrand may now be seen: a continuous complex of mines, factories and built-up areas. Turn-offs are numerous: at 72 km to Randfontein (16 km); at 74 km to Western Areas Gold Mining Company; at 87 km to Lawley (south) and Randfontein (north).

The N12 road now passes the Johannesburg municipal waterworks at Zuurbekom and then traverses the city's principal complex of African residential areas around Nancefield (95,5 km). At 98 km from Potchefstroom the road passes the Kliptown turn-off (100 km), climbs through plantations of wattle and gum trees and, 106 km from Potchefstroom, joins the great N1 trunk road of Africa coming in from the Cape on its way to the far north. This is the terminus of the Diamond Way and the entrance to the city of Johannesburg, the civic centre of which lies 10 km away (116 km from Potchefstroom).

Chapter Forty

BOTSWANA

In the extraordinary patchwork quilt of eco-systems, climatic zones, vegetational regions and landscapes which comprise Southern Africa, the area of windblown sands which makes up Botswana is so unique that it is one of the natural wonders of the world. This mantle of sand covers an area of 1,2 million square kilometres of central Southern Africa. Of this sandy region, Botswana occupies 581 730 square kilometres.

The sand mantle, the largest in the world, forms a shallow saucer tilted downwards to the north. The entire geological receptacle is a thirsty trap, a beggar's pan held out towards the north in supplication. Rainfall over the mantle of sand is erratic and skimpy. At best about 700 mm a year may fall in favoured areas, and only 200 mm or less over half of Botswana. As in most of Africa, rainfall occurs in the short 'wet' seasons of December and January, with some spit and promise in November, petering out into scattered thunderstorms in February, March and April. From May to October there is no rain.

No water remains on the surface of the sand mantle and there is no run-off. For short periods water gathers in depressions and hollows, forming shallow lakelets known as *pans*, most of them well mineralised with natural salts and lime. Without constant replenishment, however, the parched sand and atmosphere simply absorb the water which soaks down or evaporates rapidly until nothing is left. The vegetation which has blossomed amazingly with the rains reverts to drabness.

The supplicating pan, however, reaches northwards hopefully and finds Nature to be compassionate in a very ingenious way. Far to the north in the highlands of Angola, heavy rainfall of up to 2 500 mm a year finds a run-off in the form of the *Okavango* River (named after the chief Kavango of the Mbukushu tribe), one of the principal drainers of these floodwaters. Nature has caused the river to flow due south, but it does not reach the sea. Instead, the river drops down from the highlands in cascades and waterfalls. In about June each year its floodwaters are confronted by the saucer of sand.

There is no escape for the Okavango. It spreads out in a cone-shaped delta over the northern portion of the sand mantle, forming 16 000 square kilometres of an almost magical water world. Depending on the amount of rainfall in the highlands, the water pushes southwards despairingly, infiltrating every hollow and rill, groping on in the hope of finding a sudden drop in altitude to restore its flow. It becomes sluggish as it is impeded by the seemingly endless saucer of sand which eventually rises towards the southern rim. The dispirited river finally gives up. It even starts to flow in reverse as the pressure of the floods stops. The furthest points that the river reaches are Lake Ngami and the great shallow depression of Makgadikgadi, with its two main pans of Ntwetwe and Sua. This depression terminates the flow once and for all, filling with sludgy water about 250 mm in depth which covers an area of over 1 000 km in circumference. For a couple of months the morass remains, a smelly mixture of natural salts, soda and plankton which attracts prodigious numbers of aquatic birds.

Ngami (the big water) is about 2 m deep during a good season. In a poor season it too becomes a swampy puddle. In a bad season it can be completely dry. Its variations have baffled many visitors who, lured there by reports of a great lake teeming with fish, arrive to see nothing more than mirages playing on a hard floor. They leave, certain that all the descriptions of a blue-water lake so vast that it is impossible to see across to its furthest shore have simply been fabrications.

The interplay of sand and water in Botswana is a very wonderful thing to see. The vegetation and wildlife of Botswana are also magnificent, for the sand mantle is dissimilar to the face of a desert such as the dune country of the Namib or the Sahara. The annual rainfall is quite sufficient to stimulate a generous growth of vegetation. A great variety of grasses, flowering plants (especially lilies), and trees (mainly the thorny type such as various acacia species) cover the sand and provide rich grazing for antelope. Predators live on these herds of game, as do descendants of the earliest known human inhabitants of the area, the nomadic Bushmen (or basaRwa) hunters. About 10 000 pure-blooded and 20 000 mixed descendants of these pioneer people continue to roam this wilderness which they regard as their own.

African Iron Age tribes also found the area attractive and excellent for grazing cattle. The first of these people to migrate into the sand wilderness were the *Kgalagadi*, the name of whom Europeans corrupted to *Kalahari* and brought into use as the geographical name of the Kalahari Desert. About 25 000 of these people still live in the area.

The great Karanga tribe, whose main homeland lay to the north-east, in what is now Zimbabwe, also overlapped into the sand area. Their ancient skills in mining were exercised considerably when they found surface outcrops of gold on the high rim of the saucer. As with modern prospectors, the prehistoric workers were baffled by the covering of sand – a comparatively recent geological creation blanketing the same basic rock formations common to the rest of Southern Africa. These underlying rock formations could be expected to contain similar deposits of minerals, coal and other valuable treasures as in the rest of Southern Africa, if only they could be reached. However, the sand mantle makes the landscape as enigmatic as a masked human face. What lies beneath it remains a tantalising mystery. About 45 000 of the *Karanga* (or Kalanga) people live in Botswana today.

In about the 16th century a new human element migrated into the area from the north. These people spoke the language now known as *seTswana*; and tradition states that they were led by a chief named Masilo. This chief had two sons, Mohurutshe and Malope who, after their father's death, divided his following between them. Most of the descendants of Mohurutshe's section live in South Africa today, but 7 000 stay in their original homeland.

Malope's section remained. On his death, three of his sons divided his following among them, the descendants of whom are the dominant people of modern *boTswana* (Botswana). These three related tribal groups bear the names of the three sons – Kwena, Ngwato and Ngwaketse. In later years a section of the Ngwato, under a chief named Tawana, broke away and settled in the Okavango, where they now number about 45 000. The Kwena tribe number 75 000, the Ngwato 201 000, and the Ngwaketse 72 000.

Other minor tribal elements wandered into the sandy wilderness at different times, settled there and became subservient to one or other of the descendant groups of Masilo's people. Besides the basaRwa and the Kalanga, who each have their own language, about 30 separate tribal groups speak seTswana, but know themselves only by their tribal names. The present total population is 1 500 000, a population density of just over two people per square kilometre in a country 582 000 square kilometres in extent.

The generic name of Tswana was applied by foreigners to these various tribal groups, but the meaning and origin are obscure. It was convenient for the people to accept this name, originally spelt by Europeans Chuana. In its modern application seTswana is the language, baTswana the people, moTswana an individual, and boTswana (Botswana) the country. The root *Tswa* possibly originated from its application to them by Nguni (Zulu, Ndebele) people of what was their name for Bushmen.

The people of Botswana have by nature always been peaceful. They were raided in past years by such martial tribes as the Ndebele, but invariably beat them off or retired into the wilderness to hide until the trouble passed. They have always been agriculturalists and breeders of cattle, and prefer to live close together in large settlements built adjacent to water supplies.

Botswana became a British protectorate in 1884 and was known to them by the hopelessly misspelt name of Bechuanaland. The country was at first ruled directly by a High Commissioner who, strangely enough, had his headquarters in Mafikeng (then spelt Mafeking) in South Africa. Botswana was, therefore, one of the few states whose capital was situated in a foreign country. In 1960 Botswana received a representative Legislative Council, and in 1965 the centre of government was moved to Botswana itself, to Gaborone which became the capital of the country. On 30 September 1966 Botswana became an independent republic, with Sir Seretse Khama as President.

Meat is the principal agricultural product of the country, with a considerable export trade based at Lobatse in livestock and carcasses. Diamonds are mined in a great pipe at Orapa, west of Francistown. A smaller mine is situated at Letlhakane, and another mine was opened in 1982 at Jwaneng. Coal has been found at places such as Mamabula and Morupule; low-grade iron ore is mined at Chadibe; and there is a copper-nickel deposit at Selebi-Phikwe. Salt, soda ash, potash and bromides are obtained from pans such as Sua; while agates are found at Bobonong, among them a rose-coloured variety peculiar to Botswana.

A prodigious wealth of wildlife is the greatest renewable natural treasure of Botswana. Vast numbers of game animals roam across the wilderness, especially in the northern areas of Ngamiland, along the banks of the Chobe River, upstream from Kasane, and in the delta of the Okavango. Bird life is prolific and is the delight of photographers and bird-watchers.

Controlled hunting takes place under licence in most parts of Botswana. The country is divided into 36 controlled hunting areas, of which fourteen are conceded to professional safari companies, twenty are open to private hunters, two are closed, and one is under private concession.

The hunting season for most of Botswana covers the period 15 March to 15 November. At least a dozen professional companies conduct hunting or photographic safaris into the country which is today one of the principal areas in Africa for this form of sport and recreation. A variety of hunting licences are available, embracing an assortment of game animals such as elephant, crocodile, tsessebe, waterbuck, zebra, buffalo, bushbuck, hartebeest, reedbuck, wildebeest, impala, springbok, ostrich, wild pig, duiker and wart hog. Animals such as giraffe, rhino, hippo, cheetah, antbear, brown hyena, badger, klipspringer, oribi, otter, pangolin, puku and yellow-spotted dassie are totally protected. The world-record gemsbok, hartebeest and black wildebeest have been shot in Botswana. Elephants are average in stature but moderate in ivory, the Botswana record being 59,5 kg compared to the world-record of 102,5 kg taken in Kenya.

Francistown and Maun are the two principal depots for hunting safaris in Botswana which, under the auspices of professional organisations, usually last 21 days.

Game birds occur in immense numbers and may be shot under licence. Fishing is unrestricted and provides tremendous sport in the Chobe River and the Okavango, where tiger-fish abound.

Photographic and sightseeing safaris are conducted by professional companies.

There are no restrictions on private travel in Botswana, except in specific game areas, but discretion and caution are recommended. This is wild and arid country; four-wheel-drive or heavy-transport vehicles are essential if the traveller intends leaving the north–south tarmac road or the tarmac branch to Maun from Francistown.

GABORONE

A small section of the Tlokwa tribe, most of whom now live in South Africa, moved westwards into the sand wilderness. After wandering about for some years, they settled at a place called Mosaweng during the 1890s. Their leader was named Gaborone, a man who only succeeded his father in power at the age of about 60, but who remained a very well-loved chief until his death in 1932 at the estimated age of 106. The building of the railway from Vryburg in the Cape to Bulawayo in 1896–97 established Gaborone as a place-name on the map for the first time. A crossing-point for trains on the single track railway was created there and, adjoining it, a tin shanty shimmering in the heat on a rough platform of cinders. The railway was built at the record rate of 645 km in 400 days, with the erection of luxuries such as stations and conveniences simply left for more relaxed times.

The strip of ground on which the railway was constructed from north to south was actually transferred by the various chiefs to the construction company of Cecil John Rhodes. Gaborone and his people, who were living on ground by permission of the Kwena chief, overnight found themselves regarded as squatters on a railway reservation. They stayed there under tolerance until 1905 when the tract of land was transferred to the British South African Company. The Tlokwa were supposed to move. Instead, they paid the company a rental of £150 a year in order to remain as tenants. In 1933, after the death of Gaborone, the homeland of his little tribe was proclaimed the Batlokwa Native Reserve, small and congested, but at least allowing the Tlokwa to retain their identity as one of the smallest tribal units in Botswana.

Under the British Protectorate Administration, Botswana was at first very simply divided into two districts, northern and southern. Palapye was selected as the administrative centre of the northern district, and what was then called *Gaberones* (Gaborone's place) as the centre of the southern region. William Surmon was stationed there as Assistant Commissioner responsible to the Resident Commissioner in Mafikeng.

A 'camp' was erected at Gaborone, with a small fort serving as police post and government offices. Conditions were very primitive and the camp was hemmed in by thick bush. A well was dug for water and a couple of shacks were erected, but even these simple amenities disappeared at the outbreak of the Anglo-Boer War. The police and other officials were ordered to retire north to Mahalapye and to destroy Gaborone. Everything of value was removed, including a small safe which was laboriously conveyed to Bulawayo and which, when opened, was found to contain nothing more than a few small coins. Another safe, which was far too heavy to move in the general rush, was abandoned. When the Boers occupied the place they found this safe, blew it open and discovered inside it a piece of paper containing the words 'sold again'!

At the end of the war the administrative camp at Gaborone was rebuilt. With the arrival of a few traders, the place took on a more substantial appearance. The big change came in 1965 when Gaborone (instead of Mafikeng) was selected as capital of Botswana. An entire new town was planned west of the original Gaborone at the railway station. There being no shortage of level ground covered in trees, the new Gaborone was laid out on spacious lines, with a central pedestrian mall overlooked by a double row of commercial buildings. A government enclave is situated at the head of the mall. The buildings of Parliament, the splendid National Museum and art gallery, the library and university, are all handsome buildings. The museum contains a collection of superbly mounted wild animals of Botswana, and the painted dioramas are masterpieces. The museum and art gallery are open daily from 09h00 to 18h00. A national stadium and airport are situated on the western outskirts of the town, as well as a substantial dam which provides the town with water and recreational opportunities such as boating and fishing. Gaborone is spread out, with plenty of open areas planted with bush and trees. The population numbers 133 468.

From Gaborone a tarmac road leads eastwards for 15 km to the border post of *Tlokweng* (place of the Tlokwa tribe), with the South African border post of Kopfontein facing it across the frontier. The posts are open from 07h00 to 22h00. A tarmac road of 93 km links Kopfontein to Zeerust and the main road to Johannesburg.

South of Gaborone a tarmac road stretches for 68 km through well-bushed, hilly country to reach ...

LOBATSE

The situation of Lobatse – a valley surrounded by rocky hills – is pleasant. The town is named after the chief Molebatse. With a population of 28 533, the place has a similar atmosphere to a rather rough-and-ready but animated cow town of the Wild West. It is the seat of the High Court of Botswana. The abattoir of the Botswana Meat Commission is situated here, as well as a large canned-meat factory. Cattle on the hoof are driven into the town from the ranching areas, and the shops do a roaring trade with the cowboy types who ride the herds on their last long journey to the abattoir. Meat is sent by train to South Africa and exported to several countries.

Two caves containing dripstone formations and plenty of bats are situated in the vicinity of the town. However, they are difficult to enter and are therefore more suited to serious cave explorers than casual visitors. Their full length has yet to be explored.

Beyond Lobatse a tarmac road leads eastwards for 8 km to the border post of Pioneer Gate and the South African post of *Skilpadshek* (tortoise gate) across the frontier line, from where the tarmac road continues for 50 km to Zeerust in the Northern Province. The two posts are open daily from 07h00 to 20h00.

From Lobatse the tarmac road continues southwards. After 5 km a turn-off west to Kanye is reached, while the main road continues close to the railway line to Pitsane (30 km from Lobatse), and from there to the border of South Africa at Ramatlabama (50 km from Lobatse). The name *Ramatlabama* means 'one who has settled down'. The border posts are open daily from 07h00 to 20h00. Mafikeng is situated 25 km south of Ramatlabama on the tarmac road.

From the main road, 5 km south of Lobatse, a tarmac turn-off leads westwards for 47 km to ...

KANYE

The flat-topped hill of *Kanye* (the hill of the chief), a natural fortress of the kind much favoured by the Tswana people, dominates a fertile and relatively well-watered extent of the wilderness. The Ngwaketse tribe established it as the principal centre of their tribal area. Nearly 200 years ago, under the chief Makaba, a substantial town was created there.

As originally created, Kanye was a fortified settlement built on top of the hill. Stone defensive walls were constructed to reinforce the hill, and piles of rocks were kept as missiles to be used against enemies attempting to climb the slopes. The place was attacked on several occasions by people such as the Ndebele of Mzilikazi, the outlaw Jan Bloem, and others. At times the Ngwaketse were driven away, but they always returned. The old town still stands on the summit of the hill, with modern extensions built on the lower slopes.

The town, with a population of 31 354, is an interesting place to explore – a maze of pathways and passageways. Most of the habitations consist of the traditional thatched huts, generally a cluster comprising a residence, cornhouse and workhouse built around a neat courtyard with walls and floors of clay and dung. The walls are usually tastefully decorated by the women with various designs and patterns. The residence of the chief and the *kgotla* (meeting-place) is situated at Kgoseng on top of the hill. The town is still provided with water from a deep gorge known as Pharing, although there are now modern amenities such as pipes, boreholes and taps. From Kanye a track leads north to Ghanzi in the form of a cattle trail suitable only for heavy or four-wheel-drive vehicles.

From Gaborone a tarmac road stretches over level country for 66 km to Molepolole, the principal centre of the Kwena people. This is a large, sprawling village without any very notable feature, but it is an interesting place to visit. The village of huts, shacks and commercial buildings is scattered in a natural parkland of acacias. The tarmac road ends at the entrance to the Scottish Livingstone Hospital. Aloes grow in profusion around the village, and a local legend says that these plants once saved Molepolole from attack. A party of Boers – always the bogeymen of the Tswana – stole upon the place one night in 1850. In the light of the half moon they mistook the aloes for an army of warriors waiting on the defensive, and thus abandoned the attack! It is said that the name *Molepolole* originated from a curse placed on the site by a wizard. When the Kwena chief decided to build his capital on the site, the wizard was ordered to relieve the place of the curse. Hence the name, which means 'Let him undo it'.

From Malepolole a track leads north-west for 72 km to *Letlhakeng* (place of reeds), a settlement on the banks of a fossil river. From this place the track deteriorates and can only be used by four-wheel-drive vehicles. For 72 km the track winds across the face of the wilderness and then reaches the ...

KHUTSE GAME RESERVE

This reserve – proclaimed in 1971 and 2 500 square kilometres in extent – is an area of tree-covered sand plains littered with pans which hold water only during and after good rains. Hartebeest, kudu, springbok and wildebeest live in the area but tend to migrate with the rains, as they are able to sense where water is available or where some thunderstorm has benefited the grazing. A permanent population of smaller animals always remains around the pans. The area is also populated by Bushmen and Kgalagadi. A Department of Wildlife and Tourism camp is situated at Golalabadimo Pan, but no accommodation is provided. Guides may be obtained; otherwise the visitor must rely on his own resources. There are tracks leading to most parts of the reserve. The best months to visit it are July, August and September.

CENTRAL KALAHARI GAME RESERVE

This vast game reserve – 51 800 square kilometres in extent – is a complete wilderness. There are no roads and it is closed to the public unless special permission is obtained for research purposes. Nomadic Bushmen hunting groups wander through the wilderness of sandy savanna plains where innumerable pans occasionally retain water for short periods after wet seasons.

Vast herds of antelope migrate through the reserve, but their movements are unpredictable and completely dependent on the caprice of the weather. Eland, gemsbok, hartebeest and springbok sometimes form herds of up to 100 000; at other times they disperse as effectively as water evaporating in the heat, to be remembered as though simply a mirage. In the thirstland of the central Kgalagadi, life and water are so tightly interwoven that the number of inhabitants increases or decreases according to the frequency of thunderstorms and the accessibility of the scattered drinking places.

Vegetation consists of a considerable variety of grass species, acacia thorn trees, and a surprising number of flowering plants, especially lilies.

GABORONE TO FRANCISTOWN

The road from Gaborone to Francistown used to be purgatory for travellers, but it has now received a tarmac surface, making the experience of exploring Botswana a pleasure. The 439 km long road leaves Gaborone, passing after 1 km the turn-off to Molepolole, the Botswana Agricultural College at 9,5 km, and the Morwa rural centre (31 km from Gaborone). Just beyond this centre (34,5 km from Gaborone), a tarmac turn-off leads for 6 km to the village of ...

MOCHUDI

In 1871 the chief Kgamanyane led his Kgatla tribe westwards from the Transvaal and chose as a new home a pleasant site at the foot of a cluster of rocky hillocks. A considerable settlement arose, and the town was named *Motshodi*, after an individual who had pioneered the area. This name was corrupted to Mochudi.

Kgamanyane died in 1874 and was succeeded by Lentswe. For nine years his people had trouble with the Kwena tribe of Sechele, who demanded tribute from the newcomers. Raids and counter-raids made life unpleasant until peace came in 1883. In 1885 the area became part of the Bechuanaland Protectorate. In 1896 the railway was built to the north and Mochudi was served by a station named after Isang Pilane, a Kgatla chieftain who lived in the area. Lentswe died in 1924 and was succeeded by his son Lentswe II. The chief has his residence and court on the hill named *Phutadikobo* (pack your blanket).

There is an interesting museum on the summit of the hill. It is open Mondays to Fridays from 08h00 to 17h00, and Saturdays and Sundays from 14h00 to 17h00. A small store at the museum sells local handicrafts. The view from the museum is attractive.

The village, although straggling, has in it several homes built in the traditional Kgatla style with superbly thatched roofs of considerable size. Entrances are finely decorated and interesting architectural features abound. Two baobab trees growing in the village are the most southerly of their kind in Botswana.

From the turn-off to Mochudi the main tarmac road continues north over a flat, acacia-covered plain unmarked by any prominent features for 162 km until it reaches ...

MAHALAPYE

Correctly known as *Mhalatswe*, this village derives its name from the impala antelope which once frequented the area in large numbers. It is a railway and agricultural centre with a population of 28 078. West of the village, 45 km away on a gravel road, lies the old Ngwato capital of *Shoshong* (place of the thorn tree), now much smaller in size but containing relics of stone walls and signs of mining and smelting.

From Mahalapye the main tarmac road continues north for 73 km and then reaches a crossroads. To the west, 43,5 km away, lies Serowe. To the east, 5 km away is the village of ...

PALAPYE

As with Mahalapye, this village received its name (correctly spelt *Phalatswe*) from the number of impala antelope which once lived in the area. A railway and agricultural centre, it is situated near the coal-mine at Morupule, 6 km to the west. The population is 17 362.

From the crossroads at Palapye, a turn to the west crosses a level savanna. After 6 km there is a turn-off to the Moropule Colliery and, 43 km further on, the road reaches the Ngwato tribal capital of ...

SEROWE

In 1902 the Ngwato tribe moved their principal centre from the old Palapye (east of modern Palapye) to an area known as *Serowe* from the small bulbs (*Ceropegia* sp.) which grow there and are relished for their sweet flavour. A new tribal capital was created around a central tree-covered hill which serves as the burial-ground of the Khama family. The grave of Khama III is marked by a fine bronze duiker (emblem of the Ngwato tribe) sculpted by the South African artist, Anton van Wouw.

Serowe is a large, straggling village built in a natural parkland where, several hillocks provide variety of landscape and excellent viewsites for photographs. An interesting mixture of old and new may be seen in the domestic architecture, several stores, garages, public buildings, and the Sekgoma Memorial Hospital which lies at the end of the tarmac road.

The graves of the Khama family may be visited with the permission of the District Chief, whose home and offices are situated at the foot of the hill. Thathaganyana Hill is also worth climbing. On its flat summit may be seen the ruins of an 11th century settlement where there are numerous engraved holes and slides in the rocks.

Of all the Tswana villages, Serowe is probably the most photogenic. The population is 30 260.

From the turn-offs to Serowe and Palapye at the crossroads, the main tarmac road from Gaborone continues north across the level savanna, with mopane steadily taking over from the acacia as the dominant tree of the area.

At 78 km there is a tarmac turn-off leading eastwards for 56 km to the mining centre of ...

SELEBI-PHIKWE

The name of the modern mining town of Selebi-Phikwe is derived from two places. *Selebi* (place of water-holes) and *Phikwe* (a mound of sticks left after clearing land). As a result of routine geological explorations by Roan Selection Trust, a deposit of nickel was found at Selebi in 1963 and at Phikwe in 1966. Copper was found shortly afterwards at Phikwe, where there are signs of ancient workings in surface outcrops. Mining commenced at Phikwe in 1974. It is planned to develop a second mine at Selebi.

A township to serve the two mining areas was created in a parkland between the two deposits and given the combined name of Selebi-Phikwe. A dam was built in the Shashe River to supply the mines with water. The town is a bright, sun-drenched, modern little place. Mining operations are considerable, notwithstanding many technical difficulties and financial problems resulting from fluctuations in the price of base metals. The population is 39 769.

From the turn-off to Selebi-Phikwe the main tarmac road from Gaborone continues north over a mopane-covered plain – flat, hot and featureless. After 60 km the road passes the small trading centre of Shashe, with the Shashe Dam situated to the west of the railway line. A further 27 km brings the tarmac road to ...

FRANCISTOWN

Situated in a cluster of hillocks, with the Tati River flowing on the south side, Francistown originated after the discovery of gold in the area and the development of the Monarch Mine. A considerable mining industry had flourished in the area in prehistoric times. Innumerable ancient workings – shafts, adits and trenches – were sunk by early miners, presumably of the Karanga tribe. These early workers extracted a considerable amount of gold from such surface workings. However, without the aid of pumps or haulage gear, they were forced to abandon work as soon as they reached the water-level.

European hunters such as Henry Hartley observed the signs of this early mining. In 1866 Hartley showed the old gold-field to the German geologist, Karl Mauch. The reports made by Mauch stimulated the first gold-rush in Southern Africa by European miners who were attracted to the area in the hope of fortune.

Among the cosmopolitan crowd of diggers was Daniel Francis, namesake of *Francistown*.

The field never matched the expectations of the European diggers. Popular fancy had converted the place into the Ophir of the Bible, and men rushed there expecting to find vast riches. The early miners, however, had skilfully extracted most of the surface gold, the remainder being at some depth. Nevertheless, mining for gold continued in the area until 1964 when the Monarch Mine closed down. Nickel and copper deposits have been found in the area but have so far not been exploited.

Francistown started as a typical mining town, with a street of stores and pubs facing the railway line. The 1890s saw the place at its rowdiest and most opulent. After the mines closed down, the town went into a decline, but slowly revived as a trading, rail, administrative and communications centre for the northern district of Botswana.

It is still a boisterous little place where the nights are filled with the din of trains shunting and the volcanic eruption of noise from establishments such as the Sisters and Brothers open-air disco. The climate is hot and thirsty. The population is 65 244.

On the railway station stands an interesting old locomotive, a Type 15 Garratt, No 352, which saw several million kilometres of hard labour, pulling heavy trains through the heat of Botswana and Zimbabwe. Cattle, coal, copper, gold, freight, passengers – all were heaved along by the willing old puffer. Now it has been honourably retired, watching with some disdain as the modern 'growlers' (the diesels) carry out the chores of transport.

Francistown is situated at a major junction on the main road from Gaborone. To the north the road and railway continue across the savanna until, 86 km from Francistown, they reach the border of Zimbabwe at the stream known as *Ramokgwebane* (the place of the man who hunted the lesser korhaan). The border post is open daily from 07h00 to 20h00.

From the Tati River goldfields one of the most storied of all the pioneer roads of Southern Africa had its start, and can still be followed in a rugged vehicle. This romantic old trail of African pedlars, European traders, hunters, explorers and adventurers leads north-westwards through some of the most desolate country in Southern Africa.

A man of the Mlilima tribe, Mutenga by name, was a renouned ivory hunter who used this trail from his home in the south to a regular hunting base in a grove of mpanda trees *(Lonchocarpus capassa,* or rain trees) which grew near the source of the Matedzi River. This hunting camp was so pleasant an oasis in the wilderness that other hunters and European travellers also began to use the place. It became known as *Mpanda Mutenga* from the trees and the man and the 480 km long trail from Tati also took that name. Mutenga came to an unfortunate end in his grove of Mpanda trees. The Ndebele paramount chief, Lobengula, employed him as an elephant hunter. News reached the chief that Mutenga was selling ivory on the quiet to European traders. The Nyamayendlovu regiment was sent to liquidate Mutenga's enterprise. Mutenga, his family and most of his retainers were wiped out. Only a few survivors fled into the wilderness. His base camp in the grove of Mpanda trees was, however, too well established by then to be destroyed. The Mpanda trail had become the regular route to the north. It followed the line of least resistance through the wilderness and was so straight that when the modern frontier line between Botswana and Zimbabwe was drawn, the surveyor simply followed the road. The frontier line was marked as the middle of the road.

North of Mpanda Mutenga the road entered an area of tsetse fly through which ox-wagons could not go. This was an impenetrable barrier for all draught animals. Porters had to carry goods for the last 104 km to another famous landmark, a large *muzunguru (Kigelia pinnata* or sausage tree) growing on the banks of the Zambezi at a place named *Kazungula* after the tree. From here the ferrymen of the Zambezi took over transport in their canoes.

A trader named George Westbeech, partner to 'Elephant' Phillips, established a store and depot at Mpanda Mutenga in 1872 and this became a great convenience to all travellers. Wagons could be left there, porters hired, ivory sold, trade goods bartered. Westbeech even had working for him a young English doctor, Benjamin Bradshaw, formerly a ship's surgeon who, for reasons of his own, choose to spend quite a few years of his life living in this isolated but cheerful little place.

Westbeech flourished in his trading. The hunter, Frederick Selous, estimated that Westbeech each year sent down the Mpanda Mutenga trail about 25 000 lbs of ivory as well as ostrich feathers, hides, rhino horns, hippo teeth and a very profitable line in museum specimens.

All over the world, museums were hungry for exhibits from Africa. To meet the demand for bird specimens alone Westbeech even had an ex-jailer from Cape Town on his staff collecting and preserving skins for export. The slaughter of wildlife for commercial and trophy hunting purposes attracted new parties of hunters each year. Sight-seeing parties also started to use the Mpanda

Mutenga trail to reach the Victoria Falls while missionaries made their way along it northwards, with several different destinations, establishing stations in the wilderness. Mpanda Mutenga itself became the site of a Jesuit mission. As there were few Africans living in the area it was thought that the mission had the purpose of saving the traders and hunters from powerful brandy and stronger women. Females were becoming numerous, attached to travelling parties or even forming groups of their own. Westbeeck married one of these fair visitors and took her up to the Victoria Falls for a honeymoon.

The devastation of wildlife proved self-destructing to this epoch of commercial hunters. Elephants carrying worthwhile tusks became scarce. It was ivory which was the big money spinner and as heavy tusks became more difficult to secure, traffic along the Mpanda Mutenga road declined. Even missionary traffic dwindled. As a group they seemed accident prone and not too selective of sites for their mission stations without consideration of the presence of fever. The Jesuit mission station at Mpanda Mutenga was an example of such an establishment.

In June 1884, Francois Coillard, of the French Protestant Paris Evangelical mission, travelled up the Mpanda Mutenga trail. He was astonished to find the Jesuits well established at the trading station. They had erected a chapel, a simple but cosy little house, huts and sheds for store-houses, a fine poultry yard and cultivated a pretty garden. *'It is a little village which would be prosperous as a mission station'*, wrote Coillard *'if there were any evangelisation to be done here. But what can they do where there is no population?'*

Father Kroot, a Dutchman, was in charge of the station, with six European assistants. From the beginning, however, it was an ill-omened venture. One missionary died after a fall from a horse, two were drowned, two died of hunger and fatigue, one of tuberculosis, and within a couple of years the station had been abandoned to ruin.

Mpanda Mutenga was never kind to any settlers. Its founder George Westbeech, while on a visit to the Transvaal in 1888 died of the cumulative effects of years of fever. The curious collection of men who worked for him scattered, but others took their place. Since Westbeech's day there has always been a store at Mpanda Mutenga, but little else has ever flourished there. Today it is a sad and decayed little place, almost a ghost town, with a street of ruined modern houses built there after the Second World War as headquarters of a grandiose cattle-ranching scheme of the Colonial Development Corporation. The fiasco of this well-meaning project, along with the Gambia Egg Scheme and the Tanganyika Ground Nut and Wattle Schemes, left Mpanda Mutenga with the ultimate incongruity of laid-on water, sewerage, swimming pool and electrically lit streets, with the bulbs still in the lamps although the power which motivated it all has gone. Only a tin shanty police border post remains active and, of course, the store, substantially rebuilt to serve a modern community and now left forlorn. The streets outside are crowded only by memories while all around the mopane trees shimmer in the heat and the prodigious flat-land of the Kalahari stretches in solitude far away. Mpanda Mutenga may be reached by a good road branching westwards from the main road linking Hwange to the Victoria Falls in Zimbabwe.

To the west of Francistown a modern tarmac road leads across the savanna, a parkland so level that it seems endless. After 7,5 km there is a turn-off south-west leading for 260 km to the diamond-mine at Orapa. This rich diamond-bearing volcanic pipe (the second largest in the world) was found in 1967 by prospectors of De Beers. Production started in 1971 and a town has developed at the mine, with a population of 9 000 people. A second slightly smaller pipe was located 40 km south-east of Orapa at *Letlhakane* (place of reeds) where production started in 1976. A town has grown next to the mine and has a population of 8 000 people. Both mines are worked by De Beers Botswana Mining Company (Pty) Ltd, of which the Botswana Government and De Beers are equal shareholders.

From the turn-off to Orapa the tarmac road continues westwards through thickly bushed savanna country. Mopane and baobab trees dominate the flat sandy plains. Cattle posts and patches of farmlands nestle amongst the trees. At 122 km from Francistown a veterinary cordon fence is reached, where vehicles and travellers pass through a dip, a precaution against the spread of foot-and-mouth livestock disease. Numerous sellers of curios make and offer for sale their wares at the roadside.

After a further 10 km, the road reaches a turn-off to the verge of Sua Pan, one of the two main pans of the Makgadikgadi system. This sandy turn-off is negotiable by four-wheel-drive vehicles only. Beyond this turn-off the trees start to dwindle into stunted mopane. At 30 km from the Sua turn-off, to the south of the road, stands a giant baobab tree, a favourite camping spot for many travellers. The tree stands on the verge of the huge depression, an open grassy area containing in its centre the basin known as the *Makgadikgadi* or *Makharikhari* (dried-out pans).

Beyond the baobab tree the tarmac road continues west into an area of grass and tall vegetable ivory palms (*Hyphaena ventricosa*). At 17 km from the baobab tree (179 km from Francistown) the road reaches the Nata River, with the fairly large settlement of Nata situated on its banks. The *Nata* (black) River flows from the east and is one of the principal sources of water for the Sua Pan, part of the ...

MAKGADIKGADI BASIN

In the Bushman language, *sua* means salt. For generations these people have extracted salt from this shallow depression. They still use it as an article of trade with the Tswana tribes. The pan, connected to Ntwetwe Pan like a Siamese twin, is one of the natural wonders of Africa. These are the two main pans contained in the basin of the *Makgadikgadi* (area of many pans).

The entire surface of Sua Pan is only occasionally filled with water, but in the north the Nata River provides a fairly reliable flow. The delta where this river enters the pan is (especially in autumn and winter) a resort for vast numbers of aquatic birds such as flamingos.

In the south, Sua Pan is overlooked by an escarpment from where there are wide views over the whole shimmering white surface. In the south-west lies a rocky elevation 10 m high on which stands the ruins of a prehistoric stone settlement.

Ntwetwe Pan comprises a complex of islands, small depressions, large depressions containing deep water, grassy peninsulas and plains covered in grass and palm trees. These plains are favoured by game animals such as zebra and wildebeest, which migrate there during the dry months of winter, spending their summers at Nxai Pan in the north. Both Nxai Pan and the grass plains north and west of Ntwetwe are national parks. Four-wheel-drive vehicles are essential for their exploration.

At Nata the main road divides. To the north a gravel road continues to Kazungula and Kasane on the border of Zambia. Kazungula (where the famous old muzungula tree still grows) is connected by pont across the Zambezi River to Zambia. The border post is open daily from 06h00 to 18h00. *Kasane*, named after a species of tree, *Syzgium guineense*, is the gateway to the ...

CHOBE NATIONAL PARK

The 1 160 square kilometre extent of the Chobe National Park contains one of the largest concentrations of wild animals in Africa. May to September – the dry season – is the best time of year to visit this fascinating national park. Vast herds of buffalo feed in the marshes. Elephant, eland, giraffe, impala, kudu, lechwe, oribi, puku, roan, tsessebe, waterbuck, wildebeest and zebra are very numerous. Predators – lion and leopard – and scavengers roam the whole area. Hippos and crocodiles inhabit the waterways and bird life is magnificent. Rhino have been reintroduced. Wart hogs, wild pigs, baboons and monkeys abound.

The park was created in 1968 and named after the Chobe River which forms its northern boundary. The higher reaches of this river are known as the Linyanti. A fair gravel road skirts the southern side of the river for 120 km as far as Kachikau. Beyond this place, the tracks are suited to four-wheel-drive vehicles only. The visitor is well served by scenic loop roads branching off from the river road. In this area may be seen some of the largest concentrations of game animals. The riverine vegetation is luxuriant. There is a public campsite at Serondella.

South of the river lies an area of mopane forest, where there are numerous large pans which contain water and provide drinking places for an interesting variety of wild animals, including gemsbok, oribi, reedbuck and roan. There is a campsite in this area at Nogatsau.

The south-western portion of the park consists of the Mababe depression, which appears to have once been a lake. Now only enough water reaches it in time of flood from the Chobe River through the Savuti channel to maintain it as a marsh. Buffalo and various antelope graze around the verges of the marsh. There is a camping ground at Savuti. Interesting rock paintings may be seen in the area on a hill near the channel. The Magwikhwe sand ridge stretches like a disintegrating wall along the western side of the depression.

Apart from the camping grounds of the National Parks authorities, several private concerns have tented camps in the Chobe area. These camps serve as bases for conducted tours to view game, and where professional guides, boats, fishing tackle and four-wheel-drive vehicles may be hired.

Visitors to the area need to take health precautions. Tsetse flies carry sleeping sickness, mosquitoes carry malaria, and the lakes and rivers are infected with bilharzia.

From the Mababe gate at the south-western end of the Chobe National Park, a track (suitable only for four-wheel-drive vehicles) leads south for 30 km and then reaches a division. To the south the track continues for 120 km to Maun, and to the west a branch leads for 22 km to the ...

MOREMI WILDLIFE RESERVE

This spectacular 1 800 square kilometre wildlife reserve was created by the Tawana tribe in 1968 and named after their chief, Moremi. It is a pure wilderness area of great beauty, with water lily-covered lagoons, palm-covered islands, rich green vegetation and a vast population of wild animals. Bird life is magnificent. The heronries at Cakanaca and Gcodikwe are impressive towards evening, and the lagoons are always resorts for ducks, geese, ibises, jacanas, spoonbills, storks and waders.

Only very rough tracks penetrate this reserve. Visitors are allowed on foot at their own risk. Game-viewing, bird-watching and photographic possibilities are tremendous; but the area is hot, with tsetse flies and mosquitoes present. The wet season, December to April, reduces the tracks to deep mud. Visits in this season are not recommended. August and September are the best months.

NATA TO MAUN

From the settlement on the Nata River, with its two garages and stores, the main tarmac road from Francistown divides, the left branch leading west. The landscape is completely flat, a grassy plain dotted with clumps of palm trees and patches of mopane bush dominated by occasional baobab trees. The road skirts the northern end of the Makgadikgadi Basin, crossing several outlying pans and extensions of the main pan – some filled with shallow water, others dry and hard.

A few cattle posts are passed at the beginning of the drive, but the country is sparsely populated. After 40 km there is a road camp at Zorongosa and at 97 km a turn to Gweta. The road then traverses the game utilisation corridor between the ...

MAKGADIKGADI PANS GAME RESERVE AND NXAI PAN NATIONAL PARK

These two associated wildlife sanctuaries cover over 10 000 square kilometres of country, penetrable only by four-wheel-drive vehicles. No accommodation facilities are provided. The main track leading for 43 km to Nxai Pan branches north from the road to Maun at a point 164 km west of Nata.

The game population of this area is essentially migratory. From December to March a tremendous amount of wildlife is concentrated at Nxai Pan (originally an ancient lake bed), and the nearby grass plains at Kanyu. Eland and sable are less prolific; buffalo and elephant only appear during very wet seasons. Cheetah, lion, hyenas, jackals, wild dogs and bat-eared foxes are plentiful.

There are several other pans in the vicinity, such as Kgamakgama, where wildlife concentrates. The entire area is fascinating to explore. On the east shores of Kudiakam Pan a group of baobab trees known as the Sleeping Sisters grow. Originally painted by Thomas Baines, they still look the same after more than 100 years.

At the end of the rainy season – about May – the game animals migrate south from Nxai Pan across the main road to Maun and south into the Makgadikgadi Basin, where they disperse over the grassy plains on the verges of the Ntwetwe Pan. As the small pans dry up, the wildlife converge more on the Botletli (or Boteti) River which links the Makgadikgadi Basin to the Okavango swamps and supplies them with drinking-water during the dry months.

From the turn-off to Nxai Pan the main road to Maun continues west. After 49 km (213 km from Nata) the road passes a turn-off to Motopi. At 243 km a foot-and-mouth livestock-disease veterinary gate and dip are reached at Makalamobedi. A further 56 km (299 km from Nata) brings the road to the banks of the beautiful *Thamalakane* (river that goes straight). Across the river lies the town of ...

MAUN

The atmospheric, amiable and informal little town of Maun (correctly spelt *Maung,* the place of short reeds) is remote but cheerful, a surprising oasis to find in the wilderness of the Kgalagadi. Lying on the banks of the Thamalakane River, the sunny place is shaded and beautified by the tall riverine forest. The surrounding area is a proclaimed wildlife sanctuary. It is delightful to find a river in so arid a setting, with its clear water providing a home for numerous fish, aquatic birds, hippos and crocodiles. Water lilies ornament the calm surface. Mirrored on it are reflections of trees and clouds. For the fisherman and canoeist the river is fascinating. Exploring its languid, sinuous course upstream to the Okavango swamps or downstream, until it loses itself in the sand of the Kgalagadi, is a unique experience in travel.

Maun is the main gateway to the wilderness areas of sand and water of Botswana. Safari companies are based there. They conduct parties north into the swamps, south into the wilderness of the central Kgalagadi; and west to Lake Ngami, Ghanzi and the sand areas along the border with Namibia.

The town is served by shops, garages, curio and handicraft sellers, tanneries specialising in game skins, a hotel, various riverside lodges, and administrative buildings. The town is the principal centre for Ngamiland, the home of the Tawana tribe and several smaller tribal groups such as the Teti and Herero. The majority of tourists visit Maun during the winter months (mainly August and September) when the weather is cool. October and November are extremely hot prior to the rainy months of January and February when the country is at its best, especially for photography. The area is then green and cloud formations are superb. The summer months are also best for fishing. The population of Maun is estimated at 57 811.

The Thamalakane River is normally in flood from early June until October, after which, the water-level of the river starts to drop. However, local rains can cause it to flood slightly during the wet season of December to March. The safari companies provide boat trips up the river to camps in the Okavango swamps. Canoes and boats can be hired from the lodges. A delightful short trip follows the Boro tributary of the Thamalakane. Longer trips of 7 to 14 days allow for exploration of the wonders of the swamplands and the delta of the Okavango. The Thamalakane is well populated with fish, notably bream, barbel and vundu. Tiger-fish are found higher up in the actual course of the Okavango River and in the delta.

The Thamalakane River is the southern drain of the Okavango swamp world, carrying away the water which manages to penetrate the vast morass. South-west of Maun the river divides. One branch continues south-west as the Nxhabe to feed Lake Ngami; the other branch swings east as the Boteti to feed the Makgadikgadi Pans. The entire complex pattern of waterways in a sea of sand is one of the natural wonders of the world, not simply of Africa.

At present Maun forms the terminus of good roads in Botswana. Beyond lies pure safari country. It is, however, possible to reach Lake Ngami in an ordinary vehicle, 71 km along a rough but fairly firm road.

LAKE NGAMI

Ngami has always been one of the mystery lakes of Africa. Its very existence is dependent entirely on the extent of rains in Angola and the penetration of water through the swamps to the Thamalakane River, and from there through the Nxhabe to the lake. This process is quite unpredictable. If no water reaches the lake, it dries up completely, while during heavy floods it becomes an inland sea. Descriptions of the lake by olden-day travellers are understandably very varied.

The name *Ngami* apparently means 'big'. The Bushmen call it *Nxhabe* (place of giraffes); the Yei call it *Ncame* (place of reeds). During a good season it can fill to a depth of almost 2 m.

A prodigious fish population, particularly of barbel, appears with the water, feeding on rich nutrients and attracting to the lake countless aquatic birds. When the lake dries up, nothing remains except a flat floor, several mirages and the bones of unfortunate creatures which have died of thirst.

The road from Maun reaches the village of Toteng after 64 km. From here a left turn 3 km out of the village crosses the plain to the Nxhabe River on the bank of which is a campsite at a point where the river reaches the lake. From Toteng the track to Sehithwa may be followed for 20 km, after which various turn-offs lead to the lake and a fishing camp on a promontory. Bird life is impressive and views of the lake are grand at this point.

From Sehithwa a track leads northwards for 310 km to Shakawe, the border post with the Caprivi Strip of Namibia. This track is only suited to four-wheel-drive or heavy-transport vehicles. From it, turn-offs stretch to several interesting places. From the village of Tsau, 50 km north of Sehithwa, a turn-off proceeds west for 195 km to *Gcwihaba* (the hyena's hole) where, inside a rocky valley, are situated what are known as Drotsky's Caves, a series of connected caverns containing many stalactites, but few stalagmites. The main cavern is about 15 m high and 50 m long. Many bats inhabit the caves, the exploration of which is as yet incomplete. The caves are named after Marthinus Drotsky, a farmer from Ghanzi, who was led to the caves by a Bushman in June 1932. The caves were declared a national monument in 1934.

Beyond the turn-off to these caves at Tsau, the road continues to the north over sandy savanna country. Villages such as Nokaneng and Gomare are passed. At Sepupa village there is a crossing of tracks. To the east a track leads to the Okavango Fishing Lodge; to the west a track stretches for 40 km to the hills called *Tsodilo* (steep). These hills are situated in clusters known to the Bushmen as 'Man, Woman and Child'. The highest hill rises about 420 m above the savanna. These hills were occupied by man from an early period, and numerous signs of ancient villages are visible. Mining for iron ore was evidently quite a local industry. On suitable rock faces in the hills, more than 1 700 paintings may be seen in over 200 galleries. The paintings appear to be of divided origin – red paintings were probably done by the Bushmen; black paintings by the Iron Age people who displaced the Bushmen. Some paintings include several colours.

Local Bushmen act as guides for visits to the paintings but do not know anything about their origin. An Historic Monuments officer, stationed at Mbukushu village just south of the largest hill, will direct visitors and arrange guides. Pleasant camping sites are situated in the hills, and water may be obtained from springs. A landing-strip close to the hills enables aircraft to land. The hills, reputedly haunted, are atmospheric and eerie.

From Sehithwa the sandy track to the west continues for 192 km to reach the village of ...

GHANZI

This isolated little ranching centre is said to derive its name from the word *gantshi* (place of flies). The surrounding area offers fine pasturage for cattle. Nomadic pastoralist tribes moved into the region in prehistoric times and dug many wells there. In 1874 six families of Transvaal Boers, led by Hendrik van Zyl, settled there with the permission of the Tawana chief. Incessant brawls erupted with the local tribes, and extreme isolation made life very difficult. Van Zyl was eventually killed in one of the fights. Rival Europeans had settled in the area which became known as a staging post for the Thirstland Trekkers. They consisted of groups of different people who had wandered away from the Transvaal in search of some promised land of milk and honey in the west.

In 1898, 37 families made their homes in the area, each family being allocated a substantial ranch. The village of Ghanzi was founded as their centre. In the 1950s additional ranches were granted, and Ghanzi developed into a community centre with several stores, administrative buildings and a hotel. The population is 24 719.

From Ghanzi the track to the west continues for 98 km to Kalkfontein, and from there for a further 97 km to Memuno, the border post with Namibia. The post is open daily from 08h00 to 16h00. South of Ghanzi lies a track frequently used by cattlemen taking livestock to the abattoirs at Lobatse. This track leads for 271 km to Kang and for 317 km to Kanye, where it joins the tarmac road to Lobatse. From Kang a track branches off west for 109 km to Tshane, and from there swings southwards for 246 km to Tshabong, close to the border with South Africa. This track passes through the ...

MABWASEHUBE GAME RESERVE (AND GEMSBOK NATIONAL PARK)

Mabwasehube (red sands) takes its name from a dried-out pan in the northern part of the reserve. The reserve is actually an eastern extension of the Gemsbok National Park, a 9 000 square kilometre wilderness which is completely undeveloped, and best seen from the portion on the South African side west of the Nossob River which acts as the frontier line. The South African reserve is known as the Kalahari Gemsbok National Park.

Eland, gemsbok, hartebeest, springbok and other drought-resistant wild animals frequent the area, the pans in the Mabwasehube area attracting large numbers of these inhabitants of the wilderness. Predators are numerous, comprising lion, cheetah, wild dog, leopard, brown hyenas and various small wild cats.

Bushman (basaRwa) groups wander through the area among the great dunes of red-coloured sand. The hardy vegetation and the surprising number of living creatures which have adapted to the harsh conditions all make fascinating study. The area is difficult to explore and demands the use of four-wheel-drive vehicles. Water and self-reliance are essential. For such visitors, Botswana in its entirety is a world of its own, a wonderful wilderness where it is still possible, for a little while at least, to leave civilisation behind and lose oneself in a primeval landscape, to hear the sound of sweet silence, to breathe air that knows no pollution, and to see the stars at night, so vividly above a camp that one is tempted to reach upwards to touch them, and to learn whether they are hot or cold.

Chapter Forty-One
LESOTHO

Into the 30 300 square kilometres that is the diminutive state of Lesotho is concentrated some of the most spectacular scenery to be found on the continent of Africa. A full 85 per cent of the country consists of a mass of mountains while the remaining 15 per cent is comprised of lower-level viewsites from which to admire the heights. Lesotho is a delight to artists and photographers, notable for the vividness of its scenic colours: yellow, orange and red sandstone cliffs; intensely blue skies in summer with towering banks of white clouds; green grass turning brown in winter; and the transparent blueness of high basalt mountains shrouded in mantles of snow.

In addition to these rich colours, the rocks have been modelled into fantastic shapes by massive natural and unnatural erosion, giving the place the appearance of the abandoned toy room of an untidy nursery of giants. Balancing rocks, table-topped mountains, pinnacles, spires, deep ravines, dongas, cliffs, caves and almost every rock formation imaginable are littered over this landscape. The effect is bizarre, eerie and surprising.

The 1 932 879 people living in Lesotho are collectively known as *baSotho* while an individual is *moSotho*; the language is *seSotho* and the country is correctly known as *leSotho*. As with many other African peoples, the name was applied to them by foreigners. Research indicates that the name of *Sotho* or *Suthu* was given to them by the Nguni people (Zulu and Swazi) since the first people the Nguni encountered who spoke the Sotho language happened to live along the banks of the *uSuthu* or *uSutu* (dark-brown) River in Swaziland. They were from that time on referred to as the *baSuthu* and, for want of a collective name of their own, retained this appellation. The Zulu spelling, incidentally, gives English readers a correct pronunciation. The orthography of the modern Sotho language is not particularly satisfactory. With rather peculiar consequences for English readers, the language was originally reduced to the written word by French-speaking missionaries, while modern orthographers have further complicated it.

The language and customs of the Sotho are substantially the same as those of the inhabitants of Botswana. Tradition states that during the 18th century sections of the same people who had occupied Botswana wandered over the highveld plains. The men drove cattle and the women carried on their heads supplies of seeds for the cultivation of pumpkins, sorghum, beans and, later maize – the great staple crop which was introduced to Africa by the Portuguese.

These migrants, belonging to several independent clans, stumbled by chance into the beautifully fertile valley of the river they knew as the *Mohokare* (river of willow trees). Lieutenant-Colonel Richard Collins subsequently, in 1809, renamed this river the *Caledon* in honour of the Governor of the Cape, the Earl of Caledon, who had sent him north to explore the interior of Southern Africa.

Originally resident in this area were several Bushman clans, known to the Sotho collectively as *boRwa* (people of the south), or *moRwa* for an individual. Another name given to these hunter-gatherer people was ingeniously and amusingly derived from an ideophone *Qu*, imitating the unique click sounds in the Bushman language. The 'Q' is pronounced as a labial click, thus *boQu* (click people). It is from these people that the numerous sandstone caves of Lesotho shelter some of the finest galleries of polychrome rock art in the world. These cave galleries remain one of the great treasures of the country, although many are sadly mutilated by the scrawlings of vandals, the soot of fires, or by the corroding effect of water thrown on to them by people trying to revive the colours.

The newcomers to the Caledon valley, with their cattle and agricultural activity, soon drove away the herds of game animals and the Bushman hunters who lived on them. The immigrants themselves were not left in peace for long. In Zululand the human upheaval which resulted in the rise to power of Shaka and his Zulu people was developing. The shock waves of this disturbance spread all over Southern Africa in the form of raiding bands and refugees trying to find new homes for themselves as far from the Zulus as possible.

Several of these refugee clans and raiders fled over the Drakensberg and found their way into the valley of the Caledon. Then began a dismal chapter in the human story of Southern Africa. This was the time of the *Lifaqane* (migratory wars) where murder, brutality, raids, fights and cannibalism became the lot in life for many people. It was during this troubled period, however, that the Sotho nation came into being.

The flat-topped sandstone hills which are so remarkable a feature of the Caledon valley made superb natural fortresses. These hills are the remnants – like the pieces of a scattered jigsaw puzzle – of a higher plain which has been destroyed by erosion. The summit of the fragmented original plain remains in the form of small plateaus surrounded by almost unscalable cliffs. Springs surface on some of the plateau summits and there is sufficient grazing to support livestock for at least short periods. The surrounding cliff faces have restricted and easily defensible access to the summits, making these sandstone hills the Sotho equivalent of a feudal castle. Any chieftain possessing a natural stronghold such as this could survive attack and at the same time use his hill as a base from which to raid others.

Living on one of these hills in the northern end of the Caledon valley was the young chief of the section of the Kwena people known as the baMokoteli. This chief, named Lepoqo, was nicknamed *Moshweshwe* (the shaver) on account of his skill in rustling the livestock of his neighbours. To Europeans he was known as *Moshesh*.

Moshweshwe and his people had as their stronghold the hill called *Butha-Buthe* (the gatherer). On this stronghold Moshweshwe found himself having to withstand a succession of sieges by various raiding bands wandering in from Zululand. Sotho tribes such as the Tlokwa also attacked him. Unsettled by the invaders from the coast, these people were roaming about looking for a living, led by an amazon-like chieftainess named Mantatisi and her juvenile son Sigonyela.

Moshweshwe found life increasingly precarious. The Butha-Buthe stronghold was not invulnerable, and so many people were fleeing to him for protection that there was not enough room to accommodate them. At the height of his dilemma, however, one of his followers who had been hunting further south managed to reach him, giving an enthusiastic description of a sandstone hill fortress he had found and considered absolutely impregnable.

Moshweshwe decided to move to this new stronghold. Exploiting the distraction of a Zulu attack on the Tlokwa, Moshweshwe and his followers abandoned Butha-Buthe and made a forced march southwards. On the way, they ran the gauntlet of a host of thugs, bandits, renegades and cannibals who infested the mountains. There are many accounts of adventures, escapes and tragedies which occurred on this march.

Tradition has it that on an afternoon in July 1824 Moshweshwe and his followers reached the new stronghold. Moshweshwe was at first somewhat unimpressed, but as evening approached the hill seemed to gain in strength. He named it *Thaba Bosiu* (mountain of the night). Finding it unoccupied, he and his followers scrambled to the top and were delighted at the new discovery. Of all natural fortresses in the world, this is in fact one of the most remarkable.

To the undiscerning eye Thaba Bosiu (or Bosigo) simply resembles a rather inconspicuous fragment of the original plateau at the foot of the *Maluti (maLoti* or *Luteng*, meaning mountains). However, prodigious natural erosion which had shattered the plateau into pieces, left this fragment with a fairly level top which was grassy, fed by several springs, and made nearly impregnable by sharp precipice cliffs of irregular shape. It was almost impossible for a primitive army to scale these heights up the few practical paths and to be able to dislodge any resolute defenders.

Established on this natural fortress, Moshweshwe built a village above the main route of access (the Khubelu Pass), with the nearby Ramasali Pass (the back entrance, so to speak) being very convenient for secret comings and goings. From these heights Moshweshwe – intelligent and kindly, but resolute by nature – defied all attacks and personally saw to it that the members of the future Sotho nation were protected.

In 1827 the Ngwaneni people from Natal attacked the mountain, but were driven off. In 1830 the Koranna made an abortive attempt. In 1831 the Ndebele also tried and were defeated. The reputation of Moshweshwe and his invincible mountain spread far and wide and his following grew.

Europeans arrived – traders; the French Protestant missionaries, Jean-Eugéne Casalis and Thomas Arbousset; and people such as David Webber (a deserter from the British Army). He settled on the mountain. Being a good mason, he built Moshweshwe a stone house, while another deserter, John Wilks, an armourer, took charge of Moshweshwe's artillery of odd-sized cannons, obtained from various gun-runners or cast locally.

In 1852 the British, under General George Cathcart, attacked the Sotho, but on approaching Thaba Bosiu they retired without attempting to storm the place.

In 1858 the Orange Free State tried to terminate Moshweshwe's hold. Commandant F P Senekal led 1 000 men to attack Thaba Bosiu. From their camp at the bottom they sized up the impregnable fortress and its garrison of 10 000 warriors and quietly went home again.

The reputation of Moshweshwe increased steadily. More followers, including Europeans, rallied to his rule; gunsmiths, horse-traders, artisans and missionaries, including M J F Allard and C J J Gerard, the Roman Catholics who established the mission station of Roma.

In 1865 another war broke out with the Orange Free State. The mountain was besieged for two months by Commandant-General J Fick at the head of a resolute little army of 2 000 men, supported by President J H Brand. On 8 August the Free Staters set out to take Thaba Bosiu by storm. Eight men managed to reach the summit, to the consternation of the defenders, but the charge was repulsed.

On 15 August the Free Staters tried again, attacking up the Khubelu Pass. They forced a passage half-way up the pass but their commander, Louw Wepener, was killed and the men retreated. The Free Staters then laid determined siege to the mountain, hoping to starve Moshweshwe into submission.

Conditions became dismal on the summit. There were too many cattle, thousands of which died of hunger, thirst or by falling over the cliffs. However, Moshweshwe and his men remained in command of the mountain and the siege eventually dwindled. In April 1866 the so-called Peace of the Kaffircorn was arranged at a meeting held beneath the mountain. The Sotho wanted a chance to harvest their crops. With food in the larder, they resumed fighting but without notable success. The Free Staters controlled almost the whole length of the Caledon valley, apart from Thaba Bosiu itself. In March 1868, at the request of the now aged and weary Moshweshwe, the British declared the country a protectorate, and the war ended. The Sotho lost all territory west of the Caledon River (the so-called 'conquered territory'). However, they retained independent control of the strip of plains between the river and the mountain massif to the east, as well as of the mountain mass itself, hitherto uninhabited but which became increasingly settled from then on.

Moshweshwe died in 1870 and was buried on Thaba Bosiu. There is a legend that his spirit lingers about the place in a perceptible atmosphere of serenity and strength. A strange dune of red sand is blown about by the winds on the summit but, like Moshweshwe, never leaves it. It is said that even though a sample of this sand be taken away as a souvenir, it will somehow contrive to return to Thaba Bosiu.

After the death of Moshweshwe, his son Letsie succeeded him. The seat of government was moved to *Matsieng* (place of Letsie), near the French mission centre of Morija. Thaba Bosiu was retained by Masupha, another of Moshweshwe's sons, who strengthened its defences. It played one more important military role in the story of Lesotho. This was during the so-called Gun War of 1880–81.

The so-called Gun War had its origin in Lesotho on 16 October 1879. The Cape Colonial government which had charge of Lesotho informed the Sotho people that there would be an increase of taxation to cover cost of new roads and public buildings. At the same time there would be general disarmament with the surrender of all guns. Guns, ammunition and other weapons would have to be surrendered before 21 May 1880 against payment of compensation. No compensation would be payable after that date. Law enforcement and penalties would be imposed.

The Sotho protested and sent a deputation to Cape Town to present their case. The surrender date was extended to 12 July, but there was no other concession. On 3 July there was a mass tribal meeting at Thaba Bosiu. There was considerable dissension. Some were for obedience to the Government, others against. Those who surrendered their guns before the time limit, found themselves attacked, several were killed, many had their property stolen. The Cape Government hurriedly sent to Lesotho a small detachment of the Cape mounted rifles, followed by a larger force of volunteers, *burghers* (citizen force conscripts) and such professional soldiers as were available.

The dissidents started to attack the various administrative 'camps'. They were well armed and mounted on nimble Basuto ponies. Casualties were sustained on both sides. The Government forces beat off the attackers but they were inferior in numbers and very isolated. The Government by the end of 1881, had a mixed force of 19 000 men in action in Lesotho. The costs in casualties and money were increasing by the day and there seemed no end in sight to the mess. The Cape Government forces had little enthusiasm for the war. Many of them actually sympathised with the Sotho being ordered to surrender guns which they had purchased legally or been given as part of their wages for working on the diamond mines. Early in February 1880, 500 of the Government Yeomanry force simply deserted and returned home. The dissidents meanwhile were also having trouble. They had suffered losses; they wished to reap their crops and obtain more ammunition. They parleyed with the Government and won breathing space by making pretence of agreeing to terms. There was no genuine desire for peace, however, on any terms but their own. The steady dwindling through desertion of the Government force made the dissidents confident of eventual victory. Quarrels amongst the leaders were, in fact, their most serious weakness.

The war dragged on. The Cape Government found itself caught in a political quicksand. The Imperial Government was unsympathetic. They offered no support. The British public would have no enthusiasm for military involvement in a squabble which had nothing to do with them, in a remote country which many of them had never even heard of and those that had considered Lesotho to be of so little value that it was not worth fighting for.

The Cape Government tried to wriggle out of the mess. On 6 April 1882 they repealed application of the Disarmament Act to Lesotho. They had to face a humiliating defeat. A commission rubbed salt into their wounds by reporting that compensation would have to be paid to 1 507 Sothos and 82 Europeans for losses and damage. In this embarrassing period, the celebrated Major-General Charles (Chinese) Gordon was appointed commandant-general of the Cape Colonial forces. He arrived in South Africa in June 1883. For three months he busied himself in reorganising the armed forces. Then he travelled to Lesotho. There he found developing another fiasco involving two of the leading dissidents in the Gun War. Lerotholi, one of the sons of the paramount chief of Lesotho, Letsie, had quarrelled with his half-brother Masupha to such extent that they were ready for war. Lerotholi threw in his lot with the Government, announced that he would surrender the guns of his followers but only if Masupha would submit. Masupha was in command of the national stronghold of Thaba Bosiu.

While Lerotholi was trying to assemble an army to attack Masupha, General Gordon arrived in Lesotho and went to see Masupha on Thaba Bosiu. He told Masupha that he would not fight against the Sotho. He admired them and their steadfast defence of their independence. They parted good friends. General Gordon resigned his appointment and left South Africa. His death in Khartoum in the Sudan on 26 January 1885 is one of the great dramatic events in British military history.

By that date the Gun War was over. The Imperial Government was forced to intervene. The Cape Government withdrew from further control of Lesotho. With the agreement of all the chiefs of the nation (except Masupha), Lesotho was severed from the Cape Colony by an order of Queen Victoria on 18 March 1884. It became a protectorate of Great Britain, and its independence as a kingdom was confirmed. The Sotho had achieved a significant victory.

The stubborn Masupha remained on Thaba Bosiu but the brave days of its military importance were over. Its part in the fulfilment of the independence of the Sotho people, their very survival, was all pervading. Masupha after leading a truculent life was eventually defeated in a civil war in 1897 by his brother Lerotholi, the new Paramount Chief. Thus, Thaba Bosiu was abandoned to memory. It is a fascinating place to visit. Nearby stands the impressive *Qiloane* (the pinnacle), looming up like a gigantic rock sentinel, guarding Moshweshwe's mountain.

Lesotho (during that time it was known to Europeans as Basutoland) remained a British protectorate for nearly 100 years. During that period it was administered by a resident commissioner, with the descendants of Moshweshwe as the heads of state. In 1903 the country received a National Council, an advisory body of nominated members. In 1959 a Legislative Council was created, with half the members elected while the rest were chiefs and nominated members. In 1964 this council became an elected National Assembly of 60 members, with the Paramount Chief or King as head of state. The first incumbent was Motlotlehi, also known as Moshweshwe II. On 4 October 1966 Lesotho finally emerged as a fully independent state, the Kingdom of Lesotho, having seSotho and English as the two official languages.

MASERU

The capital and largest town in the Kingdom of Lesotho is *Maseru* (red sandstones). Together with its surrounding districts, it has a population of about 311 200. It originated in 1869 when the newly established British administration of the Protectorate of Basutoland required a site for their headquarters. Moshweshwe selected Maseru. Commandant James Bowker, appointed High Commissioner's agent, established his camp there. The British referred to the administrative posts of Basutoland as 'camps' since it was never expected that they would become towns. As a result, they did not benefit from proper planning or layout.

In its early years Maseru was a completely informal place. Commandant Bowker had his camp on the rocky height of red sandstone where the new Lesotho National Museum has since been built. The first trader, Richard Trower, built a store in 1869 on the most convenient level spot, the site of the present Lancer's Inn. Other traders followed, such as Irvine, Holden & Co who built a store at *Hobson's Square*, named after one of their managers, George Hobson, and the Fraser brothers who opened a store in 1880 on the site of their present retail shop in Maseru.

The site of the 'camp' was uneven and awkward, dominated on the south side by three rocky hillocks named the 'World', the 'Flesh' and the 'Devil', and hemmed in by the Caledon River on the northern and western sides. The Caledon was crossed at a fording place, from where a wagon trail led westwards into the Orange Free State. In 1880 a pont was built at the ford by an Italian, Stefano Massa, who provided the principal link with the outside world.

The years 1880 and 1881 saw the camp of Maseru under heavy attack during the Gun War. On 10 October 1880 Masupha invaded the place and destroyed several buildings. Another attack on 18 October ended in a pitched battle before the defenders held firm near the site of the present China Garden restaurant. The three overlooking hillocks, which were named by the garrison at this time, were occupied on different occasions by the attackers, with the 'World' often used by snipers as a vantage-point from which to fire at the defenders. The present site of the Lesotho Sun Hotel on this hillock was a strongpoint for the attackers.

On 18 December 1905 the pont across the Caledon was replaced by a rail and road bridge. As a result, Maseru grew considerably. The camp changed into a village where several notable buildings were built of the sandstone common to the area. The principal street, Kingsway, became the first stretch of tarmac road in Lesotho. Fronting it were buildings such as the sandstone headquarters of the British Resident Commissioner, now the office of the Prime Minister of Lesotho. At the eastern end the twin-towered sandstone Catholic Cathedral of Our Lady of Victories was built overlooking Cathedral Circle where Kingsway divides into the northern and southern highways of Lesotho. Stores, banks, offices and other places of business were erected along Kingsway. They have either been added to or replaced by modern structures. Side streets such as Palace Road lead to the royal palace, and Parliament Road leads to the Houses of Parliament. The original site of the first camp of Maseru is in Griffith Hill Road behind the Standard Bank.

Two notable modern buildings on Kingsway, one shaped like a large Sotho hat, the other in the form of a Sotho shield, display for sale the handicrafts of the Sotho people. There are also displays of traditional dancing on Saturday mornings. The Khotso Gift Shop further up Kingsway is the retail outlet for the Roma Valley Co-operative Society. The public library and the office of the Lesotho Tourist Board are also situated on Kingsway. The Royal Lesotho Tapestry Weavers, Afrotique (Afro Rugs Boutique) and Thorkild Handweaving have outlets on Moshweshwe Road, Basotho Sheepskin Products and Royal Crown Jewellers are both in Mohlomi Road. Thaba Bosigo Ceramics can be found in Motsoene Road.

Modern Maseru could hardly be described as beautiful but it is certainly animated. Traffic along Kingsway must be carefully watched, for driving standards in Lesotho are generally atrocious, although South Africa is really not much better. The old camp is now very much an adolescent town, having grown up all by itself. It is now regretting lack of early civic 'education', when the legacy of town planning might have saved a few problems.

Despite its unconventionality, Maseru is atmospheric. The numerous international aid organisations which established their headquarters in the town provided quite a cosmopolitan population. Several of these groups help by training and stimulating the Sotho people to develop their arts, crafts and home industries. Much original work is not only displayed in the shops already mentioned but is exported to many countries where it compares well with international products.

Some South African holiday-makers found Maseru attractive on account of the slight touch of salacity present in its night life. With censorship being less rigorous than in South Africa, cinema of very devious artistic merit flourished as well as literature of the lurid type, strip and cabaret shows (sometimes good, sometimes tatty). The inevitable casino opened with its one-armed bandits and gambling tables. Harmless fun is still available for those who do not take things too seriously. An occasional win against impossible odds is merely a bonanza, and the losses one can afford should be regarded as payment for entertainment.

A word of caution to visitors: Maseru is notorious for a complaint known as 'Maseru Guts', a problem seemingly caused by the drinking-water. Local doctors profit from the malady, but not visitors. The wise traveller sticks to mineral water and regards with caution some of the food in hotels whose menus are pretentious and beyond the technical skills of their chefs.

The Caledon Bridge border post is open daily from 06h00 to 22h00.

The traveller should leave Maseru as soon as possible to explore the beautiful countryside of Lesotho. The delights of Maseru can safely be exhausted in one night, but the wonders of Lesotho are endless.

The principal feature in the vicinity of Maseru is the renowned natural stronghold of Thaba Bosiu (originally spelt Bosigo) which will forever be associated with the name of Moshweshwe. To reach this interesting place drive out of Maseru on the tarmac road to Mafeteng in the south. After 4 km there is a turn-off marked Thaba Bosiu. This is the old road which can be rough for 16,5 km until a better road is joined which is known as the new Thaba Bosiu road. The new road is reached by continuing for 9,5 km on the tarmac Mafeteng road past the old turn-off to Thaba Bosiu and by taking the tarmac turn-off to Roma. At 6 km along this road (20 km from Maseru) the new Thaba Bosiu road branches off, joining the old road after 6,5 km. Thaba Bosiu is 2,5 km beyond the junction of the two roads.

Both roads include interesting features. The old road passes the strangely shaped Pack Saddle Hill and the turn-off to *Botsabelo* (place of refuge) Leper Settlement. The substantial village of Ha Makhoathi, 14 km from Maseru, is overlooked by an isolated pile of sandstone known as Boqate, a fragment of the massive Berea plateau summit to the north of the road. Boqate is worth visiting, for in its rock shelters are some fine Bushman paintings.

At 16 km from Maseru the road crosses by means of a causeway, the *Phuthiatsana* (little duiker river), also known as the Little Caledon River. About 200 m downstream from the causeway there is a confluence with a small tributary. Up this tributary (about 55 m) on the left side of a fork are numerous footprints of prehistoric creatures preserved in the stone.

Where the new road passes the school run by the Church of Lesotho, a track leads for about 1 km to the strange cave houses of *Ntlo Kholo* (the great hut), the ruins of which stand underneath a sandstone overhang. The huts, architecturally interesting and unusual, were still occupied in the 1950s.

THABA BOSIU (OR BOSIGO)

At 24 km from Maseru on the old road (29 km via the new road) lies the village of Ha Rafutho at the foot of the Khubelu Pass, the main route to the summit of Thaba Bosiu The caretaker of the mountain lives in this village, and guides are available to conduct visitors to the several places of interest on the summit, which is reached after a moderately strenuous walk. Defensive piles of stones used as missiles by the Sothos may still be seen, as well as a luck heap of pebbles deposited there by various visitors going to interview Moshweshwe (dropping a pebble on the heap was reputed to bring good luck).

The ruins of Moshweshwe's village may be seen, including the partly restored residence of the renowned chief. The cemetery contains the graves of Moshweshwe and many of his descendants and their families. There are some pieces of cannon and the outline of a foot, a memorial to a son of Moshweshwe named Mateleka, who was denied permission to marry his true love. Before jumping to his death, it is said that he carved his footprint into the rock. A delightful little spring of clear water reaches the surface. Moshweshwe took his refreshment from this spring. There is the strange red-coloured sand dune which folklore says contains the spirit of Moshweshwe. The views from the summit are superb.

From the foot of the Khubelu Pass the road continues past the Thaba Bosiu Mission and up the valley of the Phuthiatsana River. A good view may be had of the rock known as *Qiloane* (the pinnacle) which stands like a giant sentry guarding Thaba Bosiu. The road then fords the river by means of a causeway and climbs to the summit of a plateau, eventually reaching the main Maseru–Teyateyaneng road via a winding scenic route.

ROMA

The principal centre of the Roman Catholic Church in Lesotho, and the site of the University of Lesotho, is to be found at Roma. To reach it from Maseru, follow the tarmac road south towards Mafeteng. After 13 km there is a tarmac turn-off leading for 19 km to Roma.

Roma (Rome) was founded in 1862 when Moshweshwe granted the site to Bishop M J F Allard and Father Joseph Gerard. These two pioneers were joined by sisters of the Holy Family of Bordeaux, and the mission was named *Motse-oa-ma-Jesu* (village of the mother of Jesus). The mission flourished and in 1870 Father Francois le Behan built the attractive burnt-brick chapel and a double-storey building to house the members of the mission. Primary and secondary schools, a teachers' training college, seminaries, a hospital and library were added.

The church serves as a cathedral (or pro-cathedral), while in 1945 the Catholic University College, the Pius XII College, was founded with six students under Father Paul Beaule. The university college was at first linked to the University of South Africa but grew rapidly, becoming the University of Basutoland, Botswana and Swaziland. In 1964 it became fully autonomous and is now the National University of Lesotho.

THE ROAD TO RAMABANTA

Along the road to Roma, 3 km beyond the turn-off to the new road to Thaba Bosiu, a gravel turn-off provides a spectacular drive to the trading station of Ramabanta and the start of the bridle-path to Semonkong, an interesting route into the mountain heart of Lesotho.

For 7,5 km this road crosses maize fields and then joins the Koro-Koro–Maseru road which has branched off from the main Maseru–Mafeteng road 16 km from Maseru. The combined roads continue eastwards towards the mountains, with the 2 533 m high *Thaba Telle* (tall mountain) dominating the horizon. The journey is exceedingly picturesque, lined with villages, fields of maize, herds of cattle and flocks of sheep. Exotic American aloes (agaves) have been planted to form fences around the cattle corrals and villages; cosmos flower in March; and yellow-peach trees flourish quite uncared for, after pips thrown down have taken root by chance.

Caves with Bushman paintings may be seen at places such as Ha Mphotu village. This area is a great producer of reeds used for thatching, and the principal stream here is called *Malehlakana* (mother of reeds). Just across the river a track turns south for 6 km to Mofoka's village and thence on into the upper valley of the Koro-Koro stream where vast expanses of reeds grow. The *Koro-Koro* stream takes its onomatopoeic name from a curiously shaped cave near its source. Rocks dropped into this cave cause an echo to reverberate, which sounds like a gradually dwindling series of 'koro-koro' sounds.

The road crosses the wall of the dam in the Koro-Koro stream (a great place for aquatic birds) and swings southwards up the valley of the Koro-Koro. After 3 km there is a branch stretching due south to St Joseph's Mission (3 km) at the village of Mapeshoane. From here, there is a path to the fine Bushman cave of Halekokoane with its extensive gallery of paintings. The permission of the village headman and a guide should be obtained from Mapeshoane before visiting the cave.

The road to Ramabanta bears eastwards into the mountains after the turn-off to St Joseph's. After 3 km there is a track branching eastwards up the gorge of Raboshabane. There is an interesting tradition about this wild area, and a walk up the gorge is rewarding.

The track leads up a very rugged ravine choked with sandstone fragments. Keeping to the left bank of the stream, the track passes (3 km) the great cave of Mohomeng. After 1,5 km, just above the confluence of the Popa tributary stream, there looms the famed *Lefika ka Raboshabane* (the rock of Raboshabane).

THE ROCK OF RABOSHABANE

This great rock rears up about 30 m and can only be climbed on its northern side. A Sotho proverb says *'the rock of Raboshabane is slippery'*, a variant of the old *'there's many a slip 'twixt cup and lip'*. This is the story.

During the days of war and cannibalism in the first quarter of the 19th century, a racketeer named Raboshabane established himself on top of this rock where he built a cluster of huts. To the much-harassed peasantry of the district he announced that he would provide a protection service, defending them from evil upon payment of regular tributes. He also offered to store their harvest on top of the rock, supplying them on demand against payment of commission.

By intimidation and the offer of some security for the harvest, Raboshabane accumulated during that time of famine a store of food on top of his rock, growing fat and increasingly avaricious in the process. The peasants were starving and disgruntled, but had no counter to the bully. At last one of them, a scarecrow of a man named Sofeng, found the answer.

Trusting for safety on his thinness, he made his way to the stronghold of a notorious brotherhood of 28 cannibals led by a tough ruffian named Motleyoa. Sofeng pretended to be lost and appeared innocent of their reputation. He craved their hospitality for a night and regaled them with gossip very acceptable to individuals normally shunned by their fellow men. Sofeng included an account of Raboshabane, describing his fat person so lusciously that the mouths of the cannibals watered as they repeated his name and address.

And so it happened that one dark night the 28 cannibals, each carrying a club and dragging behind them a huge cooking pot, silently scaled the rock of Raboshabane. A wild fight ensued on the summit. While the peasantry watched and listened, they heard first a sudden uproar and then sounds of jollification. The glow of a great cooking fire was seen on the top of the rock. In the morning the head of Raboshabane was thrown down to the waiting peasants. From this occurrence stems the proverb and tradition of the downfall of Raboshabane.

From the turn-off to this notable rock the road to Ramabanta starts to climb steeply, reaches the top of the sandstone heights and continues over a grassy plateau where views of the mountains and the gorge of Raboshabane and the rock may be seen.

The road passes over a ridge, with Motlepu's village lying immediately beyond. From Motlepu's village, mountaineers leave the road to climb the spectacular Thaba Telle, 2 533 m high and no easy achievement. The road now loses altitude, surrounded by handsome scenery. At 30 km from the start of this gravel road on the Roma road, a junction is reached with a track coming from the Thabana li Mele pottery works and Roma, via a very rough route.

The road continues southwards, dominated to the east by the twin summits of *Thabana li Mele* (hills like teats). Passing the trading station of Thabana li Mele, the road descends to cross the *Makhalaneng* (place of little crabs) River by means of a causeway at the 36 km point. The road climbs steadily to the top of Nkesi's Pass (2 012 m), from where a superb view of the 3 096 m high Thaba Putswa (blue mountain) and its associate range may be seen.

The road descends, revealing below the cul-de-sac at Ramabanta's store, the mission station of Fatima and the site of the Catholic National Shrine of Lesotho, a scene of pilgrimage which owes its origin to events surrounding the conversion in May 1946 of the local chieftainess, Makopi Api. The road ends at Ramabanta's store, 45 km from the turn-off on the Maseru–Roma road.

The end of this road, close to the banks of the river known as *Makhaleng* (place of crabs), is the starting-point for the precipitous track to Semonkong and the 193 m high waterfall known as the *Maletsunyane* from a Bushman who once lived there. This is an exhilarating journey high over the summit of the Thaba Putswa range via Makheka's Pass and across the basalt moorland roof of Southern Africa to the trading station at *Semonkong* (place of smoke). In a gorge on the banks of the Maletsunyane River, Messrs Fraser maintain some bungalows to accommodate people viewing the Falls. Food must be taken but bedding is provided. From here, there is a short ride to the prodigious gorge of the Maletsunyane, where the river thunders down as one of the great waterfalls of the world. An eerie atmosphere and a strange confusion of sounds pervades this almost enchanted place. The journey to it is unforgettable, revealing superb views of a world of green and blue mountains. Dense masses of red-hot pokers *(Kniphofia* sp.*)* flower around March, giving the slopes a blood-stained appearance. Book at Fraser's store, Maseru, or phone (09266) 31-2601.

In winter, when most of the waterfalls in Lesotho are frozen, the Maletsunyane Falls are a fantastic sight, with towers of ice rising up from the ground to meet spirals of ice suspended from above.

From Thabana li Mele (15 km from Ramabanta) it is possible in a four-wheel-drive vehicle to return to Maseru via the alternative route through Roma. This route branches off northwards past the pottery works, continues up the valley of the Makhalaneng River, and then climbs steeply through rugged mountain country. Dominating the west are the high mountains of Popa and Popanyane, Thabana li Mele, the flat-topped Qaba and Qabanyane peaks, Furumela on whose slopes grow the famous spiral aloes (*Aloe lattifolias)* and *Thaba Tjhitja* (round mountain) from whose 2 499 m high summit, reached by a relatively easy climb, there is a stunningly beautiful view.

After 9 km the road reaches Nyakasuba village where there is a turn-off to the east over Black Nek (the starting-point for climbs to Thaba Tjhitja) to the store at Makhaleng. From this junction the road bears north-westwards, crossing the Makhaleng River after 1,5 km and traversing a plateau. After a further 1,5 km the descent of Ngakana's Pass commences. At the bottom of this pass the road stretches north-westwards, passing the Roma mission station and from there back to Maseru. The round trip, comprising 136 km, is a drive – rough and steep – that will never be forgotten by those who have completed it.

THE MOUNTAIN ROAD

The famous mountain road of Lesotho takes the traveller 124 km from Maseru over the roof of Southern Africa to the trading station at the Mantsonyane River. Named the Trans-Maluti highway, the road will continue to the valley of the Gariep (Orange) River, to Qacha's Nek and out to Matatiele in KwaZulu-Natal.

The road is perfectly usable for normal vehicles, except in rainy weather. In winter it is also blocked by snow for periods and must always be negotiated with maximum caution. Scenically the road provides a majestic and exciting experience. For mountaineers, fishermen, hikers, campers, artists and photographers, it is the key to a high world of sport and wonderful scenery hitherto only accessible by laborious walking or riding on horseback.

The mountain road branches eastwards from the main Maseru–Roma road at a point 24,5 km south of Maseru, from where it proceeds slightly north-eastwards, climbing sandstone cliffs to reach the level grassy plateau at the foot of the Maluti range. On the summit of this plateau the traveller is treated to a majestic view of the great massif of the Maluti and the handsome bulk of the 2 884 m high Machache immediately ahead. To the south are views into the valley where the Roma mission, pro-cathedral and the campus of the university are clearly visible.

After losing altitude, the road proceeds eastwards across an undulating plateau covered in maize, sorghum and grain. At 34 km from Maseru the road reaches the village of Ha Ntsi, with its stores and petrol supply. Immediately beyond this village the road crosses a stream which drains the *Mohlaka-oa-Tuka* (the marsh which burns), where underground peat fires burn incessantly.

Immediately across this stream there is a turn-off leading northwards for 3 km to Ha Khotso village. From here a track continues for a further 3 km to the gorge of the Liphiring River where, in the rock shelter known as *Ha Borwana* (place of the little Bushmen), may be seen one of the finest galleries of rock art in the world. A caretaker is stationed at the rock shelter and there is an admission charge. Visitors to these and other Bushmen caves should discourage guides from throwing water over paintings. This may brighten the colours temporarily, but it causes permanent damage.

The main gravel road meanwhile, after crossing the river from the marsh, continues towards the great mountain wall. After 5 km the road passes two rondavels and a wayside tea-room originally erected there as toll-houses for the mountain road. This is now the two-star Toll Gate House Caravan Park, with campsite and bungalows. Beyond the caravan park, passing the Machache Agricultural Station, the road arrives at the foot of the mountains and starts to climb the slopes of *Thaba Tseka* (mountain with a white mark) by means of the *Lekhalo la Borwa* (pass of the Bushmen).

The road climbs steeply for 6 km and then (46,5 km from Maseru) reaches the summit 2 268 m above sea-level. A sweeping panorama is revealed over the original zigzag bridle-path which, before the road was made, was the sole means of access to this mountain world. Until 1890 nobody lived there other than Bushmen in the valleys. Cattle posts were then established. Eventually, from about 1912, the pressure of population in the lowlands drove people to seek new homes in the valleys of the inner mountains. All the provisions and exports of these people were carried on the backs of pack animals and the famous Basuto ponies, originally of the pure Arab stock of horses brought to the Cape by the Dutch East India Co. Rustlers and horse traders passed these noble animals to the Sothos. They were stunted and made nimble, sturdy and shaggy as a result of hard usage, open-air life and the poor treatment meted out to them by owners who were horse users rather than horse lovers. They are now a breed of their own.

A complex network of bridle-paths was made over the mountains. In 1948 W K Hudson, the Government Surveyor, located this remarkable road, following the route of one of the main bridle-paths.

From the summit of Bushman's Pass the road descends steeply into the valley of the Makhaleng River. After 5 km the road crosses the river and continues up the river valley. There are fine pools in which to swim and fish, and pleasant camping sites. If a guide is obtained from one of the villages, the energetic hiker, by following the course of the Makhaleng, will eventually reach the lovely cascades of Quiloane, at the foot of which is a magnificent swimming-pool. It is a half-day return trip and the going is steep.

The road soon leaves the Makhaleng. At 53 km from Maseru a road camp is passed where there is a pretty waterfall, natural swimming-pool, fine picnic spot, and a most attractive little hotel known as Molimo Nthuse from the mountain pass above it. This two-star lodge offers snug accommodation in the high mountains. To book phone (09266) 37-0211. From the hotel the road starts to climb and after 1,5 km passes the Setibing trading station. A further 1,5 km of ascent takes the road through the pass (2 318 m) known as *Molimo Nthuse* (God help me).

The road continues up the valley of a stream abounding with crystal pools and rushing cascades. At the top of the valley (64 km from Maseru) the road reaches the summit – 2 621 m above sea-level – of the Blue Mountain Pass, named after the 2 902 m high Thaba Putswa (blue mountain) which dominates the range 1,5 km to the north.

For 9 km the road curves along the contour slopes of the range. Descending steeply, it passes a road camp in the upper reaches of the valley of the Likalaneng, 80 km from Maseru. At 1,5 km beyond the camp there is a turn-off leading down the valley for 2 km to the Likalaneng trading station, from where horses and guides may be hired for a visit to the beautiful Senqunyane Falls about 6 km away. The main gravel road passes the turn-off to the Likalaneng store and starts to climb and twist up the slopes from where sweeping views and spectacular patches of red-hot pokers flowering around March may be seen.

At 90 km from Maseru the road reaches the top of this pass, 2 621 m above sea-level. The view is superb and the panorama is forever changing as the road makes a long, curving descent into the fertile, well populated valley of the Senqunyane River where, at 99 km from Maseru, the road passes the trading station and police post of Marakabei, named after a former chief of the area. After a further 2 km the road bridges across the Senqunyane River where the pleasant tourist lodge of Messrs Fraser shelters in a grove of trees on its banks. Accommodation at the Senqunyane Lodge should be booked at Fraser's store in Maseru or phone (09266) 31-2601. Guests must take their own food, but a cook and bedding are provided.

Fishing, riding and climbing are pleasant pursuits along this crystal-clear river. Immediately across the bridge a turn-off leads down the river bank for 1,5 km to a water gauge. Camping, swimming and fishing spots are numerous. Many a fat trout has been grilled hereabouts in happy camps beneath the stars.

The Senqunyane is also known as the Little Gariep for it is one of the principal upper tributaries of the Gariep (formerly Orange), the draining river of Lesotho. Beyond the river the road climbs steeply for 9 km to the summit of the *Tshetshe* (ridge) pass, nearly 762 m above the river. The road is now at the 2 560 m level. It immediately starts to descend through a narrow valley and then emerges into the cultivated valley of the *Mantsonyane* (small black) river where, 124 km from Maseru, the road reaches the store of Messrs Collier & Yeats, a short distance above the river.

Unless a four-wheel-drive vehicle is used, most travellers turn back from here. A lasting vision remains of the wild jumble of dark basalt mountains covered with snow in winter and laced with rivers and streams, cascades of ice, ski slopes and toboggan runs. Impressions of the scarlet red-hot poker flowers linger vividly as do those of deep valleys, stupendous views and lonely cattle posts; the herdboys and the shepherds on the mountain slopes; the gentle sound of their *lesibas* (stringed musical instruments) floating on the wind; flags waving at the village huts where beer is available; the isolated stores; the horsemen in their colourful blankets on shaggy little ponies, the sheer loveliness and airy spaciousness of the high hills.

THE NORTH–SOUTH ROAD OF LESOTHO

The main road of Lesotho is the north–south highway leading down the valley of the Caledon River. Branches from this road turn into the mountains and all are being constantly being improved, with substantial lengths now under tarmac. The beginning of the road in the north is the border post of Caledon Poort Bridge, 9 km from the town of Fouriesburg in the Free State. The border post is open from 08h00 to 16h00. A most majestic entrance to Lesotho is made as the road winds its way past towering, flat-topped sandstone hills, the romantic 'castles' of the Sotho, and then reaches the border post where the *Mohokare* (or Caledon) River flows through an impressive gorge beneath high sandstone cliffs. Through this gigantic natural gateway may be seen the beautiful Maluti range, very blue in the eastern distance.

After crossing the river and passing through the border post into Lesotho, the road leads along badly eroded hill slopes for 9 km, and then enters the township of ...

BUTHA-BUTHE

Named after Moshweshwe's old mountain stronghold, *Butha-Buthe* (the gatherer) consists of a rather untidy and straggling collection of administrative buildings and trading stores. There is a small market-place, built in the form of a characteristic Sotho straw hat, where a shop sells local handicrafts. The situation of the place, as with all the early administrative posts, is picturesque, surrounded by sandstone 'castles'. The pioneer British administrative officials also had enough sense to plant trees. Consequently the place is shady, pleasant and a sharp contrast to the surroundings which are almost totally devoid of trees.

THE BUTHA-BUTHE DISTRICT

From Butha-Buthe a road stretches north-eastwards to the border post of Joel's Drift. From this road, branches lead to several places of interest, one of which is the colossal series of rock shelters known as *Sekubu* (like the hippopotamus) on account of a curious similarity between the shape of the rocks and the teats of a hippo. These caves were first occupied by Bushmen and afterwards became the lair of cannibals during the Lifaqane. Moshweshwe's followers subsequently built houses in them. Finally they became stables for livestock.

To reach these caves, take the turn-off 7 km from Butha-Buthe village on the road to Joel's Drift just after it passes Butha-Buthe hill. The turn-off leads up the left bank of the Serutle River and takes the traveller to the Sekubu Mission (4,5 km), from where guides take visitors along a 3 km footpath to the caves.

The main road to Joel's Drift, from the turn-off to the Sekubu Caves, continues north-eastwards across the Serutle River. After 5 km a turn-off west of 1 km reaches the border post at Joel's Drift.

From this turn-off to Joel's Drift a gravel road continues up the valley of the Mohokare. After 2 km (15 km from Butha-Buthe) there is a fork where one branch swings eastwards to Oxbow. The other branch continues northwards and, although rough in parts, rewards the traveller with some spectacular scenery. At 25 km from Butha-Buthe there is a turn-off to Hendrik's Drift, crossing the Mohokare into South Africa.

The main road, which serves a string of trading stations, missions and villages, continues up the left bank of the Mohokare, traversing delightful scenery. At 34 km the road passes Thakabana's store and then starts to climb, yielding fine views of mountains and across the plains to points such as Rhebokkop (2 803 m high), the highest peak in the Free State. At 50 km from Butha-Buthe the road descends to Libono store and police post with a glimpse ahead of the high Drakensberg.

OXBOW AND MOKHOTLONG

At 15 km from Butha-Buthe on the road to Libono (just described) there is a junction. The road to Libono goes northwards, a branch leads south-eastwards for 12 km to Tsime; and the Oxbow branch leads eastwards up the valley of the *Holola* (river of blue cranes). This is the beginning of one of the most spectacular road journeys in Africa. Dominated by the handsome Khatibe Mountain (2 743 m high), the road bridges across the Khukhune River tributary of the Holola. Continuing up the valley of the latter river, the road passes a number of spectacular sandstone overhangs and the countryside becomes increasingly rugged. At 34 km from Butha-Buthe there is an especially notable sandstone rock shelter known as Liphofung, with another overhang lying under the road. These shelters, watered by a fine cascade, were used by Bushmen whose gallery of polychrome paintings may be seen in the cave under the road.

The road rises steadily and approaches the main wall of the Maluti massif. At 46 km from Butha-Buthe the foot of the spectacular Moteng Pass is reached. For the next 9 km the road, twisting and climbing, rises about 762 m, reaching at the summit (56 km from Butha-Buthe) one of the highest points attained by normal two-wheel-drive vehicles on a public road in Southern Africa (2 834,6 m above sea-level).

This is the basalt roof of Southern Africa, a world of winter snows, frozen waterfalls and cascades of ice, lonely cattle posts; crisp clear air and crystal streams where fat trout dart like glints of light through deep and tranquil pools.

The road descends from the summit of the pass to the Tsehlanyane River (60 km from Butha-Buthe), climbs a ridge, and from its summit looks down on the valley of the *Malibamatso* (river of dark pools) where, just below the confluence of that river and the Tsehlanyane, the great Katse Dam has been constructed. At the site the river meanders in the shape of an oxbow, hence the name given to the area. The stored water is fed by tunnels through the mountains into the Holola valley to drive hydro-electric stations, irrigate the lowlands and supply South Africa with about 1 000 million litres of water a day, increasing to a possible 3 600 million litres a day. There will eventually be five major dams and one smaller dam, three pumping stations and 225 km of tunnels. In the process of transferring water from the highlands to the lowlands, 1 260 Gwh of hydro-electric power will be generated, making Lesotho almost self-sufficient. The water, 70 cubic metres per second, will be of high quality, and royalty payments to Lesotho will benefit its economy. From a tourist point of view this vast scheme will provide tremendous possibilities for recreation.

The road descends from the spur and at 65 km from Butha-Buthe reaches the Oxbow Camp, a great centre for trout fishermen, ski enthusiasts, and pony treks through the mountains.

Beyond the camp the road crosses the Malibamatso River, from where the road becomes a more rugged route more suited to four-wheel-drive vehicles and horsemen. This road continues over the heights for a further 46 km to the diamond-fields of Letseng la Terae and for a further 72 km (184 km from Butha-Buthe) to the isolated administrative post of *Mokhotlong* (place of the bald-headed ibis). At Mokhotlong there are trading stations, a police post and a small Government guest-house which provides accommodation. A mountaineer's chalet with five rooms is also available.

The settlement (or 'camp') of Mokhotlong has always enjoyed some renown as one of the loneliest villages in Southern Africa. For many years it could only be reached by horse and all goods were carried in by pack animals – including one 317,5 kg flywheel for a mill at Tlokoeng. The one pack mule which carried this dreadful load all the way could not be relieved of its burden and died on reaching the destination. The 56 km long track from the Sani Pass down to KwaZulu-Natal has, since October 1948, when the first four-wheel-drive vehicle did the journey, been improved into a regular route for vehicles and is a great tourist attraction. A mountaineer's chalet (the highest licensed 'hotel' in Southern Africa) is situated at the head of the Sani Pass, from where there are fine rides, climbs, ski runs in winter, and bridle-paths which lead to places such as the summit of the 3 482 m high *Thabana Ntlenyana*. Notwithstanding its incongruous name (meaning 'the little mountain which is a little nice'), this is the highest point in Southern Africa. The mountaineer's chalet has 6 rooms accommodating 22 people. Book through Sani Pass Hotel, Himeville, KwaZulu-Natal.

BUTHA-BUTHE TO MASERU

From Butha-Buthe the main trunk road of Lesotho runs south-westwards through rugged sandstone country which is densely inhabited. Climbing up to Rampai's Nek (4,5 km), the road traverses a ridge and then descends through Levi's Nek into a valley dominated on the southern and eastern sides by the sandstone heights of the extensive plateau hillock known as *Leribe* from a rock shaped like the forehead of a baboon. Strange, richly coloured rock shapes may be seen on all sides, creating the effect of a vast assembly of weird, petrified figures.

At 17 km the road passes the Roman Catholic mission of Maryland with its handsome sandstone church built close to the village of the chief, Jonathan. Colourful towering sandstone cliffs look down from the Leribe heights around which the road swings southwards. At 23 km there is a turn-off to the Leribe Mission of the Lesotho Evangelical Church nestling against the cliffs, where there is also a great rock overhang under which are the ruins of a village built by unknown people. Bushman paintings may be seen in several rock shelters.

A further 2 km (24 km from Butha-Buthe) sees a track turning off westwards just beyond the bridge over the Subeng stream, leading to the original causeway across the stream. Thirty metres downstream from this ruined causeway may be clearly seen 24 five-toed footprints of dinosaurs, well preserved in the sandstone.

The main road, now running southwards, passes the Leribe Farmers' Training Centre run by the Oxford Committee for Famine Relief, and 1,5 km further on (32 km from Butha-Buthe) reaches the village of ...

HLOTSE

The administrative centre of the Leribe district, Hlotse had its start in 1876 when Canon John Widdicombe established a mission there and built the little church which is still standing. A residency for a magistrate, Major Bell, was also built in 1877 and in the following year the small watch-tower which protected the place during the Gun War of 1880. Several attacks were made on Hlotse during this disturbance. The residency was sacked and the church damaged, but the little fort held out. During these troubles the renowned General 'Chinese' Gordon stayed in the place for three days trying to negotiate peace, but without success.

Hlotse (dead meat) received its name from the river which flows around the heights on which the mission and Government camp was erected. It is said that the name refers to the practice of travellers who, fording rivers, threw meat into the water in order to lure away crocodiles.

THE LERIBE DISTRICT

From Hlotse village a drive approaches the mountains, ending after 26 km at the trading centre of Pitseng. On the way (16 km from Hlotse) there is a turn-off to the store at Seetsa. From there a track leads to the mine at Kao where the prospector Ken Carlstein found diamonds at a point 41 km from the turn-off on the Pitseng road. Fine views of the mountains may be had from Pitseng.

Another interesting drive stretching towards the mountains in the Leribe district begins with a turn-off eastwards 15 km from Hlotse on the main road to Teyateyaneng. After 4,5 km there is a turn-off southwards to the mission station of the Immaculate Conception and to trading stations such as Mapoteng. Just before the road reaches the mission (25 km from Hlotse), an extraordinary mushroom-shaped balancing rock may be seen on the slope of an overlooking height on the eastern side of the road.

The main road from the turn-off to this rock and the mission meanwhile continues south-eastwards, passing the Corn Exchange (38 km from Hlotse) and branching to serve various trading stations close to the mountains, as well as the mission station of Santa Thérèse (48 km from Hlotse), near which may be seen some superb Bushman paintings. Guides for the short walk may be found at the mission.

This mission was the scene of one of the most extraordinary poltergeist manifestations ever to occur in Southern Africa. It all started on 11 October 1947 after the priest then in charge of the station, Father Hamel, had delivered a stiff sermon on the evils of black magic. During the course of this sermon he made some pointed comments about an individual who happened to be a member of his church. The person concerned immediately walked out of the church, exclaiming loudly that she would send her *tokoloshe* (poltergeist) to break the father's neck.

And so the game commenced. A shower of stones and other missiles regularly disrupted the work of the mission. Each sunset saw a start to proceedings, with the principal target being the private quarters of Father Hamel. Items were removed from the priest's study, letters were mixed up in locked post-bags and everybody was hit by stones. As with similar manifestations, these stones, although fist sized, did not travel through the air with speed. There was a curious deliberation about their movement as though they were being carried by an invisible hand and not being thrown. When they reached the ground, they neither bounced nor rolled.

The school was greatly disturbed by stones falling on the roof at night. The clothes of the boarders were spirited away in the dark hours, only to be found at dawn festooned so high in the branches of trees that sticks and ladders had to be used to recover them.

Several investigators and senior members of the Catholic Church went to the mission to examine this strange occurrence. The conclusion was reached that the centre of the disturbances was a hut occupied by three young boys, one of whom, Johannes, aged 12, was suspected of being host to the poltergeist. He stated that a curious-tasting sweet had been given to him by the person accused of raising the poltergeist. This magic mixture was therefore suspected of having attached the playful spirit to his person.

As an experiment, Johannes was sent away from the mission with two men being detailed to escort the boy home. Being prudent souls, the escorts presented themselves for duty wearing miners' steel helmets, souvenirs of work on the gold-fields. This was apparently too much for the poltergeist's sense of humour. The two steel helmets became targets for an accurate attack of stone throwing. The escorts ended their duties by galloping over the hills amid stones plonking down unerringly on their helmets.

Among the investigators were Father Pageau (the Provincial for Lesotho), Father Herbert (the Administrator), and Father Laydevant from Saint Rose Mission who specialised in such disturbances. Not a man to exaggerate, his description of events as given to the author, is fascinating:

> *'The stones usually fell in the open bare places where it would have been easy to notice if they had been thrown by some human being. One of them, while we were in Father Hamel's office, left his sleeping room, passed quickly through the office in a horizontal line about three feet from the ground, and dropped softly in front of the door.*
>
> *'Near the mission dispensary one evening after sunset, seven or eight of us were standing talking. We heard a heavy thud, as though of somebody falling to the ground. We looked towards the dispensary and all the witnesses, except myself, saw a man in a kind of kaross, walking slowly and disappearing in the Sisters' garden. We rushed at once to the spot where the man had disappeared, but there was no trace of anybody and the gate was locked'.*

On 3 November at 15h00, a rock weighing about 7 kg fell with a colossal crash on to the iron roof of a shed where about ten girls were washing clothes. After the squeals of terror had subsided, Father Laydevant examined the heavy stone and the roof, but there was no sign of the damage one might have expected from such a missile.

Similar manifestations continued for some time. Father Laydevant and Hamel read exorcism prayers, sprinkled holy water and resorted to everything they knew. The manifestations gradually diminished. Finally, after a special service of exorcism, they vanished altogether. But there was a strange sequel.

In December 1947 Maria Makhetha lodged a complaint with the District Commissioner of Teyateyaneng. She stated that Father Hamel had publicly accused her of being the witch responsible for the hauntings. She sued Father Hamel for damages. Although summoned, he refused to appear in court.

The complainant arrived but without her witnesses. She complained that Father Hamel had openly stated that any individual helping her with evidence or money would be expelled from the church. Father Hamel was charged with conspiring to defeat the ends of justice. Forced to appear in court, he was fined £20 damages with costs for defamation. This ended a very curious matter!

HLOTSE TO TEYATEYANENG

From Hlotse the main trunk road of Lesotho descends the ridge on which the village stands, crosses the Hlotse River and continues westwards. After 10 km there is a turn-off leading westwards across the Mohokare River to Ficksburg, 8 km away. The border post is open daily from 07h00 to 20h00. The main road continues south-westwards down the Caledon valley and after 3 km reaches the turn-off east to the Corn Exchange and Santa Thérèse Mission.

The road proceeds over the widest portion of the Lesotho plains lying between the Mohokare River and the Maluti massif. There are a few isolated hills, otherwise the landscape comprises open, undulating fields of maize. At 32 km from Hlotse the road passes through the village of Peka and then swings southwards, continuing across the open plains. After a further 23 km a turn-off leads for 32 km to Mamathes and Mapoteng. Half a kilometre beyond the turn-off (56 km from Hlotse), the road reaches the village of ...

TEYATEYANENG

The odd-sounding name of *Teyateyaneng* is taken from the river, so called on account of the shifting or quicksands in its beds. The village was founded in 1886 as the seat of the magistrate, Godfrey Lagden. An Anglican mission station was also founded there, and for nearly 50 years the well-known Father William Wrenford was in charge of the place. The thatched building in which he lived and worked remains a picturesque feature in the modern village.

Teyateyaneng is nowadays a busy trading and administrative centre for the Berea district. There is considerable local industry in weaving, while tourists can also find several fine galleries of Bushman paintings in the numerous caves and rock shelters in the area.

From Teyateyaneng the main trunk road of Lesotho descends the ridge on which the village stands and after 1 km crosses the river which gives the village its name. High sandstone cliffs containing many interesting caves overlook the river.

The tarmac road climbs a ridge, passes beneath sandstone cliffs and descends again to continue south-westwards. At 35 km there is a turn-off east to Lancer's Gap, and 4,5 km further on (40 km from Teyateyaneng) the road reaches Maseru, the capital of Lesotho, already described.

MAFETENG, MOHALE'S HOEK AND QUTHING

The tarmac main highway of Lesotho leads southwards from Maseru across a classic landscape of gigantic natural and unnatural erosion. The central mountain mass (the *Luthing* or place of mountains) recedes eastwards and the road traverses a sunny plain of maize lands, cattle herds, villages, watercourses and Sotho 'castles', the sandstone jigsaw-puzzle remnants of a once-higher plateau now eroded into fragments.

At 5 km from Maseru there is a turn-off east to Thaba Bosiu and at 15 km a turn-off east to Roma and the famous mountain road. The Roman Catholic mission named after Bishop Eugene de Mazenod stands just beyond the turn-off. One kilometre south of this mission lies another turn-off to the east leading to Ramabanta and one of the finest scenic drives in Lesotho (already described).

Yet another turn-off 24 km further on (40 km from Maseru) leads east to *Morija* (named after the Mount Morija of the Bible), the chief station of the pioneer French Protestant missions, now known as the Lesotho Evangelical Church, and also to *Matsieng* (place of Letsie, the heir of Moshweshwe who was established there in order to be near the missionaries). Since then this area has been the seat of the paramount chiefs and kings of Lesotho.

A further 9 km sees a turn-off east leading to Makhakhe, the Emmaus Mission, and over the Matelile Pass to the trading station and lodge of Malealea confronting a dreamlike view over the valley of the Makhaleng River.

Mervyn Smith, who established the trading station of Malealea, put a sign at the summit of the pass with the words '*Wayfarer, pause, behold the Gate of Paradise*'. He always stopped there for a few minutes when he was returning from some journey.

Smith died in January 1950 and was buried in the garden of his home at Malealea. He was a great character of what was then known as Basutoland. He asked that there be no headstone over his grave, for the beauty of Malealea was all around him. The sign on the top of the pass remains, with a slight change in the words, making it read '*Wayfarer, pause and look upon a gateway of Paradise*'.

From the turn-off to Malealea on the main Lesotho highway (45 km from Maseru), it is another 30 km to ...

MAFETENG

A straggling little trading and administrative centre built on a high open plateau, *Mafeteng* (place of the fat, unmarried women) has the appearance of an American cow town with its horsemen, trading stations, dusty streets and unmade pavements. A market-place offers oddments for sale but there is nothing else of note. There is a hotel.

During the Gun War of 1880, Mafeteng was attacked on several occasions but the small Government force held its own in the 'camp'.

Notwithstanding its rondescript appearance, Mafeteng has always been one of the principal trading centres of Lesotho. Traders such as William Scott, W Wilkinson, Fred and Sydney Collier, and Donald and Douglas Fraser (whose first store was close to Mafeteng, at *Liphiring*, the place of horses) all started business in this district.

From Mafeteng the main road continues south-eastwards across the open rocky plains. After 11 km there is a turn-off westwards to *Sepapushek* (Sephapo's Gate) (8 km) on the border of South Africa, while a further 10 km sees a turn-off eastwards to Lifateng. After 11 km (40 km from Mafeteng) the road crosses the Makhaleng River (known to Europeans as the Cornet Spruit), flowing from the mountains down a handsome valley. Overlooking the bridge across the Makhaleng River from the east is *Thaba Tsweu* (white mountain), notable for the petrified wood near its upper layer of white sandstone.

Five kilometres beyond this river there is a turn-off leading eastwards for 32 km into the foothills of the Maluti Range to a trading station with the odd name of *Masemouse*, derived (it is said) from a Bushman known as Masmous. This road allows access to some fine mountain scenery, with panoramic views of the Makhaleng Valley. Dominating the mountains here is the impressive *Pedlar's Peak* (2 908 m), the highest point of this part of the range. To the Sotho it is known by the name of *Thaba Putswa* (blue mountain), but Europeans have named it Pedlar in the mistaken conclusion that Masemouse (which lies at its foot) is itself derived from the Afrikaans *smous* (pedlar). The mountain is climbed from Khape's village near the end of the road. It is a day-long scramble, with a fine view as the ultimate reward.

From the turn-off to Masemouse, the main road continues southwards for 5 km and then (49 km from Mafeteng) reaches the pleasantly situated administrative centre of ...

MOHALE'S HOEK

This little place had its start in 1884 when Chief Mohale, brother of Moshweshwe, presented to the Government the beautifully situated and well-watered site for the establishment of an administrative post. The original Government 'camp' grew into a busy trading centre. With ample trees planted in the past, it is today one of the most pleasant of all the Lesotho villages.

Overlooking Mohale's Hoek is a fine example of a Sotho 'castle' known as Castle Rock. With its crumbling buttresses it looms over the golf-course. About 2 km south of Mohale's Hoek is the cave stronghold used by the notorious cannibal band led by Motlejoa during the turbulent years of the 1820s. This sinister cave is worth visiting.

The main road leaves Mohale's Hoek, travelling first westwards and then swinging to the south from the point 5 km away where a road leads for 4 km to the border post of Makhaleng Gate, and from there to Zastron 47 km away.

The main Lesotho highway continues southwards through increasingly rugged scenery and climbs steadily up a ridge to the top of the pass known as *Mesitsaneng* (place of wild beans), from where may be seen handsome views of a rugged, sun-drenched landscape. At 9 km from Mohale's Hoek the road reaches the summit, with a branch stretching eastwards to Maphutseng (10 km) and the Bethesda mission, founded by the French Protestants in 1843 close to the then residence of the renowned Chief Murosi. Near the Bethesda mission are many tracks and relics of dinosaurs. Guides are obtainable at the mission or store.

From the summit of the Mesitsaneng Pass the main road descends into the great valley of the Maphutseng River, revealing fine views of the central mountain massif.

At 23 km from Mohale's Hoek the road crosses the Maphutseng River where it flows through a deep gorge. A further 6 km takes the road across the Mekaling River, while 16 km further on (42 km from Mohale's Hoek) the road reaches the Seako bridge across the Gariep River.

The Seako bridge is the longest in Lesotho, extending for 191 m. Made in England in the 1880s, it was shipped to South Africa and then carried by wagon to Kommissiedrif on the road from Smithfield to Rouxville. Retired from this position after long service, it was sent piecemeal to Lesotho, where it was erected across the Gariep (Orange) River in 1959 to replace a pontoon that had been washed away ten years earlier.

Across the Gariep (known to the Sotho by the name of *Senqu*) the road continues for 6 km, reaching a turn-off leading westwards for 10 km to the border post of Telle Bridge, which is open from 08h00 to 16h00. A further 3 km sees a turn-off to the Masitise mission of the French Protestants with its cave house and Bushman paintings. The cave was first used by Bushmen, followed by the Phuti headman Mazitizi (after whom the mission is named), and in 1867 converted into a home by the Reverend D F Ellenberger who raised a family there.

Passing the Villa Maria Roman Catholic mission, with its training school for young priests, and just beyond it the industrial school of *Leloaleng* (place of the mill) run by the Paris mission, the road twists into the ravine of the Qomongqomong River. At 56 km from Mohale's Hoek there is a turn-off north-eastwards leading to Murosi's Mountain. The road climbs up to a shoulder of the overlooking heights, and after 3 km (58 km from Mohale's Hoek) leads into the administrative centre for the Quthing district, the 'camp' or village of ...

MOYENI (QUTHING)

The village of *Moyeni* (the windy place) was established in 1877 on the site of the present Leloaleng Industrial School. Abandoned during the Gun War of 1880, the camp was re-established in 1889 and built on the present site with its commanding views. The original buildings were then presented to the Paris Evangelical mission for their industrial school, and a water-mill was built there which gave the place its name.

Quthing is the name of the district but is also often applied to Moyeni village. The Gariep River in its upper reaches is known as the *Senqu* (place of the clicking language). The name derives from the ideophonic name *boQu* given by the Sotho to the Bushmen. It imitates the sound of the clicks in the Bushman language, the 'Q' being pronounced as a labial click. *Quthing* means, therefore, the place of clicking. The Quthing River is one of the tributaries of the Gariep reaching the great river under the northern slopes of Mount Murosi.

Moyeni 'camp' was pleasantly laid out and planted with many handsome trees whose healthy growth indicates the afforestation possibilities of the countryside. The whole of the great valley of the upper Gariep was a favourite resort for Bushmen. Their paintings may be seen in many rock shelters in the Quthing district. Beneath Moyeni village there is one gallery situated in a snug little shelter in the cliffs. More paintings, comprising several galleries, may conveniently be seen in the grounds of the Masitise mission. Particularly magnificent rock art may be found 8 km from Moyeni on the road to the Qomongqomong store in a small gorge of the Ratlayi stream situated 1 km before the store.

MOUNT MUROSI AND QACHA'S NECK

Three kilometres from the centre of Moyeni on the road to Mohale's Hoek, a turn-off leads north-eastwards to the famous stronghold of Murosi's Mountain and thence to Qacha's Neck. The road is quite practical for normal vehicles, but requires careful driving. The road crosses the Qomongqomong River immediately after the turn-off and, 250 m further on, a fenced area protects some dinosaur tracks. The road descends in an easterly direction to the Gariep (or Senqu) River 5 km from the turn-off. The road now leads up the left bank of the Gariep, with many picturesque scenes of villages, ferry boats, and the high mountains overlooking the course of the river.

At 12 km the road passes the store at *Fort Hartley,* the base camp of the Cape Mounted Rifles, named after Major Hartley, their medical officer during the assault on Murosi's Mountain. The graves of five soldiers lie nearby. Overlooking Fort Hartley is the village of Pokane, from where it is possible to reach a magnificent gallery of rock art 1 km away in the valley of the Pokane River. This is one of the finest Bushman caves in Southern Africa.

In 1967 scientists of the British Museum found fragments of the most ancient mammal so far discovered close to Fort Hartley. Lesotho seems to have been a favourite resort for these creatures of the past, especially during the final phase of the drying out of the swamplands of the Karoo.

The road climbs up the slopes of the deep valley of the Gariep. At 24 km there is a turn-off south leading to St Gabriel's Roman Catholic mission. The main road continues along the valley slopes, negotiating numerous climbs and curves. At 32 km the road crosses the important Sebapata tributary of the Gariep and, after a further 4 km of climbing, reaches a junction. The southern branch leads for 12 km to the Tosing store, beyond which a bridle-path leads to the southern border of Lesotho at Lehana's Pass.

The main road continues. At 40 km the Mount Murosi's store is reached; and at 48 km the road reaches the village of Mogalo, dominated by Mikotjomelo Mountain, a great landmark in this area.

Immediately ahead looms the height of Murosi's Mountain, looking down on the Gariep River like a toll keeper waiting for travellers.

Murosi was the chief of the Phuthi people (a section of the Zizi tribe) who settled along this stretch of the upper Gariep or Senqu River after migrating from Natal. They were not Sotho but allied themselves with Moshweshwe's followers. Murosi was a veritable prince of cattle thieves and horse rustlers; a resolute, truculent man, courageous and stubborn. Attached to Murosi's people were many Bushmen. The result of the combined talents in rustling was formidable.

In about the year 1850, Murosi first discovered this grim, sullen-looking mountain and recognised it as a stronghold of superlative strength. He settled on the summit. Over a period of ten years he fortified the mountain with stone walls and protected vantage-points. At the same time his followers raided and plundered far and wide.

In 1877 the British established the Government post at Moyeni and tried to impose law and to collect taxes in the area of the upper river. Murosi had a son named Dodo who was hardly as placid a bird as his name suggests. He was arrested by the British and incarcerated in the ramshackle gaol in Moyeni. During the night Dodo's followers broke down the gaol and fled with him to the mountain stronghold of his father.

The British authorities mustered what strength they could, marched to the mountain, and C D Griffiths (the local magistrate) sent up a demand for the surrender of Dodo. The reply was insulting. Accordingly, on the night of 8 April 1879, 250 men of the tough, professional Cape Mounted Rifles, supported by volunteer yeomanry, assembled silently at the foot of the southern side of the mountain in a rock shelter known as the Commandant's Cave, and from there launched a resolute attack on Murosi's stronghold.

Precipitous rock faces, showers of missiles and gallingly accurate rifle fire kept the attackers at bay. Dodging from rock to rock, the troopers attempted to escalade, but they had no proper ladders and Murosi's men were entrenched behind a series of parallel fortified stone walls known as *skanzen*. Thirty-four of the troopers died before the attack petered out.

Dawn came wretchedly for the troopers. There was disappointment, chagrin and angry recrimination over the parts played by the regulars and volunteers. Comrades were missing, the wounded, cruelly injured by the home-made soft lead bullets of Murosi's men, were screaming with pain under primitive surgical treatment. Up on the mountain top could be heard the hilarity of the rustlers as they celebrated victory with a colossal beerdrink. Two Victoria Crosses were awarded to men for valour in this attack.

For two months there was a stalemate situation, with raids, sniping, counter-raids and innumerable fights as the rustlers continued their activities. On the night of 29 May the rustlers surprised a piquet post overlooking the Quthing River. They poured over the protective stone wall and shot 21 of the sleeping soldiers. On another night a patrol of yeomanry was ambushed and one prisoner captured. The next morning the rustlers decapitated him in full view on the mountain top, threw his body over the cliffs and mounted his head on a pole.

Tempers reached boiling point. The British gathered reinforcements. On the night of 5 June they launched a long-planned second attack. It failed totally, with fourteen more casualties littering the mountain slopes. The surgeon, Major Hartley, had to crawl from one man to the other at such risk to his life that he received the Victoria Cross.

Winter came. The mountains slept beneath their blanket of snow and the Gariep dwindled into a sluggish shallow flow. The opposing sides warmed themselves as best they could and waited. Sir Gordon Sprigg, Prime Minister of the Cape, came to the mountain and parleyed with Murosi halfway up the slopes, but the fight continued through an icy winter.

In October the weather warmed up. Colonel Z S Bayly arrived as a new commander. He reconnoitred the mountain in great detail and commenced a persistent bombardment of its rock defences, using round 7 kg shells with delayed fuses to allow them to roll behind defence works before they exploded. In reply Murosi's men (particularly an individual nicknamed Captain Jonas by the troopers) sniped with deadly accuracy.

Bayly mustered 400 regulars of the Cape Mounted Rifles for his planned attack. They were as mixed a crowd as the French Foreign Legion: remittance men, adventurers, mercenaries, all bound together in a military unit renowned for its rugged courage and comradeship. To spur the men on, rewards of £200 were offered for Murosi or Dodo, dead or alive, and £25 for the first man to reach the mountain top.

For four days prior to the grand attack, the artillery lobbed one shell every ten minutes at the mountain. Then at 22h00 on 19 November 1879, the troopers paraded in dark clothes with their guns and bayonets blackened. At midnight the bombardment suddenly ended. Three gaudy sky-rockets rent the air above the mountain and died amid a shower of hissing stars in the water of the river. The big show was on.

All through the dark hours the men fought their way upwards. The false dawn was already lightening the sky when the scaling ladders were placed against the final cliff at a place on the eastern slopes known as Bourne's Crack.

Lieutenant Springer climbed up the first ladder. He was near the top when one of Murosi's men looked over the edge into his face. *'Don't come up here, boss,'* he said considerately in English. *'I'll shoot you'.*

'Go to hell!' replied Springer. Raising his revolver he shot the man dead, the body hurtling down into the darkness past the ladder. On all sides of the mountain arose a great clamour of combat as different approaches were tried, some determinedly, others as a diversion.

Springer clambered to the top followed by his men. Forming into a line, they swept the summit. For a few minutes it was hand to hand, but the defenders were cut down or shot where they stood. Some jumped directly over the precipices. The few who escaped did so by a miracle of rolling down the slopes and diving into the water of the river.

The mountain summit was a shambles, littered with the bodies of 200 of Murosi's men and most of their women. Murosi's body was found among the dead. Captain Jonas was discovered with fourteen bullets in his body, but with his rifle still gripped in his hands. At 05h30 Murosi's head was mounted on the selfsame pole which had carried the remains of the unfortunate patrolman. Dodo had vanished but was later found in a cave beyond the river, dying of wounds and a thigh broken during his wild escape down the mountain.

Murosi's gunpowder storehouse on the summit, containing 6 247 kg of ammunition, was exploded and the fortifications partly destroyed. The troopers went away. Forty-three soldiers had been killed and 84 wounded in that battle. Five hundred of Murosi's men, the cream of his rustlers and all his sons, had died. The rest scattered into the innermost ranges of Lesotho. There the matter ended. Only the brooding old mountain is left with its slopes still littered with cartridge cases and the bric-à-brac of battle.

Beneath the mountain the great river sweeps silently past on its way to the sea. The river and the rugged mountain are characteristic of Southern Africa itself: every inch richly storied with legends and tradition, shrouded by an atmosphere of incredible romance.

It is fairly easy to scramble to the summit of Murosi's Mountain. On the way is passed a small rock shelter, the walls of which are engraved with initials and other graffiti dating from the attack. On the summit may be seen the ruins of stone buildings, a natural reservoir in the rock which stored drinking water, and the remains of defensive walls. A panoramic view reveals sheer cliffs falling away abruptly to the Gariep and the confluence where the Quthing River joins it as a tributary. Guides are always obtainable from the village where the road passes over the saddle of land connecting Murosi's Mountain to the high ground south of the Gariep. At this point the road is 4 km from the village of Mogale and 44 km from the turn-off on the main tarmac road from Maseru to Moyeni.

From this saddle the road descends into the valley of the Quthing River. On the right-hand side of the road, 2 km below the summit of the saddle, a cluster of three cypress trees shades the common grave of soldiers killed in the attack on Mount Murosi.

The road finds a tortuous way up the gorge containing the Quthing River. The area is wild, rocky and famous for its aloes. There are many delightful places in which to camp. At 18 km from Mogale village there is a particularly beautiful site in a deep sandstone gorge with a level, grassy floor overlooked by cliffs covered in aloes which flower in October and November and also in winter.

The road continues up a valley of great scenic variety, opening up into fertile, alluvial stretches, closing again between narrow sandstone cliffs. Another fine camping site, 21 km further along the road, is situated next to a concrete causeway which carries the road across the strongly flowing river.

Beyond the causeway the road commences a zigzag climb to the top of a mountain ridge. For 20 km the road makes an involved ascent, descends again and immediately starts to climb a second pass. At 86 km from Mogale (at Murosi's Mountain) the road passes the Mopeli trading station, with the mission of Christ the King 19 km further along the road. A further 8 km takes the road past the Sekake trading store, and after 21 km the White Hill trading station is reached (134 km from Murosi's Mountain).

Nineteen kilometres beyond White Hill there is a turn-off to Tsoelike and Ramatseliso border gate. A further 10 km sees the road enter the small centre of Qacha's Nek. The entire journey of 203 km from Qacha's Nek to the junction with the tarmac Maseru road, 3 km north of Moyeni village, is dramatised by magnificent mountain scenery. The road demands a full day's travelling and should not be attempted in rainy weather. Winter snows transform the landscape while the flowers of spring are unforgettable.

QACHA'S NEK

The village of Qacha's Nek lies 2,5 km from the border post with Transkei. The border is open daily from 06h45 to 16h00. From this post the road descends the Drakensberg escarpment to Matatiele 32 km away. The name *Qacha* is a hopelessly misspelt version of the name of Ncatya, a son of the famed Murosi, who established himself there as chief of a group of rather mixed people engaged mainly in cattle-rustling in the country below the Drakensberg. The Gariep River twists into a great bend at this point. Flowing southwards from its source north of Mokhotlong, it swings westwards and sets out on its long journey to the Atlantic Ocean.

Wheat and corn are grown in the valley of the Gariep, while goats and sheep live on the rocky slopes. The village consists of a cluster of stores, administrative and police buildings, one hotel and a couple of churches, notably the Roman Catholic Church of the Most Holy Redeemer.

From Qacha's Nek, bridle-paths and a rough track lead up the valley of the Gariep to places such as the ...

SEHLABATHEBE NATIONAL PARK

This national park, 65 square kilometres in area, contains some extraordinary mountain and rock scenery. There are paths, and walking and fishing are excellent. The name *Sehlabathebe* comes from a former chief of the Phuthi tribe.

Chapter Forty-Two

MOZAMBIQUE

Maputo and the South

There is a tradition that about 1500 AD a party of African people, speaking a language allied to that of the Karanga tribe of Zimbabwe, found their way down the Nkhomati River on rafts made of papyrus and reeds. Reaching the sea, they wandered further south down the shore of what is today the great bay of Lourenzo Marques. Led by a chief named Tembe, one section of the migrants eventually settled at *Catembe (KwaTembe,* or the place of Tembe) on the southern side of the estuary which drains three large rivers into this bay. The most southerly of these rivers has ever since been known as the *Tembe* after the chief and his followers. The central river is the *umBuluzi* (river of iguanas) and the northerly one is the *Matola* named after the Madolo section of the Tembe tribe who settled there.

According to this tradition, the new arrivals found already resident in the area a few people speaking a language similar to theirs and ruled by a chief with the hereditary title of Nyaka. These people, fishermen by occupation, kept to the coast and the island still known as Inyaka after them.

Such was the beginning of the human story of the southern part of Mozambique. It is interesting to know that from those early years the inhabitants were fishermen and traders. They were not a martial people, but industrious, good craftsmen, expert carvers and skilled workers in metal.

For some reason the Zulu-speaking people in the south named Tembe's followers the *Thongas* and had a high regard for their industry and acumen in trade. Tradition has it that these people, from the site of the future *Maputo*, laid the foundations for the trade and prosperity of the city by bartering copper, iron and even gold from the inland tribes. They worked this metal into such items as hoes, spears, axes and ornamental jewellery, trading it to the less talented people in the south. With these metal goods they also carried botanical novelties such as maize, potatoes and ground nuts, which the Zulu-speaking people still know collectively as *amaNthongomane* (Thonga things) after the pedlars who introduced them to their neighbours. Like maize, the ground nut and the potato had their homes in America and were brought to Africa by the Portuguese who traded them to the Tembes.

The Tembe people had only just reached the area of the bay when the first Portuguese arrived. In the year 1501 AD João da Nova found his way into the sheltered bay into which the common estuary of the three rivers pours its waters. Europeans at that time knew nothing about the interior of Africa. From the Arabs they had heard of a great lake in the interior which was said to be the source of the Nile and other rivers. The belief was common that all the major rivers of Africa flowed from this vast inland water. The broad estuary was therefore named by the Portuguese the *Rio da Lagoa* (river of the lake) and the bay became known as the *Baia das Lagoa*. By various other nationalities, this name was corrupted into Delagoa Bay. By the end of 1502 AD the name was marked in maps produced in Portugal. The bay became known for the shelter it offered sailors at times of storms, that its population was friendly, eager to trade and offered such valuable items as ivory which was in great demand in the Indian market.

For some years the Portuguese were too busy with their new eastern possessions to be able to apply much attention to this part of Africa. Persistent reports, however, of the availability of ivory and copper eventually persuaded them to conduct a more thorough study of the coast of Southern Africa. The Governor of Mozambique, in July 1545, sent one of his captains, Lourenzo Marques by name, accompanied by Antonio Caldeira, to investigate the trade potential of the coast south of Sofala. The results were exciting. Lourenzo Marques found that copper was available for trade at Inhambane, and ivory at the Rio da Lagoa. The resident population of these places was considerable and they were all willing to trade.

Elephants in vast numbers were seen roaming over the coastal plains. The old chief, Nyaka, was so courteous and so imposing with his white beard and fine features that the Portuguese renamed him Garcia de Sa because he resembled the then captain of Malacca who had that name. Altogether the possibilities of trade seemed immense. The Portuguese king, when he received the report, was delighted. He instructed that thenceforth a trading ship be sent to the great bay at least once each year. Lourenzo Marques was appointed to command this trading venture and in his honour the name of the bay was changed to the Bahio de Lourenzo Marques while the estuary was thenceforth known as the *Rio do Santo Espirito* (river of the Holy Ghost).

No attempt was made at any permanent settlement. The visiting traders either remained on their ships, or put up temporary shacks for themselves on such islands as Inyaka, Elephant or Shefina. An average of 35 000 kg of ivory was obtained each year from the place by the traders with about 1 000 elephants killed annually to supply this amount.

Other nations also started to trade at the bay of Lourenzo Marques. The age of the great pirates, around the beginning of the eighteenth century, also saw their ships making use of the bay, to the peril of the traders. Visits to the bay, in fact, became risky. The annual Portuguese trading boat was captured by pirates. For many years no further regular calls were made by the Portuguese as the place was considered to be more dangerous than profitable. It was in this period that the Dutch became interested in the area.

In 1720 the Dutch East India Company sent an expedition to open a permanent trading station in the area of the bay. On the site of the present city the Dutchmen built a stronghold which they named Fort Lagoa. The stronghold, however, provided no safety from mosquitoes. Within two months over two-thirds of the Dutch party had died. Reinforcements were sent from the Cape but the death rate from fever was dreadful. Then, to add to the troubles of the little fort, three pirate ships, commanded by the notorious Captain George Taylor, sailed into the bay on 11 April 1772. On the 19th the pirates attacked Fort Lagoa and had no difficulty in capturing the place. Most of the Dutch were sick and eighteen of the healthiest promptly joined the pirates as a means of escape from so unsalubrious a place.

Fort Lagoa was left as a well-looted wreck by the pirates but the Dutch persisted. More reinforcements were sent from the Cape and many more men died of fever. Ivory, copper and some gold were traded from the tribal people and attempts made to explore the countryside in search of a rumoured mountain of iron, rich gold-fields and copper. There was no success to these ventures. The volume of trade remained disappointing. Sugar cane and indigo, however, were planted and grew well.

A larger fort was built, named Fort Lydzaamheid, but fever continued to levy a terrible toll. Many men deserted the place, trying to reach the Portuguese settlements further north in hope of finding their way to some healthier climate. In 1728 a third of the garrison conspired to desert and twenty-two men were executed in a most barbarous manner when their plan was discovered.

The whole history of this little settlement was sad. It was a total failure and at the end of 1730 the survivors were withdrawn to Cape Town and the fort was destroyed.

The next development came in 1776. An Englishman, Colonel William Bolts, in the name of a trading company called the Asiatic Company of Trieste, established a permanent station at the mouth of the river by then known as the Maputa (from the *Mabudu* section of the Tembe tribe). The Austrian flag was hoisted over the station and there were ambitious plans for the future. News of the venture provoked the Portuguese into retaliation. Their protests to the Austrian government resulted in the cancellation of the charter of the company and in March 1781 the Portuguese frigate *Santa Anna* was sent to eliminate the trading station. On arrival the Portuguese found that fever had already practically eliminated the settlers. The survivors were removed in the Portuguese ship and the station left in ruins.

Now at last it became the turn of the Portuguese to attempt a permanent settlement at the bay. In January 1782, Jerome de Araujo was sent there from Mozambique to erect a fort. Fever killed the commander and, most of his men being sick, the place was abandoned. The Portuguese still persisted. In 1784 another party under Peter Testeuim was sent to the place. A small fort was erected on the same site as the Dutch had used. This was named *Nossa Senhora da Conceição*. A long struggle commenced against fever and the persistent attempts of traders of other nationalities and pirates to secure the supposed wealth of the area for themselves.

In October 1796 two French frigates attacked the little settlement and totally destroyed it. Their reason was that the Portuguese were allied with the British during the Napoleonic wars. The survivors of the garrison fled for sanctuary to the bush. When the French left, the fort once again had to be rebuilt and, on 7 June 1799, Captain Louis José arrived with a party of troops and artisans. The fort was rebuilt with every intention that thenceforth the presence of Portugal in the area would be permanent.

There were many difficult days for this little fort. Fever in some years wiped out more than half of the garrison and the civilian traders. As yet there was no real knowledge of the cause of malarial fever and no cure. Mosquitoes had man in their power and they showed no mercy. The 1820s also saw great disturbances amongst the local African tribes. In the south, Shaka was establishing his Zulu nation. Raiding armies and bands of refugees made their way up the coast, with no means of living other than through murder and loot.

The Portuguese flag continued to wave at the bay of Lourenzo Marques but very limply. The handful of sick men holding it up had a precarious time. Foreign traders and whalermen continued to visit the area. In so large a bay they could always find a place to land and trade beyond the control of the Portuguese. In 1822 a British naval survey party under Captain William Owen visited the bay with credentials establishing themselves as a purely scientific expedition. Finding the countryside disturbed by raiders from the south, Captain Owen exploited the opportunity to sign treaties with the local tribespeople placing the whole area under the protection of Britain. Nothing was ever done to really give substance to these treaties. Owen, like all other visitors to the bay, neglected to sign any treaty with the mosquitoes. The deaths and sickness of many of his crew dampened any dreams of a new addition to the British Empire.

At least, however, these seafaring visitors all eventually sailed away. The emigrant bands from Zululand were the principal trouble. These invaders were generally described by the local Tembe tribespeople by the name of *vaTwa* (Bushmen) because of the clicks in their speech. Apart from the several smaller bands, there were three principal groups of invaders. One was led by a chief named Zwangendaba; a second by Nxaba and the third (and most considerable) by Soshangane. These invaders all played havoc with the Tembe people. In the general uproar the small Portuguese garrison could do little other than watch and live by its wits.

Soshangane was a particularly resolute individual. He had been the commander of the Ndwandwe army of the chief Zwide. The Zulus thoroughly defeated these people in 1818 and drove them away in confusion. Soshangane's own family name of Gaza came from one of his ancestors. In the area around the bay of Lourenzo Marques he gathered under his leadership a mixed group of renegades, refugees and tribal fragments. These people accepted him as a leader, giving him the honorific title of Manukuza (the name of one of his ancestors) and accepting for themselves the tribal name of *abakwaGaza* (the people of Gaza). The name of their chief, in the form of amaShangane, was also applied to them.

This rapidly growing tribe gave the Portuguese an increasing amount of trouble. On 22 October 1833 their army attacked the Portuguese settlement. For five days they besieged the fort. Then the Portuguese commander, Dionysio Ribeiro, fearful of being cut off from food and water, saw an opportunity during the night of the 27 October to escape with his men to Shefina Island. This was a sad mistake. With the dawn the Gaza warriors destroyed the fort and then attacked Shefina Island, using canoes to cross the bay. The entire Portuguese force was captured. The prisoners were taken back to the ruins of the fort and slaughtered there.

Once again the Portuguese Government sent men to reoccupy the bay of Lourenzo Marques. The fort was rebuilt. It was attacked again and just managed to stave off a second destruction. For years the garrison had a precarious time with Soshangane and his warriors imposing their control over the whole area from the bay of Lourenzo Marques to the Zambezi River in the north. It was during this troubled period, on 13 April 1838, that Louis Trichardt, the Voortrekker leader reached Lourenzo Marques from the interior. Most of his party died of fever at the port and the rest were evacuated to Durban. This was the start, however, of trade contacts with the Voortrekker settlers in the Transvaal.

Soshangane died in 1856. His two sons, Mzila and Mawewe, contended for the succession. Mzila went to the Portuguese on 1 December 1861 and secured their aid in exchange for promises of permanent friendship and recognition of their control of all land up to the Manisa River. An alliance was formed and on 20 August 1862 Mawewe was defeated in a battle and Mzila became chief of the Gaza people. He built a capital for himself at Tshamatshama in what is now

Zimbabwe, far from the Portuguese coastal settlements. Until his death in 1884 a measure of peace came to the area around the bay of Lourenzo Marques.

Until the alliance with Mzila the Portuguese settlement had consisted of little more than a garrison and a few officials who all lived in the fort or very close to its walls. Conditions now started to change. A stronger fort was built in 1864 and enlarged in 1867 by the addition of four small batteries. Private houses and commercial buildings started to appear around the fort. There was a steady increase in trade, particularly with the Voortrekkers of the Transvaal who regarded Lourenzo Marques as being their natural outlet to the sea.

On 29 July 1869 a commercial treaty was signed between the governments of Portugal and the South African Republic of the Transvaal. The British, fearful of losing trade through the South African ports, attempted to counter this by claiming that Captain Owen had secured cession of the whole area of the bay of Lourenzo Marques from the local tribespeople who had always been independent of the Portuguese. The dispute was given to arbitration by Marshal MacMahon, President of France. A shaky British claim was ably countered by the Portuguese consul, Viscount de Paiva Manso, who presented a detailed history of the Portuguese presence. On 24 July 1875 Marshal MacMahon announced his finding that the coastal plain as far south as the 26°30′ of latitude was definitely Portuguese territory and this included the great bay of Lourenzo Marques.

With secure title over the area, the Portuguese started to plan a railway into the interior. On 11 December 1875 they signed a comprehensive new treaty with the South African Republic allowing for free interchange of agricultural and industrial products and duty-free or duty-paid imports through Lourenzo Marques. In the following year, 1876, on 9 December the Portuguese king, Dom Luis I, proclaimed the settlement to be a town named Lourenzo Marques with its first municipality taking office on 2 September 1877. Commandante Augusto de Castilho was the first *presidente* of the Council. By the following year the population had increased from little more than the members of the garrison to a total of 458 Europeans and Asians, with an increasingly large population of Africans attracted to the place by its prospects of rapid growth.

The building of the railway to the Transvaal was the real turning point in the history of Lourenzo Marques. The line was opened to the frontier in November 1888. In the year before that Lourenzo Marques was proclaimed a city. As the railway penetrated further into the Transvaal so the volume of trade increased. After the official opening of the line to Pretoria on 8 July 1895, Lourenzo Marques reached an importance which by 1898 induced the Government to make it the capital of Mozambique, supplanting the small island trading settlement of Mozambique which had given its name to the entire colony. Vasco da Gama, the first Portuguese navigator to visit it, on his pioneer voyage to India, was welcomed there by its ruler and gave the place the Portuguese orthography of the sultan's name, Mussa Ben Mbiki.

The building of the line from Lourenzo Marques to Pretoria was one of the great sagas in the history of railway construction. More men are said to have died on the construction of this line than it has sleepers. Fever played havoc with the workers while wild animals were a constant danger. Dr Ronald Ross, working in India, had still to discover the malaria parasite in 1898 and prove that the mosquito was the carrier. It was only then that Lourenzo Marques was relieved of the curse of fever. Mosquitoes could be controlled by insecticides, drainage and hygiene, and summers thenceforth became warm but no longer lethal.

The ending of tribal disturbances among the Africans also opened the inland areas for development. The last serious spasm of trouble with the tribes came after the death of the Gaza chief, Mzila, in 1884. His successor, Ngungunyana, had military ambitions and launched his followers into a series of raids. He also demanded tribute from the Portuguese. War broke out in 1894. The Gaza (vaTwa or Shangane) army was defeated in a series of battles. Then, on 28 December 1895, Ngungunyana was surprised and taken prisoner by Captain Mouzinho d'Albuquerque at a place called Tshayimite where the chief was sacrificing to his ancestral spirits. Ngungunyana was taken captive to Lourenzo Marques, confined in the fort, then sent to Portugal. He was eventually banished to the west coast of Africa where he died in December 1906.

Lourenzo Marques had the great advantage of being wisely laid out as a city while it still had ample space to allow for wide streets, parks and viewsites. General Joaquim Machado and Major António de Araujo planned the place from its birth and they were determined to influence its growth into a beautiful, gracious, hygienic and spacious city.

To the African tribespeople, Lourenzo Marques was known as *esiLungwini (Xilunguine* in

Portuguese orthography) meaning the place of Europeans. This name correctly described the city for it was essentially European in conception, appearance and design, but blending harmoniously with its African environment of sub-tropical coast. An interesting speculation is that the word *Lungu,* which the peoples of Southern Africa adopted as their name for Europeans, was introduced to them from Lourenzo Marques. In its etymology it infers a 'ship or sea people' (*abeLungu*) and it was almost certainly the Tembe tribespeople who, encountering the Portuguese pioneers in the bay, gave them this name. spread its use to the inland tribes by means of wandering pedlars, and called the area which the early visitors frequented and then settled the 'place of the ship people'. The modern name of *Maputo* is the name, in Portuguese orthography, of a later chief of the Tembe tribe named Mabudu.

From its sheltered harbour at the mouth of the estuary which has had so many names (the *English River* to many sailors; the *Rio de Lagoa* (river of the lake) and the *Rio de Espirito Santo* or River of the Holy Ghost to the Portuguese; the Umbuluzi to the Africans), the city was laid out with avenues running parallel to the harbour. The principal thoroughfare was the Avenida Da Republica. The name celebrated the establishment of the new political regime in Portugal on 5 October 1910.

The second principal thoroughfare was the Avenida 24th De Julho. The name commemorated the day in 1875 when President MacMahon of France pronounced his arbitration in favour of Portugal against the claim of Great Britain to the ownership of the bay of Lourenzo Marques.

The third principal thoroughfare, also parallel to the two already mentioned, was named Avenida Pinheiro Chagas in honour of Manuel Pinheiro Chagas, a renowned administrator, writer and historian of Portugal.

The Avenida Da Republica led into the handsome coastal drive named the *Avenida D Manuel I* in honour of the Portuguese king who reigned from 1495–1521. With its line of tall coconut palms *(Cocos nucifero)* always bowing and swaying like a bevy of maidens at a ball, longing to dance with the preoccupied ocean which comes sweeping in from the east, this avenue leads up the shores of the bay to the *Costa Do Sol* (coast of the sun) with its beaches and shady groves of casuarina (*Casuarina equisetifolia*).

The trees of Lourenzo Marques became one of its most pleasing features. They were planned to be an extension all over the city of the central botanical garden named after Vasco da Gama, the pioneer navigator to the East. This wonderful garden, between the years 1907 and 1920, had as its director, Mr T Honey. He collected fifty-one different exotic species of trees suitable for cultivation in streets. An Arboricultural Society had been formed as far back as 1885 and plantations made of eucalyptus trees which were not only attractive and shady but also were considered to be useful in repelling mosquitoes. In the 1920s began a systematic planting of flowering trees in the streets of Lourenzo Marques. The enthusiasm of the directors of the Vasco da Gama Botanical Gardens, first Mr T Honey and later (1927–44) Senhor Guilherme J F Melquiades, gave essential impetus to the programme.

The commonest of the ornamental trees shading the streets of the city is *Delonix regia* (the poinciana, flamboyant, flame tree or peacock flower) which comes from Madagascar. This comes into bloom from September to January. They grew to perfection in the Avenida Pinheiro Chagas; the Avenida Massano de Amorim (named after a well-known general in the Portuguese army); the Avenida António Enes (named after one of the administrators of Mozambique); and the Rua do General Botha (named after the Boer general and prime minister of South Africa).

The second most popular of the ornamental trees of Lourenzo Marques is the *Cassia siamea* which comes from India, Siam and Malaya. Flowering in brilliant shades of yellow in January and February, these trees make a spectacular sight in the Avenida 24 de Julho; the Rua do Governador Simas (named after José Augusto de sá e Simas, Governor of Lourenzo Marques 1867–73); the Avenida Fernandes Tomás (named after the great Portuguese patriot who lived from 1771–1822); and the Rua de Nevala (named after the locality in the far north of Mozambique which was the scene of events in the establishment of Portuguese rule over the colony).

The third most numerous of the flowering trees is the well-loved *Jacaranda mimosifolia* which comes from Brazil. From September to December this tree displays its flowers in a purple haze in such thoroughfares as the Avenida Pinheiro Chagas; the Rua do General Botha; the Avenida Massano de Amorim; and the Avenida da Princesa Patricia (named after the daughter of the Duke of Connaught who visited Lourenzo Marques in 1900).

The fourth most numerous of the flowering trees of Lourenzo Marques is *Tabebuia pentaphylla* which comes from Brazil. A member of the Bignonia family, this abundantly and almost continuously flowering and fruiting tree with its lilac blooms of delightful perfume, may be seen to perfection in all seasons in such thoroughfares as the Avenida da Republica; the Avenida 31 de Janeiro (named in memory of the day in 1891 when the city of Porto revolted against British rule); the Avenida do General Machado (named in honour of Joaquim José Machado, a Governor-General of Mozambique); and the Avenida Manuel de Arriaga (named in honour of the first President of the Republic of Portugal).

Other notable trees planted in the gardens and streets of Lourenzo Marques include *Afzelia cuanzensis* from tropical Africa. This, the Lucky Bean tree, flowers in September and October. It may be seen in such thoroughfares as the Avenido Caldas Xavier (named after the military officer and administrator of the last century); the Avenida Lisboa (named after the capital of Portugal); the Avenida Craveiro Lopes (named after Francisco Higine de Craveiro Lopes, a military and administrative personality of Portugal); the Avenida Dr J Serrão (named after José de Oliveira Serrão, medical doctor, director of education, arts and sciences in Mozambique).

The *Aleurites moluccana* trees from Asia, also known as the Bengal walnut or candle nut trees, flower from August to November and are to be seen in the Avenida General Machado; the Avenida Caldas Xavier; and the Rua dos Lusiadas (named after the epic poem by Luis vaz de Camões).

Brachychiton discolor, from Australia, flowers from October to January and may be seen in the Rua Dr Almeida Ribeiro (named in honour of Dr Artor de Almeida Ribeiro, patriot magistrate and political personality).

Brachychiton populneum, another Australian immigrant, flowers from October to January and may be seen in such thoroughfares as the Avenida Dr Brito Camacho (named after Manuel de Brito Camacho, medical doctor, writer and political personality of Portugal).

Caryota urens is the fish-tail or toddy-palm from Malaya which makes a stately show outside the Polana Hotel in the Avenida António Enes (named after António José Enes, a Governor of Mozambique and a dominant personality in the history of the colony).

Casuarina equisetifolia, so well known in Mauritius and Madagascar as the *filaos* tree, provides shade along the verges of the beach and on the Rua dos Duques de Connaught (named in honour of the Duke of Connaught who visited Lourenzo Marques in 1906 when he was Governor-General of South Africa).

Dolichandrone alba, a flowering tree of the African bush, blooms from November to April and may be seen in the Avenida Alfonso de Albuquerque (named in honour of the Portuguese navigator and Viceroy of India).

Ficus natalensis, the wild fig of Southern Africa, attracts the attention of all visitors to the city. Growing in the central islands along the Avenida 24 de Julho, they are notable for their complex trunks, strange shapes and thousands of fruits which appear around the month of October.

Grauillea robusta, the silver oak of Australia, develops its golden flowers from August to December and may be seen in such thoroughfares as the Rua do Guerra Jungueiro (named after the writer and poet).

Guazuma ulmifolia, the bastard cedar from Mexico, flourishes in such thoroughfares as the Avenida Fernão de Magalhães (named in honour of the navigator of Portugal).

Hibiscus tiliaceus, known as *Bololo* to the local tribespeople, flowers from September to January in many places in the city, especially in the Avenida António Enes.

Melia azedaracb, the pride of India tree, may be seen in the Avenida Craveiro Lopes (named after Marshal Francisco Higino de Craveiro Lopes of the Portuguese army).

Pongamia pinnata, the Indian beach, grows in the Rua da Esperanca (the street of expectation). *Populus nigra*, the black poplar from Europe, grows in the Avenida Antóio Enes. *Roystonea oleracea* is the attractive South American palm which grows in the Avenida Pinheiro Chagas.

Spathodea campanulata is the African fountain tree, flowering at the end of summer and growing in the Rua Henrique de Sousa (named after a former Commissioner of the Lourenzo Marques police).

Trichilia emetica is the Natal mahogany tree which flowers in August to October and grows in such thoroughfares as the Avenida Paiva Manso (named in honour of Visconde de Paiva Manso, the advocate who presented Portugal's case in the arbitration conducted by President MacMahon of France).

To complete the list of the trees of this fair city, mention should be made of the common indigenous wild fig tree known to the tribespeople as the *phama*. This gives its name to that animated portion of the city where lies the African market, *esiPhamanini* (the place of the small phama tree), known in Portuguese orthography as Xipamanine.

One of the most interesting parts of the city is the old portion of the city lying between the docks and the Avenida Da Republica. Most of the really old buildings have been replaced by modern structures but some of the atmosphere of past years still lingers there. A walk by night or day through its streets is an interesting experience. The original Lourenzo Marques, as we have seen, was a child of seafaring Europeans. The first fort of Nossa Senhora da Conceicão was built to guard the harbour and rebuilt in modern times to serve as an interesting military museum. The fort is open Tuesday to Saturday 09h00 to 11h30, 14h00 to 17h00. Sundays and holidays 09h00 to 12h00. The fort still keeps watch over the entrance to the small boat harbour where a medley of fishing craft, ferry boats to Catembe and other craft make a colourful spectacle. The ferry trip to Catembe is a very pleasant outing with fine views of the port and city.

Opposite the entrance to the fort there is a pleasant square and garden, the Praca 7 De Marco whose name recorded the arrival on 7 March 1876 of Joaquim Machado, chief of the party of civil engineers sent from Portugal to lay out the city of Lourenzo Marques. The pavements around the park display some of the finest examples of the patterned stonework which is an attractive feature of Portuguese cities.

On the far side of this square, diagonally opposite the fort, on the corner of the street named Rua Consiglieri Pedroso in honour of Zofimo Consiglieri Pedroso, the Portuguese writer, professor and politician, there has been perfectly preserved a fine example of an early residence of the governors. This beautiful little building is often used to house exhibitions of works of art.

Leading into the centre of the square is the well known Rua Major Araujo, known as 'sin street'. This is the street of night-clubs, bars and late-night fun and games. From midnight on it presents a vivacious spectacle with its bars and the brightly lit entrances to night clubs. Such names as the Alto Rosa, Luso, Pinguim, Topazio, Tamila, and Cave are part of the story of old Lourenzo Marques. It has always been an atmospheric and lively little street and Major António José de Araujo, the distinguished engineer who worked on the basic planning of Lourenzo Marques, would certainly have smiled gently behind his hand at some of the antics and characters in the street which carried his name.

On its western end, the Rua Major Araujo leads into the Praca MacMahon, the square named in honour of the President of France who arbitrated the frontier dispute between Portugal and Britain. In the centre of this square stands the memorial to the First World War facing the railway station.

The portion of Maputo which we are discussing is known as the *Baixa* (lower) district. It is essentially the commercial centre of the city, dominated by the principal thoroughfare, the Avenida Da Republica. Apart from its towering commercial buildings, the *Marcado* (municipal market) is also situated on this street and provides an animated and colourful spectacle.

Let us leave the *Baixa* by following the Avenida De D Luis as it rises to the higher areas known as *Central* and *Maxaquene* (from Mashakwene, a Shangane chieftain). The avenue, named after the Portuguese king in whose twenty-three year reign Lourenzo Marques had its civic birth, leads into the handsome square dominated by the City Hall and the statue to Mouzinho de Albuquerque who defeated the Gasa tribe in the war of 1895.

The City Hall is an imposing building, housing the various municipal offices; a very beautiful reception hall (the golden room) and a conference room; a fine collection of paintings and King Louis XIV style furniture; and some superbly made dioramas of Lourenzo Marques. The building is open to the public on weekdays 07h30 to 11h30; 14h00 to 16h30. On Saturday it is open from 07h30 to 11h00. Closed on Sunday and holidays.

The Mouzinho de Albuquerque Square is notable for its decorated pavements. On its eastern side there also stands the Roman Catholic Cathedral Nossa Senhora da Conceicão, while on the south-east side lies the magnificent botanical garden named in honour of Vasco da Gama, the pioneer navigator. This is one of the great gardens of the world, especially notable for its vast collection of trees, its flowering plants, and the immense greenhouse. At the entrance to this park there stands the interesting and singular portable iron two-storey building housing the Geographical Museum. Named in honour of the pioneer Portuguese airmen who, in 1922, first flew across the

South Atlantic from Lisbon to Rio de Janeiro, Gago Coutinho and Sacadura Cabral, this museum displays a considerable collection of navigational and survey instruments. The unique building which houses the collection, the *Casa de Ferro* (house of iron) was imported in pieces from Belgium in 1893 and used as the offices of the Tribunal. In 1972 it became a museum. It is open daily 08h00 to 11h30, 14h00 to 17h30.

From the Mouzinho de Albuquerque Square the Avenida 5 de Outubro leads westwards and in the second block passes on its south side the memorial garden to the Voortrekker leader, Louis Trichardt. The avenue, whose name celebrates the date in 1910 of the revolution in Portugal which resulted in Republican government, continues westward into the Malanga district.

To the east of the Mouzinho de Albuquerque Square, the Rua Do Radio Clube leads past the entrance to the Roman Catholic Cathedral and then the imposing building housing the editorial offices of the newspaper *Diario* and the studios and administrative offices of the Mozambique Broadcasting Corporation.

The Rua Do Radio Clube then leads directly into the Avenida Do Dr Brito Camacho at the corner where stands the buildings of the British consulate. Continuing eastwards along this avenue we pass such buildings as that of the Girassol hotel in its notable round design (*girassol* means sunflower); and diagonally opposite, that home of *fado* in old Lourenzo Marques, the *Adego da Madragoa* (village of Madragoa) where performances took place on Thursday and Saturday nights.

Fado (fate) is the name given to the folk music of Portugal. It originated with the Moors but it is an intensely living art form with a stream of new compositions. To hear it at its best, go to a dimly lit cellar cafe. In such a setting a night of *Fado* is a delightful experience. The *Fadistas* (performers) and the audience have a rapport. There is a deep appreciation of superb musicianship. The room is filled with subtle combinations of shadows and sounds. The performers can be male or female. There is always a singer and generally two accompanists. The right hand player carries the melody on the Portuguese guitar; the left hand player provides the rhythm on a Spanish guitar. The songs – happy or sad – are deeply emotional. They are listened to intently. Good *Fadistas* often include extemporisations of their own, sometimes created on the spot, and referring to members of the audience in pointed terms or delicate innuendo.

The avenue continues eastwards to pass the pretty little park named after João Emilio da Silva Pereira, a government official and patriot who served Mozambique in the 1930s. From this park there are panoramic views of the city and docks. Opposite it stands the buildings of the Lyceum Salazar, and, at the intersection, across the Padrão das Descobertes Square with its memorial statue to Prince Henry the Navigator, the Museu de Historia Natural. The museum building is an excellent example of Manueline-style architecture. It houses an interesting collection of mounted game, animals, birds, marine creatures and sea shells. It is open daily 09h00 to 11h30 and 14h00 to 17h00. The Hotel Cardosa originally built by Commandante Augusto Cardosa is close to the museum down the Avenida Bartolomeu Dias, and a few blocks beyond it, the former residence of the Governor-General of Mozambique in the centre of the area known as *Ponta Vermelha* (red point) or Reuben Point.

All roads swing northwards from this point up the coast with the Avenida Bartholomeu Dias leading into the Avenida Dos Duques De Connaught with its sweeping views over the great bay. Parallel to this avenue runs the tree-shaded Avenida de António Enes which leads past such buildings as those of the Polana hotel and, just beyond it, the old Lourenzo Marques Club. From this avenue branches lead down to the beaches, the drive up the Costa do Sol, and to the Municipal camping grounds and caravan park. The church, Santo António da Polana, near the Polana hotel, is notable for extraordinary lighting effects and unusual architecture. The name *Polana* attached to this part of the city comes from a former Tembe headman who had his home there.

Among other places of interest in the city is the original bull ring where festivals of bullfights in the Portuguese manner were held, usually for two days each April (Easter), July and December. The bullring stands just off the Avenida Marschal Craveiro Lopes, named after a prestigious Portuguese military personality. This avenue leads on to the international airport named after the pioneer Gago Coutinho.

The market place in the African area of esiPhamanini is another interesting place to visit. It lies in the north-western part of the city, up the Rua dos Irmãos Roby, a picturesque street – really one long open market place – named after another notable figure in the Portuguese military history of

Angola and Mozambique. In the shops of this street, such as the Case Vipra, may be seen an enormous selection of Java cloths, the colourful and beautifully patterned materials used by African and Asian women for their dresses and scarves.

The zoo, another interesting feature of the city, lies up the Avenida de Mozambique, off the main road to Beira. It is open daily from 07h00 to 06h00.

The Museu de Geologia in the Palacia das Reparticões in the Avenida da Sagres, is open from 14h00 to 17h00 on Wednesdays and Saturdays.

Maputo, with its population of 966 000, is, in general, a city where the visitor can have a considerable amount of fun, especially if he relaxes, takes off his tie and is happy to slow down a little. The citizens are notably friendly and polite. A lot of them seem to have time on their hands to sit around talking, sipping drinks and watching girls. It is, in fact, and always has been, a great city for girl watching. The side-walk cafes are ideal for such watchers. It is a very harmless pastime, with a healthy, hearty interest and little vulgarity.

Bird watching in Lourenzo Marques, in fact, seems to do women a power of good. They get noticed, approved and admired more openly and unabashedly in this city than in most other places on earth. Even the plainest of women may have the pleasure of feeling that some hitherto hidden charm has been discovered by these bird watchers and, unless he is over-sensitive, her usual escort can share in her fun and enjoyment and learn to appreciate some aspects of his fair partner which, perhaps, familiarity has dulled to his own sense of values.

Leisure, relaxation, music, colour and the enjoyment of living and good food were always very important in Lourenzo Marques. Maputo has inherited this life-style. The weight of money does not hang as heavy in the air as it does in, say, Johannesburg. Sit down, therefore, at night at about 21h00 at one of the pavement restaurants. Order a big plate of prawns, chicken peri-peri or crabs. Listen to the pleasant natural music of people laughing and gossiping in perfect counterpoint to the more subdued rhythm of chomping, crunching, crushing, cracking and finger suckings as prawns and crabs are opened, crisp bread is broken, chicken bones snapped and long, cool drinks are swallowed in the warm air so subtly perfumed by the blossoms of innumerable lovely trees and flowering plants.

INYAKA ISLAND

Inyaka Island (also known as the Island of the Sun), that old sanctuary of the friendly chief Nyaka, is a popular holiday resort, especially for fishermen and divers. It is the most southerly place on the African coast where corals flourish to a notable extent. The reef there provides divers with a glorious spectacle of a garden beneath the sea with fish as delicately coloured as butterflies. The divers, in turn, have done the reef considerable damage by looting and vandalism of coral formations and resident marine life.

The island is an irregularly shaped remnant of the African mainland from which it is separated at its southern end by a narrow channel. The mainland projects a long finger towards it in the form of Cape Santa Maria and it is this northerly-pointing finger with the island balancing on its tip that makes the great bay of Lourenzo Marques one of the most perfectly sheltered of all natural harbours.

As a projection of the mainland, the island is home for a similar flora and fauna, with the addition that coconuts and casuarinas flourish on the salty soil and in the warm sea air. The island is hilly, with forest-covered cliffs overlooking the sea and a green and pleasant interior. The highest point, Monte Inyaka, is 116 m high. The island is 11 km long and 6 km wide. A good walker can circumnavigate the island in two days, finding the southern portion to be the prettiest stretch of coast, with some lovely little bays. The western (seaward side) is wild and seaswept, with a lighthouse guiding shipping along the coast. On the northern end there is a small, uninhabited island known as Small, Elephant or Portuguese Island. This is connected to Inyaka Island by a sandspit and provides a beautifully sheltered anchorage, very popular with international yachtsman, and the base for many deep-sea fishermen. The hotel stands on the shore at this anchorage while on the overlooking cliffs is the fort-like office of the island administration, a hospital and other official buildings.

Most of the island is a proclaimed nature reserve with its corals, mangroves, lagoons, coastline, marine and wildlife protected. Along the beach, twenty minutes walk to the west of the anchorage under the *Barreira Vermelho* (red cliffs) there is the main coral reef, while another twenty minutes brings the walker to the buildings of the Marine Biological Research Station named in honour of Almirante Moreira Rato, a former commander of the Marine Department. The cluster of buildings stands at Melville Port and houses a laboratory, museum, refectory, dormitory, electric power station and pumps feeding fresh seawater into the aquarium. It is an important research centre in marine biology and from 1963 has been part of the Institute of Scientific Research of Mozambique. Visitors are allowed during normal working hours.

The island is easy to reach from Maputo. Every Monday, Thursday and Saturday at 06h30 the hotel sends a boat to Lourenzo Marques, departing back to the island on the same day at 10h30 Messrs Empressa Fluvial de Transports also maintain a scheduled service, leaving Maputo at 07h30 every Thursday, Friday and Saturday, and departing from the island at 16h00 on the same days.

Charter companies also provide regular daily services.

Campers pitch their tents on the northern beach but there are no facilities. Meals can be had at the hotel, providing they are ordered twenty-four hours in advance. There is a bar with light snacks on the beach. Fishing boats are available for hire. Trips are organised by the hotel to all parts of the island, including the coral reef.

MAPUTO TO OURO POINT

A particularly interesting drive from Maputo leads southwards to *Ponto do Ouro* (golden point) on the border between Mozambique and South Africa. This drive starts at the car ferry to Catembe, which has its point of departure opposite the Naval Command building in the Avenida De Sagres (the passenger ferry starts from the fishing harbour). The car ferry service operates daily.

Across the estuary is Catembe, where photographers find panoramic views of the city and harbour, (very beautiful at night, especially during a summer thunderstorm); and closer scenes of a fishing village which has achieved a state of picturesque dilapidation very satisfying to artists if not to the inhabitants.

From the ferry landing pier, the gravel road finds its way past a collection of rather forlorn-looking automobiles abandoned there by owners, presumably seeking their fortune across the waters in the city. The amount of dust covering each vehicle is said locally to be a sure measure of the success of the various owners.

The smarter residential area of Catembe is passed after 5 km and the road then makes its way across level, bush-covered country for a total of 42 km before it joins the road leading from Boane (67,6 km) and then (30 km) to Maputo.

From the junction point of the Catembe–Boane roads it is one kilometre into the small town of *Bela Vista* (beautiful view) which lies on the banks of the broad Maputo River. For 18 km the road leads up the left bank of the river before finally making up its mind to cross it and reach the town of Salamanca and a turn-off to the ...

MAPUTO ELEPHANT RESERVE

The Maputo Elephant Reserve was proclaimed on 19 April 1964. At the entrance (8 km from Salamanca) there is a pleasant camp, but for the time being only four-wheel drive vehicles are able to negotiate the very sandy tracks which provide access to the game areas and the beach. The reserve is especially interesting for its elephants and for the turtles nesting on its beaches.

From the turn-off at Salamanca to the Maputo Elephant Reserve, the main gravel road continues through dense acacia bush, with fine fever trees blossoming in September. The bush peters out. There are plantations of eucalyptus trees and then the road reaches the zone of grass-covered coastal lowlands, with the clumps of lala palms characteristic of the country of the Tembe tribespeople. There is generally a great deal of merry-making in this area for the lala palms provide an endless supply of highly intoxicating free liquor from the fermented sap tapped from their stems.

At 38 km there is a turn-off leading for 10 km to the resort of Ponta Mamoli. Just beyond this turn-off lies the township of Zitundo where there is a customs post used by travellers intending to proceed into South Africa. The little town is perched on a hill overlooking a lake. These small, fresh-water lakes are a feature of an area where level country and a high coastal ridge of sand dunes block drainage into the sea.

The road continues south-eastwards. At 12 km from Zitundo there is a turn-off leading for 9 km to the coastal resort of Malongane with its beautiful beach and lake.

From the turn-off to Malongane, the gravel road continues for 6 km. Then it reaches the coast at Ponto do Ouro, where there is a spacious beach, and, on a high bush-covered sandhill, the little lighthouse which marks the border between Mozambique and South Africa. From the lighthouse hill there is a fine view of the coastline south to Kosi Bay, and north far beyond the holiday resort on the beach. The name of *Ponta do Ouro* (golden point) is all that remains of the beautiful old name, *Rio de la Medaos do Ouro* (river of the sands of gold), which early Portuguese navigators and survivors of shipwrecks applied to the gold-coloured sands of the coast of Maputo and, southwards, especially around the mouth of the Kosi chain of lakes. Fishing, swimming and the phosphorescence of the breakers at night make this area an interesting place to visit for those who like to wander free and far beyond the horizon.

Chapter Forty-Three
MOZAMBIQUE

A Journey along a Coast of Coconuts and Coral

MAPUTO TO BEIRA

The tarmac road from Maputo to Beira, more than anything else, has been the key that opened the door to many lovely beaches, spacious lagoons and interesting old-world places along the coast of Mozambique. To persons in a hurry, the journey can be completed in twelve hours. Rather take at least twelve days, meander from beach to beach. Swim, dive, fish, boat, photograph, draw, eat, sleep, indulge in a bit of dreaming (surely you haven't forgotten the art?). There is no better place in the world to do these things. Let's not spoil it by being in a hurry. Relax, take it easy. You drive carefully and look at the scenery. I'll do the talking and tell you something about the green world around us. Together, we'll have memories of sunny days and cool nights; of people and places and all those special little things which, once seen or experienced, can never be forgotten.

Four and a half kilometres on the road to Ressano Garcia and South Africa from the city centre of Maputo, the tarmac road to Beira branches northwards. For the first few kilometres it finds a way through the built-up areas of suburbs, past the zoological gardens, the outskirts of the airport, and the roadside stands of people selling such diverse things as carvings, fruit and drinks. Traffic is heavy and there is all the general bustle and flurry one expects in the immediate vicinity of a city.

Gradually buildings dwindle and the houses of the Benfica suburb give way to trees, with the level coastal plain so densely covered that it resembles a parkland. At 35 km from Maputo the road reaches the village formerly known as *Vila Luisa*, a small rural centre named after the daughter of the Governor, Antonio Enes, and notable because from here a road leads eastwards to the beach of Macaneta. It was here that Mouzinho de Albuquerque won a decisive victory over the Shangane tribe in 1895. The village stands on the banks of the Komati River. Boats take tourists up this river to view the resident population of hippos and crocodiles. The village is correctly known by its African name of Marrakwene.

North of Marrakwene the tarmac road continues through a fertile natural parkland. At intervals the road-makers have created laybys, pleasant stopping places with tables and chairs beneath shady trees. There is an especially nice example of such a layby 24 km beyond Marrakwene. The toilet facility is an interesting example of its kind and the 'engaged' sign (a miniature prohibited entry road sign) is ingenious.

Plantations of bananas, citrus and cashew nuts; fields of sugar cane and wheat alternate with patches of natural parkland. The tarmac road passes through such rural centres as Malvana (29 km from Marrakwene); Alvor (14,5 km further on); the small town of Manhica (50 km from Marrakwene); Palmeira (69 km from Marrakwene); Ingolvane (101 km from Marrakwene); and then, 119 km from Marrakwene, reaches the small town of ...

MACIA AND THE RESORT OF SÃO MARTINHO

Macia is the administrative centre for the area known as Bilene, after Bila, chief of a group of Karanga people from Zimbabwe who, after some disturbances in their original homeland, fled there about 1650 and established a sanctuary for themselves. The area is notable for the chain of fresh water lakes along the coast. High sand dunes on the coast block the drainage system of the rivers. The lakes have been formed when the rivers have been frustrated in their attempts to reach the sea. These barrier lakes, as we shall see, occur all the way up the coast as far as the area of Vilankulo. With the huge parabolic dunes between them the rivers can only reach the sea by seepage. The consequence is that the water of the sea is crystal clear and totally free of the usual mud and vegetable matter carried down by rivers. The lakes themselves are warm, sheltered and magnificent for boating and recreation.

From Macia, a tarmac road branches south-eastwards and leads for 34 km to a superb series of these barrier lakes with, on the spacious beach of the Vembje lagoon, the holiday resort of Bilene.

From Macia, the main tarmac road continues north-eastwards across level bush-covered country. After passing the rural centres of Chimonzo, Chissano and Chipenhe, the road descends into the vast flood plains of the Limpopo River where wheat and maize flourish in the rich alluvial soil. The great river is crossed by means of a toll bridge at 63 km. Immediately on the other side of the river (the left bank) lies the town of ...

XAI-XAI AND PRAIA DO XAI-XAI

Xai-Xai was named by the Portuguese *João Belo* in honour of Commandante João Belo, the Portuguese naval officer who played a part in the war with the Shangane tribe in 1897. The original African name, Xai-Xai (pronounced Tshai-Tshai), was the name of the father of the favourite wife, Sony, of the Shangane chief Ngungunyana. Until the mouth of the river silted up the town was a busy river port, with coasters bringing in trade goods and carrying out the produce of the Shangane (or Gaza) country of which João Belo became the administrative centre from the time of the ending of the Shangane war. The mouth of the Limpopo still presents an imposing sight, with fine estuary-type fishing and a rich nursery of prawns.

In 1910 a railway was built from Xai-Xai to the Shangane tribal centre of Mandlakaze. The line was extended to other places in the interior and is known as the Gaza railway. Today the town is an important communications, trade and administrative centre.

From Xai-Xai, a tarmac road leads for 11 km to the coast at the beach named by the Portuguese after one of the pioneer settler families in those parts, the Sepulvedas. It is now known as Praia Xai-Xai.

Praia Xai-Xai (Xai-Xai beach) is notable for a remarkable sandstone reef which runs parallel to the shore and provides a totally sheltered area for boats. There is a fine beach and an attractive, informal holiday resort sheltering in the shade of casuarina trees and notable for the brilliant colours of its bougainvillaea flowers.

Fishermen find the area particularly exciting. A series of deep-lying sandstone reefs further out to sea make a rich underwater fishing area. Salmon, rock cod, kingfish, barracuda, sailfish and wahoo are all taken in quantities. Sharks are also present and swimming must be done in protected areas.

From Xai-Xai, the main tarmac road continues north-eastwards. After 5,6 km it passes the turn-off to Xai-Xai beach and then continues parallel to the coast across undulating bush-covered country with patches of cultivation. It is interesting to see the cashew nut trees (*Anacardum occidentatol NV Cajueiro*) which, originally introduced from the West Indies, now grow so profusely in cultivation that vast numbers also have run wild. Mozambique, in fact, became the world's largest producer of cashew nuts, in former times exporting about 100 000 tons each year. There is a large decorticating (shelling) plant in Xai-Xai. The Gaza district generally is a real paradise for cashew trees with the well-watered, sandy soil and warm sea air which they love. During the months November to February the pulp around the ripening nuts can be converted into a drink, very pleasant and harmless when fresh and cold, but with the kick of a giraffe if fermented. Intoxication in the Gaza district is rather common during the cashew nut season.

Passing several small rural centres such as Nhamavila, Chizavane, Chidengwele, Madendere and Zandamela, the road, at 136 km from Xai-Xai reaches the small town of ...

QUISSICO

Quissico, named by the Portuguese after Kisiko, a tribal headman, is the administrative centre for the district known as *Zavala*, the hereditary name of the paramount chief of the Tshopi tribe who inhabit this part of Mozambique.

Perched on the brow of a high hill, the town has a handsome panoramic view of the coast with its lakes and lagoons. Swimming and fishing in these lakes, and on the seashore 11 km away down a gravel road, are worthwhile occupations. Quissico is particularly famous for its tribal music and dancing. The Tshopi (Chope) tribesmen are great performers on the wooden xylophones known as *marimbas*. Every Sunday at 08h00 bands of musicians gather just outside the town and entertain the tribal chief with a concert and dance. It provides an extraordinary scene of animation, colour and excitement against a majestic background of lakes and hills.

From Quissico, the main tarmac road continues its way north-eastwards up the coast. Passing the small rural centres of Guilundo and Helene, the road at 44 km crosses the western spur of the magnificent lagoon at the mouth of the Inharrime River, with a fine resting place on the north bank. The resting places or laybys along the Maputo–Beira road are very pleasant features of the journey. Several of them, such as this one, on what is known as Lake Poelela, are quite delightful. The lake (or lagoon) is one of the most beautiful in Africa with a dazzling white, gently shelving beach, water of great clarity and the most gorgeous shades of blue.

On the north shore of this lovely lake, 1,5 km beyond the bridge, the road enters the pleasant village of Inharrime. This little lake 'port' is linked to Inhambane, 91 km away, by a railway which is a joy to all lovers of steam locomotives and the clickity-clack of wheels rattling over joints and points. The railway was built in 1912 and is a real 'coconut express'. The locomotives are wood burners. They take six hours to do the journey and the drivers fortify themselves for the effort by carrying bunches of bananas and green coconuts on top of the tenders. Modern buses have, alas, largely stolen away customers from the railway, but it can still raise patronage for three return journeys a week. To see it at full speed, smoking, whistling, steaming and rattling along, with an excited babble of conversation from its two passenger coaches floating behind it in the warm air like a streamer of invisible smoke, is a most entertaining spectacle.

From Inharrime, the main tarmac road continues north-eastwards for 12 km and then reaches a turn-off to the coast 16 km away at Zavora beach. Here there are bungalows, diving and swimming in water of superb clarity.

We are now in a world quite dominated by coconuts. The stately palms grow in thousands. Their cultivation is the principal local industry with copra one of the most important exports of Mozambique. The groves of coconuts cover the undulating coastal areas with lovely green carpets, coolly shaded and very graceful to the eye.

The people living along the coast are an amiable lot. Watch (and listen to a crowd of their women at one of the community water pumps). African women generally spend a frightening amount of their lives carrying things on their heads. A few of them in these parts have discovered the wheel, or devised a technique of rolling along wooden barrels, but most of them still carry everything on their heads. Their balancing ability reaches a standard unsurpassed anywhere else in the world. Buckets of water; sacks of produce; vast bundles of firewood; tables and chairs; old-fashioned portable gramophones in the midst of playing a record, all are indiscriminately carried on the women's heads. All are so perfectly balanced that they are undisturbed by any unevenness of ground, obstructions, or a continuous din of conversation, laughter, comment and invective which emanates from the mouth of the person beneath.

Vasco da Gama, the pioneer Portuguese navigator to visit these parts, named the area *Terra da Boa Gente* (land of good people). This affable reputation has remained into modern times. Few travellers along the coastal road fail to appreciate the likable nature of both landscape and people. The journey is very pleasant. The road passes such rural centres as Cumbana, Lindela and the turn to Jangamo and its beach, 24 km to the east. A rough track ends in a bay frequented by fishermen and watched over by a lighthouse on the *Cabo das Correntes* (cape of the currents). This is a famous navigational beacon. The cape has its name from the fact that there the Mozambique Current gathers sudden velocity in its southwards flow. The Arab dhows which sailed the East African seas from early times found it dangerous to go south of this cape. They could not resist the current. The northern monsoon winds on which they relied to take them back up the coast also petered out at this latitude. Cape Correntes, therefore, marked the navigational limit of the dhows. The more southerly coast of Africa was only opened up to trade with the coming of the Portuguese. The resident African population were spared the full horror of the slave trade because the Arab dhows could not sail down the coast south of the cape. At 58 km from Inharrime, the main coastal road reaches a fork. To the right a tarmac branch leads through the coconut groves for 32 km to reach a cul-de-sac at the romantic old port of ...

INHAMBANE

Inhambane was so named from the fragment of the Karanga tribe who lived there when it was first visited by the Portuguese. Situated on a peninsula protecting a spacious bay, Inhambane was the most southerly trading point regularly used by the Arabs. From Cape Correntes northwards the atmosphere of the coast has shown a subtle change, with eastern and Arab influences playing an important part in commercial and cultural life.

The Portuguese commenced a regular trade through the port of Inhambane from 1534. One of the most important items obtained there was copper, brought down by safari traders from mines in the interior of Zimbabwe and the northern Transvaal. Mission work was started in the area in 1560 by Father da Silveira, the Jesuit missionary, and Christianity became widely accepted.

Inhambane today is still used as a coastal port, although motor transport along the tarmac road to Maputo has largely robbed it of the old trade. It remains an atmospheric relic of the past with a fine waterfront looking out across the bay to Maxixe on the far side. The white sails of dhows stand up like sheep grazing in a blue meadow and there is always a bustle of people and goods being ferried across the bay from Maxixe and other places.

Some of the buildings, such as the Cathedral of Our Lady of Conception, are handsome, while the main thoroughfare, the Avenida da Republica, is attractively planted with trees and flowers. The wood-burning puffers of the local railway still occasionally make a lumbering way down the main street to convey goods to and from the harbour. A visit to the locomotive shed is recommended to railway enthusiasts while the market also provides an interesting scene.

Boating in the great bay, swimming and fishing from the various beaches around Inhambane peninsula, are the pastimes of visitors. There are three principal beaches. Praia do Tofo is 30,5 km from the town along a tarmac road leading through groves of coconuts. There are good views of the great bay of Inhambane.

The beach is a popular resort, although it has been much eroded by massive wave action.

Praia do Barra (beach of the bar) is reached by means of a sandy track 6 km long branching off from the tarmac road leading to Praia do Tofo.

Baia dos Cocos (coconut bay), the finest of the beaches, with an interesting sandstone reef, is reached by means of a very sandy track branching off from the main Inhambane–Maputo road at a point 4,5 km from Inhambane. This track is 17 km long, leading through groves of coconuts and past several small lakes. Swimming, fishing, diving and doing nothing are good pastimes in this resort.

From the point where the road to Inhambane branched off from the main Maputo–Beira road, we continue this journey through a land of coconut palms for 25 km and then reaches the beautifully situated town of ...

MAXIXE

Maxixe (Portuguese orthography) takes its name from a local Tsonga chieftain, Mashishe. It is a busy trading and administrative centre for the Tsonga tribe, with a considerable fishing industry. Market day on Thursdays sees the place at its busiest, with a vast variety of country produce and sea foods on sale.

The town fronts on to the great bay of Inhambane. A variety of flowering trees and shrubs make a pretty garden along the verges of the shore and the municipal caravan park has a fine view. Fishing dhows make great use of Maxixe while there is a constant coming and going of ferry boats crossing the bay to Inhambane, 6 km away. A trip by ferry provides an interesting little outing. A unique feature of the local dhows is that several of them have double sails.

Fishermen use Maxixe as a base and dhows may be hired for the day. A trip to the old whaling station at Linga-Linga makes a fine outing even for non-fishermen. Big-game fishermen go for such fish as marlin during the September–December season, while barracuda, king fish, queen fish and sail fish are caught throughout the year. Power boats are available on charter.

Hunters also use Maxixe as a base for big-game safaris inland into the bush country.

From Maxixe, the main tarmac road continues northwards through groves of coconuts. Each palm produces about 22,5 kg of copra a year. The crop depends largely on proximity to the sea. The coconut thrives on warm, moist, salty sea air and the great plantations of Mozambique are all in a belt within a few miles of the coast. At current prices the copra from a single palm fetches about R20, so a large plantation is highly profitable. The palms are easy to grow, resistant to disease and fires. They start bearing at five years and have much the same life span as a human being. Every part of the palm is useful to man. The trunks make poles; the leaves are used for thatching; they withstand hurricanes and provide shelter. On a hot afternoon, their shadows make life bearable, while the milk of a green nut is a refreshing and delicious drink. Fermented, it is liquid dynamite.

Between the small rural centres of Morrumbene and Massinga, the tarmac road crosses the Tropic of Capricorn. The landscape is almost classically tropical, with vast plantations of coconuts and a vivid green vegetation. Just north of the small administrative town of Massinga (69 km from Maxixe) there is a turn-off to the coast of Praia Marungula, also known as Nelson Beach, a resort notable for its swimming, fishing, scenic beauty and the relaxed informality of its bungalow accommodation.

At 7,5 km beyond Massinga there is another turn-off leading for 52 km to the coast at Pomene, a fishermen's resort situated on a rugged promontory known as the *Ponta da Barra Falsa* (point of the false bar) where there is accommodation. Marlin and sailfish are caught here.

The main coast road continues northwards past rural centres such as Unguana, Nhachengue, Mauanza, Cheline and Mapinhane, each with a cluster of shops, post office, government buildings and community well. The coconut plantations peter out but magnificent baobab trees grow in great number. Children by the wayside offer for sale the seedpods, and also such local curiosities as bows and arrows.

At 226 km from Maxixe, the main road reaches a tarmac turn-off leading for 21 km to the coast of ...

VILANKULO

Vilankulo is named after the Tsonga clan who live in those parts as fishermen. It is a small administrative town which at night is rather deceptive, for its street lighting is generous and the place has the appearance of being substantial. There is a commercial centre and market place, garages, administration buildings and a pretty little church. But these are minor things. The great attraction to Vilanculos is its seashore, fronting on to a beautiful bay and acting as the stepping-off port for visits to the Bazaruto archipelago of islands.

The road down to the shore leads past the caravan park and ends at a point known as *Mucoque* (place of coconuts) where there is an hotel, jetty and a harbour. The harbour is filled with dhows in every state from seaworthiness to the picturesque decrepitude of literally lying dreaming on their beam ends in the shade of tall coconut palms, as though they had imbibed too freely of the fermented juice and become real beach layabouts.

Swimming, boating and fishing are all excellent at Vilankulo with, the ultimate excitement, a visit to the islands.

THE BAZARUTO ISLANDS

The Bazaruto archipelago consists of four main islands with sandstone bases surrounded by coral. The largest of the islands is Bazaruto itself, a long, narrow island with a lighthouse on its most northerly point of Don Carlos. South of this island is the smaller island known as Bwengele (or Benguerua) from a Tsonga fisherman who used it as his base. It is also known as Santo Antonio. South of Bwengele immediately opposite Vilankulo, is the still smaller island of *Margaruque*, also named after a Tsonga fisherman, and sometimes known as Santa Isabel. Inshore from Bazaruto lies the tiny island of Santa Carolina, popularly known as Paradise Island or *Perola do Indico* (pearl of the Indian Ocean). In 1971 part of the Bazaruto archipelago, including Bwengele and Margaruque islands, and a five-kilometre peripheral marine zone, was proclaimed as a marine national park especially for the protection of the dugongs, turtles, underwater grasslands, corals and marine life which make of it their home. The peninsula stub on the mainland which gave rise to the archipelago of islands is also planned as the eventual San Sebastian Maritime National Park. Sparsely inhabited by man this area, up to Ponto São Sebastiao, is a nesting place for sea turtles and flamingos. Its botany is enriched with cycads.

Altogether, the whole area of the Bazaruto archipelago deserves the strictest protection from individuals, visitors and residents who seem to have no interest other than in the slaughter of marine life and the piecemeal removal of coral reefs to the mantlepieces and display cabinets in private residences in distant cities. As it is, this area is one of the richest and most varied of all marine landscapes, with a vast population of wonderful forms of tidal and underwater life.

Even before Europeans first visited them, the islands in the archipelago were renowned among the Arab traders for the variety of their fish and for seed pearls. These little pearls were highly prized in the East for medicine purposes. They were crushed into a powder, mixed with honey or syrup, and regarded as specifics for a number of diseases. The Arabs also ate the pearls as a delicacy, especially when crushed and mixed with betel nut. They had some reputation as aphrodisiacs.

The Portuguese, when they occupied the coast, continued the trade in seed pearls, with Tsonga and baTswa divers doing the underwater work of collecting. Small settlements were made on Bazaruto and the other islands by fishermen and traders, and also by refugees from mainland disturbances among the African tribes. Persons banished by the Portuguese for political reasons were also sent to the islands. Even after the pearl trade languished there continued to be something of a permanent population.

Visually the islands are not immediately exciting. They are narrow ridges of sandstone, covered in sand and overgrown with rather nondescript shrubbery. Casuarina trees and coconut palms have been planted on them. A few groves of citrus trees, guavas, and other fruit trees are remindful of forgotten settlers of past years who probably lie buried in the nameless graves scattered in the bush. The ruins still stand on Santa Carolina Island of a small fort built there in 1855.

Notwithstanding their lack of obvious spectacle, the islands have an atmosphere and character peculiarly their own. They seem to be little worlds quite detached from the rest of the earth and absorbed entirely in their own thoughts and affairs. On them it is easy to imagine that Sinbad the Sailor himself once landed. And perhaps it was there that he found the magic bottle in which was imprisoned the mighty djinn!

Sunsets are particularly lovely on the islands. There is an indefinable quality to the light; an evanescent effervescence reflects into the sky with a luminous glow. Nights on the islands are enchanted. Then it is that the winds seem to drift in from far places, filled with aromas, murmurs and memories of mysterious lands beyond the seas. There is a languid washing of the waves on the beach, while the presence of some walker is marked by the phosphorescent sparks rising with each footstep from the zone of the tide.

A handful of Tsonga fishermen live on the islands, maintaining fish traps in the shallows and herding a few sheep and goats. There is an interesting and numerous population of birds who, by their songs, obviously enjoy life in places where they can have few natural enemies. Flamingo feathers on the beaches remind us that these gorgeous birds are living in the shallow waters of the São Sebastian peninsula, while a variety of predatory aquatic birds find a comfortable living from the teeming life of the tidal zone.

Marine life on the beaches is vigorous. Between the tides the shoreline is alive with innumerable odd-proportioned creatures, scavenging, scrounging and scuffling for food. Crabs of every size and colour seem to find the islands to be their idea of paradise. In vast hoards they run up and down the beaches keeping just ahead of the waves and feeding on the foodstuffs ceaselessly brought in by the tides.

The tidal variation is tremendous and off the islands it literally flows like a river in the ocean, richly oxygenated and laden with plankton like an endless chain of waiters carrying seafoods to a banquet table. The guests are innumerable small creatures who feed on plankton, larger creatures who feed on the smaller creatures; tropical fish galore wandering through the submarine gardens of coral like flocks of birds feeding on the insects that feed on the nectar of the flowers of the ocean.

Low tide is the time to see the coral reefs. Then they are exposed and accessible, with the water calm. The reefs encircle the islands. They are indescribably beautiful and the population of fish and crustaceans quite overwhelming. The most majestic of the reefs is *Manziture* (place of shell fish), sometimes known to visitors as 'Two Mile' or 'Three Mile' Reef. This reef lies across the channel separating Bazaruto from Bwengele Island. Even the boat journey to this reef is exhilarating. All around there is a vast seascape of islands, clouds, the distant mainland of Africa, and the eternally restless sea.

Fish such as bonito leap ahead of you. Schools of dolphins race with the boat, darting below and all around, showing off and delighting in demonstrating their complete superiority to a clumsy and smelly man-made craft. The reef itself is a fairyland. Those experts who know consider it to be at least the equal of any other coral reef in any ocean. Lovely corals, anemones and seaweeds grow here in vast variety and abundance. They are fed by the richly oxygenated tidal flow. They find a base on a bed just the right depth from the surface, and in water which is the perfect temperature for coral. At low tide the top of this reef emerges from the sea. In a dead calm, with the water as clear as glass, the submarine world is easily accessible, quite within the reach of any diver. For brilliance of colour, diversity of form, and sheer magic of surprise and discovery, there is nothing more exciting than this. It has to be seen and experienced to be really believed.

The tourist development of the islands really started about 1925 when Joaquim Alves settled in Vilankulo. Born in Portugal on 14 October 1903, he immigrated to Beira as a youth and found a job in a shop. Wages were low and he started to fish in his spare time. He was then offered the position of manager in a trading station at Vilankulo, then a very primitive little place where leopards and lions often wandered into the streets from the surrounding bush. In this setting Joaquim Alves flourished. He started fishing, used the profits to buy the shop in which he was working, and then systematically open thirty other trading stations in the district.

In the course of conducting his fishing business, Joaquim Alves visited the islands. On Bazaruta, the small baTswa fishing clan of that name traded with him and also showed him the richness of the area in marine life. On what was known as Santa Carolina, but named by Joaquim Alves *Paradise Island,* there lived at that time only a lighthouse keeper named Mafumisi. The island is still known after him *(Tshidzini kaMafumisi)* to the coast people.

Alves liked the island and soon found that many other people shared his enthusiasm. An increasing number of visitors found their way to Vilankulo and came to his door in search of accommodation. So he built a three-bedroomed hotel and bar to oblige them. More visitors came so he extended the hotel to a fifteen-roomed building and named it the *Amigo de Mozambique.* Visitors also wanted to stay on the islands, so he secured a concession from the government to build an hotel on Santa Carolina, bungalow accommodation on Bazaruta and Margaruque, and also further up the coast where a baTswa chief named Inhassoro had a fishing village.

Coconut palms, casuarina trees, Indian nuts, citrus and other trees were all planted by the indefatigable Joaquim Alves. For many years he was the general factotum of this part of the coast of Mozambique. The second hotel he built at Vilankulo, the Hotel Dona Ana, was named after his wife. It stands on a superb site looking out across the dhow harbour to the distant islands. In 1973, Joaquim Alves retired from the tourist side of his organisation. Today the various places of accommodation are run by a substantial company specialising in the tourist and hotel trade.

All visitors to the archipelago find the area of immense interest. As a marine national park it has unique possibilities. Not only is its wildlife interesting but its atmosphere is enriched with memories of old adventures and many strange human characters. Through the years, these drifters have wandered in across the Indian Ocean. They found on these little islands a sanctuary where personal problems and troubles could be forgotten. For long years no hostile force disturbed the silence of the nights and the languid passing of the days.

From the turn-off to Vilankulo, the main tarmac road continues up the coast for 58 km through densely bushed country and then reaches a turn-off leading for 15 km to the coastal resort of ...

INHASSORO

Inhassoro, named after a baTswa chieftain, is a great resort for fishermen and a good launching port for boats setting out for the big-game fishing areas of Bazaruta Island. Up the coast, as far as the fishing base of Bartolemeu Dias, there are many vantage-points for anglers. The village of Inhassoro is attractive, with Indian nut trees, casuarinas, palm trees, and a lively open-air market.

From the turn-off to Inhassoro, the main tarmac coast road continues northwards. After 8 km there is a turn-off to the village of Macovane, with a fine resting place near the road junction. The country here is densely bushed, with clumps of lala palms and baobabs. Game animals are often seen and the baTswa tribesmen use bows and arrows in their hunts for venison. Their villages and persons are interesting. In the primeval setting of the baobab-dominated wilderness they combine to a singularly harmonious picture of an African style of life.

At 46 km from the turn-off to Inhassoro, the tarmac road reaches a turn-off leading for 42 km to the small but ancient coastal resort and dhow port of Nova Mambone built at the mouth of the Save River. In former years the Save River was used by the Arabs as a trade route into the interior. Mambone (place of the king) was established at the mouth of the river and the atmosphere and some of the ruins of those early years may still be sensed and seen in this lonely and half-forgotten little place. Seafoods are rich in the estuary of the river and the small hostelry (Hotel de Mambone) can load a table very agreeably with such delectable things as prawns and crabs.

The main tarmac road, 3 km beyond the turn-off to Mambone, passes a turn-off leading through big-game country to Massangena. The 182 000 ha Zinave National Park lies between this road and the banks of the Save River. This National Park was originally a hunting concession (Coutada Official No 4) but converted into a National Park in 1973. Messrs Mozambique Safariland administer the Park with camps at Zinave and on the Save River open from April to November each year. An Ecological Research Centre is maintained in the Park.

At 39 km beyond the Mambone turn-off the road reaches the great toll bridge which crosses the Save River. This bridge, opened in 1972, replaced a precarious pontoon service across the river and made all-season road travel easy between Maputo and Beira. The Save River in flood time (about January) can be a formidable flow of water. The original ferry service was often disrupted for lengthy periods.

On the right bank (south side) of the river stands the rural centre formerly known as Vila Franco do Save where there is petrol, food and drink. A wayside shrine has been made out of a baobab tree at the entrance to the village and this is interesting to see. The river banks are well forested and the river itself wide and impressive even in the dry season.

Across the river, along its left bank lies a hunting zone (Coutada Official No 5). During the hunting season (1 April to 15 November) hunting parties are conducted into what is one of the finest big-game areas of Africa. Mozambique, generally, offers tremendous possibilities to big game hunters. Several professional hunting organisations supply the facilities of guides, camps and specialised transport.

The country north of the Save River is densely bushed and particularly handsome in September when many of the trees come into spring flower. The road crosses such broad rivers as the Repembe and the Gorongose. It finds its way steadily through the wilderness, gaining in altitude until it eventually reaches granite country covered in tall brachystegia trees.

At 401 km from Vilankulo the road finally joins the main tarmac road linking Mutare in Zimbabwe with Beira. From here it is 134 km east to Beira, or 151 km west to the frontier of Zimbabwe. From Maputo, this all-tarmac road has taken us for 956 km through a wild garden where Nature has planted countless beautiful trees and shrubs. Man, with his coconuts and casuarinas, has also managed to add substantially to the charm of a landscape of great diversity and fascination.

Chapter Forty-Four

NAMIBIA

The Northern Areas

The south-western part of the African continent, the area lying between the Gariep (formerly 'Orange') River in the south and the Kunene River in the north, is a sunbaked confection of rocky hillocks, rugged mountains, seas of sand dunes and plains so vast that a traveller half-way across them feels he is in the midst of eternity. It is these plains, some of them deserts, others prairielands of grass and still others savanna parklands covered in trees, that give the country its modern name of Namibia. In the language of the people who inhabit the southern part of the area, *Namib* means a large plain, and the people of this part of the country are generally known as the *Namaqua* (people of the plains).

The total area of Namibia is 824 292 square kilometres where live approximately 1 758 800 people – only 2,1 persons per square kilometre. Their origins and cultures range from the Late Stone Age to the plastic age of nuclear power.

The largest section of the population (913 000) consists of a group of related tribes who live in the northern section of the country where they are collectively known as the *ovaMbo* (the prefix 'ova' or 'owa' simply meaning 'the people'). The second largest section of the population (183 000) is the okaVango who live in the north-east. The third largest section consists of the Herero (130 000); next are the Nama (117 000) with the Damara also consisting of about the same number. Next are people of European origin (98 000) – a combination of Afrikaans, German and English language speakers, Caprivian (86 000), Basters (72 000), Bushmen (35 000) and Tswanas (7 800).

With a population so small living in a country of such vastness, silence and solitude predominate and there is a sense of emptiness and isolation. This widespread stillness subtly combines with the landscape which is singular in its colours full of contrasts of light and shade. Where there is water, fertility confronts the harshest aridity. Mountains rise so abruptly from the plains that they seem like jagged islands in a sea of grass or sand. Travelling through this part of Africa is an experience so full of novelty of scene and atmosphere so different from any other part of Earth that the visitor might well imagine himself to have landed on a distant planet, faced with the exciting prospect of discovering all manner of natural and unnatural wonders.

Exploring this south-western part of Africa is made easy by a magnificent network of roads, of which the construction and maintenance absorbs no less than 36 per cent of the total administrative budget of the country. The investment of this money and a prodigious amount of hard work on the part of the engineering and maintenance staff have given the country more kilometres of properly made road per head of population than in any other part of Africa, including South Africa. There are over 15 km of constructed roads in the country for every person. Those who explore this expanding network of roads, at present consisting of 41 762 km of trunk and main roads (4 382 km are tarred, 24 089 km are gravel and 13 291 km are dirt), can find themselves on long stretches so completely empty that the road seems to have been built for their use alone. These roads find their way over the plains and far away. Sometimes the only other vehicle encountered on a long journey is a road scraper patiently at work, as though maintaining a smooth surface for ghost vehicles which are seldom seen to pass.

This vast network of roads was not simply constructed as a cosmetic luxury for the country. Roads can either follow progress, providing comfort for the pioneer and support to enterprise, or they can stretch ahead into untouched spaces, tempting the explorer onwards to new farms, mines and projects. The vast per capita expenditure on such roads in a developing country is therefore an investment and a sign of confidence in the future. It is to the credit of any country's administration that so large a portion of its revenue is used on such a worthwhile asset, rather than squandered on lethal military devices and lunatic ambitions of changing the world.

The complete tarring of the main north, south, east and west trunk roads stretching from the capital, Windhoek, has made all-weather travelling possible to every main centre in the country and from the southern to the northern frontiers. The main district roads are so well maintained that, apart from dust, the traveller has no real difficulty in reaching the smaller towns, villages and rural areas. It is these untarred roads which, in fact, lead the visitor to the discovery of many remarkable places and scenes. No tourist should be reluctant to venture along these byways, for they lead to experiences and sensations which are quite enchanting.

The maintenance of these byways is the responsibility of a famous breed of man, the *padjapie* (road rustic), as he is nicknamed. They are the sun-tanned, dehydrated, dusty-looking individuals who spend their lives living in lonely camps by the wayside, maintaining about 58 000 km of by-roads and sometimes not seeing a town or village for months on end. There are 1 400 *padjapies* working on the roads of the country, operating about 800 pieces of heavy machinery with 155 grader units and several specialised work-forces.

The labours of these individuals have resulted in many notable achievements, not least of which are the unique salt roads built along the desert coast. All roads on this coast, and the streets of a town such as Swakopmund, are constructed of gypsum and salt. Gypsum, which is found in the desert, is laid down and soaked with brine extracted from brine springs far saltier than the sea. The brine compounds the gypsum into a hard surface as smooth as any tarmac, which is perfectly harmonious and suited to a climate without rain but which is misty and salty and where the wind blows incessantly.

To build and maintain roads over sand dunes, the *padjapies* use special 'sand spoor' equipment and a technique devised by the roads division. A type of sleigh is used which traverses the dunes and creates tracks in the sand which motor vehicles can follow. To keep the coastal road between Swakopmund and Walvis Bay clear of drifting sand, a special four-wheel-drive vehicle is used with hydraulically operated blades mounted in front of the vehicle to remove sand drifts of up to a metre high which are carried across the road by the winds.

One problem concerning the roads in this south-western part of Africa is the presence throughout the territory of a vast population of game animals, especially antelope such as kudu. These handsome creatures, like the kangaroo of Australia, unfortunately have very poor traffic sense. Signs urging travellers to be cautious of kudu are common along the roadsides and should be heeded. Kudu are large antelope which like to keep together in groups. They find the grazing on the road verges attractive. If one runs across a road, others will certainly follow without the slightest concern for oncoming traffic. Slow speeds are essential, especially at night, as the animals are dazzled by headlights. Other antelope, attracted by the salt in road construction, come to such roads to lick the salt and frequently collide with vehicles. Their presence at the roadside proves delightful to travellers, but they need to be carefully watched.

Along the roadsides, engineers have constructed laybys and rest places at suitable points beneath shady trees. In arid areas small thatched shelters with cement tables and seats have been erected. Such rest places are provided with litter-bins, sometimes rather overflowing with bottles. In this way, travellers can rest or relax for a while and have the chance of taking their eyes off long distances, refreshing themselves with a drink, a snack or a snooze. The road-makers must be commended for leaving many beautiful trees standing, and occasionally tolerating a bend in the road when straightening it would destroy some interesting rock or feature of the landscape.

The Department of Nature Conservation and Tourism has been responsible for many splendid features of this part of Africa. Their resorts, game sanctuaries and reserves are notable for imaginative and excellent management. The accommodation they provide is of an impeccable standard at rates which makes a holiday still possible for a family, when hotels have gone beyond the reach of many people save those fortunates travelling on professional expense accounts. The atmosphere of informal comfort and cleanliness, and the courtesy of the staff in these public resorts, is a credit to the country. The author of this book visited them all without special privilege or facility. He found them to be generally of good standard. A few exceptions are poor. For the tourist and the traveller, the discovery of Namibia is an experience which is exciting, novel, delightful and unique; a venture into a different world which should not be missed by any visitor to Southern Africa. The country will never be forgotten by any visitor for its scenes, atmosphere and people.

WINDHOEK

Handsomely situated 1 654 m above sea-level in the cul-de-sac at the head of the valley formed by a tributary of the upper Swakop River, Windhoek is surrounded by clusters of high hills and mountains well covered in trees and grass. A group of hot springs (23,9°C to 26,7°C) reaches the surface in several places in the cul-de-sac of the valley, giving the area a perennial greenness and attracting first game animals and then human beings to the site.

The Herero named the area *oTjomwuse* (the place of steam), while the Nama called it *!Ai!gams* (hot water). Several early tribes settled temporarily at the springs. At the end of 1840 Jonker Afrikaner, the renowned Nama chieftain, established himself there with his followers. He named the place *Winterhoek* in memory of his birthplace in the Cape, and built his home near the site where the most powerful spring reached the surface. The Berg Hotel was later constructed there and became the South African diplomatic headquarters.

In December 1842 the Rhenish missionaries Hans Kleinschmidt and Carl Hahn established a church and school on the site of the future city. At that time there were about 1 000 of Jonker Afrikaner's followers living in the valley. More people were being attracted to the site by the chief, who wanted to increase his following in preparation for continuing the brutal sequence of wars and outrages which had passed for the history of the south-western part of Africa over a considerable period of time.

One group of Jonker Afrikaner's followers were attached to the Wesleyan Church; and these people brought with them to the valley two missionaries, Joseph Tindall and Richard Haddy, who were invited by the chief to commence work in the area. The Rhenish Mission was then moved down the valley to oTjikango, the site of another hot spring, where they founded the station named Neu-Barmen for the benefit of the Herero people.

Traders were drawn to the valley and the first wagon trails were blazed from the coast by vehicles loaded with alcohol, guns and gunpowder – the commodities most wanted in the country. The traders who brought these goods into the country required cattle as payment, and this barter trade had already degraded most of the south-western part of Africa. To pay for guns and booze, the tribes fought one another with insensate brutality, looting, killing and rustling. Nobody ever seems to learn a lesson from the past. To settle his own debts, Jonker Afrikaner began raiding the herds of the Hereros. One raid after another simply provoked retaliation, with barbarism so appalling that an account of that period of history makes gruesome reading.

The end of the settlement of Winterhoek came on 25 August 1880. Five days previously Jonker Afrikaner's men had rustled 1 500 special oxen carefully bred by the Hereros for religious rites and sacrifice. The Hereros responded with a full-scale attack on Winterhoek. Jonker Afrikaner and his people fled southwards and the disheartened missionaries withdrew down the valley. The abandoned settlement of Winterhoek was left for the Hereros to destroy totally, and for some time only a few renegades and bandits frequented the place.

After ten years, the Germans arrived. At the beginning of October 1890, Major Curt von Francois occupied the site of Jonker Afrikaner's former settlement and renamed it Windhuk, either as a corruption of the original Winterhoek or because the Germans found the glen to be windy on their arrival. On 18 October 1890, Von Francois started building a fort on a hill commanding the upper valley. This fort survives as a handsome *beau geste* type of stronghold, turreted with white walls and shadowy verandas, courtyard and passages. This *Alte Feste* (old fort), as it is called, was completed in 1892 and became the headquarters of the *Deutsche Schutztruppe* (German Colonial Troops) and of German administration which steadily expanded control over the country.

A town grew under the protection of the fort. A narrow-gauge railway from the coast at Swakopmund reached the place in June 1902, and by 1906 Windhuk had grown sufficiently to be granted civil administration. It received a town council in 1909 and in 1910 became the seat of the newly constituted Legislative Assembly, thus confirming its position as the capital of what was known as German South West Africa.

After the invasion of the country by South African forces in 1914, Windhuk (with the spelling of its name then established as Windhoek) became the seat of the new administration when the country, as a mandate of the League of Nations, was placed under the trusteeship of South Africa. Under the new regime it developed as a centre for government, communications, trade, education and culture. On 19 October 1965, as part of the celebrations on the 75th anniversary of its establishment, Windhoek became a city. It now has 147 056 inhabitants. After a long and bitter struggle with South Africa, the South West African Peoples Organisation (Swapo) led by Sam Nujoma, won independence for the country. On 21 March 1990 Windhoek became the capital of what was named the Republic of Namibia.

Built on the floor and up the slopes of foothills and the sides of the valley, Windhoek has a pleasant range of elevation. There are viewsites, and the variety of suburban locations gives the city an attractive diversity of appearance.

The principal street, running north to south, Independence Avenue (formerly Kaiser Street), is lined with modern commercial buildings and a few interesting survivals of German colonial architecture. The municipal building is an impressive structure which faces on to this street. In the flower-beds in front of it stands a statue of Major Curt von Francois, sculpted by a South African artist, Hennie Potgieter. This statue of the father of modern Windhoek was unveiled on 19 October 1965 during the city's 75th anniversary celebrations.

Further north along Independence avenue lies a small park, formerly the zoo gardens. This is a pleasant area of lawns, trees and flowers in the centre of the city. In this garden stands a memorial erected on 5 April 1897 in memory of members of the Deutsche Schutztruppe killed during the war with the Namas under Hendrik Witbooi. Also in the garden is a display of elephant fossils recovered from the mud around one of the hot springs, and a collection of fragments of a meteorite found on the site.

The Alte Feste still stands on its hill site overlooking the city. The building is now a museum housing an interesting collection of photographs and items related to the days of German administration. Outside the museum stands a real gem of interest to railway enthusiasts – a narrow-gauge train, complete with locomotive and coaches. It is seemingly about to set off on the 373 km trip through the wild mountains and across the Namib Desert to Swakopmund, a journey which this little train made many times during its years of service.

In front of the Alte Feste stands the Rider memorial, a fine equestrian statue sculpted by Adolf Kürle of Berlin. It was unveiled on 27 January 1912 at a military parade in honour of the Kaiser's birthday. The statue is a memorial to the men of the German colonial force who died during the Herero and Nama wars between 1904 and 1908. The Alte Feste museum is open to the public Mondays to Fridays 09h00 to 18h00; Saturdays 10h00 to 13h00 and Sundays 15h00 to 18h00.

Close to the Alte Feste stands the imposing building of the German Evangelical Lutheran Church with its tall steeple providing the city with a striking landmark. There is a garden notable for its flowering trees and an avenue of olive trees behind the church. Overlooking the garden is the administrative building erected by the German administration. Popularly known as the *Tintenpalast* (palace of ink), it is still in use. Adjoining it is the modern building erected to house the Legislative Assembly. It contains numerous works of art and a superb mural decorating the front wall inside. Visitors are allowed on conducted tours on request. A small game park is situated behind the administrative buildings.

In the centre of the city, facing Leutwein Street, are the art gallery, public library, state museum, archives and the theatre used by the Namibian Performing Arts Council and other producers in the staging of drama, ballet and opera. The library has an excellent collection of books and periodicals, including many rare works dealing with this part of Africa since its early days. The state museum has social and natural science exhibits and is open Mondays to Fridays 09h00 to 18h00; Saturdays 10h00 to 13h00 and Sundays 15h00 to 18h00.

Outside the Windhoek railway station is displayed one of the narrow-gauge locomotives which worked the old line to Swakopmund. Near this locomotive is a garden and monument commemorating the lives lost in the 1916 revolt by Chief Mandume and a section of the waMbo people. Another memorial in Windhoek is the Cross of Sacrifice, erected at the southern end of Leutwein Street, opposite the military cemetery. Each year on 11 November an interdenominational service is held here, commemorating the war dead of both sides in the two world wars. The Oudstryders Memorial stands in Bismarck Street in memory of the Boer *Bittereinders* (bitter-enders or die-hards) who refused to accept the terms of the Peace of Vereeniging at the end of the Anglo-Boer War and moved to German South West Africa in order to avoid British rule.

The suburbs of Windhoek contain many fine homes and gardens. On the heights above Heinitzburg Road in the suburb of Klein Windhoek may be seen three interesting castle-like residences which were constructed in 1890. During the wars with the local African inhabitants,

Captain von Francois built a rough fortress on the site of the present Government hostel. A second fortification was built on a hill overlooking the valley. An architect named Wilhelm Sander arrived in Windhoek shortly afterwards and set up practice, designing many of the buildings of the German period, including the famous Tintenpalast.

The fortifications built by Von Francois captivated the architect. When the war was over, he secured one of the abandoned fortresses and developed it into a picturesque ruin, a *'folly'* which he named *Sperlingslust* (sparrow's longing). It was bought by Rudolf Moeller and turned into a tavern with an arched beer room filled with enormous vats of deliciously cool beer.

In 1984 when Governor von Leutwein took office, he had as a private secretary the young Graf Schwerin. This nobleman took a liking to the inn, bought it, and commissioned Sander to complete it as a castle. Timber was imported from Germany and the finished place was named *Schwerinburg* after its owner. With its tapestries, chests and crystal chandeliers, it became an outpost of German aristocracy in Africa.

In 1908 Sander created a second castle which was also bought by the Graf Schwerin and named *Heinitzburg* after his wife's family name. This castle was built on the same hill as Schwerinburg but on a lower level. It was fitted with a children's nursery decorated with a quaint frieze of nursery rhyme characters. The Graf lived in one castle and his family in the other. A path linked the two castles, along which a special messenger tramped backwards and forwards conveying messages. At the bottom of the gateway of Heinitzburg stands an oddly designed beehive-shaped construction, with windows for eyes and a nose built above a mouth which serves as an entrance.

In 1911 Sander built the third castle in Windhoek as a home for himself and named it *Sanderburg*. Like the other two castles, it has several odd touches; a fierce-looking bulldog is painted on the wall; there are pillars without purpose; useless niches and towers with unapproachable rooms. It also has living-rooms with absolutely breathtaking views over the mighty sweep of hills and mountains surrounding Windhoek.

Suburbs such as Avis, Khomasdal and Pioniers Park are residential areas. *Eros* (named after a fruit-bearing shrub which grows there) is a light industrial area and the site of an airfield for private and light planes. *Ausspannplatz* (outspan place) was the original main staging post for ox-wagons. The international airport is situated in a place with the weird name of *oNdekaremba* (the fly on the cow). The name of the industrial area and township originally built for Africans is *Katutura* (the place where we do not like to live).

Windhoek is a clean, healthy and well-ordered city. Its one disadvantage is a shortage of water – rainfall is erratic. The shops are amply stocked with the necessities and luxuries of living. Tourists will find the gemstone and curio shops very good. Fur shops are well stocked with local karakul skins. Books and photographic shops are of high standard. Meat is good but bread indifferent; fruit and dairy products come mainly from South Africa. There are some good eating-places but traditional German cooking is difficult to find. Locally-made chocolate is delicious.

Entertainment is on the quiet side, as must be expected in a small city. It has some bright features, especially during the last week of April, the first week of May and during the first week of October. These are carnival times in Windhoek when masked balls, general jollifications and parades take place and a great deal of beer is drunk.

The April–May period is especially pleasant. The rains are over; the country is green and the air cool. January is the hottest month. However, the altitude of Windhoek prevents the temperature from becoming excessively hot and there is no humidity. The maximum temperature in summer is 36°C and an average of 360 mm of rain falls each year.

Windhoek is pleasant to visit at all seasons, with its novel scenes, atmosphere and activities. Not least of these is the cosmopolitan crowd in the streets – women in sophisticated modern styles being curiously upstaged by majestic Herero ladies who promenade the town in their colourful 'missionary's wife' costumes dating from the previous century. They move with a stately gait resulting from a combination of their own weight and from the effects of a custom in past years when their feet were burdened by the heavy bangles which were fashionable. The Herero menfolk, unfortunately, are birds of far drabber plumage.

DAAN VILJOEN GAME PARK

The Daan Viljoen Game Park lies 24 km from the city. It is located in the hills overlooking Windhoek from the west, along a first-class tarmac road which leads to what is known as the Khomas Hochland (broken, high land), bounded in the west by the Namib desert and in the east by the Windhoek valley. The 3 953 ha park was proclaimed in 1962 and named after a former administrator of South West Africa, the Honourable D T du P Viljoen. The park lies 2 000 m above sea-level and has a spectacular view over the valley containing the city of Windhoek. The scene on a night when the moon is full is particularly lovely. The picture is unforgettable as the moon – large and reddish in colour – rises directly behind the city. The lights of Windhoek glitter below like a portion of the milky way fallen from heaven and now held in the embrace of the surrounding dark shapes of mountains and hills.

The park carries an interesting population of wildlife. There are about 200 different species of birds and numerous kudu, blue wildebeest, mountain zebra, oryx, eland, springbok and hartebeest. The Augeigas River is dammed in the park and provides opportunity for fishing, with pleasant picnic facilities around its verges. There is a circular drive 6,4 km in length, wilderness trails for walkers, including the 32 km long Sweet-Thorn Trail. There is a restaurant (notable for its venison), swimming-pool, bungalows and a caravan park.

THE ROAD TO BOTSWANA

From Windhoek a tarmac road (B6) leads eastwards through the hills and the valley containing the suburb of Klein Windhoek. From there the road crosses a spacious, acacia-covered plain, passing the roadside hotel of Kapps Farm and the international airport 46 km from the capital.

Beyond the airport the tarmac road continues for a total of 224 km, traversing rather dull, dry shrub and parkland country, passing small hotels at Omitara and Witvlei (where the beer is at least wet and cold), and thereafter reaching the town of ...

GOBABIS

A place which might aptly be described as a modern cow town, *Gobabis* (place of discussion) lies on the banks of the *Nossob* (black) River. It is the centre of a vast ranching district bordering Botswana, with the Kalahari just over the eastern horizon. Dawns and sunsets are rich with colours of a dusty land. A sunbaked little town, Gobabis had its origin in 1856 as the site of a Rhenish mission station. In 1895 the Germans established a military post there to guard the eastern frontier. On 6 November 1930 a railway line was opened connecting it to Windhoek. This stimulated a considerable local industry in the dispatch of beef cattle to many distant markets.

Gobabis received its first village management board in 1934, and in 1944 it became a municipality. The present population is 6 500. Today it is the site of a creamery, a point of departure for trading and hunting trips into Botswana, and a major dispatch station for cattle.

From Gobabis the B6 road continues (mainly with gravel surface) for 125 km to the border of Botswana. Beyond that point four-wheel-drive vehicles are recommended.

THE ROAD TO THE NORTH

From Windhoek, the B1 tarmac road to the north travels down the valley between the Eros and Khomas ranges, through a well-wooded parkland. This is a pleasant journey with many views of the mountains and numerous trees of a most graceful shape. The Swakop River is bridged after 64 km. Although it has only an intermittent flow, this is one of the most important watercourses in the territory. Its broad, tree-lined course can carry turbulent floods during the rainy seasons.

Three kilometres beyond the bridge there is a turn-off eastwards leading circuitously to Gobabis and (10 km away) the Fritz Gaerdes Nature Park, created by Fritz Gaerdes, a nature lover. The park contains a fine collection of indigenous plants.

One kilometre beyond this turn-off is a turn-off stretching westwards to the hot springs of Gross-Barmen. A further kilometre (69 km from Windhoek) takes the road into the town of ...

OKAHANDJA

This town is pleasantly situated on the banks of a tributary of the Swakop River. The stream is known (because of its sandy bed) as *oKahandja* (the large sand flats), from which the town received its name. The site of the town has always been attractive to human beings and has played an important part in the stormy history of this part of Africa. The Hereros made the place their tribal centre, and the graves of their early chiefs – Tjamuaha Maharero, Samuel Maharero and Friederich Maharero – may be seen beneath the trees in the municipal gardens.

In 1872 the Rhenish Missionary Society established a station at Okahandja, and the attractive and interesting church building still stands. Traders were drawn to the area and in 1894 the Germans established a garrison there, building a fort. It is accepted that the town was founded on that date.

On 21 December 1901 the narrow-gauge railway from Swakopmund on the coast to Okahandja was opened. The original railway station building is still in use. In January 1904 the war with the Herero people broke out. The inhabitants of Okahandja sheltered in the fort while shops and homes were looted and destroyed. They were besieged until 27 January 1904 when a relief force reached the town. The Hereros were defeated in a battle on the slopes of Kaiserkop and driven away from Okahandja.

Today Okahandja is a prosperous centre for ranching, and has a population of 8 000. A large creamery and meat-packing plant as well as other industries are situated in the town. Biltong locally produced by the Closwa factory is particularly renowned. Most travellers pause long enough in Okahandja at least to stock up with supplies of this delicacy. The town, set in a natural parkland, is a pleasant staging post for travellers. A privately run zoo and tea-room, situated on the northern outskirts of the town on the main road to Otjiwarongo, is open to the public daily from 08h00 to 17h30.

Each year on the last Sunday in August, the Herero people stage a memorial service dedicated to their former chiefs. Visitors are welcome to watch the procession, with the women superbly dressed in their Victorian-style dresses and the men mainly in uniform. Each grave is visited and the people take turns to touch the tombstones while prayers are said to the great leaders of the past.

The Von Bach Dam, with a capacity of 49,9 million cubic metres of water, is situated 10 km south-east of the town and, in a setting of a nature reserve, provides opportunities for recreation. There is fishing, water sports and a caravan park.

At both the exit and entrance to Okahandja the Mbangura woodcarvers' co-operative and the municipality have set up craft markets with a wonderful variety of carvings and artefacts. Some of the stall holders are equipped with cellphones and shipping schedules to allow customers to arrange dispatch of purchases to any address in the world.

GROSS-BARMEN

The hot springs and holiday resort of Gross-Barmen lie 24 km along a tarmac road which turns off 1 km from Okahandja on the main Windhoek road. Originally, this was a Rhenish mission station established in 1844 on a site known to the Hereros as *oTjikango* (the warm water depressions) but renamed *Neu-Barmen* by the missionaries, after the headquarters of their society in Germany. The mission was eventually abandoned in 1904. After lying in ruins for many years, it was taken over by the South West African administration, with the named changed to Gross-Barmen. It has been developed into a major recreational resort with bungalows, a caravan park, shop, restaurant, an outdoor tepid swimming-pool and an enclosed thermal pool with private baths for invalids.

The spring, rising from a depth of 2 500 m, reaches the surface at the rate of 6 700 *l* an hour at 65°C. The water has a high fluoride content and also contains half a gram of Glauber salts in every 500 ml, the effect of which is the same as Epsom salts. The chemical content of the spring consists of 363 mg sodium per litre; 357 mg sulphate per litre; 127 mg chloride per litre; 100 mg silica per litre; 22 mg potassium per litre; and 8,5 mg fluoride per litre. The water is extremely clear and smells of hydrogen sulphide. The temperature of the water in the thermal bath is cooled to 41°C. An earth dam filled with fish is the home of a multitude of birds. Palm trees, graves and ruins are all that remain of the original mission. Yellow, orange and red varieties of *Aloe hereroensis* flourish in the area.

From Okahandja the B1 road continues northwards. The B2 road leading westwards to the coast branches off on the outskirts of the town. The B1 road passes the old municipal rest camp and the zoo and then proceeds across an immense, flat plain covered in light bush where an occasional hill rises island-like from what is superb ranching country.

After 47 km there is a gravel turn-off to the west which stretches 121 km to Kalkfeld, passing on the way (after 91 km) a turn-off leading to some dinosaur footprints. After a further 10 km, there is a turn-off leading for 15 km to the private game reserve of the well-known professional hunter and conservationist, Jan Oelofse, whose clients secure their trophies in a spacious shooting area stocked with a considerable variety of game.

The main B1 road continues northwards past the turn-off to Kalkfeld. The road passes the rural centre of Sukses, 104 km from Okahandja. To the west of this rural centre looms a landmark likely to attract the male eye – remarkable twin heights resembling a well-shaped bosom. The mounds actually suggest another shape to the Hereros who know them as *omaTako* (the buttocks). At 153 km from Okahandja the road reaches a tarmac turn-off (C22) leading eastwards to the Waterberg Plateau Park and the Herero administrative centre with the rather odd-sounding name of *oKakarara* (the resting-place). To reach the Waterberg Plateau Park, follow the C22 tarmac for 41 km to a travel turn-off leading for 19 km to the entrance of the park.

THE WATERBERG PLATEAU PARK

The Waterberg is the relic of a sandstone layer which once covered a substantial part of Namibia. The sandstone was eroded away, leaving only fragments scattered over the plain like pieces of a jigsaw puzzle on the floor of a children's playroom. The Waterberg remnant of this lost landscape is a flat-topped plateau 48 km long and 8 km to 16 km wide. The Waterberg Plateau Park comprises 40 549 ha of this sandstone pile. It is a well-watered area covered in trees and providing a home for numerous birds and, in former years, several species of mammals such as kudu, eland, gemsbok, sable and roan antelope, tsessebe, buffalo, cheetah, leopard and white rhino.

The highest point of the Waterberg is the 7 500 m Karakuwisa Mountain on the northern side. The cliff faces of the plateau are spectacularly eroded and vividly coloured. Lichen in several colours grows on the red sandstone. In places the resulting effect is almost unreal. The sandstone was laid down about 200 million years ago. Judging by fossil relics and tracks of dinosaurs, it was a congenial home for numerous forms of life, even in those early years.

Bushman, Damara and Herero tribespeople eventually discovered the attractions of the area and settled at such places as the fountain of *oTjozondjuba* (the place of calabashes) on the southern side of the Waterberg, and in the vicinity of Karakuwisa on the northern side. Engravings of the tracks of wild animals may still be seen in the rocks surrounding the water-hole.

Europeans also settled in the area. On 11 August 1904 the Battle of Waterberg at Otjozondjuba took place, when the Germans defeated the Hereros. In 1908 a police post was established at Otjozondjuba, the depot building being known as the Rasthaus, which remained in use until 1955. It was then maintained as a guest-house for tourists until 1966, whereafter it fell into decay.

The Waterberg was first proclaimed a game reserve in 1928 but deproclaimed shortly afterwards. In 1956 the Karakuwisa Mountain was proclaimed a natural monument. In 1972 the whole plateau was proclaimed a game reserve, particularly to serve as a home for eland. Many of the animal species originally indigenous to the area are now being reintroduced.

Of particular interest in the Waterberg are smaller species such as dik-dik, klipspringer and steenbok. Cape hunting dogs, black-backed jackals and lynx are common, while bushbabies are numerous, especially in the palm and fruit trees planted at the Rasthaus. The rare Alpine swift breeds in the cliffs. At Karakuwisa there is a large colony of Cape vultures, which find their most northerly home here.

Each year on the second Sunday of August the Battle of Waterberg is commemorated at the graveyard at the battle site near the Rasthaus. There is a fine hiking trail from the camp (open throughout the year) to the plateau summit. The park is a major tourist and recreational area, as well as being a grand piece of conservation. There are bungalows and sites for campers and caravans. There is a shop, restaurant and swimming pool. The entrance gate is open from 07h00 to 19h00 for day visitors.

From the turn-off to the Waterberg Plateau Park the main tarmac B1 road continues for 28,5 km and then reaches ...

OTJIWARONGO

An important rail and road junction, *oTjiwarongo* (the pleasant place) is the centre for a considerable ranching area. Built on a gentle slope amid undulating plains, with the Waterberg range to the east, Otjiwarongo is a modern and pleasant town of 11 000 people. It had its beginning after the Herero War in 1904. In that year a police post was established on the site of the town. Two years later the narrow-gauge railway from the coast to the Otavi copper mine reached Otjiwarongo. It became a staging post and transhipment station for goods destined for Outjo and Damaraland.

In 1907 a town was laid out around the railway station and police post. On 26 June 1915 South African troops occupied the town. Under the new administration it became the seat of a magistrate. On 1 May 1939 Otjiwarongo became a municipality.

OUTJO AND THE ROAD TO ETOSHA

From Otjiwarongo the C38 tarmac road leads in a north-westerly direction over gently undulating savanna ranching country. After 69 km the road reaches the town of ...

OUTJO

This area was named by the Hereros *oHutjo* (the little hills). The town lies in a cluster of low hillocks. It is a clean and modern rural centre of 5 500 people, the terminus of a branch railway built from Otjiwarongo in 1915. It is a staging post for tourists travelling to the Etosha National Park and exploring the remarkable scenery west of the town in Damaraland and past Khorixas.

From Outjo, the tarmac road C38 leads north-westwards. After 1,5 km there is a gravel turn-off to Khorixas and the Skeleton Coast and after 10 km a tarmac turn to *Kamanjab* (place of stones). For a further 85 km the road continues through savanna ranching country and 95 km from Outjo it reaches the Andersson Gate entrance to the Etosha National Park.

OTJIWARONGO TO THE NORTH

The tarmac north road (B1) continues out of the town in a slightly easterly direction. Keeping close to the railway line, it crosses savanna ranching country, with the trees becoming taller and denser to the north. To the east may be seen the ridge of the Waterberg where many fine farms – citrus, cattle and general – prosper on the ample supplies of water from mountain streams. After 115 km the road reaches the railway junction of ...

OTAVI

The town of *oTavi* (the gushing water), with its population of 2 500, is overlooked by the 2 149 m high Otavi Mountains. Well-watered and fertile, with a rich and varied mineralisation, the area has always been desirable to human beings. Ovambo, Bushmen and Herero contended for the area over a long period, with many barbarous conflicts and murders taking place. A pile of stones close to the railway line at Ondjora is still pointed out as being the grave of the Herero chief, Nandavetu, who was killed by a poisoned arrow during a fight over the possession of one of the copper outcrops in the area.

Copper, lead, zinc, cadmium, vanadium and germanium are found in this area. Active mining in Otavi itself is no longer carried out. The town is slightly decayed, although it remains the shopping centre for outlying mines. A few kilometres from the town, along a gravel road, is the Khorab memorial which marks the place where German troops surrendered to South African forces on 9 July 1915.

From Otavi the B8 tarmac road branches off eastwards and runs through a beautiful parkland with the high ridges of the rocky and richly coloured Otavi Mountains lying on either side. After 40 km the road passes the copper mine of *Kombat (oKombahe tijnene,* the large drinking place of the giraffe). Jacaranda and poinciana trees grow well in the valley. Spring and early summer are made particularly beautiful by their blossoms. There is a gravel turn-off to Rietfontein after 58 km. The Uitkomst Research Station of the Department of Agricultural and Technical Services lies beside the road 72 km from Otavi. At 86 km there is a gravel turn-off which leads to the remarkable Hoba meteorite. After 92 km the road reaches the town of ...

GROOTFONTEIN

This town takes its name from the Afrikaans translation of the original Bushman name, *Gei-ous* (great fountain). *Grootfontein* lies on the slope of a hill and is shaded by magnificent avenues of flowering trees such as jacaranda. Bougainvillaeas grow prolifically and a vivid display of colour may be seen in September and October.

European prospectors and explorers such as Sir Francis Galton and Charles Andersson observed the African people mining and trading for copper in the area as early as 1842. Several outcrops of ore were found in the area of the Otavi Mountains. Farmers were also attracted by the fertile ground, plentiful water and ranching possibilities. In 1892 the Thirstland Trekkers – families who had crossed the Kalahari from the Transvaal – planned to create in this area a republic named Upingtonia, but nothing was established.

In 1892 the South West Africa Company was floated in London to work several concessions in the territory. It was decided to create a town to serve the mines and ranching country around the Otavi Mountains. The site of Grootfontein was selected where a small German military garrison had already been established at a place known as *oTjivanda Tongwe* (the place of the leopard). The town grew up around this stronghold.

Grootfontein was laid out in 1907 and a narrow-gauge railway was built to it from Otavi in April 1908. The place expanded into a shopping, educational and administrative centre, with social life made lively by the presence of an official distillery on the farm *Gemsboklaagte* producing an alcoholic spirit from makalani and mealies. This drink became famous amongst the miners and ranchers. In 1933 Grootfontein elected its first village management board and in September 1947 it became a municipality. Its present population is 9 400.

From Grootfontein the B8 road leads north-eastwards for 264 km to *Rundu* (high place), the administrative centre for the Kavango tribe and the gateway for journeys into the Caprivi strip. The Berg Aukas vanadium mine is reached from a turn-off 30 km along this road from Grootfontein. After 68 km there is another turn-off C44, leading eastwards for 222 km to Tsumkwe, an administrative centre in an area inhabited by Bushmen.

TSUMKWE AND THE LAST REALM OF THE HUNTER-GATHERERS

The C44 road which branches eastwards from the B8 road 68 km from Grootfontein, takes the traveller into the savanna world of baobab trees, acacia thorn trees, a diverse wildlife and an opportunity to meet the hunter-gatherer people in their retreat to the wilderness. The journey is a fascinating, very worthwhile venture, a journey where you touch the beating heart of this most ancient continent of Africa.

The road to Tsumkwe is well-used and passable at all seasons. From Tsumkwe the D3312 road branches north-westwards and leads to the 384 000 ha Khaudum Game Park, a savanna parkland bordering Botswana and the Kalahari sandveld. It was proclaimed in 1989. Roan antelope, giraffe, gemsbok, tsessebe, hartebeest, eland and reedbuck are residents. Elephants, lions, leopards, spotted hyenas, side-striped and black-backed jackals and wild dogs are common. About 320 species of birds live in the trees and grass, including varieties such as copperytailed and Senegal coucals, Bradfield's hornbills, rufousbellied tits, blackfaced babblers and sharptailed starlings. There are two small rest camps, Sikereti and Khaudum. The park is remote and no entry is allowed without reservations. Four-wheel drive vehicles are essential with a minimum of two vehicles per group and a maximum of 12 people per rest camp.

Three groups of the hunter-gatherer people inhabit this north-eastern part of Namibia, the Haixom, !Kung and Mbarankwengo. A four-wheel drive vehicle is essential to visit them.

THE CAPRIVI STRIP

In the grand imperial manner of the time, Britain, in 1893 ceded this territory, originally part of Botswana, to Germany in exchange for favours elsewhere. Empires were being formed, maps were being drawn in Europe with neat straight lines through the territory of minor nations whose rights and opinions were not much considered.

The Germans named their new possession the *Caprivi Zipfel* (Caprivi point). The eastern tip of this territorial point at Kazungula consists of a 45 metre long joint boundary with Botswana, Zambia and Zimbabwe on the Zambezi River which the Germans thought could become a waterway to the sea. They overlooked such obstructions as the Victoria Falls and its gorges. The 45 m long boundary is considered to be the shortest international boundary line in the world.

General Count Georg Leo von Caprivi di Caprara di Montecuccoli, the German soldier and politician who succeeded Bismarck as chancellor in 1890, gave his name to this curious narrow strip of tropical Africa.

From Rundu the B8 road, mainly tarmac, leads eastwards through this territorial strip which is mainly only 50 km wide except at the eastern side where it widens to double the average width to form the Liambezi area, named after a lake, with the oddly named *Katima Mulilo* (kill the fire) as its administrative centre 525 km from Rundu. The name comes from the evening winds which sweep up the Zambezi and blow out cooking fires on the river banks.

Throughout its 600 km length the Caprivi strip penetrates a part of Africa essentially dominated by water. From the highlands of Angola a vast amount of water deposited by heavy rain seeks a way to reach the distant sea. Rivers and streams follow routes of least topographical resistance. The central continental divide deflects them east to feed either the Kunene, flowing west to the Atlantic Ocean or the Zambezi flowing east to the Indian Ocean. In the centre, a considerable volume of water persists in flowing southwards until further rights of passage are denied and the water is absorbed into the great swamplands of northern Botswana and the Caprivi strip.

The B8 road leads eastwards close to the Kavango River. The river, named after the chief of the Mbukushu tribe who were the first to settle there, forms the frontier with Angola. On the north side of the river lies the Mucusso National Park. In the Caprivi strip lies the 30 000 ha Mahango Game Reserve, notable for its herds of elephant and red lechwe, all living well on a flood plain along with buffalo, sable and roan antelope, bushbuck, reedbuck, tsessebe and vast numbers of aquatic birds. The Mahango Game Reserve is easily accessible for normal vehicles. There is no accommodation but there is a pleasant picnic site at Kwetche. There are crocodiles, hippos and bilharzia in the swamps and rivers. Swimming and boating are prohibited.

Twenty-five kilometres north of the Mahango Game Reserve, at the *Popa* (waterfall), really a rapid over a ledge of rock in the Kavango River, there is a rest camp and privately run guest lodge. These resorts provide bases for visits to the Mahango Game Reserve. The reserve was proclaimed in 1989. There is a small game park at the Popa rapids with good birdwatching opportunities.

East of Popa, the B8 road crosses the Kavango River and for the next 191 km leads through the 5 715 square kilometre Caprivi Game Park. There are as yet no tourist facilities in this park and visitors are restricted to the main road. Off the main road the territory is sandy, lacking in surface water and mostly flat but with dunes up to 60 m in height. The vegetation is dominated by trees such as bushwillow species, copalwood, seringa, teak and wild raisin. It is well populated with animal life, including about 340 bird species.

The eastern boundary of the Caprivi Game Park is the Kwando River. Across the river the road passes through the small settlement of Kongola where petrol and some supplies are available. The road now enters what is known as Caprivi East, with its administration centre at Katima Mulilo 110 km further along the B8 road. Katima Mulilo is a pleasant and picturesque little town on the south bank of the Zambezi River. It is a great place for fishing with more than two dozen fish species frequenting the river. Tiger fish up to 12 kg in weight provide powerful challenges to anglers. Canoes, boats and fishing tackle are available for hire. The well-appointed river boat, *Zambezi Queen,* has its base at Katima Mulilo and cruises the Zambezi and Chobe rivers. Wildlife, especially elephants and birds abound in an environment of plentiful food and water. Elephants wander into the town itself on occasions and are always in the vicinity. Katima Mulilo is the centre for a considerable industry in carving. With ample supplies of suitable wood, the local people of East Caprivi, closely related to the Lozi of neighbouring Zambia, have a great talent for carving. Their work finds its way into many curio shops and art collections all over the world. It is lavishly displayed in Katima Mulilo. There are several guest-houses, private lodges, rest camps and other places of accommodation in Katima Mulilo. It is a good base for visiting the various game parks in the vicinity. Victoria Falls is within easy reach, and also the Chobe National Park across the nearby border with Botswana.

Malarial fever, bilharzia, crocodiles, hippos, lions and other predators must be accepted as always present in the area. Precautions must be taken to avoid unpleasant effects. There is an aircraft landing strip at Kasika. Motor vehicles of all kinds can be hired, with or without drivers. There is an office of the Namibia Ministry of Environment and Tourism in Katima Mulilo.

From Katima Mulilo a road leads south-eastwards for 60 km to Ngoma Bridge on the Chobe River frontier with Botswana. Immediately across the river lies the Chobe National Park (see Chapter Forty). The Chobe River is also known as the Linyanti. It and the Kavango feed vast quantities of water into the great wetlands of Botswana. On the Caprivi side of the border these rivers also feed wetlands. The population of wildlife is prodigious. Elephants, buffalo, roan and sable antelope, kudu, impala, oribi, Burchell's zebra, sitatunga and red lechwe may be seen grazing on the rich grasslands. Hippo, crocodiles and others live in the waterways. Birdwatchers have a particularly wonderful experience in such parks as the Mamilli National Park with its 32 000 ha of channels, reed beds, lakes and tree-covered islands. This is the largest wetland conservancy in Namibia. The park lies in the south-western end of the eastern Caprivi. During the dry season the park is accessible but in a normal rainy season 80 per cent of the area is flooded. There are two main islands in the Linyanti/Kwando River. These islands, Nkasa and Lupala, can be reached by road but only in the dry season. Bird life on these islands is magnificent.

GROOTFONTEIN TO TSUMEB AND THE HOBA METEORITE

From Grootfontein the tarmac C42 road leads north-westwards for 64 km to Tsumeb. The journey traverses a fine parkland of trees and grass with high hills. Seven kilometres from Grootfontein there is a gravel turn-off to the south-west which leads to the Hoba meteorite 21 km away. This meteorite – containing 82,4 per cent iron, 16,4 per cent nickel, and 0,76 per cent cobalt, with slight traces of copper, chromium, carbon, sulphur, germanium, gallium and iridium – was found in 1920 by Mr J H Brits, owner of the farm *Hoba* (hopeful). It was proclaimed a national monument in 1955 and is said to be the largest metal meteorite ever found. The estimated weight is 80 tons and its age about 80 000 years.

OTAVI TO TSUMEB

The main B1 road to the north from Otavi climbs and twists through a jumble of hills covered with a varied collection of tall, elegantly shaped trees. After 64 km of pleasant travel through this parkland, the road reaches one of the most famous mines in the world ...

TSUMEB

The town of Tsumeb has grown on the site of the extraordinary mine known to the Herero as *oTjisume* (the place of algae) because the surface outcrops of highly coloured copper ore reminded them of the algae covering stagnant pools. Bushmen converted this name into *Sumeb* and Europeans made it *Tsumeb*.

Tsumeb, with its population of 13 500, is a real garden town. It came into being with the development of the mine and became a municipality in 1965. Jacaranda, poinciana, bougainvillaea and various flowering trees, shrubs and creepers grow to perfection in the area. The streets are shaded and beautified by them. The visitor is advised to explore the side streets in the residential part of the town. Spring in Tsumeb is something to see.

The town is dominated by the mine and its headgear which towers over the main street. The mine produced large quantities of copper, zinc and lead and has been described by the American Mineralogical Record as the world's greatest mineral locality. In the one mine, over 184 different minerals have been found. To collectors all over the world, Tsumeb is the source of innumerable beautiful and almost unreal specimens of rocks, crystals and gemstones.

This diverse mineralisation originated in a volcanic pipe or throat which was filled to the brim with an astonishing richness of material. The pipe was first discovered in prehistoric times and worked by several different ethnic groups. When first located, the ore body protruded above the surface in the form of a low hill composed of minerals rather than rock, and of brilliantly variegated colours.

European explorers and prospectors were informed of this dazzling outcrop. On 12 January 1893 a prospector, Matthew Rogers, working for the South West Africa Company, reached the outcrop. In a report to his company, he stated: *'In the whole of my experience I have never seen such a sight as was presented before my view at Tsumeb, and I very much doubt that I shall ever see such another in any other locality'*.

Rogers negotiated with the local tribe for rights to the outcrop and began a detailed assessment of the quantity of ore, its nature and the viability of a mine in so remote a place. Financing and planning of the mine took several years. In 1900 the company formed to work concessions over the area, the Otavi Mining and Railroad Company, sent a party of 33 miners under Christopher James to commence mining. Two shafts were sunk into the hill of copper and a hint of the wonders lying beneath the surface was revealed. In the first cross-cut, a vein of pure chalcocite was encountered running through rich galena. Such was the pattern of ore in the volcanic pipe. As the miners worked into the pipe, they constantly encountered astonishing mixtures, rich veins and unexpected 'jewellery boxes' of sensationally beautiful rarities.

On 28 December 1900 the first shipment of ore was sent by ox-wagon to Swakopmund. The mine was developed in the teeth of tremendous transport difficulties while a narrow-gauge railway was constructed from the coast. The railway reached Tsumeb on 24 August 1906 and within twelve months the little narrow-gauge trains had carried 25 700 tons of ore to the coast.

Over the years, with setbacks caused by the First World War, depressions and political troubles, the Tsumeb mine continued its operations. In 1946, at the end of the Second World War, the mine and other assets of the Otavi Company were put up for sale by the Custodian of Enemy Property. A syndicate (the Tsumeb Corporation) was formed to buy the mine. It consisted of the Newmont Mining Corporation; American Metal Co; South West African Co; Selection Trust; British South Africa Co; Union Corporation and the Okiep Copper Co. The purchase price was a little over £1 000 000. The new management recommissioned the mine and developed it to a state of high productivity, with levels being worked below 1 000 m.

Drilling and testing have revealed the extraordinary geology of the mine. It is a classic example of an ore pipe. Such pipes or throats have, at various times in the Earth's relatively not-too-distant geological past, been blown up from the depths, probably as escape vents for gases under enormous pressure. Along with the gases, molten matter also surged upwards, as though taking the opportunity to escape from the infernal regions at the core of the Earth. This molten material cooled and solidified in the throat. As happens in the strange lottery of creation, among the contents of this throat was a phenomenal proportion of economic minerals; copper, lead, zinc, silver, cadmium and germanium. During the past 70 years about R700 million worth of these minerals have been extracted from the throat. If the Tsumeb mine produced only these economic minerals, it would be considered wonderful and fully equal to the celebrated Comstock lode in America. But added to the already varied economic minerals is a dazzling variety of secondary minerals created as a result of the infiltration of water and several different gases into the solid body of the throat.

The infiltrations, in a manner quite unpredictable, reacted upon the complex mother lode in the throat. At different levels, this reaction produced some of the most startling and beautiful crystals and oxides ever found. Some of these minerals were found in quantity, others in such minute amounts that they are just sufficient to be identified. Collectors of mineral specimens throughout the world regard Tsumeb as the single principal source of so vast a range of gorgeous and unusual rocks that anything near a complete collection would be a prize of incalculable value. Tsumeb can be justifiably listed among the greatest natural wonders on Earth. Of the 184 different minerals so far identified from the Tsumeb mine, 10 of them occur nowhere else in the world.

Probably the most complete collection of Tsumeb mineral specimens is in the Museum of Natural History of the Smithsonian Institute in Washington. A fine collection of specimens is also exhibited in the museum in Tsumeb, along with photographs and records of the mine since its beginning. There is also a collection of cannon retrieved from the sink-hole of Otjikoto and other places. The museum is open on weekdays 09h00 to 12h00 and 15h00 to 18h00; Saturdays 15h00 to 18h00. The museum was created by Mrs Ilse Schatz, whose enthusiasm saw the preservation of many interesting exhibits.

An open-air cultural museum has also been created in Tsumeb. Each of Namibia's cultural groups will build their own village with huts displaying traditional skills and artefacts.

Fifteen kilometres west of Tsumeb stand the masts and buildings of the Jonathan Zenneck Research Station of the Max Planck Institute for Aeronomy of Göttingen in Germany. The research station is named in honour of one of the great pioneers of radiophysics.

From Tsumeb the tarmac B1 road continues north-westwards across a tree-covered plain on which the Tsumeb Corporation established a considerable agricultural industry, producing citrus, timber, vegetables, meat and dairy products to feed the workers of the mine and the residents of Tsumeb. A herd of 200 Swiss and Simmentaler cows provided milk, while 7 000 head of cattle were ranched to provide meat.

Much of the water for this agriculture and (until 1912, for use in Tsumeb) comes from a great sink-hole in the dolomite which is passed by the main road 20 km from Tsumeb. This sink-hole is known as Lake *oTjikoto* (the deep hole) and was formed when the ceiling of a huge cavity in the dolomite rock collapsed. The lake was originally plumbed in 1851 to a depth of 55 m by the first Europeans to visit it, Sir Francis Galton and Charles Andersson. Pumping operations have reduced the depth to 36 m. The water is clear and well populated by fish of the *Tilapia guinasana* species. These fish were introduced to the lake in the 1930s and were brought from Lake Guinas 15 km away. Their origin in that lake is uncertain, but they were possibly deposited there by an ancient flood spreading over the plain. The fish are derived from the common tilapia or vleikurper.

Another fish found in the lake is an odd little mouth breeder with a name considerably larger than itself, *Pseudocrenoolabrus philander dispersus*. This dwarf bream was resident in the lake before the tilapia were introduced. It has a habit of protectively carrying its eggs and fry in its mouth. The dwarf bream live at the bottom of the lake while the tilapia live near the surface.

During the 1914 war, the Germans dumped a number of artillery pieces and transport vehicles into Lake Otjikoto. They were later retrieved by the South African forces. One of these vehicles, an ammunition wagon, is on display in the Alte Feste Museum in Windhoek. In 1927 the postal assistant of Tsumeb, Johannes Cook, drowned while swimming in the lake. His body was never recovered, giving rise to a story that there was a treacherous whirlpool in the lake. This has never been proved.

A little over 6 km north-west of Lake Otjikoto, the tarmac B1 road passes a gravel turn-off leading for 24 km through ranching country to the sink-hole known as Otjiguinas. This sink-hole is notable for its beautiful setting, with the rock faces around it covered in aloes which flower in May. The water is used to irrigate the adjoining farmlands. The sink-hole is said to be about 200 m deep and the water is clear and fresh. It is populated by *Tilapia guinasana* species of fish.

At 49 km north-east of the turn-off to Otjiguinas (75 km from Tsumeb) there is a turn-off from the main tarmac road leading for 24 km past (after 13 km) the *Mokuti* (in the bush) lodge, and then on to the Von Lindequist gate entrance to the Etosha National Park. Beyond this turn-off the B1 road continues for 185 km to Ondangwa in Ovamboland. From there it is 35 km to Oshakati and 73 km to the border of Angola.

THE ETOSHA NATIONAL PARK

The Etosha National Park conserves 22 270 square kilometres of savanna country, including the Etosha Pan itself – a vast shallow depression 130 km by 50 km in extent – which gives the park its name. This is one of the grandest and most important of all the national parks and game sanctuaries in Africa. The pan alone would be worth conserving as a classic example of its kind. It is a great, ghostly white lake dazzling with heatwaves and mirages for most of the year, filling from December to April with (at the most) a metre of slushy, muddy, algae-rich goo. This annual inundation, fed by the overflow of flooding rivers which carry the run-off of rains in Angola to the sea, and supported by 400 mm of local rainfall in the same period, attracts to the pan countless waterfowl, including pelicans and flamingos of both greater and lesser species. Depending on the extent of the floods, the pan dries out in about March, leaving a hard floor white with salt, soda and other chemicals. As the waMbo name *eTosha* indicates, it becomes once again the great, dry ghostly-white place of mirages.

The verges of the lake are well-treed and grassed, with several springs providing water for wild animals. The animals which live permanently around the pan number approximately 30 000 blue wildebeest, 25 000 springbok, 23 000 zebra, 5 000 kudu, 3 000 hartebeest, 3 000 oryx, 2 600 eland, 450 giraffe, 2 000 elephants, 260 lions, 20 black rhinos, and numerous smaller creatures. During the dry winter season considerable herds of game animals move into the area, attracted by the water and grazing.

Bird life is prodigious, with 325 species identified so far, including many lively little creatures such as the crimson-breasted shrike (the bird emblem of the territory), sometimes known as the 'German flag' because of its black, red and white colouring.

The Etosha National Park lies on approximately the same latitude as the Hwange National Park in Zimbabwe. It is its twin in atmosphere and in the magic of its game watering-pans and springs which, flavoured by various mineral salts such as lime, are very palatable to wild animals. The wise tourist simply settles himself comfortably at a shady site overlooking one of these watering-places. There, fortified by assorted refreshments and a good book with which to occupy any dull moments (there are not likely to be many), the tourist waits for action to come to him, as it surely will. This strategy is preferable to bumping about on long, hot and dusty roads, endlessly searching for some excitement which can be as elusive as the mirages on the pan.

Among the most famous of the watering-places in the Etosha National Park is the Ombika water-hole near the Andersson Gate, and Rietfontein near Halali, where the Thirstland Trekkers camped and hunted for a while in 1876. They left a few graves behind them there, including that of Mrs J E M Alberts, wife of the trek leader Gert Alberts. Other water-holes include Goas and Okevi near Namutoni and Andoni on the extreme north-eastern side of Etosha Pan. This water-hole is fed by a powerful fountain said to have been opened by a prospector searching for oil. It attracts vast numbers of zebra, oryx, wildebeest and springbok.

There are three tourist camps in the park. The camp at which the headquarters are stationed is called *Okaukuejo* (from *oKakwiyo*, place of the fertile women) and is 18 km north of the Andersson gate entrance. Dominated by a castle-like water tower which serves as an observation point, this is a substantial camp with a well laid-out complex of bungalows, caravan and camping sites, garages, restaurant, shop, community rooms, museum, swimming-pool and a floodlit water-hole enabling visitors to view the game at night from the comfort of the camp. Okaukuejo started as a veterinary post created by the Germans during a rinderpest epidemic in 1897. In 1901 a small fort was built there as a military stronghold, but has long since vanished. From Okaukuejo the south-western side of the park may be conveniently explored, including the strangely localised *Sprokieswoud* (enchanted forest) of *Moringa ovafolia* trees. These are the 'upside down' trees which fable says were weeds thrown out of the garden of Paradise. They fell to Earth upside down and, embedded in the ground, simply continued to grow with their roots pointing towards the sky.

Seventy-seven kilometres east of Okaukuejo lies the central camp of *Halali*, said to have taken its name from a German hunting camp positioned on the site in former years. At the end of each hunting season the Germans blew a traditional end-of-season *halali* on their bugle. This sound, denoting the end of all hunts and declaring peace between man and wild animals, is surely an apt name for a camp in a game sanctuary. Halali is a magnificent modern camp shaded by mopane trees, with bungalows, a restaurant, shop, garage and swimming-pool.

There is an excellent viewsite on the shores of the Etosha Pan north of Halali camp where a road is constructed for a short distance on to the floor of the pan. The turning-point reveals a tremendous panorama over the pan and its shores. The surface of the pan is a remarkable spectacle when it is dry and patterned into innumerable fragments.

The third tourist camp in Etosha is Namutoni, 74 km east of Halali. This is the classic camp of the park, made famous by the presence of the beautiful *beau geste* type fort built by the Germans as a police outpost.

The history of Namutoni is well displayed in the museum which is housed in part of the building. Initially only a strong spring bubbled up there from a swampy, reed-grown morass in a limestone basin. This spring was known to the waMbo as *oMutjamatunda* (high landmark). Travellers regularly stopped there. The first Europeans known to visit it were Charles Andersson and Sir Francis Galton. Others followed, and the waMbo name of the place began to be distorted as the various visitors mispronounced and misspelt it. Eventually it became the *Namutoni* of today.

In 1897 the rinderpest livestock disease broke out. A veterinary cordon was established along the northern border of German territory. Namutoni and Okaukuejo both became posts. At the end of the outbreak, Namutoni was maintained as a police outpost and customs post from which trade with Ovamboland was supervised. In 1903 a small fort was built at Namutoni, consisting of a rectangular building of unbaked bricks, 10 m by 24 m in extent, with battlemented walls and towers erected on its eastern and western corners.

At the outbreak of the Herero rebellion on 11 January 1904, the waMbo chief, Netshale, joined the uprising. He sent 500 warriors under the command of Shivute to attack Namutoni. The garrison of the fort was not very considerable, a sergeant, a medical orderly and two privates (of whom one was down with rheumatic fever). Three local ranchers were also at the post seeking sanctuary for their livestock.

On 28 January 1904 at 06h00, two waMbo spies arrived at the water-hole to reconnoitre. An hour later three messengers approached the fort and announced that Shivute was on a hunting trip with his warriors and intended to visit the fort. At 09h30 the 'hunting party' arrived, well armed with Martini-Henry rifles plus 5 horses and about 30 riding oxen. While the main party rested at the watering-place, Shivute and a companion approached the fort and offered to exchange a riding ox for a sack of rice. The German sergeant agreed to the barter, but the ox was not produced. The warriors gradually drew nearer to the fort. Inside the fort the Germans prepared their weapons and made arrangements for a stout defence.

At 11h00, with a stentorian shout, the warriors suddenly jumped up and rushed at the fort. They stormed into the store-room under the western tower and started looting the place while others tried to shoot the defenders who were positioned on the battlements. The Germans opened fire on their attackers, and the waMbo, not wishing to be shot, retreated, carrying their loot with them and driving away the cattle and horses belonging to the three ranchers.

Retreating into cover the waMbo began firing at the defenders. A long shooting duel ensued, lasting until 15h30 that afternoon. The waMbo then retired northwards into the bush, leaving behind about 80 dead and wounded men. By that time, the defenders had a mere 150 rounds of ammunition left and their position was grave. With the waMbo out of firing range, they descended to the ground and abandoned the fort, retreating southwards.

The waMbo spent the night taking pot-shots at the deserted fort. On discovering at dawn that the place was empty, they looted it, set it on fire and departed for home without attempting to pursue the Germans. The seven Germans, half carrying their sick comrade, made their way southwards for fourteen hours until they reached the farmhouse of *Sandhup*, which had been abandoned by two of the ranchers. The building had been looted by Bushmen but it at least provided shelter. From there the Germans sent messengers to Grootfontein with news of what had taken place. A relief force reached them on 1 February 1904.

After the defeat of the Herero on 11 August 1904 in the Battle of Waterberg, a new garrison of 30 men was sent to Namutoni. They reached the place on 29 November 1904 and found it in total ruin. The surroundings were littered with the bones of the waMbo, broken up by various scavengers. The garrison included several marines who hoisted the flag of the imperial navy to the top of a tree. The marines remained until February 1905 when they were relieved by a military garrison which shortly afterwards was placed under the command of a wealthy Silesian nobleman, Count Wilhelm von Saurma-Jettsch.

It was this nobleman who dreamed up the idea of a gleaming white fort in the wilderness. Aided by his little garrison, in whose ranks there were masons, carpenters and other artisans, he designed and built the new Namutoni. They laboured in the sun, making air-dried bricks and bringing building materials by wagon through the bush from Karibib.

The count designed the fort as an irregular quadrangle, 60 m by 68 m with four towers and three gates. Accommodation for officers and men was provided inside. There was a kitchen, a cool room for provisions, some sheds, a bakery, smithy, gunsmith's workshop, joinery, wheelwright, and even a swimming-bath outside the fort.

On 1 February 1906 Namutoni became the administrative centre for a new district and the count was appointed as the first District Commissioner. Later that year, however, when the fort was almost complete, he returned to Germany on leave. He was replaced by Lieutenant Hans Kaufman who in turn was replaced by First Lieutenant Adolf Fischer, author of the book *Menschen und Tiere in Südwest Afrika (People and Animals in South West Africa)*, and a well-known figure in the history of conservation in Africa.

Fischer led a very happy life in Namutoni. His garrison, known as Machine Gun Platoon No 1, was connected by heliograph to the outside world. It was almost self-sufficient, having amongst its complement a mixed batch of artisans and gardeners, dairymen and transport men. The fort dominated one of the principal routes into Ovamboland, controlling customs, immigration and the movement of waMbo labourers travelling south to work on farms and mines.

On 22 March 1907, Lieutenant Fischer really came into his own. On that date, Dr F von Lindequist, the then Governor of South-West Africa, proclaimed a nature reserve around the Etosha Pan. Lieutenant Fischer became the first game warden, with his garrison acting as rangers. For three years Fischer busied himself in a study of the area. He escorted visiting parties of scientists, hunters and tourists. In July 1910 Fischer was transferred to Koës, in the Kalahari, Fischer Pan, a real metropolis of birds close to Namutoni, is named after him. Namutoni itself was transferred to the police, but on 1 April 1912 was completely abandoned for economic reasons. Only on 6 July 1915 was Namutoni reoccupied, this time by South African troops after the Germans were defeated.

From then on, the fort was only occupied occasionally and gradually became dilapidated. On 1 February 1938, lightning destroyed one of the towers and the whole place became so ramshackle that it was eventually decided to demolish it. Several organisations and individuals intervened to save the fort. Dr A Pienaar (well known as an author under the pseudonym of *Sangiro*) was appointed game warden of Etosha after the First World War. He and Dr Lemmer, founder of the South West African Historical Monuments Commission, and other influential individuals campaigned to raise public support while G Kraft, a well-known architect, inspected the place and made recommendations for its reconstruction.

On 15 February 1950 Namutoni was declared an Historical Monument. Funds were allocated by the Government to rehabilitate it and to convert it into a tourist camp. In 1957 the reconstructed building was opened to tourists. In the following year it was handed over to the Department of Nature Conservation and Tourism. Immaculately maintained, Namutoni is a delight to visitors and a unique show-piece in Southern Africa. Additional accommodation, a shop, garage, caravan park and swimming-pool have been built outside the fort. The original spring still surfaces next to the fort. The reed beds and surrounding trees are roosts for countless birds. Sunset at Namutoni is a superb spectacle of colour, enlivened by the excitement of the birds drinking, squabbling and enjoying a last flight around the waters before settling down for the night. Each dawn and sunset, a flag-raising and lowering ceremony is carried out on the fort, complete with bugle calls and national anthem.

Namutoni is situated 11 km from the Von Lindequist gate, which is connected to the main B1 Tsumeb–Ovamboland road. The Etosha National Park is open all year round.

The three camps of the Etosha National Park, Okaukuejo, Halali and Namutoni, offer a variety of accommodation, from camping sites to luxury bungalows. They are all of three-star grading. Namutoni is the oldest and Halali the newest. The restaurants vary, depending on chefs. Reservations must be made through the offices of Namibia Wildlife Resorts, Private Bag 13267, Windhoek 9000. Phone 0964 61 23-6975.

THE LAND OF THE PEOPLE FROM THE PLACE CALLED MBO

Beyond the turn-off to the Etosha National Park, the B1 road continues northwards and then northwestwards to enter the homeland of the most numerous ethnic group in Namibia, the people whose traditions tell that in about 1550 they migrated south from a legendary place named Mbo, in the region of the great lakes of Central Africa where they were known as the Ajamba. They found their way through all hazards to eventually settle in the area of northern Namibia now known as owaMbo. The 'o' in front of most of their place names simply means 'the'. The 'wa' means people, thus owaMbo (the Mbo people). An individual is *omwaMbo*.

There are eight separate tribal groups collectively known as ovaMbo. The two principal of these tribes are the Kwanyama and the Ndonga, both having their own dialects of the same language. The other six tribes are the Kwambi, Ngandjera, Mbalanhu, Kwaluthi and two small groups, the Nkolonkati and the Unda. Their social system is matrilineal. They make up nearly half the population of Namibia. They are hard-working, industrious people and great traders. Their wood carvings are artistic, as is their pottery and basketry. Agriculturally their homeland is poor but they cultivate pearl millet as their staple food along with grain sorghum (kaffir corn) and beans. They make an alcoholic beverage from the wild marula fruit. They keep cattle for milk while meat is obtained mainly from goats, fowls and pigs. They fish in the shallow lakelets left by the rainy season and in the watercourses known as *oshanas*. Men and women find employment as migrant workers in mines, industries and domestic labour in the rest of Namibia.

The principal administrative centre of the waMbo country is *oNdangwa* (the somewhat sour place) 178 km up the B1 road from the entrance to the Etosha National Park. Beyond this town the B1 road leads northwards for 63 km to *oShikango* (place of one pan) on the frontier of Angola in which country live people related to the waMbo.

From Ondangwa the C46 road leads north-westwards for 35 km to *oShakati* (the place in the middle) and then for 181 km to the 120 m high waterfall of *oRuwa hakana* (the hurrying of waters) in the Kunene River. The name of the waterfall has been corrupted to *Ruacana*. The river flows southwards from the well-watered highlands of Angola. Below the waterfall, the river turns eastwards to reach the sea. In this part of the journey the river provides the frontier between Namibia and Angola. From the Namibian side it is known as the *Kunene* (right arm) because the Herero people who migrated there from Central Africa described the river as being something like a strong right arm on the northern side of the arid land in which the nomadic Himba section of their people settled and named *oKaoko* (the left-hand side).

The banks of the Kunene River, compared to the rugged wilderness of the Kaoko, are green and pleasant, beautified by baobab and wild fig trees, makalani palms and countless smaller trees, flowering plants and shrubs. A gravel road runs along the verge of the south side of the river for 148 km to reach a second waterfall, the 60 m high Epupa Falls. Rapid-shooting boats make an adventurous journey between the two waterfalls. There is accommodation for visitors at both waterfalls.

The Kaoko country, now known as the Kunene Region, tempts many people to explore it in 4 × 4 vehicles. It is a complete wilderness. There should be at least two vehicles for each party. Black rhino and desert elephants manage to live in this seemingly impossible area, 30 000 square kilometres in extent. About 16 000 people, including the Himba nomads, live there along with a surprising number of birds and game animals. The Himbo are a likeable, handsome people who still enjoy a traditional lifestyle, notable for their dress, customs, hairstyles and their red colour resultant from use of red ochre rubbed into their skin as a defence against the relentless heat.

At least a glimpse of this unique country may be had from a normal vehicle by taking the gravel road C35 which branches south from the C46 road 19 km before that road reaches the small centre of Ruacana near the Falls. The C35 road leads south for 297 km, passing a turn-off to *Opuwo* (the place of sufficiency), the only settlement of note in the Himba country. The C35 road continues down the western boundary of the Etosha National Park and reaches the administrative centre of Kamangab. From there a tarmac road, C40, continues south-eastwards for 150 km to the town of Outjo, connected by train and tarmac road to Otjiwarongo on the main B1 north–south trunk road of Namibia. The return route from the Kunene River frontier provides an unforgettable ending to any tour of Namibia. Off this road, the Kunene/Kaoko region is for 4 × 4s only and rugged vehicles at that.

Chapter Forty-Five
NAMIBIA

The Central Areas

From Okahandja, 68 km from Windhoek up the B1 road to the north, the all-tarmac B2 road to the coast branches off immediately outside the commercial centre. It leads due west over undulating savanna country, a great place for kudu. Numerous signs along the way warn travellers to beware of these antelope, as their road sense is notably poor. After 62 km there is a turn leading southwards for 70 km to the old mission station with the pleasant name of *oTjimbingwe* (the place of refreshing water). Otjimbingwe, as the name is spelled today, was one of the first places in the interior of the territory to be settled by Europeans. The original powder-tower, built in 1872 by the Rhenish missionaries for defence purposes and still standing after being attacked on at least two dozen occasions, is an historical monument.

One kilometre beyond the turn-off to Otjimbingwe is a gravel turn-off north-west leading to Omaruru. The main tarmac road to this town branches off a further 46 km down the west road. Three kilometres further on (112 km from Okahandja), the B2 road reaches the town of ...

KARIBIB

This village, the name of which means the 'place of gari plants' (*Moraea* species), had its start as a narrow-gauge railway station built in 1900 on the farm owned by Otto Hälbich. He donated 6 ha of land for the station and it became a social centre for the district. It had an excellent restaurant, post office, first and second class lounges, accommodation for the stationmaster, postmaster, and other officials. Karibib was the halfway resting place for trains and passengers making the arduous journey from Swakopmund to Windhoek. Six hotels provided accommodation. A mission station was established in Karibib after the coming of the railway and the town developed as a ranching and mining centre. Marble of excellent quality is found in the district. Lithium and mica are also mined there, while gemstones such as aquamarines, citrines (golden topaz) and tourmalines are found in the pegmatites. Sydney Pieters, one of the world's leading authorities and dealers in gemstones, extracted superb tourmalines from the Neu-Schwaben Mine located near the town. These gems find their way into collections and jewellery shops all over the world. Growing in the area are the medicinal plants, *Harpagophytum procumbens* DC and *Harpagophytum zeyheri* Deene locally known as the *Teufels Kralle* (devil's paw) because of its strange shape. A herbal tea brewed from this plant is very beneficial to sufferers of arthritis, rheumatism, liver and gallbladder complaints and various stomach malfunctions. The plant is exported to many countries.

Karibib became a municipality in 1909. Today it is an atmospheric little place housing 2 000 people. There is a tall German-style church and one long main street lined with various shops, including a fine gemstone shop run by the Henckert family who also do weaving and deal largely in 'devil's paws'. Mr Henckert is a landscape and wildlife artist of repute. He also runs the Henckert Tourist Centre where information on the area may be obtained. Several buildings dating from German times still survive and there is a marble works. Two tall chimneys and the abandoned buildings of a meat cannery and creamery are situated off the main street.

The climate of Karibib hardly makes the place a holiday resort. Hot and dry, washed by relentless sunshine rather than rain, it is nevertheless an interesting little place to explore, with gardens full of unusual plants and trees.

From Karibib the B2 road continues west for 29 km, then reaches the town of ...

USAKOS

The Nama name of this sunbaked little town situated in the valley of the Khan River is *!Us!Khos*, from which Europeans have derived the name of *Usakos*. The etymology is obscure but is said to have been originally applied to a fountain there and means 'touch the forehead'. The reason for this is unknown. The town had its origin as a station on the old narrow-gauge railway which was built in 1900. Several buildings date from this German period, including a delightful municipal office. The railway station, with an old puffer mounted outside, is also worth seeing. Usakos became a municipality in 1948. The population of the town is 3 500.

The handsome mountains known as the *Erongo* (watering-place in the midst of a plain) lie to the north of the town. This massif is renowned for the rock art found in caves such as the Philipp Cave, named after Emil Philipp who owned the farm *Ameib* on which it was found. This rock shelter is 50 m long and 20 m deep. The famous Abbé Breuil visited it in 1950 and wrote the book, *Philipp Cave*, which deals with its prehistoric art, considered by authorities to be of major importance. The Philipp Cave is 32 km from Usakos along a gravel road. Apart from the rock art which includes a great painting of a white elephant, there is a pile of stone known as the Bull's Party. Also situated there is the *Ameib* ranch which has picnic and camping sites with shade and water. Phone (064) 1111 to obtain the owner's permission before visiting the place.

From Usakos the B2 road continues westwards over a grass-covered prairie which becomes increasingly arid. The Erongo Mountains, the highest point of which is the 2 350 m Bockberg, and the extraordinary, much-photographed Spitzkoppe (1 829 m high), dominate the plain like rocky islands looming out of a dried-up sea. At 23,5 km from Usakos a turn-off north leads to Henties Bay, with a turn-off 1 km along this branch road which leads to the tin mine of Uis 101 km away. This road provides access to the Spitzkoppe, where there are several Bushman caves and deposits of artefacts and gemstones such as topaz.

The main tarmac road continues westwards across the plain where the prairie grassland gradually gives way to the gravel plains of the Namib. After 77,5 km a turn-off south leads to the Rio Tinto Mine, and at 88,5 km a turn-off takes the traveller to the uranium mine at ...

RÖSSING

When the Germans built the narrow-gauge railway from Swakopmund to the interior, they created a station in the Namib Desert and named it in honour of Nonus van Rössing, commander of the Railway Brigade in Berlin. Traces found of several minerals and gemstones such as the rare *heliodor* (gold of the sun) suggested that the area was richly mineralised. Heliodor is a topaz coloured golden by traces of uranium present in the stone. In 1928 Captain Peter (Taffy) Louw, who had come to Namibia with the Imperial Light Horse during the First World War, and had remained to become a very active prospector, found strange dark coloured rock in the Rössing area. He and his wife, Margery, suspected that the rock was pitchblende, which carried what was known in those days as radium. Margery, who had been a radiographer at Guys Hospital, London, confirmed this identification in a dark-room in Swakopmund by placing a sample of the ore on a sensitive photographic plate. From the fogging which resulted on the plate, it was evident that the rock was radioactive.

Captain Louw formed a company to prospect the area of his find. Other prospectors became interested, although no one anticipated the so-called energy crisis of the 1970s when uranium came into its own as a highly valuable mineral.

A second prospecting company found another area of uranium mineralisation about 20 km from Captain Louw's first discovery. The deposit was large, but of a low grade, so it was not developed any further. Captain Louw tried to interest mining houses in his finds. Eventually the Rio Tinto Zinc Corporation became interested. They took an option on the Rössing uranium area and began a four-year programme of testing and evaluation. As a result of this programme, the company in 1973 decided to proceed with the establishment of what was planned to be the largest uranium mine in the world.

The uranium ore of Rössing occurs in granite as opposed to other major deposits in the rest of the world which are found in softer sedimentary material. The ore is recovered from an opencast working which, it is estimated, will eventually cover about 5 square kilometres. About 900 000 tons of ore and waste are removed, and about 360 tons of uranium oxide are produced each year and exported for further processing and use as nuclear fuel.

Radioactivity levels in the mine are carefully monitored and the workers are safeguarded and under constant check to ensure that they are not exposed to harmful radiation. Employees of the mine are housed at Swakopmund and in a special township created at the railway junction with the odd name of *Arandis* (place where people get upset).

Beyond the turn-off to Rössing, the tarmac road to the west continues across the Namib gravel plain which, in these parts, is often shrouded in heavy coastal fog. After 33 km (121,5 km from Usakos) there is a turn-off to the Deblin Mining Co. A further 19 km sees a turn-off south to the Namib Desert Park, and half a kilometre further on stands the interesting historical monument known as 'Martin Luther'.

'Martin Luther' consists of the remains of a steam tractor which was brought to German South West African in 1895 by Lieutenant Edmund Troost who hoped it would prove the solution to the problem of transporting goods from the coast across the Namib to the interior. The tractor towed a train of three wagons loaded with freight, but it never seems to have had much liking for its work. After a few journeys and having carried a total of 13 605 kg, it came to a standstill so resolute that Martin Luther's celebrated statement was brought to mind: *'Here I stand; God help me, I cannot do otherwise.'*

Boiler upsets (resulting from the salty water of the Namib) were the undoing of the poor thing. Completely out of sorts, it was abandoned to the wind and sands of the desert. The tractor almost rusted away until interested parties in recent times handsomely restored and mounted it on a pedestal next to the modern tarmac B2 road where it was proclaimed an historical monument.

Three kilometres west of 'Martin Luther' (144 km from Usakos), the B2 road reaches the holiday resort (formerly a port) and most interesting town of ...

SWAKOPMUND

The name of *Swakopmund* is rather an unfortunate one, but it is certainly unique. The Topnaar people who live in the valley of the Swakop River (at whose mouth the town lies) gave the river its name on account of the evil-looking mud, flotsam and general detritus washed down during its infrequent floods, which reminded them of a very loose evacuation of the bowels!

Notwithstanding its name, the Swakop is one of the most important rivers in the south-western part of Africa. It formed the traditional boundary between the various Nama tribes and the Herero tribe and was the scene of many brutal conflicts. Like most of the other rivers in the territory, the Swakop has an extremely erratic flow. However, when it floods during seasons of exceptional rainfall in the interior, it carries such a vast quantity of sand to the sea that the entire coastline is changed until wave action partially restores the original shore and the surplus sand is blown inland, increasing still further the size of the great dunes of the Namib. Water remains below the surface of the river bed long after the river has ceased to flow. Trees and shrubs grow in the bed and on the river banks. Farmers make the most of the vegetation and water to carry out limited agricultural activity.

Swakopmund had its start through necessity. The Germans, in the process of expanding their colony in south-west Africa, needed a port, but the only natural harbour on this part of the coast was Walvis Bay, which was already annexed to the Cape. The roadstead at the mouth of the Swakop River offers little shelter to ships but at least the anchorage is good. The Germans decided to make the best of the place, creating an artificial harbour there and building a narrow-gauge railway to convey goods across the Namib to the interior.

In 1892 Captain Curt von Francois built a military post on the site of the present town and this was the beginning of Swakopmund. Soon several trading and forwarding firms established themselves there. In 1895 the building of the narrow-gauge railway began. In the following year the town was properly laid out by a surveyor. For various reasons Swakopmund only became a municipality in 1909 when it was well established as an entry port for the German colony.

In 1899 a mole was built to provide a small breakwater. From the limited shelter of this structure, Kru-boys, specially brought from West Africa for their skill in handling surfboats, landed freight and passengers. The protected basin soon silted up, however, and a wooden pier was built in 1909, thereafter being replaced by a metal pier in 1911. The new pier, originally planned to be 640 m long, had only been built 262 m into the sea when the First World War broke out. German South West Africa was taken over by South Africa and Walvis Bay automatically displaced Swakopmund as the harbour. The old wooden pier was demolished after the war but the metal one remains – a solid piece of engineering which has survived the battering of many storms. Today it is a promenade and vantage-point for fishermen.

There are several other interesting reminders of pre-war German days in Swakopmund – the lighthouse built in 1902 and several houses below it built in the same period, including the *Kabelmesse* (seat of the Eastern and South African Telegraph Company) and the building which housed the *Bezinksgericht* (District Court). This building was reconstructed after the First World War and became the holiday residence of the South African Administrator of South West Africa who, in an official capacity, spent six weeks of each year in Swakopmund.

In Bismarck Street stand the castle-like barracks which housed German soldiers. In the same street is the beautiful Woermann house and its Damara tower, built in 1905 as the quarters for crews of the largest German shipping line serving South West Africa. The tower acted as a look-out to control shipping movements. The building later became the Hofmeyr Hostel, then fell into disuse, but has now been restored and declared a national monument.

In Post Street stands the original post office, built in 1908 and now the municipal offices. In the same street may be found the Antonius Hospital, built in 1908; the Schröder House, constructed in 1904; the adjoining facade of the original Hansa Hotel (now rebuilt on another site); the Lutheran Church erected in 1910; the adjoining parsonage built in 1911 and, opposite the church, the school built in 1913.

The railway station, built in 1901 as the terminus of the narrow-gauge line, is an architectural gem of its kind, complete with a 'witch's hat' turret. It has now been converted into the Swakopmund Hotel and Entertainment Centre. The original court-house (*Amtsgericht*), built in 1905, stands in Garrisen Street, while the prison (*Gefängnis*), also built in 1905, is one of the most remarkable buildings of its kind in the world. The facade resembles, at the least, the sumptuous home of some German nobleman. It is built in a beautiful half-timbered style. The accommodation inside is not quite as elegant!

The so-called *Ritter Castle*, named after its original owner Mr T Ritter, a director of a shipping agency, was built in 1905 and is now the local office of the Ministry of Environment and Tourism. Altona House, of 1902 vintage, was the office of the Woermann Line of ships. Opposite it stand the half-timbered remains of the office of the German Colonial Company. The older Adler Apotheke, built in 1909, is still a pharmacy; and near it stands a nostalgic fragment of the once grand Bismarck Hotel, in its day the premier hotel of the territory but insolvent in 1974.

Amongst other interesting buildings dated from the German period are the *Kazerne* (barracks), built in 1904 to house railway construction workers. Hohenzollern House, a former hotel, now a block of flats; the Prinzessin Rupprecht-Heim, once a military hospital but now a private hotel; the Standard Bank building, once a hotel; Barclays Bank, once the building of the Deutsche-Afrika-Bank; and next to it the half-timbered former building of the Damara Bank. Several private homes dating from the German period also survive, especially in the southern part of the town.

The Swakopmund Museum is excellent, crammed with well-displayed exhibits on themes such as the Namib Desert, Swakopmund, the Atlantic Ocean, minerals, pioneer transport, and the culture of the indigenous peoples of Namibia. It is housed in the original German customs post and is open daily from 10h00 to 13h00 and from 14h00 to 17h00. It should not be missed.

The museum looks out across a pleasant garden to the modern building opposite which encloses an Olympic-sized, freshwater swimming-bath heated to 27°C throughout the year. It is open weekdays from 08h00 to 10h00 and from 14h30 to 20h00; Sundays from 12h00 to 19h00.

The beach in front of the enclosed pool is pleasant for sunbathing and there is swimming in the sea in the area protected by the old mole. The sea temperatures, averaging 12°C in winter and 22°C in summer, are likely to appeal only to hardy swimmers. The ocean currents are tricky in the area beyond the protection of the mole.

A promenade stretches beneath a line of palm trees from the bathing beach to the pier. At the entrance to the garden there is a monument to the marines killed in action during the Herero War of 1904.

There is a public library and reading-room in the town, and the Sam Cohen Memorial Library houses a fine collection of books, periodicals and papers dealing with all aspects of the territory. For the researcher, this library is one of the best sources of information.

Swakopmund has increased considerably in size with the development of the uranium mine at Rössing. About 1 500 people connected with this mine live in Swakopmund in two residential suburbs, *Tamariskia,* named after the wild tamarisk trees, and *Vineta,* named after the mystic underwater town in the Oder River of Germany. The total population of Swakopmund is now 15 500.

As the principal holiday resort of the territory, Swakopmund has a variety of hotels and bungalows and one of the largest caravan parks in Africa. There are several notable restaurants, including Erich's Beyern Stübchen, and Café Anton, famous for its pastries. The shopping centre is good, with a variety of food, clothing and other shops, including curio and gemstone shops of a high standard. There is also a good bookshop.

Legend has it that a commercial traveller representing a firm making traffic-control lights was once stranded in the town and could not pay his hotel bills. His range of sample traffic-lights was dumped in Swakopmund in lieu of payment. The same thing seems to have happened to a few other towns in the territory, which are equally hagridden by traffic-lights. A salesman selling four-way stop signs would have been more welcome. Incidentally, many of the street signs in Swakopmund date from German times.

Swakopmund has an average rainfall of less than 15 mm. Its water supply reaches it by pipe from underground sources in the Kuiseb and Omaruru rivers. The climate is influenced by the cold sea and, although in a desert setting, its temperature ranges from 15°C to 25°C.

From Swakopmund the coastal road to Walvis Bay stretches southwards from the town. The Swakop River is crossed by means of the longest road bridge in the territory. The bridge is 688 m long, with its foundations penetrating 30 m of sand to rest on the essential bedrock. South of the river, the road runs into dune country, and the 34 km journey along the coast to Walvis Bay can be quite an experience during a sandstorm.

The drive along a fine tarmac road is interesting at all seasons. A strange contrast exists between the cold, mist-stricken waters of the South Atlantic – rich in marine life – pounding on the shores of one of the most arid deserts in the world. Gigantic sand dunes move sluggishly with the winds which seem to blow incessantly, bringing with them a touch of the cold Antarctic if they are southerly, and the breath of a fiery dragon if they blow from the north-east. The railway maintains its right of way by means of gangs of labourers who, armed with shovels, trudge along the railway track clearing sand off the line and leaning into the wind. They remind one of the famous painting *In the Steppes of Central Asia.*

In the midst of this desolation lie the ruins of a bleak little railway siding which nevertheless can claim singular international renown. On 15 November 1962, a misguided Russian representative to the United Nations, Mr A K Gren, read to the august assembly an extract from the ebullient little twice-a-week local newspaper, published in Walvis Bay and called the *Namib Times.* In this paper, the editor featured an occasional column devoted to the doings of the fictitious Rand Rifles town council. Mr Gren quoted an interesting passage:

> *'The Municipality of Rand Rifles has issued the following directive. It had come to the attention of the council that employees have been dying on their jobs and refusing or neglecting to fall down. Any employee found dead on the job in an upright position will be dismissed.*

> 'The reluctance of its employees to move had apparently given the Rand Rifles council ground for previous concern. It had even been suggested, since it was becoming increasingly so difficult to distinguish between death and natural movement of some council men, that foremen should investigate if no movement was noticed in any two-hour spell. To hold a pay packet in front of the nose was a good test. There should at least be some involuntary effort made to grab the packet.'

Mr Gren was not amused when it was pointed out to the United Nations that the Rand Rifles municipality was a figment of the lively imagination of Paul Vincent, editor of the *Namib Times*, who used this means to poke fun at local council politics in general. The 'mayor' of Rand Rifles was a Mr P Meyer, who had once been stationed in the place as a ganger. He had long since left and Rand Rifles was simply a place of wind, sand, fog and sunshine. The name is derived from the Rand Rifles Regiment who had camped there during the First World War. The railway has now been relocated and Rand Rifles, alas, no longer exists.

A camping ground at Dolfynstrand lies 18 km from Swakopmund. At 22 km the road passes the guano platform built in 1939 by Adolf Winter over a small rocky islet which was a favourite nesting place for sea-birds such as cormorants. This platform provides a level surface for the birds. It is 548 m long and 274 m wide. It is mounted on stainless steel pillars. Mr Winter's platform is not only convenient for the birds; it is also profitable to man. Each year after the nesting season, about 1 000 tons of guano is removed from the platform and sold as fertiliser.

Twelve kilometres beyond the guano platform (34 km from Swakopmund) lies ...

WALVIS BAY

The principal port on the south-western side of Africa, *Walvis Bay* (whale bay) lies in a superb natural harbour created as part of the delta of the Kuiseb River. These days this extraordinary river has a flow of water which very seldom reaches the sea on the surface of its bed. After the river has received a copious amount of rain-water from the interior, it reaches the coastal plain of the Namib and simply soaks into a layer of sand about 61 m deep. This mass of sand acts as a natural reservoir, retaining a prodigious amount of water estimated at about 67,5 million kilolitres. Water that does eventually manage to filter to the sea is considered to take about 70 years to journey from the inland watershed to the buried mouth of the river.

Walvis Bay harbour consists of a deep-water bay sheltered from the open sea by a long, low narrow spit of land running northwards parallel to the coast and ending at Pelican Point. The bay shallows in the south where the spit is attached to the mainland. This area is the home of countless aquatic birds, particularly flamingos and pelicans. For the bird lover this area of sandbanks and shallows is an overwhelming spectacle, especially at sunset when the birds return from their day's hunt for food and settle down for the night. The road to the salt works skirts the edge of the lagoon, making the birds easily visible.

The first ship known to venture into the harbour of Walvis Bay was that of Bartholomeu Dias during the course of his voyage to discover the end of Africa and the sea route to the East. On 8 December 1487 Dias entered the bay and named it the Bay of our Lady Immaculate. The entire coast looked so barren and uninhabited that he named it the Sands of Hell. Apart from the shelter of the bay, the Portuguese found the area unattractive. There was no surface water to drink. Heat and sand were not tradable commodities. However, the riches of the sea were well observed by the Portuguese. The first chart of the coast, produced in 1489 from the discoveries of Bartholomeu Dias, called the area around Walvis Bay the *Praia dos Sardinha* (coast of sardines). By the middle of the following century the Portuguese maps were marked with the name *Bahia das Bahleas* (bay of whales). After being distorted in various ways, this name was taken up by visitors of other nationalities, becoming the *Walvis Bay* of today.

American and British sailors paid particular attention to the area. The rich nitrogen content of the Benguela Current supported such a wealth of plankton that it has been aptly described as a meadow of the ocean in which whales and vast shoals of pelagic fish – pilchards and anchovies – feed, moving about like flocks of sheep, with sea-birds and seals devouring the fish.

Whales, seals and guano attracted many ships to the coast of south-western African in the 17th century. Walvis Bay and Sandwich Harbour (another remnant of the sand-buried delta of the Kuiseb River, lying to the south of Walvis Bay) both came into irregular use as harbours for these ships. This shipping activity, and rumours of possible wealth from copper and cattle in the interior of the territory, attracted the attention of the Dutch at the Cape. The ship *Meermin*, under Captain F R Duminy, was sent to inspect the coast, and on 26 February 1793 Walvis Bay (as the captain called it) was annexed to Holland.

When the British occupied the Cape in 1795, Captain Alexander was sent up the coast where he hoisted the British flag in Walvis Bay. Apart from the visits of whalers and a little trade with the Topnaar people who lived in the valleys of the Kuiseb and Swakop rivers, nothing official resulted from these annexations. Exploration of the interior and the first actual settlement were effected essentially by private enterprise.

In April 1837 Sir James Alexander, on a scientific expedition of discovery for the Royal Geographical Society, reached Walvis Bay after journeying overland from Cape Town. This was an epic trip by ox-wagon through totally unknown country. He found the shores of the bay well littered with the spoils of whaling. A few Topnaars were in residence, living on whale meat, fish and nara melons.

The first European settlers reached the bay in June 1844 when two traders, Peter Dixon and Thomas Morris, together with their families, arrived by wagon after a tedious eight-month journey from Cape Town. They opened a store and started business by exporting cattle bartered from the inland tribes. In the following year (1845) the first missionaries arrived: first the Wesleyan Joseph Tindall on a reconnaissance, and then the Rhenish missionary H Scheppmann, who in that year established a station at Rooibank in the valley of the Kuiseb to serve the Topnaars. The Rhenish Missionary Society also built the first church in Walvis Bay in 1880. The building still stands as a national monument, but the early Rooibank Mission has long since vanished.

Walvis Bay prospered on the cattle trade and the development of copper mines in the interior. The first road in the territory was constructed in 1844 by the Nama chieftain, Jan Jonker Afrikaner. Known as the Bay road, it connected Walvis Bay to the Matchless mine and Jonker's capital of Winterhoek (now Windhoek).

The interior of south-western Africa was in a sad state of uproar during the 1870s. Rival tribes, bandits and cattle-rustlers were all involved in a lunatic series of killings and outrages. There was no supreme control of the country and many people appealed to the British Government at the Cape to intervene. A commissioner, W Coates Palgrave, was sent to the territory to investigate. As a result of his findings, the British decided that some intervention was necessary, but the apparent poverty of the area made the prospect of adding it to the British Empire unattractive. Tentatively the British decided to repeat their early annexation of Walvis Bay, delineate the area properly and establish a representative there who, by controlling imports, exports and immigration, might be able to influence the chaotic political events in the interior.

To fulfil this intention, the naval vessel *Industry* arrived in Walvis Bay on 6 March 1878. On 12 March, Commander R C Dyer formally annexed the area demarcated by him as being *'on the south by a line from a point on the coast fifteen miles south of Pelican Point to Scheppmansdorf; on the east by a line from Scheppmansdorf to the Rooibank, including the Plateau, and thence to ten miles inland from the mouth of the Swakop River; on the north by the last ten miles of the course of the said Swakop River'*. Rooibank, in the valley of the Kuiseb, was the nearest place to Walvis Bay where there was grass, trees and fresh water. The total area of this odd little enclave in the desert amounted to 750 square kilometres.

In January 1880, W Coates Palgrave was established as the first magistrate of Walvis Bay. This was the start of British administration. Unfortunately this date also marked the beginning of a major disturbance in the interior between the Herero and Nama people. For the next eight years, trade and mining in the interior was severely disrupted. Walvis Bay experienced little of the prosperity anticipated after the British annexation.

The arrival of the Germans in 1889 quietened down the disturbances in the interior. However, it was awkward that a German colony in south-western Africa should be dependent on a British-owned port for its trade. The Germans found this a difficult problem to solve but, until they managed to develop the roadstead at Swakopmund as a port, they were forced to use Walvis Bay. A short boom followed, with the first wharf being erected in 1898 to allow ships to unload cargo directly on to the shore rather than into lighters. The wooden wharf only had a draught of 3 m at low tide, with the result that large vessels still had to remain anchored further out and unload into lighters.

The conveyance of goods across the coastal belt of sand dunes was a great problem, eventually solved by the construction of a narrow-gauge railway stretching for 17,7 km to a terminus named Plum, near Rooikop on the German border. Mules and donkeys hauled 3-ton trucks along the line. In 1899 a steam locomotive named Hope was sent up by sea from the Cape. This little puffer (weighing 7 tons) worked the line until 1906 when the growth of the rival port of Swakopmund lured most of the traffic away. The line fell into disuse, became covered in sand, and Hope ran out of steam. Today the locomotive is mounted outside the Walvis Bay railway station as an interesting reminder of former days at the port.

The outbreak of the First World War transformed Walvis Bay. It became the base for the South African forces invading German territory. In 1915 a railway was hurriedly built to connect Walvis Bay to the German line from Swakopmund to the interior. Virtually overnight Swakopmund fell into disuse as a port and Walvis Bay came into its own as the principal harbour of the territory.

A second wooden wharf was erected in 1922. In 1924 work began on the dredging and construction of a first-class harbour which was opened in August 1927 by the Earl of Athlone, Governor-General of South Africa. This harbour has been still further developed and today consists of a concrete quay 1 400 m long with eight berths and a separate tanker berth 192 m long. The draught is 11 m at low water.

Water problems in Walvis Bay provide an interesting study. There is a celebrated tale of an American visiting the place who wanted to send a postcard home to show his folks something of the local scene. Caught in a sandstorm, he wandered into a hardware shop instead of a stationer. Not finding any postcards available, the American bought a piece of sandpaper, cut it to size, stamped and addressed it, and posted it off with a terse message scrawled on the back, *'Aerial view of Walvis Bay'*.

In August 1874 the hunter, Gerald McKiernan, visited the port and described it in these words:

> *'No water has flowed over the bed of the Kuiseb into the bay for twelve years, so you can imagine that water is not one of the obstacles to be met with. Sand Fountain is a pit dug in the bed of the river, and yields a scant supply of very brak water. It has not rained at the bay for 18 years but fogs are common and fleas more than common. I have never seen their equal in numbers or appetite. The only known disease at the bay is intoxication. Drinking-water is brought from Cape Town, and they will give you a bottle of English ale worth 25 cents sooner than a drink of water'.*

In 1899 a sea-water condensing plant was built by the Government. It consisted of a cluster of low glass structures resembling cucumber frames. Shallow depressions in the ground underneath these structures were filled with sea water. The sun heated the water, the moisture condensed on the glass and was caught in gutters, yielding a supply of fresh water which was perfectly drinkable but considered to be about the most expensive in the world, selling for about £5 per 5 000 *l*.

The growth of the town and the demands of ships and thirsty steam locomotives soon outstripped the output of the condensation plant. The answer to the problem, however, was there waiting for man to discover it. William MacDonald, who visited the place in 1914 and wrote a book called *Destiny of Walvis Bay*, made the matter very clear when he wrote:

> *'In my childhood days I was told the story of a vessel sailing in the mighty Amazon, while the crew lay dying of thirst, thinking they were still out in the open sea. At last, another ship hove in sight. The suffering crew signalled a message of distress. A moment later the amazing answer flashed back "dip down". This matter I leave with the authorities of Walvis Bay.'*

Nine years passed before the hint was taken. Eventually, on the advice of Professor R H Charters, the Government sank test boreholes into the bed of the Kuiseb upstream from Rooibank. The results were exciting. In 1927 Walvis Bay received from this source in the sandy bed of the Kuiseb

4 500 000 l of fresh water a day, and the cost dropped to 10s per 5 000 l. Today the Rooibank water scheme supplies Walvis Bay, Swakopmund and the uranium mine at Rössing with ample amounts of fresh water. It is estimated that the potential yield is sufficient to maintain the area for a considerable time to come.

This generous supply of water has transformed the desert towns. Waterborne sewerage systems have been introduced, and Walvis Bay and Swakopmund are now noted for their flowers, trees (especially palms), lawns and gardens. Gardeners have a special problem in that the water-table in Walvis Bay and Swakopmund is only a little over 3 m below the surface. This water is brine, with a salt content of about four and a half times that of sea water. Any plant or tree foolhardy enough to sink its roots into this liquid simply withers overnight. Consequently, everything cultivated has to be of the type which lives very close to the surface. Hardy salt-tolerant plants and trees such as casuarinas, Port Jackson and pittosporums have been successfully cultivated. A park such as the one in Walvis Bay, named after the ex-mayor, Mr J C Harris, is a splendid example of skilled work largely carried out by Mr K H Daehne, the first municipal gardener who was appointed in 1961.

Walvis Bay received a health committee in 1922, a village management board in 1925, and then achieved full municipal status on 16 March 1931. Today it is a modern desert town of 25 000 inhabitants, baked with sunshine and pestered by winds, drifting sand and an occasional strong whiff of sulphur caused by submarine disturbances in the bay. At least, however, Walvis Bay is cooled by the cold sea and its mists. The port is the coastal terminus for the railway system of the territory, and the harbour is capable of handling substantial traffic. An outstanding building in the town is the civic centre.

Fishing, particularly for pilchards, developed as a major industry in the town, with the first factory, the Walvis Bay Canning Company Ltd, being established in 1943 and managed by R Ovenstone. The success of the cannery attracted a further nine factories canning pilchards and processing fish such as snoek for export. Large fleets of foreign fishing boats accompanied by factory ships also exploited the pilchard and anchovy shoals of the Benguela Current. Consequently, this massive onslaught sadly depleted the natural resources of pilchards. Fishing – like mining – is essentially parasitic. It takes out but puts nothing back. The result is inevitable, as human beings incessantly want more and find every excuse to avoid conservation or control.

The shopping centre of Walvis Bay is second only to Windhoek's in size. There are numerous sporting facilities, including such novelties as sliding down the giant sand dunes. The bay is a fine area for yachts and waterskiers, while anglers find sport all along the coast. Fifty-six kilometres south of Walvis Bay, along a sandy track open to four-wheel-drive vehicles only, lies the great bird and angling resort of Sandwich Harbour. There are no facilities and overnight stays are not permitted. The area is also closed on Sundays, but a visit during weekdays is a unique experience for bird lovers and fishermen.

The pertinent little trilingual newspaper, *The Namib Times*, first published on 5 December 1958 by a then very youthful editor, Paul Vincent, perhaps sums up perfectly the irrepressible nature of Walvis Bay. Its setbacks, booms, peculiar difficulties and hardships are always tempered by a commendable sense of humour and an ability to see the funny side of its own predicaments. In the issue of 16 November 1962, appeared this fruity little item:

> *'Walvis Bay is not commonly regarded as the "Garden City of South West Africa" and it is certainly not "The Garden of Eden". However, on Monday a European man got his facts a bit mixed and was found strolling down at the lagoon end of 7th Street completely naked. The police were immediately summoned after the man had surprised several passers-by and housewives who happened to notice him walking down the street. It is understood he since has been committed to an institution.'*

THE NAMIB DESERT

For the connoisseur of scenery, atmosphere and the unusual, there is nothing quite like the Namib Desert. As a wilderness it is superb, a vast solitary place, harsh and primeval. Yet, it is a place where life has discovered that, even in its most austere mood, Nature still has compassion.

In creating an aeolian desert landscape such as the Namib without rain or surface water, Nature has relented. With a subtle alchemy, it has provided mists with which to sustain an astonishing number and variety of life-forms. Even in so desolate a place, ruthlessness is softened by the winds which carry fragments of vegetation into the desert, providing the sustenance which enables a chain of life-forms to begin. The brooding stillness is somehow relieved by strange harmonies murmured by the breezes as they frolic amongst the sand dunes or play a melody, using as an instrument any chance rock, stick or rusting debris which can be made to vibrate and create a sound. Even though the solitude of the place is profound, human beings cannot feel alone. Something intangible, indefinable and reflective reaches out to stir their thoughts and touch their soul. At night, through the crystal clearness of the air, the dome of the sky may be seen to blaze with light, and the Milky Way gleams like a rift in the mystery of space through which may be glimpsed the shining lights of paradise.

In the language of the Nama people *Namib* means a vast, open plain seemingly without end. In modern geographical terms, the name is applied to the entire arid coastal belt which varies in width from 80 km to 140 km. It extends from the sandveld at the northern end of the winter-rainfall region of the Cape to as far north as the area just past Mossamedes in Angola. This expanse has been conveniently divided by geographers into three parts. In the south lies the transitional Namib, extending north to approximately the line formed by the main road from Aus to Lüderitz. North of this road lies the middle Namib which the Namas call the Gobaba. This is the seemingly endless plains of the dune country, the sea of sand, the grandest part of the desert – 400 km long and 140 km wide – which ends abruptly at the valley of the Kuiseb River. North of the river lies the northern Namib, the area of arid gravel plains.

The dune sea of the middle Namib is the supreme desert. The dunes reach 275 m in height, with their nearest rivals in the empty quarter of Arabia only reaching 200 m. The Namib dunes are not only gigantic, but they are extremely beautiful, the older ones being tinted red by iron oxidation and minute fragments of garnets. The younger dunes are greyer in colour.

Where has all the sand come from which makes the mighty dunes? The birth date of the Namib was somewhere between Oligocene and Pleistocene times, about 80 million years ago. Something happened during that time to alter the weather. Perhaps the Earth received a nudge from outer space resulting in a sudden change in the sea along the south-western coast of Africa.

A powerful ocean current, a regular 'river of cold water' originating in the Antarctic, started to flow northwards up the coast. This cold stream (10°C to 20°C) is about 150 km wide and travels at about 3,5 knots an hour. The presence of this cold 'river', flowing close to the shoreline of Namibia, isolates the coast from the outer warm ocean. The prevailing westerly winds pick up moisture from the warm water but, in crossing the cold current, they are cooled. The winds are therefore unable to take up further moisture from such cold water, and the moisture they already carry is turned into a clammy mist by the sudden drop in temperature.

The mists roll over the coast and cover the Namib, causing some dampness due to condensation, but no proper rain. Any rain which does fall on the desert comes from the east coast – a long way off. Most of the moisture contained in such easterly winds is precipitated on the highlands of the interior. As these winds drop over the escarpment to the coastal regions, they warm up to an unpleasant extent, precipitation decreases, and they have a searing, dehydrating effect.

Both directions, therefore, yield little rain for the Namib, but exceptions can be caused by freak conditions. In 1934, 153 mm of rain fell in Swakopmund, a place which normally only gets 14 mm of rain a year. The floodwaters of the Swakop River transported an estimated 35 million cubic metres of sediment downriver. This extended the coastline more than 1 km into the sea. Walvis Bay, in addition to its numerous troubles, was inundated for several months, most of the town actually being below sea-level. The Kuiseb River flooded the town, pushing the sand dunes at its mouth out to sea. The sea then flowed in as the river receded, and fresh water was replaced by salt water. From January until May 1934 the only means of transportation was by boat. Snakes, washed down by the river, slithered into houses to escape drowning. Sharks swam in with the sea in search of take-aways and quick snacks. Mosquitoes bred. The supply of drinking-water was disrupted. Sanitary pails had to be collected by boat, with the result that the town could at least claim to have waterborne sewerage!

Between 30 and 31 March 1976, in the space of 36 hours, Walvis Bay, which normally receives 18 mm of rain a year, received a total of 66 mm, the equivalent of a four-year supply. The place was more than half drowned. It is said that some of its children still looked relatively clean twelve months after the event.

The Namib can obviously be capricious. Perhaps understandably, the Nama refer to the desert as a female. It is at its most contrary in its support of life. By all the accepted norms of deserts, nothing should live there. A desert is usually defined as an area where potential evaporation is at least twice as great as the average precipitation. In the Namib it is approximately 200 times greater. The potential evaporation averages 3 500 mm per year, while the average precipitation is only about 18 mm. Any liquid falling on the desert surface is therefore more than promptly snatched away like air into a vacuum. How then do so many creatures live there? The answer to most questions asked in the Namib is whispered by the winds.

Winds and the cold Benguela Current were the parents of the Namib. Hills and mountains have been steadily reduced to dust by the incessant winds which wear down the rock, already weakened by expansion and contraction due to hot days and cold nights. Flooding rivers carry sand to the sea where waves wash it back on to the beach and the wind returns it to the desert. The dune sea lies in the area of greatest wind. Consequently, it has the most sand. The huge dunes are blown into parallel ridges and valleys which run north–south, totally covering a vast plain dissected by the dried-up remains of ancient stream valleys and marked by the skeletons of island-like hills.

Even though the winds perform this work of destruction and transformation, they also bring the means of life. The east wind carries on its hot breath fragments of vegetation from the escarpment. This detritus, desiccated and seemingly unappetising, is the staff of life to primitive creatures such as silver-fish, which feed on this matter where it is caught at the foot of the dunes. About 200 different species of beetles also feed on this substance and on the silver-fish. Scorpions, spiders, geckos, chameleons, crickets, wasps and lizards devour the silver-fish, beetles and one another. The strange little 5 cm long golden moles consume everything they can catch. Side-winder snakes hunt through the sand, climbing the dunes with their peculiar sideways movement. Snake-eating eagles prey on the snakes, and jackals eat everything. So much for their eating habits, but where do they all get water?

Some of the creatures generate their own water by means of a complex process of synthesis from the provisions of dry vegetable matter. Most of the creatures, however, depend on the fog which extends about 110 km inland and is present on an average of 102 days a year. It precipitates from 35 mm to 45 mm of moisture a year, which is condensed by the desert insects, reptiles and mammals according to their own methods. The side-winder snakes simply lie in the mist and steadily lick their own bodies. Three of the nocturnal beetle species belonging to the genus *Lepidochora* build their own fog-collecting structures. As soon as they realise that fog is approaching, they trench up two parallel ridges in the sand. The height and orientation of these ridges trap the passing mist. The mist condenses into water along the ridges of the trench. The beetles wait until the ridges are nicely damp, then move along the trench between the ridges and take up the trapped moisture.

Amongst the specialised drinkers, perhaps the most remarkable is the beetle *Onymacris unguiculanis,* the celebrated 'fog-basking' beetle. This bustling little creature spends its days foraging the slip faces of the dunes and feeding on windblown seeds and other detritus. At sunset the beetle normally burrows into the sand to a level where the temperature is to its liking and goes to sleep in security. Creatures from many other different species do the same thing, each one finding its own level with the required 'air-conditioning'. A big dune is like a condominium building, with many levels providing desirable living quarters where some occupants sleep during the day, others at night.

If the fog comes, however, there is a great stirring among the beetles. They emerge from their sleeping quarters and eagerly scramble to the knife-edged crests of the dunes. There they stand heads down, facing into the wind in order to present the maximum surface of their 20 mm long bodies to the fog. The fog condenses on their bodies and the drops of water move down grooves that Nature has ingeniously provided, straight into the mouths of the beetles. Research shows that the beetle can increase its body weight by as much as 34 per cent from moisture obtained in a single fog.

The Namib has so many unique features that it deserves much study. To aid this work, the Namib Desert Research Station was founded in 1962 at *Gobabeb* (place of the fig tree), with Dr Charles Koch as its guiding spirit. Dr Koch was an outstanding entomologist and the world authority on the *Tenebrionidae* (the *tok-tokkie* beetles) which live in the Namib. He was an Austrian who became an entomologist at Vienna University, developed an interest in the tenebrionid beetles and, in order to study them, visited the deserts of Arabia and North Africa. In 1949 he transferred his interests to South Africa with a research grant from the South African Council for Industrial and Scientific Research. In 1953 he was appointed Curator of Coleoptera in the Transvaal Museum. The Namib, with its 200 tenebrionid species of beetles, always fascinated him. The idea of establishing a research station was his brainchild. To raise funds, the Namib Desert Research Association was formed. After considerable effort, enough finance was found and the South West African administration granted a site. Building commenced in 1962 and research in a number of fields began, with many interesting and rapid results. In October 1963, the historic rediscovery of the golden mole occurred. This strange little mammal, living only in the sand dunes of the Namib, had not been seen for 125 years and was thought to be extinct. It has no visible external eyes or ears and, by some freak evolutionary process, is able to breathe and live in the sand. It 'swims' rather than burrows through loose sand.

In 1966 the South African Council for Industrial and Scientific Research established a Desert Ecological Research Unit based at the Namib Desert Research Station. Dr Koch was appointed as its first director. In 1970 the Division of Nature Conservation and Tourism of the South West African administration assumed full responsibility for the buildings and material development. Unfortunately, Dr Koch died shortly afterwards on 23 February 1970, and was not destined to see the fine development of the Namib station, funded by the administration.

The South African Council for Scientific and Industrial Research continued to fund and control research activities which involved two main objectives. The first was to establish a basis for understanding the unique aspects of the Namib. Why is it that only in this desert has a fauna developed in the vegetationless area of the dunes, using windblown detritus and fog as food and moisture? While work is being done on this problem, information is being compiled to provide a sound background for those authorities regulating the development now taking place in the Namib, largely resulting from the discoveries of economic minerals such as uranium. The staff consists of a director and four permanent staff members. Various visiting scientists also carry out research at the station.

Gobabeb was selected as the site for the research station because it provides direct access to the three main desert biotopes or natural divisions. These consist of the dune sea of shifting sand (the Gobaba), which lies south of the station; the flat, gravel plain (the Namib proper) lying to the north; and the extraordinary river which effectively separates these two divisions, the Kuiseb, with its subterranean water, vegetation, wildlife and human inhabitants, the Topnaar people.

It is said that in the Nama language *Kuiseb* means a gorge. The name appears to describe the steep canyon through which the river finds a way from the interior highlands to the coastal terrace of the Namib. There is not another river in the world quite like the Kuiseb, for Nature has allocated to it several important tasks, each of considerable interest to man.

The Kuiseb only flows very intermittently on the surface. However, this occasional surface flow is of vast importance, for the river constantly has to confront the great sand dunes of the south. The dunes inexorably attempt to cross the river. Their inclination is to press northwards on to the gravel plains, but the river stubbornly blocks their march. The periodic surface floods carry the encroaching sand down towards the sea. Only at the delta of the river, where surface water seldom reaches the sea except during uncommon floods (fifteen recorded times between 1837 and 1963), do the dunes make progress. Through this one weak spot in the Kuiseb they force a passage and advance triumphantly up the coast until they reach the Swakop River which finally blocks them.

The spectacle of the great red dunes towering over the meandering valley of the Kuiseb is awesome. The sand constantly infiltrates, furtively trickling over edges or suddenly tumbling down like a minor landslide from a more aggressive and pushy dune. It seems inevitable that the dry river course must be overwhelmed. Only rains in the interior can provide it with the strength to resist and sweep away the forceful sands.

The Kuiseb has been aptly described as a linear oasis. In complete contrast to the dunes of the south and the plains of the north, its banks and course are covered in handsome trees and rich plant life. Giraffe acacias, wild figs and tamarisk trees flourish along the Kuiseb and it is a great home for the nara melon. These cucumber-like little melons provide most forms of life with food. The Topnaars, a mini nation about 200 strong under a chief named Esau Kooitjie, live along the Kuiseb with their flocks of goats. They harvest the melons from November to April, put them on the roofs of their huts to ripen, and then boil them. The seeds float to the top and are scooped off, dried and eaten, or sold in Walvis Bay. As well as being nutritious, they are claimed to be aphrodisiacs! The pulp is simply thrown on to the sand where it dries. It is then rolled up like felt and stored. It can be boiled with water and eaten at any time. It is almost the only vegetable known to the Topnaars. They value the nara so highly that clumps of the shrub are claimed by inheritance. They make no effort to cultivate the plant.

Wild animals such as oryx, springbok, baboons, jackals, hyenas and other creatures depend on the Kuiseb for their existence. The Topnaars dig wells into the sand of the river bed, as there is always water very near the surface. Wild animals also make shallow excavations in order to find water.

An important research duty of the Namib scientists is to monitor the level of the subterranean water. With vast quantities now being pumped out to supply Walvis Bay, Swakopmund and the mining areas such as Rössing, the possible depletion of the water could cause a lowering of the established water-table, with several disastrous consequences. Apart from the withering of trees and vegetation and life becoming insupportable in the valley, the river's struggle with the sand dunes could be drastically weakened. Once across the Kuiseb, the dunes would inexorably invade the gravel plains, and the consequences of such a change are difficult to visualise. It is vital that a balance be maintained and only as much water removed as can be replenished by the inland rains.

The Namib requires careful conservation. It is a curiously fragile landscape, easily damaged. Visitors driving motor vehicles at random over its gravel plain leave tracks which can scar the surface indefinitely. The presence of uranium and other minerals means exploitation by man. As a result the Namib must be understood and protected as much as possible. Too many of its plants and animals are unique. One of the very first discoveries made by the research station, along with the golden mole, was that of a new species of spider, *Leucorchestris* sp. popularly named the 'dancing spider' or the 'desert call-girl' because of its habit of leaping about in a grotesque excited dance when captured.

The strange *Welwitschia mirabilis* plants are also indigenous to the Namib. Welwitschia is a dwarf tree which simply flourishes on the moisture provided by fog. It belongs to a single species without any close relatives. Curiously enough it is very distantly related to pine and fir trees. The plant produces a turnip-like stem which can reach a width of over a metre, but which seldom projects more than a cautious few centimetres above the ground. The stem tapers off into a taproot, probing down as deep as 20 m. Two leaves are developed on opposite sides of the surface stem. The leaves are the same width as the stem. They are about 3 m long, constantly growing outwards but dying at the tips where they touch the ground. Welwitschia plants always seem bedraggled, like women who always have their hair in curlers. In the harsh conditions of wind, daytime heat and night-time cold, the leaves fray into long ribbons, giving the impression that there are several rather dilapidated leaves.

After about 20 years the welwitschia produces its first flowers, with the tenebrionid beetles providing the romantic touch of fertilisation. The life span of the plant is estimated at over 1 000 years. They were first discovered by Dr Friedrich Martin Welwitsch, an Austrian botanist appointed by the Portuguese Government in 1852 to carry out research on the flora of its then colony of Angola. During the following nine years Dr Welwitsch classified 3 227 plants, including many new species, but none more bizarre than the extraordinary *Welwitschia mirabilis*, which bears his name. It is known to the Angolan tribes as the *ntumbo*.

Dr Welwitschia found his first specimen of this plant 1,5 km inland from Cape Negro on the south coast of Angola. Almost simultaneously, Thomas Baines found and sketched the plant in the Namib south of the Kunene River where it had, in fact, been noticed but not appreciated by early hunters in the area.

The north-eastern corner of the Namib-Naukluft Park is the home of many welwitschias, including several exceptionally large specimens. The landscape in which they live is almost surrealistic – a vast, eerie gravel plain in a setting of sharply etched pegmatite hills. There is hardly any vegetation but in such an improbable setting the welwitschias flourish. One specimen growing there is estimated at over 1 500 years of age. To find it, enter the park from the entrance 3,5 km from Swakopmund on the main tarmac B2 road to Windhoek. The gravel road through the park runs for 40 km. Then, near the site of an old iron mine, there is a turn-off leading for 24 km on to a high plain where many welwitschias grow. The giant specimen lives 2 km along a signposted side track in an enclosure protected by some rusty metal posts with holes bored through them to support wires.

Quite by accident, when the wind blows in the right direction through these holes, a flute-like sound is produced, rising, falling and changing tone, creating a strange harmony of the desert – a serenade to an ancient plant.

THE NAMIB-NAUKLUFT PARK
(ORIGINALLY KNOWN AS THE MOUNTAIN ZEBRA PARK)

The Namib-Naukluft Park had its start in 1907 when the German Colonial Administration proclaimed the area between the Swakop and the Kuiseb rivers to be Game Reserve No 3. In 1941 the Sandwich area was included in this reserve in order to protect the guano islands in the lagoon. In 1956 the Welwitschia plain, Swakop valley and the Kuiseb canyon were added. The whole protected area was named the Namib Desert Park in 1968. Its size then was 14 095 square kilometres.

In 1968 the *Naukluft* farm was purchased and proclaimed as a sanctuary for Hartmann's mountain zebra. After an ecological survey in 1970 most of the Naukluft Mountain massif was purchased from various private owners. Land west of the Naukluft was added to provide a corridor for the annual migration of gemsbok between the dune country and the mountains.

In 1979 most of Diamond Area 2 south of the Kuiseb River, including Sesriem and Sossusvlei, was ceded for conservation. This area, unoccupied state land, the Namib Desert Park and the Naukluft Mountain Zebra Park were consolidated to form the 23 340 km^2 Namib-Naukluft Park. The further addition in 1986 of the remainder of Diamond Area 2 and a portion of Diamond Area 1, as far south as the Aus/Lüderitz road, made the Namib-Naukluft Park 49 768 km^2 in extent, almost the size of Belgium and Wales together, and the largest conservation area in Namibia. There is a total of 105 559 km^2 of nature reserves in Namibia.

Exploring the Park is a vintage experience for the connoisseur of travel, colour, atmosphere and scenery. The gravel roads are adequate and signposted. The tourist must simply guard against running out of petrol and carry a supply of drinking-water and food. There are a number of camping places, but facilities are limited to pit toilets. Nights in these camps are fascinating: jackals sing; the wind and the mist wander over the face of the desert; springbok, oryx and ostriches somehow find enough to eat and drink. The silence can almost be felt.

Among the camps, Bloedkoppies, Kuiseb Canyon and Homeb are particularly attractive. The Namib Desert Research Station may only be visited by special permission. It lies 85 km from the Walvis Bay entrance to the park, with the camp at Homeb 20 km further on. Visitors to Homeb are warned to be particularly careful not to proceed beyond the campsite, as the road becomes very sandy. The research station and the Homeb camp both lie on the banks of the Kuiseb. To the north lie the gravel plains with all their remarkable contrasts of light-coloured pegmatites and dark-coloured dolerite. In the south is the red dune country. The beautifully wooded river course, a unique world of its own, provides the division between two vastly different landscapes and biotopes.

The *Naukluft* (narrow cleft) consists of a massive jumble of rocky mountains carpeted with a diverse flora and abounding with perennial water, a rich bird life and a varied population of wild animals, particularly Hartmann's mountain zebra, which find the conditions to their liking. Leopards, baboons and dassies also thrive in this rugged area. Scenically, the Naukluft Mountains are grand, the rocks vividly coloured. Limestone tints the water a pale green. There are many caves, some of which contain galleries of rock art.

From the entrance the road leads for 12 km to the ranger's house and then on to the camping ground (with modern ablution block), where trees provide shade. Initially the park could only be explored on foot; a two-day 4 × 4 trail has subseqently been developed. The old farmhouse, now known as Hiker's Haven, is the base for a magnificent circular hiking route through this portion of the Namib-Naukluft Park. The route, known as the Naukluft Hiking Trail, is 120 km long and takes eight days to complete, with a shorter 17 km long version known as the Waterkloof Trail and a 10 km long Olive Trail named from the wild olive trees. Reservations for the long hike must be made well in advance. Medical certificates of fitness are essential.

A shorter but most interesting walk leads up the actual Naukluft, climbing the course of a perennial stream which tumbles down the narrow gorge in a succession of deep pools, cascades and waterfalls, The path eventually reaches the plateau summit of the mountains and continues its way while there is also a relatively easy return path to the base camp. The views are tremendous, and remnants of the old German 'cannon roads' made during the fighting with Hendrik Witbooi and his followers may be seen, as well as many lovely trees and plants. From the summit the path makes a return descent down the gorge of the Gorordsib stream, passes a Bushman cave in a spectacular cliff and several deep swimming-pools, and eventually joins the stream from the Naukluft.

Permits to enter the Namib-Naukluft Park may be obtained from the offices of Namibia Wildlife Resorts, Private Bag 13267, Windhoek 9000. Phone (0964) 61 23-6975.

THE C14 ROAD FROM WALVIS BAY TO THE B9 ROAD LINKING KEETMANSHOOP TO LÜDERITZ

The C14 road provides a diverting journey through the border country on the eastern side of the Namib-Naukluft Park. This is an exciting area of discovery for any traveller through Namibia. The road leads through the ruggedly beautiful terrace lying between the Namib coastal desert and the escarpment of the arid central highland plateau of Namibia. Benefited by at least a small rainfall for itself as well as the passage of rivers which, although erratic in their flow and dependent on rainfall on the arid central highlands, contribute to the lower-lying terrace sufficient water to make it semi-arid rather than desert. Hardy life-forms considerably different from those inhabiting the Namib Desert find it possible to exist on the terrace. Edible plants, especially *uintjies* (edible bulbous plants) such as *Moraeaedulas* and *Cyperus* sp., are especially common.

Quite an industry in this border country is developing to provide services to the growing tourist demand. Following the C14 provides a unique touring experience which few visitors will ever regret. The road is mainly gravel but maintained in good condition for all types of vehicles.

Leaving Walvis Bay the C14 road leads westwards for 189 km across the gravel plain of the Namib. At the bridge crossing the Kuiseb River there is an entrance gate to the park. The road then turns south and commences its winding way down through the western border country of the Namib. After 16 km the C28 road turns eastwards and provides a spectacular and steep route 182 km long to Windhoek.

After another 72 km the C14 road reaches an odd little place with the name of *Solitaire* (lonely), simply a trading station, a borehole, a couple of trees and a petrol pump. Several films have been produced using this solitary place as a setting for works of rather mixed quality, some of the producers being driven away by the locals after making nuisances of themselves.

After exploring the delights of Solitaire (and it is a perfectly amiable little place) the C14 road divides, one branch, the C19 road, continues southwards crosses the usually bone dry *Tsondab* (sand path) River and an arm of the Namib-Naukluft Park. After 40 km the road reaches a turn-off of the D826 road which provides access to the office of the Ministry of Environment and Tourism at *Sesriem* (six thongs). This place received its name from the deep gorge of the *Tsauchab* River. The river was so named from the ash bushes *Salsola* sp. growing there and burned to obtain lye for soap making. The gorge is so narrow and deep that it is said that s*es riem* (six thongs) were needed to lower buckets to fill with water. Apart from the administration-run camping ground, the Sossusvlei Karos lodge offers accommodation in the vicinity.

From Sesriem a road leads for 55 km into the big-dune country to reach a parking area known as Deadvlei. From here a track continues for 5 km to reach the famous Sossusvlei. A maximum of 50 vehicles only are allowed to travel to the vlei in each of three daily sessions, dawn to 10h00; 10h00 to 14h00; 14h00 to 16h00. Reservations should be made in advance (especially during school holidays) through the Namibia Wildlife Resorts office in Windhoek. There is no accommodation at Sossusvlei. No barbecues or camping are permitted and the huge dunes (reputably the highest in the world) are closely protected from damage by persons indulging in what is known as *bundu bashing* (wilderness destruction).

Sossusvlei is a marsh at the terminal point of the Tsauchab River. This river occasionally manages to bring some water down from rainfall on the central plateau. The river has the futile hope of reaching the sea but is totally frustrated when it reaches the big-dune country. Abandoning all hope of further progress the river, in seasons of good rainfall, simply expires in the dehydrated marsh. It creates for a little while a miniature lake reflecting in its mirror surface the towering dunes. They look down into it, primping in strange vanity, with complex permutations of colours – red, gold, ochre, rose. Strange shapes and shadows may be seen, elusive and haunting, seeming to belong to an eerie elder world of far away and long ago.

Throughout the day the colours and forms of the dunes change with the light. The scene is unforgettable. The visitor sighs at having to leave such a magic place and wonders whether fate will be kind enough to allow another visit some other day.

Sossusvlei is a bilingual name. *Sossus* is a Bushman word meaning a place where water gathers and *vlei* in Afrikaans meaning a marsh.

From the turn-off of the D826 to Sesriem the C19 road continues for 151 km to reach Maltahöhe where it rejoins the C14 road.

The D826 road continues its own way south and passes the 150 000 hectare Namib Rand Nature Reserve consisting of a group of nine privately owned farms with a 100 km long border with the Namib-Naukluft Park. These farms were originally surveyed in the early forties and planned to be sheep farms but this was soon found to be impossible. Domestic livestock could not flourish in a climate of heat, minimal rainfall (80 mm a year if the area is lucky) and periods of relentless total drought. The landowners turned on the wildlife – oryx, springbok and other survivors of harsh conditions – and hunted them almost to extinction in an effort to survive on the proceeds of selling venison, skins and horns.

One of the farms, *Gorrasis,* owned by Albi Brückner, a Windhoek business man, was fortunate in that its owner was also a nature lover. He bought the farm in 1984, not with any agricultural idea, but simply because of its scenic beauty. In 1988 he purchased the bordering farms *Die Duine* and *Stellarine.* He then founded Namib Rand Desert Trails (Pty) Ltd with the purpose of buying another six farms. All the farms were consolidated to form the Namib Rand Nature Reserve. The reserve was opened to the public for visits, safaris, hot-air balloon and aeroplane trips over the vast mix of desert dune country, grassveld and mountains. Mwisho camp 50 km from Sesriem is one of the tourist bases in the area. It is a comfortable tented camp beside a waterhole, a pleasant island in the surrounding sea of sand. Hot-air balloons are based at this camp.

Another 30 km south down the D826 road beyond the turn to Mwisho there is a turn leading for 20 km to the Dune Camp on the farm *Wolwedans* (dance of the hyenas) where there is a landing strip for light aircraft and a tented camp. This is the base for low-level flights over the dune desert, including Sossusvlei. Visitors have the experience of sleeping in the dunes and observing night skies completely undimmed by pollution or artificial light.

NUBIB NATURE CAMP

Remote, silent and completely wild, the *Nubib Mountains* have the name of a chieftain of a small group of Nama people who were wiped out there by the Germans. The farms below the mountains have names such as *Verweg* (far away) and *Wêreldsend* (world's end).

In 1991, one of these farms, *Nubib West* was bought by André van Rooyen whose daughter, Beandré, known as Sakkie, was a mechanical engineer in Pretoria. She enjoyed her work but she did not like city life. She asked her father to let her manage the farm, a pure wilderness area, arid and hot, without any development except for a farmhouse and a few outlying huts used by herders.

Beandré settled on the farm entirely on her own. She walked and climbed and explored the mountains. It became something of a love affair between her and the mountains. She moved away from the farmhouse into a herder's hut and installed a small portable generator to power a computer and light.

She had books and an astronomical telescope to study the stars, superbly brilliant in the unpolluted air. A few of the neighbours considered that she was daft, a mountain *klipspringer* (rock jumper) of a young woman, she'd never marry, come to a bad end.

But for everybody in this world, there is somebody else. Visiting a neighbour she met a masculine klipspringer like herself. His name was Gideon Davids. They discovered they shared a dream, to walk 150 km over the giant sand dunes to reach the sea. To do this on your own would be foolhardy. They did it together, reached the sea, decided to get married and returned home again. Together they started Nubib Adventures, offering visitors guided hikes deep into the mountains they both love so much.

Today Nubib Nature Camp offers visitors various hikes as well as a 4 × 4 drive to the summit of the mountains, a hike back down a superbly beautiful but difficult ravine, hikes into the dune country and visits to Sossusvlei.

The campsite has facilities for 10 tents/chalets, each with its own bathroom, and a restaurant.

Contact them at P O Box 25, Maltahöhe or phone (09264) 6638 and ask for Namgorab 5503.

At 27 km south of the turn to *Wolwedans* there is a turn to the research centre on *Die Duine* (the dunes). Shortly after this the D827 road turns off east and leads to Maltahöhe where it joins the C14 road. The D826 road continues southwards and passes the camp of Nubib Nature Camp. South of the entrance to Nubib Nature Camp, the D826 road continues southwards then turns westwards to reach the interesting Duwisib Castle and Duwisib Farm Rest Camp which offers very affordable self-catering camping sites with meals on request. At the castle there is a picnic area and a pleasant camp site.

The castle of *Duwisib* (a lime place without water) was built by Baron Hans Heinrich von Wolf to please his American bride, Jayta. It was designed by Wilhelm Sander, the architect who created the castles in Windhoek. It was an expensive construction. Building material, furniture, antiques, a collection of firearms, were shipped from Germany and laboriously dragged up from the harbour of Lüderitz by a fleet of twenty ox-wagons. It took two years to complete the work. Local stone was used, quarried by Italian stone masons. The building was completed in 1909. What the American bride, reputably an heiress, thought of the place and its surroundings is unknown. It was abandoned with the outbreak of the First World War in 1914. The castle is open to visitors.

The Baron bred horses on his estate and survivors of these pure-blooded animals are thought to have been the ancestors of a troop of several hundred feral horses which escaped from domestication during the First World War and still go very much their own way at Garub where they frequent a watering place just off the B4 road 100 km east of Lüderitz.

From Duwisib the D826 road continues southwards for 21 km and then joins the D831 road which leads south-eastwards and then joins the C14 road on its north–south route. The C14 road, meanwhile, continues south-eastwards from Solitaire. After 13 km, the C24 road branches off eastwards through the steep *Remhoogte* (brake-shoe) Pass and continues for 166 km to Rehoboth on the main north–south route B1 highway of Namibia.

Beyond this turn-off, the C14 road continues south-westwards for another 39 km and then reaches a turn-off 9 km long to the entrance gate of the portion of the Namib-Naukluft Park.

THE WITBOOI WAR

The trouble between the Germans and the followers of Hendrik Witbooi took place in 1894. The Witbooi people had immigrated to Namibia from Pella in South Africa. After wandering about in search of a suitable home they settled at Gibeon about 1803 and became embroiled in the interminable tribal warfare of those times. In 1880, Hendrik Witbooi claimed to have seen a vision in which he was told to unite the Nama people by leading them against the Herero tribe of the north.

Hendrik was then about 40 years of age. He had been baptised by missionaries in Gibeon in 1868. He became obsessed in what he considered to be a divine mission to wipe out the Herero people and create a Nama nation ruled by himself as king.

A long, vicious conflict commenced. In 1888 Hendrik succeeded his father, Moses, as chief of the Witbooi people. The Germans were then in process of consolidating their rule over South-West Africa, as it was then called. Hendrik refused to place himself under German rule. He left Gibeon and moved to Hornkranz. In April 1893 he was driven out of that stronghold by Curt van Francis and retreated to the Naukluft Mountains. The Germans dragged heavy cannons into the most improbable positions. Hendrik Witbooi and his men were as elusive as the leopards. Hendrik fragmented his men into small groups which slipped away into the ravines, climbed cliffs and left no tracks for pursuers to follow.

The battle of Naukluft had to end if only through the heat exhaustion of the contestants. A treaty was signed on 15 September 1894 at Tsams on the western side of the mountains. The Witbooi's were allocated more land at Gibeon. They settled there again but in October 1904 they went into revolt. Numerous German and Afrikaans settlers were killed. On 29 October 1905 Hendrik Witbooi was wounded in a clash at Vaalgras near Tses. It was a slight wound but he died of blood poisoning. The site of his grave is unknown.

The C14 road, after passing the entrance to the Park, continues its southerly way and passes the Bullspoort farm of Ernst and Johanna Sauber. This 10 000 ha farm takes its name from *Buls Poort* (bulls' pass) through the Naukluft Mountains used by ox-wagons and stock herds. The ruins of the police post which guarded this pass still stand, with a graveyard of some of the troopers who died on duty in this lonely place.

The Sauber family settled in this area in 1885. They endeavoured, like other settlers, to farm exotic domestic livestock in a totally unsuitable environment. Karakul sheep and goats were about the only farm animals which could survive but only at the expense of damaging the environment. The disastrous drought of the 1980s forced many farmers either into bankruptcy or adaptation to the realities of their environment. The Saubers converted their farmhouse into comfortable accommodation for visitors with electricity powered by a solar system. Hiking, riding and 4 × 4 trails have been opened to such places as the stone window, a spectacular arch in the mountains. Mountain scenery is magnificent.

From the turn to Bullspoort the C14 road continues southwards to reach, 114 km from the entrance to the old mountain zebra park, the village of *Maltahöhe* (Malta heights) named after Malta, wife of the District Commandant, Von Burgsdorff, and on account of the high-lying situation of the village.

From Maltahöhe the tarmac road, C19 leads for 113 km to Mariental on the main B1 north–south highway of Namibia. The C14 road continues southwards for 150 km to reach the small rural centre of Helmeringhausen. From thence there is the choice of either the C13 road for 113 km to Aus on the B4 road from Keetmanshoop to Lüderitz, or to continue south on the C19 road to Goageb, also on the B4 road (see Chapter Forty-Six).

The Naukluft mountain area of the Namib-Naukluft Park is maintained as a wilderness area. Only one party comprising between 3 and 30 visitors is allowed into the park at a time. No casual visitors are allowed and all bookings must be made through the offices of Namibia Wildlife Resorts, Private Bag 13267, Windhoek 9000, or phone (0964) 61 23-6975.

THE SKELETON COAST

The name 'Skeleton Coast' or the 'Coast of Death' is applied specifically to the desolate coast stretching between the Ugab River in the south and the Kunene River in the north. The Portuguese called this area the Sands of Hell. The Skeleton Coast was given its name in 1933 by Sam Davis, newspaperman and writer, who was reporting on the futile search for a Swiss airman, Carl Nauer, who disappeared somewhere along the coast while attempting to break the Cape Town to London solo air record.

It is an apt name, for many people have lost their lives on this formidable coast, with its mists, powerful currents, cold sea and almost totally bare gravel plains, where no rain falls and there is no surface water other than a few salty springs. Modern road construction, using the ingenious technique of soaking gypsum in brine, has opened up almost the whole coast. It is now known as the National West Coast Recreational Area. The coast north of Swakopmund is a great resort for fishermen who find the cold, misty air a tonic after the heat and dehydration of the interior. At several points up the coast the administration has created resorts for anglers, with toilets and camping sites. Today this coast is not nearly as forbidding as it used to be. Wrecks of ships, run-down mines and abandoned prospectors' claims still remain as relics of former hardships and the lost hopes of finding vast deposits of diamonds and precious minerals.

From Swakopmund, the salt road travels up the coast past the suburbs of Vineta and Tamariskia, and after 5 km passes the turn-off to the Mile 4 Caravan Park (see Swakopmund). At 9 km the road passes the salt works of the South West Africa Salt Company. Permits to visit these works may be obtained from the operating company in Swakopmund. The salt produced is largely used in the manufacture of plastics, synthetic materials and explosives. Oysters and clams are now cultivated in the pans.

At 16 km the salt road reaches the fishing site of Mile 8 and, 7 km further on, the Mile 14 caravan park where camping sites are available. After a further 7 km the salt road reaches a rather haphazard collection of seaside shacks and bungalows erected at the place known as *Wlotzkasbaken* (Wlotzka's beacon) after Paul Wlotzka, a transport rider in Swakopmund and a keen fisherman who built a hut and guided visitors here to an excellent fishing ground.

At 42,5 km from Swakopmund, the road reaches the fishing site of Mile 30 with its facilities of toilets and parking bays but where no camping is allowed. The next turn-off, after 13,5 km leads for 4 km to the camping and caravan park of Jakkalsputz. Thirteen kilometres beyond this camp, the road reaches the coastal resort of ...

HENTIES BAY

Named after Major Hentie van der Merwe who started recreational fishing there in 1929, *Henties Bay* consists of shops, tea-rooms, garages, a number of bungalows and a hotel. There is a sandy, dark-coloured beach situated at the choked-up mouth of the Omaruru River. The river valley now serves as a golf-course. Fishing and swimming (in cold water) and some amusing social life, are the season activities of the resort. Anglers secure good catches of such fish as galjoen, kabeljou, steenbras and stompneus, all of which provide excellent eating. Rock lobsters are numerous and the quality of their flesh makes them world renowned. Pilchards and anchovies have always frequented these waters in vast shoals but commercial overfishing has practically destroyed them.

From Henties Bay the branch road leads inland for 2 km to rejoin the main C34 coastal salt road. The landscape is pure Namib gravel plain – hard surface, no dunes and a few shrubs. At the junction of the Henties Bay road with the main coastal road, another road continues eastwards for 118 km to join the B2 tarmac Swakopmund–Windhoek road.

The coastal road continues northwards. After 5,5 km a turn-off, C35, leads inland for 158 km, past the Brandberg, to the Uis mine and thence to Khorixas or Omaruru. After 25 km the coastal road passes a cluster of pans and salt works, with a turn-off 3,5 km further on leading to the Strathmore Tin Mine. The area is notable for its mirages, salt pans, black basalt reefs along the coast and eroded dolerite, rutile and ilmenite gravel which covers the lighter-coloured sand.

One kilometre north of the turn-off to the Strathmore mine is the Mile 72 Caravan Park with camping sites. It was while staying in this caravan park in 1972 that Sydney Pieters, the gemstone authority from Windhoek, tired of unproductive fishing and turned his attention to some interesting-looking geological indications close to the camp. He found several aquamarines at first, and then a strange, slender hexagonal, light-blue coloured crystal, 3 cm in length, which he did not recognise. He kept the crystal for a year and then sent it to the Smithsonian Institute in Washington for identification. He might not have caught any fish on his coastal outing, but what he had found shook the mineralogists of the Smithsonian Institute. The crystal was Jeremejebite, a rarity discovered in Siberia 80 years previously, in the form of two crystals and some fragments the size of sugar grains. One crystal had found its way to the British Museum but the other vanished and no further traces of the gemstone had ever been found.

Jeremejebite is a boron mineral with a hardness of 7 on the scale of 10. The deposit at Mile 72 is blue in colour while the original Siberian crystals were white. The Russian name, pronounced with a soft 'j', is derived from a nobleman concerned with the first discovery. The crystals found at Mile 72 are in a boron-rich setting and are associated with tourmaline, muscovite and apatite deposits which occur in a weird 'lost world' landscape of dry salt pans and dark, gravel-covered hillocks looming out of the Namib plain.

Ten kilometres from the caravan park (129 km from Swakopmund) the C34 road reaches a turn-off to ...

THE CAPE CROSS SEAL RESERVE

In the year 1485 the Portuguese navigator, Diego Cão, was the first European to reach as far south down the coast of Africa as Cape Cross. In terrible isolation on a rocky crag, with the cold grey-green Atlantic to the west and the desert wilderness of the Namib to the east, he erected a cross on which was inscribed in Latin and Portuguese.

> 'Since the creation of the world 6 684 years have passed and since the birth of Christ 1 484 years and so the illustrious Don John has ordered this pillar to be erected here by Diego Cão, his knight.'

Diego Cão paid with his life for daring to sail as far as this desolate spot. He died there of some unknown cause and was buried at the height named the *Serra Padrado* (hillock of the monument) near Cape Cross. His dust remains in that place, but the cross was later removed to the Oceanographical Museum in Berlin and a granite replica now stands on the original site.

A large number of Cape fur seals (about 150 000) flourish in the cold water of the Benguela Current on the south-western coast of Africa. Along this coast are numerous islets and isolated parts of the shore which they use as nurseries for their young. Although the area is described as a seal sanctuary (6 000 ha in extent), the mammals are hunted for their pelts. The cows produce one pup each year. It is the pelts of these offspring which yield the best fur for the making of sealskin coats. The earliest commercial exploitation of any part of South West Africa was by sealers from Europe and America who discovered the seal colonies, killing many thousands of the animals each year. Sealskins remain in constant demand. Each year pelts, salted and graded according to size and quality, are packed in large barrels and shipped overseas. The carcasses are processed into bone-meal, liver oil, meat meal and fat. The fat is utilised in the perfume and margarine industries.

Breeding takes place during October and November, at which time a large seal rookery is the scene of great activity. The bulls, weighing up to 360 kg, fight for territorial rights in one of the nurseries. After many bloody battles, a bull establishes his territory but can seldom risk leaving it for fear of a competitor invading his harem. The bulls fast for about six weeks, living on their accumulated fat. Pups are born in the rookery, and mating takes place usually within five days after birth, the gestation period being 361 days. A bull in his prime can have a substantial harem of cows, but the day he weakens, either through ill health, injury or the onset of old age, a younger bull will invade his territory and take over the cows.

The diet of seals consists of cephalopods, crustaceans and fish, with an adult seal consuming about 5 kg of food a day. They hunt individually, there being no evidence of concerted planning by groups of seals. They frequent the shallows, searching the kelp beds for octopus, crabs or lobsters, but they can also dive to depths of 80 m. A curious and as-yet-unexplained habit of seals is their swallowing of stones. It has been suggested that these stones act as ballast. As many as 70 have been found in the stomach of a seal. Young seals seem to swallow more stones than adults.

Sleek and beautiful, seals are playful and friendly with swimmers and there is no record of one attacking a human being. They are hunted by sharks and have no defence against them other than flight.

The Seal Reserve is open to visitors daily from 10h00 to 17h00. There is no accommodation. Drinking water and toilets are available. No pets or motor cycles allowed.

Beyond the turn-off to Cape Cross the coastal C34 road continues for a further 24,5 km, passing (153,5 km from Swakopmund) the fishing site at Horingbaai, which has toilets and parking bays.

The road continues past several large pans. Numerous claim pegs and beacons reveal intense prospecting activity for a variety of precious minerals – somewhat surprising in a landscape which, from its dark gravel surface and black sea sand, seems to be in mourning, a real coast of death.

At 161,5 km a turn-off leads to the Brandbergwes copper mine, while a further 43,5 km brings the salt road to the Ugab River with the Skeleton Coast Park entrance gate on its south bank, 205 km from Swakopmund.

THE SKELETON COAST PARK

The Skeleton Coast Park covers an area of 1 636 000 ha, conserving a very strange landscape of fog-bound coast, gravel plains, dunes in the north, sand, persistent wind, mirages and a singularly eerie atmosphere. From the entrance gate which closes at 15h00 each day, the salt road closely follows the shoreline. It passes the remains of ships such as the *South West Sea*, wrecked in 1976, and the derelict diamond-mine known as Toscanini (51 km from the entrance gate); remnants of the *Luanda*, wrecked in 1969; and fragments of several other forgotten shipping disasters which still are found along the shoreline. A turn-off (C39), 103 km from the entrance gate, leads inland to Khorixas. Pinkish-coloured sand dunes now reappear in the Namib, the first since the Swakop River. The salt road runs northwards between them and the sea. At 10 km from the Khorixas turn-off the road reaches the seasonal fishermen's resort of Torra Bay, said to be named after the outcrop of dolerite boulders which the Damara people called *Torra*. This resort is open during the summer holiday season, with camping sites and tents available for hire. There is an admission charge for adults and children.

At 12 km north of Torra Bay the road crosses the reed-grown course of the Unjab River, with the remains of the *Atlantic,* wrecked in 1977, lying at its mouth. Springbok, oryx and other wild creatures graze in the river valley. It is a fertile example of a linear oasis in a desert. Beyond the river the salt road continues for a further 36 km and then, 161 km from the entrance gate (366 km from Swakopmund), reaches the camp and administrative centre of the Skeleton Coast Park situated at the old mine of the Desert Diamond Mining Company at Terrace Bay.

The Terrace Bay camp consists of bungalows, offices, a restaurant, shop, landing-strip, and a jumble of debris left behind after the spectacular 42 million rand bankruptcy of the celebrated Mr Ben du Preez, whose name will always be associated with lost hopes on the Skeleton Coast. From the camp the road continues for a further 80 km up the coast, ending at *Möwe Bay*, named after a German warship of former years. A special permit is needed to visit Möwe Bay, the administrative centre for the northern part of the Skeleton Coast Park which lies between the Hoanib and Kunene Rivers.

The northern portion of the park is maintained as a pure wilderness area. It was on this coast on 30 November 1942 that the *Dunedin Star* was wrecked, followed by the tug, *Sir Charles Elliot* which had been sent to rescue survivors. Later, a Ventura aircraft sent to drop supplies landed in a rescue attempt and stuck fast in the sand. Remnants of these wrecks still remain. On 13 September 1997 a sad disaster happened off this coast when a German military Tupolev aircraft, flying to Cape Town with 24 Navy personnel aboard, and an American C141 Star Lifter cargo aircraft with a crew of 9, flying from Windhoek to Ascension Island, collided at 10 600 metres altitude in an empty sky. There were no survivors.

Amethysts and agates are found in this area, especially at Sarusas. There are signs of some prehistoric settlement – mysterious circles of stone built by unknown people for unknown purposes. River courses act as linear oases, and game animals are numerous, especially in the Hoarusib canyon. Cape Fria has a large colony of fur seals and Rocky Point is the home of many sea-birds.

Fishing is good all along the Skeleton Coast, where kabeljou, steenbras, galjoen, dassie and other species may be caught. Summer is a popular season, as the cold sea and mists always keep the temperature cool along the coast, providing a complete contrast to the interior. Wind is the main problem, with the cold south-westerly prevailing. It occasionally retreats, however, especially in June and July, giving way to the hot easterly wind known on account of its moaning sound as the *Soo-Oop-Wa*.

TORRA BAY TO OUTJO

The C39 gravel road from Torra Bay to Khorixas provides a very spectacular and unusual travel experience which is at times dusty, but quite within the capability of any good driver in a normal vehicle. The turn-off to Khorixas is 9,5 km south of Torra Bay. The road is sandy at first but soon climbs on to a hard dolerite, gravel-covered plain. The temperature increases abruptly as soon as the road leaves the area influenced by coastal mists. Welwitschia plants appear, thriving in a setting abhorrent to most other plants. After travelling 25 km from the junction with the coastal salt road, the gravel road climbs a ridge of dark-brown rock, with the overlooking hillocks a pronounced purple colour.

Once over the ridge, the road reaches the shallow valley of the Koigab River. The valley is covered in shrubs and a few trees which offer shade and some convenience for man and dog. At 35 km from the coastal road the inland boundary of the Skeleton Coast Park is passed. The road climbs up a wild-looking escarpment where the air becomes considerably cooler.

At 90 km from the coastal road the gravel road linking Khorixas with Kamanjab is reached. Turning to Khorixas, the traveller is faced with a spectacular drive through a rugged mass of strangely shaped, vividly coloured hills, where many interesting rocks may be found at the roadside. The geology is complex and interesting. There is a confusion of sedimentary and igneous rocks, the combination of which produces some remarkable mixtures, metamorphoses, intrusions, changes and colours. Some of the hills are actually composed of volcanic ash spewed out from ancient eruptions and accumulated as vast heaps of debris.

At 132 km from the coast the road reaches a turn-off running 20 km through well-wooded mopane tree country to the slopes of the vividly coloured ridge of hills known as the *Verbrandeberg* (burnt mountain). At the 20 km point there is a turn-off leading to Twyfelfontein. The road continues for a further 5,5 km, passing an odd rock formation known as the Organ Pipes, and then ends at the foot of the remarkable Burnt Mountain. The mountain is a flat-topped remnant of an old plateau, extensive in size. The colours of its cliffs are almost unbelievable, with dark reds and purples predominating.

The road ends where there are piles of black cinder-like rock, resembling slag raked out of a furnace beneath the Burnt Mountain. The place gives one the uncanny impression of being a vast, phantom brick-field or pottery where various demons are employed in the baking of building materials, ceramics and large beer mugs. The Burnt Mountain is the kiln, still red hot, out of which the cinders are regularly raked, forming a pile at its foot.

TWYFELFONTEIN

On the road to the Burnt Mountain there is a 5,5 km turn-off to Twyfelfontein and the world-famous collection of rock engravings. The road ends at the ruins of a farmhouse in a valley at the foot of the Burnt Mountain plateau. The position of the engravings, indicated by arrows, is in the rocks of a steeply sloping ravine east of the farmhouse.

The valley is known in the Damara language as *Uis* (fountain). When it flows, this fountain has attracted game animals and man. Since its nature has always been erratic, Europeans have named it *Twyfelfontein* (doubtful fountain).

There are numerous well-preserved rock engravings here. Their origin is uncertain, but they are probably the work of Bushmen or Nama artists and are estimated by some to be about 5 000 years old. Engraving on rock is difficult, with no chance of erasing errors. The engravings at Twyfelfontein are so skilfully done that they must have been the work of an artist or artists who had previously learned the skill on waste rock and who made no amateurish mistakes. The engravings suggest that the artist experienced keen intellectual pleasure in executing them.

The C38 road from the Skeleton Coast to Khorixas passes the turn-off to the Burnt Mountain and Twyfelfontein and traverses a mopane parkland dotted with isolated hills and ridges. After 28,5 km (160,5 km from the coastal road) a turn-off leads for half a kilometre to the petrified forest, where a considerable number of petrified tree trunks can be seen lying on the ground. No one is certain about their origin and why they are so well preserved.

The main road continues for a further 42 km, then reaches a junction, with a left turn leading for 1,5 km to the fine tourist camp of Khorixas – a real haven in the wilderness, with accommodation, a restaurant, swimming pool and shop.

From the turn-off to the Khorixas rest camp, the C38 road continues for 2,5 km and then reaches the village of Khorixas, formerly known as Welwitschia. *Khorixas* is a corruption of the Damara name, *Gôrigas*, a species of water bush which flourishes in the area. The reason for the misspelling is not known, as 'Gôrigas' is the correct pronunciation of the name. The village is growing considerably as the administrative centre for Damaraland. It is 202 km from the salt road up the Skeleton Coast. The population is 6 500.

From Khorixas the main gravel road continues eastwards through the mopane parkland. After 8 km there is a crossroads with a turn north to Kamanjab and south to Uis. A further 23 km brings the road to a turn-off leading southwards for 18 km to the oft-photographed rock known as *Vingerklip* (finger stone). This is one of several detached pinnacles of rock remaining in the area after the erosion of an ancient landscape. It is about 35 m high and stands on a private farm whose owner charges an admission fee per car.

From the turn-off to Vingerklip the main road continues eastwards for 5,5 km, then passes a turn-off to the three-star Bambatsi holiday ranch, a popular resort with a restaurant and accommodation.

After the turn-off to Bambatsi, the C38 road stretches for 72 km, then reaches the town of Outjo 310 km from the Skeleton Coast salt road.

KALKFELD, OMARURU, UIS AND THE BRANDBERG

From Otjiwarongo a fine tarmac road, C33, leads south-westwards over an undulating plain covered with acacia and other trees. This is superb ranching country where fine herds of beef stock, mainly zebu varieties, graze on the grass and leaves. Occasional hillocks rise abruptly from the bush. After 70 km, the road passes through the small rail centre of Kalkfeld, with its cluster of stores and houses watching the trains go by. After 64 km of pleasant travelling, the tarmac road reaches the town of ...

OMARURU

Omaruru with its population of 4 000, has a Herero name, *oMaruru*, meaning 'the bitters'. The name is derived from the bitter-tasting water of the area which affected the milk of the tribal cattle herds.

The Omaruru River, on whose banks the town stands, is dry for most of the year but is formidable during its occasional floods. The river banks are lined with magnificent trees; and the town, with its long main street running parallel to the river, is well shaded and pleasant. The town is a rail, ranching and dairy centre, with a tourist camp situated beneath the trees to accommodate travellers exploring the country.

The town was originally a German police post. During the 1904 Herero War it had a few hectic experiences. The Herero laid siege to the post. The officer commanding, Captain Victor Franke, had a rough time quelling an upheaval that cost the lives of 123 German civilians and, eventually, many thousands of Herero. The war is commemorated in Omaruru by the Franke Tower, a fortification erected in 1907 which now houses a museum.

On 4 August 1905, the narrow-gauge railway reached Omaruru from the coast. After being linked to the outside world, the town started to grow, receiving its first municipal council on 22 July 1909. The narrow-gauge railway was eventually replaced by a wide-gauge line in 1961. A creamery opened there in 1928 and was the first to be registered in the territory.

From Omaruru, the main tarmac C33 road continues south-westwards. After 3 km a gravel turn-off leads to the Kranzberg mine and Paula's cave. At 60,5 km from Omaruru the road joins the main tarmac B2 Windhoek–Swakopmund road.

Another interesting drive, C36, from Omaruru leads westwards to the tin mine at Uis and also to the Brandberg. This gravel road crosses a vast plain covered with shrubs and acacia trees. The imposing heights of the Brandberg lie on the western horizon. To the south is the massive bulk of the Erongo Mountains. The landscape becomes increasingly arid towards the west. After 30 km there is a turn-off south leading to the Bushman caves and tourist resort of Etemba, where accommodation is available in a two-star ranch-style private hotel. At 115 km there is a turn-off which passes the Spitzkoppe on its way to Usakos. After a further 1,5 km (116,5 km from Omaruru), the road reaches the tin mine of ...

UIS

The name *Uis* simply means 'a spring of water' in the Damara language. The landscape is composed of many interesting varieties of pegmatites containing tin intrusions which appear as black-coloured streaks and blobs. In 1911 Dr Paul, while journeying by horse from Otjimboyo to the Brandberg, observed these signs of tin. He was an employee of the Deutsche Kolonial Gesellschaft, and the company pegged a number of claims in the area. A local farmer, Etemba Schmidt, also pegged a substantial block.

Mining commenced, but conditions were primitive and there was a serious shortage of water. The pioneers persisted, using donkeys to drag rolling barrels of water obtained from a spring known as Uis Water, 13 km away. In 1923, August Stauch, who had started the diamond rush at Kolmanskop, bought up all the tin claims and consolidated them into the Namib Tin Mines Ltd. This company, unfortunately, went bankrupt in 1930. The claims passed through various hands, with a German mining engineer, E Vaatz, working them from 1934. With the outbreak of the Second World War, he was interned. After hostilities, in 1948, the Custodian of Enemy Property sold the tin claims for £13 000 to a partnership headed by a Mr Munro. After diligent work in the area, Mr Munro and his wife were killed in an air crash in 1949. As a result of his labours, however, the Uis Tin Mining Company (SWA) Ltd was formed in 1951 and the first large-scale mining commenced. In 1958 Industrial Minerals Exploration (Pty) Ltd, a subsidiary of the South African Iron and Steel Industrial Corporation (Iscor), acquired the mineral rights of the Uis mine with associated properties and claims scattered over the Namib desert.

After investigating the various prospects, the company decided to concentrate on the Uis mine. In 1966 the Industrial Minerals Mining Corporation was formed to exploit this property. The company was a wholly owned subsidiary of Iscor which set out to develop a major mine in the area. To achieve this, the problem of water had to be solved. Adequate supplies were eventually obtained through a pipeline running all the way from the Omaruru River where considerable quantities are stored in natural reservoirs beneath the sand.

In the vicinity of Uis there are eight major outcrops of pegmatite dykes containing fairly low concentrations of tin. They vary in width from a few centimetres to about 60 m, and lengths of over 900 m are exposed on the surface. Mining is by opencast quarry. The tin is processed to a concentrate which is sent to Swakopmund where it is loaded on to trains for the long ride to a reduction plant at Vanderbijlpark in Gauteng.

A small town has been built west of the mine to house the workers. The mine lies in the Damara Okambahe Reserve.

From Uis the C36 gravel road continues westwards towards the Brandberg. After 28 km, it joins the C35 gravel road from Khorixas (127 km) to Henties Bay (120 km). This is a road which yields magnificent views of the Brandberg, the highest massif in the territory, and its principal peak, Köningstein (2 579 m high). This range of mountains is impressive from any direction. Thirteen kilometres down the road towards Henties Bay, there is a turn-off leading to the Brandberg West mine. This road is worth exploring for those who wish to photograph the Brandberg.

Fifteen kilometres up the C35 road towards Khorixas from the junction with the road from Uis, there is a turn-off leading for 30 km to the Tsisab gorge in the Brandberg, where may be seen one of the most celebrated examples of rock art.

THE WHITE LADY OF THE BRANDBERG

The rock shelter containing this famous painting lies in a superb setting. The *Tsisab* gorge is named after the leopards which live in the area. It is a wild and beautiful place where a vast jumble of rocks, remnants of many ancient landslides, choke up the gorge. When it rains, a stream somehow finds its way through this wilderness of stone. Pools of water remain well into the dry season before they sink beneath the sand to hide from the heat of the sun.

It was in 1918 that the surveyor and painter, Reinhard Maack, first found the rock shelter in this gorge and drew the attention of the world to the gallery of paintings it contained. The Abbé Breuil visited the site in 1948 and brought out a book in which the rock art of the shelter was reproduced. The book also established the fame of the central figure, named the White Lady of the Brandberg by the Abbé Breuil, who speculated that she was of Phoenician or other exotic origin.

These days, the impression is that the good Abbé was possibly romantically inclined. The painting of the figure in question is intriguing, beautiful and most interesting, but the depiction is almost certainly that of a male – probably a youth daubed in white clay for some ceremony or dance. In fact, it would be more precise to call 'her' the White Knight of the Brandberg! Whatever the identification of the central figure – and it is still controversial – this gallery of prehistoric rock art in the Maack Cave has fascinated innumerable visitors. A walk up the valley to the shelter (well marked with arrows) is an exciting experience. Please do not throw liquids of any kind over the paintings to make them clearer. Such drenchings have greatly harmed the gallery, causing the paintings to fade and decay.

Chapter Forty-Six
NAMIBIA

The Southern Areas

From Windhoek, the main tarmac B1 road and railway to the south have a lengthy, steady climb from the 1 655 m altitude at which the capital is situated to the siding of Kruin (1 922 m). The scenery comprises a rugged mass of bronze-coloured, bushy hills and the journey is attractive either by rail or road.

Once over the ridge, the railway and road commence a winding descent, passing the station, store and hotel of *Aris* (place of the steenbok) 24 km from Windhoek. From this point the road traverses a parkland of handsome trees, many of which support the unwieldy community nests of the social weaver birds. Long grass, high hills and graceful trees combine to produce a pleasant landscape. After 89 km the road reaches the town of ...

REHOBOTH

With a population of about 60 000 this is the centre for the tribe known as the *Basters*. Their origin can be traced back to about 30 Europeans who settled in the mountains south of the Gariep River, married Nama girls and fathered numerous offspring. In 1868 about 90 Baster families under the leadership of Hermanus van Wyk moved north to the site of the abandoned Rhenish mission station of Rehoboth which had been established in 1844 by the Rev H Kleinschmidt on behalf of the Swartbooi people. The mission had been destroyed during the war between the Herero and Jan Jonker Afrikaner in 1869. The Basters settled in this beautifully wooded area in 1870 and developed into the present community, with a handsome church watching over the town built among the trees.

Rehoboth has an interesting, well laid out museum, very active and innovative in research in such matters as conservation of the acacia trees on the Oanib River plain, south-east of Rehoboth. There is study in the cultivation of such drought-resistant plants as *Acanthosicyos horridus* (the Nara melon) and other valuable indigenous food producers, local and natural history, archaeological finds, traditional houses and many other subjects presented in this very worthwhile museum. It is open Monday to Friday 10h00 to 12h00; 14h00 to 16h00.

There is a mineral bath adjoining the town, with a swimming-pool, thermal bath, bungalows and caravan sites. It is a recommended stop for any traveller, especially after a long, hot drive. It is self catering.

South of Rehoboth the B1 road leads through fine parklike country made doubly attractive by a varied collection of mountains and hills lying to the north and east. After 23 km the B1 road crosses the Tropic of Capricorn. As the road continues south through good ranching and livestock country, the trees dwindle into a well-grassed savanna with low acacia thornbush. At 97 km the road passes through the small rail and trading centre of *Kalkrand* (chalk ridge).

For a further 52 km the B1 road travels south across the savanna, then reaches a point where the landscape changes notably. The road suddenly loses more than 100 m in altitude, descending an escarpment into the broad and level valley of the Fish River. At the bottom of this turn-off, 58 km from Kalkrand, a tarmac turn-off leads for 12 km to the ...

HARDAP DAM

Completed in 1963, this dam is one of the show-pieces of Namibia and is a major recreational asset to a thirsty land. The 39,2 m high dam wall in the Fish River contains a lake holding 300 million cubic metres of water covering an area of 25 square kilometres. This is the largest dam in Namibia. The dam irrigates an extensive agricultural settlement producing a considerable variety of products including table grapes and vegetables.

The administration has developed the lake and its verges into a recreational area with water sports and fishing. Bungalows, a caravan park, swimming pool, restaurant and shop have been built on a viewsite. The area surrounding the lake is a nature reserve sheltering a population of oryx, mountain zebra, eland, springbok, red hartebeest, kudu and other antelope. Black rhino have been reintroduced to the area. Bird life is prolific, including a large population of pelicans, flamingoes and fish eagles.

The lake projects 30 km upriver and contains vast quantities of fish such as large-mouth and small-mouth yellowfish, blue kurper, carp, barbel, mud mullet and mudfish. There is an aquarium in the main office block and a fish-breeding station of the Namibian Fish Institute. Excellent fish dishes are served in the restaurant. Try the bream.

The origin of the name *Hardap* is controversial, but is thought to derive from a Nama name originally applied to a big pool now flooded by the waters of the man-made lake. This pool was known as *!Narob*, referring to an iron hook used by the Nama for fishing. A perhaps more interesting etymology is that it means 'nipple' and refers to an overlooking hillock shaped like a female breast.

From the turn-off to the Hardap Dam the main tarmac B1 road continues south for a further 16 km before reaching the town of ...

MARIENTAL

Named after *Marie*, wife of H Brandt, the pioneer settler in the area, *Mariental* (Marie's valley) is the principal town of the Gibeon magisterial district and the rail and trading centre for a considerable industry in the breeding of karakul sheep. There are 6 500 people living there.

From Mariental the B1 road proceeds southwards down the level, increasingly arid floor of the broad Fish River valley. To the east lies the extraordinary flat-topped escarpment of the Weissrand, while to the west the country rises towards the Schwarzrand, 95 km away. The vegetation is notably more sparse than it is in the north.

After 52 km of travel the road passes the railway station of Gibeon, where a turn-off to the west leads to the old mission station of the same name, originally founded in 1863 for the benefit of the Witbooi tribe. The name of Gibeon is associated with meteorites. A meteorite of considerable size exploded over this area. More than 200 pieces have been found, the largest weighing 650 kg. Specimens of the so-called Gibeon shower are housed in many museums throughout the world. The date of the occurrence is uncertain.

The B1 road now traverses a vast arid plain, with only a glimpse of mountain in the west. The dullness of this landscape, however, is relieved by several features of considerable interest, one of which is a height so dominant that for 80 km of travel it provides a constant landmark on the western side of the road. This crater is known as *Mount Brukkeros*, 1 586 m high. Its strange name, meaning 'skin trousers', derives from a tribe once living on its slopes who assumed that garment. The deep crater was formerly thought to be the relic of an extinct volcano but now considered to be the scar of a collision with a meteor. It is over 2 000 m in diameter and has a flat rubble-filled floor. It was from here in 1930 that the Smithsonian Institute studied the surface of the sun in detail. The mission station of Berseba, founded in 1850 for the Nama people, lies just south of Brukkeros.

At 96 km from Mariental the road reaches the small railway centre of *Asab* (the new place). From this point a turn-off leads eastwards for 23 km to the site of what used to be the much-photographed and remarkable natural feature known as *Mukurob* (the finger of God). This formation consisted of a steep cone of slate topped with a 34 m high pillar rock which pointed towards the heavens like a gigantic admonishing finger. A small dried-out pan at the foot of the pillar and the remnant of a table-topped plateau nearby remain of interest. Mukurob, unfortunately, was so precariously balanced that, on 8 December 1988, during a high wind, it blew over and now lies prostrate. God must have had a touch of humour when He made it. Maybe He had forgotten something and had left the finger as a reminder? When He remembered, He blew it over.

Beyond the turn-off to Mukurob the main tarmac road continues south. At a distance of 144 km from Mariental the road passes the railway station, mission and administrative centre known as *Tses,* the name of which refers to a travelling stage of a day's journey.

A further 78 km (222 km from Mariental) brings the road to a gravel turn-off leading eastwards for 13 km to Koës and the farm *Gariganus* where a forest of kokerbooms (*Aloe dichotoma*) may be seen growing. These are trees which normally do not seem to like one another, therefore they grow apart. At this place, however, about 300 of them – fat, thin, short, tall, old and young – do manage to grow in close proximity. They are protected as a national monument. The name of *kokerboom* (quiver tree) comes from the Bushman practice of hollowing out the pithy interiors of the branches and using the tough outer casing of bark as quivers in which to keep their weapons.

Three kilometres south of the turn-off to the kokerboom forest (225 km from Mariental) lies the town of ...

KEETMANSHOOP

Keetmanshoop was named after a wealthy German industrialist, Johan Keetman, who actually never visited the place. He provided funds for the establishment there in 1866 of a mission station for the benefit of Hendrik Zeib's section of the Nama people. The mission flourished, despite a fiendish succession of droughts, violent floods from the usually dry Swartmodder River, and murderous disturbances among the surrounding population of tribespeople. The substantial stone mission church, built in 1895, still dominates the town and its clock continues to sound the hours with a pleasant chime. The building now houses a museum which is open Mondays to Fridays 07h30 to 12h30; 14h00 to 17h00; Saturdays 09h00 to 11h00. Closed Sundays and public holidays.

A school and hostel were attached to the mission and traders arrived. In 1894, after the German annexation of the territory, a garrison established itself there in a fort, later moving to what is now the rather picturesque castle-like police station and administrative building. Settlers began farming (largely the breeding of karakul sheep) and the town started to develop as the principal centre in the southern part of the territory.

In a climate as thirsty as this, a brewery inevitably followed, while four hotels did a roaring trade. In 1908 a narrow-gauge line was completed to the town from Lüderitzbucht on the coast. With an imposing German colonial-type railway station, Keetmanshoop became established as a trading, administrative and commercial centre for a prosperous karakul-breeding district. Political changes after the First World War did not impede the town's growth. Today it is a flourishing and busy centre, with a population of 14 000. It is a neat, clean, friendly place, with several buildings surviving from the German days. The streets are planted with poinciana trees which flower in December. The local German club is notable for its food, especially venison. Visitors are welcome.

THE KARAKUL SHEEP INDUSTRY

This industry in the southern portion of Namibia originated in 1902 when a German fur trader, Paul Thorer, visited Bukhara in Uzbekistan, Russia, during the course of his business. As an experiment he decided to buy some of the fur-producing sheep known as the *karakul* (black lake) or Persian sheep. A total of 69 sheep were shipped to Germany on his behalf, but conditions were totally unsuitable for them.

It was subsequently suggested that climatic conditions in South West Africa, then a German colony, would be similar to those of the arid natural home of the karakul in Asiatic Russia. Friedrich von Lindequist, Governor of German South West Africa at the time, received the idea with enthusiasm. The fat-tailed mutton sheep of the Nama people survived the arid local conditions, so why not karakul? Twelve karakuls were sent from Germany in 1907. Results were so encouraging that two years later Thorer shipped out 278 more sheep. An experimental farm, *Fuerstenwalde*, was established by the Government forming the basis of the present industry.

After the First World War the South African administration continued research in karakul breeding. A new experimental farm was established at *Neudam*, near Windhoek. The standard of sheep was systematically improved. In 1919 the Karakul Breeders' Association was formed and a karakul stud-book opened. As a means of identification, photographs of lambs were taken, and negotiations with international furriers were started to place the industry on a sound commercial basis.

The value of pelts steadily increased. In 1937 the industry genuinely came of age when, for the first time, over 1 million pelts were exported (1 190 212), fetching £1 222 629. In 1941 over 2 million pelts were exported and in 1976 the figure reached 2,8 million, valued at R50 million. The United States and Canada became the largest markets for the pelts. There has been a drastic decline in demand for furs in recent years.

From Keetmanshoop the B1 road continues southwards across savanna country through the range of the *Karasberge* (sharp mountains). This is a landscape of bronze and burnished colours sun-baked to such an extent that it seems never quite to have cooled since its creation. Acacia thorn trees flourish in the area. In their boughs the social weaver birds have built many communal nests where vast flocks live in a strange society of dissident chirps, whistles, scandals and gossips associated with bird life.

After 159 km the road reaches the small rail centre of *Grünau* (green meadow), rather incongruously named after one of the suburbs in Berlin. It forms the junction of a tarmac road (B3) to Karasburg (52 km away) and Upington in South Africa, and of a gravel road to the Fish River Canyon.

Grünau is at a crossroads. To the east the tarmac B3 road keeps company with the railway for 52 km and then reaches the town of ...

KARASBURG

Named after the Karasberge which look down upon the town from the north, Karasburg was proclaimed a town in 1938, at first with the unbeautiful name of Kalkfontein-Suid. This name was changed in 1939 to Karasburg at the same time as a village management board was appointed. In 1947 Karasburg became a municipality.

It is a rail centre for a karakul sheep area and lies on the well-wooded slopes of the mountains. The population is 4 000.

From Karasburg the B3 road continues eastwards with many fine trees and views of the Karasberge. After 114 km the road reaches the village of ...

ARIAMSVLEI

Named after the raisin bushes which grow around a small marsh, *Ariamsvlei* is a rail and trading centre for a farming district much plagued by drought. In this dry part of the world, however, there are still riches. South of Ariamsvlei, on the farm *Border* owned by Jurgens du Preez, there lies a deep valley known as *Oorlogskloof* (war ravine), the scene of fighting between Namas and Germans. In 1981, in the midst of a nine-year-long drought when the farm was on the verge of a forced sale, Jurgens's son, Gideon, came back from the University of Stellenbosch for a farewell look at his old home. Drought or not, he had an affection for the place. He had gone to university to study engineering but had changed to geology. It proved a fortunate change. Taking a last walk through Oorlogskloof, he noticed something lying on the valley floor at the foot of a hill. By killing off the grass, the drought had revealed the nature of some loose rocks. Gideon climbed to the summit of the hill. He found himself standing on top of a hill of solid rose quartz of very fine quality.

The farm was hastily withdrawn from sale. The family started mining. Within three years they were out of trouble and the rose quartz of Oorlogskloof was being dispatched through Ariamsvlei to many parts of the world where it finds its way into the most exquisite jewellery. An interesting stone-walled ruin named !Xamkhanaxas, and known as Namibia's Zimbabwe ruin, is in this area.

From Ariamsvlei the B3 road continues eastwards for 17 km and then reaches the border with South Africa at *Nakop* (tortoise hillock). The border post is open at all times.

Back at Grünau, a gravel road (C12) leads north-westwards on an interesting drive, with the Karasberge range on the northern side of the road. Trees of various kinds, many supporting huge community nests of the weaver birds, provide a parkland. After 38 km there is a turn-off south to Ai-Ais. After another 17 km there is a turn-off to the Fish River Canyon. For 69 km this well-kept gravel road leads across a rocky, undulating plain. With almost startling abruptness the road then reaches the main viewsite into the Fish River Canyon. This is one of the world's great views. On either side of the main viewsite a gravel road leads to other spectacular viewsites. There are toilet facilities at the main viewsite. For caravanners and campers, this is a romantic and very atmospheric place to spend a night.

From Grünau the B1 road crosses the railway and continues southwards over a spacious sandy plain dotted with isolated hills, several of which have interesting shapes. After 30 km there is a turn-off to Ai-Ais and another turn-off to the same place 99 km from Grünau. The main road then traverses a lunar-like plain with weirdly shaped hillocks and ridges of saw-toothed peaks.

There are turn-offs to several mines, such as the Seven Pillar mines, and a long steady descent into the valley of the Gariep River. Having come 140 km from Grünau, the main road reaches ...

NOORDOEWER

The small centre of *Noordoewer* (north bank) is a haven in the desert for travellers. It lies at the southern end of the vast, sparsely populated south-west African land of Namibia. Four kilometres south of Noordoewer, the road reaches the border of South Africa on the Gariep (formerly Orange) River and the bridge at Vioolsdrif which connects the two countries. The immigration post is open at all times.

THE FISH RIVER CANYON AND AI-AIS

The Fish River Canyon is one of the most staggering scenic spectacles in Africa and reputedly second only in size to the Grand Canyon of America. The canyon is 161 km long, 27 km wide at maximum, and up to 549 m deep. It is revealed with startling abruptness in an arid landscape covered with pebbles, euphorbias and small succulents.

These days, the Fish River, whose energy caused this vast gash in the landscape, flows only intermittently. Water is always contained, however, in a succession of deep pools which are full of fish such as barbel and yellowfish. Four pluvials (wet periods) seem to have occurred in the southwestern part of Africa during the last million years, resulting in the powerful run-off of water which eroded this canyon.

Several springs occur on the floor of the canyon, the most notable being *Ai-Ais*, a Nama name meaning 'very hot'. This spring has a temperature of 60°C and is rich in fluorides, sulphates and chlorides which are reputedly beneficial to people suffering from rheumatic and nervous disorders. The spring has been developed by the administration into a resort. There are indoor baths, an outdoor pool, chalets, camping and caravan grounds.

Hikers are fond of walking through the canyon, following a route which is 86 km long and normally takes four days to complete. Permits are issued each day to one group only, comprising 3 to 40 people, and then only between 1 May and the end of September. A medical certificate of fitness must be produced when applying for permission.

Ai-Ais is open from the second Friday in March to the end of October. The rest of the year is too hot for visitors.

From the main tarmac road stretching from Noordoewer to Grünau, there are two gravel turn-offs leading to Ai-Ais. The first turn-off starts 30 km south of Grünau, from where it is 62,5 km to Ai-Ais. The road descends into the Fish River valley through a jagged mass of rocks rich in rose quartz and the natural habitat of the strange plant, *Pachypodium namaquanum*, popularly known from its shape as the 'elephant trunk' or 'halfmens'.

At 12,5 km prior to reaching Ai-Ais, this road from Grünau is joined by another gravel road leading for 52,5 km to the main tarmac north–south B1 road which it joins 41 km from Noordoewer. At a point 22,5 km from Ai-Ais, on the road to Grünau, there is a turn-off which leads northwards for 55 km to the viewsites overlooking the grandest part of the canyon. There are toilets and resting-places at these viewsites. There is accommodation at the Hobas camp and at the Canon lodge on the 52 000 ha Gondwana Canon Park, a privately managed conservation area adjoining the eastern border of the Fish River Canyon Park. The lodge has been built in a picturesque setting of rocks. There are fine hiking trails known as the Fish Eagle routes. Paths down to the floor of the canyon take hikers to the starting-points of the walk to Ai-Ais. From the main viewsite there is a road along the eastern edge of the canyon which ends in a cul-de-sac after 18 km. This road reveals many magnificent views of the canyon. From the main viewsite a road stretches eastwards for 44 km to join the Grünau–Seeheim road 53 km from Grünau.

Monitor lizards, numerous birds, snakes, baboons and mountain zebra inhabit the canyon which, scenically, is awesome: a brutal scar, the unhealed wound from several lashings inflicted by Nature's rage. The impression is grand, sombre and immensely powerful. In a setting of such harsh aridity it is astounding to realise that water was the tool used by Nature to create this scene.

The Ai-Ais Hot Springs Resort, the Fish River Canyon and the gaunt Huns Mountains on the western side all form a 346 117 ha conservation area. It is hoped that one fine day they will be joined to the Richtersveld National Park in South Africa to form a unique trans-frontier conservation area.

KEETMANSHOOP TO LÜDERITZ

Two kilometres out of Keetmanshoop on the main B1 tarmac road to South Africa, a turn-off to the west (B4) leads to Lüderitz and the coast of diamonds. The tarmac road traverses a grassy plain covered with kokerbooms and various trees. At 32,5 km there is a gravel turn-off to the Naute Dam and irrigation area, a fine sight in so arid a setting. The Fish River benefits Namibia with fertility as well as the spectacle of its canyon. At 44 km along the B4 road there is a turn to Seeheim, the

Fish River Canyon and Grünau. This is an interesting way of reaching the canyon and the Gondwana Canon Park with its remarkable visitors' lodge.

The B4 road crosses the Fish River 1,5 km further on. At this stage in its course, the river flows intermittently down a broad shallow valley where there is no hint of the canyon soon to start. Forts were erected by the Germans to guard the river crossing along this road; and there are turn-offs to these historical monuments, of which very little remains. Many flat-topped hillocks may be seen in this area, with the dolerite 'umbrellas' which protect their summits.

At 105,5 km the road reaches the small railway centre known as *Goageb*, the name of which indicates that it is at the junction of two rivers. A one-star hotel and a few shops comprise the commercial area. From Goageb a tarmac road stretches for 30 km to the old mission station of Bethanie, established in 1814 by the Reverend Heinrich Schmelen for the benefit of the Nama people resident in the area. The original house belonging to the missionary and the house of Captain Josef Frederiks, chief of the Orlam Nama tribe, are preserved as historical monuments. The village comprises a one-star hotel and shops. From Bethanie (sometimes spelt Bethanien) the road continues for 82 km to the small rural centre named after the village of Helmeringhausen in Westphalia.

From Goageb (pronounced Gwa-geb) the B4 main road to Lüderitz continues over undulating savanna country. After 20 km there is a gravel turn-off to Bethanie and Maltahöhe; at 102 km a turn-off to Helmeringhausen and, after another kilometre (193 km from Goageb), a turn-off leading southwards for 163 km to the zinc mine of ...

ROSH PINAH

This great zinc ore-body was discovered by one of the most renowned prospectors of the south-western part of Africa, Mose Eli Kahan. He was a Prussian Jew who immigrated to South Africa in order to escape Nazi persecution. He became a prospector. Rumours of vast mineral riches in the south-west African wilderness attracted him to the territory. In the valley of the lower Gariep he discovered a copper deposit which he pegged and named Lorelei. The deposit was situated in remote and extremely difficult mountain country. There was, however, a track leading from Aus down to the Gariep River at *Sendelingsdrif* (missionary's ford). This track was used by a few farmers. In order to guard Sendelingsdrif the Germans had erected a police post and camel patrol station on the north bank of the river.

By dint of vast exertion, Mose Kahan improved the track and commenced mining for copper. In 1930 the price of copper fell below working costs and Kahan turned his attention to diamonds. Although his eyesight was failing and he had to use a monocle, persistence spurred him on to make several rich discoveries along the diamond coast north of Lüderitz. He found a fortune in the sands of the Namib coast, but he never forgot the mountains north of Lorelei.

In 1968 in *Namasklufd* (cleft of the Namas), where the track from Sendelingsdrif passed through the mountains, he found the deposit of zinc to which he gave the name *Rosh Pinah* (the corner-stone) because he considered the discovery to be the most important one of his life, the corner-stone of his mining endeavours. He died shortly after the discovery, but his son George successfully concluded negotiations started by his father with the South African Iron and Steel Corporation (Iscor) for a joint venture in bringing the mine into production.

Rosh Pinah became a major producer of zinc, with a village created there to house the mineworkers. The old track from Aus was developed into a first-class gravel road with an extension 22 km long leading to the Gariep River, from where the mine draws its water. The Octha Diamond Mine lies on the south bank of the river, the South African side, where Oscar Thanning found diamonds in a concession area of the Okiep Copper Company. The name *Octha* is a combination of the company name and that of the prospector. The area is renowned for its succulents.

From the turn-off to Rosh Pinah the main road to Lüderitz continues for a further 2,5 km and then, 105,5 km from Goageb, it reaches the village and railway centre of *Aus* (place of snakes), with its shops, garages, residences, and one-star Bahnhof Hotel.

Beyond Aus a first-class tarmac road takes the traveller on a fascinating journey, smoothly descending the escarpment into the magic world of the Namib desert and the *Sperrgebiet* (prohibited area). After 23 km the road passes the wire fence which marks the eastern boundary of Diamond Area No 1. From this point travellers are restricted to the tarmac main road and its immediate verges.

The surface of the Namib here is gravel, forming the transitional area to the great dune country, the start of which can be seen to the north. At first, clumps of shrub occur, but these peter out as the road continues westwards next to the railway line. Oddly shaped rock islands loom up abruptly from the plateau, while patches of pink-coloured sand creep in from different directions. This is a gorgeous stretch of desert wilderness, rich in subtle colours and forms, with wide views of vast spaces.

At 86,5 km there is a turn-off northwards to Koichab pan and, after 13,5 km, a turn-off to the south where the road to the river of diamonds begins. At 110 km the B4 road passes the Lüderitz airport and, after another kilometre, the turn-off to the ghost town of *Kolmanskop*, It may be visited by a permit obtainable from the Consolidated Diamond Mines office in Lüderitz. For a further 10 km the road winds its way through a mass of rock and then, 121 km from Aus, reaches the port of ...

LÜDERITZ

Populated by 6 000 people, this is an atmospheric, attractively faded little place whose early bustle is a past dream. Today there are almost as many empty shops and houses as those that are occupied. However, there still lingers an intangible feeling of the glamour and excitement of past events. Lüderitz has a history rich with stories of prospectors and diamonds, of fortunes made and hopes lost, of fishing and guano, strange rumours of schemes, intrigues, projects and the adventures of a colourful company of human beings.

In January 1488, the pioneer explorer, Bartholomeu Dias, sailed down the coast he called the Sands of Hell and found his way into the sheltered harbour the Portuguese named *Angra Pequena* (little bay). For five days bad weather detained Dias in the bay. On Pedestal Point he erected a stone pillar dedicated to St James. When he sailed he left a solitary Negress standing forlornly on the beach. She was one of four unfortunate women kidnapped from their home on the coast of Guinea by the Portuguese and dumped down on selected spots along the coast in order to spread the fame of Portugal to any local inhabitants who might be inclined to listen rather than run.

The Portuguese, as well as subsequent visitors, all recognised Angra Pequena as the finest natural harbour on the entire coast of south-west Africa, but its setting was repellent. Nature could not have been in a particularly good mood when the area was created. The wind blows cold with a nasty persistence; the situation is a rock wilderness composed of dark-coloured dolerite and light-coloured granite.

The shoreline is inhospitable for most of its length. Rocky cliffs – stark and sharp – rear out of the cold sea like packs of predatory animals snarling hungrily at passing ships. Mist rolls in almost daily, particularly around Dias Point where a rather battered-looking lighthouse stands in defence of the land, a small clenched fist holding the mist at bay, with a fog-horn next to it growling like a defiant watch-dog.

A number of dried-out pans lie among the rocks and there are some beaches of grey dolerite sand such as *Grosse Bucht* (great bay). Halifax Island provides a sheltered lee for Guano Bay, while Agate Beach is well protected by three islets: Flamingo, Seal and Penguin. Shark Island, connected to the mainland by a causeway, provides shelter for the Robert harbour and its yacht basin. The presence of gypsum in the sand at many places yields the strange crystal known as 'desert rose', while agates can be found on the beaches.

Sealers, whalers, fishermen and guano collectors were the first people to use the harbour, but the total absence of drinking-water was the ultimate disadvantage to life in a difficult, moody part of the world.

The man who was destined to influence the area was Adolf Lüderitz, a German trader who, searching for some new field of profitable enterprise, encountered a 20-year-old man named Heinrich Vogelsang. Vogelsang had worked for a Cape trader and was enthusiastic about prospects in south-western Africa. At the same time an out-of-work sea captain, Carl Timpe, whose experience included the south-western coast of Africa, applied to Lüderitz for employment.

Lüderitz decided on a venture. He bought the brig *Tilly* and loaded it with assorted merchandise, sending Vogelsang ahead to scout conditions. In Cape Town, while posing as the globe-trotting son of wealthy parents, Vogelsang met the missionary Dr Theophilus Hahn who drew up a report for him on the possibilities of buying Angra Pequena from the Orlam tribe at Bethanie who claimed to own the place. Vogelsang decided that Angra Pequena was a good base for trade. When the *Tilly* arrived in Cape Town at the end of March 1883, supplies were loaded, a false declaration given to the harbour authorities, and the ship sneaked off up the coast, arriving at Angra Pequena on 10 April.

At the harbour the Germans found a number of guano collectors and a man named Radford, who had lived there since 1862. The Germans landed their stores and built a prefabricated hut which they named Fort Vogelsang. Vogelsang then travelled across the Namib to Bethanie. On 1 May 1883 Captain Josef Frederiks of the Orlam tribe ceded the bay of Angra Pequena and the adjoining territory for 8 km in all directions to the firm of Adolf Lüderitz for the equivalent of £100 and 200 rifles.

Vogelsang returned to Angra Pequena in triumph. On 12 May the German flag was hoisted and Lüderitz was informed of events by means of a terse telegraph from the ship: *'Land bought from the chief with a single payment'*. On 25 August 1883 Vogelsang concluded a second agreement with Captain Frederiks in which he acquired the whole coastal area from the Gariep River to the 26th degree of south latitude extending 32 km inland. This was in exchange for another amount equivalent to £100 and 60 Wesley-Richard rifles. The area was named Lüderitzland.

British interest was stirred at news of this cession of land. Lüderitz arrived in Cape Town on 13 September 1883 and had to deal with complaints, especially from the guano-collecting company of De Pass, Spence & Co who claimed that they had bought the same area from the same Orlam people 20 years previously. Lüderitz bustled around arguing and negotiating. His Government gave him support by sending the gunboat *Nautilus* to what was now being called Lüderitz Bay, and Vogelsang commenced a booming trade by flooding the southern part of the territory with cheap guns.

Lüderitz returned to Germany and found official sympathy for his projects. The intent in Germany was belatedly to enter the current scramble for empires; therefore Lüderitz was regarded as a pioneer. In the Cape, the Colonial administration was horrified at the prospect of the Germans taking over an area which it had for years been begging the British Government to annex. However, the British were prepared to do a deal with the Germans. In exchange for favours elsewhere, notably in Egypt, they obliged the Germans at Angra Pequena and in other places. Two German corvettes were then sent to Angra Pequena. At 08h00 on 7 August 1884 the German flag was hoisted on shore, followed by a parade, and everybody, particularly Captain Josef Frederiks, becoming very merry on good beer and schnapps. This was German's first colony and the beginning of their annexation of the whole of what was called South West Africa.

Lüderitz never profited from his venture. He was forced to sell his interest to a company formed in Germany. In 1886, while prospecting down the coast in two canvas boats, he and a companion vanished without trace. The settlement which bore his name grew slowly, with a narrow-gauge railway surveyed in 1905 to cross the Namib and provide a trade link with the interior. Construction started in 1906 and the line reached Keetmanshoop on 21 June 1908. It was at that time that diamonds were discovered by railway workers and the fortunes of Lüderitz Bay really boomed. In 1909 it became a municipality and was the centre of a succession of diamond finds, a port for the shipment of supplies and the scene of great activity in share trading and fortune-seeking. Fishing, canning and the processing of rock lobsters for export also developed into a major industry.

An excellent museum in Lüderitz contains many interesting exhibits, photographs and records of the diamond-rush days, and displays of the natural history of the area. It is open on Mondays to Fridays from 16h30 to 18h00 (other times by appointment). Many buildings survive from the German period, notably the magistracy, the old post office and numerous private homes. The scenic road to Dias Point (20 km) and thereafter down the coast to Grosse Bucht (12 km) and back to Lüderitz (15 km) is filled with interesting scenes and places.

THE ROAD TO THE RIVER OF DIAMONDS

The story of the road to the river of diamonds, of the prohibited area, of the diamond discoveries, rushes and ghost towns of the south-western part of Africa, is bitter-sweet. The sands of the Namib inter the skeletons of many men who died of privation in the great loneliness of that wilderness. For many of them no one shed a tear or even wondered what had become of them.

The road to the river of diamonds, extending from Lüderitz to Oranjemund, was blazed by many feet and paved with broken hopes and the bones of forgotten men. The elusive spirit of fortune wanders along this road. Her siren call is softly carried by the winds.

Why should this spirit be feminine? Prospectors and gamblers speak about 'Lady Luck'. Only a woman could be so capricious, inconsistent, unpredictable, superficial, erratic, enigmatic, desirable, and cruel. And what of the prospectors who pursue this personification of chance? Only a man could be so lunatic, foolish, romantic, fanatical, idealistic and persistent in folly as to pursue this phantom long after all hope should have been abandoned and even then, sick or dying, alone or afraid, still try to reach out and touch the hand of an elusive spirit and whisper something as foolish as saying *'I love you'* to a dream.

It was strange how long it took men to find the desert diamonds. Many prospectors must have slipped on a diamond in the desert while their eyes were far away on something else. It was pure chance which started the whole remarkable sequence of events.

One day in April 1908 a labourer, Zacharias Lewala, while cleaning sand off the railway track near Kolmanskop, picked up a diamond. He had worked in Kimberley and therefore knew what rough diamonds looked like. He took it to his foreman, August Stauch, a German ganger who had immigrated to Lüderitz during the previous year in the hope that the dry climate would relieve his asthma. He was no prospector, but he was interested in collecting stones and knew how to identify a diamond. He tested the stone on the glass of his wrist-watch and it left a scratch.

Stauch took the discovery to two of the directors of the railway firm. With their financial help, he abandoned his job as a ganger and started to prospect. He was quickly rewarded. On 20 June 1908 he exhibited his findings in the offices of the Deutsche Kolonial Gesellschaft in Lüderitz. His discoveries caused a sensation. Nearly every able-bodied man in Lüderitz rushed out to find diamonds. All of a sudden diamonds were located in many places so obvious that people were baffled that they had failed to notice them before. It was almost as though it had rained diamonds overnight.

In the Pomona area Stauch went prospecting with a Dr Scheibe. While Stauch plotted his position on a map, he told his servants to look for diamonds. One of them simply went down on his knees, filled both hands with diamonds and even stuffed some into his mouth. The stones lay on the ground almost as thick as plums fallen from a tree. Dr Scheibe stared at the scene in amazement, repeating over and over again *'Ein marchen, ein marchen'* (a fairy-tale, a fairy-tale). Stauch named the field *Idatal* (Ida's valley) after his wife.

The pioneer discovery at *Kolmanskop,* the hill named after the transport rider, James Kolman, who habitually rested his draught animals there, became the centre of the diamond-mining field. From there the diggings spread out to places such as Charlottenthal, Central Waesche, Fiskus Waesche, Kilo 20, Elizabethbucht, and Pomona. It consisted of a rich deposit lying in the gravel bed of a dry river. A substantial mine was developed there, with a village to house the staff built on the slopes of Kolmanskop. This village survives as a perfect example of a ghost town.

The operating company built and maintained the village. In its heyday Kolmanskop was run by predominantly a German staff and labour. All housing was free, also light, water, fuel, etc. The company ran its own bakery, butchery, general dealer's store, ice factory, lemonade and soda water factory. Every household received each day a large block of ice plus soda and lemonade. One of the old iceboxes can still be seen today at Kolmanskop in the Skittle Alley. Kolmanskop had a fine hospital. It had the first X-ray plant in the whole of Southern Africa. When the mine closed down in 1940 this X-ray machine was presented to the Ovamboland authorities as a free gift. The doctor, at Kolmansdorp, Dr Kraenzle, was a great believer that every patient on the way to recovery should have a small bottle of wine or champagne and some caviar sandwiches. This must be the only hospital in the world which had its own wine cellar. The second doctor was Dr V Lossow who studied under Professor Dr Sauerbruch in Germany and was a first-class surgeon. He was also a great believer in eating a raw onion every day. It was most amusing to see the good doctor walking, whistling and chewing his raw onion.

Kolmanskop had a school up to Std 3, a very active athletic club, four skittle clubs, which had fast and furious competitions with splendid prizes. All furniture at Kolmanskop was handmade there. Painters were brought out from Germany to decorate the houses. A wonderful recreation hall was built and an orchestra was formed, which played for tea dances on Saturday and Sunday afternoons, well patronised by the people of Lüderitz. The company arranged for plays, operas, operettas and orchestras to come out from Europe to Kolmanskop. The cultural standard of the people living there was high and everything was done for them to make life in the desert as pleasant as possible. When the recreation hall was built, a man was specially brought out from Germany to advise them about the acoustics. So perfect were they that even today any visiting choir that goes to have a look at this once so lively place and, just for fun, sings in the ruined hall, vote that nowhere else because of the acoustics have they had such pleasure in singing. Children were extremely well catered for with pleasure grounds with a roundabout, swings, big wheel, etc. There was a swimming-pool on top of the hill, laid out with Italian terrazzo tiles. The water was pumped up from Elizabeth Bay, a distance of 35 kilometres and was a continuous flow, the outflow being used on the mine.

Kolmanskop got its power from Lüderitz, at that time, the biggest power station in the whole of Southern Africa and one of two places where seawater was distilled to sweet water, the other place being Aden. Kolmanskop got its water in torpedoes by rail from Garub. These containers were emptied into underground storage tanks. The water was pumped to the tanks on the hill and then fed down to be used in the houses. Kolmanskop had its own post office, police station; you name it, it was there. Every day the wind-blown sand was removed. All houses had lovely outdoor and indoor gardens. A family named Kirchoff had a tame ostrich, which was inspanned into a sleigh. It pulled passengers all over the sand dunes. This sleigh was also used at Christmas time to bring Father Christmas and at Easter time to bring the Easter Bunny.

Kolmanskop was conveniently situated next to the railway line from Lüderitz to Keetmanshoop. From this line the mining people built a private 60 cm-gauge railway running down the coast to serve a whole series of working diamond-mines. There were so many of these mines that it was sometimes said that this was the only railway in the world with stations almost as long as its total length of 95 km. Each mine had its own private platform. Petrol electric locomotives worked the line and it was in the process of being electrified when the First World War broke out.

The line ended at the great 26 m high *Bogenfels* (arched rock), where a large mine worked a diamond deposit found by Georg Klinghardt, one of the most renowned of the prospectors. Other large mines were located at Pomona and Elizabeth Bay. There were smaller workings in many remote places.

To control the activity and to market the diamonds in such a way that prices would be reasonably maintained, the German Government, in September 1908, declared the whole area as the *Sperrgebiet* (prohibited area), with licensing and discipline imposed on individuals and companies. Thousands of claims had already been pegged, with 5 million carats of diamonds having been recovered between 1908 and 1914.

The First World War totally disrupted mining. When hostilities were over, Ernest Oppenheimer went to Germany from South Africa and obtained options on the various mining groups. Ten of the largest of the former companies were amalgamated into the Consolidated Diamond Mines of South West Africa. This concern obtained exclusive diamond rights for 50 years over the area stretching 350 km north of the mouth of the Gariep (or Orange) River and 95 km inland from the coast.

The surface of the Namib will for a long time retain the footprints and vehicle tracks of its prospectors. The gravel surface, particularly, retains such trails. The footprints of men such as Georg Kinghardt, who knew the area better than any other person, might still be followed into the most inaccessible places.

The indomitable Mose Eli Kahan was also industriously prospecting for diamonds. He found a deposit 95 km north of Lüderitz in Diamond Area No 2. He registered these claims under the names of Ophir and Atlantis, and started to work them. His difficulties were typical of those encountered in mining in the Namib dune country. He tried to service the mine by boat, but the coast was dangerous and one ship was wrecked. He then organised mule trains, following the beach, but the animals took 20 days to complete the journey and most of their carrying capacity was exhausted by their having to convey their own drinking-water.

Kahan was irrepressible. He bought war-surplus Centurion tanks, but even these machines stuck in the sand. He took their tracks off and fitted war-surplus tyres made for Dakota aircraft. The tanks travelled much better but were still foiled by windstorms which made the dunes too steep. So Kahan obtained long steel cables and auxiliary motors to haul the tanks up the dunes.

Throughout this period there was great controversy surrounding the origin of the diamonds. They lay scattered on or very near the surface, especially in ancient watercourses. Their distribution was quite unpredictable and seemed entirely erratic. Apart from Kolmanskop, all major finds were along the coast, and there was a feeling that perhaps the mother lode was somewhere beneath the sea and that the diamonds had been washed up on the beach. For the diamonds to have originated in the interior, they would have required a major river to carry them down to the coast, but there was no sign of such a river being present, even in distant geological times.

Prospectors worked down the coast as far as the mouth of the Gariep, blazing the trail of the future road with immense difficulty. They found diamonds as far south as *Chamais* (lion) Bay, but south of that there seemed to be nothing. One prospector, F W Martens, wandered down the trail from Aus to Sendelingsdrif in 1909. From there he walked to the mouth of the Gariep where he found several small diamonds on the South African side. He pegged claims but the area was too remote and he never developed them.

In 1910 F C Cornell also prospected the lower Gariep, but found nothing. The idea of the Gariep being a possible source of the diamonds was dismissed by prospectors and it was left alone. In solitude near the river mouth in 1909 the Germans built a police station and camel patrol post perched on a cliff. It was named *Hohenfels* (high rock) and was regarded by its garrison as the very end of the world, where nothing ever happened save the silent flow of the river, day and night, steadily past the police post with a brooding, sullen disregard of man and his attempts to fathom the mystery of the diamonds.

Why was the mystery so elusive? Lady Luck was really feminine to be so persistent a tease. It was all there to see, but the keenest eyes seemed to be blind. Dr E Reuning, a geologist for the German Government, blazed a trail all the way down from Kolmanskop and reached the Gariep River mouth. There he met a farmer, Geel Louw, of *Sandkraal* farm on the north bank of the river, near the present bridge. Reuning asked Louw to dig a series of exploratory pits in the gravels of the river. Nothing was found. The pits still lie there filled with pebbles and flotsam. A mere 40 m away subsequent prospectors found the fabulous diamond treasure-chest in the marine gravels.

In February 1926 at Port Nolloth, F C Carstens found the first diamond south (60 km) of the Gariep River in the township reserve. The site appeared to be an ancient course of the Kamma River. A rush to the area ensued, with Dr Hans Merensky arriving on the scene from the Transvaal. He was joined by Dr Reuning and I B Celliers, who acted as assistants. Merensky noticed that, up until then, the diamonds had been found, oddly enough, in association with the shells of an extinct oyster. Oysters certainly do not produce diamonds in place of pearls, but whatever had killed the oysters had also dumped diamonds along the beach – possibly some change of current or temperature. Geologists were thus reminded that nothing is permanent. Vast colonies of rock lobsters live in the cold Benguela Current which flows up the south-west African coast. Sudden fluxes of warmer water in modern times, however, have temporarily caused a disturbance in this creepy community. The lobsters have been seen to clamber out of the water in countless numbers on to rocks and beaches in an effort to escape the warmth. A three-week blow from the warm north wind at Walvis Bay has been enough to drive the whole lobster population out of the water.

Merensky was persuaded to use the presence of oyster shells as an indication of the possible presence of diamonds. On the south bank at the mouth of the Gariep, Victor Gordon and a Mr Kaplan, were already prospecting. Near the ruins of a stone storehouse built by Sir James Alexander as a place of shipment for copper, Merensky found shingle which looked promising. He put Dr Reuning to work there, assisted by the two brothers Coetzee. They soon found diamonds. This was the start of Alexander Bay. By February 1927 the whole area was covered in claim pegs right up the Gariep as far as Sendelingsdrif. In 1928 on the north side of the river mouth, Dr Werner Beetz, consulting geologist for De Beers, found the first diamonds in a marine terrace. This was an ancient raised beach composed of pebbles and oyster shells buried under a 10 m thick layer of sand. It extended for at least 40 km up the coast. It was estimated that this strip alone contained many millions of carats of diamonds. Soon other similar terraces were found all the way up the coast as far as Bogenfels. Dr Scheibe had called it a 'fairy tale'. This was certainly a strange and eerie sort of fairyland.

In the midst of the excitement, the Wall Street crash occurred. There was a disastrous collapse in the sale of diamonds. All at once there were far too many of them and too few people with money enough to buy such jewels, however glittering. During this crisis, Ernest Oppenheimer succeeded to the chairmanship of the Consolidated Diamond Mines and with great skill steered the industry through a very difficult period. The Diamond Corporation was formed as the central selling organisation. The vast over-production of diamonds was bought up, stored away and future sales so carefully regulated that prices were controlled, gradually restored and maintained at a worthwhile level.

With marketing problems solved and the world returning to prosperity, diamond production was resumed. Work on the marine terraces was commenced in January 1935. The township of *Oranjemund* was established in 1936 to house the workers and to replace Kolmanskop as the principal centre of the diamond industry in the Sperrgebiet. The headquarters of the company were removed to *Oranjemund* (mouth of the Orange, now Gariep River) in 1943. Kolmanskop was slowly phased out of production after 1939, although it was not until 1956 that the last inhabitants were transferred elsewhere. Now the place is committed to memory and the visits of tourists. The road to the river of diamonds was built south from Kolmanskop, stretching for 288 km over the Namib gravel plain. It is perhaps the longest private road in the world, ending at Oranjemund. It carries workers and supplies to the new fairyland of gemstones. It also carries a whispered warning from the dying Kolmanskop that the sands of the Namib alone are eternal.

Kolmanskop and the chain of other diamond-mines had been relatively unsophisticated in their method of recovering diamonds from the desert. Oranjemund and its terraces at the southern end of the road were a different proposition from the start. The most advanced techniques in mechanisation were introduced. Even though there were few problems in mining the marine deposits, the sheer volume of material handled eventually made the recovery process one of the largest earth-moving operations in the world. On a normal 24-hour working day, six days a week, the marine terrace resembles a battlefield of giant earth-moving machines (the biggest fleet in Africa), including a huge bucket-wheel excavator, resembling a monstrous thing from outer space. All are busy stripping overburden, loading and hauling, supported by an antlike army of men who clean the bedrock with brushes so that not a single diamond remains. All the diamonds are conveyed in a mixture of rocks and shells to one of several conglomerate plants. Here the rock is crushed into gravel and fed to a recovery plant which identifies and sorts the diamonds by means of X-rays, optical sorters and keen-eyed humans who spot the last diamond in an annual output which, in 1977, reached a record 2 001 217 carats. The early 1980s saw a recession in diamond sales. In 1988 the recovery was 975 000 carats.

To provide the mine with a second link with the outside world, a bridge 1 km long was built over the Gariep River in 1949. It was replaced with a new structure in 1960. By the convenience of this bridge and a road link to the Cape to augment traffic on the old road from Kolmanskop to the Gariep River, the scope of mining operations was increased. Oranjemund, as the dormitory for the workers, grew rapidly into an attractive and surprising garden town conjured out of the desert by the pure magic of diamonds.

In a strange way, Oranjemund, in its desert fairyland, has become a classic example, in a setting of capitalism at its most glittering, of a town without private ownership by its residents. It is well cared for, beautified and maintained without municipality or politics, without slums, poverty or obvious extremes of wealth. It has efficient social services, minimal crime, and a superb supply of fresh vegetables, dairy products, fruit and meat produced on a vast company-run, ingeniously integrated farm named *Beauvallon* situated on the alluvial banks of the Gariep. There are recreational facilities and entertainments all dispensed by a form of benevolent company paternalism, motivated, certainly, by the need to keep employees contented in so remote a place, but revealing in the success of its application that Utopian ideals of orderly life without want or greed can be achieved by sensible organisation rather than violent confrontation. The consequence of so amiable an arrangement is obviously profitable to workers and management.

The gemstone fairyland of the Namib is the contrary setting for many surprising things. As prospectors have explored and scientists have interpreted, so the nature of the mystery of the diamonds has become better understood. The ultimate secret has still not finally been solved. Persistent exploration has shown that the diamonds only occur along the coast, not inland. On the coast they are found in a series of ancient beaches raised above the sea and usually buried under layers of windblown sand. These diamondiferous beaches extend north and south of the mouth of the Gariep, with the beaches furthest away containing the smaller stones.

Diamonds also lie beneath the sea and have been recovered in significant quantities by concerns such as the Marine Diamond Corporation, launched by S C Collins in 1961, and the Terra Marina Company which in 1966 commissioned a dredger to work the submarine gravels around Sinclair and Plumpudding islands. The effort and hazards of such recovery in the storms, mists, winds and currents of the coast made work exceedingly costly. As a result, two recovery barges were wrecked.

The largest diamond recovered so far in the coastal area weighed 230 carats and occasionally the odd gem of over 100 carats turns up. The majority are small, but are of superb quality and occur in a great variety of colours.

Careful study of diamond-size distribution indicates that the mouth of the Gariep River is the point of origin. Bartholomeu Dias called this area *Terra dos Bramidos* (the land of roarings), but did not leave any explanation for the name. It would seem that over a considerable period of time, and during successive cycles of erosion and prodigious flood, the Gariep carried diamonds to the sea. The prevailing currents and winds gradually carried the diamonds up and down the coast, washing them on to the beaches. Eroding and rebuilding the shoreline constantly changing in the unpredictable moodiness of Creation, these currents and winds reached as far inland as Kolmanskop, but for most of the forgotten years remained close to the present shoreline.

The river, then, brought the diamonds from somewhere in the far interior. Diamonds of a similar type and quality are found in the river gravels, but these are simply remnants left behind. The river seemed obsessed with taking the diamonds to the sea. The sea and wind received them, played with them along the beaches and lost them, like the toys of children left scattered in a nursery.

Still the great river flows moody and enigmatic, its ultimate mysteries still concealed. Over the face of the Namib the winds sculpt and model the dunes. The sun dazzles the gravel plains with brilliant light. The sea – cold and relentless – surges in upon beaches which sometimes seem as thin, scraggly and despondent as a woman ill used by a brutish man. The mists roll in, sometimes slowly, sometimes with unexpected speed and unpleasant effect. At night the river of diamonds is a river of stars, its surface a mirror which reflects the countless diamonds of the heavens. The ruins of the old police post of Hohenfels look upon the water in silence, the camel corral empty, the pathway stretching off into the shadows past many graves. Is it only fancy that makes one hear a call to follow, to seek and adventure, to wander into the unknown; a call inviting one to reach out, to try and seize the hand of the elusive spirit of Fortune and touch her cold lips?

Chapter Forty-Seven
SWAZILAND

A mere 17 000 square kilometres in extent, Swaziland is one of the smallest self-contained sovereign states in the world. Despite its diminutive size, the country possesses a remarkable variety of scenery, climate and atmosphere. Its inhabitants, the Swazis, are colourful and amiable. Amongst a substantial population of Europeans (known as Swazilanders) there are also a number of very picturesque characters. The total population is close to one million.

The best way to gain an overall impression of Swaziland is to climb to the rounded summit of the highest mountain, *Mlembu* (place of the spider), which rises 1 862 m above sea-level. From this vantage-point, by no means difficult to reach, may be seen practically the entire country.

The Mlembu Mountain forms part of the range known as the *Khahlamba* (broken) which lies along the western border of Swaziland, separating it from South Africa. The range consists of a jumble of mountains marking the end of the South African highveld. The scenery here is romantically beautiful. The road from Barberton to Piggs Peak, climbing and twisting high around the slopes of Mlembu, provides the most spectacular entrance to Swaziland.

Several rivers of considerable size make their way through these mountains from sources on the South African highveld. In addition, their flow is increased by over 1 000 mm of rain a year falling on the Swaziland mountains. The combination of rivers and rainfall make Swaziland one of the best-watered parts of Africa. The mountain slopes are beautifully green and crisply cool. This mountain area is known as the *Nkhangala* (open treeless country) although modern afforestation has blanketed it with trees.

East of the mountains the territory falls away into a hilly belt of middleveld foothill country with rich alluvial soil in the valleys such as that of the principal river, the *Suthu* or *Lusutfu* (dark brown). This river valley, always regarded as the heart of Swaziland, is the site of most of the principal settlements of the Swazi people.

Beyond the middleveld the country subsides still further into what is known as the *Hlanzeni* (bush country), a stretch of typical savanna bushveld linking the eastern lowveld of South Africa to the bush country of northern Zululand. Considerable numbers of game animals roamed this area in former years. Only a few remain today, but they may still be seen and are protected in certain parts.

On the eastern side of Swaziland, 145 km from the western boundary on the top of Mlembu, lies another mountain range running north to south and rising as sharply as a garden wall out of the tangled greenery of the bushveld. This range, the *Lubombo* (ridge), provides a natural boundary with Mozambique on the east. The plateau which forms its level summit is a cool and pleasant home for a considerable number of people.

The human story of Swaziland is as varied and romantic as its scenery. In the beginning Bushmen found a sanctuary in the mountain caves and hunted the animals of the bushveld. Then a few scattered clans and fragments of the Tswana tribes wandered into the country from the highveld and made their homes in areas of their choice, with many an isolated mountain summit strengthened, as was their custom, with stone walls acting as a fortress and retreat in the event of danger.

It was not until about the year 1750 that the people now known as the Swazis first made their appearance in the country. Traditional history tells us that at this period a migratory group of African people, led by a legendary hero named Dlamini and calling themselves the abaNguni, travelled down the eastern side of the Lubombo Mountains from a place far in the north called eMbo. Most of them went southwards but one small section, led by a chief named Ngwane, wandered westwards up the banks of the Phongolo River. Eventually they settled in the hills on its north bank, where Ngwane died and was buried beneath a pile of stones in a taboo forest, ever since known as *eMbilaneni* (the hallowed place).

Ngwane's people, only a few families strong, had styled themselves the *Bantu baka Ngwane* (people of Ngwane) and the country in which they settled they called *kuNgwane*, also in honour of their late chief. It was a pleasant and fertile area in which they had made their homes. They built their huts in the cool heights, looking down upon the Phongolo valley. Few traditions remain to give us any details of the mode or events of their life. As history is preoccupied with wars and troubles, so the very lack of it is symptomatic of peaceful times. Only a legacy of place names has been left behind by these early settlers, and they are tranquil enough.

There are the *maBandebande* hills, a range so close together that, as their name implies, they have almost been squeezed into one long hill. The *Mhlosheni* (white hills) and the fair valley known as *Gubuda* or *Kubutsa* (the place of trapping), where game animals were hunted in former times, both hint of carefree days in the sun and the wind. A touch of humour surely lies behind the naming of the two companion hills, the large *Hluthi* and the diminutive *Hlushwane*, both with their summit slopes so untidily streaked with bush that they resemble the stringy Swazi hairstyle of that name.

The new leader of the settlers was Ndungunya, the son of Ngwane. Like his father he made no great history, except in the manner of his death. Legend has it that he was struck by lightning. The disaster, diagnosed as the wrath of the ancestral spirits, necessitated a new taboo burial ground near the Hluthi hills, where the Ngwenya family were appointed to guard his grave. The descendants of one Ngolotsheni are appointed to the duty of guarding with their lives the original royal burial ground, the *emaKhosini* (place of the kings) around the taboo grave of Ngwane.

Ndungunya's son was named Sobhuza. He succeeded to the kingship of a tribe of not more than a few hundred people. Still, his age was that of great contemporary African nation-builders, with leaders such as Shaka rising to power in the south. Sobhuza was not remiss in launching himself upon a career of exploration and conquest. Fortunately for Sobhuza, the Tswana clans then resident in Swaziland were all so puny that they presented no strong opposition to his adventures. He soon had half the country under his control and a fine new capital kraal erected for himself close to the Phongolo and named *eShiselweni* (the place of burning).

The easy success went to the king's head. He decided that his army, swollen with conscripts from the conquered clans, was worthy of bolder deeds in the rich looting grounds of Zululand. The result was disaster. The Ndwandwe tribe, whom he selected for his attention, hit back with a force that bowled Sobhuza backwards into the heart of his country, with nothing left of his former success other than an ironic curl of smoke twisting up to the heavens from the ruins of eShiselweni.

Sobhuza moved with the survivors to the hills known as *Mankayane* (little jumps) from the chief Mankayane Sokho who lived there. From this sanctuary, he set out to recover his losses by raiding the Tswana clans who lived thereabouts, particularly along the banks of the river (the greatest in the land) known to the newcomers as *uSuthu* (the dark brown) from the muddy colour of its waters.

An interesting legend tells us that it was from this river that the people we now know as the Sotho originally took their name. The first representatives of that ethnic group encountered by Nguni people, were living along the banks of the Sutu River. These were sections of the Tswana tribes who are of the same blood as the Sotho people. They were, therefore, all dubbed *baSutu* (people of the dark brown river), for they owned to no generic name themselves. The name *baSuthu* came into general use among all Zulu and Swazi-speaking people. Just as the term *maTebele,* applied by the Tswana tribes to sundry refugees from Zululand, was accepted by them in their own language form of *Ndebele*, so the term *Sutu* was picked up by the highveld people and in modern orthography became the *Sotho* of today.

But that is simply a legend which explains an otherwise puzzling name. The fact was that Sobhuza fell upon these innocents like a lion on a lamb and swallowed them up. Once again his tribe fattened on loot and its numbers were increased with conscripts and captured women. Once again Sobhuza grew confident. He emerged from his lair in the hills and built a handsome new capital for himself in the Sutu valley, north of the old Mankayane fastness. In this place, *eLangeni* (in the sunshine) Sobhuza settled back to enjoy life and gradually weld all the conquered clanlets into a nation of his own.

He had many setbacks. Once, while his army was away on a rampage, one of his vassals named Moya rose up and attacked the capital. The place was destroyed, but Sobhuza was too expert at this sort of thing himself to be caught. He slipped away and found a sanctuary in the shadows of the *Hlatsikhulu* (great forest), a favourite refuge of his, and from there he organised retribution.

Sobhuza recalled his army from its looting expedition. He also sent ambassadors down to Lourenzo Marques (Maputo) for added reinforcements, for he had heard of the fighting prowess of Europeans. He offered ten head of cattle to every white man with a gun who would rally to his aid. In this manner, tradition has it, the first Europeans came to Swaziland. Five Portuguese traders are said to have journeyed up to view the country and investigate its worth. With their aid, and his own army, Sobhuza re-established himself. He settled accounts with a mass smelling-out and butchery of suspect vassals. The European allies received their cattle, and, before leaving, presented the people with the first seeds of maize (found by Columbus in America) which was then being introduced to the Africans all along the seaboard.

This little war was by no means the last of Sobhuza's troubles. He and his people led a precarious life, at all times exposed to the threat of Zulu raids from the south. To stave off this fate, Sobhuza tried to purchase favour by sending girls down to Shaka at various times as a token of friendship. By this discrete means Sobhuza was left in reasonable peace. Only once in Shaka's reign did a Zulu army shoulder its way across the country, like a nightmare passing through the mind of a sleeper.

It was after the death of Shaka in 1828 that Sobhuza's people really experienced the full blast of Zulu power. Early in 1836 Dingane sent his army across the Phongolo. The whole country was thoroughly looted. Sobhuza survived by hiding in the mountain caves of the Mdzimba but the experience was too much for him. He died that same year and was buried with his grandfather in the emaKhosini.

Sobhuza's heir was Mswati, known to Europeans by the Zulu form of Swazi. The name Swaziland came into use at this time by visitors to the country. Mswati inherited from his father a kingdom composed of some seventy-five different vassal clans, mainly Sotho, who were all in the process of being permanently welded into a nation with, as its own language, the so-called tekela dialect of the Nguni tongue, very similar to Zulu but with peculiar characteristics.

Mswati, at the time of his father's death, was only a youth. An uncle and a half-brother ran the tribe for him while he remained in the care of his mother, *Thandile* (the loving one), in her kraal of *eLudzidzini* (the place of mass activity). The guardians found themselves with many troubles. Dingane raided them in 1837. Then, in the following year, the Zulus were defeated by the Voortrekkers in the battle of Blood River. They were driven northwards. After a stormy few years Dingane (as a refugee) met his death at the hands of the Nyawo tribe on top of the Lubombo Mountains. In the same year (1840) Mswati was at last proclaimed king of his people.

Nervous of Zulu trouble in the south, Mswati prudently built his capital as far to the north as possible, on a ridge overlooking the stream known as the *mLumati* (turbulent little one). It was a magnificent site for a capital. The landscape was smothered in trees; it was rich in game and surrounded by superb scenery. A jumble of mountains stood all around it. The great *Khahlamba* range separated it from the Kaap valley, with high peaks such as *luFafa* (mountain of the fissure) and the broken heights of the *Gobolondo* (rugged mountain) frowning down like sentries. As a final scenic masterpiece, the *Pophonyane* (little river of the waterfall) went tumbling down nearby from the edge of the heights, in a spectacular rush that is one of the most beautiful cascades in Africa.

At this new capital, named *Hhohho,* a name said to imitate the barking of baboons in the hills, Mswati settled down to brew some mischief of his own. First of all there was a family quarrel to settle. One of the regents who had managed the tribe during Mswati's minority was his half-brother, Malambule. This individual handed over government without demur, but kept a sizeable portion of the royal herds. When Mswati tried to retrieve them, Malambule fled to the branch of the royal family known as the *ekuNene* (the right-hand section). These people lived in the southern portion of the country, along the tortuous middle reaches of the river known as the *Mkhondvo* (the erratic or zig-zag one).

Among the ekuNene people, there was living the first European to settle in the country. This was the Reverend James Allison, who had secured permission in 1838 to establish a Wesleyan mission station in the area. Allison found Malambule's presence a great embarrassment. Mswati sent a regiment down in 1841 to execute the refugee. Malambule fled to Allison for protection and the punitive regiment, in the process of killing the man, bundled the missionary and the ekuNene people out of the country for good. They fled to Natal where their descendants still live in the Biggarsberg Mountains. The name of *Mahamba* (the runaways) still lingers over the hills of the district in which they once lived. The Wesleyan mission was later re-established at Mahamba by the Reverend Daniel Msimang, who had fled to Natal with Allison.

With this retributive achievement behind him, Mswati commenced a career of large-scale raids and adventures. For his hunting ground he selected the prosperous tribal lands of the various Tswana groups in the Transvaal. There was a great slaughtering. Mswati waxed rich. The fame of his army and its crack regiments such as the *Nyathi* (buffaloes) and the *maLalane* brought terror to African homes as far afield as Zimbabwe and the plains of Mozambique.

Mswati was not left to enjoy his booty in complete peace. The 6 000 men of his army appeared terrible to the Tswana; but the Zulus regarded them as child's play. With Europeans hemming him in down in the south, Mpande, Dingane's successor, turned on Mswati's people with vigour. The Zulus never sought to settle permanently in the country but nearly every second year they came up on a spree and stripped Mswati of his possessions.

The caves in the Mdzimba mountains saved Mswati's people from extinction but even this last resort was sometimes unavailing. They were forced to send their cattle into the Transvaal each raiding season, where European farmers gave them asylum at the cost of a heavy toll.

The climax to the Zulu raids came in 1854. Mpande's heir, Cetshwayo, was in need of military instruction. Mswati's people were selected for the honour, and the rowdy Zulu army was packed off on an expedition ever afterwards known as the *ukuFunda kukaThulwana* (the learning of the Thulwanas), for this regiment contained among its host the person of Cetshwayo.

The Zulus were determined to enjoy a fight. Accordingly, they had derived a sort of secret weapon calculated to drive Mswati's people from their caves. They collected faggots of odiferous wood and commenced stinking the refugees out by lighting fires in the cave mouths.

This was too much. The Swazis survived, but when the Zulus returned home the perturbed Mswati packed off a deputation to the renowned Sir Theophilus Shepstone, the Native Commissioner in Natal. They pleaded with him for intervention with the Zulus, and as a trump card presented the surprised Sir Theophilus with one of Mswati's sisters, the princess Tifokati, as a bride.

Sir Theophilus did what was asked of him so far as the Zulus were concerned and suitably restrained them from further adventures. The princess was a bit beyond him so, with all thanks, he handed her over to his headman who knew better how to deal with her.

Thereafter Mswati was left in peace to continue his own raids into the Transvaal and indulge in political adventures by supporting the losing faction in the civil war in Portuguese East Africa when Soshangane died. After burning his fingers in that upheaval and having to provide a sanctuary for Mawewe, the losing prince in the struggle, Mswati found that times were changing.

The days of the great raids were over. If the Zulus were hemmed in by Europeans, then so were Mswati's people. An increasing number of Europeans were visiting Mswati in the heart of his own country. Seidenstecher and Martin of the Berlin Missionary Society paid him a visit, with the intention of establishing a mission in his country. Traders such as Ephraim Rathbone and his sons started making regular trading trips from Natal in the early 1860s: while several land-hungry farmers were bargaining with him for farms.

On 25 July 1846, Mswati entered into his first treaty with the Transvaal Voortrekkers. On that date he signed a treaty with a party of men from Ohrigstad. For one hundred head of cattle he ceded ownership over all the land from the Crocodile to the Olifants rivers. As he had never owned this area in the first place, he probably considered the transaction as money for nothing. All Mswati used that area for was raiding; but the fact that Europeans were now settling there meant that the principal stamping ground of his army was becoming overcrowded. A second cession of land to Europeans was made by the Swazis in 1855, when they ceded a tract of land along the Phongolo River to the Lydenburg Republic, in order to have a wedge of Europeans between themselves and the Zulus.

Another early treaty signed by Mswati was with an individual named Coenraad Vermaak. In 1860 this adventurous hunter obtained the rights to hunt and ranch in a 500 000 acre area on the southern borders of Mswati's domain. The idea of this liberal grant was once again deliberately to attract Europeans as a buffer against the Zulus. Vermaak established himself in this wilderness like a feudal baron, with a rough thatched cottage for a castle.

Six years after this cession of ground, Mswati died. Although his last years had seen him perplexed, with Europeans steadily crowding in around his domains, he at least had the satisfaction of maintaining the independence of his people in an age when the pride of nearly all the great fighting tribes was being buried deep in the dust. Mswati was buried with his father in the forest of *emaKhosini*. Behind him, he left his name to linger on over his followers, thenceforth called the *amaSwati* (people of Swati) or, by Europeans, as Swazis. A seven-year-old son named Ludonga succeeded to the throne in place of the proper heir, Mbilini, who had some time before been driven out of the country on account of sundry indiscretions.

Ludonga was established beneath the Mdzimba Mountains in a capital of his own named *Nkanini* (the place of perversity). At this centre European traders occasionally visited him, and early in 1868 the first European prospecting party wandered into his lands. A party of five prospectors, led by Captain Augustus Lindley, travelled up from the south and made their way across the Swazi bushveld from the Phongolo to the Crocodile River. They probed around in the heat below the Lubombo, but found nothing save prodigious quantities of wild animals. After shooting for a while, they wandered off into the Eastern Transvaal.

Another type of European to reach Swaziland at this time was the runaway from justice. Such people found the independent African state to be hospitable and a convenient sanctuary from legal troubles in the rest of the world. Some very curious characters reached Swaziland in this way. Most of them made their homes on top of the Lubombo, which was then one of the remotest and healthiest parts of Swaziland. There they whiled away their time in cattle rustling, stealing the pay from African mine workers returning home from the Transvaal, and generally making a curse of themselves. Charles du Pont, whose father came from Mauritius, and Bob MacNab, a Scot, were two of the most notorious.

Apart from the activities of these runaways, Ludonga's reign was not marked by great events or any successes save for his rivals. The Pedi tribe gave his raiders a good hiding for a change, when the Swazis tried to raid through the Eastern Transvaal. In the following year, on 18 March 1874, somebody fortified Ludonga's beer more than was good for his digestion. His untimely death necessitated a new burial ground. Custom does not allow an individual to be buried with his ancestors if his death has been violent. Accordingly Ludonga was carried up to the heights of the Mdzimba and laid to rest in one of the caves in which his people had so often sheltered in the past. As was customary with the Bantu, the personal belongings and treasures of the king were buried with him. Brass beads, heavy iron neckbands, anklets, and tusks accumulated for the king by the renowned elephant hunter iNyangambili, were all piled around the body in a rich treasure trove and the cave sealed up.

A first-class fight developed in the tribe after the death of Ludonga. First there was a smelling-out to find the poisoners. Then Mswati's surviving sons fought over the question of succession. For twelve months the whole country was in uproar. Some celebrated battles took place. On the island of *Mawelawela* (the place of many crossings) in the Suthu River, there was one battle which lasted all night. The river reputably turned red with blood but apart from reducing the population, the struggle reached no decisive conclusion.

Then the wise old Queen Mother of Mswati, Thandile, with her councillor Sandhlana, intervened in the slaughter and quietened down the fight. The Swazis were used to the political activities of a Queen Mother. Traditionally they had established the idea of a joint rule of the chief, styled *iNgwenyama* (the lion), and his Queen Mother, styled *iNhlopukhati* (the she-elephant). According to this custom, the two held sway in separate capitals: the young chief establishing his own residence and political centre as soon as he reached maturity. The Queen Mother's residence remained the capital for ceremony and ritual, with some restraining influence over the young chief and his people should they become too headstrong.

In July 1875 Thandile summoned the various contentious rivals to her kraal of eLudzidzini and announced that the inner council of the royal Dlamini family had selected the proper heir. Few knew his name for certain. Each jealous rival came thinking that he was sure to be the choice.

The rivals and their followers were seated in a great circle at the kraal, while 4 000 of the loyal men of the army stood in silence all around. A commando of 350 men had been invited from the Transvaal to witness the crowning of the new king and lend their weight to the young monarch as the greatest allies of the Swazis.

Into the midst of this watching gathering was led a figure shrouded in leopard skins. Sandhlana went up to it and shouted: '*You people of kuNgwane, you see your King'*. He whipped away the leopard skins. There was a surprise *'Woh!'* from the gathering. Revealed before them was a youthful, almost forgotten son of Mswati named Mbandzeni.

The gathering surveyed the youth in silence. The watching warriors took an ominous step forward. Then, raggedly, came the royal salute *'Bayete iNkhosi'* (hail king). Mbandzeni, a young man of some twenty years, was recognised as king. With his grandmother and her wise councillor to guide him, he took the helm of the Swazi nation at a time when the skies were ominous with approaching storms.

The Transvaal commando, under Gert Rudolph, congratulated him on his accession. They guaranteed the independence of the Swazis and agreed to aid them if they were attacked. In return, the Swazis acknowledged themselves to be subjects of the Republic and agreed, on their side, to supply aid in time of war.

In his lifetime, Mbandzeni was to sign innumerable treaties and concessions with Europeans. From his capital *eMbekelweni* (the place of the appointed one) beneath the Mdzimba Mountains, he was destined to live through one of the most fantastic episodes in the whole history of Southern Africa. An incredible crowd of adventurers and scallywags were preparing to rush to his country in search of fortune.

In the auspicious year of the crowning of Mbandzeni, a group of fourteen prospectors led by Tom McLachlan made their way from the Pilgrim's Rest area into the mountains of north-western Swaziland. They prospected and explored through that most beautiful wilderness. They found no gold but discovered instead all the other wealth a generous Nature had bestowed on this corner of Africa.

Thousands of wild fowl were flushed from the long green grass. The fattest of antelope lurked in the shade of the valleys and woods. It was a wonderful adventure of surprises and marvels for the prospectors. They swam swollen rivers, climbed the heights, did long hard treks, and lazed at night beneath the stars, yarning around the fire about the gold they were sure was hidden in the next valley, while from the darkness came the singing of a myriad insects and all the snuffings, growling and squeals of the African night.

The Swazis were then at the peak of their power. They welcomed the European visitors hospitably, giving them food, shelter and guidance. In return, the prospectors gave them salt and guns. Many a friendship was made between European and African in that wilderness which seemed more like a paradise to the early prospectors.

Tom McLachlan had been so impressed with the country that he decided to settle there permanently. With a partner, a former merchant marine captain by the name of Walter Carter, he moved from his home at the Mac-Mac gold-fields and built a shack in the wilds by the old footpath that wandered through the Swaziland mountains from Lourenzo Marques to the Kaap valley.

This footpath still makes its way up the course of the mLumati River, past the Pophonyane Falls; then has a tortuous time trying to find its way through the mountain massif along the Swazi border. It twists and climbs through superb scenery, has hair-raising escapes round precipice edges, and is almost defeated by the steepest of heights. Then, in a fine piece of scenic dramatics, it makes its escape by means of the *esiKhaleni seBuLembu* (pass of the spider's web), a natural bridge formed of rock choking up the neck of a vast ravine that cuts the side of *BoLembu* Mountain. Across this bridge the path finds a way safely to the Kaap valley past the range known as the *Makonjwa* (that which is pointed at), a curiously repetitive name for many African mountains, reflecting a belief that by pointing at exposed peaks rain is induced.

On 1 May 1880, the two partners received from Mbandzeni a concession giving them exclusive permission to prospect all the country north of the *Khomati* (river of cows), which drains the Swazi mountains. From their shack near the top of the Pophoyane Falls, the partners systematically searched the countryside. They soon found enough traces of gold to stimulate them to considerable activity. They attracted the aid of several other prospectors, such as G Eckersley, J McDonald, D Wright and William Pigg. It was the last named who, in January 1884, found the so-called Devil's Reef of payable gold on the summit which has ever since borne the name of Piggs Peak.

A second partnership, meanwhile, had secured exclusive prospecting rights over the mountain area south of the Khomati River. James and David Forbes secured this concession. With various members of their family from the adjoining New Scotland area, they began fossicking for gold along the eastern slopes of the two border ranges known as the Silotwane and Ngwenya hills.

Eventually, in November 1884, Alex Forbes and C I Swears, after fossicking through the hills unsuccessfully for some time, found themselves, resting on an outcrop of the reef which, in the ten years between 1886 and 1896, when it was worked by the Forbes Reef Co, yielded some £250 000 worth of gold.

This discovery along with that of Piggs Peak and a find of coal close to the Lubombo by the Forbes brothers, caused Swaziland suddenly to receive immense publicity in the outside world. The most exaggerated rumours spread abroad of rich deposits of gold. Just as it had taken the distorted rumours of Karl Mauch's discoveries of gold to start the Transvaal off on its golden revolution, so these tales of Swaziland fortunes stirred up the interest of prospectors and speculators in the outside world. It seemed to them that a fabulously wealthy area had been lying hidden in the hills all these years.

There was an immediate rush to Swaziland. Every adventurer and opportunist within miles of the place jumped on his horse and galloped off in the direction of Mbandzeni's capital intent on securing some profitable concession for himself. The normal technique of a concession hunter was first to evolve some scheme from which, if he secured an outright monopoly from the Swazi king, he hoped to enjoy a tremendous financial return, when, and if, the country was ever developed. The concession hunters were divided into three main groups. First came the seekers after grazing and agricultural rights, mostly Transvaal farmers. Then came seekers after mineral rights; and finally, seekers after commercial monopolies. The latter were the most ingenious.

Close on five hundred different concessions, covering nearly everything imaginable, were drawn up on pieces of paper and written in language which varied from something purposely vague and confusing to the most minute and involved legal document. With this scrap of paper, the would-be concessionaire would present himself at eMbekelweni. There he would mill around for a while until he made the acquaintance of some petty chief or court induna. This individual would be well bribed to arrange an interview with Mbandzeni. David Forbes Jnr has described the next step.

> 'When the interview was at last arranged with the king, your chief would take you by the hand along through the back passage of the kraal into the presence of the king, where he considered he had found a spot which was a haven of refuge from the white concession hunters.
>
> 'You would tell the king you just wanted a piece of land as big as your hand, on which you wanted the mineral rights. You would give the king some money now, but thousands of pounds later, when you discovered gold and worked it. He got £3 000 in gold when Forbes Reef was floated into a company. If your luck was in, and the king was in a good mood, he would say "Let me see your money" and never in your life did you part with your money quicker and more willingly. The king would say "where is the pen?" and it would come from your pocket, also a small bottle of ink. He would then make a cross where indicated, as his signature. Then there would be a scramble with the chiefs present to sign as witnesses, and the custom was to give each chief who signed one pound. A place was always reserved for Sandhlana and Tekuba to sign'.

In this way, concessions for an incredible variety of schemes were obtained. Almost every acre of land in the country was portioned out to concessionaires, often four and more deep, and each paying a rental varying from one goat to £500 a year. Over the same piece of ground one concession would grant the grazing rights, another would grant agricultural rights, a third plantation rights, a fifth township rights, a sixth trading rights, and so on. The confusion was astounding.

The Transvaal farmers mostly interested themselves in grazing rights, paying a couple of goats or £5 for rights to anything from 5 000 to 12 000 acres.

Mineral concessions were, of course, the most popular for the prospectors. There was intense rivalry for the best sites. The Forbes brothers had a concession over the coal deposits they had discovered. Somebody else immediately secured a concession over a narrow belt of land adjoining the coal area, so located that any road or railway would be forced to cross the property and pay heavy toll.

Alfred Henderson and Walter Shepstone secured a mineral concession over the royal grazing grounds adjoining eMbekelweni. Tom McLachlan in 1886 secured a further concession over the area of Mswati's old Hhohho capital. A £150 000 concern, the Horo Concession Exploration Co, was formed in London to exploit this concession. The so-called *Daisy* reef was found, and in 1890 a battery was laboriously dragged through the mountain to work it. The reef was patchy and refractory, however, and in any case the company went bankrupt over machinery transport costs before it ever had a real chance of working.

The commercial concessions were the most fantastic. There were concessions for banking, for printing, for importing liquor, for drilling for oil, for importing diamond drills, to name only a few. C H Verall had one concession for pawnbroking; G D Wilson drew up his monopoly for lotteries and sweepstakes; while one ingenious soul, N H Cohen, had a concession for a mint. A concession to construct a railway was soon taken out. On the strength of this, a Mrs Parr promptly obtained the monopoly for railway refreshment bars. A certain R M Campbell secured the sole concession for the generation and use of steam for £50 a year rental. The avowed purpose of this concession was to block the railway concession and compel its owner to buy the steam concession out at a high price before he could proceed with his railway.

The tough element of Swaziland's older European population also joined in the concession rush. Bob MacNab secured a concession for patent medicines. He was also active in transport riding and blazing the first road to enter Swaziland. This road, known as the Gin Road, became the principal highway of all the smugglers, bandits and concessionaires who were then flooding into Swaziland. The road started in Mozambique at Tembe Drift, the highest point in the Tembe River navigable for boats. From this river terminus the Gin Road climbed the Lubombo, passed MacNab's shack on the frontier, up the valley of the Suthu River, and ended its adventurous way at Bill Fyfe's store on the Transvaal border. This was a famous depot of those times, and the point at which a dozen paths and tracks converged on Swaziland from the Transvaal.

The old Swaziland trader Ephraim Rathbone had also left the makings of a road behind him during the course of his visits to the country. He had made Utrecht a base during the first British annexation of the Transvaal. From that little town he traded regularly with the Swazis and blazed a trail into the country from the south-west, wandering through the high hills past Joe Young's store at Mankayane and then dropping down to trade in the thickly populated valleys of the *Suthu* and *Suthwana* (Little Suthu).

Ephraim Rathbone died before the Swaziland concession rush took place, but his family continued their trading relations with the country. Thomas Rathbone, a Natal transport rider, blazed another road into Swaziland at the end of 1885. In an effort to promote trade between Durban, Swaziland and Barberton, he made a road of sorts up through Zululand and into Swaziland from the south at the farm *Rietspruit*. This road, called Rathbone's Road, forded the Suthu River at the fording place known as *isiPhofaneni*, from a tawny coloured hill nearby. It continued northwards, substantially followed by the main road of today, crossed the Gin Road, forded the *Mbuluzi* (river of iguanas), crossed the Khomati, where Bhalekana Vilakazi (*Balegane*) lived, and then swung westwards past Piggs Peak and through the mountains to Barberton.

None of these roads was made in the proper sense of the word. A few gradients were cut, and one or two fords were improved; but for the rest the roads were simply the scars tramped into the ground by the booted feet of the old adventurers, the hooves of their horses, and the rolling wheels of their wagons.

The nuclei of the first Swaziland towns came in a similarly casual manner. The establishment of a store was generally the foundation stone of future villages. The first stores all led a precarious life, plagued not only by normal commercial troubles but by all manner of wild rumours – often started playfully by Mbandzeni – that the Swazis were going to murder all traders for overcharging, or that the witchdoctors were going to smell them out. One of the early traders, Johan Colenbrander, famous in both Zululand and Zimbabwe, built a store close to Mbekelweni, just west of Mtilana. The whitewashed mud building was so clean in the sunshine that the Swazi rainmakers found it offensive. They blamed it for their current failure to make rain. A regiment was sent to destroy the place; but the alert Colenbrander forestalled them by hastily daubing the building in a more sober shade of mud tan. Later he sold out to Gideon Kannemeyer.

A former Zululand contemporary of Colenbrander's – Grosvenor Darke – had also moved to Swaziland. He established a store and hostelry at a place ever since known as Darketon. This

Darketon had its great days, when the nearby Forbes Reef was booming and a stream of concessionaires coming into Swaziland stopped at the hostelry for a drink. The bridle path from the Steynsdorp valley passed the door of Darketon, the hostelry being judiciously established on top of the long and thirsty pull from the Transvaal up the slopes of the *Ngwenya* (crocodile) range.

Beyond Darketon, the path wandered on over the hills and then dropped down with a rush to the pleasant valley of the streamlet known as *uMbabane* (the bitter little one). There Mbandzeni had his Pholonjeni grazing grounds, near where Mbabane Khunene the petty chief lived; and it was there, where the path rested awhile before it forded the stream, that an ex-artilleryman known as Bombardier Wells established an inn and store.

This Bombardier Wells was the first European to settle on the site of the present village of Mbabane. His pioneer hostelry, opened about 1888, was, truth to tell, a dreary place. Its gin was lively, but the accommodation – two mud huts – was sad. The insects were numerous, but the food was scanty. Usually some stray cur had run away with the mutton bone and a tin of canned meat was the only thing to be found.

Beyond this hostelry, the path forded the stream and went off down the rise to the middle veld and then lost itself away in the blue. This pathway was one of the busiest in Swaziland. In its time it carried many hundreds of adventurers into the country. Few of them, no matter how intently their minds were fixed on fortune, could have been oblivious to the grandeur of the scenery and the thrill of the view as the path reached the edge of the heights beyond the Mbabane stream and they saw below them the great valleys of the Suthu and Sutshwana rivers, where dwelt the bulk of the Swazi people, and where lay their great centres *Zulwini* (place of heaven) and Mbekelweni itself, the capital.

Mbekelweni, with its labyrinth of huts, was the mecca of the concession seekers. All around it were scattered the tents and shacks of the European adventurers, while the beginning of a future village came when Bob Rogers opened a store housed in a tent, built at the end of 1885 close to the banks of the Mzimunene stream. The following year, Albert Bremer and his partner Wallenstein came up from Durban in search of concessions. They bought out Bob Rogers and secured a concession giving them sole rights to import all goods into the country duty free. They erected a hotel and trading station on the site of the old tent store. The buildings stood in the lands of the chief Manzini Motha. The store and Albert Bremer both became known as *Manzini* to the Swazis. To the Europeans this was the foundation of *Bremersdorp*.

Bremer's corrugated iron pub thenceforth became the favourite gathering place of Europeans in Swaziland. There they collected in the evenings, to bargain and intrigue and give tremendous parties, while a few miles away Mbandeni sat in his capital and marvelled at the ways of white men. He was a kindly and courteous individual. While the Europeans roistered in the pub it was his delight to sit outside his hut drinking beer and chewing wild sugar cane.

Mbandeni was no drunkard, although a contemporary description tells us that he *'had as a royal seat a gin case. When at ease he was elegantly dressed in a blue and white cotton handkerchief, and drank champagne, the price of which he was sufficiently aware of seldom to offer to a visitor, except occasionally in favour of a particular friend.'*

The king's only real weaknesses were stout women and lean greyhounds. He usually had a great number of both commodities about him. He was always prepared to bargain generously for a particularly fine specimen of either kind. With these comforts and diversions he was content; the flattered, all-powerful centre of a court of warriors, fawning, courtiers, strangely dressed diviners and herbalists surrounded by cajolery, bribery, smellings out, superstition. The Europeans who crowded so carelessly within his realm, engrossed in their schemes of quick fortune and wandering blithely wherever they pleased without let or harm, little guessed the primitive dynamite smouldering beneath their feet.

At the height of the Swaziland concession mania Mbandeni received at least £1 000 a month in regular rentals. Several hundred opportunist Europeans swarmed around his capital. He was pestered by them night and day. With all manner of novel administrative demands made upon him for such things as receipts, accounts and written records, he at length resolved to employ to guide him a full-time European as *'resident adviser and agent in all matters in which white people are concerned in and about my country'* to guide him. The man eventually selected for the job was Theophilus Shepstone, called by the Swazis *uMfowethu* (our brother). Shepstone was an energetic collector of concessions himself but he secured the job because he was the son of the renowned

Sir Theophilus Shepstone of Natal, whose intercession with the Zulus on their behalf was well remembered by the Swazis.

Shepstone received his appointment on 10 December 1886. He immediately became the centre of a storm of intrigue. John Thorburn had formerly been somewhat favoured by the king as an honorary adviser, and now he felt himself deprived of a strategic position. He became a bitter enemy of Shepstone. The mineral and commercial concessionaires were about evenly divided between the two rivals. The grazing concessionaires detested them both and had as their own leader one Stoffel Towsen, a tough character, full of oaths and ill-feeling.

Shepstone and his cronies lived close to the Mdzimba Mountains in the immediate vicinity of the royal kraal. Thorburn's hotel acted as headquarters for his party. Intrigues and quarrels proceeded apace. Individuals started calling one another frauds, and the rival parties became political. All felt that if they could influence the Swazis into a particular course of action they would further their own interests. Thus, the grazing concessionaires, simmering at the mining rights complications on their pastures, attempted to persuade Mbandzeni in many a stormy meeting to hand his country over as a protectorate to the Transvaal, or at least to kick Shepstone out. Many of the mining concessionaires dreamed of establishing some sort of republic. Stoffel Towsen and his followers, a pugnacious bunch, wanted all the English ejected, and were particularly abusive. The atmosphere became increasingly uncertain and unpleasant.

Even Mbandzeni realised the need for some action. In 1887, therefore, he agreed to allow the Europeans to elect a committee for their self-government and form a police force to effect control. Mbandeni retained full authority over the Swazis, with Shepstone remaining as his personal adviser.

To support the committee, a police force of five men under S Ryan was formed. A court of two committee members was also appointed. A gaol was built; and three JPs were appointed to serve in outstations at Piggs Peak, Forbes Reef, and Ferreira's Station in the Hlatsikhulu district. To act as secretary to the committee, Allister Miller, a journalist, destined to become one of the best known of all Swazilanders, was brought from Barberton in August 1888 when the new government received its first proper charter of rights from Mbandzeni.

The formation of the committee hardly stopped the quarrelling. The grazing men, particularly, remained truculent. They were not much inclined to collaborate with a committee which consisted for the most part of the individuals they detested most – the mining concessionaires. The concessionaires were divided by their own rivalries and the persistent Shepstone–Thorburn feud with all its intrigue must have given Mbandzeni many a headache.

Shepstone was particularly jealous of his position. Friction between him and the committee had started before its election, when he refused to reveal Mbandzeni's register of concession-holders for the formation of a voters' roll. The committee struggled on to impose some order over the concessionaires. In an effort to broaden their representation, they reorganised themselves into electoral divisions. Thenceforth, the king nominated five men as his representatives. The mineral concessionaires elected five members and the grazing concessionaires had five representatives.

Apart from quarrelling within itself, this committee had much work to do. Justice, of a rough and ready pattern, had to be handed out, in the form of fines or gaol sentences for the usual petty crimes of stock theft or assault. In the midst of all this uproar, Mbandzeni fell sick with jaundice. He was very sick, and the whole of Swaziland quietened down before the storm. To the Swazi, nobody fell sick or died naturally. All such unfortunate occurrences were the results of malignant magic. The normal, expected reaction of the king to his ailment would be a smelling-out of the persons supposedly responsible.

The smelling-out came like a thunderbolt. Many great Swazi heads toppled. The blood bath took place in December 1888. Several score of the leading Swazis met a sudden end. Among them was the popular chief induna, Sandhlana, who had escorted and supported Mbandzeni when he was first shown to his people. The whole country was thrown into alarm by these killings. Only the personal popularity of Mbandzeni among the Europeans restrained them from some action against the Swazis. To them, Mbandzeni remained kindly and courteous. The only individuals who had any complaint against him were those would-be concessionaires who were denied permission for some particularly fantastic scheme.

Mbandeni well knew where the concessions were leading Swaziland. Allister Miller, the Reverend Joel Jackson and the interpreter George Eckersley had an interview with him once in

November 1888. They sought to warn him about the concessions and his liberality in handing them out. Mbandzeni listened to them attentively and discussed the question with his councillors. Then he gave them a considered reply.

'I know the concessions are bad', he said. *'But I have white men all around me. By force they have taken the countries of all my neighbours. If I do not give them rights here, they will take them. Therefore I give when they pay. Why should we not eat before we die?'*

Poor Mbandzeni. Wiser than many thought him, he could see the storm clouds all around and knew that for the Swazis there was no shelter anywhere. Europeans were crowding in on all sides. The boundaries of his domain, so boldly expanded by the Swazi armies, were being compressed and re-determined by lawyers and surveyors with hardly any reference to him save a formal request to 'make his mark' on some document. As early as 1880, Major James Alleyne of the Royal Engineers had demarcated the northern and western borders of Swaziland. He induced Mbandzeni to confirm the exclusion of the Carolina, Barberton and Komatipoort districts from Swaziland. Eight years later, just before Mbandzeni fell sick, another boundary commission was formed to finalise the eastern and southern boundaries of Swaziland.

Mbandzeni's last sickness took an increasing hold over him. The concessionaires, sensing an end to the game, milled around his court struggling for just one more favour. There were, by this time, very few possible concessions still left open. Nearly the whole of Swaziland and its commercial prospects had been monopolised by some ingenious speculator. Still, one or two extra concessions were wangled: concessions to end all concessions.

A certain John Harrington of Barberton, with a real touch of genius, secured from the sick chief a signed document irrevocably giving him and his heirs the permanent right to collect all taxes, rents, concessions, etc, in Swaziland, in return for an annual overall payment of £12 000. This concession was immediately sold, in September 1889, to the Transvaal Government.

The enterprising Thorburn was also busy. He had already secured a whole string of concessions, covering mining, banking, industry, advertising, printing and the keeping of pounds. With some cronies, he had formed the Mbandzeni Syndicate to exploit these concessions. Some of them were certainly very valuable. Thorburn had the sole right to import liquor and as the Swazilanders were consuming over £23 000 worth of alcohol a year, it meant that Thorburn reaped a rich harvest simply by imposing a royalty of 5 per cent, together with the import licence.

Now, in the last months of Mbandzeni's life, Thorburn secured two more concessions, which were really the end of the entire business. One of these concessions was the Unallotted Mineral and Forfeited or Abandoned Concessions concession. This entitled the holder to all possible mineral rights everywhere, not already portioned out by December 1888. It also granted him all concessions abandoned or lapsed. Even case-hardened concessionaires were surprised when Mbandzeni granted this concession. It even conferred rights over the very ground on which stood the royal kraal.

Thorburn's ultimate concession was the most iniquitous of all and characteristic of a man who was so fantastic that he actually christened one of his sons Lourenzo Marques Mbandzeni Thorburn. This last concession was the Unallotted Lands Concession. It conferred on its holder the right to assume possession of all land not handed out by 25 July 1889, or lapsing from the control of any other concessionaire during the next hundred years. With this concession, the holder was calculated eventually to become the owner of every acre of land in Swaziland, with the Swazis a nation of squatters living on a single giant farm. With this climax to his career, Thorburn sold out his interests to a concern styling itself the Swaziland Corporation Ltd. He then left the country, returning only once more to secure a party of Swazi warriors to appear in a circus in the British Isles.

Thorburn's two ultimate concessions marked the practical end of the crazy concession rush but a few hopefuls still buzzed around the king with some pet ideas. Mbandzeni was a weary man by then. He was only about thirty-four years of age, but his health was completely broken. The concessionaires came even to his death-bed. David Forbes Jnr was one, with his scrap of paper. The king looked at him through dim eyes.

'You too, Mahleko, son of my old friend, are you also joining the vultures that want to pick my bones before I die? I did not expect it of you.' Forbes shamefacedly tore the paper up and went away.

Mbandzeni died on 7 October 1889. Wrapped in the hide of a black bullock, his body was thoroughly cured while relays of watchers with plugged nostrils sat on guard. Periodically another black bull would be killed and its hide wrapped around the corpse until, in the end, it was enveloped in a huge ball of skins.

Then, when the noseplugs were no longer necessary, the bundle was lifted over the kraal enclosure in the darkness of night. With a bodyguard of warriors chanting the funeral song and holding their shields inverted, the bundle was steadily carried up the heights of the Mdzimba. There, beneath a pile of stones in a taboo grave, Mbandzeni joined his ill-fated brother Ludonga, to sleep in his company forever.

Behind the funeral party, Allister Miller had the task of opening up Mbandzeni's safe. There was just over £8 000 in cash there. The bulk of the fortune in concession money had been dissipated by Mbandzeni among his friends and in the purchase of trinkets, greyhounds and women. Mbandzeni was not the only monarch to squander his fortune in so congenial a manner.

Mbandzeni's heir was a fourteen-year-old youth named *Bhunu* (the boer). One of Mswati's surviving wives became regent and all the intrigues of the concessionaires were promptly transferred to her person in the new capital of *kwaNobamba (*the place of the catcher*)*.

Just prior to Mbandzeni's death, the Thorburn party in February 1889 had wangled a major victory over their rivals by influencing the king to dismiss Shepstone on the grounds of some intrigue with the Transvaal and to appoint Allister Miller in his place as advisor.

Miller immediately petitioned Britain for a protectorate over Swaziland. The grazing concessionaires reacted with a flood of protests and accusations that the petition in Mbandzeni's name was a forgery. According to them, Mbandzeni in reality wanted to hand his country over to the Transvaal. All Mbandzeni really wanted, truth to tell was to be left alone but unfortunately nobody would oblige him. The Queen Regent celebrated her accession to power by sacking Miller and reinstating Shepstone to his former post in October 1889. Shepstone gleefully dismissed the Thorburn-influenced White Committee and prepared for a long spell of absolute power.

Both the British and the Transvaal governments were well aware of the welter of rivalries in Swaziland. Shoals of letters, telegrams and petitions had been dispatched to them by their respective subjects, all seeking to advance their own interest by promoting some political intervention in Swazi affairs. The British government had little direct interest in Swaziland. Despite the claims of the concessionaires, the country's economic possibilities did not seem particularly inviting compared to the richer pickings then to be found elsewhere in Africa. The Transvaal, on the other hand, regarded the country as having some possible value, if only to provide a route to the sea. With this in view, the Republic had gone to the expense of buying up a few of the key concessions.

The death of Mbandzeni provided a suitable opportunity for the investigation of Swaziland's affairs. A joint commission was formed. The South African Republic sent Generals Joubert and Smit, with Dr Krause and Mr van Alphen. The British sent Sir Francis de Winton, Colonel Martin, Advocate Schreiner and Captain Baden-Powell. In December 1889, they settled down to their task.

After hearing all the rival claims, the commission decided to reject the old White Committee entirely, as being merely a quarrelsome racket. Instead they appointed a provisional government committee of three men to control the Europeans: Colonel Richard Martin to watch British interests, D J Esselen as Transvaal representative, and Theophilus Shepstone as Swazi representative. For its capital the committee bought Albert Bremer's hotel and lands in 1890. The hotel thenceforth became the Government offices of Swaziland, while Bremersdorp became the acknowledged capital of Swaziland, with the perpetuation of Bremer's name as one of the conditions of sale. This Triumvirate Government proved an uneasy companionship.

Eventually after prolonged haggling, the British and Boer governments signed a convention. They recognised the independence of the Swazis, confirmed the powers of the triumvirate form of government, established a chief court of three members, agreed that no more concessions be granted without the approval of the President of the South African Republic and the British High Commissioner, and existing concessions be examined by the court.

Transvaal desires for annexation were staved off with recognition of their railway concession and inclusion in the republic of the old Mbandzeni grant of the 50 000 acre area known as the Little Free State in the Piet Retief district. In exchange for these benefits Britain secured a republican guarantee not to interfere in events north of the Limpopo. The rest of Swaziland was reserved for future bargaining.

This compromise was proclaimed on 13 September 1890 in a so-called Organic Proclamation and the three judicial commissioners appointed by Britain, the Transvaal and Swazis, settled down to review the jumble of the concessions. It was a horrible mess with such fantastic concessions to consider as Grosvenor Darke's concession for all lobolo paid by the Swazi nation and Lissack's concession to apply for concessions for others. In the end three hundred and sixty-four concessions were recognised as legal and binding. The rest were too ridiculous to stand examination.

Quarrellings and bickerings instead of improving, increased. Everybody seemed to be intriguing against one another. The South African Republic was disgruntled at being fobbed off from annexation. The Swazis themselves had caught the infection and although Bhunu had officially become chief with the name of Ngwane on 5 September 1890, his court was torn with rivalry between the Queen Mother and the old Queen Regent. Periodically one or other would send off a request to Britain or the Transvaal for annexation in the hope that by this manoeuvre they would secure support for themselves.

In December, 1894, a new convention was signed. In exchange for sundry advantages Britain gave the jubilant Transvaal republic all rights of protection and administration without actual incorporation of Swaziland. Fondly the Republic imagined that dreams of a railway to the coast were coming true. But the British promptly surveyed and, in April 1895, announced the annexation of the whole coastal strip of Tongaland (Maputoland) right up to the Mozambique border, completely isolating Swaziland from the sea.

The disappointed republic took over a white elephant. Instead of an heir to fortune they found they had been left to hold a most unruly baby. Its principal inheritance of value, the route to the sea, like many an orphan's inheritance, had been neatly stripped by the lawyers. There was little compensation. In terms of their agreement the republic was even bound to recognise and support Bhunu, although as an individual he was as cruel as a cat, with a love for entertainments similar in nature to the gory delights of ancient Rome.

From its dilapidated office in Bremersdorp the Government attempted to administer the Europeans of the country. They had a Special Commissioner, a judge, a police force of some one hundred mounted burghers and half a dozen JPs. Out-stations were maintained at the old centres of the White Committee, Piggs Peak and Ferreiras Station, while a new post was established on top of the Lubombo close by the spot where, in former days, a petty chief had erected a kraal. To celebrate the building of the kraal, he had granted permission to members of his regiment to marry, always a much-longed-for honour by the bachelor warriors, and the name *iSteki* (Stegi) indicating a *Place of Much Marrying* had been applied to the site with its breathtaking view over the bushveld and Portuguese East Africa.

In so far as actual government of the Europeans went the Transvaal could do little. They were bound by treaty to respect all British rights and as these rights, the concessions, covered nearly every conceivable activity, including the keeping of pounds, the construction of roads and bridges, the levying of toll, the operation of posts and telegraphs, and most other functions normally exercised by government, the republic found its hands completely tied.

Even the right to collect taxes was ostensibly in private hands although its purchase had been stimulated by the Republic at an early stage. A certain John Harrington had negotiated this privilege. The Republic took it over from him and in the first four years during which they exercised the concession, they collected £58 000 as rentals from the concessionaires and paid the chief his regular guaranteed monthly £1 000.

Beyond exercising such concessions as they had acquired the Transvaal Government could do nothing. It was entirely hamstrung by its obligation to respect all those absurd monopolies. Before it could promulgate any act the republic had first to consider, not whether such an act was advantageous to the country in general, but rather whether it would interfere with any of the privileges it had guaranteed to respect. Under these conditions Swaziland naturally became just a backwater of the Transvaal.

One right the republic had been granted. After three years it could start levying taxes on the Swazis. In 1898 it commenced this process. Every Swazi had to pay ten shillings a hut and two shillings and sixpence road tax with two pounds per head for squatters. The levying of this inevitably provoked trouble. Times were bad. The rinderpest of 1896 had wiped out over 100 000 head of Swazi cattle and, even at the best of times, people resent paying taxes with no obviously advantageous return.

Under the triple blow of rinderpest, taxation, and the chronic sickness of their chief, the Swazis boiled. As usual given such stimulation, they relapsed into a wave of smellings-out in order to discover and liquidate the presumed supernatural instigators of their trouble.

The Europeans watched proceedings with alarm. According to treaty the Transvaal was bound to respect self-government of the Swazis as long as they did not commit any act contrary to civilised law. Bhunu had already far transgressed on this measure by his own sadism. The 1898 smellings-out were certainly well beyond the limit and culminated in Bhunu having the chief induna, Mbaba and his two attendants murdered.

The Transvaal then decided to move. An investigation was ordered and on 14 May Bhunu was summoned to appear in Bremersdorp before the commissioner, J C Krogh. After some delay Bhunu arrogantly rode down into Bremersdorp on Saturday 21 May, accompanied by some 2 000 warriors in full battle regalia and chanting war songs.

Little Bremersdorp was in a complete panic. The warriors crowded every street, whistling, shouting, and waving their shields and spears. In the court Bhunu readily admitted the killing of Mbaba. He had been a wizard, Bhunu, stated, responsible for the chief's current ills. The commissioner told him the matter would have to go further.

Bhunu's eyes flashed. *'You say the matter will go further. You say that there are others who will enquire into this matter. Who are these others? I only recognise you. I was only shown you. I am very angry with you. I am so angry that if I could I would eat you up.'*

Bhunu then, in diplomatic tradition, shook hands with the special commissioner and strode out. General alarm in Swaziland followed. Bremersdorp was hastily fortified and reinforcements were sent from Pretoria under Commandant Melt Marais. The usual opportunists started looting cattle and settling private grievances. All talk was of war. On their way to Bremersdorp the Pretoria commando was stopped on the roadside by the anxious Queen Mother with a present of beer and the question whether they came in peace or war.

With a sizeable fort built around Bremer's old hotel and the imminent arrival of Commandant-General Joubert with additional men a summons was sent to Bhunu to appear in court on a charge of murder on 5 July 1898. Bhunu promptly fled. With some twenty courtiers and a European adviser, T B Rathbone, he travelled down to Ingwavuma in Zululand and reported himself as a refugee to the British magistrate stationed there.

A complicated bickering between the Transvaal and the British followed. The British doubted whether, according to the convention, the Transvaal had the right of jurisdiction over Bhunu. Eventually they agreed to send the chief back for trial providing sundry guarantees as to his privileges were given by the Transvaal.

Thus protected, Bhunu returned and faced his trial on Monday, 5 September 1898. With the usual bickering of learned counsel, the trial dragged on for two weeks in a hot and crowded corrugated iron court room.

Bhunu was then released pending the Government's decision. He was eventually found guilty of permitting public violence. He was fined £500 together with £1 146 in costs, reprimanded, and then reinstated to his former rank to the disappointment of many, for he was hardly a popular chief.

Only political expediency had saved Bhunu from a probable hanging. Instead of that he was taken to Pretoria in April of the following year by the interpreter Mathys Grobler and, with all his courtiers, suitably lionised and impressed by meetings with President Paul Kruger and military displays. The Republic treated him so kindly in anticipation of the approaching Anglo-Boer War.

One of the immediate results of the upheaval was a protocol in 1898 to the original convention extending European jurisdiction over major crimes committed by Swazis against each other and denying the traditional right of Swazi chiefs to pronounce sentence of death or stage the iniquitous smellings-out. European control tightened its hold on the Swazis one more notch. Bremersdorp, after its wild alarms, settled back with a sigh to its habitual tranquillity – the tranquillity of a summer noon siesta with the air oppressive and the thunderclouds of the Anglo-Boer War sweeping stealthily up over the still Swazi hills.

Before the Anglo-Boer War, race relations in Swaziland were reasonably good. The 1 000 odd Europeans joined with each other in celebrating Oom Paul Kruger's birthday or the diamond jubilee of Queen Victoria with indiscriminate enthusiasm. But as the war clouds swept up from over the western horizon panic and suspicion pervaded Swaziland with the heaviness of dread that comes before a thunderstorm.

Outlying mines and ranches began to close down. With their personal treasures the English-speaking Swazilanders trekked along the roads and met together, at the kraal of chief Lomahasha on the Portuguese border. Everybody anticipated war but there was nothing the locals could do about it except take such precautionary action as they could.

On Saturday, 7 October, Allister Miller brought out the last issue of his *Times of Swaziland* the perky little newspaper which he had started in Bremersdorp on 5 June 1897. The last issue carried the sardonic proclamation of the Government two days earlier warning all Europeans to quit Swaziland. A general exodus followed.

Within a few days only a burgher garrison remained, a few Europeans of both languages who stuck to their property and Johannes Smuts, the British consul who, with a handful of his nationals, remained for a further ten days to clear up sundry business commitments. One or two others retired to the wilderness. Joseph Bennett was one. With his wife and five children he retired to the Ndzimba and lived in the hills until he had the misfortune to be taken prisoner-of-war six months later. His family then received the protection of the Swazis and acted as secretary-interpreters, being always regarded as Swazis and kindly treated in the hectic days that followed.

The Republican garrison was soon withdrawn. A few days before the proclamation to the Europeans General Joubert had sent a dispatch to Bhunu informing him of the war and of the fact that all Republican forces were to be withdrawn as they had not the men to expend in garrisoning the place and, in any case, had no wish for any fighting in Swaziland. To Bhunu was given *'power over everything, as long as the war lasts – for that time you can do as you please.'*

'Do as you please.' Bhunu's pleasure was death. He launched such a reign of terror in Swaziland as rivalled even Shaka in his heyday. Personal grievances long subdued by European control were exercised to the full. Smellings-out and eatings-up became daily occurrences. The country was bathed in blood. Bhunu was dying of his disease and he wished to kill the wizards responsible even if the entire nation perished in the process.

Over this fury of African murder the European war rolled on in almost complete oblivion. Though Swaziland never became a major arena it had its fights. At an early stage in the war the British conceived the idea of blowing up the Pretoria–Lourenzo Marques line, and the only way of approach was across Swaziland from Natal.

Several abortive attempts were made. In December, 1890, some enterprising British residents in Lourenzo Marques tried. Then in April, 1900, a small party led by David Forbes Jnr made a captain for the purpose, had a try and failed. The only result of each attempt was that the Republic increased its guard.

In the outside world the war rolled on. General Buller had become impressed with a German adventurer by the name of Sergeant Ludwig Steinacker. Buller gave this enterprising individual authority to try his hand at the Lourenzo Marques line. With six men and one pack mule laden with dynamite Steinacker rode through Swaziland. He found the great bridge over the Nkomati River too heavily guarded for interference but on 17 June 1900, he contrived to blow up a bridge near Malelane, wreck a goods train and halt traffic for fourteen days.

Steinacker rode back into the Swazi wilds. There he laid an ambush for a small party of Republicans in the kraal of the petty chief Mbudla. Several Republicans were killed and one, the commandant, Van Dam was taken prisoner. On the strength of this success Steinacker was promoted to major and allowed to raise a troop of horse, *Steinacker's Horse,* with a strength of four hundred and fifty men and the task of making as much nuisance in Swaziland and the border country as possible. In this Steinacker certainly succeeded.

In Swaziland, Steinacker made his depot at the border point of Lomahasha. On the summit of Stegi hill further south he built a small fort and helio station from which nearly all Swaziland could be seen. Then, in March, 1901, he raided Bremersdorp. He found a few Republicans and some English burghers still in residence. Eighty men were captured together with wagons. The whole village, to Steinacker's delight, was in his possession for looting.

The place was systematically ransacked. Buried in the floor of Gustav Schwab's store they found £6 000 concealed, aptly, in a gin case from the sale of which liquor to the Swazis the cash had probably been made. Roving about the country Steinacker's men also ransacked the store of B B Stuart at Oshoek. There they found £3 500 buried in the floor in some chicory tins. This treasure trove and much other loot and several captures, including the brother of the well-known Abel Erasmus, made the corps both notorious and famous with Republican and Briton alike. Most of the remaining English burghers of Swaziland were driven into surrender by the activity of

Steinacker's Horse. Their cattle raiding across the Transvaal border enraged and diverted the Republicans while their dealings with the Swazi appear not to have been very tactful. In short, Steinacker made plenty of enemies.

The republic bided its time. There is no surer way of raising hell in a farmer's heart than to rob him of his cattle. Steinacker's record in this direction was impressive. The Republicans seethed with rage and intrigued with the Swazi Queen for her support. When she at least agreed to stay neutral in any fighting, the Republic moved.

At sundown on 23 July 1901, the Ermelo commando under General Tobias Smuts set out from Belskop. There were about one hundred and fifty men muffled up in their duffel coats. All night they rode through the dark hills. They circled Bremersdorp and came in at 3 a.m. from the south. It was a surprise attack. But Steinacker was as slippery as the proverbial eel. In the night some Swazi allies had warned him of the attack.

Steinacker had considered the matter and the prospects of being hanged for cattle lifting He galloped off to Lomahasha. Only about thirty of Steinacker's men remained. When the Republicans charged down there was a brief skirmish. The garrison broke. Four of Steinacker's men were killed, four wounded and seventeen captured together with their ammunition, a maxim and supplies. Three thousand Swazi warriors watched the action from the hill on the other side of the river.

The Republicans spent the day celebrating, looting and drinking. Then they systematically set the village on fire. With the exception of the gaol and the schoolroom which were of stone, they burnt the whole place down. It burned well with all the gin and concession papers. Then they rode away. General Tobias Smuts was later court-martialled and disciplined by General Louis Botha for having destroyed the village.

Steinacker marshalled his men at Komatipoort on the eastern railway and for the duration of the war effectively blocked all communication between the Boer forces and Lourenzo Marques (see Chapter Thirty-Six).

Beyond that, a few Swazi chiefs with grudges against the Republic did a bit of murdering of isolated refugees in the southern hills. The Swazi nation as a whole was not involved. In the final clearing-up stage the British command sent a request to the Queen that she send an impi out and make a show in the mountains in order to flush any concealed Republicans. But the Swazi had no heart or enthusiasm for white men's struggles.

The war ended and the British came. Bremersdorp lay in utter ruin. Its shops were broken, its houses burnt, and even the type of the *Times of Swaziland* was scattered and rusted in the wind and rain. The British Special Commissioner, Mooney, who arrived in 1902 with a handful of police, therefore established himself at Mbabane. When the Swazilanders returned they found that tranquil little village in the high hills had become their new capital. There Allister Miller restarted his cheerful newspaper, shops were built, the picturesque bi-weekly Swazi morning market started, people settled, and snug hotels were built close by the site of Bombardier Wells's ramshackle hostelry which had sheltered so many wild and remarkable characters in the nights of not so long ago.

At the end of the Anglo-Boer War the British assumed control of Swaziland and were confronted by the absurd situation that practically the entire country was claimed by absentee owners of various concessions. If the concessions were recognised as being at all valid then, as far as land was concerned, the Swazis had been reduced to a nation of squatters living on other people's property. The Swazis claimed that the concessions were merely temporary leases, but a Government commission established to investigate the matter found otherwise. The concessions were recognised as valid as long as their owners paid their dues. However, in 1907 a third of the area of each land concession was expropriated in order to provide a home for the Swazis. Title to the remaining two-thirds of Swaziland was granted to the holders of the various concessions or leases.

It became the great desire of the Swazis to win back the rest of their country by purchase or peaceful negotiation. Sobhuza II, grandson of Mbandzeni, who was installed as Paramount Chief in 1921, dedicated himself to this great objective. As a result of persistent effort by the Swazi nation, land was steadily bought back, and today over 60 per cent of the country is once again in the possession of the Swazis.

Under the British protectorate, Swaziland was ruled by a Resident Commissioner with informal discussion held with the Paramount Chief who wielded considerable power over his own people from his seat at Lositha. In 1944, by means of the Native Administration Proclamation, the

Ngwenyama-in-Council was recognised as the native authority. In 1950 this proclamation was replaced by one recognising still wider powers.

At midnight on 5 September 1968, Swaziland became fully sovereign, with Sobhuza II being acknowledged as King. A kindly, intelligent and likeable man, Sobhuza's popularity among his people was such that, in the election for the first House of Assembly in 1967, the Mbokodvo Party (Royalists) won 79,4 per cent of the votes. Sobhuza II died in 1982 and was succeeded by Prince Makhosetive, then in his teens and being educated in Sherborne College in England. His mother, Dzeliwe, became Queen Mother and Regent until he reached maturity. A new capital named *kwaLuseni* was built for the young king near the traditional centre of *Lobamba* (the catcher). He acceded to the throne with the name of Mswati III.

Swaziland has always been a prosperous little country, richly endowed with good soil, fine grazing, plenty of water, a healthy climate, a variety of minerals, and an agreeable, happy and reasonably law-abiding population. Sugar, citrus, cotton, rice, pineapples, tobacco, cattle and timber are produced. Iron, asbestos and coal are mined.

From a tourist point of view the country has delightful scenery and atmosphere. The Swazis are tasteful woodcarvers and potters. Many of their art works are of superlative quality and they are developing an industry which will bring them considerable renown. They are also justly proud of their national dress and consequently are among the best-looking people in Africa.

The architecture of their huts is interesting, and the big centres such as Lobamba, the seat of the Queen Mother which is also the legislative capital of the country, is a fascinating place to visit.

Each year, two remarkable ceremonies take place in Lobamba in the great enclosure used as a cattle corral. From August to September, *uMhlanga* (the reed dance) is performed. A great gathering of girls superbly dressed in tribal costume takes place. Divided into age groups, they collect reeds with which to repair (as a sign of homage) the windbreaks around the residence of the Queen Mother. For four days the girls gather these reeds. On the fifth day they prepare their costumes of bead skirts, anklets, bracelets and necklaces. On the morning of the sixth day the girls bathe and dress. In the early afternoon they carry their bundles of reeds to the Queen Mother's residence and, throwing the bundles into the air, they begin to dance in a gorgeous pattern of colour and energy. At night they stop, resuming the dance the following afternoon and completing the entertainment that night with singing and feasting.

A great spectacle occurs in Swaziland at the beginning of each year when the moon is new (end of December and into January). This is the magnificent sacred ceremony known as *iNcwala*, a complex ritual of kingship, a reinforcement for the coming year of the national spirit and a celebration of the harvesting of the first fruits.

At the preceding new moon, officials known as *bemanti* fetch samples of water from all the major rivers of Swaziland, as well as from the sea. When they return to Lobamba, what is known as the Little Ncwala commences, where ceremonies and songs continue until the moon is full. At this time the next phase begins.

On the first day youths and warriors from Lobamba march to join the men of the king's residence. The combined force sing ritual songs. Towards evening the King sends the youths to gather branches of the *usekwane* trees growing at Gunundwini. In this test of endurance the youths have to march 40 km before midnight. As the full moon appears over the horizon, each boy cuts the largest branch he thinks he can carry. They then march all the way back to Lobamba, singing through the night. In the morning they deposit their branches in the cattle corral, and only then do they really rest. This ends the second day.

At dawn on the third day the boys who were too young to do the 80 km walk to fetch the lusekwane boughs, set off to collect branches of the *mbondvo* shrub, which are also deposited in the cattle corral. Using the *lusekwane* and mbondvo branches, the elders build an *nhlambelo* (bower) for the King at the western end of the great enclosure.

At about 15h00 the bemanti and the various officials of the ceremony arrive and are joined by the King. The warriors muster, dressed in their special Ncwala costumes of skins. Ritual songs (taboo for the remainder of the year) are sung and a black ox is driven into the nhlambelo and doctored. The youths have meanwhile gathered outside and excitement mounts. The black ox is suddenly driven out and is overpowered by the surging crowd who carry the dying animal back to the bower where parts of it are used in the ritual. Outside, the warriors, drawn up into a great crescent, dance backwards and forwards like the surging sea, singing the strange-sounding ritual songs.

Another black ox is caught by the youths and taken into the bower for use in certain ceremonies. It is later released.

The fourth day sees Ncwala reach its climax in the afternoon ceremony. The Swazi army in full costume is mustered in the enclosure. Official guests arrive and take their seats in a special grandstand. If a guest of honour is present, he is escorted by the King to inspect the warriors. The King then joins his warriors and a great dance begins in which the Queen Mother, her ladies and many citizens participate. Guests drink traditional beer and then depart, saying farewell to the King who, escorted by members of his royal clan, enters his bower.

The warriors dance to and fro, singing their ritual songs and pleading with the King to return to them for a further year of rule. The King, with some show of reluctance, leaves his bower, symbolically tasting the first fruits of the harvest, from which time the crops may be reaped and eaten.

The fifth day is a sacred day of seclusion, and is taboo to observers. No work is done.

On the sixth and last day the warriors march into the hills behind Lobamba to collect firewood for a huge bonfire in the centre of the cattle corral. In the afternoon this pyre is set alight and on it the warriors place items of their old costume. Dancing and singing around the fire, they beg the ancestral spirits to send rain to douse the fire as a sign of favour for the coming year. Rain actually falls on most occasions and the ceremony ends with a general celebration of feasting, dancing and singing. If no rain falls, certain ceremonies must be repeated until ancestral approval is revealed by means of rain.

Ncwala is one of the most impressive traditional ceremonies practised in the world today. Visitors are welcome for most of the ceremony, but must comply when asked to leave during taboo sections. No attempt should be made to photograph or sound record such parts of the ritual. The penalty for this is to have equipment broken.

MBABANE

The administrative capital of Swaziland, Mbabane, is handsomely situated from a visual point of view, but very awkwardly situated from a practical point of view. It is hemmed in by ancient granite mountains of what the geologists know as the Swazi Erathem, 4 000 million years old. The town lies in the valley of a stream which watered the grazing grounds of the chief, Mbabane Khunene. A trading station was established in this green setting by a man known as Bombardier Wells. His enterprise flourished on the passing trade of persons following a footpath so well used by travellers from Mozambique through Swaziland to the Transvaal that it was known as the *Ndelakayomi* (path never empty).

When the British established their protectorate over Swaziland at the end of the Anglo-Boer War, they set up their headquarters on the site of the present town and the place started to develop. Not much attention was ever given to town planning. A straggling but attractive village grew, with pretty gardens, a temperate climate and meandering streets shaded by trees.

The principal street was named after that remarkable personality of the concession rush, Allister Miller. He came to Swaziland in 1888 from Barberton where he had been a journalist. Mbandzeni, the Swazi King, had allowed the concession holders to form a committee so that it could handle their chaotic business interests on a collective basis. Allister Miller was appointed to the post of secretary to the committee. Over the years he served Swaziland as a sort of *largo factotum* involved somehow in nearly everything that was going on. He founded the newspaper *The Times of Swaziland*, writing articles with many pithy comments, editing it, setting it, printing it, soliciting advertisements, and distributing it. His personal papers became the foundation of the Swaziland archives.

The town which, together with the surrounding districts has a population of about 100 000, has a modern shopping centre, numerous shops, a hospital, hotels, a market where all manner of Swazi handicrafts may be obtained, as well as locally grown fruit and other products.

There are substantial Government administrative buildings, the studios and transmitters of the radio and television service, and an area of craft shops motivated by *Sedco* (Small Enterprises Development Company).

From Mbabane the main tarmac road to South Africa climbs out of the valley through the massive pile of granite domes with plantations of wattle trees flourishing in the mist belt. After 11 km the road reaches the top of its long climb. There is a last lingering look at the view of Mbabane in its green setting. The road then starts to descend into a grass-covered basin contained on all sides by mountains.

At 14 km from Mbabane there is a small centre at Motshane, with a turn-off north leading to the Malolotja Nature Reserve, Piggs Peak and the eastern lowveld of South Africa.

For another 2,5 km the road continues north-westwards and passes the trading centre known as *Darketon* after Grosvenor Darke, a pioneer trader of Swaziland. Beyond this old trading centre the road reaches a turn to the former iron mine of Ngwenya of the Swaziland Ore Development Company which, in 1964, constructed a railway 219 km to this point in order to export the ore through Mozambique. The railhead was called *kaDake* (the Swazi name for Grosvenor Darke). The ore was shipped at Maputo, mainly to Japan. Mining was abandoned in 1981 when declining world prices made the low grades of the mine uneconomical.

The *Ngwenya* (crocodile) Mountains were mined by prehistoric people at least as far back as 40 000 years ago. Several of their workings may still be seen. The ancient miners worked oxides and earth colouring such as red haematite, presumably using the material to paint themselves. Lion Cavern, a 10 m excavation, is probably the oldest known mine in the world. It may be visited by permission of the warden of the Malolotja Nature Reserve. Also in the area are ruins of ancient Sotho stone buildings.

Three kilometres further east from the Ngwenya mine, the road passes a beautifully constructed cluster of Swazi huts containing an interesting stock of art work and expertly made local handicrafts. The Ngwenya glass factory is just off the road. Swazi craftspeople blow and engrave exquisite artefacts in glass. Swaziland Tapestries also have their *Phumalanga* (rising sun) tapestry works in the area. Another 1,5 km takes the road to the Swazi border post of Ngwenya, with the South African post of *Oshoek* (ox glen) facing it. Both posts are open daily from 07h00 to 22h00. They are spectacularly situated at the edge of the South African highveld, with deep valleys and the grass-covered range of the Ngwenya Mountains stretching northwards along the border.

From Mbabane the main south-east tarmac road climbs out of the valley of the Mbabane stream. The road (after 2 km) reaches the summit of the rise from where the traveller is presented with a magnificent view of what is known as *eZulwini* (the place of heaven) and the valley of the great Suthu River. This is the heart of Swaziland – the site of the royal residences and Parliament, the Mlilwane wildlife sanctuary, and a cluster of hotels, casino, caravan park, curio and craft shops, a hot spring and other places of entertainment. Dominating the valley is the well-known mountain landmark of *Lugogo* (skin of a cow), known to Europeans as Sheba's Breasts.

The double-carriageway road descends steeply into the valley and is flanked by signs warning travellers about the number of fatal accidents and the need for extreme caution, especially in misty, wet conditions. At the foot of the descent, 9 km from Mbabane, stands the Mgenule motel and, 1 km further on, the *Timbali* (place of flowers) caravan park. Another kilometre takes the road past the hot magnesium spring known locally as the 'Cuddle Puddle', maintained by the Royal Swazi Sun, where there are changing rooms, saunas, facilities for massage and beauty treatments, as well as a pleasant warm-water swimming-pool. The springs are open daily from 09h00 to 20h00. In former years this was a favourite moonlight resort for Swazilanders and the name of the Cuddle Puddle dates from those halcyon days.

The Cuddle Puddle now lies in the grounds of the Royal Swazi Sun hotel, the entrance of which is 5 km further along the road. This hotel forms the centre-piece of the string of hotels built in the Ezulwini valley and is much frequented by South Africans. The hotel has a fine 18 hole golf-course and is situated in a beautiful garden. There is a theatre, used mostly for the screening of movies and where live shows are occasionally presented. The casino contains a bright assortment of one-armed bandits and gambling tables.

Situated immediately down the road from the entrance to the Royal Swazi Sun are the Ezulwini Sun and the Lugogo Sun hotels. Immediately beyond is a turn-off to the Mantenga Falls, near which is a fine craft shop, a Swazi historical village and the Smokey Mountain Village hotel further along the turn-off. A 3 km drive leads to a parking spot at the foot of the waterfall in the *Sushwana* (little uSuthu) River. This beautiful waterfall is reputedly named after a man, Mantenga, who apparently once lowered himself down the face of the waterfall to retrieve some treasure from the pool. A jealous rival is said to have cut the rope, causing Mantenga to fall to his death. It is believed that his ghost haunts the waterfall.

At 14 km along the road from Mbabane a turn-off leads to the tea-growing area, revealing views of the Mdzimba Mountains. The last hotel in the series lining the main road is the Happy Valley motel, 15 km from Mbabane. From this point there is a turn-off to the Mlilwane Wildlife Sanctuary and to Mantenga Crafts.

THE MLILWANE WILDLIFE SANCTUARY

Reached via a turn-off from the Mbabane–Manzini road 15 km from Mbabane, this sanctuary was the creation of Terence and Elizabeth Reilly whose personal enthusiasm for conservation has been the means by which at least a few of Swaziland's original wild animal inhabitants have been preserved.

Mlilwane is 4 450 ha in extent, covering an expanse of varied country that is bushy, grassy and overlooked by the granite mountain known as *Nyonyane* (place of the small bird), on the summit of which stand the ruins of stone buildings erected by early people. The name *Mlilwane* (embers) refers to the glow of fires on the mountains.

The mountain slopes needed protection as much as the remaining wildlife. A tin-mining company had secured a concession to mine the area using hydraulic sluicing. The damage done to the landscape was a fearsome example of totally uncontrolled parasitic operations. The mountain slopes were literally slashed into ghastly dongas and deep ruts. With the venality of a few individuals being the only motive, such an industry can be a curse to any country since the miners eventually quit the scene, leaving behind slag heaps, rusted machinery, corrugated iron and open excavations.

The present rejuvenation of an area once considered totally ruined is the reward of conservation which had its start in 1959. With wildlife in Swaziland rapidly declining, the Reilly family, supported by a few other enthusiasts, started an agitation for the creation of national parks in Swaziland. The help of Professor Harold Compton of the South African National Botanic Gardens, who was deeply fond of Swaziland, was enlisted and various areas were examined and recommended to the then British Administration as suitable for conservation.

The response was disappointing. The administration was apathetic and simply said that there were no funds for such conservation. Farmers were hostile and there was no support from any public or private body. The Reilly family realised that they were alone in their enthusiasm. They decided to convert their farm, *Mlilwane*, into a wildlife sanctuary. There was almost no wildlife on the farm; citrus, rice, maize and beef were being produced. In addition, there was tin mining, leaving no room in the area for wild animals.

The Reillys approached King Sothuza II for aid in re-stocking *Mlilwane*. He allowed them to translocate game animals such as impala, zebra and wildebeest from his private hunting area of Hlane. The animals flourished in their new home, but there was an immediate problem with poaching. Observing that wild animals were back in the area, the neighbours considered them fair game for hunting. Ugly incidents occurred when the Reillys and their staff defended the wildlife by arresting poachers. Petrus Ngomane, a most dedicated conservationist, was stabbed in the neck and body by a poacher and left for dead, his rifle broken over his head into four pieces and his hands imprisoned in his own handcuffs. By some miracle he survived, and for more than 35 years was head of the ranger force of Swaziland. More wire snares were seized than there were game animals surviving in the whole of Swaziland.

King Sobhuza II became aware of the struggle for conservation. He called the nation to Lobamba and arranged for the Reillys to show a film on wildlife. After the film, the King told the assembly that Mlilwane was a sanctuary for wildlife and under his protection. With this all-powerful support, the cause of conservation in Swaziland suddenly became much stronger.

Mlilwane was opened to the public in July 1969 by Hilda Stevenson-Hamilton, widow of the late warden of the Kruger National Park. Supported by the products of the farm, tin, and an overdraft from a paternal Barclays Bank, the sanctuary became a popular resort, with paying visitors helping to finance the venture. There were many continuing problems, however, such as increasing human population adjoining the sanctuary, the operation of the iron-ore railway across the property and pressure from poachers.

Nevertheless, Mlilwane was a success. King Sobhuza asked for advice on the future of his lowveld hunting-ground of Hlane and this became a protected area. The enthusiasm of the Reillys was infectious. They decided to ensure the future of Mlilwane by placing the property in a trust. Distinguished support was given to them by international conservationists such as Peter Scott and by such powerful business concerns as the Anglo American Corporation, which extended the area of Mlilwane by buying adjoining land. Dr Anton Rupert, the industrialist, also backed them in the acquisition of 1 130 ha of land. When Mlilwane was entrusted in 1969, it included a superb extent of middleveld and escarpment country dominated by Nyonyane and reaching up the spectacular valley of the Sutshwana where the waterfall of Mantenga provides a fine sight. Even the erosion left by the tin mines provided the sanctuary with an educational asset emphasising to visitors the destructive impact on nature by man when he is motivated by uncontrolled venality.

In 1972 the Swaziland National Trust Commission was formed with the purpose of creating more wildlife sanctuaries and parks. Mlilwane had proved that even in a small country it was still possible to conserve parts of the wilderness as sanctuaries and recreational areas. In 1978 the National Environmental Education Programme commenced and a lecture hall was built in Mlilwane.

Since then many parties of scholars, tourists and others have left this beautiful wildlife sanctuary with a deeper understanding of nature, as well as memories of walks, trails, drives and views, all found in an area which might well have been totally ruined if protection had not been given to it by the Reilly family and their supporters.

A delightful little rest camp was created and gravel roads made to allow visitors easy access to many interesting parts of the sanctuary, where a good number of most of the 470 known species of birds and many of the mammals indigenous to Swaziland may be seen. Maintained in the camp is the Gilbert Reynolds Memorial Garden containing a collection of aloes originally the possession of the late Mr Reynolds, the authority and standard author on aloes. The collection was presented to the sanctuary by Mr Reynolds's widow. July is the best time to see the aloes in flower.

A friendly crowd of tame birds and mammals wander through the camp. Facilities include chalets, a backpackers' lodge, large huts, a village of traditional beehive huts, and caravan park. There is a shop and recreational room overlooking a lake notable for its egrets, crocodiles, hippos and fat barbel. A camp-fire is lit at night; there is a Sibhaca dancing team, the Hippo Haunt restaurant and the Kagogo or Homestead Lodge. The atmosphere is informal and pleasant. Guided tours of the sanctuary are undertaken on horseback or in vehicles. There is also a system of self-guided walking and mountain bike trails. Mlilwane is a fine asset to Swaziland and should not be missed by visitors.

From the turn-off to the Mlilwane wildlife sanctuary the main tarmac road continues down the broad alluvial floor of the Sutshwana River. Crossing the river, the road passes after 1 km the National Stadium and the buildings of the Houses of Parliament. Behind the Houses of Parliament there is a museum which is open daily (except Mondays) from 08h30 to 16h30. The museum displays an interesting collection of archaeological and historical exhibits, Swazi dress and regimental shields. The buildings are set in a pleasant garden of indigenous trees and plants.

One kilometre beyond the turn-off to Parliament and the museum there is a turn-off to the royal residential villages of Lositha and Lobamba. There is a second turn-off to Mlilwane after a further 1,5 km and 22 km from Mbabane a tarmac turn-off to Malkerns, Bhunya and Mankayane.

The main road continues south-eastwards down the valley. After 3 km there is another turn-off to Malkerns. The road then swings eastwards, crosses the railway and the Sutshwana River and, after a further 10 km (42 km from Mbabane), reaches the principal industrial centre of Swaziland ...

MANZINI

Named after the chieftain Manzini Motha who lived there, *Manzini* had its start in 1885 as a trading station housed in a tent and run by a trader named Bob Rogers. This flourishing enterprise was bought by Albert Bremer who erected on the site a permanent store and hotel which became a busy centre during the concession rush. Mbekelweni, the royal residence of the Swazi king, Mbandzeni, was situated nearby.

To Europeans the place became known as Bremersdorp. The Swazis, however, always knew the area as Manzini, and since 1960 this has become the official name of the town.

Manzini and its industrial township of *Matsapha*, named after the plants which flourish there, are the scene of considerable commerce and trade. There is a cotton ginnery, meat-processing works, brewery, an electronics industry and other factories. The principal airport of Swaziland is also situated at Matsapha. Art work and handicrafts may be bought at a market in town.

The streets of Manzini are shaded with jacaranda, poinciana and African flame trees which flower in spring and early summer.

From Manzini the main road to the east climbs gently through a fine avenue of flowering trees. At the time of the concession rush this was known as the 'Gin Road', a highway of adventurers, cattle-rustlers, smugglers and renegades such as the famed Bob MacNab, one of the classic horse thieves of Southern Africa.

At 8 km from Manzini there is a tarmac turn-off south to Siphofaneni and South Africa. A further 8 km sees a turn-off north to Bhalekane and Tshaneni. The main road continues eastwards, descending gently into the natural parkland of the bushveld, a plain covered in long grass and stunted acacia trees. The great ridge of the Lubombo lies to the east, the wall bordering on Mozambique. At 25 km from Manzini the road passes the store known as *Ngogolo* (reedbuck ram), the name given by the Swazis to Bob MacNab who traded here for several years.

The bush thickens into great ranching country with rich grazing on sweet grass, acacia leaves and seed pods. Situated 38,5 km from Manzini is the Mpaka mine of Swaziland Colliers and 13 km further on the road divides into two important branches. The main road swings northwards, while a tarmac turn-off continues eastwards directly towards the mountain wall of the Lubombo. Just before the road begins the ascent, a turn-off leads south to Big Bend. The road climbs steeply up the Lubombo, with views over the bushveld becoming increasingly spacious as the road gains altitude. At 63 km from Manzini the road reaches ...

SITEKI

Situated in a parkland of jacaranda and tulip trees and with fine avenues of tall eucalyptus trees, the village of Siteki is a trading and administrative centre for the pleasantly cool and fertile plateau summit of the Lubombo. Situated high on the mountains, Siteki experiences a very different climate from the hot bushveld in the west and the sandy lowlands of Mozambique in the east.

In former years renegades used the area as a hideaway. Conveniently close to the border, it allowed these individuals to slip backwards and forwards if the police on either side made any attempt to apprehend them. The atmosphere of bygone days still lingers about the modern village. The name *Siteki* (the place of much marrying) conjures up some interesting possibilities.

The Mhlumeni border post between Mozambique and Swaziland is 30 km away. It is open from 07h00 to 08h00, from 08h30 to 12h00, and from 13h00 to 20h00. The Mozambique border post is at Goba, from where it is 115 km to Maputo. A rural road leads south along the top of the Lubombo for 30,5 km to Tikuba and then on to a dead end at Nkonjane. The views over the lowveld are tremendous. A track continues from Nkonjane to Abercorn on the Great Suthu River.

From the turn-off to Siteki and Big Bend the main road from Manzini continues northwards through savanna country along the foot of the Lubombo Range. After crossing the railway line, the road passes the Hlane Royal National Park on the western side. At 15 km from the turn to Siteki, the road passes the entrance to the sanctuary. The name *Hlane* means 'uninhabited place' or 'wilderness'. This is the largest wildlife sanctuary in Swaziland and is 30 000 ha in extent. It is well stocked with wild animals including elephants, lions, leopards and cheetahs. There are two camps: *Ndlovu* (elephant) and *Bhubesi* (lion). Hlane is the scene of the traditional annual royal hunt. On the eastern side it adjoins the Mlawula Nature Reserve which is 18 000 ha in extent. This reserve extends from the lowveld up the slopes of the Lubombo to the summit, and conserves an interesting transitionary range of flora. There are fine hiking trails in the two wildlife reserves.

The main road now approaches the valley of the *Mbuluzi* (iguana) River, where sugar cane is under intense cultivation. The road crosses the river and reaches a division. Straight ahead, the road continues for 19,5 km to the Swazi border post of Lomahasha and the Mozambique post known as Namaacha, both variants of the name of a man who once lived there. The posts are open to travellers from 08h00 to 16h45.

From the division at the Mbuluzi bridge, a tarmac road leads westwards through extensive sugar cane and citrus plantations. At 21,5 km from the bridge the road reaches *Mhlume,* named after the *Breonadia salicina* trees which grow nearby. This centre comprises a sugar mill and residences for employees on the extensive irrigation scheme created by the Commonwealth Development Corporation.

After a further 7,5 km of travel through the cane fields a crossroads is reached. To the north, 5 km away, is the Mananga border post and the South African post simply known as Border Gate. The posts are open to travellers from 08h00 to 18h00. Ahead stretch the Tunzini citrus orchards. Rice is also extensively cultivated in this area. A turn-off south from the crossroads leads through a 2 km long avenue of poinciana trees to ...

TSHANENI

This village, the name of which means 'at the small stone', is a centre for the extensive irrigation projects undertaken by the Commonwealth Development Corporation. The Sand River Dam near-by and the Khomati and Mbuluzi rivers provide water for this large-scale industry which produces sugar, rice and citrus. The Sand River Dam is the largest stretch of water in Swaziland and is used for boating. All water in the lowlands of Swaziland, however, is infected with bilharzia. Direct contact – swimming or paddling – should be avoided.

From Tshaneni a gravel road leads south-westwards through the rural centre of *Bhalekane* (named after Chief Bhalekane Vilakani) where there is a clinic. After 34 km, the road reaches a junction with the road descending the mountains from Piggs Peak. The road proceeds southwards for 32 km and then joins the main tarmac road from Manzini to Siteki. Turning up the road to Piggs Peak, the traveller is confronted with an involved but scenically exciting drive. This road crosses the Khomati River, passes through a superb grove of acacia trees and, after 7 km, reaches a turn-off connecting South Africa to Piggs Peak.

The road climbs steadily up bush-covered hill slopes. After a further 16 km the road arrives at a magnificent viewsite overlooking the lowveld to the east. Six kilometres on, the Endingeni store and mission is passed. Dense plantations of saligna trees stretch on either side of the road. After 10 km the road passes a sawmill, and a further 7 km brings it to Piggs Peak, 76 km from Tshaneni.

MBABANE TO PIGGS PEAK AND HAVELOCK

The all-tarmac road from Mbabane to Piggs Peak is a splendid scenic route, revealing some of the most beautiful hill country of Africa. The road starts at the trading centre of Motshane, 14 km from

Mbabane on the main tarmac road to the South African border at Ngwenya (Oshoek). The Piggs Peak road leads northwards over a rolling stretch of grass country, with rocky hills and the ranges of the Ngwenya and Silotwane mountains visible to the west.

After 10 km the road reaches the site of the old Forbes Reef gold-mine, a gold-bearing reef discovered in November 1884 by Alex Forbes and C I Swears. It was worked until 1896 and yielded a rich output of gold. Ruins of the mining village, including the hotel, may still be seen. The area is now overgrown with wattle trees.

Beyond Forbes Reef the tarmac road continues northwards across a well-watered and, in summer, intensely green landscape with numerous streams, patches of wattle trees and lovely tree ferns. The road crosses the Mbuluzi River and at 17 km passes the entrance to the ...

MALOLOTJA NATURE RESERVE

Although Swaziland occupies such a small area there are, fortunately, parts of it which are unspoilt and perfectly representative of the principal natural divisions of the country. In 1971 the Swaziland Government sought the services of an expert to advise on the establishment of national parks and nature reserves in suitable areas of the country. For this purpose, the United Nations sponsored Major Ian Grimwood, ex-Chief Game Warden of Kenya, who spent six months in Swaziland examining the country and drafting legislation to establish the National Trust Commission.

The report submitted by Major Grimwood was accepted in principle by the Government, and in 1972 the Swaziland National Trust Commission Act was promulgated. In examining Swaziland, Major Grimwood had strongly recommended that a nature reserve be created in the *Nkhangala* or treeless, open hill country on the western border. For this purpose the area watered by the river named *Malolotja* (many rapids and cascades) was ideal. It was superbly scenic, great walking country, and composed almost entirely of title-deed or privately owned land which could be obtained. There were only 63 Swazi families resident there.

King Sobhuza II appointed his Prime Minister, Chief Bhekimpi, to supervise the project. Six councillors discussed the matter of removal with the local residents. There was no difficulty: the area of the proposed nature reserve was of little agricultural value, the grazing was sour, the climate damp, misty and cold. Better ground was offered to the residents, so they moved.

On 1 September 1978 the greater part of the Malolotja area was proclaimed a nature reserve. More land was added at later stages, resulting in a total of 18 000 ha. Trails were made to the various beauty spots, a camp of five log cabins was built, and Tore Ballance appointed as warden.

It is a reserve of great geological interest, containing many signs of old-time prospecting and mining. The oldest mine so far found anywhere is reached from the reserve. Known as the Ngwenya mine, it was worked for haematite and specularite over 40 000 years ago. The various walking trails offer fine two or three day outings. Bird life is rich, the flora spectacular, and wildlife is flourishing.

Beyond the entrance to the Malolotja Nature Reserve, the tarmac road passes the small marketplace of Nkaba with its handicraft stall, and at 22 km reaches the edge of the valley of the Khomati. The scenery is on a vast scale, superbly photogenic in form and colour.

The road finds a tortuous descent for 10 km to the floor of the valley. Swazi craftsmen offer their products for sale at the side of the road. The Khomati River takes its name from the number of cows grazing along its banks. It is a strong, rushing flow of water, particularly impressive when viewed from the bridge. The Maguga Dam has been built down river from the bridge.

The road climbs the northern side of the valley, passing through the plantations of Swaziland Plantations Ltd with a timber-mill 12 km from the river crossing. A further 5 km (49 km from the turn-off to the Mbabane–Oshoek road) brings the road into the village of ...

PIGGS PEAK

In 1884 the prospector, William Pigg, found the Devil's Reef of payable gold near the site of the village named after him. The mine enjoyed a long life producing gold but was exhausted eventually. Piggs Peak then became a centre for a great industry in timber production based on afforestation started in the late 1940s by Peak Timbers.

The village is beautifully situated, with a grand view. Its one long street is shaded by an avenue of tall eucalyptus trees and is lined with stores, administrative buildings and a handicraft market. In 1958 Mrs Coral Stephens started a school of mohair weaving in Piggs Peak. As a result, the industrious students became internationally acknowledged masters of their craft, producing curtains for use in theatres and public and private buildings in many parts of the world.

From Piggs Peak a gravel road leads eastwards to join the Tshaneni–Manzini road in the lowveld. The main tarmac road continues north through plantations, past the forestry workers' residential township of Rocklands, and down to the lowveld. At 13 km from Piggs Peak the road passes near the waterfall in the Phophonyane River. This lovely waterfall is often photographed, and has been used as a location in the production of motion pictures such as *The Flame of Africa*.

The Phophonyane Nature Reserve conserves several kilometres of rapids, waterfalls and cascades in the river. There is a fine lodge and a tented camp.

The tarmac road continues northwards down the valley of the mLumati River and after 42 km reaches the customs post of Matsamo, with the South African post of Jeppe's Reef just across the border. The posts are open daily from 08h00 to 20h00.

Beyond Piggs Peak a gravel road stretches westwards for 21 km through plantations past the disused mine workings of the Devil's Reef, and (after considerable twisting, turning, rising and falling) reaches Bulembu, the site of ...

THE HAVELOCK SWAZILAND ASBESTOS MINE

This was one of the five largest asbestos mines in the world. The mine had its start in about 1923 when Gowran FitzPatrick, caretaker of the Piggs Peak mine, employed some Swazi prospectors to search the mountains for mineral samples. One of them brought him five samples of asbestos fibre found on the banks of the Tutusi stream in the old mining concession area named after Sir Arthur Havelock, a former Governor of Natal. FitzPatrick formed a syndicate and endeavoured to interest the Canadian asbestos-mining firm of Turner and Newall in the find, but they considered the area to be too remote and the find too patchy. As a result FitzPatrick abandoned his efforts.

Then, in 1928, a prospector named Izaak Holthausen, rediscovered the outcrop. With his partner, Herbert Castle, he proved the deposit and this time Turner and Newall showed interest. In 1930 they paid £240 000 for the 100 claims of the mine and began a complex process of preparation for production.

The mine lay in completely isolated mountain country. Only a bridle-path wandered over the hills from Barberton. Curving around the slopes of Bulembu, the highest mountain in Swaziland, it crosses a great gorge by means of a natural bridge of rock (the Devil's Gorge), known to the Swazis as the *esiKhaleni sebuLembu* (pass of the spider's web), and found a difficult way to the mine at Piggs Peak. This path was, however, quite useless for transport.

To solve the problem the company built a spectacular aerial ropeway which stretched over the mountains for 20 km to Barberton. It consisted of 52 pylons and 11 stations varying in height from 4,5 m to 5,41 m to carry the cables; a 25 mm carrying cable and a 15 mm traction cable. In places the ropeway was 190 m above the ground; the longest span extended 207 m across a deep valley.

From Havelock Mine (1 134 m above sea-level) the ropeway climbed to Angle station 10,5 km away, the highest point at 1 607 m. There the ropeway was deflected 4 degrees 1 193 mm and then continued to Barberton railhead, 827 m above sea-level. Two hundred and twenty-four carriers of various types rode the ropeway at a time, each carrier being spaced roughly 182 m apart from the next one and carrying 170 kg of bagged asbestos fibre. Two small electric motors of 60 horse-power, one at Havelock and one at Barberton, drove the ropeway at a steady 10,5 km an hour.

The ropeway was built by the German firm of Bleichert and Company and was a most efficient carrier. A ride on the ropeway (the author enjoyed the rare privilege) was an unforgettable experience, as it conquered the mountains with its slow, steady, giant strides.

The Havelock Mine was a model of its kind in Africa, with a neat town to house its workers laid out in a setting of tremendous scenic beauty.

One kilometre beyond the Havelock Mine the road crosses into South Africa at the customs posts of Josefdal. The posts are open from 08h00 to 16h00. After a kilometre there is a turn-off leading down to the old Diepgezet mine of African Chrysotile Asbestos Ltd. Past this turn the road curves around the towering slopes of Bulembu. The views of the mountain country at the edge of the South African highveld are superb.

Passing through the Welgelegen plantation (24 km from Havelock) and the Highlands plantation with its turn-off to the *Shiya-lo-Ngubu* (abandon your clothes) Dam (31 km from Havelock), the road makes a most spectacular descent into the mighty Kaap valley. At the bottom, the road passes the sites of the training camps of various regiments in the Second World War and then reaches the romantically situated old mining town of Barberton 42 km from Havelock. This is a wonderful drive not easily forgotten.

MBABANE TO BHUNYA

From Mbabane a tarmac road leads west and then south through spectacular granite hills into the timber country of the Usutu Pulp Company. Their plantations (mainly pine) are amongst the largest man-made forests in the world, with the mill at Bhunya having an output in excess of 100 000 tons of pulp each year.

The road climbs out of Mbabane, revealing along the way grand views into the upper reaches of the Ezulwini valley. After 18 km there is a turn-off to Meikles Mount where Murray and Nora Meikle built a holiday resort in a setting of high hills. The views are impressive and there are riding and hiking trails, and fishing in the Sutshwana River.

Beyond the turn to Meikles Mount the gravel road continues for 8,5 km and then reaches ...

MHLAMBANYATSI

Founded as a residential township for workers in the Usutu Plantations, *Mhlambanyatsi* (the swimming place of the buffaloes) is surrounded by many hectares of trees and provides a cool, pleasant retreat for people from the warmer lowlands. There is trout fishing in the rivers.

The road continues through the plantations, descending to the valley of the Suthu River where, after 14,5 km, the mill of the Usutu Pulp Company is situated at Bhunya. The mill may be visited on Thursdays. Tours start at 10h00. At Bhunya the road joins a tarmac road which has come up the valley of the Suthu for 23 km, passing Malkerns on its way from the main Mbabane–Manzini road. This road provides an interesting return route, flanked by the river flowing through a series of rapids and pools on the floor of a valley settled by peasant farmers, From Bhunya this tarmac road climbs steeply out of the valley of the Suthu and, after 32 km of passing granite boulders and plantations of trees, reaches the customs post of Sandlane and the South African post of Nerston. Both posts open daily from 08h00 to 18h00.

MBABANE TO LUVE

The road from Mbabane to Luve, where it joins the Tshaneni–Manzini road, provides a fascinating 63 km long scenic excursion (in dry weather). The road starts from the upper (northern) end of Allister Miller Street in Mbabane and follows Pine Valley Road. The road climbs into the Dlangeni hills, with a turn-off to Fonteyn leading to the radio masts and a magnificent view of Mbabane.

The road to Luve follows the valley of the Mbuluzi River whose flow is broken by several cascades, waterfalls and deep pools. This is superb walking and riding country, cool in summer and enhanced by lovely scenery.

MALKERNS TO NHLANGANO

At 22 km from Mbabane on the main tarmac road to Manzini, a tarmac turn-off leads through an agricultural area where crops such as pineapples, citrus, sugar and cotton are grown. At 1,5 km from the turn-off stands the Tisheweshwe farm stall and cottage crafts in a cluster of cottages. The cannery of Swaziland Fruit Canners (Pty) Ltd lies ahead, with its residential township and country club. There are tours of the cannery on Thursdays from 08h00 to 13h00 and 14h00 to 16h00.

At 6 km from the turn-off lies the rural centre of *Malkerns*, named after a trader, Malcolm Kerns Stuart, who ran a trading station there at the beginning of this century. At Malkerns the road joins another tarmac road which has travelled 7 km from the Mbabane–Manzini road. Five kilometres down this road stand the Nyanza stables and the wayside shop of Baobab Batik.

An interesting and surprising industry in this area is the making of decorated candles by Swazi Candles.

From the junction at Malkerns, the tarmac road continues southwards past large pineries, the Malkerns Research Station, the Swaziland Agricultural College and the University of Luyengo, built in 1966. At 5,5 km from Malkerns there is a turn-off to Mankayane. The main tarmac road carries on for 20 km up the valley of the Suthu to Bhunya.

The gravel turn-off to Mankayane is a scenic switchback railway-type route, climbing the hills on the southern side of the valley of the Suthu. After 9 km from the turn-off the road passes the Ngabeni mission with its handicrafts industry. After a further 11 km of climbing and turning, the road reaches the Mtimani forest, from where a panorama of the Suthu valley may be viewed. The road tops a high ridge and then descends through the trees, reaching at 25 km from the turn-off ...

MANKAYANE

A Swazi chief by the name of Mankayane Sokho had his residence near the site of the present village – a cluster of shops, administrative buildings and a hotel shaded by a grove of jacaranda, silver oak, eucalyptus and other trees.

From Mankayane the gravel road proceeds southwards over hill and dale through a pleasant rural countryside. At 28 km there is a junction with a road leading for 5 km to the customs post at

Sicunusa and, on the other side of the frontier, the South African post of Houtkop. The posts are open daily from 08h00 to 18h00.

The road we are following veers south-eastwards through a densely settled area of small farms interspersed with patches of wattle trees. At 15 km from the junction the rural centre of Gege is reached, from where a road leads for 5 km to the Gege customs post and the South African post of Bothashoop across the frontier. The posts are open daily from 08h00 to 16h00.

The main road continues south-eastwards through cattle and sheep country and rolling, grassy hills patched with trees. The Shiselweni plantations extend for many hectares on each side of the road. At 23 km from Gege a road branches westwards for 12 km to the customs post of Mahamba and the South African post of the same name across the frontier. The posts are open daily from 07h00 to 22h00. At 3,5 km beyond this turn-off to the frontier lies the village of ...

NHLANGANO

Once known as Goedgegun, this village was renamed *Nhlangano* (the meeting place) when King Sobhuza II met King George VI of Britain and his wife Elizabeth at the place in 1947. The village was founded in 1921 as a centre for an important agricultural and timber area. Hemmed in by trees, the village experiences a pleasantly cool climate and the air is clear. A handicraft market offers goods for sale and there are two hotels, one with a small casino and a cinema.

Nhlangano is the principal centre for a part of Swaziland of considerable historical and economic importance. In 1750 when the ancestors of the Swazi people first migrated to what is now Swaziland, they settled in this southern part of the country burying their early chiefs here in graves which are taboo. Nzama, Mlokojwa and Shiselweni are the sites of these graves.

Beyond Nhlangano the gravel road to the east passes through this area. Small trading centres are situated at places such as Mthosheni and Hluti. After 92 km the road reaches the customs post at Lavumisa and the South African post of Golela across the border.

From Nhlangano a tarmac road leads northwards, passing after 6,5 km the King's residence of emBangweni. The road finds a complex way through seemingly endless hills covered in saligna and pine trees and with many exciting views revealed. At 26,5 km the road reaches ...

HLATSIKHULU

Perched high on a ridge, this little rural centre consists of a street of shops, a hotel and a few houses, all enjoying a fine view to the north-west of what is known as Grand Valley. The name *Hlatsikhulu* means 'big bush'. The village was founded as an administrative centre for the southern hill country of Swaziland.

Five kilometres north of Hlatsikhulu the road divides. The left-hand division continues northwards, descending into the valley of the Mkhondo River and providing a fine drive for 64 km to Sidvokodvo and from there for 23 km to Manzini. The right-hand division of the road makes a winding descent through the hills for 32 km to the trading station of Kubutsa, with banana plantations covering the hill slopes. A further 14 km takes the road to Sithobela where there is a turn-off south to Maloma. The road continues northwards for 26,5 km, reaching the Suthu River at *Siphofaneni* (tawny-coloured place), where there are hot saline chloride springs on the banks of what is the largest river in Swaziland. The river crossing is picturesque. Immediately across the river the road joins the tarmac road linking Manzini (43 km away) to Big Bend, 37 km to the east.

From this road there is a turn-off north to the Mkhaya Game Reserve, a 6 250 ha refuge for endangered species and for the reintroduction of the Nguni breed of cattle. There is a tented camp for visitors. Black and white rhino have been reintroduced as well as elephant, buffalo and other wild animals. There are guided walks, and 4 × 4 excursions, with meals around the fire.

BIG BEND

The Suthu River, confronted by the barrier of the Lubombo Mountains, experienced a phase of uncertainty as to how to continue its journey. This indecision resulted in 'Big Bend' yielding ideal opportunities for the irrigation of a large area of lowveld. The village of Big Bend is the centre for sugar production, the mill there being the first (in 1960) to produce sugar in Swaziland. The gorge through which the Suthu River penetrates the Lubombo is wildly beautiful, frequented by rich bird life, crocodiles and tiger-fish. The gorge may be reached from Big Bend, either on horseback or on foot. The summers are very hot.

From Big Bend the main tarmac road to the south crosses the Suthu River after 3,5 km, finding a way through the cane fields and acacia bush, with the Lubombo range towering up immediately to the east. At 31,5 km from Big Bend the road passes the trading centre of Nsoko, and after a further 2,5 km crosses the Ngwavuma River, its banks lined with magnificent fever trees. At 31,5 km beyond the river, the road reaches the border post of Lavumisa at the southern tip of Swaziland. This is the second most important entrance to Swaziland after Oshoek–Ngwenya. It is the main link to KwaZulu-Natal. The border posts are open daily from 07h00 to 22h00. There is a handicraft market at *Lavumisa*, the name of which indicates a hot place – a claim fully justifiable in summer.

Chapter Forty-Eight
ZIMBABWE

The Central Districts

Between the river systems of the Zambezi in the north and the Limpopo in the south there lies a natural parkland 375 830 square kilometres in extent. Trees in vast numbers and considerable variety flourish in this parkland, while flowering shrubs and creepers grow in such profusion that the whole area, an extension of the African savanna, is a garden of infinite colour and form.

Running east to west through the centre of the country is a ridge which acts as a divide between the two river systems. The summit of this ridge forms a narrow linear plateau less thickly treed, more richly grassed, and cooler than the low country to the north and south. This plateau provides a fine residential area for human beings, with deep soil, a good rainfall during warm summers, cool winters, and some freedom from tropical pests such as mosquitoes.

Scattered throughout the area between the two great river systems are some of the most imposing geological features to be seen anywhere on Earth: gigantic domes and whalebacks of granite surging upwards as though they were petrified bubbles of an ancient sea of molten magma. Their age – well over 3 000 million years – makes them among the oldest datable rocks on Earth, in addition to being one of the principal natural wonders on this planet.

Animal life of great variety and profusion found a congenial home in this parkland. Man made his appearance at a very early period. Artefacts, relics and galleries of rock art provide prehistorians with an inexhaustible field of study. Bushmen hunted through the forests and savannas from ancient times. About 2 000 years ago, Iron Age people immigrated to the area from the north, displacing the Bushmen, who they called *maNdiyanerepi* (wandering vagabonds). In harmony with the granite environment they created a unique culture which embraced activities such as mining for surface metals such as copper and gold, trading with the Arabs of the east coast of Africa, and erecting stone walls for defensive purposes around their habitations.

These settlers from the north formed powerful related tribal groups – the Karanga, Rozvi and others. Their kings were known as the *mambo,* with the honorific title of *mwene mutapa* (lord conqueror). The royal residences were surrounded by particularly elaborate stone walls often skilfully decorated with various patterns. Stone units of roughly the same size, secured from the natural flaking of granite, were simply placed one on top of the other without any form of cement. The work was almost certainly carried out by the women. The results, although crude, are singularly impressive and harmonise perfectly with the vast environment of Africa. Nothing similar may be seen anywhere else in the world. The name *Zimbabwe* derives from the name given to these walled enclosures *Dzimba-dza-Mabwe* (house of stone).

Portuguese traders entered the area during the 16th century, by which time the dominant Karanga-Rozvi people seem to have passed the peak of their power and fragmented into rival factions. Invasions by various Nguni groups from the south – the Ndebele, Shangane and other people – relentlessly reduced the early inhabitants to a state of poverty, with their walled residences being overrun and their mining operations abandoned.

European ivory hunters from the south crossed the Limpopo River during the early 19th century. In the western part of the central ridge they found the chief Mzilikazi established with a heterogeneous following of Zulus and Sothos who had fled with him from troubles in the area south of the Limpopo. These people were collectively named *maTebele* (people who hide) by the Sothos. In the Zulu language this name became *Ndebele.* Europeans corrupted the name to *Matabele.* The original Karanga-Rozvi who inhabited the land between the two rivers were leading a harried existence, being raided by the Ndebele and by the Shangane people from Mozambique. To the Karango-Rozvi the Ndebele gave the derogatory name of *maShona* (bankrupt people).

The early European hunters and traders noticed the numerous signs of mining which they called 'ancient workings'. Fanciful stories spread that this must have been the Ophir of the Bible. Highly exaggerated reports of immense riches, simply waiting to be exploited, were published in Europe. Cecil Rhodes, then at the height of his remarkable career as mining magnate, financier and politician, exploited the confused tribal situation in the country. He sent agents to see Mzilikazi's son and successor, Lobengula, and obtained an exclusive concession covering mining rights to all minerals and metals in his domain. In exchange, Lobengula was offered £100 a month, 1 000 Martini-Henry rifles, 100 000 rounds of ammunition, and a steam gunboat on the Zambezi River. The concession was signed by Lobengula on 30 October 1888.

Rhodes used this mining concession as an excuse to occupy the entire eastern portion of the country. In Cape Town he persuaded Frank Johnson, a young director of the Bechuanaland Exploration Company, to organise a column of men, lead them across the Limpopo, avoid a clash with the Ndebele, construct a road, and occupy the country of the Shona people. While the Shona would certainly be surprised at the occupation of their country on the strength of mining concessions granted by the Ndebele, they would be powerless to do anything about it.

This Pioneer Column, as it was called, reached the site of Harare on 12 September 1890. The name *Fort Salisbury* was given to the place in honour of Lord Salisbury, the Prime Minister of Great Britain. The Union Jack was run up and a fort constructed. On 30 September 1890 the 180 men of the Pioneer Column were disbanded and rewarded with rights to prospect mining claims and select farms for themselves.

Although gold was found in many places, it did not match hopelessly exaggerated expectations of vast wealth. Stories then spread that the real Ophir was in the Ndebele part of the country. In 1893 the British South Africa Company of Cecil Rhodes invaded the Ndebele area, occupying Lobengula's capital of Bulawayo, and taking possession of the whole of what was named Rhodesia. Lobengula fled to the north, pursued by a section of the Company's men. The subsequent events do not provide pleasant reading. In the hope of ending the war, Lobengula sent messengers carrying 1 000 gold sovereigns as a peace offering to the Company. The messengers were intercepted by two policemen who embezzled the money.

The pursuit of Lobengula continued and ended in disaster. On the Shangani River an advance patrol led by Allan Wilson made a dash to secure Lobengula, but were instead completely annihilated by the chief's bodyguard. Lobengula fled further north and committed suicide. He is buried in the cave in which he died. As in the Shona portion of the country, gold was found in the Ndebele area, but not in the extravagant quantity anticipated.

Rhodesia, as it was called, was run by the British South Africa Company in terms of a Royal Charter until 1922 when it was annexed by Britain. In the following year it was given responsible government after having rejected a proposal of joining South Africa as a fifth province. Subsequent to the Second World War, the idea of a union of Rhodesia, Northern Rhodesia and Nyasaland was discussed. The result was the creation of a federation, with the first joint Parliament holding session in Salisbury in 1954.

The federation never settled down. Riots occurred in 1959 in Nyasaland and in 1963 in Northern Rhodesia. The three countries separated, becoming Malawi, Zambia and Rhodesia. The Rhodesian Front Party, led by Ian Smith, which held power in Rhodesia, repudiated British attempts to liberalise the regime. African leaders such as Robert Mugabe, Joshua Nkomo and Ndabaningi Sithole were detained. On 11 November 1965 Ian Smith declared a UDI (Unilateral Declaration of Independence).

In 1969 Rhodesia became a republic, but did not receive world recognition. Trade embargoes were imposed. Several attempts were made by the British Government to find solutions to the various problems, but the situation deteriorated. On 21 December 1972 the first attack on a farm was made by African guerrilla fighters. From then on, a civil war was fought between supporters of the white government and the blacks led by the African National Congress.

Despite several attempts at peace, made by such concerned people as the South African Prime Minister, John Vorster, and President Kenneth Kaunda of Zambia, and the conciliatory gesture of the release from detention of Robert Mugabe and Joshua Nkomo in 1974, the war continued. In 1976 Mugabe and Nkomo formed the Patriotic Front, comprising two separate armies, both of which fought against the Government forces: Nkomo in the west and Mugabe in the east. Casualties were heavy.

In 1978 an internal settlement was arranged between the Rhodesian Government and various African leaders, such as Bishop Abel Muzorewa, Ndabaningi Sithole and Chief Chirau. In 1979 a general election was held and Bishop Abel Muzorewa became Prime Minister. The Patriotic Front ignored the new regime and the civil war intensified. The British Conservative Government of Mrs Margaret Thatcher then intervened in a situation that was fast becoming disastrous. After a great deal of hard talking in Lancaster House, London, the rival groups at last reached a settlement. The Government of Bishop Muzorewa resigned, and Rhodesia once again became a colony, with Lord Soames sent from London as Governor.

In 1980 a general election was held in which Robert Mugabe won 57 seats, Joshua Nkomo 20, and Bishop Muzorewa 3. Twenty seats were reserved for whites. These were all won by the Rhodesian Front. On 1 April 1980 the Government of Robert Mugabe took office in a fully independent state named Zimbabwe. The population of Zimbabwe is approximately 10,4 million.

HARARE

With a population of approximately 1 184 169, Harare (formerly Salisbury) is the capital of Zimbabwe. Situated 1 471 m above sea-level, the city lies in the centre of some of the most fertile and beautiful parkland in Zimbabwe. As a result, it is a real garden city of trees and flowers, enhanced by rich soil and a summer rainfall (November to March) of 700 mm a year.

A view of the city from the toposcope on top of the overlooking hillock reveals the exact manner in which this clean and pleasant place has grown in the midst of the surrounding parkland of tall, elegantly shaped brachystegia trees. The forest has been pushed aside to make room for the city and its suburbs. In such a situation the trees and plants irrepressibly reclaim their own and spread back into the city which, as a result, has shaded pavements, beautiful public parks, private gardens and flowers blooming in every possible situation.

The hillock is known to the local Zezuru tribe as *Neharare Tshikomo* (the hillock of Neharare), one of their chiefs who was buried on its slopes. The capital city is named *Harare* after this chief.

Harare had its start as a city on 13 September 1890 when the Pioneer Column sent by Rhodes to occupy Mashonaland halted its journey, hoisted the Union Jack on the site of the memorial flagstaff in Africa Unity Square (formerly Cecil Square), and commenced the building of a fort named *Salisbury*, after the Prime Minister of Great Britain. It was there, on 30 September 1890, before the earth walls of the fort, on the square named after Cecil Rhodes, that the men of the Pioneer Column completed their contracts and were dismissed to commence the search for gold or to settle on farms. This was the beginning of what was named Rhodesia. On each anniversary of the founding of the fort descendants of the Pioneers gathered in Cecil Square (Africa Unity Square) to raise the flag once again on the tall post standing on the site of the Pioneers' flag-pole.

The fort and town were built on the banks of a small stream with the ingenious name of *Mutyisambizi* (the river where the zebra is frightened). When the place was founded, the stream divided it into two parts linked by a causeway (hence the name Causeway, applied to the portion of the modern city containing most of the administrative buildings). The stream now flows underground through large drains, and its former course is today the busy thoroughfare of Kingsway.

The wide straight streets of Harare were the result of the Pioneers' requirements for manoeuvring ox-wagon transport. Basking in brilliant sunlight and with clear air as yet unpolluted by industry, the city is clean, crisp, and well cared for, befitting its population of traders, professional men and civil servants.

Harare has several features of interest. As the capital of Zimbabwe, it is the seat of Parliament and the resort of diplomats, politicians and lobbyists, with numerous buildings housing civil service departments. A visit to Parliament while it is in session is interesting, for Zimbabwe has always made world news. Its past, preserved in the handsome and extremely well-kept National Archives, makes fascinating study. The Strangers' Gallery in Parliament is open to the public during sittings. When Parliament is not in session, visitors may be shown over the building by arrangement with the Sergeant-at-Arms or Chief Messenger. The National Archives are open Mondays to Fridays from 08h00 to 16h00, and on Saturdays from 08h00 to 13h00.

The Town House contains several treasures, such as the Blakeway Marine Shell Collection and the original medals and decorations of Frank Johnson (who led the Pioneer Column to Fort

Salisbury). Framed in the walls are the names of the men who accompanied him on his journey. Outside the Town House there is an ingenious floral clock installed in 1950 on the occasion of the Diamond Jubilee of the city. The fine modern buildings of the University and the National Gallery also grace the city. The Queen Victoria Museum is well known for its collection of Bushman paintings, relics from the various ancient ruins of Zimbabwe, and a good representative collection of the ornithology of Central Africa. The National Gallery is open daily (except Mondays) from 09h00 to 17h00, 1 April to 30 September, and from 10h00 to 18h00, 1 October to 31 March. The Queen Victoria Museum is open Mondays to Saturdays from 10h00 to 17h00, and Sundays from 14h30 to 17h00.

Harare is one of the largest tobacco markets in the world. Sales are held on the tobacco auction floors every morning, Mondays to Fridays between March and September. Visitors are welcome. The sing-song calling of the auctioneers must be heard to be believed.

Harare's greatest beauty and principal asset, however, is its magnificent parklike setting. The main Harare Public Gardens literally extend over the entire city in the form of innumerable carefully planned avenues and streets of flowering trees. The trees planted have been especially selected to ensure that there is always something in flower somewhere in the city. These trees not only beautify Harare, but provide a living link with the arboreal countryside and, notwithstanding the contrast of modern buildings, enable the city to harmonise with its surroundings.

Harare Public Gardens stand on a portion of land set aside by Cecil Rhodes for public use when he planned the city. The garden is famous for its spring displays of sweet peas and stocks, while zinnias and marigolds seem to catch fire with colour in the summer months.

A fine collection of water-lilies may be seen in the pond built in 1937 to celebrate the coronation of George VI. A great variety of trees also flourish in the gardens. There is one enormous Indian toon tree, planted a little over 30 years ago by the Duke of Connaught, which now provides shade for garden parties held for visiting dignitaries.

Another interesting tree is the *Ficus religiosa*, regarded as being so sacred in India that no metal is allowed to come into contact with it. The father of all the Mexican feather-duster trees *(Schizolobiem excelsum)* in Harare also grows in the garden. From this prolific specimen have sprung all the feather-duster trees in the city, including the one in Africa Unity Square. The popular name of these trees is very apt; each comprises a tall clean trunk topped with a bunch of feathery leaves.

In the children's section of the gardens stands a Himalayan cypress tree which is annually decorated as a Christmas tree with lights of changing colour. During the month of December a Father Christmas post-box is placed near the tree, into which children post their letters to Father Christmas. The local Toc H organisation answers the letters.

There are several memorials in the garden commemorating the uprising of 1896 and the two world wars. An interesting attraction is provided by a miniature Victoria Falls, built by a former superintendent of the park, Mr G W McGuffog. The falls are made to scale, including the gorge and the famous railway bridge. Even the rainbow may be seen in the morning sun.

Africa Unity Square in the centre of Harare is also the home of many beautiful trees and flowering plants. To symbolise the fact that Harare was the brainchild of Cecil Rhodes, then living in Cape Town, the plants in the section of the garden around the feather-duster tree all came originally from the grounds of Rhodes's cottage at Muizenberg on the Cape Peninsula.

The major feature of Africa Unity Square, however, is its fountain. This most effective, varying, automatic display of water patterns and coloured lights was built by municipal departments in Harare, and commenced playing its merry water game during the Diamond Jubilee in 1950. The fountain is particularly beautiful when it is illuminated at night.

Spring and early summer – September, October and November – are the most spectacular seasons in Harare. At that time the jacarandas are in full blossom. Bauhinias in two varieties (pink and white, and white and purple) are also in flower, as well as the Australian flame trees and the lovely yellow cassias. Bougainvillaeas glow with colours of many different shades.

From January to July the African flame trees display their beauty, while in August and September the flamboyants make a magnificent show. More sedate, but interesting, are the tall palms *Phoenix reclinata* and *Washingtonia robusta*, presented to the city in the 1920s by Pickstones, the famous nursery in the Cape closely associated with Rhodes. The graceful indigenous musasa trees grow to perfection here in their natural habitat.

Within the city limits there is a 109 ha game park, Mukuvisi Woodlands, with conducted walks and a viewing stand.

The National Botanic Gardens, 60 ha in extent, contain specimens of most of the indigenous plants and trees of Zimbabwe. It is open daily 07h45 to 18h30.

HEROES' ACRE, LAKE CHIVERO AND THE HARARE COUNTRYSIDE

The citizens of Harare are fortunate in being surrounded by a green and pleasant countryside with many interesting features, all made easily accessible by means of excellent roads. Immediately outside the city, on the Bulawayo road, is the impressive Heroes' Acre – a burial-ground, national shrine, monument and museum dedicated to the Sipra and Zanla dead of the War of Independence. Permission to visit must be obtained from the Ministry of Information, Room 514, Linguenda House, Baker Avenue, Harare.

Lake Chivero, 32 km from the city, is a major recreational area, as well as being the principal water supply for the city. Originally named after Sir Robert McIlwaine, the first chairman of the Natural Resources Board, the great dam was created in 1952, with the completion of a massive earth wall (36,5 m high, 85,3 m long and 274,3 m wide) blocking the Hunyani River in a narrow pass through a range of hills. The summer rains normally fill the dam, and the overflow pouring down the spillway of the wall provides a spectacular sight.

The surroundings of Lake *Chivero (*sharpening stone) – a brachystegia parkland dominated by a high ridge – form the McIlwaine National Park, and the recreational attractions it possesses are numerous. The northern shore has been developed with resorts, tea-rooms, and the club buildings of yachting, aquaplaning and boating enthusiasts. The numerous picnic, barbecue, caravan and camping sites are pleasant, and launches take sightseers on tours around the lake.

The southern shore of the lake consists of a game reserve, open daily from 07h00 to 18h00. Here, a considerable variety of antelope live in their natural habitat and are perfectly amenable to being admired and photographed. Bushman paintings in the rock shelters of the overlooking hills vividly reveal that in prehistoric times this area was a favourite resort for game animals and man. The lake is full of tiger-fish, bream, yellowfish, barbel and Hunyani salmon. As a result, anglers find their time pleasantly occupied. Swimming – as in most waters in the warmer parts of Africa – is not recommended on account of bilharzia.

The *Chapungu* (Bateleur eagle) Sculpture Park in Beverley East, Msasa, is a 5 ha complex of a traditional Shona village, with a large sculpture garden and workplaces for artists, jewellers and craftsmen. Traditional dancing takes place on weekends. It was said by the *Daily Telegraph* (London, 1983) that no fewer than five of the world's ten best sculptor-carvers were in Zimbabwe. Some of their work may be seen in Chapungu and in galleries in Harare. Chapungu is open daily 08h30 to 16h30. *Tengenenge* (beginning of the beginning) is another work and exhibition site for sculptors and painters. About 17 000 sculptures are displayed mostly worked on local stone such as black serpentine, steatite, spring stone or opal. Tom Blomefield, a farmer-turned-sculptor, founded this extraordinary sculptor community of artists in 1966. It and Chapungu are internationally renowned. Art lovers from all over the world visit them as though on pilgrimage to an awesome abode of genius, of the unique work of artists inspired by a reverence for stone as living rather than inanimate matter.

At 14,5 km from Harare, on the Bulawayo road, there is a snake park. The Larvon Bird Gardens, 17 km from Harare on the road to Bulawayo, shelter 400 species of birds. Also on the road to Bulawayo, 24 km from Harare, is the Lion Park, open daily from 08h30 to 17h00.

EWANRIGG NATIONAL PARK

This beautiful 285 ha garden lying to the east of Harare was the private creation of Basil Christian, owner of the farm *Ewanrigg,* which he named after his elder brother, Ewan, who was killed in the First World War. The name Ewan was combined with *rigg*, the Welsh word for a ridge. An enthusiastic gardener, Basil Christian acquired aloes and cycads from many parts of Africa, as well as trees, cacti and shrubs from all over the world. This large assembly of aloes is admirably displayed around a stream full of aquatic and marsh-loving plants. The collection is well documented and a resident curator is in charge. Mr Christian bequeathed his farm to the country on his death.

Ewanrigg is at its best during the winter months (June to August), but there is always something to be seen. To reach the garden, take the Mutoko road A2 for 8 km to the Shamva turn-off. This road should be followed for a further 18 km, after which a turn-off to the garden is reached. There are picnic sites at Ewanrigg, but no facilities for refreshments or camping are provided.

THE BALANCING ROCKS NEAR EPWORTH MISSION

As a whole, Zimbabwe is something of a giant rockery. All manner of weird and wonderfully shaped fragments (mainly granite) of hillocks, long disintegrated by the action of sun and rain, have been scattered around by Nature with gay abandon. Eleven kilometres from Harare, past the Epworth Mission, lies a particularly wonderful collection of these rocks, some balancing on each other, others of such bizarre shape that one is reminded of the strange totems and idols of long-forgotten religions. This strange area was named after Chirembe, a renowned spirit medium who once had his home there. To reach it, take the Chirembe road turn-off from the A3 Mutare road.

MAZOWE AND THE MERMAID'S POOL

An extremely interesting 200 km long circular drive leaves Harare, passing through the handsome northern suburbs of the city and continuing along what is known as the Golden Stairs road across a fertile rural area where maize and dairy farms flourish in beautiful surroundings. After 29 km the road passes the Henderson Agricultural Research Station. The tarmac road descends easily into a bushy valley and, 35 km from Harare, reaches the Mazowe Dam, which was created in 1920 by the British South Africa Company. A concrete wall blocks the passage of the *Mazowe* (river of elephants) as it passes through the Iron Mask range of hills. The impounded water is used to irrigate the Mazowe citrus estate. The Mazowe Dam is famous for the size of its carp and is a popular fishing resort.

The road passes through the Iron Mask range next to the dam wall and, after 3 km, reaches the small centre of Mazowe. One kilometre further on, the tarmac road joins the road from Concession (15 km) where H C Moore once held a mining concession. The road then swings eastwards down the valley of the Mazowe River through spacious groves of citrus trees which are in full bearing during May and June. Five kilometres from the junction the road passes the citrus estate office, beyond which the orange groves give way to maize, cotton and then to brachystegia bush. Numerous signs of mining activity, both ancient and modern, are visible. Forty-six kilometres from the junction (84 km from Harare) the tarmac road passes through the nickel-mining and agricultural centre of *Bindura* (place of trapping) built on the slopes of a hill of that name. From here, a tarmac turn-off leads north for 72 km to the administrative village of Mount Darwin, passing close to the 1 507 m high taboo mountain of *Pfuru* (the one that surpasses) which Frederick Selous incongruously renamed after Charles Darwin.

From the village of Mount Darwin the tarmac road continues north through the Mavuradonha Mountains to the frontier of Mozambique at Mkumbura. This is a fine drive.

The main road continues eastwards through fields of maize and cotton, passing a cotton-packing depot at Tafuna siding 21 km from Bindura. The road now dwindles to a narrow mat but the tarmac surface is perfectly good and leads through interesting and rugged scenery until, 27 km from Bindura, it reaches the pictureque old mining town of *Shamva,* named after the *tsamvi* (a variety of wild fig) trees which flourish there. Gold is still being mined in the area, and the signs of former mining activity will long remain in the shape of the legacy of an enormous disused opencast working on top of the hill, a substantial rubble dump and a huddle of houses. Shamva is the terminus of the branch line from Harare and is now the centre for the local Grain Marketing Board.

At Shamva the road from Bindura joins a wide tarmac road coming from Mount Darwin (77 km north). The combined roads swing southwards back to Harare. Fields of cotton stretch on either side. The picking season in May and June is beautiful. The tarmac road climbs out of the valley through hills covered in acacia and brachystegia trees. African villages and odd little mines may be seen by the wayside. The drive along a fine modern road is altogether diverting and worthwhile.

At 25 km from Shamva the road passes the impressive granite mass of Lion's Head, with a path leading to some interesting Bushman paintings. A further 25 km takes the road past a turn-off of 1 km leading to the Mermaid's Pool, a popular weekend resort, with a restaurant and a variety of accommodation clustered around a natural pool (50 m across and 5 m deep), situated at the bottom of a rock slide formed by a perennial stream.

Three kilometres beyond the Mermaid's Pool turn-off the tarmac road reaches the turn-off to the Ewanrigg National Park with its famous garden. The road now narrows for 20 km and then reaches a junction with the main road leading east to Murehwa (66 km) and Mutoko (130 km). Turning west along the main road, the traveller is taken through the suburb of Highlands and back to Harare (15 km from the junction with the Mutoko road). It is altogether a magnificent drive filled with the scenic novelty and beautiful wilderness which only Africa can offer.

HARARE TO THE ZAMBEZI

From Harare the great north–south road of Africa stretches north-west as Route A1. For the first 10 km after leaving the city centre the road penetrates the outlying suburbs and then leads north-westwards through a lovely grassy parkland where great maize lands are cultivated among the trees. Sixteen kilometres from the city, to the north of the road, may be seen the landmark of Mount Hampden, a hillock originally intended as the destination of the Pioneer Column.

Eleven kilometres further on, the tarmac road passes the Gwebi agricultural college, with its fields immaculately cultivated around the banks of the small stream whose name *Gwivi* (hairless), from the worn-out grass on its banks, has been corrupted into the European form of Gwebi.

For a further 20 km the road continues across level parkland, after which it reaches a long flat-topped ridge, well covered in trees and running north to south. This ridge is actually a surface outcrop of the Great Dyke of Zimbabwe, one of the most extraordinary geological features of Southern Africa. The Great Dyke contains an immense variety of minerals, especially chrome and asbestos. The signs of mining and prospecting may be seen throughout its length. About 2 000 million years ago an enormous subterranean eruption resulted in the intrusion of a molten mass of material between the sedimentary layers of parts of the Transvaal and Zimbabwe. In the Transvaal this disturbance resulted in the Bushveld Igneous Complex, while in Zimbabwe it produced the Great Dyke – a gigantic trough, up to 7 km wide and 500 km long running north to south for almost the full length of the country.

The road climbs over the ridge known to Europeans as the Mvukwe Range, a corruption of the Zezuru name of *Zvimvurwi* (a low, continuous range) by means of an attractive pass called the Great Dyke Pass. The road descends easily on the western side to another tree-covered but less fertile-looking plain. At 66 km from Harare there is a turn-off north leading to the Vanab mine (48 km) and Mutorashanga (38 km). Twenty-five kilometres further on, the road passes through the village of Banket, a mining and agricultural centre on the branch railway from Harare.

A further 20 km brings the road to the bridge over the Hunyani River and 1 km beyond this lies the village of Chinhoyi, a typical Zimbabwean rural centre – clean, well kept and orderly – with a fountain playing in the garden square and a line of commercial enterprises hoping to attract patronage from traffic on the main through road.

It is 8 km beyond Chinhoyi village that A1, the Great North Road, reaches the famous feature which gives the area its name ...

THE CHINHOYI CAVES

Comprising a national park, the Chinhoyi Caves lie at the foot of a long ridge of the range of tree-covered hills known as the *Mhanyami* or *Hunyani* (high land). In level ground the earth has collapsed into an enormous circular sink-hole. Looking down from the top, the viewer sees, 50 m below, the mirrow-like surface of a pool over 100 m in depth – the 'sleeping pool' containing crystal-clear water of a remarkable blue colour. A natural sloping passage leads underground to the verge of this strange pool, while a whole complex of galleries and caverns honeycombs the dolomite rock around it.

Tradition tells of an outlaw named Nyamakwere who used these caves as his stronghold and who executed many victims by throwing them down to the 'sleeping pool'. He was eventually killed there himself. The chief of the area gave the caves to his own daughter who was married to a headman named Tshinhoyi or Chinhoyi. Tshinhoyi used the caves as a sanctuary during times of raids, maintained stores of food there, and fortified the entrances. To the local people the caves are known as *Tshirodziva* (the fallen pool).

Past the Chinhoyi Caves the Great North Road (A1) finds an easy pass over the Mhanyami ridge and continues north-westwards across a savanna plain of tobacco, maize and cattle farms. After 16 km the road crosses the railway at the station of Lions Den, from where there is a turn-off to Zave (7 km), the terminus of the branch railway, and to Mhangura (47 km) with its great chrome mine.

The main A1 tarmac road continues north-westwards across a plain densely covered with brachystegia (musasa) trees and long grass. After 5 km the road crosses the Angwa River, and a further 56 km of travelling brings the road to the village of Karoi (200 km from Harare). Tradition has it that in former years a *muroyi* (witch) was punished for her spells by being drowned in the river which was thenceforth known as the *Karoyi*. The modern village of *Karoi* (which has taken its name from this event) is a centre for the mining of mica and for tobacco farming.

The A1 road continues north-westwards from Karoi across extensive tobacco fields, with the drying sheds visible on every farm. After 11 km there is a turn-off north-east to Mwami (18 km). The A1 road continues through country which becomes increasingly rugged and wild, densely covered in bush and a great variety of trees. Twenty-four kilometres from the Mwami turn-off there is a pleasant resting and barbecue site in the shade of tall wayside trees. A further 20 km brings the tarmac road to a wayside waterpump.

The country is now notably devoid of human habitation. After a further 16 km, another shady resting-place with a drinking-water supply is reached. Signs warning against wild animals appear on the road, and 9 km further on there is a tsetse fly traffic control for vehicles coming south which might have picked up some of the pestilential fly from the valley of the Zambezi River. Southbound vehicles are driven into a shed and treated to copious draughts of chemical spray.

One kilometre north-west of the tsetse control-point the Great North Road reaches the Clouds End motel and a turn-off (79 km) to Lake Kariba.

The tarmac A1 road proceeds north-westwards and approaches the edge of the Zambezi escarpment. The journey now becomes dramatic, the superbly located tarmac road making its way through a most lovely wilderness enhanced by magnificent trees and tremendous views. Sunset is the best time to make this journey. Daytime in the great Zambezi valley can be sultry, but at sunset the air starts to cool, and the far-off hills are painted in pastel shades which are indescribably lovely. When darkness comes, the headlights of passing traffic reveal many game animals – a leopard on the hunt, or a herd of elephants heading for some special place. This is indeed a wonderful portion of the diverse continent of Africa, and one of the most dramatic sections of the entire Great North Road. At 16 km from Makuti the tarmac road reaches the office of the Department of Parks and Wildlife at Morongora. Six kilometres further along the road there is a turn-off east leading for 73 km through a magnificent piece of wilderness down into the Zambezi valley to the game reserve of ...

MANA POOLS

This game reserve (375 square kilometres in extent) on the banks of the Zambezi River is one of the most fascinating in Africa. The actual pools consist of a cluster of lakelets on the flood plain of the Zambezi. Birds and game animals live around these lakes in considerable numbers, while elephant, buffalo, zebra, sable, waterbuck, impala, eland, rhino, lion, leopard, wild dogs, hippos and crocodiles all abound in the area. The pools and the river are full of fish. Anglers find considerable sport in catching tiger-fish.

The only restrictions in the Mana Pools Game Reserve are placed on shooting. Visitors may walk or drive anywhere they please, but they must keep in mind that the wild animals are dangerous. Mosquitoes, tsetse fly and heat are always present, against which precautions must be taken. All food, bedding, etc must be taken into the reserve. There are camping sites and lodges. The Mana Pools Game Reserve is open from 1 May to 31 October. Reservations can be made through the National Parks Booking Office, P O Box 8151, Harare. Phone (09263) 4 70-6077/8.

From Morongora the tarmac A1 road descends steeply into the valley of the Zambezi River. Majestic views are revealed and a magnificent collection of trees grows along the escarpment and on the broad alluvial floor of the valley. The very body fragrance of Africa itself seems to reach out from the valley (especially in May) and embrace the traveller with the earthy, warm, freshly cut potato odour of the *Phyllanthus reticulatus* shrubs which are then in fruit. Mopane trees cover the valley floor in a dense and sultry forest, with great baobab trees rearing their sinuous branches upwards like petrified land octopuses from a weird past.

At 6 km from Morongora the A1 road reaches the floor of the valley and the turn-off to the Mana Pools Game Reserve. Magnificent baobabs line the road which leads due north-west across the level floor of the valley. After a further 6 km the road crosses the Nyakasanga River. Twenty-eight kilometres of travel through this wilderness brings the tarmac road to a turn-off leading north for 3 km to the Chirundu sugar estate. Half a kilometre ahead there is another tsetse fly control-point and the cluster of buildings belonging to the Valley Services – garages, restaurant and chalets. Half a kilometre further on (58 km from Makuti and 344 km from Harare), the great A1 trunk road of Africa reaches the banks of the Zambezi – the frontier between Zimbabwe and Zambia. At this point, known as *Chirundu* from an overlooking eminence on which a man named Tshirundu once built his home in an effort to escape the relentless heat of the valley, the end of the journey up the A1 road is reached (as far as this book is concerned). Ahead, beyond the customs barrier, looms the 320 m long silver arch of the Otto Beit bridge, which spans the turbulent waters of the Zambezi and carries the road on into Zambia. The customs and immigration post at Chirundu is open daily 06h00 to 18h00.

KARIBA

The second largest man-made lake in the world, Kariba is reached via the turn-off from the A1 road at Makuti (283 km from Harare). The road descends steeply into the valley of the Zambezi through heavily wooded, rugged hill country where many magnificent baobab trees may be seen. As the road descends, so the stifling heat of the valley reaches up to envelop the traveller. Consequently, summer is not the best time for the average tourist to make the journey. For those who do drinking-water is obtainable 20 km from Makuti. Wildlife is visible at all seasons, particularly the many elephants living on the floor of the valley. A tsetse fly control-point is situated 20 km further on, and the road reaches the dam wall after a total distance of 76 km from Makuti. The dam wall, spanning the Zambezi River border with Zambia, acts as a bridge between the two countries. There are customs and immigration posts on either side. The posts at Kariba are open April to September from 06h00 to 18h00, and October to March from 06h00 to 19h00.

The dam wall of Kariba was completed in 1959 and consists of a double curvature concrete arch with a crest length of 579 m. On top of this structure runs a 12 m wide road. The six floodgates, each 9 m by 9,5 m, have a discharge capacity of 336 000 cusecs. The capacity of the lake is 865 million cubic metres and the surface area is 510 000 ha. Six 100 000 kW turbo generators on the Zimbabwe side of the dam feed their power through a 1 430 km long transmission system to various points in Zimbabwe and Zambia. The original project visualised a second set of turbo generators to be installed on the Zambian side of the dam, with a capacity of 900 000 kW. During normal rainy seasons (becoming somewhat rare nowadays) the spillway gates are open from about mid-December to the end of January. This lowers the level of the dam in order to prepare it for the seasonal influx of floodwater. Further spillway discharge depends on the scale of flood influx, but normal influx is handled by the steady flow of water through the turbines. The average annual inflow into the dam is 49 000 million cubic metres from all sources. Of this, 16 400 million cubic metres is used to drive the turbines; 20 097 million cubic metres is discharged through the spillways, and 8 600 million cubic metres is lost through evaporation. The residue is used in increase of storage, lost or discharged through the spillways. Tours of the underground hydro-electric Kariba power-station are conducted at 10h00 and 11h00 daily, except Wednesdays and Thursdays.

The dam was built at the entrance to what the Africans call a *kariba* (little trap). A township for the construction workers was built on a hilltop overlooking the dam, and this housed a population of 10 000 workers at the peak of building operations. The total construction cost of the whole project was £78 million. The principal contractors were Impresit Kariba (Pvt) Ltd of Italy.

The lake, 280 km long and 32 km wide at its maximum width, covers 5 000 square kilometres. It has been developed into a major recreational asset for Zimbabwe. Fishing for tiger-fish, bream and a variety of other species of fish provides great sport, while cruising on the dam (more like an inland sea) is popular. Swimming is inadvisable on account of bilharzia and crocodiles but most of the hotels and camps have swimming-pools. Temperature must be taken into account (especially in summer) by those susceptible to heat and the cancerous effects of excessive sunburn. April to September are the coolest months, while October and November are the hottest. Boats of many types are available for hire. There is a considerable variety of accommodation available, ranging from air-conditioned luxury hotels to picturesque fishermen's camps, several of them on islands such as Fothergill and Spurwing.

HARARE TO BEIT BRIDGE

From Harare the tarmac A4 road to the south leads through parklike country, beautifully green during summer. After 54 km the road passes the rural centre of *Beatrice* (named after the sister of the pioneer, Henry Barrow), comprising a small motel, garage and store. After a further 46 km the road passes the rural centre of Featherstone. A further 40 km (140 km from Harare) one reaches ...

CHIVHU (ENKELDOORN)

The first European settlers in this area found growing on the site of the village a particularly fine *Acacia robusta* tree known in Afrikaans as *enkeldoorn*. From this tree was derived the early name of the village which grew as the centre for a prosperous agricultural community. The place was renamed *Chivhu* in 1982.

Fifty-one kilometres south of Chivhu across the grassy savanna, the A4 road reaches the old mining and railway centre of ...

MVUMA

At Mvuma the Falcon gold-mine flourished for years, working a profitable but very recalcitrant ore. Extracting the gold required a complex oil flotation chemical recovery plant. Noxious fumes were carried out of harm's way up a 40,3 m high smoke stack which still (at least at the time of writing) provides a landmark, although the mine is no longer working. The chimney has been struck by lightning so often that its survival is something of a local wonder. The Athens mine continues in operation.

Mvuma lies on a river known as *Mumvumi* (the place of magic singing). Legend has it that there was a pool there from which could be heard emanating the sound of singing, drumming and the lowing of cattle.

The tarmac A4 road continues from Mvuma, losing altitude gently and passing the rural centre of Chiromanzu after 40 km. After a further 60 km the road reaches the town of ...

MASVINGO (FORT VICTORIA)

The oldest European-created town in Zimbabwe was Fort Victoria (now Masvingo). When the Pioneer Column made its way up Providential Pass on 13 March 1890, the men were exhilarated by the change of climate and altitude from the low country to the cooler middleveld or intermediate plateau. They made a fortified camp on the site they named *Fort Victoria* in honour of the Queen. For a few days they marshalled their resources and prepared for the next move forward. The scene, as described by Captain Sir John Willoughby, was reminiscent of an English village fair, with its tents, wagons, flags and everybody being very jolly and relaxed, playing games and holding contests.

The main Pioneer force moved on after six days. The men left behind garrisoned the earthwork Fort Victoria and it remained a major staging post on the Pioneer road. A neat little fort was eventually built to act as a stronghold, parts of which still stand in the centre of the town.

Apart from its importance as an administrative and communications centre, *Masvingo* (rocks), as it was renamed in 1982, flourishes on a rich mineral and agricultural industry. In the district asbestos, beryl, chrome, gold, copper, tin and lithium are worked, while ranches produce slaughter animals which are processed in the town in a large cold-storage plant and prepared for railage. Vast sugar-producing developments in the lowveld have also added to the prosperity of the town, while Lake Mutirikwi, built in the district to provide irrigation water for the sugar project, has added an extra recreational facility to an already important tourist area.

Masvingo became a municipality on 6 November 1953. It is a clean little town, the terminus of the branch railway from Gweru, and the centre for the famed ruins of Great Zimbabwe. Spring (September and October) sees a vivid display of poinsettias, jacarandas and bougainvillaeas.

There is an interesting museum displaying local history and geology. It is open daily. The population of the town is 51 746.

GREAT ZIMBABWE

The ruins of Great Zimbabwe are among the most famous in the world. There are few places with a more impressive atmosphere. A visit to them is a major experience in travel.

Situated 28 km south-east of Masvingo, along a good tarmac road, the ruins are easily accessible. The site is splendidly maintained and open every day from dawn to sunset. There is an excellent site museum, tea-room, and curio shop notable for its basketwork and carving of such items as the Zimbabwe bird. There is also a picnic ground. Accommodation is provided by lodges and a hotel. Staying in the area allows the visitor the unique opportunity of wandering through the ruins on a moonlit night – a memorable experience – and sleeping in the vicinity of this colossal wreck of an antique African state.

Prehistoric people lived on the site of the ruins from an early period. The site, at the head of the valley of the *Mutirikwi* (the gatherer), a river so named because it gathers to itself many tributaries, was green and parklike, a commanding position with a magnificent view and a healthy, equable climate on account of the winds whispering up the valley from the Indian Ocean. The soil was fertile enough to support a considerable population. A perennial spring provided drinking-water and was said to be the haunt of a guardian *Nzuzu* (mermaid) of surpassing beauty.

Dominating the site is a granite hill possessing several remarkable characteristics. Firstly it was easily defensible, accessible only through natural routes which could be blocked in times of danger; secondly, the summit had natural terraces and platforms among its crown of giant boulders; thirdly, there were caves, including one of quite extraordinary acoustic shape; and fourthly, its presence and appearance were awesomely impressive to any human being.

Stone Age people made their homes in the area and decorated some of the caves with their paintings. Iron Age immigrants ousted these people about 2 000 years ago; and some time, about AD 500, the people known as the Karanga reached the site. These newcomers from the north were in the process of developing a unique culture. Migrating southwards across the Zambezi River, they had found themselves in a world dominated by granite. The whole parkland between the Zambezi and Limpopo rivers lay on a shield of solid granite with giant domes and whaleback shapes exposed on the surface. The soil was granitic. Associated with the granites in fractures and reefs was a variety of economic minerals such as gold, iron and copper, exposed on the surface and fairly easy to mine. The granite, notwithstanding its hardness, also had a tendency to fracture into fragments of similar thickness as a result of the stresses of sudden expansion and contraction. After the rock had been heated by the sun, the cool shadow of a passing thunder-cloud, accompanied by cold rain or icy hail, would cause the rock suddenly to contract, then expand again when the cloud moved on, allowing the sun to reheat the rock. These stresses caused the rock to fragment. The usefulness of these fragments for building was self evident.

The Karanga people developed a real empathy with granite. They harmonised their life-style with the granite world and developed a culture influenced by the ancient rock. The hill of Great Zimbabwe attracted them. It was the ideal natural stronghold for a king. Its granite presence was almost overpowering. Apart from providing security, elevated high in the heavens, its inhabitants would be close to the inner force and mystery of something which had survived for 3 600 million years, almost since the birth of Earth. The majesty of the rock became part of their religion. The voice of *Mwari* (God) spoke to them through oracles in the caves; the granite masses personified the power and spirit of Nature.

According to tradition, the *mambo* (king) of the Karanga named Chigwagu, nicknamed *Rusvingo* (the stone man), was the individual responsible for the most impressive stonework edifice on the hill. This is the hill ruins which are regarded by the Karanga people of today as the true *Dzimba-dza-Mabwe* (house of stone). Europeans called this complex the Acropolis. The king lived there in the large forecourt, his huts surrounded by massive walls of stone 7 m high in places and topped with seven conical towers, with tall monoliths adding to the grand appearance. In this enclosure the king and his councillors met. A steep pathway (known as the Ancient Ascent), so narrow in places that only one person at a time could climb it, led up to this enclosure and entered through a low doorway. Guards could easily block this pathway. Penitents had to crawl up the pathway, and at every step prayed to the royal power for forgiveness from any transgression.

Behind the royal enclosure was the ritual enclosure, the retreat of the spirit mediums who were never seen by the common people. From behind a wall, through the voice of an oracle, they spoke to the councillors in the royal enclosure. From one of the caves, perfectly acoustical in shape, they spoke to the people in the valley below. The voice of *Mwari* boomed out from the cave, clearly audible for a great distance when the oracle harmonised its voice with the natural harmonics of the cave.

In the third, smaller enclosure, gold and metal craftsmen worked, producing jewellery, iron spears and other items. According to tradition, the king demanded that his people pay tribute to him by bringing him stones. Each person had to carry to the site at least three stones of suitable size. When fragments became hard to find, some genius discovered that granite outcrops could be artificially fractured by lighting fires on them and then pouring cold water on the heated rock.

Women performed most of the carrying and hard labour, while specialised workmen dressed the stones. These specialists are said to have been rewarded with land of their own in the Nwanezi area, where they became known as the Venda. Only walls were built. The workers never devised any method of roofing or use of mortar. They simply placed loose stones one on top of the other to form enclosures. The people, including the king, lived in the usual mud-walled black-thatched huts securely surrounded by the stone walls. The absence of cement was actually an advantage. The stone fragments could expand and contract according to temperature, without further cracking. These hundreds of thousands of stones of uniform size piled on top of one another harmonised with the vastness of Africa in a special way, where larger units would have failed. These structures are unique. The size of the stones used in building was influenced, not only by their natural fractioning through temperature variations but also by the carrying capacity of the women labourers.

Chigwagu Rusvingo reputedly lived in the early years of the 13th century. On his death the hereditary spirit medium, Dzawanda, of the Hungwe-Dziva clan, carved the famous bird, the *Hungwe* (fish eagle), which was the totem of the clan, and this was placed as a tombstone to mark the grave of the king. More birds were carved at different times.

By the time Chigwagu died, the buildings on the hill, the *Nharira ye Mambo* (place of the king), were powerfully impressive. The Karanga were at the height of their power and their king possessed the honorific title of the *Mwene Mutapa* (master of the land). Where the ancient route up the river valley from the east topped a granite outcrop, and travellers first saw the hill with its enclosures in full prominence, there is a mute reminder of the awe they must have felt. Across the pathway (and later road) there is a strange tapping line known as *Modjidjidji*. Travellers picked up a stone and tapped it across the path, murmuring prayers for safe keeping, a successful visit and a happy return home. The stone would then be deposited on a pile at the end of the tapping line. The *vivane* (luck-heaps) which the Zulu people in the south create, have a similar function.

Chigwagu was reputedly succeeded by Chidyamatamba, whose wife Mateya was a personality renowned for her rain-making, love potions and regal character. She demanded an enclosure of her own, as the hill residence was becoming overcrowded. For her the *Imba Huru* (great enclosure), called by Europeans the Temple, was built in the valley. Over 900 000 granite units were used in this elaborate construction. It became the ceremonial centre presided over by the queen. Part of the walls, sixty courses high, were decorated with a chevron pattern, probably the sign of rain and the queen's rain-making magic. Inside the enclosure a giant, solid conical tower was built in the shape of a grain basket. This was a symbol of plenty and was dedicated to the spirit of the renowned medium, Murengo Soro-Rezhou. To him the people always turned in times of trouble. In later years the uprising of 1896 and the prolonged War of Independence of the 1970s were dedicated to him.

By 1500 the Karanga were on the decline. What the Portuguese, who traded with them from the east coast, called the Monomotapa Empire was coming under increasing pressure from factions of the ruling family. The last king to rule from Great Zimbabwe is said to have been Munembire Mudadi, who was insane. His behaviour weakened the nation. Many people were driven away. The Venda stoneworkers moved south across the Limpopo and the jewellers and traders, known as the Mwenyi or Remba people, accompanied them. The Hungwe priesthood moved to the Matobo area. The nation was falling apart. To complicate matters there was a drought, said to have been caused by one of the princesses declining to have incestuous relations with her brother the king. She fled southwards with the rain-making secrets. According to tradition, she founded the Lobedu tribe in the north-eastern Transvaal and became the *Modjadji* (queen of the rain). The fertility of the Great Zimbabwe area for traditional crops had been nearly exhausted and there was a shortage of salt. Maize was also being introduced at that time by the Portuguese traders and it was rapidly becoming the staple food. It did not grow well in the area of Great Zimbabwe.

In the north, around the strange taboo mountain of *Pfuru* (the one who surpasses), called by Europeans, Mount Darwin, salt, gold and other metals were obtainable. The drought was not so severe, maize grew well in relatively virgin soil and the area was more accessible to traders from the coast. The bulk of the remaining nation moved there and the prodigious investment in stone building at Great Zimbabwe was abandoned.

At the beginning of the 19th century the upheaval occurring in Zululand sent bands of raiders and refugees northwards. These bands, led by men such as Zwangendaba and Mzilikazi, overran the walled centres of the Karanga and their latter offshoots such as the Rozvi. The places were looted and the inhabitants driven away into the wilderness. The building of stone enclosures was largely abandoned. Time and a settled life were necessary for such constructions.

When the first white hunters and prospectors came up from the south, they observed the numerous signs of ancient surface mining and the ruins of the abandoned stone enclosures. Befuddled by notions of the rediscovery of the Ophir of the Bible, of El Dorado, the land of gold, they made no serious attempt to consult the local population about the origin of the ruins. They quite simply ignored the fact that the ruins were unique, that the people they thought had built them – King Solomon, the Phoenicians, Indians, Arabs – would have used mortar, roofing and designs contemporary with the architecture of their own period.

For years the few scientists and researchers who pointed out that the most diligent investigation revealed no trace at all of exotic people, were simply scorned by persons who for various reasons seemed oblivious to the wonders of such a unique African culture. Such people constantly dreamed of some discovery to substantiate the weirdest theories. But, alas for them, the brass brassière of the Queen of Sheba has yet to be found at Great Zimbabwe. The very foundations of the various ruins have been undermined, the soil sieved and the smallest foreign objects carefully examined. A few exotic beads and coins brought in by pedlars are all that have been found, apart from signs of the presence there from early times of the selfsame people, the Karanga-speaking tribes who inhabit the area today. One might as well claim that Peter Pan and Tinkerbell had built the enclosures as a home for Wendy, for all the evidence ever produced of any exotic origin!

The Zimbabwe birds were all removed from the ruins by various visitors. W Posselt purchased one from the local headman who was guardian of the ruins. Posselt sold the bird to Cecil Rhodes, who presented it to the South African Museum in Cape Town in 1891. J T Bent, a Fellow of the Royal Geographical Society, visited the ruins in 1892. The old guardian of Great Zimbabwe, Mugabe Chiphumo, allowed him to remove a collection of objects found at the ruins, including five of the birds. These were sent on exhibition, first to London and then to the South African International Exhibition in Kimberley. After the exhibition, the Bent Collection, including the birds, were presented to the South African Museum in Cape Town. Rhodes then took back the bird he had bought from Posselt, and this was kept in his private collection in Groote Schuur.

In 1981 the five birds from the museum in Cape Town were returned to Zimbabwe in exchange for a unique collection of *Hymenoptera* (bees, wasps and ants) from the National Museum in Bulawayo. The birds are now exhibited in the site museum at Great Zimbabwe, together with one bird which had remained in the country, and the upper half of another bird. The lower half of this bird had been taken to Berlin and lost there during the Second World War. The first bird obtained by Posselt remains in Groote Schuur in Cape Town.

A likeness of the original bird, said to have been carved by Dzawanda, is now the emblem of Zimbabwe, the land which takes its name from the stone ruins, especially those on the summit of the granite hill, the *Dzimbahwe,* the residence of the king. The return of the birds was a matter of considerable emotional importance to the people of Zimbabwe, signifying the restoration of their independence and national pride.

LAKE MUTIRIKWI

Situated at the confluence of the Mutirikwi and Mshangashi rivers 32 km from Masvingo, the lake was built to supply irrigation water for the sugar and citrus estates in the lowveld of Zimbabwe. The concrete dam wall, 62 m high and 311 m long, was completed in 1961. It blocks the passage of the united rivers through a narrow gorge between granite hills. The lake was originally named *Lake Kyle* after a farm which was inundated by the waters (*kyle* being a Scottish word meaning 'a channel of water').

The Y-shaped lake covers an area of 56 square kilometres, with a shoreline of about 257 km in circumference. The lake lies in an attractive parklike setting of hills and forest. A 6 480 ha game reserve is situated on a large peninsula on the northern side of the lake. It has been stocked by translocating such game animals as square-lipped (white) rhino from Zululand, buffalo, kudu, waterbuck, giraffe, sable, zebra, eland and other smaller antelope. Hippos are also present. A fish research centre in the game reserve contains an aquarium and is managed by a resident biologist.

The lake, the second largest in Zimbabwe, (after Kariba), has been developed into a recreational area, with boating, fishing and camping in picturesque surroundings. The granite country of Zimbabwe is one of the chief scenic glories of Africa, and the environment of Lake Mutirikwi is a fine example of this type of landscape. A magnificent variety of trees and plants grow around the verges of the lake, while the whole area is ornamented with piles of granite, balancing rocks and many fanciful stone shapes.

Bushmen were fond of this area. Immediately above the rest camp may be seen a perfect example of their rock shelter homes. On top of a granite dome there stands a pile of odd-shaped rocks carefully arranged by Nature and bound by the powerful roots of a wild fig tree to make a remarkable shelter. Giant euphorbias stand nearby perhaps, as they do in Zululand, to guard the graves of forgotten chiefs. On the walls of the shelter there is a gallery of paintings. The atmosphere is so tranquil and perfect that it seems as though the Bushmen are just out visiting and will return at any moment instead of having vanished forever.

Another of these rock shelters is situated a few kilometres away above the boat club, under cool shady trees surrounded by a collection of flowering aloes, resurrection plants and ferns. Through the trees the blue waters of the man-made lake may be seen twinkling. Around the old Bushman home all is still, with only the wind and the birds providing life.

THE MUTIRIKWI NATIONAL PARK

Lying 32 km west of Masvingo, on the road to Zvishavane, this park covers 12 960 ha around the Mutirikwi lake. The lake is renowned for black bass, bream and barbel. The park is thickly wooded and is inhabited by sable, kudu, waterbuck and numerous smaller antelope. In addition, a fine Bushman rock shelter, crowned by a majestic wild fig tree whose roots festoon the rocks, may be seen in this park.

Masvingo lies on an intermediate terrace plateau, one step in altitude above the low country, one step below the central ridge. Eleven kilometres south of the town, the main tarmac A4 road reaches the site of a small wayside monument marking the top of Providential Pass, so named in August 1890 when Frederick Selous, the renowned hunter who was guiding the Pioneer Column, found by chance this easy natural gateway to the highlands. It is a beautiful wooded pass, and the verges of the road have been ornamented with poinsettias and bougainvillaeas in many lovely shades.

The road descends the pass and leads for 92 km through a parkland of trees. Turn-offs lead to the Mutirikwi National Park, and Great Zimbabwe. After 30 km the road crosses the *Tokwe* or *Tugwi* River, the name meaning 'a river that sweeps away when in flood'. A further 30 km brings the road to a turn-off leading eastwards to the sugar cane growing areas of Triangle (82 km), Hippo valley (113 km) and the Chipinda pools (161 km). Triangle was the creation of Tom McDougall, whose first experimental plantations of sugar cane were arranged in the shape of a triangle. He proved the irrigation possibilities of this part of the low country and commenced a large-scale agricultural industry. Chiredzi has grown as a centre for the area.

Scenically, this is one of the most spectacular areas of the low country. Huge granite domes surge out of the parkland. In spring the musasa trees provide a lovely spectacle. The Runde River meanders through the trees and granites. The name *Runde* means 'a river subject to great floods'. In the dry winter months this river is simply a succession of pools contained in a bed of sand and giant granite boulders. Reeds and handsome trees line the banks, and the scene resembles a still life, with hippos lazing and hardly a sign of movement in the warm air. With the arrival of the summer rains between December and March, the scene is often transformed. The river awakens in sullen fury at being roused out of its sleep by the thunder. Great surges of chocolate-coloured water sweep down with a menace and power capable of immense damage.

The road reaches this river 106 km from Masvingo. In former years a low-level bridge crossed the river and was frequently inundated by the floods. A pretty little hotel, known as the Rhino hotel, was built on the banks to shelter travellers caught by the storms, when a river crossing was often delayed for days by the floods. Now, a fine high-level bridge spans the river well above the floodwater-level. The hotel has vanished. The bridge is named after Stuart Chandler, the pioneer road builder of the country. The turn-off east to Chiredzi provides access to the ...

GONA RE ZHOU NATIONAL PARK

This national park was created in 1967, largely as the result of the enthusiasm of Allan Wright, who served as District Commissioner of the Mwenezi (formerly Nuanetsi) area from 1958 to 1968. The name *Gona re Zhou* means 'refuge of the elephant'. The park covers 4 964 square kilometres of very wild country and provides a home for nyala antelope, the very rare King Cheetah (the striped cheetah) and many elephants. *Bvekenya* (Cecil Barnard), the renowned poacher, often hunted in this area.

A giant elephant, said to be the one known as *Dhlulamithi* (taller than the trees) who features in the book on Barnard's life, *The Ivory Trail*, was shot on the border of the park in August 1967. It was later proved that the elephant was one of Dhlulamithi's sons. Its tusks are rated amongst the largest ever secured south of the Zambezi. The left tusk weighed 62 kg and the right tusk 48 kg. The park is open from 1 May to 31 October.

From the Runde River the main tarmac A4 road continues south through the trees. After 41 km the road crosses (near Rutenga station) the railway line leading to Mozambique. After a further 20 km the road crosses the Mwenezi River, with a turn-off on the north bank leading for 3 km to the administrative post of Mwenezi. A further 40 km brings the road to the Bubi River, another great hazard to cross in the days of low-level bridges. In the riverine forest on the river banks stands the Lion and Elephant motel.

South of the Bubi River the road leads through a hot, arid area of mopane trees. Rainfall is a scant 200 mm a year and the heat of summer is relentless. Baobab trees thrive in these harsh conditions, and there are many gigantic specimens visible from the road. This is ranching country, where a few game animals may still be seen.

At 75 km from the Bubi River the road joins the A6 road coming south from Bulawayo, and the combined roads then lead for a further 4 km to enter the border village of ...

BEIT BRIDGE

This is the principal southern gateway between Zimbabwe and South Africa. The village consists of a cluster of hotels, garages, stores, administrative and customs buildings standing on the northern side of the Limpopo River. A 475 m long, 14 span combined road and rail bridge crosses the river into South Africa. Alfred Beit, the mining financier and colleague of Rhodes, on his death on 16 July 1906, bequeathed the bulk of his immense personal fortune to the welfare of Southern Africa. The Beit Bridge, opened in 1929, was built with funds from the estate. The tower on the central pier carries a bronze plaque commemorating Alfred Beit. The customs post is open daily from 06h00 to 20h00.

Chapter Forty-Nine
ZIMBABWE

The Ndebele Country

BULAWAYO

With a population of approximately 620 936, Bulawayo is the administrative centre of Matebeleland, the home of the Ndebele people. Zimbabwe's principal railway junction and marshalling yard, the city is a spacious, sunny and friendly place, lying 1 356 m above sea-level on the plateau summit of the central ridge of Zimbabwe.

The history of Bulawayo began in November 1837 at the Nine Days' Battle in the Transvaal when the Voortrekkers under Hendrik Potgieter defeated Mzilikazi and his following who were known to the Sotho people as *maTebele* (refugees or runaways). Mzilikazi, already a runaway from Zululand, led his people northwards in search of a new home. After a long period of wandering in the wilderness, the maTebele or *Ndebele,* as they called themselves in their own Zulu language, found their way to the western end of the central ridge forming the watershed between the Limpopo and Zambezi rivers. There they settled, flourishing in the cool, healthy air and accumulating great herds of cattle by raiding the earlier inhabitants whom they contemptuously referred to as the *maShona* (bankrupt people).

Mzilikazi built his capital, *Hlahlandlela* (where the pathway is cut), close to the site of modern Bulawayo. On his death in 1868 his son Lobengula, after some argument, succeeded to the leadership of the Ndebele. In 1872 the young king built a new capital for himself which he named *kwaBulawayo* (place of the man who was killed), in the sense that he considered himself as having been 'killed' or persecuted by the opposition of some of the tribe to his succession to power. In Zululand the renowned chief Shaka had also given his capital this name for the same reason.

This was the beginning of the modern city. The original Bulawayo of African-type huts was dynamited and set on fire by the Ndebele in 1893 when they were conquered by the Europeans. A new Bulawayo was laid out on the site by Dr Leander Starr Jameson. It grew with phenomenal speed as a boom town of prospectors and land speculators rushing to explore the riches of what they called Matebeleland. For a while it was hoped that the place would prove to be a second Johannesburg. The bubble burst in 1895, however, but sufficient gold had been found in the area and the pastoral and agricultural richness of the locality had been proved to such an extent that the future of the town was secure.

The Ndebele uprising of 1896 caused a setback. Bulawayo was in the centre of the uprising. The market square was hastily converted into a fortified area in which the 800 women and children of the town were concentrated. Some gruesome murders occurred in the surrounding countryside, resulting in the deaths of 146 Europeans and the disappearance of a further 58, but Bulawayo itself was never attacked. A relief force from South Africa soon reached it. The little town was jammed with a crowd of men whose characters were often as picturesque as their choice of uniform. Cecil Rhodes, Robert Baden-Powell (of Boy Scout fame), Johan Colenbrander (the renowned frontiersman), prospectors such as Frank Lewis and Orlando Baragwanath; and innumerable other individuals who have played a not-insignificant part in the stormy story of Southern Africa – all rallied to the subjugation of the Ndebele.

The most spectacular fighting took place in the granite wilderness of the Matobo hills outside Bulawayo. The rebels took refuge there so successfully that the whole disturbance was only effectively ended after Cecil Rhodes held his four famous *indabas* (conferences) with the leaders of the Ndebele. He agreed to several needful improvements in their administration and treatment.

The termination of the uprising saw Bulawayo once again experiencing a surge of progress. The railway line from South Africa across Botswana, built during the rebellion at the record speed of 640 km in 400 days, reached Bulawayo on 19 October 1897. From there it was extended east to what was then Salisbury (Harare), north to the great coalfields at Hwange, and on to the Zambezi River. Cattle ranching developed at the same time. After the Anglo-Boer War, mining activity expanded considerably when the British South Africa Company (which at the time had a controlling charter over what was then Rhodesia) relaxed its demands for 50 per cent of the profits of any mines. This allowed small workers a chance of exploiting the innumerable reef outcrops and the so-called ancient workings of early African miners.

Substantial industrial development has in recent years also come to Bulawayo. Becoming a city in 1943, it is today a busy place as well as a centre for communications and tourism. State House, north of the city, occupies the original site of Lobengula's country residence. The tree which shaded meetings in the royal cattle corral still stands.

The city is notable for its wide streets and spacious planning. Amenities include two adjoining parks covering 45 ha. One of them, Centenary Park, contains a modern theatre and the fine Colosseum-style building of the National Museum which is open Mondays to Saturdays from 10h00 to 17h00, and Sundays from 14h30 to 17h00. This is a first-class museum, with many magnificent displays of mammals, including the second largest mounted elephant in the world. This elephant, shot on *Doddieburn* ranch near West Nicholson, is 353 cm high to the shoulder and weighs 5,5 tons. The tusks are 40 kg and 51 kg respectively.

Also in Centenary Park is a finely laid-out miniature railway with two steam puffers and one electric unit. The railway is run by the Round Table organisation and provides rides on weekends and public holidays. Railway enthusiasts will be interested to see a 0,6 m gauge locomotive built in Britain in 1897 and used on the first narrow-gauge railway from Beira to Mutare. There is a railway museum situated on the corner of Prospect Avenue and First Street near the railway station. Exhibits include twelve steam locomotives. It is open Tuesdays to Fridays from 09h30 to 12h00, 14h00 to 16h00; and on Sundays from 14h00 to 17h00.

The Mzilikazi Art and Craft Centre is open Mondays to Fridays from 08h30 to 12h30. There is an art gallery in the city, open from 10h00 to 17h00 daily, except Saturday afternoons and Mondays.

Also of interest is the Jairos Jiri Craft Shop, named after the Ndebele man who pioneered work for the disabled and started a profitable industry for many hundreds of handicapped persons.

The adjoining Central Park, apart from being graced by a variety of handsome trees and magnificent flowers, contains one of the best caravan parks in Southern Africa. The Borrow Street swimming-bath, one of four in Bulawayo, is situated close to the caravan park. In Central Park stands one of the finest illuminated fountains in Southern Africa, inaugurated on 4 November 1968 to mark the 75th anniversary of the city. The fountain is a skilfully designed, constantly changing pattern of water and colour, a notable feature being a rainbow which appears in the morning light.

The civic centre of Bulawayo is built on the site on the market square which was used as a stronghold during the uprising. The well which supplied water to the market square stronghold is preserved in the garden and was overlooked by a statue of Sir Charles Coghlan, the first Premier of what was then Rhodesia. Another particularly impressive statue, that of Cecil Rhodes, stood at the intersection of Eighth Avenue and Main Street. These statues are now in the garden of the museum.

At Hillside Dam, 6 km south of Bulawayo, there is a nature reserve, aviary and picnic site. The dam itself offers fishing and boating possibilities.

Bulawayo is surrounded by plenty of open land to allow for expansion. Handsome trees and gardens are an admirable feature of the city. The months of September and October are particularly lovely when jacarandas and bougainvillaeas are in full bloom.

THE KAME RUINS AND THE MATOBO HILLS

The bush-covered countryside around Bulawayo is a spacious wilderness containing many features of considerable interest. The beauty of this area culminates in the great stronghold of granite domes – one of the most impressive landscapes to be seen anywhere on Earth – known to the Africans as the *Matobo* (corrupted by Europeans into the Matopos).

Twenty-two kilometres west of Bulawayo, on a hillock overlooking the *Kame* (slow-moving) River, lies the fascinating pile of ancient stone walls and terraces of the *Kame* (originally known as Khami) ruins, a World Heritage site. This picturesque complex of ruins is all that remains of one of the most considerable stone-walled settlements of prehistoric Zimbabwe.

Whoever selected the site for this settlement had excellent taste. Surrounded by a lovely parkland, the settlement looks out over a particularly pleasant stretch of the Kame River. According to tradition, this walled settlement was one of the last to be inhabited in Zimbabwe. The Rozvi section of the Karanga tribe were reputed to have built it. Many interesting relics of their occupation have been found, including indications of the presence of a Portuguese missionary. There is a Dominican cross in stone in the middle of the enclosure where this mission was probably centred. The ruins are extensive. A day's exploration and picnicking in so remarkable and agreeable a place is not wasted. There is a site museum.

There are several magnificent drives, many fine walks and numerous recreational possibilities for visitors around the complex of granite domes known as the Matobo. The road from Bulawayo leads directly over an acacia-covered plain so level that, from the city, the traveller is surprised to see the first signs of the range looming up ahead. At this point the tarmac road passes the Matobo Dam, where there is a sailing and canoeing club and opportunities for fishing. A further 3 km takes the road past a turn-off to the Matobo Agricultural Research Station. Three kilometres further (32 km from Bulawayo) brings the road to the entrance of ...

THE MATOBO NATIONAL PARK

This National Park covers an area of 928 ha and contains some of the most majestic granite scenery to be seen anywhere on Earth. It is here that natural erosion has stripped away the central ridge of Zimbabwe and revealed an 80 km long concentration of outcrops of granite masses estimated from the disintegration of radioactive elements as being over 3 000 million years old. These old granites surging up from the secret depths of the Earth are part of the Fundamental or Basement Complex, the earliest of all geological systems.

The extraordinary shapes – domes, whalebacks, rock castles and weird fragments – which constitute the complex, as well as the beauty and unique atmosphere of the area, are so fascinating that the human imagination cannot avoid being deeply impressed. Mzilikazi, the Ndebele ruler, is said to have been particularly fond of this area. With a degree of humour and perspicacity he likened the granites to an assembly of elders, devising the apt name of *Matobo* (the bald heads). On his death in 1868 he was buried in a cave in a granite outcrop named *enThumbane (*the tomb). The earlier Karanga tribespeople had also sensed the primeval power of the ancient granites. Their priests practised there the worship of *Mwari* (God), presiding over an oracle in one of the great caves.

At the end of the uprising of 1896, Rhodes also found himself fascinated by the wonderful granites. Riding in the area at the time of the last great indaba with the Ndebele, he found by chance the colossal dome named *Marindidzimu* (the haunt of the ancestral spirits). The view from the top and the serene atmosphere of forgotten ages stretching back to the very birth of Earth gave him tremendous intellectual excitement.

'*The peacefulness of it,*' he said to his companions. '*The chaotic grandeur of it all. I call this one of the world's views. It brings home to me how very small we are.*' He sat down in the shadow of a boulder and added: '*I shall be buried here, looking in that direction.*' He pointed north.

After his death in Muizenberg in the Cape on 26 March 1902, he was buried on the summit of this gigantic rock mass, looking out, as expressed by his friend Rudyard Kipling in his poem *The Burial:*

> '*Across the world he won,*
> *The granite of the ancient north,*
> *Great spaces washed with sun'*

Rhodes had already acquired a considerable personal landholding on the verge of the Matobo, which he bequeathed to the people of Zimbabwe. The British South Africa Company added to this the area which included Rhodes's burial hill of Marindidzimu. In this way, the present National Park had its beginning.

Close to Rhodes's grave lie the graves of his stormy petrel colleague Sir Leander Starr Jameson (who died in London on 26 November 1917) and Sir Charles Coghlan, first Prime Minister of Rhodesia, who died on 14 August 1930. A slightly incongruous monument of Grecian design contains the remains of Major Allan Wilson and his men, who lost their lives in the pursuit of Lobengula when Matabeleland was occupied in December 1893.

Many of the caves in the Matobo contain superb galleries of Bushman paintings. Especially notable are the caves named Silozwane, Bambata, Gulubahwe, Nswatugi, Pomongwe, Amadizimba and the rock shelter known as the White Rhino Shelter. All are accessible and thoroughly worth visiting, not only for their prehistoric art (mainly Late Stone Age), but also for the singular beauty of their situations, each being different from the other in the setting of the granite wilderness.

The fauna of the area includes sable antelope, baboons, monkeys, numerous small antelope and other animals. A 1 012 ha game park has been created in the western portion of the Matobo around the Chintampa Dam, and this contains white and black rhino, giraffe, eland, wildebeest, zebra, kudu, sable and buffalo, as well as many varieties of smaller game. Bird life throughout the National Park is rich in variety and quantity. Lizards and reptiles also flourish in the area. All visitors to Rhodes's grave notice the brilliantly coloured rock lizards (*Platysaurus capensis*) which abound there and are extremely tame. They are quite harmless. The game park is open daily from sunrise to sunset.

Many handsome trees grow in the area. Especially notable are the musasas *(Brachystegia speciformis)*, brilliantly coloured in spring; the kaffirbooms (*Erythrina caffra*), whose blossoms are a gorgeous blood-red; the paper tree (*Commiphora marlothi*) with their peeling bark; the candelabras *(Euphorbia ingens);* the wild figs and many others. Ground orchids, ferns and flowering plants make the Matobo a garden of infinite variety of shape and colour.

This wonderful National Park is well served with roads, paths, picnic sites and rest camps.

An extraordinary dolerite dyke runs through the area, like a ruined Great Wall of China.

BULAWAYO TO BEIT BRIDGE

From Bulawayo a tarmac road A6 leads south-east over the grassy summit of the central plateau ridge of Zimbabwe. At 23 km it passes the Chipangali Wildlife Orphanage, a sanctuary for sick and injured wild animals. It is open daily, except Mondays. Reaching the end of the escarpment, 27 km from the city, the road makes a steady descent over 6 km from the 1 370 m level of the plateau to the 1 160 m level of the acacia-covered middleveld.

Eight kilometres from the bottom of the pass, the road passes through the small rural and railway centre of *Esigodini* (the place in the hollow), formerly known as Essexvale (41 km from Bulawayo), pleasantly situated in rugged country. The Ncema Dam (headquarters of the Bulawayo Power Boat Club) is 15 km away, and the popular picnic area of the Nyankuni Dam 27 km away.

Fifteen kilometres south of Esigodini there is a turn-off west leading to the Rhodes indaba site (16 km) and the picnic site of *Diana's Pool* (18 km), named after Diana Richardson, wife of a former district commissioner. The main tarmac road continues south, gradually losing altitude through well-wooded country dominated by handsome granite domes and whalebacks. Twenty-three kilometres from Esigodini (64 km from Bulawayo) the road reaches a prominent specimen of a granite dome known as *Mbalabala* from the colour and stripes on its slopes, resembling those of the antelope of that name (the greater kudu). From here, a road stretches east for 33 km to Filabusi, an old gold-mining centre, then to the asbestos-mining centre of Zvishavane (formerly Shabani) and to Masvingo (224 km).

The A6 tarmac road continues southwards through impressively beautiful granite dome country where many fine trees grow and the views are picturesque. At 62 km from Mbalabala the road reaches the village of *Gwanda,* named after a thorny type of grassy shrub growing there. Gwanda lies 985 m above sea-level (375 m below Bulawayo) on a warm, densely bushed plain. From here a scenic gravel road, practical only in dry weather, leads for 120 km through the Matobo area to

Bulawayo. Another gravel road branching off south from Gwanda leads for 140 km to the site of the old Pioneer fort at Tuli.

The A6 tarmac road swings eastwards from Gwanda and traverses a granite landscape considerably marked by the signs – active and abandoned – of mining. This has always been a great area for the famous Zimbabwean type of enterprise known as a 'small working'. Innumerable little gold-mines have flourished here. Many hardy and interesting characters have either made small fortunes or quietly gone bankrupt, labouring beneath the sun.

Twenty-five kilometres from Gwanda the A6 road reaches Colleen Bawn, where the large cement works of the United Portland Cement Company are situated. In Gaelic, *colleen bawn* means 'fair maiden'. The name was given to the limestone claims registered by John Daly on 28 March 1895.

The A6 tarmac road continues through hill country, swinging south past the rail siding of Jessie (162 km from Bulawayo) and the half-way beacon to Beit Bridge. The bric-à-brac of mining lies scattered among the hills. One kilometre further south lie the workings of the Lanninhurst Mine, while a further 7 km brings the road to the terminus of the branch railway from Bulawayo at *West Nicholson,* where the buildings of Messrs Liebigs Meat Factory dominate the scene, and the memory of Andy Nicholson, an old-time prospector, is preserved by the name.

The road is now 169 km from Bulawayo. It crosses the Mzingwani River by means of a fine bridge stretching high above the tremendous floods which sweep down during the rainy season. In winter, however, the river is almost dry and little more than a chain of pools. The road leads on southwards, gradually losing altitude through mopane bush country. After 28 km the road passes Tod's sale yards and the site of a famous hotel of former years. An interesting point is reached 20 km further south when the road crosses the route of the original trail blazed by the Pioneer Column on their way to occupy Mashonaland in 1890. The trail has long since been overgrown, but the crossing place is marked.

The modern road continues southwards through a hot wilderness of mopane trees – ranching and game country where signs warn of the presence of wild animals. At 98 km (320 km from Bulawayo) the road reaches Beit Bridge, 500 m above sea-level, on the Limpopo River frontier with South Africa. Here the customs and immigration authorities provide a service daily from 06h00 to 20h00.

BULAWAYO TO PLUMTREE

From Bulawayo the main A7 tarmac road leading west to the Botswana border at Plumtree makes its way out of the city through the industrial suburb of Belmont and the residential suburbs of Donnington and Bellevue. After 6 km, the road leaves the built-up area and continues across the acacia bush plateau.

At 26 km from the city, a turn-off south leads to the Matobo area. After 3 km, A7 reaches the Anglican Cyrene Mission, famous for its school of African art founded by Canon Edward Paterson. Nine kilometres further on (39 km from Bulawayo), the A7 road passes the small railway centre of Figtree.

Keeping company with the railway line, the main road proceeds westwards for a further 32 km, reaching the rural and railway centre of Marula. From here, a turn-off leads south for 26 km through attractive rugged bush and granite country to the Mangwe Pass, the original main route of entry for travellers in the days when Mzilikazi and his son Lobengula ruled the Ndebele country.

A further 9 km of travel west brings the A7 road to the turn-off south to a place with the rather resonant name of Mphoeings. A further 24 km to the west one reaches the village of Plumtree, with its cluster of shops, hotel, school and railway station. From here, the road leads for a further 2 km to the customs and immigration post on the border with Botswana (105 km from Bulawayo). The customs post is open daily from 06h00 to 13h00; 14h00 to 18h30; and 19h00 to 20h00.

BULAWAYO TO HARARE

From Bulawayo the A5 all-tarmac road leads north-east across the acacia-covered summit of the central plateau ridge of Zimbabwe. Twelve kilometres from the city the road passes the factory of the United Portland Cement Company and, 3 km beyond it, the turn-off to the Llewellyn barracks of the Zimbabwean army.

Immediately to the north of the road may be seen the low flat-topped hill known as *Ntaba yesinDuna* (the hill of the headman). It was there, according to tradition, that Mzilikazi settled accounts with a group of headmen who had revealed a tendency to repudiate his rule. All of them were killed there, except one, Dambisamahubo, who escaped to the east and cursed the Ndebele. Even today, when the dry east wind blows away the sorely needed rain-clouds, the curse of Dambisamahubo is said to be the cause.

The A5 tarmac road continues north-eastwards across a grassy savanna scattered with trees and clumps of bush. The road and railway keep close company, for the central ridge is narrow and falls away sharply to the low country on the north and south.

At 48 km from Bulawayo a turn-off leads south-eastwards for 40 km to the Dhlo-Dhlo ruins, one of the most beautifully constructed of all the ancient ruins of Zimbabwe. The interesting Regina ruins at Zinjanja may also be reached from this road, as well as the remnants of Fort Rixon, built on the farm of Theodore Rixon during the uprising of 1896. The A5 tarmac road continues north-eastwards. At 82 km from Bulawayo it passes the small rail centre of Insiza and after a further 17 km reaches the rail centre of Shangani, where another turn-off leads to the Dhlo-Dhlo ruins (20 km). The Shangani River is crossed 8 km further on. At an ill-fated point about 192 km downstream, Allan Wilson and his men, pursuing Lobengula in 1893, came to an unfortunate end.

A further 9 km brings the main road to a turn-off leading for 18 km to the ruins known as Nalatale. These ruins of a walled settlement, together with the nearby Dhlo-Dhlo ruins, are probably the most attractive in Zimbabwe. Although small and considerably damaged by treasure-seeking vandals, they are thoroughly worth seeing.

Forty-eight kilometres north-east of the turn-off to Nalatele, the A5 tarmac road, 168 km from Bulawayo, reaches the city of ...

GWERU

The principal centre of the midlands of Zimbabwe, Gweru, became a city on 1 October 1971. It has a population of 124 735. It is a clean and neatly laid-out place built around a long, low hill on top of which stands a tall radio mast. The name *Gweru*, formerly Gwelo, originates from the *Gweru* (dry) River which flows through the centre of the city, when it flows. Lying 320 m above sea-level, Gweru enjoys a pleasantly warm summer and a winter cold enough to waken anyone who might have gone to sleep during the sultry days.

Gweru is an army and air force training centre, as well as an important railway junction with branch lines to Masvingo and Shurugwi. A variety of industries operate in the city which is a busy place with a modern shopping area and such amenities as a handsome public park. Gardens and flowers flourish in the area, and the attractive little municipal office block boasts a notable garden of roses.

Twenty-eight kilometres south of Gweru, on the edge of the escarpment, lies the chrome-mining centre of Shurugwi. A drive to this picturesque mining town is strongly recommended, especially in spring. The musasa trees growing in that part of Zimbabwe attain such brilliance of colour – red, plum, yellow – and occur in such profusion that the spectacle is overwhelming. May is the month for poinsettias, when an immense variety of colours may be seen. In November the poincianas or flamboyant trees are in full bloom. In September and October roses, bougainvillaeas and jacarandas reach perfection.

There is a military museum in Gweru containing weapons, aircraft and armoured vehicles used in the various wars in which the country has been involved.

From Gweru the A5 tarmac road leads northwards through dense bush country, gently losing altitude. Thirty-two kilometres from Gweru the road passes the workings of the Connemara goldmine and, 3 km further on, the small rural centre of Hunters Road. The area known as *Battlefields* was named after the number of mining claims in the vicinity, all of which were named after famous battles.

The A5 road continues north. At 48 km from Gweru it bridges over the river pleasantly known to the Africans as the *Kwekwe,* from the sound made there at night by a multitude of frogs. A further 8 km brings the road to the turn-off west leading for 6 km to the Redcliff works of Ziscom (Zimbabwe Iron and Steel Company). Eight kilometres further on (63 km from Gweru), the A5 road reaches the town of ...

KWEKWE

Kwekwe is named after the river which the road crosses 16 km before reaching the town. It is a centre for a long-established mining industry in gold, chrome, iron and lime. Kwekwe had its start in 1890 when a prospector, E T Pearson, pegged an ancient gold-working, shown to him by a local African. Pearson named the outcrop the Phoenix Reef. A second prospector, Schakula by name, pegged a second outcrop 450 m away, which he named the Globe Reef. The two blocks of claims were bought in 1894 by L G Phillips and combined into what became one of the best-known and most profitable gold-mines in Zimbabwe, the Globe and Phoenix mine, which yielded 28 g (1 oz) of gold for every ton of ore mined.

The office and residence of the manager, built in 1895 of papier mâché panels, and known as the 'paper-house', is now an interesting National Museum of Gold-Mining. Permission to visit must be obtained from the mine.

Kwekwe, originally known as Que Que, was the offspring of the two mines, in the form of a commercial and administrative centre. It is a compact little town of 74 982 people. Its streets are attractively planted with poinciana trees and bougainvillaeas of numerous colours and varieties.

Recreational areas for the town are situated at the dam known as Dutchman's Pool on the Sebakwe River; the oft-photographed Sebakwe Poort; and on the Mvuma road, where the 9 000 ha Sebakwe National Park has been developed around the Sebakwe Dam. Facilities include boating, fishing, bungalows and a caravan and camping site.

From Kwekwe the A5 tarmac road continues northwards. Nine kilometres from the town the road crosses the river known as the *Sebakwe* (from *Tshibagwe,* a place of maize). The landscape is a densely wooded plain, the impression of a parkland being heightened by the consideration of the roads department in planting along the wayside patches of such flowering shrubs as poinsettia and bougainvillaea. The vivid colours provide a contrast to the green of the trees.

Thirty-one kilometres from Kwekwe the A5 road crosses the *Nyati* (buffalo) River. This river has always played an important part in the history of Zimbabwe. The great basin which forms its watershed is not only scarred with the signs of considerable early mining activity, but is also the site of many of the richest mines in modern Zimbabwe. One kilometre downriver from the road bridge stands the 140 000 kW Nyati Power-Station of the Electricity Supply Commission, which draws its water from the river. Eight kilometres further on, a turn-off leads for 67 km to the Ngezi National Park, a 10 125 ha recreational area created around a dam on the Ngezi River. Zebra, sable, waterbuck, kudu and other antelope inhabit the park, as well as hippos. Fishing and boating are pleasant. Accommodation is provided in cottages and there is a caravan park.

Eighteen kilometres beyond the turn-off to the Ngezi National Park, the A5 tarmac road crosses the *Muzvezve* (narrow) River and 16 km further on (73 km from Kwekwe) reaches the town of ...

KADOMA

With a population of 67 267 Kadoma (formerly Gatooma) is a mining and textile centre. Deposits of nickel, chrome, magnesite and iron are found in the area, while gold production amounts to nearly 50 per cent of the total output of Zimbabwe. The largest mine in the country, the Cam and Motor, is situated 5 km east of the town. The name of the town is derived from a Tonka chief, Kadoma, who once lived there. The town had its start when a Mr Godwin built a hut alongside the Bulawayo–Harare railway line and set up business as a forwarding agent. The following year the place acquired a village management board and in 1917 became a municipality.

The town is a busy agricultural centre where some notably fine bulls are bred. The David Whitehead cotton-spinning mill is situated there, with 42 000 spindles producing cotton, rayon, yarns and cotton wool. An agricultural research station stands on the town commonage.

A recreational centre for the people of Kadoma has been created around the Claw Dam, 15 km away. There are picnic sites and opportunities for catching a variety of indigenous fish.

From Kadoma the A5 tarmac road continues north-eastwards, passing the factory of Messrs Kadoma Textiles Ltd and, after 16 km, a turn-off east leading to the mining centre of Eiffel Flats (12 km).

The A5 tarmac road crosses flat savanna, maize, cotton and cattle country. At 33 km from Kadoma the road passes through the small rural centre of Chegutu (formerly Hartley), with a turn-off north leading to Chinhoyi (94 km). The A5 road then veers eastwards, traversing level agricultural and savanna country and crossing the *Mumvuri* (river of shade) after 8 km. At 67 km from Kadoma the small rural centre named after the famous hunter, Frederick Selous, is passed.

The thick, red-coloured soil, combined with the green foliage, maize fields and deep blue skies of this part of Zimbabwe, provide a scene of vivid colour. At 35 km from Selous the main road passes the industrial township of Norton, where paper and agricultural machinery are produced. Norton was named after Joseph Norton, first owner of the farm, who was killed in the Mashona uprising.

The road now finds a way alongside a ridge of hills lying to the south and east. After 7 km the *Mhanyami* (meaning 'a place of high land') River is crossed and a turn-off south is passed which leads to the wall of the Lake Chivero Dam and the McIlwaine National Park. Five kilometres further on, there is another turn to Lake Chivero and the Hunyani Hills hotel. A third turn-off close to the Harare motel, 11 km further on, also leads to Lake Chivero. The A5 road is now approaching the capital of Zimbabwe. Passing through the area of the Warren Hills, attractive parklike country, the road enters the city of Harare, 144 km from Kadoma.

HWANGE AND THE FALLS

The finely made all-tarmac road known as A8 leads north through the northern suburbs of Bulawayo and gradually begins to descend from the central ridge of the country on to the flat, forest-covered world of Kalahari sands. The road leads north through this great primeval parkland, with few features to be seen save an occasional watercourse. The trees, tall and varied, provide many a pleasant view down green and silent aisles.

Signs periodically warn the traveller to beware of wild animals, but these creatures normally keep away from the road. Humans are also seldom seen in what is essentially a world of trees; mopane, acacia, teak, brachystegia and many more. Small trading centres at places such as the Bubi River (175 km) and Halfway House (225 km) provide a landmark. At 249 km from Bulawayo the road reaches the atmospheric and pleasant hotel at *Gwayi* River, named from the wild tobacco plants growing in the valley of the river.

Eight kilometres beyond this hotel there is a tarmac turn-off leading for 24 km to the entrance of the ...

HWANGE NATIONAL PARK

This great National Park, 15 000 square kilometres in extent, is unsurpassed by any other game sanctuary. Nowhere else may a larger variety of animal life be seen and in numbers which make it impossible for visitors, even on the shortest stay, to be disappointed. Pleasant camps, good roads, a congenial atmosphere, an intelligent and courteous staff, and game-viewing platforms at several water-holes, all contribute to the success of the park.

It was in 1928 that the then Rhodesian government, spurred by the enthusiasm of such members of the Legislative Assembly as Major W Boggie, declared as a reserve what was the last principal retreat of big game animals left in Zimbabwe not under pressure from human population. In September 1928, Ted Davison, a 22-year-old official employed at the time on tsetse fly control, was offered the appointment as first warden. He accepted with alacrity. In the 33 years he remained in charge of the reserve, Ted Davison developed it to its full grandeur as a great national park. His name will forever be identified with it.

Davison found the reserve in a completely wild state, without roads or pathways and only occasionally penetrated by hunting parties of Bushmen and Europeans. Visually, it was an enormous parkland, exceedingly flat and sandy for most of its area, but hilly and stony in the north. In this part an odd recluse by the name of H G Robins had made his home, complete with an astronomical telescope mounted on a tower. On his death he bequeathed his block of farms to the national park. *Robins Camp* now houses visitors around his original home and observation tower.

The most remarkable physical features of the park are the shallow *pans* (lakelets) and the number of natural salt-licks (sodium and lime) which attract game animals from the heart of the adjoining Kalahari wilderness.

The pans comprise one of the natural wonders of Southern Africa. Most of them are 20 m to 30 m in diameter. When full after the rainy season, they reach a depth of up to 1 m of water. Strangely enough, they have been created by ants and the wildlife itself. Ants building antheaps began the process by bringing to the surface mineral salts such as lime. These salts in turn attracted the wild animals (especially elephants) which have a particular craving for them. Eating the antheaps to obtain the salts, the wild animals formed depressions in which the rain-water collected. The depressions are constantly expanded by the animals eating more of the lime-flavoured soil, drinking the water churned into mud, and carrying the mud away on their hides after wallowing in it.

The largest pans have formed in the areas of richest lime deposit such as at Main Camp, Kennedy, Ngwashli and Ngamo. The lime-flavoured water attracts heavy concentrations of wildlife. Observation platforms built at some of the pans (such as Nyamandlovu and Guvulala) allow visitors the pleasure of watching on moonlit nights an endless procession of wildlife coming to drink, bath and occasionally ambush one another in bitter dramas of life and death.

The original Wankie Game Reserve, as it was first called, was proclaimed a National Park on 27 January 1950. From that time on it was developed as a major conservation and tourist asset. Today, four camps – Main, Nantwich, Robins and Sinamatella – provide a variety of accommodation. Good roads lead to most of the interesting places in the park. The population of game animals, protected and supplied with reliable permanent watering-places by means of boreholes augmenting the natural supply in some of the pans, has increased to a spectacular extent.

Elephant as well as buffalo are particularly numerous in the park. Tremendous herds of these animals may be seen, especially at the pans during their habitual drinking time between 16h00 and 21h00. Eland also drink at this time, while zebra, giraffe and sable drink from 16h00 to 19h00; wildebeest drink at night and in the morning. Roan, sable and kudu frequent the pans during the daytime, and carnivora (lion, leopard and cheetah) drink in the early morning.

Herds of a thousand or more buffalo and several hundred elephant often may be seen in Hwange. The superb sable antelope and the kudu, surely the most handsomely horned of all game animals, are numerous. Gemsbok (oryx), impala, numerous smaller antelope varieties, wart-hogs, baboons, wild dogs, jackals, hyenas (spotted and brown), black rhino and many smaller animals may also be seen. Tsessebe and hartebeest are also present but are rare. The pans attract a great concentration of varied bird life, especially duck species during the rainy seasons.

Main Camp, Sinamatella Camp and the north-eastern part of the park are open throughout the year. The rest of the park and Robins Camp are open from 1 June to 31 October. The gates are open from sunrise to sunset. Caravans must be left in the camps which are individually accessible by separate approach roads from the main Bulawayo–Victoria Falls road. Winter is the best season to visit the park when the wild animals concentrate around the water-holes and pans. In summer the park is beautifully green but very hot, and seasonal rains allow the wild animals to scatter, as a result of which they are not so easily seen.

An excellent road leads for 145 km through the park from Main Camp to Robins Camp and thence out of the park for 68 km to the main Bulawayo Falls road at Matetsi. Apart from this road, there are at present about 400 km of game-viewing roads open to the public. Only the northern portion of the park has so far been developed for tourists. The western border of the park lies on the frontier with Botswana, where an enormous wilderness area continues deep into the Kalahari, providing safari parties with unparalleled adventure, game viewing and sport. Controlled hunting from May to September is also permitted in areas north and east of the Hwange National Park.

The A8 Bulawayo Falls road continues north-westwards from the turn-off to the Hwange National Park. After 25 km the road reaches a petrol and trading point at a junction, from where a turn-off leads westwards for 16 km to the railway station and village of *Dete* (named from the *Dete* or reedy river). A turn-off north stretches for 28 km to the tin-mining centre of Kamativi, and thence to Mlibizi (98 km) and Binga (161 km), situated on the western shores of Lake Kariba and much resorted to by fishermen.

Beyond the turn-off to these resorts, the A8 Bulawayo Falls road continues in a north-westerly direction through the mopane forest. After 25 km (310 km from Bulawayo) the road crosses the Inyantye River. Baobab trees begin to make their appearance, and the presence of huts reveals a human population more numerous than has been seen so far along the road. At 325 km the road crosses the Lukazi River, where a substantial mission station looks down at the bridge from an overlooking hillock.

The road is now in the homeland of the Nambiya section of the Rozvi tribe, whose ruler had the dynastic name of Hwange. At 11 km beyond the Lukazi bridge a turn-off leads to the railway and mining centre of ...

HWANGE

Early in 1893 a German, Albert Giese, while on a hunting trip, met an African who told him that in Hwange's country there could be found a great marvel – black stones that burned. Giese realised what this meant and eventually managed to reach the area. He found on the surface an enormous outcrop of high-grade coal. This discovery was the basis of the Wankie (Rhodesia) Coal, Railway and Exploration Company formed in 1899 to exploit the deposit – today one of the biggest coalmines in Africa. A large village grew up to house the mineworkers and provide them with facilities for trade and recreation. The village was at first named *Wankie,* a corrupted form of Hwange.

From the turn-off to Hwange the A8 Bulawayo Falls road continues through increasingly rugged country, with rocky hillocks covered in mopane trees. The signs and colours of substantial activity in coal-mining are evident all around. The heat is so heavy and oppressive, especially around October and November, that the stranger may be forgiven for wondering whether the countryside, being so substantially made of coal, may not perhaps have caught fire.

A point on the road is reached 342 km from Bulawayo, where a turn-off leads north for 48 km to the fishing resort at the confluence of the Deka and Zambezi rivers.

The main A8 road continues in a north-westerly direction past Thomson Junction and across the Deka and Matetsi rivers. At 464 km from Bulawayo a turn-off west leads for 65 km to the border of Botswana at *Mpanda Mutenga* (the rain trees of a man named Mutenga), and to Robins Camp (67 km) in the Hwange National Park. The story of Mpanda Mutenga is told in Chapter Forty.

The country becomes increasingly densely wooded. After a further 27 km (426 km from Bulawayo), the A8 road passes the Victoria Falls airport and, 6 km further on, straight ahead, the traveller can generally see the spray rising from the great waterfall. A further 5 km brings the road to the entrance of the Victoria Falls National Park, with the journey ending 11 km further on (449 km from Bulawayo) at what is surely one of the most spectacularly situated frontiers between any two countries on Earth. The customs posts of Zimbabwe and Zambia are on either side of the great bridge which spans the gorge of the Zambezi within reach of the spray of the thundering waterfall. The border posts are open 24 hours a day.

THE VICTORIA FALLS AND ZAMBEZI NATIONAL PARKS

Not only is the Victoria Falls the undisputed queen of waterfalls, but it is also without doubt one of the greatest and most unforgettable scenic spectacles. The physical nature of the waterfall is in itself astonishing, for it occurs in a country that is perfectly level. From its source in a lonely grove of trees on the borders of Zaire, the river, known in its upper reaches to the Lozi people who live on its north (left) side as the *Lwambayi* (great river) and to the Namibian people on the south (right) side as *Lokulu* also meaning 'great', meanders for 1 300 km across the wooded plateau of Zambia, eroding for itself a shallow valley in the great sheet of lava which forms the surface of this part of Africa. A few minor rapids and the small Gonye Falls alone provide some flurry of activity to the otherwise easy-going flow of the river.

Nature, however, has set a trap for the river. A series of faults in the lava sheet, in the form of vertical cracks, cross the course of the river. These cracks, filled with relatively soft matter, have literally tripped up the river in its course. Finding the lowest crack, the river scooped out the contents, tumbled into what was now a trench and promptly had to tumble out again on the far side. The river eventually found a weak spot on the lower lip of the trench and forced a passage which was steadily deepened into an exit gorge. A tremendous waterfall spectacle had now been created where the river fell headlong across the full width of an enormous trench filled with mist and thundering echoes, and then boiled out through the narrow gap.

During the last half-million years the river has scoured out no fewer than eight of these cracks across its bed, and there is every indication that there are a number of others situated higher up. In its day, each trench must have provided successively a magnificent waterfall display, for the lower lip, running the full length of the fall and broken only by the narrow escape gorge forced by the river, has always served as an ideal observation platform. So it is today, with the river falling into a scoured-out crack. The earlier cracks have been completely washed out to form 'legs' for the zigzag gorge. The powerful flow of the river forces its way out of the present crack through the Boiling Pot and the eight successive gorges.

The Victoria Falls, at present occurring where the river is 1 688 m wide, presents the spectacle of an average maximum of 550 million litres of water a minute tumbling over the upper lip of the trench in five main falls, the Devil's Cataract, Main Falls, Horseshoe Falls, Rainbow Falls, and the Eastern Cataract. Each fall is separated from the other only by slightly elevated islands of rock on the lip of the crack. The highest fall is Rainbow Falls, on an average 108 m high. A peak flood sees 750 million litres of water hurtling over the falls every minute.

Below the falls, the river receives from the Tonka tribe who live there the name of *Zambezi* which, like the name of its upper reaches, means 'the great river'. In what is now known as its middle reaches, the Zambezi flows for 800 km through some of the wildest scenery in Africa. Through the gorge of Kariba (where the great dam wall has been built) and other gorges, it eventually shoulders its way through the last barrier of the Cahora Bassa. Then, for a final 500 km in its lower reaches the river meanders across the coastal flats of Mozambique before losing itself in the Indian Ocean. It is altogether an impressive river. To the Mozambique tribes it is known as the *Kwamo* (river of great floods).

The Zambezi River is at its lowest water-level in October. It attains its peak at the end of April. It is then that the falls are staggering to see, but the spray tends to obscure the view and make photography difficult. June to September is the period of medium flow when conditions are ideal for sightseeing. In October and November the area is excessively hot. Rainbows are always visible at the falls. Full moon produces a lunar rainbow, especially clear as the moon rises in the early evening.

The banks of the Zambezi above the falls are beautifully wooded with riverine forest. Spray ceaselessly falling on the opposite side of the trough from the waterfall has given rise to a gorgeous forest. The path leading through this so-called rain forest, along the edge of the trough, is one of the world's most famous tourist promenades. Suitably attired in raincoats, countless visitors from many countries have walked along this path, spellbound by the gigantic spectacle of the falling waters revealed to them through the dripping leaves of the rain forest.

Eventually leaving the rain forest, the path traverses an open area sodden with spray and ends abruptly at Danger Point, looking down into the great gap in the trough through which the river makes its escape into the gorge. A spectacular view may be had across the gap to the Eastern Cataract. A curious indentation in the rocks at Danger Point is called Eve's Footprint.

To the Africans the waterfall is known by several names. The Sotho-speaking Kololo people of the upper reaches of the river gave it the well-known name of *Mosi o a Thunya* (smoke that rises). The Lozi people call it by the same name but translated it into 'smoke that sounds'. The Ndebele call it *aManza Thunqayo* (the water that rises like smoke). The Namibian people call it *Chinotimba* (a noise-making place like the distant sound of digging).

Dr David Livingstone, the first European to visit the falls (on 16 November 1855), reached them from upstream. Travelling down in the canoes of the friendly Kololo people, he reached the brink of the falls, first viewing them from Kazeruka (or Livingstone) Island which separates Main Falls from Rainbow Falls. To peer directly into the prodigious chasm must have been a staggering experience. Livingstone's African companions told him that the Tonka people who lived along the middle reaches of the river offered sacrifices to their ancestors at the fall in three places, each within sight of the rainbow which they considered marked the presence of God. They called the fall *Amanzi Antontora* (the water that is cold) from the spray falling down, cool and refreshing, a gift from God in so hot an environment.

Livingstone named the falls after Queen Victoria. On the island he planted a few peach and apricot stones and carved his initials and the date in a tree before setting out on the long walk to the mouth of the Zambezi, where he was picked up by the brig HMS *Frolic* on 12 July 1856. A most impressive statue of Dr Livingstone (sculpted by Sir William Reid-Dick) stands on the western side of the chasm immediately overlooking the Devil's Cataract where the river, when in flood, races past at a speed of 160 km an hour.

The combined road-rail bridge over the gorge, 200 m long and 106 m high, was opened on 12 September 1905. Its construction by the Cleveland Bridge Company of Darlington, England, had been stimulated by the discovery of copper in the north. The precise site of the bridge was selected at the express wish of Cecil Rhodes so that the spray of the waterfall would fall upon the passing trains. The centre of the bridge now marks the boundary between Zimbabwe and Zambia.

There are several interesting walks, drives, flights, canoe and launch trips in the vicinity of the waterfall. Paths lead to the second and third gorges. From Livingstone's statue visitors may follow, with the aid of chains, a path descending one-third of the way down the gorge to a spectacular viewsite from where the full length of the great trough of the waterfall is revealed. Another path from the statue finds an interesting way through the trees up the right bank of the river and leads to, among other things, an enormous baobab tree 20,4 m in circumference, 45,7 m high and about 2 000 years old.

From the falls the road follows the right bank of the river for 8 km and then enters the Zambezi National Park. Across this 56 010 ha park the road known as the Zambezi Drive continues for 48 km to the Sominungwa turn-about. Apart from fine riverine scenery all the way, the road passes through densely inhabited game country especially noted for its herds of sable antelope, elephant and buffalo. A second road into the park, known as the Chamabonda Drive, penetrates the southern portion of the area for 24 km and provides particularly fine game-viewing opportunities. The entrance is reached via a turn-off on the main Bulawayo road, 11 km south of the Victoria Falls. The park is open from 1 May to 31 October.

The village of Victoria Falls is the northern frontier village of Southern Africa. It is a relaxed and picturesque little holiday resort in a parklike setting. Hotels, stores, garages, curio shops, a rest camp, bungalows and a caravan park cluster within the shadow of the mist cloud of the waterfall. Launch cruises up the river, airflips and game-viewing flights are available. The road up the right (south) bank of the Zambezi leads for 69 km to the Botswana frontier at Kazungula and thence to Kasame.

Chapter Fifty

ZIMBABWE

The Eastern Districts

From Harare the A3 tarmac road to the eastern districts leaves the city past the suburb of Eastlea and the municipal caravan park, and then off into open country consisting of a lightly bushed plain scattered with granite boulders. The countryside is immaculately kept, spanned by a finely made road and beautified with trees and wayside patches of flowers and shrubs. There are numerous resting-places along the way where the traveller may pause and, once refreshed, find the journey as pleasant as it should be.

Twenty-five kilometres from Harare the road passes the Ruwa Country Club, with a turn-off leading north for 12 km to the administrative centre of *Garamonzi* (settle peacefully) and the beautiful Norah valley. Nine kilometres further on, the road passes the rural centre of *Bromley* (named after Bromley on the shores of Loch Lomond). The road and railway keep close company on this journey eastwards along the 1 525 m high plateau summit of the central ridge of Zimbabwe, so narrow at this point that on either side may be seen the descent to the surrounding low country. The plateau summit is a lovely, entirely rural landscape covered with hectares of rich farmland and impressive granite domes (ornamented with lichens) which loom up along the verges of the plateau as though guarding it from the encroaching valleys of the low country.

At 60 km from Harare a turn-off south leads to the administrative centre of Wedza (*Hwedza*, a place of wealth). Plantations of gum and fir trees line the road like rigid soldiers on parade while, 9,5 km further on, the road passes the Grasslands Research Station. A further 3 km (72 km from Harare) brings the tarmac road to the rural town of ...

MARONDERA

With a population of 39 601, the town takes its name from Marondera, a chief of the Zezuru people who once lived there. It is a neat agricultural town built around a large central square. Timber, cattle, grain, wine, fruit, jam, tobacco and dairy products provide the town with its prosperity. The Borradaile Trust homes for the aged, situated in the midst of a garden, may be seen as the road enters the town. The Eagle tannery is on the Harare road. There is a large abattoir in the town area.

From Marondera the A3 tarmac road continues eastwards through plantations of tall gum trees and across handsome farmlands with graceful musasa trees ornamenting the slopes of the plateau. At 9 km from Marondera the road passes Peterhouse school, and a further 22 km brings it to the rural centre of Macheke, situated in a natural rockery of granite.

The A3 road continues eastwards through gum and pine plantations. At 17 km from Macheke the road tops a rise and, from what is known as Eagles Nest, the first good view may be seen ahead of the beautiful eastern mountains of Zimbabwe.

At 59 km from Marondera the road passes the rural centre of Headlands and begins to lose altitude through a picturesque natural rockery of granite boulders and rock fragments of various odd shapes. At 91 km from Marondera the road crosses the Lesapi River with the Crocodile motel on its banks and, 1 km further on, enters the small town of ...

RUSAPE

Rusape takes its name from the *Lesapi* River, so called ('sparing of its waters') on account of its erratic flow. Rusape is a quiet agricultural town, the streets of which are shaded with flowering trees. There is a dam in the river which provides a recreational area with fishing, boating and a caravan park in an attractive setting.

From Rusape a turn-off east leads through rugged granite country for 104 km to Nyanga. The A3 tarmac road continues in a southerly direction through granite country covered in musasa trees and becoming increasingly wild in appearance. After 34 km the road crosses the Inyazura River and 35 km further on reaches the Odzi River, with a small rural centre situated on its right bank.

The A3 tarmac road has, in the meanwhile, swung eastwards and leads directly into the foothills of the eastern mountains of Zimbabwe. Thick bush covers the slopes and valleys. The climate, with the road now at a lower altitude (1 100 m), is warm and tropical. The road traverses an old gold-mining area. Ten kilometres from the Odzi River the road crosses Battery Spruit. After a further 9 km it reaches a turn-off north leading to Nyanga and the site of Old Umtali. Another kilometre through this most impressive mountain mass brings the road (81 km from Rusape) to the turn-off north leading to Penhalonga (9 km). The tarmac A3 road now starts to climb a mountain slope far more beautifully overgrown with wild flowers, shrubs and trees than any man-made garden. This is Christmas Pass, so named by the surveyor of the original road, F W Bruce, who found himself camped there over Christmas 1891.

The summit of Christmas Pass yields a superb view over the great valley in which shelters the town of Mutare, and deep into the mass of granite mountains to the east and south. Two scenic roads branch off east and west from the main road at the summit of the pass. Both lead to viewsites, the east road climbing steeply to what is known as Mutare Heights, a vantage-point nearly 1 740 m above sea-level which reveals a panorama of mountains and valley. At the start of the east road there is a garden around the memorial statue to Kingsley Fairbridge, the poet. The bronze statue was the work of W McMillan. It shows the young poet and a friend looking at the view. Kingsley Fairbridge lived from 1885 to 1924 and established the Fairbridge Farm Schools.

The main A3 road commences a steady descent past the handsomely situated Mutare municipal caravan park, down through a green forest of trees and past a nature reserve on *Murahwa's* Hill, named after an Nyika chief. Six kilometres from the summit (89 km from Rusape and 250 km from Harare) the road reaches the city of ...

MUTARE

With a population of 131 808, Mutare is one of the most beautifully situated cities in Southern Africa. Lying in the valley of the stream known as the *Sakubva* from the *Vitex payos* shrubs which grow on its banks, the city is completely dominated by a concentration of some of the most massive granite mountains in Southern Africa. The valley in which it lies forms a natural gateway between the coastal lowlands of Mozambique and the interior of Zimbabwe.

Mutare is a frontier town and railway marshalling yard on the road and rail route to Beira. Lying 1 220 m above sea-level, it experiences a warm climate which is, however, cooler than the heat and humidity of the lowlands of Mozambique.

Mutare has been described as 'the town that moved'. The first Mutare (what is known as Old Umtali) had a very lively birth in 1891 as the rough-and-ready mining settlement built on the banks of the river known as the *Mutare* (river of ore). The inhabitants of this roaring camp were more interested in gold and strong drink than in linguistics. They named their town *Umtali*, a corruption of the name of the river. Some 160 mines came into operation around the town. Old Umtali experienced a hectic social life, a renowned part of which were wild parties and the use of the main street (about the only part of the country then cleared of bush) as a playing-field for a variety of sports.

In March 1896 this boisterous little town received a sad blow. A narrow-gauge railway was being built to Zimbabwe from the port of Beira. Cecil Rhodes visited Old Umtali and informed its dismayed inhabitants that the construction engineers understandably wanted to bring the railway through the mountain barrier by means of the easiest possible natural pass, namely the valley of the Sakubva stream 17 km away and separated from Old Umtali by a high granite ridge. Rhodes was the supreme business man. It would cost a fortune to bring the railway to Old Umtali, therefore it would be far cheaper to move the town to the railway.

Rhodes literally bought Old Umtali and distributed £50 000 in cash to the residents, laying out a duplicate town on the site of the present Mutare next to the railway line in the valley of the Sakubva. Each property owner in Old Umtali was entitled to a plot in the new town. To these sites they removed piecemeal their houses, shacks and huts. In this way, in 1896 the new Umtali (or Mutare as it is now named) was born. Old Umtali was abandoned to the bush.

The new town was beautifully laid out. It was planned by its surveyor, Rhys Fairbridge, to exploit fully the superb setting, with broad, flamboyant-lined streets. Rhodes always regarded the new town as being peculiarly his own. He supervised the establishment of a spacious park and, inevitably, a stock exchange and race-track where he could relax on his visits to the area. Flowering trees in considerable quantity were planted, gardens laid out. Mutare was planned from the beginning to be what it is, a pleasant place and a friendly gateway to welcome travellers into Zimbabwe from the east coast ports of Mozambique.

Mutare became a city on 1 October 1971. Today it is lively and prosperous, with a fine theatre, concert hall, a superb civic centre, a spacious park and an aloe garden containing 140 species and 2 000 plants. John Lambert, former curator, was responsible for creating the garden. There are first-class sporting amenities, including a magnificent swimming-pool. Several industries have established themselves there, such as a refinery, a motor assembly plant, various coffee and tea packing and blending factories, canning, plywood, board and paper-mills, and other enterprises.

Christmas time sees the flame trees of Mutare at their peak of brilliance. In winter, aloes and cycads are in flower, while September and October are the months for jacarandas, bougainvillaeas and flamboyants.

The Mutare Museum houses an interesting collection of the fauna and flora of the eastern districts. The collection of antique firearms, transport vehicles (including Cecil Rhodes's coach) and early locomotives is particularly worth seeing. There is a superb aviary, a fitting example of how wild birds should be kept. The museum is open daily from 09h00 to 17h00. It is closed on Christmas and Good Friday.

Attached to the museum is *Utopia House*, the restored home of Rhys and Rosalie Fairbridge. It represents the domestic life-style of the 1910 to 1920 period. The house is open on Saturdays and Sundays from 14h30 to 16h30.

In the municipal area of Mutare, the Wildlife Society of Zimbabwe has created the fine Cecil Kop Nature Reserve on 1 100 ha of public commonage. It is open daily from 07h00 to dusk. There are observation points at water-holes and hides, and drives through beautiful forest country. The reserve was opened on 9 August 1981. Its purpose is not only to preserve the natural beauty, flora and fauna, but to educate the public as to the value of conservation.

From Mutare the A3 tarmac road continues eastwards down a heavily wooded valley hemmed in by high hills and forming a picturesque and beautiful gateway between Zimbabwe and Mozambique. After 6 km the road reaches the customs and immigration posts, where a restaurant offers refreshment to travellers before they commence the 280 km run to the coast at Beira. The border at Forbes' Post is open daily from 06h00 to 18h00.

THE BVUMBA

One of the most spectacular mountain drives in Africa leads from Mutare to the heights of what is known as the *Bvumba*, (from *Mubvumbi*, meaning 'the mountains of drizzle'), an enormous ridge of granite overlooking Mutare from the south-east.

The tarmac road leaves Mutare and climbs steeply, revealing superb views of the valley below which allows the road and railway to pass through the mountains to Mozambique. At 6 km the road reaches the Impala Arms hotel. Three kilometres further on, a gravel turn-off south provides a circular drive of 75 km around the Bvumba past the Nyachowa Falls and through the densely wooded Burma valley before rejoining the main Bvumba road.

Ahead looms a magnificent mass of granite mountains, the slopes of which are densely wooded with musasa trees, providing in spring one of the most brilliant botanical displays to be seen anywhere. Leopards, wild pigs, bushbuck and samango monkeys frequent the forests of the Bvumba. At 11 km from Mutare there is a turn-off (the Bvumba north road) leading to the White Horse Inn (2 km) and several handsome private residences built on viewsites.

The main tarmac road now begins a steep climb, with superb views visible through gaps in the forest which blankets the slopes. After 3 km (15 km from Mutare) the road reaches the summit of the climb at what is known as *Cloudlands*, the farm of the well-known late Lionel and Mary Cripps, 1 585 m above sea-level. A gravel turn-off leads eastwards from here for 75 km through the scenic Circular Drive back to the main tarmac road (5 km down the road towards Mutare).

The main road winds on over the summit of the ridge, reaching after 1 km (16 km from Mutare) a turn-off south to the old Eagle preparatory school perched on the slopes and overlooking a romantic view of hills and valleys. This is now a government training school.

A further 5 km takes the road past the grounds of the old Bvumba Heights children's hostel and school, built among the trees and overlooked by the 1 910 m Castle Beacon, the highest point of the Bvumba. It is a giant granite dome topped by the mast of a radio communication station. From the hostel there is a path with steps leading to the top of Castle Beacon, a grand viewsite. The main road twists around the slopes of this dome, tunnelling through patches of lovely indigenous forest and plantation, with panoramic views to the north-east over the lowlands of Mozambique.

At 24 km from Mutare, the main Bvumba road enters the 1 558 ha Bunga forest botanical reserve, and after 4 km a turn-off is reached leading northwards into the Bvumba Botanical Garden (see further on). The 24 ha nucleus of the Bunga forest was presented to the Zimbabwean nation on 25 February 1946 by the Honourable Lionel Cripps. A fine representative section of the original Bvumba forest, it is particularly rich in ferns (about 250 varieties).

The main road continues along the summit ridge which narrows sharply at this point. At 27 km from Mutare a superlative view to the south and north may be seen, with a footpath branching off and providing walkers with a route down to the Leopard Rock hotel. Ahead (28 km from Mutare) the road passes the former Mountain Lodge hotel and then terminates at the African school named *Mutore*, after a local headman.

The two hotels just mentioned were both built on panoramic viewsites. The Mountain Lodge was a thatched reproduction of an old English country inn, the windows of which looked towards the south at a spectacular view of the mountains lying along the eastern border. The Leopard Rock hotel can only be described as a most imaginative development on what is one of the supreme hotel sites of the world.

The hotel had its beginning in 1936 when Leslie Seymour Smith visited the eastern districts on holiday. Smith was of that happy (but rare) breed of man – an affluent small worker. Examples of non-affluent small workers are numerous in the land of El Dorado; but Smith had a profitable little mine, the Patsy mine, in Matebeleland at a hill named *Mbigo* (the look-out). Drought had brought work to a temporary halt. While waiting for rain, Smith took a holiday, during which he discovered the perennial greenness and beauty of the Bvumba. He decided to buy property there. A retired bank manager named Rutherford, who was something of an amiable crank with the habit of taking the hindquarters of leopards down to the Umtali Club to feed his friends, owned an overgrown farm named *Scandinavia* on the slopes of the Bvumba. Leslie Smith bought a portion of this farm and named it *Mbigo* after the hill overlooking his mine.

The area was a real African dreamland. A superb view; the rich greenness resulting from the misty rain and perennial water supply; magnificent trees; a unique atmosphere and a romantic past

– all contributed to make the place perfect. The mountain overlooking the farm was known to the Africans as *Tshinyakweremba* (the place of tired feet). Legend has it that a village of the Jindwi people once flourished on the slopes of the peak. An ancestral spirit in the guise of a decrepit old man is said to have visited the place. He found the drunken inhabitants so rude and inhospitable that he destroyed the village with a landslide that night, sparing only one person who had been kind to him. The village still lies buried under a huge pile of boulders. The scar on the mountain from where the landslide originated stands out in the form of a 180 m high precipice.

The scene of this legendary disaster is today a place of haunting beauty submerged beneath lovely trees filled with the whisper of the wind and the drowsy murmuring of rock pigeons and loeries. A family of leopards for a long time made their home among the fallen boulders and were often seen sunning themselves on a particular vantage-point. This was the site which Leslie Smith selected for his home. There he built one of the most individualistic of houses. Visitors thought of it as a pseudo-castle, but it was simply a development of a leopard's lair. No architect would have designed such a place. A client requesting a plan of this nature would have been referred to a lunatic asylum! Designed by Leslie Smith, the house was a projection of the fallen rock which buried the village. Using the same rock for material, the house was built over boulders and into fissures.

The original rock on which the leopards sunned themselves was enclosed to make a colossal toilet, the seat of which was actually cut into the stone. There is no other WC like it, a privy where anyone would be happy to spend a dollar rather than a penny! When the British royal family visited the place, it is said that the Queen Mother, on retiring to the privy and just before latching the door, popped her head out and observed innocently, *'Mr Seymour Smith, I see you have a throne as well'*.

The view from the house is overwhelming and the grounds of the whole estate were superbly landscaped. Huge wild fig trees, tree ferns, arum lilies, moon-flowers, hydrangeas and some particularly magnificent *Albizia gummiflora* trees are notable features of the garden.

The hotel building was also designed by Leslie Smith at the suggestion of a Salisbury architect that it would be an interesting experiment to try a building involving double-storey rondavels. The castle effect was incidental. The unique atmosphere of this 'rondavel castle' was the result of a considerable amount of thought. There was a fern room containing a grotto fountain; a lounge with a remarkable floor comprising a variety of indigenous timber and a central fireplace; a children's room with a slide designed as a miniature castle. It was one of the most amazing hotels in the world and proof of a considerable creative imagination hidden behind the rough-hewn exterior of Mr Leslie Seymour Smith.

The Leopard Rock hotel was opened in June 1946 and closed in January 1983. The mountain lodge was burned down in August 1983. The Leopard Rock hotel was re-opened as a four star resort in the early 1990s.

THE BVUMBA BOTANICAL GARDEN

This 200 ha general botanical garden contains flora of both exotic and indigenous origin. The climate and conditions on the Bvumba ridge are such that almost anything seems to grow to perfection there; from Namaqualand daisies of the arid west coast to tree ferns and cycads from tropical rain forests.

The garden originated in 1917 when Edgar Evans, who (like Leslie Smith of Leopard Rock) had made money by working a small mine, decided to retire to the cool heights of the Bvumba. His mine had been named the Kent Mine and he was jocularly called the 'Duke of Kent'. He bought the undeveloped farm *Manchester Park*, so named by its original owner, Robert Magden from Manchester. To this farm Evans built a road from *Cloudlands* and started development. Then, in 1923 Frederick John Taylor, who had emigrated from Devonshire in 1901 to work for the Meikles organisation in Zimbabwe, bought the farm. With his wife Helen he started the wonderful garden. In 1943 he retired there and worked full time on the garden. It was opened to the public in 1940. In 1958 he sold it to the government for £23 000 and the right to continue residing there for life. He died on 21 November 1961. As a botanical garden it has been developed to its present stage of magnificence and is especially notable for its gladioli, azaleas, begonias, lilies, proteas and hydrangeas. There are 193 species of trees growing in the garden, and 158 species of birds frequent the area. Samango monkeys are numerous. The smallest known species of chameleon (*Rhampholeon marshalli,* also known as Marshall's dwarf chameleon) have their home there. The females grow up to 100 mm in length; the males only up to 60 mm. These little chameleons have a tongue long enough to allow them to catch prey at a distance exceeding their body length. This length of tongue does not only apply to the females.

There is a swimming-pool, artificial lake and a 3 ha camping site with a swimming-pool. There is also a caravan park.

MUTARE TO NYANGA

Two roads lead north from Mutare into the mountain massif along the border and up to Nyanga. The longer (and rougher) road is the scenic route which will be followed first. It is a most picturesque drive, especially notable for the magnificent trees growing by the wayside.

This road branches off north from the main Mutare–Harare road opposite the Christmas Pass hotel, 8 km west of Mutare. The road immediately enters a beautifully wooded area where fine specimens of wild fig and acacia trees may be seen. After 5 km a turn-off is reached leading eastwards into the Imbeza valley for 7 km to the Imbeza Forest Estates sawmill. Tree lovers will find this short diversion worth exploring, for the valley floor shelters some of the most gracefully shaped *Acacia abasynica* trees in Africa, and several beautiful homesteads. One of these homesteads is *La Rochelle*. From 1951 to 1970 this was the home of the late Sir Stephen and Lady Virginia Courtauld. They created a garden there of supreme beauty. On 1 June 1972 this property was presented to the Zimbabwean nation and is now open to the public and managed by the National Trust of Zimbabwe. The entrance is 3 km up the Imbeza road. It is open daily. There is accommodation in the La Rochelle hotel and two self-catering chalets.

Three kilometres beyond the turn to the Imbeza valley stands a small memorial to the pioneer nurses who walked from Beira in 1891 to establish on this hillside the first hospital in the eastern districts. The signs of old mining activity are visible in many places and 1 km from the memorial the road enters the one-time boom mining village of Penhalonga. It is now dilapidated, with most of the 22 commercial enterprises lining its one street abandoned. It is still a centre for mining gold, bauxite clay and soapstone.

In its day Penhalonga (together with Old Umtali) acted as the centre for some 160 gold-mines. From it a road branches eastwards and for 8 km finds its way up a once busy mining valley in the mountains past the Imbeza Forest Estates and on until it reaches a small border post on the divide where the international frontier line runs. This was the original entry point into what was then Rhodesia. It was from here that Cecil John Rhodes, in 1891, first entered the country once named after him and saw ahead that long view of bush and mountain.

Most of the gold-mines are now exhausted, but what activity there is at least sustains a glimmer of life in Penhalonga. There is no hotel in the village, but an excellent caravan park managed by the Zimbabwe Caravan Association provides a base for the exploration of an interesting area. *Penhalonga* was named after Count Penhalonga of the Mozambique Company.

From the village the road climbs up the valley of the Mutare River with its fine cascade to the east. The road passes several handsome estates and many graceful trees. At 12 km from Penhalonga the road reaches a crossroads leading to Stapleford forest (17 km east) and to Lake Alexander, the dam in the Odzani River (6 km west) where there is a caravan and camping site. Just beyond this turn-off the road passes the small prehistoric fort of Gomo Kadzamu, marked by a sign at the roadside. The fort is on the summit of the hill on the right-hand side. The road continues its climb into the granite hills where may be seen growing some of the most gorgeously coloured musasa trees whose spring colours have a particularly vivid glow on account of the situation and climate.

On the top of this rise, 16 km from Penhalonga, a 1 km turn-off leads west to the waterfall on the Odzani River, which the main road crosses further on. A further 3 km brings the tarmac road to an end at a turn-off east to Odzani. The main road continues north through lovely patches of musasa trees, passing many tribal villages and viewsites east into the Honde valley. At 28 km from Penhalonga the road reaches the rural centre of Tzonso, situated on a high grassy plateau, and there joins the main tarmac road leading from Mutare to Nyanga.

This main tarmac road branches off from the Mutare–Harare road 9 km west of Mutare (1 km west of the turn-off to the scenic route). The road stretches north across the bushy valley of the Mutare River, with clusters of African huts enhancing the picturesque appearance of the area. After 5 km a gravel turn-off leads westwards to the site of Old Umtali where a Methodist church centre has been established.

An odd-shaped assembly of granite peaks looms ahead. The road climbs and twists towards them, penetrating a real garden of Pan, with masses of wild flowers blooming by the roadside. After 25 km the road finds a way through a natural passage in one of the granite spurs and emerges on to a plateau well populated by African people. At 28 km the road reaches the small trading centre of Tzonso, where the alternative road joins it from Mutare (48 km) through Penhalonga. Ahead lie more granite masses and there are fine views west and east into the colossal *Honde* valley (from *Muhonde*, river of euphorbia trees) where the extraordinary outcrops known as *Masimiki* (rocks that stand upright) occur.

The road climbs steadily into an area of wattle plantations. At 46 km there is a turn-off west to the mission station of Bonda. At 49 km a turn-off east follows what is known as the scenic road, leading to Nyanga (44 km) in a spectacular but rough alternative route described further on. The main tarmac road continues northwards through the plantations of the Zimbabwe Wattle Company. At 56 km the road reaches the beautiful cascade in the *Odzi* (rotting) River. Huge plantations of pine and wattle trees blanket the granite slopes while streams rush down from the heights.

At 72 km (80 km from Mutare) a junction with the road coming from Rusape is reached. The main route turns east (right) and after 1 km reaches Juliasdale with its store, garage and hotel. The road leads on, revealing fine views over a deep valley with the high granite peaks reaching off into the dim northern horizon.

At 3 km from Juliasdale there is a turn-off east to the scenic road and, 6 km further on (81 km from the start of the road and 89 km from Mutare), the road enters the Nyanga National Park. It is opportune at this point, before exploring the park, to examine the charms of ...

THE SCENIC ROAD

This route branches off from the main road to Nyanga 48 km from the start of the road (57 km from Mutare). The road is steep in places. The surface is occasionally poor and made tedious by corrugations and pot-holes caused by heavy vehicles engaged in the transport of timber. Caution is therefore necessary and this road is not suitable for caravans. Scenically, however, this alternative route to Nyanga possesses several notable features. After 1 km there is a turn-off east into the Honde valley and the tea estates 50 km down the valley – a drive which passes through wild and rugged country. One kilometre further on, a viewsite which looks down into the Honde valley is situated just off the road. It is a view worth seeing and very photogenic on a clear day.

A further 12 km brings the road to a rough turn-off leading for 9 km to the Mutarazi Falls where the stream known as the *Mutarazi* (derived from the onomatopoeic sound of water falling) makes a tremendous leap of 762 m into the Honde valley. Three kilometres further on, a short loop leads to a famous view and picnic site overlooking the valley of the *Pungwe* (an ideophone denoting the closing in and clearing of mists). From here a majestic view may be had of the oft-photographed cascade, the deep gorge and (to the north-east) the great bulk of the 2 593 m Nyangani, the highest mountain in Zimbabwe.

Beyond this viewsite the road continues for 12 km, rewarding the traveller with many handsome views as compensation for the bumps. It joins a major gravel road which links up (to the west) with the main tarmac road at Juliasdale (9 km). To the east, after 8 km, the road enters the ...

NYANGA NATIONAL PARK

This magnificent mountain National Park (34 345 ha in extent) is situated at an altitude of 1 982 m in the bracing air of an extensive mountain-top plateau. The park owes its origin to the magnanimity of Cecil Rhodes. In 1896, while arranging for the removal of Umtali to its new site, Rhodes heard of the beauty of this area. He visited it and arranged for the purchase of a 38 800 ha block of farms there. On these farms he established experimental plantations of fruit and trees. The stone farmhouse on *Fruitfield* farm became a mountain retreat for Rhodes. Preserved in much of its original state it is now the Rhodes Inyanga hotel. Rhodes stayed there in 1897 and again in 1900, on both visits recuperating from illness. On his death, the estate was bequeathed to the nation. It is today a magnificent recreational area – cool, green, close to nature, and relaxing to all who seek a release from the nervous tensions of city life. There is a museum next to the hotel.

The history of the Nyanga area is particularly fascinating. The name *Nyanga* comes from a famous *Sanyanga* (herbalist) who ruled over the mountain lands in the first half of the 19th century. Scattered over some 4 000 square kilometres of these mountains lands is a concentration of ruins of stone walls, enclosures, irrigation furrows and terraces occurring in such numbers that they must be seen to be believed.

The area of the Nyanga National Park contains a vast assortment of these ruins, apparently built by prehistoric people when times of stress drove them from their homes in the warmer lowlands. Resorting to the cold heights for security, they dug curious stone-lined pits, presumably in which to shelter their livestock, while on the aloe-covered summit of the hill known as *Nyangwe* (place of the leopard) stands a fort, crudely built but impressive in its power, glowering over the surrounding moorlands like a watch-dog. This is the centre of the area with a superb panoramic view.

The spectacle of these strange ruins left behind by a vanished people provides a curious touch of melancholy to an enchanted landscape. Exactly who the builders were remains a mystery. No relics of any exotic people have been found. The buildings were most probably the work of the same African people (a section of the Karanga) who live in the warmer lowlands today to where they doubtless removed to escape the upland cold as soon as political conditions allowed them to do so in safety. Europeans like to refer to the pits as 'slave pits' but this is romanticism. The African name for them, *Matanga epasi* (underground livestock enclosures), is more appropriate. Their small size was suited to such livestock as goats, sheep and pigs. The Karanga also had a breed of dwarf cattle. One of the pits with its surrounding huts has been perfectly restored.

The Nyanga National Park offers many fine walks and drives, with what is known as the Circular Drive providing a grand tour of the whole area. It is quite a drive, following the slopes of the great fortress-like *Nyangani* (place of horns) mountain – rising, falling, twisting and turning. There is an immense variety of flora (much of it reminiscent of the Cape), such as proteas, everlastings and ericas. Over and above this, however, looms the unique landscape – the strange and most ancient granite mountains, each with its own peculiar shape, name, legends and character. The peaks loom up through the mists like petrified giants, forgotten gods of an antique world whose brooding memory haunts this land as surely as the winds whisper through the tussock grass.

It is from the circular drive that the walker may easily reach the summit of Nyangani, from where is revealed a panorama of mountain and moorland. In spring the patches of colourful musasa trees – brown, orange, magenta and crimson – may be seen splashing the granite slopes like the stains of sacrifices made on altars of the past.

The many other pleasant features of this park include the adjoining Nyanga experimental station, the nearby Nyangombe Falls, and fishing for trout (brown and rainbow), with 85 km of streams in ideal surroundings. There are fine walks, and accommodation facilities comprise lodges and caravan and camping sites. The trout-fishing season at Mare Dam (where there is also a trout hatchery) is from 1 September to 31 May, and in the streams from 1 November to 31 May (these dates are variable). It is altogether a delightful national park.

Just across the northern border of the national park lies the village of Nyanga. The post office, shops and government administrative offices of this informal little place are all so spread-eagled over a vast area, with considerable amounts of wilderness in between each building, that it seems as though the village was laid out by people who didn't like one another.

Five kilometres beyond the north-eastern boundary of the Nyanga National Park (20 km from the Rhodes hotel and warden's office) lies the interesting and extensive area known as the ...

NYANGA DOWNS AND TROUTBECK

The inhabitants of Zimbabwe have always been notable individualists, the consequences of which characteristic are often interesting. In the story of the Bvumba area it has been seen how individuals created such places as Leopard Rock and the original Manchester Gardens. A very similar situation occurred in relation to the Nyanga Downs.

In 1926 an artilleryman, Major MacIlwaine, left the regular British army and took possession of a farm at Marondera, intending to grow tobacco under a land settlement scheme. An international rugby player (representing England twice and many times captain of the British army team), he was a versatile and purposeful character. The slump in 1930 proved ruinous to many settlers and reduced the Major to living on mealie porridge (with sausage on Sundays) and selling eggs at sixpence a dozen – his sole means of livelihood.

In this sad situation he received a letter from Charles Hanmer which contained some interesting news. Up in the highlands of the eastern districts the Anglo-French Matabeleland Company had originally acquired 27 200 ha of completely virgin and uninhabited land. Finding no use for this land, the company in 1930 sold part of it to Charles Hanmer and his brother William, who named their purchase *Inyanga Downs*. The remainder of the estate lying east of the Nyangani Mountains was procured by a syndicate who named it the *Inyangani Estates*.

The area was completely undeveloped. Charles Hanmer had to make a road to it. Then he built a house and started afforestation on the estate, but his discerning eye observed many other possibilities in the area. It was as a result of this that he wrote to Major MacIlwaine. Although Hanmer was not a fisherman himself, to his mind the Nyanga Downs, with its multitude of clear streams fed by over 1 000 mm of rain a year, looked ideal fishing country. Major MacIlwaine, a renowned trout fisherman, was therefore asked to advise on the prospects. Together with his wife he visited the area.

They were delighted with what they saw. Everything seemed perfect: the stream temperatures were ideal for trout; there was plenty of food in the water; and the only indigenous fish were small mountain barbel. Charles Hanmer asked MacIlwaine to develop the fishing, offering him his choice of 200 acres (80 ha) at 4 shillings an acre and a kilometre stretch of any of the streams. MacIlwaine was still broke, but this was a fantastic opportunity. He selected a kilometre of the stream named *Tsanga* (reedy). On his land he built a cottage which he named *Troutbeck*, after the village in Cumberland, the surroundings of which were similar to the Nyanga Downs.

The first task was to plant trees – wattle and pine – for the Nyanga Downs were devoid of indigenous trees to the point of bleakness. Transport problems made fuel excessively expensive, therefore wood was needed for fires. In 1934 the first trout ova from King William's Town in the Cape were introduced. The first two attempts failed, but the third try was successful. Two years later fishermen were throwing back everything weighing less than a half a kilogram.

Hanmer and the MacIlwaines built cottages for fishermen. Many of these visitors liked the area so much that they obtained plots for themselves. Eventually a settlement grew up around Troutbeck. After the Second World War, MacIlwaine (then a colonel) obtained more land and built a dam across the Tsanga stream. This enormous addition to the trout waters suggested the building of a hotel. No contractor during that time of post-war building boom was interested in working in so remote a situation, so MacIlwaine built the place himself with the aid of Italian workers interned during the war. It took four and a half years of effort to complete, with a minimum of technical aid, but on 1 March 1951 the Troutbeck Inn was opened – a spacious and atmospheric place that became one of Southern Africa's best hotels.

Freed from these building chores, MacIlwaine next bought 815 ha of land high above Troutbeck – scenically dramatic, cloud-covered, windswept and having staggering views of the lowland world of bush and granite hillock. In the basin-like depression on these heights MacIlwaine constructed three dams: Loch Maree, Loch Con and Loch Comb; named the area Little Connemara;

made a circular drive and started selling 2 ha 'pocket estates', each with unlimited water rights, fishing rights, fresh air, sunsets and prodigious views.

The principal viewsite, known as World's View, is 2 380 m above sea-level. With the red-flowering aloes of winter covering the foreground, this is one of Zimbabwe's most memorable outlooks. It is under the care of the Zimbabwe National Trust. The circular drive is 21 km long. From the hotel a path leads for 2,5 km to two of the pit structures built in ancient times. Five kilometres along the road to Nyamaropa (about a quarter kilometre east of the road) stands a cluster of well-preserved pit structures worth seeing.

NYAHOKWE AND THE ZIWA RUINS

In the lowlands north-west of Nyanga, a cluster of four granite mountains looms abruptly above the parkland. The principal massif is a handsomely impressive peak, 1 741 m high, known as Ziwa after a chief who lived at its foot in recent times. Attached to this peak are two smaller companions, a peak of unknown name on the eastern side, and on the western side a granite mass known as Hamba. Further east, standing on its own, is the 1 447 m high *Nyahokwe*, named after Hokwe, a former headman of the Nyama people who live in the area today.

The four granite mountains are the centre for the Ziwa ruins which occupy 80 square kilometres and constitute one of the world's greatest mysteries. This unnatural wonder has baffled all visitors. No convincing evidence has been found as to the purpose of its construction, who built it and why it was abandoned in a state so perfect that it seems as though the owners have simply gone away on holiday and will soon return.

To reach these ruins, enquire from the army depot at Nyanga, from where a permit is necessary to enter what is used as a military training ground. With this permit, take the gravel road leading to Manjoro School down to the lower plains. After 14 km the road reaches a barricade at the army training ground. Display the permit, and the barricade will be raised. Immediately there is a turn-off leading north. The main road continues to Manjoro and then on past the great granite dome of Dombo and eventually to Rusape.

The side road passes the military encampment and eventually reaches the Ngarawi River. Beyond the causeway over this river the road divides; the right turn leads to the slopes of Ziwa, meanders over the plain, and after 7,5 km passes the site of what used to be the Nyahokwe field museum, unfortunately destroyed during the troubles of the 1970s. Originally there was a reconstruction of an ancient smelting furnace, and relics were exhibited of Stone Age man (40 000 years ago) up to the ancestors of the people resident in the area today. After a further 5,5 km the road joins the main Nyanga–Mutoko road.

The left-hand division of the road, after crossing the Ngarawi River, continues for 5 km and then ends in the centre of an area densely covered in ruins, the construction of which is unique. There are numerous small, compact, fort-like structures, generally between 1 m and 2 m in height and surrounding a central pit which can be reached only through one small entrance. Through this entrance a normal-sized person can crawl or walk with a stoop. Small livestock such as pigs, goats and sheep could have entered, but the pit corrals (if that is what they are) are so small that the amount of work involved in their construction was quite disproportionate to their usefulness.

The sides of the pits are of stone. The space between these sides and the outer wall provide a circular platform on which a few huts could be built. Surrounding these odd structures are low parallel walls covering the flat country in a quite incomprehensible way. Narrow passageways lead through the walls, flanked on either side by walls about 1 m high. If the parallel walls were built for agricultural purposes, it is difficult to imagine what crops were planted within them. They had no defensive significance, for they begin and end in a completely inconsistent manner and could easily have been outflanked.

Hill slopes overlooking the plains are entirely covered in terraces which were probably used for agriculture but, again, for unknown crops. At the time when these walls were built, maize had still to be introduced to Southern Africa by the Portuguese. Most of the hill summits have larger forts built on them, some with proper parapets along which sentries could patrol. Grinding hollows for millet, stone seats and benches can be seen in many of the structures. The whole ruined complex is extremely clean. There are few fragments of pots, no large middens of ash or rubbish, and the only skeletons found have been of individuals who had apparently died of natural causes and been buried in the normal way. There are no indications of attack, destruction or the large-scale slaughter of the inhabitants.

What was the purpose of this strange settlement? Brooding over it is the dominant granite mass of Ziwa and its companions. The various sections of the Karanga people who migrated south of the Zambezi River about 2 000 years ago, developed an empathy with stones, especially granite. They harmonised their life-style accordingly. Their chiefs and kings attached themselves to granite peaks, living on the slopes or summits. The priests and spirit mediums who conducted religious affairs generally had their oracles and retreats on granite peaks.

Ziwa would impress any human being with its dominant presence. It is a mountain fit for a king, and its slopes are densely covered with ruins. On the slopes of the smaller companion peak of Hamba there is a strange pillar of granite about 7 m high and of near-perfect phallic shape. Two huge round boulders have rolled down on to the plain below it. The base of the pillar contains a cave, and the approach slopes below it are lined with low parallel walls. Fragments of pots are to be found in the cave, which has a fine natural resonance. Sound is powerfully projected to the plains below and even a normal voice is amplified. A voice of selected timbre would boom out with frightening force. From here, perhaps, spoke the voice of the oracle of *Mwari* (God).

Who built the walls, corrals and forts? Not the slightest trace of an exotic people has been found. The complex was most likely created by some section of the Karanga tribe such as the baRwe, now dispersed or largely annihilated by the invasion of the Shangane and other people at the beginning of the 19th century.

Who did the actual work? It has been said that the greatest labour-saving device the white man ever discovered was the black man, and the greatest labour-saving device the black man ever discovered was the black woman. The women, therefore, probably did the bulk of the construction.

Why was the construction done over such a vast area and much of it for so incomprehensible a purpose? One may as well ask why birds sing. Some do it to claim territorial rights, some to call a mate, and others because they enjoy it. The Karanga, when they entered the granite world between the Zambezi and Limpopo rivers, developed an empathy with the rock. They carried tributes of rocks to their leaders. They were impressed by the strength and age of granite and gathered rocks (not only confined to granite in this area) and piled them neatly, perhaps in deference to the presence of Ziwa, and through it to their king, the priesthood, to nature, to God himself.

Why did they abandon a place in which they had invested such prodigious labour? They seem to have left in about AD 1750. There are no signs of them fleeing the place after attack; no skeletons as the result of violent deaths; no remnants of shattered belongings or burned huts. The population does not seem to have been driven out; therefore some pleasant change must have lured them off to a new style of living. Perhaps it was the cultivation of maize, the new staple crop everybody wanted, which had just been introduced to Africa after its discovery in America by Christopher Columbus. Maize would not have flourished in the narrow hillside terraces, perhaps causing the population to move on to an area where the crop succeeded. The maize revolution caused profound changes to the style of living all over Africa.

It is sometimes pleasant not to know all the secrets of Earth, and to face a continuing mystery with regard to the origin of these ruins. They were formerly known as the *Van Niekerk Ruins* after Major P van Niekerk, one of the men settled by Cecil Rhodes in the so-called Dutch Settlement north of Nyanga. In 1905 he guided to the site the archaeologist, Professor D Randall MacIver, who made the first serious study of the ruins. He named them after the guide, and drew the attention of the world to this remarkable place.

From the turn to the Ziwa Ruins at the military barricade the gravel road leads westwards for 85 km to join the A3 Mutare–Harare road at Baddeley. This road passes, among other features, the gigantic granite dome of *Dombo* (the rock). In spring when the musasa trees are full of colour, the pass around this mass of rock has rewarded the author with some of the most wonderful botanical spectacles he has seen anywhere in the world. This area is a paradise for brachystegia trees.

MUTARE TO MASVINGO

From Mutare the A9 tarmac road to the south leads out of the town past the African township of Sakubu and along a hot, densely bushed valley. After 8 km a turn-off leads to the Fern valley smallholdings. A further 8 km takes the tarmac road past a turn-off east to the Ximunya township. After a further 12 km the road reaches a turn-off to the Clydesdale north road.

At 40 km from Mutare the A9 road crosses the *Mpudzi* (pumpkin) River and 3 km further on reaches a turn-off east leading to what is known as ...

HIMALAYA

The gravel road to what some surveyor named Himalaya climbs to the summit ridge of the mountains, 2 220 m above sea-level, from where a tremendous view is revealed to the north across the Burma valley to the ridge of the Bvumba. This is, in fact, the area which confronts the Bvumba and provides that mountain land with its superb view. The Bvumba fully returns the compliment to Himalaya and provides an equally fine view of itself.

The gravel road winds and climbs through rugged granite mountain country, following the valley of the river known as *Tshitora* (the taker-away) on account of the damage it causes during its floods. Musasa trees thickly blanket the valley where seed-potatoes are grown and Romney Marsh sheep flourish. Yellow arum lilies, everlastings, proteas, yellowwood and cedar trees cover the heights. In former times a footpath wandered up this valley, finding a tortuous way across the mountains. This path was known to early travellers as *Tsetsera* (hurry on), for the cold and rain-swept heights caused the death of many people caught by storms. This African name still applies to the heights of the Himalaya where skeletons of unfortunate travellers who died of exposure while making the journey have been found.

As in the Bvumba, several individualists made their homes on these heights. Fine farms, such as *Butler North, Helvetia, Engwe* (the place of the leopard) and others, line the wayside. At 48 km from its start the road reaches the summit plateau where, lying half lost in the clouds on the boundary line of Mozambique, the traveller finds the dreamlike *Tsetsera* farm established by Victor Machado de Carvalho with a homestead standing in an exquisite forest of yellowwood trees. The timber of 400 yellowwood trees was used in the construction of the homestead. Superbly furnished, romantic in design and overlooking a most serene view of the Chimanimani Mountains, this became a paradise in the wilderness of Africa. The story of the farm is fascinating.

In 1946 Senhor de Carvalho and his wife found the site of the farm. Wearying of big business in Lourenzo Marques (now Maputo), they were searching for a farm on which to retire. Travelling through the hot lowlands of Mozambique, they looked up at the cool mountains on the frontier with Zimbabwe and saw the lovely waterfalls tumbling down from the heights. Delighted at the sight, they found their way to the summit, an area proclaimed a reserve, but which was uninhabited. For the African tribesmen the mountain summits were altogether too cold, bleak and damp. With 1 000 mm of rain a year, any person residing there needed to command resources of warmth, shelter, transport and agricultural technique, if they were to survive and make a living.

Senhor de Carvalho negotiated for the Tsetsera Heights site, securing it in 1948. From the Zimbabwean side he built an involved and steeply graded road which provided the first practicable vehicle access to the heights. Only in 1958 was the spectacular road constructed up the face of the mountains from the Mozambique side. Meanwhile, Senhor de Carvalho had commenced farming on the heights, finding that the area was ideal for seed-potatoes and cattle, being high above the level of African 'coast fever'. The farm became a major agricultural enterprise, producing dairy products for Beira and seed-potatoes for the whole of Mozambique. The border gate on Tsetsera is locked and the road is not a route of entry between Zimbabwe and Mozambique.

Back on the A9 tarmac road where the Himalaya road branches off 43 km south of Mutare, the journey continues through a landscape of hillocks, odd-shaped rocks and baobab trees. After 3 km the road crosses White Waters stream, passes the turn-off to Inyarapura and then, 17 km further on, reaches a tea-room where a road turns off eastwards to Cashel (25 km) and Chimanimani (81 km). For details of this celebrated scenic drive, see further on.

The A9 road continues southwards through a landscape increasingly dominated by baobab trees. After 3 km the road crosses the pleasantly named *Mvumvumvu* (river of plenty) and traverses a densely populated area where government irrigation projects have served numerous fertile smallholdings. Bananas, tropical fruit, vegetables and baskets are offered for sale at the roadside. At the end of this settled area (81 km from Mutare) the road passes the site of the old resort known as Hot Springs, where a copious outpouring of warm mineral water attracted many visitors for the pleasure and health of swimming in the large bath or taking the waters in private.

Twelve kilometres beyond Hot Springs the tarmac road reaches another substantial irrigation settlement at *Nyanyadzi*, named after the *Munyanyadzi* (the disappearer) stream, so called because of its eroding effects on crops when in flood. Here the road leads through a handsome avenue of acacias in whose shade the peasant farmers sell bananas, farm produce and finely made baskets. Green fields stretch down to the course of the river known as the *Odzi* (the rotter) from the damage caused by its floods. The agricultural settlement was started in 1933 for the benefit of the Ndawu tribe who produce cotton, maize, beans, wheat and fruit.

The A9 road leads on through a most picturesque wilderness of trees with giant baobabs clustered in such numbers that this warm valley with its rocky soil is obviously their ideal home. At 120 km from Mutare the road reaches a junction. Straight ahead the road continues to Chipinge (56 km); Chimanimani (98 km) and Mount Selinda (88 km). The A9 road at present being followed swings sharp right. In this hot wilderness (one of the most concentrated baobab forest areas in Africa) may be seen ahead the astonishing sight of the soaring steel arch of a gigantic bridge. After 8 km of travelling through the trees the road reaches the banks of the Save River and the famous bridge which spans it.

THE BIRCHENOUGH BRIDGE AND THE SAVE RIVER

For some reason the European pioneers in Zimbabwe confused the name of the Save with that of the Sabi in the Transvaal. The proper name of this true river of the wilderness – *Save* (pronounced Sah-veh) – refers to its perennial flow. Meandering down the huge valley it has washed for itself, the river always provides an impressive sight, especially as its floods can reach gigantic proportions. Along its banks grow one of the greatest concentrations of baobab trees to be seen in Africa. Many other interesting species of flora flourish in the river valley, including the curious and beautifully flowered 'star of the Sabi' (*Adenium multiflorem).*

The Birchenough Bridge, opened in 1935, was built at a cost of £152 000 by the Beit Trust. The single-span arch is 330 m long and 88 m at its highest point, with the total length of the bridge being 378 m. The road is carried 18,25 m above the river. Designed by Ralph Freeman who designed the Sydney Harbour Bridge, it was named after Sir Henry Birchenough, at that time chairman of the Beit Trust. His ashes, together with those of his wife, were deposited in the abutment on the east side of the river.

On the right (west) bank of the river there stands a small hotel notable for the variety and brilliance of the bougainvillaeas growing in its grounds. The A9 road leads westwards past this hotel, climbing steadily out of the baobab-covered valley floor and into a world of mopane trees growing on the higher land. The strong fragrance of new-cut potatoes, issuing from the minute fruits of the *Phyllanthus reticulatus* shrubs, is characteristic of this area.

Nine kilometres from the bridge the road crosses the river known as *Devure* (the spiller) from its habit of flooding its banks. A further 15 km takes the road past a turn-off south leading for 23 km to the headquarters of the *Devuli* ranch.

The A9 road, still steadily climbing out of the valley of the Save River, now passes through a range of granite hills where baobab and mopane trees dominate the vegetation. Strangely shaped rocks lie scattered over the slopes like misshapen sculptures. The scenery here could only be seen in Africa: a wilderness of bush and rocky hillocks, with the huts of the tribespeople built on granite outcrops as a protection against termites.

At 50 km from the Birchenough Bridge there is a turn-off south to the substantial copper deposit worked by the mine known as *Umkondo* (the spear) from the ancient iron workings there where many of these weapons were made. Jim Bentley found these abandoned prehistoric workings in 1906. After numerous problems with transport and recovery, the mine became a major producer.

The road now finds a way through a series of granite domes by means of *Moodies Pass*, so named after the Moodie family who led the pioneer trek to settle the Melsetter area in 1892 and blazed the trail through this passage in the hills.

At 84 km from Birchenough Bridge there is a turn-off leading south to the administrative and mining centre of Bikita (10 km). Seventeen kilometres further on, the road reaches the tin-mining area around Glen Cova. The A9 road has now ascended to the middleveld of Zimbabwe, an undulating, lightly bushed plain. At 136 km there is a turn-off to the administrative centre of Zaka (50 km south); at 142 km to the Zimbabwean circular drive; at 144 km to Glenlivet and Lake Mutirikwi; at 152 km to Gutu; and at 158 km to the Mutirikwi National Park (18 km).

At 169 km from Birchenough Bridge (a total of 329 km from Mutare) the A9 road reaches the town of Masvingo described in Chapter Forty-Eight.

CHIMANIMANI TO MOUNT SELINDA

Sixty-four kilometres south of Mutare, on the A9 road to Birchenough Bridge, occurs the junction point of the scenic route to Chimanimani and the southern section of the eastern mountains of Zimbabwe. The road leads eastwards directly into the mountains, following the valley of the Mvumvumvu River, fertile and densely settled by peasant farmers. The river itself is a rushing, gushing, bustling type of mountain torrent liberally supplied with water from the rainfall on the heights.

After 10 km of interesting travelling, the tarmac road reaches a junction. The main road turns sharp south in a steady climb into the heights, past waterfalls and valleys, providing the shortest route to Chimanimani (72 km). The old and scenically famous road continues east up the valley. At 24 km from the Mutare road, it passes through the rural centre of *Cashel*, so named after Lieutenant-Colonel E Cashel who was a pioneer settler of those parts.

Beyond Cashel the road reaches a junction. Straight ahead a branch road continues past several farms such as *Thorn's Hope*. Eventually, after 8 km, the road reaches the border of Mozambique, revealing a fine view down into the low country. The road deteriorates at this point and is not a public route of entry into Mozambique.

At the junction outside Cashel the main road swings sharp south to Chimanimani. This is the scenic route. The road (gravel) climbs steadily up the valley of the Tandayi stream. Cascades and waterfalls are seen, while the reason for the name of the stream, *Tandayi* (the encircled one) is apparent when the road reaches its headwaters in a basin completely hemmed in by mountains.

The Tandayi basin is a rural area where cattle, barley, and fruit are produced. A small community centre named Tandayi lies beside the road 9 km from Cashel. From here a track leads for 12 km up the mountains to one of the most spectacular viewsites imaginable. It is thoroughly worth a bumpy ride. It overlooks not only the lowlands of Mozambique but also the full length of the sparkling quartzite Chimanimani Mountains – a breathtaking sight. This track actually leads to another mountain farm once owned by the enterprising Senhor Victor de Carvalho of Tsetsera. This farm is named *Tandara* and occupies the plateau summit of a great mountain buttress situated just on the Mozambique side of the watershed boundary line. The plateau is ideal for the growing of seed-potatoes and projects into one outlying peak on which stands a trigonometrical beacon. The panoramic view beyond the beacon is staggering. From the plateau a lovely waterfall leaps down to the lowlands of Mozambique. Standing guard on the verge of this fall is a solitary cedar tree, while down below a gorgeous rain forest flourishes on the spray from the falling water.

The main road leaves from the community centre of Tandayi and continues south, climbing steadily, passing after 6 km what is known as Steyn's Bank. The original coach road finds its way up the slopes on the eastern side of the modern road. At 27 km from Tandayi the road passes over a saddle of land known as Musapas Pass (2 135 m above sea-level) and reveals ahead one of the classic views of Africa. Below and to the east stretches a long valley to the slopes of the beautiful Chimanimani range. The road makes a twisting descent into the valley past various farms.

For 54 km after leaving Tandayi (95 km from the junction point on the main Mutare road) the road follows a route of superlative views, eventually reaching the village first named *Melsetter* by the Moodie family of pioneers who came from Melsetter in the Orkney islands. A pleasantly rural little place and the centre of a timber, cattle, coffee and vegetable industry, Chimanimani (as it is now called) is built on a terrace on the mountains with a sweeping view of the Chimanimani Mountains. The surroundings are green and the flora richly varied. A notable feature is the Bridal Veil Falls (known to the Africans as *Mutsarara,* from the sound of the water falling), 4 km from the village.

The village is dominated by a massive hill known as Pork Pie (Nyamzune). This is preserved as the Chimanimani wildlife sanctuary, containing a varied population of animals, including eland, zebra, bushbuck, klipspringer and grey duiker. A 5 km long road leads to the summit of the hill.

A short drive from the village of Chimanimani leads to the entrance of the ...

CHIMANIMANI NATIONAL PARK

The mountain range known to the Africans as *Mawenje* (rocky mountains) is called by Europeans *Chimanimani* from the ideophone *Tshimanimani* (to be squeezed together), which describes the narrow passage of the Musapa River through the range. Only about 50 km in length, it is singularly beautiful. In a granite world of grey-blue rock this range, with its jagged 2 240 m high peaks made up of a sugary-white quartzite sparkling in the brilliant sunshine, is a unique remnant of the water-deposited Frontier System. It presents one of the most spectacular scenes in Africa. Geologists date this rock system at about 1 700 million years.

From Chimanimani a gravel road leads to a parking and camping site known as the Base Camp, with four camping sites and an ablution block at the foot of the range. From this point a pathway provides access up the mountain slopes.

It is an ancient pathway, almost as old as man himself in Africa, a traditional route from the coast to the interior followed by countless travellers. It is a delight to the recreational hiker, but to the African travellers it suddenly brought them from the warm lowlands to the heights where, exposed to driving rain and bitter cold, death awaited many of them.

A walk through the Chimanimani along this path rewards the energetic with many unforgettable sights and scenes. From the camp the pathway climbs steadily up the slopes. The easiest path traverses what is known as Banana Grove. The other route, known as Bailey's Folly (after Bill Bailey, who used to run the Outward Bound school), is shady for most of the way and with plenty of clean mountain water to drink. There are so many interesting flowers and plants to see and so many handsome vistas unfolding on the ascent that the walker is diverted from any weariness he may feel.

To the botanist the journey is a joy on account of the diverse and lovely flora. In many respects the Chimanimani resembles the Western Cape. The quartzite erodes into sand, in this case as fine and white as salt. In this rather unlikely-looking soil flourish cedar and yellowwood trees; half a dozen different varieties of protea (some endemic to the area); golden everlastings, ericas and leucospermum. These plants serve to make the visitor from the Cape feel at home until he notices that interspersed with them are innumerable lovely plants which belong to the island continent of Madagascar which lies at the same latitude. Ferns, orchids, and aloes occur in great numbers and variety. One of the prides of the Chimanimani National Park is the *Disa ornithantha* with its gorgeous red blooms to be seen in the marshlands during January and February.

The pathways being followed reach the top of their climb and emerge on to a grassy plateau covered with odd-shaped rocks. Through this weird garden of rocks the paths meander, with the traveller left to imagine at will all manner of petrified creatures – dwarfs, giants, demons. All of a sudden the paths top a rise and the traveller is startled by a superb view of the inner valley of the mountains. Here, in a deep, thickly grassed valley, the Bundi River, with its many crystal pools in which the watching peaks are reflected, finds its source in a great natural sponge.

Looking down upon this scene, 9 km (two hours' walk) from the start of the path, is a prince of mountain huts known as *Ball's Hotel*, from a mountain enthusiast named John Ball who, for 18 months devoted his weekends to its construction, completing the task in 1955. It shelters 24 people in two big dormitories and has a communal central room, a fine fireplace, a kitchen, and the luxury (in so remote a place) of waterborne sewerage and gas lighting. Hikers and climbers use this place as a base camp, the like of which there is no better in Africa. There is a charge per adult, including the use of a sleeping-bag. The whole area (and the hut) is managed by the Department of National Parks and Wildlife. Trout fishing is permitted in the Bundi River from 1 October to 31 May.

Several paths radiate from Ball's Hotel. The main pathway descends to the floor of the valley, meanders across the grass and passes a strange pool known as *Mtseritseri* (the boiling place) where a powerful spring, as though boiling, churns up a permanent flurry of white sand from its bottom. Herds of sable and eland may often be seen grazing in the valley, while baboons and leopards roam the heights. The pathway starts to climb the far side of the valley around the slopes of the highest peak of the range, Binga Mountain (2 240 m). This pass is known as Skeleton Pass, and here the pathway reaches its highest altitude. Along the wayside the bones of several travellers have been found where they have fallen by the way.

The summit reveals a sweeping view deep into Mozambique. Now on the frontier line, the single main path separates into several branches. If you sat waiting at this point, you would see many travellers passing by from distant tribal areas: Lawi from the north, Ndawu from the east, Shangane from the south; all intent on trudging somewhere, all making use of this natural passage in the mountains. The author wrote this as he sat resting there. While he did so, three Ndawu men came along: the first bearing on his head a heavy load of home-grown tobacco to trade in Zimbabwe, the second transporting for food a couple of fowls in a wickerwork basket, the third carrying a skimpy-looking roll of blankets which must have provided scant cover for the three men if they were caught for the night on these heights. They had been walking for five days from some remote village in the bushlands. They looked rather surprised to find a white man sitting there alone wishing them a pleasant journey on their way.

From Skeleton Pass, one path veers south along the eastern slopes of the mountains and finds a way through a dramatic landscape beneath towering cliffs. Many a stream comes cascading down and crosses the path. Clumps of evergreen forest shelter in the hollows; *shoma* (the bushbuck) barks an alarm from the thickets; in the sand of the path may be seen the tracks of *khamba* (the leopard) and *nungu* (the porcupine). The droppings of baboons and the cuds and shavings of wild sugar cane – the most popular food of the road for all African wayfarers – reveal the passage of many a traveller.

Presently the path climbs on to a broad, grassy ridge which acts as a watershed. South of it the streams unite to form a handsome river, the Mubvumodzi, filled with deep pools in a grassy valley. At the end of the high-lying valley this river suddenly rushes through a barrier of rock and tumbles in a fine double leap 140 m down what is known as *Martin's Falls* (named after Gideon Martin, a pioneer of Melsetter and the first European to see them). It is a beautiful waterfall, complete with rainbow. Below it the river flows off across Mozambique on its involved way to the sea.

This is only one of the many lovely features of these handsome mountains. The walker and climber can be assured of infinite pleasure by a visit to this National Park.

From the village of Chimanimani the main road climbs steeply to what is known as Skyline Junction (17 km) where it joins the main road from Cashel and Mutare. Turning south at this junction, the road ascends the undulating hills through kilometres of wattle plantations belonging to the Zimbabwe Wattle Company, which has a factory 19 km from the junction.

Suddenly the country changes. The road twists down after 16 km (52 km from Chimanimani) to the head of the valley of the *Tanganda* (the flooding river). This was the site of *Waterfall*, the pioneer farm belonging to Thomas Moodie, who first settled in the eastern mountains in 1893 after an epic trek. His grave lies close to the road, and here a branch leads west down the valley past the tea estate to Birchenough Bridge, 48 km away.

The Tanganda valley, steep and bush-covered, was the route followed by the pioneer settlers in reaching the summit ridge of the eastern mountains. The magnificent estate, *New Year's Gift,* marks the camp where the doughty Thomas Moodie and his followers rested on New Year's Day of 1893 after a fearsome journey dragging their wagons through the wilderness. This estate eventually passed into the hands of Arthur Wood, a retired tea-planter from Assam. A pioneer of the character of Thomas Moodie, he was of the opinion that tea could be grown in the eastern districts.

Arthur Wood persuaded Grafton Phillips, another tea-planter from Assam, to migrate to Zimbabwe in 1925. The two men established on *New Year's Gift* a nursery of tea plants imported from Assam. To their consternation they then discovered that the rainfall was totally inadequate. Tea requires at least 1 200 mm of rain a year. If the two men had really studied local records they would never have started the venture. Now they were too involved to withdraw, but their precipitate action certainly paid dividends. They decided to irrigate from the Tanganda stream. Such cultivation was unique in tea growing, but it worked. In 1929 they picked their first crop of 517 kg of tea. By 1945 they had passed 453 818 kg a year, and today the Zimbabwe Tea Estates (Pvt) Ltd make a significant contribution to the economy of Southern Africa with their Tanganda and Stella teas.

The head of the Tanganda valley marks the end of the really high country of the eastern mountains. South of it the main road continues at a lower level through thickening bush. Nine kilometres from the turn-off down the valley the road passes a turn-off east leading to the eastern border road and the Ratelshoek Tea Estates. The main road continues south from 3 km and then reaches the village named *Chipinge* (the impeder) from a high buttress which blocked the early pathway. This is a picturesque half-tropical little place – a few streets lined with shops and government buildings – but it is neat, clean, and beautified with numerous flowers and flowering trees. It is a centre for dairy farming, coffee and tea, and pecan and macadamia nuts.

From Chipinge the road continues south over the middleveld bush country, scattered with cattle ranches and tea and coffee plantations. This is the administrative area known as Gasaland. After 32 km the road reaches the end of the eastern mountain. On the edge of the escarpment, facing east, is the beautiful 1 000 ha indigenous forest known as *Tshirinda* (the refuge). With its ironwoods, wild figs and red mahogany trees (one 65 m high and over 15 m in circumference), this lovely forest provides a fitting end to the scenic beauties seen so far. Butterflies and moths in prodigious numbers feed on the rotting vegetation. In spring the Tshirinda forest is a dazzling sight with the ironwood trees covered in snow-white blossoms.

In the forest stands the impressively well-built Mount Selinda mission station and next to the forest the Government forestry plantation of Gungunyana. The hills peter out into the low country. There is a border gate through which the road continues into Mozambique to the administrative post of *eSpungabera* (wood of the rock rabbits), with its one street of nondescript shops, police post, and astonishingly powerful electric lighting which makes the place literally glow at night, as though the village was a solitary city in this wilderness which sweeps up to the cool mountains as a restless sea of bush.

INDEX

4 × 4 trails 252, 264, 557, 608, 614, 853–54, 858–60, 862–63, 872, 874–75, 894, 923, 937, 941, 991
1820 Settlers National Monument 430
!Xamkhanaxas 953

A

Aasvoëlberg 663
Aasvoëlberg Hiking Trail 663
Aasvoëlkop 731
Abel Erasmus Pass 792–93, 804
Abercorn 984
Aberdeen 445
Abiquasputs 332
Abrahamsrust Pleasure Resort 642
Achterwitsenberg 247
Acornhoek 805
Acropolis, Great Zimbabwe 1003
Adderley Street 19, 35, 41
Addo 419–20
Addo Elephant National Park 418
Adelaide 460
Adendorp 426
Africa Unity Square 994
African Art Centre 526
African Window, the 745
Afrikaanse Taal Museum 188
Afrikaner Broederbond 728
Agate Beach, Lüderitz 956
Agate Terrace 494
Aggeneys 330–31
Agnes Top 780
Agricultural Museum 241
Agricultural Research Council (ARC) 747
Agterbaai 122
Ai-Ais 953–54
Ai-Ais Hot Springs Resort 954
Akkerendam Nature Reserve 320
Alanglade House Museum 785

Albany Museum 429
Albert Falls 576, 583, 608
Albert Falls Public Resort 583
Albert Hertzog tower 731
Albert Park, Durban 528
Albertinia 384
Alberton 769
Alexander Bay 267, 960
Alexander James O'Connor memorial 796
Alexander McGregor Memorial Museum 297
Alexandra Park 574
Alexandria 427, 435
Alexandria Forest Hiking Trail 435
Alexkor 269
Alfred Basin 35
Alfred County Railway 505
Alfred Dock 35
Algeria forestry station 253
Algoa Bay 415, 426
Alice 455
Alicedale 427, 436
Aliwal North Hot Springs 473
Aliwal North Museum 472–73
Aliwal Shoal 520
Aliwal Spa 473
Alkmaar 773
Allanridge 639
Alldays 681
Allemanskraal Dam Resort 634
Allesverloren 151, 200
Alphen 67
Alte Feste Fort 907
Alte Feste Museum 908
Alto 151, 173
Alvor 896
Amadizimba Cave 1011
Amalia 311, 839
Amanzimnyama Park 536
Amanzimtoti 522
Amathole Museum 454
Amatikulu Nature Reserve 544

Amatole range 455
Amersfoort 767
Amphitheatre Gardens, Durban 528
Amphitheatre Wall, Drakensberg 604
Amsterdam 761, 765
Ananda Holiday Resort 833
Anderson Gate, Etosha National Park 913
Anglican Cyrene Mission 1012
Anglican St Mary's Cathedral 733
Anglo-Boer War 591, 595, 717, 719, 726–27, 734, 742, 746, 759, 767–68, 771, 777, 782, 806, 809, 847, 852, 908, 976
Anglo-Boer War Museum 838, 842
Anglo-Boer War Museum, Perdeberg 632
Anglo-Boer War Museum, Sannapos 630
Anglo-Transvaal War 745, 755, 767–68, 831, 846
Anglo-Transvaal War of Independence 742
Anglo-Zulu War 595
Angwa River 999
Ann Bryant Art Gallery 463
Anniesfontein 264
Antonies Vlei 199
Apies (Tshwane) River 741
Apies River 748
Appie van Heerden Nature Reserve 319
apple 131, 371
Apple Express 413, 416, 449–50
apricot 132
Aquarium, Pretoria 744
Arangies Kop Trail 222
Arbeidsgenot, Oudtshoorn 351
Arcadia 742
Arcadia Park 746
Arderne Gardens 61

1039

Arend Dieperink Museum 675
Ariamsvlei 953
Aris 949
Armmansvriend 447
Arniston 240
Asab 951
Asbestos Mountains 307
Ashburton 575
Ashmead holiday camp 401
Ashton 223
Askham 336
asparagus industry, Tarlton 829
Assagay 577
Assegaaibosch Nature Reserve 169
Aston Bay 413
Athlone 366
Atlantis 117
Atteridgeville 748
Augeigas River 910
Augrabies 327
Augrabies Falls 287
Augrabies Falls National Park 327–28
Auob River 333
Aus 956
Ausspannplatz, Windhoek 909
Austin Roberts Bird Hall 744
Austin Roberts Bird Sanctuary 744
Aviation monument 297
Avis, Windhoek 909
Avondzon 754
Avontuur 392, 404, 410, 450

B

Baardskeerdersbos 237
Babalala Camp 827
Babanango 563
Baboon's Castle 506
Backsberg Wine Estate 186
Baddeley 1031
Baden 364
Baden-Baden 626
Badplaas 761–62, 764
Baia dos Cocos, Inhambane 899
Bailey's Folly 1035
Bailies Beacon 432
Bain's Kloof Pass 197
Baixa district 891
Bakens River 415, 416
Bakerville 836–37
Bakoven 27
Balancing Rocks, the 997
Balele Mountains 598
Balfour 459–60, 768

Balgowan 588
Ball's Hotel mountain huts 1036
Ballito 541
Ballito Bay 541
Balmoral 755
Balule 822
Balule Rest Camp 825
Bambata Cave 1011
Bambatsi Holiday Ranch 946
Bamboesspruit 840
Banana Express 507
Banana Grove 1035
Bandelierskop 678
Bank 848
Banke Hiking Trail 658
Banket 998
Banner's Rest 514
Bannerman, Drakensberg 612
Bantry Bay 110
baobab forest 1033
Baobab Hill 828
baobab tree 681, 802, 859, 900
Bapsfontein 754
Baragwanath 668
Barberspan 838
Barberton 742, 765, 779, 963
Barbierskraal 393
Barkly East 474
Barkly Pass 475, 478
Barkly West 299–300
Barkly West Museum 300
Barney Barnato 695
Barreira Vermelho 894
Barrydale 363
Bartholomeu Dias Museum complex 387
Bartholomeus Klip 201
Base Camp 1035
Basotho Cultural Village Museum 652
Bassonsdrif 326
Baster Footpath 475
Baths, the, Citrusdal 246
Bathurst Agricultural Museum 432
Bathurst wool mill 431–32
Batlokwa Native Reserve 851
Battery Spruit 1022
Battle of Berg-en-Dal 759
Battle of Blood River 594, 750, 965
Battle of Doornkop 718
Battle of Laing's Nek 767
Battle of Nkambule 596
Battle of Paardeberg 632
Battle of Waterberg 912, 921
Battlefields 1014

Battlefields route 560
Baviaanskloof 199, 446
Baviaanskloof Forest Reserve 446
Baviaansrivier 460
Bawa Falls 485
Baxter Theatre 57
Bayworld 415
Bazaruto Archipelago 901
Bazaruto Islands 901
Bazley Beach 518
Beachview Resort, Port Elizabeth 417
Beachwood Mangrove Nature Reserve 539
Beacon Island 406
Beatrice 1001
Beaufort West 281
Beaufort West Museum 282
Beck House 214
Beckersberg 634
Bedford 460
Bedfordview 739
Beeshoek 305
Beira 896
Beit Bridge 682
Beit Bridge customs post 682, 1007, 1012
Bekamuzi River 562
Bela Vista 894
Belfast 758, 790
Belgravia Historical Walk 298
Bell River 478
Bell, the, Drakensberg 609
Bellevue 1012
Bellingham 180
Bellville 270, 272
Belmont 293, 1012
Belvidere 398
Ben Lavin Nature Reserve 679
Ben Macdhui 477
Ben Schoeman Highway 668
Bendigo 516
Benekraal 405
Benfica 896
Benguela Current 11, 82, 99, 114, 265, 929, 960
Benoni 701
Benoni Lakes Express 702
Benoni Lane of Fame 702
Bensusan Museum of Photography 736
Berea plateau 869
Berg Mountain Marathon 647
Berg River Canoe Marathon 202
Berg River valley 132, 176
Berg-en-Dal 759

Berg-en-Dal camp 822, 824
Bergheim Holiday Resort 832
Bergkelder 151
Bergtheil House Museum 579
Bergville 605
Bergvliet 71
Berlin 462
Berlin Mission Society station, Bethany 622
Berlyn 784
Berlyn Falls 786
Bernard Price Institute of Geophysical Research 736
Bernard Price Museum of Palaeontology 736
Bernberg Fashion Museum 737
Berseba Mission station 951
Bertram House 47
Bestershoek Valley Hiking Trail 438
Bethal 760
Bethanie Mission station 955
Bethany 622
Bethelsdorp 425
Bethesda Mission 880
Bethlehem 645
Bethlehem Museum 645
Bethulie 620
Bethulie Nature Reserve and Park 620
Betty's Bay 232
Beverley East 996
Bezuidenhout Park 734
Bezuidenhout Valley 734
Bezuidenhouts Pass 650
kwaBhaca 503
Bhalekane 984–85
Bhubesi Camp 985
Bhunya 983, 988
Biddulphs Berg 644
Bidouw valley 251
Bien Donné 185
Biesiesvlei 837
Big Bend 984, 990–91
Big Hole of Kimberley 295
Biggarsberg 592
Biggarsberg Mountains 966
Bikita 1034
Bilanhlola River 513
Bilene Resort 897
Bindura 997
Binga 1017
Binga Mountain 1036
Birchenough Bridge 1033
Bird Island, Lambert's Bay 129
Bird Island, Lake St Lucia 548

Bird Rock 494
bird sanctuary, Springs 703
Birkenhead 237
Bisho 461
Bishop's Seat 559
Bishopscourt 62
Bitou River 406
Bitterfontein 257
Bizana 498
Blaauwklippen 173
Blaauwkranz massacre monument 590
Black Mfolozi River 547
Black Nek 872
Black River 18, 62
Bladgrond 329
Blakeway Marine Shell Collection 994
Blanco 391
Blesbokspruit, Springs 703
Blikkiesdorp (Dan Pienaarville) 706
Bloedkoppies Camp 937
Bloemfontein 622–26
Bloemfontein International Airport 630
Bloemhof 839–40
Bloemhof Dam 840
Blou Punt Hiking Trail 364
Bloubergstrand 2, 115
Bloukrans Pass 431
Bloukrans River 407
Bloukranspas 321
Blousteenberg 231
Blow Hole, the 486
Blue Bay 513
Blue Lagoon 513, 539
Blue Mountain Pass 873
Bluegumspoort 680
Bluff 524
Bluff Nature Reserve 529
Blybank 848
Blyde River 785
Blyde River Gorge 787
Blydepoort Holiday Resort 787
Blyderivierspoort Dam 788
Blystaanhoogte Forest Station 783
Blythedale Beach 539, 541
Blyvooruitzicht 848
Boane 894
Bobbejaangat 836
Bobbejaanskrans River 317
Bobonong 851
Boboyi River 512
Bockberg 925
Boekenhoutfontein Museum 831

Boekenhoutskloof 184
Boer Civil War 845
Boerbok Hiking Trail 222
Boereplaas Holiday Resort 313
Boesmanshoek Pass 481
Boesmanskloof Hiking Trail 223, 375
Boesmansriviere Koöperatiewe Kaasfabriek 228
Bogenfels 959
Boiling Pot, the 486
Bo-Kaap Museum 44
Boknes 434, 487
emBokodweni River 523
Boksburg 700
Bokspruit 478
Bokwa's Forest 784
BoLembu Mountain 968
Bomvu River 491
Bon Courage 224
Bonda Mission station 1027
Bonfoi 151
Bongolo Dam 470
Bonkazana 459
Bonnievale 227
Bonnievale Co-operative Wine Cellar 228
Bontebok National Park 378
Bonteheuwel 366
Bonza Bay 466
Boomslang Cave 91
Bophuthatswana 313–14
Boplaas 360
Boqate 869
Border Country 453
Border Gate 985
Boro tributary 861
Bosberg 288
Bosberg Nature Reserve 438
Bosbokrand 806
Boschendal 180
Boshof 626
Boshof Municipal Nature Reserve 627
Bosjesspruit Coal-Mine 754
Boskloof Hiking Trail, Humansdorp 411
Bosluiskloof 362
Boston 582
Bot River 373
Botanic Gardens, Durban 527
Botanic Gardens, Pietermaritzburg 574
Botanical Research Institute, Pretoria 754
Botha's Hall, Cango Caves 352

1041

Botha's Hill 577
Botha's Pass 597
Bothasdrif 287, 621
Bothashoop border post 990
Bothaville 639
Botletli River 861
Botsabelo Leper Settlement 869
Botshabelo 631
Botshabelo Open Air Museum 757
Botshabelo Trail 756
Botswana 849–63
Botswana 4 × 4 trail 851
Botterkloof 321
Boulders penguin colony 98
Boulders station, Mpumalanga 776
Bourke's Luck 787
Bourne's Crack 883
Bovlei Cellars 198
Boyden Observatory 625
Braak, die 146
Braemar 519
Brak River 457
Brakfontein 382
Brakpan 702
Brandberg 947
Brandfort 633, 635
Brandvlei 215, 322
Brandwag Mountain 274
Brandwater Hiking Trail 657
Brazen Head 492
Breakfast Rock, Table Mountain 50
Breakfast Vlei 456
Bredasdorp 240
Bredasdorp Wool Route 241
Breede River 16, 209
Breede River mouth 379
Breedtsnek 830
Bremersdorp (Manzini) 971
Brenton 398
Brenton-on Sea 398
Breyten 761, 763
Bridal Arch, Sterkfontein Caves 706
Bridal Chamber, Cango Caves 353
Bridal Veil Falls 784, 1035
Brits 832
Britstown 291, 339
Brixton 731
Broederstroom River 796
Bromley 1021
Bronkhorstspruit 755
Brooklyn 33
Brooks Hill 498
Brooks Nek 503
Bryntirion 744

Bube Pan 554
Bubi River 1007, 1015
Bucele 494
Buchuberg 266, 336–37
Buchuberg Dam Monument 337
Buffels Bay 398
Buffels River 279
Buffelsfontein 480
Buffelshoek Pass 247
Buffelsjagbaai 238
Buffelskroon Dam 792
Buffelspoort Dam 830, 832
Buffelspoort Holiday Resort 832
Buffelspruit Nature Reserve 473
Buitenverwachting 73
kwaBulawayo, Zululand 560–61
Bulawayo 1008
Bulembu Mountain 987
Bullfrog Pan Sanctuary, Benoni 701
Buls Poort 941
Bultfontein diamond mine 297
Bulugha River 467
umBuluzi River 885
Bulwer 582
Bundi River 1035
Bunga Forest Botanical Reserve 1024
Bunny Park, Benoni 701
Burgers Park, Pretoria 742
Burgersdorp 481
Burgersfort 788, 789
Burma valley 1032
Burnt Mountain 945
Bushbuck Ridge 787, 806
Bushman engravings 299
Bushman paintings 203, 217, 243–45, 250, 254, 276, 321, 342–43, 359, 380, 396, 440, 450, 471, 475–76, 478, 480–81, 585, 601, 606, 629, 658–59, 839, 869–70, 875–78, 880–81, 998, 1006, 1011
Bushman's River 427
Bushmanland 315, 329, 331
Bushmans Caves Hiking Trail 657, 668
Bushmans Kloof 250
Bushmans Kloof Wilderness Reserve 251
Bushmans Pass 613
Bushmans River 436
Bushmans River Trail, Drakensberg 613
Bushmen 211, 663, 850, 854, 915
Butha-Buthe 874

Butterworth 485
Buyskop 673
Bvekenya Memorial 828
Bvumba Botanical Garden 1025
Bvumba Mountains 1024
Bwengele Island (Santo Antonio) 901
Byrne Village 580

C

C H Mitchell Bridge 499, 515
C P Nel Museum 348
Cabo das Correntes lighthouse 899
Caesar's Camp 591
Cahora Bassa 1019
Cahora Bassa hydro-electric station 822
Cakanaca 860
Cala 479
Caledon 373
Caledon Bridge 659
Caledon Bridge border post 869
Caledon Kloof Hiking Trail 361
Caledon Museum 374
Caledon Poort Bridge border post 657, 874
Caledon River 287, 620, 866
Caledon River Museum 627
Caledon thermal springs 373
Caledon Wild Flower Garden and Reserve 374
Calitzdorp 357, 360
Calitzdorp Co-operative Cellars 360
Calitzdorp mineral baths 360
Calitzdorp Spa 361
Calvinia 320
Cambridge 463
Camden 753
Camel Rock 104
Campanile, Port Elizabeth 416
Campbell 308
Camperdown 575
Camps Bay 110
Candover Station 558
Canelands 536
Cango Angoré Rabbit Farm 351
Cango Caves 351–54
Cango Crocodile and Cheetah Ranch 351
Cango Mountain Resort 351
Cango Ostrich Farm 346
Cannibal Cave 788
Cannon Rocks 434

Canteen Koppie Nature Reserve 299
Cape Agulhas 99, 239
Cape Agulhas lighthouse 239
Cape Columbine lighthouse 126
Cape Correntes 899
Cape Cross Seal Reserve, Namibia 943
Cape Doctor 50
Cape Flats 2, 270–71
Cape Hangklip 51
Cape Hermes 494
Cape Infanta 379
Cape Medical Museum 112
Cape Minstrels' Carnival 44
Cape of Good Hope 2–3, 11, 20, 30, 99
Cape of Good Hope Nature Reserve 98, 103
Cape Padrone 415, 435
Cape Peninsula 23, 28, 52–53
Cape Point lighthouse 102
Cape Recife 415, 417
Cape Seal 406
Cape St Blaize 389
Cape St Francis 412
Cape St Francis lighthouse 411
Cape Town 1–51, 270
Cape Town Holocaust Museum 47
Cape Vidal 550
Cape Wild Coast 464
Cape Wine Academy 150
Cape-to Cairo road 270, 441, 620, 681
Caprivi Game Park 916
Caprivi Strip 862, 915
Carletonville 848
Carliesonia 837
Carlton Centre 732
Carlton Hills 441
Carnarvon 319
Carolina 758, 761, 763
Carter's Nek 614
Casa de Ferro 892
Cascade Fall 587
Cashel 1033–34
Casketts Trading Station 805
Castle Beacon 1024
Castle of Good Hope, the 25, 43
Castle Rock 880
Catalina Bay 548
Catembe 891
Cathcart 457, 469
Cathedral Peak 602, 607
Cathkin Peak 609–11
Cathkin Peak Forest Reserve 610

Catholic National Shrine of Lesotho 871
Cato Ridge 576
Cats Pass 488
Causeway 994
Cave of the Hippopotamus 663
Cavern, the 604
Cecil Kop Nature Reserve 1023
Cecil Mack Pass 556
Cecil Square 994
Cedarville 617
Cederberg 250, 253
Centane 485
Centenary Park, Bulawayo 1009
Central Gauteng Tennis Association 735
Central Kalahari Game Reserve 854
Central Waesche 958
Centurion 669
Ceres 132, 210
Ceres Nature Reserve 210
Chadibe 851
Chalumna 465
Chamais Bay 960
Chamber of Mines tours 697
Champagne Castle 609–11
Chapman's Peak 106
Chapungu Sculpture Park 996
Charlestown 599
Charlie's Pass 330
Charlo 417
Charlotte Kritzinger Shell Museum 413
Charlottenthal 958
Charter's Creek 553
Chegutu 1015
Cheline 900
Chelmsford Dam 596
cherry industry 658
Chessmen, the, Drakensberg 605
Chidengwele 898
Chimanimani 1033, 1035
Chimanimani Mountains 1032
Chimanimani National Park 1035
Chimonzo 897
Chinhoyi 998, 1015
Chinhoyi Caves 998
Chintampa Dam 1011
Chipangali Wildlife Orphanage 1011
Chipenhe 897
Chipinda Pools 1006
Chipinge 1033, 1037
Chiredzi 1006
Chirembe 997

Chiromanzu 1002
Chirundu 1000
Chirundu border post 1000
Chissano 897
Chivhu (Enkeldoorn) 1001
Chizavane 898
Chobe National Park 859, 916
Chobe (Linyanti) River 851, 916
Chris van Niekerk Museum 626
Chrissiesmeer 761
Christiana 839
Christmas Pass 1022
Church of the Good Shepherd 39
Churchhaven 119
Churchill Dam 412
Cinderella's castle 656
Cintsa 467
Cintsa Mouth East 467
Cintsa Mouth West 467
Ciskei 453, 461
citrus industry 247, 421–22, 674
Citrusdal 245
Citrusdal Museum 245
Clairmont 523
Clansthal 520
Clanwilliam 249, 252
Clarens 646, 655
Claw Dam 1015
Cleft Peak, Drakensberg 609
Cleopatra's Needle, Cango Caves 352
Clewer 755
Clifton 110
Clocolan 658
Cloetespas Pass 382
Clos Malverne 155
Clovelly 93
Clovelly Cave 91
Cockscomb 449
Cockscomb Mountain 423
Coega River 426
coelacanth 463
Coerney 418
Coffee Bay 491
Cogmans Kloof 365
Cogmans Kloof Hiking Trail 364
Cole's Kop 286
Colenso 590
Colesberg 286
Colesberg Koppie 441
Colesford Nature Reserve 617
Colesplaas 446
Coligny 842
Colleen Bawn 1012
Colley Wobbles 490
Columbine Nature Reserve 126

1043

Column, the, Drakensberg 609
Commandant's Cave 882
Commissioner Street 732
Committee's Drift 456
Company's Garden 44
Compensation Beach 541
Comrades Marathon 575
concentration camp monument, Potchefstroom 846
Concession 997
Coney Glen 399
Congella 525
Constantia 28–29, 31–32
Constantia Nek 64
Constantia Uitsig 74
Constantia Wine Route 69
Cooke's Lake 314
Cookhouse 437, 460
Cookhouse tunnel 288
Cooper Siding 382
Copper mines, Namaqualand 261
Copper mining museum 263
Copper Mountains 29
Cornelia 648
Cornet Spruit (Makhaleng River) 879
Coronation Park, Krugersdorp 705
Council of Geo-science 747
Council of Scientific and Industrial Research (CSIR) 747
Coutada Official No 5 hunting zone 904
Covie 408
eCowa Trail 475
Coward's Bush 560
Cowie's Hill 579
Cradock 439
Cradock Pass 391
Cramond 336
Croc Ranch 803
Croc World 520
Crocodile Bridge Camp 815, 822, 824
Crocodile Centre 549
Crocodile River 705, 742, 751, 771, 773, 823
Crocodile River Poort 776
Crocodile Valley Estates 774
Crooks' Corner 813, 828
Cross of Sacrifice Memorial, Windhoek 908
Crown Mines Museum 738
Crystal Pools 253
Crystal Rooms, Sudwala Caves 773
Cuddle Puddle 981

Cullinan 669, 754
Cullinan Diamond 628
Cumbana 899
Curry's Post 588
Cuyler Manor Cultural Museum 424
Cyphergat 481

D

Da Gama peak 101
Daan Viljoen Game Park 910
Dagbreek Museum 216
kaDake 981
Dal Josafat 194
Dal van Varing, Knysna Forest 404
Daleside 667
Dalton 583
Damara Okambahe Reserve 947
Damaraland 913
Dan Pienaarville 706
Danger Point 237
Danger Point lighthouse 237
Danger Point, Victoria Falls 1019
Dangers Hoek 478
Danie Joubert Dam 809
Danie Taljaard Park 702
Danielskuil 306
Dannhauser 594
Danskraal 592
Danster's Nek 663
D A P Naude Dam 796
Dargle 588
Darketon 970, 981
Darling 118
Darling Museum 118
Darnall 534
Dasklip Pass 203
Dassen Island 4, 10, 11, 14
Dassieshoek Hiking Trail 222
Dawidskraal 232
De Aar 291
De Beers Pass 650
De Dam 238
De Deur 667
De Doorns 219
De Drie Sprongh 166
De Hel 64
De Hoek 796
De Kelders 236
De Leeuwen Jagt 191
De Post Huys 89
De Rust 358
De Wetshof 151, 227
De Wildt 832

De Wildt Cheetah Research Centre 832
Deadvlei 938
Dealesville 626
Debe 455
Debegeni Waterfall 795
Delagoa Bay 885
Delaire 167
Delareyville 838
Delheim 166
Delmas 703
Delportshoop 301
Delville Wood War Memorial 743
Dendron 680
Deneysville 643
Denneboom station 749
Derdepoort 832–33
Despatch 424
Dete 1017
Devil Hill 868
Devil's Cataract, Victoria Falls 1018
Devil's Gorge 987
Devil's Knuckles, Bushmans Nek Pass 616
Devil's Knuckles, Sabiesnek 782
Devil's Peak, Table Mountain 1, 10, 50
Devil's Pulpit 792
Devil's Tooth, Drakensberg 604
Devil's Workshop, Cango Caves 353
Devon 760
Devon Valley 157
Devure River 1033
Dewetsdorp 630
Dewetshof 734
Dhlo-Dhlo ruins 1013
Diamond Coast 266
Diamond Way 290, 839, 848
diamond-fields, Lichtenburg 837
Diana's Pool 1011
Dias Point 958
Dick King monument 525–26
Dickiesberg 799
Die Berg 758
Die Bos, Prieska 339
Die Galg 375
Die Hel 203
Die Hoek, Bloemhof 840
Die Krans 360
Diepgezet 762
Diepwalle 404
Diggers' Museum 840
Dingane's Kraal 561
Dingleton 304

dinosaur park, Sudwala 772
Dirkiesdorp 767
District Six 53
Dlangeni Hills 989
Dlinza 559
Dohne 469
Dolfynstrand 929
Dombe River 516
Dombo Rock 1030
Donald Grant Nature Reserve 799
Donald McHardy Dam 593
Donkergat 119
Donkergat Whaling Station 119
Donkin Reserve 415
Donnington 1012
Doonside 522
Doorndraai Dam Nature Reserve 675
Doornfontein 734
Doornkloof 669, 830
Doornlaagte 308
Dordrecht 471, 479
Doreen Clark Nature Reserve 574
Doreen Falls 608
Doring River 317
Doringberg 339
Doringkloof 459
Doringkop 705
Dorp Street, Stellenbosch 144
Dorps River 792
Douglas 293, 308
Douglas Dam 761
Downs, the 794
Dr Siegfried Annecke Research Institute 795
Draghoender 338
Dragon's Back 611
Drakensberg 475, 477–78, 600–2, 799
Drakensberg hiking trails 616
Drakenstein 30
Drakenstein Valley 177
Draycott 612
Driekloof Dam 651
Driekop Gorge 786
Driekops Island 308
Driel barrage 650
Drizzly 474
Droërug 394
Drostdy Africana Museum 424
Drostdy Museum 377
Drostdy Wine Cellars 205
Drostdy, Tulbagh 204
Drotsky's Caves 862
Druid's Lodge Museum 221
Drummond 577

Du Toit's Kloof Pass 274
Duff's Road 531
Duggan-Cronin Gallery 298
Duiker Island 107
Duivenhoks River 380
Duiwelsberg 391
Duiwelskantoor 778
Duiwelskloof 798
Dukuduku coastal forest 548
Dukuza (kwaDukuza) 538
Dullstroom 758
Duncan Dock 36
Duncanville 667
Dundee 585, 592
Dundee Museum 592
Dune Camp 939
Durban 524–25
Durban's Sea World 528
Durbanville 272
Durbanville Nature Garden 273
Durban-Westville University 579
Dutchman's Pool 1014
Duwisib Castle 940
Duwisib Farm Rest Camp 940
Dwarskersbos 128
Dwesa Nature Reserve 490
Dzindi Fisheries and Crocodile Farm 683

E

Eagles Nest 1021
East London Aquarium 463
East London Museum 453, 462–63
East Lynn, Pretoria 669
Eastern Buttress, Drakensberg 603
Eastern Cape 410–83
Eastern Cataract, Victoria Falls 1018
Eastern Free State 644–64
Eastern Shores Nature Reserve 549
Eastlea, Harare 1021
Eastman's Peak, Drakensberg 609
Ebb and Flow 397
Ebenezer Dam 795, 797
Ecca Nature Reserve 458
Ecca Pass 458
Echo Caves 788
Ecological Research Centre 903
eCowa Trail 475
eDayizenza market 809
Edenburg 622
Edenvale 582
Edenville 654

Eendekuil 244
Eersbewoond 673
Eerste Fabrieke 754
Eerste River 25
Eerste River Valley 142
Eersteling 744
Eeufeeskloof 663
Eiffel Flats 1015
Eikendal 174
Eiland Holiday Resort 324
Eiland Mineral Baths 801
Eilandsvlei, Wilderness 397
Eileen Orpen Dam 825
ekuPhakameni 532
Elands Bay 244
Elands Cave 606
Elands Mountains 424
Elands River 770
Elands valley 778
Elandsberg 449
Elandshoek 771
Elandspad River 274
Elandsputte 836
eLangeni 964
Elephant Island 886, 893
Elephant Walk 404
Elephant's Eye 77
Elgin 132, 370
Elgin Apple Museum 372
Elim 238
Elizabeth Bay 959
Elizabethbucht 958
Elliot 475
Elliotdale (Xhora) 500
Ellis Park 735
Eloff Street, Johannesburg 732
Elsenburg 166
eLudzidzini 965
eMbekelweni 968
emBokodweni River 523
eMbumbulu 534
Emfundisweni 498
Emigrants Cabin Monument 460
Emmarentia 735
Emmaus Mission, the (Makhakhe) 879
Empangeni 545
Endingeni Mission 985
Energy–Domoina Route 760
Engcobo 470, 499
Engelhard Dam 821, 826
Enkeldoorn (Chivhu) 1001
enKovukeni 558
Enon 420
Enseleni Nature Reserve 546
Enseleni River 546

Entumeni 563
Entumeni Nature Reserve 562
Epping 366
Epupa Falls 923
Epworth Mission 997
Erfenis Dam 635
Erfenis Park 635
Eric Mayer Park 682
Ermelo 760, 784
Ermelo Mine 753–54
Ernest Robertson Dam 389
Erongo Mountains 925, 947
Eros industrial area, Windhoek 909
eShiselweni 964, 990
Eshowe 559
Eshowe Museum 559
Esigodini 1011
esiKhaleni seBuLembu Pass 968
esiPhamanini 892
Eskom 753
eSpungabera 1037
Essenbos 451
Estcourt 589
Etemba 947
Eteza 547
Etosha National Park 913, 919–22
Etosha Pan 919
Eureka City 779
Evangelina Hot Springs 682
Eve's Footprint, Victoria Falls 1019
Ewanrigg National Park 996
Execution Rock 502
Ezulweni 981

F

Faan Meintjes Nature Reserve 844
Fairview 190
Fairy Chamber, Sterkfontein Caves 706
Falcons Rugby Union 703
Fall, the, Bulawayo 1015
False Bay 2, 14, 23, 30, 80
False Bay Fire Museum 94
False Bay Reserve 549
False Bay, St Lucia 548
Famine River 478
Fanie's Island, Lake St Lucia 548
Fatima Mission station 871
Fauresmith 628
Fauresmith flyer steam locomotive 629
F C Braun park 792

F C Erasmus Forestry and Nature Reserve 807
Featherstone 1001
Felixton 545
Fernkloof Nature Reserve, Hermanus 235
Ferrobank 755
Ficksburg 657
Ficksburg border post 878
Ficksburg Museum 658
Field's Hill 577
Figtree 1012
Filabusi 1011
Fincham's Nek 470
Finger of God (Mukurob) formation 951
Fingoland 485
Firewalking Festival 573
Firgrove 366
Fischer Pan 921
Fish Hoek 93
Fish River 950
Fish River Canyon 952–54
Fish River Canyon Park 954
Fish River valley 949
Fisherman's Cove 467
Fiskus Waesche 958
Fitzsimons Snake Park 528
Flagstaff (Siphageni) 498
Flamingo Islet 956
Flesh Hill 868
Florida Lake 704
Florisbad 626
Floriskraal 279
Flotfontein 472
Fochville 847
Fonteinbos Nature Reserve 446
Fonteyn 989
Foot of Africa Marathon 241
Forbes' Post border post 1023
Fordsburg 730
Foreshore 19, 36
Forest Town 737
Fort Amiel 597
Fort Beaufort 430, 457
Fort Beaufort Museum 458
Fort Bowker 489
Fort Brown 458
Fort Cox 455
Fort Cunynghame 469
Fort Harrison 493
Fort Hartley 881
Fort Hendrina 679
Fort Klapperkop 747
Fort Klapperkop Military Museum 746

Fort Lagoa 886
Fort Lydzaamheid 886
Fort Malan 489
Fort Mistake 592
Fort Napier, Pietermaritzburg 572
Fort Selwyn battery 429
Fort Skanskop 747
Fort Victoria (Masvingo) 1002
Fortuna Mine Trail 780
Fossil Chamber, Sterkfontein Caves 706
Fossil Trail 283
Fothergill Island, Kariba 1001
Fountains recreational area 747
Four Passes Fruit Route 372
Fouriesburg 656–57
Fourteen Streams 839
four-wheel-drive trails, see 4 × 4 trails 1039
Francistown 851, 856
Frankfort 648, 653
Franklin Game Reserve 625
Franschhoek 30, 183
Fransmanshoek 385
Fraser Falls 495
Fraser's Camp 431
Fraserburg 281, 318
Fresh River 4, 8, 9, 15
Freshford House, Bloemfontein 626
Fresnaye 111
Fritz Gaerdes Nature Park 910
Frontier Museum and Art Gallery 470
Fruit Route 216
Funnystone 478
Furumela Mountain 872

G

Gaborone 851–52
Gabriel's Forest 784
Gago Coutinho Airport 892
Galeshewe 299
Gallows Hill 25, 28
Gamkas Kloof 357
Gamtoos River 413
Gamtoos River valley 447
Gansbaai 236
Garamonzi 1021
Ga-Rankuwa 741
Garbutt's Hill 583
Garcia's Pass 382
Garden Castle 602
Garden of Eden 405

Garden of Remembrance, Ottosdal 841
Garden of Remembrance, Pietermaritzburg 573
Garden Route 386–409
Gardiner's Drift 460
Gariep (Hendrik Verwoerd) Dam 288
Gariep (Orange) River 287, 324, 327–28, 336, 339, 880–81
Gariep Dam Resort 620
Garies 259
Garub 940
Gatberg 476
Gately House 463
Gates, the 486
Gates of St Johns 493
Gatyana 489
Gauteng 708
Gaza district 897
Gazankulu 683
Gcalekaland 485
Gcodikwe 860
Gcuwa River 484
Gcwihaba 862
Geelbek 121
Gege customs post 990
Gemsbokplein 333
Gemvale 494
Genadeberg 663–64
Genadendal 375
Genadendal Hiking Trail 375
General Hertzog Bridge 473, 628
General J B M Hertzog Memorial, Bloemfontein 626
Geographical Museum, Maputo 891
Geological Survey Museum, Pretoria 744
George 390
George Harrison Memorial Park 703, 739
George Museum 390
George's Valley 795, 797
Germiston 699
Germiston Lake 699
Ghaap Plateau 308
Ghanzi 853, 861, 863
Ghost Mountain 554
Giant's Castle 475, 602
Giant's Castle Game Reserve 612
Gibeon 950
Gifberg 257
Gilbert Reynolds Memorial Garden 983
Gillie Cullem Waterfall 475

Gillooly's Farm, Bedfordview 736
Gingindlovu 544
Gladstone's Nose 656
Gledhow 534
Glen, the 110
Glen Cova 1034
Glen Lynden 460
Glen Reenen 656
Glencairn 80, 94
Glencoe 593
Glenconnor 170
Glengarry 613
Glenlivet 1034
Glenmore 514
Glentana 389
Goageb 955
Goba border post 984
Gobaba area, Namib Desert 933
Gobabeb 934
Gobabis 910
God's Window 786
Godwane River 771
Goede Hoop 151
Goedverwacht 244
Goegap Nature Reserve 261
Goetz/Fleischack Museum 846
Golalabadimo Pan 854
Gold Mine Museum 703
Gold Nugget Hiking Trail 780
Gold Reef City 738
Golden Gate 646, 655
Golden Gate Highlands National Park 656
Golden Lions Rugby Union 735
Golden Valley 437
gold-fields, Free State 636
gold-mining industry, history 685–99
Golela border post 766, 990
Gomare 862
Gomo Kadzamu 1026
Gona re Zhou National Park 1007
Gondwana Canon Park 954
Gondwane River 468
Gonubie 466, 483
Gonye Falls 1018
Good Hope Centre 43
Goodhouse 330
Goodwood 271
Gordon's Bay 230
Gordonia 315, 324, 331
Gorongose River 904
Gouda 202
Goudini Spa 216
Goukamma Nature and Marine Reserve 398

Gourits River 382, 384
Government Avenue 19, 46
Graaff-Reinet 443–44
Graafwater 252
Grabouw 132, 370
Graduate School of Business, Cape Town 37
Grahamstown 428–31
Grand Parade 9, 19, 31
Grand Parade Centre 42
Grand Valley 990
Granger Bay 111–12
grapes 133–36
Grasfontein 836–37
Graskop 785–86, 808
Grasslands Research Station 1021
Gravelotte 794, 801
Graveyard, Sterkfontein Caves 706
Great Brak River 388
Great Dyke of Zimbabwe 998
Great Dyke Pass 998
Great Fish Point lighthouse 434
Great Fish River 287, 430
Great Fish River valley 436, 458
Great Karoo 315–16
Great Kei cuttings 483
Great Suthu River 984
Great Synagogue, Johannesburg 733
Great Vet River 633
Great Zimbabwe 750, 1002
Greater Brandvlei Dam 215, 219
Green Point 16, 28, 111–12
Green Point lighthouse, Clansthal 520
Greenshields Park 417
Grenshoek 798
Greylands Ostrich Farm 360
Greylingstad 768
Greyton 375
Greytown 583
Greyville Racecourse 527
Griffith Hill 868
Griqualand West 299
Griquatown 307
Grobbelaars River 347
Groblersdal 757
Groblershoop 336–37
Groendal 183
Groendal Wilderness Area, Uitenhage 424
Groenkop 646
Groenvlei, Wilderness 396
Groot Constantia 64, 66–67
Groot Marico 834
Groot River 407

Groot River Pass 447
Groot Spelonke 800
Groot Winterhoek 449
Groot Winterhoek range 423–24
Grootdraai Dam 768
Groote Kerk 31, 43
Groote Schuur 14, 58
Groote Schuur Hospital 54
Grootfontein 914
Grootjongensfontein 383
Gross-Barmen 911
Grosse Bucht 956, 958
Groutville Mission station 538
Grünau 952
grunter run 549
Guageb 941
Guano Bay 956
Guardian Peak 368
Gubu Dam 469
Gubuda (Kubutsa) valley 964
Gugulethu 366
Guilundo 898
Gulubahwe Cave 1011
Gumbandevu 820, 827
Gun War 879
Gundrift 505
Gungunyana forestry plantation 1037
Gunundwini 979
Gustav Klingbiel Nature Reserve 792
Gutu 1034
Guvulala Pan 1016
Gwanda 1011
Gwarina 450
Gwayi River 1015
Gweru 1002, 1013
Gweru Military Museum 1013
Gweru River 1013
Gweta 860
Gwivi River 998
Gxara River 486
Gydo Pass 211, 247
Gydoberg 209

H

Ha Borwana 872
Ha Khotso 872
Ha Mphotu 870
Ha Ntsi 872
Ha Rafutho 869
Haarlam 450
Haenertsburg 795, 797
Haga-Haga 467, 483

Hakwa River 374
Halali Camp, Etosha National Park 920
Halekokoane Cave 870
Halfway House 668, 1015
Half-way House 713
Halifax Island 956
Hall of Elephants, Sterkfontein Caves 706
Halle Stream 647
HaMakhoathi 869
Hamba Mountain 1030
Hambanati 538
Hamburg 466
Hammanskraal 671
Hanging Rock 506
Hangklip, False Bay 80, 231
Hangklip Forestry Reserve, Soutpansberge 680
Hangklip, Eastern Cape 471
Hangklip, Venda 680
Hankey 448
Hanover 285
Hans Merensky Nature Reserve 800
Hantam Mountains 320
Hantamsberg 320
Happy Valley, Port Elizabeth 415
Harare 993–96
Harare Public Gardens 995
Hardap Dam 950
Hardekraaltjie Caravan Park 272
Harding 504
Harkerville 405
Harkerville Coast Hiking Trail 405
Harold Porter Botanic Reserve 232
Harrismith 646
Harry's Bay 234
Harry's Huts 807
Hartbees River 323
Hartbeesfontein 843–44
Hartbeespoort Aquarium 751
Hartbeespoort Dam 751
Hartbeespoort Dam Cableway Company 751
Hartenberg 163–64
Hartenbos 387
Hartenbos River 388
Hartleyvale 56
Harts River 301, 838
Hartswater 311
Hattingspruit 594
Havelock Swaziland Asbestos Mine 987
Hawequas Nature Conservation Station 198

Hawston 233
Hazeldene Nature Reserve 615
Hazelmere Public Resort Nature Reserve 536
Hazendal 151, 163
Hazyview 808
Headlands 1021
Heads, the 399, 506
Hectorspruit 776
Heerengracht 60
Heidelberg 380, 768
Heidelberg Transport Museum 769
Heilbron 648, 654
Hekpoort 830
Hela Hela cliffs 580
Helderberg 367
Helderberg Nature Reserve 367
Helene 898
Hell's Gates 548
Helmeringhausen 941, 955
Helpmekaar 585
Helshoogte 167
Hemel-en-Aarde 234
Hemel-en-Aarde valley 235
Henderson Agricultural Research Station 997
Hendrik Verwoerd Dam, see Gariep Dam
Hendrik's Drift 875
Hendrina 758, 763
Hendrina Museum 763
Henley Dam 574, 582
Hennenman 637–38
Hennops River 669, 752
Henties Bay 942
Herbertsdale 382
Herero memorial service 911
Hermann Eckstein Park, Johannesburg 735, 738
Hermannsburg 584
Hermanus 234
Hermanus Museum 235
Hermon 200
Heroes' Acre 996
Herold's Bay 389
Heroncliff 447
Herschel 478
Hester Malan Wild Flower Garden 261
Hester Rupert Art Museum 444
Heuningberg Nature Reserve 241
Hex River Mountain Pass 275
Hex River Mountains 274
Hex River Railway Pass 275
Hex River valley 217
Hex River, Magaliesberg 830

Hibberdene 517
Hibiscus Coast 516
Higgledy-Piggledy Pass 373
Highflats 519, 581
Highgate Ostrich Farm 346, 355
Highlands 427, 998
Highveld 753
hiking trails
   Aasvoëlberg 663
   Alexandria Forest 435
   Arangies 222
   Banke 658
   Bergwaters 597
   Bestershoek Valley 438
   Bethlehem 646
   Blou Punt 364
   Blydepoort 787
   Boerbok 222
   Boesmanskloof 223, 375
   Boskloof 411
   Botshabelo 756
   Brandwater 657
   Bushmans Caves 657, 658
   Bushmans River, Drakensberg 613
   Caledon Kloof 361
   Cedarberg 253
   Chimanimani National Park 1036
   Clarens 655
   Cogmans Kloof 364
   eCowa 475
   Dassieshoek 222
   Drakensberg 616
   Du Toit's Kloof 274
   Fish River Canyon 954
   Fossil 283
   Genadendal 375
   Giant's Castle Game Reserve 613
   Gold Nugget 780
   Grahamstown 430
   Great Brak River 389
   Haenertsburg 797
   Harkerville 405
   Holkrans 597
   Hottentots Holland 370
   Jonathan's Gate 616
   Klein Aasvoëlkrans 756
   Klipspringer 329
   Knysna Forest 404
   Kologha 469
   Koranna 658
   Kosi Bay Nature Reserve 558
   Leeuwspruit 642
   Magaliesberg 829
   Malolotja Nature Reserve 986
   Maputaland 556
   Meikles Mount 988
   Middelburg 756
   Midmar Dam 588
   mKhosini 562
   Mkuze 554
   Mooivallei 228
   Moorfield 597
   Mountain 236
   Mountain Zebra 440
   Naukluft Mountains 941
   Oranjezicht 339
   Otter 408
   Oudorp 844
   Outeniqua 404
   Pietermaritzburg 574
   Pioneer 780
   Pointer 283
   Port Alfred 433
   Ravine 236
   Rhebok 656
   Rhino 678
   Riemland Eco-route 642
   Sabie 784
   Soutpansberge 680
   Suikerbosrand 667
   Sneeuberg 442
   Springbok 283
   Steve Visser 659
   Stokstert 627
   Strandloper 467
   Sugar Loaf 494
   Sweet-Thorn 910
   T'Keikamspoort 339
   Timbavati 804
   Valley of Desolation 445
   Vryheid 595
   Waterberg Plateau Park 913
   Waterfall 236
   Weza 504
   Witstinkhout 628
   Wolwedans Dam 388
Hill Crest 577
Hillbrow 708, 717, 731
Hillcrest 577
Hillcrest Berry Orchards 168
Hillside 613
Hillside Dam 1009
Hilton 585
Himalaya 1032
Himeville Museum 615
Hippo Pool 804
Hippo valley 1006
Hlane Royal National Park 985
Hlangulene picnic site 825
Hlatsikhulu 990
Hlatsikhulu Forest 965
Hlogoma Mountain 582, 615
Hlohlowane Mountain 658
Hlongwa River 520
Hlongwana River 521
Hlotse 876
Hlotse River 878
Hluhluwe Game Reserve 551
Hluhluwe River 551
Hluleka 492
Hluleka Nature Reserve 492
Hlushwane Hill 964
Hluthi Hill 964
Hluti 990
Hoba meteorite 914, 917
Hobhouse 631, 660
Hobie, Port Elizabeth 415
Hoedspruit 793, 804
Hoeko 362
Hoffman Cave 663
Hofmeyr 482
Hogsback 455–56
Hole in the Wall 491
Holela 489
Holola valley 875
Holspruit River 479
Holy Cross 497
Homeb camp 937
Homtini Pass 394
Honde valley 1027
Hondeklip Bay 260
Honoured Dead Memorial, Kimberley 296
Hopefield 122
Hopetown 292
Horse Memorial, Port Elizabeth 416
Horseshoe Bend 506
Horseshoe Bend Nature Reserve 432
Horseshoe Falls, Sabie 784
Horseshoe Falls, Victoria Falls 1018
Hosking Park, Brakpan 702
Hospital Hill 731
Hot Springs 1033
Hotagterklip 239
Hotazel 303, 305, 336
Hottentots Holland 16, 23
Hottentots Holland Hiking Trail 370
Hottentots Holland Mountains 369
Houghton 730
Houghton Estate 734
Houhoek 372

Houses of Parliament, Cape Town 19, 45
Houses of Parliament, Harare 994
Houses of Parliament, Swaziland 983
Hout Bay 21, 106
Hout Bay Museum 107
Houtbosdorp 796, 800
Houtbosloop valley 771, 781
Houtkop border post 990
Howick 585
Howick Falls 576, 585
Howick Museum 586
Howison's Poort 427
Huberta 546
Hugh Exton Photo Museum, Pietersburg 678
Hugo Naudé Art Gallery, Worcester 214
Hugo's River 274
Huguenot Memorial Museum 183
Huguenot Tunnel 274
Huisrivier Pass 361
Human Sciences Research Council (HSRC) 747
Humansdorp 407, 410
Humansdorp Park 411
Humewood, Port Elizabeth 415
Humtata 450
Huns Mountains 954
Hunter's Rest 830
Hunters Road 1014
Hunyani River 996, 998
Hutchinson 290
Hwange 1009, 1017
Hwange National Park 1016

I

Ida's Valley 167
Idutywa 485, 499
iFafa (Fafa) River 517
Ifafa Beach 517
Igoda River 464
Ilanda Wilds Nature Reserve 522
Illovo Beach 522
Imax 37
Imba Huru (the Temple) 1004
Impendle 582
Inanda 531
Inchanga 577
Inchanga Park Mobile Home Estate 577
Independence Avenue, Windhoek 908
Indumeni–Isandlwana MOTH Shellhole Museum 593
Industrigwa 647
Indwe 479
Ingeli Mountains 504
Ingolvane 896
Ingwavuma 556
Ingwelala 804
Inhambane 885, 898–99
Inharrime 898
Inharrime River 898
Inhassoro 903
iNkhongweni River 512
Inner Horn, Drakensberg 609
Inner Tower, Drakensberg 603
Insiswa Forest Reserve 503
Insiswa Mountains 503
Insiza 1013
Institute of Scientific Research of Mozambique 894
Inyaka Island 886, 893
Inyantye River 1017
Inyarapura 1033
Inyoni Rocks 522
Irene 669
Irish House, Pietersburg Museum 678
Irma Stern Museum 57
iron 303
iron forts 679
Iron Mask Hills 997
Isaac Stegmann Nature Reserve 706
Isandlwana Museum 563
Isang Pilane 854
isiHlalo sikaManyosi Mountain 561
isiPhingo River 524
isiPhofaneni Ford 970
Isipingo 523
Isipingo Flats 522
Isipingo Rail 523
Isipingo River 523
Islam Hill 27
Island Holiday Resort 210
Islands Spa 473
Iswepe 765
Itala Game Reserve 596
Itshele Juba Mission hospital 766
Ivory Trail 816
Ivy Beach 514
Ixopo 580
Iziko Museums of Cape Town 43
Izingolweni 499, 505
Izotsha River 512
Izotsha station 507

J

J C Harris Park, Walvis Bay 932
J G Strijdom Museum 673
J L B Smith Institute of Ichthyology 430
J W Pet Dam bird sanctuary 761
Jacaranda Carnival 743
Jackson's Drift 667
Jacobsdal 151, 630
Jagersfontein 622, 628
Jairos Jiri Craft Shop 1009
Jakkalsputz 942
James Hall Museum of Transport 735
Jameson's Drift 563
Jamestown 472
Jammersdrif 660
Jan Christiaan Smuts 200
Jan Kempdorp 310
Jan Marais Nature Reserve 148
Jan Smuts Park, Brakpan 702
Jan Smuts Pass 794
Jan van Riebeeck 41
Jangamo 899
Jansenville 426
Japanese water garden, Durban 528
J C le Roux Wine Estate 157
Jeffreys Bay 413
Jeppe's Reef border post 987
Jeppestown 730
Jericho Dam 761
Jessie Siding 1012
Jewish Museum, Cape Town 47
J G Strijdom tunnel 793
Jim Fouché Holiday Resort 649
Joan St Leger Lindbergh Arts Foundation 88
Joel's Drift 657
Joel's Drift border post 874
Johannesburg 708–40
Johannesburg Art Gallery 734
Johannesburg Botanical Gardens 735
Johannesburg Fort 733
Johannesburg International Airport 739
Johannesburg Public Library 736
Johannesburg Zoological Gardens 735
John Neser Dam 844
Jonathan Zenneck Research Station 918
Jonathan's Gate 616
Jongensgat 383

Jonkershoek 168
Jonkershoek Nature Reserve 169
Jordaan River 645
Jordan Winery 161
Josefdal border post 988
Josephine Mill 60–61
Joubert Park 734
Joubert's Pass 474
Joubertina 450–51
Jozini 555
Judas Peak 52
Judith's Paarl 734
Juggernathi Puri Temple 536
Jukskei River 668, 685
Juliasdale 1027
July Handicap horse-race 527
Jurieshoek 459
Jurisch Park 381
Jutten 120
Juwawa Depot 823
Jwaneng 851

K

Kaaimans River 393, 396
Kaalrug 776
Kaap River 778
Kaap Valley 764
Kaapmuiden 781
Kaapsehoop 771, 778, 780
Kachikau 859
kaDake 981
Kadoma 1015
Kafferkuils River 382
Kafferskraal Dam 764
Kaffir Kop 405
Kaga Mountains 460
Kagga Kamma 211, 254
Kakamas 326
Kalahari Desert 850
Kalahari Gemsbok National Park 331–32, 863
Kalander Kloof 407
Kalk Bay 90–91
Kalkfeld 912, 946
Kalkfontein 863
Kalkfontein Dam 629
Kalkrand 949
Kamanjab 913, 945
Kamativi 1017
Kamberg Nature Reserve 613
Kame River 1010
Kame Ruins 1009
Kamieskroon 260
Kamma River 960

Kammanassie 359, 392
Kampersrus 793, 805
Kang 863
Kanniedood Dam 827
Kanon 385
Kanoneiland 325
Kanye 853, 863
Kanyu 860
Kao 877
karakul sheep industry 951
Karakuwisa Mountain 912
Karasberge 952
Karasburg 952
Karbonkelberg 107
Karee Kloof 769
Kareeboom Route 320
Kareedouw 451
Kareedouw Pass 410
Kareekloof Holiday Resort 667
Kariba border post 1000
Karibib 924
Kariga River 427
Karkloof Fall 587
Karkloof Nature Reserve 587
Karoi 999
Karoo 280
Karoo National Botanic Garden 214
Karoo National Park 282
Karoo Nature Reserve 445
Karoo Poort 316–17
Karoo Sulphur Springs 439
Karridene 522
Kasame 1020
Kasane 851, 859
Kasika 916
Kaspersnek 788
Kassiesbaai Craft Centre 240
Kat River 457
Kat River Dam 459
Kat Valley Express 459
Katazo 560
Katbakkies 254
Katberg 455
Katberg Pass 459
Kathu 303, 305
Katima Mulilo 915
Katlehong Art and Cultural Centre 700
Katutura 909
Kavango River 915
Kayser's Beach 465
Kazeruka (Livingstone) Island 1019
Kazungula 915, 1020
Kazungula border post 857, 859

Kearsney 539
Keate's Drift 585
Keerweder 173
Keetmanshoop 951
Keetmanshoop Museum 951
Kei Mouth 468, 483
Kei River 468, 483
Keimoes 326
Keiskamma 465
Keiskamma River 453
Kelso 519
Kelvin Grove Sports Club 61
Kempton Park 739
Kendal 703, 755
Kenega Drift 619
Kenhardt 323
Kenilworth 78
Kennedy Pan 1016
Kenneth Stainbank Nature Reserve 578
Kensington 270
Kent Park, the Wanderers 735
Kenton-on-Sea 427, 434
Kerkenberg 650
Kersboschdam 122
Kershaw Park 574
Kestell 646
Keurbooms River 406
Keurbooms River Holiday Resort 407
Keurboomstrand 407
Kgalagadi 861
Kgamakgama 861
Kgoseng 853
Khahlamba Range 963
Khai-Appel Nature Reserve 305
esiKhaleni seBuLembu Pass 968
Khape's Village 880
Khatibe Mountain 875
Khaudum Camp 915
Khaudum Game Park 915
Khayelitsha 229
Khglanyoni 647
Khobongaba Point 486
Khomas Hochland 910
Khomasdal, Windhoek 909
Khomati River 968, 985
Khorab Memorial 914
Khorixas 913, 942, 944, 946
Khotso Gift Shop 868
Khubelu Pass 866, 869
Khukhune River 875
Khutse Game Reserve 854
Kidd's Beach 465
Kiepersol 809
Kilburn Dam 651

Killarney 730
Killie Campbell Africana Library and Museum 528
Kilo 20 958
Kilroe Beach 496
Kimberley 294–99
Kimberley Africana Library 298
Kimberley Mine Museum 297
King George VI Art Gallery 416
King William's Town 453–55
King's Beach, Port Elizabeth 415
King's Blockhouse 55
Kings Park rose garden, Bloemfontein 625
Kingsburgh 522
Kingston Frost Park, Brixton 735
Kingsway 994
Kirkman's Camp 807
Kirkwood 421–22
Kirstenbosch 62
Klaas Island 328, 329
Klaserie 793
Klaserie Nature Reserve 804
Klawer 254
Klein Aasvoëlkrans Trail 756
Klein Babylonstoren 186
Klein Constantia 27, 72
Klein Drakenstein Mountains 274
Klein Marico Poort Dam 834
Klein River 448
Klein Sabie Falls 784
Klein Vallei 368
Klein Windhoek 908
Klein-Hangklip 317
Kleinlopje Mine 754
Kleinmond 233
Kleinmond Coastal and Mountain Reserve 233
Kleinplasie Living Open-Air Museum 213
Kleinplasie Reptile World 213
Kleinzee 265, 268
Klerksdorp 843
Klerksdorp Museum 844
Klip River 590, 667
Klipfontein 748
Klipfontein Public Resort Nature Reserve 595
Klipspringer Trail 329
Klipstapel 763
Kloof 577
Kloppersfontein 828
Knersvlakte 257
Knysna Forest 399–402
Knysna Lagoon 399
Knysna River 394

Kobee River 257
Kobonqaba River 486
Kobus Steyn Nature Garden 228
Koeberg Nuclear Power-station 117
Koeëlbaai 231
Koekenaap 259
Koelenhof 164
Koës 951
Koffiebus 482
Koffiefontein 622, 629
Kogmanskloof 224
Koichab Pan 956
Koigab River 945
kokerboom, national monument 951
Kokstad 581
Kolmanskop 956, 958
Kologha Hiking Trail 469
Komani River 470
Komati (Nkhomati) River 763
Komati River 776, 896
Komatipoort 776
Komga 462, 469
Kommetjie 76, 104
Kompasberg 441
Kongola 916
Köningstein 947
Koopmans-de Wet House 48
Koopmansfontein 301, 306
Koopmanskloof 151
Kopfontein border post 852
Koppie Alleen 636
Koppie Nature Reserve 339
Koranna Hiking Trail 658
Koro-Koro Stream 870
Korsman Bird Sanctuary 701
Kosi Bay 549, 558, 895
Kosi Bay Coastal Forest Reserve 558
Kosi Bay Nature Reserve 558
Kosi Bay Nature Reserve Hiking Trail 558
Kosmos 751
Koster 834
Koster Dam 834
Koster River 833
Kotswana River 516
Koue Bokkeveld 132
Kouebokkeveld 209, 247
Kouga 450
Kouga Dam 448
Kouga Mountains 410
Kouga River 447
enKovukeni 558
Kowie (Qoyi) River 432

Kowie Canoe Trail 433
Kowie Nature Reserve 433
Kowyn Pass 787
Kraai River 473, 475
Kraal Kraft 810
Kraalbaai 121
Kragga Kamma 414
Krakadouw 252
kramat 26, 50, 230
Kransbrug 254
Kranshoek 403
Kransies 475
Kranskop 584, 673
Krantzkloof Nature Reserve 577
Kreef Route, see Lobster Route
Kriel 753
Krige 376
Krom River 274, 412
Krombaai 412
Kromellenboog 789
Kromellenboog Dam 835
Kronendal 107
Kroonpark Resort 640
Kroonstad 640
Kruger Bridge 768
Kruger Dam 756
Kruger National Park 801, 805, 811–28
Kruger's Nose 799
Kruger's Park (the Wanderers) 735
Krugerhof 771
Krugersdorp 704
Krugersdorp Game Reserve 705, 829
Kruis River 404
Kruisrivier 357
Kubutsa 990
Kudiakam Pan 861
Kuilsrivier 273
Kuiseb Canyon Camp 937
Kuiseb River 928, 929, 933
Kunene River 915, 922, 941
Kuruman 301
Kuruman River 336
Kwaaihoek 426
kwaBhaca 503
kwaBulawayo, Zululand 560, 561
kwaDukuza 538
Kwaggapan Reserve 831
Kwaggasnek 598
kwaMashu 531, 535
kwaMatiwane Memorial 561
kwaMbonambi 547
kwaMfazo Gaya Mabele peak, Drakensberg 612
Kwamo River 1019

Kwando River 916
KwaNdosi 523
kwaNkosinkhulu 561
kwaNogqaza (Howick) Falls 585
KwaNongoma 553
KwaZulu 544
KwaZulu-Natal, North Coast 524
KwaZulu-Natal, South Coast 504
Kwekwe 1014
Kwekwe River 1014
Kwelera River 467
Kwetche 916
KWV 190
KWV Brandy Cellar 213
Kyalami Country Club 738
Kyalami motor-racing track 738

L

L'Avenir 165
L'Ormarins 151, 182
La Bonne Esperanza 202
La Mercy beach 540
La Motte 151, 182
La Rochelle 739
Laaiplek 127
Laborie 190
Ladismith 362
Lady Grey 472, 474
Ladybrand 659
Ladysmith 590
Laing's Nek Pass 598, 767
Laingsburg 279
Lake Alexander Dam 1026
Lake Arthur 439
Lake Chivero 996
Lake Chivero Dam 1015
Lake Chrissie 761
Lake Darlington 422
Lake Eteza Nature Reserve 548
Lake Fundudzi 683
Lake Guinas 918
Lake Hlangwe 558
Lake Kariba 999, 1000, 1017
Lake Merthley 583
Lake Mutirikwi 1005, 1034
Lake Ngami 849, 861, 862
Lake oKhunwine 558
Lake oTjikoto 918
Lake Pleasant (Groenvlei) 397
Lake Poelela 898
Lake Sibaya 555–56
Lake St Lucia 548
Lake uKhalwe 558
Lakenvlei 211

Lakeside 80
Lambert's Bay 128–29
Lamont-Hussey Observatory 625
Lancer's Gap 878
Land of Waveren 204
Landdroskop 368
Landskroon 191
Lane Island, Lake St Lucia 548
Langa 366
Langebaan 119, 121, 125
Langebaan Lagoon 120
Langeberge 307, 340
eLangeni 964
Langkloofberg 368
Langleg 299
Langrietvlei 122
Langtou River 382
Langvlei, Wilderness 396
Lanzerac 170–72
Larvon Bird Gardens 996
Latter Rain Mission 702
Lavumisa 991
Lavumisa border post 990–91
Lawley 848
Lawrence de Lange Nature Reserve 470
Le Bonheur 151, 186
Le Rhône 180
Leandra 760
Lebenstraum 215
Leeu-Gamka 281
Leeuwdoringstad 843
Leeuwdoringstad Museum 843
Leeuwspruit Hiking Trail 642
Lefika ka Raboshabane (Rock of Raboshabane) 871
Lehana's Pass 881
Lehr Falls 506
Leibbrandt Kloof 655–56
Leisure Island 402
Lekhalo la Borwa Pass 873
Lekkersing 264
Leliefontein 260
Leliehoek Pleasure Resort 659
Lendlovu 418
Leribe Heights 876
Leribe Mission 876
Lesapi River 1021
Lesotho 864–88
Lesotho 4 × 4 trails 872, 874–75
Lesotho Gun War 866
Letaba Camp 822, 826
Letaba Ranch Game Reserve 801
Letaba River 795, 797, 813
Letaba valley 795, 797, 799
Letlhakane 851, 858

Letlhakeng 854
Letseng la Terae diamond-fields 875
Letsitele River 794
Levi's Nek 876
Leydsdorp 793, 802
Libanon 848
Libertas 149
Libertas (Mahlambandlovu) 744
Libode 492, 502
Libono police post 875
Lichtenburg 784, 836
Lichtenburg Museum 837
Liesbeek River 15–16, 18
Lievland 166
Lifateng 879
Likalaneng River 873
Likalaneng Trading Station 873
Limberlost 159
Limpopo River 683, 897, 1003
Lindana Memorial 825
Lindela 899
Lindley 655
Linga-Linga 900
Linyanti (Chobe) River 851, 859, 916
Lion Cavern 981
Lion Park, Harare 996
Lion's Head, Cape Town 1, 50
Lion's Head, Zimbabwe 998
Lion's River 588
Lions Den 999
Liphiring River 872
Liphofung Caves 875
Lisbon Falls 786
Lister's Point 548
Little Amanzimtoti River 522
Little Berg River 16, 205
Little Berg, Drakensberg 608
Little Bess steam train 424
Little Billy 513
Little Brak River 388
Little Caledon River 656, 869
Little Connemara 1029
Little Gariep River 874
Little Karoo 340–47
Little Olifants River, Mpumalanga 756, 758
Little Pella 330
Little Saddle, Drakensberg 609
Little Vet River 633
Llandaft Oratory 648
Llandudno 109
Lobamba 979, 983
Lobatse 851–52, 863
Lobster Route 113

Local History Museum, Durban 527
Loch Athlone Holiday Resort 645, 656
Loch Comb 1029
Loch Con 1029
Loch Maree 332, 1029
Loch Vaal 642, 666
Lochiel 761
Lodge de Goede Hoop 47
Loerie 449
Loeriesfontein 322
Loftus Versveld rugby stadium 747
Lokulu River 1018
Lomahasha border post 977, 985
Lombard's Kop 591
Londolozi Game Lodge 807
Lone Creek Falls 784
Lone Tree's Hill 780
Long Island Resort, Parys 641
Long Kloof 132, 391–92, 410, 450
Long Tom Forest Station 783
Long Tom Monument 797
Long Tom Pass 782
Longhill Nature Reserve 470
Longlands 300
Longmere Dam 809
Lookout, the 422
Lootsberg 441
Lorelei 202
Lorraine 459
Lositha 983
Loskop Dam 673, 756
Loteni Nature Reserve 614
Loteni Settlers Museum 614
Lothair 761
Louis Leipoldt 250
Louis Trichardt 679
Louis Trichardt Memorial 825
Louis Trichardt Memorial Garden 892
Louisvale 155
Lourens River 369
Lourenzo Marques (Maputo) 777
Louterwater 450
Louw's Creek 781
Louwsberg 596
Louwshoek 215
Lovers Rock Pleasure Resort 830
Lovu River 580
Lower Blinkwater 459
Lower Sabie Camp 822, 824
Lowveld 795
Lowveld Botanical Garden 774
Loxton 318
Lubombo Mountains 553, 963

Lucas Meyer House Museum 595
Luchaba Nature Reserve 501
Luckhoff 289, 630
Lüderitz 956–59
Lüderitz Museum 957
eLudzidzini 965
Lugogo Mountain 981
Lugogodo 809
Luhlaza Ridge 570
Lukazi River 1017
Lule Kop 803
Lulu Ridge 790
Lumbago Alley, Sterkfontein Caves 706
Lundeans Nek 474, 477–78
Lundy's Hill 582
Lupala Island, Caprivi 916
Lusikisiki 495
Luthing Mountain 879
Lutlamorong Village 314
Lutubeni Mission 490
Lutzputs 326, 331
Lutzville 258
Luve 989
Luvuvhu River 813, 827
Lwambasi 496
Lwambayi River 1018
Lwandile 492
Lydenburg 756, 791
Lydenburg Heads 792
Lykso 303
Lynville 755
Lyttelton 669

M

Maack Cave 948
Maartenshoek 478
Maasdorp 459
Mababe depression 859
maBandebande Hills 964
Mabibi Coastal Camp 558
Mabopane 741
Mabwasehube Game Reserve 863
Macassar 366
Macassar Beach 229
Machache Mountain 872
Machadodorp 759, 764, 770
Machavie 784
Macia 896
Mackay's Kop 479
Maclear 471, 476
Maclear's Beacon 62
Mac-Mac Pools 785
Macovane 903

Macrorie House, Pietermaritzburg 573
Madendere 898
Madragoa Village 892
Madressa Himayatil Islam Mosque 733
Mafeteng 869, 879
Mafikeng 313
Magalies River 751
Magaliesberg Mountains 741, 829
Magaliesburg 829
Magersfontein 298
Magnesite 776
Magoebaskloof 795
Magoebaskloof Pass 796
Magudu 558
Maguga Dam 986
Magusheni 498
Magwa 484
Magwa Falls 495
Magwikhwe sand ridge 860
Mahalapye 855
Mahamba border post 766, 990
Mahamba Hills 966
Mahango Game Reserve 916
Mahatma Karamchand Gandhi 531
Mahawane Dam 767
Mahera's Kloof 790
Mahlabathini 562
Mahlambandlovu (Libertas) 744
Mahlangeni, Kruger National Park 826
Maidstone 534
Main Camp 1016
Main Camp Pan 1016
Main Cave Museum 613
Main Falls, Victoria Falls 1018
Maitland, Cape Town 271
Maitland, Port Elizabeth 417
Maize Triangle of South Africa 635, 639, 653
Majola 484
Majuba Mountain 598, 767
Makalamobedi 861
Makapansgat 676
Makgadikgadi Basin 849, 859
Makgadikgadi Pans 860
Makhakhe (Emmaus Mission) 879
Makhalaneng River 871
Makhaleng 872
Makhaleng River 872, 873, 879
Makhane's Drift 557
Makheka's Pass 872
Makhollo 478
Makonjwa range 968
Makou Dam 305

Makuti 999, 1000
Makwassie 841
Malamala Game Resort 807
Malay Quarter (Bo-Kaap) 43
Malealea 879
Malehlakana Stream 870
Malelane 776
Malelane Entrance Gate 823
Maletsunyane Falls 871
Maletsunyane River 872
Malgas 120, 379
Malibali Pan 554
Malibamatso River 875
Malkerns 983, 989
Malkerns Research Station 989
Malmesbury 242
Malmesbury Museum 242
Malolotja Nature Reserve 981, 986
Maloma 990
Maloney's Eye trout hatchery 829
Malongane Resort 895
Maltahöhe 939–41
Maltese Cross 253
Maluti Mountains 865, 872
Malvana 896
Mamabula 851
Mamathes 878
Mamathwane 305
Mambone 903
Mamelodi 747
Mamilli National Park 916
Mamre 117–18
Mamusa Hill 838
Man, Woman and Child 862
Mana Pools Game Reserve 1000
Manaba Beach 512
Mananga border post 985
Mandini 544
Mandlakaze 897
Manenberg 366
manganese 303
Mangwe Pass 1012
Manhica 896
Manjoro 1030
Mankayane 983, 989
Mankelekele 772
Manteku 494
Mantenga Crafts 982
Mantenga Falls 981
Mantsonyane River 872, 874
Manyame 314
Manyeleti Game Reserve 805
Manzamnyama Stream 570
Manzini 984, 989–90
Manzini (Bremersdorp) 971
Manziture reef 902

Mapelane 547
Mapeshoane 870
Maphumulo Mission station 534
Maphutseng 880
Maphutseng River 880
Maphuzi River 491
Mapinhane 900
Mapoch's Village 672
Mapoteng 877–78
Mapungubwe 682
Maputa 558
Maputa River 886
Maputaland 555
Maputo City Hall 891
Maputo Elephant Reserve 894
Maputoland Marine Reserve 558
Mara 450, 775
Marble Hall 757
Marchand 327
Marcus 120
Mare Dam 1028
Margaret Roberts Herbal Centre 832
Margaruque Island (Santa Isabel) 901
Margate 512
Margate air show 513
Maria Moroka National Park 631
Marianhill Monastery 578
Marico Bushveld Dam 835
Marico Bushveld Nature Reserve 835
Marico River 834
Mariental 941, 950
Mariepskop 787
Marina Beach 514
Marindidzimu 1010
Marine Biological Research Station 894
Mariner's Wharf 107
Maritime Museum, Mossel Bay 387
Maritsane 313
Maritz's Forest 784
Marloth Nature Reserve 378
Maroela Nature Resort 673
Marondera 1021
Marrakwene 896
Marriamen Temple 573
Martello Tower 96
Martha and Mary hills, Tarkastad 471
Martin Melck House 48
Martin's Falls 1036
Marula 1012
Marvol Museum 163

Mary Moffat Museum 307
Marydale 338
Maryland Mission 876
Maselspoort 625, 630
Masemouse 880
Maseru 659, 868–69, 874, 878
kwaMashu 531, 535
Mashu Museum of Ethnology 528
Masimiki Rocks 1027
Masitise Mission 880
Masorini Hill 826
Massangena 903
Massinga 900
Masvingo (Fort Victoria) 750, 1002, 1005, 1011
Masvingo Museum 1002
Mataffin 773
Mata-Mata 334–35
Matatiele 617, 884
Mateku Falls 495
Matelile Pass 879
Materies Kop 618
kwaMatiwane Memorial 561
Matjiesfontein 277
Matobo Agricultural Research Station 1010
Matobo Dam 1010
Matobo Hills 1009
Matobo National Park 1010
Matola River 885
Matroosberg 219, 275
Matsamo border post 987
Matshete 682
Matsieng 879
Mauanza 900
Mauchsberg 782
Maun 851, 860–61
Mavuradonha Mountains 997
maXesibeni 503
Maxixe 900
Mayfair 717
Maynardville 78
Mayville 579
Mazenod 879
Mazeppa Bay 488
Mazowe Dam 997
Mazowe River 997
Mbabane 980
Mbabane Stream 971, 981
Mbabati River 804, 826
Mbalabala 1011
Mbango River 512
Mbashe River 483
Mbazwana 554
eMbekelweni 968
Mbilo River 579

Mbizana River 513
kwaMbonambi 547
Mbongo Hill 490
Mbotyi 495
Mbukushu Village 862
Mbuluzi Bridge 985
Mbuluzi River 970, 985, 989
eMbumbulu 534
McDougall's Bay 266
McGregor 222
McGregor Museum 298
McIlwaine National Park 996, 1015
McKommenshoek 459
Mdantsane 462
Mdloti River 534
Mdumbi River 492
Mdzimba Mountains 982
Medical Research Council (MRC) 747
Medingen Mission 799
Medunsa 747
Medwood Gardens, Durban 528
Meerendal 151
Meerlust 151, 159
Meeu Island 121
Meeurots 119
Meikles Mount 988
Meintjeskop 742
Meirings Poort 351, 358
Meiringskloof Nature Reserve 657
Mekaling River 880
Melkbosstrand 117
Melkhoutfontein 383
Melmoth 560
Melrose House 720, 746
Melsetter 1035
Melton Wold 319
Melville Koppies 735
Melville Port 894
Memel 597, 648
Memuno border post 863
Menlo Park 754
Meredale Pleasure Resort 668
Mermaid's Pool 998
Mesitsaneng Pass 880
Mesklip 260
Messina 681
Meulspruit Dam 658
Meyers Bridge 756
Meyerton 667
uMezi weZinto River 519
kwaMfazo Gaya Mabele peak, Drakensberg 612
Mfolozi River 547
Mfolozi Village 547

uMgungundlovu 561
Mhangura 999
Mhanyami Hills 998
Mhanyami River 1015
Mhlambanyatsi 988
uMhlanga River 539
Mhlangamkulu River 514
Mhlangeni River 512
Mhlatuze River 545, 560
Mhlondosi Valley 761
Mhlonhlo River 608
Mhlosheni Hills 964
Mhlume 985
Mhlumeni border post 984
Mhlungwa 517
Mhlungwane trading store 595
Mica 804
Michaelis Collection, Old Town House 47
Michaelis Collection, Pretoria Art Museum 746
Michell's Pass 209, 211
Middelberg 253
Middelburg 440, 756
Middelburg Museum 756
Middeldrift 455
Middelvlei 151, 155
Middledale Pass 650
Middleton 436
Midmar Dam 588
Midmar Dam hiking trails 588
Midmar Public Resort Nature Reserve 588
Midrand 668
Migdol 838
Mike's Pass 608
Mikotjomelo Mountain 881
military camp, Potchefstroom 846
Military Museum, Bloemfontein 625
Milk Bay 230
Miller's Point 98
Millwood 394
Milner Hall, Sterkfontein Caves 706
Milner Park 734, 736
Milnerton 115, 270
Miner's House Museum, Pilgrim's Rest 785
Misgund 450
Mitchell Park, Durban 528
Mitre, the, Drakensberg 605
Mkambati Nature Reserve 495
Mkhaya Game Reserve 990
Mkhomazi River 521
Mkhondo River 990

mKhosini Trail, Opathe Game Reserve 562
Mkomazana River 600
Mkondeni 575
Mkondo River 766
Mkuze 553
Mkuze Game Reserve 554
Mkuze hiking trails 554
Mlambonja River 605
Mlawula Nature Reserve 985
Mlazi River 523
Mlembu Mountain 963
Mlengana 502
Mlibizi 1017
Mlilwane Wildlife Sanctuary 982
Mlokojwa 990
mLumati River 968, 987
mLumati Stream 965
Mmâbatho 313
Mngababa River 521
Mngazi River 492
Mngazi Valley 502
Mngeni River 531
Mntafufu River 494
Mnweni (The Rockeries) 605
Mobeni 523
Mochudi 854
Mochudi Museum 855
Modder River 631, 635
Modderpoort 659
Modderpoort Cave church 659
Modimolle 790
Mofoka's Village 870
Mogalo 881
Mohalakwena 675
Mohale's Hoek 880
Mohlaka-oa-Tuka Stream 872
Mohlapitse Stream 794
Mohokare River 864, 875, 878
Mohomeng Cave 871
Mokhotlong 875
Mokuti Lodge 919
Molapong valley 788
Moldenhauer's Hill 485
Molenaars River 274
Molepolole 853
Molimo Nthuse Pass 873
Molopo River 836
Molteno 471, 480
Molteno Pass 319
Mon Don 225
Monk's Cowl, Drakensberg 611
Monkey Rope, Cango Caves 353
Monkey Valley 106
Monontsha 652
Mont Blois 151

Montagu 364
Montagu Museum 364
Montagu Pass 391
Mont-Aux-Sources 602
Monte Inyaka 893
Montrose Falls 771
Monzi 548
Moodies Pass 1034
Mooi River 476, 588, 845, 847
Mooi River Dam 846
Mooiplaas Camp 827
Mooi River 4 × 4 trail 588
Mooivallei Hiking Trail 228
Moor Park Nature Reserve 589
Moorddrif 675
Moordenaars River 451
Moordenaarskop 368, 483
Moordlaagte 405
Moorreesburg 243
Mopeli Trading Station 884
Moremi Wildlife Reserve 860
Moretele Park 749
Morewood Memorial Garden 533
Morgan Bay 468, 483
Morgenhof 165
Morgenzon Forestry Reserve 786
Morija 879
Morija Mission station 866
Morone Mountain 790
Morongora 999, 1000
Morupule 851
Morwa rural centre 854
Mosaweng 851
Mosega River 835
Mosego 790
Moshesh's Ford 478
Mossel Bay 386–87
Mostert's Hoek Twins 274
Mostert's Mill 54
Moteng Pass 875
Motlasedi River 804
Motlepu's Village 871
Motopi 861
Motshane 981
Motswari Game Lodge 804
Mouille Point 2, 34, 111–12
Mount Anderson 782
Mount Ayliff 503
Mount Brukkeros 950
Mount Coke 464
Mount Currie Nature Reserve 582
Mount Darwin 997, 1004
Mount Edgecombe 534
Mount Fletcher 619
Mount Frere 503
Mount Hampden 998

Mount Memory 610
Mount Pleasant 417
Mount Selinda 1033
Mount Sullivan 493
Mount Thesiger 493
Mountain Club of South Africa 49
Mountain Hiking Trail 236
mountain road of Lesotho 872
Mountain Sanctuary Park 832
Mountain Zebra National Park 439
Mountain Zebra Trail 440
Mowbray 56
Möwe Bay 944
Moyeni (Quthing) 881
Mozambique 4, 885–904
Mozambique–Agulhas Current 2, 11, 81, 82, 99, 114, 529
Mpako 491
Mpambinyoni River 520
Mpame 490
Mpanda Mutenga 1018
Mpanda Mutenga border post 857, 858
Mpande Beach 492
Mpenjati River 514
Mpharane Mountain 657
Mphoeings 1012
Mponjwana Ridge 605
Mpozolo Trading Station 490
Mpudzi River 1032
Mpumalanga 753–94
Mputi River 499
Mqanduli 490, 500
Msasa 996
Msauli River 764
Msauli Valley 764
Mshangashi River 1005
Msikaba River 495
Msimbazi River 522
Msinga Pan 554
Msunduze Canoe Marathon 574
Msunduze River 547, 554
Mtakatye River 492
Mtamvuna River 483, 515
Mtata River Mouth Resort 483, 502
Mtentu Cuttings 500
Mthatha River 492
Mthonjaneni Monument 560
Mthosheni 990
Mtimani Forest 989
Mtseritseri Pool 1036
Mtubatuba 547
Mtunzini 447, 544–45
Mtwalume 517
Mubvumodzi River 1036

Muckleneuk 528
Mucoque 901
Mucusso National Park 916
Muden 585
Muizenberg 80–83, 87–90
Muizenberg Cave 91
Muketsi 800
Mukurob (the finger of God) 951
Mukuvisi Woodlands Game Park 996
Muldersdrift Hill 705
Muldersvlei 166
Muller's Pass 597
Mumvumi River 1002
Mumvuri River 1015
Munster 514
Munyanyadzi Stream 1033
Munyengedzi River 682
Munywaneni 552
Murahwa's Hill 1022
Muratie 165
Murchison Range 793, 802
Murehwa 998
Murosi's Mountain 881, 883
Murray Park Pleasure Resort, Springs 703
Murraysburg 284
Musapas Pass 1034
Museu de Geologia 893
Museu de Historia Natural 892
Museum Africa 736
Museum of Man 788
Museum of Man and Science, Houghton 737
Museum of Science and Technology, Pretoria 746
museum, Suikerbosrand Nature Reserve 769
Mushroom, the, Cango Caves 353
Mushroom Rock, Drakensberg 608
Mutarazi Falls 1027
Mutare 997, 1022
Mutare Heights 1022
Mutare Museum 1023
Mutirikwi National Park 1006, 1034
Mutirikwi River 1002, 1005
Mutoko 997, 998
Mutorashanga 998
Mutyisambizi River 994
Muzi Swamp 557
Muzvezve River 1014
Mvoti River 538
Mvukwe Range 998
Mvuma 1001
Mvumvumvu River 1033, 1034

Mwami 999
Myrtle Rigg Church Museum 227
Mzamba craft market 515
Mzamba fossil beds 499
Mzanzene picnic site 825
Mzilikazi Art and Craft Centre 1009
Mzimayi River 517
Mzimhlava River 503, 581
Mzimkulu River 505, 511
Mzimkulwana River 505
Mzimvubu River 493
Mzingwani River 1012
Mzumbe River 516

N

Nababeep 263
Naboomspruit 674
Nagle Dam 576
Nahoon 464, 466
Nakop border post 953
Nalatale Ruins 1013
Namaacha 985
Namahadi River 603
Namaqua 4 × 4 route 331
Namaqualand 255–58
Namaqualand National Park 260
Namib Desert 114, 932–37
Namib Desert Research Station 934
Namib Rand Nature Reserve 939
Namibia 905–62
Namibia State Museum 908
Namibian Fish Institute 950
Namib–Naukluft Park 4 × 4 trail 937
Namib–Naukluft Park 938–39, 941
Namutoni Camp, Etosha 920
Namutoni Museum 920
Nancefield 848
Nantwich Camp 1016
Napier 241
Nata River 859
Natal Battlefields Route 595
Natal Lion and Game Park 575
Natal Museum, Pietermaritzburg 573
Natal North Coast Museum, Stanger 539
Natal Sharks Board 540
Natal Spa 596
Natale Labia Museum 90
National Afrikaans Literature Museum, Bloemfontein 626

National Archives, Harare 994
National Bisley Championships 627
National Botanic Gardens, Zimbabwe 996
National Cultural History Museum, Pretoria 745
National English Literary Museum 429
National Gallery, Cape Town 19
National Gallery, Zimbabwe 995
National Library of South Africa 19, 45, 747
National Museum of Gold-Mining, Kwekwe 1014
National Museum, Bloemfontein 625
National Museum, Bulawayo 1005, 1009
National Museum, Gaborone 852
National Pharmacy Museum 737
National Potato Festival 760
National Stadium 983
National West Coast Recreational Area 941
National Women's War Memorial 626
National Zoological Gardens of South Africa breeding centre 675
National Zoological Gardens of South Africa, Pretoria 744
Natural History Museum, Durban 527
Natural Sciences and History Museums, Grahamstown 429
Nature's Valley 407–8
Naudes Nek Pass 477
Naudesberg Pass 443
Naukluft Mountains 4 × 4 trail 941
Naval Hill, Bloemfontein 622
Nazareth Mission church, Bethlehem 645
Ncandu River Waterfall 597
Ncema Dam 1011
Ncera 465
Ncizele 488
Ncwanguba 490
Ndebele people 741
Ndebele Traditional Village 755
Ndebele Village, near Tsaing 671
Ndidima Dome, Drakensberg 609
Ndlovu Camp 985
Ndlozi peninsula 548
Ndlumudlumu Hills 764

Ndluzulu 492
Nduli Nature Reserve 501
Ndumeni River 608
Ndumo Game Reserve 557
Ndumo Trading Station 556
Nduzikontaba 478
Ndwe River 479
Ndwedwe 534, 536
Nederburg 149, 192
Neethlingshof 160
Neharare Hill 994
Nelson Beach (Praia Marungula) 900
Nelson Mandela 40
Nelspoort 283–84
Nelspruit 773
Nenga River 491
Nerston border post 765, 989
Neu-Barmen 911
New Bunting 492
New England 474
New Germany 578
New Guelderland 539
New Hanover 583
New Year Peak 368
Newcastle 597
Newington 807
Newlands 58
Newlands rugby ground 61
Newmarket horse-race course 769
Ngabeni Mission 989
Ngakana's Pass 872
Ngala Lodge 804
Ngamiland 861
Ngamo Pan 1016
Ngarawi River 1030
Ngezi National Park 1014
Ngezi River 1014
Ngodwane 771, 778
Ngoma Bridge 916
Ngoya 765
Ngoya Forest 545
Ngqeleni 492, 502
Ngwangwane River 617
Ngwashli Pan 1016
Ngwavuma River 991
Ngwempisi River 765
Ngweni 553
Ngwenya border post 981
Ngwenya Hills 968, 971
Ngwenya Mountains 981
Ngwenyana River 778
Ngxakaxa Stream 499
Nhachengue 900
Nhamavila 898
Nhlangano 990

Nhlazatshe Mountain 561
Niekerkshoop 307
Nietverdiend 835
Nietvoorbij 165
Nieu Bethesda 441–42
Nieuwoudt Pass 253
Nieuwoudtville 321
Nieuwoudtville Falls 321
Nieuwoudtville Wild Flower
  Reserve 321
Njambili River 516
Njesuthi Peak, Drakensberg 612
Njesuthi River 612
Nkaba 986
Nkandla 560, 563
Nkasa Island, Caprivi 916
Nkesi's Pass 871
Nkhangala area 963
Nkhomati River 885
Nkhomba River 518
Nkhombana River 518
Nkomati River 753
iNkhongweni River 512
Nkonjane 984
kwaNkosinkhulu 561
Nkwalini 560
No 7 Castle Hill Museum 416
Noah's Ark 476
Noenieput 331
Noetzie River 405
Nogatsau campsite 859
kwaNogqaza (Howick) Falls 585
Nokaneng 862
Nolangeni Mountain 503, 504
Nomlengana 478
Nongoma 553
Nonoti River 539
Nooitgedacht 299, 755
Nooitgedacht Research Station 761
Noordhoek 79, 104–5
Noordkaap 781
Noordoewer 953
Noorskloof Nature Reserve 413
Noorspoort Pass 425
Norah valley 1021
Normandien Pass 596
North End Lake, Port Elizabeth
  416
North Sands Head 515
Northcliff 731
Northern Cape 299
Northern Natal Battlefields Route
  597
Northern Province 665, 829
North-West Province 829
Norton 1015

Norvalspont 288
Nossa Senhora da Conceicáo 891
Nossob River 332, 333, 863, 910
Nossob valley 335
Nottingham Road 588
Noupoort 441, 655
Nourivier 260
Nqabara River 490
Nqadu 489
Nqwasi River 487
Nsoko 991
Nswatugi Cave 1011
Ntaba yesinDuna Hill 1013
Ntabamhlope 612
Ntabamhlope Mountain 612
Ntlo Kholo cave houses 869
Ntshabohloko River 747
Ntshala River 468
Ntshangwe Ridge 576
Ntsiri Nature Reserve 804
Ntwetwe Pan 849, 859, 861
Nubib Mountains 939
Nubib Nature Camp 940
Numbi Gate, Kruger National Park
  809, 823
Nuwejaars River 436
Nuwerus 259
Nuweveld Mountain 281, 283
Nuy 220
Nwamuriwa Hill 825
Nwandedzi Camp 822
Nwanezi area 1003
Nxai Pan 860
Nxaxo Mouth 487
Nxaxo River 487
Nxhabe River 862
Nxu River 476
Nyachowa Falls 1024
Nyahokwe Mountain 1030
Nyakasanga River 1000
Nyakasuba Village 872
Nyalazi Siding 553
Nyamandlovu Pan 1016
Nyamaropa 1030
Nyanga 366, 1022, 1027–28
Nyanga Downs 1029
Nyanga National Park 1028
Nyangani Mountain 1027
Nyangombe Falls 1028
Nyangwe Hill 1028
Nyankuni Dam 1011
Nyanyadzi 1033
Nyati River 1014
Nylstroom 673
Nylsvley Nature Reserve 675
Nyonyane Mountain 982

Nzama 990
Nzhelele valley 680

O

O'Neill's Cottage 598
Oaks Falls 375
Oberholzer 848
Observatory 56
Observatory Museum 429
Ocean View 104
Ocean View Game Park 559
Odendaalsrus 638
Odzani River 1026
Odzani Waterfall 1026
Odzi River 1022, 1027, 1033
Ofcolaco 794
Ogies 703
Ohlange Institute 531
Ohlsson's Cape Breweries 61
Ohrigstad 789
Ohrigstad Dam 792
Ohwakeni 495
oKahandja 911
oKakarara 912
Okaukuejo Camp, Etosha National
  Park 920
Okavango Delta 849
Okavango Fishing Lodge 862
Okavango River 849
Okavango swamps 861
Okiep 263
Old Bunting 492
Old Fort, Durban 528
Old House Museum, Durban 527
Old North Coast Road 531
Old Presidency, Bloemfontein 625
Old Residence, the 444
Old Town House, Cape Town 47
Old Umtali 1022
Olifants Camp 822, 826
Olifants River 245, 249, 256, 347,
  789, 825
Olifants River Dam 249
Olifantsgeraamte 782
Olifantshoek 336
Olifantskop Pass 436
Olifantsnek Dam 830
Olifantsrivierberge 203
Olijvenhoutsdrift Mission 323
Oliviershoek 652
Oliviershoek Pass 602, 649
Omaramba Holiday Resort 832
Omaruru 942, 946
Omaruru River 928, 942

Omitara 910
oNdangwa 922
oNdekaremba, Windhoek 909
Onderstepoort Veterinary Institute (OVI) 747
Ondjora 914
One Man's Pass 647
Onrus 233
Onseepkans 329
Ontmoeting 336
Oom Samie se Winkel 147
Oorlogskloof 321, 953
Op de Berg 247, 254
Op de Tradouw Pass 364
Opathe Game Reserve 562
Opathe Game Reserve 4 × 4 trail 562
Opuwo 923
Orange River, see Gariep River
Orange River Wine Cellars Co-operative 324
Orania 293
Oranjemund 961
Oranjeville Resort 643
Oranjezicht Trail 339
Orapa 851, 858
Organ Pipes, Namibia 945
Organ Pipes, Drakensberg 609
Oribi Flats 505–6
Oribi Gorge Nature Reserve 505
Orient Hills 829
Orkney 639, 844
Orpen Camp 822
Orpen Gate 805, 825, 826
oShakati 922
oShikango 922
Oshoek border post 762, 981
ostrich farming 344–45
Otavi 914
Otavi Mountains 914
Otjiguinas sink-hole 919
oTjikango 911
Otjimbingwe 924
Otjiwarongo 913
Otjozondjuba 912
Otobotii 556
Ottawa 535
Otter Trail 408
Otto Beit Bridge 1000
Otto du Plessis Pass 475
Ottosdal 841
Ottoshoop 836
Ou Kaapse Weg 79
Oude Drostdy Museum, Tulbagh 204
Oude Libertas Amphitheatre 150

Oude Pastorie Museum, Paarl 187
Oudeberg (Step) Pass 650
Oudekraal 27
Oudorp Hiking Trail, Klerksdorp 844
Oudstryders Memorial, Windhoek 908
Oudtshoorn 347–51
Our Heritage Museum 460
Ouro Point (Ponto do Ouro) 894
Ouss 260
Outeniqua Choo-Tjoe 396
Outeniqua Hiking Trail 404
Outeniqua Mountains 387, 390–91
Outeniqua Pass 359, 391
Outer Horn, Drakensberg 609
Outjo 913
Overhex 220
Owl House 442–43
Oxbow 875
Oxford Street, East London 463
Oyster Bay 411

P

P A M Brink Stadium 703
P R Owen Hall, Sudwala Caves 773
Paarden Eiland 115
Paarden Island 37
Paarl 187–92
Paarl Arboretum 190
Paarl Rock Brandy Cellar 191
Pacaltsdorp 390
Pack Ox Nek 619
Pack Saddle Hill 869
Paddagang 204
Paddock 505
Pafuri border post 828
Pafuri Camp 816
Pafuri River 813
Pageview 733
Pakhuis Pass 250, 321
Palace of Justice, Pretoria 742
Palapye 852, 855
Palm Beach 514
Palmeira 896
Palmiet Reserve, Westville 579
Palmiet River 233
Pan 784
Panbult 765
Panmure 463
Paradise Beach bird sanctuary 412
Paradise Island (Santa Carolina) 901

Paradise Valley Nature Reserve 579
Park Rynie 519
Parkview 735
Parkwood 735
Parliament Museum, Swaziland 983
Parow 270, 272
Parys 641
Patensie 416, 448
Paternoster 126
Paterson 436
Paul Budenstein Park 831
Paul Kruger 711, 742
Paul Kruger Gate 808, 825
Paul Kruger's house, Pretoria 745
Paul Roux 645
Paul Sauer Bridge 409
Paula's Cave 947
Paulpietersburg 596
Paulsberg 52
peaches 132, 326–27
pear 133
Pearly Beach 237
Pearson Park Holiday Resort 426
Pearston 438
Peddie 453
Pedestal Point 956
Pedlar's Peak 880
Peers Cave 93
Pelindaba 752
Pella 330
Pellissier House Museum 620
Penguin Islet 956
Penhalonga 1022, 1026
Penhoek Pass 471
Penicuik Siding 547
Pennington 518
Penny Ferry 35
Percy Fyfe Nature Reserve 676
Perdeberg 317
Perdeberg War Museum 632
Perdekop 767
Perola do Indico 901
Perseverance, Port Elizabeth 425
Petrus Steyn 655
Petrusburg 632
Petrusville 289
Pfuru Mountain 997, 1004
ekuPhakameni 532
Phalaborwa 801, 803
esiPhamanini 892
Phantom Pass 394
Philipp Cave 925
Philippolis 621
Philipstown 289

isiPhingo River 524
Phiphidi Waterfall 683
isiPhofaneni Ford 970
Phokeng 833
Phongolo Bush Nature Reserve 596
Phongolo River 766, 964
Phophonyane Nature Reserve 987
Phophonyane River 987
Phutadikobo 855
Phuthaditjhaba 652
Phuthiatsana River 869, 870
Pic sans Nom 368
Piekeniers Kloof Pass 244
Pienaars (Moretele) River 748, 754
Pienaarskloof 276
Pienaarsrivier 671
Pierneef Museum, Pretoria 746
Piet Retief 765
Piet Retief Mineral Baths 766
Pietermaritzburg 572–76
Pietersburg 677
Piggs Peak 776, 963, 985, 987
Piketberg 132, 243
Piketberg Museum 243
Pilanesberg 833
Pilgrim's Rest 785
Pilgrim's River 785
Pillars, the 475
Pine Creek Holiday Resort 388
Pine Forest Resort 210
pineapple 431
Pinelands 33, 366
Pinetown 578
Pineview 408
Pinnacle 786
Pioneer Gate border post 853
Pioneer Open-Air Museum, Silverton 746
Pioneer Reef 778
Pioneer Trail 780
Pioneers' Park, La Rochelle 735
Pioneers Park, Springs 703
Pioniers Park, Windhoek 909
Pirie Trout Hatcheries 461
Pitsane 853
Pitseng 876
Plaatkop 472
Plaisir de Merle 186
Planetarium, Johannesburg 737
Plaston 809
Platberg 646, 659
Platberg Nature Reserve 647
Platbos indigenous forest 408
Platteklip Gorge 3

Plessislaer 582
Plettenberg Bay 404, 406
plum 132
Plumtree 1012
Plumtree customs post 1012
Poenskop 494
Pofadder 329
Point 524
Pointer Trail 283
Pokane 881
Police Memorial, Pretoria 743
Politsi 798
Pollsmoor Prison 75
Pomene 900
Pomeroy 585
Pomona 958
Pomongwe Cave 1011
Pondoland 483, 501
Pongola 766
Pongolapoort Dam 555
Ponta Mamoli 894
Pontas do Padrão 415
Ponto do Ouro (Ouro Point) 558, 894
Ponto São Sebastiao 901
Poortjies Kloof Dam 364
Popa Falls, Caprivi 916
Popa Mountains 872
Popa Stream 871
Popanyane Mountains 872
Pophonyane Falls 968
Pork Pie Hill 1035
Port Alfred 432
Port Alfred hiking trails 433
Port Alfred Museum 433
Port Durnford 545
Port Durnford lighthouse 545
Port Edward 499, 514
Port Elizabeth 410, 414–17
Port Grosvenor 496
Port Nolloth 265
Port Shepstone 505–6
Port St Johns 493
Porterville 202
Portobello 514
Portuguese Island, Mozambique 893
Poshuli's Hoek 664
Post Office Museum, Pretoria 746
Post Retief 459
Postberg 119
Postmasburg 305
Pot River 477
Potato Express 829
Potchefstroom 845–47
Potchefstroom Museum 846

Potchefstroom University for Christian Higher Education 666, 846
Potgietersrus 675
Potties Pride Holiday Resort 676
Praca MacMahon 891
Praia do Barra, Inhambane 899
Praia do Tofo, Inhambane 899
Praia Marungula (Nelson Beach) 900
Praia Xai-Xai 897
prehistoric engravings 308
President Brand Park, Harrismith 647
President Park, Springs 703
Presley's Bay 492
Pretoria 741–52
Pretoria Art Museum 746
Pretoria National Botanic Gardens 746, 754
Pretoria Salt Pan 670
Pretoria Technikon 747
Pretoria War Memorial 743
Pretoriuskloof 645
Pretoriuskop Camp 822–23
Prieska 339
Prince Albert 280, 357
Prince Alfred's Hamlet 211
Prince Alfred's Pass 404
Prince of Wales Blockhouse 55
Pringle Bay 231
Professor Christiaan Barnard 282
Prospecton 523
Protea Heights 156
Protea Park, Groenkloof 746
Providential Pass 1006
Provost Prison 429
P T C du Plessis Dam 792
Pudimoe 839
Pullinger Kop 731
Punda Maria 816, 820, 822, 827
Pungwe River 1027
Putsonderwater 338
Pyramid 669
Pyramid, the, Drakensberg 609

Q

Qaba Mountain 872
Qabanyane Peak 872
Qacha's Nek 884
Qalweni River 608
Qhora Mouth 434
Qiloane Rock 870
Qolora Mouth 486

Qolora River 485
Qomongqomong River 881
Qora Mouth 488
Qora River 488
Qoyi (Kowie) River 432
Quanza Terrace 463
Queen Elizabeth Park 574
Queen Victoria Museum, Harare 995
Queen's Blockhouse 55
Queen's Park Zoo 463
Queens River 779
Queensburgh 578
Queenstown 470
Queenstown Collectors Museum 470
Quenera River 466
Quiloane Falls 873
Quissico 898
Quko River 468
Qumbu 503
Quthing River 881, 883

R

Raadsaal Museum, Bloemfontein 626
Raadsaal, Pretoria 742
Raboshabane 870
Railway Museum, Bulawayo 1009
Railway Museum, Kimberley 298
Railway station national monument, Paddock 505
Rain Queen, the 799
Rainbow Falls, Victoria Falls 1018
Rainbow Gorge, Drakensberg 608
Raithby Mission station 175
Ramabanta 870
Ramadipa River 796
Ramasali Pass 865
Ramatlabama border post 853
Ramatseliso border gate 884
Ramokgwebane border post 857
Rampai's Nek 876
Ramsgate 513
Ramskop Wild Flower Garden, Clanwilliam 250, 257
Rand Afrikaans University 734
Rand Club 732
Rand Show 736
Rand Stadium 739
Randburg 708, 730, 738
Randburg Waterfront 738
Randfontein 706
Randjeslaagte Beacon 708

Raphia Palm Monument 545
Rasthaus 912
Ratlayi Stream 881
Raubenheimer Dam 792
Ravine Hiking Trail 236
Rawsonville 215
Rayton 754
Red Cross War Memorial Children's Hospital 57
Reddersburg 627
Redhouse, Port Elizabeth 416, 425
Reefs End, Hibberdene 517
Regina ruins 1013
Rehoboth 940, 949
Rehoboth Museum 949
Reinet House Museum 444
Reitz 653
Rembrandt van Rijn Art Gallery 146
Remhoogte Pass 940
Renosterberg 441
Renosterhoek 782
Repembe River 904
Reptile Park, Pretoria 744
Ressano Garcia 896
Retief's Kloof 830
Retiefklip 649
Retreat 79
Reuben Point 892
Revolver Creek 781
Rhebok Hiking Trail 656
Rhebokkop 875
Rhenish Mission station, Otjikango 911
Rhino Horn, Drakensberg 616
Rhino Trail 678
Rhodes 475, 477
Rhodes Cottage 90
Rhodes Memorial 55, 58
Rhodes Park, Kensington 735
Rhodes University 428
Rhodes University Museum 429
Ribbon Falls 608
Richards Bay 546
Richards Bay Park 546
Richmond 285, 580
Richtersveld 258, 265
Richtersveld National Park 264–65
Rider Memorial 908
Riebeeck East 460
Riebeeck Lake 706
Riebeek West 200
Riebeek-Kasteel 200
Riekerts Dam 835
Riemland Eco-route 642
Riet River 294, 622, 630

Rietfontein 332–33, 914
Rietspruit Dam 842
Rietspruit Mine 754
Rietvallei 151
Rietvlei, Milnerton 115
Rietvlei Nature Reserve 752
Rio da Lagoa 885
Rio do Santo Espirito 886
Rissik Street post office 732
River Bend crocodile farm 513
River View 548
Riversdale 381
Riverton 299
Riviersonderend 376
Road to Africa 310
Roaring Sands 338
Rob Ferreira Mineral Baths 840
Robben Island 2–15, 18, 21–22, 27, 33, 37–40
Robberg 406
Robert Broom Museum 707
Robert Harbour, Lüderitz 956
Robert Jameson Park, Durban 528
Robert Sobukwe 299
Robertson 221
Robertson Co-operative Winery 221
Robins Camp, Hwange National Park 1016
Robinson Lake 706
Robinson Pass 388
Rocher Pan Nature Reserve 128
Rock of Raboshabane (Lefika ka Raboshabane) 871
rock art 859, 862, 872, 925, 945, 947
Rockeries, the 605
Rocky Bar Pier, Park Rynie 519
Roggeveld 317
Roma 869–70
Cathedral of Christ the King, Johannesburg 733
Rondebosch 14, 57
Rondebosch Common 57
Rondebult Bird Sanctuary 700
Rondegat River 253
Rondevlei, Cape Peninsula 81
Rondevlei, Wilderness 396
Roodeberg Pass 361
Roodepoort Eisteddfod 703–4
Roodezandskloof 207
Rooibank 761
Rooiberg Co-operative Winery 220
rooibos 249
rooibos tea 250, 252
Rooiels River 231

Roosfontein Nature Reserve, Westville 579
Rorke's Drift 563–64
Rose Cottage caves 659
Rosebank, Cape Town 57
Rosebank, Johannesburg 717, 730
Rosendal 657
Rosettenville 717
Rosh Pinah 955
Rosmead 482
Rössing uranium mine 925
Rouxville 628
Royal Cape Yacht Club 36
Royal Natal National Park 604
Royal Observatory 56
Ruacana Waterfall 922
Rubbervale 801
Rufane River 434
Ruiterbos 388
Rundu 915
Rusape 1022, 1027, 1030
Rust en Vreugd Museum 48
Rust en Vrede Wine Estate 173
Rustenburg 23, 29, 831
Rustenburg Kloof recreational area 832
Rustenburg Museum 832
Rustenburg Nature Reserve 831
Rust-en-Vrede Clay Museum 273
Rutenga 1007
Rutledge Park 559
Rynfield Children's Park, Benoni 701
Ryspunt 240

S

S A Dried Fruit Co-operative 324
S A Merchant Navy Academy 112
S A Police Museum 89
S A Maritime Museum 37
Sabi Sand Game Reserve 807
Sabie 783
Sabie Falls 784
Sabie River 782
Sabiesnek 782
Sacramento Trail (Sardinia Bay) 417
Safari Ostrich Farm 346, 349, 355
Sak River 320, 322
Sakubu 1032
Sakubva Stream 1022
Salamanca 894
Salamander Bay 119
Saldanha 126

Saldanha Bay 4, 11, 13, 23, 114, 119, 123–25
Salem, Eastern Cape 427
Salmondsdam Nature Reserve 236
S A Lombard Nature Reserve 840
Salt Lake 293
Salt River, Cape Town 271
Salt River, Knysna 403
Salt Rock 541
Salvation Valley 776
Sam Cohen Memorial Library, Swakopmund 928
Sammy Marks Museum 746
San Lameer 514
Sand River 637
Sand River Dam 985
Sand River Gneiss 681
Sandflats 436
Sandili's grave 461
Sandlane border post 989
iSandlwana 563
Sandrifskloof River 211
Sandton 708, 730, 738
Sandton Square 738
Sandveld 257
Sandvlei Museum 129
Sandwich Harbour 930
Sandy Bay 109
Sani Pass 614, 876
Sannaspos 630
Sannieshof 837
Santa Thérèse Mission station 877
Santarama, Johannesburg 735
São Martinho Resort 896
sardine run 529
Sardinia Bay 417
Sarel Cilliers Museum, Kroonstad 640
Sarel Cilliers, farm 640
Sarnia 578
Saron 202
Sasol 754
Sasol II 760
Sasol III 760
Sasolburg 641
Sasolburg Highveld Garden 642
Satansnek Pass 475
Satara 822, 825
Satara Camp 821
Save River 903, 1033
Savuti channel 859
Saxenburg 162
Saxonwold 730, 735, 738
Scarborough 104
Schagen 773
Schmidt's Drift 309

Schmidtsdrif 301
Schoeman's Kloof, Western Cape 351
Schoemanskloof, Mpumalanga 759, 771
Schoemansville 751
Schryvershoek 119
Schwarzrand 950
Schweizer Reneke 838
Scientia 747
Scottburgh 520
Scratch Patch (Topstones) 94
Screaming Monster, Sudwala Caves 772
Sea Acres Holiday Resort 416
Sea Point 111
Sea View 414, 417
Sea Vista 411
Seako Bridge 880
Seal Island, Mossel Bay 387
Seal Islet 956
Seaview, Transkei 494
Sebakwe Dam 1014
Sebakwe National Park 1014
Sebakwe Poort 1014
Sebakwe River 1014
Sebapata tributary 881
Secunda 760
Sedgefield 397
Seetsa 876
Sehithwa 862
Sehlabathebe National Park 616, 884
Sekake 884
Sekhukhuneland 789
Sekonyela Siding 657
Sekubu Caves 874
Sekubu Mission 874
Selebi-Phikwe 851, 856
Selous 1015
Semonkong 870–71
Sendelingsdrif 961
Sendelingspos Siding 835
Senekal 635, 644
Senqunyane Falls 873
Sentinel, Hout Bay 106
Sentinel blockhouse, Burgersdorp 481
Sentinel, Drakensberg 603
Sentinel, Witsieshoek 652
Sepapushek border post 879
Sepupa Village 862
Serfontein Bridge 287
Serondella campsite 859
Serowe 855
Serpentine, the 397

1063

Serra Padrado 943
Serutle River 874
Sesheng 302
Sesriem 938
Setibing Trading Station 873
Setlagoli 313
Settler country 426
Settlers, 1820, National Monument 430
Settlers' Park Nature Reserve 416
Seven Fountains 427
Seven Passes Road 392, 394
Seven Weeks Poort 356, 361
Seymour 459
Sezela 518
Sezela River lagoon 518
Shad Alley, Umtentweni 516
Shaka's Indaba Tree 538
Shaka's Rock 516, 541
Shakawe border post 862
Shalungwa Siyafa 828
Shamva 997
Shangani 1013
Shangani River 1013
Shangoni 821
Shark Island 956
Shashe River 856
Shawbury Mission 502
Sheba's Breasts 981
Sheepmoor 765
Shefina Island 886
Sheik Yussuf 26, 229
Sheilam cactus gardens 223
Shell Museum 387
Shelly Beach 512
Shelter Fall 587
Shiluvane Mission 794
Shingwedzi Camp 822, 827
Shingwedzi River 813
Ship Mountain 823
Shipwreck Museum 241
Shirimantanga 819
eShiselweni 964
Shiselweni 990
Shiselweni plantations 990
Shiya-lo-Ngubu Dam 988
Shongweni 577
Shongweni Dam 577
Shop Museum, Pilgrim's Rest 785
Shoshanguwe 741
Shoshong 855
Shri Gopalall Hindu Temple 535
Shurugwi 1013
Sicunusa border post 990
Sidbury 427
Sidvokodvo 990

Signal Hill 1, 6, 50
Sikereti Camp, Khaudum Game Park 915
Silaka Nature Reserve 494
Silberberg Grotto 707
Silotwane Hills, Swaziland 968
Silozwane Cave, Zimbabwe 1011
Silver Sands Bay 232
Silverhurst 65
Silvermine Nature Reserve 79
Silverton 754
Silwerstroomstrand 117
Simon's Town 30, 95
Simon's Town Museum 32, 95
Simonsig 164
Sinamatella Camp 1016
Sinclair Nature Reserve 405
Singangwana River 492
Siphageni (Flagstaff) 498
Siphofaneni 984, 990
Sir Abe Bailey Collection 46
Sir Lowry's Pass Village 369
Sir Lowry's Pass 369
Sishen 305
Siteki 984–85
Sithobela 990
Sixteen Mile Beach 120
Skaap Island 120, 121
Skeleton Coast 913, 941
Skeleton Coast Park 944
Skeleton Pass 1036
Skelmkoppie 837
Skilpad Wild Flower Reserve 260
Skilpadshek border post 853
Skoenmakers Canal 288
Skoenmakerskop 417
Skoonspruit fossil site 649
Skukuza 812, 822, 824
Skukuza airfield 808
Skurweberg 209, 596
Skyline Junction 1036
Slagtersnek 439
Slagtersnek Rebellion 436
Slangkop lighthouse 104–5
Slave Lodge 43
Sleeping Sisters baobab trees 861
Slurry 836
Small Island 893
Smithfield 627
Smithfield Dam 627
Smitswinkel 98
Sneeuberg Farm Trails 442
Sneeuberg range 420
Sneeuberge 441
Sneeukop 253, 368
Snowdon 478

Soada Forest Nature Reserve 580
Sodwana Bay National Park 555
Soekmekaar 678
Soekmekaar railway junction 800
Sol Plaatje 299
Solitaire 938
Somerset East 438
Somerset East Museum 438
Somerset West 366
Sominungwa 1019
Somkhele 547
Sonesta Holiday Resort 233
Soshanguve 748
Sossusvlei 938
South African Air Force Memorial 749
South African Astronomical Observatory 56, 318
South African Bird of Prey Trust 758
South African Bureau of Standards (SABS) 747
South African Cultural History Museum (Slave Lodge) 43
South African Library for the Blind, Grahamstown 429
South African Lion Park 705
South African Mint 747
South African Missionary Institution 48
South African Missionary Museum, King William's Town 454
South African Museum, Cape Town 19, 46
South African National Equestrian Centre 738
South African National Gallery, Cape Town 46
South African National Museum of Military History, Johannesburg 738
South African Naval Museum 95
South African Police Museum, Pretoria 746
South African Rugby Board Museum 61
South Sand Bluff 495
Southbroom 513
Southwell 434
Soutkloof 435
Soutpansberg range 678–80
Soweto 708, 739
Spaanschemat River 69
Spekboom River 783, 791
Spektakel 265

Sperrgebiet 956
Sphinx, Drakensberg 609
Spier 158–59
Spioenkop 591
Spioenkop Dam 650
Spioenkop Public Resort and Nature Reserve 591
Spitskop 404, 782, 801
Spitskop Nature Reserve 324, 331
Spitzkoppe 925, 947
Splash Rock, Umtentweni 516
Springbok 261, 263
Springbok Flats 671
Springbok Park, Pretoria 746
Springbok Trail 283
Springfield 533
Springfontein 621
Springs 702
Springs Indoor Sports Centre 703
Springs, the, Uitenhage 424
eSpungabera 1037
Spurwing Island, Kariba 1001
Sri Siva Soobramoniar Temple 573
Sri Vaithianatha Easvarar Alayam Temple 528
St Croix 426
St Francis Bay 411
St Helena Bay 3, 114, 126
St James 90
St Joseph's Church 105
St Lucia 548
St Lucia Park 549
St Michaels-on-Sea 512
St Sebastian Bay 379
Standerskop 767
Standerskop Nature Reserve 768
Standerton 767
Stanford 236
Stanger 538
Stapleford Forest 1026
Staircase, the 783
Star of South Africa 293, 754
State Theatre 743
Steelpoort River 789
Steenberg 75–76
Steenbras Dam 231
Steenbras reservoir 369
Steenbras River 231
Steinacker 805
Steinkopf 264
Stellaland flag 312
Stellenbosch 26, 28–29, 142–49
Stellenbosch Military Museum 146
Stellenbosch Village Museum 145
Stellenbosch Wine Route 155
Stellenrust 173

Stellenryck Wine Museum 146
Stellenzicht 173
Stenebrug 244
Step (Oudeberg) Pass 650
Sterboom Route 320
Sterkfontein Caves 706, 830
Sterkfontein Dam 651
Sterkspruit 478
Sterkspruit River 792
Sterkstroom 471, 480
Sterkstroom Nature Reserve 480
Stettynskloof 215
Steve Visser Hiking Trail 659
Stevenson-Hamilton Memorial Library 824
Steyn's Bank 1034
Steynsburg 482
Steynsdorp 761
Steytlerville 425
Stikland 273
Stilbaai 383
Stilfontein 845
Stofberg House 214
Stofbergsfontein 119
Stokstert Hiking Trail 627
Stompneusbaai 126
Stony Brook 184
Stormberg Peak 472
Stormberge 471
Storms River 407
Storms River mouth 408
Storms River Village 409
Stormsvlei 223, 376
Strand 230
Strandfontein 258
Strandloper Trail, Cintsa 467
Strelitzia Coast 516
Struisbaai 239
Strydenburg 292
Strydpoort Mountains 677
Stuart Chandler Bridge 1006
Stutterheim 469
Sua 851
Sua Pan 849, 858–59
Subeng Stream 876
Sudwala Caves 772
sugar cane 507
Sugar Coast 507
sugar industry 532–35, 536–38, 542–43
Sugar Loaf 368, 494
Sugar Loaf Hiking Trail 494
sugar terminal 526
Sugar Way 531
Sugarloaf, Drakensberg 609
Suikerbosrand 768

Suikerbosrand Nature Reserve 667, 769
Sukses 912
sultanas 327
Summerhill pineapple farm, Bathurst 432
Sun City 833
Sun Valley 105
Sundays River valley 418, 420–22
Sunland 422
Sunnyside, Pretoria 743
Sunrise-on-Sea 467
Surrender Hill 657
Sushwana River 982
Sutherland 56, 317
uSutu River 557, 753
Suthu River 963, 991
Sutshwana River 983, 988
Suurbraak 380
Swadini 793, 805
Swakop River 910, 926
Swakopmund 926–28
Swakopmund Museum 927
Swart River 393
Swart Kei River 470
Swartberg 617
Swartberg Pass 280, 357
Swartberge 340, 356
Swartfontein Recreational Resort 312
Swartkopfontein border post 835
Swartkoppies 330
Swartkops River 416, 426
Swartland Wine Route 242
Swartmodder River 951
Swartplaat 842
Swartrand 842
Swartruggens 832, 834
Swartvlei, Wilderness 396
Swaziland 963–91
Swaziland Agricultural College 989
Sweet-Thorn Hiking Trail 910
Swellendam 376–78
Swinburne 648
Sybrand van Niekerk Resort (Swadini) 793
Sydney-on-the-Vaal 301

T

T'Keikamspoort Trail 339
T'Numkwa 449
Tabankulu 498, 503
Table Bay 2–9, 13, 16, 19, 33–37

1065

Table Mountain 1–3, 8, 12, 15
Table Mountain Cableway 49
Table Mountain, KwaZulu-Natal 576
Tafalofeffe 488
Tafelberg, Drakensberg 475
Tafelkop, Mpumalanga 760
Tafelkop, Platberg 648
Tafuna Siding 997
Tamariskia, Swakopmund 928, 942
Tandatula Lodge 804
Tandayi Stream 1034
Tanganda River 1036
Tarkastad 460, 471
Tarlton dog-racing track 829
Tarlton Ostrich Farm 829
Tatham Art Gallery 573
Tati River 856
Taung 311
Tavern of the Sea 8, 20, 24
Teebus 482
Telle Bridge border post 478, 880
Telle River 478
Tembe Drift 970
Tembe Elephant Park 557
Tembe River 885
Tembu Pass 475
Tembuland 483
Tenbosch 776
Tengenenge 996
Terblans Walk 403
Terrace Bay 944
Teyateyaneng 877–78
Thaba Bosigo 865
Thaba Bosiu 865, 869
Thaba Nchu 631
Thaba Nchu Mountain 631
Thaba Putswa 871–73
Thaba Telle 870–71
Thaba Tjhitja 872
Thaba Tseka 873
Thaba Tswëu 880
Thabana li Mele 871–72
Thabana Ntlenyana 600, 613, 876
Thamalakane River 861, 862
Thathaganyana Hill 856
Thelema 167
thermal mineral springs, Dealesville 626
thermal sulphur baths, Machadodorp 759
Theron's Rest Camp 764
Theronsberg Pass 212
Theuniskraal 151, 205
Theunissen 635

Thohoyandou 680, 683
Thohoyandou Museum 683
Thomas River 469
Thompson Dam 475
Thompson's Bay 541
Thomson Junction 1018
Thongathi River 536
Thorn Kloof 435
Thornville 579
Thornybush Game Lodge 805
Three Anchor Bay 111
Three Sisters 284, 290
Thukela Drift Nature Reserve 590
Thukela Ferry 585
Thukela River 543
Thulamela ruins 827
Thumb, the, Drakensberg 612
Thure Lilliecrona Park 512
Tidbury's Toll 459
Tierberg Nature Reserve 326
Tiervlei 272
Tikuba 984
Timbavati Nature Reserve 804
Tina River 503, 619
Tinie Versfeld Wild Flower Reserve 118
Tinley Manor Beach 541
Tintenpalast 908
Tjaart Johannes van der Walt Memorial 447
Tjate 790
Tlokoeng 876
Tlokweng border post 835, 852
Togryers Museum 210
Tokai 79
Tokwe River 1006
Tombo 492
Tongaat 536
Tongaat Beach 541
Toorkop 362
Toorwaterpoort 358, 449
Topping 392
Toringberg 362
Torra Bay 944
Toteng 862
Totius Garden of Remembrance 846
Totius House Museum 846
Touw River 393
Touws River 276
tractor museum, Viljoenskroon 639
Tradouw Pass 363, 380
Trafalgar 514
Trafalgar Marine Reserve 514
Tragedy Hill 514

Traka 450
Trans Gariep Museum 622
Transkei 483
Trans-Maluti highway 872
Transvaal Museum 744
Trappes Valley 431
Treur River 787
Treurfontein 842
Triangle 1006
tribal and gumboot dancing 738
Trichardt 760
Trichardtsdal 794
Triplets, the 368
Trompsburg 621
Tropic of Capricorn 678, 827, 900, 949
Troutbeck 1029
Tryme Massif, Drakensberg 608
Tsanga Stream 1029
Tsau 862
Tsauchab River 938
Tsehlanyane River 875
Tseketseke River 608
Tsende River 813, 827
Tses 951
Tsetsera Heights 1032
Tshabong 863
Tshane 863
Tshaneni 984
Tshimbubfe 683
Tshinyakweremba Mountain 1025
Tshipise mineral baths 681
Tshirinda indigenous forest 1037
Tshitora River 1032
Tshlame 647
Tshokwane 820, 825
Tshontini 491
Tsisab Gorge 947
Tsitsa Valley 502
Tsitsa Waterfall 476
Tsitsikamma 407
Tsitsikamma Forest and Coastal National Park 408
Tsitsikamma Toll-Road 409
Tsodilo Hills 862
Tsoelike 884
Tsolo 502
Tsomo valley 475
Tsondab River 938
Tsumeb 917
Tsumeb Museum 918
Tsumeb Open-air Cultural Museum 918
Tsumkwe 915
Tswaing Crater Museum 670
Tugela-Vaal water scheme 650

Tugwi River 1006
Tulbagh 204
Tuli 1012
Tunnel Cave, Mossel Bay 387
Turffontein horse racing course 739
Turfloop 678
Tussen-die-Riviere Game Farm 620
Twee Jonge Gezellen 206
Twee Rivieren 331, 334
Tweedie 588
Tweeling 653
Tweespruit 631
Twelve Apostles 109
Twistniet 195
Twyfelfontein 945
Tygerberg 270
Tygerberg Nature Reserve 272
Tygerberg Zoo 273
Tzaneen 678
Tzaneen Museum 795
Tzonso 1027

U

Ubombo 555
Ugab River 941
Ugie 476
Uilenkraal River 237
Uis 947
Uitenhage 423
Uitenhage Railway Museum 424
Uiterwyk 161
Uitkomst Research Station 914
Uitkyk 151, 166, 775
Uitkyk Pass 253
Uitspanskraal 251
Ultimatum Tree, KwaZulu-Natal 543
Ulundi 562
uMbabane Stream 971
Umbogintwini 523
umBuluzi River 885
Umbulwana Hill 591
Umdloti 540
Umdoni Park 511, 519
Umdoni Road bird sanctuary 522
uMezi weZinto River 519
Umfolozi Game Reserve 547, 552
Umgeni River Bird Park 528
Umgeni Steam Museum 585
Umgeni Valley Project 586
uMgungundlovu 561
Umhlali 538

Umhlanga Lagoon Nature Reserve 540
uMhlanga River 539
Umhlanga Rocks 530, 539
Umkomaas 521
Umlalazi Nature Reserve 545
Umnini market 521
Umtamvuna Nature Reserve 515
Umtata 500
Umtentweni 516
Umvoti Vlei Nature Reserve 583
Umzimkulu 581
Umzinto 519
Umzumbe 516
Underberg 615
Unguana 900
Uniefees Dam 654
Uniefees Dam Resort 654
Union Buildings 741, 743
Uniondale 359
Uniondale Poort 450
Unitas Park 667
University of Cape Town 57–58
University of Fort Hare 456
University of Harare 995
University of Lesotho 870
University of Luyengo 989
University of Natal 574
University of Port Elizabeth 416
University of Pretoria 734, 747
University of South Africa (UNISA) 747
University of Stellenbosch 148
University of the North 678
University of the Witwatersrand 734
University of Transkei (Unitra) 501
University of Zululand 545
Unjab River 944
Upington 323
Usakos 925
uSutu River 557, 753
Utopia Holiday Resort 830
Utopia House 1023
Utrecht 598
Uvongo 512
Uvongo Beach 512
Uvongo bird park 512

V

Vaal Dam 642
Vaal Dam Nature Reserve 643, 654

Vaal River 287, 300, 641–42, 753
Vaal River Resort 667
Vaal Triangle 665
Vaal Triangle Technikon 666
Vaalbos National Park 301
Vaal-Harts Valley 310
Vaalheuningberge 252
Vaalhoek 787
Val de Grace 754
Valhalla 749
Valleiberg 368
Valley of a Thousand Hills 531, 576
Valley of Death 778
Valley of Desolation 445
Valley of Giants 828
Vals River 639
Vals River Resort, Lindley 655
Van Loveren 226
Van Meerhoff's Castle 245
Van Reenen Pass 591, 648
Van Riebeeck Karoo Garden 439
Van Ryn Brandy Cellar 158
Van Staden Mountains 424
Van Stadens Gorge 414
Van Stadens Gorge Wild Flower Reserve and Bird Sanctuary 414
Van Stadens River 414
Van Wouw House, Brooklyn 746
Van Zyl's Hall 352
Vanderbijlpark 665
Vanderkloof (P K le Roux) Dam 288–89
Vanrhynsdorp 255, 257
Vanryneveld Pass Dam 443
Vanzylsberg 475
Vanzylsrus 336
Vasco da Gama 52
Vasco da Gama Botanical Garden 891
Vegkop 654, 664
Velddrif 127
Vembje Lagoon 897
Venda country 683
Venda people 680
Venetia 681
Ventersburg 634
Venterspos 848
Venterstad 289
Verbrandeberg 945
Verdun 157
Vereeniging 666
Verena 755
Vergelegen Nature Reserve 614
Verkykerskop 648
Verlaten Kloof Pass 317

Verlorevlei 128
Vermaaklikheid 382
Verneuk Pan 322
Vernon Crookes Nature Reserve 519
Verraaiersnek 791
Versveld Pass 244
Verulam 535
Vet River 381
Victoria & Alfred Waterfront 37
Victoria Basin 35
Victoria Bay 395
Victoria Falls 858, 916, 1018
Victoria Falls airport 1018
Victoria Falls National Park 1018
Victoria Post 456
Victoria West 290
Victoria West Museum 291
Viedgesville 500
Vila Franco do Save 903
Vilankulo 900, 903
Viljoenshof 238
Viljoenskroon 639
Villiers 649
Villiersdorp 216
Villiersdorp Wild Flower Garden 216
Vincent 463
Vineta, Swakopmund 928, 942
Vingerklip 946
Vink River 220
Vioolsdrif 264
Vioolsdrif border post 953
Virginia 637
Virginia Park Resort 637
Visgat 247
Vishmarorp Temple 536
Vista University 747
Vlakfontein 748
Vlaklaagte 833
Vleesbaai 385
Vlottenburg 157
VOC-Kruithuis (Stellenbosch Military Museum) 146
Voëlvlei 202, 239, 244
Volksrust 767
Von Bach Dam 911
Von Lindequist Gate, Etosha National Park 919
Voorbaai 387
Voortrekker Monument, Pretoria 749
Voortrekker Museum, Hartenbos 388
Voortrekker Museum, Pietermaritzburg 572
Voortrekker Museum, Winburg 633
Voortrekkerhoogte 749
Vosloo Kudu Reserve 458
Vosloo's Forest 784
Vrede 648
Vrededorp 730
Vredefort 640
Vredefort Dome 641
Vredelust 153
Vredenburg 123, 174
Vredendal 258
Vredenheim 157
Vrolijkheid Nature Reserve 222
Vryburg 312
Vryheid 595
Vryheid Nature Reserve 595
Vulture's Retreat, Drakensberg 609
Vungu River 512
Vuurberg 39
Vyeboom 216

W

Waaipoort Pass 425
Waboomberg 209
Waenhuiskrans 240
Wagendrift Dam 589
Wagon Hill 591
Waldeck's Plant 300
Walker Bay 236
Wallmannsthal 669
Walmer 417
Walter Battiss Art Gallery 438
Walter Everitt sunken gardens 471
Walvis Bay 929–32
Wanderers, the 735
Wapadsberg Pass 441
war memorial, Haenertsburg 797
War Museum, Bloemfontein 626
Warden 648
Warmbaths 672
Warmbaths Resort 672
Warmbokkeveld 132, 209, 316
Warmwaterberg hot springs 363
Warner Beach 522
Warren Hills 1015
Warrenton 310, 839
Wartburg 582
Wasbank 593
Wasbank River 593
Wasgoedspruit 846
Water's Edge 848
Waterberg 673
Waterberg Plateau Park 912
Waterdown Dam 470
Waterfall Bluff 495
Waterfall Hiking Trail 236
Waterkloof 621
Waterkloof River 831
Waterkloof, Pretoria 669
Waterpoort 681
Waterval Boven 759, 770
Waterval Onder 770
Waterval Spruit 786
wattle industry 575
Waverley, Pretoria 669
Wedza 1021
Weenen 589
Weenen Museum 589
Weenen Nature Reserve 590
Weeping Cross of Delville Wood, Pietermaritzburg 573
Welgemoed 272
Welkom 638
Wellington 195
Wellington Museum 196
Welmoed 159
Weltevrede 227
Weltevreden 789
Welverdiend 848
Welwitschia mirabilis 936
Wemmer's Pan 688
Wemmershoek Dam 184
Wentzel Dam 838
Wepener 660
Wêreldend 333
West Coast 16
West Coast National Park 119–21
West Nicholson 1009, 1012
West Wits 848
Westerberg 339
Western Breakwater 34
Western Deep Levels 691
Western Province Cricket Club 61
Westoe Dam 761
Westonaria 847–48
Westville 579
Weza hiking trails 504
Weza State Forests Nature Reserve 504
Whale Rock 39
whales 235, 236, 383, 385, 389, 521
Wheat Museum 243
Whêtse's Cave 652
Whisky Spruit camping site 783
White Hill 884
White Lady of the Brandberg 948
White Mfolozi River 547
White Rhino Shelter 1011

White River 775, 809
White Waters Stream 1033
White's Folly 700
Whittlesea 457, 459
Wilcocks Poort 627
Wild Coast 483
Wild Coast Sun hotel and casino 499
Wilderness 393, 396
Wilds Garden, the, Houghton 735
Wilfred Bauer Nature Reserve 618
Wilge River 646
Wilger River 643
Wilgerivier 755
Wilgespruit Gorge 686
Willem Pretorius Game Reserve 634
Willem Prinsloo Agricultural Museum 754
William Campbell Furniture Museum 528
William Fehr Collection 43
William Humphreys Art Gallery 298
Williston 320
Willowglen, Port Elizabeth 417
Willowgrange 588
Willowgrove, Port Elizabeth 417
Willowmore 446
Willowmore Park, Benoni 701
Willows 754
Willows, the, Port Elizabeth 417
Willowvale 489, 499
Winburg Museum 633
Windhoek 907
Windhoek International Airport 909
Windsor Castle, Drakensberg 609
Windsor Dam 591
Windsorton 309
Windvoëlberg 469
Windy Corner 591
Wines of the Cape 136
Winkelshoek 244
Winklespruit 522
Winterton 609
Witbank 747, 755
Witbank Dam 755
Witblits Festival 622
Witbooi War, the 940
Witch, the, Drakensberg 609
Witdraai 336
Witels River 210
Witpoortjie 704
Witput 293

Witsand 337, 379
Witsand Holiday Resort 338
Witsenberg 209
Witsieshoek 652
Witsieshoek Mountain Resort 646, 651
Witstinkhout Hiking Trail 628
Witteberge 472, 478
Witvlei 910
Witwatersrand 668, 684–99, 742
Wlotzkasbaken 942
Wolfberg Arch 253
Wolfberg Cracks 254
Wolhuterskop Nature Reserve 646, 656
Wolkberg 795, 799
Wolkberg Caves 797
Wolmaransstad 841
Wolraad Woltemade 33
Wolseley 212
Woltemade Cemetery 33
Wolwedans Dam Hiking Trail 388
Wonder Cave, Cango Caves 354
Wonderboom 669
Wonderboom Nature Reserve 747
Wonderboomnek 741
Wonderfontein 847
Wondergat 264
Wonderhoek 481
Woodbridge Island 115
Woodbush 784, 796
Woodhouse Fall 587
Woodstock 3, 53
Woodstock Dam 651
Woodville 393
Woody Island Resort, Parys 641
Worcester 213
Worcester Museum 214
World End 335
World Hill 868
World of Birds 109
World's View 574, 705, 799, 1030
Wreck of the Grosvenor 496
Wuppertal 250, 251
Wylie Park 574
Wylie's Poort 681
Wynberg 28, 62, 78

X

!Xamkhanaxas 953
Xai-Xai 897
Xalanga 475, 479
Xhenib River 608

Xhora (Elliotdale) 500
Ximunya township 1032

Y

Yengele Forest 514
Yzerfontein 119

Z

Zambezi National Park 1018–19
Zambezi River 915, 1000, 1003, 1009, 1019
Zambezi River border post 1018
Zandamela 898
Zandvliet 151
Zangozolo tented camp 544
Zastron 660–63
Zavala district 898
Zave 999
Zavora beach 898
Zebediyela 674
Zeekoebaardsdrif 337
Zeekoevlei 229
Zeerust 834, 837
Zeerust Museum 834
Zeraatsfontein 755
Zevenwacht 162
Zimbabwe 992–1037
Zinave National Park 903
zinc mine 955
Zinjanja 1013
Zinkwazi Beach 541
Zion City Moria 678
Zion City Moria Nature Reserve 678
Zitundo customs post 895
Ziwa Peak 1030
Ziwa Ruins 1030
Zoetendalvlei 239
Zoo Lake 735
Zoological Gardens, Ashburton 575
Zululand 544–64
Zululand game reserves 565
Zungwini Mountain 596
Zuuranys 451
Zuurbekom 848
Zuurberge 418, 436
Zvishavane (Shabani) 1006, 1011
Zwartkop Air Force station 749
Zwartkoppies Hall 746
Zwelitsha 455